Ounces	9×12 envelope, 9×12 SASE number of pages	9×12 SASE (for return trips) number of pages	First Class Postage	Third Class Postage	Postage from U.S. to Canada
under 2	. . .	1 to 2	$.39*	$.39*	$.63*
2	1 to 4	3 to 8	.52	.52	.73
3	5 to 10	9 to 12	.75	.75	.86
4	11 to 16	13 to 19	.98	.98	1.09
5	17 to 21	20 to 25	1.21	1.21	1.32
6	22 to 27	26 to 30	1.44	1.21	1.55
7	28 to 32	31 to 35	1.67	1.33	1.78
8	33 to 38	36 to 41	1.90	1.33	2.01
9	39 to 44	42 to 46	2.13	1.44	2.24
10	45 to 49	47 to 52	2.36	1.44	2.47
11	50 to 55	53 to 57	2.59	1.56	2.70

* This cost includes a 10¢ assessment for oversized mail that is light in weight.

1992 Writer's Market

1992
Writer's Market

Where & How
To Sell What You Write

Editor: **Mark Kissling**

Assistant Editor: **Roseann Shaughnessy**

Writer's
Digest
Books

Cincinnati, Ohio

Distributed in Canada by
McGraw-Hill Ryerson
300 Water St.
Whitby, Ontario L1N 9B6

Distributed in Australia by
Kirby Book Co.
Private Bag No. 19
Alexandria NSW 2015

Distributed in New Zealand by
David Bateman
P.O. Box 100-242
N. Shore Mail Centre
Auckland 10

Managing Editor, Market Books Department:
Constance J. Achabal

Assistant Managing Editor:
Glenda Tennant Neff

Library of Congress Catalog Number
31-20772
International Standard Serial Number
0084-2729
International Standard Book Number
0-89879-498-6

U.S. Postage by the Page by Carolyn Hardesty;
Canadian Postage by the Page by Barbara Murrin

Contents

The Writing Profession

From the Editors **1**

How to Use *Writer's Market* **3**

Key to Symbols and Abbreviations **5**

The Interview and Its Uses, *by Michael Schumacher* **6**
Knowing different interview methods and how to use them is an important step in the writing process. This veteran writer shares insight on when to interview in person, by phone or mail, to get the best results for your book or article.

Writing an Irresistible Book Proposal, *by Michael Larsen* **11**
Excellent detail and organization in a proposal are essential to a book's chances for publication. This author and literary agent spells out the essential elements for an offer publishers can't refuse.

The Business of Writing **16**

Marketing your manuscripts 16	Mailing submissions 27
Writing tools 17	Recording submissions 28
Approaching markets...........................19	Bookkeeping 29
Sample magazine query 21	Tax information.................................29
Sample book query 22	Rights and the writer.......................30
Exploring the Self-Publishing Option ..25	Copyrighting your writing 32
Manuscript mechanics 26	How much should I charge? 35

Special Business Feature: Publishers' Roundtable **45**
Four professionals from small and large publishing houses discuss what happens behind the scenes from the time an initial query is received until books are printed.
The 22 Kinds of Editors 52

The Markets

Book Publishers **55**

Close-up 137
Mark Richard, Author
Openings of stories, methods of following narrative lines and talking a story out are just a few things addressed by this award-winning author.
Close-up 161
Dan Frank, Pantheon
A little extra research can make a world of difference in getting your book published, says this senior editor.

Canadian and International Book Publishers **216**

Close-up 222
Susanne Alexander, Goose Lane Editions
This managing editor is seeking a balance of literary nonfiction, fiction and poetry—all with a Canadian connection.

Small Presses *236*
Close-up 241
Constance Hunting, Puckerbrush Press
A close and personal rapport with authors is what this literary small press editor offers.

Special Feature: First Bylines *244*
Three book authors share experiences from research to publication on their first books.

Book Packagers and Producers *248*

Subsidy Publishers 253
Other Book Publishers and Packagers 253

Consumer Publications *255*

Animal....................................256
Art and Architecture 265
Associations............................270
Astrology, Metaphysical and
   New Age 275
Automotive and Motorcycle 278
Aviation..................................285
Business and Finance 287
Career, College and Alumni......297
Child Care and Parental
   Guidance..........................305
Comic Books 312
Consumer Service and Business
   Opportunity 314
Contemporary Culture 316
Close-up 317
Jay Walljasper, *Utne Reader*
The reprint market is largely untapped, this editor says, and he tells writers how to take advantage of it.
Detective and Crime.................319
Disabilities 320
Entertainment.........................323
Ethnic/Minority 331
Food and Drink.......................339
Games and Puzzles 342
General Interest 344
Close-up 351
Lewis H. Lapham, *Harper's*
Strong voices are what this long-time editor wants in articles and stories selected for publication in his prestigious monthly.
Health and Fitness 357
History....................................365
Hobby and Craft 372
Home and Garden....................399
Close-up 405
Katie Tamony, *Northern California Home and Garden*

People-oriented articles that complement a visual format are important to home and garden magazines, says this managing editor.
Humor.....................................408
Inflight 410
Juvenile 413
Literary and "Little" 427
Close-up 437
Dorian Gossey, *Indiana Review*
Experimental writing contributes to the diverse vision of this literary magazine, says this associate editor.
Men's 448
Military...................................453
Music......................................458
Mystery 464
Nature, Conservation and
   Ecology 464
Personal Computers.................473
Photography............................478
Politics and World Affairs.........479
Psychology and
   Self-Improvement..............483
Regional 484
Relationships 538
Religious.................................543
Retirement...............................570
Romance and Confession 575
Rural.......................................577
Science 580
Science Fiction, Fantasy
   and Horror 583
Sports.....................................589
Archery and Bowhunting, Baseball, Bicycling, Boating, Bowling, Gambling, General Interest, Golf, Guns, Horse Racing, Hunting and Fishing, Martial Arts, Miscellaneous, Skiing and Snow Sports, Soccer, Tennis, Water Sports, Wrestling

Close-up 629
Bob Wischnia, *Runner's World*
*Research and thorough familiarity with
the magazine are the essentials to
breaking into highly specialized markets*

*such as this well-known magazine for
runners.*

Teen and Young Adult 636
Travel, Camping and Trailer......643
Women's 658

Special Feature: First Bylines 670

*Getting that first story or article published is a milestone for any writer. Three writers discuss
their writing, their first sales and what has followed.*

Other Consumer Publications 673

Trade, Technical and Professional Journals 675

Advertising, Marketing
   and PR 676
Art, Design and Collectibles 679
Auto and Truck 683
Aviation and Space 686
Beverages and Bottling 686
Book and Bookstore..................689
Brick, Glass and Ceramics 690
Building Interiors 690
Business Management 691
Church Administration and
   Ministry...............................698
Clothing 701
Coin-Operated Machines..........702
Confectionery and
   Snack Foods 703
Construction and Contracting ..704
Dental......................................707
Drugs, Health Care and
   Medical Products 708
Education and Counseling 710

Close-up 715
Holly Brady,
Technology & Learning

*Technical material can also be
readable, and this trade journal editor
offers advice on cutting through the
jargon.*

Electronics and
   Communication....................716
Energy and Utilities..................720
Engineering and Technology 722
Entertainment and
   the Arts................................725
Farm...728
   Agricultural Equipment, Crops and
   Soil Management, Dairy Farming,
   Livestock, Management, Miscel-
   laneous, Regional
Finance.....................................738
Fishing......................................742
Florists, Nurseries and
Landscaping 742
Government and
   Public Service 744
Groceries and Food Products....750
Hardware..................................754
Home Furnishings and
   Household Goods 755
Hospitals, Nursing and
   Nursing Homes....................757
Hotels, Motels, Clubs, Resorts
   and Restaurants 758
Industrial Operations 761
Information Systems 763
Insurance..................................768
International Affairs..................770
Jewelry 771
Journalism and Writing 771
Law 781
Leather Goods 786
Library Science 786
Lumber.....................................788
Machinery and Metal 789
Maintenance and Safety...........789
Management and Supervision ..791
Marine and Maritime
   Industries 795
Medical.....................................796
Music..802
Office Environment and
   Equipment 804
Paper..804
Pets 805
Photography Trade 806
Plumbing, Heating, Air Condi-
   tioning and Refrigeration 808
Printing 809
Real Estate 810
Resources and
   Waste Reduction 812
Selling and Merchandising 813
Sport Trade...............................816

Stone, Quarry and Mining 820
Toy, Novelty and Hobby 822
Transportation 823
Travel.................................824
Veterinary............................825
Other Trade Journals 826

Scriptwriting *828*

Business and Educational Writing...828
Playwriting 837
Close-up 841
Thom Atkinson, Playwright
A young playwright with a background in fiction offers advice on plotting, revising and developing characters.
Close-up 857
Lloyd Richards, National Playwrights Conference
This artistic director discusses the opportunities select playwrights have to improve their plays at this prestigious conference.
Screenwriting 865
Close-up 871
Bruce Joel Rubin, Screenwriter
The award-winning screenwriter of "Ghost" says persistence was his key to achieving commercial success while producing scripts with a message.
Other Scriptwriting Markets...873

Syndicates *874*

Close-up 885
Caroline Marshall, PEN Syndicated Fiction Project
Fiction with a high narrative profile, appropriate for radio broadcast and newspaper syndication, is what this project director is seeking.
Other Syndicates..886

Greeting Card Publishers *887*

Other Greeting Card Publishers 896

Resources

Contests and Awards *897*

Other Contests and Awards 937

Organizations of Interest *938*

Publications of Interest *939*

Glossary *940*

Book Publishers Subject Index *946*

Check the categories for publishers that most closely match what you write.
Fiction 946
Nonfiction 949

Index *970*

The Writing Profession

From the Editors

One of the wonderful aspects of writing is its ability to fulfill your life in many different ways. Writing can be a profession, a part-time hobby, an artistic outlet and a means of learning and self-discovery.

Although their reasons for writing vary, most writers want to be published so they can share their work with others. Getting published requires more than just your talent for putting words to paper, however. It requires a professional approach to targeting markets, selling your work and keeping up with publishing trends.

This, the 63rd edition of *Writer's Market*, will enable you to do that and more. Two articles provide insight into interviewing and book proposal writing. Michael Schumacher's The Interview and Its Uses details different kinds of interviews, their relative advantages and when to use them. Prospective authors who are ready to propose their book ideas to publishers but are not familiar with the intricacies of the task will want to read Writing an Irresistible Book Proposal by Michael Larsen.

For an inside look at the book publishing process, from your first contact to printed books, turn to the Publishers' Roundtable. As part of the Roundtable we surveyed 686 book publishers for information on their submission procedures and the role of agents in the process. Representatives of four book publishers also provide in-depth information about the publishing process at their houses, and they offer opinions on ways writers can improve their chances with book publishers. A reference guide to types of editors is included in the Roundtable. If you've ever been confused about what an acquisitions editor does or why your manuscript has been turned over to a production editor, this guide will help you through the maze. In addition, we've included more information about book publishers' imprints in our listings, so you can identify them quickly and better target your submissions.

Six newly published writers are featured again in First Bylines. Three have recently published their first books, and three, their first articles or stories. They share their experiences and offer advice to new and younger writers eager to follow their leads.

With this edition, author's agents are no longer listed in *Writer's Market*. The volume of mail about agents made it clear to us that the small section of agents' listings was not sufficient to meet writers' needs. In response to the demand for expanded listings and more articles on approaching, evaluating and dealing with author's agents, Writer's Digest Books has developed *Guide to Literary Agents and Art/Photo Reps*. The move gives *Writer's Market* more room for magazine and book publisher listings, along with titles and organizations of interest and a guide to proofreading and copyediting marks.

New to this edition are listings for closed markets. Because of their high profile in the industry, a number of book publishers and consumer magazines are listed with just names, addresses and the information that they declined full listings. We wanted to include these abbreviated listings to let you know the policies of some leading book publishers and magazines. Many of these markets specified why they are closed to submissions and when they did so, we have passed that information along. These listings are intended to keep you informed about the marketplace, not to encourage submissions. We hope you'll respect their desire not to receive unsolicited queries and manuscripts.

Also new to this edition is a section of Canadian and International Book Publishers. Some of the listings previously appeared in the general Book Publishers section, but many are new markets. Writers should be aware of the different policies and procedures of many Canadian and international companies; these are specified in that section. Authors with book proposals best suited for international publishers now have a new, more focused starting point.

Fourteen Close-up interviews with writers and editors will inform, and we hope, inspire you to greater achievements in 1992.

The publishing industry is always changing, with mergers, moves, start-ups and failures. Policies change, too, especially with a change in editor or publisher. We make corrections and updates until the book is sent to the printer, but for information after that time, consult *Writer's Digest* magazine, which records updates to *Writer's Market* listings.

We want your input and ideas to make *Writer's Market* a better resource for you. If you learn of paying markets not listed, let us know about them. If you know someone who could be featured in our First Bylines sections, we'd also like to hear about it. As always, if you learn of new policies or have a complaint about nonpayment or lack of response from a market listed, please write to us about it. Always enclose a self-addressed, stamped envelope with your letter if you expect a reply.

Whatever your writing pursuit, professional or personal, we hope this edition of *Writer's Market* will bring you many opportunities and successes in 1992.

Mark Kissling

Roseann Shaughnessy

How to Use Writer's Market

Before beginning your search for markets to send your writing to, take a moment to read this section. It will help you make full use of the individual listings and will explain the symbols and abbreviations used throughout the book.

The Table of Contents should be your next stop. That way, you'll know where to find all the publishing opportunities for your work.

Check the Glossary for unfamiliar words. Specific symbols and abbreviations are explained in the table on page 5. The most important abbreviation is SASE—self-addressed, stamped envelope. *Always* enclose one when you send unsolicited queries or manuscripts to editors or publishers. This requirement is not included in the individual market listings because it's a "given" that you must follow if you expect to receive a reply.

Review the following sample listing and the explanation section that accompanies it.

(1) BRITISH CAR, P.O. Box 9099, Canoga Park CA 91309. **(2)** (818)710-1234. FAX:(818)710-1877. **(3)** Editor: Dave Destler. **(4)** 50% freelance written. **(5)(6)** A bimonthly magazine covering British cars. "We focus upon the cars built in Britain, the people who buy them, drive them, collect them, love them. Writers must be among the aforementioned. Written by enthusiasts for enthusiasts." **(7)** Estab. 1985. **(8)** Circ. 30,000. **(9)** Pays on publication. Publishes ms an average of 3 months after acceptance. Byline given. Buys all rights, unless other arrangements made. **(10)** Submit seasonal/holiday material 4 months in advance. Query for electronic submissions. **(11)** Reports in 1 month. **(12)** Sample copy $2.95; writer's guidelines for #10 SASE.

(13) Nonfiction: (14) Historical/nostalgic; how-to (on repair or restoration of a specific model or range of models, new techniques or process); humor (based upon a realistic nonfiction situation); interview/profile (famous racer, designer, engineer, etc.); photo feature and technical. "No submissions so specific as to appeal or relate to a very narrow range of readers; no submissions so general as to be out-of-place in a specialty publication." **(15)** Buys 30 mss/year. **(16)** Send complete ms. "Include SASE if submission is to be returned." **(17)** Length: 750-4,500 words. **(18)** Pays $2-5/column inch for assigned articles; pays $2-3/column inch for unsolicited articles. **(19)**

(20)Photos: Send photos with submission. Reviews transparencies and prints. Offers $15-17/photo. Captions and identification of subjects required. Buys all rights, unless otherwise arranged.

(21)Columns/Departments: Update (newsworthy briefs of interest, not too timely for bimonthly publication), approximately 50-175 words. Buys 20 mss/year. Send complete mss.

(22)Tips: "Thorough familiarity of subject is essential. *British Car* is read by experts and enthusiasts who can see right through superficial research. Facts are important, and must be accurate. Writers should ask themselves, 'I know I'm interested in this story, but will most *British Car*'s readers appreciate it?' "

(1) Symbols, names and addresses. One or more symbols (*, ‡, □) may precede the name and address of the publication or market; check the key on page 5 for their meanings. (A double dagger signifies a new listing.) We differentiate between post office and other boxes. Post office boxes are listed as P.O. Box.

(2) Phone and FAX numbers. A phone number or fax number in a listing does not mean the market accepts phone queries. Make a phone query only when your story's timeliness would be lost by following the usual procedures. As a rule, don't call or fax information unless you have been invited to do so.

(3) Contact names. In most listings, names of contact persons are given in the first paragraph or under the bold subheadings. Address your query or submission to a specific name when possible. If the name is not easily recognizable by gender, use the full name (e.g., Dear Dale Smith:). If no contact name is given, consult a sample copy. As a last resort, you can address your query to "Articles Editor" or what is appropriate. For more information, read Approaching Markets in the Business of Writing.

(4) Size of market. A market's general openness to writers is indicated by the percentage of freelance material used or by the percentage of published manuscripts from new, un-agented writers.

(5) Copyright information. Because most publications are copyrighted, the information is only given in this spot when the publication is *not* copyrighted. For information on copyrighting your own work, see Rights and the Writer in the Business of Writing.

(6) Emphasis and readership. A description of the market provides the focus and audience.

(7) Established date. We attempt to include the established date for *all* listings. Book publishers and magazines with older established dates tend to be more stable markets.

(8) Circulation. The figures listed are the sum of subscriptions plus shelf sales.

(9) Rights purchased. General business policies give information about rights purchased and time of payment. **Pays on acceptance** is a policy we favor, so we highlight it in the listings with bold lettering. Book publishers list average royalty rates. See Rights and the Writer in the Business of Writing for more information.

(10) Submission requirements. Submission requirements include how far in advance to submit seasonal material and whether or not previously published material will be considered. Send manuscripts or queries to one market at a time unless it indicates simultaneous submissions are OK. If you send your manuscript to more than one market at a time, mention in your cover letter that it is a simultaneous submission. Electronic submissions are mentioned only if the market accepts them. See Writing Tools in the Business of Writing for more information.

(11) Reporting time. Reporting times indicate how soon a market will respond to your query or manuscript, but times listed are approximate. Quarterly publications, book publishers, literary magazines and all new listings may be slower to respond. Wait three weeks beyond the stated reporting time before you send a polite inquiry. If no reporting time is listed, wait 2 months for a reply.

(12) Writer's guidelines and sample copies. If you're interested in writing for a particular market, request the writer's guidelines and/or a sample copy if the market indicates availability. "Writer's guidelines for SASE" means that a business-size envelope (#10) with one first class stamp will be adequate. You should request a sample copy if you are unable to find the publication at a newsstand or library. A sample copy or book catalog is often available for a 9 × 12 self-addressed envelope with a specified number of stamps or International Reply Coupons. Most publishers will send, at no extra charge, writer's guidelines with sample copies if you request them.

(13) Subheads. Subheads in bold (Nonfiction, Photos, etc.) guide you to requirements for those types of materials.

(14) Types of nonfiction needed. The specific material desired (and often material *not* desired) is listed. Follow the guidelines. Do not send fiction to a publication that only uses nonfiction; do not send a children's book manuscript to a publisher of men's adventure novels.

(15) Manuscripts purchased. The number of manuscripts purchased per issue or per year will give you an idea of how easy or difficult it may be to sell your work to a particular market. With new listings, these figures may change dramatically depending on the submissions they receive or changes in policy.

(16) Submission information. If the market wants to see queries, that's what you should send. The same goes for outlines and sample chapters, etc. Don't send a complete manuscript unless the listing indicates it's acceptable.

(17) Word length. Editors know the length of most material they buy; follow their range of words or pages. If your manuscript is longer or shorter (by a wide margin) than the stated requirements, find another market.

(18) Payment rates. Payment ranges tell you what the market usually paid at the time *Writer's Market* was published.

(19) Expenses. Whether a market sometimes or usually pays expenses of writers on assignment is listed. No mention is made when a market does *not* pay expenses.

(20) Photos and (21) Columns/departments, fiction, poetry and fillers. Needs, rates and policies for specified material.

(22) Tips. Helpful suggestions are listed under the subhead Tips in many listings. They describe the best way to submit manuscripts or give special insight into needs and preferences of the market.

Key to Symbols and Abbreviations

‡ New listing in all sections
* Subsidy publisher in Book Publishers section
☐ Cable TV market in Scriptwriting section
ms-manuscript; **mss**-manuscripts
b&w-black and white (photo)
SASE-self-addressed, stamped envelope
SAE-self-addressed envelope
IRC-International Reply Coupon, for use on reply mail in countries other than your own.
FAX-a communications system used to transmit documents over the telephone lines.

(See Glossary for definitions of words and expressions used in writing/publishing.)

The Interview and Its Uses

by Michael Schumacher

People. It's difficult to imagine any work of nonfiction without them.

They add motion and sound and color and life to nonfiction. They flesh out the most skeletal of ideas. They give readers someone to listen to, empathize or disagree with, identify with or believe in. They're measuring sticks, sounding boards. Even inanimate objects come to life when they are surrounded by people.

Interviews bring people into nonfiction. Through interviews we exchange information, listen to opinions, enjoy anecdotes and learn more about other people's characters—all of which we are able to pass along to our readers. In every sense, interviews are literary conduits.

Meeting people and making some kind of art out of their remarks is the core of interviewing. By art, I don't necessarily mean that you should be soliciting comments or quotations that are highbrow or stylistically mind-boggling; to enter into any conversation with those goals in mind is both arrogant and silly, and you are likely to leave the interview with the tinny echo of prepared or predictable statements ringing in your ears. What I mean is that there is an art to preparing for a formal interview, carrying on that conversation, and extracting from it remarks that reflect well upon you, on the person speaking and on the topic being addressed.

Writers use interviews in a myriad of ways, but let us look at four main uses for interviews:

- **support quotes** for news stories, features, magazine articles and nonfiction books;
- **research and background information;**
- **personality profiles;** and
- **the question/answer interview.**

The greatest percentage of interviews are conducted for the first two categories on this list. For example, if you are a journalist assigned to write an article about a new method of cancer treatment, you will want to talk to a number of experts on every aspect of that treatment. Not only will those authorities provide you with important information that gives you a better understanding of the treatment itself, but you will also be able to use their words, in direct quotation, to support what you write about in the narrative of your text. No writer can possibly be an authority on every topic he or she chooses to write about, and even if it were possible, readers would demand a feeling of consensus—or, with controversial or provocative issues, a sense of argument—before they would accept what the writer was presenting in the article.

Support quotes

Support quotes provide that sense of consensus or argument. For example, before Mark Dowie wrote *We Have A Donor*, his study of organ transplantation practices today, he interviewed a number of internationally recognized authorities on numerous aspects of transplantation. Much of the discussion was used for research purposes—for gathering

Michael Schumacher has interviewed and written profiles on Raymond Carver (Carver's last interview, out of which developed a warm friendship), Norman Mailer, Joseph Heller, Mike Royko, Bob Greene, Kurt Vonnegut and many others. His work has appeared in Playboy, Writer's Digest, Chicago Tribune, Chicago Sun Times, local newspapers and little/literary magazines. This article is excerpted from his book, Creative Conversations (Writer's Digest Books).

information needed for the author to discuss the history and nature of transplantation — but when Dowie addressed the controversial legal and ethical issues associated with transplantation in his book, he needed authoritative voices to passionately discuss the issues.

"Altogether, I talked to about 100 people for the book," Dowie says, adding that many of his conversations were very brief, often amounting to his asking only a question or two. Using support quotes for a book, he says, is different from employing the same kind of quotes in magazine articles. "You have to be more selective when you're writing for magazines. You use fewer quotes. In the book, I used all of the quotes that were good."

In their published form, support quotes should be attributed to the speaker. Without attribution, the speaker's words lose much of their credibility and punch. Unfortunately, in the post-Watergate era of investigative reporting, attribution has become the focus of a major debate. Sources will occasionally agree to speak for the record only on the condition that their names not be used in the published article. This issue is problematic: Editors, understandably squeamish about off-the-record or confidential sources at a time when journalists and publications are losing landmark libel cases, nevertheless encourage their reporters to bring back the BIG story, which so often hinges on information provided by a confidential source. This is an issue debated often by writers.

Background information

Unlike interviews conducted for support quotes, interviews intended for research or background information may result in a source's not being quoted at all. Let's say your local newspaper has asked you to write a feature story on the topic of growing raspberries. You don't know the first thing about raspberries (other than the fact that they're dark red or black, and you like them on French vanilla ice cream), so you decide to contact several area growers. For the most part, your interview will be conducted for the purpose of gathering information on where raspberries grow best, how one cultivates them, and so on. In writing your article, you will use the information you obtained in the interviews, but to attribute a direct quote of the obvious ("Raspberries taste good on French vanilla ice cream," says Mrs. Smith) is not only pointless, but it can undermine your story by making you look as if you're "talking down" to your readers.

On other occasions, you might be using these interviews as research for other interviews. If, for example, you've been asked to write a profile of rock star Mick Jagger, you might want to interview Keith Richards, his longtime band member and co-writer of most of his songs, for insights into Jagger's life and personality. Some of what Richards tells you may wind up being the foundation for the questions you would eventually ask Jagger himself. You may also quote Richards in your article (his love/hate relationship with Jagger has been the spice of many articles about Jagger, Richards or the Rolling Stones), or you may agree to use him as "deep background," that is, an unattributed source of information. Either way, his insights would be invaluable to your article.

Personality profile

The third main use for interviews, the personality or celebrity profile, has become one of the most popular forms of nonfiction in the newspaper and magazine businesses. People seem never to grow tired of reading about the actions or thoughts of people in the public light. The profile focuses on one person, attempting to show as many sides of that person as is possible within a limited amount of space.

Writing a profile today can be quite a challenge, since editors are calling for short articles, such as those found in magazines like *People*, more than they are soliciting the lengthy, in-depth profiles featured in publications like *The New Yorker*. With television competing for coverage of the same profile subjects, the writer is put in the position of finding something original or new to say about a profile subject in very little space. As a result, the writer must be creative in approach, well versed on the person being profiled and adept at gaining the kind of quotes necessary for a fresh, interesting angle to the profile.

A newspaper once asked me to write a 750-word profile of Norman Mailer for its Sunday book review section. As anyone who has interviewed this author can tell you, Mailer, an eloquent interviewee, is quite capable of spending more than 750 words in answering a *single question* in a clear, concise and interesting way. The trick to my writing a successful profile for this paper was to find a very specific angle, interview Mailer on that angle, and break down his answers in a reasonable mixture of narrative, indirect quotes and direct quotes, as well as to find a way to provide the color and setting to give the sense that the reader was sitting in on our conversation.

Q&A

The question/answer interview, designed to read like a typescript of a conversation, was an immensely popular form of the published interview in the 1970s. Though it is not as favored today as it was during that decade, the question/answer interview still offers reader benefits that might be unavailable in the profile or feature article. For one thing, it is more direct, so the reader is seeing more of the person's words than would be the case if the writers were filling space with description and background. In longer Q&A's, the topic focus doesn't have to be so tight. Readers draw their own conclusions more in this format than in profiles, where author interpretation is an integral part of the writing.

To be effective, question/answer-style interviews must be conducted with people already in the public eye, or on topics already familiar to a majority of readers, since very little space in this format is devoted to introductory remarks or background information. Interviewers assume that their readers know something about their subject, and they proceed to use the interview to build upon what the public already knows or to fill in the blanks in areas that may be unfamiliar to the reader.

Question/answer interviews present their own unique challenges to the writer. They have to flow smoothly and "sound" as if they are direct transcriptions of a single, relatively short conversation, even if they are the result of many hours of interviews involving several sessions. Transitions in the conversation have to be crisp, and each answer has to be complete. In this use of the interview, the writer employs an editor's skills as well as those of a writer.

How you intend to use the material you gather from your interview will influence the way you design and conduct the interview itself. For an in-depth profile, you would ask a broader range of questions than you might ask if you were looking for support quotes focusing on one topic. For a question/answer interview, you would probably solicit more detailed, quotable anecdotes than you might look for if you were gathering only background information. Despite the different uses, the basic interviewing techniques vary only slightly from one use to another.

How interviews are conducted

As we will see, how, when and where interviews are conducted can greatly influence the information or quotes you gather during an interview. For the most part, interviewers have only a marginal say in these factors, but with good planning and experience, how you conduct your interviews should not affect your pursuit of strong, creative results.

Interviews can be conducted in three ways:
- **In person.** The in-person or on-location interview finds the interviewer and interviewee meeting face to face at an agreed-upon location (or at the site of a news event) for the purpose of formally discussing topics of interest to a general readership. Because it affords the interviewer the opportunity to see as well as hear an interview subject in a given setting, the in-person conversation is the optimum method of conducting an interview. Unless

special arrangements are made prior to the interview, it should be "for the record," with the mutual understanding that any information obtained by the interviewer will be used in one form or another for publication.

● **Telephone.** The telephone interview employs the same basic techniques as in-person conversation; it is preferable when time or distance factors make a personal visit impractical or impossible. In many cases, the telephone interview is ideal when the interviewer is checking facts, looking for a single piece of research, or searching for a brief quotation or two; it can also be employed when the interviewer is asking brief follow-up questions to those addressed during an initial in-person interview.

● **Mail.** The mail interview, which may be written or taped, involves the interviewer's sending an interviewee questions to which he or she responds. Questionnaires and surveys, used primarily for research or round-up style articles, are the most popular forms of mail interviews, although entire question/answer interviews have been conducted in this manner.

An interviewer doesn't have to choose one particular method of conducting an interview for each article he or she is writing. It's quite common for a writer to use two or even all three methods when working on a single article. For example, I used all three methods in an interview I conducted with novelists Louise Erdrich and Michael Dorris. I talked with Erdrich in person for an hour in Chicago before we were joined by her husband, and then I talked with Erdrich and Dorris together for another hour. I followed up those conversations with separate telephone interviews. Finally, still needing to have another question or two answered and a few clarified, I mailed them the needed questions, as well as an edited transcript of our prior conversations for their review. Since I was not pressed by a tight deadline on the interview, I was afforded the chance to make the conversation, to be published in question/answer format, as in-depth and conclusive as possible. Using all three methods of interviewing gave me a chance to follow up my questions, and my subjects the opportunity to color in or clarify their answers. The result was an interview that was satisfactory to all of us.

Types of interviewers

All successful interviewers have their own styles of preparing for, conducting and writing up interviews, those styles dependent upon factors such as the interviewers' personalities and the publications they are writing for. A writer for *The Saturday Evening Post*, for instance, might take an entirely different approach to interviewing a profile subject from that of a writer for *Mother Jones*; not only do the two publications take different approaches to the profiles they publish, but it could be argued that the publications attract different types of writers.

Some interviewers thrive on hard-line questioning and almost combative interviews, while others are loath to ask a semipointed question. An investigative reporter's approach to an interview will differ from that taken by a writer of "puff" pieces or soft news features; this will be quite evident when you're researching a potential interview subject and witness the different angles and approaches to that subject taken by different writers.

To be effective, it is crucial that you have as good an understanding as possible of who you are as an interviewer and writer. Part of this knowledge will be the result of your professional experiences, while another part will be inextricably connnected to your personality and temperament, as well as to your values and goals as a writer. This is not to imply that you should be content to stand pat as a writer or person; the best writers are always seeking ways to expand their artistic and creative horizons by taking on new challenges in style and content. However, it's important that you know yourself and approach an interview on your own terms. If you're not the type of person who is able to pose tough questions, over and over, to reluctant or hostile interviewees, you should not propose and research an article on area politicians suspected of taking bribes; you may get the assignment, but you won't turn into a Mike Wallace overnight, and the interview you conduct will probably disappoint an editor. Editors have long memories and are quick to categorize their contributors, and if you disappoint them once, it's unlikely that you'll get a chance to redeem yourself. Conversely, if you satisfy them by submitting well-written pieces on topics that you're comfortable writing about, you will be on the way to a lasting, profitable relationship with those editors.

Writing an Irresistible Book Proposal

by Michael Larsen

Would you like to be paid to produce a book that you would also love to write? If this is an offer you can't refuse, then you have to offer publishers a proposal they can't refuse.

No one technique for writing a proposal can encompass the broad range of nonfiction books: how-tos, exposes, issue books, biographies, photography, humor and reference books. This approach has evolved during the 19 years that my partner, Elizabeth Pomada, and I have been agents, and it continues to evolve.

Although it can be shorter or longer, a proposal generally ranges from 35-70 pages, and its primary functions are as a selling tool and a writing tool.

As a selling tool, the proposal uses as few words as possible to generate as much enthusiasm as possible for your book. It has to answer every question an editor or anyone else in the house may have about you. Your proposal must give a publisher as many ways as possible to say yes to your book, but not a single reason to say no.

As a writing tool, a proposal is a map. Preparing a solid outline will enable you and your editor to see where you are going. Writing one or two sample chapters will enable you to see whether you can and really want to write the book—while also giving you an idea of how long it will take.

Books are sold in one of two ways. A complete manuscript is usually required for novels, especially first novels. But if you prove that you can research, organize and write nonfiction, you can sell a book with a proposal consisting of an introduction, a chapter-by-chapter outline and one or two sample chapters.

Keep in mind that this is the order in which the proposal will be read, not the order in which you have to write it.

The introduction

The introduction has three parts: the Overview, Resources Needed to Complete the Book, and About the Author.

The overview may be the most important part of the proposal, making or breaking your chances for further consideration.

Ideally, the first page should only have two paragraphs. Start half way down the page, and hook the editor to the subject with the single most exciting, compelling thing that you can say about the subject: a quote, event, anecdote, statistic, idea or joke. You may not figure out what this subject hook is until you have almost finished writing the proposal.

The second paragraph of the proposal, the book hook, includes the title, selling handle and length. These hook editors to the book by giving them the essence of the book and why it will sell.

The title and, if you need one, subtitle, must tell and *sell*. They must say what the book is and give book buyers an irresistible reason for purchasing it.

Michael Larsen *is a partner in Michael Larsen/Elizabeth Pomada Literary Agents, the San Francisco Bay Area's oldest literary agency. Since 1972, the agency has sold books to more than 30 publishers. He is the author of* How to Write a Book Proposal *and* How to Write with a Collaborator *(Writer's Digest Books), in collaboration with Hal Bennett. Paragon House will publish a revised and updated edition of his book,* Literary Agents: How to Get and Work with the Right One for You, *in Fall 1992.*

The book's selling handle is crucial to its success. One sales representative estimated that he spent an average of 14 seconds selling a book to a bookseller. Just as sales reps need one line of copy that will convince booksellers to take a chance, editors need a short description to "sell" the book inhouse. The *best* selling handle is a sentence that begins: "(The title of the book) will be the first book to . . ." If you have a difficult time summarizing your book this way, it may be an indication that you haven't really narrowed down your subject.

The next sentence should read: "The complete manuscript will contain XXX pages and XX illustrations" (if it will have illustrations). You will estimate these numbers as you write the outline. Most nonfiction runs 200-400 pages at 250 words per page or 50,000-100,000 words.

A list of the book's other special features should include elements such as tone, structure, anecdotes, checklists, exercises or sidebars. If it's appropriate, use humor; funny is money.

Include identification of a well-known authority who will write the introduction if you will use one. Editors look for authoritative and experienced writers to tackle subjects. If, for example, you want to write a health book and you're not a doctor, try to collaborate with one. If that's not possible, get an introduction from someone whose name will add to the book's credibility and salability.

If the book will raise technical or legal questions, add a sentence about what you have done to answer them.

If the book's on a specialized subject, find an expert to verify it for you and mention who the person is. Publishers are extremely concerned about lawsuits, so if your book will present legal problems, give the name of the experienced literary attorney you hired to go over it.

Include information about any back matter—appendices, glossary, bibliography, notes, or an index—that will add to the book's value as a research tool.

Then list the groups of readers waiting for your book, starting with the largest one. Be sure to include any information about large clubs or organizations that have members who would be interested in the book's subject. (For instance, a book on single parenting might be marketed to members of Parents Without Partners.) If your book will have adoption potential, list the courses and the teachers who said they will adopt it.

To enhance your book's commercial potential, describe any subsidiary rights possibilities: book clubs (listed in the trade directory *Literary Market Place*), movies, audio and videocassettes, foreign sales, electronic rights. If you use an agent, your agent will try to keep as many of these rights as possible for you. Nonetheless, make the book sound recyclable in as many forms and media as possible.

Publishers don't like literary one-night stands. If your book can be a series or lends itself to sequels, mention the other books. This might lead to a multi-book deal that will make you and your project more important to the house.

A list of what you will do to promote the book can also be an important part of the proposal. Create a marketing plan that you will carry out to promote the book. This list can't be too long. If the book lends itself, one of the best openers may be: "To coincide with the publication of the book, the author will present seminars (or lectures) in the following X cities: . . ." Follow this with a list of the major cities around the country you can get yourself to, and the number of copies you think you can sell at these events.

A list of books that will compete with and complement yours is important because the editor must have that information to make a decision on your manuscript. List the books that will compete with yours—title, author, publisher, year—and in a phrase or sentence, say what each book does and fails to do. End this list with a statement of how your book will be different or better than the competition. A list of books on the same subject that don't compete with yours will prove that there's interest in the subject.

Resources needed to complete the book

Starting on a new page, list out-of-pocket expenses such as travel, illustrations, permissions, or an introduction, and a round figure for how much they will cost. Don't include normal expenses such as typing and phone calls. If the book will require updating, indicate when this will happen.

The last sentence should read: "The manuscript will be completed X months after the receipt of the advance." If time is the only resource you need, add this sentence to the end of the overview.

About the author

Your bio is your opportunity to prove that you are qualified to write the book. On one new page (most of us have led one-page lives), tell editors everything you want them to know about you in order of importance to the sale of your book.

Include any media experience. If you have an audio or videocassette of yourself in action, mention it. If you will go to New York at your expense to meet with interested editors, say so. It will add to an editor's sense of your commitment to the book.

To avoid a page full of "I's" and to suggest modesty, write your bio in the third person. The exception to this rule: Write your bio in the first person if you want to describe your personal sense of mission about the project.

On a blank page behind the bio, affix a 5×7 or 8×10 personal photograph if appropriate to your proposal.

The chapter-by-chapter outline

The chapter-by-chapter outline for most books starts with a page listing the chapters in the book and the page of the proposal the outline is on. Some exceptions:

If you're proposing an encyclopedia, the outline will be the list of entries.

If you want to write a guidebook to 10 great cities, list the cities and what each chapter will cover.

Most books require no more than a page of outline in prose for every chapter of the book. Aim for one line of outline for every page of text you envision. If your chapters will range from 20 to 40 pages each, provide the editor with about one page of information (in three or four paragraphs) for every chapter. Give each chapter a sense of structure in one of two ways:

● Start the outline with a sentence saying the chapter is divided into X parts, then write about each part.

● Divide the chapter into parts *as* you write it by using the following phrases:

The chapter starts, opens, begins with . . .

The next or following part or segment of the chapter . . .

The chapter ends, concludes, closes with . . .

Here are three tips to help ease your way through the outline:

● Write about what will be in the chapter. Don't write about the subject. That's what the sample chapters are for.

● Use "outline" verbs such as describe, explain, examine, discuss and analyze. Vary the verbs as much as possible.

● Find the right hooks for the beginning and end of every chapter to entice readers into the chapter and to encourage them to go on to the next one.

After you have the written the outline, go back through and guess how long each part of the chapter will be. Add these numbers up to arrive at the length of the chapter.

If the book will have illustrations, add "photo" or "drawing" after every person, event or instruction to be illustrated. Put the number of pages and illustrations on the same line as the title of the chapter.

Start each chapter on a new page that begins:

Chapter X
How to Write an Outline (XX pages, X photos)
After you have finished the outline, add up the number of pages and illustrations in the book. These are the numbers you will use in the book hook. These numbers will probably change in the course of writing the book, but being definite will help convince an editor that you have thought the project through.

Sample chapters

You may not need any sample chapters if you have already written a book or one or more articles on the subject that are long enough and strong enough to convince an editor that you can write the book.

If you're writing a reference book, submit at least 10% of the text.

If you're planning a book of photography, submit the introduction to the book, 20% of the prints and captions, and if possible, sheets of duplicate slides for as much of the book as you can prepare. If you are able, send four sample pages with text and illustrations so an editor can get a feeling for your vision of the book.

If you want to write a humor book, send at least 30% of the text.

If you want to write a guidebook to 10 great cities, you only need one sample chapter.

For most books, editors like to see two chapters or 40-50 pages of sample material. One might be an introductory chapter, the other a chapter representative of the rest of the book. Send the two chapters you can write best and feel will most excite an editor about the book. If you're writing an inspirational story that should read like a novel and will have the greatest impact if the editor sees all of it, have the complete manuscript ready to submit if you can. If you send the complete manuscript, you can send a one-page synopsis instead of an outline with it.

Poetry and carpentry

The most thrilling writing is an inseparable, indistinguishable blend of poetry and carpentry, art and craft, vision and fact. It's also the result of many drafts. As Mario Puzo once said: "The art of writing is rewriting."

Keep revising your proposal until you're convinced it's as well conceived and crafted as you can make it. Your goal is to keep readers turning the pages by making your proposal as enjoyable as it is informative.

Getting feedback

Share your proposal with your professional network before you send it to an agent or editor. Five kinds of readers can help in evaluating your proposal:

- Friends and family will tell you that they love it, which is fine because you deserve encouragement.
- Potential buyers of the book can also help evaluate content. Would they buy it if they saw the book in a store?
- Literate, objective readers will help ensure that your proposal is well written.
- Experts on the subject can make an informed judgment about the content of your proposal.
- Finally, a devil's advocate is highly desirable. Their ability to spot every word, sentence, paragraph, chapter, punctuation, character and idea that can either be improved or removed make devil's advocates worth their weight in royalties.

The joys of nonfiction

Once you've written one book, you're no longer just a writer with an idea, you're an author! Once you've joined the club, you can go more easily from book to book and from advance to advance. You may want every book you write to be on a different topic, but if you choose the right angle, you can carve a career out of it.

This is what one of our writers, Jay Conrad Levinson, is doing with his Guerrilla Marketing series for entrepreneurs (which also has excellent advice about promoting books). His Guerrilla Marketing books have led to collaborations on Guerrilla Financing and Guerrilla Selling, which in turn are generating sequels.

To be a successful writer, you—with the creative suggestions of your agent and editor— have to keep brainstorming new ideas and writing proposals. Once you have proven that you can write a book, your editor won't need as elaborate a proposal as the one described above.

Thinking big

To make the most of the opportunities in writing nonfiction books:

● Think globally. As with many other American industries, fewer than 10 companies control more than half the publishing industry. They are all international conglomerates looking for books that will be of interest around the world.

● Think multimedia. Bernie Rath, the president of the American Booksellers Association, envisions the day when hardcovers, paperbacks, graphic novels, audiocassettes, videocassettes, CD-ROMs and laser disks of the same book will be sold on the same shelf. So when you're considering what to write about, try to find ideas for books that you can promote and recycle in as many media as possible.

The word multimedia has another meaning for the 90s. It is now possible to combine words, images, graphics, audio and video on a computer. The creative and financial potential of this fusion are unexplored and incalculable.

The Business of Writing

Trends in the publishing industry over the past year continue to be mixed for writers. Whether or not there was or is a recession, advertising revenues for magazines are generally down. This has resulted in the demise of several consumer publications, including a few high-budget recent launches.

Some international conglomerates are also wondering what has happened to profit margins in trade book sales. Discouraged by an always unpredictable market, many are turning to textbooks and business publications for more acceptable profit levels.

Bret Easton Ellis' shocker, *American Psycho*, was dropped by Simon & Schuster despite a hefty advance paid to and kept by the author. Public reaction to early released excerpts was varied, but Simon & Schuster may have been worried about complaints against the author's treatment of women, the homeless and other controversial subjects. In any case, Vintage picked up *American Psycho*, and the book was published after all.

More consumer publications are changing their policies for fiction submission and acceptance. Due to the volume some magazines are facing, they have begun to respond *only* on acceptance. Submissions are not sent back when rejected. Writers should follow submission guidelines in these individual listings; enclosing a SASE is unnecessary.

Most freelance writers concentrate on their writing and overlook the business side. While writing is your main pursuit, as a writer you should also keep an eye on business developments, such as the above examples, that will affect your livelihood. Plan to invest some time in managing the business side of your writing even if you just want to make a little extra money with it. The following information will help you keep current with the industry's latest developments and help you better manage your writing.

Marketing your manuscripts

Writers often find interesting stories to write about and then begin to look for a suitable publisher or magazine. While this approach is common, it reduces your chances of success. Instead, try choosing categories that interest you and study those sections in *Writer's Market*. Select several listings that you consider good prospects for your type of writing. Sometimes the individual listings will help you generate ideas too.

Next, make a list of the potential markets for each idea. Make the initial contact with markets using the method stated in the market listings.

If you exhaust your list of possibilities, don't give up. Reevaluate the idea, revise it, or try another angle. Continue developing ideas and approaching markets with them. Identify and rank potential markets for an idea and continue the process, but don't approach a market a second time until you've received a response to your first submission.

Prepare for rejection and the sometimes lengthy process that publishing takes. When a submission is returned, check the file folder of potential markets for that idea. Cross off the current market and immediately mail an appropriate submission to the next market on your list. If the editor has given you suggestions or reasons as to why the manuscript was not accepted, you might want to incorporate these when revising your manuscript. In any event, remember the first editor didn't reject *you*, but simply chose not to buy your product. A rejection only means that your particular piece did not fit the needs of the publisher at that time. Veteran writers also find it helpful to have several projects going at once to avoid dwelling on the one that's out for consideration.

Writing tools

Like anyone involved in a trade or business, you need certain tools and supplies to produce your product or provide your service. While writers compose their work in a variety of ways—ranging from pencil and legal pad to expensive personal computers—there are some basics you'll need for your writing business. We've also included information about some you may want in the future.

Typewriter. Many writers use electric or electronic typewriters that produce either pica or elite type. Pica type has 10 characters to a horizontal inch and elite has 12; both have six single-spaced, or three double-spaced lines to a vertical inch. The slightly larger pica type is easier to read and many editors prefer it, although they don't object to elite.

Editors do dislike, and often refuse to read, manuscripts that are single-spaced, typed in all caps or in an unusual type style like script, italic or Old English. Reading these manuscripts is hard on the eyes. You should strive for clean, easy-to-read manuscripts and correspondence that reflect a professional approach to your work and consideration for your reader.

Use a good black (never colored) typewriter ribbon and clean the keys frequently. If the enclosures of the letters a, b, d, e, g, o, etc., become inked in, a cleaning is overdue.

Even the best typists make errors. *Occasional* retyping over erasures is acceptable, but strikeovers give your manuscript a sloppy, careless appearance. Hiding typos with large splotches of correction fluid makes your work look amateurish; use it sparingly. Some writers prefer to use typing correction film for final drafts. Better yet, a self-correcting electric typewriter with a correction tape makes typos nearly invisible. Whatever method you use, it's best to retype a page that has several noticeable corrections. Sloppy typing is taken by many editors as a sign of sloppy work habits—and the possibility of careless research and writing.

Personal computers and word processors. More and more writers are working on personal computers. A personal computer can make a writer's work much more efficient. Revising and editing are usually faster and easier on a computer than on a typewriter, and it eliminates tedious retyping. Writers also can rely on their computers to give them fresh, readable copy as they revise rough drafts into finished manuscripts. For some writers, a fairly inexpensive word processor is adequate to produce manuscripts and letters; others may have additional uses and want computers with more capabilities.

When a manuscript is written on a computer, it can come out of the computer in three ways: as hard copy from the computer's printer; stored on a removable 5¼″ floppy disk or 3½″ diskette that can be read by other computers; or as an electronic transfer over telephone lines using a modem (a device that allows one computer to transmit to another).

● Hard copy—Most editors are receptive to computer printout submissions if they look like neatly-typed manuscripts. Some older and cheaper printers produce only a low-quality dot-matrix printout with hard-to-read, poorly shaped letters and numbers. Many editors are not willing to read these manuscripts. (In addition, most editors dislike copy with even, or justified, right margins.) New dot-matrix printers, however, produce near letter-quality (NLQ) printouts that are almost indistinguishable from a typewritten manuscript. These are acceptable to editors, along with true letter-quality submissions. Remember that readability is the key. Whether you use a $100 24-pin dot-matrix printer or a $1,000 laser printer doesn't matter to the editor. He just wants to be able to read your manuscript easily.

When you submit hard copy to an editor, be sure to use quality paper. Some computer printers use standard bond paper that you'd use in a typewriter. Others are equipped with a tractor-feed that pulls continuous form paper with holes along the edges through the machine. If you use continuous form paper, be sure to remove the perforated tabs on each side and separate the pages.

• Disk—You'll find that more publishers are accepting or even requesting submissions on disk. A few publishers pay more for electronic submissions, and some won't accept anything but submissions on disk. Eventually, industry observers say electronic submissions will be the norm, just as typewritten submissions became the norm over handwritten manuscripts earlier in the century.

• Modem—Some publishers who accept submissions on disk also will accept electronic submissions by modem. This is the fastest method of getting your manuscript to the publisher. When you receive an assignment, ask about the editor's computer requirements. You'll need to work out submission information before you send something by modem, but you'll probably find that even computer systems you thought were incompatible can communicate easily by modem.

Because most editors also want hard copy along with an electronic submission, you may wonder why you should even consider using a disk or modem. Editors like electronic submissions because they can revise manuscripts quickly as well as save typesetting expenses. Most want a backup hard copy in case there is a problem with a computer submission, while others prefer to edit the hard copy first and then revise the electronic version from it. If you have a particularly timely topic or a manuscript that needs to be submitted quickly, a disk or modem submission is an asset that also can save you and the editor time on deadline.

Publishers who accept submissions by disk or modem have this phrase in their listings: Query for electronic submissions. We give the information this way because you'll need to speak with someone before you send anything by these methods. Also, many magazines and publishers change system requirements each year as equipment and software is updated. Instead of listing information that you may find is outdated when you begin to send the submission, we have put just general information in the listing.

Facsimile machines and boards. Publishers' facsimile machine numbers are in listings. These machines, known commonly as fax machines, transmit copy across phone lines. Those publishers who wanted to list their facsimile machine numbers have done so.

Between businesses, the fax has come into standard daily use for materials that have to be sent quickly. In addition, some public fax machines are being installed in airports, hotels, libraries and even grocery stores. Unfortunately, the convenience of the machines has also given rise to "junk" fax transmissions, including unwanted correspondence and advertisements.

The information we have included is not to be used to transmit queries or entire manscripts to editors, unless they specifically request it. Although some machines transmit on regular bond paper, most still use a cheaper grade that is difficult to write on, making it unsuitable for editing. In most cases, this paper also fades with time, an undesirable characteristic for a manuscript. Writers should continue to use traditional means for sending manuscripts and queries and use the fax number we list only when an editor asks to receive correspondence by this method.

Some computer owners also have fax boards installed to allow transmissions to their computer screens or computer printers. Unless the fax board can operate independently from the computer's main processor, an incoming fax forces the user to halt whatever work is in process until the transmission ends. You should never send anything by this method without calling or arranging with the editor for this type of transmission.

Types of paper. The paper you use must measure 8½×11 inches. That's a standard size and editors are adamant—they don't want unusual colors or sizes. There's a wide range of white 8½×11 papers. The cheaper ones are made from wood pulp. They will suffice, but are not recommended. Editors also discourage the use of erasable bond for manuscripts; typewriter ribbon ink on erasable bond tends to smear when handled and is difficult to write on. Don't use less than a 16 lb. bond paper; 20 lb. is preferred. Your best bet is paper with a 25% cotton fiber content. Its texture shows type neatly and it holds up under erasing and corrections.

You don't need fancy letterhead for your correspondence with editors. Plain bond paper is fine; just type your name, address, phone number and the date at the top of the page — centered or in the right-hand corner. If you want letterhead, make it as simple and business-like as possible. Many quick print shops have standard typefaces and can supply letterhead stationery at a relatively low cost. Never use letterhead for typing your manuscripts; only the first page of queries, cover letters and other correspondence should be typed on letterhead.

Photocopies. Always make copies of your manuscripts and correspondence before putting them in the mail. Don't learn the hard way, as many writers have, that manuscripts get lost in the mail and publishers sometimes go out of business without returning submissions.

You might want to make several copies of your manuscript while it is still clean and crisp. Some writers keep their original manuscript as a file copy and submit good quality photocopies. Submitting copies can save you the expense and effort of retyping a manuscript if it becomes lost in the mail. If you submit a copy, it's a good idea to explain to the editor whether or not you are making a simultaneous (or multiple) submission to several markets. Follow the requirements in the individual listings, and see Approaching Markets later in this article for more detailed information about simultaneous submissions.

Some writers include a self-addressed postcard with a photocopied submission and suggest in their cover letter that if the editor is not interested in the manuscript, it may be tossed out and a reply returned on the postcard. This practice is recommended when dealing with markets outside your country. If you find that your personal computer generates copies more cheaply than you can pay to have them returned, you might choose to send disposable manuscripts. Submitting a disposable manuscript costs the writer some photocopy or computer printer expense, but it can save on large postage bills.

The cost of personal photocopiers is coming down — some run about $500 — but they remain too expensive for many writers to consider purchasing. If you need to make a large number of photocopies, you should ask your print shop about quantity discounts. One advantage of owning a personal computer and printer is that you can quickly print copies of any text you have composed and stored on it.

Assorted supplies. Where will you put all your manuscripts and correspondence? A two- or four-drawer filing cabinet with file folders is a good choice, but some writers find they can make do with manila envelopes and cardboard boxes. It's important to organize and label your correspondence, manuscripts, ideas, submission records, clippings, etc., so you can find them when you need them. See sections on Recording Submissions and Bookkeeping for other helpful hints on keeping records.

You will also need stamps and envelopes; see Mailing Submissions in this section and the U.S. and Canadian Postage by the Page tables on the inside covers of the book. If you decide to invest in a camera to increase your sales, you'll find details on submitting and mailing photos in the sections on Approaching Markets and Mailing Submissions.

Approaching markets

Before submitting a manuscript to a market, be sure you've done the following:

● Familiarize yourself with the publication or other type of market that interests you. Your first sales probably will be to markets you already know through your reading. If you find a listing in *Writer's Market* that seems a likely home for an idea you've been working on, study a sample copy or book catalog to see if your idea fits in with their current topics. If you have a magazine article idea, you may also want to check the *Reader's Guide to Periodical Literature* to be sure the idea hasn't been covered with an article in the magazine during the past year or two. For a book idea, check the *Subject Guide to Books in Print* to see what other books have been published on the subject.

• Always request writer's guidelines if they're available. Guidelines give a publication's exact requirements for submissions and will help you focus your query letter or manuscript. If a publication has undergone editorial changes since this edition of *Writer's Market* went to press, those changes will usually be reflected in its writer's guidelines. Some publications also have theme or other special issues, or an editorial calendar planned in advance that will be included in its guidelines. The response to your request for guidelines or an editorial calendar can also let you know if a publication has folded or if it has an unreasonably long response time.

• Check submission requirements. A publication that accepts only queries may not respond at all to a writer who submits an unsolicited complete manuscript. Don't send an unpublished manuscript to a publication that publishes only reprints, and if you're submitting photos, be sure the publication reviews prints or slides, and find out if they require model releases and captions.

• Always look at the latest issues of a magazine before submitting. You'll find out about focus, article length and have a chance to double-check the editor's name and the publication's address. An editor also is impressed when a writer carefully studies a publication and its requirements before making a submission.

• With unsolicited submissions or correspondence, enclose a self-addressed, stamped envelope (SASE). Editors appreciate the convenience and the savings in postage. Some editorial offices deal with such a large volume of mail that their policies do not allow them to respond to mail without SASEs. If you submit to a market outside your country, enclose a self-addressed envelope (SAE) with International Reply Coupons (IRCs) purchased from the post office. (You don't need to send a SASE if you send a disposable manuscript or your manuscript is an assignment, but be sure you mention in your cover letter if it's a disposable manuscript. If it's an assignment, your cover letter should be short and should state that.)

Those are the basics; now you're ready to learn the details of what you should send when you contact an editor.

Query letters. A query letter is a brief, but detailed letter written to interest an editor in your manuscript. Some beginners are hesitant to query, thinking an editor can more fairly judge an idea by seeing the entire manuscript. Actually, most editors of nonfiction prefer to be queried.

Do your best writing when you sit down to compose your query. There is no query formula that guarantees success, but there are some points to consider when you begin:

• Queries are single-spaced business letters, usually limited to one page. Address the current editor by name, if possible. (If you cannot tell whether an editor is male or female from the name in the listing, address the editor by a full name: Dear Robin Jones:). Don't show unwarranted familiarity by immediately addressing an editor by a first name; follow the editor's lead when responding to your correspondence.

• Your major goal is to convince the editor that your idea would be interesting to the publication's readership and that you are the best writer for the job. Mention any special training or experience that qualifies you to write the article—either as an assignment or on speculation. If you have prior writing experience, you should mention it; if not, there's no need to call attention to the fact. Some editors will also ask to look at clips or tearsheets—actual pages or photocopies of your published work. If possible, submit something related to your idea, either in topic or style.

• Be sure you use a strong opening to pique the editor's interest. Some queries begin with a paragraph that approximates the lead of the intended article.

• Briefly detail the structure of the article. Give some facts and perhaps an anecdote and mention people you intend to interview. Give editors enough information to make them want to know more, but don't feel the need to give them details of the whole story. You want to sell the sizzle now and save the steak for later.

[Address and date]

[Magazine's
name and
address]

Dear Mr. Larson:

If you haven't already prepared it for your "Current News" section, would you be interested in a 500 word item about the new International Women's Air and Space Museum in Centerville, Ohio? It's just opened two rooms of a historic house owned by the Wright Brothers' uncle, Asahel Wright.

Its president, Nancy Hopkins Tier, is one of the last active flyers of the original "99's" group of female pilots whose president was Amelia Earhart when the group was formed in 1929.

I am a freelance writer (female) and private pilot whose latest books include OCEANS OF THE WORLD: Our Essential Resource and THE PRIVATE PILOT'S DICTIONARY AND HANDBOOK, a revision of my first edition published in 1974.

Sincerely,

Kirk Polking

P.S. Although Nancy Tier lives in Connecticut she visits this area for board meetings periodically and a feature article on her career as an early woman pilot might offer more opportunity for human interest material and the museum could be described in a sidebar.

Magazine query. This sample query for a magazine article presents the author's idea and qualifications effectively. Reprinted with permission. Copyright © 1986 by Kirk Polking.

[Address and date]

[Publisher's
name and
address]

Dear Ms. Hill:

The excellent article in TWA's Ambassador magazine, "Small
Presses Flex Big Muscles" gave new hope to all of us who've
written midlist books and have heard the gloomy and oft-re-
preated statement, "The midlist is dead."

By coincidence, CRAZY LADIES is one of the books I brought
home from the ABA. It is a wonderful, literary story--beauti-
fully written, all the characters so vivid!

The manuscript I'm writing you about is a nonfiction called
HIGHER THAN EAGLES, the story of my son, a hang gliding
champion, who overcomes a difficult childhood to accomplish
everything he set out to do in life. Though he died at twenty-
six, we realized later it might not be the length of a man's life
that matters so much, but whether he lived life very well.

The story contrasts the difficult, early years of a stubborn, sin-
gle-minded boy beset by asthma, with his years of triumph,
when he became the U.S., Canadian and British hang gliding
champion. He is the flyer who did all the hang gliding sequences in the Smithsonian Institution's epic, "To Fly," and
he was the subject of a Sports Illustrated article on hang gliding. Though the book focuses on my oldest son, Bobby, it is a
family story told by me and my second son, Chris.

My credits include six published books: four category fiction
and two nonfiction. MANBIRDS: HANG GLIDERS & HANG
GLIDING (Prentice-Hall, 1981) was listed by Library Journal
as one of the 100-best in Science and Technology and FUN
GAMES FOR GREAT PARTIES (Price/Stern/Sloan, 1988) went
into an immediate second printing.

If you'd like to see HIGHER THAN EAGLES, the manuscript
is ready to send.

Very Sincerely,

Maralys Wills

Book query. This sample query for a book presents the author's idea, interest in the book and the author's qualifications. Reprinted with permission. Copyright © 1990 by Maralys Wills.

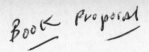
Book Proposal

- If photos are available to accompany the manuscript, let the editor know, but never send original photos, transparencies or artwork on your initial contact with a publisher. Send photocopies or contact sheets instead. You should always have duplicates, so if your material is lost, you haven't lost your only copy.
- Your closing paragraph should include a direct request to do the article; it may specify the date the manuscript can be completed and an approximate length. Don't discuss fees or request advice from the editor at this time. Editors are put off by presumption that they are beyond the point of consideration and to the point of negotiation. Treat the query like a short introductory job interview. You wouldn't presume to discuss money at this early a stage in a job interview; treat the query the same way.
- Fiction is sometimes queried but most fiction editors don't like to make a final decision until they see the complete manuscript. The majority of editors will want to see a synopsis and sample chapters for a book, and a complete manuscript of a short story. If a fiction editor does request a query, briefly describe the main theme and story line, including the conflict and resolution of your story.
- Some writers state politely in their query letters that after a specified date (slightly beyond the listed reporting time), they will assume the editor is not currently interested in their topic and will submit their query elsewhere. It's a good idea to do this only if your topic is a timely one that will suffer if not considered quickly.

For more information about writing query letters and biographical notes, read *How to Write Irresistible Query Letters*, by Lisa Collier Cool (Writer's Digest Books).

Cover letters. A brief cover letter enclosed with your manuscript is helpful in personalizing a submission. If you have previously queried the editor on the article or book, the note should be a brief reminder: "Here is the piece on toxic waste dumping, which we discussed previously. I look forward to hearing from you at your earliest convenience." Don't use the letter to make a sales pitch. Your manuscript must stand on its own at this point.

If you are submitting to a market that considers unsolicited complete manuscripts, your cover letter should tell the editor something about your manuscript and about you—your publishing history and any particular qualifications you have for writing the enclosed manuscript.

Once your manuscript has been accepted, offer to get involved in the editing process. This process varies from magazine to magazine. Most magazine editors don't send galleys to authors before publication. If the magazine regularly sends authors copies of the edited versions of their manuscripts, you should return the galleys as promptly as possible after you've reviewed them. If the editors don't regularly send galleys, you should ask to be involved in the editing process and offer to rewrite your article to the magazine's specifications. Writers almost always prefer to rework their own prose rather than have someone else do it.

Book proposals. Most nonfiction books are sold by book proposal, a detailed look at what you plan to write. Most fiction is sold either by complete manuscript, especially for first-time authors, or by two or three sample chapters.

The nonfiction book proposal includes some combination of a cover or query letter, a synopsis, an outline, author's information sheet and sample chapters. Increasingly, editors also want to see information about the audience for your book and about titles that compete with your proposed book.

Take a look at individual listings to see what submission method editors prefer. If they have not specified, send as much of the following information as you can.

- The cover or query letter should be a short introduction to the material you include in the proposal.
- A synopsis is a brief summary of your book. For nonfiction, it should detail your book's theme and give an overview of the scope of material. If you're sending a synopsis of a novel, cover the basic plot.

- An outline covers your book chapter by chapter. The outline should include all major points covered in each chapter. Some outlines are done in traditional outline form, while others are written in paragraph form. Use whichever form you feel works best for your topic.
- An author's information sheet will give the editor background on you as a writer and on your qualifications to write about the subject.
- Many editors like to see sample chapters, especially for your first book. In fiction it's essential to them; in nonfiction, they like to see sample chapters to see how well you write and develop the ideas from your outline.
- Marketing information is becoming very important in the decision-making process. If you can provide information about the audience for your book and ways the book publisher can reach those people, you will have a better chance of acceptance. If you've written a book on public relations strategies, for instance, you could note that the Public Relations Society of America, with 13,000 members, would be interested. The book publisher could send a review copy or press release to the organization's newsletter editor to let members know about your book.

Editors also want to know what books in the marketplace compete with yours. Look in the *Subject Guide to Books in Print* for titles on the topic of your book. Then check out those titles and write a one- or two-sentence synopsis for each. Be sure to mention how your book will be different from the other titles.

For more tips on putting together a book proposal, see the article Writing an Irresistible Book Proposal, by Michael Larsen, on page 11.

Reprints. You can get more mileage—and money—out of your research and writing time by marketing your previously published material for reprint sales. You may use a photocopy of your original manuscript and/or tearsheets from the publication in which it originally appeared. With your reprint submission, be sure to inform the editor that you are marketing the article as a reprint, especially if you send a photocopy without tearsheets. The editor will also need to know when and in what publication it appeared.

If you market for reprint an article that has not yet been published by the original purchaser, inform editors that it cannot be used before it has made its initial appearance. Give them the intended publication date and be sure to inform them if any changes take place. Note: You can only market these rights if you have not already sold them. See Rights and the Writer for more information.

Photographs and slides. The availability of good quality photos can be a deciding factor when an editor is considering a manuscript. Most publications also offer additional pay for photos accepted with a manuscript. When submitting black and white prints, editors usually want to see 8 × 10 glossy photos, unless they indicate another preference in the listing. The universally accepted format for transparencies is 35mm; few buyers will look at color prints.

On all your photos and slides, you should stamp or print your copyright notice and "Return to:" followed by your name, address and phone number. Rubber stamps are preferred for labeling photos since they are less likely to cause damage. You can order them from many stationery or office supply stores. If you use a pen to write this information on the back of your photos, be careful not to damage the print by pressing too hard or by allowing ink to bleed through the paper. A felt tip pen is best, but you should take care not to put photos or copy together before the ink dries, or it will smear.

- Captions can be typed on a sheet of paper and taped to the back of the prints. Some writers, when submitting several transparencies or photos, number the photos and type captions (numbered accordingly) on a separate 8½ × 11 sheet of paper.
- Submit prints rather than negatives or consider having duplicates made of your slides or transparencies. Don't risk having your original negative or slide lost or damaged when you submit it.

Exploring the Self-Publishing Option

by Tom and Marilyn Ross

As merger mania continues to engulf the publishing industry, markets for book manuscripts shrink even more. There are simply fewer trade publishers today. And because many are now owned by huge conglomerates interested in bottom line profits, they are less likely to take a chance on an unknown writer. Must this necessarily paint a gloomy picture? Not at all. In fact, it may be a blessing in disguise.

Many authors are opting to take control of their destinies and publish their own work. Some enormously popular books began this way: *What Color is Your Parachute?*, *How to Heal Your Life*, and *The Personal Computer Book*, for instance.

But self-publishing isn't for every book or every person. It's tough for fiction and poetry. And even a good nonfiction book may be difficult to independently publish unless it is slanted for a specific niche. Therein lies the secret.

You need a narrowly focused topic to reach your market. A book on dog training, for example, is better than one on animals because you can find and penetrate your target audience. Dog trainers, breeders, pet shops, dog shows—all are rich hunting grounds. Perhaps you can merchandise the book to a dog food manufacturer for a giveaway.

To prosper in self-publishing you must have certain personal characteristics. Writing is only the beginning. Marketing is critical. You must be willing to acquire this knowledge or hire someone who possesses it. Self-discipline is also important because you'll be wearing many hats. A self-publisher is writer, editor, book designer, typesetter, printer, business manager, bookkeeper, order fulfillment clerk and publicist. Although you'll sub-contract some of these functions, you'll act as the construction superintendent. Ultimately, it's your project. It takes time, money and energy.

Be sure your motivation is clear. Most self-publishing ventures are undertaken because the author wants to make a profit. That's fine. Done properly, this can be very lucrative. (Done improperly, you can lose your shirt.) We know self-publishers who earn a whopping 80% on their books. But they work hard for it.

Perhaps your goal is to influence people about a subject you feel strongly about, so you want to do a "cause" book. Or maybe you just hanker to see your name in print. Today many of our clients publish a book as a business-building strategy. These are professionals, corporate executives or entrepreneurs who seek to position themselves as "experts." A book gives them new visibility and credibility.

But whatever your reason, do it right! Educate yourself by reading. When you elect to self-publish, you're going into business. If you expect to compete in the marketplace, do your homework.

Also learn about printing. It's your biggest expense. Having a few hundred copies done at your local print shop may make sense for a family history. But to become cost-effective you need to print a minimum of 2,000 to 3,000 copies of most books, and you should work with a book manufacturer or print broker who will look out for your best interests.

Self-publishing can be profitable, fun and exciting. If you're the type of person who likes to be behind the wheel, rather than just along for the ride, it may be the perfect alternative for getting your book into print.

Tom and Marilyn Ross *have been leaders in the self-publishing field for 14 years. They have published seven books and tape programs of their own. Through their Buena Vista, Colorado-based consulting firm, About Books, Inc., they've helped thousands of writers, professionals and entrepreneurs launch their own work. They are frequent contributors to national magazines and are the authors of* The Complete Guide to Self-Publishing *(Writer's Digest Books).*

Manuscript mechanics

Your good writing may be hurt by your presentation if it's not done in correct form. Follow these rules of manuscript mechanics to present your work at its best.

Manuscript format. Do not use a cover sheet or title page. Use a binder only if you are submitting a play or a television or movie script. You can use a paper clip to hold pages together, but never use staples.

The upper corners of the first page of an article manuscript contain important information about you and your manuscript. This information is always single-spaced. In the upper left corner list your name, address, phone number and Social Security number (publishers must have this to file accurate payment records with the government). If you are using a pseudonym for your byline, your legal name still must appear in this space. In the upper right corner, indicate the approximate word count of the manuscript, the rights you are offering for sale and your copyright notice (© 1992 Chris Jones). A handwritten copyright symbol is acceptable. For a book manuscript the same information except rights is necessary. Do not number the first page of your manuscript.

Many writers of short fiction and poetry do not feel it necessary to put the rights or word count on manuscripts they submit to literary magazines. Some writers also consider the copyright notice unnecessary or think editors will consider it amateurish. Others use it only when they submit unsolicited complete manuscripts and not when they send assigned or solicited manuscripts. A copyright notice is not required to obtain copyright protection or to avoid losing it, but persons who use protected works without authorization can claim "innocent infringement" if the notice is not on the manuscript. U.S. copyright owners also must register their works with the U.S. Copyright Office before they file a copyright infringement lawsuit; otherwise, registration is not necessary.

Center the title in capital letters one-third of the way down the page. To center, set the tabulator to stop halfway between the right and left edges of the page. Count the letters in the title, including spaces and punctuation, and backspace half that number. Type the title. Set your typewriter to double-space. Type "by" centered one double-space under your title, and type your name or pseudonym centered one double-space beneath that.

After the title and byline, drop down two double-spaces, paragraph indent, and begin the body of your manuscript. Always double-space your manuscript and use standard paragraph indentations of five spaces. Margins should be about 1¼ inches on all sides of each full page of typewritten manuscript. You may lightly pencil in a line to remind you when you reach the bottom margin of your page, but be sure to erase it before submitting your manuscript.

On every page after the first, type your last name, a dash and the page number in either the upper left or right corner. (This is sometimes called the slug line.) The title of your manuscript may, but need not, be typed on this line or beneath it. Page number two would read: Jones—2. If you are using a pseudonym, type your real name, followed by your pen name in parentheses, then a dash and the page number: Jones (Smith)—2. Then drop down two double-spaces and continue typing. Follow this format throughout your manuscript.

If you are submitting novel chapters, leave the top one-third of the first page of each chapter blank before typing the chapter title. Subsequent pages should include the author's last name, the page number, and a shortened form of the book's title: Jones—2—Skating. (In a variation on this, some authors place the title before the name on the left side and put the page number on the right-hand margin.)

When submitting poetry, the poems should be typed single-spaced (double-space between stanzas), one poem per page. For a long poem requiring more than one page, paper clip the pages together.

On the final page of your manuscript, after you've typed your last word and period, skip three double-spaces and center the words "The End." Some nonfiction writers use ### or the old newspaper symbol -30- to indicate the same thing. Further information on formats for books, articles, scripts, proposals and cover letters, with illustrated examples, is available in *The Writer's Digest Guide to Manuscript Formats*, by Dian Dincin Buchman and Seli Groves (Writer's Digest Books).

Estimating word count. For a quick estimate, multiply 250 words (an average) by the number of pages in your manuscript. To get a more precise count, add the number of characters and spaces in an average line and divide by 6 for the average words per line. Then count the number of lines of type on a representative page. Multiply the words per line by the lines per page to find out the average number of words per page. Then count the number of manuscript pages (fractions should be counted as fractions, except in book manuscript chapter headings, which are counted as a full page). Multiply the number of pages by the number of words per page you already determined. This will give you the approximate number of words in the manuscript. For short manuscripts, it's often quicker to count each word on a representative page and multiply by the total number of pages.

Mailing submissions

No matter what size manuscript you're mailing, always include sufficient return postage and a self-addressed envelope large enough to contain your manuscript if it is returned.

A manuscript of fewer than six pages may be folded in thirds and mailed as if it were a letter using a #10 (business-size) envelope. The enclosed SASE should be a #10 folded in thirds (though these are sometimes torn when a letter opener catches in one of the folds), or a #9 envelope which will slip into the mailing envelope without being folded. Some editors also appreciate the convenience of having a manuscript folded into halves in a 6 × 9 envelope.

For longer manuscripts, use 9 × 12 envelopes for both mailing and return. The return SASE may be folded in half.

A book manuscript should be mailed in a sturdy, well-wrapped box. Your typing paper, computer paper or envelope box is a suitable mailer. Enclose a self-addressed mailing label and paper clip your return postage stamps or International Reply Coupons to the label.

Always mail photos and slides First Class. The rougher handling received by Fourth Class mail could damage them. If you are concerned about losing prints or slides, send them certified or registered mail. For any photo submission that is mailed separately from a manuscript, enclose a short cover letter of explanation, separate self-addressed label, adequate return postage and an envelope. Never submit photos or slides mounted in glass.

To mail up to 20 prints, you can buy photo mailers that are stamped "Photos—Do Not Bend" and contain two cardboard inserts to sandwich your prints. Or use a 9 × 12 manila envelope, write "Photos—Do Not Bend" and devise your own cardboard inserts. Some photography supply shops also carry heavy cardboard envelopes that are reusable.

When mailing a number of prints, say 25 to 50 for a book with illustrations, pack them in a sturdy cardboard box. A box for typing paper or photo paper is an adequate mailer. If, after packing both manuscript and photos, there's empty space in the box, slip in enough cardboard inserts to fill the box. Wrap the box securely.

To mail transparencies, first slip them into protective vinyl sleeves, then mail as you would prints. If you're mailing a number of sheets, use a cardboard box as for photos.

Types of mail service

● First Class is the most expensive way of mailing a manuscript, but many writers prefer it. First Class mail generally receives better handling and is delivered more quickly. Mail sent First Class is forwarded for one year if the addressee has moved, and is returned automatically if it is undeliverable.

● Fourth Class rates are available for packages but you must pack materials carefully when mailing Fourth Class because they will be handled roughly. If a letter is enclosed with your Fourth Class package, write "First Class Letter Enclosed" on the package and add adequate First Class postage for your letter. To make sure your package will be returned to you if it is undeliverable, print "Return Postage Guaranteed" under your address.

• Certified Mail must be signed for when it reaches its destination. If requested, a signed receipt is returned to the sender. There is an $1 charge for this service, in addition to the required postage, and a $1 charge for a return receipt.

• Registered Mail is a high security method of mailing. The package is signed in and out of every office it passes through, and a receipt is returned to the sender when the package reaches its destination. This service begins at $4.40 in addition to the postage required for the item. If you obtain insurance for the package, the cost begins at $4.50.

• United Parcel Service may be slightly cheaper than First Class postage if you drop the package off at UPS yourself. UPS cannot legally carry First Class mail, so your cover letter needs to be mailed separately. Check with UPS in your area for current rates. The cost depends on the weight of your package and the distance to its destination.

• Overnight and two-day mail services are provided by both the U.S. Postal Service and several private firms. These services can be useful if your manuscript or revisions *must* be at an editor's office quickly. More information on next day service is available from the U.S. Post Office in your area, or check your Yellow Pages under "Delivery Services."

Other important details

• Money orders should be used if you are ordering sample copies or supplies and do not have checking services. You'll have a receipt and money orders are traceable. Money orders for up to $35 can be purchased from the U.S. Postal Service for a 75¢ service charge; the cost is $1 for a maximum $700 order. Banks, savings and loans, and some commercial businesses also carry money orders; their fees vary. *Never* send cash through the mail for sample copies.

• Insurance is available for items handled by the U.S. Postal Service but is payable only on typing fees or the tangible value of the item in the package—such as typing paper—so your best insurance when mailing manuscripts is to keep a copy of what you send. Insurance is 75¢ for $50 or less, and goes up to a $5 maximum charge.

• When corresponding with publications and publishers in other countries, International Reply Coupons (IRCs) must be used for return postage. Surface rates in other countries differ from those in the U.S., and U.S. postage stamps are of no use there. Currently, one IRC costs 95¢ and is sufficient for one ounce traveling at surface rate; two must be used for airmail return. Canadian writers pay $1.50 for IRCs.

Because some post offices don't carry IRCs, many writers dealing with international mail send photocopies and tell the publisher to dispose of them if they're not appropriate. When you use this method, it's best to set a deadline for withdrawing your manuscript from consideration, so you can market it elsewhere. For the benefit of both U.S. and international writers, U.S. stamps also can be ordered by phone using a VISA credit card. Call 1-800-782-6724. If 800 service is not available in your area, you can call (816)455-4880 to place orders between 8 a.m. and 5 p.m. Central Standard Time. There is a $5 service charge for all foreign orders.

• International money orders are also available from the post office for a $3 charge.

• See U.S. and Canadian Postage by the Page on the inside covers for specific mailing costs. All charges were current at press time but subject to change during the year.

Recording submissions

A number of writers think once they've mailed a manuscript, the situation is out of their hands; all they can do is sit and wait. But submitting a manuscript doesn't mean you've lost control of it. Manage your writing business by keeping copies of all manuscripts and correspondence, and by recording the dates of submissions.

One way to keep track of your manuscripts is to use a record of submissions that includes the date sent, title, market, editor and enclosures (such as photos). You should also note the date of the editor's response, any rewrites that were done, and, if the manuscript was accepted, the publication date and payment information. You might want to keep a similar record just for queries.

Also remember to keep a separate file for each manuscript or idea along with its list of potential markets. You may want to keep track of expected reporting times on a calendar, too. Then you'll know if a market has been slow to respond and you can follow up on your query or submission.

Bookkeeping

Whether or not you are profitable in your writing, you'll need to keep accurate financial records. These records are necessary to let you know how you're doing, and, of course, the government is also interested in your financial activities.

If you have another source of income, you should plan to keep separate records for your writing expenses and income. Some writers open separate checking accounts for their writing-related expenses.

The best financial records are the ones that get used, and usually the simpler the form, the more likely it will be used regularly. Get in the habit of recording every transaction related to your writing. You can start at any time; it doesn't need to be on Jan. 1. Because you're likely to have expenses before you have income, start keeping your records whenever you make your first purchase related to writing—such as this copy of *Writer's Market*.

A simple bookkeeping system. For most freelance writers, a simple type of single-entry book-keeping is adequate. The heart of the single-entry system is the journal, an accounting book available at any stationery or office supply store. You record all of the expenses and income of your writing business in the journal.

The single-entry journal's form is similar to a standard check register. Instead of withdrawals and deposits, you record expenses and income. You'll need to describe each transaction clearly—including the date, the source of the income (or the vendor of your purchase), a description of what was sold or bought, whether the payment was by cash, check or credit card, and the amount of the transaction.

Your receipt file. Keep all documentation pertaining to your writing expenses or income. This is true whether you have started a bookkeeping journal or not. For every payment you receive, you should have a check stub from the publisher's check, a letter of agreement or contract stating the amount of payment, or your own bank records of the deposit. For every check you write to pay business expenses, you should have a record in your check register as well as a cancelled check. Keep credit card receipts, too. And for every cash purchase, you should have a receipt from the vendor—especially if the amount is over $25. For small expenses, you can usually keep a list if you don't record them in a journal.

Tax information

Freelance writers, artists and photographers have a variety of concerns about taxes that employees don't have, including deductions, self-employment tax and home office credits. A subsection has been added to the Internal Revenue Code that exempts freelance authors, photographers and artists from having to capitalize "qualified creative expenses" incurred while in the business as a freelancer. The expenses can be allowed as deductions instead. Individuals who are involved in related but separate business and freelance activities, such as self-publishers who are writers and publishers, probably will have to keep the expenses separate and capitalize expenses related to publishing, while they deduct expenses from freelancing.

There also is a home office deduction that can be used if an area in your home is used strictly for business. Contact the IRS for information on requirements for this deduction. The deduction is limited to net income after all other deductions have been made; you cannot declare a loss on deductions from your business. The law also requires a business to be profitable three out of five years to avoid being treated as a hobby.

If your freelance income exceeds your expenses, regardless of the amount, you must declare that profit. If the profit is $400 or more, you also must pay quarterly Self-Employment Social Security Tax and fill out that self-employment form on your 1040 tax form. While we cannot offer you tax advice or interpretations, we can suggest several sources for the most current information.

• Call your local IRS office. Look in the white pages of the telephone directory under U.S. Government – Internal Revenue Service. Someone will be able to respond to your request for IRS publications and tax forms or other information. Ask about the IRS Tele-tax service, a series of recorded messages you can hear by dialing on a touch-tone phone. If you need answers to complicated questions, ask to speak with a Taxpayer Service Specialist.

• Obtain the basic IRS publications. You can order them by phone or mail from any IRS office; most are available at libraries and some post offices. Start with *Your Federal Income Tax* (Publication 17) and *Tax Guide for Small Business* (Publication 334). These are both comprehensive, detailed guides – you'll need to find the regulations that apply to you and ignore the rest. You may also want to get a copy of *Business Use of Your Home* (Publication 587) and *Self-Employment Tax* (Publication 533).

• Consider other information sources. Many public libraries have detailed tax instructions available on tape. Some colleges and universities offer free assistance in preparing tax returns. And if you decide to consult a professional tax preparer, the fee is a deductible business expense on your tax return.

Rights and the writer

We find that writers and editors sometimes define rights in different ways. To eliminate any misinterpretations, read the following definitions of each right – and you'll see the definitions upon which editors updated the information in their listings.

Occasionally, we hear from a writer who is confused because an editor claims never to acquire or buy rights. The truth is, any time an editor buys a story or asks you for permission to publish a story, even without payment, the editor is asking you for rights. In some cases, however, editors will reassign those rights to the author after publishing the story.

Sometimes people start magazines in their areas of expertise but don't have extensive knowledge of publishing terms and practices. And sometimes editors simply don't take the time to specify the rights they are buying. If you sense that an editor is interested in getting stories but doesn't seem to know what his and the writer's responsibilities are regarding rights, be wary. In such a case, you'll want to explain what rights you're offering (preferably one-time rights only) and that you expect additional payment for subsequent use of your work. Writers may also agree to sell first rights, for example, to a magazine but then never receive a check for the manuscript. Subsequent inquiries bring no response. In a case like this, we recommend that the writer send a certified letter, return receipt requested, notifying the magazine that the manuscript is being withdrawn from that publication for submission elsewhere. There is no industry standard for how long a writer should wait before using this procedure. The best bet is to check the *Writer's Market* listing for what the magazine lists as its usual reporting time and then, after about one month, institute the withdrawal.

For a complete discussion about book and magazine agreements and information on rights and negotiations, see *A Writer's Guide to Contract Negotiations*, by Richard Balkin (Writer's Digest Books).

Selling rights to your writing. The Copyright Law that went into effect Jan. 1, 1978, said writers were primarily selling one-time rights to their work (plus any revision of that collective work and any later collective work in the same series) unless they – and the publisher – agreed otherwise in writing. In some cases, however, a writer may have little say in the rights sold to an editor; some companies and publications have standard rights they buy and never deviate. In this case, if negotiating isn't possible, you must decide whether selling those rights is in your best interests.

As a writer acquires skill, reliability and professionalism on the job, he becomes more valued by editors—and rights become a more important consideration. Though a beginning writer will accept modest payment just to get in print, an experienced writer cannot afford to give away good writing just to see a byline. At this point the writer must become concerned with selling reprints of articles already sold to one market, using previously published articles as chapters in a book on the same topic, seeking markets for the same material overseas, or offering rights to TV or the movies.

You should strive to keep as many rights to your work as you can from the outset, because before you can resell any piece of writing, you must own the rights to negotiate. If you have sold all rights to an article, for instance, it can be reprinted without your permission and without additional payment to you. Some writers will not deal with editors who buy all rights. What an editor buys will determine whether you can resell your own work. Here is a list of the rights most editors and publishers seek. (Book rights will be covered by the contract submitted to the writer by a book publisher.)

• First Serial Rights—First serial rights means the writer offers the newspaper or magazine the right to publish the article, story or poem for the first time in any periodical. All other rights to the material belong to the writer. Variations on this right are, for example, first North American serial rights. Some magazines use this purchasing technique to obtain the right to publish first in both the U.S. and Canada since many U.S. magazines are circulated in Canada. If an editor had purchased only first U.S. serial rights, a Canadian magazine could come out with prior or simultaneous publication of the same material. When material is excerpted from a book scheduled to be published and it appears in a magazine or newspaper prior to book publication, this is also called first serial rights.

• One-Time Rights—This differs from first serial rights in that the buyer has no guarantee he will be the first to publish the work. One-time rights often apply to photos, but also apply to writing sold to more than one market over a period of time. See also Simultaneous Rights.

• Second Serial (Reprint) Rights—This gives a newspaper or magazine the opportunity to print an article, poem or story after it has already appeared in another newspaper or magazine. The term is also used to refer to the sale of part of a book to a newspaper or magazine after a book has been published, whether or not there has been any first serial publication. Income derived from second serial rights to book material is often shared 50/50 by author and book publisher.

• All Rights—Some magazines buy all rights because of the top prices they pay for material or the exclusive nature of the publication; others have book publishing interests or foreign magazine connections. (Some will call this world rights.)

A writer who sells an article, story or poem to a magazine under these terms forfeits the rights to use his material in its present form elsewhere. If he signs a work-for-hire agreement, he signs away all rights and the copyright to the company making the assignment.

If the writer thinks he may want to use his material later (perhaps in book form), he must avoid submitting to such markets or refuse payment and withdraw his material if he discovers it later. Ask the editor whether he is willing to buy only first rights instead of all rights before you agree to an assignment or sale. Some editors will reassign rights to a writer after a given period, such as one year. It's worth an inquiry in writing.

• Simultaneous Rights—This term covers articles and stories sold to publications (primarily religious magazines) that do not have overlapping circulations. A Catholic publication, for example, might be willing to buy simultaneous rights to a Christmas story they like very much, even though they know a Presbyterian magazine may be publishing the same story in its Christmas issue. Publications that buy simultaneous rights indicate this fact in their listings in *Writer's Market*.

Always advise an editor when the material you are sending is a simultaneous submission to another market. Some writers put the information in their cover letters while others also add it to the upper right-hand corner of the first page of the manuscript under the word count.

● Foreign Serial Rights—Can you resell a story you had published in the U.S. or North America to an international magazine? If you sold only first U.S. serial rights or first North American rights, yes, you are free to market your story abroad. Of course, you must contact a magazine that buys material that has previously appeared in the U.S. or North American periodicals. Books with these markets include *International Literary Market Place*, by R.R. Bowker and *International Writers' and Artists' Yearbook*, by A&C Black Ltd.

● Syndication Rights—This is a division of serial rights. For example, a book publisher may sell the rights to a newspaper syndicate to print a book in 12 installments in each of 20 U.S. newspapers. If they did this after book publication, they would be syndicating second serial rights to the book. In either case, the syndicate would be taking a commission on the sales it made to newspapers, so the remaining percentage would split between author and publisher.

● Subsidiary Rights—The rights, other than book publication rights, that should be specified in a book contract. These may include various serial rights, dramatic rights, translation rights, etc. The contract lists what percentage of these sales goes to the author and what percentage to the publisher. Be careful when signing away these rights. If the publisher is unlikely to market them, you may be able to retain them and market them yourself or through an agent.

● Dramatic, Television and Motion Picture Rights—This means the writer is selling his material for use on the stage, in television or in the movies. Often a one-year option to buy such rights is offered (generally for 10% of the total price). The interested party then tries to sell the idea to other people—actors, directors, studios or television networks, etc.—who become part of the project, which then becomes a script. Some properties are optioned over and over again, but most fail to become dramatic productions. In such cases, the writer can sell his rights again and again—as long as there is interest in the material. Though dramatic, TV and motion picture rights are more important to the fiction writer than the nonfiction writer, producers today are increasingly interested in nonfiction material; many biographies, topical books and true stories are being dramatized.

Communicate and clarify. Before submitting material to a market, check its listing in this book to see what rights are purchased. Most editors will discuss rights they wish to purchase before any exchange of money occurs. Some buyers are adamant about what rights they will accept; others will negotiate. In any case, the rights purchased should be stated specifically in writing sometime during the course of the sale, usually in a contract, memo or letter of agreement. If the editor doesn't put this information in writing, you should. Summarize what you talked about and send a copy to the editor.

Give as much attention to the rights you haven't sold as you do to the rights you have sold. Be aware of the rights you retain with an eye for additional sales.

Regardless of the rights you sell or keep, be sure all parties involved in any sale understand the terms of the sale. Keep in mind, too, that if there is a change in editors or publishers, the rights purchased may also change. Communication, coupled with these guidelines and some common sense, will preclude misunderstandings with editors over rights.

Copyrighting your writing

The copyright law, effective since Jan. 1, 1978, protects your writing, unequivocally recognizes the creator of the work as its owner, and grants the creator all the rights, benefits and privileges that ownership entails.

In other words, the moment you finish a piece of writing—whether it is a short story, article, novel or poem—the law recognizes that only you can decide how it is to be used.

This law gives writers power in dealing with editors and publishers, but they should understand how to use that power. They should also understand that certain circumstances can complicate and confuse the concept of ownership. Writers must be wary of these circumstances or risk losing ownership of their work. Here are answers to frequently asked questions about copyright law:

To what rights am I entitled under copyright law? The law gives you, as creator of your work, the right to print, reprint and copy the work; to sell or distribute copies of the work; to prepare "derivative works"—dramatizations, translations, musical arrangement, novelizations, etc.; to record the work; and to perform or display literary, dramatic or musical works publicly. These rights give you control over how your work is used, and assure you (in theory) that you receive payment for any use of your work.

If, however, you create the work as a "work-for-hire," you do not own any of these rights. The person or company that commissioned the work-for-hire owns the copyright.

When does copyright law take effect, and how long does it last? A piece of writing is copyrighted the moment it is put to paper and you indicate your authorship with the word Copyright or the ©, the year and your name. Protection lasts for the life of the author plus 50 years, thus allowing your heirs to benefit from your work. For material written by two or more people, protection lasts for the life of the last survivor plus 50 years. The life-plus-50 provision applies if the work was created or registered with the Copyright Office after Jan. 1, 1978, when the updated copyright law took effect. The old law protected works for a 28-year term and gave the copyright owner the option to renew the copyright for an additional 28 years at the end of that term. Works copyrighted under the old law that are in their second 28-year term automatically receive an additional 19 years of protection (for a total of 75 years). Works in their first term also receive the 19-year extension beyond the 28-year second term, but must still be renewed when the first term ends.

If you create a work anonymously or pseudonymously, protection lasts for 100 years after the work's creation, or 75 years after its publication, whichever is shorter. The life-plus-50 coverage takes effect, however, if you reveal your identity to the Copyright Office any time before the original term of protection runs out.

Works created on a for-hire basis are also protected for 100 years after the work's creation or 75 years after its publication, whichever is shorter. But the copyright is held by the publisher, not the writer.

Must I register my work with the Copyright Office to receive protection? No. Your work is copyrighted whether or not you register it, although registration offers certain advantages. For example, you must register the work before you can bring an infringement suit to court. You can register the work *after* an infringement has taken place, and *then* take the suit to court, but registering after the fact removes certain rights from you. You can sue for actual damages (the income or other benefits lost as a result of the infringement), but you can't sue for statutory damages and you can't recover attorney's fees unless the work has been registered with the Copyright Office *before* the infringement took place. Registering before the infringement also allows you to make a stronger case when bringing the infringement to court.

If you suspect that someone might infringe on your work, register it. If you doubt that an infringement is likely (and infringements are rare), you might save yourself the time and money involved in registering the material.

I have an article that I want to protect fully. How do I register it? Request the proper form from the Copyright Office. Send the completed form, the registration fee, and one copy (if the work is unpublished; two if it's published) of the work to the Register of Copyrights, Library of Congress, Washington DC 20559. You needn't register each work individually. A group of articles can be registered simultaneously if they meet these requirements: They must be assembled in orderly form (simply placing them in a notebook binder is sufficient);

they must bear a single title ("Works by Chris Jones," for example); they must represent the work of one person (or one set of collaborators); and they must be the subject of a single claim to copyright. No limit is placed on the number of works that can be copyrighted in a group.

If my writing is published in a "collective work"—such as a magazine—does the publication handle registration of the work? Only if the publication owns the piece of writing. Although the copyright notice carried by the magazine covers its contents, you must register any writing to which *you* own the rights if you want the additional protection registration provides.

Collective works are publications with a variety of contributors. Magazines, newspapers, encyclopedias, anthologies, etc., are considered collective works. If you sell something to a collective work, state in writing what rights you're selling. If you don't specify rights, the law allows one-time rights plus publication in any revision of the collective work and any later collective work in the same series. For example, a publishing company could reprint a contribution from one issue in a later issue of its magazine without paying you. The same is true for other collective works, so always detail in writing what rights you are selling before actually making the sale.

When contributing to a collective work, ask that your copyright notice be placed on or near your published manuscript (if you still own the manuscript's rights). Prominent display of your copyright notice on published work has two advantages: It signals to readers and potential reusers of the piece that it belongs to you, and not to the collective work in which it appears; and it allows you to register all published work bearing such notice with the Copyright Office as a group for a single fee. A published work *not* bearing notice indicating you as copyright owner can't be included in a group registration.

Display of copyright notice is especially important when contributing to an uncopyrighted publication—that is, a publication that doesn't display a copyright symbol and doesn't register with the Copyright Office. When the United States joined the Berne Copyright Convention on March 1, 1989, mandatory notice of copyright was no longer required and failure to place a notice of copyright on copies no longer results in loss of copyright. It can still be important to display a copyright notice so no one will innocently infringe on your copyright, however.

Official notice of copyright consists of the symbol ©, the word "Copyright," or the abbreviation "Copr."; the name of the copyright owner or owners; and the year date of first publication (for example, "© 1992 by Chris Jones"). A hand-drawn copyright symbol is acceptable.

Under what circumstances should I place my copyright notice on unpublished works that haven't been registered? Place official copyright notice on the first page of a manuscript if you decide to use it. This procedure is not intended to stop a buyer from stealing your material (editorial piracy is very rare, actually), but to demonstrate to the editor that you understand your rights under copyright law, that you own that particular manuscript, and that you want to retain your ownership after the manuscript is published.

How do I transfer copyright? A transfer of copyright, like the sale of any property, is simply an exchange of the property for payment. The law stipulates, however, that the transfer of any exclusive rights (and the copyright is the most exclusive of rights) must be made in writing to be valid. Various types of exclusive rights exist, as outlined above. Usually it is best not to sell your copyright. If you do, you lose control over the use of the manuscript and forfeit future income from its use.

What is a "work-for-hire assignment"? This is a work that another party commissions you to do. Two types of work-for-hire works exist: Work done as a regular employee of a company, and commissioned work that is specifically called "work for hire" in writing at the time of assignment. The phrase "work for hire" or something close must be used in the written agreement, though you should watch for similar phrasings. The work-for-hire provision was included in the new copyright law so that no writer could unwittingly sign away his copyright. The phrase "work for hire" is a bright red flag warning the writer that the agreement he is about to enter into will result in loss of rights to any material created under the agreement.

Some editors offer work-for-hire agreements when making assignments and expect writers to sign them routinely. By signing them, you forfeit the potential for additional income from a manuscript through reprint sales or sale of other rights. Be careful, therefore, in signing away your rights in a "work-for-hire" agreement. Many articles written as works for hire or to which all rights have been sold are never resold, but if you retain the copyright, you might try to resell the article—something you couldn't do if you forfeited your rights to the piece.

Can I get my rights back if I sell all rights to a manuscript, or if I sell the copyright itself? Yes. You or your heirs can terminate the transfer of rights 40 years after the grant was made or, in the case of publication, 35 years after publication—whichever comes first. You can do this by serving written notice, within specified time limits, to the person to whom you transferred rights. Consult the Copyright Office for the procedural details.

Must all transfers be in writing? Only work-for-hire agreements and transfers of exclusive rights *must* be in writing. However, getting any agreement in writing before the sale is wise. Beware of other statements about what rights the buyer purchases that may appear on checks, writer's guidelines or magazine mastheads. If the publisher makes such a statement elsewhere, you might insert a phrase like "No statement pertaining to purchase of rights other than the one detailed in this letter—including masthead statements or writer's guidelines—applies to this agreement" into the letter that outlines your rights agreement. Some publishers put their terms in writing on the back of a check that, when endorsed by the writer, becomes in their view a "contract." If the terms on the back of the check do not agree with the rights you are selling, contact the editor to discuss this difference in rights.

Are ideas and titles copyrightable? No. Nor can facts be copyrighted. Only the actual expression of ideas or information can be copyrighted. You can't copyright the idea to do a solar energy story, and you can't copyright lists of materials for building solar energy converters. But you can copyright the article that results from that idea and that information.

Where can I get more information about copyright? Write the Copyright Office (Library of Congress, Washington, DC 20559) for a free Copyright Information Kit. Call (not collect) the Copyright Public Information Office at (202)479-0700 weekdays between 8:30 a.m. and 5 p.m. if you need forms for registration of a claim to copyright. The Copyright Office will answer specific questions but won't provide legal advice.

How much should I charge?

To reap financial reward as a writer, you must not only be talented, but immensely creative. You must be aware that there are literally thousands of outlets for the written word (including brochures, newsletters, customer letters, catalog copy, proposals, speeches, advertising, signage, software manuals and contracts), and *someone* has to write them! While the magazine writing market remains a prime market for your writing (see the Consumer and Trade magazine section introductions), other markets can serve as significant money-making alternatives.

Some of the best alternative markets for your writing may be in your own city. Manufacturing companies, health care organizations, service industries, retail businesses and nonprofit organizations often prefer to hire freelancers to write copy for them. By not hiring an employee for this duty, they are able to avoid overhead and employee benefit costs.

Before approaching businesses and organizations with your portfolio, familiarize yourself with the type of material they publish. You can generally obtain sample newsletters, brochures, press releases, etc. via a quick phone call or personal visit to the director of publications, of corporate communications or of public relations (this title varies according to the company). Use this opportunity to introduce yourself as a freelancer interested in contributing material to that particular firm. When you have read the samples and determined that your ideas are congruent with the material they publish, query the contact person with your ideas. With your query, enclose a portfolio containing your best clips to demonstrate your qualifications as a professional freelancer.

If you fail to receive a response from a business or organization, don't consider this an outright rejection. It is possible that they have no need for freelance writers at that time, but are keeping your portfolio on file for future reference. Communicate with the contact person periodically in order to "keep your foot in the door." At the same time, establish contact with other local businesses and organizations. For more information about writing for alternative markets, consult *The Writer's Essential Desk Reference* (Writer's Digest Books).

When setting your freelance fees, keep these factors in mind: pay rates in your area; amount of competition; how much you think the client is willing or able to pay for the job; and how much you want to earn for your time. One way to figure your hourly rate is to determine what an annual salary might be for a staff person to do the same job you are bidding on, and base an hourly wage on that. If, for example, you think the buyer would have to pay a staff person $24,000 per year, divide that by 2,000 (approximately 40 hours per week for 50 weeks) and you will arrive at $12 per hour. Then add another 20% to cover the amount of fringe benefits that an employer normally pays (but you must now absorb) in Social Security, unemployment insurance, paid vacations, hospitalization, retirement funds, etc. Then add another dollars-per-hour figure to cover your actual overhead expense for office space, equipment, supplies; plus time spent on professional meetings, readings, and making unsuccessful proposals. (To get this figure, add up one year's expenses and divide by the number of hours per week you work on freelancing. In the beginning—when you may have large one-time expenses—you may have to adjust this to avoid pricing yourself out of the market.)

Example:

$24,000 (salary) ÷ 2,000 (hours) = $12.00	per hour	
	+ 2.40	(20% to cover fringe benefits, taxes, etc.)
	+ 2.00	(overhead based on annual expenses of $4,000)
	$16.40	per hour charge

Regardless of the method by which you arrive at your fee for the job, be sure to get a letter of agreement signed by both parties covering the work to be done and the fee to be paid.

If there is any question about how long the project will take you, be sure the agreement indicates that you are estimating the time and your project fee is based on X hours. If more time is required, you should be able to renegotiate with the client. This is a good reason to require partial payment as parts of the job are completed, so both you and the client have a better idea of the time involved.

You will, of course, from time to time handle certain jobs at less than desirable rates because they are for a cause you believe in, allow you to get your foot in the door, or because the job offers additional experience or exposure to some profitable client for the future.

Some clients pay hourly rates; others pay flat fees for jobs. Both kinds of rates are in the following list so you have as many pricing options as possible. Please note that the categories often encompass a wide range due to responses from various areas and from writers with various levels of experience.

A

Advertising copywriting: Advertising agencies and the advertising departments of large companies need part-time help in rush seasons. Newspapers, radio and TV stations also need copywriters for their small business customers who do not have agencies.

Depending on the client, the locale and the job, the following rates could apply: $20-100 per hour, $250 and up per day, $500 and up per week, $1,000-2,000 as a monthly retainer. Flat-fee-per-ad rates could range from $100 and up per page depending upon size and kind of client.

Annual reports: A brief report with some economic information and an explanation of figures, $20-35 per hour; 12-page report, $600-1,500; a report that must meet Securities and Exchange Commission (SEC) standards and reports that use legal language could bill at $40-65 per hour. Some writers who provide copywriting and editing services charge flat fees ranging from $5,000-10,000.

Anthology editing: Variable advance plus 3-15% of royalties. Advance should cover reprint fees or fees handled by publisher. Flat-fee-per-manuscript rates could range from $500-5,000 or more if it consists of complex, technical material.

Article manuscript critique: 3,000 words, $40.

Arts reviewing: For weekly newspapers, $15-35; for dailies, $45 and up; for Sunday supplements, $100-400; regional arts events summaries for national trade magazines, $35-100.

Associations: Miscellaneous writing projects, small associations, $15-25 per hour; larger groups, up to $85 per hour; or a flat fee per project, such as $550-900 for 10-12 page magazine articles, or $1,200-1,800 for a 10-page booklet.

Audiocassette scripts: $10-50 per scripted minute, assuming written from existing client materials, with no additional research or meetings; otherwise $75-100 per minute, $750 minimum.

Audiovisuals: For writing, $250-350 per requested scripted minute; includes rough draft, editing conference with client, and final shooting script. For consulting, research, producing, directing, soundtrack oversight, etc., $400-600 per day plus travel and expenses. Writing fee is sometimes 10% of gross production price as billed to client.

B

Book, as-told-to (ghostwriting): Author gets full advance and 50% of author's royalties; subject gets 50%. Hourly rate for subjects who are self-publishing ($25-50 per hour).

Book, ghostwritten, without as-told-to credit: For clients who are either self-publishing or have no royalty publisher lined up, $5,000 to $35,000 (plus expenses) with one-fourth down payment, one-fourth when book half finished, one-fourth at three quarters mark and last fourth of payment when manuscript completed; or chapter by chapter.

Book content editing: $12-50 per hour and up; $600-5,000 per manuscript, based on size and complexity of the project.

Book copyediting: $9-22 per hour and up.

Book indexing: $10-22.50 per hour; $25 per hour using computer indexing software programs that take fewer hours; $1.50-6 per printed book page; 40-70¢ per line of index; or flat fee of $250-500, depending on length.

Book jacket copywriting: From $100-600 for front cover jacket plus flaps and back jacket copy summarizing content and tone of the book.

Book manuscript criticism: $160 for outline and first 20,000 words; $300-500 for up to 100,000 words.

Book manuscript reading, nonspecialized subjects: $20-50 for a half page summary and recommendation. **Specialized subject:** $250-500 and up, depending on complexity of project.

Book proofreading: $8.50-25 per hour and up; sometimes $1.50-3 per page.

Book proposal consultation: $25-50 per hour, or flat rate, $100-250.

Book proposal writing: $300-1,000 or more depending on length and whether client provides full information or writer must do some research.

Book query critique: $50 for letter to publisher and outline.

Book research: $10-30 per hour and up, depending on complexity.

Book reviews: For byline and the book only, on small newspapers; to $35-300 on larger publications.

Book rewriting: $18-50 per hour; sometimes $5 per page. Some writers have combination ghostwriting and rewriting short-term jobs for which the pay could be $350 per day and up. Some participate in royalties on book rewrites.

Book summaries for book clubs, film producers: $50-100/ book. Note: You must live in the area where the business is located to get this kind of work.

Book summaries for business people: $400 for 4-8 printed pages.

Brochures: $200-7,500 and up depending on client (small nonprofit organization to large corporation), length, and complexity of job.

Business booklets, announcement folders: Writing and editing, $100-1,000 depending on size, research, etc.

Business facilities brochure: 12-16 pages, $1,000-4,000.

Business letters: Such as those designed to be used as form letters to improve customer relations, $100 per letter for small businesses; $500 and up per form letter for corporations.

Business meeting guide and brochure: 4 pages, $200; 8-12 pages, $400.

Business writing: On the local or national level, this may be advertising copy, collateral materials, speechwriting, films, public relations or other jobs—see individual entries on these subjects for details. General business writing rates could range from $25-60 per hour; $100-200 per day, plus expenses.

Business writing seminars: $250 for a half-day seminar, plus travel expenses.

C

Catalogs for business: $25-40 per hour or $60-75 per printed page; more if many tables or charts must be reworked for readability and consistency.

Church history: $200-1,000 for writing 15 to 50 pages.

Collateral materials for business: See Business booklets, Catalogs for business, etc.

Comedy writing for night club entertainers: Gags only, $2-25 each. Routines, $100-1,000 per minute. Some new comics may try to get a five-minute routine for $150; others will pay $2,500 for a five-minute bit from a top writer.

Comics writing: $35-50 per page and up for established comics writers.

Commercial reports for businesses, insurance companies, credit agencies: $6-10 per page; $5-20 per report on short reports.

Company newsletters and inhouse publications: Writing and editing 2-4 pages, $200-500; 4-8 pages, $500-1,000; 12-48 pages, $1,000-2,500. Writing, $20-60 per hour; editing, $15-40 per hour.

College/university history: $35 per hour for research through final ms.

Consultant to publishers: $25-50 per hour.

Consultation on communications: $250 per day plus expenses for nonprofit, social service and religious organizations; $400 per day to others.

Consultation on magazine editorial: $1,000-1,500 per day plus expenses.

Consultation to business: On writing, PR, $25-50 per hour.

Consumer complaint letters: $25 each.

Contest judging: Short manuscripts, $5 per entry; with one-page critique, $15-25. Overall contest judging: $100-500.

Copyediting and content editing for other writers: $10-50/hour or $2 per page. (See also Manuscript consultation and Manuscript criticism.)

Copyediting for advertising: $25 per hour.

Copyediting for book publishers: see Book copyediting.

Copyediting for nonprofit organizations: $15 per hour.

Copywriting for book club catalogs: $85-200.

Corporate comedy: Half-hour show, $300-800.
Corporate history: $1,000-20,000, depending on length, complexity and client resources.
Corporate profile: Up to 3,000 words, $1,250-2,500.

D

Dance criticism: $25-400 per article. (See also Arts reviewing.)
Direct-mail catalog copy: $75-100 per item; $400-500 per page.
Direct-mail packages: Copywriting direct mail letter, response card, etc., $1,500-10,000 depending on writer's skill, reputation, and the client.
Direct response card on a product: $250.
Drama criticism: Local, newspaper rates; non-local, $50 and up per review.

E

Editing: See Book copyediting, Company newsletters, Magazine editing, etc.
Educational consulting and educational grant and proposal writing: $250-750 per day and or $25-75 per hour.
Encyclopedia articles: Entries in some reference books, such as biographical encyclopedias, 500-2,000 words; pay ranges from $60-80 per 1,000 words. Specialists' fees vary.
English teachers — lay reading for: $6 per hour.
Executive biography: (based on a resume, but in narrative form): $100.

F

Fact checking: $17-25 per hour.
Family histories: See Histories, family.
Financial presentation for a corporation: 20-30 minutes, $1,500-4,500.
Flyers for tourist attractions, small museums, art shows: $50 and up for writing a brief bio, history, etc.
Fund-raising campaign brochure: $5,000 for 20 hours' research and 30 hours to write a major capital campaign brochure, get it approved, lay out and produce with a printer. For a standard fund-raising brochure, many fund-raising executives hire copywriters for $50-75 an hour to do research which takes 10-15 hours and 20-30 hours to write/produce.

G

Gags: see Comedy writing for nightclub entertainers.
Genealogical research: $25 per hour.
Ghostwriting: $25-100 per hour; $200 per day plus expenses. Ghostwritten professional and trade journal articles under someone else's byline, $400-4,000. Ghostwritten books: see Book, as-told-to (ghostwriting) and Book, ghostwritten, without as-told-to credit.
Ghostwriting a corporate book: 6 months' work, $13,000-25,000.
Ghostwriting a religious book: $6,000-15,000. 50% of flat fee in advance and 50% upon completion of accepted ms.
Ghostwriting article for a physician: $2,500-3,000.
Ghostwriting speeches: See Speechwriting.
Government public information officer: Part-time, with local governments, $25 per hour; or a retainer for so many hours per period.
Grant appeals for local non-profit organizations: $50 an hour or flat fee.
Grant proposals: $40 per hour.
Greeting card verse: $150/sentiment for humor; $100/sentiment for conventional.

H

Histories, family: Fees depend on whether the writer edits already prepared notes or does extensive research and writing; and the length of the work, $500-15,000.

Histories, local: Centennial history of a local church, $25 per hour for research through final manuscript for printer.

House organ editing: See Company newsletters and inhouse publications.

I

Industrial product film: $125-150/minute; $500 minimum flat fee.

Industrial promotions: $15-40 per hour. See also Business writing.

J

Job application letters: $20-40.

L

Lectures to local librarians or teachers: $50-100.

Lectures to school classes: $25-75; $150 per day; $250 per day if farther than 100 miles.

Lectures at national conventions by well-known authors: $2,500-20,000 and up, plus expenses; less for panel discussions.

Lectures at regional writers' conferences: $300 and up, plus expenses.

M

Magazine, city, calendar of events column: $150.

Magazine column: 200 words, $25. Larger circulation publications pay fees related to their regular word rate.

Magazine editing: Religious publications, $200-500 per month; $15-30 per hour.

Magazine stringing: 20¢-$1 per word based on circulation. Daily rate: $100-200 plus expenses; weekly rate: $750 plus expenses. Also $7.50-35 per hour plus expenses.

Manuscript consultation: $25-50 per hour.

Manuscript criticism: $25 per 16-line poem; $40-60 per article or short story of up to 3,000 words; book outlines and sample chapters of up to 20,000 words, $160.

Manuscript typing: Depending on ms length and delivery schedule, $1.25-2 per page with one copy; $15 per hour.

Market research survey reports: $15-30 per hour; writing results of studies or reports, $500-1,200 per day.

Medical editing: $25-65 per hour.

Medical proofreading: $12-30 per hour.

Medical writing: $25-100 per hour; manuscript for pharmaceutical company submitted to research journal, $4,500-5,000.

Movie novelization: $3,500-15,000, depending on writer's reputation, amount of work to be done, and amount of time writer is given.

N

New product release: $300-500 plus expenses.

News release: See Press release.

Newsletters: See Company newsletters and Retail business newsletters.

Newspaper ads for small business: $25 for a small, one-column ad, or $10 per hour and up.

Newspaper column, local: $10 for a weekly; $15 for dailies of 4,000-6,000 circulation; $20 for 7,000-10,000 dailies; $25 for 11,000-25,000 dailies; and $30 and up for larger dailies.

Newspaper feature: $15-30 per article for a weekly; $70-80 for a daily.

Newspaper feature writing, part-time: $1,000 a month for an 18-hour week.

Newspaper reviews of art, music, drama: See Arts reviewing.

Newspaper stringing: Sometimes flat rate of $15-30 to cover meeting and write article; sometimes additional mileage payment.

Novel synopsis for film producer: $150 for 5-10 pages typed single-spaced.
Novel synopsis for literary agent: $150 for 5-10 pages typed single-spaced.

O

Obituary copy: Where local newspapers permit lengthier than normal notices paid for by the funeral home (and charged to the family), $15. Writers are engaged by funeral homes.

Opinion research interviewing: $4-6 per hour or $15-25 per completed interview.

P

Party toasts, limericks, place card verses: $1.50 per line.

Permission fees to publishers to reprint article or story: $75-500; 10-15¢ per word; less for charitable organizations.

Photo brochures: $700-15,000 flat fee for photos and writing.

Photo research: $12-25 per hour.

Poetry criticism: $25 per 16-line poem.

Political writing: See Public relations and Speechwriting.

Press background on a company: $500-1,200 for 4-8 pages.

Press kits: $500-3,000.

Press release: 1-3 pages, $85-300.

Printers' camera-ready typeset copy: Negotiated with individual printers, but see also Manuscript typing.

Product literature: Per page, $100-150.

Programmed instruction consultant fees: $300-700 per day; $50 per hour.

Programmed instruction materials for business: $50 per hour for inhouse writing and editing; $500-700 a day plus expenses for outside research and writing. Alternate method: $2,000-5,000 per hour of programmed training provided, depending on technicality of subject.

Proofreading: $7.50-12 per hour.

Public relations for business: $200-500 per day plus expenses.

Public relations for conventions: $500-1,500 flat fee.

Public relations for libraries: Small libraries, $5-10 per hour; larger cities, $35 an hour and up.

Public relations for nonprofit or proprietary organizations: Small towns, $100-500 monthly retainers.

Public relations for politicians: Small town, state campaigns, $10-50 per hour; incumbents, congressional, gubernatorial, and other national campaigns, $25-100 per hour; up to 10% of campaign budget.

Public relations for schools: $15-20 per hour and up in small districts; larger districts have full-time staff personnel.

R

Radio advertising copy: $20-65 per script; $200-225 per week for a four- to six-hour day; larger cities, $250-400 per week.

Radio continuity writing: $5 per page to $150 per week, part-time.

Radio documentaries: $200 for 60 minutes, local station.

Radio editorials: $10-30 for 90-second to two-minute spots.

Radio interviews: For National Public Radio, up to 3 minutes, $25; 3-10 minutes, $40-75; 10-60 minutes, $125 to negotiable fees. Small radio stations would pay approximately 50% of the NPR rate; large stations, double the NPR rate.

Readings by poets, fiction writers: $25-600 depending on the author.

Record album cover copy: $100-250 flat fee.

Recruiting brochure: 8-12 pages, $500-1,500.

Research for individuals: $5-30 per hour, depending on experience, geographic area and nature of the work.

Research for writers or book publishers: $15-40 an hour and up; $15-200 per day and all expenses. Some quote a flat fee of $300-500 for a complete and complicated job.

Restaurant guide features: Short article on restaurant, owner, special attractions, $20; interior, exterior photos, $25.

Résumé writing: $25-250 per résumé.

Retail business newsletters for customers: $175-300 for writing four-page publications. Some writers work with a local printer and handle production details as well, billing the client for the total package. Some writers also do their own photography.

Rewriting: Copy for a local client, $25-40 per hour.

S

Sales brochure: 12-16 pages, $750-3,000.

Sales letter for business or industry: $350-1,000 for one or two pages.

Science writing: For newspapers $150-600; magazines $2,000-5,000; encyclopedias $1 per line; textbook editing $40 per hour; professional publications $500-1,500 for 1,500-3,000 words.

Script synopsis for agent or film producer: $75 for 2-3 typed pages, single-spaced.

Scripts for nontheatrical films for education, business, industry: Prices vary among producers, clients, and sponsors and there is no standardization of rates in the field. Fees include $75-120 per minute for one reel (10 minutes) and corresponding increases with each successive reel; approximately 10% of the production cost of films that cost the producer more than $1,500 per release minute.

Services brochure: 12-18 pages, $1,250-2,000.

Shopping mall promotion: $500 monthly retainer up to 15% of promotion budget for the mall.

Short story manuscript critique: 3,000 words, $40-60.

Slide film script: See Audiovisuals.

Slide presentation: Including visual formats plus audio, $1,000-1,500 for 10-15 minutes.

Slide/single image photos: $75 flat fee.

Slide/tape script: $75-100 per minute, $750 minimum.

Software manual writing: $35-50 per hour for research and writing.

Special news article: For a business's submission to trade publication, $250-400 for 1,000 words.

Special occasion booklet: Family keepsake of a wedding, anniversary, Bar Mitzvah, etc., $115 and up.

Speech for government official: $4,000 for 20 minutes plus up to $1,000 travel and miscellaneous expenses.

Speech for local political candidate: $250 for 15 minutes; for statewide candidate, $375-500.

Speech for national congressional candidate: $1,000 and up.

Speech for owners of a small business: $100 for six minutes.

Speech for owners of larger businesses: $500-3,000 for 10-30 minutes.

Speech for statewide candidate: $500-800.

Speechwriting: $20-75 per hour.

Syndicated newspaper column, self-promoted: $5-10 each for weeklies; $10-25 per week for dailies, based on circulation.

T

Teaching adult education course: $10-60 per class hour; fee usually set by school, not negotiated by teachers.

Teaching adult seminar: $350 plus mileage and per diem for a 6- or 7-hour day; plus 40% of the tuition fee beyond the sponsor's breakeven point.

Teaching business writing to company employees: $60 per hour.

Teaching college course or seminar: $15-70 per class hour.

Teaching creative writing in school: $15-70 per hour of instruction, or $1,500-2,000 per 12-15 week semester; less in recessionary times.

Teaching elementary and middle school teachers how to teach writing to students: $75-120 for a 1-1½ hour session.

Teaching home-bound students: $5-15 per hour.

Teaching journalism in high school: Proportionate to salary scale for full-time teacher in the same school district.

Technical editing: $15-60 per hour.

Technical typing: $1-4 per double-spaced page.

Technical writing: $35 per ms page or $35-75 per hour, depending on degree of complexity and type of audience.

Textbook copyediting: $14-20 per hour, depending on el-hi, college, technical, non-technical.

Textbook editing: $15-30 per hour.

Textbook proofreading: $9-18.50 per hour.

Textbook writing: $14-50 per hour.

Trade journal ad copywriting: $250-500.

Trade journal feature article: For business client, $400-1,000.

Translation, commercial: Final draft from one of the common European languages, $115-120 per thousand words.

Translation for government agencies: Up to $125 per 1,000 foreign words into English.

Translation, literary: $50-100 per thousand English words.

Translation through translation agencies: Less 33⅓% (average) for agency commission.

Translation, technical: $125 per thousand words.

Tutoring: $25 per 1-1½ hour private session.

TV documentary: 30-minute 5-6 page proposal outline, $250 and up; 15-17 page treatment, $1,000 and up; less in smaller cities.

TV editorials: $35 and up for 1-minute, 45 seconds (250-300 words).

TV home shopping: Local ad copy: $6 an hour. Writing, misc. freelance: $15-85 per hour; $.50-1 per word.

TV information scripts: Short 5- to 10-minute scripts for local cable TV stations, $10-15 per hour.

TV instruction taping: $150 per 30-minute tape; $25 residual each time tape is sold.

TV news film still photo: $3-6 flat fee.

TV news story: $16-25 flat fee.

TV filmed news and features: From $10-20 per clip for 30-second spot; $15-25 for 60-second clip; more for special events.

TV, national and local public stations: $35-100 per minute down to a flat fee of $100-500 for a 30- to 60-minute script.

TV scripts: (Teleplay only), 60 minutes, prime time, Writers Guild rates: $11,780; 30 minutes, $8,733.

V

Video script: See Audiovisuals.

W

Writer-in-schools: Arts council program, $130 per day; $650 per week. Personal charges plus expenses vary from $25 per day to $100 per hour depending on school's ability to pay.

Writer's workshop: Lecturing and seminar conducting, $50-150 per hour to $750 per day plus expenses; local classes, $35-50 per student for 10 sessions.

Publishers' Roundtable

by Mark Kissling

The book publishing process seems, to many writers, a mystical process. (Writing a book is often mystical enough.) When the time comes to find a publisher, writers are often confused and don't know where to begin. And those not knowledgeable about the process may not ask questions, for fear they will expose their naivete.

In an effort to demystify the book publishing process, the editors of *Writer's Market* interviewed professionals from four companies of varying size. We asked them to comment on the book publishing process, from a writer's initial contact to seeing a finished book. We also conducted a survey of all the book publishers listed in the 1991 edition. The results confirmed some expectations and illuminated other trends.

What the survey said

The last decade brought swift and sweeping changes in many industries. Book publishing was certainly among them. Corporate mergers and takeovers resulted in many publishers streamlining their workforces. The most common practice was to cut back in editorial staff, especially those responsible for reading unsolicited manuscripts sent in over the transom. In many large publishing houses the dreaded "slush pile" grew at such a rate that many changed policy on dealing with unsolicited manuscripts. Today there are few large firms that will accept and read such submissions. They tend now to rely more and more on agented material.

In our survey, we polled 686 book publishers. Of the 441 editors replying, 343 (78%) receive fewer than 10% of their submissions from agents. Of these, 117 (27%) report receiving no agented submissions. These are most often smaller or specialized firms that are also much more likely to read unsolicited manuscripts. Indeed, of those receiving 10% or fewer agented submissions, 111 (32%) stated that at least 50% of their books were originally unsolicited manuscripts. Seventy-five (17%) reported that 90% or more of their books had originated over the transom.

Only 40 (9%) of those to respond said 50% or more of submissions they consider are from agents. These tend to be the larger companies, which will not accept or read unsolicited manuscripts. (We should point out that we had more success in receiving responses from smaller publishers than larger ones, and that 10 or 15 conglomerates place the overwhelming majority of books in bookstores.) From this data, we can deduce that agents tend to concentrate on sending their clients' material to the larger houses. This should not come as a surprise: Larger book publishers are capable of higher print runs, in-depth marketing and larger advances. Greater advances and higher sales, in turn, mean more income for the agent.

Therefore, writers should be aware that the competition to publish with a large firm has never been greater, and that most of these firms are interested only in agented material. Writers interested in breaking into this level most often need an agent to be competitive. However, not every publisher shares the policies of the conglomerates. Indeed, the majority can still be reached without an agent. It should be pointed out that agents are also experts in contract negotiation and other useful areas and can help writers beyond initial contact.

For more information on agents, look into *Guide to Literary Agents and Art/Photo Reps* (Writer's Digest Books).

Niche publishing

While it may not be entirely fair to refer to Canadian publishers and university presses as filling a niche, their publishing activity compared to the conglomerates is on a much smaller scale. They tend not to deal with agents or receive agented submissions, and many of them are more than willing to deal directly with writers.

Twenty-eight Canadian book publishers responded to our poll. Of these, 23 (82%) reported they receive 10% or fewer submissions from agents. This is fairly close to the 78% figure among all book publishers polled. Eight (29%) stated that 75% or more of their books originated as unsolicited manuscripts. This is also close to the overall percentage of 17%, given the small size of the sample. From this we can conclude that book publishing is not radically different in Canada in terms of the role of agents and unsolicited manuscripts.

Twenty university presses also responded. All 20 stated that 10% or fewer of their submissions were from agents. This is no surprise when one considers that university presses tend to pay low royalties and offer small or no advances. Only four (20%) reported that 75% or more of their books started in the slush pile. While this, too, is a small sample, it does indicate that in this niche, manuscripts are often solicited from specific writers, usually scholars.

Authors covering special subjects should take note that they will not be competing so much with agents, but that the road to publication is not nearly as easy as sending a manuscript in blind.

First readers

It may come to a surprise to some writers, or offer others comfort, that not everyone who reads a manuscript for the first time is an overworked, eye-strained, low-on-the-totem-pole staffer. We asked the publishing houses: "If you accept unsolicited manuscripts, who reads them?" The most common answers among respondents were, as expected, "editor," "editorial assistant/assistant editor," "acquisitions editor" and "managing editor." Also common were "freelance reader" and "outside reader." (See page 52 for a list and explanation of types of editors.) However, among small and medium-sized firms, there were a significant number of answers of "president," "publisher" and "owner." Clearly, in some smaller houses, a proposal or manuscript goes straight to the top.

In fact, the range of answers was quite wide. It would require a few pages just to list each job title we encountered with this one question. Cropping up often enough to merit interest were "editorial committee," "editorial board," and answers with multiple titles, suggesting that a manuscript is, at some companies, read by more than one person. Also interesting were the number of times "marketing director" and "promotional manager" were mentioned. This indicates that these companies' first-round decisions are based largely on a book's market potential.

Regardless of the first reader's title, writers should take note that the best approach for initial contact is to address material to a name, not a job title. Use the contact name given in the individual listings. If the listing does not provide a name (a few don't), query for a name. Dan Frank, senior editor at Pantheon Books, could not stress enough the importance of addressing material to a specific person at a book publisher. "It stuns me that people send off their queries and manuscripts blind or to a job title," he says. "Seek out books edited by specific editors at publishing houses you're interested in," he says. A little research makes "a world of difference."

The process, in brief

The following is a sample of responses to the question, "What is the process between your interest in a manuscript and contract signing?" The answers were quite varied and often complex, but some patterns did emerge. Marketability plays a large role for most publishers; usually, the bigger the company, the larger the role. Also, once a writer's proposal has convinced one editor, that editor must often convince others of the book's potential success. In essence, the book is sold more than once. Finally, a writer must be willing to rewrite and be open to editorial changes. Writing the book may have been a mystical experience, but to get it published, one cannot guard a manuscript as though it were an unalterable sacred text.

From a smaller publisher: "We like writers to send a query letter with synopsis, contents and chapter outlines. The writer should also identify the market for the book. Manuscripts are reviewed inhouse, then sent to other readers. The decision to publish is based on favorable reviews, need, budget and market."

From a medium-size company: "The manuscript is sent to the senior editor and other readers. They take one month to six weeks. If the manuscript gets the OK, we ask the author if she will make the suggested changes. If the author agrees, we submit the book to a feasability study by the business manager, marketing manager, editor and publisher. A decision is made on pricing, on the season in which to publish it, and costs. If it passes the feasability study, we send a contract. The entire process takes about three months."

From a large firm: "If a book manuscript is of sufficient interest to be considered for publication, it is discussed in an acquisitions meeting. Editors and marketing personnel discuss the prospects for the success of such a book. If they are convinced of its merit, they contract for the book. This can take several months. At times this group asks the author to submit additional material or revise his manuscript."

From a Canadian publisher: "The manuscript is given a first reading, then recommended for a second reading by an editor. If still favorable, the manuscript is considered by the editorial board and judged from the vantage of literary quality, marketability, financial viability, risk, conforming to the company mandate, etc. If a favorable decision is reached, we send the contract."

The process, in detail

In addition to the survey responses from editors, we also sought the experience of four publishing professionals. Their in-depth answers will help to enlighten you on what goes on behind the scenes as a manuscript becomes a book. The participants are:

Jane Hill, senior editor, Longstreet Press, first worked in publishing as a freelance editor and manuscript screener for Peachtree Press. Since 1985 she has acquired and/or edited more than 35 books of fiction and nonfiction. Longstreet Press was established in 1988 in Marietta, Georgia, and averages 20 titles per year.

Victoria Klose works for William Morrow & Company, Inc./Publishers, a New York publisher of 200 titles per year. Klose started as a freelance copy editor at Morrow and was later chief copy editor at Random House. She has come full circle back to Morrow as director of editorial services.

Steve Lane, editorial director, school division, Prentice-Hall Canada Inc., is a former teacher, sales representative and acquiring editor. He has worked in publishing since 1972 and has held his current position for four years. Prentice-Hall Canada was incorporated in 1960 and its school division was formed in 1965. It is one of the largest publishers in Canada.

Jim Pruett has worked in publishing for 10 years. He has been involved in promotion and marketing as well as acquisitions and editorial. He is currently publisher of Pruett Publishing Company, founded by his father 35 years ago. Their emphasis is on books covering aspects of the American West and they average 12 titles per year.

Please rank your preference on a writer's method of first contacting your company.

JH: For fiction my preferences would be ranked this way: 1) Complete manuscript 2) Query and sample chapters 3) Query letter only. Agents generally send the complete manuscript or call and inquire before sending. For nonfiction: 1) Query letter only 2) Query and outline 3) Complete manuscript. Many, in fact most, nonfiction books are not complete manuscripts at the time of inquiry.

VK: Morrow does not accept unsolicited manuscripts, so our preference is to receive a query from an agent.

SL: 1) Query and outline (nonfiction) or sample chapters (fiction) 2) Query letter only 3) Query from writer's agent 4) Complete manuscript.

JP: Query and outline or sample chapters.

If a writer or agent makes a submission, who reads it first and who makes the decision to advance it along?

JH: Normally, a query will be opened by the person to whom it is addressed. If it is addressed to the Editorial Department, an editorial assistant will open the letter and screen it, handling it himself or routing it to the editor he deems most appropriate. Thus, such decisions are at times made by the editorial assistant.

VK: Most agents will submit material directly to editors with whom they deal. If an unknown writer sends material to no one in particular at a house, the grim reality is that the material will go to whomever is reading the dreaded slush pile. This person is most likely an editorial assistant to one of the senior editors. That editorial assistant makes the decision to pursue such a manuscript.

SL: The editorial director and/or director of research and marketing would be the first to read the submission. A manuscript would not be read unless the subject matter fit our publishing mandate. If we are interested, the project is passed along to the sponsoring editor for that subject area and then that editor would make contact with the author.

JP: I read everything that comes through the door. The first step is to look for manuscripts that fit our list and return those that don't.

How are manuscripts and proposals rejected? Is there a form letter? Are agented submissions rejected differently?

JH: Most manuscripts and proposals are rejected with a form letter or with what I like to call an enhanced form letter. That means that we give constructive advice when we have time and when we have it to give—other markets, directions for an idea, brief critiques. Generally, an agented submission would receive, at the very least, an enhanced letter. Depending on my relationship with the agent and/or author, I might do an extensive critique. But the extensive response has as often been done on books not represented by agents, I suspect.

VK: Agented submissions are rejected differently from unsolicited manuscripts in that the complete manuscript has been read (which is not always the case with unsolicited manuscripts) and the letter would be addressed directly to the agent who submitted it and it would have a personal tone. Most houses use a form rejection letter for unsolicited material.

SL: A basic form letter is used, and this is modified to fit the circumstances.

JP: We have used a form rejection letter in the past but will answer all proposals with a personal note in the future. We see very few proposals from agents and treat them as we would any other project.

When you receive the complete manuscript of a proposal you expressed interest in, how often is rewriting necessary and how much of the manuscript generally needs to be rewritten?

JH: I have never asked that a manuscript be rewritten until after we have bought the book. If I think something needs enough reworking that I can't commit to it, I return it to the author. If I have constructive suggestions regarding the reworking, I make them. If the project interests me, I sometimes invite the author to resubmit after revising, if he wishes. But that resubmission would be handled as if it were the first time I had seen the material, by which I mean that invitation is never an implied acceptance of the reworked material. Because authors often take it as such, I am very sparing with such invitations.

VK: The quality of a manuscript is in the eye of the beholder. Two equally skillful and successful editors might very well differ in their opinions of the same material. One might think the material is ready to roll while another might feel drastic rewrite is necessary.

SL: In almost all cases, rewriting is necessary in order to better shape the manuscript to meet the needs of the marketplace. If the entire manuscript was written before the author made contact with the publisher, the amount of rewriting could be substantial. However, if the author works with the publisher from the beginning, revisions to the manuscript after the first draft stage should be less substantial.

JP: Manuscripts and book proposals vary so much that there is no general comment that would apply here.

Who is involved in approving a book? How long does the process take from initial interest to the book coming off the press?

JH: Once I make a decision that I'd like to acquire a book, I speak with the president of the company about the book, how it fits with our overall publishing plan and about the terms of the offer I want to make. When he and I are agreed upon the approach and the offer, I negotiate with the agent or the author. I also generally try, at the time of acquisition, to get a base of inhouse support for the book because that's important to its ultimate success. That, however, is not a formal part of the process. The time to finished book varies, usually from six to 18 months.

VK: The people involved in approving a book are the editor to whom the manuscript was submitted, the editor-in-chief and the president or CEO. In some houses, the approval people vary according to the money involved; usually the higher the price on a book, the more people involved. If an editor thinks the manuscript is perfect as is, a contract could be drawn up and approved within a matter of weeks. The author signs it and turns over the manuscript to the editor, who in turn hands it over to copyediting. From that point on, like a baby, it should take nine months to produce bound books.

SL: The sponsoring editor summarizes the outline, sample chapter(s), reviews, and financial assessments and seeks final approval from the president of the school division, the president of the company (if the project required a large investiture of upfront money), the editorial director, the director of research and marketing, the director of sales and the business manager. The time can vary between two and three years depending on the magnitude of the project.

JP: Those involved in the decision are the publisher, business manager, director of marketing and sales and the CEO. The time varies for this process, but it normally takes six months to a year for the writer to complete the manuscript and nine months to a year for us to produce the book.

Who decides the author's advance, if any?

JH: The editor who buys the book, in consultation with the company president, determines the advance according to reasonable expectations regarding the book's performance. If the author has previously published books with the company or if information about previous books with another house is available, the sales information is certainly a part of the reasonable expectations formula. The company's size and resources are also obviously a consideration. My personal philosophy is to make the most generous reasonable offer that I can, serving both the company's and the author's interests. Whether the writer has an agent or not is not a significant factor.

VK: The writer's advance is a joint decision among the author, the agent and the publisher and this agreement is clearly spelled out in the contract.

SL: In school publishing, the advances are usually very small (between $1,000-3,000 Canadian). The sponsoring editor makes a recommendation for an advance to the editorial director and the president of the school division. These people approve the advance.

JP: The business manager, sales and marketing director and the publisher make the decision.

How many people is a writer likely to deal with when publishing a book with your company? What happens to the writer and his book when the book is orphaned (the editor of the book leaves the company)?

JH: 1) An editor—the person who buys and edits the book, and in some cases, also line edits the manuscript; 2) An associate editor or editorial assistant—if the editor does not line edit the book, one of these people will. He will also supervise proofreading, corrections, etc., and deal with the writer on these matters, under the supervision of the book's editor; 3) A publicist will work with the writer on promotion and advertising plans, appearances, etc.; 4) The director of sales or an assistant will keep the writer informed of developments in this area and answer questions the writer may have. In our short history we've never had an orphaned book.

VK: The two most involved people will be the acquisitions editor who bought the manuscript and his assistant. Beyond that, an author might have contact with the copyeditor, who checks for spelling, grammar and punctuation. An author would talk with a publicist or a book marketer. Depending on the terms of the contract, an author might also talk to the jacket designer and the interior book designer, but the primary contacts are the editor and the assistant. No book is ever orphaned for long. If an editor leaves a house, his books are reassigned within a matter of weeks and those new editors make contact with the author and agent soon thereafter.

SL: An author would deal with the sponsoring editor, the research and marketing manager, a developmental editor (as the project is being written/revised), and a production editor (in the final stages leading to publication). Because we have large subject area teams, an author should never feel his project would become an orphan.

JP: A writer would deal with me (the publisher) and the sales and marketing director while the book is being created. After that, the writer would probably talk with our publicist to help get the word out.

What are the most common mistakes writers make throughout the process of publishing a book with your company?

JH: The most common mistake is probably having unrealistic expectations about their book's performance. By this I mean that writers often judge what will happen with their book by what happened with Stephen King's last book. It won't, unfortunately. Most books will not have the advertising and promotion budgets that Mr. King's books have. Most will not become major motion pictures or translated into 40 languages. And so on. Writers also tend to be uninformed about how books are actually bought and sold in this country and how the review process works at major review outlets, print and electronic. There is a tremendous amount of luck involved in every step once the book leaves the publisher's warehouse, even when the publisher is doing an exemplary job.

VK: Some authors think of the process as adversarial, which it definitely is not. Some send in material and then assume it's been received and that "no news is good news." They don't check to see if the material has arrived or find out what the editor thinks of it.

SL: In school publishing, the most common pitfall is having an author feel that he knows more than the publisher about what the marketplace really wants. Successful publishing results when the author and the publisher work together. The author provides subject and pedagogical expertise, and the publisher provides a solid base of market research that gives the author a clear understanding of what readers are looking for. In addition, of course, the publisher also provides editorial assistance and marketing expertise.

JP: The most common mistake is wanting to change words after the type has been set.

To sum up, editors stress that writers owe it to themselves to find out as much about the book publishing process as they can. The knowledge will enable them to make informed choices in seeking and working with a publisher. Ignorance is not always bliss. Knowing what to do and what to expect could give you the edge that puts your book over the top. "Good writers, professional writers, should ask questions," says Jane Hill. "Good publishers will give the best, most honest answers they can. That's what I try to do. The writers who are best to work with are the ones who ask and then really listen."

The 22 Kinds of Editors

1. Acquisitions (or Acquiring) Editor. Primarily responsible for soliciting, evaluating, purchasing and (usually) editing manuscripts.

2. Assistant Editor, Associate Editor, Associate Department Editor, etc. Ambiguous. Can be anything from a secretary to a copy editor to an acquisitions editor.

3. Book Packager. A person or organization that provides publishing services (such as design or production), finished manuscripts, and, in some cases, printed, bound books to large book publishers. The term book producer is synonymous.

4. Consulting Editor. Usually a freelance editor hired to offer advice and expertise. Occasionally oversees a project. In some cases the title is honorary, given to a well known figure to add prestige to the publication.

5. Contributing Editor. 1) Someone who writes regularly for a publication and has some editing duties as well 2) Someone who writes regularly for a publication but does no actual editing; the title is honorary and is awarded as a perk.

6. Copy Editor. Reads through manuscripts word by word, making changes and corrections. Sometimes called manuscript editor.

7. Department Editor. A person in charge of the editorial content of one department, genre, series or section.

8. Editor. A generic term; can refer to anyone involved in the editorial function of publishing.

9. Editor-at-large. 1) A staff editor who handles a variety of tasks and wears several different hats, depending on the circumstances; 2) A freelance editor; 3) A consulting editor.

10. Editor-in-Chief. Someone in charge of the entire editing function at a publication—or of one entire line, area, imprint, or division at a book publishing house. The term editorial director is synonymous.

11. Editorial Assistant or Editorial Associate. Usually an editor's assistant; duties may range from those of a secretary to those of a full-fledged editor.

12. Editorial Board Member. Part of a board that, as a group, selects manuscripts for publication. This person may also help determine editorial policy. Editorial boards are common among literary magazines and professional, technical and scholarly journals; they are rare elsewhere. Occasionally the title is honorary (see consulting editor).

13. Executive Editor. Ambiguous. Synonymous with either senior editor, editor-in-chief or managing editor, depending on the publisher or publication.

14. Freelance Editor. Hired by a publisher as an independent contractor to serve as an editor on a project-by-project basis.

15. Managing Editor. Oversees the day-to-day operations of a publication, publishing firm, or editorial department; often serves as the editor-in-chief's right-hand person.

16. Production Editor. In charge of the physical production of a publication, including printing, design, etc.

17. Project Editor. Supervises a particular publishing project.

18. Proofreader. Reads manuscripts and/or typeset material to check for errors in spelling, grammar, typesetting, etc. Does little or no editing.

19. Publisher. The person in charge of everything that goes on at a publication or publishing firm. Oversees the editorial department and all other functions.

20. Reader. Screens unsolicited manuscripts (those in the "slush pile"); rejects most and passes on the more promising ones to an editor. Sometimes called manuscript reader or first reader.

21. Senior Editor. Usually an acquisitions editor with a good deal of decision-making (and sometimes policy-making power).

22. Supervising Editor. Ambiguous. Synonymous with either managing editor or (more often) project editor.

From *The Writer's Book of Checklists*, by Scott Edelstein (Writer's Digest Books).

Important Listing Information

Listings are based on editorial questionnaires and interviews. They are not advertisements; publishers do not pay for their listings. The markets are not endorsed by Writer's Market *editors.*

● *All listings have been verified before publication of this book. If a listing has not changed from last year, then the editor told us the market's needs have not changed and the previous listing continues to accurately reflect its policies. We require documentation in our files for each listing and never run a listing without its editorial office's approval.*

● Writer's Market *reserves the right to exclude any listing.*

● *When looking for a specific market, check the index. A market may not be listed for one of these reasons.*

   1. *It doesn't solicit freelance material.*

   2. *It doesn't pay for material.*

   3. *It has gone out of business.*

   4. *It has failed to verify or update its listing for the 1992 edition.*

   5. *It was in the middle of being sold at press time, and rather than disclose premature details, we chose not to list it.*

   6. *It hasn't answered* Writer's Market *inquiries satisfactorily. (To best of our ability, and with our readers' help, we try to screen out fraudulent listings.)*

   7. *It buys few manuscripts, thereby constituting a very small market for freelancers.*

● *See the index of additional markets at the end of each major section for specific information on individual markets not listed.*

The Markets

Book Publishers

Publishers Weekly reported that among recent bestsellers, fiction sales outpaced nonfiction by a wide margin. The top 15 fiction sellers were written by established authors (such as Scott Turow), who tend to produce a bestseller every year. The three leading nonfiction books had a connection with television (*The Civil War*, for example). Celebrity status from entertainment, sports, politics and journalism helped to catapult several nonfiction books into sales of more than 250,000 copies.

These trends suggest that some of the large publishing houses have come to rely on established authors and celebrity status for their bestsellers. This should not imply that only big name writers, movie stars, sports heroes and former presidents can publish books. Their books, however, will get the highest advertising and promotion budgets that help to make bestsellers possible.

Although bestsellers and other books from the conglomerate publishing houses tend to dominate shelf space in most bookstores, there are a host of medium and smaller companies that publish and distribute very fine books. Some publishers are interested only in specific areas, such as science fiction, while others consider a broad range of general interest topics. You'll find that some houses pursue mass market bestsellers only, while others want to produce literary novels or specialized books.

In 1991, the American Booksellers Association began to recognize and reward worthy midlist books with the innauguration of the Abby Awards. *The Education of Little Tree* by Forrest Carter (University of New Mexico Press) won $5,000 for this first, annual award. Soon after, it made *The New York Times* trade paperback bestseller list.

A few publishers have started receiving submissions electronically, either by modem or computer disk, while others still prefer hard copy. Some want both. Information in the individual listings, as well as researching publisher's new titles, will help you keep up with the changing business of book publishing. For an inside look at the book publishing industry, small to large, and the process by which a proposal and manuscript become a book, read the Publishers' Roundtable on page 45.

Hot topics

No one can predict with certainty what topics and types of books will be strong sellers. Book publishers plan their titles months to several years in advance, and general trends such as the aging population and the new baby boom will undoubtedly affect their choice of manuscripts. Current events and their possible future effects also influence editors' choices. Writers, especially those marketing nonfiction, should make it a practice to keep up with recent information and events to make their manuscripts as timely and salable as possible.

Here are some industry trends that may affect what editors buy in the coming year:

- A number of publishing houses have created more imprints. This has allowed increased flexibility to acquire different types of books, and has balanced out the inefficiency that often follows publishing mergers. Imprints have varying degrees of independence from the rest of the company and may be more open to particular topics and unsolicited submissions.

● Children's books remain a strong category, although publishers are becoming increasingly selective. Many schools are now using children's trade books instead of textbooks as classroom readers. For more information about the children's book market and interviews with two children's writers, see First Bylines at the end of this section.

● Sports books remain popular, particularly those about baseball, basketball and golf. Sports personalities, fitness, and instructional books all enjoy good sales.

● Environmental topics have been a big hit among both adults and children. Books on conservation techniques and environmental concerns are selling well.

● True crime remains very popular. See First Bylines at the end of this section for an interview with a writer of true crime books.

● Books of comic strips are also doing well of late. Renewed interest in prime time cartoons has made this a hot topic.

Other strong categories include travel, gardening, science fiction, parenting, cooking, business, celebrity and humor. While these categories are popular, writers should keep in mind that editors are always looking for something new and different.

Book markets

Give your book the best publisher possible by analyzing your manuscript and studying the market. For some writers, the best is a publisher whose books regularly appear on the bestseller lists. For others, the best is a small press where each author gets personal attention from the editor. For publishers who produce fewer than four titles per year, see the Small Presses section. For more information on small presses, contact the Small Press Writers and Artists Organization, 1210 Greer Ave., Holbrook AZ 86025.

No matter what type of book you've written, the Book Publishers section can help you. You'll find more than 800 publishers listed. Not all of them buy the kind of work you write, but studying the listing subheads for nonfiction and fiction in the Book Publishers Subject Index will tell you which ones do.

When you read the detailed listings of publishers, choose two or three that buy what you're writing. Send for their catalogs and writer's guidelines. You'll learn the most current information about the books they've published, as well as their preferences for receiving manuscripts. Try to read a few of the publishers' books; a visit to the library is all that's necessary.

You will find publishers prefer different types of submissions. Some will read only a query letter; some want a query with an outline or synopsis; others want a proposal. If editors accept submissions only through agents, don't send material directly.

Most editors like specific information in query letters. (See the Business of Writing for a sample book query letter.) Show that you understand their concerns by mentioning the audience for your book, the competition, and why your book is different. The editor also will want to know if you have previous publishing experience or special training relevant to the book's subject. Do not claim to have written the next blockbuster bestseller—even if you think you have.

Remember that only a fraction of today's writers sell a book to the first publisher to which it's submitted. Prepare a list of at least a dozen publishers that might be interested in your book. Learn more about them; send for catalogs and guidelines a few at a time. If your submission comes back with a rejection, don't lose heart. An editor who rejected the manuscript of *Lolita* was quoted in *Rotten Rejections* (Pushcart Press) as having written back to author Vladimir Nabokov, "The book would serve no purpose of any kind and should be buried under a large stone for a thousand years."

Send your work to the next publisher on your list. You may be able to speed up this process with simultaneous submissions of your query letter or manuscript. It's usually acceptable to send queries to several editors at the same time—as long as each letter is individually addressed. Never send a form letter as a query. If more than one editor responds favorably, you may be able to submit your manuscript simultaneously. Some publishers, however, refuse to consider simultaneous submissions; their *Writer's Market* listings and their guidelines will tell you their policies. Otherwise, you can send your manuscript to two or more publishers at the same time—but you should notify the editors that it's a simultaneous submission.

Be sure to address every letter and proposal to a specific person at a publisher. Unsolicited manuscripts marked "Editorial Department" will end up in the slush pile, a region from which few books emerge, especially at larger companies. Agents are playing a greater role at such companies, who are coming to rely on agents to screen material for them. For more information on these topics and the book publishing process in general, see the Publishers' Roundtable in The Business of Writing section.

Subsidy publishing

We receive many calls and letters asking about subsidy publishing and self-publishing. As you read more about the publishing industry, you'll undoubtedly find advertisements and articles describing these alternatives. Be cautious. Know what you want from your writing.

Most writers want to make money from the books they write. Those who aspire to be professional writers know that it may take years to perfect a book, find the right publisher and receive royalty payments. They are willing to invest their time and efforts to meet that goal.

Some writers are more impatient. They've tried to sell a book and have met only rejection—encouraging rejection, maybe, but still rejection. They know they haven't written bestsellers, but they don't believe their books can be improved by further revision. They believe a specific market exists, and they want the book published.

Other writers simply write for their own satisfaction or for the pleasure of family and friends. Their writing may be just a hobby, but because of some encouragement they wonder why they can't get published. They haven't tried to market a manuscript before and are confused about the differences between royalty publishers, subsidy publishers and self-publishing. For more information on self-publishing see Exploring the Self-Publishing Option in The Business of Writing section.

We encourage you to work with publishers that pay writers. Most publishers do this through a royalty arrangement, paying the author 3-25% of the wholesale or retail price. These publishers actively market their books; you'll find them in bookstores and libraries, read about them in the newspaper and sometimes see their authors on TV. Whenever a copy of one of these books is sold, both the writer and the publisher make money.

Subsidy publishers, on the other hand, expect writers to pay part or all of the cost of producing a book. They may ask for $1,000 or sometimes as much as $25,000, explaining that current economic conditions in the industry necessitate authors paying the costs of publishing. Subsidy publishers rarely market books as effectively as major publishing companies. Subsidy publishers make money by selling their services to writers, not by selling their products to bookstores and libraries. Some subsidy publishers offer royalties but expect the writer to pay for promotion expenses.

Problems can arise when writers don't understand the policies and terms of a subsidy publisher's proposal or contract. Don't sign anything unless you understand and are comfortable with the terms. If you are willing to pay to have your book published, you should be willing to hire an attorney to advise you on a contract.

Subsidy publishers are sometimes called "vanity" publishers because the companies appeal to a writer's ego in wanting to have his book published. Most subsidy publishers are offended when they are called vanity presses, but we don't distinguish between the two.

Any publishing effort that asks the writer to pay all or part of the cost is identified as a subsidy publisher. Companies that ask authors to pay subsidies on more than 50% of the books they publish each year are listed in the Subsidy Publishers section.

This doesn't mean that subsidy publishing is always a bad choice. In Canada, for example, books are often subsidized by government grants. In the U.S., a special interest book may be subsidized by the writer's friends, a foundation or church. Sometimes a royalty publisher or university press will offer a subsidy arrangement to a writer whose talent outweighs the marketing potential of the book. Companies that do this 50% of the time or less are identified with an asterisk (*) before the listings.

Selling your work

If you receive a number of rejections, don't give up. Many successful writers submit a manuscript to dozens of publishers before finding one to publish their book. Others rely on agents to market their manuscripts. Three writers who recently published their first books all recommend having agents submit manuscripts to publishers, especially those by new writers.

First, be sure you've done everything to improve your book's chances. Study writing and revision techniques and continue to study the markets. Many writers also find classes and writer's groups helpful in putting them in touch with other people who share their interest in writing.

No matter which method you choose, remember that the writing of the book comes first. Think of your book as a manuscript in transition and help it evolve into the best book it can be while you search for the best possible publisher.

For a list of publishers according to their subjects of interest, see the nonfiction and fiction sections of the Book Publishers Subject Index. Information on some book publishers and packagers not included in this edition of *Writer's Market* can be found in the Other Book Publishers and Packagers at the end of the Subsidy Publishers section.

AASLH, American Association for State and Local History, Suite 202, 172 2nd Ave. N., Nashville TN 37201. (615)255-2971. FAX: (615)255-2979. Estab. 1940. Publishes hardcover and softcover originals and reprints. Averages 6 titles/year; receives 20-30 submissions annually. 50% of books from first-time authors; 100% of books from unagented writers. Pays 10% royalty on retail price. Publishes book an average of 1 year after acceptance. Reports in 3 months on submissions. Free book catalog.
Nonfiction: How-to, reference, collections, preservation, and textbook. "We publish books, mostly technical, that help people do effective work in historical societies, sites and museums, or do research in, or teach, history. No manuscripts on history itself—that is, on the history of specific places, events, people." Submit outline/synopsis and sample chapters. Reviews artwork/photos.
Recent Nonfiction Title: *Landscapes and Gardens for Historic Buildings*, by Rudy J. and Joy P. Favretti.
Tips: "The American Association for State and Local History provides leadership for and service to those who priactice and support history in North America: historical societies, museums, historic sites, parks, libraries, archives, historic preservation organizations, schools, colleges, and other educational organizations."

ABBEY PRESS, Publishing Division, St. Meinrad IN 47577. (812)357-8011. Publisher: Keith McClellan O.S.B. Estab. 1867. Publishes mass market paperback originals. Averages 10 titles/year. Receives 200 submissions/year. 40% of books from first-time authors; 100% of books from unagented writers. Pays 10% royalty on retail price. Publishes book an average of 1 year after acceptance. Reports in 1 month on queries; 6 weeks on mss. Ms guidelines for SASE.
Nonfiction: Abbey publications focus in three general areas: marriage, parenting and family life; pastoral care and spiritual growth. These materials include inspirational, self-help, gift, and personal/professional enrichment titles. They are distinguished by a gently spiritual and religious dimension. Query with outline/synopsis and sample chapters.
Recent Nonfiction Title: *Children Facing Grief*, by Janis Romond.
Tips: "Abbey publications are designed to offer practical, supportive and uplifting materials for people challenged by the demands of vocation, career and ordinary day-to-day living."

ABBOTT, LANGER & ASSOCIATES, 548 1st St., Crete IL 60417. (312)672-4200. President: Dr. Steven Langer. Publishes trade paperback originals and loose-leaf books. Averages 14 titles/year; receives 25 submissions annually. 15% of books from first-time authors; 100% of books from unagented writers. Pays 10-15% royalty; no advance. Publishes book an average of 18 months after acceptance. Query for electronic submissions. Book catalog for 6×9 SAE with 2 first class stamps. Reports in 2 weeks on queries; 2 months on mss.
Nonfiction: How-to, reference, technical on some phase of personnel administration, industrial relations, sales management, etc. Especially needs "a very limited number (3-5) of books dealing with very specialized topics in the field of personnel management, wage and salary administration, sales compensation, training, recruitment, selection, labor relations, etc." Publishes for personnel directors, wage and salary administrators, training directors, sales/marketing managers, security directors, etc. Query with outline. Reviews artwork/photos.
Recent Nonfiction Title: *How to Build a Motivated Work Force Using Non-Monetary Incentives*, by Lynn Grensing.
Tips: "A how-to book in personnel management, sales/marketing management or security management has the best chance of selling to our firm."

ABINGDON PRESS, Imprint of The United Methodist Publishing House, 201 8th Ave. S., P.O. Box 801, Nashville TN 37202. (615)749-6301. Editor-in-Chief: Neil M. Alexander. Editor Trade Books: Mary Catherine Dean. Senior Editor Academic Books: Rex Mathews. Senior Editor Church Resources: Ronald P. Patterson. Editor Professional Books: Paul Franklyn. Editor Reference Books: Jack Keller. Estab. 1789. Other imprints are Cokesbury and Kingswood Books. Publishes paperback originals and reprints; church supplies. Receives approximately 2,500 submissions annually. Published 85 titles last year. Few books from first-time authors; 90-95% of books from unagented writers. Average print order for a writer's first book is 4,000-5,000. Pays royalty. Publishes book an average of 18 months after acceptance. Query for electronic submissions. Ms guidelines for SASE. Reports in 2 months.
Nonfiction: Religious-lay and professional, children's religious books and academic texts. Length: 32-300 pages. Query with outline and samples only. Reviews artwork/photos.
Recent Nonfiction Title: *Last Rights*, by Joseph B. Ingle.

HARRY N. ABRAMS, INC., Subsidiary of Times Mirror Co., 100 5th Ave., New York NY 10011. (212)206-7715. President, Publisher and Editor-in-Chief: Paul Gottlieb. Publishes hardcover and "a few" paperback originals. Averages 100 titles/year. "We are one of the few publishers who publish almost exclusively illustrated books. We consider ourselves the leading publishers of art books and high-quality artwork in the U.S." Offers variable advance. Publishes book an average of 1-2 years after acceptance. Reports in 3 months. Book catalog for $5.
Nonfiction: Art, nature and science, and outdoor recreation. Requires illustrated material for art and art history, museums. Submit outline/synopsis and sample chapters and illustrations. Reviews artwork/photos as part of ms package.
Tips: "We publish *only* high-quality illustrated art books, i.e., art, art history, museum exhibition catalog, written by specialists and scholars in the field. Once the author has signed a contract to write a book for our firm the author must finish the manuscript to agreed-upon high standards within the schedule agreed upon in the contract."

ACADEMY CHICAGO, 213 W. Institute Place, Chicago IL 60610. (312)751-7302. FAX: (312)751-7306. Editorial Director/Senior Editor: Anita Miller. Estab. 1975. Publishes hardcover and paperback originals and reprints. Averages 25–30 titles/year; receives approximately 2,000 submissions annually. 10% of books from first-time authors; 25% of books from unagented writers. Average print order for a writer's first book 1,500-5,000. Pays 7-10% royalty; modest advances. Publishes book an average of 18 months after acceptance. Book catalog for 8½×11 SAE with 3 first class stamps; guidelines for #10 SASE. Submit cover letter with first four chapters. Reports in 2 months.
Nonfiction: Adult, travel, true crime and historical. No how-to, cookbooks, self-help, etc. Query and submit first four consecutive chapters. Reviews artwork/photos.
Recent Nonfiction Title: *Conquest of Eden*, by Michael Paiewonsky.
Fiction: "Mysteries, mainstream novels." No "romantic," children's, young adult, religious or sexist fiction; nothing avant-garde.
Recent Fiction Title: *In a Dark Wood Wandering*, by Hella S. Haasse.
Tips: "At the moment, we are looking for good nonfiction, although we certainly want excellent original fiction."

ACCENT BOOKS, Division of Accent Publications, 12100 W. 6th Ave., P.O. Box 15337, Denver CO 80215. (303)988-5300. Executive Editor: Mary B. Nelson. Estab. 1947. Publishes evangelical Christian paperbacks, the majority of which are nonfiction. Guidelines available for #10 SASE. Averages 10-

15 titles/year. 30% of books from first-time authors; 100% of books from unagented writers. Pays royalty on cover price. Publishes book an average of 1 year after acceptance. Query or submit 3 sample chapters with a brief synopsis and chapter outline. Do not submit full ms unless requested. Reports in 3 months. Book catalog for 9 × 12 SAE with 4 first class stamps.

Recent Nonfiction Title: *Ordinary Heroes*, by David R. Walls.

Fiction: "Fiction titles have strong evangelical message woven throughout plot. Main characters are Christians. Books are either contemporary mystery/romance or frontier romance."

Recent Fiction Title: *The Fire Within*, by B.J. Hansen.

Tips: "How-to books designed for personal application of biblical truth and/or dealing with problems/ solutions of philosophical, societal, and personal issues from a biblical perspective have the best chance of selling to our firm. We also consider books for the professional and volunteer in church ministries."

‡**ACCESS PUBLISHERS,** 1078 E. Otero Ave., Littleton CO 80122. (303)797-2821. Editor: Kathy Fanchi. Publishes mass market originals on DOS readable disks. Division averages 6 titles/year. Receives 20-25 submissions/year. 100% of books are from first-time authors. 100% from unagented writers. Pays 10% royalty. No advances. Publishes book an average of 3 months after acceptance. Simultaneous submissions OK. Query for electronic submissions. Submissions on DOS readable disk(s) preferred. Reports in 3 weeks on queries; in 2 months on mss. Book catalog and manuscript guidelines for #10 SASE.

Fiction: Adventure, fantasy, historical, humor, mainstream/contemporary, mystery, romance, science fiction, suspense, western and young adult. "We are looking for highly readable manuscripts dealing with mainstream/contemporary issues or science fiction. Do not send pornographic material or books requiring graphics." Submit complete ms on DOS readable disk(s) in standard ASCII format.

Recent Fiction Title: *Preemie*, by Fran Richards (contemporary).

Tips: "We are interested in highly readable books written for the mainstream or science fiction audience. Our audience consists of literate computer users (and their families) with an interest in contemporary issues and/or future trends in science and technology. If I were a writer trying to market a book today I would want a publisher who is willing to let the market determine the fate of my book."

ACE SCIENCE FICTION, The Berkley Publishing Group, 200 Madison Ave., New York NY 10016. (212)686-9820. Estab. 1953. Publishes paperback originals and reprints. Publishes 120 titles/year. Writer's guidelines for #10 SASE.

Fiction: Science fiction and fantasy. Query with synopsis and first 3 chapters. Reports in 3 months.

Recent Fiction Title: *Orbital Decay*, by Allen Steele.

ACS PUBLICATIONS, INC., P.O. Box 34487, San Diego CA 92163-4487. (619)297-9203. Editorial Director: Maritha Pottenger. Estab. 1977. Publishes trade paperback originals and reprints. Averages 8 titles/year; receives 400 submissions annually. 50% of books from first-time authors; 95% of books from unagented writers. Average print order for a writer's first book is 3,000. Pays 15% royalty "on monies received through wholesale and retail sales." No advance. Publishes book an average of 2 years after acceptance. Query for electronic submissions. Reports in 1 month on queries; 2 months on mss. Book catalog and guidelines for 9 × 12 SAE with 3 first class stamps.

Nonfiction: New Age. Subjects include astrology, useful metaphysics. "Our most important market is astrology. We are seeking pragmatic, useful, immediately applicable contributions to field; prefer psychological approach. Specific ideas and topics should enhance people's lives. Research also valued. No determinism ('Saturn made me do it.') No autobiographies. No airy-fairy 'space cadet' philosophizing. Keep it grounded, useful, opening options (not closing doors) for readers." Query or submit outline and 3 sample chapters.

Recent Nonfiction Title: *The Book of Neptune*, by Marilyn Waram.

Tips: "The most common mistake writers make when trying to get their work published is to send works to inappropriate publishers. We get too many submissions outside our field or contrary to our world view."

BOB ADAMS, INC., 260 Center St., Holbrook MA 02343. (617)767-8100. Managing Editor: Brandon Toropov. Publishes hardcover and trade paperback originals. Averages 25 titles/year. Receives 1,000 submissions/year. 25% of books from first-time authors; 25% of books from unagented writers. Variable royalty "determined on case-by-case basis." Publishes book an average of 12-18 months after acceptance. Reports in 2 months "if interested. We accept no responsibility for unsolicited manuscripts." Book catalog for 9 × 12 SAE and 10 first class stamps.

Nonfiction: Reference books on careers, self-help and business. Query with SASE.

Recent Nonfiction Title: *Why Love is Not Enough*, by Sol Gordon.

ADDISON-WESLEY PUBLISHING CO., INC., General Books Division, Jacob Way, Reading MA 01867. Publisher: David C. Miller. Contact: Editorial Dept. Estab. 1942. Publishes hardcover and paperback originals. Publishes 125-150 titles/year. Pays royalty. Simultaneous submissions OK. Reports in 6 weeks. Free book catalog.
Nonfiction: Biography, history, business/economics, health, how-to, politics, psychology and science, cookbooks, computer books. Query, then submit outline/synopsis and 1 sample chapter.
Recent Nonfiction Title: *Iron John*, by Robert Bly.
Tips: "We will accept submissions for cookbooks, computer books and general nonfiction." Queries/ mss will be routed to the appropriate editors in the publishing group.

ADVOCACY PRESS, Division of Advocates for Girls, P.O. Box 236, Santa Barbara CA 93102. (805)962-2728. Editor: Penelope C. Paine. Estab. 1983. Non-profit press publishes hardcover and trade paperback originals with an equity/self-esteem focus. Does not publish adult or young adult fiction. Children's picture books must focus on specific concepts, e.g. leadership, self-reliance, etc. Publishes average 4 titles/year. Receives 100-150 submissions/year. 25% from first-time authors; 100% from unagented writers. Publishes ms an average of 6 months after acceptance. Simultaneous submissions OK. Reports in 6 weeks.
Nonfiction: Biography, juvenile, self-help. Subjects include education, psychology and women's issues/studies. "Children's picture books needed. Non-sexist, issue-oriented adult and young adult materials." Submit outline/synopsis and sample chapters.
Recent Nonfiction Title: *More Choices*, by Bingham/Stryker (young adult self-help).
Fiction: Adventure, feminist, historical, juvenile, picture books. Submit outline/synopsis and sample chapters.
Recent Fiction Title: *Mother Nature Nursery Rhymes*, by Stryker.

‡AFCOM PUBLISHING, P.O. Box H, Harbor City CA 90710-0330. (213)377-4951. FAX: (213)544-2314. Manager: Greg Cook. Estab. 1988. Publishes mass market paperback originals and reprints. 80% of books are originals; 20% are reprints. Firm averages 5 titles/year. Receives 50 submissions/year. 50% of books from first-time authors. 100% from unagented writers. Pays 5-15% royalty on wholesale price. Offers $200 average advance. Publishes book an average of 6 months after acceptance. Simultaneous submissions OK. Reports in 2 months on queries; 3 months on mss.
Nonfiction: How-to, juvenile, reference, self-help, textbook. Subjects include business, education, hobbies, recreation, sports, books on total quality management and children's books. "We are looking for how-to books, total quality management, books on projects to entertain children and business textbooks." Submit outline/synopsis and sample chapters or complete ms. Reviews artwork/photos as part of freelance ms package.
Recent Nonfiction Title: *Over 101 Inexpensive Ways to Entertain Children*, by Juanita Ferry.
Fiction: Humor, juvenile. Submit complete ms.
Recent Fiction Title: *The 12 Powers of Animals*, by Eloise Dickis (Juvenile).
Tips: "Writers have the best chance selling us how-to books with an easily reachable market and any books related to total quality management, or business related improvement books including books on quality function deployment, design of experiments, statistical process controls, cycle-time management, value engineering, benchmarking and/or teambuilding. If I were a writer trying to market a book today, I would concentrate on books that have a target market or books that would interest libraries."

AGLOW PUBLICATIONS, Women's Aglow Fellowship International, P.O. Box 1548, Lynnwood WA 98046-1557. (206)775-7282. FAX: (206)778-9615. Editor: Gloria Chisholm. Estab. 1969. Publishes trade paperback originals. Averages 10 titles/year; receives 1,000 submissions annually. 50% of books from first-time authors; 95% of books from unagented writers. Average print order of a writer's first book is 10,000. Pays up to 10% maximum royalty on retail price. Buys some mss outright. Publishes book 18 months after acceptance. Reports in 1 month on queries; 2 months on mss. Book catalog and guidelines for 9 × 12 SAE with 3 first class stamps.
Nonfiction: Biblically-oriented support group books, self-help and inspirational. Subjects include religion (Christian only). "Familiarize yourself with our materials before submitting. Our needs and formats are very specific." Query or submit outline/synopsis and first 3 sample chapters.
Recent Nonfiction Title: *Love and Its Counterfeits*, by Barbara Cook.
Tips: "The writer has the best chance of selling our firm a book that shows some aspect of the Christian life."

ALA BOOKS, Subsidiary of American Library Association, 50 E. Huron St., Chicago IL 60611. (312)280-1544. Senior Editor: Herbert Bloom. Publishes hardcover and paperback originals. Firm averages 35-40 titles/year. Receives approximately 100 submissions/year. 60% of books from first-time authors; 100% from unagented writers. Pays royalty of "not more than 15% of our receipts from sales." Publishes ms an average of 7 months after acceptance. Reports in 2 weeks on queries; 2 months on mss. Free ms guidelines.

Nonfiction: Reference. Subjects include library science, child and adult guidance, education, library service. Professional and reference books for librarians. "We are looking for guides to information, management of information centers; and application of electronic technologies to such management particularly." Query.

Recent Nonfiction Title: *Movie Characters of Leading Performers*, by Nowlan (general reference).

Tips: "Think analytically, but write simply."

‡ALASKA NORTHWEST BOOKS, Division of GTE Discovery Publications, 22026 20th Ave. SE, Bothell WA 98041-3007. (206)487-6100. Contact: Acquisitions Editor. Estab. 1959. Publishes hardcover and trade paperback originals and reprints. Firm averages 20 titles/year. Receives hundreds of submissions/year. 50% of books from first-time authors. 80% from unagented writers. Pays 10-15% royalty on wholesale price. Buys mss outright (rarely). Offers $4,000 average advance. Publishes book an average of 1 year after acceptance. Simultaneous submissions OK. Reports in 6 months on queries. Book catalog and manuscript guidelines free on request.

Nonfiction: "All written for a general readership, not for experts in the subject." Subjects include nature and natural history, travel, cookbooks, Native American culture, adventure, outdoor recreation and sports, the arts, and children's books. "Our book needs are as follows: one-quarter Alaskan focus, one-quarter Northwest, one-quarter Pacific coast, one-quarter national (looking for logical extensions of current subjects)." Submit outline/synopsis and sample chapters.

Recent Nonfiction Title: *Wild Echoes: Encounters With the Most Endangered Animal in North America*, by Charles Bergman.

Tips: "Writers have the best chance selling us books that are professionally written and polished, with a clear market. We are looking for originality. We publish a wide range of books for a wide audience. Some of our books are clearly for travelers, others for those interested in outdoor recreation or a specific art form. If I were a writer trying to market a book today, I would research the competition (existing books) for what I have in mind, and clearly (and concisely) express why my idea is different and better. I would describe the bookbuyers (and readers)—where they are, how many of them are there, how they can be reached (organizations, publication), why they want or need my book."

THE ALBAN INSTITUTE, INC., 4125 Nebraska Ave. NW, Washington DC 20016. (202)244-7320. Director of Publications: Celia A. Hahn. Publishes trade paperback originals. Averages 7 titles/year; receives 100 submissions annually. 100% of books from unagented writers. Pays 7% royalty on books; $50 on publication for 2- to 8-page articles relevant to congregational life—practical—ecumenical. Publishes book an average of 1 year after acceptance. Reports in 2 months. Proposals must be submitted. No unsolicited manuscripts. Book catalog and ms guidelines for 9 × 12 SAE and 3 first class stamps.

Nonfiction: Religious—focus on local congregation—ecumenical. Must be accessible to general reader. Research preferred. Needs mss on the task of the ordained leader in the congregation, the career path of the ordained leader in the congregation, problems and opportunities in congregational life, and ministry of the laity in the world and in the church. No sermons, devotional, children's titles, inspirational type or prayers. Query: write for guidelines.

Recent Nonfiction Title: *The Inviting Church: A Study of New Member Assimilation*, by Roy Oswald and Speed Leas.

Tips: "Our audience is comprised of intelligent, probably liberal mainline Protestant and Catholic clergy and lay leaders, executives and seminary administration/faculty—people who are concerned with the local church at a practical level and new approaches to its ministry. We are looking for titles on Problems and Opportunities in Congregational Life, The Clergy Role and Career, and The Ministry of the Laity in the Church and in the World."

ALLEN PUBLISHING CO., 7324 Reseda Blvd., Reseda CA 91335. (818)344-6788. Owner/Publisher: Michael Wiener. Estab. 1979. Publishes mass market paperback originals. Firm averages 4 titles/year. Receives 50-100 submissions/year. 50% of books from first-time authors. 100% from unagented writers. Buys mss outright for negotiable sum. Publishes book an average of 6 months after acceptance. Simultaneous submissions OK. Reports in 2 weeks. Book catalog for #10 SASE.

Nonfiction: How-to and self-help. Subjects include business and economics and money/finance. "We want self-help material, 25,000 words approximately, aimed at wealth-builders, opportunity seekers, aspiring entrepreneurs. We specialize in material for people who are relatively inexperienced in the world of business and have little or no capital to invest. Material must be original and authoritative, not rehashed from other sources. All our books are marketed exclusively by mail, in soft-cover, 8½ × 11 format. We are a specialty publisher and will not consider anything that does not exactly meet our needs." Query. Reviews artwork/photos as part of ms package.

Recent Nonfiction Title: *How To Win Multi-Million Dollar State Lotteries*, by Doug Freeman.
Tips: "There are more and more people who call themselves writers but who do not have the expertise to write nonfiction books on the subjects they choose. We prefer books by people who really know their subjects. Choose a very specialized subject, learn all you can about it, and write."

ALMAR PRESS, 4105 Marietta Dr., Vestal NY 13850. (607)722-0265. FAX: (607)722-0265. Editor-in-Chief: A.N. Weiner. Managing Editor: M.F. Weiner. Estab. 1977. Publishes hardcover and paperback originals and reprints. Averages 8 titles/year; receives 200 submissions annually. 75% of books from first-time authors; 100% of books from unagented writers. Average print order for a writer's first book is 2,000. Pays 10% royalty; no advance. Publishes book an average of 6 months after acceptance. Prefers exclusive submissions; however, simultaneous (if so indicated) submissions OK. Query for electronic submissions. Reports in 1 month. Book catalog for 8½×11 SAE with 2 first class stamps. *"Submissions must include SASE for reply and return of manuscript."*
Nonfiction: Publishes business, technical, regional and consumer books and reports. "These main subjects include general business, financial, travel, career, technology, personal help, North-East regional, hobbies, general medical, general legal, and how-to. *Almar Reports* are business and technology subjects published for management use and prepared in 8½×11 and book format. Publications are printed and bound in soft covers as required. Reprint publications represent a new aspect of our business." Submit outline/synopsis and sample chapters. Reviews artwork/photos as part of ms package. Looks for information in the proposed book that makes it different or unusual enough to attract book buyers. Reviews artwork/photos.
Recent Nonfiction Title: *A Picture Postcard History of U.S. Aviation*, by Jack W. Legenfelder.
Tips: "We're adding a new series of postcard books for various topics where the picture postcards are illustrated and the captions describe the scene on the postcard and the history related to it. Approximately 225 illustrations per book. We are open to any suggested topic. This type of book will be important to us. We look for timely subjects. The type of book the writer has the best chance of selling to our firm is something different or unusual—*no* poetry or fiction, also *no* first-person travel or family history. The book must be complete and of good quality."

*ALPINE PUBLICATIONS, INC., 214 19th St. SE, Loveland CO 80537. (303)667-9317. Publisher: B.J. McKinney. Estab. 1975. Publishes hardcover and trade paperback originals. Averages 6 titles/year. Subsidy publishes 2% of books when "book fits into our line but has a market so limited (e.g., rare dog breed) that we would not accept it on royalty terms." Occasional small advance. Pays 7-15% royalty. Publishes book an average of 1½ years after acceptance. Reports in 3 weeks on queries; 2 months on mss. Writer's guidelines for #10 SAE with 2 first class stamps.
Nonfiction: How-to books about animals. "We need comprehensive breed books on the more popular AKC breeds, books for breeders on showing, breeding, genetics, gait, new training methods, and cat and horse books. No fiction or fictionalized stories of real animals; no books on reptiles; no personal experience stories except in case of well-known professional in field." Submit outline/synopsis and sample chapters or complete ms. Reviews artwork/photos as part of manuscript package.
Recent Nonfiction Title: *201 Ways to Enjoy Your Dog*, by E. Milon.

ALYSON PUBLICATIONS, INC., 40 Plympton St., Boston MA 02118. (617)542-5679. Publisher: Sasha Alyson. Estab. 1979. Publishes trade paperback originals and reprints. Averages 20 titles/year; receives 500 submissions annually. 30% of books from first-time authors; 80% of books from unagented writers. Average print order for a writer's first book is 6,000. Pays 8-15% royalty on net price; offers $1,000-3,000 advance. Publishes book an average of 15 months after acceptance. Reports in 2 weeks on queries; 5 weeks on mss. Looks for "writing ability and content suitable for our house." Book catalog and ms guidelines for #10 SAE and 3 first class stamps.
Nonfiction: Gay/lesbian subjects. "We are especially interested in nonfiction providing a positive approach to gay/lesbian issues." Accepts nonfiction translations. Submit one-page synopsis. Reviews artwork/photos as part of ms package.
Recent Nonfiction Title: *The Trouble with Harry Hay*, by Stuart Timmons.
Fiction: Gay novels. Accepts fiction translations. Submit one-page synopsis.
Recent Fiction Title: *Vampires Anonymous*, by Jeffrey McMahan.
Tips: "We publish many books by new authors. The writer has the best chance of selling to our firm well-researched, popularly-written nonfiction on a subject (e.g., some aspect of gay history) that has not yet been written about much. With fiction, create a strong storyline that makes the reader want to find out what happens. With nonfiction, write in a popular style for a non-academic audience. Actively soliciting manuscripts aimed at kids of lesbian and gay parents."

AMACOM BOOKS, Imprint of American Management Association, 135 W. 50th, New York NY 10020. (212)903-8081. Director, Weldon P. Rackley. Publishes hardcover and trade paperback originals and trade paperback reprints. Firm averages 50 titles/year. Receives 200 submissions/year. 50%of books from first-time authors. 90% from unagented writers. Pays 10-15% royalty on net receipts by the publisher. Publishes book an average of 10 months after acceptance. Query for electronic submissions. Reports in 2-3 weeks on queries. Free book catalog and manuscript guidelines.

Nonfiction: How-to, reference, self-help, textbook and retail bookstore market. Subjects include business, computers, education/business, business books of all types. Query. Submit outline/synopsis and sample chapters.

Tips: "Our audience consists of people in the business sector looking for very applied books on business."

AMERICA WEST PUBLISHERS, P.O. Box 986, Tehachapi CA 93581. (805)822-9655. FAX: (805)822-9658. Review Editor: George Green. Estab. 1986. Publishes hardcover and trade paperback originals and hardcover and trade paperback reprints. Averages 5 titles/year. Receives 50 submissions/year. 30% of books from first-time authors. 90% from unagented writers. Pays 10% on wholesale price. Offers $300 average advance. Publishes book an average of 6 months after acceptance. Simultaneous submissions OK. Reports in 2 weeks on queries; 3 months on mss. Free book catalog and manuscript guidelines.

Nonfiction: UFO—metaphysical. Subject includes health/medicine (holistic self-help). Submit outline/synopsis and sample chapters. Reviews artwork/photos as part of ms package.

Recent Nonfiction Title: *The Energy Grid*, by Bruce Cathie.

Tips: "We currently have materials in all bookstores that have areas of UFO's and also metaphysical information and New Age."

AMERICAN ASTRONAUTICAL SOCIETY, Univelt, Inc., Publisher, P.O. Box 28130, San Diego CA 92198. (619)746-4005. Editorial Director: H. Jacobs. Estab. 1970. Publishes hardcover originals. Averages 8 titles/year; receives 12-15 submissions annually. 5% of books from first-time authors; 5% of books from unagented writers. Average print order for a writer's first book is 600-2,000. Pays 10% royalty on actual sales; no advance. Publishes book an average of 4 months after acceptance. Simultaneous submissions OK. Reports in 1 month. Book catalog and ms guidelines for 9 × 12 SAE and 3 first class stamps.

Nonfiction: Proceedings or monographs in the field of astronautics, including applications of aerospace technology to Earth's problems. "Our books must be space-oriented or space-related. They are meant for technical libraries, research establishments and the aerospace industry worldwide." Submit outline/synopsis and 1-2 sample chapters. Reviews artwork/photos as part of ms package.

Recent Nonfiction Title: *Soviet Space Programs 1980-1985*, by N.L. Johnson.

AMERICAN BUSINESS CONSULTANTS, INC., 1540 Nuthatch Lane, Sunnyvale CA 94087-4999. (408)738-3011. President: Wilfred Tetreault. Estab. 1979. Publishes trade paperback originals. Averages 30 titles/year. Receives 2 submissions/year. 100% of books from first-time authors. Buys mss outright. Publishes book an average of 1 month after acceptance. Simultaneous submissions OK. Query for electronic submissions. Reports in 1 month.

Nonfiction: Appraising, buying and selling any kind of business fraud and ripoffs. Query.

Recent Nonfiction Title: *Buying & Selling Business Opportunities*, by W. Tetreault (business how-to paperback).

Tips: "Writers have the best chance selling us books on business frauds. Our audience consists of buyers, sellers of businesses and business brokers."

AMERICAN CATHOLIC PRESS, 16160 S. Seton Dr., South Holland IL 60473. (312)331-5845. Editorial Director: Fr. Michael Gilligan, Ph.D. Estab. 1967. Publishes hardcover originals and hardcover and paperback reprints. "Most of our sales are by direct mail, although we do work through retail outlets." Averages 4 titles/year. Pays by outright purchase of $25-100; no advance. Publishes book an average of 8 months after acceptance. Simultaneous submissions OK. Reports in 2 months.

Nonfiction: "We publish books on the Roman Catholic liturgy—for the most part, books on religious music and educational books and pamphlets. We also publish religious songs for church use, including Psalms, as well as choral and instrumental arrangements. We are interested in new music, meant for use in church services. Books, or even pamphlets, on the Roman Catholic Mass are especially welcome. We have no interest in secular topics and are not interested in religious poetry of any kind." Query.

Recent Nonfiction Title: *Psalter*, by Jeanette Dandurand.

The double dagger before a listing indicates that the listing is new in this edition. New markets are often more receptive to freelance submissions.

‡**AMERICAN CORRECTIONAL ASSOCIATION**, 8025 Laurel Lakes Ct., Laurel MD 20707. (301)206-5100. Managing Editor: Elizabeth Watts. Publishes hardcover and trade paperback originals. Firm averages 20 titles/year. Receives 20 submissions/year. 90% of books from first-time authors. 100% from unagented writers. Pays 10% royalty on net sales. Publishes book an average of 1 year after acceptance. Query for electronic submissions. Reports in 1 month on queries; 3 months on mss. Free book catalog and manuscript guidelines.

Nonfiction: How-to, reference, technical, textbook, correspondence courses. "We are looking for practical, how-to texts or training materials written for the corrections profession. No true-life accounts of current or former inmates or correctional officers, theses or dissertations." Query. Submit outline/synopsis and sample chapters, complete ms. Reviews artwork/photos as part of ms package.

Recent Nonfiction Title: *Getting High and Doing Time: What's the Connection*, by Edward Read and Dennis Daley (recovery guide).

Tips: "People in the field want practical information, as do academics to a certain extent. Our audience is made up of criminal justice students and corrections professionals. If I were a writer trying to market a book today, I would contact publishers while developing my manuscript to get a better idea of the publishers' needs."

AMERICAN HOSPITAL PUBLISHING, INC., American Hospital Association, 211 E. Chicago Ave., Chicago IL 60611. (312)440-6800. Vice President, Books: Brian Schenk. Estab. 1979. Publishes trade paperback originals. Firm averages 20-30 titles/year. Receives 20 submissions/year. 20% of books from first-time authors; 100% from unagented writers. Pays 10-12% royalty on retail price. Offers $1,000 average advance. Publishes book an average of 1 year after acceptance. Reports in 1 month on queries; 6 weeks on mss. Book catalog and manuscript guidelines for #10 SASE.

Nonfiction: Reference, technical, textbook. Subjects include business and economics (specific to health care institutions); health/medicine (never consumer oriented). Need field-based, reality-tested responses to changes in the health care field directed to hospital CEO's, planners, boards of directors, or other senior management. No personal histories, untested health care programs or clinical texts. Query.

Recent Nonfiction Title: *Restructuring for Ambulatory Care*, by Ted Matson, Ed.

Tips: "The successful proposal demonstrates a clear understanding of the needs of the market and the writer's ability to succinctly present practical knowledge of demonstrable benefit that comes from genuine experience that readers will recognize, trust and accept. The audience is senior and middle management of health care institutions."

AMERICAN SOCIETY OF CIVIL ENGINEERS, Book Publishing Program, 345 E. 47th St., New York NY 10017. (212)705-7689. Book Acquisitions Editor: Zoe G. Foundotos. Estab. 1988. Imprint averages 5 titles/year. 80% of books from first time authors; 100% from unagented writers. Pays 10% royalty. No advances available. Simultaneous submissions OK. Query for electronic submissions. Reports in 1 month on queries; 3 months on mss. Free book catalog and manuscript guidelines.

Nonfiction: Civil engineering. We are looking for "topics that are useful and instructive to the engineering practitioner." Query with outline/synopsis and sample chapters.

Recent Nonfiction Title: *Sons of Martha*, by Augustine J. Fredrich, Ed.

AMHERST MEDIA, 418 Homecrest Dr., Amherst NY 14226. (716)874-4450. FAX: (716)874-4450. Publisher: Craig Alesse. Estab. 1974. Publishes hardcover and trade paperback originals and reprints. Averages 7 titles/year. Receives 20 submissions/year. 80% of books from first-time authors; 100% from unagented writers. Pays 5-8% royalty. Publishes book an average of 3-6 months after acceptance. Simultaneous submissions OK. Reports in 3 weeks. Book catalog for #10 SAE and 3 first class stamps. Manuscript guidelines free on request.

Nonfiction: How-to. Subjects include photography, astronomy and video. We are looking for well-written and illustrated photo, video and astronomy books. Query. Reviews artwork/photos as part of ms package.

Recent Nonfiction Titles: *Basic Camcorder Guide*, by Steve Bryant.

Tips: "Our audience is made up of beginning to advanced photographers. If I were a writer trying to market a book today, I would fill the need of a specific audience and edit in a tight manner."

ANCESTRY INCORPORATED, P.O. Box 476, Salt Lake City UT 84110. (801)531-1790. FAX: (801)531-1798. Managing Editor: Robert J. Welsh. Estab. 1982. Publishes hardcover and mass market paperback originals. Averages 10 titles/year; receives 10-20 submissions annually. 70% of books from first-time authors; 100% of books from unagented writers. Pays 8-12% royalty or purchases mss outright. Advances are discouraged but considered if necessary. Publishes book an average of 1 year after acceptance. Simultaneous submissions OK. Query for electronic submissions. Reports in 1 month on queries; 2 months on mss. Free book catalog and ms guidelines.

Nonfiction: How-to, reference and genealogy. Subjects include Americana; history (family and local); and hobbies (genealogy). "Our publications are aimed exclusively at the genealogist. We consider everything from short monographs to book length works on immigration, migration, record collections and heraldic topics are considered." No mss that are not genealogical or historical. Query, or submit outline/synopsis and sample chapters, or complete ms. Reviews artwork/photos.

Recent Nonfiction Title: *The Library of Congress*, by James C. Neagles.

Tips: "Genealogical reference, how-to, and descriptions of source collections have the best chance of selling to our firm. Be precise in your description. Please, no family histories or genealogies."

‡ANCHORAGE PRESS, INC., P.O. Box 8067, New Orleans LA 70182. (504)283-8868. Editor: Orlin Corey. Publishes hardcover originals. Firm averages 10 titles/year. Receives 450-900 submissions/year. 50% of books from first-time authors. 80% from unagented writers. Pays 10-15% royalty on retail price. Playwrights also receive 50-70% royalties. Publishes book an average of 1 year after acceptance. Reports in 3 weeks on queries; 4 months on mss. Free book catalog and manuscript guidelines.

Nonfiction: Textbook and plays. Subjects include education, language/literature and plays. "We are looking for play anthologies; and texts for teachers of drama/theater (middle school and high school.)" Query. Reviews artwork/photos as part of ms package.

Recent Nonfiction Title: *The Creative Drama Book: 3 Approaches*, by Judith Kase-Polisini.

Fiction: Juvenile, literary, plays of juvenile/young people's interest. Query.

ANDERSON PUBLISHING CO., 2035 Reading Rd., Cincinnati OH 45202. (513)421-4142. Vice President of Editorial: Dale Hartig. Estab. 1887. Publishes hardcover, paperback originals, journals and software and reprints. Publishes 13-15 titles/year. Pays 15-18% royalty; "advance in selected cases." Publishes book an average of 7 months after acceptance. Simultaneous submissions OK. Reports in 2 months. Book catalog for 8½ × 11 SASE; guidelines for SASE.

Nonfiction: Law and law-related books, law school, paralegal and criminal justice criminology texts (justice administration legal series). Query or submit outline/chapters with vitae.

Recent Nonfiction Title: *Paralegal Resource Manual*, by Charles Nemeth.

ANDREWS AND McMEEL, 4900 Main St., Kansas City MO 64112. Editorial Director: Donna Martin. Publishes hardcover and paperback originals. Averages 30 titles/year. Pays royalty on retail price. "Query only. No unsolicited manuscripts. Areas of specialization include humor, how-to, and consumer reference books, such as *The Universal Almanac*, edited by John W. Wright."

APPALACHIAN MOUNTAIN CLUB BOOKS, 5 Joy St., Boston MA 02108. (617)523-0636. FAX: (617)523-0722. Editor: Gordon Hardy. Estab. 1897. Publishes hardcover and trade paperback originals. Averages 8 titles/year; receives 100 submissions annually. 50% of books from first-time authors;. 95% of books from unagented writers. Publishes book an average of 6 months after receipt of acceptable manuscript. Simultaneous submissions OK. Query for electronic submissions. Reports in 1 month on queries; 4 months on mss. Book brochure for 6 × 9 SAE.

Nonfiction: How-to, reference, field guides and guidebooks. Subjects include history (Northeast, mountains), nature, outdoor recreation, and travel. "We want manuscripts about the environment, mountains and their history and culture, and outdoor recreation (such as hiking, climbing, skiing, canoeing, kayaking, bicycling)." No physical fitness manuals. Query or submit outline/synopsis and sample chapters.

Recent Nonfiction Title: *Sea Kayaking Along the New England Coast*, by Tamsin Venn.

Tips: "We are expanding into travel throughout the U.S. that offers opportunities for outdoor recreation. We have also begun to publish children's books on outdoor recreation, nature, and environmentally related subjects."

APPLEZABA PRESS, P.O. Box 4134, Long Beach CA 90804. (213)591-0015. Publisher: D.H. Lloyd. Estab. 1977. Publishes hardcover and trade paperback originals. Firm averages 4 titles/year. Receives 1,000 submissions/year. 5% of books from first-time authors; 95% from unagented writers. Pays 8-15% royalty on retail price. Publishes book average of 3 years after acceptance. Simultaneous submissions OK. Reports in 2 weeks on queries; 3 months on mss. Free book catalog; mss guidelines for #10 SASE.

Nonfiction: Cookbook. Subjects include cooking, foods and nutrition. Query or submit complete ms. Reviews artwork/photos as part of ms package.

Recent Nonfiction Title: *College Quickies Survival Cookbook*, by Sandy Sieg.

Fiction: Literary and short story collections. Query or submit outline/synopsis and sample chapters.

Recent Fiction Title: *Horse Medicine*, by Raefael Zepeda.

Recent Poetry Title: *The Dr. Poems*, by Lyn Lifshin.

ARCHITECTURAL BOOK PUBLISHING CO., INC., 268 Dogwood Lane, Stamford CT 06903. (203)322-1460. Editor: Walter Frese. Estab. 1891. Averages 10 titles/year; receives 400 submissions annually. 80% of books from first-time authors; 95% of books from unagented writers. Average print order for a writer's first book is 5,000. Royalty is percentage of retail price. Publishes book an average of 10 months after acceptance. Prefers queries, outlines and 2 sample chapters with number of illustrations. Reports in 2 weeks.
Nonfiction: Publishes architecture, decoration, and reference books on city planning and industrial arts. Accepts nonfiction translations. Also interested in history, biography, and science of architecture and decoration. Reviews artwork/photos.

ARCHWAY/MINSTREL BOOKS, Imprint of Pocket Books, 1230 Avenue of the Americas, New York NY 10020. (212)698-7268. Executive Editor: Patricia MacDonald. Publishes mass market paperback originals and reprints. Averages 60 titles/year. Receives 1,000 submissions/year. Pays royalty. Publishes book an average of 2 years after acceptance. Reports in 1 month on queries; 3 months on mss. SASE for all material necessary or query not answered.
Nonfiction: Middle grade and young adult. Subjects include current popular subjects or people, sports. Query/SASE. Submit outline/synopsis and sample chapters. Reviews artwork/photos as part of ms package.
Fiction: Middle grade, young adult. Suspense thrillers for YA; mysteries, school stories, funny/scary stories, animal stories for middle grade readers. No picture books. Query/SASE. Submit outline/synopsis and sample chapters.
Recent Fiction Title: *Witch*, by Christopher Pike (YA novel).

ARCsoft PUBLISHERS, P.O. Box 132, Woodsboro MD 21798. (301)845-8856. Publisher: Anthony R. Curtis. Estab. 1980. Publishes trade paperback originals. Averages 20 titles/year. "We now offer only 'buyout' contracts in which all rights are purchased. Typically, an advance of 20 percent is paid at contract signing and 80 percent at acceptable completion of work. Royalties are no longer offered because writers suffer under royalty contracts for small-volume technical books." Offers variable advance. Publishes book an average of 6 months after acceptance. Reports in 1 month on queries; 10 weeks on mss. Free book catalog.
Nonfiction: Technical. "We publish technical books including space science, desktop publishing, personal computers and hobby electronics, especially for beginners." Accepts nonfiction translations. Query or submit outline/synopsis and 1 sample chapter. Reviews artwork/photos as part of ms package.
Recent Nonfiction Title: *Space Almanac*, by A.R. Curtis.
Tips: "We look for the writer's ability to cover our desired subject thoroughly, writing quality and interest."

‡ARDEN PRESS INC., P.O. Box 418, Denver CO 80201. (303)239-6155. Publisher: Susan Holte. Estab. 1980. Publishes hardcover and trade paperback originals and reprints. 95% of books are originals; 5% are reprints. Firm averages 4-6 titles/year. Receives 50 submissions/year. 20% of books from first-time authors. 80% from unagented writers. Pays 8½-15% royalty on wholesale price. Offers $2,000 average advance. Publishes book an average of 6 months after acceptance. Simultaneous submissions OK. Query for electronic submissions. Reports in 2 weeks on queries. Manuscript guidelines free on request.
Nonfiction: Biography, reference, textbooks. Subjects include women's issues/studies (history, biography, politics, guides). "We are looking for additional volumes for the Women & Modern Revolution Series. They need to be by recognized subject specialists on specific countries. Any women's history or biography, practical guides." Query. Submit outline/synopsis and sample chapters. Reviews artwork/photos as part of ms package.
Recent Nonfiction Title: *Emergence of the Modern Mexican Woman*, by Shirlene Soto (women's history).
Tips: "Writers have the best chance selling us nonfiction on women's subjects. Our audience consists of general and women's bookstores, course adoptions for colleges and universities, public and academic libraries. If I were a writer trying to market a book today, I would learn as much as I could about publishers' profiles, request catalogs—*then* contact publishers who publish similar works."

*M. ARMAN PUBLISHING, INC., P.O. Box 785, Ormond Beach FL 32175. (904)673-5576. Contact: Mike Arman. Estab. 1978. Publishes trade paperback originals, reprints and software. Averages 6-8 titles/year; receives 20 submissions annually. 20% of books from first-time authors; 100% of books from unagented writers. Average print order for a writer's first book is 2,500. Subsidy publishes 20% of books. Pays 10% royalty on wholesale price. No advance. Publishes book (on royalty basis) an average of 8 months after acceptance; 6 weeks on subsidy basis. Query for electronic submissions. Reports in 1 week on queries; 3 weeks on mss. Book catalog for #10 SASE.

Nonfiction: How-to, reference, technical, and textbook. "Motorcycle technical books only." Accepts nonfiction translations. Publishes for enthusiasts. Submit complete ms. Reviews artwork/photos as part of ms package.

Recent Nonfiction Title: *V-Twin Thunder*, by Carl McClanahan (motorcycle performance manual).

Tips: "The type of book a writer has the best chance of selling to our firm is how-to fix motorcycles — specifically Harley-Davidsons. We have a strong, established market for these books."

‡JASON ARONSON INC., 230 Livingston St., Northvale NJ 07647. (201)767-4093. Vice President: Arthur Kurzweil. Publishes hardcover originals and reprints. 90% of books are originals; 10% are reprints. Firm averages 50 titles/year. 50% of books from first-time authors. 95% from unagented writers. Pays 10-15% royalty on retail price. Publishes book an average of 1 year after acceptance. Reports in 3 weeks on queries. Free book catalog.

Nonfiction: How-to, reference, technical. Subjects include psychology and religion. "We publish in two fields: psychotherapy and Judaica. We are looking for high quality books in both fields." Query. Reviews artwork/photos as part of ms package.

Recent Nonfiction Title: *Psychotherapy: The Art of Wooing Nature*, by Sheldon Roth, M.D. (Psychoanalysis).

ART DIRECTION BOOK COMPANY, 10 E. 39th St., 6th Floor, New York NY 10016. (212)889-6500. Editorial Director: Dan Barron. Senior Editor: Loren Bliss. Imprint is Infosource Publications. Publishes hardcover and paperback originals. Publishes 10 titles/year. Pays 10% royalty on retail price; offers average $1,000 advance. Publishes book an average of 1 year after acceptance. Reports in 3 months. Book catalog for 6×9 SAE.

Nonfiction: Commercial art, ad art how-to and textbooks. "We are interested in books for the professional advertising art field — that is, books for art directors, designers, etc.; also entry level books for commercial and advertising art students in such fields as typography, photography, paste-up, illustration, clip-art, design, layout and graphic arts." Query with outline/synopsis and 1 sample chapter. Reviews artwork/photos as part of ms package.

Recent Nonfiction Title: *American Corporate Identity #4*, by D.E. Carter.

‡ASHER-GALLANT PRESS, Division of Caddylak Systems, Inc., 131 Heartland Blvd., Box W, Brentwood NY 11717-0698. FAX: (516)254-2018. Contact: Submissions Editor. Publishes softcover and loose-leaf format originals (sold mostly through direct marketing). Averages 20 titles/year; receives 150 submissions annually. 50% of books from first-time authors; 95% of books from unagented writers. "Many of our authors are first-time authors when they begin working with us, but write several subsequent books for us. Payment for each project is treated individually, but generally, the rights to smaller works (up to about 25,000 words) are purchased on a flat fee basis, and rights to larger works are purchased on a royalty basis." Advance varies by project. Publishes books an average of 6 months after acceptance. Simultaneous submissions OK. Ms returned only if requested. "We prefer to keep a writer's sample on file for possible future assignments." Reports negative results in 2 weeks on queries; 1 month on mss. Free book catalog.

Nonfiction: How-to, reference, audio cassette programs and business directories. Subjects include business (general) and management topics. "We plan to do 35 to 40 new titles during the next two years. The list will consist of individual business titles, more technical management reports, and longer, more comprehensive books that will be published in binder format. All subject matter must be appropriate to our broad audience of middle-level corporate managers. No sensational, jazzy nonfiction without solid research behind it." Submit outline/synopsis and sample chapters.

Recent Nonfiction Title: *Words for Telemarketing*, by Steven R. Isaac.

Tips: "The deciding factors in whether or not we publish a certain book are: (1) we believe there will be a very sizeable demand for the book, (2) the outline we review is logically structured and very comprehensive, and (3) the sample chapters are concisely and clearly written and well-researched."

ASIAN HUMANITIES PRESS, P.O. Box 3523, Fremont CA 94539. (415)659-8272. Editor: Lew Lancaster. Estab. 1976. Publishes hardcover and trade paperback originals. Firm averages 12 titles/year. Receives 150 submissions/year. 80% of books from unagented authors. Pays up to 8% royalty on retail price. Publishes book an average of 1 year after acceptance. Query for electronic submissions. Reports on queries in 1 month; 3 months on mss. Free book catalog.

Nonfiction: Reference, textbooks and general trade books. Subjects include language/literature (Asian), philosophy/religion (Asian and East-West), psychology/spirituality (Asian and East-West), art/culture (Asian and East-West), deep ecology, holistic healing, vegetarianism and pacifism. Submit complete ms with SASE. Reviews artwork/photos as part of ms package.

Recent Nonfiction Title: *New Mahayana: Buddhism for a Post Modern World*, by Akizuki Ryonsin.

ATHENEUM CHILDREN'S BOOKS, Imprint of Macmillan, Inc., 866 3rd Ave., New York NY 10022. (212)702-7894. Editorial Director: Jonathan J. Lanman. Editors: Marcia Marshall and Gail Paris. Publishes hardcover originals. Averages 60 titles/year; receives 7,000-8,000 submissions annually. 8-12% of books from first-time authors; 50% of books from unagented writers. Pays 10% royalty on retail price; offers average $2,000-3,000 advance. Publishes book an average of 18 months after acceptance. Reports in 2 weeks on queries; 3 months on outline and sample chapters. Book catalog and ms guidelines for 7×10 SAE and 2 first class stamps.

Nonfiction: Biography, how-to, humor, illustrated book, juvenile (pre-school through young adult) and self-help, all for juveniles. Subjects include: Americana, animals, art, business and economics, cooking and foods, health, history, hobbies, music, nature, philosophy, photography, politics, psychology, recreation, religion, sociology, sports, and travel, all for young readers. "Do remember, most publishers plan their lists as much as two years in advance. So if a topic is 'hot' right now, it may be 'old hat' by the time we could bring it out. It's better to steer clear of fads. Some writers assume juvenile books are for 'practice' until you get good enough to write adult books. Not so. Books for young readers demand just as much 'professionalism' in writing as adult books. So save those 'practice' manuscripts for class, or polish them before sending them." Query, submit outline/synopsis and sample chapters. Reviews artwork/photos as part of ms package; prefers photocopies of artwork.

Recent Nonfiction Title: *Dead Serious*, by Jane Mersky Leder (teenage suicide).

Fiction: Adventure, ethnic, experimental, fantasy, gothic, historical, horror, humor, mainstream, mystery, romance, science fiction, suspense, and western, all in juvenile versions. "We have few specific needs except for books that are fresh, interesting and well written. Again, fad topics are dangerous, as are works you haven't polished to the best of your ability. (The competition is fierce.) We've been inundated with dragon stories (misunderstood dragon befriends understanding child), unicorn stories (misunderstood child befriends understanding unicorn), and variations of 'Ignatz the Egg' (Everyone laughs at Ignatz the egg [giraffe/airplane/accountant] because he's square [short/purple/stupid] until he saves them from the eggbeater [lion/storm/I.R.S. man] and becomes a hero). Other things we don't need at this time are safety pamphlets, ABC books, and rhymed narratives. In writing picture book texts, avoid the coy and 'cutesy.' " Query, submit outline/synopsis and sample chapters for novels; complete ms for picture books.

Recent Fiction Title: *The Return*, by Sonia Levitin (young adult novel).

Poetry: "At this time there is a growing market for children's poetry. However, we don't anticipate needing any for the next year or two, especially rhymed narratives."

Tips: "Our books are aimed at children from pre-school age, up through high school. Our young adult novels and much of our science fiction and fantasy also cross over into adult markets."

‡ATHENEUM PUBLISHERS, Imprint of Macmillan, Inc., 866 3rd Ave., New York NY 10022. Editor-in-Chief: Mr. Lee Goerner. Receives 10,000 submissions annually. 5% of books from first-time authors; 1% of books from unagented writers. Average print order for a writer's first book is 7,000. Publishes book an average of 1 year after acceptance. Simultaneous submissions OK. Electronic submissions OK, but requires hard copy also. Reports in 2 months on queries.

Nonfiction: General trade material dealing with politics, psychology, history, cookbooks, sports, biographies and general interest. Length: 40,000 words minimum. Query or submit outline/synopsis and a sample chapter.

AVALON BOOKS, Imprint of Thomas Bouregy & Co., Inc., 401 Lafayette St., New York NY 10003. Vice President and Publisher: Barbara J. Brett. Estab. 1950. Publishes 60 titles/year. Pays $600 for first book, $800 for the second, and $1,000 thereafter, which is applied against sales of the first 3,500 copies of the book (initial run is 2,100 copies). Reports in 3 months. Writer's guidelines for #10 SASE.

Fiction: "We publish wholesome adult romances, and adult westerns that are sold to libraries throughout the country. Our books are read by adults as well as teenagers, and their characters are all adults. All the romances are contemporary; all the westerns are historical." Length: 40,000 to 50,000 words. Submit first chapter and a brief, but complete summary of the book, or, if you are sure the book fits our requirements, submit the complete manuscript. Enclose manuscript size SASE.

Recent Fiction Title: *Heart Games*, by Lynn Bulock.

Tips: "We do not want old-fashioned, predictable, formula-type books. We are looking for contemporary characters and fresh, contemporary plots and storylines. Every heroine should have an interesting career or profession."

‡AVANYU PUBLISHING INC., P.O. Box 27134, Albuquerque NM 87125. (505)266-6128. FAX: (505)256-9243. President: J. Brent Ricks. Estab. 1984. Publishes hardcover and trade paperback originals and reprints. Firm averages 6 titles/year. Receives 8 submissions/year. 50% of books from first-time authors. 90% from unagented writers. Pays 8% maximum royalty on wholesale price. No advance. Publishes book an average of 1 year after acceptance. Query for electronic submissions. Reports in 6 weeks. Book catalog for #10 SASE.

Nonfiction: Biography, illustrated book, reference, Southwest Americana. Subjects include Americana, anthropology/archaeology, art/architecture, ethnic, history, photography, regional, sociology. Query. Submit complete ms. Reviews artwork/photos as part of ms package.

Recent Nonfiction Title: *Tonita Pena*, by Sam Grey (biography of Indian painter).

Fiction: Adventure, historical, Western. Query. Submit complete ms.

Tips: "Writers have the best chance selling us history oriented books with lots of pictures, or contemporary Indian/Western art. Our audience consists of libraries, art collectors, history students and interests."

AVERY PUBLISHING GROUP, 120 Old Broadway, Garden City Park NY 11040. (516)741-2155. Contact: Managing Editor. Estab. 1976. Publishes hardcover and trade paperback originals. Averages 40 titles/year. Receives 200-300 submissions/year. 90% of books from first-time authors; 95% from unagented writers. Pays 10% royalty on wholesale price. Publishes book an average of 9 months after acceptance. Simultaneous submissions OK. Reports in 1 week. Book catalog free on request.

Nonfiction: Cookbook, how-to, reference and textbook. Subjects include business and economics, child guidance/parenting, cooking, foods & nutrition, health/medicine, history, military/war, nature/environment, child birth and alternative health. Query.

Recent Nonfiction Title: *Empty Harvest*, by Dr. Bernard Jensen and Mark Anderson (ecology/health).

AVON BOOKS, Division of the Hearst Corp., 1350 Avenue of the Americas, New York NY 10019. FAX: (212)532-2172. Publisher: Carolyn Reidy. Associate Publisher, trade paperbacks: Mark Gompertz. Editor-in-Chief: Robert Mecoy. Estab. 1941. Publishes trade and mass market paperback originals and reprints. Averages 400 titles/year. Pay and advance are negotiable. Publishes ms an average of 2 years after acceptance. Simultaneous submissions OK. Reports in 2 months. Book catalog for SASE.

Nonfiction: How-to, popular psychology, self-help, health, history, war, sports, business/economics, biography and politics. No textbooks.

Recent Nonfiction Title: *It's Always Something*, by Gilda Radner (mass market).

Fiction: Romance (contemporary), historical romance, science fiction, fantasy, men's adventure, suspense/thriller, mystery, and western. Submit query letter only.

Recent Fiction Title: *Spartina*, by John Casey (trade paperback).

AVON FLARE BOOKS, Young Adult Imprint of Avon Books, Division of the Hearst Corp., 105 Madison Ave., New York NY 10016. (212)481-5609. FAX: (212)532-2172. Editorial Director: Ellen Krieger. Publishes mass market paperback originals and reprints. Imprint publishes 18-20 new titles annually. 25% of books from first-time authors; 15% of books from unagented writers. Pays 6-8% royalty; offers minimum $2,500 advance. Publishes book an average of 15 months after acceptance. Simultaneous submissions OK. Reports in 10 weeks. Book catalog and manuscript guidelines for 8×10 SAE and 5 first class stamps.

Nonfiction: General. Submit outline/synopsis and sample chapters. "*Very* selective with young adult nonfiction."

Fiction: Adventure, ethnic, humor, mainstream, mystery, romance, suspense and contemporary. "Very selective with mystery." Mss appropriate to ages 12-18. Query with sample chapters and synopsis.

Recent Fiction Title: *Live From New York*, by Alan Gelb.

Tips: "The YA market is not as strong as it was 5 years ago. We are very selective with young adult fiction. Avon does not publish picture books."

BACKCOUNTRY PUBLICATIONS, Imprint of The Countryman Press, Inc., P.O. Box 175, Woodstock VT 05091. (802)457-1049. Contact: Managing Editor. Estab. 1981. Publishes trade paperback originals. Averages 12 titles/year. 50% of books from first-time authors; 95% from unagented writers. Pays 5-10% royalty on retail price. Offers $500 average advance. Publishes book average of 9 months after acceptance. Simultaneous submissions OK. Reports on queries in 2 weeks; on mss in 6 weeks. Free book catalog.

Nonfiction: Reference. Subjects include recreation. "We're looking for regional guides to hiking, walking, bicycling, cross-country skiing, canoeing, and fishing for all parts of the country." Submit outline/synopsis and sample chapters. Reviews artwork/photos as part of ms package.

Market conditions are constantly changing! If this is 1993 or later, buy the newest edition of Writer's Market at your favorite bookstore or order directly from Writer's Digest Books.

Recent Nonfiction Title: *Fifty Hikes in Lower Michigan*, by Jim DuFresne.

BAKER BOOK HOUSE COMPANY, P.O. Box 6287, Grand Rapids MI 49516-6287. FAX: (616)676-9573. Director of Publications: Allan Fisher. Publishes hardcover and trade paperback originals. Averages 120 titles/year. 10% of books from first-time authors; 85% of books from unagented writers. Queries and proposals only. No unsolicited mss. Pays 14% royalty on net receipts. Publishes book within 1 year after acceptance. Simultaneous submissions (if so identified) OK. Reports in 1 month. Book catalog for 9×12 SAE and 6 first class stamps.
Nonfiction: Contemporary issues, women's concerns, parenting, singleness, self-help, recovery, children's books, Bible study, Christian doctrine, reference books, books for pastors and church leaders, textbooks for Christian colleges and seminaries.
Recent Nonfiction Title: *Televangelism and American Culture: The Business of Popular Religion*, by Quentin J. Schultze.
Fiction: Novels focusing on women's concerns, mysteries.
Tips: "Most of our authors and readers are evangelical Christians, and our books are purchased from Christian bookstores, mail-order retailers, and school bookstores."

BALE BOOKS, Division of Bale Publications, P.O. Box 2727, New Orleans LA 70176. Editor-in-Chief: Don Bale Jr. Estab. 1963. Publishes hardcover and paperback originals and reprints. Averages 10 titles/year; receives 25 submissions annually. 50% of books from first-time authors; 90% of books from unagented writers. Average print order for a writer's first book is 1,000. Offers standard 10-12½-15% royalty contract on wholesale or retail price; sometimes purchases mss outright for $500. Offers no advance. Publishes book an average of 3 years after acceptance. "Send manuscript by registered or certified mail. Be sure copy of manuscript is retained." Book catalog for SAE and 2 first class stamps.
Nonfiction: Numismatics. "Our specialties are coin and stock market investment books; especially coin investment books and coin price guides. Most of our books are sold through publicity and ads in the coin newspapers. We are open to any new ideas in the area of numismatics. The writer should write for a teenage through adult level. Lead the reader by the hand like a teacher, building chapter by chapter. Our books sometimes have a light, humorous treatment, but not necessarily." Looks for "good English, construction and content, and sales potential." Submit outline and 3 sample chapters.
Recent Nonfiction Title: *Out of Little Coins Big Fortunes Grow*, by Bale.

BALLANTINE, See listing for Random House, Inc.

BANKS-BALDWIN LAW PUBLISHING CO., 1904 Ansel Rd., Cleveland OH 44106. (216)721-7373. FAX: (216)721-8055. Editor-in-Chief: P.J. Lucier. Estab. 1804. Publishes law books and services in a variety of formats. Averages approximately 10 new titles/year; receives 10-15 submissions annually. 5% of books from first-time authors; 90% of books from unagented writers. "Most titles include material submitted by outside authors." Pays 8-16% on net revenue, or fee. Offers advance not to exceed 25% of anticipated royalty or fee. Publishes book an average of 18 months after acceptance, 3 months after receipt of ms. Query for electronic submissions. Reports in 3 weeks on queries; 6 weeks on submissions. Free book catalog; ms guidelines for SASE.
Nonfiction: Reference, law/legal. Query.
Recent Nonfiction Title: *Arizona Juvenile Law*, by Thomas A. Jacobs (handbook).
Tips: "We publish books for attorneys, government officials and professionals in allied fields. Trends in our field include more interest in handbooks, less in costly multi-volume sets; electronic publishing. Writer has the best chance of selling us a book on a hot new topic of law. Check citations and quotations carefully."

BANTAM BOOKS, Subsidiary of Bantam Doubleday Dell, 666 5th Ave., New York NY 10103. (212)765-6500. Imprints are Spectra, Crime Line, New Age, Bantam Classics, Bantam New Fiction, Loveswept, New Sciences, Bantam Electronic Publishing, Books for Young Readers. Publishes hardcover, trade paperback and mass market paperback originals, trade paperback, mass market paperback reprints and audio. Publishes 650 titles/year. Buys no books from unagented writers. Pays 4-15% royalty. Publishes book an average of 1 year after ms is accepted. Simultaneous submissions OK. Reports in 3 weeks on queries; 1 month on ms.
Nonfiction: Biography, coffee table book, how-to, cookbook, humor, illustrated book, juvenile and self-help. Subjects include Americana, anthropology/archaelogy, business/economics, child guidance/parenting, computers and electronics, cooking, foods and nutrition, gay/lesbian, government/politics, health/medicine, history, language/literature, military/war, money/finance, music/dance, philosophy, psychology, religion, science, sociology, sports and travel. Query or submit outline/synopsis or complete ms through agent only. All unsolicited mss are returned unopened.

Recent Nonfiction Title: *Homecoming*, by John Bradshaw.
Fiction: Adventure, fantasy, feminist, gay/lesbian, historical, horror, juvenile, literary, mainstream/ contemporary, mystery, romance, science fiction, suspense, western, young adult. Query or submit outline/synopsis or complete ms through agent only. All unsolicited mss are returned unopened.
Recent Fiction Title: *Skinny Legs and All*, by Tom Robbins.

BANTAM DOUBLEDAY DELL, 666 5th Ave., New York NY 10103. Divisions include Bantam Books, Doubleday Books, and Dell Books. Imprints include Delacorte Books for Young Readers, Delacorte Press, and Delta Books.

BARRON'S EDUCATIONAL SERIES, INC., 250 Wireless Blvd., Hauppauge NY 11788. FAX: (516)434-3723. Director of Acquisitions: Grace Freedson. Publishes hardcover and paperback originals and software. Publishes 170 titles/year. 10% of books from first-time authors; 90% of books from unagented writers. Pays royalty, based on both wholesale and retail price. Publishes book an average of 1 year after acceptance. Simultaneous submissions OK. Reports in 3 months. Free catalog.
Nonfiction: Adult education, art, business, cookbooks, crafts, foreign language, review books, guidance, pet books, travel, literary guides, parenting, health, juvenile, young adult sports, test preparation materials and textbooks. Reviews artwork/photos as part of package. Query or submit outline/synopsis and 2-3 sample chapters. Accepts nonfiction translations.
Recent Nonfiction Title: *Great American Bake Sale*, by Alison Boteeler.
Tips: "The writer has the best chance of selling us a book that will fit into one of our series."

BEACON HILL PRESS OF KANSAS CITY, Book division of Nazarene Publishing House, P.O. Box 419527, Kansas City MO 64141. Coordinator: Paul Martin. Estab. 1912. Publishes hardcover and paperback originals. Averages 65-70 titles/year. Offers "standard contract (sometimes flat rate purchase). Advance on royalty is paid on first 1,000 copies at publication date. On standard contract, pays 10% on first 10,000 copies and 12% on subsequent copies at the end of each calendar year." Publishes book an average of 2 years after acceptance. Reports in up to 8 months unless immediately returned. "Book Committee meets quarterly to select from the manuscripts which will be published."
Nonfiction: Inspirational, Bible-based. Doctrinally must conform to the evangelical, Wesleyan tradition. Conservative view of Bible. No autobiography, poetry, devotional collections, or children's picture books. Accent on holy living; encouragement in daily Christian life. Contemporary issues. Popular style books usually under 128 pages. Query. Textbooks "almost exclusively done on assignment." Full ms or outline/sample chapters. Length: 20,000-40,000 words.
Recent Nonfiction Title: *A Matter of Life and Death: Bioethics for the Christian*, by Albert Truesdale.

BEACON PRESS, 25 Beacon St., Boston MA 02108. (617)742-2110. FAX: (617)723-3097. Director: Wendy J. Strothman. Estab. 1902. Publishes hardcover originals and paperback reprints. Averages 60 titles/year; receives 4,000 submissions annually. 10% of books from first-time authors; 70% of books from unagented writers. Average print order for a writer's first book is 3,000. Offers royalty on net retail price; advance varies. Publishes book an average of 1 year after acceptance. Simultaneous submissions OK. Return of materials not guaranteed without SASE. Reports in 2 months. Query or submit outline/synopsis and sample chapters to Editorial Department.
Nonfiction: General nonfiction including works of original scholarship, religion, women's studies, philosophy, current affairs, literature, communications, sociology, psychology, history, political science, art, anthropology, children's books, environmental concerns.
Recent Nonfiction Title: *The Global Ecology Handbook*, World Resources Institute.
Tips: "We probably accept only one or two manuscripts from an unpublished pool of 4,000 submissions per year. No fiction or poetry submissions invited. Authors should have academic affiliation."

BEAR AND CO., INC., Drawer 2860, Santa Fe NM 87504-2860. (505)983-9868. Vice President Editorial: Barbara Clow. Publishes trade paperback originals. Averages 12 titles/year. Receives 6,000 submissions/year. 20% of books from first-time authors; 80% of books from unagented writers. Pays 10% royalty on net. Publishes book an average of 18 months after acceptance. Query for electronic submissions. Reports in 1 month on queries; 3 months on mss. "No response without SASE." Free book catalog.
Nonfiction: Illustrated books, science, theology, mysticism, religion and ecology. "We publish books to 'heal and celebrate the earth.' Our interest is in New Age, western mystics, new science, ecology. We are not interested in how-to, self-help, etc. Our readers are people who are open to new ways of looking at the world. They are spiritually oriented but not necessarily religious; interested in healing of the earth, peace issues, and receptive to New Age ideas." Query or submit outline/synopsis and sample chapters. Reviews artwork/photos as part of ms package.
Recent Nonfiction Title: *Crying for a Dream*, by Richard Erdoes.

BEAU LAC PUBLISHERS, P.O. Box 248, Chuluota FL 32766. Estab. 1968. Publishes hardcover and paperback originals.
Nonfiction: "Military subjects. Specialist in social side of service life." Query.

*BEAVER POND PUBLISHING & PRINTING, P.O. Box 224, Greenville PA 16125. (412)588-3492. Owner: Richard E. Faler, Jr. Estab. 1989. Publishes 95% mass market paperback originals, 5% reprints. Averages 5 titles/year. Receives 20 submissions/year. 20% of books from first-time authors. 20% from unagented writers. Subsidy publishes 10% of books. Determines subsidy "if we don't wish to take on the book as publisher, but the author still wants us to print it." Pays 5-15% royalty on net sales. Buys mss outright for $100-1,000 on booklets. Publishes book an average of 6 months after acceptance. Simultaneous submissions OK. Reports in 1 month. Manuscript guidelines for #10 SASE.
Nonfiction: How-to. Subjects include animals, natural history of wildlife, hobbies particularly on exotic pets (snakes instead of dogs), nature/environment, photography especially of wildlife, recreation, hunting, fishing. "We want to see manuscripts suitable for 24 page booklets through 200 page books that are written with authority on very specific topics and that are how-to. Example: "Photographing Birds in Flight." Query. Submit outline/synopsis and sample chapters and complete ms. Reviews artwork/photos as part of ms package.
Recent Nonfiction Title: *Seining and Trapping Minnows*, by Rich Faler (booklet).
Tips: "We're looking for very specific topics in both consumptive and non-consumptive animal use that are too specific for larger publishers. There are experts out there with valuable information. We want to make that information available. Our primary audiences are hunters, fishermen and photographers. If I were a writer trying to market a book today, I would look for a niche, fill that niche, and attempt to fill it with a work that would be difficult, if not impossible, for someone to duplicate or do better."

BEHRMAN HOUSE INC., 235 Watchung Ave., W. Orange NJ 07052. (201)669-0447. FAX: (201)669-9769. Subsidiary includes Rossel Books. Managing Editor: Adam Bengal. Estab. 1921. Publishes trade paperback originals and reprints. Averages 20 titles/year. Receives 200 submissions/year. 20% of books from first-time authors; 95% from unagented writers. Pays 2-10% on wholesale price or retail price. Buys mss outright for $500-10,000. Offers $1,000 average advance. Publishes book an average of 18 months after acceptance. Simultaneous submissions OK. Reports in 2 weeks on queries; 1 month on mss. Free book catalog and manuscript guidelines.
Nonfiction: Juvenile (1-18), reference and textbook. Subjects include religion. "We want Jewish textbooks for the El-Hi market." Query. Submit outline/synopsis and sample chapters.

ROBERT BENTLEY, INC., Automotive Publishers, 1000 Massachusetts Ave., Cambridge MA 02138. (617)547-4170. Publisher: Michael Bentley. Estab. 1949. Publishes hardcover and trade paperback originals and reprints. Publishes 15-20 titles/year. 20% of books are from first-time authors; 90% from unagented writers. Pays 10-15% royalty on net price; or makes outright purchase. Advances negotiable. Publishes book an average of 10-12 months after acceptance. Query for electronic submissions. Reports in 1 month. Book catalog and ms guidelines for 6×9 SAE and 4 first class stamps.
Nonfiction: How-to, technical, theory of operation, coffee table. Automotive subjects only; this inlcudes motor sports. Query or submit outline/synopsis and sample chapters or complete ms. Reviews artwork/photos as part of manuscript package.
Recent Nonfiction Title: *Bosch Fuel Injection and Engine Management Including High Performance Tuning*, by Charles Probst, SAE (automotive).
Tips: "We are excited about the possibilities and growth in the automobile enthusiast book market. Our audience is composed of serious and intelligent automobile, sports car, or racing enthusiasts, automotive technicians and high performance tuners."

THE BERKLEY PUBLISHING GROUP, Publishers of Berkley/Berkley Trade Paperbacks/Jove/Diamond/Pacer/Ace Science Fiction, 200 Madison Ave., New York NY 10016. (212)951-8800. Editor-in-Chief: Leslie Gelbman. Publishes paperback originals and reprints. Publishes approximately 800 titles/year. Pays 4-10% royalty on retail price; offers advance. Publishes book an average of 18-24 months after acceptance.
Nonfiction: How-to, inspirational, family life, business, biographies, autobiographies and nutrition.
Recent Nonfiction Title: *High Treason*, by Robert Groden and Harrison Edward Livingstone.
Fiction: Adventure, historical, mainstream men's adventure, young adult, suspense, western, occult, romance and science fiction. Submit outline/synopsis and first 3 chapters (for Ace Science Fiction only).
Recent Fiction Title: *Bittersweet*, by LaVyrle Spencer.
Young Adult Fiction Title: *The Sword of the Sun*, by Joe Dever and John Grant.

BETHANY HOUSE PUBLISHERS, Subsidiary of Bethany Fellowship, Inc., 6820 Auto Club Rd., Minneapolis MN 55438. (612)829-2500. Editorial Director: Carol Johnson. Estab. 1956. Publishes hardcover and paperback originals and reprints. "Contracts negotiable." Averages 60 titles/year; receives 2,000 submissions annually. 5% of books from first-time authors; 95% of books from unagented writers. Publishes book an average of 9-18 months after acceptance. Simultaneous submissions OK. Query for electronic submissions. Reports in 2 months. Book catalog and ms guidelines for 9×12 SASE and 5 first class stamps.

Nonfiction: Publishes reference (lay-oriented); devotional (evangelical, charismatic); and personal growth books. Submit outline and 2-3 sample chapters. Looks for "provocative subject, quality writing style, authoritative presentation, unique approach, sound Christian truth." Reviews artwork/photos as part of ms package. SASE required.

Recent Nonfiction Title: *Married Lovers, Married Friends*, by Steve and Annie Chapman.

Fiction: Well written stories with a Christian message. No poetry. Submit synopsis and 2-3 sample chapters with SASE to Manuscript Review Editor. Guidelines available.

Recent Fiction Title: *Munich Signature*, by Bodie Thoene.

Tips: "The writer has the best chance of selling our firm a book that will market well in the Christian bookstore. In your query, list other books in your subject category (price, length, main thrust), and tell how yours is better or unique."

BETHEL PUBLISHING, Subsidiary of Missionary Church, Inc., 1819 S. Main St., Elkhart IN 46516 (219)293-8585. FAX: (219)522-5670. Executive Director: Rev. Richard Oltz. Estab. 1903. Publishes trade paperback originals and reprints. Averages 5 titles/year. Receives 150 submissions/year. 20% of books from first-time authors, 90% from unagented writers. Pays 5-10% royalties. Offers $250 average advance. Publishes book an average of 1 year after acceptance. Simultaneous submissions OK. Reports in 2 weeks on queries; 3 months on mss. Free book catalog and manuscript guidelines.

Nonfiction: Reference. Subjects include religion. Reviews artwork/photos as part of ms package. Query or submit complete ms.

Recent Nonfiction Title: *We Have An Advocate*, by Ringenberg (religious).

Fiction: Adventure, religious, suspense, young adult. Books must be evangelical in approach. No occult, gay/lesbian, erotica. Query or submit complete ms.

Recent Fiction Title: *Deadline*, by Stahl (mystery).

Tips: "Our audience is made up of Christian families with children. If I were a writer trying to market a book today, I would find out what publisher specializes in the type of book I have written."

BETTER HOMES AND GARDENS BOOKS, Division of the Meredith Corporation, 1716 Locust St., Des Moines IA 50336. FAX: (515)284-3697. Managing Editor: David A. Kirchner. Estab. 1930. Publishes hardcover and trade paperback originals. Averages 40 titles/year. "The majority of our books are produced by on-staff editors, so we very rarely buy book-length manuscripts from outside authors. But we often use freelance writers on assignment for sections or chapters of books already in progress." Reports in 6 weeks.

Nonfiction: "We publish nonfiction in many family and home-service categories, including gardening, decorating and remodeling, crafts, money management, handyman's topics, cooking and nutrition, Christmas activities, and other subjects of home-service value. Emphasis is on how-to and on stimulating people to action. We require concise, factual writing. Audience is comprised of readers with home and family as their main center of interest. Style should be informative and lively with a straightforward approach. Stress the positive. Emphasis is entirely on reader service. Because most of our books are produced by on-staff editors, we're less interested in book-length manuscripts than in hearing from freelance writers with solid expertise in gardening, do-it-yourself, health/fitness, and home decorating. We have no need at present for cookbooks or craft books. The Managing Editor recommends careful study of specific Better Homes and Gardens Books titles before submitting material." Prefers outline and sample chapters. *"Please include SASE with appropriate return postage."*

Recent Nonfiction Title: *Step-by-Step Landscaping*.

Tips: "Writers often fail to familiarize themselves with the catalog/backlist of the publishers to whom they are submitting. We expect heavier emphasis on health/fitness, gardening and do-it-yourself titles. But, again, we're most interested in hearing from freelance writers with subject expertise in these areas than in receiving queries for book-length manuscripts. Queries/mss may be routed to other editors in the publishing group."

‡BETTERWAY PUBLICATIONS, INC., P.O. Box 219, Crozet VA 22932. (804)823-5661. Senior Editor: Hilary Swinson. Imprint is Shoe Tree Press. Publishes hardcover and trade paperback originals. Averages 40 titles/year; receives 1,200 submissions annually. 70% of books from first-time authors; 90% of books from unagented writers. Pays royalty on wholesale price; offers $500-1,500 advance. Publishes book an average of 8 months after acceptance. Simultaneous submissions OK. Query for electronic submissions. Reports in 6 weeks on queries; 2 months on mss. Book catalog for 9 × 12 SAE and 5 first class stamps.

Nonfiction: How-to, illustrated book, juvenile (see listing for Shoe Tree Press), reference, and self-help on business and economics, cooking and foods, gardening, hobbies, sociology, genealogy, small businesses, all aspects of homebuilding and ownership ("e.g., contracting your own home, remodeling, decorating, painting, buying/selling real estate, etc."). "We are seeking to expand our list in small and home-based business guides or handbooks, parenting books, genealogy books (advanced how-to), theater crafts books, popular music/jazz reference books, 'collectibles' source books." No cookbooks, diet/exercise, psychology self-help or health books. Submit outline/synopsis and sample chapters. Reviews artwork/photos.

Recent Nonfiction Title: *So You Want to Build a House*, by J. Rodney Taylor.

Tips: "We are continuing our emphasis on small and home business books and all aspects of housing/home ownership. We're also looking for distinctive (if not unique) how-to books, like *Gameplan — The Game Inventor's Handbook*, *The Theater Props Handbook*, and *Garage Sale Mania!*."

‡**BICYCLE BOOKS, INC.**, P.O. Box 2038, Mill Valley CA 94941. (415)381-2515. Editor: Rob van der Plas. Imprint is Velo Press. Publishes hardcover and trade paperback originals. Firm averages 4 titles/year. Receives 20 submissions/year. 20% of books are from first-time authors. 50% from unagented writers. Pays 7½-15% royalty. Publishes book an average of 1 year after acceptance. Simultaneous submissions OK. Query for electronic submissions. Reports in 2 months. Book catalog free on request.

Nonfiction: How-to and technical. Subjects include recreation, sports, travel and bicycle-related titles only. "Bicycle travel manuscripts must include route descriptions and maps. Please, do not send anything outside the practical how-to field." Submit complete ms. Artwork/photos essential as part of the freelance manuscript package.

Recent Nonfiction Title: *Tour de France*, by Samule Abt.

Tips: "Writers have a good chance selling us books with better and more illustrations and a systematic treatment of the subject. Our audience: sports/health/fitness conscious adults; cyclists and others interested in technical aspects. If I were a writer trying to market a book today, I would first check what is on the market and ask myself whether I am writing something that is not yet available and wanted."

*****BINFORD & MORT PUBLISHING**, 1202 NW 17th Ave., Portland OR 97209. (503)221-0866. Publisher: James Gardenier. Estab. 1891. Publishes hardcover and paperback originals and reprints. Receives 500 submissions annually. 60% of books from first-time authors; 90% of books from unagented writers. Average print order for a writer's first book is 5,000. Pays 10% royalty on retail price; offers variable advance (to established authors). Publishes about 10-12 titles annually. Occasionally does some subsidy publishing (10%), at author's request. Publishes book an average of 1 year after acceptance. Reports in 4 months.

Nonfiction: Books about the Pacific Coast and the Northwest. Subjects include Western Americana, biography, history, nature, maritime, recreation, reference, and travel. Query with sample chapters and SASE. Reviews artwork/photos as part of ms package.

Recent Nonfiction Title: *Barbey: The Story of a Pioneer Columbia River Salmon Packer*, by Roger T. Tetlow and Graham J. Barbey.

BLACK SPARROW PRESS, 24 10th St., Santa Rosa CA 95401. (707)579-4011. Assistant to Publisher: Julie Curtiss Voss. Estab. 1966. Publishes hardcover and trade paperback originals and reprints. Averages 12 titles/year. 0% of books from first-time authors; 75% from unagented writers. Pays 5-10% royalty on retail price. Publishes book an average of 1 year after acceptance. Simultaneous submissions OK. Reports in 1 month on queries; 2 months on mss. Book catalog free on request.

Nonfiction: Subjects include language/literature. No how-to, cookbook, juvenile, self-help. Query.

Recent Nonfiction Title: *Creatures of Habit*, Wyndham Lewis (essays on art and literature).

Fiction: Literary, feminist, gay/lesbian, short story collections. We generally solicit from authors we are interested in. "We only publish 12 new books a year so our schedule is quickly filled." No genre such as romance, westerns, etc. Query.

Recent Fiction Title: *Homesick*, by Lucia Berlin (stories).

Poetry: "We generally solicit from authors we are interested in." No light verse, nonsense verse, limmerick, traditional rhymed verse. Submit 5 samples.

Recent Poetry Title: *The Engendering Flood*, by William Everson.

JOHN F. BLAIR, PUBLISHER, 1406 Plaza Dr., Winston-Salem NC 27103. (919)768-1374. Editor: Stephen Kirk. Estab. 1954. Publishes hardcover originals and trade paperbacks; receives 1,000 submissions annually. 20-30% of books from first-time authors; 90% of books from unagented writers. Average print order for a writer's first book is 3,500-5,000. Royalty to be negotiated. Publishes book an average of 1-1½ years after acceptance. Query for electronic submissions. Reports in 3 months. Book catalog and ms guidelines for 9×12 SAE and 5 first class stamps.

Nonfiction: Especially interested in well-researched adult biography and history. Preference given to books dealing with Southeastern United States. Also interested in environment, travel and Americana; query on other nonfiction topics. Looks for utility and significance. Submit synopsis/outline and first 3 chapters or complete ms. Reviews artwork/photos as part of ms package.

Recent Nonfiction Title: *Touring the Western North Carolina Backroads,* by Carolyn Sakowski (travel).

Fiction: "We are most interested in serious novels of substance and imagination. Preference given to material related to Southeastern United States." No category fiction, juvenile fiction, picture books or poetry.

Recent Fiction Title: *The Legend of Nance Dude,* by Maurice Stanley.

‡BLOCKBUSTER BOOKS, INC., 2131 Hollywood Blvd., Hollywood FL 33020. (305)925-5242. FAX: (305)925-5244. Acquisitions Editor: Donald L. Lessne. Estab. 1943. Imprints include Fell Publishers, Inc., Compact Books, Inc. Publishes trade paperback originals and hardcover and trade paperback reprints. Firm averages 20 titles/year. Receives 2,000 submissions/year. 50% of books from first-time authors. 75% from unagented writers. Pays 6-10% royalty. Publishes book an average of 1 year after acceptance. Reports in 2 months on queries. Book catalog for 8½×11 SAE and 4 first class stamps. Manuscript guidelines for #10 SASE.

Nonfiction: Coffee table book, cookbook, how-to, self-helf. Subjects include animals, business and economics, child guidance/parenting, cooking, foods & nutrition, month/finance, religion, sports. "Blockbuster has published over 1,500 books to date. We are looking for mass market topics published in trade format. We are interested only in the eight topics of specialization that Blockbuster is known for." Reviews artwork/photos as part of freelance ms package.

Recent Nonfiction Title: *Secret of Mind Power,* by Harry Lorayne (self-help).

BLUE BIRD PUBLISHING, #306, 1713 E. Broadway, Tempe AZ 85282. (602)982-9003. FAX: (602)983-7319. Publisher: Cheryl Gorder. Publishes trade paperback originals. Firm averages 6 titles/year. 50% of books from first-time authors. 100% from unagented writers. Pays 10% royalty on wholesale price; 15% on retail price. Publishes book an average of 9 months after acceptance. Simultaneous submissions OK. Reports in 6 weeks. Book catalog and manuscript guidelines for #10 SASE.

Nonfiction: How-to and reference. Subjects include child guidance/parenting, education (especially home education) and sociology (current social issues). "The home schooling population in the U.S. is exploding. We have a strong market for anything that can be targeted to this group: home education manuscripts, parenting guides, home business ideas. We would also like to see complete nonfiction manuscripts in current issues, how-to topics." Submit complete ms. Reviews artwork/photos as part of ms package.

Recent Nonfiction Title: *Green Earth Resource Guide.*

Tips: "We are interested if we see a complete manuscript that is aimed toward a general adult nonfiction audience. We are impressed if the writer has really done his homework and the manuscript includes photos, artwork, graphs, charts, and other graphics."

BLUE DOLPHIN PUBLISHING, INC., P.O. Box 1908, Nevada City CA 95959. (916)265-6923. FAX: (916)265-0787. President: Paul M. Clemens. Estab. 1985. Publishes hardcover and trade paperback originals. Firm averages 8 titles/year. Receives over 2,000 submissions/year. 75% of books from first-time authors. 90% from unagented writers. Pays 10% on wholesale price. Publishes book an average of 6-9 months after acceptance. Simultaneous submissions OK. Query for electronic submissions. Reports in 1 month on queries; 3 months on mss. Plese send SASE with query. Free book catalog.

Nonfiction: Biography, cookbook, how-to, humor and self-help. Subjects include anthropology/archaeology, cooking, foods and nutrition, ecology, education, foods and nutrition, health/medicine, psychology and comparative religion. "We are interested primarily in self-help psychology, health and the environment, comparative spiritual traditions, including translations." Submit outline/synopsis and sample chapters with SASE. Reviews artwork as part of package.

Recent Nonfiction Title: *Turning to the Source: An Eastern View of Western Mind,* by V.R. Dhiravamsa.

Poetry: "We will only consider previously published authors of some merit or translations of noted works." Submit complete ms.

Recent Poetry Title: *Mahamudra: Boundless Joy and Freedom,* by Ole Nydahl.

Tips: "The concerned person interested in self-growth and awareness for oneself and the planet is our audience."

BLUE HERON PUBLISHING, Rt. 3 Box 376, Hillsboro OR 97124. (503)621-3911. President: Dennis Stovall. Vice President: Linny Stovall. Estab. 1985. Imprints include Media Weavers. Publishes trade paperback originals and reprints. Firm averages 5 titles/year. Free book catalog on request.

Fiction: Juvenile, young adult. "We are doing reprints of well known authors, but will also consider strong ethnic multi-cultural fiction or strong adventure with environmental values."
Recent Fiction Title: *DeathWalk*, by Walt Morey (YA/juvenile).

BNA BOOKS, Division of The Bureau of National Affairs, Inc., 1250 23rd St. NW, Washington DC 20037. (202)452-4400. FAX: (202)452-9186. Contact: Acquisitions Manager. Estab. 1929. Publishes hardcover and softcover originals. Averages 35 titles/year. Receives 200 submissions/year. 20% of books from first-time authors; 95% of books from unagented writers. Pays 5-15% royalty on net cash receipts; offers $1,000 average advance. Simultaneous submissions OK. Publishes book an average of 1 year after acceptance. Reports in 2 months on queries; 3 months on mss. Free book catalog and ms guidelines.
Nonfiction: Reference and professional/scholarly. Subjects include business law and regulation, environment and safety, legal practice, labor relations and human resource management. No biographies, bibliographies, cookbooks, religion books, humor or trade books. Submit detailed table of contents or outline.
Recent Nonfiction Title: *Supreme Court Practice*, sixth edition, by Stern, Gressman and Shapiro (law).
Tips: "Our audience is made up of practicing lawyers and business executives; managers, federal, state, and local government administrators; unions; and libraries. We look for authoritative and comprehensive works on subjects of interest to executives, professionals, and managers, that relate to the interaction of government and business."

*BONUS BOOKS, INC., 160 E. Illinois St., Chicago IL 60611. (312)467-0580. Editor: Larry Razbadouski. Estab. 1985. Publishes hardcover and trade paperback originals and reprints. Averages 30 titles/year. Receives 400-500 submissions/year. 40% of books from first-time authors; 60% from unagented writers. Subsidy publishes 5% of books. Determines subsidy "when some synergism exists." Pays 6-10% royalty on wholesale price. Advances are not frequent. Publishes book an average of 6 months after acceptance. Simultaneous submissions OK "if informed they are such." Query for electronic submissions. Reports in 1 month on queries; 5 weeks on mss. Book catalog free on request. All submissions and queries must include SASE.
Nonfiction: Biography, coffee table book, how-to, self-help. Subjects include business and economics, foods and nutrition, government/politics, health/medicine, money/finance, recreation, sports and women's issues/studies. Query with outline/synopsis and sample chapters. Reviews artwork/photos as part of ms package.
Recent Nonfiction Title: *William Heirens: His Day in Court*, by Dolores Kennedy (true crime).

BOOKCRAFT, INC., 1848 W. 2300 S., Salt Lake City UT 84119. (801)972-6180. Editorial Manager: Cory H. Maxwell. Estab. 1942. Publishes (mainly hardcover) originals and reprints. Pays standard 7½-10-12½-15% royalty on retail price; rarely gives a royalty advance. Averages 40-45 titles/year; receives 500-600 submissions annually. 20% of books from first-time authors; virtually 100% of books from unagented writers. Publishes book an average of 6 months after acceptance. Reports in about 2 months. Will send general information to prospective authors on request; ms guidelines for #10 SASE.
Nonfiction: "We publish for members of The Church of Jesus Christ of Latter-Day Saints (Mormons) and do not distribute to the national market. All our books are closely oriented to the faith and practices of the LDS church, and we will be glad to review such mss. Mss which have merely a general religious appeal are not acceptable. Ideal book lengths range from about 80 to 240 pages or so, depending on subject, presentation, and age level. We look for a fresh approach—rehashes of well-known concepts or doctrines not acceptable. Mss should be anecdotal unless truly scholarly or on a specialized subject. We do not publish anti-Mormon works. We also publish short and moderate length books for Mormon youth, about ages 14 to 19, mostly nonfiction. These reflect LDS principles without being 'preachy'; must be motivational. 30,000-45,000 words is about the right length, though good, longer mss are not entirely ruled out. This is a tough area to write in, and the mortality rate for such mss is high. We publish only 2 or 3 new juvenile titles annually. No poetry, plays, personal philosophiz-

An asterisk preceding a listing indicates that subsidy publishing or co-publishing (where author pays part or all of publishing costs) is available. Firms whose subsidy programs comprise more than 50% of their total publishing activities are listed at the end of the Book Packagers and Producers section.

ings, or family histories." Query. "Include contents page with manuscript."
Recent Nonfiction Title: *Let Not Your Heart Be Troubled*, by Boyd K. Packer.
Fiction: Must be closely oriented to LDS faith and practices.
Recent Fiction Title: *The Work and the Glory: Pillar of Light*, by Gerald N. Land.

THE BORGO PRESS, P.O. Box 2845, San Bernardino CA 92406. (714)884-5813. Editor: Mary A. Burgess. Estab. 1975. Publishes hardcover and paperback originals. Averages 150 titles/year, of which 120 are imported or distributed books; receives 500 submissions annually. 5% of books from first-time authors; 100% of books from unagented writers. Pays royalty on retail price: "10% of gross." No advance. Publishes book an average of 3 years after acceptance. "99% of our sales go to the academic library market; we do not sell to the trade (i.e., bookstores)." Query for electronic submissions. Reports in 3 months. Book catalog and writer's guidelines for 8½×11 SAE and 5 first class stamps.
Nonfiction: Publishes literary critiques, bibliographies, historical research, film critiques, theatrical research, interview volumes, biographies, social studies, political science, and reference works for the academic library market only. Query with letter or outline/synopsis and 1 sample chapter. "All of our proprietary books, without exception, are published in open-ended, numbered, monographic series. Do not submit proposals until you have looked at actual copies of recent Borgo Press publications (*not our catalog*). We are *not* a market for fiction, poetry, popular nonfiction, artwork, or anything else except scholarly monographs in the humanities and social sciences. We discard unsolicited manuscripts from outside of our subject fields that are not accompanied by SASE. The vast majority of proposals we receive are clearly unsuitable and are a waste of both our time and the prospective author's."
Recent Nonfiction Title: *First Century Palestinian Judaism: A Bibliography of Works in English*, by David R. Bourquin.
Tips: "We are currently buying comprehensive, annotated bibliographies of twentieth-century writers; these must be produced to a strict series format (available for SASE and 3 first class stamps). Proposals for *The Milford Series: Popular Writers of Today* series of literary critiques should go to the series editor, Dr. Dale Salwak, Dept. of English, Citrus College, 1000 W. Foothill Blvd., Glendora CA 91740."

*DON BOSCO MULTIMEDIA, 475 N. Ave., Box T, New Rochelle NY 10802. (914)576-0122. Publisher: James Hurley. Subsidiaries include Salesiana Publishers. Publishes hardcover and trade paperback originals. Averages 10-20 titles/year; receives 50 submissions annually. 15% of books from first-time authors; 100% of books from unagented writers. Average print order for a writer's first book is 2,500. Subsidy publishes 10% of books. Subsidy publishes (nonauthor) 30% of books. "We judge the content of the manuscript and quality to be sure it fits the description of our house. We subsidy publish for nonprofit and religious societies." Pays 5-10% royalty on retail price; offers average $100 advance. Publishes book an average of 10 months after acceptance. Reports in 6 weeks on queries; 3 months on mss. Free book catalog.
Nonfiction: Biography, juvenile and textbook on Roman Catholic religion. "Biographies of outstanding Christian men and women of today. We are a new publisher with wide experience in school marketing, especially in religious education field." Accepts nonfiction translations from Italian and Spanish. Query or submit outline/synopsis and 2 sample chapters. Occasionally reviews artwork/photos as part of ms package.
Recent Nonfiction Title: *Catholic Families: Growing and Sharing in Faith*, by John Roberts.
Tips: Queries/mss may be routed to other editors in the publishing group.

BOWLING GREEN STATE UNIVERSITY POPULAR PRESS, Bowling Green State University, Bowling Green OH 43403. (419)372-7866. Editor: Ms. Pat Browne. Estab. 1967. Publishes hardcover and trade paperback originals and reprints. Averages 25-30 titles/year. Receives 150-200 submissions/year. 50% of books from first-time authors; 95% from unagented writers. Pays 5-12½% royalty on wholesale price; buys mss outright. Publishes book an average of 12 months after acceptance. Reports in 1 week on queries; 3 months on mss. Book catalog and manuscript guidelines free on request.
Nonfiction: Biography, reference and textbook. Subjects include Americana, anthropology/archaeology, art/architecture, history, language/literature, photography, regional, religion, sociology, sports and women's issues/studies. Submit outline/synopsis and sample chapters.
Recent Nonfiction Title: *The Monster With a Thousand Faces*, by Brian J. Frost (reference).
Tips: "Our audience includes university professors, students, and libraries."

*THE BOXWOOD PRESS, 183 Ocean View Blvd., Pacific Grove CA 93950. (408)375-9110. Editor: Dr. Ralph Buchsbaum. Imprints include Viewpoint Books, Free Spirit Books. Publishes hardcover and trade paperback originals. Firm averages 5 titles/year. Receives 25 submissions/year. Subsidy publishes 25% of books. Determines subsidy by high merit; low market. Pays 10% royalty. Publishes book an average of 10 months after acceptance. Query for electronic submissions. Reports in 6 weeks on queries; 2 months on mss. Book catalog free on request.

Nonfiction: Biography, technical and textbook. Subjects include biology (plants and animals), health/medicine, history, nature/environment, philosophy, psychology, regional or area studies and other science. Submit complete ms. Reviews artwork/photos as part of ms package.
Recent Nonfiction Title: *Beyond Birding*, by Grubb (text).
Tips: "Writers have the best chance selling us sound science and natural history books. Our audience is high school and college, general and educated. If I were a writer trying to market a book today, I would know my subject, readership and do my clearest writing."

BOYD & FRASER PUBLISHING COMPANY, Division of South-Western Publishing Company, Suite 1405, 20 Park Plaza, Boston MA 02116. (617)426-2292. Acquisitions Editor: James Edwards. Publishes hardcover and paperback originals primarily for the college textbook market; some trade sales of selected titles. Averages 25-30 titles/year. Receives 100 submissions/year. 50% of books from first-time authors; 100% from unagented writers. Pays 15% royalty on wholesale price. Advance is negotiated individually. Publishes book an average of 1 year after acceptance. Simultaneous submissions OK. Query for electronic submissions. Reports in 1 month on queries; 2 months on mss. Book catalog and manuscript guidelines free on request.
Nonfiction: Textbook. Subjects include computer information systems and application software. Query or submit outline/synopsis first; unsolicited mss not invited. Reviews artwork/photos as part of ms package.
Recent Nonfiction Title: *Database Systems, Management and Design*, by Phillip J. Pratt.
Tips: "Writers have the best chance sending us proposals for college-level textbooks in computer education. Our audience consists of students enrolled in business oriented courses on computers or computer application topics."

‡BOYDS MILLS PRESS, Subsidiary of *Highlights for Children*, 910 Church St., Honesdale PA 18431. (717)253-1080. Manuscript Coordinator: Juanita Galuska. Imprints include Caroline House, Bell Books, Wordsong. Publishes hardcover, trade paperback and mass market paperback originals. Publishes 73 titles/year. Receives 7,800 queries and mss/year. 80% of books are from first-time authors; 75% from unagented writers. Pays 4-10% royalty on retail price. Offers varying advance. Publishes ms an average of 9 months after acceptance. Simultaneous submissions OK. Reports in 1 month. Free book catalog and ms guidelines.
Nonfiction: Juvenile on all subjects. "Boyds Mills Press is not interested in mss depicting violence, explicit sexuality, racism of any kinds or which promotes hatred." Submit outline/synopsis and sample chapters or complete ms. Reviews artwork/photos as part of ms package.
Recent Nonfiction Title: *Amazon*, by Peter Lourie (chronicle of changes in Amazon River basin).
Fiction: Juvenile in all genres. Also publishes boardbooks, puzzle books, gamebooks and poetry. Submit outline/synopsis and sample chapters or complete ms.
Recent Fiction Title: *The Cows are Going to Paris*, by Allen Woodman and David Kirby (picture book).
Tips: "Our audience is pre-school to young adult. Concentrate first on you writing. Polish it. Then—and only then—select a market."

BRADBURY PRESS, Affiliate of Macmillan, Inc., 866 3rd Ave., New York NY 10022. (212)702-9809. Editorial Director: Barbara Lalicki. Publishes hardcover originals for children and young adults. Averages 30 titles/year. Pays royalty and offers advance. Reports in 3 months. Book catalog and ms guidelines for 9 × 12 SAE with 4 first class stamps.
Recent Nonfiction Title: *The Great American Gold Rush*, by Rhoda Blumburg.
Fiction: Picture books, concept books, photo essays and novels for elementary school children. Also "stories about real kids; special interest in realistic dialogue." No adult ms. No religious material. Submit complete ms.
Recent Fiction Title: *Miss Penny and Mr. Grubbs*, by Lisa Campbell Ernst.
Tips: "We're looking for books that will get kids excited about reading."

BRANDEN PUBLISHING CO., INC., 17 Station St., Box 843, Brookline Village MA 02147. Subsidiaries include International Pocket Library and Popular Technology, Four Seas and Brashear. Publishes hardcover and trade paperback originals, reprints and software. Averages 15 titles/year; receives 1,000 submissions annually. 80% of books from first-time authors; 90% of books from unagented writers. Average print order for a writer's first book is 3,000. Pays 5-10% royalty on net; offers $1,000 maximum advance. Publishes book an average of 10 months after acceptance. Query for electronic submissions. Reports in 1 week on queries; 2 months on mss.
Nonfiction: Biography, illustrated book, juvenile, reference, technical and textbook. Subjects include Americana, art, computers, health, history, music, photography, politics, sociology, software and classics. Especially looking for "about 10 manuscripts on national and international subjects, including biographies of well-known individuals." No religion or philosophy. Prefers paragraph query with au-

thor's vita and SASE; no unsolicited mss. Reviews artwork/photos as part of ms package.

Recent Nonfiction Title: *Barbra—An Actress Who Sings.*

Fiction: Ethnic (histories, integration); mainstream (emphasis on youth and immigrants); religious (historical-reconstructive); romance (novels with well-drawn characters). No science, mystery or pornography. Paragraph query with author's vita and SASE; no unsolicited mss.

Recent Fiction Title: *The Dance of the 12 Apostles,* by P.J. Carisella (historical novel).

Tips: "Branden publishes only manuscripts determined to have a significant impact on modern society. Our audience is a well-read general public, professionals, college students, and some high school students. If I were a writer trying to market a book today, I would thoroughly investigate the number of potential readers interested in the content of my book. We like books by or about women."

BREVET PRESS, INC., P.O. Box 1404, Sioux Falls SD 57101. Publisher: Donald P. Mackintosh. Managing Editor: Peter E. Reid. Estab. 1972. Publishes hardcover and paperback originals and reprints. Receives 40 submissions annually. 50% of books from first-time authors; 100% of books from unagented writers. Average print order for a writer's first book is 5,000. Pays 5% royalty; advance averages $1,000. Publishes book an average of 1 year after acceptance. Simultaneous submissions OK. Reports in 2 months. Free book catalog.

Nonfiction: Specializes in business management, history, place names, and historical marker series. Americana (A. Melton, editor); business (D.P. Mackintosh, editor); history (B. Mackintosh, editor); and technical books (Peter Reid, editor). Query; "after query, detailed instructions will follow if we are interested." Reviews artwork/photos; send copies if photos/illustrations are to accompany ms.

Tips: "Write with market potential and literary excellence. Keep sexism out of the manuscripts by male authors."

*BRIARCLIFF PRESS PUBLISHERS, 11 Wimbledon Ct., Jericho NY 11753. Editorial Director: Trudy Settel. Senior Editor: J. Frieman. Estab. 1980. Publishes hardcover and paperback originals. Averages 5-7 titles/year; receives 250 submissions annually. 10% of books from first-time authors; 60% of books from unagented writers. Average print order for a writer's first book is 5,000. Subsidy publishes 20% of books. Pays $4,000-5,000 for outright purchase; offers average of $1,000 advance. Publishes book an average of 6 months after acceptance. "We do not use unsolicited manuscripts. Ours are custom books prepared for businesses, and assignments are initiated by us."

Nonfiction: How-to, cookbooks, sports, travel, fitness/health, business and finance, diet, gardening and crafts. "We want our books to be designed to meet the needs of specific businesses." Accepts nonfiction translations from French, German and Italian. Query. Submit outline and 2 sample chapters. Reviews artwork/photos as part of ms package.

Recent Nonfiction Title: *Nail Care,* by Kristi Wells.

BRICK HOUSE PUBLISHING CO., P.O. Box 2134, 11 Thoreau Rd, Acton MA 01720. (508)635-9800. Publisher: Robert Runck. Estab. 1976. Publishes hardcover and trade paperback originals. Averages 12 titles/year; receives 200 submissions annually. 20% of books from first-time authors; 100% of books from unagented writers. Pays 10-15% royalty on wholesale price. Offers average $1,000 advance. Publishes book an average of 6 months after acceptance. Simultaneous submissions OK. Query for electronic submissions. Reports in 2 weeks on queries; 3 months on mss. Book catalog and ms guidelines for 8½ × 11 SAE with 4 first class stamps.

Nonfiction: How-to, reference, technical and textbook. Subjects include business and consumer advice. "We are looking for writers to do books in the following areas: New England regional topics, energy and environment, practical information for people running small businesses, consumer trade books on job search and career building, and college business textbooks." Query with synopses.

Recent Nonfiction Title: *Get the Job You Want,* by Signe Dayhoff.

Tips: "A common mistake writers make is not addressing the following questions in their query/proposals: What are my qualifications for writing this book? Why would anyone want the book enough to pay for it in a bookstore? What can I do to promote the book?"

BRISTOL PUBLISHING ENTERPRISES, INC., P.O. Box 1737, 14692 Wicks Blvd., San Leandro CA 94577. (415)895-4461. Chairman: Patricia J. Hall. President: Brian Hall. Imprints include Bristol Nitty Gritty Cookbooks. Publishes 12-14 titles/year. Receives 250 proposals/year. 25% of books from first-time authors; 100% from unagented writers. Pays 6-9% royalty on wholesale price. Average advance $100. Publishes within 1 year of acceptance. Reports in 2 months. Book catalog for SAE with 2 first class stamps.

Nonfiction: Cookbooks. Nonfiction books for readers over 50 years of age. Submit outline/synopsis and sample chapters.

Recent Nonfiction Title: *The Encyclopedia of Grandparenting,* by Rosemary Dalton.

‡BRITISH AMERICAN PUBLISHING, 19B British American Blvd., Latham NY 12110. (518)786-6000. Managing Editor: Kathleen Murphy. Imprint is The Paris Review Editions. Publishes hardcover and trade paperback originals and hardcover reprints. Firm averages 15 titles/year. Receives 500 submissions/year. 10% of books from first-time authors. 10% from unagented writers. Pays royalties. Publishes book an average of 1 year after acceptance. Simultaneous submissions OK. Query for electronic submissions. Free book catalog and manuscript guidelines.

Nonfiction: Biography, humor, self-help, how-to. Subjects include business and economics, child guidance/parenting, cooking, foods & nutrition, education, government/politics, history, language/literature, psychology, recreation, regional, sports and travel. Submit complete ms.

Recent Nonfiction Title: *Marion Barry: The Politics of Race*, by Jonathan I. Z. Agnosky (cloth/bio).

Fiction: Adventure, confession, experimental, fantasy, feminist, historical, horror, humor, literary, mainstream/contemporary, mystery, religious, romance, short story collections and suspense. Submit complete ms.

Recent Fiction Title: *Shine Hawk*, by Charlie Smith.

Poetry: Submit complete ms.

Recent Poetry Title: *Imaginary Paintings*, by Charles Baxter.

BROADWAY PRESS, 12 W. Thomas St., P.O. Box 1037, Shelter Island NY 11964. (516)749-3266. FAX: (516)749-3267. Publisher: David Rodger. Estab. 1985. Publishes trade paperback originals. Averages 5-10 titles/year; receives 20-30 submissions annually. 50% of books from first-time authors; 75% of books from unagented writers. Pays negotiable royalty. Publishes book an average of 18 months after acceptance. Simultaneous submissions OK. Reports in 1 month on queries.

Nonfiction: Reference and technical. Subjects include theatre, film, television and the performing arts. "We're looking for professionally-oriented and authored books." Submit outline/synopsis and sample chapters.

Recent Nonfiction Title: *Stock Scenery Construction Handbook*, by Bill Raoul.

Tips: "Our readers are primarily professionals in the entertainment industries. Submissions that really grab our attention are aimed at that market."

BUCKNELL UNIVERSITY PRESS, Lewisburg PA 17837. (717)524-3674. Director: Mills F. Edgerton, Jr. Publishes hardcover originals. Averages 20 titles/year; receives 150 submissions annually. 20% of books from first-time authors; 99% of books from unagented writers. Pays royalty. Publishes book an average of 2 years after acceptance. Query for electronic submissions. Reports in 1 month on queries; usually 6 months on mss. Free book catalog.

Nonfiction: Subjects include scholarly art, history, literary criticism, music, philosophy, politics, psychology, religion and sociology. "In all fields, our criterion is scholarly presentation; manuscripts must be addressed to the scholarly community." Query.

Recent Nonfiction Title: *Claudio Rodriguez and the Language of Poetic Vision*, by Jonathan Mayhew.

Tips: "An original work of high-quality scholarship has the best chance of selling to us. We publish for the scholarly community."

BULL PUBLISHING CO., 110 Gilbert, Menlo Park CA 94025. (415)332-2855. FAX: (415)327-3300. Publisher: David Bull. Estab. 1974. Publishes hardcover and trade paperback originals. Averages 4-8 titles/year. Receives 100 submissions/year. 40-50% of books from first-time authors; 99% from unagented writers. Pays 14-16% royalty on wholesale price (net to publisher). Publishes ms an average of 6 months after acceptance. Simultaneous submissions OK. Query for electronic submissions. Reports in 6 weeks. Book catalog free on request.

Nonfiction: How-to, self-help. Subjects include foods and nutrition, fitness, child health and nutrition, health education, sports medicine. "We look for books that fit our area of strength: responsible books on health that fill a substantial public need, and that we can market primarily through professionals." Submit outline/synopsis and sample chapters. Reviews artwork/photos as part of ms package.

Recent Nonfiction Title: *Nutrition for the Chemotherapy Patient*, by Rosenbaum/Ramstack.

BUSINESS & LEGAL REPORTS, INC., 64 Wall St., Madison CT 06443. (203)245-7448. FAX: (203)245-2559. Editor-in-Chief: Stephen D. Bruce, Ph.D. Estab. 1978. Publishes loose leaf and soft cover originals. Averages 20 titles/year. Receives 100 submissions/year. Pays 2½-5% royalty on retail price; buys mss outright for $1,000-5,000. Offers $1,500-3,000 average advance. Publishes book an average of 6 months after acceptance. Simultaneous submissions OK. Query for electronic submissions. Book catalog free on request.

Nonfiction: Reference. Subjects include human resources, management, human resources, safety, environmental management. Query.

Recent Nonfiction Title: *Supervisor's Safety Meeting Guide*, by Barbara Kelly.

‡C Q INC., Imprint of Congressional Quarterly, Inc., 1414 22nd St. NW, Washington DC 20037. (202)887-8642. Acquisitions Editor: Jeanne Ferris. Publishes 30-40 hardcover and paperback titles/ year. 95% of books from unagented writers. Pays royalties on net receipts. Sometimes offers an advance. Publishes book an average of 6-12 months after acceptance. Simultaneous submissions OK. Reports in 3 months. Free book catalog.

Nonfiction: Reference books, information directories and monographs on federal and state governments, national elections, politics and governmental issues. Public affairs paperbacks on developing issues and events. Submit prospectus, writing sample and curriculum vitae.

Recent Nonfiction Title: *The U.S. Supreme Court: A Bibliography*, by Fenton Martin and Robert Goehlert.

Tips: "Our books present important information on American government and politics, and related issues, with careful attention to accuracy, thoroughness and readability."

C Q PRESS, Imprint of Congressional Quarterly, Inc., 1414 22nd St. NW, Washington DC 20037. (202)887-8641. Acquisitions Editor: Brenda Carter. Publishes 20-30 hardcover and paperback original titles annually. 95% of books from unagented writers. Pays standard college royalty on wholesale price; offers college text advance. Publishes book an average of 5 months after acceptance of final ms. Simultaneous submissions OK. Reports in 3 months. Free book catalog.

Nonfiction: College text. All levels of political science texts. "We are one of the most distinguished publishers in the areas of American government, public administation and international relations textbooks." Submit proposal, outline and sample chapter.

Recent Nonfiction Title: *Divided Democracy: Cooperation and Conflict Between the President and Congress*, James A. Thurber, Editor.

*C.S.S. PUBLISHING COMPANY, 628 S. Main St., Lima OH 45804. (419)227-1818. Editorial Director: Fred Steiner. Estab. 1970. Imprints include Fairway Press. Publishes trade paperback originals. Publishes 50 titles/year. Receives 300 mss/year. 65% of books from first-time authors; 100% from unagented writers. Subsidy publishes 20%. "If books have limited market appeal and/or deal with basically same subject matter as title already on list, we will consider subsidy option." Pays 6-8% royalty on wholesale price or outright purchase of $25-400. Publishes book 1-2 years after acceptance. Simultaneous submissions OK. Query for electronic submissions. Reports on mss in 6 months. Book catalog free on request; ms guidelines for #10 SASE.

Nonfiction: Humor (religious) and self-help (religious). Subjects include religion: "Christian resources for mainline Protestant denominations; some Catholic resources. We are interested in sermon and worship resources, preaching illustrations, sermon seasonings, some Bible study, inspirationals, pastoral care, plays, practical theology, newsletter and bulletin board blurbs, church growth, success stories, teacher helps/training helps, church program material. Also sermon and worship resources based on the three-year lectionary; marriage helps and wedding services." Reviews photos/artwork as part of ms package.

Recent Nonfiction Title: *Is The Cross Still There?*, by George M. Bass.

Tips: "Books that sell well for us are seasonal sermon and worship resources; books aimed at clergy on professional growth and survival; also books of children's object lessons; seasonal plays (Christmas/ Lent/Easter etc.). Our primary market is the clergy in all mainline denominations; others include church leaders, movers and shakers, education directors, Sunday school teachers, women's groups, youth leaders; to a certain extent we publish for the Christian layperson. Write something that makes Christianity applicable to the contemporary world, something useful to the struggling, searching Christian. The treatment might be humorous, certainly unique. We have published a few titles that other houses would not touch—with some degree of success. We are open to new ideas and would be pleased to see anything new, different, creative, and well-written that fits our traditional markets."

CALGRE PRESS, Subsidiary of Calgre, Inc., P.O. Box 711, Antioch CA 94509. (415)754-4916. Editor: Diane Power. Estab. 1988. Publishes hardcover and trade paperback originals. Firm averages 4 titles/ year. 70% of books from first-time authors; 90% from unagented writers. Pays 5-15% royalty on retail price. Publishes book an average of 9 months after acceptance. Simultaneous submissions OK. Reports in 2 weeks on queries; 2 months on mss. Book catalog and manuscript guidelines for #10 SASE.

Nonfiction: How-to, reference, self-help. Subjects include child guidance/parenting, education. Submit outline/synopsis and sample chapters. Reviews artwork/photos as part of ms package.

Recent Nonfiction Title: *The Defiant Ones: A Manual For Raising Kids*, by Jeffery M. Bruns.

Tips: "The writer has the best chance with how-to and self-help books, also books dealing with education and our educational system. Our audience includes adults, parents, teachers, business oriented adults in search of behavior motivation for higher productivity. If I were a writer trying to market a book today, I would contact small publishing firms specializing in the field that my book covers. An alternative is to contact literary agents hoping that they'll accept it for on

CAMBRIDGE CAREER PRODUCTS, P.O. Box 2153, Charleston WV 2532
(304)344-5583. Subsidiaries include: Cambridge Home Economics, Camb
Health. President: Edward T. Gardner, Ph.D. Estab. 1980. Publishes ha
originals. Firm averages 12 titles/year. Receives 20 submissions/year.
authors. 90% from unagented writers. Pays 6-15% on wholesale price, $
Offers $1,200 average advance. Publishes book an average of 8 months
submissions OK. Reports in 2 weeks on queries; 1 month on mss. Free bo
guidelines.
Nonfiction: How-to, juvenile and self-help. Subjects include child guidance/parenting, cooking,
and nutrition, education, health/medicine, money/finance, recreation and sports. "We need high quality books written for young adults (13 to 24 years old) on job search, career guidance, educational
guidance, personal guidance, home economics, physical education, coaching, recreation, health, personal development, substance abuse, and sports. We only publish books written for young adults and
primarily sold to libraries, schools, etc. We do not seek books targeted to adults or written at high
readability levels." Query or submit outline/synopsis and sample chapters or send complete ms. Reviews artwork/photos as part of ms package.
Recent Nonfiction Title: *Job Search Guide,* by J. Lupia.
Tips: "We encourage the submission of high-quality books on timely topics written for young adult
audiences at moderate to low readability levels. Call and request a copy of all our current catalogs,
talk to the management about what is timely in the areas you wish to write on, thoroughly research
the topic, and write a manuscript that will be read by young adults without being overly technical. Low
to moderate readability yet entertaining, informative and accurate."

CAMBRIDGE UNIVERSITY PRESS, 40 W. 20th St., New York NY 10011. Director: Alan Winter.
Estab. 1534. Publishes hardcover and paperback originals. Publishes 1,2000 titles/year; receives 1,000
submissions annually. 50% of books from first-time authors; 99% of books from unagented writers.
Subsidy publishes (nonauthor) 8% of books. Pays 10% royalty on receipts; 8% on paperbacks; no
advance. Publishes book an average of 1 year after acceptance. Query for electronic submissions.
Reports in 4 months.
Nonfiction: Anthropology, archeology, economics, life sciences, mathematics, psychology, physics, art
history, upper-level textbooks, academic trade, scholarly monographs, biography, history, and music.
Looking for academic excellence in all work submitted. Department Editors: Frank Smith (history,
social sciences); Ellen Shaw (English as second language); Michael Agnes (reference); Lauren Cowles
(mathematics, computer science); Scott Parris (economics); Julia Hough (developmental and social
psychology, cognitive science); Emily Loose (politics, sociology); Beatrice Rehl (fine arts); Robin
Smith (life sciences); Alan Harvey, (applied mathematics); Florence Padgett, (engineering, materials
science); and Terence Moore (philosophy). Query. Reviews artwork/photos.
Recent Nonfiction Title: *Frederick Douglass: New Literary and Historical Essays,* edited by Erick J.
Sundquist.

‡CAMDEN HOUSE, INC., P.O. Drawer 2025, Columbia SC 29202. (803)736-9455. Editor: James N.
Hardin. Publishes hardcover originals and reprints. Publishes 25-30 titles/year. 75% of books from
first-time authors. 100% from unagented writers. Pays 5-10% royalties on retail price. Publishes ms
an average of 6 months after acceptance. Query for electronic submissions. Reports on queries in 2
weeks. Book catalog and ms guidelines free on request.
Nonfiction: Reference, technical and textbook. Subjects include health/medicine, language/litera-
ture, music/dance. "We are looking for medical books for the layperson: diet, stress management,
etc." Query. Reviews artwork/photos as part of ms package.
Recent Nonfiction Title: *Music, Love, Death and Mann's Doctor Faustus,* by John Fetzer (literary
criticism).

CAMELOT BOOKS, Children's Book Imprint of Avon Books, Division of the Hearst Corp., 105 Madison Ave., 8th Floor, New York NY 10016. (212)481-5609. FAX: (212)532-2172. Editorial Director:
Ellen Krieger. Publishes paperback originals and reprints. Averages 60-70 titles/year; receives 1,000-
1,500 submissions annually. 10-15% of books from first-time authors; 75% of books from unagented
writers. Pays 6-8% royalty on retail price; offers minimum advance of $2,000. Publishes book an

*For information on book publishers' areas of interest, see
the nonfiction and fiction sections in the Book Publishers
Subject Index.*

months after acceptance. Simultaneous submissions OK. Reports in 10 weeks. Free og and ms guidelines for 8×10 SAE and 5 first class stamps.

Subjects include adventure, fantasy, humor, juvenile (Camelot, 8-12 and Young Camelot, 7- ainstream, mystery, ("very selective with mystery and fantasy") and suspense. Avon does not sh picture books. Submit entire ms or 3 sample chapters and a brief "general summary of the ory, chapter by chapter."

Recent Fiction Title: *A Haunting in Williamsburg*, by Lou Kassem.

CAMINO BOOKS, INC., P.O. Box 59026, Philadelphia PA 19102. (215)732-2491. Publisher: E. Jutkowitz. Estab. 1987. Publishes hardcover and trade paperback originals. Averages 5 titles/year. Receives 100 submissions/year. 20% of books from first-time authors. Pays 6-12% royalty on net price. Offers $1,000 average advance. Publishes book an average of 1 year after acceptance. Reports in 2 weeks on queries; 1 month on mss.
Nonfiction: Biography, cookbook, how-to, humor and juvenile. Subjects include agriculture/horticulture, Americana, art/architecture, child guidance/parenting, cooking, foods and nutrition, ethnic, gardening, government/politics, history, regional and travel. Query or submit outline/synopsis and sample chapters.
Recent Nonfiction Title: *A Guide to the Caves of the Middle Atlantic States*, by Silverman.
Tips: "The books must be on interest to readers in the Middle Atlantic states."

C&T PUBLISHING, 5021 Blum Rd., #1, Martinez CA 94553. (415)370-9600. FAX: (415)370-1576. Editor-in-Chief: Diane Pederson. Estab. 1983. Publishes hardcover and trade paperback originals. Publishes 6-8 titles/year; receives 24 submissions/year. Buys 10% from first-time authors; 100% from unagented writers. Pays 5-10% royalty on retail price. Offers $1,000 average advance. Publishes book an average of 9 months after acceptance. Simultaneous submissions OK. Reports in 3 weeks on queries; 2 months on mss. Free book catalog and ms guidelines.
Nonfiction: Quilting books, primariy how-to, occasional quilt picture books, children's books relating to quilting, quilt-related crafts, wearable art, other books relating to fabric crafting. "Please submit ms with color photos of your work."
Recent Nonfiction Title: *Crazy Quilt Odyssey*, by Judith Montano.
Tips: "In our industry, we find that how-to books have the longest selling life. The art quilt is coming into its own as an expression by women. Quiltmakers, sewing enthusiasts and fiber artists are our audience."

‡**CAPSTONE PRESS, INC.**, P.O. Box 669, North Mankato MN 56001. (507)387-4992. Contact: Acquisitions Editor. Publishes hardcover originals. Firm averages 48-96 titles/year. Buys by outright purchase. Publishes book an average of 6 months after acceptance. Reports in 2 weeks. Book catalog free on request.
Nonfiction: Juvenile. Subjects include Americana, animals, history, hobbies, science, sports and travel. Query. Reviews artwork/photos as part of ms package.
Fiction: Adventure, fantasy, historical, horror, humor, juvenile, mainstream/contemporary, mystery, picture books, romance, science fiction, suspense and western. Query.

‡*ARISTIDE D. CARATZAS, PUBLISHER**, Box 210/30 Church St., New Rochelle NY 10801. (914)632-8487. FAX: (914)636-3650. Managing Editor: John Emerich. Publishes hardcover originals and reprints. Averages 20 titles/year; receives 100 submissions annually. 35% of books from first-time authors; 80% of books from unagented writers. Subsidy publishes 25% of books. "We seek grants/subsidies for limited run scholarly books; granting organizations are generally institutions or foundations." Pays royalty; offers $1,500 average advance. Publishes book an average of 18 months after acceptance. Simultaneous submissions OK. Query for electronic submissions. Reports in 1 month on queries; 3 months on mss. Free book catalog.
Nonfiction: Reference, technical and textbook. Subjects include art, history (ancient, European, Russian), politics, religion, travel, classical languages (Greek and Latin), archaeology and mythology. Nonfiction book ms needs for the next year include "scholarly books in archaeology; mythology; ancient and medieval history; and art history." Query or submit outline/synopsis and sample chapters. Reviews artwork/photos as part of ms package.
Recent Nonfiction Title: *The Coroplast's Art*, by Jarmee Uhlenbrock (art history).

THE CAREER PRESS INC., 180 5th Ave., P.O. Box 34, Hawthorne NJ 07507. (201)427-0229. FAX: (201)427-2037. President: Ron Fry. Estab. 1985. Imprints include Career Directory Series and Internships Series. Publishes trade paperback originals. Averages 12-18 titles/year. Receives 150 submissions/year. 50% of books from first-time authors; 50% from unagented writers. Pays 10-15% royalty on wholesale price. Publishes book an average of 6 months after acceptance. Simultaneous submissions OK. Query for electronic submissions. Reports in 3 weeks. Book catalog free on request.

Nonfiction: How-to, reference and self-help. Subjects include business and economics, child guidance/parenting, education, money/finance and career/job search/resume. Submit complete ms. Reviews artwork/photos as part of ms package.

Recent Nonfiction Title: *How to Strengthen Your Winning Business Personality*, by B. Smith (business/management).

CAREER PUBLISHING, INC., P.O. Box 5486, Orange CA 92613-5486. (714)771-5155. FAX: (714)532-0180. Editor-in-Chief: Marilyn M. Martin. Publishes paperback originals and software. Averages 6-20 titles/year; receives 300 submissions annually. 80% of books from first-time authors; 90% of books from unagented writers. Average print order for a writer's first book is 5,000-10,000. Pays 10% royalty on actual amount received; no advance. Publishes book an average of 6 months after acceptance. Simultaneous submissions OK (if so informed with names of others to whom submissions have been sent). Query for electronic submissions. Reports in 2 months. Book catalog for 8½ × 11 SAE with 2 first class stamps; ms guidelines for 9 × 12 SASE.

Nonfiction: Microcomputer material, educational software, word processing, guidance material, allied health, dictionaries, etc. "Textbooks should provide core upon which class curriculum can be based: textbook, workbook or kit with 'hands-on' activities and exercises, and teacher's guide. Should incorporate modern and effective teaching techniques. Should lead to a job objective. We also publish support materials for existing courses and are open to unique, marketable ideas with schools in mind. Reading level should be controlled appropriately—usually 8th-9th grade equivalent for vocational school and community college level courses. Any sign of sexism or racism will disqualify the work. No career awareness masquerading as career training." Submit outline/synopsis, 2 sample chapters and table of contents or complete ms. Reviews artwork/photos as part of ms package. If material is to be returned, enclose SAE and return postage.

Recent Nonfiction Title: *Truck Driver's Guide to CDL*, by Robert M. Calvin.

Tips: "Authors should be aware of vocational/career areas with inadequate or no training textbooks and submit ideas and samples to fill the gap. Trends in book publishing that freelance writers should be aware of include education—especially for microcomputers."

CAROL PUBLISHING, 600 Madison Ave., New York NY 10022. (212)486-2200. Imprints include Lyle Stuart, Birch Lane Press, Citadel Press, and University Books. Firm publishes hardcover originals, and trade paperback originals and reprints. Firm averages 80 titles/year. Receives 1,000 submissions/year. 5% of books from first-time authors; 5% from unagented writers. Pays 10-15% royalty on retail price. Publishes book an average of 1 year after acceptance. Simultaneous submissions OK. Reports in 2 months.

Nonfiction: Biography, how-to, humor, illustrated book and self-help. Subjects include Americana, animals, art/architecture, business and economics, child guidance/parenting, computers and electronics, cooking, foods and nutrition, ethnic, gay/lesbian, health/medicine, history, hobbies, money/finance, music/dance, nature/environment, philosophy, psychology, recreation, regional, science, sports, travel and women's issues/studies. Submit outline/synopsis and sample chapters.

Recent Nonfiction Title: *A Woman Named Jackie*, by C. David Heymann.

Fiction: Adventure, confession, fantasy, horror, humor, literary, mystery, science fiction. Submit outline/synopsis and sample chapters.

Recent Fiction Title: *A Reasonable Madness*, by Fran Borf.

CAROLRHODA BOOKS, INC., 241 1st Ave. N., Minneapolis MN 55401. (612)332-3344. Submissions Editor: Rebecca Poole. Estab. 1969. Publishes hardcover originals. Averages 25-35 titles/year. Receives 1,500 submissions/year. 15% of books from first-time authors; 95% of books from unagented writers. Pays 4-6% royalty on wholesale price, makes outright purchase, or negotiates cents per printed copy. Publishes book an average of 18 months after acceptance. Simultaneous submissions OK. Reports in 3 months. Book catalog and ms guidelines for 9 × 12 SASE.

Nonfiction: Publishes only children's books. Subjects include biography, animals, art, history, music and nature. Needs "biographies in story form on truly creative individuals—25 manuscript pages in length." Send full ms. Reviews artwork/photos as part of ms package.

Recent Nonfiction Title: *Harp Seals*, by Olga Cossi.

Fiction: Children's historical. No anthropomorphized animal stories. Submit complete ms.

Recent Fiction Title: *A Dinosaur for Gerald*, by Helena Clare Pittman.

Tips: "Our audience consists of children ages four to eleven. We publish very few picture books. Nonfiction science topics, particularly nature, do well for us, as do biographies, photo essays, and easy readers. We prefer manuscripts that can fit into one of our series. Spend time developing your idea in a unique way or from a unique angle; avoid trite, hackneyed plots and ideas."

CARROLL & GRAF PUBLISHERS, INC., 260 5th Ave., New York NY 10001. (212)889-8772. Contact: Kent Carroll. Publishes hardcover, trade and mass market paperback originals, and trade and mass market paperback reprints. Averages 125 titles/year; receives 1,000 submissions annually. 10% of books from first-time authors; 10% of books from unagented writers. Pays 6-15% royalty on retail price. Publishes book an average of 9 months after acceptance. Reports in 3 weeks on queries; 1 month on mss. Book catalog for 6×9 SASE.

Nonfiction: Biography, history, psychology, current affairs. Query. Reviews artwork/photos as part of ms package.

Recent Nonfiction Title: *Bernstein Remebered: A Life in Photographs*, by Donel Henahan.

Fiction: Literary, erotica, mainstream, mystery, science fiction, horror/fantasy and suspense. Query with SASE.

CARSTENS PUBLICATIONS, INC., Hobby Book Division, P.O. Box 700, Newton NJ 07860. (201)383-3355. Publisher: Harold H. Carstens. Publishes paperback originals. Averages 8 titles/year. 75% of books from unagented writers. Pays 10% royalty on retail price; offers average advance. Publishes book an average of 1 year after acceptance. Query for electronic submissions. Book catalog for SASE.

Nonfiction: Model railroading, toy trains, model aviation, railroads and model hobbies. "We have scheduled or planned titles on several railroads as well as model railroad and model airplane books. Authors must know their field intimately because our readers are active modelers. Our railroad books presently are primarily photographic essays on specific railroads. Writers cannot write about somebody else's hobby with authority. If they do, we can't use them." Query. Reviews artwork/photos as part of ms package.

Tips: "No fiction. We need lots of good b&w photos. Material must be in model, hobby, railroad and transportation field only."

CASSANDRA PRESS, P.O. Box 868, San Rafael CA 94915. (415)382-8507. FAX: (415)382-7758. President: Gurudas. Estab. 1985. Publishes trade paperback originals. Averages 6 titles/year. Receives 200 submissions/year. 50% of books from first-time authors; 50% from unagented writers. About 10% agented. Pays 6-8% maximum royalty on retail price. Advance rarely offered, but to $4,000. Publishes book an average of 1 year after acceptance. Simultaneous submissions OK. Reports in 3 weeks on queries; 2 months on mss. Free book catalog and manuscript guidelines.

Nonfiction: New Age, cookbook, how-to, self-help. Subjects include cooking, foods and nutrition, health/medicine (holistic health), philosophy, psychology, religion (New Age) and metaphysical. "We like to do around six titles a year in the general New Age, metaphysical and holistic health fields so we continue to look for good material. No children's books." Submit outline/synopsis and sample chapters or complete ms. Reviews artwork/photos as part of ms package.

Recent Nonfiction Title: *Spiritual Wisdom of the Native Americans*, by John Heinerman, Ph.D.

Tips: "Not accepting fiction or children's book submissions."

CASSELL PUBLICATIONS, Cassell Communications Inc., P.O. Box 9844, Ft. Lauderdale FL 33310. (305)485-0795. FAX: (305)485-0806. Executive Editor: Dana K. Cassell. Estab. 1982. Firm publishes trade paperback originals. Publishes 8 titles/year; receives 300 submissions/year. 50% from first-time authors; 100% from unagented writers. Pays 10% royalty on retail price. Pays $500 average advance. Publishes book an average of 6 months after acceptance. Simultaneous submissions OK. Query for electronic submissions. Reports in 1 month on queries; 2 months on mss. Ms guidelines for #10 SASE.

Nonfiction: How-to, reference. Subjects include small business, freelance writing, publishing. Wants books covering writing, advertising, promotion, marketing and how-to treatments for freelance writers, professionals and independent retailers and services businesses. Query or submit outline/synopsis and sample chapters, competitive analysis, market analysis. Reviews artwork/photos as part of ms package.

Recent Nonfiction Title: *Nuts & Bolts Writer's Manual*, by Loma Davies.

‡CATBIRD PRESS, 44 N. 6th Ave., Highland Park NJ 08904. (908)572-0816. Publisher: Robert Wechsler. Estab. 1987. Imprints include Garrigue Books. Publishes hardcover and trade paperback originals and trade paperback reprints. Firm averages 5-6 titles/year. Receives 100 submissions/year. 10% of books from first-time authors. 100% from unagented writers. Pays 2½-10% royalty on retail price. Offers $1,500 average advance. Publishes book an average of 1 year after acceptance. Simultaneous submissions OK. Reports in 2 weeks on nonfiction queries if receives SASE. Book catalog free on request. Manuscript guidelines for #10 SASE.

Nonfiction: Humor, reference, travel writing. "We are looking for up-market humor, travel humor, legal humor books. No New Age or joke books." Submit outline/synopsis and sample chapters.

Recent Nonfiction Title: *The Giver's Guide: Making Your Charity Dollars Count*, by P. Mackey (reference/consumer).

Fiction: Humor, literary, mainstream/contemporary. "We are looking for well-written literature that takes a different approach and is not genre-oriented or obscurely experimental. No genre fiction." Submit outline/synopsis and sample chapters.

Recent Fiction Title: *Three Novels*, by Karel Capek.
Tips: "Our audience is generally up-market. If I were a writer trying to market a book today, I would learn about the publishing industry just as a musician learns about night clubs. If you play jazz, you should know the jazz clubs. If you write children's books, you should learn the children's book publishers. Writing is just as much an art and a business as jazz."

CATHOLIC UNIVERSITY OF AMERICA PRESS, 620 Michigan Ave. NE, Washington DC 20064. (202)319-5052. Director: Dr. David J. McGonagle. Marketing Manager: Marla Bucy. Averages 15-20 titles/year; receives 100 submissions annually. 50% of books from first-time authors; 100% of books from unagented writers. Average print order for a writer's first book is 1,000. Pays variable royalty on net receipts. Publishes book an average of 1 year after acceptance. Query for electronic submissions. Reports in 2 months. Book catalog for SASE.
Nonfiction: Publishes history, biography, languages and literature, philosophy, religion, church-state relations, political theory and social sciences. No unrevised doctoral dissertations. Length: 200,000-500,000 words. Query with sample chapter plus outline of entire work, along with *curriculum vitae* and list of previous publications. Reviews artwork/photos.
Recent Nonfiction Title: *The Italian Refuge: Rescue of Jews During the Holocaust*.
Tips: Freelancer has best chance of selling us "scholarly monographs and works suitable for adoption as supplementary reading material in courses."

CATO INSTITUTE, 224 2nd St. SE, Washington DC 20003. (202)546-0200. Executive Vice President: David Boaz. Estab. 1977. Publishes hardcover originals, trade paperback originals and reprints. Averages 12 titles/year. Receives 50 submissions/year. 25% of books from first-time authors; 90% from unagented writers. Buys mss by outright purchase for $1,000-10,000. Publishes book an average of 9 months after acceptance. Simultaneous submissions OK. Reports in 3 weeks on queries; 3 months on mss. Book catalog free on request.
Nonfiction: Public policy. Subjects include business and economics, education, government/politics, health/medicine, military/war, money/finance, sociology. "We want books on public policy issues from a free-market or libertarian perspective." Query.
Recent Nonfiction Title: *The Excluded Americans: Homelessness and Housing Policy*, by William Tucker.

THE CAXTON PRINTERS, LTD., 312 Main St., Caldwell ID 83605. (208)459-7421. FAX: (208)459-7450. Vice President: Gordon Gipson. Estab. 1895. Publishes hardcover and trade paperback originals. Averages 6-10 titles/year; receives 250 submissions annually. 50% of books from first-time authors; 60% of books from unagented writers. Audience includes Westerners, students, historians and researchers. Pays royalty; advance is $500-2,000. Publishes book an average of 18 months after acceptance. Simultaneous submissions OK. Reports in 2 weeks on queries; 2 months on mss. Book catalog for 9×12 SASE.
Nonfiction: Coffee table, Americana and Western Americana. "We need good Western Americana, especially the Northwest, preferably copiously illustrated with unpublished photos." Query. Reviews artwork/photos as part of ms package.
Recent Nonfiction Title: *Tiger on the Road: A Biography of Vardis Fisher*, by Woodward.

CCC PUBLICATIONS, 20306 Tau Place, Chatsworth CA 91311. (818)407-1661. Contact: Editorial Dept. Estab. 1983. Publishes trade paperback originals and mass market paperback originals. Averages 10-15 titles/year; receives 400-600 mss/year. 50% of books from first-time authors; 50% of books from unagented writers. Pays 5-10% royalty on wholesale price. Publishes book an average of 1 year after acceptance. Simultaneous submissions OK. Reports in 1 month on queries; 3 months on mss.
Nonfiction: Humorous how-to/self-help. "We are looking for *original*, *clever* and *current* humor that is not too limited in audience appeal or that will have a limited shelf life. All of our titles are as marketable 5 years from now as they are today. No rip-offs of previously published books, or too special interest mss." For best results: Query first with SASE; will review complete ms only. Reviews artwork/photos as part of ms package.
Recent Nonfiction Title: *Hormones from Hell*, by Jan King.
Tips: "Humor—we specialize in the subject and have a good reputation with retailers and wholesalers for publishing super-impulse titles. SASE is a must!"

CENTER FOR APPLIED LINGUISTICS, 1118 22nd St. NW, Washington DC 20007. (202)429-9292. Editor/Publications Coordinator: Ms. Whitney Stewart. Estab. 1965. Publishes scholarly monographs. Firm averages 4 titles/year. 100% of books from unagented writers. Pays $500 maximum for outright purchase. Publishes book an average of 6 months after acceptance. Appreciates computer disk with manuscript submission. Reports in 1 month.

Nonfiction: Textbook on language in education. Subjects include child language, literacy, computers and language, linguistics, teaching foreign languages, learning English-as-a-foreign language. "We want texts on teaching foreign languages; texts on special education; texts on bilingual education; texts on child language acquisition. NO FOREIGN LANGUAGE TEXTBOOKS. We want only theoretical information and practical methodology on language instruction." Query.

Recent Nonfiction Title: *Pigeon-birds and Rhyming Words: The Parental Role in Language Learning*, by Naomi S. Baron.

Tips: "We need manuscripts of 100-200 pages—texts on classroom theory and practice—written for the teacher, the parent, or the linguistics student. We want theory but with an emphasis on practical application. Authors/specialists must be leaders in the field, writing up-to-date theoretical works."

‡*CHALICE PRESS, (formerly CBP Press), P.O. Box 179, St. Louis MO 63166. (314)231-8500. Editor: David P. Polk. Publishes trade paperback originals. Firm averages 16-20 titles/year; Receives 125-150 submissions/year. 15-20% of books by first-time authors. 100% from unagented writers. Subsidy publishes 5% of books. Determines subsidy by importance of work vs. low expected sales. Pays 12-17% royalty on wholesale price. Publishes book an average of 9 months after acceptance. Simultaneous submissions OK. Query for electronic submissions. "*Accepted* manuscripts *must* also be on computer disk." Reports in 1 week on queries; 3 months on mss. Free book catalog and manuscript guidelines.

Nonfiction: Religious. Subjects include religion. "Our ms needs for the next year are very low. Most likely, new titles are already in the pipeline." No poetry or biography. Submit outline/synopsis and sample chapters. Reviews artwork/photos as part of the ms package.

Recent Nonfiction Title: *Hope for the Mainline Church*, by Charles Bayer (religion).

Tips: "Ours are books for a thinking church. Our primary audience is clergy and laity in mainline churches. Academic community is secondary."

CHARLESBRIDGE PUBLISHING, 85 Main St., Watertown MA 02172. (617)926-0329. Vice President: Elena Dworkin Wright. Estab. 1980. Publishes school programs and hardcover and trade paperback originals. Averages 100 titles/year. Receives 1,000 submissions/year. 10% of books from first-time authors; 100% from unagented writers. Buys by outright purchase. Publishes books an average of 1 year after acceptance. Query for electronic submissions. Reports in 1 month on mss. Markets through schools, book stores and specialty stores at museums, science centers, etc.

Nonfiction: Juvenile. "We look for nature/science books that teach about the world from a perspective that is relevant to a young child." Submit outline/synopsis and sample chapter or complete ms.

Recent Nonfiction Title: *The Underwater Alphabet*, by Jerry Pallotta (juvenile).

Fiction: Early readers: nature/science themes.

*CHATHAM PRESS, Box A, Old Greenwich CT 06870. FAX: (203)622-6688. Contact: Editor. Estab. 1971. Publishes hardcover and paperback originals, reprints and anthologies relating to New England and the Atlantic coastline. Averages 15 titles/year; receives 50 submissions annually. 25% of books from first-time authors; 75% of books from unagented writers. Subsidy publishes mainly poetry or ecological topics (nonauthor) 10% of books. "Standard book contract does not always apply if the book is heavily illustrated. Average advance is low." Publishes book an average of 6 months after acceptance. Query for electronic submissions. Reports in 2 weeks. Book catalog and ms guidelines for 6×9 SAE with 10 first class stamps.

Nonfiction: Publishes mostly "regional history and natural history, involving mainly Northeast seaboard to the Carolinas, mostly illustrated, with emphasis on conservation and outdoor recreation." Accepts nonfiction translations from French and German. Query with outline and 3 sample chapters. Reviews artwork/photos as part of ms package.

Recent Nonfiction Title: *Beachcomber's Companion*, by Wesemann.

Recent Poetry Title: *Weapons Against Chaos*, by M. Ewald.

Tips: "Illustrated New England-relevant titles have the best chance of being sold to our firm. We have a slightly greater (15%) skew towards cooking and travel titles."

CHELSEA GREEN, P.O. Box 130, Post Mills VT 05058. (802)333-9073. Editor: Ian Baldwin Jr. Fiction Editor: Jim Schley. Estab. 1984. Publishes hardcover and paperback trade originals. Averages 10 titles/year.

ALWAYS submit unsolicited manuscripts or queries with a self-addressed, stamped envelope (SASE) within your country or a self-addressed envelope with International Reply Coupons (IRC) purchased from the post office for other countries.

Nonfiction: Biography, nature, politics, travel, art and history. Query only and include SASE.
Recent Nonfiction Title: *Strangers Devour the Land*, by Boyce Richardson.
Fiction: "Serious contemporary fiction originating in northern New England or set in northern New England, as well as fiction that deals with the contemporary global environmental crisis. Please submit query with SASE."
Recent Fiction Title: *Judevine*, by David Budbill.

CHICAGO REVIEW PRESS, 814 N. Franklin, Chicago IL 60610. (312)337-0747. Editorial Director: Amy Teschner. Estab. 1973. Imprints include Lawrence Hill Books, A Capella Books and Ziggurat Books. Publishes hardcover and trade paperback originals. Averages 15 titles/year; receives 375 submissions annually. 60% of books from first-time authors; 90% of books from unagented writers. Pays 10-15% royalty. Offers average $1,000 advance. Publishes book an average of 1 year after acceptance. Simultaneous submissions OK. Query for electronic submissions. Reports in 2 months on queries; 3 months on mss. Book catalog for 9 × 12 SAE and 7 first class stamps.
Nonfiction: How-to, guidebooks, architecture, specialty cookbooks, popular science, Native American culture, feminism, recreation, regional titles. Needs regional Chicago and the Midwest material and how-to, popular science, books on Native American culture, and nonfiction project books in the arts and sciences for ages 10 and up. Query or submit outline/synopsis and sample chapters. Reviews artwork/photos.
Recent Nonfiction Title: *The Spark in the Stone: Skills and Projects from the Native American Tradition*, by Peter Goodchild.
Tips: "The audience we envision for our books is comprised of adults and young people 15 and older, educated readers with special interests, do-it-yourselfers. Right now, we also are very excited about our series called Ziggurat Books, hands-on books for kids 10 and up on subjects such as astronomy, architecture and creative writing."

‡CHINA BOOKS & PERIODICALS, INC., 2929 24th St., San Francisco CA 94110. (415)282-2994. FAX: (415)282-0994. Senior Editor: Bob Schildgen. Estab. 1960. Publishes hardcover and trade paperback originals. Firm averages 10 titles/year. Receives 300 submissions/year. 10% of books from first-time authors. 95% from unagented writers. Pays 8-10% royalty on retail price. Offers $1,500 average advance. Publishes book an average of 1 year after acceptance. Simultaneous submissions OK. Query for electronic submissions. Reports in 1 month on queries. Book catalog free on request. Manuscript guidelines for #10 SASE.
Nonfiction: Biography, coffee table book, cookbook, how-to, juvenile, self-helf, textbook. Subjects include agriculture/horticulture, art/architecture, business and economics, cooking, foods and nutrition, ethnic, gardening, government/politics, history, language/literature, nature/environment, religion, sociology, translation, travel, women's issues studies. "*Important: All* books *must* be on topics related to China or East Asia, or Chinese-Americans. Books on China's history, politics, environment, women, art, architecture; language textbooks, acupuncture and folklore." Query. Submit outline/ synopsis and sample chapters. Reviews artwork/photos as part of ms package.
Recent Nonfiction Title: *China's Unfinished Revolution*, by James M. Ethridge (Contemporary history and politics).
Fiction: Ethnic, experimental, feminist, gay/lesbian, historical, literary, religious. "*Must* have Chinese, Chinese-American or East Asian theme. We are looking for high-quality fiction with a Chinese theme or translated from Chinese that makes a genuine literary breakthrough and seriously treats life in contemporary China or Chinese Americans. No fiction that is too conventional in style or treats hackneyed subjects. No fiction without Chinese or Chinese-American or East Asian themes, please." Query. Submit outline/synopsis and sample chapters.
Recent Fiction Title: *Old Well*, by Zheng Yi (translation).
Poetry: "Must be *outstanding* poetry with Chinese or Chinese-American theme, either by a contemporary poet or translation of a classic Chinese poet." Submit 10 samples. "You have to produce work on the cutting edge, and it must be readable as excellent modern poetry."
Tips: "I have noticed that publishers are less willing to take risks on books because of the economic recession. We look for a well-researched, well-written book on China or East Asia that contains fresh insights and appeals to the intelligent reader. Our audience consists of educated and curious readers of trade books, academics, students, travelers, government officials, business people and journalists. If I were a writer trying to market a book today, I would attempt to cultivate personal relationships with pubishers, because it seems as if the only way you get someone's attention is to know him or her personally. That's a shame. It would definitely help to have an agent, because the agent today is, in essence, the screening person for the publisher. I would also make sure to submit queries to the *smaller* publishers, especially those in your home region, because they will treat your work more seriously."

CHOSEN BOOKS PUBLISHING CO., LTD., Imprint of the Gleneida Publishing Group, 120 White Plains Rd., Tarrytown NY 10591. (914)332-8500. FAX: (914)332-8661. Editor: Jane Campbell. Estab. 1971. Publishes hardcover and trade paperback originals. Averages 16 titles/year; receives 600 submissions annually. 15% of books from first-time authors; 99% of books from unagented writers. Pays royalty on retail price. Publishes book an average of 1 year after acceptance. Simultaneous submissions OK. Reports in 2 months. Manuscript guidelines for #10 SASE.

Nonfiction: How-to, self-help, and a very limited number of first-person narratives. "We publish books reflecting the current acts of the Holy Spirit in the world, books with a charismatic Christian orientation." No New Age, poetry, fiction, academic or children's books. Submit synopsis, chapter outline and SASE. No complete mss. No response without SASE.

Recent Nonfiction Title: *And God Changed His Mind*, by Brother Andrew.

Tips: "In expositional books we look for solid, practical advice for the growing and maturing Christian from authors with professional or personal experience platforms. Narratives must have a strong theme and reader benefits. No conversion accounts or chronicling of life events, please. State the topic or theme of your book clearly in your cover letter."

*THE CHRISTOPHER PUBLISHING HOUSE, 24 Rockland St., Commerce Green, Hanover MA 02339. (617)826-7474. FAX: (617)826-5556. Managing Editor: Nancy Lucas. Estab. 1910. Publishes hardcover and trade paperback originals. Averages 10-20 titles/year; receives 300-400 submissions annually. 30% of books from first-time authors; 100% of books from unagented writers. Subsidy publishes 15% of books. Pays 5-30% royalty on net proceeds; offers no advance. Publishes book an average of 12-15 months after acceptance. Simultaneous submissions OK. Query for electronic submissions. Reports in 1 month. Book catalog for #10 SAE with 2 first class stamps; ms guidelines for SASE.

Nonfiction: Biography, how-to, reference, self-help, textbook and religious. Subjects include Americana, animals, art, business and economics, cooking and foods (nutrition), health, history, philosophy, politics, psychology, religion, sociology and travel. "We will be glad to review all nonfiction manuscripts, particularly college textbook and religious-oriented." Submit complete ms. Reviews artwork/photos as part of ms package.

Recent Nonfiction Title: *Toynbee at Home*, by John W. Smurr.

Poetry: "We will review all forms of poetry." Submit complete ms.

Recent Poetry Title: *The Sea Cries over My Shoulder*, by Jonathan Russell.

Tips: "Our books are for a general audience, slanted toward college-educated readers. There are specific books targeted toward specific audiences when appropriate."

CHRONICLE BOOKS, Chronicle Publishing Co., 275 5th St., San Francisco CA 94103. (415)777-7240. FAX: (415)777-8887. Executive Editor: Nion McEvoy. Editor, fiction: Jay Schaefer. Editor, children's: Victoria Rock. Publishes hardcover and trade paperback originals. Averages 100 titles/year; receives 1,500 submissions annually. 10% of books from first-time authors; 15% of books from unagented writers. Pays 5-10% royalty on retail price. Buys by outright purchase for $500-5,000. Publishes book an average of 1½ years after acceptance. Simultaneous submissions OK. Reports in 1 month on queries; 3 months on mss. Book catalog for 11 × 14 SAE with 5 first class stamps.

Nonfiction: Coffee table book, cookbook, and regional California on art, cooking and foods, design, gardening, health and medicine, nature, photography, recreation, and travel. Query or submit outline/synopsis and sample chapters. Reviews artwork/photos with ms package.

Recent Nonfiction Title: *Frida Kahlo*, by Martha Zamora.

Fiction: Juvenile, picture books, novels and short story collections. Query or submit outline/synopsis and sample chapters.

Recent Fiction Title: *C is for Curious*, by Woodleigh Hubbard.

CITADEL PRESS, Imprint of Carol Publishing Group, 120 Enterprise, Secaucus NJ 07094. FAX: (201)866-8159. Editorial Director: Allan J. Wilson. Estab. 1945. Other imprints are Lyle Stuart, Birch Lane Press and University Books. Publishes hardcover originals and paperback reprints. Averages 60-80 titles/year. Receives 800-1,000 submissions annually. 7% of books from first-time authors; 50% of books from unagented writers. Average print order for a writer's first book is 5,000. Pays 10% royalty on hardcover, 5-7% on paperback; offers average $10,000 advance. Publishes book an average of 1 year after acceptance. Simultaneous submissions OK. Reports in 2 months. Book catalog for $1.

Nonfiction and Fiction: Biography, film, psychology, humor and history. Also seeks "off-beat material," but no "poetry, religion, politics." Accepts nonfiction and fiction translations. Query. Submit outline/synopsis and 3 sample chapters. Reviews artwork/photos as part of ms package.

Recent Nonfiction Title: *Boxing Babylon*, by Nigel Collins.

Recent Fiction Title: *The Rain Maiden*, by Jill M. Phillips.

Tips: "We concentrate on biography, popular interest, and film, with limited fiction (no romance, religion, poetry, music)."

CITY LIGHTS BOOKS, 261 Columbus Ave., San Francisco CA 94133. (415)362-1901. Editor and Publisher: Lawrence Ferlinghetti. Publishes trade paperback originals and reprints. Averages 15 titles/year. Receives 500 submissions/year. 25% of books from first-time authors; 75% from unagented writers. Pays 6-10% royalty on retail price. Offers $1,000 average advance. Publishes book an average of 1 year after acceptance. Simultaneous submissions OK. Reports in 1 month on queries; 2 months on mss. Free book catalog and manuscript guidelines.
Nonfiction: Subjects include anthropology/archaeology, gay/lesbian, philosophy, translation, women's issues/studies. Query.
Fiction: Ethnic, gay/lesbian, literary, mainstream/contemporary, plays. Query.

CLARION BOOKS, Imprint of Houghton Mifflin Company, 215 Park Ave. S., New York NY 10003. Editor and Publisher: Dorothy Briley. Executive Editor: Dinah Stevenson. Estab. 1965. Publishes hardcover originals. Averages 50 titles/year. Pays 5-10% royalty on retail price; $1,000-3,000 advance, depending on whether project is a picture book or a longer work for older children. No multiple submissions. Reports in 2 months. Publishes book an average of 18 months after acceptance. Ms guidelines for #10 SASE.
Nonfiction: Americana, biography, holiday, humor, nature, photo essays and word play. Prefers books for younger children. Reviews artwork/photos as part of ms package. Query.
Recent Nonfiction Title: *The Boys' War*, by Jim Murphy.
Fiction: Adventure, humor, mystery, strong character studies, and suspense. "We would like to see more humorous contemporary stories that young people of 8-12 or 10-14 can identify with readily." Accepts fiction translations. Send complete ms. Looks for "freshness, enthusiasm—in short, life" (fiction and nonfiction).
Recent Fiction Title: *Summer Endings*, by Sollace Hotze.

*ARTHUR H. CLARK CO. , P.O. Box 14707, Spokane WA 99214. (509)928-9540. Editorial Director: Robert A. Clark. Estab. 1902. Publishes hardcover originals. Averages 8 titles/year; receives 40 submissions annually. 40% of books from first-time authors; 100% of books from unagented writers. Subsidy publishes 15% of books based on whether they are "high-risk sales." Subsidy publishes (nonauthor) 5% of books. Pays 10% minimum royalty on wholesale price. Publishes book an average of 9 months after acceptance. Reports in 1 week on queries; 6 months on mss. Book catalog for 6×9 SASE.
Nonfiction: Biography, reference and historical nonfiction. Subjects include Americana and history. "We're looking for documentary source material in Western American history." Query or submit outline/synopsis with SASE. Looks for "content, form, style." Reviews artwork/photos as part of ms package.
Recent Nonfiction Title: *The Californios vs Jedediah Smith 1826-1827*, by David Weber.
Tips: "Western Americana (nonfiction) has the best chance of being sold to our firm."

CLARKSON POTTER, Imprint of Crown Publishers, Division of Random House, 201 E. 50th St., New York NY 10022. (212)572-6160. FAX: (212)572-6192. Editor: Carol Southern, associate publisher, Crown. Imprint is Griffin Paperbacks. Publishes hardcover and trade paperback originals. Averages 55 titles/year; receives 1,500 submissions annually. 18% of books from first-time authors, but many of these first-time authors are well-known and have had media coverage. Pays 10% royalty on hardcover; 5-7½% on paperback; 5-7% on illustrated hardcover, varying escalations; advance depends on type of book and reputation or experience of author. No unagented mss can be considered. Book catalog for 7×10 SASE. No manuscript guidelines available.
Nonfiction: Publishes art, autobiography, biography, cooking and foods, design, how-to, humor, juvenile, nature, photography, self-help, style and annotated literature. Accepts nonfiction translations. "Manuscripts must be cleanly typed on 8½×11 nonerasable bond; double-spaced. *Chicago Manual of Style* is preferred." Query or submit outline/synopsis and sample chapters. Reviews artwork/photos as part of ms package.
Recent Nonfiction Title: *Jackson Pollock*, by Steven Naifeh and Gregory White Smith.
Fiction: Will consider "quality fiction."
Recent Fiction Title: *Doctors and Women*, by Susan Cheever.

*CLEANING CONSULTANT SERVICES, INC., 1512 Western Ave., P.O. Box 1273, Seattle WA 98101. (206)682-9748. President: William R. Griffin. Publishes trade paperback originals and reprints. Averages 4-6 titles/year; receives 15 submissions annually. 75% of books from first-time authors; 100% of books from unagented writers. Subsidy publishes 5% of books. "If they (authors) won't sell it and won't accept royalty contract, we offer our publishing services and often sell the book along with our books." Pays 5-15% royalty on retail price or outright purchase, $100-2,500, depending on negotiated agreement. Publishes book an average of 6-12 months after acceptance. Reports in 6 weeks on queries; 3 months on mss. Free book catalog; ms guidelines for SASE.

Nonfiction: How-to, illustrated book, reference, self-help, technical, textbook and directories. Subjects include business, health, and cleaning and maintenance. Needs books on anything related to cleaning, maintenance, self-employment or entrepreneurship. Query or submit outline/synopsis and sample chapters or complete ms. Reviews artwork/photos as part of ms package.

Recent Nonfiction Title: *Food Service, Health, Sanitation and Safety*, by William R. Griffin and Bruce Jackson.

Tips: "Our audience includes those involved in cleaning and maintenance service trades, opportunity seekers, schools, property managers, libraries — anyone who needs information on cleaning and maintenance. How-to and self-employment guides are doing well for us in today's market. We are now seeking books on fire damage restoration and also technical articles for *Cleaning Business Magazine*, a quarterly."

CLEIS PRESS, P.O. Box 14684, San Francisco CA 94114. FAX: (415)864-3385. Co-editor, Acquisitions Coordinator: Frederique Delacoste. Publishes trade paperback originals and reprints. Publishes 4 titles/year. 75% of books are from first-time authors; 90% from unagented writers. Royalties vary on retail price. Publishes book an average of 1 year after acceptance. Simultaneous submissions OK "only if accompanied by an original letter stating where and when ms was sent." Query for electronic submissions. Reports in 1 month. Books catalog for #10 SAE and 2 first class stamps.

Nonfiction: Human rights, feminist. Subjects include gay/lesbian, government/politics, sociology (of women), women's issues/studies. "We are interested in books that: will sell in feminist and progressive bookstores, and will sell in Europe (translation rights). We are interested in books by and about women in Latin America; on lesbian and gay rights; and other feminist topics which have not already been widely documented. We do not want religious/spiritual tracts; we are not interested in books on topics which have been documented over and over, unless the author is approaching the topic from a new viewpoint." Query or submit outline/synopsis and sample chapters or submit complete ms.

Recent Nonfiction Title: *Susie Sexpert Lesbian Sex World*, by Susie Bright.

Fiction: Feminist, gay/lesbian, literary. "We are looking for high quality novels by women. We are especially interested in translations of Latin American women's fiction. No romances!" Submit complete ms.

Recent Fiction Title: *Night Train to Mother*, by Ronit Lentin (novel).

Tips: "An anthology project representing the work of a very diverse group of women . . . an anthology on a very hot, very unique, risk-taking theme. These books sell well for us; they're our trademark. If I were trying to market a book today, I would become very familiar with the presses serving my market. More than reading publishers' catalogs, I think an author should spend time in a bookstore whose clientele closely resembles her intended audience; be absolutely aware of her audience; have researched potential market; present fresh new ways of looking at her topic; avoid 'PR' language in query letter."

*CLEVELAND STATE UNIVERSITY POETRY CENTER, R.T. 1815, Cleveland State University, Cleveland OH 44115. (216)687-3986. FAX: (216)687-9366. Editor: Leonard M. Trawick. Estab. 1962. Publishes trade paperback and hardcover originals. Averages 5 titles/year; receives 400 queries, 900 mss annually. 60% of books from first-time authors; 100% of books from unagented writers. 30% of titles subsidized by CSU, 30% by government subsidy. CSU poetry series pays one-time, lump-sum royalty of $200-400 plus 50 copies; Cleveland Poetry Series (Ohio poets only) pays 100 copies. $1,000 prize for best manuscript each year. No advance. Publishes book an average of 1 year after acceptance. Simultaneous submissions OK. Reports in 2 weeks on queries; 6 months on mss. Book catalog for 6×9 SAE with 2 first class stamps; ms guidelines for SASE.

Poetry: No light verse, "inspirational," or greeting card verse. ("This does not mean that we do not consider poetry with humor or philosophical/religious import.") Query — ask for guidelines. Submit only December-February. Reviews artwork/photos if applicable (e.g., concrete poetry).

Recent Poetry Title: *Inland, Thinking of Waves*, by Sarah Provost.

Tips: "Our books are for serious readers of poetry, i.e. poets, critics, academics, students, people who read *Poetry, Field, American Poetry Review, Antaeus*, etc." Trends include "movement from 'confessional' poetry; greater attention to form and craftsmanship. Try to project an interesting, coherent personality; link poems so as to make coherent unity, not just a miscellaneous collection." Especially needs "poems with *mystery*, i.e., poems that reflect profound thought, but do not tell all — suggestive, tantalizing, enticing."

CLIFFHANGER PRESS, P.O. Box 29527, Oakland CA 94604-9527. (415)763-3510. Editor: Nancy Chirich. Estab. 1986. Publishes quality trade paperback originals. Averages 3 titles/year. Pays 8% royalty on retail price. Publishes book an average of 18 months after acceptance. Simultaneous submissions OK. Reports in 3 weeks on 2-3 sample chapters and one-page synopsis. Do not send full ms unless requested. Writers' guidelines and catalog for #10 SASE.

Fiction: Mystery and suspense. "Manuscripts should be about 75,000 words, heavy on American regional or foreign atmosphere. No cynical, hardboiled detectives or spies." Submit synopsis/outline and 2-3 sample chapters. "No returns without SASE."
Recent Fiction Title: *Beecher*, by Virginia O'Neal.
Tips: "Mystery/suspense is our specialty. Have believable characters, a strong, uncomplicated story and heavy regional or foreign atmosphere. No justified right margins on manuscripts submitted. They're very hard to read at length. Please send for writer's guidelines before submitting *anything*."

CLIFFS NOTES, INC., P.O. Box 80728, Lincoln NE 68501. (402)423-5050. General Editor: Michele Spence. Notes Editor: Gary Carey. Estab. 1958. Publishes trade paperback originals. Averages 20 titles/year. 100% of books from unagented writers. Pays royalty on wholesale price. Buys some mss outright; "full payment on acceptance of ms." Publishes book an average of 1 year after acceptance. Reports in 1 month. "We provide specific guidelines when a project is assigned."
Nonfiction: Self-help and textbook. "We publish self-help study aids directed to junior high through graduate school audience. Publications include *Cliffs Notes*, *Cliffs Test Preparation Guides*, *Cliffs Teaching Portfolios*, and other study guides. Most authors are experienced teachers, usually with advanced degrees. Some books also appeal to a general lay audience. Among these are those in a new series, *Bluffer's Guides*, published under our Centennial Press imprint. The books are both informative and humorous and cover a wide range of subject areas." Query.
Recent Nonfiction Title: *Bluff Your Way in Gourmet Cooking*, by Joseph T. Straub.

‡COFFEE HOUSE PRESS, Suite 400, 27 N. 4th St., Minneapolis MN 55401. (612)338-0125. FAX: (612)338-4004. Editorial Assistant: Michael L. Wiegers. Publishes trade paperback originals. Publishes 10-12 titles/year; receives 2,000 queries and mss/year. 95% of books are from unagented writers. Pays 8% royalty on retail price. Offers average $500 advance. Publishes book an average of 18 months after acceptance. Reports in 6 weeks on queries, 6 months on mss. Free book catalog; ms guidelines for #10 SASE.
Fiction: Ethnic, literary, short story collections. Looking for novels, but not genre. Submit complete ms.
Recent Fiction Title: *Donald Duk*, by Frank Chin (novel).

COLLECTOR BOOKS, Division of Schroeder Publishing Co., Inc., 5801 Kentucky Dam Rd., P.O. Box 3009, Paducah KY 42001. FAX: (502)898-8890. Editor: Steve Quertermous. Estab. 1974. Publishes hardcover and paperback originals. Publishes 35 titles/year. 50% of books from first-time authors; 100% of books from unagented writers. Average print order for a writer's first book is 5,000-10,000. Pays 5% royalty on retail; no advance. Publishes book an average of 8 months after acceptance. Reports in 1 month. Book catalog for 9 × 12 SAE and 4 first class stamps. Ms guidelines for #10 SASE.
Nonfiction: "We only publish books on antiques and collectibles. We require our authors to be very knowledgeable in their respective fields and have access to a large representative sampling of the particular subject concerned." Query. Accepts outline and 2-3 sample chapters. Reviews artwork/photos as part of ms package.
Recent Nonfiction Title: *Schroeder's Antiques Price Guide*.
Tips: "Common mistakes writers make include making phone contact instead of written contact and assuming an accurate market evaluation."

*COLLEGE PRESS PUBLISHING CO., INC., 205 N. Main, P.O. Box 1132, Joplin MO 64802. (417)623-6280. Contact: Steven F. Jennings. Estab. 1958. Publishes hardcover and trade paperback originals and reprints. Publishes 25 titles/year. Receives 150 submissions/year. 25% of books are from first-time authors; 100% from unagented writers. Subsidy publishes 5% of books. Subsidy considered "if we really want to publish a book, but don't have room in schedule at this time or funds available." Pays 10% royalty on net receipts. Publishes book an average of 1 year after acceptance. Simultaneous submissions OK. Reports on queries in 1 month; on ms in 3 months. Free book catalog.
Nonfiction: Bible commentaries, topical Bible studies. (Christian church, Church of Christ.) Query.
Recent Nonfiction Title: *Beyond a Reasonable Doubt*, by Herbert Casteel.
Fiction: Religious. Query.
Tips: "Topical Bible study books have the best chance of being sold to our firm. Our audience consists of Christians interested in reading and studying Bible-based material."

COMPUTER SCIENCE PRESS, Imprint of W.H. Freeman and Company, 41 Madison Ave., New York NY 10010. (212)576-9400. FAX: (212)689-2383. Publisher: William B. Gruener. Estab. 1974. Publishes hardcover and paperback originals. Averages 10 titles/year. 25% of books from first-time authors; 98% of books from unagented writers. All authors are recognized subject area experts. Pays royalty on net price. Publishes book an average of 6-9 months after acceptance. Reports ASAP.

Nonfiction: "Technical books in all aspects of computer science, computer engineering, computer chess, electrical engineering, and telecommunications. Both text and reference books. Will also consider public appeal 'trade' books in computer science, manuscripts and diskettes." Query or submit complete ms. Requires 3 copies of manuscripts. Looks for "technical accuracy of the material and the reason this approach is being taken. We would also like a covering letter stating what the author sees as the competition for this work and why this work is superior."
Recent Nonfiction Title: *A First Course in Computer Science with Turbo PASCAL*, by Carmony-Holliday.

CONARI PRESS, 1339 61st St., Emeryville CA 94608. (415)596-4040. Editor: Mary Jane Ryan. Publishes hardcover and trade paperback originals. Firm averages 10 titles/year. Receives 200 submissions/year. 50% of books from first-time authors. 50% from unagented writers. Pays 8-12% royalty on list price. Offers $1,500 average advance. Publishes book an average of 9 months after acceptance. Simultaneous submissions OK. Query for electronic submissions. Reports in 1 month. Free book catalog. Manuscript guidelines for #10 SASE.
Nonfiction: Psychology/self-help, business psychology, women's issues, some consumer guides. We are looking for any well thought out and written nonfiction in areas that haven't been over done. No travel books or cookbooks. Submit outline/synopsis and sample chapters or complete ms. Reviews artwork/photos as part of ms package.
Recent Nonfiction Title: *True Love: How to Make Your Relationship Sweeter, Deeper and More Passionate*, by Daphne Rose Kingman (psychology/self help).
Tips: "Writers should send us well targeted, specific and focused manuscripts."

CONCORDIA PUBLISHING HOUSE, 3558 S. Jefferson Ave., St. Louis MO 63118. (314)664-7000. Contact: Product Development. Estab. 1869. Publishes hardcover and trade paperback originals. Averages 50 titles/year. Receives 1,000 submissions/year. 10% of books from first-time authors; 95% from unagented writers. Pays royalty or buys by outright purchase. Publishes book an average of 1 year after acceptance. Simultaneous submissions OK. Query for electronic submissions. Reports in 1 month on queries; 2 months on mss. Manuscript guidelines for #10 SASE.
Nonfiction: Juvenile. Subjects include child guidance/parenting (in Christian context), religion. "We publish Protestant, inspirational, theological, family and juveniles. All manuscripts must conform to the doctrinal tenents of The Lutheran Church—Missouri Synod. Authors should query before submitting a manuscript." Query.
Recent Nonfiction Title: *Renewing the Family Spirit*, by David J. Ludwig (family relationships).
Fiction: Juvenile. "We will consider preteen and children's fiction and picture books. All books must contain Christian content. No adult Christian fiction." Query.
Recent Fiction Title: *Treasure at Morning Gulch*, by Joan Biggar (juvenile fiction).

THE CONSULTANT PRESS, Subsidiary of The Photographic Arts Center, Ltd., 163 Amsterdam Ave., #201, New York NY 10023. FAX: (212)873-7065. Publisher: Bob Persky. Estab. 1980. Publishes hardcover and trade paperback originals. Firm averages 7 titles/year; Receives 10 submissions/year. 50% of books from first-time authors. 100% from unagented writers. Buys mss outright for $1,000-2,500. Publishes book an average of 6 months after acceptance. Simultaneous submissions OK. Reports in 2 weeks on queries; 1 month on mss. Free book catalog.
Nonfiction: Subjects include the business of art, art books, and photography. "We want books filling needs of artists, photographers and galleries—business oriented. No books of pictures or books on how to take pictures or paint pictures."
Recent Nonfiction Title: *How To Publish Your Poster and Cards*, by Harold Davis.
Tips: "Artists, photographers, galleries, museums, curators and art consultants are our audience."

CONSUMER REPORTS BOOKS, Subsidiary of Consumers Union, 101 Truman Ave., Yonkers NY 10703. FAX: (914)378-2903. Contact: Sarah Uman. Estab. 1936. Publishes trade paperback originals and reprints. Averages 30-35 titles/year; receives 1,000 submissions annually. Most of books from agented writers. Pays variable royalty on retail price; buys some mss outright. Publishes book an average of 1½ years after acceptance. Simultaneous submissions OK. Reports in 6 weeks on queries; 2 months on mss. Free book list and writer's manuscript guidelines on request.
Nonfiction: Cookbook, how-to, reference, self-help and automotive and how-to books for children. Subjects include money and finance, cooking and foods, health and medicine, consumer guidance, home owners reference. Submit outline/synopsis and 1-2 sample chapters.

 The double dagger before a listing indicates that the listing is new in this edition. New markets are often more receptive to freelance submissions.

CONTEMPORARY BOOKS, INC., 180 N. Michigan Ave., Chicago IL 60601. (312)782-9182. Editorial Director: Nancy J. Crossman. Publishes hardcover originals and trade paperback originals and reprints. Averages 75 titles/year; receives 2,500 submissions annually. 25% of books from first-time authors; 25% of books from unagented writers. Pays 6-15% royalty on retail price. Publishes book an average of 10 months after acceptance. Query for electronic submissions. Simultaneous submissions OK. Reports in 3 weeks. Ms guidelines for SASE.
Nonfiction: Biography, cookbook, how-to, humor, reference and self-help. Subjects include business, finance, cooking, health, fitness, psychology, sports, real estate, nutrition, popular culture and women's studies. Submit outline/synopsis and sample chapters. Reviews artwork/photos as part of ms package.
Recent Nonfiction Title: *Arnold, An Unauthorized Biography*, by Wendy Leigh.
Tips: "The New Age market has become saturated. Also, competition in cookbooks mean we need professional, accomplished cooks instead of amateurs to write them."

‡DAVID C. COOK PUBLISHING CO., 850 N. Grove Ave., Elgin IL 60120. (708)741-2400. Managing Editor: Cathy Davis. Imprints include Chariot Books and Life Journey Books. Publishes hardcover originals and trade paperback originals and reprints. Firm averages 100 titles/year. 10% of books from first-time authors. 95% from unagented writers. Pays 8-18% royalty on wholesale price. Offers $2500 average advance. Publishes book an average of 1 year after acceptance. Simultaneous submissions OK. Reports in 4 months on mss. Book catalog for 9×12 SAE and 10 first class stamps. Manuscript guidelines for #10 SASE.
Fiction: Adventure, historical, mainstream/contemporary, mystery, religious, young adult. "Contemporary stories and young adult manuscripts will be given priority. Any category must have Christian emphasis to be appropriate for our market." Submit outline/synopsis and sample chapters.
Recent Fiction Title: *With Wings as Eagles*, by Elaine Schulte.
Tips: "We prefer fresh approaches to popular topics rather than imitation of already successful books. Our audience consists of readers with some degree of Christian background/experience."

CORNELL MARITIME PRESS, INC., Imprint of Tidewater Publishers, P.O. Box 456, Centreville MD 21617. Contact: Associate Editor. Estab. 1938. Publishes hardcover originals and quality paperbacks for professional mariners and yachtsmen. Averages 7-9 titles/year; receives 150 submissions annually. 41% of books from first-time authors; 99% of books from unagented writers. Payment is negotiable but royalties do not exceed 10% for first 5,000 copies, 12½% for second 5,000 copies, 15% on all additional. Royalties for original paperbacks and regional titles are invariably lower. Revised editions revert to original royalty schedule. Publishes book an average of 1 year after acceptance. Query for electronic submissions. Send queries first, accompanied by writing samples and outlines of book ideas. Reports in 1 month. Free book catalog and ms guidelines.
Nonfiction: Marine subjects (highly technical); manuals; and how-to books on maritime subjects. Tidewater imprint publishes books on regional history, folklore and wildlife of the Chesapeake Bay and the Delmarva Peninsula.
Recent Nonfiction Title: *Watchstanding Guide for the Merchant Officer*, by Robert J. Meurn.

THE COUNTRYMAN PRESS, INC., P.O. Box 175, Woodstock VT 05091. (802)457-1049. Fiction: Louis Kannenstine, president. Nonfiction: Carl Taylor, vice president. Estab. 1973. Imprints include Foul Play Press and Backcountry Publications. Publishes hardcover and trade paperback originals and paperback reprints. Publishes 20-25 titles/year. Receives 150 submissions/year. 50% of books from first-time authors; 75% from unagented writers. Pays 5-10% royalty on retail price. Offers $500 average advance. Publishes book an average of 1 year after acceptance. Simultaneous submissions OK. Reports in 1 month on queries; in 2 months on mss. Free book catalog.
Nonfiction: Cookbook, how-to, travel guides. Subjects include cooking, foods and nutrition, adult fitness, history, nature/environment, recreation, fishing, regional (New England, especially Vermont), travel. "We want good 'how-to' books, especially those related to rural life." Submit outline/synopsis and sample chapters. Review artwork/photos as part of ms package.
Recent Nonfiction Title: *Fishing Small Streams with a Fly Rod*, by Charles R. Meck.
Fiction: Mystery. Submit inquiries, or outline, sample chapter, and SASE.
Recent Fiction Title: *Dream of Darkness*, by Reginald Hill writing as Patrick Ruell (suspense).

‡CRAFTSMAN BOOK COMPANY, 6058 Corte Del Cedro, P.O. Box 6500, Carlsbad CA 92008. (619)438-7828 or (800)829-8123. FAX (619)438-0398. Editor-in-Chief: Laurence D. Jacobs. Publishes paperback originals. Averages 12 titles/year; receives 50 submissions/year. 85% of books from first-time authors; 98% of books from unagented writers. Pays 7½-12½% royalty on wholesale price or retail price. Publishes book an average of 18 months after acceptance. Simultaneous submissions OK. Query for electronic submissions. Reports in 1 month on queries; 2 months on mss. Free book catalog and ms guidelines.

Nonfiction: How-to and technical. All titles are related to construction for professional builders. Query. Reviews artwork/photos as part of ms package.
Recent Nonfiction Title: *Remodeling Contractor's Handbook*, by D. Wong.
Tips: "The book should be loaded with step-by-step instructions, illustrations, charts, reference data, forms, samples, cost estimates, rules of thumb, and examples that solve actual problems in the builder's office and in the field. The book must cover the subject completely, become the owner's primary reference on the subject, have a high utility-to-cost ratio, and help the owner make a better living in his chosen field."

CREATIVE PUBLISHING CO., The Early West, Box 9292, College Station TX 77840. (409)775-6047. Contact: Theresa Earle. Publishes hardcover originals. Receives 20-40 submissions/year. 50% of books from first-time authors; 100% from unagented writers. Royalty varies on wholesale price. Publishes book an average of 8 months after acceptance. Reports in "several" week on queries; "several" months on mss. Free book catalog.
Nonfiction: Biography. Subjects include Americana (western), history. No mss other than 19th century western America. Query. Reviews artwork/photos as part of ms package.
Recent Nonfiction Title: *Garrett & Roosevelt*, by Jack DeMattos.

‡CRISP PUBLICATIONS, INC., 95 1st St., Los Altos CA 94022. (415)949-4888. Managing Editor: Kathleen Barcos. Publishes trade paperback originals. Firm averages 25-30 titles/year. Pays roylaty on retail price. Publishes book an average of 6 months after acceptance. Free book catalog.
Nonfiction: How-to and self-help. Subjects include art/architecture, business and economics, education, health/medicine and money/finance. Submit outline/synopsis and sample chapters.

THE CROSSING PRESS, 97 Hangar Way, Watsonville CA 95076. (408)722-0711. Co-Publishers: Elaine Goldman Gill, John Gill. Publishes hardcover and trade paperback originals. Averages 30 titles/year; receives 1,600 submissions annually. 10% of books from first-time authors; 90% of books from unagented writers. Pays royalty. Publishes book an average of 18 months after acceptance. Simultaneous submissions OK. Reports in 6 weeks on queries; 3 months on mss. Free book catalog.
Nonfiction: Cookbook, how-to, men's studies, literary and feminist. Subjects include cooking, health, gays, mysteries, sci-fi. Submissions to be considered for the feminist series must be written by women. Submit outline and sample chapter.
Recent Nonfiction Title: *All Women Are Healers*, by Diane Stein.
Fiction: Good literary material. Submit outline and sample chapter.
Recent Fiction Title: *Married Life & Other True Adventures*, by Binnie Kirshenbaum.
Tips: "Simple intelligent query letters do best. No come-ons, no cutes. It helps if there are credentials. Authors should research the press first to see what sort of books it publishes."

CROSSWAY BOOKS, Subsidiary of Good News Publishers, 1300 Crescent St., Wheaton IL 60187. Acquisitions Editor: Jennifer Nahrstadt. Estab. 1938. Publishes hardcover and trade paperback originals. Averages 35 titles/year; receives 2,000 submissions annually. 10% of books from first-time authors; 80% of books from unagented writers. Average print order for a writer's first book is 3,000. Pays negotiable royalty; offers negotiable advance. Publishes book an average of 1 year after acceptance. No phone queries! Reports in 9 months. Book catalog and ms guidelines for 9×12 SAE and 6 first class stamps.
Nonfiction: Subjects include issues on Christianity in contemporary culture, Christian doctrine, and church history. "All books must be written out of Christian perspective or world view." Query with synopsis.
Recent Nonfiction Title: *A Quest for Godlines*, by J.I. Packer.
Fiction: Mainstream; science fiction; fantasy (genuinely creative in the tradition of C.S. Lewis, J.R.R. Tolkien and Madeleine L'Engle); and juvenile (10-14; 13-16). No formula romance. No short stories. No poetry. No true stories. Query with synopsis. "All fiction must be written from a genuine Christian perspective."
Recent Fiction Title: *The Hawk and the Dove*, by Penelope Wilcock.
Tips: "The writer has the best chance of selling our firm a book which, through fiction or nonfiction, shows the practical relevance of biblical doctrine to contemporary issues and life."

CROWN PUBLISHING GROUP, Division of Random House, 201 E. 50th St., New York NY 10022. (212)572-6190. Estab. 1933. Imprints include Clarkson N. Potter, Orion Books, and Harmony. Publishes 200 titles/year. Simultaneous submissions OK. Reports in 2 months.
Nonfiction: Americana, animals, art, biography, cookbooks/cooking, health, history, hobbies, how-to, humor, military history, nature, photography, politics, psychology, recreation, reference, science, self-help and sports. Query with letter only.
Recent Nonfiction Title: *Lee Bailey's Southern Food.*

DANCE HORIZONS, Imprint of Princeton Book Co., Publishers, P.O. Box 57, 12 W. Delaware Ave., Pennington NJ 08534. (609)737-8177. Managing Editor: Debi Elfenbein. Publishes hardcover and paperback originals and paperback reprints. Averages 10 titles/year; receives 50-75 submissions annually. 50% of books from first-time authors; 100% of books from unagented writers. Pays 10% royalty on net receipts; offers no advance. Publishes book an average of 10 months after acceptance. Simultaneous submissions OK. Reports in 3 months. Free book catalog.
Nonfiction: "Anything dealing with dance." Query first. Reviews artwork/photos.
Recent Nonfiction Title: *The Pointe Book: Shoes, Training & Technique*, by Janice Barringer and Sarah Schlesinger.

JOHN DANIEL AND COMPANY, PUBLISHERS, Imprint of Daniel & Daniel, Publishers Inc., P.O. Box 21922, Santa Barbara CA 93121. (805)962-1780. Publisher: John Daniel. Estab. 1985. Publishes trade paperback originals. Averages 10 titles/year; receives 1,000 submissions annually. 50% of books from first-time authors; 100% of books from unagented writers. Pays 10% royalty on wholesale price. Publishes book an average of 8 months after acceptance. Simultaneous submissions OK. Query for electronic submissions. Reports in 3 weeks on queries; 2 months on mss. Book catalog and ms guidelines for #10 SASE.
Nonfiction: Autobiography, biography, literary memoir and essays. "We'll look at anything, but are particularly interested in books in which literary merit is foremost—as opposed to books that simply supply information. No libelous, obscene, poorly written or unintelligent manuscripts." Query or submit outline and sample chapters.
Recent Nonfiction Title: *Making Faces: Memoirs of a Caricaturist*, by Alice Fruhauf (memoir).
Fiction: Novels and short story collections. "We do best with books by authors who have demonstrated a clear, honest, elegant style. No libelous, obscene, poorly written, or boring submissions." Query or submit synopsis and sample chapters.
Recent Fiction Title: *Rats in the Trees*, by Jess Mowry (stories).
Poetry: "We're open to anything, but we're very cautious. Poetry's hard to sell." Submit complete ms.
Recent Poetry Title: *Letter from Los Angeles*, by Charles Gullans.
Tips: "If I were a writer trying to market a book today, I would envision my specific audience and approach publishers who demonstrate that they can reach that audience. Writing is not always a lucrative profession; almost nobody makes a living off of royalties from small press publishing houses. That's why the authors we deal with are dedicated to their art and proud of their books—but don't expect to appear on the Carson show. Small press publishers have a hard time breaking into the bookstore market. We try, but we wouldn't be able to survive without a healthy direct-mail sale."

DANTE UNIVERSITY OF AMERICA PRESS, INC., Box 843, Brookline VA 02147. Contact: Manuscripts Editor. Publishes hardcover originals and reprints, and trade paperback originals and reprints. Averages 5 titles/year; receives 50 submissions annually. 50% of books from first-time authors; 50% of books from unagented writers. Average print order for a writer's first book is 3,000. Pays royalty; offers negotiable advance. Publishes book an average of 10 months after acceptance. Simultaneous submissions OK. Query for electronic submissions. Reports in 2 weeks on queries only; 2 months on mss.
Nonfiction: Biography, reference, reprints, and nonfiction and fiction translations from Italian and Latin. Subjects include general scholarly nonfiction, Renaissance thought and letter, Italian language and linguistics, Italian-American history and culture, and bilingual education. Query first with SASE. Reviews artwork/photos as part of ms package.
Poetry: "There is a chance that we would use Renaissance poetry translations."
Recent Poetry Title: Dante's *Inferno* (new translation, 34 illustrations).

MAY DAVENPORT, PUBLISHERS, 26313 Purissima Rd., Los Altos Hills CA 94022. (415)948-6499. Editor/Publisher: May Davenport. Estab. 1975. Imprint is md Books (nonfiction and fiction). Publishes hardcover and trade paperback originals. Averages 4 titles/year; receives 1,000-2,000 submissions annually. 95% of books from first-time authors; 5% from professional writers. Pays 15% royalty on retail price; no advance. Publishes book an average of 1-3 years after acceptance. Reports in 3 weeks. Ms guidelines for #10 SASE.
Nonfiction: Juvenile (13-17). Subject art, music to interest ages 13-17. "Our readers are students in elementary and secondary public school districts, as well as correctional institutes of learning, etc. No hack writing." Query.
Recent Nonfiction Title: *The Fancy Fish Coloring Book*, by Julie Donohue.
Fiction: Adventure, fantasy. "We're overstocked with picture books and first readers; prefer literature for TV-oriented teenagers. Be entertaining while informing." No sex or violence. Query with SASE.
Recent Fiction Title: *Chase of the Sorceress*, by P.R. Johnson.
Tips: "If you can't entertain with words, make people laugh some other way."

DAVIS PUBLICATIONS, INC., 50 Portland St., Worcester MA 01608. (508)754-7201. FAX: (508)753-3834. Managing Editor: Wyatt Wade. Estab. 1901. Averages 5-10 titles/year. Pays 10-15% royalty. Publishes book an average of 1 year after acceptance. Write for copy of guidelines for authors.
Nonfiction: Publishes technique-oriented art, design and craft books for the educational market. Accepts nonfiction translations. "Keep in mind the intended audience. Our readers are visually oriented. All illustrations should be collated separately from the text, but keyed to the text. Photos should be good quality transparencies and black and white photographs. Well-selected illustrations should explain, amplify, and enhance the text. We average 2-4 photos/page. We like to see technique photos as well as illustrations of finished artwork, by a variety of artists, including students. Recent books have been on papermaking, airbrush painting, jewelry, design, puppets, and watercolor painting." Submit outline, sample chapters and illustrations. Reviews artwork/photos as part of ms package.
Recent Nonfiction Title: *Computers in the Artroom*, by Deborah Greh.

DAW BOOKS, INC., 375 Hudson St., 3rd Floor, New York NY 10014-3658. Submissions Editor: Peter Stampfel. Estab. 1971. Publishes science fiction and fantasy hardcover and paperback originals and reprints. Publishes 60-80 titles/year. Pays in royalties with an advance that is negotiable on a book-by-book basis. Sends galleys to author. Simultaneous submissions "returned at once, unread unless prior arrangements are made by agent." Reports in 6 weeks "or longer, if a second reading is required." Free book catalog.
Fiction: "We are interested in science fiction and fantasy novels only. We do not publish any other category of fiction. We accept both agented and unagented ms. We are not seeking collections of short stories or ideas for anthologies. We do not want any nonfiction manuscripts." Submit complete ms.

‡DCI PUBLISHING, Suite 250, 13911 Ridgedale Dr., Minneapolis MN 55343. (612)541-0239. Director of Publishing: George Cleveland. Publishes hardcover and trade paperback originals. Firm averages 16-20 titles/year. Receives 200 submissions/year. 30% of books are from first-time authors. 60% from unagented writers. Pays 6-12% royalties on retail price, or buys outright. Publishes ms an average of 6 months after acceptance. Simultaneous submissions OK. Query for electronic submissions. Reports in 3 weeks on queries; 2 weeks on mss. Book catalog and ms guidelines free.
Nonfiction: Cookbook and self-help. Subjects include cooking, foods and nutrition, health/medicine and psychology. "We are seeking anything relating to health, from fitness to family psychology from authoritative sources. No New Age material." Submit outline/synopsis and sample chapters and complete ms.
Recent Nonfiction Title: *When You're Sick and Don't Know Why*, by Linda Hanner and John Witek, M.D. (health).

IVAN R. DEE, INC., 1332 N. Halsted St., Chicago IL 60622. (312)787-6262. FAX: (312)787-6269. President: Ivan R. Dee. Estab. 1988. Imprints include Elephant Paperbacks. Publishes hardcover originals and trade paperback originals and reprints. Averages 25 titles/year. 10% of books from first-time authors; 75% from unagented writers. Pays royalty. Publishes book an average of 9 months after acceptance. Reports in 2 weeks on queries; 6 weeks on mss. Book catalog free on request.
Nonfiction: Biography. Subjects include anthropology/archaeology, art/architecture, business and economics, government/politics, health/medicine, history, language/literature, military/war, psychology, religion, sociology, women's issues/studies. Submit outline/synopsis and sample chapters or complete ms. Reviews artwork/photos as part of ms package.
Recent Nonfiction Title: *Culture in an Age of Money*, by Nicolaus Mills.
Tips: "We publish for an intelligent lay audience and college course adoptions."

DEL REY BOOKS, Imprint of Ballantine Books, Division of Random House, 201 E. 50th St., New York NY 10022. (212)572-2677. Vice President and Editor-in-Chief: Owen Lock. Vice President and Fantasy Editor: Lester del Rey. Estab. 1977. Publishes hardcover, trade paperback and mass market originals and mass market paperback reprints. Averages 60 titles/year; receives 1,900 submissions annually. 10% of books from first-time authors; 40% of books from unagented writers. Pays royalty on retail price. Offers competitive advance. Publishes book an average of 1 year after acceptance. Reporting time slow. Writer's guidelines for #10 SASE.
Fiction: Fantasy ("should have the practice of magic as an essential element of the plot") and science fiction ("well-plotted novels with good characterization, exotic locales, and detailed alien cultures. Novels should have a 'sense of wonder' and be designed to please readers"). Will need "80 original fiction manuscripts of science fiction and fantasy suitable for publishing over the next two years. No flying-saucers, Atlantis, or occult novels." Submit complete ms or detailed outline and first three chapters.
Recent Fiction Title: *The Seeress of Kell*, by David Eddings.
Tips: "Del Rey is a reader's house. Our audience is anyone who wants to be pleased by a good entertaining novel. Pay particular attention to plotting and a satisfactory conclusion. It must be/feel believable. That's what the readers like."

DELACORTE PRESS, Imprint of Dell Publishing, Division of Bantam Doubleday Dell, 666 5th Ave., New York NY 10103. (212)765-6500. Editorial Director: Brian deFiore. Publishes hardcover originals. Publishes 36 titles/year. Royalty and advance vary. Publishes book an average of 1 year after acceptance, but varies. Simultaneous submissions OK. Reports in 2 months. Book catalog and guidelines for 6×9 SASE.
Nonfiction and Fiction: *Query, outline, first 3 chapters or brief proposal.* No mss for children's or young adult books accepted in this division.
Recent Nonfiction Title: *Riders of the Storm*, by John Densmore.
Recent Fiction Title: *Circle of Friends*, by Maeve Binchy.

DELL BOOKS, Division of Bantam Doubleday Dell, 666 5th Ave., New York NY 10103. Did not want to be listed.

DELTA BOOKS, Division of Bantam Doubleday Dell Publishing Co., 666 5th Ave., New York NY 10103. (212)765-6500. Editorial Director: Brian deFiore. Publishes trade paperback reprints and originals. Averages 20 titles/year. Pays variable royalty; offers variable advance. Simultaneous submissions OK. Reports in 2 months. Book catalog for 8½×11 SASE.
Nonfiction: Biography, childcare, film, music, New Age, popular culture, popular psychology, science. "We are expanding our base of strong childcare and New Age titles, while also looking for good books on popular culture (film, music, television). Query or submit outline/synopsis and sample chapters. *Prefers submissions through agents.*"
Recent Nonfiction Title: *When You and Your Mother Can't Be Friends*, by Victoria Secunda.

THE DENALI PRESS, P.O. Box 021535, Juneau AK 99802. (907)586-6014. FAX: (907)463-6780. Contact: Sally Silvas-Ottumwa. Estab. 1986. Publishes trade paperback originals. Averages 5 titles/year. Receives 20-40 submissions/year. 50% of books from first-time authors; 80% from unagented writers. Pays 10-15% royalty on wholesale price; buys mss by outright purchase. Publishes book an average of 9-12 months after acceptance. Simultaneous submissions OK. Query for electronic submissions. Reports in 3 weeks on queries; 6 weeks on mss. Book catalog free on request.
Nonfiction: Reference. Subjects include Americana, Alaskana, anthropology, ethnic, government/politics, history, recreation, regional, sports and travel. "We need reference books—ethnic, refugee and minority concerns." Query with outline/synopsis and sample chapters; all unsolicited mss are returned unopened.
Recent Nonfiction Title: *Refugee and Immigrant Resource Directory 1990-1991*, by Alan Edward Schorr.

T.S. DENISON & CO., INC., 9601 Newton Ave. S., Minneapolis MN 55431. (612)888-1460. FAX: (612)888-9641. Editor-in-Chief: Sherrill B. Flora. Acquisitions Editor: Baxter Brings. Estab. 1876. Publishes teacher aid materials; receives 500 submissions annually. 90% of books from first-time authors; 100% of books from unagented writers. Average print order for a writer's first book is 3,000. Royalty varies; no advance. Publishes book an average of 1-2 years after acceptance. Reports in 1 month. Book catalog and ms guidelines for SASE.
Nonfiction: Specializes in early childhood and elementary school teaching aids. Send prints if photos are to accompany ms. Submit complete ms. Reviews artwork/photos as part of ms package.
Recent Nonfiction Title: *Famous Children's Authors*, by Shirly Norby and Greg Ryan.
Recent Fiction Title: *Mr. Wiggle Goes to the Library*, by Paula Craig.

‡DENLINGERS PUBLISHERS, LTD., P.O. Box 2300, Centreville VA 22020. (703)830-4646. FAX: (703)830-5303. Publisher: William W. Denlinger. Estab. 1926. Publishes hardcover and trade paperback originals and reprints. Averages 12 titles/year; receives 250 submissions annually. 10% of books from first-time authors; 85% of books from unagented writers. Average print order for a writer's first book is 3,000. Pays variable royalty. No advance. Publishes book an average of 1 year after acceptance. Simultaneous submissions OK. Query for electronic submissions. Reports in 1 week on queries; 6 weeks on mss. Book catalog for SASE.
Nonfiction: How-to and technical books; dog-breed books only. Query. Reviews artwork/photos as part of ms package.
Recent Nonfiction Title: *German Shepherd Dog*, by Chris Walkawitz.

*DEVIN-ADAIR PUBLISHERS, INC., 6 N. Water St., Greenwich CT 06830. (203)531-7755. Editor: Jane Andrassi. Estab. 1911. Imprints are Patriot Press, Flag Press, Irish Book Society, and Photography Associates. Publishes hardcover and paperback originals, reprints and software. Averages 20 titles/year; receives up to 500 submissions annually. 30% of books from first-time authors; 70% of books from unagented writers. Average print order for a writer's first book is 7,500. Subsidy publishes 5% of books. Royalty on sliding scale, 5-25%; "average advance is low." Publishes book an average of 9 months after acceptance. No simultaneous submissions. Query for electronic submissions. Book catalog and guidelines for 6×9 SAE and 5 first class stamps.

Nonfiction: Publishes Americana, business, how-to, conservative politics, history, medicine, nature, economics, sports and travel books. New line: photography books. Accepts translations. Query or submit outline/synopsis and sample chapters. Looks for "early interest, uniqueness, economy of expression, good style, and new information." Reviews artwork/photos as part of ms package.

Recent Nonfiction Title: *Exploring Old Block Island*, by H. Whitman and R. Fox.

Tips: "We seek to publish books of high quality manufacture. We spend 8% more on production and design than necessary to ensure a better quality book. Trends include increased specialization and a more narrow view of a subject. General overviews are now a thing of the past. Better a narrow subject in depth than a wide superficial one."

*DEVONSHIRE PUBLISHING CO., P.O. Box 85, Elgin IL 60121-0085. (708)242-3846. Vice President: Don Reynolds. Estab. 1988. Publishes hardcover and trade paperback originals. Averages 4 titles/year; receives 1,000 submissions annually. 85% of books from first-time authors; 75% of books from unagented writers. Subsidy publishes 20% of books. "Although we do not generally subsidy publish we will enter into 'cooperative publishing agreements' with an author if the subject matter is of such limited appeal that we doubt its profitability, or if the author desires a more extravagant finished product than we planned to produce." Pays 10-15% royalty on retail price. "Royalty would be higher if author engaged in cooperative venture." Offers negotiable advance. Publishes book an average of 1 year after acceptance. Simultaneous submissions OK. Reports in 1 month on queries; 2 months on submissions. Book catalog and guidelines for #10 SASE.

Nonfiction: Reference, technical and textbook. Subjects include business and economics, history, hobbies, nature, psychology, religion and sociology. "We will be looking for books that have an impact on the reader. A history or religious book will have to be more than just a recitation of past events. Our books must have some relation to today's problems or situations." No works of personal philosophy or unverifiable speculation. Query and/or submit outline/synopsis.

Recent Nonfiction Title: *The Way We Were*, by Mace Crandall Erandall (history).

Fiction: Erotica, experimental, historical, horror, religious and science fiction. "All works must have some relevance to today's reader and be well written. We hope to produce one or two titles, but our main thrust will be in the nonfiction area. However, if a work is thought-provoking and/or controversial, we may give it priority." Query and/or submit outline/synopsis.

Recent Fiction Title: *The Dew of Hermon*, by Janis Fedor (historical fiction).

Tips: "Because we are a small publishing company, we can aim for the smaller, more specialized market. We envision that the audience for our books will be well educated with a specific area of interest. We can afford to look at work that other publishers have passed over. Although we are not looking for works that are controversial just for the sake of controversy, we are looking for topics that go beyond the norm." At deadline *Writer's Market* **editors learned that Devonshire is no longer operating at this address and phone.**

DIAL BOOKS FOR YOUNG READERS, Division of NAL Penguin Inc., 375 Hudson St., 3rd Floor, New York NY 10014. (212)366-2800. Submissions Editor: Phyllis J. Fogelman. Imprints include Dial Easy-to-Read Books and Dial Very First Books. Publishes hardcover originals. Averages 80 titles/year; receives 8,000 submissions annually. 10% of books from first-time authors. Pays variable royalty and advance. Simultaneous submissions OK, but not preferred. Reports in 2 weeks on queries; 4 months on mss. Book catalog and ms guidelines for 9×12 SASE and 4 first class stamps.

Nonfiction: Juvenile picture books and young adult books. Especially looking for "quality picture books and well-researched young adult and middle-reader mss." Not interested in alphabet books, riddle and game books, and early concept books. Query with outline/synopsis and sample chapters. Reviews artwork/photos.

An asterisk preceding a listing indicates that subsidy publishing or co-publishing (where author pays part or all of publishing costs) is available. Firms whose subsidy programs comprise more than 50% of their total publishing activities are listed at the end of the Book Packagers and Producers section.

Recent Nonfiction Title: *Ryan White: My Own Story*, by Ryan White with Ann Marie Cunningham.
Fiction: Juvenile picture books and young adult books. Adventure, fantasy, historical, humor, mystery, romance (appropriate for young adults), and suspense. Especially looking for "lively and well written novels for middle grade and young adult children involving a convincing plot and believable characters. The subject matter or theme should not already be overworked in previously published books. The approach must not be demeaning to any minority group, nor should the roles of female characters (or others) be stereotyped, though we don't think books should be didactic, or in any way message-y." No "topics inappropriate for the juvenile, young adult, and middle grade audiences. No plays." Submit complete ms. Also publishes Pied Piper Book (paperback Dial reprints) and Pied Piper Giants (1½ feet tall reprints).
Recent Fiction Title: *Pillow of Clouds*, by Marc Talbert.
Tips: "Our readers are anywhere from preschool age to teenage. Picture books must have strong plots, lots of action, unusual premises, or universal themes treated with freshness and originality. Humor works well in these books. A very well thought out and intelligently presented book has the best chance of being taken on. Genre isn't as much of a factor as presentation."

DILLON PRESS, INC., 242 Portland Ave. S., Minneapolis MN 55415. (612)333-2691. Editorial Director: Uva Dillon. Senior Editor: Tom Schneider. Publishes hardcover originals. Averages 30-40 titles/year; receives 3,000 submissions annually. 30% of books from first-time authors; 90% of books from unagented writers. Average print order for a writer's first book is 5,000. Pays royalty or by outright purchase. Publishes book an average of 18 months after acceptance. Reports in 6 weeks. Book catalog for 10×12 SAE with 4 first class stamps.
Nonfiction: "We are actively seeking mss for the juvenile educational market." Subjects include world and U.S. geography, international festivals and holidays, U.S. states and cities, contemporary and historical biographies for elementary and middle grade levels, unusual approaches to science topics for primary grade readers, unusual or remarkable animals, and contemporary issues of interest and value to young people. Submit complete ms or outline and 2 sample chapters; query letters if accompanied by book proposal. Reviews artwork/photos as part of ms package.
Recent Nonfiction Title: *Sneakers, The Shoes We Choose*, by Robert Young.
Tips: "Before writing, authors should check out the existing competition for their book idea to determine if it is really needed and stands a reasonable chance for success, especially for a nonfiction proposal."

‡DISTINCTIVE PUBLISHING CORPORATION, P.O. Box 17868, Plantation FL 33318-7868. (305)975-2413. Editor: K. Ancona. Estab. 1986. Publishes hardcover and trade paperback originals and trade paperback reprints. Firm averages 15 titles/year. Receives 200 submissions/year. 60% of books from first-time authors. 80% from unagented writers. Pays 6-10% royalty on retail price. Publishes book an average of 1 year after acceptance. Simultaneous submissions OK. Reports in 3 months on queries. Book catalog and manuscript guidelines free on request.
Nonfiction: How-to, humor, reference, self-help, technical, textbook. Subjects inculde art/architecture, child guidance/parenting, education, health/medicine, music/dance, psychology, regional, sociology. Submit complete ms. Reviews artwork/photos as part of ms package.

DOUBLEDAY BOOKS, Division of Bantam Doubleday Dell, 666 5th Ave., New York NY 10103. (212)765-6500. Imprints are Anchor Books, Nan A. Talese, Image, Currency Books, Perfect Crime, Dolphin Books, Double D Western, Spy Books and Zephyr Books. Publishes hardcover and trade paper originals. Offers royalty on retail price and variable advance. Reports in 2½ months. Doubleday accepts fiction and nonfiction through agents. Will not read unsolicited material. Send proposal/synopsis to Perfect Crime Editor, or Loveswept Editor as appropriate. Sufficient postage for return via fourth class mail must accompany manuscript.

DOWN EAST BOOKS, Division of Down East Enterprise, Inc., P.O. Box 679, Camden ME 04843. Managing Editor: Karin Womer. Estab. 1954. Publishes hardcover and trade paperback originals and trade paperback reprints. Averages 10-14 titles/year; receives 300 submissions annually. 50% of books from first-time authors; 90% of books from unagented writers. Average print order for a writer's first book is 3,000. Pays 10-15% on receipts. Offers average $200 advance. Publishes book an average of 1 year after acceptance. Simultaneous submissions OK. Reports in 2 weeks on queries; 2 months on mss. Ms guidelines for 9×12 SAE with 3 first class stamps.
Nonfiction: Books about the New England region, Maine in particular. Subjects include Americana, cooking and foods, history, nature, crafts and recreation. "All of our books must have a Maine or New England emphasis." Query. Reviews artwork/photos as part of ms package.

Recent Nonfiction Title: *Mr. Rockefeller's Roads: The Untold Story of Acadia's Carriage Roads and Their Creator,* by Ann R. Roberts.
Fiction: "We generally publish no fiction except for an occasional juvenile title (average 1/year) but are now keeping alert for good general-audience novels—same regional criteria apply."
Recent Fiction Title: *Sunny's Mittens: Learn to Knit Lovikka Mittens,* by Robin Hansen.

DRAMA BOOK PUBLISHERS, 260 5th Ave., New York NY 10001. (212)725-5377. FAX: (212)725-8506. Contact: Ralph Pine or Judith Holmes. Estab. 1967. Publishes hardcover and paperback originals and reprints. Averages 4-15 titles/year; receives 420 submissions annually. 70% of books from first-time authors; 90% of books from unagented writers. Royalty varies; advance varies; negotiable. Publishes book an average of 18 months after acceptance. Reports in 2 months.
Nonfiction: Texts, guides, manuals, directories, reference—for and about performing arts theory and practice: acting, directing; voice, speech, movement, music, dance, mime; makeup, masks, wigs; costumes, sets, lighting, sound; design and execution; technical theatre, stagecraft, equipment; stage management; producing; arts management, all varieties; business and legal aspects; film, radio, television, cable, video; theory, criticism, reference; playwriting; theatre and performance history. Accepts nonfiction, drama and technical works in translations also. Query; accepts 1-3 sample chapters; no complete mss. Reviews artwork/photos as part of ms package.
Fiction: Professionally produced plays and musicals.

*DUQUESNE UNIVERSITY PRESS, 600 Forbes Ave., Pittsburgh PA 15282. (412)434-6610. FAX: (412)434-5780. Contact: Acquisitions Editor. Estab. 1924. Averages 9 titles/year; receives 400 submissions annually. 25% of books from first-time authors; 100% of books from unagented writers. Average print order for a writer's first book is 1,000. Subsidy publishes 20% of books. Pays 10% royalty on net sales; no advance. Publishes book an average of 1 year after acceptance. Query for electronic submissions. Query. Reports in 3 months.
Nonfiction: Scholarly books in the humanities, social sciences for academics, libraries, college bookstores and educated laypersons. Length: open. Looks for scholarship. No unsolicited mss. Query.
Recent Nonfiction Title: *The Bible of the Poor [Biblia Pauperum],* by Albert C. Labriola and John W. Smeltz.

DURST PUBLICATIONS LTD., 29-28 41st Ave., Long Island City NY 11101. (718)706-0303. FAX: (718)706-0891. Owner: Sanford Durst. Publishes hardcover and trade paperback originals and reprints. Averages 20 titles/year; receives 100 submissions annually. Average print order for first book is 2,500. Pays variable royalty. Publishes book an average of 6 months after acceptance. Reports in 1 month. Book catalog for #10 SAE and 4 first class stamps.
Nonfiction: How-to and reference. Subjects include Americana, art, business and economics, cooking and foods, hobbies-primarily coin collecting, stamp collecting, antiques and legal. Especially needs reference books and how-to on coins, medals, tokens, paper money, art, antiques-illustrated with valuations or rarities, if possible. Publishes for dealers, libraries, collectors and attorneys. Submit outline/synopsis and sample chapters. Reviews artwork/photos as part of ms package.
Recent Nonfiction Title: *Buying & Setting Country Land,* by D. Reisman (practical/legal).
Tips: "Write in simple English. Do not repeat yourself. Present matter in logical, orderly form. Try to illustrate."

DUSTBOOKS, Box 100, Paradise CA 95967. (916)877-6110. Publisher: Len Fulton. Publishes hardcover and paperback originals. Averages 7 titles/year. Offers 15% royalty. Simultaneous submissions OK if so informed. Reports in 2 months. Free book catalog; writer's guidelines for #10 SASE.
Nonfiction: "Our specialty is directories of small presses, poetry publishers, and a monthly newsletter on small publishers (*Small Press Review*)." Submit outline/synopsis and sample chapters.

DUTTON CHILDREN'S BOOKS, Division of Penguin USA, 375 Hudson St., New York NY 10014. (212)366-2000. Editor-in-Chief: Lucia Monfried. Estab. 1852. Firm publishes hardcover originals. Publishes 70 titles/year. 15% from first-time authors. Pays royalty on retail price. Simultaneous submissions OK. Reports in 1 month on queries; 4 months on mss. Book catalog for 9½×11 SAE with 6 first class stamps. Ms guidelines for #10 SASE. "Please send query letter first on all except picture book manuscripts."
Nonfiction: For preschoolers to middle-graders; including animals/nature, U.S. history, general biography, sciene and photo essays.
Recent Nonfiction Title: *It's an Armadillo!,* by Bianca Lavies (photo essay).
Fiction: Dutton Children's Books has a complete publishing program that includes picture books; easy-to-read books; and fiction for all ages, from "first-chapter" books to young adult readers.
Recent Fiction Title: *Eye of the Needle,* by Teri Sloat (picture book).

E.P. DUTTON, Imprint of Penguin USA, 375 Hudson St., New York NY 10014. (212)725-1818. Publisher: Elaine Koster. Estab. 1852. Publishes hardcover originals. Firm averages 120 titles/year. Does not read unsolicited manuscripts.
Nonfiction: Biography, self-help, serious nonfiction, politics, psychology, science.
Fiction: Mainstream/contemporary. "We don't publish genre romances or westerns."

DUTTON/NEW AMERICAN LIBRARY, Division of Penguin USA, 375 Hudson St., New York NY 10014. Did not want to be listed.

*EDICIONES UNIVERSAL, 3090 SW 8th St., Miami FL 33135. (305)642-3355. FAX: (305)642-7978. Director: Juan M. Salvat. Estab. 1965. Publishes trade paperback originals in Spanish. Publishes 50 titles/year; receives 150 submissions/year. 40% of books from first-time authors. 90% of books from unagented writers. Subsidy publishes 10% of books. Pays 5-10% royalty on retail price. Publishes book an average of 9 months after acceptance. Simultaneous submissions OK. Reports in 1 month on queries; 2 months on mss. Book catalog free.
Nonfiction: Biography, cookbook, humor and reference. Subjects include cooking and foods, philosophy, politics, psychology and sociology. "We specialize in Cuban topics." All manuscripts must be in Spanish. Submit outline/synopsis and sample chapters. Reviews artwork/photos as part of ms package.
Recent Nonfiction Title: *Cultura Afro Cubana, Vol. 2.*
Fiction: "We will consider everything as long as it is written in Spanish." Submit outline/synopsis and sample chapters.
Recent Fiction Title: *El Circulo del Alacran*, by Luis Zalamea.
Poetry: "We will consider any Spanish-language poetry." Submit 3 or more poems.
Recent Poetry Title: *Antologia De Poesia Infantil*, by Ana Rosa Nunez.
Tips: "Our audience is composed entirely of Spanish-language readers. This is a very limited market. Books on Cuban or Latin American topics have the best chance of selling to our firm."

*EDUCATION ASSOCIATES, Division of The Daye Press, Inc., P.O. Box 8021, Athens GA 30603. (404)542-4244. Editor, Text Division: D. Keith Osborn. Estab. 1974. Publishes hardcover and trade paperback originals. Averages 2-6 titles/year; receives 300 submissions annually. 1% of books from first-time authors; 100% of books from unagented writers. Subsidy publishes 5% of books. "We may publish a textbook that has a very limited audience and is of unusual merit . . . but we still believe that the book will make a contribution to the educational field." Buys mss "on individual basis." Publishes book an average of 9 months after acceptance. Do not send mss; query first. No reponse without SASE. Reports in 1 month on queries.
Nonfiction: How-to, textbook, lab manuals. Subjects include psychology and education. "Books in the fields of early childhood and middle school education. No basic textbooks. Rather, are interested in more specific areas of interest in above fields. We are more interested in small runs on topics of more limited nature than general texts." Query only with one-page letter. If interested will request synopsis and sample chapters. Absolutely no reply unless SASE is enclosed. No phone queries.
Recent Nonfiction Title: *Observation Guide for Child Study*, by L. Paquio.
Tips: "We are not taking any unsolicited college textbook manuscripts. We will consider small runs of college study guides or study manuals that are used by a professor at his/her own college or university. Will consider any college academic field for a small run lab manual."

*WILLIAM B. EERDMANS PUBLISHING CO., 255 Jefferson Ave. SE, Grand Rapids MI 49503. (616)459-4591. FAX: (616)459-6540. Editor-in-Chief: Jon Pott. Managing Editor: Charles Van Hof. Children's Book Editor: Amy Eerdmans. Publishes hardcover and paperback originals and reprints. Averages 65-70 titles/year; receives 3,000-4,000 submissions annually. 25% of books from first-time authors; 95% of books from unagented writers. Average print order for a writer's first book is 4,000. Subsidy publishes 1% of books. Pays 7½-10% royalty on retail price; usually no advance. Publishes book an average of 1 year after acceptance. Simultaneous submissions OK if noted. Reports in 3 weeks for queries; 4 months for mss. Looks for "quality and relevance." Free book catalog.
Nonfiction: Reference, textbooks and tourists guidebooks. Subjects include children's religious literature, history, philosophy, psychology, religion, sociology, regional history and geography. "Approximately 80% of our publications are religious—specifically Protestant—and largely of the more academic or theological variety (as opposed to the devotional, inspirational or celebrity-conversion books). Our history and social studies titles aim, similarly, at an academic audience; some of them are documentary histories. We prefer that writers take the time to notice if we have published anything at all in the same category as their manuscript before sending it to us." Accepts nonfiction translations. Query. Include SASE for return of ms. Accepts outline/synopsis and 2-3 sample chapters. Reviews artwork/photos.
Recent Nonfiction Title: *Dancing in the Dark*, by Roy Avker, et al.

EES PUBLICATIONS, 1120 Royal Palm Beach Blvd., Box 216, Royal Palm Beach FL 33411. (407)795-7475. Director: Candace Brown. Publishes trade paperback originals. Firm averages 3-6 titles/year. 10% of books from first-time authors. Pays 10-15% royalty on retail price. Negotiable outright purchase. Publishes book an average of 6 months after acceptance. Reports generally in 2 weeks on queries; 1 month on mss. Free book catalog and ms guidelines, "just send legible address."

Nonfiction: How-to, reference, technical and textbook. Subjects include education (EMS field only) and health/medicine (EMS related only). "We're interested in specialized EMS and law enforcement topics. Authors must be properly credentialed for the topic." No pictorial history, how to read an EKG, general topic initial education textbooks, or nursing topics. Query or submit outline/synopsis and sample chapters.

Recent Nonfiction Title: *How to Bitch Effectively: An Officers Guide to Selling an Idea to the Brass*, by Clarence E. Jones.

Tips: "Writers have the best chance of selling us a specialized topic about which the author is acutely knowledgeable and properly credentialed-i.e., an EMT should not attempt to write on an ALS level. EMTs, paramedics, rescue personnel, students and educators in EMS/rescue and law enforcement are our audience."

‡ELYSIUM GROWTH PRESS, 5436 Fernwood Ave., Los Angeles CA 90027. (213)455-1000. FAX: (213)455-2007. Publishes hardcover and paperback originals and reprints. Averages 4 titles/year; receives 20 submissions/year. 20% of books from first-time authors; 100% of books from unagented writers. Pays $5,000 average advance. Publishes book an average of 18 months after acceptance. Query for electronic submissions. Reports in 2 weeks on queries; 6 weeks on submissions. Book catalog free on request.

Nonfiction: Illustrated book, self-help and textbook. Subjects include health, nature, philosophy, photography, psychology, recreation, sociology and travel. A nudist, naturist, special niche publisher. Needs books on "body self-image, body self-appreciation, world travel and subjects depicting the clothing-optional lifestyle." Query. All unsolicited mss are returned unopened. Reviews artwork/photos as part of ms package.

Recent Nonfiction Title: *The Importance of Wearing Clothes*, by Lawrence Langner.

ENTELEK, Ward-Whidden House/The Hill, Box 1303, Portsmouth NH 03801. Editor-in-Chief: Albert E. Hickey. Publishes paperback originals. Offers royalty on retail price of 5% trade; 10% textbook. No advance. Averages 5 titles/year. Simultaneous submissions OK. Submit outline and sample chapters or submit complete ms. Reports in 1 week. Book catalog for SASE.

Nonfiction: Publishes computer books and software of special interest to educators. Length: 3,000 words minimum.

Recent Nonfiction Title: *Sail Training for Young Offenders*, edited by A. Hickey (education).

‡ENTERPRISE PUBLISHING CO., INC., 725 N. Market St., Wilmington DE 19801. (302)654-0110. FAX: (302)654-0277. Publisher: T.N. Peterson. Publishes hardcover and paperback originals, "with an increasing interest in newsletters and periodicals." Averages 8 titles/year; receives 150 submissions annually. 50% of books from first-time authors; 90% of books from unagented writers. Pays royalty on wholesale or retail price. Offers $1,000 average advance. Publishes book an average of 6 months after acceptance. Simultaneous submissions OK, but "let us know." Query for electronic submissions. Catalog and ms guidelines for SASE.

Nonfiction: "Subjects of interest to small business executives/entrepreneurs. They are highly independent and self-sufficient, and of an apolitical to conservative political leaning. They need practical information, as opposed to theoretical: self-help topics on business, including starting and managing a small enterprise, advertising, marketing, raising capital, public relations, tax avoidance and personal finance. Business/economics, legal self-help and business how-to." Queries only. All unsolicited mss are returned unopened. Reviews artwork/photos.

Recent Nonfiction Title: *43 Proven Ways to Raise Capital For Your Business*, by Ted Nicholas.

PAUL S. ERIKSSON, PUBLISHER, Battell-on-the-Otter, Suite 208, Middlebury VT 05753. (802)388-7303; Summer: Forest Dale VT 05745. (802)247-8415. Publisher/Editor: Paul S. Eriksson. Associate Publisher/Co-Editor: Peggy Eriksson. Estab. 1960. Publishes hardcover and paperback trade originals and paperback trade reprints. Averages 5-10 titles/year; receives 1,500 submissions annually. 25% of books from first-time authors; 95% of books from unagented writers. Average print order for a writer's first book is 3,000-5,000. Pays 10-15% royalty on retail price; advance offered if necessary. Publishes book an average of 6 months after acceptance. Catalog for #10 SASE.

Nonfiction: Americana, birds (ornithology), art, biography, business/economics, cookbooks/cooking/foods, health, history, hobbies, how-to, humor, nature, politics, psychology, recreation, self-help, sociology, sports and travel. Query.

Recent Nonfiction Title: *Book Banning in America*, by William Noble.
Fiction: Mainstream. Query.
Recent Fiction Title: *Zachary*, by Ernest Pintoff.
Tips: "We look for intelligence, excitement and salability."

LAWRENCE ERLBAUM ASSOCIATES, INC., 365 Broadway, Hillsdale NJ 07642. (201)666-4110. FAX: (201)666-2394. Vice President, Editorial: Judith Amsel. Estab. 1974. Publishes hardcover and paperbacks originals. Firm averages 100 titles/year. Receives 300 submissions/year. 5-10% of books from first-time authors. 100% from unagented writers. Pays 10-15% royalty on net receipts. Offers $400 average advance. Publishes book an average of 9 months after acceptance. Simultaneous submissions OK. Query for electronic submissions. Reports in 2 weeks on queries; 3 months on mss. Free book catalog and manuscript guidelines.
Nonfiction: Technical, textbook and scholarly. Subjects include computer science (AI, HCI), communications, education, health/medicine (behaviorial), psychology, science (neuroscience), women's issues/studies and statistics.Growing lists in theoretical and applied cognitive and behavioral sciences (monographs and some edited collections). Professional-level books, upper-level college texts and alternative media (video, software). No trade-audience oriented. Submit outline/synopsis and sample chapters. Reviews artwork/photos as part of ms package.
Recent Nonfiction Title: *The Complete Guide to Graduate School Admission: Psychology and Related Fields*, by P. Keith-Spiegel.
Tips: "Writers have the best chance with multidisciplinary titles that are appropriate for many of our markets on the increase. List increasingly includes books on applications developed from recent research, such as industrial/organizational psychology and neural networks are needed. Clean, focused writing always works better. Our audience consists of academics and professionals in the behavioral, social and cognitive sciences. If I were a writer trying to market a book today, I would go to those publishers whose books I most respect and want to have in my own library."

ETC PUBLICATIONS, 700 E. Vereda Sur, Palm Springs CA 92262. (619)325-5352. Editorial Director: LeeOna S. Hostrop. Senior Editor: Dr. Richard W. Hostrop. Estab. 1972. Publishes hardcover and paperback originals. Averages 6-12 titles/year; receives 100 submissions annually. 75% of books from first-time authors; 90% of books from unagented writers. Average print order for a writer's first book is 2,500. Offers 5-15% royalty, based on wholesale and retail price. No advance. Publishes book an average of 9 months after acceptance. Reports in 3 weeks.
Nonfiction: Educational management, gifted education, futuristics and textbooks. Accepts nonfiction translations in above areas. Submit complete ms with SASE. Reviews artwork/photos as part of ms package.
Recent Nonfiction Title: *The Effective School Administrator*, by Richard W. Hostrop.
Tips: "ETC will seriously consider textbook manuscripts in any knowledge area in which the author can guarantee a first-year adoption of not less than 500 copies. Special consideration is given to those authors who are capable and willing to submit their completed work in camera-ready, typeset form."

M. EVANS AND CO., INC., 216 E. 49 St., New York NY 10017. FAX: (212)486-4544. Editor-in-Chief: George C. deKay. Publishes hardcover originals. Royalty schedule to be negotiated. Averages 30-40 titles/year. 5% of books from unagented writers. Publishes book an average of 8 months after acceptance. "No mss should be sent unsolicited. A letter of inquiry is essential." Reports in 2 months.
Nonfiction and Fiction: "We publish a general trade list of adult fiction and nonfiction, cookbooks and semireference works. The emphasis is on selectivity because we publish only 30 titles a year. Our general fiction list, which is very small, represents an attempt to combine quality with commercial potential. We also publish westerns and romance novels. Our most successful nonfiction titles have been related to health and the behavioral sciences. No limitation on subject. A writer should clearly indicate what his book is all about, frequently the task the writer performs least well. His credentials, although important, mean less than his ability to convince this company that he understands his subject and that he has the ability to communicate a message worth hearing." Reviews artwork/photos.
Tips: "Writers should review our catalog (available for 9 × 12 envelope with 3 first class stamps) or the *Publishers Trade List Annual* before making submissions."

For explanation of symbols, see the Key to Symbols and Abbreviations on Page 5. For unfamiliar words, see the Glossary.

EVERGREEN COMMUNICATIONS, INC., 2085-A Sperry Ave., Ventura CA 93003. (805)650-9248. Co-publisher/Managing Editor: Mary Beckwith. Estab. 1989. Publishes trade paperback originals. Averages 4-6 titles/year. 50% of books from first-time authors; 90% from unagented writers. Pays 12% royalty on wholesale price. Offers $500 average advance. Publishes book an average of 18 months after acceptance. Simultaneous submissions OK. Reports in 2 weeks on queries; 2 months on mss. Manuscript guidelines for #10 SAE and 2 first class stamps.

Nonfiction: Coffee table book, how-to, juvenile, reference, self-help, devotionals, personal experience. Subjects include child guidance/parenting, Christianity women's issues/studies, inspirational. Submit outline/synopsis and sample chapters. Reviews artwork/photos as part of ms package.

Recent Nonfiction Title: *Help for Hurting Moms*, by Kathy Collard Miller.

Fiction: Adventure, juvenile, mystery, Christian, romance, young adult. Submit outline/synopsis and sample chapters.

Tips: "We believe there's a trend to get back to the basics. We want to see manuscripts that speak to the needs of everyday people, written in a basic, easy-to-read style; that offer encouragement, through solid—yet basic—teaching, and good family entertainment, with values based on Christian-Judeo standards. Research the market, send for publisher submission guidelines, then submit the most complete, professional proposal possible. First impressions count."

FABER & FABER, INC., Division of Faber & Faber, Ltd., London, England; 50 Cross St., Winchester MA 01890. (617)721-1427. Contact: Editorial Assistant. Estab. 1976. Publishes hardcover and trade paperback originals, and trade paperback reprints. Averages 20 titles/year; receives 600 submissions annually. 10% of books from first-time authors; 25% of books from unagented writers. Pays 10% royalty on wholesale or retail price; advance varies. Publishes book an average of 1 year after acceptance. Simultaneous submissions OK. Reports in 6 weeks on queries; 3 months on mss. Book catalog for 9×12 SAE and 4 first class stamps; writer's guidelines for #10 SASE.

Nonfiction: Anthologies, biography, contemporary culture, film and screenplays, history and natural history. Subjects include Americana, animals, pop/rock music, New England, and sociology. Query with synopsis and outline with SASE. Reviews artwork/photos as part of ms package.

Recent Nonfiction Title: *Tula Hatti: The Last Great Elephant*, by Byrne.

Fiction: Collections, ethnic, experimental, juvenile (8-12), and regional. No historical/family sagas or mysteries. Query with synopsis and outline with SASE.

Recent Fiction Title: *Life After Death and Other Stories*.

Tips: "We are concentrating on subjects that have consistently done well for us. These include popular culture; serious, intelligent rock and roll books; anthologies; and literary, somewhat quirky fiction. Please do not send entire ms; please include SASE for reply."

FACTS ON FILE, INC., 460 Park Ave. S., New York NY 10016. (212)683-2244. Associate Publisher: Gerard Helferich. Estab. 1941. Publishes hardcover originals and reprints. Averages 125 titles/year; receives approximately 2,000 submissions annually. 25% of books from unagented writers. Pays 10-15% royalty on retail price. Offers average $10,000 advance. Simultaneous submissions OK. Query for electronic submissions. No submissions returned without SASE. Reports in 6 weeks on queries. Free book catalog.

Nonfiction: Reference and other informational books on business and economics, cooking and foods (no cookbooks), health, history, hobbies (but no how-to), entertainment, natural history, philosophy, psychology, recreation, religion, language and sports. "We need serious, informational books for a targeted audience. All our books must have strong library interest, but we also distribute books effectively to the book trade." No computer books, technical books, cookbooks, biographies, pop psychology, humor, do-it-yourself crafts, fiction or poetry. Query or submit outline/synopsis and a sample chapter.

Recent Nonfiction Title: *Shakespeare A to Z*, by Charles Boyce.

Tips: "Our audience is school and public libraries for our more reference-oriented books and libraries, schools and bookstores for our less reference-oriented informational titles."

*FAIRLEIGH DICKINSON UNIVERSITY PRESS, 285 Madison Ave., Madison NJ 07940. (201)593-8564. Director: Harry Keyishian. Estab. 1967. Publishes hardcover originals. Averages 30 titles/year; receives 300 submissions annually. 33% of books from first-time authors; 100% of books from unagented writers. Average print order for a writer's first book is 1,000. "Contract is arranged through Associated University Presses of Cranbury, New Jersey. We are a *selection* committee only." Subsidy publishes (nonauthor) 2% of books. Publishes book an average of 18 months after acceptance. Reports in 2 weeks on queries; 4 months average on mss.

Nonfiction: Reference and scholarly books. Subjects include art, business and economics, Civil War, film, history, Jewish studies, literary criticism, music, philosophy, politics, psychology, sociology and women's studies. Looking for scholarly books in all fields. No nonscholarly books. Query with outline/synopsis and sample chapters. Reviews artwork/photos as part of ms package.

Recent Nonfiction Title: *Reading Shakespeare in Performance*, by James P. Lusardi and June Schlueter.

Tips: "Research must be up to date. Poor reviews result when authors' bibliographies and notes don't reflect current research. We follow *Chicago Manual of Style* style in scholarly citations."

*FALCON PRESS PUBLISHING CO., INC., P.O. Box 1718, Helena MT 59624. (406)442-6597. FAX: (406)442-2995. Publisher: Bill Schneider. Estab. 1978. Imprint is Skyhouse Publications. Publishes hardcover and trade paperback originals. Averages 20-30 titles/year. Subsidy publishes 20% of books. Pays 8-15% royalty on net price or pays flat fee. Publishes book an average of 6 months after ms is in final form. Reports in 1 month on queries. Free book catalog.

Nonfiction: "We're primarily interested in ideas for recreational guidebooks and books on regional outdoor subjects for either adults or children.We can only respond to submissions that fit these categories." No fiction or poetry. Query only; do not send ms.

Recent Nonfiction Title: *The Hiker's Guide to California*.

*THE FAMILY ALBUM, Rt. 1, Box 42, Glen Rock PA 17327. (717)235-2134. FAX: (717)235-8042. Contact: Ron Lieberman. Estab. 1969. Publishes hardcover originals and reprints and software. Averages 4 titles/year; receives 150 submissions annually. 30% of books from first-time authors; 100% of books from unagented writers. Average print order for a writer's first book is 1,000. Subsidy publishes 20% of books. Pays royalty on wholesale price. Publishes book an average of 10 months after acceptance. Simultaneous submissions OK. Query for electronic submissions. Reports in 2 months. Include SASE for ms return.

Nonfiction: "Significant works in the field of (nonfiction) bibliography. Worthy submissions in the field of Pennsylvania history, biography, folk art and lore. We are also seeking materials relating to books, literacy, and national development. Special emphasis on Third World countries, and the role of printing in international development." No religious material. Submit outline/synopsis and sample chapters.

FARRAR, STRAUS AND GIROUX, INC., 19 Union Sq. W., New York NY 10003. Publisher, Books for Young Readers: Stephen Roxburgh. Editor-in-Chief, Books for Young Readers: Margaret Ferguson. Publishes hardcover originals. Receives 5,000 submissions annually. Pays royalty; advance. Publishes book an average of 18 months after acceptance. Reports in 3 months. Catalog for #10 SAE and 3 first class stamps.

Nonfiction and Fiction: "We are primarily interested in fiction picture books and novels for children and middle readers and in nonfiction—both in picture book and longer formats." Submit outline/synopsis and sample chapters. Reviews copies of artwork/photos as part of ms package.

Recent Fiction Title: *Celine*, by Brock Cole.

Recent Picture Book Title: *Carl's Christmas*, by Alexandra Day.

Tips: "Study our style and our list."

FAWCETT JUNIPER, Imprint of Ballantine/Del Rey/Fawcett/Ivy, Division of Random House, 201 E. 50th St., New York NY 10022. (212)751-2600. Editor-in-Chief, Vice President: Leona Nevler. Publishes 24 titles/year. Pays royalty. Publishes book an average of 1 year after acceptance. Simultaneous submissions OK. Reports in 2 months on queries; in 4 months on mss. Free book catalog.

Nonfiction: Adult books.

Recent Nonfiction Title: *All I Need to Know I Learned in Kindergarten*, by Robert Fulghum.

Fiction: Juvenile, mainstream/contemporary, young adult. Query.

Recent Fiction Title: *Seven Against the Dealer*, Cynthia Voigt.

FEARON/JANUS PUBLISHERS, Subsidiary of Simon & Schuster, 500 Harbor Blvd., Belmont CA 94002. (415)592-7810. Publisher: Carol Hegarty. Averages 100-120 titles/year. Pays royalty or fee outright. Reports in 1 month. Book catalog and ms guidelines for $1.50.

Nonfiction: Educational. Query or submit synopsis.

Recent Nonfiction Title: *Our Century Magazine*, (social studies).

Fiction: "We are looking for easy-to-read fiction suitable for middle school and up. We prefer the major characters to be young adults or adults."

Recent Fiction Title: *An American Family*, by Bledsoe/Jones.

‡J.G. FERGUSON PUBLISHING COMPANY, Suite 250, 200 West Monroe, Chicago IL 60606. Editorial Director: C.J. Summerfield. Publishes hardcover originals. Firm averages 4-8 titles/year. Pays by project. Reports in 3 months on queries.

Nonfiction: Reference. "We publish work specifically for the high school/college library reference market. Nothing is a single-author project. They are mainly encyclopedic in nature. We mainly publish medical and career encyclopedias. No mass market, scholarly, or juvenile books, please." Query or submit outline/synopsis and one sample chapter.

Recent Nonfiction Title: *The Encyclopedia of Career and Vocational Guidance.*

‡FIESTA BOOKS INC., P.O. Box 51234, Phoenix AZ 85076. (602)820-4771. Acquisitions Editor: Amber Lee. Estab. 1987. Publishes trade paperback originals. Firm averages 5 titles/year. 80% of books from first-time authors. Pays royalty (varies) on wholesale price. Publishes book an average of 1 year after acceptance. Reports in 3 months on queries. Book catalog and manuscript guidelines for #10 SASE.

Nonfiction: How-to, self-help. Subjects include business, child guidance/parenting, health/medicine, regional, travel. "We are primarily a regional (Southwest) publisher, expanding to include a line of health and family related books. Please ask yourself 'Who would be willing to spend $10-20 to buy this book?' If you can specifically identify and describe those buyers we may be interested." Query. Submit outline/synopsis and sample chapters.

Recent Nonfiction Title: *The Truth Just Changed*, by Gary Fagg.

Tips: "If I were a writer trying to market a book today, I would prepare a detailed marketing strategy, including statistical information on the potential audience."

‡*FILTER PRESS, P.O. Box 5, Palmer Lake CO 80133. (719)481-2523. President: Gilbert L. Campbell. Publishes trade paperback originals and reprints. Firm averages 6-7 titles/year. Receives 100 submissions/year. 5% of books are from first time authors. 100% from unagented writers. Subsidy publishes 10% of books, "if the book has merit, but it is not one we would commission." Pays 6-10% royalties on wholesale price. Publishes ms an average of 6-8 months after acceptance. SASE. Reports in 2 weeks on queries.

Nonfiction: Cookbook and how-to. Subjects include Americana, anthropology/archaeology, cooking, foods and nutrition, ethnic, hobbies, regional and travel. "We will consider some Western Americana, up to 72 pages. We do not want family diaries. Most of our works are reprints of 19th century published things on Indians, Gold rushes, western exploration, etc. Very rarely do we use unsolicited material. I dream up a project, find an author in 90% of them." Query. Review artwork/photos as part of ms package.

Recent Nonfiction Title: *West on Wood*, by Choda (collections of old engravings).

FINANCIAL SOURCEBOOKS, Division of Sourcebooks, Inc., P.O. Box 313, Naperville IL 60566. (312)961-2161. Publisher: Dominique Raccah. Estab. 1987. Publishes hardcover and trade paperback originals. Firm averages 15 titles/year. 50% of books from first-time authors; 100% from unagented writers. Pays 5-15% royalty on wholesale price, or buys mss outright. Publishes book an average of 6 months after acceptance. Simultaneous submissions OK. Query for electronic submissions. Reports in 1 month on queries. "We do not want to see complete manuscripts." Book catalog free for SASE.

Nonfiction: Reference, technical and textbook. Subjects include business and finance, computers, money management, small business and economics/banking. "We publish books, directories and newsletters for financial executives. We also publish more general books, particularly in business and finance. We are now looking for additional projects. The books of interest to us will establish a standard in their domain. We look for books with a well-defined, strong market such as reference works or books with a technical, informative bent." Query or submit outline/synopsis and sample chapters (2-3 chapters, not the first). Reviews artwork/photos as part of ms package.

Recent Nonfiction Title: *Future Vision: The 189 Most Important Trends of the 1990s.*

Tips: "Executives today are bombarded with information in most every form through much of their working day. Writers can easily sell us books that will help a busy professional deal with the workload more productively. That means books that 1.) compile otherwise difficult to obtain (but useful) information; or 2.) develop new concepts or ideas that will help executives "work smarter"; or 3.) reformat concepts or information executives need into some more useful or digestible form (e.g. graphics, tutorials, etc.)."

DONALD I. FINE, INC., 19 W. 21st St., New York NY 10010. (212)727-3270. Imprints include Primus Library of Contemporary Americana. Publishes hardcover originals and trade paperback originals and reprints. Firm averages 75-80 titles/year. Receives 1,000 submissions/year. 30% of books from first-time authors. Pays royalty on retail price. Advance varies. Publishes book an average of 1 year after acceptance. Book catalog for #10 SASE.

Nonfiction: Biography, cookbook, humor, self-help. Subjects include history, military/war and sports. All unsolicited mss are returned unopened. Reviews artwork/photos as part of ms package.
Recent Nonfiction Title: *April Fool's: An Insider's Account of the Rise and Fall of Drexel Burnham*, by Dan G. Stone.
Fiction: Adventure, ethnic, fantasy, historical, horror, humor, literary, mainstream/contemporary, mystery, science fiction, suspense and western. All unsolicited mss are returned unopened.
Recent Fiction Title: *Hammerheads*, by Dale Brown.

FIREBRAND BOOKS, 141 The Commons, Ithaca NY 14850. (607)272-0000. Publisher: Nancy K. Bereano. Estab. 1985. Publishes hardcover and trade paperback originals. Averages 8-10 titles/year; receives 300-400 submissions annually. 50% of books from first-time authors; 90% of books from unagented writers. Pays 7-9% royalty on retail price, or makes outright purchase. Publishes book an average of 18 months after acceptance. Simultaneous submissions OK "with notification." Reports in 2 weeks on queries; 2 months on mss. Free book catalog.
Nonfiction: Criticism and essays. Subjects include feminism and lesbianism. Submit complete ms.
Recent Nonfiction Title: *A Burst of Light*, by Audre Lorde.
Fiction: Will consider all types of feminist and lesbian fiction.
Recent Fiction Title: *Trash*, by Dorothy Allison.
Recent Poetry Title: *Crime Against Nature*, by Minnie Bruce Pratt.
Tips: "Our audience includes feminists, lesbians, ethnic audiences, and other progressive people."

FISHER BOOKS, P.O. Box 38040, Tucson AZ 85740-8040. (602)292-9080. Contact: Editorial Submissions Director. Estab. 1987. Publishes trade paperback originals and trade paperback reprints. Firm averages 20 titles/year. 25% of books from first-time authors; 50% from unagented writers. Pays 10-15% royalty on wholesale price. Simultaneous submissions OK. Reports in 1 month. Book catalog for 3 first class stamps.
Nonfiction: Automotive, cookbook, how-to and self-help. Subjects include automotive, cooking, foods and nutrition, gardening, health/medicine, psychology. Submit outline/synopsis and sample chapters. Include return postage.
Recent Nonfiction Title: *Cookbook for the 90s*, by Helen V. Fisher.

J. FLORES PUBLICATIONS, P.O. Box 163001, Miami FL 33116. Editor: Eli Flores. Estab. 1982. Publishes trade paperback originals and reprints. Averages 10 titles/year. 99% of books from unagented writers. Pays 10-15% royalty on net sales; no advance. Publishes book an average of 1 year after acceptance. Simultaneous submissions OK. Reports in 1 month on queries; 6 weeks on mss. Book catalog and ms guidelines for 6 × 9 SAE with 2 first class stamps.
Nonfiction: How-to, illustrated book and self-help. "We need original nonfiction manuscripts on outdoor adventure, military science, weaponry, current events, self-defense, true crime (especially need mss on true crime for new line), and military history. How-to manuscripts are given priority." No pre-Vietnam material. Query with outline and 2-3 sample chapters. Reviews artwork/photos. "Photos are accepted as part of the manuscript package and are strongly encouraged."
Recent Nonfiction Title: *The Force Option*, by Brett Woods.
Tips: "Trends include illustrated how-to books on a specific subject. Be thoroughly informed on your subject and technically accurate."

FOCAL PRESS, Subsidiary of Butterworth-Heinemann Publishers, Division of Reed Publishing (USA) Inc., 80 Montvale Ave., Stoneham MA 02180. (617)438-8464. Senior Editor: Karen M. Speerstra. Estab. 1972. Imprint publishes hardcover and paperback originals and reprints. Other imprint is Butterworth Architecture. Averages 30-35 UK-US titles/year; entire firm averages 60-70 titles/year; receives 500-700 submissions annually. 25% of books from first-time authors; 90% of books from unagented writers. Pays 10-12% royalty on wholesale price; offers $1,500 average advance. Publishes book an average of 1 year after acceptance. Simultaneous submissions OK. Reports in 2 months. Free book catalog and ms guidelines.
Nonfiction: How-to, reference, technical and textbooks in media arts: photography, film and cinematography, broadcasting theater and performing arts. High-level scientific/technical monographs are also considered. We generally do not publish collections of photographs or books composed primarily of photographs. Our books are text-oriented, with artwork serving to illustrate and expand on points in the text." Query preferred, or submit outline/synopsis and sample chapters or complete ms. Reviews artwork/photos as part of ms package.
Recent Nonfiction Title: *Photojournalism: The Professional's Approach, 2nd Ed.*, by Ken Kobre.

FORMAN PUBLISHING, INC., Suite 201, 2932 Wilshire Blvd., Santa Monica CA 90403. FAX: (213)453-4663. President: Len Forman. Executive Vice President: Claudia Forman. Estab. 1982. Publishes hardcover and trade paperback. Averages 6 titles/year; receives 1,000 submissions/year. 100% of books from first-time authors. 90% of books from unagented writers. Pays 6-15% royalty. Simultaneous submissions OK. Publishes book an average of 18 months after acceptance. Reports in 1 month on queries; 3 months on mss. Book catalog for 9×12 SASE.

Nonfiction: Cookbooks, how-to and self-help. Subjects include art, business and economics, cooking and foods, health, nature and psychology. Submit outline/synopsis and sample chapters. Reviews artwork/photos as part of ms package.

Recent Nonfiction Title: *Epouste Flunt*, by David Snyder (interior design).

FOUR WALLS EIGHT WINDOWS, P.O. Box 548, New York NY 10014. Estab. 1987. Publishes hardcover and trade paperback originals and trade paperback reprints. Averages 18 titles/year. Receives 1,000 submissions/year. 20% of books from first-time authors. 66% from unagented writers. Pays royalty (depends—negotiated contract) on retail price. Offers $2,000 average advance. Publishes book an average of 10 months after acceptance. Reports in 2 weeks on queries; 4 months on mss. Free book catalog.

Nonfiction: Political, investigative. Subjects include art/architecture, cooking, foods and nutrition, government/politics, history, language/literature, nature/environment, science, travel. We do not want New Age works. Query first. Submit outline with SASE. All sent without SASE returned unopened.

Recent Nonfiction Title: *Harvey Wasserman's History of The U.S.*, by Harvey Wasserman (history).

Fiction: Erotica, ethnic, experimental, feminist, horror, literary, mystery, science fiction. "No romance, popular." Query first. Submit outline with SASE.

Recent Fiction Title: *Man with The Golden Arm*, by Nelson Algren (novel).

Tips: "Send us something original, unusual, off-beat, possibly 'alternative.' "

‡FPMI COMMUNICATIONS, INC., 3322 S. Memorial Pkwy., Suite 40, Bldg. 400, Huntsville AL 35801. (205)882-3042. FAX: (205)882-1046. President: Ralph Smith. Publishes trade paperback originals. Averages 4-6 titles/year. Receives 4-5 submissions/year. 60% of books from first-time authors; 100% from unagented writers. Pays 15% on retail price. Publishes book an average of 1 year after acceptance. Simultaneous submissions OK. Query for electronic submissions. Reports in 3 weeks on queries; 2 months on mss. Free book catalog.

Nonfiction: Technical. Subjects include government/politics, labor relations and personnel issues. "We will be publishing books for government and business on topics such as sexual harassment, drug testing, and how to deal with leave abuse by employees. Our books are practical, how-to books for a supervisor or manager. Scholarly theoretical works do not interest our audience." Submit outline/synopsis and sample chapters or send complete ms.

Recent Nonfiction Title: *Federal Manager's Guide to TQM*, by Dr. Jean G. Lamkin.

Tips: "We are interested in books that are practical, easy-to-read and less than 150 pages. Primary audience is federal managers and supervisors—particularly first and second level. If I were a writer trying to market a book today, I would emphasize practical topics with plenty of examples in succinct, concrete language."

SAMUEL FRENCH, INC., 45 W. 25th St., New York NY 10010. (212)206-8990. FAX: (212)206-1429. Editor: Lawrence Harbison. Estab. 1830. Subsidiaries include Samuel French Ltd. (London); Samuel French (Canada) Ltd. (Toronto); Samuel French, Inc. (Hollywood); and Baker's Plays (Boston). Estab. 1830. Publishes paperback acting editions of plays. Averages 100-120 titles/year; receives 1,200 submissions annually, mostly from unagented playwrights. About 10% of publications are from first-time authors; 20% from unagented writers. Pays 10% book royalty on retail price. Pays 90% stock production royalty; 80% amateur production royalty. Offers variable advance. Publishes book an average of 6 months after acceptance. Simultaneous submissions OK. Reports immediately on queries; from 6 weeks to 8 months on mss. Book catalog $1.50; ms. Guidelines $4.

Nonfiction: Acting editions of plays.

Tips: "Broadway and Off-Broadway hit plays, light comedies and mysteries have the best chance of selling to our firm. Our market is theater producers—both professional and amateur—and actors. Read as many plays as possible of recent vintage to keep apprised of today's market; write small-cast plays with good female roles; and be one hundred percent professional in approaching publishers and producers (see Guidelines)."

‡FROMM INTERNATIONAL, 560 Lexington Ave., New York NY 10022. (212)308-4010. FAX: (212)371-5187. Managing Editor: Thomas Thornton. Estab. 1982. Publishes hardcover originals and trade paperback reprints. 50% of books are original; 50% are reprints. Firm averages 8-10 titles/year. Receives 100-150 submissions/year. Pays 10-15% royalty on retail price. Offers $3,000-3,500 average advance. Publishes book an average of 9 months after acceptance. Reports in 1 month on queries. Book catalog free on request. Manuscript guidelines not available (follow *Chicago Manual of Style*).

Nonfiction: Biography, textbook. Subjects include history, music/dance, psychology, translation, cultural history. Query. Submit outline/synopsis and sample chapters.
Recent Nonfiction Title: *Architects of Fortune*, by Elaine Hochman (history).
Fiction: Literary. "We publish four to six fiction titles per year, including translations from European languages. We have one fiction title for Spring 92 and are currently considering a couple of submissions. No mainstream fiction." Query. Submit outline/synopsis and sample chapters.
Recent Fiction Title: *The Couple*, by Thomas Huerlimann (belles lettres translation).
Tips: "Placing first novels has become increasingly difficult, but we are still looking for good fiction. While we are not looking for experimental prose, we definitely don't want mass-market novels. A 'European touch' is preferred. Our audience consists of educated readers who love literature, read some classics once in a while but also want to keep abreast of what is currently going on in the world outside as well as inside. We like good stories but never for the sake of merely being commercial. If I were a writer trying to market a book today, I would write a good book, rewrite it, try to analyze as best as possible my target readership, and with that readership in mind, rewrite the book again. Then I'd look for an agent or publisher, writing a well thought-out outline and a query letter, keeping in mind what an editor looks for (and thus proving that I can write what I have to say but at the same time am able to write for a specific market—in this case, the editorial market). For example, I would *not* put into a query letter that I'm the greatest writer since Solomon (which has happened to me); editors like to judge for themselves."

GALLAUDET UNIVERSITY PRESS, 800 Florida Ave. NE, Washington DC 20002. (202)651-5488. Publishing Assistant: Ann Kammerer. Estab. 1980. Imprints include Kendall Green Publications, Clerc Books, Gallaudet University Press. Publishes hardcover originals, and trade paperback and mass market paperback originals and reprints. Firm averages 15 titles/year. Receives 450 submissions/year. 50% of books from first-time authors; 95% from unagented writers. Pays 10-15% royalty on wholesale price (net). Publishes book an average of 12-18 months after acceptance. Simultaneous submissions OK. Query for electronic submissions. Reports in 3 months. Free manuscript guidelines.
Nonfiction: Biography, illustrated book, juvenile, reference, self-help, technical, textbook and sign language. All topics must relate to hearing impairment/deafness in some way (through topic doesn't have to focus on hearing impairment/deafness). Subjects include child guidance/parenting, education, health/medicine, history, language/literature, psychology, regional, science, sociology, sports, translation and travel. "Because of the press's mission to publish books for and about deafness/hearing impairment, we'll accept books as long as they're somehow related." Submit outline/synopsis and sample chapters or complete ms. Reviews artwork/photos as part of ms package.
Recent Nonfiction Title: *Deaf Sport: The Impact of Sports Within the Deaf Community*, by David Stewart.
Fiction: For children/young adults only, adventure, ethnic, fantasy, historical, humor, literary, mainstream/contemporary, mystery, picture books, plays, science fiction, short story collections, suspense. Do not publish adult fiction. (Most categories are considered as long as they relate to hearing impairment in some way.) "We need fiction for 8 to 12-year-olds and young adults with hearing-impaired character(s), although the hearing-impairment does not need to be the focus of the story." Submit outline/synopsis and sample chapters or complete ms.
Recent Fiction Title: *Clerc: The Story of His Early Years*, by Cathryn Carroll (fictionalized biography).
Tips: "The market is wide open and growing for books relating to hearing impairment due especially to an increased awareness of deafness and sign language among the public. Individuals in our audience come from many walks of life and include every age group. The common denominator among them is an interest and /or openness to learn more about hearing impairment/deafness."

*GARDNER PRESS, INC., 19 Union Square W., New York NY 10003. (212)924-8293. FAX: (212)242-6339. Publisher: Gardner Spungin. Estab. 1975. Imprint is Gestalt Institute of Cleveland Press. Publishes hardcover and paperback originals and reprints. Firm averages 15 titles/year. Receives 150 submissions/year. 10% of books from first-time authors; 90% from unagented writers. Subsidy publishes 10% of books. Pays 6-15% royalty on net price. Publishes book an average of 8-10 months after acceptance. Simultaneous submissions OK. Reports in 3 weeks. Free book catalog.
Nonfiction: Reference, self-help and textbook. Subjects include child guidance/parenting, education, health/medicine, psychology, recreation, religion, sociology, sports, translation and women's issues/studies. Query.
Recent Nonfiction Title: *Woman and Alcohol: The Journey Back*, by M. Ellen Stammer, Ed.D.

GARRETT PARK PRESS, P.O. Box 190, Garrett Park MD 20896. Publisher: Robert Calvert. Estab. 1967. Publishes trade paperback originals. Firm averages 6 titles/year. Receives 15 submissions/year. 20% of books from first-time authors. 100% from unagented writers. Pays 10-15% royalty on wholesale or retail price. Publishes book an average of 8 months after acceptance. Reports in 1 month on queries; 2 months on mss. Free book catalog.

Nonfiction: Reference. Subjects include education, ethnic. Query.

GASLIGHT PUBLICATIONS, 626 N. College Ave., Bloomington IN 47404. (812)332-5169. Publisher: Jack Tracy. Estab. 1979. Imprints include McGuffin Books. Publishes hardcover originals. Averages 6 titles/year. Receives 15-20 submissions/year. 75% of books from first-time authors; 90% from un-agented writers. Pays 10% royalty on retail price. Publishes book an average of 1 year after acceptance. Simultaneous submissions OK. Reports in 1 month. Free book catalog.
Nonfiction: "We publish specialized studies of the mystery genre and related fields: biography, criticism, analysis, reference, film. Submissions should be serious, well-researched, not necessarily for the scholar, but for readers who are already experts in their own right. 12,000 words minimum." Query, submit outline/synopsis and sample chapters or send complete ms. Reviews artwork/photos as part of ms package.
Recent Nonfiction Title: *Nova 57 Minor: The Waxing and Waning of the 61st Adventure of Sherlock Holmes,* by Jon L. Lellenberg.
Tips: "Our purchasers tend to be public libraries and knowledgeable mystery aficionados."

GAY SUNSHINE PRESS AND LEYLAND PUBLICATIONS, P.O. Box 410690, San Francisco CA 94141. (415)824-3184. Editor: Winston Leyland. Estab. 1970. Publishes hardcover and trade paperback originals and trade paperback reprints. Averages 10 titles/year. Pays royalty or makes outright purchase. Reports in 3 weeks on queries; 1 month on mss. Book catalog $1.
Nonfiction: How-to and gay lifestyle topics. "We're interested in innovative literary nonfiction which deals with gay lifestyles." No long personal accounts, academic or overly formal titles. Query. "After query is returned by us, submit outline/synopsis and sample chapters. All unsolicited mss are returned unopened."
Recent Nonfiction Title: *Gay Roots: Twenty Years of Gay Sunshine, An Anthology of Gay History, Sex, Politics and Culture.*
Fiction: Erotica, ethnic, experimental, historical, mystery, science fiction and gay fiction in translation. "Interested in well-written novels on gay themes; also short story collections. We have a high literary standard for fiction." Query. "After query is returned by us, submit outline/synopsis and sample chapters. All unsolicited mss are returned unopened."
Recent Fiction Title: *Crystal Boys,* by Pai Hsien-yung (translated by Howard Goldblatt).

*GENEALOGICAL PUBLISHING CO., INC., 1001 N. Calvert St., Baltimore MD 21202. (301)837-8271. FAX: (301)752-8492. Editor-in-Chief: Michael H. Tepper, Ph.D. Estab. 1959. Publishes hardcover originals and reprints. Subsidy publishes 10% of books. Averages 80 titles/year; receives 400 submissions annually. 50% of books from first-time authors; 100% of books from unagented writers. Average print order for a writer's first book is 2,000-3,000. Offers straight 10% royalty on retail price. Publishes book an average of 6 months after acceptance. Reports "immediately." Enclose SAE and return postage.
Nonfiction: Reference, genealogy, and immigration records. "Our requirements are unusual, so we usually treat each author and his subject in a way particularly appropriate to his special skills and subject matter. Guidelines are flexible, but it is expected that an author will consult with us in depth. Most, though not all, of our original publications are offset from camera-ready typescript. Since most genealogical reference works are compilations of vital records and similar data, tabular formats are common. We hope to receive more ms material covering vital records and ships' passenger lists. We want family history compendia, basic methodology in genealogy, heraldry, and immigration records." Prefers query first, but will look at outline and sample chapter or complete ms. Reviews artwork/photos as part of ms package.
Recent Nonfiction Title: *The Researcher's Guide to American Genealogy,* by Val Greenwood.

‡GENERAL HALL, INC., 5 Talon Way, Dix Hills NY 11746. (516)243-0155. President: Ravi Mehra. Publishes hardcover and trade paperback originals. Firm averages 10-12 titles/year. Receives 75-100 submissions/year. 20% of books are from first-time authors. 100% from unagented writers. Pays 10% royalties on wholesale price. Publishes book 8 months after acceptance. Simultaneous submissions OK. Query for electronic submission. Reports in 2 months on queries. Book catalog for 8×10 SAE and 6 first class stamps.

For information on book publishers' areas of interest, see the nonfiction and fiction sections in the Book Publishers Subject Index.

Nonfiction: Subjects include education, ethnic, gay/lesbian, government/politics, sociology and women's issues/studies. "We publish only college textbooks." Submit outline/synopsis and sample chapters.
Recent Nonfiction Title: *A New Look at Black Families*, by Charles V. Willie.
Tips: "We are looking for basic textbooks. College students comprise our audience. If I were a writer trying to market a book today, I would study my competition first."

GIFTED EDUCATION PRESS, The Reading Tutorium, 10201 Yuma Ct., P.O. Box 1586, Manassas VA 22110. (703)369-5017. Publisher: Maurice D. Fisher. Estab. 1981. Publishes paperback originals for school districts and libraries. Averages 5 titles/year; receives 50 submissions annually. 100% of books from first-time authors; 100% of books from unagented writers. Pays royalty of $1 per book. Publishes book an average of 6 months after acceptance. Simultaneous submissions OK. Reports in 4 months. Book catalog and ms guidelines for #10 SAE with 2 first class stamps. Send letter of inquiry first. No unsolicited manuscripts will be accepted.
Nonfiction: How-to. Subjects include philosophy, psychology, education of the gifted; and how to teach adults to read. "Need books on how to educate gifted children—both theory and practice, and adult literacy. Also, we are searching for books on using computers with the gifted, and teaching the sciences to the gifted. Need rigorous books on procedures, methods, and specific curriculum for the gifted. Send letter of inquiry only. Do not send manuscripts or parts of manuscripts."
Recent Nonfiction Title: *Teaching Shakespeare to Gifted Students*, by Michael E. Walters.
Tips: "If I were a writer trying to market a book today, I would develop a detailed outline based upon intensive study of my field of interest. Present creative ideas in a rigorous fashion. Be knowledgeable about and comfortable with ideas. We are looking for books on using computers with gifted students; books on science and humanities education for the gifted; and books on how to teach adults to read."

GLENBRIDGE PUBLISHING LTD., 4 Woodland Lane, Macomb IL 61455. (309)833-5104. Editor: James A. Keene. Estab. 1986. Publishes hardcover originals and reprints, and trade paperback originals. Publishes 6 titles/year. Pays 10% royalty. Publishes book an average of 1 year after acceptance. Simultaneous submissions OK. Reports in 1 week on queries; 1 month on mss. Ms guidelines for #10 SASE.
Nonfiction: Reference and textbook. Subjects include Americana, business and economics, history, music, philosophy, politics, psychology and sociology. Query or submit outline/synopsis and sample chapters. Include SASE.
Recent Nonfiction Title: *Teachers Talk*, by John Godar.

THE GLOBE PEQUOT PRESS, INC., 138 W. Main St., Chester CT 06412. (203)526-9571. Managing Editor: Bruce Markot. Editorial Contact Person: Andrea Fuller. Imprints are Voyager Books and East Woods Books. Publishes hardcover and paperback originals and paperback reprints. Averages 70 titles/year; receives 1,500 submissions annually. 30% of books from first-time authors; 60% of books from unagented writers. Average print order for a writer's first book is 5,000-7,500. Offers 7½-10% royalty on net price; offers advances. Publishes book an average of 1 year after acceptance. Simultaneous submissions OK. Reports in 10 weeks. Book catalog for 9×12 SASE.
Nonfiction: Travel guidebooks (regional OK), natural history, outdoor recreation, gardening, carpentry, how-to, Americana, biography, and cookbooks. No doctoral theses, genealogies, or textbooks. Submit outline, table of contents, sample chapter(s), and resume/vita. Complete mss accepted. Reviews artwork/photos.

GLOBE PRESS BOOKS, P.O. Box 2045, Madison Square Station, New York NY 10159. (914)962-4614. Publisher: Joel Friedlander. Imprint is Fourth Way Books. Publishes hardcover and trade paperback originals. Averages 4 titles/year; receives 12 submissions/year. 25% of books from first-time authors. 50% of books from unagented writers. Pays royalty on retail price. Publishes book an average of 1 year after publication. Simultaneous submissions OK. Query for electronic submissions. Reports in 6 weeks. Book catalog for #10 SASE.
Nonfiction: Self-help and esoteric psychology. Subjects include history, philosophy and psychology. "We want manuscripts on east/west psychology and esoteric thought. No economics, politics or how-to books." Query or submit outline/synopsis and sample chapters. Reviews artwork/photos as part of ms package.
Recent Nonfiction Title: *Body of Light*, by John Mann and Lar Short.
Tips: "Well written, well thought-out mss on esoteric approaches to psychology, art, literature and history are needed."

DAVID R. GODINE, PUBLISHER, INC., 300 Masachusetts Ave., Boston MA 02115. (617)536-0761. Contact: Verba Mundi or Debbie Zeidenberg. Estab. 1970. Imprints are Nonpareil Books and Godine Storytellers. Publishes hardcover and trade paperback originals and reprints. Publishes 35 titles/year. 30% of books from first-time authors; 5-10% from unagented writers. Pays royalty on retail price.

Publishes ms an average of 18 months after acceptance. Simultaneous and photocopied submissions OK. Reports in 6 weeks.

Nonfiction: Biography, cookbooks, illustrated books, juvenile. Subjects include Americana, art/architecture, cooking, gardening, history, language/literature, music/dance, nature, photography, translation, travel. Needs more history and biography, less photography. No genealogies, sports books, college theses, celebrity address books, adventure/suspense, or romances. Query or submit ms. Reviews artwork/photos as part of complete ms package.

Recent Nonfiction Title: *Broken Vessels*, by Andre Dubus.

Fiction: Literary, mystery and translated fiction. No science fiction, fantasy, adventure, or religious books. Query or submit complete ms.

Recent Fiction Title: *The Bride Price*, by Grete Weil.

Tips: "In fiction, literary works appeal to us the most; that is, books that are thoughtful and well written as well as original in plot and intent."

‡GOLDEN WEST BOOKS, Box 80250, San Marino CA 91118. (213)283-3446. Editor-in-Chief: Donald Duke. Managing Editor: Vernice Dagosta. Publishes hardcover and paperback originals. Averages 4 titles/year. Receives 50 submissions annually. 50% of books from first-time authors; 100% of books from unagented writers. Pays 10% royalty contract; no advance. Publishes book an average of 3 months after acceptance. Simultaneous submissions OK. Reports in 1 month. Free book catalog.

Nonfiction: Publishes selected Western Americana and transportation Americana. Query or submit complete ms. "Illustrations and photographs will be examined if we like manuscript."

GOLDEN WEST PUBLISHERS, 4113 N. Longview, Phoenix AZ 85014. (602)265-4392. Editor: Hal Mitchell. Estab. 1973. Publishes trade paperback originals. Averages 5-6 titles/year; receives 200 submissions annually. 50% of books from first-time authors; 100% of books from unagented writers. Average print order for a writer's first book is 5,000. Pays 6-10% royalty on retail price. No advance. Publishes book an average of 6 months after acceptance. Simultaneous submissions OK. Query for electronic submissions. Reports in 2 weeks on queries; 1 month on mss. Book catalog for #10 SASE.

Nonfiction: Cookbooks, books on the Southwest and West. Subjects include cooking and foods, southwest history and outdoors, and travel. Query or submit outline/synopsis and sample chapters. Prefers query letter first. Reviews artwork/photos as part of ms package.

Recent Title: *Hiking Arizona*, by Don Kiefer.

Tips: "We are interested in Arizona and Southwest material, and cookbooks, and welcome material in these areas."

GOSPEL PUBLISHING HOUSE, Imprint of Assemblies of God General Council, 1445 Boonville Ave., Springfield MO 65802-1894. (417)862-2781. Book Editor: Glen Ellard. Estab. 1914. Firm publishes hardcover, trade and mass market paperback originals. Publishes 18 titles/year. Receives 380 submissions/year. 90% of books from first-time authors; 90% from unagented writers. Pays 10% royalty on retail price. Publishes book an average of 18 months after acceptance. Simultaneous submissions OK. Reports in 2 weeks on queries; 2 months on mss. Free book catalog and ms guidelines.

Nonfiction: Biography and self-help. Subjects include education (Christian or deaf), history (Assemblies of God), religion (Bible study, Christian living, devotional, doctrinal, evangelism, healing, Holy Spirit, missionary, pastoral, prophecy). "Gospel Publishing House is owned and operated by the Assemblies of God. Therefore, the doctrinal viewpoint of all books published is required to be compatible with our denominational positions." Query or submit outline/synopsis and sample chapters.

Recent Nonfiction Title: *Going It Alone*, by Bette Carter.

Tips: "We no longer publish fiction."

GOVERNMENT INSTITUTES, INC., 4 Research Place, Rockville MD 20850. (301)251-9250. Director of Acquisitions: Roland W. Schumann III. Estab. 1973. Imprint is State Environmental Law Compliance Center. Publishes hardcover and softcover originals. Averages 45 titles/year; receives 20 submissions annually. 50% of books from first-time authors; 100% of books from unagented writers. Pays variable royalty or fee. No advance. Publishes book an average of 2 months after acceptance. Simultaneous submissions OK. Reports in 1 month on queries; 2 months on mss. Book catalog available on request.

Nonfiction: Reference and technical. Subjects include environmental law, health, safety and real estate. Needs professional-level titles in those areas. Also looking for international environmental topics. Submit outline and sample chapters.

Recent Nonfiction Title: *Environmental Law Handbook, 10th Edition*, by J. Gordon Arbuckle, et al. (professional).

‡*GOWER PUBLISHING COMPANY, Old Post Rd., Brookfield VT 05036. (802)276-3162. FAX: (802)276-3837. President: James W. Gerard. Estab. 1978. Imprints include Avebury, Scolar Press, Edward Elgar and Wildwood House. Publishes hardcover originals and reprints and trade paperback originals. Averages 250 titles/year. Receives 100 submissions/year. 25% of books from first-time authors; 100% from unagented writers. Subsidy publishes 10% of books. Pays royalty on retail price or buys mss outright. Publishes book an average of 3 months after acceptance. Simultaneous submissions OK. Query for electronic submissions. Reports in 1 week on queries; 1 month on mss. Free book catalog and manuscript guidelines.

Nonfiction: Reference, technical and textbook. Subjects include agriculture/horticulture, art/architecture, business and economics, government/politics, money/finance, philosophy, religion and sociology. Submit outline/synopsis and sample chapters.

GRAPEVINE PUBLICATIONS, INC., P.O. Box 2449, Corvallis OR 97339. (503)754-0583. FAX: (503)754-6508. Managing Editor: Christopher M. Coffin. Developmental Editor: Daniel R. Coffin. Estab. 1983. Publishes trade paperback originals. Averages 6-10 titles/year; receives 200-300 submissions/year. 20% of books from first-time authors; 100% of books from unagented writers. Pays 6-9% royalty on retail price. Publishes book an average of 6 months after acceptance. Simultaneous submissions OK. Query for electronic submissions. Reports in 2 weeks on queries; 1 month on mss.

Nonfiction: Tutorials on technical subjects written for the layperson, innovative curricula or resources for math and science teachers. Subjects include math, science, computers, calculators, software, video, audio and other technical tools. Submit complete ms.

Recent Nonfiction Title: *Problem-Solving Situations: A Resource Book for Teachers of the 90s*, by Greenberg.

Tips: "We place heavy emphasis on readability, visual presentation, clarity, and reader participation. We will insist on numerous diagrams and illustrations, loosely-spaced text, large, easy-to-read formats, friendly, conversational writing, but tight, well-designed instruction. We disguise top-flight teaching as merely refreshing reading. The writer must be first and foremost a teacher who holds an engaging one-on-one conversation with the reader through the printed medium."

GRAPHIC ARTS CENTER PUBLISHING CO., 3019 NW Yeon Ave., P.O. Box 10306, Portland OR 97210. (503)226-2402. FAX: (503)223-1410. General Manager and Editor: Douglas Pfeiffer. Estab. 1968. Publishes hardcover originals. Averages 10 titles/year. Makes outright purchase, averaging $3,000.

Nonfiction: "All titles are pictorials with text. Text usually runs separately from the pictorial treatment. Authors must be previously published and are selected to complement the pictorial essay." Query.

Recent Nonfiction Title: *Utah*, by Ann Zwinger.

GRAPHIC ARTS TECHNICAL FOUNDATION, 4615 Forbes Ave., Pittsburgh PA 15213-3796. (412)621-6941. FAX: (412)621-3049. Editor-in-Chief: Thomas M. Destree. Assistant Editor: Pamela J. Groff. Estab. 1924. Publishes trade paperback originals. Firm averages 10 titles/year. Receives 15 submissions/year. 50% of books from first-time authors; 100% from unagented writers. Pays 5-15% royalty on average price. Publishes book an average of 1 year after acceptance. Query for electronic submissions. Reports in 1 month on queries; 2 months on mss. Book catalog for 9 × 12 SASE; manuscript guidelines for #10 SASE.

Nonfiction: How-to, reference, technical and textbook. Subjects include printing/graphic arts. "We want textbook/reference books about printing and related technologies, providing that the content does not overlap appreciably with any other GATF books in print or in production. Although original photography is related to printing, we do not anticipate publishing any books on that topic." Query or submit outline/synopsis and sample chapters. All queries and samples submitted must include ample return postage and appropriate return envelope to ensure a response. Reviews artwork/photos as part of ms package.

Recent Nonfiction Title: *Tone and Color Correction*, by Gary Field.

Tips: "Our typical audience would be students in high schools and colleges as well as trainees in the printing industry."

GRAYWOLF PRESS, Suite 203, 2402 University Ave., St. Paul MN 55114. Contact: Assistant Editor. Estab. 1974. Publishes hardcover and trade paperback originals and hardcover and trade paperback reprints. Averages 12-16 titles/year. Receives 2,000 submissions/year. 20% of books from first-time authors. Pays 6-12½% royalty on retail price; royalty advance varies. Publishes book an average of 9 to 18 months after acceptance. Simultaneous submissions OK but discouraged. Reports in 1 month on queries. Free book catalog.

Nonfiction: Literary essays and memoirs. "We do not publish mainstream romance novels, thrillers, science fiction, or mysteries." Query first.

Fiction: Literary novels and short story collections. Query first.

Recent Fiction Title: *Skywater*, by Melinda Worth Popham.

GREAT NORTHWEST PUBLISHING AND DISTRIBUTING COMPANY, INC., P.O. Box 10-3902, Anchorage AK 99510-3902. (907)373-0122. FAX: (907)376-0826. President: Marvin H. Clark Jr. Estab. 1979. Imprint is Alaska Outdoor Books. Publishes hardcover and trade paperback originals. Averages 5 titles/year; receives 22-25 submissions annually. 30% of books from first-time authors; 100% of books from unagented writers. Pays 10% royalty. Publishes book an average of 1 year after acceptance. Simultaneous submissions OK. Query for electronic submissions. Reports in 2 weeks on queries; 2 months on mss. Free book catalog.

Nonfiction: Biography and how-to. Subjects include Alaska and hunting. "Alaskana and hunting books by very knowledgeable hunters and residents of the Far North interest our firm." Query.

Recent Nonfiction Title: *Alaska Safari*, by Harold Schetzle.

Tips: "Pick a target audience first, subject second. Provide crisp, clear journalistic prose."

WARREN H. GREEN, INC., 8356 Olive Blvd., St. Louis MO 63132. FAX: (314)997-1788. Editor: Warren H. Green. Estab. 1966. Imprint is Fireside Books. Publishes hardcover originals. Offers "10-20% sliding scale of royalties based on quantity distributed. All books are short run, highly specialized, with no advance." Subsidy publishes about 1% of books, e.g., "books in philosophy and those with many color plates." Averages 30 titles/year; receives 200 submissions annually. 15% of books from first-time authors; 100% of books from unagented writers. "37% of total marketing is overseas." Catalog available on request. Publishes book an average of 10 months after acceptance. Simultaneous submissions OK. Query or submit outline and sample chapters. "Publisher requires 300-500 word statement of scope, plan, and purpose of book, together with curriculum vitae of author." Reports in 4 months.

Nonfiction: Medical and scientific. "Specialty monographs for practicing physicians and medical researchers. Books of 160 pages upward. Illustrated as required by subject. Medical books are non-textbook type, usually specialties within specialties, and no general books for a given specialty. For example, separate books on each facet of radiology, and not one complete book on radiology. Authors must be authorities in their chosen fields and accepted as such by their peers. Books should be designed for all doctors in English speaking world engaged in full or part time activity discussed in book. We would like to increase publications in the fields of radiology, anesthesiology, pathology, psychiatry, surgery and orthopedic surgery, obstetrics and gynecology, and speech and hearing." Also interested in books on health, philosophy, psychology and sociology. Reviews artwork/photos as part of ms package.

Recent Nonfiction Title: *Drug And Alcohol Abuse*, by Herrington.

GREENHAVEN PRESS, INC., P.O. Box 289009, San Diego CA 92128-9009. Senior Editor: Bonnie Szumski. Estab. 1970. Publishes hard and softcover educational supplementary materials and (non-trade) juvenile nonfiction. Averages 20-30 juvenile manuscripts published/year; all are works for hire; receives 100 submissions/year. 50% of juvenile books from first-time authors; 100% of juvenile books from unagented writers. Makes outright purchase for $1,500-3,500. Publishes book an average of 1 year after acceptance. Simultaneous (if specified) submissions OK. Book catalog for 9×12 SAE with 2 first class stamps.

Nonfiction: Juvenile. "We produce tightly formatted books for young people grades 4-6 and 7-9. Each series has specific requirements: Great Mysteries (5th-8th grade); Overviews (5th-8th grade); Opposing Viewpoints Juniors (5th-6th grade). Encyclopedia of Discovery and Invention (5th-8th grade). Potential writers should familiarize themselves with our catalog and senior high material. No unsolicited manuscripts." Query or submit outline/synopsis and sample chapters. Reviews artwork/photos as part of manuscript package.

Recent Nonfiction Title: *Garbage*, by Karen O'Connor.

Nonfiction Juvenile: *Pearl Harbor*, by Deborah Bacharach.

GROSSET & DUNLAP PUBLISHERS, Imprint of the Putnam Berkley Publishing Group, 200 Madison Ave., New York NY 10016. Editor-in-Chief: Jane O'Connor. Estab. 1898. Imprint includes Platt & Munk. Publishes hardcover and paperback originals. Averages 75 titles/year; receives more than 3,000 submissions annually. Publishes book an average of 18 months after acceptance. Simultaneous submissions OK. Reports in 10 weeks.

Nonfiction: Juveniles. Submit proposal or query first. Nature and science are of interest. Looks for new ways of looking at the world of a child.

Fiction: Juveniles, picture books for 3-7 age group and some higher. Submit proposal or query first.

Recent Fiction Title: *Whiskerville Board Books*, by Joanne Barkan.

Tips: "Nonfiction that is particularly topical or of wide interest in the mass market; a new concept for novelty format for preschoolers; and very well-written fiction on topics that appeal to parents of preschoolers have the best chance of selling to our firm. We want something new — a proposal for a new series for the ordinary picture book. You have a better chance if you have new ideas."

GROVE WIEDENFELD, Division of Grove Press Inc., 841 Broadway, New York NY 10003-4793. Did not want to be listed.

*GULF PUBLISHING CO., Book Division, P.O. Box 2608, Houston TX 77252-2608. (713)529-4301. FAX: (713)520-4438. Vice President: C.A. Umbach Jr. Editor-in-Chief: William J. Lowe. Estab. 1916. Imprints include Gulf, (sci-tech and business/management), Lone Star Books (regional Texas books) and Pisces Books, (travel and outdoor recreation line). Publishes hardcover and large format paperback originals and software. Averages 35 titles/year; receives 200 submissions annually. 1% of books from first-time authors; 100% of books from unagented writers. Subsidy publishes 5% of books. Pays 10% royalty on net income. Publishes book an average of 10 months after acceptance. Simultaneous submissions OK. Query for electronic submissions. Reports in 2 months. Free book catalog; ms guidelines for SASE.
Nonfiction: Popular science, business, management, reference, regional trade, scientific and technical. Submit outline/synopsis and 1-2 sample chapters. Reviews artwork/photos as part of ms package.
Recent Nonfiction Title: *Handbook of Business Quotations*, by Charles Lightfoot.
Tips: "Common mistakes writers make include calling first, not having a marketing plan of their own, and not matching publishers with their subject. Tell us the market, and how it can be reached at *reasonable* cost."

HALF HALT PRESS, INC., 6416 Burkittsville Rd., Middletown MD 21769. (301)371-9110. Publisher: Elizabeth Carnes. Estab. 1985. Publishes hardcover and trade paperback originals and reprints (90% originals, 10% reprints). Firm averages 8 titles/year. Receives 25 submissions/year. 50% of books from first-time authors. 50% from unagented authors. Pays 10-12½% royalty on retail price. Offers advance by agreement. Publishes book an average of 1 year after acceptance. Reports in 1 month on queries; 4 months on mss. Free book catalog.
Nonfiction: Instructional: Horse and equestrian related subjects only. Subjects include horses only. We need serious instructional works by authorities in the field on horse-related topics, broadly defined. Query. Reviews artwork/photos as part of ms package.
Recent Nonfiction Title: *Dancing With Your Horse*, by Mary Campbell (freestyle dressage).
Tips: "Writers have the best chance selling us well written, unique works that teach serious horse people how to do something better. If I were a writer trying to market a book today, I would offer a straightforward presentation, letting work speak for itself, without hype or hard sell. Allow publisher to contact writer, without frequent calling to check status. They haven't forgotten the writer but may have many different proposals at hand; frequent calls to 'touch base,' multiplied by the number of submissions, become an annoyance. As the publisher/author relationship becomes close and is based on working well together, early impressions may be important, even to the point of being a consideration in acceptance for publication."

ALEXANDER HAMILTON INSTITUTE, 197 W. Spring Valley Ave., Maywood NJ 07607. (201)587-7050. Editor-in-Chief: Brian L.P. Zevnik. Estab. 1909. Publishes 3-ring binder and paperback originals. Averages 18 titles/year; receives 150 submissions annually. 40% of books from first-time authors; 90% of books from unagented writers. "We pay advance against negotiated royalty or straight fee (no royalty)." Offers average $3,000 advance. Publishes book an average of 10 months after acceptance. Simultaneous submissions OK. Reports in 1 month on queries; 2 months on mss.
Nonfiction: Executive/management books for two audiences. One is overseas, upper-level manager. "We need how-to and skills building books. *No* traditional management texts or academic treatises." The second audience is U.S. personnel executives and high-level management. Subject is legal personnel matters. "These books combine court case research and practical application of defensible programs." Query or submit outline or synopsis. Preferred form is outline, three paragraphs on each chapter, examples of lists, graphics, cases.
Recent Nonfiction Title: *Management Advancement Program*, by James M. Jenks.
Tips: "We sell exclusively by direct mail to managers and executives around the world. A writer must know his/her field and be able to communicate practical systems and programs."

HANCOCK HOUSE PUBLISHERS LTD., 1431 Harrison Ave., Blaine WA 98230. (604)538-1114. FAX: (604)538-2262. Publisher: David Hancock. Estab. 1971. Publishes hardcover and trade paperback originals and reprints. Averages 12 titles/year; receives 400 submissions annually. 50% of books from

Market conditions are constantly changing! If this is 1993 or later, buy the newest edition of Writer's Market at your favorite bookstore or order directly from Writer's Digest Books.

first-time authors; 100% of books from unagented writers. Pays 10% maximum royalty on wholesale price. Simultaneous submissions OK. Publishes book an average of 6 months after acceptance. Reports in 6 months. Book catalog free on request. Ms guidelines for SASE.

Nonfiction: Biography, cookbook, how-to and self-help. Subject include Americana; cooking and foods; history (Northwest coast Indians); nature; recreation (sports handbooks for teachers); sports; and investment guides. Query with outline/synopsis and sample chapters. Reviews artwork/photos.

Recent Nonfiction Title: *Spirit Quest*, by Carol Batdorf.

HARBINGER HOUSE, INC., 2802 N. Alvernon Way, Tucson AZ 85712. (602)326-9595. Publisher: Laurel Gregory. Estab. 1987. Publishes hardcover originals and trade paperback originals and reprints. Averages 20 titles/year. Receives 400 submissions/month. Only 5% of published books were unsolicited submissions. Pays 8-15% royalty on net receipts. Offers $1,500 average advance. Publishes book an average of 10 months after acceptance. Simultaneous submissions OK. Reports in 1 month on queries; 4 months on mss. Book catalog for 7½ × 10½ SAE and 4 first class stamps. Manuscript guidelines for #10 SASE.

Nonfiction: Social issues, personal growth. Subjects include child guidance/parenting, nature/environment, psychology, sociology and women's issues/studies. Submit outline/synopsis and 2 sample chapters, resume and SASE for return of materials.

Recent Nonfiction Title: *Mystical Sex: Love, Ecstasy and the Mystical Experience*, by Louis William Meldman, Ph.D.

Fiction: Children's Books: picture books; stories for middle readers. For short children's books, send ms. No adult fiction. Artwork reviewed as part of ms package. Include SASE for return of materials.

Recent Children's Title: *Lissa and the Moon's Sheep*, by Eli Goldblatt.

HARCOURT BRACE JOVANOVICH, 6277 Sea Harbor Dr., Orlando FL 32887. Divisions include Harcourt Brace Jovanovich Children's Books Division and Holt, Rinehart & Winston. Did not want a listing for their Adult Trade Books Division. "The trade division of Harcourt Brace Jovanovich does not accept any unsolicited manuscripts. The children's division is the only one open to unsolicited submissions."

HARCOURT BRACE JOVANOVICH, Children's Books Division, 1250 Sixth Ave., San Diego CA 92101. (619) 699-6810. FAX: (619)699-6777. Contact: Manuscript Submissions. Imprints include HBJ Children's Books, Gulliver Books, Voyager and Odyssey Paperbacks, and Jane Yolen Books. Publishes hardcover originals and trade paperback reprints. Division publishes 75 hardcover originals/year and 40-50 paperback reprints/year. Royalty varies. Advance varies. Publishes ms an average of 2 years after acceptance. Reports in 6 weeks on queries; 2 months on mss. Book catalog for 9 × 12 SAE with 3 first class stamps. Manuscript guidelines for #10 SAE wth 1 first class stamp.

Nonfiction: Juvenile. Query. Reviews artwork/photos as part of ms package "but requests that no originals are sent."

Fiction: Query or submit outline/synopsis and sample chapters for middle-grade and young-adult novels; or complete ms for picture books.

HARPER SAN FRANCISCO, Division of HarperCollins, Icehouse One #401, 151 Union St., San Francisco CA 94111-1299. (415)477-4400. FAX: (415)477-5865. Editorial Director: Thomas Grady. Estab. 1817. Firm publishes hardcover and trade paperback originals and trade paperback reprints. Publishes 180 titles/year. Receives about 10,000 submissions/year. 5% of books from first-time authors; 50% from unagented writers. Pays royalty. Publishes book an average of 18 months after acceptance. Simultaneous (if notified) submissions OK. Reports in 2 months on queries; 6 months on mss. Free book catalog and ms guidelines.

Nonfiction: Biography, how-to, reference, self-help. Subjects include addiction/recovery, philosophy, psychology, religion, women's issues/studies, theology, New Age. Query or submit outline/synopsis and sample chapters.

Recent Nonfiction Title: *Co-Dependent No More*, by Melody Beattie.

HARPERCOLLINS CHILDREN'S BOOKS PACIFIC NORTHWEST, Division of HarperCollins Publishers, Suite 154, 8948 SW Barbur Blvd., Portland OR 97219. Publisher: Marilyn Kriney. Executive Editor, Pacific Northwest: Linda Zuckerman. Publishes hardcover originals. Averages 15 titles/year; receives 2,400 submissions annually. 10% of books from first-time authors. 40% of books from unagented writers. Pays royalty on invoice price. Advance negotiable. Publishes book an average of 2 years after acceptance. Simultaneous submissions OK. Reports in 3 months. Does not accept applications for freelance manuscript readers. Book catalog and guidelines from New York office (HarperCollins Publishers, 10 E. 53rd St., New York NY 10022) for 10 × 13 SASE with 5 first class stamps.

Nonfiction: Juvenile. Query or submit complete ms. Reviews artwork/photos as part of ms package.
Recent Nonfiction Title: *Eight Hands Round*, by Ann Whitford Paul.
Fiction: Juvenile. Submit complete ms only. No queries.
Recent Fiction Title: *The Planetoid of Amazement*, by Mel Gilden.
Poetry: No Dr. Seuss-type verse. Submit complete ms.
Recent Poetry Title: *Under the Sunday Tree*, by Eloise Greenfield.
Tips: "Our market is children, ages 3-6; 4-8; 8-12; 10-14; 12-16. Read contemporary children's books at all age levels; try to take some writing or children's literature courses; talk to children's librarians and booksellers in independent bookstores; read *Horn Book*, *Booklist*, *School Library Journal* and *Publishers Weekly*; take courses in book illustration and design."

HARPERCOLLINS PUBLISHERS, 10 E. 53rd St., New York NY 10022. (212)207-7000. Managing Editor: Tracy Behar. Imprints include Harper San Francisco (religious books only); Harper Perennial Library; and Harper Torchbooks. Publishes hardcover and paperback originals, and paperback reprints. Trade publishes over 400 titles/year. Pays standard royalties; advances negotiable. No unsolicited queries or mss. Reports on solicited queries in 6 weeks.
Nonfiction: Americana, animals, art, biography, business/economics, cookbooks, health, history, how-to, humor, music, nature, philosophy, politics, psychology, reference, religion, science, self-help, sociology, sports and travel.
Recent Nonfiction Title: *Barbarians at the Gate*.
Fiction: Adventure, fantasy, gothic, historical, mystery, science fiction, suspense, western and literary. "We look for a strong story line and exceptional literary talent."
Recent Fiction Title: *Magic Hour*.
Tips: "Strongly suggest that you go through a literary agent before submitting any ms. Any unsolicited query or ms will be returned unread."

‡HARROW AND HESTON, Stuyvesant Plaza, P.O. Box 3934, Albany NY 12203. (518)456-4894. Editor-in-Chief: Graeme Newman. Estab. 1985. Publishes hardcover and trade paperback originals and paperback reprints. Averages 4 titles/year; receives 10-20 submissions annually. 80% of books from first-time authors; 100% of books from unagented writers. Pays 10% royalty on wholesale price. Publishes book an average of 3 months after acceptance. Simultaneous submissions OK. Query for electronic submissions. Reports in 2 months on queries; 6 months on mss.
Nonfiction: Textbooks on sociology and criminal justice. Query.
Recent Nonfiction Title: *A Primer in the Sociology of Law*, by Dragan Milovanovic.
Tips: "Submissions must be clearly written with no jargon, and directed to upper undergraduate or graduate criminal justice students, on central criminal justice topics."

‡HARTLEY & MARKS, P.O. Box 147, Point Roberts WA 98281. (206)945-2017. Editorial Director: Sue Tauber. Publishes hardcover and trade paperback originals. Averages 8-10 titles/year. Receives 700 submissions/year. 80% of books from first-time authors; 100% from unagented writers. Pays 7-10% royalty on retail price. Reports in 1 month on queries; 2 months on mss. Free book catalog.
Nonfiction: How-to, self-help and technical. Subjects include agriculture/horticulture (organic), architecture, healthy cooking, gardening (organic), holistic health and medicine, crafts, nature/environment (practical how-to), psychology self-help, translations of previous subjects. No metaphysical books, autobiography or cookbooks. Query or submit outline/synopsis and sample chapters.
Recent Nonfiction Title: *Making Twig Furniture*, by Abby Ruoff (how-to).

THE HARVARD COMMON PRESS, 535 Albany St., Boston MA 02118. (617)423-5803. President: Bruce P. Shaw. Imprint is Gambit Books. Publishes hardcover and trade paperback originals and reprints. Averages 6 titles/year. Receives "thousands" of submissions annually. 75% of books from first-time authors; 75% of books from unagented writers. Average print order for a writer's first book is 7,500. Pays royalty; offers average $1,500 advance. Publishes book an average of 9 months after acceptance. Simultaneous submissions OK. Reports in 1 month. Book catalog for 9 × 12 SAE and 3 first class stamps; ms guidelines for SASE.
Nonfiction: Travel, cookbook, how-to, reference and self-help. Emphasis on travel, family matters and cooking. "We want strong, practical books that help people gain control over a particular area of their lives, whether it's family matters, business or financial matters, health, careers, food or travel. An increasing percentage of our list is made up of books about travel and travel guides; in this area we are looking for authors who are well traveled, and who can offer a different approach to the series guidebooks. We are open to good nonfiction proposals that show evidence of strong organization and writing, and clearly demonstrate a need in the marketplace. First-time authors are welcome." Accepts nonfiction translations. Submit outline/synopsis and 1-3 sample chapters. Reviews artwork/photos.
Recent Nonfiction Title: *The Insider's Guide to Santa Fe*, by Bill Jamison and Cheryl Alters Jamison (travel).

HARVEST HOUSE PUBLISHERS, 1075 Arrowsmith, Eugene OR 97402. (503)343-0123. FAX: (503)342-6410. Vice President of Editorial: Eileen L. Mason. Estab. 1974. Publishes hardcover, trade paperback and mass market originals and reprints. Averages 55-60 titles/year; receives 1,200 submissions annually. 10% of books from first-time authors; 90% of books from unagented writers. Pays 14-18% royalty on wholesale price. Publishes book an average of 1 year after acceptance. Simultaneous submissions OK. Reports in 10 weeks. Book catalog for 8½ × 11 SAE with 2 first class stamps; manuscript guidelines for SASE.

Nonfiction: How-to, illustrated book, juvenile (picture books ages 2-8; ages 9-12), reference, self-help, counseling, curent issues, women's and family on evangelical Christian religion. No cookbooks, theses, dissertations or music.

Recent Nonfiction Title: *Too Old, Too Soon,* by Doug Fields.

Fiction: Historical, mystery and religious. No short stories. Query or submit outline/synopsis and sample chapters.

Recent Fiction Title: *The Heart Remembers,* by June Masters Bacher.

Tips: "Audience is women ages 25-40 and high school youth—evangelical Christians of all denominations."

*HAWKES PUBLISHING, INC., 5947 South 350 West, Murray UT 84107. (801)266-5555. President: John Hawkes. Publishes hardcover and trade paperback originals. Averages 24 titles/year; receives 200 submissions annually. 70% of books from first-time authors; 90% of books from unagented writers. Subsidy publishes 25-50% of books/year based on "how promising they are." Pays varying royalty of 10% on retail price to 10% on wholesale; no advance. Publishes book an average of 6 months after acceptance. Letters preferred describing book. Reports in 1 month on queries; 3 months on mss. Free book catalog.

Nonfiction: Cookbook, how-to and self-help. Subjects include cooking and foods, health, history, hobbies and psychology. Query or submit outline/synopsis and sample chapters. Reviews artwork/photos.

‡HAY HOUSE, INC., P.O. Box 2212, Santa Monica CA 90407. (213)394-7445. Editorial Director: Dan Olmos. Imprint is Lulu's Library (children's division). Publishes hardcover and trade paperback originals, and trade paperback reprints. Firm averages 10 titles/year; imprint averages 10 titles/year. Receives approximately 250 submissions/year. 20% of books are from first-time authors. 25% from unagented writers. Pays 8-12% royalty. Offers $3-10,000 average advance. Publishes book an average of 8-15 months after acceptance. Simultaneous submissions OK. Reports in 3 weeks on queries; 2 months on manuscripts. Free book catalog.

Nonfiction: Biography, how-to, humor, juvenile, reference and self-help. Subjects include ecology, healing power of pets, business and economics/self-help, cooking, foods and nutrition, education/self-help, gardening/environment, gay/lesbian, health/medicine, money/finance/self-help, nature/environment/ecology, philosophy/New Age, psychology/self-help, recreation, religion, science/self-help, sociology/self-help and women's issues/studies. "Hay House is interested in a variety of subjects so long as they have a positive self-help/metaphysical slant to them. No poetry or negative concepts that are not conducive to helping/healing ourselves or our planet." Query or submit outline/synopsis and sample chapters. Reviews artwork/photos as part of ms package if duplicate.

Recent Nonfiction Title: *You Can Heal You Life,* by Louise L. Hay (metaphysics/self-help).

Tips: "Our audience is concerned with ecology, our planet, the healing properties of love, self-help, and teaching children loving principles. Hay House has noticed that our readers are interested in taking more control of his/her life. A writer has a good chance of selling us a book with a unique, positive, and healing message. If I were a writer trying to market a book today, I would research the market thoroughly to make sure that there weren't already too many books on the subject I was interested in writing about. Then I would make sure that I had a unique slant on my idea."

 An asterisk preceding a listing indicates that subsidy publishing or co-publishing (where author pays part or all of publishing costs) is available. Firms whose subsidy programs comprise more than 50% of their total publishing activities are listed at the end of the Book Packagers and Producers section.

HEALTH ADMINISTRATION PRESS, Foundation of the American College of Healthcare Executives, 1021 East Huron St., Ann Arbor MI 48104. (313)764-1380. FAX: (313)763-1105. Director: Daphne M. Grew. Estab. 1972. Imprints include Health Administration Press, Association for Health Services Research/Health Administration Press and ACHE Management Series. Publishes hardcover and trade paperback originals. Publishes 12 titles/year. Pays 10-15% royalty on net revenue from sale of book. Occasionally offers small advance. Publishes book an average of 10 months after acceptance. Query for electronic submissions. Reports in 6 weeks on queries; 5 months on mss. Book catalog free on request.

Nonfiction: Professional or textbook. Subjects include business and economics, government/politics, health/medicine, sociology, health administration. "We are always interested in good, solid texts and references, and we are adding to our management series; books in this series offer health services CEOs and top managers immediately useful information in an accessible format." Submit outline/ synopsis and sample chapters.

Recent Nonfiction Title: *The Well-Managed Community Hospital*, by John R. Griffith.

Tips: "We publish books primarily for an audience of managers of health care institutions and researchers and scholars in health services administration. The books we like to see have something to say and say it to our audience."

HEALTH COMMUNICATIONS, INC., 3201 SW 15th St., Deerfield Beach FL 33442. (305)360-0909. FAX: (305)360-0054. Book Editor: Marie Stilkind. Estab. 1982. Publishes trade paperback originals. Publishes 35 titles/year. Receives 520 submissions/year. 20% of books from first-time authors. 90% from unagented writers. Pays 15% royalty on wholesale price. Publishes book an average of 9 months after acceptance. Reports in 1 month on queries; 6 weeks on mss. Free book catalog and ms guidelines.

Nonfiction: Self-help recovery. Subjects include adult child and co-dependent issues, psychology and recovery/addiction. We are looking for recovery trends in self-help format. Submit outline/synopsis and sample chapters. Reviews artwork/photos as part of ms package.

Recent Nonfiction Title: *Healing the Shame That Binds You*, by John Bradshaw.

*HEART OF THE LAKES PUBLISHING, P.O. Box 299, Interlaken NY 14847-0299. (607)532-4997. Contact: Walter Steesy. Estab. 1976. Imprints include Empire State Books and Windswept Press. Publishes hardcover and trade paperback originals and reprints. Averages 20-25 titles/year; receives 200 submissions annually. 100% of books from unagented writers. Average print order for a writer's first book is 500-1,000. Subsidy publishes 10% of books, "depending on type of material and potential sales." 15% author subsidized; 35% nonauthor subsidized. Payment is "worked out individually." Publishes book an average of 1-2 years after acceptance. Simultaneous submissions OK. Query for electronic submissions. Reports in 1 week on queries; 2 weeks on mss. Current books flyer for #10 SAE and 2 first class stamps.

Nonfiction: New York state and regional, history and genealogy source materials. Query. Reviews artwork/photos.

Recent Nonfiction Title: *Cheese Making in New York State*, by Eunice Stamm.

Fiction: Will be done only at author's expense.

HEINLE & HEINLE PUBLISHERS, INC., Division of Wadsworth, Inc., 20 Park Plaza, Boston MA 02216. (617)451-1940. FAX: (617)426-4379. Publisher: Stanley Galek. Estab. 1980. Publishes books, video and software. Averages 15-20 titles/year. 50% of books from first-time authors; 100% of books from unagented writers. Pays 6-13% royalty on net price. Publishes book an average of 1 year after acceptance. Query for electronic submissions. Reports immediately on queries; 2 weeks on mss. Free book catalog; ms guidelines for SASE.

Nonfiction: Textbook. "Foreign language and English as a second or foreign language text materials for the college and secondary market. Before writing the book, submit complete prospectus along with sample chapters, and specify market and competitive position of proposed text."

Recent Nonfiction Title: *Intercambios*, by Hendrickson.

Tips: "Introductory and intermediate and educational textbooks in foreign languages and English as a second language (ESL) and foreign language textbooks have the best chance of selling to our firm. A common mistake writers make is planning the project and/or writing the book without first reviewing the market and product concept with the publisher."

HENDRICK-LONG PUBLISHING CO., INC., P.O. Box 25123, Dallas TX 75225-1123. (214)358-4677. Contact: Joann Long. Estab. 1969. Publishes hardcover and trade paperback originals and hardcover reprints. Firm averages 8 titles/year. Receives 100 submissions/year. 90% from unagented writers. Pays royalty on selling price. Publishes book an average of 18 months after acceptance. Reports in 2 weeks on queries; 2 months on mss. Manuscript guidelines for #10 SASE.

Nonfiction: Biography, juvenile and textbook. Subject mainly Texas focused material for children and young adults. Query or submit outline/synopsis and sample chapters. Reviews artwork/photos as part of ms package; copies of material are acceptable.
Recent Nonfiction Title: *Clues from the Past*, by Pam Wheat and Brenda Whorton.
Fiction: Adventure (Texas juvenile), historical (Texas Juvenile), juvenile (Texas), mystery (Texas juvenile) and western (Texas juvenile). Query or submit outline/synopsis and sample chapters.
Recent Fiction Title: *My Dear Mollie: Love Letters of a Texas Sheep Rancher*, by Agnesa Reeve.

HENDRICKSON PUBLISHERS, INC., 137 Summit St., P.O. Box 3473, Peabody MA 01961-3473. Acquisitions Editor: Dr. A. Sterling Quatsch, III. Publishes hardcover and trade paperback originals and reprints. Averages 8-12 titles/year; receives 100-125 submissions annually. 3% of books from first-time authors; 100% of books from unagented writers. Publishes book an average of 8 months after acceptance. Simultaneous (if so notified) submissions OK. Free book catalog. Ms returned only with SASE. Ms guidlines for SASE.
Nonfiction: Religious, principally academic. "We will consider any quality mss within the area of religion specifically related to biblical studies and related fields. Popularly written manuscripts, poetry, plays or fiction are not acceptable." Submit outline/synopsis and sample chapters or complete ms.
Recent Nonfiction Title: *1 and 2 Timothy*, by Gordon D. Fee, Ph.D.

VIRGIL W. HENSLEY, INC., 6116 E. 32nd St., Tulsa OK 74135. (918)644-8520. Editor: Terri Kalfas. Estab. 1964. Publishes hardcover originals. Publishes 5 titles/year (will increase that number). Receives 100 submissions/year. 50% of books from first-time authors; 50% from unagented writers. Pays 5% minimum royalty on retail price or outright purchase of $250 minimum for study aids. Publishes ms an average of 18 months after acceptance. Reports in 6 weeks on queries; 2 months on mss. Book catalog for 9×12 SAE and $1 postage. Manuscript guidelines for #10 SASE.
Nonfiction: Bible study curriculum. Subjects include child guidance/parenting, money/finance, religion, women's issues/studies. "We look for subjects that lend themselves to long-term Bible studies—prayer, prophecy, family, faith, etc. We do not want to see anything non-Christian." Query with brief synopsis then submit outline/sample chapters or complete ms.
Recent Nonfiction Title: *7 Steps to Bible Skills for Youth*, by Dorothy Hellstern.
Tips: "Submit something that crosses denominational lines; Bible studies which are directed toward the large Christian market, not small specialized groups; heavy emphasis on student activities and student involvement. We serve an interdenominational market—churches of all sizes and Christian persuasions. Our books are used by both pastors and Christian education leaders in Bible studies, Sunday Schools, home Bible studies, and school classrooms."

‡HERALD PRESS, Imprint of Mennonite Publishing House, 616 Walnut Ave., Scottdale PA 15683. (412)887-8500. FAX: (412)887-3111. General Book Editor: David Garber. Estab. 1908. Publishes hardcover, trade and mass market paperback originals, trade paperback and mass market paperback reprints. Averages 30 titles/year; receives 900 submissions annually. 15% of books from first-time authors. 95% of books from unagented writers. Pays minimum royalty of 10% retail, maximum of 12% retail. Advance seldom given. Publishes book an average of 14 months after acceptance. Query for electronic submissions. Reports in 3 weeks on queries; 2 months on submissions. Book catalog 50¢.
Nonfiction: Christian inspiration, Bible study, current issues, missions and evangelism, peace and justice, family life, Christian ethics and theology, ethnic (Amish, Mennonite), self-help and juveniles (mostly ages 9-14). No drama or poetry. Query or submit outline/synopsis and 2 sample chapters. Reviews artwork/photos as part of ms package.
Recent Nonfiction Title: *Surviving Without Romance*, by Mary Lou Cummings (African women).
Fiction: Religious. Needs some fiction for youth and adults reflecting themes similar to those listed in nonfiction, also "compelling stories that treat social and Christian issues in a believable manner." No fantasy. Query or submit outline/synopsis and sample chapters.
Recent Fiction Title: *Daniel*, by Mary Christner Borntrager (Amish family-hardship).

HERALD PUBLISHING HOUSE, Division of Reorganized Church of Jesus Christ of Latter Day Saints, 3225 South Noland Rd., P.O. Box HH, Independence MO 64055. (816)252-5010. FAX: (816)252-3976. Editorial Director: Roger Yarrington. Estab. 1860. Imprints include Independence Press and Graceland Park Press. Publishes hardcover and trade paperback originals and reprints. Averages 30 titles/year; receives 700 submissions annually. 20% of books from first-time authors; 100% of books from unagented writers. Pays 5% maximum royalty on retail price. Offers average $400 advance. Publishes book an average of 14 months after acceptance. Reports in 3 weeks on queries; 2 months on mss. Book catalog for 9×12 SASE.
Nonfiction: Self-help and religious (RLDS Church). Subjects include Americana, history and religion. Herald House focus: history and doctrine of RLDS Church. Independence Press focus: regional studies (Midwest, Missouri). No submissions unrelated to RLDS Church (Herald House) or to Mid-

west regional studies (Independence Press). Query. Use *Chicago Manual of Style*. Reviews artwork/photos as part of ms package.

Recent Nonfiction Title: *Missouri: Folk Heroes of the 19th Century*, by F. Mark McKiernan and Roger D. Launius (eds).

Tips: "The audience for Herald Publishing House is members of the Reorganized Church of Jesus Christ of Latter Day Saints; for Independence Press, persons living in the Midwest or interested in the Midwest; for Graceland Park Press, readers interested in academic and exploratory studies on religious topics."

HERE'S LIFE PUBLISHERS, INC., Subsidiary of Campus Crusade for Christ, P.O. Box 1576, San Bernardino CA 92404. (714)886-7981. FAX: (714)886-7985. President: Les Stobbe. Editorial Director: Dan Benson. Estab. 1977. Publishes hardcover and trade paperback originals. Averages 25 titles/year; receives 400 submissions annually. 40% of books from first-time authors; 100% of books from unagented writers. Average print order for a writer's first book is 5,000. Pays 15% royalty on wholesale price. Publishes book an average of 1 year after acceptance. Simultaneous proposal submissions OK. Query for electronic submissions. Reports in 1 month on queries; 3 months on mss. Ms guidelines for 8½×11 SAE with 2 first class stamps.

Nonfiction: Biography, how-to, reference and self-help. Needs "books in the areas of evangelism, Christian growth and family life; must reflect basic understanding of ministry and mission of Campus Crusade for Christ. No metaphysical or missionary biography." Query or submit outline/synopsis and sample chapters. Reviews artwork/photos.

Recent Nonfiction Title: *When Victims Marry*, by Don and Jan Frank.

Tips: "The writer has the best chance of selling our firm a sharply focused how-to book that provides a Biblical approach to a felt need."

*HERITAGE BOOKS, INC., 1540-E Pointer Ridge Pl., Bowie MD 20716. (301)390-7708. Editorial Director: Laird C. Towle. Estab. 1978. Publishes hardcover and paperback originals and reprints. Averages 100 titles/year; receives 100 submissions annually. 25% of books from first-time authors; 100% of books from unagented writers. Subsidy publishes 5% or less of books. Pays 10% royalty on retail price; no advance. Publishes book an average of 6 months after acceptance. Simultaneous submissions OK. Reports in 1 month. Book catalog for SAE.

Nonfiction: "We particularly desire nonfiction titles dealing with history and genealogy including how-to and reference works, as well as conventional histories and genealogies. Ancestries of contemporary people are not of interest. The titles should be either of general interest or restricted to Eastern U.S. Material dealing with the present century is usually not of interest. We prefer writers to query or submit an outline/synopsis." Reviews artwork/photos.

Recent Nonfiction Title: *Missouri: Genealogical Records and Abstracts, Vol. 1: 1766-1839*, by Sherida K. Eddlemon.

Tips: "The quality of the book is of prime importance; next is its relevance to our fields of interest."

HEYDAY BOOKS, Box 9145, Berkeley CA 94709. (415)549-3564. Publisher: Malcolm Margolin. Publishes hardcover and trade paperback originals, trade paperback reprints. Averages 4-9 titles/year; receives 200 submissions annually. 50% of books from first-time authors; 75% of books from unagented writers. Pays 8-10% royalty on retail price; offers average $1,000 advance. Publishes book an average of 8 months after acceptance. Reports in 1 week on queries; up to 5 weeks on mss. Book catalog for 7×9 SAE and 2 first class stamps.

Nonfiction: Books about California only; how-to and reference. Subjects include Americana, history, nature and travel. "We publish books about native Americans, natural history, history, and recreation, with a strong California focus." Query with outline and synopsis. Reviews artwork/photos.

Recent Nonfiction Title: *Jack London and His Daughters*, by Joan London.

Tips: "Give good value, and avoid gimmicks. We are accepting *only* nonfiction books with a California focus."

‡LAWRENCE HILL BOOKS, Imprint of Chicago Review Press, Suite 6A, 230 Park Pl., Brooklyn NY 11238. (718)857-1015. Director: Shirley A. Cloyes. Estab. 1972. Publishes hardcover and trade paperback originals and trade paperback reprints. Firm averages 25 titles/year; imprint averages 8 titles/year. 25% of books from first-time authors. 75% from unagented writers. Pays 7½% minimum for paper, 10% minimum for hardcover on net sales. Offers $3,500-5,000 average advance. Publishes book an average of 9 months after acceptance. Simultaneous submissions OK. Query for electronic submissions. Reports in 2 weeks on queries. Free book catalog and manuscript guidelines.

Nonfiction: Adult nonfiction. Subjects include ethnic, government/politics, women's issues/studies and Middle East. "We are interested in politically-progressive books in the fields of African-American and African studies, the Middle East, the Third World, international politics and women's studies that appeal to both general and academic audiences." Query.

Recent Nonfiction Title: *The False Prophet: Rabbi Meir, Kahane—From FBI Informant to Knesset Member*, by Robert I. Friedman (biography/Middle East).
Tips: "Our audience ranges from general to academic to activist."

HIPPOCRENE BOOKS INC.,171 Madison Ave., New York NY 10016. (212)685-4371. President: George Blagowidow. Estab. 1971. Publishes hardcover and trade paperback originals. Averages 100 titles/year. Receives 250 submissions annually. 10% of books from first-time authors; 95% of books from unagented writers. Pays 6-10% royalty on retail price. Offers "few thousand" dollar advance. Publishes book an average of 16 months after acceptance. Simultaneous submissions OK. Ms guidelines for #10 SASE.
Nonfiction: Reference. Subjects include Americana, language, military/war, regional (travel), history, recreation and travel. Submit outline/synopsis and 2 sample chapters.
Recent Nonfiction Titles: *The Elephant & the Tiger: The Full Story of the Vietnam War*, by Wilbur H. Morrison, Peter Deriabin and T.H. Bagley.
Tips: "Our recent successes in publishing general books considered midlist by larger publishers is making us more of a general trade publisher. We continue to do well with travel books and reference books like dictionaries, atlases and language studies. We ask for proposal, sample chapter, and table of contents. We then ask for material if we are interested."

‡HOLLOWBROOK PUBLISHING, P.O. Box 757, Stoneham Rd., Wakefield NH 03872. (603)522-3338. FAX: (603)522-6305. Editor-in-Chief: Wyatt Benner. Estab. 1981. Publishes hardcover and quality paperback originals and hardcover and trade paperback reprints. Firm averages 30 titles/year. Receives 100 submissions/year. 25% of books from first-time authors. 90% from unagented writers. Publishes book an average of 1 year after acceptance. Simultaneous submissions OK. Reports in 1 month on queries; 2 months on mss. Free book catalog and manuscript guidelines.
Nonfiction: Scholarly works of all kinds. Subjects include education, history, language/literature, music/dance, philosophy, science, women's issues/studies, literary criticism and Asian studies. "We publish primarily scholarly books of high quality aimed at academics and college libraries. We'll consider all topics for which there is an academic audience. That eliminates coffee table books, juvenile books, cookbooks, how-to books, etc." Submit complete ms and vita as part of ms package.
Recent Nonfiction Title: *Hobbes: Theory of Obligation.*

HOLT, RINEHART & WINSTON, Division of Harcourt Brace Jovanovich, 6277 Sea Harbor Dr., Orlando FL 32887. Did not want to be listed.

HOMESTEAD PUBLISHING, Box 193, Moose WY 83102. Editor: Carl Schreier. Publishes hardcover and trade paperback originals and trade paperback reprints. Averages 5 titles/year; receives 100 submissions annually. 30% of books from first-time authors. 90% of books from unagented writers. Pays 8-12% royalty on net receipts; offers $1,000 average advance. Publishes book an average of 1 year after acceptance. Simultaneous submissions OK. Query for electronic submissions. Reports in 2 weeks on queries; 2 months on submissions. Book catalog for #10 SAE with 2 first class stamps.
Nonfiction: Biography, coffee table book, illustrated book, juvenile and reference. Subjects include animals, art, history, nature, photography and travel. Especially needs natural history and nature books for children. No textbooks. Query; or submit outline, synopsis and sample chapters or complete ms. Reviews artwork/photos as part of ms package.
Recent Nonfiction Title: *Yellowstone: Selected Photographs 1870-1960.*
Tips: "Illustrated books on natural history are our specialty. Our audiences include professional, educated people with an interest in natural history, conservation, national parks, and western art. Underneath the visual aspects, a book should be well written, with a good grasp of the English language. We are looking for professional work and top quality publications."

HOUGHTON MIFFLIN CO., Adult Trade Division, 2 Park St., Boston MA 02108. (617)725-5000. Submissions Editor: Janice Harvey. Estab. 1832. Hardcover and paperback originals and paperback reprints. Royalty of 6-7½% on retail price for paperbacks; 10-15% on sliding scale for standard fiction and nonfiction; advance varies widely. Publishes book an average of 18 months after acceptance.

ALWAYS submit unsolicited manuscripts or queries with a self-addressed, stamped envelope (SASE) within your country or a self-addressed envelope with International Reply Coupons (IRC) purchased from the post office for other countries.

Publishes 100 titles/year. Simultaneous queries OK. SASE required with all queries and submissions. Reports in 2 months. Book catalog for 8½×11 SAE with 5 first class stamps.
Nonfiction: Natural history, biography, health, history, current affairs, psychology and science. Query.
Recent Nonfiction Title: *The Spiritual Life of Children*, by Robert Coles.
Fiction: Literary. Query.
Recent Fiction Title: *Symposium*, by Muriel Spark.
Tips: "No unsolicited manuscripts will be read. Submit query letter and outline or synopsis, with SASE, to Submissions Editor. (Include one sample chapter for fiction.) The query letter should be short and to the point—that is, it should *not* incorporate the book's synopsis. The letter should say who the writer is (including information on previous publications) and the subject of the book."

HOUGHTON MIFFLIN CO., Children's Trade Books, 2 Park St., Boston MA 02108. Editor: Stephanie Welch. Publishes hardcover originals and trade paperback reprints (some simultaneous hard/soft). Averages 45-50 titles/year. Pays standard royalty; offers advance. Reports in 1 month on queries; 2 months on mss. Free book catalog.
Nonfiction: Submit outline/synopsis and sample chapters. Reviews artwork/photos as part of ms package.
Recent Nonfiction Title: *Families*, by Aylette Jenness.
Fiction: Submit complete ms.
Recent Fiction Title: *Black and White*, by David Macaulay.

HOWELL PRESS, INC., Suite B, 700 Harris St., Charlottesville, VA 22901. (804)977-4006. Senior Editor: Kathleen D. Valenzi. Estab. 1985. Publishes hardcover originals. Firm averages 6 titles/year. Receives 500 submissions/year. 10% of books from first-time authors. 80% from unagented writers. Pays 5-7% on net retail price. "We generally offer an advance, but amount differs with each project and is generally negotiated with authors on a case-by-case basis." Publishes book an average of 18 months after acceptance. Reports in 2 months. Book catalog for 9×12 SAE with 4 first class stamps.
Nonfiction: Coffee table book, illustrated book. Subjects include aviation, military history, maritime history, motorsports, gardening, sports history. "Generally open to most ideas, as long as writing is not scholarly (easily accessible to average adult reader) and can be heavily illustrated in some fashion with photography or art. While our line is esoteric, it would be advisable to look over our catalog before querying to better understand what Howell Press does." Query. Submit outline/synopsis and sample chapters. Reviews artwork/photos as part of ms package. Mss submitted without return postage will not be returned.
Recent Nonfiction Title: *Special Forces at War: An Illustrated History, Southeast Asia 1959-1975*, by Shelby L. Stanton.
Tips: "We're looking for books with built-in buyers (aviation enthusiasts, motorsports fans, etc.); books that can be beautifully illustrated with four-color art/photography."

HRD PRESS, INC., 22 Amherst Rd., Amherst MA 01002. (413)253-3488. FAX: (800)822-2801. Publisher: Robert W. Carkhuff. Estab. 1970. Publishes hardcover and trade paperback originals. Averages 15-20 titles/year. Receives 30-40 submissions/year. 25% of books from first-time authors. 100% from unagented writers. Pays 10-15% royalty on wholesale price. Offers $1,000 average advance. Publishes book an average of 6 months after acceptance. Simultaneous submissions OK. Reports in 2 weeks on queries; 2 months on mss. Free book catalog and ms guidelines.
Nonfiction: Juvenile, reference, self-help, software, technical. Subjects include business, child guidance/parenting, psychology. We are looking for mostly business oriented titles; we will consider child guidance/parenting and psychology. Submit outline/synopsis and samples chapters.
Recent Nonfiction Title: *Too Smart For Trouble*, by Sharon Scott (child guidance/parenting).
Tips: "Books must be practical and useful."

HUDSON HILLS PRESS, INC., Suite 1308, 230 5th Ave., New York NY 10001-7704. (212)889-3090. President/Editorial Director: Paul Anbinder. Estab. 1978. Publishes hardcover and paperback originals. Averages 10 titles/year; receives 50-100 submissions annually. 15% of books from first-time authors; 90% of books from unagented writers. Average print order for a writer's first book is 3,000. Offers royalties of 5-8% on retail price. Average advance: $5,000. Publishes book an average of 1 year after acceptance. Simultaneous submissions OK. Reports in 1 month. Book catalog for SAE with 2 first class stamps.
Nonfiction: Art and photography. "We are only interested in publishing books about art and photography, including monographs." Query first, then submit outline/synopsis and sample chapters. Reviews artwork/photos as part of ms package.
Recent Nonfiction Title: *Impressionism*, by Gerstein.

HUMAN KINETICS PUBLISHERS, INC., P.O. Box 5076, Champaign IL 61825-5076. (217)351-5076. FAX: (217)351-2674. Publisher: Rainer Martens. Imprints are Leisure Press and Human Kinetics Books. Publishes hardcover and paperback text and reference books and trade paperback originals. Averages 80 titles/year; receives 300 submissions annually. 50% of books from first-time authors; 97% of books from unagented writers. Pays 10-15% royalty on net income. Publishes book an average of 18 months after acceptance. Simultaneous submissions OK. Query for electronic submissions. Reports in 2 months. Free book catalog.
Nonfiction: How-to, reference, self-help, technical and textbook. Subjects include health, recreation, sports, sport sciences and sports medicine, and physical education. Especially interested in books on wellness, including stress management, weight management, leisure management, and fitness; books on all aspects of sports technique or how-to books and coaching books; books which interpret the sport sciences and sports medicine, including sport physiology, sport psychology, sport pedagogy and sport biomechanics. No sport biographies, sport record or statistics books or regional books. Submit outline/synopsis and sample chapters. Reviews artwork/photos as part of ms package.
Recent Nonfiction Title: *Successful Coaching*, by Rainer Martens.
Tips: "Books which accurately interpret the sport sciences and health research to coaches, athletes and fitness enthusiasts have the best chance of selling to us."

‡**HUMAN SERVICES INSTITUTE, INC.,** Subsidiary of TAB Books, Division of McGraw-Hill, Inc., P.O. Box 14610, Bradenton FL 34280-4610. (813)746-7088. Senior Editor: Dr. Lee Marvin Joiner. Publishes hardcover and trade paperback originals. Firm averages 10-12 titles/year. Receives 100 submissions/year. 95% of books are from first-time authors. 100% from unagented writers. Pays 7-15% royalties on wholesale price. Publishes book an average of 9 months after acceptance. Query for electronic submissions. Reports in 2 weeks on queries. Free book catalog and manuscript guidelines.
Nonfiction: Self-help. Subjects include child guidance/parenting, psychology and women's issues/studies. "We are looking for books on divorce, cocaine, cults, sexual victimization, alternative medicine, mental health, secular recovery and violence. No autobiographical accounts." Query or submit outline/synopsis and sample chapters.
Recent Nonfiction Title: *Too Old to Cry*, by Ackerman and Graham.
Tips: "Our audience is made up of clinics, hospitals, prisons, mental health centers, human service professionals and general readers. If I were a writer trying to market a book today, I would write a video script (30 minute) first. This should contain the book's message in a compressed format."

HUMANICS PUBLISHING GROUP, 1482 Mecaslin St. NW, Atlanta GA 30309. President: Gary B. Wilson. Contact: Robert Grayson Hall, Executive Editor. Estab. 1976. Publishes softcover, educational and trade paperback originals. Averages 12 titles/year; receives 500 submissions annually. 20% of books from first-time authors; 100% of books from unagented writers. Average print order for a writer's first book is 5,000. Pays average 10% royalty on net sales; buys some mss outright. Publishes book an average of 1 year after acceptance. Reports in 4 months. Book catalog and ms guidelines for SASE.
Nonfiction: Self-help, teacher resource books and psychological assessment instruments for early education. Subjects include health, psychology, sociology, education, business and New Age. Submit outline/synopsis and at least 3 sample chapters. Reviews artwork/photos as part of ms package.
Recent Nonfiction Title: *Empowerment*, by William B. Cunningham Ph.D.
Tips: "Be resourceful, bold and creative. But be sure to have the facts and expertise in hand to back up your work."

*****HUMANITIES PRESS INTERNATIONAL, INC.,** 165 1st Ave., Atlantic Highlands NJ 07716. (908)872-1441. FAX: (908)872-0717. President: Keith M. Ashfield. Estab. 1951. Imprints are Humanities Press and Ashfield Press. Publishes hardcover originals and trade paperback originals and reprints. Averages 35-50 titles/year. Receives 500 submissions/year. 5% of books from first-time authors. 80% from unagented writers. Subsidy publishes 2% of books. Pays 5-12½% royalty on retail price. Offers $500 average advance. Publishes book an average of 1 year after acceptance. Reports in 3 weeks on queries; 10 weeks on mss. Free book catalog.
Nonfiction: Subjects include politics (international/theory), philosophy (continental, cultural theory), history (European Early Modern to Modern), and sociology. "We want books for senior level undergraduates and upward."
Recent Nonfiction Title: *Cosmos and Anthropos: A Philosophical Interpretation of the Anthropic Cosmological Principle*, by Errol E. Harris.
Tips: "We want well-written contributions to scholarly investigation or synthesis of recent thought. Serious students and scholars are our audience."

CARL HUNGNESS PUBLISHING, P.O. Box 24308, Speedway IN 46224. (317)244-4792. Editorial Director: Carl Hungness. Publishes hardcover and paperback originals. Pays "negotiable" outright purchase. Reports in 3 weeks. Free book catalog.

Nonfiction: Stories relating to professional automobile racing. No sports car racing or drag racing material. Query.

‡**HUNTER PUBLISHING, INC.**, 300 Raritan Center Pkwy., Edison NJ 08818. President: Michael Hunter. Estab. 1985. Averages 100 titles/year; receives 300 submissions annually. 10% of books from first-time authors. 75% of books from unagented writers. Pays royalty; offers $0-2,000 average advance. Publishes book on average 9 months after acceptance. Simultaneous submissions OK. Query for electronic submissions. Reports in 3 weeks on queries; 1 month on submissions. Book catalog for #10 SAE with 4 first class stamps.
Nonfiction: Reference. Subjects include travel. "We need travel guides to areas covered by few competitors: Caribbean Islands, Pacific Islands, Canada, Mexico, regional U.S. from an active 'adventure' perspective. Walking and climbing guides to all areas—from Australia to India." No personal travel stories or books not directed to travelers. Query or submit outline/synopsis and sample chapters. Reviews artwork/photos as part of ms package.
Recent Nonfiction Title: *Charming Small Hotels of Italy*.
Tips: "Study what's out there, pick some successful models, and identify ways they can be made more appealing. We need active adventure-oriented guides and more specialized guides for travelers in search of the unusual."

‡**IDEALS PUBLISHING CORP.**, Suite 800, 565 Marriott Dr., Nashville TN 37210. (615)885-8270. Publisher: Patricia Pingry. Publishes trade children's titles. Firm averages 30-50 titles/year. Payment varies. Simultaneous submissions OK. Reports in 2 months. Manuscript guidelines free on request.
Nonfiction: Coffee table book and juvenile. Query. Reviews artwork/photos as part of ms package.
Recent Nonfiction Title: *The Easter Story*, by Carol Heyer (juvenile).

***IEEE PRESS**, Subsidiary of The Institute of Electrical and Electronics Engineers, 445 Hoes Ln., P.O. Box 1331, Piscataway NJ 08855. (201)562-3969. Executive Editor: Dudley R. Kay. Publishes hardcover and softcover originals and reprints. Averages 15-20 titles/year. Receives 50-60 submissions/year. 70% of books from first-time authors. 100% from unagented writers. Subsidy publishes 10% of books. Pays 5-18% royalty on wholesale price. Publishes book an average of 6-9 months after acceptance. Simultaneous submissions OK. Query for electronic submissions. Reports in 3 weeks on queries; 2 months on mss. Free book catalog and ms guidelines.
Nonfiction: Technical reference and textbooks. Subjects include computers and electronics. "We need advanced texts and references in electrical engineering, especially telecommunications. *Major push is on original, authored works* rather than edited collections and reprints. No trade/consumer orientation books in electronics and computers. We publish for the professional and advanced student in engineering." Query. Submit outline/synopsis and sample chapters.
Recent Nonfiction Title: *Real-World Engineering: A Guide to Career Success*, by L. Kamm.
Tips: "Professional reference books have flourished due to changing technologies and need to keep current. However, technical writers are few. Engineers and scientists should consider trained technical writers as co-authors. Our audience consists of engineers—largely at management and project leader levels. "If I were a writer trying to market a book today, I would work with a good agent or other experienced writer with contacts and knowledge of the 'system.' Authors expend too much energy, and endure unnecessary frustration, because they don't know how to match a good idea and respectable proposal with the *appropriate* publishers."

ILR PRESS, Division of The New York State School of Industrial and Labor Relations, Cornell University, Ithaca NY 14851-0952. (607)255-3061. Director: E. Benson. Estab. 1945. Publishes hardcover and trade paperback originals and reprints. Averages 5-10 titles/year. Pays royalty. Reports in 1 month on queries; 4 months on mss. Free book catalog.
Nonfiction: All titles relate to industrial and labor relations. Biography, reference, technical, and academic books. Subjects include history, sociology of work and the workplace, and business and economics. Book manuscript needs for the next year include "manuscripts on workplace problems, employment policy, women and work, personnel issues, and dispute resolution that will interest academics and practitioners." Query or submit outline/synopsis and sample chapters or complete ms.
Recent Nonfiction Title: *Holding the Line: Women in the Great Arizona Mine Strike of 1983*, by Barbara Kingsolver.
Tips: "We are interested in manuscripts that address topical issues in industrial and labor relations that concern both academics and the general public. These must be well documented to pass our editorial evaluation, which includes review by academics in the industrial and labor relations field."

IMAGINE, INC., P.O. Box 9674, Pittsburgh PA 15226. (412)571-1430. President: R.V. Michelucci. Estab. 1982. Publishes trade paperback originals. Averages 3-5 titles/year; receives 50 submissions annually. 50% of books from first-time authors; 75% of books from unagented writers. Pays 6-10%

royalty on retail price. Offers average $500 advance. Publishes book an average of 1 year after acceptance. Reports in 2 weeks on queries; 2 months on mss. Book catalog for #10 SASE. SASE's are a *must* for all replies.

Nonfiction: Coffee table book, how-to, illustrated book and reference. Subjects include films, science fiction, fantasy and horror films. Submit outline/synopsis and sample chapters or complete ms with illustrations and/or photos.

Recent Nonfiction Title: *Bruno Sammartino, An Autobiography of Wrestling's Living Legend*, by Bob Michelucci and Paul McCullough.

Tips: "If I were a writer trying to market a book today, I would research my subject matter completely before sending a manuscript. Our audience is between ages 18-45 and interested in film, science fiction, fantasy and the horror genre. We do not solicit nor publish fiction *novels*."

IN DEPTH PUBLISHERS, 3412 Milwaukee Ave., #408, Northbrook IL 60062. (708)803-1567. Publisher: Kathryn Dokas. Publishes trade paperback originals. Averages 5 titles/year. Receives 10 submissions/year. 100% of books from first-time authors; 100% from unagented writers. Pay negotiated on author by author basis, generally 5-10%, no advance. Publishes book an average of 6 months after acceptance. Simultaneous submissions OK. Reports in 3 months on queries; 6 months on mss.

Nonfiction: How-to. Subjects include senior issues, insurance and consumer-medical. "We are looking for books on senior citizen, medical and health care issues and health insurance. Very specific, how-to books written by experts with inside information. If it isn't within the above paremeters, please don't send it!" Submit outline/synopsis and sample chapters. Send return postage.

Recent Nonfiction Title: *Hassle Free Health Insurance*, by Border (how-to).

Tips: "We are looking for experts in their field as opposed to freelance writers. We want insider, in-depth information for our books. Our audience consists of consumers, older Americans, business owners. Check your proposals for spelling punctuation and grammar. Errors send your proposal immediately to the garbage. If you can't send a clear, consice, error free proposal—you won't deliver a valuable manuscript and we are not interested."

‡*INDIANA UNIVERSITY PRESS, 10th and Morton Sts., Bloomington IN 47405. (812)337-4203. FAX: (812)855-7931. Director: John Gallman. Estab. 1951. Publishes hardcover and paperback originals and paperback reprints. Averages 150 titles/year. 30% of books from first-time authors. 98% from unagented writers. Average print order for a writer's first book is 1,000. Subsidy publishes (nonauthor) 9% of books. Pays maximum 10% royalty on retail price; offers occasional advance. Publishes book an average of 1 year after acceptance. Reports in 2 months. Free book catalog and ms guidelines.

Nonfiction: Scholarly books on humanities, history, philosophy, religion, Jewish studies, Black studies, translations, semiotics, public policy, film, music, linguistics, philanthropy, social sciences, regional materials, African studies, Soviet and East European Studies, women's studies, and serious nonfiction for the general reader. Query or submit outline/synopsis and sample chapters. "Queries should include as much descriptive material as is necessary to convey scope and market appeal to us." Reviews artwork/photos.

Recent Nonfiction Title: *The Limits of Writer Interpretation*, by Umberto Eco.

INDUSTRIAL PRESS INC., 200 Madison Ave., New York NY 10016. (212)889-6330. FAX: (212)545-8327. Editorial Director: Woodrow Chapman. Estab. 1884. Publishes hardcover originals. Averages 12 titles/year; receives 25 submissions annually. 2% of books from first-time authors; 100% of books from unagented writers. Publishes book an average of 1 year after acceptance of finished ms. Query for electronic submissions. Reports in 1 month. Free book catalog.

Nonfiction: Reference and technical. Subjects include business and economics, science and engineering. "We envision professional engineers, plant managers, on-line industrial professionals responsible for equipment operation, professors teaching manufacturing, engineering, technology related courses as our audience." Especially looking for material on manufacturing technologies and titles on specific areas in manufacturing and industry. Computers in manufacturing are a priority. No energy-related books or how-to books. Query.

Recent Nonfiction Title: *Statistical Process Control*, by Leonard A. Doty.

‡*INFO NET PUBLISHING, 34233 Via Santa Rosa, Capistrano Beach CA 92624. (714)489-9267. FAX: (714)489-9595. President: Herb Wetenkamp. Estab. 1985. Publishes trade and mass market paperback originals. Firm averages 5 titles/year. Receives 25-30 submissions/year. 85% of books from first-time authors. 85% from unagented writers. Subsidy publishes 5% "subsidy determined case by case." Pays 5-10% on wholesale price. Buys mss outright $1,000-7,500. Combination purchse/royalty. Offers $1,000 average advance. Publishes book an average of 10 months after acceptance. Simultaneous submissions OK. Reports in 5 weeks on queries. Book catalog for #10 SAE with 2 first class stamps. Manuscript guidelines for #10 SASE.

Nonfiction: Cookbook, how-to, reference, self-help, bicycling and technical. Subjects include business and economics, cooking, foods and nutrition, history, hobbies, military/war, recreation, sports, travel and small retailer. "We are seeking specialty authors in vertical market how-tos, specific industry oriented overviews and senior how-tos and self-helps. No cookbooks without a theme, or travel books with too much goo." Query. Submit outline/synopsis and sample chapters. Reviews artwork/photos as part of ms package.

Recent Nonfiction Title: *Principles of Bicycle Retailing*, by Randy W. Kirk (retail how-to).

Fiction: Adventure and historical. "We are open to unique adventure and/or history first person accounts. No romance." Query. Submit outline/synopsis and sample chapters.

Tips: "We have noticed an increase in audience served by specialty pubishers, more targeted marketing, vertical publishing. If I were a writer trying to market a book today, I would expect to participate fully in *marketing* the book. No author can expect to be successful unless he/she *sells* the book after writing it."

INNER TRADITIONS INTERNATIONAL, One Park St., Rochester VT 05767. (802)767-3174. FAX: (802)767-3726. Managing Editor: Leslie Colket. Estab. 1975. Imprints include Inner Traditions, Destiny Books, Healing Arts Press, Park Street Press. Publishes hardcover and trade paperback originals and reprints. Averages 40 titles/year. Receives 300 submissions/year. 5% of books from first-time authors. 5% from unagented writers. Pays 8-10% royalty on retail price. Offers $1,000 average advance. Publishes book an average of 9 months after acceptance. Query for electronic submissions. Reports in 3 months on queries; 3 months on mss. Free book catalog and ms guidelines.

Nonfiction: Biography, coffee table book, cookbook, illustrated book, self-help, textbook. Subjects include anthropology/archaeology, art/architecture, business and economics, child guidance/parenting, cooking, foods and nutrition, ethnic, health/alternative medicine, history, music/dance, nature/environment, esoteric philosophy, psychology, religion, travel, women's issues/studies, New Age. Query. Submit outline/synopsis and sample chapters with return postage. Reviews artwork/photos as part of ms package.

Recent Nonfiction Title: *The Phoenix Cards: Reading and Interpreting Past-Life Influences with the Phoenix Deck*, by Susan Sheppard.

‡INNOVATIA PRESS, Subsidiary of Innovatia 90© Writing Group, 1425 Maryland Dr., Irving TX 75062. (214)438-5825. Senior Editor: Ray Bell. Estab. 1990. Publishes trade and mass market paperback originals. Firm averages 3 titles/year from outside sources (3 from group). 67% of books from first-time authors. 100% from unagented writers. Pays 25-35% royalty on wholesale price. Buys mss outright for $50-1,500. Offers $50-500 average advance. Publishes book an average of 1 year after acceptance. Reports in 2 weeks on queries. Manuscript guidelines for #10 SAE with 2 first class stamps.

Nonfiction: Biography and humor. Subjects include history, military/war (except Vietnam) and religion. "We are looking for biography or autobiography of person(s) persecuted by authorities for political beliefs. We hope to publish 2 of these. No pornographic on mystery tales based on true stories." Query. Submit outline/synopsis and sample chapters. All unsolicited mss are returned unopened. Reviews artwork/photos as part of ms package.

Recent Nonfiction Title: *The Fifth Gospel*, by Joseph Lunova and Jim Hrabal (personal account).

Fiction: Adventure, fantasy, historical, humor, mystery, religious and short story collections. "Success of work in progress and quality of submissions will dictate. No pornography, explicit language or sex. No Vietnam War stories." Query. Submit outline/synopsis and sample chapters.

Recent Fiction Title: *Conquest of the Holy Land*, by David Lusk.

Tips: "We are looking for well written stories that have a plot or informative format. Not heavily interested in mainstream, copy-cat work. Our audience consists of mature adults with at least one year of college, a concern for mankind and a love of good literature. If I were a writer trying to market a book today, I would be sure that I knew the basic tenets of story construction, had defined the audience I was trying to reach and continued trying until I found a publisher."

INSIGHT BOOKS, Subsidiary of Plenum Publishing Corp., 233 Spring St., New York NY 10013. (212)620-8000. FAX: (212)463-0742. Executive Editor: Norma Fox. Estab. 1946. Publishes hardcover and trade paperback originals. Averages 12 titles/year. Receives 250 submissions/year. 50% of books from first-time authors. 75% from unagented writers. Pays royalty. Advance varies. Publishes book an average of 1 year after acceptance. Simultaneous submissions OK. Query for electronic submissions. Reports in 1 week on queries; 6 weeks on mss. Free book catalog and ms guidelines.

Nonfiction: Self-help, how-to, monographs, treatises, essays, biography. Subjects include anthropology/archaeology, art/architecture, business and economics, child rearing and development, education, ethnic, government/politics, health/medicine, language/literature, money/finance, nature/environment, philosophy, psychology, parenting, religion, science, sociology and women's issues/studies. Submit outline/synopsis and sample chapters.

Recent Nonfiction Title: *Baby Talk: The Art of Communicating with Infants and Toddlers*, by Monica Devine.

Tips: "Writers have the best chance selling thoughtful quality self-help offering well-written serious information in areas of health, mental health, social sciences, education and child-rearing. Our audience consists of informed general readers as well as professionals and students in human and life sciences. If I were a writer trying to market a book today, I would say something interesting, important and useful, and say it well."

INTERCULTURAL PRESS, INC., P.O. Box 700, Yarmouth ME 04096. (207)846-5168. FAX: (207)846-5181. Contact: Margaret D. Pusch. Estab. 1980. Publishes hardcover and trade paperback originals. Averages 5-7 titles/year; receives 50-80 submissions annually. 50% of books from first-time authors; 95% of books from unagented writers. Pays royalty; occasionally offers small advance. Publishes book an average of 2 years after acceptance. Simultaneous submissions OK. Reports in "several weeks" on queries; 2 months on mss. Free book catalog and ms guidelines.

Nonfiction: How-to, reference, self-help, textbook and theory. Subjects include business and economics, philosophy, politics, psychology, sociology, travel, or "any book with an international or domestic intercultural, multicultural or cross-cultural focus, i.e., a focus on the cultural factors in personal, social, political or economic relations. We want books with an international or domestic intercultural or multicultural focus, especially those on business operations (how to be effective in intercultural business activities) and education (textbooks for teaching intercultural subjects, for instance). Our books are published for educators in the intercultural field, business people who are engaged in international business, and anyone else who works in an international occupation or has had intercultural experience. No manuscripts that don't have an intercultural focus." Accepts nonfiction translations. Query "if there is any question of suitability (we can tell quickly from a good query)," or submit outline/synopsis. Do not submit mss unless invited.

Recent Nonfiction Title: *Breaking the Language Barrier*, by H. Douglas Brown.

INTERNATIONAL FOUNDATION OF EMPLOYEE BENEFIT PLANS, P.O. Box 69, Brookfield WI 53008-0069. (414)786-6700. FAX: (414)786-2990. Director of Publications: Dee Birschel. Publishes hardcover and trade paperback originals. Averages 30 titles/year; receives 10 submissions annually. 15% of books from first-time authors. 80% of books from unagented writers. Pays 5-15% royalty on wholesale and retail price. Publishes book an average of 1 year after acceptance. Reports in 3 months on queries. Book catalog free on request; ms guidelines for SASE.

Nonfiction: Reference, technical, consumer information and textbook. Subjects include health care, pensions, retirement planning, business and employee benefits. "We publish general and technical monographs on all aspects of employee benefits—pension plans, health insurance, etc." Query with outline.

Recent Nonfiction Title: *Flexible Benefits—A How-to Guide*, 3rd Ed., by Richard E. Johnson.

Tips: "Be aware of interests of employers and the marketplace in benefits topics, for example, how AIDS affects employers, health care cost containment."

INTERNATIONAL PUBLISHERS CO., INC., P.O. Box 3042, New York NY 10116. (212)685-2864. FAX: (212)366-9820. President: Betty Smith. Estab. 1924. Publishes hardcover and trade paperback originals and trade paperback reprints. Averages 10-15 titles/year; receives 100 submissions annually. 10% of books from first-time authors. Pays 5-7½% royalty on paperbacks; 10% royalty on cloth. No advance. Publishes book an average of 6 months after acceptance. Simultaneous submissions OK. Reports in 1 month on queries; send SASE. 6 months on mss. Book catalog and ms guidelines for SASE with 2 first class stamps.

Nonfiction: Biography, reference and textbook. Subjects include Americana, economics, history, philosophy, politics, social sciences, and Marxist-Leninist classics. "Books on labor, black studies and women's studies based on Marxist science have high priority." Query or submit outline and sample chapters. Reviews artwork/photos as part of ms package.

Recent Nonfiction Title: *Counter Revolution: U.S. Foreign Policy*, by Ed and Regula Boorstein.

Fiction: "We publish very little fiction." Query or submit outline and sample chapters.

INTERNATIONAL WEALTH SUCCESS, P.O. Box 186, Merrick NY 11566. (516)766-5850. Editor: Tyler G. Hicks. Estab. 1967. Averages 10 titles/year; receives 100 submissions annually. 100% of books from first-time authors; 100% of books from unagented writers. Average print order for a writer's first book "varies from 500 and up, depending on the book." Pays 10% royalty on wholesale or retail price. Buys all rights. Usual advance is $1,000, but this varies, depending on author's reputation and nature of book. Publishes book 4 months after acceptance. Query for electronic submissions. Reports in 1 month. Book catalog and ms guidelines for 9×12 SAE with 3 first class stamps.

Nonfiction: Self-help and how-to. "Techniques, methods, sources for building wealth. Highly personal, how-to-do-it with plenty of case histories. Books are aimed at the wealth builder and are highly sympathetic to his and her problems." Financing, business success, venture capital, etc. Length: 60,000-70,000 words. Query. Reviews artwork/photos as part of ms package.

Recent Nonfiction Title: *Money Agency Planning Guide*, by Brisky.

Tips: "With the mass layoffs in large and medium-size companies there is an increasing interest in owning your own business. So we will focus on more how-to hands-on material on owning—and becoming successful in—one's own business of any kind. Our market is the BWB—Beginning Wealth Builder. This person has so little money that financial planning is something they never think of. Instead, they want to know what kind of a business they can get into to make some money without a large investment. Write for this market and you have millions of potential readers. Remember—there are a lot more people *without* money than *with* money."

*INTERSTATE PUBLISHERS, INC., 510 N. Vermilion St., P.O. Box 50, Danville IL 61834-0050. (217)446-0500. FAX: (217)446-9706. Acquisitions/Vice President-Editorial: Ronald L. McDaniel. Estab. 1914. Hardcover and paperback originals and software. Publishes about 50 titles/year. 50% of books from first-time authors; 100% of books from unagented writers. Subsidy publishes 5% of books; 3% nonauthor subsidy. Usual royalty is 10%; no advance. Markets books by mail and exhibits. Publishes book an average of 9-12 months after acceptance. Reports in 4 months. Book catalog for 9×12 SAE. "Our guidelines booklet is provided only to persons who have submitted proposals for works in which we believe we might be interested. If the booklet is sent, no self-addressed envelope or postage from the author is necessary."

Nonfiction: Publishes high school and undergraduate college-level texts and related materials in agricultural education (production agriculture, agriscience and technology, agribusiness, agrimarketing, horticulture). Also publishes items in correctional education (books for professional training and development and works for use by and with incarcerated individuals in correctional facilities). "We favor, but do not limit ourselves to, works that are designed for class-quantity rather than single-copy sale." Query or submit synopsis and 2-3 sample chapters. Reviews artwork/photos as part of ms package.

Recent Nonfiction Title: *Animal Science*, 9th Ed., by M.E. Ensminger.

Tips: "Freelance writers should be aware of strict adherence to the use of nonsexist language; fair and balanced representation of the sexes and of minorities in both text and illustrations; and discussion of computer applications and career opportunities wherever applicable. Writers commonly fail to identify publishers who specialize in the subject areas in which they are writing. For example, a publisher of textbooks isn't interested in novels, or one that specializes in elementary education materials isn't going to want a book on auto mechanics."

INTERURBAN PRESS/TRANS ANGLO BOOKS, P.O. Box 6444, Glendale CA 91225-0444. (818)240-9130. President: Mac Sebree. Publishes hardcover and trade paperback originals. Averages 10-12 titles/year; receives 50-75 submissions yearly. 35% of books from first-time authors; 99% of books from unagented writers. Average print order for a writer's first book is 2,000. Pays 5-10% royalty on gross receipts; offers no advance.Reports in 2 weeks on queries; 2 months on mss. Free book catalog.

Nonfiction: Western Americana and transportation. Subjects include Americana, history, hobbies and travel. "We are interested mainly in manuscripts about railroads, local transit, local history, and Western Americana (gold mining, logging, early transportation, etc.). Also anything pertaining to preservation movement, nostalgia." Query. Reviews artwork/photos.

Recent Nonfiction Title: *The Surfliners—50 Years of the San Diegan*, by Dick Stephenson.

Tips: "Our audience is comprised of hobbyists in the rail transportation field ('railfans'); those interested in Western Americana (logging, mining, etc.); and students of transportation history, especially railroads and local rail transit (streetcars)."

*INTERVARSITY PRESS, Division of InterVarsity Christian Fellowship, P.O. Box 1400, Downers Grove IL 60515. (708)964-5700. FAX: (708)964-1251. Editorial Director: Andrew T. LePeau. Estab. 1954. Publishes hardcover and paperback originals and reprints. Averages 60 titles/year; receives 1200 submissions annually. 25% of books from first-time authors; 95% of books from unagented writers. Subsidy publishes (nonauthor) 6% of books. Pays average 10% royalty on retail price; negotiable advance. Sometimes makes outright purchase for $600-2,500. Publishes book an average of 1 year after acceptance of final draft. "Indicate simultaneous submissions." Reports in 3 months. Writer's guidelines for SASE.

Nonfiction: "InterVarsity Press publishes books geared to the presentation of Biblical Christianity in its various relations to personal life, art, literature, sociology, psychology, philosophy, history and so forth. Though we are primarily publishers of trade books, we are cognizant of the textbook market at the college, university and seminary level within the general religious field. The audience for which the books are published is composed primarily of adult Christians. Stylistic treatment varies from topic to topic and from fairly simple popularizations to scholarly works primarily designed to be read by scholars." Accepts nonfiction translations. Query or submit outline/synopsis and 2 sample chapters.

Recent Nonfiction Title: *Adult Children of Legal or Emotional Divorce*, by Jim Conway (Christian Living).

Fiction: Fantasy, humor, mainstream, murder mysteries, religious, science fiction. "While fiction need not be explicity Christian or religious, it should rise out of a Christian perspective." Submit outline/ synopsis and sample chapters.

Recent Fiction Title: *The Last Christmas*, by John Bibee (juvenile fantasy).

Tips: "Religious publishing has become overpublished. Books that fill niches or give a look at a specific aspect of a broad topic (such as marriage or finances or Christian growth) are doing well for us. Also, even thoughtful books need lower reading levels, more stories and illustrative materials. If I were a writer trying to market a book today, I would read William Zinsser's *On Writing Well* and do as he says. Writers commonly send us types of mss that we don't publish, and act as if we should publish their work—being too confident of their ideas and ability."

‡INTERWEAVE PRESS, 306 N. Washington Ave., Loveland CO 80537. (303)669-7672. Book Coordinator: Barbara Liebler. Estab. 1975. Firm publishes hardcover and trade paperback originals. Publishes 8 titles/year; receives 50 submissions/year. 60% from first-time authors; 98% from unagented writers. Pays 10% royalty on net receipts. Offers $500 average advance. Publishes book an average of 1 year after acceptance. Simultaneous (if clearly identified) submissions OK. Query for electronic submissions. Reports in 2 months. Free book catalog and ms guidelines.

Nonfiction: How-to, technical. Subjects include fiber arts—basketry, spinning, knitting, dyeing and weaving. Submit outline/synopsis and sample chapters, or send complete ms. Reviews artwork/photos as part of ms package.

Recent Nonfiction Title: *Splint Woven Basketry*, by Robin Daughtery (basketry how-to).

Tips: "We are looking for very clear, informally written, technically correct manuscripts, generally of a how-to nature, in our specific fiber fields. Our audience includes a variety of creative self-starters who like fibers and appreciate inspiration and clear instruction. They are often well educated and skillful in many areas."

*IOWA STATE UNIVERSITY PRESS, 2121 S. State Ave., Ames IA 50010. (515)292-0140. FAX: (515)292-3348. Director: Richard Kinney. Assistant Director and Chief Editor: Bill Silag. Estab. 1934. Hardcover and paperback originals. Averages 85 titles/year; receives 450 submissions annually. 98% of books from unagented writers. Average print order for a writer's first book is 2,000. Subsidy publishes (nonauthor) 25% of titles, based on sales potential of book and contribution to scholarship on trade books. Pays 10-12½-15% royalty for trade books on wholesale price; no advance. Publishes book an average of 1 year after acceptance. Simultaneous submissions OK, if advised. Query for electronic submissions. Reports in 4 months. Free book catalog; ms guidelines for SASE.

Nonfiction: Publishes biography, history, scientific/technical textbooks, the arts and sciences, statistics and mathematics, economics, aviation, and medical and veterinary sciences. Accepts nonfiction translations. Submit outline/synopsis and several sample chapters, preferably not in sequence; must be double-spaced throughout. Looks for "unique approach to subject; clear, concise narrative; and effective integration of scholarly apparatus." Send contrasting b&w glossy prints to illustrate ms. Reviews artwork/photos.

Recent Nonfiction Title: *Roadside America: The Automobile in Design and Culture*, edited by Jan Jennings.

‡IRON CROWN ENTERPRISES, P.O. Box 1605, Charlottesville VA 22902. (804)295-3917. Managing Editor: Coleman Charlton. Estab. 1980. Imprint is Hero Games. Publishes 8½×11 paperback and mass market paperback originals. Averages 30-40 titles/year; receives 200 submissions annually. 25% of books from first-time authors; 75% of books from unagented writers. Pays 2-6% royalty on wholesale price, or makes outright purchase for $1,000-2,500. Offers average $600 advance. Publishes book an average of 1 year after acceptance. Reports in 1 month on queries; 3 months on mss. Book catalog and ms guidelines for #10 SASE.

For explanation of symbols, see the Key to Symbols and Abbreviations on Page 5. For unfamiliar words, see the Glossary.

Fiction: Fantasy, science fiction and role-playing supplements. Query. "We do not accept unsolicited manuscripts."
Recent Fiction Title: *Death Valley Free Prison*, by Brain Booker (game).
Tips: "Our basic audience for gaming books is role-players, who are mostly ages 12-25. Iron Crown Enterprises publishes only a very specific sub-genre of fiction, namely fantasy role-playing supplements. We own the exclusive worldwide rights for such material based on J.R.R. Tolkien's *Hobbit* and *Lord of the Rings*. We also have a line of science fiction supplements and are planning a line of fantasy books of our own. We are currently concentrating on a very specific market, and potential submissions must fall within stringent guidelines. Due to the complexity of our needs, please query."

*ISHIYAKU EUROAMERICA, INC., (IEA Publishers), 716 Hanley Industrial Court, St. Louis MO 63144. (314)644-4322. FAX: (314)644-9532. Editor-in-Chief: Dr. Gregory Hacke. Estab. 1983. Publishes hardcover originals. Averages 15 titles/year; receives 50 submissions annually. Subsidy publishes (nonauthor) 100% of books. 75% of books from first-time authors; 100% of books from unagented writers. Average print order for a writer's first book is 3,000. Pays 10% minimum royalty on retail price or pays 35% of all foreign translation rights sales. Offers average $1,000 advance. Simultaneous submissions OK. Query for electronic submissions. Reports in 2 weeks on queries; 1 week on mss. Free book catalog; ms guidelines for SASE.
Nonfiction: Reference and medical/nursing textbooks. Subjects include health (medical and dental); psychology (nursing); and psychiatry. Especially looking for "all phases of nursing education, administration and clinical procedures. Query, or submit outline/synopsis and sample chapters or complete ms. Reviews artwork/photos as part of ms package.
Recent Nonfiction Title: *Emotion Buffers: Quality in Health Care*, by Larry Hynson, Jr., Ph.D. (nursing, medicine).
Tips: "Medical authors often feel that their incomplete works deserve to be published; dental authors have a tendency to overstress facts, thereby requiring considerable editing. We prefer the latter to the former."

JALMAR PRESS/B.L. WINCH & ASSOCIATES, 45 Hitching Post Dr., Bldg. 2, Rolling Hills Estates CA 90274. (213)547-1240. FAX: (213)547-1644. Editorial Director: B.L. Winch. Estab. 1973. Publishes hardcover and trade paperback originals. Averages 4-8 titles/year. Pays 5-15% royalty on net sales. Publishes book an average of 18 months after acceptance. Simultaneous submissions OK. Query for electronic submissions. Reports in 3 months. Book catalog for 8½×11 SAE with 4 first class stamps.
Nonfiction: Positive self-esteem materials for parenting and teaching; right-brain/whole-brain learning materials; peacemaking skills activities for parenting and teaching; and inspirational titles on self-concept and values. Reviews artwork/photos as part of ms package. "Prefer completed ms."
Recent Nonfiction Title: *Feel Better Now*, by Dr. Chris Schriner.
Tips: "A continuing strong effort is being made by Jalmar in the areas of positive self-esteem, right brain/whole brain learning, peaceful conflict resolution and drug and alcohol abuse prevention."

JIST WORKS, INC., 720 N. Park Ave., Indianapolis IN 46202. (317)264-3720. FAX: (317)264-3709. Editor: Sara Hall. Estab. 1981. Publishes trade paperback originals and reprints. Receives 25-30 submissions/year. 60% of books from first time authors; 100% from unagented writers. Pays 5-12% royalty on wholesale price or outright purchase (negotiable). Publishes ms an average of 6-12 months after acceptance. Simultaneous submissions OK. Query for electronic submissions. Reports in 1 month on queries. Book catalog and ms guidelines for SASE.
Nonfiction: How-to, reference, self-help, software, textbook. Specializes in job search and career related topics. "We want text/workbook formats that would be useful in a school or other institutional setting. We also publish trade titles. All reading levels. Will consider books for professional staff and educators, appropriate software and videos." Reviews artwork/photos as part of ms package. Nonfiction areas are career topics: assessment, job search, resumes, job survival, etc.; reference books and professional materials for career and vocational instruction; low reading, remediation, and adult education materials.
Recent Nonfiction Title: *The Resume Solution*.
Tips: "Institutions and staff who work with people making career and life decisions or who are looking for jobs are our audience as well as persons with low reading and academic skills."

JOHNSON BOOKS, Johnson Publishing Co., 1880 S. 57th Ct., Boulder CO 80301. (303)443-1576. FAX: (303)443-1679. Estab. 1979. Editorial Director: Rebecca L. Herr. Imprint is Spring Creek Press. Publishes hardcover and paperback originals and reprints. Publishes 10-12 titles/year; receives 500 submissions annually. 30% of books from first-time authors; 90% of books from unagented writers. Average print order for a writer's first book is 5,000. Royalties vary. Publishes book an average of 1 year after acceptance. Reports in 2 months. Book catalog and ms guidelines for 9×12 SAE with 4 first class stamps.

Nonfiction: General nonfiction, books on the West, environmental subjects, natural history, paleontology, geology, archaeology, travel, guidebooks, and outdoor recreation. Accepts nonfiction translations. "We are primarily interested in books for the informed popular market, though we will consider vividly written scholarly works. As a small publisher, we are able to give every submission close personal attention." Query first or call. Accepts outline/synopsis and 3 sample chapters. Looks for "good writing, thorough research, professional presentation and appropriate style. Marketing suggestions from writers are helpful." Reviews artwork/photos.
Recent Nonfiction Title: *Biologic: Environmental Protection by Design*, by David Wann.
Tips: "We are looking for nature titles with broad national, not just regional, appeal."

JONATHAN DAVID PUBLISHERS, 68-22 Eliot Ave., Middle Village NY 11379. (718)456-8611. Editor-in-Chief: Alfred J. Kolatch. Publishes hardcover and paperback originals. Averages 15 titles/year; receives 750-1,000 submissions annually. 50% of books from first-time authors; 90% of books from unagented writers. Pays standard royalty. Publishes book an average of 18 months after acceptance. Reports in 2 weeks on queries; 2 months on ms.
Nonfiction: Adult nonfiction books for a general audience. Cookbooks, cooking and foods, how-to, baseball, reference, self-help, Judaica. Query with SASE.
Recent Nonfiction Title: *Completely Cheese*, by Anita May Pearl.

JUDSON PRESS, P.O. Box 851, Valley Forge PA 19482-0851. (215)768-2118. Director: Kristy Arnesen Pullen. Estab. 1824. Publishes hardcover and paperback originals. Averages 10-15 titles/year; receives 750 queries annually. Average print order for a writer's first book is 3,500. Pays royalty or flat fee. Publishes book an average of 15 months after acceptance. Simultaneous submissions acceptable. Reports in 6 months. Enclose return postage. Book catalog for 9 × 12 SASE and 4 first class stamps; ms guidelines for SASE.
Nonfiction: Adult religious nonfiction of 30,000-80,000 words. "Our audience is mostly church members who seek to have a more fulfilling personal spiritual life and want to serve Christ in their churches and other relationships." Query with outline and 1 sample chapter.
Recent Nonfiction Title: *Prayers for All Occasions*, by Roy Pearson.
Tips: "Writers have the best chance selling us practical books assisting clergy or laypersons in their ministry and personal lives. Our audience consists of Protestant church leaders and members. Be sensitive to our workload and adapt to the market's needs. Books on multicultural issues are very welcome."

KALMBACH PUBLISHING CO., 21027 Crossroads Circle, P.O. Box 1612, Waukesha WI 53187. FAX: (414)796-0126. Books Editor: Bob Hayden. Publishes hardcover and paperback originals and paperback reprints. Averages 6-8 titles/year; receives 25 submissions annually. 85% of books from first-time authors; 100% of books from unagented writers. Offers 5-8% royalty on retail price. Average advance is $1,000. Publishes book an average of 18 months after acceptance. Reports in 2 months.
Nonfiction: Hobbies, how-to, and recreation. "Our book publishing effort is in railroading and hobby how-to-do-it titles *only*." Query first. "I welcome telephone inquiries. They save me a lot of time, and they can save an author a lot of misconceptions and wasted work." In written query, wants to see "a detailed outline of two or three pages and a complete sample chapter with photos, drawings, and how-to text." Reviews artwork/photos as part of ms package.
Recent Nonfiction Title: *Milwaukee Road Remembered*, by Jim Scribbins.
Tips: "Our books are about half text and half illustrations. Any author who wants to publish with us must be able to furnish good photographs and rough drawings before we'll consider contracting for his book."

KAR-BEN COPIES INC., 6800 Tildenwood Ln., Rockville MD 20852. (301)984-8733 or 1-800-4KAR-BEN. FAX: (301)881-9195. President: Judye Groner. Estab. 1975. Publishes hardcover and trade paperback originals. Averages 8-10 titles/year; receives 150 submissions annually. 25% of books from first-time authors; 100% from unagented writers. Average print order for a writer's first book is 5,000. Pays 6-8% royalty on net receipts; makes negotiable outright purchase; offers average $1,000 advance. Publishes book an average of 1 year after acceptance. Reports in 1 week on queries; 1 month on mss. Free book catalog; ms guidelines for 9 × 12 SAE with 2 first class stamps.
Nonfiction: Jewish juvenile (ages 1-12). Especially looking for books on Jewish life-cycle, holidays, and customs for children — "early childhood and elementary." Send only mss with Jewish content. Query with outline/synopsis and sample chapters or submit complete ms. Reviews artwork/photos as part of ms package.
Recent Nonfiction Title: *Two By Two: Favorite Bible Stories*, by Harry Araten.
Fiction: Adventure, fantasy, historical and religious (all Jewish juvenile). Especially looking for Jewish holiday and history-related fiction for young children. Submit outline/synopsis and sample chapters or complete ms.

Recent Fiction Title: *Daddy's Chair*, by Sandy Lanten.
Tips: "We envision Jewish children and their families, and juveniles interested in learning about Jewish subjects, as our audience."

*KENT STATE UNIVERSITY PRESS, Kent State University, Kent OH 44242. (216)672-7913. FAX: (216)672-3104. Director: John T. Hubbell. Editor: Julia Morton. Estab. 1965. Publishes hardcover and paperback originals and some reprints. Averages 20-25 titles/year. Subsidy publishes (nonauthor) 20% of books. Standard minimum book contract on net sales; rarely offers advance. "Always write a letter of inquiry before submitting manuscripts. We can publish only a limited number of titles each year and can frequently tell in advance whether or not we would be interested in a particular manuscript. This practice saves both our time and that of the author, not to mention postage costs. If interested we will ask for complete manuscript. Decisions based on in-house readings and two by outside scholars in the field of study." Reports in 10 weeks. Enclose return postage. Free book catalog.
Nonfiction: Especially interested in "scholarly works in history and literary studies of high quality, any titles of regional interest for Ohio, scholarly biographies, archaeological research, the arts, and general nonfiction."
Recent Nonfiction Title: *The Remarkable Case of Dorothy L. Sayers*, by Catherine Kenney.

MICHAEL KESEND PUBLISHING, LTD., 1025 5th Ave., New York NY 10028. (212)249-5150. Director: Michael Kesend. Estab. 1979. Publishes hardcover and trade paperback originals and reprints. Averages 4-6 titles/year; receives 150 submissions annually. 50% of books from first-time authors; 50% of books from unagented writers. Pays 3-12½% royalty on wholesale price or retail price, or makes outright purchase for $500 minimum. Advance varies. Publishes book an average of 18 months after acceptance. Reports in 2 months on queries; 3 months on mss. Guidelines for #10 SASE.
Nonfiction: Biography, how-to, illustrated book, self-help and sports. Subjects include animals, health, history, hobbies, nature, sports, travel, the environment, and guides to several subjects. Needs sports, health self-help and environmental awareness guides. No photography mss. Submit outline/synopsis and sample chapters. Reviews artwork/photos as part of ms package.
Recent Nonfiction Title: *Swee' Pea and Other Playground Legends, Tales of Drugs, Violence and Basketball*, by John Valenti with Ron Naclerio.
Fiction: Literary fiction only. No science fiction or romance. No simultaneous submissions. Submit outline/synopsis and 2-3 sample chapters.
Recent Fiction Title: *Season of Migration to the North*, by Tayeb Salih.
Tips: "We are now more interested in nature-related topics and also regional guides and sports nonfiction."

KINSEEKER PUBLICATIONS, P.O. Box 184, Grawn MI 49637. (616)276-6745. Editor: Victoria Wilson. Estab. 1986. Publishes trade paperback originals. Averages 6 titles/year. 100% of books from unagented writers. Pays 10-25% royalty on retail price. Publishes book an average of 8 months after acceptance. Simultaneous submissions OK. Reports in 2 weeks. Book catalog and manuscript guidelines for #10 SASE.
Nonfiction: Reference books. Subjects include history and genealogy. Query or submit outline/synopsis and sample chapters. Reviews artwork/photos as part of ms package.
Recent Nonfiction Title: *Yours in Love, The Birmingham Civil War Letters*, by Zoe vonEnde Lappin.

B. KLEIN PUBLICATIONS, P.O. Box 8503, Coral Springs FL 33075. (305)752-1708. FAX: (305)752-2547. Editor-in-Chief: Bernard Klein. Estab. 1946. Publishes hardcover and paperback originals. Specializes in directories, annuals, who's who books, bibliography, business opportunity, reference books. Averages 5 titles/year. Pays 10% royalty on wholesale price, "but we're negotiable." Advance "depends on many factors." Markets books by direct mail and mail order. Simultaneous submissions OK. Reports in 2 weeks. Book catalog for #10 SASE.
Nonfiction: Business, hobbies, how-to, reference, self-help, directories and bibliographies. Query or submit outline/synopsis and sample chapters or complete ms.
Recent Nonfiction Title: *Mail Order Business Directory*, by Bernard Klein.

KNIGHTS PRESS, INC., P.O. Box 6737, Stamford CT 06901. Publisher: Elizabeth G. Gershman. Estab. 1983. Publishes trade paperback originals. Averages 12 titles/year; receives 500 submissions annually. 50% of books from first-time authors; 50% of books from unagented writers. Publishes book an average of 18 months after acceptance. Reports in 1 month on queries; 3 months on mss. Book catalog and/or ms guidelines for #10 SASE.
Nonfiction "We are looking for well-written, nonfiction of interest to gay men or discussing gay lifestyles for the general public."
Fiction: "We publish *only* gay men's fiction; must show a positive gay lifestyle or positive gay relationship." No young adult or children's; no pornography; no formula plots, especially no formula romances; no lesbian fiction. Query a must. Do not submit complete manuscript unless requested.

Recent Fiction Title: *Some Dance to Remember,* by Jack Fritscher.
Tips: "We are interested in well-written, well-plotted gay fiction. We are looking only for the highest quality gay literature."

ALFRED A. KNOPF, INC., Division of Random House, 201 E. 50th St., New York NY 10022. (212)751-2600. Senior Editor: Ashbel Green. Children's Book Editor: Ms. Frances Foster. Publishes hardcover and paperback originals. Averages 200 titles annually. 15% of books from first-time authors; 30% of books from unagented writers. Royalties and advance "vary." Publishes book an average of 10 months after acceptance. Simultaneous (if so informed) submissions OK. Reports in 1 month. Book catalog for 7×10 SAE with 5 first class stamps.
Nonfiction: Book-length nonfiction, including books of scholarly merit. Preferred length: 50,000-150,000 words. "A good nonfiction writer should be able to follow the latest scholarship in any field of human knowledge, and fill in the abstractions of scholarship for the benefit of the general reader by means of good, concrete, sensory reporting." Query. Reviews artwork/photos as part of ms package.
Recent Nonfiction Title: *Means of Ascent,* by Robert Caro (biography).
Fiction: Publishes book-length fiction of literary merit by known or unknown writers. Length: 40,000-150,000 words. Submit complete ms.
Recent Fiction Title: *Jurassic Park,* by Michael Crichton.

KNOWLEDGE BOOK PUBLISHERS, Suite 100, 3863 SW Loop 820, Fort Worth TX 76133-2076. (817)292-4270. FAX: (817)294-2893. Editor/Publisher: Dr. O.A. Battista. Estab. 1976. Publishes hardcover, trade paperback and mass market paperback originals. Firm averages 4-6 titles/year. Receives 50-100 submissions/year. 75% of books from first-time authors. 0% from unagented writers. Pays 10-15% royalty on wholesale price. Advance varies. Publishes book an average of 1 year after acceptance. Query for electronic submissions. Reports in 1 month on queries; 2 months on mss. Manuscript guidelines for #10 SASE.
Nonfiction: How-to, humor, juvenile, technical. Subjects include Americana, health/medicine, science. Submit through agent only.
Recent Nonfiction Title: *Research for Profit,* by O. A. Battista.
Fiction: Juvenile. Submit through agent only.
Tips: "Our audience is a general audience interested in *new* knowledge useful in everyday life. If I were a writer trying to market a book today, I would do intense research on a new knowledge data that the general public can use to their *personal* benefit in everyday life."

‡KNOWLEDGE INDUSTRY PUBLICATIONS, INC., 701 Westchester Ave., White Plains NY 10604. (914)328-9157. FAX: (914)328-9093. Senior Vice President: Janet Moore. Publishes hardcover and paperback originals. Averages 10 titles/year; receives 30 submissions annually. 25% of books from first-time authors; 100% of books from unagented writers. Average print order for a writer's first book is 2,500. Offers negotiable advance. Publishes book an average of 1 year after acceptance. Query for electronic submissions. Reports in 2 weeks. Free book catalog; ms guidelines for SASE.
Nonfiction: Business and economics, also corporate, industrial video, interactive video. Especially needs TV and video. Query first, then submit outline/synopsis and sample chapters. Reviews artwork/photos as part of ms package.
Recent Nonfiction Title: *Secrets of Video Training,* by Steve Cartwright.

KODANSHA INTERNATIONAL U.S.A., Subsidiary of Kodansha International (Tokyo), 114 5th Ave., New York NY 10011. (212)727-6460. Contact: Assistant Editor. Publishes hardcover and trade paperback originals (70%); hardcover and trade paperback reprints (30%). Averages 10-20 titles/year. Receives 300 submissions/year. 10% of books from first-time authors; 70% from unagented writers. Pays 6-15% royalty on retail price. Offers $10,000 average advance. Publishes book an average of 9 months after acceptance. Simultaneous submissions OK. Reports in 1 month. Book catalog for 8×13 SAE and 6 first class stamps.
Nonfiction: Biography, topical books-current events. Subjects include anthropology/archaeology, art/architecture, business and economics, cooking, foods and nutrition, ethnic, gardening, government/politics, health/medicine, history, hobbies, language/literature, military/war, music/dance, nature/environment, philosophy, psychology, religion, science, sociology, translation, travel and Asian subjects. We are looking for distinguished critical books on international subjects; Asian-related subjects; serious new consciousness New Age books. No pop psychology, how-to, true crime, regional. Query. Reviews artwork/photos as part of ms package.
Recent Nonfiction Title: *Inside the Robot Kingdom: Japan, Mechatronics, and the Coming Robotopia,* by Frederik L. Schodt (science, sociology).
Tips: "Writers have the best chance selling us well-researched, well-written nonfiction about the current state of the world or a specific area of knowledge about which the author is an expert. Our audience is the intellectually-curious bookreader or student who is a bit of world traveler. If I were a

Close-up

Mark Richard
Author

Photo by Bill Hayward

"The openings of short stories are very important," says author Mark Richard. He learned this from Gordon Lish, an editor at Alfred A. Knopf and mentor to many of today's successful writers. "Short stories are competing against an incessant blitz of stimuli, and you must get the attention of the reader right away."

Richard's collection of stories, *The Ice at the Bottom of the World*, published by Knopf, reflects this philosophy. "What's more, when you have a premise in the beginning of a story, you must render it so completely that by the end, the same group of words will have a whole new meaning," he says. "There will be an irony or a change or movement on the part of the narrator or characters."

The Ice at the Bottom of the World won the PEN-Ernest Hemingway Foundation Award for best first fiction book of 1989. Richard's stories have appeared in *Esquire, Harper's, The Atlantic Monthly* and *The New Yorker* and have been reprinted in *The Best American Short Stories* and *The Pushcart Prize*. He is currently working on a novel. "Something that's helped me a lot with the novel is reducing the printed pages and pasting them on a large poster board," he says. "I took some different colored highlighters and where I see certain thematic things happening, I color blue. Where a character shows up often, orange. After a while, you can see the narrative lines."

Richard has never attempted a novel before, and has come to realize that to be successful at it, he must write almost every day. "When you're young and starting out with a little bit of talent and a lot of determination, you can write stories in bursts," he says. "But after a dozen stories, those bursts will be expended. The heat is still there, though it may not burn so intensely. And you need to stay close to that heat by writing every day." Richard says he has been working on the novel almost every day, so he can write at home, in a car; it's not important. "Once the fever's on you, you can write anywhere. But when the fever's not on you, you must have a place to go where you can write without distraction."

Writers must do their storytelling through writing, according to Richard, not through talking about a story. "Talking about a story before writing it can jinx the story," he says. "There's a certain amount of pressure to tell a story and a good way to ruin one is to talk it out. The most important thing is your discovering the story as you write." You can resurrect yourself out of having talked out a story, however, by writing the story anyway. "I'll bet it doesn't turn out the way it did when you were telling it," contends Richard. "Also, it's not always bad to talk out a story, because it's easier to tell the obvious story. Maybe if you've talked it out you've told the obvious story."

Sometimes Richard thinks he's a writer in the same way he was an aerial photographer or a modular furniture assembler. "Being a writer is great and it's a great way to chronicle your life and the age we live in," he says. "I think I write best, though, when I don't see myself as A Writer. I write best when I see writing as a part of my life, not everything in my life." He's certain he will always write, but he wants to live this life. "It's only when you look at your writing askance that you're going to get your best work done."

—Mark Kissling

writer trying to market a book today, I would spend a lot of time in bookstores checking out what is available and from whom."

‡KRIEGER PUBLISHING COMPANY, Box 9542, Melbourne FL 32902-9542. (407)724-9542. FAX (407)951-3671. Executive Assistant: Marie Bowles. Imprints are Orbit Series, Anvil Series and Public History. Publishes hardcover and paperback originals and reprints. Averages 120 titles/year; receives 50-60 submissions annually. 30% of books from first-time authors; 100% of books from unagented writers. Pays royalty on net realized price. Publishes book an average of 8 months after acceptance. Reports in 1 month. Free book catalog.
Nonfiction: College reference, technical, and textbook. Subjects include history, music, philosophy, psychology, space science herpetology, chemistry, physics, engineering and medical. Reviews artwork/photos as part of ms package.
Recent Nonfiction Title: *Introduction to Space: The Science of Spaceflight*, by Thomas D. Damon.

*KUMARIAN PRESS, INC., Suite 119, 630 Oakwood Ave., West Hartford CT 06110-1529. (203)953-0214. Editor: Jenna Dixon. Publishes hardcover and paperback originals and paperback reprints. Averages 8-12 titles/year. Receives 50-100 submissions/year. 10% of books from first-time authors. 100% from unagented writers. Subsidy publishes 25% of books. Determines subsidy by financial viability. Pays 0-10% royalty on net. Publishes book an average of 9 months after acceptance. Query for electronic submissions. Reports in 2 weeks on queries; 2 months on mss. Free book catalog and ms guidelines.
Nonfiction: Professional. Subjects include agriculture/horticulture, business and economics, government/politics, nature/environment, relition, sociology, women's issues/studies, international development. We are looking for mss that address the practical needs of international development community; specific topics include: women in development, natural resource management, private vs. voluntary organizations, and effective and accountable public service. Query. Submit outline/synopsis and sample chapters and cover letters.
Recent Nonfiction Title: *Women's Ventures: Assistance to the Informal Sector in Latin America*, by Marguerite Berger and Mayra Burinic.
Tips: "Authors have the best chance selling us well written mss that are specifically targeted to addressing the issues faced by the international development community. Our audience is the international development community."

*PETER LANG PUBLISHING, Subsidiary of Verlag Peter Lang AG, Bern, Switzerland, 62 W. 45th St., New York NY 10036. (212)302-6740. FAX: (212)302-7574. Managing Director: Christopher S. Myers; Senior Acquisitions Editor: Michael Flamini; Associate Acquisitions Editor: Kathryn Earle; San Francisco Acquisitions Editor: Heidi Burns. Estab. 1952. Publishes mostly hardcover originals. Averages 200 titles/year. 75% of books from first-time authors; 98% of books from unagented writers. Subsidy publishes 25% of books. All subsidies are guaranteed repayment plus profit (if edition sells out) in contract. Subsidy published if ms is highly specialized and author relatively unknown. Pays 10-20% royalty on net price. Translators get flat fee plus percentage of royalties. No advance. Publishes book an average of 1 year after acceptance. Reports in 1 month on queries; 2 months on mss. Free book catalog and ms guidelines.
Nonfiction: General nonfiction, reference works, and scholarly monographs. Subjects include literary criticism, Germanic and Romance languages, art history, business and economics, American and European political science, history, music, philosophy, psychology, religion, sociology and biography. All books are scholarly monographs, textbooks, reference books, reprints of historic texts, critical editions or translations. "We are expanding and are receptive to any scholarly project in the humanities and social sciences." No mss shorter than 200 pages. Submit complete ms. Fully refereed review process.
Fiction and Poetry: "We do not publish original fiction or poetry. We seek scholarly and critical editions only. Submit complete ms."
Tips: "Besides our commitment to specialist academic monographs, we are one of the few U.S. publishers who publish books in most of the modern languages. A major advantage for Lang authors is international marketing and distribution of all titles. Translation rights sold for many titles."

LARSON PUBLICATIONS/PBPF, 4936 Rt. 414, Burdett NY 14818. (607)546-9342. Director: Paul Cash. Estab. 1982. Publishes hardcover and trade paperback originals. Averages 4-6 titles/year. Receives 1,000 submissions/year. 8% of books from first-time authors. Pays 7½-10% royalty on retail price; or 10% cash received. Offers $1,000 average advance. Publishes book an average of 9 months after acceptance. Simultaneous submissions OK. Reports in 4 months on queries. Unsolicited mss not accepted; queries only. Free book catalog.

Nonfiction: Self-help and spiritual philosophy. Subjects include philosophy, psychology and religion. We are looking for studies of comparative spiritual philosophy or personal fruits of independent (transsectarian viewpoint) spiritual research/practice. Query or submit outline/synopsis and sample chapters. Reviews artwork/photos as part of ms package.

Recent Nonfiction Title: *At the Leading Edge*, by Michael Toms.

MERLOYD LAWRENCE BOOKS, Imprint of Addison-Wesley, 102 Chestnut St., Boston MA 02108. President: Merloyd Lawrence. Estab. 1982. Publishes hardcover and trade paperback originals. Averages 7-8 titles/year. Receives 400 submissions/year. 25% of books from first-time authors. 20% from unagented writers. Pays royalty on retail price. Publishes book an average of 1 year after acceptance. Simultaneous submissions OK. Reports in 3 weeks on queries; no unsolicited ms read. All queries with SASE read and answered. Book catalog available from Addison Wesley.

Nonfiction: Biography. Subjects include child development/parenting, health/medicine, nature/environment, psychology. Query with SASE.

Recent Nonfiction Title: *Mindfulness*, by Ellen Langer, Ph.D. (psychology).

LEISURE BOOKS, Division of Dorchester Publishing Co., Inc., Suite 1008, 276 5th Ave., New York NY 10001. (212)725-8811. Editor: Frank Walgren. Estab. 1970. Publishes mass market paperback originals and reprints. Averages 144 titles/year; receives thousands of submissions annually. 20% of books from first-time authors; 40% of books from unagented writers. Pays royalty on retail price. Advance negotiable. Publishes book an average of 18 months after acceptance. Reports in 1 month on queries; up to 2 months on mss. Book catalog and ms guidelines for #10 SASE.

Nonfiction: "Our needs are minimal as we publish perhaps four nonfiction titles a year." Query.

Fiction: Historical (90,000 words); Gothics (75,000 words); futuristic romance (80,000 words). "We are strongly backing historical romance. No sweet romance, science fiction, western, erotica, contemporary women's fiction, mainstream or male adventure." Query or submit outline/synopsis and sample chapters. "No material will be returned without SASE."

Recent Fiction Title: *Lacey's Way*, by Madeline Baker (historical romance).

Tips: "Historical romance is our strongest category."

LEISURE PRESS, Imprint of Human Kinetics Publishers, P.O. Box 5076, Champaign IL 61820. (217)351-5076. FAX: (217)351-2674. Director: Brian Holding. Estab. 1974. Other imprint is Human Kinetics Books. Publishes hardcover, trade paperback and mass market paperback originals. Averages 30 titles/year; receives 200-250 submissions annually. 25% of books from first-time authors; 95% from unagented writers. Pays 10-15% royalty on wholesale price. Offers average $1,000 advance. Publishes ms an average of 9 months after acceptance. Simultaneous submissions OK. Query for electronic submissions. Reports in 2 weeks on queries; 6 weeks on ms. Free book catalog; writer's guidelines for SASE.

Nonfiction: How-to, reference, technical. Subjects include sports, fitness and wellness. "We want coaching-related books, technique books on sports and fitness. No fitness or coaching books that are not based on sound physical education principles and research." Reviews artwork/photos as part of ms package. Query or submit outline/synopsis and sample chapters.

Recent Nonfiction Title: *Drugs, Sport, and Politics*, by Robert Voy, M.D.

Tips: "Our audience is comprised of coaches, athletes, physical education students and fitness enthusiasts."

LEXIKOS, P.O. Box 296, Lagunitas CA 94938. (415)488-0401. Editor: Mike Witter. Estab. 1981. Imprint is Don't Call It Frisco Press. Publishes hardcover and trade paperback originals and trade paperback reprints. Averages 8 titles/year; receives 200 submissions annually. 50% of books from first-time authors; 90% of books from unagented writers. Average print order for a writer's first book is 5,000. Royalties vary from 8-12½% according to books sold. "Authors asked to accept lower royalty on high discount (50% plus) sales." Offers average $1,000 advance. Publishes book an average of 10 months after acceptance. Simultaneous submissions OK. Reports in 1 month. Book catalog and ms guidelines for 6×9 SAE and 2 first class stamps.

Nonfiction: Coffee table book, illustrated book. Subjects include regional, outdoors, oral histories, Americana, history and nature. Especially looking for 50,000-word "city and regional histories, anecdotal in style for a general audience; books of regional interest about *places*; adventure and wilderness books; annotated reprints of books of Americana; Americana in general." No health, sex, European travel, diet, broad humor, fiction, quickie books (we stress backlist vitality), religion, children's or nutrition. Submit outline/synopsis and sample chapters. Reviews artwork/photos as part of ms package.

Recent Nonfiction Title: *A Short History of Portland*, by Gordon DeMarco.
Tips: "A regional interest or history book has the best chance of selling to Lexikos. Submit a short, cogent proposal; follow up with letter queries. Give the publisher reason to believe you will help him *sell* the book (identify the market, point out the availability of mailing lists, distinguish your book from the competition). Avoid grandiose claims."

LIBERTY HALL PRESS, Imprint of McGraw-Hill, Inc., 11 W. 19th St., 3rd Floor, New York NY 10011. Vice President/Editorial Director: David J. Conti. Estab. 1964. Publishes hardcover originals and trade paperback originals and reprints. Publishes 25 titles/year. Receives 300 submissions/year. 40% of books from first-time authors; 50% from unagented writers. Pays 5-15% royalty on wholesale price. Offers $3,000 average advance. Publishes book an average of 9 months after acceptance. Simultaneous submissions OK. Reports on queries in 2 weeks; on ms in 1 month. Book catalog free on request; writer's guidelines for #10 SASE.
Nonfiction: Subjects include investing, real estate, personal finance, business finance, small business/entrepreneurship, legal self-help. "We're engaged in a wide-ranging business publishing program. We publish for professionals as well as the general public." Submit outline/synopsis and sample chapter.
Recent Nonfiction Title: *Understanding Corporate Bonds*, by Harold Kerzner.
Tips: "We publish very practical, results-oriented books. Study the competition, study the market, then submit a proposal."

LIBERTY PUBLISHING COMPANY, INC., 440 S. Federal Hwy., Deerfield Beach FL 33441. (305)360-9000. Publisher: Jeffrey B. Little. Subsidiaries include LPC Software. Publishes hardcover and trade paperback originals. Averages 5-10 titles/year. Receives 300-800 submissions/year. 90% of books from first-time authors; 95% of books from unagented writers. Pays 5-12% royalty on wholesale. Buys mss outright for $300-2,000. Offers $400 average advance. Publishes book an average of 9-18 months after acceptance. Simultaneous submissions OK. Reports in 3 weeks on queries; 2 months on mss. Book catalog for 9×12 SAE with 4 first class stamps. Manuscript guidelines for #10 SASE.
Nonfiction: Cookbook, how-to, reference, self-help. Subjects include business and economics, cooking, foods and nutrition, hobbies, money/finance, recreation, sports especially horseracing, travel. "Liberty Publishing Company seeks only titles that can become *the* leading book in its respective area. The author should have credibility in his/her field of expertise. Seeking new ideas (e.g., retirement community guides, highly specialized cooking, etc.) No mind-benders, please. No psychology, religious, or esoteric clap-trap. Prefer only useful, hands-on, practical material." Query. Submit complete ms. "We are only interested in completed mss." Reviews artwork/photos as part of ms package.
Recent Nonfiction Title: *Ten Steps to Winning*, by Danny Holmes (guide for racing fans).
Tips: "We favor nonfiction books that offer the reader an immediate and obvious benefit. Books that answer the book-buyer's initial question. 'Why should I buy this book?' Price is not the major consideration. This is one reason why horse race handicapping titles do well for us. Adults seeking to learn a specific piece of information, and less concerned about the price of the book. The potential bookbuyer probably recognizes the value of the book's message before it leaves the bookstore. The message is practical and useful, and maybe profitable. If I were a writer trying to market a book today, I would make a point of knowing the *market* for the book and know something about the expected *audience* for the work. We also favor books that can be sold in specialty markets and we are seeking tie-ins with software and videos."

*LIBRA PUBLISHERS, INC., Suite 383, 3089C Clairemont Dr., San Diego CA 92117. (619)581-9449. Contact: William Kroll. Estab. 1960. Publishes hardcover and paperback originals. Specializes in the behavioral sciences. Averages 15 titles/year; receives 300 submissions annually. 60% of books from first-time authors; 85% of books from unagented writers. 10-15% royalty on retail price; no advance. "We will also offer our services to authors who wish to publish their own works. The services include editing, proofreading, production, artwork, copyrighting, and assistance in promotion and distribution." Publishes book an average of 8 months after acceptance. Reports in 2 weeks. Free book catalog; writer's guidelines for #10 SASE.
Nonfiction: Mss in all subject areas will be given consideration, but main interest is in the behavioral sciences. Prefers complete manuscript but will consider outline/synopsis and 3 sample chapters. Reviews artwork/photos as part of ms package.
Recent Nonfiction Title: *Highway Robbery: The Truth About America's Auto Dealers*, by Sherman Ruthmay.
Recent Fiction Title: *Tarnished Hero*, by Steve Berman.

LIBRARIES UNLIMITED, P.O. Box 3988, Englewood CO 80155-3988. FAX: (303)220-8843. Editor-in-Chief: Bohdan S. Wynar. Estab. 1964. Imprints are Teacher Ideas Press and Ukranian Academic Press. Publishes hardcover and paperback originals. Averages 50 titles/year; receives 100-200 submissions annually. 10-20% of books from first-time authors. Average print order for a writer's first book is

2,000. 10% royalty on net sales; advance averages $500. Publishes book an average of 1 year after acceptance. Reports in 2 months. Free book catalog and ms guidelines.
Nonfiction: Publishes reference and library science textbooks, teacher resource and activity books also software. Looks for professional experience. Query or submit outline and sample chapters; state availability of photos/illustrations with submission. All prospective authors are required to fill out an author questionnaire.
Recent Nonfiction Title: *Handbook of Business Information*, by Diane Strauss.

LIBRARY RESEARCH ASSOCIATES, INC., RD #5, Box 41, Dunderberg Rd., Monroe NY 10950. (914)783-1144. President: Matilda A. Gocek. Estab. 1968. Imprint is Empire State Fiction. Publishes hardcover and trade paperback originals. Averages 4 titles/year; receives about 300 submissions annually. 100% of books from first-time authors; 100% of books from unagented writers. Pays 10% maximum royalty on retail price. Offers 20 copies of the book as advance. Publishes book an average of 14 months after acceptance. Reports in 3 weeks on queries; 3 months on mss. Book catalog free on request.
Nonfiction: Biography, how-to, reference, technical and American history. Subjects include Americana, business and economics, history and politics. "Our nonfiction book manuscript needs for the next year or two will include books about historical research of some facet of American history, and definitive works about current or past economics or politics." No astrology, occult, sex, adult humor or gay rights. Submit outline/synopsis and sample chapters.
Recent Nonfiction Title: *American Woman: Her Role During the Revolutionary War*, by Dianne McKinstrie.
Fiction: Send fiction to Empire State Fiction, Dianne D. McKinstrie, senior editor. Adventure (based in an authentic NY location); historical (particularly in or about New York state); mystery; and suspense. "I try to publish at least three novels per year. Characterization is so important! The development of people and plot must read well. The realism of world events (war, terrorism, catastrophes) is turning readers to a more innocent world of reading for entertainment with less shock value. Free speech (free *everything!*) is reviving old values. Explicit sex, extreme violence, vile language in any form will not be considered." Submit outline/synopsis and sample chapters.
Recent Fiction Title: *Tales from an Irish Wake*, by Armstrong.
Tips: "Our audience is adult, over age 30, literate and knowledgeable in business or professions. The writer has the best chance of selling our firm historical fiction or nonfiction and scientific texts. If I were a writer trying to market a book today, I would try to write about people in a warm human situation—the foibles, the loss of self, the unsung heroism—angels with feet of clay."

LINCH PUBLISHING, INC., Suite 106, 2431 Aloma Ave., Winter Park FL 32792. (407)679-4446. Vice President: Debbie Williams. Editor: Peggy H. Maddox. Estab. 1983. Publishes hardcover and trade paperback originals. Averages 10 titles/year. Pays 6-8% royalty on retail price. Rarely pays advances. Publishes book an average of 9 months after acceptance. Simultaneous submissions OK. Reports in 6 weeks. Book catalog for $1 and #10 SAE with 2 first class stamps.
Nonfiction: Publishes books only on estate planning and legal how-to books which must be applicable in all 50 states. "We are interested in a book on getting through probate, settling an estate, and minimizing federal estate and/or state inheritance taxes." Query editor by phone before submitting mss—"we could have already accepted a manuscript and be in the process of publishing one of the above."
Recent Nonfiction Title: *It's Easy to Avoid Probate*, by Barbara R. Stock.
Tips: "Currently interest is mainly estate planning and avoiding probate how-to."

LION PUBLISHING CORPORATION, 1705 Hubbard Ave., Batavia IL 60510. (708)879-0707. Editor: Robert Bittner. Estab. 1967. Publishes hardcover and trade paperback originals. Firm averages 15 titles/year. Pays royalty. Publishes book an average of 18 months after acceptance. Reports in 1 month on queries; 2 months on mss. Book catalog for 9 × 12 SAE and 4 first class stamps. Manuscript guidelines for #10 SAE and 2 first class stamps.
Nonfiction: Subjects include child guidance/parenting, biography and religion. "We are especially interested in manuscripts on relationships and on spirituality. We do not want Bible studies or sermons." Query or submit outline/synopsis and sample chapters.
Recent Nonfiction Titles: *In Search of Happiness*, by James Houston.
Fiction: Fantasy, literary historical, and YA. "Stories that create meaty, believable characters, not puppets or simplistic representations of certain values or beliefs. Give us a story that anyone would be intrigued with—and write it from a Christian perspective." Submit complete ms.
Recent Fiction Titles: *The Paradise War*, by Stephen Lawhead.
Tips: "All Lion books are written from a Christian perspective. However, they must speak to a general audience. Because Lion's approach is unique, we strongly recommend that every potential author request our guidelines."

LITTLE, BROWN AND CO., INC., Division of Time Warner Inc., 34 Beacon St., Boston MA 02108. Contact: Editorial Department, Trade Division. Estab. 1837. Imprint is Bullfinch Press. Publishes hardcover and paperback originals and paperback reprints. Averages 100 titles/year. "Royalty and advance agreements vary from book to book and are discussed with the author at the time an offer is made. Submissions only from authors who have had a book published or have been published in professional or literary journals, newspapers or magazines." Reports in 5 months for queries/proposals.
Nonfiction: "Some how-to books, distinctive cookbooks, biographies, history, popular science and nature, and sports." Query or submit outline/synopsis and sample chapters.
Recent Nonfiction Title: *The Cat and the Curmudgeon*, by Cleveland Amory.
Fiction: Contemporary popular fiction as well as fiction of literary distinction. Query or submit outline/synopsis and sample chapters.
Recent Fiction Title: *The Last Voyage of Somebody the Sailor*, by John Barth.

LLEWELLYN PUBLICATIONS, Subsidiary of Llewellyn Worldwide, Ltd., P.O. Box 64383, St. Paul MN 55164. (612)291-1970. FAX: (612)291-1908. Acquisitions Manager: Nancy J. Mostad. Estab. 1901. Publishes trade and mass market paperback originals. Averages 60 titles/year. Receives 500 submissions/year. 30% of books from first-time authors; 90% from unagented writers. Pays 10% royalty on moneys received both wholesale and retail. Publishes book an average of 1 year after acceptance. Simultaneous submissions OK. Query for electronic submissions. Reports in 2 weeks on queries; 3 months on mss. Book catalog for #10 SASE. Manuscript guidelines free on request.
Nonfiction: How-to and self-help. Subjects include nature/environment, metaphysical/magick, psychology and women's issues/studies. Submit outline/synopsis and sample chapters. Reviews artwork/photos as part of ms package.
Recent Nonfiction Title: *Goddesses and Heroines*, by Patricia Monaghan.

LODESTAR BOOKS, Imprint of Dutton Children's Books, Division of Penguin USA, 375 Hudson St., New York NY 10014. (212)366-2627. Editorial Director: Virginia Buckley. Senior Editor: Rosemary Brosnan. Publishes hardcover originals. Publishes juveniles, young adults, fiction and nonfiction; and picture books. Averages 30 titles/year; receives 1,000 submissions annually. 10-20% of books from first-time authors; 25-30% of books from unagented writers. Average print order for a writer's first novel or nonfiction is 5,000-6,000; picture book print runs are higher. Pays royalty on invoice list price; advance offered. Publishes book an average of 18 months after acceptance. Reports in 4 months. Ms guidelines for SASE.
Nonfiction: Query or submit outline/synopsis and 2-3 sample chapters including "theme, chapter-by-chapter outline, and 1 or 2 completed chapters." State availability of photos and/or illustrations. Queries/mss may be routed to other editors in the publishing group. Reviews artwork/photos as part of ms package.
Recent Nonfiction Title: *Christopher Columbus: Voyager to the Unknown*, by Nancy Smiler Levinson.
Fiction: Publishes for young adults (middle grade) and juveniles (ages 5-17): multicultural, adventure, fantasy, historical, humorous, contemporary, mystery, science fiction, suspense and western books, also picture books. Submit complete ms.
Recent Fiction Title: *Lyddie*, by Katherine Paterson.
Tips: "A young adult or middle-grade novel that is literary, fast-paced, well-constructed (as opposed to a commercial novel); well-written nonfiction on contemporary issues, photographic essays, and nonfiction picture books have been our staples. We have now expanded into the picture book market as well."

LONE EAGLE PUBLISHING CO., Suite 9, 2337 Roscomare Rd., Los Angeles CA 90077. (213)471-8066. FAX: (213)471-4969. Toll Free: 1-800-FILMBKS. President: Joan V. Singleton. Estab. 1982. Publishes hardcover and trade paperback originals. Averages 8 titles/year; receives 20-30 submissions annually. 100% of books from unagented writers. Pays 10% royalty minimum on net income wholesale and retail. Offers $100-250 average advance. Publishes a book an average of 1 year after acceptance. Simultaneous submissions OK. Query for electronic submissions. Reports in 1 month on queries; 3 months on mss. Book catalog for #10 SAE and 2 first class stamps.
Nonfiction: Self-help, technical, how-to, and reference. Subjects include movies. "We are looking for technical books in the motion picture and video field by professionals. No unrelated topics or biographies." Submit outline/synopsis and sample chapters. Reviews artwork/photos as part of ms package.
Recent Nonfiction Title: *The Film Editing Room Handbook*, by Norman Hollyn.
Tips: "A well-written, well-thought-out book on some technical aspect of the motion picture (or video) industry has the best chance: for example, script supervising, editing, special effects, costume design, production design. Pick a subject that has not been done to death, make sure you know what you're

talking about, get someone well-known in that area to endorse the book and prepare to spend a lot of time publicizing the book."

LONGMAN PUBLISHING GROUP, 95 Church St., White Plains NY 10601. (914)993-5000. FAX: (914)997-8115. President: Bruce S. Butterfield. Estab. 1974. Publishes hardcover and paperback originals. Publishes 200 titles/year. Pays variable royalty; offers variable advance. Reports in 6 weeks.
Nonfiction: Textbooks only (elementary/high school, college and professional): world history, political science, economics, communications, social sciences, sociology, education, English, Latin, foreign languages, English as a second language. No trade, art or juvenile.

LONGSTREET PRESS, INC., Suite 102, 2150 Newmarket Parkway, Marietta GA 30067. (404)980-1488. Associate Editor: John Yow. Estab. 1988. Publishes hardcover and trade paperback originals. Averages 20 titles/year. Receives 250 submissions/year. 25-30% of books from first-time authors. 60% from unagented writers. Pays royalty. Publishes book an average of 1 year after acceptance. Simultaneous submissions OK. Reports in 6 weeks on queries; 6 months on mss. No electronic submissions via disk or modem. Book catalog for 9 × 12 SAE with 4 first class stamps. Manuscript guidelines for #10 SASE.
Nonfiction: Biography, coffee table book, cookbook, humor, illustrated book, reference. Subjects include Americana, cooking, foods and nutrition, gardening, history, language/literature, nature/environment, photography, regional, sports, women's issues/studies. "We want serious journalism-oriented nonfiction on subjects appealing to a broad, various audience. No poetry, how-to, religious or inspirational, scientific or highly technical, textbooks of any kind, erotica." Query. Submit outline/synopsis and sample chapters. Reviews artwork as part of ms package.
Recent Nonfiction Title: *Broken Pledges: The Deadly Rite of Hazing*, by Hank Nuwer.
Fiction: Literary, mainstream/contemporary. "We are looking for solid literary fiction with appeal to a general reader. No juvenile or young adult literature, science fiction, mysteries, supernatural/horror, action/adventure/thriller, romance, historical fiction and romances." Query. Submit outline/synopsis and sample chapters.
Recent Fiction Title: *Heat Storm*, by Linda Chandler Munson (novel).
Tips: "Midlist books have a harder time making it. The nonfiction book, serious or humorous, with a clearly defined audience has the best chance. The audience for our books has a strong sense of intellectual curiosity and a functioning sense of humor. If I were a writer trying to market a book today, I would do thorough, professional work aimed at a clearly defined and reachable audience."

LOOMPANICS UNLIMITED, P.O. Box 1197, Port Townsend WA 98368. Book Editor: Michael Hoy. Estab. 1975. Publishes trade paperback originals. Publishes 20 titles/year; receives 100 submissions annually. 40% of books from first-time authors; 100% of books from unagented writers. Average print order for a writer's first book is 1,000. Pays 7½-15% royalty on wholesale or retail price or makes outright purchase of $100-1,200. Offers average $500 advance. Publishes book an average of 10 months after acceptance. Simultaneous submissions OK. Reports in 6 weeks. Free book catalog and author guidelines.
Nonfiction: How-to, reference and self-help. Subjects include business and economics, philosophy, politics, travel, and "beat the system" books. "We are looking for how-to books in the fields of espionage, investigation, the underground economy, police methods, how to beat the system, crime and criminal techniques. No cookbooks, inspirational, travel, or cutesy-wutesy stuff." Query, or submit outline/synopsis and sample chapters. Reviews artwork/photos.
Recent Nonfiction Title: *Building with Junk*, by Jim Broadstreet (how-to).
Tips: "Our audience is young males looking for hard-to-find information on alternatives to 'The System.'"

LOS HOMBRES PRESS, P.O. Box 632729, San Diego CA 92163-2729. (619)234-6710 or (619)688-1023. Contact: Jim Kitchen. Estab. 1989. Publishes trade paperback originals. Averages 4 titles/year. 50% of books from first-time authors. Most from unagented writers. Pays 7-10% royalty on retail price. Publishes book an average of 1 year after acceptance. Query for electronic submission.
Nonfiction: Subjects include gay/lesbian. Query. Reviews artwork/photos as part of ms package.
Recent Nonfiction Title: *The Vinyl Closet, Gays in the Music World*, by Boze Hadleigh.
Fiction: Gay/lesbian. "We want gay oriented mystery novels, short story collections including mysteries and science fiction and "mainstream" type novels with gay characters. Emphasis on good writing, not on explicit sex. No pornography. Query.
Recent Fiction: *The Search for Sebastian*, by Judston Crown.
Poetry: "We are interested *only* in haiku."
Recent Poetry Title: *The Rise & Fall of Sparrows*, by Alexis Rotella, Ed (haiku).

LOTHROP, LEE & SHEPARD BOOKS, Imprint of William Morrow and Company, 105 Madison Ave., New York NY 10016. (212)889-3050. Editor-in-Chief: Susan Pearson. Estab. 1859. Other children's imprints are Morrow Junior Books, Greenwillow Books and Tambourine Books. Publishes hardcover original children's books only. Royalty and advance vary according to type of book. Averages 60 titles/year. Less than 2% of books from first-time authors; 25% of books from unagented writers. Average print order for a writer's first book is 6,000. Publishes book an average of 2 years after acceptance. Does *not* accept unsolicitied manuscripts.

Fiction and Nonfiction: Publishes picture books, general nonfiction, and novels. Juvenile fiction emphasis is on novels for the 8-12 age group. Looks for "organization, clarity, creativity, literary style." Does *not* read unsolicited manuscripts.

Recent Nonfiction Title: *Portrait of a Tragedy: America and the Vietnam War*, by James A. Warren.

Recent Fiction Title: *The Outside Child*, by Nina Bawden.

Tips: "Trends in book publishing that freelance writers should be aware of include the demand for books for children under age three and the shrinking market for young adult books, especially novels."

LOUISIANA STATE UNIVERSITY PRESS, Baton Rouge LA 70893. (504)388-6294. Editor-in-Chief: Margaret Fisher Dalrymple. Estab. 1935. Publishes hardcover originals and hardcover and trade paperback reprints. Averages 60-70 titles/year. Receives 500 submissions/year. 33% of books from first-time authors. 90% from unagented writers. Pays royalty on wholesale price. Publishes book an average of 1 year after acceptance. Simultaneous submissions OK. Reports in 2 weeks on queries; 6 weeks on mss. Free book catalog and ms guidelines.

Nonfiction: Biography. Subjects include anthropology/archaeology, art/architecture, ethnic, government/politics, history, language/literature, military/war, music/dance, philosophy, photography, regional, sociology, women's issues/studies. Query. Submit outline/synopsis and sample chapters.

Fiction: Literary, novels, poetry collections and short story collections. Query. Submit outline/synopsis and sample chapters.

Tips: "Our audience includes scholars, intelligent laymen, general audience."

*LOYOLA UNIVERSITY PRESS, 3441 N. Ashland Ave., Chicago IL 60657. (312)281-1818. FAX: (312)281-0555. Editorial Director: Rev. Joseph F. Downey. Estab. 1927. Imprints are Campion Books, Values & Ethics. Publishes hardcover and trade paperback originals and reprints. Averages 12 titles/year; receives 100 submissions annually. 40% of books from first-time authors; 95% of books from unagented writers. Subsidy publishes 2% of books. Pays 10% royalty on wholesale price; offers no advance. Publishes book an average of 1 year after acceptance. Simultaneous submissions acceptable. Query for electronic submissions. Reports in 1 month. Book catalog for 6×9 SASE.

Nonfiction: Biography and textbook. Subjects include art (religious); history (church); and religion. The four subject areas of Campion Books include Jesuitica (Jesuit history, biography and spirituality); Literature-Theology interface (books dealing with theological or religious aspects of literary works or authors); contemporary Christian concerns (books on morality, spirituality, family life, pastoral ministry, prayer, worship, etc.); and Chicago/art (books dealing with the city of Chicago from historical, artistic, architectural, or ethnic perspectives, but with religious emphases). Query before submitting ms. Reviews artwork/photos.

Recent Nonfiction Titles: *Models of Faith—Biblical Spirituality for Our Time*, by Carlos G. Valles.

Tips: "Our audience is principally the college-educated reader with a religious, theological interest."

LUCENT BOOKS, P.O. Box 289011, San Diego CA 92128-9011. (619)485-7424. Managing Editor: Bonnie Szumski. Publishes hardcover originals and reprints. Publishes 50 titles/year; receives 75 submissions/year. 50% from first-time authors; 90% from unagented writers. Buys by outright purchase of $2,000-3,000. Offers average advance of 1/3 of total fee. Publishes book an average of 9 months after acceptance. Simultaneous submissions OK. Reports in 2 weeks on queries; 2 months on mss. Book catalog and ms guidelines for 9×12 SAE with 3 first class stamps.

An asterisk preceding a listing indicates that subsidy publishing or co-publishing (where author pays part or all of publishing costs) is available. Firms whose subsidy programs comprise more than 50% of their total publishing activities are listed at the end of the Book Packagers and Producers section.

Nonfiction: Juvenile. Subjects include controversial issues, discoveries and inventions, anthropology/ archaelogy, business and economics, computers and electronics, government/politics, history, military/ war, nature/environment, science, sports, women's issues/studies. All on the juvenile level. Submit outline/synopsis and sample chapters. All unsolicited mss are returned unopened. Reviews artwork/ photos as part of ms package.

Recent Nonfiction Title: *World Disasters*.

Tips: "A well-organized book at the juvenile reading level has the best chance of being sold to our firm. The trend is toward more interesting nonfiction at the 5-9th grade level. The more you know about a publisher the better chance you have of finding a home for your book."

LURAMEDIA, P.O. Box 261668, 10227 Autumnview Lane, San Diego CA 92126. (619)578-1948. FAX: (619)578-7560. Editorial Director: Lura Jane Geiger. Estab. 1982. Publishes trade paperback originals and reprints. Averages 6 titles/year; receives 250 submissions annually. 75% of books from first-time authors. 90% of books from unagented writers. Pays 10-15% royalty on wholesale price. Publishes book an average of 9 months after acceptance. Query for electronic submissions. Reports in 1 month. Book catalog and ms guidelines for #10 SASE.

Nonfiction: Self-help. Subjects include health, spirituality, psychology, and creativity. "Books on renewal: body, mind, spirit; using the right brain and relational material. Books on creativity, journaling, women's issues, black Christian, relationships. I want well digested, thoughtful books. No 'Jesus Saves' literature; books that give all the answers; poetry; or strident politics." Submit outline/synopsis, biography and sample chapters. Reviews artwork/photos as part of ms package.

Recent Nonfiction Title: *Circle of Stones: Woman's Journey to Herself*, by Judith Duerk.

Tips: "Our audience are people who want to grow and change; who want to get in touch with their spiritual side; who want to relax; who are creative and want creative ways to live."

LYONS & BURFORD, PUBLISHERS, INC., 31 W. 21 St., New York NY 10010. (212)620-9580. Publisher: Peter Burford. Estab. 1984. Publishes hardcover and trade paperback originals and hardcover and trade paperback reprints. Averages 30-40 titles/year. 50% of books from first-time authors. 75% from unagented writers. Pays varied royalty on retail price. Publishes book an average of 1 year after acceptance. Simultaneous submissions OK. Reports in 2 weeks on queries. Free book catalog.

Nonfiction: Subjects include agriculture/horticulture, Americana, animals, art/architecture, cooking, foods and nutrition, gardening, hobbies, nature/environment, science, sports and travel. Query.

Recent Nonfiction Title: *Eiger Dreams*, by Jon Krakauer (essays).

Tips: "We want practical, well written books on any aspect of the outdoors."

McCUTCHAN PUBLISHING CORPORATION, 2940 San Pablo Ave., Berkeley CA 94702. (415)841-8616. FAX: (415)841-7787. Editor: Kim Sharrar. Estab. 1963. Publishes 5 titles/year. Receives 60 submissions/year. 30% of books from first-time authors; 100% from unagented writers. Pays 12-15% royalty on wholesale price. Publishes book an average of 8 months after acceptance. Reports in 6 weeks. Book catalog and ms guidelines free on request.

Nonfiction: Textbook. Subjects include education, food service and criminal justice. Submit outline/ synopsis and sample chapters.

Recent Nonfiction Title: *Purchasing for Food Service Managers*, by Warfel and Cremer (food service).

Tips: "Professors and instructors of education, food service and criminal justice are our audience."

MARGARET K. McELDERRY BOOKS, Imprint of Macmillan Children's Book Group, Inc., Division of Macmillan Publishing Co., 866 3rd Ave., New York NY 10022. Editor: Margaret K. McElderry. Publishes hardcover originals. Publishes 20-25 titles/year; receives 3,000-3,500 submissions annually. 8% of books from first-time authors; 45% of books from unagented writers. The average print order is 6,000-7,500 for a writer's first teen book; 10,000-15,000 for a writer's first picture book. Pays royalty on retail price. Publishes book an average of 1½ years after acceptance. Reports in 3 months. Ms guidelines for #10 SASE.

Nonfiction and Fiction: Quality material for preschoolers to 16-year-olds, but publishes only a few YAs. Looks for "originality of ideas, clarity and felicity of expression, well-organized plot and strong characterization (fiction) or clear exposition (nonfiction); quality." Reviews artwork/photos as part of ms package.

Recent Title: *We're Going on a Bear Hunt*, by Michael Rosen, illustrated by Helen Oxenbury.

Tips: "There is not a particular 'type' of book that we are interested in above others though we always look for humor. Rather, we look for superior quality in both writing and illustration. Freelance writers should be aware of the swing away from teen-age novels to books for younger readers and of the growing need for beginning chapter books for children just learning to read on their own."

McFARLAND & COMPANY, INC., PUBLISHERS, P.O. Box 611, Jefferson NC 28640. (919)246-4460. President and Editor-in-Chief: Robert Franklin. Business Manager: Rhonda Herman. Assistant Editor: Lisa Camp. Estab. 1979. Publishes mostly hardcover and a few "quality" paperback originals; a non-"trade" publisher. Averages 110 titles/year; receives 1000 submissions annually. 70% of books from first-time authors; 95% of books from unagented writers. Average first print order for a book is 1,000. Pays 10-12½% royalty on net receipts; no advance. Publishes book an average of 8 or 9 months after acceptance. Reports in 1 week.

Nonfiction: Reference books and scholarly, technical and professional monographs. Subjects include Americana, art, business, chess, drama/theatre, cinema/radio/TV (very strong), health, history, librarianship (very strong), music, sociology, sports/recreation (very strong) women's studies (very strong), and world affairs (very strong). "We will consider *any* scholarly book—with authorial maturity and competent grasp of subject." Reference books are particularly wanted—fresh material (i.e., not in head-to-head competition with an established title). "We don't like manuscripts of fewer than 200 double-spaced typed pages. Our market consists mainly of libraries." No New Age material, memoirs, poetry, children's books, devotional/inspirational works or personal essays. Query or submit outline/synopsis and sample chapters. Reviews artwork/photos as part of ms package.

Recent Nonfiction Title: *Women's Rights in International Documents: A Sourcebook with Commentary*, edited by Winston E. Langley.

Tips: "We do *not* accept novels or fiction of any kind or personal Bible studies. Don't worry about writing skills—we have editors. What we want is well-organized *knowledge* of an area in which there is not good information coverage at present, plus reliability so we don't feel we have to check absolutely everything."

McGRAW-HILL INC., 1221 Avenue of the Americas, New York NY 10020. Divisions include McGraw-Hill Ryerson (Canada), Osborne/McGraw-Hill, and TAB Books. Did not want a listing for their Adult Trade Books Division.

MACMILLAN PUBLISHING COMPANY, Division of Macmillan Inc., 866 3rd Ave., New York NY 10022. Imprints include Atheneum, Bradbury Press, Charles Scribner's Sons, and Margaret K. McElderry Books. Did not want a listing for their Adult Trade Books Division.

MADISON BOOKS, 4720 Boston Way, Lanham MD 20706. (301)459-5308. FAX: (301)459-2118. Publisher: James E. Lyons. Estab. 1984. Publishes hardcover originals and trade paperback originals and reprints. Averages 20 titles/year. Receives 750 submissions/year. 15% of books from first-time authors; 50% from unagented writers. Pays 10-20% royalty on wholesale price. Offers average advance of $2,500. Publishes ms an average of 1 year after acceptance. Book catalog and manuscript guidelines for 9×12 SAE and 4 first class stamps.

Nonfiction: History, biography, contemporary affairs, popular culture and trade reference. Query or submit outline/synopsis and sample chapter. No complete mss.

Recent Nonfiction Title: *The Cambridge Spies*, by Verne W. Newton (history/politics).

‡MARK PUBLISHING, 5400 Scotts Valley Dr., Scotts Valley CA 95066. (408)438-7668. Editor: Bill Myers. Publishes hardcover and trade paperback originals. Firm averages 20 titles/year. Receives 100 submissions/year. 20% of books from first-time authors. 100% from unagented writers. Pays 5-10% royalty on wholesale price. No advance offered. Publishes book an average of 6 months after acceptance. Simultaneous submissions OK. Query for electronic submissions. Reports in 1 month on queries. Free book catalog and manuscript guidelines.

Nonfiction: Coffee table book and how-to. Subjects include art/architecture, hobbies, craft and sewing. "We are looking for quilting and home decorating books." Query. Submit outline/synopsis and sample chapters.

Recent Nonfiction Title: *Silk Flowers*, by Geller (how-to).

Poetry: "We are looking for poetry on love and relationships. No political or social poetry." Submit 1 sample.

Recent Poetry Title: *Our Lives Were Meant to be Shared*, by Finn (love poetry).

Tips: "Our audience consists mostly of women."

‡MARKETSCOPE BOOKS, 119 Richard Ct., Aptos CA 95003. (408)688-7535. Editor-in-Chief: Ken Albert. Publishes hardcover and trade paperback originals. Firm averages 10 titles/year. 50% of books from first-time authors. 50% from unagented writers. Pays 10-15% royalty on wholesale price. Publishes book an average of 4-6 months after acceptance. Simultaneous submissions OK. Reports in 1 months on queries; 1 month on mss.

Nonfiction: Biography, how-to, humor, self-help. Subjects include anthropology/archaeology, child guidance/parenting, gay/lesbian, health/medicine, hobbies, money/finance, nature/environment, recreation, regional, religion, sociology. Submit outline/synopsis and sample chapters. Reviews artwork/photos as part of the freelance ms package.

Recent Nonfiction Title: *Bass Fishing in California*, by Kovach (recreation).

MARLOR PRESS, INC., 4304 Brigadoon Dr., St. Paul MN 55126. (612)483-1588. Editor: Marlin Bree. Estab. 1981. Publishes mostly quality trade paperback originals and a few hardcover books. Averages 6 titles/year; receives 100 submissions annually. Pays 10% royalty on net sales. Publishes book an average of 8 months after final acceptance. Reports in 3 months on personal queries.
Nonfiction: Travel books. Query or submit outline/synopsis and sample chapters. Do not send full ms. Reviews artwork/photos as part of ms package.
Recent Nonfiction Title: *South to the Pole by Ski,* by Joseph E. Murphy.
Tips: "We primarily publish travel guidebooks, fact books and travel directories to major vacation and travel areas in the U.S., Canada and Western Europe. No advice, personal reminiscences or anecdotal manuscripts. We are broadening our line to include some nonfiction children's books."

‡MASTERS PRESS, 5025 28th St. SE, Grand Rapids MI 49512. (616)957-4704. Managing Editor: Amy Wolterstorff. Publishes hardcover and trade paperback originals. Firm averages 6-10 titles/year. Receives 50 submissions/year. 70% of books are from first-time authors. 50% from unagented writers. Pays 10-20% royalty on retail price. Publishes ms an average of 7 months after acceptance. Simultaneous submissions OK. Query for electronic submissions. Reports in 1 month on queries. Free book catalog.
Nonfiction: Biography (sports). Subjects include recreation and sports. "We are interested in well-researched and well-written books on organized sports, and on well-known sports figures, as well as books about current topics in spots. We do not want to see anything unrelated to sports." Submit outline/synopsis and sample chapters. Reviews artwork/photos as part of ms package.
Recent Nonfiction Title: *Coaching Basketball,* Jerry Krause, editor.
Tips: "Writers have their best chance of selling us thorough, well-written, well-researched books about an aspect of sports that is currently popular. We have a general audience: those interested in organized sports, those who participate in sports, and coaches."

MEDIA FORUM INTERNATIONAL, LTD., RFD 1, P.O. Box 107, W. Danville VT 05873. (802)592-3444. Or P.O. Box 65, Peacham VT 05862. (802)592-3310. Managing Director: D.K. Bognár. Estab. 1969. Imprint: Media Forum Books; Division: Ha' Penny Gourmet. Publishes hardcover and trade paperback originals. Averages 4 titles/year. Pays 10% minimum royalty.
Nonfiction: Biography, cookbook, humor and reference. Subjects include cooking, ethnic, broadcast/film and drama. "All mss are assigned."
Recent Nonfiction Title: *The Signal Book* (broadcasting and film).

‡MEDIA PUBLISHING/MIDGARD PRESS, Division of Westport Publishers, Inc., Suite 202, 2440 O Street, Lincoln NE 68510. (402)474-2676. President: Leonard Strauss. Publishes hardcover originals and trade paperback originals and reprints. Averages 9-12 titles annually. Receives 200 submissions/year. 60% of books from first-time writers; 95% from unagented writers. Pays 2-15% royalty based on net sales. Makes some work-for-hire assignments. "Midgard Press is contract publishing; Media Publishing is trade publishing." Publishes book an average of 6 months after acceptance. Simultaneous submissions OK. Query for electronic submissions. Reports in 1 month. Book catalog (as available) for #10 SASE.
Nonfiction: Biography, how-to, reference, self-help, textbook. Subjects include Americana, history, politics and general interest. "We will consider manuscripts of general interest with good commercial appeal to regional or special interest markets." Query or submit outline/synopsis and sample chapters or submit complete ms. Reviews artwork/photos as part of ms package.
Recent Nonfiction Title: *Love and Glory: Women of The Old West,* by Larry Underwood.

MEERAMMA PUBLICATIONS, 26 Spruce Lane, Ithaca NY 14850. (607)257-1715. Editor: Christine Cox. Publishes hardcover and trade paperback originals. Averages 6 titles/year. 50% of books from first-time authors; 50% from unagented writers. Pays 8-10% royalty on retail price. Advance varies. Publishes book an average of 5 months after acceptance. Simultaneous submissions OK. Reports in 2 weeks on queries; 1 month on mss. Free book catalog.
Nonfiction: Women's spirituality, philosophical and mystical literature. Subjects include art, health/medicine, aging, philosophy, psychology, religion and women's issues/studies. Seeking 10 high quality manuscripts on mystical, religious, or philosophical topics, per year. Submit outline/synopsis and sample chapters with SASE. Reviews artwork/photos as part of ms package.
Recent Nonfiction Title: *Speaking Flame,* by Andrew Harvey (mystical literature).
Fiction: Mystical religious and philosophical. Seeking 1 philosophical novel per year. Submit sample chapter with SASE.
Tips: "Writers have the best chance selling us books on the Divine Mother or Goddess, biography or novelization of the lives of mystics and philosophers, or self-help/psychology with spiritual outlook. Our audience has an interest in spirituality."

MENASHA RIDGE PRESS, INC., 3169 Cahaba Heights Rd., Birmingham AL 35243. (205)967-0566. FAX: (205)967-0580. Publisher: R.W. Sehlinger. Estab. 1981. Publishes hardcover and trade paperback originals. Averages 10-15 titles/year; receives 600-800 submissions annually. 50% of books from first-time authors; 90% of books from unagented writers. Average print order for a writer's first book is 4,000. Pays 10% royalty on wholesale price or purchases outright; offers average $1,000 advance. Publishes book an average of 8 months after acceptance. Simultaneous submissions OK. Query for electronic submissions. Reports in 1 month. Book catalog for 9 × 12 SAE and 4 first class stamps; ms guidelines for SASE.
Nonfiction: How-to, reference, self-help, consumer, outdoor recreation, travel guides and small business. Subjects include business and economics, health, hobbies, recreation, sports, travel and consumer advice. No biography or religious copies. Submit outline/synopsis. Reviews artwork/photos.
Recent Nonfiction Title: *Whitewater Sourcebook*, by Richard Penny.
Tips: "Audience: age 25-60, 14-18 years' education, white collar and professional, $30,000 median income, 75% male, 75% east of Mississippi River."

METAMORPHOUS PRESS, P.O. Box 10616, Portland OR 92710. (503)228-4972. FAX: (503)223-9117. Publisher: David Balding. Acquisitions Editor: Gene Radeka. Estab. 1982. Publishes hardcover and trade paperback originals and reprints. Averages 4-5 titles/year; receives 800 submissions annually. 90% of books from first-time authors; 90% of books from unagented writers. Average print order for a writer's first book is 2,000-5,000. Pays minimum 10% profit split on wholesale prices. No advance. Publishes book an average of 8 months after acceptance. Simultaneous submissions OK. Query for electronic submissions. Free book catalog; ms guidelines for #24 SASE.
Nonfiction: How-to, illustrated book, reference, self-help, technical and textbook—all related to behavioral science and personal growth. Subjects include business and sales, health, psychology, sociology, education, children's books, science and new ideas in behavioral science. "We are interested in any well-proven new idea or philosophy in the behavioral science areas. Our primary editorial screen is 'will this book further define, explain or support the concept that we are responsible for our reality or assist people in gaining control of their lives.' " Submit idea, outline, and table of contents only. Reviews artwork/photos as part of ms package.
Recent Nonfiction Title: *Self Rescue*, by John C. Kiley, M.D.

THE MGI MANAGEMENT INSTITUTE, INC., 378 Halstead Ave., Harrison NY 10528. (914)835-5790. FAX: (914)835-4824. President: Dr. Henry Oppenheimer. Estab. 1968. Averages 5-10 new titles/year; receives 40 submissions annually. 50% of books from first-time authors; 100% of those books from unagented writers. Pays 4% royalty on retail price of correspondence course or training manual (price is usually in $100 range). Does not publish conventional books. Publishes course or manual an average of 6 months after acceptance. Query for electronic submissions. Reports in 2 weeks.
Nonfiction: How-to, technical and correspondence courses. Subjects include business and economics, engineering, computer, and manufacturing-related topics. Needs correspondence courses in management, purchasing, manufacturing management, production and inventory control, quality control, computers and marketing professional services. Reviews artwork/photos.
Recent Nonfiction Title: *Space Planning for the NCIDQ Exam*, by Dr. Mark Karlen.
Tips: "Our audience includes quality and inventory control managers, purchasing managers, graduate engineers and architects, manufacturing supervisors and managers, real estate investors, and interior designers."

MICHIGAN STATE UNIVERSITY PRESS, Room 25, 1405 S. Harrison Rd., East Lansing MI 48823-5202. (517)355-9543. Director: Fred Bohm. Editor-in-Chief: Julie Loehr. Estab. 1947. Publishes hardcover and softcover originals. Averages 15 titles annually. Receives 150 submissions/year. 95% of books from first-time writers; 100% from unagented writers. Pays 10% royalty on net sales. Publishes ms an average of 9 months after acceptance. Query for electronic submissions. Book catalog and manuscript guidelines for #10 SASE.
Nonfiction: Reference, technical, and scholarly. Subjects include African Studies, agriculture, American Studies, business and economics, Canadian Studies, history, literature, philosophy, politics and religion. Looking for "scholarly publishing representing strengths of the university." Query with outline/synopsis and sample chapters. Reviews artwork/photos.
Recent Nonfiction Title: *Dangerous Society*, by Carl S. Taylor.

MICROTREND BOOKS, Imprint of Slawson Communications, Inc., 165 Vallecitos de Oro, San Marcos CA 92069. (619)744-2299. Editorial Director: Lance A. Leventhal, Ph.D. Estab. 1963. Other imprints are Avant, Health Media, and Mad Hatter. Publishes only computer books as trade paperback originals. Imprint averages 24 titles/year. Receives 150 submissions/year. 50% of books from first-time authors; 80% from unagented writers. Pays 12-15% royalty on net price. Advance amount determined by subject. Publishes book an average of 4 months after acceptance. Simultaneous submissions OK. Reports in 2 weeks. Book catalog for $2.

Nonfiction: Technical. Subjects include computers and electronics. No entry level computer book manuscripts. Query or submit outline/synopsis and sample chapters. Reviews artwork/photos as part of ms package.

Recent Nonfiction Title: *Clipper Programming Guide*, by Rick Spence (computer).

Tips: "Our audience is make up of mid to advanced computer users. If I were a writer trying to market a book today, I would know the computer trade."

MILKWEED EDITIONS, P.O. Box 3226, Minneapolis MN 55403. (612)332-3192. Editor: Emilie Buchwald. Estab. 1980. Publishes hardcover originals and paperback originals and reprints. Averages 10-12 titles/year. Receives 1,560 submissions/year. 30% of books from first-time authors; 70% from unagented writers. Pays 10% royalty on wholesale price. Offers average advance of $500. Publishes work an average of 1 year after acceptance. Simultaneous submissions OK. Reports in 3 weeks on queries; 3 months on mss. Book catalog and ms guidelines for SASE.

Nonfiction: Illustrated book. Subjects include anthropology/archaeology, art/architecture, government/politics, history, language/literature, nature/environment, photography, regional, sports, women's issues/studies. Query. Reviews artwork/photos as part of ms package.

Recent Nonfiction Title: *Coming Home Crazy*, by Bill Holm (essays).

Recent Fiction Title: *Blue Taxis*, by Eileen Drew.

Tips: "We are looking for excellent writing in fiction, nonfiction and poetry. Write for our fiction contest guidelines. Twelve books will be chosen for our 1992 list."

MILLS & SANDERSON, PUBLISHERS, Suite 201, 41 North Rd., Bedford MA 01730. (617)275-1410. Publisher: Georgia Mills. Estab. 1986. Publishes trade paperback originals. Publishes 6-8 titles/year; receives 400 submissions annually. 50% of books from first-time authors; 80% of books from unagented writers. Pays 12½% royalty on net price; offers average $1,000 advance. Publishes book 1 year after acceptance. Simultaneous submissions OK. Reports in 6 weeks on queries; 2 months on mss. Ms guidelines for #10 SASE.

Nonfiction: Self-help. Subjects include health, lifestyle issues, travel and parenting. "All our books are aimed at improving the individual's life in some way. No religion, music, art or photography." Query.

Recent Nonfiction Title: *The 50 Healthiest Places to Live and Retire in the United States*, by Norman D. Ford.

Tips: "We only publish nonfiction with broad general consumer appeal because it normally is less chancy than fiction. It must be an interesting subject with broad appeal by an author whose credentials indicate he/she knows a lot about the subject, be well researched and most importantly, must have a certain uniqueness about it."

MODERN LANGUAGE ASSOCIATION OF AMERICA, 10 Astor Pl., New York NY 10003. (212)475-9500. FAX: (212)477-9863. Head, Publications Division: A. Joseph Hollander. Estab. 1883. Publishes hardcover and paperback originals. Averages 20 titles/year; receives 125 submissions annually. 100% of books from unagented writers. Pays 5-10% royalty on net proceeds. Publishes book an average of 1 year after acceptance. Query for electronic submissions. Reports in 3 weeks on mss. Book catalog free on request.

Nonfiction: Reference and professional. Subjects include language and literature. Needs mss on current issues in research and teaching of language and literature. No critical monographs. Query or submit outline/synopsis and sample chapters.

Recent Nonfiction Title: *Literary Research Guide*, by James L. Harner

‡MONITOR BOOK CO., INC., Box 9078, Palm Springs CA 92263. Editor-in-Chief: Alan F. Pater. Hardcover originals. Pays 10% minimum royalty or by outright purchase, depending on circumstances; no advance. Reports in 4 months. Book catalog for SASE.

Nonfiction: Americana, biographies (only of well-known personalities), law and reference books. Send prints if photos and/or illustrations are to accompany ms.

MOON PUBLICATIONS, INC., 722 Wall St., Chico CA 95928. (916)345-5473. Senior Editor: Mark Morris. Estab. 1973. Publishes trade paperback originals. Publishes average of 15 titles/year; receives 75-100 submissions/year. 50% of books from first-time authors; 95% from unagented writers. Pays royalty on wholesale price; offers advance of up to $7,000. Publishes book an average of 18 months after acceptance. Simultaneous submissions OK. Query for electronic submissions. Reports in 3 weeks on queries and ms. Book catalog and ms guidelines for #10 SASE.

Nonfiction: "We specialize in travel guides to Asia and the Pacific Basin, the western United States, Canada, the Caribbean, and Latin America, and favor these areas, but are open to new ideas. Our guides include in-depth cultural and historical background, as well as recreational and practical travel information. We prefer comprehensive guides to entire countries, states, and regions over more narrowly defined areas such as cities, museums, etc. Writers should write first for a copy of our guidelines. Query with outline/synopsis, table of contents, and writing sample. Author should also be prepared to provide photos, artwork and base maps. No fictional or strictly narrative travel writing; no how-to guides." Reviews artwork/photos as part of ms package.

Recent Nonfiction Title: *Southeast Asia Handbook*, by Carl Parkes.

Tips: "Moon Travel Handbooks are designed by and for independent, do-it-yourself travelers seeking the most rewarding travel experience possible. Our Handbooks appeal to all travelers because they are the most comprehensive and honest guides available."

*MOREHOUSE PUBLISHING CO., Suite 204, 871 Eathan Allen Hgwy., Ridgefield CT 06887. (203)431-3927. FAX: (203)431-3964. Publisher: E. Allen Kelley. Senior Editor: Deborah Graham-Smith. Children's Editor: Jill Weaver. Academic Advisor: Theodore A. McConnell. Estab. 1884. Publishes hardcover and paperback originals. Averages 45 titles/year; receives 500 submissions annually. 40% of books from first-time authors; 75% of books from unagented writers. Pays 10% royalty on retail price. Publishes book an average of 8 months after acceptance. Book catalog for 9 × 12 SAE with 4 first class stamps.

Nonfiction: Specializes in Christian publishing (with an Anglican emphasis). Theology, ethics, church history, pastoral counseling, liturgy, religious education and children's books (preschool-teen). No poetry or drama. Accepts outline/synopsis and 1-2 sample chapters. Reviews artwork/photos as part of ms package.

Recent Nonfiction Title: *Technique of Icon Painting*, by Guillem Ramos-Poqui (techniques of painting).

WILLIAM MORROW AND COMPANY, INC., 1350 Avenue of the Americas, New York NY 10019. (212)889-3050. FAX: (212)689-9139. Publisher: James D. Landis. Managing Editor: Susan VanOmmeren. Imprints include Beech Tree Books (juvenile), Paulette Kaufmann, editor-in-chief. Fielding Travel Books, Randy Ladenheim-Gil, editor. Greenwillow Books (juvenile), Susan Hirschman, editor-in-chief. Hearst Books (trade), Ann Bramson, editorial director. Hearst Marine Books (nautical), Connie Roosevelt, editor. Lothrop, Lee & Shepard (juvenile), Susan Pearson, editor-in-chief. Morrow Junior Books (juvenile), David Reuther, editor-in-chief. Mulberry Books (juvenile), Paulette Kaufmann, editor-in-chief. Quill Trade Paperbacks, Andrew Dutter, editor. Tambourine Books (juvenile), Paulette Kaufmann, editor-in-chief. Estab. 1926. Publishes 200 titles/year. Receives 10,000 submissions annually. 30% of books from first-time authors; 5% of books from unagented writers. Payment is on standard royalty basis on retail price. Advance varies. Publishes book an average of 1-2 years after acceptance. Reports in 3 months. Query letter on all books. *No* unsolicited mss or proposals.

Nonfiction and Fiction: Publishes adult fiction, nonfiction, history, biography, arts, religion, poetry, how-to books and cookbooks. Length: 50,000-100,000 words. Query only; mss and proposals should be submitted only through an agent.

Recent Nonfiction Title: *You Just Don't Understand*, by Deborah Tanner.

Recent Fiction Title: *Father Melancholy's Daughter*, by Gail Godwin.

MORROW JUNIOR BOOKS, Division of William Morrow and Company, Inc., 1350 Avenue of the Americas, New York NY 10019. (212)261-6691. Editor-in-Chief: David L. Reuther. Executive Editor: Meredith Charpentier. Senior Editor: Andrea Curley. Publishes hardcover originals. Publishes 50 titles/year. All contracts negotiated separately; offers variable advance. Book catalog and guidelines for 9 × 12 SAE with 2 first class stamps.

Nonfiction: Juveniles (trade books). No textbooks. Query. Reviews artwork/photos as part of ms package.

Recent Nonfiction Title: *My Puppy Is Born*, by Joanna Cole.

Fiction: Juveniles (trade books).

Recent Fiction Title: *School's Out*, by Johanna Hurwitz.

Tips: "We are no longer accepting unsolicited manuscripts."

MOSAIC PRESS MINIATURE BOOKS, 358 Oliver Rd., Cincinnati OH 45215. (513)761-5977. Publisher: Miriam Irwin. Estab. 1977. Publishes hardcover originals. Averages 4 titles/year; receives 150-200 submissions annually. 49% of books from first-time authors. Average print order for a writer's first book is 2,000. Buys mss outright for $50. Publishes book an average of 30 months after acceptance. Reports in 2 weeks; "but our production, if manuscript is accepted, often takes 2 or 3 years." Book catalog $3. Writer's guidelines for #10 SAE and 2 first class stamps.

Nonfiction: Biography, cookbook, humor, illustrated book and satire. Subjects include Americana, animals, art, business and economics, cooking and foods, health, history, hobbies, music, nature, sports and travel. Interested in "beautifully written, delightful text. If factual, it must be extremely correct and authoritative. Our books are intended to delight, both in their miniature size, beautiful bindings and excellent writing." No occult, pornography, science fiction, fantasy, haiku, or how-to. Query or submit outline/synopsis and sample chapters or complete ms. Reviews artwork/photos as part of ms package.

Recent Nonfiction Title: *Paisley*, by Suzanne Crowley.

Tips: "I want a book to tell me something I don't know."

MOTHER COURAGE PRESS, 1533 Illinois St., Racine WI 53405. (414)634-1047. Executive Editor: Barbara Lindquist. Estab. 1981. Publishes trade paperback and hardcover originals. Averages 4 titles/ year; receives 500-600 submissions annually. 100% of books from first-time authors; 100% of books from unagented writers. Pays 10-15% royalty on wholesale and retail price; offers $250 average advance. Publishes book an average of 1 year after acceptance. Simultaneous submissions OK. Query for electronic submissions. Reports in 1 month on queries; 2 months on mss. Book catalog for #10 SASE.

Nonfiction: Biography, how-to and self-help. Subjects include health, psychology and sociology. "We are looking for books on women's spirituality, feminist issues, humor and books about courageous women." Submit outline/synopsis and sample chapters. Reviews artwork/photos as part of ms package.

Recent Nonfiction Title: *Women at the Helm*, by Jeannine Talley.

Fiction: Lesbian, adventure, fantasy, historical, humor, mystery, romance, science fiction. "We are looking for lesbian/feminist themes. Don't send male-oriented fiction of any kind." Submit outline/ synopsis and sample chapters or complete ms.

Recent Fiction Title: *Singin' the Sun Up*, by Ocala Wings (lesbian romance).

Tips: "We like to do books that have 'Women of Courage' as the theme."

MOTORBOOKS INTERNATIONAL PUBLISHERS & WHOLESALERS, Imprint of Chronicle Publishing, P.O. Box 2, Osceola WI 54020. FAX: (612)439-5627. Director of Publications: Tim Parker. Managing Editor: Barbara K. Harold. Estab. 1973. Hardcover and paperback originals. Averages 60 titles/year. 90% of books from unagented writers. Offers 7-12% royalty on net receipts. Offers $2,000 average advance. Publishes book an average of 1 year after acceptance. Simultaneous submissions OK. Query for electronic submissions. Reports in 3 months. Free book catalog; ms guidelines for #10 SASE.

Nonfiction: Biography, history, how-to, photography (as they relate to cars, trucks, motorcycles, R/ C modeling, motor sports, aviation—domestic, foreign and military. Accepts nonfiction translations. Submit outline/synopsis, 1-2 sample chapters and sample of illustrations. "State qualifications for doing book." Reviews artwork/photos as part of ms package.

Recent Nonfiction Title: *Corvette Grand Sport*, by Lowell C. Paddock and Dave Friedman.

‡**MOUNTAIN PRESS PUBLISHING COMPANY**, P.O. Box 2399, Missoula MT 59806. (406)728-1900. FAX: (406)728-1635. Series Editor: Danial Greer. Estab. 1948. Imprints are Roadside Geology Series, Roadside History Series, Classics of the Fur Trade. Publishes hardcover and trade paperback originals. Averages 15 titles/year. Receives 250 submissions/year. 50% of books from first-time authors. 90% of books from unagented writers. Pays 7-15% on wholesale price. Publishes book an average of 1 year after acceptance. Simultaneous submissions OK. Query for electronic submissions. Reports in 1 month on queries. Free book catalog.

Nonfiction: Nontechnical. Subjects include Americana, nature/environment, recreation, regional, science, travel. "We are expanding our Roadside Geology and Roadside History series (done on a state by state basis.) We would also be interested in how-to books (related to horses). Also well written regional outdoor guides—plant, flower and bird. No personal histories or journals." Query or submit outline/synopsis and sample chapters or complete ms. Reviews artwork/photos as part of ms package.

Tips: "It is obvious that small- to medium-size publishers are becoming more important, while the giants are becoming harder and less accessible. If I were a writer trying to market a book today, I would find out what kind of books a publisher was interested in and tailor my writing to them. Research markets and target my audience. Research other books, on the same subjects. Make yours different. Don't present your manuscript to a publisher—*sell* it to him. Give him the information he needs to make a decision on a title."

The double dagger before a listing indicates that the listing is new in this edition. New markets are often more receptive to freelance submissions.

THE MOUNTAINEERS BOOKS, The Mountaineers, Suite 107, 1011 SW Klickitat Way, Seattle WA 98134. (206)285-2665. Director: Donna DeShazo. Estab. 1961. Publishes hardcover and trade paperback originals (95%) and reprints (5%). Averages 25 titles/year; receives 150-250 submissions annually. 25% of books from first-time authors; 98% of books from unagented writers. Average print order for a writer's first book is 5,000-7,000. Offers royalty based on net sales. Offers advance on occasion. Publishes book an average of 1 year after acceptance. Reports in 2 months. Book catalog and ms guidelines for 9 × 12 SAE with 2 first class stamps.
Nonfiction: Adventure travel, recreation, conservation/environment, non-competitive sports, and outdoor how-to books. "We specialize in books dealing with mountaineering, hiking, backpacking, skiing, snowshoeing, canoeing, bicycling, etc. These can be either how-to-do-it, where-to-do-it (guidebooks)." Does *not* want to see "anything dealing with hunting, fishing or motorized travel." Submit outline/synopsis and minimum of 2 sample chapters. Accepts nonfiction translations. Looks for "expert knowledge, good organization."
Recent Nonfiction Title: *Best Short Hikes in California's Southern Sierra*, by Karen and Terry Whitehill (guidebook).
Fiction: "We might consider an exceptionally well-done book-length manuscript on mountaineering." Does *not* want poetry or mystery. Query first.
Tips: "The type of book the writer has the best chance of selling our firm is an authoritative guidebook (*in our field*) to a specific area not otherwise covered; or a how-to that is better than existing competition (agin, *in our field*)."

JOHN MUIR PUBLICATIONS, P.O. Box 613, Santa Fe NM 87504. (505)982-4078. President: Steven Cary. Estab. 1969. Publishes trade paperback originals and reprints. Averages 45 titles/year. Receives 300 submissions/year. 30% of books from first-time authors. 85% of books from unagented writers. Pays 8-12% on wholesale price. Offers $750-1,000 average advance. Publishes book an average of 1 year after acceptance. Simultaneous submissions OK. Reports in 1 month. Free book catalog.
Nonfiction: Travel for adults and children. Lively children's nonfiction for trade and to supplement texts in school market. We want "unique and/or original treatments of ideas which inform, enlighten and stimulate our independent readers." Query or submit outline/synopsis and sample chapters. Reviews artwork/photos as part of ms package.
Recent Nonfiction Title: *Rads, Eags and Cheeseburgers: The Kids' Guide to Energy and the Environment*.

MULTNOMAH PRESS, Division of Multnomah School of The Bible, 10209 SE Division St., Portland OR 97266. (503)257-0526. Contact: Manuscript Review Editor. Publishes hardcover and trade paperback originals, and a limited number trade paperback reprints. Averages 40 titles/year; receives 1,200 submissions annually. 20% of books from first-time authors; 100% of books from unagented writers. Pays royalty on wholesale price. Publishes books an average of 9 months after acceptance. Query for electronic submissions. Reports in 6 weeks on queries; 10 weeks on mss. Book catalog and ms guidelines for SASE.
Nonfiction: Coffee table book and self-help. Subjects include religion. "We publish issue-related books linking social/ethical concerns and Christianity; books addressing the needs of women from a Christian point of view; books addressing the needs of the traditional family in today's society; illustrated books for children; and books explaining Christian theology in a very popular way to a lay audience." No daily devotional, personal experience, scripture/photo combinations or poetry. Submit outline/synopsis and sample chapters.
Recent Nonfiction Title: *Six Hours One Friday*, by Mars Lucado.
Fiction: Realistic fiction with a Christian world view for the middle reader (8-11-year-olds).
Tips: "We have a reputation for tackling tough issues from a Biblical view; we need to continue to deserve that reputation. Avoid being too scholarly or detached. Although we like well-researched books, we do direct our books to a popular market, not just to professors of theology."

*MUSEUM OF NORTHERN ARIZONA PRESS, Subsidiary of Museum of Northern Arizona, Box 720, Rt. 4, Flagstaff AZ 86001. (602)774-5211. Publisher: Diana Clark Lubick. Publishes hardcover and trade paperback originals, and quarterly magazine. Averages 10-12 titles/year; receives 35 submissions annually. 10% of books from first-time authors; 100% of books from unagented writers. Subsidy publishes (nonauthor) 15% of books. Pays one-time fee on acceptance of ms. No advance. Publishes book an average of 1 year after acceptance. Queries only. Query for electronic submissions. Reports in 1 month. Book catalog for 9 × 12 SAE and ms guidelines for #10 SASE.
Nonfiction: Coffee table book, reference and technical. Subjects include Southwest, art, nature, science. "Especially needs manuscripts on the Colorado Plateau that are written for a well-educated general audience." Query or submit outline/synopsis and 3-4 sample chapters. Reviews artwork/photos as part of ms package.
Recent Nonfiction Title: *A Separate Vision*, by Linda Eaton (ethnology and art).

MUSTANG PUBLISHING CO., P.O. Box 3004, Memphis TN 38173. (901)521-1406. President: Rollin Riggs. Estab. 1983. Publishes nonfiction hardcover and trade paperback originals. Averages 6 titles/year; receives 1,000 submissions annually. 50% of books from first-time authors; 90% of books from unagented writers. Pays 6-8% royalty on retail price. Publishes book an average of 1 year after acceptance. Simultaneous submissions OK. No electronic submissions. No phone calls, please. Reports in 1 month. SASE a must. Book catalog available from address above—include #10 SASE for catalog.
Nonfiction: How-to, humor and self-help. Subjects include Americana, hobbies, recreation, sports and travel. "Our needs are very general—humor, travel, how-to, nonfiction, etc.—for the 18-to 40-year-old market." Query or submit synopsis and sample chapters.
Recent Nonfiction Title: *Australia: Where the Fun Is*, by Goodyear and Skinner.
Tips: "From the proposals we receive, it seems that many writers never go to bookstores and have no idea what sells. Before you waste a lot of time on a nonfiction book idea, ask yourself, 'How often have my friends and I actually *bought* a book like this?' Know the market, and know the audience you're trying to reach."

THE MYSTERIOUS PRESS, Subsidiary of Warner Books, 129 W. 56th St., New York NY 10019. (212)765-0901. FAX: (212)265-5478. Editor-in-Chief: William Malloy. Subsidiaries include Penzler Books (non-mystery fiction by mystery authors) and *The Armchair Detective* (magazine). Publishes hardcover originals, trade paperback reprints and mass market paperback reprints. Averages 40-50 titles/year; receives 750 submissions annually. 10% of books from first-time authors. *Accepts no unagented mss.* Pays standard, but negotiable, royalty on retail price; amount of advance varies widely. Publishes book an average of 1 year after acceptance. Reports in 2 months. Book catalog and guidelines for 9×12 SAE with 4 first class stamps.
Nonfiction: Reference books on criticism and history of crime fiction. Submit complete ms. Reviews artwork/photos as part of ms package.
Recent Nonfiction Title: *Sleep with the Devil, A Jim Thompson Biography*, by Michael McCauley.
Fiction: Mystery, suspense and espionage. "We will consider publishing any outstanding crime/espionage/suspense/detective novel that comes our way. No short stories." Submit complete mss.
Recent Fiction Title: *Twilight at Mac's Place*, by Ross Thomas.
Tips: "We no longer read unagented material. Agents only, please."

THE NAIAD PRESS, INC., P.O. Box 10543, Tallahassee FL 32302. (904)539-5965. FAX: (904)539-9731. Editorial Director: Barbara Grier. Estab. 1973. Publishes paperback originals. Averages 24 titles/year; receives 700 submissions annually. 20% of books from first-time authors; 99% of books from unagented writers. Average print order for a writer's first book is 12,000. Pays 15% royalty on wholesale or retail price; no advance. Publishes book an average of 18 months after acceptance. Reports in 4 months. Book catalog and ms guidelines for #10 SAE and 2 first class stamps.
Fiction: "We publish lesbian fiction, preferably lesbian/feminist fiction. We are not impressed with the 'oh woe' school and prefer realistic (i.e., happy) novels. We emphasize fiction and are now heavily reading manuscripts in that area. We are working in a lot of genre fiction—mysteries, science fiction, short stories, fantasy—all with lesbian themes, of course." Query.
Recent Fiction Title: *Murder by Tradition*, by Katherine V. Forrest.
Tips: "There is tremendous world-wide demand for lesbian mysteries from lesbian authors published by lesbian presses, and we are doing several such series. Ms under 60,000 words have twice as good a chance as over 60,000."

‡NATIONAL PRESS, INC., Suite 212, 7200 Wisconsin Ave., Bethesda MD 20814. (301)657-1616. Editorial Director: G. Edward Smith. Publishes hardcover and trade paperback originals. Firm averages 23 titles/year. Receives 1500 submissions/year. 70% of books are from first-time authors. 80% from unagented writers. Pays 5-10% royalty on wholesale or retail price. Also makes outright purchases, minimum $10. Offers flexible average advance. Publishes book an average of 8 months after acceptance. Simultaneous submissions OK. Reports in 2 months. Book catalog and manuscript guidelines for 7×9 SAE and 4 first class stamps.
Nonfiction: Biography, cookbook and self-help. Subjects include business and economics, child guidance/parenting, cooking, foods and nutrition, government/politics, history, money/finance, psychology, regional and sports. Query or submit outline/synopsis and sample chapters. Reviews artwork/photos as part of ms package.
Recent Nonfiction Title: *Silverado*, by Steve Wilmsen.

NATIONAL TEXTBOOK CO., Imprint of NTC Publishing Group, 4255 W. Touhy Ave., Lincolnwood IL 60646. (708)679-5500. FAX: (708)679-2494. Editorial Director: Leonard I. Fiddle. Publishes originals for education and trade market, and software. Averages 100-150 titles/year; receives 200 submissions annually. 10% of books from first-time authors; 80% of books from unagented writers. Mss purchased on either royalty or buy-out basis. Publishes book an average of 1 year after acceptance.

Reports in 4 months. Book catalog and ms guidelines for SAE and 2 first class stamps.
Nonfiction: Textbook. Major emphasis being given to foreign language and language arts classroom texts, especially secondary level material, and business and career subjects (marketing, advertising, sales, etc.). Raymond B. Walters, Language Arts Editor. Michael Ross, Foreign Language and ESL. Michael Urban, Career Guidance. Anne Knudsen, Business Books. Send sample chapter and outline or table of contents.
Recent Nonfiction Title: *Sports in Literature*, by Bruce Emra.

NATUREGRAPH PUBLISHERS, INC., P.O. Box 1075, Happy Camp CA 96039. (916)493-5353. Editor: Barbara Brown. Imprint is Prism Editions. Estab. 1946. Averages 3 titles/year; receives 300 submissions annually. 75% of books from first-time authors; 100% of books from unagented writers. Average print order for a writer's first book is 2,500. "We offer 10% of wholesale; 12½% after 10,000 copies are sold." Publishes book an average of 18 months after acceptance. Reports in 2 months. Book catalog and ms guidelines for #10 SAE with 3 first class stamps.
Nonfiction: Primarily publishes nonfiction for the layman in 7 general areas: natural history (biology, geology, ecology, astronomy); American Indian (historical and contemporary); outdoor living (backpacking, wild edibles, etc.); land and gardening (modern homesteading); crafts and how-to; holistic health (natural foods and healing arts); and Prism Editions (Baha'i and other New Age approaches to harmonious living). All material must be well-grounded; author must be professional, and in command of effective style. Our natural history and American Indian lines can be geared for educational markets. "To speed things up, queries should include summary, detailed outline, comparison to related books, 2 sample chapters, availability and samples of any photos or illustrations, and author background. Send manuscript only on request." Reviews artwork/photos as part of ms package.
Recent Nonfiction Title: *Give Peas a Chance*, by Peter Barbarow.

THE NAUTICAL & AVIATION PUBLISHING CO., Suite 314, 101 West Read St., Baltimore MD 21201. (301)659-0220. President/Publisher: Jan Snouck-Hurgronje. Estab. 1979. Publishes hardcover originals and reprints. Averages 8-10 titles/year. Receives 20-25 submissions/year. Pays 10-15% royalty on net selling price. Offers $500-1,000 average advance. Publishes book an average of 6 weeks after acceptance. Simultaneous submissions OK. Free book catalog.
Nonfiction: Reference. Subjects include history, military/war. Submit complete ms. Reviews artwork/ photo as part of package.
Recent Nonfiction Title: *Soldiers of the Sea, the USMC from 1775 to 1962*, by Col. Robert D. Heinl, Jr. (History of U.S. Marine Corps).
Fiction: Historical. "No techno thrillers *a la* Clancy." Submit outline/synopsis and sample chapters or complete ms.
Recent Fiction Title: *South to Java*, by Admiral Mack.

NAVAL INSTITUTE PRESS, Annapolis MD 21402. Manager of Acquisitions: Paul Wilderson. Press Director: Thomas F. Epley. Estab. 1873. Averages 60 titles/year; receives 400-500 submissions annually. 70% of books from first-time authors; 70% of books from unagented writers. Average print order for a writer's first book is 3,000. Pays 14-21% royalty based on net sales; advance. Publishes book an average of 1 year after acceptance. Reports in 2 weeks on queries; 2 months on other submissions. Free book catalog; ms guidelines for SASE.
Nonfiction: "We are interested only in naval and maritime subjects: tactics, strategy, navigation, naval history, biographies of naval leaders and naval aviation." Reviews artwork/photos as part of ms package.
Recent Nonfiction Title: *In Love and War*, by Jim and Sybil Stockdale.
Fiction: Limited, very high quality fiction on naval and maritime themes.
Recent Fiction Title: *Flight of the Intruder*, by Stephen Coonts.

‡NAVPRESS, Division of The Navigators, P.O. Box 6000, Colorado Springs CO 80934. (719)598-1212. Editorial Director: Bruce Nygren. Publishes hardcover and trade paperback originals and software. Averages 40 titles/year. Receives 300-350 submissions/year. 25% of books from first-time authors; 90% from unagented writers. Pays royalty on wholesale price. Publishes book an average of 18 months after acceptance. Simultaneous submissions OK. Reports in 1 month on queries; 10 weeks on mss. Free book catalog and manuscript guidelines.
Nonfiction: Juvenile and Christian instruction. Subjects include business and economics, child guidance/parenting, money/finance, psychology, religion and women's issues/studies. Query or submit outline/synopsis and sample chapters.
Recent Nonfiction Title: *Parenting with Love and Logic*, by Foster Cline and Jim Fay.
Tips: "We want fresh insights on the relevancy of the Christian faith in contemporary society; books that creatively respond to felt needs. Aggressively study existing books and seek to find niches in the market where specific needs of significant groups of readers are not being met."

THOMAS NELSON PUBLISHERS, Nelson Place at Elm Hill Pike, P.O. Box 141000, Nashville TN 37214. (615)889-9000. FAX: (615)391-5225. Managing Editor: Larry D. Hampton. Estab. 1798. Imprints are Oliver-Nelson and Generoux. Publishes hardcover and paperback originals and reprints. Averages 120 titles/year. Pays royalty or makes outright purchase. Publishes book an average of 1 year after acceptance. Send proposal to Book Editorial. Reports in 2 months. SASE must accompany submissions or unable to return proposals.
Nonfiction: Adult inspirational/motivational Christian trade books and reference books on the Bible and Christianity. Accepts outline/synopsis and 3 sample chapters.
Recent Nonfiction Title: *Love Hunger: Recovery from Food Addiction*, by Drs. Frank Minirth, Paul Meier, Robert Hemfelt, and Sharon Sneed.
Fiction: Seeking high quality novels with Christian themes for adults and teens.

‡**NELSON-HALL PUBLISHERS**, 111 N. Canal St., Chicago IL 60606. (312)930-9446. Editorial Director: Harold Wise, Ph.D. Estab. 1909. Publishes hardcover and paperback originals. Averages 90 titles/year. 90% of books submitted by unagented writers. Pays 15% maximum royalty on retail price; offers average advance. Reports in 1 month. Free book catalog.
Nonfiction: Textbooks and general scholarly books in the social sciences. Query.
Recent Nonfiction Title: *Men and Society*, by Clyde W. Franklin, II.

NEW LEAF PRESS, INC., P.O. Box 311, Green Forest AR 72638. FAX: (501)438-5120. Contact: Editorial Board. Estab. 1975. Publishes hardcover and paperback originals. Specializes in charismatic books. Publishes 15 titles/year; receives 236 submissions annually. 15% of books from first-time authors; 90% of books from unagented writers. Average print order for a writer's first book is 10,000. Pays 10% royalty on first 10,000 copies, paid once per year; no advance. Send photos and illustrations to accompany ms. Publishes book an average of 10 months after acceptance. Simultaneous submissions OK. Reports in 3 months. Book catalog and guidelines for 9×12 SAE with 5 first class stamps.
Nonfiction: Biography and self-help. Charismatic books; life stories, and how to live the Christian life. Length: 100-400 pages. Submit complete ms. Reviews artwork/photos as part of ms package.
Recent Nonfiction Title: *Prophecy 2000*, by David Allen Lewis.
Tips: "Biographies, relevant nonfiction, and Bible-based fiction have the best chance of being sold to our firm. Honest and real-life experience help make a book or query one we can't put down."

NEW READERS PRESS, Division of Laubach Literacy International, P.O. Box 131, Syracuse NY 13210. FAX: (315)422-6369. Editor-in-Chief: Laura Martin. Estab. 1959. Publishes paperback originals. Averages 30 titles/year; receives 200 submissions/year. 40% of books by first-time authors; 95% of books by unagented writers. Average print order for a writer's first book is 5,000. "Most of our sales are adult basic education programs, with some sales to volunteer literacy programs, private human services agencies, prisons, and libraries with outreach programs for poor readers." Pays royalty on retail price, or by outright purchase. Rate varies according to type of publication and length of manuscript. Advance is "different in each case, but does not exceed projected royalty for first year." Publishes book an average of 1 year after acceptance. Query for electronic submissions. Reports in 2 months. Free book catalog and authors' brochure.
Nonfiction: "Our audience is adults and older teenagers with limited reading skills (6th grade level and below). We publish basic education and ESL literacy materials in reading and writing, math, social studies, health, science, and English as a second language for double illiterates. We are particularly interested in materials that fulfill curriculum requirements in these areas. Manuscripts must be not only easy to read (3rd-6th grade level) but mature in tone and concepts. We are not interested in anything at all written for children." Submit outline and 1-3 sample chapters.
Recent Nonfiction Title: *Reading in the Content Areas*, by Laura Johnson.
Fiction: Short novels (12,000-15,000 words) at third grade reading level on themes of interest to adults and older teenagers. Submit synopsis.
Recent Fiction Title: *Kaleidoscope*, by Sara Hoskinson Frommer.

NEW VICTORIA PUBLISHERS, P.O. Box 27, Norwich VT 05055. (802)649-5297. Editor: Claudia Lamperti. Estab. 1976. Publishes trade paperback originals. Averages 5-6 titles/year; receives 100 submissions/year. 50% of books from first-time authors; 100% of books from unagented writers. Pays 10% royalty on wholesale price. Publishes book an average of 1 year after acceptance. Prefers electronic submissions. Reports on queries in 2 weeks; on mss in 1 month. Free book catalog.
Nonfiction: History. "We are interested in feminist history or biography and interviews with or topics relating to lesbians. No poetry." Submit outline/synopis and sample chapters.
Recent Nonfiction Title: *Radical Feminists of Hetereodoxy*, by Judith Schwarz (feminist history).
Fiction: Adventure, erotica, fantasy, historical, humor, mystery, romance, science fiction and western. "We will consider most anything if it is well written and appeals to lesbian/feminist audience." Submit outline/synopsis and sample chapters.

Recent Fiction Title: *Captive in Time,* by Sarah Dreher.

Tips: "Try to appeal to a specific audience and not write for the general market."

NEWCASTLE PUBLISHING CO., INC., 13419 Saticoy, North Hollywood CA 91605. (213)873-3191. FAX: (213)780-2007. Editor-in-Chief: Alfred Saunders. Estab. 1970. Publishes trade paperback originals and reprints. Averages 10 titles/year; receives 300 submissions annually. 70% of books from first-time authors; 95% of books from unagented writers. Average print order for a writer's first book is 3,000-5,000. Pays 5-10% royalty on retail price; no advance. Publishes book an average of 8 months after acceptance. Simultaneous submissions OK. Reports in 3 weeks on queries; 6 weeks on mss. Free book catalog; ms guidelines for SASE.

Nonfiction: How-to, self-help, metaphysical, New Age and practical advice for older adults. Subjects include health (physical fitness, diet and nutrition), psychology and religion. "Our audience is made up of college students and college-age nonstudents; also, adults ages 25 and up and older adults of above average education. They are of above average intelligence and are fully aware of what is available in the bookstores." No biography, travel, children's books, poetry, cookbooks or fiction. Query or submit outline/synopsis and sample chapters. Looks for "something to grab the reader so that he/she will readily remember that passage."

Recent Nonfiction Title: *Lighten Up Your Body, Lighten Up Your Life,* by Lucia Capacchione.

Tips: "Check the shelves in the larger bookstores on the subject of the manuscript being submitted. A book on life extension, holistic health, or stress management has the best chance of selling to our firm along with books geared for older adults on personal health issues, etc."

THE NOBLE PRESS, INCOPORATED, Suite 508, 213 W. Institute Pl., Chicago IL 60610. (312)642-1168. Editor: Mark Harris. Estab. 1988. Firm publishes hardcover and trade paperback originals. Publishes 15 titles/year; receives 200 submissions/year. 50% of books from first-time authors; 80% from unagented writers. Pays 5-15% royalty on retail price. Advance varies. Publishes book an average of 8 months after acceptance. Simultaneous submissions OK. Reports in 6 weeks. Free ms guidelines; book catalog for 2 first class stamps.

Nonfiction: Biography, how-to, illustrated book, reference, self-help. Subjects include education, ethnic, government/politics, history, nature/environment, philosophy, sociology, women's issues/studies. No cookbooks, technical manuals, texts in full. Query of submit outline/synopsis and 1 sample chapter.

Recent Nonfiction Title: *The U.S. Peace Movement from the Cold War to Desert Storm,* by Roger Peace III.

Tips: "The writer has the best chance of selling us a nonfiction book that addresses contemporary issues of importance to our society. Many of our books take subjects often explored in academic arenas, and we translate them in such a way that mainstream readers can understand and become involved in them."

‡NORDICPRESS, NordicTrack, Inc., 141 Jonathan Blvd. N., Chaska MN 55318. (612)448-6987. Acquisitions Editor: Nathan Unseth. Publishes trade paperback originals. Averages 6-8 titles/year. Pays 6-10% roaylty on wholesale or retail price, or offers outright purchase for $2,500-5,000. Offers average $2,500 advance. Publishes book an average of 9 months after acceptance of ms. Simultaneous submissions OK. Reports in 1 month.

Nonfiction: Cookbook, how-to, self-help. Subjects include nutrition, health/medicine, and recreation. "We're looking for books that promote the fitness lifestyle and our message of balanced fitness programs." Submit outline/synopsis and sample chapters. Reviews artwork/photos as part of ms package.

Recent Nonfiction Title: *The New Fitness Formula of the 90's* (how-to/exercise).

NORTH LIGHT BOOKS, Imprint of F&W Publications, 1507 Dana Ave., Cincinnati OH 45207. Editorial Director: David Lewis. Publishes hardcover and trade paperback originals. Averages 30-35 titles/year. Pays 10% royalty on net receipts. Offers $3,000 advance. Simultaneous submissions OK. Reports in 3 weeks on queries; 2 months on mss. Book catalog for 9 × 12 SAE with 6 first class stamps.

Nonfiction: Art and graphic design instruction books. Interested in books on watercolor painting, oil painting, basic drawing, pen and ink, airbrush, markers, basic design, computer graphics, desktop publishing, desktop design, color, layout and typography. Do not submit coffee table art books without how-to art instruction. Query or submit outline/synopsis and examples of artwork (transparencies and photographs of artwork are OK).

Recent Nonfiction Titles: *Getting Started in Computer Graphics.*

NORTHERN ILLINOIS UNIVERSITY PRESS, DeKalb IL 60115. (815)753-1826/753-1075. Director: Mary L. Lincoln. Estab. 1965. Pays 10-15% royalty on wholesale price. Free book catalog.
Nonfiction: "The NIU Press publishes mainly history, social sciences, philosophy, literary criticism and regional studies. It does not consider collections of previously published articles, essays, etc., nor do we consider unsolicited poetry." Accepts nonfiction translations. Query with outline/synopsis and 1-3 sample chapters.
Recent Nonfiction Title: *Guns for the Tsar: Technology Transfer and the Small Arms Industry in Nineteenth Century Russia*, by Joseph Bradley.

NORTHLAND PUBLISHING CO., INC., P.O. Box N, Flagstaff AZ 86002. (602)774-5251. FAX: (602)774-0592. Editorial Director: Susan McDonald. Estab. 1958. Publishes hardcover and trade paperback originals. Firm averages 20 titles/year. Receives 250 submissions/year. 30% of books from first-time authors. 75% from unagented writers. Pays 8-15% royalty (on net receipts), depending upon terms. Offers $1,000 average advance. Publishes book an average of 10 months after acceptance. Simultaneous submissions OK. Reports in 1 month on queries; 2 months on mss. Free book catalog and manuscript guidelines.
Nonfiction: Biography, coffee table, cookbook, how-to and illustrated books. Subjects include animals, anthropology/archaeology, art/architecture, history, nature/environment, photography and regional (American west/Southwest). "We are seeking authoritative, well-written manuscripts on natural history subjects. We do not want to see poetry, general fiction, or New Age/science fiction material." Query or submit outline/synopsis and sample chapters. Reviews artwork/photos as part of ms package.
Recent Nonfiction Title: *R.C. Gorman: A Retrospective*, by Doris Monthan.
Tips: "In general, our audience is composed of general interest readers and those interested in specialty subjects such as Native American culture and crafts. It is not necessarily a scholarly market, but is sophisticated."

‡**NORTHWORD PRESS, INC.**, P.O. Box 1360, Minocqua WI 54548. (715)356-9800. Editor: Tom Klein. Imprints are Willow Creek and Heartland Press. Publishes hardcover and trade paperback originals. Firm averages 30 titles/year; imprints average 20 titles/year. Receives 200 submissions/year. 50% of books are from first time authors. 90% are from unagented writers. Pays 5-15% royalty on wholesale price. Offers $3,000 average advance. Publishes book an average of 9 months. Simultaneous submissions OK. Query for electronic submissions. Reports in 3 weeks on queries; 2 months on mss. Book catalog for 8½×11 SAE and 2 first class stamps. Ms guidelines for SASE.
Nonfiction: Coffee table book, how-to, illustrated book, juvenile. Subjects include nature/environment (exclusive). "We are seeking nature topics only with special attention to wildlife. Environmental issue (green books) a new area of interest." Submit outline/synopsis and sample chapters. Reviews artwork/photos as part of ms package.
Recent Nonfiction Title: *Open Spaces*, by Jim Dale Vickery (nature essays).

W.W. NORTON CO., INC., 500 5th Ave., New York NY 10110. (212)354-5500. Editor: Liz Malcolm. Imprints include Norton Paperback Fiction. Publishes 300 titles/year; receives 5,000 submissions annually. Often publishes new and unagented authors. Royalty varies on retail price; advance varies. Publishes book an average of 1 year after acceptance. Simultaneous submissions OK. Submit outline and/or 2-3 sample chapters for fiction and nonfiction. Not responsible for return of material sent without return packaging and postage. Reports in 2 months. Book catalog and guidelines for 9×12 SAE with 2 first class stamps.
Nonfiction and Fiction: "General, adult fiction and nonfiction of the highest quality possible. No occult, paranormal, religion, genre fiction, formula romances, science fiction or westerns, cookbooks, arts and crafts, young adult or children's books. Last year there were 100 book club rights sales; 36 mass paperback reprint sales; and innumerable serializations, second serial, syndication, translations, etc. Looks for clear, intelligent, creative writing on original subjects or with original characters."
Recent Nonfiction Title: *The Search for Modern China*, by Jonathan Spence.
Recent Fiction Title: *The Indian Lawyer*, by James Welch.
Tips: "Long novels are too expensive—keep them under 350 (manuscript) pages."

NTC PUBLISHING GROUP, 4255 W. Touhy Ave., Lincolnwood IL 60646-1975. (708)679-5500. FAX (708)679-2494. Imprints include National Textbook Company, Passport Books, NTC Business Books, VGM Career Books. Foreign Language and English as a Second Language/Editorial Director: Michael Ross. Language Arts Editor: Raymond Walters. Passport Books Editorial Director: Michael Ross. NTC Business Books Manager: Anne Knudsen. VGM Career Books Editor: Michael Urban. Estab. 1960. Publishes hardcover and trade paperback originals and reprints. Averages 150 titles/year. Receives 800 submissions/year. 98% of books from unagented writers. Pays royalty or buys by outright purchase. Offers varying advance. Publishes book an average of 8 months after acceptance. Simultane-

ous submissions OK. Query for electronic submissions. Reports in 2 months. Book catalog free on request.
Nonfiction: Textbook, travel, foreign language, reference, advertising and marketing busines books. Subjects include business, education, language/literature, photography, travel. Query. Reviews artwork/photos as part of ms package.
Recent Nonfiction Title: *New York on $1,000 a Day*, by Ferne Kadish and Shelley Clark.

OCTAMERON ASSOCIATES, 1900 Mt. Vernon Ave., Alexandria VA 22301. (703)836-5480. Editorial Director: Karen Stokstad. Estab. 1976. Publishes trade paperback originals. Averages 15 titles/year; receives 100 submissions annually. 10% of books from first-time authors; 100% of books from unagented writers. Average print order for a writer's first book is 8,000-10,000. Pays 7½% royalty on retail price. Publishes book an average of 6 months after acceptance. Simultaneous submissions OK. Query for electronic submissions. Reports in 2 weeks. Book catalog for 2 first class stamps.
Nonfiction: Reference, career and post-secondary education subjects. Especially interested in "paying-for-college and college admission guides." Query. Submit outline/synopsis and 2 sample chapters. Reviews artwork/photos as part of ms package.
Recent Nonfiction Title: *College Match: A Blueprint for Choosing the Best School for You*, by Steven R. Antonoff and Marie A. Friedemann.

ODDO PUBLISHING, INC., P.O. Box 68, Redwine Rd., Fayetteville GA 30214. (404)461-7627. Managing Editor: Genevieve Oddo. Estab. 1964. Publishes hardcover and paperback originals. Averages 4 titles/year; receives 300 submissions annually. 25% of books from first-time authors; 100% of books from unagented writers. Average print order for a writer's first book is 3,500. Makes outright purchase. "We judge all scripts independently." Royalty considered for special scripts only. Publishes book an average of 2-3 years after acceptance. Reports in 4 months. Book catalog for 9 × 12 SAE with 5 first class stamps.
Nonfiction and Fiction: Publishes juvenile books (ages 4-10) in language arts, workbooks in math, writing (English), photophonics, science (space and oceanography), and social studies for schools, libraries, and trade. Interested in children's supplementary readers in the areas of language arts, math, science, geography, social studies, etc. "Texts run from 1,500 to 3,500 words. Ecology, space, patriotism, oceanography and pollution are subjects of interest. Manuscripts must be easy to read, general, and not set to outdated themes. They must lend themselves to full color illustration. No stories of grandmother long ago. No love angle, permissive language, or immoral words or statements." Submit complete ms. Reviews artwork/photos as part of ms package.
Recent Fiction Title: *Wrongway Santa*, by Rae Oetting.
Tips: "We are currently expanding our line to include materials more acceptable in the trade market. To do so, we are concentrating on adding titles to our top selling series in lieu of developing new series; however, we will consider other scripts."

OHARA PUBLICATIONS, INC., 24715 Ave. Rockefeller, P.O. Box 918, Santa Clarita CA 91380-9018. (805)257-4066. FAX: (805)257-3028. Contact: Editor. Estab. 1968. Publishes trade paperback originals. Averages 12 titles/year. Pays royalty. Write for guidelines. Reports in 3 weeks on queries; 2 months on mss.
Nonfiction: Martial arts. "We decide to do a book on a specific martial art, then seek out the most qualified martial artist to author that book. 'How to' books are our mainstay, and we will accept no manuscript that does not pertain to martial arts systems (their history, techniques, philosophy, etc.)." Query first, then submit outline/synopsis and sample chapter. Include author biography and copies of credentials.
Recent Nonfiction Title: *Wing-Chun/Feet Kune Do*, by Wn Cheung and Ted Wong.

‡OHIO STATE UNIVERSITY PRESS, 1070 Carmack Rd., Columbus OH 43210. (614)292-6930. Director: Peter J. Givler. Pays royalty on wholesale or retail price. Averages 30 titles/year. Reports in 3 months; ms held longer with author's permission.
Nonfiction: Publishes history, biography, philosophy, the arts, political science, law, literature, criminology, education, sociology, urban studies, regional titles and general scholarly nonfiction. Query with outline and sample chapters.
Recent Nonfiction Title: *Justifiable Homicide: Battered Women, Self-Defense, and the Law*, by Cynthia K. Gillespie.
Tips: "Publishes some poetry and fiction.".

ONCE UPON A PLANET, INC., 65-28 Fresh Meadow Lane, Fresh Meadows NY 11365. (718)961-9240. President: Charles Faraone. Estab. 1978. Imprint is Planet Books. Publishes humorous, novelty 32-page books for the international gift and stationery market. Publishes 12-20 titles/year. Pays authors 5-15% royalty on wholesale price, outright $500-3,000 purchase or flat amount per book printed or

per book sold. Offers average advance of $500-1,500. Publishes ms an average of 4 months after acceptance. Simultaneous submissions OK. Reports in 2 weeks on queries and 3 weeks on mss. Book catalog and ms guidelines for #10 SASE.
Nonfiction: Humor, illustrated books. Query or submit outline/synopsis and sample chapters.
Fiction: Humor. "We'd like to find 10-15 funny books each year to fit our format." Query or submit outline/synopsis and sample chapters.
Recent Fiction Title: *Golfer's Prayer Book*.

OPEN COURT PUBLISHING CO., P.O. Box 599, Peru IL 61354. Publisher: M. Blouke Carus. President: Dr. André W. Carus. Estab. 1887. Averages 15 titles/year; receives 300 submissions annually. 20% of books from first-time authors; 80% of books from unagented writers. Royalty contracts negotiable for each book. Publishes book an average of 18 months after acceptance. Query for electronic submissions. Guidelines for 9×12 SAE.
Nonfiction: Philosophy, psychology, Jungian analysis, science and history of science, mathematics, public policy, comparative religion, education, studies in Oriental thought and related scholarly topics. Accepts nonfiction translations. "This is a publishing house run as an intellectual enterprise, to reflect the concerns of its staff and as a service to the world of learning." Query or submit outline/synopsis and 2-3 sample chapters. Reviews artwork/photos as part of ms package.
Recent Nonfiction Title: *Myth and Philosophy*, by Lawrence J. Hatab.

*OREGON HISTORICAL SOCIETY PRESS, Oregon Historical Society, 1230 SW Park, Portland OR 97205. (503)222-1741. FAX: (503)221-2035. Director—Publications: Bruce Taylor Hamilton. Estab. 1873. Publishes hardcover originals, trade paperback originals and reprints and a quarterly historical journal, *Oregon Historical Quarterly*. Publishes 12-14 titles/year. Receives 300 submissions/year. 75% of books from first-time authors; 100% from unagented writers. Subsidy publishes 70% (nonauthor) of books. Pays royalty on wholesale price or makes outright purchase. Publishes book an average of 18 months after acceptance. Simultaneous submissions OK. Query for electronic submissions. Reports in 1 week on queries; 3 months on mss. Free book catalog. Ms guidelines for #10 SASE.
Nonfiction: Subjects include Americana, art/architecture, biography, business history, ethnic, government/politics, history, nature/environment, North Pacific Studies, photography, reference, regional juvenile, women's. Query or submit outline/synopsis and sample chapters or submit complete ms. Reviews artwork/photos as part of ms package.
Recent Nonfiction Title: *Sowing Good Seeds: The Northwest Suffrage Campaigns of Susan B. Anthony*, by G. Thomas Edwards.

*OREGON STATE UNIVERSITY PRESS, 101 Waldo Hall, Corvallis OR 97331. (503)737-3166. Contact: Managing Editor. Estab. 1961. Publishers hardcover and paperback originals. Averages 6 titles/year; receives 100 submissions annually. 75% of books from first-time authors; 100% of books from unagented writers. Average print order for a writer's first book is 1,500. Subsidy publishes (nonauthor) 40% of books. Pays royalty on net receipts. No advance. Publishes book an average of 1 year after acceptance. Query for electronic submissions. Reports in 1 month. Book catalog for 6×9 SAE with 2 first class stamps.
Nonfiction: Publishes scholarly books in history, biography, geography, literature, life sciences and natural resource management, with strong emphasis on Pacific or Northwestern topics. Submit outline/synopsis and sample chapters.
Recent Nonfiction Title: *William L. Finley: Pioneer Wildlife Photographer*, by Worth Mathewson (biography/photos).

OSBORNE/MCGRAW-HILL, Subsidiary of McGraw-Hill Inc., 2600 10th St., Berkeley CA 94710. (415)548-2805. (800)227-0900. Editor-in-Chief: Jeff Pepper. Estab. 1979. Publishes trade paperback originals. Averages 65 titles/year. Receives 120 submissions/year. 30% of books from first-time authors; 99% from unagented writers. Pays 10-15% royalty on wholesale price. Offers $5,000 average advance. Publishes book an average of 6 months after acceptance. Simultaneous submissions OK. Query for electronic submissions. Reports in 1 week on queries; 2 weeks on mss. Book catalog and manuscript free on request.
Nonfiction: Software and technical. Subjects include computers. Query with outline/synopsis and sample chapters. Reviews artwork/photos as part of ms package.
Recent Nonfiction Title: *Dvorak's Guide to PC Telecommunications*, by John C. Dvorak/Nick Anis.

OUR SUNDAY VISITOR, INC., 200 Noll Plaza, Huntington IN 46750. (219)356-8400. President/Publisher: Robert Lockwood. Editor: Jacquelyn Eckert. Estab. 1912. Publishes paperback originals and reprints. Averages 20-30 titles a year; receives 75 submissions annually. 10% of books from first-time authors; 90% of books from unagented writers. Pays variable royalty on net receipts; offers average $500 advance. Publishes book an average of 1 year after acceptance. Query for electronic submissions.

Reports in 1 month on most queries and submissions. Author's guide and catalog for SASE.

Nonfiction: Catholic viewpoints on current issues, reference and guidance, Bibles and devotional books, and Catholic heritage books. Prefers to see well-developed proposals as first submission with "annotated outline, three sample chapters, and definition of intended market." Reviews artwork/photos as part of ms package.

Recent Nonfiction Title: *The Catholic Answer Book*, by Fr. Peter M.J. Stravinskas.

Tips: "Solid devotional books that are not first person, well-researched church histories or lives of the saints and self-help for those over 55, have the best chance of selling to our firm. Make it solidly Catholic, unique, without pious platitudes."

THE OVERLOOK PRESS, Distributed by Viking/Penguin, 149 Wooster St., New York NY 10012. Contact: Editorial Department. Imprints include Tusk Books. Publishes hardcover and trade paperback originals and hardcover reprints. Averages 40 titles/year; receives 300 submissions annually. Pays 3-15% royalty on wholesale or retail price. Submissions accepted only through literary agents. Reports in 2 months. Free book catalog.

Nonfiction: How-to and reference. Subjects include Americana, business and economics, history, nature, recreation, sports, and travel. No pornography.

Recent Nonfiction Title: *Wild Flora of the Northeast*.

Fiction: Adventure, ethnic, fantasy/science fiction, historical, mainstream, mystery/suspense. "We tend not to publish commercial fiction."

Recent Fiction Title: *The Universe and Other Fictions*, by Paul West.

Poetry: "We like to publish poets who have a strong following—those who read in New York City regularly or publish in periodicals regularly." No poetry from unpublished authors. Submit complete ms.

Recent Poetry Title: *Disappearances*, by Paul Auster.

Tips: "We are a very small company. If authors want a very quick decision, they should go to another company first and come back to us. We try to be as prompt as possible, but it sometimes takes many months for us to get to a final decision."

PACIFIC BOOKS, PUBLISHERS, P.O. Box 558, Palo Alto CA 94302. (415)965-1980. Editor: Henry Ponleithner. Estab. 1945. Averages 6-12 titles/year. Royalty schedule varies with book. No advance. Send complete ms. Reports "promptly." Book catalog and guidelines for 9 × 12 SASE.

Nonfiction: General interest, professional, technical and scholarly nonfiction trade books. Specialties include western Americana and Hawaiiana. Looks for "well-written, documented material of interest to a significant audience." Also considers text and reference books for high school and college. Accepts artwork/photos and translations.

Recent Nonfiction Title: *Growing Up While Growing Older*, by Jon Eisenson.

PACIFIC PRESS PUBLISHING ASSOCIATION, Book Division, Seventh-Day Adventist Church, P.O. Box 7000, Boise ID 83707. (208)465-2595. FAX: (208)465-2531. Vice President for Editorial Development: B. Russell Holt. Estab. 1874. Publishes hardcover and trade paperback originals and reprints. Averages 35 titles/year; receives 600 submissions and proposals annually. Up to 50% of books from first-time authors; 100% of books from unagented writers. Pays 8-14% royalty on wholesale price. Offers average $300-500 advance depending on length. Publishes books an average of 6 months after acceptance. Query for electronic submissions. Reports in 1 month on queries; 2 months on mss. Ms guidelines for #10 SASE.

Nonfiction: Biography, cookbook (vegetarian), how-to, juvenile, self-help and textbook. Subjects include cooking and foods (vegetarian only), health, nature, religion, and family living. "We are an exclusively religious publisher. We are looking for practical, how-to oriented manuscripts on religion, health, and family life that speak to human needs, interests and problems from a Biblical perspective. We can't use anything totally secular or written from other than a Christian perspective." Query or submit outline/synopsis and sample chapters. Reviews artwork/photos as part of ms package.

Recent Nonfiction Title: *Deceived by the New Age*, by Will Baron.

Tips: "Our primary audiences are members of our own denomination (Seventh-Day Adventist), the general Christian reading market, and the secular or nonreligious reader. Books that are doing well for us are those that relate the Biblical message to practical human concerns and those that focus more on the experiential rather than theoretical aspects of Christianity."

‡PANTHEON BOOKS, Division of Random House, Inc., 201 E. 50th St., 27th Floor, New York NY 10022. Publishes quality fiction and nonfiction. Send query letter first, addressed to Adult Editorial Department.

*PARAGON HOUSE PUBLISHERS, 90 5th Ave., New York NY 10011. (212)620-2820. Editor-in-Chief: Ken Stuart. Estab. 1983. Publishes hardcover and trade paperback originals and reprints. Averages 100 titles/year; receives 1,000 submissions annually. 10-20% of nonfiction from first-time authors; 50%

Close-up

Dan Frank
Senior Editor
Pantheon

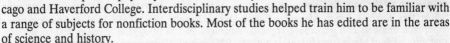

"Essentially I act as a surrogate for the general reader," says Pantheon Senior Editor Dan Frank. "It's my job to make sure a book can be and will want to be read by the public." Frank has edited many books for many publishers, including Harcourt Brace Jovanovich, Alfred A. Knopf, New American Library and Viking Penguin.

Frank was a philosophy major at the University of Chicago and Haverford College. Interdisciplinary studies helped train him to be familiar with a range of subjects for nonfiction books. Most of the books he has edited are in the areas of science and history.

One very interesting book Frank developed while an executive editor at Viking Penguin was a recent bestseller entitled *Chaos: Making a New Science*. After reading an article in *The New York Times Sunday Magazine* by author James Gleick, Frank became intrigued by the concept that there is an order to chaos, and that the study of chaos can give an important perspective to the earth and the universe. He contacted Gleick and discussed his idea that this new frontier of science could make for an interesting book. "I worked on the organization of the book," Frank says. "The whole process took a little over a year."

Frank's experience with conglomerate publishers is extensive. Despite their ownership by international corporations, he says there is not excessive pressure to pick books that will earn huge profits. "I have always had a strong commitment to quality writing," Frank says. "The sales basically take care of themselves."

One area Frank has noticed that has changed over the past few years is the role of agents among big name book publishers. "In this area there has been a sea change as a result of conglomeration," he says. "No longer are writers in personal contact with publishers so much as agents are. My main contacts the past few years have been with agents, and it is with the agent all the way through the publishing process for a book."

Frank suggests that writers seek out books edited by specific editors at publishing houses they are interested in selling to. "It stuns me that people send off their queries and manuscripts blind or to a job title," he says. A little research on the writer's part would make "a world of difference." He is also a great believer in the small and university presses. "Writers should definitely take them seriously. Investigate what is happening in the regional small and university presses in your area. They are publishing books of real quality." They are able to do this, according to Frank, "because their nets are much finer."

Another thing writers should know is that the huge advances occasionally reported in newspapers and magazines are the overwhelming exceptions in comparison with most advances. "Those million dollar advances are greatly misleading," Frank says. "Ninety-eight percent of advances are under $25,000, and what's more, 90% of all books sell under 15,000 copies."

Sadly, he notes, many books that do get published fall into oblivion, but that should not dissuade a determined writer. "Track down books by an editor and target your book accordingly," Frank says. "You'll be a world ahead of the majority."

—Mark Kissling

of books from unagented writers. Subsidy publishes 2% of books/year (mostly translations). Whether an author is subsidy published is determined by "how much subsidy there is, as well as how much market." Royalty and advance negotiable. Simultaneous submissions OK. Query for electronic submissions. Reports in 1 month on queries; 2 months on mss. Book catalog free on request.

Nonfiction: Biography, reference and college textbook. Subjects include Americana, history, philosophy, politics, religion. Especially needs history, biography and serious nonfiction. No diet, gardening, crafts or humor. Query or submit outline/synopsis and sample chapters. Reviews artwork/photos as part of ms package.

Recent Nonfiction Title: *Spiritual Parenting*, by David Carroll.

Poetry: No new or unestablished writers.

Recent Poetry Title: *New and Collected Poems*, by Leo Conellan.

PASSPORT PRESS, P.O. Box 1346, Champlain NY 12919. (514)937-3868. Publisher: Jack Levesque. Estab. 1975. Publishes trade paperback originals. Averages 4 titles/year. 25% of books from first-time authors; 100% from unagented writers. Pays 8-12% royalty on retail price. Publishes book an average of 9 months after acceptance. Send query only. Unsolicited manuscripts or samples and non-travel material will not be returned even if accompanied by postage.

Nonfiction: Travel books only. Especially looking for manuscripts on practical travel subjects and travel guides on specific countries. Query. Reviews artwork/photos as part of ms package.

Recent Nonfiction Title: *Honduras and the Bay Islands*, by J.P. Panet.

‡*PAULIST PRESS, 997 Macarthur Blvd., Mahwah NJ 07430. (201)825-7300. FAX: (201)825-8345. Editor: Rev. Kevin A. Lynch. Managing Editor: Donald Brophy. Estab. 1865. Publishes hardcover and paperback originals and paperback reprints. Averages 90-100 titles/year; receives 500 submissions annually. 5-8% of books from first-time authors; 95% of books from unagented writers. Subsidy publishes (nonauthor) 1-2% of books. Pays royalty on retail price. Usually offers advance. Publishes book an average of 10 months after acceptance. Query for electronic submissions.

Nonfiction: Philosophy, religion, self-help and textbooks (religious). Accepts nonfiction translations from German, French and Spanish. "We would like to see theology (Catholic and ecumenical Christian), popular spirituality, liturgy, and religious education texts." Submit outline/synopsis and 2 sample chapters. Reviews artwork/photos as part of ms package.

Recent Nonfiction Title: *What is Religion?*, by John Haught.

PBC INTERNATIONAL INC., 1 School St., Glen Cove NY 11542. (516)676-2727. FAX: (516)676-2738. Publisher: Mark Serchuck. Estab. 1980. Imprints are Library of Applied Design (nonfiction), Great Graphics Series (nonfiction) and Design In Motion Series (nonfiction). Publishes hardcover and trade paperback originals. Averages 15 titles/year; receives 100-200 submissions annually. Most of books from first-time authors and unagented writers done on assignment. Pays royalty and/or flat fees. Simultaneous submissions OK. Book catalog for 9 × 12 SASE.

Nonfiction: Subjects include design, graphic art, architecture/interior design and photography. The Library of Applied Design needs books that show the best in current design trends in all fields. No submissions not covered in the above listed topics. Query with outline/synopsis and sample chapters. Reviews artwork/photos as part of ms package.

Recent Nonfiction Title: *CLIO Awards—A Tribute to Thirty Years of Advertising Excellence*, by The CLIO Awards.

PEACHTREE PUBLISHERS, LTD., 494 Armour Circle NE, Atlanta GA 30324. (404)876-8761. Contact: Managing Editor. Estab. 1977. Publishes hardcover and trade paperback originals. Averages 20-25 titles/year; receives up to 4-5,000 submissions annually. 50% of books from first-time authors; 75% of books from unagented writers. Average print order for a writer's first book is 5,000-10,000. Publishes book an average of 1 year after acceptance. Reports in 3 weeks on queries; 5 months on mss. Book catalog for SAE with 3 first class stamps.

Nonfiction: General and humor. Subjects include cooking and foods, history, recreation and travel. No technical, reference, art, juvenile or animals. Submit outline/synopsis and sample chapters. Reviews artwork/photos as part of ms package.

Recent Nonfiction Title: *Side Orders: Small Helpings of Southern Culture and Cookery*, by John Egerton.

Fiction: Literary, humor and mainstream. "We are particularly interested in fiction with a Southern feel." No fantasy, juvenile, science fiction or romance. Submit sample chapters.

Recent Fiction Title: *To Dance with the White Dog*, by Terry Kay.

Tips: "We're looking for mainstream fiction and nonfiction of general interest; although our books are sold throughout North America. We consider ourselves the national publisher with a Southern accent."

PELICAN PUBLISHING COMPANY, 1101 Monroe St., P.O. Box 189, Gretna LA 70053. (504)368-1175. FAX: (504)368-1195. Editor: Nina Kooij. Estab. 1926. Publishes hardcover, trade paperback and mass market paperback originals and reprints. Averages 40-50 titles/year; receives 3,000 submissions annually. 20% of books from first-time authors; 97% of books from unagented writers. Pays royalty on publisher's actual receipts. Publishes book an average of 18 months after acceptance. Reports in 1 month on queries; 4 months on mss. Writer's guidelines for SASE.

Nonfiction: Travel, biography, coffee table book (limited), cookbook, how-to, humor, illustrated book, juvenile, self-help, motivational, inspirational, and Scottish. Subjects include Americana (especially Southern regional, Ozarks, Texas and Florida); business and economics (popular how-to and motivational); cooking and food; health; history; music (American artforms: jazz, blues, Cajun, R&B); politics (special interest in conservative viewpoint); recreation; religion (for popular audience mostly, but will consider others); and travel. *Travel*: Regional and international (especially areas in Pacific). *Motivational*: with business slant. *Inspirational*: author must be someone with potential for large audience. *Cookbooks*: "We look for authors with strong connection to restaurant industry or cooking circles, i.e. someone who can promote successfully." *How-to*: will consider broad range. Query. "We require that a query be made first. This greatly expedites the review process and can save the writer additional postage expenses." Does not consider multiple queries or submissions. Reviews artwork/photos as part of ms package.

Recent Nonfiction Title: *The Maverick Guide to Thailand*, by Len Rutledge.

Fiction: Historical, humor, mainstream, Southern, and juvenile. "Fiction needs are *very* limited. We are most interested in Southern novels. We are also looking for good mainstream juvenile works." No young adult, romance, science fiction, fantasy, gothic, mystery, erotica, confession, horror; no sex or violence. Submit outline/synopsis and sample chapters.

Recent Fiction Title: *Holt and the Teddy Bear*, by Jim McCafferty.

Tips: "We do extremely well with travel, motivational, cookbooks, and children's titles. We will continue to build in these areas. The writer must have a clear sense of the market and this includes knowledge of the competition. A query letter should describe the project briefly, give the author's writing and professional credentials, and promotional ideas. Include an SASE."

*PENDRAGON PRESS, Imprint of Camelot Publishing Co., Inc., R.R. 1, Box 159, Ferry Rd., Stuyvesant NY 12173-9720. (518)828-3008. FAX: (518)828-2368. Managing Editor: Robert Kessler. Estab. 1972. Publishes hardcover originals and reprints. Averages 12-15 titles/year. Receives 100 submissions/year. 50% of book from first-time authors; 99.9% from unagented writers. Subsidy publishes 30% of books. "If the book is of such special interest that sales will not cover publishing expenses, we subsidy publish." Pays 8-12% royalty on retail price. Publishes book an average of 15 months after acceptance. Simultaneous submissions OK. Query for electronic submissions. Reports in 2 weeks on queries; 2 months on mss. Book catalog and manuscript guidelines free on request.

Nonfiction: Reference. Subjects include music/dance and sociology (of music). "We deal specifically with scholarly material, for study and research." Submit outline/synopsis and sample chapters. Reviews artwork/photos as part of ms package.

Recent Nonfiction Title: *The History of Orchestral Conducting*, by Elliot W. Galkin (musicology).

Tips: "In our field, music history, there is a trend toward exploring interdisciplinary studies, such as aesthetics in music, sociology of music, ethomusicology, etc."

PENGUIN USA, 375 Hudson St., New York NY 10014. Imprints include Dial Books for Young Readers, E. P. Dutton, Dutton Juvenile, Dutton/New American Library, and Viking Penguin. Did not want a listing for their Adult Trade Books Division.

PENNSYLVANIA HISTORICAL AND MUSEUM COMMISSION, The official history agency for the Commonwealth of Pennsylvania, P.O. Box 1026, Harrisburg PA 17108-1026. (717)787-8312. FAX: (717)783-1073. Chief, Marketing, Sales and Publications Division: Diane Reed. Estab. 1913. Publishes hardcover, and paperback originals and reprints. Averages 6 titles/year; receives 25 submissions annually. May pay 5-10% royalty on wholesale or retail price. May make outright purchase of $500-1,000; sometimes makes special assignments; may offer $350 average advance. Publishes book an average of 18 months after acceptance. Simultaneous submissions OK. Query for electronic submissions. Reports in 6 weeks on queries; 3 months on mss. Manuscripts prepared according to the *Chicago Manual of Style*.

Nonfiction: All books must be related to Pennsylvania, its history or culture: biography, coffee table, how-to, illustrated book, cookbook, reference, technical, visitor attractions and historic travel guidebooks. "The Commission seeks manuscripts on Pennsylvania in general, but more specifically on archaeology, history, art (decorative and fine), politics, religion, travel, photography, nature, sports history, and cooking and food." Query or submit outline/synopsis and sample chapters.

Recent Nonfiction Title: *Guide to the State Historical Markers of Pennsylvania*, by George R. Beyer.
Tips: "Our audience is diverse—students, specialists and generalists—all of them interested in one or more aspects of Pennsylvania's history and culture. Manuscripts must be well researched and documented (footnotes not necessarily required depending on the nature of the manuscript) and interestingly written. Because of the expertise of our reviewers, manuscripts must be factually accurate, but in being so, writers must not sacrifice style. We have a tradition of publishing scholarly and reference works, and although we continue to do so, we want to branch out with more popularly styled books that will reach an even broader audience."

THE PERMANENT PRESS/SECOND CHANCE PRESS, RD 2, Noyac Rd., Sag Harbor NY 11963. (516)725-1101. FAX: (516)725-1101. Editor: Judith Shepard. Estab. 1978. Publishes hardcover originals and reprints. Second Chance Press devotes itself exclusively to re-publishing fine books that are out of print and deserve continued recognition. Permanent Press publishes original fiction and some books of social and/or political significance. Averages 10 titles/year; receives 3,000 submissions annually. 35% of books from first-time authors; 75% of books from unagented writers. Average print order for a writer's first book is 2,000. Pays 10% royalty on wholesale price; offers $1,000 advance for Permanent Press books and royalty only on Second Chance Press titles. Publishes book an average of 18 months after acceptance. Simultaneous submissions OK. Reports in 2 weeks on queries; 3 months on mss. Book catalog for $2 postage.
Nonfiction: Biography, autobiography, historical and current events. No scientific and technical material or academic studies. Query.
Recent Nonfiction Title: *City of Discontent*, by Mark Harris.
Fiction: Adventure, confession, ethnic, experimental, fantasy, historical, humor, mainstream, mystery, and suspense. Especially looking for fiction with a unique point of view—"original and arresting" suitable for college literature classes. No mass market romance. Query.
Recent Fiction Title: *Postcards from Pinsk*, by Larry Duberstein.

PERSPECTIVES PRESS, P.O. Box 90318, Indianapolis IN 46290-0318. (317)872-3055. Publisher: Pat Johnston. Estab. 1982. Publishes hardcover and trade paperback originals. Averages 4 titles/year; receives 200 queries annually. 95% of books from first-time authors. 95% of books from unagented writers. Pays 5-15% royalty on net sales. Publishes book an average of 8 months after acceptance. Simultaneous submissions OK. Reports in 2 weeks on queries. Book catalog and writer's guidelines for #10 SAE and 2 first class stamps.
Nonfiction: How-to, juvenile and self-help books on health, psychology and sociology—all related to adoption or infertility. Query.
Recent Nonfiction Title: *Sweet Grapes: How to Stop Being Infertile and Start Living Again*, by Mike and Jean Carter.
Fiction: Adoption/infertility for adults or children. Query.
Recent Fiction Title: *Where the Sun Kisses the Sea*, by Susan Gabel.
Tips: "For adults we are seeking infertility and adoption decision-making materials, books dealing with parenting issues, books to use with children, books to share with others to help explain infertility or adoption or foster care, special programming or training manuals, etc. For children we will consider adoption or foster care related manuscripts that are appropriate for preschoolers, for early elementary, for later elementary or middle school children, for high schoolers. While we would consider a manuscript from a writer who was not personally or professionally involved in these issues, we would be more inclined to accept a manuscript submitted by an infertile person, an adoptee, a birthparent, an adoptive parent, a professional working with any of these."

PETER PAUPER PRESS, INC., 202 Mamaroneck Ave., White Plains NY 10601. (914)681-0144. FAX: (914)681-0389. Co-Publisher: Nick Beilenson. Estab. 1928. Publishes hardcover originals. Averages 12 titles/year; receives 100 submissions annually. Buys some mss outright for $1,000. Offers no advance. Publishes ms an average of 9 months after acceptance. Simultaneous submissions OK. Reports in 2 weeks. Book catalog for #10 SAE with 2 first class stamps.
Nonfiction: Subjects include Americana, humor, holidays and inspirational. *No* cookbooks, fiction, or children's books. Submit complete ms. Reviews artwork as part of ms package.
Recent Nonfiction Title: *The Little Birthday Book*, by Suzanne Beilenson.
Tips: "Books on women's subjects have done well for Peter Pauper Press."

PETERSON'S, P.O. Box 2123, Princeton NJ 08543. (800)338-3282. Publisher/President: Peter W. Hegener. Executive Vice President: Karen C. Hegener. Estab. 1966. Publishes paperback originals and software (for the educational/career market). Averages 55-75 titles/year. Receives 200-250 submissions annually. 30% of books from first-time authors; 90% from unagented writers. Average print order for a writer's first book is 10,000-15,000. Pays 8-10% royalty on net sales; offers advance. Publishes book an average of 1 year after acceptance. Responds in 3 weeks. Free catalog.

Nonfiction: Educational and career reference and guidance works for professionals, libraries, and trade. Submit complete ms or detailed outline and sample chapters. Looks for "appropriateness of contents to our market, accuracy of information, author's credentials, and writing style suitable for audience." Reviews artwork/photos as part of ms package.
Recent Nonfiction Title: *Who's Going to Run General Motors?*, by Daniel Seymour and Kenneth Green.

PFEIFFER & COMPANY, (formerly University Associates, Inc.), 8517 Production Ave., San Diego CA 92121. (619)578-5900. FAX: (619)578-2042. President: J. William Pfeiffer. Estab. 1968. Publishes paperback and hardback originals and reprints. Averages 25 titles/year. Specializes in practical materials for human resource development, consultants, etc. Pays average 10% royalty; no advance. Publishes book an average of 6 months after acceptance. Markets books by direct mail. Simultaneous submissions OK. Reports in 4 months. Book catalog and guidelines for SASE.
Nonfiction: Richard Roe, Vice President, Publications. Publishes (in order of preference) human resource development and group-oriented material, management education, personal growth, and business. No materials for grammar school or high school classroom teachers. Use *American Psychological Association Style Manual*. Query. Send prints or completed art or rough sketches to accompany ms.
Recent Nonfiction Title: *The 1991 Annual: Developing Human Resources*, J.W. Pfeiffer, editor.

PHAROS BOOKS, Publisher of *The World Almanac*, 200 Park Ave., New York NY 10166. (212)692-3824. Editor-in-Chief: Hana Umlauf Lane. Editor: Eileen Schlesinger. Assistant Editor: Sharilyn K. Jee. Publishes hardcover and trade paperback originals. Averages 50 titles/year. Pays 6-15% on retail price. Publishes book an average of 1 year after acceptance. Reports in 3 weeks. Free book catalog.
Nonfiction: "We look for books under three imprints: Pharos Books for nonfiction with strong consumer interest; World Almanac for innovative trade reference books; Topper for humor books. We expect at least a synopsis/outline and sample chapters, and would like to see the completed manuscript." Reviews artwork/photos as part of ms package.

PICADILLY BOOKS, (formerly Polka-Dot Press), Java Publishing Co., P.O. Box 25203, Colorado Springs CO 80936. (719)548-1844. Publisher: Bruce Fife. Estab. 1985. Firm publishes hardcover and trade paperback originals and trade paperback reprints. Publishes 3-8 titles/year; receives 120 submissions/year. 70% of books from first-time authors; 95% from unagented writers. Pays 5-10% royalty on retail price, or buys ms for $250-5,000 outright. Offers $250 average advance. Publishes book an average of 9 months after acceptance. Simultaneous submissions OK. Reports in 1 month on queries; 2 months on mss. Book catalog of 6×9 SAE and 2 first class stamps; ms guidelines for #10 SASE.
Nonfiction: Biography, how-to, humor, self-help. Subjects include hobbies, recreation, sports, entertainment and performing arts. Submit complete ms. Reviews artwork/photos as part of ms package.
Recent Nonfiction Title: *Strutter's Complete Guide to Clown Makeup*, by Jim Roberts.
Fiction: Humor. Submit complete ms.

‡THE PILGRIM PRESS, United Church Board for Homeland Ministries, 700 Prospect Ave. E., Cleveland OH 44115-1100. (216)736-3700. Publishes trade paperback originals. Firm averages 20 titles/year. 40% of books from first-time authors. 100% from unagented writers. Pays 7½-8% royalty on retail price. No advance. Publishes book an average of 18 months after acceptance. Reports in 2 months on queries. Book catalog and ms guidelines free on request.
Nonfiction: Subjects include biblical, theological, pastoral and worship resources, social issues in Christian context. Query or submit outline/synopsis and sample chapters. All unsolicited mss are returned unopened.
Recent Nonfiction Title: *Gender and the Name of God: The Trinitarian Baptismal Formula*, by Ruth C. Duck (Theology).
Tips: "Writers should send books about contemporary social issues in a Christian context. Our audience is liberal, open-minded, socially aware, feminist, educated lay church members and clergy, teachers and seminary professors."

PILOT BOOKS, 103 Cooper St., Babylon NY 11702. (516)422-2225. President: Sam Small. Estab. 1959. Publishes paperback originals. Averages 20-30 titles/year; receives 300-400 submissions annually. 20% of books from first-time authors; 90% of books from unagented writers. Average print order for a writer's first book is 3,000. Offers standard royalty contract based on wholesale or retail price. Usual advance is $250, but this varies, depending on author's reputation and nature of book. Publishes book an average of 8 months after acceptance. Reports in 1 month. Book catalog and guidelines for SASE.
Nonfiction: Financial, business, travel, career, personal guides and training manuals. "Our training manuals are utilized by America's major corporations as well as the government. Directories and books on travel and moneymaking opportunities. Wants clear, concise treatment of subject matter."

Length: 8,000-30,000 words. Send outline. Reviews artwork/photos as part of ms package.
Recent Nonfiction Title: *The Budget Traveler's Guide to Great Off-Beat Vacations*, by Paige Palmer.

PINEAPPLE PRESS, INC., Drawer 16008, Southside Station, Sarasota FL 34239. (813)952-1085. Editor: June Cussen. Estab. 1982. Publishes hardcover and trade paperback originals. Averages 12 titles/year; receives 600 submissions annually. 20% of books from first-time authors; 80% of books from unagented writers. Pays 6½-15% royalty on retail price. Seldom offers advance. Publishes book an average of 1 year after acceptance. Simultaneous submissions OK. Query for electronic submissions. Reports in 1 month on queries; 6 weeks on mss. Book catalog for 9×12 SAE and 2 first class stamps.
Nonfiction: Biography, how-to, reference, nature. Subjects include animals, history, gardening and nature. "We will consider most nonfiction topics. We are seeking quality nonfiction on diverse topics for the library and book trade markets." No pop psychology or autobiographies. Query or submit outline/brief synopsis and sample chapters with SASE.
Recent Nonfiction Title: *Growing and Using Exotic Foods*, by Marian Van Atta.
Fiction: Literary, historical and mainstream. No romance, science fiction, or children's. Submit outline/brief synopsis and sample chapters.
Recent Fiction Title: *Princess of the Everglades*, by Charles Mink.
Tips: "If I were a writer trying to market a book today, I would learn everything I could about book publishing and book publicity and agree to actively participate in promoting my book. A query on a novel without a brief sample seems useless."

PIPPIN PRESS, 229 E. 85th St., Gracie Station, P.O. Box 92, New York NY 10028. (212)288-4920. Publisher/President: Barbara Francis. Estab. 1987. Publishes hardcover originals. Publishes 6-8 titles/year; receives 3,000 submissions/year. 80% of books from unagented writers. Pays royalty. Publishes book an average of 9-18 months after acceptance. Simultaneous submissions OK. Reports in 3 weeks on queries; 2 months on mss. Book catalog for 6×9 SASE; ms guidelines for #10 SASE.
Nonfiction: Children's books: biography, humor, juvenile, picture books. Animals, history, language/literature, nature, science. General nonfiction for children ages 4-12. Query. Reviews copies of artwork/photos as part of ms package.
Recent Nonfiction Title: *Pass the Quill: I'll Write a Draft: A Story of Thomas Jefferson*, by Robert Quackenbush (humorous).
Fiction: Adventure, fantasy, historical, humor, juvenile, mystery, picture books, suspense. Wants humorous fiction for ages 7-11. Query.
Recent Fiction Title: *Lost in the Amazon: A Miss Mallard Mystery*, written and illustrated by Robert Quaekenked.
Tips: "Read as many of the best children's books published in the last five years as you can. I would pay particular attention to children's books favorably reviewed in *School Library Journal*, *The Booklist*, *The New York Times Book Review*, *Publishers Weekly*."

PLAYERS PRESS, INC., P.O. Box 1132, Studio City CA 91614. (818)789-4980. Vice President, Editorial: Robert W. Gordon. Estab. 1965. Publishes hardcover and trade paperback originals, and trade paperback reprints. Averages 15-25 titles/year; receives 75-300 submissions annually. 10% of books from first-time authors; 90% of books from unagented writers. Pays royalty on retail price. Publishes book an average of 20 months after acceptance. Reports in up to 1 year. Book catalog and guidelines for 6×9 SAE and 3 first class stamps.
Nonfiction: Juvenile and theatrical drama/entertainment industry. Subjects include the performing arts. Needs quality plays and musicals, adult or juvenile. Send query. Reviews artwork/photos as part of package.
Recent Nonfiction Title: *Survival*, by William-Alan Landes.
Fiction: Subject matter of plays include adventure, confession, ethnic, experimental, fantasy, historical, horror, humor, mainstream, mystery, religious, romance, science fiction, suspense and western. Submit complete ms for theatrical plays only. "No novels are accepted. We publish plays, musicals and books on theatre, only."
Recent Fiction Title: *A Dusty Echo*, by Ev Miller.
Tips: "Plays, entertainment industry texts and children's story books have the only chances of selling to our firm."

PLENUM PUBLISHING, 233 Spring St., New York NY 10013. (212)620-8000. Senior Editor, Trade Books: Linda Greenspan Regan. Estab. 1946. Publishes hardcover originals. Averages 350 titles/year; trade division publishes 12. Receives 250 submissions annually. 35% of books from first-time authors. 60% of books from unagented writers. Publishes book an average of 8 months after acceptance. Simultaneous submissions OK. Query for electronic submissions. Reports in several months on queries and mss.

Nonfiction: Subjects include trace science, criminology, sociology, psychology, and health. "We need popular books in the sciences and social sciences." Query only.
Recent Nonfiction Title: *Colliding Galaxies: The Universe in Turmoil*, by Barry Parker.
Tips: "Our audience consists of intelligent laymen and professionals. Authors should be experts on subject matter of book. They must compare their books with competitive works, explain how theirs differs, and define the market for their books."

POCKET BOOKS, Division of Simon & Schuster, 1230 Avenue of the Americas, New York NY 10020. Imprints include Pocket Star Books, Washington Square Press (high-quality mass market), Archway and Minstrel (juvenile/YA imprints). Publishes paperback originals and reprints, mass market and trade paperbacks and hardcovers. Averages 300 titles/year; receives 750 submissions annually. 15% of books from first-time authors. 100% of submissions are from agented writers. Pays royalty on retail price. Publishes book an average of 1 year after acceptance. *No unsolicited mss or queries.* "All submissions must go through a literary agent."
Nonfiction: History, biography, reference and general nonfiction, cookbooks, humor, calendars.
Fiction: Adult (mysteries, thriller, psychological suspense, Star Trek ® novels, romance, westerns).

PORTER SARGENT PUBLISHERS, INC., 11 Beacon St., Suite 1400, Boston MA 02108. (617)523-1670. FAX: (617)523-1021. Coordinating Editor: Heather Joy Lane. Estab. 1914. Imprints are Sargent's Handbook Series and Extending Horizons Books. Publishes hardcover and paperback originals, reprints, translations and anthologies. Averages 4 titles/year. Pays royalty on retail price. "Each contract is dealt with on an individual basis with the author." Book catalog for SASE.
Nonfiction: Reference, special education and academic nonfiction. "Handbook Series and Special Education Series offer standard, definitive reference works in private education and writings and texts in special education. The Extending Horizons Series is an outspoken, unconventional series that presents topics of importance in contemporary affairs and the social sciences." This series is particularly directed to the college adoption market. Accepts nonfiction translations from French and Spanish. Send query with brief description, table of contents, sample chapter and information regarding author's background.
Recent Nonfiction Title: *Handbook of Private Schools*.

‡POSEIDON PRESS, Division of Simon & Schuster, 1230 Avenue of the Americas, New York NY 10020. (212)698-7290. Vice President/Publisher: Ann E. Patty. Publishes hardcover and trade paperback originals. Averages 20 titles/year; receives 1,000 submissions annually. 20% of books from first-time authors; none from unagented writers. Pays 10-15% royalty on hardcover retail price. Publishes book an average of 1 year after acceptance. Computer printout submissions acceptable; no dot-matrix. Does not accept unsolicited material.
Nonfiction: Autobiography, biography and self-help. Subjects include business and economics, culture, history, politics, psychology and biography, autobiography and self-help. No religious/inspirational, cookbooks, diet or exercise.
Recent Nonfiction Title: *Signs of the Times*, by David Lehman.
Fiction: Literary, historical, contemporary and mainstream.
Recent Fiction Title: *Two Girls, Fat and Thin*, by Mary Gaitskill.

POTENTIALS DEVELOPMENT FOR HEALTH & AGING SERVICES, 775 Main St., Buffalo NY 14203. (716)842-2658. Editor: J.A. Elkins. Publishes paperback originals. Averages 4 titles/year; receives 30-40 submissions annually. 90% of books from first-time authors; 100% of books from unagented writers. Average print order for a writer's first book is 500. Pays 5% royalty on sales of first 3,000 copies; 8% thereafter. Publishes book an average of 1 year after acceptance. Reports in 6 weeks. Book catalog and ms guidelines for #10 SASE.
Nonfiction: "We seek material of interest to those working with elderly people in the community and in institutional settings. We need tested, innovative and practical ideas." Query or submit outline/synopsis and 3 sample chapters. Looks for "suitable subject matter, writing style and organization."
Recent Nonfiction Title: *Moving for Life*, by Leslie Van Houten.
Tips: "The writer has the best chance of selling us materials of interest to those working with elderly people in nursing homes, senior and retirement centers. Our major market is activity directors. Give us good reasons why activity directors would want or need the material submitted."

PRAKKEN PUBLICATIONS, INC., P.O. Box 8623, Ann Arbor MI 48107. (313)769-1211. FAX: (313)769-8383. Publisher: George Kennedy. Estab. 1934. Publishes educational hardcover and paperback originals as well as educational magazines. Averages 4 titles/year; receives 50 submissions annually. 20% of books from first-time authors; 95% of books from unagented writers. Pays 10% royalty on net price of book (negotiable, with production costs). Publishes book an average of 6 months after acceptance. Simultaneous submissions OK. Reports in 3 weeks on queries; 6 months on mss. Book catalog for #10 SASE.

Nonfiction: Vocational and technology education and related areas, and general educational reference. "We are interested in manuscripts with broad appeal in any of the specific subject areas of industrial arts, vocational-technical education, and reference for the general education field." Submit outline/synopsis and sample chapters. Reviews artwork/photos as part of ms package.

Recent Nonfiction Title: *Oral Communication Skills for Vo-Tech Students: A Competency-Based Approach*, by C.S. Mester and R.T. Tanber.

Tips: "We have a continuing interest in magazine and book manuscripts which reflect emerging policy issues in education, especially vocational, industrial, and technical education."

PRENTICE HALL PRESS, Imprint of Simon & Schuster, Trade Division, 15 Columbus Circle, 15th Flr., New York NY 10023. Publisher: Elizabeth Perle. Publishes nonfiction hardcover and trade paperback originals. Publishes book an average of 10 months after acceptance. Will not consider unsolicited submissions.

Nonfiction: Categories include: literary nonfiction, history, self-help, New Age, psychology, business, health, diet, fitness, travel, sports, nature, the environment and science. Does not publish fiction, poetry, romances, westerns or other fiction genres.

Recent Nonfiction Title: *The Day America Told the Truth*, by Jim Patterson and Peter Kim.

THE PRESERVATION PRESS, Imprint of the National Trust for Historic Preservation, 1785 Massachusetts Ave. NW, Washington DC 20036. FAX: (202)673-4172. Director: Buckley C. Jeppson. Estab. 1975. Publishes nonfiction books on historic preservation (saving and reusing the "built environment"). Averages 12 titles/year; receives 100 submissions annually. 40% of books from first-time authors; 50% of books from unagented writers. Books are often commissioned by the publisher. Publishes book an average of 2 years after acceptance. Query for electronic submissions. Book catalog for 9 × 12 SASE.

Nonfiction: Subject matter encompasses architecture and architectural history, building restoration and historic preservation. No local history. Looks for "relevance to national preservation-oriented audience; educational or instructional value; depth; uniqueness; need in field." Query. Reviews artwork/photos as part of ms package.

Recent Nonfiction Title: *Lighting for Historic Buildings*, by Roger W. Moss.

Tips: "The writer has the best chance of selling our press a book clearly related to our mission — historic preservation — that covers new ideas and is unique and practical. If it fills a clear need, we will know immediately."

‡PRESIDIO PRESS, 31 Pamaron Way, Novato CA 94949. (415)883-1373. Editor-in-Chief: Dale Wilson. Senior Editor: Joan Griffin. Estab. 1974. Imprint is Lyford Books. Publishes hardcover originals and reprints. Firm averages 25 titles/year. Receives 700 submissions/year. 10% of books from first-time authors. 30% from unagented writers. Pays 15-20% royalty on net price. Offers various advances. Publishes book an average of 1 year after acceptance. Reports in 1 month on queries. Free book catalog and manuscript guidelines. Distributes books for other publishers in the military category.

Nonfiction: Biography (military only), (military history, equipment, units, etc.). Subjects include history (military only) and military/war. "We are looking for books on military history, theory (strategy, operational art and tactics), equipment, units, procedures. Primarily we market to interested civilians, but we also publish works for the military audience. No author's personal tour in Vietnam unless he was with a unit on which nothing has been published and the book is primarily about the unit and not about the author. Same applies to Korea, WWII, etc." Query. Submit outline/synopsis and sample chapters. Reviews artwork/photos as part of ms package. "Prefer photocopies with initial submission, not originals."

Recent Nonfiction Title: *The Art of Maneuver*, by Robert R. Leonhard (military-operational art).

Fiction: Adventure (military) and historical (military). "We are looking for technothrillers, military procedurals, historical military fiction. No fictionalized versions of author's tour in Vietnam (World War II, Korea, etc.)." Query. Submit outline/synopsis and sample chapters.

Recent Fiction Title: *Rules of Engagement*, by Joe Weber (technothriller).

Tips: "What we most need are informative, popular expositions of military matters such as new technology, special units, historical operations. Our audience consists of civilians interested in the military, military history buffs, wargamers, some professional military. If I were a writer trying to market a book

For information on book publishers' areas of interest, see the nonfiction and fiction sections in the Book Publishers Subject Index.

today, I would study the market. Find out what publishers are publishing, what they say they want and so forth. Then write what the market seems to be asking for, but with some unique angle that differentiates the work from others on the same subject."

‡**THE PRESS AT CALIFORNIA STATE UNIVERSITY, FRESNO**, Shaw and Cedar Avenues, Fresno CA 93740. (209)278-7082. General Manager: Carla Millar. Publishes hardcover and trade paperback originals. Averages 5 titles/year; receives 75 submissions/year. 50% of books from first-time authors; 100% from unagented writers. Offers average $1,000 advance. Publishes book an average of 3 months after acceptance. Simultaneous submissions OK. Reports in 2 weeks. Free book catalog.
Nonfiction: Biography, coffee table book, scholarly books. Subjects include art/architecture, business and economics, government/politics, history, music/dance, film. "We are looking for mss of significant general interest that are competently and professionally done. We have published books on art, architecture, music, film, drama, business and New Age politics." Query or submit outline/synopsis and sample chapters. Reviews artwork/photos as part of ms package.
Recent Nonfiction Title: *Flamenco, Body and Soul*, by Juan Serrano (music).

PREVENTION HEALTH BOOKS, Subsidiary of Rodale Press, Inc., 33 E. Minor St., Emmaus PA 18098. (215)967-5171. Assistant to the Editor-in-Chief: Cynthia Nickerson. Estab. 1940. Publishes hardcover originals and tradepaperback originals and reprints. Imprint averages 10 titles/year. Receives 300 submissions/year. 25% of books from first-time authors; 10% from unagented writers. Pays 2-15% royalty on retail price; buys mss outright for $2,000-25,000. Offers $15,000 average advance. Publishes book an average of 8 months after acceptance. Simultaneous submissions OK. Query for electronic submissions. Reports in 3 weeks on queries; 6 weeks on mss.
Nonfiction: Cookbook, how-to, self-help, health. Subjects include cooking, foods and nutrition, health/medicine, fitness. "Our needs are innovative health and nutrition books by M.D.'s or other health professionals. No child care and parenting or relationships." Submit outline/synopsis and sample chapters. Reviews artwork/photos as part of ms package.
Recent Nonfiction Title: *The Healing Herbs*, by Michael Castleman.
Tips: "Our audience is largely women aged 45-65 who are concerned about their health and their spouse's health. Most are pretty well-informed, but not terribly active. Very interested in diet, nutrition, self-care techniques. If I were a writer trying to market a book today, I would make sure I was familiar with what's hot, what's selling well and what's passé."

‡**PRICE STERN SLOAN INC., PUBLISHERS**, Suite 650, 11150 Olympic Blvd., Los Angeles CA 90064. Contact: Editorial Director. Estab. 1969. Imprints include Serendipity Books, Wee Sing, Troubador Press and Laughter Library. Publishes trade paperback originals. Averages 85 titles/year; receives 2,000 submissions annually. 20% of books from first-time authors; 50% of books from unagented writers. Pays royalty on wholesale price, or by outright purchase. Offers small or no advance. Publishes book an average of 1 year after acceptance. Reports in 3 months. Ms guidelines for SASE.
Nonfiction: Subjects include humor, calendars and satire (limited). Juveniles (all ages). Query *only*. "Most titles are unique in concept as well as execution and are geared for the so-called gift market." Reviews artwork/photos as part of ms package. "Do not send original artwork."
Tips: "Humor and satire were the basis of the company's early product and are still the mainstream of the company."

PRIMA PUBLISHING, P.O. Box 1260, Rocklin CA 95677. (916)624-5718. Publisher: Ben Dominitz. Estab. 1984. Publishes hardcover and trade paperback originals and trade paperback reprints. Publishes 90 titles/year. Receives 750 queries/year. Buys 10% of books from first-time authors; 50% from unagented writers. Pays 15-20% royalty on wholesale price. Advance varies. Publishes books an average of 6-9 months after acceptance. Simultaneous submissions OK. Query for electronic submissions. Reports in 2 months. Catalog for 9×12 SAE with 7 first class stamps; writer's guidelines for #10 SASE.
Nonfiction: Biography, cookbook, how-to, self-help. Subjects include business and economics, cooking and foods, health, music, politics and psychology. "We want books with originality, written by highly qualified individuals. No fiction at this time." Query.
Recent Nonfiction Title: *Other Losses: The Shocking Truth Behind the Mass Deaths of Disarmed German Soldiers and Civilians Under General Eisenhower's Command*, by James Bacque.
Tips: "Prima strives to reach the primary and secondary markets for each of its books. We are known for promoting our books aggressively. Books that genuinely solve problems for people will always do well if properly promoted. Try to picture the intended audience while writing the book. Too many books are written to an audience that doesn't exist."

***PRINCETON ARCHITECTURAL PRESS**, 37 E. 7th St., New York NY 10003. (212)995-9620. FAX: (212)995-9454. Estab. 1983. Publishes hardcover and trade paperback originals and hardcover reprints. Averages 20 titles/year; receives 50 submissions annually. 50% of books from first-time authors; 100%

of books from unagented writers. Subsidy publishes 10% of books; subsidy publishes (nonauthor) 20% of books. Pays 6-10% royalty on wholesale price. Simultaneous submissions OK. Query for electronic submissions. Reports in 1 month. Book catalog and guidelines for 9 × 12 SAE with 3 first class stamps. "Manuscripts will not be returned unless SASE is enclosed."

Nonfiction: Illustrated book and textbook. Subjects include architecture, landscape architecture and design. Needs texts on architecture, landscape architecture, architectural monographs, and texts to accompany a possible reprint, architectural history and urban design. Submit outline/synopsis and sample chapters or complete ms. Reviews artwork/photos as part of ms package.

Recent Nonfiction Title: *Surface and Symbol: Giuseppe Terragni and the Architecture of Italian Rationalism*, by Thomas Schumacher.

Tips: "Our audience consists of architects, designers, urban planners, architectural theorists, and architectural-urban design historians, and many academicians and practitioners. We are still focusing on architecture and architectural history but would like to increase our list of books on design."

*PRINCETON BOOK COMPANY, PUBLISHERS, P.O. Box 57, Pennington NJ 08534. (609)737-8177. President: Charles H. Woodford. Estab. 1975. Imprint is Dance Horizons. Publishes hardcover originals, trade paperback originals and reprints. Firm averages 15 titles/year. Receives 100 submissions/year. 25% of books from first-time authors. 100% from unagented writers. Pays 10% royalty on wholesale price. Publishes book an average of 10 months after acceptance. Simultaneous submissions OK. Reports in 2 weeks on queries; 1 month on mss. Free book catalog.

Nonfiction: How-to, reference, self-help and textbook. Subjects include dance. "We're looking for textbooks in the field of dance." Query or submit outline/synopsis and sample chapters. Reviews artwork/photos as part of manuscript package.

Recent Nonfiction Title: *People Who Dance*, by John Gruen (dance trade book).

Tips: "Books that have appeal to both trade and text markets are of most interest to us. Our audience is made up of dance professors, students and professionals. If I were a writer trying to market a book today, I would write with a clear notion of the market in mind. Don't produce a manuscript without first considering what is needed in your field."

‡PROBUS PUBLISHING CO., 1925 N. Clybourn St., Chicago IL 60614. (312)868-1100. FAX: (312)868-6250. Senior Editor: Pamela van Giesen. Estab. 1983. Imprints are Probus Trade, Bankers Publishing Co., Probus/Mortgage Bankers Association. Publishes hardcover and paperback originals and trade paperback reprints. Averages 80 titles/year; receives 250 submissions annually. 50% of books from first-time authors; 100% of books from unagented writers. Pays 10-15% royalty on wholesale price; advance varies. Publishes book an average of 5 months after acceptance. Simultaneous submissions OK. Reports in 1 week on queries; 1 month on mss. Free book catalog; ms guidelines for SASE.

Nonfiction: How-to and technical. Subjects include business, economics and investments. Query or submit outline/synopsis and sample chapters.

Recent Nonfiction Title: *The Informed Investor: How to Use the Money Media to Improve Investment Performance*, by Ray Vicker.

PROFESSIONAL PUBLICATIONS, INC., 1250 5th Ave., Belmont CA 94002. (415)593-9119. FAX: (415)592-4519. Acquisitions Editor: Wendy Nelson. Estab. 1975. Publishes hardcover and paperback originals. Averages 6 titles/year; receives 20-50 submissions annually. Pays 8-12% royalty on wholesale price; offers $1,000 average advance. Sometimes makes outright purchase for $1,000-2,000. Publishes book an average of 6-18 months after acceptance. Simultaneous submissions OK. Query for electronic submissions. Reports in 2 weeks on queries; 1 month on mss. Free book catalog.

Nonfiction: Reference, technical and textbook. Subjects include business and economics, mathematics, engineering, accounting, architecture, contracting and building. Especially needs "licensing examination review books for general contractors and lawyers." Query or submit outline/synopsis and sample chapters or complete ms. Reviews artwork/photos as part of ms package.

Recent Nonfiction Title: *Sample Building and Site Design Exam Problems*, by David Ballast.

Tips: "We specialize in books for working professionals: engineers, architects, contractors, accountants, etc. The more technically complex the manuscript is the happier we are. We love equations, tables of data, complex illustrations, mathematics, etc. In technical/professional book publishing, it isn't always obvious to us if a market exists. We can judge the quality of a ms, but the author should make some effort to convince us that a market exists. Facts, figures, and estimates about the market—and marketing ideas from the author—will help sell us on the work. Besides our interest in highly technical materials, we will be trying to broaden our range of titles in each discipline. Specifically, we will be looking for career guides for accountants and architects, as well as for engineers."

‡PRUETT PUBLISHING, 2928 Pearl St., Boulder CO 80301. (303)449-4919. Publisher: Jim Pruett. Publishes hardcover originals and trade paperback originals and reprints. Firm averages 10-12 titles/year. 60% of books are from first-time authors. 100% from unagented writers. Pays 5-15% royalty on net income. Publishes book an average of 18 months after acceptance. Simultaneous submissions OK. Reports in 2 weeks on queries. Free book catalog and manuscript guidelines.

Nonfiction: Biography, coffee table book, illustrated book and textbook. Subjects include agriculture/horticulture (western), Americana (western), animals (western), archaeology (Native American), child guidance/parenting, cooking, foods and nutrition, ethnic (Native American), gardening (western), history, nature/environment, recreation (outdoor), regional, sports (cycling, hiking, flyfishing), travel (armchair and guides, both) and railroad histories. "We are looking for nonfiction manuscripts and guides that focus on the rocky mountain west." Reviews artwork/photos as part of ms package.

Recent Nonfiction Title: *Magpie Rising*, by Merrill Gilfillan (essays on the Great Plains).

Tips: "There has been a movement away from large publisher's mass market books and towards small publisher's regional interest books, and in turn distributors and retail outlets are more interested in small publishers. Author's don't need to have a big-name to have a good publisher. Look for similar books that you feel are well produced—consider design, editing, overall quality and contact those publishers. Get to know several publishers, and find the one that feels right—trust your instincts."

PSI RESEARCH, 300 N. Valley Dr., Grants Pass OR 97526. (503)479-9464. FAX: (503)476-1479. Editor: Rosanno Alejandro. Estab. 1975. Imprint is Oasis Press. Firm publishes hardcover, trade paperback and binder originals. Publishes 20-30 books/year; receives 90 submissions/year. 60% from first-time authors; 90% from unagented writers. Pays royalty. Publishes ms an average of 6-12 months after acceptance. Simultaneous submissions OK. Reports in 2 weeks (initial feedback) on queries. Free book catalog and ms guidelines.

Nonfiction: How-to, reference, self-help, textbook. Subjects include business and economics, computers and electronics, education, money/finance, retirement, exporting, franchise, finance, marketing and public relations, relocations. Needs information-heavy, readable manuscripts written by professionals in their subject fields. Interactive where appropriate. Authorship credentials less important than hands-on experience qualifications. Must relate to either small business or to individuals who are entrepreneurs, owners or managers of small business (1-300 employees). Query for unwritten material or to check current interest in topic and orientation. Submit outline/synopsis and sample chapters. Reviews artwork/photos as part of freelance ms package.

Recent Nonfiction Title: *Franchise Bible*, by Erwin J. Keup.

Tips: "Best chance is with practical, step-by-step manuals for operating a business, with worksheets, checklists. The audience is made up of entrepreneurs of all types: small businesses and those who would like to be; attorneys, accountants and consultants who work with small businesses; college students; dreamers. Make sure your information is valid and timely for its audience, also that by virtue of either its content quality or viewpoint, it distinguishes itself from other books on the market."

‡PUBLISHERS ASSOCIATES, P.O. Box 160361, Las Colinas TX 75106. (214)686-5332. Senior Editor: Belinda Buxjom. Estab. 1979. Imprints are The Liberal Press, Liberal Arts Press, Minuteman Press, Monument Press, Nichole Graphics, Scholars Books, Tagelwüld. Publishes trade paperback originals. Receives 1,500 submissions/year. 40% of books from first-time authors. 100% from unagented writers. Pays 4% and up royalty on retail price. Publishes book an average of 4 months after acceptance. Reports in 1 months on queries. Book catalog for 6×9 SAE with 4 first class stamps. Manuscript guidelines for #10 SAE with 2 first class stamps.

Nonfiction: Textbook (scholarly). Subjects include gay lesbian, government politics (liberal), history, religion (liberation/liberal) and women's issues/studies. "We are looking for gay/lesbian history, pro-choice/feminist studies and liberal politics. Quality researched gay/lesbian history will have beginning royalty of 7% and up. Academics are encouraged to submit. No biographies, evangelical fundamentalism/bible, conservative politics, New Age studies or homophobic. No fiction or poetry." Query. Reviews artwork/photos as part of ms package.

Recent Nonfiction Title: *Homophobia and the Judaeo-Christian Tradition*, by Stemmeler/Clark (religion/gay/lesbian).

Tips: "Writers have the best chance with gender free/nonsexist, liberal academic studies. We sell primarily to libraries and to scholars. Our audience is highly educated, politically and socially liberal, if religious they are liberational. If I were a writer trying to market a book today, I would compare my manuscript with books already published by the press I am seeking to submit to."

THE PUTNAM BERKLEY GROUP, Divisions include Ace Science Fiction & Fantasy, Berkley Books, and Grosset & Dunlap. See The Berkley Publishing Group.

‡*QED PRESS, Subsidiary of Comp-type, Inc., 155 Cypress St., Fort Bragg CA 95437. (707)964-9520. Senior Editor: John Fremont. Publishes hardcover originals and trade paperback originals and reprints. Averages 10 titles/year; receives 500 submissions/year. 75% of books from first-time authors; 75% from unagented writers. Subsidy publishes 10% of books. Decision made upon evaluation of ms. Pays 6-12% royalty on retail price. Publishes ms an average of 10-12 months after acceptance.

Simultaneous submissions OK. Query for electronic submissions. Reports in 1 months on queries; 2 months on mss. Book catalog for 9×12 SAE and 2 first class stamps.

Nonfiction: Biography, cookbook, how-to, humor, self-help. "We seek books on the aging process, coping with aging, careers for older people, investments, etc." No juvenile, illustrated, photography, travel. Submit outline/synopsis and sample chapters.

Recent Nonfiction Title: *Hyla Doc*, ed. by Elsie Landstrom (biography).

Fiction: Adventure, ethnic, experimental, fantasy, feminist, historical, literary, mainstream/contemporary, mystery, science fiction, short story collections, suspense. "Our thrust will be the acquisition of translated fiction by contemporary European, African and South American authors." Submit outline/synopsis and sample chapters.

Recent Fiction Title: *Tales from the Mountain*, by Miguel Torga (translation).

Poetry: Minimal needs for poetry. No traditional, religious, rhymed or derivative poetry. Submit 3 samples.

Recent Poetry Title: *Messages*, by Luke Breit (romantic).

Tips: "Our audience is older, literary, literate, involved and politically aware."

QUE CORPORATION, Imprint of Macmillan Computer Publishing, 11711 N. College Ave., Carmel IN 46032. (317)573-2500. FAX: (317)573-2585. Acquisitions Manager: Terrie Lynn Solomon. Acquisitions Editor: Mike LaBonne. Estab. 1983. Imprint is New Readers Publishing. Publishes tutorials and application books on popular business software, and trade paperback originals, programming languages and systems and technical books. Receives 500 submissions/year. 80% of books from first-time authors; 90% of books from unagented writers. Pays 2-15% escalating royalty on net price. Many work-for-hire titles are paid a flat fee. Publishes book an average of 4 months after acceptance. Simultaneous (if so advised) submissions OK. Reports in 1 month. Free book catalog.

Nonfiction: How-to, technical, and reference books relating to microcomputers; textbooks on business use of microcomputers; software user's guides and tutorials; operating systems user's guides; computer programming language reference works; books on microcomputer systems, spreadsheet software business applications, word processing, data base management, time management, popular computer programs for the home, computer graphics, networking, communications, languages, educational uses of microcomputers, computer-assisted instruction in education and business and course-authoring applications. "We will consider books on specific subjects relating to microcomputers." Query or submit outline/synopsis and sample chapters. Reviews artwork/photos as part of ms package.

Recent Nonfiction Title: *Using Windows 3, 2nd Ed.*, by QUE Corporation.

QUILL, Imprint of William Morrow and Co., Inc., Subsidiary of The Hearst Corporation, 105 Madison Ave., New York NY 10016. (212)889-3050. Editor: Andrew Dutter. Publishes trade paperback originals and reprints. Averages 40 titles/year; receives over 2,000 submissions annually. 25% of books from first-time authors; 5% of books from unagented writers. Pays royalty on retail price. Offers variable advance. Publishes ms an average of 1 year after acceptance. Simultaneous submissions OK. No unsolicited mss or proposals; mss and proposals should be submitted through a literary agent. Reports in 3 months.

Nonfiction: Biography and trade books. Subjects include history, music, psychology, science, light reference and military history. Needs nonfiction trade paperbacks with enduring importance; books that have backlist potential and appeal to educated people with broad intellectual curiosities. No fiction, poetry, fitness, diet, how-to, self-help or humor. Query.

Recent Nonfiction Title: *How to Make the World a Better Place*, by Jeffrey Hollender.

RAINBOW BOOKS, P.O. Box 1069, Moore Haven FL 33471. (813)946-0293. Associate Editor: B. A. Lampe. Estab. 1979. Publishes hardcover, trade paperback originals, video (VHS) and audio tapes. Averages 10-20 titles/year; receives 600 submissions annually. 70% of books from first-time authors; 50% of books from unagented writers. Publishes book an average of 8 months after acceptance. Reports in 2 weeks on queries. Book catalog for 6×9 SAE and 3 first class stamps; ms guidelines for #10 SAE and 2 first class stamps.

Nonfiction: Reference, self-help, how-to and resource books. Prefer query first on all books. Interested in seeing all nonfiction books.

Recent Nonfiction Title: *The Food Bible*, by Jayne Benkendorf.

Tips: "Send queries only with SASE. We are interested these days in seeing any and all nonfiction books."

*R&E PUBLISHERS, P.O. Box 2008, Saratoga CA 95070. (408)866-6303. FAX: (408)866-0825. Publisher: R. Reed. Estab. 1967. Publishes hardcover and trade paperback originals. Averages 30 titles/year. Receives 300 submissions/year. 80% of books from first-time authors. 80% from unagented writers. Subsidy publishes 5% of books. Pays 10-20% on wholesale price. Publishes book an average

of 6 months after acceptance. Simultaneous submissions OK. Query for electronic submissions. Reports in 2 months. Free book catalog and manuscript guidelines.
Nonfiction: How-to, humor, illustrated book, reference, self-help, software, technical and textbook. Subjects include business and economics, child guidance/parenting, computers and electronics, cooking, foods and nutrition, education, ethnic, government/politics, health/medicine, history, money/finance, music/dance, nature/environment, philosophy, psychology, regional, science, sociology, travel and women's issues/studies. Query or submit outline/synopsis and sample chapters. Reviews artwork as part of package.
Recent Nonfiction Title: *The Mourning After: Managing Grief Wisely*, by Stanley Cornils.

RANDOM HOUSE, INC., Subsidary of Advance Publications, 201 E. 50th St., 11th Floor, New York NY 10022. (212)572-2600. Random House Trade Division publishes 180 titles/year; receives 3,000 submissions annually. Other imprints within the Random House Trade Division include Villard Books, Times Books, and Turtle Bay Books. Other subsidiaries of Random House, Inc., include Alfred A. Knopf, Inc., Pantheon Books, Vintage Books, Crown Publishers, Clarkson Potter, Inc., Harmony Books, Orion Books, Random House Reference, Fodor's Travel Publications, Inc., and Ballantine/Del Rey/Fawcett/Ivy Books. See individual imprint listings for further information. Some imprints have chosen not to be listed. Pays royalty on retail price. Simultaneous submissions OK. Reports in 3 weeks on queries; 6 weeks on mss. Free book catalog; ms guidelines for #10 SASE.
Nonfiction: Biography, cookbook, humor, illustrated book, self-help. Subjects include Americana, art, business and economics, cooking and foods, health, history, music, nature, politics, psychology, religion, sociology and sports. No juveniles or textbooks (separate division). Query with outline/synopsis and at least 3 sample chapters.
Fiction: Adventure, confession, experimental, fantasy, historical, horror, humor, mainstream, mystery, and suspense. Submit outline/synopsis and at least 3 sample chapters. "SASE is helpful."
Tips: "If I were a writer trying to market a book today, I would get an agent."

RANDOM HOUSE, INC. JUVENILE BOOKS, 225 Park Ave. S., New York NY 10003. (212)254-1600. Subsidiaries include Knopf Children's Books, Knopf Children's Paperbacks (Bullseye Books, Dragonfly Books and Borzoi Sprinters), Random House Children's Books, Crown Children's Books. Juvenile Division: J. Schulman, Publisher. Managing Editor: R. Abend. Alfred A. Knopf: S. Spinner, Executive Editor. Random House Juvenile: Kate Klimo, Editor-in-Chief. Crown: S. Boughton, Executive Editor. Firm publishes hardcover, trade paperback and mass market paperback originals, and mass market paperback reprints. Publishes 300 titles/year. Simultaneous submissions OK.
Nonfiction: Biography, humor, illustrated book, juvenile. Subjects include animals, nature/environment, recreation, science, sports. Query or submit outline/synopsis and sample chapters. Submit ms through agent only.
Recent Nonfiction Title: *175 More Science Experiments to Amuse and Amaze Your Friends*, by T. Cash and B. Taylor.
Fiction: Adventure, confession (young adult), fantasy, historical, horror, humor, juvenile, mystery, picture books, science fiction (juvenile/young adult), suspense, young adult. Submit through agent only.
Recent Fiction Title: *Aliens for Lunch*, by J. Etra and S. Spinner.
Tips: Books for children 6 months to 15 years old.

REFERENCE SERVICE PRESS, Suite 9, 1100 Industrial Rd., San Carlos CA 94070. (415)594-0743. FAX: (415)594-0411. Acquisitions Editor: Stuart Hauser. Publishes hardcover originals. Firm averages 5 titles/year. 100% of books from unagented writers. Pays 10% or higher royalty. Publishes book an average of 3-6 months after acceptance. Simultaneous submissions OK. Query for electronic submissions. Reports in 1 week on queries; 3 weeks on mss. Book catalog for #10 SASE.
Nonfiction: Reference. Subjects include education, ethnic, military/war, women's issues/studies and disabled. We are interested only in directories and monographs dealing with financial aid. Submit outline/synopsis and sample chapters.
Recent Nonfiction Title: *Financial Aid for the Disabled & Their Families*, by Schlachter and Weber (directory).
Tips: "Our audience consists of librarians, counselors, researchers, students, reentry women, scholars and other fundseekers."

REGAL BOOKS, Imprint of Gospel Light Publications, 2300 Knoll Dr., Ventura CA 93003. FAX: (805)644-4729. Managing Director, Acquisitions: Linda Holland. Estab. 1965. Publishes hardcover and paperback originals. Averages 25 titles/year. Receives 5,000 submissions annually. 20% of books from first-time authors; 90% of books from unagented writers. Average print order for writer's first book is 2,500. Pays 15% net royalty on paperback titles, 10% net for curriculum books. Publishes book an average of 11 months after acceptance. Buys all rights. Reports in 3 months. Book catalog and ms guidelines for 9×12 SAE and 8 first class stamps.

Nonfiction: Fiction Christian living, counseling (self-help), contemporary concerns, evangelism (church growth), marriage and family, youth, inspirational/devotional, Bible studies (Old and New Testament), communication resources, teaching enrichment resources, Bible commentary for Laymen Series, and missions. Query or submit detailed outline/synopsis and 2-3 sample chapters; no complete mss.

Recent Nonfiction Title: *Always Daddy's Girl*, by H. Norman Wright.
Recent Fiction Title: *Children of the Furor*, by Roger Elwood.

REGNERY/GATEWAY, INC., Suite 600, 1130 17th St., N.W., Washington DC 20036. Editor: Harry Crocker. Estab. 1947. Imprint is Gateway Editions. Publishes hardcover and paperback originals and paperback reprints. Averages 15 titles/year. Pays royalty. "Responds only to submissions in which we have interest."

Nonfiction: Business and politics. Queries preferred. Looks for "expertise of the author, salability of the proposed work, and built-in, guaranteed markets."

Recent Nonfiction Title: *The Hollow Men: Politics and Corruption in Higher Education*, by Charles J. Sykes.

RELIGIOUS EDUCATION PRESS, 5316 Meadow Brook Rd., Birmingham AL 35242. (205)991-1000. FAX: (205)991-9669. Editor: James Michael Lee. Estab. 1974. Imprint is R.E.P. Books. Publishes trade paperback and hardback originals. Averages 5 titles/year; receives 280 submissions annually. 40% of books from first-time authors; 100% of books from unagented writers. Pays 10% royalty on actual selling price. "Many of our books are work for hire. We do not have a subsidy option." Offers no advance. Query for electronic submissions. Reports 2 months on queries and mss. Free book catalog.

Nonfiction: Technical and textbook. Scholarly subjects on religion and religious education. "We publish serious, significant and scholarly books on religious education and pastoral ministry." No mss under 200 pages, no poetry, books on Biblical interpretation, or "popular" books. Query. Reviews artwork/photos as part of ms package.

Recent Nonfiction Title: *Handbook of Faith*, by James Michael Lee.
Tips: "Write clearly, reason exactly and connectively, and meet deadlines. We do not return unsolicited mss unless accompanied by return postage."

‡RENAISSANCE HOUSE PUBLISHERS, Subsidiary of Jende-Hagan, Inc., Box 177, 541 Oak St., Frederick CO 80530. (303)833-2030. Editor: Eleanor Ayer. Publishes hardcover and trade paperback originals and trade paperback reprints. Averages 8 titles/year; receives 125 submissions annually. 60% of books from first-time authors; 75% of books from unagented writers. Pays 8-12% royalty on net receipts. Offers average advance of 10% of anticipated first printing royalties. May consider work for hire by experts in specific fields of interest. Publishes book an average of 18 months after acceptance. Simultaneous submissions OK. Query for electronic submissions. Reports in 1 month on queries; 2 months on mss. Book catalog free on request.

Nonfiction: Subjects include regional guidebooks. No fiction, personal reminiscences, general traditional philosophy, children's books, general cookbooks, books on topics totally unrelated to subject areas specified above. Submit outline/synopsis and sample chapters. Reviews artwork/photos as part of ms package.

Recent Nonfiction Title: *Indians of Arizona* in *The Arizona Traveler* (series).
Tips: "We rely exclusively on in-house generation of book concepts and then find authors who will write for hire to our specifications."

*RESOURCE PUBLICATIONS, INC., Suite 290, 160 E. Virginia St., San Jose CA 95112. Editorial Director: Kenneth E. Guentert. Publishes paperback originals. Publishes 14 titles/year; receives 100-200 submissions annually. 30% of books from first-time authors; 99% of books from unagented writers. Average print order for a writer's first book is 2,000. Subsidy publishes 10% of books. "If the author can present and defend a personal publicity effort or otherwise demonstrate demand and the work is in our field, we will consider it." Pays 8% royalty; occasionally offers advance in the form of books. Publishes book an average of 18 months after acceptance. Query for electronic submissions. Reports in 2 months.

Nonfiction: "We look for imaginative but practical books relating to celebration, professional growth, and spirituality. How-to books, especially for contemporary religious art forms, are of particular interest (dance, mime, drama, choral reading, singing, music, musicianship, bannermaking, statuary, or any visual art form). No heavy theoretical, philosophical, or theological tomes. Query or submit outline/synopsis and sample chapters. "Prepare a clear outline of the work and an ambitious schedule of public appearances to help make it known and present both as a proposal to the publisher. With our company a work that can be serialized or systematically excerpted in our periodicals is always given special attention." Accepts translations. Reviews artwork/photos as part of ms package.

Recent Nonfiction Title: *Symbols For All Seasons*, by Katherine Krier.

Fiction: "We are not interested in novels or collections of short stories in the usual literary sense. But we look for storytelling resources and collections of short works in the area of drama, dance, song, and visual art, especially if related to worship celebrations, festivals, or mythology." Query or submit outline/synopsis and sample chapters.

Tips: "Books that provide readers with practical, usable suggestions and ideas pertaining to worship, celebration, education, and the arts have the best chance of selling to our firm. We've moved more clearly into the celebration resources field and are looking for resources on popular — as well as little known — celebrations, feasts, and rituals to complement our strong backlist of worship resources."

REVIEW AND HERALD PUBLISHING ASSOCIATION, 55 West Oak Ridge Dr., Hagerstown MD 21740. Acquisitions Editor: Penny Estes Wheeler. Imprint is Autumn House. Publishes hardcover and paperback originals. Specializes in religious-oriented books. Averages 30-40 titles/year; receives 300 submissions annually. 15% of books from first-time authors; 100% of books from unagented writers. Average print order for a writer's first book is 5,000-7,500. Pays 14% of retail price, hardcover; 12% of retail price, softcover; offers average $500 advance. Publishes book an average of 1 year after acceptance. Encourages computer submissions by disk. Reports in 3 months. Free brochure; ms guidelines for SASE.

Nonfiction: Juveniles (religious-oriented only), nature, and religious, all 20,000-60,000 words; 128 pages average. Query or submit outline/synopsis and 2-3 sample chapters. Prefers to do own illustrating. Looks for "literary style, constructive tone, factual accuracy, compatibility with Adventist theology and lifestyle, and length of manuscript." Reviews artwork/photos as part of ms package.

Recent Nonfiction Title: *My Grieving Heart*, by Joyce Rigsby.

Recent Fiction Title: *Plain, Plain, Melissa Jane*, by Colleen Reece.

Tips: "Familiarize yourself with Adventist theology because Review and Herald Publishing Association is owned and operated by the Seventh-day Adventist Church. We are accepting fewer but better-written manuscripts. Many of our books were written on assignment."

‡RICHBORO PRESS, Box 1, Richboro PA 18954. (215)364-2212. Editor: George Moore. Publishes hardcover, trade paperback originals and software. Averages 6 titles/year. Receives 500 submissions annually. 90% of books from unagented writers. Pays 10% royalty on retail price. Pubilshes book an average of 1 year after acceptance. Query for electronic submissions. Reports in 6 weeks on queries; 3 months on mss. Free book catalog; ms guidelines for $1 and #10 SASE.

Nonfiction: Cookbook, how-to and gardening. Subjects include cooking and foods. Query.

Recent Nonfiction Title: *Classified Advertising, 5th Ed.*, by Blair.

*RONIN PUBLISHING INC., P.O. Box 1035, Berkeley CA 94701. (415)540-6278. Publisher: Sebastian Orfali. Estab. 1984. Imprint is And/Or Books. Publishes originals and trade paperback reprints. Averages 6-8 titles/year; mostly repackages previously published books.

Nonfiction: How-to (business), humor, 20th century visionaries. Subjects include business and psychology (psychoactive). Query. No unsolicited manuscripts.

Recent Nonfiction Title: *Controlled Substances: Chemical and Legal Guide to the Federal Drug Laws*, by Alexander Shulgen, Ph.D.

THE ROSEN PUBLISHING GROUP, 29 E. 21st St., New York NY 10010. (212)777-3017. President: Roger Rosen. Estab. 1950. Imprint is Pelion Press (music titles). Publishes hardcover originals. Entire firm averages 46 titles/year; young adult division averages 35 titles/year. 45% of books from first-time authors; 80% of books from unagented writers. Pays royalty or makes outright purchase. Publishes book an average of 9 months after acceptance. Simultaneous submissions OK. Reports in 1 month. Book catalog and guidelines for 9×12 SAE with 3 first class stamps.

Nonfiction: Young adult, reference, self-help and textbook. Subjects include art, health (coping), and music. "Our books are geared to the young adult audience whom we reach via school and public libraries. Most of the books we publish are related to career guidance and personal adjustment. We also publish material on music and art, as well as journalism for schools. Interested in supplementary material for enrichment of school curriculum. We have begun a high/low division and are interested in material that is supplementary to the curriculum written at a 4 reading level for teenagers who are reluctant readers." Mss in the young adult nonfiction areas include vocational guidance, personal and social adjustment, journalism. For Pelion Press, mss on classical music, emphasis on opera and singing. Query or submit outline/synopsis and sample chapters. Reviews artwork/photos as part of ms package.

Recent Nonfiction Title: *Coping with Sexual Abuse*, by Judith Cooney.

Tips: "The writer has the best chance of selling our firm a book on vocational guidance or personal social adjustment, or high-interest, low reading level material for teens."

ROSS BOOKS, P.O. Box 4340, Berkeley CA 94704. FAX: (415)841-2695. President: Franz Ross. Estab. 1979. Publishes hardcover and paperback originals, paperback reprints, and software. Averages 4-6 titles/year; receives 200 submissions annually. 90% of books from first-time authors; 99% of books from unagented writers. Average print order for a writer's first book is 5,000-10,000. Offers 8-12% royalty on net price. Offers average advance of 2% of the first print run. Publishes book an average of 1 year after acceptance. Simultaneous submissions OK. Query for electronic submissions. Reports in 1 month. Book catalog for 6×9 SAE with 2 first class stamps.
Nonfiction: Popular how-to on science, business, general how-to. No political, religious or children's books. Accepts nonfiction translations. Submit outline or synopsis of no more than 3 pages and 1 sample chapter with SASE. Reviews artwork/photos as part of ms package.
Recent Nonfiction Title: *Holography Marketplace 2nd Ed.*, ed. by F. Ross and E. Yerkes.
Tips: "We are looking for books on holography and desktop publishing."

‡ROUTLEDGE, CHAPMAN & HALL, INC., 29 W. 35th St., New York NY 10001. (212)244-3336. 30 subject editors in the U.K. Editorial Director (New York): William P. Germano, editor for media, literary criticism, cultural studies, classical studies, and theater arts. Editor for philosophy and psychoanalysis: Maureen MacGrogan. Editor for history and politics: Cecilia Cancellaro. Editor for education: Jayne Fargnoli. Editor for life sciences: Gregory Payne. Editor for chemistry: Barbara Goldman. Editor for statistics: Beatrice Shube. Science books published under Chapman and Hall. Humanities and social sciences published under Routledge. New corporate name comprises former imprints Methuen; Routledge & Kegan Paul; Croom Helm; Tavistock. Also publishers of Theatre Arts Books. Chapman & Hall list includes scientific and technical books in life and physical sciences, statistics, allied health, science reference. Routledge list includes humanities, social sciences, business and economics, reference. Monographs, reference works, hardback and paperback upper-level texts, academic general interest. Averages 800 titles/year; receives 5,000 submissions annually. 10% of books from first-time authors; 95% of books from unagented authors. Average royalty 10% net receipts; advances. No simultaneous submissions. Reports in 6 weeks on queries. Do not send manuscripts at initial stage. No replies to unsolicited inquiries without SASE.
Nonfiction: Academic subjects include philosophy, literary criticism, psychoanalysis, social sciences, business and economics, history, psychology, women's studies, lesbian and gay studies, political science, anthropology, geography, education, reference. Scientific subjects include biology, ecology, statistics, materials science, chemistry.

ROXBURY PUBLISHING CO., P.O. Box 491044, Los Angeles CA 90049. (213)653-1068. Executive Editor: Claude Teweles. Publishes hardcover and paperback originals and reprints. Averages 10 titles/year. Pays royalty. Simultaneous submissions OK. Reports in 2 months.
Nonfiction: College-level textbooks only. Subjects include business and economics, humanities, speech, English, developmental studies, social sciences and sociology. Query, submit outline/synopsis and sample chapters, or submit complete ms.
Recent Nonfiction Title: *The Writing Cycle*, by Clela Allphin-Hoggatt.

‡RUSSELL SAGE FOUNDATION, 112 E. 64 St., New York NY 10021. (212)750-6037. FAX: (212)371-4761. Director of Publications: Lisa Nachtigall. Estab. 1907. Publishes hardcover and trade paperback originals. Averages 20 titles/year. Receives 50 submissions/year. "Usually, payment is through grant support; book is end result." Publishes book an average of 9 months after acceptance.
Nonfiction: Social science research. Subjects include business and economics, education, ethnic, government, history, psychology, sociology, women's issues/studies, public policy. Query or submit outline/synopsis and sample chapters.
Recent Nonfiction Titles: *New People In Old Neighborhoods*, by Louis Winnick (immigrants, society).

RUTLEDGE HILL PRESS, 513 3rd Ave. S, Nashville TN 37210. (615)244-2700. FAX: (615)244-2978. President: Lawrence Stone. Vice President: Ron Pitkin. Estab. 1982. Publishes hardcover and trade paperback originals and reprints. Averages 25 titles/year; receives 300 submissions annually. 40% of books from first-time authors; 90% of books from unagented writers. Pays 10-20% royalty on wholesale price. Publishes book an average of 1 year after acceptance. Reports in 6 weeks on queries; 3 months on mss. Book catalog for 9×12 SAE and 3 first class stamps.
Nonfiction: Biography, cookbook, humor, reference and self-help. "The book must have an identifiable market, preferably one that is geographically limited." Submit outline/synopsis and sample chapters. Reviews artwork/photos as part of ms package.
Recent Nonfiction Title: *Great Stories of the American Revolution*, by Webb Garrison.

ST. ANTHONY MESSENGER PRESS, 1615 Republic St., Cincinnati OH 45210. FAX: (513)241-0399. Editor-in-Chief: The Rev. Norman Perry, O.F.M. Managing Editor: Lisa Biedenbach. Estab. 1970. Publishes paperback originals. Averages 14 titles/year; receives 250 submissions annually. 10% of books from first-time authors; 100% of books from unagented writers. Pays 10-12% royalty on net receipts of sales. Offers $600 average advance. Publishes book an average of 1 year after acceptance. Books are sold in bulk to groups (study clubs, high school or college classes, and parishes) and in bookstores. No simultaneous submissions. Query for electronic submissions. Book catalog and ms guidelines for 9×12 SAE with 2 first-class stamps.

Nonfiction: Religion. "We try to reach the Catholic market with topics near the heart of the ordinary Catholic's belief. We want to offer insight and inspiration and thus give people support in living a Christian life in a pluralistic society. We are not interested in an academic or abstract approach. Our emphasis is on popular writing with examples, specifics, color and anecdotes." Length: 25,000-40,000 words. Query or submit outline and 2 sample chapters. Reviews artwork/photos as part of ms package.

Recent Nonfiction Title: *Why Be Catholic? Understanding Our Experience and Tradition*, by Richard Rohr and Joseph Martos.

Tips: "We are looking for aids to parish ministry, prayer, spirituality, scripture, liturgy and the sacraments. Also, we are seeking manuscripts that deal with the Catholic identity—explaining it, identifying it, understanding it. The book cannot be the place for the author to think through a subject. The author has to think through the subject first and then tell the reader what is important to know. Style uses anecdotes, examples, illustrations, human interest, 'colorful' quotes, fiction techniques of suspense, dialogue, characterization, etc. Address practical problems, deal in concrete situations, free of technical terms and professional jargon. We do not publish fiction, poetry, autobiography, personal reflections, academic studies, art or coffee-table books."

‡*ST. BEDE'S PUBLICATIONS, Subsidiary of St. Scholastica Priory, Box 545, Petersham MA 01366. (508)724-3407. FAX: (508)724-3574. Editorial Director: Sr. Scholastica Crilly, OSB. Estab. 1977. Publishes hardcover originals, trade paperback originals and reprints. Averages 8-12 titles/year; receives 100 submissions annually. 30-40% of books from first-time authors; 90% of books from unagented writers. Subsidy publishes (nonauthor) 10% of books. Pays 5-10% royalty on wholesale price or retail price. No advance. Publishes book an average of 2 years after acceptance. Simultaneous submissions OK. Query for electronic submissions. Unsolicited mss are not returned unless accompanied by sufficient return postage. Reports in 2 weeks on queries; 3 months on mss. Book catalog and ms guidelines for #10 SAE and 2 first class stamps.

Nonfiction: Textbook (theology), religion, prayer, spirituality, hagiography, theology, philosophy, church history and related lives of saints fields. "We are always looking for excellent books on prayer, spirituality, liturgy, church or monastic history. Theology and philosophy are important also. We publish English translations of foreign works in these fields if we think they are excellent and worth translating." No submissions unrelated to religion, theology, spirituality, etc. Query or submit outline/synopsis and sample chapters.

Recent Nonfiction Title: *Hammer and Fire*, by Raphael Simon.

Fiction: Historical (only if religious) and religious. "Generally we don't do fiction—but we are willing to look over a manuscript if it fits into our categories." No fiction submissions unrelated to religion. Query or submit outline/synopsis and sample chapters.

Tips: "There seems to be a growing interest in monasticism among lay people and we will be publishing more books in this area during the next couple of years. For our theology/philosophy titles our audience is scholars, colleges and universities, seminaries, etc. For our other titles (i.e. prayer, spirituality, lives of saints, etc.) the audience is above-average readers interested in furthering their knowledge in these areas. Theology seems to be swinging back to studying more conservative lines. We're finding a lot of excellent books being published in France and are getting the rights to translate these. Also, there's a great, general interest in prayer and spirituality so we try to publish really excellent titles in these areas, too. New material, or newly translated material, gets priority."

*ST. LUKE'S PRESS, Division of The Wimmer Companies, 4210 B.F. Goodrich Blvd., Memphis TN 38118. (901)362-8923. FAX: (901)795-9806. Director: Phyllis Tickle. Other imprints are Iris Press and Tradery House. Averages 8-10 titles/year; receives 3,000 submissions annually. 90% of books from unagented writers. Average print order for a writer's first book is 5,000. Pays 10% minimum royalty on monies received; offers average $1,000-5,000 advance. Publishes book an average of 2 years after acceptance. Reports in 3 months. Book catalog $1.

Recent Nonfiction Title: *At the River I Stand*, by Joan Turner Beifuss.

Fiction: Submit story line and 3 sample chapters.

Tips: "We publish primarily nonfiction and within the food experience—the sacredness."

ST. MARTIN'S PRESS, 175 5th Ave., New York NY 10010. Averages 1,100 titles/year; receives 3,000 submissions annually. 15-20% of books from first-time authors; 30% of books from unagented writers. Query for electronic submissions. Reports "promptly."

Nonfiction and Fiction: General, college texts, scholarly, reference, and mass market books. Publishes general fiction and nonfiction; major interest in adult fiction and nonfiction, history, self-help, political science, popular science, biography, scholarly, popular reference, etc. Query. Reviews artwork/photos as part of ms package. "It takes very persuasive credentials to prompt us to commission a book or outline."

Recent Title: *The Silence of the Lambs*, by Thomas Harris.

Tips: "We do almost every kind of book there is — trade, textbooks, reference and mass market. Crime fiction has the best chance of selling to our firm — over twenty percent of all the trade books we published are this category."

ST. PAUL BOOKS AND MEDIA, Daughters of St. Paul, 50 St. Paul's Ave., Boston MA 02130. (617)522-8911. FAX: (617)522-4081. Director, Editorial Department: Sister M. Eileen, FSP. Estab. 1948. Firm publishes hardcover, trade paperback originals, and reprints. Average 20 titles/year; receives approximately 900 proposals/year. Pays authors 7-12% royalty on net sales. Publishes ms an average of 2-3 years after acceptance. Reports in 1 month on queries; in 2 months on mss. Book catalog free; ms guidelines for #10 SASE.

Nonfiction: Biography, juvenile, self-help. Subjects include child guidance/parenting, devotionals, psychology and religion. "No strictly secular manuscripts." Query or submit outline/synopsis and 2-3 sample chapters.

Recent Nonfiction Title: *Do Whatever He Tells You*, by Henry P. Libersat.

Fiction: Juvenile, religious, young adult. "We want books promoting moral values for children, adolescents and young adults." Query or submit outline/synopsis and 2-3 sample chapters.

Tips: "We are looking for books with a religious and/or moral orientation. No New Age."

*ST. VLADIMIR'S SEMINARY PRESS, 575 Scarsdale Rd., Crestwood NY 10707. (914)961-8313. Managing Director: Theodore Bazil. Publishes hardcover and trade paperback originals and reprints. Averages 15 titles/year. Subsidy publishes 20% of books. Market considerations determine whether an author should be subsidy published. Pays 7% royalty on retail price. Simultaneous submissions OK. Reports in 3 months on queries; 9 months on mss. Free book catalog and ms guidelines.

Nonfiction: Religion dealing with Eastern Orthodox theology. Query. Reviews artwork/photos as part of ms package.

Tips: "We have an interest in books that stand on firm theological ground; careful writing and scholarship are basic."

SANDHILL CRANE PRESS, INC., P.O. Box 1702-100, Gainesville FL 32602. (904)371-9858. FAX: (904)373-9749. Publisher: Ross H. Arnett, Jr. Estab. 1947. Imprints are Flora & Fauna Publiclations and Natural Science Publiclations. Publishes hardcover and trade paperback originals. Entire firm publishes 350 annually; imprint averages 10-12 titles/year; receives 70 submissions annually. 50% of books from first-time authors; 100% of books from unagented writers. Average print order for a writer's first book is 500. Pays 10% royalty on list price; negotiable advance. Publishes book an average of 1 year after acceptance. Query for electronic submissions. Reports in 2 weeks on queries; 3 months on mss.

Nonfiction: Reference, technical, textbook, and directories. Subjects include plants and animals (for amateur and professional biologists), and natural history. Looking for "books dealing with kinds of plants and animals; new nature guide series underway. No nature stories or 'Oh My' nature books." Query with outline and 2 sample chapters. Reviews artwork/photos as part of ms package.

Recent Nonfiction Title: *Biogeography of the West Indies*, by Charles A. Woods.

Tips: "Well-documented books, especially those that fit into one of our series, have the best chance of selling to our firm — biology, natural history, no garden books."

SAS INSTITUTE INC., SAS Campus Dr., Cary NC 27513-8000. (919)677-8000. FAX: (916)677-8166. Acquisitions Editor: David D. Baggett. Estab. 1976. Publishes hardcover and trade paperback originals. Firm averages 40 titles/year. Receives 10 submissions/year. 50% of books from first-time authors. 100% from unagented writers. Payment negotiable. Offers negotiable advance. Query for electronic submissions. Reports in 2 weeks on queries; 6 weeks on mss. Free book catalog and manuscript guidelines.

Nonfiction: Software, technical, textbook and statistics. "SAS Institute's Publications Division publishes books developed and written in-house. In the past, we've also worked with non-Institute authors to publish books on a variety of topics relating to SAS software, especially to supplement our statistical documentation. We want to publish more books written by non-Institute authors on an even wider range of topics. We want to provide our users with additional titles to supplement our primary documentation and to enhance the users' ability to use the SAS System effectively. We're interested in publishing manuscripts that describe or illustrate using any of SAS Institute's software products. Books must be aimed at SAS software users, either new or experienced. Tutorials are particularly attractive, as are descriptions of user-written applications for solving real-life business, industry or academic problems. Books on programming techniques using the SAS language are also desirable. Manuscripts must reflect current or upcoming software releases, and the author's writing should indicate an understanding of the SAS System and the technical aspects covered in the manuscript." Query. Submit outline/synopsis and sample chapters. Reviews artwork/photos as part of ms package.

Recent Nonfiction Title: *SAS Sytem for Linear Models, Third Edition*, by Rudolf J. Freund, Ph.D. and Ramon C. Littell, Ph.D.

Tips: "Our readers are SAS software users, both new and experienced. If I were a writer trying to market a book today, I would concentrate on developing a manuscript that teaches or illustrates a specific concept or application that SAS software users will find beneficial in their own environments or can adapt to their own needs."

SASQUATCH BOOKS, 1931 2nd Ave., Seattle WA 98101. (206)441-5555. FAX: (206)441-6213. Managing Editor: Anne Depue. Estab. 1975. Firm publishes regional hardcover and trade paperback originals. Averages 6-8 titles/year. 25% of books from first-time authors; 95% from unagented writers. Pays authors 5-12% royalty on cover price. Offers wide range of advances. Publishes ms an average of 6 months after acceptance. Simultaneous submissions OK. Query for electronic submissions. Reports in 1 month. Free book catalog.

Nonfiction: Subjects include regional art/architecture, business and economics, cooking, foods and nutrition, gardening, government/politics, history, nature/environment, photography, recreation, sports and travel. "We are seeking quality nonfiction works by, about, or for people of the Pacific Northwest region. In this sense we are a regional publisher, but we do distribute our books nationally, depending on the title." Submit outline/synopsis and sample chapters.

Recent Nonfiction Title: *Mount St. Helens: The Eruption and Recovery of a Volcano*, by Rob Carson.

Tips: "We sell books through a range of channels in addition to the book trade. Our audience consists of active, literate residents of the Pacific Northwest."

SCARBOROUGH HOUSE/PUBLISHERS, 901-B Taylor St., P.O. Box 459, Chelsea MI 48118. (313)475-1210. Contact: Editorial Department. Publishes hardcover and trade paperback originals and trade paperback reprints. Firm averages 35 titles/year. 20% of books are from first-time authors. 60% from unagented writers. Pays advance against standard royalty. Publishes book an average of 9-12 months after acceptance. Simultaneous submissions OK. Reports in 2 months on queries; 3 months on mss.

Nonfiction: Biography, cookbook, how-to, reference and self-help. Subject include Americana, animals, anthropology/archaeology, business and economics, child guidance/parenting, cooking, foods and nutrition, education, ethnic, gardening, government/politics, health/medicine, history, hobbies, language/literature, military/war, money/finance, psychology, recreation, popular science, sports and travel. We are looking for quality general-interest books with a clearly definable market. Query. Submit outline/synopsis and sample chapters.

Recent Nonfiction Title: *Sumter: The First Day of The Civil War*, by Robert Hendrickson.

SCARECROW PRESS, INC., Imprint of Grolier, 52 Liberty St., P.O. Box 4167, Metuchen NJ 08840. Vice President, Editorial: Norman Horrocks. Senior Editor: Barbara Lee. Estab. 1950. Publishes hardcover originals. Averages 110 titles/year; receives 600-700 submissions annually. 70% of books from first-time authors; 100% of books from unagented writers. Average print order for a writer's first book is 1,000. Pays 10% royalty on net of first 1,000 copies; 15% of net price thereafter. 15% initial royalty on camera-ready copy. Offers no advance. Publishes book 6-18 months after receipt of ms. Query for electronic submissions. Reports in 2 weeks. Free book catalog.

Nonfiction Needs reference books and meticulously prepared annotated bibliographies, indexes and books on women's studies, music, movies and stage. Query. Occasionally reviews artwork/photos as part of ms package.

Recent Nonfiction Title: *Dictionary of American Immigration History*, ed. by Francesco Cordasco.

Tips: "Essentially we consider any scholarly title likely to appeal to libraries. Emphasis is on reference material, but this can be interpreted broadly, provided author is knowledgeable in the subject field."

‡SCHIFFER PUBLISHING LTD., 1469 Morstein Rd., West Chester PA 19380. (215)696-1001. FAX: (215)344-9765. President: Peter Schiffer. Estab. 1972. Imprints are Canal Press and Whitford Press. Publishes hardcover and trade paperback originals and reprints. Firm averages 50 titles/year; imprint averages 40 titles/year. Receives 500 submissions/year. 90% of books from first-time authors. 95% from unagented writers. Royalty on wholesale price. Publishes book an average of 6 months after acceptance. Simultaneous submissions OK. Reports in 2 weeks on queries. Free book catalog.

Nonfiction: Coffee table book, how-to, illustrated book, reference and textbook. Subjects include Americana, art/architecture, history, hobbies, military/war and regional. "We want books on collecting, hobby carving, military, architecture, aeronautic history and natural history." Query. Submit outline/synopsis and sample chapters. Reviews artwork/photos as part of ms package.

Recent Nonfiction Title: *American Wristwatches*, by Faber & Unger, (history of American wristwatch).

SCHIRMER BOOKS, Imprint of Macmillan Publishing Co., 866 3rd Ave., New York NY 10022. FAX: (212)605-9368. Editor-in-Chief: Maribeth Anderson Payne. Associate Editor: Robert Axelrod. Assistant Editor: Brian Edwards. Publishes hardcover and paperback originals, related audio recordings, paperback reprints and some software. Averages 20 books/year; receives 250 submissions annually. 25% of books from first-time authors; 75% of books from unagented writers. Submit photos and/or illustrations only "if central to the book, not if decorative or tangential." Publishes book an average of 1 year after acceptance. Query for electronic submissions. Reports in 4 months. Book catalog and ms guidelines for SASE.
Nonfiction: Publishes college texts, biographies, scholarly, reference, and trade on the performing arts specializing in music, film and theatre. Submit outline/synopsis and sample chapters and current vita. Reviews artwork/photos as part of ms package.
Recent Nonfiction Title: *Opening Night on Broadway*, by Steven Suskin.
Tips: "The writer has the best chance of selling our firm a music book with a clearly defined, reachable audience, either scholarly or trade. Must be an exceptionally well-written work of original scholarship prepared by an expert in the field who has a thorough understanding of correct manuscript style and attention to detail (see the *Chicago Manual of Style*)."

SCHOLASTIC, INC., 730 Broadway, New York NY 10003. (212)505-3000. Executive Editor: Ann Reit. Estab. 1920. Publishes trade paperback originals and hardcovers. Pays royalty on retail price. Reports in 3 months. Ms guidelines for #10 SASE.
Nonfiction: Publishes general nonfiction.
Recent Nonfiction Title: *Nelson Mandela*, by Barry Devenberg.
Fiction: Family stories, mysteries, school, and friendships for ages 8-12, 35,000 words. YA fiction, romance, family and mystery for ages 12-15, 40,000-45,000 words for average to good readers. Query or submit entire manuscripts.
Tips: Queries/mss may be routed to other editors in the publishing group.

SCHOLASTIC PROFESSIONAL BOOKS, 730 Broadway, New York NY 10003. Publishing Director: Claudia Cohl. Editor-in-Chief: Terry Cooper. Buys 20-35 manuscripts/year from published or unpublished writers. Buys all rights. Writer should have "Background working in the classroom with elementary or middle school children and developing quality, appropriate, and innovative learning experiences and/or solid background in developing supplementary educational materials for these markets." Catalog for 8½×11 SAE.
Nonfiction: Elementary and middle-school level enrichment—all subject areas, whole language, theme units, integrated materials, writing process, management techniques, teaching strategies based on personal/professional experience in the classroom. Model and strategies for restructuring—site-based management, shared decision-making. Production is limited to printed matter: resource and activity books, professional development materials, reference titles. Length: 6,000-12,000 words. Query should include TOC. Standard contract.

CHARLES SCRIBNER'S SONS, Children's Books Department, Imprint of Macmillan Publishing Co., 866 3rd Ave., New York NY 10022. (212)702-7885. Editorial Director, Children's Books: Clare Costello. Estab. 1846. Other children's book imprints are Atheneum, Margaret K. McElderry Books, Bradbury Press, Four Winds, Crestwood and Aladdin. Publishes hardcover originals and paperback reprints of own titles. Averages 20-25 titles/year. Pays royalty on retail price; offers advance. Publishes book an average of 1 year after acceptance. Reports in 2 weeks on queries; 10 weeks on mss. Free book catalog and ms guidelines.
Nonfiction: Subjects include animals, biography, health, history, nature, science, self-help, sports for ages 3-14. Query. Reviews artwork/photos as part of ms package.
Recent Nonfiction Title: *Desert of Ice: Life and Word in Antarctica*, by W. John Hackwell.
Fiction: Adventure, fantasy, historical, humor, mystery, picture books, science fiction and suspense. Submit outline/synopsis and sample chapters.
Recent Fiction Title: *A Woman of Her Tribe*, by Margaret Robinson.

ALWAYS submit unsolicited manuscripts or queries with a self-addressed, stamped envelope (SASE) within your country or a self-addressed envelope with International Reply Coupons (IRC) purchased from the post office for other countries.

‡**SEMAPHORE PRESS**, P.O. Box 628, Chatham MA 02633. (508)945-5678. Publisher: Jack Warner. Imprint is Charles River Books. Publishes hardcover and trade paperback originals and reprints. Firm averages 14 titles/year. Receives 40 submissions/year. 10% of books are from first-time authors. 40% from unagented writers. Pays 5-10% royalty on retail price. Offers $3,000 average advance. Publishes book an average of 1 year after acceptance. Reports in 1 month on queries. Free book catalog and ms guidelines.
Nonfiction: Biography, how-to, illustrated book, self-help, textbook. Subjects include art/architecture, ethnic, history, hobbies, music/dance, psychology, recreation, sociology, sports and translations. "No cookbooks or diet books." Query. All unsolicited mss are returned unopened. Reviews artwork/photos as part of ms package.
Recent Nonfiction Title: *Off The Beaten Track*, by Auduson.

SERVANT PUBLICATIONS, 840 Airport Blvd., Box 8617, Ann Arbor MI 48107. (313)761-8505. Editorial Director: Ann Spangler. Estab. 1972. Imprint is Vine Books, "especially for evanglical Protestant readers." Publishes hardcover, trade and mass market paperback originals and trade paperback reprints. Averages 35 titles/year. 5% of books from first-time authors; 95% of books from unagented writers. Pays 7-10% royalty on retail price. Publishes book an average of 1 year after acceptance. Reports in 2 months. Free book catalog for 9 × 12 SASE.
Nonfiction: "We're looking for practical Christian teaching, biblical psychology, recovery, fiction, scripture, current problems facing the Christian church, and inspiration." No heterodox or non-Christian approaches. Query or submit brief outline/synopsis and 1 sample chapter. All unsolicited mss are returned unopened. Reviews artwork/photos as part of ms package.
Recent Nonfiction Title: *Against the Night*, by Chuck Colson.

SEVEN LOCKS PRESS, INC., P.O. Box 27, Cabin John MD 20818. (301)320-2130. President/Publisher: James McGrath Morris. Estab. 1975. Imprint is Isidore Staphanus Sons Publishing. Publishes hardcover and trade paperback originals and reprints. Averages 6 titles/year; receives 100 submissions annually. 50% of books from first-time authors; 50% of books from unagented writers. Pays 8-15% royalty of retail price on hardbacks 6-12% on paperbacks. Simultaneous submissions OK. Reports in 1 month on queries; 3 months on mss. Free book catalog.
Nonfiction: Biography, reference and textbook. Subjects include Americana, business and economics, history, international relations, nature, politics, religion and sociology. Especially needs "books that promise to enlighten public policy." Query or submit outline/synopsis and sample chapters. Reviews artwork/photos as part of ms package.
Recent Nonfiction Title: *Global Dumping Ground: The International Traffic in Hazardous Waste*, by Center for Investigative Reporting and Bill Moyers.
Tips: "Literate, intelligent, socially conscious men and women are our readers."

‡*****SHAPOLSKY PUBLISHERS**, 136 W. 22nd St., New York NY 10011. (212)633-2022. FAX: (212)633-2123. Editorial Director: Isaac Mozeson. Estab. 1983. Publishes hardcover and paperback originals and reprints. 75% originals and 25% reprints. Subsidy publishes 5% of books. Pays 5-10% royalty on retail price. Offers average $1,000 advance. Publishes ms an average of 15 months after acceptance. Simultaneous submissions OK. Reports on queries with SASE in 3 weeks. No unsolicited mss will be read.
Nonfiction: "The major thrust of our list is business, how-to, true crime and some light and lively Judaica. No memoirs." Query or submit outline/synopsis and sample chapters. Reviews artwork/photos as part of package.
Recent Nonfiction Title: *The Place I Call Home: Faces and Voices Of Homeless Teens*, by Lois Stavsky.
Tips: "60% of our books are general interest; 40% are Jewish interest."

HAROLD SHAW PUBLISHERS, 388 Gundersen Dr., P.O. Box 567, Wheaton IL 60189. (708)665-6700. Director of Editorial Services: Ramona Cramer Tucker. Estab. 1967. Imprint is Northcote Books. Publishes hardcover and trade paperback originals and reprints. Averages 32 titles/year; receives 4,000 submissions annually. 10% of books from first-time authors; 90% of books from unagented writers. Offers 5-10% royalty on retail price. Sometimes makes outright purchase for $1,000-2,500. Publishes book an average of 12-15 months after acceptance. Reports in 1 month on queries; 6 weeks on mss. Book catalog and ms guidelines for 9 × 12 SAE with 5 first class stamps.
Nonfiction and Fiction: Juvenile (13 and up), reference and self-help. Subjects include history (of religious movements/evangelical/charismatic), psychology (self-help) and religion (Bible study guides and general religion). "We are looking for general nonfiction, with different twists—self-help manuscripts on issues and topics with fresh insight and colorful, vibrant writing style. We already have how to forgive yourself and how to deal with screaming, cancer, death and handicaps. No autobiographies or biographies accepted. Must have an evangelical Christian perspective for us even to review the ms." Query. Reviews artwork/photos as part of ms package.

Recent Nonfiction Title: *Choices Are Not Child's Play*, by Pat Hold and Grace Ketterman, M.D.
Tips: "Get an editor who is not a friend or a spouse who will tell you honestly whether your book is marketable. It will save a lot of your time and money and effort. Then do an honest evaluation. Who would actually read the book other than yourself? If it won't sell at least 5,000 copies, it's not very marketable and most publishers wouldn't be interested."

THE SHEEP MEADOW PRESS, P.O. Box 1345, Riverdale-on-Hudson NY 10471. (212)549-3321. Publisher/Editor: Stanley Moss. Associate Editor: Sharon Kraus. Estab. 1978. Publishes trade paperback originals. Firm averages 8-9 titles/year. Receives 1,000 submissions/year. 75% of books from first-time authors. 100% from unagented writers. Pays royalty. Reports in 3 weeks on queries; 3 months on mss. Book catalog for 6×9 SASE.
Poetry: "We are always in the market for original manuscripts." Submit complete ms.
Recent Poetry Title: *A Quarter Turn*, by Debra Nystrom.

‡SHELBY PUBLISHING CO., 155 Federal St., Boston MA 02110. (617)423-0978. Editorial Director: W.R. Roof. Imprints are John Liner and FRP Books. Publishes trade paperback originals. Firm averages 5 titles/year. Receives 10 submissions/year. 50% of books are from first-time authors. 100% from unagented writers. Pays 10-12% royalty on retail price. Offers $5,000 average advance. Publishes book an average of 1 year after acceptance. Query for electronic submissions. Reports in 2 weeks. Book catalog and manuscript guidelines free on request.
Nonfiction: Reference and technical. Subjects include business and economics, money/finance, and insurance. "We are looking for 4 to 6 titles on technical, how-to subjects. No self-help books, please."
Recent Nonfiction Title: *Risk Management and Insurance Audit Techniques*, by Dwight Levich.
Tips: "Our audience consists of practicing insurance professionals."

THE SHOE STRING PRESS, 925 Sherman Ave., P.O. Box 4327, Hamden CT 06514. (203)248-6307. President: James Thorpe III. Estab. 1952. Imprints are Archon, Library Professional Publications and Linnet Books. Publishes hardcover and trade paperback originals. Publishes 30 titles/year; receives 700 submissions annually. 15% of books from first-time authors; 95% of books from unagented writers. Pays escalating royalty scale. Publishes book an average of 1 year after acceptance. Query for electronic submissions. Reports in 1 month on queries; 4 months on mss. Book catalog and ms guidelines for SASE.
Nonfiction: Biography, reference and general. Subjects include Americana, children's books, history, nature, philosophy, politics, religion, literature and military. Will consider "any good scholarly or general nonfiction, reference, children's fiction or nonfiction or professional library literature. No flying saucers, reincarnation, or inspiration." Submit outline/synopsis and sample chapters. Reviews artwork/photos as part of ms package.
Recent Nonfiction Title: *Understanding Shakespeare's England: A Companion for the American Reader*, by Jo McMurtry (reference).

‡SHOE TREE PRESS, Imprint of Betterway Publications, P.O. Box 219, Crozet VA 22932. (804)823-5661. Associate Editor: Susan Lewis. Publishes juvenile/hardcover and trade paperback originals. Averages 10 titles/year. Pays 12-16% royalty on wholesale price. Offers $1,500 average advance. Publishes book an average of 8 months after acceptance. Simultaneous submissions OK. Reports in 6 weeks. Book catalog for 9×12 SAE with 5 first class stamps.
Nonfiction: "We are looking for nonfiction books for ages 8-12 and the young adult markets: biographies and useful books that kids can learn from and also enjoy. No picture books or books for children under age 7." Query or submit outline and sample chapters.
Recent Nonfiction Title: *Market Guide for Young Writers, 3rd Ed.*, by Kathy Henderson (reference).
Fiction: Juvenile. "We are looking for young adult fiction, ages 10 and up, historical fiction and novels that teach through compelling stories." Query. Submit synopsis and sample chapters.
Recent Fiction Title: *With Secrets to Keep*, by Rose Levit.

SIERRA CLUB BOOKS, 100 Bush St., San Francisco CA 94104. (415)291-1600. FAX: (415)291-1602. Editor-in-Chief: Daniel Moses. Publishes hardcover and paperback originals and reprints. Averages 20 titles/year; receives 1,000 submissions annually. 50% of books from unagented writers. Royalties vary by project. Offers average $3,000-5,000 advance. Publishes book an average of 12-18 months after acceptance. Reports in 2 months. Free book catalog.
Nonfiction: Animals; health; history (natural); how-to (outdoors); juveniles; nature; philosophy; photography; recreation (outdoors, nonmechanical); science; sports (outdoors); and travel (by foot or bicycle). "The Sierra Club was founded to help people to explore, enjoy and preserve the nation's forests, waters, wildlife and wilderness. The books program looks to publish quality trade books about the outdoors and the protection of natural resources. Specifically, we are interested in nature, environmental issues such as nuclear power, self-sufficiency, natural history, politics and the environment,

and juvenile books with an ecological theme." Does *not* want "personal, lyrical, philosophical books on the great outdoors; proposals for large color photographic books without substantial text; how-to books on building things outdoors; books on motorized travel; or any but the most professional studies of animals." Query first, submit outline/synopsis and sample chapters. Reviews artwork/photos ("duplicates, not originals") as part of ms package.

Recent Nonfiction Title: *Global Warming*, by Stephen H. Schneider.

Fiction: Adventure, historical, mainstream and ecological fiction. "We do very little fiction, but will consider a fiction manuscript if its theme fits our philosophical aims: the enjoyment and protection of the environment." Does *not* want "any manuscript with animals or plants that talk; apocalyptic plots." Query first, submit outline/synopsis and sample chapters, or submit complete ms.

SILHOUETTE BOOKS, Division of Harlequin Enterprises, 300 E. 42nd St., New York NY 10017. (212)682-6080. Editorial Manager, Silhouette Books, Harlequin historicals: Isabel Swift. Estab. 1979. Other divisions are Harlequin Books, Gold Eagle Books and Worldwide Library. Publishes mass market paperback originals. Averages 316 titles/year; receives 4,000 submissions annually. 10% of books from first-time authors; 25% of books from unagented writers. Pays royalty. Publishes book an average of 1 year after acceptance. No unsolicited mss. Send query letter; 2 page synopsis and SASE to head of imprint. Ms guidelines for #10 SASE.

Imprints: Silhouette Romances (contemporary adult romances), Valerie Hayward, Senior Editor; 53,000-58,000 words. Silhouette Special Editions (contemporary adult romances), Tara Gavin, Senior Editor; 75,000-80,000 words. Silhouette Desires (contemporary adult romances), Lucia Macro, Senior Editor; 55,000-60,000 words. Silhouette Intimate Moments (contemporary adult romances), Leslie Wainger, Senior Editor and Editorial Coordinator; 80,000-85,000 words. Harlequin Historicals (adult historical romances), Tracy Farrell, Senior Editor; 95-105,000 words.

Fiction: Romance (contemporary and historical romance for adults). "We are interested in seeing submissions for all our lines. No manuscripts other than the types outlined above. Ms should follow our general format, yet have an individuality and life of its own that will make it stand out in the readers' minds."

Recent Fiction Title: *To Mother with Love*, by Curtis Ann Matlock, Linda Shaw, and Carol Halston.

Tips: "The romance market is constantly changing, so when you read for research, read the latest books and those that have been recommended to you by people knowledgeable in the genre. We are actively seeking new authors for all our lines, contemporary and historical."

SILVER BURDETT PRESS, Imprint of Simon & Schuster, 190 Sylvan Ave., Englewood Cliffs NJ 07632. FAX: (201)461-8178. President: Carole Cushmore. Editor-in-Chief: Bonnie Brook. Imprints are Julian Messner (science, teen issues and current affairs) and Silver Press (preschool and primary fiction and nonfiction). Publishes hardcover and paperback originals. Averages 65-80 titles/year; does not accept unsolicited manuscripts. Publishes book an average of one year after acceptance. Offers variable advance. Free book catalog.

Nonfiction: Juvenile and young adult reference. Subjects include Americana, science, history, nature, and geography. "We're primarily intersted in nonfiction for students on subjects which supplement the classroom curricula, but are graphically appealing and, in some instances, have commercial as well as institutional appeal."

Recent Nonfiction Title: *History of the Civil Rights Movement*, introduction by Andrew Young.

Tips: "Our books are primarily bought by school and public librarians for use by students and young readers. Virtually all are nonfiction and done as part of a series."

SILVER PRESS, Imprint of Silver Burdett Press, 190 Sylvan Ave., Englewood Cliffs NJ 07632. (201)461-6257. Editor-in-Chief: Bonnie Brook. Publishes hardcover and trade paperback originals. Publishes 40 titles/year; receives 100 submissions/year. 10% from first-time authors; 50% from unagented writers. Pays 5-7½% royalty on retail price or assigns work-for-hire. Publishes book an average of 1 year after acceptance. Simultaneous submissions OK. Reports in 1 month on queries; 6 months on mss. Free book catalog.

Nonfiction: Juvenile. Subjects include animals, ethnic, history, hobbies, language/literature. Need good photo essays with simple science subjects. Submit complete ms.

Recent Nonfiction Title: *More than Just a Flower Garden*, by Dwight Kuhn (photo essay).

Fiction: Juvenile, picture books. Submit complete ms.

Recent Fiction Title: *Bears, Bears, Bears*, by Mary Pope Osborne (anthology of bear literature).

Tips: "Preschool and primary (ages 3-8) are our audience."

SIMON & SCHUSTER, Trade Books Division, 1230 Avenue of the Americas, New York NY 10020. Imprints and divisions include Pocket Books, Prentice Hall, and Silver Burdett Press. "We do not accept unsolicited manuscripts. Only manuscripts submitted by agents will be considered. In such cases, our requirements are as follows: Manuscripts must be typewritten, double-spaced, on one side of the sheet only. We suggest margins of about one and one half inches all around and the standard 8½×11 typewriter paper."

Nonfiction and Fiction: "Simon and Schuster publishes books of general adult fiction, history, biography, science, philosophy, the arts and popular culture, running 50,000 words or more. Our program does not, however, include school textbooks, extremely technical or highly specialized works, or, as a general rule, poetry or plays. Exceptions have been made, of course, for extraordinary manuscripts of great distinction or significance."

SKIDMORE-ROTH PUBLISHING, 207 Cincinnati Ave., El Paso TX 79902. (915)544-3150. President: Linda Roth. Publishes trade paperback originals and reprints. Firm averages 10/year. Receives 250 submissions/year. 50% first time writers. 100% from unagented writers. Pays 5-12½% royalty on wholesale price. Publishes book an average of 9 months after acceptance. Simultaneous submissions OK. Reports in 3 weeks on queries; 2 months on mss. Free book catalog.

Nonfiction: Self-help, technical, textbook. Subject include child guidance/parenting, health/medicine and psychology. We are currently searching for manuscripts in the following areas: geriatric nursing, consumer health, self-improvement, psychology, parenting, allied health. Nothing on religion, history, music/dance, travel, sports, agriculture, computers, military, politics, gay/lesbian or literature. Query. Reviews artwork/photos as part of ms package.

Recent Nonfiction Title: *Mom, I'm Pregnant,* by Lovely Free-Smith, M.D. and Melissa Baker, R.N. (health).

Tips: "Anything on consumer health is more likely to be published. Our audience is largely a geriatric population, also single women with small children, professionals in the field of medicine, nursing, allied health. If I were a writer trying to market a book today, I would look for an area that has been completely overlooked by other writers and write on that subject."

‡SLAWSON COMMUNICATIONS, INC., 165 Vallecitos de Oro, San Marcos CA 92069-1436. (619)744-2299. President: Leslie S. Smith. Computer Book Editor: Lance A. Leventhal. Subsidiaries include Avant Books®, Microtrend®, Health Media of America®. Publishes hardcover and trade paperback originals and trade paperback reprints. Firm averages 24 titles/year. Receives 100 submissions/year. 60% of books are from first-time authors. 90% from unagented writers. Pays 10-15% royalty on wholesale price. Offers $1,000-10,000 average advance. Publishes book an average of 6 months after acceptance. Simultaneous submissions OK. Reports in 2 weeks on queries; 1 month on manuscripts. Book catalog for $2.50.

Nonfiction: Software, technical and businesses. Subjects include businesses and economics, computers and electronics, health/medicine, money/finance. Submit outline/synosis and sample chapters. Reviews artwork/photos as part of ms package.

Recent Nonfiction Title: *The Achievement Factors,* by B. Eugene Griessman (Ph.D. business).

GIBBS SMITH, PUBLISHER, P.O. Box 667, Layton UT 84041. (801)544-9800. Editorial Director: Madge Baird. Fiction Editor: Steve Chapman. Estab. 1969. Imprint is Peregrine Smith Books. Publishes hardcover and paperback originals and reprints. Averages 25-30 titles/year; receives 2,000 submissions annually. 25% of books from first-time authors; 40% of books from unagented writers. Average print order for a writer's first book is 3,000-4,000. Starts at 10% royalty on wholesale price. Offers average $1,000 advance. Publishes book an average of 1½ years after acceptance. Reports in 2 months. Book catalog for 6×9 SAE and 3 first class stamps; ms guidelines for #10 SASE.

Nonfiction: "Subjects include western American history, natural history, architecture, art history, and fine arts. We consider biographical, historical, descriptive and analytical studies in all of the above. Emphasis is also placed on pictorial content." Query. Reviews artwork/photos as part of ms package.

Recent Nonfiction Title: *Entering the Grove,* text by Kim Stafford, photos by Gary Braasch.

Fiction: "We publish contemporary literary fiction. Looks for style, readable, intelligent, careful writing, contribution to the social consciousness of our time." Query.

Recent Fiction Title: *The Light Possessed,* by Alan Cheuse.

Tips: "We're looking for art books (visual arts and architecture) on the leading edge of our culture. In fiction we are interested in work with literary merit, work that demonstrates a control of subject with a distinctive and original voice will be seriously considered. We are not interested in potboilers, bodice-rippers, science fiction, techno-thrillers or anything that deals with a subject that claims to be 'as current as today's headlines.' "

SOHO PRESS, INC., 853 Broadway, New York NY 10003. (212)260-1900. Editor-in-Chief: Juris Jurjevics. Estab. 1986. Publishes hardcover and trade paperback originals. Firm averages 12 titles/year. Receives 4,000 submissions/year. 75% of books from first-time authors. 50% of books from unagented writers. Pays 10-15% on retail price. Publishes book an average of 1 year after acceptance. Simultaneous submissions OK. Reports in 1 month on queries; 2 months on mss. Book catalog for SASE.

Nonfiction: Biography. "We want literary non-fiction: travel, autobiography, biography, etc. No self-help." Submit outline/synopsis and sample chapters or complete ms with SASE.
Recent Nonfiction Title *O Come Ye Back to Ireland*, by Niall Williams and Christine Breen, (travel and biography).
Fiction: Adventure, ethnic, feminist, historical, literary, mainstream/contemporary, mystery and suspense. Submit complete ms with SASE.
Recent Fiction Title: *Me and You*, by Margaret Diehl.

SOUTHFARM PRESS, Haan Graphic Publishing Services, Ltd., P.O. Box 1296, Middletown CT 06457. (203)344-9137. Publisher: Walter J. Haan. Estab. 1983. Publishes trade paperback originals. Firm averages 5 titles/year. 100% from first-time authors; 100% from unagented writers. Pays 5-10% royalty on retail price. Offers $500 average advance. Publishes book an average of 1 year after acceptance. Simultaneous submissions OK. Reports in 1 month. Free book catalog.
Nonfiction: Subjects include history and military/war. Submit outline/synopsis and sample chapters.
Recent Nonfiction Title: *Ghost Ship: The Confederate Raider Alabama*, by Norman C. Delaney.

‡SPARROW PRESS, 103 Waldron St., West Lafayette IN 47906. (317)743-1991. Editor/Publisher: Felix Stefanile. Estab. 1954. Imprints are Sparrow Poverty Pamphlets and Vagrom Chap Books. Publishes trade paperback originals. Averages 3 pamphlets and 1-3 chapbooks/year; receives 1,200 submissions annually. 25% of books from first-time authors; 100% of books from unagented writers. Pays $30 advance on royalties, 20% of profits after cost is recovered. No simultaneous submissions. Publishes book an average of 10 months after acceptance. Reports in 1 month on queries; 6 weeks on mss. We publish by invitation only. Send SASE with all correspondence. Sample pamphlet $2; book catalog for 50¢.
Poetry: "We need the best poetry we can find. We plan at least three volumes per year. We are not interested in seeing any humor, or religious verse. We don't want prose poems. We do not want cut-up prose confessional poems." 28 page typescript only, one poem/page. "If we want to see more, we'll ask." *No* queries answered without SASE.
Recent Poetry Title: *Here*, by Alice Monks Mears.
Tips: "Our readers are contemporary-minded fellow poets, creative writing students, serious readers and teachers. Poetry is becoming more formal again, more literate. The better poets write out of their hearts, and find their own genuine, if not too large, following. Recent Sparrow poets have won the Guggenheim, the Carl Sandburg Memorial Award, etc. Under no circumstances do we return submitted manuscripts not accompanied by SASE."

THE SPEECH BIN, INC., 1766 20th Ave., Vero Beach FL 32960. (407)770-0007. FAX: (407)770-0006. Senior Editor: Jan Binney. Estab. 1984. Publishes trade paperback originals. Publishes 10-20 titles/ year. Receives 200-250 manuscripts per year. 50% of books from first-time authors; 90% from unagented writers. Pays negotiable royalty on wholesale price. Publishes ms average of 6 months after acceptance. Query for electronic submissions. Reports in one month on queries, six weeks on manuscripts. Book catalog for 9 × 12 SASE.
Nonfiction: How-to, illustrated book, juvenile (preschool-teen), reference, textbook, educational material and games. Subjects include health, communication disorders and education for handicapped persons. Query or submit outline synopsis and sample chapters. Reviews artwork/photos as part of ms package. Do not send original artwork; photocopies only please.
Recent Nonfiction Title: *Calendar Capers*, by Pamela Meza Steckbeck.
Fiction: Booklets or books "for children and adults about handicapped persons, especially with communication disorders." Query or submit outline/synopsis and sample chapters. "This is a potentially new market for The Speech Bin."
Tips: "Our audience is made up of special educators, speech-language pathologists and audiologists, parents, caregivers, and teachers of children and adults with developmental and post-trauma disabilities. Books and materials must be research-based, clearly presented, well written, competently illustrated, and unique. We'll be adding books and materials for use by occupational and physical therapists and other allied health professionals."

SPINSTERS BOOK COMPANY, P.O. Box 410687, San Francisco CA 94141. (415)558-9586. Editors: Sherry Thomas and Joan Pinkvoss. Publishes trade paperback originals and reprints. Averages 6-8 titles/year; receives 200 submissions annually. 50% of books from first-time authors; 95% of books from unagented writers. Pays 7-11% royalty on retail price. Publishes book an average of 1 year after acceptance. Reports in 3 weeks on queries; 6 months on mss. Free book catalog; ms guidelines for SASE.
Nonfiction: Self-help and feminist analysis for positive change. Subjects include women's issues. "We are interested in books that not only name the crucial issues in women's lives, but show and encourage change and growth. We do not want to see work by men, or anything that is not specific to women's

lives (humor, childrens' books, etc.). We do not want genre fiction (romances, etc.)." Query. Reviews artwork/photos as part of ms package.

Recent Nonfiction Title: *Lesbians at Midlife.*

Fiction: Ethnic, women's, lesbian. Submit outline/synopsis and sample chapters.

Recent Fiction Title: *Final Session*, by Mary Morrell (lesbian mystery).

Poetry: Minimal. Submit complete ms.

Recent Poetry Title: *We Say We Love Each Other*, by Minnie Bruce Pratt (Southern lesbian).

ST PUBLICATIONS, INC., Signs of the Times Publishing Co., Book Division, 407 Gilbert Ave., Cincinnati OH 45202. (513)421-4050. FAX: (513)421-5144. Book Division Manager: George B. Harper. Estab. 1957. Publishes hardcover and trade paperback originals and hardcover reprints. Averages 6 titles/year; receives 15-20 submissions annually. 50% of books from first-time authors; 100% of books from unagented writers. Pays royalty on wholesale price: 10% until recovery of production costs; 12½% thereafter; and 15% on straight reprints. Publishes book an average of 9 months after acceptance. Reports in 6 weeks on queries; 2 months on mss. Free book catalog and ms guidelines.

Nonfiction: How-to, reference, technical and textbook. Subjects include art (collections of copyright-free artwork suitable for sign, display or screen printing industries). "We need technical how-to books for professionals in three specific industries: the sign industry, including outdoor advertising, electric and commercial signs; the screen printing industry, including the printing of paper products, fabrics, ceramics, glass and electronic circuits; and the visual merchandising and store design industry. We are not interested in submissions that do not relate specifically to those three fields." Submit outline/synopsis and sample chapters. Reviews artwork/photos as part of ms package.

Recent Nonfiction Title: *Screen Printing Production Management*, by Richard C. Webb, Jr.

Tips: "The writer has the best chance of selling our firm how-to books related to our industries: signs, screen printing, and visual merchandising. These are the fields our marketing and distribution channels are geared to. Request copies of, and thoroughly absorb the information presented in, our trade magazines (*Signs of the Times*, *Visual Merchandising*, and *Screen Printing*). Our books are permanent packages of this type of information. We are taking a closer look at submissions that we can sell outside our primary range of customers, yet still confining our subject interests to sign painting and design, visual merchandising, display and store design, and screen printing (both technical and art aspects)."

STACKPOLE BOOKS, Company of Commonwealth Communications Services, P.O. Box 1831, Harrisburg PA 17105. FAX: (717)234-1359. Editorial Director: Judith Schnell. Estab. 1930. Publishes hardcover and paperback originals. Publishes 50 titles/year. Publishes book an average of 1 year after acceptance.

Nonfiction: Outdoor-related subject areas—fishing, hunting, wildlife, adventure, outdoor skills, gardening, decoy carving/woodcarving, outdoor sports, crafts, military guides, military history. Reviews artwork/photos as part of ms package.

Recent Nonfiction Title: *Shadows on the Tundra*, by Tom Walker.

Tips: "Stackpole seeks well-written, authoritative manuscripts for specialized and general trade markets. Proposals should include chapter outline, sample chapter and illustration, and author's credentials."

STANDARD PUBLISHING, Division of Standex International Corp., 8121 Hamilton Ave., Cincinnati OH 45231. (513)931-4050. Publisher/Vice President: Eugene H. Wigginton. Estab. 1866. Publishes hardcover and paperback originals and reprints. Specializes in religious books for children. Publishes book an average of 18 months after acceptance. Reports in 3 months. Ms guidelines for #10 SASE.

Nonfiction: Publishes how-to; crafts (to be used in Christian education); juveniles; Christian education; quiz; puzzle. All mss must pertain to religion. Query.

Recent Nonfiction Title: *Message in Motion: Simulation Games for Teens*, by Tim Jones.

Fiction: Religious, contemporary for ages 8-11 or 12-15.

Recent Fiction Title: *Two of a Kind*, by Kristi Holl.

Tips: "Children's books (picture books, ages 4-7), juvenile fiction (8-11 and 12-15), Christian education, activity books, and helps for Christian parents and church leaders are the types of books writers have the best chance of selling to our firm."

*STANFORD UNIVERSITY PRESS, Stanford University, Stanford CA 94305-2235. (415)723-9598. Editor: William W. Carver. Estab. 1925. Averages 65 titles/year; receives 1,200 submissions annually. 40% of books from first-time authors, 95% of books from unagented writers. Subsidy (nonauthor) publishes 65% of books. Pays up to 15% royalty ("typically 10%, often none"); sometimes offers advance. Publishes book an average of 1 year after acceptance. Query for electronic submissions. Reports in 3 weeks on queries; 5 weeks on mss. Free book catalog.

Nonfiction: Scholarly books in the humanities, social sciences, and natural sciences: history and culture of China, Japan, and Latin America; European history; biology, natural history, and taxonomy; anthropology, linguistics, and psychology; literature, criticism, and literary theory; political science and sociology; archaeology and geology; and medieval and classical studies. Also high-level textbooks and books for a more general audience. Query. "We like to see a prospectus and an outline." Reviews artwork/photos as part of ms package.

Recent Nonfiction Title: *The Butterflies of North America*, by James A. Scott.

Tips: "The writer's best chance is a work of original scholarship with an argument of some importance and an appeal to a broad audience."

‡STAR BOOKS INC., 408 Pearson St., Wilson NC 27893. (919)237-1591. President: Irene Burk Harrell. Firm averages 9-15 titles/year. 90% of books from first-time authors. 100% from unagented writers. Pays 10-15% royalty on retail price. Offers no advance. Publishes book an average of 1 year after acceptance. Reports in 1 week on queries; 1 month on mss. Book catalog for #10 SAE with 2 first class stamps. Manuscript guidelines for #10 SASE.

Nonfiction: Biography, humor, juvenile, self-help. Subjects include abortion, alcoholism, biography, Christian testimony, cartoons (Christian), devotionals, divorce, personal experiences (specifically Christian), novels (biblical or contemporary Christian), poetry (with Christian focus), prayer (devotional books), rape, short stories (Christian). "We are looking for first-person accounts (testimonies) by persons who have found God's answers for the difficult problems of life. No third-person, impersonal, researched material." Submit complete ms. Reviews artwork/photos (b&w only) as part of ms package.

Recent Nonfiction Title: *Won't Somebody Help Me!*, by Janice Gravely (adventure/biography).

Fiction: Adventure, confession, ethnic, fantasy, humor, juvenile, picture books (b&w only), religious, romance, short story collections, young adult. All must have strong Christian focus. "We don't want to see anything that is not specifically Christian or is too esoteric." Submit complete ms.

Recent Fiction Title: *Shatterings*, by Ralph Filicchia (short stories).

Recent Poetry Title: *Wayfarer*, by Gennet Emery (Christian verse).

*STARBURST PUBLISHERS, Subsidiary of Starburst Inc., P.O. Box 4123, Lancaster PA 17604. (717)293-0939. Editorial Director: Ellen Hake. Estab. 1982. Publishes hardcover and trade paperback originals and trade paperback reprints. Averages 15-20 titles/year. Receives 1,000 submissions/year. 75% of books by first-time authors. 75% from unagented writers. Subsidy publishes 11% of books. Pays 6-15% royalty on net price to retailer. Publishes book an average of 1 year after acceptance. Reports in 1 month on queries; 2 months on mss. Book catalog for 9 × 12 SAE with 2 first class stamps. Manuscript guidelines for #10 SASE.

Nonfiction: Biography, cookbook, how-to, juvenile, self-help, Christian. Subjects include business and economics, child guidance/parenting, cooking, foods and nutrition, government/politics, health/medicine, military/war, money/finance, psychology, religion. "We are looking for contemporary issues facing Christians. General—how-to, business, self-help and family." Submit outline/synopsis, 3 sample chapters, bio, photo and SASE. Reviews artwork/photos as part of ms package.

Recent Nonfiction Title: *Teenage Mutant Ninja Turtles Exposed!*, by Joan Hake Robie (issues).

Fiction: Adventure, historical, juvenile, mainstream/contemporary, religious, young adult. We are looking for good, wholesome fiction that could either be Christian or general. Submit outline/synopsis, 3 sample chapters, bio, photo and SASE.

Tips: "75% our line goes into the Christian marketplace; 25% into the general marketplace. Write on an issue that slots you on talk shows and thus establish your name as an expert and writer."

STARRHILL PRESS, P.O. Box 32342, Washington DC 20007. (202)686-6703. Co-presidents: Liz Hill and Marty Starr. Publishes trade paperback originals. Firm averages 4 titles/year. Receives 10 submissions/year. 90% of books from first-time authors. 100% from unagented writers. Pays 5-10% royalty on retail price. Publishes book an average of 1 year after acceptance. Simultaneous submissions OK. Reports in 2 weeks on queries. Book catalog for #10 SASE.

Nonfiction: Reference. Subjects include art/architecture, music/dance, nature/environment and travel. "American arts, decoration, literary guide books, performing arts, short nonfiction (with line drawings only) are our needs. No popular junk, coffee table books or expensive artwork." Query or submit outline/synopsis and sample chapters. Reviews artwork/photos as part of manuscript package.

Recent Nonfiction Title: *Look Again! Clues to Modern Painting*, by Sally Montanari.

‡STEMMER HOUSE PUBLISHERS, INC., 2627 Caves Rd., Owings Mills MD 21117. (301)363-3690. President: Barbara Holdridge. Publishes hardcover originals. Averages 12 titles/year; receives 500 submissions annually. 10% of books from first-time authors; 90% of books from unagented writers. Average print order for a writer's first book is 4,000-10,000. Pays royalty on wholesale price. Publishes

book an average of 1 year after acceptance. Reports in 2 weeks on queries; 3 months on mss. Book catalog for 9×12 SAE and 4 first class stamps.

Nonfiction: Biography, cookbook, illustrated book, juvenile (ages 4-14) and design books. Subjects include Americana, animals, art, cooking and foods, history and nature. Especially looking for "quality biography, history, and art and design." No humor. Query or submit outline/synopsis and sample chapters.

Recent Nonfiction Title: *Henrietta Maria*, by Rosalind K. Marshall.

Fiction: Adventure, ethnic, historical, mainstream and philosophical. "We want only manuscripts of sustained literary merit. No popular-type manuscripts written to be instant bestsellers." Query.

Recent Fiction Title: *The Fringe of Heaven*, by Margaret Sutherland (contemporary novel).

Tips: "We are interested in finding original manuscripts on gardens and gardening. If I were a writer trying to market a book today, I would not imitate current genres on the bestseller lists, but strike out with a subject of intense interest to me. Freelancer has best chance of selling a book with a universal theme, either for adults or children, exceptionally well written, and marketable internationally. Our goal is a list of perennial sellers of which we can be proud."

STERLING PUBLISHING, 387 Park Ave. S., New York NY 10016. (212)532-7160. Acquisitions Manager: Sheila Anne Barry. Estab. 1949. Publishes hardcover and paperback originals and reprints. Averages 80 titles/year. Pays royalty; offers advance. Publishes book an average of 8 months after acceptance. Reports in 6 weeks. Guidelines for SASE.

Nonfiction: Alternative lifestyle, fiber arts, games and puzzles, health, how-to, business, foods, hobbies, how-to, children's humor, children's science, nature and activities, militaria, New Age, pets, recreation, reference, sports, technical, wine and woodworking. Query or submit complete chapter list, detailed outline/synopsis and 2 sample chapters with photos if necessary. Reviews artwork/photos as part of ms package.

Recent Nonfiction Title: *Cars Detroit Never Built*, by Edward Janicki.

STIPES PUBLISHING CO., 10-12 Chester St., Champaign IL 61820. (217)356-8391. FAX: (217)356-5753. Contact: Robert Watts. Estab. 1925. Publishes hardcover and paperback originals. Averages 15-30 titles/year; receives 150 submissions annually. 50% of books from first-time authors; 100% of books from unagented writers. Pays 15% maximum royalty on retail price. Publishes book an average of 4 months after acceptance. Reports in 2 weeks on queries; 2 months on mss.

Nonfiction: Technical (some areas), textbooks on business and economics, music, chemistry, agriculture/horticulture, and recreation and physical education. "All of our books in the trade area are books that also have a college text market." No "books unrelated to educational fields taught at the college level." Submit outline/synopsis and 1 sample chapter.

Recent Nonfiction Title: *Graphics for Engineers*, by D. C. O'Bryant and J.S. Dobrolvolny.

STOEGER PUBLISHING COMPANY, 55 Ruta Court, S. Hackensack NJ 07606. (201)440-2700. FAX: (201)440-2707. Publisher: Robert E. Weise. Estab. 1925. Publishes trade paperback originals. Averages 12-15 titles/year. Royalty varies, depending on ms. Simultaneous submissions OK. Reports in 1 month on queries; 3 months on mss. Book catalog for SASE.

Nonfiction: Specializing in reference and how-to books that pertain to hunting, fishing and appeal to gun enthusiasts. Submit outline/synopsis and sample chapters.

Recent Nonfiction Title: *Great Shooters of the World*, by Sam Fadala.

STORMLINE PRESS, P.O. Box 539, Urbana IL 61801. (217)328-2665. Publisher: Raymond Bial. Estab. 1985. Publishes hardcover and trade paperback originals. Averages 2-3 titles/year. Receives 1,250 submissions/year. Pays standard royalties. Publishes book an average of 1 year after acceptance. Book catalog for #10 SASE.

Nonfiction: Biography, humor, illustrated book and juvenile. Subjects include agriculture, Americana, art, ethnic, history, photography and regional. "We are interested in fiction and nonfiction of the highest literary quality only. Do not send unsolicited manuscripts. We consider queries in November and December only. For complete guidelines, send SASE."

For explanation of symbols, see the Key to Symbols and Abbreviations on Page 5. For unfamiliar words, see the Glossary.

Recent Nonfiction Title: *Living With Lincoln: Life and Art in the Heartland*, by Dan Guillory (essays on life in the Midwest).
Fiction: "We are interested in considering carefully-crafted manuscripts of the highest literary quality. Nearly all books have some connection with the American Midwest. Please query first with SASE."
Recent Fiction Title: *Dim Tales*, by John Knoepfle.
Tips: "Do not submit unsolicited manuscripts. Please query in November and December *only* with a brief description of your work. Writers should also study other publications of our press, most of which are available at their local public library."

‡SUCCESS PUBLISHING, 2812 Bayonne Dr., Palm Beach Gardens FL 33410. (407)626-4643. President: Allan H. Smith. Publishes trade paperback originals. Averages 6 titles/year. Receives 200 submissions annually. 75% of books from first-time authors. 100% of books from unagented writers. Pays 7% royalty. Publishes book an average of 3 months after acceptance. Simultaneous submissions OK. Reports in 2 weeks on queries. Book catalog and manuscript guidelines for #10 SAE and 2 first class stamps.
Nonfiction: How-to, humor and self-help. Business and economics, hobbies and money/finance. "We are looking for books on how-to subjects such as home business and sewing." Query.
Recent Nonfiction Title: *Making Money at A&C Shows*, by Herbison (how-to).
Tips: "Our audience is made up of housewives, hobbyists and owners of home-based businesses. If I were a writer trying to market a book today, I would read books about how to market a self-written book."

SUNFLOWER UNIVERSITY PRESS, Subsidiary of Journal of the West, Inc., 1531 Yuma, Box 1009, Manhattan KS 66502-4228. (913)539-1888. Associate Publisher: Carol A. Williams. Publishes trade paperback originals and reprints. Averages 8-15 titles/year. Receives 50-75 submissions/year. 75% of books from first-time authors. 80% of books from unagented writers. Pays 10% royalty after first printing. Publishes book an average of 8 months after acceptance and contract. Reports in 3 weeks on queries; 3 months on mss. Free book catalog.
Nonfiction: Biography, illustrated books, reference. Subjects include agriculture/horticulture, Americana, anthropology/archaeology, business and economics, ethnic, government/politics, health/medicine, history, language/literature, military/war, money/finance, music/dance, nature/environment, photography, recreation, regional, religion, science, sociology, sports, women's issues/studies. Our field of specialization lies in memoirs and histories of the West, and of the military, naval, and air fields; perhaps some specialized collectors' books. Query. Reviews artwork/photos as part of the ms package (photocopies acceptable).
Recent Nonfiction Title: *Passages to Freedom: A Story of Capture and Escape*, by Joseph S. Frelinghuysen (military).
Fiction: Historical, western, military. We need narratives that are historically accurate and shed light on historical incidents or events. No X-rated, juvenile, stream of consciousness. Query.
Recent Fiction Title: *Tiger Tales*, by Milt Miller (military fiction).
Tips: "Our audience is the informed aviation, military, or Western American history enthusiast."

SUNSTONE PRESS, Imprint of Sunstone Corporation, P.O. Box 2321, Santa Fe NM 87504-2321. (505)988-4418. FAX: (505)988-1025. Editor-in-Chief: James C. Smith Jr. Estab. 1971. Other imprint is Sundial Publications. Publishes paperback originals; few hardcover originals. Averages 20 titles/year; receives 400 submissions annually. 70% of books from first-time authors; 100% of books from unagented writers. Average print order for writer's first book is 2,000-5,000. Pays royalty on wholesale price. Publishes book an average of 1 year after acceptance. Reports in 2 months.
Nonfiction: How-to series craft books. Books on the history and architecture of the Southwest. Looks for "strong regional appeal (Southwestern)." Reviews artwork/photos as part of ms package.
Recent Nonfiction Title: *Rural Architecture*, by Myrtle Stedman.
Fiction: Publishes material with Southwestern theme.
Recent Fiction Title: *Of Arms I Sing*, by Joseph J. Bohnaker.
Poetry: Traditional or free verse. Poetry book not exceeding 64 pages. Prefers Southwestern theme.
Recent Poetry Title: *Signature of the Spiral*, by Daniel Schreck.

SYBEX, INC., 2021 Challenger Dr., Alameda CA 94501. (415)523-8233. FAX: (415)523-2373. Editor-in-Chief: Dr. Rudolph S. Langer. Acquisitions Manager: Dianne King. Acquisitions Editor: David J. Clark. Estab. 1976. Publishes paperback originals. Averages 100 titles/year. Royalty rates vary. Offers average $3,000 advance. Publishes book an average of 3 months after acceptance. Simultaneous submissions OK. Query for electronic submissions. Reports in 2 months. Free book catalog.
Nonfiction: Computers and computer software. "Manuscripts most publishable in the field of personal computers, desktop computer business applications, hardware, programming languages, and telecommunications." Submit outline/synopsis and 2-3 sample chapters. Looks for "clear writing;

technical accuracy; logical presentation of material; and good selection of material, such that the most important aspects of the subject matter are thoroughly covered; well-focused subject matter; and well-thought-out organization that helps the reader understand the material." Reviews artwork/photos as part of ms package.

Recent Nonfiction Title: *Mastering WordPerfect 5.1.*

Tips: Queries/mss may be routed to other editors in the publishing group.

*SYRACUSE UNIVERSITY PRESS, 1600 Jamesville Ave., Syracuse NY 13244-5160. (315)443-5534. FAX: (315)443-5545. Director: Charles Backus. Estab. 1943. Averages 40 titles/year; receives 400 submissions annually. 40% of books from first-time authors; 95% of books from unagented writers. Subsidy publishes (nonauthor) 20% of books. Pays royalty on net sales. Publishes book an average of 10-12 months after acceptance. Simultaneous submissions OK "if we are informed." Reports in 2 weeks on queries; "longer on submissions." Book catalog and ms guidelines for SASE.

Nonfiction: "Special opportunity in our nonfiction program for freelance writers of books on New York state. We have published regional books by people with limited formal education, but authors were thoroughly acquainted with their subjects, and they wrote simply and directly about them. Provide precise descriptions about subjects, along with background description of project. The author must make a case for the importance of his or her subject." Query. Accepts outline/synopsis and at least 2 sample chapters. Reviews artwork/photos as part of ms package.

Recent Nonfiction Title: *The Town That Started the Civil War*, by Nat Brandt (history).

TAB BOOKS, Division of McGraw-Hill, Inc., Blue Ridge, Summit PA 17214. (717)794-2191. FAX: (717)794-2080. Director of Acquisitions: Ron Powers. Estab. 1964. Imprint is Windcrest (microcomputer books). Publishes hardcover and paperback originals and reprints. Publishes 275 titles/year; receives 600 submissions annually. 50% of books from first-time authors; 85% of books from unagented writers. Average print order for writer's first book is 10,000. Pays variable royalty; buys some mss outright for a negotiable fee. Offers advance. Query for electronic submissions. Reports in 6 weeks. Free book catalog and ms guidelines.

Nonfiction: TAB publishes titles in such fields as computer hardware, computer software, business, solar and alternate energy, marine line, aviation, automotive, music technology, consumer medicine, electronics, electrical and electronics repair, amateur radio, shortwave listening, model railroading, toys, hobbies, drawing, animals and animal power, woodworking, practical skills with projects, building furniture, basic how-to for the house, building large structures, calculators, robotics, telephones, model radio control, TV servicing, audio, recording, hi-fi and stereo, electronic music, electric motors, electrical wiring, electronic test equipment, video programming, CATV, MATV and CCTV, broadcasting, photography and film, appliance servicing and repair, advertising, antiques and restoration, bicycles, crafts, farmsteading, hobby electronics, home construction, license study guides, mathematics, metalworking, reference books, schematics and manuals, small gasoline engines, two-way radio and CB, military fiction, and woodworking. Accepts nonfiction translations. Query with outline/synopsis. Reviews artwork/photos as part of ms package.

Recent Nonfiction Title: *Abused No More*, by Robert J. Ackerman.

Tips: "Many writers believe that a cover letter alone will describe their proposed book sufficiently; it rarely does. The more details we receive, the better the chances are that the writer will get published by us. We expect a writer to tell us what the book is about, but many writers actually fail to do just that."

TAYLOR PUBLISHING COMPANY, Subsidiary of Insilco, 1550 W. Mockingbird Ln., Dallas TX 75235. (214)637-2800. Contact: Editorial Assistant, Trade Books Division. Estab. 1981. Publishes hardcover and softcover originals. Averages 30 titles/year; receives 1,000 submissions annually. 25% of books from first-time authors; 10% of books from unagented writers. Buys some mss outright. Publishes book 1½ years after acceptance. Simultaneous submissions OK. Reports in 2 months. Book catalog and ms guidelines for 8½×11 SASE.

Nonfiction: True crime, cookbook, humor, gardening, coffee table books, nature/outdoors, regional (South), sports, self-help and trivia. Submit outline/synopsis and sample chapters. Also submit author bio as it pertains to the proposed subject matter. Reviews artwork/photos as part of ms package.

Recent Nonfiction Title: *Best Home Hints from the Superhandyman*, by Al Carrell.

TEACHERS COLLEGE PRESS, 1234 Amsterdam Ave., New York NY 10027. (212)678-3929. FAX: (212)678-4149. Director: Carole P. Saltz. Estab. 1904. Publishes hardcover and paperback originals and reprints. Averages 40 titles/year. Pays royalty. Publishes book an average of 1 year after acceptance. Reports in 1 year. Free book catalog.

Nonfiction: "This university press concentrates on books in the field of education in the broadest sense, from early childhood to higher education: good classroom practices, teacher training, special education, innovative trends and issues, administration and supervision, film, continuing and adult education, all areas of the curriculum, computers, guidance and counseling and the politics, economics, philosophy, sociology and history of education. The Press also issues classroom materials for students at all levels, with a strong emphasis on reading and writing and social studies." Submit outline/synopsis and sample chapters.

Recent Nonfiction Title: *The Reflective Turn: Case Studies In and On Educational Practice*, by Donald Schön, Ed.

‡**TECHNICAL COMMUNICATIONS ASSOCIATES, INC.**, Suite 210, 1250 Oakmead Pkwy., Sunnyvale CA 94088. (408)737-2665. Contact: Frank Patrinostro. Publishes trade paperback originals. Firm averages 10 titles/year. 10% of books from first-time authors; 10% from unagented writers. Pays royalty. Publishes book an average of 3 months after acceptance. Simultaneous submissions OK. Query for electronic submissions. Reports in 2 weeks on queries. Free book catalog.

Nonfiction: Reference, software, technical, textbook. Subjects include computers and electronics and science. "We will consider only these categories listed." Reviews artwork/photos as part of ms package.

Tips: "Writers have the best chance selling us books on computer systems management. Our audience consists of computer professionals and technical writers."

‡**TEMPLE UNIVERSITY PRESS**, Broad and Oxford Sts., Philadelphia PA 19122. (215)787-8787. FAX: (215)787-4719. Editor-in-Chief: Michael Ames. Publishes 60 titles/year. Pays royalty of up to 10% on wholesale price. Publishes book an average of 1 year after acceptance. Query for electronic submissions. Reports in 3 months. Free book catalog.

Nonfiction: American history, sociology, women's studies, health care, philosophy, labor studies, photography, urban studies, Latin American studies, Afro-American studies, Asian American studies, public policy and regional (Philadelphia area). "All books should be scholarly. Authors are generally connected with a university. No memoirs, fiction or poetry." Uses *Chicago Manual of Style*. Reviews artwork/photos as part of ms package. Query.

Recent Nonfiction Title: *The Boss: J. Edgar Hoover and the Great American Inquisition*, by Athan Theoharis and John Stuart Cox.

‡**TEN SPEED PRESS**, P.O. Box 7123, Berkeley CA 94707. (415)845-8414. Acquisitions Editor: Nichole Geiger. Estab. 1971. Imprints are Celestial Arts and Double Elephant Books. Publishes trade paperback originals and reprints. Firm averages 60 titles/year; imprint averages 40 titles/year. 25% of books from first-time authors. 75% from unagented writers. Pays 8-12% royalty on retail price. Offers $2,500 average advance. Publishes book an average of 1 year after acceptance. Simultaneous submissions OK. Reports in 2 months on queries. Book catalog for 9 × 12 SAE with 6 first class stamps. Manuscript guidelines for #10 SASE.

Nonfiction: Cookbook, how-to, reference and self-help. Subjects include business and economics, child guidance/parenting, cooking, foods and nutrition, gardening, gay/lesbian, health/medicine, money/finance, nature/environment, recreation and science. "We mainly publish innovative how-to books. We are always looking for cookbooks from a proven, tested sources—successful restaurants, etc. *Not* 'grandma's favorite recipies.' Books about the 'new science' interest us. No biographies or autobiographies, first-person travel narratives, fiction or humorous treatments of just about anything." Query. Submit outline/synopsis and sample chapters.

Recent Nonfiction Title: *A Woman's Guide to Cycling*, by Susan Weaver (women's how-to, sports).

Tips: "We like books from people who really know their subject, rather than people who think they've spotted a trend to capitalize on. We like books that will sell for a long time, rather than nine-day wonders. Our audience consists of a well-educated, slightly weird group of people who like food, the outdoors and take a light but serious approach to business and careers. If I were a writer trying to market a book today, I would really study the backlist of each publisher I was submitting to, and tailor my proposal to what I perceive as their needs. Nothing gets a publisher's attention like someone who knows what he or she is talking about, and nothing gets flat like someone who obviously has no idea who he or she is submitting to."

***TEXAS A&M UNIVERSITY PRESS**, Drawer C, College Station TX 77843. (409)845-1436. FAX: (409)847-8752. Director: John F. Stetter. Estab. 1974. Publishes 30 titles/year. Subsidy publishes (nonauthor) 15% of books. Pays in royalties. Publishes book an average of 1 year after acceptance. Query for electronic submissions. Reports in 1 week on queries; 1 month on submissions. Free book catalog.

Nonfiction: Natural history, American history, environmental history, military history, women's studies, economics and regional studies.

Recent Nonfiction Title: *The American Crow and the Common Raven*, by Lawrence Kilham.

***TEXAS CHRISTIAN UNIVERSITY PRESS**, P.O. Box 30783, TCU, Fort Worth TX 76129. (817)921-7822. FAX: (817)921-7333. Director: Judy Alter. Editor: A.T. Row. Estab. 1966. Publishes hardcover originals, some reprints. Averages 8 titles/year; receives 100 submissions annually. 10% of books from first-time authors; 75% of books from unagented writers. Subsidy publishes (nonauthor) 10% of books. Pays royalty. Publishes book an average of 16 months after acceptance. Reports "as soon as possible."

Nonfiction: American studies, juvenile (Chaparral Books, 10 and up), Texana, literature and criticism. "We are looking for good scholarly monographs, other serious scholarly work and regional titles of significance." Query. Reviews artwork/photos as part of ms package.

Recent Nonfiction Title: *Between the Enemy and Texas*, by Anne Bailey.

Fiction: Adult and young adult regional fiction. Query.

Recent Fiction Title: *The Heirs of Franklin Woodstock*, by Benjamin Capps.

Tips: "Regional and/or Texana nonfiction or fiction have best chance of breaking into our firm."

TEXAS WESTERN PRESS, Imprint of The University of Texas at El Paso, El Paso TX 79968-0633. (915)747-5688. Director: Dale L. Walker. Estab. 1952. Imprint is Southwestern Studies. Publishes hardcover and paperback originals. Publishes 7-8 titles/year. "This is a university press, 40 years old; we do offer a standard 10% royalty contract on our hardcover books and on some of our paperbacks as well. We try to treat our authors professionally, produce handsome, long-lived books and aim for quality, rather than quantity of titles carrying our imprint." Free book catalog and ms guidelines. Reports in 3 months.

Nonfiction: Scholarly books. Historic and cultural accounts of the Southwest (West Texas, New Mexico, northern Mexico and Arizona). Occasional technical titles. "Our *Southwestern Studies* use manuscripts of up to 30,000 words. Our hardback books range from 30,000 words up. The writer should use good exposition in his work. Most of our work requires documentation. We favor a scholarly, but not overly pedantic, style. We specialize in superior book design." Query with outlines. Follow *Chicago Manual of Style*.

Recent Nonfiction Title: *The Wars of Peggy Hull*, by Wilda M. Smith and Eleanor A. Bogart.

Tips: "Texas Western Press is interested in books relating to the history of Hispanics in the U.S., will experiment with photo-documentary books, and is interested in seeing more 'popular' history and books on Southwestern culture/life."

THEATRE ARTS BOOKS, Imprint of Routledge, Chapman & Hall, Inc., 29 W. 35th St., New York NY 10001. (212)244-3336. Editorial Director: William P. Germano. Publishes hardcover and trade paperback originals. Pays royalty. Publishes ms an average of 1 year after acceptance. Reports in 6 weeks. Use *Chicago Manual of Style* for ms guidelines.

Nonfiction: Drama and theater. Subjects include acting, directing, lighting, costume, dance, staging, etc. "We publish only books of broad general interest to actors, directors and theater technicians, especially books that could be useful in college classrooms. Most of our authors have had long experience in professional theater. Topics that are very narrowly focused (a costume book on women's shoes in the eighteenth century, for example) would not be acceptable. We no longer publish original plays." Query with outline, synopsis and author's qualifications.

THE THEOSOPHICAL PUBLISHING HOUSE, Subsidiary of The Theosophical Society in America, 306 W. Geneva Rd., Wheaton IL 60187. (708)665-0130. FAX: (708)665-8791. Senior Editor: Shirley Nicholson. Estab. 1968. Imprint is Quest Books. Publishes trade paperback originals. Averages 12 titles/year; receives 750-1,000 submissions annually. 50-60% of books from first-time authors; 95% of books from unagented writers. Average print order for a writer's first book is 5,000. Pays 12½% royalty on net price; offers average $1,500 advance. Publishes book an average of 9 months after acceptance. Simultaneous submissions OK. Reports in 2 weeks on queries, 2 months on mss. Free book catalog; ms guidelines for SASE.

Nonfiction: Subjects include self-development, self-help, philosophy (holistic), psychology (transpersonal), Eastern and Western religions, comparative religion, holistic implications in science, health and healing, yoga, meditation and astrology. "TPH seeks works that are compatible with the theosophical philosophy. Our audience includes the 'New Age' community, seekers in all religions, general public, professors, and health professionals. No submissions that do not fit the needs outlined above." Accepts nonfiction translations. Query or submit outline/synopsis and sample chapters. Reviews artwork/photos as part of ms package.

Recent Nonfiction Title: *Music: Physician for Times to Come*, by Don G. Campbell.

Tips: "The writer has the best chance of selling our firm a book that illustrates a connection between spiritually-oriented philosophy or viewpoint and some field of current interest."

THOMAS PUBLICATIONS, Subsidiary of Thomas Graphics, Inc., Box 33244, Austin TX 78764. (512)832-0355. Contact: Ralph D. Thomas. Publishes trade paperback originals and reprints. Averages 8-10 titles/year; receives 20-30 submissions annually. 90% of books from first-time authors; 90% of books from unagented writers. Pays 10-15% royalty on wholesale or retail price, or makes outright purchase of $500-2,000. Publishes book an average of 1 year after acceptance. Simultaneous submissions OK. Reports in 2 weeks on queries; 1 month on mss. Book catalog $1.

Nonfiction: How-to, reference and textbook. Subjects include sociology and investigation and investigative techniques. "We are looking for hardcore investigative methods books, manuals on how to make more dollars in private investigation, private investigative marketing techniques, and specialties in the investigative professions." Query or submit outline/synopsis and sample chapters. Reviews artwork/photos as part of ms package.

Recent Nonfiction Title: *How to Investigate by Computer: 1990*, by Ralph Thomas and Leroy Cook.

Tips: "Our audience includes private investigators, those wanting to break into investigation, related trades such as auto repossessors, private process servers, news reporters, and related security trades."

*THREE CONTINENTS PRESS, 1901 Pennsylvania Ave. NW, Washington DC 20006. Publisher/Editor-in-Chief: Donald E. Herdeck. General Editor: Usha Nagarajan. Estab. 1973. Publishes hardcover and paperback originals and reprints. Averages 20-30 titles/year. Receives 200 submissions annually. 15% of books from first-time authors; 100% of books from unagented writers. Average print order for a writer's first book is 1,000. Subsidy publishes (nonauthor) 5% of books. Pays 10% royalty; advance "only on delivery of complete manuscript which is found acceptable; usually $300." Simultaneous submissions OK. State availability of photos/illustrations. Reports in 2 months. Book catalog and guidelines for 9×12 SAE.

Nonfiction and Fiction: Specializes in African, Caribbean, Middle Eastern (Arabic and Persian) and Asian-Pacific literature, criticism and translation, Third World literature and history. Scholarly, well-prepared mss; creative writing. Fiction, poetry, criticism, history and translations of creative writing. "We search for books that will make clear the complexity and value of non-western literature and culture, including bilingual texts (Arabic language/English translations). We are always interested in genuine contributions to understanding non-western culture." Length: 50,000-125,000 words. Query. "Please do not submit manuscript unless we ask for it. We prefer an outline, and an annotated table of contents, for works of nonfiction; and a synopsis, a plot summary (one to three pages), for fiction. For poetry, send two or three sample poems." Reviews artwork/photos as part of ms package.

Recent Nonfiction Title: *The Imperishable Empire: A Study of British Fiction on India*, by Rashna B. Singh.

Recent Fiction Title: *The Fantasy Eaters, Stories from Fiji*, by Subramani.

Tips: "We need a *polished* translation, or original prose or poetry by non-Western authors *only*."

THUNDER'S MOUTH PRESS, #45, 54 Greene St., New York NY 10013. (212)226-0277. Publisher: Neil Ortenberg. Publishes hardcover and trade paperback originals and reprints. Averages 15 titles/year; receives 1,000 submissions annually. 10% of books from unagented writers. Average print order for a writer's first book is 7,500. Pays 5-10% royalty on retail price; offers average $5,000 advance. Publishes book an average of 8 months after acceptance. Reports in 3 months on queries. Does not consider unsolicited manuscripts.

Nonfiction: Biography, politics, popular culture. Publishes 5-10/year. Query only.

Fiction: Query only.

TICKNOR & FIELDS, Imprint of Houghton-Mifflin, 215 Park Ave. S., New York NY 10003. (212)410-5800. Editorial Director: John Herman. Estab. 1980. Publishes hardcover originals. Firm averages 14 titles/year; imprint averages 30 titles/year. Receives 500 submissions/year. 10% of books from first-time authors; 100% of submissions from agents. Does *not* accept unsolicited mss. Pays royalty.

Nonfiction and Fiction: General subjects. Query.

TIDEWATER PUBLISHERS, Imprint of Cornell Maritime Press, Inc., P.O. Box 456, Centreville MD 21617. (301)758-1075. Contact: Associate Editor. Estab. 1938. Publishes hardcover and paperback originals. Imprint averages 7-9 titles/year. Receives 150 submissions/year. 41% of books from first-time authors. 99% from unagented writers. Pays 7½-15% royalty on retail price. Publishes book an average of 1 year after acceptance. Simultaneous submissions OK. Query for electronic submissions. Reports in 2 weeks on queries; 1 month on mss. Free book catalog and manuscript guidelines.

Nonfiction: Coffee table books, cookbook, how-to, illustrated book, juvenile, reference, self-help, technical, textbook. Subjects include regional. Query. Submit outline/synopsis and sample chapters. Reviews artwork/photos as part of ms package.

Recent Nonfiction Title: *Harvesting the Chesapeake*, by Larry S. Chowning.

Fiction: Nothing other than regional juvenile fiction. Query. Submit outline/synopsis and sample chapters.

Recent Fiction Title: *Oswald and the Timberdoodles*, by Priscilla Cummings, with illustrations by A.R. Cohen (juvenile).

Tips: "Our audience is made up of readers interested in works that are specific to the Chesapeake Bay and Delmarva Peninsula area."

TIMBER PRESS, INC., 9999 SW Wilshire, Portland OR 97225. (503)292-0745. FAX: (503)292-6607. Publisher: Robert B. Conklin. Estab. 1976. Imprints are Dioscorides Press (botany), Amadeus Press (music) and Areopagitica Press (history). Publishes hardcover and paperback originals. Publishes 40 titles/year; receives 300-400 submissions annually. 90% of books from first-time authors; 100% of books from unagented writers. Pays 10-15% royalty; sometimes offers advance to cover costs of artwork and final ms completion. Publishes book an average of 1 year after acceptance. Query for electronic submissions. Reports in 2 months. Book catalog for 9 × 12 SAE with 3 first class stamps.

Nonfiction: Horticulture (ornamental and economic), botany, plant sciences, natural history, Northwest regional material, forestry, serious music and history. Accepts nonfiction translations from all languages. Query or submit outline/synopsis and 3-4 sample chapters. Reviews artwork/photos as part of ms package.

Recent Nonfiction Title: *Enrico Caruso*, by Caruso and Farkas.

Tips: "The writer has the best chance of selling our firm good books on botany, plant science, horticulture, forestry, agriculture, serious music and history."

TIME-LIFE BOOKS INC., Division of Time Warner Inc., 777 Duke St., Alexandria VA 22314. (703)838-7000. Managing Editor: Tom Flaherty. Publishes hardcover originals. Averages 40 titles/year. Books are almost entirely staff-generated and staff-produced, and distribution is primarily through mail order sale. Query to the Director of Corporate Development.

Nonfiction: "General interest books. Most books tend to be heavily illustrated (by staff), with text written by assigned non-staff authors. We very rarely accept mss or book ideas submitted from outside our staff." Length: open.

Recent Nonfiction Title: *Mysteries of the Unknown* (series).

TIMES BOOKS, Imprint of Random House, Inc., 201 E. 50 St., New York NY 10022. (212)872-8110. Vice President and Publisher: Peter Osnos. Editorial Director: Steve Wasserman. Publishes hardcover and paperback originals and reprints. Publishes 45 titles/year. Pays royalty; average advance. Publishes book an average of 1 year after acceptance.

Nonfiction: Business/economics, science and medicine, history, biography, women's issues, the family, cookbooks, current affairs and sports. Accepts only solicited manuscripts. Reviews artwork/photos as part of ms package.

Recent Nonfiction Title: *The American Heart Association Low Fat Low Cholesterol Diet*, by Scott Grundy M.D.

TOR BOOKS, Subsidiary of St. Martin's Press, 49 W. 24th St., 9th Floor, New York NY 10010. (212)741-3100. Publisher: Tom Doherty. Estab. 1981. Publishes mass market, hardcover and trade paperback originals and reprints. Averages 250 books/year. Pays 6-8% royalty; offers negotiable advance. Book catalog for 9 × 12 SASE.

Fiction: Science fiction, fantasy, horror, technothrillers, "women's" suspense, American historicals. "We prefer an extensive chapter-by-chapter synopsis and the first 3 chapters complete." Prefers agented mss or proposals.

Recent Fiction Title: *The Great Hunt*, by Robert Jordan (fantasy).

Tips: "We're never short of good sci fi or fantasy, but we're always open to solid, technologically knowledgeable hard science fiction or thrillers by writers with solid expertise."

*TRANSACTION BOOKS, Rutgers University, New Brunswick NJ 08903. (201)932-2280. FAX: (201)932-3138. President: I.L. Horowitz. Publisher: Scott Bramson. Book Division Director: Mary E. Curtis. Publishes hardcover and paperback originals and reprints. Specializes in scholarly social science books. Averages 135 titles/year; receives 800 submissions annually. 15% of books from first-time authors; 85% of books from unagented writers. Average print order for a writer's first book is 1,000. Subsidy publishes 10% of books. Royalty "depends on individual contract; we've gone anywhere from 2% edited to 15% authored." No advance. Publishes book an average of 10 months after acceptance. Electronic submissions OK, but requires hard copy also. Reports in 4 months. Book catalog and ms guidelines for SASE.

Nonfiction: Americana, biography, economics, history, law, medicine and psychiatry, music, philosophy, politics, psychology, reference, scientific, sociology, technical and textbooks. "All must be scholarly social science or related." Strong emphasis on applied social research. Query or submit outline/synopsis. "Do not submit sample chapters. We evaluate complete manuscripts only." Accepts nonfiction translations. Use *Chicago Manual of Style*. Looks for "scholarly content, presentation, methodology, and target audience." State availability of photos/illustrations and send one photocopied example. Reviews artwork/photos as part of ms package.

Recent Nonfiction Title: *Authority in Islam*, by Hamid Dabashi (religion/sociology).

TRANSPORTATION TRAILS, Imprint of National Bus Trader, Inc., 9698 W. Judson Rd., Polo IL 61064. (815)946-2341. FAX: (815)946-2347. Editor: Larry Plachino. Estab. 1977. Publishes hardcover, trade paperback and mass market paperback originals. Firm averages 8 titles/year. Receives 10 submissions/year. 50% of books from first-time authors. 100% from unagented writers. Pays 10-15% on retail price. Publishes book an average of 1 year after acceptance. Simultaneous submissions OK. Reports in 2 weeks on queries; 2 months on mss. Free book catalog and manuscript guidelines.
Nonfiction: Subject includes travel. "We are only interested in transportation history—prefer electric interurban railroads or trolley lines but will consider steam locomotives, horsecars, buses, aviation and maritime." Query. Reviews artwork/photos as part of ms package.
Recent Nonfiction Title: *Sunset Lines—The Story of the Chicago Aurora and Elgin Railroads*, by Larry Plachno.

TRAVEL KEYS, P.O. Box 160691, Sacramento CA 95816. (916)452-5200. Publisher: Peter B. Manston. Estab. 1984. Publishes hardcover and trade paperback originals. Averages 4 titles/year; receives 35 submissions annually. 60% of books from first-time authors; 90% of books from unagented writers. Pays 6-15% royalty or work for hire. Offers minimum advance. Publishes book an average of 1 year after acceptance. Simultaneous submissions OK if mentioned in initial proposal. Query for electronic submissions. Reports in 1 month. Book catalog for #10 SAE with 2 first class stamps.
Nonfiction: Travel, antiques and flea market guides, and home security. "We need carefully researched, practical travel manuscripts." Full disclosure of sponsored travel is required. Submit outline/synopsis and sample chapters. Reviews artwork/photos as part of ms package.
Recent Nonfiction Title: *Disneyworld for Kids of All Ages*, by Maria Saine.

‡TREND BOOK DIVISION, P.O. Box 611, St. Petersburg FL 33731. (813)821-5800. Chairman: Andrew Barnes. President: Andrew Corty. Publisher: Paul Tash. Estab. 1958. Publishes paperback originals and reprints. Specializes in books on Florida—all categories. Pays royalty; no advance. Books are marketed through *Florida Trend* magazine. Publishes book an average of 8 months after acceptance. Reports in 1 month.
Nonfiction: Business, economics, history, law, politics, reference, textbooks and travel. "All books pertain to Florida." Query. Reviews artwork/photos as part of ms package.
Tips: "We are shifting to more emphasis on books of a Florida business/economics nature."

‡TROUBADOR PRESS, Imprint of Price Stern Sloan, Inc., Suite 650, 11150 Olympic Blvd., Los Angeles CA 90064. Contact: Editorial Assistant. Estab. 1969. Other imprints are HP Books and Doodle Art. Publishes paperback originals. Averages 4 titles/year; receives 300 submissions annually. 95% of books from unagented writers. Average print order for a writer's first book is 10,000. Pays royalty. Offers average $500 advance. Publishes book an average of 6 months after acceptance. Reports in 3 months. Book catalog and ms guidelines for SASE.
Nonfiction: "Troubador Press publishes mainly, but is not limited to, children's activity books: coloring, cut-out, mazes, games, paper dolls, etc. All titles feature original art and exceptional graphics. Age range varies. We like books which have the potential to develop into series." Query or submit outline/synopsis and 2-3 sample chapters with conciseness and clarity of a good idea. Reviews artwork as part of ms package. "Do not send original artwork."
Recent Nonfiction Title: *Zoo Animals Action Set 2*, by M. Whyte and artist Dan Smith (play book and environment dictionary).
Tips: "We continue to publish new authors along with established writers/artists. We feel the mix is good and healthy. Queries/mss may be routed to other editors in the publishing group."

TSR, INC., P.O. Box 756, Lake Geneva WI 53147. (414)248-3625. Managing Editor: Mary Kirchoff. Estab. 1975. Imprints are TSR™ Books, Buck Rogers®/XXVc™ Books, Dragonlance® Books, Forgotten Realms™ Books, Spelljammer™ Books, Ravenloft™ Books, and Dark Sun™ Books. Publishes trade paperback originals. Firm averages 70-80 titles/year; imprint averages 20-25 titles/year. Receives 250 submissions/year. 30-40% of books from first-time authors. 5% from unagented authors. Pays 4% royalty on retail price. Offers $4,000 average advance. Publishes book an average of 1 year after acceptance. Simultaneous submissions OK. Reports in 1 month on queries; 6 weeks on mss.
Nonfiction: "All of our nonfiction books are generated in-house."
Fiction: Fantasy, horror, mystery and science fiction. "We have a very small market for good science fiction and fantasy for the TSR Book line, but also need samples from writers willing to do work-for-hire for our other lines. We do not need occult, new age, or adult theme fiction. Nor will we consider excessively violent or gory fantasy, science fiction or horror." Query and write for guidelines. Submit outline/synopsis and sample chapters or ms.
Recent Fiction Title: *The Parched Sea*, by Troy Denning.
Tips: "Our audience is comprised of highly imaginative 12-40 year-old males."

‡**TWAYNE PUBLISHERS**, Division of G.K. Hall & Co., Subsidiary of Macmillan, Inc., 70 Lincoln St., Boston MA 02111. (617)423-3990. Publishes hardcover and paperback originals. Publishes 100 titles/year; receives 1,000 submissions annually. 5% of books from first-time authors; 90% of books from unagented writers. Pays royalty. Reports in 3 months on queries.
Nonfiction: Publishes scholarly books and volumes in and out of series for the general reader. Literary criticism, biography, history, women's studies, art history, performing arts, current affairs and social science. Query only.
Recent Nonfiction Title: *Henry R. Luce and The Rise of the American News Media*, by James L. Baughman.
Tips: "Queries may be routed to other editors in the publishing group. Unsolicited mss will not be read."

TWIN PEAKS PRESS, P.O. Box 129, Vancouver WA 98666. (206)694-2462. President: Helen Hecker. Estab. 1984. Publishes hardcover originals and reprints and trade paperback originals and reprints. Averages 7-10 titles/year. Receives 1,000 submissions/year. 25% of books from first-time authors. 100% from unagented writers. Payment varies—individual agreement. Publishes book an average of 6 months after acceptance. Simultaneous submissions OK. Does not report unless interested. Do *not* send unsolicited mss.
Nonfiction: Cookbook, how-to, reference and self-help. Subjects include business and economics, cooking, foods and nutrition, health/medicine, hobbies, recreation, sociology, sports and travel. Query with outline in writing only.
Recent Nonfiction Title: *All About Sewing Machines*, by Robert Johanson.

*****UAHC PRESS**, Union of American Hebrew Congregations, 838 5th Ave., New York NY 10021. (212)249-0100. Managing Director: Stuart L. Benick. Trade Acquisitions Editor: Aron Hirt-Manheimer. Text Acquisitions Editor: David Kasakove. Estab. 1873. Publishes hardcover and trade paperback originals. Averages 15 titles/year. 60% of books from first-time authors; 90% of books from unagented writers. Subsidy publishes 40% of books. Pays 5-15% royalty on wholesale price. Publishes book an average of 9 months after acceptance. Simultaneous submissions OK. Book catalog and ms guidelines for SASE.
Nonfiction: Illustrated, juvenile and Jewish textbooks. "Looking for authors that can share an enthusiasm about Judaism with young readers. We welcome first-time authors." Reviews artwork/photos as part of ms package.
Fiction: Jewish religion. "We publish books that teach values."

ULI, THE URBAN LAND INSTITUTE, 1090 Vermont Ave. NW, Washington DC 20005. (202)289-8500. Staff Vice President of Publications: Frank H. Spink, Jr. Estab. 1936. Publishes hardcover and trade paperback originals. Averages 15-20 titles/year. Receives 20 submissions annually. No books from first-time authors; 100% of books from unagented writers. Pays 10% royalty on gross sales. Offers advance of $1,500-2,000. Publishes book an average of 6 months after acceptance. Query for electronic submissions. Book catalog and writer's guidelines for 9×12 SAE.
Nonfiction: Technical books on real estate development and land planning. "The majority of mss are created in-house by research staff. We acquire two or three outside authors to fill schedule and subject areas where our list has gaps. We are not interested in real estate sales, brokerages, appraisal, making money in real estate, opinion, personal point of view, or mss negative toward growth and development." Query. Reviews artwork/photos as part of ms package.
Recent Nonfiction Title: *Carrots and Sticks: New Downtown Zoning*, by Terry Jill Lassar.

ULTRALIGHT PUBLICATIONS, INC., P.O. Box 234, Hammelstown PA 17036. (717)566-0468. Editor: Michael A. Markowski. Estab. 1981. Publishes hardcover and trade paperback originals. Averages 6 titles/year; receives 30 submissions annually. 50% of books from first-time authors; 100% of books from unagented writers. Average print order for a writer's first book is 5,000. Pays 10-15% royalty on

An asterisk preceding a listing indicates that subsidy publishing or co-publishing (where author pays part or all of publishing costs) is available. Firms whose subsidy programs comprise more than 50% of their total publishing activities are listed at the end of the Book Packagers and Producers section.

wholesale price; buys some mss outright. Offers average $1,000-1,500 advance. Publishes book an average of 9 months after acceptance. Simultaneous submissions OK. Reports in 3 weeks on queries; 2 months on mss. Book catalog and ms guidelines for #10 SAE with 2 first class stamps.

Nonfiction: How-to, technical on hobbies (model airplanes, model cars, and model boats) and aviation. Publishes for "aviation buffs, dreamers and enthusiasts. We are looking for titles in the homebuilt, sport and general aviation fields. We are interested in how-to, technical and reference books of short to medium length that will serve recognized and emerging aviation needs." Also interested in popular health, medical, and fitness for the general public, self-help, motivation and success. Query or submit outline/synopsis and 3 sample chapters. Reviews artwork/photos as part of ms package.

Recent Nonfiction Title: *Canard: A Revolution in Flight*, by Lennon (aviation history).

UMBRELLA BOOKS, Imprint of Epicenter Press Inc., 18821 64th Ave. NE, Seattle WA 98155. (206)485-6822. Publishes 4-6 titles/year. Pays royalty on retail price. Publishes book an average of 6 months after acceptance. Simultaneous submissions OK. Query for electronic submissions. Reports in 1 month on queries. Manuscript guidelines for #10 SASE.

Nonfiction: Travel (Pacific Northwest). Query; do *not* send photos.

Recent Nonfiction Title: *Umbrella Guide to Bicycling the Oregon Coast*.

UNION SQUARE PRESS, Imprint of NJ Sambul & Co., Inc., 5 E. 16th St., New York NY 10003. (212)924-2800. FAX: (212)675-5479. Publisher: Nathan J. Sambul. Estab. 1987. Publishes trade paperback originals. Firm averages 4 titles/year. 50% of books from first-time authors. 90% from unagented writers. Pays 10% on list price. Offers $500-1,000 average advance. Publishes book an average of 1 year after acceptance. Simultaneous submissions OK. Query for electronic submissions. Reports in 3 months.

Nonfiction: How-to, reference and technical. Subjects include business and economics, science (broadcast engineering) and media. Submit outline/synopsis and sample chapters. Reviews artwork/photos as part of ms package.

Recent Nonfiction Titles: *HDTV: The Politics, Policies, and Economics of Tomorrow's Television*, by John F. Rice.

‡UNITED RESOURCE PRESS, 4521 Campus Dr. #388, Irvine CA 92715. General Manager: Sally Black. Publishes trade paperback and mass market paperback originals. Publishes 6 titles/year. 50% of books from first-time authors. 50% from unagented writers. Pays 3-7% on retail price. Publishes book an average of 1 year after acceptance. Simultaneous submissions OK. Query for electronic submissions. Reports in 2 months.

Nonfiction: Personal finance. Subjects include money/finance. "For next two years we will focus on personal finance (primary)." Submit outline/synopsis and sample chapters and complete ms.

Recent Nonfiction Title: *Marriage and Money*.

Tips: "Write for or buy samples of the publishers' best selling or favorite titles to see what they want."

*UNIVELT, INC., P.O. Box 28130, San Diego CA 92198. (619)746-4005. Publisher: H. Jacobs. Estab. 1970. Imprints are American Astronautical Society, National Space Society, and Lunar & Planetary Institute. Publishes hardcover originals. Averages 8 titles/year; receives 20 submissions annually. 5% of books from first-time authors; 5% of books from unagented writers. Subsidy publishes (nonauthor) 10% of books. Average print order for a writer's first book is 1,000-2,000. Pays 10% royalty on actual sales; no advance. Publishes book an average of 4 months after acceptance. Reports in 1 month. Book catalog and ms guidelines for SASE.

Nonfiction: Publishes in the field of aerospace, especially astronautics and technical communications, but including application of aerospace technology to Earth's problems, also astronomy. Submit outline/synopsis and 1-2 sample chapters. Reviews artwork/photos as part of ms package.

Recent Nonfiction Title: *To Catch a Flying Star, A Scientific Theory of UFOs*.

Tips: "Writers have the best chance of selling manuscripts on the history of astronautics (we have a history series) and astronautics/spaceflight subjects. We publish for the American Astronautical Society. Queries/mss may be routed to other editors in the publishing group."

UNIVERSITY OF ALABAMA PRESS, Box 870380, Tuscaloosa AL 35487. Director: Malcolm MacDonald. Estab. 1945. Publishes hardcover originals. Averages 40 titles/year; receives 200 submissions annually. 80% of books from first-time authors; 100% of books from unagented writers. "Pays maximum 10% royalty on wholesale price; no advance." Publishes book an average of 16 months after acceptance. Free book catalog; ms guidelines for SASE.

Nonfiction: Biography, history, philosophy, politics, religion, literature and anthropology. Considers upon merit almost any subject of scholarly interest, but specializes in linguistics and philology, political science and public administration, literary criticism and biography, philosophy and history. Accepts nonfiction translations. Reviews artwork/photos as part of ms package.

Recent Nonfiction Title: *Until Justice Rolls Down: The Birmingham Church Bombing Case*, by Frank Sikora.

UNIVERSITY OF ALASKA PRESS, 1st Floor Gruening Bldg., UAF, Fairbanks AK 99775-1580. (907)474-6389. FAX: (907)474-7225. Manager: Debbie Van Stone. Estab. 1927. Imprints are Ramuson Library Historical Translation Series, Oral Biographies, and Classic Reprints. Publishes hardcover originals and trade paperback originals and reprints. Averages 5-10 titles/year. Receives 100 submissions/year. 0% of books from first-time authors; 100% from unagented writers. Pays 7½-10% royalty on net sales. Publishes book an average of 2 years after acceptance. Simultaneous submissions OK. Query for electronic submissions. Reports in 6 weeks. Book catalog free on request.
Nonfiction: Biography, reference, technical, textbook, scholarly nonfiction relating to Alaska-circum-polar north. Subjects include agriculture/horticulture, Americana (Alaskana), animals, anthropology/archaeology, art/architecture, education, ethnic, government/politics, health/medicine, history, language, military/war, nature/environment, regional, science and translation. Nothing that isn't northern or circumpolar. Query or submit complete ms. Reviews artwork/photos as part of ms package.
Recent Nonfiction Title: *Birds of the Seward Peninsula*, by Brina Kessel (reference).
Tips: "Writers have the best chance with scholarly, nonfiction relating to Alaska, the circumpolar north and North Pacific Rim. Our audience is made up of scholars, historians, students, libraries, universities, individuals."

UNIVERSITY OF ARIZONA PRESS, 1230 N. Park Ave., No. 102, Tucson AZ 85719. (602)621-1441. Director: Stephen Cox. Estab. 1959. Publishes hardcover and paperback originals and reprints. Averages 50 titles/year; receives 300-400 submissions annually. 30% of books from first-time authors; 95% of books from unagented writers. Average print order is 1,500. Royalty terms vary; usual starting point for scholarly monograph is after sale of first 1,000 copies. Publishes book an average of 1 year after acceptance. Query for electronic submissions. Reports in three months. Book catalog for 9 × 12 SAE; ms guidelines for #10 SASE.
Nonfiction: Scholarly books about anthropology, Arizona, American West, archaeology, environmental science, global change, Latin America, Native Americans, natural history, space sciences and women's studies. Query and submit outline, list of illustrations and sample chapters. Reviews artwork/photos as part of ms package.
Recent Nonfiction Title: *The View from Officers' Row*, by Sherry Smith.
Tips: "Perhaps the most common mistake a writer might make is to offer a book manuscript or proposal to a house whose list he or she has not studied carefully. Editors rejoice in receiving material that is clearly targeted to the house's list, 'I have approached your firm because my books complement your past publications in. . .,' presented in a straightforward, businesslike manner."

THE UNIVERSITY OF ARKANSAS PRESS, Fayetteville AR 72701. (501)575-3246. FAX: (501)575-6044. Director: Miller Williams. Estab. 1980. Publishes hardcover and trade paperback originals and hardcover reprints. Averages 36 titles/year; receives 4,000 submissions annually. 30% of books from first-time authors; 90% of books from unagented writers. Pays 10% royalty on net receipts. Publishes book an average of 18 months after acceptance. Simultaneous (if so informed) submissions OK. Query for electronic submissions. Reports in 3 weeks on queries; 6 weeks on mss. Ms guidelines for #10 SAE and 2 first class stamps.
Nonfiction: Biography and literature. Subjects include Americana, history, humanities, nature, general politics and history of politics, and sociology. "Our current needs include literary criticism—especially on contemporary authors, history and biography. We won't consider manuscripts for texts, juvenile or religious studies, or anything requiring a specialized or exotic vocabulary." Query or submit outline/synopsis and sample chapters.
Recent Nonfiction Title: *The Cape of Storms*, by Anthony Heard.
Fiction: "Works of high literary merit; short stories; rarely novels. No genre fiction." Query.
Recent Fiction Title: *Plato at Scratch Daniel's*, by Ed Falco.
Poetry: "Because of small list, query first." Arkansas Poetry Award offered for publication of first book. Write for contest rules.
Recent Poetry Title: *The Collected Poems of Henri Coulette*.

UNIVERSITY OF CALIFORNIA PRESS, 2120 Berkeley Way, Berkeley CA 94720. Director: James H. Clark. Assistant Director: Lynne E. Withey. Estab. 1893. Los Angeles office: 405 Hilgard Ave., Los Angeles CA 90024-1373. New York office: Room 513, 50 E. 42 St., New York NY 10017. London office: University Presses of California, Columbia, and Princeton, Avonlea, 10 Watlington Rd., Cowley, Oxford OX4 5NF England. Publishes hardcover and paperback originals and reprints. "On books likely to do more than return their costs, a standard royalty contract beginning at 7% on net receipts is paid; on paperbacks it is less." Publishes 200 titles/year. Queries are always advisable, accompanied by outlines or sample material. Accepts nonfiction translations. Send to Berkeley address. Reports vary, depending on the subject. Enclose return postage.

Nonfiction: "Most of our publications are hardcover nonfiction written by scholars." Publishes scholarly books including art, literary studies, social sciences, natural sciences and some high-level popularizations. No length preferences.

Recent Nonfiction Title: *Alexander to Actium, The Historical Evolution of the Hellenistic Age*, by Peter Green.

Fiction and Poetry: Publishes fiction and poetry only in translation, usually in bilingual editions.

*UNIVERSITY OF ILLINOIS PRESS, 54 E. Gregory, Champaign IL 61820. (217)333-0950. FAX: (217)244-8082. Director/Editor: Richard L. Wentworth. Estab. 1918. Publishes hardcover and trade paperback originals and reprints. Averages 90-100 titles/year. 50% of books from first-time authors; 95% of books from unagented writers. Subsidy publishes (nonauthor) 30% of books. Pays 0-10% royalty on net sales; offers average $1,000-1,500 advance (rarely). Publishes book an average of 1 year after acceptance. Query for electronic submissions. Reports in 1 week on queries; 3 months on mss. Free book catalog.

Nonfiction: Biography, reference and scholarly books. Subjects include Americana, business and economics, history (especially American history), music (especially American music), politics, sociology, sports and literature. Always looking for "solid scholarly books in American history, especially social history; books on American popular music, and books in the broad area of American studies." Query with outline/synopsis.

Recent Nonfiction Title: *Crazeology: The Autobiography of a Chicago Jazzman*, by Bud Freeman.

Fiction: Ethnic, experimental and mainstream. "We publish 2-4 collections of stories by individual writers each year. We do not publish novels." Query.

Recent Fiction Title: *Falling Free*, by Barry Targan (stories).

Tips: "Serious scholarly books that are broad enough and well-written enough to appeal to non-specialists are doing well for us in today's market. Writers of nonfiction whose primary goal is to earn money (rather than get promoted in an academic position) are advised to try at least a dozen commercial publishers before thinking about offering the work to a university press."

UNIVERSITY OF IOWA PRESS, 119 W. Park Rd., Iowa City IA 52242. (319)335-2000. FAX: (319)335-2055. Director: Paul Zimmer. Estab. 1969. Publishes hardcover and paperback originals. Averages 30 titles/year; receives 300-400 submissions annually. 30% of books from first-time authors; 95% of books from unagented writers. Average print order for a writer's first book is 1,200-1,500. Pays 7-10% royalty on net price. "We market mostly by direct mailing of flyers to groups with special interests in our titles and by advertising in trade and scholarly publications." Publishes book an average of 1 year after acceptance. Query for electronic submissions. Reports within 4 months. Free book catalog and ms guidelines.

Nonfiction: Publishes anthropology, archaeology, British and American literary studies, history (Victorian, U.S., German, medieval, Latin American), aviation history, history of photography and natural history. Currently publishes the Iowa Short Fiction Award and Edwin Ford Piper Poetry Award selections. "Please query regarding poetry or fiction before sending manuscript. Looks for evidence of original research; reliable sources; clarity of organization, complete development of theme with documentation and supportive footnotes and/or bibliography; and a substantive contribution to knowledge in the field treated." Query or submit outline/synopsis. Use *Chicago Manual of Style*. Reviews artwork/photos as part of ms package.

Recent Nonfiction Title: *The Letters of Rudyard Kipling*.

UNIVERSITY OF MASSACHUSETTS PRESS, P.O. Box 429, Amherst MA 01004. (413)545-2217. FAX: (413)545-1226. Director: Bruce Wilcox. Estab. 1963. Publishes hardcover and paperback originals, reprints and imports. Averages 30 titles/year; receives 600 submissions annually. 20% of books from first-time authors; 90% of books from unagented writers. Average print order for a writer's first book is 1,500. Royalties generally 10% of net income. Advance rarely offered. No author subsidies accepted. Publishes book an average of 1 year after acceptance. Query for electronic submissions. Preliminary report in 1 month. Free book catalog.

Nonfiction: Publishes Afro-American studies, art and architecture, biography, criticism, history, natural history, philosophy, poetry, public policy, sociology and women's studies in original and reprint editions. Accepts nonfiction translations. Submit outline/synopsis and 1-2 sample chapters. Reviews artwork/photos as part of ms package.

Recent Nonfiction Title: *Seabrook Station: Citizen Politics and Nuclear Power*, by Henry F. Bedford.

‡UNIVERSITY OF MICHIGAN PRESS, 839 Greene St., Ann Arbor MI 48106. (313)764-4388. FAX: (313)936-0456. Director: Colin Day. Editors: Mary C. Erwin, LeAnn Fields, Joyce Harrison, Ellen Bauerle. Estab. 1930. Imprint is Ann Arbor Paperbacks. Publishes hardcover and paperback originals and reprints. Averages 70-80 titles/year. Pays royalty on net price; offers advance. Query for electronic submissions. Reports in 2 months. Free book catalog.

Nonfiction: Archaeology, advanced textbooks, anthropology, classics, economics, English as a second language, Great Lakes regional, history, law, literary criticism, music, political science, reference, theater, women's studies. Query first.

UNIVERSITY OF NEBRASKA PRESS, 901 N. 17th St., Lincoln NE 68588-0520. Editor-in-Chief: Willis G. Regier. Estab. 1941. Publishes hardcover and paperback originals and reprints. Specializes in scholarly nonfiction, some regional books; reprints of Western Americana; and natural history. Averages 50 new titles, 50 paperback reprints (*Bison Books*)/year; receives more than 1,000 submissions annually. 25% of books from first-time authors; 95% of books from unagented writers. Average print order for a writer's first book is 1,000. Royalty is usually graduated from 10% on wholesale price for original books; no advance. Reports in 4 months. Book catalog and guidelines for 9 × 12 SAE with 5 first class stamps.

Nonfiction: Publishes Americana, biography, history, nature, photography, psychology, sports, literature, agriculture and American Indian themes. Accepts nonfiction and fiction translations but no original fiction. Query. Accepts outline/synopsis, 2 sample chapters and introduction. Looks for "an indication that the author knows his subject thoroughly and interprets it intelligently." Reviews artwork/photos as part of ms package.

Recent Nonfiction Title: *Billy the Kid*, by Robert Utley.

Recent Fiction Title: *Mad Love*, by André Breton (translation).

UNIVERSITY OF NEVADA PRESS, Reno NV 89557. (702)784-6573. FAX: (702)784-1300. Director: Thomas R. Radko. Estab. 1961. Publishes hardcover and paperback originals and reprints. Averages 20 titles/year. 20% of books from first-time authors; 99% of books from unagented writers. Average print order for a writer's first book is 2,000. Pays average of 10% royalty on net price. Publishes book an average of 1 year after acceptance. Preliminary report in 2 months. Free book catalog and ms guidelines.

Nonfiction: Specifically needs regional history and natural history, literature, current affairs, ethnonationalism, gambling and gaming, anthropology, biographies and Basque studies. "We are the first university press to sustain a sound series on Basque studies – New World and Old World." No juvenile books. Submit complete ms. Reviews photocopies of artwork/photos as part of ms package.

Recent Nonfiction Title: *A Time We Knew: Images of Yesterday in the Basque Homeland*, photographs by William Albert Allard, text by Robert Laxalt.

Recent Fiction Title: *That Constant Coyote: California Stories*, by Gerald Haslam.

‡UNIVERSITY OF NEW MEXICO PRESS, 1720 Lomas Blvd. NE, Albuquerque NM 87131-1591. (505)277-2346. Editor: Jeffrey Grathwohl. Publishes hardcover originals and trade paperback originals and reprints. Firm averages 50 titles/year. Receives 500 submissions/year. 12% of books from first-time authors. 90% from unagented writers. Pays up to 15% royalty on wholesale price. Publishes book an average of 1 year after acceptance. Reports in 2 weeks on queries. Free book catalog.

Nonfiction: Biography, illustrated book and scholarly books. Subjects include anthropology/archaeology, art/architecture, ethnic, history and photography. "No how-to, humor, juvenile, self-help, software, technical or textbook." Query. Reviews artwork/photos as part of ms package. Prefer to see photocopies first.

Recent Nonfiction Title: *Recovering the Past*, by Richard A. Gould (archaeology).

Tips: "Most of our authors are academics. A scholarly monograph by an academic has a better chance than anything else. Our audience is a combination of academics and interested by readers."

THE UNIVERSITY OF NORTH CAROLINA PRESS, P.O. Box 2288, Chapel Hill NC 27515-2288. (919)966-3561. Editor-in-Chief: Kate Douglas Torrey. Publishes hardcover and paperback originals. Specializes in scholarly books and regional trade books. Averages 65 titles/year. 70% of books from first-time scholarly authors; 90% of books from unagented writers. Royalty schedule "varies." Occasional advances. Query for electronic submissions. Publishes book an average of 1 year after acceptance. Reports in 5 months. Free book catalog; ms guidelines for SASE.

Nonfiction: "Our major fields are American history, American studies and Southern studies." Also, scholarly books in legal history, Civil War history, literary studies, classics, oral history, folklore, political science, religious studies, historical sociology, Latin American studies. In European studies, focus is on history of the Third Reich, 20th-century Europe, and Holocaust history. Special focus on general interest books on the lore, crafts, cooking, gardening and natural history of the Southeast. Submit outline/synopsis and sample chapters; must follow *Chicago Manual of Style*. Looks for "intellectual excellence and clear writing. We do *not* publish poetry or original fiction." Reviews artwork/photos as part of ms package.

Recent Nonfiction Title: *Walking the Blue Ridge: A Guide to the Trails of the Blue Ridge Parkway*, by Leonard M. Adkins.

UNIVERSITY OF OKLAHOMA PRESS, 1005 Asp Ave., Norman OK 73019. (405)325-5111. FAX: (405)325-4000. Editor-in-Chief: John Drayton. Estab. 1928. Imprint is Oklahoma Paperbacks. Publishes hardcover and paperback originals and reprints. Averages 70 titles/year. Pays royalty comparable to those paid by other publishers for comparable books. Publishes book an average of 12-18 months after acceptance. Query for electronic submissions. Reports in 3 months. Book catalog $1.

Nonfiction: Publishes American Indian studies, Western U.S. history, literary theory, and classical studies. No unsolicited poetry and fiction. Query, including outline, 1-2 sample chapters and author résumé. Use *Chicago Manual of Style* for ms guidelines. Reviews artwork/photos as part of ms package.

Recent Nonfiction Title: *It's Your Misfortune and None of My Own: A History of the American West*, by Richard White.

*UNIVERSITY OF PENNSYLVANIA PRESS, 418 Service Dr., Philadelphia PA 19104. (215)898-6261. FAX: (215)898-0404. Director: Thomas M. Rotell. Estab. 1860. Publishes hardcover and paperback originals and reprints. Averages 70 titles/year; receives 650 submissions annually. 10-20% of books from first-time authors; 99% of books from unagented writers. Subsidy publishes (nonauthor) 4% of books. Subsidy publishing is determined by evaluation obtained by the press from outside specialists; approval by Faculty Editorial Committee and funding organization. Royalty determined on book-by-book basis. Publishes book an average of 9 months after delivery of completed ms. Query for electronic submissions. Reports in 3 months. Do not send unsolicited mss.

Nonfiction: Publishes Americana, biography, business, economics, history, medicine, biological sciences, computer science, physical sciences, law, anthropology, folklore and literary criticism, linguistics, art history, architecture. "Serious books that serve the scholar and the professional." Follow the *Chicago Manual of Style*. Query with outline and letter describing project, state availability of photos and/or illustrations to accompany ms, with copies of illustrations. Do not send ms with query.

Recent Nonfiction Title: *Behind the Disappearances: Argentina's Dirty War Against Human Rights and the U.N.*, by Ian Guest.

Tips: Queries/mss may be routed to other editors in the publishing group.

UNIVERSITY OF PITTSBURGH PRESS, 127 N. Bellefield Ave., Pittsburgh PA 15260. (412)624-4110. FAX: (412)624-7380. Managing Editor: Catherine Marshall. Estab. 1936. Publishes hardcover and trade paperback originals and reprints. Averages 45 titles/year. 5% of books from first-time authors; 100% from unagented writers. Pays royalties on retail price (per contract). Publishes books an average of 1 year after acceptance. Query for electronic submissions. Reports in 3 weeks on queries; 2 months on mss. Book catalog free on request. Manuscript guidelines for contests for #10 SASE.

Nonfiction: Biography, reference, textbook, scholarly monographs. Subjects include anthropology/archaeology, art/architecture, business and economics, ethnic, government/politics, health/medicine, history, language/literature, music/dance, philosophy, regional, Latin American studies, Russian and East European studies, social and labor history, Milton studies. Query. Reviews artwork/photos as part of ms package.

Recent Nonfiction Title: *Creating America: George Horace Lorimer and the Saturday Evening Post*, by Jan Cohn (history).

Fiction: Literary. "One title per year, winner of the Drue Heinz Literature Prize." No novels. Submit complete ms via contest, send SASE for rules.

Recent Fiction Title: *Cartographies*, by Maya Sonenberg (short fiction collection).

Poetry: 6 titles per year; 1 from previously unpublished author. Submit complete ms via contest, send SASE for rules; authors with previous books send direct to press in Sept. and Oct.

Recent Poetry Title: *Captivity*, by Toi Derricotte (contemporary).

*THE UNIVERSITY OF TENNESSEE PRESS, 293 Communications Bldg., Knoxville TN 37996-0325. FAX: (615)974-6435. Contact: Acquisitions Editor. Estab. 1940. Averages 30 titles/year; receives 300 submissions annually. 50% of books from first-time authors; 99% of books from unagented writers. Average print order for a writer's first book is 1,250. Subsidy publishes (nonauthor) 10% of books. Pays negotiable royalty on retail price. Publishes book an average of 1 year after acceptance. Reports in 1 month. Book catalog for $1 and 12×16 SAE; ms guidelines for SASE.

Nonfiction: American history, cultural studies, religious studies, vernacular architecture and material culture, literary criticism, Black studies, women's studies, Caribbean, anthropology, folklore and regional studies. Prefers "scholarly treatment and a readable style. Authors usually have Ph.D.s." Submit outline/synopsis, author vita, and 2 sample chapters. No fiction, poetry or plays. Reviews artwork/photos as part of ms package.

Recent Nonfiction Title: *The Feminine and Faulkner: Reading (Beyond) Sexual Differences*, by Minrose C. Gwin.

Tips: "Our market is in several groups: scholars; educated readers with special interests in given scholarly subjects; and the general educated public interested in Tennessee, Appalachia and the South. Not all our books appeal to all these groups, of course, but any given book must appeal to at least one of them."

UNIVERSITY OF TEXAS PRESS, P.O. Box 7819, Austin TX 78713-7819. FAX: (512)320-0668. Executive Editor: Theresa May. Estab. 1952. Averages 60 titles/year; receives 1,000 submissions annually. 50% of books from first-time authors; 99% of books from unagented writers. Average print order for a writer's first book is 1,000. Pays royalty usually based on net income; occasionally offers advance. Publishes book an average of 18 months after acceptance. Query for electronic submissions. Reports in 2 months. Free book catalog and writer's guidelines.
Nonfiction: General scholarly subjects: astronomy, natural history, American, Latin American and Middle Eastern studies, native Americans, classics, films, biology, contemporary architecture, archeology, anthropology, geography, ornithology, ecology, Chicano studies, linguistics, 20th-century and women's literature. Also uses specialty titles related to Texas and the Southwest, national trade titles, and regional trade titles. Accepts nonfiction and fiction translations (Middle Eastern or Latin American fiction). Query or submit outline/synopsis and 2 sample chapters. Reviews artwork/photos as part of ms package.
Recent Nonfiction Title: *William Wayne Justice*, by Frank Kemerer.
Recent Fiction Translation: *Goodbyes and Stories*, by Juan Carlos Onetti (translated from Spanish).
Tips: "It's difficult to make a manuscript over 400 double-spaced pages into a feasible book. Authors should take special care to edit out extraneous material. Looks for sharply focused, in-depth treatments of important topics."

UNIVERSITY OF WISCONSIN PRESS, 114 N. Murray St., Madison WI 53715. (608)262-4928. Director: Allen N. Fitchen. Acquisitions Editor: Barbara J. Hanrahan. Estab. 1937. Publishes hardcover and paperback originals and reprints. Averages 50 titles/year. Pays standard royalties on retail price. Reports in 3 months.
Nonfiction: Publishes general nonfiction based on scholarly research. Looks for "originality, significance, quality of the research represented, literary quality, and breadth of interest to the educated community at large." Follow *Chicago Manual of Style*. Send letter of inquiry and prospectus.

UNIVERSITY PRESS OF AMERICA, INC., 4720 Boston Way, Lanham MD 20706. (301)459-3366. Publisher: James E. Lyons. Estab. 1975. Publishes hardcover and paperback originals and reprints. Averages 450 titles/year. Pays 5-15% royalty on net receipts; occasional advance. Reports in 6 weeks. Book catalog and guidelines for SASE.
Nonfiction: Scholarly monographs, college, and graduate level textbooks in history, economics, business, psychology, political science, African studies, Black studies, philosophy, religion, sociology, music, art, literature, drama and education. No juvenile, elementary or high school material. Submit outline or request proposal questionnaire.
Recent Nonfiction Title: *Thomas Jefferson: A Strange Case of Mistaken Identity*, by Alf J. Mapp Jr. (biography).

UNIVERSITY PRESS OF COLORADO, (formerly Colorado Associated University Press), P.O. Box 849, Niwot CO 80544. (303)530-5337. Director: Luther Wilson. Estab. 1965. Publishes hardcover and paperback originals. Averages 25 titles/year; receives 350 submissions annually. 50% of books from first-time authors; 99% of books from unagented writers. Average print order for a writer's first book is 1,500-2,000. Pays 10-12½-15% royalty contract on net price; no advances. Publishes book an average of 9 months after acceptance. Electronic submissions encouraged. Reports in 3 months. Free book catalog.
Nonfiction: Scholarly, regional and environmental subjects. Length: 250-500 pages. Query first with table of contents, preface or opening chapter. Reviews artwork/photos as part of ms package.
Recent Nonfiction Title: *Boomtown Blues*, by Andrew Gulliford.
Tips: "Books should be solidly researched and from a reputable scholar, because we are a university press. We have a new series on world resources and environmental issues."

UNIVERSITY PRESS OF KANSAS, 2501 W. 15th St., Lawrence KS 66049. (913)864-4154. FAX: (913)864-4586. Editor: Cynthia Miller. Estab. 1946. Publishes hardcover and paperback originals. Averages 35-40 titles/year; receives 500-600 submissions annually. 25% of books from first-time authors; 95% of books from unagented writers. Royalties negotiable; occasional advances. Markets books by advertising, direct mail, publicity, and sales representation to the trade; 55% of sales to bookstores. "State availability of illustrations if they add significantly to the manuscript." Publishes book an average of 10 months after acceptance. Reports in 4 months. Free book catalog; ms guidelines for #10 SASE.

Nonfiction: Publishes biography, history, sociology, philosophy, politics, military studies, regional subjects (Kansas, Great Plains, Midwest), and scholarly. Reviews artwork/photos as part of ms package. Query first.

Recent Nonfiction Title: *Feminist Ethics*, edited by Claudia Card (philosophy).

UNIVERSITY PRESS OF KENTUCKY, 663 S. Limestone, Lexington KY 40508-4008. (606)257-2951. Associate Director: Jerome Crouch. Estab. 1951. Publishes hardcover originals and hardcover and trade paperback reprints. Averages 35 titles/year; receives 200 submissions annually. 25-50% of books from first-time authors; 98% of books from unagented writers. Pays 10-15% royalty on wholesale price. "As a nonprofit press, we generally exclude the first 1,000 copies from royalty payment." No advance. Publishes ms an average of 1 year after acceptance. Reports in 1 month on queries; 3 months on mss. Free book catalog.

Nonfiction: Biography, reference and monographs. Subjects include Americana, history, politics and sociology. "We are a scholarly publisher, publishing chiefly for an academic and professional audience. Strong areas are history, literature, political science, folklore, anthropology, and sociology. Our books are expected to advance knowledge in their fields in some measure. We would be interested in the treatment of timely topics in the fields indicated, treatments that would be solid and substantial but that would be readable and capable of appealing to a general public. No textbooks; genealogical material; lightweight popular treatments; how-to books; and generally books not related to our major areas of interest." Query. Reviews artwork/photos, but generally does not publish books with extensive number of photos.

Recent Nonfiction Title: *Hitler and Spain: The Nazi Role in the Spanish Civil War*, by Robert H. Whealey.

Tips: "Most of our authors are drawn from our primary academic and professional audience. We are probably not a good market for the usual freelance writer, unless his work fits into our special requirements. Moreover, we do not pay advances and income from our books is minimal; so we cannot offer much financial reward to a freelance writer."

UNIVERSITY PRESS OF MISSISSIPPI, 3825 Ridgewood Rd., Jackson MS 39211. (601)982-6205. FAX: (601)982-6217. Director: Richard Abel. Acquisitions Editor: Seetha Srinivasan. Estab. 1970. Imprint is Muscadine Books (regional trade). Publishes hardcover and paperback originals and reprints. Averages 40 titles/year; receives 500 submissions annually. 20% of books from first-time authors; 95% of books from unagented writers. "Competitive royalties and terms." Publishes book an average of 1 year after acceptance. Reports in 3 months. Free book catalog.

Nonfiction: Americana, biography, history, politics, folklife, literary criticism, ethnic/minority studies, natural sciences and popular culture with scholarly emphasis. Interested in southern regional studies and literary studies. Submit outline/synopsis and sample chapters and *curriculum vita* to Acquisitions Editor. "We prefer a proposal that describes the significance of the work and a chapter outline." Reviews artwork/photos as part of ms package.

Recent Nonfiction Title: *Photographs*, by Eudora Welty.

Fiction: Commissioned trade editions by prominent writers.

Recent Fiction Title: *Homecomings*, by Willie Morris.

UNIVERSITY PRESS OF NEW ENGLAND, (Includes Wesleyan University Press), 17½ Lebanon St., Hanover NH 03755. (603)646-3349. FAX: (603)643-1540. Director: Thomas L. McFarland. Editors: Jeanne West, Scott Mahler and Terry Cochran. Estab. 1970. "University Press of New England is a consortium of university presses. Some books—those published for one of the consortium members—carry the joint imprint of New England and the member: Wesleyan, Dartmouth, Brandeis, Brown, Tufts, Clark, Universities of Connecticut, New Hampshire, Vermont, Rhode Island and Middlebury." Publishes hardcover and trade paperback originals and trade paperback reprints. Averages 60 titles/year. Subsidy publishes (nonauthor) 80% of books. Pays standard royalty; occasionally offers advance. Query for electronic submissions. Reports in 1 month. Book catalog and guidelines for SASE.

Nonfiction: Americana (New England), art, biography, history, music, nature, politics, psychology, reference, science, sociology, and regional (New England). No festschriften, memoirs, unrevised doctoral dissertations, or symposium collections. Submit outline/synopsis and 1-2 sample chapters.

Recent Nonfiction Title: *Ethics at the Bedside*, edited by Charles M. Culver, M.D.

‡*UNLIMITED PUBLISHING CO.,** Rt. 17K, P.O. Box 240, Bullville NY 10915. (914)361-1299. Publisher: John J. Prizzia, Jr. Estab. 1982. Publishes trade paperback originals. Averages 12 titles/year; receives 25 submissions annually. 90% of books from first-time; 95% of books from unagented writers. Subsidy publishes 20% of books. Pays 10-40% royalty on retail price or makes outright purchase for $500-4,000; offers $1,000 average advance. Publishes book an average of 1 year after acceptance.

Reports in 1 month on queries; 1 year on submissions. Book catalog for SASE.

Nonfiction: Biography, cookbook, how-to, humor, illustrated book, reference, self-help and technical. Subjects include business and economics, cooking and foods, hobbies, nature and sociology. "Prefers self-help and how-to books pertaining to cooking, traveling, hobbies, small business, advertising for small business, start your own business, etc." Submit outline/synopsis and sample chapters or complete ms.

Recent Nonfiction Title: *The Little People of Guadalcanal,* by Joseph T. Webber, M.D.

Fiction: Adventure, experimental, historical, humor and mystery. "War stories, adventures of successful business people, the beginnings of millionaires, etc." Submit outline/synopsis and sample chapters or complete ms.

*UTAH STATE UNIVERSITY PRESS, Logan UT 84322-7800. (801)750-1362. Director: Linda Speth. Publishes hardcover and trade paperback originals and reprints. Averages 6 titles/year; receives 170 submissions annually. 8% of books from first-time authors. Average print order for a writer's first book is 1,000. Subsidy publishes 10% of books; subsidy publishes (nonauthor) 45% of books. Pays royalty on net price; no advance. Publishes book an average of 18 months after acceptance. Electronic submissions OK on Word Perfect 5.1, but requires hard copy also. Reports in 2 weeks on queries; 2 months on mss. Free book catalog; ms guidelines for SASE.

Nonfiction: Biography, reference and textbook on folklore, Americana (history and politics). "Particularly interested in book-length scholarly manuscripts dealing with folklore, Western history, Western literature. All manuscript submissions must have a scholarly focus." Submit complete ms. Reviews artwork/photos as part of ms package.

Recent Nonfiction Title: *Creative Ethncity,* by Stephen Stern and John Allan Cicala.

Poetry: "At the present time, we have accepted several poetry manuscripts and will not be reading poetry submissions for one year."

Recent Poetry Title: *Only Morning In Her Shoes,* edited by Leatrice Lifshitz.

THE VESTAL PRESS, LTD., 320 N. Jensen Rd., P.O. Box 97, Vestal NY 13851-0097. (607)797-4872. Publisher: Grace L. Houghton. Estab. 1961. Publishes hardcover and trade paperback originals and reprints. Averages 6-8 titles/year; receives 50-75 submissions annually. 20% of books from first-time writers; 95% of books from unagented authors. Pays 10% maximum royalty on net sales. Publishes books an average of 1 year after acceptance. Simultaneous submissions OK. Usually reports in 2 weeks. Book catalog for $2.

Nonfiction: Technical antiquarian hobby topics in antique radio, mechanical music (player pianos, music boxes, etc.), reed organs, carousels, antique phonographs, early cinema history, regional history based on postcard collections. Query or submit outline/synopsis and sample chapters or submit complete ms.

Recent Nonfiction Title: *Philadelphia in Picture Postcards, 1900-1930.*

VGM CAREER HORIZONS, Imprint of NTC Publishing Group, 4255 W. Touhy Ave., Lincolnwood IL 60646-1975. (708)679-5500. FAX: (708)679-2494. Editorial Director: Michael Urban. Estab. 1960. Publishes hardcover and paperback originals. Averages 30-40 titles/year; receives 150-200 submissions annually. 10% of books from first-time authors; 95% of books from unagented writers. Pays royalty or makes outright purchase. Advance varies. Publishes book an average of 1 year after acceptance. Simultaneous submissions OK. Query for electronic submissions. Reports in 3 weeks. Book catalog and ms guidelines for 9×12 SAE with 5 first class stamps.

Nonfiction: Textbook and general trade on careers and jobs. Nonfiction book manuscript needs are for careers in visual arts, medicine, business, etc. Query or submit outline/synopsis and sample chapters. Reviews artwork/photos as part of ms package.

Recent Nonfiction Title: *Career Planning for College Students,* by John Steele and Marily Morgan.

Tips: "Our audience is made up of job seekers, career planners, job changers, and students and adults in education and trade markets. Study our existing line of books before sending proposals."

VICTOR BOOKS, Division of Scripture Press Publications, Inc. 1825 College Ave., Wheaton IL 60187. (708)668-6000. FAX: (708)668-3806. Contact: Acquisitions Editor. Estab. 1934. Imprints are SonFlower, Winner, SonPower. Publishes hardcover and trade paperback originals. Firm averages 75 titles/year. Receives 1,400 submissions/year. 5% of books from first-time authors; 98% from unagented writers. Royalty negotiable on retail price. Publishes book an average of 18 months after acceptance.

For information on book publishers' areas of interest, see the nonfiction and fiction sections in the Book Publishers Subject Index.

Simultaneous submissions OK. Reports in 1 month on queries; 2 months on mss. Ms guidelines for #10 SASE; 4 first class stamps for a catalog and guidelines.

Nonfiction: Juvenile, reference and self-help. Subjects include child guidance/parenting, psychology, life-related Bible study and women's issues/studies. "We are interested in manuscripts with a fresh approach to Bible study and Christian living/leadership topics, written from an evangelical perspective. Issues-type books are also welcome." Query or submit outline/synopsis and sample chapters.

Recent Nonfiction Title: *The Complete Financial Guide for Single Parents,* by Larry Burkett.

Fiction: For ages 2-12. "We are looking for simple Bible-related stories that could be developed into picture books for the preschooler or young reader. For the 8-12-year-old, we are interested in action stories with a Christian take-away message. Fiction should also be series oriented." Submit outline/synopsis and sample chapters or submit complete ms.

Recent Fiction Title: *Lost Beneath Manhattan,* by Sigmund Brouwer.

Tips: "Too many books rehash the same topic and there are many shallow books that require no thinking. A writer has the best chance of selling Victor a well-conceived and imaginative manuscript that helps the reader apply Christianity to his/her life in practical ways. Christians active in the local church and their children are our audience."

VIKING PENGUIN, Division of Penguin USA, 375 Hudson St., New York NY 10014. Did not want to be listed.

‡VILLARD BOOKS, Random House, 201 E. 50th St., New York NY 10022. (212)572-2720. Publisher and Editorial Director: Peter Gethers. Estab. 1983. Publishes hardcover and trade paperback originals. Averages 40-45 titles/year. 95% of books are agented submissions. Reports in 3 weeks. Pays varying advances and royalties; negotiated separately. Simultaneous submissions OK. Query for electronic submissions.

Nonfiction and Fiction: Looks for commercial nonfiction and fiction. Submit outline/synopsis and up to 50 pages in sample chapters.

Recent Nonfiction Title: *Life is Too Short* (autobiography).

WADSWORTH PUBLISHING COMPANY, Imprint of Wadsworth, Inc., 10 Davis Dr., Belmont CA 94002. (415)595-2350. FAX: (415)592-3342. Editor-in-Chief: Stephen D. Rutter. Estab. 1956. Other divisions include Brooks/Cole Pub. Co., PWS/Kent Pub. Co. and Heinle & Heinle Publishing Co. Publishes hardcover and paperback originals and software. Publishes 350 titles/year. 35% of books from first-time authors; 99% of books from unagented writers. Pays 5-15% royalty on net price. Advances not automatic policy. Publishes ms an average of 1 year after acceptance. Simultaneous submissions OK. Query for electronic submissions. Reports in 1 week. Book catalog (by subject area) and ms guidelines available.

Nonfiction: Textbook: higher education only. Subjects include mathematics, music, social sciences, economics, philosophy, religious studies, speech and mass communications, English, history, social work and other subjects in higher education. "We need books that use fresh teaching approaches to all courses taught at schools of higher education throughout the U.S. and Canada. We specifically do not publish textbooks in art." Query or submit outline/synopsis and sample chapters.

Recent Nonfiction Title: *Biology: Concept and Applications,* by Cecie Starr.

WAKE FOREST UNIVERSITY PRESS, P.O. Box 7333, Winston-Salem NC 27109. (919)759-5448. Director: Dillon Johnston. Manager: Candide Jones. Estab. 1976. Publishes hardcover and trade paperback originals. Press averages 5 titles/year. Receives 80 submissions/year. Pays 10% on retail price. Offers $500 average advance. Publishes book an average of 6 months after acceptance. Reports in 1 month on queries; 3 months on mss. Free book catalog.

Nonfiction: Subjects include language/literature and photography. "We publish exclusively poetry, photography, and criticism of the poetry of Ireland and bilingual editions of contemporary French poetry." Query.

Recent Nonfiction Title: *The Magdale Sermon and Earlier Poems,* by Eilean Ni Chuilleanain (Irish poetry).

Tips: "Readers of contemporary poetry and of books of Irish interest or French interest are our audience."

J. WESTON WALCH, PUBLISHER, P.O. Box 658, Portland ME 04104. (207)772-2846. FAX: (207)772-3105. Managing Editor: Richard S. Kimball. Editor: Jane Carter. Math/Science Editor: Eric Olson. Computer Editor: Robert Crepeau. Estab. 1927. Publishes paperback originals and software. Averages 110 titles/year; receives 300 submissions annually. 10% of books from first-time authors; 95% of books from unagented writers. Average print order for a writer's first book is 700. Offers 10-15% royalty on gross receipts; buys some titles by outright purchase for $100-2,500. No advance. Publishes book an average of 18 months after acceptance. Query for electronic submissions. Reports in 6 weeks. Book catalog for 9×12 SAE with 5 first class stamps; ms guidelines for #10 SASE.

Nonfiction: Subjects include art, business, computer education, economics, English, foreign language, government, health, history, mathematics, music, physical education, psychology, science, social science, sociology and special education. "We publish only supplementary educational material for grades six to twelve in the U.S. and Canada. Formats include books, posters, master sets, card sets, cassettes, filmstrips, microcomputer courseware, video and mixed packages. Most titles are assigned by us, though we occasionally accept an author's unsolicited submission. We have a great need for author/artist teams and for authors who can write at third- to tenth-grade levels. We do *not* want basic texts, anthologies or industrial arts titles. Most of our authors—but not all—have secondary teaching experience. I cannot stress too much the advantages that an author/artist team would have in approaching us and probably other publishers." Query first. Looks for "sense of organization, writing ability, knowledge of subject, skill of communicating with intended audience." Reviews artwork/photos as part of ms package.

Recent Nonfiction Title: *Living on Your Own: An Independent Living Simulation*, by Jean Bunnell.

WALKER AND CO., Division of Walker Publishing Co., 720 5th Ave., New York NY 10019. FAX: (212)307-1764. Contact: Submissions Editor. Estab. 1959. Hardcover and trade paperback originals and reprints of British books. Averages 100 titles/year; receives 3,500 submissions annually. 50% of books from first-time authors; 50% of books from unagented writers. Pays varying royalty or makes outright purchase. Advance averages $1,000-3,000 "but could be higher or lower." Do not telephone submissions editors. Material without SASE will not be returned. Book catalog and guidelines for 8½×11 SAE with 3 first class stamps.

Nonfiction: Publishes biography, business, histories, science and natural history, health, music, nature, parenting, reference, popular science, and self-help books. Query or submit outline/synopsis and sample chapter. Reviews artwork/photos as part of ms package (photographs). Do not send originals.

Recent Nonfiction Title: *March of the Millenia*, by Isaac Asimov.

Fiction: Mystery/suspense, juvenile (ages 5 and up), regency romance, western, thriller/adventure.

Recent Fiction Title: *No Sign of Murder*, by Alan Russell.

Tips: "We also need preschool to young adult nonfiction, science fiction, historical novels, biographies and middle-grade novels. Query."

‡WARNER BOOKS, Warner Publishing Inc., 666 5th Ave., New York NY 10103. (212)484-2900. Vice President and Senior Editor: Fredda Isaacson. Publishes hardcover, trade and mass market paperback originals and reprints. 20% of books are from first-time authors. Royalty varies on retail price. Advance varies by book and author. Reports in 2 months.

Nonfiction: Celebrity biography, cookbook, how-to, humor, illustrated book, reference, self-help. Need self-help, true crime, business and reference books. Query or submit outline/synopsis and sample chapters with letter. Reviews artwork/photos if crucial to ms package.

*WASHINGTON STATE UNIVERSITY PRESS, Pullman WA 99164-5910. (509)335-3518. FAX: (509)335-8568. Director: Thomas H. Sanders. Estab. 1928. Publishes hardcover originals, trade paperback originals and reprints. Averages 6-10 titles/year; receives 75-150 submissions annually. 50% of books from first-time writers; 100% of books from unagented authors. Subsidy publishes 20% of books. "The nature of the manuscript and the potential market for the manuscript determine whether it should be subsidy published." Pays 10% royalty on second printing. Publishes book an average of 18 months after acceptance. Simultaneous submissions OK. Query for electronic submissions. Reports on queries in 1 month; on submissions in 4 months.

Nonfiction: Biography, academic and scholarly. Subjects include Americana, art, business and economics, history (especially of the American West and the Pacific Northwest), nature, philosophy, politics, psychology, and sociology. Needs for the next year are "quality manuscripts that focus on the development of the Pacific Northwest as a region, and on the social and economic changes that have taken place and continue to take place as the region enters the 21st century. No romance novels, historical fiction, how-to books, gardening books, or books specifically written as classroom texts." Submit outline/synopsis and sample chapters. Reviews artwork/photos as part of ms package.

Recent Nonfiction Title: *North Bank Road: The Spokane, Portland and Seattle Railway*, by John T. Gaertner (NW history).

Tips: "Our audience consists of scholars, specialists and informed general readers who are interested in well-documented research presented in an attractive format. Writers have the best chance of selling to our press completed manuscripts on regional history. We have developed our marketing in the direction of regional and local history and have attempted to use this as the base around which we hope to expand our publishing program. In regional history, the secret is to write a good narrative—a good story—that is substantiated factually. It should be told in an imaginative, clever way. Have visuals (photos, maps, etc) available to help the reader envision what has happened. Tell the local or regional history story in a way that ties it to larger, national, and even international events. Weave it into the large pattern of history."

‡FRANKLIN WATTS, INC., Division of Grolier, Inc., 387 Park Ave. S, New York NY 10016. (212)686-7070. Editorial Director: Jeanne Vestal. Publishes hardcover originals. Entire firm publishes 200 titles/year; trade and professional division publishes 40. 10% of books from first-time authors; 2% of books from unagented writers. Pays royalty on wholesale or retail price. Simultaneous queries OK. Reports in 1 month on queries. Free book catalog.

Nonfiction: Biography and history. Subjects include Americana, politics and sports. No humor, coffee table books, cookbooks or gardening books. Query.

Fiction: Mainstream, mystery and science fiction. Query.

‡WAYFINDER PRESS, P.O. Box 217, Ridgway CO 81432. (303)626-5452. Owner: Marcus E. Wilson. Publishes trade paperback originals. Firm averages 8 titles/year. Receives 20 submissions/year. 30% of books are from first-time authors. 90% from unagented writers. Pays 8-12% royalty on retail price. Publishes book an average of 6 months after acceptance. Simultaneous submissions OK. Reports in 2 weeks on queries. Free book catalog and manuscript guidelines.

Nonfiction: Biography, cookbook, illustrated book, reference, self-help and technical. Subjects include Americana, cooking, foods and nutrition, government/politics, history, nature/environment, photography, recreation, regional, sociology and travel. "We are looking for books on western Colorado, Southwest U.S.A. interest books: history, sociology, cooking, nature, recreation, photo, and travel. No books on subjects outside our geographical area of specialization." Query or submit outline/synopsis and sample chapters. Reviews artwork/photos as part of ms package.

Recent Nonfiction Title: *The Way It Was*, by David Bachman & Tod Bacigalupi (historical narrative).

Fiction: Adventure, historical, humor, mystery, picture books, and short story collections. "We are looking for fiction with a specific Colorado or Southwest U.S.A. perspective." Query or submit outline/synopsis and sample chapters.

Tips: "Writers have the best chance selling us tourist oriented books. The local population and tourists comprise our audience."

‡*WEBB RESEARCH GROUP, P.O. Box 314, Medford OR 97501. (503)664-5205. Editor-in-Chief: Bert Webber. Publishes hardcover and trade paperback originals. Firm averages 11 titles/year. Receives 25 submissions/year. 10% of books are from first-time authors. "We decline to deal with agents." Subsidy publishes 20% of books. "Subsidy based on subject and authorship." Pays 10% royalty on wholesale price; also negotiates outright purchase. Publishes book an average of 1 year after acceptance. Reports in 2 weeks on queries. Book catalog for #10 SAE and 2 first class stamps.

Nonfiction: Biography and reference. Subjects include Americana (limited to Pacific Northwest and Oregon Trail), history (Pacific Northwest), military/war (WWII Japanese attack against mainland of USA only), recreation, religion, travel, and Japanese-American relocation in WWII. "We are always on the lookout for photographically illustrated manuscripts on aspects of the history of the Pacific Northwest and along the Oregon Trail. We have enough books on Indians for now. We never do restaurant or camping guides." Query with SASE; all unsolicited mss are returned unopened C.O.D. mail. Reviews artwork/photos as part of ms package. "Submit copies of photos with query."

Recent Nonfiction Title: *Oregon Covered Bridges: An Oregon Documentary in Pictures*, by Webber.

Tips: "Writers have the best chance selling us books with first-hand knowledge of history of the Pacific Northwest or pioneer period Oregon Trail (1843-1869). We do limited postal history for specialist philatelists. Our books are aimed at reference librarians who want accurate answers recorded in popular language. All books have biblio and index and we seek 9th grade readability to suit the all-American public. If I were a writer trying to market a book today, I would know what I'm writing about, not fake it, and support with a suitable bibliography. I would also have suitable quality photographs."

SAMUEL WEISER, INC., P.O. Box 612, York Beach ME 03910. (207)363-4393. Editor: Susan Smithe. Estab. 1956. Publishes hardcover originals and trade paperback originals and reprints. Publishes 18-20 titles/year; receives 200 submissions annually. 50% of books from first-time authors; 98% of books from unagented writers. Pays 10% royalty on wholesale or retail price; offers average $500 advance. Publishes book an average of 1½ years after acceptance. Query for electronic submissions. Reports in 3 months. Free book catalog.

Nonfiction: How-to and self-help. Subjects include health, music, philosophy, psychology and religion. "We look for strong books in our specialty field—written by teachers and people who know the subject. Don't want a writer's rehash of all the astrology books in the library, only texts written by people with strong background in field. No poetry or novels." Submit complete ms. Reviews artwork/photos as part of ms package.

Recent Nonfiction Title: *Inner Journeys*, by Jay Earley, Ph.D.

Tips: "Most new authors do not check permissions, nor do they provide proper footnotes. If they did, it would help. We specialize in oriental philosophy, metaphysics, esoterica of all kinds (tarot, astrology, qabalah, magic, etc.) and our emphasis is still the same. We still look at all manuscripts submitted to us. We are interested in seeing freelance art for book covers."

WESTERN PUBLISHING, 1220 Mound Ave., Racine WI 53404. Divisions include Golden Books—Books for Children. Did not want a listing for Golden Books or for their Adult Trade Books Division.

WESTERNLORE PRESS, Box 35305, Tucson AZ 85740. Editor: Lynn R. Bailey. Publishes 6-12 titles/year. Pays standard royalties on retail price "except in special cases." Query. Reports in 2 months. Enclose return postage with query.

Nonfiction: Publishes Western Americana of a scholarly and semischolarly nature: anthropology, history, biography, historic sites, restoration, and ethnohistory pertaining to the greater American West. Re-publication of rare and out-of-print books. Length: 25,000-100,000 words.

WESTPORT PUBLISHERS, INC., 4050 Pennsylvania, Kansas City MO 64111. (816)756-1490. FAX: (816)756-0159. Managing Editor: Terry Faulkner. Estab. 1982. Subsidiaries include Media Publishing, Midgard Press, Media Periodicals, and Test Corporation of America. Publishes hardcover originals and trade paperback originals. Averages 10-12 titles/year. Receives 100 submissions/year. 50% of books from first-time authors. 100% from unagented writers. Pays royalty. Publishes book an average of 9 months after acceptance. Reports in 1 month on queries; 6 weeks on mss. Send SASE with queries and mss.

Nonfiction: Coffee table book, cookbook, and reference works. Subjects include child guidance/parenting, cooking, foods and nutrition, psychology, recreation, biographies, reference and regional studies. "Topics to consider are child guidance/parenting; psychology related; regional topics; family issues. However, we will consider all topics except books with sensational topics (mass murderers, etc.)" Submit complete ms. Reviews artwork/photos as part of ms package.

Recent Nonfiction Title: *Little People: Guidelines for Commonsense Childrearing*, by Edward R. Christophersen (parenting).

Tips: "Books with a well-defined audience have the best chance of succeeding. An author must have demonstrated expertise in the topic on which he or she is writing."

‡*WHITAKER HOUSE, 580 Pittsburgh St., Springdale PA 15144. (412)274-4440. Editor: Debra Petrosky. Estab. 1970. Publishes trade and mass market paperback originals and reprints. Averages 3 new titles/year. Subsidy publishes (author and nonauthor) 25% of books. "We publish only Christian books for the adult reader." Book catalog for 9 × 12 SAE with 2 first class stamps. Ms guidelines for SASE.

Nonfiction: How-to and personal growth books centered on biblical teaching and related to everyday life—especially topics of interest to women and related to diet, health, and exercise. Looking for teaching books supported by author's research and personal experience. Wants typewritten copy or computer printout, double-spaced, 50,000-90,000 words. Prefers synopsis of chapters with query letter. Interested in receiving queries from Christian leaders with a recognized ministry. No booklets, poetry, or children's books considered.

Recent Nonfiction Title: *Exploring the World of Dreams*, by Benny Thomas.

WHITE CLIFFS MEDIA COMPANY, P.O. Box 561, Crown Point IN 46307-0561. (219)322-5537. Owner: Larry W. Smith. Estab. 1985. Publishes hardcover and trade paperback originals. Averages 5-10 titles/year. 75% of books from first-time authors; 75% from unagented writers. Pays 5-15% royalty. Publishes book an average of 1 year after acceptance. Query for electronic submissions. Reports in 3 months. Book catalog for #10 SASE.

Nonfiction: Biography, software, technical, textbook. Subjects include anthropology, education, ethnic, music/dance, sociology. "We are looking for ethnic music performance, music sociology/biography (more pop/mass oriented), books on computer/desktop publishing." Query. Reviews artwork/photos as part of ms package.

Recent Nonfiction Title: *The New Folk Music*, by Craig Harris (trade).

Tips: "Trend—distribution is more difficult due to the large number of publishers. Writers should send proposals that have potential for mass markets as well as college texts, and that will be submitted and completed on schedule. Our audience reads college texts, general interest trade publications. If I were a writer trying to market a book today, I would send a book on music comparable in quality, mass appeal, and readibility to a book like Stephen Hawking's *A Brief History of Time*."

‡WHITFORD PRESS, Imprint of Schiffer Publishing, Ltd., 1469 Morstein Rd., West Chester PA 19380. (215)696-1001. Managing Editor: Ellen Taylor. Estab. 1985. Publishes trade paperback originals. Averages 3-4 titles/year; receives 400-500 submissions annually. 50% of books from first-time authors; 90%

of books from unagented writers. Pays royalty on wholesale price; no advances. Publishes on an average of 9-12 months after acceptance and receipt of complete ms. Simultaneous submissions OK. Reports in about 1 month. Free book catalog; ms guidelines for SASE.

Nonfiction: How-to, self-help, reference. Subjects include astrology, metaphysics, New Age topics. "We are looking for well written, well-organized, originals books on all metaphysical subjects (except channeling and past lives). Books that empower the reader or show him/her ways to develop personal skills are preferred. New aproaches, techniques, or concepts are best. No personal accounts unless they directly relate to a general audience. No moralistic, fatalistic, sexist or strictly philosophical books. Query first or send outline. Enclose SASE large enough to hold your submission if you want it returned."

Recent Nonfiction Title: *Planets in Signs*.

Tips: "Our audience is knowledgeable in metaphysical fields, well-read and progressive in thinking. Please check bookstores to see if your subject has already been covered thoroughly. Expertise in the field is not enough; your book must be clean, well written and well organized. A specific and unique marketing angle is a plus. No Sun-sign material; we prefer more advanced work. Please don't send entire ms unless we request it, and be sure to include SASE. Let us know if the book is available on computer diskette and what type of hardware/software. Mss should be between 60,000 and 110,000 words."

‡ALBERT WHITMAN AND CO., 6340 Oakton St., Morton Grove IL 60053-2723. (708)581-0033. Executive Editor: Kathleen Tucker. Publishes hardcover originals. Firm averages 25 titles/year. Receives 2,000 submissions/year. 12% of books from first-time authors. 88% from unagented writers. Pays 10% royalty. Publishes book an average of 18 months after acceptance. Simultaneous submissions OK. Reports in 1 month on queries; 3 months on mss. Book catalog for 8×10 SAE and 2 first class stamps. Manuscript guidelines for #10 SASE.

Nonfiction: "All books are for ages 2-12." Biography, humor, and concept books which are about special problems children have. Subjects include agriculture/horticulture, animals, anthropology/archaeology, art/architecture, computers and electronics, cooking, foods and nutrition, ethnic, gardening, health/medicine, history, hobbies, language/literature, music/dance, nature/environment, photography, recreation, religion, science, sports and travel. "We are looking for picture books for young children. No adult subjects, please." Submit outline/synopsis and sample chapters (novels) and complete ms (picture books). Reviews artwork/photos as part of ms package. "We may accept the manuscript and reject the artwork."

Recent Nonfiction Title: *Theodore Roosevelt Takes Charge*, by Nancy Whitelaw (biography).

Fiction: "All books are for ages 2-12." Adventure, ethnic, fantasy, historical, humor, mystery, picture books and concept books (to help children deal with problems and concerns). "We need historical fiction and picture books. No young adult and adult books." Submit outline/synopsis and sample chapters (novels) and complete ms (picture books).

Recent Fiction Title: *If All the World Were Paper*, by Miriam Nerlove (fantasy).

Tips: "There is a trend toward highly visual books. The writer can most easily sell us a strong picture book text that has good illustration possibilities. We sell mostly to libraries, but our bookstore sales are growing. The books are all for children somewhere between the ages of 2 and 12. If I were a writer trying to market a book today, I would study published picture books."

THE WHITSTON PUBLISHING CO., P.O. Box 958, Troy NY 12181. (518)283-4363. Editorial Director: Jean Goode. Estab. 1969. Publishes hardcover originals. Averages 20 titles/year; receives 100 submissions annually. 50% of books from first-time authors; 100% of books from unagented writers. Pays 10% royalty on wholesale price; no advance. Publishes book an average of 30 months after acceptance. Reports in 1 year. Book catalog for $1.

Nonfiction: "We publish scholarly and critical books in the arts, humanities and some of the social sciences. We also publish reference books, bibliographies, indexes, checklists and monographs. We will consider author bibliographies. We are interested in scholarly monographs and collections of essays." Query or submit complete ms. Reviews artwork/photos as part of ms package.

Recent Nonfiction Title: *A Melville Encyclopedia: The Novels*, by Kathleen Kier.

*WILDERNESS ADVENTURE BOOKS, P.O. Box 968, Fowlerville MI 48836. FAX: (517)223-8290. Editor: Clayton Klein. Estab. 1983. Publishes hardcover and trade paperback originals and reprints. Firm averages 6 titles/year. Receives 120 submissions/year. 90% of books from first-time authors. 90% from unagented writers. Subsidy publishes 25% of books. Pays 5-10% royalty on retail price. Offers $100 average advance. Publishes book an average of 10 months after acceptance. Simultaneous submissions OK. Reports in 2 weeks on queries; 6 weeks on mss. Free book catalog.

Nonfiction: Biography, how-to and illustrated book. Subjects include Americana, animals, anthropology/archaeology, history, nature/environment, regional, sports and travel. Query. Submit outline/synopsis and sample chapters. Reviews artwork/photos as part of ms package.

Recent Nonfiction Title: *Bambo*, by Gary Lawton Hargis.
Fiction: Adventure, historical and young adult. Query. Submit outline/synopsis and sample chapters or complete ms.
Recent Fiction Title: *Terror and Triumph*, by Rear Adm. John Harllee.
Poetry: Submit samples.
Recent Poetry Title: *Expressions in Poetry*, by Marie Blue Powell.

WILDERNESS PRESS, 2440 Bancroft Way, Berkeley CA 94704. (415)843-8080. FAX: (415)548-1355. Editorial Director: Thomas Winnett. Estab. 1967. Publishes paperback originals. Averages 5 titles/year; receives 150 submissions annually. 20% of books from first-time authors; 95% of books from unagented writers. Average print order for a writer's first book is 5,000. Pays 8-10% royalty on retail price; offers average $1,000 advance. Publishes book an average of 6 months after acceptance. Reports in 2 weeks. Book catalog for 9×12 SASE.
Nonfiction: "We publish books about the outdoors. Most of our books are trail guides for hikers and backpackers, but we also publish how-to books about the outdoors and perhaps will publish personal adventures. The manuscript must be accurate. The author must thoroughly research an area in person. If he is writing a trail guide, he must walk all the trails in the area his book is about. The outlook must be strongly conservationist. The style must be appropriate for a highly literate audience." Query, submit outline/synopsis and sample chapters, or submit complete ms demonstrating "accuracy, literacy, and popularity of subject area." Reviews artwork/photos as part of ms package.
Recent Nonfiction Title: *Afoot and Afield in Los Angeles County*, by Jerry Schad.

JOHN WILEY & SONS, 605 3rd Ave., New York NY 10158. Did not want to be listed.

WILLIAMSON PUBLISHING CO., P.O. Box 185, Church Hill Rd., Charlotte VT 05445. (802)425-2102. Editorial Director: Susan Williamson. Estab. 1983. Publishes trade paperback originals. Averages 12 titles/year; receives 450 submissions annually. 50% of books from first-time authors; 80% of books from unagented writers. Average print order for a writer's first book is 5,000-10,000. Pays 10-12% royalty on sales dollars received or makes outright purchase if favored by author. Advance negotiable. Publishes book an average of 1 year after acceptance. Simultaneous submissions OK. Reports in 1 month on queries; 3 months on mss. Book catalog for 6×9 SAE and 3 first class stamps.
Nonfiction: Subjects include business, children's activity books, education, gardening, careers, home crafts, parenting, building, animals, cooking and foods, hobbies, nature, landscaping, and children. "Our areas of concentration are children's activity books, people-oriented business and psychology books, women's issues, cookbooks, international marketing, gardening, small-scale livestock raising, family housing (all aspects), health and education." No children's fiction books, photography, politics, religion, history, art or biography. Query with outline/synopsis and sample chapters. Reviews photos as part of ms package.
Recent Nonfiction Title: *The Kids' Nature Book: 365 Indoor/Outdoor Activities*, by Susan Milord.
Tips: "We're most interested in authors who are experts in their fields—doers, not researchers. Give us a good, solid manuscript with original ideas and we'll work with you to refine the writing. We also have a highly skilled staff to develop the high quality graphics and design of our books."

‡WILLOW CREEK PRESS, Imprint of NorthWord Press, Inc., P.O. Box 1360, Minocqua WI 54548. (715)356-9800. Editor: Tom Klein. Publishes hardcover originals and reprints and trade paperback originals. Firm averages 30 titles/year; imprint averages 10 titles/year. Receives 50 submissions/year. 25% of books are from first-time authors. 100% from unagented writers. Pays 5-15% royalty on wholesale price. Offers $3,000 average advance. Publishes book an average of 9 months after acceptance. Simultaneous submissions OK. Query for electronic submissions. Reports in 3 weeks on queries; 2 months on mss. Book catalog for 8½×11 SAE and 2 first class stamps. Manuscript guidelines for #10 SASE.
Nonfiction: Coffee table book, humor, illustrated book. Subjects include sports (outdoor, hunting and fishing related). "We are seeking hunting and fishing projects with strong visual potential." Submit outline/synopsis and sample chapters.
Recent Nonfiction Title: *Wild Turkey Country*, by Lovett Williams (illustrated natural history).
Tips: "The Willow Creek imprint will publish classy illustrated titles on hunting and fishing topics for upscale sportsman."

‡WILLOWISP PRESS, INC., Subsidiary of SBF Services, Inc., 10100 SBF Drive, Pinellas Park FL 34666. (813)578-7600. Editorial Secretary: Eileen Haley. Publishes trade paperback originals. 10% of books are from first-time authors. 80% from unagented writers. Pays royalty or buys by outright purchase. Offers varying average advance. Publishes book an average of 6-12 months after acceptance. Simultaneous submissions OK. Electronic submissions "only upon request." Reports in 5 weeks on queries;

2 months on mss. Book catalog for 9×12 SAE and 5 first class stamps. Manuscript guidelines for #10 SASE.
Nonfiction: Illustrated book and juvenile. Subjects include animals, science and sports. Query with outline. Reviews artwork/photos as part of ms package "rarely."
Recent Nonfiction Title: *Auto Thrill Shows*, by Ed Perez (car racing).
Fiction: (K through Middle School only). Adventure, fantasy, horror (mild), humor, juvenile, literary, contemporary, mystery, picture books, romance, science fiction, short story collections, suspense, western and young adult. "3-6 grade level a prime market for both fiction and nonfiction. Nothing directed at high school; no poetry or religious orientation."
Recent Fiction Title: *The Scariest Stories You've Ever Heard, Part III*, by Tracey E. Dils (scary/mystery).

WILSHIRE BOOK CO., 12015 Sherman Rd., North Hollywood CA 91605. (818)765-8579. Editorial Director: Melvin Powers. Estab. 1947. Publishes paperback originals and reprints. Publishes 50 titles/year; receives 5,000 submissions annually. 80% of books from first-time authors; 75% of books from unagented writers. Average print order for a writer's first book is 5,000. Pays standard royalty; offers variable advance. Reports in 1 month. Book catalog for SASE.
Nonfiction: Health, hobbies, horsemanship, how-to, psychology, recreation, self-help, entrepreneurship, how to make money, and mail order. "We are always looking for self-help and psychological books such as *Psycho-Cybernetics, The Magic of Thinking Big* and *Guide to Rational Living*. We need manuscripts teaching mail order and entrepreneur techniques. All that I need is the concept of the book to determine if the project is viable. I welcome phone calls to discuss manuscripts or book ideas with authors." Synopsis or detailed chapter outline, 3 chapters and SASE required. Reviews artwork/photos as part of ms package.
Recent Nonfiction Title: *The Knight in Rusty Armor*, by Robert Fisher (adult fable).
Tips: "We are looking for such books as *Jonathan Livingston Seagull, The Little Prince*, and *The Greatest Salesman in the World*."

WINDSOR BOOKS, Subsidiary of Windsor Marketing Corp., P.O. Box 280, Brightwaters NY 11718. (516)321-7830. Managing Editor: Stephen Schmidt. Estab. 1968. Publishes hardcover and trade paperback originals, reprints, and very specific software. Averages 8 titles/year; receives approximately 40 submissions annually. 60% of books from first-time authors; 90% of books from unagented writers. Pays 10% royalty on retail price; 5% on wholesale price (50% of total cost); offers variable advance. Publishes book an average of 6 months after acceptance. Simultaneous submissions OK. Reports in 2 weeks on queries; 3 weeks on mss. Free book catalog and ms guidelines.
Nonfiction: How-to and technical. Subjects include business and economics (investing in stocks and commodities). Interested in books on strategies, methods for investing in the stock market, options market, and commodity markets. Query or submit outline/synopsis and sample chapters. Reviews artwork/photos as part of ms package.
Recent Nonfiction Title: *The World's Most Valuable Investment Strategy*, by B. Becker Fisher, Jr.
Tips: "Our books are for serious investors; we sell through direct mail to our mailing list and other financial lists. Writers must keep their work original; this market tends to have a great deal of information overlap among publications."

WINE APPRECIATION GUILD LTD., 155 Connecticut St., San Francisco CA 94107. (514)864-1202. FAX: (514)864-0377. Director: Maurice Sullivan. Estab. 1973. Imprints are Vintage Image and Wine Advisory Board (nonfiction). Publishes hardcover and trade paperback originals, trade paperback reprints, and software. Averages 12 titles/year; receives 30-40 submissions annually. 30% of books from first-time authors; 100% of books from unagented writers. Pays 5-15% royalty on wholesale price or makes outright purchase. Publishes book an average of 18 months after acceptance. Simultaneous submissions OK. Query for electronic submisstions. Reports in 2 months. Book catalog for $2.
Nonfiction: Cookbook and how-to—wine related. Subjects include wine, cooking and foods and travel. Must be wine-related. Submit outline/synopsis and sample chapters. Reviews artwork/photos as part of ms package.
Recent Nonfiction Title: *Winery Technology and Operations*, by Yair Margalit, Ph.D.
Tips: "Our books are read by wine enthusiasts—from neophytes to professionals, and wine industry and food industry people. We are interested in anything of a topical and timely nature connected with wine, by a knowledgeable author. We do not deal with agents of any type. We prefer to get to know the author as a person and to work closely with him/her."

WINGBOW PRESS, Subsidiary of Bookpeople, 2929 5th St., Berkeley CA 94710. (415)549-3030. Editor: Randy Fingland. Estab. 1971. Publishes trade paperback originals. Averages 4 titles/year; receives 450 submissions annually, "mostly fiction and poetry, which we aren't even considering." 50% of books from first-time authors; 100% of books from unagented writers. Pays 7-10% royalty on retail price; offers average $250 advance. Publishes book an average of 15 months after acceptance. Query for

electronic submissions. Reports in 2 weeks on queries; 2 months on mss. Book catalog for #10 SASE.
Nonfiction: Reference and self-help. Subjects include philosophy/metaphysics, psychology and women's issues. "We are currently looking most seriously at women's studies; religion/metaphysics/ philosophy; psychology and personal development. Our readers are receptive to alternative/New Age ideas. No business/finance how-to." Query or submit outline/synopsis and sample chapters.
Recent Nonfiction Title: *The Heart of the Goddess*, by Hallie Islehart Austen.

*WINSTON-DEREK PUBLISHERS, INC., Pennywell Dr., Box 90883, Nashville TN 37209. (615)329-1319/321-0535. FAX: (615)329-4811. Publisher: James W. Peebles. Estab. 1976. Imprints are Scythe Books and One Horn Press. Publishes hardcover, trade, and mass market paperback originals. Averages 70-75 titles/year; receives 3,500 submissions annually. 5% of books are reprints. 60% of books from first-time authors; 75% of books from unagented authors. Average print order for writer's first book is 3,000-5,000. "We will co-publish exceptional works of quality and style only when we reach our quota in our trade book division." Subsidy publishes 25% of books; more likely to subsidy publish juvenile books and poetry. Pays 10-15% of the net amount received on sales. Advance varies. Simultaneous submissions OK. Queries and mss without SASE will be discarded. Reports in 6 weeks on queries; 2 months weeks on mss. Book catalog and guidelines for 9×12 SASE.
Nonfiction: Biography (current or historically famous), behavioral science and health (especially interested in mss of this category for teenagers and young adults). Subjects include Americana, theology, philosophy (nontechnical with contemporary format), religion (noncultist), and inspirational. Length: 65,000-85,000 words or less. Submit outline and first 2 or 4 chapters. Reviews artwork/photos as part of ms package.
Recent Nonfiction Title: *I Choose to Live*, by Beverly D. Brown.
Fiction: Ethnic (non-defamatory); religious (theologically sound); suspense (highly plotted); and Americana (minorities and whites in positive relationships). Length: 85,000 words or less. "We can use fiction with a semi-historical plot; it must be based or centered around actual facts and events — Americana, religion, and gothic. We are looking for juvenile books (ages 9-15) on relevant aspects of growing up and understanding life's situations. No funny animals talking." Children's/juvenile books must be of high quality. Submit complete ms for children and juvenile books with illustrations, which are optional.
Recent Fiction Title: *The Mengele Hoax*, by Ray V. Waymire.
Poetry: Should be inspirational and with meaning. Poetry dealing with secular life should be of excellent quality. "We will accept unusual poetry books of exceptional quality and taste. We do not publish avant-garde poetry." Submit complete ms. No single poems.
Recent Poetry Title: *Light of the Sun*, by T. Benton Young.
Tips: "We do not publish material that advocates violence or is derogatory of other cultures or beliefs. There is now a growing concern for books about seniors, aging, and geriatic care. Outstanding biographies are quite successful, as are books dealing with the simplicity of man and his relationship with his environment. Our imprint Scythe Books for children needs material for adolescents within the 9-13 age group. These manuscripts should help young people with motivation for learning and succeeding at an early age, goal setting and character building. Biographies of famous women and men as role models are always welcomed. Always there is a need for books about current minority, scholars, issues and concerns. Stories must have a new twist and be provocative."

WIZARDS BOOKSHELF, P.O. Box 6600, San Diego CA 92166. (619)297-9879. Contact: R.I. Robb. Estab. 1972. Publishes hardcover and trade paperback originals and reprints. Firm averages 5 titles per year. Pays royalty or buys mss outright. Publishes book an average of 1 year after acceptance. Reports in 1 month on queries; 1 month on mss. Free book catalog and manuscript guidelines.
Nonfiction: Hermetic philosophy. Subjects include translation and antiquities. Submit outline/synopsis and sample chapters.
Recent Nonfiction Title: *Books of Kiu-Te, or The Tibetan Buddhist Tantras*, by David Reigle.
Tips: "Theosophists, Masons, Rosicrucians and neoplatonists are our audience."

WOODBINE HOUSE, 5615 Fishers Ln., Rockville MD 20852. (301)468-8800. FAX: (301)468-5784. Editor: Susan Stokes. Estab. 1985. Publishes hardcover and trade paperback books from first-time authors; 80% of books from unagented writers. Pays royalty; buys some mss outright. Publishes book an average of 18 months after acceptance. Simultaneous submissions OK. Query for electronic submissions. Reports in 1 month on queries; 3 months on mss. Free book catalog; ms guidelines for 6×9 SAE and 3 first class stamps.
Nonfiction: Subjects include reference, health, history, hobbies, natural history, science, education, consumer issues. Especially needs parents' guides for special needs children and the professionals who work with them. No personal accounts. Submit outline/synopsis and sample chapters. Reviews artwork/photos as part of ms.

Recent Nonfiction Title: *The Writer's Guide to Metropolitan Washington*, by Beth DeFrancis.
Tips: "Before querying, familiarize yourself with the types of books we publish and put some thought into how your book could be marketed (aside from in bookstores). Otherwise, you are wasting your time and ours."

WOODBRIDGE PRESS, P.O. Box 6189, Santa Barbara CA 93160. (805)965-7039. Contact: Howard Weeks. Imprint includes Banquo Books. Estab. 1971. Publishes hardcover and trade paperback originals. Firm averages 4-5 titles/year. Receives 250 submissions/year. 60% of books from first-time authors. 80% from unagented writers. Pays 10-15% on wholesale price. Publishes book an average of 8 months after acceptance. Simultaneous submissions OK. Reports as expeditiously as possible. Free book catalog.
Nonfiction: Cookbook (vegetarian) and self-help. Subjects include agriculture/horticulture, cooking, foods, and nutrition, gardening, health/medicine, nature/environment and psychology (popular). Query. Submit outline/synopsis and sample chapters or complete ms. Reviews artwork/photos as part of ms package.
Recent Nonfiction Title: *Artistically Cultivated Herbs*, by Elise Felton (gardening).

*WOODSONG GRAPHICS, INC., P.O. Box 304, Lahaska PA 18931-0304. (215)794-8321. Editor: Ellen P. Bordner. Estab. 1977. Publishes hardcover and trade paperback originals. Averages 6-8 titles/year; receives 2,500-3,000 submissions annually. 40-60% of books from first-time authors; 100% of books from unagented writers. Average print order for writer's first book is 2,500-5,000. Will occasionally consider subsidy publishing based on "quality of material, motivation of author in distributing his work, and cost factors (which depend on the type of material involved), plus our own feelings on its marketability." Subsidy publishes 50% of books. Pays royalty on net price; offers average $100 advance. Publishes book an average of 1 year after acceptance. Simultaneous submissions OK. Reports in 1 month on queries; reports on full mss *can* take several months, depending on the amount of material already in house. "We do everything possible to facilitate replies, but we have a small staff and want to give every manuscript a thoughtful reading." Book catalog for #10 SASE. "Manuscripts not returned unless SASE enclosed."
Nonfiction: Biography, cookbook, how-to, humor, illustrated book, juvenile, reference, and self-help. Subjects include cooking and foods, hobbies, philosophy and psychology. "We're happy to look at anything of good quality, but we're not equipped to handle lavish color spreads at this time. Our needs are very open, and we're interested in seeing any subject, provided it's handled with competence and style. Good writing from unknowns is also welcome." No pornography; only minimal interest in technical manuals of any kind. Query or submit outline/synopsis and at least 2 sample chapters. Reviews artwork/photos as part of ms package.
Recent Nonfiction Title: *Dogs and You*, by Doris Phillips.
Fiction: Adventure, experimental, fantasy, gothic, historical, humor, mainstream, mystery, romance, science fiction, suspense and western. "In fiction, we are simply looking for books that provide enjoyment. We want well-developed characters, creative plots, and good writing style." No pornography or "sick" material. Submit outline/synopsis and sample chapters.
Recent Fiction Title: *Snowflake Come Home*, by John A. Giegling.
Tips: "Good nonfiction with an identified target audience and a definite slant has the best chance of being sold to our firm. We rarely contract in advance of seeing the completed manuscript. We prefer a synopsis, explaining what the thrust of the book is without a chapter-by-chapter profile. If the query is interesting enough, we'll look at the full manuscript for further details. Partial subsidy program available for authors with a serious interest in promoting their own books."

WRITER'S DIGEST BOOKS, Imprint of F&W Publications, 1507 Dana Ave., Cincinnati OH 45207. Editorial Director: William Brohaugh. Publishes hardcover and paperback originals. Pays 10% royalty on net receipts. Simultaneous (if so advised) submissions OK. Publishes book an average of 1 year after acceptance. Enclose return postage. Book catalog for 9×12 SAE with 6 first class stamps.
Nonfiction: Writing, photography, music, and other creative pursuits, as well as general-interest subjects. "We're seeking up-to-date how-to treatments by authors who can write from successful experience. Our books stress results and how—very specifically—to achieve them. Should be well-researched, yet lively and readable. Query or submit outline/synopsis and sample chapters. Be prepared to explain how the proposed book differs from existing books on the subject. We are also very interested in republishing self-published nonfiction books and good instructional or reference books that have gone out of print before their time. No fiction or poetry. Send sample copy, sales record, and reviews if available. If you have a good idea for a book that would be updated annually, try us. We're willing to consider freelance compilers of such works." Reviews artwork/photos as part of ms package.
Recent Nonfiction Title: *The Writer's Book of Checklists*.

WYRICK & COMPANY, 12 Exchange St., Charleston SC 29401. (803)722-0881. FAX: (803)722-6771. Editor: C.L. Wyrick, Jr. Estab. 1986. Imprints are Ampthill Books and Southern Images. Publishes hardcover and trade paperback originals. Averages 6-12 titles/year. Receives 300-500 submissions/year. 90% of books from first-time authors; 100% from unagented writers. Pays 6-10% royalty. Offers $500 average advance. Publishes book an average of 9-12 months after acceptance. Simultaneous submissions OK. Query for electronic submissions. Reports in 1 month on queries; 6 months on mss. Book catalog for 9×12 SAE and 4 first class stamps. Manuscript guidelines for #10 SASE.
Nonfiction: Biography, humor, illustrated book. Subjects include art/architecture, gardening, language/literature, photography, regional and travel. Submit complete ms. Reviews artwork/photos as part of ms package.
Recent Nonfiction Title: *Nets and Doors*, by Jack Leigh.
Fiction: Humor, literary, mainstream/contemporary. Submit complete ms.
Recent Fiction Title: *Things Undone*, by Max Childers (adult).

YANKEE BOOKS, (formerly Lance Tapley, Publisher, Inc.), P.O. Box 1248, Camden ME 04843. (207)236-0933. FAX: (207)236-0941. President: Lance Tapley. Estab. 1989. Imprint is Heron Books. Publishes hardcover and trade paperbacks of New England interest. Firm averages 20-30 titles/year. Receives over 1,000 submissions/year. 50% of books from first-time authors. 90% from unagented writers. Pays 5-15% royalty on wholesale price or retail price. Offers negotiable advance. Publishes book an average of 6 months after acceptance. Simultaneous submissions OK. Reports in 2 weeks on queries and 4 months on mss. Free book catalog.
Nonfiction: Biography, coffee table book, cookbook, how-to, humor, illustrated book, juvenile, reference, self-help. Subjects include Americana, animals, anthropology/archaeology, art/architecture, child guidance/parenting, cooking, foods and nutrition, government/politics, history, language/literature, nature/environment, photography, recreation, regional, religion and sports. Query before sending ms. Reviews artwork/photos as part of ms package.
Recent Nonfiction Title: *Those Eccentric Yankees.*
Fiction: Short stories of New England interest. No erotica. Query.
Recent Fiction Title: *Wife or Spinster: Stories by Nineteenth-Century Women.*

‡*YE GALLEON PRESS, P.O. Box 287, Fairfield WA 99012. (509)283-2422. Owner: Glen C. Adams. Firm averages 25 titles/year. Subsidy publishes 25% of books. "Subsidy based on sales probabilities." Pays 5-10% royalties based on moneys actually received. No advance. Publishes book an average of 9 months after acceptance. Reports in 2 weeks on queries. Free book catalog.
Nonfiction: Biography (if sponsored). Subjects include Americana and history. Query. Reviews artwork/photos as part of ms package.
Recent Nonfiction Title: *Saga of Coeur d'Alene Indians, an Account of Chief Joseph Seltice*, by Joseph Seltice (historical).
Fiction: Historical. "I print historical fiction only if paid to do so and even then it needs to be pretty good." Query.
Tips: "We are looking for books on native Americans written from an Indian point of view. Our audence is general. A probable reader is male, college educated, middle aged or past, wearing glasses or collector of rare western U.S. history."

ZEBRA BOOKS, Imprint of Kensington Publishing Corp., 475 Park Ave. S., New York NY 10016. (212)889-2299. Publishes hardcovers, mass market paperback originals and reprints. Averages 600 titles/year; receives thousands of submissions annually. 50% of books from first-time authors. Pays royalty on retail price or makes outright purchase. Publishes book an average of 12-18 months after acceptance. Simultaneous submissions OK. Reports in 3 months on queries; 4 months on mss.
Nonfiction: Biography, how-to, humor, self-help, true crime, first-person Vietnam experience. Subjects include health, history and psychology. "We are open to many areas, especially self-help, stress, money management, child-rearing, health, war (WWII, Vietnam), and celebrity biographies." No nature, art, music, photography, poetry, religion or philosophy. Query or submit outline/synopsis and sample chapters.
Fiction: Adventure, men's action, confession, erotica, gothic, historical, horror, humor, mainstream, regencies, medical novels, westerns, romance and suspense. Tip sheet on historical romances, gothics, family sagas, adult romances and women's contemporary fiction is available. No poetry or short story collections. Query with synopsis and several sample chapters. SASE is a must.

‡ZOLAND BOOKS, INC., P.O. Box 2766, Cambridge MA 02238. (617)864-6252. FAX: (617)661-4998. Publisher: Roland Pease, Jr. Managing Editor: Peter Nielsen. Marketing Manager: John Howell. Publishes hardcover and trade paperback originals. Averages 4-6 titles/year. Receives 400 submissions/year. 33% of books from first-time authors. 75% from unagented writers. Pays 7% royalty on retail price. Publishes book an average of 1½ years after acceptance. Reports in 2 months on mss. Book catalog for 6½×9½ SASE with 2 first class stamps.

Nonfiction: Biography, coffee table book. Subjects include art/architecture, language/literature, nature/environment, photography, regional, translation, travel, women's issues/studies. Query or submit complete ms. Reviews artwork/photos as part of ms package.

Recent Nonfiction Title: *The Old Marlborough Road*, by Ken Wolgemuth, (environmental literature).

Fiction: Literary and short story collections. Submit complete ms.

Recent Poetry Title: *Don't Think: Look*, by William Corbett.

Tips: "We are most likely to publish books which provide original, thought-provoking ideas, books which will captivate the reader, and are evocative."

THE ZONDERVAN CORP., 1415 Lake Drive SE, Grand Rapids MI 49506. (616)698-6900. Contact: Manuscript Review Editor. Estab. 1931. Publishes hardcover and trade paperback originals and reprints. Averages 130 titles/year; receives 3,000 submissions annually. 20% of books from first-time authors; 80% of books from unagented writers. Average print order for a writer's first book is 5,000. Pays royalty of 14% of the net amount received on sales of cloth and softcover trade editions and 12% of net amount received on sales of mass market paperbacks. Offers variable advance. Reports in 10 weeks on proposals. Book catalog for 9×12 SASE. Recommend ms guidelines for #10 SASE. To receive a recording with submission information call (616)698-3447.

Nonfiction and Fiction: Biography, autobiography, self-help, devotional, Bible study resources, references for lay audience; some adult fiction; youth and children's ministry, teens and children. Academic and Professional Books: college and seminary textbooks (biblical studies, theology, church history, the humanities); preaching, counseling, discipleship, worship, and church renewal for pastors, professionals, and lay leaders in ministry; theological and biblical reference books; variety of books written from the Wesleyan perspective. All from religious perspective (evangelical). Immediate needs listed in guidelines. Submit outline/synopsis, 1 sample chapter, and SASE for return of materials.

Recent Nonfiction Title: *Tom Landry: An Autobiography*, by Tom Landry with Gregg Lewis.

Recent Fiction Title: *Children in the Night*, by Harold Myra.

Canadian and
International Book Publishers

This section is new to *Writer's Market*. It lists book publishers whose addresses of principal contact lie outside the United States. Some of the publishers listed in this section also have editorial offices in the U.S., however. Some of the publishers listed in the previous section also are worldwide conglomerates, and are "international" in the subject matters of the books they publish, as well as the locations in which they acquire and distribute these books.

The Canadian and International Book Publishers section was separated from the previous section for several reasons. Essentially, users of this section now have more information, an additional starting point. Writers whose ideas and books are better suited to the Canadian or international marketplace may now target their queries to the publishers in this section. Finally, the guidelines, requirements and arrangements of these book publishers are different from their U.S. counterparts.

For example, "Editors don't have the kind of power within the firm as their U.S. and British colleagues," says Joanne Kellock, a literary agent in Edmonton. "Acceptance of a manuscript is a decision made by the entire firm." The role of agents is not different, however. "Agents act the same way they do in every English language country of the world," says Kellock.

Government support of the book publishing industry in Canada is carried out on a greater scale than in the U.S. Many national and provincial arts agencies make funds available to subsidize book publishing. Writers should note that subsidy publishing contracts in Canada are most often different from those in the U.S. in that the funds originate with these agencies, not with the author. Nevertheless, there are still a few author subsidy publishers in Canada. Hopeful writers should know the difference and proceed with care when negotiating a contract.

Vibrant as the book publishing industry is in Canada, it still tends to be dominated by publishers from the United States. "About 70% of books in Canadian bookstores are from U.S. publishers," says Susanne Alexander, managing editor of Goose Lane Editions, in Fredericton, New Brunswick. "Canadian book publishers find the competition very strong, and many concentrate on publishing Canadian authors or books with Canadian themes." Again, writers should be aware of these needs. Some Canadian publishers will only publish Canadian writers.

The same holds for publishers in England, Ireland, Japan, Australia and New Zealand. Check with each individual publisher for its requirements. Canadian writers may want to look at *The Canadian Writer's Guide* (Fitzhenry & Whiteside) and *The Canadian Writer's Market* (McClelland & Stewart). *The Writer's Essential Desk Reference* (Writer's Digest Books), includes a chapter on publishing in Canada. Also of use to writers are *International Literary Market Place* (R.R. Bowker & Co., New York), and *International Writer's and Artist's Yearbook* (A&C Black Ltd., London).

Whatever your nation of residence may be, enclose International Reply Coupons (IRC's) with all correspondence to publishers outside of your country. Postage stamps from your country are not valid on letters and parcels originating elsewhere. Publishers receiving SASE's and manuscripts with stamps from other countries are likely not to return or respond to the material, as international mailing costs are a considerable expense. To defer a portion of this expense otherwise paid by you, consider sending disposable (photocopied or computer generated) outlines, synopses, sample chapters or manuscripts. This eliminates the cost of having an entire manuscript package returned. One IRC will cover the publisher's reply. They are available at post offices all over the world and can be redeemed for stamps of any country. Please note that the cost for items such as catalogs is expressed in the currency of the country in which the publisher is located.

APA PUBLICATIONS, Vigilant House, 120 Wilton Rd., London SW1V 1JZ England. Editorial Director: Brian Bell. Estab. 1970. Imprints include Insight Guides, Apa City Guides and Apa Pocket Guides. Publishes hardcover and trade paperback originals. Publishes 50 titles/year. Receives 100 submissions/ year. "We assign books and parts of books to writers and photographers. We have a strong journalistic orientation, and apply magazine criteria to both text and photography. We pay authors outright — $6,000 for editing a book, plus minor expenses; 25¢/word for writing." Publishes books an average of 10 months after assignment. Query for electronic submissions. Reports on queries in 1 month. No unsolicited mss. Book catalog and ms guidelines free on request (also see *Insight Guides*, distributed by Prentice-Hall for guidance).
Nonfiction: Travel guides. "We need writers, photographers and project editors for an enormous variety of city and country books." Query along with resume, clips and statement of area of expertise. Reviews artwork/photos as part of ms package.
Recent Nonfiction Title: *Insight Guide to Bermuda*, by Zenfell, et al (trade paper guidebook).
Tips: "We're embarking on an ambitious publishing program in the next two years to add to our list of travel titles and update existing titles. We therefore require researchers and fact-checkers in many areas."

AQUARIAN PRESS, Imprint of HarperCollins, 77-85 Fullham Palace Rd., Hammersmith, London W6 8JB England. FAX: 081-307-4440. Publishing Director: Eileen Campbell. Estab. 1952. Other imprint is Thorsons. Publishes hardcover and paperback originals. Firm averages 50-60 titles/year. Pays 7½-10% royalty. Reports in 2 months. Free book catalog.
Nonfiction: "We publish a broad-based New Age list covering the Western tradition, astrology, divination, psychic awareness and the paranormal." Sub-imprint is Mandala Books, which "is a qualty New Consciousness list covering the Eastern tradition, psychology and therapy, religion and spirituality, philosophy and the new science." Length: 50,000-100,000 words.
Recent Nonfiction Title: *Visions of Another World*.

BETWEEN THE LINES INC., 394 Euclid Ave., Toronto, Ontario M6G 2S9 Canada. (416)925-8260. FAX: (416)324-8268. Editor: Ian Rashid. Estab. 1977. Publishes trade paperback originals. Averages 9-10 titles/year. Receives 150 submissions/year. 75% of books are from first-time authors; 100% from unagented writers. Pays 8-15% royalty. Publishes ms an average of 10 months after acceptance. Simultaneous submissions OK. Query for electronic submissions. Reports in 2 months on queries; 3 months on mss. Free book catalog. Ms guidelines for #10 SASE. No U.S. stamps, please.
Nonfiction: Subjects include agriculture/horticulture, business and economics, education, culture, ethnic, gay/lesbian, government/politics, health/medicine, women's issues/studies. Query or submit outline/synopsis and sample chapters. Reviews artwork/photos as part of ms package.
Recent Nonfiction Title: *Sultans of Sleaze*, by Joyce Nelson (culture/politics).

BOREALIS PRESS, LTD., 9 Ashburn Dr., Nepean, Ontario K2E 6N4 Canada. Editorial Director: Frank Tierney. Senior Editor: Glenn Clever. Estab. 1972. Imprint is The Tecumseh Press. Publishes hardcover and paperback originals. Averages 4 titles/year; receives 400-500 submissions annually. 80% of books from first-time authors; 95% of books from unagented writers. Pays 10% royalty on retail price; no advance. Publishes book an average of 18 months after acceptance. "No multiple submissions or electronic printouts on paper more than 8½ inches wide." Reports in 8 months. Book catalog $2 with SAE and IRCs.
Nonfiction: "Only material Canadian in content." Query. Reviews artwork/photos as part of ms package. Looks for "style in tone and language, reader interest, and maturity of outlook."
Recent Nonfiction Title: *The Community Doukhobors: A People in Transition*, by John Friesen and Michael Veregin.
Fiction: "Only material Canadian in content and dealing with significant aspects of the human situation." Query.
Recent Fiction Title: *Annie*, by Hortie (novel).
Tips: "Ensure that creative writing deals with consequential human affairs, not just action, sensation, or cutesy stuff."

THE BOSTON MILLS PRESS, 132 Main St., Erin, Ontario N0B 1T0 Canada. (519)833-2407. FAX: (519)833-2195. President: John Denison. Estab. 1975. Publishes hardcover and trade paperback originals. Averages 16 titles/year; receives 100 submissions annually. 75% of books from first-time authors; 90% of books from unagented writers. Pays 6-10% royalty on retail price; no advance. Publishes book an average of 8 months after acceptance. Simultaneous submissions OK. Query for electronic submissions. Reports in 2 weeks on queries; 1 month on mss. Free book catalog.

Nonfiction: Illustrated book. Subjects include history. "We're interested in anything to do with Canadian or American history—especially transportation. We like books with a small, strong market." No autobiographies. Query. Reviews artwork/photos as part of ms package.

Recent Nonfiction Title: *Next Stop Grand Central*, by Stan Fischler (railway history).

Tips: "We can't compete with the big boys so we stay with short-run specific market books that bigger firms can't handle. We've done well this way so we'll continue in the same vein."

‡*BROADVIEW PRESS LTD.**, P.O. Box 1243, Peterborough, Ontario K9J 7H5 Canada. (705)743-8990. Senior Editor: Don LePan. Publishes hardcover and trade paperback originals. Firm averages 10-12 titles/year. Receives 250 submissions/year. 40% of books from first-time authors. 100% from unagented writers. Subsidy pubishes 5%. Subsidy determined "if the market is minimal and the book has scholarly significance." Royalty varies and negotiable. Advance negotiable. Publishes book 3-12 months after acceptance. Simultaneous submissions OK. Query for electronic submissions. Reports in 2 months. Free book catalog.

Nonfiction: Biography, reference, self-help, textbook, general nonfiction. Subjects include anthropology/archaeology, art/architecture, business and economics, government/politics, health/medicine, history, language/literature, money/finance, nature/environment, philosophy, psychology, sports, travel, women's issues/studies. "We specialize in university/college supplementary textbooks which often have both a trade and academic market. Nothing in the form of a nonfiction novel." Submit outline/synopsis and sample chapters. Sometimes reviews artwork/photos as part of ms package.

Recent Nonfiction Title: *Winter: A Natural History*, by D. Sadler (nature/coffee table).

Tips: "Publishing has become more concentrated in specific areas, with small print runs and more cost effective production. The days of large advances and long runs are overs. If I were a writer trying to market a book today, I would believe whole-heartedly in my work and not get discouraged by rejection. After all, *Gone With the Wind* was rejected 19 times."

‡**CAMDEN HOUSE PUBLISHING**, Telemedia Publishing Inc., 7 Queen Victoria Rd., Camden East, Ontario K0K 1J0 Canada. (613)378-6661. Editor: Tracy Read. Publishes hardcover originals and reprints. Averages 4-8 titles/year. Receives 75-100 submissions annually. 20% of books from first-time authors; 90% from unagented writers. Pays 7-14% royalty on retail price. Offers average $5,000 advance. Publishes book an average of 18 months after acceptance. Reporting time varies. Free book catalog.

Nonfiction: Coffee table book, cookbook, how-to, juvenile, reference. Subjects include agriculture/horticulature, animals, cooking, foods and nutrition, gardening, hobbies, nature/environment, photography, recreation, regional, travel, women's issues/studies. No New Age material. Submit outline/synopsis and sample chapters. Reviews artwork/photos as part of ms package.

Recent Nonfiction Title: *Portraits of the Rainforest*, by Adrian Forsyth (essays on an ecosystem/coffee table format).

Fiction: Humor and short story collections. Submit outline/synopsis and sample chapters.

Recent Fiction Title: *From the Country: Writings about Rural Canada*, Ed. by Wayne Grady (anthology).

CANADIAN INSTITUTE OF UKRAINIAN STUDIES PRESS, 352 Athabasca Hall, University of Alberta, Edmonton, Alberta T6G 2E8 Canada. (403)492-2972. Managing Editor: Myroslav Yurkevich. Estab. 1976. Publishes hardcover and trade paperback originals and reprints. Press averages 10-15 titles/year. Receives 10 submissions/year. Subsidy publishes 20-30% of books. (Subsidies from granting agencies, not authors.) Pays 0-2% on retail price. Publishes book an average of 2 years after acceptance. Query for electronic submissions. Reports in 1 month on queries; 3 months on mss. Free book catalog and manuscript guidelines.

Nonfiction: Scholarly. Subjects include education, ethnic, government/politics, history, language/literature, religion, sociology and translation. We publish scholarly works in the humanities and social sciences dealing with the Ukraine or Ukrainians in Canada. Query or submit complete ms. Reviews artwork/photos as part of ms package.

Recent Nonfiction Title: *The Ukrainian Religious Experience,* by David J. Goa (history/social science).
Fiction: Translations of Ukrainian literary works. We do not publish fiction, except translations of Ukrainian literary works that have scholarly value.
Recent Fiction Title: *Night and Day,* by Volodymyr Gzhytsky (autobiographical novel).
Tips: "We are a scholarly press and do not normally pay our authors. Our audience consists of University students and teachers; general public interested in Ukrainian and Ukrainian-Canadian affairs."

CANADIAN PLAINS RESEARCH CENTER, University of Regina, Regina, Saskatchewan S4S 0A2 Canada. (306)585-4795. FAX: (306)586-9862. Coordinator: Brian Mlazgar. Estab. 1974. Publishes scholarly paperback originals and some casebound originals. Averages 3-4 titles/year; receives 10-15 submissions annually. 35% of books from first-time authors. Subsidy publishes 80% (nonauthor) of books. Determines whether an author should be subsidy published through a scholarly peer review. Publishes book an average of 2 years after acceptance. Query for electronic submissions. Reports in 2 months. Free book catalog and ms guidelines. Also publishes *Prairie Forum,* a scholarly journal.
Nonfiction: Biography, coffee table book, illustrated book, technical, textbook and scholarly. Subjects include animals, business and economics, history, nature, politics and sociology. "The Canadian Plains Research Center publishes the results of research on topics relating to the Canadian Plains region, although manuscripts relating to the Great Plains region will be considered. Material *must* be scholarly. Do not submit health, self-help, hobbies, music, sports, psychology, recreation or cookbooks unless they have a scholarly approach. For example, we would be interested in acquiring a pioneer manuscript cookbook, with modern ingredient equivalents, if the material relates to the Canadian Plains/Great Plains region." Submit complete ms. Reviews artwork/photos as part of ms package.
Recent Nonfiction Title: *The Political Economy of Manitoba,* Ed. by James Silver and Jeremy Hull.
Tips: "Pay great attention to manuscript preparation and accurate footnoting, according to the *Chicago Manual of Style.*"

‡COACH HOUSE PRESS, 401 Huron St., Toronto, Ontario M4S 2G5 Canada. (416)979-7374. FAX: (416)979-7506. Publisher: Margaret McClintock. Publishes trade paperback originals. Averages 13 titles/year. Pays 10-15% royalty on retail price. Publishes book an average of 1 year after acceptance. Simultaneous submissions OK. Reports on mss in 6 months. Free book catalog and ms guidelines.
Nonfiction: Illustrated book, criticism and essays. Subjects include art/architecture, language/literature, photography. Submit ms through agent only.
Recent Nonfiction Title: *Language in Her Eye,* Ed. by Libby Scheier et al (essays).
Fiction: Experimental, feminist, gay/lesbian, literary, short story collections. Submit through agent only.
Recent Fiction Title: *Miss You Like Crazy,* by Eliza Clark.

COTEAU BOOKS, Imprint of Thunder Creek Publishing Cooperative, Suite 401, 2206 Dewdney Ave., Regina, Saskatchewan S4R 1H3 Canada. (306)777-0170. FAX: (306)565-8505. Managing Editor: Shelley Sopher. Estab. 1975. Publishes hardcover, trade paperback and mass market paperback originals. Publishes 10 titles/year; receives approximately 500 queries and mss/year. 60% of books from first-time authors; 95% from unagented writers. Pays 10% royalty on retail price or outright purchase of $50-200 for anthology contributors. Publishes book an average of 18-24 months after acceptance. Reports in 1 month on queries; 4 months on ms. Book catalog send free with SASE or IRC.
Nonfiction: Humor, illustrated book, juvenile, reference, desk calendars. Subjects include art/architecture, ethnic, history, language/literature, photography, regional and women's issues/studies. "We publish only Canadian authors; **we will consider NO American manuscripts.** We are interested in history for our region and books on multicultural themes pertaining to our region." Reviews artwork/photos as part of ms package.
Recent Nonfiction Title: *On Air: Radio in Saskatchewan,* by Wayne Schmalz.
Fiction: Ethnic, experimental, fantasy, feminist, humor, juvenile, literary, mainstream/contemporary, picture books, plays, short story collections. "No popular, mass market sort of stuff. We are a literary press." Submit complete ms. **We only publish fiction and poetry from Canadian authors.**
Recent Fiction Title: *The Last India Overland,* by Craig Grant.

HARRY CUFF PUBLICATIONS LIMITED, 94 LeMarchant Rd., St. John's, Newfoundland A1C 2H2 Canada. (709)726-6590. FAX: (709)726-0902. Editor: Harry Cuff. Managing Editor: Douglas Cuff. Estab. 1980. Publishes hardcover and trade paperback originals. Averages 10 titles/year; receives 50

Some Canadian publishers will consider book proposals by Canadian authors only. Please check each listing carefully for this restriction.

submissions annually. 50% of books from first-time authors; 100% of books from unagented writers. Pays 10% royalty on retail price. No advance. Publishes book an average of 8 months after acceptance. Reports in 6 months on mss. Book catalog for 6×9 SASE.

Nonfiction: Biography, humor, reference, technical, and textbook, all dealing with Newfoundland. Subjects include history, photography, politics and sociology. Query.

Recent Nonfiction Title: *A History of the Newfoundland Railway, Volume II* (1923-1988) by A.R. Penney.

Fiction: Ethnic, historical, humor and mainstream. Needs fiction by Newfoundlanders or about Newfoundland. Submit complete ms.

Recent Fiction Title: *Persons*, by Grace Butt.

Tips: "We are currently dedicated to publishing books about Newfoundland. We will return 'mainstream' manuscripts from the U.S. unread."

DUNDURN PRESS LTD., 2181 Queen St. E., Toronto, Ontario M4E 1E5 Canada. (416)698-0454. FAX: (416)698-1102. Publisher: Kirk Howard. Estab. 1972. Publishes hardcover, trade paperback and hardcover reprints. Averages 20 titles/year; receives 500 submissions annually. 45% of books from first-time authors; 90% of books from unagented writers. Average print order for a writer's first book is 2,000. Pays 10% royalty on retail price; 8% royalty on some paperback children's books. Publishes book an average of 1 year after acceptance. Query for electronic submissions.

Nonfiction: Biography, coffee table books, juvenile (12 and up), literary and reference. Subjects include Canadiana, art, history, hobbies, Canadian history and literary criticism. Especially looking for Canadian biographies. No religious or soft science topics. Query with outline/synopsis and sample chapters. Reviews artwork/photos as part of ms package.

Recent Nonfiction Title: *Double Take: The Story of the Elgin & Winter Garden Theatres*, by Hilary Russell.

Tips: "Publishers want more books written in better prose styles. If I were a writer trying to market a book today, I would visit bookstores and watch what readers buy and what company publishes that type of book 'close' to my manuscript."

ECW PRESS, 307 Coxwell Ave., Toronto, Ontario M4L 3B5 Canada. (416)694-3348. President: Jack David. Estab. 1979. Publishes hardcover and trade paperback originals. Publishes 20-25 titles/year; receives 120 submissions annually. 50% of books from first-time authors; 80% of books from unagented writers. Subsidy publishes (nonauthor) up to 5% of books. Pays 10% royalty on retail price. Simultaneous submissions OK. Query for electronic submissions. Reports in 2 weeks. Free book catalog.

Nonfiction: Reference and Canadian literary criticism. "ECW is interested in all Canadian literary criticism aimed at the undergraduate and graduate university market." Query. Reviews artwork/photos as part of ms package.

Recent Nonfiction Title: *Canadian Writers and Their Works*, by W.J. Keith.

Tips: "The writer has the best chance of selling literary criticism to our firm because that's our specialty and the only thing that makes us money. ECW does not publish fiction or poetry."

FITZHENRY & WHITESIDE, LTD., 91 Granton Dr., Richmond Hill, Ontario L4B 2N5 Canada. (416)764-0030. FAX: (416)764-7156. Vice President: Robert Read. Estab. 1966. Publishes hardcover and paperback originals and reprints. Royalty contract varies; advance negotiable. Publishes 50 titles/ year, text and trade. Reports in 3 months. Enclose return postage.

Nonfiction: "Especially interested in topics of interest to Canadians, and by Canadians." Textbooks for elementary and secondary schools, also biography, business, history, health, fine arts. Submit outline and sample chapters. Length: open.

Recent Title: *Canada Exploring New Directions*.

THE FRASER INSTITUTE, 626 Bute St., Vancouver, British Columbia V6E 3M1 Canada. (604)688-0221. FAX: (604) 688-8539. Assistant Director: Sally Pipes. Estab. 1974. Publishes trade paperback originals. Averages 4-6 titles/year; receives 30 submissions annually. Pays honorarium. Publishes book an average of 6 months after acceptance. Simultaneous submissions OK. Query for electronic submissions. Reports in 6 weeks. Free book catalog; ms guidelines for SAE and IRC.

Nonfiction: Analysis, opinion, on economics, social issues and public policy. Subjects include business and economics, politics, religion and sociology. "We will consider submissions of high-quality work on economics, social issues, economics and religion, public policy, and government intervention in the economy." Submit complete ms.

Recent Nonfiction Title: *Economics and the Environment: A Reconciliation*, edited by Walter Block.

Tips: "Our books are read by well-educated consumers, concerned about their society and the way in which it is run and are adopted as required or recommended reading at colleges and universities in Canada, the U.S. and abroad. Our readers feel they have some power to improve society and view our books as a source of the information needed to take steps to change unproductive and inefficient ways of behavior into behavior which will benefit society. Recent trends to note in book publishing include affirmative action, banking, broadcasting, insurance, health care and religion. A writer has the best chance of selling us books on government, economics, finance, or social issues."

GOOSE LANE EDITIONS, 248 Brunswick St., Fredericton, New Brunswick E3B 1G9 Canada. Acquisitions Editor: John Timmins. Firm averages 12-14 titles/year. Receives 350 submissions/year. 20% of books are from first-time authors. 75-100% from unagented writers. Pays royalty on retail price. Offers $250-500 average advance. Simultaneous submissions OK. Reports in 3 queries. Book catalog and manuscript guidelines free on request.
Nonfiction: Biography, coffee table book, cookbook, illustrated book, reference, literary history (Canadian). Subjects include art/architecture, cooking, foods and nutrition, history, language/literature, nature/environment, photography, translation, women's issues/studies. Query or submit outline/synopsis and sample chapters. Reviews artwork/photos as part of ms package.
Recent Nonfiction Title: *The Real Klondike Kate*, by T. Ann Brennan (historical biography).
Fiction: Experimental, feminist, historical, literary and short story collections. "Our needs in fiction never change: substantial, character-centred literary fiction (either as novel or collection of short stories) which shows more interest in the craft of writing (i.e. use of language, credible but clever plotting, shrewd characterization) than in cleaving to tired, mainstream genre-conventions." No mainstream, mass market, genre, mystery, thriller, or sci-fi fiction, please." Query or submit complete ms.
Recent Fiction Title: *A Guide to Animal Behavior*, by Douglas Glover (contemporary short stories).
Tips: "Trends we have noticed are continuing cutbacks, close-downs, belt-tightening, and drying-up of funds and state support for the arts. Writers should send us books that show a very well-read author who has thought long and deeply about the art of writing and, in either fiction or nonfiction, has something of Canadian relevance to offer. Our audience is literate, thoughtful, well-read, non-mainstream. If I were a writer trying to market a book today, I would contact the targeted publisher with a query letter, and synopsis, request book catalogue, and manuscript guidelines. Purchase a book (recent) from the publisher in relevant area, if possible. Never send a complete ms blindly to a publisher without first investigating it. Never send a ms without IRC's or sufficient return postage (valid in that country if outside U.S.)."

GUERNICA EDITIONS, Box 633, Station N.D.G., Montreal, Quebec H4A 3R1 Canada. (514)987-7411. FAX: (514)982-9793. President/Editor: Antonio D'Alfonso. Publishes trade paperback originals, reprints and software. Averages 20 titles/year; receives 1,000 submissions annually. 5% of books from first-time authors. Average print order for a writer's first book is 1,000. Subsidy publishes (nonauthor) 50% of titles. "Subsidy in Canada is received only when the author is established, Canadian-born and active in the country's cultural world. The others we subsidize ourselves." Pays 3-10% royalty on retail price. Makes outright purchase of $200-5,000. Offers 10¢/word advance for translators. IRCs required. "American stamps are of no use to us in Canada." Reports in 1 month on queries; 6 weeks on mss. Book catalog for SASE.
Nonfiction: Biography, juvenile. Subjects include art, film, history, music, philosophy, politics, psychology, religion and Canadiana.
Recent Nonfiction Title: *Conscience and Coercion: Ahmadi Muslims and Orthodoxy in Pakistan*, by Antonio Gualtieri.
Fiction: Ethnic, historical, mystery. "We wish to open up into the fiction world. No country is a country without its fiction writers. Canada is producing some fine fiction writers. We'd like to read you. No first novels." Query.
Poetry: "We wish to have writers in translation. Any writer who has translated Italian poetry is welcomed. Full books only. Not single poems by different authors, unless modern, and used as an anthology. First books will have no place in the next couple of years." Submit samples.
Recent Poetry Title: *Nomadic Trajectory*, by Pasquale Verdicchio.
Tips: "We are seeking less poetry, more modern novels, and translations into the English or French."

‡HARLEQUIN ENTERPRISES, LTD., Subsidiary of Torstar Corporation, Home Office: 225 Duncan Mill Rd., Don Mills, Ontario M3B 3K9 Canada. (416)445-5860. President and Chief Executive Officer: Brian E. Hickey. Vice President and Editor-in-Chief: Horst Bausch. Editorial divisions: Harlequin Books (Editorial Manager: Karin Stoecker); Silhouette Books (Editorial Manager: Isabel Swift; for editorial requirements, see separate listing, under Silhouette Books); and Worldwide Library/Gold Eagle Books (Editorial Director and Assistant to the Editor-in-Chief: Randall Toye; see separate listing under Worldwide Library). Imprints: Harlequin Romance and Harlequin Presents (Paula Eykelhof, Editor); Harlequin Superromance (Marsha Zinberg, Senior Editor); Harlequin Temptation (Birgit Davis-Todd, Senior Editor); Harlequin Regency Romance (Marmie Charndoff, Editor); Harlequin Intrigue and Harlequin American Romance (Debra Matteucci, Senior Editor and Editorial Coordinator); Harlequin Historicals (Tracy Farrell, Senior Editor). Estab. 1949. Submissions for Harlequin Intrigue, Harlequin American Romance and Harlequin Historicals should be directed to the desig-

Close-up

Susanne Alexander
Managing Editor
Goose Lane Editions

In 1956 Fred Cogswell founded Fiddlehead Poetry Books as a forum for Canada's emerging poets. Cogswell, a professor of literature at The University of New Brunswick in Fredericton, self-financed the small press for 25 years. During that period, Cogswell published some 300 books of poetry. In the early 1980s, control of Fiddlehead transferred to Peter Thomas, and the small press became Goose Lane Editions. Thomas introduced innovative fiction and regional nonfiction to Fiddlehead's well-established line of poetry and made the publishing house more viable. Goose Lane publishes award-winning authors such as Helen Weinzweig, Douglas Glover and Dorothy Roberts, and promising newcomers Yvonne Trainer, Bradd Burningham and Herb Curtis.

Susanne Alexander signed on as managing editor at Goose Lane Editions in 1989, and the once small poetry press has never been more active. With an academic background in English literature and theater, and experience in radio and print media journalism, Alexander moved to Fredericton to take a job with the Performing Arts Council of the provincial government. Alexander then brought her administrative training to Goose Lane Editions.

"All of our books have a Canadian connection," Alexander says. "Many have a New Brunswick focus." Goose Lane Editions has struck a working balance, publishing one-third nonfiction, one-third fiction and one-third poetry. "We have published books by a couple of writers from the U.S. in recent years, but their books have been on subjects of interest to Canadians."

Subject areas of Goose Lane's books range from folklore and history to humor, biography and literary criticism. Their fiction and poetry needs are for literary works of merit and substance. Many of their books are regional, focusing on New Brunswick or the other maritime provinces. All of them appeal to the Canadian reader and discerning readers looking for excellent literature.

Goose Lane Editions receives nearly 400 submissions each year, a little less than half coming from the United States. "My advice to all writers interested in publishing their books with us, especially U.S. writers, is to investigate the company, write a query and ask for our guidelines and catalog. Our areas of interest are evident from the catalog."

Decisions are made at bimonthly editorial board meetings. A panel of five, which includes Alexander, looks for a track record. "Writers should have published their work in journals before contacting us," she says. "That's a fairly standard order of things in this business." The board seeks to maintain the balance of nonfiction, fiction and poetry with works of substance and high literary merit. Beyond that their primary interest is in Canadian writers. "We feel a certain responsibility in that area," Alexander says.

Although Goose Lane Editions is deeply rooted in the tradition of Fiddlehead Poetry Books, they do not publish chapbooks. Nor do they publish genre fiction, New Age material or mass market books of any kind. Goose Lane Editions distributes books in English and French by several associated book publishers: York Press, New Ireland Press & Non-Entity Press, Four East Publications, Acadiensis Press, Owl's Head Press & Percheron Press and Editions d'Acadie.

The staff of Goose Lane Editions (from left to right): Susanne Alexander, Helen Thomas, John Timmins, Gary Stairs, Julie Scriver, Tanya Flinn and Peter Thomas. (The geese in the foreground are Evinrude and The Perfessor.)

Alexander advises writers to gain experience with writing by having their colleagues read and critique their work. "Also, don't exaggerate the merits of your work in the query letter," she says. "Simple, straightforward queries are best." Writers from the United States hoping to join the few who have published a book with Goose Lane Editions should, of course, enclose a sufficient number of International Reply Coupons with their queries and submissions. This practice is not a courtesy, but a necessity when writers expect a reply from a publisher outside their country of origin.

—Mark Kissling

nated editor and sent to Harlequin Books, 300 E. 42nd St., New York NY 10017 (212)682-6080. All other submissions should be directed to the Canadian address. Publishes mass market paperback originals. Averages 780 titles/year; receives 10,000 submissions annually. 10% of books from first-time authors; 20% of books from unagented writers. Pays royalty. Offers advance. Publishes book an average of 1 year after acceptance. Reports in 2 weeks on queries; 3 months on submissions. Free writer's guidelines.

Fiction: Adult contemporary and historical romance, including novels of romantic suspense (Intrigue), short contemporary romance (Presents and Romance), long contemporary romance (Superromance), short contemporary sensuals (Temptation), period historical (Regency) and adult historical romance (Historicals). "We welcome submissions to all of our lines. Know our guidelines and be familiar with the style and format of the line you are submitting to. Stories should possess a life and vitality that makes them memorable for the reader."

Tips: "Harlequin's readership comprises a wide variety of ages, backgrounds, income and education levels. The audience is predominantly female. Because of the high competition in women's fiction, readers are becoming very discriminating. They look for a quality read. Read as many recent romance books as possible in all series to get a feel for the scope, new trends, acceptable levels of sensuality, etc."

‡THE FREDERICK HARRIS MUSIC CO., LIMITED, 529 Speers Rd., Oakville, Ontario L6K 2G4 Canada. (416)845-3487. Managing Editor: Trish Sauerbrei. Publishes trade paperback originals. Firm averges 30 titles/year. Receives 90 submissions/year. Pays royalty on retail price. Publishes book an average of 1-2 years after acceptance. Simultaneous submissions OK. Reports in 1 month on queries; 3 months on mss. Free book catalog and manuscript guidelines.

Nonfiction: Juvenile (piano methods) textbooks, music repertoire collections (piano, vocal and violin, classical only). Subjects include music only. "We are looking for albums of contemporary piano (original compositions). No religious or choral music or pop music of any kind." Query. Submit outline/synopsis and sample chapters (for texts) and complete ms (for music). Reviews artwork/photos as part of ms package.

Recent Nonfiction Title: *Study Guides for Piano*, (8 vols.) by Royal Conservatory of Music, Toronto, Canada (student's and teacher's guide).

‡HERALD PRESS CANADA, Subsidiary of Mennonite Publishing House, 490 Dutton Dr., Waterloo, Ontario N2L 6H7 Canada. (412)887-8500. Book Editor: S. David Garber. Firm publishes hardcover and trade paperback originals and reprints. Firm averages 34 titles/year (a few are by Congregational Literature Division); division publishes 30 titles/year. Receives 900 submissions/year. 15% of books are from first-time authors. 98% from unagented writers. Subsidy publishes 5% of books. "Specialized volumes for church agencies. This is not an option for an individual author, only for a church agency." Pays 10-12% royalty on retail price. Publishes book an average of 1 year after acceptance. Accepts electronic submissions only with hard copy. SASE. Reports in 3 weeks on queries; 2 months on mss. Book catalog 60¢. Manuscript guidelines free on request.

Nonfiction: Coffee table book, cookbook, illustrated book, juvenile, reference, self-help, textbook. Subjects include child guidance/parenting, cooking, foods and nutrition, education, Christian, ethnic, Mennonite, Amish, history, language/literature, money/finance, stewardship, nature/environment, psychology, counseling, self-help, recreation, lifestyle, missions, justice, peace. "We will be seeking books on Christian inspiration, medium-level Bible study, current issues of peace and justice, family life, Christian ethics and lifestyle, and earth stewardship." Does not want to see war, politics, or the end of the world. Query or submit outline/synopsis and sample chapters. Reviews artwork/photos as part of ms package.

Recent Nonfiction Title: *Dancing in the Dark*, by Elsie K. Neufeld (personal grief experience).

Fiction: Ethnic (Mennonite/Amish), historical (Mennonite/Amish), humor, juvenile (Christian orientation), literary, picture books, religious, romance (Christian orientation), short story collections and young adult. Does not want to see war, gangsters, drugs, explicit sex, or cops and robbers. Query or submit outline/synopsis and sample chapters.

Recent Fiction Title: *Sara's Summer*, by Naomi R. Stucky (teen visits Hutterites).

‡HORSDAL & SCHUBART PUBLISHERS LTD., Box 1, Ganges, British Columbia V0S 1E0 Canada. (604)537-4334. Editor: Marlyn Horsdal. "We consider any well-written, useful work of biography or history, mainly for western Canada."

ALWAYS submit unsolicited manuscripts or queries with a self-addressed, stamped envelope (SASE) within your country or a self-addressed envelope with International Reply Coupons (IRC) purchased from the post office for other countries.

HOUNSLOW PRESS, Subsidiary of Anthony R. Hawke Limited, 124 Parkview Ave., Willowdale, Ontario M2N 3Y5 Canada. (416)225-9176. President: Tony Hawke. Estab. 1972. Publishes hardcover and trade paperback originals. Firm averages 8 titles/year. Receives 250 submissions/year. 10% of books from first-time authors. 95% from unagented writers. Pays 10-12½% royalty on retail price. Offers $500 average advance. Publishes book an average of 1 year after acceptance. Reports in 1 month on queries; 2 months on mss. Free book catalog.

Nonfiction: Biography, coffee-table book, cookbook, how-to, humor, illustrated book and self-help. Subjects include animals, art/architecture, business and economics, child guidance/parenting, cooking, foods and nutrition, health/medicine, history, money/finance, photography, translation and travel. "We are looking for controversial manuscripts and business books." Query.

Recent Nonfiction Title: *Holy Grail Across the Atlantic*, by Michael Bradley (history).

Fiction: Literary and suspense. "We really don't need any fiction for the next year or so." Query.

Poetry: "We do not need any poetry in the next few years."

Tips: "If I were a writer trying to market a book today, I would try to get a good literary agent to handle it."

‡INSTITUTE OF PSYCHOLOGICAL RESEARCH, INC./INSTITUT DE RECHERCHES PSYCHOLO-GIQUES, INC., 34 Fleury St. W., Montréal, Québec H3L 1S9 Canada. (514)382-3000. President and General Director: Jean-Marc Chevrier. Publishes hardcover and trade paperback originals and reprints. Firm averages 12 titles/year. Receives 15 submissions/year. 10% of books from first-time authors. 100% from unagented writers. Pays 10-12% royalty. Publishes book an average of 6 months after acceptance. Reports in 2 months on mss.

Nonfiction: Textbook, psychological tests. Subjects include philosophy, psychology, science and translation. "We are looking for psychological tests in French or English." Submit complete ms.

Recent Nonfiction Title: *Épreuve individuelle d'habileté mentale*, by Jean-Marc Chevrier (intelligence test).

Tips: "Psychologists, guidance counsellors, professionals. Schools, school boards, hospitals, teachers, government agencies and industries comprise our audience."

INTERNATIONAL SELF-COUNSEL PRESS, LTD., 1481 Charlotte Rd., North Vancouver, British Columbia V7J 1H1 Canada. (604)986-3366. President: Diana R. Douglas. Managing Editor: Ruth Wilson. Publishes trade paperback originals. Averages 15 titles/year; receives 1,000 submissions annually. 80% of books from first-time authors; 95% of books from unagented writers. Average print order for a writer's first book is 4,000. Pays 10% royalty on wholesale price. Publishes book an average of 9 months after submission of contracted ms. Simultaneous submissions OK. Query for electronic submissions. Reports in 2 months. Free book catalog and manuscript guidelines.

Nonfiction: Specializes in self-help and how-to books in law, business, reference, and psychology for the lay person. Query or submit outline and sample chapters. Follow *Chicago Manual of Style*.

Recent Nonfiction Title: *Start and Run a Successful Home-Based Business*.

‡JESPERSON PRESS LTD., 39 James Lane, St. John's, Newfoundland A1E 3H3 Canada. (709)753-0633. FAX: (709)753-5507. Publishing Assistant: Shellie Dawe. Publishes hardcover and trade paperback originals. Firm averages 10 titles/year. Receives 30 submissions/year. 100% of books from unagented writers. Pays 10% royalty. Publishes book an average of 9 months after acceptance. Simultaneous submissions OK. Query for electronic submissions. Reports in 1 month on queries; 3 months on mss. Free book catalog.

Nonfiction: Biography, cookbook, humor, illustrated book, juvenile, reference, technical and textbook. Subjects include animals, cooking, foods and nutrition, education, ethnic, history, language/literature, military/war, music/dance, nature/environment, regional, religion and translation. "We deal mainly with mss centering around the Newfoundland culture. No books on the history of flying in Newfoundland or Canada." Submit complete ms. "Prefers to receive all photos/artwork after acceptance of mss."

Recent Nonfiction Title: *Window of Agates*, by Dr. D.G. Pitt (history of church).

Fiction: Adventure, historical, humor, mainstream/contemporary, mystery, romance, short story collections and young adult. "We, for the most part, publish Newfoundland authors." Submit complete ms.

Recent Fiction Title: *A Dream Come True*, by Janice Stuckless (young adult/romance).

LONE PINE PUBLISHING, #206 10426 81st Ave., Edmonton, Alberta T6E 1X5 Canada. (403)433-9333. Editor-in-Chief: Gary Whyte. Estab. 1980. Imprints are Lone Pine, Pine Bough, Home World, Pine Candle and Pine Cone. Publishes hardcover and trade paperback originals and reprints. Averages 12-20 titles/year. Receives 200 submissions/year. 45% of books from first-time authors; 95% from unagented writers. Pays royalty. Simultaneous submissions OK. Reports in 1 month on queries; 2 months on mss. Free book catalog.

Nonfiction: Biography, how-to, juvenile and nature/recreation guide books. Subjects include animals, anthropology/archaeology, art/architecture, business and economics, cooking, foods and nutrition, gardening, government/politics, history, nature/environment (this is where most of our books fall), photography, sports, travel (another major category for us). We publish recreational and natural history titles, and some historical biographies. Most of our list is set for the next year and a half, but we are interested in seeing new material. Submit outline/synopsis and sample chapters. Reviews artwork/photos as part of ms package.

Recent Nonfiction Title: *Inside Outer Canada*, by David Kilgour.

Tips: "Writers have their best chance with recreational or nature guidebooks. If I were a writer trying to market a book today, I would query first, to save time and money, and possibly even contact prospective publishers before the book is completed. Always send material with SASE or IRC's, and make the ms clean and easy to read."

‡**McCLELLAND & STEWART INC.**, Suite 900, 481 University Ave., Toronto, Ontario M5G 2E9 Canada. (416)598-1114. Contact: Editorial Assistant. Publishes hardcover, trade paperback, and mass market paperback originals, and mass market paperback reprints. Firm averages 100 titles/year. Receives 3,000 submissions/year. 1% of books is from first-time authors. 30% from unagented writers. Pays 10-15% royalties on retail price. Offers $10,000 average advance. Publishes book an average of 1 year after acceptance. Simultaneous submissions OK. Reports in 1 month on queries.

Nonfiction: Biography, coffee table book, cookbook, how-to, humor, illustrated book and self-help. Subjects include art/architecture, business and economics, child guidance/parenting, cooking, foods and nutrition, gardening, government/politics, health/medicine, history, hobbies, language/literature, military/war, money/finance, music/dance, nature/environment, photography, psychology, recreation, religion, sports, travel. "We are looking for material of special interest to Canadian readers. No unsolicited manuscripts, please." Query. All unsolicited mss are returned unopened. Reviews artwork/photos as part of ms package.

Recent Nonfiction Title: *Canadian Impressionism*, by Duval (art).

Fiction: Adventure, historical, literary, mainstream/contemproary, short story collections and suspense. "We are looking for books by major Canadian writers. Again, no unsolicited manuscripts, please." Query. All unsolicitd mss are returned unopened.

Recent Fiction Title: *Friend of My Youth*, by Alice Munro (short stories).

Poetry: "No further poetry at this time."

Recent Poetry Title: *The Woman on the Shore*, by Al Purdy.

McGRAW-HILL RYERSON LIMITED, Division of McGraw-Hill, 300 Water St., Whitby, Ontario L1N 9B6 Canada. Senior Editor: Mr. Glen Ellis. Publishes hardcover and trade paperback originals and trade paperback reprints. 75% of books are originals; 25% are reprints. Firm averages 120 titles/year; imprint averages 45 titles/year. 15% of books from first-time authors. 85% from unagented writers. Pays 7½-15% royalty on retail price. Offers $4,000 average advance. Publishes book an average of 1 year after acceptance. Simultaneous submissions OK. Reports in 1 month on queries.

Nonfiction: Biography, cookbook, how-to, reference, self-help, software, technical. Subjects include Canadiana, business and economics, computers and electronics, cooking, foods and nutrition, military/war, money/finance, photography (aviation), sports, aviation. "We are looking for books on Canadian small business, and personal finance. No books and proposals that are primarily American in focus. We publish for the Canadian market." Query. Submit outline and sample chapters.

Recent Nonfiction Title: *Canadian Wings*, by John McQuarrie (Canadian military aircraft/photography).

Tips: "Writers have the best chance selling us well-priced nonfiction, usually trade paper format. Our audience consists of consumers who need current information. If I were a writer trying to market a book today, I would test market ideas and research relevant potential publishers."

‡**MACMILLAN OF CANADA**, Canada Publishing Corp., 29 Birch Ave., Toronto, Ontario M4V 1ER Canada. (416)963-8830. Editorial Assistant: Joanne Ashdown. Publishes hardcover and trade paperback originals and reprints. Averages 30-50 titles/year; receives 2,000 submissions annually. Less than 25% of books from first-time authors; less than 15% from unagented writers. 10% subsidy published; must meet Ontario/Canada Arts Council requirements. Pays 8-12% royalty on retail price. Offers average $2,000-3,000 advance. Publishes book an average of 6-7 months after acceptance. Simultaneous submissions OK. Query for electronic submissions. Reports in 1 month on queries; 3 months on mss. Ms guidelines for #10 SASE.

Nonfiction: Biography, cookbook, how-to, humor, reference, self-help and software. Subjects include child guidance/parenting, computers and electronics, cooking, foods and nutrition, gardning, government/politics, health/medicine, history, language/literature, military/war, money/finance, psychology, recreation, religion, science, sports, women's issues/studies. Query or submit outline/synopsis and sample chapters.

Recent Nonfiction Title: *Lighthearted Everyday Cooking,* by Anne Lindsay.
Tips: "If I were a writer trying to market a book today, I would do preliminary research an competition, special sales potential, and ways of gaining an international readership."

THE MERCURY PRESS, Imprint of Aya Press, Box 446, Stratford, Ontario N5A 6T3 Canada. Editor: Beverley Daurio. Publishes trade paperback originals and reprints. Averages 8 titles/year. Receives 200 submissions/year. 10% of books from first-time authors; 99% from unagented writers. Pays 10% royalty on retail price. Publishes book an average of 1 year after acceptance. Query for electronic submissions. Reports in 2 months. Free book catalog.
Nonfiction: Biography. Subjects include art/architecture, government/politics, history, language/literature, music/dance, sociology and women's issues/studies. Query.
Recent Nonfiction Title: *City Hall & Mrs. God,* by Cary Fagan (social issues).
Fiction: Feminist, literary, mainstream/contemporary and short story collections. No genre fiction. Submit complete ms.
Recent Fiction Title: *Hannah B.,* by Veronica Ross.
Poetry: No unsolicited mss until 1992. No traditional, rhyme, confessional. Submit complete ms.
Recent Poetry Title: "Sky, A Poem in Four Pieces," by Libby Scheier.
Tips: "If I were a writer trying to publish a book today, I would study markets objectively, listen to feedback, present mss professionally, and use IRC's plus SAE for submissions to Canada."

‡*NETHERLANDIC PRESS, P.O. Box 396, Station A, Windsor, Ontario N9A 6L7 Canada. (519)944-2171. Editor: Hendrika Ruger. Publishes various nonfiction, fiction and poetry by and about Dutch-Canadians.

NEWEST PUBLISHERS LTD., #310, 10359 Whyte Ave., Edmonton, Alberta T6E 1Z9 Canada. (403)432-9427. FAX: (403)432-9429. General Manager: Liz Grieue. Estab. 1977. Publishes trade paperback originals. Averages 8 titles/year. Receives 100 submissions/year. 40% of books from first-time authors; 90% from unagented writers. Pays 10% royalty. Publishes book an average of 2 years after acceptance. Simultaneous submissions OK. Reports in 2 weeks on queries; 3 months on mss. Book catalog for 9×12 SAE and 4 first class stamps.
Nonfiction: Literary/essays. Subjects include art/architecture, ethnic, government/politics (Western Canada), history (Western Canada) and Canadiana. Query.
Recent Nonfiction Title: *Home Place,* by Stan Rowe (ecology).
Fiction: Literary and short story collections. We are looking for Western Canadian authors. Submit outline/synopsis and sample chapters.
Recent Fiction Title: *Grace Lake,* by Glen Huser.
Tips: "Our audience consists of people interested in the west and north of Canada; teachers, professors. If I were a writer trying to market a book today, I would study publisher's catalogues and their recent titles. I'd always include a SASE."

‡NIMBUS PUBLISHING LIMITED, Subsidiary of H.H. Marshall Ltd., Box 9301, Station A, Halifax, Nova Scotia B3K 5N5 Canada. (902)454-8381. Contact: Dorothy Blythe. Estab. 1980. Publishes hardcover and trade paperback originals and trade paperback reprints. Averages 12 titles/year; receives 60 submissions annually. 50% of books from first-time authors; 100% of books from unagented writers. Average print order for a writer's first book is 3,000. Pays 10% royalty on retail price. Publishes book an average of 2 years after acceptance. Query for electronic submissions. Computer printout submissions acceptable. Reports in 2 months on queries; 4 months on mss. Free book catalog.
Nonfiction: Biography, coffee table books, cookbooks, illustrated books, juvenile and books of national and regional interest. Subjects include cooking and foods, history, nature, travel and regional. "We do some specialized publishing, otherwise our audience is the trade market and tourist in Canada." Query or submit outline/synopsis and a minimum of 1 sample chapter. Reviews artwork/photos as part of ms package.
Tips: "Titles of regional interest, with potential for national or international sales, have the best chance of selling to our firm."

‡*OISE PRESS, Subsidiary of Ontario Institute for Studies in Education, 252 Floor, W., Toronto, Ontario M5S 1V6 Canada. (416)923-6641, ext. 2531. FAX: (416)926-4725. Editor-in-Chief: Hugh Oliver. Publishes trade paperback originals. Averages 25 titles/year; receives 100 submissions annually. 20% of books from first-time authors; 90% of books from unagented writers. Subsidy publishes (nonauthor) 5% of books. Pays 10-15% royalty; rarely offers an advance. Simultaneous submissions OK. Query for electronic submissions. Reports in 1 week on queries; 2 months on submissions. Free book catalog and guidelines.

Nonfiction: Textbooks and educational books. "Our audience includes educational scholars; educational administrators, principals and teachers and students. In the future, we will be publishing fewer scholarly books and more books for teachers and students." Submit complete ms. Reviews artwork/photos as part of ms package.

Recent Nonfiction Title: *Education Lost*, by David Solway.

‡**OOLICHAN BOOKS**, P.O. Box 10, Lantzville, British Columbia V0R 2H0 Canada. (604)390-4839. Publisher: Ron Smith. Publishes hardcover originals and trade paperback originals and reprints; 99% of books are originals; 1% are reprints. Firm averages 10 titles/year. Receives 1000 submissions/year. 40% of books from first-time authors. 90% from unagented writers. Pays 6-10% royalty on retail price. Publishes book an average of 18 months after acceptance. "At present, we are booked two years in advance." Simultaneous submissions OK. Query for electronic submissions; does not accept without hard copy. Reports in 1 month on queries; 3 months on mss. Book catalog for 9×12 SAE and 2 first class stamps. Manuscript guidelines for #10 SASE.

Nonfiction: Biography and history. Subjects include ethnic, government/politics, history, language/literature, regional western Candian, religion, translation and native issues. "We are interested in considering western Canadian regional history and autobiography. However, our list is now booked two years in advance (to the end of 1992, at present). Any manuscripts we accepted would not be published until at least 1993. No how-to books, including cookbooks; no military, Americana, art/architecture, or business." Query or submit outline/synopsis and sample chapters. Reviews artwork/photos as part of ms package occasionally.

Recent Nonfiction Title: *Indian Government: Its Meaning in Practice*, by Frank Cassidy (native issues).

Fiction: Ethnic, experimental, feminist, humor, literary and short story collections. "Our list is now booked two years in advance. However, we are always interested in new fiction, either short story collections or novels. We are no longer publishing children's, juvenile, or young adult titles." Query or submit outline/synopsis and sample chapters.

Recent Fiction Title: *A Planet of Eccentrics*, by Ven Begamudré (short story collection).

Poetry: "We are seeking contemporary poetry—poets should be aware of current aesthetics. Our list is booked two years in advance; any manuscripts considered would be for publication in 1993 or 1994. We do not want to see doggerel, card verse, or verse that proselytizes." Submit 10-15 samples.

Recent Poetry Title: *Woman At Mile Zero*, by Linda Rogers (prose poem).

Tips: "Oolichan is a literary press interested in fiction, poetry and regional history. Our decision to publish is ultimately based on the quality of the writing."

ORCA BOOK PUBLISHING LTD., P.O. Box 5626 Stn. B., Victoria, British Columbia V8R 6S4 Canada. (604)380-1229. Publisher: R. Tyrrell. Estab. 1984. Publishes hardcover and trade paperback originals. Publishes 15-20 titles/year; receives 500-600 submissions/year. 50% from first-time authors; 80% from unagented writers. Pays 10-12 ½% royalty on retail price. Offers average $500 advance. Publishes ms and average of 9-12 months after acceptance. Reports in 3 weeks on queries; 2 months on mss. Book catalog for 9×12 SAE and $1 (Canadian) postage; ms guidelines for SASE.

Nonfiction: Biography, illustrated book, travel guides, children's. Subjects include history, nature/environment, recreation, sports, and travel. Needs history (West Coast Canadian), biography, and young children's book. Query or submit outline/synopsis and sample chapters. All unsolicited mss are returned unopened. Reviews artwork/photos as part of ms package.

Recent Nonfiction Title: *Penny Candy, Bobskates and Frozen Roadapples*, by R. Thompson (memoir/biography).

Fiction: Juvenile, literary, mainstream/contemporary. Needs West Coast Canadian contemporary fiction; illustrated children's books, 3-6-year-old range. Query or submit outline/synopsis and sample chapters. All unsolicited mss are returned unopened.

Recent Fiction Title: *Maxine's Tree*, by D. Leger-Haskell (children's).

PEGUIS PUBLISHERS LIMITED, 520 Hargrave St., Winnipeg, Manitoba R3A 0X8 Canada. (204)956-1486. Vice President, Acquisitions: Judy Norget. Educational paperback originals. Averages 20 titles/year. Receives 150 submissions/year. 80% of books from first-time authors; 100% from unagented writers. Pays 10% average royalty on educational net (trade less 20%). Publishes book an average of 1-2 years after acceptance. Simultaneous submissions OK. Electronic submissions only if accompanied by hard copy. Reports in 2 months on queries; 1 month on mss if quick rejection, up to 1 year if serious consideration. Free book catalog.

Nonfiction: Educational (focusing on teachers' resource material for primary education, integrated whole language, guidance). Submit outline/synopsis and sample chapters or complete ms preferably.

Recent Nonfiction Title: *The Learners' Way*, by Forester/Reinhard (teacher's resource K-3).

Fiction: Children's books for whole-language classrooms only.

Recent Fiction Title: *Lion in the Lake*, by Oberman (bilingual, French/English, alphabet book).

Tips: "Writers have the best chance selling us quality educational resource materials. Our audience consists of educators (teachers, counsellors, administrators) and school children."

PLAYWRIGHTS CANADA PRESS, Imprint of Playwrights Union of Canada, 54 Wolseley St., 2nd floor, Toronto, Ontario M5J 1A5 Canada. (416)947-0201. FAX: (416)947-0159. Contact: Editorial Board. Estab. 1972. Publishes paperback originals and reprints of plays by Canadian citizens or landed immigrants, whose plays have been professionally produced on stage. Receives 100 member submissions/year. 50% of plays from first-time authors; 50% from unagented authors. Pays 10% royalty on list price. Publishes about 1 year after acceptance. Simultaneous submissions OK. Free play catalog and ms guidelines. Non-members should query. Accepts children's plays.
Recent Fiction Title: *Scientific Americans*, by John Mighton (play).

‡POLESTAR PRESS LTD., RR #1, Winlaw, British Columbia V0G 2J0 Canada. (604)226-7670. Editor: Michelle Benjamin. Publishes hardcover originals and trade paperback originals and reprints. Publishes 12 titles/year. Receives 300 submissions/year. 50% of books are from first-time authors. 100% from unagented writers. Subsidy publishes 35% of books. Literary quality as determined by the publisher and the Canada Council. Pays 10% royalty on retail price. Offers $300 average advance. Publishes book an average of 6 months after acceptance. Simultaneous submissions OK. Reports in 6 weeks on queries; 3 months on mss. Book catalog for 9 × 6 SAE and 60¢ Canadian postage. Manuscript guidelines for business size SAE and 40¢ Canadian postage.
Nonfiction: Humor, hockey and history. Subjects include history, nature/environment, regional (B.C. railways), sports, women's issues/studies and engagement calendars. "Our list is filled for the next year." Submit outline/synopsis and sample chapters.
Recent Nonfiction Title: *Seeing the Forest Among the Trees: The Case For Wholistic Forest Use*, by Herb Hammond (forestry/ecology).
Fiction: Feminist, humor, literary, short story collections and young adult. "Accessible and well-crafted, sophisticated sense of language, strong narrative. Humor is always appreciated. One or two fiction titles are published annually." Submit outline/synopsis and sample chapters.
Recent Fiction Title: *Rapid Transits and Other Stories*, by Holley Rubinsky (short fiction). "Our poetry needs are filled for the next two years."
Tips: "Write provocative, political, wickedly funny, lucid, poignant prose with brilliant language."

PORCÉPIC BOOKS, 4252 Commerce Circle, Victoria, British Columbia V8Z 4M2 Canada. (604)727-6522. Estab. 1971. Publishes trade paperback originals. Averages 12 titles/year; receives 300 submissions annually. 40% of books from first-time authors. 70% of books from unagented writers. Pays 10% royalty on retail price; offers $600 average advance. Publishes ms an average of 1 year after acceptance. Simultaneous (if so advised) submissions OK. Reports in 2 months on queries; 3 months on mss.
Nonfiction: Biography (regional), juvenile and young adult. Subjects include history (regional) and regional (Pacific Northwest). Intersted only in areas mentioned above. Submit outline and sample chapters.
Recent Nonfiction Title: *The Brother XII*, by Charles Lillard (regional biography).
Fiction: Experimental, science fiction and speculative fiction. "Anticipate no need for fiction in next year."
Recent Fiction Title: *Tesseracts³*, edited by Candas Jane Dorset.
Tips: "Make sure the manuscript is well written. We see so many mss that only the unique and excellent can't be put down."

PRENTICE-HALL CANADA, INC., College Division, Subsidiary of Simon & Schuster, 1870 Birchmount Road, Scarborough, Ontario M1P 2J7 Canada. (416)293-3621. FAX: (416)299-2539. Editorial Director: Cliff Newman. Estab. 1960. Publishes hardcover and paperback originals and software. Averages 50 titles/year. Receives 200-300 submissions annually. 30-40% of books from first-time authors; 100% of books from unagented writers. Pays 10-15% royalty on net price. Publishes book an average of 14 months after acceptance. Prefer submission on disk with hard copy accompanying.
Nonfiction: The College Division publishes textbooks suitable for the community college and large university market. Most submissions should be designed for existing courses in all disciplines of study. Will consider software in most disciplines, especially business, technology and sciences. Canadian content is important. The division also publishes textbooks and reference books in computer science, technology and mathematics.
Recent Nonfiction Title: *Psychology*, by D. Martin.
Tips: "Manuscripts of interest to Canadians and/or by authors resident in Canada should be forwarded to above address. All other manuscripts should be sent to Prentice-Hall, Inc., Englewood Office, N.J. 07632."

PRENTICE-HALL CANADA, INC., School Division, Subsidiary of Simon & Schuster, 1870 Birchmount Road, Scarborough, Ontario M1P 2J7 Canada. (416)293-3621. FAX: (416)299-2529. President: Rob Greenaway. Director of Research and Marketing: MaryLynne McSchino. Estab. 1960. Imprint is Globe/Modern Curriculum Press. Averages 30 titles annually.

Nonfiction: Publishes texts, workbooks, and instructional media including computer courseware, video disks, and filmstrips for elementary grades and junior and senior high schools. Subjects include geography, history, language arts, science, social studies, health and French as a second language. Query.
Recent Nonfiction Title: *The Law in Canada*, by Barnhorst/Zetzl.

PRENTICE-HALL CANADA, INC., Trade Division, Subsidiary of Simon & Schuster, 1870 Birchmount Road, Scarborough, Ontario M1P 2J7 Canada. (416)293-3621. Managing Editor: Tanya Long. Estab. 1960. Publishes hardcover and trade paperback originals. Averages 25-30 titles/year; receives 750-900 submissions annually. 30% of books from first-time authors; 40% of books from unagented writers. Negotiates royalty and advance. Publishes book an average of 9 months after acceptance. Query for electronic submissions. Reports in 10 weeks. Ms guidelines for #10 SAE and 1 IRC.
Nonfiction: Subjects of Canadian and international interest; art, politics and current affairs, sports, business, travel, health and food. Send outline and sample chapters. Reviews artwork/photos as part of ms package.
Recent Nonfiction Title: *Wilderness of Mirrors: The Life of Gerald Bull*, by Dale Grant (current affairs).
Tips: Needs general interest nonfiction books on topical subjects. "Present a clear, concise thesis, well-argued with a thorough knowledge of existing works. We are looking for more books on social and political issues."

‡PRESS GANG PUBLISHERS, Feminist Co-Operative, 603 Powell St., Vancouver, British Columbia V6A 1H2 Canada. (604)253-2537. Editor: Barbara Kuhne. Publishes nonfiction, fiction and poetry, giving priority to Canadian women and women of color.

‡RED DEER COLLEGE PRESS, 56 Ave. and 32 St., Box 5005, Red Deer, Alberta T4N 5H5 Canada. Managing Editor: Dennis Johnson. Subsidiaries include Northern Lights Books for Children, Discovery Books, Writing West. Publishes hardcover and trade paperback originals. Firm averages 10-12 titles/year. Receives 1,200 submissions/year. 25% of books are from first-time authors. 50% from unagented writers. Pays 7-12% royalty on retail price. Offers $500-7,500 average advance (depends heavily on genre). Publishes book an average of 12-18 months after acceptance. Simultaneous submissions OK. Reports in 3 weeks on queries; 3 months on mss. Book catalog for 8½×11 SAE. Manuscript guidelines not available.
Nonfiction: Biography, coffee table book, cookbook, illustrated book, juvenile. Subjects include cooking, foods and nutrition, language/literature, and science (natural history only). Reviews artwork/photos as part of ms package.
Recent Nonfiction Title: *The Last Great Dinosaurs*, by Monty Reid (adult illustrated).
Fiction: Juvenile, literary, picture books, short story collections and young adult. "We are seeking quality literary novels and short story collections." No sci-fi or romance. Query or submit outline/synopsis and sample chapters. All unsolicited mss are returned unopened.
Recent Fiction Title: *The Hockey Fan Came Riding*, by Birk Sprokton and Kristian Gunnars (short fiction).
Poetry: Long or serial poem sequences, experimental poetry, prose poetry. No confessional verse, nothing that rhymes. Submit 6 samples.
Recent Poetry Title: *Vanity Shades*, by Mary Howes (serial poetry).

‡*REIDMORE BOOKS, INC., 012, 11523-100 Ave., Edmonton, Alberta T5K 0J8 Canada. (403)488-5091. Editor-in-Chief: Nancy Mackenzie. Publishes hardcover originals. Firm averages 10-12 titles/year. Receives 18-20 submissions/year. 60% of books from first-time authors. 100% from unagented writers. Subsidy publishes 5-10% of books. Pays royalty. Offers $1,500 average advance. Publishes book an average of 8 months after acceptance. Query for electronic submissions. Reports in 1 month on queries. Free book catalog.
Nonfiction: Textbook. Subjects include ethnic, government/politics, history. Query. All unsolicited mss are returned unopened. Reviews artwork/photos as part of ms package.
Recent Nonfiction Title: *Families Around the World*, by Don Massey (educational text).

‡SIMON & PIERRE PUBLISHING CO. LTD., Suite 404, 815 Danforth Ave., Toronto, Ontario M4J 1L2 Canada. (416)463-0313. Director of Operations: Jean Paton. Publishes hardcover and trade paperback originals and reprints. Firm averages 6-10 titles/year. Receives 300 submissions/year. 50% of books are from first-time authors. 85% from unagented writers. Trade book royalty 10% sliding to 15% on retail price. Education royalty is 8% of net. Offers $500 average advance. Publishes book an average of 1 year after acceptance. Simultaneous submissions OK. Reports in 3 weeks on queries. Free book catalog and ms guidelines.

Nonfiction: *Canadian authors only.* Biography, reference and drama. Subjects include language/literature, music/dance (drama) and Sherlockian literature criticism. "We are looking for Canadian drama and drama related books." Query or submit outline/synopsis and sample chapters. Sometimes reviews artwork/photos as part of ms package.

Recent Nonfiction Title: *The Actor's Survival Kit*, by Miriam Newhouse and Peter Messaline (the business side of acting in Canada).

Fiction: Adventure, historical, literary, mainstream/contemporary, mystery, plays (Canadian; must have had professional production.), short story collections and young adult. "No romance, sci-fi or experimental." Query or submit outline/synopsis and sample chapters.

Recent Fiction Title: *An Emerald for Imanja*, by Michael Jacot (novel).

Recent Poetry Title: *Singed Leaves, A Book of Haiku*, by Marshall Hryciuk.

Tips: "We are looking for Canadian themes by Canadian authors. Special interest in drama and drama related topics; also Sherlockian. If I were a writer trying to market a book today, I would check carefully the types of books published by a publisher before submitting manuscript; books can be examined in bookstores, libraries, etc.; should look for a publisher publishing the type of book being marketed. Clean manuscripts essential; if work is on computer disk, give the publisher that information. Send information on markets for the book, and writer's resume, or at least why the writer is an expert in the field. Covering letter is important first impression."

*THISTLEDOWN PRESS, 668 East Place, Saskatoon, Saskatchewan S7J 2Z5 Canada. (306)244-1722. Editor-in-Chief: Patrick O' Rourke. Estab. 1975. Publishes trade paperback originals by resident Canadian authors *only.* Averages 10-12 titles/year; receives 150 submissions annually. 10% of books from first-time authors; 90% of books from unagented writers. Average print order for a writer's first (poetry) book is 500 or (fiction) 1,000. Subsidy publishes (nonauthor) 100% of books. Pays standard royalty on retail price. Publishes book an average of 18-24 months after acceptance. Reports in 2 weeks on queries; 2 months on poetry mss; 3 months on fiction mss. Book catalog and guidelines for #10 SASE.

Fiction: Juvenile (ages 8 and up), literary. Interested in fiction mss from resident Canadian authors only. Minimum of 30,000 words. Accepts no unsolicited work. Query first.

Recent Fiction Title: *Paradise Cafe and Other Stories*, by Martha Brooks (young adult).

Poetry: "The author should make him/herself familiar with our publishing program before deciding whether or not his/her work is appropriate." No poetry by people *not* citizens and residents of Canada. Submit complete ms. Minimum of 60 pages. Prefers poetry mss that have had some previous exposure in literary magazines. Accepts no unsolicited work. Query first.

Recent Poetry Title: *Calling Texas*, by Bert Almon.

Tips: "We prefer to receive a query letter first before a submission. We're looking for quality, well-written literary fiction—for children and young adults and for our adult fiction list as well."

‡THORSONS, Imprint of HarperCollins, 77-85 Fullham Palace Rd., Hammersmith, London W6 8JB, England. FAX: 081-307-4440. Publishing Director: Eileen Campbell. Estab. 1930. Other imprint is Aquarian Press. Publishes hardcover and paperback originals. Firm averages 50-60 titles/year. Pays 7½-10% royalty. Reports in 2 months. Free book catalog.

Nonfiction: Publishes books on health and lifestyle, environmental issues, business, popular psychology, self-help, and positive thinking.

Recent Nonfiction Title: *Food Combining for Health.*

*CHARLES E. TUTTLE PUBLISHING COMPANY, INC., 2-6 Suido 1-Chome, Tokyo 112, Japan. FAX: 03-5689-4926. Managing Editor: Ray Furse. Imprint is Yenbooks (less serious Asia-related books). Publishes hardcover and trade paperback originals and reprints. Averages 36 titles/year. Receives 750 submissions/year. 10% of books from first-time authors; 80% from unagented writers. Subsidy publishes 5% of books. Pays 6-10% on wholesale price. Offers $1,000 average advance. Publishes book an average of 8-12 months after acceptance. Simultaneous submissions OK. Query for electronic submissions. Reports in 2 weeks on queries; 2 months on manuscripts. Free book catalog and manuscript guidelines.

Nonfiction: Cookbook, how-to, humor, illustrated book and reference. Subjects include art/architecture, business and economics, cooking, foods and nutrition, government/politics, history, language/literature, money/finance, philosophy, regional, religion, sports and travel. "We want Asia-related, but specifically Japan-related manuscripts on various topics, particularly business, martial arts, language, etc." Query with outline/synopsis and sample chapters. Reviews artwork as part of ms package.

Recent Nonfiction Title: *Japan: The Art of Living,* by Amy Katoh and Shin Kimura.
Fiction: Literature of Japan or Asia in English translation. Query with outline/synopsis and sample chapters.
Recent Fiction Title: *The Square Persimmon and Other Stories,* by Takashi Atoda.
Poetry: Submit samples.
Tips: "Readers with an interest in Japan and Asia—culture, language, business, foods, travel, etc.—are our audience."

THE UNIVERSITY OF ALBERTA PRESS, 141 Athabasca Hall, Edmonton, Alberta T6G 2E8 Canada. (403)492-3662. FAX: (403)492-0719. Director: Norma Gutteridge. Estab. 1969. Imprint is Pica Pica Press. Publishes hardcover and trade paperback originals, and trade paperback reprints. Averages 10 titles/year; receives 100-200 submissions annually. 60% of books from first-time authors; majority of books from unagented writers. Average print order for a writer's first book is 1,000. Pays 10% royalty on retail price. Publishes book an average of 1 year after acceptance. Query for electronic submissions. Reports in 1 week on queries; 3 months on mss. Free book catalog and ms guidelines.
Nonfiction: Biography, how-to, reference, technical, textbook, and scholarly. Subjects include art, history, nature, philosophy, politics, and sociology. Especially looking for "biographies of Canadians in public life, and works analyzing Canada's political history and public policy, particularly in international affairs. No pioneer reminiscences, literary criticism (unless in Canadian literature), reports of narrowly focused studies, unrevised theses." Submit complete ms. Reviews artwork/photos as part of ms package.
Recent Nonfiction Title: *The Buffalo People: Prehistoric Archaeology on the Canadian Plains,* by Liz Bryan.
Tips: "We are interested in original research making a significant contribution to knowledge in the subject."

*THE UNIVERSITY OF CALGARY PRESS, 2500 University Drive NW, Calgary, Alberta T2N 1N4 Canada. (403)220-7578. FAX: (403)282-6837. Director: L. D. Cameron. Estab. 1981. Publishes scholarly hard cover and paperback originals. Averages 12-16 titles/year; receives 120 submissions annually. 50% of books from first-time authors; 99% of books from unagented authors. Subsidy publishes (nonauthor) 100% of books. "As with all Canadian University presses, UCP does not have publication funds of its own. Money must be found to subsidize each project. We do not consider publications for which there is no possibility of subvention." Publishes book average of 1 year after acceptance. Pays negotiable royalties. "Ms must pass a two tier review system before acceptance." Query for electronic submissions. Reports in 2 weeks on queries; 2 months on mss. Free book catalog and guidelines.
Nonfiction: "UCP has developed an active publishing program that includes up to 12 new scholarly titles each year and 8 scholarly journals. (For UCP's purposes works of scholarship are usually required to be analytical in nature with unity of purpose and unfolding argument and aimed primarily at an audience of specialists.) UCP publishes in a wide variety of subject areas and is willing to consider any innovative scholarly manuscript. The intention is not to restrict the publication list to specific areas."
Recent Nonfiction Title: *Applied Inorganic Chemistry,* by T. W. Swaddle.
Tips: "If I were trying to interest a scholarly publisher, I would prepare my manuscript on a word processor and submit a completed prospectus, including projected market, to the publisher."

‡THE UNIVERSITY OF OTTAWA PRESS, 603 Cumberland, Ottawa, Ontario K1N 6N5 Canada. (613)564-9287. Editor, English Publications: Janet Shorten. Publishes trade paperback originals. Firm averages 28 titles/year; 15 titles/year in English. Receives 70 submissions/year. 20% of books from first-time authors. 95% from unagented writers. Determines subsidy by preliminary budget. Pays 5-15% royalty on net price. Publishes book an average of 2 years after acceptance. Reports in 2 months on queries; 4 months on mss. Free book catalog and manuscript guidelines.
Nonfiction: Reference, textbook, scholarly. Subjects include education, Canadian government/politics, Canadian history, language/literature, nature/environment, philosophy, religion, sociology, translation, women's issues/studies. "We are looking for scholarly mss by academic authors resident in Canada." No trade books. Submit outline/synopsis and sample chapters.
Recent Nonfiction Title: *How to Write an Executive Summary,* by Ed and Judi Jewinski (self-help for government and business).
Tips: "Envision audience of academic specialists and (for some books) educated public."

VANWELL PUBLISHING LIMITED, 1 Northrup Cres., P.O. Box 2131 Stn. B, St. Catharines, Ontario L2M 6P5 Canada. (416)937-3100. General Editor: Ms. Lynn J. Hunt. Publishes trade paperback originals and reprints. Firm averages 5-7 titles/year. Receives 100 submissions/year. 85% of books from first-time authors. 100% from unagented writers. Pays 5-12% royalty on wholesale price. Offers $200 average advance. Publishes book an average of 1 year after acceptance. Query for electronic submis-

sions. Reports in 1 month on queries; 6 months on mss. Free book catalog.
Nonfiction: Biography. Subjects include education, military/war and regional. All military/history related. Reviews artwork/photos as part of ms package.
Tips: "The writer has the best chance of selling a manuscript to our firm which is in keeping with our publishing program, well written and organized. Our audience: Older male, history buff, war veteran; regional tourist; students. Military/aviation and Canadian history have the best chance with us. However, we have reduced our publishing program for the next few years."

‡**VEHICULE PRESS**, Box 125, Place du Parc Station, Montreal, Quebec H2W 2M9 Canada. (514)844-6073. President/Publisher: Simon Dardick. Imprints include Signal Editions (poetry) and Dossier Quebec (history, memoirs). Publishes trade paperback originals by Canadian authors *only*. Averages ten titles/year; receives 250 submissions annually. 20% of books from first-time authors; 95% of books from unagented writers. Pays 10-15% royalty on retail price; offers $200-500 advance. Publishes book an average of 1 year after acceptance. Query for electronic submissions. Computer printout submissions acceptable; prefers letter-quality. "We would appreciate receiving an IRC with SAE rather than U.S. postage stamps which we cannot use." Reports in 1 month on queries; 2 months on mss. Book catalog for 9×12 SAE with IRCs.
Nonfiction: Biography and memoir. Subjects include Canadiana, history, politics, social history and literature. Especially looking for Canadian social history. Query. Reviews artwork/photos as part of ms package.
Recent Nonfiction Title: *Swinging in Paradise: The Story of Jazz in Montreal,* by John Gilmore.
Poetry: Contact Michael Harris, editor. Looking for Canadian authors only. Submit complete ms.
Recent Poetry Title: *Infinite Worlds: The Poetry of Louis Dudek.*
Recent Fiction Title: *A Private Performance,* by Kenneth Radu.
Tips: "We are only interested in Canadian authors."

*****VESTA PUBLICATIONS, LTD.**, Box 1641, Cornwall, Ontario K6H 5V6 Canada. (613)932-2135. FAX: (613)932-1641. Editor-in-Chief: Stephen Gill. Estab. 1976. Publishes trade paperback and mass market paperback originals. Pays 10% minimum royalty on wholesale price. Subsidy publishes 5% of books. "We ask a writer to subsidize a part of the cost of printing; normally, it is 50%. We do so when we find that the book does not have a wide market, as in the case of university theses and the author's first collection of poems. The writer gets 25 free copies and 10% royalty on paperback editions." No advance. Publishes 4 titles/year; receives 350 submissions annually. 80% of books from first-time authors; 100% of books from unagented writers. Simultaneous submissions OK if so informed. Query for electronic submissions. Reports in 3 weeks. Send SAE with IRCs. Free book catalog.
Nonfiction: Publishes Americana, biography, ethnic, government/politics, philosophy, language/literature, money/finance, reference, and religious books. Accepts nonfiction translations. Query or submit complete ms. Reviews artwork/photos. Looks for knowledge of the language and subject. "Query letters and mss should be accompanied by synopsis of the book and biographical notes." State availability of photos and/or illustrations to accompany ms.
Recent Nonfiction Title: *Rethinking History,* by Dr. H. Crum.
Fiction: Ethnic and literary. Query.
Poetry: Submit 5-6 samples.
Recent Poetry Title: *We Flowers of Thirst,* by Stephen Gill (love poems).

WALL & EMERSON, INC., 6 O'Connor Dr., Toronto, Ontario M4K 2K1 Canada. (416)467-8685. FAX: (416)696-2460. President: Byron E. Wall. Imprints are Wall & Thompson and Wall Editions. Publishes hardcover and trade paperback originals and reprints. Firm averages 5-10 titles/year. 50% of books from first-time authors. 100% from unagented writers. Subsidy publishes 10% of books. Only subsidies provided by external granting agencies accepted. Generally these are for scholarly books with a small market. Pays royalty of 8-15% on wholesale price. Publishes book an average of 1 year after acceptance. Simultaneous submissions OK. Prefers electronic submissions. Reports in 1 month on queries; 3 months on mss. Free book catalog.
Nonfiction: Reference and textbook. Subjects include business and economics, computers and electronics, education, government/politics, health/medicine, history, language/literature, nature/environment, philosophy, psychology, sociology, science and mathematics. "We are looking for any undergraduate college text that meets the needs of a well-defined course in colleges in the U.S. and Canada." Submit outline/synopsis and sample chapters.

Some Canadian publishers will consider book proposals by Canadian authors only. Please check each listing carefully for this restriction.

Recent Nonfiction Title: *Children of Prometheus: A History of Science and Technology*, by James MacLachlan (textbook).
Tips: "We are most interested in textbooks for college courses; books that meet well defined needs and are targeted to their audiences are best. Our audience consists of college undergraduate students and college libraries. If I were a writer trying to market a book today, I would identify the audience for the book and write directly to the audience throughout the book. I would then approach a publisher that publishes books specifically for that audience."

‡WEIGL EDUCATIONAL PUBLISHERS LTD., 2114 College Ave., Regina, Saskatchewan S4P 1C5 Canada. (306)569-0766. Publisher: Linda Weigl. Publishes hardcover originals and reprints. Firm averages 6-7 titles/year. Receives 50-100 submissions/year. 75% of books are from first-time authors. 100% from unagented writers. Pays 5-12% royalty on retail price. Publishes book an average of 2 years after acceptance. Query for electronic submissions. Reports in 1 week on queries; 1 month on ms. Free book catalog.
Nonfiction: Biography, how-to, juvenile, reference, self-help and textbook. Subjects include agriculture/horticulture, animals, child guidance/parenting, education, ethnic and language/literature. Submit outline/synopsis and sample chapters. Reviews artwork/photos as part of ms package.
Recent Nonfiction Title: *Technology and Change in Canada*, by David Evans et al (school).
Fiction: Ethnic, historical, and juvenile.
Tips: "Audience is school students."

WESTERN PRODUCER PRAIRIE BOOKS, P.O. Box 2500, Saskatoon, Saskatchewan S7K 2C4 Canada. Publishing Director: Jane McHughen. Estab. 1954. Publishes hardcover and paperback originals and reprints. Averages 18 titles/year; receives 400-500 submissions annually. 20% of books from first-time authors; 80% of books from unagented writers. Average print order for a writer's first book is 4,000. Pays negotiable royalty on list price. Publishes book an average of 1 year after acceptance. Query for electronic submissions. Reports in 3 months. Free book catalog; ms guidelines for SAE with IRCs.
Nonfiction: Publishes coffee table books, humor, illustrated books, juvenile, art/architecture, gardening, history, nature, photography, biography, reference, agriculture, economics and politics. No textbooks. "We are looking for natural history, western biography and history." Submit outline, synopsis and 2-3 sample chapters with contact sheets or prints if illustrations are to accompany ms.
Recent Nonfiction Title: *Prairie Dreams*, by Courtney Milne (photography).

*WOOD LAKE BOOKS, INC., P.O. Box 700, Winfield, British Columbia V0H 2C0 Canada. (604)766-2778. FAX: (604)766-2736. Editor: Jim Taylor. Estab. 1979. Publishes trade paperback originals. Firm averages 6-10 titles/year. Receives 200 submissions/year. 75% of books from first-time authors. 99% from unagented writers. Subsidy publishes 5% of books. If subsidy is available, we will accept it. But the decision is first made on the manuscript—*then* we consider additional funding. Pays 7% minimum royalty on retail price, depends on situation. Publishes book an average of 9 months after acceptance. Simultaneous submissions OK. Query for electronic submissions. We decide on titles at editorial meetings 2 times a year, May and November. Waiting period therefore varies. Rejections take less time than acceptances. Free book catalog.
Nonfiction: We are looking for mss that approach religion from the perspective of personal experience, anecdotal style; religion that makes common sense, is open to new insights and has practical application in daily life. No academic or theoretical mss; anything based on biblical inerrancy; anything that promotes ill feeling against any race, religion, sex, etc.; anything dealing with prophecy about the future. Query. Submit outline/synopsis and sample chapters. Reviews artwork/photos as part of ms package.
Recent Nonfiction Title: *Christian Parenting*, by Donna Sinclair and Yvonne Stewart.
Tips: "Our audience includes people who struggle to make their beliefs relevant to daily living, without having to park their minds on a shelf. If I were a writer trying to market a book today, I would ask myself how many people I know personally who would be willing to pay to get their hands on the book. If it's less than, say, 75% of the people I know well, I would quit now."

‡WORLDWIDE LIBRARY, Division of Harlequin Enterprises Ltd., 225 Duncan Mill Rd., Don Mills, Ontario M3B 3K9 Canada. (416)445-5860. Editorial Director: Randall Toye. Imprints are Gold Eagle Books, Worldwide Mysteries. Publishes mass market paperback originals and reprints. Averages 72 titles/year; receives 1,100 submissions annually. 20% of books from first-time authors; 25% of books from unagented writers. Offers negotiable royalty on retail price; offers average $3,000-7,000 advance. Publishes book an average of 1 year after acceptance. Reports in 1 month on queries; 2 months on mss.
Fiction: Action-adventure and mystery. Prefers complete ms; will accept synopsis and first 3 chapters. Query Senior Editor: Feroze Mohammed for action-adventure and Dianne Moggy for mystery.
Recent Fiction Title: *Murder on Safari*, by Hillary Waugh.
Tips: "We are an excellent market for action-adventure and near-future fiction."

YORK PRESS LTD., P.O. Box 1172, Fredericton, New Brunswick E3B 5C8 Canada. (506)458-8748. General Manager/Editor: Dr. S. Elkhadem. Estab. 1975. Publishes trade paperback originals. Averages 10 titles/year; receives 50 submissions annually. 10% of books from first-time authors; 100% of books from unagented writers. Pays 10-20% royalty on wholesale price. Publishes book an average of 6 months after acceptance. Reports in 1 week on queries; 1 month on ms. Free book catalog; ms guidelines for $2.50.

Nonfiction and Fiction: Reference, textbook and scholarly. Especially needs literary criticism, comparative literature and linguistics and fiction of an experimental nature by well-established writers. Query.

Recent Nonfiction Title: *Tennessee Williams: Life, Work and Criticism*, by F. Londré.

Recent Fiction Title: *Red White & Blue*, by Ben Stoltzfus.

Tips: "If I were a writer trying to market a book today, I would spend a considerable amount of time examining the needs of a publisher *before* sending my manuscript to him. Scholarly books and creative writing of an experimental nature are the only kinds we publish. The writer must adhere to our style manual and follow our guidelines exactly."

Small Presses

Following are listings of small presses that publish three or fewer titles per year or new presses that had not published four books by the time they completed a questionnaire for a listing in this edition of *Writer's Market*. This means the publishing opportunity is more limited, but these companies are still legitimate markets and have expressed an interest in being listed in *Writer's Market*. Writers should query for more information when first contacting a small press.

Please note that our use of the term *small press* is not an inherent statement about the size of these companies or the books they publish. Many of the publishers listed in previous sections consider themselves small presses even though they publish 10 or more books in a year. We use the term to describe publishers that publish three or fewer titles per year.

These presses operate in much the same way as their larger counterparts and share many similar problems and concerns. Just because they publish three or fewer titles per year does not mean they have the time to look at more manuscripts. In fact, the opposite is often true. Editors tell us, for example, that many writers are sending unsolicited complete manuscripts. Writers should send for small press catalogs, and approach the presses with queries, synopsis/outlines and sample chapters, just as they would the larger houses.

ACORN PUBLISHING, P.O. Box 7067W, Syracuse NY 13261. (315)689-7072. Editor: Mary O. Robb. Estab. 1985. Publishes trade paperback originals on health, recreation, sports and general fitness.

AHSAHTA PRESS, Boise State University, Dept. of English, 1910 University Dr., Boise ID 83725. (208)385-1246. Co-Editor: Tom Trusky. Publishes Western American poetry in trade paperback. Reads SASE samplers annually, January through March.

‡ARDOR PUBLISHING, 7804 Vicksburg Ave., Los Angeles CA 90045. (213)645-7571. Manager: W. Kane. Publishes trade paperback originals.

‡ASTARTE SHELL PRESS, P.O. Box 10453, Portland ME 04104. (207)871-1817. Partner: Eleanor H. Haney. New press looking for manuscripts on feminist spirituality, politics and justice.

‡AUTO BOOK PRESS, P.O. Bin 711, San Marcos CA 92069. (619)744-3582. Editorial Director: William Carroll. Estab. 1955. Publishes hardcover and paperback originals. Automotive material only: technical or definitive how-to.

BARN OWL BOOKS, P.O. Box 226, Vallecitos NM 87581. (505)582-4226. Estab. 1983. Imprint is Amazon Press. Nonfiction and fiction on women's, gay/lesbian, feminist and mainstream topics. Query first.

‡BARTON & BRETT, PUBLISHERS, INC., P.O. Box 421, Sea Cliff NY 11579. Publisher: Barbara J. Brett. Publishes general interest books on timely subjects.

‡BERKSHIRE TRAVELLER PRESS, P.O. Box 297, Stockbridge MA 01262. (413)298-3636. FAX: (413)298-5323. Editor: Virginia Rowe. Estab. 1966. Publishes travel and recreation guides, Americana, Shaker books, Berkshire history, cookbooks, popular psychology.

‡BLACK BEAR PUBLICATIONS, 1916 Lincoln St., Croydon PA 19021-8026. (215)788-3543. Editor: A. Jeanne. Publishes poetry collections reflective of the world and our environment.

‡BLACK TIE PRESS, P.O. Box 440004, Houston TX 77244-0004. (713)789-5119. Publisher: Peter Gravis. Estab. 1986. Imprints are Deluxe, Matineé and Plain Editions. Publishes fiction and poetry.

CAROUSEL PRESS, P.O. Box 6061, Albany CA 94706. (415)527-5849. Editor/Publisher: Carole T. Meyers. Estab. 1976. Publishes nonfiction, family-oriented travel books.

CHALLENGER PRESS, Suite 8, 540 Alisal Rd., Solvang CA 93463. (805)688-4439. FAX: (805)686-1340. Project Director: Marilyn White-Munn. Estab. 1989. Publishes self-help books.

CLARITY PRESS INC., 3277 Roswell Rd. NE, #469, Atlanta GA 30305. (404)231-0649. FAX: (404)231-3899. Editorial Committee Contact: Annette Gordon. Estab. 1984. Publishes manuscripts on minorities, human rights in US, Middle East and Africa.

CLOTHESPIN FEVER PRESS, 5529 N. Figueroa, Los Angeles CA 90042. (213)254-1373. Contact: Jenny Wrenn. Estab. 1986. Publishes lesbian fiction and nonfiction.

‡COLORMORE INC., P.O. Box 111249, Carrollton TX 75011-1249. (316)636-9326. President: Susan C. Koch. Publishes travel guides for kids to specific U.S. and Canadian cities.

CORKSCREW PRESS, Suite 234, 4470-107 Sunset Blvd., Los Angeles CA 90027. Editorial Director: J. Croker Norge. Estab. 1988. Publishes trade humor and humorous how-to books.

CREATIVE WITH WORDS PUBLICATIONS, P.O. Box 223226, Carmel CA 93922. (408)649-1682. Publisher/Editor: Brigitta Geltrich. Estab. 1975. Publishes poetry and prose.

‡DAEDALUS PRESS, Subsidiary of *Whole Notes Magazine*, P.O. Box 1374, Las Cruces NM 88004. (505)382-7446. Editor: Nancy Peters Hastings. Publishes poetry chapbooks.

DIAMOND PRESS, Box 2458, Doylestown PA 18901. (215)345-6094. Marketing Director: Paul Johnson. Publishes trade paperback originals on softball and antiques.

DIMI PRESS, 3820 Oak Hollow Lane SE, Salem OR 97302. (503)364-7698. FAX: (503)364-9727. President: Dick Lutz. Estab. 1981. Trade paperback originals of health and psychology, also certain other nonfiction titles.

‡DUSTY DOG CHAPBOOK SERIES, P.O. Box 1103, Zuni NM 87327. (505)782-4958. Editor: John Pierce. Estab. 1990. Looking for high caliber, well crafted poetry. Not interested in rhyme, light verse or haiku. Publishes three poetry chapbooks per year.

‡FALLEN LEAF PRESS, P.O. Box 10034, Berkeley CA 94709. (415)848-7805. Owner: Ann Basart. Publishes books on music and music scores.

FIESTA CITY PUBLISHERS, P.O. Box 5861, Santa Barbara CA 93150-5861. (805)733-1984. President: Frank E. Cooke. Publishes how-to, health cookbooks and music books.

‡FORD-BROWN & CO., PUBLISHERS, P.O. Box 2764, Boston MA 02208-2764. Publisher: Steven Ford Brown. Publishes poetry and poetry criticism.

FROG IN THE WELL, P.O. Box 170052, San Francisco CA 94117. (415)431-2113. Editor: Susan Hester. Estab. 1980. Publishes fiction and nonfiction on women's issues.

FRONT ROW EXPERIENCE, 540 Discovery Bay Blvd., Byron CA 94514. (415)634-5710. Editor: Frank Alexander. Estab. 1974. Imprint is Kokono. Publishes teacher/educator edition paperback originals. Only wants submissions for "Movement Education" and related areas.

‡GMS PUBLICATIONS, 11659 Doverwood Dr., Riverside CA 92505-3216. Publisher: G. Michael Short. Imprints are Dragon's Den Publishing, DDP Deluxe Editions and New Horizons Press. Looking for New Age fiction and nonfiction.

GREEN TIMBER PUBLICATIONS, P.O. Box 3884, Portland ME 04104. (207)797-4180. President: Tirrell H. Kimball. Estab. 1987. Publishes trade paperback originals in juvenile nonfiction, fiction and poetry.

GURZE BOOKS, P.O. Box 2238, Carlsbad CA 92008. (619)434-7533. FAX: (619)434-5476. Editor: Lindsey Hall. Estab. 1980. "We are primarily interested in new approaches to eating disorders and related issues of self-improvement for lay readers or professional therapists (without a clinical orientation)."

‡*HAYPENNY PRESS, 211 New St., West Paterson NJ 07424. Contact: Dawn Conti. Publishes novellas, story collections, teen/young adult novels and unusual or unique how-to or self-help. Subsidy arrangements possible.

‡HELIX PRESS, 4410 Hickey, Corpus Christi TX 78413. (512)852-8834. Editor: Aubrey R. McKinney. Estab. 1984. Publishes hardcover originals on science for adults.

HEMINGWAY WESTERN STUDIES SERIES, Boise State University, 1910 University Dr., Boise ID 83725. (208)385-1999. Editor: Tom Trusky. Publishes Rocky Mountain nonfiction and popular scholarship. Write for author's guidelines and catalog.

‡HOHM PRESS, P.O. Box 2501, Prescott AZ 86302. (602)778-9189. Senior Editor: Regina Sara Ryan. Estab. 1975. Publishes books on holistic health, transformational psychology, the performing arts, and world philosophies.

ILLUMINATIONS PRESS, #B, 2110 9th St., Berkeley CA 94710-2141. (415)849-2102. Editor/Publisher: Norm Moser. Estab. 1965. Publishes poetry and plays.

‡INVERTED-A, INC., 401 Forrest Hill, Grand Prairie TX 75051. (214)264-0066. Editors: Amnon Katz and Aya Katz. Publishes nonfiction books on a range of subjects, novellas, short story collections and poetry.

JAMENAIR LTD., P.O. Box 241957, Los Angeles CA 90024-9757. (213)470-6688. Publisher: P.K. Studner. Estab. 1986. Publishes originals and reprints on business and economics, computers and electronics, education and career-advancement/job search.

‡ALICE JAMES BOOKS, Imprint of Alice James Poetry Cooperative, 33 Richdale Ave., Cambridge MA 02140. (617)354-1408. Program Administrator: Jean Amaral. Publishes books of poetry.

JASON & NORDIC PUBLISHERS, P.O. Box 441, Hollidaysburg PA 16648. (814)696-2920. General Manager: Norma McPhee. "We want entertaining stories, well-plotted with the main character a child who is handicapped. The stories are told from this child's viewpoint. The goals must be attainable."

LAHONTAN IMAGES, P.O. Box 1093, Susanville CA 96130. (916)257-6747. Owner: Tim I. Purdy. Estab. 1986. Publishes books pertaining to Northeastern California and Western Nevada.

LANDMARK EDITIONS, INC., 1402 Kansas Ave., P.O. Box 4469, Kansas City MO 64127. (816)241-4919. Editorial Coordinator: Nan Thatch. "We accept manuscripts written and illustrated by students, ages six to nineteen, through our annual National Written and Illustrated by . . . Awards Contest for Students."

LAVENDER TAPES, 1125 Veronica Springs Rd., Santa Barbara CA 93105. Publisher: Deby DeWeese. Estab. 1990. Produces lesbian books-on-cassette for a lesbian market. Produces approximately 2 tapes/year. Buys audio rights only.

‡LAWCO LTD., P.O. Box 2009, Manteca CA 95336. (209)239-6006. Editor: Bill Thompson. Subsidiaries include Moneytree Publishing. Publishes nonfiction books on billiards and small business marketing.

‡LIBERTY BELL PRESS, Suite 3-183, 4700 S. 900 E, Salt Lake City UT 84117. (801)943-8573. Publisher: Ron Jorgenson. Estab. 1988. Actively seeking anti-establishment books on divorce and family law.

LINCOLN SPRINGS PRESS, P.O. Box 269, Franklin Lakes NJ 07417. Contact: M. Gabrielle. Estab. 1958. Nonfiction subjects include Americana, ethnic, government/politics, history, language/literature, military/war, sociology and women's issues/studies. Fiction: ethnic, feminist, gothic, historical, literary, mainstream/contemporary, mystery, romance, short story collections.

‡LINTEL, Box 8609, Roanoke VA 24014. (703)345-2886. Editorial Director: Walter James Miller. Publishes nonfiction, fiction and poetry.

‡MADWOMAN PRESS, P.O. Box 690, Northboro MA 01532. (508)393-3447. Editor and Publisher: Diane Benison. Publishes lesbian fiction and nonfiction. Query for further information.

MARADIA PRESS, 228 Evening Star Dr., Naugatuck CT 06770. (203)723-0758. Vice President: Peter A. Ciullo. Estab. 1990. Publishes well researched consumer-related issue books; especially interested in unique, balanced treatments of health topics.

‡**MARKGRAF PUBLICATIONS GROUP**, The Robots Inc., P.O. Box 936. Menlo Park CA 94025. FAX: (415)940-1299. Publisher: James Hall. Estab. 1987. Publishes nonfiction books on history, government and international affairs and seriously-researched historical fiction.

‡**MAUPIN HOUSE PUBLISHING**, P.O. Box 90148, Gainesville FL 32607. (904)336-9290. Co-Publisher: Julia Graddy. Publishes nonfiction books on horticulture, education, regional (Florida) and travel.

MERRY MEN PRESS, 274 Roanoke Rd., El Cajon CA 92020. (619)442-5541. Contact: Robin Hood. Estab. 1984. Publishes science fiction/fantasy, erotica in a book anthology.

****MEYERBOOKS, PUBLISHER**, Box 427, Glenwood IL 60425. (708)757-4950. Publisher: David Meyer. Imprint is David Meyer Magic Books. History, reference and self-help works published on subjects of Americana, cooking and foods, health and nature.

MISTY HILL PRESS, 5024 Turner Rd., Sebastopol CA 95472. (415)892-0789. Managing Editor: Sally C. Karste. Estab. 1984. Publishes trade paperback biography and historical fiction.

‡**MOUNTAIN AUTOMATION CORPORATION**, P.O. Box 6020, Woodland Park CO 80866. (719)687-6647. President: Claude Wiatrowski. Estab. 1976. Publishes illustrated souvenir books and videos for specific tourist attractions.

‡**MOUNTAIN HOUSE PRESS**, Box 353, Philo CA 95466. (707)895-3241. Publisher: J.D. Colfax. Estab. 1988. Publishes books on education, politics, folklore and alternative agriculture.

MYSTIC SEAPORT MUSEUM, 50 Greenmanville Ave., Mystic CT 06355-0990. (203)572-0711. Publication Director: Gerald E. Morris. Imprint is American Maritime Library. "We need serious, well-documented biographies, studies of economic, social, artistic, or musical elements of American maritime (not navel) history; books on traditional boat and ship types and construction (how-to)."

NAR PUBLICATIONS, P.O. Box 233, Barryville NY 12719. (914)557-8713. FAX: (914)557-6770. Editor: Monique E. Dubacher. Estab. 1977. Imprints are Teacher Update, Brandon Books and Education Guide. Publishes trade paperback originals on business and economics, child guidance/parenting, education, gardening, government/politics, health/medicine, hobbies, money/finance, recreation, sports and consumer.

NATIONAL PUBLISHING COMPANY, P.O. Box 8386, Philadelphia PA 19101-8386. (215)732-1863. FAX: (215)735-5399. Editor: Peter F. Hewitt. Estab. 1863. Publishes Bibles, New Testament and foreign language New Testaments.

NATURE'S DESIGN, P.O. Box 255, Davenport CA 95017. (408)426-8205. Publisher/Editor: Frank S. Balthis. Estab. 1982. Publishes guides to parks and books on nature, wildlife and the environment. Query with SASE.

‡**NEWSAGE PRESS**, P.O. Box 41029, Pasadena CA 91114-8029. (213)641-8912. Publisher: Maureen Michelson. Publishes hardcover and trade paperback originals.

‡**NIGHTSHADE PRESS**, P.O. Box 76, Troy ME 04987. (207)948-3427. Co-Editors: Carolyn Page and Roy Zarucchi. Estab. 1988. Publishes mostly poetry chapbooks.

C. OLSON & CO., P.O. Box 5100, Santa Cruz CA 95063-5100. (408)458-3365. Owner: C. Olson. Estab. 1981. "We are looking for nonfiction books that can be sold at natural food stores and small independent bookstores on health and on how to live a life which has less negative impact on the earth's environment." Queries first only, and please enclose SASE.

‡**OPEN HAND PUBLISHING, INC.**, P.O. Box 22048, Seattle WA 98122. (206)323-3868. Publisher: P. Anna Johnson. Publishes fiction and nonfiction about African-American issues.

OUT WEST PUBLISHING, P.O. Box 4278, Alburquerque NM 87196. (505)889-3745. Publisher: Robert Spiegel. Publishes cookbooks, gardening and travel on specific cuisines: Asian, Cajun, Southwestern, "with an eye to the spicy." Also publishes consumer magazine *The Chile Pepper*.

PAN-EROTIC REVIEW, P.O. Box 2992, Santa Cruz CA 95063. (408)426-7082. Editor: David Steinberg. Publishes quality erotic books of photography and fiction.

‡PANTEX INTERNATIONAL LTD., P.O. Box 17322, Irvine CA 92713. (714)497-5681. Manager: Jess E. Dines. Estab. 1990. Publishes nonfiction books on handwriting analysis.

‡PAPIER-MACHE PRESS, 795 Via Manzana, Watsonville CA 95076. (408)726-2933. Owner/Editor: Sandra Martz. Publishes mostly fiction and poetry about women's issues. Query first.

PARADISE PUBLICATIONS, 8110 SW Wareham, Portland OR 97223. (503)246-1555. President: Christie Stilson. Publishes specific location travel guides.

PARTNERS IN PUBLISHING, P.O. Box 50374, Tulsa OK 74150. (918)584-5906. Editor: P.M. Fielding. Estab. 1976. Publishes biography, how-to, reference, self-help, technical and textbooks on learning disabilities, special education.

PC PRESS, Imprint of Scandinavian PC Systems Inc., Suite 1101, 51 Monroe St., Rockville MD 20850. (301)294-7450. FAX: (301)251-1053. Publication Manager: Barbara Marsh. Estab. 1989. "We're looking for material relating to personal computers and the use of personal computers in business."

PEEL PRODUCTIONS, P.O. Box 185-M, Molalla OR 97038. (503)829-6849. Managing Editor: S. DuBosque. Estab. 1985. Publishes how-to, picture books, juvenile books and children's plays. Query first with outline/synopsis, sample chapters and SASE.

THE PERFECTION FORM CO., 10520 New York Ave., Des Moines IA 50322. (515)278-0133. Estab. 1926. Imprint is Magic Key. Publishes supplemental educational material grades K-12, including quarterly newsletter with students' responses to reading.

PERIVALE PRESS & AGENCY, 13830 Erwin St., Van Nuys CA 91401. (818)785-4671. Publisher: Lawrence P. Spingarn. Managing Editor: Barbara Rhys-Davies. Estab. 1968. Publishes West Coast oriented works, translations, poetry chapbooks, and short story collections.

‡POPULAR MEDICINE PRESS, P.O. Box 1212, San Carlos CA 94070. (415)594-1855. Vice President: John Bliss. Publishes books on nutrition, health and medicine.

‡PRARIE OAK PRESS, 2577 University Ave., Madison WI 53705. (608)238-1685. FAX: (608)238-0500. President: Jerry Minnich. Publishes nonfiction biography, history, regional and travel books.

PUBLISHERS SYNDICATION INTERNATIONAL, Suite 856, 1377 K Street NW, Washington DC 20005. President: A.P. Samuels. Estab. 1987. Estab. 1971. Publishes books on military history.

PUCKERBRUSH PRESS, 76 Main St., Orono ME 04473. (207)581-3832/866-4808. Publisher/Editor: Constance Hunting. Estab. 1971. Publishes trade paperback originals of literary fiction and poetry.

‡QUIKREF PUBLISHING, 913 N. Sanborn Ave., Los Angeles CA 90029. (213)913-1430. FAX: (213)913-1066. Senior Editor: Claudia O'Keefe. Estab. 1989. Imprint is Dodo Bird Books (juvenile). Publishes nonfiction books, reference and how-to, juveniles pertaining to animals, both fiction and nonfiction.

‡RED ALDER BOOKS, P.O. Box 2992, Santa Cruz CA 95063. (408)426-7082. Owner: David Steinberg. Estab. 1977. Publishes non-pornographic erotic writing and photography of exceptional imagination and quality.

REFERENCE PUBLICATIONS, INC., 218 St. Clair River Dr., P.O. Box 344, Algonac MI 48001. (313)794-5722. FAX: (313)794-7463. Estab. 1975. Publishes Africana, Americana, and botany reference books.

RESOLUTION BUSINESS PRESS, Suite 208, 11101 NE 8th St., Bellevue WA 98004. (206)455-4611. Contact: John Spilker. Estab. 1987. "We publish computer industry reference books, including directories on job, sales and product development opportunities in the industry."

‡RHOMBUS PUBLISHING CO., P.O. Box 806, Corrales NM 87048. (505)897-3700. Editor/Publisher: Jeff Radford. Estab. 1984. Publishes nonfiction books on anthropology/archaeology, biography, government/politics, nature/environment, regional and travel.

Close-up

Constance Hunting
Publisher
Puckerbrush Press

Before founding Puckerbrush Press, Editor/Publisher Constance Hunting had already established herself as a writer and poet. The author of several books of poetry and literary fiction, she resolved to start a small press in 1971 with the royalties from her first book, published by Charles Scribner's Sons.

The press evolved "slowly and in a small way," Hunting says, and she prefers to keep it small to reduce complications. "I am the staff, and that makes for a certain efficiency." She singlehandedly selects and edits all of the publishable manuscripts, but calls upon a commercial printer to handle the production aspects. The press publishes both fiction and poetry titles (an average of 2-3 per year) that are distributed by Inland Books.

One of the most encouraging aspects of Puckerbrush Press is its commitment to publishing promising new writers. Hunting gives equal consideration to both solicited and unsolicited works and admits to still being excited by the discovery of new talent. "I like very much to publish first works. It is interesting to follow the careers of young, unknown writers. A few have gone on to become well-known." Among such writers whose first works were published by Puckerbrush Press are Scots poet James Kelman and writer Mary Gray Hughes.

While Hunting will read "just about anything," she admits she is on the lookout for "something out of the ordinary, something fresh. This freshness comes off of the page." She also expresses a preference for works of a "certain literary quality. I'm not interested in commercial works. I don't publish blockbuster novels. I couldn't afford to."

There are no specific submission guidelines for Puckerbrush Press, but Hunting advises writers not to submit material on disk. She says that, while she does receive some fascinating queries and cover letters, she is wary of gimmicks. "It is interesting to read the places where a writer has been published, but that does not tip the scale." She contends that she must ultimately be impressed by the work itself.

A fundamental advantage of small press publishing has always been the close rapport it offers between publisher and author. Hunting attempts to maintain such a relationship with authors publishing works through Puckerbrush Press. "I do have personal contact with the authors. They are not involved in the production process, but I do consult with them about their preferences."

While the small size offers definite advantages, Hunting admits that it also presents certain obstacles. "The only major obstacle I have had in maintaining Puckerbrush Press is the ongoing minor problem of money." She curtails this by teaching creative writing classes at the University of Maine and by giving occasional readings of her own work.

Hunting expresses optimism for the future of small presses, and maintains that they fulfill a vital function in the procurement of fine literature. "I think the outlook for small presses is excellent. Small presses will continue to be where literature is coming from. Not exclusively, of course, but it's a spring that is continually bubbling forth."

—Roseann Shaughnessy

‡THE RYDAL PRESS, P.O. Box 2247, Santa Fe NM 87504. (505)983-1680. FAX: (505)982-9105. Publisher: Clark Kimball. Estab. 1930. Publishes fiction and nonfiction relevant to the modern Southwest.

ST. JOHN'S PUBLISHING, INC., 6824 Oaklawn Ave., Edina MN 55435. (612)920-9044. President: Donna Montgomery. Estab. 1986. Publishes nonfiction books on parenting.

‡SAND RIVER PRESS, 1319 14th St., Los Osos CA 93402. (805)528-7347. Publisher: Bruce Miller. Estab. 1987. Publishes mostly nonfiction titles on Americana, cooking, history, literature, Native Americans, regional (California) and some literary fiction.

SANDPIPER PRESS, P.O. Box 286, Brookings OR 97415. (503)469-5588. Editor: Marilyn Riddle. Estab. 1979. Plans an anthology of true Native American visions and prophesies submitted by verified Native Americans only.

‡SILVERCAT PUBLICATIONS, Suite C, 4070 Goldfinch St., San Diego CA 92103-1865. (619)299-6774. Editor: Robert Outlaw. Estab. 1988. Publishes consumer-oriented nonfiction on topics of current interest.

‡SMOOTH STONE PRESS, P.O. Box 19875, St. Louis MO 63144. (314)968-2596. Editor: Maryann Hibbs. Looking for "a unique perspective" within a range of nonfiction subjects.

SOUND VIEW PRESS, 170 Boston Post Rd., Madison CT 06443. President: Peter Hastings Falk. Estab. 1985. Publishes hardcover and trade paperback originals, dictionaries, exhibition records, and price guides on 19th-mid 20th century American art.

‡SPHERIC HOUSE, Subsidiary of Southwest H.E.R.M. Inc., P.O. Box 40877, Tucson AZ 85717. (602)623-5577. Editors: Joanie Gurgon/Seth Linthicum. Publishes a variety of nonfiction and children's fiction.

‡STONE BRIDGE PRESS, P.O. Box 8208, Berkeley CA 94707. (415)524-8732. Publisher: Peter Goodman. Publishes books on working and communicating with the Japanese, Japanese garden and design related books, Japan related literary fiction, language learning, and translations.

STONE WALL PRESS, INC., 1241 30th St. NW, Washington DC 20007. President/Publisher: Henry Wheelwright. Estab. 1972. Publishes hardcover and trade paperback originals of how-to, natural history, adventure travel, environmental/outdoor instruction and literature.

‡SWORD & QUILL, P.O. Box 3088, Grand Junction CO 81502-3088. (303)242-3402. Associate Editor: Tamara James. Publishes books on what teens want and need to know.

‡TAMBRA PUBLISHING, P.O. Box 14161, Las Vegas NV 89114. (702)876-4232. FAX: (702)876-5252. Editor: Tambra Campbell. Publishes how-to books on handwriting analysis and movie scriptwriting.

TECHNICAL ANALYSIS OF STOCKS & COMMODITIES, Technical Analysis, Inc., 3517 SW Alaska St., Seattle WA 98126-2730. (206)938-0570. Editor: Thom Hartle. Technical Editor: John Sweeney. Publishes business and economics books and software about using charts and computers to trade stocks, options, mutual funds or commodity futures.

TESSERA PUBLISHING, INC., 9561 Woodridge Circle, Eden Prairie MN 55347. (612)941-5053. Secretary/Treasurer: Pat Bell. Estab. 1989. Publishes nonfiction books on "uncommon stories of common people." Queries and sample chapters must be accompanied by SASE to ensure suspense.

‡TRAFALGAR SQUARE PUBLISHING, P.O. Box 257, N. Pomfret VT 05053. (802)457-1911. Editor: Caroline Robbins. Publishes nonfiction books about horses.

‡UCLA-AMERICAN INDIAN STUDIES CENTER, 3220 Campbell Hall, 405 Hilgard Ave., Los Angeles CA 90024-1548. (213)825-7315. Editor: Duane Champagne. Publishes nonfiction how-to and reference books on anthropology, education, ethnic, government/politics, history, language/literature, and sociology themes.

VICTORY PRESS, 543 Lighthouse Ave., Monterey CA 93940-1422. (408)883-1725. Editor: Eileen Hu. Estab. 1988. Interested in topics on Chinese philosophy and medicine; martial arts books that fit in with the philosophy of Buddhism and Taoism.

VORTEX COMMUNICATIONS, Box 1008, Topanga CA 90290. (213)455-7221. President: Cynthia Riddle. Articles on health care, exercise, fitness, nutrition, spiritual well being from a holistic perspective, 1,000 to 2,500 words.

‡WASATCH PUBLISHERS, 4460 Ashford Dr., Salt Lake City UT 84124. (801)278-5826. Publisher: John Veranth. Estab. 1973. Publishes books on outdoor recreation in the intermountain west.

‡WATERFRONT BOOKS, 98 Brookes Ave., Burlington VT 05401. (802)658-7477. Publisher: Sherrill N. Musty. Estab. 1983. Publishes books on children's issues, books that empower children, books on prevention, mental health, environmental concerns, and whatever addresses increasing opportunities for children. Fiction or non-fiction.

‡WAYFARER BOOKS, P.O. Box 5927, Concord CA 94524. Managing Editor: Michael Clark. Estab. 1990. Publishes nonfiction books on cooking, spiritual subjects, travel and Thailand.

WESTERN TANAGER PRESS, 1111 Pacific Ave., Santa Cruz CA 95060. (408)425-1111. Publisher: Hal Morris. Estab. 1979. Publishes biography, hiking and biking guides and regional history hardcover and trade paperback originals and reprints.

First Bylines

by Mark Kissling

Nineteen ninety-one was another encouraging year for new writers. B. Dalton Booksellers continued its marketing strategy, "Discover—Great New Writers." *The New York Times* and *Library Journal* featured new novelists and nonfiction writers with special editions or columns. The PEN-Ernest Hemingway Foundation Award, The St. Lawrence Prize and The PEN/Martha Albrand Award for Nonfiction all rewarded writers of first books.

A writer's first book is often difficult to write and more challenging to sell. After distilling a lifetime of ideas and experiences into book form, a writer must then compete against colleagues with track records. Many book publishers are reluctant to take on a new writer, as established writers tend to have more predictable sales potential. Some break in, of course, every year. Three who have recently published first books are interviewed here.

Evelyn Clarke Mott is a writer of young children's books. Harry Spiller has written a memoir of the Vietnam War and life afterwards. Carla R. Heymsfeld writes juvenile fiction and nonfiction. Their advice is useful to writers interested in their particular fields, and those in other areas was well.

Evelyn Clarke Mott
Steam Train Ride (Walker & Company)

Photo by Frank Pronesti

"If you don't know anyone in publishing, chances are good that someone you know does," says Evelyn Clarke Mott. "A great source of publishing contacts is your local librarian. Through my local librarians, the manuscript for my book, *Steam Train Ride*, ended up in the hands of a retired children's book editor." A year later, that editor sold *Steam Train Ride* to Walker & Company.

Mott was born in Port Chester, New York, and attended Thomas Edison College. Her degree in marketing "helped a great deal," she says, when it came to marketing her manuscript for *Steam Train Ride*. She is married and has one child, Christopher, whose passion for children's books, particularly books about steam trains, was Mott's driving influence in writing and publishing *Steam Train Ride*.

"The book carries the reader along with a young boy on his journey along America's oldest short-line," says Mott. "He meets the engine crew, visits the station and takes an exciting ride on the train." The photos and text, both done by Mott, capture the thrill of the steam train era.

As a girl, Mott entered two writing contests, but did not attempt to publish anything in high school or college. She learned the craft of children's book writing by reading aloud to her son. "There are so many great children's book writers out there," she says. Margaret Wise Brown, author of *Goodnight Moon* (Harper Junior), and Virginia Lee Burton, author of *Mike Mulligan and His Steam Shovel* (Houghton Mifflin) are two of her major influences.

Mott says she had the idea for *Steam Train Ride* for two years before she began to write it. "I lacked confidence at first," she says. After checking out the competition in *Books in Print*, she found confidence when nothing filled her niche. "I wrote to the president of the Strassberg line railroad for permission, then took the photographs I would need."

She put together a dummy of the book and presented it to her library's children's book coordinator, who, in turn, suggested Barbara Bates, a retired field editor of children's books. Bates suggested several changes, including a shift in point-of-view from first to third person. Mott rewrote the book twice during several months of correspondence. "Finally, the book was ready, and Walker & Company agreed to publish it," Mott says.

New and younger writers should take note of Mott's research, persistence and especially her willingness to take advice from a professional in the field. Her hard work paid off with a sale to the first company she approached. However, her manuscript had been revised considerably beforehand. Mott considers the period of revision with Bates the turning point in her career so far.

"People do get published without agents," says Mott. "Especially in the field of children's books. The money is not there for agents. Small advances and short print runs turn most of them away. But that is 15% more I get to keep." Without agents, however, writers must market themselves and their books. Mott credits Ellen Roberts' *The Children's Picture Book: How to Write It, How to Sell It* (Writer's Digest Books) for her successful and professional submission of the manuscript for *Steam Train Ride*.

Mott advises writers to read widely on how to write and sell manuscripts. "To make a sale, it's important to learn how to write and submit professionally." She also suggests writers join a manuscript critique group. "If you can't find one, start one," she says. "I couldn't find a children's critique group in my area, so I started my own: Lakeside Writers for Young People. We now have eight loyal, supportive and committed members."

Writer's conferences are helpful, too. "Conferences are wonderful places that provide inspiration, information and a chance to make contacts." Along those lines, Mott encourages hopefuls to join the Society of Children's Book Writers for its helpful newsletter and the conferences they sponsor. "*Children's Writer's and Illustrator's Market* also helped a great deal," Mott says. "The interview with Amy Shields of Walker & Company in the 1990 edition gave me a lot of insight."

She is now working on a companion to *Steam Train Ride* called *Balloon Ride*. "Don't be in it for the money," she says. "Love what you're doing and do what you love."

Harry Spiller
Death Angel (McFarland & Co., Publishers)

In a letter to the editors of *Writer's Market*, Harry Spiller wrote, "On January 25, 1991, I received the dream come true for any new writer—my first contract. McFarland Publishers is going to publish my Vietnam memoir, *Death Angel*." During a time when Vietnam stories are proliferating in books and films, Spiller found his niche by covering a new area. The memoir is from the point-of-view of a soldier whose unenviable task is delivering death messages to families. "A good portion of the book does not involve combat," Spiller says. "Not everyone is buried in Arlington."

A native of Marion, Illinois, Spiller now teaches criminal justice at John A. Logan College in nearby Carterville. He is a veteran of the Vietnam War, a doctoral candidate and now, a published author. "I've always read a tremendous amount," he says. "I like various types of books, but I suppose I read more nonfiction than fiction." Joe McGinnis' *Fatal Vision* (Putnam) and Anne Rule's *The Stranger Beside Me*

(NAL) are two books that have influenced Spiller a great deal. "McGinnis has a wonderful sense of organization and a good style," he says. "Rule's writing really holds my interest."

Following a path that has worked for many writers and is suggested by many book publishers, Spiller sent his first stories to "little" and literary magazines. He has published many true crime pieces in *Official Detective*. "This is an important step in a writer's career," he says. "The first few publications build your confidence and give you a track record."

Spiller began writing *Death Angel* in 1983 as a work of fiction. "It took me a few years," he says. "I started sending it out in 1986, and got a lot of rejections." One of the companies he contacted was McFarland & Co., Publishers. They told Spiller they didn't publish fiction, but that they would look at the book again in nonfiction form. A playwright friend suggested the same change. Spiller rewrote and resubmitted the book as nonfiction to McFarland and they accepted it. "Don't take suggestions for changes and rewrites personally," he says. "I am happier with the book being nonfiction. It is a true story after all."

Spiller advises new and younger writers to try to write every day. "If you're going to be a writer, you can't give in to excuses like 'I don't have time,'" he says. "Try to develop good work habits. Set aside some time to write. Make time to write."

Most importantly, Spiller believes, a writer must believe in himself. "If you're sincere about being a writer, you must be prepared for rejection," he says. "And that creates a potential to lose confidence." Perseverance and willingness to completely rework a fictional story into a nonfiction memoir helped carry Spiller through to a contract.

"I hope having a contract will open doors for me," he says. He considers it the turning point of his career. "Now I have a track record with books as well as magazines." Spiller has already written two novels. *Cops Are People Too* is based on his experience as a small town sheriff. "It attempts to take the sunglasses off small town police," Spiller says. *Murder on Central School Road* is a mystery set in nearby St. Charles, Missouri. "True crime and mystery have always been popular," he says. "Serial murders are in at the moment."

Spiller sold *Death Angel* without an agent, but he is looking for one to market his other two books. "One of the rejection slips from *Death Angel* said I needed an agent," he says. "I made an effort to get one, but you don't absolutely have to have one to get published."

The little things count a lot in Spiller's experience. "When you're not a published writer, things like the query letter become that much more important," he says. "That first letter must be good. It sets the impression of you in the publisher's mind." The rest is good habits, openness to revision and perseverence.

Carla R. Heymsfeld
The Fourth Grade Baseball Project (Bradbury Press)

"Something has happened recently in education," says Carla R. Heymsfeld. "There has been a major shift from using textbooks to trade books. Interest, variety, styles and reading levels have made trade books more appealing to teachers." Heymsfeld should know. She is a reading specialist for elementary school children in Washington, D.C. Teacher and writer, Heymsfeld has a keen insight into trends of today's juvenile fiction and nonfiction.

"Multi-cultural literature is extremely popular at the moment," she says. "especially in fiction. This presents a problem for writers because people who are not of a culture cannot often write authentically about other cultures." This should not dissuade writers from including these groups, however, she says.

Heymsfeld was born in Brooklyn, New York, and educated at Brandeis University. She married while in college and moved to Washington soon after. "A solid liberal arts education is useful for many things, writing included," she says. Her work as a teacher moved her to write. Teaching, reading, writing, as well as teaching reading and writing: All are related for Heymsfeld.

The core story of her book, *The Fourth Grade Baseball Project*, is autobiographical. A couple of years ago, Heymsfeld had to participate in a faculty-sixth grade softball game, an activity she was less than thrilled about. Apparently her talents are not on display in the arena of a baseball diamond. The book is a fictional account of a class that teaches its teacher how to play ball. Jane O'Conor illustrated Heymsfeld's text.

"Initially, the book was not written for publication," Heymsfeld says. "But my writing group liked it, so I sent it out as a short story." Rejections led her to rewrite the story with a new protagonist for a younger audience. The whole process took more than five years. She credits *The Art of Fiction* (Random House) by John Gardner, workshops and the Society of Children's Book Writers for valuable instruction.

"I don't write every day, so I cannot recommend it as a method I use," says Heymsfeld. "I would like to, though. When I'm involved in a project, I get up early on weekends and try to do as much writing as I can. Otherwise, I have no rigid routine." Like many writers, Heymsfeld has discovered that computers can be excellent tools, including one for creation. "The computer was a liberating experience for me," she says. "I can't imagine writing without one."

A writing group has also been invaluable for Heymsfeld, now a six-year veteran of one. "They're useful not only for feedback, but for support," she says. "I couldn't have gotten this far by myself." She considers her growth as a writer more as a staircase than one involving a turning point. "The process of change has been more gradual for me."

Heymsfeld has had two agents and her experience with them has been less than positive. "I had an image of my agent having lunch with editors and talking up my book," she says. "In fact, what they did was send the book out and collect it back. After a number of rejections, they did not wish to represent me any longer." Heymsfeld admits an agent can be helpful with contract negotiations, but she does not have one at the moment. "Don't give up when you confront adversity," Heymsfeld says. "Concentrate on writing and you're on your way."

In the meantime she has written two other books, *George Mason: Father of the Bill of Rights*, is a sixth to ninth grade level biography, co-authored by Joan Lewis. It required scholarly research and will be published by the Patriotic Educational Corporation. *Where Was George Washington?* is a picture book for young children, illustrated by Jennifer Koury, to be published by Mt. Vernon.

Book Packagers and Producers

Book packaging is a relatively new opportunity for writers in North America. While it originated in England in the 1940s, the trend didn't pick up in the U.S. on a large scale until the 1970s. Originally known as book packagers, today many firms prefer to be called book producers or book developers. They provide a book publisher with services ranging from hiring writers, photographers or artists, to editing and delivering finished books.

One British book producer has recently taken up publishing books in New York, under its own imprint, after 15 years of packaging. They will publish only nonfiction titles, and many of their books are heavily illustrated. Nonfiction works involving a great deal of artwork and photography are common types of books for packagers to produce.

In most instances, a book packager or producer develops a book proposal, assembles the writers, illustrators and editors to prepare it and submits it to a publisher. When a proposal is accepted by a publisher, the producer serves several functions. When the manuscript is in preparation, the producer is an editor. As the manuscript and illustrations or photo package are put together, the function changes to managing editor. Then the producer takes over coordination of production and may also serve as a sales consultant for the project. In other cases, a book publisher will contract with a book packager or producer to perform one or more of these functions.

In some cases, however, the packager even delivers bound books to the publisher. This means the packager must also arrange the printing and binding of the books. The amount of involvement a packager has in a project depends on the individual arrangement and is a very flexible business.

The term book developer may be used to refer to a book packager or producer, or it may apply to a literary agent who joins with writers to provide writing and editorial services. An agent who functions as a book packager or developer often provides additional writing support for the author as they work together to produce a proposal. Then the agent uses his contacts within the industry to sell the work like any other book.

Speed and specialties make book packagers' and producers' services attractive to publishers. Many publishers with small editorial staffs use packagers and producers as extensions of their companies. An inhouse staff member can provide 20% of the work on the book and rely on the packager to produce the remaining 80%. This frees the staff member to move on to other projects. In some cases, publishers ask packagers to provide resources or knowledge the publisher doesn't need fulltime, but does need for a specific book. Many book packagers and producers also are experts at producing high quality illustrated books, an area where small publishers may lack inhouse expertise.

Writers who want to work in the field should be aware of differences between book publishers and book packagers. Publishers accept book proposals and ideas for books submitted to them by writers. Book packagers and agents who act as book packagers most often assign topics to writers. Occasionally, a packager will develop an idea brought in by a writer, but this is rare. When you submit material, packagers most often want to see a query with your writing credentials and list of areas of expertise. Writers who are trying to establish themselves in the industry may consider this an attractive option but should be aware that it doesn't always provide you with credit for your writing because many books require several writers. Book producers and packagers also make outright purchases of writing, contract on work-for-hire agreements or offer a large advance and low royalty percentage.

On the other hand, some writers do receive credit for the books they have worked on. The packager or agent provides details of the project and contacts experts for the writer to interview. The freelancer is not writing on speculation, so he will not worry about having to market his writing. Writing for a packager may also be a good way to obtain that first book credit.

Don't expect to receive a book catalog from a book producer or book packager; they produce books for other publishers' catalogs. If you ask for a sample of titles they've produced, however, you may be surprised to find some bestsellers on the list.

More than 150 book packagers, producers and agents work in the field but most prefer to make their own contacts with writers and do not accept unsolicited queries. In this section, we've only included those who say they are interested in being contacted by writers. For a list of other book packagers and producers, see the latest edition of *Literary Market Place* in your local library.

‡ARCHETYPE PRESS, INC., 2828 10th St., NE, Washington DC 20017. (202)832-2828. FAX: (202)832-6304. President: Diane Maddex. Estab. 1990. Firm produces hardcover and trade paperback originals for publication by trade and other publishers. Averages 10 titles/year. Works with 50% first-time authors; 95% unagented writers. Offers variable advance. All manuscripts must be on disks. Reports in 2 weeks.
Nonfiction: Coffee table books, illustrated books, cookbooks. Subjects include Americana, art/architecture, gardening, photography, travel and historic preservation. Submit proposal. Submit resume, publishing history and clips. Reviews artwork/photos as part of freelance ms package.
Recent Nonfiction Titles: *The Wright Style* for Simon & Schuster (coffee-table).

‡ATTICUS PRESS, 1100 20th St., Birmingham AL 35205. (205)933-8886. FAX: (205)933-8463. Managing Editor: Amanda Adams. Firm produces hardcover originals. Averages 10 titles/year. Pays royalty (varies). Offers advance (varies). Reports in 1 month.
Nonfiction: Biography, coffee table book, how-to, illustrated book, self-helf. Subjects include Americana, art/architecture, business and economics, cooking, foods and nutrition, gardening, history, language/literature, nature/environment, photography, regional, sports. Submit proposal. Reviews artwork/photos as part of freelance ms package.
Recent Nonfiction Title: *Faulkner's Mississippi*, for Oxmoor Press (art/photography).
Fiction: Adventure, historical, literary, mainstrea, picture books, religious, romance, suspense. Submit resume, publishing history and clips.

‡BLACKBIRCH GRAPHICS, INC., 1 Bradley Rd., #205, Woodbridge CT 06525. (203)387-7525. FAX: (203)389-1596. Editor-in-Chief: Bruce Glassman. Estab. 1979. Imprint is Blackbirch Press. Firm produces hardcover originals. Averages 70 titles/year. Works with 20% first-time authors; 85% unagented writers. Pays 5-10% on net receipts. Makes outright purchase for $1,000-5,000. Offers $1,500 average advance. Query for electronic submissions. Does not return submissions, even those accompanied by SASE. Reports in 2 months.
Nonfiction: Biography, self-help, illustrated book, juvenile, how-to and reference. Subjects include child guidance/parenting, education, money/finance and nature/environment. Submit proposal. Reviews artwork/photos as part of freelance ms package.
Tips: "Young adult publishing means *series* work quite often. This means small advances and budgets on a *per book* basis but often enables authors to get commitments on 4-8 titles at a time."

BOOKWORKS, INC., 119 S. Miami St., West Milton OH 45383. (513)698-3619. FAX: (513)698-3651. President: Nick Engler. Estab. 1984. Firm averages 6 titles/year. Receives 1-10 submissions/year. 20-40% of books from first-time authors. 100% from unagented writers. Pays 2½-5% royalty on retail price. Buys mss outright for $3,000-10,000. Offers $7,500-25,000 advance. Publishes book an average of 8-18 months after acceptance. Simultaneous submissions OK. Reports in 6 weeks on queries; 2 months on mss.
Nonfiction: How-to. Subjects include hobbies, woodworking and home improvement. Nothing other than crafts/woodworking/home improvement. Query or submit outline/synopsis and sample chapters. Reviews artwork/photos as part of manuscript package.
Recent Nonfiction Title: *American Country Furniture*, by Engler.
Tips: "In the how-to field, there is more emphasis on projects, less emphasis on techniques and methods. We publish how-to books for do-it-yourselfers, hobbyists and craftsmen."

CARPENTER PUBLISHING HOUSE, Suite 4602, 175 E. Delaware Place, Chicago IL 60611. (312)787-3569. President: Allan Carpenter. Estab. 1962. Develops hardcover originals. "We develop our products or theirs on contract for major publishers. We assign work to authors and artists." Negotiates fee. Reports promptly on queries.

Nonfiction: Biography, juvenile, reference and supplementary texts. Subjects include Americana, history and directory/resource annuals. "We do not solicit mss. We specialize in books in large series." Query. All unsolicited mss are returned unopened.

Recent Nonfiction Title: *Our Fascinating America*, 50-volume series.

MICHAEL FRIEDMAN PUBLISHING GROUP, 15 W. 26th St., New York NY 10010. (212)685-6610. FAX: (212)685-1307. Editorial Director: Karla Olson. Estab. 1975. Packages hardcover originals working with all major publishers. Firm averages 75 packages/year. "We work with many first-time authors and almost exclusively with unagented authors." Buys mss outright. Produces book an average of 1 year after acceptance; Friedman group responsible for all illustrative material included in book. Query for electronic submissions. Free book catalog.

Nonfiction: Illustrated coffee table book, cookbook, how-to craft book. Subjects include Americana, animals, anthropology/archaeology, art/architecture, cooking, foods and nutrition, gardening, health and fitness, hobbies, nature/environment, recreation and sports. Query.

Recent Nonfiction Title: *Discovery*, by Eric Flaum.

HELENA FROST ASSOCIATES, Maple Rd., Brewster NY 10509. (914)279-7923 or 301 E. 21st St., New York NY 10010. (212)475-6642. FAX: (212)353-2894. President: Helena Frost. Estab. 1986. Packages approximately 50 titles/year. Receives approximately 100 queries/year. Authors paid by flat or hourly fees or on freelance assignments. Query for electronic submissions. Reports in 3 weeks. Completed projects list available; ms guidelines available per project.

Nonfiction: Textbook ancillaries, some general trade titles. Subjects include business and economics, education, government/politics, health/medicine, history, language/literature, psychology. Query.

Tips: "Although we are not interested in over-the-transom mss, we do request writers' and editors' resumes with publication history and will review school-related proposals and outlines for submission to major publishers."

THE K S GINIGER COMPANY INC., Suite 519, 250 W. 57th St., New York NY 10107. (212)570-7499. President: Kenneth S. Giniger. Estab. 1964. Publishes hardcover, trade paperback and mass paperback originals. Averages 8 titles/year; receives 250 submissions annually. 25% of books from first-time authors; 75% of books from unagented writers. Pays 5-15% royalty on retail price; offers $3,500 average advance. Publishes book an average of 18 months after acceptance. Reports in 2 weeks on queries.

Nonfiction: Biography, coffee table book, illustrated book, reference and self-help. Subjects include business and economics, health, history, religion and travel. "No religious books, cookbooks, personal histories or personal adventure." Query with SASE. All unsolicited mss are returned unread (if postage is enclosed for return of ms).

Recent Nonfiction Title: *How To Defeat Saddam Hussein*, by Col. Trevor N. Dupuy (USA, Ret.).

Tips: "We look for a book whose subject interests us and which we think can achieve success in the marketplace. Most of our books are based on ideas originating with us by authors we commission, but we have commissioned books from queries submitted to us."

LAING COMMUNICATIONS INC., Suite 1050, 500-108th NE, Bellevue WA 98004. (206)451-9331. FAX: (206)646-6515. Vice President/Editorial Director: Christine Laing. Estab. 1985. Imprint is Laing Research Series (industry monographs). Firm produces hardcover and trade paperback originals. Averages 6-10 titles/year. Works with 20% first-time authors; 100% unagented writers. Payment "varies dramatically since all work is sold to publishers as royalty-inclusive package." Reports in 1 month.

Nonfiction: Biography, coffee table book, cookbook, how-to, illustrated book, juvenile, reference, software, technical, textbook. Subjects include Americana, anthropology, business and economics, computers/electronics, history, science, travel. Query. Reviews artwork/photos as part of freelance ms package.

Recent Nonfiction Titles: *Behind the Blue and Gray—The Soldier's Life in the Civil War*, for Dutton/Lodestar Books (juvenile, history).

LAMPPOST PRESS INC., 253 E. 62 St., New York NY 10021. (212)935-6030. President: Roseann Hirsch. Estab. 1988. Firm produces hardcover, trade paperback and mass market paperback originals. Averages 25 titles/year. Works with 50% first-time authors; 85% unagented writers. Pays 50% royalty or by outright purchase.

Nonfiction: Biography, cookbook, how-to, humor, illustrated book, juvenile, self-help. Subjects include child guidance/parenting, cooking, foods and nutrition, gardening, health, money/finance, women's issues. Query or submit proposal. Reviews artwork/photos as part of freelance ms package.
Recent Nonfiction Titles: *New Kids on the Block*, for Bantam.
Fiction: Gothic, historical, humor, juvenile, mainstream, mystery, picture books, romance, young adult. Query or submit proposal.
Recent Fiction Titles: *Legal Affairs*, for Simon & Schuster (modern romance).
Tips: "Call first."

LUCAS-EVANS BOOKS, 1123 Broadway, New York NY 10010. (212)929-2583. Contact: Barbara Lucas. Estab. 1984. Packages hardcover, trade paperback originals and mass market paperback originals for major publishers. Averages 10 titles/year. 20% of books from first-time authors. Pays 1-10% royalty, "depends on our contract agreement with publisher." Makes work-for-hire assignments. Offers $3,000 on up average advance. Reports in 1 week on queries; 6 weeks on mss.
Nonfiction: "We are looking for series proposals and selected single juvenile books: preschool through high school." Submit query letter with credentials, discussing proposed subject.
Recent Nonfiction Title: *A Six-Book Series on Natural Disasters* for Crestwood House.
Fiction: Preschool through high school. Prefers picture books and early chapter books.
Recent Nonfiction Title: *Sing for a Gentle Rain*, by J. Alison James for Atheneum.

‡MEGA-BOOKS OF NEW YORK, INC., 116 E. 19th St., New York NY 10003. (212)598-0909. FAX: (212)979-5074. President: Pat Fortunato. Firm produces trade paperback originals and mass market paperback originals. Averages 95 titles/year. Works with 30% first-time authors; 75% unagented writers. Makes outright purchase for $3,000 and up or makes work-for-hire assignment. Offers 50% average advance. Free ms guidelines.
Fiction: Juvenile, mystery and young adult. Submit resume, publishing history and clips.
Recent Fiction Titles: *Nancy Drew, Hardy Boys* and *Bobbsey Twins*, for Simon & Schuster (mass market paperback).
Tips: "Please be sure to obtain a current copy of our writers guidelines before writing. Please do not submit an unsolicited completed manuscript."

MOUNT IDA PRESS, 4 Central Ave., Albany NY 12210. (518)426-5935. President: Diana S. Waite. Estab. 1984. Firm publishes and packages hardcover and trade paperback originals. Averages 5 titles/year. Works with 50% first-time authors; 100% unagented writers. Pays royalty. Query for electronic submissions, "if hard copy also is available." Reports in 1 month. Catalog for #10 SASE.
Nonfiction: Illustrated book and reference. Subjects include art/architecture, history, regional and commemorative histories. Query. Reviews artwork/photos as part of freelance ms package.
Recent Nonfiction Title: *Ornamental Ironwork: Two Centuries of Craftsmanship in Albany and Troy, New York*, by Diana S. Waite.

NEW ENGLAND PUBLISHING ASSOCIATES, INC., P.O. Box 5, Chester CT 06412. (203)345-4976. FAX: (203)345-3660. President: Elizabeth Frost Knappman. Vice President/Treasurer: Edward W. Knappman. Estab. 1983. Firm originates hardcover and trade paperback originals. Works with 25% first-time authors. Reports in 1 month.
Recent Nonfiction Title: *The Lion in Literature*, by Nancy Frazier (publishers in Germany, Italy, France).
Tips: "We prefer a phone call first, followed by an outline and sample chapter."

OTTENHEIMER PUBLISHERS, INC., 300 Reisterstown Rd., Baltimore MD 21208. (301)484-2100. FAX: (301)486-8301. Chairman of the Board: Allan T. Hirsh Jr. President: Allan T. Hirsh III. Vice President: Edward Davis. Estab. 1890. Publishes hardcover and paperback originals and reprints. Publishes 250 titles/year; receives 500 submissions annually. 20% of books from first-time authors; 100% of books from unagented writers. Average print order for a writer's first book is 15,000. Negotiates royalty and advance, sometimes makes outright purchase for $25-3,000. Publishes book an average of 6 months after acceptance. Reports in 3 months.
Nonfiction: Cookbooks, reference, gardening, home repair and decorating, children's nonfiction activities, automotive and medical for the layperson. Submit outline/synopsis and sample chapters or complete ms. Reviews artwork/photos as part of ms package.
Recent Nonfiction Title: *The Illustrated Children's Bible*.
Tips: "We're looking for nonfiction adult books in the how-to information area, for mass market — we're a packager."

‡**RETAIL REPORTING CORP.**, 101 5th Ave., New York NY 10003. (212)255-9595. FAX: (212)243-9822. Publisher: Larry Fuersich. Firm produces hardcover originals. Works with 30% first-time authors; 50% unagented writers. Pays royalty or makes outright purchase. Offers $1,000-3,000 average advance. Query for electronic submissions. Reports in 2 months. Free catalog.
Nonfiction: Technical. Subjects include art/architecture, business and economics, design and graphic. Submit proposal. Reviews artwork/photos as part of freelance ms package.

TENTH AVENUE EDITIONS, 625 Broadway, New York NY 10012. (212)529-8900. Managing Editor: Rose Hass. Estab. 1984. Firm produces hardcover, trade paperback and mass market paperback originals. Averages 6 titles/year. Pays advance paid by publisher less our commission. Query for electronic submissions. Reports in 2 months.
Nonfiction: Biography, how-to, illustrated book, juvenile, catalogs. Subjects include music/dance, photography, women's issues/studies, art. Query. Reviews artwork/photos as part of freelance ms package.
Recent Nonfiction Titles: *Lovingly Georgia: Georgia O'Keefe.*
Tips: "Send query with publishing background."

‡**DANIEL WEISS ASSCIATES, INC.**, 33 W. 17th St., New York NY 10011. Contact: Ann Brashares. Firm produces hardcover and mass market paperback originals. Averages 120 titles/year. Works with 20% first-time authors; 20% unagented writers. Pays 1-4% royalty on retail price; or outright puchase $2,500 minimum "depending on author's experience." Offers $4,000 average advance. Reports in 6 weeks. Free ms guidelines.
Nonfiction: Juvenile. Submit proposal. Reviews artwork/photos as part of freelance ms package.
Fiction: Juvenile, picture books, young adult. Query.

THE WHEETLEY COMPANY, INC., Suite 1100, 4709 Golf Rd., Skokie IL 60076. (708)675-4443. FAX: (708)675-4489. Human Resources Manager: Linda Rogers. Estab. 1986. Firm produces hardcover originals for publishers of school, college and professional titles. Pays by the project. Query for electronic submissions. Does not return submissions, even those accompanied with SASE.
Nonfiction: Technical, textbook. Subjects include animals, anthropology, art/architecture, business and economics, child guidance/parenting, computers/electronics, cooking, foods and nutrition, education, government/politics, health, history, language/literature, money/finance, music/dance, nature/environment, philosophy, psychology, recreation, regional, religion, science, sociology, sports, translation. Submit resume and publishing history. Reviews artwork/photos as part of freelance ms package.
Recent Nonfiction Titles: Kept confidential.

WIESER & WIESER, INC., 118 E. 25th St. New York NY 10010. (212)260-0860. FAX: (212)505-7186. Producer: George J. Wieser. Estab. 1976. Firm produces hardcover, trade paperback and mass market paperback originals. Averages 25 titles/year. Works with 10% first-time authors; 90% unagented writers. Makes outright purchase for $5,000 or other arrangement. Offers $5,000 average advance. Reports in 2 weeks.
Nonfiction: Coffee table book. Subjects include Americana, cooking, foods and nutrition, gardening, health, history, hobbies, military/war, nature/environment, photography, recreation, sports and travel. Query. Reviews artwork/photos as part of freelance ms package.
Recent Nonfiction Title: *Desert Storm: The Weapons of War*, by Brenner, Harwood and UPI for Crown.
Tips: "Have an original idea and develop it completely before contacting us."

WINGRA WOODS PRESS, P.O. Box 9601, Madison WI 53715. Acquisitions Editor: M.G. Mahoney. Estab. 1983. Publishes trade paperback originals. Averages 6-10 titles/year; receives 200 submissions annually. 70% of books from first-time authors; 100% of books from unagented writers. Pays 10-12% royalty on retail price, sometimes makes outright purchase of $500-10,000. Publishes book an average of 18 months after acceptance. Simultaneous submissions OK. Reports in 6 weeks.
Nonfiction: Coffee table book, cookbook, how-to, juvenile, self-help. Subjects include Americana, popular history and science, animals, art, psychology, nature and environment. Especially looking for popularized book-length treatments of specialized knowledge; interested in proposals from academics and professionals. Query with outline/synopsis. Do not send complete ms. Reviews artwork/photos as part of ms package.
Recent Nonfiction Title: *The Christmas Cat.*
Tips: "Put your 'good stuff' in the very first paragraph . . . tell us why we should care. Consider page 1 of the query as distilled flap copy. Then follow up with facts and credentials."

Subsidy Publishers

The following publishers produce more than 50% of their books on a subsidy or cooperative basis. What they charge and what they offer to each writer varies, so you'll want to judge each publisher on its own merit. Because subsidy publishing can cost you several thousand dollars, be sure the number of books, the deadlines and services offered by the publisher are detailed in your contract. If you are willing to pay to have your book published, you should also be willing to hire an attorney to review the contract. This step prevents misunderstandings between you and your prospective publisher. Never agree to terms you don't understand in a contract. There are a growing number of editorial services that offer services similar to those performed by subsidy publishers. Companies offering editorial services are not listed in *Writer's Market*. Consult the Book Publishers introduction for more information on subsidy publishing.

Aegina Press, Inc.
59 Oak Lane, Spring Valley
Huntington WV 25704

Authors' Unlimited
3324 Barham Blvd.
Los Angeles CA 90068

Brunswick Publishing Company
P.O. Box 555
Lawrenceville VA 23868

Carlton Press, Inc.
11 W. 32nd St.
New York 10001

De Young Press
Box 76, Rt 1
Stark KS 66775

Fairway Press
C.S.S. Publishing Company, Inc.,
628 S. Main St.
Lima OH 45804

Fithian Press
P.O. Box 1525
Santa Barbara CA 93102

The Golden Quill Press
Avery Rd.
Francestown NH 03043

Peter Randall Publisher
500 Market St., P.O. Box 4726
Portsmouth NH 03802

Reflected Images Publishers
P.O. Box 314
Medford OR 97501

Rivercross Publishing, Inc.
127 E. 59th St.
New York NY 10022

Ronin Publishing, Inc.
P.O. Box 1035
Berkeley CA 94701

San Diego Publishing Company
San Diego CA 92169-0222

Silex Publishing
P.O. Box 65284
Washington DC 20035

Vantage Press
516 W. 34th St.
New York NY 10001

Other Book Publishers and Packagers

The following book publishers and packagers were listed in the 1991 edition but do not have listings in this edition of *Writer's Market*. The majority did not respond to our request to update their listings or return a questionnaire for a new listing. If a reason was given for their exclusion, we have included it in parentheses after the listing name.

ABC-Clio, Inc.
Accelerated Development Inc.
African American Images
Alba House
Amadeus Publishing Company
American Atheist Press
American Library Association
The American Psychiatric
    Press, Inc.

American References Inc.
American Showcase, Inc.
American Studies Press, Inc.
    (asked to be deleted; company is cutting back to 1-2 volumes/year and not accepting freelance submissions)
The Amwell Press

And Books
Anderson McLean, Inc.
Auto Book Press (asked to be deleted)
Aviation Book Co.
Baen Publishing Enterprises
Bear Flag Books
The Benjamin Company, Inc.
Bennett & McKnight Publish-

ing Co.
Bookmakers Guild, Inc.
Breakwater Books (asked to be deleted)
Broadman Press
Cadmus Editions
Cambridge Career Products
Capra Press
Cay-Bel Publishing Company
Center for Thanatology Research (asked to be deleted; cutbacks in production due to budget changes)
Child Welfare League of America
Chilton Book Co.
The College Board
Compute! Books
The Countrywoman's Press
Coventure Press (no longer uses freelance writing)
Crown Publishers, Inc.
Davis Publishing Company/ Law Enforcement Division
Steve Davis Publishing (asked to be deleted; not currently soliciting manuscripts)
Dembner Books
Diamond Editions
Digital Press
Dry Canyon Press
English Mountain Publishing Company (out of business)
Fairchild Books & Visuals
Five Star Publications (asked to be deleted; operates an editorial service and no longer accepts manuscript submissions)
Flockophobic Press (asked to be deleted; received too many manuscripts)
Flying Pencil Publications
Fordham University Press
Franciscan Herald Press
The Free Press
Free Spirit Publishing Inc.
Fulcrum, Inc. (asked to be deleted; receiving too many unsuitable manuscripts)
Garber Communications, Inc. (not considering manuscripts for one year)
Gem Guides Book Company
Gessler Publishing Company, Inc.
The J. Paul Getty Museum
Global Business and Trade (no longer publishing books)
Great Ocean Publishers

Green Tiger Press Inc.
Max Hardy-Publisher
Hazelden Educational Materials
Helm Publishing
Hermes House Press
Higgs Publishing Corporation (not publishing in 1992)
Holloway House Publishing Co.
Holmes & Meier Publishers, Inc.
Horizon Publishers & Distributors
Hunter House, Inc., Publishers (moving; updated information not available at press time)
Huntington House, Inc.
Information Resources Press
Instrument Society of America
Integrated Press, Inc. (backlogged with manuscripts)
Intergalactic Publishing Co.
Interlink Publishing Group, Inc.
International Marine Publishing Co.
International Resources
ISHI Press International
Jones 21st Century, Inc.
Sue Katz & Associates, Inc.
Learning Publications Inc.
Longman Financial Services Publishing
MCN Press
Medical Economics Books
Mennonite Publishing House, Inc.
Mercury House Inc.
Miller Books
National Book Company
National Gallery of Canada (asked to be deleted; publishing only solicited manuscripts)
The New England Press, Inc.
New Seed Press (asked to be deleted; receiving inappropriate submissions)
Nichols Publishing
Noyes Data Corp.
Oak Tree Publications
Old Army Press
Orbis Books
Paladin Press
Parker-Griffin Publishing Co.
Parkside Publishing Corporation
Peacock Books
The Pickering Press

V. Pollard Press
Potomac-Pacific Press
Praeger Publishers
Press of MacDonald & Reinecke
Princeton University Press
Puma Publications
Q.E.D. Information Sciences, Inc.
Q.E.D. Press of Ann Arbor, Inc.
The Riverdale Company, Inc., Publishers
Rocky Top Publications (accepting no unsolicited material)
Rutgers University Press
San Francisco Press, Inc.
Sandlapper Publishing, Inc.
Schenkman Books Inc.
Schuettge & Carleton (asked to be deleted)
Science Tech Publishers, Inc. (asked to be deleted)
Self-Counsel Press
Sentinel Books
Sigo Press (asked to be deleted; backlogged with submissions)
Gordon Soules Book Publishers Ltd.
Gareth Stevens, Inc.
Stillpoint Publishing
Surfside Publishing
Synesis Press (no longer accepting new titles)
Jeremy P. Tarcher, Inc. (asked to be deleted; receives too many unsolicited submissions)
TGNW Press (asked to be deleted)
Transnational Publishers, Inc.
Trillium Press
Tyndale House Publishers, Inc.
Universe Books
University of Minnesota Press (asked to be deleted)
University of Utah Press
Vance Bibliographies
Wallace-Homestead Book Co.
Welcome Enterprises, Inc.
Westgate Press
Westview Press
Whitney Library of Design
Word Books Publisher (asked to be deleted)
Wordware Publishing, Inc.

Consumer Publications

The past year has been a difficult one for the consumer magazine industry. In the midst of a recession and the Persian Gulf War, many magazines were forced to cut staff and decrease the number of issues published annually due to declines in advertising sales. More than 40 magazines listed in last year's edition of *Writer's Market* went out of business during the year. Five others have temporarily suspended publication while revamping the magazines or seeking additional funding. Twelve are no longer accepting freelance submissions and are going primarily with staff-written material. Even some prominent magazines such as *Savvy Woman*, *Business Month*, *Manhattan, inc.* and *Egg* were forced to cease publication.

While this sounds discouraging, freelancers may actually benefit from these cutbacks. "In a recession, some magazines will cut back on staff and use freelancers," says Keith Kelly, executive editor of *Magazine Week*. "They may have a staff of three editors and rely on freelancers for the rest. When this happens, they really have to find reliable freelancers. It's up to the freelancer to work harder on the marketing side when the market is in turmoil."

In order to keep abreast of the flux in the consumer magazine business, writers should frequent newsstands, bookstores and libraries to note startups and closings. In addition, they should peruse publications such as *Writer's Digest*, *Magazine Week* and *Folio* to note changes in magazines since this edition of *Writer's Market* went to press.

Notable trends to date include drop-offs in the growth of computer, regional and men's magazines, and continued growth in the area of environmental publications. According to Kelly, "The older magazines like *Sierra* are getting better, and there are more articles about the environment in the mainstream press. It's being picked up everywhere." Finally, with widespread focus on the education and child care agendas, there is a potential for growth in these areas.

In the area of nonfiction, editors continue to look for shorter feature articles covering specialized topics. Thus, the writer who can provide expertise in the form of a well-researched, "tight" article may have an advantage over a writer of long, general interest pieces. This will become increasingly important as magazines continue to define more specific editorial focuses. Many magazines, particularly those that have undergone budget cuts in the art and photography areas, seek freelancers who can provide quality photographs with their manuscript packages.

Before submitting articles to magazines, writers should always obtain sample copies, writer's guidelines and editorial calendars (if available) to apprise themselves of the specific types of material those magazines are seeking.

With regard to fiction, established magazines such as *Gentleman's Quarterly*, *Esquire* and *Lear's* remain prime markets, while newer publications such as *American Short Fiction* and *Vox* are also looking for short stories. Writers should keep in mind, however, that most consumer magazines receive far more fiction than they can publish and, for that reason, often do not respond to writers unless interested in using a story. Examine the categories in the Fiction subhead—science fiction, mystery, romance, men's, women's, juvenile, teen and literary—for a listing of fiction requirements for consumer magazines. More comprehensive information on the field of fiction can be found in *Novel & Short Story Writer's Market* (Writer's Digest Books).

Although articles submitted on disk seldom generate higher payment than their typewritten counterparts, most freelancers agree that personal computers save them time in editing and revising. The most commonly used word processing programs among publishers are ASCii, WordPerfect, XyWrite and Microsoft Word. Most publishers want submissions on disk in generic or ASCii format.

To make the most of their writing time, writers should expand the number of publications for which they write. Selling any unsold rights enables writers to market their articles to other magazines after they have been published the first time and allows them to make more money without investing more writing time. In addition, submitting to magazines that accept simultaneous submissions helps writers decrease the amount of time it takes to sell an article. Introductions in this section and the section introductions under Trade, Technical and Professional Journals provide related topics and publications for which writers may write or adapt articles.

When submitting material, writers should heed requirements of the magazines listed in *Writer's Market*. For example, when an editor specifically requests queries, as most do, entire manuscripts should not be sent. Manuscript length is also important to editors who must fit space requirements for their publications.

Information on publications not included in *Writer's Market* may be found in Other Consumer Publications, located at the end of this section.

Animal

The publications in this section deal with pets, racing and show horses, and other pleasure animals and wildlife. Magazines about animals bred and raised for the market are classified in the Farm category. Publications about horse racing can be found in the Sports section.

‡**ANIMAL HOUSE MAGAZINE**, Suite 179, 6914 Katella Ave., Cypress CA 90630. (714)891-2937. Senior Copy Editor: John Chadwell. Copy Editor: Todd Jarett. 40% freelance written. Monthly magazine for pet enthusiasts. "*Animal House* is a pet magazine with across-the-board appeal. We are looking for stories which show animals interacting with people, whether the animals are tame or wild." Estab. 1991. Circ. 30,000. Pays on publication. Publishes ms an average of 4 months after acceptance. Byline given. Buys first North American serial rights. Submit seasonal/holiday material 3 months in advance. Accepts simultaneous and previously published submissions. Query for electronic submissions. Reports in 1 week on queries; 2 weeks on mss.
Nonfiction: Essays, historical/nostalgic, how-to, interview/profile, new product, personal experience, photo feature. Buys 20 mss/year. Send complete ms. Length: 300-1,500 words. Pays 4-10¢/word. Sometimes pays expenses of writers on assignment.
Photos: Send photos with submission. Offers no additional payment for photos accepted with ms. Captions required. Buys one-time rights.
Tips: "Look for odd and unique animal slant. For instance, stories on a top breeder in your region, or a prominent local animal celebrity always work as do bigger scope items on trends in the pet industry."

ANIMAL TALES, 2113 W. Bethany Home Rd., Phoenix AZ 85015. (602)246-7144. Editor: Berta Cellers. Bimonthly magazine covering animals and their relationships with humans. Estab. 1989. Pays on publication. Byline given. Buys first rights. Reports in 2 months. Writer's guidelines for #10 SASE. Sample copy $4.95. Subscription: $19.95/year.
Fiction: Adventure, fantasy, historical, humorous, mystery. "Animals must be the primary focus of interest." Send complete ms. Length: 2,000-6,000 words. Pays $10-50.
Poetry: Light verse and traditional. Pays $5-20.
Fillers: Facts and short humor. Pays $5-20.
Tips: "Artwork and cartoons are also accepted. All must have animal theme. Submissions should appeal to all age groups."

‡**ANIMALS**, Massachusetts Society for the Prevention of Cruelty to Animals, 350 S. Huntington Ave., Boston MA 02130. (617)522-7400. FAX: (617)522-4885. Editor: Joni Praded. Managing Editor: Paula Abend. 90% freelance written. Bimonthly magazine covering animals. "*Animals* publishes articles on wildlife (American and international), domestic animals, balanced treatments of controversies involving animals, conservation, animal welfare issues, pet health and pet care." Circ. 70,000. Pays on

publication. Publishes ms an average of 5 months after acceptance. Byline given. Offers negotiable kill fee. Buys one-time rights or makes work-for-hire assignments. Submit seasonal/holiday material 6 months in advance. Reports in 6 weeks. Sample copy $2.50 with 9×12 SAE and 4 first class stamps. Writer's guidelines for #10 SASE.

Nonfiction: Essays, expose, general interest, how-to, opinion and photo feature on animal and environmental issues and controversies, plus practical pet-care topics. "*Animals* does not publish breed-specific domestic pet articles or 'favorite pet' stories. Poetry and fiction are also not used." Buys 6 mss/year. Query with published clips. Length: 3,000 words maximum. Pays $300 maximum. Sometimes pays the expenses of writers on assignment.

Photos: State availability of photos with submission. Reviews contact sheets, 35mm transparencies and 5×7 or 8×10 prints. Payment depends on usage size and quality. Captions, model releases and identification of subjects required. Buys one-time rights.

Columns/Departments: Books (book reviews of books on animals and animal-related subjects), 300 words. Buys 18 mss/year. Query with published clips. Length: 300 words maximum. Pays $75 maximum.

Tips: "Present a well-researched proposal. Be sure to include clips that demonstrate the quality of your writing. Stick to categories mentioned in *Animals'* editorial description. Combine well-researched facts with a lively, informative writing style. Feature stories are written almost exclusively by freelancers. We continue to seek proposals and articles that take a humane approach. Articles should concentrate on how issues affect animals, rather than humans."

‡**APPALOOSA JOURNAL**, Appaloosa Horse Club, 5070 Hwy. 8 West, P.O. Box 8403, Moscow ID 83843. (208)882-5578. Editor: Debbie Pitner Moors. 20-30% freelance written. Monthly magazine covering Appaloosa horses. Estab. 1946. Circ. 16,000. Pays on publication. Publishes ms an average of 3 months after acceptance. Byline given. Buys first North American serial rights. Query for electronic submissions. Reports in 2 weeks on queries; 2 months on mss. Free sample copy and writer's guidelines.

Nonfiction: Essays, historical/nostalgic, how-to, humor, interview/profile, horse health, personal experience, photo feature. Buys 6-7 mss/year. Query with or without published clips, or send complete ms. Length: 400-3,000 words. Pays $100-400 for assigned articles; $400 maximum for unsolicited articles. Sometimes pays expenses of writers on assignment.

Photos: Send photos with submission. Payment varies. Captions and identification of subjects required.

Tips: "Articles by writers with horse knowledge, news sense and photography skills are in great demand. If it's a good story about an Appaloosa, the writer has a pretty good chance of publication. Features and race-related articles are needed. A good understanding of the breed and the industry is helpful."

AQUARIUM FISH MAGAZINE, Fancy Publications, Box 6050, Mission Viejo CA 92690. (714)855-8822. FAX: (714)855-3045. Editor: Edward Bauman. 100% freelance written. Monthly magazine on aquariums, tropical fish, ponds and pond fish. "We need well-written feature articles, preferably with color transparencies, dealing with all aspects of the hobby and directed toward novices and experienced hobbyists." Estab. 1988. Circ. 70,000. Pays on publication. Buys first North American serial rights. ASCII files by disk or modem. Reports in 2 weeks on queries; 1 month on mss. Sample copy $3.50 Free writer's guidelines.

Nonfiction: "Articles on biology, care and breeding of aquarium and pond fish; pond and aquarium set-up and maintenance. No pet fish stories." Buys 45-60 mss/year. Query. Length: 1,500-3,500 words. Pays $100-300 for assigned articles.

Photos: Send slides with submission. Reviews contact sheets and transparencies. Offers $50-150 for color; up to $25 for b&w. Buys one-time rights.

Tips: "Know the subject; write tight, well-organized copy. Avoid 'my first aquarium' type of articles. Too many writers avoid adequate research. Many readers are knowledgeable about hobby and want solid information."

ARABIAN HORSE TIMES, Adams Corp., Rt. 3, Waseca MN 56093. (507)835-3204. FAX: (507)835-5138. Editor: Joyce Denn. 20% freelance written. Works with a small number of new/unpublished writers each year. Monthly magazine about Arabian horses. Editorial format includes hard news (veterinary, new products, book reports, etc.), lifestyle and personality pieces, and bloodline studies. Estab. 1969. Circ. 22,000. Pays on publication. Publishes ms an average of 6 months after acceptance. Byline given. Buys first serial rights. Submit seasonal/holiday material 3 months in advance. Simultaneous queries OK. Sample copy and writer's guidelines upon request.

Nonfiction: General interest, how-to, interview/profile, new product and photo feature. Buys at least 12 mss/year. Query with published clips. Length: 1,000-3,000 words. Sometimes pays expenses of writers on assignment.

Photos: Prefers color prints. Payment depends on circumstances. Captions and identification of subjects required. Buys one-time rights.

Fiction: Will look at anything about Arabians except erotica. Buys 1-2 mss/year. Send complete ms. Length: 1,500-5,000 words.

Tips: "As our periodical is specific to Arabian horses, we are interested in anyone who can write well and tightly about them. Send us something timely. Also, narrow your topic to a specific horse, event, incident, person or problem. 'Why I Love Arabians' will not work."

BIRD TALK, Dedicated to Better Care for Pet Birds, Fancy Publications, Box 6050, Mission Viejo CA 92690. (714)855-8822. FAX: (714)855-3045. Editor: Karyn New. 85% freelance written. Works with about 60 new/unpublished writers each year. Monthly magazine covering the care and training of cage birds for men and women who own any number of pet or exotic birds. Circ. 170,000. Pays latter part of month in which article appears. Publishes ms an average of 6 months after acceptance. Byline given. Buys first North American serial rights. Submit seasonal/holiday material 7 months in advance. Previously published submissions OK. No simultaneous submissions. Reports in 3 weeks on queries; 2 months on mss. Sample copy $4; writer's guidelines for #10 SASE.

Nonfiction: General interest (anything to do with pet birds); historical/nostalgic (of bird breeds, owners, cages); how-to (build cages, aviaries, playpens and groom, feed, breed, tame); humor; interview/profile (of bird and bird owners); new product; how-to (live with birds—compatible pets, lifestyle, apartment adaptability, etc.); personal experience (with your own bird); photo feature (humorous or informative); travel (with pet birds or to see exotic birds); and articles giving behavioral guidelines, medical information, legal information, and description of species. No juvenile or material on wild birds not pertinent to pet care; everything should relate to *pet* birds. Buys 150 mss/year. Query or send complete ms. Length: 500-3,000 words. Pays 10-15¢/word.

Photos: State availability of photos or include in ms. Reviews b&w contact sheets; prefers prints. Pays $50-150 for color transparencies; $15 minimum for 5×7 b&w prints. Model release and identification of subjects preferred. Buys one-time rights.

Columns/Departments: Editorial (opinion on a phase of owning pet birds) and Small Talk (short news item of general interest to bird owners). Buys 20 mss/year. Send complete ms. Length: 300-1,200 words. Pays 10-15¢/word and up.

Fiction: "Only fiction with pet birds as primary focus of interest." Adventure, fantasy, historical, humorous, mystery, suspense. No juvenile, and no birds talking unless it's their trained vocabulary. Buys 1 ms/year. Send complete ms. Length: 2,000-3,000 words. Pays 7¢/word and up.

Tips: "Send grammatical, clean copy on a human-interest story about a pet bird or about a medical, behavioral or health-related topic. We also need how-tos on feather crafts; cage cover making; aviary, perch and cage building; and planting plants in aviaries safe and good for birds. Keep health, nutrition, lack of stress in mind regarding pet birds. Study back issues to learn our style."

CALIFORNIA HORSE REVIEW, P.O. Box 2437, Fair Oaks CA 95628. (916)638-1519. FAX: (916)638-1784. Editor: Jennifer Meyer. Managing Editor: Cleann McGuire. Monthly magazine covering equestrian interests. "*CHR* covers a wide spectrum—intensive veterinary investigation, fashion and showing trends, trainer 'how-to' tips, breeding research up-dates, personality profiles, nutritional guidance. Editorial also devotes effort to reporting news and large state and national show results." Estab. 1963. Circ. 10,000. **Pays on acceptance.** Byline given. Buys first North American serial rights. Previously published submissions OK. Free sample copy and writer's guidelines.

Nonfiction: General interest (West Coast equine emphasis), how-to (training, breeding, horse care, riding), interview/profile (West Coast horse people *only*), technical (riding, training). "No fiction or anything *without* a strong focal point of interest for *West Coast equestrians*." Buys 25-40 mss/year. Query with published clips. Length: 500-2,500 words. Pays $50-200 for assigned articles; $25-150 for unsolicited articles. Sometimes pays expenses of writers on assignment.

Photos: Send photos with submission. Reviews 3×5 or larger prints. Offers no additional payment for photos accepted with ms. Captions required. Buys one-time rights.

Tips: "Be accurate, precise and knowledgeable about horses. Our readers are not beginners but sophisticated equestrians. Elementary, overly-basic how-tos are not appropriate for us. *See* what we publish! Personality profiles of well-known West Coast equestrians are the best way to break in. Use a lot of direct quotes; include at least one good photo. Not overly lengthy, but enough detail to provide interest."

CAT FANCY, Fancy Publications, Inc., Box 6050, Mission Viejo CA 92690. (714)855-8822. FAX: (714)855-3045. Editor: K. E. Segnar. 80-90% freelance written. Monthly magazine for men and women of all ages interested in all phases of cat ownership. Estab. 1965. Circ. 317,000. Pays after publication. Publishes ms an average of 6 months after acceptance. Buys first North American serial rights. Byline given. Submit seasonal/holiday material 4 months in advance. Reports in 6 weeks. Sample copy $4; writer's guidelines for SASE.

Nonfiction: Historical, medical, how-to, humor, informational, personal experience, photo feature and technical. Buys 5 mss/issue. Query or send complete ms. Length: 500-3,000 words. Pays 5¢/word; special rates for photo/story packages.

Photos: Photos purchased with or without accompanying ms. Pays $15 minimum for 8×10 b&w glossy prints; $50-150 for 35mm or 2¼×2¼ color transparencies. Send prints and transparencies. Model release required.

Fiction: Adventure, fantasy, historical and humorous. Nothing written with cats speaking. Buys 1 ms/issue. Send complete ms. Length: 500-3,000 words. Pays 5¢/word.

Fillers: Newsworthy or unusual; items with photo and cartoons. Buys 10/year. Length: 100-500 words. Pays $20-35.

Tips: "We receive more filler-type articles than we can use. It's the well-researched, hard information articles that we need."

CATS MAGAZINE, Cats Magazine Inc., P.O. Box 290037, Port Orange FL 32129. (904)788-2770. Editor: Linda J. Walton. 50% freelance written. A monthly magazine for cat lovers, veterinarians, breeders and show enthusiasts. Estab. 1945. Circ. 149,000. Pays on publication. Byline given. Buys one-time rights. Submit seasonal/holiday material 7 months in advance. Reports in 1 month on queries; 3 months on manuscripts (sometimes longer depending on the backlog). Sample copy and writer's guidelines with 9×12 SAE and $1.25 postage.

Nonfiction: Book excerpts; general interest (concerning cats); how-to (care for cats); humor; interview/profile (on cat owning personalities); new product; personal experience; photo feature; and technical (veterinarian writers). No talking cats. Buys 36 mss/year. Send complete ms. Length 800-2,500 words. Pays $25-300.

Photos: Send photos with submission. Reviews transparencies. Offers $5-25/photo, $150 for cover. Identification of subjects required. Buys one-time rights.

Fiction: Fantasy, historical, mystery, science fiction, slice-of-life vignettes and suspense. "We rarely use fiction, but are not averse to using it if the cat theme is handled in smooth, believable manner. All fiction must involve a cat or relationship of cat and humans, etc." No talking cats. Send complete ms. Length: 800-2,500 words. Pays $25-300.

Poetry: Avant-garde, free verse, haiku, light verse and traditional. Length: 4-64 lines. Pays 50¢/line.

Tips: "Well researched articles are the freelancer's best bet. Writers must at least like cats. Writers who obviously don't miss the mark."

THE CHRONICLE OF THE HORSE, P.O. Box 46, Middleburg VA 22117. (703)687-6341. FAX: (703)687-3937. Editor: John Strassburger. Managing Editor: Nancy Comer. 80% freelance written. Weekly magazine about horses. "We cover English riding sports, including horse showing, grand prix jumping competitions, steeplechase racing, foxhunting, dressage, endurance riding, handicapped riding and combined training. We are the official publication for the national governing bodies of many of the above sports. We feature news of the above sports, and we also publish how-to articles on equitation and horse care, and interviews with leaders in the various fields." Estab. 1937. Circ. 24,500. Pays for features on acceptance; news and other items on publication. Publishes ms an average of 3 months after acceptance. Byline given. Buys first North American rights and makes work-for-hire assignments. Submit seasonal/holiday material 3 months in advance. Reports in 3 weeks. Sample copy for 9×12 SAE and $2; writer's guidelines for #10 SASE.

Nonfiction: General interest; historical/nostalgic (history of breeds, use of horses in other countries and times, art, etc.); how-to (trailer, train, design a course, save money, etc.); humor (centered on living with horses or horse people); interview/profile (of nationally known horsemen or the very unusual); technical (horse care, articles on feeding, injuries, care of foals, shoeing, etc.); and news (of major competitions, clear assignment with us first). Special issues include Steeplechasing; Grand Prix Jumping; Combined Training; Dressage; Hunt Roster; Junior and Pony; and Christmas. No Q&A interviews, clinic reports, Western riding articles, personal experience, or wild horses. Buys 300 mss/year. Query or send complete ms. Length: 300-1,225 words. Pays $25-200.

Photos: State availability of photos. Accepts prints or color slides. Accepts color for b&w reproduction. Pays $15-30. Identification of subjects required. Buys one-time rights.

Columns/Departments: Dressage, Combined Training, Horse Show, Horse Care, Racing over Fences, Young Entry (about young riders, geared for youth), Horses and Humanities, and Hunting. Query or send complete ms. Length: 300-1,225 words. Pays $25-200.

Poetry: Light verse and traditional. No free verse. Buys 30/year. Length: 5-30 lines. Pays $15.

Fillers: Anecdotes, short humor, newsbreaks and cartoons. Buys 300/year. Length: 50-175 lines. Pays $10-25.

Tips: "Get our guidelines. Our readers are sophisticated, competitive horsemen. Articles need to go beyond common knowledge. Freelancers often attempt too broad or too basic a subject. We welcome well-written news stories on major events, but clear the assignment with us."

DOG FANCY, Fancy Publications, Inc., P.O. Box 6050, Mission Viejo CA 92690. (714)855-8822. Editor: Kim Thornton. 75% freelance written. Eager to work with unpublished writers. "We'd like to see a balance of both new and established writers." Monthly magazine for men and women of all ages interested in all phases of dog ownership. Circ. 150,000. Pays on publication. Publishes ms an average of 6 months after acceptance. Buys one-time rights. Byline given. Submit seasonal/holiday material 6 months in advance. Reports in 6-8 weeks. Sample copy $4; writer's guidelines for #10 SASE.
Nonfiction: Historical, medical, how-to, humor, informational, interview, personal experience, photo feature, profile and technical. We'll be looking for (and paying more for) high quality writing/photo packages. Interested writers should query with topics." Buys 5 mss/issue. Query or send complete ms. Length: 500-3,000 words. Pays 5¢/word, 10¢/word with photos.
Photos: Photos purchased without accompanying ms. Pays $15 minimum for 8×10 b&w glossy prints; $50-150 for 35mm or 2¼×2¼ color transparencies. Send prints or transparencies. Model release required.
Tips: "We're looking for the unique experience that communicates something about the dog/owner relationship—with the dog as the focus of the story, not the owner. Articles that provide hard information (medical, etc.) through a personal experience are appreciated. Note that we write for a lay audience (non-technical), but we do assume a certain level of intelligence: no talking down to people. If you've never seen the type of article you're writing in *Dog Fancy*, don't expect to."

THE GREYHOUND REVIEW, P.O. Box 543, Abilene KS 67410. (913)263-4660. FAX: (913)263-4689. Editor: Gary Guccione. Managing Editor: Tim Horan. 20% freelance written. A monthly magazine covering greyhound breeding, training and racing. Estab. 1911. Circ. 7,000. **Pays on acceptance.** Byline given. Buys first rights. Submit seasonal/holiday material 2 months in advance. Query for electronic submissions. Reports in 2 weeks on queries; 1 month on mss. Sample copy $2.50. Free writer's guidelines.
Nonfiction: How-to, interview/profile and personal experience. "Articles must be targeted at the greyhound industry: from hard news, special events at racetracks to the latest medical discoveries." Do not submit gambling systems. Buys 24 mss/year. Query. Length: 1,000-10,000 words. Pays $85-150 for assigned articles; $85-150 for unsolicited articles. Sometimes pays the expenses of writers on assignment.
Photos: State availability of photos with submission. Reviews 35mm transparencies and 8×10 prints. Offers $10-50 per photo. Identification of subjects required. Buys one-time rights.

HORSE AND HORSEMAN, Gallant Charger Publications, Inc., 34249 Camino Capistrano, P.O. Box HH, Capistrano Beach CA 92624. (714)493-2101. Editor: Jack Lewis. Managing Editor: Jeri Van Duzen. Monthly magazine on horses. Estab. 1972. Circ. 92,000. **Pays on acceptance.** Publishes ms an average of 3-4 months after acceptance. Byline given. Buys first North American serial rights. Submit seasonal/holiday material 5 months in advance. Sample copy for 9×12 SAE with 6 first class stamps; writer's guidelines for #10 SASE.
Nonfiction: General interest, how-to, humor, interview/profile, personal experience, photo feature, travel. Buys 60 mss/year. Query. Length: 250-3,000 words. Pays $25-250. Sometimes pays expenses of writers on assignment.
Photos: Send photos with submission. Reviews contact sheets, transparencies and prints. Offers no additional payment for photos accepted with ms. Captions required. Buys one-time rights.
Tips: "As our main audience is comprised of pleasure horse owners, we present material of interest to them for the most part. We do, however, cover the rest of the equine world, from rodeo to dressage, on a somewhat lesser scale. We do not publish puzzles, poems or sketches, unless the latter supports a story. The likelihood that we will purchase and use a given article is strongly affected by the amount and quality of the artwork accompanying it."

HORSE ILLUSTRATED, The Magazine for Responsible Horse Owners, Fancy Publications, Inc., P.O. Box 6050, Mission Viejo CA 92690. (714)855-8822. FAX: (714)855-3045. Managing Editor: Sharon Ralls Lemon. 90% freelance written. Prefers to work with published/established writers but eager to work with new/unpublished writers. Monthly magazine covering all aspects of horse ownership. "Our readers are adult women between the ages of 18 and 40; stories should be geared to that age group and reflect responsible horse care." Circ. 125,000. Pays on publication. Publishes ms an average of 8 months after acceptance. Byline given. Buys one-time rights. Submit seasonal/holiday material 6 months in advance. Reports in 6 weeks on queries; 2 months on mss. Sample copy $3.50. Writer's guidelines for #10 SASE.
Nonfiction: How-to (horse care, training, veterinary care), humor, personal experience and photo feature. No "little girl" horse stories, "cowboy and Indian" stories or anything not *directly* relating to horses. "We are beginning to look for longer, more in-depth features on trends and issues in the horse industry. Such articles must be queried first with a detailed outline of the article and clips." Buys 100 mss/year. Query or send complete ms. Length: 1,000-2,500 words. Pays $100-250 for assigned articles.

Pays $50-200 for unsolicited articles. Sometimes pays telephone bills for writers on assignment.

Photos: Send photos with submission. Reviews contact sheet, 35mm transparencies and 5×7 prints. Occasionally offers additional payment for photos accepted with ms.

Tips: "Freelancers can break in at this publication with feature articles on Western and English training methods and trainer profiles (including training tips); veterinary and general care how-to articles; and horse sports articles. While we use personal experience articles (six to eight times a year), they must be extremely well-written and have wide appeal; humor in such stories is a bonus. Submit photos with training and how-to articles whenever possible. We have a very good record of developing new freelancers into regular contributors/columnists. We are always looking for fresh talent, but certainly enjoy working with established writers who 'know the ropes' as well."

HORSE WORLD USA, Garri Publications, Inc., 114 West Hills Rd., P.O. Box 249, Huntington Station NY 11746. (516)423-0620. FAX: (516)423-0567. Editor: Diana DeRosa. 25% freelance written. A magazine published 13 times per year about horses. Estab. 1978. Circ. 16,500. Pays on publication. Byline given. Buys first North American serial rights. Submit seasonal/holiday material 6 months in advance. Query for electronic submissions. Reports in 3 months on queries. Sample copy for 9×12 SAE, and 6 first class stamps. Writer's guidelines for #10 SASE.

Nonfiction: "Anything horse-related (see topics listed in columns/departments section below)." Buys 25 mss/year. Query with published clips. Length: 100-2,000 words. Pays $5-125 or offers complimentary ad in directory or in classifieds as payment.

Photos: State availability of photos with submission or send photos with submission. Reviews 5×7 prints. Offers $5-10 per photo. Captions, model releases and identification of subjects required. Buys one-time rights. "No name on front of photo; give credit line."

Columns/Departments: Stable Management/Horse Care, Puzzles, Equine Spotlight, Equestrian Spotlight, Celebrity Corner, Diet/Health/Fitness, Horoscopes, The Judge's Corral, From The Horse's Mouth, The Foal's Paddock (does not pay). "Remember these must all be related to horses or horse people." Features: Horse Show, Driving, Dressage, Polo, Racing, Side-Saddle, Eventing, Breeding, Gift Mart, Grand Prix, Western, Youth, Saratoga in August. Query with published clips. Length: 500-1,000 words. Pays $25-75 maximum.

Fillers: Cartoons, gags to be illustrated by cartoonist. Buys 18/year. Pays $5.

Tips: "We are an information center for horse people. Write for guidelines. We like to work with writers and artists who are new and are not necessarily looking for money but rather a chance to be published. When writing please specify whether payment is required."

HORSEMEN'S YANKEE PEDLAR NEWSPAPER, 785 Southbridge St., Auburn MA 01501. (508)832-9638. Publisher: Nancy L. Khoury. Managing Editor: Jane Sullivan. 40% freelance written. "All-breed monthly newspaper for horse enthusiasts of all ages and incomes, from one-horse owners to large commercial stables. Covers region from New Jersey to Maine." Circ. 15,000. Pays on publication. Buys all rights for one year. Submit seasonal/holiday material 3 months in advance of issue date. Query for electronic submissions. Publishes ms an average of 5 months after acceptance. Reports in 1 month. Sample copy $3.75.

Nonfiction: Humor, educational and interview about horses and the people involved with them. Pays $2/published inch. Buys 100 mss/year. Query or submit complete ms or outline. Length: 1,500 words maximum.

Photos: Purchased with ms. Captions and photo credit required. Submit b&w prints; for return include SASE. Pays $5.

Columns/Departments: Area news column. Buys 85-95/year. Length: 1,200-1,400 words. Query.

Tips: "Query with outline of angle of story, approximate length and date when story will be submitted. Stories should be people oriented and horse focused. Send newsworthy, timely pieces, such as stories that are applicable to the season, for example: foaling in the spring or how to keep a horse healthy through the winter. We like to see how-tos, features about special horse people and anything that has to do with the preservation of horses and their rights as creatures deserving a chance to survive."

‡HORSES ALL, Box 9, Hill Spring, Alberta T0K 1E0 Canada. (403)626-3344. FAX: (403)626-3600. Editor: Jacki French. 30% freelance written. Eager to work with new/unpublished writers. Monthly tabloid for horse owners, 75% rural, 25% urban. Circ. 11,200. Pays on publication. Publishes ms an average of 6 months after acceptance. Buys one-time rights. Phone queries OK. Submit seasonal material 3 months in advance. Simultaneous, photocopied (if clear), and previously published submissions OK. Reports on queries in 5 weeks; on mss in 6 weeks. Sample copy for 9×12 SAE and $2.

Nonfiction: Interview, humor and personal experience. Query. Pays $20-100. Sometimes pays the expenses of writers on assignment.
Photos: State availability of photos. Captions required.
Columns/Departments: Open to suggestions for new columns/departments. Send query to Doug French. Length: 1-2 columns.
Fiction: Historical and western. Query. Pays $20-100.
Tips: "We use more short articles. The most frequent mistakes made by writers in completing an article assignment for us are poor research, wrong terminology, and poor (terrible) writing style."

‡**I LOVE CATS,** Grass Roots Publishing, Inc., 950 3rd Ave., 16th Fl., New York NY 10022. (212)888-1855. Editor: Lisa Maddock-Sheets. 75% freelance written. Bimonthly magazine covering cats. "*I Love Cats* is a general interest cat magazine for the entire family. It caters to cat lovers of all ages. The stories in the magazine include fiction and nonfiction, how-to, humorous and columns for the cat lover." Estab. 1989. Circ. 250,000. **Pays on acceptance.** Publishes ms an average of 9-12 months after acceptance. Byline given. No kill fee. Buys one-time rights. Submit seasonal material 6 months in advance. Previously published submissions OK. Query for electronic submissions; IBM compatible. Reports in 1 month. Sample copy $3. Free writer's guidelines.
Nonfiction: Book excerpts, essays, how-to, humor, inspirational, interview/profile, new product, opinion (does not mean letters to the editor), personal experience and photo feature. No poetry. Buys 50 mss/year. Send complete ms. Length: 100-1,500 words. Pays $25-200, or in contributor copies or other premiums "if requested." Sometimes pays expenses of writers on assignment. Send photos with submission. Offers no additional payment for photos accepted with ms. Identification of subjects required. Buys one-time rights.
Fiction: Adventure, fantasy, historical, humorous, mainstream, mystery, novel excerpts, slice-of-life vignettes, suspense. "This is a family magazine. No graphic violence, pornography or other inappropriate material. *I Love Cats* is strictly 'G-rated.'" Buys 100 mss/year. Send complete ms. Length: 500-2,000 words. Pays $25-200.
Fillers: Gags to be illustrated by cartoonist and short humor, Buys 25/year. Pays $10-35. "Please keep stories short and concise. Send complete ms with photos, if possible. I buy lots of first-time authors. Nonfiction pieces are always in short supply. With the exception of the standing columns, the rest of the magazine is open to free-lancers. Be witty, humorous or take a different approach to writing."

THE INTERNATIONAL HORSE DIGEST, (formerly *The Horse Digest*), Equine Excellence Management Group, P.O. Box 3039, Berea KY 40403. (606)986-4644. FAX: (606)986-1770. Editor: Thomas A. Watson. 75% freelance written. Monthly magazine on the US equine trade. Estab. 1987. Circ. 15,000. Pays on publication. Byline given. Offers negotiable kill fee. Buys first North American serial rights. Reports in 1 month on queries. Sample copy and writer's guidelines $4.
Nonfiction: Exposé (business oriented), how-to (should be serious, useable, business information), interview/profile (with industry people). No girl-and-her-horse, how-to clean your tack, or historical pieces. Also, we do not want "great horse" profiles. We are not a "backyard," casual interest horse magazine. No fiction. Buys 60 mss/year. Query with published clips. Length: 1,000-2,500 words. Payment based on piece and the information and value of the article. Rarely pays expenses of writers on assignment.
Photos: State availability of photos with submission or send photos with submission. Reviews 3½×5 prints. Offers $5-15 per photo (negotiable). Captions or model releases required. Buy one-time rights.
Columns/Departments: International (international, overseas business-interest pieces), 1,000 words; The Entrepreneurs (stories about business success in the equine industry), 1,000 words. Buys 10 mms/year. Query with published clips. Pays $50-100.
Tips: "Read *THD* and *other* trade publications. Understand that we serve the professional business community and not the casual horse owner. Understand the U.S. horse industry. If you write informative articles for business, gear your articles that way. People in the equine trade are like other business-people; they have employees, need insurance, they travel, own computers, advertise, need basic and not so basic information like other business-people."

MUSHING, Stellar Communications, Inc., P.O. Box 149, Ester AK 99725. (907)479-0454. Editor: Todd Hoener. Bimonthly magazine. "We cover all aspects of dog driving activities. We include information (how-to), nonfiction (entertaining), news and history stories." Estab. 1987. Circ. 6,000. Pays on publication. Publishes ms an average of 4 months after acceptance. Byline given. Buys first North American serial rights and second serial (reprint) rights. Submit seasonal/holiday material 4 months in advance. Query for electronic submissions. Reports in 3 weeks. Sample copy $3.50; free writer's guidelines.
Nonfiction: Book excerpts, general interest, historical, how-to, humor, interview/profile, new product, personal experience, photo feature, technical, travel. Themes are: December/January—Christmas, beginning race season, winter trips; February/March—travel, main dog sled race, recreation and work season; April/May—breeding, puppies, breakup; June/July—dog packing, carting, and health and

nutrition; August/September—Equipment, get ready for gear up; October/November—winter schedules, skijoring. Query with or without published clips, or send complete ms. Length: 500-3,000 words. Pays $50-250 for articles. Sometimes pays expenses of writers on assignment.

Photos: Send photos with submission. Reviews contact sheets, transparencies, prints. Offers $20-150/photo. Captions, model releases, identification of subjects required. Buys one-time and second reprint rights.

Fillers: Anecdotes, facts, gags to be illustrated by cartoonist, newsbreaks, short humor. Length: 100-250 words. Pays $35.

Tips: "Read our magazine. Know something about the sport."

PAINT HORSE JOURNAL, American Paint Horse Association, P.O. Box 961023, Fort Worth TX 76161. (817)439-3412. FAX: (817)439-1509. Editor: Bill Shepard. 10% freelance written. Works with a small number of new/unpublished writers each year. For people who raise, breed and show Paint horses. Monthly magazine. Estab. 1966. Circ. 13,000. **Pays on acceptance.** Publishes ms an average of 3 months after acceptance. Buys first North American serial rights plus reprint rights occasionally. Pays negotiable kill fee. Byline given. Phone queries OK, but prefers written query. Submit seasonal/holiday material 3 months in advance. Previously published submissions OK. Reports in 1 month. Sample copy for 9×12 SAE and 5 first class stamps; writer's guidelines for #10 SASE.

Nonfiction: General interest (personality pieces on well-known owners of Paints); historical (Paint horses in the past—particular horses and the breed in general); how-to (train and show horses); photo feature (Paint horses); and articles on horse health. Now seeking informative well-written articles on recreational riding. Buys 4-5 mss/issue. Send complete ms. Pays $50-250.

Photos: Send photos with ms. Offers no additional payment for photos accepted with accompanying ms. Uses 3×5 or larger b&w glossy prints; 35mm or larger color transparencies. Captions required.

Tips: "*PHJ* needs breeder-trainer articles, Paint horse marketing and timely articles from areas throughout the U.S. and Canada. We are looking for more horse health articles, recreational and how-to articles. We are beginning to cover more equine activity outside the show ring. This can include such things as trail riding, orienteering and other outdoor events. Photos with copy are almost always essential. Well-written first person articles are welcomed. Submit well-written items that show a definite understanding of the horse business. Be sure you understand precisely what a Paint horse is as defined by the American Paint Horse Association. Use proper equine terminology and proper grounding in ability to communicate thoughts."

PETS MAGAZINE, Moorshead Publications, 1300 Don Mills Rd., Toronto Ontario M3B 3M8 Canada. (416)445-5600. FAX: (416)445-8149. Editor: Caroline Butler. Editorial Director/Veterinarian: Dr. Tom Frisby. 50% freelance written. Bimonthly magazine on pets. Circ. 67,000 distributed by vet clinics; 5,500 personal subscriptions. Pays on publication. Publishes ms an average of 4 months after acceptance. Buys all rights. Submit seasonal/holiday material 4 months in advance. Previously published submissions OK (sometimes). Query for electronic submissions. Sample copy for #10 SAE with 95¢ IRC or Canadian stamps. Free writer's guidelines.

Nonfiction: General interest, historical, how-to (train, bathe/groom, build dog houses, make cat toys and photograph pets), breed profile and photo feature. No "I remember Fluffy. No poetry, no fiction." Buys 40 mss/year. Query with outline. Length: 300-2,000 words. Pays 10-18¢ (Canadian)/ word.

Photos: State availability of photos with submission. Reviews prints 3×5 and larger, b&w preferred. Offers $25 maximum per photo. Identification of subjects required. Buys all rights.

Fillers: Facts. Query with samples. Buys 1-2/year. Length: 100-400 words. Pays 10-15¢(Canadian)/ word. "Always call or send topic outline first; we always have a backlog of freelance articles waiting to be run. Prefers factual, information pieces, not anecdotal or merely humorous, but can be written with humor; we do not cover controversial areas such as product testing, vivisection, puppy mills, pound seizure."

PURE-BRED DOGS/AMERICAN KENNEL GAZETTE, American Kennel Club, 51 Madison Ave., New York NY 10010. (212)696-8331. Executive Editor: Elizabeth Bodner, D.V.M. 80% freelance written. Monthly association publication on pure-bred dogs. "Material is slanted to interests of fanciers of pure-bred dogs as opposed to commercial interests." Estab. 1889. Circ. 58,000. **Pays on acceptance.** Publishes ms an average of 6 months after acceptance. Byline given. Offers 30% kill fee. Buys first North American serial rights. Submit seasonal/holiday material 6 months in advance. Reports in 3 weeks. Sample copy and writer's guidelines for 9×12 SAE and 11 first class stamps.

Nonfiction: General interest, historical, how-to, humor, photo feature, travel. No profiles, poetry, tributes to individual dogs, or fiction. Buys about 75 mss/year. Query with or without published clips, or send complete ms. Length: 1,000-2,500 words. Pays $100-300. Sometimes pays expenses of writers on assignment.

Photos: Send photos with submission. Reviews tranparencies and prints. Offers $25-100/photo. Captions required. Buys one-time rights. (Photo contest guidelines for #10 SASE).
Fiction: Annual short fiction contest only. Guidelines for #10 SASE. Twelve annual contest winners are anthologized in separate booklet.
Tips: "Contributors should be involved in dog fancy or be expert in the area they write about (veterinary, showing, field trialing, obedience, training, dogs in legislation, dog art or history or literature). All submissions are welcome but the author must be credible. Veterinary articles must be written by or with veterinarians. Humorous features are personal experiences relative to pure-bred dogs. For features generally, know the subject thoroughly and be conversant with jargon peculiar to dog sport."

THE QUARTER HORSE JOURNAL, Box 32470, Amarillo TX 79120. (806)376-4811. FAX: (806)376-8364. Editor-in-Chief: Audie Rackley. 10% freelance written. Prefers to work with published/established writers. Official publication of the American Quarter Horse Association. Monthly magazine. Circ. 70,000. **Pays on acceptance.** Publishes ms an average of 3 months after acceptance. Buys first North American serial rights. Submit seasonal/holiday material 2 months in advance. Reports in 2 weeks. Free sample copy and writer's guidelines.
Nonfiction: Historical ("those that retain our western heritage"); how-to (fitting, grooming, showing, or anything that relates to owning, showing, or breeding); informational (educational clinics, current news); interview (feature-type stories—must be about established horses or people who have made a contribution to the business); personal opinion; and technical (equine updates, new surgery procedures, etc.). Buys 20 mss/year. Length: 800-2,500 words. Pays $50-250.
Photos: Purchased with accompanying ms. Captions required. Send prints or transparencies. Uses 5×7 or 8×10 b&w glossy prints; 2¼×2¼ or 4×5 color transparencies. Offers no additional payment for photos accepted with accompanying ms.
Tips: "Writers must have a knowledge of the horse business. We will be purchasing more material on quarter horse racing."

REPTILE & AMPHIBIAN MAGAZINE, RD3, P.O. Box 3709, Pottsville PA 17901. (717)622-1098. Editor: Norman Frank, D.V.M. 80% freelance written. Full-color digest size bimonthly magazine covering reptiles and amphibians. Devoted to the amateur herpetologist who is generally college-educated and familiar with the basics of herpetology. Estab. 1989. Circ. 6,000. **Pays on acceptance.** Publishes ms an average of 4 months after acceptance. Byline given. Buys first North American serial, one-time and second serial (reprint) rights (occasionally). Previously published submissions OK. Reports in 6 weeks. Sample copy $4. Writer's guidelines for #10 SASE.
Nonfiction: General interest, photo feature, technical. No first-person narrative, me-and-Joe stories or articles by writers unfamiliar with the subject matter. Buys 30 mss/year. Send complete ms. Length: 1,500-2,000 words. Pays $75-100. Sometimes pays expenses of writer on assignment.
Photos: Send photos with submission. Reviews 35mm slide transparencies, 5×7 and 8×10 glossy prints. Offers $10-25 per photo. Captions, model releases and identification of subjects required. Buys one-time rights.
Columns/Departments: Photo Dept., 750-1,000 words; Book Review, 750-1,000 words. Buys 12 mss/year. Send complete ms. Pays $50-75.
Tips: "Note your personal qualifications, such as experience in the field or advanced education. Writers have the best chance selling us feature articles—know your subject and supply high quality color photos."

TROPICAL FISH HOBBYIST, "The World's Most Widely Read Aquarium Monthly," TFH Publications, Inc., 211 W. Sylvania Ave., Neptune City NJ 07753. (201)988-8400. Editor: Ray Hunziker. Managing Editor: Neal Pronek. 75% freelance written. Monthly magazine covering the tropical fish hobby. "We favor articles well illustrated with good color slides and aimed at both the neophyte and veteran tropical fish hobbyist." Circ. 60,000. **Pays on acceptance.** Publishes ms an average of 4 months after acceptance. Byline given. Buys all rights. Submit seasonal/holiday material 4 months in advance. Reports in 2 weeks. Sample copy $3; writer's guidelines for #10 SASE.
Nonfiction: General interest, how-to, photo feature, technical, and articles dealing with beginning and advanced aspects of the aquarium hobby. No "how I got started in the hobby" articles that impart little solid information. Buys 20-30 mss/year. Length: 500-2,500 words. Pays $25-100.
Photos: State availability of photos or send photos with ms. Pays $10 for 35mm transparencies. Identification of subjects required. "Originals of photos returned to owner, who may market them elsewhere."
Fiction: "On occasion, we will review a fiction piece relevant to the aquarium hobby."
Tips: "We cater to a specialized readership—people knowledgeable in fish culture. Prospective authors should be familiar with subject; photography skills are a plus. It's a help if an author we've never dealt with queries first or submits a short item."

‡**THE WESTERN HORSE**, 321 Kalili Place, Kapa'a HI 96746. Editor: Richard Gibson. (808)822-7466. FAX: (808)822-7713. 95% freelance written. Bimonthly magazine covering horses. "Audience is young women 18-50" Estab. 1977. Circ. 80,000. Pays on publication. Publishes ms an average of 1-3 months after acceptance. Byline given. Offers no kill fee. Buys first North American serial and second serial (reprint) rights. Previously published submissions OK. Query for electronic submissions. Reports in 2 weeks. Sample copy for 9×12 SAE. Writer's guidelines for #10 SAE.

Nonfiction: General interest, how-to (train, breed, feed, care, shoe), humor, interview/profile, personal experience, photo feature and travel. No fiction or poetry. Buys 150 mss/year. Send complete ms. Length: 1,000-2,500 words. Pays 5-10¢/word for assigned articles. Send photos with submission. Reviews 4×5 prints. Offers no additional payment for photos accepted with ms. Buys one-time rights.

Fillers: Gags to be illustrated by cartoonist and short humor. Buys 100/year. Pays $10.

THE WESTERN HORSEMAN, World's Leading Horse Magazine Since 1936, Western Horseman, Inc., P.O. Box 7980, Colorado Springs CO 80933. (719)633-5524. Editor: Pat Close. 50% freelance written. Works with a small number of new/unpublished writers each year. Monthly magazine covering western horsemanship. Estab. 1936. Circ. 180,598. **Pays on acceptance.** Publishes ms an average of 5 months after acceptance. Buys one-time, North American serial rights. Byline given. Submit seasonal/holiday material 6 months in advance. Reports in 2 weeks. Sample copy $5; free writer's guidelines. Send SASE.

Nonfiction: How-to (horse training, care of horses, tips, ranch/farm management, etc.); and informational (on rodeos, ranch life, historical articles of the West emphasizing horses). Buys 100 mss/year. Length: 500-2,000 words. Payment begins at $35-300; "sometimes higher by special arrangement."

Photos: Send photos with ms. Offers no additional payment for photos. Uses 5×7 or 8×10 b&w glossy prints and 35mm transparencies. Captions required.

Tips: "Submit clean copy with professional quality photos. All copy, including computer copy, should be double-spaced. Stay away from generalities. Writing style should show a deep interest in horses coupled with a wide knowledge of the subject."

Art and Architecture

Listed here are publications about art, art history, specific art forms and architecture written for art patrons, architects and artists. Publications addressing the business and management side of the art industry are listed in the Art, Design and Collectibles category of the Trade section. Trade publications for architecture can be found in Building Interiors and Construction and Contracting sections.

‡**THE AMERICAN ART JOURNAL**, Kennedy Galleries, Inc. 40 W. 57th St., 5th Floor, New York NY 10019. (212)541-9600. FAX: (212)333-7451. Editor-in-Chief: Jane Van N. Turano . Prefers to work with published/established writers; works with a small number of new/unpublished writers each year. Scholarly magazine of American art history of the 17th, 18th, 19th and 20th centuries, including painting, sculpture, architecture, decorative arts, etc., for people with a serious interest in American art, and who are already knowledgeable about the subject. Readers are scholars, curators, collectors, students of American art, or persons who have a strong interest in Americana. Semi-annual magazine; 96 pages. Circ. 2,000. **Pays on acceptance.** Publishes ms an average of 6 months after acceptance. Buys all rights, but will reassign rights to a writer. Byline given. Reports in 2 months. Sample copy $11.

Nonfiction: "All articles are about some phase or aspect of American art history." No how-to articles or reviews of exhibitions. No book reviews or opinion pieces. No human interest approaches to artists' lives. No articles written in a casual or "folksy" style. *Writing style must be formal and serious.* Buys 25-30 mss/year. Submit complete ms "with good cover letter." No queries. Length: 2,500-8,000 words. Pays $300-600.

Photos: Purchased with accompanying ms. Captions required. Uses b&w only. Offers no additional payment for photos accepted with accompanying ms.

Tips: "Articles *must be* scholarly, thoroughly documented, well-researched, well-written, and illustrated. Whenever possible, all manuscripts must be accompanied by b&w photographs which have been integrated into the text by the use of numbers."

‡**AMERICAN INDIAN ART MAGAZINE**, American Indian Art, Inc., 7314 E. Osborn Dr., Scottsdale AZ 85251. (602)994-5445. Managing Editor: Roanne P. Goldfein. 97% freelance written. Works with a small number of new/unpublished writers each year. Quarterly magazine covering Native American art, historic and contemporary, including new research on any aspect of Native American art. Circ. 15,000. Pays on publication. Publishes ms an average of 3 months after acceptance. Byline given. Buys one-time and first rights. Simultaneous queries OK. Reports in 2 weeks on queries; 2 months on mss. Writer's guidelines for #10 SASE.

Nonfiction: New research on any aspect of Native American art. No previously published work or personal interviews with artists. Buys 12-18 mss/year. Query. Length: 1,000-2,500 words. Pays $75-300.
Tips: "The magazine is devoted to all aspects of Native American art. Some of our readers are knowledgeable about the field and some know very little. We seek articles that offer something to both groups. Articles reflecting original research are preferred to those summarizing previously published information."

ART TIMES, A Cultural and Creative Journal, P.O. Box 730, Mount Marion NY 12456-0730. (914)246-6944. Editor: Raymond J. Steiner. 10% (just fiction and poetry) freelance written. Prefers to work with published/established writers; works with a small number of new/unpublished writers each year; will work with new/unpublished writers. Monthly tabloid covering the arts (visual, theatre, dance, etc.). "*Art Times* covers the art fields and is distributed in locations most frequented by those enjoying the arts. Our 15,000 copies are sold at newsstands and are distributed throughout upstate New York counties rich in the arts as well as in most of the galleries in Soho, 57th Street and Madison Avenue in the metropolitan area; locations include theaters, galleries, museums, cultural centers and the like. Subscriptions come from across U.S. and abroad. Our readers are mostly over 40, affluent, art-conscious and sophisticated." Estab. 1984. Circ. 15,000. Pays on publication. Publishes ms an average of 1 year after acceptance. Byline given. Buys first serial rights. Submit seasonal/holiday material 8 months in advance. Simultaneous queries and simultaneous submissions OK. Reports in 3 months on queries; 6 months on mss. Sample copy for 9 × 12 SAE and 6 first class stamps; writer's guidelines for #10 SASE.
Fiction: "We're looking for short fiction that aspires to be *literary*. No excessive violence, sexist, off-beat, erotic, sports, or juvenile fiction." Buys 8-10 mss/year. Send complete ms. Length: 1,500 words maximum. Pays $15 maximum (honorarium) and 1 year's free subscription.
Poetry: Poet's Niche. Avant-garde, free verse, haiku, light verse and traditional. "We prefer well-crafted 'literary' poems. No excessively sentimental poetry." Buys 30-35 poems/year. Submit maximum 6 poems. Length: 20 lines maximum. Offers contributor copies and 1 year's free subscription.
Tips: "Be advised that we are presently on an approximate two year lead. We are now receiving 300-400 poems and 40-50 short stories per month. We only publish 2-3 poems and one story each issue. Competition is getting very great. We only pick the best. Be familiar with *Art Times* and its special audience. *Art Times* has literary leanings with articles written by a staff of scholars knowledgeable in their respective fields. Our readers expect quality. Although an 'arts' publication, we observe no restrictions (other than noted) in accepting fiction/poetry other than a concern for quality writing—subjects can cover anything and not specifically arts."

THE ARTIST'S MAGAZINE, F&W Publications, Inc., 1507 Dana Ave., Cincinnati OH 45207. Editor: Michael Ward. 80% freelance written. Works with a small number of new/unpublished writers each year. Monthly magazine covering primarily two-dimensional art instruction for working artists. "Ours is a highly visual approach to teaching the serious amateur artist techniques that will help him improve his skills and market his work. The style should be crisp and immediately engaging." Circ. 250,000. **Pays on acceptance.** Publishes ms an average of 4 months after acceptance. Byline given; bionote given for feature material. Offers 20% kill fee. Buys first North American serial rights and second serial (reprint) rights. Simultaneous queries and previously published submissions OK "as long as noted as such." Reports in 6 weeks. Sample copy $2.50 with 9 × 12 SAE and 3 first class stamps; writer's guidelines for #10 SASE.
Nonfiction: Instructional only—how an artist uses a particular technique, how he handles a particular subject or medium, or how he markets his work. "The emphasis must be on how the reader can learn some method of improving his artwork, or the marketing of it." No unillustrated articles; no seasonal/holiday material; no travel articles; no profiles of artists (except for "The Artist's Life," below). Buys 60 mss/year. Query first; all queries must be accompanied by slides, transparencies, prints or tearsheets of the artist's work as well as the artist's bio, and the writer's bio and clips. Length: 1,000-2,500 words. Pays $100-350 and up. Sometimes pays the expenses of writers on assignment.
Photos: "Transparencies are required with every accepted article since these are essential for our instructional format. Full captions must accompany these." Buys one-time rights.
Departments: Two departments are open to freelance writers: The Artist's Life and P.S. The Artist's Life (profiles and brief items about artists and their work. Also, art-related games and puzzles and art-related poetry). Query first with samples of artist's work for profiles; send complete ms for other items. Length: 600 words maximum. Pays $50 and up for profiles; up to $25 for brief items and poetry. P.S. (a humorous look at art from the artist's point of view, or at least sympathetic to the artist). Send complete ms. Pays $50 and up.
Tips: "Look at several current issues and read the author's guidelines carefully. Remember that our readers are fine and graphic artists."

THE ARTS JOURNAL, 324 Charlotte St., Asheville NC 28801. (704)255-7888. Editor: Richard James. Monthly tabloid of literary, performing and visual arts. "Our purpose is to link North Carolina artists and shows with their audiences. In our reviews and interviews we try to use language that is clear to artists and non-artists." Estab. 1975. Circ. 5,000. Pays on publication. Byline given. Offers $25 kill fee. Buys one-time rights. Submit seasonal/holiday material 2 months in advance. Reports in 2 weeks. Sample copy $2 with 8×10 SAE and 4 first class stamps.

Nonfiction: Art reviews, interviews. Buys 60 mss/year. Query. Length: 500-2,000 words. Pays $25-100.

Photos: State availability of photos with submission. Offers no additional payment for photos accepted with ms.

Fiction: Fiction Editor: J.W. Bonner. Experimental, historical, mainstream, slice-of-life vignettes. Buys 12 mss/year. Send complete ms. Length: 500-2,500 words. Pays $20-75.

Poetry: Poetry Editor: J.W. Bonner. Avant-garde, free verse, traditional. Uses 45/year. Submit up to 6 poems at 1 time. Length: 40 lines maximum. Pays in copies for poetry.

Tips: "State expertise in one of the areas we cover and give evidence of writing ability."

EQUINE IMAGES, The National Magazine of Equine Art, Equine Images Ltd., P.O. Box 916, Fort Dodge IA 50501. (800)247-2000, ext. 218. Editor: Kelly Rawlings. Publisher: Susan Badger. 20% freelance written. A quarterly magazine of equine art. "*Equine Images* serves collectors and equine art enthusiasts. We write for a sophisticated, culturally-oriented audience." Circ. 35,000. Pays on publication. Byline given. Offers $25 kill fee. Publication copyrighted. Buys first rights and makes work for hire assignments. Previously published submissions OK. Reports in 3 weeks. Sample copy for 9×12 SAE and $7.50; writer's guidelines for #10 SASE.

Nonfiction: Historical/nostalgic (history of the horse in art), how-to (art and art collections), interview/profile (equine artists, galleries, collectors), personal experience (of equine artists and collectors), photo feature (artworks or collections). "No articles about horses in general—just horse art." Buys 4-8 mss/year. Query with published clips. Length: 500-3,000 words. Pays $150-400 for assigned articles; $100-350 for unsolicited articles.

Photos: State availability of photos with submission. Writer responsible for sending visuals with finished manuscript. Reviews contact sheets, transparencies, prints. Offers no additional payment for photos accepted with ms. Identification of subjects required. Buys one-time rights.

Tips: "We are interested only in art-related subjects. We are looking for stories that help art collectors better understand, expand or protect their collections. The most promising categories for writers are profiles of prominent artists and equine galleries or museums. Send a good query letter with accompanying visuals, along with published clips or writing samples."

‡EXHIBIT, Allied Publications, Inc., 1776 Lake Worth Rd., Lake Worth FL 33460. (407)582-2099. Assiciate Editor: Karl H. Meyer. 5% freelance written. Bimonthly magazine covering fine art exhibits in museums and galleries. "*Exhibit* is a very limited market for freelancers. All articles are prepared by experts in their fields, or reprinted from catalogs." Estab. 1945. Circ. 105,000. Pays on publication. Publishes ms an average of 6 months after acceptance. Byline given. Offers no kill fee. Buys one-time or second serial (reprint) rights. Submit seasonal/holiday material 6-8 months in advance. Simultaneous and previously published submissions OK. Query for electronic submissions. Reports in 2 weeks to 3 months on mss. Sample copy for $1. Writer's guidelines for #10 SAE and 1 first class stamp.

Nonfiction: "No highly technical or cutesy material; no vulgar, obscene language. No jeremiads. Think positively." Buys 216 mss/year. Query with or without published clips, or send complete ms. "I often reject query and purchase clips submitted." Length: 300-1,500 words. Pays $25 maximum for unsolicited articles at 30¢ per published line. Pays in contributor copies or other premiums (only if author requests).

Photos: State availability of photos with submission. Offers $5 per photo. Model releases and identification of subjects required. Photographer must have model releases on file; do not send.

Tips: "All areas of the magazine open to freelancers. I enjoy working with new writers, and have been the first to publish the work of many new writers who show skill at handling words and ideas, and who are receptive to my ideas."

METROPOLIS, The Urban Magazine of Architecture and Design, Bellerophon Publications, 177 E. 87th St., New York NY 10128. (212)722-5050. Editor: Susan S. Szenasy. Managing Editor: Eric Brand. 75% freelance written. A monthly (except bimonthly January/February and July/August) magazine for consumers interested in architecture and design. Estab. 1981. Circ. 30,000-40,000. **Pays on**

 The double dagger before a listing indicates that the listing is new in this edition. New markets are often more receptive to freelance submissions.

acceptance. Publishes ms an average of 6 months after acceptance. Byline given. Buys first rights or makes work-for-hire assignments. Submit calendar material 6 weeks in advance. Reports in 4 weeks on queries and mss. Sample copy $4.50 including postage.

Nonfiction: Book excerpts; essays (ideas, design, residential interiors); and profile (only well-known international figures). No profiles on individuals or individual architectural practices, technical information, information from public relations firms, or fine arts. Buys approximately 30 mss/year. Query with published clips. Length: 1,500-4,000 words. Pays $500-1,200.

Photos: State availability, or send photos with submission. Reviews contact sheets, 35mm or 4×5 transparencies, or 8×10 b&w prints. Payment offered for certain photos. Captions required. Buys one-time rights.

Columns/Departments: Insites (miscellany: information on design and architecture), 100-600 words; pays $150-300; In Print (book review essays), 1,000-2,000 words; The Metropolis Observed (NY architecture and city planning news features and opinion) 750-1,500 words; pays $300-500; Visible City (historical aspects of cities), 1,500-2,500 words; pays $600-800; By Design (product design), 1,000-2,000 words; pays $600-800. Buys approximately 40 mss/year. Query with published clips.

Tips: "We're looking for ideas, what's new, the obscure or the wonderful. Keep in mind that we are interested *only* in the consumer end of architecture and design. Send query with examples of photos explaining how you see illustrations working with article. Also, be patient and don't expect an immediate answer after submission of query."

MUSEUM & ARTS/WASHINGTON, Museum & Arts/Washington, Inc., Suite 222, 1707 L St. NW, Washington D.C. 20036. (202)659-5973. Publisher: Anne Abramson. Editor-in-Chief: John Strand. 50% freelance written. Bimonthly magazine on the arts and culture. "*Museum & Arts/Washington* is a lively guide to the arts in the Washington area. It seeks to interest and enliven its readers appreciation of art and artists in the capitol city." Estab. 1985. Circ. 50,000. Pays on publication. Publishes ms an average of 2 months after acceptance. Byline given. Offers 33⅓% kill fee. Buys first North American serial rights and makes work-for-hire assignments. Submit seasonal/holiday material 4 months in advance. Query for electronic submissions. Reports in 2 weeks. Sample copy for 11×13 SAE with $2 first class postage.

Nonfiction: Submit to Mary Gabriel, executive editor. Book excerpts, essays, exposé, historical, interview/profile, opinion, personal experience and technical. Does *not* want anything that does not clearly relate to the Washington cultural scene. Length: 300-6,000 words. Pays $75-2,500 for assigned articles. Sometimes pays expenses of writers on assignment.

Photos: State availability of photos with submission or send photos with submission. Reviews transparencies. Payment negotiable. Identification of subjects required. Buys one-time rights.

THE ORIGINAL ART REPORT, P.O. Box 1641, Chicago IL 60690. Editor and Publisher: Frank Salantrie. Emphasizes "visual art conditions from the visual artists' and general public's perspectives." Newsletter; 6-8 pages. Estab. 1967. Pays on publication. Reports in 2 weeks. Sample copy $1.50 and 1 first class stamp.

Nonfiction: Expose (art galleries, government agencies ripping off artists, or ignoring them); historical (perspective pieces relating to now); humor (whenever possible); informational (material that is unavailable in other art publications); inspirational (acts and ideas of courage); interview (with artists, other experts; serious material on visual art conditions; no profiles); personal opinion; technical (brief items to recall traditional methods of producing art); travel (places in the world where artists are welcomed and honored); philosophical, economic, aesthetic, and artistic. "We would like to receive investigative articles on government and private arts agencies, and nonprofits, too, perhaps hiding behind status to carry on for business entities. Exclusive interest in visual fine art condition as it affects individuals, society and artists and as they affect it. Must take advocacy position. Prefer controversial subject matter and originality of treatment. Also artist's position on non-art topics. No vanity profiles of artists, arts organizations and arts promoters' operations." Buys 4-5 mss/year. Query or submit complete ms. Length: 1,000 words maximum. Pays 1¢/word.

Columns/Departments: In Back of the Individual Artist. Artists express their views about non-art topics. After all, artists are in this world, too. WOW (Worth One Wow), Worth Repeating, and Worth Repeating Again. Basically, these are reprint items with introduction to give context and source, including complete name and address of publication. Looking for insightful, succinct commentary. Submit complete ms. Length: 500 words maximum and copy of item. Pays ½¢/word.

Tips: "We have a stronger than ever emphasis on editorial opinion or commentary, based on fact, of the visual art condition: economics, finances, politics and manufacture of art and the social and individual implications of and to fine art."

‡SF, The Magazine of Design & Style, California Magazines Partnership, 1045 Sansome St., #110, San Francisco CA 94111. (415)986-4940. Editor: Ms. Lee Ryder. Executive Editor: Leslie Plummer Clagett. 95% freelance written. Monthly magazine covering design—architecture, food and fashion.

Estab. 1989. Circ. 95,000. Pays on acceptance. Publishes ms an average of 6 months after acceptance. Byline given. Buys first North American serial rights. Submit seasonal/holiday material 6 months in advance. Reports in 3 weeks. Free sample copy and writer's guidelines.

Nonfiction: Seeking articles about collectors and artists' studios. Buys 120 mss/year. Query with published clips. Length: 1,500-2,500 words. Pays $200-750 for assigned articles. Sometimes pays expenses of writers on assignment. State availability of photos with submissions. Reviews transparencies and prints.

‡**SITE SOUND,** The Society for the Advancement of Regionalism in the Arts Inc., 163 Mill Street, P.O. Box 23015, London, Ontario N6A 5N9 Canada. (519)432-9211. Editor: Robert C. McKenzie. 80% freelance written. Bimonthly magazine covering the arts. "Our circulation is primarily in Southwestern Ontario. Our editorial aim is to promote the cultural resources of our region, and to inform our readers of cultural activities elsewhere in a way which makes these matters relevant to our readers." Estab. 1988. Circ. 5,000. Pays on publication. Publishes ms an average of 1 month after acceptance. Byline given. Offers 50% kill fee. Buys first North American serial rights. Submit seasonal/holiday material 3 months in advance. Query for electronic submissions. Reports in 2 weeks. Sample copy for 9 × 12 SAE with 3 first class International Reply Coupons.

Nonfiction: Essays, historical/nostalgic, interview/profile, opinion (does not mean letters to the editor). "No opinion unsupported by expert knowledge." Buys 30 mss/year. Length: 1,000-5,000. Pays $100-500. Sometimes pays expenses of writers on assignment.

Photos: Send photos with submission. Reviews 8 × 10 prints. Identification of subjects required. Buys one-time rights.

Columns/Departments: Book Reviews (new books dealing with some aspect of the arts), 250-1,500; Compact Disc Reviews (new releases of 'serious' music — classical, opera, jazz, etc.), 100-500. Buys 40 mss/year. Send complete ms. Pays $50-150.

Tips: "We are looking for writers who can communicate in readable language and who possess the knowledge and skill to supply serious critical writing in one or more of the arts (painting, opera, theater, etc.)."

‡**SOUTHWEST ART**, Collector's Preference, CBH Publishing, P.O. Box 460535, Houston TX 77256-0535. (713)850-0990. FAX: (713)850-1314. Editor-in-Chief: Susan H. McGarry. Managing Editor: Jacqueline M. Pontello. 60% freelance written. Consumer publication. Monthly fine arts magazine. "*SWA* is directed to art collectors interested in artists, market trends, art history of the American West." Estab. 1971. Circ. 70,413. **Pays on acceptance.** Publishes ms an average of 6 months after acceptance. Byline given. Offers $125 kill fee. All rights negotiable. Submit seasonal/holiday material 8 months in advance. Accepts simultaneous submissions. Free sample copy and writer's guidelines.

Nonfiction: Book excerpts, interview/profile, opinion (does not mean letters to the editor). Does not want to see fiction or poetry. Buys 72 mss/year. Query with published clips. Length 1,800-3,000 words. Pays $300-400 for assigned articles; $300 for unsolicited articles. Send photos with submission.

Photos: Reviews transparencies (35mm, 2¼, 4 × 5) and 8 × 10 prints. Captions and identification of subjects required. Buys one-time rights.

WESTART, P.O. Box 6868, Auburn CA 95604. (916)885-0969. Editor-in-Chief: Martha Garcia. Emphasizes art for practicing artists and artists/craftsmen; students of art and art patrons. Semimonthly tabloid; 20 pages. Estab. 1961. Circ. 5,000. Pays on publication. Buys all rights. Byline given. Phone queries OK. Free sample copy and writer's guidelines.

Nonfiction: Informational, photo feature and profile. No hobbies. Buys 6-8 mss/year. Query or submit complete ms. Include SASE for reply or return. Length: 700-800 words. Pays 50¢/column inch.

Photos: Purchased with or without accompanying ms. Send b&w prints. Pays 50¢/column inch.

Tips: "We publish information which is current — that is, we will use a review of an exhibition only if exhibition is still open on the date of publication. Therefore, reviewer must be familiar with our printing and news deadlines."

‡**WILDLIFE ART NEWS, The International Magazine of Wildlife Art**, Pothole Publications, Inc. 3455 Dakota Ave. S., P.O. Box 16246, St. Louis Park MN 55416. (612)927-9056. Editor: Robert Koenke. Associate Editor: Rebecca Hakala. 80% freelance written. Bimonthly magazine of wildlife art and conservation. "*Wildlife Art News* is the world's largest wildlife art magazine. Features cover interviews on living artists as well as wildlife art masters, illustrators and conservation organizations. Audience is publishers, collectors, galleries, museums, show promoters worldwide." Estab. 1982. Circ. 48,000. Pays on publication. Publishes ms an average of 4 months after acceptance. Byline given. Negotiable kill fee. Buys second serial (reprint) rights. Query for electronic submissions. Reports in 2 months. Sample copy for 9 × 12 SAE with 10 first class stamps. Writer's guidelines for #10 SASE. Buys 40 mss/year. Query with published clips. Length: 800-5,000 words. Pays $150-1,000 for assigned articles.

Columns/Departments: Buys up to 6 mss/year. Pays $100-300.

WOMEN ARTISTS NEWS, Midmarch Arts Press, P.O. Box 3304, Grand Central Station, New York NY 10163. Editor: Judy Seigel. 70-90% freelance written. Eager to work with new/unpublished writers. Bimonthly magazine for "artists and art historians, museum and gallery personnel, students, teachers, crafts personnel, art critics and writers." Estab. 1975. Circ. 5,000. Buys first serial rights only when funds are available. "Token payment as funding permits." Publishes ms an average of 2 months after acceptance. Byline given. Submit seasonal material 2 months in advance. Reports in 1 month. Sample copy $3.
Nonfiction: Features, informational, historical, interview, opinion, personal experience, photo feature and technical. Query or submit complete ms. Length: 500-2,500 words.
Photos: Used with or without accompanying ms. Query or submit contact sheet or prints. Pays $5 for 5 × 7 b&w prints when money is available. Captions required.

Associations

Association publications allow writers to write for national audiences while covering local stories. If your town has a Kiwanis, Lions or Rotary Club chapter, one of its projects might merit a story in the club's magazine. If you are a member of the organization, find out before you write an article if the publication pays members of the organization for stories; some associations do not. In addition, some association publications gather their own club information and rely on freelancers solely for outside features. Be sure to find out what these policies are before you submit a manuscript. Club-financed magazines that carry material not directly related to the group's activities are classified by their subject matter in the Consumer and Trade sections.

‡**THE ASSOCIATION EXECUTIVE, An Independent News Magazine Serving Association, Hospitality and Meeting Executives,** Special Editions Publishing, Inc. 450 Wymore Rd., Winter Park FL 32789. (407)644-0031. Editor: Lisa McDuffie. 1% freelance written. Monthly tabloid on association and hospitality news. "We are primarily a news magazine, with special sections for features and news features. Our magazine is read by people who run associations. They are interested in things that affect their members and their associations." Circ. 4,600. Pays on publication on an individual basis. Byline given. Submit seasonal/holiday material 2 months in advance. Simultaneous, photocopied and previously published submissions OK. Query for electronic submissions. Reports in 1 month on queries; 1 month (usually much faster) on mss. Sample copy and writer's guidelines for 8½ × 11 SAE with 4 first class stamps.
Nonfiction: Opinion (the effect of current affairs on the association industry), travel (especially cities with convention facilities) and legislative. Feature sections on convention facilities in: May: Carolinas, August: Georgia, October: Florida, November: Tennessee and December: Association Services. Buys 1 ms/year. Query with or without published clips, or send complete ms. Length: 500-2,500 words. Pays $1-50 for unsolicited articles.
Photos: Send photos with submission. Reviews transparencies (1 × 1¼) and 4 × 5 prints. Offers no additional payment for photos accepted with ms. Buys all rights.
Columns/Departments: Executive to Executive (ways and ideas for effective managament). Buys 1 ms/year. Send complete ms. Length: 500-1,500 words. Pays $1-50.
Tips: "Our magazine is easy to break into. Either a phone call or a query letter will be answered right away, with explanations on our readers' interests. Make sure that it relates to the interests of the association or convention planning industries. It can also effect business. Example: legislation, taxes, union movement."

CALIFORNIA HIGHWAY PATROLMAN, California Association of Highway Patrolmen, 2030 V St., Sacramento CA 95818-1730. (916)452-6751. Editor: Carol Perri. 80% freelance written. Will work with established or new/unpublished writers. Monthly magazine. Circ. 20,000. Pays on publication. Publishes ms an average of 1 year after acceptance. Buys one-time rights. Submit seasonal/holiday material 6 months in advance. Reports in 3 months. Sample copy and writer's guidelines for 9 × 12 SAE and 4 first class stamps.
Nonfiction: Publishes articles on transportation safety, driver education, consumer interest, California history, humor and general interest. "Topics can include autos, boats, bicycles, motorcycles, snowmobiles, recreational vehicles and pedestrian safety. We are also in the market for California travel pieces and articles on early California. We are *not* a technical journal for teachers and traffic safety experts, but rather a general interest publication geared toward the layman." Pays 2½¢/word, or $50 minimum.

Photos: "Illustrated articles always receive preference." Pays $5/b&w photo; no transparencies. Captions required.
Tips: "If a writer feels the article idea, length and style are consistent with our magazine, submit the manuscript for me to determine if I agree. We are especially looking for articles for specific holidays."

COMEDY WRITERS ASSOCIATION NEWSLETTER, P.O. Box 023304, Brooklyn NY 11202-0066. (718)855-5057. Editor: Robert Makinson. 10% freelance written. Quarterly newsletter on comedy writing for association members. Estab. 1989. **Pays on acceptance.** Publishes ms an average of 3 months after acceptance. Byline given. Buys all rights. Reports in 2 weeks on queries; 1 month on mss. Sample copy $4; writer's guidelines for #10 SASE.
Nonfiction: How-to, humor, opinion, personal experience. "No exaggerations about the sales that you make and what you are paid. Be accurate." Query. Length: 250-500 words. Pays 3¢/word.
Photos: State availability of photos with submission. Offers no additional payment for photos accepted with ms.
Fillers: Facts. Length: 100 words maximum. Pays 3¢/word.
Tips: "The easiest way to be mentioned in the publication is to submit short jokes. (Payment is $1-3 per joke.)"

‡DISCOVERY YMCA, YMCA of the USA, 101 N. Wacker Dr., Chicago IL 60606. (312)269-1126. Editor: Anthony Ripley. 40% freelance written. Quarterly magazine covering the YMCA movement in 50 states. "We concentrate on challenges and accomplishments of YMCAs and on issues facing the movement." Estab. 1982. Circ, 86,000. **Pays on acceptance.** Publishes ms an average of 1-2 months after acceptance. Byline given. Offers no kill fee. Makes work-for-hire assignments. Free sample copy and writer's guidelines.
Nonfiction: Historical/nostalgic, humor, inspirational, interview/profile, opinion, personal experience, photo feature, religious. "No testimonies on how wonderful the YMCA is." Buys 10-12 mss/year. Query. Length: 1,500-2,500 words. Pays $450-550 for assigned articles; $300 for unsolicited articles. Pays expenses of writers on assignment.
Tips: "Send 3 or 4 pieces that you are really proud of having written. I don't need to see breadth of coverage but style and complete grasp of the subject."

FEDCO REPORTER, A Publication Exclusively for FEDCO Members, Box 2605, Terminal Annex, Los Angeles CA 90051. (213)946-2511. Editor: Michele A. Brunmier-Scianna. 90% freelance written. Works with a small number of new/unpublished writers each year. A monthly catalog/magazine for FEDCO department store members. Estab. 1940. Circ. 2 million. **Pays on acceptance.** Publishes ms an average of 4 months after acceptance. Byline given. Offers $50 kill fee. Buys first rights. Query for electronic submissions. Reports in 6 weeks. Sample copy for 9×12 SAE with 4 first class stamps; writer's guidelines for SASE.
Nonfiction: General interest, historical. The magazine publishes material on historical events, personalities, anecdotes and little-known happenings (especially relating to California); general interest stories on common, everyday items with an unusual background or interesting use. Seasonal stories (especially relating to California); and stories about Southern California wildlife. No first person narrative. Buys 75 mss/year. Query with or without published clips, or send complete manuscript. Length: 450 words. Pays $100.
Photos: State availability of photos. Reviews b&w and color slides. Pays $25.
Tips: "We will publish excellent writing that is well-researched regardless of prior writings. Articles should be tightly written and not stray from subject."

KIWANIS, 3636 Woodview Trace, Indianapolis IN 46268. FAX: (317)879-0204. Executive Editor: Chuck Jonak. 85% of feature articles freelance written. Buys about 50 manuscripts annually. Magazine published 10 times/year for business and professional persons and their families. Estab. 1915. Circ. 285,000. **Pays on acceptance.** Buys first serial rights. Pays 40% kill fee. Publishes ms an average of 6 months after acceptance. Byline given. Reports within 2 months. Sample copy and writer's guidelines for 9×12 SAE and 5 first class stamps.
Nonfiction: Articles about social and civic betterment, small-business concerns, science, education, religion, family, sports, health, recreation, etc. Emphasis on objectivity, intelligent analysis and thorough research of contemporary issues. Positive tone preferred. Concise, lively writing, absence of cliches, and impartial presentation of controversy required. When applicable, information and quotation from international sources are required. Avoid writing strictly to a U.S. audience. "We have a continuing need for articles of international interest. In addition, we are very interested in proposals that concern helping youth, particularly prenatal through age five: infant mortality, day care, developmentally appropriate education, early intervention for at-risk children, parent education, safety and pediatric trauma." Length: 2,500-3,000 words. Pays $400-1,000. "No fiction, personal essays, profiles, travel pieces, fillers or verse of any kind. A light or humorous approach is welcomed where the subject

is appropriate and all other requirements are observed." Usually pays the expenses of writers on assignment. Query first. Must include SASE for response.

Photos: "We accept photos submitted with manuscripts. Our rate for a manuscript with good photos is higher than for one without." Model release and identification of subjects required. Buys one-time rights.

Tips: "We will work with any writer who presents a strong feature article idea applicable to our magazine's audience and who will prove he or she knows the craft of writing. First, obtain writer's guidelines and a sample copy. Study for general style and content. When querying, present detailed outline of proposed manuscript's focus, direction, and editorial intent. Indicate expert sources to be used for attribution, as well as article's tone and length. Present a well-researched, smoothly written manuscript that contains a 'human quality' with the use of anecdotes, practical examples, quotations, etc."

THE LION, 300 22nd St., Oak Brook IL 60521-8842. (708)571-5466. Editor-in-Chief: Mark C. Lukas. Senior Editor: Robert Kleinfelder. 35% freelance written. Works with a small number of new/unpublished writers each year. Covers service club organization for Lions Club members and their families. Monthly magazine. Estab. 1918. Circ. 670,000. **Pays on acceptance.** Publishes ms an average of 5 months after acceptance. Buys all rights. Byline given. Phone queries OK. Reports in 2 weeks. Free sample copy and writer's guidelines.

Nonfiction: Informational (stories of interest to civic-minded individuals) and photo feature (must be of a Lions Club service project). No travel, biography, or personal experiences. No sensationalism. Prefers anecdotes in articles. Buys 4 mss/issue. Query. Length: 500-2,200. Pays $50-750. Sometimes pays the expenses of writers on assignment.

Photos: Purchased with or without accompanying ms or on assignment. Captions required. Query for photos. B&w and color glossies at least 5×7 or 35mm color slides. Total purchase price for ms includes payment for photos, accepted with ms. "Be sure photos are clear and as candid as possible."

Tips: "Incomplete details on how the Lions involved actually carried out a project and poor quality photos are the most frequent mistakes made by writers in completing an article assignment for us. We are geared increasingly to an international audience."

THE MODERN WOODMEN, Public Relations Department, 1701 1st Ave., Rock Island IL 61201. (309)786-6481. Editor: Gloria Bergh. Contact: Beth T. Fratzke, public relations assistant. 5-10% freelance written. Works with both published and new writers. "Our publication is for families who are members of Modern Woodmen of America. Modern Woodmen is a fraternal life insurance society, and most of our members live in smaller communities or rural areas throughout the United States. Various age groups read the magazine." Quarterly magazine. Circ. 350,000. Not copyrighted. **Pays on acceptance.** Keeps a file of good manuscripts to meet specific future needs and to balance content. Buys one-time rights or second serial (reprint) rights to material. Simultaneous submissions OK. Reports in 1 month if SASE included. Sample copy and guidelines for 9×12 SAE and 2 first class stamps; writer's guidelines for #10 SASE.

Nonfiction: For children and adults. "We seek lucid style and rich content. We need manuscripts that center on family-oriented subjects, human development, and educational topics."

Fiction: "Publishes an occasional fiction story for children and teens. We stress plot and characterization. A moral is a pleasant addition, but not required." Length: about 1,200 words. Pays $50 minimum.

Tips: "We want articles that appeal to young families, emphasize family interaction, community involvement, and family life. We also consider educational, historical, patriotic, and humorous articles. We don't want religious articles, teen romances, or seasonal material. Focus on people, whether the article is about families or is educational, historical or patriotic or humorous."

THE NEIGHBORHOOD WORKS, Resources for Urban Communities, Center for Neighborhood Technology, 2125 West North Ave., Chicago IL 60647. (312)278-4800. FAX: (312)278-3840. Editor: Mary O'Connell. 15-25% freelance written. A bimonthly magazine on community organizing, housing, energy, environmental and economic issues affecting city neighborhoods. "Writers must understand the importance of empowering people in low- and moderate-income city neighborhoods to solve local problems in housing, environment and local economy." Estab. 1978. Circ. 2,500. Pays on publication. Publishes ms an average of 2 months after acceptance. Byline given. Buys all rights. Submit seasonal/holiday material 2 months in advance. Previously published submissions OK. Reports in 1 month on queries; 2 months on mss. Sample copy and writer's guidelines for 9×12 SAE and 2 first class stamps.

Nonfiction: Exposes, historical (neighborhood history), how-to (each issue has "reproducible feature" on such topics as organizing a neighborhood block watch, a community garden, recycling, etc.), interview/profile ("of someone active on one of our issues"), personal experience ("in our issue areas, e.g, community organizing"), technical (on energy conservation and alternative energy, environmental issues). Buys 6-10 mss/year. Query with or without published clips or send complete ms. Length: 750-2,000 words. Pays $100-500. "We pay professional writers (people who make a living at it). We don't pay nonprofessionals and students but offer them a free subscription." Pays expenses of writers on assignment by previous agreement.

Photos: State availability of photos with submission. Reviews contact sheets and prints. Offers $10-35/photo. Captions and identification of subjects required. Buys one-time rights.

Columns/Departments: Reproducible features (how-to articles on issues of interest to neighborhood organizations), 1,000-2,000 words. Query with published clips. Pays $100-250.

Tips: "We are increasingly interested in stories from cities other than Chicago (our home base)."

RECREATION NEWS, Official Publication of the League of Federal Recreation Associations, Inc., Icarus Publishers, Inc., P.O. Box 32335, Washington DC 20007. (202)965-6960. Editor: Sam Polson. 85% freelance written. A monthly guide to leisure activities for federal workers covering outdoor recreation, travel, fitness and indoor pastimes. Estab. 1979. Circ. 100,000. Pays on publication. Publishes ms an average of 6 months after acceptance. Byline given. Buys first rights and second serial (reprint) rights. Submit seasonal/holiday material 8 months in advance. Simultaneous queries and simultaneous and previously published submissions OK. Reports in 1 month. Sample copy and writer's guidelines for 9×12 SAE with $1.05 postage.

Nonfiction: Articles Editor. General interest and travel (on recreation, outdoors); historical/nostalgic (Washington-related); and personal experience (with recreation, life in Washington). Special issues feature skiing (December); education (August). Query with clips of published work. Length: 500-2,000 words. Pays $35-300.

Photos: Photo editor. State availability of photos with query letter or ms. Reviews contact sheets, transparencies, and 5×7 b&w prints. Pays $25/b&w photo ordered from contact sheet, $50-125 for color. Captions and identification of subjects required.

Tips: "Our writers generally have a few years of professional writing experience and their work runs to the lively and conversational. We'll need more manuscripts in a wider range of recreational topics, including the off-beat. The areas of our publication most open to freelancers are general articles on travel and sports, both participational and spectator, also historic in the DC area."

REVIEW, A Publication of North American Benefit Association, 1338 Military St., P.O. Box 5020, Port Huron MI 48061-5020. (313)985-5191, ext. 77. Editor: Janice U. Whipple. Associate Editor: Patricia Pfeifer. 10-15% freelance written. Prefers to work with published/established writers, and works with a small number of new/unpublished writers each year. Quarterly trade journal on insurance/fraternal deeds. Family magazine. Estab. 1895. Circ. 42,000. **Pays on acceptance.** Publishes ms an average of 2 years after acceptance. Byline given. Not copyrighted. Buys one-time rights, simultaneous rights, and second serial (reprint) rights. Submit seasonal/holiday material 6 months in advance. Simultaneous and previously published submissions OK. Reports in 2 months. Sample copy for 9×12 SAE with 4 first class stamps; writer's guidelines for #10 SASE.

Nonfiction: General interest, nature, historical/nostalgic, how-to (improve; self-help); humor; inspirational; personal experience; and photo feature. No political/controversial. Buys 4-10 mss/year. Send complete ms. No queries, please. Length: 600-1,500 words. Pays 3-5¢/word.

Photos: Prefers ms with photos if available. Send photos with ms. Reviews 5×7 or 8×10 b&w prints and color slides or prints. Pays $10-15. Model release and identification of subjects required. Buys one-time rights.

Fiction: Adventure, humorous and mainstream. Buys 2-4 mss/year. Send complete ms. Length: 600-1,500 words. Pays 3-5¢/word. "No queries please."

Tips: "We like articles with accompanying color photos; articles that warm the heart; stories with gentle, happy humor. Give background of writer as to education and credits. Manuscripts and art material will be carefully considered, but received only with the understanding that North American Benefit Association shall not be responsible for loss or injury."

THE SAMPLE CASE, The Order of United Commercial Travelers of America, 632 N. Park St., Box 159019, Columbus OH 43215. (614)228-3276. FAX: (614)228-1898. Editor: Sam Perdue. Bimonthly magazine covering news for members of the United Commercial Travelers. Emphasizes fraternalism for its officers and active membership. Estab. 1889. Circ. 140,000. Pays on publication. Buys one-time rights. Submit seasonal/holiday material 6 months in advance. Simultaneous queries and submissions OK. Free sample copy.

Nonfiction: Articles on travel in the U.S. and Canada; food/cuisine; health/fitness/safety; hobbies/entertainment; fraternal/civic activities; business finance/insurance.

Photos: David Knapp, art director. State availability of photos with ms. Pays minimum $20 for 5×7 b&w or larger prints; $30 for 35mm or larger transparencies used inside (more for cover). Captions required.

‡SCOUTING, Boy Scouts of America, 1325 W. Walnut Hill Ln., P.O. Box 15015, Irving TX 75015-2079. (214)580-2355. FAX: (214)580-2079. Editor: Ernest Doclar. Executive Editor: Jon Halter. 90% freelance written. A bimonthly magazine on Scouting activities for adult leaders of the Boy Scouts.

Estab. 1913. Circ. 1 million. **Pays on acceptance.** Publishes ms an average of 4 months after acceptance. Byline given. Buys first North American serial rights. Submit seasonal/holiday material 4 months in advance. Reports in 2 weeks. Sample copy for #10 SAE with $1 postage; writer's guidelines for #10 SAE with 1 first class stamp.

Nonfiction: Buys 60 mss/year. Query with published clips. Length: 1,500-2,000 words. Pays $300-600 for assigned articles; pays $200-500 for unsolicited articles. Pays expenses of writers on assignment.

Photos: State availability of photos with submission. Reviews contact sheets and transparencies. Identification of subjects required. Buys one-time rights.

Columns/Departments: Family Quiz (quiz on topics of family interest), 1,000 words; and Way it Was (Scouting history), 1,200 words. Buys 6 mss/year. Query. Pays $200-300.

THE SONS OF NORWAY VIKING, Sons of Norway, 1455 W. Lake St., Minneapolis MN 55408. (612)827-3611. FAX: (612)827-0658. Editor: Gaelyn Beal. 50% freelance written. Prefers to work with published/established writers. A monthly membership magazine for the Sons of Norway, a fraternal and cultural organization, covering Norwegian culture, heritage, history, Norwegian-American topics, modern Norwegian society, genealogy and travel. "Our audience is Norwegian-Americans (middle-aged or older) with strong interest in their heritage and anything Norwegian. Many have traveled to Norway." Estab. 1903. Circ. 70,000. Pays on publication. Publishes ms an average of 8 months after acceptance. Byline given. Offers $25 kill fee. Buys first North American serial rights and second serial (reprint) rights. Submit seasonal/holiday material 6 months in advance. Previously published submissions OK. Reports in 6 weeks on queries; 8 weeks on mss. Free sample copy and writer's guidelines on request.

Nonfiction: General interest, historical/nostalgic, humor, interview/profile, and travel—all having a Norwegian angle. "Articles should not be personal impressions nor a colorless spewing of facts, but well-researched and conveyed in a warm and audience-involving manner. Does it entertain *and* inform?" Buys 30 mss/year. Query. Length: 1,500-3,000 words. Pays $75-250.

Photos: Reviews transparencies and prints. Pays $10-20/photo; pays $100 for cover color photo. Identification of subjects required. Buys one-time rights.

Tips: "Show familiarity with Norwegian culture and subject matter. Our readers are somewhat knowledgeable about Norway and quick to note misstatements. Articles about modern Norway are most open to freelancers—the society, industries—but historical periods also okay. Call before a scheduled trip to Norway to discuss subjects to research or interview while there."

THE TOASTMASTER, Toastmasters International, 23182 Arroyo Vista, Rancho Santa Margarita CA 92688 or P.O. Box 9052, Mission Viejo, CA 92690-7052. (714)858-8255. FAX: (714)858-1207. Editor: Suzanne Frey. Associate Editor: Brian Richard. 50% freelance written. A monthly magazine on public speaking, leadership and club concerns. "This magazine is sent to members of Toastmasters International, a nonprofit educational association of men and women throughout the world who are interested in developing their communication and leadership skills. Members range from novice speakers to professional orators and come from a wide variety of backgrounds." Estab. 1932. Circ. 160,000. **Pays on acceptance.** Publishes ms an average of 8-10 months after acceptance. Byline given. Buys second serial (reprint) rights, first-time or all rights. Submit seasonal/holiday material 3 months in advance. Simultaneous and previously published submissions OK. Query for electronic submissions. Reports in 6 weeks on queries; 1 month on mss. Sample copy for 9 × 12 SAE and 2 first class stamps; writer's guidelines for #10 SASE.

Nonfiction: Book excerpts, how-to (communications related), humor (only if informative; humor cannot be off-color or derogatory), interview/profile (only if of a very prominent member or former member of Toastmasters International or someone who has a valuable perspective on communication and leadership). Buys 50 mss/year. Query. Length: 1,000-2,500 words. Pays $75-250. Sometimes pays expenses of writers on assignment. "Toastmasters members are requested to view their submissions as contributions to the organization. Sometimes asks for book excerpts and reprints without payment, but original contribution from individuals outside Toastmasters will be paid for at stated rates."

Photos: Reviews b&w prints. Offers no additional payment for photos accepted with ms. Captions are required. Buys all rights.

Tips: "We are looking primarily for 'how-to' articles on subjects from the broad fields of communications and leadership which can be directly applied by our readers in their self-improvement and club programming efforts. Concrete examples are useful. Avoid sexist or nationalist language."

‡VFW AUXILIARY MAGAZINE, Ladies Auxiliary to the Veterans of Foreign Wars, 406 W. 34th St., Kansas City MO 64111. (816)561-7663. Editor: Marilyn Ebersole. 20% freelance written. 8 issues each year. **Pays on acceptance.** Publishes ms an average of 2 months after acceptance. Buys one-time rights. Reports in 4 weeks.

Nonfiction: "We are a general interest publication, so we look at everything as long as it is good and wholesome." Query. Pays a maximum of $300.

VFW MAGAZINE, Veterans of Foreign Wars of the United States, Suite 523, 34th and Broadway, Kansas City MO 64111. (816)968-1171. FAX: (816)968-1169. Editor: Rich Kolb. 75% freelance written. Monthly magazine on veterans' affairs. *"VFW Magazine* goes to its members worldwide, all having served honorably in the armed forces overseas during periods of conflict or war and earning a campaign medal." Circ. 2.1 million. **Pays on acceptance.** Publishes ms 6 months after acceptance. Offers 100% kill fee. Buys first rights. Submit seasonal/holiday material 6 months in advance. Query for electronic submissions. Reports in 1 month on queries; 6 weeks on mss. Free sample copy.
Nonfiction: Interview/profile and veterans' affairs. Buys 10-15 mss/year. Query. Length: 500-3,000 words. Pays $200-750.
Photos: Send photos with submission. Reviews contact sheets, negatives, transparencies and prints. Captions, model releases and identification of subjects required. Buys all rights.

WOODMEN OF THE WORLD MAGAZINE, 1700 Farnam St., Omaha NE 68102. (402)271-7860. FAX: (402)271-6270. Editor: George M. Herriott. 10% freelance written. Works with a small number of new/unpublished writers each year. Published by Woodmen of the World Life Insurance Society for "people of all ages in all walks of life. We have both adult and child readers from all types of American families." Monthly. Circ. 480,000. Not copyrighted. Buys 10 mss/year. **Pays on acceptance.** Byline given. Buys one-time rights. Publishes ms an average of 2 months after acceptance. Will consider simultaneous submissions. Submit seasonal material 3 months in advance. Reports in 5 weeks. Free sample copy.Writer's guidelines for #10 SASE.
Nonfiction: "General interest articles which appeal to the American family—travel, history, art, new products, how-to, sports, hobbies, food, home decorating, family expenses, etc. We want more 'consumer type' articles, humor, historical articles, think pieces, nostalgia, photo articles." Buys 15-10 unsolicited mss/year. Submit complete ms. Length: 1,500 words or less. Pays $10 minimum, 10¢/word.
Photos: Purchased with or without mss; captions optional "but suggested." Uses 8 × 10 glossy prints, 4x5 transparencies ("and possibly down to 35mm"). Payment "depends on use." Color and b&w prices vary according to use and quality.
Fiction: Humorous and historical short stories. Length: 1,500 words or less. Pays "$10 minimum or 10¢/word."

Astrology, Metaphysical and New Age

Magazines in this section carry articles ranging from the occult to holistic healing. The following publications regard astrology, psychic phenomena, metaphysical experiences and related subjects as sciences or as objects of serious study. Each has an individual personality and approach to these phenomena. If you want to write for these publications, be sure to read them carefully.

BODY, MIND & SPIRIT, Island Publishing Co. Inc., P.O. Box 701, Providence RI 02901. (401)351-4320. FAX: (401)272-5767. Publisher and Editor-in-Chief: Paul Zuromski. Editor: Carol Kramer. 75% freelance written. Prefers to work with published/established writers; works with many new/unpublished writers each year. Bimonthly magazine covering New Age, natural living, and metaphysical topics. "Our editorial is slanted toward assisting people in their self-transformation process to improve body, mind and spirit. We take a holistic approach to the subjects we present. They include spirituality, health, healing, love, relationships, prosperity, nutrition, new ideas, interviews, travel, books and music. We avoid sensationalizing and try to present material objectively to allow the individual to decide what to accept or believe." Estab. 1982. Circ. 150,000. Pays on publication. Publishes ms an average of 6 months after acceptance. Byline given. Offers negotiable kill fee. Buys first North American serial rights. Submit seasonal/holiday material 8 months in advance. Simultaneous queries OK. Reports in 2 months on queries; 4 months on mss. Sample copy for 9 × 12 SAE and 6 first class stamps. Writer's guidelines for #10 SASE stamp.
Nonfiction: Book excerpts, how-to (develop psychic abilities, health, healing, proper nutrition, etc., based on holistic approach); inspirational; interview/profile (of New Age people); new product (or services offered in this field—must be unique and interesting); opinion (on any New Age, natural living or metaphysical topic); and travel (example: to Egypt based on past life research). Don't send "My life as a psychic" or "How I became psychic" articles. Buys 30-40 mss/year. Query with published clips. Length: 2,000-4,000 words. Pays $100-300. Sometimes pays the expenses of writers on assignment.
Photos: State availability of photos with query. Pays $10-20 for b&w contact sheets. Captions, model releases and identification of subjects required. Buys one-time rights.
Fillers: Clippings, anecdotes or newsbreaks on any interesting or unusual New Age, natural living, or metaphysical topic. Buys 10-20 fillers/year. Length: 500 words maximum. Pays $10-40.
Tips: "Examine our unique approach to the subject matter. We avoid sensationalism and overly strange or unbelievable stories. Reading an issue should give you a good idea of our approach to the subject."

FATE, Llewellyn Worldwide, Ltd., P.O. Box 64383, St. Paul MN 55164-0383. FAX: (612)291-1908. Editor: Donald Michael Kraig. 70% freelance written. Estab. 1948. Buys all rights; occasionally first serial rights only. Byline given. Pays on publication. Sample copy $3. Query. Reports in 2 months.
Nonfiction and Fillers: Personal psychic and magical experiences, 300-500 words. Pays $25. Articles on parapsychology, occultism, witchcraft, magic, spiritual healing, flying saucers, new frontiers of science, and mystical aspects of ancient civilizations, 2,000-3,000 words. *Must* include complete authenticating details. Prefers interesting accounts of single events rather than roundups. "We very frequently accept manuscripts from new writers; the majority are individual's first-person accounts of their own psychic/magical/spiritual experiences. We do need to have all details, where, when, why, who and what, included for complete documentation. We ask for a notarized statement attesting to truth of the article." Pays minimum of 5¢/word. Fillers must be be fully authenticated also, and on similar topics. Length: 100-300 words.
Photos: Buys good glossy prints with mss. Pays $10.
Tips: "For the past several years *Fate* has moved toward archeological and debunking types of articles. We will be moving back to the original concept of *Fate*—looking at the unusual in the world—the things that science doesn't like to talk about. Our focus will be more New Age-oriented, including more parapsychology, spirituality, divination, magic, UFO's, etc."

‡**MAGICAL BLEND, the Transformative Journey**, P.O. Box 11303, San Francisco CA 94101. (415)673-1001. Editor: Julie Marchasin. Managing Editor: Jerry Snider. 30% freelance written. Quarterly magazine covering new age/metaphysics/psychology/visionary art. Estab. 1980. Circ. 45,000. Pays on publication. Publishes ms an average of 6 months after acceptance. Byline given. No kill fee. Buys first North American serial rights. Query for electronic submissions. Requires hard copy to accompany submission. Reports in 3-7 months. Sample copy $3. Writer's guidelines for standard SAE with 1 first class stamp.
Nonfiction: General interest, how-to (related to new age/metaphysics/creativity/psychology), inspirational, interview/profile, personal experience, religious, travel and planetary ecology and holistic health. No downbeat/satanic/doomsday scenarios. Buys 10 mss/year. Send complete ms. Length: 1,000-8,000 words. Pays $5-100; "depends on agreement with writer." State availability of photos with submission. Reviews transparencies and prints. Offers no additional payment for photos accepted with ms. Model releases and identification of subjects required. Buys one-time rights.
Tips: "The best approach is to read the current issue and recent back issues to get a sense of what kind and quality of material we're looking for. Please send clean copy, with a cover letter and an SASE. We are most receptive to interviews with big-name people about their spiritual and creative practices and beliefs."

‡**MEDITATION**, Vision to Reality, Intergroup for Planetary Oneness, 17211 Orozco St., Granada Hills CA 91344. (818)366-5441. FAX: (818)360-2059. Executive Editors: Patrick Harbula and Tricia Harbula. 50% freelance written. Bimonthly magazine covering alternative psychology, health, living and metaphysics. "Submissions should reflect alternative spiritual philosophies and practical methods of integrating spiritual principles with daily living." Estab. 1985. Circ. 30,000. Pays on publication. Byline given. No kill fee. Buys first North American serial rights. Submit seasonal/holiday material 3 months in advance. Simultaneous and previously published submissions OK. Reports in 1 month on queries; 2 months on mss. Free sample copy and writer's guidelines.
Nonfiction: Book excerpts, essays, exposé, general interest, historical/nostalgic, how-to, humor, inspirational, interview/profile, new product, opinion (does not mean letters to the editor), personal experience, photo feature, religious, technical. "No purely promotional material." Buys 15 mss/year. Query with or without published clips, or send complete ms. Length 900-3,000 words. Pays $50-150 for assigned articles; $50-100 for unsolicited articles.
Photos: State availability of photos with submission. Reviews transparencies (any) and prints (any). Identification of subjects required. Buys one-time rights.
Columns/Departments: New Economy (socially and environmentally responsible viewpoints), 1,250; Health and Nutrition (whole person and preventitive), 1,250. Buys 24 mss/year. Query with published clips or send complete ms. Length 900-1,250 words. Pays $50.
Fiction: Adventure, confession, erotica, ethnic, experimental, fantasy, historical, humorous, mainstream, mystery, novel excerpts, religious, romance, science fiction, slice-of-life vignettes, suspense, Western. Buys 1 mss/year. Query. Length: 900-1,500 words. Pays $50-100.
Poetry: Avant-garde, free verse, haiku, light verse, traditional. "No epic poetry." Submit maximum 5 poems.
Tips: "We welcome innovative approaches to editorial purpose and would be happy to speak with interested contributors. We are open to interviews with prominent people or articles that research data supporting positive effects of metaphysical practice. The interviews can center around the personal experiences or life triumphs of these people from the political and entertainment fields."

RAINBOW CITY EXPRESS, Adventures on the Spiritual Path, P.O. Box 8447, Berkeley CA 94707. Editor: Helen B. Harvey. 75-95% freelance written. Quarterly magazine on "spiritual awakening and evolving consciousness, especially feminist spirituality and women's issues. We take an eclectic, mature and innovative approach to the topics of spiritual awakening and evolution of consciousness. A positive, constructive, healing tone is required, not divisive, separatist slant." Estab. 1988. Circ. 1,000. Pays on publication. Byline given. Buys first North American serial rights or second serial (reprint) rights. Submit seasonal/holiday material 4-6 months in advance. Previously published (only when full publishing information accompanies ms showing where previously published) submissions OK. Reports in 2 months on queries; 3 months on mss. Sample copy $6 postpaid. Writer's guidelines for #10 SAE and 2 first class stamps.

Nonfiction: Book excerpts, essays, general interest, historical/nostalgic, how-to, humor, inspirational, interview/profile, opinion, personal experience, religious, travel. "No get-rich-quick or how-to channel spirits, how-to manipulate the cosmos/others, occult/voodoo/spellcasting diatribes and no glorification of victimization/scapegoating or addictions." Buys 50-100 mss/year. Query with or without published clips, or send complete ms. Length: 250-2,000 words. Pays $5-50 per piece, negotiated individually.

Columns/Departments: Book Reviews (spirituality, goddess consciousness, New Age topics), 250-500 words; Readers' Forum. Acquires 30 mss/year. Send complete ms. Pays in contributor copies.

Fiction: Adventure, fantasy, historical, religious. "Fiction should relate directly to our slant which is about spiritual/consciousness evolution. No science fiction, thriller, sex, drugs or violence mss." Acquires about 12 mss/year. Query. Length: 500-1,000 words. Pays in contributor copies.

Poetry: Avant-garde, free verse, haiku, light verse, traditional. *No* rhyming poetryd! Acquires about 30/year. Submit 3 poems maximum. Length: 8-30 lines.

Fillers: Anecdotes, short humor. "Fillers must relate to our spirituality slant."

Tips: "We feature true life experiences and accounts of spiritual awakenings/attendant phenomena, and consciousness evolution. Readers/writers who have experienced some of these phenomena and know what they're talking about are likely to be well received. We are particularly interested in actual experiences with Kundalini activation and archetypal stirring. We aim to demonstrate the often unsuspected connections between spiritual awakening and everyday realities. Note: *Please* obtain and study sample copy prior to submitting mss! No mss read or returned without SASE. Also sponsors writing contests. Send SASE for details. All material submitted on speculation."

TRANSFORMATION TIMES, Life Resources Unlimited, P.O. Box 425, Beavercreek OR 97004. (503)632-7141. Editor: Connie L. Faubel. Managing Editor: E. James Faubel. 100% freelance written. A tabloid covering new age, metaphysics, and natural health, published 10 times/year. Estab. 1983. Circ. 8,000. Pays on publication. Publishes ms an average of 2 months after acceptance. Byline given. Buys one-time rights. Submit seasonal/holiday material 2 months in advance. Simultaneous and previously published submissions OK. Query for electronic submissions. Sample copy and writer's guidelines for 9×12 SAE and 5 first class stamps.

Nonfiction: Book excerpts, inspirational, interview/profile, women's issues, metaphysical. "No articles with emphasis on negative opinions and ideas." Buys 60 mss/year. Send complete ms. Length: 500-1,000 words. Pays 1¢/word.

Photos: Send photos with submission. Reviews 3×5 prints. Captions and identification of subjects required. Buys one-time rights.

Columns/Departments: Woman's Way (women's issues) 500-1,000 words. Buys 20 mss/year. Send complete ms. Pays 1¢/word.

Tips: "In addition to present interests, we plan on adding articles on environmental quality issues and socially responsible investing."

‡UFO MAGAZINE, A Forum on Extraordinary Theories and Phenomena, California UFO, P.O. Box 1053, Sunland CA 91041-1053. (818)951-1250. Co-Publishers: Vicki Cooper and Sherie Stark. 50% freelance written. Bimonthly magazine covering UFO phenomena, events and theories. "*UFO Magazine* is the only newsstand-quality publication applying journalistic standards to the UFO subject. It is the most legitimate vehicle for UFO news and information now available to the general public." Pays on publication. Publishes ms and average of 2-6 months after acceptance. Byline given. Offers no kill fee. Buys one-time rights. Submit seasonal/holiday material 6 months in advance. Previously published submissions OK. Query for electronic submissions. Reports in 2 months on queries. Will not return unsolicited mss. Sample copy $4.50. Free writer's guidelines.

Nonfiction: Vicki Cooper, editor. Book excerpts, essays, exposé, general interest, historical/nostalgic, interview/profile, opinion (does not mean letters to the editor), personal experience, photo feature, technical. "Please, no fiction or fanatical material!" Buys 15-20 mss/year. Query. Length: 500-3,500 words. Pays $25-100 for assigned articles, or "more in some cases;" $25 maximum for unsolicited articles. UFO researchers, previously unpublished, are paid with copies unless other arrangements are made." Sometimes pays expenses of writers on assignment.

Photos: Send photos with submission. Reviews contact sheets, transparencies and 5×7 prints. Offers no additional payment for photos accepted with ms from writers. Offers $5-25 per photo from professional photographers only. "Reprints can be given with credit to *UFO Magazine.*"

Columns/Departments: Forum (opinion pieces based on factual UFO cases), 500-2,000 words; Encounter: First Hand (first-hand accounts of contact with UFO phenomena and/or aliens), 500-2,500 words; The Blue File (news briefs and special aspects of UFO phenomena), 500-1,500 words. Buys 15-20 mss/year. Send complete ms.

Fillers: Facts and newsbreaks. Buys 3-4/year. Pays $5-10.

Tips: "Our best submissions come from writers who have a working familiarity with the UFO subject and the research that has ensued in the modern UFO era (since 1947). But many potential contributors could also be those who have an abiding *private* fascination with UFOs along with exceptional writing skills! *UFO Magazine* is in constant need of comprehensive news-features on vital cases and/or issues concerning UFOs and related topics. The UFO subject is inextricably linked to the policies and practices of the U.S. military and intelligence agencies, so our magazine will venture into those sensitive avenues at times."

Automotive and Motorcycle

Publications in this section detail the maintenance, operation, performance, racing and judging of automobiles and recreational vehicles. Publications that treat vehicles as means of shelter instead of as a hobby or sport are classified in the Travel, Camping and Trailer category. Journals for service station operators and auto and motorcycle dealers are located in the Trade Auto and Truck section.

AMERICAN MOTORCYCLIST, American Motorcyclist Association, P.O. Box 6114, Westerville OH 43081-6114. (614)891-2425. Executive Editor: Greg Harrison. For "enthusiastic motorcyclists, investing considerable time and money in the sport. We emphasize the motorcyclist, not the vehicle." Monthly magazine. Estab. 1942. Circ. 165,000. Pays on publication. Rights purchased vary with author and material. Pays 25-50% kill fee. Byline given. Query with SASE. Submit seasonal/holiday material 4 months in advance. Reports in 1 month. Free sample copy and writer's guidelines.

Nonfiction: How-to (different and/or unusual ways to use a motorcycle or have fun on one); historical (the heritage of motorcycling, particularly as it relates to the AMA); interviews (with interesting personalities in the world of motorcycling); photo feature (quality work on any aspect of motorcycling); and technical or how-to articles. No product evaluations or stories on motorcycling events not sanctioned by the AMA. Buys 20-25 mss/year. Query. Length: 500 words minimum. Pays minimum $5.50/published column inch.

Photos: Purchased with or without accompanying ms, or on assignment. Captions required. Query. Pays $30 minimum per published photo.

Tips: "Accuracy and reliability are prime factors in our work with freelancers. We emphasize the rider, not the motorcycle itself. It's always best to query us first and the further in advance the better to allow for scheduling."

AMERICAN WOMAN MAGAZINE, (formerly *American Woman Road Riding*), Ladylike Enterprises, Inc. #5, 1038 7th St., Santa Monica CA 90403. (213)395-1171. Publisher: Courtney Caldwell. Editor: Jamie Elvidge. 40% freelance written. Bimonthly magazine on women in motorcycling and other adventure sports. "We are geared towards career, family and/or goal-oriented women who enjoy the sport of motorcycling. The magazine is upscale and is dedicated to image enhancement." Estab. 1988. Circ. 20,000. Pays on publication an average of 2 months after acceptance. Byline sometimes given. Buys first rights, second serial (reprint) rights or makes work-for-hire assignments. Submit seasonal/holiday material 4 months in advance. Previously published submissions OK. Query for electronic submissions. Reports in 2 months. Free sample copy.

Nonfiction: Humor, inspirational, interview/profile, new product, photo feature, travel and lifestyle. No articles depicting women in motorcycling or professions that are degrading, negative or not upscale. Buys 30 mss/year. Send complete ms. Length 250-1,000 words. Pays $30-50 for assigned articles; $20-

---

***ALWAYS** submit unsolicited manuscripts or queries with a self-addressed, stamped envelope (SASE) within your country or a self-addressed envelope with International Reply Coupons (IRC) purchased from the post office for other countries.*

35 for unsolicited articles. Sometimes pays expenses of writers on assignment.

Photos: Send photos with submission. Reviews contact sheets. Black and white or Kodachrome 64 preferred. Offers $10-50 per photo. Captions, model releases and identification of subjects required. Buys all rights.

Columns/Departments: Man of the Month (highlight and profile select gentlemen who ride motorcycles and are making positive contributions to industry and community), 500-1,000 words.

Fillers: Anecdotes, facts, gags to illustrated by cartoonist, newsbreaks and short humor. Buys 12/year. Length: 25-100 words. Pays $10-25.

Tips: "It helps if the writer is into motorcycles. It is a special sport. If he/she doesn't ride, he/she should have a positive point of view of motorcycling and be willing to learn more about the subject. We are a lifestyle type of publication more than a technical magazine. Positive attitudes wanted."

AUTOMOBILE, Murdoch Magazines, 120 E. Liberty, Ann Arbor MI 48104. Did not want to be listed.

BRITISH CAR, P.O. Box 9099, Canoga Park CA 91309. (818)710-1234. FAX: (818)710-1877. Editor: Dave Destler. 50% freelance written. A bimonthly magazine covering British cars. "We focus upon the cars built in Britain, the people who buy them, drive them, collect them, love them. Writers must be among the aforementioned. Written by enthusiasts for enthusiasts." Estab. 1985. Circ. 30,000. Pays on publication. Publishes ms an average of 3 months after acceptance. Byline given. Buys all rights, unless other arrangements made. Submit seasonal/holiday material 4 months in advance. Query for electronic submissions. Reports in 1 month. Sample copy $2.95; writer's guidelines for #10 SASE.

Nonfiction: Historical/nostalgic; how-to (on repair or restoration of a specific model or range of models, new technique or process); humor (based upon a realistic nonfiction situation); interview/profile (famous racer, designer, engineer, etc.); photo feature and technical. "No submissions so specific as to appeal or relate to a very narrow range of readers; no submissions so general as to be out-of-place in a specialty publication. Buys 30 mss/year. Send complete ms. "Include SASE if submission is to be returned." Length: 750-4,500 words. Pays $2-5/column inch for assigned articles; pays $2-3/column inch for unsolicited articles.

Photos: Send photos with submission. Reviews transparencies and prints. Offers $15-75/photo. Captions and identification of subjects required. Buys all rights, unless otherwise arranged.

Columns/Departments: Update (newsworthy briefs of interest, not too timely for bimonthly publication), approximately 50-175 words. Buys 20 mss/year. Send complete ms.

Tips: "Thorough familiarity of subject is essential. *British Car* is read by experts and enthusiasts who can see right through superficial research. Facts are important, and must be accurate. Writers should ask themselves 'I know I'm interested in this story, but will most of *British Car's* readers appreciate it?' "

‡CAA'S AUTOPINION ANNUAL, Canadian Automobile Association, 1775 Courtwood Crescent, Ottawa, Ontario K2C 3J2 Canada. (613)226-7631. Editor: David Steventon. 75% freelance written. Annual magazine covering new and used car purchasing. "Contains features relating to what's new in cars and automotive technology, and to the car buying process including: leasing and factors to consider (size, intended use of vehicle, towing, etc); new vehicle profiles; results of annual vehicle durability survey." Estab. 1988. Circ. 45,000. Pays on publication. Byline given. No kill fee. Buys all rights. Previously published submissions. Query for electronic submissions.

Nonfiction: General interest (automotive), historical/nostalgic (auto), interview/profile, new product (automotive), and technical (automotive). Buys 5 mss/year. Query with or without published clips, or send complete ms. Length: 2,500-4,000 words. Pays $250-500. Send photos with submission. Reviews transparencies. Offers no additional payment for photos accepted with ms. Captions, model releases and identification of subjects required. Buys one-time rights.

Tips: "Contact editor, submit clippings of recent work, verify type of material needed for next edition (topics, etc.)."

CAR AND DRIVER, 2002 Hogback Rd., Ann Arbor MI 48105. (313)971-3600. Editor: William Jeanes. For auto enthusiasts; college-educated, professional, median 24-35 years of age. Monthly magazine. Estab. 1961. Circ. 950,000. **Pays on acceptance.** Rights purchased vary with author and material. Buys all rights or first North American serial rights. "Unsolicited manuscripts are not accepted. Query letters may be addressed to the editor. Rates are generous.

Nonfiction: Non-anecdotal articles about automobiles, new and old. Automotive road tests, informational articles on cars and equipment; some satire and humor. Personalities, past and present, in the automotive industry and automotive sports. "Treat readers as intellectual equals. Emphasis on people as well as hardware." Informational, humor, historical, think articles, and nostalgia.

Photos: Color slides and black and white photos sometimes purchased with accompanying mss.
Tips: "It is best to start off with an interesting query and to stay away from nuts-and-bolts ideas because that will be handled in-house or by an acknowledged expert. Our goal is to be absolutely without flaw in our presentation of automotive facts, but we strive to be every bit as entertaining as we are informative."

CAR AUDIO AND ELECTRONICS, AvCom Publishing, Suite 1600, 21700 Oxnard St., Woodland Hills CA 91367. (818)593-3900. FAX: (818)593-2274. Editor: William Neill. Managing Editor: Doug Newcomb. 80-90% freelance written. Monthly magazine on electronic products designed for cars. "We help people buy the best electronic products for their cars. The magazine is about electronics, how to buy, how to use, and so on: *CA&E* explains complicated things in simple ways. The articles are accurate, easy, and fun." Estab. 1988. Circ. 225,000. **Pays on acceptance.** Publishes ms an average of 3-5 months after acceptance. Byline given. Offers 50% kill fee. Buys all rights. Submit seasonal/holiday material 3-4 months in advance. Simultaneous submissions OK. Query for electronic submissions. Reports in 1 week on queries; 1 week on mss. Sample copy $3.95 with 9 × 12 SAE and 4 first class stamps; writer's guidelines for #10 SASE.
Nonfiction: How-to (buy electronics for your car), interview/profile, new product, opinion, photo feature and technical. Buys 60-70 mss/year. Query with or without published clips, or send complete ms. Length: 500-1,700 words. Pays $300-1,000. Sometimes pays expenses of writers on assignment.
Photos: Send photos with submission. Review transparencies, any size.
Fillers: Gags to be illustrated by cartoonist and cartoons. Pays $20-50.
Tips: "Write clearly and knowledgeably about car electronics."

CAR CRAFT, Petersen Publishing Co., 8490 Sunset Blvd., Los Angeles CA 90069. (213)854-2320. Editor: Jim McGowan. For men and women, 18-34, "enthusiastic owners of 1949 and newer muscle cars." Monthly magazine. Circ. 400,000. Study past issues before making submissions or story suggestions. Pays generally on publication, on acceptance under special circumstances. Buys all rights. Buys 2-10 mss/year. Query.
Nonfiction: How-to articles ranging from the basics to fairly sophisticated automotive modifications. Drag racing feature stories and some general car features on modified late model automobiles. Especially interested in do-it-yourself automotive tips, suspension modifications, mileage improvers and even shop tips and homemade tools. Length: open. Pays $100-200/page.
Photos: Photos purchased with or without accompanying text. Captions suggested, but optional. Reviews 8 × 10 b&w glossy prints; 35mm or 2¼ × 2¼ color. Pays $30 for b&w, color negotiable. "Pay rate higher for complete story, i.e., photos, captions, headline, subtitle: the works, ready to go."

‡CHEVY HIGH PERFORMANCE, Petersen Publishing Co., 8490 Sunset Blvd., Los Angeles CA 90069. (213)854-2250. Editor: Chuck Coyne. Managing Editor: Rochelle Shapiro Konoff. 85% freelance written. Bimonthly magazine covering Chevrolet vehicles. "Covers all aspects of street, racing, restored high performance Chevrolet vehicles." Estab. 1985. Circ. 125,000. Pays on acceptance. Byline given. Offers no kill fee. Buys all rights. Submit seasonal/holiday material 6 months in advance. Simultaneous submissions OK. Query for electronic submissions. Reports in 2 weeks. Free writer's guidelines.
Nonfiction: How-to, new product, photo feature, technical. Buys 50 mss/year. Query. Length: 500-2,000 words. Pays $150-1,000. Sometimes pays expenses of writers on assignment.
Photos: Send photos with submission. Reviews contact sheets, any transparencies and any prints. Offers no additional payment for photos accepted with ms. Model releases required. Buys all rights.
Columns/Departments: Buys 12 mss/year. Query. Length: 100-1,500. Pays $150-500.

CYCLE, Diamandis Communications, Inc., 1499 Monrovia Ave., Newport Beach CA 92663. Did not want to be listed.

CYCLE WORLD, Hachette Magazines, Inc., 853 W. 17th St., Costa Mesa CA 92627. (714)720-5300. Editor: David Edwards. 20% freelance written. For active motorcyclists, "young, affluent, educated, very perceptive." Subject matter includes "road tests (staff-written), features on special bikes, customs, racers, racing events; technical and how-to features involving mechanical modifications." Monthly. Circ. 245,000. **Pays on acceptance.** Publishes ms an average of 3 months after acceptance. Buys all rights. Query for electronic submissions. Reports in 2 weeks on queries; 1 month on mss. Sample copy $2; free writer's guidelines.
Nonfiction: Buys informative, well-researched, technical, theory and how-to articles; interviews; profiles; humor; and historical pieces. Buys 20 mss/year. Query. Length: 1,000-2,000 words. Pays variable rates. Sometimes pays the expenses of writers on assignment.
Photos: Purchased with or without ms, or on assignment. Reviews contact sheets and transparencies. Pays $75 minimum. Buys one-time rights and reprint rights.
Tips: "Area most open to freelancers is short nonfiction features. They must contain positive and fun experiences regarding motorcycle travel, sport and lifestyle."

‡**EUROPEAN CAR**, Argus Publishing Corp., 12100 Wilshire, #250, Los Angeles CA 90025. (213)820-3601. Editor: Greg Brown. Managing Editor: Stephanie Wolfe. 50% freelance written. Magazine published 10 times/year covering European cars. Estab. 1969. Circ. 90,000. Pays on publication. Publishes ms an average of 3-6 months after acceptance. Byline given. Offers 40% kill fee. Buys one-time and second serial (reprint) rights. Submit seasonal/holiday material 4-5 months in advance. Simultaneous submissions OK. Query for electronic submissions. Reports in 2 months on queries. Sample copy $3.75. Writer's guidelines for #10 SASE.

Nonfiction: Historical/nostalgic, how-to, interview/profile, new product, photo feature, technical, travel. Query. Length: 500 words average. Pays $50-75 per ms page. Sometimes pays expenses of writers on assignment.

Photos: Send photos with submission. Reviews contact sheets, negatives, 35mm, 2¼ × 2¼ transparencies, 5 × 7 prints. Payment depends on quality. Captions, model releases and identification of subjects required.

FOUR WHEELER MAGAZINE, 6728 Eton Ave., Canoga Park CA 91303. (818)992-4777. FAX: (818)992-4979. Editor: John Stewart. 20% freelance written. Works with a small number of new/unpublished writers each year. Emphasizes four-wheel-drive vehicles, competition and travel/adventure. Monthly magazine; 164 pages. Estab. 1963. Circ. 355,466. Pays on publication. Publishes ms an average of 4 months after acceptance. Buys all rights. Submit seasonal/holiday material at least 4 months in advance. Query for electronic submissions. Writer's guidelines for #10 SAE.

Nonfiction: 4WD competition and travel/adventure articles, technical, how-tos, and vehicle features about unique four-wheel drives. "We like the adventure stories that bring four wheeling to life in word and photo: mud-running deserted logging roads, exploring remote, isolated trails, or hunting/fishing where the 4 × 4 is a necessity for success." See features Gary Wescott, Matt Conrad and Dick Stansfield for examples. Query with photos before sending complete ms. Length: 1,200-2,000 words; average 4-5 pages when published. Pays $100/page minimum for complete package. Sometimes pays the expenses of writers on assignment.

Photos: Requires professional quality color slides and b&w prints for every article. Captions required. Prefers Kodachrome 64 or Fujichrome 50 in 35mm or 2¼ formats. "Action shots a must for all vehicle features and travel articles."

Tips: "Show us you know how to use a camera as well as the written word. The easiest way for a new writer/photographer to break in to our magazine is to read several issues of the magazine, then query with a short vehicle feature that will show his or her potential as a creative writer/photographer."

‡**HOT ROD**, Petersen Publishing Co., 8490 Sunset Blvd., Los Angeles CA 90069. (213)854-2222. Editor: Jeff Smith. 5% freelance written. Monthly magazine. Pays on publication. Publishes ms an average of 3 months after acceptance. Kill fee varies. Buys exclusive rights. Reports in 1 month. Send complete ms. Length and payment vary.

KEEPIN' TRACK OF VETTES, P.O. Box 48, Spring Valley NY 10977. (914)425-2649. FAX: (914)638-3864. Editor: Shelli Finkel. 70% freelance written. Works with a small number of new/unpublished writers each year. Monthly magazine for Corvette owners and enthusiasts. Estab. 1976. Circ. 38,000. Pays on publication. Publishes ms an average of 3 months after acceptance. Buys all rights. Byline given. Submit seasonal/holiday material 3 months in advance. Reports in 1 month. $3 for sample copy and writer's guidelines.

Nonfiction: Expose (telling of Corvette problems with parts, etc.); historical (any and all aspects of Corvette developments); how-to (restorations, engine work, suspension, race, swapmeets); humor; informational; interview (query); nostalgia; personal experience; personal opinion; photo feature; profile (query); technical; and travel. Buys 1-2 mss/issue. Query or submit complete ms. Pays $50-200. Sometimes pays the expenses of writers on assignment.

Photos: Send photo with ms. Pays $10-35 for b&w contact sheets or negatives; $10-50 for 35mm color transparencies; offers no additional payment for photos with accompanying ms.

Tips: The writer "must have more than a passing knowledge of Corvettes specifically and automobiles in general. We're looking for more material covering '53-'67 Corvettes—as they appreciate in value, interest in those years is rising."

MOPAR MUSCLE, Dobbs Publishing Group, 3816 Industry Blvd., Lakeland FL 33811. (813)644-0449. Editor: Greg Rager. 25% freelance written. Bimonthly magazine covering Chrysler Corp. performance vehicles. "Our audience has a knowledge of and interest in Chrysler vehicles." Estab. 1987. Circ. 75,000. Pays within 30 days of publication. Byline given. Buys first rights. Submit seasonal/holiday material 6 months in advance. Query for electronic submissions. Reports in 2 weeks. Free sample copy and writer's guidelines.

Nonfiction: Historical/nostalgic, how-to/technical, humor, interview/profile, new product, personal experience, photo feature, technical. Buys 20-25 mss/year. Query with published clips. Sometimes pays expenses of writers on assignment.
Photos: Send photos with submission. Reviews contact sheets and transparencies. Model release required. Buys one-time rights.
Columns/Departments: Moparts (new products), 50 words; Mopar Scene (news for Chrysler devotees), varies. Buys 20-25 mss/year. Query.
Fiction: Historical, humorous. Query.

MOTOR TREND, Petersen Publishing Co., 8490 Sunset Blvd., Los Angeles CA 90069. (213)854-2222. Editor: Jeff Karr. 5-10% freelance written. Prefers to work with published/established writers. For automotive enthusiasts and general interest consumers. Monthly. Circ. 800,000. Publishes ms an average of 3 months after acceptance. Buys all rights. "Fact-filled query suggested for all freelancers." Reports in 1 month.
Nonfiction: Automotive and related subjects that have national appeal. Emphasis on domestic and imported cars, roadtests, driving impressions, auto classics, auto, travel, racing, and high-performance features for the enthusiast. Packed with facts. Freelancers should confine queries to photo-illustrated exotic drives and other feature material; road tests and related activity handled inhouse.
Photos: Buys photos, particularly of prototype cars and assorted automotive matter. Pays $25-500 for transparencies.

MUSTANG MONTHLY, Dobbs Publications, Inc., P.O. Box 7157, Lakeland FL 33807. (813)646-5743. Editor: Tom Corcoran. Technical Editor: Earl Davis. 50% freelance written. A monthly magazine covering concours 1964½ through 1973 Ford Mustang, and mildly modified late-'80s Mustang. "Our average reader makes over $35,000 annually, and is 35 years of age." Estab. 1977. Circ. 85,000. Pays on publication. Publishes ms an average of 4 months after acceptance. Byline given. Buys first North American rights. No simultaneous submissions. Reports in 6 weeks on mss. Writers guidelines available.
Nonfiction: How-to and technical. Color car features. No seasonal, holiday, humor, fiction or first-person nostalgia material. Buys 35 mss/year. Query with or without published clips, or send complete ms. Freelancers should write for guidelines first. Length: 2,500 words maximum. Pays 15¢/word for first 500 words; 10¢/word to 2,500-limit. Generally uses ms within 6 months of acceptance.
Photos: Send photos with submission; photography will make or break articles. Reviews contact sheets, negatives and transparencies. No color prints. Offers $100/page color pro-rated to size, $25 minimum; $10/photo b&w, $25 minimum. Captions, model releases, (on our forms) "required."
Tips: "*Mustang Monthly* is looking for color features on trophy-winning original Mustangs and well-researched b&w how-to and technical articles. Our format rarely varies. A strong knowledge of early Mustangs is essential."

NATIONAL DRAGSTER, Drag Racing's Leading News Weekly, National Hot Rod Association, 2035 Financial Way, Glendora CA 91740. (818)963-8475. FAX: (818)335-4307. Editor: Phil Burgess. Managing Editor: Vicky Walker. 50% freelance written. Weekly tabloid of NHRA drag racing. "Covers NHRA drag racing—race reports, news, performance industry news, hot racing rumors—for NHRA members. Membership included with subscription." Estab. 1960. Circ. 80,000. Pays on publication. Publishes ms 1 month after acceptance. Byline given. Buys all rights. Submit seasonal/holiday material 2 months in advance. Simultaneous submissions OK. Query for electronic submissions. Reports in 2 weeks. Free sample copy.
Nonfiction: General interest, historical/nostalgic, how-to, humor, interview/profile, new product, personal experience, photo feature, technical. Buys 20 mss/year. Query. Pay is negotiable. Sometimes pays expenses of writers on assignment.
Photos: State availability of photos with submission. Reviews 5×7 prints. Offers no additional payment for photos accepted with ms. Captions, model releases and identification of subjects required. Buys all rights.
Columns/Departments: On the Run (first-person written, ghost written by drag racers), 900-1,000 words. Buys 52 mss/year. Query. Pay is negotiable.
Tips: "Feature articles on interesting drag racing personalities or race cars are most open to freelancers."

ON TRACK, The Auto Racing Magazine of Record, OT Publishing, Inc., Box 8509, Fountain Valley CA 92728. (714)966-1131. FAX: (714)556-9776. Editor: Craig Fischer, Andrew Crask. 90% freelance written. Biweekly magazine on auto racing (no drag racing, sprint cars, etc.). Circ. 40,000. Pays on publication. Publishes ms an average of 2 months after acceptance. Byline given. Buys first North American serial rights. Query for electronic submissions. Reports on queries. Sample copy $2.50. Free writer's guidelines.

Nonfiction: Interview/profile and technical. Stories about race drivers with quotes from driver. Buys 3-4 mss/year. Query with published clips, or send complete ms. Length: 800-2,000 words. Pays $5/column inch. Sometimes pays expenses of writers on assignment.

Photos: State availability of photos with submission. Review 5×7 prints. Offers $10 per photo when used. Captions and identification of subjects required. Buys one-time rights.

Columns/Departments: Inside Line (look at subjects affecting trends, safety rules, etc.), 850 words; Broadcast Booth (TV, radio), 850 words. Buys 40 mss/year. Send complete ms. Pays $5.25 per column inch.

Tips: "Show some knowledge on the subject. Our readers are very knowledgeable and are quick to spot mistakes that get by us. Most of the magazine is done by a select few, but there are openings."

OPEN WHEEL MAGAZINE, General Media, Box 715, Ipswich MA 01938. (508)356-7030. FAX: (508)356-2492. Editor: Dick Berggren. 80% freelance written. Monthly magazine. "*OW* covers sprint cars, midgets, supermodifieds and Indy cars. *OW* is an enthusiast's publication that speaks to those deeply involved in oval track automobile racing in the United States and Canada. *OW*'s primary audience is a group of men and women actively engaged in competition at the present time, those who have recently been in competition and those who plan competition soon. That audience includes drivers, car owners, sponsors and crew members who represent perhaps 50-70 % of our readership. The rest who read the magazine are those in the racing trade (parts manufacturers, track operators and officials) and serious fans who see 30 or more races per year." Circ. 150,000. Pays on publication. Publishes ms an average of 6 months after acceptance. Byline given. Buys all rights. Submit seasonal material 2 months in advance. Reports in 3 weeks on queries. Sample copy for 9×12 SAE and 7 first class stamps. Writer's guidelines for #10 SASE.

Nonfiction: General interest, historical/nostalgic, how-to, humor, interview/profile, new product, photo feature and technical. "We don't care for features that are a blow-by-blow chronology of events. The key word is interest. We want features which allow the reader to get to know the main figure very well. Our view of racing is positive. We don't think all is lost, that the sport is about to shut down and don't want stories that claim such to be the case, but we shoot straight and avoid whitewash." Buys 125 mss/year. Query with complete ms.

Photos: State availability of photos with submission. Reviews contact sheets, negatives, transparencies and prints. Buys one-time rights.

Fillers: Anecdotes, facts and short humor. Buys 100/year. Length: 1-3 pages, double-spaced. Pays $35.

Tips: "Virtually all our features are submitted without assignment. An author knows much better what's going on in his backyard than we do. We ask that you write to us before beginning a story theme. Judging of material is always a combination of a review of the story and its support illustrations. Therefore, we ask for photography to accompany the manuscript on first submission. We're especially in the market for tech."

PETERSEN'S 4-WHEEL, (formerly *4-Wheel & Off-Road*), Petersen Publishing Co., 8490 Sunset Blvd., Los Angeles CA 90069. (213)854-2360. Editor: Drew Hardin. A monthly magazine covering four-wheel-drive vehicles, "devoted to new-truck tests, buildups of custom 4×4s, coverage of 4WD racing, trail rides and other competitions." Circ. 330,000. **Pays on acceptance.** Publishes ms an average of 4 months after acceptance. Byline given. Pays 20% kill fee. Buys first North American serial rights or all rights. Submit seasonal/holiday material 4 months in advance. Reports in 3 weeks. Writer's guidelines for #10 SASE.

Nonfiction: How-to (on four-wheel-drive vehicles—engines, suspension, drive systems, etc.), new product, photo feature, technical and travel. Buys 12-16 mss/year. Send complete ms. Length: 1,000-2,500 words. Pays $200-600.

Photos: Send photos with submission. Reviews transparencies and b&w prints. Offers no additional payment for photos accepted with ms. Captions, model releases and identification of subjects required. Buys all rights.

Fillers: Anecdotes, facts, gags, newsbreaks and short humor. Buys 12-16/year. Length: 50-150 words. Pays $15-50.

Tips: "Attend 4×4 events, get to know the audience. Present material only after full research. Manuscripts should contain *all* of the facts pertinent to the story. Technical/how-to articles are most open to freelancers."

ROAD KING MAGAZINE, Box 250, Park Forest IL 60466. Editor-in-Chief: George Friend. 10% freelance written. Eager to work with new/unpublished writers. Truck driver leisure reading publication. Bimonthly magazine. Circ. 218,000. **Pays on acceptance.** Publishes an average of 2 months after acceptance. Usually buys all rights; sometimes buys first rights. Byline given "always on fiction—if requested on nonfiction." Submit seasonal/holiday material 3 months in advance. Sample copy for 7×10 SAE and 98¢ postage or get free sample copy at any Unocal 76 truck stop; writer's guidelines for #10 SASE.

Nonfiction: Trucker slant or general interest, humor, and photo feature. No articles on violence or sex. Name and quote release required. No queries. Submit complete ms. Length: 500-1,200 words. Pays $50-400.

Photos: Submit photos with accompanying ms. No additional payment for b&w contact sheets or 2¼×2¼ color transparencies. Captions preferred. Buys first rights. Model release required.

Fiction: Adventure, historical, humorous, mystery, rescue-type suspense and western. Especially about truckers. No stories on sex and violence. "We're looking for quality writing." Buys 4 mss/year. Submit complete ms. Length: approximately 1,200 words. Pays up to $400. Writer should quote selling price with submission.

Fillers: Jokes, gags, anecdotes and short humor about truckers. Buys 20-25/year. Length: 50-500 words. Pays $5-100.

Tips: "No collect phone calls or postcard requests. Never phone for free copy as we will not handle such phone calls. We don't appreciate letters we have to answer. Do not submit manuscripts, art or photos using registered mail, certified mail or insured mail. Publisher will not accept such materials from the post office. Publisher will not discuss refusal with writer. Nothing personal, just legal. Do not write and ask if we would like such and such article or outline. We buy only from original and complete manuscripts submitted on speculation. Do not ask for writer's guidelines. See above and/or get a copy of the magazine and be familiar with our format before submitting anything. We are a trucker publication whose readers are often family members and sometimes Bible Belt. We refrain from violence, sex, nudity, etc."

STOCK CAR RACING MAGAZINE, General Media, Box 715, Ipswich MA 01938. Editor: Dick Berggren. 80% freelance written. Eager to work with new/unpublished writers. For stock car racing fans and competitors. Monthly magazine. Circ. 400,000. Pays on publication. Publishes ms an average of 3 months after acceptance. Buys all rights. Byline given. Query for electronic submissions. Reports in 6 weeks. Free writer's guidelines.

Nonfiction: General interest, historical/nostalgic, how-to, humor, interviews, new product, photo features and technical. "Uses nonfiction on stock car drivers, cars, and races. We are interested in the story behind the story in stock car racing. We want interesting profiles and colorful, nationally interesting features. We are looking for more technical articles, particularly in the area of street stocks and limited sportsman." Query with or without published clips, or submit complete ms. Buys 50-200 mss/year. Length: 100-6,000 words. Pays up to $450.

Photos: State availability of photos. Pays $20 for 8×10 b&w photos; up to $250 for 35mm or larger transparencies. Captions required.

Fillers: Anecdotes and short humor. Buys 100 each year. Pays $35.

Tips: "We get more queries than stories. We just don't get as much material as we want to buy. We have more room for stories than ever before. We are an excellent market with 12 issues per year. Virtually all our features are submitted without assignment. An author knows much better what's going on in his backyard than we do. We ask that you write to us before beginning a story theme. If nobody is working on the theme you wish to pursue, we'd be glad to assign it to you if it fits our needs and you are the best person for the job. Judging of material is always a combination of a review of the story and its support illustration. Therefore, we ask for photography to accompany the manuscript on first submission."

‡**SUPER CYCLE**, LFP Inc., # 300, 9171 Wilshire Blvd., Beverly Hills CA 90210. (213)274-7684. Editor: Elliot Borin. 95% freelance written. Monthly magazine covering motorcycles—Harley Davidson. "Motorcycle events, parties, fiction stories about bikers, no Jap bike stuff, (no 'bad-biker' stuff) motorcycle legislation." Circ. 100,000. Pays on publication. Publishes ms an average of 6 months after acceptance. Byline sometimes given. Offers no kill fee. Buys first rights. Submit seasonal/holiday material 6 months in advance. Query for electronic submissions. Reports in 2 months. Sample copy $4 with 9×12 SAE.

Nonfiction: Interview/profile (bike builder races, etc.), personal experience (bike rally), photo feature (super customized bike with model), travel (motorcycling). "No Jap bikes, no poetry." Buys 50 mss/year. Query with or without published clips, or send complete ms. Length: 200-1,500 words. Pays $200-400 for assigned articles; $200-300 for unsolicited articles. Pays in contributor copies or other premiums in trade for motorcycle painting, parts, work.

Photos: Send photos with submission. Reviews 2×2 transparencies and 3×5 or 4×6 prints. Offers no additional payment for photos accepted with ms. Offers $35-50 per photo with no ms. Model release required. Buys all rights.

Columns/Departments: Elliot Borin. Gearheads (technical advice on motorcycles), 100-1,000 words; On Target (guns), 1,000 words; Tattoo Time (tattoos), 1,000 words. Buys 50 mss/year. Send complete ms. Pays $200-400.

Fiction: Adventure, humorous, mystery, romance, science fiction, Vietnam, tattoo (must all pertain to bikers.) "No stories about 'bad guy' bikers." Buys 15 mss/year. Send complete ms. Length: 200 words maximum. Pays $200-400.

Tips: "Writers must be literate, understand bikers, type, photograph, be better than the rest!"

‡**3 & 4 WHEEL ACTION,** Hi-Torque Publications, 10600 Sepulveda, Mission Hills CA 91345. (818)365-6831. Editor: Steve Casper. Managing Editor: John Howell. 20% freelance written. Monthly magazine on off-road all-terrain vehicles (3 & 4 wheelers). "Nearly 100% male readers, mostly in the 18-24 age group—the magazine is designed to inform ATV enthusiasts on new products, machines, races and riding areas." Circ. 50,000. Pays on publication. Byline given. Buys one-time rights. Submit seasonal/holiday material 3 months in advance. Free sample copy.
Nonfiction: How-to (technical stories on ATVs), personal experience, photo features, technical, travel (to great riding areas); all about ATV's. Query. Length: 500-1,250 words. Pays $40-120.
Photos: Send photos with submission. Reviews negatives, 35mm transparencies and 5×7 prints. Offers $15-40 per photo. Buys one-time rights.
Tips: "What we need from other areas of the country are photo features on scenic riding spots and hunting and fishing on your ATV stories. These stories can also have a personal slant to them. A writer's best bet is to contact a local ATV club or enthusiast (the local dealers should know these people) and go on a scenic *legal* ride with them and take good photographs of the trip—same goes for hunting and fishing."

VETTE MAGAZINE, CSK Publishing, Inc., 299 Market St., Saddle Brook NJ 07662. (201)712-9300. FAX: (201)712-9899. Editor: D. Randy Riggs. Managing Editor: Peter Easton. 60% freelance written. Monthly magazine. All subjects related to the Corvette automobile. "Our readership is extremely knowledgeable about the subject of Corvettes. Therefore, writers must know the subject thoroughly and be good at fact checking." Estab. 1976. Circ. 60,000. Offers 50% kill fee. Buys first North American serial rights. Submit seasonal/holiday material 3 months in advance. Query for electronic submissions. Reports in 3 weeks on queries and mss. Sample copy for 9×12 SAE with $1.67 postage; writer's guidelines for #10 SASE.
Nonfiction: General interest, historical/nostalgic, how-to, interview/profile, new product, personal experience, photo feature, technical and travel. Buys 120 mss/year. Query with published clips. Length: 4pp-2,700 words. Pays $150-750 for assigned articles; $100-350 for unsolicited articles. Sometimes pays expenses of writers on assignment.
Photos: State availability of photos with submission. Reviews contact sheets. Offers no additional payment for photos accepted with ms. Captions and model releases are required. Buys one-time rights.
Columns/Departments: Reviews (books/videos), 400-500 words. Buys 12 mss/year. Query. Pays $50-150.
Fiction: Adventure, fantasy and slice-of-life vignettes. Buys 4 mss/year. Query with published clips. Length: 400-2,500 words. Pays $100-500.

Aviation

Professional and private pilots and aviation enthusiasts read the publications in this section. Editors want material for audiences knowledgable about commercial aviation. Magazines for passengers of commercial airlines are grouped in the In-flight category. Technical aviation and space journals and publications for airport operators, aircraft dealers and others in aviation businesses are listed under Aviation and Space in the Trade section.

AIR & SPACE/SMITHSONIAN MAGAZINE, 370 L'Enfant Promenade S.W., 10th Floor, Washington DC 20024. (202)287-3733. FAX: (202)287-3163. Editor: George Larson. Managing Editor: Tom Huntington. 80% freelance written. Prefers to work with published/established writers. A bimonthly magazine covering aviation and aerospace for a non-technical audience. "Features are slanted to a technically curious, but not necessarily technically knowledgeable audience. We are looking for unique angles to aviation/aerospace stories, history, events, personalities, current and future technologies, that emphasize the human-interest aspect." Circ. 310,000. **Pays on acceptance.** Byline given. Offers kill fee. Buys first North American serial rights. Reports in 5 weeks. Sample copy for $3.50 plus 9½×13 SASE; free writer's guidelines.
Nonfiction: Book excerpts, essays, general interest (on aviation/aerospace), historical/nostalgic, how-to, humor, interview/profile, photo feature and technical. Buys 50 mss/year. Query with published clips. Length: 1,500-3,000 words. Pays $2,000 maximum. Pays the expenses of writers on assignment.
Photos: State availability of illustrations with submission. Reviews 35mm transparencies.
Columns/Departments: Above and Beyond (first person), 2,000-2,500 words; Flights and Fancy (whimsy, insight), approximately 1,200 words; Oldies & Oddities (weird, wonderful and old), 1,200 words; Groundling's Notebook (looking upward), length varies. Buys 25 mss/year. Query with published clips. Pays $1,000 maximum. Soundings (brief items, timely but not breaking news), 500-800 words. Pays $300.

Tips: "Soundings is the section most open to freelancers. We will be buying more stories about space flight than aviation now that space program is heating up again."

AIR LINE PILOT, Air Line Pilots Association, 535 Herndon Parkway, P.O. Box 1169, Herndon VA 22070. (703)689-4176. Editor: Esperison Martinez, Jr. 10% freelance written. Prefers to work with published/established writers; works with a small number of new/unpublished writers each year. A monthly magazine for airline pilots covering "commercial aviation industry information—economics, avionics, equipment, systems, safety—that affects a pilot's life in professional sense." Also includes information about management/labor relations trends, contract negotiations, etc. Estab. 1931. Circ. 60,000. **Pays on acceptance.** Publishes ms an average of 6 months after acceptance. Offers 50% kill fee. Buys all rights. Submit seasonal/holiday material 6 months in advance. Query for electronic submissions. Reports in 2 months. Sample copy $2; writer's guidelines for #10 SASE.
Nonfiction: Humor, inspirational, photo feature and technical. "We are backlogged with historical submissions and prefer not to receive unsolicited submissions at this time." Buys 20 mss/year. Query with or without published clips, or send complete ms. Length: 700-3,000 words. Pays $200-600 for assigned articles; pays $50-600 for unsolicited articles.
Photos: Send photos with submission. Reviews contact sheets, 35mm transparencies and 8 × 10 prints. Offers $10-25/photo. Identification of subjects required. Buys one-time rights.
Tips: "For our feature section, we seek aviation industry information that affects the life of a professional airline pilot from a career standpoint. We also seek material that affects his life from a job security and work environment standpoint. Any airline pilot featured in an article must be an Air Line Pilot Association member in good standing."

‡CAREER PILOT, Future Aviation Professionals of America, 4959 Massachusetts Blvd., Atlanta GA 30337. (404)997-8097. Editor: Teresa Greer. Director of Editorial/Publications: Carol Vernon. 60% freelance written. Monthly magazine covering aviation. "A career advisory magazine as a service to FAPA members. Readers largely are career pilots who are working toward their professional goals. Articles cover topics such as recent developments in aviation law and medicine, changes in the industry, job interview techniques and how to get pilot jobs." Estab. 1983. Circ. 17,486. **Pays on acceptance.** Publishes ms an average of 3-4 months after acceptance. Byline given. Offers 50% kill fee. Buys all rights. Simultaneous submissions and previously published submissions. Query for electronic submissions. Reports in 6 weeks.
Nonfiction: How-to (get hired by an airline), interview/profile (aviation related), personal experience (aviation related). Special issues: October-Corporate Aviation, January-Helicopters. "No humor, cartoons or fiction." Buys 50 mss/year. Send complete ms. Length: 2,000-2,500 words. "Pays 18¢/word with $50 bonus for meeting deadlines." Sometimes pays expenses of writers on assignment.
Photos: State availability of photos with submission. Reviews prints. Offers no additional payment for photos accepted with ms. Captions and identification of subjects required.
Tips: "Send articles and clips that are aviation/business related. Express your interest in writing for our publication on a semi-regular basis. Writers have a good chance selling us how to get started articles and airline profiles."

‡FLYING, Diamandis Communications, Inc., 550 W. Putnam Ave., 2nd Floor, Greenwich CT 06830. (203)622-2701. Editor: J. MacClellan. 10% freelance written. Monthly magazine. **Pays on acceptance.** Publishes ms an average of 3 months after acceptance. Buys first North American serial rights, but with exclusivity for 2 years. Reports in 3 weeks on queries; 5 weeks on mss. "Writers should be pilots and know first-hand what they are writing about." Query, query with published clips or send complete ms. Length: 4 pages typeset maximum. Pay varies; $1,200 maximum.

GENERAL AVIATION NEWS & FLYER, N.W. Flyer, Inc., P.O. Box 98786, Tacoma WA 98498-0786. (206)588-1743. FAX: (206)588-4005. Editor: Dave Sclair. 30% freelance written. Prefers to work with published/established writers. Biweekly tabloid covering general aviation. Provides "coverage of aviation news, activities, regulations and politics of general and sport aviation with emphasis on timely features of interest to pilots and aircraft owners." Estab. 1949. Circ. 35,000. Pays 1 month after publication. Publishes ms an average of 3 months after acceptance. Byline given. Buys one-time rights and first North American serial rights, on occasion second serial (reprint) rights. Submit seasonal/holiday material 2 months in advance. Simultaneous queries and previously published submissions from noncompetitive publications OK but must be identified. Query for electronic submissions. Reports in 2 weeks on queries; 1 month on mss. Sample copy $3.50; writer's guidelines, style guidelines for #10 SASE.
Nonfiction: Features of current interest about aviation businesses, developments at airports, new products and services, safety, flying technique and maintenance. "Good medium-length reports on current events—controversies at airports, problems with air traffic control, FAA, etc. We want solid news coverage of breaking stories." Query first on historical, nostalgic features and profiles/interviews.

Many special sections throughout the year; send SASE for list. Buys 100 mss/year. Query or send complete ms. Length: 500-2,000 words. Pays up to $3/printed column inch maximum. Rarely pays the expenses of writers on assignment.

Photos: "Good pics a must." Send photos (b&w or color prints preferred, no slides) with ms. All photos must have complete captions and carry photographer's ID. Pays $10/b&w photo used.

Tips: "We always are looking for features on places to fly and interviews or features about people and businesses using airplanes in unusual ways. Travel features must include information on what to do once you've arrived, with addresses from which readers can get more information. Get direct quotations from the principals involved in the story. We want current, first-hand information."

PRIVATE PILOT, Fancy Publications Corp., Box 6050, Mission Viejo CA 92690. (714)855-8822. Editor: Mary F. Silitch. 75% freelance written. Works with a small number of new/unpublished writers each year. For owner/pilots of private aircraft, for student pilots and others aspiring to attain additional ratings and experience. "We take a unique, but limited view within our field." Circ. 105,000. Buys first North American serial rights. Pays on publication. Publishes manuscript average of 6 months after acceptance. No simultaneous submissions. Query for electronic submissions. Reports in 2 months. Sample copy $4; writer's guidelines for SASE.

Nonfiction: Material on techniques of flying, developments in aviation, product and specific airplane test reports, travel by aircraft, development and use of airports. All must be related to general aviation field. No personal experience articles. Buys about 60-90 mss/year. Query. Length: 1,000-4,000 words. Pays $75-300.

Photos: Pays $25 for 8×10 b&w glossy prints purchased with mss or on assignment. Pays $200 for color transparencies used on cover.

Columns/Departments: Business flying, homebuilt/experimental aircraft, pilot's logbook. Length: 1,000 words. Pays $75-250.

Tips: "Freelancer must know the subject about which he is writing; use good grammar; know the publication for which he's writing; remember that we try to relate to the middle segment of the business/pleasure flying public. We see too many 'first flight' type of articles. Our market is more sophisticated than that. Most writers do not do enough research on their subject. We would like to see more material on business-related flying, more on people involved in flying."

PROFESSIONAL PILOT, Queensmith Communications, 3014 Colvin St., Alexandria VA 22314. (703)370-0606. FAX: (703)370-7082. Editor: Clifton Stroud. 75% freelance written. A monthly magazine on major and regional airline, corporate, military and various other types of professional aviation. "Our readers are commercial pilots with highest ratings and the editorial content reflects their knowledge and experience." Estab. 1967. Circ. 32,000. **Pays on acceptance.** Publishes ms an average of 3 months after acceptance. Byline given. Kill fee negotiable. Buys all rights. Free sample copy.

Nonfiction: How-to (avionics and aircraft flight checks), humor, interview/profile, personal experience (if a lesson for professional pilots), photo feature, technical (avionics, weather, engines, aircraft). All issues have a theme such as regional airline operations, maintenance, jet aircraft, helicopters, etc. Buys 40 mss/year. Query. Length: 750-2,500. Pays $200-750. Sometimes pays expenses of writers on assignment.

Photos: Send photos with submission. Prefers transparencies. Offers no additional payment for photos accepted with ms. Captions and identification of subjects required. Buys all rights.

Columns/Departments: Pireps (aviation news), 300-500 words. Buys 12 mss/year. Query. Pays $100-250.

Tips: Query first. "Freelancer should have background in aviation that will make his articles believable to highly qualified pilots of commercial aircraft. We are placing a greater emphasis on airline operations, management and pilot concerns."

Business and Finance

Business publications give executives and consumers a range of information from local business news and trends to national overviews and laws that affect them. National and regional publications are listed below in separate categories. Magazines that have a technical slant are in the Trade section under Business Management, Finance or Management and Supervision categories.

National

BARRON'S, National Business and Financial Weekly, Dow Jones and Co. Inc., 200 Liberty St., New York NY 10281. (212)416-2700. FAX: (212)416-2829. Editor: Alan Abelson. Managing Editor: Kathryn M. Welling. 10% freelance written. Weekly tabloid covering the investment scene. "*Barron's* is written for active participants in and avid spectators of the investment scene. We require top-notch reporting *and* graceful, intelligent and irreverent writing." Estab. 1921. Circ. 241,319. Pays on publication. Byline given. Offers 25% kill fee. Buys all rights. Reports in 2 months. Writer's guidelines for SASE.

Nonfiction: Book excerpts, general financial interest and interview/profile. Publishes quarterly mutual fund sections. Buys 50 mss/year. Query with published clips. Length: 1,500-2,000 words. Pays $500-2,000 for assigned articles. Pays expenses of writers on assignment.

Photos: State availability of photos with submission. Reviews contact sheets, negatives and 8×10 prints. Offers $150-300/photo (day rate). Model releases and identification of subjects required. Buys one-time rights.

‡BUSINESS TO BUSINESS MAGAZINE, 129 E. Park Avenue, P.O. Box 6085, Tallahassee FL 32314. (904)222-6996. Editor: Robert Mellon Singer. 100% freelance written. Monthly magazine covering business. Estab. 1980. Circ. 20,000. Pays on publication. Publishes ms an average of 3 months after acceptance. Byline sometimes given. No kill fee. Buys one-time rights, "depends on article." Submit seasonal/holiday material 3 months in advance. Simultaneous and previously published submissions OK. Reports in 3 weeks. Free sample copy and writer's guidelines with SASE and $1.50 in 1st class postage.

Nonfiction: Book excerpts, exposé, historical/nostalgic, how-to, humor, inspirational, interview/profile, new product, technical, travel. "We are looking for articles on controversial issues (drugs, politics, environmental, crime) in small towns." Buys 250 mss/year. Query with or without published clips, or send complete ms. Length: 300-2,500 words. Pays $50-500 for assigned articles; $25-200 for unsolicited articles. Sometimes pays expenses of writers on assignment. Offers variable payment. Identification of subjects required. Buys one-time rights.

Colunmns/Departments: Tax $$ at Work (misuse/abuse and good use of tax money); Local Politics (interview with local politician); Limited Warranty (unique business opportunity/in/out of business stories dealing with customers, clients, other business). Buys 12 mss/year. Query with published clips or send complete ms. Length: 300-2,500 words. Pays $50-250.

Fillers: Anecdotes, facts, gags to be illustrated by cartoonist, newsbreaks, short humor. Buys 24/year.

Tips: "Writers should have a positive approach toward business and business education!"

BUSINESS WEEK, McGraw-Hill, 1221 Ave. of the Americas, New York NY 10020. Staff written. Did not want to be listed.

‡CONSUMER SENSE, Consumer Sense Marketing, 177 Pine St., P.O. Box 2065, Natick MA 01760. (508)653-2168. Editor: Ronald M. Weinberg. 30% freelance written. Quarterly company publication for marketing. "Writers should address marketing issues using a creative and practical approach. Our audience wants thoughtful insight to help and guide them." Estab. 1990. Circ. over 2,000. Pays on acceptance and publishes ms an average of 6 months after acceptance. Byline sometimes given. Not copyrighted. Buys all rights. Reports in 3 weeks on queries; 4 weeks on manuscripts. Free sample copy and writer's guidelines.

Nonfiction: Inspirational, how-to, opinion, and personal experience. Buys 15 manuscripts each year. Length: 600-1500 words. Pays $25-75 for assigned articles; $25-50 for unsolicited articles.

Columns/Departments: In The News (newspaper marketing issues), 750 words. Buys 1-2 mss/year. Query with published clips. Length 750-900 words. Pays $25-50.

D&B REPORTS, The Dun & Bradstreet Magazine for Small Business Management, Dun & Bradstreet, 299 Park Ave., 24th Floor, New York NY 10171. (212)593-6723. Editor: Patricia W. Hamilton. 10% freelance written. Works with a small number of new/unpublished writers each year. A bimonthly magazine for small business. "Articles should contain useful information that managers of small businesses can apply to their own companies. *D&B Reports* focuses on companies with $15 million in annual sales and under." Estab. 1954. Circ. 76,000. **Pays on acceptance.** Publishes ms an average of 2 months after acceptance. Byline given. Buys first North American serial rights. Query for electronic submissions. Reports in 3 weeks on manuscripts. Free sample copy and writer's guidelines.

Nonfiction: How-to (on management); and interview/profile (of successful entrepreneurs). Buys 5 mss/year. Query. Length: 1,500-2,500 words. Pays $500 minimum. Sometimes pays expenses of writers on assignment.

Photos: State availability of photos with submission. Identification of subjects required. Buys one-time rights.

Tips: "The area of our publication most open to freelancers is profiles of innovative companies and managers."

EXECUTIVE FEMALE, NAFE, 127 W. 24th St., 4th Fl., New York NY 10011. (212)645-0770. Editor-in-Chief: Diane P. Burley. Editor: Ingrid Eisenstadter. Emphasizes "useful career and financial information for the upwardly mobile female." 60% freelance written. Prefers to work with published/

established writers; works with a small number of new/unpublished writers each year. Bimonthly magazine. Estab. 1975. Circ. 200,000. Byline given. Pays on publication. Publishes ms an average of 2 months after acceptance. Submit seasonal/holiday material 6 months in advance. Buys first rights and second serial (reprint) rights to material originally published elsewhere. Previously published submissions OK. Query for electronic submissions. Reports in 2 months. Sample copy $2.50; writer's guidelines for #10 SASE.

Nonfiction: "Articles on any aspect of career advancement and financial planning are welcomed." Needs how-tos for managers and articles about coping on the job, trends in the workplace, financial planning, trouble shooting, business communication, time and stress management, career goal-setting and get-ahead strategies. "We would also like to receive humorous essays dealing with aspects of the job/workplace." Written queries only. Submit photos with ms (b&w prints or transparencies), or include suggestions for artwork. Length: 800-1,000 words. Pays $50-400. Pays for local travel and telephone calls.

Columns/Departments: Money (savings, financial advice, economic trends, interesting tips); Competitive Edge (tips on managing people, getting ahead); Risk (entrepreneurial stories). Buys 20 mss/year. Query with published clips or send complete ms. Department length: 500-1,000 words. Pays $50-100.

FINANCIAL WORLD, Financial World Partners, 1328 Broadway, New York NY 10001. Staff written. Did not want to be listed.

‡HOMEWORKING MOTHERS, Mothers' Home Business Network, Box 423, East Meadow NY 11554. (516)997-7394. Editor: Georganne Fiumara. 80% freelance written. Eager to work with new/unpublished writers. Quarterly newsletter "written for mothers who have home businesses or would like to. These mothers want to work at home so that they can spend more time with their children." Circ. 10,000. Pays on publication. Publishes ms an average of 3-6 months after acceptance. Byline given. Buys one-time rights. Submit seasonal/holiday material 8 months in advance. Simultaneous, photocopied and previously published submissions OK. Reports in 1 month on queries; 6 weeks on mss. Sample copy $2 with #10 SAE and 65¢ postage.

Nonfiction: Book excerpts, essays, how-to, humor, inspirational, personal experience and technical— home business information "all relating to working at home or home-based businesses." Special issues feature excerpts and reviews of books and periodicals about working at home (spring) and tax-related articles (winter). No articles about questionable home business opportunities. Buys 16-20 mss/year. Query with published clips, or send complete ms. Length: 300-1,000 words. Payment varies. Sometimes pays writers with contributor copies or in advertising or promoting a writer's business if applicable. "We would like to receive in-depth descriptions of one home business possibility, i.e., bookkeeping, commercial art, etc.—at least 3,000 words to be published in booklet form. (Pays $150 and buys all rights)."

Columns/Departments: It's My Business (mothers describe their businesses, how they got started, and how they handle work and children at the same time); Advice for Homeworking Mothers (business, marketing and tax basics written by professionals); Considering the Possibilities (ideas and descriptions of legitimate home business opportunities); A Look at a Book (excerpts from books describing some aspect of working at home or popular work-at-home professions); and Time Out for Kids (inspirational material to help mothers cope with working at home). Length: Varies, but average is 500 words. Buys 4 mss/year. Send complete ms.

Poetry: Free verse, light verse and traditional. "About being a mother working at home or home business." Submit maximum 5 poems. Pays $5.

Fillers: Facts and newsbreaks "about working at home for 'Take Note' page." Length: 150 words maximum. Pays $10.

Tips: "We prefer that the writer have personal experience with this lifestyle or be an expert in the field when giving general home business information. It's My Business and Time Out for Kids are most open to freelancers. Writers should read *HM* before trying to write for us."

I.B. (Independent Business), America's Small Business Magazine, F/S Publishing Inc., #211, 875 S. Westlake Blvd., Westlake Village CA 91361. (805)496-6156. Editor: Daniel Kehrer. Editorial Director: Don Phillipson. 75% freelance written. Bimonthly magazine for small and independent business. "We publish only practical articles of interest to small business owners all across America; also some small business owner profiles." Estab. 1989. Circ. 560,000. **Pays on acceptance.** Publishes ms an average of 4 months after acceptance. Byline given. Offers 25% kill fee. First and non-exclusive reprint rights. Simultaneous queries OK. Do not send manuscripts. Reports in 2 months. Sample copy for $4. Writer's guidelines for #10 SAE and 1 first class stamp.

Nonfiction: Book excerpts, how-to, interview/profile, new product, photo feature. No "generic" business article; no articles on big business; no general articles on economic theory. Buys 80-100 mss/year. Query with bio/resume. Length: 1,000-2,000 words. Pays $500-1,500 for assigned articles. Pays expenses of writers on assignment.

Columns/Departments: Fast Track (short items on small business interests), 50-200 words. Tax Tactics, Small Business Computing, Marketing Moves, Ad-visor, Managing Money, Banking & Finance, Business Cost-Savers; all 500-1,500 words. Buys 40-50 mss/year. Query with resume and published clips. Pays $100-1,500.

Fillers: Anecdotes, facts, short humor; must relate to running a small business.

Tips: "Talk to small business owners anywhere in America about what they want to read, what concerns or interests them in running a business. All areas open, but we use primarily professional business writers with top credentials in the field."

INDIVIDUAL INVESTOR, Financial Data Systems, Inc., 4th Fl., 38 E. 29th St., New York NY 10016. (212)689-2777. Editor: Jonathan Steinberg. Senior Editor: Gordon T. Anderson. 60% freelance written. Monthly magazine. We publish company profiles, designed to highlight possible stock investments for individuals. Estab. 1981. Circ. 50,000. Pays on publication. Publishes ms an average of 1 month after acceptance. Byline given. Offers 40% kill fee. Buys all rights. Query for electronic submissions. Free sample copy and writer's guidelines.

Nonfiction: Financial/business. Buys 60 mss/year. Query with published clips. Length: 1,200-1,500 words. Pays $350-450 for assigned articles.

Columns/Departments: Buys 30 mss/year. Query with published clips. Length: 1,200-1,500 words. Pays $350-450.

Tips: "Because we do not accept unsolicited articles, queries are essential. We are very open to freelancers, especially those who understand the stock market."

‡MODERN OFFICE, Allied Publications, Inc., 1776 Lake Worth Rd., Lake Worth FL 33460. (407)582-2099. Associate Editor: Karl H. Meyer. 85% freelance written. Bimonthly magazine covering the world of business. "Our audience is the total spectrum of the business world, from business school students to secretaries to corporate officers. How to do it better, faster, more efficiently; workplace relationships." Estab. 1945. Circ. (combined) 105,000. Pays on publication. Publishes ms an average of 6 months after acceptance. Byline given. Offers no kill fee. Buys one-time rights and second serial (reprint) rights. Submit seasonal/holiday material 6-8 months in advance. Simultaneous and previously published submissions OK. Query for electronic submissions. Reports 2 weeks to 3 months on mss. Sample copy $1. Writer's guidelines for #10 SAE with 1 first class stamp.

Nonfiction: "No highly technical or cutesy material, vulgar or obscene language; no jeremiads. Think positively." Buys 216 mss/year. Query with or without published clips, or send complete ms. "I often reject query and purchase clips submitted." Length: 300-1,500 words. Pays $25 maximum for unsolicited articles at 30¢ per published line. Pays in contributor copies or other premiums only if author requests. State availability of photos with submission.

Tips: "Study an issue or two, then write and submit. If rejected, it's not because I don't like you, or even your writing. I might love it, but have no place for it for some reason (usually does not fit with other articles). Write something else and submit. Do not call me on phone a month after you submit to check status—it will be returned pronto! All areas of magazine are open to freelancers. I enjoy working with new writers, and have been the first to publish the work of many new writers who show skill at handling words and ideas, and who are receptive to my ideas."

MONEY, Entertainment Weekly, Inc., 1675 Broadway, Rockefeller Center, New York NY 10019. Staff written. Did not want to be listed.

MONEY MAKER, Your Guide to Financial Security and Wealth, Consumers Digest Inc., 5705 N. Lincoln Ave., Chicago IL 60659. (312)275-3590. Editor: Dennis Fertig. 90% freelance written. A bimonthly magazine on personal investing. "We cover the broad range of topics associated with personal finance—the strongest emphasis is on traditional investment opportunities." Estab. 1979. Circ: 165,000. **Pays on acceptance.** Publishes ms an average of 2 months after acceptance. Byline given. Offers 50% kill fee. Buys first rights and second serial (reprint) rights. Reports in 3 months on queries. Do not send computer disks. Sample copy for 8½×11 SAE with $1 postage; writer's guidelines for #10 SASE.

Nonfiction: How-to. "No personal success stories or profiles of one company." Buys 25 mss/year. Send complete ms or query and clips. Include stamped, self-addressed postcard for more prompt response. Length: 1,500-3,000 words. Pays 25¢/word for assigned articles. Pays expenses of writers on assignment.

Tips: "Know the subject matter. Develop real sources in the investment community. Demonstrate a reader-friendly style that will help make the sometimes complicated subject of investing more accessible to the average person."

‡**MONEY WORLD,** World Perspective Communications, Inc. 3443 Parkway Center Ct., Orlando FL 32808. (407)290-9600. FAX: (407)290-9622. Editor: G. Patrick Charuhas. 90% freelance written. Bimonthly new magazine on financial/economic/investment news. "*Money World* reaches astute business leaders and serious investors. Writers must be knowledgeable about world economic affairs and write in an interesting fashion." Circ. 140,000. Pays 1 month after publication. Byline given. Buys all rights. Submit seasonal/holiday material 3 months in advance. Simultaneous and photocopied submissions OK. Reports in 2 weeks on queries; 3 weeks on mss. Free sample copy and writer's guidelines.
Nonfiction: Essays, exposé how-to ("consumer reports" investments strategies), interview/profile (with successful people) and other investing news. No "advertorials" for products or companies. Buys 100 mss/year. Query with published clips. Length: 1,500-2,500 words.
Photos: Send photos with submission. Reviews negatives, transparencies and prints. Prefers negatives. Offers $10-25 per photo. Captions required. Buys one-time rights.
Tips: "We encourage new writers, with the understanding that there are plenty of unpublished writers who will become tomorrow's 'stars', but we do scrutinize vehemently."

NATION'S BUSINESS, U.S. Chamber of Commerce, 1615 H. St., N.W., Washington DC 20062. (202)463-5650. Editor: Robert T. Gray. Deputy Editor: Ripley Hotch. 50% freelance written. Monthly magazine covering management of small businesses. Estab. 1912. Circ. 865,000. **Pays on acceptance.** Publishes ms an average of 6 months after acceptance. Byline given. Kill fee negotiable. Buys all rights. Query for electronic submissions. Reports in 1 month. Sample copy $2.50. Free writer's guidelines.
Nonfiction: Book excerpts, how-to, new product and personal experience. No opinion or corporate personnel. Buys 100 mss/year. Query. Length: 250-3,000 words. Pays $100-2,000. Sometimes pays expenses of writers on assignment.

NEW BUSINESS OPPORTUNITIES, Entrepreneur Group, Inc., 2392 Morse Ave., Irvine CA 92714. (714)261-2083. Editor: Rieva Lesonsky. 20-25% freelance written. Monthly magazine on small business. "Provides how-to information for starting a small business and profiles of entrepreneurs who have started small businesses." Estab. 1989. Circ. 200,000. **Pays on acceptance.** Byline given. Offers 20% kill fee. Buys first time worldwide rights. Submit seasonal/holiday material 6 months in advance. Reports in 2 months on queries. Sample copy $3. Writer's guidelines for SASE.
Nonfiction: "We are especially seeking how-to articles for starting a small business. Please read the magazine and writer's guidelines first before querying." Interview/profiles on entrepreneurs. Query. Length: 500-2,000 words. Pays $150-350.
Photos: State availability of photos with submission. Identification of subjects required.

TECHNICAL ANALYSIS OF STOCKS & COMMODITIES, The Trader's Magazine, 3517 S.W. Alaska St., Seattle WA 98126-2730. (206)938-0570. Publisher: Jack K. Hutson. 75% freelance written. Eager to work with new/unpublished writers. Magazine covers methods of investing and trading stocks, bonds and commodities (futures), options, mutual funds, and precious metals. Estab. 1982. Circ. 26,000. Pays on publication. Publishes ms an average of 3 months after acceptance. Byline given. Offers 50% kill fee. Buys all rights; however, second serial (reprint) rights revert to the author, provided copyright credit is given. Previously published submissions OK. Query for electronic submissions. Reports in 3 weeks on queries; 1 month on mss. Sample copy $5; detailed writer's guidelines for #10 SAE and 1 first class stamp.
Nonfiction: Thomas R. Hartle, editor. Reviews (new software or hardware that can make a trader's life easier; comparative reviews of software books, services, etc.); how-to (trade); technical (trading and software aids to trading); utilities (charting or computer programs, surveys, statistics or information to help the trader study or interpret market movements); humor (unusual incidents of market occurrences, cartoons). No newsletter-type, buy-sell recommendations. The article subject must relate to trading psychology, technical analysis, charting or a numerical technique used to trade securities or futures. Virtually requires graphics with every article. Buys 150 mss/year. Query with published clips if available, or send complete ms. Length: 1,000-4,000 words. Pays $100-500. (Applies per inch base rate and premium rate—write for information). Sometimes pays expenses of writers on assignment.
Photos: Christine M. Morrison, photo editor. State availability of photos. Pays $20-150 for 5 × 7 b&w glossy prints or color slides. Captions, model releases and identification of subjects required. Buys one-time and reprint rights.

Columns/Departments: Buys 24 mss/year. Query. Length: 800-1,600 words. Pays $50-300.
Fillers: Karen Webb, fillers editor. Jokes and cartoons on investment humor. Must relate to trading stocks, bonds, options, mutual funds or commodities. Buys 20/year. Length: 500 words. Pays $20-50.
Tips: "Describe how to use technical analysis, charting or computer work in day-to-day trading of stocks, bonds, mutual funds, options or commodities. A blow-by-blow account of how a trade was made, including the trader's thought processes, is, to our subscribers, the very best received story. One of our prime considerations is to instruct in a manner that the lay person can comprehend. We are not hyper-critical of writing style. The completeness and accuracy of submitted material are of the utmost consideration. Write for detailed writer's guidelines."

WORKING MOTHER MAGAZINE, Lang Communications, 230 Park Ave., New York NY 10169. (212)551-9500. Editor: Judsen Culbreth. Executive Editor: Mary McLaughlin. 90% freelance written. Prefers to work with published/established writers; works with a small number of new/unpublished writers each year. For women who balance a career with the concerns of parenting. Monthly magazine. Circ. 700,000. **Pays on acceptance.** Publishes ms an average of 4 months after acceptance. Byline given. Buys first North American Serial Rights and all rights. Pays 20% kill fee. Submit seasonal/holiday material 6 months in advance. Reports in 6 weeks. Sample copy $1.95; writer's guidelines for SASE.
Nonfiction: Service, humor, child development, material pertinent to the working mother's predicament. "Don't just go out and find some mother who holds a job and describe how she runs her home, manages her children and feels fulfilled. Find a working mother whose story is inherently dramatic." Send query to attention of *Working Mother Magazine.* Buys 9-10 mss/issue. Length: 750-2,000 words. Pays $300-1,800. "We pay more to people who write for us regularly." Pays the expenses of writers on assignment.
Tips: "We are looking for pieces that help the reader. In other words, we don't simply report on a trend without discussing how it specifically affects our readers' lives and how they can handle the effects. Where can they look for help if necessary?"

Regional

‡ADCOM MAGAZINE New England's Advertising and Marketing Magazine, Johnson Communications Group, Inc., 18 Imperial Pl., Providence RI 02903. (401)751-6550. Managing Editor: Jim Johnson. 30% freelance written. Monthly magazine covering advertising, marketing, media, PR. "*Adcom Magazine* provides information and features on advertising, marketing, media, PR and related fields—within New England. Primary freelance need: case studies and strategies. Readership: ad agencies, corporate advertising staff." Estab. 1976. Circ. 7,000. Pays 30 days after publication. Publishes ms an average of 2 months after acceptance. Byline given. No kill fee. Buys first rights or second serial (reprint) rights. Submit seasonal/holiday material 3 months in advance. Simultaneous and previously published submissions OK. Query for electronic submissions. Reports in 2 weeks on queries; 3 weeks on manuscripts. Sample copy for 9×12 SAE with 6 first class stamps.
Nonfiction: How-to, opinion, strategies, case studies, industry overviews. Buys 25 mss/year. Query with published clips. Length: 500-3,000 words. Pays $75-350 for assigned articles; $25-200 for unsolicited articles. Sometimes pays expenses of writers on assignment.
Photos: State availability of photos with submission. Reviews contact sheets, transparencies and 5×7 prints. Offers $10-20 per photo. Captions, model releases and identification of subjects required. Buys one-time rights.
Columns/Departments: Case study (case study of a company's advertising/marketing program. Must be a New England company), 1,200-3,000 words; Strategies ("How to" or explanatory articles that relate to advertising, PR, marketing, direct marketing, media), 400-700 words; Industry overview (an overview of marketing/advertising within specific industries in New England), 700-2,500 words. Buys 15 mss/year. Query with published clips. Length: 400-3,000 words. Pays $50-350.
Tips: "Call the editor. When he's not on deadline he's happy to brainstorm with prospective contributors. Best to send him a letter with clips first, though. Remember—submissions must have New England focus. Good luck!"

BOSTON BUSINESS JOURNAL, P&L Publications, 451 D St., Boston MA 02210-1907. (617)330-1000. FAX: (617)330-1016. Editor: Bennie DiNardo. 20% freelance written. Weekly newspaper covering business in Greater Boston. "Our audience is top managers at small, medium and Fortune 500 companies." Circ. 26,000. Pays on publication. Publishes ms an average of 2 weeks after acceptance. Byline given. Offers 50% kill fee. Buys all rights. Submit seasonal/holiday material 1 month in advance. Query for electronic submissions. Reports in 1 week on queries; in 2 weeks on mss.
Nonfiction: Expose, humor, interview/profile, opinion, and photo features. Special focus on hotels, health care, real estate, construction, computers and the office. Buys 50 mss/year. Query with published clips. Length: 600-1,500 words. Pays $125-250 for assigned articles; $125-150 for unsolicited articles. Pays expenses of writers on assignment.

Photos: State availability of photos with submission. Reviews 8 × 10 prints. Pays $40-75 per photo. Identification of subjects required. Buys one-time rights and reprint rights.

Tips: "Read *Wall Street Journal*. Look for hard news angle versus feature angle. Use 'numbers' liberally in the story. We prefer submissions on computer disk (call for specifics). We are only interested in local stories."

BOULDER COUNTY BUSINESS REPORT, #200, 4885 Riverbend Rd., Boulder CO 80301-2617. (303)440-4950. FAX: (303)440-8954. Editor: Jerry W. Lewis. 75% freelance written. Prefers to work with published/established writers; works with a small number of new/unpublished writers each year. Monthly newspaper covering Boulder County business issues. Offers "news tailored to a monthly theme and read primarily by Colorado businesspeople and by some investors nationwide. Philosophy: Descriptive, well-written articles that reach behind the scene to examine area's business activity." Estab. 1982. Circ. 18,000. Pays on publication. Publishes ms an average of 1 month after acceptance. Byline given. Buys one-time rights and second serial (reprint) rights. Simultaneous queries OK. Query for electronic submissions. Reports in 1 month on queries; 2 weeks on mss. Sample copy free on request.

Nonfiction: Interview/profile, new product, examination of competition in a particular line of business. "All our issues are written around one or two monthly themes. No articles are accepted in which the subject has not been pursued in depth and both sides of an issue presented in a writing style with flair." Buys 120 mss/year. Query with published clips. Length: 250-2,000 words. Pays $50-300.

Photos: State availability of photos with query letter. Reviews b&w contact sheets. Pays $10 maximum for b&w contact sheet. Identification of subjects required. Buys one-time rights and reprint rights.

Tips: "It would be difficult to write for this publication if a freelancer were unable to localize a subject. In-depth articles are written by assignment. The freelancer located in the Colorado area has an excellent chance here."

CALIFORNIA BUSINESS, Suite 400, 4221 Wilshire Blvd., Los Angeles CA 90010. (213)937-5820. Editor: Michael Kolbenschlag. 10% freelance written. Monthly business publication covering California. Includes Pacific rim and Mexico. Estab. 1965. Circ. 130,000. **Pays on acceptance.** Publishes ms an average of 3 months after acceptance. Byline given. Pays 15% kill fee. Buys first North American serial rights. Submit seasonal/holiday material 6 months in advance. Query for electronic submissions. Reports in 1 month. Sample copy for 8½ × 11 SAE with 4 first class stamps. Writer's guidelines for #10 SASE.

Nonfiction: Book excerpts, expose, interview/profile. Buys 50 mss/year. Query. Length: 2,000-4,000 words. Pays $750-2,500 for assigned articles. Pays reasonable expenses of writers on assignment.

Photos: State availability of photos with submission. Reviews transparencies. Captions, model releases required. Buys one-time rights.

Tips: "Follow written query with phone call."

‡**CORPORATE CLEVELAND,** Business Journal Publishing Co., 3rd floor, 1720 Euclid Ave., Cleveland OH 44115. (216)621-1644. FAX: (216)621-5918. Editor: Robert W. Gardner. Managing Editor: Michael E. Moore. 10% freelance written. Prefers to work with published/established writers. A monthly magazine covering general business topics. "*Corporate Cleveland* serves Northeast Ohio. Readers are business executives in the state engaged in manufacturing, agriculture, mining, construction, transportation, communications, utilities, retail and wholesale trade, services, and government." Circ. 31,000. Pays for features on acceptance; news on publication. Publishes ms an average of 4 months after acceptance. Byline sometimes given. Kill fee can be negotiated. Buys first serial rights; depends on projects. Submit seasonal/holiday material 3-4 months in advance. Simultaneous queries, and simultaneous, photocopied, and previously published submissions OK. Reports in 2 weeks on queries; 1 month on mss. Sample copy $2; writer's guidelines for SAE and 1 first class stamp.

Nonfiction: Book excerpts, general interest, how-to, interview/profile, opinion and personal experience. "In all cases, write with an Northeast Ohio executive in mind. Stories should give readers useful information on business within the state, trends in management, ways to manage better, or other developments which would affect them in their professional careers." Buys 14-20 mss/year. Query with published clips. Length: 800-2,500 words. Pays $100 minimum. Sometimes pays expenses of writers on assignment.

Always check the most recent copy of a magazine for the address and editor's name before you send in a query or manuscript.

Photos: State availability of photos. Reviews b&w and color transparencies and prints. Captions and identification of subjects required. Buys variable rights.

Columns/Departments: News; People (profiles of business execs). Query with published clips. Length: 100-600 words. Pay varies.

Tips: "Features are most open to freelancers. Come up with new ideas or information for our readers: executives in manufacturing and service industries. Writers should be aware of the trend toward specialization in magazine publishing with strong emphasis on people in coverage."

CRAIN'S DETROIT BUSINESS, Crain Communications, Inc., 1400 Woodbridge, Detroit MI 48207. (313)446-0460. FAX: (313)393-0997. Editor: Mary Kramer. Managing Editor: Dave Guilford. 20% freelance written. Weekly tabloid covering Detroit area businesses. *"Crain's Detroit Business* reports the activities of local businesses. Our readers are mostly executives; many of them own their own companies. They read us to keep track of companies not often reported about in the daily press—privately held companies and small public companies. Our slant is hard news and news features. We do not report on the auto companies, but other businesses in Wayne, Oakland, Macomb, and Washtenaw counties are part of our turf." Estab. 1985. Circ. 35,000. Pays on publication. Byline given. Offers negotiable kill fee. Buys first rights and "the right to make the story available to the other 25 Crain publications, and the right to circulate the story through the Crain News Service." Query for electronic submissions. Sample copy 50¢; writer's guidelines for SASE.

Nonfiction: Cindy Goodaker, articles editor. No "how-tos, new product articles, or fiction." Looking for local and statewide news. Buys 200 mss/year. Query. Length: 800 words average. Pays $6/inch and expenses for assigned articles. Pays $6/inch without expenses for unsolicited articles. Pays expenses of writers on assignment.

Tips: "What we are most interested in are specific news stories about local businesses. The fact that Widget Inc. is a great company is of no interest to us. However, if Widget Inc. introduced a new product six months ago and sales have gone up from $20 million to $30 million, then that's a story. The same is true if sales went down from $20 million to $10 million. I would strongly encourage interested writers to contact me directly. Although we don't have a blanket rule against unsolicited manuscripts, they are rarely usable. We are a general circulation publication, but we are narrowly focused. A writer not familiar with us would have trouble focusing the story properly, In addition writers may not have a business relationship with the company they are writing about."

‡FLORIDA TREND, Magazine of Florida Business and Finance, Box 611, St. Petersburg FL 33731. (813)821-5800. (813)822-5083. Editor and Publisher: Paul Tash. Executive Editor: Matt Walsh. A monthly magazine covering business economics and public policy for Florida business people and investors. Circ. 50,000. Pays on final acceptance. Byline given. Buys first North American serial rights. Computer printout submissions acceptable. Reports in 1 month. Sample copy $3.50.

Nonfiction: Business and finance. Buys 10-12 mss/year. Query with or without published clips. Length: 1,200-2,500 words.

INDIANA BUSINESS MAGAZINE, 6502 Westfield Blvd., Indianapolis IN 46220. (317)252-2737. FAX: (317)252-2738. Editor: Steve Kaelble. 50% freelance written. Statewide publication focusing on business in Indiana. "We are a general business publication that reaches 30,000 top executives in Indiana, covering all business categories." Circ. 35,000. Pays on publication. Publishes ms an average of 2 months after acceptance. Rights negotiable. Byline given. Reports in 1 month. Sample copy $2.

Nonfiction: Expose; interview/profile; and opinion. No first person experience stories. "Stories planned on assignment basis. Unsolicited mss usually not accepted. All articles must relate to Indiana business and must be of interest to a broad range of business and professional people. We are especially interested in profiles of Indiana executives. We would like to hear about business success stories but only as they pertain to current issues, trends (i.e., a real estate company that has made it big because they got in on the Economic Development Bonds and invested in renovation property)." Buys 60 mss/year. Submit clips with query. Length: 500-2,500 words. Pay negotiable. Pays expenses of writers on assignment.

Photos: State availability of photos. Reviews contact sheets, negatives, transparencies and 5 × 7 prints. Pay negotiable for b&w or color photos. Captions, model releases and identification of subjects required.

Fillers: Anecdotes and newsbreaks. Length: 125-250 words.

Tips: "Give us a concise query telling us not only why we should run the article but why you should write it. Be sure to indicate available photography or subjects for photography or art. We look first for good ideas. Our readers are sophisticated business people who are interested in their peers as well as how they can run their businesses better. We will look at non-business issues if they can be related to business in some way."

MEMPHIS BUSINESS JOURNAL, Mid-South Communications, Inc., Suite 102, 88 Union, Memphis TN 38103. (901)523-1000. Editor: Barney DuBois. Weekly tabloid covering industry, trade, agribusiness and finance in west Tennessee, north Mississippi, east Arkansas, and the Missouri Bootheel. "Articles should be timely and relevant to business in our region." Estab. 1979. Circ. 14,500. **Pays on acceptance.** Byline given. Pays $50 kill fee. Buys one-time rights, and makes work-for-hire assignments. Free sample copy.

Nonfiction: Exposé, historical/nostalgic, interview/profile, business features and trends. "All must relate to business in our area." Query with or without clips of published work, or send complete ms. Length: 750-2,000 words. Pays $100-250. Sometimes pays the expenses of writers on assignment.

Photos: State availability of photos or send photos with ms. Pays $25-50 for 5 × 7 b&w prints. Identification of subjects required. Buys one-time rights.

Tips: "We are interested in news—and this means we can accept short, hard-hitting work more quickly. We also welcome freelancers who can do features and articles on business in the smaller cities of our region. We are a weekly, so our stories need to be timely."

‡**METRO TORONTO BUSINESS JOURNAL, Business Journal**, Metro Toronto Board of Trade, 3 1st Canadian Place 60, Toronto Ontario M5X 1C1 Canada. (416)366-6811. FAX: (416)366-5620. Editor: Peter Carter. Managing Editor: John Greenwood. 90% freelance written. Monthly magazine on Toronto business. Circ. 46,000. **Pays on acceptance.** Offers 50% kill fee. Buys first North American serial rights. Computer printout submissions OK; prefers letter-quality. Reports in 2 weeks on queries; 1 week on mss. Free sample copy.

Nonfiction: Book excerpts, essays, exposé, general interest, historical/nostalgic, humor, interview/ profile, opinion, personal experience and photo feature. Buys 300 mss/year. Query. Length: 150-3,000 words. Pays $150-2,500 for assigned articles. Sometimes pays expenses of writers on assignment.

Photos: State availability of photos with submission. Reviews contact sheets. Captions required. Buys all rights.

Columns/Departments: City Business (Toronto related, innovative business ideas, personalities), 50-300 words; Landmarks (Toronto business landmarks, historic sites), 900 words; In Progress (changing Toronto landscapes), 900 words. Buys 300 mss/year. Query. Pays $150-500.

OREGON BUSINESS, Media America Publications, Suite 407, 921 SW Morrison, Portland OR 97205. (503)223-0304. Editor: Robert Hill. 60% freelance written. Works with a small number of new/unpublished writers each year. Monthly magazine covering business in Oregon. Estab. 1981. Circ. 20,000. Pays on publication. Publishes ms an average of 4 months after acceptance. Byline given. Buys first rights. Submit seasonal/holiday material 3 months in advance. Previously published submissions OK. Reports in 1 month. Sample copy for 9 × 12 SAE and 5 first class stamps.

Nonfiction: General interest (real estate, business, investing, small business); interview/profile (business leaders); and new products. Special issues include tourism, world trade, finance. "We need articles on real estate or small business in Oregon, outside the Portland area." Buys 50 mss/year. Query with published clips. Length: 900-2,000 words. Pays 10¢/word minimum. Sometimes pays expenses of writers on assignment.

ORLANDO MAGAZINE, Orlando Media Affiliates, P.O. Box 2207, Suite 290, 341 N. Maitland Ave., Orlando FL 32802. (407)539-3939. FAX: (407)539-0553. 10% freelance written. Monthly magazine covering city growth, development and business and lifestyle. Estab. 1946. Circ. 35,000. Pays on publication. Publishes ms an average of 2 months after acceptance. Byline given. Offers negotiable kill fee. Submit seasonal/holiday material 3 months in advance. Simultaneous submissions OK. Reports in 3 weeks. Free sample copy and writer's guidelines.

Nonfiction: Exposé, how-to (business), and interview. Buys 12-15 mss/year. Send complete ms. Length: 1,000-2,500 words. Pays $100-450 for assigned articles.

Photos: State availability of photos with submission. Reviews transparencies. Offers $5 per photo. Captions and identification of subjects required. Buys one-time rights.

Columns/Departments: Virtually all business topics. Length: 1,200-1,500. Buys 12-15 mss/year. Pays $100-200.

REGARDIES: THE MAGAZINE OF WASHINGTON BUSINESS, 1010 Wisconsin Ave., NW, Washington DC 20007. (202)342-0410. Editor: Brian Kelly. 80% freelance written. Works with a small number of new/unpublished writers each year. Monthly magazine covering business and general features in the Washington DC metropolitan area for Washington business executives. Circ. 60,000. Pays within 30 days after publication. Publishes ms an average of 2 months after acceptance. Byline given. Offers variable kill fee. Buys first serial rights and second serial (reprint) rights. Submit seasonal/holiday material 3 months in advance. Reports in 3 weeks. Sample copy for $8 and 9 × 12 SAE.

Nonfiction: Profiles (of business leaders), investigative reporting, real estate, advertising, politics, lifestyle, media, retailing, communications, labor issues and financial issues—all on the Washington business scene. "If it is not the kind of story that could just as easily run in a good city magazine or a national magazine like *Harper's*, *Atlantic*, *Esquire*, etc., I don't want to see it." Also buys book mss for excerpt. No how-to. Narrative nonfiction only. Buys 90 mss/year. Length: 4,000 words average. Buys 5-6/issue. Pays negotiable rate. Pays the expenses of writers on assignment.

Columns/Departments: Length: 1,500 words average. Buys 8-12/issue. Pays negotiable rates.

Tips: "The most frequent mistake writers make is not including enough information and data about business which, with public companies, is easy enough to find. This results in flawed analysis and a willingness to accept the 'official line.' "

ROCHESTER BUSINESS MAGAZINE, Rochester Business, Inc., 1600 Lyell Ave., Rochester NY 14606. (716)458-8280. Editor: Douglas Sprei. 25% freelance written. Monthly magazine. "*RBM* is a colorful tutorial business publication targeted specifically toward business owners and upper level managers in the Rochester metropolitan area. Our audience is comprised of upscale decision-makers with keen interest in the 'how-to' of business. Some features deal with lifestyle, travel, cultural focus, etc." Circ. 17,000. Pays on publication. Publishes ms an average of 2-6 months after acceptance. Byline given. Buys all rights. Previously published submissions OK. Reports in 1 month. Sample $2.

Nonfiction: Essays, historical/nostalgic, how-to, humor, interview/profile and personal experience, all with business slant. Buys 12-24 mss/year. Query with published clips. Length: 1,500 words maximum. Pays $50-100. Pays barter (trade dollars) to interested writers.

Photos: State availability of photos with submission. Offers no additional payment for photos accepted with ms. Captions required.

SAN FRANCISCO BUSINESS TIMES, 325 Fifth St., San Francisco CA 94107. (415)777-9355. FAX: (415)777-4558. Editor: Tim Clark. Focus Editor: Jackie Taub. 10% freelance written. Weekly tabloid of Bay Area business news and issues. "The *San Francisco Business Times* is a publication targeted to small business owners, mid- and top-level managers of corporations throughout the Bay Area. The stories must be written in non-technical, jargon-free literate style." Estab. 1986. Circ. 16,000. Pays on publication. Publishes ms an average of 1 month after acceptance. Byline given. Negotiated kill fee. Query for electronic submission.

Nonfiction: "Focus" section. Length: 800-1,000 words. Pays $150.

Tips: "Become aware of the trends in the business community and prepare a brief outline of your proposed submission. Include sources that may be contacted for the story. The Focus section concentrates on issues and concerns to Bay Area business community. There is a need to relate material to local and national scene."

‡VERMONT BUSINESS MAGAZINE, Manning Publications, Inc., Brattleboro Professional Center, P.O. Box 6120, Brattleboro VT 05301. (802)257-4100. FAX: (802)257-5266. Editor: Timothy McQuiston. 80% freelance written. A monthly tabloid covering business in Vermont. Estab. 1972. Circ. 15,000. Pays on publication. Publishes ms an average of 1 month after acceptance. Byline given. Offers kill fee. Not copyrighted. Buys one-time rights. Simultaneous submissions OK. Query for electronic submissions. Free sample copy.

Nonfiction: Business trends and issues. Buys 200 mss/year. Query with published clips. Length: 800-1,800 words. Pays $50-150. Pays the expenses of writers on assignment.

Photos: Send photos with submission. Reviews contact sheets. Offers $10-35 per photo. Identification of subjects required.

Tips: "Read daily papers and look for business angles for a follow-up article. We look for issue and trend articles rather than company or businessman profiles. Note: Magazine accepts Vermont-specific material *only*. The articles *must* be about Vermont."

VICTORIA'S BUSINESS REPORT, Monday Publications Ltd., 1609 Blanshard St., Victoria, British Columbia V8W 2J5 Canada. (604)382-7777. FAX: (604)381-2662. Editor: Gery Lemon. 20% freelance written. Monthly magazine that covers Victoria business. "*Victoria's Business Report* focuses on business on Victoria and southern Vancouver Island." Pays on publication. Publishes ms an average of 2 months after acceptance. Byline given. Buys first North American serial rights. Simultaneous and previously published submissions OK. Query for electronic submissions. Reports in 3 weeks on queries. Sample copy $2.75.

Nonfiction: Length: 500-2,000 words. Pays $50-400 for assigned articles. Sometimes pays expenses of writers on assignment.

Photos: State availability of photos with submission. Offers $10-35 per photo. Captions and identification of subjects required. Buys one-time rights.

Career, College and Alumni

Three types of magazines are listed in this section: university publications written for students, alumni and friends of a specific institution; publications about college life for students; and publications on career and job opportunities.

AIM, A Resource Guide for Vocational/Technical Graduates, Communications Publishing Group, 3100 Broadway, 225 PennTower, Kansas City MO 64111. (816)756-3039. FAX: (816)756-3018. Editor: Georgia Clark. 40% freelance written. A bi-annual educational and career source guide "designed to assist experienced voc/tech students in their search for career opportunities and aid in improving their life survival skills. For Black and Hispanic young adults—ages 21-35." Estab. 1982. Circ. 350,000. Pays on publication. Byline sometimes given. Buys second serial (reprint) rights or makes work-for-hire assignments. Submit seasonal/holiday material 6 months in advance. Simultaneous and previously published submissions OK. Reports in 2 months. Sample copy for 9 × 10 SASE with 4 first class stamps. Writer's guidelines for #10 SASE.

Nonfiction: Book excerpts or reviews, general interest, how-to (dealing with careers or education), humor, inspirational, interview/profile (celebrity or "up and coming" young adult), new product (as it relates to young adult market), personal experience, photo feature, technical, travel. Query or send complete ms. Length: 750-2,000 words. Pays $150-400 for assigned articles; 10¢/word for unsolicited articles. Sometimes pays expenses of writers on assignment.

Photos: State availability of photos with submission. Prefers transparencies. Offers $20-25/photo. Captions, model releases and identification of subjects required. Buys all rights.

Columns/Departments: Profiles of Achievement (striving and successful minority young adult ages 21-35 in various technical careers). Buys 15 mss/year. Send complete ms. Length: 500-1,000 words. Pays $50-250.

Fiction: Adventure, ethnic, historical, humorous, mainstream, slice-of-life vignettes. Buys 3 mss/year. Send complete ms. Length: 1,000-5,000 words. Pays $100-400.

Poetry: Free verse. Buys 5 poems/year. Submit up to 5 poems at one time. Length: 10-25 lines. Pays $10-50.

Fillers: Anecdotes, facts, gags to be illustrated by cartoonist, newsbreaks, short humor. Buys 10/year. Length: 25-250 words. Pays $25-100.

Tips: "For new writers, submit full manuscript that is double spaced; clean copy only. Include on first page of manuscript your name, address, phone, Social Security Number and number of words in article. Need to have clippings of previous published works and resume. Resume should tell when available to write. Most open are profiles of successful and striving Black or Hispanic young adults (age 21-35). Include photo."

ALCALDE, P.O. Box 7278, Austin TX 78713. (512)471-3799. FAX: (512)471-8088. Editor: Ernestine Wheelock. 20% freelance written. Works with a small number of new/unpublished writers each year. Bimonthly magazine. Estab. 1913. Circ. 50,000. Pays on publication. Publishes ms an average of 6 months after acceptance. Buys all rights. Submit seasonal/holiday material 5 months in advance. Query for electronic submissions. Reports in 1 month. Sample copy 8½ × 11 and $1.30 postage. Writer's guidelines for #10 SASE.

Nonfiction: General interest; historical (University of Texas, research and faculty profile); humor (humorous Texas subjects); nostalgia (University of Texas traditions); profile (students, faculty, alumni); and technical (University of Texas research on a subject or product). No subjects lacking taste or quality, or not connected with the University of Texas. Buys 12 mss/year. Query. Length: 1,000-2,400 words. Pays according to importance of article.

THE BLACK COLLEGIAN, The Career & Self Development Magazine for African American Students, Black Collegiate Services, Inc., 1240 S. Broad St., New Orleans LA 70125. (504)821-5694. FAX: (504)821-5713. Editor: K. Kazi-Ferrouillet. 25% freelance written. Magazine for African-American college students and recent graduates with an interest in career and job information, African-American cultural awareness, personalities, history, trends and current events. Published bimonthly during school year (4 times/year). Estab. 1970. Circ. 121,000. Buys one-time rights. Byline given. Pays on publication. Submit seasonal and special interest material 2 months in advance of issue date (Careers, September; Computers/Grad School and Travel/Summer programs, November; Engineering and Black History programs, January; Finance and Jobs, March). Reports in 2 months on queries; 3

months on mss. Sample copy for 9 × 12 SAE and $4. Writer's guidelines for #10 SASE.

Nonfiction: Material on careers, sports, black history, news analysis. Articles on problems and opportunities confronting African-American college students and recent graduates. Book excerpts, expose, general interest, historical/nostalgic, how-to (develop employability), opinion, personal experience, profile, inspirational, humor. Buys 40 mss/year (6 unsolicited). Query with published clips or send complete ms. Length: 500-1,500 words. Pays $50-500.

Photos: State availability of photos with query or ms, or send photos with query or ms. Black and white photos or color transparencies purchased with or without ms. 8 × 10 prints preferred. Captions, model releases and identification of subjects required. Pays $35/b&w; $50/color.

Tips: "Career features area is most open to freelancers."

CAREER FOCUS, For Today's Professional, Communications Publishing Group, Inc., Suite 225, 3100 Broadway, Kansas City MO 64111. (816)756-3039. FAX: (816)756-3018. Editor: Georgia Clark. 40% freelance written. Bimonthly magazine "devoted to providing positive insight, information, guidance and motivation to assist Blacks and Hispanics (ages 21-35) in their career development and attainment of goals." Estab. 1988. Circ. 250,000. Pays on publication. Byline often given. Buys second serial (reprint) rights and makes work-for-hire assignments. Submit seasonal/holiday material 6 months in advance. Simultaneous and previously published submissions OK. Reports in 2 months. Sample copy for 9 × 12 SASE and 4 first class stamps; writer's guidelines for #10 SASE.

Nonfiction: Book excerpts, general interest, historical, how-to, humor, inspirational, interview/profile, personal experience, photo feature, technical, travel. Length: 750-2,000 words. Pays $150-400 for assigned articles; pays 10¢/word for unsolicited articles. Sometimes pays expenses of writers on assignment.

Photos: State availability of photos with submission. Reviews transparencies. Pays $20-25/photo. Captions, model releases and identification of subjects required. Buys all rights.

Columns/Departments: Profiles (striving and successful Black and Hispanic young adult, ages 21-35). Buys 15 mss/year. Send complete ms. Length: 500-1,000 words. Pays $50-250.

Fiction: Adventure, ethnic, historical, humorous, mainstream, slice-of-life vignettes. Buys 3 mss/year. Send complete ms. Length: 1,500-5,000 words. Pays $100-400.

Poetry: Free verse. Buys 4/year. Length: 10-25 lines. Pays $10-50.

Fillers: Anecdotes, facts, gags to be illustrated by cartoonist, newsbreaks, short humor. Buys 10/year. Length: 25-250 words. Pays $25-100.

Tips: "For new writers: Submit full manuscript that is double-spaced; clean copy only. Need to have clippings and previously published works and resume. Should also tell when available to write. Most open to freelancers are profiles of successful and striving persons including photos. Profile must be of a Black or Hispanic adult living in the U.S. Include on first page of manuscript your name, address phone, Social Security number and number of words in article."

CAREER WOMAN, For Entry-Level and Professional Women, Equal Opportunity Publications, Inc., 44 Broadway, Greenlawn NY 11740. (516)261-8917. FAX: (516)261-8935. Editor: Eileen Nester. 80% freelance written. Works with small number of new/unpublished writers each year. Magazine published 3 times/year (fall, winter, spring) covering career-guidance for college women. Strives to "aid women in developing career abilities to the fullest potential; improve job hunting skills; present career opportunities; provide personal resources; help cope with discrimination." Audience is 92% college juniors and seniors; 8% working graduates. Circ. 10,500. Controlled circulation, distributed through college guidance and placement offices. Pays on publication. Publishes ms an average of 3-12 months after acceptance. Byline given. Buys first North American rights. Simultaneous queries and submissions OK. Sample copy and writer's guidelines for five first-class stamps and a 9 × 12 SASE.

Nonfiction: "We want career-related articles describing for a college-educated woman the how-tos of obtaining a professional position and advancing her career." Looks for practical features detailing self-evaluation techniques, the job-search process, and advice for succeeding on the job. Emphasizes role-model profiles of succesful career women. Needs manuscripts presenting information on professions offering opportunities to young women—especially the growth professions of the future. Special issues emphasize career opportunities for women in fields such as health care, communications, sales, marketing, banking, insurance, finance, science, engineering, and computers. Query first.

Photos: Send with ms. Prefers 35mm color slides, but will accept b&w prints. Captions and identification of subjects required. Buys all rights.

Tips: "Articles should focus on career-guidance, role model, and industry prospects for women and should have a snappy, down-to-earth writing style."

CARNEGIE MELLON MAGAZINE, Carnegie Mellon University, 5017 Forbes Ave., Pittsburgh PA 15213. (412)268-2900. FAX: (412)268-6929. Editor: Ann Curran. Alumni publication issued fall, winter, spring, summer covering university activities, alumni profiles, etc. Circ, 52,000. **Pays on acceptance.** Byline given. Not copyrighted. Reports in 1 month.

Nonfiction: Book reviews (faculty alumni), general interest, humor, interview/profile, photo feature. "We use general interest stories linked to CMU activities and research." No unsolicited mss. Buys 5 features and 5-10 alumni profiles/year. Query with published clips. Length: 800-2,000 words. Pays $100-400 or negotiable rate. Sample copy for 9×12 SAE and $2.

Poetry: Avant-garde or traditional. No previously published poetry. No payment.

CIRCLE K MAGAZINE, 3636 Woodview Trace, Indianapolis IN 46268. FAX: (317)879-0204. Executive Editor: Nicholas K. Drake. 60% freelance written. "Our readership consists almost entirely of above-average college students interested in voluntary community service and leadership development. They are politically and socially aware and have a wide range of interests." Publishes 5 times/year. Circ. 14,000. **Pays on acceptance.** Normally buys first North American serial rights. Byline given. Submit seasonal/holiday material 6 months in advance. Reports in 1 month. Sample copy and writer's guidelines for large SAE with 3 first class stamps.

Nonfiction: Articles published in *Circle K* are of two types—serious and light nonfiction. "We are interested in general interest articles on topics concerning college students and their lifestyles, as well as articles dealing with careers, community concerns and leadership development." No "first person confessions, family histories or travel pieces." Query. Length: 2,000-2,500 words. Pays $225-350.

Photos: Purchased with accompanying ms. Captions required. Total purchase price for ms includes payment for photos.

Tips: "Query should indicate author's familiarity with the field and sources. Subject treatment must be objective and in-depth, and articles should include illustrative examples and quotes from persons involved in the subject or qualified to speak on it. We are open to working with new writers who present a good article idea and demonstrate that they've done their homework concerning the article subject itself, as well as concerning our magazine's style. We're interested in college-oriented trends, for example, entrepreneur schooling is now a major shift; more awareness of college crime; health issues."

COLLEGE MONTHLY, New England, Lapierre & Associates, Suite 805, 332 Main St., Worcester MA 01608. (508)753-2550. Editor: Maureen Castillo. Managing Editor: Randy Cohen. 25% freelance written. College lifestyle and entertainment magazine published 8 times/year. Estab. 1986. Circ. 73,000. Pays on publication. Byline given. Offers $5 kill fee. Buys one-time rights. Query for electronic submissions. Free sample copy and writer's guidelines.

Nonfiction: Humor, interview/profile, opinion, personal experience and travel. Query with published clips. Length: 500-2,000 words. Pays $25-100 for assigned articles; $5-25 for unsolicited articles. Sometimes pays the expenses of writers on assignment.

Photos: State availability of photos with submission. Offers no additional payment for photos accepted with ms. Caption required. Buys one-time rights.

Columns/Departments: Fashion (trends in the college market for clothes); Lifestyle (off-the-wall things students do); Sports (national sports and college); Politics (national level/hot social issues), all 500-750 words.

Fillers: Newsbreaks, short humor. Length: 100 words. Pays $5-25.

COLLEGE PREVIEW, A Guide for College-Bound Students, Communications Publishing Group, 3100 Broadway, 225 PennTower, Kansas City MO 64111. (816)756-3039. FAX: (816)756-3018. Editor: Georgia Clark. 40% freelance written. A bi-annual educational and career source guide. "Contemporary guide is designed to inform and motivate Black and Hispanic young adults, ages 16-21 years old about college preparation, career planning and life survival skills." Estab. 1982. Circ. 600,000. Pays on publication. Byline often given. Buys second serial (reprint) rights or makes work-for-hire assignments. Submit seasonal/holiday material 6 months in advance. Simultaneous and previously published submissions OK. Reports in 2 months. Sample copy for 9×10 SASE with 4 first class stamps. Writer's guidelines for #10 SASE.

Nonfiction: Book excerpts or reviews, general interest, how-to (dealing with careers or education), humor, inspirational, interview/profile (celebrity or "up and coming" young adult), new product (as it relates to young adult market), personal experience, photo feature, technical, travel. Send complete ms. Length: 750-2,000 words. Pays $150-400 for assigned articles; 10¢/word for unsolicited articles. Sometimes pays expenses of writers on assignment.

Photos: State availability of photos with submission. Reviews transparencies. Offers $20-$25/photo. Captions, model releases and identification of subjects required. Buys all rights.

Columns/Departments: Profiles of Achievement (striving and successful minority young adults ages 16-35 in various careers). Buys 15 mss/year. Send complete ms. Length: 500-1,500. Pays $50-250.

Fiction: Adventure, ethnic, historical, humorous, mainstream, slice-of-life vignettes. Buys 3 mss/year. Send complete ms. Length: 1,000-5,000 words. Pays $100-400.

Poetry: Free verse. Buys 5 poems/year. Submit up to 5 poems at one time. Length: 10-25 lines. Pays $10-50.

Fillers: Anecdotes, facts, gags to be illustrated by cartoonist, newsbreaks, short humor. Buys 10/year. Length: 25-250 words. Pays $25-100.

Tips: For new writers—Send complete manuscript that is double spaced; clean copy only. If available, send clippings of previous published works and resume. Should state when available to write. Include on first page of manuscript your name, address, phone, Social Security number and word count.

‡DIRECTIONS, A Guide to Career Alternatives, Communications Publishing Group, 3100 Broadway, 225 PennTower, Kansas City MO 64111. (816)756-3039. Editor: Georgia Clark. 40% freelance written. A bi-annual magazine that focuses on evaluating career possibilities and enhancement of life survival skills for Black and Hispanic young adults, ages 18-25. Circ. 500,000. Pays on publication. Byline often given. Buys second serial (reprint) rights or makes work-for-hire assignments. Submit seasonal/holiday material 6 months in advance. Simultaneous, photocopied and previously published submissions OK. Reports in 2 months. Sample copy for 9 × 12 SASE with 4 first class stamps. Writer's guidelines for #10 SASE.

Nonfiction: Book excerpts or reviews, general interest, how-to (dealing with careers or education), humor, inspirational, interview/profile (celebrity or "up and coming" young adult), new product (as it relates to young adult market), personal experience, photo feature, technical, travel. Send complete ms. Length: 750-2,000 words. Pays $150-400 for assigned articles; 10¢/word for unsolicited articles. Sometimes pays expenses of writers on assignment.

Photos: State availability of photos with submission. Reviews transparencies. Offers $20-25/photo. Captions, model releases and identification of subjects required. Buys all rights.

Columns/Departments: Profiles of Achievement (striving and successful minority young adult age 16-35 in various careers). Buys 15 mss/year. Send complete ms. Length: 500-1,500. Pays $50-250.

Fiction: Adventure, ethnic, historical, humorous, mainstream, slice-of-life vignettes. Buys 3 mss/year. Send complete ms. Length: 1,000-5,000 words. Pays $100-400.

Poetry: Free verse. Buys 5 poems/year. Submit up to 5 poems at one time. Length: 10-25 lines. Pays $10-50.

Fillers: Anecdotes, facts, gags to be illustrated by cartoonist, newsbreaks, short humor. Buys 10/year. Length: 25-250 words. Pays $25-100.

Tips: "For new writers—Send complete manuscript that is double spaced; clean copy only. If available, send clippings of previous published works and resume. Should state when available to write. Must include on first page of ms—name, address, phone, Social Security and number of words in article."

EQUAL OPPORTUNITY, The Nation's Only Multi-Ethnic Recruitment Magazine for Black, Hispanic, Native American & Asian American College Grads, Equal Opportunity Publications, Inc., 44 Broadway, Greenlawn NY 11740. (516)261-8917. FAX: (516)261-8935. Executive Editor: James Schneider. 50% freelance written. Prefers to work with published/established writers. Magazine published 3 times/year (fall, winter, spring) covering career guidance for minorities. "Our audience is 90% college juniors and seniors; 10% working graduates. An understanding of educational and career problems of minorities is essential." Estab. 1967. Circ. 15,000. Controlled circulation, distributed through college guidance and placement offices. Pays on publication. Publishes ms an average of 2 months after acceptance. Byline given. Buys first rights. Deadline dates: fall, August 10; winter, November 15: spring, February 1. Simultaneous queries and previously published submissions OK. Sample copy and writer's guidelines for 9 × 12 SAE and 5 first class stamps.

Nonfiction: Book excerpts and articles (on job search techniques, role models), general interest (on specific minority concerns), how-to (on job-hunting skills, personal finance, better living, coping with discrimination); humor (student or career related), interview/profile (minority role models), opinion (problems of minorities), personal experience (professional and student study and career experiences), technical (on career fields offering opportunities for minorities), travel (on overseas job opportunities), and coverage of Black, Hispanic, Native American and Asian American interests. Special issues include career opportunities for minorities in industry and government in fields such as banking, insurance, finance, communications, sales, marketing, engineering, computers, military and defense. Query or send complete ms. Length: 1,000-1,500 words. Sometimes pays expenses of writers on assignment. Pays 10¢/word.

Photos: Prefers 35mm color slides and b&w. Captions and identification of subjects required. Buys all rights at $15 per photo use.

Tips: "Articles must be geared toward questions and answers faced by minority and women students."

ETC MAGAZINE, Student Media—University of North Carolina at Charlotte, Cone University Center UNCC, Charlotte NC 28223. (704)547-2146. Editor: Ann Larrow. A semiannual magazine on collegiate lifestyle. "*Etc. Magazine* is a student publication serving the University of North Carolina at Charlotte that features general interest articles dealing with collegiate lifestyles." Estab. 1986. Circ. 5,000. Pays on publication. Byline given. Buys one-time rights. Previously published material OK. Reports in 6 months. Free sample copy and writer's guidelines.

Nonfiction: 2,000 word general interest cover story covering topical issues in university setting and 1,000 word general interest feature articles. Magazine departments (1,000 words): Lifeline—helping students cope with stress and changes associated with college life; Skyline—highlighting university's important ties to the Charlotte community; Aspects—focusing on diverse ethnic groups which form large part of university community; Passport—interesting travel ideas for students on limited budgets. Special issues—Freshman orientation issue and graduate section. Issue-oriented articles average 1,000 words. Pays no more than $10.

Photos: State availability of photos with submission or send photos with submission. Stipend of no more than $10 will be paid upon publication.

‡**FIRST OPPORTUNITY, A Guide for Vocational/Technical Students,** Communications Publishing Group, 3100 Broadway, 225 PennTower, Kansas City MO 64111. (816)756-3039. Editor: Georgia Clark. 40% freelance written. A bi-annual resource publication focusing on advanced voc/tech educational opportunities and career preparation for Black and Hispanic young adults, ages 16-21. Circ. 500,000. Pays on publication. Byline sometimes given. Buys second serial (reprint) rights or makes work-for-hire assignments. Submit seasonal/holiday material 6 months in advance. Simultaneous, photocopied and previously published submissions OK. Reports in 2 months. Sample copy for 9 × 12 SASE with 4 first class stamps. Writer's guidelines for #10 SASE.

Nonfiction: Book excerpts or reviews, general interest, how-to (dealing with careers or education), humor, inspirational, interview/profile (celebrity or "up and coming" young adult), new product (as it relates to young adult market), personal experience, photo feature, technical, travel. Length: 750-2,000 words. Pays $150-400 for assigned articles; 10¢/word for unsolicited articles. Sometimes pays expenses of writers on assignment.

Photos: State availability of photos with submission. Prefers transparencies. Offers $20-25/photo. Captions, model releases and identification of subjects required. Buys all rights.

Columns/Departments: Profiles of Achievement (striving and successful minority young adult, age 16-35 in various vocational or technical careers). Buys 15 mss/year. Send complete ms. Length: 500-1,500. Pays $50-250.

Fiction: Adventure, ethnic, historical, humorous, mainstream, slice-of-life vignettes. Buys 3 mss/year. Send complete ms. Length: 1,000-5,000 words. Pays $100-400.

Poetry: Free verse. Buys 5 poems/year. Submit up to 5 poems at one time. Length: 10-25 lines. Pays $10-50.

Fillers: Anecdotes, facts, gags to be illustrated by cartoonist, newsbreaks, short humor. Buys 10/year. Length: 25-250 words. Pays $25-100.

Tips: For new writers—Send complete manuscript that is double spaced; clean copy only. If available, send clippings of previous published works and resume. Should state when available to write. Include on first page your name, address, phone, Social Security number and number of words in article.

FLORIDA LEADER, P.O. Box 14081, Gainesville FL 32604. (904)373-6907. Publisher: W.H. "Butch" Oxendine, Jr. Editor: Patricia Sprott. Nearly 80% freelance written. "Florida's college magazine, feature oriented, especially activities, events, interests and issues pertaining to college students." Published 6 times/year. Estab. 1981. Circ. 28,000. Publishes ms an average of 2 months after acceptance. Byline given. Submit seasonal/holiday material 6 months in advance. Query for electronic submissions. Reports in 1 month on queries. Sample copy and writer's guidelines for 9 × 12 SAE with 5 first class stamps.

Nonfiction: How-to, humor, interview/profile, and feature—all Florida college related. Special issues include careers and majors (January and June) and high school edition (August and January). Query. Length: 500 words or less. Payment varies. Sometimes pays expenses of writers on assignment.

Photos: State availability of photos with submission. Reviews negatives and transparencies. Captions, model releases and identification of subjects requested.

FORDHAM MAGAZINE, Fordham University, 113 West 60th St., Suite 313, New York NY 10023. (212)841-5360. FAX: (212)765-2976. Editor: Michael Gates. 50% freelance written. A quarterly magazine on Fordham University and its alumni. "We are heavy on feature and personality profiles on our alumni: e.g. actor Denzel Washington, author Mary Higgins Clark, and how education influenced their careers." **Pays on acceptance.** Publishes ms an average of 8 months after acceptance. Byline given. Offers $25 kill fee. Makes work-for-hire assignments. Submit seasonal/holiday material 10 months in advance. Previously published submissions OK. Reports in 1 month on queries; 2 months on mss. Free writer's guidelines for SAE and 2 first class stamps.

Nonfiction: Book excerpts, essays, historical/nostalgic, humor, inspirational, interview/profile (alumni, faculty, students); photo feature. All must be specific to Forham University or its alumni. Buys 12 mss/year. Query with published clips. Length: 1,00-2,500. Pays $500-1,250 for assigned articles; $50-500 for unsolicited articles. Sometimes pays expenses of writers on assignment.

Photos: State availability of photos with submission. Reviews contact sheets, transparencies, prints. Offers additional payment for photos accepted with ms. Model releases and identification of subjects required.

Fillers: Anecdotes, facts, newsbreaks, short humor. "All must be specific to Fordham University." Buys 1-2/year. Length: 150-350 words. Pays $25-50.

Tips: "Have a good familiarity with alumni publications in general: research some of the schools and see what they use, what they look for. Research alumni of the school and see if there is a noted personality you might interview—someone who might live in your area. Be prepared to narrow the proposed idea down to the publication's very specific needs. Feature articles and personality profiles are most open to freelancers. These include interviews with famous or interesting alumni and faculty or students, as well as in-depth analytical articles on trends in university life today (pertinent to Fordham) and features on student life in New York. This includes articles on ways that our school interacts with the community around it."

JOURNEY, A Success Guide for College and Career Bound Students, Communications Publishing Group, 3100 Broadway, 225 PennTower, Kansas City MO 64111. (816)756-3039. FAX: (816)756-3018. Editor: Georgia Clark. 40% freelance written. A bi-annual educational and career source guide for Asian-American high school and college students who have indicated a desire to pursue higher education through college, vocational and technical or proprietary schools. For students ages 16-25. Estab. 1982. Circ. 200,000. Pays on publication. Byline sometimes given. Buys second serial (reprint) rights or makes work-for-hire assignments. Submit seasonal/holiday material 6 months in advance. Simultaneous and previously published submissions OK. Reports in 2 months. Sample copy for 9 × 12 SASE with 4 first class stamps. Writer's guidelines for #10 SASE.

Nonfiction: Book excerpts or reviews, general interest, how-to (dealing with careers or education), humor, inspirational, interview/profile (celebrity or "up and coming" young adult), new product (as it relates to young adult market), personal experience, photo feature, technical, travel and sports. First time writers with *Journey* must submit complete manuscript for consideration. Length: 750-2,000 words. Pays $150-400 for assigned articles; 10¢/word for unsolicited articles. Sometimes pays expenses of writers on assignment.

Photos: State availability of photos with submission. Prefers transparencies. Offers $20-25/photo. Captions, model releases and identification of subjects required. Buys all rights or one-time rights.

Columns/Departments: Profiles of Achievement (striving and successful minority young adult, age 16-35 in various careers). Buys 15 mss/year. Send complete ms. Length: 500-1,500. Pays $50-200.

Fiction: Adventure, ethnic, historical, humorous, mainstream, slice-of-life vignettes. Buys 3 mss/year. Send complete ms. Length: 1,000-3,000 words. Pays $100-400.

Poetry: Free verse. Buys 5/year. Submit up to 5 poems at one time. Length: 10-25 lines. Pays $10-50.

Fillers: Anecdotes, facts, gags to be illustrated by cartoonist, newsbreaks, short humor. Buys 10/year. Length: 25-250 words. Pays $25-100.

Tips: For new writers—Must submit complete manuscript that is double spaced; clean copy only. If available, send clippings of previous published works and resume. Should state when available to write. Include on first page your name, address, phone, Social Security number and number of words in article.

NOTRE DAME MAGAZINE, University of Notre Dame, Room 415, Administration Bldg., Notre Dame IN 46556. (219)239-5335. FAX: (219)239-6947. Editor: Walton R. Collins. Managing Editor: Kerry Temple. 75% freelance written. Quarterly magazine covering news of Notre Dame and education and issues affecting the Roman Catholic Church. "We are interested in the moral, ethical and spiritual issues of the day and how Christians live in today's world. We are universal in scope and Catholic in viewpoint and serve Notre Dame alumni, friends and other constituencies." Estab. 1972. Circ. 110,000. **Pays on acceptance.** Publishes ms an average of 1 year after acceptance. Byline given. Kill fee negotiable. Buys first rights. Simultaneous queries OK. Query for electronic submissions. Computer printout submissions acceptable; prefers letter-quality. Reports in 1 month. Free sample copy.

Nonfiction: Opinion, personal experience, religion. "All articles must be of interest to Christian/Catholic readers who are well educated and active in their communities." Buys 35 mss/year. Query with clips of published work. Length: 600-3,000 words. Pays $500-1,500. Sometimes pays the expenses of writers on assignment.

Photos: State availability of photos. Reviews b&w contact sheets, transparencies, and 8 × 10 prints. Model releases and identification of subjects required. Buys one-time rights.

OLD OREGON, The Magazine of the University of Oregon, University of Oregon, 101 Chapman Hall, Eugene OR 97403. (503)346-5047. FAX: (503)346-2537. Editor: Tom Hager. 50% freelance written. A quarterly university magazine of people and ideas at the University of Oregon. Estab. 1919. Circ. 90,000. Pays on publication. Publishes ms an average of 3 months after acceptance. Byline given.

Offers 33% kill fee. Buys first North American serial rights. Query for electronic submissions. Reports in 3 weeks. Sample copy for 9×12 SAE with 2 first class stamps.
Nonfiction: Historical/nostalgic, interview/profile, personal experience relating to U.O. issues and alumni. Buys 30 mss/year. Query with published clips. Length: 750-3,000 words. Pays $75-300. Sometimes pays expenses of writers on assignment.
Photos: State availability of photos with submission. Reviews 8×10 prints. Offers $10-25/photo. Identification of subjects required. Buys one-time rights.
Tips: "Query with strong, colorful lead; clips."

PICTURE PERFECT, (formerly *IFMT Magazine*), International Fashion Model & Talent, Aquino Productions, Inc., Suite 206, 159 Main St., P.O. Box 15760, Stamford CT 06901. (203)967-2512. Editor: Elaine Hallgren. Managing Editor: Andres Aquino. 50% freelance written. Bimonthly magazine covering fashion, photography, modeling, entertainment. Estab. 1989. Circ. 140,000. Pays on publication. Publishes ms an average of 3 months after acceptance. Offers 50% kill fee. Buys first North American serial rights or all rights. Submit seasonal/holiday material 4 months in advance. Simultaneous submissions OK. Reports in 3 weeks on queries; 6 weeks on mss. Sample copy $4. Writer's guidelines for SAE and 2 first class stamps.
Nonfiction: Book excerpts, how-to, interview/profile, new product, personal experience, photo feature and travel. Buys 36-48 mss/year. Send complete ms. Length 250-1,500 words. Pays 20¢/word for assigned articles; 15¢/word for unsolicited articles. Sometimes pays expenses of writers on assignment.
Photos: Send photos with submission. Reviews contact sheets, 2×2 transparencies and 4×6 prints. Offers $25-200 per photo. Captions, model releases and identification of subjects required. Buys one-time rights or First North American Rights.

‡THE PURDUE ALUMNUS, Purdue Alumni Association, Purdue Memorial Union 160, West Lafayette IN 47907. (317)494-5184. FAX: (317)494-9179. Editor: Gay L. Totten. 30% freelance written. Prefers to work with published/established writers; works with small number of new/unpublished writers each year. Magazine published 9 times/year (except February, June, August) covering subjects of interest to Purdue University alumni. Estab. 1912. Circ. 72,000. Pays on publication. Publishes ms an average of 2 months after acceptance. Byline given. Buys first rights and makes work-for-hire assignments. Submit seasonal/holiday material 3 months in advance. Simultaneous queries, and simultaneous and previously published submissions OK. Reports in 1 week on queries; 2 weeks on mss. Sample copy for 8½×11 SAE and 2 first class stamps.
Nonfiction: Book excerpts, general interest, historical/nostalgic, humor, interview/profile, personal experience. Focus is on campus news, issues, opinions of interest to 72,000 members of the Alumni Association. Feature style, primarily university-oriented. Issues relevant to education. Buys 12-20 mss/year. Length: 1,500-2,500 words. Pays $25-250. Sometimes pays expenses of writers on assignment.
Photos: State availability of photos. Reviews b&w contact sheet or 5×7 prints.
Tips: "We are still aiming to be more broadly issue-focused, moving away from the rah-rah type of traditional alumni magazine article. We are interested in issues of concern to educated people, with a university perspective. We want carefully researched, in-depth material, and would prefer, if at all possible, that it somehow include a Purdue authority, alumnus, or citation. For instance, in a recent article on Nicaragua, we cited some 25 sources for information, two were Purdue-related."

RIPON COLLEGE MAGAZINE, P.O. Box 248, Ripon WI 54971. (414)748-8115. Editor: Loren J. Boone. 15% freelance written. "*Ripon College Magazine* is a quarterly publication that contains information relating to Ripon College. It is mailed to alumni and friends of the college." Estab. 1851. Circ. 13,000. Pays on publication. Publishes ms an average of 3 months after acceptance. Byline given. Not copyrighted. Makes work-for-hire assignments. Query for electronic submissions. Reports in 2 weeks.
Nonfiction: Historical/nostalgic and interview/profile. Buys 4 mss/year. Query with or without published clips, or send complete ms. Length: 250-1,000 words. Pays $25-350.
Photos: State availability of photos with submission. Reviews contact sheets. Offers no additional payment for photos accepted with ms. Captions and model releases are required. Buys one-time rights.
Tips: "Story ideas must have a direct connection to Ripon College."

‡RUTGERS MAGAZINE, Rutgers University, Alexander Johnston Hall, New Brunswick NJ 08903. (908)932-7315. Executive Editor: Patrick Sarver. 50% freelance written. Quarterly university magazine of "general interest, but articles must have a Rutgers tie-in." Circ. 137,000. **Pays on acceptance.** Publishes ms an average of 4 months after acceptance. Byline given. Pays 30-35% kill fee. Buys first North American serial rights. Submit seasonal/holiday material 6-8 months in advance. Query for electronic submissions. Reports in 1 month. Sample copy $3 with 9×12 SAE and 5 first class stamps.
Nonfiction: Book excerpts, essays, general interest, historical/nostalgic, humor, interview/profile, personal experience, photo feature. No articles without a Rutgers connection. Buys 15-20 mss/year. Query with published clips. Pays 25-40¢/word. Pays expenses of writers on assignment.

Photos: State availability of photos with submission. Payment varies. Identification of subjects required. Buys one-time rights.

Columns/Departments: Business (related to Rutgers), 1,600-1,800 words. Buys 4-6 mss/year. Query with published clips. Length: 1,500-2,000 words. Pays 25-40¢/word.

Tips: "Send ideas. We'll evaluate clips and topic for most appropriate use."

SCORECARD, Falsoft, Inc., 9509 US Highway 42, P.O. Box 385, Prospect KY 40059. (502)228-4492. FAX: (502)228-5121. Editor: John Crawley. 50% freelance written. Prefers to work with published/established writers. A weekly sports fan tabloid covering University of Louisville sports only. Estab. 1982. Circ. 7,500. Pays on publication. Publishes ms an average of 1 month after acceptance. Byline given. Buys first rights. Submit seasonal/holiday material 1 month in advance. Previously published submissions OK "rarely." Reports in 2 weeks. Free sample copy and writer's guidelines.

Nonfiction: Assigned to contributing editors. Buys 100 mss/year. Query with published clips. Length: 750-1,500 words. Pays $20-50. Sometimes pays expenses of writers on assignment.

Photos: State availability of photos.

Columns/Departments: Notes Page (tidbits relevant to University of Louisville sports program or former players or teams). Buys 25 mss/year. Length: Approximately 100 words. Pay undetermined.

Tips: "Be very familiar with history and tradition of University of Louisville sports program. Contact us with story ideas. Know the subject."

‡SHIPMATE, U.S. Naval Academy Alumni Association Magazine, Alumni House, Annapolis MD 21402. (301)263-4469. Editor: Col. J.W. Hammond, Jr., USMC (retired). 100% freelance written. A magazine published 10 times a year by and for alumni of the U.S. Naval Academy. Estab. 1938. Circ. 34,000. Pays on publication. Byline given. Buys first North American serial rights. Submit seasonal/holiday material 10 months in advance. Reports in 1 week. Sample copy for 8½×11 SAE and 6 first class stamps.

Nonfiction: Buys 50 mss/year. Send complete ms. Length: 2,000-7,500 words. Pays $100 for unsolicited articles.

Photos: Send photos with submission. Offers no additional payment for photos accepted with ms. Identification of subjects required. Buys one-time rights.

Tips: "The writer should be a Naval Academy alumnus (not necessarily a graduate) with first-hand experience of events in the Naval Service."

THE STUDENT, 127 9th Ave. N., Nashville TN 37234. FAX: (615)251-3953. Editor: Milt Hughes. 10% freelance written. Works with a small number of new/unpublished writers each year. Publication of Student Ministry Department of the Southern Baptist Convention. For college students; focusing on freshman and sophomore levels. Published 12 times during the school year. Estab. 1922. Circ. 45,000. Buys all rights. **Payment on acceptance.** Publishes ms an average of 10 months after acceptance. Mss should be double-spaced on white paper with 50-space line, 25 lines/page. Reports usually in 6 weeks. Sample copy and guidelines for 8×10 SAE.

Nonfiction: Contemporary questions, problems, and issues facing college students viewed from a Christian perspective to develop high moral and ethical values. Cultivating interpersonal relationships, developing self-esteem, dealing with the academic struggle, coping with rejection, learning how to love, developing a personal relationship with Jesus Christ. Prefers complete ms rather than query. Length: 1,000 words maximum. Pays 5½¢/word after editing with reserved right to edit accepted material. Extra payment for use of computer diskette.

Fiction: Satire and parody on college life, humorous episodes; emphasize clean fun and the ability to grow and be uplifted through humor. Contemporary fiction involving student life, on campus as well as off. Length: 900 words. Pays 5½¢/word.

‡VISIONS, A Success Guide for Native American Students, Communications Publishing Group, 3100 Broadway, 225 Penntower, Kansas City MO 64111. (816)756-3039. Editor: Georgia Clark. 40% freelance written. A bi-annual education and career source guide designed for Native American students who want to pursue a higher education through colleges, vocational and technical schools, or proprietary schools, to focus on insight, motivational and career planning informations. For young adults, ages 16-25. Circ. 100,000. Pays on publication. Byline sometimes given. Buys second serial (reprint) rights or makes work-for-hire assignments. Submit seasonal/holiday material 6 months in advance. Simultaneous, photocopied and previously published submissions OK. Reports in 2 months. Sample copy for 9x10 SASE with 4 first class stamps; writer's guidelines for #10 SASE.

Nonfiction: Book excerpts or reviews, general interest, how-to, humor, inspirational, interview/profile, new product, personal experience, photo feature, technical, travel and sports. Query or send complete ms. Length: 750-2,000 words. Pays $150-400 for assigned articles; 10¢/word for unsolicited articles. Sometimes pays expenses of writers on assignment.

Photos: State availability of photos with submission. Reviews transparencies. Offers $20-25/photo. Captions, model releases, and identification of subjects required. Buys all rights.

Columns/Departments: Profiles of Achievement (striving and successful Native American young adults, age 16-35, in various careers). Length: 500-1,500 words. Buys 15 mss/year. Send complete ms. Pays $50-250.

Fiction: Adventure, ethnic, historical, humorous, mainstream, slice-of-life vignettes. Buys 3 mss/year. Send complete ms. Length: 1,000-5,000 words. Pays $100-400.

Poetry: Free verse. Buys 5 poems/year. Submit up to 5 poems at one time. Length: 10-25 lines. Pays $10-50.

Fillers: Anecdotes, facts, gags to be illustrated by cartoonist, newsbreaks, short humor. Buys 10 fillers/year. Length: 25-250 words. Pays $25-100.

Tips: For new writers—Submit complete manuscript that is double spaced; clean copy only. If available, send clippings of previous published works and resume. Should state when available to write. Include on first page of manuscript your name, address, phone, Social Security number and number of words in article.

WPI JOURNAL, Worcester Polytechnic Institute, 100 Institute Rd., Worcester MA 01609. FAX: (508)831-5483. Editor: Michael Dorsey. 20% freelance written. A quarterly alumni magazine covering science and engineering/education/business personalities for 19,000 alumni, primarily engineers, scientists, managers, parents of students, national media. Estab. 1897. Circ. 22,500. Pays on publication. Publishes ms an average of 6 months after acceptance. Byline given. Buys one-time rights. Submit seasonal/holiday material 6 months in advance. Simultaneous queries, and simultaneous and previously published submissions OK. Query for electronic submissions. Requires hard copy also. Reports in 1 month on queries.

Nonfiction: Book excerpts; general interest; historical/nostalgic; interview/profile (people in engineering, science); photo feature; and technical (with personal orientation). Query with published clips. Length: 1,000-4,000 words. Pays negotiable rate. Sometimes pays the expenses of writers on assignment.

Photos: State availability of photos with query or ms. Reviews b&w contact sheets. Pays negotiable rate. Captions required.

Tips: "Submit outline of story and/or ms of story idea or published work. Features are most open to freelancers. Keep in mind that this is an alumni magazine, so most articles focus on the college and its community."

Child Care and Parental Guidance

Readers of today's parenting magazines are starting families later and having fewer children but they want more information on pregnancy, infancy, child development and parenting research. Child care magazines address these and other issues from many different perspectives: Some are general interest parenting magazines while others for child care providers combine care information with business tips. Other markets that buy articles about child care and the family are included in the Education, Religious and Women's sections.

AMERICAN BABY MAGAZINE, For Expectant and New Parents, 475 Park Ave. S., New York NY 10016. (212)689-3600. Editor: Judith Nolte. 90% freelance written. Prefers to work with published/established writers; works with a small number of new/unpublished writers each year. A monthly magazine covering pregnancy, child care and parenting. "Our readership is composed of women in late pregnancy and early new motherhood. Most readers are first-time parents; some have older children. A simple, straightforward, clear approach is mandatory." Estab. 1938. Circ. 1,150,000. **Pays on acceptance.** Publishes ms an average of 6 months after acceptance. Byline given. Buys first North American serial rights. Submit seasonal holiday material 6 months in advance. Simultaneous and previously published submissions OK. Reports in 4 weeks on queries; 2 months on mss. Sample copy for 9×12 SAE with 6 first class stamps. Writer's guidelines for SASE.

Nonfiction: Book excerpts, how-to (on some aspect of pregnancy or child care), humor and personal experience. "No 'hearts and flowers' or fantasy pieces." Buys 60 mss/year. Query with published clips, or send complete ms. Length: 1,500-2,500 words. Pays $350-1,000 for assigned articles; pays $300-500 for unsolicited articles. Pays the expenses of writers on assignment.

Photos: State availability of photos with submission. Reviews transparencies and prints. Model release and identification of subjects required. Buys one-time rights.

Columns/Departments: My Own Experience (an opinion or personal experience essay on some aspect of pregnancy, birth or parenting), 1,000 words. Buys 12 mss/year. Send complete ms.

Tips: "Articles should either give 'how to' information on some aspect of pregnancy or child care, cover some common problem of child raising, along with solutions, or give advice to the mother on some psychological or practical subject."

CHRISTIAN PARENTING TODAY, Good Family Magazines, P.O. Box 3850, 548 Sisters Parkway, Sisters OR 97759. (503)549-8261. Editor: David Kopp. Managing Editor: Kathleen Stephens. 50% freelance written. Bimonthly magazine covering parenting today's children. "*Christian Parenting Today* is a positive, practical magazine that targets real needs of the contemporary family with authoritative articles based on fresh research and the timeless truths of the Bible. *CPT*'s readers represent the broad spectrum of Christians who seek intelligent answers to the new demands of parenting in the 90s." Estab. 1988. Circ. 200,000. **Pays on acceptance.** Byline given. Buys first North American serial or second serial (reprint) rights. Submit seasonal/holiday material 6 months in advance. Query for electronic submissions. Reports in 2 months. Sample copy for 8×11 SAE with 5 first class stamps. Free writer's guidelines.

Nonfiction: Book excerpts, how-to, humor, inspirational and religious. Buys 50 mss/year. Query. Length: 750-2,000 words. Pays $175-500 for assigned articles; $115-300 for unsolicited articles. Sometimes pays expenses of writers on assignment.

Photos: State availability of photos with submission. Reviews transparencies. Model release required. Buys one-time rights.

Columns/Departments: Parent Exchange (family-tested parenting ideas from our readers), 25-100 words; Life In Our House (entertaining, true, humorous stories about your family), 25-100 words. Buys 120 mss/year. Send complete ms. Pays $25-40.

Poetry: Free verse. Buys 3/year. Pays $25 minimum.

Fillers: Anecdotes and short humor. Buys 75/year. Length: 25-750 words. Pays $25-175.

Tips: "Our readers are active evangelical Christians from the broad spectrum of Protestant and Roman Catholic traditions. We are *not* interested in advocating any denominational bias. Our readers want authority, conciseness, problem-solving, entertainment, encouragement and surprise. They also require a clear biblical basis for advice."

‡EXPECTING, Gruner + Jahr USA Publishing, 685 Third Ave., New York NY 10017. Editor: Evelyn Podsiadlo. 80% freelance written. Quarterly magazine covering pregnancy, birth and the newborn. "*Expecting* covers subjects that are of interest to expectant and new parents. Articles must be authoritative and reassuring." Estab. 1967. Circ. 1,250,000 per quarter. **Pays on acceptance.** Byline given. No kill fee. Buys one-time rights. Submit seasonal/holiday material 6 months in advance. Reports in 1-2 months. Writer's guidelines for 4×9" SAE with 29¢ postage.

Nonfiction: Book excerpts, humor, personal experience, health, nutrition, and financial subjects related to pregnancy, birth, and the newborn. "No essays or inspirational pieces." Buys 32 to 40 mss/year. Query with published clips. Length: 1,000-2,500 words. Pays $400-750 for assigned articles. Pays $300-600 for unsolicited articles.

Columns/Departments: Happenings (short, humorous anecdotes related to pregnancy, birth, or new parenthood), 50-100 words; Your Turn (personal experience related to pregnancy, birth, or new parenthood), 500-750 words. Buys 12-16 for Happenings; 2-3 for Your Turn. Send complete ms. "Happenings pays $25 on publication and manuscripts are not returned. Your Turn pays $250 on acceptance and manuscripts are returned."

Tips: "Much of the information in *Expecting* is health-related, so we prefer experienced health writers or writers who work well with doctors, nurses and other health professionals. Expertise in the areas of pregnancy, birth, and the newborn is also a plus. All areas of substance are open to freelancers. Articles must be authoritative."

GROWING PARENT, Dunn & Hargitt, Inc., 22 N. 2nd St., P.O. Box 620, Lafayette IN 47902. (317)423-2624. FAX: (317)423-4495. Editor: Nancy Kleckner. 40-50% freelance written. Works with a small number of new/unpublished writers each year. "We do receive a lot of unsolicited submissions but have had excellent results in working with some unpublished writers. So, we're always happy to look at material and hope to find one or two jewels each year." A monthly newsletter which focuses on parents—the issues, problems, and choices they face as their children grow. "We want to look at the parent as an adult and help encourage his or her growth not only as a parent but as an individual."

For information on setting your freelance fees, see How Much Should I Charge? in the Business of Writing section.

Estab. 1967. **Pays on acceptance.** Publishes ms an average of 6 months after acceptance. Byline given. Buys first North American serial rights; maintains exclusive rights for three months. Submit seasonal/holiday material 6 months in advance. Previously published submissions OK. Reports in 2 weeks. Sample copy and writer's guidelines for 5×8 SAE with 2 first class stamps.

Nonfiction: "We are looking for informational articles written in an easy-to-read, concise style. We would like to see articles that help parents deal with the stresses they face in everyday life—positive, upbeat, how-to-cope suggestions. We rarely use humorous pieces, fiction or personal experience articles. Writers should keep in mind that most of our readers have children under three years of age." Buys 15-20 mss/year. Query. Length: 1,500-2,000 words; will look at shorter pieces. Pays 8-10¢/word (depends on article).

Tips: "Submit a very specific query letter with samples."

HEALTHY KIDS: BIRTH-3/HEALTHY KIDS: 4-10, Cahners Publishing, 475 Park Ave. S., New York NY 10016. (212)689-3600. FAX: (212)779-5790. Editor: Phyllis Steinberg. 90% freelance written. Birth-3 published 4 times/year; 4-10 published 3 times/year. Both magazines cover children's health. Estab. 1989/1990. Circ. 1.5 million/2 million. **Pays on acceptance.** Byline given. Buys first rights. Submit seasonal/holiday material 6 months in advance. Reports in 1 month on queries. Free sample copy and writer's guidelines for SASE.

Nonfiction: How-to help your child develop as a person, keep safe, keep healthy, and personal experience. No poetry, fiction, travel or product endorsement. Buys 30 mss/year. Query. Length: 1,500-2,000 words. Pays $500-1,000. Pays expenses of writers on assignment.

Columns/Departments: Buys 30 mss/year. Query. Length: 1,500-2,000 words. Pays $500-1,000.

HOME EDUCATION MAGAZINE, P.O. Box 1083, Tonasket WA 98855. Editors: Mark J. Hegener and Helen E. Hegener. 80% freelance written. Eager to work with new/unpublished writers each year. A bimonthly magazine covering home-based education. "We feature articles which address the concerns of parents who want to take a direct involvement in the education of their children—concerns such as socialization, how to find curriculums and materials, testing and evaluation, how to tell when your child is ready to begin reading, what to do when home schooling is difficult, teaching advanced subjects, etc." Estab. 1983. Circ. 5,500. Pays on publication. Publishes ms an average of 6 months after acceptance. Byline given. ("Please include a 30-50 word credit with your article.") Buys first North American serial rights, first rights, one-time rights, second serial (reprint) rights, simultaneous rights, all rights, and makes work-for-hire assignments. Submit seasonal/holiday material 6 months in advance. Simultaneous and previously published submissions OK. Query for electronic submission requirements. Reports in 2 months. Sample copy $4.50; writer's guidelines for #10 SASE.

Nonfiction: Book excerpts, essays, how-to (related to home schooling), humor, inspirational, interview/profile, personal experience, photo feature and technical. Buys 40-50 mss/year. Query with or without published clips, or send complete ms. Length: 750-3,500 words. Pays $10 per final typeset page, (about 750 words). Sometimes pays expenses of writers on assignment.

Photos: Send photos with submission. Reviews 5×7, 35mm prints and b&w snapshots. Write for photo rates. Identification of subjects required. Buys one-time rights.

Tips: "We would like to see how-to articles (that don't preach, just present options); articles on testing, accountability, working with the public schools, socialization, learning disabilities, resources, support groups, legislation and humor. We need answers to the questions that home schoolers ask."

HOME LIFE, Sunday School Board, 127 9th Ave. N., Nashville TN 37234. (615)251-2271. Editor-in-Chief: Charlie Warren. 60-70% freelance written. Prefers to work with published/established writers; eager to work with new/unpublished writers. Emphasizes Christian marriage and Christian family life. For married adults of all ages, but especially newlyweds and middle-aged marrieds. Monthly magazine. Estab. 1947. Circ. 680,000. **Pays on acceptance.** Publishes ms an average of 15 months after acceptance. Buys first rights, first North American serial rights and all rights. Byline given. Phone queries OK, but written queries preferred. Submit seasonal/holiday material 1 year in advance. Reports in 6 weeks. Sample copy $1; writer's guidelines for #10 SASE.

Nonfiction: How-to (good articles on marriage and family life); informational (about some current family-related issue of national significance such as "Television and the Christian Family" or "Whatever Happened to Family Worship?"); personal experience (informed articles by people who have solved marriage and family problems in healthy, constructive ways). "No column material. We are not interested in material that will not in some way enrich Christian marriage or family life." Buys 150-200 mss/year. Query or submit complete ms. Length: 600-1,800 words. Pays up to 5½¢/word.

Fiction: "Fiction should be family-related and should show a strong moral about how families face and solve problems constructively." Buys 12-20 mss/year. Submit complete ms. Length: 600-1,800 words. Pays up to 5½¢/word.

Tips: "Study the magazine to see our unique slant on Christian family life. We prefer a life-centered case study approach, rather than theoretical essays on family life. Our top priority is marriage enrichment material."

L.A. PARENT, The Magazine for Parents in Southern California, P.O. Box 3204, Burbank CA 91504. (818)846-0400. FAX: (818)841-4380. Editor: Jack Bierman. 80% freelance written. Prefers to work with published/established writers, and works with a small number of new/unpublished writers each year. Monthly tabloid covering parenting. Estab. 1980. Circ. 120,000. Pays on publication. Publishes ms an average of 4 months after acceptance. Byline given. Buys first rights and reprint rights. Submit seasonal/holiday material 3 months in advance. Simultaneous queries and previously published submissions OK. Query for electronic submissions. Reports in 1 month. Sample copy and writer's guidelines for $2.

Nonfiction: David Jameison, articles editor. General interest, how-to. "We focus on generic parenting for ages 0-10 and southern California activities for families, and do round-up pieces, i.e., a guide to private schools, fishing spots." Buys 60-75 mss/year. Query with clips of published work. Length: 700-1,200 words. Pays $200 plus expenses.

Tips: "We will be using more contemporary articles on parenting's challenges. If you can write for a 'city magazine' in tone and accuracy, you may write for us. The 'Baby Boom' has created a need for more generic parenting material."

LIVING WITH CHILDREN, Baptist Sunday School Board, 127 9th Ave. N., Nashville TN 37234. (615)251-2229. Editor: Phillip H. Waugh. 50% freelance written. Works with a small number of new/unpublished writers each year. Quarterly magazine covering parenting issues for parents of elementary-age children (ages 6 through 11). "Written and designed from a Christian perspective." Estab. 1892. Circ. 50,000. **Pays on acceptance.** Publishes ms an average of 2 years after acceptance. Byline given. "We generally buy all rights to mss; first serial rights on a limited basis. First and reprint rights may be negotiated at a lower rate of pay." Submit seasonal/holiday material 1 year in advance. Previously published submissions (on limited basis) OK. Reports in 1 month on queries; 2 months on mss. Sample copy for 9 × 12 SASE; free writer's guidelines.

Nonfiction: How-to (parent), humor, inspirational, personal experience, and articles on child development. No highly technical material or articles containing more than 15-20 lines quoted material. Buys 60 mss/year. Query or send complete ms (queries preferred). Length: 800-1,450 words. Pays 5½¢/word.

Photos: "Submission of photos with mss is strongly discouraged."

Fiction: Humorous (parent/child relationships); and religious. "We have very limited need for fiction." Buys maximum of 4 mss/year. Length: 800-1,450 words. Pays 5½¢/word.

Poetry: Light verse and inspirational. "We have limited need for poetry and buy only all rights." Buys 15 poems/year. Submit maximum 3 poems. Length: 4-30 lines. Pays $1.75 for 1-7 lines, plus $1.25 for each additional line; pays $5.40 for 8 lines or more plus 75¢ each additional line with $24 maximum.

Fillers: Jokes, anecdotes and short humor. Buys 15/year. Length: 100-400 words. Pays $5 minimum, 5½¢/word.

Tips: "Articles must deal with an issue of interest to parents. A mistake some writers make in articles for us is failing to write from a uniquely Christian perspective; that is very necessary for our periodicals. Material should be 850 or 1,450 in length. All sections, particularly articles, are open to freelance writers. Only regular features are assigned."

LIVING WITH PRESCHOOLERS, Baptist Sunday School Board, 127 9th Ave. N., Nashville TN 37234. (615)251-2229. Editor: Phillip H. Waugh. 50% freelance written. Works with a small number of new/unpublished writers each year. Quarterly magazine covering parenting issues for parents of preschoolers (infants through 5-year-olds). The magazine is "written and designed from a Christian perspective." Estab. 1892. Circ. 152,000. **Pays on acceptance.** Publishes manuscript an average of 2 years after acceptance. Byline given. "We generally buy all rights to manuscripts. First and reprint rights may be negotiated at a lower rate of pay." Submit seasonal/holiday material 2 years in advance. Previously published submissions (on limited basis) OK. Reports in 1 month on queries; 2 months on mss. Sample copy for 9 × 12 SASE; free writer's guidelines.

Nonfiction: How-to (parent), humor, inspirational, personal experience and articles on child development. No highly technical material or articles containing more than 15-20 lines quoted material. Buys 60 mss/year. Query or send complete ms (queries preferred). Length: 800-1,450 words. Pays 5½¢/word for manuscripts offered on all-rights basis.

Photos: "Submission of photos with mss is strongly discouraged."
Fiction: Humorous (parent/child relationships); and religious. "We have very limited need for fiction." Buys maximum of 4 mss/year. Length: 800-1,450 words. Pays 5½¢/word.
Poetry: Light verse and inspirational. "We have limited need for poetry and buy only all rights." Buys 15 poems/year. Submit maximum 3 poems. Length: 4-30 lines. Pays $2.10 for 1-7 lines, plus $1.25 for each additional line; pays $5.40 for 8 lines or more plus 75¢ each additional line with $24 maximum.
Fillers: Jokes, anecdotes or short humor. Buys 15/year. Length: 100-400 words. Pays $5 minimum, 5½¢/word maximum.

Tips: "Articles must deal with an issue of interest to parents. A mistake some writers make in writing an article for us is failing to write from a uniquely Christian perspective; that is very necessary for our periodicals. Material should be 850 or 1,450 words in length. All sections, particularly articles, are open to freelance writers. Only regular features are assigned."

‡**LONG ISLAND PARENTING NEWS**, RDM Publishing, P.O. Box 214, 4584 Austin Blvd., Island Park NY 11558. (516)889-5510. FAX: (516)889-5513. Editor: Pat Simms-Elias. Managing Editor: Andrew Elias. 70% freelance written. Free community newspaper published monthly covering parenting, children and family issues. "A publication for concerned parents with active families and young children. Our slogan is: 'For parents who care to know.'" Estab. 1989. Circ. 40,000. Pays on publication. Publishes ms an average of 1-3 months after acceptance. Byline given. (Also 1-3 line bio, if appropriate.) No kill fee. Buys one-time rights. Simultaneous and previously published submissions OK. Reports in 2 months. Sample copy $3. Free writer's guidelines.
Nonfiction: Book excerpts, essays, general interest, humor, interview/profile, travel, other. Will need articles covering childcare, childbirth/maternity, schools and camps and back-to-school. Buys 20-30 mss/year. Query with or without published clips, or send complete ms. Length: 350-2,000 words. Pays $25-150. "Sometimes trade article for advertising space." Sometimes pays expenses of writers on assignment.
Photos: Send photos with submission. Reviews 4 × 5 prints. Offers $5-50 per photo. Captions required. Buys one-time rights.
Columns/Departments: Off The Shelf (book reviews); Toy Report (toy reviews and game reviews); KidVid (reviews of kids' video); The Beat (reviews of kids' music); Monitor (reviews of computer hardware and software for kids); Big Screen (reviews of kids' films). Buys 20-30 mss/year. Send complete ms. Length: 500-1,000 words. Pays 25-150.
Fiction: Stories for children. Buys 1-4 mss/year. Send complete ms. Length: 500-2,000 words. Pays $25-150.
Fillers: Facts and newsbreaks. Buys 10-20/year. Length: 200-500. Pays $10-25.

PARENTING MAGAZINE, 501 Second St., #110, San Francisco CA 94107. (415)546-7575. Executive Editor: Lornora Weiner. Managing Editor: Bruce Raskin. Editor: David Markus. Magazine published 10 times/year. "Edited for parents of children from birth to ten years old, with the most emphasis put on the under-sixes." Estab. 1987. **Pays on acceptance.** Byline given. Offers 25% kill fee. Buys first rights. Query for electronic submissions. Reports in 6 weeks to 3 months. Sample copy $1.95 with 9 × 12 SAE and $1.20 postage. Writer's guidelines for SASE.
Nonfiction: Rachel Grossman, articles editor. Book excerpts, humor, investigative reports, personal experience and photo feature. Buys 20-30 mss/year. Query with or without published clips, or send complete ms. Length: 1,000-3,500 words. Pays $500-2,000. Sometimes pays expenses of writers on assignment.
Columns/Departments: Extra (news items relating to children/family), 100-400 words; Care and Feeding (health, nutrition, new products and service stories), 100-500 words; Passages (parental rites of passage), 850 words; Up in Arms (opinion, 850 words. Buys 50-60 mss/year. Pays $50-350.

PARENTS CARE, PARENTS COUNT NEWSLETTER, P.O. Box 1563, 44321 Calston Ave., Lancaster CA 93539. (805)945-2360. Editor: Marilyn Anita Dalrymple. 100% freelance written. Bimonthly newsletter for parents of addictive or disruptive children. "Writing must be done with empathy towards parents. No 'it's your fault' aimed at parent *or* child. Articles must contain message of 'I was there, and I survived,' or 'This helped me . . . .' **Pays on acceptance.** Byline given. Buys one-time rights. Submit seasonal/holiday material 4 months in advance. Simultaneous and previously published submissions OK. Reports in 2 weeks. Sample copy $1.25. Writer's guidelines for #10 SAE with 1 first class stamp.
Nonfiction: Humor, inspirational, personal experience and news updates concerning family/drugs. No how to be a "perfect" parent, or raise a "perfect child." Length: 750 words maximum. Pays $2.50-7.50 for unsolicited articles.

Columns/Departments: Have You Read (book reviews); Have You Heard (audio/visual tapes); News Reports. Buys 18 mss/year. Length: 250 words. Send complete ms. Pays $2.50.

Poetry: Avant-garde, free verse, haiku, light verse, traditional. Buys 18/year. Submit maximum 5 poems. Length: 2-16 lines. Pays $2.50.

Fillers: Anecdotes, facts and newsbreaks. Length: 250 words maximum. Pays $2.50.

Tips: "Let me know you've been there, either as the child (addict), parent or professional who works with these families. Honesty is a must. Where technical data is concerned (laws, treatments, etc.), need verification. Freelancers are welcome to contribute to all departments."

PARENTS MAGAZINE, 685 3rd Ave., New York NY 10017. FAX: (212)867-4583. Editor-in-Chief: Ann Pleshette Murphy. 25% freelance written. Monthly. Estab. 1925. Circ. 1,740,000. **Pays on acceptance.** Publishes ms an average of 8 months after acceptance. Usually buys first serial rights or first North American serial rights; sometimes buys all rights. Pays 25% kill fee. Reports in approximately 6 weeks. Writer's guidelines for #10 SASE.

Nonfiction: "We are interested in well-documented articles on the development and behavior of preschool, school-age and adolescent children and their parents; good, practical guides to the routines of baby care; articles that offer professional insights into family and marriage relationships; reports of new trends and significant research findings in education and in mental and physical health; and articles encouraging informed citizen action on matters of social concern. Especially need articles on women's issues, pregnancy, birth, baby care and early childhood. We prefer a warm, colloquial style of writing, one which avoids the extremes of either slang or technical jargon. Anecdotes and examples should be used to illustrate points which can then be summed up by straight exposition." Query. Length: 2,500 words maximum. Payment varies. Sometimes pays the expenses of writers on assignment.

‡PARENTS' PRESS, The Monthly Newspaper for Bay Area Parents, 1454 Sixth St., Berkeley CA 94710. (415)524-1602. Editor: Dixie M. Jordan. Managing Editor: Deborah Haeseler. 50% freelance written. Monthly tabloid for parents. Estab. 1980. Circ. 75,000. Pays within one month of publication. Publishes ms an average of 1-3 months after acceptance. Kill fee varies (individually negotiated). Buys first rights, second serial (reprint) rights, and almost always Northern California Exclusive rights. Submit seasonal material 3-6 months in advance. Reports in 1-4 weeks on queries; 2-8 weeks on mss. Sample copy $3. Writer's guidelines for SAE and 1 first class stamp.

Nonfiction: Book excerpts (family, children), how-to (parent, raise children, nutrition, health, etc.), humor (family life, children), interview/profile (of Bay Area residents, focus on their roles as parents), travel (family), and family resources and family activities. "Annual issues include Pregnancy and Birth, Travel, Back-to-School, Children's Health; write for planned topic, or suggest one. While we publish researched articles which spring from personal experience, we do not publish strictly personal essays. Please, no birth stories." Buys 30-50 mss/year. Query with or without published clips, or send complete ms. Length: 300-3,000 words; 1,500-2,000 average. Pays $50-150 for assigned articles; $25-125 for unsolicited articles. State availability of photos with submission. Reviews prints, any size, b&w only. Offers $15/photo. Model release and identification of subject required. Buys one-time rights.

Columns/Departments: Books (reviews of parenting and children's books, preferably by San Francisco Bay Area authors, publishers). Buys 12-24 mss/year. Send complete ms. Length: 100-750 words. Pays $15-25.

Tips: "All sections of Parents' Press are open to freelancers, but we are protective of our regular columnists' turf (children's health, women's health, infant and child behavior), so we ask writers to query whether a topic has been addressed in the last three years. Best bets to break in are family activities, education, nutrition, family dynamics and issues. While we prefer articles written by experts, we welcome well-researched journalism."

PEDIATRICS FOR PARENTS, The Newsletter for Caring Parents, Pediatrics for Parents, Inc., P.O. Box 1069, Bangor ME 04402-1069. (207)942-6212. FAX: (207)947-3134. Editor: Richard J. Sagall, M.D. 20% freelance written. Eager to work with new/unpublished writers. Monthly newsletter covering medical aspects of rearing children and educating parents about children's health. Estab. 1981. Circ. 2,000. Pays on publication. Publishes ms an average of 3-4 months after acceptance. Byline given. Buys first North American serial rights, first and second rights to the same material, and second (reprint) rights to material originally published elsewhere. Rights always include right to publish article in our books on "Best of . . ." series. Submit seasonal/holiday material 6 months in advance. Simultaneous queries and previously published submissions OK. Query for electronic submissions. Reports in 1 month on queries; 6 weeks on mss. Sample copy for $2; writer's guidelines for #10 SAE and 2 first class stamps.

Nonfiction: Book reviews; how-to (feed healthy kids, exercise, practice wellness, etc.); new product; technical (explaining medical concepts in shirtsleeve language). No general parenting articles. Query with published clips or submit complete ms. Length: 25-1,000 words. Pays 2-5¢/edited word.

Columns/Departments: Book reviews; Please Send Me (material available to parents for free or at nominal cost); Pedia-Tricks (medically-oriented parenting tips that work). Send complete ms. Pays $15-250. Pays 2¢/edited word.

Tips: "We are dedicated to taking the mystery out of medicine for young parents. Therefore, we write in clear and understandable language (but not simplistic language) to help people understand and deal intelligently with complex disease processes, treatments, prevention, wellness, etc. Our articles must be well researched and documented. Detailed references must always be attached to any article for documentation, but not for publication. We strongly urge freelancers to read one or two issues before writing."

‡SEATTLE'S CHILD, P.O. Box 22578, Seattle WA 98122. (206)322-2594. Editor: Ann Bergman. 85% freelance written. Works with a small number of new/unpublished writers each year. Monthly tabloid of articles related to being a parent of children age 12 and under. Directed to parents and professionals involved with children 12 and under. Circ. 20,000. Pays on publication. Publishes ms an average of 6 months after acceptance. Byline given. Offers 50% kill fee. Buys first North American serial rights or all rights. Submit seasonal/holiday material 6 months in advance. Simultaneous queries and submissions OK. Query for electronic submissions. Reports in 1 month on queries; 3 months on mss. Sample copy $1.50 with 10×13 envelope; writer's guidelines for #10 SAE and 1 first class stamp.

Nonfiction: Needs reports on political issues affecting families. Exposé, general interest, historical/nostalgic, how-to, humor, interview/profile, new product, opinion, personal experience, travel, record, tape and book reviews, and educational and political reviews. Articles must relate to parents and parenting. Buys 120 mss/year. Send complete ms (preferred) or query with published clips. Length: 400-2,500 words. Pays 10¢/word.

Tips: "We prefer concise, critical writing and discourage overly sentimental pieces. Don't talk down to the audience. Consider that the audience is sophisticated and well-read."

‡SESAME STREET MAGAZINE, Parent's Guide, Children's Television Workshop, One Lincoln Plaza, New York NY 10023. (212)595-3456. FAX: (212)595-3650. Editor-in-Chief: Ira Wolfman. Senior Editors: Sima Bernstein and Diane O'Connell. 60% freelance written. A monthly magazine for parents of preschoolers. Circ. 1.3 million. **Pays on acceptance.** Byline given. Offers 33% kill fee. Buys all rights. Submit seasonal/holiday material 7 months in advance. Reports in 1 month on queries. Sample copy for 9×12 SAE with 6 first class stamps. Writer's guidelines for #10 SAE.

Nonfiction: Child development/parenting, book excerpts, essays, how-to (practical tips for parents of preschoolers), interview/profile, personal experience, photo feature and travel (with children). Buys 40 mss/year. Query with published clips, or send complete ms. Length: 800-2,000 words. Pays $300-1,000 for assigned articles. Pays $250-600 for unsolicited articles.

Photos: State availability of photos with submission. Model releases and identification of subjects required. Buys one-time rights or all rights.

THE SINGLE PARENT, Parents Without Partners, Inc., 8807 Colesville Rd., Silver Spring MD 20910. (301)588-9354. FAX: (301)588-9216. Editor: Allan N. Glennon. 60% freelance written. Works with small number of new/unpublished writers each year. Magazine, published 6 times/year; 48 pages. Emphasizes single parenting, family, divorce, widowhood and children. Distributed to members of Parents Without Partners, plus libraries, universities, psychologists, psychiatrists, subscribers, etc. Estab. 1957. Circ. 120,000. Pays on publication. Publishes ms an average of 9 months after acceptance. Buys one-time rights. Simultaneous and previously published submissions OK. No electronic submissions. Reports in 2 months. Sample copy $1, writer's guidelines for #10 SASE.

Nonfiction: Informational (parenting, legal issues, single parents in society, programs that work for single parents, children's problems); how-to (raise children alone, travel, take up a new career, cope with life as a new or veteran single parent; short lists of how-to tips). No first-hand accounts of bitter legal battles with former spouses. No "poor me" articles. Buys 50 unsolicited mss/year. Query not required. Mss not returned unless SASE is enclosed. Length: 1,000-3,000 words. Payment $50-150, based on content, not length. Fillers to 500-700 words, $25-50.

Fiction: Publishes two short stories (800-1500 words) per issue for children. Stories may·be aimed at any age group from toddlers through teens. Prefers stories about children in single parent households, coping with or learning from their situations. No anthropomorpics. Payment $35-75.

Columns/Departments: F.Y.I., for short news items, reports on research, tips on how to do things better, and new products, Letters to Editor column.

Photos: Purchased with accompanying ms. Also, uses freelance stock shots. Query. Pays negotiable rates. Model release required.

Tips: "Be familiar with our magazine and its readership before trying to write for us. We publish constructive, upbeat articles that present new ideas for coping with and solving the problems that confront single parents. Articles on origins of Halloween customs, tribal behavior in Ghana, or how to predict the weather have little likelihood of acceptance unless there is a clear tie-in to single parent issues."

TWINS, The Magazine for Parents of Multiples, P.O. Box 12045, Overland Park KS 66212. (913)722-1090. FAX: (913)722-1767. Editor: Barbara C. Unell. 100% freelance written. Eager to work with new/unpublished writers. A bimonthly international magazine designed to give professional guidance to help multiples, their parents and those professionals who care for them learn about twin facts and research. Estab. 1984. Circ. 50,000. Pays on publication. Publishes ms an average of 6 months after acceptance. Byline given. Buys all rights. Submit seasonal/holiday material 10 months in advance. Simultaneous and previously published submissions OK. Reports in 6 weeks on queries; 2 months on mss. Sample copy $4.50 plus $1.50 postage and handling; writer's guidelines for #10 SASE.
Nonfiction: Book excerpts, general interest, how-to, humor, interview/profile, personal experience and photo feature. "No articles that substitute the word 'twin' for 'child' – those that simply apply the same research to twins that applies to singletons without any facts backing up the reason to do so." Buys 150 mss/year. Query with or without published clips, or send complete ms. Length: 1,250-3,000 words. Payment varies; sometimes pays in contributor copies or premiums instead of cash. Sometimes pays the expenses of writers on assignment.
Photos: Send photos with submission. Reviews contact sheets, 4×5 transparencies and all size prints. Captions, model releases and identification of subjects required. Buys all rights.
Columns/Departments: Resources, Supertwins, Prematurity, Family Health, Twice as Funny, Double Focus (series from pregnancy through adolescence), Personal Perspective (first-person accounts of beliefs about a certain aspect of parenting multiples), Over the Back Fence (specific tips that have worked for the writer in raising multiples), Consumer Matters, Feelings on Fatherhood, Research, On Being Twins (first-person accounts of growing up as a twin), On Being Parents of Twins (first-person accounts of the experience of parenting twins), Double Takes (fun photographs of twins), and Education Matters. Buys 70 mss/year. Query with published clips. Length: 1,250-2,000 words. Payment varies.
Fillers: Anecdotes and short humor. Length: 75-750 words. Payment varies.
Tips: "Features and columns are both open to freelancers. Columnists write for *Twins* on a continuous basis, so the column becomes their column. We are looking for a wide variety of the latest, well-researched practical information. There is no other magazine of this type directed to this market. We are interested in personal interviews with celebrity twins or celebrity parents of twins, tips on rearing twins from experienced parents and/or twins themselves, and reports on national and international research studies involving twins."

‡WEE CARE FOR KIDS, Box 12407, San Luis Obispo CA 93406. (805)544-8609. Editor: Rhonda Jones. 60% freelance written. Bimonthly newsletter on information, newsbriefs, craft and activities, and reviews written for family daycare providers nationwide. Estab. 1991. Circ. 5,000. Pays on publication. Publishes ms an average of 6 months after acceptance. Byline given. Buys first rights or second serial (reprint) rights. Submit seasonal/holiday material 6 months in advance. Reports in 4 months. Sample copy for $2 with 9×12 SAE with 5 first class stamps; writer's guidelines brochure for #10 SASE.
Nonfiction: Professional, how-to, in-depth features all related to operating a successful daycare business. Examples: Taxes, teaching reading, avoiding burnout, effective discipline. 500-1,200 words. Pays $1/column inch.
Columns/Departments: News Briefs (current issues and legislation affecting the daycare industry), 200-600 words. Provider Profile: (interviews family day care providers to discover how they got started, daily operations and other unique aspects of their business) 600-1,000 words. Arts, Crafts & Fun Learning Activities: (craft, art, outdoor, games and educational activities for children 12 and under) 50-500 words, $2.50. Reviews: (books, music, videos, preschool curriculum and programs), 100-600 words. Pays $1/column inch.

Comic Books

Comic books aren't just for kids. Today, this medium also attracts a reader who is older and wants stories presented visually on a wide variety of topics. In addition, some instruction manuals, classics and other stories are using a comic book format.

This doesn't mean you have to be an artist to write for comic books. Most of these publishers want to see a synopsis of one to two double-spaced pages. Highlight the story's beginning, middle and end, and tell how events will affect your main character emotionally. Be concise. Comics use few words and rely on graphics as well as words to forward the plot.

Once your synopsis is accepted, either an artist will draw the story from your plot, returning these pages to you for dialogue and captions, or you will be expected to write a script. Scripts run approximately 23 typewritten pages and include suggestions for artwork as well as dialogue. Try to imagine your story on actual comic book pages and divide your script accordingly. The average comic has six panels per page, with a maximum of 35 words per panel.

If you're submitting a proposal to Marvel or DC, your story should center on an already established character. If you're dealing with an independent publisher, characters are often the property of their creators. Your proposal should be for a new series. Include a background sheet for main characters who will appear regularly, listing origins, weaknesses, powers or other information that will make your character unique. Indicate an overall theme or direction for your series. Submit story ideas for the first three issues. If you're really ambitious, you may also include a script for your first issue. As with all markets, read a sample copy before making a submission. The best markets may be those you currently read, so consider submitting to them even if they aren't listed in this section. Writer's Digest Books now publishes a market book specifically for humorous writers and illustrators, *Humor and Cartoon Markets*.

AMAZING HEROES, Fantagraphics Books, 7563 Lake City Way, Seattle WA 98115. FAX: (206)524-2014. Editor: Thomas Harrington. 80% freelance written. Eager to work with new/unpublished writers. A monthly magazine for comic book fans of all ages and backgrounds. "*Amazing Heroes* focuses on both historical aspects of comics and current doings in the industry." Estab. 1981. Circ. 10,000. Pays on publication. Publishes ms an average of 2 months after acceptance. Byline given. Offers $25 kill fee on solicited ms. Buys first North American serial rights and second serial (reprint) rights. Submit seasonal/holiday material 3 months in advance. Previously published submissions OK. Reports in 2 weeks on queries; 1 month on mss. Sample copy for 7½ × 10½ SAE and $2.50.
Nonfiction: Essays, historical/nostalgic, interview/profile, new product. Query with published clips and interests. Length: 300-7,500 words. Pays $5-125 for assigned articles; pays $5-75 for unsolicited articles. Pays writers with double payment in Fantagraphics book merchandise if requested. Sometimes pays the expenses of writers on assignment.
Photos: State availability of photos on profile pieces and interviews.
Tips: "Recently, there has been a renaissance, though some refer to it as a glut, of new material and new publishers in the comic book industry. This has called for a greater need for more writers who are not just interested in super-heroes or just books produced by DC and Marvel. There is now, more than ever, a need to be open-minded as well as critical. Writers for *Amazing Heroes* must have a much broader knowledge of the entire, ever-widening spectrum of the comic book industry."

CARTOON WORLD, P.O. Box 30367, Dept. WM, Lincoln NE 68503. Editor: George Hartman. 100% freelance written. Works with published/established writers and a small number of new/unpublished writers each year. "Monthly newsletter for professional and amateur cartoonists who are serious and want to utilize new cartoon markets in each issue." Buys only from paid subscribers. Circ. 150-300. **Pays on acceptance.** Publishes ms an average of 2 months after acceptance. Byline given. Buys second (reprint) rights to material originally published elsewhere. Not copyrighted. Submit seasonal/holiday material 3 months in advance. Simultaneous submissions OK. Reports in 1 month. Sample copy $5.
Nonfiction: "We want only positive articles about the business of cartooning and gag writing." Buys 10 mss/year. Query. Length: 1,000 words. Pays $5/page.

COMICS SCENE, Starlog Group, 475 Park Ave. S., 8th Floor, New York NY 10016. (212)689-2830. FAX: (212)889-7933. Editor: David McDonnell. Magazine published 9 times/year on comic books, strips, cartoons, those who create them and TV/movie adaptations of both. Estab. 1981. Pays on publication. Byline given. Offers 25% kill fee. Buys all rights or second serial (reprint) rights. Submit seasonal/holiday material 6 months in advance. Simultaneous and previously published submissions OK if noted. Reports in 6 weeks on queries; 2 months on mss. Sample copy $4.50; writer's guidelines for #10 SASE. *No* queries by phone.
Nonfiction: Book excerpts, historical/nostalgic, interview/profile, new product, personal experience. Buys 90 mss/year. Query with published clips. Length: 750-3,500 words. Pays $125-200. Sidebars $50-75. Does *not* publish fiction.
Photos: State availability of photos and comic strip/book/animation artwork with submission. Reviews contact sheets, transparencies, 8 × 10 prints. Offers $5-25 for original photos. Captions, model releases, identification of subjects required. Buys all rights.

Columns/Departments: The Comics Scene (interviews with comic book artists, writers and editors on upcoming projects and new developments), 100-350 words; The Comics Reporter ("newsy" interviews with writer, director, producer of TV series/movie adaptations of comic books and strips). Buys 25 mss/year. Query with published clips. Length: 100-750 words. Pays $15-50.

Tips: "We really need small department items, re: independent comics companies' products and creators. We need interviews with specific comic strip creators. Comics are hot and comics-based movies (thanks to *Batman*) should be even hotter in '92. Most any writer can break in with interviews with hot comic book writers and artists—and with comic book creators who don't work for the big two companies. We do *not* want nostalgic items or interviews. Do not burden us with your own personal comic book stories or artwork. Get interviews we can't get or haven't thought to pursue. Out-thinking overworked editors is an almost certain way to sell a story."

ECLIPSE COMICS, P.O. Box 1099, Forestville CA 95436. (707)887-1521. Publisher: Dean Mullaney. Editor-in-Chief: Catherine Yronwode. 100% freelance written. Works with a small number of new/unpublished writers each year. Publishers of various four-color comic books, graphic albums, and trading cards. *Eclipse* publishes comic books with high-quality paper and color reproduction, geared toward the discriminating comic book fan and sold through the "direct sales" specialty store market. Estab. 1978. Circ. varies (35,000-100,000). **Pays on acceptance** (net 1 month). Publishes ms an average of 6 months after acceptance. Byline given. Buys first North American serial rights, second serial (reprint) rights with additional payment, and first option on collection and non-exclusive rights to sell material to South American and European markets (with additional payments). Simultaneous queries and submissions OK. Reports in 2 months. Sample copy $2; writer's guidelines for #10 SASE.

Fiction: "Most of our comics are fictional." Adventure, fantasy, mystery, science fiction, horror. "No sexually explicit material, please." Buys approximately 200 mss/year (mostly from established comics writers).

Tips: "At the present time we are publishing both adventure and super-heroic series but we are currently scheduling fewer 32-page periodical adventure comics and more 48-96 page graphic albums, some of which are nonfiction current events journalism in graphic format. We are moving into the arena of political and social commentary and current events in graphic form. We have also expanded our line of classic newspaper strip reprints and political satire non-sports trading cards sets. Because all of our comics are creator-owned, we do not buy fill-in plots or scripts for our periodicals. Plot synopsis less than a page can be submitted; we will select promising concepts for development into full script submissions. All full script submissions should be written in comic book or 'screenplay' form for artists to illustrate. Writers who are already teamed with artists stand a better chance of selling material to us, but if necessary we'll find an artist. Our special needs at the moment are for heroic, character-oriented series with overtones of humanism, morality, political opinion, philosophical speculation, and/or social commentary. Comic book adaptations (by the original authors) of previously published science fiction and horror short stories are definitely encouraged. Queries about current events/nonfiction albums and non-sports trading card sets should be discussed with us prior to a full-blown submission."

MARVEL COMICS, 387 Park Ave. S., New York NY 10016. (212)576-9200. Editor-in-Chief: Tom DeFalco. 99% freelance written. Publishes 60 comics and magazines per month, 6-12 graphic novels per year, and specials, storybooks, industrials, and paperbacks for all ages. Over 9 million copies sold/month. Pays a flat fee for most projects, plus a royalty type incentive based upon sales. Also works on advance/royalty basis on many projects. **Pays on acceptance.** Publishes manuscript an average of 6 months after acceptance. Byline given. Offers variable kill fee. Rights purchased depend upon format and material. Submit seasonal/holiday material 1 year in advance. Simultaneous submissions OK. Reports in 6 months. Writer's guidelines for #10 SASE. Additional guidelines on request.

Fiction: Super hero, action-adventure, science fiction, fantasy, and other material. No noncomics. Buys 600-800 mss/year. Query with brief plot synopses only. Do not send scripts, short stories or long outlines. A plot synopsis should be less than two typed pages; send two synopses at most. Pays expenses of writers on assignment. *Marvel Comics no longer accepts unsolicited manuscripts.*

Consumer Service and Business Opportunity

Some of these magazines are geared to investing earnings or starting a new business; others show how to make economical purchases. Publications for business executives and consumers interested in business topics are listed under Business and Finance. Those on how to run specific businesses are classified by category in the Trade section.

CHANGING TIMES, The Kiplinger Magazine, 1729 H St. NW, Washington DC 20006. Editor: Ted Miller. Less than 10% freelance written. Prefers to work with published/established writers. For general, adult audience interested in personal finance and consumer information. Monthly. Estab. 1947.

Circ. 1 million. **Pays on acceptance.** Publishes ms an average of 2 months after acceptance. Buys all rights. Reports in 1 month. Query for electronic submissions. Thorough documentation required for fact-checking.

Nonfiction: "Most material is staff-written, but we accept some freelance." Query with clips of published work. Pays expenses of writers on assignment.

Tips: **Magazine has changed name to** *Kiplinger's Personal Finance Magazine.*

CONSUMER ACTION NEWS, Suite 216, 1106 E. High St., Springfield OH 45505. (513)325-2001. Editor: Victor Pence. 10% freelance written. Eager to work with new/unpublished writers. A monthly newsletter circulated in the state of Ohio for readers who are interested in knowing that problems can be solved without legal action and when other protection agencies could not solve them, or refused to handle them. "We handle consumer complaints and publish results in newsletter." Estab. 1980. **Pays on acceptance.** Byline given. Buys one-time rights. Simultaneous queries, and simultaneous and previously published submissions OK. Reports in 6 weeks.

Nonfiction: Send complete ms. Length: 1,000 words or less. Pays $10-25.

Tips: "We want only experiences with complaints that were solved when the usual protection sources couldn't solve them. Creative ways of finding solutions without legal actions. If the problem has not been solved, we will offer possible solutions to the problem anywhere in the U.S., Canada or Mexico at no charge."

ECONOMIC FACTS, The National Research Bureau, Inc., 424 N. 3rd St., P.O. Box 1, Burlington IA 52601-0001. FAX: (319)752-3421. Editor: Rhonda Wilson. Editorial Supervisor: Doris J. Ruschill. 25% freelance written. Eager to work with new/unpublished writers; works with a small number of new/unpublished writers each year. Published 4 times/year. Estab. 1948. Pays on publication. Publishes ms an average of 1 year after acceptance. Buys all rights. Byline given. Previously published submissions OK. Reports in 1 week. Writer's guidelines for #10 SASE; sample for 6½×9½ envelope and 55¢ postage.

Nonfiction: General interest (private enterprise, government data, graphs, taxes and health care). Buys 3-5 mss/year. Query with outline of article. Length: 400-600 words. Pays 4¢/word.

FDA CONSUMER, 5600 Fishers Lane, Rockville MD 20857. (301)443-3220. Editor: Judith Levine Willis. 30% freelance written. Prefers to work with experienced health and medical writers. Monthly magazine. January/February and July/August issues combined. For general public interested in health issues. A federal government publication (Food and Drug Administration). Circ. 25,000. Pays after acceptance. Publishes ms an average of 3 months after acceptance. Byline given. Not copyrighted. Pays 50% kill fee. "All purchases automatically become part of public domain." Buys 15-20 freelance mss a year. "We cannot be responsible for any work by writer not agreed upon by prior contract." Query for electronic submissions. Free sample copy.

Nonfiction: "Upbeat feature articles of an educational nature about FDA regulated products and specific FDA programs and actions to protect the consumer's health and pocketbook. Articles based on health topics with the proviso that the subjects be connected to food, drugs, medicine, medical devices, and other products regulated by FDA. All articles subject to clearance by the appropriate FDA experts as well as acceptance by the editor. All articles based on prior arrangement by contract." Query. Length: 2,000-2,500 words. Pays $800-950 for first-timers, $1,200 for those who have previously published in *FDA Consumer.* Sometimes pays the expenses of writers on assignment.

Photos: Black and white photos are purchased on assignment only.

Tips: "Besides reading the feature articles in *FDA Consumer,* a writer can best determine whether his/her style and expertise suit our needs by submitting a query letter, resume and sample clips for our review."

INCOME PLUS MAGAZINE, Opportunity Associates, Suite 303, 73 Spring St., New York NY 10012. (212)925-3180. FAX: (212)925-3108. Editor: Donna Ruffini. 33-50% freelance written. Monthly magazine on small business and money-making ideas. Provides "hands-on service to help small business owners, home office owners and entrepreneurs successfully start up and run their enterprises. Focus on franchising, mail order." Estab. 1989. Circ. 200,000. Pays on publication. Byline given. Offers 20% kill fee. Buys first North American serial rights. Query for electronic submissions. Reports in 6 weeks. Sample copy $2 with 1 first class stamp; writer's guidelines for 1 first class stamp.

Nonfiction: How-to (business, finance, home office, technical start-up). Buys 48 mss/year. Query with published clips. Length: 1,500-2,500 words. Pays $50-750. Sometimes pays expenses of writers on assignment.

Photos: State availability of photos with submission. Offers no additional payment for photos accepted with ms.

Columns/Departments: Legal and You The Boss (original reporting with real example of business owners to back up point of story); Home Business Marketing (service with easily and immediately applicable advice. Frequent use of bullets); 1,200 words. Buys 24 mss/year. Query with published clips. Pays $50-350.

‡**PROFIT, The Magazine for Canadian Entrepreneurs**, CB Media Limited, 70 The Esplanade, 2nd Fl., Toronto, ON M5E 1R2 Canada. (416)364-4760. Editor: Rick Spence. Managing Editor: John Southerst. 80% freelance written. Monthly magazine covering small and medium business. "We specialize in specific, useful information that helps our readers manage their businesses better. We want Canadian stories only." Estab. 1982. Circ. 110,000. **Pays on acceptance.** Publishes ms an average of 1-2 months after acceptance. Byline given. Kill fee varies. Buys first North American serial rights and database rights. Submit seasonal/holiday material 6 months in advance. Query for electronic submissions. Reports in 1 month on queries; 2-6 weeks on mss. Sample copy for 9×12 SAE and 84¢ postage (Canadian). Free writer's guidelines.

Nonfiction: How-to (business management tips), strategies and Canadian business profiles. Buys 50 mss/year. Query with published clips. Length: 800-2,000 words. Pays $500-2,000 (payment in Canadian dollars). Pays expenses of writers on assignment. State availability of photos with submission.

Columns/Departments: Innovators (interesting new Candian products, inventions or services), 200 words; Your People (hints for better human-resource management), 700 words; Finance (info on raising capital in Canada), 700 words; Marketing (marketing strategies for independent business), 700 words. Buys 80 mss/year. Query with published clips. Length: 200-800 words. Pays $150-600 (Canadian dollars).

Tips: "We're wide open to freelancers with good ideas and some knowledge of business. Read the magazine and understand it before submitting your ideas."

TOWERS CLUB, USA NEWSLETTER, The Original Information-By-Mail, Direct-Marketing Newsletter, Towers Club Press, P.O. Box 2038, Vancouver WA 98668. (206)574-3084. Editor: Jerry Buchanan. 5-10% freelance written. Works with a small number of new/unpublished writers each year. Newsletter published 10 times/year (not published in May or December) covering entrepreneurism (especially selling useful information by mail). Estab. 1974. Circ. 8,000. Pays on publication. Publishes ms an average of 2 months after acceptance. Byline given. Buys one-time rights. Submit seasonal/holiday material 10 weeks in advance. Simultaneous and previously published submissions OK. Query for electronic submissions. Reports in 2 weeks. Sample copy for $5 and 6×9 SAE; writer's guidelines for $1 and #10 SAE.

Nonfiction: Exposé (of mail order fraud); how-to (personal experience in self-publishing and marketing); book reviews of new self-published nonfiction how-to-do-it books (must include name and address of author). "Welcomes well-written articles of successful self-publishing/marketing ventures. Must be current, and preferably written by the person who actually did the work and reaped the rewards. There's very little we will not consider, *if* it pertains to unique money-making enterprises that can be operated from the home." Buys 10 mss/year. Send complete ms. Length: 500-1,500 words. Pays $150-250. Pays extra for b&w photo and bonus for excellence in longer manuscript.

Tips: "The most frequent mistake made by writers in completing an article for us is that they think they can simply rewrite a newspaper article and be accepted. That is only the start. We want them to find the article about a successful self-publishing enterprise, and then go out and interview the principal for a more detailed how-to article, including names and addresses. We prefer that writer actually interview a successful self-publisher. Articles should include how idea first came to subject; how they implemented and financed and promoted the project; how long it took to show a profit and some of the stumbling blocks they overcame; how many persons participated in the production and promotion; and how much money was invested (approximately) and other pertinent how-to elements of the story. Glossy photos (b&w) of principals at work in their offices will help sell article."

Contemporary Culture

These magazines combine politics, gossip, fashion and entertainment in a single package. Their approach to institutions is typically irreverent and the target is primarily a young adult audience. Although most of the magazines are centered in large metropolitan areas, some have a following throughout the country.

BOSTON REVIEW, 33 Harrison Ave., Boston MA 02111. (617)350-5353. Editor: Margaret Ann Roth. 100% freelance written. Works with a small number of new/unpublished writers each year. Bimonthly magazine of the arts, politics and culture. Estab. 1975. Circ. 10,000. **Pays on acceptance.** Publishes ms

Close-up

Jay Walljasper
Editor
Utne Reader

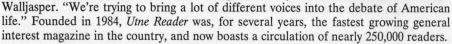

Jay Walljasper, editor of *Utne Reader*, a bimonthly, Minne-
apolis-based publication, reprints the best work from the
thousands of alternative publications currently on the market. In his quest to find the best of the alternative press,
Walljasper reviews more than 2,000 publications.

"We're looking for something that offers a different,
fresher point of view than in mainstream magazines," says
Walljasper. "We're trying to bring a lot of different voices into the debate of American
life." Founded in 1984, *Utne Reader* was, for several years, the fastest growing general
interest magazine in the country, and now boasts a circulation of nearly 250,000 readers.

As the *"Reader's Digest* of the alternative press," *Utne Reader* publishes few original
pieces, and these are written by a regular group of freelancers. The magazine is mostly
made up of reprints. Walljasper prefers to contact the publication concerning reprints, but
he believes there are other markets for reprints that writers can seek out.

"I think reprinting is something that is going on more and more in the United States."
The market is not, however, a wide-open one, he adds. His advice: find out which magazines
are willing to publish reprints before sending off queries.

The most common strategy in marketing reprints is to sell an article to a local publication, then to resell it to a regional or national one. The submission process is the same for
reprints as for first-time sales, says Walljasper, who advises writers to include a cover letter,
resume, and clips along with the reprint. He believes writers should either revise the piece
before submitting it – to define or eliminate local references – or they should state in the
cover letter their willingness to revise.

The editor's main worry in buying a reprint is not knowing where or when the article
appeared previously, says Walljasper. To eliminate the chance of buying an article printed
previously by a competitor, editors may avoid reprints. Walljasper therefore advises writers
to be open in the cover letter about an article's publication history. In addition, a writer
must be aware of the rights previously sold. (For a complete description of rights and the
writer, see The Business of Writing.)

"In general, it's a tricky business," he says. "It's best to be up front. The more you can
clear up the uncertainty and reduce risks for the editors, the easier it will be to sell your
reprint." The writer, he adds, also has an obligation to the publication that buys an article
first. "You need to make sure the reprint doesn't scoop the original article," he says.

Though the market for reprints is growing, it is not an especially lucrative one, Walljasper concedes. "Payment for reprints tends to be lower than you'd think," he says. At
Utne Reader, he buys one-time rights, which revert back to the writer after the article is
published, freeing the writer to sell it again. But no matter what the price, he finds that
writers are thrilled to have their work reprinted. A writer himself, Walljasper feels that
any sale after the first one is "gravy."

—Jack Heffron

an average of 2 months after acceptance. Buys first American serial rights. Byline given. Simultaneous submissions OK. Reports in 2 months. Sample copy $4; writer's guidelines for #10 SASE.

Nonfiction: Critical essays and reviews, natural and social sciences, literature, music, painting, film, photography, dance and theatre. Buys 20 unsolicited mss/year. Length: 1,000-3,000 words. Sometimes pays expenses of writers on assignment.

Fiction: Length: 2,000-4,000 words. Pays according to length and author, ranging from $50-200.

Poetry: Pays according to length and author.

Tips: "Short (500 words) color pieces are particularly difficult to find, so we are always on the lookout for them. We look for in-depth knowledge of an area, an original view of the material, and a presentation which makes these accessible to a sophisticated reader who will be looking for more and better articles which anticipate ideas and trends on the intellectual and cultural frontier."

‡**CANADIAN DIMENSION**, Dimension Publications Inc., #707-228 Notre Dame Ave., Winnipeg, Manitoba, R3B 1N7 Canada. FAX: (204)943-4617. 80% freelance written. A magazine that makes sense of the world. We bring a socialist perspective to bear on events across Canada and around the world. Our contributors provide in-depth coverage on popular movements, peace, labour, women, aboriginal justice, environment, third world, eastern Europe. Published 8 times/year. Estab. 1963. Circ. 5,000. Pays on publication. Publishes ms an average of 6 months after acceptance. Copyrighted by CD after publication. Simultaneous submissions OK. Reports in 6 weeks on queries. Sample copy $1; writer's guidelines for #10 SAE.

Nonfiction: Interview/profile, opinion, reviews, political commentary and analysis, journalistic style. Buys 8 mss/year. Length: 500-2,000 words. Pays $25-100.

‡**CRISIS MAGAZINE**, Crisis Publishing Co., 260 5th Ave., 6th Fl., New York NY 10016. (212)481-4100. Editor: Fred Beauford. 75% freelance written. Monthly magazine covering current events and the arts. Estab. 1910. Circ. 400,000. Pays on publication. Publishes ms an average of 3 months after acceptance. Byline given. Buys first North American serial rights, makes work-for-hire assignments. Reports in 2 weeks on queries; 3 weeks on mss. Free sample copy.

Nonfiction: Exposé, general interest, interview/profile, travel. Buys 50 mss/year. Query. Length: 500-5,000 words. Pays $75-500. Pays expenses of writers on assignment.

Photos: Send photos with submission. Reviews 5×7 transparencies; 5×7 prints. Offers $35-300 per photo. Captions, model releases and identification of subjects required. Buys one-time rights.

Columns/Departments: Books, Visual Arts, Theatre, Dance, Arts Organizations, Music. Buys 50 mss/year. Query. Length: 500-750 words. Pays $75-100.

‡**FRANCE TODAY**, FrancePress Inc., 1051 Divisadero St., San Francisco CA 94115. (415)921-5100. Editor: Anne Prah-Perochon. Managing Editor: Allyn Kaufmann. 90% freelance written. Tabloid covering contemporary France; published 10 times/year. "*France Today* is a feature publication on contemporary France including sociocultural analysis, economics, business, trends, current events and travel." Estab. 1989. Circ. 5,000. Pays on publication. Publishes ms an average of 1-3 months after acceptance. Byline given. Buys first North American serial rights, first rights and second serial (reprint) rights. Submit seasonal/holiday material 4 months in advance. Simultaneous submissions OK. Free sample copy and writer's guidelines.

Nonfiction: Essays, exposé, general interest, historical, humor, interview/profile, personal experience and travel. "No travel pieces about well-known tourist attractions." Buys 90% mss/year. Query with or without published clips, or send complete ms. Length: 500-2,000 words. Pays $175-425. Pays expenses of writers on assignment "if actually assigned. Not for unsolicited pieces." Offers $25-40/photo. Identification of subjects required. Buys one-time rights.

Columns/Departments: Letter from Paris (current issues, trends, tones of Paris), 1100 words; In Any Event (noteworthy performances, exhibits in Paris), 1100. Query with published clips and send complete ms. Length: 500-1,100 words. Pays $150-275.

HIGH TIMES, Trans High Corp., Floor 20, 211 E. 43rd St., New York NY 10017. (212)972-8484. Editor: Steve Hager. Executive Editor: John Holmstrom. 75% freelance written. Monthly magazine covering marijuana and the counterculture. Circ. 250,000. Pays on publication. Byline given. Offers 20% kill fee. Buys one-time rights, all rights, or makes work-for-hire assignments. Submit seasonal/holiday material 6 months in advance. Simultaneous submissions OK. Reports in 1 month on queries; 2 months on mss. Sample for $5 and SASE; writer's guidelines for SASE.

Nonfiction: Book excerpts, expose, humor, interview/profile, new product, personal experience, photo feature and travel. Special issues include indoor Growers issue in September. No stories on "my drug bust." Buys 30 mss/year. Send complete ms. Length: 1,000-10,000 words. Pays $150-400. Sometimes pays in trade for advertisements. Sometimes pays expenses of writers on assignment.

Photos: Send photos with submission. Pays $50-300. Captions, model releases and identification of subjects required. Buys all rights or one-time use.
Columns/Departments: Steve Bloom, news editor. Drug related books; drug related news. Buys 10 mss/year. Query with published clips. Length: 100-2,000 words. Pays $25-300.
Fiction: Adventure, fantasy, humorous and stories on smuggling. Buys 5 mss/year. Send complete ms. Length: 2,000-5,000 words. Pays $250-400.
Fillers: Gags to be illustrated by cartoonist, newsbreaks and short humor. Buys 10/year. Length: 100-500 words. Pays $10-50. Cartoon Editor: John Holmstrom.
Tips: "All sections are open to good, professional writers."

QUALITY LIVING, A Magazine for the Study of Values, Quality Living Publications, Inc. P.O. Box 1, Valle Crucis NC 28691. (704)963-7051. Editor: Rick Herrick. Quarterly magazine. "Reflections on what deepens the best qualities in our living." Estab. 1986. Circ. 1,000. **Pays on acceptance**. Publishes ms an average of 6 months after acceptance. Byline given. Buys first North American serial rights. Submit seasonal/holiday material 6 months in advance. Reports in 3 weeks on queries; 2 months on mss. Writer's guidelines for #10 SASE.
Nonfiction: Essays, inspirational, interview/profile, opinion, personal experience, book reviews and movie reviews. "No pure problem-presentation, no cynicism, no highly technical, no exposé." Buys 30 mss/year. Query with or without published clips, or send complete ms. Length: 1,000-1,700 words. Pays $50 maximum.
Columns/Departments: Quality Reviews (of book or movies, from standpoint of their positive contribution to quality in life, or their exploration of this question). Buys 12 mss/year. Send complete ms. Length: 1,000 words. Pays $50 maximum.
Tips: "Essays are most open to freelancers. Our audience is well educated, yet not academic. Style and vocabulary should be comfortable, not complex, highly readable. Ideas can be challenging if clearly handled. We like some sparkle!"

SPY, Spy Publishing Partners, 5 Union Sq. W., 8th Floor, New York NY 10003. (212)633-6550. Editor: K. Andersen and G. Carter. 50% freelance written. "*Spy* is a non-fiction satirical magazine published 10 times a year." Circ. 150,000. **Pays on acceptance**. Publishes ms an average of 3 months after acceptance. Byline given. Offers 25% kill fee. Buys first and second North American serial rights, non-exclusive anthology rights. Submit seasonal/holiday material 6 months in advance. Simultaneous submissions OK. Query for electronic submissions. Reports in 2 weeks on queries; 1 month on mss. Sample copy $4.
Nonfiction: Susan Morrison, executive editor. Jamie Malanowski, national editor. Book excerpts, essays, exposé, humor, interview/profile, opinion. Buys 100 mss/year. Query with published clips. Length: 200-4,000 words. Pays $50-2,000. Sometimes pays expenses of writers on assignment.
Photos: State availability of photos with submission. Reviews contact sheets. Offers $40-200/photo. Model release and identification of subjects required. Buys one-time rights.

UTNE READER, Suite 330, 1624 Harmon Place, Minneapolis MN 55403. Does *not* accept unsolicited material.

Detective and Crime

Fans of detective stories want to read accounts of actual criminal cases, detective work and espionage. The following magazines specialize in nonfiction, but a few buy some fiction. Markets specializing in crime fiction are listed under Mystery publications.

INSIDE DETECTIVE, Official Detective Group, R.G.H. Publishing Corp., 460 W. 34th St., New York NY 10001. (212)947-6500. Editor-in-Chief: Rose Mandelsberg. Managing Editor: Christofer Pierson. Magazine published 7 times per year. Circ. 90,000. **Pays on acceptance**. Publishes ms an average of 3 months after acceptance. Byline given. Buys first rights and one-time world rights. Query for electronic submissions. Reports in 2 weeks. Free writer's guidelines.
Nonfiction: Buys 120 mss/year. Query. Pays $250. Length: 5,000-6,000 words (approx. 20 typed pages).

P. I. MAGAZINE, Fact and Fiction about the World of Private Investigators, 755 Bronx, Toledo OH 43609. (419)382-0967. Editor: Bob Mackowiak. 75% freelance written. "Not a trade journal. Audience includes professional investigators and mystery/private eye fans. We're America's Consumer Private Eye Magazine." Estab. 1988. Circ. 700. Pays on publication. Publishes ms an average of 3 months after acceptance. Buys one-time rights. Submit seasonal/holiday material 3 months in advance. Simultaneous submissions OK. Reports in 3 months on queries; 4 months on mss. Sample copy $4.75.

Nonfiction: Interview/profile, new product and personal experience (investigators only). Buys 4-10 mss/year. Send complete ms. Length: 500+ words. Pays $10-25 for unsolicited articles.

Photos: Send photos with submission. May offer additional payment for photos accepted with ms. Model releases and identification of subjects required. Buys one-time rights.

Columns/Departments: Profile (personality stories—what makes this person different from other investigators), 1,000-2,000 words. Buys 4-8 mss/year. Send complete ms. Pays $25.

Fiction: Adventure, humorous and mystery (Main character *must* be a private detective—not police detective, spy, or little old lady who happens to solve murders on the side.) Buys 16-20 mss/year. Length: 2,000-5,000 words. Send complete ms. Pays $25.

Tips: "The best way to get published in *P.I.* is to write a detailed story about a professional private detective's true-life case."

Disabilities

These magazines are geared toward disabled persons and those who care for or teach them. A knowledge of disabilities and lifestyles is important for writers trying to break in to this field; editors regularly discard material without a realistic focus. Some of these magazines will accept manuscripts only from disabled persons or those with a background in caring for disabled persons.

ARTHRITIS TODAY, Arthritis Foundation, 1314 Spring St., N.W., Atlanta GA 30309. (404)872-7100. FAX: (404)872-7100. Editor: Cindy T. McDaniel. 70% freelance written. A bimonthly magazine about living with arthritis; latest in research/treatment. "*Arthritis Today* is written for the 37 million Americans who have arthritis and for the millions of others whose lives are touched by an arthritis-related disease. The editorial content is designed to help the person with arthritis live a more productive, independent and painfree life. The articles are upbeat and provide practical advice, information and inspiration." Estab. 1987. Circ. 500,000. Buys first North American serial rights but requires unlimited reprint rights in Arthritis Foundation publications. Submit seasonal/holiday material 6 months in advance. Simultaneous and previously published submissions OK. Reports in 1 month on queries; 6 weeks on mss. Sample copy for 9×11 SAE with 4 first class stamps. Writer's guidelines for #10 SASE.

Nonfiction: General interest, arts and entertainment, how-to (tips on any aspect of living with arthritis), humor, inspirational, interview/profile, new product, opinion, personal experience, photo feature, technical and travel. Buys 45 mss/year. Query with published clips. Length: 1,000-2,500. Pays $300-950. Sometimes pays expenses of writers on assignment.

Photos: State availability of photos with submission. Reviews 3x5 transparencies and 5×7 prints. Offers $75-200 per photo. Captions, model releases and identification of subjects required. Buys one-time rights or all rights.

Columns/Departments: Quick Takes (general news and information); Personality Profiles (upbeat profiles of people living positively in spite of arthritis); Scientific Frontier (research news about arthritis) 200-600 words. Buys 16-20 mss/year. Query with published clips. Pays $250-400.

Fillers: Anecdotes, facts, newsbreaks and short humor. Buys 2-4/year. Length: 75-150 words. Pays $75-200.

Tips: "In addition to articles specifically about living with arthritis, we look for articles to appeal to an older audience on subjects such as travel, history, arts and entertainment, hobbies, general health, etc."

CAREERS & THE DISABLED, Equal Opportunity Publications, 44 Broadway, Greenlawn, NY 11740. (516)261-8917. FAX: (516)261-8935. Executive Editor: James Schneider. 60% freelance written. A career guidance magazine published three times a year that is distributed through college campuses for disabled college students and professionals. "The magazine offers role-model profiles and career guidance articles geared toward disabled college students and professionals." Pays on publication. Publishes ms an average of 6 months after acceptance. Circ. 10,000. Byline given. Buys first rights. Simultaneous and previously published submissions OK. Reports in 2 weeks. Sample copy and writer's guidelines for 7×10 SAE and $1.45 postage.

Nonfiction: General interest, interview/profile, opinion and personal experience. Buys 15 mss/year. Query. Length: 1,000-1,500 words. Pays 10¢ per word. Sometimes pays the expenses of writers on assignment.

Photos: State availability of photos with submission. Reviews prints. Offers $15 per photo and/or color slides. Captions. Buys one-time rights.

Tips: "Be as targeted as possible. Role model profiles which offer advice to disabled college students are most needed."

‡**DIABETES SELF-MANAGEMENT**, R.A. Rapaport Publishing, Inc., Suite 800, 150 West 22nd St., New York NY 10011. (212)989-0200. Editor: James Hazlett. 40% freelance written. Bimonthly magazine about diabetes. "We publish how-to health care articles for motivated, intelligent readers who have diabetes and who are actively involved in their own health care management. All articles must have immediate application to their daily living." Estab. 1983. Circ. 197,000. Pays on publication. Publishes ms an average of 3 months after acceptance. Byline given. Offers 20% kill fee. Buys all rights. Submit seasonal/holiday material 6 months in advance. Query for electronic submissions. Reports in 1 month. Sample copy $2 with 9×12 SAE and 6 first class stamps. Writer's guidelines for #10 SAE with 1 first class stamp.

Nonfiction: How-to (exercise, nutrition, diabetes self-care product surveys), technical (reviews of products available, foods sold by brand name), travel (considerations and prep for people with diabetes). Buys 10-12 mss/year. Query with published clips. Length: 2,000-4,000 words. Pays $400-600 for assigned articles; $ 200-600 for unsolicited articles.

Tips: "The rule of thumb for any article we publish is that it must be clear, concise, useful and instructive, and it must have immediate application to the lives of our readers."

INDEPENDENT LIVING, The Health Care Magazine Serving Dealers, Rehabilitation Facilities and Their Clients, Equal Opportunity Publications, Inc. 44 Broadway, Greenlawn NY 11740. (516)-261-8917. Editor: Anne Kelly. 75% freelance written. Quarterly magazine on home health care, rehabilitation and disability issues. "*Independent Living* magazine is written for persons with disabilities and the home care dealers, manufacturers, and health care professionals who serve their special needs." Circ. 35,000. Pays on publication. Byline given. Buys all rights. Simultaneous submissions OK. Reports in 1 month. Free sample copy and writer's guidelines.

Nonfiction: Essays, how-to, humor, inspirational, interview/profile, new product, opinion, personal experience, cartoons and travel. Buys 40 mss/year. Query. Length: 500-2,500 words. Pays 10¢/word.

Photos: Send photos with submission. Reviews prints. Offers $15 per photo. Prefers 35mm color slides. Captions and identification of subjects required. Buys all rights.

Tips: "The best way to have a manuscript published is to first send a detailed query on a subject related to the health care and independent lifestyles of persons who have disabilities. We need articles on innovative ways that home health care dealers are meeting their clients needs."

KALEIDOSCOPE: International Magazine of Literature, Fine Arts, and Disability, Kaleidoscope Press, 326 Locust St., Akron OH 44302. (216)762-9755; (216)379-3349 (TDD only). FAX: (216)762-0912. Editor: Darshan C. Perusek, Ph.D. 75% freelance written. Works with a small number of new/unpublished writers each year; eager to work with new/unpublished writers. Semiannual magazine with international collection of disability-related literature and art by disabled/nondisabled people. Estab. 1979. Circ. 1,500. Pays on publication. Publishes ms an average of 6 months after acceptance. Byline given. Buys first North American serial rights. Simultaneous queries OK. Previously published submissions "at editor's discretion." Reports in 6 months. Sample copy $2. Writer's guidelines for #10 SASE.

Nonfiction: Disability-related literary criticism, book reviews, personal experience essays, interview/profiles/photo features on literary and/or art personalities. Publishes 8-10 mss/year. Payment $25-50 for up to 2,500 words. Maximum 3,500 words. Feature length ms (15-20 pp) up to $100. All contributors receive 2 complimentary copies.

Photos: Pays up to $25/photo. Reviews 3×5, 5×7, 8×10 b&w and color prints. Captions and identification of subjects required.

Fiction: Short stories, excerpts. Traditional and experimental. Theme generally disability-related, occasional exceptions. Publishes 8-10 mss/year. Length: 5,000 words maximum. Pays $25; editor's discretion for higher payment. Two complimentary copies.

Poetry: Traditional and experimental. Theme: experience of disability. Submit up to 12 poems. Publishes 16-20/year. Payment up to $25 for multiple publication.

Tips: "*Kaleidoscope* is interested in work that captures and reflects the experience of disability. We seek works that challenge stereotypical perceptions of people with disabilities by offering balanced, realistic images. We do not, however, limit ourselves to such subject matter. Become familiar with *Kaleidoscope* (sample copy very helpful). Always send photocopies."

MAINSTREAM, Magazine of the Able-Disabled, Exploding Myths, Inc., 2973 Beech St., San Diego CA 92102. (619)234-3138. Editor: Cyndi Jones. 100% freelance written. Eager to develop writers who have a disability. A magazine published 10 times/year (monthly except January and June) covering disability-related topics, written for disabled consumers. Estab. 1975. Circ. 15,500. Pays on publication. Publishes ms an average of 3 months after acceptance. Byline given. Buys all rights. Submit seasonal/holiday material 4 months in advance. Reports in 2 months. Sample copy $4.25 or 9x12 SAE with $3 and 5 first class stamps. Writer's guidelines for #10 SASE.

Nonfiction: Book excerpts, exposé, how-to (daily independent living tips), humor, interview/profile, personal experience (dealing with problems/solutions), photo feature, technical, travel, politics and legislation. "All must be disability-related, directed to disabled consumers." *NO* articles on " 'my favorite disabled character', 'my most inspirational disabled person', 'poster child stories.' " Buys 50 mss/year. Query with or without published clips and send complete ms. Length: 6-12 pages. Pays $50-150. May pay subscription if writer requests.

Photos: State availability of photos with submission. Reviews contact sheets, 1½ × ¾ transparencies and 5 × 7 or larger prints. Offers $5-35 per b&w photo. Captions and identification of subjects required. Buys all rights.

Columns/Departments: Creative Solutions (unusual solutions to common aggravating problems); Personal Page (deals with personal relations: dating, meeting people). Buys 10 mss/year. Send complete ms. Length: 500-800 words. Pays $25-50.

Fiction: Humorous. Must be disability-related. Buys 4 mss/year. Send complete ms. Length: 800-1,200 words. Pays $50-100.

Tips: "It seems that politics and disability are becoming more important. Please include your phone number on cover page. We accept 5¼ or 3½ floppy discs — ASCII, Wordperfect, Wordstar-IBM."

‡**PARAPLEGIA NEWS,** Paralyzed Veterans of America, Suite 111, 5201 North 19th Ave., Phoenix AZ 85015. (602)246-9426. Editor: Cliff Crase. Monthly magazine covering news and information for the wheelchair-user. "An official organ of the Paralyzed Veterans of America, PN is published in the interest of and for the benefit of paraplegics (civilians and veterans) all over the world. It is dedicated to the presentation of all news concerning paraplegics and wheelchair living." Estab. 1946. Circ. 25,000. Pays on publication. Publishes ms an average of 3 months after acceptance. Byline given. Offers no kill fee. Buys first rights or second serial (reprint) rights. Submit seasonal/holiday material 4 months in advance. Simultaneous submissions OK. Query for electronic submissions. Reports in 1 month on queries; 2 weeks on mss. Free sample copy and writer's guidelines.

Nonfiction: Susan Robbins. Travel, accessible housing, employment of people with disabilities (wheelchair users). No fiction or poetry. Buys 5 mss/year. Query with or without published clips, or send complete ms. Length: 1,500-3,000 words. Pays $25-200. All authors receive 10-20 complimentary copies of issue. Sometimes pays the expenses of writers on assignment.

Photos: Send photos with submission. Reviews contact sheets, transparencies and 4 × 6 or larger prints. Offers $10-50 per photo. Captions and identification of subjects required. Buys one-time rights.

Fillers: Newsbreaks and cartoons. Buys 25-50/year (cartoons only). Pays $10.

Tips: "Keep in mind that we do not write for all disabilities: wheelchair users only. We do not use condescending language in referring to people with disabilities (they are not victims, confined to a wheelchair, etc.). We are most open to feature articles. Include photos or illustrations. Best if wheelchair user in photos, to show how this article is applicable to them. Illustration OK, too. Write for a disabled audience."

‡**PEOPLENET,** "Where People Meet People," P.O. Box 897, Levittown NY 11756. (516)579-4043. Editor: Robert Mauro. 20% freelance written. Networking newsletter for *disabled* singles. Published 3 times/year. "Covers relationships, mainly of disabled singles. I am looking for articles, poems and short shorts about disabled singles — people who want to meet people for friendship and romance." Estab. 1987. Circ. 200. Pays on acceptance. Publishes ms an average of 8 months after acceptance. Byline given. No kill fee. Buys first rights. Submit seasonal/holiday material 8 months in advance. Query for electronic submission. Reports in 3 weeks. Sample copy $2 with #10 SAE and 2 first class stamps. Writer's guidelines for 1 SAE with 1 first class stamp.

Nonfiction: How-to deal with (rejection, low self-esteem), humor, other (disabled singles and relationships). Does not want to see articles on "super-crips." Buys 3-6 mss/year. Send complete ms. Length: 500-750 words. Pays $5-7.50 for unsolicited articles. Besides check, gets 1 copy of issue with his or her work.

Columns/Departments: Dating Scene (ways and means and problems of dating), 500-750 words; Coping Scene (coping with rejection, low self-esteem, low energy), 500-750 words. Buys 3-6 mss/year. Send complete ms. Length: 500-750 words. Pays $5-7.50.

Fiction: Experimental, fantasy, humorous, romance, slice-of-life vignettes. Does not want to see "Anything that does not have a disabled character in it. All fiction must have a disabled character in it." Buys 3-6 mss/year. Send complete ms. Length: 500-1,000 words. Pays $5-10.

Poetry: Avant-garde, free verse, haiku, light verse and traditional. "Anything that is romantic." Buys 3-6 poems/year. Submit maximum 4 poems. Length: 4-20 lines. Pays $1-5.

Fillers: Gags, short humor. Buys 3-6 mss/year. Length: 100-500 words.

Tips: "We want professionally submitted pieces. I'd love to see some good cartoons on *the dilemmas of dating for the disabled*. All areas are open. But we want good material that will instruct, entertain and make a reader *think*."

‡**SPORTS 'N SPOKES, The Magazine for Wheelchair Sports and Recreation**, Paralyzed Veterans of America, Suite 111, 5201 North 19th Ave., Phoenix AZ 85015. (602)246-9426. FAX: (602)242-6862. Editor: Cliff Crase. Bimonthly magazine covering sports and recreation for the wheelchair user. "*Sports 'n Spokes* covers wheelchair competitive sports and recreation primarily for those with spinal cord injury, spina bifida, amputation and some congenital defects. Articles on wheelchair sports, recreation, equipment, personalities and related topics." Estab. 1975. Circ. 10,000. Pays on publication. Publishes ms an average of 5 months after acceptance. Byline given. Offers no kill fee. Buys first rights or second serial (reprint) rights. Submit seasonal/holiday material 5 months in advance. Query for electronic submissions. Reports in 6 weeks on queries; 1 month on mss. Free sample copy and writer's guidelines.
Nonfiction: Survey of lightweight-wheelchair manufacturers, People in Sports (personal profile). No fiction, poetry or anything not relating to sports and recreation. Buys 10 mss/year. Query with or without published clips, or send complete ms. Length: 1,500-3,000 words. Pays $25-200. All authors receive 10-20 complimentary copies of issue. Sometimes pays the expenses of writers on assignment.
Photos: Send photos with submission. Reviews negatives, transparencies and 4×6 or larger prints. Offers $10-50 per photo. Captions and identification of subjects required. Buys one-time rights.
Fillers: Buys 20-30/year (cartoons only). Pays $10. "Keep in mind that our readers are primarily wheelchair users. We do not use condescending language in referring to people with disabilities (they are not 'victims,' 'confined to a wheelchair,' etc.). Articles must have something to do with sports and recreation for the wheelchair user. We are most open to feature articles. Include photos or illustrations. Best is wheelchair users shown in photos, showing how this article is applicable to them. Write for disabled audience."

Entertainment

This category's publications cover live, filmed or videotaped entertainment, including home video, TV, dance, theater and adult entertainment. Besides celebrity interviews, most publications want solid reporting on trends and upcoming productions. Magazines in the Contemporary Culture section also use articles on entertainment. For those publications with an emphasis on music and musicians, see the Music section.

AMERICAN FILM MAGAZINE, Billboard, Suite 1514, 6671 Sunset Blvd., Hollywood CA 90028. (213)856-5350. Editor: Wolf Schneider. Managing Editor: Randall Tierney. Senior Editor: Shawn Levy. Monthly magazine. Estab. 1975. Circ. 130,000. Pays on acceptance. Byline given. Offers 25% kill fee. Buys first North American serial rights. Submit seasonal/holiday material 6 months in advance. Query for electronic submissions. Reports in 3 months. Sample copy for $2.50 with SAE.
Nonfiction: Book excerpts, essays, exposé, general interest, historical/nostalgic, humor, interview/profile, and new product. Buys 100 mss/year. Query with published clips. Length: 300-4,000 words. Pays $100-2,500 for assigned articles. Pays expenses of writers on assignment.
Photos: State availability of photos with submission. Reviews transparencies. Payment negotiated. Identification of subjects required. Buys one-time rights and occasionally all rights for some, such as cover shots.
Columns/Departments: Illuminations (a collection of essays and issues), 200-600 words; Epilogue (last page—humorous or provocative, or both). Buys 100 mss/year. Query with published clips or send complete ms. Pays $100-750.
Tips: "Know the magazine. Know film; know good writing. We look for thinking writers who do their homework and don't take shortcuts. 'Illumination's' columns—pithy and intriguing entries, short and sweet—are the best way to break in."

AMERICAN SQUAREDANCE, Burdick Enterprises, P.O. Box 488, Huron OH 44839. (419)433-2188. FAX: (419)433-5043. Editors: Stan and Cathie Burdick. 10% freelance written. Works with a small number of new/unpublished writers each year. Monthly magazine of interviews, reviews, topics of interest to the modern square dancer. Circ. 20,000. Pays on publication. Publishes ms an average of 6 months after acceptance. Byline given. Buys all rights. Submit seasonal/holiday material 3 months in advance. Reports in 2 weeks on queries. Sample copy for 6×9 SAE with $1.21 postage; writer's guidelines for #10 SASE.
Nonfiction: General interest, historical/nostalgic, humor, inspirational, interview/profile, new product, opinion, personal experience, photo feature, travel. Must deal with square dance. Buys 6 mss/year. Send complete ms. Length: 1,000-1,500 words. Pays $2/column inch.
Photos: Send photos with ms. Reviews b&w prints. Captions and identification of subjects required.
Fiction: Subject related to square dancing only. Buys 1-2 mss/year. Send complete ms. Length: 1,500-2,000 words. Pays $2/column inch.
Poetry: Avant-garde, free verse, haiku, light verse, traditional. Square dancing subjects only. Buys 6 poems/year. Submit maximum 3 poems. Pays $2 for first 4 lines; $2/verse thereafter.

‡**APPLAUSE, The Magazine of WHYY**, Public Broadcast Publishers, Inc. and WHYY, Inc., WHYY/ 150 N. 6th St., Philadelphia PA 19106. (215)351-0539. Editor: Eileen Fisher. 70% freelance written. Monthly magazine covering public broadcast subjects, arts and regional culture. "*Applause* is designed for the Delaware Valley public broadcast subscriber. Features expand on and amplify each month's public broadcast subjects. Style is sophisticated but lively. Emphasizes local and cultural." Estab. 1984. Circ. 145,000. Pays on publication. Byline given. Offers 33% kill fee. Buys first rights. Submit seasonal/ holiday material 6 months in advance. Query; on-disc submissions preferred. Reports in 2 months. Free sample copy.

Nonfiction: Essays, general interest, historical/nostalgic, humor, interview/profile, photo feature. Buys 30-35 features/year. "Specific ideas related to a public broadcast subject not necessary. Can send clips and description of writer's interests/specializations." Length: 1,500-2,000 words. Pays $400-500.

Columns/Departments: "Address by subject (Food Editor, etc.)" Books (reviews current major fiction and nonfiction releases), 1,500 words; Critic's Choice (monthly performing arts previews; generally use contributing editors), 500 words; Food & Wine, Smart $, Better Homes, Health (lifestyle topics covered in an informal style; by contributing editors), 11-1,200 words. Buys 150 mss/year. Query with published clips. Pays $300-350.

Fillers: Contact: Opening Lines Editor. Regional focus anecdotes, facts, short humor, short profiles. Buys 20-30/year. Length: 200-500 words. Pays $75-175.

Tips: "Don't hesitate because you don't have advance knowledge of specific shows on which to base your query. Start with an 'Opening Lines' or column query (these topics are independent of programming). Or, send clips with a list of your interests/specializations; include a story idea related to a subject often covered on public broadcasting—drama, psychology, etc.—if you have one to offer."

CINEASTE, America's Leading Magazine on the Art and Politics of the Cinema, Cineaste Publishers, Inc., #1320, 200 Park Ave. S., New York NY 10003. (212)982-1241. Managing Editor: Gary Crowdus. 50% freelance written. A quarterly magazine on motion pictures, offering "social and political perspective on the cinema." Estab. 1967. Circ. 7,000. Pays on publication. Publishes ms an average of 3 months after acceptance. Byline given. Offers 50% kill fee. Buys first North American serial rights. Reports in 3 weeks on queries; 1 month on mss. Sample copy $2. Writer's guidelines for #10 SASE.

Nonfiction: Essays, interview/profile, criticism. Buys 40-50 mss/year. Query with or without published clips, or send complete ms. Length: 3,000-6,000 words. Pays $20.

Photos: State availability of photos with submissions. Reviews prints. Offers no additional payment for photos accepted with ms. Identification of subjects required.

CINEFANTASTIQUE MAGAZINE, The review of horror, fantasy and science fiction films, P.O. Box 270, Oak Park IL 60303. (708)366-5566. Editor: Frederick S. Clarke. 100% freelance written. Eager to work with new/unpublished writers. A bimonthly magazine covering horror, fantasy and science fiction films. Estab. 1970. Circ. 60,000. Pays on publication. Publishes ms an average of 6 months after acceptance. Byline given. Buys all magazine rights. Simultaneous queries OK. Sample copy for $7 and 9×12 SAE. Reports in 2 months or longer.

Nonfiction: Historical/nostalgic (retrospects of film classics); interview/profile (film personalities); new product (new film projects); opinion (film reviews, critical essays); technical (how films are made). Buys 100-125 mss/year. Query with published clips. Length: 1,000-10,000 words. Sometimes pays the expenses of writers on assignment.

Photos: State availability of photos with query letter or ms.

Tips: "Study the magazine to see the kinds of stories we publish. Develop original story suggestions; develop access to film industry personnel; submit reviews that show a perceptive point of view."

COUNTRY AMERICA, Meredith Publishing Corporation, Locust at 17th, Des Moines IA 50336. (515)284-3790. FAX: (515)284-3035. Editor: Danita Allen. Managing Editor: Bill Eftink. Magazine covering country entertainment/lifestyle published 10 times/year. Estab. 1989. Circ. 700,000. **Pays on acceptance.** Byline given. Buys all rights (lifetime). Submit seasonal/holiday material 8 months in advance. Previously published submissions OK "if notified." Free writer's guidelines.

Nonfiction: General interest, historical/nostalgic, how-to (home improvement), garden/food, interview/profile country music entertainers, photo feature, travel. Special Christmas, travel, wildlife/conservation, country music issues. Buys 130 mss/year. Query. Pays $100-1,000 for assigned articles. Sometimes pays expenses of writers on assignment.

Photos: State availability of photos with submission. Reviews contact sheets, negatives, 35mm transparencies. Offers $50-500/photo. Captions and identification of subjects required. Buys all rights.

Fillers: Short humor. Country curiosities that deal with animals, people, crafts, etc.

Tips: "Think visually. Our publication will be light on text and heavy on photos. Be general; this is a general interest publication meant to be read by every member of the family. We are a service-oriented publication; please stress how-to sidebars and include addresses and phone numbers to help readers find out more."

DANCE CONNECTION, Alberta Dance Alliance, 603, 815 1st St. S.W., Calgary AB T2P IN3 Canada. (403)263-3232 or (403)237-7327. Editor: Heather Elton. 75% freelance written. Published five times per year. Magazine devoted to dance with a broad editorial scope reflecting a deep commitment to a view of dance that embaces its diversity of style and fuction. Articles have ranged in subject matter from the changing role of dance in Plains Indian culture from the buffalo days to the modern powwow, to the history of belly dancing, to postmodern dance. Estab. 1983. Circ. 5,000. Pays on publication. Byline given. Buys first rights or second serial (reprint) rights. Submit material 3 months in advance. Simultaneous and previously published submissions OK. Query for electronic submissions. Sample copy for 8½ × 11 SAE with IRCs.
Nonfiction: A variety of writing styles including criticism, essay, exposé, general interest, historical/ nostalgic, humor, opinion, interview, performance review, forum debate, literature and photo feature. Query with published clips, or send complete ms. Length 800-2,500 words. Pays $5-150.
Fiction: Literature and poetry relating to dance. No poems about ballet.
Columns/Departments: Education, Children in Dance, Multiculturalism and Movement.

DANCE MAGAZINE, 33 W. 60th St., New York NY 10023. (212)245-9050. FAX: (212)956-6487. Editor-in-Chief: Richard Philp. 25% freelance written. Monthly magazine covering dance. Estab. 1927. Circ. 51,000. Pays on publication. Byline given. Offers up to $150 kill fee (varies). Makes work-for-hire assignments. Submit seasonal/holiday material 4 months in advance. Reports in "weeks." Sample copy and writer's guidelines for 8 × 10 SAE.
Nonfiction: Interview/profile. Buys 50 mss/year. Query with or without published clips, or send complete ms. Length: 300-1,500 words. Pays $15-350. Sometimes pays expenses of writers on assignment.
Photos: State availability of photos with submission. Reviews transparencies and prints. Offers $15-285/photo. Captions and identification of subjects required. Buys one-time rights.
Columns/Departments: Presstime News (topical, short articles on current dance world events) 150-400 words. Buys 40 mss/year. Query with published clips. Pays $20-75.
Tips: Writers must have "thorough knowledge of dance and take a sophisticated approach."

DRAMATICS MAGAZINE, International Thespian Society, 3368 Central Pkwy., Cincinnati OH 45225. (513)559-1996. Editor-in-Chief: Donald Corathers. 70% freelance written. Works with small number of new/unpublished writers. For theater arts students, teachers and others interested in theater arts education. Magazine published monthly, September through May. Estab. 1929. Circ. 35,000. **Pays on acceptance.** Publishes ms an average of 3 months after acceptance. Buys first North American serial rights. Byline given. Submit seasonal/holiday material 3 months in advance. Simultaneous and previously published submissions OK. Query for electronic submissions. Reports in 1 month. Sample copy for $2 and a 9 × 12 SAE with 5 first class stamps; free writer's guidelines.
Nonfiction: How-to (technical theater), informational, interview, photo feature, humorous, profile and technical. Buys 30 mss/year. Submit complete ms. Length: 750-3,000 words. Pays $30-200. Rarely pays expenses of writers on assignment.
Photos: Purchased with accompanying ms. Uses b&w photos and transparencies. Query. Total purchase price for ms usually includes payment for photos.
Fiction: Drama (one-act plays). No "plays for children, Christmas plays or plays written with no attention paid to the conventions of theater." Prefers unpublished scripts that have been produced at least once. Buys 5-9 mss/year. Send complete ms. Pays $50-200.
Tips: "The best way to break in is to know our audience—drama students, teachers and others interested in theater—and to write for them. Writers who have some practical experience in theater, especially in technical areas, have a leg-up here, but we'll work with anybody who has a good idea. Some freelancers have become regular contributors. Others ignore style suggestions included in our writer's guidelines."

‡**EAST END LIGHTS**, The Quarterly Magazine for Elton John Fans, Voice Communications Corp., P.O. Box 760, 31950 23 Mile Road, New Baltimore MI 48047. (313)949-7900. FAX: (313)949-2217. Editor: Tom Stanton. 70% freelance written. Quarterly magazine covering British rock star Elton John. "In one way or another, a story must relate to Elton John, his activities or associates (past and present). We appeal to discriminating Elton fans. No gushing fanzine material. No concert reviews." Estab. 1990. Circ. 500. Pays 3 weeks after acceptance. Publishes ms an average of 2-3 months after acceptance. Byline given. Offers 100% kill fee. Buys first rights and second serial (reprint) rights. Submit seasonal material 2-3 months in advance. Reports in 2 weeks. Sample copy $2. Free writer's guidelines.
Nonfiction: Book excerpts, essays, exposé, general interest, historical/nostalgic, humor, interview/ profile. "No superficial, gushing fan pieces." Buys 20 mss/year. Query with or without published clips or send complete ms. Length: 400-1,000 words. Pays $50-150 for assigned articles; $40-100 for unsolicited articles. Pays with contributor copies only if the writer requests. Sometimes pays the expenses of writers on assignment.

Photos: State availability of photos with submission. Reviews negatives and 5×7 prints. Offers $10-75 per photo. Identification of subjects required. Buys one-time rights and all rights.
Columns/Departments: Clippings (non-wire references to Elton John in other publications), max. 200 words. Buys 12 mss/year. Send complete ms. Length: 50-200 words. Pays $10-20.
Tips: "Approach with a well-thought-out story idea. We'll provide direction. All areas equally open. We prefer interviews with Elton-related personalities—past or present."

‡**EMMY MAGAZINE,** Academy of Television Arts & Sciences, Suite 700, 3500 W. Olive, Burbank CA 91505-4628. (818)953-7575. FAX: (818)953-4182. Editor and Publisher: Hank Rieger. Managing Editor: Daphne Tanyol. 100% freelance written. Works with a small number of new/unpublished writers each year. Bimonthly magazine on television—a "provocative, critical—though not necessarily fault-finding—treatment of television and its effects on society." Circ. 12,000. Pays on publication. Publishes ms an average of 3 months after acceptance. Byline given. Offers 20% kill fee. Buys first North American serial rights. Computer printout submissions acceptable; no dot-matrix. Reports in 1 month. Sample copy for 9×12 SAE with 5 first class stamps.
Nonfiction: Provocative and topical articles, nostalgic, humor, interview/profile, opinion—all dealing with television. Buys 40 mss/year. Query with published clips. Length: 1,500-2,000 words. Pays $500-900. Sometimes pays expenses of writers on assignment.
Columns/Departments: Opinion or point-of-view columns dealing with TV. Buys 18-20 mss/year. Query with published clips. Length: 800-1,200 words. Pays $250-550.
Tips: "Query in writing with a thoughtful description of what you wish to write about. Please do not call. The most frequent mistake made by writers in completing an article for us is that they misread the magazine and send fan-magazine items."

FANGORIA: Horror in Entertainment, Starlog Group, 475 Park Ave. S., 8th Floor, New York NY 10016. (212)689-2830. FAX: (212)889-7933. Editor: Anthony Timpone. 95% freelance written. Works with a small number of new/unpublished writers each year. Published 10 times/year. Magazine covering horror films, TV projects, comics, videos and literature and those who create them. Estab. 1979. Pays on publication. Publishes ms an average of 3 months after acceptance. Byline given. Buys all rights. Submit seasonal/holiday material 6 months in advance. Simultaneous queries OK. Query for electronic submissions. Reports in 6 weeks. "We provide an assignment sheet (deadlines, info) to writers, thus authorizing queried stories that we're buying." Sample copy $4.50; writers' guidelines for #10 SASE.
Nonfiction: Book excerpts, interview/profile of movie directors, makeup FX artists, screenwriters, producers, actors, noted horror novelists and others—with genre credits. No "think" pieces, opinion pieces, reviews (excluding books), or sub-theme overviews (i.e., vampire in the cinema). Buys 100 mss/year. Query with published clips. Length: 1,000-3,000 words. Pays $100-225. Rarely pays the expenses of writers on assignment. Avoids articles on science fiction films—see listing for sister magazine *Starlog* in *Writer's Market* science fiction magazine section.
Photos: State availability of photos. Reviews b&w and color prints and transparencies. "No separate payment for photos provided by film studios." Captions and identification of subjects required. Photo credit given. Buys all rights.
Columns/Departments: Monster Invasion (news about new film productions; must be exclusive, early information; also mini-interviews with filmmakers and novelists). Query with published clips. Length: 300-500 words. Pays $25-50.
Fiction: "We do *not* publish any fiction. *Don't* send any."
Tips: "Other than recommending that you study one or several copies of *Fangoria*, we can only describe it as a horror film magazine consisting primarily of interviews with technicians and filmmakers in the field. Be sure to stress the interview subjects' words—not your own opinions as much. We're very interested in small, independent filmmakers working outside of Hollywood. These people are usually more accessible to writers, and more cooperative. *Fangoria* is also sort of a *de facto* bible for youngsters interested in movie makeup careers and for young filmmakers. We are devoted only to *reel* horrors— the fakery of films, the imagery of the horror fiction of a Stephen King or a Clive Barker—*we do not* want nor would we *ever* publish articles on real-life horrors, murders, etc. A writer must *like* and *enjoy* horror films and horror fiction to work for us. If the photos in *Fangoria* disgust you, if the sight of (*stage*) blood repels you, if you feel 'superior' to horror (and its fans), you aren't a writer for us and we certainly aren't the market for you. *Fangoria*'s frequency has increased over the last years and, with an editorial change reducing staff written articles, this has essentially doubled the number of stories we're buying. In 1991-92, we expect such opportunities only to increase for freelancers. *Fangoria* will also try for a lighter, irreverent, more 'Gonzo' tone in the year ahead, plus an expansion in horror comics coverage."

FILM QUARTERLY, University of California Press, Berkeley CA 94720. (415)642-6333. FAX: (415)643-7127. Editor: Ernest Callenbach. 100% freelance written. Eager to work with new/unpublished writers. Quarterly. Buys all rights. Byline given. Pays on publication. Publishes ms an average of 3 months after acceptance. Query. Sample copy and writer's guidelines for SASE.

Nonfiction: Articles on style and structure in films, articles analyzing the work of important directors, historical articles on development of the film as art, reviews of current films and detailed analyses of classics, book reviews of film books. Must be familiar with the past and present of the art; must be competently, although not necessarily breezily, written; must deal with important problems of the art. "We write for people who like to think and talk seriously about films, as well as simply view them and enjoy them. We use no personality pieces or reportage pieces. Interviews usually work for us only when conducted by someone familiar with most of a filmmaker's work. (We don't use performer interviews.)" Length: 6,000 words maximum. Pay is about 2¢/word.

Tips: "*Film Quarterly* is a specialized academic journal of film criticism, though it is also a magazine (with pictures) sold in bookstores. It is read by film teachers, students, and die-hard movie buffs, so unless you fall into one of those categories, it is very hard to write for us. Currently, we are especially looking for material on independent, documentary, etc. films not written about in the national film reviewing columns."

‡**HOLLYWOOD MAGAZINE, The City, the Dream,** Roosevelt Hotel, Cabena 9, 7000 Hollywood Blvd., Hollywood CA 90028. (213)856-9022. Editor: Kim Williamson. Associate Editor: Heidi Siegmund. 75% freelance written. Bimonthly magazine covering the city of Hollywood and the creative industries. "For residents of Hollywood and an international audience interested in film, TV, music, art, video." Estab. 1988. **Pays on acceptance.** Publishes ms an average of 2-6 months after acceptance. Offers 25% kill fee. Buys first North American serial rights. Submit seasonal/holiday material 6 months in advance. Query for electronic submissions. Sample copy $2. Writer's guidelines for letter-sized SAE with 1 first class stamp.

Nonfiction: Book excerpts, essays, historical/nostalgic, interview/profile, photo feature, business: on film, music, other creative industries. "Each issue contains a special report section on one of the 'cities of Hollywood'—Hollywood, Venice, Burbank, Beverly Hills, Santa Monica, etc." No first-person, non-classically journalistic pieces. Buys 60 mss/year. Query with published clips. Length: 1,500-2,500 words. Pays $100-400.

Photos: Send photos with submission. Reviews b&w contact sheets, color transparencies. Offers $25-50 per photo (on occastion). Buys first North American serial rights.

Fiction: Mainstream, novel excerpts, slice-of-life vignettes. "All fiction must have Hollywood theme, setting or element, however glancing." "No stories without human heft." Buys 6 mss/year. Send complete ms. Length 500-2,500 words. Pays $35-200.

Poetry: Avant-garde and free verse. Buys 12 poems/year. Submit maximum 4 poems. Length: 5-40 lines. Pays $35-50.

Tips: "Submit clips covering a range of subject matter showing your knowledge of the Hollywood industry or Hollywood the city. Include cover letter briefly describing your topic interests. Know the current industry and coming developments."

‡**INSIDE HOLLYWOOD,** World Publishing, 990 Grove St., Evanston IL 60201. (708)491-6440. Editor: Robert Meyers. Managing Editor: James Turano. 90% freelance written. Bimonthly magazine covering movies, celebrity interviews, industry trends. Estab. 1991. Circ. 200,000. Pays on acceptance. Byline given. Offers $100 kill fee. Buys first North American serial rights. Submit seasonal/holiday material 6 months in advance. Simultaneous and previously published submissions OK. Reports in 3 weeks. Sample copy $2.50 with 9×12 SAE. Free writer's guidelines.

Nonfiction: Interview/profile, opinion (does not mean letters to the editor), photo feature. Query with published clips. Length: 800-2,000 words. Pays $250-400.

Photos: State availability of photos with submission or send photos with submission. Reviews negatives. Offers no additional payment for photos accepted with ms. Identification of subjects required. Buys all rights.

JET, Johnson Publishing Co., 820 S. Michigan, Chicago IL 60605. Staff written. Did not want to be listed.

‡**KPBS On Air,** San Diego's Guide to Public Broadcasting, KPBS-TV/FM, Suite 235, 2727 Camino Del Rio So., San Diego CA 92108. (619)293-3490. Editor: Michael Good. Managing Editor: Deanna Mackey. 15% freelance written. Monthly magazine on public broadcasting programming, San Diego arts. "Our readers are very intelligent, very sophisticated and rather mature. Your writing should be, too." Estab. 1970. Circ. 62,000. Pays on publication. Publishes ms an average of 1 month after acceptance. Byline given. Pays 50% kill fee. Not copyrighted. Buys first North American serial rights. Submit seasonal/holiday material 3 months in advance. Previously published submissions OK. Query for electronic submissions. Reports in 3 weeks. Sample copy for 9×12 SAE with 4 first class stamps.

Nonfiction: Book excerpts, essays, general interest, interview/profile, opinion, profiles of public TV and radio personalities, backgrounds on upcoming programs. Nothing over 1,500 words. Buys 60 mss/ year. Query with published clips. Length: 300-1,500 words. Pays $45-300. Sometimes pays expenses of writers on assignment

Photos: State availability of photos with submission. Reviews transparencies and 5×7 prints. Offers $30-300 per photo. Identification of subjects required. Buys one-time rights.

Columns/Departments: On the Town (upcoming arts events in San Diego), 800 words; Short Takes (backgrounds on public TV shows), 500 words; Radio Notes (backgrounds on public radio shows), 500 words. Buys 35 mss/year. Query or query with published clips. Length: 300-800 words. Pays $45-160.

Tips: "Feature stories for national writers are most open to freelancers. Arts stories for San Diego writers are most open. Read the magazine, then talk to me."

THE MAYBERRY GAZETTE, The World Authority on Mayberry, NC, Wake Forest University, 8955 Reynolds Station, Winston-Salem NC 27109. (919)998-2860. Editor: John Meroney. 50% freelance written. Quarterly paper. "The audience is broad-based." Estab. 1986. Circ. 5,000. Publishes ms an average of 2 months after acceptance. Byline sometimes given. Buys all rights. Submit seasonal/holiday material 4 months in advance. Simultanous and previously published submissions OK. Reports in 1 month. Sample copy $3. Writer's guidelines for large 9×12 SASE.

Nonfiction: Essays, historical/nostalgic, humor, interview/profile, new product, personal experience and photo feature. Buys 8 mss/year. Query with published clips. Length: 25-1,080 words. Pays in contributor copies or other premiums depending on individual situation; please inquire. Sometimes pays expenses of writers on assignment.

Photos: Send photos with submission. Reviews 8×10 prints. Offers no additional payment for photos accepted with ms. Identification of subjects required. Will make determination about rights upon seeing photographs.

Columns/Departments: Mayberry Alumni (Deals with individuals, on-screen and off, who were involved in some facet with the show), 250-300 words; Mayberry After Midnite (update column on numerous aspects of Mayberry lore), 900-1,080 words. Query with published clips.

Fiction: Humorous and slice-of-life vignettes. "We suggest that the individual writer be very clear and specific in their initial query as to what they plan to do." Buys 8 mss/year. Query with published clips. Length: 250-1,080 words.

Poetry: Light verse and traditional. Submit maximum 4 poems.

Fillers: Anecdotes, facts, gags to be illustrated by cartoonist and short humor. Length: 50-250 words.

Tips: "We suggest that writers be very familiar with the subjects they are writing about. The fictional town of Mayberry, North Carolina, as presented through television's "Andy Griffith Show" (CBS, 1960-1968) has become a permanent fixture in Americana. The publication maintains the original mood and theme expressed in the series. Writers should look to the program and issues of the publication for direction."

‡MOVIE MARKETPLACE, World Publishing, 990 Grove St., Evanston IL 60201. (708)491-6440. Editor: Robert Meyers. Managing Editor: James Turano. 90% freelance written. Bimonthly magazine featuring video and movie subjects. Estab. 1987. Circ. 100,000. **Pays on acceptance.** Byline given. Offers $100 kill fee. Buys first North American serial rights. Submit seasonal/holiday material 6 months in advance. Simultaneous and previously published submissions OK. Reports in 3 weeks. Sample copy $2.50 with 9×11 SAE.

Nonfiction: Interview/profile, movie-video topics. Query with published clips. Length: 800-1,500 words. Pays $100-200 for assigned articles. State availability of photos with submission or send photos with submission. Reviews contact sheets. Offers no additional payment for photos accepted with ms. Identification of subjects required. Buys first North American serial rights only.

‡NEW YORK NIGHTLIFE, MJC Publishers, 5550 Merrick Rd., Massapequa NY 11758. (516)797-0250. Editor: Cheryl Ann Meglio. Managing Editor: Allison A. Whitney. 60% freelance written. Monthly magazine covering entertainment: all facets. "*N.Y. and L.I. Nightlife* magazines cover regional entertainment interests as well as national interests." Estab. 1980. Circ. 35,000. Pays on publication. Publishes ms an average of 4 months after acceptance. Byline given. Buys all rights. Submit seasonal/ holiday material 4 months in advance. Query for electronic submissions. Reports in 10 weeks on queries. Free sample copy and writer's guidelines.

Nonfiction: General interest, humor, interview/profile, new product, travel. Buys 60 mss/year. Query with published clips. Length: 250-1,500 words. Pays $35-100.

Photos: State availability of photos with submission. Offers $25 maximum per photo. Captions, model releases and identification of subjects required.

Columns/Departments: Nightcap (humor piece), 700 words. Query with published clips. Pays $35-100.

Fiction: Humorous. Buys 8 mss/year. Length: 700 maximum words. Pays $75 maximum.

PEOPLE MAGAZINE, Time-Warner, Inc., 1675 Broadway, Rockefeller Center, New York NY 10019. Did not want to be listed.

THE PLAY MACHINE, P.O. Box 330507, Houston TX 77233-0507. Editor: Norman Clark Stewart Jr. 90% freelance written. Quarterly tabloid of recreation/adult play. Our publication is dedicated to reviving the spirit of playfulness in a workaholic world. Estab. 1990. Circ. 1,000. Pays on publication. Byline given. Buys first North American, one-time or second serial (reprint) rights. Submit seasonal/ holiday material 8 months in advance. Simultaneous and previously published submissions OK. Reports in 8 months on mss. Sample copy with 9 × 12 SAE and 4 first class stamps. Writer's guidelines for #10 SAE with 2 first class stamps.
Nonfiction: How-to (play or have fun), humor (not satire—playful), interview/profile (with pranksters/jokers or genius in relation to fun), new product (recreational/hobby, etc.). Nothing that is not fun, playful or related to recreation—nothing serious. Buys 20-100 mss/year. Send complete ms. Length: 3,500 words maximum. Pays $50 maximum for unsolicited articles.
Photos: Send photos with submission. Offers no additional payment for photos accepted with ms. Model releases and identification of subjects required. Buys one-time rights.
Fillers: Anecdotes, facts, gags to be illustrated by cartoonist, short humor. Buys 200/year. Pays $5 maximum.
Tips: "Have fun writing the submissions."

PLAYBILL, Playbill Inc., Suite 320, 71 Vanderbilt Ave., New York NY 10169. (212)557-5757. Editor: Joan Alleman. 50% freelance written. Monthly magazine covering NYC, Broadway and Off-Broadway theater. Estab. 1884. Circ. 1.75 million. **Pays on acceptance.** Publishes ms an average of 2 months after acceptance. Byline given. Buys all rights. Reports in 2 months.
Nonfiction: Book excerpts, humor, interview/profile, personal experience—must all be theater related. Buys approximately 10 mss/year. Query with published clips. Length: 1,500-1,800 words. Pays $250-500.
Photos: State availability of photos with submission. Offers no additional payment for photos accepted with ms. Identification of subjects required.
Fillers: Anecdotes, facts and short humor. Buys 10 mss/year. Length: 350-700 words. Pays $50-100. Must all be theater related.

PREMIERE, Murdoch Publications, Inc., 2 Park Ave., 4th Fl, New York NY 10016. (212)725-7927. Editor: Susan Lyne. Monthly magazine. "Monthly magazine for young adults (18-34 years old) that takes readers behind the scenes of movies in release and in production." **Pays on acceptance.** Byline given. Offers 25% kill fee. Buys first North American serial rights and world rights for 3 months. Submit seasonal/holiday material 4 months in advance. Reports in 4-5 weeks on queries.
Nonfiction: Film. Video issue (January), Year-End Issue (February), Academy Award Issue (April), Summer Preview Issue (June), Fall Preview Issue (October). Query with published clips. Maximum length 2,500 words. Pays $1/word maximum. Pays expenses of writers on assignment.
Columns/Departments: Maximum length 1,000 word. Pays $1/word maximum.
Fillers: Features, columns etc. Maximum length 500 words. Pays 50¢/word maximum.
Tips: "*Premiere* looks for articles that go behind the scenes of movies in release and in production; that answer questions about creative strategy, development, financing and distribution as well as focusing on the producers, directors and stars who create the films. Feature articles include interviews, profiles and film commentary and analysis. Monthly departments look for coverage of the movie business, video technology and hardware, home video, movie music/scoring and books."

‡SATELLITE ORBIT, Commtek Communications Corp., Suite 600, 8330 Boone Blvd., Vienna VA 22182. (703)827-0511. Publisher: David Wolford. Editor: Michael Doan. 10% freelance written. Monthly magazine. **Pays on acceptance.** Publishes ms an average of 3 months after acceptance. Kill fee varies. Reports in 1 month.
Nonfiction: "Wants to see articles on satellite programming, equipment, television trends, celebrity interviews. Query with published clips. Length: 700 words. Pay varies.

‡SOAP OPERA DIGEST, News America, 45 W. 25 St., New York NY 10010. Editor: Meredith Berlin. Managing Editor: Lynn Leahey. 20% freelance written. Bimonthly magazine covering soap operas. "Extensive knowledge of daytime and prime time soap operas is required." Estab. 1975. Circ.

For explanation of symbols, see the Key to Symbols and Abbreviations on Page 5. For unfamiliar words, see the Glossary.

1,000,000+. **Pays on acceptance.** Publishes ms an average of 3 months after acceptance. Byline given. Offers 30% kill fee. Buys first North American serial rights and second serial (reprint) rights. Submit seasonal/holiday material 4 months in advance. Reports in 1 month. Writer's guidelines for #10 SAE with 1 first class stamp.

Nonfiction: Interview/profile. No essays. Buys 30 mss/year. Query with published clips. Length: 1,000-2,000 words. Pays $250-500 for assigned articles; $150-250 for unsolicited articles. Sometimes pays expenses of writers on assignment.

Photos: Offers no additional payment for photos accepted with ms. Buys all rights.

TDC, The Magazine of the Discovery Channel, Discovery Publishing, Inc., 7700 Wisconsin Ave., Bethesda MD 20814. (301)986-1999. Editor: Rebecca Farwell. Managing Editor: Kathy H. Davis. A monthly magazine that amplifies and develops—but does not review or retell—the topics covered on the channel including science and technology, nature and ecology, human adventure, history, people and places. 90% freelance written. Estab. 1985. Circ. 150,000. **Pays on acceptance.** Articles commissioned by staff, though queries sometimes considered. Buys first North American rights. Reports in 3 weeks. Writer's guidelines for SASE. Sample copy $2.50 with 10×12 SAE and 3 first class stamps.

Nonfiction: Adventure, nature, history; health, science and technology; people, places, culture; human interest, world events and trends, photo features, book excerpts—all with an eye for the experiential "small" story in an effort to say something about a "larger" issues. Buys 70-80 mss/year. Send letter of introduction with published clips and resume. No phone queries. Length 100-4,000 words. Pays range of fees from 25¢-$1/word, depending on assignment.

Photos: State availability of photos, if any, with submission.

Columns/Departments: Roundabout (nonfictional notes and musings), Once Upon a Time (history), Heart and Soul (health and medicine), American Pie (Americana), Local Hero (extraordinary deeds by ordinary people), Global Links (intriguing but overlooked connections is a shrinking world), Because It's There (adventure), and Eureka! (science and technology). Length: 100-1,200 words.

Tips: "Our objective is to approach nonfiction subjects in a literary style. We hope to entertain as well as educate. We are always looking for writing with a strong 'you are there' presence."

TDR; The Drama Review: A Journal of Performance Studies, New York University, 721 Broadway, 6th Floor, New York NY 10003. (212)998-1626. Editor: Richard Schechner. 95% freelance written. Works with a small number of new/unpublished writers each year. "Emphasis not only on theater but also dance, ritual, musical performance, mime, and other facets of performative behavior. For avantgarde community, students and professors of anthropology, performance studies and related fields. Political material is welcome." Quarterly magazine. Estab. 1954. Circ. 7,000. Pays on publication. Submit material 4 months in advance. Previously published (if published in another language) submissions OK. Reports in 2 months. Publishes ms an average of 6 months after acceptance. Sample copy $8 (from MIT Press); free writer's guidelines.

Nonfiction: Barbara Harrington, managing editor. Buys 10-20 mss/issue. Query by letter only. Pays 3¢/word.

Photos: Barbara Harrington, managing editor. State availability of photos with submission. 5×7 b&w photos preferred. Captions required.

Tips: "*TDR* is a place where contrasting ideas and opinions meet. A forum for writing about performances and the social, economic and political contexts in which performances happen. The editors want interdisciplinary, intercultural, multivocal, eclectic submissions."

VIDEO MAGAZINE, Reese Communications, 460 West 34 St., New York NY 10001. (212)947-6500. FAX: (212)947-6727. Monthly magazine on home video in all its aspects. Estab. 1977. Circ. 450,000. **Pays on acceptance.** Publishes ms an average of 2-4 months after acceptance. Byline given. Buys first North American serial rights. Submit seasonal/holiday material 5 months in advance. Query for electronic submissions. Reports in 2-4 weeks on queries; 1-2 weeks on mss. Sample copy for 8x11 SAE.

Nonfiction: Art Levis. Book excerpts (pre-publication galleys), how-to (editing and camera shooting), interview/profile, personal experience and technical. Buys 50-60 mss/year. Query with published clilps. Length: 1,000-2,500 words. Pays $400-750 for assigned articles. Pays expenses of writers on assignment.

Photos: State availability of photos with submission. Captions, model releases and identification of subjects required. Buys one-time rights.

Columns/Departments: Camcorner (How-to shoot/edit home videos), 1,200 words; Technically Speaking (Technical aspects of home video gear), 1,200; Gazette (Celebrity interviews/offbeat video applications), 200-500 words. Query with published clips. Length: 700-1,800 words. Pays $100-500.

Fillers: Brent Butterworth. Facts. Length: 100-200 words. Pays $25.

VIDEOMANIA, "The Video Collector's Newspaper," Legs Of Stone Publishing Co., P.O. Box 47, Princeton WI 54968. Editor: Bob Katerzynske. 70% freelance written. Eager to work with new/unpublished writers. A monthly tabloid for the home video hobbyist. "Our readers are very much 'into' home video: they like reading about it—including both video hardware and software—98% also collect video (movies, vintage TV, etc.)." Estab. 1981. Circ. 5,000. Pays on publication. Publishes ms an average of 3 months after acceptance. Byline given. Buys all rights; may reassign. Submit seasonal/holiday material 6 months in advance. Reports in 3 weeks on mss. Sample copy for 9×12 SAE and $2.50 postage; writer's guidelines for #10 SASE .

Nonfiction: Book excerpts, videotape and book reviews, expose, general interest, historical/nostalgic, how-to, humor, interview/profile, new product, opinion, personal experience, photo feature, technical and travel. "All articles should deal with video and/or film. We always have special holiday issues in November and December." No *complicated* technical pieces." Buys 24 mss/year. Send complete ms. Length: 500-800 words. Pays $2.50 maximum. "Contributor copies also used for payment."

Photos: Send photos with submissions. Reviews contact sheets and 3×5 prints. Offers no additional payment for photos accepted with ms. Model releases and identification of subjects required. Buys all rights; may reassign.

Fiction: Adventure, horror and humorous. "We want short, video-related fiction only on an occasional basis. Since we aim for a general readership, we do not want any pornographic material." Buys 5 mss/year. Send complete ms. Length: 400 words. Pays $2.50 maximum plus copies.

Tips: "We want to offer more reviews and articles on offbeat, obscure and rare movies, videos and stars. Write in a plain, easy-to-understand style. We're not looking for a highhanded, knock-'em-dead writing style . . . just something good! We want more short video, film and book reviews by freelancers."

Ethnic/Minority

Ethnic magazines, especially for Hispanics, have started up and done well during the past year. Some ethnic magazines seek material that unites people of all races. Ideas, interests and concerns of nationalities and religions are covered by publications in this category. General interest lifestyle magazines for these groups are also included. Many ethnic publications are locally-oriented or highly specialized and do not wish to be listed in a national publication such as *Writer's Market*. Query the editor of an ethnic publication with which you're familiar before submitting a manuscript, but do not consider these markets closed because they are not listed in this section. Additional markets for writing with an ethnic orientation are located in the following sections: Career, College and Alumni; Juvenile; Men's; Women's; and Teen and Young Adult.

AFRICA ABROAD, 232 Valeside #F, P.O. Box 1096 Massillon, OH 44646-1096. (216)830-1277. Editor/Publisher: Isaiah Jackson. Managing Editor: John Misha. 95% freelance written. Monthly newspaper covering news that affects Africa, Africans and the entire Black race. Estab. 1989. Circ. 5,000. Pays on publication. Publishes ms an average of 3 months after acceptance. Byline given. Not copyrighted. Buys all rights. Submit seasonal/holiday material 4 months in advance. Free writer's guidelines, SASE required.

Nonfiction: Exposé, general interest, historical/nostalgic, humor, inspirational, interview/profile, opinion, personal experience, photo feature, travel, food, political and economy. Buys 36 mss/year. Send complete ms. Length: 500-3,000 words. Pays $20-200 for assigned articles; $20-100 for unsolicited articles. Sometimes pays expenses of writers on assignment.

Photos: Send photos with submission or state availability of photos with submission. Reviews 5×7 transparencies and prints. Offers $5 per photo. Captions, model releases and identification of subjects required. Buys all rights.

Columns/Departments: Food (cooking and review African food and restaurants), Marriage, Political and Economy, all 250-400 words. Send complete ms. Length: 250-400 words. Pays $15.

Poetry: Traditional. Submit maximum 2 poems. Pays $10.

Fillers: Facts and short humor. Offers no payment.

Tips: "Submit with a note about interest in African affairs."

AFRICAN-AMERICAN HERITAGE, Dellco Publishing Company, Suite 103, 8443 S. Crenshaw Blvd., Inglewood CA 90305. (213)752-3706. Editor: Dennis W. DeLoach. 30% freelance written. Bimonthly magazine looking for "positive, informative, educational articles that build self-esteem, pride and an appreciation for the richness of culture and history." Estab. 1978. Circ. 25,000. Pays on publication. Publishes ms an average of 3-6 months after acceptance. Byline given. Offers 25% kill fee. Buys First North American serial rights, one-time rights or simultaneous rights. Submit seasonal/holiday material 6 months in advance. Simultaneous and previously published submissions OK. Reports in 1 month on queries; two months on mss. Free sample copy. Writer's guidelines for 1 SAE with 4 first class stamps.

Nonfiction: Book excerpts, essays, general interest, historical/nostalgic, how-to, humor, inspirational, interview/profile, new product, opinion, personal experience, photo feature, religious and travel. Black History Month (February). Buys 6 mss/year. Query. Length: 200-2,500 words. Pays $25-300 for assigned articles. Sometimes pays expenses of writers on assignment.

Photos: State availability of photos with submission. Reviews 5×7 prints. Offers no additional payment for photos accepted with ms. Identification of subject required. Buys one-time rights.

Columns/Departments: History (historical profiles); Commentary (letters to the editor) 2,500 max.; Interviews (personalities, unusual careers, positive experiences) 2,500 max.; Short Stories (well written, entertaining) 2,500 max. Buys 12 mss/year. Query. Pays $25-300.

Fiction: Adventure, ethnic, historical, humorous, mystery, religious, romance and slice-of-life vignettes. "No erotica, horror, fantasy." Buys 6 mss/year. Query. Length: 200-2,500 words. Pays $25-300.

Poetry: Avant-garde, free verse, haiku, light verse and traditional. Buys 60 poems/year. Submit maximum 5 poems. Length: 4-36 lines. Pays $10-25.

Fillers: Anecdotes and facts. Buys 12/year. Length: 10-200 words. Pays $25-100.

AIM MAGAZINE, AIM Publishing Company, 7308 S. Eberhart Ave., Chicago IL 60619. (312)874-6184. Editor: Ruth Apilado. Managing Editor: Dr. Myron Apilado. 75% freelance written. Works with a small number of new/unpublished writers each year. Quarterly magazine on social betterment that promotes racial harmony and peace for high school, college and general audience. Circ. 10,000. Pays on publication. Publishes ms an average of 3 months after acceptance. Offers 60% of contract as kill fee. Not copyrighted. Buys one-time rights. Submit seasonal/holiday material 6 months in advance. Simultaneous queries and submissions OK. Reports in 6 weeks on queries. Sample copy and writer's guidelines for $3.50, 8½×11 SAE and 4 first class stamps.

Nonfiction: Exposé (education); general interest (social significance); historical/nostalgic (Black or Indian); how-to (create a more equitable society); and profile (one who is making social contributions to community); and book reviews and reviews of plays "that reflect our ethnic/minority orientation." No religious material. Buys 16 mss/year. Send complete ms. Length: 500-800 words. Pays $25-35.

Photos: Reviews b&w prints. Captions and identification of subjects required.

Fiction: Ethnic, historical, mainstream, and suspense. Fiction that teaches the brotherhood of man. Buys 20 mss/year. Send complete ms. Length: 1,000-1,500 words. Pays $25-35.

Poetry: Avant-garde, free verse, light verse. No "preachy" poetry. Buys 20 poems/year. Submit maximum 5 poems. Length: 15-30 lines. Pays $3-5.

Fillers: Jokes, anecdotes and newsbreaks. Buys 30/year. Length: 50-100 words. Pays $5.

Tips: "Interview anyone of any age who unselfishly is making an unusual contribution to the lives of less fortunate individuals. Include photo and background of person. We look at the nations of the world as part of one family. Short stories and historical pieces about blacks and Indians are the areas most open to freelancers. Subject matter of submission is of paramount concern for us rather than writing style. Articles and stories showing the similarity in the lives of people with different racial backgrounds are desired."

THE AMERICAN CITIZEN ITALIAN PRESS, 13681 V St., Omaha NE 68137. (402)896-0403. FAX: (402)895-7820. Publisher/Editor: Diana C. Failla. 80% freelance written. Quarterly newspaper of Italian-American news/stories. Estab. 1923. Circ. 8,490. Pays on publication. Publishes ms an average of 3 months after acceptance. Byline given. Not copyrighted. Buys first North American serial rights. Submit seasonal/holiday material 2 months in advance. Previously published submissions OK. Reports in 1 month. Sample copy for 10×13 SAE and $1.50 postage; writer's guidelines for #10 SAE with 2 first class stamps.

Nonfiction: Book excerpts, general interest, historical/nostalgic, opinion, photo feature, celebrity pieces, travel, fashions, profiles and sports (Italian players). Query with published clips. Length: 400-600 words. Pays $15-25. Pays more for in-depth pieces.

Photos: State availability of photos. Reviews b&w prints. Pays $5. Captions and identification of subjects required. Buys all rights.

Columns/Departments: Query.

Fiction: Query. Pays $15-20.

Poetry: Submit maximum 5 poems. Pays $5-10.

Tips: "Human interest stories are the most open to freelancers. We like work dealing with current issues involving those of Italian/American descent."

AMERICAN DANE, The Danish Brotherhood in America, 3717 Harney St., Omaha NE 68131-3844. (402)341-5049. FAX: (402)341-0830. Editor: Jerome L. Christensen. Managing Editor: Jennifer C. Denning. 50% freelance written. Prefers to work with published/ established writers; works with a small number of new/unpublished writers each year. The monthly magazine of the Danish Brotherhood in America. All articles must have Danish ethnic flavor. Estab. 1916. Circ. 10,000. Pays on publication. Publishes ms an average of 1 year after acceptance. Byline given. Not copyrighted. Buys first rights. Submit seasonal/holiday material 1 year in advance. Reports in 2 weeks on queries. Sample copy for 9½×4 SAE and 3 first class stamps; writer's guidelines for #10 SASE.

Nonfiction: Historical, humor, inspirational, personal experience, photo feature and travel, all with a Danish flavor. Buys 12 mss/year. Query. Length: 1,500 words maximum. Pays $50 maximum for unsolicited articles.

Photos: Send photos with submission. Reviews prints. Offers no additional payment for photos accepted with ms. Captions and identification of subjects required. Buys one-time rights.

Fiction: Adventure, historical, humorous, mystery, romance and suspense, all with a Danish flavor. Buys 6-12 mss/year. Query with published clips. Length: 1,500 words maximum. Pays $50 maximum.

Poetry: Traditional. Buys 1-6 poems/year. Submit maximum 6 poems. Pays $35 maximum.

Fillers: Anecdotes and short humor. Buys up to 12/year. Length: 300 words maximum. Pays $15 maximum.

Tips: "Feature articles are most open to freelancers. Reviews unsolicited manuscripts in August only."

AMERICAN JEWISH WORLD, AJW Publishing Inc., 4509 Minnetonka Blvd., Minneapolis MN 55416. (612)920-7000. Managing Editor: Marshall Hoffman. 10% freelance written. Weekly Jewish newspaper covering local, national and international stories. Estab. 1912. Circ. 6,500. Pays on publication. Publishes ms an average of 1-4 months after acceptance. Byline given. Publication copyrighted. Makes work-for-hire assignments. Submit seasonal/holiday material 3 months in advance. Simultaneous and photocopied submissions OK. Free sample copy and writer's guidelines.

Nonfiction: Essays, expose, general interest, historical/nostalgic, humor, inspirational, interview/profile, opinion, personal experience, photo feature, religious, travel. Buys 30-50 mss/year. Query with or without published clips, or send complete ms. Length: 1,000 words maximum. Pays $10-75. Sometimes pays expenses of writers on assignment.

Photos: State availability of photos with submission. Reviews prints. Pays $5 per photo. Identification of subjects required. Buys one-time rights.

‡AMERICAN VISIONS, The Magazine of Afro-American Culture, Warwick Communications, 1538 9th St. NW, Washington DC 20001. (202)462-1779. Managing Editor: Joanne Harris. 75% freelance written. Bimonthly magazine on African-American art, culture and history. "Editorial is reportorial, current, objective, 'pop-scholarly'. Audience is ages 25-54, mostly black, college educated." Estab. 1986. Circ. 102,000. Pays 30 days after publication. publishes mss an average of 2 months after acceptance. Byline given. Offers 25% "contract agreement." Buys first North American, one-time and second serial (reprint) rights. Submit seasonal/holiday material 5 months in advance. Simultaneous and previously published submissions OK. Query for electronic submissions. Reports in 2 months. Free sample copy and writer's guidelines.

Nonfiction: Book excerpts, general interest, historical/nostalgic, interview/profile, photo feature, travel. Publishes travel supplements—domestic, Africa, Europe, Canada, Mexico. No fiction, poetry, personal experience or opinion. Buys about 55 mss/year. Query with or without published clips, or send complete ms. Length: 500-2,500 words. Pays $100-750 for assigned articles; $100-600 for unsolicited articles. Sometimes pays expenses of writers on assignment.

Photos: State availability of photos with submission. Reviews contact sheets, 3×5 transparencies, and 3×5 or 8×10 prints. Offers $15 minimum. Identification of subjects required. Buys one-time rights.

Columns/Departments: Cuisine, Film, Music, Profile, 750-1,500 words. Buys about 40 mss/year. Query or send complete ms. Pays $100-400.

Tips: "Little-known but terribly interesting information about black history and culture is desired. Aim at an upscale audience. Send ms with credentials."

‡ARARAT, 585 Saddle River Rd., Saddle Brook NJ 07662. Editor-in-Chief: Leo Hamalian. 80% freelance written. Emphasizes Armenian life and culture for Americans of Armenian descent and Armenian immigrants. "Most are well-educated; some are Old World." Quarterly magazine. Circ. 2,200. Pays on publication. Publishes ms an average of 1 year after acceptance. Buys first North American serial rights and second (reprint) rights to material originally published elsewhere. Submit seasonal/holiday material at least 3 months in advance. Photocopied and previously published submissions OK. Reports in 6 weeks. Sample copy $7 plus 4 first class stamps.

Nonfiction: Historical (history of Armenian people, of leaders, etc.); interviews (with prominent or interesting Armenians in any field, but articles are preferred); profile (on subjects relating to Armenian life and culture); personal experience (revealing aspects of typical Armenian life); and travel (in Armenia and Armenian communities throughout the world and the US). Buys 3 mss/issue. Query. Length: 1,000-6,000 words. Pays $25-100.

Columns/Departments: Reviews of books by Armenians or relating to Armenians. Buys 6/issue. Query. Pays $25. Open to suggestions for new columns/departments.
Fiction: Any stories dealing with Armenian life in America or in the old country. Buys 4 mss/year. Query. Length: 2,000-5,000 words. Pays $50-100.
Poetry: Any verse that is Armenian in theme. Buys 6/issue. Pays $10.
Tips: "Read the magazine, and write about the kind of subjects we are obviously interested in, e.g., Kirlian photography, Aram Avakian's films, etc. Remember that we have become almost totally ethnic in subject matter, but we want articles that present (to the rest of the world) the Armenian in an interesting way. The most frequent mistake made by writers in completing an article for us is that they are not sufficiently versed in Armenian history/culture. The articles are too superficial for our audience. We also accept articles or stories dealing with Armenia's neighboring nations and adopted homelands."

‡ARMENIAN INTERNATIONAL MAGAZINE, Suite 305, 109 E. Harvard St., Glendale CA 91205. (818)546-2246. FAX: (818)546-2283. Editor: Charles Nazarian. Managing Editor: Vartan Oskanian. 75% freelance written. Monthly ethnic news magazine about Armenians worldwide. "Uplifting articles about Armenians and issues concerning Armenians—politics, business, education, culture, profiles, etc." Estab. 1989. Circ. 30,000. Pays on publication. Publishes ms an average of 3 months after acceptance. Bylines sometimes given. Offers 20% kill fee. Buys all rights. Submit seasonal/holiday material 2 months in advance. Query for electronic submissions. Reports in 2 weeks on queries; 6 weeks on mss.
Nonfiction: General interest, historical/nostalgic, humor, inspirational, interview/profile, photo feature and religious. Buys 120 mss/year. Query with published clips. Length: 600-1,200 words. Pays $100-400 for assigned articles; $50-200 for unsolicited articles. Sometimes pays expenses of writers on assignment. State availability of photos with submission. Reviews negatives, transparencies and prints. Offers $10-50 per photo. Captions and identification of subjects required. Buys all rights.
Fillers: "Report any major development (commercial, cultural or political) involving Armenians in any part of the world, especially Soviet Armenia."

THE B'NAI B'RITH INTERNATIONAL, JEWISH MONTHLY, 1640 Rhode Island Ave. NW, Washington DC 20036. (202)857-6645. Editor: Jeff Rubin. 50% freelance written. Magazine covering Jewish affairs published 10 times per year. Estab. 1886. Circ. 185,000. **Pays on acceptance.** Publishes ms an average of 5 months after acceptance. Byline given. Kill fee depends on rate of payment. Buys first North American serial rights. Submit seasonal/holiday material 6 months in advance. Query for electronic submissions. Reports in 2 weeks. Sample copy $1 with 9×13 SAE and 2 first class stamps. Free writer's guidelines.
Nonfiction: Book excerpts, essay, exposé, general interest, historical/nostalgic, humor, inspirational, interview/profile, new product, personal experience, photo feature, travel. Buys 40-50 mss/year. Query with published clips. Length: 250-3,000 words. Pays $50-1,000 for assigned articles; $50-500 for unsolicited articles. Sometimes pays expenses of writers on assignment.
Photos: State availability of photos with submission. Reviews contact sheets, 2×3 transparencies and prints. Payment depends on quality and type of photograph. Identification of subjects required. Buys one-time rights.
Columns/Departments: Generations (senior citizens and parenting) and Arts (theater, movie, book reviews). Buys 10 mss/year. Query. Length: 500-750 words. Pays $60-200.
Fiction: "We publish very few works of fiction each year and strongly discourage writers from submitting such material to us. Short stories should present truly novel perspectives on Jewish life and should be of the highest caliber of writing. Fiction based on personal anecdotes or the Holocaust will not be reviewed." Buys 1-2 mss/year. Send complete ms. Length: 1,000-3,000 words. Pays $200-500.
Tips: "Writers should submit clips with their queries. The best way to break in to the *Jewish Monthly* is to submit a range of good story ideas accompanied by clips. We aim to establish relationships with writers and we tend to be loyal. All sections are equally open."

‡BRITISH HERITAGE, Cowles Magazine, 2245 Kohn Rd., Harrisburg PA 17105. (717)657-9555. Editor: Gail Huganir. Managing Editor: Bruce Heydt. 80% freelance written. Consumer magazine covering the United Kingdom. "*British Heritage* is for anglophiles. We cover places of interest in Great Britain, profiles of British historical figures, new British products, British foods and crafts." Estab. 1979. Circ. 110,000. **Pays on acceptance.** Bylines sometimes given. Buys first North American and all rights—in most cases. Submit seasonal/holiday material 6 months in advance. Simultaneous submissions OK. Reports in 4 months. Sample copy $3.95; free writer's guidelines.
Nonfiction: Historical, interview/profile, travel. No fiction. Buys 60 mss/year. Query. Length: 1,000-2,000 words. Pays $100-400 for assigned articles; $100-200 for unsolicited articles.
Photos: State availability of photos with submission. Pays $50-250 for photos. Identification of subjects required. Buys one-time rights.

‡CANADIAN INDIE STAR, C.C. Publications, 1429 Dufferin St., Toronto, Ontario M6H 4C7. (416)533-8243. Editor: S. Singh. Managing Editor: T.S. Gill. 5% freelance written. Bimonthly newsletter covering minority rights, particularly Sikhs in India/around the world. Estab. 1974. Circ. 3,000. Pays on publication. Publishes ms an average of 1-2 months after acceptance. Byline sometimes given. Not copyrighted. Buys one-time rights. Submit seasonal/holiday material 2 months in advance. Sample copy $1 with SAE and 1 first class stamp.

Nonfiction: General interest, opinion (does not mean letters to the editor), religious, travel, minority languages. Nothing promoting wars or brain washing. Query with published clips. Length: 100-500 words. Pays $25-100 for assigned articles; $25-75 for unsolicited articles. Pays in contributor copies or other premiums if desired by writers. Sometimes pays expenses of writers on assignment.

Photos: State availability of photos with submission or send photos with submission. Reviews contact sheets and prints. Offers no additional payment for photos accepted with ms. Captions required. Buys one-time rights.

Columns/Departments: S. Simph. Query with published clips. Length: 100-500 words. Pays $25-100.

Fiction: T. Gill. Ethnic, experimental, historical, religious. Buys 50-60 mss/year. Query with published clips. Length: 100-500 words. Pays $25-100.

Poetry: Free verse, Haiku, light verse, traditional. Buys 20-30 poems/year. Submit maximum 1-5 poems. Pays $10-25.

Fillers: Anecdotes, facts. Buys 50-150/year. Length: 50-150 words. Pays $5-15.

CONGRESS MONTHLY, American Jewish Congress, 15 E. 84th St., New York NY 10028. (212)879-4500. Editor: Maier Deshell. 90% freelance written. Magazine published 7 times/year covering topics of concern to the American Jewish community representing a wide range of views. Distributed mainly to the members of the American Jewish Congress; readers are intellectual, Jewish, involved. Estab. 1933. Circ. 35,000. Pays on publication. Publishes ms an average of 3 months after acceptance. Byline given. Buys one-time rights. Submit seasonal/holiday material 2 months in advance. No previously published submissions. Reports in 2 months.

Nonfiction: General interest ("current topical issues geared toward our audience"). No technical material. Send complete ms. Length: 2,000 words maximum. Pays $100-150/article.

Photos: State availability of photos. Reviews b&w prints. "Photos are paid for with payment for ms."

Columns/Departments: Book, film, art and music reviews. Send complete ms. Length: 1,000 words maximum. Pays $100-150/article.

EBONY MAGAZINE, 820 S. Michigan Ave., Chicago IL 60605. (312)322-9200. Editor: John H. Johnson. Senior Staff Editor: Charles F. Whitaker. 10% freelance written. For Black readers of the U.S., Africa, and the Caribbean. Monthly. Circ. 1.8 million. Buys first North American serial rights and all rights. Buys about 10 mss/year. Pays on publication. Publishes ms an average of 3 months after acceptance. Submit seasonal material 2 months in advance. Query. Reports in 1 month.

Nonfiction: Achievement and human interest stories about, or of concern to, Black readers. Interviews, profiles and humor pieces are bought. Length: 1,500 words maximum. "Study magazine and needs carefully. Perhaps one out of 50 submissions interests us. Most are totally irrelevant to our needs and are simply returned." Pays $200 minimum. Sometimes pays the expenses of writers on assignment.

Photos: Purchased with mss, and with captions only. Buys 8×10 glossy prints, color transparencies, 35mm color. Submit negatives and contact sheets when possible. Offers no additional payment for photos accepted with mss.

GREATER PHOENIX JEWISH NEWS, Phoenix Jewish News, Inc., P.O. Box 26590, Phoenix AZ 85068. (602)870-9470. FAX: (602)870-0426. Executive Editor: Flo Eckstein. Managing Editor: Leni Reiss. 10% freelance written. Prefers to work with published/established writers. Weekly tabloid covering subjects of interest to Jewish readers. Estab. 1948. Circ. 7,000. Publishes ms an average of 3 months after acceptance. Byline given. Submit seasonal/holiday material 3 months in advance. Simultaneous queries, and simultaneous and previously published submissions OK. Sample copy $1.

Nonfiction: General interest, issue analysis, interview/profile, opinion, personal experience, photo feature and travel. Special sections include Fashion and Health, House and Home, Back to School, Summer Camps, Party Planning, Bridal, Travel, Business and Finance, and Jewish Holidays. Send complete ms. Length: 1,000-2,500 words. Pays $15-75 for simultaneous rights; $1.50/column inch for first serial rights.

Photos: Send photos with query or ms. Pays $10 for 8×10 b&w prints. Captions required.

Tips: "We are looking for lifestyle and issue-oriented pieces of particular interest to Jewish readers. Our newspaper reaches across the religious, political, social and economic spectrum of Jewish residents in this burgeoning southwestern metropolitan area. We stay away from cute stories as well as ponderous submissions."

HERITAGE FLORIDA JEWISH NEWS, 207 O'Brien Rd. P.O. Box 300742, Fern Park FL 32730. (407)834-8787. Associate Editor: Edith Schulman. Publisher/Editor: Jeffrey Gaeser. 30% freelance written. Weekly tabloid on Jewish subjects of local, national and international scope, except for special issues. "Covers news of local, national and international scope of interest to Jewish readers and not likely to be found in other publications." Estab. 1976. Circ. 10,000. Pays on publication. Publishes ms an average of 2 months after acceptance. Byline given. Buys first North American serial rights, first rights, one-time rights, second serial (reprint) rights or simultaneous rights. Submit seasonal/holiday material 2 months in advance. Photocopied and previously published submissions OK. Sample copy 50¢.
Nonfiction: General interest, interview/profile, opinion (does not mean letters to the editor), photo feature, religious and travel. "Especially needs articles for these annual issues: Rosh Hashanah, Financial, Chanukah, Celebration (wedding and bar mitzvah), Passover, Health and Fitness, Education and House and Home. No fiction, poems, first-person experiences." Buys 50 mss/year. Send complete ms. Length: 500-1,000 words. Pays $15-30. Sometimes pays expenses of writers on assignment.
Photos: State availability of photos with submission. Reviews 5 × 7 prints. Offers $5 per photo. Captions and identification of subjects required. Buys one-time rights.

THE HIGHLANDER, Angus J. Ray Associates, Inc., P.O. Box 397, Barrington IL 60011. (708)382-1035. Editor: Angus J. Ray. Managing Editor: Ethyl Kennedy Ray. 50% freelance written. Works with a small number of new/unpublished writers each year. Bimonthly magazine covering Scottish history, clans, genealogy, travel/history, and Scottish/American activities. Estab. 1930. Circ. 40,000. **Pays on acceptance.** Publishes ms an average of 6 months after acceptance. Byline given. Buys first North American serial rights and second serial (reprint) rights to material originally published elsewhere. Submit seasonal/holiday material 6 months in advance. Previously published submissions OK. Reports in 1 month. Sample copy for $2 and 9 × 12 SAE. Free writer's guidelines.
Nonfiction: Historical/nostalgic. "No fiction; no articles unrelated to Scotland." Buys 50 mss/year. Query. Length: 750-2,000 words. Pays $75-150. Sometimes pays the expenses of writers on assignment.
Photos: State availability of photos. Pays $5-10 for 8 × 10 b&w prints or transparencies. Reviews b&w contact sheets. Identification of subjects required. Buys one-time rights.
Tips: "Submit something that has appeared elsewhere."

HISPANIC, Hispanic Publishing Corporation, Suite 410, 111 Massachusetts Ave. NW, Washington DC 20001. (202)682-3000. FAX: (202)682-4901. Editor: Alfredo J. Estrada. Associate Editor: Ana Maria Arias. 90% freelance written. Monthly magazine for the Hispanic community. "*HISPANIC* is a general interest, lifestyle, entertainment, upbeat, role model publication." Estab. 1987. Circ. 150,000. Pays on publication. Publishes ms an average of 4 months after acceptance. Byline given. Offers 20% kill fee. Buys all rights. Submit seasonal/holiday material 4 months in advance. Free sample copy and writer's guidelines.
Nonfiction: General interest, historical/nostalgic, humor, interview/profile, opinion, personal experience, photo feature, travel. Buys 200 mss/year. Query. Length: 50-3,000 words. Pays $50-600. Pays writers "phone, travel and lunch expenses," but these must be cleared with editors first.
Photos: State availability of photos with submission. Reviews transparencies. Offers $25-600 per photo. Captions, model releases and identification of subjects required. Buys one-time rights.
Columns/Departments: Forum (political opinion and analysis), 600 words; La Merienda (humor), 50-200 words.

‡INDIA CURRENTS, America's Magazine of Indian Arts, Entertainment & Dining, P.O. Box 21285, San Jose CA 95151. (408)274-6966. Publisher: Ashok Jethanandani. Editor: Arvind Kumar. 70% freelance written. Monthly magazine covering East Indian culture in America. "We take the mystery and exoticism out of India and make it accessible and understandable." Estab. 1987. Circ. 27,500. Pays on publication. Publishes ms an average of 6 months after acceptance. Byline given. Buys first North American serial rights. Submit seasonal/holiday material 6 months in advance. Simultaneous submissions OK. Query for electronic submissions. Reports in 1 month on queries; 2 months on mss. Sample copy for 9 × 12 SAE with 4 first class stamps. Writer's guidelines for #10 SASE.
Nonfiction: Book excerpts, essays, general interest, humor, interview/profile, opinion, music reviews, film reviews, recipes, comic strips, fiction, personal experience, photo feature, religious, travel. Buys 60 mss/year. Send complete ms. Length: 300-1,500 words/Pays $10-30. "Free subscription for all accepted manuscripts."
Photos: Send photos with submission. Reviews 3 × 5 prints. Offers $5-10 per photo. Captions and identification of subjects required. Buys one-time rights.
Columns/Departments: Opinion (editorials about Indian life in the U.S.), 800 words; Audio Review (review of new releases of Indian music), 300 words; Film (review of new releases of Indian films), 300 words; Travel (a personal account of a trip to India), 750 words. Buys 50 mss/year. Send complete ms. Pays $10-20.

Fiction: Ethnic (Indian), historical, humorous, mainstream. "No pieces in which India is only a backdrop, where Indians are mere wallflowers." Buys 12 mss/year. Send complete ms. Length: 750-1,000 words. Pays $10-20.

Fillers: Anecdotes, facts, gags to be illustrated by cartoonist, newsbreaks, short humor. Length: 50 words maximum. Pays $5-10.

Tips: "We look for any special insights into India, Indians, their culture. We look for articles which show how Indian culture has contributed to American culture. Our readership is 50% Indian, 50% Indophile. Writers have the best chance selling us fiction, travel and audio review pieces. If you feel passionately about India, let it show in your writing."

INSIDE, The Jewish Exponent Magazine, Jewish Federation of Greater Philadelphia, 226 S. 16th St., Philadelphia PA 19102. (215)893-5700. FAX: (215)546-3957. Editor: Jane Biberman. Managing Editor: Linda Belsky Zamost. 95% freelance written (by assignment). Works with published/established writers and a small number of new/unpublished writers each year. Quarterly Jewish community magazine — for a general interest Jewish readership 25 years of age and older. Estab. 1979. Circ. 75,000. **Pays on acceptance.** Publishes ms an average of 2 months after acceptance. Byline given. Offers 20% kill fee. Buys first rights. Submit seasonal/holiday material 3 months in advance. Simultaneous queries OK. Reports in 2 weeks on queries; 3 weeks on mss. Sample copy for 9 × 12 SAE and $3; writer's guidelines for #10 SASE.

Nonfiction: Book excerpts, general interest, historical/nostalgic, humor, interview/profile. Philadelphia angle desirable. No personal religious experiences or trips to Israel. Buys 82 unsolicited mss/year. Query. Length: 600-3,000 words. Pays $200-1,000. Pays the expenses of writers on assignment.

Fiction: Short stories. Query.

Tips: "Personalities — very well known — and serious issues of concern to Jewish community needed."

‡**IRISH AMERICAN MAGAZINE,** Irish America Inc., 432 Park Ave. S., 10th Fl., New York NY 10016. (212)684-3366. Editor: Patricia Harty. Managing Editor: Niall O'Dowd. Monthly magazine covering Irish American issues. Estab. 1985. Circ. 56,000. Pays on publication. Byline given. Offers 50% kill fee. Buys one-time rights. Submit seasonal/holiday material 3 months in advance. Reports in 1 month.

Nonfiction: Special issue for St. Patrick's Day. Buys 2 mss/year. Send complete ms. Length: 1,000 words minimum. Pays $100-350 for assigned articles. Sometimes pays expenses of writers on assignment.

Photos: State availability of photos with submission. Offers $50-200 per photo. Identification of subjects required. Buys one-time rights.

Tips: "Well written feature articles on major Irish American figures have the best chance of being published."

‡**JEWISH ACTION,** Union of Orthodox Jewish Congregations of America, 45 West 36 St., 9th Fl., New York NY 10018. (212)244-2011. Editor: Heidi T. Pekarsky. Managing Editor: Tziporah Spear. 20% freelance written. "Quarterly magazine covering Jewish history, topics and literature." Circ. 80,000. Pays on publication. Publishes ms an average of 3 months after acceptance. Byline given. Offers 50% kill fee. Submit seasonal/holiday material 6 months in advance. Sample copy for 8½ × 11 SAE.

Nonfiction: Books excerpts, essays, historical/nostalgic, humor, inspirational, interview/profile, new product, personal experience, religious. "No articles about religions other than Judaism or articles that do not pertain to Judaism at all." Query with published clips. Length: 1,500-2,500 words. Pays $100-300 for assigned articles; $100-150 for unsolicited articles. Sometimes pays the expenses of writers on assignment.

Photos: Send photos with submission. Offers no additional payment for photos accepted with ms. Captions and identification of subjects required.

Columns/Departments: Jewish Living Section (consumer and lifestyle information), 1,500-2,000 words. Buys 10 mss/year. Query with published clips. Pays $100-300.

Fiction: Matis Greenblatt. Historical, humorous, religious. Buys 2 mss/year. Query with published clips.

‡**MIDSTREAM, A Monthly Jewish Review,** 110 E. 59 St., New York NY 10022. Editor: Joel Carmichael. 90% freelance written. Works with a small number of new/unpublished writers each year. Monthly. Circ. 10,000. Buys first North American serial rights. Byline given. Pays after publication. Publishes ms an average of 6 months after acceptance. Reports in 2 months. Fiction guidelines for SAE with 1 first class stamp.

Nonfiction: "Articles offering a critical interpretation of the past, searching examination of the present, and affording a medium for independent opinion and creative cultural expression. Articles on the political and social scene in Israel, on Jews in Russia, the U.S. and elsewhere; generally it helps to have a Zionist orientation." Buys historical and think pieces, primarily of Jewish and related content. Pays 5¢/word.

Fiction: Primarily of Jewish and related content. Pays 5¢/word.

Tips: "A book review is a good way to start. Send us a sample review or a clip, let us know your area of interest, suggest books you would like to review. For longer articles, give a brief account of your background or credentials in this field. Send query describing article or ms with cover letter. Since we are a monthly, we look for critical analysis rather than a 'journalistic' approach."

‡NATIVE PEOPLES MAGAZINE, The Arts and Lifeways, 1833 North 3rd St., Phoenix AZ 85004. (602)252-2236. FAX: (602)252-6180. Editor: Gary Avey. Quarterly magazine on Native Americans. "The primary purpose of this magazine is to offer a sensitive portrayal of the arts and lifeways of native peoples of the Americas." Estab. 1987. Circ. 40,000. Pays on publication. Byline given. Buys one-time rights. Query for electronic submissions. Reports in 1 month on queries; 2 weeks on mss. Sample copy for 8½ × 11 SAE with 5 first class stamps. Free writer's guidelines. Extremely high quality reproduction with full-color throughout.

Nonfiction: Book excerpts, historical/nostalgic, interview/profile, personal experience, photo feature. Buys 35 mss/year. Query with published clips. Length: 1,400-2,000 words. Pays 25-50¢/word. Sometimes pays expenses of writer's on assignment.

Photos: State availability of photos with submission. Reviews transparencies (all formats). Offers $75-150 per-page rates. Identification of subjects required. Buys one-time rights.

POLISH AMERICAN JOURNAL, Polonia's Voice, Panagraphics, Inc., 774 Fillmore Ave., Buffalo NY 14212. (716)852-8211. FAX: (716)852-8230. Editor: Mark A. Kohan. Managing Editor: Paulette Kulbacki. 20% freelance written. Monthly tabloid for Polonia (Polish and Polish-American events, people, etc.). "Stories should be about Polish-Americans active in their community on either a local or national level. Prefer biographies/histories of these people or essays on their accomplishments." Estab. 1911. Circ. 20,000. Pays at end of publication quarter (March, June, Sept., Dec.). Publishes ms 3-4 months after acceptance. Byline given. Offers $2 kill fee. Not copyrighted. Buys one-time rights. Submit seasonal/holiday material 3 months in advance. Previously published submissions OK. Query for electronic submissions. Sample copy for 9 × 12 SAE with 3 first class stamps.

Nonfiction: Exposé (story on Polish-Americans), general interest (community news), historical/nostalgic (retrospectives on events), how-to (organize groups, etc.), interview/profile (background on local Pol-Ams), opinion (historical observations, anti-defamation, etc.), personal experience (growing up Polish-American). Special issues on Easter and Christmas celebrations—how practiced in other areas; travel to Poland, airfare and comparisons, etc.; salute to prominent Polish-American business leaders, clergy, media personalities, etc. Buys 6-8 mss/year. Query. Length: 200-1,000 words. Pays $10-25. Sometimes pays expenses of writers on assignment.

Photos: State availability of photos with submission. Reviews 8½ × 11 prints. Offers $2-7.50 per solicited photo. Identification of subjects required. Buys one-time rights.

Columns/Departments: Forum/Viewpoints (observations on recent decisions/events), 750 words maximum; culture (music/art developments), 750 words maximum; scholarships/studies (grants and programs available), 750 words maximum. Buys 6 mss/year. Query. Pays $10-25.

Fillers: Anecdotes, facts, gags to be illustrated by cartoonist, newsbreaks and short humor. Buys 10/year. Length: 50-250 words. Pays $2-10.

Tips: "With the recent changes in Poland and within the Polish-American community, we have been flooded with hard news. There are some stories that are 'on deck,' i.e. need writers. We look to freelancers for lighter, human interest, humorous and/or reminiscent articles and essays."

THE UKRAINIAN WEEKLY, Ukrainian National Association, 30 Montgomery St., Jersey City NJ 07302. (201)434-0237. Editor: Roma Hadzewycz. 30% freelance written (mostly by a corps of regular contributors). A weekly tabloid covering news and issues of concern to Ukrainian community. Estab. 1933. Circ. 9,200. Pays on publication. Publishes ms an average of 1-2 months after acceptance. Byline given. Buys first North American serial rights, second serial (reprint) rights or makes work-for-hire assignments. Submit seasonal/holiday material 1 month in advance. Reports in 1 month. Free sample copy.

Nonfiction: Book excerpts, essays, exposé, general interest, historical/nostalgic, interview/profile, opinion, personal experience, photo feature and news events. Special issues include Easter, Christmas, anniversary of Helsinki Accords, anniversary of Ukrainian Helsinki monitoring group, student scholarships, anniversary of Chernobyl nuclear accident and year-end review of news. Buys 80 mss/year. Query with published clips. Length: 500-2,000 words. Pays $45-100 for assigned articles. Pays $25-100 for unsolicited articles. Sometimes pays the expenses of writers on assignment.

Photos: Send photos with submission. Reviews contact sheets, negatives and 3×5, 5×7 or 8×10 prints. Offers no additional payment for photos accepted with ms.
Columns/Departments: News & Views (commentary on news events), 500-1,000 words. Buys 10 mss/year. Query. Pays $25-50.
Tips: "Become acquainted with the Ukrainian community in the U.S. and Canada. The area of our publication most open to freelancers is community news—coverage of local events. We'll put more emphasis on events in Ukraine during this period in the USSR."

‡**VISTA, The Hispanic Magazine,** Suite 600, 999 Ponce de Leon Blvd., Coral Gables FL 33134. (305)442-2462. FAX: (305)443-7650. Editor, Publisher, CEO: Dilys Tosteson Garcia. Managing Editor: Judith C. Faerron. 95% freelance written. Prefers to work with published/established writers. An English-language weekly directed at Hispanic Americans. It appears as a supplement to 24 newspapers across the country with acombined circulation of one million in cities with large Latin populations. Pays on publication. Publishes ms an average of 4 months after acceptance. Byline given. Offers 25% of original price kill free. Buys first rights. Submit seasonal/holiday material 6 months in advance. Reports in 2 weeks on queries; 1 month on mss. Sample copy and writer's guidelines for $11\frac{1}{2} \times 12\frac{1}{2}$ SAE with 3 first class stamps.
Nonfiction: General interest, historical/nostalgic, inspirational, interview/profile, opinion and travel. No articles without a Hispanic American angle. Buys 90 mss/year. Query with published clips. Length: 100-1,500 words. Pays $50-500. Sometimes pays the expenses of writers on assignment.
Photos: State availability of photos with submission. Reviews contact sheets, negatives, transparencies and prints. Offers negotiable payment per photo. Identification of subjects required. Buys one-time rights.
Columns/Departments: Vistascopes and Newsnotes (Hispanic people in the news), 25 words; Cameo (profile of a Hispanic notable for his/her accomplishments), 500-750 words; Voices (personal views on matters affecting Hispanic Americans), 500 words. Buys 48 mss/year. Query with published clips. Length: 100-750 words. Pays $50-200.
Fiction: Slice-of-life vignettes. Buys 2 mss/year. Send complete ms. Length: 1,000 words maximum. Pays 20¢ per word.
Tips: "Be aware of topics and personalities of interest to Hispanic readers. We need profiles of Hispanic Americans in unusual or atypical roles and jobs. Anticipate events; profiles should tell the reader what the subject will be doing at the time of publication. Keep topics upbeat and positive: no stories on drugs, crimes. A light, breezy touch is needed for the profiles. Express your opinion in the Voices pages but be scrupulously impartial and accurate when writing articles of general interest."

Food and Drink

Magazines appealing to gourmets are classified here. Journals aimed at food processing, manufacturing and retailing are in the Trade section. Many magazines in General Interest and Women's categories also buy articles on food topics.

‡**BEST RECIPES MAGAZINE,** Grit Publishing Group, 208 W. Third Street, Williamsport PA 17701. (717)326-1771. Production Manager: Joseph A. Subarton. Editor: Michael Rafferty. 5% freelance written. Bimonthly magazine covering recipes, food, cooking and cooking tips. "*Best Recipes* seeks articles about creative people in cooking; profiles with recipe samples of ordinary people cooking features. No fancy recipes using exotic foods. *Best Recipes* theme is "simple cooking" for average housewives, cooks." Estab. 1987. Circ. 150,000. Pays on publication. Byline given. No kill fee. Not copyrighted. Buys one-time or second serial (reprint) rights. Submit seasonal/holiday material 6 months in advance. Previously published submissions OK. Reports in 2 weeks. Sample copy $4. Free writer's guidelines.
Nonfiction: How-to, interview/profile. "Do not send anything not related to foods, recipes, cooking tips and ideas." Buys 6-8 mss/year. Query. Length 500-1,500 words. Pays $75-200 for unsolicited articles.
Photos: State availability of photos with submission. Send photos with submission. Reviews contacts sheets, negatives, slides, 8×10 or 5×8 prints. Offers $25-75 per photo. Captions required. Buys one-time rights.
Tips: "Have a good knowledge of cooking and baking and be able to write features on such subjects or do profile articles about such people . . . Two or three recipes required with feature article. Recipes should be related directly to the article."

CHILE PEPPER, The Magazine of Spicy Foods, (formerly *The Whole Chile Pepper*), Out West Publishing Company, 5106 Grand NE, P.O. Box 4278, Albuquerque NM 87196. (505)266-8322. 25-30% freelance written. Bimonthly magazine on spicy foods. "The magazine is devoted to spicy foods, and most articles include recipes. We have a very devoted readership who love their food hot!" Estab. 1986. Circ. 60,000. Pays on publication. Offers 50% kill fee. Buys first and second rights. Submit seasonal/ holiday material 6 months in advance. Previously published submissions OK. Query for electronic submissions. Reports in 1 month on queries. Sample copy for 9×12 SAE with 5 first class stamps. Writer's guidelines for #10 SASE.

Nonfiction: Book excerpts (cookbooks), how-to (cooking and gardening with spicy foods), humor (having to do with spicy foods), new product (hot products), travel (having to do with spicy foods). Buys 20 mss/year. Query. Length: 1,000-3,000 words. Pays $150 minimum for assigned articles; $100 minimum for unsolicited articles. Sometimes pays expenses of writers on assignment.

Photos: State availability of photos with submission. Reviews contact sheets, negatives, transparencies and prints. Offers $25 minimum per photo. Captions and identification of subjects required. Buys one-time rights.

Fillers: Newsbreaks, short humor. Buys 5/year. Length: 100 minimum. Pays $25 minimum.

Tips: "We're always interested in queries from *food* writers. Articles about spicy foods with six to eight recipes are just right."

COOKING LIGHT, The Magazine of Food and Fitness, Southern Living, Inc. P.O. Box 1748, Birmingham AL 35201. (205)877-6000. Editor: Katherine M. Eakin. Managing Editor: B. Ellen Templeton. 75% freelance written. Bimonthly magazine on healthy recipes and fitness information. "*Cooking Light* is a positive approach to a healthier lifestyle. It's written for healthy people on regular diets who are counting calories or trying to make calories count toward better nutrition. Moderation, balance and variety are emphasized. The writing style is fresh, upbeat and encouraging, emphasizing that eating a balanced, varied, lower-calorie diet and exercising regularly do not have to be boring." Estab. 1987. Circ. 800,000. **Pays on acceptance.** Publishes ms an average of 12 months after acceptance. Byline sometimes given. Offers 25% of original contract fee as kill fee. Buys all rights. Submit seasonal/ holiday material 12 months in advance.

Nonfiction: Personal experience on nutrition, healthy recipes, fitness/exercise. Buys 150 mss/year. Query with published clips. Length: 400-2,000 words. Pays $250-2,000 for assigned articles. Pays expenses of writers on assignment.

Columns/Departments: Profile (an incident or event that occurred in one's life that resulted in a total lifestyle change), 2,000-2500 words; Children's Fitness (emphasis on prevention and intervention in regard to fitness, exercise, nutrition), 1,000-1,500 words; Taking Aim (a personal account of progression from desire to obstacle to achievement for incorporating exercise into one's routine schedule), 1,000-1,500 words and Downfall (a humorous personal account of desire to obstacle to the continuing struggle to overcome a particular food habit or addiction), 1,000-1,500 words. Buys 30 mss/year. Query. Length: 1,000-2,000 words. Pays $250-2,000.

Tips: "Emphasis should be on achieving a healthier lifestyle through food, nutrition, fitness, exercise information. In submitting queries, include information on professional background. Food writers should include examples of healthy recipes which meet the guidelines of *Cooking Light*."

‡EATING WELL, The Magazine of Food and Health, Telemedia Communications (U.S.) Inc., Ferry Rd., Charlotte VT 05445. (802)425-3961. Editor: Barry Estabrook. Sr. Editor: Rux Martin. 90% freelance written. Bimonthly magazine covering food and health. Estab. 1989. Circ. 405,000. Pays 45 days after acceptance. Publishes ms an average of 6 months after acceptance. Byline given. Offers 25% kill fee. Buys first North American serial rights and second serial (reprint) rights. Submit seasonal/holiday material 1 year in advance. Reports in 2 months.

Nonfiction: Kathleen Hackett. Book excerpts, nutrition, cooking, interview/profile, food and travel. Query with published clips. Length: 1,500-6,000 words. Pays $1,000-3,000. Pays expenses of writers on assignment. State availability of photos with submission. Reviews transparencies. Offers $50-250 per photo. Captions and identification of subjects required. Buys one-time rights.

Columns/Departments: Allison Cleary. Nutrition Letter (timely nutrition research news), 150-400 words; Observer (current news in the food world), 150-400 words. Buys 60 mss/year. Query. Pays $200-300.

Tips: "We invite experienced, published science writers to do nutrition features."

FOOD & WINE, American Express Publishing Corp., 1120 Avenue of the Americas, New York NY 10036. (212)382-5618. Editor: Carole Lalli. Managing Editor: Warren Picower. Monthly magazine for "active people for whom eating, drinking, entertaining, dining out, travel and all the related equipment and trappings are central to their lifestyle." Estab. 1978. Circ. 800,000. **Pays on acceptance.** Byline given. Offers 25% kill fee. Buys first world rights. Submit seasonal/holiday material 9 months in advance. Query for electronic submissions. Reports in 3 weeks on queries; 2 weeks on mss. Sample copy $3. Free writer's guidelines.

Nonfiction: Essays, how-to, humor, kitchen and dining room design, and travel. Query with published clips. Buys 125 mss/year. Length: 1,000-3,000 words. Pays $800-2,000. Pays expenses of writers on assignment.
Photos: State availability of photos with submission. No unsolicited photos or art. Offers $100-450 page rate per photo. Model releases and identification of subjects required. Buys one-time rights.
Columns/Departments: What's New, Eating Out, The Traveler. Buys 120 mss/year. Query with published clips. Length: 800-3,000 words. Pays $800-2,000.
Tips: "Good service, good writing, up-to-date information, interesting article approach and appropriate point of view for *F&W*'s audience are important elements to keep in mind. Look over several recent issues before writing query."

GOURMET, Condé Nast, 560 Lexington Ave., New York NY 10022. Did not want to be listed.

KASHRUS MAGAZINE, The Bimonthly for the Kosher Consumer and the Trade, Yeshiva Birkas Reuven, P.O. Box 204, Parkville Station, Brooklyn NY 11204. (718)998-3201. Editor: Rabbi Yosef Wikler. 25% freelance written. Prefers to work with published/established writers, and is eager to work with new/unpublished writers. Bimonthly magazine covering kosher food industry and food production. Estab. 1980. Circ. 10,000. **Pays on acceptance.** Publishes ms an average of 2 months after acceptance. Byline given. Offers 50% kill fee. Buys first or second serial (reprint) rights. Submit seasonal/holiday material 2 months in advance. Simultaneous and previously published submissions OK. Prefers submissions in major word processing programs on disk with accompanying hard copy. Reports in 1 week on queries; 2 weeks on mss. Sample copy and writer's guidelines for $2. Professional discount on subscription: $15/10 issues (regularly $27).
Nonfiction: General interest, interview/profile, new product, personal experience, photo feature, religious, technical and travel. Special issues feature International Kosher Travel (October) and Passover (March). Buys 8-12 mss/year. Query with published clips. Length: 1,000-2,000 words. Pays $100-250 for assigned articles; pays up to $100 for unsolicited articles. Sometimes pays the expenses of writers on assignment.
Photos: State availability of photos with submission. Offers no additional payment for photos accepted with ms. Buys one-time rights.
Columns/Departments: Book Review (cook books, food technology, kosher food), 250-500 words; People in the News (interviews with kosher personalities), 1,000-1,500 words; Regional Kosher Supervision (report on kosher supervision in a city or community), 1,000-2,000 words; Food Technology (new technology or current technology with accompanying pictures), 1,000-1,500 words; Travel (international, national), must include Kosher information and Jewish communities, 1,000-1,500 words; Regional Kosher Cooking, 1,000-1,500 words.Buys 8-12 mss/year. Query with published clips. Pays $50-250.
Tips: "*Kashrus Magazine* will do more writing on general food technology, production, and merchandising as well as human interest travelogs and regional writing in 1992 than we have done in the past. Areas most open to freelancers are interviews, food technology, regional reporting and travel. We welcome stories on the availability and quality of Kosher foods and services in communities across the U.S. and throughout the world."

NATURAL FOOD & FARMING, Natural Food Associates, Highway 59, Box 210, Atlanta TX 75551. (214)796-3612. 80% freelance written. Eager to work with an experienced writer. Executive Director: Bill Francis. A bimonthly magazine covering organic gardening, natural foods, preventive medicine, vitamins and supplements. Estab. 1953. Circ. 50,000. **Pays on acceptance.** Publishes ms an average of 3 months after acceptance. Byline given. Not copyrighted. Buys first rights or second serial (reprint) rights. Submit seasonal/holiday material 2-3 months in advance. Simultaneous, photocopied and previously published submissions OK. Computer printout submissions acceptable. Free sample copy and writer's guidelines.
Nonfiction: Book excerpts; exposé; how-to (gardening, recipes and canning), new product; opinion; personal experience (organic gardening) and photo feature. Buys approximately 150 mss/year. Query with or without published clips, or send complete ms. Length: 1,000-3,000 words. Pays $100-200; sometimes pays in free advertising for company, books or products. Sometimes pays the expenses of writers on assignment.
Photos: State availability or send photos with submission.
Columns/Departments: Bugs, Weeds & Free Advice (organic gardening), 800 words; Food Talk (tips on cooking and recipes), 300-1,500 words; Of Consuming Interest (shorts on new developments in field), 800-1,500 words; and The Doctor Prescribes (questions and answers on preventive medicine),

For information on setting your freelance fees, see How Much Should I Charge? in the Business of Writing section.

800-1,500 words. Buys 96 mss/year. Send complete ms. Pays $100 (negotiable).
Fillers: Facts and short humor.
Tips: "Articles on subjects concerning gardening organically or cooking with natural foods are most open to freelancers."

‡**WINE ENTHUSIAST**, P.O. Box 39, Pleasantville NY 10570. (914)747-9830. Editor: W.R. Tish. 35% freelance written. Bimonthly magazine covering wine, food, travel and lifestyle. Estab. 1988. Circ. 75,000. Pays on publication. Byline given. Offers 50% kill fee. Buys first North American serial rights. Query for electronic submissions. Reports in 1 month on queries.
Nonfiction: Essays, historical/nostalgic, humor, interview/profile, photo feature, travel with wine interest. "No junket-related pieces, please." Buys 10-15 mss/year. Query. Length: 1,000-2,500 words. Pays $250-500. Payment in wine storage equipment possible. Sometimes pays expenses of writers on assignment.
Photos: State availability of photos with submission. Offer $50-100 per photo. Identification of subjects required. Buys one-time rights.
Columns/Departments: *Wine's Little-Seen* (hidden treasures of interest to wine lovers), 750-1,500 words; *Enthusiasts' Guide* (focus on specific wine region, type, style), 750-1,500 words; *Food* (food, with wine angle included), 750-1,500 words. Pays $200-300.

THE WINE SPECTATOR, M. Shanken Communications, Inc., Opera Plaza, Suite 2014, 601 Van Ness Ave., San Francisco CA 94102. (415)673-2040. Managing Editor: Jim Gordon. 20% freelance written. Prefers to work with published/established writers. Twice monthly consumer news magazine covering wine. Estab. 1976. Circ. 105,000. Pays within 30 days of publication. Publishes ms an average of 2 months after acceptance. Byline given. Buys all rights and makes work-for-hire assignments. Submit seasonal/holiday material 4 months in advance. Query for electronic submissions. Reports in 3 weeks. Sample copy $2.50; free writer's guidelines.
Nonfiction: General interest (news about wine or wine events); interview/profile (of wine, vintners, wineries); opinion; and photo feature. No "winery promotional pieces or articles by writers who lack sufficient knowledge to write below just surface data." Query. Length: 100-2,000 words average. Pays $50-500.
Photos: Send photos with ms. Pays $75 minimum for color transparencies. Captions, model releases and identification of subjects required. Buys all rights.
Tips: "A solid knowledge of wine is a must. Query letters essential, detailing the story idea. New, refreshing ideas which have not been covered before stand a good chance of acceptance. *The Wine Spectator* is a consumer-oriented *news magazine* but we are interested in some trade stories; brevity is essential."

WINE TIDINGS, Kylix Media Inc., 5165 Sherbrooke St. W., 414, Montreal, Quebec H4A 1T6 Canada. (514)481-5892. Publisher: Judy Rochester. Editor: Barbara Leslie. 90% freelance written. Works with small number of new/unpublished writers each year. Magazine published 8 times/year primarily for men with incomes of more than $50,000. "Covers anything happening on the wine scene in Canada." Circ. 28,000. Pays on publication. Publishes ms an average of 3-4 months after acceptance. Byline given. Buys all rights. Submit seasonal/holiday material 3 months in advance. Reports in 1 month.
Nonfiction: General interest; historical; humor; interview/profile; new product (and developments in the Canadian and U.S. wine industries); opinion; personal experience; photo feature; and travel (to wine-producing countries). "All must pertain to wine or wine-related topics and should reflect author's basic knowledge of and interest in wine." Buys 20-30 mss/year. Send complete ms. Length: 500-1,200 words. Pays $35-300.
Photos: State availability of photos. Pays $20-100 for color prints; $10-25 for b&w prints. Identification of subjects required. Buys one-time rights.

Games and Puzzles

These publications are written by and for game enthusiasts interested in both traditional games and word puzzles and newer role-playing adventure, computer and video games. Additional home video game publications are listed in the Entertainment section. Other puzzle markets may be found in the Juvenile section.

‡**bePUZZLED, Mystery Jigsaw Puzzles**, 45 Wintonbury Ave., Bloomfield CT 06002. (203)286-4222. Editor: Mary Ann Lombard. Managing Editor: Luci Seccareccia. 100% freelance written. Mystery jigsaw puzzle used short mystery stories published 4-12 times/year. Covers mystery, suspense, romance, adventure for children and adults. Estab. 1987. Pays on completion. Publishes ms an average of 9 months after acceptance. Byline given (sometimes pen name required). Buys all rights. Submit sea-

sonal/holiday material 9 months in advance. Simultaneous submissions OK. Reports in 2 weeks on queries; 3 months on mss. Sample copy for $10. (Mystery Jigsaw Puzzle retails at $18). Free writer's guidelines.

Fiction: Luci Seccareccia. Adventure, humorous, mainstream, mystery, romance and suspense (*exact* subject within genre above is released to writers as available.) Buys 10 mss/year. Query. Length: 3,500-5,500 words. Pays $250-600.

Fillers: "Writers must follow submission format as outlined in writer's guidelines. We incorporate short mystery stories and jigsaw puzzles into a game where the clues to solve the mystery are cleverly hidden in both the short story and the puzzle picture. Writer must be able to integrate the clues in the written piece to these to appear in puzzle picture. Playing one of our games helps to clarify how we like to "marry" the story clues and the visual clues in the puzzle."

‡CHESS LIFE, United States Chess Federation, 186 Route 9W, New Windsor NY 12550. (914)562-8350. Editor: Glenn Petersen. 15% freelance written. Works with a small number of new/unpublished writers each year. Monthly magazine covering the chess world. Circ. 60,000. Pays variable fee. Publishes ms an average of 5 months after acceptance. Byline given. Offers kill fee. Buys first or negotiable rights. Submit seasonal/holiday material 8 months in advance. Simultaneous queries, and simultaneous and previously published submissions OK. Reports in 1 month. Sample copy and writer's guidelines for 9×11 SAE.

Nonfiction: General interest, historical, interview/profile, and technical—all must have some relation to chess. No "stories about personal experiences with chess." Buys 30-40 mss/year. Query with samples "if new to publication." Length: 3,000 words maximum. Sometimes pays the expenses of writers on assignment.

Photos: Reviews b&w contact sheets and prints, and color prints and slides. Captions, model releases and identification of subjects required. Buys all or negotiable rights.

Fiction: "Chess-related, high quality." Buys 1-2 mss/year. Pays variable fee.

Tips: "Articles must be written from an informed point of view—not from view of the curious amateur. Most of our writers are specialized in that they have sound credentials as chessplayers. Freelancers in major population areas (except New York and Los Angeles, which we already have covered) who are interested in short personality profiles and perhaps news reporting have the best opportunities. We're looking for more personality pieces on chessplayers around the country; not just the stars, but local masters, talented youths, and dedicated volunteers. Freelancers interested in such pieces might let us know of their interest and their range. Could be we know of an interesting story in their territory that needs covering."

DRAGON® MAGAZINE, TSR, Inc., P.O. Box 111, 201 Sheridan Springs Rd., Lake Geneva WI 53147. (414)248-3625. FAX: (414)248-0389. Editor: Roger E. Moore. Monthly magazine of fantasy and science-fiction role-playing games. 90% freelance written. Eager to work with published/established writers as well as new/unpublished writers. "Most of our readers are intelligent, imaginative teenage males." Estab. 1976. Circ. about 100,000, primarily across the United States, Canada and Great Britain. Byline given. Offers kill fee. Submit seasonal/holiday material 8 months in advance. Pays on publication for articles to which all rights are purchased; pays on acceptance for articles to which first/worldwide rights in English are purchased. Publishing dates vary from 1-24 months after acceptance. Writer's guidelines for #10 SAE and 1 first-class stamp or International Reply Coupon.

Nonfiction: Articles on the hobby of science fiction and fantasy role-playing. No general articles on gaming hobby; "our article needs are *very* specialized. Writers should be experienced in gaming hobby and role-playing. No strong sexual overtones or graphic depictions of violence." Buys 120 mss/year. Query. Length: 1,000-8,000 words. Pays $50-500 for assigned articles; pays $5-400 for unsolicited articles.

Fiction: Barbara G. Young, fiction editor. Fantasy only."No strong sexual overtones or graphic depictions of violence." Buys 12 mss/year. Send complete ms. Length: 2,000-8,000 words. Pays 6-8¢/word.

Tips: "*Dragon® Magazine* is *not* a periodical that the 'average reader' appreciates or understands. A writer must *be* a reader and must share the serious interest in gaming our readers possess."

GIANT CROSSWORDS, Scrambl-Gram, Inc., Puzzle Buffs International, 1772 State Road, Cuyahoga Falls OH 44223. (216)923-2397. Editors: C.J. Elum and C.R. Elum. 40% freelance written. Eager to work with new/unpublished writers. Crossword puzzle and word game magazines issued quarterly. Estab. 1970. **Pays on acceptance.** Publishes ms an average of 10 days after acceptance. No byline given. Buys all rights. Simultaneous queries OK. Reports in several weeks. "We furnish constructors' kits, master grids and clue sheets and offer a 'how-to-make-crosswords' book for $37.50 postpaid."

Nonfiction: Crosswords only. Query. Pays according to size of puzzle and/or clues.
Tips: "We are expanding our syndication of original crosswords and our publishing schedule to include new titles and extra issues of current puzzle books."

General Interest

General interest magazines need writers who can appeal to a varied audience – teens and senior citizens, wealthy readers and the unemployed. Each magazine still has a personality that suits its audience – one that a writer should study before sending material to an editor. Other markets for general interest material are in these Consumer categories: Ethnic/Minority, In-flight, Men's, Regional and Women's.

AMERICAN ATHEIST, American Atheist Press, P.O. Box 140195, Austin TX 78714-0195. (512)458-1244. Editor: R. Murray-O'Hair. Managing Editor: Jon Garth Murray. 20-40% freelance written. Monthly magazine covering atheism and topics related to it and separation of State and Church. Estab.1959. Circ. 50,000. Publishes ms an average of 6 months after acceptance. Byline given. Buys one-time and all rights. Submit seasonal/holiday material 3 months in advance. Simultaneous queries and simultaneous and previously published submissions OK. Query for electronic submissions. Reports in 6 weeks on queries; 3 months on mss. Publishes ms an average of 4 months after acceptance. Sample copy and writer's guidelines for 9 × 12 SAE.
Nonfiction: Book excerpts, expose, general interest, historical, how-to, humor, interview/profile, opinion, personal experience and photo feature, but only as related to State/Church or atheism. "We receive a great many Bible criticism articles – and publish very few. We would advise writers not to send in such works. We are also interested in fiction with an atheistic slant." Buys 40 mss/year. Send complete ms. Length: 400-10,000 words. Pays in free subscription or 15 copies for first-time authors. Repeat authors paid $15 per 1,000 words. Sometimes pays the expenses of writers on assignment.
Columns/Departments: Atheism, Church/State separation and humor. Send complete ms. Length: 400-10,000 words.
Poetry: Avant-garde, free verse, haiku, light verse and traditional. Submit unlimited poems. Length: open. Pays $10 per thousand words maximum.
Fillers: Jokes, short humor and newsbreaks. Length: 800 words maximum, only as related to State/Church separation or atheism.
Tips: "We are primarily interested in subjects which bear directly on atheism or issues of interest and importance to atheists. This includes articles on the atheist lifestyle, on problems that confront atheists, the history of atheism, personal experiences of atheists, separation of state and church, theopolitics and critiques of atheism in general and of particular religions. We are starting to have issues which focus on lifestyle topics relevant to atheism. We would like to receive more articles on current events and lifestyle issues. Critiques of *particular* religions would also be likely candidates for acceptance."

THE AMERICAN LEGION MAGAZINE, P.O. Box 1055, Indianapolis IN 46206. (317)635-8411. Editor-in-Chief: Daniel S. Wheeler. Monthly. 95% freelance written. Prefers to work with published/established writers, eager to work with new/unpublished writers, and works with a small number of new/unpublished writers each year. Estab. 1919. Circ. 2.85 million. Buys first North American serial rights. Reports on submissions "promptly." **Pays on acceptance.** Publishes ms an average of 6 months after acceptance. Byline given. Sample copy for 9 × 12 SAE and 6 first class stamps. Writer's guidelines for #10 SASE.
Nonfiction: Query first, but will consider unsolicited mss. "Prefer an outline query. Relate your article's thesis or purpose, tell why you are qualified to write it, the approach you will take and any authorities you intend to interview. War-remembrance pieces of a personal nature (vs. historic in perspective) should be in ms form." Uses current world affairs, topics of contemporary interest, 20th century war-remembrance pieces, and 750-word commentaries on contemporary problems and points of view. No personality profiles or regional topics. Buys 75 mss/year. Length: 1,500 words maximum. Pays $300-2,000. Pays phone expenses of writers on assignment.
Photos: On assignment.
Tips: Query should include author's qualifications for writing a technical or complex article, and samples of published work. Also include thesis, length, outline and conclusion. "Send a thorough query. Submit material that is suitable for us, showing that you have read several issues. *The American Legion Magazine* considers itself 'the magazine for a strong America.' Any query that reflects this theme (which includes strong economy, educational system, moral fiber, infrastructure and armed forces) will be given priority. No longer accepting unsolicited cartoons or jokes."

THE AMERICAN SCHOLAR, The Phi Beta Kappa Society, 1811 Q Street NW, Washington DC 20009. (202)265-3808. Editor: Joseph Epstein. Managing Editor: Jean Stipicevic. 100% freelance written. Intellectual quarterly. "Our writers are specialists writing for the college educated public." Estab.

1932. Circ. 26,000. Pays after author has seen edited piece in galleys. Byline given. Offers ½ kill fee. Buys first rights. Submit seasonal/holiday material 6 months in advance. Reports in 2 weeks on queries; 2 months on ms. Sample copy for $5.75. Writer's guidelines for #10 SASE.

Nonfiction: Book excerpts (prior to publication only), essays, historical/nostalgic, humor. Buys 40 mss/year. Query. Length: 3,000-5,000 words. Pays $500.

Columns/Departments: Buys 16 mss/year. Query. Length: 3,000-5,000 words. Pays $500.

Poetry: Sandra Costich, poetry editor. Buys 20/year. Submit maximum 3 poems. Length: 75 lines. Pays $50. "Write for guidelines."

Tips: "The section most open to freelancers is the book review section. Query and send samples of reviews written."

ANGLO-AMERICAN SPOTLIGHT, Spotlight Verlag, Freihamer Strasse 4b (Box 1629), D-8032 Gräfelfing/Munich, Germany, (049)898548221. FAX: (049)898548223. Editor: Kevin Perryman. 30% freelance written. Monthly magazine on current events, travel, personalities and history in English-speaking countries only. "*Spotlight* is a general interest magazine for German-speakers who are trying to brush up and improve their English. In general we prefer an informal newsy style with relatively simple sentence structure and vocabulary." Estab. 1983. Circ. 75,000. Pays on publication. Byline given. Offers no kill fee. Buys one-time rights for Germany, Austria, Switzerland. Submit seasonal/holiday material 6 months in advance. Simultaneous and previously published submissions OK. Reports within 6 months. Free sample copy.

Nonfiction: General interest, historical/nostalgic, interview/profile, photo feature and travel. No pieces unrelated to the English-speaking world. Buys at least 20 mss/year. Query with published clips. Length: 1,000-2,000 words. Pays DM 1 per printed column line, (about seven words). Sometimes pays expenses of writers on assignment.

Photos: State availability of photos with submission. Reviews color transparencies and b&w prints. Offers $25-100 per photo. Buys one-time rights.

Tips: "Try a travel story (a national park, a state, an event), a city portrait (history, current problems, travel info), an article about a current issue or trend, interview or article about a well-known person. Please type flush left, 40 characters per line, triple space. It's best from an 'insider's' point of view. Tell our German readers something beyond what they can already find in travel brochures. Fill the story with anecdotes, honest information and advice about what to do and what not to do."

THE ATLANTIC MONTHLY, 745 Boylston St., Boston MA 02116. (617)536-9500. Editor: William Whitworth. Managing Editor: Cullen Murphy. Monthly magazine of arts and public affairs. Circ. 470,000. Pays on publication. Byline given. Buys first North American serial rights. Simultaneous submissions discouraged. Reporting time varies.

Nonfiction: Book excerpts, essays, general interest, humor, personal experience, religious, travel. Query with or without published clips or send complete ms. Length: 1,000-6,000 words. Payment varies. Sometimes pays expenses of writers on assignment.

Fiction: C. Michael Curtis, fiction editor. Buys 15-18 mss/year. Send complete ms. Length: 2,000-6,000 words preferred. Payment varies.

Poetry: Peter Davison, poetry editor. Buys 40-60 poems/year.

A BETTER LIFE FOR YOU, The National Research Bureau, Inc., 424 N. 3rd St., P.O. Box 1, Burlington IA 52601-0001. (319)752-5415. FAX: (319)752-3421. Editor: Rhonda Wilson. Editorial Supervisor: Doris J. Ruschill. 75% freelance written. Works with a small number of new/unpublished writers each year, eager to work with new/unpublished writers. Quarterly magazine. Estab. 1948. Pays on publication. Publishes ms an average of 1 year after acceptance. Buys all rights. Submit seasonal/holiday material 7 months in advance of issue date. Previously published submissions OK. Reports in 3 weeks. Writer's guidelines for #10 SASE; sample for 6½"×9½" envelope with 55¢ postage.

Nonfiction: General interest (steps to better health, on-the-job attitudes); and how-to (perform better on the job, do home repair jobs, and keep up maintenance on a car). Buys 10-12 mss/year. Query or send outline. Length: 400-600 words. Pays 4¢/word.

Tips: "Writers have a better chance of breaking in at our publication with short articles."

CAPPER'S, Stauffer Communications, Inc., 616 Jefferson St., Topeka KS 66607. (913)295-1108. Editor: Nancy Peavler. 25% freelance written. Works with a small number of new/unpublished writers each year. Emphasizes home and family for readers who live in small towns and on farms. Biweekly tabloid. Estab. 1879. Circ. 375,000. Pays for poetry on acceptance; articles on publication. Publishes ms an average of 6 months after acceptance. Buys first serial rights only. Submit seasonal/holiday material at least 2 months in advance. Reports in 3 months; 8 months for serialized novels. Sample copy 85¢; writer's guidlelines for #10 SASE.

Nonfiction: Historical (local museums, etc.), inspirational, nostalgia, travel (local slants) and people stories (accomplishments, collections, etc.). Buys 50 mss/year. Submit complete ms. Length: 700 words maximum. Pays $1/inch.

Photos: Purchased with accompanying ms. Submit prints. Pays $5-10 for 8×10 or 5×7 b&w glossy prints. Total purchase price for ms includes payment for photos. Limited market for color photos (35mm color slides); pays $20-25 each.

Columns/Departments: Heart of the Home (homemakers' letters, recipes, hints), and Hometown Heartbeat (descriptive). Submit complete ms. Length: 300 words maximum. Pays $1-7.

Fiction: "We have begun to buy very few fiction pieces—longer than short stories, shorter than novels." Adventure and romance mss. No explicit sex, violence or profanity. Buys 4-5 mss/year. Query. Pays $75-250.

Poetry: Free verse, haiku, light verse, traditional, nature and inspiration. "The poems that appear in *Capper's* are not too difficult to read. They're easy to grasp. We're looking for everyday events, and down-to-earth themes." Buys 4-5/issue. Limit submissions to batches of 5-6. Length: 4-16 lines. Pays $3-6.

Tips: "Study a few issues of our publication. Most rejections are for material that is too long, unsuitable or out of character for our paper (too sexy, too much profanity, etc.). On occasion, we must cut material to fit column space."

‡CATHOLIC FORESTER, 425 W. Shuman Blvd., P.O. Box 3012, Naperville IL 60566-7012. (708)983-4920. Editor: Barbara Cunningham. 75% freelance written. Bimonthly general interest magazine. Estab. 1883. Circ. 150,000. **Pays on acceptance.** Publishes ms an average of 3-6 months after acceptance. Byline given. Buys one-time, second serial (reprint), or simultaneous rights. Submit seasonal/holiday material 6 months in advance. Simultaneous and previously published submissions OK. Reports in 1 month on mss. Sample copy for 9×11 SAE with 3 first class stamps. Prefer SASE. Writer's guidelines for SASE. Will include with sample copy if requested.

Nonfiction: Essays, general interest, historical/nostalgic, humor, interview/profile, opinion, photo feature, travel. "No violence, bloody, explicit sex." Send complete ms. "No queries please." Length: 500-2,000 words. Pays 5-20¢/word for unsolicited articles.

Photos: Send photos with submission. Reviews 4×5 prints. Offers $10-20 per photo. Captions and identification of subjects required. Buys one-time rights.

Columns/Departments: *View Point* (No special slant; I do like light, amusing pieces), 600-700; *Observations* (Thoughts on contemporary life, personal life, what's going on in the world), 600-700. Buys 20 mss/year. Send complete ms. Length: 500-700 words. Pays 5-20¢/word.

Fiction: Adventure, humorous, mainstream, mystery, slice-of-life vignettes, suspense. Buys 2-3 mss/year. Send complete ms. Length: 1,000-2,500 words. Pays 5-20¢/word.

Poetry: Free verse, light verse. "No long, serious poetry: romantic, religious, inspirational." Buys 5-10 poems/year. Submit maximum 4 poems. Length: 4-6 lines. Pays $10-25.

Fillers: Anecdotes, facts, short humor—jokes. Buys 20/year. Length: 50-150 words. Pays $10-25.

Tips: "I look for interesting subjects and writing style, good grammar, good spelling, proper punctuation and careful typing. Informative, amusing, contemporary and unusual subjects get my attention. Everything should be double-spaced with article word count and author's name and address on first page, name and title of article on all pages. I do appreciate photos accompanying ms, if possible. I do not want queries."

THE CHRISTIAN SCIENCE MONITOR, 1 Norway St., Boston MA 02115. (617)450-2303. Contact: Submissions. International newspaper issued daily except Saturdays, Sundays and holidays in North America; weekly international edition. Circ. 104,314. Buys all newspaper rights for 3 months following publication. Buys limited number of mss, "top quality only." Publishes original (exclusive) material only. Pays on acceptance or publication, "depending on department." Reports in 1 month. Submit complete original ms or letter of inquiry. Writer's guidelines available.

Nonfiction: David Holmstrom, feature editor. In-depth features and essays. Please query by mail before sending mss. "Style should be bright but not cute, concise but thoroughly researched. Try to humanize news or feature writing so reader identifies with it. Avoid sensationalism, crime and disaster. Accent constructive, solution-oriented treatment of subjects." Home Forum page buys essays of 400-900 words. Pays $70-140. Education, people, books, food and science pages will consider articles not usually more than 800 words appropriate to respective subjects." Pays $100-150.

Poetry: Traditional, blank and free verse. Seeks non-religious poetry of high quality and of all lengths up to 75 lines. Pays $25 average.

Tips: "We prefer neatly typed originals. No handwritten copy. Enclosing an SAE and postage with ms is a must."

‡**CLIFTON MAGAZINE,** The Communications Board of the University of Cincinnati, 204 Tangeman University Center, University of Cincinnati, Cincinnati OH 45221. (513)556-6378. Editor: Rich Roell. Managing Editor: Tina McMahon. 10-20% freelance written. Quarterly general interest magazine with extensive literary section. Estab. 1972. Circ. 30,500. Pays on publication. Publishes ms an average of 1 month after acceptance. Byline given. Buys first rights and one-time rights. Submit seasonal/holiday material 3 months in advance. Simultaneous and previously published submissions OK. Reports in 2 weeks. Sample copy for $1. Free writer's guidelines.

Nonfiction: Tina McMahon. Essays, exposé, general interest, humor, interview/profile, opinion, personal experience and travel. Buys 4-6 mss/year. Query with or without published clips, or send complete ms. Length: 1,500-5,000 words. Pays $60. "3 contributor copies in addition to cash payment." Sometimes pays expenses of writers on assignment. State availability of photos with submissions. Reviews 8½×11 prints. Offers $5-10 per photo. Model releases and identification of subjects required. Buys one-time rights.

Columns/Departments: Humor columns–Solomon Davidoff; all others–Tina McMahon. Music Review (reviews of music and bands with college audience), 1,500-2,000 words; Essay (any topic), 1,500-2,000; Humor (any topic, but spare us the racial slurs), 1,500-2,000 words. Send complete ms. Pays $25-50.

Fiction: Solomon Davidoff. Adventure, erotica, ethnic, experimental, fantasy, historical, horror, humorous, mainstream, mystery, religious, romance, science fiction, suspense, western, cyberpunk. "No stories in which nothing happens or social issues *without* research or correct information." Buys 8 mss/year. Send complete ms. Length: 6,000 words maximum. Pays 3 copies.

Poetry: Geoffrey Woolf. Avante-garde, free verse, Haiku, light verse, traditional. Buys 20 poems/year. Submit maximum 5 poems. Length: 5-100 lines. Pays with contributor copies–3 copies.

Fillers: Tina McMahon. Facts, gags to be illustrated by cartoonist, newsbreaks and short humor. Buys 5-7/year. Length: 750-1,000 words. Pays $15-25. "In query letter make sure you list any published work. Write with college community in mind (not just students but faculty and staff). Letters to the Editor, Guest Essay, Humor: Be fair in your approach. Make sure your facts are justified and verified."

THE CONNOISSEUR, The Hearst Corp., 1790 Broadway, 18th Fl., New York NY 10019. (212)492-1300. Editor-in-Chief: Gael Love. Executive Editor: Spencer Beck. Managing Editor: Robert Sabat. 90% freelance written. Prefers to work with published/established writers. Monthly magazine of the arts—fine, decorative and performing—with a focus on personal ties. "*Connoisseur* is informed by lively scholarship, a keen critical eye, and a civilized sense of fun. It covers a wide range of subjects and provides our audience with first-hand access to our topics and pertinent service data." Circ. 320,000. **Pays on acceptance.** Offers 25% kill fee. Buys first English language rights. Query for electronic submissions.

Nonfiction: Travel; the arts—fine, decorative, performing; food; wine; architecture; fashion and jewelry. Buys 120 mss/year. Query with published clips. Length: 1,500-5,000 words. Usually pays $1/word.

Photos: Pamela Hassell, photo editor. Captions, model releases and identification of subjects required. Buys one-time rights.

Tips: "A freelancer can best break in to our publication with a strong, original proposal backed by good clips. Be aware of what we *have been doing*—read the magazine."

DIVERSION, Hearst Professional Management, 60 E. 42nd St., New York NY 10165. All writing is commissioned. Did not want to be listed.

‡**DIVERSITY,** One of a Kind, P.O. Box 268805, Chicago IL 60626-8805. (312)285-7972. Editors: Deborah and Michael Brownstein. 100% freelance written. Estab. 1990. Circ. 1,000. Pays on publication. Publishes ms an average of 2 months after acceptance. Byline given. Not copyrighted. Buys first and second serial (reprint) rights. Submit seasonal/holiday material 6 months in advance. Reports in 1 month on mss. Sample copy for $3 and 9×12 SAE with 4 first class stamps; writer's guidelines for #10 SASE.

Nonfiction: Essays, expose, general interest, historical/nostalgic, how-to, humor, inspirational, interview/profile, new product, opinion, personal experience, photo feature, travel. No fiction or poetry. Buys 100 mss/year. Send complete mss. Length: 2,000 words maximum. Pays $5-200. Sometimes pays expenses of writers on assignment.

Photos: State availability of photos with submission. Reviews contact sheets, transparencies and 5×7 prints. Pays $5-200 for photos. Captions, model releases and identification of subjects required. Buys all rights.

Fillers: Anecdotes, facts, gags to be illustrated by cartoonist, short humor. Buys 200/year. Length: 100 words maximum. Pays $5.

Tips: "Write as if you are explaining something you care about a lot to other people who you would like to interest in your topic."

EQUINOX: THE MAGAZINE OF CANADIAN DISCOVERY, Equinox Publishing, 7 Queen Victoria Dr., Camden East, Ontario K0K 1J0 Canada. (613)378-6661. Editor: Bart Robinson. Bimonthly magazine. "We publish in-depth profiles of people, places and wildlife to show readers the real stories behind subjects of general interest in the fields of science and geography." Estab. 1982. Circ. 166,000. **Pays on acceptance.** Byline given. Offers 50% kill fee. Buys first North American serial rights only. Submit seasonal queries 1 year in advance. Reports in 6 weeks. Sample copy $5; free writer's guidelines, include SASE.

Nonfiction: Book excerpts (occasionally), geography, science, art, natural history and environment. No travel articles. Buys 40 mss/year. Query. "Our biggest need is for science stories. We do not touch unsolicited feature manuscripts." Length: 5,000-10,000 words. Pays $1,500-negotiated.

Photos: Send photos with ms. Reviews color transparencies—must be of professional quality; no prints or negatives. Captions and identification of subjects required.

Columns/Departments: Nexus (current science that isn't covered by daily media) and Habitat (Canadian environmental stories not covered by daily media). Buys 80 mss/year. Query with clips of published work. Length: 200-800 words. Pays $200-500.

Tips: "Submit Habitat and Nexus ideas to us—the *only* route to a feature is through these departments if writers are untried."

FORD TIMES, 1 Illinois Center, Suite 1700, 111 E. Wacker Dr., Chicago IL 60601. No longer freelance written.

FRIENDLY EXCHANGE, Meredith Publishing Services, Locust at 17th, Des Moines IA 50336. Publication Office: (515)284-2008. Editor: (702)786-7419. Editor: Adele Malott. 80% freelance written. Works with a small number of new/unpublished writers each year. Quarterly magazine exploring travel and leisure topics of interest to active Western families. For policyholders of Farmers Insurance Group of Companies. "These are traditional families (median adult age 39) who live in the area bounded by Ohio on the east and the Pacific Ocean on the west." Estab. 1981. Circ. 4.8 million. **Pays on acceptance.** Publishes ms an average of 5 months after acceptance. Offers 25% kill fee. Buys all rights. Submit seasonal/holiday material 1 year in advance. Simultaneous queries OK. Query for electronic submissions. Reports in 2 months. Sample copy for 9 × 12 SAE and 5 first class stamps; writer's guidelines for #10 SASE.

Nonfiction: "Travel and leisure topics of interest to the Western family can be addressed from many different perspectives, including health and safety, consumerism, heritage and education. Articles offer a service to readers and encourage them to take some positive action such as taking a trip. Style is colorful, warm, and inviting, making liberal use of anecdotes and quotes. The only first-person articles used are those assigned; all others in third person. Domestic locations in the Midwest and West are emphasized." Buys 8 mss/issue. Query. Length: 600-1,800 words. Pays $300-800/article, plus agreed-upon expenses.

Photos: Jann Williams, art director. Pays $150-250 for 35mm color transparencies; and $50 for b&w prints. Cover photo payment negotiable. Pays on publication.

Columns/Departments: All columns and departments rely on reader-generated materials; none used from professional writers.

Tips: "We are now concentrating exclusively on the travel and leisure hours of our readers. Do not use destination approach in travel pieces—instead, for example, tell us about the people, activities, or events that make the location special. We prefer to go for a small slice rather than the whole pie, and we are just as interested in the cook who made it or the person who will be eating it as we are in the pie itself. Concentrate on what families can do together."

FUTURIFIC MAGAZINE, 280 Madison Ave., New York NY 10016. (212)684-4913. Editor-in-Chief: Balint Szent-Miklosy. 50-75% freelance written. Monthly. "Futurific, Inc. "Foundation for Optimism," is an independent, nonprofit organization set up in 1976 to study the future, and *Futurific Magazine* is its monthly report on findings. We report on what is coming in all areas of life from international affairs to the arts and sciences. Readership cuts across all income levels and includes leadership, government, corporate and religious circles." Circ. 10,000. Pays on publication. Publishes ms an average of 1 month after acceptance. Byline given in most cases. Buys one-time rights and will negotiate reprints. Reports within 1 month. Sample copy for $5 and 9 × 12 SAE. Writer's guidelines for #10 SASE.

Nonfiction: All subjects must deal with the future: book, movie, theater and software reviews, general interest, how to forecast the future—seriously, humor, interview/profile, new product, photo feature and technical. No historical, opinion or gloom and doom. Send complete ms. Length: 5,000 words maximum. Payment negotiable.

Photos: Send photos with ms. Reviews b&w prints. Pay negotiable. Identification of subjects required.

Columns/Departments: Medical breakthroughs, new products, inventions, book, movie, theater and software reviews, etc. "Anything that is new or about to be new." Send complete ms. Length: 5,000 words maximum.

Poetry: Avant-garde, free verse, haiku, light verse and traditional. "Must deal with the future. No gloom and doom or sad poetry." Buys 6/year. Submit unlimited number of poems. Length: open. Pays in copies.

Fillers: Clippings, jokes, gags, anecdotes, short humor, and newsbreaks. "Must deal with the future." Length: open. Pays in copies.

Tips: "It's not who you are, it's what you have to say that counts with us. We seek to maintain a light-hearted, professional look at forecasting. Be upbeat and show a loving expectation for the marvels of human achievement. Take any subject or concern you find in regular news magazines and extrapolate as to what the future will be. Use imagination. Get involved in the excitement of the international developments, social interaction. Write the solution—not the problem."

GOOD READING, for Everyone, Henrichs Publications, Inc., P.O. Box 40, Sunshine Park, Litchfield IL 62056. (217)324-3425. Editor: Peggy Kuethe. 85% freelance written. Works with a small number of new/unpublished writers each year, and is eager to work with new/unpublished writers. A monthly general interest magazine with articles and stories based on a wide range of current or factual subjects. Estab. 1968. Circ. 7,500. **Pays on acceptance.** Publishes ms an average of 6 months after acceptance. Byline given. Buys first North American serial rights. Submit seasonal/holiday material 5 months in advance. Reports in 2 months. Sample copy for 50¢, 6×10 SAE and 2 first class stamps; writer's guidelines for #10 SASE.

Nonfiction: General interest, historical/nostalgic, humor, photo feature and travel. Also stories about annual festivals, trends, people who make a difference. "No material that deals with the sordid side of life, nothing about alcohol, smoking, drugs, gambling. Nothing that deals with the cost of travel, or that is too technical." Send complete ms. Length: 100-1,000 words. Pays $20-100 for unsolicited articles.

Photos: Send photos with submission. Reviews contact sheets and 3×5, 5×7, or 8×10 b&w prints. No color photos accepted. Offers additional payment for photos accepted with ms. Identification of subjects required. Buys one-time rights.

Columns/Departments: Youth Today (directed at young readers), 100 words maximum. Buys 6-9 mss/year. Send complete ms. Pays $10-50.

Poetry: Light verse. No limit to number of poems submitted at one time. Length: 4-16 lines. Pays in copies.

Fillers: Anecdotes, facts and short humor. Length: 50-150 words. Pays $10-30.

Tips: "The tone of *Good Reading* is wholesome; the articles are short. Keep writing informal but grammatically correct. *Good Reading* is general interest and directed at the entire family—so we accept only material that would be of interest to nearly every age group."

GRIT, America's Family Magazine, Grit Publishing Group, 208 W. 3rd St., Williamsport PA 17701. (717)326-1771. Editor: Michael R. Rafferty. 30% freelance written. "*Grit* is aimed at what is good about America. Its audience is generally older and conservative. We also look for stories about unusual people, places and things." Estab. 1882. Circ. 550,000. Pays on publication. Publishes ms an average of 2 months after acceptance. Byline given. Offers 15¢/word kill fee. Buys first or second rights or makes work-for-hire assignments. Submit seasonal/holiday material 8 months in advance. Simultaneous and previously published submissions OK. Query for electronic submissions. Reports in 3 weeks on queries; 1 month on mss. Sample copy for 11×14 SAE with 4 first class stamps. Writer's guidelines for #10 SASE.

Nonfiction: General interest, how-to (car care, home and household repairs), humor, inspirational, interview/profile. "No crime, violence, alcohol, drug or tabacco uses, sex." Query. Send complete ms. Length: 600-1,500 words. 15-22¢/word for assigned articles; 12-15¢/word for unsolicited articles. Sometimes pays expenses of writers on assignment.

Photos: Send photos with submission. Reviews 35mm transparencies and 8×10 prints. Offers $40-175 per photo. Model releases and identification of subjects required. "We purchase first and subsequent-use rights."

Poetry: Joanne Decker, poetry editor. Buys 150/year. Submit maximum 20 poems. Length: 4-20 lines. Pays $6 for first four lines, 50¢ per line thereafter.

Fillers: Al Elmer, fillers editor. Short humor. Buys 150/year. Length: 50-150 words. Pays 12-15¢/word.

Tips: "Keep in mind *Grit* is looking for the uplifting and the unusual. If it might offend somebody's grandma, *don't* send it to *Grit*."

HARPER'S MAGAZINE, 666 Broadway, 11th Floor, New York NY 10012. (212)614-6500. FAX: (212)228-5889. Editor: Lewis H. Lapham. 40% freelance written. For well-educated, socially concerned, widely read men and women who value ideas and good writing. Monthly. Estab. 1850. Circ. 190,000. Rights purchased vary with author and material. Pays negotiable kill fee. **Pays on acceptance.** Reports in 2 weeks. Publishes ms an average of 3 months after acceptance. Sample copy $2.95.

Nonfiction: "For writers working with agents or who will query first only, our requirements are: public affairs, literary, international and local reporting, and humor." No interviews; no profiles. Complete mss and queries must include SASEs. No unsolicited poems will be accepted. Publishes one major report per issue. Length: 4,000-6,000 words. Publishes one major essay per issue. Length: 4,000-6,000 words. "These should be construed as topical essays on all manner of subjects (politics, the arts, crime, business, etc.) to which the author can bring the force of passionately informed statement." Publishes one short story per month. Generally pays 50¢-$1/word.

Photos: Deborah Rust, art director. Occasionally purchased with mss; others by assignment. Pays $50-500.

KNOWLEDGE, Official Publication of the World Olympiads of Knowledge, Knowledge, Inc., 3863 Southwest Loop 820, S 100, Ft. Worth TX 76133-2076. (817)292-4272. FAX: (817)292-2893. Editor: Dr. O.A. Battista. Managing Editor: N.L. Matous. 90% freelance written. For lay and professional audiences of all occupations. Quarterly magazine; 60 pages. Estab. 1985. Circ. 3,000. Pays on publication. Publishes ms an average of 6 months after acceptance. Buys all rights. "We will reassign rights to a writer after a given period." Byline given. Submit seasonal/holiday material 6 months in advance. Reports in 1 month. Sample copy $5; writer's guidelines for #10 SASE.

Nonfiction: Informational—original new knowledge that will prove mentally or physically beneficial to all readers. Buys 30 unsolicited mss/year. Query. Length: 1,500-2,000 words maximum. Pays $100 minimum. Sometimes pays the expenses of writers on assignment.

Columns/Departments: Journal section uses maverick and speculative ideas that other magazines will not publish and reference. Payment is made, on publication, at the following minimum rates: Why Don't They, $50; Salutes, $25; New Vignettes, $25; Quotes To Ponder, $10; and Facts, $5.

Tips: "The editors of *Knowledge* welcome submissions from contributors. Manuscripts and art material will be carefully considered but received *only* with the unequivocal understanding that the magazine will not be responsible for loss or injury. Material from a published source should have the publication's name, date and page number. Submissions cannot be acknowledged and will be returned only when accompanied by a SASE having adequate postage."

LEFTHANDER MAGAZINE, Lefthander International, P.O. Box 8249, Topeka KS 66608. (913)234-2177. Managing Editor: Suzan Ireland. 80% freelance written. Eager to work with new/unpublished writers. Bimonthly. "Our readers are lefthanded people of all ages and interests in 50 U.S. states and 12 foreign countries. The one thing they have in common is an interest in lefthandedness." Estab. 1975. Circ. 26,000. Pays on publication. Publishes ms an average of 4 months after acceptance. Byline usually given. Offers 25% kill fee. Rights negotiable. Simultaneous queries OK. Reports on queries in 6 weeks. Sample copy for 8½ × 11 SAE and $2. Writer's guidelines for #10 SASE.

Nonfiction: Interviews with famous lefthanders; features about lefthanders with interesting talents and occupations; how-to features (sports, crafts, hobbies for lefties); research on handedness and brain dominance; exposé on discrimination against lefthanders in the work world; features on occupations and careers attracting lefties; education features relating to ambidextrous right brain teaching methods. Length: Buys 50-60 mss/year. 750-1,000 words for features. Buys 6 personal experience shorts/year. Query with SASE. Length 750 words. Pays $25. Pays expenses of writer on assignment.

Photos: State availability of photos for features. Pays $10-15 for good contrast b&w glossies. Rights negotiable.

Tips: "All material must have a lefthanded hook. We prefer quick, practical, self-help and self-awareness types of editorial content; keep it brief, light and of general interest. More of our space is devoted to shorter pieces. A good short piece gives us enough evidence of writer's style, which we like to have before assigning full-length features."

LEISURE WORLD, Ontario Motorist Publishing Company, 1215 Ovellette Ave., Box 580, Windsor, Ontario N9A 6N3 Canada. (519)971-3208. FAX: (519)977-1197. Editor: Douglas O'Neil. 30% freelance written. Bimonthly magazine. "*Leisure World* is distributed to members of the Canadian Automobile Association in Southwestern Ontario and the Atlantic provinces. Editorial content is focused on travel, entertainment and leisure time pursuits of interest to CAA members." Estab. 1988. Circ. 280,000. Pays on publication. Publishes ms an average of 2 months after acceptance. Buys first rights and second serial (reprint) rights. Submit seasonal/holiday material 4 months in advance. Sample copy $2. Free writer's guidelines.

Close-up

Lewis H. Lapham
Editor
Harper's

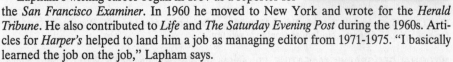

"Everybody on the *Harper's* staff writes," says Editor Lewis H. Lapham. "We try to get as many voices in the magazine as possible. That way we can achieve a degree of diversity." Voice has everything to do with *Harper's*, according to Lapham. "What do *you* care about?" asks Lapham. "That's what we want to put into every issue of *Harper's*."

Lapham's writing career began in 1957 as a reporter for the *San Francisco Examiner*. In 1960 he moved to New York and wrote for the *Herald Tribune*. He also contributed to *Life* and *The Saturday Evening Post* during the 1960s. Articles for *Harper's* helped to land him a job as managing editor from 1971-1975. "I basically learned the job on the job," Lapham says.

He became editor in 1976 and brought with him "a writer's prejudices," he says. When the ownership of *Harper's* changed hands in 1980, Lapham soon after was fired. He was rehired in 1983 as the editor, making him "the Grover Cleveland of the magazine business." He still empathizes with writers and produces a monthly column for the magazine.

Harper's is read closely by agents and publishers both for its fiction and nonfiction. Many writers got their first big break in the magazine: Annie Dillard, T.C. Boyle and others. For a while, more than half of the submissions to *Harper's* were being made by agents. "This is becoming less the case, though," says Lapham. "Magazines are a small market for agents and they don't make enough in commissions."

Perhaps *Harper's* is best known for its unique "Harper's Index," a collection of unusual and poignant data, often corresponding to subjects addressed by the articles. The magazine also features a regular column of "Readings". These are reprints of interesting articles, letters, transcripts and ad copy from a variety of sources. Given the range it covers — nonfiction articles, short fiction and occasional poetry, the Index and Readings — *Harper's* provides an interesting forum for all types of writers and readers.

Nonfiction writers should know they need an inroad, a personal connection to an editor on the staff — no matter how remote — for their queries. Otherwise, letters not addressed to a specific person end up in the slush pile. The same applies for fiction: Send it to any editor, but be sure to address it to a name, not just a title.

Lapham estimates that 40% of the writing for *Harper's* is accepted over the transom. Sixty percent is commissioned on the strength of queries. Nothing is written on spec, according to Lapham, because "it's not worth it for the writer." Prospective contributors to *Harper's* should realize that the editorial offices receive thousands of manuscripts and queries every year. "I try to read as much as I can," says Lapham, but much of the time, he concedes, he can only read the first three pages of some manuscripts.

"We want to hear the writer in the work," says Lapham. "When you care about something, let your voice be heard."

— Mark Kissling

Nonfiction: General interest, historical/nostalgic, humor, new product and travel. Buys 20 mss/year. Send complete ms. Length: 800-1,500 words. Pays $50-200.

Photos: Reviews negatives. Offers $15-40 per photo. Captions and model releases required. Buys one-time rights.

Columns/Departments: Query with published clips. Length: 400-800 words. Pays $40-60.

Tips: "We are most interested in travel destination articles that offer a personal, subjective and positive point of view on international (including US) destinations. Good quality color slides are a must."

‡**LIFE**, Time & Life Bldg., Rockefeller Center, New York NY 10020. (212)522-1212. Managing Editor: James R. Gaines. Articles: Assist Managing Editor: Jay D. Lovinger. 10% freelance written. Prefers to work with published/established writers, and works with a small number of new/unpublished writers each year. Monthly general interest picture magazine for people of all ages, backgrounds and interests. Circ. 1.5 million. Average issue includes one short and one long text piece. **Pays on acceptance.** Publishes ms an average of 3 months after acceptance. Byline given. Buys first North American serial rights. Submit seasonal material 4 months in advance. Simultaneous and photocopied submissions OK. Reports in 6 weeks.

Nonfiction: "We've done articles on anything in the world of interest to the general reader and on people of importance. It's extremely difficult to break in since we buy so few articles. Most of the magazine is pictures. We're looking for very high quality writing. We select writers whom we think match the subject they are writing about." Query with clips of previously published work. Length: 2,000-6,000 words.

MACLEAN'S, Canada's Weekly News Magazine, Maclean Hunter Ltd., 777 Bay St., Toronto, Ontario M5W 1A7 Canada. No longer freelance written.

NATIONAL GEOGRAPHIC MAGAZINE, 17th and M Sts. NW, Washington DC 20036. Editor: William Graves. Approximately 50% freelance written. Prefers to work with published/established writers, and works with a small number of new/unpublished writers each year. For members of the National Geographic Society. Monthly. Estab. 1888. Circ. 10 million.

Nonfiction: *National Geographic* publishes general interest, illustrated articles on science, natural history, exploration politics and geographical regions. Almost half of the articles are staff-written. Of the freelance writers assigned, most are experts in their fields; the remainder are established professionals. Fewer than one percent of unsolicited queries result in assignments. Query (500 words) by letter, not by phone, to Senior Assistant Editor Robert Poole (Contract Writers). Do not send manuscripts. Before querying, study recent issues and check a *Geographic Index* at a library since the magazine seldom returns to regions or subjects covered within the past ten years. Pays expenses of writers on assignment.

Photos: Photographers should query in care of the Illustration Division.

THE NEW YORKER, 20 W. 43rd St., New York NY 10036. Editor: Robert Gottlieb. Weekly. Circ. 600,000. Reports in 2 months. **Pays on acceptance.**

Nonfiction, Fiction, Poetry and Fillers: Long fact pieces are usually staff-written. So is "Talk of the Town," although freelance submissions are considered. Pays good rates. Uses fiction, both serious and light. About 90% of the fillers come from contributors with or without taglines (extra pay if the tagline is used).

‡**OUT WEST, America's On the Road Newspaper**, 10522 Brunswick Rd., Grass Valley CA 95945. (916)477-9378. Editor: Chuck Woodbury. Submissions editor: Mike Randolph. 15% freelance written. Quarterly tabloid for general audience. Estab. 1987. Circ. 17,000. Pays on acceptance or publication (negotiated). Byline given. Buys one-time or reprint rights. Submit seasonal/holiday material 4 months in advance. Simultaneous and previously published submissions OK. Reports in 6 weeks. Sample copy $2; writer's guidelines for #10 SASE.

Nonfiction: Essays, historical, humor, photo feature, profiles, travel, but always relating to the rural West. Readers are travelers and armchair travelers interested in what's along the back roads and old two-lane highways of the non-urban West. Articles about old cafes, motels, hotels, roadside trading posts, drive-in theaters, highways of yesteryear like Route 66 and good roadtrips are especially welcome. No foreign travel. Query or send complete ms. Length: 300-1,000 words. Pays $25-125.

For information on setting your freelance fees, see How Much Should I Charge? in the Business of Writing section.

Photos: Black and white only; prefers 5×7 or 8×10 prints. Buys stand-alone photos of funny things and signs along the road. Pays $5-30.

Columns/Departments: Western wildlife, roadfood, roadtrips, rural museums and attractions, tourist railroads. Length: 400-600 words. Pays $30-50.

Fillers: Anecdotes, short humor, unusual Western historical facts, funny small business slogans, cartoons, travel tips. Length 25-150 words. Pays $5-20.

Pays $2-12.

Tips: "It's very important to read the publication before submitting work. No how-to articles. Our West is not an RV or senior publication."

PARADE, Parade Publications, Inc., 750 3rd Ave., New York NY 10017. (212)573-7000. Editor: Walter Anderson. Weekly magazine for a general interest audience. 90% freelance written. Circ. 37 million. **Pays on acceptance.** Publishes ms an average of 3 months after acceptance. Kill fee varies in amount. Buys first North American serial rights. Reports in 5 weeks on queries. Writer's guidelines for #10 SAE.

Nonfiction: General interest (on health, trends, social issues, business or anything of interest to a broad general audience); interview/profile (of news figures, celebrities and people of national significance); and "provocative topical pieces of news value." Spot news events are not accepted, as *Parade* has a 6-week lead time. No fiction, fashion, travel, poetry, quizzes or fillers. Address three-paragraph queries to Articles Editor. Length: 800-1,500 words. Pays $1,000 minimum. Pays expenses of writers on assignment.

Tips: "Send a well-researched, well-written query targeted to our market. Please, no phone queries. We're interested in well-written exclusive manuscripts on topics of news interest. The most frequent mistake made by writers in completing an article for us is not adhering to the suggestions made by the editor when the article was assigned."

READER'S DIGEST, Pleasantville NY 10570. Monthly. Circ. 16.5 million. Publishes general interest articles "as varied as all human experience." The *Digest* does not read or return unsolicited mss. Address proposals and tearsheets of published articles to the editors. Considers only previously published articles; pays $1,200/*Digest* page for World Digest rights. (Usually split 50/50 between original publisher and writer.) Tearsheets of submitted article must include name of original publisher and date of publication.

Columns/Departments: "Original contributions become the property of *Reader's Digest* upon acceptance and payment. Life-in-these-United States contributions must be true, unpublished stories from one's own experience, revealing adult human nature, and providing appealing or humorous sidelights on the American scene. Length: 300 words maximum. Pays $400 on publication. True and unpublished stories are also solicited for Humor in Uniform, Campus Comedy and All in a Day's Work. Length: 300 words maximum. Pays $400 on publication. Towards More Picturesque Speech—the first contributor of each item used in this department is paid $50 for original material, $35 for reprints. Contributions should be dated, and the source must be given. For items used in Laughter, the Best Medicine, Personal Glimpses, Quotable Quotes, and elsewhere in the magazine payment is as follows; to the *first* contributor of each from a published source, $35. For original material, $30 per *Digest* two-column line, with a minimum payment of $50. Send complete anecdotes to excerpt editor."

‡READER'S DIGEST (CANADA), 215 Redfern, Westmount, Quebec H3Z 2V9 Canada. (514)934-0751. Editor: Alexander Farrell. Managing Editor: Robert Cameron. 10-24% freelance written. Monthly magazine of general interest articles and subjects. Estab. 1948. Circ. 1.3 million. **Pays on acceptance** for original works. Pays on publication for "pickups." Byline given. Offers $500 kill fee (Canadian funds). Buys one-time rights (for Pickups), all rights (for Original articles). Submit seasonal/holiday material 4-5 months in advance. Previously published submissions OK. Query for electronic submissions. Reports in 3 weeks on queries. Writer's guidelines for #10 SASE with Canadian postage or #10 SAE with 1 IRC.

Nonfiction: General interest, how-to (general interest), inspirational, personal experience. "No fiction, poetry or articles too specialized, technical or esoteric—read *Reader's Digest* to see what kind of articles we want." Query with published clips to Managing Editor. Length: 3,000-5,000 words. Pays $2,500-3,200 (Canadian) for assigned articles to writers with *Digest* experience. Pays expenses of writers on assignment.

Photos: State availability of photos with submission.

Tips: "*Reader's Digest* usually finds its freelance writers through other well-known publications in which they have previously been published. There are guidelines available and writers should read *Reader's Digest* to see what kind of stories we look for and how they are written. WE DO NOT ACCEPT UNSOLICITED MANUSCRIPTS."

READERS REVIEW, The National Research Bureau, Inc., 424 N. 3rd St., P.O. Box 1, Burlington IA 52601-0001. FAX: (319)752-3421. Editor: Rhonda Wilson. Editorial Supervisor: Doris J. Ruschill. 75% freelance written. Works with a small number of new/unpublished writers each year, and is eager to work with new/unpublished writers. Quarterly magazine. Estab. 1948. Pays on publication. Publishes ms an average of 1 year after acceptance. Buys all rights. Previously published submissions OK. Submit seasonal/holiday material 7 months in advance of issue date. Reports in 3 weeks. Writer's guidelines for #10 SASE; sample for 6½ × 9½ envelope with 55¢ postage.
Nonfiction: General interest (steps to better health, attitudes on the job); how-to (perform better on the job, do home repairs, car maintenance); and travel. Buys 10-12 mss/year. Query with outline or submit complete ms. Length: 400-600 words. Pays 4¢/word.
Tips: "Writers have a better chance of breaking in at our publication with short articles."

REAL PEOPLE, The Magazine of Celebrities and Interesting People, Main Street Publishing Co., Inc., 950 Third Ave. 16th Fl., New York NY 10022-2705. (212)371-4932. FAX: (212)838-8420. Editor: Alex Polner. 75% freelance written. Bimonthly magazine focusing on celebs, but also human interest, true crime, people and their strange occupations and behaviors, profiles, and self-help articles for audience, ages 35 and up. Estab. 1988. Circ. 165,000. Pays on publication. Byline given. Pays 33% kill fee. Buys all rights except in some specific cases. Submit seasonal/holiday material 6 months in advance. Reports in 1 month. Sample copy for $3.50 with 6 × 9 SAE and 75¢ postage. Writer's guidelines for #10 SASE.
Nonfiction: Book excerpts, how-to, interview/profile. Buys 60 mss/year. Query (and SAE) with published clips. Length: 500-1,200 words. Pays $150-250 for assigned articles; $100-200 for unsolicited articles.
Photos: State availability of photos with submissions. Reviews 5 × 7 prints. Offers no additional payment for photos accepted with ms. Captions, model releases and identification of subjects required. Buys one-time rights.

‡THE ROBB REPORT, The Magazine for Connoisseurs, 1 Acton Place, Acton MA 01720. (508)263-7749. Editor: Robert Feeman. Managing Editor: Janice Stillman. 60% freelance written. Monthly magazine. "We are a lifestyle magazine geared toward active, affluent readers." Addresses upscale autos, luxury travel, boating, technology, lifestyles, personal style, sports, investments, collectibles. Estab. 1975. Circ. 80,000. Pays on publication. Byline given. Offers 50% kill fee. Buys all rights or first North American serial rights. Submit seasonal/holiday material 5 months in advance. Query for electronic submissions. Reports in 6 weeks on queries; 1 month on mss. Sample copy $6; free writer's guidelines.
Nonfiction: General interest (autos, lifestyle, etc.), interview/profile (business), new product (autos, boats, consumer electronics), travel (prefer domestic). No essays, personal travel experiences, bargain travel. Buys 60 mss/year. Query with or without published clips, or send complete ms. Length: 2,500-3,500 words. Pays $600-800. Sometimes pays expenses of writers on assignment.
Photos: State availability of photos with submission. Payment depends on article. Buys one-time rights.
Tips: "Study the magazine. We are geared exclusively to affluent readers. All article submissions should be targeted at that audience."

‡THE ROOSTER & THE RAVEN, Mike & Paul's Publishing, Suite 102, 1057 Solano Ave., Albany CA 94706. (415)527-2172. Editor: Paul Gould. 80% freelance written. Works primarily with new/unpublished writers. Twice monthly magazine, publishing quality fiction, nonfiction, poetry, music articles and reviews and comics. Circ. 16,000. **Pays on acceptance.** Publishes 2 months after acceptance. Byline given. Buys first rights. Reports in 6 weeks. Free sample copy.
Nonfiction: Narrative, descriptive essays/stories. No news stories or vacation accounts. Pays minimum $20 plus copies. Illustrations frequently accompany copy.
Columns/Departments: Solicits reviews of alternative trends in popular music: Rock, Funk, Thrash, Rap, Jazz, Classical. No New Age. Also interested in interviews with music world figures, and stories about independent labels, new musical forms, etc. Pays minimum $20.
Fiction: We print a wide variety of manuscripts and excerpts of varying length. Well written, original stories. No EN 101 material, please. No pornography, racism or sexism or gratuitous anything. Pays minimum of $20 plus copies. Illustration frequently accompany copy.
Poetry: Any format, any topic. Pays $10 minimum.
Tips: "We publish for the sake of publishing skilled and unpublished writers. We are a forum for the up-and-coming, but our standards are high. We love brilliant, insightful writing, but are content with quality stories and poetry that inform, interest and occasionally amuse."

‡THE SATURDAY EVENING POST, The Saturday Evening Post Society, 1100 Waterway Blvd., Indianapolis IN 46202. (317)636-8881. Editor: Cory SerVaas, M.D. Managing Editor: Ted Dreiter. 30% freelance written. General interest magazine published 8 times/year. "A family-oriented magazine focusing on physical fitness, preventive medicine." Estab. 1728. Circ. 570,000. Pays on publication. Publishes ms an average of 3 months after acceptance. Byline given. Buys second serial (reprint) rights and all rights. Submit seasonal/holiday material 4 months in advance. Simultaneous and previously published submissions OK. Query for electronic submissions. Reports in 1 month on queries; 6 weeks on mss. Writer's guidelines for #10 SASE.

Nonfiction: Book excerpts, general interest, how-to (gardening, home improvement), humor, interview/profile, travel. "No political articles or articles containing sexual innuendo or hypersophistication." Buys 50 mss/year. Query with or without published clips, or send complete ms. Length: 750-2,500 words. Pays $100 minimum, negotiable maximum for assigned articles. Sometimes pays expenses of writers on assignment.

Photos: State availability of photos with submission. Reviews negatives and transparencies. Offers $50 minimum, negotiable maxmimu per photo. Model release and identifiction required. Buys one-time rights or all rights.

Columns/Departments: Travel (destinations), 750-1,500. Buys 16 mss/year. Query with published clips or send complete ms. Length: 750-1,500 words. Pays $100 minimum, negotiable maximum.

Fiction: Fiction Editor: Sue Gordon. Historical, humorous, mainstream, mystery, science fiction, western. "No sexual innuendo or profane expletives." Send somplete ms. Length: 1,000-2,500 words. Pays $150 minimum, negotiable maximum.

Poetry: Light verse.

Fillers: PostScripts Editor: Chuck Mason. Anecdotes, short humor. Buys 200/year. Length 300 words. Pays $15.

Tips: "Areas most open to freelancers are Post Scripts and Travel. For travel we like text-photo packages, pragmatic tips, side bars and safe rather than exotic destinations. Query by mail, not phone. Send clips."

SELECTED READING, The National Research Bureau, Inc., 424 N. 3rd St., P.O. Box 1, Burlington IA 52601-0001. FAX: (319)752-3421. Editor: Rhonda Wilson. Editorial Supervisor: Doris J. Ruschill. 75% freelance written. Eager to work with new/unpublished writers, works with a small number of new/unpublished writers each year. Quarterly magazine. Estab. 1948. Pays on publication. Publishes ms an average of 1 year after acceptance. Buys all rights. Previously published submissions OK. Submit seasonal/holiday material 7 months in advance of issue date. Reports in 3 weeks. Writer's guidelines for #10 SASE; sample for 6½×9½ envelope with 55¢ postage.

Nonfiction: General interest (economics, health, safety, working relationships); how-to; and travel (out-of-the way places). No material on car repair. Buys 10-12 mss/year. Query. A short outline or synopsis is best. Lists of titles are no help. Length: 400-600 words. Pays 4¢/word.

Tips: "Writers have a better chance of breaking in at our publication with short articles."

SMITHSONIAN MAGAZINE, 900 Jefferson Dr., Washington DC 20560. Articles Editor: Marlane A. Liddell. 90% freelance written. Prefers to work with published/established writers. For "associate members of the Smithsonian Institution; 85% with college education." Monthly. Circ. 3 million. Buys first North American serial rights. "Payment for each article to be negotiated depending on our needs and the article's length and excellence." **Pays on acceptance.** Publishes ms an average of 6 months after acceptance. Submit seasonal material 3 months in advance. Reports in 2 months. Writer's guidelines for #10 SASE.

Nonfiction: "Our mandate from the Smithsonian Institution says we are to be interested in the same things which now interest or should interest the Institution: cultural and fine arts, history, natural sciences, hard sciences, etc." Query. Length: 750-4,500 words. Payment negotiable. Pays expenses of writers on assignment.

Photos: Purchased with or without ms and on assignment. Captions required. Pays $400/full color page.

‡SOUTHERN LIVING, Southern Progress Corp., 2100 Lakeshore Dr., Birmingham AL 35209. (205)877-6000. Editor: John A. Floyd, Jr. Managing Editor: William McDougal. 5% freelance written. Monthly magazine. **Pays on acceptance.** Publishes ms an average of 2-3 months after acceptance. Kill fee "varies with article." Buys all rights or other negotiated rights. Reports in 2 months.

Nonfiction: "No essays about Southern life written by freelancers are used for our columns." Query with or without published clips, but prefers completed mss. Length: 500-900 words. Payment negotiated individually.

THE STAR, 660 White Plains Rd., Tarrytown NY 10591. (914)332-5000. FAX: (914)332-5043. Editor: Richard Kaplan. Executive Editor: Bill Ridley. Managing Editor: Steve LeGrice. 40% freelance written. Prefers to work with published/established writers. "For every family; all the family—kids, teenagers, young parents and grandparents." Weekly magazine; 48 pages. Estab. 1974. Circ. 3.5 million. Publishes ms an average of 1 month after acceptance. Buys first North American serial rights, occa-

sional second serial book rights. Query for electronic submissions. Pays expenses of writers on assignment.
Nonfiction: Exposé (government waste, consumer, education, anything affecting family); general interest (human interest, consumerism, informational, family and women's interest); how-to (psychological, practical on all subjects affecting readers); interview (celebrity or human interest); new product; photo feature; profile (celebrity or national figure); health; medical; and diet. No first-person articles. Query or submit complete ms. Length: 500-1,000 words. Pays $50-1,500.
Photos: Alistair Duncan, photo editor. State availability of photos with query or ms. Pays $25-100 for 8×10 b&w glossy prints, contact sheets or negatives; $150-1,000 for 35mm color transparencies. Captions required. Buys one-time or all rights.

‡SUN, Globe Communications Corp., 5401 NW Broken Sound Blvd., Boca Raton FL 33487. (407)997-7733. 60% freelance written. Weekly publication. Pays on publication. Publishes ms an average of 3-4 months after acceptance. Kill fee varies with original assignment. Buys first or second serial (reprint) rights. Reports in 2 weeks.
Nonfiction: Prefers to see human interest stories. Query with or without published clips. Length and payment vary.

‡THE SUN, A Magazine of Ideas, The Sun Publishing Company, 107 N. Roberson St., Chapel Hill NC 27516. (919)942-5282. Editor: Sy Safransky. 90% freelance written. Monthly general interest magazine. "We are open to all kinds of writing, though we favor work of a personal nature." Estab. 1974. Circ. 15,000. Pays on publication. Publishes ms an average of 6 months after acceptance. Byline given. Buys one-time rights. Simultaneous and previously published submissions OK. Reports in 1 month on queries; 3 months on mss. Sample copy $3. Free writer's guidelines.
Nonfiction: Book excerpts, essays, expose, general interest, humor, interview/profile, opinion, personal experience, religious and travel. Buys 24 mss/year. Send complete ms. Length: 10,000 words maximum. Pays $100-200. "Complimentary subscription is given in addition to payment." Sometimes pays expenses of writers on assignment.
Photos: Send photos with submission. Reviews prints. Offers $25 per photo. Model releases required. Buys one-time rights.
Fiction: Erotica, ethnic, experimental, historical, humorous, mainstream, novel excerpts, religious, serialized novels. Buys 30 mss/year. Send complete ms. Length: 10,000 words maximum. Pays $100.
Poetry: Avant-garde, free verse, haiku, light verse and traditional. Buys 24 poems/year. Submit 6 poems maximum. Pays $25.

SUNSHINE MAGAZINE, Henry F. Henrichs Publications, P.O. Box 40, Sunshine Park, Litchfield IL 62056. (217)324-3425. Editor: Peggy Kuethe. 95% freelance written. Eager to work with new/unpublished writers. A monthly magazine. "Primarily human interest and inspirational in its appeal, *Sunshine Magazine* provides worthwhile reading for all the family." Estab. 1924. Circ. 70,000. **Pays on acceptance.** Publishes ms an average of 6 months after acceptance. Byline given. Buys first North American serial rights or one-time rights. Submit seasonal/holiday material 6 months in advance. Reports in 2 months. Sample copy for 50¢, 6×9 SAE and 2 first class stamps; writer's guidelines for #10 SASE.
Nonfiction: Essays, nostalgic, inspirational and personal experience. "No material dealing with specifically religious matters or that is depressing in nature (divorce, drug abuse, alcohol abuse, death, violence, child abuse)." Send complete ms. Length: 200-900. Pays $10-100.
Columns/Departments: Extraordinary Experience (personal experience), 500 words; Let's Reminisce (reminiscent, nostalgia), 500 words; Guidelines (inspirational), 200 words; and Favorite Meditation (inspirational essay), 200 words. Buys 85-90 mss/year. Send complete ms. Pays $15-50.
Fiction: Inspirational and human interest. Buys 75-80 mss/year. Send complete ms. Pays $30-75, maximum length 1,250 words.
Poetry: Light verse and traditional. No avant-garde, free verse or haiku. Buys 12-15 poems/year. No limit to the number of poems submitted at one time. Length: 4-16 lines. Pays $20, or may pay in copies.
Fillers: Anecdotes and short humor. Buys 1-5/year. Length: 50-150 words. Pays $10-20.
Tips: "Make a note that *Sunshine* is not religious—but it is inspirational. After reading a sample copy, you should know that we do not accept material that is very different from what we've been doing for over 60 years. Don't send a manuscript that is longer than specified or that is 'different' from anything else we've published—that's not what we're looking for. The whole magazine is written primarily by freelancers. We are just as eager to publish new writers as they are to get published."

TIME, Time & Life Bldg., Rockefeller Center, New York NY 10020-1393. Did not want to be listed.

WHAT MAKES PEOPLE SUCCESSFUL, The National Research Bureau, Inc., 424 N. 3rd St., P.O. Box 1, Burlington IA 52601-0001. FAX: (319)752-3421. Editor: Rhonda Wilson. Editorial Supervisor: Doris J. Ruschill. 75% freelance written. Eager to work with new/unpublished writers, and works with a small number of new/unpublished writers each year. Published quarterly. Estab. 1948. Pays on publication. Publishes ms an average of 1 year after acceptance. Buys all rights. Previously published submissions OK. Submit seasonal/holiday material 8 months in advance of issue date. Reports in 3 weeks. Writer's guidelines for #10 SASE; sample copy for 6½ × 9½ envelope with 55¢ postage.

Nonfiction: How-to (be successful); general interest (personality, employee morale, guides to successful living, biographies of successful persons, etc.); experience; and opinion. No material on health. Buys 3-4 mss/issue. Query with outline. Length: 400-600 words. Pays 4¢/word.

Tips: Short articles (rather than major features) have a better chance of acceptance because all articles are short.

THE WORLD & I, A Chronicle of Our Changing Era, News World Communications, Inc., 2800 New York Ave. NE, Washington DC 20002. (202)635-4000. FAX: (202)269-9353. Editor: Morton A. Kaplan. Executive Editor: Michael Marshall. 90% freelance written. Publishing more than 100 articles each month, this is a broad interest magazine for the thinking person. Estab. 1986. Circ. 30,000. **Pays on acceptance.** Publishes ms an average of 4 months after acceptance. Byline given. Offers 20% kill fee. Buys all rights. Submit seasonal/holiday material 5 months in advance. Query for electronic submissions. Reports in 6 weeks on queries; 10 weeks on mss. Writer's guidelines for #10 SASE. Description of Sections: Current Issues: Politics, economics and strategic trends covered in a variety of approaches, including special report, analysis, commentary and photo essay. The Arts: International coverage of music, dance, theater, film, television, design, architecture, photography, poetry, painting and sculpture—through reviews, features, essays and a 10-page Gallery of full-color reproductions. Life: Human interest section on children, family, garden, home, sports, beauty, fashion, health, adventure, humor and more. Natural Science: Covers the latest in science and technology, relating it to the social and historical context, under these headings: At the Edge, Impacts, Nature Walk, Science and Spirit, Science and Values, Scientists: Past and Present, Crucibles of Science and Science Essay. Book World: Excerpts from important, timely books (followed by commentaries) and 10-12 scholarly reviews of significant new books each month, including untranslated works from abroad. Covers current affairs, intellectual issues, contemporary fiction, history, moral/religious issues and the social sciences. Currents in Modern Thought: Examines scholarly research and theoretical debate across the wide range of disciplines in the humanities and social sciences. Featured themes are explored by several contributors. Investigates theoretical issues raised by certain current events, and offers contemporary reflection on issues drawn from the whole history of human thought. Culture: Surveys the world's people in these subsections: Peoples (their unique characteristics and cultural symbols), Crossroads (changes brought by the meeting of cultures), Patterns (photo essay depicting the daily life of a distinct culture), Folk Wisdom (folklore and practical wisdom and their present forms), and Heritage (multicultural backgrounds of the American people and how they are bound to the world. Photo Essay: The 10-page Life and Ideals dramatizes a human story of obstacles overcome in the pursuit of an ideal. Three other photo essays appear each month: Focus (Current Issues), Gallery (The Arts), and Patterns (Culture).

Nonfiction: "No *National Enquirer*-type articles." Buys 1,200 mss/year. Query with published clips. Length: 1,000-15,000 words. Pays 10-20¢/word. Sometimes pays expenses of writers on assignment. First-person work is discouraged.

Poetry: Query arts editor. Avant-garde, free verse, haiku, light verse and traditional. Buys 6-12 poems/year. Submit maximum 5 poems. Pays $25-50.

Photos: State availability of photos with submission. Reivews contact sheets, transparencies and prints. Payment negotiable. Model releases and identification of subjects required. Buys one-time rights.

Tips: "Send a short query letter with a viable story idea (no unsolicited mss, please!) for a specific section and/or subsection."

WORLD'S FAIR, World's Fair, Inc., P.O. Box 339, Corte Madera CA 94976. (415)924-6035. Editor: Alfred Heller. 50% freelance written. Quarterly magazine covering fairs and expositions (past, present and future). "The people, politics and pageantry of fairs and expositions, in historical perspective; lively, good-humored articles of fact and analysis." Estab. 1981. Circ. 5,000. **Pays on acceptance.** Publishes ms an average of 3 months after acceptance. Byline given. Offers 50% kill fee. Buys all rights. Reports in 3 weeks. Free sample copy and writer's guidelines.

Nonfiction: Essays, historical/nostalgic, humor, interview/profile, personal experience and photo feature, related to international fairs and expositions. Buys 8-10 mss/year. Query with published clips. Length: 750-3,000 words. Pays $50-400. Sometimes pays expenses of writers on assignment.

Photos: State availability of photos or line drawings with submission. Reviews contact sheets and 8 × 10 b&w prints. Identification of subjects required. Buys one-time rights.

Tips: Looking for "correspondents in cities planning major expositions, in the US and abroad."

Health and Fitness

The magazines listed here specialize in covering health and fitness topics for a general audience. Many focus not as much on exercise as on general "healthy lifestyle" topics.

Magazines covering health topics from a medical perspective are listed in the Medical category of Trade. Also see the Sports/Miscellaneous section where publications dealing with health and particular sports may be listed. Many general interest publications are also potential markets for health or fitness articles.

ACCENT ON LIVING, Box 700, Bloomington IL 61702. (309)378-2961. FAX: (309)378-4420. Editor: Betty Garee. 75% freelance written. Eager to work with new/unpublished writers. For physically disabled persons and rehabilitation professionals. Quarterly magazine. Circ. 20,000. Buys first rights and second (reprint) rights to material originally published elsewhere. Byline usually given. Buys 50-60 unsolicited mss/year. Pays on publication. Publishes ms an average of 6 months after acceptance. Reports in 2 weeks. Sample copy with writer's guidelines for $2.50, 6×8 SAE and four first class stamps; writer's guidelines alone for #10 SAE and 1 first class stamp.
Nonfiction: Articles about new devices that would make a disabled person with limited physical mobility more independent; should include description, availability, and photos. Medical breakthroughs for disabled people. Intelligent discussion articles on acceptance of physically disabled persons in normal living situations; topics may be architectural barriers, housing, transportation, educational or job opportunities, organizations, or other areas. How-to articles concerning everyday living, giving specific, helpful information so the reader can carry out the idea himself/herself. News articles about active disabled persons or groups. Good strong interviews. Vacations, accessible places to go, sports, organizations, humorous incidents, self improvement, and sexual or personal adjustment—all related to physically handicapped persons. No religious-type articles. "We are looking for upbeat material." Query. Length: 250-1,000 words. Pays 10¢/word for article as it appears in magazine (after editing and/or condensing by staff).
Photos: Pays $10 minimum for b&w photos purchased with accompanying captions. Amount will depend on quality of photos and subject matter. Pays $50 and up for four-color slides used on cover. "We need good-quality transparencies or slides with submissions—or b&w photos."
Tips: "Ask a friend who is disabled to read your article before sending it to *Accent*. Make sure that he/she understands your major points and the sequence or procedure."

BETTER HEALTH, Better Health Press, 1450 Chapel St., New Haven CT 06511. (203)789-3974. FAX: (203)789-4053. Pubilshing Director: James F. Malerba. 75% freelance written. Prefers to work with published/established writers; will consider new/unpublished writers. A bimonthly magazine devoted to health and wellness issues, as opposed to medical issues. Estab. 1979. Circ. 110,000. Pays on publication. Byline given. Offers $50 kill fee. Buys all rights. Query. Sample copy $2. Writer's guidelines for #10 SASE.
Nonfiction: Wellness/prevention issues are of prime interest. New medical techniques or similar topics are not considered. No fillers, poems, quizzes, seasonal, heavy humor, inspirational or personal experience. Length: 1,200-2,500 words. Pays $150-300. Does not offer additional payment for photos, research costs, etc.
Tips: "Please do not submit 'how-I-overcame-my-painful-illness' articles. We look for upbeat health and wellness features of interest to a general audience, such as new developments in exercise techniques, infertility, senior housing options and so forth. We want a reader to say, "I didn't know that!" Absolutely no 'cute' humor or articles that are not well-researched through medical doctors or similar authorities. Our audience demands the best wellness news available. Queries or proposed articles not accompanied with an SASE be consigned to the wastebasket, unread."

‡CHANGES, For and About Adult Children, the U.S. Journal, Inc., 3201 SW 15th St., Deerfield Beach FL 33442. (800)851-9100. Managing Editor: Jeffrey Faign. Associate Editor: Andrew Meacham. 10% freelance written. Bimonthly magazine covering self-help, therapy for adults reared in dysfunctional homes. "*Changes* is intended to offer a mixture of information, entertainment and emotional support for adults engaged in a recovery process, primarily from a history of negative messages and unhealthy family patterns." Estab. 1986. Circ. 30,000. Pays on publication. Publishes ms an average of 4 months after acceptance. Byline given. Pays $25 kill fee. Buys first North American serial rights. Submit seasonal/holiday material 3 months in advance. Simultaneous and previously published submissions OK. Query for electronic submissions. Reports in 1 month. Sample copy $3.75; free writer's guidelines.
Nonfiction: Humor, opinion, personal experience, recovery/therapy, practices/issues. No interview (unless we have approved), lengthy personal experience (over 1,000 words), religious material, self-advertisements, reviews of books. Buys 8-12 mss/year. Query with or without published clips, or send complete ms. Length: 500-2,000 words. Pays 15¢/word. Sometimes pays poetry and personal experience pieces with contributor's copies or other premiums. Pays telephone expenses only.

Photos: State availability of photos with submission. Reviews 5 × 7 prints. Payment negotiable. Model releases required. Buys one-time rights.

Fiction: Confession, experimental, humorous, romance. "We look for insightful fiction which casts the magazine's serious subjects in unique ways. No morbid stories, stream-of-rage, fairy tales or fantasies, drug war cliches about people who hit bottom and found salvation."

Poetry: Avant-garde, free verse and light verse. Avoid rhyme and meter. Pays in contributor's copies.

Tips: "Query by mail, preferably. Show a willingness and skill for talking to a variety of sources, going to the library, tying in a current event, if applicable. Use a friendly, conversational style, but don't assume your readers are disinterested in the deeper aspects of your story. Do it right and they won't be. Don't interview a friend of yours and call that an article. The first-peson departments are most open to freelancers. Can be personal experience or opinion/observation. Doesn't have to be upbeat, but if you're going to be gloomy, at least keep us in suspense or surprise us somehow."

IN HEALTH, Suite 225, 475 Gate 5 Rd., Sausalito CA 94965. (415)332-5866. FAX: (419)332-1606. Editor: Eric Schrier. Managing Editor: Michael Gold. 75% freelance written. A bimonthly magazine on health and medicine. "Articles should be written with wit, reflection and authority." Estab. 1986. Circ. 800,000. **Pays on acceptance.** Publishes ms an average of 6 months after acceptance. Offers 25% kill fee. Buys first North American serial rights.

Nonfiction: Essays, general interest, how-to, interview/profile, photo feature. Query with published clips. Length: 2,000-5,000 words. Pays $2,000-4,500. Pays approved expenses of writers on assignment.

Columns/Departments: Leslie Talmadge, editorial assistant. Food, Family, Fitness, Drugs, Vanities, Mind, all about 1,200 words. Buys 12 mss/year. Query with published clips. Pays about $1,200.

Fillers: Clippings: verbatim from other publications or book, $50 each *used*; nothing if unused.

Tips: "Send sharply focused queries with the proposed style and sources clearly defined. Departments are the best place to start. Queries can run to 250 words per topic and should demonstrate the finished story's structure and character. Departments are Food, Family, Fitness, Drugs, Vanities and Mind. Tightly focused stories, with real voices and touches of humor used. *Always* query first. The magazine for M.D.'s is still entitled *Hippocrates*. General public receives *In Health*."

LET'S LIVE MAGAZINE, Hilltopper Publications, Inc., 444 N. Larchmont Blvd., Box 74908, Los Angeles CA 90004. (213)469-8379. FAX: (213)469-9597. Editor: Debra Jenkins Robinson. Emphasizes nutrition. 15% freelance written. Works with a small number of new/unpublished writers each year. Monthly magazine. Estab. 1933. Circ. 140,000. Pays on publication. Publishes ms an average of 4 months after acceptance. Buys first North American serial rights. Byline given. Submit seasonal/holiday material 6 months in advance. Reports in 1 month on queries; 8 weeks on mss. Sample copy for $2.50 and 10 × 13 SAE with 5 first class stamps; writer's guidelines for SAE and 1 first class stamp.

Nonfiction: General interest (effects of vitamins, minerals and nutrients in improvement of health or afflictions); historical (documentation of experiments or treatment establishing value of nutrients as boon to health); how-to (acquire strength and vitality, improve health of adults and/or children and prepare tasty health-food meals); interview (benefits of research in establishing prevention as key to good health); personal opinion (views of orthomolecular doctors or their patients on value of health foods toward maintaining good health); and profile (background and/or medical history of preventive medicine, M.D.s or Ph.D.s, in advancement of nutrition). Manuscripts must be well-researched, reliably documented, and written in a clear, readable style. Buys 2-4 mss/issue. Query with published clips. Length: 1,000-1,200 words. Pays $150. Sometimes pays expenses of writers on assignment.

Photos: State availability of photos with ms. Pays $17.50 for 8 × 10 b&w glossy prints; $35 for 8 × 10 color prints and 35mm transparencies. Captions and model releases required.

Tips: "We want writers with experience in researching nonsurgical medical subjects and interviewing experts with the ability to simplify technical and clinical information for the layman. A captivating lead and structural flow are essential. The most frequent mistakes made by writers are in writing articles that are too technical; in poor style; written for the wrong audience (publication not thoroughly studied), or have unreliable documentation or overzealous faith in the topic reflected by flimsy research and inappropriate tone."

LONGEVITY, General Media International, Inc., 1965 Broadway, New York NY 10023. (212)496-6100. FAX: (212)580-3693. Editor-in-Chief: Rona Cherry. A monthly magazine on medicine, health, fitness and life extension research. "*Longevity* is written for an audience with a median age of 40 who want to prolong their ability to lead a productive, vibrant, healthy life, and to look as good as they feel at their best." Estab. 1989. Circ. 300,000. **Pays on acceptance.** Publishes ms an average of 2 months after acceptance. Byline given. Offers 25% kill fee. Makes work-for-hire assignments. Query for electronic submissions.

Nonfiction: Consumer trends in anti-aging, new products, health. Query. Length: 150-950 words. Pays $100-2,500. Pays expenses of writers on assignment.
Columns/Departments: Antiaging News; Outer Limits; Looks Savers; Eat For Life; Childwise; Air, Earth & Water; Marketing Youth.

‡MASSAGE MAGAZINE, Keeping Those Who Touch—In Touch, Noah Publishing Co., P.O. Box 1500, Davis CA 95617-1500. (916)757-6033. Editor: Robert Calvert. Managing Editor: Melissa B. Bower. 80% freelance written. Prefers to work with published/established writers, and works with a small number of new/unpublished writers each year. A bimonthly magazine on massage-bodywork and related healing arts. Circ. 45,000. Pays on publication. Publishes ms an average of 6 months after acceptance. Byline given. Buys first North American rights. Previously published submissions OK. Query for electronic submissions. Reports in 2 months on queries; 3 months on mss. Sample copy $5. Free writer's guidelines.
Nonfiction: Book excerpts, essays, general interest, historical/nostalgic, how-to, humor, inspirational, interview/profile, new product, photo feature, technical and travel. Length: 600-2,000 words. Pays $50-100 for assigned articles; $25-50 for unassigned. Sometimes pays the expenses of writers on assignment.
Photos: Send photos with submission. Offers $10-25 per photo. Identification of subjects required. Buys one-time rights.
Columns/Departments: Business; Touching Tales (experiential); Insurance; Table Talk (news briefs); Kneading Advice; In Touch with Associations (convention highlights); In Review/On Video (product, book, music and video reviews); and Convention Calendar (association convention listings). Query. Length: 800-1,200 words. Pays $25-50.
Fillers: Anecdotes, facts, newsbriefs and short humor. Buys 5/year. Length: 100 words. Pays $25 maximum.
Tips: "For first articles accepted, we don't pay much, but as a writer establishes with us, we pay more. Wholesome stories with facts, interviews and industry insight are welcomed."

MEN'S FITNESS, Men's Fitness, Inc., 21100 Erwin St., Woodland Hills CA 91367. (818)884-6800. Executive Editor: Jim Rosenthal. Associate Editor: Ted Mason. 50% freelance written. Works with small number of new/unpublished writers each year. A monthly magazine for health-conscious men between the ages of 18 and 45. Provides reliable, entertaining guidance for the active male in all areas of lifestyle. Writers often share bylines with professional experts. Pays 1 month after acceptance. Publishes ms an average of 6 months after acceptance. Offers 20% kill fee. Buys all rights. Submit seasonal material 4 months in advance. Reports in 1 month. Writer's guidelines for 8½×11 SAE.
Nonfiction: Service, informative, inspirational, scientific studies written for men. Few interviews, regional news unless extraordinary. Query with published clips. Buys 50 mss/year. Length: 2,000-3,000 words. Pays $300-600. Occasionally buys mss devoted to specific fitness programs, including exercises, e.g. 6-week chest workout, aerobic weight-training routine. Buys 10-15 mss/year. Pays $250-300.
Columns/Departments: Nutrition, Mind Fitness, Grooming, Sex, Prevention, Health. Length: 1,250-2,000 words. Buys 40-50 mss/year. Pays $250-400.
Tips: "Articles are welcomed in all facets of men's health; they must be well-researched, entertaining and intelligent."

MEN'S HEALTH, Rodale Press, 33 E. Minor St., Emmaus PA 18098. (215)967-5171. Editor: Michael Lafavore. Managing Editor: Steve Slon. 90% freelance written. Bimonthly magazine. "We publish health articles with a male slant. We take a broad view of health to encompass the physical and emotional." Circ. 250,000. **Pays on acceptance.** Publishes ms an average of 2 months after acceptance. Byline given. Offers 15% kill fee. Buys first North American serial rights or second serial (reprint) rights. Submit seasonal/holiday material 6-8 months in advance. Previously published submissions OK. Query for electronic submissions. Reports in 2 weeks. Sample copy $2.95 with SAE and postage.
Nonfiction: Book excerpts, essays, exposé, interview/profile, personal experience and travel. Buys 50 mss/year. Query with published clips. Length: 100-2,000 words. Pays 25-50¢/word. Sometimes pays expenses of writers on assignment.
Photos: State availability of photos with submission. Offers no additional payment for photos accepted with ms. Model releases required. Buys one-time rights.
Columns/Departments: Eating Right (nutrition); Couples (relationships); Clinic (deals with a specific health problem) and Malegrams (short news items). Buys 10 mss/year. Query. Length: 800-1,000 words. Pays 25-60¢/word.

‡MICHIGAN ARTS, Command Your Mind, Body and Spirit, Michigan Arts Promotion Association, 5139 S. Clarendon St., Detroit MI 48204-2926. Editor: Shannon Roxborough. 100% freelance written. Quarterly newsletter covering oriental and western health and fitness methods, medical therapies, diet/nutrition, spiritual practices and related topics. Estab. 1989. Circ. 5,000. **Pays on acceptance.** Publishes ms an average of 2 months after acceptance. Byline given. Buys all rights. Submit season/

holiday material 6 months in advance. Simultaneous submissions OK. Reports in 2 weeks on queries; 1 month on mss. Sample copy $3 with SAE and 3 first class stamps. Writer's guidelines for 1 first class stamp.

Nonfiction: General interest, historical/nostalgic, how-to (yoga, martial arts, TaiChi, Chi Kung, exercise) interview/profile, photo feature. "No technical pieces." Buys 25-35 mss/year. Query with or without published clips, or send complete mss. Length: 500-1,800 words. Pays $10-50 for assigned articles; $5-35 for unsolicited articles. Send photos with submission. Reviews negatives and prints. Offers $1-10 per photo. Captions required. Buys all rights.

Fillers: Buys 25-35/year. Length: 100-500 words. Pays $5-25. "New and unpublished writers are especially welcome. Exotic and lesser-known subjects are welcomed. We buy all rights. We're interested in new trends or new ways of looking at old topics."

MUSCLE & FITNESS, Brute Enterprises Inc., 21100 Erwin St., Woodland Hills CA 91367. Did not want to be listed.

MUSCLE MAG INTERNATIONAL, 52 Bramsteele Rd., Unit 2, Brampton, Ontario L6W 3M5 Canada. Editor: Robert Kennedy. 80% freelance written. "We do not care if a writer is known or unknown; published or unpublished. We simply want good instructional articles on bodybuilding." For 16- to 50-year-old men and women interested in physical fitness and overall body improvement. Monthly magazine. Circ. 225,000. Buys all rights. **Pays on acceptance.** Publishes ms an average of 4 months after acceptance. Byline given. Buys 80 mss/year. Sample copy $4 and 9×12 SAE. Reports in 1 month. Submit complete ms with IRCs.

Nonfiction: Articles on ideal physical proportions and importance of supplements in the diet, training for muscle size. Should be helpful and instructional and appeal to young men and women who want to live life in a vigorous and healthy style. "We would like to see articles for the physical culturist on new muscle building techniques or an article on fitness testing." Informational, how-to, personal experience, interview, profile, inspirational, humor, historical, exposé, nostalgia, personal opinion, photo, spot news, new product, and merchandising technique articles. "Also now actively looking for good instructional articles on Hardcore Fitness." Length: 1,200-1,600 words. Pays 10¢/word. Sometimes pays the expenses of writers on assignment.

Columns/Departments: Nutrition Talk (eating for top results) and Shaping Up (improving fitness and stamina). Length: 1,300 words. Pays 20¢/word.

Photos: B&w and color photos are purchased with or without ms. Pays $20 for 8×10 glossy exercise photos; $20 for 8×10 b&w posing shots. Pays $200-400 for color cover and $30 for color used inside magazine (transparencies). More for "special" or "outstanding" work.

Fillers: Newsbreaks, puzzles, quotes of the champs. Length: open. Pays $5 minimum.

Tips: "The best way to break in is to seek out the muscle-building 'stars' and do in-depth interviews with biography in mind. Color training picture support essential. Writers have to make their articles informative in that readers can apply them to help gain bodybuilding success. Specific fitness articles should quote experts and/or use scientific studies to strengthen their theories."

NEW BODY, The Magazine of Health & Fitness, GCR Publishing Group, Inc., 1700 Broadway, 34th Floor, New York NY 10019. (212)541-7100. Editor: Nayda Rondon. Managing Editor: Sandra Kosherick. 75% freelance written. Works with a small number of new/unpublished writers each year. A bimonthly magazine covering fitness and health for young, middle-class women. Circ. 125,000. Pays on publication. Publishes ms an average of 6 months after acceptance. Byline given. Offers negotiable kill fee. Buys all rights. Submit seasonal/holiday material 6 months in advance. Simultaneous submissions OK. Reports in 2 months.

Nonfiction: Health, exercise, psychology, relationships, diet, celebrities, and nutrition. "We do not cover bodybuilding—please no queries." No articles on "How I do exercises." Buys 75 mss/year. Query with published clips. Length: 800-1,500 words. Pays $100-300 for assigned articles; $50-150 for unsolicited articles.

Photos: Reviews contact sheets, transparencies and prints. Model releases and identification of subjects required. Buys all rights.

Columns/Departments: How I Lost It. Readers can submit "before" and "after" success stories along with color slides or photos. Pays $75.

Tips: "We are moving toward more general interest women's material on relationships, emotional health, nutrition, etc. We look for a fresh angle—a new way to present the material. Celebrity profiles, fitness tips, and health news are good topics to consider. Make a clean statement of what your article is about, what it would cover—not why the article is important. We're interested in new ideas, new trends or new ways of looking at old topics."

‡PERSONAL FITNESS AND WEIGHT LOSS, NordicTrack, 141 Jonathan Blvd. N., Chaska MN 55318. (612)449-6987. Editor: Charles Wetherall. Managing Editor: Nathan Unseth. 95% freelance written. Quarterly magazine on fitness and weight loss, with strong exercise emphasis. Reader is over 35, well educated, upscale, interested in a fitness lifestyle. Estab. 1989. Circ. 25,000. Pays on publication. Byline given. Buys first North American, second serial (reprint) rights or makes work-for-hire assignments. Previously published submissions OK. Reports in 1 month. Sample copy for $2, 9 × 12 SAE and 7 first class stamps.

Nonfiction: How-to, inspirational/motivational, new product. Buys 40-50 mss/year. Query. Length: 1,000-2,000 words. Pays $200-600. Sometimes pays expenses of writers on assignment.

Photos: State availability of photos with submission. Model releases required. Buys one-time rights.

‡**THE PHOENIX, Recovery, Renewal and Growth**, 2464 Arona St., Roseville MN 55113. (612)636-6241. FAX: (612)636-6241 (call ahead). Editor: Rosanne Bane. Managing Editor: Michael Kelberer. 100% freelance written. Monthly tabloid covering recovery and personal growth. Estab. 1981. Circ. 100,000. Pays on publication. Byline given. Offers 50% kill fee. Buys one-time rights or simultaneous rights. Submit seasonal/holiday material 2 months in advance. Simultaneous and previously published submissions. Query for electronic submissions. Sample copy for 9 × 12 SAE with 4 first class stamps. Writer's guidelines for #10 SAE with 1 first class stamp.

Nonfiction: Essays, how-to, humor, inspirational, interview/profile, opinion. Buys 60 mss/year. Query. Length: 800-2,000 words. Pays $35-150. Sometimes pays expenses of writers on assignment. Send photos with submission. Payment for photos accepted with ms. Identification of subjects required.

Tips: "We like articles/interviews which contain useful, practical information on recovery and personal growth. Avoid promotional pieces."

SHAPE MAGAZINE, Weider Enterprises, 21100 Erwin St., Woodland Hills CA 91367. (818)595-0593. Editor: Barbara Harris. 10% freelance written. Prefers to work with published/established writers, but is eager to work with new/unpublished writers. Monthly magazine covering women's health and fitness. Circ. 785,000. Pays on publication. Publishes ms an average of 6 months after acceptance. Offers 1/3 kill fee. Buys all rights and reprint rights. Submit seasonal/holiday material 8 months in advance. Reports in 2 months.

Nonfiction: Book excerpts; expose (health, fitness related); how-to (get fit); interview/profile (of fit women); travel (spas). "We use health and fitness articles written by professionals in their specific fields. No articles which haven't been queried first." Query with clips of published work. Length: 500-2,000 words. Pays negotiable fee. Pays expenses of writers on assignment.

SOBER TIMES, The Recovery Magazine, Sober Times Inc., 3601 30th St., San Diego CA 92104. (619)295-5377. Editor: J.S. Rudolf, Ph.D. Managing Editor: Milt Schwartz. 70% freelance written. Monthly tabloid on recovery from addictions. "*Sober Times* provides information about recovery from drug, alcohol and other addictive behavior, and it champions sober, sane and healthy lifestyles." Estab. 1987. Circ. 42,000. Pays on publication. Publishes ms an average of 2 months after acceptance. Byline given. Buys all rights and makes work-for-hire assignments. Submit seasonal/holiday material 3 months in advance. Reports in 3 weeks. Send SASE for writer's guidelines. Sample copy $3.

Nonfiction: Essays, general interest, humor, interview/profile, opinion, personal experience and photo feature. "No fiction or poetry will be considered. No medical or psychological jargon." Buys 90 mss/year. Send complete ms. Length: 900-2,000 words. Pays $100-300.

Photos: Send photos with submission. Reviews prints only. Offers no additional payment for photos accepted with ms. Identification of subjects required. Buys one-time rights.

Tips: "Send in finished ms with any prints. They will be returned if accompanied with self-addressed stamped envelope. Most accepted articles are under 1,000 words. Celebrity interviews should focus on recovery from addiction."

TOTAL HEALTH, Body, Mind and Spirit, Trio Publications, Suite 300, 6001 Topanga Cyn Blvd., Woodland Hills CA 91367. (818)887-6484. FAX: (818)887-7960. Editor: Robert L. Smith. Managing Editor: Rosemary Hofer. Prefers to work with published/established writers. 80% freelance written. A bimonthly magazine covering fitness, diet (weight loss), nutrition and mental health—"a family magazine about wholeness." Circ. 90,000. Pays on publication. Publishes ms an average of 2 months after acceptance. Byline given. Buys first rights. Submit seasonal/holiday material 4 months in advance. Reports in 1 month. Sample copy $1 with 9 × 12 SAE and 5 first class stamps; writer's guidelines for SAE.

Nonfiction: Exposé; how-to (pertaining to health and fitness); and religious (Judeo-Christian). Especially needs articles on skin and body care and power of positive thinking articles. No personal experience articles. Buys 48 mss/year. Send complete ms. Length: 1,500-2,000 words. Pays $50-75. Sometimes pays the expenses of writers on assignment.

Photos: State availability of photos with submission. Offers no additional payment for photos accepted with ms. Captions, model releases and identification of subjects required.
Columns/Departments: Query with or without published clips. Length: 1,000 words maximum. Pays $50-75 maximum.
Tips: "Feature-length articles are most open to freelancers. We are looking for more self help, prevention articles."

VEGETARIAN JOURNAL, Box 1463, Baltimore MD 21203. (301)366-VEGE. Editors: Charles Stahler/ Debra Wasserman. A bimonthly journal on vegetarianism and animal rights. *"Vegetarian* issues include health, nutrition, animal rights and world hunger. Articles related to nutrition should be documented by established (mainstream) nutrition studies." Estab. 1982. Circ. 13,000. **Pays on acceptance.** Publishes ms an average of 3-5 months after acceptance. Byline given. Makes work-for-hire assignments. Submit seasonal/holiday material 6 months in advance. Reports in 1 month. Sample copy $3; writer's guidelines for SASE.
Nonfiction: Book excerpts, expose, how-to, interview/profile, new products, travel. "At present we are only looking for in-depth articles on selected nutrition subjects from registered dietitians or M.D.'s. Please query with your background. Possibly some in-depth practical and researched articles from others. No miracle cures or use of supplements." Buys 1-5 mss/year. Query with or without published clips or send complete ms. Length: 2,500-8,250 words. Pays $100-300. Sometimes pays writers with contributor copies or other premiums "if not a specific agreed upon in-depth article." Sometimes pays the expenses of writers on assignment.
Photos: State availability of photos with submission. Reviews prints. Offers additional payment for photos accepted with ms. Identification of subjects required. Buys one-time rights.
Poetry: Avant-garde, free verse, haiku, light verse, traditional. "Poetry should be related to vegetarianism, world hunger, or animal rights. No graphic animal abuse. We do not want to see the word, blood, in any form." Pays in copies.
Tips: "We are most open to vegan-oriented medical professionals or vegetarian/animal rights activists who are new to freelancing."

VEGETARIAN TIMES, Box 570, Oak Park IL 60303. (312)848-8100. FAX: (312)848-8175. Executive Editor: Sally Cullen. 30% freelance written. Prefers to work with published/established writers; works with small number of new/unpublished writers each year. Monthly magazine. Circ. 170,000. Rights purchased vary with author and material. Buys first serial rights or all rights. Byline given unless extensive revisions are required or material is incorporated into a larger article. **Pays on acceptance.** Publishes ms an average of 6 months after acceptance. Submit seasonal material 6 months in advance. Reports in 1 month. Query. Sample copy $3; writer's guidelines for #10 SASE.
Nonfiction: Features articles inform readers about how vetetarianism relates to diet, cooking, lifestyle, health, consumer choices, natural foods, environmental concerns and animal welfare. "All material should be well-documented and researched, and written in a sophisticated yet lively style." Informational, how-to, personal experience, interview, profile. Length: average 2,000 words. Pays 20¢/word and up, though a flat rate may be negotiated. Will also use 500-word items for new digest. Sometimes pays expenses of writers on assignment.
Photos: Pays $40 for b&w; $40 for color photos used.
Tips: "You don't have to be a vegetarian to write for *Vegetarian Times,* but it is VITAL that your article has a vegetarian slant. The best way to pick up that slant is to read several issues of the magazine (no doubt a tip you've heard over and over). We are very particular about the articles we run and thus tend to ask for rewrites. The best way to break in is by querying us on a well-defined topic that is appropriate for our news digest section. Make sure your idea is well thought out before querying."

VIBRANT LIFE, A Magazine for Healthful Living, Review and Herald Publishing Assn., 55 W. Oak Ridge Dr., Hagerstown MD 21740. (301)791-7000. 20% freelance written. Enjoys working with published/established writers; works with a small number of new/unpublished writers each year. Bimonthly magazine covering health articles (especially from a prevention angle and with a Christian slant). Estab. 1849. Circ. 50,000. **Pays on acceptance.** "The average length of time between acceptance of a freelance-written manuscript and publication of the material depends upon the topics; some immediately used; others up to 2 years." Byline always given. Offers 25% kill fee. Buys first serial rights, first North American serial rights, or sometimes second serial (reprint) rights. Submit seasonal/ holiday material 6 months in advance. Reports in 2 months. Sample copy $1; free writer's guidelines for #10 SASE.
Nonfiction: Interview/profile (with personalities on health). "We seek practical articles promoting better health and a more fulfilled life. We especially like features on breakthroughs in medicine, and most aspects of health." Buys 20-25 mss/year. Send complete ms. Length: 750-1,800 words. Pays $125-250. Pays the expenses of writers on assignment.

Photos: Send photos with ms. Needs 35mm transparencies. Not interested in b&w photos.

Tips: *"Vibrant Life* is published for baby boomers, particularly women and young professionals, age 30-45. Therefore articles must be written in an interesting, easy-to-read style. Information must be reliable; no faddism. We are more conservative than other magazines in our field. Request a sample copy, and study the magazine and writer's guidelines."

‡**VIM & VIGOR, America's Family Health Magazine,** Suite 11, 8805 N. 23rd Ave., Phoenix AZ 85021. (602)395-5850. Editor: Fred Petrovsky. 75% freelance written. Quarterly magazine covering health and healthcare. Estab. 1985. Circ. 524,000. **Pays on acceptance.** Publishes ms an average of 3 months after acceptance. Byline given. Offers no kill fee. Buys all rights. Query for electronic submissions. Reports in 2 weeks on queries. Sample copy for 9 × 12 SAE with 8 first class stamps. Writer's guidelines for #10 SASE.

Nonfiction: Health, diseases and healthcare. "Don't send complete manuscripts. All articles are assigned to freelance writers. Send samples of your style." Buys 25 mss/year. Query with published clips. Length: 2,000-4,000 words. Pays $450. Pays expenses of writers on assignment.

Photos: State availability of photos with submission. Reviews contact sheets and any size transparencies. Offers no additional payment fo photos accepted with ms. Captions, model releases and identification of subjects required. Buys one-time rights.

Tips: "We rarely accept suggested story ideas. Writers have the best chance selling us natural articles. Write technical articles so the lay consumer can understand them."

‡**THE WALKING MAGAZINE,** Raben Publishing Co. 9-11 Harcourt St., Boston MA 02116. (617)266-3322. Editor: Bradford W. Ketchum, Jr. 50% freelance written. Bimonthly publication. Pays on final acceptance. Publishes ms an average of 3-4 months after acceptance. Buys first North American serial rights. Reports in 1 month.

Nonfiction: "We want to see articles on travel, health, fitness, nutrition, general infomation on walking and newsy fitness items." Query. Length: 300-1,200 words for departments; 1,500-2,500 for features. Pays $100-600 for departments; $500-1,000 for features.

WEIGHT WATCHERS MAGAZINE, 360 Lexington Ave., 11th Floor, New York NY 10017. FAX: (212)687-4398. Editor-in-Chief: Lee Haiken. Health & Fitness Editor: Susan Rees. 50% freelance written. Works with a small number of new/unpublished writers each year. Monthly publication for those interested in weight loss and weight maintenance through sensible eating and health/nutrition guidance. Estab. 1968. Circ. 1 million. Buys first North American serial rights only. **Pays on acceptance.** Publishes ms an average of 6 months after acceptance. Sample copy and writer's guidelines for 8½ × 11 SAE and $1.95.

Nonfiction: "We are interested in general health and medical articles; nutrition pieces based on documented research results; fitness stories that feature types of exercises that don't require special skills or excessive financial costs; and weight loss stories that focus on interesting people and situations. While our articles are authoritative, they are written in a light, upbeat style; a humorous tone is acceptable as long as it is in good taste. To expedite the fact-checking process, we require a second copy of your manuscript that is annotated in the margins with the telephone numbers of all interview subjects, and with citations from such written sources as books, journal articles, magazines, newsletters, newspapers, or press releases. You must attach photocopies of these sources to the annotated manuscript with relevant passages highlighted and referenced to your margin notes. We will be happy to reimburse you for copying costs." Send detailed queries with published clips and SASE. No full-length mss; send feature ideas, as well as before-and-after weight loss story ideas dealing either with celebrities or "real people" Length: 750-1,000 words. Pays $250-500.

Tips: "Though we prefer working with established writers, *Weight Watchers Magazine* welcomes new writers as well. As long as your query is tightly written, shows style and attention to detail, and gives evidence that you are knowledgeable about your subject matter, we won't reject you out-of-hand just because you don't have three clips attached. When developing a story for us, keep in mind that we prefer interview subjects to be medical professionals with university appointments who have published in their field of expertise."

THE YOGA JOURNAL, California Yoga Teachers Association, 2054 University Ave., Berkeley CA 94704. (415)841-9200. Editor: Stephan Bodian. 75% freelance written. Bimonthly magazine covering yoga, holistic health, conscious living, spiritual practices, and nutrition. "We reach a middle-class, educated audience interested in self-improvement and higher consciousness." Estab. 1975. Circ. 60,000. Pays on publication. Publishes ms an average of 6 months after acceptance. Byline given. Offers $50 kill fee. Buys first North American serial rights only. Submit seasonal/holiday material 4 months in advance. Simultaneous queries OK. Reports in 6 weeks on queries; 2 months on mss. Sample copy $3; free writer's guidelines.

Nonfiction: Book excerpts; how-to (exercise, yoga, massage, etc.); inspirational (yoga or related); interview/profile; opinion; photo feature; and travel (if about yoga). "Yoga is our main concern, but our principal features in each issue highlight other New Age personalities and endeavors. Nothing too far-out and mystical. Prefer stories about Americans incorporating yoga, meditation, etc., into their normal lives." Buys 40 mss/year. Query. Length: 750-3,500 words. Pays $150-400.

Photos: Lawrence Watson, art director. Send photos with ms. Pays $200-300 for cover transparencies; $15-25 for 8×10 b&w prints. Model release (for cover only) and identification of subjects required. Buys one-time rights.

Columns/Departments: Forum; Cooking; Bodywork; Meditation; Well-Being; Psychology; Profiles; Music (reviews of New Age music); and Book Reviews. Buys 12-15 mss/year. Pays $50-150 for columns; $35-60 for book reviews.

Tips: "We always read submissions. We are very open to freelance material and want to encourage writers to submit to our magazine. We're looking for out-of-state contributors, particularly in the Midwest and East Coast."

YOUR HEALTH, Globe Communications Corp., 5401 NW Broken Sound Blvd., Boca Raton FL 33487. (407)997-7733. Editor: Susan Gregg. Associate Editor: Lisa Rappa. 50% freelance written. Semi-monthly magazine on health and fitness. "*Your Health* is a lay-person magazine covering the entire gamut of health, fitness and medicine." Estab. 1962. Circ. 50,000. Pays on publication. Byline given. Offers $10 kill fee. Buys first North American serial rights and second serial (reprint) rights. Submit seasonal/holiday material 3 months in advance. Previously published submissions OK. Reports in 1 month on queries; 6 weeks on mss. Free sample copy and writer's guidelines.

Nonfiction: Book excerpts, exposé, general interest, how-to (on general health and fitness topics), inspirational, interview/profile, new product and personal experience. "No general articles, such as 'Why vitamins are good for you.' Give us something new and different." Buys 75-100 mss/year. Query with published clips or send complete ms. Length: 300-1,000 words. Pays $15-75. Sometimes pays expenses of writers on assignment.

Photos: Send photos with submission. Reviews contact sheets, negatives, transparencies and prints. Offers $50-100 per photo. Captions, model releases and identification of subjects required. Buys one-time rights.

Tips: "We are especially interested in profiles and features on common people and celebrities who have conquered illness or who participate in a unique physical fitness regimen. Freelancers can best break in by offering us stories of national interest that we won't find through other channels, such as wire services."

YOUR HEALTH & FITNESS, General Learning Corp., 60 Revere Dr., Northbrook IL 60062-1563. (312)205-3000. Executive Editor: Laura Ruekberg. Managing Editor: Carol Lezak. 90-95% freelance written. Prefers to work with published/established writers. A bimonthly magazine covering health and fitness. Needs "general, educational material on health, fitness and safety that can be read and understood easily by the layman." Estab. 1969. Circ. 1 million. Pays within 30 days after acceptance. Publishes ms an average of 6 months after acceptance. No byline given. Offers 50% kill fee. *Buys all rights.* Submit seasonal/holiday material 6 months in advance.

Nonfiction: General interest. "All article topics assigned. No queries; if you're interested in writing for the magazine, send a cover letter, resume, curriculum vitae and writing samples. All topics are determined a year in advance of publication by editors; no unsolicited manuscripts." Buys approximately 65 mss/year. Length: 350-1,400 words. Pays $100-700 for assigned articles. Sometimes pays the expenses of writers on assignment.

Photos: Offers no additional payment for photos accepted with ms.

Tips: "Write to a general audience that has only a surface knowledge of health and fitness topics. Possible subjects include exercise and fitness, psychology, nutrition, safety, disease, drug data, and health concerns."

History

Listed here are magazines and other periodicals written for historical collectors, genealogy enthusiasts, historic preservationists and researchers. Editors of history magazines look for fresh accounts of past events in a readable style. Some publications cover an era, such as the Civil War, or a region while others specialize in historic preservation.

AMERICAN HERITAGE, 60 5th Ave., New York NY 10011. Editor: Richard Snow. 70% freelance written. Published 8 times/year. Estab. 1954. Circ. 290,000. Usually buys first North American rights or all rights. Byline given. **Pays on acceptance.** Publishes ms an average of 6-12 months after acceptance. Before submitting material, "check our index to see whether we have already treated the

subject." Submit seasonal material 1 year in advance. Reports in 1 month. Guidelines for #10 SASE.
Nonfiction: Wants "historical articles by scholars or journalists intended for intelligent lay readers rather than for professional historians." Emphasis is on authenticity, accuracy and verve. "Interesting documents, photographs and drawings are always welcome. Query." Style should stress "readability and accuracy." Buys 30 unsolicited mss/year. Length: 1,500-5,000 words. Sometimes pays the expenses of writers on assignment.
Tips: "We have over the years published quite a few 'firsts' from young writers whose historical knowledge, research methods and writing skills met our standards. The scope and ambition of a new writer tell us a lot about his or her future usefulness to us. A major article gives us a better idea of the writer's value. Everything depends on the quality of the material. We don't really care whether the author is 20 and unknown, or 80 and famous, or vice versa."

AMERICANA MAGAZINE, Americana Magazine, Inc., 29 W. 38th St., New York NY 10018. (212)398-1550. Editor: Sandra Wilmot. Senior Editor: Helen Dunn. 80% freelance written. Bimonthly magazine taking a contemporary approach to American history. Estab. 1973. Circ. 200,000. Pays on publication. Byline given. Offers $150 kill fee. Buys first North American serial rights. Submit seasonal/holiday material 3 months in advance. Reports in 3 months on queries. Sample copy for 8 × 10 SAE and 5 first class stamps. Free writer's guidelines.
Nonfiction: Book excerpts, how-to restoration and preservation, interview/profile, photo feature, travel. No straight historical articles without a contemporary angle. Buys 20-30 mss/year. Query with published clips, or send complete ms. Length: 500-2,500 words. Pays $75-600. Pays expenses of writers on assignment. Send photos with submission. Reviews negatives and transparencies. Offers $25-300 per photo. Buys one-time rights.
Columns/Departments: Sampler (newsy articles), 500 words. Query with published clips. Pays $75.
Tips: "Query one idea at a time and be patient. Stress the contemporary, not historical angle. Include photographs with query."

‡AMERICA'S CIVIL WAR, Empire Press, A Cowles Media Co. Affiliate, Suite 300, 602 S. King St., Leesburg VA 22075. (703)771-9400. Editor: Roy Morris, Jr. 95% freelance written. Bimonthly magazine of "popular history and straight historical narrative for both the general reader and the Civil War buff." Estab. 1988. Circ. 75,000. Pays on publication. Publishes ms up to 2 years after acceptance. Byline given. Buys first North American serial rights. Query for electronic submissions. Reports in 3 months on queries; 6 months on mss. Sample copy $3.95; writer's guidelines for #10 SAE with 1 first class stamp.
Nonfiction: Book excerpts, historical, travel. No fiction or poetry. Buys 48 mss/year. Query. Length: 4,000 words maximum. Pays $300 maximum.
Photos: State availability of photos with submission. Payment for photos negotiable. Captions and identification of subjects required. Buys one-time rights.
Columns/Departments: Personality (probes); Ordnance (about weapons used); Commands (about units); Travel (about appropriate historical sites). Buys 24 mss/year. Query. Length: 2,000 words. Pays up to $150.

ANCESTRY NEWSLETTER, Ancestry, Inc., P.O. Box 476, Salt Lake City UT 84110. (801)531-1790. Editor: Robb Barr. 95% freelance written. Eager to work with new/unpublished writers. A bimonthly newsletter covering genealogy and family history. "We publish practical, instructional, and informative pieces specifically applicable to the field of genealogy. Our audience is the active genealogist, both hobbyist and professional." Estab. 1984. Circ. 8,200. Pays on publication. Publishes ms an average of 9 months after acceptance. Byline given. Buys first North American serial rights or all rights. Submit seasonal/holiday material 4 months in advance. Simultaneous submissions OK. Reports in 2 weeks. Sample copy and writer's guidelines for 3 first class stamps.
Nonfiction: General interest (genealogical); historical; how-to (genealogical research techniques); instructional; and photo feature (genealogically related). No unpublished or published family histories, genealogies, the "story of my great-grandmother," or personal experiences. Buys 25-30 mss/year. Send complete ms. Length: 1,500-4,000 words. Pays $50.
Photos: Send photos with submission. Reviews contact sheets and 5 × 7 prints. Offers no additional payment for photos accepted with ms. Identification of subjects required. Buys one-time rights.
Tips: "You don't have to be famous, but you must know something about genealogy. Our readers crave any information which might assist them in their ancestral quest."

Market conditions are constantly changing! If this is 1993 or later, buy the newest edition of Writer's Market at your favorite bookstore or order directly from Writer's Digest Books.

THE ARTILLERYMAN, Cutter & Locke, Inc., Publishers, 4 Water St., P.O. Box C, Arlington MA 02174. (617)646-2010. FAX: (617)643-1864. Editor: C. Peter Jorgensen. 60% freelance written. Quarterly magazine covering antique artillery, fortifications, and crew-served weapons 1750 to 1900 for competition shooters, collectors and living history reenactors using artillery; "emphasis on Revolutionary War and Civil War but includes everyone interested in pre-1900 artillery and fortifications, preservation, construction of replicas, etc." Estab. 1979. Circ. 2,600. Pays on publication. Publishes ms an average of 3-6 months after acceptance. Byline given. Not copyrighted. Buys one-time rights. Simultaneous queries and simultaneous and previously published submissions OK. Reports in 3 weeks. Sample copy and writer's guidelines for 8½ × 11 SAE and 4 first class stamps.
Nonfiction: Historical; how-to (reproduce ordnance equipment/sights/implements/tools/accessories, etc.); interview/profile; new product; opinion (must be accompanied by detailed background of writer and include references); personal experience; photo feature; technical (must have footnotes); and travel (where to find interesting antique cannon). Interested in "artillery *only*, for sophisticated readers. Not interested in other weapons, battles in general." Buys 24-30 mss/year. Send complete ms. Length: 300 words minimum. Pays $20-60. Sometimes pays the expenses of writers on assignment.
Photos: Send photos with ms. Pays $5 for 5 × 7 and larger b&w prints. Captions and identification of subjects required.
Tips: "We regularly use freelance contributions for Places-to-Visit, Cannon Safety, The Workshop and Unit Profiles departments. Also need pieces on unusual cannon or cannon with a known and unique history. To judge whether writing style and/or expertise will suit our needs, writers should ask themselves if they could knowledgeably talk *artillery* with an expert. Subject matter is of more concern than writer's background."

CANADIAN WEST, P.O. Box 3399, Langley, British Columbia V3A 4R7 Canada. (604)534-9378. Editor-in-Chief: Garnet Basque. 80-100% freelance written. Works with a small number of new/unpublished writers each year. Emphasizes pioneer history, primarily of British Columbia, Alberta and the Yukon. Quarterly magazine. Estab. 1985. Circ. 8,000. Pays on publication. Publishes ms an average of 6 months after acceptance. Buys first North American serial rights. Phone queries OK. Query for electronic submissions. Previously published submissions OK. Reports in 2 months. Sample copy and writer's guidelines for $1.50 and 9 × 12 SAE.
Nonfiction: How-to (related to gold panning and dredging); historical (pioneers, shipwrecks, massacres, battles, exploration, logging, Indians, ghost towns, mining camps, gold rushes and railroads). Interested in an occasional U.S. based article from states bordering B.C. when the story also involves some aspect of Canadian history. No American locale articles. Buys 28 mss/year. Submit complete ms. Length: 2,000-3,500 words. Pays $100-300.
Photos: All mss must include photos or other artwork. Submit photos with ms. Pays $10 per b&w photo and $20 per color photo. Captions preferred. "Photographs are kept for future reference with the right to re-use. However, we do not forbid other uses, generally, as these are historical prints from archives."
Columns/Departments: Open to suggestions for new columns/departments.

‡CHICAGO HISTORY, The Magazine of the Chicago Historical Society, Chicago Historical Society, Clark St. at North Ave., Chicago IL 60614. (312)642-4600. FAX: (312)266-2077. Editor: Russell Lewis. Associate Editor: Claudia Lamm Wood. Assistant Editors: Rosemary Adams, Patricia Bereck Weikersheimer. 100% freelance written. Works with a small number of new/unpublished writers each year. Quarterly magazine covering Chicago history: cultural, political, economic, social, architectural. Estab. 1945. Circ. 9,500. Pays on publication. Publishes ms an average of 6-12 months after acceptance. Byline given. Buys all rights. Submit seasonal/holiday material 9 months in advance. Query for electronic submissions. Reports in 6 weeks. Sample copy $3.25; free writer's guidelines.
Nonfiction: Book excerpts, essays, historical/nostalgic, interview/profile and photo feature. Articles to be "analytical, informative, and directed at a popular audience with a special interest in history." No "cute" articles. Buys 16-20 mss/year. Query; send complete ms. Length: approximately 4,500 words. Pays $250.
Photos: State availability of photos with submission and submit photocopies. Would prefer no originals. Offers no additional payment for photos accepted with ms. Identification of subjects required.
Tips: "A freelancer can best break in by 1) calling to discuss an article idea with editor; and 2) submitting a detailed outline of proposed article. All sections of *Chicago History* are open to freelancers, but we suggest that authors do not undertake to write articles for the magazine unless they have considerable knowledge of the subject and are willing to research it in some detail. We require a footnoted manuscript, although we do not publish the notes."

CIVIL WAR TIMES ILLUSTRATED, 2245 Kohn Rd., P.O. Box 8200, Harrisburg PA 17105. (717)657-9555. FAX: (717)657-9526. Editor: John E. Stanchak. 90% freelance written. Works with a small number of new/unpublished writers each year. Magazine published bimonthly. Estab. 1961. Circ.

164,000. **Pays on acceptance.** Publishes ms an average of 12-18 months after acceptance. Buys all rights, first rights or one-time rights, or makes work-for-hire assignments. Submit seasonal/holiday material 1 year in advance. Query for electronic submissions. Reports in 2 weeks on queries; 3 months on mss. Sample copy $3; free writer's guidelines.

Nonfiction: Profile, photo feature, and Civil War historical material. "Positively no fiction or poetry." Buys 20 freelance mss/year. Length: 2,500-5,000 words. Query. Pays $75-450. Sometimes pays the expenses of writers on assignment.

Photos: W. Douglas Shirk, art director. State availability of photos. Pays $5-50 for 8×10 b&w glossy prints and copies of Civil War photos; $400-500 for 4-color cover photos; and $100-250 for color photos for interior use.

Tips: "We're very open to new submissions. Query us after reading several back issues, then submit illustration and art possibilities along with the query letter for the best 'in.' Never base the narrative solely on family stories or accounts. Submissions must be written in a popular style but based on solid academic research. Manuscripts are required to have marginal source annotations."

GHOST TOWN QUARTERLY, McLean Enterprises, P.O. Box 714, Philipsburg MT 59858. (406)859-3365. Editor: Donna B. McLean. 90% freelance written. Quarterly magazine on ghost towns and abandoned sites—U.S., Canada and Mexico. "Materials should be factual yet interesting to the general public. We want to present history in such a manner that we are a human-interest magazine yet valuable to historians." Estab. 1988. Circ. 6,000. Byline given. Buys first North American serial rights, first rights and one-time rights. Submit seasonal/holiday material 1 year in advance. Reports in 3 weeks on queries; 3-6 months on mss. Sample copy for $3.50. Writer's guidelines for SAE with 1 first class stamp.

Nonfiction: General interest, historical/nostalgic, interview/profile, interesting, unusual up-coming events of a historical nature. Buys 80 mss/year. Send complete ms. Length: 300-3,500 words. Pays 5¢/word. Pays in contributor copies only if requested by the writer.

Photos: Send photos with submission. Reviews 5×7 prints, smaller or larger also OK. Also review picture postcards (old). Offers $5-50 per photo (cover photo). Captions required. Buys one-time rights.

Columns/Departments: Student's Corner (materials submitted by students from kindergarten through 12th grade. 2 pages reserved in each issue for this feature. Follow same guidelines as for adult contributors. Photos, artwork, poetry, and articles acceptable, 1,500 words maximum. Buys 30 mss/year. Send complete ms. Pays 5¢/word.

Poetry: Avant-garde, free verse, haiku, light verse and traditional. Must be relevant to our themes. No foul language or lewdness. No extreme negativism unless it has an important purpose relevant to our themes. Buys 20 poems/year. Submit maximum 3 poems. Pays 5¢/word.

Fillers: Cartoons. Buys 16/year. Pays $10.

Tips: "If submitting an article, research facts and include bibliographical information. Interview people who may have first-hand knowledge, and include interesting facts you uncover, quotes from diaries, photocopies of old documents and historical photographs when available. We like to feature the unusual, things people may not have realized before—such as silver being found in petrified wood."

GOOD OLD DAYS, America's Premier Nostalgia Magazine, House of White Birches, 306 E. Parr Rd., Berne IN 46711. (219)589-8741. Editor: Rebekah Montgomery. Managing Editor: Bettina Miller. 75% freelance written. A monthly magazine of first person nostalgia, 1900-1955. "We look for strong narratives showing life as it was in the first part of this century. Our readership is comprised of nostalgia buffs, history enthusiasts, and the people who actually lived and grew up in this era." Pays on publication. Publishes ms an average of 8 months after acceptance. Byline given. Buys all rights, first North American serial rights or one-time rights. Submit seasonal/holiday material 8 months in advance. Reports in 3 weeks. Sample copy $2; writer's guidelines for #10 SASE.

Nonfiction: Historical/nostalgic, humor, interview/profile, personal experience, photo feature. Instructional (how to cane a chair, how to hand-bundle a shock of corn, etc.). Buys 300 mss/year. Query or send complete ms. Length: 4,000 words maximum. Pays 2-4¢/word or more, depending on quality and photos.

Photos: Send photos with submission. Offers $5/photo. Identification of subjects required. Buys one-time or all rights.

MEDIA HISTORY DIGEST, Media History Digest Corp., % Editor and Publisher, 11 W. 19th St., New York NY 10011. Editor: Hiley H. Ward. 100% freelance written. Semiannual (will probably return to being quarterly) magazine. Estab. 1980. Circ. 2,000. Pays on publication. Publishes ms an average of 4 months after acceptance. Byline given. Buys first or second serial (reprint) rights. Submit seasonal/holiday material 8 months in advance. Previously published submissions OK. Reports in 2 months. Sample copy $3.75.

Nonfiction: Historical/nostalgic (media); humor (media history); and puzzles (media history). Buys 15 mss/year. Query. Length: 1,500-3,000 words. Pays $125 for assigned articles; pays $100 for unsolicited articles. Pays in contributor copies for articles prepared by university graduate students. Sometimes pays the expenses of writers on assignment.

Photos: Send photos with submission. Buys first or reprint rights.

Columns/Departments: Quiz Page (media history) and "Media Hysteria" (media history humor). Query. Pays $50-125 for humor; $25 for puzzles.

Fillers: Anecdotes and short humor on topics of media history.

Tips: "Present in-depth enterprising material targeted for our specialty—media history, pre-1970."

MHQ, The Quarterly Journal of Military History, MHQ, Inc., 29 West 38th St., New York NY 10018. (212)398-1550. FAX: (212)840-6790. Editor: Robert Cowley. Managing Editor: Barbara Benton. 95% freelance written. Quarterly hardcover magazine on military history. "Our readers are people with a special interest in military history that is scholarly (well researched), yet written in a lively and imaginative style." Estab. 1988. Circ. 30,000. **Pays on acceptance.** Publishes ms an average of 6 months after acceptance. Byline given. Kill fee varies. Buys first rights and second serial (reprint) rights. Reports in 1 month on queries; 3 months on mss. Sample copy $20. Writer's guidelines not available.

Nonfiction: Book excerpts, essays, exposé, interview/profile and personal experience. "No articles weighted down with professional jargon." Buys 40 mss/year. Query with or without published clips, or send complete ms. Length: 2,000-4,000 words. Pays $300-1,200 for assigned articles; $200-800 for unsolicited articles. Sometimes pays expenses of writers on assignment.

Photos: State availability of photos with submission. Reviews contact sheets, negatives, transparencies and prints. Offers no additional payment for photos accepted with ms. Buys one-time rights.

Columns/Departments: Tactical Exercises (military tactics), 1,500 words; Experience of War (personal memoirs), 800-1,000 words; Arms and Men (weaponry), 1,500 words; and In Review (reviews recent publications in military history), 1,500 words. Buys 16 mss/year. Query with published clips. Pays $250-600.

Tips: "Most of our contributors are experts in the field of military history. We will consider any article on any aspect of military history that is well researched, well written, and approaches its subject from a fresh angle. Acceptance may also depend on our needs of a particular moment."

MILITARY HISTORY, Empire Press, 602 S. King St. #300, Leesburg VA 22075. (703)771-9400. Editor: C. Brian Kelly. 95% freelance written. Circ. 200,000. "We'll work with anyone, established or not, who can provide the goods and convince us as to its accuracy." Bimonthly magazine covering all military history of the world. "We strive to give the general reader accurate, highly readable, often narrative popular history, richly accompanied by period art." Pays on publication. Publishes ms 1-2 years after acceptance. Byline given. Buys all rights. Submit anniversary material 1 year in advance. Reports in 3 months on queries; 6 months on mss. Sample copy $3.95; writer's guidelines for SASE.

Nonfiction: Historical; interview (military figures of commanding interest); personal experience (only occasionally). Buys 18 mss, plus 6 interviews/year. Query with published clips. "To propose an article, submit a short, self-explanatory query summarizing the story proposed, its highlights and/or significance. State also your own expertise, access to sources or proposed means of developing the pertinent information." Length: 4,000 words. Pays $400.

Columns/Departments: Espionage, weaponry, personality, travel (with military history of the place) and books—all relating to military history. Buys 24 mss/year. Query with published clips. Length: 2,000 words. Pays $200.

Tips: "We would like journalistically 'pure' submissions that adhere to basics, such as full name at first reference, same with rank, and definition of prior or related events, issues cited as context or obscure military 'hardware.' Read the magazine, discover our style, and avoid subjects already covered. Pick stories with strong art possibilities (*real* art and photos), send photocopies, tell us where to order the art. Avoid historical overview, focus upon an event with appropriate and accurate context. Provide bibliography. Tell the story in popular but elegant style."

MILITARY IMAGES, RD 1, Box 99A, Lesoine Dr., Henryville PA 18332. Editor: Harry Roach. 100% freelance written. A bimonthly journal reaching a broad spectrum of military historians, antiquarians, collectors and dealers. *MI* covers American military history from 1839 to 1900, with heavy concentration on the Civil War. Circ. 3,000. Pays on publication. Byline given. Buys first North American serial rights. Submit seasonal/holiday material 2 months in advance. Query for electronic submissions. Reports in 2 weeks on queries; 1 month on mss. Sample copy for $3; free writer's guidelines.

Nonfiction: Book excerpts, historical, humor, interview/profile, photo feature and technical. No articles not tied to, or illustrated by, period photos. Buys 36 mss/year. Query. Length: 1,000-12,000 words. Pays $40-200.

Photos: State availability of photos with submission, or send photocopy with query. Reviews 5×7 or larger b&w prints. Offers no additional payment for photos accepted with ms. Captions required.

Columns/Departments: The Darkroom (technical, 19th-century photo processes, preservation), 1,000 words. Buys 6 mss/year. Query. Length: 1,000-3,000 words. Pays $20-75.

Tips: "Concentrate on details of the common soldier, his uniform, his equipment, his organizations. We do not publish broad-brush histories of generals and campaigns. Articles must be supported by period photos."

OLD MILL NEWS, Society for the Preservation of Old Mills, 604 Ensley Dr., Rt. 29, Knoxville TN 37920. (615)577-7757. Editor: Michael LaForest. 40% freelance written. Quarterly magazine covering "water, wind, animal, steam power mills (usually grist mills)." Estab. 1972. Circ. 2,500. **Pays on acceptance.** Byline given. Buys first North American serial rights or first rights. Simultaneous submissions OK. Reports in 2 weeks. Sample copy $3.

Nonfiction: Historical and technical. "No poetry, recipes, mills converted to houses, commercial or alternative uses, nostalgia." Buys 8 mss/year. Query with or without published clips, or send complete ms. Length: 400-1,000 words. Pays $15-50.

Photos: Send photos with submission. "At least one recent photograph of subject is highly recommended." Uses b&w or color prints only; no transparencies. Offers $5-10 per photo. Identification of subjects required. Buys one-time rights.

Fillers: Short humor. Buys 3-4/year. Length: 50-200 words. Pays $10 maximum.

Tips: "An interview with the mill owner/operator is usually necessary. Accurate presentation of the facts and good English are required."

PERSIMMON HILL, 1700 NE 63rd St., Oklahoma City OK 73111. FAX: (405)478-4714. Editor: M.J. Van Deventer. 70% freelance written. Prefers to work with published/established writers and works with a small number of new/unpublished writers each year. For an audience interested in Western art, Western history, ranching and rodeo, including historians, artists, ranchers, art galleries, schools, and libraries. Publication of the National Cowboy Hall of Fame and Western Heritage Center. Quarterly. Estab. 1965. Circ. 15,000. Buys first rights. Byline given. Buys 15-20 mss/year. Pays on publication. Publishes ms an average of 6 months after acceptance. Reporting time on mss varies. Sample copy $5 plus 5 first class stamps; writer's guidelines for #10 SASE.

Nonfiction: Historical and contemporary articles on famous Western figures connected with pioneering the American West, Western art, rodeo, cowboys, etc. (or biographies of such people), stories of Western flora and animal life, and environmental subjects. "We want thoroughly researched and historically authentic material written in a popular style. May have a humorous approach to subject. No broad, sweeping, superficial pieces; i.e., the California Gold Rush or rehashed pieces on Billy the Kid, etc." Length: 2,000-3,000 words. Query with clips. Pays $100-250; special work negotiated.

Photos: B&w glossy prints or color transparencies purchased with ms, or on assignment. Pays according to quality and importance for b&w and color photos. Suggested captions required.

Tips: "Excellent illustrations for articles are essential!"

PRESERVATION NEWS, National Trust for Historic Preservation, 1785 Massachusetts Ave. NW, Washington DC 20036. (202)673-4075. Editor: Arnold M. Berke. 30% freelance written. Prefers to work with published/established writers. A monthly tabloid covering preservation of historic buildings in the U.S. "We cover proposed or completed preservation projects and controversies involving historic buildings and districts. Most entries are news stories, features or opinion pieces." Circ. 200,000. Pays on publication. Publishes ms an average of 1 month after acceptance. Byline given. Offers variable kill fee. Buys one-time rights. Simultaneous queries and previously published submissions OK. Reports in 2 months on queries. Sample copy for $1 and 10×14 SAE with 56¢ postage; writer's guidelines for SAE and 1 first class stamp.

Nonfiction: News, interview/profile, opinion, humor, personal experience, photo feature and travel. Buys 12 mss/year. Query with published clips. Length: 500-1,200 words. Pays $150-400. Sometimes pays the expenses of writers on assignment.

Photos: State availability of photos with query or ms. Reviews b&w contact sheet. Pays $25-100. Identification of subjects required.

Columns/Departments: "We seek an urban affairs reporter who can give a new slant on development conflict throughout the United States. We also are looking for foreign coverage, and profiles of preservation craftspersons." Buys 6 mss/year. Query with published clips. Length: 600-1,200 words. Pays $150-250.

Tips: "Do not send or propose histories of buildings, descriptive accounts of cities or towns or long-winded treatises on any subjects. This is a *newspaper*. Proposals for coverage of fast-breaking events are especially welcome."

TIMELINE, Ohio Historical Society, 1982 Velma Ave., Columbus OH 43211. (614)297-2360. Editor: Christopher S. Duckworth. 90% freelance written. Works with a small number of new/unpublished writers each year. A bimonthly magazine covering history, natural history, archaeology, and fine and decorative arts. Estab. 1984. Circ. 11,000. **Pays on acceptance.** Publishes ms an average of 1 year after acceptance. Byline given. Offers $75 minimum kill fee. Buys first North American serial rights or all rights. Submit seasonal/holiday material 6 months in advance. Query for electronic submissions. Reports in 3 weeks on queries; 6 weeks on manuscripts. Sample copy $5 and 8½×11 SAE. Writer's guidelines for #10 SASE.
Nonfiction: Book excerpts, essays, historical, profile (of individuals) and photo feature. Buys 22 mss/year. Query. Length: 500-6,000 words. Pays $100-900.
Photos: State availability of photos with submission. Will not consider submissions without ideas for illustration. Reviews contact sheets, transparencies, and 8×10 prints. Captions, model releases, and identification of subjects required. Buys one-time rights.
Tips: "We want crisply written, authoritative narratives for the intelligent lay reader. An Ohio slant may strengthen a submission, but it is not indispensable. Contributors must know enough about their subject to explain it clearly and in an interesting fashion. We use high-quality illustration with all features. If appropriate illustration is unavailable, we can't use the feature. The writer who sends illustration ideas with a manuscript has an advantage, but an often-published illustration won't attract us."

TRACES OF INDIANA AND MIDWESTERN HISTORY, Indiana Historical Society, 315 W Ohio St., Indianapolis IN 46202. (317)232-1884. FAX: (317)233-3109. Executive Editor: Thomas Mason. Managing Editor: Kent Calder. 100% freelance written. Quarterly magazine on Indiana and Midwestern history. Estab. 1989. Circ. 9,000. **Pays on acceptance.** Publishes ms an average of 6 months after acceptance. Byline given. Buys one-time rights. Submit seasonal/holiday material 1 year in advance. Previously published submissions OK. Reports in 3 months on mss. Sample copy $5; free writer's guidelines.
Nonfiction: Book excerpts, essays, historical/nostalgic and photo feature. Buys 20 mss/year. Send complete ms. Length: 2,000-5,000 words. Pays $100-500.
Photos: State availability of photos with submission. Reviews contact sheets, transparencies and prints. Offers $10-30 per photo. Captions, model releases and identification of subjects required. Buys one-time rights.
Columns/Departments: Focus; Destination Indiana; Hoosier Home (Editors seek short articles on significant people, places, and artifacts in Indiana and Midwestern history.), 750-1,500 words. Query. Pays $50-100.
Tips: "Freelancers should be aware of prerequisites for writing history in general and popular history in particular. Should have some awareness of other magazines of this type published by midwestern and western historical societies. Preference is given to subjects with an Indiana connection. Quality of potential illustration is also important."

TRUE WEST, Western Periodicals, Inc., P.O. Box 2107, Stillwater OK 74076. (405)743-3370. Editor: John Joerschke. 100% freelance written. Works with a small number of new/unpublished writers each year. Magazine on Western American history before 1940. "We want reliable research on significant historical topics written in lively prose for an informed general audience." Circ. 30,000. **Pays on acceptance.** Publishes ms an average of 4 months after acceptance. Byline given. Buys first North American serial rights. Submit seasonal/holiday material 6 months in advance. Simultaneous queries OK. Reports in 1 month on queries; 6 weeks on mss. Sample copy for 8½×11 SAE and $2; writer's guidelines for #10 SASE.
Nonfiction: Historical/nostalgic, how-to, photo feature and travel. "We do not want rehashes of worn-out stories, historical fiction, or history written in a fictional style." Buys 150 mss/year. Query. Length: 500-4,500 words. Pays 3-6¢/word.
Photos: Send photos with accompanying query or manuscript. Pays $10 for b&w prints. Identification of subjects required. Buys one-time rights.
Columns/Departments: Western Roundup—200-300-word short articles on historically oriented places to go and things to do in the West. Should include one b&w print. Buys 12-16 mss/year. Send complete ms. Pays $35.
Tips: "Do original research on fresh topics. Stay away from controversial subjects unless you are truly knowledgeable in the field. Read our magazines and follow our guidelines. A freelancer is most likely to break in with us by submitting thoroughly researched, lively prose on relatively obscure topics. First person accounts rarely fill our needs."

VIRGINIA CAVALCADE, Virginia State Library and Archives, Richmond VA 23219-3491. (804)786-2312. Primarily for readers with an interest in Virginia history. 90% freelance written. "Both established and new writers are invited to submit articles." Quarterly magazine. Estab. 1951. Circ. 9,000.

Buys all rights. Byline given. **Pays on acceptance.** Publishes ms an average of 6-12 months after acceptance. Rarely considers simultaneous submissions. Submit seasonal material 15-18 months in advance. Reports in 1-1½ months. Sample copy $2; free writer's guidelines.

Nonfiction: "We welcome readable and factually accurate articles that are relevant to some phase of Virginia history. Art, architecture, literature, education, business, technology and transportation are all acceptable subjects, as well as political and military affairs. Articles must be based on thorough, scholarly research. We require foot- or end notes but do not publish them. Any period from the age of exploration to the mid-20th century, and any geographical section or area of the state may be represented. Must deal with subjects that will appeal to a broad readership. Articles must be suitable for illustration, although it is not necessary that the author provide the pictures. If the author does have pertinent illustrations or knows their location, the editor appreciates information concerning them." Buys 12-15 mss/year. Query. Length: 3,500-4,500 words. Pays $100.

Photos: Uses 8×10 b&w glossy prints; transparencies should be at least 4×5.

Tips: "*Cavalcade* employs a narrative, anecdotal style. Too many submissions are written for an academic audience or are simply not sufficiently gripping."

WILD WEST, Empire Press, 602 S. King St. #300, Leesburg VA 22075. (703)771-9400. Editor: William M. Vogt. 95% freelance written. Bimonthly magazine on history of the American West. "*Wild West* covers the popular (narrative) history of the American West—events, trends, personalities, anything of general interest." Estab. 1988. Circ. 75,000. Pays on publication. Byline given. Buys all rights. Submit seasonal/holiday material 1 year in advance. Query for electronic submissions. Sample copy $3.95; writer's guidelines for #10 SASE.

Nonfiction: Historical/nostalgic, humor, travel. No fiction or poetry—nothing current. Buys 24 mss/year. Query. Length: 4,000 words. Pays $300.

Photos: State availability of photos with submission. Captions and identification of subjects required. Buys one-time rights or all rights.

Columns/Departments: Travel; Gun Fighters & Lawmen; Personalities; Warriors & Chiefs; Books Reviews. Buys 16 mss/year. Length: 2,000. Pays $150 for departments, by the word for book reviews.

YESTERDAY'S MAGAZETTE, The Magazine of Memories, Independent Publishing Co., P.O. Box 15126, Sarasota FL 34277. (813)922-7080. Editor: Ned Burke. Managing Editor: Gail Haborak. 95% freelance written. Bimonthly magazine of nostalgia. Estab. 1973. Circ. 2,500. Pays on publication. Publishes ms an average of 6 months after acceptance. Byline given. Buys first rights. Submit seasonal/holiday material 4 months in advance. Reports in 2 weeks on queries; 2 months on mss. Sample copy for $2. Free writer's guidelines.

Nonfiction: General interest, historical/nostalgic, humor, inspirational, interview/profile ('yesterday' celebrities), opinion, personal experience, photo feature and photo. Special "Christmas" issue, deadline Nov. 15, featuring "My Favorite Christmas Memory." Plus special traditional poetry issue in May, deadline April 15. "No current topics and events." Buys 100 mss/year. Send complete ms. Length: 100-1,500 words. Pays $5-25 for unsolicited articles. Pays for most short articles, poems, etc.

Photos: Send photos with submission. Reviews 5×7 prints. Offers no additional payment for photos accepted with ms. Identification of subjects required. Buys one-time rights.

Columns/Departments: The Way We Were (a look at certain period of time—40s, 50s, etc.); When I Was a Kid (childhood memories); In A Word (objects from the past—'ice box', etc.); Yesterday Trivia (quiz on old movie stars, TV shows, etc.). All 300-750 words. Buys 12 mss/year. Send complete ms. Length: 500-750 words. Pays $5-10.

Fiction: Historical, humorous, slice-of-life vignettes. "No modern settings." Buys 4 mss/year. Send complete ms. Length: 750-2,500 words. Pays $5-25.

Poetry: Traditional. Nothing other than traditional. Buys 50 poems/year. Submit maximum 5 poems. Length: 4-32 lines. Pays $5 and contributor copies.

Fillers: Anecdotes, short humor. Buys 5/year. Length: 50-250 words. Pays $5 and contributor copies.

Tips: "We would like to see more 40s, 50s and 60s pieces, especially with photos. It's hard to reject any story with a good photo. All areas are open, especially 'Plain Folks Page' which uses letters, comments and opinions of readers."

Hobby and Craft

Magazines in this category range from home video to cross stitch. Craftspeople and hobbyists who read these magazines want new ideas while collectors need to know what is most valuable and why. Collectors, do-it-yourselfers and craftspeople look to these magazines for inspiration, research and information. Publications covering antiques and miniatures are also listed here, while additional publications for electronics and radio hobbyists are included in the Science classification.

THE AMERICAN COLLECTORS JOURNAL, P.O. Box 407, Kewanee IL 61443. (308)852-2602. Editor: Carol Savidge. 55% freelance written. Eager to work with new/unpublished writers. A bimonthly tabloid covering antiques and collectibles. Estab. 1963. Circ. 51,841. Pays on publication. Publishes ms an average of 8 months after acceptance. Byline given. Not copyrighted. Buys first North American serial rights. Submit seasonal/holiday material 6 months in advance. Reports in 3 weeks. Sample copy for 6×9 SAE with 4 first class stamps.
Nonfiction: Carol Harper, articles editor. General interest, interview/profile, photo feature and technical. Buys 12-20 mss/year. Query or send complete ms. Pays $10-35 for unsolicited articles.
Photos: Send photos with submission. Reviews 5×7 prints. Offers no additional payment for photos accepted with ms. Captions required. Buys one-time rights.
Tips: "We are looking for submissions with photos in all areas of collecting and antiquing, unusual collections, details on a particular kind of collecting or information on antiques."

ANTIQUE REVIEW, P.O. Box 538, Worthington OH 43085. Editor: Charles Muller. (614)885-9757. FAX: (614)885-9762. 60% freelance written. Eager to work with new/unpublished writers. For an antique-oriented readership, "generally well-educated, interested in folk art and other early American items." Monthly tabloid. Estab. 1975. Circ. 9,500. Pays on publication date assigned at time of purchase. Publishes ms an average of 3 months after acceptance. Buys first North American serial rights, and second (reprint) rights to material originally published in dissimilar publications elsewhere. Byline given. Phone queries OK. Reports in 1 month. Free sample copy and writer's guidelines for #10 SASE.
Nonfiction: "The articles we desire concern history and production of furniture, pottery, china, and other quality Americana. In some cases, contemporary folk art items are acceptable. We are also interested in reporting on antique shows and auctions with statements on conditions and prices. We do not want articles on contemporary collectibles." Buys 5-8 mss/issue. Query with clips of published work. Query should show "author's familiarity with antiques, an interest in the historical development of artifacts relating to early America and an awareness of antiques market." Length: 200-2,000 words. Pays $100-200. Sometimes pays the expenses of writers on assignment.
Photos: State availability of photos with query. Payment included in ms price. Uses 3×5 or larger glossy b&w prints. Color acceptable. Captions required. Articles with photographs receive preference.
Tips: "Give us a call and let us know of specific interests. We are more concerned with the background in antiques than in writing abilities. The writing can be edited, but the knowledge imparted is of primary interest. A frequent mistake is being too general, not becoming deeply involved in the topic and its research. We are interested in primary research into America's historic material culture."

THE ANTIQUE TRADER WEEKLY, P.O. Box 1050, Dubuque IA 52001. (319)588-2073. FAX: (319)588-0888. Editor: Kyle D. Husfloen. 50% freelance written. Works with a small number of new/unpublished writers each year. For collectors and dealers in antiques and collectibles. Weekly newspaper. Estab. 1957. Circ. 90,000. Publishes ms an average of 1 year after acceptance. Buys all rights. Payment at beginning of month following publication. Simultaneous submissions OK. Submit seasonal/holiday material 4 months in advance. Sample copy 50¢; free writer's guidelines.
Nonfiction: "We invite authoritative and well-researched articles on all types of antiques and collectors' items and in-depth stories on specific types of antiques and collectibles. No human interest stories. We do not pay for brief information on new shops opening or other material printed as a service to the antiques hobby." Buys about 60 mss/year. Query or submit complete ms. Pays $25-100 for feature articles; $100-200 for feature cover stories.
Photos: Submit a liberal number of good b&w photos to accompany article. Uses 35mm or larger color transparencies for cover. Offers no additional payment for photos accompanying mss.
Tips: "Send concise, polite letter stating the topic to be covered in the story and the writer's qualifications. No 'cute' letters rambling on about some 'imaginative' story idea. Writers who have a concise yet readable style and know their topic are always appreciated. I am most interested in those who have personal collecting experience or can put together a knowledgeable and informative feature after interviewing a serious collector/authority."

BANK NOTE REPORTER, Krause Publications, 700 E. State St., Iola WI 54990. (715)445-2214. FAX: (715)445-4087. Editor: David Harper. 30% freelance written. Works with a small number of new/unpublished writers each year. Monthly tabloid for advanced collectors of U.S. and world paper money. Circ. 5,000. Pays on publication. Publishes ms an average of 3 months after acceptance. Byline given. Buys first North American serial rights and reprint rights. Query for electronic submissions. Reports in 2 weeks. Sample copy for 8½×11 SAE and postage.
Nonfiction: "We review articles covering any phase of paper money collecting including investing, display, storage, history, art, story behind a particular piece of paper money and the business of paper money." News items not solicited. "Our staff covers the hard news." Buys 6 mss/issue. Send complete ms. Length: 500-3,000 words. Pays 3¢/word to first-time contributors; negotiates fee for later articles.

Photos: Pays $5 for 5×7 b&w glossy prints. Captions and model releases required.
Tips: "The writer has a better chance of breaking in at our publication with short articles due to the technical nature of the subject matter and sophistication of our readers. Material about bank notes used in a writer's locale would be interesting, useful, encouraged. We like new names."

BASEBALL CARDS, Krause Publications, 700 E. State St., Iola WI 54990. (715)445-2214. FAX: (715)445-4087. Editor: Kit Kiefer. 50% freelance written. A monthly magazine covering sports memorabilia collecting. "Geared for the novice collector or general public who might become interested in the hobby." Estab. 1981. Circ. 345,000. Pays on publication. Publishes an average of 6 months after acceptance. Byline given. Buys first North American serial rights and second serial (reprint) rights. Submit seasonal/holiday material 6 months in advance. Reports in 2 weeks. Sample copy for 8½×11 SAE with 3 first class stamps. Writer's guidelines for #10 SASE.
Nonfiction: General interest, historical/nostalgic, how-to (enjoy or enhance your collection) and photo feature. No personal reminiscences of collecting baseball cards as a kid or articles that relate to baseball, rather than cards. Buys 36-50 mss/year. Query. Length: 1,000-3,000 words. Pays up to $650.
Photos: Send photos with submission. Reviews contact sheets and transparencies. Payment negotiated. Identification of subjects required.
Tips: "We would like to receive knowledgeable features on specific collectibles: card sets, team items, etc. We want to identify the collecting trends of the 90s and be the first to report on them."

BECKETT BASEBALL CARD MONTHLY, Statabase, Inc., Suite 200, 4887 Alpha Rd., Dallas TX 75244. (214)991-6657. FAX: (214)991-8930. Editor: Dr. James Beckett. Managing Editor: Pepper Hastings. 85% freelance written. Monthly magazine on baseball card and sports memorabilia collecting. "Our readers expect our publication to be entertaining and informative. Our slant is that hobbies are fun and rewarding. Especially wanted are how-to collect articles." Estab. 1984. Circ. 679,000. **Pays on acceptance.** Publishes ms an average of 4 months after acceptance. Byline given. Pays $50 kill fee. Buys first North American serial rights. Submit seasonal/holiday material 6 months in advance. "No simultaneous submissions, please!" Reports in 1 month. Sample copy $2.50; free writer's guidelines.
Nonfiction: Book excerpts, historical/nostalgic, how-to, humor, interview/profile, new product, opinion, personal experience, photo feature, technical. Special issues include: March (spring training/new card sets issued); July (Hall of Fame/All Star Game issue); October (World Series issue); November (autograph special issue). No articles that emphasize speculative prices and investments. Buys 145 mss/year. Send complete ms. Length: 300-2,000 words. Pays $100-400 for assigned articles; $50-200 for unsolicited articles. Sometimes pays expenses of writers on assignment.
Photos: Send photos with submission. Reviews 35mm transparencies, 5×7 or larger prints. Offers $10-300 per photo. Captions, model releases and identification of subjects required. Buys one-time rights.
Columns/Departments: Jay Johnson, editor. Autograph Experiences (memorable experience with baseball star), 50-400 words; Prospects (players on the verge of major league stardom), 300-500 words; Collecting Tips (basic but overlooked helpful hints), 300-500 words; Trivia (major league baseball odd or humorous facts), 20-50 words; Player Vignettes (general baseball articles featuring emerging or proven superstars). Buys 60 mss/year. Send complete ms. Length: 50-400 words. Pays $25-100.
Fiction: Humorous only.
Tips: "A writer for *Becket Baseball Card Monthly* should be an avid sports fan and/or a collector with an enthusiasm for sharing his/her interests with others. Articles must be factual, but not overly statistical-laden. First person (not research) articles presenting the writer's personal experiences told with wit and humor, and emphasizing the stars of the game, are *always* wanted. Acceptable articles must be of interest to our two basic reader segments: teenaged boys and their middle-aged fathers who are reexperiencing a nostalgic renaissance of their own childhoods. Prospective writers should write down to neither group!"

‡BECKETT BASKETBALL MONTHLY, Statabase, Inc., Suite 200, 4887 Alpha Rd., Dallas TX 75244. (214)991-6657. FAX: (214)991-8930. Editor: Dr. James Beckett. Managing Editor: Pepper Hastings. 85% freelance written. Monthly magazine on basketball card and sports memorabilia collecting. "Our readers expect our publication to be entertaining and informative. Our slant is that hobbies are fun and rewarding. Especially wanted are articles dealing directly with the hobby of basketball card collecting." Estab. 1990. Circ. 300,000. **Pays on acceptance.** Publishes ms an average of 4 months after acceptance. Byline given. Pays $50 kill fee. Buys first North American serial rights. Submit seasonal/holiday material 6 months in advance. "No simultaneous submissions, please!" Reports in 1 month. Sample copy $2.95; free writer's guidelines.
Nonfiction: Book excerpts, historical/nostalgic, how-to, humor, interview/profile, new product, opinion, personal experience, photo feature, technical. Special issues include: February (All-Star Game); June (playoffs); September (new card sets issued). No articles that emphasize speculative prices and

investments. Buys 145 mss/year. Send complete ms. Length: 300-2,000 words. Pays $100-400 for assigned articles; $100-200 for unsolicited articles. Sometimes pays expenses of writers on assignment.

Photos: Send photos with submission. Reviews 35mm transparencies, 5×7 or larger prints. Offers $10-300 per photo. Captions, model releases and identification of subjects required. Buys one-time rights.

Columns/Departments: Randy Cummings, assistant editor. Autograph Experiences (memorable experience with NBA star), 50-400 words; Prospects (players on the verge of NBA stardom), 300-500 words; Collecting Tips (basic but overlooked helpful hints), 300-500 words; Trivia (NBA odd or humorous facts), 20-50 words; Player Vignettes (general articles featuring emerging or proven NBA superstars). Length: 50-400 words. Pays $25-100. Buys 60 mss/year. Send complete ms.

Fiction: Humorous only.

Tips: "A writer for *Beckett Basketball Monthly* should be an avid sports fan and/or a collector with an enthusiasm for sharing his/her interests with others. Articles must be factual, but not overly statistical laden. First person (not research) articles presenting the writer's personal experiences told with wit and humor, and emphasizing the stars of the game, are *always* wanted. Acceptable articles must be of interest to our two basic reader segments: late teenaged boys and their fathers who are re-experiencing a nostalgic renaissance of their own childhoods. Prospective writers should write down to neither group!"

‡BECKETT FOCUS ON FUTURE STARS, Statabase, Inc., Suite 200, 4887 Alpha Rd., Dallas TX 75244. (214)991-2630. FAX: (214)991-8930. Editor: Dr. James Beckett. Managing Editor: Pepper Hastings. 85% freelance written. Monthly magazine offering superstar coverage of young, outstanding players in baseball (major league rookies, minor league stars and college), basketball (college) and football (college), with an emphasis on collecting sports cards and memorabilia. "Our readers expect our publication to be entertaining and informative. Our slant is that hobbies are fun and rewarding. Especially wanted are how-to collect articles." Estab. 1991. Circ. 100,000. **Pays on acceptance.** Publishes ms an average of 4 months after acceptance. Byline given. Pays $50 kill fee. Buys first North American serial rights. Submit seasonal/holiday material 8 months in advance. "No simultaneous submissions, please!" Reports in 1 month. Sample copy $2.95; free writer's guidelines.

Nonfiction: Book excerpts, historical/nostalgic, how-to, humor, interview/profile, new product, opinion, personal experience, photo feature, technical. Special issues include: March (spring training/new card sets issued); April (NFL Draft); June (Baseball Draft); July (NBA Draft); September (Major League call-ups). No articles that emphasize speculative prices and investments on cards. Buys 145 mss/year. Send complete ms. Length: 300-2,000 words. Pays $100-400 for assigned articles; $50-200 for unsolicited articles. Sometimes pays expenses of writers on assignment.

Photos: Send photos with submission. Reviews 35mm transparencies, 5×7 or larger prints. Offers $25-300 per photo. Captions, model releases and identification of subjects required. Buys one-time rights.

Columns/Departments: Gary Santaniello, editor. I Remember . . . (stories from major league stars about their days in the minors or college), 300-500 words; Player Vignettes (general baseball articles featuring emerging superstars), 50-400 words. Pays $25-100. Buys 60 mss/year. Send complete ms.

Fiction: Humorous only.

Tips: "A writer for *Beckett Focus on Future Stars* should be an avid sports fan and/or a collector with an enthusiasm for sharing his/her interests with others. Articles must be factual, but not overly statistical laden. First person (not research) articles presenting the writer's personal experiences told with wit and humor, and emphasizing the stars of the game, are *always* wanted. Acceptable articles must be of interest to our two basic reader segments: teenaged boys and their middle-aged fathers who are reexperiencing a nostalgic renaissance of their own childhoods. Prospective writers should write down to neither group!"

‡BECKETT FOOTBALL MONTHLY, Statabase, Inc., Suite 200, 4887 Alpha Rd., Dallas TX 75244. (214)991-6657. FAX: (214)991-8930. Editor: Dr. James Beckett. Managing Editor: Pepper Hastings. 85% freelance written. Monthly magazine on football card and sports memorabilia collecting. "Our readers expect our publication to be entertaining and informative. Our slant is that hobbies are fun and rewarding. Especially wanted are how-to collect articles." Estab. 1989. Circ. 300,000. **Pays on acceptance.** Publishes ms an average of 4 months after acceptance. Byline given. Pays $50 kill fee. Buys first North American serial rights. Submit seasonal/holiday material 6 months in advance. "No simultaneous submissions, please!" Reports in 1 month. Sample copy $2.95; free writer's guidelines.

Nonfiction: Book excerpts, historical/nostalgic, how-to, humor, interview/profile, new product, opinion, personal experience, photo feature, technical. Special issues include: January (Super Bowl); February (Pro Bowl); April (NFL Draft); September (Preview). No articles that emphasize speculative prices and investments. Buys 145 mss/year. Send complete ms. Length: 300-2,000 words. Pays $100-400 for assigned articles; $50-200 for unsolicited articles. Sometimes pays expenses of writers on assignment.

Photos: Send photos with submission. Reviews 35mm transparencies, 5×7 or larger prints. Offers $10-300 per photo. Captions, model releases and identification of subjects required. Buys one-time rights.

Columns/Departments: Randy Cummings, assistant editor. Autograph Experiences (memorable experience with football star), 50-400 words; Prospects (players on the verge of major league stardom), 300-500 words; Collecting Tips (basic but overlooked helpful hints), 300-500 words; Trivia (NFL odd or humorous facts), 20-50 words; Player Vignettes (general football articles featuring emerging or proven superstars), 50-400 words. Pays $25-100. Buys 60 mss/year. Send complete ms.

Fiction: Humorous only.

Tips: "A writer for *Beckett Football Card Monthly* should be an avid sports fan and/or a collector with an enthusiasm for sharing his/her interests with others. Articles must be factual, but not overly statistical-laden. Acceptable articles must be of interest to our two basic reader segments: teenaged boys and their middle-aged fathers who are re-experiencing a nostalgic renaissance of their own childhoods. Prospective writers should write down to neither group!"

‡**BECKETT HOCKEY MONTHLY**, Statabase, Inc., Suite 200, 4887 Alpha Rd., Dallas TX 75244. (214)991-6657. FAX: (214)991-8930. Editor: Dr. James Beckett. Managing Editor: Pepper Hastings. Associate Editor: E.J. Hradek. 85% freelance written. Monthly magazine on hockey, hockey card and memorabilia collecting. "Our readers expect our publication to be entertaining and informative. Our slant is that hobbies are for fun and rewarding. Especially wanted are how-to collect articles." Estab. 1990. Paid circ. 225,000. **Pays on acceptance.** Publishes ms an average of 3 months after acceptance. Byline given. Pays $50 kill fee. Buys first North American serial rights. Submit seasonal/holiday material 6 months in advance. "No simultaneous submissions, please!" Reports in 1 month. Sample copy $2.95; free writer's guidelines.

Nonfiction: Book excerpts, historical/nostalgic, how-to, humor, interview/profile, new product, opinion, personal experience, photo feature, technical. Special issues include: October (training camp/new card sets issued); January (All-Star Game); April & May (Stanley Cup Playoff); June (Draft). No articles that emphasize speculative prices and investments. Buys 145 mss/year. Send complete ms. Length: 300-2,000 words. Pays $100-400 for assigned articles; $50-200 for unsolicited articles. Sometimes pays expenses of writers on assignment.

Photos: Send photos with submission. Reviews 35mm transparencies, 5×7 or larger prints. Offers $10-300 per photo. Captions, model releases and identification of subjects required. Buys one-time rights.

Columns/Departments: E.J. Hradek, associate editor. Autograph Experiences (memorable experience with hockey star), 50-400 words; Prospects (players on the verge of major junior or college stardom), 300-500 words; Collecting Tips (basic but overlooked helpful hints), 300-500 words; Trivia (NHL odd or humorous facts), 20-50 words; Player Vignettes (general hockey articles featuring emerging or proven superstars), 50-400 words. Pays $25-100. Buys 60 mss/year. Send complete ms.

Fiction: Humorous only.

Tips: "A writer for *Beckett Hockey Monthly* should be an avid sports fan and/or a collector with an enthusiasm for sharing his/her interests with others. Articles must be factual, but not overly statistical laden. Acceptable articles must be of interest to our two basic reader segments: teenaged boys and their middle-aged fathers who are re-experiencing a nostalgic renaissance of their own childhoods. Prospective writers should write down to neither group!"

‡**THE BLADE MAGAZINE, BLADE TRADE**, Box 22007, Chattanooga TN 37422. Editor: J. Bruce Voyles. 90% freelance written. For knife enthusiasts who want to know as much as possible about quality knives and edged weapons. Bimonthly magazine. Pays on publication. Publishes ms an average of 6 months after acceptance. Buys all rights. Submit seasonal/holiday material 6 months in advance. Previously published submissions OK. Reports in 2 months. Sample copy $2.95; writer's guidelines for #10 SASE.

Nonfiction: How-to; historical (on knives and weapons); adventure on a knife theme; interview (knifemakers); celebrities who own knives; knives featured in movies with shots from the movie, etc.; new product; nostalgia; personal experience; photo feature; profile and technical. "We would also like to receive articles on knives in adventuresome life-saving situations." No poetry. Buys 75 unsolicited mss/year. "We evaluate complete manuscripts and make our decision on that basis." Length: 1,000-2,000 words. Pays 5¢/word minimum, more for better writers. "We will pay top dollar in the knife market." Sometimes pays the expenses of writers on assignment.

Photos: Send photos with ms. Pays $5 for 8×10 b&w glossy prints, $25-75 for 35mm color transparencies. Captions required.

Tips: "We are always willing to read submissions from anyone who has read a few copies and studied the market. The ideal article for us is a piece bringing out the romance, legend, and love of man's oldest tool—the knife. We like articles that place knives in peoples' hands—in life saving situations, adventure modes, etc. (Nothing gory or with the knife as the villain). People and knives are good copy. We are getting more and better written articles from writers who are reading the publication beforehand. That makes for a harder sell for the quickie writer not willing to do his homework."

THE COIN ENTHUSIAST'S JOURNAL, Masongate Publishing, P.O. Box 1383, Torrance CA 90505. Editor: William J. Cook. 40% freelance written. Prefers to work with published/established writers, and works with a small number of new/unpublished writers each year. Monthly newsletter covering numismatics (coin collecting) and bullion trading. "Our purpose is to give readers information to help them make sound investment decisions in the areas we cover and to help them get more enjoyment out of their hobby." Estab. 1984. Circ. 2,000. Pays on publication. Publishes ms an average of 2 months after acceptance. Byline given. Offers $25 kill fee. Buys all rights. Submit seasonal/holiday material 3 months in advance. Simultaneous queries and submissions OK. Reports in 3 weeks. Sample copy for $3 and #10 SAE with 2 first class stamps (must mention *Writer's Market*). Guidelines sent free with sample *when requested*.
Nonfiction: How-to (make money from your hobby and be a better trader); opinion (what is the coin market going to do?); personal experience (insiders' "tricks of the trade"); and technical (why are coin prices going up [or down]?). No "crystal ball" predictions, e.g., "I see silver going up to to $50 per ounce by mid-1992." Query with published clips. Length: 500-2,500 words. Buys 18-30 mss/year. Pays mostly $50-150. Also looking for "staff writers" who will submit material each month or bi-monthly.
Photos: State availability of photos with query. Pays $5-25 for b&w prints. Buys one-time rights.
Tips: "Occasionally we buy cartoons. We are buying a few more short articles but the majority are longer articles (i.e. 1,500 words and up). We are also buying more 'human interest' and humorous articles. More entertainment as opposed to just technical information. Try to make articles interesting—we get *too* much dry, boring stuff."

COINS, Krause Publications, 700 E. State St., Iola WI 54990. (715)445-2214. FAX: (715)445-4087. Editor: Arlyn G. Sieber. 50% freelance written. Eager to work with new/unpublished writers. Monthly magazine about U.S. and foreign coins for all levels of collectors, investors and dealers. Estab. 1952. Circ. 71,000. Free sample copy and writer's guidelines.
Nonfiction: "We're looking for stories that are going to help coin collectors pursue their hobby in today's market. Stories should include what's available in the series being discussed, its value in today's market, and tips for buying that material." Buys 2-4 mss/issue. Send complete ms. Length: 500-3,000 words. Pays 3¢/word to first-time contributors; fee negotiated for later articles. Sometimes pays the expenses of writers on assignment.
Photos: Pays $5 minimum for b&w prints. Pays $25 minimum for 35mm transparencies used. Captions and model releases required. Buys first rights.

COLLECTOR EDITIONS, Collector Communications Corp., 170 5th Ave., New York NY 10010. (212)989-8700. FAX: (212)645-8976. Editor: Joan Muyskens Pursley. 40% freelance written. Works with a small number of new/unpublished writers each year. Bimonthly magazine on porcelain and glass collectibles. "We specialize in contemporary (post-war ceramic and glass) collectibles, including reproductions, but also publish articles about antiques, if they are being reproduced today and are generally available." Estab. 1973. Circ. 70,000. Rights purchased vary with author and material. Buys first North American serial rights and sometimes second serial (reprint) rights. "First assignments are always done on a speculative basis." Pays within 30 days of acceptance. Publishes ms an average of 6 months after acceptance. Reports in 2 months. Sample copy $2; writer's guidelines for #10 SASE.
Nonfiction: "Short features about collecting, written in tight, newsy style. We specialize in contemporary (postwar) collectibles. Values for pieces being written about should be included." Informational, how-to, interview, profile, exposé and nostalgia. Buys 8-10 mss/year. Query with sample photos. Length: 500-2,500 words. Pays $100-300. Sometimes pays expenses of writers on assignments.
Columns/Departments: Columns cover porcelain, glass, auction reports and artist profiles. Query. Length: 750 words. Pays $75.
Photos: B&w and color photos purchased with accompanying ms with no additional payment. Captions are required. "We want clear, distinct, full-frame images that say something."
Tips: "Unfamiliarity with the field is the most frequent mistake made by writers in completing an article for us."

COLLECTORS NEWS & THE ANTIQUE REPORTER, 506 2nd St., Box 156, Grundy Center IA 50638. (319)824-6981. FAX: (319)824-3414. Editor: Linda Kruger. 20% freelance written. Works with a small number of new/unpublished writers each year. A monthly tabloid covering antiques, collectibles and nostalgic memorabilia. Circ. 15,000. Byline given. Pays on publication. Publishes ms an average of 1 year after acceptance. Buys first rights and makes work-for-hire assignments. Submit seasonal material (holidays) 3 months in advance. Reports in 2 weeks on queries; 6 weeks on mss. Sample copy for $2 and 9×12 SAE; free writer's guidelines.

Nonfiction: General interest (any subject re: collectibles, antique to modern); historical/nostalgic (relating to collections or collectors); how-to (display your collection, care for, restore, appraise, locate, add to, etc.); interview/profile (covering individual collectors and their hobbies, unique or extensive; celebrity collectors, and limited edition artists); technical (in-depth analysis of a particular antique, collectible or collecting field); and travel (coverage of special interest or regional shows, seminars, conventions—or major antique shows, flea markets; places collectors can visit, tours they can take, museums, etc.). Special issues include January and June show/flea market issues; and usual seasonal emphasis. Buys 100 mss/year. Query with sample of writing. Length: 1,200-1,600 words. Pays 75¢/column inch; $1/column inch for color features.

Photos: Reviews b&w prints and 35mm color slides. Payment for photos included in payment for ms. Captions required. Buys first rights.

Tips: Articles most open to freelancers are on celebrity collectors; collectors with unique and/or extensive collections; music collectibles; transportation collectibles; advertising collectibles; bottles; glass, china and silver; primitives; furniture; toys; political collectibles; and movie memorabilia.

COLLECTORS' SHOWCASE, America's Premier Collecting Magazine, Sports Magazines of America, #210, 7130 S. Lewis, Tulsa OK 74136. (918)496-7405. FAX: (918)496-7485. Editorial Coordinator: James Brackin. 90% freelance written. Collectibles magazine published 12 times/year. "Our readers collect in general, but we focus editorially on antique dolls, toys, advertising and Americana." Estab. 1981. Circ. 15,000. **Pays on acceptance.** Publishes ms an average of 1-2 months after acceptance. Byline given. Buys first North American serial rights. Submit seasonal/holiday material 3 months in advance. Query for electronic submissions. Reports in 2 weeks. Sample copy for 9×12 SAE with 5 first class stamps; writer's guidelines for #10 SASE.

Nonfiction: Book excerpts, essays, general interest, how-to, interview/profile, new product, photo feature. "No modern or contemporary collectibles, no coins, no plates, no reproductions." Buys 50-70 mss/year. Query with or without published clips, or send complete ms. Length: 750-2,000 words. Pays $100-250. Sometimes pays expenses of writers on assignment.

Photos: Send photos with submission. Reviews negatives, 35mm and larger transparencies and 3×5 prints. Payment negotiable. Captions and identification of subjects required. Buys one-time rights.

Columns/Departments: Showtime (recap of show or convention), 200 words; Auction Report, 100-500 words; Museum News (museum exhibits), 100-500 words. Buys 10-15 mss/year. Send complete ms. Pays $25-100.

Tips: "Under new management, *Collectors' Showcase* is moving away from fluff and toward informative, factual and well written features. Contact in writing or over the phone with James Brackin is encouraged. Photos are very important."

‡CRAFTS MAGAZINE, PJS Publications Inc., News Plaza, Box 1790, Peoria IL 61656. (309)682-6626. Editor: Judith Brossart. Monthly magazine. **Pays on acceptance.** Publishes ms an average of 3 months after acceptance. Offers 100% kill fee. Buys all rights. Reports in 2 weeks. "We do how-to only; we don't have special features in our magazine." Send query with photo or sketch first. Pays $75-250.

CREATIVE WOODWORKS & CRAFTS, MSC Publishing Co., 70 Sparta Ave., CN 1003, Sparta NJ 07871. (201)729-4477. Editor: Laurice Brazell. 90% freelance written. Bimonthly magazine on woodworking. "Simple weekend projects for the veteran woodworker and woodcrafter are presented in how-to format. For designs from fine furnishings to handpainted collectibles folk art, toys and other wood items." Estab. 1989. Pays on publication. Publishes ms an average of 4-6 months after acceptance. Byline given. Buys first rights and all rights. Submit seasonal/holiday material 6 months in advance. Reports in 6 weeks on queries; 10 weeks on mss. Sample copy for 9×12 SAE with $1.25 postage. Writer's guidelines for #10 SAE with 1 first class stamp.

Nonfiction: How-to. Buys 8-10 mss/year. Query. Length: 500-2,000 words. Pays 7-10¢/word. Sometimes pays expenses of writers on assignment.

Photos: State availability of photos with submission. Reviews all sizes of transparencies and prints. Pays negotiable rates. Captions, model releases and identification of subjects required. Rights negotiable.

Fillers: Woodworking tips. Buys 6-12/year. Length: 50-100 words. Pays $5-10.

Tips: "Send original designs appropriate to our subject i.e., woodcrafts and woodworking."

CROCHET FANTASY, All American Crafts, Inc., 70 Sparta Ave., CN 1003, Sparta NJ 07871. (201)729-4477. Editorial Director: Camille Pomaco. Editor: Janice Edsall. Crochet magazine published 8 times/year. Estab. 1982. "Each issue includes a variety of sweaters, doilies, afghans and other items." Pays on publication. Publishes ms an average of 6 months after acceptance. Byline given. Buys first rights, second serial (reprint) rights or all rights. Submit seasonal/holiday material 8 months in advance. Query for electronic submissions. Reports in 2 months on queries. Sample copy for 9×12 SAE. Writer's guidelines for #10 SASE.

Nonfiction: How-to, humor, personal experience and technical. Buys 2 mss/year. Query. Length: 500-3,000 words. Pays 7-10¢/word for assigned articles.
Photos: Send photos with submission. Reviews all sizes transparencies and prints. Offers no additional payment for photos accepted with ms. Model releases required. Buys all rights.
Columns/Departments: Stitch Wit (crochet hints, crochet anecdotes, etc.), 50-500 words. Pays $5 per published hint.

CROSS STITCH SAMPLER, Sampler Publications, #7, Olde Ridge Village, Chadds Ford PA 19317. (215)358-9242. Quarterly magazine on needlework and counted thread. Estab. 1983. Circ. 118,000. Pays on publication. Publishes ms an average of 3 months after acceptance. Byline given. Buys all rights. Simultaneous and previously published submissions OK. Sample copy for 9 × 12 SAE with $1.77 in stamps.
Nonfiction: General interest, historical/nostalgic, inspirational, interview/profile, personal experience, photo feature. Buys 4-6 mss/year. Send complete ms. Pays $75-300.
Photos: Send photos with submission. Reviews contact sheets, 4 × 5 transparencies, and 3 × 5 prints. Offers no additional payment for photos accepted with ms. Captions and identification of subjects required. Buys one-time rights.

‡CROSS-STITCH PLUS, House of White Birches, 306 E. Parr Rd., Berne IN 46711. (219)589-8741. Editor: Läna Schurb. 85% freelance written. Bimonthly magazine covering cross-stitch and, to a lesser degree, other needle crafts. "We print high-quality original cross-stitch designs of varying degrees of difficulty, aimed at novices and experienced needleworkers. We also feature, in each issue, one or two projects of another needle medium, designed to expand our readers' horizons." Estab. 1985. Circ. 75,000. Pays "Whenever possible, shortly after acceptance. No later than publication." Byline sometimes given (name is always used, sometimes in accompanying copy rather than as a byline). Buys first rights, all rights, or makes work-for-hire assignments. Submit seasonal/holiday material 7 months in advance. Query for electronic submission. Reports in 2 weeks. Free sample copy and writer's guidelines.
Nonfiction: Historical (*limited* number of background pieces on specific types of needlework), how-to (cross-stitch and needlework), new product, technical (technical aspects of stitching). "We do not want to see humor, knitting or crocheting; reviews of shows or books." Query with or without published clips, or send complete ms. Pays $20-300. Offers no additional payment for photos accepted with ms (except in rare instances).
Columns/Departments: Product Review (A complete project which uses specific product. An accurate, unslanted opinion of the product frames, fibers, etc.) Send complete ms. Pays $40-150.
Fillers: Gags to be illustrated by cartoonist. Buys 6/year. Pays $50-100. "A writer can best approach *Cross-Stitch Plus* by exhibiting excellence in their stitchery and by following our writer's guides (typed manuscripts, etc.). We are flexible and will work with beginners *if* their stitchery is good enough."

DECORATIVE ARTIST'S WORKBOOK, F&W Publications, Inc., 1507 Dana Ave., Cincinnati OH 45207. Editorial Director: Michael Ward. 50% freelance written. Bimonthly magazine covering decorative painting and related crafts and home decor. Offers "straightforward, personal instruction in the techniques of decorative painting, crafting and decorating." Circ. 100,000. **Pays on acceptance.** Byline given. Offers 20% kill fee. Buys first North American serial rights. Submit seasonal/holiday material 8 months in advance. Reports in 1 month. Sample copy for $3.65 with 9 × 12 SAE and sufficient first class postage.
Nonfiction: How-to (related to decorative painting, crafting and home decor), new product and technical. Artist/crafter profiles and/or general craft topics. Buys 30 mss/year. Query with slides or photos. Length: 1,200-1,800 words. Pays 10-12¢/word.
Photos: State availability of photos and slides with submission or send photos with submission. Reviews 35mm, 4 × 5 transparencies and quality photos. Offers no additional payment for photos accepted with ms. Captions required. Buys one-time rights.
Fillers: Anecdotes, facts and short humor. Buys 15/year. Length: 50-200 words. Pays $10-25.
Tips: "The more you know—and can prove you know—about decorative painting, crafting and home decor, the better your chances. I'm looking for experts in the field who, through their own experience, can artfully describe the techniques involved. How-to articles are most open to freelancers. Be sure to query with slides or transparencies, and show that you understand the extensive graphic requirements for these pieces and are able to provide progressives—slides that show works in progress."

ALWAYS submit unsolicited manuscripts or queries with a self-addressed, stamped envelope (SASE) within your country or a self-addressed envelope with International Reply Coupons (IRC) purchased from the post office for other countries.

DOLLS, The Collector's Magazine, Collector Communications Corp., 170 5th Ave., New York NY 10010. (212)989-8700. FAX: (212)645-8976. Editor: Joan Muyskens Pursley. 75% freelance written. Works with a small number of new/unpublished writers each year. Magazine published 8 times/year covering doll collecting "for collectors of antique, contemporary and reproduction dolls. We publish well-researched, professionally written articles illustrated with photographs of high quality, color or b&w." Estab. 1982. Circ. 85,000. Pays within 1 month of acceptance. Publishes ms an average of 6 months after acceptance. Byline given. "Almost all first manuscripts are on speculation. We rarely kill assigned stories, but fee would be about 33% of article fee." Buys first North American serial rights, second serial rights if piece has appeared in a non-competing publication. Submit seasonal/holiday material 6 months in advance. Previously published submissions OK. Reports in 2 months. Sample copy $2; writer's guidelines for #10 SASE.

Nonfiction: Book excerpts; historical (with collecting angle); interview/profile (on collectors with outstanding collections); new product (just photos and captions; "we do not pay for these, but regard them as publicity"); opinion ("A Personal Definition of Dolls"); technical (doll restoration advice by experts only); and travel (museums and collections around the world). "No sentimental, uninformed 'my doll collection' or 'my grandma's doll collection' stories or trade magazine-type stories on shops, etc. Our readers are knowledgeable collectors." Query with clips. Length: 500-2,500 words. Pays $100-350. Sometimes pays expenses of writers on assignment.

Photos: Send photos with accompanying query or ms. Reviews 4×5 transparencies; 4×5 or 8×10 b&w prints and 35mm slides. "We do not buy photographs submitted without manuscripts unless we have assigned them; we pay for the manuscript/photos package in one fee." Captions required. Buys one-time rights.

Columns/Departments: Doll Views—a miscellany of news and views of the doll world includes reports on upcoming or recently held events. "*Not* the place for new dolls, auction prices or dates; we have regular contributors or staff assigned to those columns." Query with clips if available or send complete ms. Length: 200-500 words. Pays $25-75. Doll Views items are rarely bylined.

Fillers: "We don't use fillers but would consider them if we got something good. Hints on restoring, for example, or a nice illustration." Length: 500 words maximum. Pays $25-75.

Tips: "We need experts in the field who are also good writers. The most frequent mistake made by writers in completing an article assignment for us is being unfamiliar with the field; our readers are very knowledgeable. Freelancers who are not experts should know their particular story thoroughly and do background research to get the facts correct. Well-written queries from writers outside the NYC area are especially welcomed. Non-experts should stay away from technical or specific subjects (restoration, price trends). Short profiles of unusual collectors or a story of a local museum collection, with good photos, might catch our interest. Editors want to know they are getting something from a writer they cannot get from anyone else. Good writing should be a given, a starting point. After that, it's what you know."

EARLY AMERICAN LIFE, Cowles Magazines, Inc. Box 8200, Harrisburg PA 17105. FAX: (717)657-9526. Editor: Frances Carnahan. 60-70% freelance written. Bimonthly magazine for "people who are interested in capturing the warmth and beauty of the 1600 to 1840 period and using it in their homes and lives today. They are interested in arts, crafts, travel, restoration and collecting." Estab. 1970. Circ. 150,000. Buys first North American serial rights. **Pays on acceptance.** Publishes ms an average of 1 year after acceptance. Sample copy and writer's guidelines for 9×12 SAE and 4 first class stamps. Reports in 1 month. Query or submit complete ms with SASE.

Nonfiction: "Social history (the story of the people, not epic heroes and battles), travel to historic sites, country inns, antiques and reproductions, refinishing and restoration, architecture and decorating. We try to entertain as we inform. While we're always on the lookout for good pieces on any of our subjects, the 'travel to historic sites' theme is most frequently submitted. Would like to see more on how real people did something great to their homes." Buys 40 mss/year. Query or submit complete ms. Length: 750-3,000 words. Pays $100-600. Pays expenses of writers on assignment.

Photos: Pays $10 for 5×7 (and up) b&w photos used with mss, minimum of $25 for color. Prefers 2¼×2¼ and up, but can work from 35mm.

Tips: "Our readers are eager for ideas on how to bring early America into their lives. Conceive a new approach to satisfy their related interests in arts, crafts, travel to historic sites, and especially in houses decorated in the early American style. Write to entertain and inform at the same time, and be prepared to help us with illustrations, or sources for them."

‡EDGES, The Official Publication of the American Blade Collectors Association, American Blade, Inc., 2835 Hickory Valley Rd., Chattanooga TN 37421. Editor: J. Bruce Voyles. Bimonthly magazine covering the knife business and knife collecting. Circ. 20,000. Pays on publication. Byline given. Buys all rights. Submit seasonal/holiday material 6 months in advance. Simultaneous queries, and photocopied and previously published submissions OK "as long as they are exclusive to our market." Reports in 5 months. Acknowledges receipt of queries and ms in 2 months. Sample copy $1.

Nonfiction: "Emphasis on pocket knives and folders." Book excerpts, expose, general interest, historical (well-researched), how-to, humor, new product, opinion, personal experience, photo feature, and technical. "We look for articles on all aspects of the knife business, including technological advances, profiles, knife shows, and well-researched history. Ours is not a hard market to break into if the writer is willing to do a little research. To have a copy is almost a requirement." Buys 150 mss/year. Send complete ms. Length: 50-3,000 words "or more if material warrants additional length." Pays 5¢/word.
Photos: Pays $5 for 5×7 b&w prints. Captions and model release required (if persons are identifiable).
Fillers: Clippings, anecdotes and newsbreaks.
Tips: "If writers haven't studied the publication they shouldn't bother to submit an article. If they have studied it, we're an easy market to sell to." Buys 80% of the articles geared to "the knife business."

FIBERARTS, The Magazine of Textiles, Altamont Press, 50 College St., Asheville NC 28801. (704)253-0467. FAX: (704)253-7952. Editor: Ann Batchelder. 100% freelance written. Eager to work with new/unpublished writers. Magazine appears 5 times/year, covering textiles as art and craft (weaving, quilting, surface design, stitchery, knitting, fashion, crochet, etc.) for textile artists, craftspeople, hobbyists, teachers, museum and gallery staffs, collectors and enthusiasts. Estab. 1975. Circ. 23,000. Pays 60 days after publication. Publishes ms an average of 4 months after acceptance. Byline given. Buys first rights. Editorial guidelines and style sheet available. Sample copy $4.50 and 10×12 SAE with 2 first class stamps; writer's guidelines for #10 SAE with 2 first class stamps.
Nonfiction: Historical; artist interview/profile; opinion; photo feature; technical; travel (for the textile enthusiast, e.g., collecting rugs in Turkey); and education, trends, exhibition reviews and textile news. Query. "Please be very specific about your proposal. Also an important consideration in accepting an article is the kind of photos—35mm slides and/or b&w glossies—that you can provide as illustration. We like to see photos in advance." Length: 250-1,200 words. Pays $40-300, depending on article. Rarely pays the expenses of writers on assignment.
Tips: "Our writers are very familiar with the textile field, and this is what we look for in a new writer. Familiarity with textile techniques, history or events determines clarity of an article more than a particular style of writing. The writer should also be familiar with *Fiberarts*, the magazine. We outline our upcoming agenda in each issue far enough in advance for a prospective writer to be aware of our future needs."

‡FINE WOODWORKING, The Taunton Press, 63 S. Main St., Box 5506, Newtown CT 06470-5506. (203)426-8171. FAX: (203)426-3434. Editor: Dick Burrows. Bimonthly magazine on woodworking in the small shop. "All writers are also skilled woodworkers. It's more important that a contributor be a woodworker than a writer. Our editors (also woodworkers) will fix the words." Circ. 292,000. Pays on publication. Byline given. Kill fee varies; "editorial discretion." Buys first rights and rights to republish in anthologies and use in promo pieces. Submit seasonal/holiday material 6 months in advance. Simultaneous and photocopied submissions OK. Query for electronic submissions. Reports in 2 months. Sample copy $4.95.
Nonfiction: How-to (woodworking). Buys 120 mss/year. "No specs—our editors would rather see more than less." Pays $150 per magazine page. Sometimes pays expenses of writers on assignment.
Photos: Send photos with submission. Reviews contact sheets, negatives, transparencies and prints. Captions, model releases and identification of subjects required. Buys one-time rights.
Columns/Departments: Notes & Comment (topics of interest to woodworkers); Question & Answer (woodworking Q & A); Follow-Up (information on past articles/readers' comments); and Methods of Work (shop tips). Buys 400 items/year. Length varies. Pays $10 minumum-150/published page.
Tips: "Send for authors guidelines and follow them. Stories about woodworking reported by non-woodworkers *not* used. Our magazine is essentially reader-written by woodworkers."

FINESCALE MODELER, Kalmbach Publishing Co., 21027 Crossroads Circle, P.O. Box 1612, Waukesha WI 53187. (414)796-8776. Editor: Bob Hayden. 80% freelance written. Eager to work with new/unpublished writers. Magazine published 8 times/year "devoted to how-to-do-it modeling information for scale model builders who build non-operating aircraft, tanks, boats, automobiles, figures, dioramas, and science fiction and fantasy models." Circ. 80,000. **Pays on acceptance.** Publishes ms an average of 14 months after acceptance. Byline given. Buys all rights. Reports in 6 weeks on queries; 3 months on mss. Sample copy for 9×12 SAE and 3 first class stamps; free writer's guidelines.
Nonfiction: How-to (build scale models); and technical (research information for building models). Query or send complete ms. Length: 750-3,000 words. Pays $30/published page minimum.
Photos: Send photos with ms. Pays $7.50 minimum for transparencies and $5 minimum for 5×7 b&w prints. Captions and identification of subjects required. Buys one-time rights.
Columns/Departments: *FSM* Showcase (photos plus description of model); and *FSM* Tips and Techniques (model building hints and tips). Buys 25-50 Tips and Techniques/year. Query or send complete ms. Length: 100-1,000 words. Pays $5-100.

Tips: "A freelancer can best break in first through hints and tips, then through feature articles. Most people who write for *FSM* are modelers first, writers second. This is a specialty magazine for a special, quite expert audience. Essentially, 99% of our writers will come from that audience."

HANDWOVEN, Interweave Press, 201 E. 4th St., Loveland CO 80537. (303)669-7672. FAX: (303)667-8317. Editor: Jane Patrick. 75% freelance written. Bimonthly magazine (except July) covering hand-weaving, spinning and dyeing. Audience includes "practicing textile craftsmen. Article should show considerable depth of knowledge of subject, although tone should be informal and accessible." Estab. 1975. Circ. 35,000. Pays on publication. Publishes ms an average of 10 months after acceptance. Byline given. Pays 50% kill fee. Buys first North American serial rights. Simultaneous queries OK. Sample copy $4.50; writer's guidelines for #10 SASE.
Nonfiction: Historical and how-to (on weaving and other craft techniques; specific items with instructions); and technical (on handweaving, spinning and dyeing technology). "All articles must contain a high level of in-depth information. Our readers are very knowledgeable about these subjects." Query. Length: 500-2,000 words. Pays $35-150.
Photos: State availability of photos. Identification of subjects required.
Tips: "We prefer work written by writers with an in-depth knowledge of weaving. We're particularly interested in articles about new weaving and spinning techniques as well as applying these techniques to finished products."

HOME MECHANIX, 2 Park Ave., New York NY 10016. (212)779-5000. Editor: Michael Morris. Executive Editor: Michael Chotiner. 50% freelance written. Prefers to work with published/established writers. "If it's good, and it fits the type of material we're currently publishing, we're interested whether writer is new or experienced." Magazine, published 10 times/year, for the active home and car owner. "Articles emphasize an active, home-oriented lifestyle. Includes information useful for maintenance, repair and renovation to the home and family car. Information on how to buy, how to select products useful to homeowners/car owners. Emphasis in home-oriented articles is on good design, inventive solutions to styling and space problems, useful home-workshop projects." Estab. 1905. Circ. 1.2 million. **Pays on acceptance.** Publishes ms an average of 6 months after acceptance. Byline given. Buys first North American serial rights. Query.
Nonfiction: Feature articles relating to homeowner/car owner, 1,500-2,500 words. "This may include personal home-renovation projects, professional advice on interior design, reports on different or unusual construction methods, energy-related subjects, outdoor/backyard projects, etc. We are no longer interested in high-tech subjects such as aerospace, electronics, photography or military hardware. Most of our automotive features are written by experts in the field, but fillers, tips, how-to repair, or modification articles on the family car are welcome. Articles on construction, tool use, refinishing techniques, etc., are also sought. Pays $300 minimum for features; fees based on number of printed pages, photos accompanying mss., etc." Pays expenses of writers on assignment.
Photos: Photos should accompany mss. Pays $600 and up for transparencies for cover. Inside color: $300/1 page, $500/2, $700/3, etc. Captions and model releases required.
Fillers: Tips and fillers useful to tool users or for general home maintenance. Pays $25 and up for illustrated and captioned fillers.
Tips: "The most frequent mistake made by writers in completing an article assignment for *Home Mechanix* is not taking the time to understand its editorial focus and special needs."

‡THE HOME SHOP MACHINIST, 2779 Aero Park Dr., Box 1810, Traverse City MI 49685. (616)946-3712. FAX: (616)946-3289. Editor: Joe D. Rice. 95% freelance written. Bimonthly magazine covering machining and metalworking for the hobbyist. Circ. 24,000. Pays on publication. Publishes ms an average of 18 months after acceptance. Byline given. Buys first North American serial rights only. Simultaneous submissions OK. Reports in 3 weeks. Free sample copy and writer's guidelines for 9 × 12 SASE.
Nonfiction: How-to (projects designed to upgrade present shop equipment or hobby model projects that require machining); and technical (should pertain to metalworking, machining, drafting, layout, welding or foundry work for the hobbyist). No fiction. Buys 50 mss/year. Query or send complete ms. Length: open—"whatever it takes to do a thorough job." Pays $40/published page, plus $9/published photo; $70/page for camera-ready art; and $40 for b&w cover photo.
Photos: Send photos with ms. Pays $9-40 for 5 × 7 b&w prints. Captions and identification of subjects required.
Columns/Departments: Sheetmetal; Book Reviews; New Product Reviews; Micro-Machining; and Foundry. "Writer should become familiar with our magazine before submitting. Query first." Buys 25-30 mss/year. Length: 600-1,500 words. Pays $40-70/page.

Fillers: Machining tips/shortcuts. No news clippings. Buys 12-15/year. Length: 100-300 words. Pays $30-48.

Tips: "The writer should be experienced in the area of metalworking and machining; should be extremely thorough in explanations of methods, processes—always with an eye to safety; and should provide good quality b&w photos and/or clear drawings to aid in description. Visuals are of increasing importance to our readers. Carefully planned photos, drawings and charts will carry a submission to our magazine much farther along the path to publication."

INTERNATIONAL DOLL WORLD, The doll lover's magazine, House of White Birches, 306 E. Parr Rd., Berne IN 46711. (219)589-8741. FAX: (219)589-8093. Editor: Rebekah Montgomery. Managing Editor: Läna Schurb. 90% freelance written. Bimonthly magazine covering doll collecting, restoration. "Our readers collect dolls because they enjoy them. Some do as investments, but most consider them decorative." Estab. 1979. Circ. 85,000. Pays on publication. Publishes ms an average of 8 months after acceptance. Byline given. Buys first North American serial or one-time rights. Submit seasonal/holiday material 1 year in advance. Simultaneous submissions OK. Reports in 2 weeks on queries. Sample copy $2.50. Writer's guidelines for SASE.

Nonfiction: Historical/nostalgic, how-to, interview/profile and technical. Special issue forthcoming on teddy bear and doll patterns. No articles about people and their doll collections. Buys 90 mss/year. Query with or without published clips, or send complete ms. Length: 5,000 words maximum. Pays $35-250.

Photos: Send photos with submission. Offers $5-50 per photo. Captions and identification of subjects required. Buys one-time or all rights.

Tips: "Choose a specific manufacturer and talk about his dolls or a specific doll—modern or antique—and explore its history and styles made."

JUGGLER'S WORLD, International Jugglers Association, Box 443, Davidson NC 28036. (704)892-1296. FAX: (704)892-2526. Editor: Bill Giduz. 25% freelance written. A quarterly magazine on juggling. "*Juggler's World* publishes news, feature articles, fiction and poetry that relates to juggling. We also encourage 'how-to' articles describing how to learn various juggling tricks." Circ. 3,500. **Pays on acceptance.** Publishes ms an average of 6 months after acceptance. Byline given. Buys all rights. Submit seasonal/holiday material 6 months in advance. Simultaneous and previously published submissions OK. Query for electronic submissions. Reports in 1 week. Sample copy for 8½×11 SAE with 5 first class stamps. Writer's guidelines for #10 SASE.

Nonfiction: Essays, general interest, historical/nostalgic, how-to, humor, interview/profile, opinion, personal experience, photo feature and travel. Buys 3 mss/year. Query. Length: 500-2,000 words. Pays $50-100 for assigned articles. Pays expenses of writers on assignment.

Photos: State availability of photos with submission. Reviews contact sheets, negatives and prints. Offers no additional payment for photos accepted with ms. Captions required. Buys one-time rights.

Fiction: Ken Letko, fiction editor. Adventure, fantasy, historical, humorous, science fiction and slice-of-life vignettes. Buys 2 mss/year. Query. Length: 250-1,000 words. Pays $25-50.

Tips: "The best approach is a feature article on or an interview with a leading juggler. Article should include both human interest material to describe the performer as an individual and technical juggling information to make it clear to a knowledgeable audience the exact tricks and skits performed."

KITPLANES, For designers, builders and pilots of experimental aircraft, Fancy Publications, P.O. Box 6050, Mission Viejo CA 92690. (714)240-6001. FAX: (714)855-3045. Editor: Dave Martin. 70% freelance written. Eager to work with new/unpublished writers. Monthly magazine covering self-construction of private aircraft for pilots and builders. Estab. 1972. Circ. 52,000. Pays on publication. Publishes ms an average of 3 months after acceptance. Byline given. Offers negotiable kill fee. Buys first North American serial rights. Submit seasonal/holiday material 6 months in advance. Query for electronic submissions. Reports in 2 weeks on queries; 6 weeks on mss. Sample copy $3; free writer's guidelines.

Nonfiction: How-to, interview/profile, new product, personal experience, photo feature, technical and general interest. "We are looking for articles on specific construction techniques, the use of tools, both hand and power, in aircraft building, the relative merits of various materials, conversions of engines from automobiles for aviation use, installation of instruments and electronics." No general-interest aviation articles, or "My First Solo" type of articles. Buys 80 mss/year. Query. Length: 500-5,000 words. Pays $100-400 including story photos.

Photos: Send photos with query or ms, or state availability of photos. Pays $250 for cover photos. Captions and identification of subjects required. Buys one-time rights.

Tips: "*Kitplanes* contains very specific information—a writer must be extremely knowledgeable in the field. Major features are entrusted only to known writers. I cannot emphasize enough that articles must be directed at the individual aircraft builder. We need more 'how-to' photo features in all areas of homebuilt aircraft."

‡**THE LEATHER CRAFTERS JOURNAL**, 4307 Oak Dr., Rhinelander WI 54501. (715)362-5393. Editor: William R. Reis. Managing Editor: Dorothea Schulze. 100% freelance written. Bimonthly hobby and craft magazine. "Aid to craftsmen using leather as the base medium. All age groups and skill levels from beginners to master carvers and artisans." Estab. 1990. Circ. 6,000. Pays on publication. Publishes ms an average of 2 months after acceptance. Byline given. "All assigned articles subject to review for acceptance by editor." Buys first North American serial rights and second serial (reprint) rights. Reprints at one-half original price. Submit seasonal/holiday material 6 months in advance. Simultaneous and previously published submissions OK. Reports in 1 month. Sample copy for $3 with SAE and 1 first class stamp. Writer's guidelines for SAE with 1 first class stamp.

Nonfiction: How-to (crafts and arts and any other projects using leather. "I do not want articles that omit hands-on, step-by-step, how-to information." Buys 75 mss/year. Send complete ms. Length: 500-2,500 words. Pays $20-200 for assigned articles; $20-150 for unsolicited articles. Send good contrast color print photos and full size patterns and/or full-size photo-carve patterns with submission. Lack of these reduces payment amount. Captions required. Buys one-time and reprints at one-half original price. No previously published submissions.

Columns/Departments: Beginners, Intermediate, Artists, Western Design, International Design, Letters (the open exchange of all information between all peoples), 500-2,500 on all). Buys 75 mss/year. Send complete ms. Pays 5¢ per word.

Poetry: Dorothea Schulze. No non-humorous. Buys 6 poems/year. Submit maximum 6 poems. Pays $5-10.

Fillers: Anecdotes, facts, gags to illustrated by cartoonist, newsbreaks. Length: 25-200 words. Pays $3-10.

Tips: "We want to work with people who understand and know leathercraft and are interested in passing on their knowledge to others. We would prefer to interview people who have achieved a high level in leathercraft skill."

LINN'S STAMP NEWS, Amos Press, 911 Vandemark Rd., P.O. Box 29, Sidney OH 45365. (513)498-0801. FAX: (513)498-0814. Editor: Michael Laurence. Managing Editor: Elaine Boughner. 50% freelance written. Weekly tabloid on the stamp collecting hobby. "All articles must be about philatelic collectibles." Estab. 1928. Circ. 75,000. Pays on publication. Publishes ms an average of 1 month after acceptance. Byline given. Buys first North American serial rights. Submit seasonal/holiday material 2 months in advance. Reports on queries; 2 weeks on mss. Free sample copy. Writer's guidelines for #10 SAE with 2 first class stamps.

Nonfiction: General interest, historical/nostalgic, how-to, interview/profile and technical. "No articles merely giving information on background of stamp subject. Must have philatelic information included." Buys 300 mss/year. Send complete ms. Length: 500 words maximum. Pays $10-50. Rarely pays expenses of writers on assignment.

Photos: State availability of photos with submission. Prefers glossy b&w prints. Offers no additional payment for photos accepted with ms. Captions required. Buys all rights.

‡**LIVE STEAM**, Live Steam, Inc., 2779 Aero Park Dr., Box 629, Traverse City MI 49685. (616)941-7160. Editor: Joe D. Rice. 90% freelance written. Eager to work with new/unpublished writers. Monthly magazine covering steam-powered models and full-size engines (i.e., locomotives, traction, cars, boats, stationary, etc.) "Our readers are hobbyists, many of whom are building their engines from scratch. We are interested in anything that has to do with the world of live steam-powered machinery." Circ. 12,800. Pays on publication. Publishes ms an average of 18 months after acceptance. Byline given. Buys first North American serial rights only. Reports in 3 weeks. Free sample copy and writer's guidelines.

Nonfiction: Historical/nostalgic; how-to (build projects powered by steam); new product; personal experience; photo feature; and technical (must be within the context of steam-powered machinery or on machining techniques). No fiction. Buys 50 mss/year. Query or send complete ms. Length: 500-3,000 words. Pays $30/published page—$500 maximum. Sometimes pays the expenses of writers on assignment.

Photos: Send photos with ms. Pays $50/page of finished art. Pays $8 for 5×7 b&w prints; $40 for cover (color). Captions and identification of subjects required.

Columns/Departments: Steam traction engines, steamboats, stationary steam, and steam autos. Buys 6-8 mss/year. Query. Length: 1,000-3,000 words. Pays $20-50.

Tips: "At least half of all our material is from the freelancer. Requesting a sample copy and author's guide will be a good place to start. The writer must be well-versed in the nature of live steam equipment and the hobby of scale modeling such equipment. Technical and historical accuracy is an absolute must. Often, good articles are weakened or spoiled by mediocre to poor quality photos. Freelancers must learn to take a *good* photograph."

‡**LOOSE CHANGE**, Mead Publishing Co., 1515 S. Commerce St., Las Vegas NV 89102-2703. (702)387-8750. Publisher: Daniel R. Mead. 10-20% freelance written. Eager to work with new/unpublished writers. Magazine covering gaming and coin-operated machines; published 10 times/year. Slot machines; trade stimulators; jukeboxes; gumball and peanut vendors; pinballs; scales, etc. "Our audience is predominantly male. Readers are all collectors or enthusiasts of coin-operated machines, particularly slot machines and jukeboxes. Subscribers are, in general, not heavy readers." Circ. 3,000. **Pays on acceptance.** Publishes ms an average of 2-3 months after acceptance. Byline given. Prefers to buy all rights, but also buys first and reprint rights. "We may allow author to reprint upon request in noncompetitive publications." Previously published submissions must be accompanied by complete list of previous sales, including sale dates. Query for electronic submissions. Reports in 1 month on queries; 6 weeks on mss. Sample copy $1.50; writer's guidelines for #10 SASE.
Nonfiction: Historical/nostalgic, how-to, interview/profile, opinion, personal experience, photo feature and technical. "Articles illustrated with clear, black and white photos are always considered much more favorably than articles without photos (we have a picture-oriented audience). The writer must be knowledgeable about subject matter because our readers are knowledgeable and will spot inaccuracies." Buys up to 50 mss/year. Length: 900-6,000 words; 3,500-12,000 for cover stories. Pays $100 maximum, inside stories; $200 maximum, cover (feature) stories.
Photos: "Captions should tell a complete story without reference to the body text." Send photos with ms. Reviews 8 × 10 and 5 × 7 b&w glossy prints. Captions required. "Purchase price for articles includes payment for photos."
Fiction: "All fiction must have a gambling/coin-operated-machine angle. Very low emphasis is placed on fiction. Fiction must be exceptional to be acceptable to our readers." Buys maximum 4 mss/year. Send complete ms. Length: 800-2,500 words. Pays $60 maximum.

LOST TREASURE, P.O. Box 1589, Grove OK 74344. Managing Editor: Deborah Williams. 95% freelance written. Monthly magazine for treasure hunting hobbyists, relic collectors, amateur prospectors and miners. Estab. 1966. Circ. 55,000. Buys all rights. Byline given. Buys 100 mss/year. Pays on publication. No simultaneous submissions. Reports in 2 months. Submit complete ms. Sample copy and writer's guidelines for 9 × 12 SASE.
Nonfiction: How-to articles about treasure hunting, coinshooting, personal profiles, and stories about actual hunts, stories that give an unusual twist to treasure hunting—using detectors in an unorthodox way, odd sidelights on history, unusual finds. *Avoid* writing about the more famous treasures and lost mines. No bottle hunting stories. Length: 1,000-2,000 words. "If an article is well-written and covers its subject well, we'll buy it—regardless of length." Pays 4¢/word.
Photos: B&w glossy prints with mss help sell your story. Pays $5 for each photo published. Cover photos pay $100 each (35mm color slides). Captions required.
Tips: "Read *Lost Treasure* before submitting your stories. We are especially interested in stories that deal with the more unusual aspects of treasure hunting and metal detecting. Try to avoid the obvious—give something different. Good photos and graphics are a *must*."

‡**MAINLINE MODELER & N-SCALE**, Hundman Publishing, 5115 Monticello Dr., Edmonds WA 98020. (206)743-2607. FAX: (206)743-2607 (call first). Editor: Robert L. Hundman. 80% freelance written. Monthly magazines on railroad history and modeling. "Must have accurate information on the history of railroads or details on modeling techniques." Estab. 1979. Circ. 14,000 for each magazine. Pays within 1 month after publication. Byline given. Buys all rights. Submit seasonal/holiday material 3-6 months in advance. No simultaneous submissions.
Nonfiction: Historical/nostalgic, how-to, interview/profile, personal experience, photo feature and technical. Buys 250 mss/year. Send complete ms. Length: 500-6,000 words. Pays $100-600.
Photos: Send photos or photocopies with submission. Captions, model releases and identification of subjects required.

MANUSCRIPTS, The Manuscript Society, Department of History, University of South Carolina, Columbia SC 29208. (803)777-6525. Editor: David R. Chesnutt. 10% freelance written. A quarterly magazine for collectors of autographs and manuscripts. Estab. 1948. Circ. 1,500. **Pays on acceptance.** Publishes ms an average of 6-18 months after acceptance. Byline given. Buys first publication rights. Query for electronic submissions. Reports in 2 weeks on queries; 1 month on mss.
Nonfiction: Historical, personal experience and photo feature. Buys 4-6 mss/year. Query. Length: 1,500-3,000 words. Pays $50-250 for unsolicited articles. Sample copy for 6½ × 9½ SAE and 5 first class stamps.
Photos: State availability of photos with submission. Reviews contact sheets and prints. Offers $15-30/photo. Captions and identification of subjects required. Buys one-time rights.
Tips: "The Society is a mix of autograph collectors, dealers and scholars who are interested in manuscripts. Good illustrations of manuscript material are essential. Unusual documents are most often the basis of articles. Scholarly apparatus may be used but is not required. Articles about significant

collections of documents (or unusual collections) would be welcomed. Please query first."

‡MINIATURE QUILTS, Chitra Publications, 301 Church St., Box 437, New Milford PA 18834. (717)465-3306. FAX: (717)465-7187. Editor: Patti Bachelder. 40% freelance written. Quarterly magazine on miniature quilts. "We seek patterns and articles of an instructional nature (all techniques), profiles of talented quiltmakers and informational articles on all aspects of miniature quilts. Miniatures defined as quilts made up of blocks smaller than five inches." Estab. 1990. Circ. 50,000. Pays on publication. Publishes ms an average of 6 months after acceptance. Byline given. Buys second serial (reprint) rights. Submit seasonal/holiday material 6-8 months in advance. Query for electronic submissions. Reports in 2 months on queries and mss. Free sample copy and writer's guidelines.

Columns/Departments: A Quilter's Dollhouse (patterns to scale). Loving Stitches (how-to for beginners, currently written by one writer). Book and product reviews (focused on miniature quilts, currently written by one writer). Length: 800-1,600 words.

Photos: Send photos with submission. Reviews transparencies. Offers $20 per photo. Captions, model releases and identification of subjects required. Buys all rights.

Tips: "Publication hinges on good photo quality. Query with ideas; send samples of prior work."

MINIATURES SHOWCASE, Kalmbach Publishing Co., 21027 Crossroads Circle, Waukesha WI 53186. Editor: Geraldine Willems. 65% freelance written. A quarterly magazine about dollhouse miniatures. "We feature a different decorating theme each issue—our articles support the miniature room scene we focus on." Circ. 48,000. Pays on publication. Publishes ms an average of 3 months after acceptance. Byline given. Buys all rights. Submit seasonal/holiday material 4 months in advance. Query for electronic submissions. Reports in 1 month. Sample copy $3; writer's guidelines for SASE.

Nonfiction: Historical/social. Buys 12 mss/year. Query. Length: 100-1,500 words. Pays 10¢/word.

Photos: State availability of photos with submission. Reviews contact sheets, negatives, transparencies and 4-color prints only. Offers no additional payment for photos accepted with ms. Captions and identification of subjects required.

Tips: "Our articles are all assigned—a freelancer should query before sending in anything. Our features are open to freelancers—each issue deals with a different topic, often historical."

MODERN GOLD MINER AND TREASURE HUNTER, Modern Gold Miner's Association, Inc., 114 Druey Rd., P.O. Box 47, Happy Camp CA 96039. (916)493-2062. FAX: (916)493-2095. Editor: Maria McCracken. Managing Editor: David McCracken. Bimonthly magazine on small-scale gold mining and treasure hunting. "We want interesting fact and fiction stories and articles about small-scale mining, treasure hunting, camping and the great outdoors." Estab. 1987. Circ. 50,000. Pays on publication. Buys all rights. Submit seasonal/holiday material 4 months in advance. Query for electronic submissions. Reports in 2 weeks on queries. Sample copy for 9×12 SAE with $1.35 postage. Free writer's guidelines.

Nonfiction: How-to, humor, inspirational, interview/profile, new product, personal experience, photo feature, travel. "No promotional articles concerning industry products." Buys 125 mss/year. Send complete ms. Length: 1,500-2,500 words. Pays $25-150.

Photos: Send photos with submission. Reviews any size transparencies and prints. Pays $10-50 per photo. Captions are required. Buys all rights.

Fiction: Adventure, experimental, fantasy, historical, horror, humorous, mystery, suspense, western.

Tips: "Our general readership is comprised mostly of individuals who are actively involved in gold mining and treasure hunting, or people who are interested in reading about others who are active and successful in the field. True stories of actual discoveries, along with good color photos—particularly of gold—are preferred. Also, valuable how-to information on new and workable field techniques, preferably accompanied by supporting illustrations and/or photos."

MOUNTAIN STATES COLLECTOR, Spree Publishing, P.O. Box 2525, Evergreen CO 80439. FAX: (303)674-1253. Editor: Carol Rudolph. Managing Editor: Peg DeStefano. 85% freelance written. A monthly tabloid covering antiques and collectibles. Estab. 1970. Circ. 8,000. Pays on publication. Publishes ms an average of 3-6 months after acceptance. Byline given. Not copyrighted. Buys first rights, one-time rights or second serial (reprint) rights to material published elsewhere. Submit seasonal/holiday material at least 3 months in advance. Simultaneous and previously published submissions OK. Reports in 10 weeks. Sample copy for 9×12 SAE with 4 first class stamps; writer's guidelines for SASE.

Nonfiction: About antiques and/or collectibles—book excerpts, historical/nostalgic, how-to (collect), interview/profile (of collectors) and photo feature. Buys 75 mss/year. Query with or without published clips, or send complete ms. Length: 500-1,500 words. Pays $15. Sometimes pays the expenses of writers on assignment (mileage, phone—not long distance travel).

Photos: Send photos with submission. Reviews contact sheets, and 5×7 b&w prints. Offers $5/photo used. Captions preferred. Buys one-time rights.

Tips: "Writers should know their topics well or be prepared to do in-depth interviews with collectors. We prefer a down-home approach. We need articles on antiques, collectors and collections; how-to articles on collecting; how a collector can get started; or clubs for collectors. We would like to see more articles with high-quality b&w photos."

THE NEW YORK ANTIQUE ALMANAC, The New York Eye Publishing Co., Inc., Box 335, Lawrence NY 11559. (516)371-3300. Editor-in-Chief: Carol Nadel. Tabloid published 10 times/year. Emphasizes antiques, art, investments and nostalgia. 20% freelance written. Circ. 62,000. Pays on publication. Buys all rights. Byline given. Phone queries OK. Previously published submissions OK but must advise. Reports in 6 weeks. Publishes ms an average of 6 months after acceptance. Free sample copy.

Nonfiction: Humor only. Buys 1 ms/issue. Query or submit complete ms. Length: 3,000 words maximum. Pays $15-75.

THE NUMISMATIST, American Numismatic Association, 818 N. Cascade Ave., Colorado Springs CO 80903-3279. (719)632-2646. FAX: (719)634-4085. Editor: Barbara Gregory. Monthly magazine "for collectors of coins, medals, tokens and paper money." Estab. 1888. Circ. 31,000. Pays on publication. Publishes ms an average of 1 year after acceptance. Byline given. Buys first North American serial rights or second serial (reprint) rights. Submit seasonal/holiday material 1 year in advance. Previously published submissions OK. Reports in 2 months. Free sample copy and writer's guidelines for 9×11″ envelope and $1.40 postage.

Nonfiction: Essays, exposé, general interest, historical/nostalgic, humor, interview/profile, new product, opinion, personal experience, photo feature and technical. No articles that are lengthy or non-numismatic. Buys 48-60 mss/year. Send complete ms. Length: 1,000-3,500 words. Pays "on rate-per-published-page basis." Sometimes pays the expenses of writers on assignment.

Photos: Send b&w photos with submission. Reviews contact sheets and 4×5 or 5×7 prints. Offers $2.50-5/photo. Captions and identification of subjects required. Buys one-time rights.

Columns/Departments: Buys 6 mss/year. Length: 775-2,000 words. "Pays negotiable flat fee per column."

NUTSHELL NEWS, For creators and collectors of scale miniatures, Kalmbach Publishing Co., 21027 Crossroads Circle, Waukesha WI 53187. (414)796-8776. Editor: Sybil Harp. 50% freelance written. Monthly magazine covering dollhouse scale miniatures. *Nutshell News* is aimed at serious, adult hobbyists. Our readers take their miniatures seriously and do not regard them as toys. "We avoid 'cutesiness' and treat our subject as a serious art form and/or an engaging leisure interest." Estab. 1971. Circ. 35,000. **Pays on acceptance.** Byline given. Offers $25 kill fee. Buys all rights but will revert rights by agreement. Submit seasonal/holiday material 1 year in advance. Reports in 3 weeks on queries; 2 months on mss. Sample copy $3.50; writer's guidelines.

Nonfiction: How-to miniature projects in 1″, ½″, ¼″ scales, interview/profile—artisans or collectors, photo feature—dollhouses, collections, museums. Annual special issues: May—smaller scales annual (½″, ¼″ or smaller scales); August—kitcrafting—customizing kits or commercial miniatures, a how-to issue. No articles on miniature shops or essays. Buys 120 mss/year. Query. Length: 1,000-2,000 words. Pays 10-12¢/word for assigned articles; 10¢/word for unsolicited articles. Sometimes pays expenses of writers on assignment.

Photos: Send photos with submission. Requires 35mm slides and larger, 3×5 prints. Pay $10-50. Captions preferred; identification of subjects required. Buys all rights.

Tips: "It is essential that writers for *Nutshell News* be active miniaturists, or at least very knowledgeable about the hobby. Our readership is intensely interested in miniatures and will discern lack of knowledge or enthusiasm on the part of an author. A writer can best break in to *Nutshell News* by convincing me that he/she knows and is interested in miniatures, and by sending photos and/or clippings to substantiate that. Photographs are extremely important. They must be sharp and properly exposed to reveal details. A writer must convince me that he/she can provide good photos. For articles about subjects in the Chicago/Milwaukee area, we can usually send our staff photographer."

OLD CARS NEWS & MARKETPLACE, (formerly *Old Cars Weekly*), Krause Publications, 700 E. State St., Iola WI 54990. (715)445-2214. FAX: (715)445-4087. Editor: Brad Bowling. 50% freelance written. Weekly tabloid. Estab. 1952. Circ. 80,000. Pays on publication. Publishes ms an average of 2 months after acceptance. Buys all rights. Phone queries OK. Byline given. Reports in 2 weeks. Free sample copy and writer's guidelines.

Nonfiction: Short (2-3 pages) timely news reports and features on old car hobby with photos. Buys 5-10 mss/issue. Query. Pays 3¢/word.

Photos: Pays $5 for 5×7 b&w glossy prints. Captions required. Buys all rights.

Tips: "We purchase both news and feature articles, especially interesting stories from our readers who own old cars. Will accept articles on cars, trucks, buses, toys and pedal cars, 1975 model year and older."

PAPER COLLECTORS MARKETPLACE, Watson Graphic Designs, Inc., P.O. Box 128, Scandinavia WI 54977-0128. (715)467-2379. Editor: Doug Watson. 100% freelance written. A monthly magazine on paper collectibles. "All articles must relate to the hobby in some form. Whenever possible values should be given for the collectibles mentioned in the article." Estab. 1983. Circ. 4,000. Pays on publication. Byline given. Offers 25% kill fee on commissioned articles. Buys first North American serial rights. Submit seasonal/holiday material 2 months in advance. Reports in 2 weeks. Free sample copy; writer's guidelines for #10 SASE.

Nonfiction: Historical/nostalgic, how-to, photo feature, technical. Buys 60 mss/year. Query with published clips. Length: 1,000-2,000 words. Pays 3-5¢/words.

Photos: Send photos with submissions. Offers no additional payment for photos accepted with ms. Captions, model releases and identification of subjects required. Buys one-time rights.

Tips: "We presently publish three special issues per year: February (December 1 deadline) Mystery/Detective; April (Feb. 1 deadline), Spring Postcard Special; Oct. (Aug. 1 deadline), Fall Postcard Special."

THE PEN AND QUILL, Universal Autograph Collectors Club (UACC), P.O. Box 6181, Washington DC 20044-6181. (202)332-7388. Editor: Bob Erickson. 20% freelance written. Bimonthly magazine of autograph collecting. All articles must advance the hobby of autograph collecting in some manner. Estab. 1966. Circ. 1,700. Pays on publication. Publishes ms an average of 6 months after acceptance. Byline given. Buys first North American serial rights. Submit seasonal/holiday material 4 months in advance. Sample copy $3.50.

Nonfiction: General interest, historical/nostalgic, interview/profile. Buys 4 mss/year. Send complete ms. Length: 500-2,500 words. Pays $20-100.

Photos: Send photos with submission. Offers no additional payment for photos accepted with ms. Captions and identification of subjects required. Buys one-time rights.

POPULAR ELECTRONICS, (formerly *Hands-On-Electronics*), Gernsback Publications, Inc., 500B Bi-County Blvd., Farmingdale NY 11735. (516)293-3000. Editor: Carl Laron. 100% freelance written. Monthly magazine covering hobby electronics—"features, projects, ideas related to audio, CB, radio, experimenting, test equipment, antique radio, communications, state-of-the-art, etc." Circ. 87,877. **Pays on acceptance.** Byline given. Buys all rights. Submit seasonal/holiday material 6 months in advance. Query for electronic submissions. Reports in 2 weeks. Free sample copy, "include label." Writer's guidelines for SASE.

Nonfiction: General interest, how-to, photo feature and technical. Buys 200 mss/year. Query or send complete ms. Length: 1,000-3,500 words. Pays $100-350.

Photos: Send photos with submission. "Wants b&w glossy photos." Offers no additional payment for photos accepted with ms. Captions required. Buys all rights.

Tips: "All areas are open to freelancers. Project-type articles and other 'how-to' articles have best success."

‡**POPULAR ELECTRONICS HOBBYIST'S HANDBOOK**, Gernsback Publications, Inc., 500 B Bi-County Blvd., Farmingdale NY 11735. (516)293-3000. Editor: Carl Laron. 100% freelance written. Annual magazine on hobby electronics. Estab. 1989. Circ. 125,000. **Pays on acceptance.** Byline given. Buys all rights. Submit seasonal/holiday material 5-6 months in advance. Query for electronic submissions. Reports in 2 weeks. Free sample copy and writer's guidelines.

Nonfiction: General interest, historical/nostalgic, how-to (build projects, fix consumer products, etc., all of which must "have a wire in it!"), photo feature and technical. "No product reviews!" Buys 5-6 mss/year. Send complete ms. Length: 1,000-5,000 words. Pays $100-500 for assigned articles; $100-400 for unsolicited articles. Sometimes pays expenses of writers on assignment.

Photos: Send photos with submission. "We want b&w glossy photos." Reviews 5×7 or 8×10 b&w prints. Offers no additional payment for photos accepted with ms. Captions and model releases are required. Buys all rights.

Tips: "Read the magazine. Know and understand the subject matter. Write it. Submit it."

‡**POPULAR MECHANICS**, Hearst Corp., 224 W. 57th St., 3rd Floor, New York NY 10019. (212)649-2000. Editor: Joe Oldham. Managing Editor: Deborah Frank. 50% freelance written. Monthly magazine on automotive, home improvement, science, boating, outdoors, electronics. "We are a men's

service magazine that tries to address the diverse interests of today's male, providing him with information to improve the way he lives. We cover stories from do-it-yourself projects to technological advances in aerospace, military, automotive and so on." Estab. 1902. Circ. 1.6 million. **Pays on acceptance.** Publishes ms an average of 6 months after acceptance. Byline given. Offers 25% kill fee. Buys all rights. Submit seasonal/holiday material 6 months in advance. Query for electronic submissions. Reports in 2 weeks on queries; 1 month on mss. Free sample copy and writer's guidelines.

Nonfiction: General interest; how-to (shop projects, car fix-its); new product; technical. Special issues: January, Design and Engineering Awards. February, Boating Guide. April, Home Improvement Guide. May, Car Care Guide. October, Automotive Parts & Accessories Guide. November, Woodworking Guide. No historical, editorial or critique pieces. Buys 24 mss/year. Query with or without published clips or send complete ms. Length: 500-3,000 words. Pays $500-1,500 maximum for assigned articles; $15-1,000 for unsolicited articles. Sometimes pays expenses of writers on assignment.

Photos: Send photos with submission. Reviews 5×7 transparencies and prints. Offers no additional payment for photos accepted with ms. Captions, model releases and identification of subjects required. Buys first and exclusive publication rights in the U.S. during on-sale period of issue in which photos appear plus 90 days after.

Columns/Departments: New Cars (latest and hottest cars out of Detroit and Europe); Car Care (Maintenance basics; How It Works; Fix-Its; New products. Send to Tony Swan. Electronics; Audio; Home Video; Computers; Photography; send to Frank Vizard. Boating (new equipment, how-tos, fishing tips); Outdoors (gear, vehicles, outdoor adventures); send to Joe Skorupa. Home & Shop Journal; send to Steve Willson. Science (latest developments); Tech Update (breakthroughs); and Aviation (sport aviation, homebuilt aircraft, new commercial aircraft, civil aeronautics); send to Abe Dane. All columns are about 1,000 words.

Tips: "We have a hotline set up between 3 and 5 p.m. Eastern time, every Wednesday, so readers may speak directly to the editors. The phone numbers of each editor for these specific hours only are published in every issue. Freelancers should contact the editor of the department they are interested in writing for and propose any ideas directly to that editor. Tech Update is most accessible to freelancers. Any articles about the newest discoveries or technological advancements are accepted. The best places to find such information are colleges and universities, research and developments departments at various companies and manufacturers."

POSTCARD COLLECTOR, Joe Jones Publishing, P.O. Box 337, Iola WI 54945. (715)445-5000. FAX: (715)445-4053. Editor: Deb Lengkeek. 70% freelance written. Monthly magazine. "Publication is for postcard collectors; all editorial content relates to postcards in some way." Estab. 1986. Circ. 6,000. Pays on publication. Publishes ms an average of 6 months after acceptance. Byline given. Buys one-time rights, first rights or second serial rights. Submit seasonal/holiday material 3 months in advance. Previously published submissions OK. Reports in 2 weeks on queries; 1 month on mss. Free sample copy and writer's guidelines.

Nonfiction: General interest, historical/nostalgic, how-to (e.g. preservatives), new product, opinion, personal experience, photo feature and travel. Buys 60 mss/year. Send complete ms. Length: 200-1,800 words. Pays 5-8¢/word for assigned articles; 3-5¢/word for unsolicited articles.

Photos: State availability of postcards with submission. Offers $1-3/photo. Captions and identification of subjects required. Buys perpetual, but nonexclusive rights.

Columns/Departments: 50-150 words. Buys 60 mss/year. Query. Pay is negotiable.

Tips: "We publish information about postcards written by expert topical specialists. The writer must be knowledgeable about postcards and have acquired 'expert' information. We plan more complete listings of postcard sets and series—old and new." Areas most open to freelancers are feature-length articles on specialized areas (600-1,800 words) with 1 to 10 illustrations.

THE PROFESSIONAL QUILTER, Oliver Press, P.O. Box 75277, St. Paul MN 55175-0277. (612)426-9681. Editor: Jeannie M. Spears. 80% freelance written. Works with a small number of new/unpublished writers each year. Quarterly magazine on the quilting business. Emphasis on small business, preferably quilt related. Estab. 1983. Circ. 2,000. Payment negotiated. Publishes ms an average of 6 months after acceptance. Byline given. Buys first North American serial rights, first serial rights and second serial (reprint) rights. Simultaneous queries and previously published submissions OK. Reports in 2 weeks on queries; 1 month on mss. Sample copy for 9×12 SAE with 4 first class stamps and $5; writer's guidelines for #10 SASE.

Nonfiction: How-to (quilting business); interview/profile; new product; opinion; and personal experience (of problems and problem-solving ideas in a quilting business). No quilting or sewing *techniques* or quilt photo spreads. Buys 20 mss/year. Query or send complete ms. Length: 500-1,500 words. Pays $25-75.

Tips: "Each issue will focus in depth on an issue of concern to the professional quilting community, such as ethics, art vs. craft, professionalism, etc. We would also like to receive articles on time and space (studio) organization, stress and family relationships. Remember that our readers already know that quilting is a time-honored tradition passed down from generation to generation, that quilts reflect the life of the maker, that quilt patterns have revealing names, etc. Ask yourself: If my grandmother had been running a quilting business for the last 5 years, would she have found this article interesting? Send a letter describing your quilt, craft or business experience with a query or manuscript."

QST, American Radio Relay League, Inc., 225 Main St., Newington CT 06111. (203)666-1541. FAX: (203)665-7531. Editor: Paul L. Rinaldo. Managing Editor: Mark Wilson. 20% freelance written. Monthly magazine covering amateur radio, general interest, technical activities. "Ours are topics of interest to radio amateurs and persons in the electrical and communications fields." Estab. 1914. Circ. 160,000. Pays on publication. Publishes ms an average of 4 months after acceptance. Byline given. Buys all rights. Submit seasonal/holiday material 4-5 months in advance. Query for electronic submissions. Reports in 3 weeks on queries. Free sample copy and writer's guidelines.

Nonfiction: General interest, how-to, humor, new products, personal experience, photo feature, technical (anything to do with amateur radio). Buys 50 mss/year. Query with or without published clips, or send complete ms. Length: no minimum or maximum. Pays $50 per published page. Sometimes pays expenses of writers on assignment.

Photos: Send photos with submission. Offers no additional payment for photos accepted with ms. Captions, model releases and identification of subjects required. Buys all rights.

Columns/Departments: Hints and Kinks (hints/time saving procedures/circuits/associated with amateur radio), 50-200 words. Buys 100 mss/year. Send complete ms. Length: 50-200 words. Pays $20.

Tips: "Write with an idea, ask for sample copy and writer's guide. Technical and general interest to amateur operators, communications and electronics are most open."

QUICK & EASY CRAFTS, For Today's Crafty Women, House of White Birches, 306 E. Parr Rd., Berne IN 46711. (219)589-8741. FAX: (219)589-8093. Editor: Beth Schwartz. Managing Editor: Läna Schurb. 90% freelance written. Bimonthly magazine covering crafts that are upscale but easily and quickly done. "Our audience does not mind spending money on craft items to use in their projects but they don't have lots of time to spend." Estab. 1979. Circ. 90,000. Pays on publication. Byline given. Buys first, one-time or all rights. Submit seasonal/holiday material 1 year in advance. Reports in 2 weeks on queries. Sample copy $2; free writer's guidelines.

Nonfiction: How-to. Upcoming special issue for Christmas. No profiles of other crafters. Buys 150 mss/year. Send complete ms. Pays $25-250.

Tips: "Send good, clear photo with ms. Ms should include complete instructions for project."

QUILT WORLD, House of White Birches, 306 E. Parr Rd., Berne IN 46711. (219)589-8741. Editor: Sandra L. Hatch. 100% freelance written. Works with a small number of new/unpublished writers each year. Bimonthly magazine covering quilting. "We publish articles on quilting techniques, profile of quilters and coverage of quilt shows. Reader is 30-70 years old, midwestern." Circ. 130,000. Pays on publication. Publishes ms an average of 6 months after acceptance. Byline given. Buys all rights, first rights, one-time rights and second serial (reprint) rights. Submit seasonal/holiday material 9 months in advance. Previously published submissions OK. Query for electronic submissions. Reports in 3 weeks. Sample copy $3; writer's guidelines for SASE.

Nonfiction: How-to, interview/profile (quilters), technical, new product (quilt products) and photo feature. Buys 18-24 mss/year. Query. Length: open. Pays $35-100.

Photo: Send photos with submission. Reviews transparencies and prints. Offers $15/photo (except covers). Identification of subjects required. Buys all rights or one-time rights.

Tips: "Send list of previous articles published with resume and a SASE. List ideas which you plan to base your articles around."

QUILTER'S NEWSLETTER MAGAZINE, P.O. Box 394, Wheatridge CO 80033. FAX: (303)420-7358. Editor: Bonnie Leman. Monthly. Estab. 1969. Circ. 200,000. Buys first North American serial rights or second rights. Buys about 15 mss/year. Pays on publication, sometimes on acceptance. Reports in 5 weeks. Free sample copy.

Nonfiction: "We are interested in articles on the subject of quilts and quiltmakers *only*. We are not interested in anything relating to 'Grandma's Scrap Quilts' but could use fresh material." Submit complete ms. Pays 5¢/word minimum, usually more.

Photos: Additional payment for photos depends on quality.

Fillers: Related to quilts and quiltmakers only.

Tips: "Be specific, brief, and professional in tone. Study our magazine to learn the kind of thing we like. Send us material which fits into our format but which is different enough to be interesting. Realize that we think we're the best quilt magazine on the market and that we're aspiring to be even better, then send us the cream off the top of your quilt material."

QUILTING INTERNATIONAL, All American Crafts, Inc., 70 Sparta Ave., CN 1003, Sparta NJ 07871. (201)729-4477. FAX: (201)729-5426. Editorial Director: Camille Pomaco. Editor: Mitzi Roberts. 50% freelance written. Quilts and quilting magazine published 6 times/year. "We try to offer both inspirational and instructive material for every level of quilter." Estab. 1987. Pays on publication. Publishes ms an average of 4-6 months after acceptance. Byline given. Buys first North American serial rights or all rights. Submit seasonal/holiday material 6 months in advance. Reports in 1 month on queries; 2 months on mss. Sample copy for 9×12 SAE with $1.25 postage. Free writer's guidelines for SASE.
Nonfiction: Quilts and patterns; quilt exhibits, international and local quilt events, historical, how-to, humor, inspirational, interview/profile, new product, opinion, personal experience, photo feature, technical, travel (all as related to quilts and quilting). Buys 20 or more mss/year. Send complete ms. Length: 800-1500 words. Pays 7-10¢/word.
Photos: Send photos with submission. Reviews 4×5 transparencies or slides. Pays $15 and up. Model releases and identification of subjects required. Buys one-time rights and all rights.
Columns/Departments: Quickie (a fast project using some facet of quilting); Small Treasures (portable project). "Always open to innovative subjects for new columns. Send complete ms or directions with templates for projects."
Poetry: Buys 5 poems/year. Submit maximum 4 poems. Length: 4-30 lines. Pays $5-15.
Fillers: Anecdotes, gags to be illustrated by cartoonist, short humor. Buys 6-12/year. Length: 100-300 words. Pays 10¢/word.
Tips: "Good quality slides or chromes of beautiful quilts are highly desirable. We want articles about specific quilts and the quilters involved."

‡QUILTING TODAY MAGAZINE, The International Quilt Magazine, Chitra Publications, 301 Church St., P.O. Box 437, New Milford PA 18834. (717)465-3306. FAX: (717)465-7187. Editor: Patti Bachelder. 80% freelance written. Bimonthly magazine on quilting, traditional and contemporary. "We seek articles that will cover one or two full pages (800 words each); informative to the general quilting public, present new ideas, interviews, instructional, etc." Estab. 1986. Circ. 90,000. Pays on publication. Publishes ms an average of 6 months after acceptance. Byline given. Buys second serial (reprint) rights and makes work-for-hire assignments. Submit seasonal/holiday material 6-8 months in advance. Query for electronic submissions. Reports in 1 month on queries; 2 months on mss. Free sample copy and writer's guidelines.
Nonfiction: Books excerpts, essays, how-to (for various quilting techniques), humor, interview/profile, new product, opinion, personal experience and photo feature. "No articles about family history related to a quilt or quilts unless the quilt is a masterpiece of color and design, impeccable workmanship." Buys 20-30 mss/year. Query with or without published clips, or send complete mss. Length: 800-1,600 words. Pays $50-75/page. Sometimes pays expenses of writers on assignment.
Photos: Send photos with submission. Reviews 35mm slides and larger transparencies. Offers $20 per photo. Captions, identification of subjects required. Buys all rights unless rented from a museum.
Columns/Departments: Book and product reviews, 300 words maximum. Quilters Lesson Book (instructional), 800-1,600 words. Buys 10-12 ms/year. Send complete ms. Pays up to $75/column.
Fiction: Fantasy, historical and humorous. Buys 1 mss/year. Send complete ms. Length: 300-1,600 words. Pays $50-75/page.
Tips: "Query with ideas; send samples of prior work so that we can assess and suggest assignment. Our publications appeal to traditional quilters (generally middle-aged) who use the patterns in each issue. Must have excellent photos."

RADIO-ELECTRONICS, Gernsback Publicaitons, Inc., 500 B Bi-County Blvd., Farmingdale NY 11735. (516)293-3000. Editor: Brian C. Fenton. 75% freelance written. Monthly magazine on electronics technology. "*Radio-Electronics* presents features on electronics technology and electronics construction." Estab. 1948. Circ. 185,026. **Pays on acceptance.** Publishes ms an average of 4 months after acceptance. Byline given. Buys all rights. Submit seasonal/holiday material 5-6 months in advance. Simultaneous submissions OK. Query for electronic submissions. Reports in 2 months on queries; 4 months on mss. Free sample copy and writer's guidelines.
Nonfiction: How-to (electronic project construction), humor (cartoons) and new product. Buys 150-200 mss/year. Send complete ms. Length: 1,000-10,000 words. Pays $200-800 for assigned articles; $100-800 for unsolicited articles.
Photos: Send photos with submission. Offers no additional payment for photos accepted with ms. Captions, model releases and identification of subjects required. Buys all rights.

RAILROAD MODEL CRAFTSMAN, Box 700, Newton NJ 07860. (201)383-3355. FAX: (201)383-4064. Editor: William C. Schaumburg. 75% freelance written. Works with a small number of new/unpublished writers each year. For model railroad hobbyists, in all scales and gauges. Monthly. Circ. 97,000. Buys all rights. Buys 50-100 mss/year. Pays on publication. Publishes ms an average of 9 months after acceptance. Submit seasonal material 6 months in advance. Sample copy $2; writer's and photographer's guidelines for SASE.

Nonfiction: "How-to and descriptive model railroad features written by persons who did the work are preferred. Almost all our features and articles are written by active model railroaders. It is difficult for non-modelers to know how to approach writing for this field." Pays minimum of $1.75/column inch of copy ($50/page).

Photos: Purchased with or without mss. Buys sharp 8×10 glossy prints and 35mm or larger transparencies. Pays minimum of $10 for photos or $2/diagonal inch of published b&w photos, $3 for color transparencies and $100 for covers, which must tie in with article in that issue. Caption information required.

Tips: "We would like to emphasize freight car modeling based on actual prototypes, as well as major prototype studies of them."

SCOTT STAMP MONTHLY, P.O. Box 828, Sidney OH 45365. (513)498-0802. FAX: (513)498-0808. Editor: Richard L. Sine. 60% freelance written. Works with a small number of new/unpublished writers each year. For stamp collectors, from the beginner to the sophisticated philatelist. Monthly magazine. Estab. 1873. Circ. 22,000. Rights purchased vary with author and material; usually buys first North American serial rights. Byline given. Buys 96 unsolicited mss/year. Pays on publication. Publishes ms an average of 5 months after acceptance. Submit seasonal or holiday material at least 6 months in advance. Query for electronic submissions. Reports in 1 month. Sample copy for $1.50.

Nonfiction: "We are in the market for articles, written in an engaging fashion, concerning the remote byways and often-overlooked aspects of stamp collecting. Writing should be clear and concise, and subjects must be well-researched and documented. Illustrative material should also accompany articles whenever possible." Query. Pays about $100.

Photos: State availability of photos. Offers no additional payment for b&w photos used with mss.

Tips: "It's rewarding to find a good new writer with good new material. Because our emphasis is on lively, interesting articles about stamps, including historical perspectives and human interest slants, we are open to writers who can produce the same. Of course, if you are an experienced philatelist, so much the better. We do not want stories about the picture on a stamp taken from a history book or an encyclopedia and dressed up to look like research. If an idea is good and not a basic rehash, we are interested."

SEW NEWS, The Fashion Magazine for People Who Sew, PJS Publications, Inc., News Plaza, P.O. Box 1790, Peoria IL 61656. (309)682-6626. FAX: (309)682-7394. Editor: Linda Turner Griepentrog. 90% freelance written. Works with a small number of new/unpublished writers each year. Monthly magazine covering fashion-sewing. "Our magazine is for the beginning home sewer to the professional dressmaker. It expresses the fun, creativity and excitement of sewing." Estab. 1980. Circ. 230,000. **Pays on acceptance.** Publishes ms an average of 6 months after acceptance. Byline given. Buys all rights. Submit seasonal/holiday material 6 months in advance. Reports in 2 months. Sample copy $3; writer's guidelines for #10 SAE and 2 first class stamps.

Nonfiction: How-to (sewing techniques) and interview/profile (interesting personalities in home-sewing field). Buys 200-240 ms/year. Query with published clips. Length: 500-2,000 words. Pays $25-400. Rarely pays expenses of writers on assignment.

Photos: State availability of photos. Prefers b&w contact sheets and negatives. Payment included in ms price. Identification of subjects required. Buys all rights.

Tips: "Query first with writing sample. Areas most open to freelancers are how-to and sewing techniques; give explicit, step-by-step instructions plus rough art."

SHUTTLE SPINDLE & DYEPOT, Handweavers Guild of America, 120 Mountain Road, Bloomfield CT 06002. (203)243-3982. Editors: Bobbie Miller and Sandy Bowles. 60% freelance written. A quarterly magazine covering handweaving, spinning and dyeing. "We take the practical and aesthetic approach to handweaving, handspinning, and related textile arts." Estab. 1969. Pays on publication. Publishes ms 4-15 months after acceptance. Byline given. Buys first North American serial rights. Submit seasonal/holiday material 1 year in advance. Rarely accepts previously published submissions. Reports in 1 month on queries; 2 months on mss. Sample copy $6.50; free writer's guidelines.

Nonfiction: How-to, interview/profile, personal experience, photo feature and technical. "We want interesting, practical, technical information in our field." Buys 30 mss/year. Query with or without published clips, or send complete ms. Length: 500-1,500 words. Pays $25-100.

Photos: Send photos or state availability of photos with submission. Reviews contact sheets and transparencies.

Tips: "We read all submissions, especially from weavers and weaving teachers."

‡SPIN-OFF, Interweave Press, 306 N. Washington, Loveland CO 80537. (303)669-7672. Editor: Deborah Robson. 10-20% freelance written. Quarterly magazine covering handspinning, dyeing, techniques and projects for using handspun fibers. Audience includes "practicing textile/fiber craftsworkers. Article should show considerable depth of knowledge of subject, although the tone should be informal and accessible." Circ. 10,000. Pays on publication. Publishes ms an average of 6-12 months after acceptance. Byline given. Buys first North American serial rights. Simultaneous queries and photocopied submissions OK. Sample copy $4.50 and 8½×11 SAE; free writer's guidelines for #10 SAE and 2 ounces' worth of postage.

Nonfiction: Historical and how-to (on spinning; knitted, crocheted, woven projects from handspun fibers with instructions); interview/profile (of successful and/or interesting fiber workers); and technical (on spinning, dyeing or fiber technology, use, properties). "All articles must contain a high level of in-depth information. Our readers are very knowledgeable about these subjects." Query. Length: 2,000 words. Pays $15-100.

Photos: State availability of photos. Identification of subjects required.

Tips: "You should display an in-depth knowledge of your subject, but you can tailor your article to reach beginning, intermediate or advanced spinners. Try for thoughtful organization, a personal informal style and an article or series segment that is self-contained. New approaches to familiar topics are welcomed."

‡**SPORTS COLLECTORS DIGEST**, Krause Publications, 700 E. State St., Iola WI 54990. (715)445-2214. FAX: (715)445-4087. Editor: Tom Mortenson. 60% freelance written. Eager to work with new/unpublished writers; works with a small number of new/unpublished writers each year. Sports memorabilia magazine published weekly. "We serve collectors of sports memorabilia—baseball cards, yearbooks, programs, autographs, jerseys, bats, balls, books, magazines, ticket stubs, etc." Circ. 52,000. Pays after publication. Publishes ms an average of 3 months after acceptance. Byline given. Buys first North American serial rights only. Submit seasonal/holiday material 3 months in advance. Simultaneous queries and photocopied submissions OK. Reports in 5 weeks on queries; 2 months on mss. Free sample copy; writer's guidelines for #10 SASE.

Nonfiction: General interest (new card issues, research on older sets); historical/nostalgic (old stadiums, old collectibles, etc.); how-to (buy cards, sell cards and other collectibles, display collectibles, ways to get autographs, jerseys and other memorabilia); interview/profile (well-known collectors, ball players—but must focus on collectibles); new product (new card sets) and personal experience ("what I collect and why"-type stories). No sports stories. "We are not competing with *The Sporting News*, *Sports Illustrated* or your daily paper. Sports collectibles only." Buys 200-300 mss/year. Query. Length: 300-3,000 words; prefers 1,000 words. Pays $50-125.

Photos: Unusual collectibles. State availability of photos. Pays $5-15 for b&w prints. Identification of subjects required. Buys all rights.

Columns/Departments: "We have all the columnists we need but welcome ideas for new columns." Buys 100-150 mss/year. Query. Length: 600-3,000 words. Pays $60-80.

Tips: "If you are a collector, you know what collectors are interested in. Write about it. No shallow, puff pieces; our readers are too smart for that. Only well-researched articles about sports memorabilia and collecting. Some sports nostalgia pieces are OK. Write only about the areas you know about."

‡**STAMP COLLECTOR, For People Who Love Philately**, Division of Van Dahl Publications, Capital Cities/ABC, Inc., P.O. Box 10, Albany OR 97321. (503)928-3569. FAX: (503)967-7262. Editor: David M. Schiller, Jr. Managing Editor: Patricia Hainline. 70% freelance written. Weekly tabloid covering philately. "Stamp Collector is dedicated to promoting the growth and enjoyment of philately through the exchange of information and ideas. All shades of opinion are published to provide the widest possible view of the hobby." Estab. 1931. Circ. 18,500. Pays on publication. Byline given. Buys all rights. Submit seasonal/holiday material 1½ months in advance. Query for electronic submissions. Call for details. Reports in 2 weeks. Free sample copy and writer's guidelines upon request. Send SASE with unsolicited mss.

Nonfiction: "No general articles on world history, world geography, lengthy articles about one particular stamp; puzzles, games, quizzes, etc." Buys 500 mss/year. Query. Pays $30-50. Sometimes pays the expenses of writers on assignment. Send photos, stamps, or clear photocopies with submission. Buys all rights.

Columns/Departments: Guest Editorials (guest editorials), 1,000 words. Buys 15 mss/year. Send complete ms. Pays $30.

Tips: "Be a stamp collector or stamp dealer with some specific area of interest and/or expertise. Find a subject (stamps of a particular country, time period, designer, subject matter portrayed, printing method, etc.) that you are interested in and knowledgeable about, and in which our average reader would be interested. Our average reader is well-educated, intelligent, professional with diverse interests in postal services, printing methods, politics, geography, history, anthropology, economics, arts, etc."

SUNSHINE ARTISTS USA, The Voice Of The Nation's Artists and Craftsmen, Sun Country Enterprises, 1700 Sunset Dr., Longwood FL 32750. (407)323-5937. Editor: Joan L. Wahl. Managing Editor: 'Crusty' Sy. A monthly magazine covering art and craft shows in the United States. "We are a top marketing magazine for professional artists, craftspeople and photographers working street and mall shows. We list 10,000 shows a year, critique many of them and publish articles on marketing, selling and improving arts and crafts." Circ. 16,000. Pays on publication. Publishes ms an average of 3 months after acceptance. Byline given. Buys first North American serial rights. Reports in 2 weeks on queries; 6 weeks on manuscripts. Sample copy $2.50.

Nonfiction: "We are interested in articles that relate to artists and craftsmen traveling the circuit. Although we have a permanent staff of 40 writers, we will consider well-written, thoroughly researched articles on successful artists making a living with their work, new ways to market arts and crafts. Attend some art shows. Talk to the exhibitors. Get ideas from them." No how-tos. Buys 20 mss/year. Query. Length: 550-2,000 words. Pays $15-50 for assigned articles.

Photos: State availability of photos with submission. Black & white photos only. Offers no additional payment for photos accepted with ms. Captions, model releases and identification of subjects required.

TEDDY BEAR REVIEW, Collector Communications Corp., 170 Fifth Ave., New York NY 10010. (212)989-8700. Editor: A. Christian Revi. 75% freelance written. Works with a small number of new/unpublished writers each year. A quarterly magazine on teddy bears. Pays 30 days after acceptance. Byline given. Buys first North American serial rights. Submit seasonal/holiday material 6 months in advance. Reports in 2 months. Sample copy and writer's guidelines for $2 and 9 × 12 SAE.

Nonfiction: Book excerpts, historical, how-to and interview/profile. No nostalgia on childhood teddy bears. Buys 20 mss/year. Query with published clips. Length: 500-1,500 words. Pays $75-200. Sometimes pays the expenses of writers on assignment "if approved ahead of time."

Photos: Send photos with submission. Reviews transparencies and b&w prints. Offers no additional payment for photos accepted with ms. Captions required. Buys one-time rights.

Tips: "We are interested in good, professional writers around the country with a strong knowledge of teddy bears. Historical profile of bear companies, profiles of contemporary artists and knowledgeable reports on museum collections are of interest."

TRADITIONAL QUILTER, The Leading Teaching Mag for Creative Quilters, MSC Publishing Co., 70 Sparta Ave., CN 1003, Sparta NJ 07871. (201)729-4474. Editorial Director: Camille Pomaco. Editor: Phyllis Barbieri. 45% freelance written. Bimonthly magazine on quilting. Estab. 1988. Pays on publication. Byline given. Buys first rights or all rights. Submit seasonal/holiday 6 months in advance. Reports in 2 months. Sample copy for 9 × 12 SAE with $1.10 postage. Writer's guidelines for #10 SASE.

Nonfiction: Quilts and quilt patterns with instructions, quilt-related projects, historical/nostalgic, humor, interview/profile, opinion, personal experience, photo feature, travel — all quilt related. Query with published clips. Length: 350-1,000 words. Pays 7-10¢/word.

Photos: Send photos with submission. Reviews all size transparencies and prints. Offers $10-15 per photo. Captions and identification of subjects required. Buys one-time or all rights.

Columns/Departments: Feature Teacher (qualified quilt teachers with teaching involved — with slides), 1,000 words; Remnants (reports on conventions, history — humor). Length: 1,000 words maximum. Pays 7-10¢/word. Around the Quilting Frame (reports on quilting guild activities, shows, workshops, and retreats), 1,000 words maximum. Pays 7-10¢/word.

Fillers: Anecdotes, facts, short humor. Buys 24/year. Length: 75-500 words. Pays 10-15¢/word.

‡TRADITIONAL QUILTWORKS, The Pattern Magazine for Innovative Quilters, Chitra Publications, 301 Church St., Box 437, New Milford PA 18834. (717)465-3306. Editor: Patti Bachelder. 60% freelance written. Bimonthly magazine on quilting. "We seek articles of an instructional nature, profiles of talented teachers, articles on the history of specific areas of quiltmaking (patterns, fiber, regional, etc.)." Estab. 1988. Circ. 90,000. Pays on publication. Publishes ms an average of 6 months after acceptance. Byline given. Buys second serial (reprint) rights. Submit seasonal/holiday material 6-8 months in advance. Query for electronic submissions. Reports in 6-8 weeks on queries and mss. Free sample copy and writer's guidelines.

Nonfiction: Historical, instructional and quilting education. "No light-hearted entertainment." Buys 12-18 mss/year. Query with or without published clips, or send complete ms. Length: 1,600 words maximum. Pays $75/page.

Photos: Send photos with submission. Reviews transparencies (color). Offers $20 per photo. Captions, model releases and identification of subjects required. Buys all rights.

Tips: "Query with ideas; send samples of prior work so that we can assess and suggest assignment. Our publications appeal to traditional quilters, generally middle-aged and mostly who use the patterns in the magazine. Publication hinges on good photo quality."

‡**TREASURE**, Jess Publishing Co., Inc., #105, 1111 Rancho Conejo Blvd., Newberry Park CA 91320. (805)375-1474 or (619)367-3531. FAX: (805)498-5925. Editor: Jim Williams. Emphasizes treasure hunting and metal detecting. 90% freelance written. Eager to work with new/unpublished writers. Monthly magazine. Circ. 40,000. Pays 2-3 months after publication. Publishes ms an average of 6 months after acceptance. Buys all rights. Byline given. Phone queries OK. Submit seasonal/holiday material 4 months in advance. Previously published submissions OK. Query for electronic submissions. Reports in 2 months. Sample copy for 8½×11 SAE and $1.05 postage; writer's guidelines for SAE and $1.

Nonfiction: Lee Chandler, articles editor. How-to (coinshooting and treasure hunting tips); informational and historical (location of lost treasures with emphasis on the lesser-known); interviews (with treasure hunters); profiles (successful treasure hunters and metal detector hobbyists); personal experience (treasure hunting); technical (advice on use of metal detectors and metal detector designs). "We would like more coverage of archaeological finds, both professional and amateur, and more reports on recently found caches, whether located purposefully or accidentally—both types should be accompanied by photos of the finds." Buys 6-8 mss/issue. Send complete ms. Length: 300-3,000 words. Pays $30-200. "Our rate of payment varies considerably depending upon the proficiency of the author, the quality of the photographs, the importance of the subject matter, and the amount of useful information given."

Photos: Offers no additional payment for 5×7 or 8×10 b&w glossy prints used with mss. Pays $75 minimum for color transparencies (35mm or 2¼×2¼). Color for cover only. "Clear photos and other illustrations are a must." Model release required.

Tips: "We hope to increase our news coverage of archaeological digs and cache finds, opening the doors to writers who would like simply to use their journalistic skills to report a specific event. No great knowledge of treasure hunting will be necessary. The most frequent mistakes made by writers in completing an article for *Treasure* are failure to list sources of information and to supply illustrations or photos with a story."

TREASURE CHEST, The Information Source & Marketplace for Collectors and Dealers, Venture Publishing Co., Suite 211A, 253 West 72nd St., New York NY 10023. (212)496-2234. Editor: Howard E. Fischer. 60% freelance written. Monthly newspaper on antiques and collectibles. Estab. 1988. Circ. 50,000. Pays on publication. Publishes ms an average of 2 months after acceptance. Byline given. Buys first rights and second serial (reprint) rights. Previously published submissions OK. Reports in 1 month on queries; 2 months on mss. Sample copy for 9×12 SAE with $1; writer's guidelines for #10 SASE.

Nonfiction: Exposé, general interest, historical/nostalgic, how-to (detect reproductions, find new sources of items, etc.), humor, interview/profile, personal experience and photo feature. Buys 20-35 mss/year. Query with published clips. Length: 700-1,000 words. Pays $20-50. Payment in contributor copies or other premiums negotiable.

Photos: State availability of photos with submission. Reviews contact sheets, 5×7 and 8×10 prints. Offers no additional payment for photos accepted with ms. Captions and identification of subjects required. Buys one-time rights.

Columns/Departments: Investing in Antiques & Collectibles (what's hot; investing tips, etc.) and Sold! (antiques and collectibles sold recently at auctions, shows, etc and their prices). Query with published clips.

Fillers: Anecdotes, facts, gags to be illustrated by cartoonist and short humor. Buys 12-30/year. Length: 30-200 words. Pays $10-25.

THE TRUMPETER, Croatian Philatelic Society, 1512 Lancelot, Borger TX 79007. (806)273-7225. Editor: Eck Spahich. 80% freelance written. Eager to work with new/unpublished writers. A quarterly magazine covering stamps, coins, currency, military decorations and collectibles of the Balkans, and of central Europe. Circ. 800. Pays on publication. Publishes ms an average of 9 months after acceptance. Byline given. Buys first and one-time rights. Submit seasonal/holiday material 6 months in advance. Simultaneous submissions OK. Reports in 2 months on queries; 1 month on mss. Sample copy $4; free writer's guidelines with #10 SASE.

Nonfiction: Book excerpts, general interest, historical/nostalgic, how-to (on detecting forged stamps, currency etc.) interview/profile, photo feature and travel. Buys 15-20 mss/year. Send complete ms. Length: 500-1,500 words. Pays $25-50 for assigned articles; pays $5-25 for unsolicited articles. Sometimes pays the expenses of writers on assignment.

Photos: State availability of photos with submission. Reviews 3×5 prints. Offers $5-10/photo. Captions and identification of subjects required. Buys one-time rights.

Columns/Departments: Book Reviews (stamps, coins, currency of Balkans), 200-400 words; Forgeries (emphasis on pre-1945 period), 500-1,000 words. Buys 10 mss/year. Send complete ms. Length: 100-300 words. Pays $5-25.

Fillers: Facts. Buys 15-20/year. Length: 20-50 words. Pays $1-5.

Tips: "We desperately need features on Zara, Montenegro, Serbia, Bulgaria, Bosnia, Croatia, Romania and Laibach."

‡TUFF STUFF, The Complete Sports Price Guide Publication, 2309 Hungary Rd., Richmond VA 23228. (804)266-0140. FAX: (804)266-6874. Editor: Ronda Faries. 80% freelance written. Monthly magazine covering sports memorabilia. "Our focus is on the sports memorabilia collecting hobby and the hobbyists, not on sports in general. We like articles that balance the two to attract the largest audience possible." Estab. 1984. Pays on publication. Publishes ms an average of 2 months after acceptance. Byline given. Buys first rights and all rights. Submit seasonal/holiday material 3 months in advance. Simultaneous submissions OK. Send queries to the attention of the Assistant Editor, Tucker Freeman Smith. Reports in 3 weeks. Free sample copy and writer's guidelines.

Nonfiction: Historical/nostalgic, how-to, humor, interview/profile, new product, technical. No articles that do not somehow incorporate the sports memorabilia market. Buys 50 mss/year. Query with published clips. Length: 300-3,000 words. Pays $75-200 for assigned articles; $40-150 for unsolicited articles. State availability of photos with submission. Reviews 3×5 prints. Offers no additional payment for photos accepted with ms. Buys first or all rights.

Fiction: Sports memorabilia—related considered. "Not interested in fiction that is not sports and/or collecting related." Buys 2 mss/year. Query with published clips. Length: 500-3,000 words. Pays $40-100.

Poetry: Avant-garde, free verse, light verse, traditional. "Not interested in poetry that isn't sports/collecting related." Buys 5-10 poems/year. Length: 10-100 lines. Pays $10-50.

Tips: "Try to submit timely and seasonable articles. For example, we do not run a basketball article as our feature in July when baseball is king. Collecting knowledge, well-researched and documented facts or stats a must. Nonfiction articles on sports and sports memorabilia collecting that share knowledge, give pointers, enlarge perspective and tell 'how-to' are most often in demand."

VIDEOMAKER™, The Video Camera User's Magazine, Videomaker Inc., P.O. Box 4591, Chico CA 95927. (916)891-8410. FAX: (916)891-8443. Editor: Bradley Kent. 75% freelance written. A monthly magazine on video production. "Our audience encompasses video camera users ranging from broadcast and cable TV producers to special-event videographers to video hobbyists . . . labeled professional, industrial, 'prosumer,' and consumer. Editorial emphasis is on video*making* (production and exposure), *not* reviews of commercial videos. Personal video phenomenon is a young 'movement'—readership encouraged to participate—get in on the act, join the fun." Estab. 1986. Circ. 75,000. Pays on publication. Publishes ms an average of 4-6 months after acceptance. Byline given. Buys all rights. Submit seasonal/holiday material 6 months in advance. Simultaneous and previously published submissions OK. Query for electronic submissions. Reports in 1 month. Sample copy for 9×12 SAE with 9 first class stamps. Free writer's guidelines.

Nonfiction: How-to (tools, tips, techniques for better videomaking), interview/profile (notable videomakers), product probe (review of latest and greatest or innovative), personal experience (lessons to benefit other videomakers), technical (state-of-the-art audio/video). Articles with comprehensive coverage of product line or aspect of videomaking preferred. Buys 70 mss/year. Query with or without published clips or send complete ms. Length: open. Pays $150-300, negotiable.

Photos: Send photos and/or other artwork with submissions. Reviews contact sheets, transparencies and prints. Captions required. Payment for photos accepted with ms included as package compensation. Buys one-time rights.

Columns/Departments: Computer Video (state-of-the-art products, applications, potentials for computer-video interface); Profile (highlights videomakers using medium in unique/worthwhile ways); Book/Tape Mode (brief reviews of current works pertaining to video production); Videocrafts (projects, gadgets, inventions for videomaking); Video for Hire (money-making opportunities); Edit Points (tools and techniques for successful video editing). Buys 40 mss/year. Pays $35-200.

Fillers: Anecdotes, facts, cartoons, newsbreaks, short humor. Negotiable pay.

Tips: "Comprehensiveness a must. Article on shooting tips covers *all* angles. Buyer's guide to special-effect generators cites *all* models available. Magazine strives for an 'all-or-none' approach. Most topics covered once (twice tops) per year, so we must be thorough. Manuscript/photo package submissions helpful. *Videomaker* wants videomaking to be fulfilling and fun."

The double dagger before a listing indicates that the listing is new in this edition. New markets are often more receptive to freelance submissions.

WESTERN & EASTERN TREASURES, People's Publishing Co., Inc., P.O. Box 1095, Arcata CA 95521. FAX: (707)822-0973. Editor: Rosemary Anderson. Monthly magazine emphasizing treasure hunting and metal detecting for all ages, entire range of education, coast-to-coast readership. 90% freelance written. Estab. 1966. Circ. 70,000. Pays on publication. Publishes ms an average of 1 year after acceptance. Buys all rights. Sample copy and writer's guidelines for $2 and 9 × 12 SAE.

Nonfiction: How-to "hands on" use of metal detecting equipment, how to locate coins, jewelry and relics, prospect for gold, where to look for treasures, rocks and gems, etc., "first-person" experiences. "No purely historical manuscripts or manuscripts that require two-part segments or more." Buys 200 unsolicited mss/year. Submit complete ms. Length: maximum 1,500 words. Pays 2¢/word—negotiable.

Photos: Purchased with accompanying ms. Captions required. Submit b&w prints (preferred), color prints or 35mm Kodachrome transparencies. Pays $5 maximum for 3×5 and up b&w glossy prints; $50 and up for 35mm Kodachrome cover slides. Model releases required.

Tips: "The writer has a better chance of breaking in at our publication with short articles and fillers as these give the readers a chance to respond to the writer. The publisher relies heavily on reader reaction. Not adhering to word limit is the main mistake made by writers in completing an article for us. Writers must clearly cover the subjects described above in 1,500 words or less."

‡**WOMEN'S HOUSEHOLD CROCHET**, House of White Birches, Inc., P.O. Box 776, Henniker NH 03242. Editor: Susan Hankins Foster. 99% freelance written. A quarterly magazine. "We appeal to crochet lovers—young and old, city and country, thread and yarn lovers alike. Our readers crochet for necessity as well as pleasure. Articles are 99% pattern-oriented. We need patterns for all expertise levels—beginner to expert. No knit patterns please." Circ. 75,000. Pays on publication. Publishes ms an average of 3 months to 1 year after acceptance. Byline given. Buys all rights. Submit seasonal/ holiday material 6 months in advance. Reports in 1 month on queries; 6 weeks on mss. Sample copy for $2; free writer's guidelines.

Photos: Buys no photos. Must send crocheted item for staff photography.

Columns/Departments: Designer's Debut Contest (1st and 2nd prizes chosen each issue for crochet design). Buys 8 mss/year. Send complete ms. Length: 500-2,000 words. Pays competitive designer rates.

Poetry: Light verse and traditional. "No long poems over 20 lines. None of a sexual nature." Buys 6 poems/year. Submit maximum 2 poems. Length: 5-20 lines. Pays $5-20.

Fillers: Anecdotes, crochet cartoons, facts and short humor. Buys 4-6/year. Length: 35-70 words. Pays $5-20.

Tips: "We only buy crochet patterns. No longer interested in non-pattern mss."

WOODSHOP NEWS, Soundings Publications Inc., 35 Pratt St., Essex CT 06426. (203)767-8227. Editor: Ian C. Bowen. Senior Editor: Thomas Clark. 20% freelance written. Monthly tabloid "covering woodworking for professionals and hobbyists. Solid business news and features about woodworking companies. Feature stories about interesting amateur woodworkers. Some how-to articles." Estab. 1986. Circ. 100,000. Pays on publication. Publishes ms an average of 2 months after acceptance. Byline given. Offers 25% kill fee. Buys first North American serial rights. Submit seasonal/holiday material 4 months in advance. Simultaneous submissions OK. Query for electronic submissions. Reports in 3 weeks on queries; 1 month on mss. Free sample copy and writer's guidelines.

Nonfiction: How-to—query first, interview/profile, new product, opinion, personal experience, photo feature. No general interest profiles of "folksy" woodworker. Buys 50-75 mss/year. Query with published clips. Length: 100-1,800 words. Pays $30-400 for assigned articles; $30-200 for unsolicited articles. Pays expenses of writers on assignment. Send photos with submission.

Photos: Reviews contact sheets and prints. Offers $20-35 per photo. Captions and identification of subjects required. Buys one-time rights.

Columns/Departments: Pro Shop (business advice, marketing, employee relations, taxes etc. for the professional written by an established professional in the field), 1,200-1,500 words; Tech Talk (technical how-to, written by experts in the topic), 1,200-1,500 words. Buys 24 mss/year. Query. Pays $200-350.

Tips: "The best way to start is a profile of a business or hobbyist woodworker in your area. Find a unique angle about the person or business and stress this as the theme of your article. Avoid a broad, general-interest theme that would be more appropriate to a daily newspaper. Our readers are woodworkers who want more depth and more specifics than would a general readership. If you are profiling a business, we need standard business information such as gross annual earnings/sales, customer base, product line and prices, marketing strategy, etc. Black and white 35 mm photos are a must."

WOODWORK, A magazine for all woodworkers, Ross Periodicals, P.O. Box 1529, Ross CA 94957. (415)382-0580. FAX: (415)382-0587. Editor: Terrie Noll. Publisher: Tom Toldrian. 90% freelance written. Bimonthly magazine covering woodworking. "We are aiming at a broad audience of woodworkers, from the home enthusiast/hobbyist to more advanced." Estab. 1986. Circ. 100,000. Pays on publication. Byline given. Buys first North American serial rights and second serial (reprint) rights. Reports in 2 months. Sample copy $3 with 9×12 SAE and 6 first class stamps. Writer's guidelines for #10 SASE.

Nonfiction: How-to (simple or complex, making attractive furniture), interview/profile (of established woodworkers that make attractive furniture), photo feature (of interest to woodworkers), technical (tools, techniques). "Do not send a how-to unless you are a woodworker." Buys 40 mss/year. Query first. Length: 1,500-3,000 words. Pays $150/published page.

Photos: Send photos with submission. Reviews 35mm slides. Offers no additional payment for photos accepted with ms. Captions and identification of subjects required. Buys one-time rights.

Columns/Departments: Feature articles (from non-woodworking freelancers, we use interview/profiles of established woodworkers. Bring out woodworker's philosophy about the craft, opinions about what is happening currently. Good photos of attractive furniture a must. Section on how-to desirable.), 1,500-3,000 words. Query with published clips. Pays $600-1,500 at $150 per published page.

Fillers: Anecdotes, facts, newsbreaks, short humor. Length: 1,000 words. Pays $150 maximum.

Tips: "If you are not a woodworker, the interview/profile is your best, really only chance. Good writing is essential as are good photos. The interview must be intertaining, but informative and pertinent to woodworkers' interests."

WOODWORKING ASSOCIATION OF NORTH AMERICA MONTHLY BONUS PACKET, P.O. Box 706, Rt. 3 and Cummings Hill Rd., Plymouth NH 03264. (603)536-3876. Managing Director: Sheri Ball. Buys first time North American one-time reprint rights. Monthly newsletter on woodworking for hobbyists and professionals. It is strongly suggested that illustrations and/or photographs accompany project and construction plans. Estab. 1984. Simultaneous submissions OK. Reports in 6 weeks.

Nonfiction: Project plans on all aspects of woodworking, furniture making, woodturning, antique repair, restoration, musical instrument construction, miniatures, wooden crafts, jigs and accessories. Woodworking projects plans need to be of the level that can be completed in the home shop. Readers are of the advanced amateur level. Buys 25 mss/year. Will respond to queries but mss preferred. Pays $25-250 which includes illustrations.

Photos: Send photos with submission. Reviews 3×5 or larger prints, no transparencies. Caption, model releases and identification of subjects required. Buys first time North American one-time reprint rights.

THE WORKBASKET, 4251 Pennsylvania Ave., Kansas City MO 64111. FAX: (816)531-3873. Editor: Roma Jean Rice. Issued six times per year. Buys first rights. **Pays on acceptance.** Reports in 6 weeks.

Nonfiction: Step-by-step directions for craft and needlework projects (400-500 words) and gardening articles (200-500 words). Query. Pays 7¢/word.

Photos: Color photos only. Pays negotiable fee.

WORKBENCH, 4251 Pennsylvania Ave., Kansas City MO 64111. (816)531-5730. FAX: (816)531-3873. Executive Editor: Robert N. Hoffman. 75% freelance written. Prefers to work with published/established writers; works with a small number of new/unpublished writers each year. For woodworkers and home improvement do-it-yourselfers. Estab. 1957. Circ. 909,000. **Pays on acceptance.** Publishes ms an average of 1 year after acceptance. Byline given. Buys all rights. Reports in 2 months. Sample copy for 8½×11 SAE and 6 first class stamps; free writer's guidelines.

Nonfiction: "We have continued emphasis on do-it-yourself woodworking, home improvement and home maintenance projects. We provide in-progress photos, technical drawings and how-to text for all projects. We are very strong in woodworking, cabinetmaking and classic furniture construction. Projects range from simple toys to reproductions of furniture now in museums. We would like to receive woodworking projects that can be duplicated by both beginning do-it-yourselfers and advanced woodworkers." Query. Pays $175/published page or more depending on quality of submission. Additional payment for good color photos. "If you can consistently provide good material, including photos, your rates will go up and you will get assignments."

Columns/Departments: Shop Tips bring $25 with a line drawing and/or b&w photo. Workbench Solver pays $75 to experts providing answers to readers' problems related to do-it-yourself projects and home repair.

Tips: "Our magazine focuses on woodworking, covering all levels of ability and home improvement projects from the do-it-yourselfer's viewpoint, emphasizing the most up-to-date materials and procedures. We would like to receive articles on home improvements and remodeling, and/or simple contemporary furniture. We place a heavy emphasis on projects that are both functional and classic in design. We can photograph projects worthy for publication, so feel free to send snapshots."

WORLD COIN NEWS, Krause Publications, 700 E. State, Iola WI 54990. (715)445-2214. FAX: (715)445-4087. Editor: David C. Harper. 30% freelance written. Works with a small number of new/unpublished writers each year. Weekly newsmagazine about non-U.S. coin collecting for novices and advanced collectors of foreign coins, medals, and other numismatic items. Circ. 10,000. Pays on publication. Publishes ms an average of 1 month after acceptance. Byline given. Buys first North American serial rights and reprint rights. Submit seasonal material 2 months in advance. Simultaneous submissions OK. Reports in 2 weeks. Free sample copy.

Nonfiction: "Send us timely news stories related to collecting foreign coins and current information on coin values and markets." Send complete ms. Buys 30 mss/year. Length: 500-2,000 words. Pays 3¢/word to first-time contributors; fees negotiated for later articles.

Photos: Send photos with ms. Pays $5 minimum for b&w prints. Captions and model release required. Buys first rights and reprint rights.

YESTERYEAR, Yesteryear Publications, P.O. Box 2, Princeton WI 54968. (414)787-4808. Editor: Michael Jacobi. 5% freelance written. Prefers to work with published/established writers. For antique dealers and collectors, people interested in collecting just about anything, and nostalgia buffs. Monthly tabloid. Estab. 1976. Circ. 7,000. Pays on publication. Publishes ms an average of 2-3 months after acceptance. Buys one-time rights. Byline given. Submit seasonal/holiday material 3 months in advance. Simultaneous and previously published submissions OK. Reports in 1 month. Sample copy $2.

Nonfiction: General interest (basically, anything pertaining to antiques, collectible items or nostalgia in general); historical (again, pertaining to the above categories); and how-to (refinishing antiques, how to collect). The more specific and detailed, the better. "We do not want personal experience or opinion articles." Buys 10 mss/year. Send complete ms. Pays $5-25. Pays expenses of writers on assignment.

Photos: Send photos with ms. Pays $5 for 5×7 b&w glossy or matte prints; $5 for 5×7 color prints. Captions preferred.

Columns/Departments: "We will consider new column concepts as long as they fit into the general areas of antiques and collectibles." Buys 1 ms/issue. Send complete ms. Pays $5-25.

Home and Garden

Some magazines here concentrate on gardens; others on the how-to of interior design. Still others focus on homes and gardens in specific regions of the country. Be sure to read the publication to determine its focus before submitting a manuscript or query.

AMERICAN HORTICULTURIST, Publication of the American Horticultural Society, 7931 E. Blvd. Dr., Alexandria VA 22308. (703)768-5700. FAX: (703)765-6032. Editor: Kathleen Fisher. 90% freelance written. Bimonthly magazine covering gardening. Estab. 1922. Circ. 25,000. Pays on publication. Publishes ms an average of 6 months after acceptance. Byline given. Offers 20% kill fee. Buys first North American serial rights. Submit seasonal/holiday material 6 months in advance. Query for electronic submissions. Reports in 2 months on queries. Sample copy $2.50; free writer's guidelines.

Nonfiction: Book excerpts, historical, how-to (grow unusual plants, garden under difficult conditions), humor, interview/profile, personal experience, technical (explain science of horticulture to lay audience). Buys 40-50 mss/year. Query with published clips. Length: 1,000-2,500 words. Pays $100-400. Pays with contributor copies or other premiums when other horticultural organizations contribute articles.

Photos: Send photos with submission. Reviews transparencies. Offers $50-75 per photo. Captions required. Buys one-time rights.

Tips: "We are read by sophisticated gardeners, but also want to interest beginning gardeners. Subjects should be unusual plants, recent breakthroughs in breeding, experts in the field, translated for lay readers."

ARCHITECTURAL DIGEST, Knapp Communications, 5900 Wilshire Blvd., Los Angeles CA 90036. Did not want to be listed.

BACKWOODS HOME MAGAZINE, Word Publishing, P.O. Box 2630, Ventura CA 93002. (805)647-9341. Editor: Dave Duffy. 80% freelance written. Bimonthly magazine covering house building, alternate energy, gardening and health. "We write for the person who values self-independence above all else. Our readers want to build their own homes, generate their own electricity, grow their own food and in general stand on their own two feet." Estab. 1989. Circ. 40,000. Pays on publication. Publishes ms an average of 2 months after acceptance. Byline given. Offers $15 kill fee. Buys first rights and second serial (reprint) rights or makes work-for-hire assignments. Submit seasonal/holiday material 6 months in advance. Simultaneous and previously published submissions OK. Query for electronic submissions. Reports in 2 weeks. Sample copy for $1 with 9×12 SAE and $1.05 in postage. Writer's guidelines for #10 SASE.

Nonfiction: Historical/nostalgic, how-to (about country things, alternate energy), humor (country humor), interview/profile (of independent people), new product (alternate energy), personal experience, photo feature (about country things) and technical (about alternate energy production, building a house). "No opinion, exposé or religious articles." Buys 50 mss/year. Query with or without published clips, or send complete ms. Length: 300-3,000 words. Pays $15.

Photos: State availability of photos with submission. Reviews 3×5 or larger prints. Offers $5 per photo. Identification of subjects required. Buys one-time rights.

Columns/Departments: Book Review (alternate energy/house building/gardening), 300-400 words; Recipes (country cooking), 150 words; Alternate Energy (solar cells, hydro, generator), 600-3,000 words; Gardening (organic), 600-1,800 words; Home Building (do-it-yourself), 600-1,800 words. Buys 30-40 mss/year. Send complete ms. Pays $15.

Fiction: Historical, humorous, slice-of-life vignettes and western. "No erotica, confession, religious, fantasy or romance fiction." Buys 6 mss/year. Send complete ms. Length: 1,800-3,600. Pays $15.

Poetry: Free verse, haiku, light verse, traditional. Buys 15 poems/year. Length: 3-25 lines. Pays $5.

Fillers: Anecdotes, facts, short humor. Buys 9-12/year. Length: 25-150. Pays $5.

Tips: "We insist on accuracy in nonfiction articles. Writers must know the subject. We are basically a country magazine that tries to show people how to do things that make country life more pleasant."

BETTER HOMES AND GARDENS, 1716 Locust St., Des Moines IA 50336. (515)284-3000. Editor (Building): Joan McCloskey. Editor (Furnishings): Denise Caringer. Editor (Foods): Nancy Byal. Editor (Travel): Editor. Editor (Garden Outdoor Living): Doug Jimerson. Editor (Health & Education): Paul Krantz. Editor (Money Management, Automotive, Features): Margaret Daly. 10-15% freelance written. **Pays on acceptance.** Buys all rights. "We read all freelance articles, but much prefer to see a letter of query rather than a finished manuscript."

Nonfiction: Travel, education, health, cars, money management, and home entertainment. "We do not deal with political subjects or with areas not connected with the home, community, and family." Pays rates "based on estimate of length, quality and importance."

Tips: Direct queries to the department that best suits your story line.

CANADIAN WORKSHOP, The Do-It-Yourself Magazine, Camar Publications (1984) Inc., 130 Spy Ct., Markham, Ontario L3R 5H6 Canada. (416)475-8440. Editor: Erina Kelly. 90% freelance written; half of these are assigned. Monthly magazine covering the "do-it-yourself" market including woodworking projects, renovation and restoration, and maintenance. Canadian writers only. Circ. 130,000. Payment in two installments. Half when received, half the month following. Byline given. Offers 75% kill fee. Rights are negotiated with the author. Submit seasonal/holiday material 6 months in advance. Simultaneous queries OK. Reports in 3 weeks. Sample copy for 8×11 SASE; free writer's guidelines with #10 SASE.

Nonfiction: How-to (home maintenance, renovation projects, woodworking projects and features). Buys 40-60 mss/year. Query with clips of published work. Length: 1,500-4,000 words. Pays $225-600. Pays expenses of writers on assignment.

Photos: Send photos with ms. Payment for photos, transparencies negotiated with the author. Captions, model releases, and identification of subjects required.

Tips: "Freelancers must be aware of our magazine format. Products used in how-to articles must be readily available across Canada. Deadlines for articles are 5 months in advance of cover date. However tos should be detailed enough for the amateur but appealing to the experienced. A frequent mistake made by writers is not directing the copy toward our reader. Stories sometimes have a tendency to be too basic."

COLONIAL HOMES, Hearst Corp., 1700 Broadway, 28th Fl., New York NY 10019. Staff written. Did not want to be listed.

‡COLORADO HOMES & LIFESTYLES, 7009 S. Potomac St., Englewood CO 80112. (303)397-7600. FAX: (303)397-7619. Editor: Anne McGregor Parsons. 50% freelance written. Bimonthly magazine covering Colorado homes and lifestyles for upper-middle-class and high income households as well as designers, decorators and architects. Circ. 30,000. **Pays on acceptance.** Publishes ms an average of 4 months after acceptance. Byline given. Buys all rights. Submit seasonal/holiday material 6 months in advance. Simultaneous queries and photocopied submissions OK. Query for electronic submissions. Reports in 1 month.

Nonfiction: Fine homes and furnishings, regional interior design trends, interesting personalities and lifestyles, gardening and plants—all with a Colorado slant. Buys 30 mss/year. Send complete ms. Length: 1,000-1,500 words. "For unique, well-researched feature stories, pay is $150-200. For regular departments, $125-140." Sometimes pays the expenses of writers on assignment.

Photos: Send photos with ms. Reviews 35mm, 4×5 and 2¼ color transparencies and b&w glossy prints. Identification of subjects required.

Tips: "The more interesting and unique the subject the better. A frequent mistake made by writers is failure to provide material with a style and slant appropriate for the magazine, due to poor understanding of the focus of the magazine."

‡**COTTAGE LIFE,** Quarto Communications, Ste. 408, 111 Queen St. E., Toronto, Ontario M5C 152 Canada. (416)360-6880. Editor: Ann Vanderhoof. Managing Editor: David Zimmer. 80% freelance written. Bimonthly magazine covering cottaging in Ontario. "Cottage Life is written and designed for the people who own and spend time at cottages on Ontario's lakes." Estab. 1988. Circ. 75,000. **Pays on acceptance.** Publishes ms an average of 2 months after acceptance. Byline given. Buys first North American serial rights. Query for electronic submissions.

Nonfiction: Send queries to Ann Vanderhoor. Book excerpts, exposé, historical/nostalgic, how-to, humor, interview/profile, personal experience, photo feature and technical. Buys 90 mss/year. Query with published clips. Length: 150-3,500 words. Pays $100-2,200 for assigned articles. Pays $50-1,000 for unsolicited articles. Sometimes pays expenses of writers on assignment. Query first.

Columns/Departments: Cooking, Real Estate, Fishing, Nature, 150-1200 words. Query with published clips. Length: 150-1500 words. Pays $100-750.

COUNTRY HOME, Meredith Corp., 750 3rd Ave., New York NY 10017. Did not want to be listed.

COUNTRY LIVING, Reiman Publications, Inc., 5400 S. 60th St., Box 643, Greendale WI 53129. Did not want to be listed.

DECORATING REMODELING, New York Times Company Magazine Group, 110 5th Ave., New York NY 10011. Did not want to be listed.

‡**FAMILY LIVING, The Trade Magazine for Homeowners,** #448, 14742 Beach Blvd., La Mirada CA 90638. (714)521-4681. Editor: Marie Madera. 10% freelance written. Bimonthly magazine for the homeowner market. Estab. 1980. Circ. 1,000,000. Pays on publication. Byline given. Makes work-for-hire assignments. Submit seasonal/holiday material 4 months in advance. Simultaneous and previously published submissions OK. Sample copy $1.

Nonfiction: General interest, how-to, new product and travel. "No political or fiction material." Buys 1-2 mss/year. Query. Length: 100-600 words. Pays $50-150 for assigned articles. Sometimes pays the expenses of writers on assignments.

Photos: State availability of photos with submission. Offers no additional payment for photos accepted with ms. Identification of subjects required. Buys one-time rights.

FLORIDA HOME & GARDEN, Suite 500, 800 Douglas Rd., Coral Gables Fl 33134. (305)445-4500. FAX: (305)445-4600. Editor: Kathryn Howard. Managing Editor: James Watson. 20% freelance written. Works with a small number of new/unpublished writers each year. Monthly magazine of Florida homes, interior design, architecture, landscape architecture, gardens, cuisine, travel, lifestyles and home entertainment. "We want beautiful, practical coverage of the subjects listed as they relate to Florida." Estab. 1984. Circ. 65,000. Pays on publication. Publishes ms an average of 3 months after acceptance. Byline given. Offers $25 kill fee by pre-agreement only. Buys first North American serial rights for one year, plus unlimited reuse in our magazine (no resale). Submit seasonal/holiday material 6 months in advance. Sample copy $3; writer's guidelines for #10 SASE.

Nonfiction: General interest (photos and articles about Florida homes); and travel Caribbean/Florida (home architecture or garden destinations only). Buys 36 mss/year. Query with published clips. Length: 1,000-2,000 words. Pays $200-400. Pays expenses of writers on assignment by prior agreement only.

Photos: State availability of photos or send photos with query. Reviews 35mm, 4×5 or 2×4 transparencies, Polaroids, prints. Captions and identification of subjects required. Buys one-time rights plus unlimited editorial re-use of magazine's separations.

Columns/Departments: How-to (specific home how-to); Garden Care; What's Hot (Florida products); Real Estate; Cuisine; Travel (Florida, Mexico's Gulf Coast; Caribbean); Books (reviews). Buys 20 mss/year. Query with published clips. Length: 750-1,500 words. Pays $150-300.

Tips: "We're looking for stories that visually show the beauty of Florida and impart practical information to our readers. Must relate to Florida's tropicality in all subjects."

FLOWER AND GARDEN MAGAZINE, 4251 Pennsylvania, Kansas City MO 64111. FAX: (816)531-3873. Editor: Kay Melchisedech Olson. 50% freelance written. Works with a small number of new/unpublished writers each year. For home gardeners. Bimonthly picture magazine. Estab. 1957. Circ. 600,000. Buys first rights only. Byline given. **Pays on acceptance.** Publishes ms an average of 6-12 months after acceptance. Reports in 6 weeks. Sample copy $2.95 and 9½×12½ SAE; writer's guidelines for SASE.

Nonfiction: Interested in illustrated articles on how to do certain types of gardening and descriptive articles about individual plants. Flower arranging, landscape design, house plants, patio gardening are other aspects covered. "The approach we stress is practical (how-to-do-it, what-to-do-it-with). We emphasize plain talk, clarity and economy of words. An article should be tailored for a national audience." Buys 20-30 mss/year. Query. Length: 500-1,500 words. Rates vary depending on quality and kind of material.

Photos: Pays up to $12.50/5×7 or 8×10 b&w prints, depending on quality, suitability. Also buys transparencies, 35mm and larger. "We are using more four-color illustrations." Pays $30-125 for these, depending on size and use. Photos are paid for on publication.

Tips: "The prospective author needs good grounding in gardening practice and literature. Offer well-researched and well-written material appropriate to the experience level of our audience. Use botanical names as well as common. Illustrations help sell the story. Describe special qualifications for writing the particular proposed subject."

‡**GARDEN DESIGN**, Suite 500, 4401 Connecticut Ave. NW, Washington DC 20008. (202)686-2752. Executive Editor: Deborah Papier. 90% freelance written. Eager to work with new writers. A bimonthly devoted to the fine art of garden design. Circ. 100,000. Pays 2 months after acceptance. Byline given. Offers 20-30% kill fee. Buys first North American rights. Submit seasonal/holiday material 6 months in advance. Query for electronic submissions. Reports in 2 months. Sample copy $5. Writer's guidelines for #10 SASE.

Nonfiction: "We look for literate writing on a wide variety of garden-related topics—art, architecture, food, furniture, decorating, travel, shopping, personalities." Buys 100-120 mss/year. Query with published clips. Length: 800-2,000 words. Pays approx. 50¢ per word. Sometimes pays expenses of writer or photographer on assignment.

Photos: Submit scouting photos when proposing article on a specific garden. Offers $75-150 per photo or day rate for assigned shoot. Buys one-time rights.

Tips: "Our greatest need is for extraordinary private gardens. Scouting locations is a valuable service freelancers can perform, by contacting designers and garden clubs in the area, visiting gardens and taking snapshots for our review. All departments of the magazine are open to freelancers. Writing should be as stylish as the gardens we feature."

THE HERB COMPANION, Interweave Press, 201 E. 4th St., Loveland CO 80537. (303)669-7672. Editor: Linda Ligon. 80% freelance written. Bimonthly magazine about herbs: culture, history, culinary use, crafts, medicinal. Audience includes a wide range of herb enthusiasts. Circ. 35,000. Pays on publication. Byline given. Buys first North American serial rights. Sample copy $4; writer's guidelines for #10 SASE. Query. Length: 10-16 pages. Typical payment is $100 per published page.

Photos: State availability of photos.

Tips: "Articles must show depth and working knowledge of the subject, though tone should be informal and accessible."

HERB QUARTERLY, P.O. Box 548, Boiling Springs PA 17007. FAX: (717)258-4465. Publisher: Linda Sparrowe. 80% freelance written. Quarterly magazine for herb enthusiasts. Estab. 1978. Circ. 25,000. Pays on publication. Publishes ms an average of 1 year after acceptance. Buys first North American serial rights and second (reprint) rights to previously published submissions. Query for electronic submissions. Query letters recommended. Reports in 1 month. Sample copy $5 and 9×12 SASE; writer's guidelines for #10 SASE.

Nonfiction: Gardening (landscaping, herb garden design, propagation, harvesting); herb businesses; medicinal and cosmetic use of herbs; crafts; cooking; historical (folklore, focused piece on particular period—*not* general survey); interview of a famous person involved with herbs or folksy herbalist; personal experience; and photo essay ("cover quality" 8×10 b&w prints). "We are particularly interested in herb garden design, contemporary or historical." No fiction. Send double-spaced ms. Length: 1,000-3,500 words. Pays $50-200.

Tips: "Our best submissions are narrowly focused on herbs with much practical information on cultivation and use for the experienced gardener."

‡**HOME**, Allied Publications, Inc., 1776 Lake Worth Rd., Lake Worth FL 33460. (407)582-2099. Associate Editor: Karl H. Meyer. 85% freelance written. Bimonthly general interest magazine for homeowners. "We cover home finances, insurance, repairs, recipes, kids, crafts, hobbies, domestic travel, almost anything of interest to adults in home situations. Light pieces and always good." Estab. 1945. Circ. (combined) 105,000. Pays on publication. Publishes ms an average of 6 months after acceptance. Byline given. Buys one-time rights and second serial (reprint) rights. Submit seasonal/holiday material 6-8 months in advance. Simultaneous and previously published submissions OK. Query for electronic

submissions. Reports in 2 weeks-3 months on mss. Sample copy $1. Writer's guidelines for #10 SAE with 1 first class stamp.

Nonfiction: "No highly technical of 'cutesy' material. No vulgar or obscene language. No jeremiads. Think posivitely." Buys 216 mss/year. Query with or without published clips, or send complete ms. "I often reject query and purchase clips submitted." Length: 300-1,500 words. Pays $25 maximum for unsolicited articles at 36¢ per published line. Pays in contributor copies or other premiums only if author requests.

Photos: State availability of photos with submission. Offers $5 per photo. Model releases and identification of subjects required. Photographer must have model releases on file; do not send.

‡**HOME MAGAZINE, The Magazine of Remodeling and Decorating,** 5900 Wilshire Blvd, 15 Floor, Los Angeles CA 90036. (213)932-1400. Editor Director: Channing Dawson. 50% freelance written. Monthly magazine covering remodeling, decorating, architecture entertaining, building and gardens. Circ. 925,000. **Pays on acceptance.** Publishes ms an average of 6-18 months after acceptance. Offers negotiable kill fee. Buys all rights. Submit seasonal/holiday material 6-13 months in advance. Query for electronic submissions. Reports in 6 weeks. Free sample copy and writer's guidelines.

Nonfiction: Anne Colby. Book excerpts, essays, how-to, interview/profile, new product, personal experience, photo feature, technical, travel. Buys 100-150 mss/year. Query with published clips. Length: 100-3,500 words. Pays 75¢-$1.

HOMEOWNER, Family Media Inc., 3 Park Ave., New York NY 10016. Editor-in-chief: Joe Carter. Managing Editor: Michael Hartnett. 75% freelance written. Monthly (combined Jan/Feb; July/Aug) magazine on home improvement, including remodeling, landscaping, maintenance and repair. Aimed at men and women with helpful information of planning, design options, new products and do-it-yourself techniques. Circ. 775,000. **Pays on acceptance.** Publishes ms an average of 4 months after acceptance. Byline given. Offers kill fee. Buys first North American serial rights. Reports in 1 month. Sample copy on request; writer's guidelines for #10 SASE.

Nonfiction: Remodeling, landscaping, design ideas, home repair and maintenance, how-to; some technical information on products, materials, how things work. Length: 1,500 maximum. Rates start at $400 for short articles plus some expenses of writers on assignment.

LOG HOME LIVING, Home Buyer Publications Inc., P.O. Box 220039, Chantilly VA 22022. (703)222-9411. Editor: Roland Sweet. Less than 10% freelance written. Bimonthly magazine covering contemporary log homes. "*Log Home Living* is for people who own or are planning to build contemporary manufactured and handcrafted kit log homes. Our audience comprises married couples 35-50 years old." Estab. 1989. **Pays on acceptance.** Publishes ms an average of 6 months after acceptance. Byline given. Offers $100 kill fee. Buys one-time rights. Submit seasonal/holiday material 9-12 months in advance. Reports in 6-8 weeks. Sample copy $3.25. Writer's guidelines for SAE with 1 first class stamp.

Nonfiction: How-to (buy or build log home), interview/profile (log home owners), photo feature (log homes) and technical (design/decor topics). "We do not want historical/nostalgic material." Buys 2-3 mss/year. Query with published clips. Length: 750-1,500 words. Pays $100-500. Sometimes pays expenses of writers on assignment.

Photos: Send photos with submission. Reviews contact sheets, 2½×2½ transparencies and 5×7 prints. Offers $50-100 per photo. Captions, model releases and identification of subjects required. Buys one-time rights.

Tips: "Owner profiles are most open to freelancers. Reveal how they planned for, designed and bought/built their dream home; how they decorated it; how they like it; advice for others thinking of buying."

MIDWEST LIVING, Meredith Corp., 1716 Locust St., Des Moines IA 50036. Did not want to be listed.

‡**NATIONAL GARDENING,** National Gardening Association, 180 Flynn Ave., Burlington VT 05401. (802)863-1308. FAX: (802)863-5962. Editor: Warren Schultz. Managing Editor: Emily Stetson. 75% freelance written. Willing to work with new/unpublished writers. Bimonthly magazine covering all aspects of food gardening and ornamentals. "We publish not only how-to garden techniques, but also news that affects gardeners, like science advances. Detailed, experienced-based articles with carefully worked-out techniques for planting, growing, harvesting and using garden fruits and vegetables sought. Our material is for both experienced and beginning gardeners." Estab. 1978. Circ. 200,000. **Pays on acceptance.** Publishes ms an average of 9 months after acceptance. Byline given. Buys first serial rights and occasionally second (reprint) rights to material originally published elsewhere. Submit seasonal/holiday material 8 months in advance. Reports in 1 month. Sample copy for 8½×11 SAE and $1; writer's guidelines for #10 SASE.

Nonfiction: How-to, humor, inspirational, interview/profile, new product, pest patrol, opinion, personal experience, photo feature and technical. Buys 80-100 mss/year. Query first. Length: 500-3,000 words. Pays $30-500/article. Sometimes pays the expenses of writers on assignment; must have prior approval.

Photos: Vicky Congdon, Associate Editor. Send photos with ms. Pays $20-40 for b&w photos; $50 for color photos. Captions, model releases and identification of subjects required.

Tips: "Wordiness is a frequent mistake made by writers. Few writers understand how to write 'tight'. We have increased coverage of ornamentals, although primary focus will remain food gardening."

NEW HOME, Gilford Publishing, P.O. Box 2008, Village West, Laconia NH 03247. FAX: (603)524-0643. Managing Editor: Steven Maviglio. 90% freelance written. Bimonthly magazine. *"New Home* is mailed to homebuyers (new and existing within one month of filing the deed). The magazine goes to those who have purchased homes costing $100,000 or more. The first few months of living in a new house means decorating, remodeling and buying products. We show them how to make quality decisions." Estab. 1986. Circ. 300,000. Pays within 60 days of acceptance. Publishes ms an average of 2 months after acceptance. Byline given. Kill fee varies. Buys all rights. Submit seasonal/holiday material 6 months in advance. Simultaneous submissions OK. Reports in 2 weeks. Sample copy for $5 and 8½×11 SAE with 6 first class stamps. Free writer's guidelines.

Nonfiction: Essays, how-to, interview/profile, new product, technical. No articles on "How I Dealt with My New Kitchen," "Why Moving Is So Terrible." Buys 50 mss/year. Query with published clips. Pays $200-1,500 for articles. Sometimes pays expenses of writers on assignment.

Photos: State availability of photos with submission. Reviews transparencies (5×7) and slides. Offers $50-250/photo. Captions, model release and identification of subjects required. Buys all rights.

Columns/Departments: Out-of-Doors (lawn and garden, landscaping) 1,000-1,500 words; The Kitchen (kitchen cabinets, countertops, small appliances); The Bath (new tubs, working with color, Victorian baths); Details (do-it-yourself, fun projects); Back Porch (essay of a new home experience). Buys 50 mss/year. Query with published clips. Length: 250-2,000 words. Pays $200-1,500.

Fillers: "Homefront" (news and trends). Facts. Buys 20 mss/year. Length: 50-250 words. Pays up to $250.

Tips: "We assign nearly all of our stories. But it doesn't hurt for a writer to query with samples and present their idea in a one-page letter. No unsolicited manuscripts except for our Back Porch section."

‡NORTHERN CALIFORNIA HOME AND GARDEN, Westar Media, 656 Bair Island Rd., Redwood City CA 94063. (415)368-8800. Editor: Ann Bertelsen. Managing Editor: Katie Tamony. 50% freelance written. Monthly magazine on architecture, interior decorating and gardening. Estab. 1987. Circ. about 50,000. Pays on acceptance. Publishes ms an average of 3 months after acceptance. Byline given. Offers 30% kill fee. Buys first North American serial rights. Submit seasonal/holiday material 5 months in advance. Simultaneous submissions OK. Writer's guidelines for #10 SASE.

Nonfiction: General interest (within our scope of interest), interview/profile (with an architect/designer and his home), personal experience (building/remodeling home. "Our July issue is devoted to remodeling; March is gardens. No how-to, technical articles on mundane topics." Buys 25 mss/year. Query with published clips. Length: 1,200-2,000 words. Pays $400-600. Sometimes pays expenses of writers on assignment.

Photos: State availability of photos or send photos with submission. Reviews contact sheets and 4x5 transparencies. Buys one-time rights. All photography/art assigned by art director.

Columns/Departments: Antiques; Real Estate, Elements (glasswork, concrete "coloring," "rescued" lumber, etc.) Query with pbulished clips. Length: 1,200-1,500 words. Pays $150-250.

Tips: "The best approach for new freelancers is through columns/departments. We hardly ever assign a feature to a freelance that we don't know. Suggest several ideas. You must be familiar with Northern California. Writers should speak to an upscale homeowner with a variety of interests in art and design."

1,001 HOME IDEAS, Family Media, Inc., 3 Park Ave., New York NY 10016. (212)779-6200. Editor: Ellen Frankel. Executive Editor: Errol Croft. 40% freelance written. Prefers to work with published/established writers. A monthly magazine covering home furnishings, building, remodeling and home equipment. "We are a family shelter magazine edited for young, mainstream homeowners, providing ideas for decorating, remodeling, outdoor living, and at-home entertaining. Emphasis on ideas that are do-able and affordable." Estab. 1945. Circ. 1.5 million. **Pays on acceptance.** Publishes ms an average of 6 months after acceptance. Byline given. Offers 25% kill fee. Buys first North American serial rights, second serial (reprint) rights, or makes work-for-hire assignments. Submit seasonal/holiday material 12 months in advance. Reports in 1 month. Sample copy $2.50; writer's guidelines for #10 SASE.

Nonfiction: Book excerpts (on interior design and crafts only); how-to (on decorating, remodeling and home maintenance); interview/profile (of designers only); new product; photo feature (on homes only); crafts; home equipment; and home furnishings and decor. No travel, religious, technical or

Close-up

Katie Tamony
Managing Editor
Northern California Home and Garden

"I would say 30-50% of the magazine is freelance—at least one feature and several of the longer departments each month." This good news for freelancers comes from Katie Tamony, managing editor of *Northern California Home and Garden* magazine.

Begun in 1987, *NCH&G*'s circulation figures have already topped 50,000. "We are the flagship magazine of the company," Tamony explains. *NCH&G* is the largest and fastest-growing magazine of Westar Media, the publishing group that produces *Peninsula*, *Southern California Home and Garden* and *Pacific Guest Books*.

Writers benefit from the corporate link. Queries directed to editor David Gorn, for example, at the lifestyle magazine *Peninsula*, may be forwarded to *NCH&G*. In addition, *NCH&G* occasionally develops features with the editor of *Southern California Home and Garden*, Leslie Gregory. Tamony remarks, "We might decide that (an idea) fits both magazines—our remodeling issue in July is a joint venture."

Tamony certainly knows her own turf. Upon graduation from the University of California, Berkeley, she landed her first journalism job at *NCH&G* in 1988 as an editorial assistant. A year later she became an associate editor, and in 1990, Tamony was appointed managing editor. Despite the recent slowdown in the national economy, *NCH&G* continues to grow and fatter issues mean more pages for freelance writing. How do freelancers tap this market?

"Queries for departments are easier to decide on," Tamony asserts. "If a person sends a query, an outline, and mentions how it would fit our magazine, I'd talk about the idea. If we agreed on how the article should go, I'd send out a contract," probably within two weeks. A feature concept requires a longer process with complete staff review. Freelancers typically have 6-8 weeks to finish a piece.

Savvy freelancers know *NCH&G*'s editorial calendar. Writers who create articles with "the right mix"—neither overly technical nor too "breezy"—have the best chance for repeat assignments. Freelancers must dovetail writing with visual design. "When a writer queries, we ask to see visuals," says Tamony. A snapshot sent with a story idea may lock in that assignment.

California-based sources and clips are essential to underscore familiarity with one's subject. A publication's reputation is not as important to Tamony, however, as quality writing and a knowledge of "people-oriented" stories.

Tamony encourages writers to approach lesser-known magazines—with one caution. "You can't expect to walk in and be a feature writer or a top editor. You have to plug away at some of the smaller jobs first." Then, when opportunity knocks, prepared freelancers are primed to answer the call.

—Lynn Narlesky

exposés. Buys 25 mss/year. Query with or without published clips, or send complete ms. Length: 300-2,000 words. Pays $100-750 for assigned articles; pays $100-500 for unsolicited articles. Sometimes pays the expenses of writers on assignment.

Photos: State availability of photos with submission. Reviews transparencies and prints. Offers $10-125/photo. Captions, model releases, and identification of subjects required. Buys one-time rights.

Columns/Departments: Kathie Robitz, column/department editor. 1,001 Ways to Save $$$ (consumer buymanship, housing, finance, home furnishings, products, etc.) 1,500 words. Buys 12 mss/year. Query. Pays $350-450.

Tips: "The idea is what sells an article to us . . . good ideas for decorating, remodeling and improving the home, and well-researched information on how-to, with any necessary directions and patterns, to help the reader carry out the idea. The department, 1,001 Ways to Save, is the area most open to freelance writers. We also look for features which we can turn into photo features on decorating, remodeling and improving the home."

ORGANIC GARDENING, Rodale Press, 33 E. Minor, Emmaus PA 18098. (215)967-5171. Managing Editor: Matt Damsker. 30% freelance written. Appears 9 times/year. Pays between acceptance and publication. Buys all rights. Reports in 2 months on queries; 1 month on mss.

Nonfiction: "Our title says it all. We seem to put more emphasis on the gardening aspect." Query with published clips and outline. Pays 50¢/word.

PRACTICAL HOMEOWNER, Practical Homeowner Publishing Co., 27 Unquowa, Fairfield CT 06430. (203)259-9877. Editor: Joe Provey. 40% freelance written. Works with a small number of new/unpublished writers each year. Magazine published 9 times/year about well-designed remodelings, home improvements and new home construction. Estab. 1988. Circ. 760,000. **Pays on acceptance.** Publishes ms an average of 3 months after acceptance. Submit seasonal material at least 1 year in advance. Query for electronic submissions. Reports in 6 weeks.

Nonfiction: "*Practical Homeowner* is a home improvement magazine for people who want to create a safe, efficient and healthy home environment. Its aim is to put the reader in control of all decisions affecting his home, which may mean simplifying day-to-day maintenance and improving an existing structure or the more involved overseeing of new home construction." Feature articles relating to the home, including—but not limited to—remodeling, home repair, home management, improving energy efficiency, landscaping, home design, construction techniques, building materials and technology, home ownership trends, and home health issues. Length: 1,000-1,500 words. Buys all rights. Payment $400-2,500.

Photos: Horst Weber, art director. State availability of photos. Pays $35-100 for b&w; $75-400 for transparencies or 35mm slides, depending on size and use. Captions and model releases required. Buys one-time rights.

Columns/Departments: Healthy Home (maintaining a safe, healthy home environment), Financial Advisor (managing home and home improvement finances), Well-Crafted Home (projects for the intermediate to advanced do -it-yourselfer), Trade Secrets (professional tradesmen explain techniques), Practical Products (building supplies, home furnishings, tools) and Life at My House (anecdotal essays on life at home). Length: 600-1,000 words. All columns are on assignment basis. Pays: $150-600.

‡SOUTHERN ACCENTS, Southern Progress Corp., 2100 Lakeshore Dr., Birmingham AL 35209. (205)877-6000. Editor: Karen Irons. Managing Editor: Lynn Carter. 50-75% freelance written. Published 10 times/year. Pays on acceptance of finished manuscript. Publishes ms an average of 3 months after acceptance. Buys first and second serial (reprint) rights. Reports in 2 months.

Nonfiction: Query with published clips and resume. "We do not accept completed articles unless we assign them." Length: 1,000-1,200 words. Payment varies according to assignment and experience of writer.

Tips: "Read the magazine to see what we are publishing. This is the best way to find out what we want and what we don't."

‡SOUTHERN HOMES, Atlanta's Magazine for Better Living, Haas Group, Inc., Georgia regional office: 3146 Reps Miller Rd., Norcross GA 30071. (404)446-6585. FAX: (404)446-0197. Editor: Gina Schreiber. Managing Editor: Ann A. Elstad. 80% freelance written. Bimonthly magazine on shelter design, lifestyle in the home. "*Southern Homes* is designed for the achievement-oriented, well-educated reader who is concerned about the quality of his/her shelter, its design and construction, its environment, and how to best enjoy living and entertaining in it." Estab. 1983. **Pays on acceptance.** Byline given. Publishes ms an average of 6 months after acceptance. Pays 25% kill fee. Buys all rights. Reports in 3 months. Sample copy.

Nonfiction: Frances Schultz, senior editor. Historical/nostalgic, interview/profile, new product, well-designed homes, antiques, photo feature, gardens, local art, remodeling, food and entertaining. "We do not want articles outside respective market area, not written for magazine format, or that are excessively controversial, investigative or that cannot be appropriately illustrated with attractive photography." Buys 35 mss/year. Query with published clips. Length: 800-1,200 words. Pays $375-450. Sometimes pays expenses of writers on assignment "if agreed upon in advance of assignment."

Photos: State availability of photos with submission "but, most photography is assigned." Reviews transparencies. Offers $50/photo. Captions, model releases, and identification of subjects required. Buys one-time rights.

Columns/Departments: Antiques, Quick Fix (simple remodeling ideas), Cheap Chic (stylish decorating that is easy on the wallet), Digging In (outdoor solutions from Atlanta's gardeners), Home Ecology, Home Technology, Real Estate News, Interior Elements (hot new furnishings on the market). Query with published clips. Buys 25-30 mss/year. Length: 350-900 words. Pays $50-300.

SPROUTLETTER, Sprouting Publications, P.O. Box 62, Ashland OR 97520. (503)488-2326. Editor: Michael Linden. 50% freelance written. Bimonthly newsletter covering sprouting, live foods and indoor food gardening. "We emphasize growing foods (especially sprouts) indoors for health, economy, nutrition and food self-sufficiency. We also cover topics related to sprouting, live foods and holistic health." Estab. 1980. Circ. 2,500. Pays on publication. Publishes ms an average of 3 months after acceptance. Byline given. Buys North American serial rights and second (reprint) rights. Submit seasonal/holiday material 4 months in advance. Previously published submissions OK. Reports in 2 weeks on queries; 3 weeks on mss. Sample copy $2.50.

Nonfiction: General interest (raw foods, algae, sprouting, holistic health); how-to (grow sprouts, all kinds of foods indoors; build devices for sprouting or indoor gardening); personal experience (in sprouting or related areas); and technical (experiments with growing sprouts). No common health food/vitamin articles or growing ornamental plants indoors (as opposed to food producing plants). Buys 4-6 mss/year. Query. Length: 500-2,400 words. Pays $15-50. Trades for merchandise are also considered.

Columns/Departments: Book Reviews (books oriented toward sprouts, nutrition or holistic health). Reviews are short and informative. News Items (interesting news items relating to sprouts or live foods); Recipes (mostly raw foods). Buys 5-10 mss/year. Query. Length: 100-450 words. Pays $3-10.

Fillers: Short humor and newsbreaks. Buys 3-6/year. Length: 50-150 words. Pays $2-6.

Tips: "Writers should have a sincere interest in holistic health and in natural whole foods. We like tight writing which is optimistic, interesting and informative. Consumers are demanding more thorough and accurate information. Articles should cover any given subject in depth in an enjoyable and inspiring manner. A frequent mistake is that the subject matter is not appropriate. Also buys cartoon strips and singles. Will consider series."

‡**TEXAS GARDENER, The Magazine for Texas Gardeners, by Texas Gardeners,** Suntex Communications, Inc., Box 9005, Waco TX 76714. (817)772-1270. Editor: Chris S. Corby. 80% freelance written. Works with a small number of new/unpublished writers each year. Bimonthly magazine covering vegetable and fruit production, ornamentals and home landscape information for home gardeners in Texas. Circ. 37,000. Pays on publication. Publishes ms an average of 4 months after acceptance. Byline given. Buys first North American serial rights and all rights. Submit seasonal/holiday material 6 months in advance. Query for electronic submissions. Reports in 6 weeks. Sample copy $2.75; writer's guidelines for business size SASE.

Nonfiction: How-to, humor, interview/profile and photo feature. "We use feature articles that relate to Texas gardeners. We also like personality profiles on hobby gardeners and professional horticulturists who are doing something unique." Buys 50-100 mss/year. Query with clips of published work. Length: 800-2,400 words. Pays $50-200.

Photos: "We prefer superb color and b&w photos; 90% of photos used are color." State availability of photos. Pays negotiable rates for 2¼, 35mm color transparencies and 8 × 10 b&w prints and contact sheets. Model release and identification of subjects required.

Tips: "First, be a Texan. Then come up with a good idea of interest to home gardeners in this state. Be specific. Stick to feature topics like 'How Alley Gardening Became a Texas Tradition.' Leave topics like 'How to Control Fire Blight' to the experts. High quality photos could make the difference. We would like to add several writers to our group of regular contributors and would make assignments on a regular basis. Fillers are easy to come up with in-house. We want good writers who can produce accurate and interesting copy. Frequent mistakes made by writers in completing an article assignment for us are that articles are not slanted toward Texas gardening, show inaccurate or too little gardening information or lack good writing style. We will be doing more 'people' features and articles on ornamentals."

TWENTYONE® MAGAZINE, The Magazine of the Century 21® Preferred Client Club, The Quarton Group, Suite 200, 2155 Butterfield, Troy MI 48084. (313)649-1110. Editor: Dee Ann Maki. 90% freelance written. Bimonthly magazine on home ownership. "Our readers have all either recently purchased or are about to purchase a new home. We're here to make that experience more productive and enjoyable." Circ. 500,000+. **Pays on acceptance.** Publishes ms an average of 4 months after acceptance. Byline given. Offers 25% kill fee. Buys first North American serial and second serial (reprint) rights. Submit seasonal/holiday material 6 months in advance. Query for electronic submissions. Reports in 2 months. Sample copy for 9×12 SAE with 8 first class stamps. Writer's guidelines for #10 SAE with 2 first class stamps.

Nonfiction: Book excerpts, how-to, interview/profile, new product, photo feature and technical. "No food stories. We are strictly a home-owning and real estate investment publication." Buys 42 mss/year. Query with published clips. Length: 300-2,000 words. Pays $350-1,000 for assigned articles. Sometimes pays expenses of writers on assignment.

Photos: Send photos with submission. Reviews transparencies (any size). Offers $25-100 per photo. Model releases and photo captions required. Buys one-time rights.

Columns/Departments: Home Finds (potpourri of home-related items), length open; Dollars & Sense (home-buying/investment/tax tips), 1200-1500 words; Home Library (book and video reviews), length open. Buys 20 mss/year. Query with published clips. Pays $100-500.

Humor

Publications listed here specialize in gaglines or prose humor, some just for readers and others for performers or speakers. Other publications that use humor can be found in nearly every category in this book. Some have special needs for major humor pieces; some use humor as fillers; many others are interested in material that meets their ordinary fiction or nonfiction requirements but also has a humorous slant. The majority of humor articles must be submitted as complete manuscripts on speculation because editors usually can't know from a query whether or not the piece will be right for them. For more information and markets for humor, see *Humor and Cartoon Markets* (Writer's Digest Books).

CURRENT COMEDY, Suite 4D, 165 West 47th St., New York NY 10036. Editor: Gary Apple. For "speakers, toastmasters, business executives, public officials, educators, public relations specialists and communication professionals." Estab. 1955. Pays on publication (at end of month material published). Buys all rights. Writer's guidelines for SASE.

Fillers: "We are looking for funny, performable one-liners and short jokes that deal with happenings in the news, fads, trends, and other topical subjects. The accent is on laugh-out-loud comedy. We are particularly interested in material that can be used by speakers and toastmasters: lines for beginning a speech, ending a speech, acknowledging an introduction, specific speaking occasions—any clever, original comments that would be of use to a person making a speech. We are also in the market for jokes used to respond to specific speaking situations (microphone feedback, broken air conditioning, hecklers). Short, sharp comment on business trends and events is also desirable. No puns, poems, sexist or stereotype jokes." Pays $12/joke.

Tips: "The material *must be original*. Do not send jokes you have heard, only those from your own creativity. We have a constant need for good comedy writers. Please send only your strongest material. We'd rather receive 5 truly funny jokes than 50 so-so ones. If you're not sure that your jokes are funny, try them out on some friends before trying them out on us. Please enclose a #10 SASE for the return of your material."

LATEST JOKES, P.O. Box 3304, Brooklyn NY 11202-0066. (718)855-5057. Editor: Robert Makinson. Estab. 1974. 20% freelance written. Monthly newsletter of humor for TV and radio personalities, comedians and professional speakers. **Pays on acceptance.** Byline given. Buys all rights. Submit seasonal/holiday material 3 months in advance. Reports in 1 month. Sample copy $3 and 1 first class stamp.

Nonfiction: Humor (short jokes). No "stupid, obvious, non-funny vulgar humor. Jokes about human tragedy also unwelcome." Send complete ms. Pays $1-3 for each joke.

Fiction: Humorous jokes. Pays $1-3.

Poetry: Light verse (humorous). Submit maximum 3 poems at one time. Line length: 2-8 lines. Pays 25¢/line.

Tips: "No famous personality jokes. Clever statements are not enough. Be original and surprising."

MAD MAGAZINE, 485 Madison Ave., New York NY 10022. (212)752-7685. Editors: Nick Meglin and John Ficarra. 100% freelance written. Magazine published 8 times/year. Estab. 1952. Circ. 1 million. **Pays on acceptance.** Publishes ms an average of 6 months after acceptance. Byline given. Buys all rights. Submit seasonal/holiday material 6 months in advance. Reports in 6 weeks. Writer's guidelines for #10 SASE.

Nonfiction: Satire, parody. "We're always on the lookout for new ways to spoof and to poke fun at hot trends — music, computers, fashions etc. We're *not* interested in formats we're already doing or have done to death like... 'you know you're a ... when ...' " Buys 400 ms yearly. Submit a premise with 3 or 4 examples of how you intend to carry it through, describing the action and visual content. Rough sketches are not necessary. Pays minimum $350/*MAD* page. One-page gags: 2-8 panel cartoon continuities in the style and tradition of *MAD*. Buys 30 yearly. Pays minimum of $350/*MAD* page. Don't send riddles, advice columns, TV or movie satires, book manuscripts, articles about Alfred E. Neuman or text pieces.

Tips: "Have fun! We're interested in anything and everything that you think is funny. Remember to think visually! Freelancers can best break in with nontopical material. If we see even a germ of talent, we will try to work with that person. We like outrageous, silly and/or satirical humor."

NATIONAL LAMPOON, National Lampoon Inc., 155 Avenue of the Americas, New York NY 10013. (212)645-5040. Editor-in-Chief: George Burkin. 50% freelance written. Works with small number of new/unpublished writers each year. A monthly magazine of "offbeat, irreverent satire." Circ. 250,000. **Pays on acceptance.** Publishes ms an average of 4 months after acceptance. Byline given. Offers 20% kill fee. Buys first North American serial rights. Simultaneous submissions OK. Reports in 3 months. Sample copy $2.95 with SAE.

Nonfiction: Humor. Buys 60 mss/year. Query with published clips. Length: approximately 2,000 words maximum. Pays 50-70¢/word. Pays the expenses of writers on assignment.

Columns/Departments: John Bendel, column/department editor. True Facts (weird true-life stories). Buys 240/year. Send complete ms. Length: 200 words maximum. Offers T-shirt for items, $10 and T-shirt for photos.

Tips: "We use very few new freelancers for major articles." True Facts section is most open to freelancers.

THE ONION, Suite 270, 33 University Square, Madison WI 53715. (608)256-1372. Editor: Rich Dahm. 80% freelance written. Weekly humor-entertainment newspaper. "*The Onion* is an irreverent humor publication with witty and outrageous stories, articles and cartoons satirizing college life, or any subject of interest to a college audience." Estab. 1988. Circ. 25,000. Pays on publication. Publishes manuscript an average of 1 month after acceptance. Byline given. Buys one-time rights. Submit seasonal/holiday material 3 months in advance. No simultaneous, photocopied or previously published submissions. Reports in 1 month. Sample copy and writer's guidelines for 9 × 12 SASE.

Nonfiction: Humor, personal experience and mean-spirited parodies. Buys 20 mss/year. Send complete ms. Length: 50-400 words. Pays $10.

Photos: Send photos with submission. Offers $5. Buys one-time rights.

Columns/Departments: "We do not publish columns for which freelancers may write; we publish columns by freelancers willing to create their own column of engaging, original and humorous thoughts. Buys 2 mss/year. Send complete ms. Length: 50-300. Pays $10.

Fiction: Humorous, slice-of-life vignettes and humorous, shocking and offbeat stories. Buys 180 mss/year. Send complete ms. Length: 50-1,000. Pays $10.

Tips: "Hip, funny and unconventional submissions are always taken seriously. First-time writers are welcome. We plan to expand to other cities around the country, and we'd like creative, witty and reliable writers to expand with us. We are most interested in short short stories and satirical articles of interest to a college audience. Our tone is sharp, intelligent and irreverent, but deviations for comic effect are encouraged. We're sick of traditional comedy."

‡WE ARE THE WEIRD, Briggs Museum of American Culture, P.O. Box 2002, Dallas TX 75221. (214)692-8601. FAX: (214)368-2310. Editor: Jo Bob Briggs. Managing Editor: Mindy Irvin. 5% freelance written. Weekly newsletter/fanzine covering Joe Bob Briggs, popular culture, film. "Radical humor in the spirit of syndicated columnist and TV personality Joe Bob Briggs." Estab. 1985. Circ. 3,500. Pays on publication. Publishes ms an average of 1 month after acceptance. Byline given. Buys first North American serial rights and second serial (reprint) rights. Submit seasonal/holiday material 2-3 months in advance. Simultaneous and previously published submissions OK. Query for electronic submissions. Free sample copy.

Nonfiction: Essays, humor, opinion, personal experience. Buys 10 mss/year. Send complete ms. Length: 2,000 words maximum. Pays $25 maximum for unsolicited articles. Pays in contributor copies or other premiums when the writer requests it. Send photos with submission. Offers $5-25 per photo. Model releases and identification of subjects required. Buys all rights.

Fiction: Fantasy, horror, humorous, slice-of-life vignettes. Buys 5 mss/year. Send complete ms. Length: 2,000 maximum words. Pays $25 maximum.
Poetry: Avant-garde, free verse, Haiku, light verse, traditional. Buys 5 poems/year. Pays $25 maximum.
Fillers: Anecdotes, facts and short humor. Buys 5/year. Length: 25 maximum words.
Tips: "Anything that makes us laugh will get our attention. We are most open to poems or short essays (500 words or less). They should be humorous or deal with popular culture, especially the fields of movies, music and stand-up comedy."

Inflight

Most major inflight magazines cater to business travelers and vacationers who will be reading, during the flight, about the airline's destinations and other items of general interest. Airline mergers and acquisitions continue to decrease the number of magazines published in this area. The writer should watch for airline announcements in the news and in ads and read the latest sample copies and writer's guidelines for current information.

ABOARD, North-South Net, Inc., Suite 220, 100 Almeria, Coral Gables FL 33134. (305)441-9744. Editor: Marisella Veiga. 20% freelance written. Bimonthly magazine. Estab. 1976. Circ. 89,000. Pays on publication. Byline given. Buys one-time rights, simultaneous rights or makes work-for-hire assignments. Submit seasonal/holiday material 4 months in advance. Simultaneous and previously published submissions OK. Query for electronic submissions.
Nonfiction: General interest, historical/nostalgic, humor, new product, personal experience, photo feature, technical, travel. "No controversial or political material." Buys 50 mss/year. Length: 1,200-1,500 words. Pays $100-150. Sometimes pays expenses of writers on assignment.
Photos: Send photos with submission. Reviews transparencies. Offers no additional payment for photos accepted with ms. Offers $20 minimum per photo. Identification of subjects required. Buys one-time rights.
Fillers: Facts, short humor. Buys 6/year. Length: 800-1,200 words. Pays $100.
Tips: "Send article with photos. We need lots of travel material on Chile, Ecuador, Bolivia, El Salvador, Honduras, Peru, Guatemala and the Dominican Republic."

AMERICA WEST AIRLINES MAGAZINE, Skyword Marketing, Inc., Suite 240, 7500 N. Dreamy Draw Dr., Phoenix AZ 85020. (602)997-7200. Editor: Michael Derr. 80% freelance written. Works with small number of new/unpublished writers each year. A monthly "general interest magazine emphasizing the western and southwestern U.S. Some midwestern, northwestern and eastern subjects also appropriate. We look for ideas and people that celebrate opportunity, and those who put it to positive use." Estab. 1986. Query with published clips and SASE. Pays on publication. Publishes ms an average of 4 months after acceptance. Byline given. Offers 15% kill fee. Buys first North American rights. Submit seasonal/holiday material 6-8 months in advance. Simultaneous submissions OK, "if indicated as such." Query for electronic submissions. Reports in 1 month on queries; 5 weeks on mss. Sample copy for $3; writer's guidelines for 9 × 12 SAE with 3 first class stamps.
Nonfiction: General interest, creative leisure, profile, photo feature, science, sports, business issues, entrepreneurs, nature, health, history, arts, book excerpts, travel and trends. Also considers essays and humor. No puzzles, reviews or highly controversial features. Buys 130-140 mss/year. Length: 500-2,200. Pays $200-750. Pays some expenses.
Photos: State availability of original photography. Offers $50-250/photo. Captions, model releases and identification of subjects required. Buys one-time rights.

AMERICAN WAY, P.O. Box 619640, Dallas/Fort Worth Airport TX 75261-9640. (817)967-1804. FAX: (817)967-1571. Editor: Doug Crichton. 98% freelance written. Prefers to work with published/established writers. Fortnightly inflight magazine for passengers flying with American Airlines. Estab. 1966. **Pays on acceptance.** Publishes ms an average of 4 months after acceptance. Buys first serial rights.
Nonfiction: Business and CEO profiles, the arts and entertainment, sports, personalities, technology, food, science and medicine and travel. "We are amenable to almost any subject that would be interesting, entertaining or useful to a passenger of American Airlines." Also humor, trivia, trends, and will consider a variety of ideas. Buys 450 mss/year. Query with published clips. Length: 1,000-4,000 words.

For explanation of symbols, see the Key to Symbols and Abbreviations on Page 5. For unfamiliar words, see the Glossary.

Pays $850 and up. Usually pays the expenses of writers on assignment.

‡**CANADIAN, Inflight Magazine of Canadian Airlines Int'l,** Airstream Inflight Marketing Inc., Suite 306, 1305 11 Ave., S.W., Calgary, Alberta T3C 3P6 Canada. (403)244-7516. Editor: Alister Thomas. 75% freelance written. Monthly magazine covering travel and business. Estab. 1988. Circ. 141,000. **Pays on acceptance.** Byline given. Offers 50% kill fee. Buys first North American serial rights. Submit seasonal/holiday material 6 months in advance. Query for electronic submissions. Reports in 6 weeks on queries. Sample copy $2 for 9 × 12 SAE and 3 first class stamps. Writer's guidelines for SAE.

Nonfiction: General interest and travel. Query with published clips. Length: 600-1,500 words. Pays 40¢/word and up. Pays expenses of writers on assignment. State availability of photos with submission. Identification of subjects required.

‡**MIDWAY MAGAZINE,** Skies America Publishing Co., Suite 310, 9600 S.W. Oak St., Portland OR 97223. (503)244-2299. Editor: Terri J. Wallo. 50% freelance written. Monthly magazine. Circ. approximately 40,000. Pays on publication. Publishes ms an average of 2 months after acceptance. Byline given. Submit seasonal/holiday material 6 months in advance. Simultaneous submissions OK. Reports in 1 month. Sample copy for 8½ × 11 SAE $3; writer's guidelines only, include #10 SASE.

Nonfiction: Interview/profile, photo feature and travel. "Business features should be timely, well-researched and well-focused. Corporate profiles and personality profiles are encouraged. Travel destination pieces should be original, detailed and lively. No stale pieces that sound like canned promotions." Buys 24 mss/year. Query with published clips. Length: 1,000-2,500 words. Pays $150-400 for assigned articles; pays $150-250 for unsolicited articles. Sometimes pays the expenses of writers on assignment.

Photos: Send photos with submission. Reviews color transparencies and 8 × 10 b&w prints. Offers no additional payment for photos accepted with ms. Identification of subjects required. Buys one-time rights.

Tips: "The cities we focus on are: New York; Boston; Chicago; Indianapolis; Miami; Pittsburgh; Columbus; New Orleans; all Florida cities; New York; Minneapolis; Dallas; Cleveland; Detroit; New Orleans; Washington, D.C.; Virgin Islands; Cincinnati; Kansas City; Philadelphia; Las Vegas; Denver and Atlanta. Write to us with specific ideas relating to these cities. A fresh, original idea with excellent photo possibilities will receive our close attention. Areas most open to freelancers are corporate profiles; destination travel pieces with an unusual slant; personality profiles on businessmen and women, entrepreneurs."

SKIES AMERICA PUBLISHING, Compass Readings, (formerly *Northwest Airlines*), Skies America Publishing Co., 7730 S.W. Mohawk, Tualatin OR 97062. (503)691-1955. Editor: Terri J. Wallo. Managing Editor: Kelly Kearns. 75% freelance written. Monthly magazine of business and leisure. Estab. 1969. Circ. 425,000. Pays on publication. Publishes ms an average of 2 months after acceptance. Byline given. Offers 100% kill fee. Buys first rights. Submit seasonal/holiday material 6 months in advance. Simultaneous submissions OK. Reports in 1 month. Sample copy $3. Writer's guidelines for #10 SAE with 1 first class stamp.

Nonfiction: General interest, interview/profile, personal experience, photo feature, travel. No poetry, new product, controversial, fiction, religious, fillers. Buys 5 mss/year. Query. Length: 2,000-3,000 words. Pays $850-1,000. Pays expenses of writers on assignment.

Photos: State availability of photos with submission. Offers $200 maximum per photo. Captions and identification of subjects required. Buys one-time rights.

Tips: "Query letter only. No ms. No phone calls. Study structure of magazine. Freelancers have the best chance breaking in with articles on adventure sports, corporate profiles or sports profiles."

SKY, Inflight Magazine of Delta Air Lines, Halsey Publishing Co., 12955 Biscayne Blvd., N. Miami FL 33181. (305)893-1520. Editor: Lidia De Leon. Managing Editor: Barbara Mlotek Cloudman. 90% freelance written. Monthly magazine. "Delta *SKY* is a general interest, nationally/internationally-oriented magazine with the main purpose to entertain and inform business and leisure travelers aboard Delta Air Lines." Estab. 1971. Circ. 410,000. **Pays on acceptance.** Publishes ms an average of 2 months after acceptance. Byline given. Offers 100% kill fee when cancellation is through no fault of the writer. Buys one-time rights. Submit seasonal/holiday material 9 months in advance. Simultaneous submissions OK. Query for electronic submissions. Reports in 1 month. Sample copy for 9 × 12 SAE; free writer's guidelines for SASE.

Nonfiction: General interest and photo feature. "No excerpts, essays, personal experience, opinion, religious, reviews, poetry, fiction or fillers." Buys 200-250 mss/year. Query with published clips. Length: 1700-2500 words. Pays $500-700 for assigned articles; pays $400-500 for unsolicited articles. Pays expenses of writers on assignment.

Photos: State availability of photos with submission. Reviews transparencies (4×5) and prints (5×7). Offers $25-50/photo. Captions, model releases and identification of subject required. Buys one-time rights.

Columns/Departments: Management (managerial techniques, methods of topical nature); Language (word origins, usage, international comparisons); Finance (personal finance, tips). Buys 50-60 mss/year. Query. Length: 1500-1700 words. Pays $300-450.

Tips: "Send a well detailed query tied in to one of the feature or column categories of the magazine. Since our lead times call for planning of editorial content 6-9 months in advance, that should also be kept in mind when proposing story ideas. All feature story and column/department categories are open to freelancers, with the exceptions of Travel (areas are predetermined by the airline) and the executive Profile Series (which is also predetermined)."

‡**TRADEWIND**, Caribbean Travel and Life, Inc., Suite 830, 8403 Colesville Rd., Silver Spring MD 20910. (301)588-2300. Editor: Norie Quintos. 75% freelance written. Quarterly magazine covering destinations of ALM Antillean Airlines (Aruba, Bonaire, Curaçao, Jamaica, Guyana, Venezuela, Columbia). "*TradeWind* is the inflight magazine for ALM Antillean Airlines, the airline of the Dutch Caribbean. We publish articles on travel to the Dutch Caribbean and other ALM destinations. Our audience is the airline traveler on ALM." Estab. 1987. Circ. 22,000. Pays on publication. Publishes ms an average of 4 months after acceptance. Byline given. Offers 25% kill fee. Buys first North American serial rights, one-time rights and second serial (reprint) rights. Submit seasonal material 6 months in advance. Simultaneous and previously published submissions OK. Query for electronic submissions. Reports in 2 months. Sample copy for 9×12 SAE with 5 first class stamps. Writer's guidelines for #10 SASE.

Nonfiction: General interest (related to ALM destinations) and travel. "No superficial pieces, or pieces on destinations not on airline route." Buys 10 mss/year. Query with or without published clips, or send complete ms. Length: 800-1,000 words. Pays $35-150.

Photos: Send photos with submission. Reviews all sizes of transparencies. Offers $35-200/photo. Identification of subjects required. Buys one-time rights.

Columns/Departments: Panorama (short pieces on travel news, new books, tours), 400-600 words; Sugar & Spice (food column on Caribbean food), 600-800 words. Buys 4 mss/year. Query with published clips or send complete ms. Pays $35-100.

Tips: "We are in particular need of story ideas on some of ALM's more exotic destinations: Caracas and Valencia, Venezuela; Georgetown, Guyana; Paramibo, Surinam. Recent freelance pieces have been: Glassblowers of Caracas. Though our rates are on the low end, we're willing to work with new freelancers who have good ideas and skills."

USAIR MAGAZINE, Pace Communications, 1301 Carolina St., Greensboro NC 27401. (919)378-6065. Editor: Maggie Oman. Associate Editor: Terri Barnes. 95% freelance written. Prefers to work with published/established writers. A monthly general interest magazine published for airline passengers, many of whom are business travelers, male, with high incomes and college educations. Circ. 475,000. Pays before publication. Publishes ms an average of 4 months after acceptance. Buys first rights only. Submit seasonal material 4 months in advance. Reports in 6 weeks. Sample copy $5; free writer's guidelines with SASE.

Nonfiction: Travel, business, sports, health, food, nature, the arts, science/technology and photography. Buys 100 mss/year. Query with clips of previously published work. Length: 1,500-2,800 words. Pays $400-800. Pays expenses of writers on assignment, if requested.

Photos: Send photos with ms. Pays $75-150/b&w print, depending on size; color from $100-250/print or slide. Captions preferred; model release required. Buys one-time rights.

Columns/Departments: Sports, food, health, business, living and science. Buys 8-10 mss/issue. Query. Length: 1,200-1,800 words. Pays $300-500.

Tips: "Send irresistible ideas and proof that you can write. It's great to get a clean manuscript from a good writer who has given me exactly what I asked for. Frequent mistakes are not following instructions, not delivering on time, etc."

WASHINGTON FLYER MAGAZINE, #111, 11 Canal Center Plaza, Alexandria VA 22314. (703)739-9292. Editor: Brian T. Cook. Assistant Editors: Laurie McLaughlin, Stephen Soltis. 90% freelance written. Bimonthly in-airport magazine for business and pleasure travelers at Washington National and Washington Dulles International airports. "Primarily affluent, well-educated audience that flies frequently in and out of Washington, D.C." Estab. 1989. Circ. 160,620. **Pays on acceptance.** Byline given. Buys first North American or second serial (reprint) rights. Submit seasonal/holiday material 4 months in advance. Previously published submissions OK, preferably out of market. Query for electronic submissions. Reports in 6-8 weeks. Free sample copy, writer's guidelines with appropriate SASE.

Nonfiction: General interest, historical/nostalgic, how-to, interview/profile, personal experience, travel. Buys 30-40 mss/year. Query with published clips. Length: 500-3,500 words. Pays $100-600. Sometimes pays expenses of writers on assignment.

Photos: State availability of photos with submission. Reviews negative and transparencies. Will consider additional payment for top-quality photos accepted with ms. Identification of subjects required. Buys one-time rights.

Tips: "Know the Washington market and issues relating to frequent business/pleasure travelers as we move toward a global economy."

Juvenile

Just as children change and grow, so do juvenile magazines. Children's magazine editors stress that writers must read recent issues. This section lists publications for children ages 2-12. Magazines for young people 13-19 appear in the Teen and Young Adult category. Many of the following publications are produced by religious groups and, where possible, the specific denomination is given. For the writer with a story or article slanted to a specific age group, the following children's index is a quick reference to markets for each age group. A book of juvenile markets, *Children's Writer's and Illustrator's Market*, is available from Writer's Digest Books.

Juvenile publications classified by age

Two- to Five-Year-Olds: *Chickadee, The Friend, Humpty Dumpty, Stone Soup, Story Friends, Turtle, Wee Wisdom.*

Six- to Eight-Year-Olds: *Boys' Life, Chickadee, Children's Album, Children's Playmate, Cricket, The Dolphin Log, The Friend, Highlights for Children, Hopscotch, Humpty Dumpty, Jack and Jill, Kid City, Ladybug, Odyssey, Owl, Pockets, R-A-D-A-R, Ranger Rick, Sports Illustrated for Kids, Stone Soup, Story Friends, 3-2-1 Contact, Touch, Wee Wisdom, Wonder Time.*

Nine- to Twelve-Year-Olds: *Boys' Life, Calliope, Children's Album, Children's Digest, Clubhouse, Cobblestone, Cricket, Crusader, Current Health 1, The Dolphin Log, The Friend, High Adventure, Highlights for Children, Hopscotch, Jack and Jill, Kid City, Odyssey, On the Line, Owl, Pockets, R-A-D-A-R, Ranger Rick, Scouting, Sports Illustrated for Kids, Stone Soup, 3-2-1 Contact, Touch, Venture, Wee Wisdom, The World of Business Kids.*

BOYS' LIFE, Boy Scouts of America, P.O. Box 152079, 1325 Walnut Hill Lane, Irving TX 75015-2079. Editor-in-Chief: William B. McMorris. 75% freelance written. Prefers to work with published/established writers; works with small number of new/unpublished writers each year. Monthly magazine covering activities of interest to all boys ages 8-18. Most readers are Scouts or Cub Scouts. Estab. 1911. Circ 1.4 million. **Pays on acceptance.** Publishes ms an average of 6-12 months after acceptance. Buys one-time rights. Reports in 2 weeks. Sample copy for 9×12 SAE and $2.50. Writer's guidelines for #10 SASE.

Nonfiction: Major articles run 1,000-1,200 words. Preferred length is about 1,000 words including sidebars and boxes. Pays minimum $500 for major article text. Uses strong photo features with about 500 words of text. Separate payment or assignment for photos. "Much better rates if you really know how to write for our market." Buys 60 major articles/year. Also needs how-to features and hobby and crafts ideas. "We pay top rates for ideas accompanied by sharp photos, clean diagrams, and short, clear instructions." Query first in writing. Buys 30-40 how-tos/year. Query all ideas in writing. Pays expenses of writers on assignment. Also buys freelance comics pages and scripts. Query first.

Columns: "Food, Health, Pets, Bicycling and Magic Tricks are some of the columns for which we use 400-600 words of text. This is a good place to show us what you can do. Query first in writing." Pays $150 minimum. Buys 75-80 columns/year.

Fiction: Short stories 1,000-1,500 words; occasionally longer. Send complete ms. Pays $500 minimum. Buys 15 short stories/year.

Tips: "We strongly recommend reading at least 12 issues of the magazine and learning something about the programs of the Boy Scouts of America before you submit queries. We are a good market for any writer willing to do the necessary homework."

CALLIOPE: The World History Magazine for Young People, Cobblestone Publishing, Inc., 30 Grove St., Peterborough NH 03458. (603)924-7209. Editor-in-Chief: Carolyn P. Yoder. Editors: Rosalie and Charles Baker. Assistant Editor: Sarah E. Hale. 80% freelance written. Prefers to work with published/

established writers. A magazine published 5 times/year covering world history through 1800 AD for 9- to 15-year-olds. Articles must relate to the issue's theme. Pays on publication. Byline given. Buys all rights. Simultaneous submissions OK. Previously published submissions rarely accepted. Sample copy 7½×10½ SAE with 5 first class stamps and $3.95; writer's guidelines for SASE.

Nonfiction: Essays, general interest, historical/nostalgic, how-to (activities), recipes, humor, interview/profile, personal experience, photo feature, technical and travel. Articles must relate to the theme. No religious, pornographic, biased or sophisticated submissions. Buys approximately 30-40 mss/year. Query with published clips. Length: 250-1,000 words. Pays up to 15¢/word.

Photos: State availability of photos with submission. Reviews contact sheets, color slides and b&w prints. Offers $10/photo. Buys one-time rights.

Fiction: All fiction must be theme-related. Buys 10 mss/year. Query with published clips. Length: 500-1,000 words. Pays 10-15¢/word.

Poetry: Light verse and traditional. No religious or pornographic poetry or poetry not related to the theme. Submit maximum 1 poem. Pays on individual basis.

Tips: "Writers must have an appreciation and understanding of world history. Writers must not condescend to our readers."

CHICKADEE MAGAZINE, For Young Children from *OWL*, The Young Naturalist Foundation, 56 The Esplanade, Suite 306, Toronto, Ontario M5E 1A7 Canada. (416)868-6001. Editor: Catherine Ripley. 25% freelance written. Magazine published 10 times/year (except July and August) for 4-9-year-olds. "We aim to interest young children in the world around them in an entertaining and lively way." Estab. 1979. Circ. 110,000 Canada and U.S. Pays on publication. Byline given. Buys all rights. Submit seasonal/holiday material up to 1 year in advance. Reports in 2½ months. Sample copy for $3.50 and SAE; writer's guidelines for SAE.

Nonfiction: How-to (arts and crafts, easy experiments for children); personal experience (real children in real situations); and photo feature (wildlife features). No articles for older children; no religious or moralistic features. Sometimes pays the expenses of writers on assignment.

Photos: Send photos with ms. Reviews 35mm transparencies. Identification of subjects required.

Fiction: Adventure (relating to the 4-9-year-old), humor. No science fiction, fantasy, talking animal stories or religious articles. Send complete ms with $1 money order for handling and return postage. No IRCs. Pays $100-300.

Tips: "A frequent mistake made by writers is trying to teach too much—not enough entertainment and fun."

‡THE CHILDREN'S ALBUM, EGW Publishing Co., Box 6086, Concord CA 94524. (415)671-9852. Editor: Margo M. Lemas. Managing Editor: Wayne Lin. 95% freelance written. A bimonthly magazine of stories and poems written by children ages 8-14. "Adult input includes discussion of writing techniques, terms and examples, book reviews and fillers (anagrams, cartoons, etc.) on literature, writing or other topics of general education." Pays on publication. Publishes ms an average of 1 year after acceptance. Byline given. Buys all rights. Submit seasonal/holiday material 6 months in advance. Simultaneous and photocopied submissions OK. Reports in 2 months on mss. Sample copy $3; writer's guidelines for letter-size SASE.

Nonfiction: *Open to all adults.* How-to (on improving your writing, overcoming writer's block); technical (writing tips); book reviews and literary terms defined and exemplified. "We cannot accept any articles on creative writing that are too erudite. Our readers are children ages 8-14." Buys 15 mss/year. Send complete ms. Length: 100-800 words. Payment varies per contract.

Columns/Departments: Write On! (tips for writing better fiction and poetry; thinking like a writer/poet; unblocking writer's block; stimulating creativity); Send complete ms. Length: 100-800 words.

Fiction: *Open to only children 6-14.* Adventure, ethnic, experimental, fantasy, horror, humorous, mainstream, mystery, romance, science fiction, slice-of-life vignettes, suspense and western. Length: 50-1,000 words.

Fillers: Anecdotes, facts, short humor, crossword puzzles, mazes, quizzes, sayings, anagrams and cartoons. Length: 100-100 words. Pays $5-20.

Tips: "We are writer-friendly. We review each submission carefully and encourage new writers. Children—use your imagination. Adults—remember we are geared to children 8-14."

CHILDREN'S DIGEST, Children's Better Health Institute, P.O. Box 567, Indianapolis IN 46206. (317)636-8881. Editor: Elizabeth Rinck. 85% freelance written. Works with a small number of new/unpublished writers each year. Magazine published 8 times/year covering children's health for preteen children. Estab. 1950. Pays on publication. Publishes ms an average of 1 year after acceptance. Byline given. Buys all rights. Submit seasonal/holiday material 8 months in advance. Submit *only* complete manuscripts. "No queries, please." Reports in 2 months. Sample copy for 75¢; writer's guidelines for #10 SASE.

Nonfiction: Historical, interview/profile (biographical), craft ideas, health, nutrition, hygiene, fitness and safety. "We're especially interested in factual features that teach readers about the human body or encourage them to develop better health habits. We are *not* interested in material that is simply rewritten from encyclopedias. We try to present our health material in a way that instructs *and* entertains the reader." Buys 15-20 mss/year. Send complete ms. Length: 500-1,200 words. Pays 10¢/word. Sometimes pays the expenses of writers on assignment.

Photos: State availability of full color or b&w photos. Payment varies. Model releases and identification of subjects required. Buys one-time rights.

Fiction: Adventure, humorous, mainstream and mystery. Stories should appeal to both boys and girls. "We need some stories that incorporate a health theme. However, we don't want stories that preach, preferring instead stories with implied morals. We like a light or humorous approach." Buys 15-20 mss/year. Length: 500-1,500 words. Pays 10¢/word.

Poetry: Pays $10 minimum.

Tips: "Many of our readers have working mothers and/or come from single-parent homes. We need more stories that reflect these changing times while communicating good values."

CHILDREN'S PLAYMATE, 1100 Waterway Blvd., P.O. Box 567, Indianapolis IN 46206. (317)636-8881. Editor: Elizabeth Rinck. 75% freelance written. Eager to work with new/unpublished writers. "We are looking for articles, stories, and activities with a health, safety, fitness or nutritionally oriented theme. Primarily we are concerned with preventative medicine. We try to present our material in a positive—not a negative—light, and we try to incorporate humor and a light approach wherever possible without minimizing the seriousness of what we are saying." For children ages 6-8. Magazine published 8 times/year. Estab. 1928. Buys all rights. Byline given. Pays on publication. Publishes ms an average of 1 year after acceptance. Submit seasonal material 8 months in advance. Reports in 2 months. Sometimes may hold mss for up to 1 year, with author's permission. Write for guidelines. "Material will not be returned unless accompanied by a self-addressed envelope and sufficient postage." Sample copy 75¢; free writer's guidelines with SASE.

Nonfiction: 600 words maximum. A feature may be an interesting presentation on animals, people, events, objects or places, especially about good health, exercise, proper nutrition and safety. Include number of words in articles. Buys 30 mss/year. "We do not consider outlines. Reading the whole manuscript is the only way to give fair consideration. The editors cannot criticize, offer suggestions, or review unsolicited material that is not accepted." No queries. Pays about 10¢/word.

Fiction: Short stories for beginning readers, not over 700 words. Seasonal stories with holiday themes. Humorous stories, unusual plots. "We are interested in stories about children in different cultures and stories about lesser-known holidays (not just Christmas, Thanksgiving, Halloween, Hanukkah)." Vocabulary suitable for ages 6-8. Submit complete ms. Pays about 10¢/word. Include number of words in stories.

Fillers: Puzzles, dot-to-dots, color-ins, hidden pictures and mazes. Buys 30 fillers/year. Payment varies.

Tips: Especially interested in stories, poems and articles about special holidays, customs and events.

CLUBHOUSE, Your Story Hour, P.O. Box 15, Berrien Springs MI 49103. (616)471-3701. Editor: Elaine Trumbo. 75% freelance written. Works with a small number of new/unpublished writers each year. Magazine published 6 times/year covering many subjects with Christian approach, though not associated with a church. "Stories and features for fun for 9-14 year-olds. Main objective: To provide a psychologically 'up' magazine that lets kids know that they are acceptable, 'neat' people." Estab. 1951. Circ. 10,000. Pays on acceptance within about 6 months. Publishes ms an average of 1 year after acceptance. Byline given. Buys first serial rights or first North American serial rights, one-time rights, simultaneous rights, and second serial (reprint) rights. Simultaneous queries, and simultaneous and previously published submissions OK. Reports in 4-8 weeks. Sample copy for 6×9 SAE and 3 first class stamps; writer's guidelines for #10 SASE.

Nonfiction: How-to (crafts), personal experience and recipes (without sugar or artificial flavors and colors). "No stories in which kids start out 'bad' and by peer or adult pressure or circumstances are changed into 'good' people." Send complete ms. Length: 750-800 words ($25); 1,000-1,200 words ($30); feature story, 1,200 words ($35).

Photos: Send photos with ms. Pays on publication according to published size. Buys one-time rights.

Columns/Departments: Body Shop (short stories or "ad" type material that is anti-smoking, drugs and alcohol and pro-good nutrition, etc.); and Jr. Detective (secret codes, word search, deduction problems, hidden pictures, etc.). Buys 12/year. Send complete ms. Length: 400 words maximum for Jr. Detective; 1,000 maximum for Body Shop. Pays $10-30.

Fiction: Adventure, historical, humorous and mainstream. "Stories should depict bravery, kindness, etc., without a preachy attitude." No science fiction, romance, confession or mystery. Cannot use Santa-elves, Halloween or Easter Bunny material. Buys 30 mss/year. Send query or complete ms (prefers ms). Length: 750-800 words ($20); 1,000-1,200 words ($30); lead story ($35).

Poetry: Free verse, light verse and traditional. Buys 6-10/year. Submit maximum 5 poems. Length: 4-24 lines. Pays $5-20.

Fillers: Cartoons. Buys 18/year. Pay $12 maximum.

Tips: "Send all material during March or April. (Not accepting material until April 1992.) By the middle of June acceptance or rejection notices will be sent. Material chosen will appear the following year. Basically, kids are more and more informed and aware of the world around them. This means that characters in stories for *Clubhouse* should not seem too simple, yet maintain the wonder and joy of youth."

COBBLESTONE: The History Magazine for Young People, Cobblestone Publishing, Inc., 30 Grove St., Peterborough NH 03458. (603)924-7209. Editor-in-Chief: Carolyn P. Yoder. Editor: Beth Turin Weston. 80% freelance written (approximately 2 issues/year are by assignment only). Prefers to work with published/established writers. Monthly magazine covering American history for children ages 8-14. "Each issue presents a particular theme, from different angles, making it exciting as well as informative. Half of all subscriptions are for schools." Circ. 45,000. Pays on publication. Publishes ms an average of 4 months after acceptance. Byline given. Buys all rights; makes work-for-hire assignments. All material must relate to monthly theme. Simultaneous and previously published submissions OK. Sample copy for 7½ × 10½ SAE with 5 first class stamps and $3.95; writer's guidelines for SASE.

Nonfiction: Historical/nostalgic, how-to, interview, plays, biography, recipes, activities and personal experience. "Request a copy of the writer's guidelines to find out specific issue themes in upcoming months." No material that editorializes rather than reports. Buys 5-8 mss/issue. Length: 800-1,200 words. Supplemental nonfiction 200-800 words. Query with published clips, outline and bibliography. Pays up to 15¢/word.

Fiction: Adventure, historical, humorous and biographical fiction. "Has to be very strong and accurate." Buys 1-2 mss/issue. Length: 800-1,200 words. Request free editorial guidelines that explain upcoming issue themes and give query deadlines. "Message" must be smoothly integrated with the story. Query with written samples. Pays up to 15¢/word.

Poetry: Free verse, light verse and traditional. Submit maximum 2 poems. Length: 5-100 lines. Pays on an individual basis.

Tips: "All material is considered on the basis of merit and appropriateness to theme. Query should state idea for material simply, with rationale for why material is applicable to theme. Request writer's guidelines (includes themes and query deadlines) before submitting a query. Include SASE."

CRICKET, The Magazine for Children, Carus Publishing Co., 315 5th St., P.O. Box 300, Peru IL 61354. (815)224-6643. Publisher and Editor-in-Chief: Marianne Carus. Monthly magazine. Estab. 1973. Circ. 120,000. Pays on publication. Byline given. Buys first North American serial rights. Submit seasonal/holiday material 1 year in advance. Previously published submissions OK. Reports in 3-4 months. Sample copy $2; writer's guidelines for SASE.

Nonfiction: Historical/nostalgic, lively science, personal experience and travel. Send complete ms. Length: 200-1,200 words. Pays up to 25¢/word.

Fiction: Adventure, ethnic, fantasy, historical, humorous, mystery, novel excerpts, science fiction, suspense and western. No didactic, sex, religious or horror stories. Buys 24-36 mss/year. Send complete ms. Length: 200-1,500 words. Pays up to 25¢/word.

Poetry: Buys 8-10 poems/year. Length: 100 lines maximum. Pays up to $3/line on publication.

CRUSADER MAGAZINE, P.O. Box 7259, Grand Rapids MI 49510. FAX: (616)241-5558. Editor: G. Richard Broene. 40% freelance written. Works with a small number of new/unpublished writers each year. Magazine published 7 times/year. "*Crusader Magazine* shows boys (9-14) how God is at work in their lives and in the world around them." Estab. 1958. Circ. 13,000. Buys 20-25 mss/year. **Pays on acceptance.** Byline given. Publishes ms an average of 8 months after acceptance. Rights purchased vary with author and material; buys first serial rights, one-time rights, second serial (reprint) rights, and simultaneous rights. Submit seasonal material (Christmas, Easter) at least 5 months in advance. Simultaneous submissions OK. Reports in 1 month. Free sample copy and writer's guidelines for 9 × 12 SAE and 3 first class stamps.

Nonfiction: Articles about young boys' interests: sports, outdoor activities, bike riding, science, crafts, etc., and problems. Emphasis is on a Christian multi-racial perspective, but no simplistic moralisms. Informational, how-to, personal experience, interview, profile, inspirational and humor. Submit complete ms. Length: 500-1,500 words. Pays 2-5¢/word.

Photos: Pays $4-25 for b&w photos purchased with mss.

Fiction: "Considerable fiction is used. Fast-moving stories that appeal to a boy's sense of adventure or sense of humor are welcome. Avoid preachiness. Avoid simplistic answers to complicated problems. Avoid long dialogue and little action." Length: 900-1,500 words. Pays 2¢/word minimum.

Fillers: Uses short humor and any type of puzzles as fillers.

‡CURRENT HEALTH 1, The Beginning Guide to Health Education, General Learning Corporation, 60 Revere Dr., Northbrook IL 60062-1563. (312)564-4070. Executive Editor: Laura Ruekberg. Managing Editor: Nancy Dreher. 95% freelance written. An educational health periodical. Published monthly 9 times per year. September-May. "Our audience is fourth through seventh grade health education students. Articles should be written at a fifth grade reading level. As a curriculum supplementary publication, info should be accurate, timely, accessible and highly readable." Estab. 1976. Circ. 100,000. Pays on publication. Publishes ms an average of 9 months after acceptance. Buys all rights.
Nonfiction: General interest, interview/profile, new product, and educational. Buys 100 mss/year. "We accept no queries or unsolicited mss. *Articles are on assignment only.* Send introductory letter, resume and clips." Length: 800-2,000 words. Pays $100-400 for assigned articles.
Tips: "We are looking for good writers with an education and health background preferably, who can write for the age group in a firm, accessible, and medically/scientifically accurate way. Ideally, the writer should be an expert in the area in which he or she is writing. Topics open to freelancers are disease, drugs, fitness and exercise, psychology, safety, nutrition and personal health."

THE DOLPHIN LOG, The Cousteau Society, 8440 Santa Monica Blvd., Los Angeles CA 90069. (213)656-4422. Editor: Pamela Stacey. 30-40% freelance written. Prefers to work with published/established writers; works with a small number of new/unpublished writers each year. Bimonthly magazine covering marine biology, ecology, environment, natural history, and water-related stories. "The *Dolphin Log* is an educational publication for children ages 7-15 offered by The Cousteau Society. Subject matter encompasses all areas of science, history and the arts which can be related to our global water system. The philosophy of the magazine is to delight, instruct and instill an environmental ethic and understanding of the interconnectedness of living organisms, including people." Estab. 1981. Circ. 110,000. Pays on publication. Publishes ms an average of 1 year after acceptance. Byline given. Buys one-time and translation rights. Reports in 1 month. Sample copy for $2 with 9 × 12 SAE and 3 first class stamps; writer's guidelines for SASE. (Make checks payable to The Cousteau Society.)
Nonfiction: General interest (per guidelines); how-to (water-related crafts or science); and photo feature (marine subject). "Of special interest are articles on specific marine creatures, and games involving an ocean/water-related theme which develop math, reading and comprehension skills. Experiments that can be conducted at home and demonstrate a phenomenon or principle of science are wanted as are clever crafts or art projects which also can be tied to an ocean theme. No "talking" animals. First-person accounts are discouraged, as are fictional narratives and articles that address the reader. Buys 8-12 mss/year. Query or send complete ms. Length: 500-1,000 words. Pays $50-150.
Photos: Send photos with query or ms (duplicates only). Prefers underwater animals, water photos with children, photos that explain text. Pays $25-100/photo. Identification of subjects required. Buys one-time and translation rights.
Columns/Departments: Discovery (science experiments or crafts a young person can easily do at home), 50-500 words; Creature Feature (lively article on one specific marine animal), 500-700 words. Buys 1 mss/year. Send complete ms. Pays $25-150.
Poetry: No "talking" animals or dark or religious themes. Buys 1-2 poems/year. Pays $10-100.
Tips: "Find a lively way to relate scientific facts to children without anthropomorphizing. We need to know material is accurate and current. Articles should feature an interesting marine creature and yet contain factual material that's fun to read. We will be increasingly interested in material that draws information from current scientific research."

THE FRIEND, 50 East North Temple, Salt Lake City UT 84150. Managing Editor: Vivian Paulsen. 60% freelance written. Eager to work with new/unpublished writers as well as established writers. Appeals to children ages 3-11. Monthly publication of The Church of Jesus Christ of Latter-Day Saints. Circ. 205,000. **Pays on acceptance.** Buys all rights. Submit seasonal material 8 months in advance. Sample copy and writer's guidelines for 8½ × 11 SAE with 98¢ postage.
Nonfiction: Subjects of current interest, science, nature, pets, sports, foreign countries, and things to make and do. Special issues for Christmas and Easter. "Submit only complete ms—no queries, please." Length: 1,000 words maximum. Pays 8¢ and up/word minimum.
Fiction: Seasonal and holiday stories and stories about other countries and their children. Wholesome and optimistic; high motive, plot, and action. Character-building stories preferred. Length: 1,200 words maximum. Stories for younger children should not exceed 250 words. Pays 8¢ and up/word minimum.
Poetry: Serious, humorous and holiday. Any form with child appeal. Pays $15.
Tips: "Do you remember how it feels to be a child? Can you write stories that appeal to children ages 3-11 in today's world? We're interested in stories with an international flavor and those that focus on present-day problems. Send material of high literary quality slanted to our editorial requirements. Let the child solve the problem—not some helpful, all-wise adult. No overt moralizing. Nonfiction should be creatively presented—not an array of facts strung together. Beware of being cutesy."

HIGH ADVENTURE, Assemblies of God, 1445 Boonville, Springfield MO 65802. (417)862-2781, ext. 4178. FAX: (417)862-8558. Editor: Marshall Bruner. Eager to work with new/unpublished writers. Quarterly magazine "designed to provide boys with worthwhile, enjoyable, leisure reading; to challenge them in narrative form to higher ideals and greater spiritual dedication; and to perpetuate the spirit of the Royal Rangers program through stories, ideas and illustrations." Estab. 1971. Circ. 87,000. **Pays on acceptance.** Byline given. Buys one-time rights. Submit seasonal/holiday material 9 months in advance. Simultaneous queries, and simultaneous and previously published submissions OK. Reports in 1 month. Sample copy for 9 × 12 SAE with 3 first class stamps; free writer's guidelines.
Nonfiction: Historical/nostalgic, how-to, humor and inspirational. Buys 25-50 mss/year. Query or send complete ms. Length: 800-1,200 words. Pays 3¢/word.
Photos: Reviews b&w negatives, color transparencies and prints. Identification of subjects required. Buys one-time rights.
Fiction: Adventure, historical, humorous, religious and western. Buys 25-50 mss/year. Send complete ms. Length: 1,000 words maximum. Pays 3¢/word.
Fillers: Jokes, gags and short humor. Pays $2-4 for jokes; $12-20 for cartoons; others vary.

HIGHLIGHTS FOR CHILDREN, 803 Church St., Honesdale PA 18431. Editor: Kent L. Brown Jr. 80% freelance written. Magazine published 11 times/year for children ages 2-12. Estab. 1946. Circ. 2.8 million. **Pays on acceptance.** Buys all rights. Reports in about 2 months. Free sample copy; writer's guidelines for #10 SASE.
Nonfiction: "We need articles on science, technology and nature written by persons with strong backgrounds in those fields. Contributions always welcomed from new writers, especially engineers, scientists, historians, teachers, etc., who can make useful, interesting facts accessible to children. Also writers who have lived abroad and can interpret the ways of life, especially of children, in other countries in ways that will foster world brotherhood. Sports material, biographies and articles of general interest to children. Direct, original approach, simple style, interesting content, not rewritten from encyclopedias. State background and qualifications for writing factual articles submitted. Include references or sources of information. Length: 900 words maximum. Pays $75 minimum. Also buys original party plans for children ages 7-12, clearly described in 300-800 words, including drawings or samples of items to be illustrated. Also, novel but tested ideas in crafts, with clear directions and made-up models. Projects must require only free or inexpensive, easy-to-obtain materials. Especially desirable if easy enough for early primary grades. Also, fingerplays with lots of action, easy for very young children to grasp and to dramatize. Avoid wordiness. We need creative-thinking puzzles that can be illustrated, optical illusions, brain teasers, games of physical agility and other "fun" activities. Pays minimum $35 for party plans; $20 for crafts ideas; $25 for fingerplays.
Fiction: Unusual, meaningful stories appealing to both girls and boys, ages 2-12. Vivid, full of action. "Engaging plot, strong characterization, lively language." Prefers stories in which a child protagonist solves a dilemma through his or her own resources. Seeks stories that the child ages 8-12 will eagerly read, and the child ages 2-7 will begin to read and/or will like to hear when read aloud (400-800 words). "We publish stories in the suspense/adventure/mystery, fantasy and humor category, all requiring interesting plot and a number of illustration possiblities. Also need rebuses (picture stories 150 words or under), stories with urban settings, stories for beginning readers (100-400 words), sports and horse stories and retold folk tales. We also would like to see more material of 1-page length (300-500 words), both fiction and factual. War, crime and violence are taboo. Pays $65 minimum.
Tips: "We are pleased that many authors of children's literature report that their first published work was in the pages of *Highlights*. It is not our policy to consider fiction on the strength of the reputation of the author. We judge each submission on its own merits. With factual material, however, we do prefer that writers be authorities in their field or people with first-hand experience. In this manner we can avoid the encyclopedic article that merely restates information readily available elsewhere. We don't make assignments. Query with simple letter to establish whether the nonfiction *subject* is likely to be of interest. A beginning writer should first become familiar with the type of material which *Highlights* publishes. Include special qualifications, if any, of author. Write for the child, not the editor."

HOPSCOTCH, The Magazine for Girls, Hopscotch, Inc., P.O. Box 1292, Saratoga Springs NY 12866. (518)587-2268. Editor: Donald P. Evans. 90% freelance written. Bimonthly magazine on basic subjects of interest to young girls. "*HOPSCOTCH* is a digest-size magazine with a four-color cover and two-color format inside. It is designed for girls ages 6 to 12 and features pets, crafts, hobbies, games, science, fiction, history, puzzles, careers, etc." Estab. 1989. Pays on publication. Publishes ms an average of 4 months after acceptance. Byline given. Offers 50% kill fee. Buys first and second rights. Submit seasonal/holiday material 6-8 months in advance. Simultaneous and previously published submissions OK. Reports in 3 weeks on queries; 1 month on mss. Sample copy $3. Writer's guidelines for #10 SAE with 1 first class stamp.

Nonfiction: Book excerpts, general interest, historical/nostalgic, how-to (crafts), humor, inspirational, interview/profile, personal experience, pets, games, fiction, careers, sports, cooking. "No fashion, hairstyles, sex or dating articles." Buys 60 mss/year. Send complete ms. Length: 400-1,100 words. Pays $30-100. Sometimes pays expenses of writers on assignment.

Photos: Send photos with submission. Reviews negatives, transparencies and 5×7 prints. Offers $7.50-10 per photo. Captions, model releases and identification of subjects required. Buys one-time rights.

Columns/Departments: Science—nature, crafts, pets, cooking—(basic), 400-1,000 words. Send complete ms. Pays $25-60.

Fiction: Adventure, fantasy, historical, humorous, mainstream, mystery, novel excerpts, suspense. Buys 15 mss/year. Send complete ms. Length: 600-1,000 words. Pays $30-70.

Poetry: Free verse, light verse and traditional. "No experimental or obscure poetry." Submit maximum 6 poems. Pays $10-30.

Tips: "Almost all sections are open to freelancers. Freelancers should remember that *HOPSCOTCH* is a bit old fashioned, appealing to *young* girls (6 to 12). We cherish nonfiction pieces that have a young girl or young girls directly involved in unusual and/or worthwhile activities. Any piece accompanied by decent photos stands an even better chance of being accepted."

HUMPTY DUMPTY'S MAGAZINE, Children's Better Health Institute, 1100 Waterway Blvd., Box 567, Indianapolis IN 46206. Editor: Christine French Clark. 90% freelance written. "We try not to be overly influenced by an author's credits, preferring instead to judge each submission on its own merit." Magazine published 8 times/year stressing health, nutrition, hygiene, exercise and safety for children ages 4-6. Combined issues: January/February, April/May, July/August, October/November. Pays on publication. Publishes ms at least 8 months after acceptance. Buys all rights. Submit seasonal material 8 months in advance. Reports in 10 weeks. Sample copy 75¢; writer's guidelines for SASE.

Nonfiction: "We are open to nonfiction on almost any age-appropriate subject, but we especially need material with a health theme—nutrition, safety, exercise, hygiene. We're looking for articles that encourage readers to develop better health habits without preaching. Very simple factual articles that creatively teach readers about their bodies. We use simple crafts, some with holiday themes. We also use several puzzles and activities in each issue—dot-to-dot, hidden pictures and other activities that promote following instructions, developing finger dexterity and working with numbers and letters. Submit complete ms. "Include number of words in manuscript and Social Security number." Length: 600 words maximum. Pays minimum 10¢/word.

Fiction: "We use some stories in rhyme and a few easy-to-read stories for the beginning reader. All stories should work well as read alouds. Currently we need sports/fitness stories and seasonal stories with holiday themes. We use contemporary stories and fantasy, some employing a health theme. We try to present our health material in a positive light, incorporating humor and a light approach wherever possible. Avoid stereotyping. Characters in contemporary stories should be realistic and up-to-date. Remember, many of our readers have working mothers and/or come from single-parent homes. We need more stories that reflect these changing times but at the same time communicate good, wholesome values." Submit complete ms. "Include number of words in manuscript and Social Security number." Length: 600 words maximum. Pays about 10¢/word.

Poetry: Short, simple poems. Pays $10 minimum.

Tips: "Writing for *Humpty Dumpty* is similar to writing picture book manuscripts. There must be a great economy of words. We strive for at least 50% art per page (in stories and articles), so space for text is limited. Because the illustrations are so important, stories should lend themselves well to visual imagery."

JACK AND JILL, 1100 Waterway Blvd., Box 567, Indianapolis IN 46206. (317)636-8881. Editor: Steve Charles. 85% freelance written. Magazine published 8 times/year for children ages 7-10. Pays on publication. Publishes ms an average of 8 months after acceptance. Buys all rights. Byline given. Submit seasonal material 8 months in advance. Reports in 10 weeks. May hold material seriously being considered for up to 1 year. "Material will not be returned unless accompanied by self-addressed envelope with sufficient postage." Sample copy 75¢; writer's guidelines for SASE.

Nonfiction: "Because we want to encourage youngsters to read for pleasure and for information, we are interested in material that will challenge a young child's intelligence *and* be enjoyable reading. Our emphasis is on good health, and we are in particular need of articles, stories, and activities with health, safety, exercise and nutrition themes. We are looking for well-written articles that take unusual approaches to teaching better health habits and scientific facts about how the body works. We try to present our health material in a positive light—incorporating humor and a light approach wherever possible without minimizing the seriousness of what we are saying." Straight factual articles are OK if they are short and interestingly written. "We would rather see, however, more creative articles to the straight factual article. For instance, we'd be interested in seeing a health message or facts presented in articles featuring positive role models for readers. Many of the personalities children admire—athletes, musicians, and film or TV stars—are fitness or nutrition buffs. Many have kicked drugs, alcohol or smoking habits and are outspoken about the dangers of these vices. Color slides, transparencies, or black and white photos accompanying this type of article would greatly enhance salability." Buys 25-30 nonfiction mss/year. Length: 500-1,200 words. Pays approximately 8¢ a word.

Photos: When appropriate, photos should accompany ms. Reviews sharp, contrasting b&w glossy prints. Sometimes uses color slides, transparencies, or good color prints. Pays $10 for b&w, $20 for color, $50 for cover. Buys one-time rights.

Fiction: May include, but is not limited to, realistic stories, fantasy adventure—set in past, present or future. All stories need a well-developed plot, action and incident. Humor is highly desirable. "Currently we need stories with holiday themes. Stories that deal with a health theme need not have health as the primary subject. We would like to see more biographical fiction." Length: 500-1,500 words, short stories; 1,500 words/installment, serials of two parts. Pays approximately 8¢ a word. Buys 20-25 mss/year.

Fillers: Puzzles (including various kinds of word and crossword puzzles), poems, games, science projects, and creative craft projects. Instructions for activities should be clearly and simply written and accompanied by models or diagram sketches. "We also have a need for recipes. Ingredients should be healthful; avoid sugar, salt, chocolate, red meat, and fats as much as possible. In all material, avoid references to eating sugary foods, such as candy, cakes, cookies and soft drinks."

Tips: "We are constantly looking for new writers who can tell good stories with interesting slants— stories that are not full of out-dated and time-worn expressions. Our best authors are writers who know what today's children are like. Keep in mind that our readers are becoming 'computer literate', living in an age of rapidly developing technology. They are exploring career possibilities that may be new and unfamiliar to our generation. They are faced with tough decisions about drug and alcohol use. Many of them are latch-key children because both parents work or they come from single-parent homes. We need more stories and articles that reflect these changing times but that also communicate good, wholesome values. Obtain *current* issues of the magazines and *study* them to determine our present needs and editorial style."

KID CITY™, Children's Television Workshop, 1 Lincoln Plaza, New York NY 10023. (212)595-3456. Editor: Maureen Hunter-Bone. Associate Editor: Lisa Rao. 10% freelance written. Works with small number of new/unpublished writers each year. Magazine published 10 times/year. "We are a humor/ reading/activity magazine for children 6-10 years old." Estab. 1969. Circ. 275,000. **Pays on acceptance.** Publishes ms an average of 8 months after acceptance. Byline given. Offers 50% kill fee. Buys all rights. Submit seasonal/holiday material at least 6 months in advance. Simultaneous submissions OK. Reports in 6 weeks. Sample copy for 9 × 12 SAE with 6 first class stamps and $1.50.

Nonfiction: General interest, humor and photo feature. Buys 3-4 mss/year. Query with or without published clips, or send complete ms. Length: 500 words maximum. Pays $25-350.

Photos: State availability of photos with submission. Model releases and identification of subjects required.

Fiction: Adventure, fantasy, historical, humorous, mystery and western. "No stories with heavily didactic, preachy moral messages or those whose main focus is child abuse, saying 'no,' divorce, etc." Buys 3 mss/year. Query or send complete ms. Length: 250-700 words. Pays $400 maximum.

Tips: "Just think about what you liked to read about when you were a kid and write it down. No stories about doggies, bunnies or kitties. No stories with heavy moral message. We're looking for more interesting items about *real* kids who have done something newsworthy or exceptional."

‡LADYBUG, the Magazine for Young Children, Carus Publishing Corporation, P.O. Box 300, 315 Fifth St., Peru IL 61354. (815)224-6643. Publisher and Editor-in-Chief Marianne Carus. Managing Editor: Theresa Gaffey. 100% freelance written. Children's magazine (for ages 2-7). Monthly general interest magazine for children (ages 2-7). "We look for quality writing—quality literature, no matter the subject." Estab. 1990. Circ. 130,000. Pays on publication. Byline given. All accepted manuscripts are published. First North American serial rights. Submit seasonal/holiday material 1 year in advance. Simultaneous submissions OK. Reports in 3 months on mss. Sample copy for $2. Writer's guidelines for #10 SAE with 1 first class stamp. Do not query; send completed ms.

Nonfiction: Submissions Editor. Book excerpts, general interest, historical/nostalgic, how-to (any type of crafts or recipes 1-2 pages), humor, interview/profile, personal experience, technical, science, science fiction book reviews, crossword puzzles. Buys approximately 35 mss/year. Send complete ms. Length: 750 maximum words. Pays 25¢ per word. Send photos with submission. Reviews prints. Offers no additional payment for photos accepted with ms. Identification of subjects required. Buys one-time rights.

Columns/Departments: Recipes, 1 page; Crafts, 2 pages; Crosswords, 1 page; Can You Do This?, 2-3 pages; The World Around You, 2-3 pages. Buys 35 mss/year. Send complete ms. Length: 250 maximum words.

Fiction: Adventure, ethnic, fantasy, historical, humorous, mainstream, mystery, novel excerpts, science fiction, slice-of-life vignettes, suspense. Buys 200 mss/year. Send complete ms. Length: 750 maximum words. Pays up to 25¢ per word.

Poetry: Avant-garde, free verse, Haiku, light verse, traditional. Buys 20 poems/year. Submit maximum 5 poems. Length: 20 lines maximum. Pays up to $3 per line.

Fillers: Anecdotes, facts and short humor. Buys 10/year. Length: 250 (appr.) maximum words. Pays up to 25¢ per word.

Tips: "Reread a manuscript *before* sending it in. The more polished a manuscript the more likely it will be accepted. Be sure to keep within specified word limits."

ODYSSEY, Kalmbach Publishing Co., 21027 Crossroads Circle, Waukesha WI 53186. (414)796-8776. FAX: (414)796-0126. Editor: Nancy Mack. 50% freelance written. Works with a small number of new/unpublished writers each year. Monthly magazine emphasizing astronomy and outer space for children ages 8-12. Estab. 1979. Circ. 86,000. Pays on publication. Publishes ms an average of 8 months after acceptance. Buys one-time rights. Submit seasonal/holiday material 4 months in advance. Previously published submissions OK. Reports in 2 months. "Material with little news connection may be held up to one year." Sample copy and writer's guidelines for 10 × 13 SAE and 5 first class stamps.

Nonfiction: General interest (astronomy, outer space, spacecraft, planets, stars, etc.); how-to (astronomy projects, experiments, etc.); and photo feature (spacecraft, planets, stars, etc.). "We like short, off-beat articles with some astronomy or space-science tie-in. A recent example: an article about a baseball game that ended with the explosion of a meteorite over the field. Study the styles of the monthly columnists. No general overview articles; for example, a general article on the Space Shuttle, or a general article on stars. We do not want science fiction articles." Buys 12 mss/year. Query with published clips. Length: 750-2,000 words. Pays $100-350 depending on length and type of article. Sometimes pays expenses of writers on assignment.

Photos: State availability of photos. Buys one-time rights. Captions preferred; model releases required. Payment depends upon size and placement.

Tips: "Because I am overstocked and have a stable of regular writers, a query is very important. I often get several manuscripts on the same subject and must reject them. Write a very specific proposal and indicate why it will interest kids. If the subject is very technical, indicate your qualifications to write about it. Frequent mistakes writers make are trying to fudge on material they don't understand, using outdated references, and telling me their articles are assignments for the Institute of Children's Literature."

ON THE LINE, Mennonite Publishing House, 616 Walnut Ave., Scottdale PA 15683-1999. (412)887-8500. Editor: Mary Clemens Meyer. 95% freelance written. Works with a small number of new/unpublished writers each year. Weekly magazine for children ages 10-14. Circ. 10,000. **Pays on acceptance.** Publishes ms an average of 1 year after acceptance. Byline given. Buys one-time rights. Submit seasonal/holiday material 6 months in advance. Simultaneous and previously published submissions OK. Reports in 1 month. Sample copy for 8½ × 11 SAE and 2 first class stamps.

Nonfiction: How-to (things to make with easy-to-get materials); and informational (500-word articles on wonders of nature, people who have made outstanding contributions). Buys 95 unsolicited mss/year. Send complete ms. Length: 500-900 words. Pays $10-30.

Photos: Photos purchased with or without ms. Pays $10-25 for 8 × 10 b&w photos. Total purchase price for ms includes payment for photos.

Fiction: Adventure, humorous and religious. Buys 52 mss/year. Send complete ms. Length: 800-1,200 words. Pays 2-4¢/word.

Poetry: Light verse and religious. Length: 3-12 lines. Pays $5-15.

Tips: "Study the publication first. We need short well-written how-to and craft articles. Don't send query; we prefer to see the complete manuscript."

‡OWL MAGAZINE, The Discovery Magazine for Children, The Young Naturalist Foundation, 56 The Esplanade, Suite 306, Toronto, Ontario M5E 1A7 Canada. (416)868-6001. FAX: (416)868-6009. Editor: Debora Pearson. 25% freelance written. Works with small number of new writers each year. Magazine published 10 times/year (no July or August issues) covering science and nature. Aims to interest children in their environment through accurate, factual information about the world around them presented in an easy, lively style. Estab. 1976. Circ. 160,000. Pays on publication. Publishes ms an average of 3 months after acceptance. Byline given. Buys all rights. Submit seasonal/holiday material 1 year in advance. Reports in 10 weeks. Sample copy $2.50; free writer's guidelines. Send SAE (large envelope if requesting sample copy) and a money order for $1 to cover postage (no stamps please).

Nonfiction: How-to (activities, crafts); personal experience (real life children in real situations); photo feature (natural science, international wildlife, and outdoor features); and science and environmental features. No problem stories with drugs, sex or moralistic views, or talking animal stories. "We accept short, well-written articles about up-to-the-minute science discoveries or developments for our HOOT CLUB News section." Query with clips of published work.

Photos: State availability of photos. Reviews 35mm transparencies. Identification of subjects required. Send for photo package before submitting material.

Tips: "Write for editorial guidelines first. Review back issues of the magazine for content and style. Know your topic and approach it from an unusual perspective. Our magazine never talks down to children." Also publishes *Chickadee* for 4-9-year-olds.

‡**PENNYWHISTLE PRESS**, Gannett Co., Inc., 1000 Wilson Blvd., Arlington VA 22229-0002. (800)368-3553 ext. 3796. Editor: Anita Sama. 25% freelance written. Weekly newspaper for children. Estab. 1981. Circ. 2,000,000. **Pays on acceptance.** Byline given. Buys all rights. Submit seasonal/holiday material 6 months in advance. "We accept no queries. We do not return manuscripts." Sample copy 75¢ with 10×12 SAE and 2 first class stamps. Free writer's guidelines.

Nonfiction: Travel. Buys 3 mss/year. Send complete ms. Length: 300-500 words. Pays $50-125. Sometimes pays expenses of writers on assignment.

Fiction: Children's fiction. No fairy tales, stories with talking animals or religious overtones. Buys 12 mss/year. Send complete ms. Length: 400-800 words. Pays $75-125.

Poetry: "Any style, as long as geared toward children." Buys 6 poems/year. Submit maximum 3 poems. Pays $25-75.

POCKETS, The Upper Room, 1908 Grand Ave., P.O. Box 189, Nashville TN 37202. (615)340-7333. Editor: Janet R. McNish. 50% freelance written. Eager to work with new/unpublished writers. A monthly themed magazine (except combined January and February issues) covering children's and families spiritual formation. "We are a Christian, non-denominational publication for children 6 to 12 years of age." Estab. 1981. Circ. 70,000. **Pays on acceptance.** Byline given. Offers 4¢/word kill fee. Buys first North American serial rights. Submit seasonal/holiday material 1 year in advance. Previously published submissions OK. Reports in 10 weeks on manuscripts. Sample copy for 7×9 SAE with 4 first class stamps; writer's guidelines and themes for #10 SASE.

Nonfiction: Learmond Chapman, articles editor. Interview/profile, religious (retold scripture stories) and personal experience. List of themes for special issues available with SASE. No violence or romance. Buys 5 mss/year. Send complete ms. Length: 600-1,500 words. Pays 7¢-10¢/word.

Photos: Send photos with submission. Prefer no photos unless they accompany an article. Reviews contact sheets, transparencies and prints. Offers $25-50/photo. Buys one-time rights.

Columns Departments: Refrigerator Door (poetry and prayer related to themes), 25 lines; Pocketsful of Love (family communications activities), 300 words; and Peacemakers at Work (profiles of people, particularly children, working for peace, justice and ecological concerns), 300-600 words. Buys 20 mss/year. Send complete ms. Pays 7¢-10¢/word; recipes $25.

Fiction: Adventure, ethnic and slice-of-life. "Stories should reflect the child's everyday experiences through a Christian approach. This is often more acceptable when stories are not preachy or overtly Christian." Buys 22 mss/year. Send complete ms. Length: 750-1,600 words. Pays 7-10¢/word.

Poetry: Buys 8 poems/year. Length: 4-25 lines. Pays $25-50.

Tips: "Theme stories, role models and retold scripture stories are most open to freelancers. Poetry is also open, but we rarely receive an acceptable poem. It's very helpful if writers send for our themes. These are *not* the same as writer's guidelines."

R-A-D-A-R, 8121 Hamilton Ave., Cincinnati OH 45231. (513)931-4050. Editor: Margaret Williams. 75% freelance written. Prefers to work with published/established writers; works with a small number of new/unpublished writers each year. Weekly for children in grades 3-6 in Christian Sunday schools. Estab. 1866 (publishing house). Rights purchased varies with author and material; prefers buying first serial rights, but will buy second (reprint) rights. Occasionally overstocked. **Pays on acceptance.** Publishes ms an average of 1 year after acceptance. Submit seasonal material 1 year in advance. Reports in 2 months. Free sample copy; writer's guidelines for #10 SASE.

Nonfiction: Articles on hobbies and handicrafts, nature, famous people, seasonal subjects, etc., written from a Christian viewpoint. No articles about historical figures with an absence of religious implication. Length: 500-1,000 words. Pays 3-7¢/word maximum.

Fiction: Short stories of heroism, adventure, travel, mystery, animals and biography. True or possible plots stressing clean, wholesome, Christian character-building ideas, but not preachy. Make prayer, church attendance and Christian living a natural part of the story. "We correlate our fiction and other features with a definite Bible lesson. Writers who want to meet our needs should send for a theme list." No talking animal stories, science fiction, Halloween stories or first-person stories from an adult's viewpoint. Length: up to 1,000 words. Pays 3-7¢/word maximum.

RANGER RICK, National Wildlife Federation, 1400 16th St. NW, Washington DC 20036. (703)790-4274. Editor: Gerald Bishop. 30% freelance written. Works with a small number of new/unpublished writers each year. Monthly magazine for children from ages 6-12, with the greatest concentration in the 7-10 age bracket. Buys all world rights unless other arrangements made. Byline given "but occasionally, for very brief pieces, we will identify author by name at the end. Contributions to regular columns usually are not bylined." Estab. 1967. **Pays on acceptance.** Publishes ms an average of 18 months after acceptance. Reports in 6 weeks. "Anything written with a specific month in mind should be in our hands at least 10 months before that issue date." Writer's guidelines for #10 SASE.

Nonfiction: "Articles may be written on anything related to nature, conservation, the outdoors, environmental problems or natural science." Buys 25-35 unsolicited mss/year. Query. Pays from $50-550, depending on length, quality and content (maximum length, 900 words).

Fiction: "Same categories as nonfiction plus fantasy and science fiction. The attributing of human qualities to animals is limited to our regular feature, 'The Adventures of Ranger Rick,' so please do not humanize wildlife. The publisher, The National Wildlife Federation, discourages keeping wildlife as pets."

Photos: "Photographs, when used, are paid for separately. It is not necessary that illustrations accompany material."

Tips: "In your query letter, include details of what manuscript will cover; sample lead; evidence that you can write playfully and with great enthusiasm, conviction and excitement (formal, serious, dull queries indicate otherwise). Think of an exciting subject we haven't done recently, sell it effectively with query, and produce a manuscript of highest quality. Read past issues to learn successful styles and unique approaches to subjects. If your submission is commonplace, we won't want it."

SCOUTING, Boy Scouts of America, 1325 West Walnut Hill Lane, Box 152079, Irving TX 75015. (214)580-2355. Editor: Ernest Doclar. 90% freelance written. Published bimonthly. **Pays on acceptance.** Publishes ms an average of 3-4 months after acceptance. Buys first North American serial rights. Reports in 3 weeks on queries; 2 weeks on mss.

Nonfiction: Prefers to see success stories of scouting in the U.S.A. Query with or without published clips. Length: 1,600-1,800 words. Pays $500 maximum.

SPORTS ILLUSTRATED FOR KIDS, Time-Warner, Time & Life Building, New York NY 10020. (212)522-5437. FAX: (212)522-0120. Managing Editor: Craig Neff. 50% freelance written. Monthly magazine on sports for children eight years old and up. Content is divided 50/50 between sports as played by kids, and sports as played by professionals. Estab. 1989. **Pays on acceptance.** Publishes ms an average of 3 months after acceptance. Byline given. Offers 25% kill fee. Buys all rights. Sample copy $1.95. Writer's guidelines for SAE.

Nonfiction: Patricia Berry, articles editor. Games, general interest, how-to, humor, inspirational, interview/profile, photo feature and puzzles. Buys 30 mss/year. Query with published clips. Length: 100-1,500 words. Pays $75-1,000 for assigned articles; $75-800 for unsolicited articles. Pays expenses of writers on assignment.

Photos: State availability of photos with submission. Buys one-time rights.

Columns/Departments: The Worst Day I Ever Had (tells about day in pro athlete's life when all seemed hopeless), 500-600 words; Hotshots (young [8-15] athlete getting good things out of sports), 100-250 words; and Home Team (son, daughter, brother, sister of famous athlete), 500-600 words. Buys 30-40 mss/year. Query with published clips. Pays $75-600.

STONE SOUP, The Magazine by Children, Children's Art Foundation, P.O. Box 83, Santa Cruz CA 95063. (408)426-5557. Editor: Ms. Gerry Mandel. 100% freelance written. A bimonthly magazine of writing and art by children, including fiction, poetry, book reviews, and art by children through age 13. Estab. 1973. Audience is children, teachers, parents, writers, artists. "We have a preference for writing and art based on real-life experiences; no formula stories or poems." **Pays on acceptance.** Publishes ms an average of 3 months after acceptance. Buys all rights. Submit seasonal/holiday material 6 months in advance. Reports in 2 weeks on queries; 1 month on mss. Sample copy $4. Free writer's guidelines.

Nonfiction: Book reviews. Buys 10 mss/year. Query. Pays $15 for assigned articles.

Fiction: Adventure, ethnic, experimental, fantasy, historical, humorous, mystery, science fiction, slice-of-life vignettes and suspense. "We do not like assignments or formula stories of any kind." Accepts 35 mss/year. Send complete ms. Pays $10 for stories. Authors also receive 2 copies and discounts on additional copies and on subscriptions.

Poetry: Avant-garde and free verse. Accepts 20 poems/year. Pays $10 per poems. (Same discounts apply.)

Tips: "We can't emphasize enough how important it is to read a couple of issues of the magazine. We have a strong preference for writing on subjects that mean a lot to the author. If you feel strongly about something that happened to you or something you observed, use that feeling as the basis for your story or poem. Stories should have good descriptions, realistic dialogue and a point to make. In a poem, each word must be chosen carefully. Your poem should present a view of your subject and a way of using words that are special and all your own."

STORY FRIENDS, Mennonite Publishing House, 616 Walnut Ave., Scottdale PA 15683. (412)887-8500. FAX: (412)887-3111. Editor: Marjorie Waybill. 80% freelance written. Monthly story paper in weekly parts for children ages 4-9. "*Story Friends* is planned to provide wholesome Christian reading for the 4- to 9-year-old. Practical life stories are included to teach moral values and remind the children that God is at work today. Activities introduce children to the Bible and its message for them." Estab. 1905. Circ. 10,500. **Pays on acceptance.** Publishes ms an average of 1 year after acceptance. Byline given. Publication not copyrighted. Buys one-time rights and second serial (reprint) rights. Submit seasonal/holiday material 6 months in advance. Simultaneous submissions and previously published material OK. Sample copy for 8½ × 11 SAE with 2 first class stamps. Writer's guidelines for #10 SASE.
Nonfiction: How-to (craft ideas for young children), photo feature. Buys 20 mss/year. Send complete ms. Length: 300-500 words. Pays 3-5¢/word.
Photos: Send photos with submission. Reviews 8½ × 11 b&w prints. Offers $20-25/photo. Model releases required. Buys one-time rights.
Fiction: See writer's guidelines for *Story Friends*. Buys 50 mss/year. Send complete ms. Length: 300-800 words. Pays 3-5¢/word.
Poetry: Traditional. Buys 20 poems/year. Length: 4-16 lines. Pays $5-10/poem.
Tips: "Send stories that children from a variety of ethnic backgrounds can relate to; stories that deal with experiences similar to all children. For example, all children have fears but their fears may vary depending on where they live."

3-2-1 CONTACT, Children's Television Workshop, One Lincoln Plaza, New York NY 10023. (212)595-3456. FAX: (212)580-3845. Editor-in-Chief: Jonathan Rosenbloom. Senior Editor: Curtis Slepian. 40% freelance written. Magazine published 10 times/year covering science and technology for children ages 8-14. Estab. 1979. Circ. 400,000. **Pays on acceptance.** Publishes ms an average of 6 months after acceptance. Buys all rights "with some exceptions." Submit seasonal material 8 months in advance. Simultaneous and previously published submissions OK if so indicated. Reports in 1 month. Sample copy $1.75 with 8½ × 11 SAE; writer's guidelines for SASE.
Nonfiction: General interest (space exploration, the human body, animals, computers and the new technology, current science issues); profile (of interesting scientists or children involved in science or with computers); photo feature (centered around a science theme); and role models of women and minority scientists. No articles on travel not related to science. Buys 5 unsolicited mss/year. Query with published clips. Length: 700-1,000 words. Pays $150-500. Sometimes pays expenses of writers on assignment.
Photos: Do *not* send photos on spec.
Tips: "I prefer a short query, without manuscript, that makes it clear that an article is interesting. When sending an article, include your telephone number. Don't call us, we'll call you. Many submissions we receive are more like college research papers than feature stories. We like articles in which writers have interviewed kids or scientists, or discovered exciting events with a scientific angle. Library research is necessary; but if that's all you're doing, you aren't giving us anything we can't get ourselves. If your story needs a bibliography, chances are, it's not right for us."

TOUCH, Box 7259, Grand Rapids MI 49510. Editor: Joanne Ilbrink. 80% freelance written. Prefers to work with published/established writers. Monthly magazine. Purpose of publication is to show girls ages 7-14 how God is at work in their lives and in the world around them. "The May/June issue annually features the material written by our readers." Estab. 1972. Circ. 15,500. **Pays on acceptance.** Publishes ms an average of 1 year after acceptance. Byline given. Buys second serial (reprint) rights and first North American serial rights. Submit seasonal/holiday material 9 months in advance. Simultaneous and previously published submissions OK. Reports in 2 months. Free sample copy and writer's guidelines for 9 × 12 SAE and 3 first class stamps.
Nonfiction: How-to (crafts girls can make easily and inexpensively); informational (write for issue themes); humor (need much more); inspirational (seasonal and holiday); interview; multicultural materials; travel; personal experience (avoid the testimony approach); and photo feature (query first). "Because our magazine is published around a monthly theme, requesting the letter we send out twice a year to our established freelancers would be most helpful. We do not want easy solutions or quick character changes from bad to good. No pietistic characters. Constant mention of God is not necessary if the moral tone of the story is positive. We do not want stories that always have a good ending."

For information on setting your freelance fees, see How Much Should I Charge? in the Business of Writing section.

Buys 36-45 unsolicited mss/year. Submit complete ms. Length: 100-1,000 words. Pays 2½¢/word, depending on the amount of editing.

Photos: Purchased with or without ms. Reviews 5×7 clear b&w (only) glossy prints. Appreciate multicultural subjects. Pays $20-30 on publication.

Fiction: Adventure (that girls could experience in their hometowns or places they might realistically visit); humorous; mystery (believable only); romance (stories that deal with awakening awareness of boys are appreciated); suspense (can be serialized); and religious (nothing preachy). Buys 50 mss/year. Submit complete ms. Length: 300-1,000 words. Pays 2½¢/word.

Poetry: Free verse, haiku, light verse and traditional. Buys 10/year. Length: 30 lines maximum. Pays $5-15 minimum.

Fillers: Puzzles, short humor and cartoons. Buys 3/issue. Pays $7-15.

Tips: "Prefers not to see anything on the adult level, secular material or violence. Writers frequently over-simplify the articles and often write with a Pollyanna attitude. An author should be able to see his/her writing style as exciting and appealing to girls ages 7-14. The style can be fun, but also teach a truth. The subject should be current and important to *Touch* readers. We would like to receive material that features a multi-cultural slant."

TURTLE MAGAZINE FOR PRESCHOOL KIDS, Children's Better Health Institute, Benjamin Franklin Literary & Medical Society, Inc., 1100 Waterway Blvd., Box 567, Indianapolis IN 46206. (317)636-8881. Editor: Christine French Clark. 90% freelance written. Monthly magazine (bimonthly Jan/Feb, April/May, July/Aug, Oct.-Nov). General interest, interactive magazine with the purpose of helping preschoolers develop healthy minds and healthy bodies. Pays on publication. May hold manuscripts for up to one year before acceptance/publication. Byline given. Buys all rights. Submit seasonal/holiday material 8 months in advance. Reports in 10 weeks. Sample copy 75¢; writer's guidelines for #10 SASE.

Fiction: Fantasy, humorous and realistic stories. All should have single-focus story lines and work well as read-alouds. Most of the stories we use will have a character-building bent, but they should not be preachy or overly moralistic. We are in constant need of stories that will help a preschooler grow to a greater appreciation of his/her body and what it can do; stories that encourage active, vigorous play; stories that teach fundamental lessons about good health without being too heavy-handed. We're no longer buying many stories about "generic" turtles and would like to see instead some mini-adventure stories featuring our own Turtle character; authors must study current issues to familiarize themselves with this character's personality. All stories featuring our own Turtle character; authors must study current issues to familiarize themselves with this character's personality. All stories should "move along" and lend themselves well to illustration. Writing should be energetic, enthusiastic and creative—like preschoolers themselves.

Poetry: We're especially looking for action rhymes to foster creative movement in preschoolers. We also use original finger plays, stories in rhyme and short verse.

Tips: "We are trying to include more material for our youngest readers. We'd like to see some well-executed ideas for teaching basic concepts to two- and three-year-olds. We're open to counting and alphabet stories, but they must be handled in a new, fresh way. All material must first be entertaining; otherwise all efforts to teach will be wasted."

VENTURE, Christian Service Brigade, P.O. Box 150, Wheaton IL 60189. (708)665-0630. Editor: Deborah Christensen. 15% freelance written. Works with a small number of new/unpublished writers each year. "Venture is a bimonthly company publication published to support and compliment *CSB's* Stockade and Battalion programs. We aim to provide wholesome, entertaining reading for boys ages 10-15." Estab. 1959. Circ. 22,000. Pays on publication. Publishes ms an average of 4-6 months after acceptance. Byline given. Offers $35 kill fee. Buys first North American serial, one-time and second serial (reprint) rights. Submit seasonal/holiday material 6 months in advance. Previously published submissions OK. Reports in 2 weeks. Sample copy $1.85 with 9×12 SAE and 4 first class stamps; writer's guidelines for #10 SASE.

Nonfiction: Exposé, general interest, historical/nostalgic, humor, inspirational, interview/profile, personal experience, photo feature and religious. Buys 10-12 mss/year. Send complete ms. Length: 1,000-1,500 words. Pays $75-150 for assigned articles; pays $40-100 for unsolicited articles. Sometimes pays expenses of writers on assignment.

Photos: Send photos with submission. Reviews contact sheets and 5×7 prints. Offers $35-125/photo. Buys one-time rights.

Fiction: Adventure, humorous, mystery and religious. Buys 10-12 mss/year. Send complete ms. Length: 1,000-1,500 words. Pays $40-125.

Tips: "Talk to young boys. Find out the things that interest them and write about those things. We are looking for material relating to our theme: Building Men to Serve Christ. We prefer shorter (1,000 words) pieces."

WEE WISDOM, Unity Village MO 64065. FAX: (816)251-3550. Editor: Ms. Judy Gehrlein. 90% freelance written. "We are happy to work with any freelance writers whose submissions and policies match our needs." Magazine published 10 times/year "for children aged 13 and under, dedicated to the truth that each person has an inner source of wisdom, power, love and health that can be applied in a practical manner to everyday life." Estab. 1893. Circ. 175,000. Publishes ms an average of 8 months after acceptance. Submit seasonal/holiday material 10-12 months in advance. **Pays on acceptance.** Byline given. Buys first North American serial rights only. Sample copy and editorial policy for 6×9 SAE and 4 first class stamps.

Fiction: Character-building stories that encourage a positive self-image. Although entertaining enough to hold the interest of the older child, they should be readable by the third grader. "Characters should be appealing; plots should be imaginative but plausible, and all stories should be told without preaching. Life combines fun and humor with its more serious lessons, and our most interesting and helpful stories do the same thing. Language should be universal, avoiding the Sunday school image." Length: 500-800 words. Rates vary, depending on excellence.

Poetry: Limited. Prefers short, seasonal and general poems for children. Pays $15 minimum, 50¢ per line after 15 lines. Rhymed prose (read aloud) stories are paid at about the same rate as prose stories, depending on excellence. Poetry by children published in "Writer's Guild" section not eligible for payment.

Fillers: Pays $8-10 for puzzles and games.

WONDER TIME, 6401 The Paseo, Kansas City MO 64131. (816)333-7000. Editor: Evelyn Beals. 75% freelance written. "Willing to read and consider appropriate freelance submissions." Published weekly by Church of the Nazarene for children ages 6-8. Estab. early 1900s. **Pays on acceptance.** Publishes ms an average of 1 year after acceptance. Byline given. Buys rights to reuse without furthur payment and all rights for curriculum assignments. Sample copy and writer's guidelines for 9×12 SAE with 3 first class stamps.

Fiction: Buys stories portraying Christian attitudes without being preachy. Uses stories for special days—stories teaching honesty, truthfulness, kindness, helpfulness or other important spiritual truths, and avoiding symbolism. Also, stories about real life problems children face today. "God should be spoken of as our Father who loves and cares for us; Jesus, as our Lord and Savior." Buys 52/mss year. Length: 350-550 words. Pays $25 on acceptance.

Poetry: Uses verse which has seasonal or Christian emphasis. Length: 4-8 lines. Pays 25¢/line, minimum $3.

Tips: "Any stories that allude to church doctrine must be in keeping with Nazarene beliefs. Any type of fantasy must be in good taste and easily recognizable. We are overstocked now with poetry and stories with general themes. We plan to reprint more than before to save art costs, therefore we will be more selective and purchase fewer new manuscripts."

THE WORLD OF BUSINE$$ KIDS, Busine$$ Kids/America's Future, Lemonade Kids, Inc., Suite 330, 301 Almeria Ave., Coral Gables FL 33134. (305)445-8869. Editor: Jacky Robinson. Monthly tabloid on business, specifically young entrepreneurs. "We cover stories about young entrepreneurs, how teens and preteens can become entrepreneurs, and useful information for effective business operation and management." Estab. 1988. Circ. 75,000. **Pays on acceptance.** Publishes ms an average of 6 months after acceptance. All writers, including teens are listed as contributors. Buys all rights. Submit seasonal/holiday material 1 year in advance. Reports in 10 weeks on mss. Free sample copy and writer's guidelines.

Nonfiction: Any nonfiction pertaining to teens in the business world. How-to choose, build, improve, market or advertise a business. Profiles of successful young entrepreneurs. The latest in any field, entertainment, sports, medicine, etc., where teens are making megabucks or just movie money. Articles on the stock market, bonds, precious metals, taxes, how to invest/save money, news releases, cartoons, puzzles, games, poetry, new products and companies. "No articles with inappropriate language; any mention of alcohol, drugs or tobacco, religious articles; product advertising; inappropriate themes for teens; cheesecake; inappropriate photo backgrounds." Buys 50 mss/year. Send complete ms. Length: 200-600 words. Pays 15¢/word.

Photos: Send photos with submission. Reviews 5×7 b&w prints or 35mm transparencies. Offers $5-10 per photo. Captions, model releases and identification of subjects required. Buys all rights.

Columns/Departments: Corporate Champs (corporations in community affairs); News-Worthy (companies with new and innovative products or services); Klever Kids (opinion/interview); Bright Busine$$ Idea; Biz Quiz (games); Biz Blasts (movie, book, TV and video reviews) Inside Fax (international business news). Parentally Speaking (book review or advice for parents, what teens should know about money). Send complete ms. Length: 200-400 words.

Poetry: Avant-garde, free verse, haiku, light verse and traditional. Nothing unrelated to business. Buys 8-10 poems/year. No limit on number of poem submissions. Length: open. Pays $15-20.

Fillers: Cartoons, puzzles and games. Buys 8-10/year. Length: 25-100 words. Pays cartoons $15-20; puzzles and games $35-50.

Tips: "Write thoroughly researched, entertaining, factual and *positive* how-tos. No sermonettes or abstract concepts. Understanding teens is a prerequisite. Study our guidelines. Use words economically, and submit clean copy with SASE."

Literary and "Little"

Literary and "little" magazines contain fiction, poetry, book reviews, essays and literary criticism. Many are published by colleges and universities and have a regional or scholarly focus.

Literary magazines launch many writers into print. Serious writers will find great opportunities here; some agents read the magazines to find promising potential clients, and many magazines also sponsor annual contests. Writers who want to get a story printed may have to be patient. Literary magazines, especially semiannuals, will buy good material and save it for future editions. When submitting work to literary magazines, the writer may encounter frequent address changes or long response times. On the other hand, some editors carefully read submissions several times and send personal notes to writers.

Many literary magazines do not pay writers or pay in contributor's copies. Only paying literary magazines are included in *Writer's Market* listings. However, *Novel and Short Story Writer's Market*, published by Writer's Digest Books, includes nonpaying fiction markets and has indepth information about fiction techniques and markets. Literary and "little" magazine writers will notice that *Writer's Market* does not have a Poetry section, although Poetry subheads can be found in this section and in many consumer magazine listings. Writer's Digest Books also publishes *Poet's Market*, edited by Judson Jerome, with detailed information for poets.

‡**ACM (Another Chicago Magazine)**, Another Chicago Press, 3709 N. Kenmore, Chicago IL 60613. (312)524-1289. Editor: Barry Silesky. 98% freelance written. Open to new/unpublished writers. Literary journal published biannually and funded partially by the National Endowment for the Arts. Estab. 1977. Circ. 1,100. **Pays on acceptance.** Publishes ms an average of 6 months after acceptance. Byline given. Buys first serial rights. Simultaneous queries, and simultaneous and photocopied submissions OK. No electronic submissions. Reports in 6-10 weeks. Sample copy $6; writer's guidelines for #10 SASE and 1 first class stamp.

Nonfiction: Interview (contemporary poets and fiction writers), essays (contemporary literature) and reviews of small press publications. Buys 5-6 mss/year. Query. Length: 1,000-20,000 words. Pays $5-25.

Fiction: Sharon Solwitz, fiction editor. Ethnic, experimental and serious fiction. Buys 10-20 mss/year. Send complete ms. Length: 50-10,000 words. Pays $5-25.

Poetry: Serious poetry. No light verse or inspirational. Buys 50 poems/year. Length: 1-1,000 lines. Pays $5-25.

‡**ADVENTURES IN HELL, Vietnam War Stories by Vietnam Veterans**, Ritz Publishing. 202 W. 5th Ave., Ritzville WA 99169. (509)659-4336. Editor: David A. Andersen. 100% freelance written. Annual book of Vietnam War stories and poems. "Author must be Vietnam Veteran: focus on life at war." Estab. 1990. Pays on publication. Publishes ms an average of 9 months after acceptance. Byline given. Buys one-time rights. Simultaneous submissions OK. Reports on queries in 3 months. Sample copy $11.95.

Nonfiction: Personal experience. Buys 4 mss/year. Query. Length: 500-10,000 words. Pays $50-500. "Pays writers with contributor copies when negotiated."

Fiction: Experimental, fantasy, historical, novel excerpts, serialized novels, slice-of-life vignettes. Buys 4 mss/year. Query. Length: 500-10,000 words. Pays $50-500.

Poetry: Avant-garde, free verse. Buys 2 poems/year. Submit maximum 3 poems. Length: 12-60 lines. Pays $50-500.

ALASKA QUARTERLY REVIEW, College of Arts & Sciences, University of Alaska Anchorage, Dept. of English, 3221 Providence Dr., Anchorage AK 99508. (907)786-1731. Executive Editors: Ronald Spatz and James Liszka. 100% freelance written. Prefers to work with published/established writers;

eager to work with new/unpublished writers. A semiannual magazine publishing fiction and poetry, both traditional and experimental styles, and literary criticism and reviews, with an emphasis on contemporary literature. Estab. 1982. Circ. 1,000. Pays honorariums on publication when funding permits. Publishes ms an average of 6 months after acceptance. Byline given. Buys first North American serial rights. Upon request, rights will be transferred back to author after publication. Reports in 4 months. Sample copy $3 and 8×10 SASE; writer's guidelines for SASE.

Nonfiction: Essays, literary criticism, reviews and philosophy of literature. Buys 1-5 mss/year. Query. Length: 1,000-20,000 words. Pays $50-100 subject to funding; pays in copies when funding is limited.

Fiction: Ronald Spatz, fiction editor. Experimental and traditional literary forms. No romance, children's or inspirational/religious. Buys 10-20 mss/year. Send complete ms. Length: 500-20,000 words. Pays $50-150 subject to funding; sometimes pays in contributor's copies only.

Poetry: Thomas Sexton, poetry editor. Avant-garde, free verse, haiku and traditional. No light verse. Buys 10-30 poems/year. Submit maximum 10 poems. Pays $10-50 subject to availability of funds.

Tips: "All sections are open to freelancers. We rely exclusively on unsolicited manuscripts. *AQR* is a non-profit literary magazine and does not always have funds to pay authors."

AMELIA MAGAZINE, Amelia Press, 329 E St., Bakersfield CA 93304. (805)323-4064. Editor: Frederick A. Raborg Jr. 100% freelance written. Eager to work with new/unpublished writers. "*Amelia* is a quarterly international magazine publishing the finest poetry and fiction available, along with expert criticism and reviews intended for all interested in contemporary literature. *Amelia* also publishes three supplements each year: *Cicada*, which publishes only high quality traditional or experimental haiku and senryu plus fiction, essays and cartoons pertaining to Japan; *SPSM&H*, which publishes the highest quality traditional and experimental sonnets available plus romantic fiction and essays pertaining to the sonnet; and the annual winner of the Charles William Duke long poem contest." Circ. 1,250. **Pays on acceptance.** Publishes ms an average of 6 months after acceptance. Byline given. Offers 50% kill fee. Buys first North American serial rights. Submit seasonal/holiday material 2 months in advance. Reports in 2 months on mss. Sample copy $7.95 (includes postage); writer's guidelines for #10 SASE. Sample copy of any supplement $4.50.

Nonfiction: Historical/nostalgic (in the form of belles lettres); humor (in fiction or belles lettres); interview/profile (poets and fiction writers); opinion (on poetry and fiction only); personal experience (as it pertains to poetry or fiction in the form of belles lettres); travel (in the form of belles lettres only); and criticism and book reviews of poetry and small press fiction titles. "Nothing overtly slick in approach. Criticism pieces must have depth; belles lettres must offer important insights into the human scene." Buys 8 mss/year. Send complete ms. Length: 1,000-2,000 words. Pays $25 or by arrangement. "Ordinarily payment for all prose is a flat rate of $25/piece, more for exceptional work." Sometimes pays the expenses of writers on assignment.

Fiction: Adventure; book excerpts (original novel excerpts only); erotica (of a quality seen in Anais Nin or Henry Miller only); ethnic; experimental; fantasy; historical; horror; humorous; mainstream; mystery; novel excerpts; science fiction; suspense; and western. "We would consider slick fiction of the quality seen in *Redbook* and more excellent submissions in the genres—science fiction, wit, Gothic horror, traditional romance, stories with complex *raisons d'être*; avant-garde ought to be truly avant-garde." No pornography ("good erotica is not the same thing"). Buys 24-36 mss/year. Send complete ms. Length: 1,000-5,000 words. Pays $35 or by arrangement for exceptional work.

Poetry: Avant-garde, free verse, haiku, light verse and traditional. "No patently religious or stereotypical newspaper poetry." Buys 100-160 poems/year depending on lengths. Prefers submission of at least 3 poems. Length: 3-100 lines. Pays $2-25; additional payment for exceptional work, usually by established professionals. *Cicada* pays $10 each to three "best of issue" poets; *SPSM&H* pays $14 to two "best of issue" sonnets; winner of the long poem contest receives $100 plus copies and publication.

Tips: "*Have something to say* and say it well. If you insist on waving flags or pushing your religion, then do it with subtlety and class. We enjoy a good cry from time to time, too, but sentimentality does not mean we want to see mush. Read our fiction carefully for depth of plot and characterization, then try very hard to improve on it. With the growth of quality in short fiction, we expect to find stories of lasting merit. I also hope to begin seeing more critical essays which, without sacrificing research, demonstrate a more entertaining obliqueness to the style sheets, more 'new journalism' than MLA. In poetry, we also often look for a good 'storyline' so to speak. Above all we want to feel a sense of honesty and value in every piece. As in the first issue of *Amelia*, 'name' writers are used, but newcomers who have done their homework suffer no disadvantage here. So often the problem seems to be that writers feel small press publications allow such a sloughing of responsibility. It is not so."

‡AMERICAN SHORT FICTION, University of Texas Press, Parlin 14, Dept. of English, Austin TX 78712-1164. (512)471-4531. Editor: Laura Furman. 100% freelance written. Quarterly fiction magazine. "*American Short Fiction* carries fiction of all lengths up to and including the novella, and is aimed at a general readership. No special slant or philosophy is required in writing for our readers." Estab. 1991. **Pays on acceptance.** Publishes mss an average of 6 months after acceptance. Buys first North

American serial rights. Sample copy $7.95 plus $1.50 for foreign postage if necessary.

Fiction: "Stories are selected for their originality and craftsmanship. No condensed novels or slice-of-life vignettes, please." Buys 30-40 mss/year. Send complete ms. Pays $500-1,000.

Tips: "Manuscripts are only accepted Sept. 1-May 31."

THE AMERICAN VOICE, 332 W. Broadway, Louisville KY 40202. (502)562-0045. Editor: Frederick Smock. Works with small number of new/unpublished writers each year. A quarterly literary magazine "for readers of varying backgrounds and educational levels, though usually college-educated. Radical, feminist, unpredictable, we publish new writers' work along with the more radical work of established writers. Avant-garde, open-minded." Circ. 2,000. Pays on publication. Publishes ms an average of 4 months after acceptance. Byline given. Offers 50% kill fee. Buys first North American serial rights. Reports in 1 month on queries; 2 months on mss. Sample copy $5.

Nonfiction: Essays, opinion, and criticism. Buys 25 mss/year. Send complete ms. Length: 10,000 words maximum. Pays $400/essay; $150 to translator.

Fiction: Buys 15 mss/year. Send complete ms. Pays $400/story; $150 to translator.

Poetry: Avant-garde and free verse. Buys 35 poems/year. Submit maximum 10 poems. Pays $150/poem; $75 to translator.

Tips: "We are looking only for vigorously original fiction, poetry and essays, from new and established writers, and will consider nothing that is in any way sexist, racist or homophobic."

‡ANTAEUS, The Ecco Press, 26 West 17th St., New York NY 10011. (212)645-2214. Editor: Daniel Halpern. Administrative Director: Chris Kingsley. Managing Editor: Cathy Jewell. Assistant Editor: Stephen Morrow. Semiannual literary magazine. Estab. 1970. Pays on publication. Publishes ms an average of 6 months after acceptance. Byline given. Buys first North American serial rights, trade edition reprint rights. Submit seasonal/holiday material 1 year in advance. Reports in 2-4 months. Sample copy $10-15. Writer's guidelines for legal SAE with 1 first class stamp.

Nonfiction: Essays, historical/nostalgic, interview/profile, travel. No book reviews. Buys up to 2 mss/year. Query with published clilps. Pays $10/page. Pays in contributor copies or other premiums.

Photos: State availability of photos with submission. Offers no additional payment for photos accepted with ms. Buys one-time rights.

Fiction: Adventure, experimental, historical, humorous, mainstream, novel excerpts, science fiction. Buys 10-20 mss/year. Send complete ms. Pays $10/page.

Poetry: Avant-garde, free verse, Haiku, light verse, traditional. Buys 20-60 poems/year. Pays $10/page.

‡ANTIETAM REVIEW, 82 W. Washington St., 3rd Floor, Hagerstown MD 21740. (301)791-3132. Editors: Susanne Kass and Ann Knox. 100% freelance written. Annual magazine of fiction (short stories), poetry and b&w photography. Estab. 1982. Circ. 1500. Pays on publication. Byline given. Reports in 1 week on queries; 2 months on mss. Sample copy $3. Free writer's guidelines.

Fiction: Novel excerpts, short stories of a literary quality. No religious, romance, erotica, confession, horror or condensed novels. Buys 8 mss/year. Query or send complete ms. Length: 5,000 words. Pays $100.

Poetry: Crystal Brown. Avant-garde, free verse, traditional. Does not want to see haiku, religious and most rhyme. Buys 12-15 poems/year. Submit 5 poems maximum. Pays $25.

ANTIOCH REVIEW, P.O. Box 148, Yellow Springs OH 45387. Editor: Robert S. Fogarty. 80% freelance written. Quarterly magazine for general, literary and academic audience. Estab. 1941. Buys all rights. Byline given. Pays on publication. Publishes ms an average of 10 months after acceptance. Reports in 6 weeks. Sample copy for $5; writer's guidelines for #10 SASE.

Nonfiction: "Contemporary articles in the humanities and social sciences, politics, economics, literature and all areas of broad intellectual concern. Somewhat scholarly, but never pedantic in style, eschewing all professional jargon. Lively, distinctive prose insisted upon." Length: 2,000-8,000 words. Pays $15/published page.

Fiction: Quality fiction only, distinctive in style with fresh insights into the human condition. No science fiction, fantasy or confessions. Pays $15/published page.

Poetry: Concrete visual imagery. No light or inspirational verse. Contributors should be familiar with the magazine before submitting.

BAD HAIRCUT, 3115 SW Roxbury, Seattle WA 98126. Editors: Ray Goforth and Kim Goforth. 99% freelance written. Estab. 1987. Circ. 2,000. Pays on publication. Byline given. Buys first North American serial rights. Submit seasonal/holiday material 4 months in advance. Simultaneous and previously published submissions OK. Reports in 1 week on queries; 1 month on mss. Sample copy $4; writer's guidelines for #10 SASE.

Nonfiction: Essays, expose (government), general interest, interview/profile (political leaders, activists), opinion, photo feature. No pornography or hate-oriented articles. Buys 6 mss/year. Query with or without published clips, or send complete ms. Length: 500-5,000. Pays copies and small cash amount. Sometimes pays writers with contributor copies or other premiums rather than a cash payment.

Fiction: Adventure, experimental, historical, science fiction. Buys 6 mss/year. Send complete ms. Length: 500-5,000 words. Pays $50 maximum, (usually copies).

Poetry: Avant-garde, free verse. Buys 300 poems/year. Submit up to 10 poems at one time. Length: 1-100 lines. Pays with copies or small cash amount.

Fillers: Anecdotes, facts, newsbreaks. Buys 20 mss/year. Length: 7-100 words. Pays $2.

Tips: "There is a rising tide of activism—a caring for others and the common future we all share. Tap into this—let your heart guide you along the path to peace."

BLACK MOUNTAIN REVIEW, Lorien House, P.O. Box 1112, Black Mountain NC 28711-1112. (704)669-6211. Editor: David A. Wilson. 100% freelance written. Annual magazine covering literary figures. Each issue is dedicated to a writer. For example, #8 (1992) is on Ernest Hemingway, #9 (1993) is on Tennessee Williams. Estab. 1987. Circ. 200. Byline given. Buys one-time rights. Previously published submissions OK. Reports in 1 week on queries, 2 weeks on mss. Sample copy for $4; writer's guidelines for #10 SAE with 1 first class stamp.

Nonfiction: Essays, historical/nostalgic. Upcoming issues: #8 "On Ernest Hemingway." No violence, sex, or general material not related to the theme. Buys 3-4 mss/year. Query. Length: 500-2,000 words. Payment: $15 articles.

Photos: State availability of photos with submission. Reviews prints (5×7). Offers $5. Model release and identification of subjects required. Buys one-time rights.

Fiction: Historical, mainstream, slice-of-life vignettes. Buys 1-2 mss/year. Must relate to theme. Query. Length: 500-2,000 words. Pays $15.

Poetry: Free verse, traditional. Buys 2 poems/year. Submit maximum 3 poems. Length: 60 lines maximum. Pays $5.

Tips: "Each issue is a specific theme, and by getting into some aspect of the theme, a writer has a very good chance of being published. The greatest problem is receiving general material which does not relate to the theme. A query first saves everyone time, energy and postage. Nonfiction is most needed, and well-researched material has the best chance of publication."

BLACK WARRIOR REVIEW, P.O. Box 2936, Tuscaloosa AL 35486. (205)348-4518. Editor, volume 18: Glenn Mott. Managing Editor: Dale Prince. 95% freelance written. A semiannual magazine of fiction and poetry. Estab. 1974. Circ. 2,000. Pays on publication. Publishes ms an average of 6 months after acceptance. Byline given. Buys first rights. Reports in 2 weeks on queries; 3 months on mss. Sample copy $5; writer's guidelines for #10 SASE.

Nonfiction: Interview/profile and book reviews. Buys 5 mss/year. Query or send complete ms. No limit on length. Payment varies.

Photos: State availability of photos with submission. Offers no additional payment for photos accepted with ms. Identification of subjects required. Buys one-time rights.

Fiction: Nicola Williams, fiction editor. Buys 10 mss/year.

Poetry: James H.N. Martin, poetry editor. Submit 3-6 poems. Long poems encouraged. Buys 50 poems/year.

Tips: "Read the *BWR* before submitting; editor changes each year. Send us your best work. Submissions of photos and/or artwork is encouraged. We sometimes choose unsolicited photos/artwork for the cover. Address all submissions to the appropriate genre editor."

‡BLOOMSBURY REVIEW, A Book Magazine, Owaissa Communications Co., Inc., 1028 Bannock, Denver CO 80204. (303)892-0620. FAX: (303)892-5620. Publisher/Editor-in-chief: Tom Auer. 75% freelance written. Tabloid covering books and book-related matters published 8 times a year. "We publish book reviews, interviews with writers and poets, literary essays and original poetry. Our audience consists of educated, literate, *non-specialized* readers." Estab. 1980. Circ. 50,000. Pays on publication. Publishes ms an average of 4 months after acceptance. Byline given. Buys first rights or one-time rights. Reports in 1 month on queries; 3 months on mss. Sample copy $3.50; writer's guidelines for #10 SASE.

Nonfiction: Essays, interview/profile and book reviews. "Summer issue features reviews, etc. about the American West." No academic or religious articles. Buys 60 mss/year. Query with published clips or send complete ms. Length 500-1,500 words. Pays $10-20. Sometimes pays writers with contributor copies or other premiums "if writer agrees."

Photos: State availability of photos with submissions. Reviews prints. Offers no additional payment for photos accepted with ms. Buys one-time rights.

Columns/Departments: Book reviews and essays. Buys 6 mss/year. Query with published clips or send complete ms. Length: 500-1,500 words. Pays $10-20.

Poetry: Ray Gonzalez, poetry editor. Avant-garde, free verse, haiku, light verse and traditional. Buys 20 poems/year. Submit up to 5 poems at one time. Pays $5-10.

Tips: "We appreciate receiving published clips and/or completed manuscripts. Please—no rough drafts. Book reviews should be of new books (within 6 months of publication)."

‡**BOING-BOING, The World's Greatest Neurozine,** P.O. Box 12311, Boulder CO 80303. Editor: Mark Frauenfelder. 90% freelance written. Consumer publication. Quarterly consumer magazine providing cognition enhancement and fun for neophiles. "Writers must be skeptical yet open to new ideas. Would like to see positive articles about using new technologies and paradigms for individual and social freedom and well-being." Estab. 1989. Circ. 1,000. Pays on publication. Publishes ms an average of 4 months after acceptance. Byline given. Offers 20% kill fee. Buys one-time rights. Submit seasonal/holiday material 6 months in advance. Simultaneous and previously published submissions OK. Query for electronic submissions. Reports in 2 weeks on queries; 1 month on mss. Sample copy $3.95. Writer's guidelines for #10 SASE.

Nonfiction: Book excerpts, essays, exposé, humor, interview/profile, new product, opinion (does not mean letters to the editor), personal experience, technical (computer technology, mind machines), software, science fiction and book reviews. Buys 32 mss/year. Query with or without published clips or send complete ms. Length: 500-5,000 words. Pays $5-35. Pays in contributor copies or other premiums "If requested by the writer." State availability of photos with submission. Reviews prints. Offers $5 maximum per photo. Buys one-time rights.

Columns/Departments: Exciting News (fake news stories satirizing current events), 100-500. Buys 8 mss/year. Send complete ms. Pays $1-15.

Fiction: Erotica, experimental, fantasy, humorous, science fiction, slice-of-life vignettes. Buys 12 mss/year. Send complete ms. Length: 100-5,000 words. Pays $5-20.

Fillers: Anecdotes, facts, newsbreaks, short humor. Buys 12/year. Length: 20-200 words. Pays $1-5.

Tips: "Scan computer bulletin boards to learn about cutting-edge developments in brain/mind research, computer technology, popular culture and science fiction. Read fanzines and attend lectures and workshops held by people with unusual ideas. Send articles and essays about new technologies and paradigms, as well as their ramifications and possibilities."

‡**BOULEVARD,** Opojaz, Inc., #2208, 2400 Chestnut St., Philadelphia PA 19103. Editor: Richard Burgin. Managing Editor: Linda Harris. 100% freelance written. Literary magazine covering fiction, poetry and essays; published 3 times/year. "*Boulevard* is a diverse triquarterly literary magazine presenting original creative work by well-known authors, as well as by writers of exciting promise." Estab. 1984. Circ. 2,500. Pays on publication. Publishes ms an average of 3-12 months after acceptance. Byline given. Offers no kill fee. Buys first North American serial rights. Simultaneous submissions OK. Reports in 2 weeks on queries; 2 months on mss. Sample copy $6. Writer's guidelines for SAE with 1 first class stamp.

Nonfiction: Book excerpts, essays, interview/profile. "No pornography, science fiction, children's stories or westerns." Buys 4 mss/year. Send complete ms. Length: 8,000 words maximum. Pays $50-150 (sometimes higher).

Fiction: Confession, experimental, mainstream, novel excerpts. "We do not want erotica, science fiction, romance, western or children's stories." Buys 20 mss/year. Send complete ms. Length: 8,000 words maximum. Pays $50-150 (sometimes higher).

Poetry: Avant-garde, free verse, Haiku, traditional. "Do not send us light verse." Buys 80 poems/year. Submit maximum 5 poems. Length: up to 200 lines. Pays $25-150 (sometimes higher).

Tips: "Read the magazine first. The work *Boulevard* publishes is generally recognized as among the finest in the country. Send only your best work."

‡**CALIFORNIA QUARTERLY,** University of California at Davis, 100 Sproul Hall, Davis CA 95616. (916)752-2729. Acting Editor: Jack Hicks. Managing Editor: Michael Ishii. 95% freelance written. Magazine of short fiction and poetry published 3 times/year. "We publish experimental, contemporary and literary short fiction and poetry and suggest that would-be contributors read our magazine to get a feel for its style." Estab. 1971. Circ. 600. Pays on publication. Publishes ms an average of 1 year after acceptance. Byline given. Buys first North American serial rights. Reports 3 weeks on queries; 2 months on mss. Sample copy $4. Writer's guidelines for #10 SASE.

Fiction: Mark Wisniewski. Ethnic, experimental, horror, humorous, mystery, novel excerpts, suspense. "We do not want to see any genre fiction." Buys 15 mss/year. Send complete ms. Pays $3/page.

Poetry: Jordan Jones. Avant-garde, free verse, haiku. "Again, nothing but the highest quality." Buys 50 poems/year. Submit maximum 5 poems. Pays $4/page.

CANADIAN FICTION MAGAZINE, Box 946, Station F, Toronto, Ontario M4Y 2N9 Canada. Editor: Geoffrey Hancock. Quarterly magazine. Publishes only Canadian fiction, short stories and novel excerpts. Circ. 1,800. Pays on publication. Buys first North American serial rights. Byline given. Reports in 6 weeks. Back issue $6; current issue $9.95 plus 7% tax (in Canadian funds).

Nonfiction: Interview (must have a definite purpose, both as biography and as a critical tool focusing on problems and techniques) and book reviews (Canadian fiction only). Looking for a critical series featuring speculation on the future of fiction. Buys 35 mss/year. Query. Length: 1,000-3,000 words. Pays $10/printed page plus 1-year subscription.

Photos: Purchased on assignment. Send prints. Pays $10 for 5×7 b&w glossy prints; $50 for cover. Model releases required.

Fiction: "No restrictions on subject matter or theme. We are open to experimental and speculative fiction as well as traditional forms. Style, content and form are the author's prerogative. Novellas and instant fiction also considered. We also publish self-contained sections of novel-in-progress and French-Canadian fiction in translation, as well as an annual special issue on a single author such as Mavis Gallant, Leon Rooke, Robert Harlow or Jane Rule. Please note that *CFM* is an anthology devoted *exclusively* to Canadian fiction. We publish only the works of writers and artists residing in Canada and Canadians living abroad." Pays $10/printed page.

Tips: "Prospective contributors must study several recent issues carefully. *CFM* is a serious professional literary magazine whose contributors include the finest writers in Canada."

CANADIAN LITERATURE, #223-2029 West Mall, University of British Columbia, Vancouver, British Columbia V6T 1W5 Canada. Editor: W.H. New. 70% freelance written. Works with "both new and established writers depending on quality." Quarterly. Estab. 1959. Circ. 2,000. Not copyrighted. Buys first Canadian rights only. Pays on publication. Publishes ms an average of 2 years after acceptance. Query "with a clear description of the project." Sample copy and writer's guidelines for $7.50 (Canadian) and 7×10 SAE with $4.30 Canadian postage.

Nonfiction: Articles of high quality only on Canadian books and writers written in French or English. Articles should be scholarly and readable. Length: 2,000-5,500 words. Pays $5/printed page.

‡CHAKRA, Freelance Press, P.O. Box 8551, Dept. 1010, FDR Station, New York NY 10022. Editor: Liz Camps. 100% freelance written. Literary magazine covering speculative arts and sciences, published 2-3 times/year. "*Chakra* seeks cyberotic art for a magickal world: erotica, mysticism, psychedelia, philosophy, esoteric sociopolitics, sf/fantasy. Fiction, essays, plays, poetry, reviews, interviews, etc." Estab. 1988. Circ. 200. Pays on publication. Publishes ms an average of 6 months after acceptance. Byline sometimes given. Offers kill fee of ½ publication fee. Buys one-time rights. Submit seasonal/holiday material 6 months in advance. Simultaneous and previously published submissions OK. Query for electronic submissions. Reports in 3 weeks or less on queries; 3 months or less on mss. Sample copy for $2.25. Writer's guidelines for #10 SAE with 1 first class stamp.

Nonfiction: Book excerpts, essays, humor, interview/profile, opinion, religious. Buys 2-6 mss/year. Query with or without published clips, or send complete ms. Length: 3,000 maximum words. Pays $1-30. Pays in contributor copies or other premiums "if requested." Send photos with submission. Offers $1 minimum per photo. Buys one-time rights.

Fiction: Richard Behrens. Condensed novels, erotica, experimental, fantasy, humorous, novel excerpts, religious, science fiction. Buys 4-6 mss/year. Send complete ms. Length: 3,000 maximum words. Pays $1-30.

Poetry: Richard Behrens. Avant-garde, free verse, Haiku, light verse, traditional. Buys 4-8 poems/year. Pays $1-15.

Tips: "Request a copy of our guidelines, which are very detailed. When submitting please include a cover letter telling us a little about yourself. All departments open to freelancers."

THE CHARITON REVIEW, Northeast Missouri State University, Kirksville MO 63501. (816)785-4499. Editor: Jim Barnes. 100% freelance written. Semiannual (fall and spring) magazine covering contemporary fiction, poetry, translation and book reviews. Circ. 600. Pays on publication. Publishes ms an average of 6 months after acceptance. Byline given. Buys first North American serial rights. Reports in 1 week on queries; 2 weeks on mss. Sample copy for $2.50, 7×10 SAE and $1 postage.

Nonfiction: Essays and essay reviews of books. Buys 2-5 mss/year. Send complete ms. Length: 1,000-5,000. Pays $15.

Fiction: Ethnic, experimental, mainstream, novel excerpts and traditional. "We are not interested in slick material." Buys 6-10 mss/year. Send complete ms. Length: 1,000-6,000 words. Pays $5/page.

Poetry: Avant-garde, free verse and traditional. Buys 50-55 poems/year. Submit maximum 10 poems. Length: open. Pays $5/page.

Tips: "Read *Chariton* and similar magazines. Know the difference between good literature and bad. Know what magazine might be interested in your work. We are not a trendy magazine. We publish only the best. All sections are open to freelancers. Know your market or you are wasting your time—

and mine. Do *not* write for guidelines; the only guideline is excellence in all matters."

‡**CLOCKWATCH REVIEW, (a journal of the arts)**, Dept. of English, Illinois Wesleyan University, Bloomington IL 61702. (309)556-3352. Editor: James Plath. 85% freelance written. Semiannual literary magazine. Estab. 1983. Circ. 1,400. **Pays on acceptance.** Byline given. Buys first North American serial rights. Submit seasonal/holiday material 6 months in advance. Reports in 1 months on queries; 2 weeks to 2 months on mss. Sample copy $4. Writer's guidelines for #10 SAE with 1 first class stamp.
Nonfiction: Essays (only literary) and interviews with writers, musicians, artists. Buys 1 mss/year. Query with or without published clips. Length: 1,500-4,000 words. Pays $50. State availability of photos with submission. Reviews contact sheets, negatives, transparencies. Offers no additional payment for photos accepted with ms. Buys one-time rights.
Fiction: Experimental, humorous, mainstream, novel excerpts. "Literary quality genre stories that break the mold. No straight mystery, fantasy, sci-fi, romance or western." Buys 6 mss/year. Send complete ms. Length: 1,500-4,000 words. Pays $50.
Poetry: Avant-garde, free verse, light verse, traditional. Buys 30 poems/year. Submit maximum 6 poems. Length: 32 lines maximum. Pays $10.

‡**COLORADO REVIEW A Journal of Contemporary Literature**, Department of English, Colorado State University, Ft. Collins CO 80523. (303)491-6428. Fiction: David Milofsky. Managing Editor: Bill Tremblay (also edits Poetry section). Translations: Mary Crow. Biannual magazine of contemporary human experience and literature. "Our journal is dedicated to contemporary literature as a fine art; we print only the best writing we can find." Estab. 1977. Circ. 1,100. Pays on publication. Byline given. Buys first North American serial rights. Simultaneous submissions OK. Reports in 3 months. Sample copy $5; free writer's guidelines.
Nonfiction: Essays; interviews with writers, poets; literary essays on contemporary work. Send complete ms. Length: 2,000-4,000 words.
Fiction: "No formula writing. We want stories with believable characters we can care about in a language and a narrative style that is engaging, interesting." Length: 5,000 words maximum. Pays $20 per printed page.
Poetry: "We print good poetry, regardless of its form." Buys 40-50 poems/year. Submit maximum 6 poems at a time. Length: 60 lines maximum. Pays $20 per printed page.

‡**CONFRONTATION, A Literary Journal**, Long Island University, Brookville NY 11548. (516)299-2391. Editor: Martin Tucker. 75% freelance written. Semiannual literary magazine. "We are eclectic in our taste. Excellence of style is our dominant concern." Estab. 1968. Circ. 2,000. Pays on publication. Publishes ms an average of 6 months after acceptance. Byline given. "We rarely offer kill fee." Buys first North American serial rights, first rights, one-time rights, all rights. Simultaneous submissions OK. Reports in 3 weeks on queries; 6-8 weeks on mss. Sample copy $3.
Nonfiction: Essays, personal experience. Buys 15 mss/year. Send complete ms. Length: 1,500-5,000 words. Pays $100-300 for assigned articles; $15-300 for unsolicited articles.
Photos: State availability of photos with submission. Offers no additional payment for photos accepted with ms. Buys one-time rights.
Fiction: Julian Mates. Experimental, mainstream, science fiction, slice-of-life vignettes. "We judge on quality, so genre is open." Buys 60-75 mss/year. Send complete ms. Length 6,000 words maximum. Pays $25-250.
Poetry: Katherine Hill-Miller. Avant-garde, free verse, Haiku, light verse, traditional. Buys 60-75 poems/year. Submit maximum 6 poems. Length open. Pays $10-100.
Tips: "Most open to fiction and poetry."

‡**THE CONNECTICUT POETRY REVIEW**, P.O. Box 3783, New Haven CT 06525. Editors: J. Claire White and J. Wm. Chichetto. 100% freelance written. Annual poetry journal. Estab. 1981. Circ. 500. **Pays on acceptance.** Submit seasonal material 3 months in advance. Reports in 3 months. Sample copy $3.50. Writer's guidelines for #10 SASE.
Poetry: Avant-garde, free verse and traditional. "No previously published work." Buys 30 poems/ year. Submit maximum 5 poems. Length: 4-30 lines. Pays $5.

‡**CRAZYHORSE**, University of Arkansas at Little Rock, English Dept., 2801 S., Little Rock AR 72204. (501)569-3160. Managing Editor: Zabelle Stodola. 100% freelance written. Semiannual literary magazine covering poetry and fiction. Estab. 1960. Circ. 1,000. Pays on publication. Publishes book an average of 6-12 months after acceptance. Reports in 1-4 months. Sample copy $5.
Fiction: Fiction Editor: Judy Troy. Experimental and mainstream. "Serious quality fiction of any kind." Buys approximately 10 mss/year. Send complete ms. Pays $10 per page—$500 Annual Fiction Prize.

Poetry: Poetry Editor: Ralph Burns. Traditional. Buys 50 poems/year. Pays $10 per page. $500 Annual Poetry Prize.

THE DENVER QUARTERLY, University of Denver, Dept. of English, Denver CO 80208. (303)871-2892. Editor: Donald Revell. 100% freelance written. Works with a small number of new/unpublished writers. Quarterly magazine for generally sophisticated readership. Estab. 1966. Circ. 1,000. Pays on publication. Publishes ms an average of 6-12 months after acceptance. Buys first North American serial rights. Reports in 3 months. Sample copy $5.
Nonfiction: "Most reviews are solicited; we do publish a few literary essays in each number. Use non-sexist language, please." Send complete ms. Pays $5/printed page.
Fiction: Buys 10 mss/year. Send complete ms. Pays $5/printed page.
Poetry: Buys 50 poems/year. Send poems. Pays $5/printed page.
Tips: "We decide on the basis of quality only. Prior publication is irrelevant. Promising material, even though rejected, may receive some personal comment from the editor; some material can be revised to meet our standards through such criticism. I receive more good stuff than *DQ* can accept, so there is some subjectivity and a good deal of luck involved in any final acceptance. *DQ* is becoming interested in issues of aesthetics and *lucid* perspectives and performances of the avant-garde. We are also interested in topics and translations in the literature of Eastern Europe. Please look at a *recent* issue before submitting. Reading unsolicited mss during academic year only; we do *not* read between May 15 and Sept. 15."

EPOCH, Cornell University, 251 Goldwin Smith, Ithaca NY 14853. (607)255-3385. Editor: Michael Koch. 50-98% freelance written. Works with a small number of new/unpublished writers each year. Literary magazine of original fiction and poetry published 3 times/year. Estab. 1947. Circ. 1,000. Pays on publication. Publishes ms an average of 2-12 months after acceptance. Byline given. Buys first North American serial rights. Sample copy $4.
Fiction: "Potential contributors should *read* a copy or two. There is *no other way* for them to ascertain what we need or like." Buys 15-20 mss/year. Send complete ms. Pays $5/page.
Nonfiction: Essays. Buys 3-6 mss/year.
Poetry: "Potential contributors should read magazine to see what type of poetry is used." Buys 20-30 poems/year. Pays 50¢/line.
Tips: Mss received over the summer (May 15 - Sept 15) will be returned unread.

EROTIC FICTION QUARTERLY, EFQ Publications, Box 4958, San Francisco CA 94101. Editor: Richard Hiller. 100% freelance written. Small literary magazine (published irregularly) for thoughtful people interested in a variety of highly original and creative short fiction with sexual themes. **Pays on acceptance.** Byline given. Buys first rights. Writer's guidelines for SASE.
Fiction: Heartfelt, intelligent erotica, any style. Also, stories—not necessarily erotic—about some aspect of authentic sexual experience. No standard pornography or men's magazine-type stories; no contrived or formula plots or gimmicks; no broad satire or parody. We do not publish poetry. Send complete ms. Length: 500-5,000 words, average 1,500 words. Pays $50 minimum.
Tips: "What we especially need and do not see enough of is truly interesting and original erotica, whether graphic or subtle, as well as literary-quality fiction that depends on sexual insight. No particular 'slant' is required. Stories should reflect real life, not media ideas."

EVENT, Douglas College, Box 2503, New Westminster, British Columbia V3L 5B2 Canada. FAX: (604)527-5095. Managing Editor: Bonnie Bauder. 100% freelance written. Works with a small number of new/unpublished writers each year. Triannual magazine (March, July and November) for "those interested in literature and writing." Estab. 1970. Circ. 1,000. Uses 80-100 mss/year. Small payment and contributor's copy only. Publishes ms an average of 3 months after acceptance. Buys first North American serial rights. Byline given. Reports in 4 months. Submit complete ms with IRCs.
Nonfiction: "High quality work." Reviews of Canadian books and essays.
Fiction: Short stories and drama.
Poetry: Submit complete ms. "We are looking for high quality modern poetry."

‡FICTION QUARTERLY, The Tampa Tribune, P.O. Box 191, Tampa FL 33601. (813)272-7600. Editor: Rick Wilber. 75% freelance written. Quarterly newspaper fiction and poetry supplement. "We have a general newspaper readership, so we are touchy about explicit sex, rough language and the like." Estab. 1988. Circ. 400,000. Pays on publication. Byline given. Buys first North American serial rights. Reports in 3 months on mss.
Fiction: Adventure, confession, ethnic, experimental, fantasy, historical, horror, humorous, mainstream, mystery, novel excerpts, religious, romance, science fiction, slice-of-life vignettes, suspense and western. Buys 8-12 mss/year. Send complete ms. Length: 2,000-2,500 words. Pays $100-200.

Poetry: Free verse and narrative poetry. Buys 8-10 poems/year. Submit 4 or 5 poems maximum. Length: 20 lines maximum. Pays $40.

THE FIDDLEHEAD, University of New Brunswick, Campus House, P.O. Box 4400, Fredericton, New Brunswick E3B 5A3 Canada. (506)453-3501. FAX: (506)453-4599. Editor: Don MacKay. 90% freelance written. Eager to work with new/unpublished writers. Quarterly magazine covering poetry, short fiction, drawings and photographs and book reviews. Estab. 1945. Circ. 1,100. Pays on publication. Publishes ms an average of 6-12 months after acceptance. Not copyrighted. Buys first North American serial rights. Submit seasonal/holiday material 6 months in advance. Simultaneous queries OK. Reports in 3 weeks on queries; 2 months on mss. Sample copy $6.
Fiction: K.E. Thompson, Anthony Boxill, Diana Austin, fiction editors. "Stories may be on any subject—acceptance is based on quality alone. Because the journal is heavily subsidized by the Canadian government, some preference is given to Canadian writers." Buys 24 mss/year. Pays $12/page.
Poetry: Robert Gibbs, Robert Hawkes, Don MacKay, poetry editors. "Poetry may be on any subject—acceptance is based on quality alone. Because the journal is heavily subsidized by the Canadian government, some preference is given to Canadian writers." Buys average of 60 poems/year. Submit maximum 10 poems. Pays $12/page; $100 maximum.
Tips: "Quality alone is the criterion for publication. Return postage (Canadian, or IRCs) should accompany all manuscripts."

‡FRANK: An International Journal of Contemporary Writing & Art, B.P. 29, Frank Books, 94301 Vincennes Cedex, France. (33)1-43-65-64-05. FAX: (33)1-43-65-33-02. Editor: David Applefield. 50% freelance written. Semiannual literary and arts magazine. "We are seeking writing that responds to the world—well-crafted but also conveys a sense of necessity. Work that takes risks and is non-ethnocentric." Estab. 1983. Circ. 4,000. Pays on publication. Publishes ms an average of 2-6 months after acceptance. Byline given. Buys one-time rights. Query for electronic submissions. Reports in 2 weeks on queries; 2 months on mss. Sample copy $8. Free writer's guidelines.
Nonfiction: Interview/profile. Buys 3 mss/year. Query. Length: 500-3,000 words. Pays $10-150 for assigned articles; $5/page plus two copies. Sometimes pays expenses of writers on assignment. Send photos with submission. Reviews 8 × 10 prints. Offers $10-25/photo. Identification of subjects required. Buys one-time rights.
Poetry: Avant-garde, translations and free verse. "No sentimental poetry." Buys 10-20 poems/year. Submit maximum 10 poems. Length: 1-200 lines. Pays $5-100.

THE GAMUT, A Journal of Ideas and Information, Cleveland State University, 1983 E. 24th St., #FT 1218, Cleveland OH 44115-2440. (216)687-4679. FAX: (216)687-9366. Editor: Louis T. Milic. Managing Editor: Susan Grimm Dumbrys. 50-60% freelance written. Triannual magazine. Estab. 1980. Circ. 1,000. Pays on publication. Publishes ms an average of 6 months after acceptance. Byline given. Buys one-time rights. Submit seasonal/holiday material 6 months in advance. Simultaneous submissions OK. Reports in 1 month on queries; 3 months on mss. Sample copy $2.50; writer's guidelines for #10 SASE.
Nonfiction: Essays, general interest, historic/nostalgic, opinion, personal experience, photo feature and technical. Buys 15-20 mss/year. Query with or without published clips, or send complete ms. Length: 1,000-6,000 words. Pays $25-250. Pays authors associated with the university with contributor copies.
Photos: State availability of photos with submission. Offers no additional payment for photos accepted with ms. Captions, model releases and identification of subjects required. Buys one-time rights.
Columns/Departments: Languages of the World (linguistic). Length: 2,000-4,000. Buys 1-2 mss/year. Query with published clips or send complete ms. Pays $75-125.
Fiction: Ethnic, experimental, historical, humorous, mainstream, novel excerpts and science fiction. No condensed novels or genre fiction. Buys 1-2 mss/year. Send complete ms. Length: 1,000-3,000 words. Pays $25-150.
Poetry: Leonard Trawick, poetry editor. Buys 6-15 poems/year. Submit up to 10 at one time. Pays $25-75.
Tips: "Get a fresh approach to an interesting idea or subject; back it up with solid facts, analysis, and/or research. Make sure you are writing for an educated, but general and not expert reader."

HANSON'S, A Magazine of Literary and Social Interest, CIRE Publishing, 113 Merryman Ct., Annapolis MD 21401. (410)626-0744. Editor: Eric Hanson. 80% freelance written. Semiannual literary magazine. "Hanson's is a magazine of literary and social interest appealing to the larger community of readers who enjoy stimulating thought communicated through excellent writing." Estab. 1988. Circ. 3,000. **Pays on acceptance.** Publishes ms an average of 4 months after acceptance. Byline given. Buys first North American serial rights or one-time rights. Reports in 2 weeks on queries; 3 weeks on mss. Sample copy $4. Writer's guidelines for #10 SAE with 2 first class stamps.

Nonfiction: Essays, general interest, historical/nostalgic, humor, interview/profile, opinion, personal experience, travel. Buys 8 mss/year. Send complete ms. Length: 1,000-4,000 words. Pays $50-200 for assigned articles; $40-100 for unsolicited articles. Sometimes pays expenses of writers on assignment.
Columns/Departments: Column/Department Editor: Daniel Sentso. Wordly Wisdom (history and derivation of interesting words), 2,000 words; Ask Auntie Em (humorous parody of advice columnists), 2,000 words; "Fable Nonce" (stories with a moral, done in a simple, 'fable' style), 2,000 words; Other Shoes (examinations of unusual lifestyles and situations); "A Backward Glance" (oral history), 3,000 words. Buys 8 mss/year. Pays $40-100.
Fiction: Eric Hanson, fiction editor. Erotica, experimental, fantasy, humorous, mainstream, mystery, suspense. Buys 15 mss/year. Send complete ms. Length: 1,500-4,000 words. Pays $50-200.
Poetry: Shannon Rogowski, poetry editor. Avant-garde, free verse and traditional. Buys 50 poems/year. Submit maximum 5 poems. Length: 4-100 lines. Pays $20-50.
Tips: "Because of our unique format, it is a tremendous help to review a sample copy before submitting. Not to be discounted as a good foot in the door is a short, well-written cover letter."

‡**HIGH PLAINS LITERARY REVIEW**, Suite 250, 180 Adams St., Denver CO 80206. (303)320-6828. Editor: Robert O. Greer, Jr. Managing Editor: Phyllis A. Harwell. 80% freelance written. Literary magazine published three times per year. The *High Plains Literary Review* publishes short stories, essays, poetry, reviews and interviews "bridging the gap between commercial quarterlies and academic reviews." Estab. 1986. Circ. 1200. Pays on publication. Byline given. Buys first North American serial rights. Simultaneous submissions OK. Reports in 2 months. Sample copy $4. Writer's guidelines for #10 SASE.
Nonfiction: Essays and reviews. Buys 20 mss/year. Send complete ms. Length: 10,000 words maximum. Pays $5/page.
Fiction: Ethnic, historical, humorous, mainstream, other. Buys 12 mss/year. Send complete ms. Length: 10,000 words maximum. Pays $5/page.
Poetry: Buys 45 poems/year. Pays $10/page.

‡**HOBO JUNGLE, A Quarterly Journal of New Writing**, 33 Rucum Rd., Roxbury CT 06783. (203)354-4359. Editors: Marc Erdrich/Ruth Boerger. 100% freelance written. Quarterly literary magazine. "*HJ* is a quarterly literary journal of new writing by published and unpublished writers. There is only one fiat: good writing. We are trying to reach a mass audience through a policy of free distribution in certain markets." Estab. 1987. Distribution 11,000. Pays on publication. Byline given. Buys one-time rights. Submit seasonal/holiday material 6 months in advance. Simultaneous submissions OK. Query for electronic submissions. Reports in 3-4 months on mss. Free writer's guidelines. Sample copy $3.
Nonfiction: Essays, humor, opinion. Send complete ms. Pays $10 for published articles.
Fiction: Erotica, ethnic, experimental, fantasy, historical, humorous, mainstream, novel excerpts, science fiction, serialized novels, suspense. "We have no specific subject matter requirements; however, we are not accepting children's stories though we *do* accept manuscripts *from* young writers (under 15) for publication in our 'Young Hobos' section." Buys 10 mss/year. Send complete ms. Pays $10 for published work.
Poetry: No sentimental poetry. Buys 200 poems/year. Submit maximum 5 poems. Pays $10 for any number of author's work published in one issue.
Fillers: We publish musical scores, drawings, dance notation, cartoons, i.e., anything written!

THE HUDSON REVIEW, 684 Park Ave., New York NY 10021. Managing Editor: Ronald Koury. Quarterly. Estab. 1948. Pays on publication. Buys first world serial rights in English. Reports in 2 months.
Nonfiction: Articles, translations and reviews. Length: 8,000 words maximum.
Fiction: Uses "quality fiction." Length: 10,000 words maximum. Pays 2½¢/word.
Poetry: 50¢/line for poetry.
Tips: Unsolicited mss will be read according to the following schedule: *Nonfiction:* Jan. 1-March 31, and Oct. 1-Dec. 31; *Poetry:* April 1-Sept. 30; *Fiction:* June 1-Nov. 30.

INDIANA REVIEW, Indiana University, 316 N. Jordan, Bloomington IN 47405. (812)855-3439. Editor: Allison Joseph. Associate Editor: Dorian Gossey. 100% freelance written. Magazine published 3 times/year. "We publish fine innovative fiction and poetry. We're interested in energy, originality and careful attention to craft. While we publish many well-known writers, we also publish new and emerging poets and fiction writers." Estab. 1982. Circ. 600. **Pays on acceptance.** Byline given. Buys first North American serial rights. Reports in 2 weeks on queries; 3 months on mss. Sample copy $5; free writer's guidelines.

Close-up

Dorian Gossey
Associate Editor
Indiana Review

"I'm intrigued by fiction that isn't afraid to take on the world—to reach beyond the four walls of a yuppie family or a stagnant relationship for its material," says *Indiana Review* Associate Editor Dorian Gossey. The journal began in the mid-70s as *Indiana Writes*, a magazine devoted to publishing experimental literature. In 1983 it became *Indiana Review*, and "while we consider and encourage experimental work, we are by no means confined to it," she says.

Gossey, who previously served as production editor at Harper & Row, San Francisco, collaborates with current editor Allison Joseph on administrative duties at the Indiana University-affiliated journal. Gossey has been writing fiction for three years and editing it for 10 and, with that experience, devotes her time to selecting and editing fiction. Joseph, a published poet and MFA candidate, selects and edits all poetry for the journal. Upon Joseph's graduation, Gossey will assume the editorship and will hire a new associate editor to handle poetry. "The magazine's rotating student editorship (staffed entirely by MFA students at Indiana University) ensures a kind of diversity that I think lends it the freshness it has. We read hundreds of manuscripts per month, and what we take reflects the singularity of our combined, varied vision."

Although the editors give special consideration to works by Indiana writers, *Indiana Review* has a nationwide audience. Material is selected from both solicited and unsolicited manuscripts, thus creating a balanced representation of both well-known and emerging writers. Gossey advises writers who are interested in submitting to *Indiana Review* to become familiar with the journal's standards of quality and to keep correspondence to a minimum when sending work. "Please don't query. Just send the manuscript. Don't make the cover letter a direct mail piece by trying to interest the editor in the manuscript. Just make it simple and indicate what you'd like done with the manuscript if we don't take it. It's fine to just put in a standard business-size SASE for the response; we do recycle paper."

A story must undergo a comprehensive screening process before actually appearing in *Indiana Review*. Interns and volunteers screen the first round of unsolicited manuscripts. The selection process is then coordinated by the genre editor and involves three fiction editors who all read the same manuscript and discuss its merits. Any manuscript published has most likely been read six or seven times. "What grabs me when I read a story from the slush pile is a strong sense of voice and a firm grip on language, a sense of command. The writer is in charge of the story and not at the mercy of some clichéd convention of what a story is," says Gossey. "I like to see work that has a sense of place in the world. Not just a physical place, though that is important, but also a connectedness to larger issues and ideas."

She encourages writers to be innovative in their approaches to writing and persistent in their publishing endeavors: "Innovative fiction has verve and takes risks. Innovative fiction isn't afraid to make mistakes and try again. We do cultivate authors who have promise and seem to be trying new things. The trick is to be persistent."

—Roseann Shaughnessy

Nonfiction: Essays. No pornographic or strictly academic articles dealing with the traditional canon. Buys 3 mss/year. Query. Length: 5,000 maximum. Pays $25-200.
Fiction: Experimental and mainstream. No pornography. Buys 18 mss/year. Send complete ms. Length: 250-15,000. Pays $5/page.
Poetry: Avant-garde and free verse. "No pornography and no slavishly traditional poetry." Buys 60 mss/year. Submit up to 5 poems at one time. Length: 5 lines minimum. Pays $5/page.
Tips: "Read us before you submit. Often reading is slower in summer months."

THE IOWA REVIEW, 369 EPB, The University of Iowa, Iowa City IA 52242. (319)335-0462. Editor: David Hamilton, with the help of colleagues, graduate assistants, and occasional guest editors. Magazine published 3 times/year. Buys first serial rights. Reports in 3 months.
Nonfiction, Fiction and Poetry: "We publish essays, stories and poems and would like for our essays not always to be works of academic criticism." Buys 65-85 unsolicited mss/year. Submit complete ms. Pays $1/line for verse; $10/page for prose.

JAPANOPHILE, Box 223, Okemos MI 48864. Editor: Earl Snodgrass. 80% freelance written. Works with a small number of new/unpublished writers each year. Quarterly magazine for literate people who are interested in Japanese culture anywhere in the world. Pays on publication. Publishes ms an average of 5 months after acceptance. Buys first North American serial rights. Previously published submissions OK. Reports in 1 month. Sample copy $4, postpaid. Writer's guidelines with #10 SASE.
Nonfiction: "We want material on Japanese culture in *North America or anywhere in the world*, even Japan. We want articles, preferably with pictures, about persons engaged in arts of Japanese origin: a Michigan naturalist who is a haiku poet, a potter who learned raku in Japan, a vivid 'I was there' account of a Go tournament in California. We use some travel articles if exceptionally well-written, but we are *not* a regional magazine about Japan. We are a little magazine, a literary magazine. Our particular slant is a certain kind of culture wherever it is in the world: Canada, the U.S., Europe, Japan. The culture includes flower arranging, haiku, sports, religion, art, photography, fiction, etc. It is important to study the magazine." Buys 8 mss/issue. Query preferred but not required. Length: 1,600 words maximum. Pays $8-20.
Photos: State availability of photos. Pays $10-20 for 8×10 b&w glossy prints.
Fiction: Experimental, mainstream, mystery, adventure, science fiction, humorous, romance and historical. Themes should relate to Japan or Japanese culture. Length: 1,000-6,000 words. Contest each year pays $100 to best short story. (Reading fee $5.) Should include one or more Japanese and non-Japanese characters in each story.
Columns/Departments: Regular columns and features are Tokyo Scene and Profile of Artists. "We also need columns about Japanese culture in American cities." Query. Length: 1,000 words. Pays $20 maximum.
Poetry: Traditional, avant-garde and light verse related to Japanese culture or in a Japanese form such as haiku. Length: 3-50 lines. Pays $1-100.
Fillers: Newsbreaks, clippings and short humor of up to 200 words. Pays $1-5.
Tips: "We prefer to see more articles about Japanese culture in the U.S., Canada and Europe." Lack of convincing fact and detail is a frequent mistake.

‡**THE JOURNAL**, Ohio State University, 421 Denney Hall, 164 W. 17th Ave., Columbus OH 43210. (614)292-4076. Editor: Kathy Fagan and Michelle Herman. Managing Editor: Jackie Spangler. 100% freelance written. Semiannual literary magazine. "We're open to all forms; we tend to favor work that gives evidence of a mature and sophisticated sense of the language." Estab. 1972. Circ. 1,200. Pays on publication. Byline given. Buys first North American serial rights. Reports in 2 weeks on queries; 2 months on mss. Sample copy $5; writer's guidelines for #10 SASE.
Nonfiction: Essays, interview/profile. Buys 2 mss/year. Query. Length: 2,000-4,000 words. Pays $25 maximum and contributor's copies.
Photos: State availability of photos with submission. Offers no additional payment for photos accepted with ms. Identification of subjects required. Buys one-time rights.
Columns/Departments: Reviews of contemporary poetry, 2,000-4,000 words. Buys 2 mss/year. Query. Pays $25.
Fiction: Novel excerpts, literary short stories.
Poetry: Avant-garde, free verse, traditional. Buys 100 poems/year. Submit maximum 5 poems/year. Pays $25.

LIGHTHOUSE, P.O. Box 1377, Auburn WA 98071-1377. Editor: Tim Clinton. 100% freelance written. A bimonthly literary magazine. Estab. 1986. Circ. 300. Pays on publication. Byline given. Buys first North American serial rights and first rights. Reports in 2 months. Sample copy and writer's guidelines for $3; writer's guidelines only for #10 SASE.

Fiction: Lynne Trindl, fiction editor. Adventure, humorous, mainstream, mystery, romance, science fiction, suspense, western. "No murder mysteries or anything not G-rated." Buys 66 mss/year. Send complete ms. Length: 5,000 words maximum. Pays up to $50.

Poetry: Lorraine Clinton, poetry editor. Free verse, light verse, traditional. Buys 24 poems/year. Submit up to 5 poems at one time. Pays up to $5.

Tips: "Both fiction and poetry are open to freelancers. Just follow the guidelines."

LITERARY MAGAZINE REVIEW, KSU Writers Society, English Dept., Denison Hall, Kansas State University, Manhattan KS 66506. (913)532-6106. Editor: G.W. Clift. 98% freelance written. "Most of our reviewers are recommended to us by third parties." A quarterly literary magazine devoted almost exclusively to reviews of the current contents of small circulation serials publishing some fiction or poetry. Estab. 1951. Circ. 500. Pays on publication. Publishes ms an average of 1 month after acceptance. Byline given. Buys first rights. Query for electronic submissions. Reports in 2 weeks. Sample copy $4.

Nonfiction: Buys 60 mss/year. Query. Length: 1,500 words. Pays $25 maximum for assigned articles and two contributor's copies. Sometimes pays expenses of writers on assignment.

Photos: State availability of photos with submission. Identification of subjects required.

Tips: Interested in "omnibus reviews of magazines sharing some quality, editorial philosophy, or place of origin and in articles about literary magazine editing and the literary magazine scene."

LITERARY SKETCHES, P.O. Box 810571, Dallas TX 75381-0571. (214)243-8776. Editor: Olivia Murray Nichols. 33% freelance written. Willing to work with new/unpublished writers. Monthly newsletter for readers with literary interests; all ages. Estab. 1961. Circ 500. Byline given. Pays on publication. Publishes ms an average of 1 year after acceptance. Reports in 1 month. Sample copy for #10 SASE.

Nonfiction: Interviews of well-known writers and biographical material of more than common knowledge on past writers. Concise, informal style. Centennial pieces relating to a writer's birth, death or famous works. Buys 4-6 mss/year. Submit complete ms. Length: up to 1,000 words. Pays ½¢/word, plus copies.

Tips: "Articles need not be footnoted, but a list of sources should be submitted with the manuscript. We appreciate fillers of 100 words or less if they concern some little known information on an author or book."

LOS ANGELES TIMES BOOK REVIEW, Times Mirror, Times Mirror Sq., Los Angeles CA 90053. (213)237-7777. Editor: Jack Miles. 70% freelance written. Weekly tabloid reviewing current books. Estab. 1881. Circ. 1.5 million. Pays on publication. Publishes ms an average of 3 weeks after acceptance. Byline given. Offers variable kill fee. Buys first North American serial rights. Accepts no unsolicited book reviews or requests for specific titles to review. "Query with published samples—book reviews or literary features." Buys 500 mss/year. Length: 200-1,500 words. Pays approx 35¢/word.

LOST CREEK LETTERS, Lost Creek Publications, Box 373A, Rushville MO 64484. Editor: Pamela Montgomery. 100% freelance written. Quarterly magazine. "We seek mature, thoughtful fiction, poetry and essays. Nothing trite, sentimental or didactic. We publish material on any subject. Our audience is generally college educated." Estab. 1988. Pays on publication. Publishes ms an average of 4 months after acceptance. Byline given. Buys one-time rights. Simultaneous and previously published submissions OK. Query for electronic submissions. Sample copy $4 with 6×9 SAE and 3 first class stamps. Writer's guidelines for #10 SAE with 1 first class stamp.

Nonfiction: Essays, humor, personal experience. "No religious or inspirational articles." Buys 50 mss/year. Send complete ms. Length: 500-2,500 words. Pays $5.

Fiction: Ethnic, experimental, fantasy, historical, humorous, mainstream, science fiction, slice-of-life vignettes, surrealism. "No religious or romance." Buys 8-10 mss/year. Send complete ms. Length: 200-3,000 words. Pays $5.

Poetry: Avant-garde, free verse, haiku, light verse, traditional. No "Hallmark card" poems. Buys 50-100 poems/year. Submit maximum 20 poems. Pays $2.

Tips: "Study literature which has withstood the test of time. Have something to say and say it *once very well*. Keep in mind our audience of college educated mature adults. We prefer no cover letter at all and no credit lists, only the manuscript and SASE. If you feel you must send a cover letter, keep it very brief; do not use it to explain the manuscript intent or how it was inspired. The best submissions need no explanation or explication. Above all, find out what a literary magazine is. We get many submissions that are totally unsuited for a litmag, wasting your precious writing time and a lot of expensive postage. Invest in a sample copy and share it with your writing friends, then submit material you believe to conform to our tastes."

THE MALAHAT REVIEW, The University of Victoria, P.O. Box 3045, Victoria, British Columbia V8W 3P4 Canada. Contact: Editor. 100% freelance written. Eager to work with new/unpublished writers. Magazine published 4 times/year covering poetry, fiction, drama and criticism. Estab. 1967. Circ. 1,700.

Pays on acceptance. Publishes ms up to 1 year after acceptance. Byline given. Offers 100% kill fee. Buys first serial rights. Reports in 2 weeks on queries; 3 months on mss. Sample copy $6.
Nonfiction: Interview/profile (literary/artistic). Buys 2 mss/year. Query first. Length: 1,000-8,000. Pays $35-175.
Photos: Pays $25 for b&w prints. Captions required. Pays $100 for color print used as cover. 4/year.
Fiction: Buys 20 mss/year. Send complete ms. Length: no restriction. Pays $40/1,000 words.
Poetry: Avant-garde, free verse and traditional. Buys 100/year. Pays $20/page.

THE MASSACHUSETTS REVIEW, Memorial Hall, University of Massachusetts, Amherst MA 01003. (413)545-2689. Editors: Mary Heath, Jules Chametzky and Paul Jenkins. "As pleased to consider new writers as established ones." Quarterly. Pays on publication. Publishes ms 6-18 months after acceptance. Buys first North American serial rights. Reports in 3 months. Mss will not be returned unless accompanied by SASE. Sample copy for $4.50 plus 50¢ postage.
Nonfiction: Articles on literary criticism, women, public affairs, art, philosophy, music and dance. Length: 6,500 words average. Pays $50.
Fiction: Short stories or chapters from novels when suitable for independent publication. Length: max. 25 typed pages (approx.). Pays $50.
Poetry: 35¢/line or $10 minimum.
Tips: No fiction manuscripts are considered from June to October.

MICHIGAN QUARTERLY REVIEW, 3032 Rackham Bldg., University of Michigan, Ann Arbor MI 48109. Editor: Laurence Goldstein. 75% freelance written. Prefers to work with published/established writers; works with a small number of new/unpublished writers each year. Quarterly. Estab. 1962. Circ. 2,000. Publishes ms an average of 1 year after acceptance. Pays on publication. Buys first serial rights. Reports in 1 month for mss submitted in September-May; in summer, 2 months. Sample copy $2 with 2 first class stamps.
Nonfiction: "*MQR* is open to general articles directed at an intellectual audience. Essays ought to have a personal voice and engage a significant subject. Scholarship must be present as a foundation, but we are not interested in specialized essays directed only at professionals in the field. We prefer ruminative essays, written in a fresh style and which reach interesting conclusions. We also like memoirs and interviews with significant historical or cultural resonance." Length: 2,000-5,000 words. Pays $100-150, sometimes more.
Fiction and Poetry: No restrictions on subject matter or language. "We publish about 10 stories a year and are very selective. We like stories which are unusual in tone and structure, and innovative in language." Send complete ms. Pays $10/published page.
Tips: "Read the journal and assess the range of contents and the level of writing. We have no guidelines to offer or set expectations; every manuscript is judged on its unique qualities. On essays – query with a very thorough description of the argument and a copy of the first page. Watch for announcements of special issues, which are usually expanded issues and draw upon a lot of freelance writing. Be aware that this is a university quarterly that publishes a limited amount of fiction and poetry; that it is directed at an educated audience, one that has done a great deal of reading in all types of literature."

MID-AMERICAN REVIEW, Dept. of English, Bowling Green State University, Bowling Green OH 43403. (419)372-2725. Editor: Ken Letko. 100% freelance written. Eager to work with new/unpublished writers. Semiannual literary magazine of "the highest quality fiction, poetry and translations of contemporary poetry and fiction." Also publishes critical articles and book reviews of contemporary literature. Estab. 1972. Pays on publication. Publishes ms an average of 3-6 months after acceptance. Byline given. Buys one-time rights. Reports in 4 months or less. Current issue $5, back issues for $4; rare back issues $10.
Fiction: Character-oriented, literary. Buys 12 mss/year. Send complete ms; do not query. Pays $7/page up to $50.
Poetry: Strong imagery, strong sense of vision. Buys 60 poems/year. Pays $7/page up to $50.
Tips: "We are seeking translations of contemporary authors from all languages into English; submissions must include the original; essays in feminist criticism."

NEW ENGLAND REVIEW, (formerly *New England Review/Bread Loaf Quarterly*), Middlebury College, Middlebury VT 05753. (802)388-3711, Ext 5075. Editors: T.R. Hummer and Devon Gersild. Office Editor: Toni Best. 99% freelance written. Quarterly magazine covering contemporary literature. "We print a wide range of contemporary poetry, fiction, essays and reviews. Our readers tend to be literary and intellectual, but we're not academic, over-refined or doctrinaire." Circ. 3,200. Pays on publication. Publishes ms an average of 6 months after acceptance. Byline given. Buys first-time rights. Reports in 1 week on queries; 2 months on ms. Sample copy $6; writer's guidelines for #10 SASE.

Nonfiction: Book excerpts, essays, general interest, humor and personal experience. Buys 10 mss/year. Send complete ms. Length: 500-6,000 words. Pays $10/page, $20 minimum.

Photos: Also accepts drawings, woodcuts and etchings. Send with submission. Reviews transparencies and prints. Offers $60 minimum for cover art. Captions and identification of subjects required. Buys one-time rights.

Fiction: Ethnic, experimental, mainstream, novel excerpts, slice-of-life vignettes. Buys 30 mss/year. Send complete ms. Pays $10/page, $20 minimum.

Poetry: Avant-garde, free verse and traditional. Buys 75 poems/year. Submit up to 6 at one time. Pays $10/page, $20 minimum.

Tips: "Read at least one issue to get an idea of our range, standards and style. Don't submit simultaneously to other publications. All sections are open. We look for writing that's intelligent, well informed and well crafted."

THE NEW RENAISSANCE, An International Magazine of Ideas and Opinions, Emphasizing Literature and the Arts, 9 Heath Road, Arlington MA 02174. Editor: Louise T. Reynolds. 95% freelance written. Works with a small number of new/unpublished writers each year. Only accepts mss from Jan. 2-June 30 each year. International biannual literary magazine covering literature, visual arts, ideas and opinions for a general literate, sophisticated public. Estab. 1968. Circ. 1,500. Pays after publication. Publishes ms 18-23 months after acceptance. Buys all rights. Does not read any ms without SASE or IRCs. Answers no queries without SASE, IRCs or stamped postcards. Does not read mss from July 1 through December 31 of any year. Reports in 1 month on queries; 7 months on prose mss. Sample copy $5.65 for back issues; $4.80 recent issue; $7.40 current issue (all rates apply to U.S. submission; add 50¢ for foreign requests). Subscriptions: $12.50 U.S.; $14.50-Europe, Canada, Mexico.

Nonfiction: Interview/profile (literary/performing artists); opinion; and literary/artistic essays. "We prefer expert opinion in a style suitable for a literary magazine (i.e., *not* journalistic). Send complete manuscript or essays. Because we are biannual, we prefer to have writers query us, with outlines, etc., on political/sociological articles and give a sample of their writing." Buys 3-6 mss/year. Query for political/sociological pieces with published clips or 2 pg. sample writing. SASE and IRC. Length: 11-35 pages. Pays $32-135.

Photos: State availability of photos or send photos with query. Do not send slides; do not send originals without SASE. Pays $5-11 for 5×7 b&w prints. Captions, model releases and identification of subjects required, if applicable. Buys one-time rights.

Fiction: Quality fiction, well-crafted, literary and "serious"; occasionally, experimental or light. No "formula or plotted stories; no pulp or woman's magazine fiction; no academic writing. We are looking for writing with a personal voice and with something to say." Buys 5-12 mss/year. Send complete ms. Length: 2-35 pages. Send only one ms. Pays $30-70.

Poetry: James E. S. Woodbury, poetry editor. Avant-garde, free verse, light verse, traditional and translations (with originals). No obviously "academic" poetry; "we publish occasional light verse but do not want to see 'Hallmark Card' writing." Submit maximum 6 average length poems; 1-2 long poems. Reports in 4 months. Buys 12-25 poems/year. Pays $13-30. "Now backlogged through Jan. 1993."

Tips: "Know your markets. We still receive manuscripts that, had the writer any understanding of our publication, would have been directed elsewhere. Don't submit to independent small magazines unless you've bought and studied an issue. *tnr* is unique and should be *carefully* perused. Close reading of one or two issues will reveal that we have a classicist philosophy and want manuscripts that hold up to re-readings. Fiction and poetry are completely open to freelancers. Writers most likely to break in to *tnr* are 'serious' writers, poets, those who feel 'compelled' to write. We don't want to see 'pop' writing, trendy or formula writing. Nor do we want writing where the 'statement' is imposed on the story, or writing where the author shows off his superior knowledge or sensibility. Respect the reader and do not 'explain' the story. If we've rejected your work and our comments make some sense to you, keep on submitting to us. Always send your best work. New writers frequently don't know how to structure or organize for greatest impact, or sometimes they attempt ambitious statements that they need more skill or expertise to bring off. Do not submit anything from July 1 through December 31. Submissions during those months will be returned unread. We now are working with a backlog of material."

THE NORTH AMERICAN REVIEW, University of Northern Iowa, Cedar Falls IA 50614. (319)273-6455. Editor: Robley Wilson. 50% freelance written. Quarterly. Circ. 5,000. Buys all rights for nonfiction and North American serial rights for fiction and poetry. Pays on publication. Publishes ms an average of 1 year after acceptance. Familiarity with magazine helpful. Reports in 10 weeks. Sample copy $4.

Nonfiction: No restrictions, but most nonfiction is commissioned by magazine. Query. Rate of payment arranged.

Fiction: No restrictions; highest quality only. Length: open. Pays minimum $10/page. Fiction department closed (no mss read) from April 1 to December 31.

Poetry: Peter Cooley, department editor. No restrictions; highest quality only. Length: open. Pays 50¢/line minimum.

THE OHIO REVIEW, Ellis Hall, Ohio University, Athens OH 45701-2979. (614)593-1900. Editor: Wayne Dodd. 40% freelance written. Published 3 times/year. "A balanced, informed engagement of contemporary American letters, with special emphasis on poetics." Circ. 2,000. Publishes ms an average of 8 months after acceptance. Rights acquired vary with author and material; usually buys first serial rights or first North American serial rights. Submit complete ms. Unsolicited material will be read only September-May. Reports in 10 weeks.

Nonfiction, Fiction and Poetry: Buys essays of general intellectual and special literary appeal. Not interested in narrowly focused scholarly articles. Seeks writing that is marked by clarity, liveliness, and perspective. Interested in the best fiction and poetry. Buys 75 unsolicited mss/year. Pays minimum $5/page, plus copies.

Tips: "Make your query very brief, not gabby—one that describes some publishing history, but no extensive bibliographies. We publish mostly poetry—short fiction, some book reviews."

THE PARIS REVIEW, 45-39 171st Place, Flushing NY 11358. Submit mss to 541 E. 72nd St., New York NY 10021. Editor: George A. Plimpton. Quarterly. Buys all rights. Pays on publication. Reporting time varies. Address submissions to proper department. Sample copy $7. Writer's guidelines for #10 SASE (from Flushing Office).

Fiction: Study publication. No length limit. Pays up to $600. Awards $1,000 in annual Aga Khan fiction contest and $1,500 in John Train Humor Prize contest.

Poetry: Patricia Storace, poetry editor. Study publication. Pays $50/1-24 lines; $65/25-59 lines; $100/60-99 lines; and $150-170/100 lines and over. Awards $1,000 in Bernard F. Conners Poetry Prize contest.

‡PASSAGES NORTH, Kalamazoo College, 1200 Academy St., Kalamazoo MI 49007. (916)383-8473. Editor: Ben Mitchell. Managing Editor: Leslie Roberts. 100% freelance written. Eager to work with emerging writers. A semiannual tabloid of poetry, fiction and graphic arts. Circ. 2,000. Pays on publication. Publishes ms an average of 2-4 months after acceptance. Byline given. Buys first rights. Computer printout submissions acceptable. Reports in 1 month on queries; 3 months on manuscripts. Sample copy $3; writer's guidelines for #10 SASE.

Fiction: "High quality" fiction. Buys 6-8 mss/year. Send complete ms. Length: 4,000 words maximum. Pays 3 copies minimum, $50 maximum.

Poetry: No "greeting card" or sentimental poetry and no song lyrics. Buys 80 poems/year. Submit maximum 4 poems. Length: prefers 40 lines maximum. Pays 3 copies minimum, $20 maximum.

Tips: "We want poems and stories of high quality that make the reader see, imagine and experience."

PIG IRON MAGAZINE, Pig Iron Press, P.O. Box 237, Youngstown OH 44501. (216)783-1269. Editors-in-Chief: Jim Villani and Naton Leslie. 95% freelance written. Annual magazine emphasizing literature/art for writers, artists and intelligent lay audience interested in popular culture. Circ. 1,500. Buys one-time rights. Pays on publication. Publishes ms an average of 6-18 months after acceptance. Byline given. Photocopied and previously published submissions OK. Reports in 3 months. Sample copy $3; writer's guidelines and current theme with #10 SASE.

Nonfiction: General interest, personal opinion, criticism, new journalism and lifestyle. Buys 3 mss/year. Query. Length: 8,000 words maximum. Pays $5/page minimum.

Photos: Submit photo material with query. Pays $5 minimum for 5×7 or 8×10 b&w glossy prints. Buys one-time rights.

Fiction: Narrative fiction, psychological fiction, environment, avant-garde, experimental, metafiction, satire and parody. Buys 4-12 mss/issue. Submit complete ms. Length: 8,000 words maximum. Pays $5 minimum.

Poetry: Avant-garde and free verse. Buys 25-50/issue. Submit in batches of 5 or less. Length: open. Pays $5 minimum.

Tips: "Looking for fiction and poetry that is sophisticated, elegant, mature and polished. Interested in literary works that are consistent with the fundamental characteristics of modern and contemporary literature, including works that address alienation, the unconscious, loss, despair and historical discontinuity."

‡THE PINEHURST JOURNAL, P.O. Box 360747, Milpitas CA 95036. (408)945-0986. Editor: Michael K. McNamara. Contributing Editor: Kathleen M. McNamara. Poetry Editor: Virginia L. Bell. 90% freelance written. Quarterly magazine of fiction, nonfiction and poetry. "For an educated audience appreciative of polished, thought provoking work. Audience is 25-75." Estab. 1990. Circ. 150. Pays on publication. Publishes ms an average of 1-4 months after acceptance. Byline given. ($5 plus contributor copy). Buys one-time rights. Submit seasonal/holiday material 6 months in advance. Simultaneous submissions, if identified as such, OK. Offers 100% kill fee. Reports in 1-2 months. Sample copy $4.50. Writer's guidelines for #10 SAE with 1 first class stamp.

Nonfiction: Book or theater reviews, essays, historical/nostalgic, profile, environmental or political/social problems and general interest. Buys 8-10 mss/year. Query (reviews and profiles). Send complete ms. Length: 750-4,000 words. Pays $5 plus 1 contributor copy. Needs b&w artwork, not photos.

Fiction: mild erotica, experimental, lite fantasy, gay, historical, horror, wry humor, lesbian, mainstream, mystery, slice-of-life vignettes, suspense. No formula romance or western. No hard sci-fi, occult, swords and sorcery, slasher, porno, travel or religious. Buys 35-40 mss/year. Send complete ms. Length: 750-4,000 words. Pays $5 plus 1 contributor copy.

Poetry: Avant-garde, free verse, Haiku, light verse, traditional. Buys 40-50 poems/year. Submit maximum 6 poems. Length: 2-24 lines. Pays contributor copy.

Fillers: Anecdotes and short humor. Length: 200-400 words. Pays contributor copy.

Tips: "Try to make each word pull its own weight but not at the expense of warmth. Spend the extra 25 words, but don't overly embellish. Polish and punctuation are very important to us. Please enclose a 20-40 word bio. This can be publishing success or whatever you're comfortable with. All areas are equally open although nonfiction might be the hardest to crack because of the limited number of topics."

PLOUGHSHARES, Emerson College, Dept. M, 100 Beacon St., Boston MA 02116. Executive Director: DeWitt Henry. Quarterly magazine for "readers of serious contemporary literature: students, educators, adult public." Circ. 3,800. Pays on publication. Publishes ms an average of 6 months after acceptance. Buys first North American serial rights. Reports in 5 months. Sample/back issue $6; writer's guidelines for SASE.

Nonfiction: Personal and literary essays. Length: 5,000 words maximum. Pays $50. Reviews (assigned). Length: 500 words maximum. Pays $10/page, $50 maximum.

Fiction: Literary and mainstream. Buys 25-35 unsolicited mss/year. Length: 300-6,000 words. Pays $10/page, $50 maximum.

Poetry: Traditional forms, blank verse, free verse and avant-garde. Length: open. Pays $10/poem minimum, $5/page per poem over 2 printed pages, $50 maximum.

Tips: "Because of our policy of rotating editors, we suggest writers check the current issue for news of reading periods and upcoming editors and/or themes."

POETRY, The Modern Poetry Association, 60 W. Walton St., Chicago IL 60610. (312)280-4870. Editor: Joseph Parisi. Managing Editor: Helen Lothrop Klaviter. 100% freelance written. A monthly poetry magazine. Estab. 1912. Circ. 7,000. Pays on publication. Byline given. Buys all rights. "Copyright assigned to author on request." Submit seasonal/holiday material 6 months in advance. Reports in 2 months. Sample copy $3.50. Writer's guidelines for #10 SASE.

Poetry: All styles and subject matter. Buys 180-250 poems/year. Submit maximum 6 poems. All lengths considered. Pays $2/line.

THE PRAIRIE JOURNAL of Canadian Literature, P.O. Box 997, Station G, Calgary, Alberta T3A 3G2 Canada. Editor: A. Burke. 100% freelance written. A semiannual magazine of Canadian literature. Estab. 1983. Circ. 400. Pays on publication; "honorarium depends on grant." Byline given. Buys first North American serial rights. Reports 1 month on queries. Sample copy $3 and IRCs.

Nonfiction: Interview/profile and scholarly. Buys 5 mss/year. Query with published clips. "Include IRC." Pays $25 maximum. Pays contributor copies or honoraria for literary work.

Photos: Send photos with submission. Offers no additional payment for photos accepted with ms. Identification of subjets required. Buys one-time rights.

Fiction: Literary. Buys 10 mss/year. Send complete ms.

Poetry: Avant-garde and free verse. Buys 10 poems/year. Submit maximum 6-10 poems.

Tips: "Commercial writers are advised to submit elsewhere. Art needed, b&w pen and ink drawings or good-quality photocopy. We are strictly small press editors interested in highly talented, serious artists. We are oversupplied with fiction but seek more high-quality poetry, especially the contemporary long poem or sequences from longer works."

PRISM INTERNATIONAL, Department of Creative Writing, Buch E462, 1866 Main Mall, University of British Columbia, Vancouver, British Columbia V6T 1Z1 Canada. Editor-in-Chief: Rodger Cove. Executive Editor: Patricia Gabin. 100% freelance written. Eager to work with new/unpublished writers. Quarterly magazine emphasizing contemporary literature, including translations. For university and public libraries, and private subscribers. Estab. 1959. Circ. 1,000. Pays on publication. Publishes ms an average of 3 months after acceptance. Buys first North American serial rights. Reports in 3 months. Sample copy $4. Writer's guidelines for #10 SAE with 1 first class Canadian stamp (Canadian entries) or 1 IRC (U.S. entries).

Nonfiction: Memoirs, belles-lettres, etc. "*Creative* nonfiction that possibly reads like fiction." No reviews, tracts or scholarly essays.

Fiction: Francie Green Slade, fiction editor. Experimental and traditional. Buys 3-5 mss/issue. Send complete ms. Length: 5,000 words maximum. Pays $20/printed page and 1-year subscription.

Poetry: Vivian Marple, poetry editor. Avant-garde and traditional. Buys 30 poems/issue. Submit maximum 6 poems. Pays $20/page printed page and 1-year subscription.

Drama: One-acts preferred. Pays $20/page printed page and 1-year subscription.

Tips: "We are looking for new and exciting fiction. Excellence is still our number one criterion. As well as poetry, imaginative nonfiction and fiction, we are especially open to translations of all kinds, very short fiction pieces and drama which works well on the page. This year we plan to publish an issue that focuses on the theme of sexuality."

‡QUARRY, Quarry Press Inc. P.O. Box 1061, Kingston, Ontario K7L 4Y5. (613)548-8423. Editor: Steven Heighton. Managing Editor: Melanie Dugan. 100% freelance written. Quarterly literary magazine. Estab. 1952. Circ. 1,250. Pays after publication. Publishes ms an average of 10 months after acceptance. Buys first North American serial rights. Reports in 3 weeks on queries; 4 months on mss. Sample copy $5 (Canadian).

Fiction: Adventure, erotica, ethnic, experimental, fantasy, historical, humorous, mainstream, novel excerpts, religious. Buys 20 mss/year. Send complete ms. Length: 6,000 words maximum. Pays $10 per published page.

Poetry: Avant-garde, free verse, haiku, traditional. Buys 150 poems/year. Submit maximum 8 poems at one time. Pays $15 per poem.

RENOVATED LIGHTHOUSE, Renovated Lighthouse Publications, P.O. Box 100, Riparius NY 12862. Editor: R. Allen Dodson. 90% freelance written. Bimonthly literary magazine covering New Age, poetry, fiction, markets and chapbooks. Our publications are intended to be entertaining, enlightening and informative to the serious freelancer: poetic, musical, artistic and literary. Estab. 1986. Circ. 200. Pays on publication. Publishes ms an average of 6-10 months after acceptance. Byline given. Buys one year, one-time rights or makes work-for-hire assignments. Reports in 1 week on queries; 2 weeks on mss. Sample copy for $2.90.

Nonfiction: Essays, exposé, general interest, historical/nostalgic, how-to (related to writing), humor, inspirational (non-religious), interview/profile (query first), opinion. Query first, maximum 2,250 words. Pays in money, copies or premiums.

Columns/Departments: Review columns by assignment. Query. Pay ranges from contributor copy to $10. Buys 12 mss/year. Send complete ms. Pays $2.50 minimum.

Fiction: Adventure, fantasy, mystery, science fiction, slice-of-life vignettes. Buys 12 mss/year. Send complete ms. Length: 2,250 maximum. Pays $2.50 minimum.

Tips: "Purchase of application (free) and sample copy required before submitting. Although we will work with beginners, professionalism is a must."

SING HEAVENLY MUSE!, Women's Poetry and Prose, Sing Heavenly Muse! Inc., Box 13320, Minneapolis MN 55414. (612)822-8713. 100% freelance written. Prefers to work with published/established writers; eager to work with new/unpublished writers. A semi-annual journal of women's literature. Circ. 1,500. Pays on publication. Publishes ms an average of 6 months after acceptance. Byline given. Buys first North American serial rights. Reports in 3 months. Sample copy $4; writer's guidelines for #10 SASE.

Fiction: Women's literature, journal pieces, memoir. Buys 15-20 mss/year. Length: 5,000 words maximum. Pays $15-25; contributors receive 2 free copies.

Poetry: Avant-garde, free verse, haiku, light verse and traditional. Accepts 75-100 poems/year. No limit on length. Pays $15-25.

Tips: "To meet our needs, writing must be feminist and women-centered. We read manuscripts generally in April and September. Issues are often related to a specific theme; writer should always query for guidelines and upcoming themes before submitting manuscripts. We occasionally hold contests. Writers should query for contest guidelines."

THE SOUTH FLORIDA POETRY REVIEW, South Florida Poetry Institute, 7190 NW 21st St., Ft. Lauderdale FL 33313. (305)742-5624. Editor: S.A. Stirnemann. Associate Editors: Carole Borges-Rosen and Virginia Wells. Managing Editor: Shirley Blum. 100% freelance written. Quarterly magazine on poetry. "*SFPR* invites submissions of contemporary poetry of the highest literary quality. We are also interested in essay-reviews of books of poetry published in previous year, Q&A interviews with established poets, and essays on current American poetry." Estab. 1983. Circ. 750. Pays on publication.

Publishes ms an average of 3-12 months after acceptance. Byline given. Buys first rights. Reports in 3 months on ms. Sample copy $3.50. Writer's guidelines for #10 SASE.

Nonfiction: Essays (reviews and American poetry), interview/profile (Q&A). Do not want to see "anything that is *not* related to poetry." Buys 16 mss/year. Query. Length: 300-2,000 words. Pays $5-25 for unsolicited articles.

Poetry: Avant-garde, free verse and traditional. Buys 125 poems/year. Submit maximum 6 poems.

Tips: "All sections are open to freelancers. They should be familiar with contemporary American poetry as it is defined in most national literary journals."

THE SOUTHERN REVIEW, 43 Allen Hall, Louisiana State University, Baton Rouge LA 70803. (504)388-5108. Editors: James Olney and Dave Smith. 75% freelance written. Works with a moderate number of new/unpublished writers each year. Quarterly magazine for academic, professional, literary, intellectual audience. Estab. 1965. Circ. 3,100. Buys first serial rights only. Byline given. Pays on publication. Publishes ms an average of 18 months after acceptance. No queries. Reports in 2 to 3 months. Sample copy $5. Writer's guidelines for #10 SASE.

Nonfiction: Essays with careful attention to craftsmanship, technique and to seriousness of subject matter. "Willing to publish experimental writing if it has a valid artistic purpose. Avoid extremism and sensationalism. Essays exhibit thoughtful and sometimes severe awareness of the necessity of literary standards in our time." Emphasis on contemporary literature, especially Southern culture and history. Minimum number of footnotes. Buys 45 mss/year. Length: 4,000-10,000 words. Pays $12/page for prose.

Fiction and Poetry: Short stories of lasting literary merit, with emphasis on style and technique. Length: 4,000-8,000 words. Pays $12/page for prose; $20/page for poetry.

‡SOUTHWEST REVIEW, 6410 Airline Rd., Southern Methodist University, Dallas TX 75275. (214)373-7440. Editor: Willard Spiegelman. 100% freelance written. Works with a small number of new/unpublished writers each year. Quarterly magazine for "adults and college graduates with literary interests and some interest in the Southwest, but subscribers are from all over America and some foreign countries." Circ. 1,500. Pays on publication. Publishes ms an average of 1 year after acceptance. Buys first North American serial rights. Byline given. Buys 65 mss/year. Reports immediately or within 3 months. Sample copy $5.

Nonfiction: "Literary essays, social and political problems, history (especially Southwestern), folklore (especially Southwestern), the arts, etc. Articles should be appropriate for literary quarterly; no feature stories. Critical articles should consider writer's whole body of work, not just one book. History should use new primary sources or new perspective, not syntheses of old material." Interviews with writers, historical articles. Query. Length: 3,500-7,000 words.

Fiction: No limitations on subject matter for fiction; high literary quality is only criterion. Prefers stories of experimental and mainstream. Submit complete ms. Length: 1,500-7,000 words. The John H. McGinnis Memorial Award of $1,000 made annually for fiction and nonfiction pieces that appeared in *SWR* during preceding year.

Poetry: No limitations on subject matter. Not particularly interested in broadly humorous, religious or sentimental poetry. Free verse, some avant-garde forms; open to all serious forms of poetry. "There are no arbitrary limits on length, but we find shorter poems are easier to fit into our format." The Elizabeth Matchett Stover Memorial Award of $100 made annually for a poem published in *SWR*.

Tips: "The most frequent mistakes we find in work that is submitted for consideration are lack of attention to grammar and syntax and little knowledge of the kind of thing we're looking for. Writers should look at a couple of issues before submitting."

SPECTRUM, Spectrum/Anna Maria College, Box 72-F, Sunset Lane, Paxton MA 01612. (508)757-4586. Editor: Robert H. Goepfert. Managing Editor: Robert Lemieux. A literary magazine, "*Spectrum* is a multidisciplinary national publication aimed particularly at scholarly generalists affiliated with small liberal arts colleges." Estab. 1985. Circ. 1,000. Pays on publication. Publishes ms an average of 6 months after acceptance. Byline given. Publication copyrighted. Buys first North American serial rights. Reports in 3 weeks on queries; 6 weeks on ms. Sample copy $3. Writer's guidelines for #10 SASE.

Nonfiction: Louise N. Soldani, articles editor. Essays, general interest, historical/nostalgic, inspirational, opinion and interdisciplinary. Buys 8 mss/year. Send complete ms. Length: 3,000-15,000 words. Pays $20 for unsolicited articles. State availability of photos with submission. Prints (8 × 10) b&w only. Offers no additional payment for photos accepted with ms. Model releases and identification of subjects required. Buys one-time rights.

Columns/Departments: Sandra Rasmussen, reviews and correspondence editor. Reviews (books/recordings/audiovisual aids), 300-500 words; (educational computer software), up to 2,000 words. Buys 2 mss/year. Send complete ms. Length: 300-2,000 words. Pays $20.

Fiction: Joseph Wilson, fiction editor. Ethnic, experimental, fantasy, historical, humorous, mainstream, romance and slice-of-life vignettes. "No erotica, mystery, western or science fiction." Buys 2 ms/year. Send complete ms. Length: 3,000 words. Pays $20.

Poetry: Joseph Wilson, poetry editor. Avant-garde, free verse, light verse and traditional. No long poems (over 100 lines). Buys 8 poems/year. Submit maximum 6 poems.

Tips: "We welcome short fiction and poetry, as well as short-to medium-length articles that are interdisciplinary or that deal with one discipline in a manner accessible to the scholarly-generalist reader. Articles referring to or quoting work of other authors should be footnoted appropriately. All areas are equally open to freelancers. In general, originality and relative brevity are paramount, although we will occasionally publish longer works (e.g., articles) that explore ideas not subject to a briefer treatment."

STORY, F&W Publications, Inc., 1507 Dana Ave., Cincinnati OH 45207. (513)531-2222. Editor: Lois Rosenthal. Associate Editor: Jack Heffron. 100% freelance written. Quarterly literary magazine of short fiction. "We want short stories and self-inclusive novel excerpts of general interest that are extremely well-written. Our audience is sophisticated and accustomed to the finest imaginative writing by new and established writers." Estab. 1931. Circ. 30,000. **Pays on acceptance.** Byline given. Buys first North American serial rights. Reports in 1 month. Sample copy $5 with 9 × 12 SAE and 10 first class stamps. Writer's guidelines for #10 SASE.

Fiction: Novel excerpts, experimental and mainstream. No genre fiction. Buys 40-50 mss/year. Send complete ms. Length: 1,000-8,000 words. Pays $250.

Tips: "No replies without SASE."

‡**STORYTELLING MAGAZINE**, National Association for the Preservation and Perpetuation of Storytelling, NAPPS, P.O. Box 309, Jonesborough TN 37659. (615)753-2171. Editor: Mary C. Weaver. 80% freelance written. Quarterly magazine on storytelling, oral history and tradition, folklore. Estab. 1989. Circ. 6,750. Pays within 30 days of acceptance. Byline given. Offers 35% kill fee. Buys first North American serial rights and second serial (reprint) rights. Submit seasonal/holiday material 6 months in advance. Simultaneous and previously published submissions OK. Query for electronic submissions. Reports in 3 months. Sample copy for 10 × 13 SAE with $1.67 in first class stamps; free writer's guidelines.

Nonfiction: Book excerpts, essays, general interest (within our subject matter), interview/profile, novel or interesting uses of storytelling. No fiction, poetry, how-tos, nostalgia, personal experiences. Buys 8-12 feature-length articles/year. Query with published clips if available. Length: 1,500-3,200 words. Pays $75-320. Pays expenses of writers on assignment.

Photos: State availability of photos with submission. Payment varies. Identification of subjects required. Buys one-time rights.

Columns/Departments: Gleanings (interesting ways performers, teachers, others are using the art of storytelling), 600-800 words; Profiles (storytellers, writers, other performers, teachers, ministers), 600-800 words; Traditions (essay on roots of stories, folklore, myth, etc.), 800 words. Buys 36 mss/year. Query with published clips. Pays $30-80.

Tips: "Send clear, detailed queries. Keep the audience in mind: Our readers are largely teachers, librarians, and others in the helping professions who use storytelling in their work. Don't tell readers what they already know: that storytelling is enjoying a renaissance, that it can build children's creative skills, that ancient tales contain timeless psychological themes, etc. Gleanings and Profiles are most open to freelancers. Emphasize what's unique about the subject. My judgment of the writer's ability is based mostly on the quality of the query."

TAMPA REVIEW, Humanities Division, University of Tampa, Tampa FL 33606. (813)253-3333. Editor of Fiction: Andy Solomon, Box 135F. Editors of Poetry: Don Morrill, Box 115F; Kathy Van Spanckeren, Box 16F. 100% freelance written. Annual magazine of literary fiction and poetry. Estab. 1988. Circ. 5,000. Pays on publication. Publishes ms an average of 4 months after acceptance. Byline given. Buys first North American serial rights. Reports in 6 weeks on mss. Sample copy $9.

Fiction: Experimental, mainstream. "We are far more concerned with quality than genre." Buys 4-6 mss/year. Send complete ms. Length: 1,000-6,000 words; slight preference for mss less than 20 pp. Pays $10/printed page.

Poetry: Buys 30 poems/year. Submit up to 5 poems at one time. Pays $10/printed page.

‡**THEMA**, Box 74109, Metairie LA 70033-4109. (504)887-1263. Editor: Virginia Howard. 100% freelance written. Quarterly literary magazine covering a different theme for each issue. "Journal is designed to stimulate creative thinking by challenging writers with unusual themes. Appeals to writers, teachers of creative writing and general reading audience." Estab. 1988. Circ. 350. **Pays on acceptance.** Byline given. Buys one-time rights. Reports in 2 weeks on queries; 1½ months on mss (after deadline for particular issue). Sample copy $5. Writer's guidelines for #10 SAE with 1 first class stamp.

Fiction: Adventure, ethnic, experimental, fantasy, historical, humorous, mainstream, mystery, religious, science fiction, slice-of-life vignettes, suspense, western, different theme for each issue. "No alternate lifestyle or erotica." Buys 48 mss/year. Send complete ms and (*specify theme* for which it is intended.) Pays $10-25.

Poetry: Avant-garde, free verse, Haiku, light verse, traditional. No erotica. Buys 32 poems/year. Submit maximum 3 poems. Length: 4-50 lines. Pays $10.

Tips: "Be familiar with the themes—*Don't submit* unless you have an upcoming theme in mind. Specify the target theme on the first page of your manuscript or in a cover letter. Put your name on *first* page of manuscript only. (All submissions are judged in blind review after the deadline for a specified issue.) Most open to fiction and poetry. Don't be hasty when you consider a theme—mull it over and let it ferment in your mind. We appreciate interpretations that are carefully constructed, clever, subtle, well thought out."

THE THREEPENNY REVIEW, Box 9131, Berkeley CA 94709. (415)849-4545. Editor: Wendy Lesser. 100% freelance written. Works with small number of new/unpublished writers each year. A quarterly literary tabloid. "We are a general interest, national literary magazine with coverage of politics, the visual arts and the performing arts as well." Circ. 8,000. **Pays on acceptance.** Publishes ms an average of 1 year after acceptance. Byline given. Buys first North American serial rights. Reports in 1 month on queries; 2 months on mss. Sample copy for 10×13 SAE, 5 first class stamps and $5; writer's guidelines for SASE.

Nonfiction: Essays, exposé, historical, interview/profile, personal experience, book, film, theater, dance, music and art reviews. Buys 40 mss/year. Query with or without published clips, or send complete ms. Length: 1,500-4,000 words. Pays $100.

Fiction: No fragmentary, sentimental fiction. Buys 10 mss/year. Send complete ms. Length: 800-4,000 words. Pays $100.

Poetry: Free verse and traditional. No poems "without capital letters or poems without a discernible subject." Buys 30 poems/year. Submit maximum 10 poems. Pays $50.

Tips: Nonfiction (political articles, memoirs, reviews) is most open to freelancers.

TRIQUARTERLY, 2020 Ridge Ave., Northwestern University, Evanston IL 60208. (312)491-3490. Editors: Reginald Gibbons and Susan Hahn. 70% freelance written. Eager to work with new/unpublished writers. Published 3 times/year. Publishes fiction, poetry, and essays, as well as artwork. Pays on publication. Publishes ms an average of 1 year after acceptance. Buys first serial rights and nonexclusive reprint rights. Reports in 3 months. Study magazine before submitting. Sample copy $4. Writer's guidelines for #10 SASE.

Nonfiction: Query before sending essays (no scholarly or critical essays except in special issues).

Fiction and Poetry: No prejudice against style or length of work; only seriousness and excellence are required. Buys 20-50 unsolicited mss/year. Pays $40/page.

UNIVERSITY OF TORONTO QUARTERLY, University of Toronto Press, Suite 700, 10 St. Mary St., Toronto, Ontario M4Y 2W8 Canada. Editor-in-Chief: Alan Bewell. 66% freelance written. Eager to work with new/unpublished writers. Quarterly magazine focused on interdisciplinary theory and criticism in literature and the humanities for the university community. Estab. 1933. Pays on publication. Publishes ms an average of 1 year after acceptance. Acquires all rights. Byline given. Sample copy $8.95, SAE and IRCs.

Nonfiction: Scholarly articles on the humanities; literary criticism and intellectual discussion. Buys 12 unsolicited mss/year. Pays $50 maximum.

‡UNIVERSITY OF WINDSOR REVIEW, Windsor, Ontario N9B 3P4 Canada. (519)253-4232. Editor: Joseph A. Quinn. Biannual for "the literate layman, the old common reader." Circ. 300+. Buys first North American serial rights. Reports in 4-6 weeks. Sample copy $5 plus postage. Enclose SAE, IRCs.

Fiction: Alistair MacLeod, department editor. Publishes mainstream prose with open attitude toward themes. Length: 2,000-6,000 words. Pays $25.

Poetry: John Ditsky, department editor. Accepts traditional forms, blank verse, free verse and avant-garde. No epics. Pays $10.

WEBSTER REVIEW, Webster University, 470 E. Lockwood, Webster Groves MO 63119. (314)432-2657. Editor: Nancy Schapiro. 100% freelance written. An annual magazine. "*Webster Review* is an international literary magazine publishing fiction, poetry, essays and translations of writing in those categories. Our subscribers are primarily university and public libraries, and writers and readers of quality fiction and poetry." Circ. 1,000. Pays on publication. Publishes ms an average of 1 year after acceptance. Byline given. Buys first North American serial rights. Simultaneous submissions OK. Reports in 6 weeks on manuscripts. Sample copy for 9½×6½ SAE with 4 first class stamps.

Nonfiction: Essays. Send complete ms.
Fiction: Will consider all types of literature. Buys 6 mss/year. Send complete ms. Pays $25-50, (if funds are available).
Poetry: Pamela White Hadas, poetry editor. Buys 100 poems/year. Pays $10-50 (if funds are available).

‡**THE YALE REVIEW,** P.O. Box 1902A Yale Station, New Haven CT 06520. Editor: Penelope Laurans. Managing Editor: Wendy Wipprecht. 20% freelance written. Buys first North American serial rights. Estab. 1911. Pays on publication. Publishes ms an average of 1 year after acceptance. Writer's guidelines for #10 SASE.
Nonfiction and Fiction: Authoritative discussions of politics, literature and the arts. Buys quality fiction. Pays $100. Length: 3,000-5,000 words.

YELLOW SILK, Journal of Erotic Arts, verygraphics, Box 6374, Albany CA 94706. (415)644-4188. Editor: Lily Pond. 90% freelance written. Prefers to work with published/established writers; works with a small number of new/unpublished writers each year. A quarterly magazine of erotic literature and visual arts. "Editorial policy: All persuasions; no brutality." Our publication is artistic and literary, not pornographic or pandering. Humans are involved: heads, hearts and bodies—not just bodies alone; and the quality of the literature is as important as the erotic content." Circ. 15,000. Pays on publication. Publishes ms an average of 6 months after acceptance. Byline given. Buys all publication rights for one year, at which time they revert to author; and reprint and anthology rights for duration of copyright. Reports in 3 months on manuscripts. Sample copy $7.
Nonfiction: Book excerpts, essays, humor and reviews. "We often have theme issues, but non-regularly and usually not announced in advance. No pornography, romance-novel type writing, sex fantasies. No first-person accounts or blow-by-blow descriptions. No articles. No novels." Buys 5-10 mss/year. Send complete ms. All submissions should be typed, double-spaced, with name, address and phone number on each page; always enclose SASE. No specified length requirements. Pays minimum $10 and 3 contributor copies and subscription.
Photos: Photos may be submitted independently, not as illustration for submission. Reviews photocopies, contact sheets, transparencies and prints. We accept 4-color and b&w artwork. Offers varying payment for series of 8-20 used, plus copies. Buys one-time rights and reprint rights.
Columns/Departments: Reviews (book, movie, art, dance, food, music, anything). "Erotic content and how it's handled is focus of importance. Old or new does not matter. We want to bring readers information of what's out there." Buys 8-10 mss/year. Send complete ms or query. Pays minimum of $10 plus copies.
Fiction: Erotica, including ethnic, experimental, fantasy, humorous, mainstream, novel excerpts and science fiction. See "Nonfiction." Buys 12-16 mss/year. Send complete ms. Pays $1/printed column inch, plus copies.
Poetry: Avant-garde, free verse, haiku, light verse and traditional. "No greeting-card poetry." Buys 80-100 poems/year. No limit on number of poems submitted, "but don't send book-length manuscripts." Pays .375¢/line, plus copies.
Tips: "The best way to get into *Yellow Silk* is produce excellent, well-crafted work that includes eros freshly, with strength of voice, beauty of language, and insight into character. I'll tell you what I'm sick of and have, unfortunately, been seeing more of lately: the products of 'How to Write Erotica' classes. This is not brilliant fiction; it is poorly written fantasy and not what I'm looking for."

Men's

Men's magazines have been able to stabilize the downward spiral that has affected them during the past several years, but few are prospering. Not many new magazines in this category have succeeded, but those that have are focusing either on information, service or fashion. Magazines that also use material slanted toward men can be found in Business and Finance, Relationships, Military and Sports sections.

CAVALIER, Suite 600, 2600 S. Douglas Rd., Coral Gables FL 33134. (305)443-2378. Editor: Douglas Allen. 80% freelance written. Works with published/established and new/unpublished writers each year. Monthly magazine for "young males, ages 18-29, 80% college graduates, affluent, intelligent, interested in current events, sex, sports, adventure, travel and good fiction." Estab. 1960. Circ. 100,000. Pays on publication. Publishes ms an average of 3 months after acceptance. Byline given. Buys first serial and second serial (reprint) rights. Buys 30 or more mss/year. See past issues for general approach to take. Submit seasonal material at least 3 months in advance. Reports in 5 weeks. Sample issue $3. Writer's guidelines for #10 SAE.
Nonfiction: Personal experience, interview, humor, think pieces, exposé and new product. "Be frank—we are open to dealing with controversial issues. No timely material (have 4 month lead time). Prefers 'unusual' subject matter as well as sex-oriented (but serious) articles." Query. Length: 2,800-

3,500 words. Pays maximum $500 with photos. Sometimes pays the expenses of writers on assignment.
Photos: Photos purchased with or without captions. No cheesecake.
Fiction: Nye Willden, department editor. Mystery, science fiction, humorous, adventure and contemporary problems "with at least one explicit sex scene per story." Send complete ms. Length: 2,500-3,500 words. Pays $250 maximum, higher for special.
Tips: "Our greatest interest is in originality—new ideas, new approaches; no tired, overdone stories—both feature and fiction. We do not deal in 'hack' sensationalism but in high quality pieces. Keep in mind the intelligent 18- to 29-year-old male reader. We will be putting more emphasis upon articles and fiction with sexual themes. We prefer serious articles. Pornography—fiction can be very imaginative and sensational."

‡**CHIC MAGAZINE,** Larry Flynt Publications, Suite 300, 9171 Wilshire Blvd., Beverly Hills CA 90210. FAX: (213)275-3857. Executive Editor: Doug Oliver. 40% freelance written. Prefers to work with published/established writers. Monthly magazine for men, ages 20-35 years, college-educated and interested in current affairs, entertainment and sports. Circ. 100,000. Pays 1 month after acceptance. Publishes ms an average of 3 months after acceptance. Buys all rights. Pays 20% kill fee. Byline given unless writer requests otherwise. Reports in 2 months. Writer's guidelines for #10 SASE.
Nonfiction: Sex-related topics of current national interest; interview (personalities in news and entertainment); and celebrity profiles. Buys 12-18 mss/year. Query. Length: 3,000 words. Pays $750. Sometimes pays the expenses of writers on assignment.
Columns/Departments: Odds and Ends (front of the book shorts; study the publication first), 100-300 words. Pays $50. Third Degree (short Q&As) columns, 2,000 words. Pays $350.
Fiction: "At present we are buying stories with emphasis on erotic themes. These may be adventure, action, mystery, horror or humorous stories, but the tone and theme must involve sex and eroticism. The erotic nature of the story should not be subordinate to the characterizations and plot; the sex must grow logically from the people and the plot, not be contrived or forced."
Tips: "We do not buy poetry or non-erotic science fiction. Refrain from stories with drug themes, sex with minors, incest and bestiality."

ESQUIRE, 1790 Broadway, New York NY 10019. (212)459-7500. Editor-in-Chief: Lee Eisenberg. Editor: Terry McDonell. 99% freelance written. Monthly. Estab. 1933. **Pays on acceptance.** Publishes ms an average of 6 months after acceptance. Usually buys first serial rights. Reports in 3 weeks. "We depend chiefly on solicited contributions and material from literary agencies. We are unable to accept responsibility for unsolicited material." Query.
Nonfiction: Articles vary in length, but features usually average 3,000-7,000 words. Articles should be slanted for sophisticated, intelligent readers; however, not highbrow in the restrictive sense. Wide range of subject matter. Rates run roughly between $300 and $3,000, depending on length, quality, etc. Sometimes pays expenses of writers on assignment.
Photos: Alison Morley, photo editor. Payment depends on how photo is used, but rates are roughly $300 for b&w; $500-750 for color. Guarantee on acceptance. Buys first periodical publication rights.
Fiction: L. Rust Hills, fiction editor. "Literary excellence is our only criterion." Discourages genre fiction (horror, science fiction, murder mystery, etc.). Length: about 1,000-6,000 words. Payment: $1,000-5,000.
Tips: The writer sometimes has a better chance of breaking in at *Esquire* with short, lesser-paying articles and fillers (rather than with major features) "because we need more short pieces."

FLING, Relim Publishing Co., Inc., 550 Miller Ave., Mill Valley CA 94941. (415)383-5464. Editor: Arv Miller. Managing Editor: Ted Albert. 30% freelance written. Prefers to work with published/established writers; works with a small number of new/unpublished writers each year. Bimonthly magazine in the men's sophisticate field. Young male audience of adults ages 18-34. Sexual-oriented field. Estab. 1957. Circ. 100,000. **Pays on acceptance.** Publishes ms an average of 3 months after acceptance. Buys first North American serial rights and second serial (reprint) rights; makes work-for-hire assignments. Submit seasonal/holiday material 8 months in advance. Does not consider multiple submissions. Reports in 1 week on queries; 2 weeks on mss. Sample copy $5; writer's guidelines for SASE.
Nonfiction: Exposé; how-to (better relationships with women, better lovers); interview/profile; personal experience; photo feature; and taboo sex articles. Buys 15 mss/year. Query. Length: 1,500-3,000 words. Pays $150-250. Sometimes pays expenses of writers on assignment.
Photos: Send photos with query. Reviews b&w contact sheets and 8×10 prints; 35mm color transparencies. Pays $10-25 for b&w; $20-35 for color. Model releases required. Buys one-time rights.
Columns/Departments: Buys 12 mss/year. Query or send complete ms. Length: 100-200 words. Pays $15-125.
Fiction: Sexually oriented, strong male-female relationship. Lots of written detail about female's abundant chest-size a must. No science fiction, western, plotless, private-eye, "dated" or adventure. Buys 20 mss/year. Send complete ms. Length: 2,000-3,000 words. Pays $135-200.

Fillers: Clippings. Buys 50/year. Length: 100-500 words. Pays $5-15.

Tips: "Nonfiction and fiction are wide open areas to freelancers. Always query with one-page letter to the editor before proceeding with any writing. Also send a sample photocopy of published material, similar to suggestion."

‡FORUM, The International Journal of Human Relations, Penthouse International, 1965 Broadway, New York NY 10023. (212)496-6100. Editor: Don Myrus. 100% freelance written. Works with small number of new/unpublished writers each year. A monthly magazine. "*Forum* is the only serious publication in the U.S. to cover human sexuality in all its aspects for the layman—not only the erotic, but the medical, political, legal, etc." Circ. 300,000. **Pays on acceptance.** Publishes an average of 4-6 months after acceptance. Byline given. "Pseudonym mandatory for first-person sex stories." Offers 25% kill fee. Buys all rights. Submit seasonal/holiday material 6 months in advance. Query for electronic submissions. Reports in 1 month on queries.

Nonfiction: Book excepts, personal experience and essays or articles on all aspects of sex and sexuality. Buys 100 mss/year. Query or send complete ms. Length: 2,000-3,000 words. Pays 75¢ per word up to a max. of $1,875. Sometimes pays expenses of writers on assignment.

Fiction: "Well-developed erotic fiction is considered. However, letters detailing sexual adventures are sent in by our readers, and we make no payment for them. We do not publish poetry."

Photos: State availability of photos with submission. Reviews transparencies and 8x11 prints. Offers $50 minimum/photo. Captions, model releases and identification of subjects required.

GALLERY MAGAZINE, Montcalm Publishing Corp., 401 Park Ave. S., New York NY 10016-8802. (212)779-8900. FAX: (212)725-7215. Editorial Director: Barry Janoff. Managing Editor: Peter R. Emshwiller. 50% freelance written. Prefers to work with published/established writers. Monthly magazine "focusing on features of interest to the young American man." Estab. 1972. Circ. 500,000. Pays 50% on acceptance, 50% on publication. Byline given. Pays 25% kill fee. Buys first North American serial rights; makes work-for-hire assignments. Submit seasonal/holiday material 6 months in advance. Reports in 1 month on queries; 2 months on mss. Sample copy $3.50 plus $1.75 postage and handling. Free writer's guidelines with SASE.

Nonfiction: Investigative pieces, general interest, how-to, humor, interview, new products and profile. "We *do not* want to see pornographic articles." Buys 4-5 mss/issue. Query or send complete mss. Length: 1,000-3,000 words. Pays $300-2,000. "Special prices negotiated." Sometimes pays expenses of writers on assignment.

Photos: Send photos with accompanying mss. Pay varies for b&w or color contact sheets and negatives. Buys one-time rights. Captions preferred; model release required.

Fiction: Adventure, erotica (special guidelines available), experimental, humorous, mainstream, mystery and suspense. Buys 1 ms/issue. Send complete ms. Length: 1,000-3,000 words. Pays $350-1,000.

‡GENESIS, Jakel Corp., 1776 Broadway, 20th Floor, New York NY 10019. (212)265-3500. Editor: Michael Banka. 85% freelance written. Men's magazine published 13 times/year. "We are interested in headline and behind-the-headlines articles on sexual or controversial subjects of interest to men." Estab. 1973. Circ. 425,000. Pays after acceptance. Publishes ms an average of 2 months after acceptance. Byline given. Offers 25% kill fee. Buys second serial (reprint) rights and English worldwide (may revert to writer upon request). Submit seasonal/holiday material 5 months in advance. Simultaneous submissions OK. Reports in 2 weeks. Sample copy for 9 × 12 SAE with $2 postage. Writer's guidelines for 4 × 9½ SAE with 1 first class stamp.

Nonfiction: Exposé, humor, interview/profile, photo feature, erotica; comment on contemporary relationships; automotive. "Writers must keep in mind that, with the exception of one exposé-style piece and one automotive article per month, all editorial in *Genesis* has a sexual orientation." Buys 60 mss/year. Query with published clips. Length: 1,500-3,000 words. Pays $300-700 for assigned articles; $200-500 for unsolicited articles. State availability of photos with submission. Reviews transparencies (no fixed size requirements) and prints. Offers $50-100 per photo. Model releases and identification of subjects required. English worldwide and second serial (reprint).

Columns/Departments: Dear Prunella (humorous sexual advice), 500 words; Shared Secrets (brief sexual confessions with provocative angles), 400-500 words; On the Couch (sexual confessions from woman's point of view), 1,500-1,800 words. Buys 65 mss/year. Query with published clips. Pays $75-350.

Tips: Query with clips. "Because we accept only a small number of nonsex-related articles, freelancers' best chance to break in is to write sex features or contribute to the departments. When writing about sexual issues or lifestyles, writers should offer their own opinions on the subject rather than provide drably objective overviews. 'On the Couch' and 'Shared Secrets' are the sections most open to freelancers. Writing must be sexually explicit with a minimum amount of 'lead in.' "

GENTLEMEN'S QUARTERLY, Condé Nast, 350 Madison Ave., New York NY 10017. (212)880-8800. Editor-in-Chief: Arthur Cooper. Managing Editor: Eliot Kaplan. 60% freelance written. Circ. 675,000. Monthly magazine emphasizing fashion, general interest and service features for men ages 25-45 with a large discretionary income. **Pays on acceptance.** Byline given. Pays 25% kill fee. Submit seasonal/holiday material 6 months in advance. Reports in 1 month.

Nonfiction: Politics, personality profiles, lifestyles, trends, grooming, nutrition, health and fitness, sports, travel, money, investment and business matters. Buys 4-6 mss/issue. Query with published clips. Length: 1,500-4,000 words. Pay varies.

Columns/Departments: Eliot Kaplan, managing editor. Body & Soul (fitness, nutrition and grooming); Private Lives; Health; Games (sports); All About Adam (nonfiction by women about men). Query with published clips. Length: 1,000-2,500 words. Pay varies.

Tips: "Major features are usually assigned to well-established, known writers. Pieces are almost always solicited. The best way to break in is through the columns, especially Male Animal, All About Adam, Games, Health or Humor."

‡GUYS, First Hand Ltd., P.O. Box 1314, Teaneck NJ 07666. (201)836-9177. Editor: Bob Harris. 80% freelance written. Monthly magazine of erotica for gay men. "A positive, romantic approach to gay sex." Estab. 1988. Circ. 60,000. Pays on publication. Publishes ms an average of 12 months after acceptance. Byline given. Buys first North American serial rights or all rights. Submit seasonal/holiday material 10 months in advance. Reports in 2 weeks on queries; 2 months on mss. Sample copy $5. Writer's guidelines for 1 SAE with 1 first class stamp.

Columns/Departments: Starstruck (Hollywood with a gay angle), 1,250-1,500 words. Buys 12 mss/year. Query. Pays $75-100.

Fiction: Erotica. Buys 72 mss/year. Length: 1,000-10,000 words. Pays $75-250.

OPTIONS, AJA Publishing, P.O. Box 470, Port Chester NY 10573. (914)939-2111. Editor: Don Stone. Assistant Editor: Diana Sheridan. Mostly freelance written. Sexually explicit magazine for and about bisexuals and homosexuals, published 10 times/year. "Articles, stories and letters about bisexuality. Positive approach. Safe-sex encounters unless the story clearly pre-dates the AIDS situation." Estab. 1977. Circ. 100,000. Pays on publication. Publishes mss an average of 4-10 months after acceptance. Byline given. Buys all rights. Submit seasonal/holiday material 6-8 months in advance; buys very little seasonal material. Reports in 3 weeks. Sample copy $2.95 with 6×9 SAE and 5 first class stamps. Writer's guidelines for SASE.

Nonfiction: Essays (occasional), how-to, humor, interview/profile, opinion and (especially) personal experience. All must be bisexually related. Does not want "anything not bisexually related, anything negative, anything opposed to safe sex, anything dry/boring/ponderous/pedantic. Write even serious topics informally if not lightly." Buys 70 mss/year. Send complete ms. Length: 2,000-3,000. Pays $100.

Photos: Reviews transparencies and prints. Pays $20 for b&w photos; $200 for full color. B&w or color sets $150. Previously published photos acceptable.

Fiction: "We don't usually get enough true first-person stories and need to buy some from writers. They must be bisexual, usually man/man, hot and believable. They must not read like fiction." Buys 60 ms/year. Send complete ms. Length: 2,000-3,000. Pays $100.

Tips: "We use many more male/male pieces than female/female. Use only one serious article per issue. A serious/humorous approach is good here, but only if it's natural to you; don't make an effort for it. No longer buying 'letters'. We get enough real ones."

PLAYBOY, 680 N. Lakeshore Dr., Chicago IL 60611. (312)751-8000. 50% freelance written. Prefers to work with published/established writers; works with a small number of new/unpublished writers each year. Monthly. **Pays on acceptance.** Publishes ms an average of 6 months after acceptance. Offers 20% kill fee. Buys first serial rights and others. Reports in 1 month. Writer's guidelines for #10 SASE.

Nonfiction: John Rezek, articles editor. "We're looking for timely, topical pieces. Articles should be carefully researched and written with wit and insight. Little true adventure or how-to material. Check magazine for subject matter. Pieces on outstanding contemporary men, sports, politics, sociology, business and finance, music, science and technology, games, all areas of interest to the contemporary urban male." Query. Length: 3,000-5,000 words. Pays $3,000 minimum. *Playboy* interviews run between 10,000 and 15,000 words. After getting an assignment, the freelancer outlines the questions, conducts and edits the interview, and writes the introduction. Pays $5,000 minimum. For interviews contact John Rezek, Executive Editor, 747 3rd Ave., New York NY 10017. Pays expenses of writers on assignment.

Photos: Gary Cole, photography director, suggests that all photographers interested in contributing make a thorough study of the photography currently appearing in the magazine. Generally all photography is done on assignment. While much of this is assigned to *Playboy*'s staff photographers, approximately 50% of the photography is done by freelancers, and *Playboy* is in constant search of creative new talent. Qualified freelancers are encouraged to submit samples of their work and ideas. All assignments made on an all rights basis with payments scaled from $600/color page for miscellaneous features such as fashion, food and drink, etc.; $300/b&w page; $1,000/color page for girl features; cover, $1,500. Playmate photography for entire project: $10,000-13,000. Assignments and submissions handled by senior editor: Jeff Cohen and associate editors: James Larson and Michael Ann Sullivan, Chicago; Marilyn Grabowski and Linda Kenney, Los Angeles. Assignments made on a minimum guarantee basis. Film, processing, and other expenses necessitated by assignment honored.

Fiction: Alice Turner, fiction editor. Both light and serious fiction. "Entertainment pieces are clever, smoothly written stories. Serious fiction must come up to the best contemporary standards in substance, idea and style. Both, however, should be designed to appeal to the educated, well-informed male reader." General types include comedy, mystery, fantasy, horror, science fiction, adventure, social-realism, "problem" and psychological stories. Fiction lengths are 3,000-6,000 words; short-shorts of 1,000 to 1,500 words are used. Pays $2,000; $1,000 short-short. Rates rise for additional acceptances.

Fillers: Party Jokes are always welcome. Pays $100 each. Also interesting items for Playboy After Hours section (check it carefully before submitting). The After Hours front section pays $75 for humorous or unusual news items (submissions not returned). Send to After Hours editor. Has regular movie, book and record reviewers. Ideas for Playboy Potpourri pay $75. Query to John Rezek, Chicago. Games, puzzles and travel articles should be addressed to New York office.

SCREW, P.O. Box 432, Old Chelsea Station, New York NY 10113. Managing Editor: Manny Neuhaus. 95% freelance written. Eager to work with new/unpublished writers. Weekly tabloid newspaper for a predominantly male, college-educated audience; ages 21 through mid-40s. Estab. 1968. Circ. 125,000. Pays on publication. Publishes ms an average of 3 months after acceptance. Byline given. Buys all rights. Reports in 3 months. Free sample copy and writer's guidelines.

Nonfiction: "Sexually-related news, humor, how-to articles, first-person and true confessions. Frank and explicit treatment of all areas of sex; outrageous and irreverent attitudes combined with hard information, news and consumer reports. Our style is unique. Writers should check several recent issues." Buys 150-200 mss/year. Will also consider material for Letter From . . ., a consumer-oriented wrap-up of commercial sex scene in cities around the country; submit complete ms or query. Length: 1,000-3,000 words. Pays $100-250. Also, My Scene, a sexual true confession. Length: 1,000-2,500 words. Pays $40.

Photos: Reviews b&w glossy prints (8×10 or 11×14) purchased with or without manuscripts or on assignment. Pays $10-50.

Tips: "All mss get careful attention. Those written in *Screw* style on sexual topics have the best chance. I anticipate a need for more aggressive, insightful political humor."

SWANK, GCR Publishing Corp., 1700 Broadway, New York NY 10019. (212)541-7100. Editor: Michael Wilde. 75% freelance written. Works with new/unpublished writers. Monthly magazine on "sex and sensationalism, lurid. High quality adult erotic entertainment." Audience of men ages 18-38, high school and some college education, medium income, skilled blue-collar professionals, union men, some white-collar. Circ. 400,000. Pays on publication. Publishes ms an average of 4 months after acceptance. Byline given; pseudonym, if wanted. Buys first North American serial rights. Submit seasonal/holiday material 6 months in advance. Reports in 3 weeks on queries; 8 weeks on mss. Sample copy $5.95; writer's guidelines for SASE.

Nonfiction: Exposé (researched) and adventure must be accompanied by photographs. "We buy articles on sex-related topics, which don't need to be accompanied by photos." Interested in lifestyle (unusual) pieces. Buys photo pieces on autos, action, adventure. Buys 34 mss/year. Query with or without published clips. Pays $350-500. Sometimes pays the expenses of writers on assignment. "It is strongly recommended that a sample copy is reviewed before submitting material."

Photos: Bruce Perez, photo editor. State availability of photos. "If you have good photographs of an interesting adventure/lifestyle subject, the writing that accompanies is bought almost automatically." Model releases required.

Tips: "Don't even bother to send girl photos unless you are a published professional." Looks for "lifestyle and adventure pieces that are accompanied by color 35mm chromes and articles about sex-related topics. We carry one photo/journalism piece about automobiles or related subjects per issue."

TURN-ON LETTERS, AJA Publishing, P.O. Box 470, Port Chester NY 10573. Editor: Julie Silver. Magazine published 9 times/year covering sex. "Adult material, must be positive, no pain or degradation. No incest, no underage." Estab. 1977. Circ. 100,000. Pays on publication. Publishes mss an average of 4-6 months after acceptance. Buys all rights. No byline. No kill fee; "assigned mss are not killed unless they do not fulfill the assignment and/or violate censorship laws." Reports in 3 weeks. Sample copy $2.50 with 6×9 SAE and 4 first class stamps. Writer's guidelines for #10 SASE.

Fiction: Sexually explicit material in the format of a letter. Buys 441 "letters"/year. Send complete ms. Length: 500-750 words (2-3 typed pages). Pays $15.

Photos: Reviews transparencies and prints. Buys b&w for $20 and full color cover for $200, and b&w or color sets for $150. Previously published pictures OK. Buys all rights.

Tips: "When you write, be different, be believable."

Military

These publications emphasize military or paramilitary subjects or other aspects of military life. Technical and semitechnical publications for military commanders, personnel and planners, as well as those for military families and civilians interested in Armed Forces activities are listed here.

AMERICAN SURVIVAL GUIDE, McMullen Publishing, Inc., 2145 W. La Palma Ave., Anaheim CA 92801. (714)635-9040. FAX: (714)533-9979. Editor: Jim Benson. 50% freelance written. Monthly magazine covering "self-reliance, defense, meeting day-to-day and possible future threats—survivalism for survivalists." Circ. 72,000. Pays on publication. Publishes ms up to 1 year after acceptance. Byline given. Submit seasonal/holiday material 5 months in advance. Sample copy $3.50; writer's guidelines for SASE.

Nonfiction: Expose (political); how-to; interview/profile; personal experience (how I survived); photo feature (equipment and techniques related to survival in all possible situations); emergency medical; health and fitness; communications; transportation; food preservation; water purification; self-defense; terrorism; nuclear dangers; nutrition; tools; shelter; etc. "No general articles about how to survive. We want specifics and single subjects." Buys 60-100 mss/year. Query or send complete ms. Length: 1,500-2,000 words. Pays $140-350. Sometimes pays some expenses of writers on assignment.

Photos: Send photos with ms. "One of the most frequent mistakes made by writers in completing an article assignment for us is sending photo submissions that are inadequate." Captions, model releases and identification of subjects mandatory. Buys all rights.

Tips: "Prepare material of value to individuals who wish to sustain human life no matter what the circumstance. This magazine is a text and reference."

ARMY MAGAZINE, 2425 Wilson Blvd., Arlington VA 22201. (703)841-4300. FAX: (703)525-9039. Editor-in-Chief: L. James Binder. Managing Editor: Mary Blake French. 80% freelance written. Prefers to work with published/established writers; eager to work with new/unpublished writers. Monthly magazine emphasizing military interests. Estab. 1904. Circ. 146,000. Pays on publication. Publishes ms an average of 6 months after acceptance. Buys all rights. Byline given except for back-up research. Submit seasonal/holiday material 3 months in advance. Sample copy and writer's guidelines for 8½ × 12 SAE with $1 postage.

Nonfiction: Historical (military and original); humor (military feature-length articles and anecdotes); interview; new product; nostalgia; personal experience dealing especially with the most recent conflicts in which the U.S. Army has been involved (Desert Storm, Panama, Grenada); photo feature; profile; and technical. No rehashed history. "We would like to see more pieces about little-known episodes involving interesting military personalities. We especially want material lending itself to heavy, contributor-supplied photographic treatment. The first thing a contributor should recognize is that our readership is very savvy militarily. 'Gee-whiz' personal reminiscences get short shrift, unless they hold their own in a company in which low military service, heroism and unusual experiences are commonplace. At the same time, Army readers like a well-written story with a fresh slant, whether it is about an experience in a foxhole or the fortunes of a corps in battle." Buys 12 mss/issue. Submit complete ms. Length: 4,500 words, but shorter items, especially in 1,500 to 2,500 range, often have better chance of getting published. Pays 12-18¢/word.

Photos: Submit photo material with accompanying ms. Pays $15-50 for 8 × 10 b&w glossy prints; $35-150 for 8 × 10 color glossy prints or 2¼ × 2¼ transparencies, will also accept 35mm. Captions preferred. Buys all rights. Pays $35-50 for cartoon with strong military slant.

Columns/Departments: Military news, books, comment (*New Yorker*-type "Talk of the Town" items). Buys 8/issue. Submit complete ms. Length: 1,000 words. Pays $40-150.

ASIA-PACIFIC DEFENSE FORUM, Commander-in-Chief, U.S. Pacific Command, Box 13, Camp H.M. Smith HI 96861. (808)477-0760/1454. Editor-in-Chief: Lt. Col. (Ret.) Paul R. Stankiewicz. Editor: Major Robyn Blanpied. 12% (maximum) freelance written. Quarterly magazine for foreign military officers in 51 Asian-Pacific, Indian Ocean and other countries; all services—Army, Navy, Air Force and Marines. Secondary audience—government officials, media and academicians concerned with defense issues. "We seek to keep readers abreast of current status of U.S. forces and of U.S. national security policies in the Asia-Pacific area, and to enhance regional dialogue on military subjects."

Estab. 1976. Circ. 34,000. **Pays on acceptance.** Publishes ms an average of 4 months after acceptance. Byline given. Buys simultaneous rights, second serial (reprint) rights or one-time rights. Simultaneous and previously published submissions OK. Requires only a self-addressed label. Reports in 3 weeks on queries; at most 10 weeks on mss. Free sample copy and writer's guidelines (send self-addressed label).

Nonfiction: General interest (current type forces and weapons systems, strategic balance and regional security issues and Asian-Pacific armed forces); historical (rarely used); how-to (training, leadership, force employment procedures, organization); interview and personal experience (rarely used). "We do not want overly technical weapons/equipment descriptions, overly scholarly articles, controversial policy, or budget matters; nor do we seek discussion of in-house problem areas. We do not deal with military social life, base activities or PR-type personalities/job descriptions." Buys 2-4 mss/year. Query or send complete ms. Length: 1,000-3,000 words. Pays $100-300.

Photos: State availability of photos with query or ms. "We provide nearly all photos; however, we will consider good quality photos with manuscripts." Reviews color, b&w glossy prints or 35mm color transparencies. Offers no additional payment for photos accompanying mss. Photo credits given. Captions required. Buys one-time rights.

Tips: "Don't write in a flashy, Sunday supplement style. Our audience is relatively staid, and fact-oriented articles requiring a newspaper/journalistic approach are used more than a normal magazine style. Provide material that is truly foreign audience-oriented and easily illustrated with photos."

FAMILY MAGAZINE, The Magazine for Military Wives, 169 Lexington Ave., New York NY 10016. (212)532-0660. Editor: Susan Fritz. 100% freelance written. Works with a small number of new/unpublished writers each year. A monthly magazine for military wives who are young, high school educated and move often. Estab. 1969. Circ. 545,000. Pays on publication. Publishes ms an average of 6-12 months after acceptance. Byline given. Buys first North American serial rights. Submit seasonal/holiday material 6 months in advance. Simultaneous submissions OK. Reports in 6 weeks. Sample copy $1.25; writer's guidelines for SASE.

Nonfiction: Humor, personal experience, photo feature and travel, of interest to military wives. No romance, anything to do with getting a man or aging. Buys 30 mss/year. Send complete ms. Length: 2,000 words maximum. Pays $75-200.

Photos: Send photos with submissions. Reviews contact sheets, transparencies and prints. Offers $25-100/photo. Identification of subjects required. Buys one-time rights.

Fiction: Humorous, mainstream and slice-of-life vignettes. No romance or novel excerpts. Buys 5 mss/year. Length: 2,000 words maximum. Pays $75-150.

MARINE CORPS GAZETTE, Professional Magazine for United States Marines, Marine Corps Association, P.O. Box 1775, Quantico VA 22134. (703)640-6161. FAX: (703)640-0823. Editor: Col. John E. Greenwood, USMC (Ret.). FAX: (703)640-0823. Managing Editor: Lt. Col. Steven M. Crittenden, USMC (Ret.). Less than 5% freelance written. "Will continue to welcome and respond to queries, but will be selective due to large backlog from Marine authors." Monthly magazine. "*Gazette* serves as a forum in which serving Marine officers exchange ideas and viewpoints on professional military matters." Estab. 1916. Circ. 37,900. Pays on publication. Publishes ms an average of 6 months after acceptance. Byline given. Buys all rights. Reports in 3 weeks on queries; 2 months on mss. Free sample copy and writer's guidelines.

Nonfiction: Historical/nostalgic (Marine Corps operations only); and technical (Marine Corps related equipment). "The magazine is a professional journal oriented toward hard skills, factual treatment, technical detail—no market for lightweight puff pieces—analysis of doctrine, lessons learned goes well. A very strong Marine Corps background and influence are normally prerequisites for publication." Buys 4-5 mss/year from non-Marine Corps sources. Query or send complete ms. Length: 2,500-5,000 words. Pays $200-400.

Photos: "We welcome photos and charts." Payment for illustrative material included in payment forms. "Photos need not be original, nor have been taken by the author, but they must support the article."

Columns/Departments: Book Reviews (of interest and importance to Marines); and Ideas and Issues (an assortment of topical articles, e.g., opinion or argument, ideas of better ways to accomplish tasks, reports on weapons and equipment, strategies and tactics, etc., also short vignettes on history of Corps). Buys 60 book reviews/year; pays $25-50 plus book for 750-word book review. Buys 150 Ideas and Issues mss/year; pays $50-100 for these short features.

Tips: "Book reviews or short articles (500-1,500 words) on Marine Corps related hardware or technological development are the best way to break in. Sections/departments most open to freelancers are Book Reviews and Ideas & Issues sections—query first. We are not much of a market for those outside U.S. Marine Corps or who are not closely associated with current Marine activities."

MILITARY REVIEW, U.S. Army Command and General Staff College, Fort Leavenworth KS 66027-6910. (913)684-5642. FAX: (913)684-4647. Editor-in-Chief: Lt. Col. Steven F. Rausch. Managing Editor: Maj. Chris LeBlanc. Associate Editor: Lt. Col. Donald G. Rhodes. 75% freelance written. Eager to work with new/unpublished writers. Monthly journal (printed in three languages; English, Spanish and Brazilian Portuguese), emphasizing the military for military officers, students and scholars. Estab. 1922. Circ. 27,000. Pays on publication. Publishes ms an average of 8 months after acceptance. Byline given. Buys first serial rights and reserves right to reprint for training purpose. Phone queries OK. Query for electronic submissions. Reports in 1 month. Writer's guidelines for #10 SASE.

Nonfiction: Operational level of war, military history, international affairs, tactics, new military equipment, strategy and book reviews. Buys 100-120 mss/year. Query. Length: 2,000-3,000 words. Pays $50-200.

Tips: "We need more articles from military personnel experienced in particular specialties. Examples: Tactics from a tactician, military engineering from an engineer, etc. By reading our publication, writers will quickly recognize our magazine as a forum for any topic of general interest to the U.S. Army. They will also discover the style we prefer: concise and direct, in the active voice, with precision and clarity, and moving from the specific to the general."

‡**NAVY TIMES**, Times Journal, 6883 Commercial Dr., Springfield VA 22159. (703)750-8636. Editor: Thomas Philpott. Managing Editor: John Grady. Weekly newspaper covering sea services. News and features of men and women in the Navy, Coast Guard and Marine Corps. Estab. 1950. Circ. 90,000. **Pays on acceptance.** Byline given. Buys first North American serial rights or second serial (reprint) rights. Submit seasonal/holiday material 2 months in advance. Reports in 2 months. Free writer's guidelines.

Nonfiction: Historical/nostalgic, opinion. No poetry. Buys 20 mss/year. Query. Length: 500-2,000 words. Pays $50-500 for unsolicited articles. Sometimes pays expenses of writers on assignment.

Photos: State availability of photos with submission. Offers $20-100 per photo. Captions and identification of subjects required. Buys one-time rights.

‡**OFF DUTY MAGAZINE**, Suite C-2 3303 Harbor Blvd., Costa Mesa CA 92626. (714)549-7172. FAX: (714)549-4222. Editor: Gary Burch. Managing Editor: Jim Shaw. 30% freelance written. Monthly magazine covering the leisure-time life of the military community. "Our audience is solely the military members and their families; many of our articles could appear in other consumer magazines, but we always start them toward the military; i.e. where to get a military discount for traveler." Estab. 1970. Circ. 700,000. **Pays on acceptance.** Publishes ms an average of 3 months after acceptance. Byline given. Buys one-time rights. Submit seasonal/holiday material 4 months in advance. Simultaneous submissions OK. Reports in 1-2 months on queries. Sample copy for 9 × 11 SAE with $1.75 postage. Free writer's guidelines.

Nonfiction: Historical/nostalgic (military), humor (military), interview/profile (music & entertainment), travel (U.S. destinations), finance and lifestyle (with a military angle). "Nothing from somebody who does not know *OFF DUTY* and its needs." Buys 20 mss/year. Query. Length: 800-2,100 words. Pays $160-420 for assigned articles. State availability of photos with submission. Reviews contact sheets and 35mm transparencies. Offers $75-200 per photo. Captions and identification of subjects required. Buys one-time rights.

Tips: "Get to know the military community and its interests beyond the stereotypes. Travel—query with the idea of getting on our next year's editorial calendar. We choose our primary topics at least 6 months prior to its start."

OVERSEAS!, Military Consumer Today, Inc., Kolpingstr 1, 6906 Leimen, West Germany 011-49-6224-7060. FAX: 011-49-6224-70616. Editorial Director: Charles L. Kaufman. Managing Editor: Greg Ballinger. 95% freelance written. Eager to work with new/unpublished writers; "we don't get enough submissions." Monthly magazine. "*Overseas!* is aimed at the U.S. military in Europe. It is the leading military lifestyle magazine slanted toward living in Europe." Estab. 1973. Circ. 83,000. Pays on publication. Publishes ms an average of 3 months after acceptance. Byline given. Publishes photos, bio of new writers in editor's column. Offers kill fee depending on circumstances and writer. Buys one-time rights. Submit seasonal/holiday material at least 4 months in advance. Simultaneous queries and simultaneous and previously published submissions OK. Reports in 2 weeks on queries; 1 month on mss. Sample copy for SAE and 4 IRCs; writer's guidelines for SAE and 1 IRC.

Nonfiction: General interest (lifestyle for men and other topics); how-to (use camera, buy various types of video, audio, photo and computer equipment); interview/profile (music, personality interviews; current music stars for young audience); technical (video, audio, photo, computer; how to purchase and use equipment); travel (European, first person adventure; write toward male audience). "We need freelancers with solid background in travel; that's where we turn to them most. We have regular columnists for several of our columns." Also men's cooking and men's fashion/lifestyle. Special issues include Video, Audio, Photo, and Military Shopper's Guide. Needs 250-750-word articles on video, audio, photo and computer products. Published in September every year. No articles that are drug- or sex-related. No cathedrals or museums of Europe stories. Buys 30-50 mss/year "but would buy more if we got better quality and subjects." Query with or without published clips or send complete ms. Length: 750-2,000 words. Pays 10¢/word. Usually pays expenses of writers on assignment; negotiable.

Photos: Send photos with accompanying query or ms. Pays $20 minimum, b&w; $35 transparencies, 35mm or larger. Photos must accompany travel articles—color slides.

Tips: "We would like more submissions on travel in Europe. Writing should be lively, interesting, with lots of good information. We anticipate a change in the length of articles. Articles will be shorter and livelier with more sidebars because readers don't have time to read longer articles. *Overseas!* magazine is the *Travel and Leisure/GQ/Esquire* of this market; any articles that would be suitable for these magazines would probably work in *Overseas!*"

PARAMETERS: U.S. ARMY WAR COLLEGE QUARTERLY, U.S. Army War College, Carlisle Barracks PA 17013. (717)245-4943. Editor: Col. Lloyd J. Matthews, U.S. Army Retired. Quarterly. 100% freelance written. Prefers to work with published/established writers or experts in the field. Readership consists of senior leadership of U.S. defense establishment, both uniformed and civilian, plus members of the media, government, industry and academia interested in national and international security affairs, military strategy, military leadership and management, art and science of warfare, and military history (provided it has contemporary relevance). Most readers possess a graduate degree. Estab. 1971. Circ. 10,000. Not copyrighted; unless copyrighted by author, articles may be reprinted with appropriate credits. Buys first serial rights. Byline given. Pays on publication. Publishes ms an average of 6 months after acceptance. Reports in 1 month. Free writer's guidelines.

Nonfiction: Articles are preferred that deal with current security issues, employ critical analysis and provide solutions or recommendations. Liveliness and verve, consistent with scholarly integrity, appreciated. Theses, studies and academic course papers should be adapted to article form prior to submission. Documentation in complete endnotes. Submit complete ms. Length: 4,500 words average, preferably less. Pays $150 average (including visuals).

Tips: "Make it short; keep it interesting; get criticism and revise accordingly. Tackle a subject only if you are an authority."

PERIODICAL, Council on America's Military Past, 4970 N. Camino Antonio, Tucson AZ 85718. Editor-in-Chief: Dan L. Thrapp. 90% freelance written. Works with a small number of new/unpublished writers each year. Quarterly magazine emphasizing old and abandoned forts, posts and military installations; military subjects for a professional, knowledgeable readership interested in one-time defense sites or other military installations. Circ. 1,500. Pays on publication. Publishes ms an average of 6 months after acceptance. Buys one-time rights. Simultaneous and previously published (if published a long time ago) submissions OK. Reports in 3 weeks. Writer's guidelines for #10 SASE.

Nonfiction: Historical, personal experience, photo feature and technical (relating to posts, their construction/operation and military matters). Buys 4-6 mss/issue. Query or send complete ms. Length: 300-4,000 words. Pays $2/published page minimum.

Photos: Purchased with or without ms. Query. Reviews glossy, single-weight b&w prints. Offers no additional payment for photos accepted with accompanying ms. Captions required.

Tips: "We plan more emphasis on appeal to professional military audience and military historians."

R&R SHOPPERS NEWS, (formerly *R&R Entertainment Digest*), R&R Communications GmbH, 1 Kolpingstrasse, 6906 Leimen, W. Germany 06224-7060. FAX: 06224-70616. Editor: Tory Billard. 50% freelance written. Monthly entertainment magazine for military and government employees and their families stationed in Europe "specializing in travel in Europe, audio/video/photo information, music and the homemaker scene. Aimed exclusively at military/DoD based in Europe—Germany, Britain and the Mediterranean." Estab. 1969. Circ. 100,000. Pays on publication. Publishes ms an average of 2-6 months after acceptance. Byline given. "We offer 50% of payment as a kill fee, but this rarely happens—if story can't run in one issue, we try to use it in a future edition." Buys first serial rights for military market in Europe only. "We will reprint stories that have run in stateside publications if applicable to us." Submit seasonal/holiday material 3 months in advance. Simultaneous queries, and simultaneous and previously published submissions OK. Reports in 2 months. Sample copy and writer's guidelines available for #10 SAE and 5 IRCs.

Nonfiction: Travel (always looking for good travel in Europe features). "We want readers to use our travel articles as a handy guide as well as be entertained by them. We buy only articles by writers who have been to or lived in the destination on which they write. Not interested in "by-the-book" tourist articles. Our readers live in Europe, average age 26.5, married with 2 children. Over 50% travel by car. Annual vacation is 1 week or more. Weekend trips are also popular. Should always include specific details: restaurant/clubs/hotel recommendations as well as prices. Looking for bargains." Humor (limited amount used—dealing with travel experiences in Europe) is accepted. No interviews of singers, historical pieces, album/movie/book reviews, or technical stories. Buys 15-20 mss/year. Query with published clips or send complete ms. Length: 900-2,000 words. Pays in Deutsche Marks—DM 120/page; partial payment for partial page.

Photos: State availablility of photos or send photos with query or mss. Pays DM 80 for 35mm transparencies. Captions required. "We pay once for use with story but can reuse at no additional cost."

Tips: "Best chance would be a tie-in travel or first-person (personalized) story with an American holiday: Mother's Day in Paris, Labor Day, Thanksgiving, St. Pat's Day in Europe, etc. Stories must be written with an American military member and family in mind—young married, 2 children with car, 2 weeks annual leave, several 3-day weekends. Sports/adventure travel stories and 'walking tours' of a city are popular with our readers."

THE RETIRED OFFICER MAGAZINE, 201 N. Washington St., Alexandria VA 22314. (800)245-8762. FAX: (703)838-8173. Editor: Col. Charles D. Cooper, USAF-Ret. 60% freelance written. Prefers to work with published/established writers. Monthly for officers of the 7 uniformed services and their families. Estab. 1929. Circ. 370,000. **Pays on acceptance.** Publishes ms an average of 9-12 months after acceptance. Byline given. Buys first serial rights. Submit seasonal material (holiday stories with a military theme) at least 9-12 months in advance. Reports on material accepted for publication within 2 months. Sample copy and writer's guidelines for 9×12 SAE with 5 first class stamps.

Nonfiction: Current military/political affairs, health and wellness, recent military history, travel, second-career job opportunities and military family lifestyle. Also, upbeat articles on aging, issues pertinent to a retired military officer's milieu. "We rarely accept unsolicited mss. We look for detailed query letters with resumé and sample clips attached. We do not publish poetry or fillers." Buys 48 mss/year. Length: 800-2,000 words. Pays up to $500.

Photos: Query with list of stock photo subjects. Reviews 8×10 b&w photos (normal halftone). Pays $20. Original slides or transparencies must be suitable for color separation. Pays up to $125 for inside color; up to $200 for cover.

Tips: "Our readers are 55-65. We never write about them as senior citizens, yet we look for upbeat stories that take into consideration the demographic characteristics of their age group. An author who can submit a complete package of story and photos is valuable to us."

SOLDIER OF FORTUNE, The Journal of Professional Adventurers, Omega Group, Ltd., P.O. Box 693, Boulder CO 80306. (303)449-3750. FAX: (303)444-5617. Managing Editor: John W. Coleman. 50% freelance written. A monthly magazine covering military, paramilitary, police, combat subjects and action/adventure. "We are an action-oriented magazine; we cover combat hot spots around the world such as Afghanistan, Central America, Angola, etc. We also provide timely features on state-of-the-art weapons and equipment; elite military and police units; and historical military operations. Readership is primarily active-duty military, veterans and law enforcement." Estab. 1975. Circ. 175,000. Byline given. Offers 25% kill fee. Buys all rights; will negotiate. Submit seasonal/holiday material 5 months in advance. Reports in 3 weeks on queries; 1 month on mss. Sample copy $5; writer's guidelines for #10 SASE. Send ms to articles editor; queries to managing editor.

Nonfiction: Exposé; general interest; historical/nostalgic; how-to (on weapons and their skilled use); humor; profile; new product; personal experience; photo feature ("number one on our list"); technical; travel; combat reports; military unit reports and solid Vietnam and operation Desert Storm articles. "No 'How I won the war' pieces; no op-ed pieces *unless* they are fully and factually backgrounded; no knife articles (staff assignments only). *All* submitted articles should have good art; art will sell us on an article." Buys 75 mss/year. Query with or without published clips, or send complete ms. Length: 2,000-3,000 words. Pays page rate of $150-250. Sometimes pays the expenses of writers on assignment.

Photos: Send photos with submission (copies only, no originals). Reviews contact sheets and transparencies. Offers no additional payment for photos accepted with ms. Pays $500 for cover photo. Captions and identification of subjects required. Buys one-time rights.

Columns/Departments: Address to articles editor. Combat craft (how-to military and police survival skills) and I Was There (first-person accounts of the arcane or unusual based in a combat or law enforcement environment), all 600-800 words. Buys 16 mss/year. Send complete ms. Length: 600-800 words. Combat craft pays $200; I was There pays $100.

Fillers: Bulletin Board editor. Newsbreaks; military/paramilitary related, "*has* to be documented." Length: 100-250 words. Pays $25.

Tips: "Submit a professionally prepared, complete package. All artwork with cutlines, double-spaced typed manuscript win 5¼" or 3½" IBM-compatible disc, if available, cover letter including synopsis of article, supporting documentation where applicable, etc. Manuscript must be factual; writers have to do their homework and get all their facts straight. One error means rejection. We will work with authors over the phone or by letter, tell them if their ideas have merit for an acceptable article, and help them fine-tune their work. I Was There is a good place for freelancers to start. Vietnam features, if carefully researched and art heavy, will always get a careful look. Combat reports, again, with good art, are number one in our book and stand the best chance of being accepted. Military unit reports from around the world are well received as are law enforcement articles (units, police in action). If you write for us, be complete and factual; pros read *Soldier of Fortune*, and are *very* quick to let us know if we (and the author) err. We will be Operation Desert Storm-oriented for years to come, in terms of first-person accounts and incisive combat reports. Read a current issue to see where we're taking the magazine in the 1990s."

VIETNAM, Empire Press, 602 S. King St., #300, Leesburg VA 22075. (703)771-9400. Editor: Colonel Harry G. Summers, Jr. Managing Editor: Kenneth Phillips. 80-90% freelance written. Quarterly magazine on military aspects of the Vietnam War. "Without debating the wisdom of U.S. involvement, pro or con, our objective is to tell the story of the military events, weaponry and personalities of the war, as it happened." Estab. 1988. Circ. 140,000. Pays on publication. Publishes ms up to 2 years after acceptance. Byline given. Buys all rights. Query for electronic submissions. Reports in 3 months on queries; 6 months on mss. Sample copy $3.95. Writer's guidelines for #10 SASE.

Nonfiction: Book excerpts (if original), historical, interview, personal/experience, military history. "Absolutely no fiction or poetry; we want straight history, as much personal narrative as possible, but not the gung-ho, shoot-em-up variety, either." Buys 50 mss/year. Query. Length: 4,000 words maximum. Pays $300 for features.

Photos: State availability of photos with submission. Pays up to $100/photo, depending on use. Identification of subjects required. Buys one-time rights.

Columns/Departments: Arsenal (about weapons used, all sides); Personality (profiles of the players, all sides), Fighting Forces (about various units or types of unites: air, sea, rescue); Perspectives. Query. Length: 2,000 words. Pays $150.

WORLD WAR II, Empire Press, 602 S. King St. #300, Leesburg VA 22075. (703)771-9400. Editor: C. Brian Kelly. 95% freelance written. Prefers to work with published/established writers. A bimonthly magazine covering "military operations in World War II – events, personalities, strategy, national policy, etc." Estab. 1983. Circ. 200,000. Pays on publication. Publishes ms an average of 1-2 years after acceptance. Byline given. Buys all rights. Submit anniversary-related material 1 year in advance. Reports in 3 months on queries; 6 months or more on mss. Sample copy $4; writer's guidelines for #10 SASE.

Nonfiction: World War II military history. No fiction. Buys 24 mss/year. Query. Length: 4,000 words. Pays $200.

Photos: State availability of art and photos with submission. (For photos and other art, send photocopies and cite sources. "We'll order.") Sometimes offers additional payment for photos accepted with ms. Captions and identification of subjects required. Buys one-time rights.

Columns/Department: Undercover (espionage, resistance, sabotage, intelligence gathering, behind the lines, etc.); Personalities (WW II personalities of interest); and Armaments (weapons, their use and development), all 2,000 words. Book reviews, 300-750 words. Buys 18 mss/year (plus book reviews). Query. Pays $100.

Tips: "List your sources and suggest further readings in standard format at the end of your piece – as a bibliography for our files in case of factual challenge or dispute. All submissions are on speculation. When the story's right, but the writing isn't, we'll pay a small research fee for use of the information in our own style and language."

Music

Music fans follow the latest music industry news in these publications. Types of music and musicians or specific instruments are the sole focus of some magazines. Publications geared to music industry and professionals can be found in the Trade Music section. Additional music and dance markets are included in the Entertainment section.

‡THE ABSOLUTE SOUND, The Journal of The High End, Box 115, Sea Cliff NY 11579. (516)676-2830. Editor-in-Chief: Harry Pearson, Jr. Managing Editor: Laura Dearborn. 10% freelance written. Works with a small number of new/unpublished writers each year. Bimonthly magazine covering the music reproduction business, audio equipment and records for "up-scale, high tech men and women

ALWAYS submit unsolicited manuscripts or queries with a self-addressed, stamped envelope (SASE) within your country or a self-addressed envelope with International Reply Coupons (IRC) purchased from the post office for other countries.

between the ages of 20 and 100, serious music lovers." Pays on publication. Byline given. Buys all rights. Query for electronic submissions. Sample copy $7.50.

Nonfiction: Exposé (of bad commercial audio practices); interview/profile (famous recording engineers, famous conductors); new product (audio); opinion (audio and record reviews); and technical (how to improve your stereo system). Special Recordings issue. No puff pieces about industry. No newspaper clippings. Query with published clips. Length: 250-5,000 words. Pays $125-1,000. Sometimes pays the expenses of writers on assignment.

Columns/Departments: Audio Musings (satires) and Reports from Overseas (audio shows, celebrities, record companies). Buys 6 mss/year. Length: 250-750 words. Pays $125-200.

Tips: "Writers should know about audio, recordings and the engineering of same, as well as live music. The approach is *literate*, witty, investigative, good journalism."

BAM, Rock and Video/the California Music Magazine, BAM Publications, 5951 Canning St., Oakland CA 94609. (415)652-3810. Editors: Steve Stolder and Bill Holdship. 60% freelance written. Bi-weekly tabloid. Circ. 110,000. Pays on publication. Publishes ms an average of 1 month after acceptance. Byline given. Offers negotiable kill fee. Buys first North American serial rights. Submit seasonal/holiday material 3 months in advance. Reports in 3 weeks. Sample copy $2.

Nonfiction: Book excerpts, interview/profiles, record reviews and new product reviews. Buys 100 mss/year. Query with published clips. Length: 1,500-5,000 words. Pays $40-300. Sometimes pays expenses of writers on assignment.

Tips: "*BAM*'s focus is on both the personality and the craft of musicians. Writers should concentrate on bringing out their subject's special traits and avoid bland, clichéd descriptions and quotes. Clear, crisp writing is essential. Many potential *BAM* writers try to be too clever and end up sounding stupid. Also, it helps to have a clear focus. Many writers tend to ramble and simply string quotes together."

BANJO NEWSLETTER, Box 364, Greensboro MD 21639. (301)482-6278. Editor: Hub Nitchie. 10% freelance written. Monthly magazine covering the "instructional and historical treatment of the 5-string banjo. Covers all aspects of the instrument. Tablature is used for musical examples." Circ. 7,000. Pays on publication. Byline given. Buys one-time rights. Query for electronic submissions. Reports in 1 month on queries. Sample copy for $1.

Nonfiction: Interviews with 5-string banjo players, banjo builders, shop owners, etc. No humorous fiction from anyone unfamiliar with the popular music field. Buys 6 mss/year. Query. Length: 500-4,000 words. Pays $20-100. Sometimes pays writers with contributor copies or other premiums "if that is what writer wants." Very seldom pays expenses of writers on assignment. "We can arrange for press tickets to musical events."

Photos: State availability of photos with submission. Reviews b&w prints. Offers $10-40/photo. Captions and identification of subjects required whenever possible. Buys one-time rights.

Columns/Departments: Buys 60 mss/year. Query. Length: 500-750 words. Payment varies.

Poetry: Don Nitchie, poetry editor: Rt. 1, Box 289, Chilwark MA 02535. Buys 2 poems/year. Submit maximum 1 poem at one time.

Tips: "The writer should be motivated by being a student of the 5-string banjo or interested in the folk or bluegrass music fields where 5-string banjo is featured. Writers should be able to read and write banjo tablature and know various musicians or others in the field."

BLUEGRASS UNLIMITED, Bluegrass Unlimited, Inc., P.O. Box 111, Broad Run VA 22014. (703)349-8181. Editor: Peter V. Kuykendall. 80% freelance written. Prefers to work with published/established writers. Monthly magazine on bluegrass and old-time country music. Estab. 1966. Circ. 21,500. Pays on publication. Publishes ms an average of 4 months after acceptance. Byline given. Kill fee negotiated. Buys first North American serial rights, one-time rights, all rights and second serial (reprint) rights. Submit seasonal/holiday material 4 months in advance. Reports in 2 weeks on queries; 2 months on mss. Free sample copy and writer's guidelines for #10 SASE.

Nonfiction: General interest, historical/nostalgic, how-to, interview/profile, personal experience, photo feature and travel. No "fan" style articles. Buys 75-80 mss/year. Query with or without published clips. No set word length. Pays 6-8¢/word.

Photos: State availability of photos or send photos with query. Reviews 35mm transparencies and 3×5, 5×7 and 8×10 b&w and color prints. Pays $50-150 for transparencies; $25-50 for b&w prints; and $50-150 for color prints. Identification of subjects required. Buys one-time rights and all rights.

Fiction: Ethnic and humorous. Buys 3-5 mss/year. Query. No set word length. Pays 6-8¢/word.

Tips: "We would prefer that articles be informational, based on personal experience or an interview with lots of quotes from subject, profile, humor, etc."

CD REVIEW, WGE Publishing, Forest Road, Box 278, Hancock NH 03449. (603)525-4201. FAX: (603)525-4423. Editorial Director: Dick Lewis. Executive Editor: Larry Canale. 50% freelance written. Monthly magazine on compact disc recordings and hardware. Estab. 1984. Circ. 120,000. Pays on publication. Publishes ms an average of 3 months after acceptance. Byline given. Offers 20% kill fee. Buys first North American serial rights. Submit seasonal/holiday material 3 months in advance. Query for electronic submissions. Reports in 2 weeks. Sample copy for 8½×11 SAE; writer's guidelines for #10 SASE.

Nonfiction: Interview/profile. Buys 50 mss/year. Query with published clips. Length: 500-2,500 words. Pays $50-600. Sometimes pays expenses of writers on assignment.

Photos: State availability of photos with submission. Reviews contact sheets and transparencies. Offers $50-100 per photo. Identification of subjects required. Buys one-time rights.

Columns/Departments: Classical Critique; Rock Report; World Beat. Buys 12 mss/year. Query with published clips. Length: 750-1,000 words. Pays $250-350.

COUNTRY MUSIC, Silver Eagle Publishers, 342 Madison Ave. #2118, New York NY 10173-0002. Staff written. Did not want to be listed.

GUITAR PLAYER MAGAZINE, GPI Publications, 20085 Stevens Creek, Cupertino CA 95014. (408)446-1105. Contact: Editor. 70% freelance written. Monthly magazine for persons "interested in guitars, guitarists, manufacturers, guitar builders, bass players, equipment, careers, etc." Circ. 150,000. Buys first serial and limited reprint rights. **Pays on acceptance.** Publishes ms an average of 3 months after acceptance. Byline given. Reports in 6 weeks. Free sample copy; writer's guidelines for #10 SASE.

Nonfiction: Publishes "wide variety of articles pertaining to guitars and guitarists: interviews, guitar craftsmen profiles, how-to features—anything amateur and professional guitarists would find fascinating and/or helpful. On interviews with 'name' performers, be as technical as possible regarding strings, guitars, techniques, etc. We're not a pop culture magazine, but a magazine for musicians." Also buys features on such subjects as a guitar museum, role of the guitar in elementary education, personal reminiscences of past greats, technical gadgets and how to work them, analysis of flamenco, etc. Buys 30-40 mss/year. Query. Length: open. Pays $100-300. Sometimes pays expenses of writers on assignment.

Photos: Reviews b&w glossy prints. Pays $50-100. Buys 35mm color transparencies. Pays $250 (for cover only). Buys one time rights.

HIT PARADER, Charlton Publishing, 441 Lexington Ave. #900, New York NY 10017. (212)370-0986. Editor: Andy Secher. Managing Editor: Anne Leighton. 5% freelance written. Monthly magazine covering heavy metal music. "We look for writers who have access to the biggest names in heavy metal music." Estab. 1948. Circ. 200,000. Pays on publication. Publishes ms an average of 4 months after acceptance. Byline given. Negotiable kill fee. Buys all right. Submit seasonal material 4 months in advance. Reports in 1 month on queries. Sample copy for 9×12 SAE with 5 first class stamps.

Nonfiction: General interest and interview/profile. Buys 3-5 mss/year. Query with published clips. Length: 600-800 words. Pays $75-140. Lifestyle-oriented and hardball pieces. "Study and really know the bands to get new angles on story ideas."

Photos: Reviews transparencies, 5×7 and 8×10 b&w prints and Kodachrome 64 slides. Offers $25-200 per photo. Buys one-time rights.

Tips: "Interview big names in metal, get published in other publications. We don't take chances on new writers."

ILLINOIS ENTERTAINER, Suite 150, 2250 E. Devon, Des Plaines IL 60018. (708)298-9333. FAX: (708)298-7973. Editor: Michael C. Harris. 95% freelance written. Prefers to work with published/established writers but open to new writers with "style." Monthly tabloid covering music and entertainment for consumers within 100-mile radius of Chicago. Estab. 1975. Circ. 80,000. Pays on publication. Publishes ms an average of 2 months after acceptance. Byline given. Offers 10% kill fee. Buys one-time rights. Simultaneous queries OK. Reports in 1 month on queries; 2 months on mss. Sample copy $5.

Nonfiction: Interview/profile (of entertainment figures). No Q&A interviews. Buys 75 mss/year. Query with published clips. Length: 500-2,000 words. Pays $15-100. Sometimes pays expenses of writers on assignment.

Photos: State availability of photos. Pays $20-30 for 5×7 or 8×10 b&w prints; $125 for color cover photo, both on publication only. Captions and identification of subjects required.

Columns/Departments: Spins (record reviews stress record over band or genre). Buys 50 mss/year. Query with published clips. Length: 150-250 words. Pays $6-20.

Tips: "Send clips (published or unpublished) with phone number, and be patient. Full staff has seniority, but if you know the ins and outs of the entertainment biz, and can balance that knowledge with a broad sense of humor, then you'll have a chance. Also, *IE* is more interested in alternative music than the pop-pap you can hear/read about everywhere else."

INTERNATIONAL MUSICIAN, American Federation of Musicians, Suite 600, Paramount Building, 1501 Broadway, New York NY 10036. (212)869-1330. Editor: Stephen R. Sprague. 10% freelance written. Prefers to work with published/established writers. Monthly magazine for professional musicians. Estab. 1900. **Pays on acceptance.** Publishes ms an average of 3 months after acceptance. Byline given. Reports in 2 months.
Nonfiction: Articles on prominent instrumental musicians (classical, jazz, rock or country). Send complete ms. Length: 1,500 words.

THE MISSISSIPPI RAG, "The Voice of Traditional Jazz and Ragtime," 6500 Nicollet Ave. S, Minneapolis MN 55423. (612)861-2446 or (612)920-0312. Editor: Leslie Johnson. 70% freelance written. Works with small number of new/unpublished writers each year, "but most of our writers have been with us for years." Monthly tabloid covering traditional jazz and ragtime. Estab. 1973. Paid circ. 4,000; readership 12,000. Pays on publication. Publishes ms an average of 4 months after acceptance. Byline given. Buys all rights, "but writer may negotiate if he wishes to use material later." Submit seasonal/holiday material 3 months in advance. Sample copy and writer's guidelines for 9×12 SAE with 98¢ postage.
Nonfiction: Historical, interview/profile, personal experience, photo features, current jazz and ragtime, festival coverage, book reviews and record reviews. Reviews are always assigned. No "longwinded essays on jazz or superficial pieces on local ice cream social Dixieland bands." Buy 24-30 mss/year. Query with or without published clips, or send complete ms. Length: 1,500-4,000 words. Pays 2¢/word.
Photos: Send photos with submission. Prefers b&w 5×7 or 8×10 prints. Offers $5 minimum per photo. Identification of subjects required. Buys one-time rights.
Columns/Departments: Book and Record reviews. Buys 60 assigned mss/year. Query with published clips. Pays 2¢/word.
Tips: "Become familiar with the jazz world. The *Rag* is read by musicians, jazz/ragtime writers, historians and jazz/ragtime buffs. We want articles that have depth—solid facts and a good basic grasp of jazz and/or ragtime history. Not for the novice jazz writer. Interviews with jazz and ragtime performers are most open to freelancers. It's wise to query first because we have already covered so many performers."

MODERN DRUMMER, 870 Pompton Ave., Cedar Grove NJ 07009. (201)239-4140. Editor-in-Chief: Ronald Spagnardi. Features Editor: William F. Miller. Managing Editor: Rick Van Horn. Monthly for "student, semi-pro and professional drummers at all ages and levels of playing ability, with varied specialized interests within the field." 60% freelance written. Circ. 85,000. Pays on publication. Publishes ms an average of 3 months after acceptance. Buys all rights. Previously published submissions OK. Reports in 1 month. Sample copy $3.95; free writer's guidelines.
Nonfiction: How-to, informational, interview, new product, personal experience and technical. "All submissions must appeal to the specialized interests of drummers." Buys 20-30 mss/year. Query or submit complete ms. Length: 5,000-8,000 words. Pays $200-500.
Photos: Purchased with accompanying ms. Reviews 8×10 b&w prints and color transparencies.
Columns/Departments: Jazz Drummers Workshop, Rock Perspectives, In The Studio, Show Drummers Seminar, Teachers Forum, Drum Soloist, The Jobbing Drummer, Strictly Technique, Book Reviews and Shop Talk. "Technical knowledge of area required for most columns." Buys 40-50 mss/year. Query or submit complete ms. Length: 500-2,500 words. Pays $25-150.

‡MUSIC CITY NEWS, Suite 601, 50 Music Square West, Nashville TN 37203. (615)329-2200. Editor/General Manager: John Sturdivant. Managing Editor: Lydia Dixon Harden. 15% freelance written. Monthly magazine covering different aspects of country music and its entertainers. "The magazine deals with all aspects of country music and its entertainers. Often use feature stories on entertainers, their home lives, hobbies, interests, etc." Estab. 1963. Circ. 500,000. Pays on publication. Byline given. Offers no kill fee. Buys one-time rights. Submit seasonal/holiday material 3 months in advance. Reports in 2 months on queries. Free sample copy.
Nonfiction: General interest, humor, interview/profile, personal experience. "No meeting a star backstage stories." Buys 12 mss/year. Query with published clips. Length: 200-1,000 words. Pays $75-200 for assigned articles; $75-100 for unsolicited articles.
Photos: State availability of photos with submission. Reviews contact sheets. Offers no additional payment for photos accepted with ms. Identification of subjects required. Buys one-time rights.

MUSIC EXPRESS, Rock Express Communications., 47 Jefferson Ave., Toronto, Ontario M6K 1Y3 Canada. (416)538-7500. FAX: (416)538-7503. Editor: Mary Dickie. 50% freelance written. Monthly magazine on contemporary music. "A contemporary consumer music magazine covering all forms of popular music slanted at a demographic between 18-25 with equal appeal for male and female readers." Estab. 1975. Circ. 350,000. Pays 45 days after publication. Byline given. Offers 50% kill fee. Buys first North American serial rights. Submit seasonal/holiday material 2 months in advance.

Nonfiction: Humor, interview/profile and photo feature. Buys 20 mss/year. Query. Length: 500-3,000 words. Pays $75-1,000. Sometimes pays expenses of writers on assignment.

Photos: State availability of photos with submission. Reviews transparencies and 5×7 and 8×10 prints. Offers $35-500 per photo. Captions, model releases and identification of subjects required. Buys one-time rights.

Columns/Departments: Regional (local news); Video (latest releases); Specific Music Columns (jazz, country, blues, hard rock); album reviews; concert reviews; and Film (latest movie releases). Buys 80 mss/year. Query. Length: 200-500 words. Pays $60-250.

MUSICAL AMERICA, 825 7th Ave., New York NY 10019. FAX: (212)586-1364. Editor: Shirley Fleming. 50% freelance written. Bimonthly. Estab. 1898. Circ. 20,000. Pays on publication. Publishes ms an average of 3-4 months after acceptance. Buys all rights. Free sample copy and writer's guidelines.

Nonfiction: Articles on classical music and classical record reviews are generally prepared by acknowledged writers and authorities in the field, but uses freelance material. Query with published clips. Length: 2,000 words maximum. Pays $300 minimum.

Photos: New b&w and color photos of musical personalities, events, etc.

MUSICIAN, Billboard Publications, 1515 Broadway, 39th Floor, New York NY 10036. (212)536-5208. Editor: Bill Flanagan. Senior Editors: Matt Resnicoff and Tony Scherman. 85% freelance written. Monthly magazine covering contemporary music, especially rock, pop and jazz. Estab. 1976. Circ. 170,000. Pays on publication. Byline given. Offers kill fee of 25-33%. Buys first North American serial rights. Submit seasonal/holiday material 3 months in advance.

Nonfiction: All music-related: book excerpts, exposé, historical, how-to (recording and performing), humor, interview/profile, new product and technical. Buys 150 mss/year. Query with published clips. Length: 300-10,000 words. Payment negotiable. Pays expenses of writers on assignment.

Photos: Assigns photo shoots. Uses some stock. Offers $50-300 per photo.

Columns/Departments: Jazz (jazz artists or works), 1,000-5,000 words; Reviews (record reviews), 300-500 words; Faces (short, newsy stories), 300 words; and Working Musician (technical "trade" angles on musicians), 1,000-3,000 words. Query with published clips. Length 300-1,500 words.

Tips: "Be aware of special music writers' style; don't gush, be somewhat skeptical; get the best quotes you can and save the arcane music criticism for reviews; know and apply Strunk and White; be interesting. Please send *published* clips; we don't want to be anyone's first publication. Our writing is considered excellent (in all modesty), even though we don't pay as much as we'd like. We recognize National Writers Union."

ONE SHOT, Attentive Writing for Neglected Rock 'N' Roll, One Shot Enterprises, Contract Station 6, P.O. Box 145, 125 Sherman St., Denver CO 80203. Editor: Steve Rosen. 80% freelance written. Eager to work with new/unpublished writers. "*One Shot* is a quarterly magazine dedicated to remembering now-obscure or under-appreciated performers of rock and related musics; expecially the one-hit wonders. Uses interviews, essays and journalism." Estab. 1985. Circ. 200. **Pays on acceptance.** Publishes ms up to 1 year after acceptance. Byline given. Buys one-time, second serial (reprint) or simultaneous rights, and makes work-for-hire assignments. Simultaneous and previously published submissions OK. Reports in 1 month. Sample copy $3. Writer's guidelines for #10 SASE.

Nonfiction: Book excerpts, essays, exposé, general interest, historical/nostalgic, interview/profile, opinion, personal experience and travel. No religious/inspirational articles. Buys 16 mss/year. Query. Length: 2,500 maximum words. Pays up to $100 for most articles, will pay more for longer features. Sometimes pays expenses of writers on assignment.

Photos: State availability of photos with submission. Reviews contact sheets and 8½×11 prints. Offers additional payment for photos accepted with ms. Buys one-time rights.

Columns/Departments: Speak, Memory! (personal experiences with now-obscure rock, etc., performers); and Travel (update on a place that once figured in a rock song, or performer's career, such as "Hitsville USA" studios in Detroit). Buys 10 mss/year. Query with or without published clips or send complete ms. Length: 1,000 maximum words. Pays up to $100.

Tips: "*One Shot* needs 'Where are They Now' articles on obscure and neglected rock performers who were once popular. Those pieces should include interviews with the performer and others; and provide a sense of 'being there'. *One Shot* will pay for such stories. Just send me a note explaining your interests, and I'll respond with detailed suggestions. I won't disqualify anyone for not following procedures; I want to encourage a body of work on this topic. Also looking for remembrances, travel pieces, concerning neglected rock."

OPERA CANADA, Suite 433, 366 Adelaide St. E., Toronto, Ontario M5A 3X9 Canada. (416)363-0395. Editor: Harvey Chusid. 80% freelance written. Prefers to work with published/established writers. Quarterly magazine for readers who are interested in serious music; specifically, opera. Estab. 1960.

Circ. 8,000. Pays on publication. Byline given. Not copyrighted. Buys first serial rights. Simultaneous submissions OK. Reports on material accepted for publication within 1 year. Sample copy $4.50.

Nonfiction: "Because we are Canada's only opera magazine, we like to keep 75% of our content Canadian, i.e., by Canadians or about Canadian personalities and events. We prefer informative and/or humorous articles about any aspect of music theater, with an emphasis on opera. The relationship of the actual subject matter to opera can be direct or indirect. We accept interviews with major operatic personalities. Please, no reviews of performances; we have staff reviewers." Query or submit complete ms. Length (for all articles except reviews of books and records): 1,000-3,000 words. Pays $50-200.

Photos: Photos with cutlines (i.e. captions) to accompany mss are welcome. No additional payment for photos used with mss. Captions required.

Tips: "We are interested in articles with an emphasis on current or controversial issues in opera."

ROCK & ROLL DISC, TAG Enterprises, P.O. Box 17601, Memphis TN 38187-0601. Editor: Tom Graves. 20% freelance written. A monthly magazine devoted to reviews and news about compact discs. "We review current compact discs relating to rock and roll. Our market is CD buyers who listen to rock and roll primarily. *Rock & Roll Disc* wants to publish the most informed and inspired music writing possible." Estab. 1987. Circ. 6,500. Pays on publication. Publishes ms an average of 2 months after acceptance. Byline given. Buys all rights. Submit seasonal/holiday material 3 months in advance. Reports in 1 month on queries and manuscripts only if accompanied by SASE. Sample copy mailed for three first class stamps.

Nonfiction: Interviews with rock personalities and reviews of compact discs, plus special features. Buys 100 mss/year. Query with two published music-related clips. Length: 200-2,000 words. Pays $10-50 depending on assignment.

Tips: "The writer needs to know the compact disc market and know rock music intimately. Don't bother if you don't, because knowledge can't be faked. Don't overwhelm editor with too many writing samples. Send only two and make sure they are music-related. Also, many writers don't bother to include an SASE. When that happens we don't bother to reply. Including a checklist on queries is most helpful since it saves the editor valuable time."

‡SOUNDTRACK, The Journal of the Independent Music Association, SoundTrack Publishing, P.O. Box 609, Ringwood NJ 07456. (201)831-1317. Editor: Don Kulak. 60% freelance written. Bimonthly music and acoustics magazine. Estab. 1988. Circ. 10,000. **Pays on acceptance.** Publishes ms an average of 3-4 months after acceptance. Byline sometimes given. Buys first and second serial (reprint) rights. Submit seasonal/holiday material 4 months in advance. Simultaneous and previously published submissions OK. Reports in 1 week on queries; 3 weeks on mss. Free sample copy and writer's guidelines for 9 × 12 SAE and $2 postage.

Nonfiction: Book excerpts, expose, how-to, interview/profile, new product, opinion, technical. Buys 36 mss/year. Query with published clips. Length: 1,500-5,000 words.. Pays $50-200 for assigned articles; $20-75 for unsolicited articles. Sometimes pays writers with contributor copies or other premiums rather than cash by "mutually beneficial agreement." Sometimes pays expenses of writers on assignment.

Photos: State availability of photos with submissions. Offers $10-20 per photo. Buys all rights.

Columns/Departments: The Business of Music (promotion, distribution, forming a record label; alternative markets—film scores, jingles, etc.; how-to's on generating more income from own music); Sound Input (in-depth and objective reporting on audio equipment and technology, emphasizing acoustical ramifications, also, cassette, record and CD manufacturing); Acousticraft (in-depth articles on acoustics in general, including acoustic instruments, concert halls, hearing). Buys 24 mss/year. Query with published clips. Length: 1,500-3,500 words.

Tips: "Write a letter explaining background, interests, and areas of special study and what you hope to get out of writing for our publication. All sections are open to freelancers. Writing should be fluid and direct. When describing music, the writing should paint an aural picture with good use of metaphors, and not be overly critical or pretentious. Technical writing should be well documented."

STEREO REVIEW, Hachette Magazines, Inc., 1633 Broadway, New York NY 10019. (212)767-6000. Editor-in-Chief: Louise Boundas. Executive Editor: Michael Riggs. Classical Music Editor: Robert Ripps. Popular Music Editor: Steve Simels. 65% freelance written, almost entirely by established contributing editors, and on assignment. A monthly magazine. Estab. 1958. Circ. 600,000. **Pays on acceptance.** Publishes ms an average of 5 months after acceptance. Byline given. Buys first North American rights or all rights. Sample copy for 9 × 12 SAE with $3 postage.

Nonfiction: Equipment and music reviews, how-to-buy, how-to-use, stereo and interview/profile. Buys approximately 25 mss/year. Query with published clips. Length: 1,500-3,000 words. Pays $500-800 for assigned articles.

TRADITION, Prairie Press, Box 438, Walnut IA 51577. (712)366-1136. Editor: Robert Everhart. 20% freelance written. Bimonthly magazine emphasizing traditional country music and other aspects of pioneer living. Circ. 2,500. Pays on publication. Not copyrighted. Byline given. Buys one-time rights. Submit seasonal/holiday material 6 months in advance. Simultaneous queries, and simultaneous and previously published submissions OK. Reports in 1 month. Sample copy for $1 to cover postage and handling.

Nonfiction: Historical (relating to country music); how-to (play, write, or perform country music); inspirational (on country gospel); interview (with traditional country performers,); nostalgia (pioneer living); personal experience (country music); and travel (in connection with country music contests or festivals). Query. Length: 800-1,200 words. Pays $10-15.

Photos: State availability of photos with query. Payment included in ms price. Reviews 5×7 b&w prints. Captions and model releases required. Buys one-time rights.

Poetry: Free verse and traditional. Buys 4 poems/year. Length: 5-20 lines. Submit maximum 2 poems with SASE. Pays $2-5.

Fillers: Clippings, jokes and anecdotes. Buys 5/year. Length: 15-50 words. Pays $5-10.

Tips: "Material must be concerned with what we term 'real' country music as opposed to today's 'pop' country music. Freelancer must be knowledgable of the subject; many writers don't even know who the father of country music is, let alone write about him."

Mystery

These magazines buy fictional accounts of crime, detective work and mystery. Additional mystery markets can be found in the Literary and "Little" section. Skim through other sections to identify markets for fiction; some will consider mysteries.

ALFRED HITCHCOCK'S MYSTERY MAGAZINE, Davis Publications, Inc., 380 Lexington Ave., New York NY 10017. (212)557-9100. Editor: Cathleen Jordan. Magazine published 13 times/year emphasizing mystery fiction. Circ. 225,000. **Pays on acceptance.** Byline given. Buys first serial rights, second serial (reprint) rights and foreign rights. Submit seasonal/holiday material 7 months in advance. Reports in 2 months. Writer's guidelines for SASE.

Fiction: Original and well-written mystery and crime fiction. Length: up to 14,000 words.

ELLERY QUEEN'S MYSTERY MAGAZINE, Davis Publications, Inc., 380 Lexington Ave., New York NY 10017. Editor: Eleanor Sullivan. 100% freelance written. Magazine published 13 times/year. Estab. 1941. Circ. 375,000. **Pays on acceptance.** Publishes ms an average of 6 months after acceptance. Byline given. Buys first serial rights or second serial (reprint) rights. Submit seasonal/holiday material 7 months in advance. Simultaneous and previously published submissions OK. Reports in 1 month. Writer's guidelines for #10 SASE.

Fiction: Special consideration will be given to "anything timely and original. We publish every type of mystery: the suspense story, the psychological study, the deductive puzzle—the gamut of crime and detection from the realistic (including stories of police procedure) to the more imaginative (including 'locked rooms' and impossible crimes). We always need detective stories, and do not want sex, sadism or sensationalism-for-the-sake-of-sensationalism." No gore or horror; seldom publishes parodies or pastiches. Buys up to 13 mss/issue. Length: 6,000 words maximum; occasionally higher but not often. Pays 3-8¢/word.

Tips: "We have a Department of First Stories to encourage writers whose fiction has never before been in print. We publish an average of 13 first stories a year."

Nature, Conservation and Ecology

These publications—probably the fastest-growing category during the past year—promote reader awareness of the natural environment, wildlife, nature preserves and ecosystems. Many of these "green magazines" also concentrate on recycling and related issues. They do not publish recreation or travel articles except as they relate to conservation or nature. Other markets for this kind of material can be found in the Regional; Sports; and Travel, Camping and Trailer categories, although magazines listed there require that nature or conservation articles be slanted to their specialized subject matter and audience. Some juvenile and teen publications also buy nature-related material for young audiences.

AMERICAN FORESTS, American Forestry Association, 1516 P St. NW, Washington DC 20005. (202)667-3300. FAX: (202)667-7751. Editor: Bill Rooney. 70% freelance written. Bimonthly magazine. "The magazine of trees and forests, published by a citizens' organization for the advancement of intelligent management and use of our forests, soil, water, wildlife and all other natural resources necessary for an environment of high quality." Circ. 30,000. **Pays on acceptance.** Publishes ms an average of 8 months after acceptance. Byline given. Buys one-time rights. Phone queries OK but written queries preferred. Submit seasonal/holiday material 5 months in advance. Reports in 2 months. Sample copy $1.20; writer's guidelines for SASE.

Nonfiction: General interest, historical, how-to, humor and inspirational. All articles should emphasize trees, forests, forestry and related issues. Buys 7-10 mss/issue. Query. Length: 2,000 words. Pays $300-700.

Photos: State availability of photos. Offers no additional payment for photos accompanying ms. Uses 8 × 10 b&w glossy prints; 35mm or larger transparencies, originals only. Captions required. Buys one-time rights.

Tips: "Query should have honesty and information on photo support."

THE AMICUS JOURNAL, Natural Resources Defense Council, 40 N. 20th St., New York NY 10011. (212)727-2700. Editor: Francesca Lyman. 80% freelance written. Quarterly magazine covering national and international environmental policy. *"The Amicus Journal* is intended to provide the general public with a journal of thought and opinion on environmental affairs, particularly those relating to policies of national and international significance." Estab. 1979. Circ. 120,000. **Pays on acceptance.** Publishes ms an average of 6 months after acceptance. Byline given. Offers 50% kill fee. Buys first North American serial rights. Submit seasonal/holiday material 6 months in advance. Query for electronic submissions. Reports in 6 weeks. Sample copy for 9 × 12 SAE with 5 first class stamps. Writer's guidelines for #10 SASE.

Nonfiction: Exposé and interview/profile. No articles not concerned with environmental issues of national or international policy significance. Buys 25 mss/year. Query with published clips. Length: 200-1,500 words. Payment negotiable. Sometimes pays expenses of writers on assignment.

Photos: State availability of photos with submssion. Reviews contact sheets, negatives, transparencies and 8 × 10 prints. Offers negotiable payment for photos. Captions, model releases and identification of subjects required. Buys one-time rights.

Columns/Departments: News and Comment (summary reporting of environmental issues, usually tied to topical items), 200-500 words; Articles (in-depth reporting on issues and personalities), 750-1,500 words; Book Reviews (well-informed essays on books of general interest to environmentalists interested in policy and history), 500-1,000 words. Buys 25 mss/year. Query with published clips. Payment negotiable.

Poetry: Brian Swann, poetry editor. Avant-garde and free verse. All poetry should be rooted in nature. Buys 20 poems/year. Pays $25.

Tips: "Except for editorials, all departments are open to freelance writers. Queries should precede manuscripts, and manuscripts should conform to the *Chicago Manual of Style*. Writers are asked to be sensitive to tone. As a policy magazine, we do not publish articles of a personal or satirical nature."

APPALACHIAN TRAILWAY NEWS, Appalachian Trail Conference, P.O. Box 807, Harpers Ferry WV 25425. (304)535-6331. 50% freelance written. Bimonthly magazine "subject matter must relate to Appalachian Trail." Estab. 1925. Circ. 26,000. **Pays on acceptance.** Byline given. Buys first North American serial rights or second serial (reprint) rights. Previously published submissions OK. Reports in 1 month. Sample copy includes guidelines for $2.50; guidelines only for SASE.

Nonfiction: Essays, general interest, historical/nostalgic, how-to, humor, inspirational, interview/profile, photo feature, technical and travel. No poetry or religious materials. Buys 15-20 mss/year. Query with or without published clips, or send complete ms. Length: 250-3,000 words. Pays $25-300. Pays expenses of writers on assignment. Publishes, but does not pay for "hiking reflections."

Photos: State availability of b&w photos with submission. Reviews contact sheets, negatives and 5 × 7 prints. Offers $25-125 per photo. Identification of subjects required. Negotiates future use by ATC.

Tips: "Contributors should display an obvious knowledge of or interest in the Appalachian Trail. Those who live in the vicinity of the Trail may opt for an assigned story and should present credentials and subject in which interested to the editor."

‡ARCHIPELAGO, The Society for Ocean Studies, P.O. Box 266, Key Colony Beach FL 33051. (305)743-6155. Editor: Robert O. Stafford. Managing Editor: Phil Edwards. Quarterly newsletter covering the oceans. "Our readers are educated, upscale laymen with an interest in marine matters. We run informative stories on just about any subject related to the sea." Estab. 1986. Circ. 100. Pays on publication. Publishes ms an average of 3 months after acceptance. Byline given. Buys first North American serial rights. Simultaneous submissions OK. Reports in 1 week. Sample copy for 4½ × 9½ SAE with 1 first class stamp. Writer's guidelines for 4½ × 9½ SAE with 1 first class stamp.

Nonfiction: "No high tech material with specialized jargon, highly localized interest or very broad subject matter." Buys 2-3 mss/year. Query. Length: 700-1,500 words. Pays $50.

Photos: State availability of photos with submission. Offers no additional payment for photos accepted with ms. Buys one-time rights.

Tips: "We are looking for general interest articles related to marine matters: oceanography, biology, chemistry, archaeology, history, meteorology, etc."

THE ATLANTIC SALMON JOURNAL, The Atlantic Salmon Federation, Suite 1030, 1435 St. Alexandre, Montreal, Quebec H3A 2G4 Canada. (514)842-8059. Editor: Terry Davis. 50-68% freelance written. Works with a small number of new/unpublished writers each year. A quarterly magazine covering conservation efforts for the Atlantic salmon. Caters to "affluent and responsive audience – the dedicated angler and conservationist of the Atlantic salmon." Circ. 20,000. Pays on publication. Publishes ms an average of 3-6 months after acceptance. Byline given. Buys first serial rights to articles and one-time rights to photos. Submit seasonal/holiday material 3 months in advance. Simultaneous queries and submissions OK. Query for electronic submissions. Reports in 2 months. Sample copy for 9 × 12 SAE and $1 (Canadian), or SAE with IRC; free writer's guidelines.

Nonfiction: Exposé, historical/nostalgic, how-to, humor, interview/profile, new product, opinion, personal experience, photo feature, technical, travel, conservation, cuisine, science, research and management. "We are seeking articles that are pertinent to the focus and purpose of our magazine, which is to inform and entertain our membership on all aspects of the Atlantic salmon and its environment, preservation and conservation." Buys 15-20 mss/year. Query with published clips and state availability of photos. Length: 1,500-3,000 words. Pays $150-300. Sometimes pays the expenses of writers on assignment.

Photos: State availability of photos with query. Pays $50 for 3×5 or 5×7 b&w prints; $50-100 for 2¼×3¼ or 35mm color slides. Captions and identification of subjects required.

Columns/Departments: Adventure Eating (cuisine) and First Person (nonfiction, anecdotal, from first-person viewpoint, can be humorous). Buys about 6 mss/year. Length: 1,000-1,500 words. Pays $150.

Fiction: Adventure, fantasy, historical, humorous and mainstream. "We don't want to see anything that does not deal with Atlantic salmon directly or indirectly. Wilderness adventures are acceptable as long as they deal with Atlantic salmon." Buys 3 ms/year. Query with published clips. Length: 3,000 words maximum. Pays $150-300.

Fillers: Clippings, jokes, anecdotes and short humor. Length: 100-300 words average. Does not pay. Cartoons, single panel, $25-50.

Tips: "Articles must reflect informed and up-to-date knowledge of Atlantic salmon. Writers need not be authorities, but research must be impeccable. Clear, concise writing is a plus, and submissions must be typed. Anecdote, River Log and photo essays are most open to freelancers. The odds are that a writer without a background in outdoors writing and wildlife reporting will not have the 'informed' angle I'm looking for. Our readership is well-read and critical of simplification and generalization."

AUDUBON, The Magazine of the National Audubon Society, National Audubon Society, 950 Third Ave., New York NY 10022. FAX: (212)755-3752. Editor: Les Line. 85% freelance written. Bimonthly magazine on conservation, environment and natural history. "We are edited for people who delight in, care about and are willing to fight for the protection of wildlife, natural resources, and the global environment." Estab. 1887. Circ. 430,000. **Pays on acceptance.** Byline given. Buys first North American serial rights; second serial (reprint) rights on occasion. Query before submission. Reports in 2-3 months. Sample copy $4 with 8½ × 11 SAE and postage ($3 for first class). Free writer's guidelines.

Nonfiction: Essays, investigative, historical, humor, interview/profile, opinion and photo feature and book excerpts (well in advance of publication). "No poorly written, ill-researched or duplicative articles or things that sound as if they were written for a small-town newspaper or encyclopedia." Length: 250-4,000 words. Pays $250-2,500. Pays expenses of writers on assignment.

Photos: Query with photographic idea before submitting slides. Reviews 35mm transparencies. Offers page rates per photo on publication. Caption info and identification of subjects required. Write for photo guidelines.

Fiction: Appropriate to our audience. Send complete ms. Length: 500-3,000 words. Pays $250-2,000.

Tips: "Because we are presently overstocked, we are not actively soliciting freelance submissions. However, a *good* story, *well* written, always seems to find room. But, please, study the magazine carefully before querying. And be advised that we have recently shifted the emphasis away from nature appreciation and natural history and toward environmental issues."

BIRD WATCHER'S DIGEST, Pardson Corp., P.O. Box 110, Marietta OH 45750. Editor: Mary Beacom Bowers. 60% freelance written. Works with a small number of new/unpublished writers each year. Bimonthly magazine covering natural history – birds and bird watching. "*BWD* is a nontechnical magazine interpreting ornithological material for amateur observers, including the knowledgeable birder, the serious novice and the backyard bird watcher; we strive to provide good reading and good ornithology." Estab. 1978. Circ. 80,000. Pays on publication. Publishes ms an average of 1 year after acceptance. Byline given. Buys one-time rights, first serial rights and second serial (reprint) rights. Submit seasonal/ holiday material 6 months in advance. Previously published submissions OK. Reports in 6 weeks. Sample copy $3; writer's guidelines for #10 SASE.

Nonfiction: Book excerpts, how-to (relating to birds, feeding and attracting, etc.), humor, personal experience and travel (limited—we get many). "We are especially interested in fresh, lively accounts of closely observed bird behavior and displays and of bird watching experiences and expeditions. We often need material on less common species or on unusual or previously unreported behavior of common species." No articles on pet or caged birds; none on raising a baby bird. Buys 75-90 mss/year. Send complete ms. Length: 600-3,500 words. Pays $25-50 minimum.

Photos: Send photos with ms. Pays $10 minimum for b&w prints; $25 minimum for transparencies. Buys one-time rights.

Poetry: Avant-garde, free verse, light verse and traditional. No haiku. Buys 12-18 poems/year. Submit maximum 3 poems. Length 8-20 lines. Pays $10.

Tips: "We are aimed at an audience ranging from the backyard bird watcher to the very knowledgeable birder; we include in each issue material that will appeal at various levels. We always strive for a good geographical spread, with material from every section of the country. We leave very technical matters to others, but we want facts and accuracy, depth and quality, directed at the veteran bird watcher and at the enthusiastic novice. We stress the joys and pleasures of bird watching, its environmental contribution, and its value for the individual and society."

BIRDER'S WORLD, The Magazine Exploring Wild Birds and Birding, 720 E. 8th St., Suite 4, Holland MI 49423. (616)396-5618. Editor: Eldon D. Greij. 80% freelance written. Bimonthly magazine on wild birds, birding and bird-watching. *"Birder's World* is designed for people with a broad interest in wild birds and birding. Readers have varying degrees of experience in the world of birds, ranging from the absolute novice to the studied ornithologist. They are well educated, curious readers." Estab. 1987. Circ. 55,000. Publishes ms an average of 1 year after acceptance and pays on publication. Byline given. Buys first North American serial rights. Sample copy for $3.50. Writer's guidelines for #10 SASE.

Nonfiction: Species profiles, birding trips, historical, interview/profile, personal experience, photo essay, and photo/technical. Buys 30-40 mss/year. Query with sample introduction, outline of proposed article and published clips if available. No poetry or fiction please. Length: 2,200-2,800 words. Pays $300-400 for feature articles. Sometimes pays expenses of writers on assignment.

Photos: State availability of photos with submission. Reviews transparencies and prints. Offers $75-100 per inside photo; $150 for a two-page spread; and $200 for covers. Model releases and identification of subjects required. Buys one-time rights.

Columns/Departments: Attracting Birds (how-to, backyard habitat); Birding Hot Spots (prefer North American); and Birds and Art (carvers, painters, sculptors). Buys 20 mss/year. Length: 2,200-2,800 words. Pays $300-400.

Fillers: Humor, opinion, personal experience. Length: 1,000-2,000 words. Buys fewer than 5 mss/year. Book reviews. Query with book title and published clips. Buys fewer than 10 mss/year. Limit length to 500 words.

Tips: "We strongly encourage interested writers to send for our writer's guidelines before submitting work."

BUZZWORM, The Environmental Journal, Buzzworm Inc., 2305 Canyon Blvd., #206, Boulder CO 80302. Editor: Joseph E. Daniel. Managing Editor: Elizabeth Darby Junkin. 75% freelance written. Bimonthly magazine. Estab. 1988. Circ. 75,000. Pays 2-3 months after off-sale date of publication. Byline given. Buys first world serial rights, first rights or all rights. Submit seasonal/holiday material 6 months in advance. Reports in 1 month on queries; 2 months on mss. Sample copy $4 with 9 × 11 SAE and 6 first class stamps. Writer's guidelines for #10 SAE with 1 first class stamp. "Care is taken, but no responsibility accepted for unsolicited mss and photos."

Nonfiction: Book excerpts, essays, expose, interview/profile, photo feature, environmental. Buys 18-20 mss/year. Query with published clips. Length: 100-3,500 words. Pays $50-1,500 for assigned articles; $25-1,500 for unsolicited articles. Sometimes pays expenses of writers on assignment.

Photos: Send photos with submission. Offers additional payment for photos accepted and published. Captions, model releases and identification of subjects required. Buys all rights.

Columns/Departments: Eco Voice Editor/Eco Business Editor/Urban Biology Editor. Eco Voice (personal view), 1,250-1,700 words; Eco Business (green/environmental business column), 1,250-1,500 words; Urban Ecology (city environment issues), 1,200-1,500 words. Buys 3-4 mss/year. Query with published clips or send complete ms. Pays $100-350.

Fiction: Fiction Editor. Environmental only. Buys 3 mss/year. Send complete ms. Length: 3,500+ words. Pays $750.

Poetry: Poetry Editor. Free verse and haiku. Buys 1-2 poems/year. Submit maximum 5 poems. Pays $25-50.

Fillers: Notes, New and Reviews Editor. Newsbreaks. Buys 10-20/year. Length: 250 words. Pays $50.

Tips: "Know what has been covered, read the magazine and read the guidelines!"

ENVIRONMENT, Heldref Publications, 4000 Albemarle St. NW, Washington DC 20016. Managing Editor: Barbara T. Richman. 2% freelance written. For scientists, business and government executives, teachers, citizens, high school and college students and teachers interested in environment or effects of technology and science in public affairs. Magazine published 10 times/year. Estab. 1958. Circ. 16,000. Buys all rights. Byline given. Pays on publication to professional writers. Publishes ms an average of 4 months after acceptance. Reports in 2 months. Query or submit 3 double-spaced copies of complete ms. Sample copy $4.50.

Nonfiction: Scientific and environmental material, and effects of technology on society. Preferred length: 2,500-4,500 words for full-length article. Pays $100-300, depending on material. Also accepts shorter articles (1,000-1,700 words) for "Overview" section. Pays $100. "All full-length articles must be annotated (referenced), and all conclusions must follow logically from the facts and arguments presented." Prefers articles centering around policy-oriented, public decision-making, scientific and technological issues.

ENVIRONMENTAL ACTION, 1525 New Hampshire Ave. NW, Washington DC 20036. (202)745-4870. FAX: (202)745-4880. Editor: Hawley Truax. 30% freelance written. Bimonthly magazine on environmental news and policy. "*Environmental Action* provides balanced reporting on key environmental issues facing the U.S. – particularly at a national level. Articles are written for a general audience – we don't assume any knowledge of environmental conditions or problems." Estab. 1970. Circ. 16,000. Pays on publication. Publishes ms an average of 2 months after acceptance. Kill fee negotiated. Byline given. Buys first North American serial rights or second serial (reprint) rights. Simultaneous submissions OK if noted. Reports in 4 months. Sample copy for 9×12 SAE with 4 first class stamps; free writer's guidelines.

Nonfiction: Exposé, profile, news feature, political analysis, book reviews. No nature appreciation, personal history, adventure in nature, academic/journal articles, or opinion articles. Buys 20 mss/year. Query with published clips and résumé, or send complete ms. Length: 250-3,000 words. Pays $50-500. Sometimes pays expenses of writers on assignment.

Photos: State availability of photos (b&w prints preferred) with submission. Reviews contact sheets, negatives and prints. Offers $25/photo, $50/cover. Captions required. Buys one-time rights.

FORESTS & PEOPLE, Official Publication of the Louisiana Forestry Association, Louisiana Forestry Association, P.O. Drawer 5067, Alexandria LA 71307. (318)443-2558. Editor: Georgiann Gullett. 50% freelance written. Works with a small number of new/unpublished writers each year. Quarterly magazine covering Louisiana forests, forest industry, wood-related stories, wildlife for general readers, both in and out of the Louisiana forest industry. Estab. 1951. Circ. 7,500, readership 39,000. Pays on publication. Byline given. Not copyrighted. Simultaneous submissions and queries OK. Sample copy $2; writer's guidelines for #10 SASE.

Nonfiction: General interest (recreation, wildlife, crafts with wood, festivals); historical/nostalgic (logging towns, historical wooden buildings, forestry legends); interview/profile (of forest industry execs, foresters, loggers, wildlife managers, tree farmers); photo feature (of scenic forest, wetlands, logging operations); and technical (innovative equipment, chemicals, operations, forestland studies, or industry profiles). No research papers. Articles may cover a technical subject but must be understandable to the general public. Stories must be of interest to Louisiana readers." Buys 12 mss/year. Query with published clips. Length: open. Pays $100.

Photos: State availability of photos. Reviews b&w and color slides. Identification of subjects required.

INTERNATIONAL WILDLIFE, National Wildlife Federation, 8925 Leesburg Pike, Vienna VA 22184. Editor: Jonathan Fisher. 85% freelance written. Prefers to work with published/established writers. Bimonthly for persons interested in natural history, outdoor adventure and the environment. Estab. 1971. Circ. 650,000. **Pays on acceptance.** Publishes ms an average of 4 months after acceptance. Usually buys all rights to text. "We are now assigning most articles but will consider detailed proposals for quality feature material of interest to a broad audience." Reports in 6 weeks. Writer's guidelines for #10 SASE.

Nonfiction: Focuses on world wildlife, environmental problems and peoples' relationship to the natural world as reflected in such issues as population control, pollution, resource utilization, food production, etc. Stories deal with non-U.S. subjects. Especially interested in articles on animal behavior and other natural history, first-person experiences by scientists in the field, well-reported coverage

of wildlife-status case studies which also raise broader themes about international conservation, and timely issues. Query. Length: 2,000-2,500 words. Also in the market for short, 750-word "one pagers." Examine past issue for style and subject matter. Pays $1,200 minimum. Sometimes pays expenses of writers on assignment.
Photos: Purchases top-quality color photos; prefers packages of related photos and text, but single shots of exceptional interest and sequences also considered. Prefers Kodachrome or Fujichrome transparencies. Buys one-time rights.

MICHIGAN NATURAL RESOURCES MAGAZINE, State of Michigan Department of Natural Resources, P.O. Box 30034, Lansing MI 48909. (517)373-9267. Editor: N.R. McDowell. Managing Editor: Richard Morscheck. 60% freelance written. Works with a small number of new/unpublished writers each year. Bimonthly magazine covering natural resources in the Great Lakes area. Estab. 1931. Circ. 120,000. **Pays on acceptance.** Publishes ms an average of 6 months after acceptance. Byline given. Offers 100% kill fee. Buys first rights. Submit seasonal/holiday material 1 year in advance. Reports in 1 month. Sample copy for $3 and 9 × 12 SAE; writer's guidelines for #10 SASE.
Nonfiction: "All material must pertain to this region's natural resources: lakes, rivers, wildlife, flora and special features. No personal experience, domestic animal stories or animal rehabilitation." Buys 24 mss/year. Query with clips of published work. Length: 1,000-3,000 words. Pays $150-400. Sometimes pays the expenses of writers on assignment.
Photos: Gijsbert (Nick) vanFrankenhuyzen, photo editor. "Photos submitted with an article can help sell it, but they must be razor sharp in focus." Send photos with ms. Pays $50-200 for 35mm transparencies; Fuji or Kodachrome preferred. Model releases and identification of subjects required. Buys one-time rights.
Tips: "We hope to exemplify why Michigan's natural resources are valuable to people and vice versa."

NATIONAL PARKS, 1015 31st St., Washington DC 20007. (202)944-8565. FAX: (202)944-8535. Senior Editor: Sue Dodge. 75% freelance written. Prefers to work with published/established writers. Bimonthly magazine for a highly educated audience interested in preservation of National Park System units, natural areas and protection of wildlife habitat. Estab. 1917. Circ. 300,000. **Pays on acceptance.** Publishes ms an average of 6 months after acceptance. Buys first North American serial rights and second serial (reprint) rights. Submit seasonal/holiday material 5 months in advance. Query for electronic submissions. Reports in 10 weeks. Sample copy $3; writer's guidelines for SASE.
Nonfiction: Exposé (on threats, wildlife problems to national parks); descriptive articles about new or proposed national parks and wilderness parks; brief natural history pieces describing park geology, wildlife, or plants; "adventures" in national parks (cross country skiing, bouldering, mountain climbing, kayaking, canoeing, backpacking); and travel tips to national parks. All material must relate to national parks. No poetry or philosophical essays. No first person narratives. Buys 6-10 unsolicited mss/year. "We prefer queries rather than unsolicited stories." Length: 1,000-1,500 words. Pays $75-800.
Photos: State availability of photos or send photos with ms. Pays $25-50 for 8 × 10 b&w glossy prints; $35-150 for transparencies. Captions required. Buys first North American serial rights.

NATIONAL WILDLIFE, National Wildlife Federation, 8925 Leesburg Pike, Vienna VA 22184. (703)790-4510. Editor-in-Chief: Bob Strohm. Editor: Mark Wexler. 90% freelance written. Works with a small number of new/unpublished writers each year. Bimonthly magazine on wildlife, natural history and environment. "Our purpose is to promote wise use of the nation's natural resources and to conserve and protect wildlife and its habitat. We reach a broad audience that is largely interested in wildlife conservation and nature photography. We avoid too much scientific detail and prefer anecdotal, natural history material." Estab. 1963. Circ. 950,000. **Pays on acceptance.** Publishes ms an average of 1 year after acceptance. Offers 25% kill fee. Buys all rights. Submit seasonal/holiday material 8 months in advance. Reports in 6 weeks. Sample copy for 9 × 12 SAE and 4 first class stamps; writer's guidelines for #10 SASE.
Nonfiction: General interest (2,500-word features on wildlife, new discoveries, behavior, or the environment); how-to (an outdoor or nature related activity); personal experience (outdoor adventure); photo feature (wildlife); and short 700-word features on an unusual individual or new scientific discovery relating to nature. Buys 50 mss/year. Query with or without published clips. Length: 750-2,500 words. Pays $500-2,000. Sometimes pays expenses of writers on assignment.
Photos: John Nuhn, photo editor. State availability of photos or send photos with query. Reviews 35mm transparencies. Pays $250-750. Buys one-time rights.
Tips: "Writers can break in with us more readily by proposing subjects (initially) that will take only one or two pages in the magazine (short features)."

NATURAL HISTORY, Natural History Magazine, Central Park West at 79th St., New York NY 10024. Editor: Alan Ternes. Over 75% freelance written. Monthly magazine for well-educated, ecologically aware audience: professional people, scientists and scholars. Circ. 520,000. Pays on publication. Publishes ms an average of 3 months after acceptance. Byline given. Buys first serial rights and becomes agent for second serial (reprint) rights. Submit seasonal material at least 6 months in advance.

Nonfiction: Uses all types of scientific articles except chemistry and physics—emphasis is on the biological sciences and anthropology. Prefers professional scientists as authors. "We always want to see new research findings in almost all the branches of the natural sciences—anthropology, archeology, zoology and ornithology. We find that it is particularly difficult to get something new in herpetology (amphibians and reptiles) or entomology (insects), and we would like to see material in those fields. We lean heavily toward writers who are scientists. We expect high standards of writing and research. We favor an ecological slant in most of our pieces, but do not generally lobby for causes, environmental or other. The writer should have a deep knowledge of his subject, then submit original ideas either in query or by manuscript. Acceptance is more likely if article is accompanied by high-quality photographs." Buys 60 mss/year. Query or submit complete ms. Length: 2,000-4,000 words. Pays $750-1,000, plus additional payment for photos used.

Photos: Rarely uses 8×10 b&w glossy prints; pays $125/page maximum. Much color is used; pays $300 for inside and up to $500 for cover. Buys one-time rights.

Tips: "Learn about something in depth before you bother writing about it."

‡**OCEAN REALM, Magazine of the Sea,** 342 W. Sunset Rd., San Antonio TX 78209. (512)824-8099. Editors: Charlene deJori and Cheryl Schorp. 90% freelance written. Quarterly magazine covering all subjects relating to the sea—scuba diving, natural history, travel, adventure, science, ecology, oceanography, geography, people and cultures, seafood—all with emphasis on expanding some awareness of the ocean. Circ. 40,000. Pays on publication. Reports in 1 month on queries. Sample copy $5.95 with 9×12 SASE; writer's guidelines for #10 SASE.

Nonfiction: Historical/nostalgic, personal experience, travel, science and anything relating to the sea. Query with or without published clips, or send complete ms. Length: 3,000-4,000 words. Pays $50 per page for articles and photographs.

Photos: Send photos with submission, registered—return postage for photos a must. Offers $25 per photo, purchased with or without ms.

Columns/Departments: Marine Life (sea animals), 1,000 words; Ocean Art (artists of marine subjects), 500 words; Ocean Profile (unsung heroes working in the sea), 1,000 words; Marine Cuisine (seafood and seafood industry), 1,000-1,500 words.

Tips: "This is an excellent market for new, untried writers who have something to say about places they've gone and things they've seen. We're as much interested in personal experience and unusual approaches to a foreign land and culture as we are in the scenery underwater; the influence of the ocean on the land, however, should be a central point of a story."

OUTDOOR AMERICA, 1401 Wilson Blvd., Level B, Arlington VA 22209. (703)528-1818. FAX: (703)528-1836. Editor: Kristin Merriman. 30% freelance written. Prefers to work with published/established writers. Quarterly magazine about natural resource conservation and outdoor recreation for sports enthusiasts and local conservationists who are members of the Izaak Walton League. Estab. 1922. Circ. 55,000. Pays half on receipt of manuscript, half on publication. Publishes ms an average of 4 months after acceptance. Byline and brief biography given. Buys one-time North American rights, depending on arrangements with author. "Considers previously published material if there's not a lot of audience overlap." Query first. Submit seasonal material 6 months in advance. Reports in 1 month. Sample copy $1.50 with 9×12 SAE; writer's guidelines for SASE.

Nonfiction: "We are interested in thoroughly researched, well-written pieces on current natural resource and recreation issues of national importance (threats to water, fisheries, wildlife habitat, air, public lands, soil, etc.); articles on wildlife management controversies, and first-person essays and humor pieces on outdoor recreation themes (fishing, hunting, camping, ethical outdoor behavior, etc.)." Length: 1,500-2,500 words. Payment: 20¢/word; 10¢/word for reprints.

Photos: Reviews 5×7 b&w glossy prints and 35mm and larger transparencies. Additional payment for photos with ms negotiated. Pays $225 for covers. Captions and model releases required. Buys one-time rights.

Tips: "Writers should obtain guidelines and sample issue *before* querying us. They will understand our needs and editorial focus much better if they've done this. Queries submitted without the writer having read the guidelines are *almost always* off base and almost always rejected."

PACIFIC DISCOVERY, California Academy of Sciences, Golden Gate Park, San Francisco CA 94118. (415)750-7116. FAX: (415)750-7106. Editor: Keith Howell. 100% freelance written. Prefers to work with published/established writers. "A journal of nature and culture in California, the West, the Pacific and Pacific Rim countries read by scientists, naturalists, teachers, students, and others having a keen interest in knowing the natural world more thoroughly." Published quarterly by the California Academy of Sciences. Estab. 1948. Circ. 30,000. Buys first North American serial rights on articles; one-time rights on photos. Pays on publication. Query for electronic submissions. Usually reports within

1 month. Sample copy for 9×12 SAE and $1.25 postage; writer's guidelines for #10 SASE.

Nonfiction: "Subjects of articles include behavior and natural history of animals and plants, ecology, evolution, anthropology, geology, paleontology, biogeography, taxonomy and related topics in the natural sciences. Occasional articles are published on the history of natural science, exploration, astronomy and archaeology. Emphasis is on current research findings. Authors need not be scientists; however, all articles must be based, at least in part, on firsthand fieldwork. Accuracy is crucial." Query with 100-word summary of projected article for review before preparing finished ms. Length: 800-4,000 words. Pays 25¢/word.

Photos: Send photos with submission "even if an author judges that his own photos should not be reproduced. Referrals to professional photographers with coverage of the subject will be greatly appreciated." Reviews 35mm, 4×5 or other transparencies or 8×10 b&w glossy prints. Offers $75-175 and $200 for the cover. Buys one-time rights.

SEA FRONTIERS, 4600 Rickenbacker Causeway, P.O. Box 499900, Virginia Key, Miami FL 33149. (305)361-4888. Editor: Bonnie Bilyeu Gordon. Executive Editor: Jean Bradfisch. 80% freelance written. Works with a small number of new/unpublished writers each year. Bimonthly. "For anyone interested in the sea, its conservation, and the life it contains. Our audience is the general public with an interest in the ocean." Circ. 65,000. **Pays on acceptance.** Publishes ms an average of 4-10 months after acceptance. Byline given. Buys first serial rights. Reports on submissions in 2 months. Sample copy $3; writer's guidelines for SASE.

Nonfiction: "Articles (with illustrations) covering interesting and little known facts about the sea, marine life, chemistry, geology, physics, fisheries, mining, engineering, navigation, influences on weather and climate, ecology, conservation, explorations, discoveries or advances in our knowledge of the marine sciences, or describing the activities of oceanographic laboratories or expeditions to any part of the world. Emphasis should be on research and discoveries rather than personalities involved." Buys 40-50 mss/year. Query. Length: 1,000-3,000 words. Pays 25¢/word minimum.

Photos: Reviews 8×10 b&w glossy prints and 35mm (or larger) color transparencies. Pays $100 minimum per full page.

Tips: "Query should include a paragraph or two that tells the subject, the angle or approach to be taken, and the writer's qualifications for covering this subject."

SIERRA, 730 Polk St., San Francisco CA 94109. (415)923-5656. FAX: (415)776-0350. Editor-in-Chief: Jonathan F. King. Managing Editor: Annie Stine. Senior Editor: Joan Hamilton. Senior Editor: Reed McManus. 80% freelance written. Works with a small number of new/unpublished writers each year. Bimonthly magazine emphasizing conservation and environmental politics for people who are well educated, activist, outdoor-oriented and politically well informed with a dedication to conservation. Estab. 1893. Circ. 413,000. **Pays on acceptance.** Publishes ms an average of 4 months after acceptance. Byline given. Buys first North American serial rights. Query for electronic submissions. Reports in 2 months. Writer's guidelines for SAE and 2 first class stamps.

Nonfiction: Exposé (well-documented on environmental issues of national importance such as energy, wilderness, forests, etc.); general interest (well-researched nontechnical pieces on areas of particular environmental concern); historical (relevant to environmental concerns); how-to and equipment pieces (on camping, climbing, outdoor photography, etc.); profiles (of environmental activists); interview (with very prominent figures in the field); photo feature (photo essays on threatened or scenic areas); and journalistic treatments of semi-technical topics (energy sources, wildlife management, land use, waste management, etc.). No "My trip to . . ." or "why we must save wildlife/nature" articles; no poetry or general superficial essays on environmentalism and local environmental issues. Buys 10-15 mss/issue. Query with published clips. Length: 300-3,000 words. Pays $75-1,500. Sometimes pays limited expenses of writers on assignment.

Photos: Silvana Nova, art and production manager. State availability of photos. Pays $300 maximum for transparencies; more for cover photos. Buys one-time rights.

Columns/Departments: Book reviews. Buys 20-25 mss/year. Length: 750-1,000 words. Pays $100; submit queries to Mark Mardon, assistant editor. For Younger Readers, natural history and conservation topics presented for children ages 8 to 13. Pays $200-500; submit queries to Reed McManus, senior editor. Afield, short (250-300 word) punchy pieces for graphic-heavy front-of-book section.

Tips: "Queries should include an outline of how the topic would be covered and a mention of the political appropriateness and timeliness of the article. Familiarity with Sierra Club positions and policies is recommended. Statements of the writer's qualifications should be included. We don't have fillers in our format."

SNOWY EGRET, The Fair Press, P.O. Box 9, Bowling Green IN 47833. (812)829-4339. Editors: Karl Barnebey and Michael Aycock. 95% freelance written. Semiannual magazine of natural history from literary, artistic, philosophical and historical perspectives. "We are interested in works that celebrate the abundance and beauty of nature, encourage a love and respect for the natural world, and examine the variety of way, both positive and negative, through which human beings interact with the environment." Circ. 500. Pays on publication. Publishes ms an average of 6 months after acceptance. Buys first North American serial rights and one-time rights. Submit seasonal/holiday material 6 months in advance. Simultaneous and photocopied submissions OK. Reports in 2 weeks on queries; 1 month on mss. Sample copy $8 with 9 × 12. Prospectus with recently published work and writer's guidelines for 6 × 9 SASE.

Nonfiction: Essays, general interest, historical, how-to, humor, inspirational, interview/profile, opinion, personal experience and travel. "No topical, dated articles, highly scientific or technical pieces." Buys 20 mss/year. Send complete ms. Length: 500-10,000. Pays $2/page.

Fiction: Literary with natural history orientation. "No popular and genre fiction." Buys up to 10 mss/year. Send complete ms. Length: 500-10,000. Pays $2/page.

Poetry: Nature-oriented: avant-garde, free verse, haiku, light verse and traditional. Buys 20 poems/year. Pays $2/poem to $4/page.

Tips: "Make sure that all general points, ideas, messages, etc. are thoroughly rooted in detailed observations, shared wtih the reader through description, dialogue, and narrative. The reader needs to see what you've seen, live what you've lived. Whenever possible the subject shown should be allowed to carry its own message, to speak for itself. We look for book reviews, essays, poetry, fiction, conservation and environmental studies based on first-hand observations of plants and animals that show an awareness of detail and a thorough-going familiarity with the organisms or habitats in question."

‡**SUMMIT, The Mountain Journal**, 111 Schweitz Rd., Fleetwood PA 19522. (215)682-1701. Editor: John Harlin. 100% freelance written. Quarterly magazine covering mountain culture, environment and sport. "Sophisticated, inspired, introspective and passionate writing for an educated audience with high literary standards. The writing must relate to the mountain world, but this can be treated broadly." Estab. 1990. Circ. 20,000. **Pays on acceptance.** Publishes ms an average of 3-9 months after acceptance. Byline given. Offers 25% kill fee. Buys first North American serial rights, first rights, second serial (reprint) rights or simultaneous rights. Submit seasonal/holiday material 3-12 months in advance. Simultaneous and previously published submissions OK. Query for electronic submissions. Reports in 1 month. Sample copy $3 with 9 × 12 SAE and 10 first class stamps "or send $5.40 w/SAE and we'll stamp." Writer's guidelines for SAE with 1 first class stamp.

Nonfiction: Book excerpts, essays, exposé, general interest, historical/nostalgic, humor, inspirational, interview/profile, opinion, personal experience, photo feature and travel. "No service pieces, or what-I-did stories that don't have strong literary content." Buys 30 mss/year. Query with or without published clips, or send complete ms. Length: 500-5,000 words. Pays $200-800.

Photos: State availability of photos with query or ms. Send photos with submission. Reviews contact sheets, transparencies and prints. Offers $50-175 per photo. Identification of subjects required. Buys one-time rights.

Columns/Departments: Mountain Times (news on mountain world), 500-1,000 words; Reviews (essay on several books of a genre within the mountain world), 800-1,200 words. Buys 8 mss/year. Query with published clips or send complete ms. Pays $100-250.

Fiction: Adventure, ethnic, experimental, historical, humorous, novel excerpts. Buys 1-4 mss/year. Send complete ms. Length: 500-5,000 words. Pays $200-800.

Poetry: Avant-garde, free verse, Haiku, light verse, traditional. Pays $50-200.

Fillers: Facts and short humor. Pays $50 minimum.

Tips: "If we don't know the writer, submitting complete manuscripts or partial manuscripts helps. Published clips help, but we distrust them because they've already been edited. Know the magazine, *know your subject* and *know your writing*. Mountain Times news pieces can be about any place and anything in the mountain world but they tend to stress environment issues. The report should be timeless even though there is a newsy hook."

WILDLIFE CONSERVATION, New York Zoological Society, 185 St. and Southern Blvd., Bronx NY 10460. (212)220-5121. FAX: (212)584-2625. Editor-in-Chief: Eugene J. Walter, Jr. Executive Editor: Penny O'Prey. 90% freelance written. Bimonthly magazine covering wildlife. Estab. 1895. Circ. 141,858. **Pays on acceptance.** Publishes ms an average of 1 year or more after acceptance. Byline given. Buys first North American serial rights. Submit seasonal/holiday material 1 year in advance. Simultaneous submissions OK. Reports on 1 month on queries; 3 months on mss. Sample copy $2.95 with 9 × 12 and 6 first class stamps. Free writer's guidelines with SASE.

The double dagger before a listing indicates that the listing is new in this edition. New markets are often more receptive to freelance submissions.

Nonfiction: Nancy Simmons, senior editor. Essays, personal experience and wildlife articles. No pet or any domestic animal stories. Buys 12 mss/year. Query. Length 1,500-2,500 words. Pays $750-3,000 for assigned articles; $500-1,000 for unsolicited articles.

Photos: State availability of photos with submission. Reviews transparencies. Buys one-time rights.

Personal Computers

Personal computer magazines continue to change and evolve. The most successful have a strong focus on a particular family of computers or widely-used applications and carefully target a specific type of computer use. Magazines serving MS-DOS and Macintosh families of computers are expected to grow, while new technology will also offer opportunities for new titles. Some of the magazines offer an on-line service for readers in which they can get the magazine alone or with a supplement on computer disk. Be sure you see the most recent issue of a magazine before submitting material.

AMAZING COMPUTING, PiM Publications, Inc., 1 Currant Place, Box 869, Fall River MA 02720. (508)678-4200. Submissions Editor: Elizabeth G. Fedorzyn. Managing Editor: Donald D. Hicks. 90% freelance written. Monthly magazine for the Commodore Amiga computer system user. Circ. 35,000. Pays on publication. Publishes ms an average of 2-4 months after acceptance. Byline given. Buys all rights. Query for electronic submissions. Sample copy for $5; free writer's guidelines.

Nonfiction: How-to, new product, technical, reviews and tutorials. Buys 200 mss/year. Query. Length: 1,000 words minimum. Pays $65/page.

Photos: Send photos with submission. Reviews 4×5 prints. Offers $25 per photo. Captions required. Buys all rights.

Columns/Departments: Reviews, Programs. Buys 100 mss/year. Query. Length: 1,000-5,000 words.

‡ATARI EXPLORER, The Official Atari Journal, Jainschigg Communications, 29-05 Broadway, Astoria NY 11106. Editor: John B. Jainschigg. 50% freelance written. A b-imonthly magazine about Atari computers, game systems, and information appliances. "Our audience consists of users of all Atari products: computers, game systems, peripherals, etc., and our objective is to help them get the most out of their Atari investment." Circ. 70,000. **Pays on acceptance.** Publishes ms an average of 4 months after acceptance. Byline given. Offers 20% kill fee. Buys all rights. Query for electronic submissions. Reports in 6 weeks. Sample copy $3 with 9×13 SAE and $1.67 postage.

Nonfiction: How-to (applications), interview/profile (of people who use Atari products in interesting ways), product reviews. No fiction, opinion. Buys 50 mss/year. Send query. Length: 750-4,000 words. Pays $50-600. Sometimes pays the expenses of writers on assignment.

Tips: "Writers must have access to and use Atari products. All submissions must be relevant to Atari users."

BYTE MAGAZINE, 1 Phoenix Mill Lane, Peterborough NH 03458. (603)924-9281. Editor: Fred Langa. Monthly magazine covering personal computers for college-educated, professional users of computers. 50% freelance written. Estab. 1975. Circ. 461,000. **Pays on acceptance.** Byline given. Buys all rights. Reports on rejections in 6 weeks; 3 months if accepted. Electronic submissions accepted, IBM or Macintosh compatible. Sample copy $3.50; writer's guidelines for #10 SASE.

Nonfiction: News, reviews, and in-depth discussions of topics related to microcomputers or technology. Buys 160 mss/year. Query. Length: 1,500-5,000 words. Pay is $50-1,000 + for assigned articles; $500-750 for unassigned.

Tips: "Read several issues of BYTE to see what we cover, and how we cover it. Read technical journals to stay on the cutting edge of new technology and trends. Send us a proposal with a short outline of an article explaining some new technology, software trend, and the relevance to advanced business users of personal computers. Our readers want accurate, useful, technical information; not fluff and not meaningless data presented without insight or analysis."

CLOSING THE GAP, INC., P.O. Box 68, Henderson MN 56044. (612)248-3294. Managing Editor: Paul M. Malchow. 40% freelance written. Eager to work with new/unpublished writers. Bimonthly tabloid covering microcomputers for handicapped readers, special education and rehabilitation professionals. "We focus on currently available products and procedures written for the layperson that incorporate microcomputers to enhance the educational opportunities and quality of life for persons with disabilities." Estab. 1982. Circ. 10,000. Pays on publication. Publishes ms an average of 2 months after acceptance. Byline given. Buys first serial rights. Simultaneous queries and simultaneous submissions OK. Query for electronic submissions. Reports in 2 weeks. Free sample copy and writer's guidelines.

Nonfiction: How-to (simple modifications to computers or programs to aid handicapped persons); interview/profile (users or developers of computers to aid handicapped persons); new product (computer products to aid handicapped persons); personal experience (by a handicapped person or on use of microcomputer to aid a handicapped person); articles of current research on projects on microcomputers to aid persons with disabilities; and articles that examine current legislation, social trends and new projects that deal with computer technology for persons with disabilities. No highly technical "computer hobbyist" pieces. Buys 25 mss/year. Query. Length: 500-2,000 words. Pays $25 and up (negotiable). "Many authors' material runs without financial compensation."

Tips: "Knowledge of the subject is vital, but freelancers do not need to be computer geniuses. Clarity is essential; articles must be able to be understood by a layperson. All departments are open to freelancers. We are looking for new ideas. If you saw it in some other computer publication, don't bother submitting. *CTG*'s emphasis is on increasing computer user skills in our area of interest, not developing hobbyist or technical skills. The most frequent mistakes made by writers in completing an article for us is that their submissions are too technical—they associate 'computer' with hobbyist, often their own perspective—and don't realize our readers are not hobbyists or hackers."

COMPUTER LANGUAGE, Miller Freeman Publications, 600 Harrison St., San Francisco CA 94107. (415)905-2501. Editor: Larry O'Brien. Managing Editor: Brett Warren. 100% freelance written. Monthly magazine covering programming languages and software design. Estab. 1902. Circ. 65,000. Pays on publication. Byline given. Buys first rights. Query for electronic submissions. Free sample copy and writer's guidelines. Query author's BBS: (415)882-9915 (300/1,200 baud).

Nonfiction: Interview/profile, new product, technical how-to and product reviews. Buys 150 mss/year. Query. Length: 1,500-4,000. Pays $100-650.

Columns/Departments: Product Wrap-Up (in-depth comparative software review); Software Review. Buys 24 mss/year. Query only.

Tips: "Introduce idea for article and/or send manuscripts to editor; propose to become software reviewer. Current hot topics: object-oriented programming, OS/2, multitasking, 80386, TSRs, C, Pascal, Ada, BASIC. Communicate with editors via online edition on CompuServe. 'Go CLMFORUM' to access the Forum; address editor Larry O'Brien."

COMPUTERCRAFT, The Practical Magazine for Personal Computers & Microcontrollers, (formerly *Modern Electronics*), CQ Communications, 76 N. Broadway, Hicksville NY 11801. (516)681-2922. FAX: (516)681-2926. 90% freelance written. Monthly magazine covering single-board computers, microcontrolled electronic devices, software, personal computers, electronic circuitry, construction projects and technology for readers with a technical affinity. Estab. 1984. Circ. 50,000. **Pays on acceptance.** Publishes ms an average of 3 months after acceptance. Byline given. Offers 25% kill fee. Buys first North American serial rights. Query for electronic submissions. Reports in 2 weeks on queries; 3 weeks on mss. Sample copy for 9×12 SAE and $1; writer's guidelines for #10 SASE.

Nonfiction: How-to (construction projects, applications, computer enhancements, upgrading and troubleshooting); new product (reviews); opinion (experiences with computer products); technical (features and tutorials: circuits, applications). "Articles must be technically accurate. Writing should be 'loose,' not textbookish." No long computer programs. Buys 125 mss/year. Query. Length: 500-4,000 words. Pays $90-150/published page. Sometimes pays expenses of writers on assignment.

Photos: Send photos with query or ms. Reviews transparencies and 5×7 b&w prints. Captions, model releases, and identification of subjects required. Buys variable rights depending on mss.

Tips: "The writer must have technical or applications acumen and well-researched material. Articles should reflect the latest products and technology. Sharp, interesting photos are helpful, as are rough, clean illustrations for re-drawing. Cover useful improvements to existing personal computers. Areas most open to freelancers include feature articles, technical tutorials, and projects to build. Some writers exhibit problems with longer pieces due to limited technical knowledge and/or poor organization. We can accept more short pieces."

COMPUTOREDGE, San Diego's Computer Magazine, The Byte Buyer, Inc., P.O. Box 83086, San Diego CA 92138. (619)573-0315. FAX: (619)573-0205. Editors: Tina Rathbone and Wally Wang. 90% freelance written. A weekly magazine on computers. "We cater to the novice/beginner/first-time computer buyer. Humor is welcome." Estab. 1983. Circ. 70,000. Pays on publication. Net 30 day payment after publication. Byline given. Offers $15 kill fee. Buys first North American serial rights. Submit seasonal/holiday material 2 months in advance. Query for electronic submissions. Reports in 2 months. Writer's guidelines for #10 SASE "or call (619)573-1675 with your modem and download writer's guidelines. Read sample issue on-line." Sample issue for $1.75 postage.

Nonfiction: General interest (computer), how-to, humor and personal experience. Buys 80 mss/year. Send complete ms. Length: 300-1,200 words. Pays 8-10¢/word for assigned articles. Pays 5-10¢/word for unsolicited articles. State availability of photos with submission. Captions and identification of subjects required. Buys one-time rights.

Columns/Departments: Beyond Personal Computing (a reader's personal experience). Buys 80 mss/year. Send complete ms. Length: 500-1,000 words. Pays $50.
Fiction: Confession, fantasy and slice-of-life vignettes. Buys 5 mss/year. Send complete ms. Length: 500-1,200 words. Pays 8-10¢/word.
Tips: "Be relentless. Convey technical information in an understandable, interesting way. We like light material, but not fluff. Write as if you're speaking with a friend. Avoid the typical 'Love at First Byte' article. Avoid the 'How My Grandmother Loves Her New Computer' article. Avoid sexual innuendoes/metaphors. Reading a sample issue is advised."

‡ELECTRONIC COMPOSITION AND IMAGING, Youngblood Publishing, Suite 102, 505 Consumers Rd., Willowdale, Ontario M2J 4V8 Canada. (416)492-5777. FAX: (416)492-7595. Editor: Chris Dickman. 70% freelance written. Bimonthly magazine on desktop publishing, computer graphics, video and animation. Circ. 25,000. Pays on publication. Publishes ms an average of 2 months after acceptance. Byline given. Offers $100 kill fee. Buys first North American serial rights. Query for electronic submissions. Reports in 1 week on queries; 2 weeks on mss. Free sample copy and writer's guidelines.
Nonfiction: How-to (computers and graphics or publishing), interview/profile, new product, technical. "No humor." Buys 60 mss/year. Query with published clips. Length: 1,000-3,000 words. Pays $200-600 for assigned articles; $100-300 for unsolicited articles.
Photos: Sometimes pays the expenses of writers on assignment. State availability of photos with submission. Reviews negatives, 4×5 transparencies and 4×5 prints. Offers $10-50 per photo. Captions required. Buys one-time rights.
Tips: "Call to discuss article ideas, or fax query, or mail. Writers must know their areas of electronic composition and imaging in depth."

GENEALOGICAL COMPUTING, Ancestry Inc., P.O. Box 476, Salt Lake City UT 84110. (801)531-1790. FAX: (801)531-1798. Editor: Robert Passaro. 50% freelance written. Quarterly magazine on genealogy, using computers. Designed for genealogists who use computers for records management. "We publish articles on all types of computers: PC, Macintosh, Apple II, etc." Estab. 1981. Circ. 3,000. Pays on publication. Publishes ms an average of 4 months after acceptance. Byline given. Buys all rights. Query for electronic submissions. Reports in 2 months.
Nonfiction: New product, personal experience (with software), technical (telecommunications, data exchange, data base development) how-to, reviews, opinion and programming. "Articles on pure genealogy cannot be accepted; this also applies to straight computer technology." Query with outline/summary. Length: 1,300-4,000 words. Pays $100.
Tips: "We need how-to articles describing methods of managing genealogical information with your computer. We accept a *limited* number of pertinent BASIC programs or programming ideas for publication."

HOME OFFICE COMPUTING, Scholastic Inc., 730 Broadway, New York NY 10003. Editor-in-Chief: Claudia Cohl. Editor: Bernadette Grey. 75% freelance written. Monthly magazine on home/small business and computing. Estab. 1983. Circ. 375,000. **Pays on acceptance.** Publishes ms an average of 6 weeks after acceptance. Byline given. Offers 25% kill fee. Buys all rights or makes work-for-hire assignments. Submit seasonal/holiday material 6 months in advance. Simultaneous submissions OK. Query for electronic submissions. Free sample copy and writer's guidelines for 8½×11 SAE.
Nonfiction: How-to, interview/profile, new product, technical, reviews. "No fiction, humor, opinion." Buys 30 mss/year. Query with published clips. Length: 200-4,000 words. Pays $100-2,000.
Photos: Sometimes pays the expenses of writers on assignment. State availability of photos with submission.
Columns/Departments: Sales & Marketing, Desktop Publishing, Business Opportunities, Resources, Profiles, Hardware/Software Reviews. Length: 500-1,000 words. Pays $100-2,000.
Tips: "Submission must be on disk or telecommunicated."

MICROAGE QUARTERLY, MicroAge Computer Stores, Inc., Box 1920, Tempe AZ 85281. (602)968-3168. Managing Editor: David Lucas. 90% freelance written. Prefers to work with published/established writers. A quarterly magazine for business users of microcomputers. Circ. 200,000. **Pays on acceptance.** Publishes ms an average of 3 months after acceptance. Byline given. Offers kill fee. Buys first North American serial rights, one-time rights and second serial (reprint) rights. Sample copy and writer's guidelines for 9×12 SAE with $1.50 postage.
Nonfiction: Query with published clips. Length: 800-2,000 words. Pays $200-1,200. Pays the phone expenses of writers on assignment.
Columns/Departments: Changing Market (changes in uses of business-oriented microcomputer equipment—what affects the market, and how it changes); Changing Technology (changes/improvements in microcomputer technology that affect the business user); and Changing Industry (adaptations in the microcomputer industry); all 1,000-2,000 words.

Tips: "We're looking for problem-solving articles on office automation and microcomputer applications oriented toward small- and medium-sized businesses. We're willing to discuss ideas with experienced business or computer-literate writers. Please, no queries on home-computer subjects."

MICROpendium, Covering the TI99/4A, Myarc 9640 compatibles, Burns-Koloen Communications Inc., P.O. Box 1343, Round Rock TX 78664. (512)255-1512. Editor: Laura Burns. 40% freelance written. Eager to work with new/unpublished writers. A monthly magazine for users of the "orphaned" TI99/4A. "We are interested in helping users get the most out of their home computers." Estab. 1984. Circ. 6,000. Pays on publication. Publishes ms an average of 2-3 months after acceptance. Byline given. Buys second serial rights. Previously published submissions OK. Query for electronic submission. Reports in 2 weeks on queries; 2 months on manuscripts. Free sample copy and writer's guidelines.

Nonfiction: Book excerpts; how-to (computer applications); interview/profile (of computer "personalities," e.g. a software developer concentrating more on "how-to" than personality); and opinion (product reviews, hardware and software). Buys 30-50 mss/year. Query with or without published clips, or send complete ms. "We can do some articles as a series if they are lengthy, yet worthwhile." Pays $10-150, depending on length. No pay for product announcements. Sometimes pays the expenses of writers on assignment.

Photos: Send photos with submission. Reviews contact sheets, negatives, transparencies, and prints (b&w preferred). Buys negotiable rights.

Columns/Departments: User Notes (tips and brief routines for the computer) 100 words and up. Buys 35-40 mss/year. Send complete ms. Pays $10.

Tips: "We have more regularly scheduled columnists, which may reduce the amount we accept from others. The area most open to freelancers is product reviews on hardware and software. The writer should be a sophisticated TI99/4A computer user. We are more interested in advising our readers of the availability of good products than in 'panning' poor ones. We are interested in coverage of the Geneve 9640 by Myarc. We are not at all interested in general computer or technology-related articles unrelated to TI or Myarc computers."

PC COMPUTING, Ziff-Davis Publishing Co., 950 Tower Ln., 20th Fl., Foster City CA 94404. (415)578-7000. Executive Editors: Ron White, Chris Shipley, Ed Bott, Sandy Reed. Monthly magazine on personal computing. Estab. 1988. Circ. 650,000. Pays on publication. Byline given. Offers negotiable kill fee. Makes work-for-hire assignments. Query for electronic submissions. Reports in 1 month. Sample copy for $2.95; writer's guidelines for #10 SASE.

Nonfiction: Book excerpts, how-to, interview/profile, new product, technical. Query with published clips. Payment negotiable. Sometimes pays expenses of writers on assignment.

Tips: "We prefer electronic mail for queries. Query the specific editor for each department. You may contact us on MCI Mail as follows: Ed Botts, 349-1742, Help and consumer education section; Ron White, 329-1704, news and reviews; Jean Atelsek, features editor; Sandy Reed, 382-6179, Working Smarter. Either name or number can be used for the online address."

PCM, The Personal Computing Magazine for Tandy Computer Users, Falsoft, Inc., Falsoft Bldg., 9509 U.S. Highway 42, Box 385, Prospect KY 40059. (502)228-4492. FAX: (502)228-5121. Editor: Lawrence C. Falk. Managing Editor: Judy Hutchinson. 75% freelance written. A monthly (brand specific) magazine for owners of the Tandy Model 100, 200 and 600 portable computer and the Tandy 1000, 1200, 2000 and 3000, 4000 and 5000. Estab. 1983. Circ. 54,874. Pays on publication. Publishes ms an average of 3 months after acceptance. Byline given. Buys full rights, and rights for disk service reprint. Submit seasonal/holiday material 4 months in advance. Query for electronic submissions. Reports in 2 months. Free writer's guidelines.

Nonfiction: Tony Olive, submissions editor. How-to. "We prefer articles with programs." No general interest material. Buys 80 mss/year. Send complete ms. "Do not query." Length: 300 words minimum. Pays $40-50/page.

Photos: State availability of photos. Rarely uses photos.

Tips: "At this time we are only interested in submissions for the Tandy MS-DOS and portable computers. Strong preference is given to submissions accompanied by brief program listings. All listings must be submitted on tape or disk as well as in hard copy form."

‡PORTABLE 100, Tandy Laptop Computing, Portable Computing International Corp., 145 Grove St. Ext., P.O. Box 428, Peterborough NH 03458. (603)924-9455. FAX: (603)924-9441. Editor: Terry Kepner. 80% freelance written. Eager to work with new/unpublished writers. Monthly magazine covering laptop computers, their software and peripherals. Estab. 1986. Pays on publication. Publishes ms an average of 4 months after acceptance. Byline given. Offers 30% kill fee. Buys first North American serial rights and the right to use the article again in a yearbook, compendium or "best of . . ." magazine or book. Submit seasonal/holiday material 6 months in advance. Previously published submissions OK.

Query for electronic submissions. Reports in 2 weeks. Sample copy $3.95 with 9×12 SAE and 5 first class stamps; writer's guidelines for #10 SASE.

Nonfiction: General interest, humor (April), interview/profile, new product reviews and technical. No articles on how to write programs in BASIC, "my first computer," etc. Buys 60 mss/year. Query with published clips, or send complete ms. Length: 1,000-4,000 words. Pays $22-330 for assigned articles; pays $22-264 for unsolicited articles. Sometimes pays the expenses of writers on assignment.

Photos: Send photos with submission. Especially reviews 8×10 prints; 3x5 prints acceptable. Offers $10-16.50 per photo. Identification of subjects required. Buys one-time and reprint rights.

Columns/Departments: "Columns are arranged case by case; some are written in-house, some are written by freelance authors." Send complete ms. Length: 700-1,000 words. Pays $52-82.50.

Fiction: Humorous (April). Buys 2-3 mss/year. Query. Length: 500-1,000 words. Pays $33-66.

Tips: "We want *application* stories: how lap top computers are being integrated into business and society. In general, the easiest way to break in is via a review of some software or hardware. You must write in first person."

PUBLISH, The Magazine for Graphic Communicators, MultiMedia Communications, Inc., 501 Second St., San Francisco CA 94107. (415)546-7722. Editor-in-Chief: Sandra Rosenzweig. Managing Editor: Leslie Steere. 80% freelance written. Monthly magazine on desktop publishing and presentations. "*Publish!* helps communications professionals learn to effectively use desktop publishing. The emphasis is on practical hands-on advice for computer novice and publishing professional alike." Estab. 1986. Circ. 107,000. **Pays on acceptance.** Publishes ms an average of 3 months after acceptance. Byline given. Buys first international rights. Query for electronic submissions. Reports in 3 weeks. Free writer's guidelines.

Nonfiction: Book excerpts, product reviews, how-to (publishing topics), interview/profile, news, new products, technical tips. Buys 120 mss/year. Query with published clips to Leslie Steere. Length: 300-2,500 words. Pays $300-2,000. Sometimes pays expenses of writers on assignment.

Photos: State availability of photos with submission. Reviews contact sheets. Captions and identification of subjects required.

WANG IN THE NEWS, an independent newspaper for Wang Computer Users, Publications and Communications, Inc., 12416 Hymeadow Dr., Austin TX 78750-1896. (512)250-9023. FAX: (512)331-6779. Editor: Larry Storer. 30-40% freelance written. Works with small number of new/unpublished writers each year. A monthly newspaper of technical articles relating to all Wang computer applications. Estab. 1987. Circ. 22,000. Pays on publication. Publishes ms an average of 1 month after acceptance. Byline given. Buys first North American serial rights and reprints from other PCI magazines. Simultaneous submissions OK. Query for electronic submissions. Sample copy and writer's guidelines for 9×12 SASE.

Nonfiction: How-to, interview/profile, new product, opinion and technical on Wang-related articles only. Query with or without published clips, or send complete ms. Length 500-1,500 words. Fees negotiable upon assignment, acceptance. Occasionally pays with subscription or other premiums; will negotiate. Sometimes pays the expenses of writers on assignment.

Photos: State availability of photos with submissions. Reviews contact sheets, transparencies, and prints. Offers $10 maximum/photo. Captions, model releases and identification of subjects required. Buys one-time rights.

Tips: "We accept submissions from Value Added Resellers of Wang and solicit material on all Wang computers and applications."

WORDPERFECT, THE MAGAZINE, WordPerfect Publishing Co., 270 W. Center St., Orem UT 84057. (801)226-5555. FAX: (801)226-8804. Editor: Clair F. Rees. 85% freelance written. Monthly magazine of "how-to" articles for users of various WordPerfect computer software. "Easy-to-understand articles written with *minimum* jargon. Articles should provide readers good, useful information about word processing and other computer functions." Estab. 1988. Circ. 200,000. Publishes ms an average of 6-8 months after acceptance. Byline given. Negotiable kill fee. Buys first world rights. Submit seasonal/holiday material 8 months in advance. Query for electronic submissions only (WordPerfect 4.2, 5.0 or 5.1). Reports in 2 months. Sample copy for 9×12 SAE with $1.25 postage. Free writer's guidelines.

Nonfiction: How-to, step-by-step applications (with keystrokes), humor, interview/company profile, new product and technical. Buys 120-160 mss/year. Query with or without published clips. Length: 800-1,800 words.

Photos: State availability of photos with submission. Reviews transparencies (35mm or larger). Offers no additional payment for photos accepted with ms. Captions and identification of subjects required. Buys one-time rights.

Columns/Departments: Macro Magic (WordPerfect macros), 1,000-1,400 words; Back to Basics (tips for beginners), 1,000-1,400 words; Final Keystrokes (humor), 800 words. Buys 90-120 mss/year. Query with published clips. Pays $400-700, on acceptance.

Tips: "Studying publication provides best information. We're looking for writers who can both inform *and* entertain our specialized group of readers."

Photography

Readers of these magazines use their cameras as a hobby and for weekend assignments. Magazines geared to the professional photographer can be found in the Photography Trade section.

AMERICAN PHOTO, (formerly *American Photographer*), Hatchette Magazines, Inc., 1633 Broadway, New York NY 10019. (212)767-6273. Editor: David Schonauer. Managing Editor: Sudie Redmond. Bimonthly magazine for advanced amateur, sophisticated general interest and pro-photographers. **Pays on acceptance.** Byline given. Buys first North American serial rights. Sample copy $3.50. Writer's guidelines for #10 SASE.

Nonfiction: Length: 500-2,500 words. Query. Sometimes pays writers expenses on assignment (reasonable).

Columns/Departments: Buys 10-30 mss/year. Length: 700 words maximum.

CAMERA & DARKROOM MAGAZINE, (formerly *Darkroom Photography Magazine*), Suite 300, 9171 Wilshire Blvd., Beverly Hills CA 90210. (213)858-7100. FAX: (213)274-7985. Editorial Director: Thom Harrop. Senior Editor: Anna Ercegovac. Editorial Assistant: Maggie Devcich. A photography magazine with darkroom emphasis, published 12 times/year for both professional and amateur photographers "interested in what goes on after the picture's been taken: processing, printing, manipulating, etc." Estab. 1979. Circ. 80,000. Pays on publication; pays regular writers on acceptance. Byline given. Buys one-time rights. Query for electronic submissions. Reports in 6 weeks. Sample copy and writer's guidelines for 8½ × 11 SASE.

Nonfiction: Historical/nostalgic (some photo-history pieces); how-to (darkroom equipment build-its); interview/profile (famous photographers); and technical (articles on darkroom techniques, tools, and tricks). No stories on shooting techniques, strobes, lighting, or in-camera image manipulation. Query or send complete ms. Length: varies. Pays $50-500, depending on project.

Photos: State availability or send photos with query or ms. Reviews transparencies and prints. "Supporting photographs are considered part of the manuscript package."

Columns/Departments: Darkroom Basics, Tools & Tricks, Special Effects, Making Money and Larger Formats. Query or send complete ms. Length: 800-1,200 words. "Published darkroom-related 'tips' receive free one-year subscriptions." Length: 100-150 words.

DARKROOM & CREATIVE CAMERA TECHNIQUES, Preston Publications, Inc., P.O. Box 48312, 7800 Merrimac Ave., Niles IL 60648. (708)965-0566. FAX: (708)965-7639. Publisher: Seaton Preston. Editor: David Alan Jay. 85% freelance written. Bimonthly publication covering the most technical aspects of photography: photochemistry, lighting, optics, processing and printing, Zone System, special effects, sensitometry, etc. Aimed at advanced workers. Estab. 1979. Circ. 45,000. Prefers to work with experienced photographer-writers; happy to work with excellent photographers whose writing skills are lacking. "Article conclusions often require experimental support." Pays within about 2 weeks of publication. Publishes ms an average of 6 months after acceptance. Byline given. Buys one-time rights. Query for electronic submissions. Sample copy $4.50; writer's guidelines with #10 SASE.

Nonfiction: Special interest articles within above listed topics; how-to, technical product reviews and photo features. Query or send complete ms. Length open, but most features run approximately 2,500 words or 3-4 magazine pages. Pays $100/published page for well-researched technical articles.

Photos: "Don't send photos with ms. Will request them at a later date." Ms payment includes photo payment. Prefers transparencies and 8 × 10 b&w prints. Captions, model releases (where appropriate) and technical information required. Buys one-time rights.

Tips: "We like serious photographic articles with a creative or technical bent. Successful writers for our magazine are doing what they write about. Also, any ms that addresses a serious problem facing many photographers will get our immediate attention."

PHOTO TRAVELER, (formerly *Western Photo Traveler*), Photo Traveler Publications, P.O. Box 39912, Los Angeles CA 90039. (213)660-0473. Editor: Nadine Orabona. 40% freelance written. Bimonthly newsletter on photo travel. "Travel articles on places or events in North America written from a photographer's point of view. Audience is amateur and professional photographers." Estab. 1985. Circ. 2,000. Pays on publication. Publishes ms an average of 3-6 months after acceptance. Byline given. Buys first, one-time or second serial (reprint) rights. Submit seasonal/holiday material 6 months in advance. Simultaneous and previously published submissions OK. Query for electronic submissions. Reports in 1 month on queries; 6 weeks on mss. Sample copy $5; writer's guidelines for SASE.

Nonfiction: Travel. "No regular travel articles." Buys 18 mss/year. Query with or without published clips, or send complete ms. Length: 500-2,500 words. Pays $25 for feature articles of more than 1,500 words and $10 for short articles of under 1,500 words.

Tips: "Writer should know photography and should visit the site or event. We want specifics such as best photo spots, best time of day or year, photo tips, recommended equipment, etc., but not a lot of technical advice. We like maps showing best photo spots."

POPULAR PHOTOGRAPHY, 1633 Broadway, New York NY 10019. Editorial Director: Jason Schneider. 20% freelance written. Monthly. "The magazine is designed for advanced amateur and professional photographers." Estab. 1937. Circ. 950,000. **Pays on acceptance.** Publishes ms an average of 4 months after acceptance. Byline given. "Rights purchased vary occasionally but are usually one-time." Submit material 4 months in advance. Reports in 1 month. SASE.

Nonfiction: "This magazine is mainly interested in instructional articles on photography that will help photographers improve their work. This includes all aspects of photography, from theory to camera use and darkroom procedures. Utter familiarity with the subject is a prerequisite to acceptance. It is best to submit article ideas in outline form since features are set up to fit the magazine's visual policies. Style should be easily readable but with plenty of factual data when a technique story is involved." Buys how-to, pictorial/technical pieces, historical articles. Query. Length: 500-2,000 words. Pays $250/page.

Photos: Monica Cipnic, picture editor. Interested in seeing portfolios in b&w and color of highest quality in terms of creativity, imagination and technique.

WILDLIFE PHOTOGRAPHY, P.O. Box 224, Greenville PA 16125. (412)588-3492. Editor: Rich Faler. 90% freelance written. Eager to work with new/unpublished writers. Quarterly magazine. "We are dedicated to the pursuit and capture of wildlife on film. Emphasis on how-to." Estab. 1985. Circ. 3,000. **Pays on acceptance.** Publishes ms an average of 1 year after acceptance. Byline given. Buys first rights, one-time rights or second serial (reprint) rights. Submit seasonal/holiday material 4 months in advance. Simultaneous and previously published submissions OK. Reports in 2 weeks on queries; 6 weeks on mss. Sample copy for $2 and 9 × 12 SAE; free writer's guidelines.

Nonfiction: Book excerpts; how-to (work with animals to take a good photo); interview/profile (of professionals); new product (of particular interest to wildlife photography); personal experience (with cameras in the field); and travel (where to find superb photo opportunities of plants and animals). No fiction or photography of pets, sports and scenery. Buys 30 mss/year. Query or send complete ms. Length: 500-3,000 words. Pays $30-100.

Photos: Send sharp photos with submission. Reviews contact sheets, negatives, transparencies and 5 × 7 prints as part of ms package. Photos not accepted separate from ms. Offers no additional payment for photos accepted with ms. Captions and identification of subjects required. Buys one-time rights.

Fillers: Anecdotes and facts. Buys 12/year. Length: 50-200 words. Pays $5-15.

Tips: "Give solid how-to info on how to photograph a specific species of wild animal. Send photos, not only of the subject, but of the photographer and his gear in action. The area of our publication most open to freelancers is feature articles."

Politics and World Affairs

These publications cover politics for the reader interested in current events. Other publications that will consider articles about politics and world affairs are listed under Business and Finance, Contemporary Culture, Regional and General Interest. For listings of publications geared toward the professional, see Government and Public Service and International Affairs in the Trade section.

AFRICA REPORT, 833 United Nations Plaza, New York NY 10017. (212)949-5666. FAX: (212)682-6421. Editor: Margaret A. Novicki. 60% freelance written. Prefers to work with published/established writers. A bimonthly magazine for U.S. citizens and residents with a special interest in African affairs for professional, business, academic or personal reasons. Not tourist-related. Circ. 10,500. Pays on publication. Publishes ms an average of 2 months after acceptance. Rights purchased vary with author and material; usually buys all rights, very occasionally first serial rights. Byline given unless otherwise requested. Sample copy for $4.50; free writer's guidelines.

Nonfiction: Interested in "African political, economic and cultural affairs, especially in relation to U.S. foreign policy and business objectives. Style should be journalistic but not academic or light. Articles should not be polemical or long on rhetoric but may be committed to a strong viewpoint. I do not want tourism articles." Would like to see in-depth topical analyses of lesser known African countries, based on residence or several months' stay in the country. Buys 15 unsolicited mss/year. Pays $150-250.

Photos: Photos purchased with or without accompanying mss with extra payment. Reviews b&w only. Pays $25. Submit 12×8 "half-plate."

Tips: "Read *Africa Report* and other international journals regularly. Become an expert on an African or Africa-related topic. Make sure your submissions fit the style, length and level of *Africa Report*."

CALIFORNIA JOURNAL, 1714 Capitol Ave., Sacramento CA 95814. (916)444-2840. Editor: Richard Zeiger. Managing Editor: A.G. Block. 50% freelance written. Prefers to work with published/established writers. Monthly magazine that emphasizes analysis of California politics and government. Estab. 1970. Circ. 20,000. Pays on publication. Publishes ms an average of 2 months after acceptance. Byline given. Buys all rights. Query for electronic submissions. Writer's guidelines for #10 SASE.

Nonfiction: Profiles of state and local government and political analysis. No outright advocacy pieces. Buys 25 unsolicited mss/year. Query. Length: 900-3,000 words. Pays $150-500. Sometimes pays the expenses of writers on assignment.

‡CURRENT WORLD LEADERS, Biography & News/Speeches & Reports, International Academy at Santa Barbara, Suite D, 800 Garden St., Santa Barbara CA 93101. (805)965-5010. Editorial Director: Thomas S. Garrison. Assistant Editor: Cathy McNamara. 25% freelance written. Bimonthly magazine covering international and comparative politics. "We cover several perspectives for each issue topic. We welcome papers which present a particular point of view on current international political issues. Our main audience is college-level teachers and students." Pays on publication. Publishes ms an average of 4 months after acceptance. Byline given. Offers no kill fee. Buys first rights. Simultaneous and previously published submissions OK. Query for electronic submissions. Reports in 3 weeks on queries. Free sample copy and writer's guidelines.

Nonfiction: Essays (political), opinion (political) and photo feature. "No articles that do not have a political theme." Buys 3-5 mss/year. Length: 4,500-13,500 words. Pays $25-100.

Photos: State availability of photos with submission. Reviews 4×5 prints. Offers no additional payment for photos accepted with ms. Captions and identification of subjects required. Buys one-time rights.

Tips: "Write and ask for our writers guidelines and our annual Call for Papers. Know your topic."

EMPIRE STATE REPORT, The magazine of politics and public policy in New York State, State Report Network, 545 8th Ave., 16th Fl., New York NY 10018. (212)239-9797. FAX: (212)564-0196. Editor: Alex Storozynski. 50% freelance written. Monthly magazine covering politics and public policy in NY State. "We provide timely political and public policy features for local and statewide public officials in New York State. Anything that would be of interest to them is of interest to us." Estab. 1983. Circ. 12,000. Pays 2 months after publication. Byline given. Buys first North American serial rights. Query for electronic submissions. Reports in 1 month on queries; 2 weeks on mss. Sample copy $3.50 with #10 SASE.

Nonfiction: Essays, exposé, interview/profile, opinion. Writers should send for our editorial calendar. Buys 48 mss/year. Query with published clips. Length: 750-3,000 words. Pays $35-400 for assigned articles. Sometimes pays expenses of writers on assignment.

Photos: State availability of photos with submission. Reviews any size prints. Offers $50-100 per photo. Identification of subjects required. Buys one-time rights.

Columns/Departments: "Notes and Asides" (short gossip pieces about state politics), 200 words maximum; Perspective (opinion pieces), 750-800 words. Buys 24 mss/year. Query. Length: 750-1,000 words. Pays $50-100.

Tips: Send us a query. If we are not already working on the idea, and if the query is well written, we might work something out with the writer. Writers have the best chance selling something for "Notes and Asides."

EUROPE, 2100 M St. NW, 707, Washington DC 20037. (202)862-9555. Editor: Robert Guttman. 50% freelance written. Magazine published 10 times a year for anyone with a professional or personal interest in Western Europe and European/U.S. relations. Circ. 25,000. **Pays on acceptance.** Publishes ms an average of 2 months after acceptance. Buys first serial rights and all rights. Submit seasonal material 3 months in advance. Reports in 1 month.

Nonfiction: Interested in current affairs (with emphasis on economics, business and politics), the Common Market and Europe's relations with the rest of the world. Publishes occasional cultural pieces, with European angle. "High quality writing a must. We publish articles that might be useful to people with a professional interest in Europe." Query or submit complete ms or article outline. Include résumé of author's background and qualifications. Length: 500-2,000 words. Pays $75-150.

Photos: Photos purchased with or without accompanying mss. Buys b&w and color. Pays $25-35 for b&w print, any size; $100 for inside use of transparencies; $450 for color used on cover; per job negotiable.

‡**FREEDOM MAGAZINE,** Investigative Reporting in the Public Interest, the Church of Scientology, Suite 1200, 6331 Hollywood Blvd., Los Angeles CA 90028. (213)663-2058. Editor: Thomas G. Whittle. 20% freelance written. Monthly magazine with emphasis on hard news, current events and investigative reporting. Estab. 1968. Circ. 100,000. Pays on publication. Publishes ms an average of 3 months after acceptance. Rights purchased vary with author and material. Submit seasonal material 4 months in advance. Responds in 4-6 weeks.
Nonfiction: National and international news, investigative reporting, business news. Recent articles have exposed misconduct and abuses by Internal Revenue Service officials. Harmful effects of psychiatric drugs such as Prozac have been probed in depth. Features individuals who are championing the causes of human rights in a special "Human Rights Advocate of the Month" department. Query with detailed outline, including statement of whether the information has appeared elsewhere. Enclosing clips of other stories you have published may help your chances of acceptance. Length 800-3,000 words. Pays $100-250, occasionally more.
Photos: Send photos with submission. Color: 35-mm slides, but prefers 2¼-inch transparencies. B&w 8×10 or 5×7 prints. Offers $20-100 per photo. Captions required. Buys one-time rights.
Columns/Departments: Book Reviews (600-1,000 words). Pays $50-150. Guest Commentary: (1,000 to 1,200 words). Pays $250.

THE FREEMAN, 30 S. Broadway, Irvington-on-Hudson NY 10533. (914)591-7230. FAX: (914)591-8910. Senior Editor: Brian Summers. 85% freelance written. Eager to work with new/unpublished writers. Monthly for "the layman and fairly advanced students of liberty." Buys all rights, including reprint rights. Byline given. Estab. 1946. Pays on publication. Publishes ms an average of 5 months after acceptance. Sample copy for 7½×10½ SASE with 4 first class stamps.
Nonfiction: "We want nonfiction clearly analyzing and explaining various aspects of the free market, private enterprise, limited government philosophy. Though a necessary part of the literature of freedom is the exposure of collectivistic clichés and fallacies, our aim is to emphasize and explain the positive case for individual responsibility and choice in a free economy. Especially important, we believe, is the methodology of freedom – self-improvement, offered to others who are interested. We try to avoid name-calling and personality – clashes and find satire of little use as an educational device. Ours is a scholarly analysis of the principles underlying a free market economy. No political strategy or tactics." Buys 100 mss/year. Length: 3,500 words maximum. Pays 10¢/word. Sometimes pays expenses of writers on assignment.
Tips: "It's most rewarding to find freelancers with new insights, fresh points of view. Facts, figures and quotations cited should be fully documented, to their original source, if possible."

MOTHER JONES MAGAZINE, The Foundation for National Progress, 1663 Mission St., Second Floor, San Francisco CA 94103. (415)558-8881. Editor: Doug Foster. Managing Editor: Peggy Orenstein. 90% freelance written. Bimonthly magazine with focus on progressive politics and culture. Specializes in investigative reporting. "*Mother Jones* is the largest magazine of political opinion in the United States." Estab. 1976. Circ. 200,000. **Pays on acceptance.** Byline given. Offers 33% kill fee. Buys first North American serial rights. Submit seasonal/holiday material 4 months in advance. Sample copy $5; free writer's guidelines for #10 SASE. Send all unsolicited material to: Editorial Coordinator.
Nonfiction: Book excerpts, essays, exposé, interview/profile, personal experience and photo feature. Buys 35 mss/year. Query with published clips. Length: 1,500-5,000 words. Pays $1,500-2,000. Pays expenses of writers on assignment.
Photos: State availablility of photos with submission. Reviews contact sheets, negatives, transparencies and prints. Offers $75 minimum/photo. Captions, model releases and identification of subjects required. Buys one-time rights.
Columns/Departments: Latest Thinking (essays), Hot Spots (foreign coverage), Trips (travel for non-ugly American), Buys 10 mss/year. Length: 1,000-2,500 words. Query with published clips. Pays $500-900.
Fiction: "Please read our magazine to get a feel for our fiction." No western, romance or confession. Buys 3 mss/year. Send complete ms. Length: 1,500-5,000 words. Pays $400-2,000.
Fillers: Outfront (short profiles), Previews (reviews and arts coverage – Peggy Orenstein, editor). Buys 20 mss/year. Length: 100-600 words. Pays $75-200.
Tips: "Read an issue before you query us. We have a 3-month lead time. Think ahead."

THE NATION, 72 5th Ave., New York NY 10011. FAX: (212)463-9712. Editor: Victor Navasky. 75% freelance written. Works with a small number of new/unpublished writers each year. Weekly. Buys first serial rights. Query for electronic submissions. Free sample copy and writer's guidelines for 6×9 SASE.

Nonfiction: "We welcome all articles dealing with the social scene, from an independent perspective." Queries encouraged. Buys 100 mss/year. Length: 2,500 words maximum. Modest rates. Sometimes pays expenses of writers on assignment.

Tips: "We are firmly committed to reporting on the issues of labor, national politics, business, consumer affairs, environmental politics, civil liberties and foreign affairs."

NATIONAL REVIEW, National Review Inc., 150 E. 35th St., New York NY 10016. (212)679-7330. Editor: John O'Sullivan. Managing Editor: Linda Bridges. 60% freelance written. Biweekly political and cultural journal of conservative opinion. "While we sometimes publish symposia including liberal or even leftist opinion, most of what we publish has a conservative or libertarian angle." Estab. 1955. Circ. 150,000. Pays on publication. Byline given. Offers 50% kill fee "on pieces definitely accepted." Buys first, one-time, second serial or simultaneous rights. Submit seasonal/holiday material 2 months in advance. Reports in 2 weeks on queries; 3 months on mss. Free sample copy.

Nonfiction: Mark Cunningham, articles editor. Essays, exposés (of government boondoggles), interview/profile, religious. No editorial-type pure opinion. Buys 130 mss/year. Query. Length: 500-3,000 words. Pays $100-1,000 for assigned articles; $100-600 for unsolicited articles. Sometimes pays expenses of writers on assignment.

Columns/Departments: Book reviews (conservative political where applicable); arts pieces. Buys 130 mss/year. Query. Length: 800-1,200 words. Pays $225-300.

Tips: "Query—although if a writer already has a manuscript ready, he may as well send it in instead. We accept phone queries. Double-space manuscripts. For the book section, always query before sending manuscript. We expect a fairly conservative point of view, but don't want a lot of editorializing. And we prefer pieces that are a bit more essayistic than a standard newspaper report."

NEWSWEEK, 444 Madison Ave., New York NY 10022. (212)350-4000. Contact: My Turn Editor. Although staff written, accepts unsolicited mss for My Turn, a column of opinion. The 1,000- to 1,100-word essays for the column must be original and contain verifiable facts. Payment is $1,000, on publication. Buys first rights. Reports in 6 weeks with SASE.

THE PRAGMATIST, A Utilitarian Approach, P.O. Box 392, Forest Grove PA 18922. Editor: Jorge Amador. Publisher: Hans G. Schroeder. 67% freelance written. Bimonthly magazine on politics and current affairs. *"The Pragmatist* is a free-market magazine with a social conscience. We explore the practical benefits of tolerance, civil liberties and the market order, with emphasis on helping the poor and the underprivileged." Estab. 1983. Circ. 1,550. Pays on publication. Publishes ms an average of 4 months after acceptance. Byline given. Publication not copyrighted "but will run copyright notice for individual author on request." Buys first rights and/or second serial (reprint) rights. Submit seasonal/holiday material 6 months in advance. Previously published submissions OK. Query for electronic submissions. Reports in 2 months. Sample copy $3; writer's guidelines for #10 SASE.

Nonfiction: Essays, humor, opinion. *"The Pragmatist* is solution-oriented. We seek facts and figures, no moralizing or abstract philosophy, and focus on the issues, not personalities. Recent articles have explored alternatives to socialized military defense and examined the hazards of drug prohibition." Buys 35 mss/year. Query with published clips or send complete ms. Length: 500-2,500 words. Pays 1¢/published word plus copies.

Columns/Departments: Book Review (history/current affairs, dealing with the dangers of power or the benefits of civil liberties and market relations). Buys 10-15 mss/year. Query with published clips or send complete ms. Length: 1,000-1,500 words. Pays 1¢/published word plus copies.

Fiction: "We use very little fiction, and then only if it makes a political point."

Tips: "We welcome new writers. Most of our authors are established, but the most important article criteria are clear writing and sound reasoning backed up by facts. Write for an educated lay audience, not first-graders or academics. Polite correspondence gets answered first. No phone calls, please. Don't get discouraged by initial rejections; keep working on your writing and your targeting."

THE PROGRESSIVE, 409 E. Main St., Madison WI 53703. (608)257-4626. FAX: (608)257-3373. Editor: Erwin Knoll. 75% freelance written. Monthly. Estab. 1909. Pays on publication. Publishes ms an average of 6 weeks after acceptance. Byline given. Buys all rights. Reports in 2 weeks. Sample copy for 8½×11 SAE and $1.05 postage. Writer's guidelines for #10 SASE.

Nonfiction: Primarily interested in articles which interpret, from a progressive point of view, domestic and world affairs. Occasional lighter features. *"The Progressive* is a *political* publication. General-interest material is inappropriate." Query. Length: 3,000 words maximum. Pays $75-250.

Tips: "Display some familiarity with our magazine, its interests and concerns, its format and style. We want query letters that fully describe the proposed article without attempting to sell it—and that give an indication of the writer's competence to deal with the subject."

REASON MAGAZINE, Suite 1062, 2716 Ocean Park Blvd., Santa Monica CA 90405. (213)392-0443. Editor: Virginia I. Postrel. 50% freelance written. "Strongly prefer experienced, published writers." A monthly public-affairs magazine with a classical liberal/libertarian perspective. Estab. 1968. Circ. 40,000. **Pays on acceptance.** Publishes ms an average of 2 months after acceptance. Rights purchased vary with author and material. Byline given. Offers kill fee by pre-arrangement. Query for electronic submissions. Reports in 2 months. Sample copy for $3 and 9×12 SAE with $1.24 postage.
Nonfiction: *"Reason* deals with social, economic and political issues, supporting both individual liberty and economic freedom. We are looking for politically sophisticated analysis, solid reporting, and excellent writing. Authors should not submit manuscripts without reviewing at least one recent issue." Query. Buys 50-70 mss/year. Length: 1,000-5,000 words. Sometimes pays expenses of writers on assignment.

‡REPORT ON THE AMERICAS, North American Congress on Latin America, 475 Riverside Dr., Room 454, New York NY 10115. (212)870-3146. Editor: Mark Fried. Associate Editor: Elizabeth Oglesby. 75% freelance written. A bimonthly magazine on Latin America and Caribbean U.S. foreign policy. Estab. 1966. Circ. 11,000. Pays on publication. Byline given. Offers ¼ kill fee. Buys one-time rights. Simultaneous and photocopied submissions OK. Query for electronic submissions. Sample copy $5.
Nonfiction: Exposé, opinion, and photo feature. Buys 25 mss/year. Query with published clips or send complete ms. Length: 1,000-2,500 words. Pays $75-150.
Photos: State availability of photos with submission. Reviews contact sheets and prints (5×7). Pays $25 minimum. Identification of subjects required. Buys one-time rights.

WASHINGTON MONTHLY, 1611 Connecticut Ave., Washington DC 20009. (202)462-0128. FAX: (202)332-8413. Editor-in-Chief: Charles Peters. 35% freelance written. Works with a small number of new/unpublished writers each year. For "well-educated, well-read people interested in politics, the press and government." Monthly. Circ. 30,000. Rights purchased depend on author and material; buys all rights, first rights, or second serial (reprint) rights. Buys 20-30 mss/year. Pays only for publication. Sometimes does special topical issues. Query or submit complete ms. Tries to report in 2 months. Publishes ms an average of 2-6 weeks after acceptance. Sample copy $4.
Nonfiction: Responsible investigative or evaluative reporting about the U.S. government, business, society, the press and politics. "No editorial comment/essays." Also no poetry, fiction or humor. Length: "average 2,000-6,000 words." Pays 10¢/word.
Photos: Buys b&w glossy prints.
Tips: "Best route is to send 1-2 page proposal describing article and angle. The most rewarding aspect of working with freelance writers is getting a solid piece of reporting with fresh ideas that challenge the conventional wisdom."

WORLD POLICY JOURNAL, World Policy Institute, 777 UN Plaza, New York NY 10017. (212)490-0010. FAX: (212)986-1482. Editor: Sherle Schwenninger. Estab. 1983. 10% freelance written. "We are eager to work with new or unpublished writers as well as more established writers." A quarterly journal covering international politics, economics and security issues. "We hope to bring a new sense of imagination, principle and proportion, as well as a restored sense of reality and direction to America's discussion of its role in the world." Circ. 10,000. **Pays on acceptance.** Publishes ms an average of 3 months after acceptance. Byline given. Offers variable kill fee. Buys all rights. Reports in 2 months. Sample copy for 9×12 SAE, 10 first class stamps and $5.75.
Nonfiction: Articles that "define policies that reflect the shared needs and interests of all nations of the world." Query. Length: 30-40 pages (8,500 words maximum). Pays variable commission rate. Sometimes pays the expenses of writers on assignment.
Tips: "By providing a forum for many younger or previously unheard voices, including those from Europe, Asia, Africa and Latin America, we hope to replace lingering illusions and fears with new priorities and aspirations. Articles submitted on speculation very rarely suit our particular needs."

Psychology and Self-Improvement

These publications focus on psychological topics, how and why readers can improve their own outlooks, and how to understand people in general. Many General Interest, Men's and Women's publications also publish articles in these areas.

CELEBRATE LIFE, The Magazine of Positive Living, Unimedia Corp., P.O. Box 247, Indian Rocks Beach FL 34635. (813)595-4141. Editor: Marty Johnson. 75% freelance written. Quarterly magazine covering motivational, positive lifestyles. Estab. 1989. Circ. 10,000. Pays on publication. Publishes ms an average of 3 months after acceptance. Byline given. Buys first North American serial rights, all rights or make work-for-hire assignments. Submit seasonal/holiday material 6 months in advance.

Simultaneous and previously published submissions OK "if notified." Query for electronic submissions. Reports in 2 months. Sample copy $2 with 9 × 12 SAE and 6 first class stamps. Writer's guidelines for #10 SAE with 1 first class stamp.

Nonfiction: How-to (self-improvement), humor, inspirational, interview/profile, personal experience, photo feature, religious (new thought), travel, natural lifestyles (i.e. holistic health). "Each issue is thematic. This is an upbeat, positive publication." Query with or without published clips, or send complete ms. Length: 400-2,000 words. Pays $25-75 for assigned articles. Complimentary copies to $25 or more for unsolicited material. "Rarely" pays expenses of writers on assignment.

Photos: State availability or send photos with submission. Reviews contact sheets, transparencies and prints. Captions, model releases and identification of subjects required. Buys one-time rights.

Columns/Departments: Books and Tapes (must be assigned), 100 words; Humor (new thought, reflections), 200 words. Query with published clips or send complete ms. Pays $10-20.

Poetry: Light verse. Submit maximum 3 poems. Length: 8-24 lines. Pays $5 maximum. "Usually for byline only."

Fillers: Anecdotes, facts, gags, newsbreaks, short humor. Length: 1-100 words. Pays $5-20.

Tips: "We are very specific about what we want in each upcoming issue. Read the magazine first. Nothing outside these parameters will fit. Interviews/profiles of leaders of positive change are wanted."

JOURNAL OF GRAPHOANALYSIS, 111 N. Canal St., Chicago IL 60606. (312)930-9446. Editor: William R. Harms. For an audience interested in self-improvement. Monthly magazine. Buys all rights. Pays negotiable kill fee. Byline given. **Pays on acceptance.** Reports on submissions in 1 month.

Nonfiction: Self-improvement material helpful for ambitious, alert, mature people. Applied psychology and personality studies, techniques of effective living, etc., all written from intellectual approach by qualified writers in psychology, counseling and teaching, preferably with advanced degrees. Length: 2,000 words. Pays 10¢/word, minimum.

Regional

Many regional publications rely on staff-written material, but others accept work from freelance writers who live in or know the region. Many of these magazines are among the bestselling magazines in a particular area and are read carefully, so writers must be able to supply accurate, up-to-date material. The best regional publication is usually the one in your hometown, whether it's a city or state magazine or a Sunday supplement in a newspaper. (Since you are familiar with the region, it is easier to propose suitable story ideas.)

Listed first are general interest magazines slanted toward residents of and visitors to a particular region. Next, regional publications are categorized alphabetically by state, followed by Canada. Publications that report on the business climate of a region are grouped in the regional division of the Business and Finance category. Recreation and travel publications specific to a geographical area are listed in the Travel, Camping and Trailer section. Regional publications are not listed if they only accept material from a select group of freelancers in their area or if they did not want to receive the number of queries and manuscripts a national listing would attract. If you know of a regional magazine that is not listed, approach it by asking for writer's guidelines before you send unsolicited material.

General

AMERICAS, Organization of American States, Editorial Offices, General Secretariat Bldg., 1889 F Street NW, Washington DC 20006. FAX: (201)458-6421. Managing Editor: Rebecca Read Medrano. 80% freelance written. Official magazine of Organization of American States. Editions published in English and Spanish. Bimonthly. Estab. 1948. Circ. 60,000. Buys first publication and reprint rights. Byline given. Pays on publication. Queries preferred. Articles received on speculation only. Include cover letter with writer's background.

Nonfiction: Articles of general New World interest on history, art, literature, theatre, development, archaeology, etc. Emphasis on modern, up-to-date Latin America. "Photos are not required, but are a big plus." Buys 6-10 unsolicited mss/year. Length: 2,500 words maximum. Pays $400 for features.

Tips: "Send excellent photographs in both color and b&w. Address an international readership, not a local or national one. We want something insightful culturally."

BLUE RIDGE COUNTRY, Leisure Publishing, 3424 Brambleton Ave. SW, P.O. Box 21535, Roanoke VA 24018-1535. (703)989-6138. FAX: (703)989-7663. Editor: Kurt Rheinheimer. 75% freelance written. Bimonthly magazine on the Blue Ridge region from Maryland to Georgia. "The magazine is designed to celebrate the history, heritage and beauty of the Blue Ridge region. It is aimed at the adult, upscale readers who enjoy living or traveling in the mountain regions of Virginia, North Carolina, West Virginia, Maryland, Kentucky, Tennessee, South Carolina and Georgia." Estab. 1988. Circ. 55,000. Pays on publication. Publishes ms an average of 6-8 months after acceptance. Byline given. Offers $50 kill fee for commissioned pieces only. Buys first and second serial (reprint) rights. Submit seasonal/holiday material 6 months in advance. Query for electronic submissions. Reports in 5 weeks. Sample copy for 9×12 SAE with $2.50 postage. Writer's guidelines for #10 SASE.

Nonfiction: General interest interest, historical/nostalgic, interview/profile, personal expeerience, photo feature, travel, history. Buys 25-30 mss/year. Query with or without published clips or send complete ms. Length: 500-2,500 words. Pays $50-350 for assigned articles; $25-250 for unsolicited articles.

Photos: State availability of photos with submission. Prefers transparencies. Offers $10-25 per photo and $100 for cover photo. Identification of subjects required. Buys all rights.

Columns/Departments: Country Roads (stories on people, events, ecology, history, antiques, books); Mountain Living (profiles of cooks and their recipes, garden tips, weather info); 50-300 words. Buys 12-24 mss/year. Query. Pays $10-25.

Tips: Freelancers needed for departmental shorts and "macro" issues affecting whole region. Need field reporters from all areas of Blue Ridge region. "Also, we need updates on the Blue Ridge Parkway, Appalachian Trail, national forests, ecological issues, preservation movements."

INLAND, The Magazine of the Middle West, Inland Steel Co., 18 S. Home Ave., Park Ridge IL 60068. Managing Editor: Sheldon A. Mix. 35-50% freelance written. Prefers to work with published/established writers, but eager to work with new/unpublished writers. Quarterly magazine that emphasizes steel products, services and company personnel. Circ. 8,000. **Pays on acceptance.** "Articles assigned are published within 4 months usually, but pieces in the inventory may remain years without being published." Buys first North American serial rights. Byline given. Submit seasonal/holiday material at least 1 year in advance. Query for electronic submissions. Tries to report in 4 months. Free sample copy. No writers' guidelines.

Nonfiction: Essays, humorous commentaries, profile, historical, think articles, personal opinion and photo essays. "We encourage individuality." At least half of each issue deals with staff-written steel subjects; half with widely ranging nonsteel matter. Articles and essays related somehow to the Midwest (Illinois, Wisconsin, Minnesota, Michigan, Missouri, Iowa, Nebraska, Kansas, North Dakota, South Dakota, Indiana and Ohio) in such subject areas as business, entertainment, history, folklore, sports, humor, current scene generally. But subject is less important than treatment. We like perceptive, thoughtful writing, and fresh ideas and approaches. Please don't send slight, rehashed historical pieces or any articles of purely local interest." Buys 5-10 unsolicited mss/year. Length: 1,200-5,000 words. Payment depends on individual assignment or unsolicited submission (usual range: $300-750).

Photos: Purchased with or without mss. Captions required. "Payment for pictorial essay same as for text feature."

Tips: "We are overstocked with nostalgia and are not looking for folksy treatments of family life and personal experiences. Our publication particularly needs humor that is neither threadbare nor in questionable taste, and shorter pieces (800-1,500 words) in which word choice and wit are especially important. The most frequent mistake made by writers in completing an article for us is untidiness in the manuscript (inattentiveness to good form, resulting in errors in spelling and facts, and in gaping holes in information). 'The Education of a Steel Hauler's Daughter'; 'Adventures of a Young Balzac' (Vincent Starrett's early newspaper days in Chicago); 'Chicago Introduces Lincoln'; articles on the gold rush to Pikes Peak in 1859; homestead movement; first steamboat in the Middle West; Illinois-Michigan Canal National Heritage Corridor; Jane Addams; Garrison Keillor; the birth of night baseball; pioneer women; origins of unusual place names in the Middle West; the Battle of Lake Erie (1812) are recent article examples."

INTERNATIONAL LIVING, Agora Publishing, 824 E. Baltimore St., Baltimore MD 21202. (301)234-0515. FAX: (301)837-3879. Editor: Kathleen Peddicord. 60% freelance written. "We prefer established writers and unpublished writers with original, first-hand experience." Monthly newsletter covering international lifestyles, travel, retirement, education, employment and investment for Americans. Aimed at affluent and not-so-affluent dreamers to whom the romance of living overseas has a strong appeal, especially when it involves money-saving angles. Estab. 1980. Circ. 55,000. Pays within 1 month

Market conditions are constantly changing! If this is 1993 or later, buy the newest edition of Writer's Market at your favorite bookstore or order directly from Writer's Digest Books.

of publication. Publishes ms an average of 6 months after acceptance. Byline given. Buys all rights. Submit seasonal/holiday material 2 months in advance. Query for electronic submissions. Reports in 1 month on queries; 6 weeks on mss. Sample copy $2.50; writer's guidelines for #10 SASE.

Nonfiction: Book excerpts (overseas, travel, retirement, investment, save money overseas, invest overseas); how-to (save money, find a job overseas); interview/profile (famous people and other Americans living abroad); personal experience; travel (unusual, imaginative destinations—give how-to's and costs); and other (humor, cuisine). "We want pithy, fact-packed articles. No vague, long-winded travel articles on well-trodden destinations. No articles on destinations in the United States." Buys 100 mss/year. Query with published clips or send complete ms. Length: 200-1,500 words. Pays $50-400.

Tips: "We are looking for writers who can combine original valuable information with a style that suggests the romance of life abroad. Break in with highly specific, well-researched material combining subjective impressions of living in a foreign country or city with information on taxes, cost of living, residency requirements, real estate, employment and entertainment possibilities. We do heavy rewrites and usually reorganize because of tight space requirements. We are moving toward more how-to and source lists."

ISLANDS, An International Magazine, Islands Publishing Company, 3886 State St., Santa Barbara CA 93105. FAX: (805)569-0349. Editor: Joan Tapper. 95% freelance written. Works with established writers. Bimonthly magazine covering islands throughout the world. "We cover accessible and once-in-a-lifetime islands from many different perspectives: travel, culture, lifestyle. We ask our authors to give us the essence of the island and do it with literary flair." Estab. 1981. Circ. 150,000. **Pays on acceptance.** Publishes ms an average of 8 months after acceptance. Byline given. Buys all rights. Query for electronic submissions. Reports in 1 month on queries; 6 weeks on ms. Sample copy for $5.25; writer's guidelines with #10 SASE.

Nonfiction: General interest, historical/nostalgic, interview/profile, personal experience, photo feature, technical, and any island-related material. "Each issue contains 3 or 4 feature articles of roughly 2,000-4,000 words, and 4 or 5 topical articles for departments, each of which runs approximately 750-1,500 words. Any authors who wish to be commissioned should send a detailed proposal for an article, an estimate of costs (if applicable) and samples of previously published work." Buys 25 mss/year. "The majority of our manuscripts are commissioned." Query with published clips or send complete ms. Length: 500-3,000 words. Pays $100-3,000. Pays expenses of writers on assignment.

Photos: State availability or send photos with query or ms. Pays $75-300 for 35mm transparencies. "Fine color photography is a special attraction of *Islands*, and we look for superb composition, technical quality and editorial applicability." Label slides with name and address, include captions, and submit in protective plastic sleeves. Identification of subjects required. Buys one-time rights.

Columns/Departments: "Columns and departments are generally assigned, but we have accepted short features for our Island Hopping department or very short items for our Logbook section. These should be highly focused on some specific aspect of islands." Buys 50 mss/year. Query with published clips. Length: 500-1,500 words. Pays $100-700.

Tips: "A freelancer can best break in to our publication with short (500-1,000 word) features or departments that are highly focused on some aspect of island life, history, people, etc. Stay away from general, sweeping articles. We are always looking for topics for our Islanders and Logbook pieces. These are a good place to break in. We will be using big name writers for major features; will continue to use newcomers and regulars for columns and departments."

NOW AND THEN, Center for Appalachian Studies and Services, East Tennessee State University, Box 19180A, Johnson City TN 37614. (615)929-5348. FAX: (615)929-5770. 80% freelance written. A tri-annual regional magazine. Estab. 1984. Circ. 1,500. Pays on publication. Publishes ms an averge of 6 months after acceptance. Byline given. Buys one-time rights. Simultaneous and previously published submissions OK. Reports in 1 month on queries; 4 months on mss. Sample copy $3.50; writer's guidelines for #10 SASE.

Nonfiction: Book excerpts, essays, historical, humor, interview/profile, personal experience, photo feature. "We do have a special focus in each issue—we've featured Appalachian Blacks, Cherokees, women, music and veterans. Write for future themes. Stereotypes (especially granny rocking on the front porch), generalizations, sentimental writing are rejected. It must have to do with Appalachia." Buys 8 mss/year. Query with or without published clips, or send complete ms. Length: 2,500 words. Pays $15-60 for assigned articles; $10-60 for unsolicited articles. Sometimes pays expenses of writers on assignment.

Photos: Send photos with submission. Reviews contact sheets and prints. Offers no additional payment for photos accepted with ms. Captions, model releases and identification of subjects required. Buys one-time rights.

Fiction: Ethnic, experimental, historical, humorous, novel excerpts, slice-of-life vignettes. "Everything we publish has to be by or about Appalachians. No stereotypes, generalizations, or sentimentality." Buys 3 mss/year. Send complete ms. Length: 2,500 words maximum. Pays $10-50.

Poetry: Avant-garde, free verse. "Must have something to do with the Appalachian region. Avoid stereotypes, generalizations and sentimentality." Buys 30-35 poems/year. Pays 2 contributor's copies and a year subscription. Send no more than 5 poems at a time.

Tips: "Everything we publish has something to do with life in Appalachia present and past. Profiles of people living and working in the region, short stories that convey the reality of life in Appalachia (which can include malls, children who wear shoes and watch MTV) are the kinds of things we're looking for."

RURALITE, P.O. Box 558, Forest Grove OR 97116. (503)357-2105. Editor-in-Chief: Rod O'Dell. 80% freelance written. Works with new, unpublished writers "who have mastered the basics of good writing." Monthly magazine aimed at members of a consumer-owned electric utilities throughout 13 western states, including Alaska. Publishes 54 regional editions. Estab. 1954. Circ. 265,000. Buys first rights, sometimes reprint rights. Rights may be reassigned. Byline given. **Pays on acceptance.** Query first, unsolicited manuscripts submitted without request rarely read by editors. Sample copy and writer's guidelines for 10×13 SASE and $1.

Nonfiction: Looking for well-written nonfiction, (occasional fiction piece) dealing primarily with human interest topics. Must have strong Northwest perspective and be sensitive to Northwest issues and attitudes. Wide range of topics possible, from energy-related subjects to little-known travel destinations to unusual businesses located in areas served by consumer-owned electric utilities. "About half of our readers are rural and small town residents; others are urban and suburban. Topics with an obvious 'big-city' focus not accepted. Family-related issues, Northwest history (no encyclopedia re-writes) people and events, unusual tidbits that tell the Northwest experience are best chances for a sale. Nostalgia, dripping sentimental pieces rejected out of hand." Buys 12-15 mss/yr. Length 900-1500 words. Pays $140-400; quality photos may increase upper pay limit for "polished stories with impact."

Photos: "Illustrated stories are the key to a sale. Stories without art rarely make it, with the exception of humor pieces. Black-and-white prints, color slides, all formats, accepted with 'razor-sharp' focus. Fuzzy, low-contrast photos may lose the sale."

Tips: We need solid writers and photographers who can relate to the Northwest attitude and convey that sensibility in their stories. Magazine is repositioning as regional four-color publication and will cover a wider range of topics. Recent coverage included regional health care (obstetrics); forest fire fighting; dog sled racing; finding a job in a recession economy. Look at a recent copy. We're looking for regular contributors to whom we can assign topics from our story list after they've proven their ability to deliver quality mss."

SUNDAY JOURNAL MAGAZINE, Providence Journal Co., 75 Fountain St., Providence RI 02902. (401)277-7349. Editor: Elliot Krieger. 50% freelance written. Weekly Sunday supplement magazine about news of Rhode Island and New England. Estab. 1860. Circ. 250,000. Pays on publication. Byline given. Buys first North American serial rights. Submit seasonal/holiday 3 months in advance. Simultaneous submissions OK. Query for electronic submissions. Reports in 2 weeks on queries.

Nonfiction: Book excerpts, exposé, general interest, historical/nostalgic, interview/profile and photo feature. "We are strictly a regional news magazine." No fiction, poetry or personal opinion. Buys 100 mss/year. Query. Length: 750-5,000. Pays $100-1,000.

Photos: State availability of photos with submission. Offers $25-100/photo. Captions and identification of subjects required.

SUNSET, Lane Publishing Co., 80 Willow Rd., Menlo Park CA 90010. Did not want to be listed.

Alabama

ALABAMA HERITAGE, University of Alabama, Box 870342, Tuscaloosa AL 35487-0342. (205)348-7467. Editor: Suzanne Wolfe. Managing Editor: G. Ward Hubbs. 50% freelance written. Quarterly magazine on Alabama history and culture. "*Alabama Heritage* is a nonprofit historical quarterly published by the University of Alabama for the intelligent lay reader. We are interested in lively, well written and thoroughly researched articles on Alabama/Southern history and culture. Readability and accuracy are essential." Estab. 1986. Pays on publication. Byline given. Buys first rights and second serial (reprint) rights. Query for electronic submissions. Reports in 1 month. Sample copy $5. Writer's guidelines for #10 SASE.

Nonfiction: Historical. "We do not want fiction, poetry, book reviews, articles on current events or living artists and personal/family reminiscences." Buys 10 mss/year. Query. Length: 1,500-5,000 words. Pays $100 minimum. Pays 10 copies to each author plus one-year subscription.

Photos: Reviews contact sheets. Identification of subjects required. Buys one-time rights.

Tips: "Authors need to remember that we regard history as a fascinating subject, not as a dry recounting of dates and facts. Articles that are lively and engaging, in addition to being well researched, will find interested readers among our editors. No term papers, please. All areas of our magazine are open to freelance writers. Best approach is a written query."

Alaska

ALASKA, The Magazine of Life on the Last Frontier, Suite 200, 808 E. St., Anchorage AK 99501. (907)272-6070. Editor: Grant Sims. 60% freelance written. Eager to work with new/unpublished writers. A monthly magazine covering topics "uniquely Alaskan." Estab. 1935. Circ. 235,000. **Pays on acceptance.** Publishes ms an average of 6 months after acceptance. Byline given. Buys first rights or one-time rights. Submit seasonal/holiday material 1 year in advance. Query for electronic submissions. Reports in 1 month on queries; 2 months on manuscripts. Sample copy $3; writer's guidelines for #10 SASE.

Nonfiction: Historical/nostalgic, how-to (on anything Alaskan), humor, interview/profile, personal experience and photo feature. Also travel articles and Alaska destination stories. Does not accept fiction or poetry. Buys 60 mss/year. Query. Length: 100-2,500 words. Pays $100-1,250. Pays expenses of writers on assignment.

Photos: Send photos with submission. Reviews 35mm or larger transparencies. Captions and identification of subjects required.

ALASKA OUTDOORS MAGAZINE, Swensen's Alaska Outdoors Corporation, Suite 200, 400 "D" St., P.O. Box 190324, Anchorage AK 99519. (907)276-2672. FAX: (907)258-6027. Editor: Evan Swensen. 90% freelance written. Monthly magazine on outdoor recreation in Alaska. Estab. 1978. Circ. 55,000. Pays 30 days after publication. Publishes ms an average of 4 months after acceptance. Byline given. Offers 50% kill fee. Buys first North American serial rights. Submit seasonal/holiday material 4 months in advance. Query for electronic submissions. Reports in 3 weeks on queries; 4 weeks on mss. Sample copy $1 with 8½×11 SAE and 3 first class stamps. Free writer's guidelines.

Nonfiction: Essays, how-to (outdoor recreation), humor, personal experience, photo feature and travel. Buys 150-175 mss/year. Query with or without published clips or send complete ms. Length: 800-2,400 words. Pays $75-200.

Photos: Send photos with submission. Reviews transparencies and prints. Offers no additional payment for photos accepted with ms (except cover). Captions, model releases and identification of subjects required. Buys one-time rights.

Arizona

ARIZONA HIGHWAYS, 2039 W. Lewis Ave., Phoenix AZ 85009. (602)258-6641. FAX: (602)254-4505. Managing Editor: Richard G. Stahl. 90% freelance written. Prefers to work with published/established writers. State-owned magazine designed to help attract tourists into and through the state. Estab. 1925. **Pays on acceptance.** Publishes ms an average of 6 months after acceptance. Writer's guidelines for SASE.

Nonfiction: Contact managing editor. Subjects include narratives and exposition dealing with contemporary events, popular geography, history, anthropology, nature, special things to see and do, outstanding arts and crafts, travel, etc.; all must be oriented toward Arizona and the Southwest. Buys 6 mss/issue. Buys first serial rights. Query with "a lead paragraph and brief outline of story. We deal with professionals only, so include list of current credits." Length: 600-2,000 words. Pays 35-50¢/word. Sometimes pays expenses of writers on assignment. Writer's guidelines available.

Photos: "We will use transparencies of 2¼, 4×5 or larger, and 35mm when it displays exceptional quality or content. We prefer Kodachrome in 35mm. Each transparency *must* be accompanied by information attached to each photograph: where, when, what. No photography will be reviewed by the editors unless the photographer's name appears on *each* and *every* transparency." Pays $80-350 for "selected" transparencies. Buys one-time rights.

Tips: "Writing must be of professional quality, warm, sincere, in-depth, well-peopled and accurate. Avoid themes that describe first trips to Arizona, the Grand Canyon, the desert, Colorado River running, etc. Emphasis is to be on Arizona adventure and romance as well as flora and fauna, when appropriate, and themes that can be photographed. Double check your manuscript for accuracy."

‡**PHOENIX,** Arizona Television Company, 4707 N. 12th St., Phoenix AZ 85014. (602)248-8900. Executive Editor: Richard S. Vonier. Managing Editor: Beth Deveny. 70% freelance written. Monthly magazine covering southwest, state of Arizona, metro Phoenix. Estab. 1966. Circ. 33,600. Pays on acceptance or publication. Publishes ms and average of 2-3 months after acceptance. Byline gvien. Negotiable kill

fee. Buys first North American serial rights and one-time rights. Submit seasonal material 3-4 months in advance. Simultaneous and previously published submissions OK. Query for electronic submissions. Sample copy $1.95 with 9×12 SAE and $1.25 postage.

Nonfiction: Book excerpts, essays, investigative, general interest, historical/nostalgic, how-to, humor, inspirational, interview/profile, opinion, personal experience, photo feature, religious, technical, travel and other. "No material dealing with travel outside the region or other subjects that don't have an effect on the area." Buys 75-100 mss/year. Query with published clips. Pays $50-1,500 for assigned articles; $50-500 for unsolicited articles. Sometimes pays expenses of writers on assignment. State availability of photos with submissions. Reviews contact sheets, negatives, transparencies and prints. Offers $25-100/photo. Captions, model releases and identification of subjects required. Buys one-time rights.

Fiction: Adventure, condensed, ethnic, fantasy, historical, humorous, mainstream, novel excerpts, slice-of-life vignettes and western. No poetry. Buys 4-8 mss/year. Send complete ms. Length: 5,000 words. Pays $50-1,000.

Tips: "We have no published guidelines. Articles should be of local or regional interest with vivid descriptions that put the reader in the story and present new information or a new way of looking at things. We are not afraid of opinion."

‡THE SCOTTSDALE PROGRESS, Cowles Media Group, 7320 E. Earll Dr., Scottsdale AZ 85251. (602)941-2300. Editor: Steve Wilson. Features Editor: Karlin McCarthy. 30% freelance written. Daily newspaper w/weekly arts magazine. "Covers general news and features for resort area/growth market." Estab. 1948. **Pays on acceptance.** Publishes ms an average of 1 month after acceptance. Byline given. Offers $25 kill fee. Submit seasonal/holiday material 2 months in advance. Query for electronic submissions. Reports in 2 weeks. Sample copy $2. Free writer's guidelines.

Nonfiction: Essays (regional), exposé, general interest (lifestyle), how-to (relationships, lifestyle), humor (local/regional), inspirational (religious section), interview/profile (*locals* — Arizona), new product, personal experience (health lifestyle, travel fashion, food), photo feature, travel. Home and garden, seniors, food, personal finance. No poetry or articles written in the 1st person. Buys 150 mss/year. Query with published clips. Send complete ms. Length: 300-1,500 words. Pays $25-125 for assigned articles. Sometimes pays expenses of writers on assignment.

Photos: State availability of photos with submission. Reviews transparencies and prints. Offers negotiable payment. Identification of subjects required. Buys one-time rights.

Columns/Departments: At Home (high profile people interviewed at their home), 800 words; Weekenders (travel getaways — regional), 500 words; A la Carte (food industry news), 200 words; Fashion. Buys 25 mss/year. Query with published clips. Length: 200-800 words. Pays $25-125.

Tips: "Read the newspapers and articles about writing for newspapers and magazines; always *write* first, then call to query."

TUCSON LIFESTYLE, Old Pueblo Press, Suite 11, 7000 E. Tanque Verde Rd., Tucson AZ 85715. (602)721-2929. FAX: (602)721-8665. Editor-in-Chief: Sue Giles. 90% freelance written. Prefers to work with published/established writers. A monthly magazine covering city-related events and topics. Estab. 1982. Circ. 32,000. **Pays on acceptance.** Publishes ms an average of 6 months after acceptance. Byline given. Buys first rights and second serial (reprint) rights. Submit seasonal/holiday material 1 year in advance. Previously published submissions OK. Reports in 2 months. Sample copy $3; free writer's guidelines.

Nonfiction: All stories need a Tucson angle. Historical/nostalgic, humor, interview/profile, personal experience, travel and local stories. Special Christmas issue (December). "We do not accept *anything* that does not pertain to Tucson or Arizona." Buys 100 mss/year. Query. Length: open. Pays $50-300. Sometimes pays expenses of writers on assignment.

Photos: Reviews contact sheets, 2¼×2¼ transparencies and 5×7 prints. Offers $25-100/photo. Identification of subjects required. Buys one-time rights.

Columns/Departments: In Business — articles on Tucson businesses and business people; Southwest Homes (environmental living in Tucson: homes, offices). Buys 36 mss/year. Query. Length: open. Pays $100-200.

Tips: Features are most open to freelancers. " 'Style' is not of paramount importance; good, clean copy with interesting lead is a 'must.' "

Arkansas

ARKANSAS TIMES, Arkansas Writers' Project, Inc., Box 34010, Little Rock AR 72203. (501)375-2985. Editor: Richard Martin. 50% freelance written. Monthly magazine. "We are an Arkansas magazine. We seek to appreciate, enliven and, where necessary, improve the quality of life in the state." Estab. 1974. Circ. 32,000. **Pays on acceptance.** Publishes ms an average of 3 months after acceptance. Byline given. Buys first serial rights. Submit seasonal/holiday material 5 months in advance. Simultaneous and previously published submissions OK. Reports in 2 weeks on queries; 1 month on mss. Sample copy $3.50; writer's guidelines for SASE.

Nonfiction: Book excerpts; exposé (in investigative reporting vein); general interest; historical/nostalgic; humor; interview/profile; opinion; recreation; and entertainment, all relating to Arkansas. "The Arkansas angle is all-important." Buys 24 mss/year. Query. Length: 250-6,000 words. Pays $100-500. Sometimes pays the expenses of writers on assignment.

Photos: Melissa James, art director. State availability of photos. Pays $25-75. Identification of subjects required. Buys one-time rights.

Columns/Departments: Mike Trimble, column editor. In Our Times (articles on people, places and things in Arkansas or with special interest to Arkansans). "This is the department that is most open to freelancers." Buys 15 mss/year. Query. Length: 250-1,000 words. Pays $100-150.

Tips: "The frustrating aspect of freelance submissions is that so many of the writers have obviously never seen our magazine. Only writers who know something about Arkansas should send us mss."

California

CALIFORNIA MAGAZINE, 11601 Wilshire Blvd., Los Angeles CA 90025. (213)479-6511. Editor: Neal Travis. Managing Editor: Rebecca Levy. 90% freelance written. Monthly magazine about California — lifestyle, the arts, politics, business, crime, education, technology, etc. Estab. 1976. Circ. 363,000. **Pays on acceptance.** Publishes ms an average of 3 months after acceptance. Byline given. Offers variable kill fee. Buys first North American serial rights. Reports in 6 weeks on queries. Sample copy $2 and 9 × 12 SAE.

Nonfiction: Stewart Weiner, Ed Gierke and David Weir (San Francisco office), features editors. Exposé (environment, government, education, business), general interest, historical/nostalgic, humor, interview/profile, new product, photo feature and travel; *all* must pertain to California. Length: 800-4,000 words. Pays expenses of writers on assignment.

Photos: Assigns most photos; reviews portfolios. Captions, model releases and identification of subjects required. Buys one-time rights.

Columns/Departments: Open to freelance: Travel, New West. Query with published clips. Length: 750-2,000 words. Pays $450-1,500.

Tips: "Query first with clips. *Read* the magazine."

‡THE CITY, San Francisco's Magazine, All of US in De, Inc., 312, 1095 Market St., San Francisco CA 94103. (415)252-1391. Editor: Fred Dodsworth. Managing Editor: Wanda Hoberg. 80% freelance written. Monthly magazine covering San Francisco city and county. Estab. 1989. Circ. 30,000. Pays on publication. Publishes ms an average of 2 months after acceptance. Byline given. Buys first rights. Submit seasonal/holiday material 4 months in advance. Query for electronic submissions. Reports in 4 weeks. Sample copy for 8 × 10 SAE with $1.65. Writer's guidelines for 9½ × 4 SAE with 25¢.

Nonfiction: Exposé, general interest, humor, interview/profile, photo feature, "anything specific to San Francisco." "We do not want to see anything not related to San Francisco or reviews." Buys 100 mss/year. Query with published clips. Length: 300-3,000 words. Pays $30-300 for assigned articles. Payment is 10¢ to 25¢ per published word. State availability of photos with submission. Reviews contact sheets, all transparencies and all prints. Offers $35-150/photo. Model releases and identification of subjects required. Buys first-time rights.

Columns/Departments: Inside the City (San Francisco briefs—social, political, cultural, odd), 100-300 words; Comedy Spotlight (San Francisco comedian professional written stand-up piece), 500-600 words; Portrait of a Chef (profile of a San Franciscan Chef with recipe), 800 words; Emperor Norton (profile of a San Franciscan character, slightly offbeat), 400 words. Query with published clips. Length: 200-600 words. Pays $30-80.

Tips: "Send for writers guidelines, send written query and then follow up with phone call to editor or managing editor, and be prepared to send manuscripts on a speculation basis. Be specific in queries, i.e., writer has contacted sources, estimated completion time, length, and knowledge of proposed topic. All areas open to freelancers on spec basis."

LOS ANGELES MAGAZINE, ABC/Capital Cities, 1888 Century Park East, Los Angeles CA 90067. (213)557-7569. Editor: Lew Harris. 98% freelance written. Monthly magazine about southern California. "The primary editorial role of the magazine is to aid a literate, upscale audience in getting the most out of life in the Los Angeles area." Estab. 1960. Circ. 174,000. Pays on publication. Publishes ms an average of 4 months after acceptance. Byline given. Offers 30% kill fee. Buys first North American serial rights. Submit seasonal/holiday material 3-6 months in advance. Reports in 6 weeks. Sample copy $5; writer's guidelines for #10 SASE.

Nonfiction: Rodger Claire, executive editor. Book excerpts (about L.A. or by famous L.A. author); exposé (any local issue); general interest; historical/nostalgic (about L.A. or Hollywood); and interview/profile (about L.A. person). Buys 400 mss/year. Query with published clips. Length: 250-3,500 words. Pays $50-1,200. Sometimes pays expenses of writers on assignment.
Photos: Rodger Claire, photo editor. State availability of photos.
Columns/Departments: Rodger Claire, executive editor. Buys 170 mss/year. Query with published clips. Length: 250-1,200 words. Pays $50-500.

LOS ANGELES READER, Suite 301, 5550 Wilshire Blvd., Los Angeles CA 90036. (213)933-0161. Editorial Director: Eric Mankin. 85% freelance written. Weekly tabloid of features and reviews for "affluent young Los Angelenos interested in politics, the arts and popular culture." Circ. 70,000. Pays on publication. Publishes ms an average of 6 weeks after acceptance. Byline given. Buys one-time rights. Reports in 1 month. Sample copy $1 and 9 × 12 SAE.
Nonfiction: General interest, journalism, interview/profile, personal experience and photo features—all with strong local slant. Buys "dozens" of mss/year. Send complete ms or query. Length: 200-3,500 words. Pays $25-300.
Tips: "Break in with submissions for our Cityside page which uses short (400-800 word) news items on Los Angeles happenings. personalities and trends. Try to have some conflict in submissions: 'x exists' is not as good a story as 'x is struggling with y over z.' "

LOS ANGELES TIMES MAGAZINE, Los Angeles Times, Times Mirror Sq., Los Angeles CA 90053. (213)237-7000. Editor: Linda Mathews. 50% freelance written. Weekly magazine of regional general interest. Circ. 1 million. Payment schedule varies. Publishes ms an average of 2 months after acceptance. Byline given. Buys first North American serial rights. Submit seasonal/holiday material 3 months in advance. Simultaneous queries and submissions OK. Reports in 1 month. Sample copy for 9 × 12 SAE and 6 first class stamps. Writer's guidelines for SAE and 2 first class stamps.
Nonfiction: General interest, historical/nostalgic, interview/profile, personal experience and photo feature. Must have California tie-in, but no need to be set in California. Query with published clips. "We welcome all queries." Length: 400-1,800 words. Pays $400-2,000. Sometimes pays the expenses of writers on assignment.
Photos: Query first. Reviews color transparencies and b&w prints. Payment varies. Captions, model releases and identification of subjects required. Buys one-time rights.
Tips: "The writer should know the subject well or have researched it adequately. As for style, the best style is when the writer goes to the trouble of employing proper English and self-edits an article prior to submission."

‡METRO, Metro Publishing Ltd., 410 S. First St., San Jose CA 95113. (408)298-8000. Editor: Dan Pulcrano. Managing Editor: Sharan Street. 35-50% freelance written. Weekly general interest tabloid. "*Metro* is for sophisticated urban audience—stories must be more in-depth with an unusual slant not covered in daily newspapers." Estab. 1985. Circ. 65,000. Pays on publication (varies considerably, from one week to two months). Byline given. Offers 50% kill fee. Buys first North American serial rights and second serial (reprint) rights—non-exclusive. Submit seasonal/holiday material 2-3 months in advance. Query for electronic submissions. Reports in 3-4 weeks on queries; 2-3 months on mss. Sample copy $3. Writer's guidelines for SAE with 1 first class stamp.
Nonfiction: Book excerpt, essays, exposé, general interest, humor, interview/profile (particularly entertainment oriented), personal experience. Wedding Feature, Health & Fitness. Buys 75 mss/year. Query with published clips. Length: 500-4,000 words. Pays $50-300 for assigned articles; $25-200 for assigned articles. Sometimes pays expenses of writers on assignment.
Photos: State availability of photos with submission. Reviews contact sheets, negatives, any size transparencies and prints. Offers $25-50 per photo. Captions, model releases and identification of subjects required. Buys one-time rights.
Columns/Departments: Metro Menu (copy related to food, dining out), 500-1,000 words; Metro Guide (entertainment features, interviews), 500-1,500 words. Buys 100 mss/year. Query with published clips. Pays $25-75.
Tips: "Humor, seasonal features and personal essays are the most open, but we take only the best stuff. Material must be very well written, sophisticated and aimed at an urban audience and demonstrate an acute understanding of social and cultural trends."

ORANGE COAST MAGAZINE, The Magazine of Orange County, O.C.N.L., Inc., 245-D Fischer, Costa Mesa CA 92626. (714)545-1900. Editor: Palmer Thomason Jones. Managing Editor: Erik Himmelsbach. Associate Editor: Lynn Allison. 95% freelance written. Monthly. "*Orange Coast* is designed to inform and enlighten the educated, upscale residents of affluent Orange Country, California and is highly graphic and well-researched." Estab. 1974. Circ. 40,000. **Pays on acceptance.** Publishes ms an average of 5 months after acceptance. Byline given. Buys first serial rights. Submit seasonal/holiday material 6 months in advance. Simultaneous queries and submissions OK. Query for electronic submissions. Reports in 2 months. Sample copy $2.50 with 10 × 12 SAE and $2.25 postage; writer's guidelines for SASE.

Nonfiction: Expose (Orange Country government, refugees, politics, business, crime); general interest (with Orange County focus); historical/nostalgic; guides to activities and services; interview/profile (Orange County prominent citizens); local sports; lifestyle features and travel. Special issues include Dining (March); Health and Beauty (January); Resort Guide (October); Home and Garden (June); and Holiday (December). Buys 100 mss/year. Query or send complete ms. No phone queries. Length: 1,000-4,000 words. Pays $250 maximum.

Columns/Departments: Local Consumer, Investments, Business, Health, Profiles, Adventure, and Destination. Not open for submission are: Music, Art, Medicine, Film, Sports, Insight, Couples, Parents, Restaurant Review ("we have regular reviewers"). Buys 200 mss/year. Query or send complete ms; no phone queries. Length: 1,000-2,000 words. Pays $100 maximum.

Fiction: Buys only under rare circumstances. Send complete ms. Length: 1,000-5,000 words. Must have an Orange County setting. Pays $150 maximum.

Tips: "Most features are assigned to writers we've worked with before. Don't try to sell us 'generic' journalism. *Orange Coast* prefers well-written stories with specific and unusual angles that in some way include Orange County. Be professional and write manuscripts that present you as a stylized, creative writer. A lot of writers miss the Orange County angle. Our writers *must* concentrate on the local angle. We get far too many generalized manuscripts."

PALM SPRINGS LIFE, Desert Publications, Inc., Indian Canyon Dr., P.O. Box 2724, Palm Springs CA 92263. (619)325-2333. FAX: (619)325-7008. Editor: Jamie Pricer. Estab. 1959. 30% freelance written. Monthly magazine covering "affluent resort/southern California/Coachella Valley. Printed in full color on the highest quality 70 lb. paper. *Palm Springs Life* is a luxurious magazine aimed at the 'affluence' market. Surveys show that our readership has a median age of 50.1, a median household income of $190,000, a primary home worth $275,150 and a second home worth $190,500." Circ. 75,000. Pays on publication. Publishes ms an average of 3 months after acceptance. Byline given. Buys universal (all) rights (negotiable). Submit seasonal/holiday material 4 months in advance. Simultaneous and previously published submissions OK. Query for electronic submissions. Reports in 2 weeks. Sample copy $5.

Nonfiction: Book excerpts, general interest, historical/nostalgic, humor, interview/profile, new product, photo feature and travel. Special issues include Real Estate (May); Home and Garden (June); Health (July); Desert Living Animal/Coachella Valley focus (September); Beauty and Style (April); Desert Progress (October); Arts & Culture (November); Holiday Shopping (December). Query with published clips. Length: 700-1,200 words. Pays 20¢/word. Sometimes pays the expenses of writers on assignment.

Photos: Reviews 2¼ × 2¼, 4 × 5 and 35mm transparencies. Offers $50-500 (for cover). Captions, model releases and identification of subjects required.

Tips: "*Palm Springs Life* publishes articles about dining, fashion, food, wine, beauty, health, sports (especially tennis and golf) and the lifestyle of the powerful, rich and famous. We are always interested in new ways to enjoy wealth, display luxury and consume it. We want to hear what's 'in' and what's 'out,' what's new in Palm Springs and the Coachella Valley, and how to solve problems experienced by our readers."

PENINSULA MAGAZINE, 656 Bair Island Rd., 2nd Fl., Redwood City CA 94063. (415)368-8800. FAX: (415)368-6251. Editor: David Gorn. Managing Editor: Dale Conour. 50% freelance written. A monthly magazine on San Mateo and Santa Clara counties. "We have an educated and affluent readership, so we need stories with a little bite." Estab. 1985. Circ. 40,000. **Pays on acceptance.** Publishes ms an average of 2 months after acceptance. Byline given. Offers 30% kill fee. Buys first rights. Submit seasonal/holiday material 4 months in advance. Simultaneous and previously published submissions OK. Query for electronic submissions. Reports in 2 months. Sample copy for 9 × 12 SAE with $4 postage. Writer's guidelines for #10 SAE with 2 first class stamps.

Nonfiction: Exposé, general interest, interview/profile, photo feature, environment, innovations, power and money, the arts, history, fashion, finance, food, health, fitness and medicine. Buys 30 mss/year. Send complete ms. Length: 2,000-4,000 words. Pays $125-600 for assigned articles. Pays $75-350 for unsolicited articles. Sometimes pays the expenses of writers on assignment.

Photos: State availability of photos with submission or send photos with submission. Reviews transparencies and prints. Offers $10-100 per photo. Model releases and identification of subjects required. Buys one-time rights.

RANCH & COAST, L.A. West Media Magazine, Inc., #302, 462 Stevens Ave., Solana Beach CA 92075. (619)481-7659. FAX: (619)481-6205. Publisher/Editor-in-Chief: Jan Loomis. Editor: Kit Ladwig. "Mostly" freelance written. Monthly magazine targeted at a sophisticated, upper-income readership, in San Diego County and surrounding areas. Most articles have a strong San Diego County focus. Circ. 30,000. Pays on publication. The vast majority of feature articles and departments are written on assignment; very few unsolicited mss are purchased. Queries with published clips are preferred to complete mss as the magazine's needs are very specific. Sample copy $2.50; writer's guidelines for SASE.

Photos: Availability of top-quality photos is helpful.

Tips: "Familiarity with *Ranch & Coast* in its current form is strongly advised."

SACRAMENTO MAGAZINE, 1021 2nd St., Sacramento CA 95812. FAX: (916)446-1238. Editor: Jan Haag. 80-90% freelance written. Works with a small number of new/unpublished writers each year. Monthly magazine emphasizing a strong local angle on politics, local issues, human interest and consumer items for readers in the middle to high income brackets. Estab. 1975. Pays on publication. Publishes ms an average of 3 months after acceptance. Rights vary; generally buys first North American serial rights, rarely second serial (reprint) rights. Original mss only (no previously published submissions). Reports in 2 months. Sample copy $3.50; writer's guidelines for #10 SASE.

Nonfiction: Local issues vital to Sacramento quality of life. Buys 15 unsolicited feature mss/year. Query first; no phone queries. Length: 1,500-3,000 words, depending on author, subject matter and treatment. Sometimes pays expenses of writers on assignment.

Photos: State availability of photos. Payment varies depending on photographer, subject matter and treatment. Captions (including IDs, location and date) required. Buys one-time rights.

Columns/Departments: Business, home and garden, media, parenting, first person essays, regional travel, gourmet, profile, sports and city arts (1,000-1,800 words); City Lights (250-400 words).

SAN FRANCISCO BAY GUARDIAN, 520 Hampshire St., San Francisco CA 94110. (415)255-3100. Editor/Publisher: Bruce Brugmann. 60% freelance written. Works with a small number of new/unpublished writers each year. An urban newsweekly specializing in investigative, consumer and lifestyle reporting for a sophisticated, urban audience. Circ. 80,000. Pays 1 month after publication. Publishes ms an average of 2 months after acceptance. Byline given. Buys 200 mss/year. Buys first rights. No simultaneous or multiple submissions. Query for electronic submissions.

Nonfiction: Vince Bielski, city editor; Eileen Ecklund, arts and entertainment editor; also features and book editor. Publishes "incisive local news stories, investigative reports, features, analysis and interpretation, how-to, consumer and entertainment reviews. Most stories have a Bay Area angle." Freelance material should have a "public interest advocacy journalism approach." Sometimes pays the expenses of writers on assignment.

Photos: John Schmitz, photo editor. Purchased with or without mss.

Tips: "Work with our volunteer and intern projects in investigative, political and consumer reporting. We teach the techniques and send interns out to do investigative research. We like to talk to writers in our office before they begin doing a story."

‡SAN FRANCISCO FOCUS, The City Magazine for the San Francisco Bay Area, 680 8th St., San Francisco CA 94103. (415)553-2800. Editor: Mark K. Powelson. Managing Editor: Rick Clogher. 80% freelance written. Prefers to work with published/established writers. A monthly city/regional magazine. Circ. 200,000. **Pays on acceptance.** Publishes ms an average of 2 months after acceptance. Byline given. Offers 33% kill fee. Buys one-time rights. Submit seasonal/holiday material 5 months in advance. Simultaneous queries and previously published submissions OK. Query for electronic submissions. Reports in 6 weeks. Sample copy $2.50; free writer's guidelines.

Nonfiction: Expose, humor, interview/profile, the arts, politics, public issues and travel. All stories should relate in some way to the San Francisco Bay Area (travel excepted). Query with published clips or send complete ms. Length: 750-4,000 words. Pays $75-750. Sometimes pays the expenses of writers on assignment.

THE SAN GABRIEL VALLEY MAGAZINE, Miller Books, 2908 W. Valley Blvd., Alhambra CA 91803. (213)284-7607. Editor-in-Chief: Joseph Miller. 75% freelance written. Bimonthly magazine. For middle- to upper-income people who dine out often at better restaurants in Los Angeles County. Estab. 1962. Circ. 3,400. Pays on publication. Publishes ms an average of 45 days after acceptance. Buys simultaneous rights, second serial (reprint) rights and one-time rights. Phone queries OK. Submit seasonal/holiday material 1 month in advance. Simultaneous and previously published submissions OK. Reports in 2 weeks. Sample copy $1.

Nonfiction: Exposé (political); informational (restaurants in the Valley); inspirational (success stories and positive thinking); interview (successful people and how they made it); profile (political leaders in the San Gabriel Valley); and travel (places in the Valley). Interested in 500-word humor articles. Buys 18 unsolicited mss/year. Length: 500-10,000 words. Pays 5¢/word.

Columns/Departments: Restaurants, Education, Valley News and Valley Personality. Buys 2 mss/issue. Send complete ms. Length: 500-1,500 words. Pays 5¢/word.
Fiction: Historical (successful people) and western (articles about Los Angeles County). Buys 2 mss/issue. Send complete ms. Length: 500-10,000 words. Pays 5¢/word.
Tips: "Send us a good personal success story about a Valley or a California personality. We are also interested in articles on positive thinking."

VALLEY MAGAZINE, World of Communications, Inc., Suite 275, 16800 Devonshire St., Granada Hills CA 91344. (818)368-3353. Editor: Barbara Wernik. 90% freelance written. Monthly magazine covering topics and people of interest to the San Fernando, Santa Clarita, Simi, Conejo and San Grabriel Valleys. Estab. 1978. Circ. 40,000. Pays within 2 months of acceptance. Publishes ms an average of 3 months after acceptance. Byline given. Offers 20% kill fee. Buys first North American serial rights. Submit seasonal/holiday material 6 months in advance. Simultaneous and previously published submissions OK. Reports in 2 weeks. Sample copy for $3 and 10×13 SAE; writer's guidelines for #10 SASE.
Nonfiction: Book excerpts, education, business, essays, general interest, how-to, humor, interview/profile, personal experience and travel. "General interest articles range from health to business to personality profiles. There must be a Valley slant. Audience is upscale, mature professionals." Special issues include Dining, Travel, Health and Local Business. Buys 130 mss/year. Query with published clips. Length: 750-2,000 words. Pays $50-350 for assigned articles; pays $25-250 for unsolicited articles.
Photos: State availability of photos with submission. Reviews transparencies. Captions, model releases and identification of subjects required.

VENTURA COUNTY & COAST REPORTER, VCR Inc., Suite 213, 1583 Spinnaker Dr., Ventura CA 93001. (805)658-2244; (805)656-0707. Editor: Nancy Cloutier. 12% freelance written. Works with a small number of new/unpublished writers each year. Weekly tabloid covering local news. Circ. 35,000. Pays on publication. Publishes ms an average of 2 weeks after acceptance. Byline given. Buys first North American serial rights. Reports in 3 weeks.
Nonfiction: General interest (local slant), humor, interview/profile and travel (local—within 500 miles). Local (Ventura County) slant predominates. Length: 2-5 double-spaced typewritten pages. Pays $10-25.
Photos: State availability of photos with ms. Reviews b&w contact sheet.
Columns/Departments: Entertainment, Sports, Dining News, Real Estate and Boating Experience (Southern California). Send complete ms. Pays $10-25.
Tips: "As long as topics are up-beat with local slant, we'll consider them."

Colorado

ASPEN MAGAZINE, Ridge Publications, P.O. Box G3, Aspen CO 81612. (303)920-4040. FAX: (303)920-4044. Editor: Janet C. O'Grady. Managing Editor: Carolyn Ely Hines. 85% freelance written. Bimonthly magazine covering Aspen and the Roaring Fork Valley. Estab. 1974. Circ. 15,000. Pays on publication. Byline given. Kill fee varies. Buys first North American serial rights. Query for electronic submissions. Sample copy for 9×12 SAE with 10 first class stamps. Free writer's guidelines.
Nonfiction: Essays, historical/nostalgic, interview/profile, new product, photo feature, travel, sports, outdoors and arts. "We do not publish general interest articles without an Aspen hook. We do not publish 'theme' (skiing in Aspen) or anniversary (40th year of Aspen Music Festival)." Buys 30-60 mss/year. Query with published clips. Length: 50-5,000 words. Pays $50-1,000. Sometimes pays expenses of writers on assignment.
Photos: State availability of photos with submission. Reviews contact sheets, negatives, transparencies and prints. ASMP standard minimum useage fees. Model release and identification of subjects required.
Columns/Departments: Discoveries (favorite spot: sense of place; enterprise: business; made in Aspen: crafts; then and now: history/present), 300-1,000. Query with published clips. Pays $50-150.

Connecticut

CONNECTICUT MAGAZINE, Communications International, 789 Reservoir Ave., Bridgeport CT 06606. (203)374-5488. FAX: (203)371-6561. Editor: Charles Monagan. Managing Editor: Dale Salm. 80% freelance written. Prefers to work with published/established writers who know the state and live/have lived here. A monthly magazine covering the state of Connecticut. "For an affluent, sophisticated, suburban audience. We want only articles that pertain to living in Connecticut." Estab. 1971. Circ. 90,000. Pays on publication. Publishes ms an average of 3-4 months after acceptance. Byline given. Offers 20% kill fee. Buys first North American serial rights. Submit seasonal/holiday material 4 months in advance. Reports in 6 weeks on queries. Writer's guidelines for #10 SASE.

Nonfiction: Book excerpts, expose, general interest, interview/profile and other topics of service to Connecticut readers. No personal essays. Buys 50 mss/year. Query with published clips. Length: 2,500-4,200 words. Pays $600-1,200. Sometimes pays the expenses of writers on assignment.

Photos: State availability of photos with submission. Reviews contact sheets and transparencies. Offers $50 minimum/photo. Model releases and identification of subjects required. Buys one-time rights.

Columns/Departments: Business, Health, Politics, Connecticut Guide, Arts, Gardening, Environment, Education, People, Sports, Law and Courts, Media and From the Past. Buys 50 mss/year. Query with published clips. Length: 1,500-2,500 words. Pays $300-600.

Fillers: Around and About editor—Valerie Schroth, senior editor. Short pieces about trends, curiosities, interesting short subjects, etc. Buys 50/year. Length: 150-400 words. Pays $75.

Tips: "Make certain that your idea is not something that has been covered to death by the local press and can withstand a time lag of a few months. Free-lancers can best break in with Around and About; find a Connecticut story that is offbeat and write it up in a fun, lighthearted, interesting manner. Again, we don't want something that has already received a lot of press."

‡HARTFORD MONTHLY, Hartford Monthly, Inc. 486 New Park Ave., West Hartford CT 06110. (203)236-7272. Editor: Mara Braverman. 85% freelance written. Monthly magazine on Greater Hartford area. Estab. 1988. Circ. 31,000. Pays on publication. Publishes ms an average of 3 months after acceptance. Byline given. Offers 15% kill fee. Buys first North American serial rights. Submit holiday/seasonal material 6 months in advance. Reports in 3 weeks on queries and mss. Sample copy for 8½ × 11 SAE with $3.85 postage.

Nonfiction: Essays, exposé, historical/nostalgic, how-to (gardening, cooking, decorating, etc.), humor, interview/profile, opinion, personal experience and photo feature. Buys 80-90 mss/year. Query with published clips. Send complete ms only for "Lasting Impressions" page. Length: 300-4,000 words. Pays $100-600. Sometimes pays expenses of writers on assignment. "Usually, we use writers based in Connecticut."

Photos: State availability of photos with submission or send photos with submission. Reviews 4 × 5 transparencies and 5 × 7 prints. Model releases and identification of subjects required. Buys one-time rights.

Fiction: Only interested in short stories by Connecticut writers.

HW, Gamer Publishing, 20 Isham Rd., West Hartford CT 06107. (203)231-7777. FAX: (203)233-2080. Editor: Donna Sicuranza. Circ. 40,000. Pays on publication. Publishes ms an average of 3 months after acceptance. Byline given. Offers 50% kill fee. Buys first rights and reprint rights. Submit seasonal/holiday material 3 months in advance. Simultaneous (unless within our geographic area), and previously published submissions OK. Reports in 2-3 weeks on queries; 1 month on mss. Sample copy for 11 × 14 SAE and $1.25 postage; writer's guidelines for #10 SASE.

Nonfiction: Essays of opinion, humorous, serious or reflective. Essays: "Hers," "His" and "Ours." Buys 3/month. Length: 750 words. Pays $35-50.

Poetry: Any topic. No set length. Buys 1-3/month. Pays $25-50.

Tips: "Send complete manuscripts. No phone calls, please. Manuscripts must be submitted with SASE if return is requested. We are looking for fresh ideas, innovative twists on old topics." Queries welcome for feature articles.

NORTHEAST MAGAZINE, *The Hartford Courant*, 285 Broad St., Hartford CT 06115. (203)241-3700. FAX: (203)520-6906. Editor: Lary Bloom. 50% freelance written. Eager to work with new/unpublished writers. Weekly magazine for a Connecticut audience. Estab. 1982. Circ. 300,000. **Pays on acceptance.** Publishes ms an average of 10 months after acceptance. Byline given. Buys one-time rights. Reports in 3 months.

Nonfiction: General interest (has to have strong Connecticut tie-in); in-depth investigation of stories behind news (has to have strong Connecticut tie-in); historical/nostalgic; interview/profile (of famous or important people with Connecticut ties); and personal essays (humorous or anecdotal). No poetry. Buys 75-100 mss/year. Length: 750-2,500 words. Pays $200-1,500.

For explanation of symbols, see the Key to Symbols and Abbreviations on Page 5. For unfamiliar words, see the Glossary.

Photos: Most assigned; state availability of photos. "Do not send originals."

Fiction: Well-written, original short stories. Length: 750-1,500 words.

Tips: "Less space available for all types of writing means our standards for acceptance will be much higher. We can only print 3-4 short stories a year."

District of Columbia

THE WASHINGTON POST, 1150 15th St. NW, Washington DC 20071. (202)334-7591. Travel Editor: Linda L. Halsey. 60% freelance written. Works with small number of new/unpublished writers each year. Prefers to work with published/established writers. Weekly newspaper travel section (Sunday). Pays on publication. Publishes ms an average of 3-6 months after acceptance. Byline given. "We are now emphasizing staff-written articles as well as quality writing from other sources. Stories are rarely assigned; all material comes in on speculation; there is no fixed kill fee." Buys first North American serial rights. Usually reports in 3 weeks.

Nonfiction: Emphasis is on travel writing with a strong sense of place, color, anecdote and history. Query with published clips. Length: 1,500-2,500 words, plus sidebar for practical information.

Photos: State availability of photos with ms.

THE WASHINGTON POST MAGAZINE, *The Washington Post,* 1150 15th St. NW, Washington DC 20071. Managing Editor: Linton Weeks. 40% freelance written. Prefers to work with published/established writers. Weekly magazine featuring articles of interest to Washington readers. Circ. 1.2 million (Sunday). Average issue includes 2 feature articles. **Pays on acceptance.** Publishes ms an average of 2 months after acceptance. Byline given. Buys all rights or first North American serial rights, depending on fee. Submit seasonal material 4 months in advance. Reports in 6 weeks on queries and mss. Sample copy for 9 × 12 SAE and 2 first class stamps.

Nonfiction: Controversial and consequential articles with a strong Washington angle. Query with published clips. Length: 1,500-6,500 words. Pays $100-up; competitive with major national magazine rates. Pays expenses of writers on assignment.

Photos: Reviews 4 × 5 or larger b&w glossy prints and 35mm or larger color transparencies. Model releases required.

Tips: "Always send SASE for return of material."

THE WASHINGTONIAN MAGAZINE, 1828 L St. NW, Washington DC 20036. FAX: (202)785-1822. Editor: John A. Limpert. 20% freelance written. Prefers to work with published/established writers who live in the Washington area. For active, affluent and well-educated audience. Monthly magazine. Estab. 1965. Circ. 166,891. Buys first rights only. Pays on publication. Publishes ms an average of 2 months after acceptance. Simultaneous submissions OK. Reports in 6 weeks. Sample copy for $3 and 9 × 12 SAE; writer's guidelines for #10 SASE.

Nonfiction: *"The Washingtonian* is written for Washingtonians. The subject matter is anything we feel might interest people interested in the mind and manners of the city. The only thing we ask is thoughtfulness and that no subject be treated too reverently. Audience is literate. We assume considerable sophistication about the city, and a sense of humor." Buys how-to, personal experience, interview/profile, humor, think pieces and exposes. Buys 75 mss/year. Length: 1,000-7,000 words; average feature 4,000 words. Pays 50¢/word. Sometimes pays the expenses of writers on assignment. Query or submit complete ms.

Photos: Photos rarely purchased with mss.

Fiction and Poetry: Howard Means, department editor. Must be Washington-oriented. No limitations on length for fiction; poetry not to exceed 30 lines. Pays 30¢/word for fiction; $35 on acceptance for poetry.

Florida

‡BAREFOOT REPORTER, Suncoast Publishing Group, P.O. Box 236, Pinellas Park FL 34664-0236. Editor: Nancy Dempsey Yost. 25% freelance written. Prefers to work with published/established writers. A weekly newspaper for beach communities. Circ. 15,000. Pays on publication. Publishes ms an average of 3 months after acceptance. Byline given. Buys one-time rights. Submit seasonal/holiday material 3 months in advance. Simultaneous and previously published submissions OK. Reports in 1 month. Sample copy $1 with 10 × 13 SAE and 5 first class stamps.

Nonfiction: Exposé, general interest, historical/nostalgic, how-to, humor, inspirational, interview/profile, opinion, photo feature, travel, health and finance, all slanted to a beach resident or visitor readership. Buys 10 mss/year. Query or send complete ms. Length: 300-600 words. Pays $15.

Photos: Send photos with submission. Reviews 3×5 color and 5×7 b&w prints. Identification of subjects required.

Columns/Departments: Travel, Profiles. Buys 10 mss/year. Send complete ms. Length: 300-600 words. Pays $15.

Fillers: Anecdotes, facts, cartoons, gags to be illustrated by cartoonist, and short humor. Buys 10/year. Length: 150-250 words. Pays $10.

Tips: "We serve the beach communities along the Florida Gulf Coast. Our sub-head is 'Life's a Beach.' A breezy, relaxed, conversational voice is just about right for us. Photos are important. Copy must be clean and concise."

BOCA RATON MAGAZINE, JES Publishing, Suite 100, 6413 Congress Ave., Boca Raton FL 33487. (407)997-8683. FAX: (407)997-8909. Editor: Darrell Hofheinz. 70% freelance written. Bimonthly magazine covering Boca Raton lifestyles. "Ours is a lifestyle magazine devoted to the residents of South Florida, featuring fashion, interior design, food, people, places and issues that shape the affluent South Florida market." Estab. 1981. Circ. 18,000. Pays on publication. Publishes ms an average of 2 months after acceptance. Byline given. Offers $25 kill fee. Buys second serial (reprint) rights. Submit seasonal/holiday material 7 months in advance. Simultaneous and previously published submissions OK. Query for electronic submission. Reports in 1 month. Sample copy $3.50 with 10×13 SAE and 10 first class stamps. Writer's guidelines for #10 SAE with one first class stamp.

Nonfiction: General interest, historical/nostalgic, humor, interview/profile, photo feature, travel. Query with or without published clips, or send complete ms. Length: 800-2,500 words. Pays $50-500 for assigned articles; $50-300 for unsolicited articles. Sometimes pays expenses of writers on assignment.

Photos: State availability of photos with submission.

Columns/Departments: Body & Soul (health, fitness and beauty column, general interest), 1,000 words; Family Room (family and social interactions), 1,000 words; Humor (South Florida topics), 600-1,200 words. Buys 6 mss/year. Query with published clips or send complete ms. Length: 600-1,500 words. Pays $50-250.

Fiction: Adventure, humorous, mainstream, romance, slice-of-life vignettes. "This is still a new category for us. We especially would like submissions that have South Florida setting or theme." Buys 3 mss/year. Query with published clips or send complete ms. Length: 1,000-2,000 words. Pays $50-200.

CORAL SPRINGS MONTHLY/PLANTATION MONTHLY, 10762 Wiles Rd., P.O. Box 8783, Coral Springs FL 33076. (305)344-8090. Executive Editor: Karen King. Monthly lifestyle magazines catering to residents of Coral Springs and Plantation. Residents are well-educated and interested in timely, innovative subjects. The magazines offer a variety of topics each month, among them health, fashion, classic cars, interior design, etc. Estab. 1986. Cir. 8,000. Pays on publication. Publishes ms an average of 2-3 months after acceptance. Byline given. Buys first rights and second serial (reprint) rights; all rights for an assigned story. Submit seasonal/holiday material 5-6 months in advance. Reports in 3 months. Sample copy $1.95.

Nonfiction: General interest, how-to, home decorating, gardening, fashion and beauty, humor, interview/profile, new products and travel. Buys 60 mss/year. Send complete ms; will return if unused. Length: 900-1,500 words. Pays $55-75.

Photos: Send photos with submission. Reviews transparencies (2½×2½ or 4×5); 5×7 b&w prints. Captions, model releases and identification of subjects required. Pay is negotiable.

Columns/Departments: On the Light Side (humorous slants on life, raising children, etc.); Classic Cars; Vital Signs (timely health news); Innovations (new consumer electronic products).

Tips: "Send completed manuscript. Any subject that might appeal to families will be considered. Our residents love to travel, like to learn about new ideas and services, and are interested in world and community issues."

‡FLORIDA LIVING, North Florida Publishing Co. Inc., Suite 1, 102 NE 10th Ave., Gainesville FL 32601. (904)372-8865. Editor: John Paul Jones. Managing Editor: Holly M. Hays. Monthly magazine covering Florida subjects for Floridians and would be Floridians. "We are a lifestyle magazine for Floridians and those interested in Florida. We have a rather large circulation outside of Florida." Estab. 1981. Circ. 22,000. Publishes ms an average of 3-6 months after acceptance. Byline given. No kill fee. Buys one-time rights. Submit seasonal/holiday material 3-12 months in advance. Sample copies and writer's guidelines for 9×12 SAE.

Nonfiction: General Florida interest, historical/nostalgic, interview/profile, personal experience, travel, other (out-of-the-way Florida places). Buys 50-60 mss/year. Query. Length: 500-1,500 words. Pays $25-200 for assigned articles; $25-100 for unsolicited articles. Send photos with submission. Reviews 3×5 prints. Offers $2.50-7.50 per photo. Captions required. Buys one-time rights.

Fiction: Historical. Buys 2-3 mss/year. Send complete ms. Length: 1,000-3,000 words. Pays $50-200.

GULF COAST, The Magazine of Southwest Florida, Gulfcoast Media Affiliates, 205 S. Airport Rd., Naples FL 33942. (813)643-4232. FAX: (813)643-6253. Editor: Barbara Amrhein. 65% freelance written. Monthly magazine. "We reach an affluent, literate readership, providing information on Florida's Gulf Coast." Estab. 1987. Circ. 22,000. Pays within 30 days of acceptance. Byline given. Offers $50 kill fee. Buys first North American serial rights, one-time rights or makes work-for-hire assignments. Submit seasonal/holiday material 4 months in advance. Query for electronic submissions. Reports in 3 weeks on queries; 2 months on mss. Sample copy for 9 × 12 SAE with 6 first class stamps. Writer's guidelines for #10 SASE.

Nonfiction: General interest and interview/profile. "We are heavily regional and use very little material that is not written by area writers." Buys 15-24 mss/year. Query. Length: 800-3,000 words. Pays $200-750 for assigned articles.

Photos: State availability of photos with submission. Reviews contact sheets, 35mm to 4 × 5 transparencies and prints. Pays $25 minimum per photo. Captions, model releases and identification of subjects required. Buys one-time rights.

Columns/Departments: Business, Health, Sports, Environment, Finance, Media, The Arts, People, and Insiders, 150-1,200 words. Buys 50 mss/year. Query. Pays $50-200.

GULFSHORE LIFE, 2975 S. Horseshoe Dr., Naples FL 33942. (813)643-3933. FAX: (813)643-5017. Editor: Janis Lyn Johnson. 30% freelance written. 10 times per year lifestyle magazine of southwest Florida. Estab. 1970. Circ. 20,000. Pays on publication. Publishes ms an average of 4 months after acceptance. Byline given. Offers ¼-⅓ kill fee. Buys first North American serial rights. Submit seasonal/holiday material 8 months in advance. Simultaneous and previously published submissions OK. Query for electronic submissions. Reports in 6 weeks. Sample copy for 8½ × 11 SAE with 10 first class stamps.

Nonfiction: Historical/nostalgic (SW Florida), interview/profile (SW Florida), travel/unusual Florida destinations. No articles that have absolutely nothing to do with SW Florida. Buys 40 mss/year. Query with published clips. Length: 1,200-3,000 words. Pays $150-450 for assigned articles. Sometimes pays expenses of writers.

Photos: State availability of photos with submission. Reviews 35mm transparencies and 5 × 7 prints. Pays $25-50. Captions, model releases and identification of subjects required. Buys one-time rights.

Fiction: SW Florida orientation. Can't exceed 3,000 words. Pays $150-300.

Tips: "Send me a superb query letter offering a must-use story idea. Tell me about a SW Florida place or person we don't already know about!"

ISLAND LIFE, The Enchanting Barrier Islands of Florida's Southwest Gulf Coast, Island Life Publications, P.O. Box 929, Sanibel FL 33957. Editor: Joan Hooper. Editorial Associate: Susan Shores. 40% freelance written. Prefers to work with published/established writers, but works with a small number of new/unpublished writers each year. Quarterly magazine of the Barrier Islands Sanibel, Captiva, Marco, for upper-income residents and vacationers of Florida's Gulf Coast area. Estab. 1980. Circ. 20,000. Pays on publication. Publishes ms an average of 1 year after acceptance. Byline given. Buys first serial rights and second serial (reprint) rights. Simultaneous queries and submissions OK. Reports in 1 month on queries; 3 months on mss.

Nonfiction: General interest, historical. "Travel and interview/profile done by staff. Our past use of freelance work has been heavily on Florida wildlife (plant and animal), Florida cuisine, and Florida parks and conservancies. We are a regional magazine. No fiction or first-person experiences. No poetry. Our editorial emphasis is on the history, culture, wildlife, art, scenic, sports, social and leisure activities of the area." Buys 10-20 mss/year. Query with ms and photos. Length: 500-1,500 words. Pays 3-8¢/word.

Photos: Send photos with ms. No additional payment. Captions, model releases, and identification of subjects required.

Tips: "Submissions are rejected, most often, when writer sends other than SW Florida focus."

PALM BEACH LIFE, Palm Beach Newspapers Inc./Cox Enterprises, 265 Royal Poinciana Way, Palm Beach FL 33486. (407)820-4750. FAX: (407)655-4594. Editor: Joyce Harr. 100% freelance written. Monthly magazine, a regional publication for Palm Beach County and South Florida. Estab. 1906. Circ. 19,971. **Pays on acceptance.** Publishes ms an average of 3 months after acceptance. Byline given. Buys first North American serial rights. Submit seasonal/holiday material 6 months in advance. Query for electronic submission. Reports in 1 month.

Nonfiction: Essays, exposé, general interest, historical/nostalgic, humor, interview/profile, photo feature and travel. Buys 100 mss/year. Query with published clips. Length: 900-5,000 words. Pays $150-700 for assigned articles; $75-400 for unsolicited articles. Sometimes pays expenses of writers on assignment (depending on agreed-upon fee).

Photos: Send photos with submission. Reviews transparencies. Offers $35-200 per photo. Captions, model releases and identification of subjects required. Buys one-time rights.

Columns/Departments: Traveler's Journal (specifically focused topical travel pieces), 1,500 words; High Profile (profiles of people of interest to readers in our region), 2,500 words. Buys 36 mss/year. Query with published clips. Pays $75-300.

‡**SENIOR VOICE OF FLORIDA**, Florida's Leading Newspaper for Active Mature Adults, (formerly Senior Voice Newspaper), Suncoast Publishing Group, P.O. Box 236, Pinellas Park FL 34664-0236. Publisher: Gerald R. Castellanos. Editor: Nancy Dempsey Yost. 25% freelance written. Prefers to work with published/established writers. A monthly newspaper for mature adults 50 years of age and over. Circ. 50,000. Pays on publication. Publishes ms an average of 3 months after acceptance. Byline given. Buys one-time rights. Submit season/holiday material 3 months in advance. Simultaneous and previously published submissions OK. Reports in 1 month. Sample copy $1 with 10×13 SAE and 5 first class stamps.

Nonfiction: Exposé, general interest, historical/nostalgic, how-to, humor, inspirational, interview/profile, opinion, photo feature, travel, health and finance, all slanted to a senior audience. Buys 10 mss/year. Query or send complete ms. Length: 300-600 words. Pays $15.

Photos: Send photos with submission. Reviews 3×5 color and 5×7 b&w. Identification of subjects required.

Columns/Departments: Travel (senior slant); V.I.P. Profiles (mature adults). Buys 10 mss/year. Send complete ms. Length: 300-600 words. Pays $15.

Fillers: Anecdotes, facts, cartoons, gags to be illustrated by cartoonist and short humor. Buys 10/year. Length: 150-250 words. Pays $10.

Tips: "Our service area is the Florida Gulf Coast, an area with a high population of resident retirees and repeat visitors who are 50 plus. We are interested primarily in serving their needs. In writing for that readership, keep their interests in mind. What they are interested in, we are interested in. We like a clean, concise writing style. Photos are important."

SOUTH FLORIDA, Florida Media Affiliates, Suite 500, 800 Douglas Rd., Coral Gables FL 33134. (305)445-4500. FAX: (305)445-4600. Editor: Marilyn A. Moore. 90% freelance written. Monthly magazine; general interest, must relate to Miami, Fort Lauderdale, the Florida Keys or Palm Beach County. Circ. 43,000. Pays 30 days after acceptance. Publishes ms an average of 3 months after acceptance. Byline given. Buys first North American serial rights, one-time rights or second serial (reprint) rights. Submit seasonal/holiday material 4 months in advance. Simultaneous and previously published submissions OK. Query for electronic submissions. Reports in 6 weeks on queries. Sample copy $3 plus $1 for postage. Florida residents add 6% sales tax. Writer's guidelines for #10 SASE.

Nonfiction: Exposé, general interest, humor, interview/profile, photo feature, South Florida Lifestyles and travel. Buys 120 mss/year. Query with or without published clips, or send complete ms. Length: 3,500 words maximum. Pays $100-750 for assigned articles. Sometimes pays expenses of writers on assignment.

Photos: State availability of photos with submission. Identification of subjects required. Buys one-time rights.

Columns/Departments: Business, Media, Arts, Home and "Lunch With" (profile of a locally connected celebrity). Buys 12 mss/year. Query with published clips. Length: 1,100-1,500 words. Pays $200-400.

SUNSHINE: THE MAGAZINE OF SOUTH FLORIDA, The News & Sun-Sentinel Co., 200 E. Las Olas Blvd., Fort Lauderdale FL 33301-2293. (305)356-4685. Editor: John Parkyn. 50% freelance written. Prefers to work with published/established writers, and works with a small number of new/unpublished writers each year. A general interest Sunday magazine for the *Sun-Sentinel's* 800,000 readers in South Florida. Circ. 325,000. Pays within 1 month of acceptance. Publishes ms an average of 2 months after acceptance. Byline given. Offers 25% kill fee for assigned material. Buys first serial rights or one-time rights in the state of Florida. Submit seasonal/holiday material 2 months in advance. Simultaneous queries, and simultaneous and previously published submissions OK. Reports in 2 weeks on queries; 1 month on mss. Free sample copy and writer's guidelines.

Nonfiction: General interest, interview/profile and travel. "Articles must be relevant to the interests of adults living in South Florida." Buys about 100 mss/year. Query with published clips. Length: 1,000-3,000 words; preferred length 1,500-2,500 words. Pays 20-25¢/word to $1,000 maximum.

Photos: State availability of photos. Pays negotiable rate for 35mm and 2¼ color slides and 8×10 b&w prints. Captions and identification of subjects required; model releases required for sensitive material. Buys one-time rights for the state of Florida.

Tips: "Do not phone, but do include your phone number on query letter. Keep your writing tight and concise—readers don't have the time to wade through masses of 'pretty' prose. We are always in the market for first-rate profiles, human-interest stories and travel stories (which must spotlight destinations within easy access of South Florida, e.g. S.E. U.S., Caribbean, Central America. Be as sophisticated and stylish as you can—Sunday magazines have come a long way from the Sunday supplements of yesteryear."

TAMPA BAY LIFE, The Bay Area's Magazine, Tampa Bay Media Affiliates, Inc., Suite 990, 6200 Courtney Campbell Causeway, Tampa FL 33607. (813)281-8855. FAX: (813)281-1920. Editorial Director: Larry Marscheck. 90% freelance written. Monthly magazine on Tampa Bay area lifestyle. "All material must be relevant to Tampa Bay area readers, whether it is trendy lifestyle material or serious environmental, social or political material." Estab. 1988. Circ. 25,000. Pays on publication. Publishes ms an average of 3 months after acceptance. Offers 25% kill fee. Buys first North American serial rights. Submit seasonal/holiday material 5 months in advance. Query for electronic submissions. Sample copy $2.50 with $2.50 postage. Writer's guidelines for #10 SAE with 1 first class stamp.
Nonfiction: Exposé, general interest, historical, humor, interview/profile. Buys 100 mss/year. Query with published clips. Length: 800-3,000 words. Pays $125-600. Sometimes pays expenses of writers on assignment.
Photos: State availability of photos with submission. Reviews contact sheets, transparencies and prints. Captions, model releases and identification of subjects required. Buys one-time rights.
Columns/Departments: Business (trends, personalities, company—big or small—profiles); Health (trends, topics, personalities, true-life stories); Travel (specific destinations people from the Tampa Bay area are likely to visit); Lively Arts (arts of all types, personalities, trends); Sporting Life (sports relevant to area, personalities, trends); Epicure (gourmet slant to anything edible, especially Florida edibles). Buys 48 mss/year. Query with published clips. Length: 1,030-1,400 words. Pays $150-300.
Fiction: Adventure, historical, mainstream, mystery, slice-of-life vignettes. "It should be noted that we have bought only two fiction pieces since publication began—we are open to buying more, if it is relevant to our area and extremely well written." Buys 1 or more ms/year. Query with published clips. Length: 800-3,000 words. Pays $200-450.
Tips: "We are a writer's magazine, therefore we demand writing that tells a story with flair. While the whole magazine is open to freelancers (we rely on them for ideas and treat them with TLC because we need them as much as they need us), new writers can break in via: Front Pages—bright briefs about the Tampa Bay area and its people; Journal—again, relevant to the Tampa Bay area on an unlimited range of subjects, but copy must be cogent, plunge the reader immediately into the story and make its sound point within 830 words."

TROPIC MAGAZINE, Sunday Magazine of the Miami Herald, Knight Ridder, 1 Herald Plaza, Miami FL 33132. (305)376-3432. Executive Editor: Bill Rose. Editor: Tom Shroder. 20% freelance written. Works with small number of new/unpublished writers each year. Weekly magazine covering general interest, locally oriented topics for local readers. Circ. 500,000. Pays on publication. Publishes ms an average of 2 months after acceptance. Byline given. Buys first serial rights. Submit seasonal/holiday material 2 months in advance. Reports in 6 weeks. Sample copy for 11 × 14 SAE.
Nonfiction: General interest; interview/profile (first person); and personal experience. No fiction or poetry. Buys 20 mss/year. Query with published clips or send complete ms with SASE. Length: 1,500-3,000 words. Pays $200-1,000/article.
Photos: Philip Brooker, art director. State availability of photos.

‡WATERFRONT NEWS, Ziegler Publishing Co., Inc., 1224 S.W. 1st Ave., Ft. Lauderdale FL 33315. (305)524-9450. FAX: (305)524-9464. Editor: John Ziegler. 75% freelance written. A monthly tabloid covering marine and boating topics for the Greater Ft. Lauderdale waterfront community. Circ. 35,000. Pays on publication. Publishes ms an average of 2 months after acceptance. Byline given. Buys first serial rights; second serial (reprint) rights or simultaneous rights in certain circumstances. Submit seasonal/holiday material 3 months in advance. Reports in 1 month on queries. Sample copy for 9 × 12 SAE and 4 first class stamps; free writer's guidelines.
Nonfiction: Historical/nostalgic (nautical or Southern Florida); new marine products; opinion (on marine topics); technical (on marine topics); and marine travel. Buys 50 mss/year. Query with or without published clips, or send complete ms. Length: 500-1,000 words. Pays $50-200 for assigned articles; pays $25-200 for unsolicited articles. Sometimes pays the expenses of writers on assignment.
Photos: State availability of photos or send photos with submission. Reviews contact sheets and 3 × 5 or larger prints. Offers $5/photo. Buys one-time rights.
Columns/Departments: Query with published clips. Length 500-1,000 words. Pays $25-100.
Fillers: Anecdotes, facts, nautical one-liners to be illustrated by cartoonist, newsbriefs and short humor. Buys 12/year. Length 100-500 words. Pays $10-200.
Tips: "Nonfiction marine, nautical or South Florida stories are more likely to be published than fiction or poetry. Keep it under 1,000 words. Photos or illustrations help. Send for a sample copy of *Waterfront News* so you can acquaint yourself with our water publication and our unique audience."

Georgia

NORTH GEORGIA JOURNAL, Legacy Communications, Inc., 110 Hunter's Mill, Woodstock GA 30188. (404)928-7739. Editor: Olin Jackson. 75% freelance written. A quarterly magazine of feature-length history articles, leisure lifestyles, and of travel opportunities to historic sites in the North Georgia area. Estab. 1984. Pays on publication. Publishes ms an average of 6 months after acceptance. Byline given. Buys first publication rights or all rights. Reports in 6 weeks. Sample copy $3.95 with 9×12 SAE and 8 first class stamps; free writer's guidelines.

Nonfiction: Historical/nostalgic personal experiences; photo features, travel. "I'm interested primarily in a first-person account of experiences involving the exploration of unique historic sites and travel opportunities indigenous to north Georgia and areas contiguous to north Georgia in other states." Buys 20-30 mss/year. Query. Length: 2,000-4,000 words. Pays $75-250.

Photos: Send photos with submission. "Photos are crucial to the acceptance of submissions." Reviews contact sheets and 8×10 and 5×7 prints. Offers no additional payment for photos accepted with ms. Captions and identification of subjects required. Buys first publication rights or all rights.

Tips: "We're interested in first-person accounts of experiences involving travel to and exploration of unique and interesting historic sites, travel opportunities and lifestyles indigenous to the Appalachian Mountains of north Georgia and areas contiguous to north Georgia in Tennessee, North Carolina, South Carolina and Alabama. An approach similar to that taken by submissions in *National Geographic* magazine is most desired. Subject matter of particular interest includes gold mining; pioneers in the area; Indian/early settlements/communities; catastrophic events and occurrences; and travel subject matter related to present-day opportunities at scenic and historic sites such as historic bed and breakfast/mountain inns, etc. Unique present-day mountain lifestyles features and featurettes with a historic twist are also highly desired."

Hawaii

ALOHA, THE MAGAZINE OF HAWAII AND THE PACIFIC, Davick Publishing Co., 49 S. Hotel St., #309, Honolulu HI 96813. (808)523-9871. FAX: (808)533-2055. Editor: Cheryl Tsutsumi. 50% freelance written. *Aloha* is a bimonthly regional magazine of international interest. "Most of our readers do not live in Hawaii, although most readers have been to the Islands at least once. Even given this fact, the magazine is directed primarily to residents of Hawaii in the belief that presenting material to an immediate critical audience will result in a true and accurate presentation that can be appreciated by everyone. *Aloha* is not a tourist publication and is not geared to such a readership, although travelers will find it to be of great value." Estab. 1977. Circ. 65,000. Pays on publication. Publishes ms an average of 6 months after acceptance; unsolicited ms can take a year or more. Byline given. Offers variable kill fee. Buys first-time rights. Submit seasonal/holiday material 1 year in advance. Reports in 2 months. Sample copy $2.95 with $2.90 first-class postage; writer's guidelines for SASE.

Nonfiction: Book excerpts; historical/nostalgic (historical articles must be researched with bibliography); interview/profile; and photo features. Subjects include the arts, business, flora and fauna, people, sports, destinations, food, interiors and history of Hawaii. "We don't want stories of a tourist's experiences in Waikiki or odes to beautiful scenery. We don't want an outsider's impressions of Hawaii, written for outsiders." Buys 24 mss/year. Query with published clips. Length: 1,000-4,000 words. Pay ranges from $200-400. Sometimes pays expenses of writers on assignment.

Photos: State availability of photos with query. Pays $25 for b&w prints; prefers negatives and contact sheets. Pays $60 for 35mm (minimum size) color transparencies used inside; $125 for double-page bleeds; $175 for color transparencies used as cover art. "*Aloha* features Beautiful Hawaii, a collection of photographs illustrating that theme, in every issue. A second photo essay by a sole photographer on a theme of his/her own choosing is also run occasionally. Queries are essential for the sole photographer essay." Model releases and identification of subjects required. Buys one-time rights.

Fiction: Ethnic and historical. "Fiction depicting a tourist's adventures in Waikiki is not what we're looking for. As a general statement, we welcome material reflecting the true Hawaiian experience." Buys 2 mss/year. Send complete ms. Length: 1,000-2,500 words. Pays $300.

Poetry: Haiku, light verse and traditional. No seasonal poetry or poetry related to other areas of the world. Buys 6 poems/year. Submit maximum 6 poems. Prefers "shorter poetry"—15 lines or less. Pays $25.

Tips: "Read *Aloha*. Be meticulous in research and have good illustrative material available to accompany your text."

HAWAII MAGAZINE, Fancy Publications, Inc., P.O. Box 6050, Mission Viejo CA 92690. (714)855-8822. Editor: Dennis Shattuck. Managing Editor: Julie Applebaum. 60% freelance written. Bimonthly magazine covering The Islands of Hawaii. "Hawaii magazine is written for people all over the world who visit and enjoy the culture, people and places of the Hawaiian Islands." Estab. 1984. Circ. 65,000.

Pays on publication. Byline given. Buys first North American serial rights. Submit seasonal/holiday material 6 months in advance. Query for electronic submissions. Reports in 4 weeks on queries; 6 weeks on mss. Sample copy for $3.95. Free writer's guidelines.

Nonfiction: General interest, historical/nostalgic, how-to, interview/profile, personal experience, photo feature and travel. "No articles on the following: first trip to Hawaii—How I discovered the Islands, the Hula, Poi, or Luaus." Buys 66 mss/year. Query with or without published clips or send complete ms. Length: 4,000 words maximum. Pays $100-500 for assigned articles.

Photos: Send photos with submission. Reviews contact sheets and transparencies. Offers $25-150 per photo. Identification of subjects preferred. Buys one-time rights.

Columns/Departments: Backdoor Hawaii (humorous look at the islands), 800-1,200 words; Hopping the Islands (news, general interest items), 100-200 words. Buys 6-12 mss/year. Query. Length: 800-1,500 words. Pays $100-200.

Tips: "Freelancers must be knowledgeable about Island subjects, virtual authorities on them. We see far too many first-person, wonderful-experience types of gushing articles. We buy articles only from people who are thoroughly grounded in the subject on which they are writing."

HONOLULU, Honolulu Publishing Co., Ltd., 36 Merchant St., Honolulu HI 96813. (808)524-7400. FAX: (808)531-2306. Editor: Ed Cassidy. Managing Editor: Janice Otaguro. 20% freelance written. Prefers to work with published/established writers. Monthly magazine covering general interest topics relating to Hawaii. Estab. 1888. Circ. 75,000. **Pays on acceptance.** Publishes ms an average of 4 months after acceptance. Byline given. Offers $50 kill fee. Buys first serial rights. Submit seasonal/holiday material 5 months in advance. Simultaneous queries and simultaneous submissions OK. Sample copy $2 with 9×12 SAE and $2.40 postage; free writer's guidelines.

Nonfiction: Exposé, general interest, historical/nostalgic, and photo feature—all Hawaii-related. "We run regular features on fashion, interior design, travel, etc., plus other timely, provocative articles. No personal experience articles." Buys 10 mss/year. Query with published clips if available. Length: 2,000-4,000 words. Pays $500. Sometimes pays expenses of writers on assignment.

Photos: Teresa Black, photo editor. State availability of photos. Pays $15 maximum for b&w contact sheet; $25 maximum for 35mm transparencies. Captions and identification of subjects required. Buys one-time rights.

Columns/Departments: Calabash (light, "newsy," timely, humorous column on any Hawaii-related subject). Buys 15 mss/year. Query with published clips or send complete ms. Length: 250-1,000 words. Pays $35.

KAU KAU KITCHEN NEWSLETTER, Yuen Media Services, 372 Haili St., Hilo HI 96720. (808)961-3984. Editor: Leilehua Yuen. 50% freelance written. Quarterly newsletter on regional-Hawaii cooking, food, beverage and nutrition. "Food is meant to be enjoyed. Cooking is fun. Hawaii's food is special and deserves preservation. *Kau Kau Kitchen* gives a taste of Hawaii's culture—past and present." Estab. 1988. Circ. 100. Publishes ms an average of 3-6 months after acceptance. Byline given. Offers kill fee by arrangement with author. Buys one-time rights. Submit seasonal/holiday material 6 months in advance. Simultaneous and previously published submissions OK. Reports in 2 months. Sample copy $2. Writer's guidelines for #10 SASE with 1 first class stamp.

Nonfiction: Book excerpts, how-to (cooking techniques), travel (with food/family slant—either traveling in Pacific region or Pacific people visiting other areas), humor (related to cooking), interview/profile (of interesting Hawaii cooks, not necessarily chefs) and new product. "No fiction, anything blatantly opinionated on vegetarianism or any other 'ism'." Query with or without published clips, or send complete ms. Length: 50-800 words. Pays $5 minimum for assigned articles. Pays in advertising space, subscriptions. Sometimes pays expenses of writers on assignment.

Columns/Departments: TuTu's Tips (kitchen and household tips with Hawaii slant) and Keiki Kitchen (kitchen and household with children's slant). Query or send complete ms. Length: 300-800 words. Pays $5 minimum.

Poetry: Avant-garde, free verse, haiku, light verse and traditional. Hawaii slant on food, household or family. "No erotic or non-food/household/family." Buys 30-50 poems/year. Submit maximum 10 poems. Should fit a 40 character by 20 line space. "Please, please, please stop sending poetry on rolling New England oceans, and God's glory over the Appalachians. If it doesn't touch the Pacific Ocean, we don't want it."

Fillers: Anecdotes, facts, newsbreaks and cartoons if well drawn. Length: 50 words maximum.

Tips: "Love what you write about and the people you write for. *Kau Kau Kitchen* is very informal. Technically perfect writing is not as desirable as honestly talking with the reader. Yes, I occasionally end sentences with prepositions, but my readers *know* what I'm saying. We're all sitting around the kitchen table. It's not the place for dissertations."

Idaho

OH! IDAHO, The Idaho State Magazine, P.O. Box 925, Hailey ID 83333. (208)788-4500. FAX: (208)788-5098. Editor: Laurie Sammis. 80% freelance written. Quarterly magazine on Idaho related topics. Estab. 1988. Circ. 20,000. Pays on publication. Publishes ms an average of 3 months after acceptance. Byline given. Buys first North American serial rights. Submit seasonal/holiday material 6 months in advance. Simultaneous submissions and previously published submissions (if not in an Idaho publication within same year) OK. Query for electronic submissions. Reports in 6 weeks. Sample copy $3 with 8½ × 11 SAE. Writer's guidelines for #10 SASE.

Nonfiction: Buys 15-20 mss/year. Query. Length: 1,500-2,500 words. Pays $100-250 (more for *top quality*).

Photos: Send photos in response to want list (generated 4 times/year). Reviews transparencies. Offers $25-200 per photo, more for cover shot. Captions, model releases and identification of subjects required. Buys one-time rights.

Columns/Departments: Education (exciting topics from Idaho universities or schools), food; general interest; interview/profile; new product; opinion; and travel, all Idaho related. "No descriptions of small business unless it has an Idaho base and a national impact." Buys 30-40 mss/year. Query or send complete ms. Length: 900-1,500 words. Pays $90-150, more for top quality.

Tips: "All articles must specifically be related to Idaho. Most willing to consider all queries and submissions. Writing should *sparkle* and avoid journalistic approach."

Illinois

‡CHAMPAIGN-URBANA MAGAZINE, Faucett Communications, Inc., Suite 511, 44 Main St., Champaign IL 61820. (217)351-9105. Editor: Philip M. Faucett. Monthly magazine for readers in five central Illinois counties surrounding the Champaign-Urbana metropolitan area. Circ. 15,000. **Pays on acceptance.** Byline given. Offers 20% kill fee. Submit seasonal/holiday material 2 months in advance. Reports in 2 weeks on queries; 1 month on mss. Free sample copy and writer's guidelines.

Nonfiction: Exposé, general interest, historical/nostalgic, how-to, humor, interview/profile, new product, opinion, personal experience, photo feature, travel. Special issues include anniversary issues: Back-to-School, City/Regional Guide, Christmas Issue, Spring Issue. No religious, technical writing, fiction or poetry. Buys 50 mss/year. Query. Length: 1,000-3,000 words. Pays $75 minimum for 1,500 published words.

Photos: State availability. Pays $10-60 for b&w contact sheet and negatives; $10-75 for b&w prints.

Columns/Departments: Film Reviews, Dining Out, Astronomy, Food/Cooking, Financial, Around Town, Weather, Shopping, Health, etc. Buys 50 mss/year. Query. Length: 500 words minimum. Pays $25 minimum.

Fillers: Clippings, anecdotes, short humor. Buys 72/year. Length: 250-350 words. Pays $15 minimum.

Tips: "We encourage writers to submit ideas of their choosing. The slant should be to the point, informative, nonfictional and sharp."

‡CHICAGO LIFE, Box 11311, Chicago IL 60611-0311. Editor: Pam Berns. 95% freelance written. A bimonthly magazine on Chicago Life. Circ. 60,000. Pays on publication. Byline given. Kill fee varies. Submit seasonal/holiday material 8 months in advance. Simultaneous and previously published submissions OK. Reports in 3 months. Sample copy for 9 × 12 SAE with 7 first class stamps.

Nonfiction: Book excerpts, essays, exposé, how-to, photo feature and travel. Buys 50 mss/year. Send complete ms. Length: 400-1,200 words. Pays $30 for unsolicited articles. Sometimes pays the expenses of writers on assignment. Send photos with submission. Reviews contact sheets, negatives, transparencies and prints. Offers $15-30 per photo. Buys one-time rights.

Columns/Departments: Law, Book Reviews, Travel and Fashion. Send complete ms. Length: 500 words. Pays $30.

Fillers: Facts. Pays $15-30.

Tips: "Please send work with visuals (photos, if possible). Topics open include travel, self improvement, how-to-do almost anything, entrepreneurs, how to get rich, beautiful, more well-informed."

CHICAGO MAGAZINE, 414 N. Orleans, Chicago IL 60610. Managing Editor: Joanne Trestrail. 40% freelance written. Prefers to work with published/established writers; works with a small number of new/unpublished writers each year. Monthly magazine for an audience which is "95% from Chicago area; 90% college-trained; upper income; overriding interests in the arts, politics, dining, good life in the city and suburbs. Most are in 25-50 age bracket, well-read and articulate." Circ. 210,000. Buys first serial rights. **Pays on acceptance.** Publishes ms an average of 6 months after acceptance. Submit seasonal material 4 months in advance." Reports in 2 weeks. Query; indicate "specifics, knowledge of city and market, and demonstrable access to sources." For sample copy, send $3 to Circulation Dept.; writer's guidelines for #10 SASE.

Nonfiction: "On themes relating to the quality of life in Chicago: past, present, and future." Writers should have "a general awareness that the readers will be concerned, influential longtime Chicagoans reading what the writer has to say about their city. We generally publish material too comprehensive for daily newspapers." Personal experience and think pieces, profiles, humor, spot news, historical articles and exposés. Buys about 50 mss/year. Length: 500-6,000 words. Pays $100-$2,500. Pays expenses of writers on assignment.

Photos: Reviews b&w glossy prints, 35mm color transparencies or color prints. Usually assigned separately, not acquired from writers.

Tips: "Submit detailed queries, be business-like and avoid clichéd ideas."

THE CHICAGO TRIBUNE MAGAZINE, Chicago Tribune Co., 435 N. Michigan Ave., Chicago IL 60611. (312)222-3232. Editor: Denis Gosselin. Managing Editor: John S. Wade. 35% freelance written. A weekly Sunday magazine. "*Sunday* looks for unique, compelling, all researched, elequently written articles on subjects of general interest." Circ. 1 million. Pays on publication. Publishes ms an average of 2 months after acceptance. Offers 35-50% kill fee. Buys one-time rights. Submit seasonal/holiday material 6 months in advance. Query for electronic submissions. Reports in1 month on queries; 6 weeks on manuscripts.

Nonfiction: Book excerpts, exposé, general interest, interview/profile, photo feature, technical and travel. No humor, first person or casual essays. Buys 35 mss/year. Query or seen complete ms. Length: 2,500-5,000 words. Pays $1,000. Sometimes pays the expenses of writers on assignment. State availability of photos with submission. Offer varies for photos. Captions and identification of subjects required. Buys one-time rights.

Columns/Departments: First Person (Chicago area subjects only, talking about their occupations), 1,000 words. Buys 52 mss/year. Query. Pays $250.

‡FOX VALLEY LIVING, Sampler Publications, Inc. 707 Kautz Rd., St. Charles IL 60174. (708)377-7570. Editor: Francie Graham Smith. Associate Editor: Becky Moorehead Hoag. 50% freelance written. Bimonthly magazine for the Fox River Valley of Illinois. "Family-oriented regional lifestyle publication." Estab. 1989. Circ. 35,000. **Pays on acceptance.** Publishes ms an average of 4 months after acceptance. Byline given. Offers 33% kill fee. Buys all rights (but gives permission for reprints in noncompeting publications). Submit seasonal/holiday material at least 6 months in advance. Query for electronic submissions. Reports in 10 weeks on queries; 2 months on mss. Sample copy $2; free writer's guidelines.

Nonfiction: Book excerpts, general interest, historical/nostalgic, how-to (recipes, crafts, gardening, decorating), humor, interview/profile, opinion, personal experience, photo feature, travel. "All must be related to the Fox Valley area. Writers should write for editorial calendar." Buys 40-50 mss/year. Query with or without published clips. Length: 600 words maximum preferred. Pays $100-350 for assigned articles; $50-250 for unsolicited articles. Sometimes pays expenses of writers on assignment.

Photos: State availability of photos with submission. Reviews contact sheets, negatives, transparencies or prints. Offers $50-150 for photos. Model releases and indentification of subjects required. Buys one-time rights.

Columns/Departments: Almanac (history, helpful info), 50-250 words; Environment (how to help), 100-300 words; Heritage (Fox Valley people or places), 200-600 words. "Treatment" preferred. Pays $50-200.

Fiction: Holds a student short fiction contest. Would consider work of a published author from the Fox Valley. Query. Length: 1,000 words or less.

Poetry: Haiku, light verse, traditional. Buys 3-6 poems/year. Submit maximum of 10 poems at one time. Length: 36 lines maximum. Pays $50-150.

Fillers: Anecdotes, facts, newsbreaks, short humor. Buys 6-10/year. Length: 50-300 words. Pays $50-200.

Tips: "Query with 3-6 ideas. We prefer slant and treatment. Be as specific as possible. Writing samples are much more useful than a list of credits. State any expertise on the subjects you query about. Home and gardens, and recreation and leisure are easiest areas for freelancers to break in."

ILLINOIS MAGAZINE, The Magazine of the Prairie State, Sunshine Park, P.O. Box 40, Litchfield IL 62056. (217)324-3425. Editor: Peggy Kuethe. 85% freelance written. Works with a small number of new/unpublished writers each year, and is eager to work with new/unpublished writers. A bimonthly magazine devoted to the heritage of the state. Emphasizes history, current interest and travel in Illinois for historians, genealogists, students and others who are interested in the state. Estab. 1964. Circ. 16,000. Pays on publication. Publishes ms an average of 6 months after acceptance. Byline given. Buys first North American serial rights or one-time rights. Submit seasonal/holiday material 6 months in advance. Reports in 2 months on queries; 4 months on mss. Include SASE with submission. Sample copy for 10×12 SAE and 5 first class stamps; writer's guidelines for #10 SASE.

Nonfiction: Essays, general interest, historical/nostalgic, interview/profile, photo feature and travel. Also, festivals (annual events), biography, points of interest, botany, animals, scenic areas that would be of interest to travelers. "We do not want to see family history/family tree/genealogy articles." Buys 75-85 mss/year. Send complete ms. Length: 100-1,500 words. Pays $20-100.

Photos: Send photos with submission. Reviews contact sheets, 35mm or 4×5 transparencies using slow film and 3×5, 5×7 and 8×10 b&w prints. Offers $5-50 photo. Captions, model releases, and identification of subjects required. Buys one-time rights. Length: 50-200 words. Pays $10-$25.

Fillers: Anecdotes, facts and short humor. Buys 3-5/year. Length: 50-200 words. Pays $10-$25.

Tips: "Be sure to include a phone number where you can be reached during the day. Also, try if at all possible to obtain photographs for the article if it requires them. And don't forget to include sources or references for factual material used in the article."

‡**INSIDE CHICAGO**, Signature Publishing, 2501 W. Peterson Ave., Chicago IL 60659. (312)784-0800. FAX: (312)784-6094. Editor: Barbara J. Young. 90% freelance written. Bimonthly magazine. Estab. 1987. Circ. 70,000. Pays within 30 days of publication. Byline given. Offers 20% kill fee. Buys first rights. Submit seasonal/holiday material 3 months in advance. Query for electronic submissions. Reports in 1 month. Sample copy $4.40; writer's guidelines for SASE.

Nonfiction: Business, general and special interest, humor, interview/profile, photo feature, travel, music, art, theatre, design and political. "Send only material with an offbeat, local angle." Buys 60 mss/year. Query with published clips.

Columns/Departments: Music, Art, Nightlife, Travel, Dining, Accent/Lifestyle, Neighborhoods, Books and Film. Length: approximately 1,000 words. Pays $200 and up.

Fillers: Needs short pieces for The Front and Power Play. Buys 30/year. Length: 300-400 words.

‡**NORTH SHORE, The Magazine of Chicago's Northern Suburbs**, PB Communications, 874 Green Bay Rd., Winnetka IL 60093. (708)441-7892. Publisher: Asher Birnbaum. Managing Editor: Karen Titus. 75% freelance written. Monthly magazine. "Our readers are a diverse lot, from middle-class communities to some of the country's wealthiest ZIP codes. But they all have one thing in common — our proximity to Chicago." Pays on publication. Publishes ms an average of 3 months after acceptance. Byline given. 50% kill fee. Buys first North American serial rights. Submit seasonal/holiday material 5 months in advance. Photocopied and previously published submissions OK. Reports in 1 month on queries; 1 month on mss. Free writer's guidelines.

Nonfiction: Book excerpts, exposé, general interest, how-to, interview/profile, photo feature and travel. Fitness — February; Weddings — January, July; Homes/Gardens — March, June, September, December; Weekend Travel — May; Nursing/Retirement Homes — August; Dining and Nightlife — October. Buys 50 mss/year. Query with published clips. Length: 500-4,000 words. Pays $100-800. Sometimes pays expenses of writers on assignment.

Photos: State availability of photos with submission. Reviews contact sheets, negatives, transparencies and prints. Offers $25-100 per photo. Identification of subjects required. Buys one-time rights.

Columns/Departments: "Prelude" (shorter items of local interest), 400-900 words. Buys 12 mss/year. Query with published clips. Pays $50-100.

Tips: "We're always looking for something of local interest that's fresh and hasn't been reported elsewhere. Look for local angle. Offer us a story that's exclusive in the crowded Chicago-area media marketplace. Well-written feature stories have the best chance of being published. We cover all of Chicago's north and northwest suburbs together with some Chicago material, not just the North Shore."

ROCKFORD MAGAZINE, Northwest Publishing, 331 E. State St., Rockford IL 61105. (815)961-2400. Editor: Elaine Johnson. 50% freelance written. Monthly magazine covering the city of Rockford. Stories must concern, or be of interest to, the people of the Rockford area. Estab. 1986. Circ. 22,000. **Pays on acceptance.** Publishes ms an average of 2 months after acceptance. Byline given. Offers 15% kill fee. Buys first rights. Submit seasonal/holiday material 2 months in advance. Query for electronic submissions. Sample copy for $2.95. Free writer's guidelines.

Nonfiction: General interest and interview/profile. "No personal experiences, poetry or fiction." Buys 20 mss/year. Send complete ms. Length: 1,200-3,000 words. Pays $100-300 for assigned articles. Sometimes pays expenses of writers on assignment.

Photos: State availability of photos with submission. Captions and model releases required. Buys one-time rights.

Columns/Departments: Eats (food, restaurant); Nightbeat (entertainment), Destinations (day-trips in Rockford area). Buys 20 mss/year. Send complete ms. Length: 1,300-1,800 words. Pays $75-125.

Tips: "The difficulty is that freelancers must generally be from this area. We're open to them in most departments of the magazine."

Indiana

ARTS INDIANA, Arts Indiana, Inc. Suite 701, 47 S. Pennsylvania, Indianapolis IN 46204-3622. (317)632-7894. Editor: Richard J. Roberts. 95% freelance written. Monthly, Sept.-June magazine on artists and arts organizations working in Indiana—literary, visual and performing. Circ. 12,000. Pays on publication. Publishes ms an average of 3-6 months after acceptance. Byline given. Offers 50% kill fee. Buys first North American serial rights. Submit seasonal/holiday material 4 months in advance. Reports in 3 months. Free sample copy and writer's guidelines.
Nonfiction: Essays, historical/nostalgic, interview/profile, opinion, photo feature and interviews with reviews; Q & A format. "No straight news reportage." Query with published clips. Length: 1,000-3,000 words. Pays $50-250 for assigned articles; $50-150 for unsolicited articles. Complimentary one-year subscription is given in addition to cash payment. Sometimes pays expenses of writer on assignment.
Photos: Send photos with submission. Reviews 5×7 or larger prints. Offers no additional payment for photos accepted with ms. Captions and identification of subjects required. Buys one-time rights.
Tips: "We are looking for people-oriented and issue-oriented articles. Articles about people should reveal the artist's personality as well as describe his artwork. Contributors must reside in Indiana."

‡INDIANAPOLIS MONTHLY, Emmis Publishing Corp., Suite 1200, 950 N. Meridian St., Indianapolis IN 46204. (317)237-9288. Editor: Deborah Paul. Managing Editor: Sam Stall. 20% freelance written. Prefers to work with published/established writers. A monthly magazine of "upbeat material reflecting current trends. Heavy on lifestyle, homes and fashion. Material must be regional in appeal." Circ. 50,000. Pays on publication. Publishes ms an average of 2 months after acceptance. Byline given. Offers 50% kill fee in some cases. Buys first North American serial rights and makes work-for-hire assignments. Submit seasonal/holiday material 3 months in advance. Reports in 1 month. Sample copy for 9×12 SAE and $3.05; writer's guidelines for #10 SASE.
Nonfiction: General interest, historical/nostalgic, interview/profile and photo feature. Special issue is the 500 Mile Race issue (May). No poetry, domestic humor or stories without a regional angle. "We prefer stories with a timely or topical angle or 'hook' as opposed to topics plucked out of thin air." Buys 50 mss/year. Query with published clips or send complete ms. Length: 200-5,000 words. Pays $50-500. Sometimes pays the expenses of writers on assignment.
Photos: Send photos with submission. Reviews 35mm or 2¼ transparencies. Offers $25 minimum/photo. Identification of subjects required. Buys one-time rights.
Columns/Departments: Business (local made-goods), Sport (heroes, trendy sports), Health (new specialties, technology) and Retrospect (regional history), all 1,000 words. Buys 6-9 mss/year. Query with published clips or send complete mss. Pays $100-300.
Tips: "Monthly departments are open to freelancers. We also run monthly special sections—write for editorial special section lineups."

Kansas

KANSAS!, Kansas Department of Economic Development, 400 W. 8th, 5th Floor, Topeka KS 66603. (913)296-3479. Editor: Andrea Glenn. 90% freelance written. Quarterly magazine. Emphasizes Kansas "people and places for all ages, occupations and interests." Estab. 1945. Circ. 54,000. **Pays on acceptance.** Publishes ms an average of 1 year after acceptance. Byline given. Buys one-time rights. Submit seasonal/holiday material 8 months in advance. Reports in 2 months. Free sample copy and writer's guidelines.
Nonfiction: "Material must be Kansas-oriented and have good potential for color photographs. We feature stories about Kansas people, places and events that can be enjoyed by the general public. In other words, events must be open to the public, places also. People featured must have interesting crafts, etc." General interest, interview, photo feature and travel. Query. "Query letter should clearly outline story in mind. I'm especially interested in Kansas freelancers who can supply their own photos." Length: 3-5 pages double-spaced, typewritten copy. Pays $100-200. Sometimes pays expenses of writers on assignment.
Photos: "We are a full-color photo/manuscript publication." State availability of photos with query. Pays $50-75 (generally included in ms rate) for transparencies. Captions required.

For information on setting your freelance fees, see How Much Should I Charge? in the Business of Writing section.

Tips: "History and nostalgia stories do not fit into our format because they can't be illustrated well with color photography."

Kentucky

BACK HOME IN KENTUCKY, Greysmith Publishing Inc., 128 Holiday Ct., P.O. Box 681629, Franklin TN 37068-1629. (615)794-4338. FAX: (615)790-6188. Editor: Nanci P. Gregg. 90% freelance written. Bimonthly magazine covering Kentucky heritage, peoples, places, events. We reach Kentuckians and "displaced" Kentuckians living outside the state. Estab. 1977. Pays on publication. Publishes ms an average of 8 months after acceptance. Byline given. Buys first North American serial rights. Submit seasonal/holiday material 8 months in advance. Query for electronic submissions. Reports in 2 months. Sample copy for $2.50 with 9×12 SAE and 5 first class stamps. Writer's guidelines for #10 SAE with 1 first class stamp.
Nonfiction: Historical (Kentucky related), how-to (might be gardening or crafts), interview/profile (noted or unusual Kentuckians), photo feature (Kentucky places and events), travel (Kentucky places). No inspirational or religion—all must be Kentucky related. Buys 50 mss/year. Query with or without published clips or send complete ms. Length: 500-2,000 words. Pays $25-100 for assigned articles; $15-50 for unsolicited articles. "In addition to normal payment, writers receive 4 copies of issue containing their article and 1 year subscription." Sometimes pays expenses of writers on assignment.
Photos: Send photos with submission. Reviews transparencies and 5×7 prints. Offers no additional payment for photos accepted with ms. Model releases and identification of subjects required. Rights purchased depends on situation.
Columns/Departments: Kentucky travel, Kentucky crafts and Kentucky gardening. Buys 10-12 mss/year. Query with published clips. Length: 500-750 words. Pays $15-40.
Tips: "We recently purchased this magazine and are trying to organize and departmentalize its content. We work mostly with unpublished writers who have a feel for Kentucky—its people, places, events, etc. The areas most open to freelancers are travel—places in Kentucky, history, and profiles of interesting, unusual Kentuckians."

KENTUCKY LIVING, P.O. Box 32170, 4515 Bishop Lane, Louisville KY 40232. (502)451-2430. Editor: Gary W. Luhr. Mostly freelance written. Prefers to work with published/established writers. Monthly feature magazine primarily for Kentucky residents. Estab. 1948. Circ. 340,000. **Pays on acceptance.** Publishes ms on average of 2-8 months after acceptance. Byline given. Buys first serial rights for Kentucky. Submit seasonal/holiday material at least 6 months in advance. Will consider previously published and simultaneous submissions (if previously published and/or simultaneous submissions outside Kentucky). Reports in 2 weeks. Sample copy for 8½×11 SAE and 4 first class stamps.; writer's guidelines for #10 SASE.
Nonfiction: Prefers Kentucky-related profiles (people, places or events), history, biography, recreation, travel, leisure or lifestyle articles or book excerpts; articles on contemporary subjects of general public interest and general consumer-related features including service pieces. Publishes some humorous and first-person articles of exceptional quality and opinion pieces from qualified authorities. No general nostalgia. Buys 24-36 mss/year. Query or send complete ms. Pays $75 to $125 for "short" features (600-800 words) used in section known as "Kentucky Fare." For major articles (800-2,000 words) pays $150 to $300. Sometimes pays the expenses of writers on assignment.
Photos: Send photos with submission. Reviews color slides and b&w prints. Identification of subjects required. Payment for photos included in payment for ms. Pays extra if photo used on cover.
Tips: "The quality of writing and reporting (factual, objective, thorough) is considered in setting payment price. We prefer well-documented pieces filled with quotes and anecdotes. Avoid boosterism. Well-researched, well-written feature articles, particularly on subjects of a serious nature, are given preference over light-weight material."

Louisiana

‡LOUISIANA LIFE MAGAZINE, Ardmont Publishing Group, Suite 220, 4200 S. I-10 Service Rd., P.O. Box 308, Metairie LA 70004. (504)456-2220. Editor: Maria Ward McIntosh. 95% freelance written. Bimonthly general interest magazine. "We report on the people, places and events that make Louisiana unique." Estab. 1981. Circ. 35,000. Pays on publication. Publishes ms an average of 3-6 months after acceptance. Byline given. $25-100 kill fee. Buys first North American serial rights. Submit seasonal/holiday material 6 months in advance. Query for electronic submissions. Reports in 4 weeks. Sample copy $3.
Nonfiction: General interest, historical/nostalgic, interview/profile, photo feature and travel. "No articles on subjects we've covered before!" Buys 150 mss/year. Query with published clips. Length: 200-4,000 words. Pays $25-800. Pays expenses of writer on assignment. State availability of photos with

submission. Review contact sheets and transparencies. Offers $50-135/photo. Captions, model releases and identification of subjects required. Buys one-time rights.

SUNDAY ADVOCATE MAGAZINE, P.O. Box 588, Baton Rouge LA 70821. (504)383-1111, ext. 319. FAX: (504)388-0371. Editor: Larry Catalanello. 5% freelance written. "We are backlogged but still welcome submissions." Byline given. Estab. 1925. Pays on publication. Publishes ms up to 1 year after acceptance. Query for electronic submissions.
Nonfiction and Photos: Well-illustrated, short articles; must have local, area or Louisiana angle, in that order of preference. Also interested in travel pieces. Photos purchased with mss. Rates vary.
Tips: Styles may vary. Subject matter may vary. Local interest is most important. No more than 4-5 typed, double-spaced pages.

Maine

GREATER PORTLAND MAGAZINE, Greater Portland Publications, 477 Congress St., Portland ME 04101. (207)773-5000. Editor: Shirley Jacks. 75% freelance written. Works with a small number of new/unpublished writers each year. "We enjoy offering talented and enthusiastic new writers the kind of editorial guidance they need to become professional freelancers." A bimonthly magazine covering metropolitan and island lifestyles of Greater Portland. "We cover the arts, night life, islands, people and progressive business in and around Greater Portland." Estab. 1990. Circ. 7,000. Pays on publication. Publishes ms an average of 2 months after acceptance. Byline given. Buys first serial rights. Submit seasonal/holiday material 6 months in advance. Query for electronic submissions. Reports in 1 week on queries; 2 weeks on mss. Sample copy $3; writer's guidelines for #10 SASE.
Nonfiction: Articles about people, places, events, institutions and the arts in greater Portland. "*Greater Portland* is largely freelance written. We are looking for well-researched, well-focused essayistic features. First-person essays are welcome." Buys 20 mss/year. Query with published clips. Length: 1,000-2,000 words. Pays 10¢/word maximum.
Photos: Buys b&w and color slides with ms. Captions required.
Tips: "Send some clips with several story ideas. We're looking for informal, essayistic features structured around a well-defined point or theme. A lively, carefully crafted presentation is as important as a good subject. We enjoy working closely with talented writers of varying experience to produce a literate (as opposed to slick or newsy) magazine."

ISLESBORO ISLAND NEWS, Islesboro Publishing, HCR 227, Islesboro ME 04848. (207)734-6745. FAX: (207)734-2262. Publisher: Agatha Cabaniss. 20% freelance written. Monthly tabloid on Penobscot Bay islands and people. Estab. 1985. **Pays on acceptance.** Byline given. Buys one-time rights. Sample copy $2; writer's guidelines for #10 SAE with 3 first class stamps.
Nonfiction: Articles about contemporary issues on the islands, historical pieces, personality profiles, arts, lifestyles and businesses on the islands. Any story must have a definite Maine island connection. No travel pieces. Query or send complete ms. Pays $20-50.
Photos: State availability of photos with submission.
Tips: "Writers must know the Penobscot Bay Islands. We are not interested in pieces of a generic island nature unless they relate to development problems, or the viability of the islands as year round communities. We do not want 'vacation on a romantic island,' but we are interested in island historical pieces."

MAINE MOTORIST, AAA Maine, P.O. Box 3544, Portland ME 04104. (207)780-6800. Editor: Ellen Kornetsky. 1% freelance written. Bimonthly tabloid on travel, car care, AAA news. "Our readers enjoy learning about travel opportunities in the New England region and elsewhere. In addition, they enjoy topics of interest to automobile owners." Estab. 1910. Circ. 122,500. Pays on publication. Publishes ms an average of 3 months after acceptance. Byline given. Not copyrighted. Buys simultaneous rights; makes work-for-hire assignments. Submit seasonal/holiday material 4 months in advance. Simultaneous submissions OK. Free sample copy and writer's guidelines.
Nonfiction: Historical/nostalgic (travel); how-to (car care, travel); humor (travel); and travel (New England, U.S. and foreign). No exotic travel destinations that cost a great deal. Send complete ms. Length: 500-1,000 words. Pays $50-100.
Photos: State availability of photos. Reviews 5×7 transparencies. Pays $10-25 for b&w; $25-100 for color. Captions required. Buys one-time rights.
Tips: "Travel (particularly New England regional) material is most needed. Interesting travel options are appreciated. Humorous flair sometimes helps."

Maryland

BALTIMORE MAGAZINE, Suite 1000, 16 S. Calvert St., Baltimore MD 21202. (301)752-7375. Editor: Stan Heuisler. Managing Editor: Kay MacIntosh. 30-40% freelance written. Monthly magazine covering the Baltimore area. "Pieces must address an educated, active, affluent reader and must have a very strong Baltimore angle." Estab. 1907. Circ. 54,369. Pays on publication. Byline given. Offers 30% kill fee. Buys first rights, second serial (reprint) rights, all rights or makes work-for-hire assignments. Submit seasonal/holiday material 4 months in advance. Query for electronic submissions. Reports in 2 months on queries; 2 weeks on assigned mss; 3 months on unsolicited mss. Sample copy $2.05 with 9×12 SAE and $2.40 postage. Writer's guidelines for 1 first class stamp.

Nonfiction: Mark Cohen. Book excerpt (Baltimore subject or Baltimore author), essays (Baltimore subject), exposé (Baltimore subject), humor (Baltimore focus), interview/profile (w/Baltimorean), personal experience (Baltimore focus), photo feature, travel (local and regional to Maryland *only*). "Nothing that lacks a strong Baltimore focus or angle." Query with published clips or send complete ms. Length: 200-6,000 words. Pays $25-1,500 for assigned articles; $25-500 for unsolicited articles. Sometimes pays expenses of writers on assignment.

Photos: State availability of photos with submission. Reviews contact sheets, 4×5 transparencies, 5×7 or 8×10 transparencies. Model releases and identification of subjects required. Rights purchased depend on assignment.

Columns/Departments: Being There (descriptive piece on B'more person or place), 1,600 words; Living Well (short consumer pieces [fashion, food, homestyle], with emphasis on photos), 280-480 words; UpFront (newsy or off-beat items), 200-600 words. Query with published clips. Pays $100-350.

Tips: "Writers who live in the Baltimore area can send resume and published clips to be considered for first assignment. Must show an understanding of writing that is suitable to an educated magazine reader and show ability to write with authority, describe scenes, help reader experience the subject. Too many writers send us newspaper-style articles, instead. We are seeking: 1) *Human interest features* — strong, even dramatic profiles of Baltimoreans of interest to our readers. 2) *First person accounts* of experience in Baltimore, or experiences of a Baltimore resident. 3) *Consumer* — according to our editorial needs, and with Baltimore sources."

CHESAPEAKE BAY MAGAZINE, Suite 157, 1819 Bay Ridge Ave., Annapolis MD 21403. (301)263-2662. Editor: Jean Waller. 40% freelance written. Works with a small number of new/unpublished writers each year. "*Chesapeake Bay Magazine* is a monthly regional publication for those who enjoy reading about the Chesapeake and its tributaries. Our readers are yachtsmen, boating families, fishermen, ecologists — anyone who is part of Chesapeake Bay life." Circ. 30,000. Pays on publication. Publishes ms an average of 10-14 months after acceptance. Buys first North American serial rights and all rights. Submit seasonal/holiday material 6-8 months in advance. Reports in 2 months. Sample copy $2.50; writer's guidelines for SASE.

Nonfiction: "All material must be about the Chesapeake Bay area — land or water." How-to (fishing and sports pertinent to Chesapeake Bay); general interest; humor (welcomed, but don't send any "dumb boater" stories where common safety is ignored); historical; interviews (with interesting people who have contributed in some way to Chesapeake Bay life: authors, historians, sailors, oystermen, etc.); and nostalgia (accurate, informative and well-paced — no maudlin ramblings about "the good old days"); personal experience (drawn from experiences in boating situations, adventures, events in our geographical area); photo feature (with accompanying ms); profile (on natives of Chesapeake Bay); technical (relating to boating, fishing); and Chesapeake Bay folklore. "We do not want material written by those unfamiliar with the Bay area, or general sea stories. No personal opinions on environmental issues or new column (monthly) material and no rehashing of familiar ports-of-call (e.g., Oxford, St. Michaels)." Buys 25-40 unsolicited mss/year. Query or submit complete ms. Length: 1,000-2,500 words. Pays $100-150.

Photos: Chris Gill, art director. Submit photo material with ms. Reviews 8×10 b&w glossy prints and color transparencies. Pays $200 for 35mm, 2¼×2¼ or 4×5 color transparencies used for cover photos; $50, $30 or $15 for color photo used inside. Captions and model releases required. Buys one-time rights with reprint permission.

Fiction: "All fiction must deal with the Chesapeake Bay and be written by persons familiar with some facet of bay life." Adventure, fantasy, historical, humorous, mystery and suspense. "No general stories with Chesapeake Bay superimposed in an attempt to make a sale." Buys 2-3 mss/year. Query or submit complete ms. Length: 1,000-2,500 words. Pays $100-150.

Tips: "We are a regional publication entirely about the Chesapeake Bay and its tributaries. Our readers are true 'Bay' lovers, and look for stories written by others who obviously share this love. We are particularly interested in material from the Lower Bay (Virginia) area and the Upper Bay (Maryland/Delaware) area. We are looking for personal experience Chesapeake boating articles/stories, especially from power boaters."

‡MARYLAND MAGAZINE, Department of Economic and Employment Development, 30 Hudson St., Annapolis MD 21401. (301)974-7024. Publisher/Editorial Director: D. Patrick Hornberger. 95% freelance written. Prefers to work with published/established writers. Quarterly magazine promoting the state of Maryland. Circ. 45,000. **Pays on acceptance.** Publishes ms 8-12 months after acceptance. Byline given. Offers 25% kill fee. Buys all rights. Submit seasonal/holiday material 1 year in advance. Reports in 2 months. Sample copy $2.25; writer's guidelines for #10 SASE.
Nonfiction: General interest, historical/nostalgic, humor, interview/profile, photo feature and travel. Articles on any facet of Maryland life. No poetry, fiction or controversial material or any topic *not* dealing with the state of Maryland; no trendy topics, or one that has received much publicity elsewhere. Buys 32 mss/year. Query with published clips or send complete ms. Length: 900-2,200 words. Pays $175-400. Pays expenses of writers on assignment.
Tips: "All sections are open to freelancers. Thoroughly research your topic and give sources (when applicable)."

Massachusetts

BOSTON GLOBE MAGAZINE, *Boston Globe,* Boston MA 02107. Editor-in-Chief: Ms. Ande Zellman. 50% freelance written. Weekly magazine; 72 pages. Circ. 805,099. **Pays on acceptance.** Publishes ms an average of 2 months after acceptance. No reprints of any kind. Buys first serial rights. Submit seasonal/holiday material 3 months in advance. SASE must be included with ms or queries for return. Reports in 1 month.
Nonfiction: Expose (variety of issues including political, economic, scientific, medical and the arts); interview (not Q&A); profile; and book excerpts (first serial rights only). No travelogs. Buys up to 100 mss/year. Query. Length: 3,000-5,000 words. Payment negotiable.
Photos: Purchased with accompanying ms or on assignment. Reviews contact sheets. Pays standard rates according to size used. Captions required.

BOSTONIA, The Magazine of Culture & Ideas, Boston University, 10 Lenox St., Brookline MA 02146. (617)353-3081. FAX: (617)353-6488. Publisher/Editor: Keith Botsford. 90% freelance written. Bimonthly magazine on culture and ideas. Circ. 138,000. **Pays on acceptance.** Publishes ms an average of 2 months after acceptance. Byline given (except for Commonwealth Avenue). Offers 20% kill fee. Buys first rights. Simultaneous submissions OK. Query for electronic submissions. Reports in 1 month. Free sample copy and writer's guidelines.
Nonfiction: National, international issues, the arts, profiles, social issues. Primarily commissioned but will consider queries with published clips. Length: 2,000-5,000 words. Pays up to $1,250 plus expenses.
Photos: Portfolios with proposals to Art Director. All must be identified.
Columns/Departments: Commonwealth Avenue, 300-1,000 words. $150 per acceptance.
Fiction: No length restrictions, internationally-known writers are preferred; will read new writers. Pays up to $1,500.
Tips: "Freelancers' best way in is Commonwealth Avenue column."

CAPE COD HOME & GARDEN, Cove Communications Corp., 60 Munson Meeting, Chatham MA 02633. (508)945-3542. Editor: John C. Whitmarsh. Managing Editor: Donald Davidson. 90% freelance written. A magazine published 4 times/year about fine homes and gardens on Cape Cod, Martha's Vineyard and Nantucket. Estab. 1989. Circ. 20,000. Pays on publication. Publishes ms an average of 2 months after acceptance. Byline given. Offers variable kill fee. Buys first North American serial rights or one-time rights. Reports in 1 month. Sample copy $4; writer's guidelines for #10 SAE.
Nonfiction: Colorful features and regular columns on interior design and architecture, art and antiques, gardening and landscaping, cooking and dining, restoration and remodeling. Articles must be of interest to primary and second homeowners in this unique geographic region. We do not publish first-person articles, poetry, fiction, history or memoirs. Buys 60 mss/year. Query with published clips or send complete ms. Length: 2,000-2,500 words. Pays $150-400 for assigned articles.
Photos: Send photos with submission, if any. Reviews transparencies. Offers $70/photo. Model releases and identification of subjects required. Buys one-time rights.
Tips: "We welcome submissions from published writers who are familiar with the unique living environment on Cape Cod and the Islands. Our readers are upscale homeowners with a serious interest in their homes and an appreciation of their natural environment. Both features and columns must have a strong 'local angle.' "

‡CAPE COD LIFE, Including Martha's Vineyard and Nantucket, Cape Cod Life, Inc., Box 222, Osterville MA 02655. (508)428-5706. FAX: (508)420-0208. Editor: Brian F. Shortsleeve. Managing Editor: Marc Swan. 80% freelance written. Magazine published 6 times/year, focusing on "area life-

style, history and culture, people and places, business and industry, and issues and answers." Readers are "year-round and summer residents of Cape Cod as well as non-residents who spend their leisure time on the Cape." Circ. 32,000. Pays within 30 days of publication. Byline given. Offers 20% kill fee. Buys first North American serial rights; makes work-for-hire assignments. Submit seasonal/holiday material 6 months in advance. Simultaneous queries and photocopied submissions OK. Reports in 6 weeks on queries; 2 months on mss. Sample copy $3; writer's guidelines for #10 SASE.

Nonfiction: General interest, historical, gardening, interview/profile, photo feature, travel, marine, nautical, nature, arts and antiques. Buys 20 mss/year. Query with or without published clips. Length: 1,000-4,000 words. Pays $100-400.

Photos: State availability of photos with query. Pays $7.50-20 for photos. Captions and identification of subjects required. Buys first rights with right to reprint.

Tips: "Freelancers submitting *quality* spec articles with a Cape Cod angle have a good chance at publication. We do like to see a wide selection of writer's clips before giving assignments. We accept more spec work written about Cape and Islands history than any other area."

Michigan

ABOVE THE BRIDGE MAGAZINE, P.O. Box 416, Marquette MI 49855. Editor: Jacqueline J. Miller. Managing Editor: Judith A. Hendrickson. 100% freelance written. A quarterly magazine on the upper peninsula of Michigan. "Most material, including fiction, has an upper peninsula of Michigan slant. Our readership is past and present upper peninsula residents." Circ. 2,000. Pays on publication. Publishes ms an average of 6 months after acceptance. Byline given. Offers 50% kill fee. Buys one-time rights. Submit seasonal/holiday material 6 months in advance. Previously published submissions. Query for electronic submissions. Reports in 2 months. Sample copy for $3.50. Writer's guidelines for #10 SASE.

Nonfiction: Book excerpts (books on upper peninsula or UP writer), essays, historical/nostalgic (UP), interview/profile (UP personality or business) personal experience, photo feature (UP). Note: Travel by assignment only. "This is a family magazine; therefore, no material in poor taste." Buys 60 mss/ year. Send complete ms. Length: 1,000-2,500 words. Pays 2¢/word. Send photos with submission. Reviews prints (5×7 or larger). Offers $5 ($15-20 if used for cover). Captions, model releases and identification of subjects required. Buys one-time rights.

Fiction: Ethnic (UP heritage), humorous, mainstream and mystery. No horror or erotica. "Material set in UP has preference for publication. Accepts children's fiction." Buys 12 mss/year. Send complete ms. Length: 2,000 words (1,000 maximum for children's). Pays 2¢/word.

Poetry: Free verse, haiku, light verse and traditional. No erotica. Buys 20 poems/year. Shorter poetry preferred. Pays $5.

Fillers: Anecdotes and short humor. Buys 25/year. Length: 100-500 words. Pays $5 or 2¢/word maximum.

Tips: "Material on the shorter end of our requirements has a better chance for publication. We're very well-stocked at the moment, so if we receive a submission that might not be published for a year of more, we'll pay on acceptance. As the budget allows we're attempting to eventually pay for all material on acceptance. We can't use material by out-of-state writers with content not tied to upper peninsula of Michigan. Know the area and people, read the magazine. Most material received is too long. Stick to our guidelines. We love to publish well written material by previously unpublished writers."

ANN ARBOR OBSERVER, Ann Arbor Observer Company, 201 E. Catherine, Ann Arbor MI 48104. FAX: (313)769-3375. Editor: John Hilton. 50% freelance written. Works with a small number of new/ unpublished writers each year. Monthly magazine featuring stories about people and events in Ann Arbor. Estab. 1976. Circ. 53,000. Pays on publication. Publishes ms an average of 2 months after acceptance. Byline given. Buys one-time rights. Query for electronic submissions. Reports in 3 weeks on queries; 1 month on mss. Sample copy for 12½×15 SAE and $3 postage; free writer's guidelines.

Nonfiction: Historical, investigative features, profiles and brief vignettes. Must pertain to Ann Arbor. Buys 75 mss/year. Length: 100-7,000 words. Pays up to $1,000/article. Sometimes pays expenses of writers on assignment.

Tips: "If you have an idea for a story, write up a 100-200-word description telling us why the story is interesting. We are most open to intelligent, insightful features of up to 5,000 words about interesting aspects of life in Ann Arbor."

‡THE DETROIT FREE PRESS MAGAZINE, *The Detroit Free Press*, 321 W. Lafayette Blvd., Detroit MI 48231. (313)222-6558. 20% freelance written. Prefers to work with published/established writers; works with a small number of new/unpublished writers each year. For a general newspaper readership; urban and suburban. Weekly magazine. Circ. 1.2 million. Pays within 6 weeks of publication. Publishes ms an average of 2-3 months after acceptance. Buys first or second serial rights. Byline given. Query for electronic submissions. Reports in 6 weeks.

Nonfiction: "Seeking quality magazine journalism on subjects of interest to Detroit and Michigan readers: lifestyles and better living, trends, behavior, business and political intrigue, crime and cops, money, success and failure, sports, fascinating people, arts and entertainment. *DFP Magazine* is bright and cosmopolitan in tone. Most desired writing style is literate but casual—the kind you'd like to read—and reporting must be unimpeachable." Buys 75-100 mss/year. Query or submit complete ms. "If possible, the letter should be held to one page. It should present topic, organizational technique and writing angle. It should demonstrate writing style and give some indication as to why the story would be of interest to us. It should not, however, be an extended sales pitch." Length: 1,000 to 5,000 words maximum. Pays $150-2,500. Sometimes pays the expenses of writers on assignment.

Photos: Purchased with or without accompanying ms.

DETROIT MONTHLY, Crain Communications, 1400 Woodbridge, Detroit MI 48207. (313)446-6000. Editor: John Barron. 50% freelance written. Monthly magazine. "We are a city magazine for educated, reasonably well-to-do, intellectually curious Detroiters." Circ. 100,000. **Pays on acceptance.** Byline given. Offers negotiable kill fee. Buys first North American serial rights. Submit seasonal/holiday material 4 months in advance. Query for electronic submissions. Reports in 6 weeks.

Nonfiction: Book excerpts, exposé and travel. Buys 25 mss/year. Query with published clips. Length: 1,000-5,000 words. Pays $100-1,200. Sometimes pays the expenses of writers on assignment.

Photos: State availability of photos with submission.

GRAND RAPIDS MAGAZINE, Suite 1040, Trust Bldg., 40 Pearl St., NW, Grand Rapids MI 49503. (616)459-4545. FAX: (616)459-4800. Publisher: John H. Zwarensteyn. Editor: Carole Valade Smith. 70% freelance written. Eager to work with new writers. Monthly general feature magazine serving western Michigan. Estab. 1964. Circ. 12,000. Pays on 15th of month of publication. Publishes ms an average of 4 months after acceptance. Buys first serial rights. Phone queries OK. Submit seasonal material 3 months in advance. Previously published submissions OK. Query for electronic submissions. Reports in 2 months. Sample copy $2 and 6 first class stamps.

Nonfiction: Western Michigan writers preferred. Western Michigan subjects only: government, labor, investigative, criminal justice, environment, health/medical, education, general interest, historical, interview/profile and nostalgia. Inspirational and personal experience pieces discouraged. No breezy, self-centered "human" pieces or "pieces not only light on style but light on hard information." Humor appreciated but must be specific to region. "If you live here, see the managing editor before you write. If you don't, send a query letter with published clips, or phone." Length: 500-4,000 words. Pays $35-200. Sometimes pays the expenses of writers on assignment.

Photos: State availability of photos. Pays $25 minimum for 5×7 glossy print and $35 minimum for 35 or 120mm transparency. Captions and model releases required.

Tips: "Television has forced city/regional magazines to be less provincial and more broad-based in their approach. People's interests seem to be evening out from region to region. The subject matters should remain largely local, but national trends must be recognized in style and content. And we must *entertain* as well as inform."

MICHIGAN COUNTRY LINES, Michigan Electric Cooperative Association, 400 North Walnut, Lansing MI 48933. (517)484-5022. Editor: Michael Buda. Managing Editor: Michelle Smith. 20% freelance written. Bimonthly magazine covering rural Michigan. Estab. 1980. Circ. 165,000. Pays on publication. Publishes ms an average of 4 months after acceptance. Byline given. Buys one-time rights and second serial (reprint) rights. Submit seasonal/holiday material 3 months in advance. Query for electronic submissions. Reports in 2 weeks. Free sample copy.

Nonfiction: Historical/nostalgic, how-to (rural living) and photo feature. No product or out-of-state. Buys 6 mss/year. Send complete ms. Length: 700-1,500 words. Pays $100-200 for assigned articles; $100-150 unsolicited articles. Pays expenses of writers on assignment.

Photos: Send photos with submission. Reviews contact sheets, 35mm transparencies and 3×5 prints. Offers $10-15 per photo. Captions, model releases and identification of subjects required. Buys one-time rights.

Tips: "Features are most open to freelancers."

Minnesota

LAKE SUPERIOR MAGAZINE, Lake Superior Port Cities, Inc., P.O. Box 16417, Duluth MN 55816-0417. (218)722-5002. FAX: (218)722-1341. Editor: Paul L. Hayden. 60% freelance written. Works with a small number of new/unpublished writers each year. A bimonthly regional magazine covering contemporary and historic people, places and current events around Lake Superior. Estab. 1979. Circ.

20,000 (subscribers in all states and 56 foreign countries). Pays on publication. Publishes ms an average of 8-10 months after acceptance. Byline given. Offers $25 kill fee. Buys first North American serial rights and some second rights. Submit seasonal/holiday material 8-12 months in advance. Query for electronic submissions. Reports in 3 months on manuscripts. Sample copy $4.95 and 5 first class stamps; writer's guidelines for #10 SASE.

Nonfiction: Book excerpts, general interest, historic/nostalgic, humor, interview/profile (local), personal experience, photo feature (local), travel (local), city profiles, regional business, some investigative. Buys 45 mss/year. Query with published clips. Length 300-2,200 words. Pays $80-400 maximum. Sometimes pays the expenses of writers on assignment.

Photos: Quality photography is our hallmark. State availability of photos with submission. Reviews contact sheets, 2×2 transparencies and 4×5 prints. Offers $20 for b&w and $35 for color transparencies. Captions, model releases and identification of subjects required.

Columns/Departments: Current events and things to do (for Events Calendar section) short, under 300 words; Lake Watch (media reviews and short pieces on Lake Superior or Great Lakes environmental or issues themes), up to 200 words; I Remember (nostalgic lake-specific pieces), up to 1,100 words; Shore Lines (letters and short pieces on events and highlights of the Lake Superior Region), up to 150 words; Life Lines (single personality profile with b&w), up to 700 words. Buys 20 mss/year. Query with published clips. Pays $10-75.

Fiction: Ethnic, historic, humorous, mainstream, slice-of-life vignettes and ghost stories. Must be regionally targeted in nature. Buys 2-3 mss/year. Query with published clips. Length: 300-2,500 words. Pays $1-200.

Tips: "Well-researched queries are attended to. We actively seek queries from writers in Lake Superior communities. We prefer manuscripts to queries. Provide enough information on why the subject is important to the region and our readers, or why and how something is unique. We want details. The writer must have a thorough knowledge of the subject and how it relates to our region. We prefer a fresh, unused approach to the subject which provides the reader with an emotional involvement. Almost all of our articles feature quality photography, color or black and white. It is a prerequisite of all nonfiction. All submissions should include a *short* biography of author/photographer."

MPLS. ST. PAUL MAGAZINE, Suite 400, 12 S. 6th St., Minneapolis MN 55402. (612)339-7571. FAX: (612)339-5806. Editor: Brian Anderson. Executive Editor: Sylvia Paine. Managing Editor: Claude Peck. 80% freelance written. Monthly general interest magazine covering the metropolitan area of Minneapolis/St. Paul and aimed at college-educated professionals who enjoy living in the area and taking advantage of the cultural, entertainment and dining out opportunities. Reports on people and issues of importance to the community. Circ. 62,000. **Pays on acceptance.** Publishes ms an average of 3 months after acceptance. Byline given. Offers 25% kill fee. Buys first North American serial rights. Submit seasonal/holiday material 5 months in advance. Query for electronic submissions. Reports in 1 month. Sample copy $4.

Nonfiction: Book excerpts; general interest; historical/nostalgic; interview/profile (local); new product; photo feature (local); and travel (regional). Buys 250 mss/year. Query with published clips. Length: 1,000-4,000 words. Pays $100-1,200. Sometimes pays expenses of writers on assignment.

Photos: Chris Greco, photo editor.

Columns/Departments: Nostalgia—Minnesota historical; Home—interior design, local. Query with published clips. Length: 750-2,000 words. Pays $100-400.

Tips: "People profiles (400 words) and Nostalgia are areas most open to freelancers."

Mississippi

MISSISSIPPI, Downhome Publications, 254 Highland Village, P.O. Box 16445, Jackson MS 39236. (601)982-8418. Editor: Ann Becker. 95% freelance written. Bimonthly magazine covering Mississippi. "Our magazine focuses almost exclusively on positive aspects of Mississippi—people, places, events." Estab. 1982. Circ. 25,000. Pays on publication. Publishes ms an average of 6 months after acceptance. Byline given. Offers $75 kill fee. Buys one-time rights. Submit seasonal/holiday material 1 year in advance. Query for electronic submissions. Reports in 3 months. Sample copy for $2.50. Free writer's guidelines.

Nonfiction: Essays, general interest, historical/nostalgic, interview/profile, personal experience, photo feature and travel. No essays on Southern accents or Southerners in the North. Buys 72 mss/year. Query with published clips. Length: 500-2,000 words. Pays $50-500.

Photos: Send photos with submission. Reviews contact sheets, 2¼×2¼ transparencies and 4×5 prints. Offers $25-100 per photo. Captions, model releases and identification of subjects required. Buys one-time rights.

Columns/Departments: Travel, People, Music, Heritage, Sports, Business, Art, Outdoors, Homes and Gardens (focuses on Mississippi people, places or events), 1,500 words each. Buys 35 mss/year. Query with published clips. Length: 500-1,500 words. Pays $125.

Tips: "Query by mail. Query should give some idea of how story would read. Including a lead is good. Be patient. Be aware of past articles—we only feature a subject once. All departments are good starting points. Be sure subject has *state*wide interest. Be sure subject has good reputation in field."

Missouri

‡KANSAS CITY LIVE!, 201 East Armour, Kansas City MO 64111. (816)968-LIVE. Editor: Tracey Mershon. 90% freelance written. Monthly magazine covering Kansas City and surrounding area. "*Kansas City Live!* is a city/lifestyle magazine with an emphasis on health." Estab. 1990. Circ. 105,000. **Pays on acceptance.** Byline given. 10% kill fee. Buys first North American serial rights. Submit seasonal material 4 months in advance. Previously published submissions OK. Query for electronic submissions. Sample copy $1.95. Free writer's guidelines.
Nonfiction: How-to (home, gardening), interview/profile, personal finance, photo feature (midwest), sports, health/wellness, travel (only Kansas City topics). "No articles about international travel. We prefer query letter over manuscripts." Buys 12 mss/year. Query with published clips. Length: 1,000-2,000 words. Pays $250-500 for assigned articles; $250-300 for unsolicited articles. Sometimes pays the expenses of writers on assignment. State availability of photos with submission. Reviews contact sheets and transparencies. Offers $50-80/photo. Captions, model releases and identification of subjects required. Buys one-time rights.

MISSOURI MAGAZINE, 22 N. Euclid Ave., St Louis MO 63108. (314)367-0907. Editor: Jeanne Lafser. Quarterly magazine covering Missouri-oriented topics. "We prefer human-interest articles unique to Missouri—from historical pieces to profiles of people and places in Missouri today." Estab. 1974. Circ. 15,000. Pays on publication. Publishes ms an average of 6 months after acceptance. Byline given. Offers $25 kill fee. Buys first rights. Submit seasonal/holiday material 3 months in advance. Simultaneous submissions OK. Query for electronic submissions. Reports in 1 month queries; 3 months on mss. Sample copy for $4.95. Free writer's guidelines.
Nonfiction: General interest, historical/nostalgic, interview/profile, photo feature, travel, Missouri geology, natural history and wildlife. No fiction. Buys 28 mss/year. Send complete ms. Length: 1,500-3,000 words. Pays $150-300 for assigned articles; $75-200 for unsolicited articles. Sometimes pays in trade out with ads. Sometimes pays expenses of writers on assignment.
Photos: State availability of photos with submission. Reviews 2¼ × 2¼ transparencies. Offers $10-25 per photo. Captions, model releases and identification of subjects required. Buys one-time rights.
Columns/Departments: Bed & Breakfast Review (reviews B&Bs in Missouri—unique, 'quality' establishments), 300 words; Best Foot Forward (listing of exemplary establishments or services in Missouri), 50-100 words. Buys 28 mss/year. Send complete ms. Length 50-300 words. Pays $10-25.
Fillers: Facts. Buys 40/year. Length: 50-100 words. Pays $5-25.
Tips: "Send complete manuscript—professionally written with photos of excellent quality."

SPRINGFIELD! MAGAZINE, Springfield Communications Inc., P.O. Box 4749, Springfield MO 65808. (417)882-4917. Editor: Robert C. Glazier. 85% freelance written. Works with a small number of new/unpublished writers each year; eager to work with new/unpublished writers. Monthly magazine. "This is an extremely local and provincial magazine. No *general* interest articles." Estab. 1979. Circ. 10,000. Pays on publication. Publishes ms an average of 6 months after acceptance. Byline given. Buys first serial rights. Submit seasonal/holiday material 6-12 months in advance. Simultaneous queries OK. Reports in 3 months on queries; 6 months on mss. Sample copy for $2.50 and 9½ × 12½ SAE.
Nonfiction: Book excerpts (by Springfield authors only); expose (local topics only); historical/nostalgic (top priority but must be local history); how-to (local interest only); humor (if local angle); interview/profile (needs more on females than on males); personal experience (local angle); photo feature (local photos); and travel (1 page per month). No material that could appeal to any magazine anywhere. Buys 150 mss/year. Query with published clips or send complete ms. Length: 500-5,000 words. Pays $25-250. Sometimes pays expenses of writers on assignment.
Photos: State availability of photos or send photos with query or ms. Reviews b&w and color contact sheets; 4 × 5 color transparencies; and 5 × 7 b&w prints. Pays $5-35 for b&w; $10-50 for color. Captions, model releases, and identification of subjects required. Buys one-time rights.
Columns/Departments: Buys 250 mss/year. Query or send complete ms. Length varies widely but usually 500-2,500 words. Pays scale.
Tips: "We prefer that a writer read eight or ten copies of our magazine prior to submitting any material for our consideration. The magazine's greatest need is for features which comment on these times in Springfield. We are overstocked with nostalgic pieces right now. We also are much in need of profiles about young women and men of distinction."

‡ST. LOUIS MAGAZINE, P.O. Box 88908, St. Louis MO 63118. (314)231-7200. FAX: (314)231-6902. Editor: Steve Friedman. Managing Editor: Jeanette Batz. 80% freelance written. A monthly magazine about St. Louisans and St. Louis events. **Pays on acceptance.** Publishes ms an average of 2 months after acceptance. Byline given. Buys first rights; makes work-for-hire assignments. Submit seasonal/holiday material 4 months in advance. Reports in 2 months on queries; 3 months on mss.
Nonfiction: Historical, interview/profile, photo feature and travel. Query with published clips. Length: 250-4,000 words. Pays $25-500. Sometimes pays the expenses of writers on assignment.
Photos: State availability of photos with submission.
Columns/Departments: Travel, Arts, Health, Money, Sports, Entertaining. Buys 36 mss/year. Query with published clips. Length: 500-1,250 words. Pays $150 maximum.
Tips: "Columns and upfronts are the best ways to break in."

Nevada

NEVADA MAGAZINE, 1800 E. Hwy. 50, Carson City NV 89710. (702)687-5416. FAX: (702)687-6159. Editor: David Moore. 50% freelance written. Works with a small number of new/unpublished writers each year. Bimonthly magazine published by the state of Nevada to promote tourism in the state. Circ. 100,000. Pays on publication. Publishes ms an average of 6 months after acceptance. Byline given. Buys first North American serial rights. Phone queries OK. Submit seasonal/holiday material at least 6 months in advance. Query for electronic submissions. Reports in 1 month. Sample copy $1; free writer's guidelines.
Nonfiction: Nevada topics only. Historical, nostalgia, photo feature, people profile, recreational, travel and think pieces. "We welcome stories and photos on speculation." Buys 40 unsolicited mss/year. Submit complete ms or queries to Associate Editor Cliff Glover. Length: 500-2,000 words. Pays $75-300.
Photos: Jim Crandall, art director. Send photo material with accompanying ms. Pays $10-50 for 8 × 10 glossy prints; $15-75 for color transparencies. Name, address and caption should appear on each photo or slide. Buys one-time rights.
Tips: "Keep in mind that the magazine's purpose is to promote tourism in Nevada. Keys to higher payments are quality and editing effort (more than length). Send cover letter, no photocopies. We look for a light, enthusiastic tone of voice without being too cute; articles bolstered by amazing facts and thorough research; and unique angles on Nevada subjects."

New Hampshire

‡NEW HAMPSHIRE LIFE, Masthead Communications, Inc., Box 1200, North Hampton NH 03862. (603)964-2121. Fiction Editor: John A. Meng. 85% freelance written. A bimonthly magazine covering southern Maine, seacoast New Hampshire and northeast Massachusetts. Estab. 1985. Circ. 20,000. Pays 30 days after publication. Byline given. Buys first and second rights. Submit seasonal/holiday material 4 months in advance. Simultaneous submissions OK. Query for electronic submissions. Reports in 2 months. Publishes ms an average of 4 months after acceptance. Sample copy for 9 × 12 SAE with 4 first class stamps; writer's guidelines for #10 SAE with 2 first class stamps.
Nonfiction: Exposé, general interest, historical/nostalgic, humor, interview/profile, photo feature. Buys 25 mss/year. Send complete ms. Length: 1,200-4,500 words. Pays $50-1,000. Does not pay expenses separately. Expenses should be considered by writer during pay negotiations.
Photos: State availability of photos with submission. Reviews contact sheets, transparencies and prints. Offers $25-150 per photo. Captions, model releases and identification of subjects required. Negotiates rights purchased.
Columns/Departments: Food (recipes/seasonal); Business, Real Estate (market trends). Busy 150 mss/year. Query. Length: 800-2,000 words. Pays $100-300.
Fiction: Adventure, historical, humorous, mainstream, mystery, romance, slice-of-life vignettes, suspense and other. No erotica. Buys 6 mss/year. Send complete ms. Length: 1,500-4,000 words. Pays $100-350.
Tips: "Our readership is highly educated, critical of shabby work and loves good fiction. Our readers love to read. Writers should be patient. We will read and reply to all submissions."

NEW HAMPSHIRE PROFILES, Isle of Shoals Publishing, P.O. Box 370, Stratham NH 03885. (603)772-5252. Editor: Suki Casanave. 90% freelance written. Prefers to work with published/established writers; works with small number of new/unpublished writers each year. Bimonthly magazine; articles concentrate on audience ages 25 and up, consumer-oriented readers who want to know more about the quality of life in New Hampshire. **Pays on publication.** Publishes ms an average of 4 months after acceptance. Offers 25% kill fee. Buys first North American serial rights. Submit seasonal/holiday material 9 months in advance. Query for electronic submissions. Reports in 2 months. Sample copy $3.50 with 9½×12 SAE. Writer's guidelines for #10 SASE.

Nonfiction: Interview, profile, photo feature and interesting activities for and about the state of New Hampshire and people who live in it. Buys 75 mss/year. Query with published clips or send complete ms. Length varies from 1,000-3,000 words, depending on subject matter. Pays $100-500. Sometimes pays expenses of writers on assignment.

Photos: Uses seasonal stock and makes some assignments. Pays $50-150.

Columns/Departments: Buys 40 mss/year. Query with published clips. Length: 1,000-1,500 words. Pays $100-275.

Tips: "Query before submitting manuscript, and don't send us your only copy of the manuscript—photocopy it. Familiarity with magazine is essential."

New Jersey

‡ATLANTIC CITY MAGAZINE, P.O. Box 2100, Pleasantville NJ 08232-1924. (609)272-7900. FAX: (609)272-7910. Editor: Ken Weatherford. 80% freelance written. Works with small number of new/unpublished writers each year. Monthly city magazine covering issues pertinent to the South Jersey area. Circ. 50,000. Pays on publication. Publishes ms an average of 4 months after acceptance. Byline given. Buys one-time rights. Offers variable kill fee. Submit seasonal/holiday material 6 months in advance. Reports in 1 month. Sample copy $3; free writer's guidelines for SASE.

Nonfiction: Entertainment, general interest, recreation, history, lifestyle, interview/profile, photo feature and trends. "No travel pieces or any article without a South Jersey shore area/Atlantic City slant." Query. Length: 100-5,000 words. Pays $50-800 for assigned articles; pays $50-500 for unsolicited articles. Sometimes pays the expenses of writers on assignment.

Photos: State availability of photos. Reviews contact sheets, negatives, 2¼×2¼ transparencies and 8×10 prints. Pay varies. Captions, model releases and identification of subjects required. Buys one-time rights.

Columns/Departments: Art, Business, Entertainment, Sports, Dining, History, Style and Real Estate. Query with published clips. Length: 500-2,500 words. Pays $150-400.

Tips: "Our readers are a broad base of local residents and visiting tourists. We need stories that will appeal to both audiences."

NEW JERSEY MONTHLY, 55 Park Place, P.O. Box 920, Morristown NJ 07963-0920. (201)539-8230. Editor: Jan Bresnick. 50% freelance written. Monthly magazine covering New Jersey. "Almost anything that's New Jersey related." Estab. 1976. Circ. 106,000. Pays on completion of fact-checking. Byline given. Offers 10-30% kill fee. Buys first rights. Submit seasonal/holiday material 6 months in advance. Query for electronic submissions. Reports in 6 weeks. Sample copy $5.95; writer's guidelines for #10 SASE.

Nonfiction: Book excerpts, essays, exposé, general interest, historical, humor, interview/profile, opinion, personal experience and travel. Special issue features Dining Out (Feb. and Aug.); Real Estate (March); Home & Garden (April); Great Weekends (May); Holiday Shopping & Shore Guide (June); Fall Getaways (Oct.); Entertaining (Nov.). "No experience pieces from people who used to live in New Jersey or general pieces that have no New Jersey angle." Buys 96 mss/year. Query with published magazine clips and SASE. Length: 200-3,000 words. Pays 30¢/word and up. Pays reasonable expenses of writers on assignment with prior approval.

Photos: State availability of photos with submission. Payment negotiated. Identification of subjects and return postage required. "Submit dupes only. Drop off for portfolios on Wednesdays only. The magazine accepts no responsibility for unsolicited photography, artwork or cartoons." Buys one-time rights.

Columns/Departments: New Jersey Success (company profile, trends, individual profiles); Health & Fitness (trends, how-to, personal experience, service); Home & Garden (homes, gardens, how-tos, trends, profiles, etc.); Travel (in and out-of-state). Buys 36 mss/year. Query with published clips. Length: 750-1,500 words. Pays 30¢ and up per word.

Tips: "To break in, we suggest contributing briefs to our front-of-the-book section, 'Upfront' (light, off-beat items, trends, people, things; short service items, such as the 10 best NJ-made ice creams; short issue-oriented items; gossip; media notes). We pay a flat fee, from $50-150. This is the only section we pay for on publication."

THE SANDPAPER, Newsmagazine of the Jersey Shore, The SandPaper, Inc., 1816 Long Beach Blvd., Surf City NJ 08008. (609)494-2034. FAX: (609)494-1437. Editor: Curt Travers. Freelance Submissions Editor: Gail Travers. 20% freelance written. Weekly tabloid covering subjects of interest to Jersey shore residents and visitors. "*The SandPaper* publishes three editions covering many of the Jersey Shore's finest resort communities. Each issue includes a mix of hard news, human interest features, opinion columns and entertainment/calendar listings." Circ. 85,000. Pays on publication. Publishes ms an average of 1 month after acceptance. Byline given. Offers 100% kill fee. Buys first rights or all rights. Submit seasonal/holiday material 3 months in advance. Simultaneous and previously published submissions OK. Reports in 1 month.

Nonfiction: Essays, general interest, historical/nostalgic, humor, opinion and environmental submissions relating to the ocean, wetlands and pinelands. Must pertain to New Jersey shore locale. Also, arts and entertainment news and reviews if they have a Jersey shore angle. Buys 25 mss/year. Send complete ms. Length: 200-2,000 words. Pays $15-100. Sometimes pays the expenses of writers on assignment.

Photos: State availability of photos with submission. Offers $6-25/photo. Buys one-time rights or all rights.

Columns/Departments: SpeakEasy (opinion and slice-of-life; often humorous); and Commentary (forum for social science perspectives); all 500-1,500 words, preferably with local or Jersey shore angle. Buys 50 mss/year. Send complete ms. Pays $15-35.

Tips: "Anything of interest to sun worshippers, beach walkers, nature watchers, water sports lovers is of potential interest to us. There is an increasing coverage of environmental issues. The opinion page and columns are most open to freelancers. We are steadily increasing the amount of entertainment-related material in our publication."

New Mexico

‡**NEW MEXICO MAGAZINE**, Joseph Montoya State Bldg., 1100 St. Francis Drive, Santa Fe NM 87503. Editor-in-Chief: Emily Drabanski. Editor: Jon Bowman. Associate Editor: Arnold Vigil. Copy Editor: Walter K. Lopez. 85% freelance written. Monthly magazine. Emphasizes New Mexico for a college-educated readership, above average income, interested in the Southwest. Circ. 120,000. **Pays on acceptance.** Publishes ms an average of 6 months after acceptance. Buys first North American serial rights. Submit seasonal/holiday material 8 months in advance. Reports in 8 weeks. Sample copy for $2.75; free writer's guidelines.

Nonfiction: New Mexico subjects of interest to travelers. Historical, cultural, humorous, and informational articles. "We are looking for more short, light and bright stories for the 'Asi Es Nuevo Mexico' section." No columns, cartoons, poetry or non-New Mexico subjects. Buys 5-7 mss/issue. Query with 3 published writing samples. Length: 250-2,000 words. Pays $80-450.

Photos: Purchased with accompanying ms or on assignment. Query or send contact sheet or transparencies. Pays $50-80 for 8×10 b&w glossy prints; $50-150 for 35mm—prefers Kodachrome; (photos in plastic-pocketed viewing sheets). Captions and model releases required. Buys one-time rights.

Tips: "Send a superb short (300 words) manuscript on a little-known person, event, aspect of history or place to see in New Mexico. Faulty research will ruin a writer's chances for the future. Good style, good grammar. No generalized odes to the state or the Southwest. No sentimentalized, paternalistic views of Indians or Hispanics. No glib, gimmicky 'travel brochure' writing. We're always looking for well-researched pieces on unusual aspects of New Mexico history. Lively writing."

‡**ON THE SCENE MAGAZINE**, 3507 Wyoming NE, Albuquerque NM 87111. (505)299-4401. Editor: Gail Skinner. 40% freelance written. Will work with new/unpublished writers. Monthly tabloid covering lifestyles for all ages. Pays on publication. Publishes ms an average of 6 months after acceptance. Byline given. Submit seasonal/holiday material 3 months in advance. Query for electronic submissions. Reports in 3 months. Sample copy $3. Writer's guidelines for #10 SASE.

Nonfiction: General interest; how-to; humor; inspirational; opinion; personal experience; relationships; consumer guide; travel; parenting; and astrology. No suggestive or pornographic material. Buys 100 mss/year. Send complete ms. "Ms returned only if adequate SASE is included." Also publishes some fiction. Length: 300-1,500 words. Pays $20-60. Sometimes pays expenses of writers on assignment.

Photos: State availability of photos with ms. Captions, model releases, and identification of subjects required.

Tips: "We are looking for articles that deal with every aspect of living—whether on a local or national level. Our readers are of above-average intelligence, income and education. The majority of our articles are chosen from 'relationships' and 'humor' submissions. Expanded format from 'singles only' to general readership."

SOUTHWEST PROFILE, Whitney Publishing Co., P.O. Box 1236, Santa Fe NM 87504-1236. (505)984-1773. Editor: Stephen Parks. 50% freelance written. Magazine on the Southwest, published 4 times per year. "*Southwest Profile* is a guide to travel and adventure, art and culture, and living and leisure in the Southwest, with special emphasis on Arizona and New Mexico." Estab. 1978. Circ. 20,000. Pays on publication. Publishes ms an average of 2 months after acceptance. Byline given. Offers 50% kill fee. Buys first North American serial rights. Submit seasonal/holiday material 6 months in advance.

Query for electronic submissions. Reports in 2 months. Sample copy for 9 × 12 SAE with $1.25 postage; writer's guidelines for #10 SASE.

Nonfiction: General interest, interview/profile, photo feature, travel and art. Buys 10 mss/year. Query with published clips. Length: 1,000-2,500 words. Pays $150-300.

Photos: Send photos with submission. Reviews 35mm or larger transparencies and 5 × 7 prints. Offers $25-50 per photo. Captions required. Buys one-time rights.

New York

ADIRONDACK LIFE, Route 9N, P.O. Box 97, Jay NY 12941. FAX (518)946-7461. Editor: Tom Hughes. 50% freelance written. Prefers to work with published/established writers; works with a small number of new/unpublished writers each year. Emphasizes the Adirondack region and the North Country of New York State in articles concerning outdoor activities, history, and natural history directly related to the Adirondacks. Bimonthly magazine. Estab. 1970. Circ. 50,000. **Pays on acceptance.** Publishes ms an average of 6 months after acceptance. Buys one-time rights. Byline given. Submit seasonal/holiday material 1 year in advance. Reports in 1 month. Sample copy for 9 × 12 SAE and $1.65 postage; writer's guidelines for #10 SASE.

Nonfiction: *Adirondack Life* attempts to capture the unique flavor and ethos of the Adirondack mountains and North Country region through feature articles directly pertaining to the qualities of the area and through department articles examining specific aspects. Example: Barkeater: personal essay; Special Places: unique spots in the Adirondacks; Working: careers in the Adirondacks; Wilderness: environmental issues, personal experiences. Buys 10-16 unsolicited mss/year. Query. Length: for features, 3,000 words maximum; for departments, 1,500 words. Pays up to 25¢/word. Sometimes pays expenses of writers on assignment.

Photos: All photos must have been taken in the Adirondacks. Each issue contains a photo feature. Purchased with or without ms or on assignment. All photos must be identified as to subject or locale and must bear photographer's name. Submit color slides or b&w prints. Pays $25 for b&w prints; $50 for transparencies; $300 for cover (color only, vertical in format). Credit line given.

Tips: "We are looking for clear, concise, well-organized manuscripts, written with flair. Indices of previously covered subjects are available."

BUFFALO SPREE MAGAZINE, Spree Publishing Co., Inc., 4511 Harlem Rd., P.O. Box 38, Buffalo NY 14226. (716)839-3405. Editor: Johanna V. Shotell. 90% freelance written. A quarterly literary, consumer-oriented, city magazine. Estab. 1967. Circ. 21,000. Pays on publication. Publishes ms an average of 6-12 months after acceptance. Byline given. Buys first North American serial rights. Submit seasonal/holiday material 9-12 months in advance. Reports in 6 months on mss. Sample copy $2 with 9 × 12 SAE and $2.40 postage.

Nonfiction: Essays, interview/profile, historical/nostalgic, humor, personal experience and travel. Buys 50 mss/year. Send complete ms. Length: 600-1,800 words. Pays $75-125 for unsolicited articles.

Photos: State availability of photos with submission. Reviews prints (any size). Offers no additional payment for photos accepted with ms. Captions required. Buys one-time rights.

Fiction: Experimental, mainstream. "No pornographic or religious manuscripts." Buys 60 mss/year. Send complete ms. Length: 500-2,000 words. Pays $75-100.

Poetry: Janet Goldenberg, poetry editor. Buys 24 poems/year. Submit maximum 4 poems. Length: 50 lines maximum. Pays $25.

‡CITY GUIDE MAGAZINE, Bill of Fare, Inc., Suite 1A, 853 Seventh Ave., New York NY 10019. (212)315-0800. Editor: Peter Insalaco. Managing Editor: Joyce Snadecky. 90% freelance written. Weekly magazine. Circ. 42,500. **Pays on acceptance.** Byline given. Submit seasonal/holiday material 3 months in advance. Query for electronic submissions. Free sample copy.

Nonfiction: General interest. All articles should pertain to New York City. Query. Length: 750 words maximum. Pays with restaurant certificates and theatre tickets.

Photos: Send photos with submission. Reviews contact sheets. Offers no additional payment for photos accepted with ms. Captions required.

CITY LIMITS, City Limits Community Information Service, Inc., 40 Prince St., New York NY 10012. (212)925-9820. FAX: (212)996-3407. Editor: Doug Turetsky. Associate Editor: Lisa Glazer. 50% freelance written. Works with a small number of new/unpublished writers each year. A monthly magazine covering housing and related urban issues. "We cover news and issues in New York City as they relate to the city's poor, moderate and middle-income residents. We are advocacy journalists with a progressive or 'left' slant." Estab. 1976. Circ. 5,000. Pays on publication. Publishes ms an average of 1-2 months after acceptance. Byline given. Buys first North American serial rights, one-time rights, or second serial (reprint) rights. Query for electronic submissions. Reports in 3 weeks. Sample copy $2.

Nonfiction: Expose, interview/profile, opinion, hard news and community profile. "No fluff, no propaganda." Length: 600-2,500 words. Pays $50-150. Sometimes pays expenses of writers on assignment.
Photos: Reviews contact sheets and 5×7 prints. Offers $10-40/photo, cover only. Identification of subjects required. Buys one-time rights.
Columns/Departments: Short Term Notes (brief descriptions of programs, policies, events, etc.), 250-400 words; Book Reviews (housing, urban development, planning, etc.), 250-600 words; Pipeline (covers community organizations, new programs, government policies, etc.), 600-800 words; People (who are active in organizations, community groups, etc.), 600-800 words; and Organize (groups involved in housing, job programs, health care, etc.), 600-800 words. Buys 50-75 mss/year. Query with published clips or send complete ms. Pays $25-100.
Tips: "We are open to a wide range of story ideas in the community development field. If you don't have particular expertise in housing, urban planning etc., start with a community profile or pertinent book or film review. Short Term Notes is also good for anyone with reporting skills. We're looking for writing that is serious and informed but not academic or heavy handed."

FACETS OF NEW YORK, Room 945, 100 Church St., New York NY 10007. (212)513-9405. FAX: (212)513-9788. Editor: Wayne J. Mitchell. 50% freelance written. Quarterly magazine on New York City culture, people and events. Estab. 1987. **Pays on acceptance.** Byline given. Buys one-time rights. Submit seasonal/holiday material 6 months in advance. Simultaneous and previously published submissions OK. Query for electronic submissions. Reports in 2 weeks on queries; 1 month on mss. Free sample copy and writer's guidelines.
Nonfiction: Expose, general interest, humor, interview/profile, personal experience, photo feature, travel to New York City. No fiction or New York put-downs. Buys 20 mss/year. Query with or without published clips, or send complete ms. Length: 500-2,000 words. Pays 10-25¢/word. Sometimes pays expenses of writers on assignment.
Photos: State availability of photos with submision. Offers no additional payment for photos accepted with ms. Captions and model releases required. Buys one-time rights.
Columns/Departments: New York sports, theatre, dining, sightseeing, entertainment, shopping. Sights & Sounds (things to do in New York, odd events). Buys 20 mss/year. Query. Length: 500-1,000 words. Pays 10-25¢/word.
Tips: "*Facets* is published for the New York visitor—usually a young 40ish who visits NYC 10+ times a year. He or she is in tune with New York so don't write about the Circle Line or the Empire State Building. Delve into the more offbeat things that make New York great."

FINGER LAKES MAGAZINE, Grapevine Press, Inc., 108 S. Albany St., P.O. Box O, Ithaca NY 14851. (607)272-3470. FAX: (607)272-0587. Editor: Linda McCandless. 95% freelance written. A bimonthly magazine covering Finger Lakes Region of New York State. Estab. 1974. Circ. 20,000. Pays 1 month after publication. Publishes ms an average of 6-12 months after acceptance. Byline given. Offers negotiable kill fee. Buys first North American serial rights. Submit seasonal/holiday material 8 months in advance. Simultaneous submissions OK. Reports in 1 month on queries; 2 months on mss. Sample copy for 9×12 SAE and 8 first class stamps; writer's guidelines for #10 SASE.
Nonfiction: Investigative reporting, expose, general interest, historical/nostalgic, humor, interview/profile, recreation and photo feature. Buys 30 mss/year. Query with published clips. Length: 600-2,400 words. Pays $40-200.
Columns/Departments: Lake Takes (profile on person of interest). Query with published clips. Length: 100-300 words. Pays $20-40. Excursions (day trip). Query with published clips. Length: 300-400 words. Pays $30-40.
Fiction: Needs 2-3 "Fiends of The Finger Lakes" each year; one crime for the past 200 years in Central New York reconstructed in colorful detail. Buys 4 mss/year. Query with published clips or send complete ms. Length: 1,200-1,500 words. Pays $75.

N.Y. HABITAT, For Co-op, Condominium and Loft Living, Carol Group Ltd., Suite 1105, 928 Broadway, New York NY 10010. (212)505-2030. FAX: (212)254-6795. Editor: Carol Ott. Managing Editor: Lloyd Chrein. 75% freelance written. Publishes 8 issues/year. "*N.Y. Habitat* is a magazine directed to owners, board members, and potential owners of co-ops and condos. All articles should be instructive to these readers, offering them information in an easy-to-read and entertaining manner." Circ. 10,000. Pays on publication. Byline given. Offers 50% kill fee. Buys one-time rights. Submit seasonal/holiday material 6 months in advance. Reports in 2 weeks on queries; 1 month on mss. Sample copy $5; writer's guidelines for #10 SASE.
Nonfiction: How-to (run a co-op); interview/profile (of co-op/condo managers, board members, etc.); personal experience; news stories on trends in co-ops and condos. Special issues include Annual Management Issue (July/August). No articles on lifestyles or apartment furnishings. Buys 30 mss/year. Query with published clips. Length: 500-2,000 words. Pays $75-800 for assigned articles. Pays expenses of writers on assignment.

Photos: State availability of photos with submission. Reviews contact sheets. Offers $50-75 per photo. Captions, model releases and identification of subjects required. Buys one-time rights.

Columns/Departments: Hotline (short, timely news items about co-op and condo living), 500 words; Finances (financial information for buyers and owners), 1000-1500 words. Westchester Report (news, profiles, management. stories pertaining to Westchester County), 1,000-1,500 words. Buys 15 mss/year. Query with published clips. Pays $100.

Tips: "The Hotline section is the most accessible to freelancers. This calls for light (but informative) news and personality pieces pertaining to co-op/condo concerns. If you have ideas for our other columns, however, query, as most of them are completely freelance written."

‡**NEW YORK ALIVE, The Magazine of Life and Work in the Empire State**, Chase Communications Group, Ltd., P.O. Box 9001, Mt. Vernon NY 10552. FAX: (914)699-2025. Editor: Michelle Eldredge. 50% freelance written. Works with a small number of new/unpublished writers each year. Bimonthly magazine about New York State—people, places, events, history. "Devoted to promoting the culture, heritage and lifestyle of New York state. Aimed at people who enjoy living and reading about the New York state experience. All stories must be positive in tone and slanted toward promoting the state." Circ. 35,000. Pays within 45 days of acceptance. Publishes ms an average of 8 months after acceptance. Byline given. Offers 25% of agreed-upon purchase price as kill fee. Buys one-time rights. Submit seasonal/holiday material 4 months in advance. Simultaneous queries and previously published submissions OK. Query for electronic submissions. Reports in 3 months on queries; 1 month on mss. Sample copy $2.50; writer's guidelines for #10 SASE.

Nonfiction: Historical, humor, interview/profile, personal experience, and travel. In all cases subject must be a New York state person, place, event or experience. No stories of general nature (e.g. nationwide trends); political; religious; non New York state subjects. Query with published clips. Buys 30-40 mss/year. Length: 1,500-3,000 words. Pays $200-350. Pays expenses of writers on assignment.

Photos: State availability of photos. Reviews b&w contact sheets, 35mm color transparencies, and b&w prints. Pays $15-30 for b&w and $30-250 for color. Model releases and identification of subjects required.

Columns/Departments: Buys 80-100 mss/year. Query with published clips. Length: 500-1,000 words. Pays $50-150.

Tips: "We buy more short articles. The writer should enjoy and feel comfortable with writing straightforward, promotional type of material."

NEW YORK DAILY NEWS, Travel Section, 220 E. 42 St., New York NY 10017. (212)210-1699. FAX: (212)661-4675. Travel Editor: Gunna Biteé. 30% freelance written. Prefers to work with published/established writers. Weekly tabloid. Circ. 1.8 million. "We are the largest circulating newspaper travel section in the country and take all types of articles ranging from experiences to service oriented pieces that tell readers how to make a certain trip." Pays on publication. Publishes ms an average of 3 months after acceptance. Byline given. Submit seasonal/holiday material 4 months in advance. Contact first before submitting electronic submissions; requires hard copy also. Reports "as soon as possible." Writer's guidelines for #10 SASE.

Nonfiction: General interest, historical/nostalgic, humor, inspirational, personal experience and travel. "Most of our articles involve practical trips that the average family can afford—even if it's one you can't afford every year. We put heavy emphasis on budget saving tips for all trips. We also run stories now and then for the Armchair Traveler, an exotic and usually expensive trip. We are looking for professional quality work from professional writers who know what they are doing. The pieces have to give information and be entertaining at the same time. No 'How I Spent My Summer Vacation' type articles. No PR hype." Buys 60 mss/year. Query with SASE. Length: 1,500 words maximum. Pays $75-150.

Photos: "Good pictures always help sell good stories." State availability of photos with ms. Reviews contact sheets and negatives. Captions and identification of subjects required. Buys all rights.

Columns/Departments: Short Hops is based on trips to places within a 300-mile radius of New York City. Length: 800-1,000 words. Travel Watch gives practical travel advice.

Tips: "A writer might have some luck gearing a specific destination to a news event or date: In Search of Irish Crafts in March, for example, but do it well in advance."

NEW YORK MAGAZINE, News America Publishing, Inc., 755 2nd Ave., New York NY 10017. (212)880-0700. Editor: Edward Kosner. Managing Editor: Laurie Jones. 25% freelance written. Weekly magazine focusing on current events in the New York metropolitan area. Circ. 433,813. **Pays on acceptance.** Offers $150-250 kill fee. Buys first North American serial rights. Submit seasonal/holiday material 2 months in advance. Reports in 1 month. Sample copy for $3.50 if the individual has the copy mailed. Otherwise, the charge is $2.25. Free writer's guidelines.

Nonfiction: Exposé, general interest, profile, new product, personal experience, travel. Query. Pays 75¢-$1.25/word. Pays expenses of writers on assignment.

Tips: "Submit a detailed query to Laurie Jones, *New York*'s managing editor. If there is sufficient interest in the proposed piece, the article will be assigned."

NEW YORK NIGHTLIFE, MJC Publishers, 5550 Merrick Rd., Massapequa NY 11758. (516)797-0250. Editor: Cheryl Ann Meglio. Managing Editor: Allison A. Whitney. 60% freelance written. Monthly magazine covering entertainment: all facets. "*N.Y. and L.I. Nightlife* magazines cover regional entertainment intersets as well as national interests." Estab. 1980. Circ. 35,000. Pays on publication. Publishes ms an average of 4 months after acceptance. Byline given. Buys all rights. Submit seasonal/holiday material 4 months in advance. Query for electronic submissions. Reports in 10 weeks on queries.

Nonfiction: General interest, humor, interview/profile, new product, travel. Query with published clips. Length: 250-1,500 words. Pays $35-100.

Photos: State availability of photos with submission. Offers $25 maximum per photo. Captions, model releases and identification of subjects required.

Columns/Departments: Nightcap (humor piece), 700 words. Query with published clips. Pays $35-100.

NEWSDAY, Melville NY 11747-4250. Viewpoints Editor: James Lynn. Opinion section of daily newspaper. Byline given.

Nonfiction: Seeks "opinion on current events, trends, issues—whether national or local, government or lifestyle. Must be timely, pertinent, articulate and opinionated. Preference for authors within the circulation area including New York City." Length: 600-1,000 words. Pays $150-300.

Tips: "The writer has a better chance of breaking in at our publication with short articles since the longer essays are commissioned from experts and well-known writers."

‡**OUR TOWN**, East Side/West Side Communications Corp., 451 E. 83rd St., New York NY 10028. (212)439-7800. Editor: Ed Kayatt. 80% freelance written. Eager to work with new/unpublished writers. Weekly tabloid covering neighborhood news of Manhattan (96th St.-14th St.). Circ. 119,000. Pays on publication. Publishes ms an average of 1 month after acceptance. Byline given. Buys first serial rights. Submit seasonal/holiday material 1 month in advance.

Nonfiction: Expose (especially consumer ripoffs); historical/nostalgic (Manhattan, 14th St.-96th St.); interview/profile (of local personalities); photo feature (of local event); and animal rights. "We're looking for local news (Manhattan only, mainly 14th St.-96th St.). We need timely, lively coverage of local issues and events, focusing on people or exposing injustice and good deeds of local residents and business people. (Get *full names, spelled correctly*.)" Special issues include Education (January, March and August); and Summer Camps (March). Query with published clips. Length: 1,000 words maximum. Pays "70¢/20-pica column-inch as published." Sometimes pays expenses of writers on assignment.

Photos: Pays $2-5 for 8 × 10 b&w prints. Buys all rights.

Tips: "Come by the office and talk to the editor. (Call first.) Bring samples of writing."

North Carolina

SOUTHERN EXPOSURE, P.O. Box 531, Durham NC 27702. (919)688-8167. Contact: Editor. Quarterly journal for well educated Southerners of all ages interested in "left-liberal" political perspective and the South. Estab. 1970. Circ. 7,500. Pays on publication. Buys all rights. Offers kill fee. Byline given. Will consider simultaneous submissions. Submit seasonal material 6 months in advance. Reports in 3 months. "Query is appreciated, but not required." Sample copy $4. Writer's guidelines for #10 SASE.

Nonfiction: "Ours is one of the few publications about the South *not* aimed at business or upper-class people; it appeals to all segments of the population. *And*, it is used as a resource—sold as a magazine and then as a book—so it rarely becomes dated." Needs investigative articles about the following subjects as related to the South: politics, energy, institutional power from prisons to universities, women, labor, black people and the economy. Informational interview, profile, historical, think articles, exposé, opinion and book reviews. Length: 4,500 words maximum. Pays $50-200. Smaller fee for short items.

Photos: "Very rarely purchase photos, as we have a large number of photographers working for us." 8 × 10 b&w preferred; no color. Payment negotiable.

Tips: "Because we will be publishing shorter issues on a quarterly basis, we will be looking for clear and thoughtful writing, articles that relate specific experiences of individual Southerners or grass roots groups to larger issues."

THE STATE, Down Home in North Carolina, Suite 2200, 128 S. Tryon St., Charlotte NC 28202. Managing Editor: Angela Terez. 90% freelance written. Monthly. Circ. 21,000. Publishes ms an average of 6-12 months after acceptance. Byline given. No kill fee. Buys first serial rights. Pays on publication. Submit seasonal/holiday material 8-12 months in advance. Sample copy $3.
Nonfiction: General articles about places, people, events, history, nostalgia and general interest in North Carolina. Emphasis on travel in North Carolina. Will use humor if related to region. Length: 700-2,000 words average. Pays $125-150 for assigned articles; $75-125 for unsolicited articles.
Photos: State availability of photos with submission. Reviews contact sheets and transparencies. Offers no additional payment for photos. Captions, model release and identification of subjects required. Buys one-time rights.
Columns/Departments: The State We're In (newsbriefs about current events in NC; most have travel, historic or environmental slant) 150-500 words. Buys 5 mss/year. Pays $25.

Ohio

BEACON MAGAZINE, Akron Beacon Journal, P.O. Box 640, 44 E. Exchange St., Akron OH 44309-0640. (216)996-3586. Editor: Ann Sheldon Mezger. 25% freelance written. Works with a small number of new/unpublished writers each year. Sunday newspaper magazine of general interest articles with a focus on Northeast Ohio. Circ. 225,000. Pays on publication. Publishes ms an average of 2 months after acceptance. Byline given. Offers 50% kill fee. Buys one-time rights, simultaneous rights and second serial (reprint) rights. Submit seasonal/holiday material 3 months in advance. Simultaneous queries, and simultaneous and previously published submissions OK. Reports in 1 month. Free sample copy and writer's guidelines.
Nonfiction: General interest, historical/nostalgic, short humor and interview/profile. Buys 50 mss/year. Query with or without published clips. Include Social Security number with story submission. Length: 500-3,000 words. Pays $75-450. Sometimes pays expenses of writers on assignment.
Photos: State availability of photos. Pays $25-50 for 35mm color transparencies and 8 × 10 b&w prints. Captions and identification of subjects required. Buys one-time rights.

BEND OF THE RIVER® MAGAZINE, 143 W. Third St., P.O. Box 39, Perrysburg OH 43552. (419)874-7534. FAX: (419)874-1466. Publishers: R. Lee Raizk or Christine Raizk Alexander. 90% freelance written. Works with a small number of new/unpublished writers each year, and eager to work with new/unpublished writers. "We buy material that we like whether by an experienced writer or not." Monthly magazine for readers interested in Ohio history, antiques, etc. Estab. 1972. Circ. 3,500. Pays on publication. Publishes ms an average of 6 months after acceptance. Byline given. Buys one-time rights. Submit seasonal material 2 months in advance; deadline for holiday issue is October 15. Reports in 6 weeks. Sample copy $1.
Nonfiction: "We deal heavily in Northwestern Ohio history. We are looking for well-researched articles about local history and modern day pioneers doing the unusual. We'd like to see interviews with historical (Ohio) authorities; travel sketches of little-known but interesting places in Ohio; articles about grass roots farmers, famous people from Ohio like Doris Day, Gloria Steinem, etc. and preservation. Our main interest is to give our readers happy thoughts and good reading. We strive for material that says 'yes' to life, past and present." No personal reflection or nostalgia unless you are over 65. Buys 75 unsolicited mss/year. Submit complete ms or send query. Length: 1,500 words. Pays $10-25. Sometimes pays the expenses of writers on assignment.
Photos: Purchases b&w or color photos with accompanying mss. Pays $2 minimum. Captions required.
Tips: "Any Toledo area, well-researched history will be put on top of the heap. Send us any unusual piece that is either cleverly humorous, divinely inspired or thought provoking. We like articles about historical topics treated in down-to-earth conversational tones. We pay a small amount (however, we're now paying more) but usually use our writers often and through the years. We're loyal."

CINCINNATI MAGAZINE, 409 Broadway, Cincinnati OH 45202. (513)421-4300. Editorial Director: Felix Winternitz. Monthly magazine emphasizing Cincinnati living. Circ. 32,000. **Pays on acceptance.** Byline given. Offers 33% kill fee. Buys first rights. Submit seasonal/holiday material 4 months in advance. Simultaneous and previously published submissions OK. Reports in 5 weeks.
Nonfiction: Informational, interview, humor, profile and travel. Buys 4-5 mss/issue. Query. Length: 2,000-4,000 words. Pays $150-400.
Columns/Departments: Travel, people, politics and sports. Buys 5 mss/issue. Query. Length: 750-1,500 words. Pays $75-150.
Tips: "We do special features each month. January: Home section; February: Dining out-restaurants; March: Health; April: Home and Fashion; May: Commercial real estate and gold; June: Health; July: Food and homes; August: Fashion; September: Homes; October: Automotive guide; November:

Fashion; December: City guide. We also have a special issue in August where we feature a fiction contest. Call or write for contest instructions."

COLUMBUS MONTHLY, 171 E. Livingston Ave., Columbus OH 43215. (614)464-4567. Editor: Lenore E. Brown. 20-40% freelance written. Prefers to work with published/established writers; works with a small number of new/unpublished writers each year. Monthly magazine emphasizing subjects specifically related to Columbus and central Ohio. Pays on publication. Publishes ms an average of 2 months after acceptance. Byline given. Buys all rights. Query for electronic submissions. Reports in 1 month. Sample copy $3.57.
Nonfiction: No humor, essays or first person material. "I like query letters which are well-written, indicate the author has some familiarity with *Columbus Monthly*, give me enough detail to make a decision and include at least a basic biography of the writer." Buys 4-5 unsolicited mss/year. Query. Length: 400-4,500 words. Pays $50-400. Sometimes pays the expenses of writers on assignment.
Photos: State availability of photos. Pay varies for b&w or color prints. Model release required.
Columns/Departments: Art, business, food and drink, movies, politics, sports and theatre. Buys 2-3 columns/issue. Query. Length: 1,000-2,000 words. Pays $100-175.
Tips: "It makes sense to start small—something for our Around Columbus section, perhaps. Stories for that section run between 400-1,000 words."

OHIO MAGAZINE, Ohio Magazine, Inc., Subsidiary of Dispatch Printing Co., 62 E. Broad St., Columbus OH 43215. Editor: Ellen Stein Burbach. 40% freelance written. Works with a small number of new/unpublished writers each year. Monthly magazine. Emphasizes news and feature material of Ohio for an educated, urban and urbane readership. Estab. 1978. Circ. 103,327. Pays on publication. Publishes ms an average of 5 months after acceptance. Buys all rights, second serial (reprint) rights, one-time rights, first North American serial rights or first serial rights. Byline given except on short articles appearing in sections. Submit seasonal/holiday material minimum 5 months in advance. Previously published submissions OK. Reports in 2 months. Sample copy $3 and 9 × 12 SAE; writer's guidelines for #10 SASE.
Nonfiction: Features: 2,000-8,000 words. Pays $350-950. Cover pieces $650-1,000; Columns: Ohioans (should be offbeat with solid news interest; 1,000-2,000 words, pays $200-500); Business (covering business related news items, profiles of prominent people in business community, personal finance—all Ohio angle; 1,000 words and up, pays $200-500); and Environment (isues related to Ohio and Ohioans, 1,000-2,000 words, pays $200-500). Send submissions for features/columns to Ellen Stein Burbach, editor; Diners' Digest to Lynn Campbell. Buys minimum 40 unsolicited mss/year. Sometimes pays expenses of writers on assignment.
Columns/Departments: Ellen Stein Burbach, editor.
Photos: Brooke Wenstrup, editorial designer. Rate negotiable.
Tips: "Freelancers should send a brief prospectus if complete one is not ready for submission. All articles should have a definite Ohio application."

PLAIN DEALER MAGAZINE, Plain Dealer Publishing Co., 1801 Superior Ave., Cleveland OH 44114. (216)344-4546. FAX: (216)694-6354. Editor: Clint O'Connor. 50% freelance written. A general interest Sunday newspaper magazine focusing on (but not limited to) Cleveland and Ohio. Circ. 550,000. Pays on publication. Publishes ms an average of 2-3 months after acceptance. Byline given. Buys first or one-time rights. Submit seasonal/holiday material 3 months in advance. Reports in 4 weeks on queries; 2 months on mss. Sample copy $1.
Nonfiction: Profiles, in-depth features, essays, exposé, historical/nostalgic, humor, personal experience and travel. Buys 20 mss/year. Query with published clips, or send complete ms. Manuscripts must be double-spaced, and should include a daytime telephone number. Length: 800-3,000 words. Pays $150-500.
Photos: State availability of photos with submission. Buys one-time rights.
Fiction: Buys 6 mss/year. Send complete ms. Length: 1,000-3,000 words. Pays $150-400.
Tips: "We're always looking for good writers and good stories."

TOLEDO MAGAZINE, The Blade, 541 Superior St., Toledo OH 43660. (419)245-6121. Editor: Sue Stankey. 40% freelance written. Prefers to work with published/established writers and works with a small number of new/unpublished writers each year. Weekly general interest magazine that appears in the Sunday newspaper. Circ. 225,000. Pays on publication. Publishes ms an average of 3 months after acceptance. Byline given. Buys one-time rights. Submit seasonal/holiday material 4-6 months in advance. Simultaneous queries and submissions OK. Reports in 2 weeks on queries; 1 month on mss. Sample copy for 9 × 12 SASE.

Nonfiction: General interest, historical/nostalgic, humor, interview/profile and personal experience. Buys 50 mss/year. Query with or without published clips. Length: 500-6,000 words. Pays $50-500.
Photos: State availability of photos. Reviews b&w and color contact sheets. Payment negotiable. Captions, model release and identification of subjects required. Buys one-time rights.
Tips: "Submit a well-organized story proposal and include copies of previously published stories."

Oklahoma

OKLAHOMA TODAY, Oklahoma Department of Tourism and Recreation, P.O. Box 53384, Oklahoma City OK 73152. Editor-in-Chief: Sue Carter. Managing Editor: Jeanne Devlin. 99% freelance written. Works with a small number of new/unpublished writers each year. Bimonthly magazine covering travel and recreation in the state of Oklahoma. "We are interested in showing off the best Oklahoma has to offer; we're pretty serious about our travel slant but will also consider history, nature and personality profiles." Estab. 1956. Circ. 45,000. **Pays on acceptance.** Publishes ms an average of 3 months after acceptance. Byline given. Buys first serial rights. Submit seasonal/holiday material 1 year in advance "depending on photographic requirements." Simultaneous queries OK. Reports in 2 months. Sample copy $2.50 with 8½×11 SASE; writer's guidelines for #10 SASE.
Nonfiction: Book excerpts (pre-publication only, on Oklahoma topics); photo feature and travel (in Oklahoma). "We are a specialized market; no first-person reminiscences or fashion, memoirs, though just about any topic can be used if given a travel slant." Buys 35-40 mss/year. Query with published clips; no phone queries. Length: 1,000-1,500 words. Pays $150-250.
Photos: High-quality transparencies, b&w prints. "We are especially interested in developing contacts with photographers who either live in Oklahoma or have shot here. Send samples and price range." Free photo guidelines with SASE. Pays $50-100 for b&w and $50-250 for color; reviews 2¼ and 35mm color transparencies. Model releases, identification of subjects and other information for captions required. Buys one-time rights plus right to use photos for promotional purposes.
Tips: "The best way to become a regular contributor to *Oklahoma Today* is to query us with one or more story ideas, each developed to give us an idea of your proposed slant. We're looking for *lively* writing, writing that doesn't need to be heavily edited and is not newspaper style. We have a two-person editorial staff, and freelancers who can write and have done their homework get called again and again."

Oregon

CASCADES EAST, 716 NE 4th St., P.O. Box 5784, Bend OR 97708. (503)382-0127. Editor: Geoff Hill. 90% freelance written. Prefers to work with published/established writers. Quarterly magazine for "all ages as long as they are interested in outdoor recreation in central Oregon: fishing, hunting, sight-seeing, golf, tennis, hiking, bicycling, mountain climbing, backpacking, rockhounding, skiing, snowmobiling, etc." Estab. 1972. Circ. 10,000 (distributed throughout area resorts and motels and to subscribers). Pays on publication. Publishes ms an average of 6 months after acceptance. Buys all rights. Byline given. Submit seasonal/holiday material 6 months in advance. Reports in 6 weeks. Sample copy and writer's guidelines for $4 and 9×12 SAE.
Nonfiction: General interest (first person experiences in outdoor central Oregon—with photos, can be dramatic, humorous or factual); historical (for feature, "Little Known Tales from Oregon History," with b&w photos); and personal experience (needed on outdoor subjects: dramatic, humorous or factual). "No articles that are too general, sight-seeing articles that come from a travel folder, or outdoor articles without the first-person approach." Buys 20-30 unsolicited mss/year. Query. Length: 1,000-3,000 words. Pays 3-10¢/word.
Photos: "Old photos will greatly enhance chances of selling a historical feature. First-person articles need black and white photos, also." Pays $10-25 for b&w; $15-100 for transparencies. Captions preferred. Buys one-time rights.
Tips: "Submit stories a year or so in advance of publication. We are seasonal and must plan editorials for summer '93 in the spring of '92, etc., in case seasonal photos are needed."

‡NORTHWEST TRAVEL, Spooner Industries Inc., 1870 Highway 126, P.O. Box 18000, Florence OR 97439. (800)727-8401. Editors: Alicia and Rob Spooner. Managing Editors: Dave Peden and Judy Fleagle. 95% freelance written. Bimonthly magazine of Northwest living. Estab. 1991. Circ. 32,000. Pays on publication. Publishes ms an average of 6 months after acceptance. Byline given. Offers ⅓ kill fee. Buys one-time rights. Submit seasonal/holiday material 6 months in advance. Query for electronic submissions. Reports in 1 month on queries; 3 months on manuscripts. Sample copy $3.50. Writer's guidelines for #10 SAE with 2 first class stamps.
Nonfiction: Nature as pertains to Pacific Northwest. "Any article not related to the Pacific Northwest will be returned." Query with published clips. Length: 500-2,000 words. Pays $50-200. "Along with payment comes 5 copies."

Photos: Send photos with submission. Preferred 35mm or larger transparencies, 3×5 or larger prints. Captions and identification of subjects required. Buys one-time rights.

Poetry: Poetry Editor, Vickie Nelson. Free verse, haiku, light verse and traditional. "If it does not relate to the Pacific Northwest, it will be returned." Buys 15 poems/year. Submit maximum 4 poems. Length: 60 lines. Pays 5 copies in which work appears.

Fillers: Newsbreaks (no-fee basis) and short articles. Buys 30/year. Byline given. Length: 300-500 words. Pays $35-50.

Tips: "Slant article for readers who do not live in the Pacific Northwest. At least one historical article and at least two travel articles will be used in each issue. City and town profiles, special out-of-the-way places to visit, will also be used in each issue. An occasional restaurant review will be used. Short articles with photos (transparencies preferred) will be easiest to fit in. Query first. After go-ahead, send cover letter with manuscript/photo package. Photos often make the difference in deciding which article gets published."

OREGON COAST, The Bi-Monthly Magazine of Coastal Living, 1870 Highway 126, P.O. Box 18000, Florence OR 97439. (800)727-8401. FAX: (503)997-1124. Editor: Alicia Spooner. Managing Editor: Judy Fleagle. 70% freelance written. Bimonthly magazine covering the Oregon Coast. Estab. 1982. Circ. 65,000. Pays on publication. Publishes ms an average of 6-8 months after accpetance. Byline given. Offers ⅓ kill fee. Buys one-time rights. Submit seasonal/holiday material 5 months in advance. Query for electronic submissions. Reports in 3 months. Sample copy $3.50. Writer's guidelines for #10 SAE with 2 first class stamps.

Nonfiction: General interest, historical/nostalgic, humor, interview/profile, personal experience, photo feature, travel, nature as pertains to Oregon Coast. Buys 60 mss/year. Query with published clips. Length: 500-2,000 words. Pays $50-200.

Photos: Send photos with submission. Reviews 35mm or larger transparencies and 3×5 or larger prints. Offers no additional payment for photos accepted with ms. Captions and identification of subjects required. Buys one-time rights.

Poetry: Vickie Nelson, Free verse, haiku, light verse, traditional. Nothing unrelated to the Northwest Coast. Buys 15 poems/year. Submit maximum 4 poems. Length: 60 lines maximum. Pays 5 copies in which work appears.

Fillers: Newsbreaks (no-fee basis) and short articles. Buys 12/year. Length: 300-500 words. Pays $35-50.

Tips: "Slant article for readers who do not live at the Oregon Coast. At least one historical article is used in each issues. Manuscript/photo packages are preferred over manuscripts with no photos. List photo credits and captions for each print or slide. Check all facts, proper names and numbers carefully."

‡OREGON COAST GETAWAY GUIDE, Monthly Magazine of Coastal Activities, Spooner Industries Inc., 1870 Highway 126, P.O. Box 18000, Florence OR 97439. (800)727-8401. Editor: Alicia Spooner. Managing Editor: Dave Peden. 40% freelance written. Monthly magazine covering Oregon Coast activities and places. Estab. 1990. Circ. 6,000. Pays on publication. Publishes ms an average of 3-4 months after acceptance. Offers ⅓ fill fee. Buys one-time rights. Submit seasonal/holiday material 4 months in advance. Query for electronic submissions. Reports in 1 month on queries; 2 months on manuscripts. Sample copy for $2.50 SAE; writer's guidelines for SAE with 2 first class stamps.

Nonfiction: General interest, how-to, interview/profile, personal experience, travel, places and activities on Oregon Coast. "Any article not related to the Oregon Coast will be returned." Buys 60 mss/year. Query with published clips. Length: 500-1,500 words. Pays $50-200 and 5 copies.

Photos: Send photos with submission. Reviews 35mm transparencies and (preferred) 3×5 or larger prints. Offers no additional payment for photos accepted with ms. Captions and identification of subjects required. Buys one-time rights.

Fillers: Short articles, Buys 24/year. Length: 300-500 words. Pays $35-50.

Tips: "No matter what length—short or regular feature—photos (prints) would be appreciated. Query first. After go-ahead, send cover letter with manuscript/photo package. Photos often make the difference in deciding which article gets published. Glossy black-and-white photos work best but color prints with good contrast also work well."

Pennsylvania

PENNSYLVANIA, Pennsylvania Magazine Co., Box 576, Camp Hill PA 17001-0576. (717)761-6620. Editor: Albert E. Holliday. Managing Editor: Joan Holliday. 90% freelance written. Bimonthly magazine. Circ. 40,000. Pays on acceptance for assigned articles. Publishes ms an average of 6-12 months after acceptance. Byline given. Offers 33% kill fee. Buys first North American serial rights or one-time rights. Reports in 4-6 weeks on queries; 3 weeks on mss. Sample copy $2.95 and 9×12 SAE; writer's guidelines for #10 SASE.

Nonfiction: General interest, historical/nostalgic, photo feature and travel—all dealing with or related to Pennsylvania. Nothing on Amish topics, hunting or skiing. Buys 50-75 mss/year. Query. Length: 250-2,500 words. Pays $25-250. Sometimes pays the expenses of writers on assignment. All articles must be illustrated; send photocopies of possible illustrations with query.

Photos: Reviews 35mm and 2¼ color transparencies and 5×7 to 8×10 color and b&w prints. Pays $15-50 for b&w; $15-100 for color. Captions required. Buys one-time rights.

Columns/Departments: Panorama—short items about people, unusual events; Made in Pennsylvania-short items about family and individually owned consumer-related businesses. Scrapbook (short historical items).

PENNSYLVANIA HERITAGE, Pennsylvania Historical and Museum Commission, P.O. Box 1026, Harrisburg PA 17108-1026. (717)787-7522. Editor: Michael J. O'Malley III. 90% freelance written. Prefers to work with published/established writers. Quarterly magazine. *"Pennsylvania Heritage* introduces readers to Pennsylvania's rich culture and historic legacy, educates and sensitizes them to the value of preserving that heritage and entertains and involves them in such as way as to ensure that Pennsylvania's past has a future. The magazine is intended for intelligent lay readers." Circ. 10,000. **Pays on acceptance.** Publishes ms an average of 8-12 months after acceptance. Byline given. Buys all rights. Simultaneous queries and submissions OK. Reports in 6 weeks on queries; 10 weeks on mss. Sample copy for 9×12 SAE and $3; free writer's guidelines for #10 SASE.

Nonfiction: Art, science, biographies, industry, business, politics, transportation, military, historic preservation, archaeology, photography, etc. No articles which in no way relate to Pennsylvania history or culture. "Our format requires feature-length articles. Manuscripts with illustrations are especially sought for publication." Buys 20-24 mss/year. Query. Length: 2,000-3,500 words. Pays $300-500.

Photos: State availability or send photos with query or ms. Pays $25-100 for transparencies; $5-10 for b&w photos. Captions and identification of subjects required. Buys one-time rights.

Tips: "We are looking for well-written, interesting material that pertains to any aspect of Pennsylvania history or culture. Potential contributors should realize that, although our articles are popularly styled, they are not light, puffy or breezy; in fact they demand strident documentation and substantiation (sans footnotes). The most frequent mistake made by writers in completing articles for us is making them either too scholarly or too nostalgic. We want material which educates, but also entertains. Authors should make history readable and entertaining."

PHILADELPHIA MAGAZINE, 1500 Walnut St., Philadelphia PA 19102. (215)545-3500. Editor: Ron Javers. 40% freelance written. Prefers to work with published/established writers; works with a small number of new/unpublished writers each year. Monthly magazine for sophisticated middle- and upper-income people in the Greater Philadelphia/South Jersey area. Circ. 152,272. **Pays on acceptance.** Publishes ms an average of 2 months after acceptance. Buys first serial rights. Pays 20% kill fee. Byline given. Reports in 1 month. Writer's guidelines for SASE.

Nonfiction: Laurene Stains, articles editor. "Articles should have a strong Philadelphia (city and suburbs) focus but should avoid Philadelphia stereotypes—we've seen them all. Submit lifestyles, city survival, profiles of interesting people, business stories, music, the arts, sports and local politics, stressing the topical or unusual. Intelligent, entertaining essays on subjects of specific local interest. No puff pieces. We offer lots of latitude for style." Buys 50 mss/year. Length: 1,000-7,000 words. Pays $100-2,000. Sometimes pays expenses of writers on assignment.

PITTSBURGH MAGAZINE, Metropolitan Pittsburgh Public Broadcasting, Inc., 4802 5th Ave., Pittsburgh PA 15213. (412)622-1360. FAX: (412)622-1488. Editor-in-Chief: Bruce VanWyngarden. 60% freelance written. Prefers to work with published/established writers; works with a small number of new/unpublished writers each year. "The magazine is purchased on newsstands and by subscription and is given to those who contribute $35 or more a year to public TV in western Pennsylvania." Estab. 1970. Circ. 65,000. Pays on publication. Publishes ms an average of 2 months after acceptance. Buys first North American serial rights and second serial (reprint) rights. Pays kill fee. Byline given. Submit seasonal/holiday material 6 months in advance. Query for electronic submissions. Reports in 2 months. Publishes ms an average of 2 months after acceptance. Sample copy $2.

Nonfiction: Expose, lifestyle, sports, informational, service, interview, nostalgia and profile. Query or send complete ms. Length: 2,500 words. Pays $50-500. Query for photos. Model releases required. Sometimes pays the expenses of writers on assignment.

Columns/Departments: Art, books, films, dining, health, sports and theatre. "All must relate to Pittsburgh or western Pennsylvania."

‡THE PITTSBURGH PRESS SUNDAY MAGAZINE,The Pittsburgh Press Co., 34 Boulevard of the Allies, Pittsburgh PA 15230. (412)263-1510. Editor: Ed Wintermantel. 10% freelance written. Prefers to work with published/established writers. A weekly general interest newspaper magazine for a general

audience. Circ. 544,402. Pays on publication. Publishes ms an average of 2 months after acceptance. Byline given. Not copyrighted. Buys first serial rights in circulation area. Simultaneous queries acceptable. Query for electronic submissions. Reports in 1 month. Writer's guidelines for #10 SASE.
Nonfiction: Regional or local interest, humor and interview/profile. No hobbies, how-to or timely events. Buys 40-50 mss/year. Query. "When submitting a manuscript, writer must include his or her social security number. This is a requirement of the Internal Revenue Service since payments for published stories must be reported." Length: 1,000-3,000 words. Pays $100-400.

Rhode Island

RHODE ISLAND MONTHLY, 18 Imperial Place, Providence RI 02903. (401)421-2552. FAX: (401)831-5624. Editor: Dan Kaplan. Managing Editor: Vicki Sanders. 90% freelance written. Monthly magazine on Rhode Island living. Estab. 1988. Circ. 26,000. Pays on publication. Publishes ms an average of 2 months after acceptance. Byline given. Kill fee varies. Buys first rights. Submit seasonal/holiday material 4 months in advance. Query for electronic submissions. Reports in 1 month. Sample copy $1.95 with 9 × 12 SAE with $1.20 postage.
Nonfiction: Profiles, human interest features, exposé, photo feature. "We do not want material unrelated to Rhode Island." Buys 48 mss/year. Query with published clips. Length: 200-6,000 words. Pays $100-1,000. Pays expenses of writers on assignment for stories over $400.
Photos: State availability of photos with submission. Reviews contact sheets and 5 × 7 prints. Offers $50-200. Captions, model releases and identification of subjects required. Buys one-time rights.

South Carolina

‡CHARLESTON MAGAZINE, P.O. Box 21770, Charleston SC 29413. (803)769-2323. Editor: Katharine W. Cart. Managing Editor: Sally Sun. 95% freelance written. Monthly magazine covering the Lowcountry South Carolina, the South as a region. "Consumer magazine with a literary bent. Our aim is to become the *New Yorker* of the South where we will at once reach upscale consumers and the Southern intelligentia." Estab. 1987. Circ. 20,000. Pays on publication. Publishes ms and average of 3 months after acceptance. Byline given. Buys one-time rights. Submit seasonal/holiday material 4 months in advance. Simultaneous submissions and previously published submissions OK. Query for electronic submissions. Sample copies for 9 × 12 SAE with 5 first class stamps. Free writer's guidelines.
Nonfiction: Book excerpts, essays, exposé, general interest, historical/nostalgic, humor, interview/profile, new product, opinion, personal experience, photo feature, travel. ("Each issue has a focus—these themes are listed in our writer's guidelines. Not interested in general interest articles. Must pertain to the Charleston area or, at their broadest scope, the south as a region. Buys 120 mss/year. Query with published clips. Length: 150-2,000 words. Pays 10¢/printed word. Sometimes pays expenses of writers on assignment.
Photos: Send photos with submission. Reviews contact sheets, transparencies and slides. Offers $35 maximum per photo. Captions and identification of subjects required. Buys one-time rights.
Columns/Departments: Channel Markers (general interest) 50-250 words; Hindsight (historical perspectives and local low country interest) 1,000-1,500 words; First Person (profile—people of local interest) 1,000-1,500 words; Art (features an successful organization or innovative articles) 1,000-1,500; Business (developments in regional or local economy) 1,000-1,500 words. Buys 90 mss/year. Query with published clips. Pays 3-10¢/word.
Fiction: Adventure, historical, humorous, mainstream, mystery, novel excerpts. Buys 12 mss/year. Send complete ms. Length: 2,000 words maximum. Pays $100 flat rate.
Poetry: Avant-garde, free verse, haiku, light verse, traditional. Buys 12 poems/year. Pays $35 maximum.
Fillers: Anecdotes, facts, short humor. Buys 100/year. Length: 25-250 wrods. Pays 10¢/printed word.
Tips: "Follow our writer's guidelines. Areas most open to freelancers are Fiction and Columns/Departments and features. Should be of local or Southern interest."

SANDLAPPER, The Magazine of South Carolina, RPW Publishing Corp, P.O. Box 1108, Lexington SC 29071. (803)359-9954. FAX: (803)957-8226. Editor: Robert P. Wilkins. Managing Editor: Daniel E. Harmon. 70% freelance written. A semiannual feature magazine focusing on the positive aspects of South Carolina. Estab. 1989. Circ. 20,000. Pays during the dateline period. Publishes ms an average of 4 months after acceptance. Byline given. Buys first North American serial rights and the right to reprint. Submit seasonal material 6 months in advance. Query for electronic submissions. Reports in 1 month on queries; 2 months on mss. Free writer's guidelines.
Nonfiction: Feature articles and photo essays about South Carolina's interesting people, places, cuisine, things to do. Occasional history articles. Query. Length: 600-5,000 words. Pays $50-500. Sometimes pays the expenses of writers on assignment.

Tips: "We're not interested in articles about topical issues, politics, crime or commercial ventures. Humorous angles are encouraged. Avoid first-person nostalgia and remembrances of places that no longer exist."

South Dakota

DAKOTA OUTDOORS, South Dakota, Hipple Publishing Co., P.O. Box 669, 333 W. Dakota, Pierre SD 57501. (605)224-7301. FAX: (605)224-9210. Editor: Kevin Hipple. 50% freelance written. Monthly magazine on Dakota outdoor life. Estab. 1975. Circ. 4,150. Pays on publication. Publishes ms an average of 2 months after acceptance. Byline given. Submit seasonal/holiday material 3 months in advance. Simultaneous and previously published submissions (if notified) OK. Query for electronic submissions. Sample copy for 9 × 12 SAE with 2 first class stamps.
Nonfiction: General interest, how-to, humor, interview/profile, new product, opinion, personal experience, photo feature and technical (all on outdoor topics – prefer in Dakotas). Buys 50 mss/year. Query with or without published clips, or send complete ms. Length: 200-1,000 words. Pays $5-40 for assigned articles; $40 maximum for unsolicited articles. Pays in contributor copies or other premiums (inquire).
Photos: Send photos with submission. Reviews 5 × 7 prints. Offers no additional payment for photos accepted with ms. Identification of subjects preferred. Buys one-time rights.
Fillers: Anecdotes, facts, gags to be illustrated by cartoonist, newsbreaks and short humor. Buys 4/year. Also publishes line drawings of fish and game. Prefers 5 × 7.
Tips: "Submit samples of manuscript or previous works for consideration; photos or illustrations with manuscript are helpful."

Tennessee

MEMPHIS, MM Corporation, P.O. Box 256, Memphis TN 38101. (901)521-9000. FAX: (901)521-0129. Editor: Leanne Kleinmann. 60% freelance written. Works with a small number of new/unpublished writers. Estab. 1976. Circ. 21,917. **Pays on acceptance.** Publishes ms an average of 3 months after acceptance. Byline given. Buys first North American serial rights. Offers 20% kill fee. Simultaneous and previously published submissions OK. Reports in 6 weeks. Sample copy for 9 × 12 SAE and $2.50 postage; writer's guidelines for SASE.
Nonfiction: Exposé, general interest, historical, how-to, humor, interview and profile. "Virtually all of our material has strong mid-South connections." Buys 25 freelance mss/year. Query or submit complete ms or published clips. Length: 1,500-5,000 words. Pays $100-1,000. Sometimes pays expenses of writers on assignment.
Tips: "The kinds of manuscripts we most need have a sense of story (i.e., plot, suspense, character), an abundance of evocative images to bring that story alive, and a sensitivity to issues at work in Memphis. The most frequent mistakes made by writers in completing an article for us are lack of focus, lack of organization, factual gaps and failure to capture the magazine's style. Tough investigative pieces would be especially welcomed."

THE TENNESSEE MAGAZINE, Tennessee Electric Cooperative Assn., P.O. Box 100912, Nashville TN 37224. Staff written. Did not want to be listed.

Texas

"D" MAGAZINE, American Express Publishing Corporation, A subsidiary of American Express Travel Related Services Co., Inc., Suite 1200, 3988 N. Central Expressway, Dallas TX 75204. (214)827-5000. FAX: (214)827-8844. Editor: Ruth Miller Fitzgibbons. 25% freelance written. Monthly magazine. "We are a general interest magazine with emphasis on events occuring in Dallas." Estab. 1974. Circ. 102,000. **Pays on acceptance.** Publishes ms an average of 3 months after acceptance. Byline given. Offers 25% kill fee. Buys first North American serial rights. Submit seasonal/holiday material 3 months in advance. Query for electronic submissions. Reports in 1 month. Sample copy $2.50 with SAE and 5 first class stamps; free writer's guidelines.
Nonfiction: Essays, exposé, historical/nostalgic, how-to, interview/profile and travel. Buys 20-30 mss/year. Query with published clips. Length: 1,000-5,000 words. Pays $75-750 for assigned articles; pays $50-500 for unsolicited articles. Pays expenses of writers on assignment.

Photos: State availability of photos with submission. Reviews transparencies and 35mm prints. Offers $50-75 per photo. Captions required. Buys one-time rights.

Columns/Departments: Business, Politics, Travel and Relationships. Query with published clips or send complete ms. Length: 1,500-2,000 words. Pays $250-500.

Tips: "Tell us something about our city that we have not written about. We realize that is very difficult for someone outside of Dallas to do—that's why 90% of our magazine is written by people who live in the North Texas area."

‡DALLAS LIFE MAGAZINE, Sunday Magazine of *The Dallas Morning News*, Communications Center, P.O. Box 655237, Dallas TX 75265. (214)745-8432. Managing Editor: Mike Maza. Weekly magazine. "We are a lively, topical, sometimes controversial city magazine devoted to informing, enlightening and entertaining our urban Sunbelt readers with material which is specifically relevant to Dallas lifestyles and interests." **Pays on acceptance.** Byline given. Buys first North American serial rights or simultaneous rights. Simultaneous queries and submissions OK ("if not competitive in our area"). Reports in 1 month on queries; 6 weeks on mss.

Nonfiction: General interest; humor (short); interview/profile. "All material must, repeat *must*, have a Dallas metropolitan area frame of reference." Special issues include: spring and fall home furnishings theme and travel. Buys 5-10 unsolicited mss/year. Query with published clips or send complete ms. Length: 1,200-3,000 words. Pays $200-750.

HOUSTON METROPOLITAN MAGAZINE, City Home Publishing, P.O. Box 25386, Houston TX 77265. (713)524-3000. Editorial Director: Gabrielle Cosgriff. Managing Editor: Mike Peters. 85% freelance written. A monthly city magazine. Estab. 1974. Circ. 87,500. **Pays on acceptance.** Publishes ms an average of 3 months after acceptance. Byline given. Offers 25% kill fee. Buys first North American serial rights. Submit holiday/seasonal material 6 months in advance. Query for electronic submissions. Simultaneous and photocopied submissions OK. Reports in 2 weeks on queries; 1 month on mss. Sample copy for 9½×12 SAE and 8 first class stamps.

Nonfiction: Issue-oriented features, profiles, lifestyle/entertainment, food features, visual stories, and humorous features about Houston or Houstonians. Query with published clips or send complete ms. Length: 300-2,500 words. Pays $50-1,000.

Photos: Fernande Bondarenko, Art Dept. State availability of photos with submission. Buys one-time rights. "Also assigns photographers at day or job rates."

Columns/Departments: About Town Column. Must have strong Houston-area slant. Length: 300-500 words. Pays $50-200.

Tips: "Submit clips demonstrating strong writing and reporting skills with detailed queries, bearing in mind that this is a city magazine. Our intent is to be a lively, informative city book, addressing the issues and people who affect our lives objectively and fairly. But also with affection and, where suitable, a sense of humor. Only those familiar with the Houston metropolitan area should approach us."

ULTRA, Suite 305, 1400 Post Oak Blvd., Houston TX 77056. (713)622-1967. FAX: (713)622-8716. Executive Editor: Lagay Sonnier-Varoutsos. 70% freelance written. Bimonthly magazine covering connoisserhip in the arts, architecture, design, food, fashion in Texas. Estab. 1982. Circ. 100,000. Pays on publication. Publishes ms an average of 3 months after acceptance. Byline given. Offers 25% kill fee. Buys first North American serial rights. Query for electronic submissions. Reports in 2 months. Sample copy $4 with 11×14 SAE and 6 first class stamps.

Nonfiction: Book excerpts, essays, general interest, historical, photo feature and travel. Buys 100 mss/year. Query with published clips. Pays expenses of writers on assignment.

Photos: State availability of photos with submission. Reviews transparencies. Captions, model releases and identification of subjects required. Buys one-time rights.

Utah

‡SALT LAKE CITY, Suite A, 1270 West 2320 South, Salt Lake City UT 84119. (801)975-1927. Editor: Renon K. Hulet. Managing Editor: Amy Albo. 75% freelance written. Bimonthly magazine. "Ours is a lifestyle magazine, focusing on the people, issues and places that make Utah and the Intermountain West unique. Our audience is mainly educated, affluent, ages 25-55. Our pieces are generally positive, or at the very least suggestive of solutions. Again, we focus heavily on people!" Estab. 1990. Circ. 15,000. Pays on publication. Publishes ms an average of 3-6 months after acceptance. Byline given. Offers $25 kill fee. Buys first North American serial rights or second serial (reprint) rights. Submit seasonal/holiday material 6 months in advance. Simultaneous and previously published submissions OK. Query for electronic submissions. Reports in 1 month on queries; 6 weeks on mss. Free sample copy and writer's guidelines.

Nonfiction: Essays (health, family matters, financial), general interest, historical/nostalgic (pertaining to Utah and Intermountain West), humor, interview/profile (famous or powerful people associated with Utah business, politics, media); personal experience, photo feature (fashion available in Utah stores or cuisine of anywhere in world); travel (anywhere exotic in the world). "Every year in November-December issue we publish a fiction section with two short stories and several poems pertaining to the holidays. No movie reviews or current news subjects, please." Buys 5 mss/year. Query with published clips or send complete ms. Length: 800-2,000 words. Pays $75-400 for assigned articles; $75-250 for unsolicited articles. "A major feature is negotiable." Sometimes pays expenses of writers on assignment.

Photos: State availability of photos with submission. Reviews transparencies (size not important). Captions, model releases and identification of subjects required. Payment and rights negotiable.

Columns/Departments: Up Close (standard personality profile) 1,200-1,500 words; Travel (exotic world travel/preferable to include excellent photography) 2,500-3,000; (Q and A question and answer of famous person) 1,200-1,500 words; Executive Signature (profile, business slant of major Utah entrepeneur); Food (recipes must be included) 1,000-1,500 words. Buys 5-10 mss/year. Query with published clips or send complete ms. Pays $75-150.

Fiction: Adventure, fantasy, historical, humorous, mainstream, mystery, romance, science fiction, slice-of-life vignettes, suspense, western. "No pornography." Buys 3 mss/year. Query with published clips or send complete ms. Length: 1,000-1,500 words. Pays $75-250.

Poetry: Free verse, haiku, light verse, traditional. Buys 5 poems/year. Submit maximum 5 poems. Pays $75-150.

Tips: "Well-written, neatly typed, well-researched complete manuscripts that come across my desk are most likely to be published if they fit our format. They are a God send! Writers have the best chance of selling us humor, eye-openers, family topics and small features on topics of general interest to Utahns and American western living. For example, we have done mountainwest recreation, child abuse, drugs, earthquakes and Native American issues."

UTAH HOLIDAY MAGAZINE, Utah, Tuesday Publishing Co., 807 E. South Temple, #200, Salt Lake City UT 84102. (801)532-3737. FAX: (801)532-3742. Editor: Bruce Lee. Managing Editor: Mildred Evans. 100% freelance written. Monthly magazine on Utah oriented—subjects newspapers do not print, provocative opinion. Theatre, art, movie reviews. Estab. 1971. Circ. 10,000. Pays on 15th of month of publication. Byline given. Buys first North American serial rights. Submit seasonal/holiday material 3 months in advance. Query for electronic submissions. Reports in 3 weeks on queries. Sample copy for 10×12 SAE and 5 first class stamps; writer's guidelines for #10 SASE.

Nonfiction: Essays, exposé, interview/profile, opinion and personal experience. "No travel outside Utah, humor or personal essays." Buys 1 ms/year. Query with or without published clips, or send complete ms. Length: 2,500-8,000 words. Pays $90-350 for assigned articles. Also pays in contributor copies or other premiums. Sometimes pays expenses of writers on assignment.

Photos: State availability of photos with submission. Send photos with submission. Reviews contact sheets and transparencies. Offers $15-70 per photo. Identification of subjects required. Buys one-time rights.

Columns/Departments: Movie Reviews, Opera, Theatre, Ballet and Art (all slanted to current Utah productions), 1,500 words. Buys 10 mss/year. Query with published clips. Pays $90-120.

Vermont

VERMONT LIFE MAGAZINE, 61 Elm St., Montpelier VT 05602. (802)828-3241. Editor-in-Chief: Thomas K. Slayton. 90% freelance written. Prefers to work with published/established writers. Quarterly magazine. Circ. 110,000. Publishes ms an average of 9 months after acceptance. Byline given. Offers kill fee. Buys first serial rights. Submit seasonal/holiday material 1 year in advance. Simultaneous queries, and simultaneous and previously published submissions OK. Reports in 1 month. Writer's guidelines for #10 SASE.

Nonfiction: Wants articles on today's Vermont, those which portray a typical or, if possible, unique aspect of the state or its people. Style should be literate, clear and concise. Subtle humor favored. No Vermont dialect attempts as in "Ayup," outsider's view on visiting Vermont, or "Vermont clichés"—maple syrup, town meetings or stereotyped natives. Buys 60 mss/year. Query by letter essential. Length: 1,500 words average. Pays 20¢/word. Seldom pays expenses of writers on assignment.

Photos: Buys photographs with mss; buys seasonal photographs alone. Prefers b&w contact sheets to look at first on assigned material. Color submissions must be 4×5 or 35mm transparencies. Rates on acceptance: $75-150 inside, color; $200 for cover. Gives assignments but only with experienced photographers. Query in writing. Captions, model releases, and identification of subjects required. Buys one-time rights, but often negotiates for re-use rights.

Tips: "Writers who read our magazine are given more consideration because they understand that we want authentic articles about Vermont. If a writer has a genuine working knowledge of Vermont, his or her work usually shows it. Vermont is changing and there is much concern here about what this state will be like in years ahead. It is a beautiful, environmentally sound place now and the vast majority of residents want to keep it so. Articles reflecting such concerns in an intelligent, authoritative, non-hysterical way will be given very careful consideration. The growth of tourism makes *Vermont Life* interested in intelligent articles about specific places in Vermont, their history and attractions to the traveling public."

‡VERMONT MAGAZINE, 14 School St., Box 288, Bristol VT 05443. (802)453-3200. Editor: John S. Rosenberg. Bimonthly magazine about Vermont. Buys first North American serial rights. Submit all material 5-6 months in advance; prefer queries first. Photocopied submissions OK. Query for electronic submissions. Reports in 2 weeks. Writer's guidelines for #10 SASE.
Nonfiction: Journalism and reporting, book excerpts, essays, expose, general interest, historical, how-to, humor, interview/profile, photo feature, calendar. Buys 50 mss/year. Query with published clips, or send complete ms. Length: 900-3,500 words. Pays $200-800. Sometimes pays expenses of writers on assignment.
Photos: Send photos with submission. Reviews contact sheets, 35mm transparencies and 8 × 10 b&w prints. Captions, model releases (if possible) and identification of subjects required. Buys one-time rights.
Tips: "Our readers *know* their state well, and they know the 'real' Vermont can't be slipped inside a glib and glossy brochure. We're interested in serious journalism on major issues, plus coverage of arts, outdoors, living, nature, architecture."

Virginia

‡NOVASCOPE, Novascope, Inc., P.O. Box 1590, Middleburg VA 22117. (703)687-3314. FAX: (703)687-4113. Editor: Mark Smith & Joy Smith. 75% freelance written. Monthly magazine on human interest, environmental issues, history and events pertinent to northern Virginia. Estab. 1985. Circ. 50,000. Pays on publication. Byline given. Buys first North American serial rights. Submit seasonal/holiday material 3 months in advance. Simultaneous submissions OK. Reports in 2 weeks. Free sample copy and writer's guidelines.
Nonfiction: General interest, historical and interview/profile, all pertinent to Northern Virginia. Buys 50 mss/year. Query with published clips. Length: 1,000 words maximum. Pays $50 maximum for unsolicited articles. Sometimes pays expensese of writers on assignment.
Photos: State availability of photos with submission. Reviews 35mm transparencies. Offers $10 maximum per photo. Identification of subjects required. Buys one-time rights.

RICHMOND SURROUNDINGS, Target Communications Inc., Suite 110, 7814 Carousel Ln., Richmond VA 23294. (804)346-4130. FAX: (804)965-0083. Editor: Frances C. Helms. 90% freelance written. Bimonthly magazine covering the metropolitan Richmond area. *"Richmond Surroundings* is a city magazine with an editorial mix of news and features which appeal to our upscale audience, ages 30-55. We want to inform as well as entertain." Estab. 1979. Circ. 20,000. Pays on publication. Publishes ms an average of 2 months after acceptance. Negotiable kill fee. Buys first rights, one-time rights, second serial (reprint) rights and makes work-for-hire assignments. Submit seasonal/holiday material 6 months in advance. Simultaneous submissions OK. Query for electronic submissions. Reports in 2 weeks. Sample copy $2. Free writer's guidelines.
Nonfiction: Investigative, general interest, historical/nostalgic, humor, interview/profile, personal experience, photo feature and travel. Upcoming special issue: Newcomers Edition, each February. Information pertinent to newcomers to the metro Richmond area. "No articles not about Virginians or not pertinent to Virginia in general and Richmond in particular." Buys 150 mss/year. Query with published clips. Length: 250-5,000 words. Pays 10-15¢/word for assigned articles.
Photos: Send photos with submission. Reviews contact sheets and 5 × 7 prints or slides. Offers $25-75 per photo (more for special assignments). Identification of subjects required. Buys one-time rights or all rights.
Tips: "Make a personal contact by phone first, then in person; let us see your work; call and suggest a topic; write on spec. Be able to produce on a short deadline. Our entire publication is open to freelancers. Let us know your specialty (travel, profiles, investigative, etc.)."

Always check the most recent copy of a magazine for the address and editor's name before you send in a query or manuscript.

THE ROANOKER, Leisure Publishing Co., 3424 Brambleton Ave., P.O. Box 21535, Roanoke VA 24018. (703)989-6138. FAX: (703)989-7603. Editor: Kurt Rheinheimer. 75% freelance written. Works with a small number of new/unpublished writers each year. Monthly magazine covering people and events of Western Virginia. "*The Roanoker* is a general interest city magazine edited for the people of Roanoke, Virginia, and the surrounding area. Our readers are primarily upper-income, well-educated professionals between the ages of 35 and 60. Coverage ranges from hard news and consumer information to restaurant reviews and local history." Estab. 1974. Circ. 14,000. Pays on publication. Publishes ms an average of 4 months after acceptance. Byline given. Buys all rights; makes work-for-hire assignments. Submit seasonal/holiday material 4 months in advance. Simultaneous queries OK. Reports in 2 months. Sample copy for $2 and 9 × 12 SAE with $2.50 postage; writer's guidelines for #10 SASE.
Nonfiction: Exposé; historical/nostalgic; how-to (live better in western Virginia); interview/profile (of well-known area personalities); photo feature; and travel (Virginia and surrounding states). "Were looking for more 'sex, drugs and murder' stories based in Western Virginia. We place special emphasis on consumer-related issues and how-to articles." Periodic special sections on fashion, real estate, media, banking, investing. Buys 60 mss/year. Query with published clips or send complete ms. Length: 3,000 words maximum. Pays $35-200.
Photos: Send photos with ms. Reviews color transparencies. Pays $5-10 for 5 × 7 or 8 × 10 b&w prints; $10 maximum for 5 × 7 or 8 × 10 color prints. Captions and model releases required. Rights purchased vary.
Tips: "It helps if freelancer lives in the area. The most frequent mistake made by writers in completing an article for us is not having enough Roanoke-area focus: use of area experts, sources, slants, etc."

Washington

‡NORTHWEST LIVING!, Northwest Living Company, 130 2nd Ave., S., Edmonds WA 98020. (206)774-4111. Editor: Terry W. Sheely. 85% freelance written. A bimonthly magazine publishing information on "people, places of the Northwest from Montana west to Washington, north to Alaska south to Northern California. Country-style information." Circ. 30,000. Pays on publication. Publishes ms an average of 1 year after acceptance. Byline given. Buys one-time rights. Submit queries 1 year in advance. Previously published submissions OK. Computer printout submissions OK; double-space; no dot-matrix. Reports in 1 month on queries. Sample copy for 10 × 13 SAE and $1. Writer's guidelines for SASE (required!).
Nonfiction: How-to, interview/profile, living style, photo feature and travel, garden and kitchen. No poetry or fiction. Buys 120 mss/year. Length: 500-1,200 words.
Photos: Send photos with query. Reviews 35mm transparencies and 5 × 7 prints. Offers no additional payment for photos accepted with ms. Buys one-time rights.
Fillers: Regional shorts. See brief section. Buys 25/year. Length: 25-300 words.
Tips: "Query in detail with specific Northwest-oriented material. Include photo support if available. No telephone queries."

PACIFIC NORTHWEST, Pacific Northwest Media, Inc., Suite 101, 701 Dexter Ave. N., Seattle WA 98109. (206)284-1750. FAX: (206)284-2550. Editor: Ann Naumann. 80% freelance written. "*Pacific Northwest* is a monthly magazine directed primarily at longtime residents of Oregon, Washington, Idaho and British Columbia." Estab. 1966. Circ. 81,300. Pays on publication. Publishes ms an average of 3 months after acceptance. Byline given. Offers kill fee. Buys first North American serial rights. Submit seasonal/holiday material 6 months in advance. Simultaneous submissions OK. Query for electronic submissions. Reports in 5 weeks on queries; 6 weeks on mss. Sample copy $3. Free writer's guidelines.
Nonfiction: Book excerpts (Northwest), essays, exposé, general interest, historical/nostalgic, humor, interview/profile, personal experience, photo feature, travel, business, arts. No self-help. Buys 180 mss/year. Query with published clips. Length: 800-2,500 words. Pays $100-1,000 for assigned articles. Sometimes pays expenses of writers on assignment.
Photos: State availability of photos with submission. Reviews contact sheets. Offers $50-250 per photo. Identification of subjects required. Buys one-time rights.
Columns/Departments: EcoHeroes (regional environmental leader profiles), 1,000 words; Outside Moves (outdoor activity how-to), 1,000 words; Weekends (regional getaways), 500-1,200 words. Buys 90 mss/year. Query with published clips. Pays $150-400.

THE SEATTLE WEEKLY, Sasquatch Publishing, 1931 2nd Ave., Seattle WA 98101. (206)441-5555. FAX: (206)441-6213. Editor: David Brewster. 20% freelance written. Eager to work with new/unpublished writers, especially those in the region. Weekly tabloid covering arts, politics, food, business, sports and books with local and regional emphasis. Estab. 1976. Circ. 33,000. Pays 1 week after publication. Publishes ms an average of 1 month after acceptance. Byline given. Offers variable kill fee. Buys first North American serial rights. Submit seasonal/holiday material minimum 2 months in advance. Simultaneous queries OK. Reports in 1 month. Sample copy $2; writer's guidelines for #10 SASE.

Nonfiction: Book excerpts; expose; general interest; historical/nostalgic (Northwest); how-to (related to food and health); humor; interview/profile; opinion; travel; and arts-related essays. Buys 6-8 cover stories/year. Query with resume and published clips. Length: 700-4,000 words. Pays $75-800. Sometimes pays the expenses of writers on assignment.

Tips: "The *Seattle Weekly* publishes stories on Northwest politics and art, usually written by regional and local writers, for a mostly upscale, urban audience; writing is high quality magazine style."

West Virginia

WONDERFUL WEST VIRGINIA, State of West Virginia Department of Natural Resources, 1900 Kanawha Blvd. E., Bldg. 3, State Capital Complex, Charleston WV 25305. (304)348-9152. Editor: Nancy Clark. 85% freelance written. Monthly magazine. "A general interest, show-piece quality, magazine portraying a positive image of West Virginia, with emphasis on outdoor/natural resources subjects." Estab. 1970. Circ. 85,000. **Pays on acceptance.** Publishes ms an average of 18 months after acceptance. Byline given. Offer 5¢/word kill fee. Buys first or second rights. Submit seasonal/holiday material 6 months in advance. Previously published submissions OK. Reports in 1 month. Sample copy $3.25. Free writer's guidelines.

Nonfiction: General interest, historical/nostalgic, photo feature, travel. "No outsider's views of West Virginia and its people; nothing negative or about poor, ignorant 'hillbilly' types of people or places. No Me and Joe hunting and fishing stories." Buys 50 mss/year. Query. Length: 500-3,000 words. Pays $50-300.

Photos: Photos are taken by staff photographer, if feasible. Will consider photos with submission. Reviews 35mm or larger transparencies. Offers $75 per color photo. Captions, model releases and identification of subjects required. Buys one-time rights.

Tips: "Read Guidelines for Writers. Write an article especially for readers who love West Virginia about an interesting place or event in West Virginia. Entire publication is open to freelancers. We have only recently started buying professionally written articles and welcome submissions from all writers with a personal knowledge of West Virginia subjects."

Wisconsin

MADISON MAGAZINE, P.O. Box 1604, Madison WI 53701. Editor: James Selk. 50% freelance written. Prefers to work with published/established writers. Monthly magazine. General city magazine aimed at upscale audience. Estab. 1978. Circ. 21,500. Pays on publication. Publishes ms an average of 2 months after acceptance. Buys all rights. Reports on material accepted for publication 10 days after acceptance. Returns rejected material immediately. Query. Sample copy $3 and 9×12 SAE.

Nonfiction: General human interest articles with strong local angles. Buys 100 mss/year. Length: 1,000-5,000 words. Pays $25-500. Pays the expenses of writers on assignment.

Photos: Offers no additional payment for b&w photos used with mss. Captions required.

‡MILWAUKEE MAGAZINE, 312 E. Buffalo St., Milwaukee WI 53202. (414)273-1101. Editor: David A. Fryxell. 40% freelance written. Monthly magazine covering Milwaukee and surrounding region. "We publish stories about Milwaukee, of service to Milwaukee-area residents and exploring the area's changing lifestyle, business, arts, politics, dining." Circ. 50,000. Pays on publication. Publishes ms an average of 2 months after acceptance. Byline given. Offers 20% kill fee. Buys first rights. Submit seasonal/holiday material 5-6 months in advance. Query for electronic submissions. Reports in 6 weeks on queries. Sample copy $4.

Nonfiction: Book excerpts, essays, exposé, general interest, historical/nostalgic, interview/profile, photo feature, travel, food and dining, other services. "No articles without a strong Milwaukee or Wisconsin angle." Buys 30-50 mss/year. Query with published clips. Length: 1,500-5,000 words. Pays $600-1,000. Sometimes pays expenses of writers on assignment.

Photos: State availability of photos with submission. Reviews contact sheets, negatives, any transparencies and any prints. Offers no set rate per photo. Identification of subjects required. Buys one-time rights.

Columns/Departments: Steve Filmanowicz. Insider (inside information on Milwaukee), 200-700 words. Buys 60 mss/year. Query with published clips. Pays $30-125.

Tips: "Pitch something for the Insider, or suggest a compelling profile we haven't already done and submit clips that prove you can do the job. The department most open is Insider. Think short, lively, offbeat, fresh, people-oriented."

WISCONSIN, *The Milwaukee Journal Magazine,* P.O. Box 661, Milwaukee WI 53201. (414)224-2341. FAX: (414)224-2047. Editor: Alan Borsuk. 20% freelance written. Prefers to work with published/ established writers. Weekly general interest magazine appealing to readers living in Wisconsin. Estab. 1969. Circ. 520,000. Pays on publication. Publishes ms an average of 4 months after acceptance. Byline given. Buys first serial rights. Submit seasonal/holiday material 4 months in advance. Simultaneous queries OK. Reports in 1 month on queries; 6 months on mss. Free sample copy; writer's guidelines for 9×12 SASE.

Nonfiction: Expose, general interest, humor, interview/profile, opinion, personal experience and photo feature. No nostalgic reminiscences. Buys 50 mss/year. Query. Length: 150-2,500 words. Pays $75-600. Sometimes pays expenses of writers on assignment.

Photos: State availability of photos.

Columns/Departments: Opinion, Humor and Essays. Buys 50 mss/year. Length: 300-1,000 words. Pays $100-200.

Tips: "We are primarily Wisconsin-oriented and are becoming more news-oriented."

‡WISCONSIN TRAILS, Box 5650, Madison WI 53705. (608)231-2444. Managing Editor: Geri Nixon. 70% freelance written. Prefers to work with published/established writers; works with a small number of new/unpublished writers each year. Bimonthly magazine for readers interested in Wisconsin; its contemporary issues, personalities, recreation, history, natural beauty; and the arts. Circ. 55,000. Buys first serial rights, and one-time rights sometimes. Pays on publication. Submit seasonal material at least 1 year in advance. Publishes ms an average of 6 months after acceptance. Byline given. Reports in 1 month. Writer's guidelines for #10 SASE.

Nonfiction: "Our articles focus on some aspect of Wisconsin life; an interesting town or event, a person or industry, history or the arts and especially outdoor recreation. We do not use first-person essays or biographies about people who were born in Wisconsin but made their fortunes elsewhere. No poetry. No articles that are too local for our regional audience, or articles about obvious places to visit in Wisconsin. We need more articles about the new and little-known." Buys 3 unsolicited mss/ year. Query or send outline. Length: 1,000-3,000 words. Pays $100-400 (negotiable), depending on assignment length and quality. Sometimes pays expenses of writers on assignment.

Photos: Purchased with or without mss or on assignment. Uses 35mm transparencies; larger format OK. Color photos usually illustrate an activity, event, region or striking scenery. Prefer photos with people in scenery. B&w photos usually illustrate a given article. Pays $50 each for b&w on publication. Pays $50-75 for inside color; $100-200 for covers. Captions preferred.

Tips: "We're looking for active articles about people, places, events and outdoor adventures in Wisconsin. We want to publish one in-depth article of state-wide interest or concern per issue, and several short (1,000-word) articles about short trips, recreational opportunities, restaurants, inns and cultural activities. We will be looking for more articles about out-of-the-way places in Wisconsin that are exceptional in some way."

Canada

CANADIAN GEOGRAPHIC, 39 McArthur Ave., Ottawa, Ontario K1L 8L7 Canada. (613)745-4629. FAX: (613)744-0947. Editor: Ian Darragh. Managing Editor: Eric Harris. 90% freelance written. Works with a small number of new/unpublished writers each year. Circ. 215,000. Bimonthly magazine. **Pays on acceptance.** Publishes ms an average of 3 months after acceptance. Buys first Canadian rights; interested only in first-time publication. Sample copy for 9×12 SAE and $5; free writer's guidelines.

Nonfiction: Buys authoritative geographical articles, in the broad geographical sense, written for the average person, not for a scientific audience. Predominantly Canadian subjects by Canadian authors. Buys 30-45 mss/year. Always query first in writing. Length: 1,500-3,000 words. Pays 30¢/word minimum. Usual payment for articles ranges between $500-2,500. Higher fees reserved for commissioned articles. Sometimes pays the expenses of writers on assignment.

Photos: Reviews 35mm slides, 2¼ transparencies or 8×10 glossies. Pays $75-400 for color photos, depending on published size.

THE GEORGIA STRAIGHT, Vancouver Free Press Publishing Corp., 2nd Floor, 1235 W. Pender St., Vancouver, British Columbia V6E 2V6 Canada. (604)681-2000. FAX: (604)681-0272. Managing Editor: Charles Campbell. 90% freelance written. Weekly tabloid on arts/entertainment/lifestyle/civic issues. Circ. 75,000. Pays on publication. Byline given. Offers 75-100% kill fee. Buys first North American serial rights or second serial (reprint) rights. Simultaneous and previously published submissions OK. Reports in 1 month. Sample copy for 9×12 SAE and $1.

Nonfiction: General interest, humor, interview/profile, travel, and arts and entertainment. Buys 600 mss/year. Query with published clips. Length: 250-4,000 words. Pays $20-300. Sometimes pays expenses of writers on assignment.

Photos: Send photo with submission. Reviews, contact sheets, transparencies and 8 × 10 prints. Offers $30-70 per photo. Captions, model releases and identification of subjects required. Buys one-time rights.
Tips: "Be aware of entertainment events in the Vancouver area and expansion of our news coverage. Most stories relate to those events."

THE MIRROR, The Mirror-Northern Report, P.O. Box 269, High Prairie, Alberta T0G 1E0 Canada. (403)523-3706. Editor: Al Burger. 25% freelance written. Weekly magazine of northern Alberta news and features. Estab. 1986. Circ. 2,000. Pays on publication. Publishes ms an average of 3 months after acceptance. Byline given. Publication not copyrighted. Buys one-time rights. Simultaneous and previously published submissions OK. Reports in 3 months. Sample copy for 9 × 12 SAE and $2.
Nonfiction: Buys 20 mss/year. Send complete ms. Length: 2,000 words maximum. Pays 1¢/word.
Photos: Send photos with submission. Reviews prints. Offers no additional payment for photos accepted with ms. Captions and identification of subjects required. Buys one-time rights.
Fiction: Buys 10 mss/year. Send complete ms. Length: 1,500 words.

‡ONTARIO OUT OF DOORS, 227 Front St. E., Toronto, Ontario M5A 1E8 Canada. (416)368-0815. FAX: (416)941-9113. Editor-in-Chief: Burton J. Myers. 80% freelance written. "We prefer a blend of both experienced and new writers." Emphasizes hunting, fishing, camping, and conservation. Monthly magazine; 80 pages. Circ. 60,230. **Pays on acceptance.** Publishes ms an average of 6 months after acceptance. Buys first North American serial rights. Phone queries OK. Submit seasonal/holiday material 5 months in advance of issue date. Reports in 6 weeks. Free sample copy and writer's guidelines; mention *Writer's Market* in request.
Nonfiction: Exposé of conservation practices; how-to (improve your fishing and hunting skills); humor; photo feature (on wildlife); travel (where to find good fishing and hunting); and any news on Ontario. "Avoid 'Me and Joe' articles or funny family camping anecdotes." Buys 20-30 unsolicited mss/year. Query. Length: 150-3,500 words. Pays $35-500. Sometimes pays the expenses of writers on assignment.
Photos: Submit photo material with accompanying query. No additonal payment for b&w contact sheets and 35mm color transparencies. "Should a photo be used on the cover, an additional payment of $350-500 is made."
Fillers: Outdoor tips. Buys 100 mss/year. Length 20-50 words. Pays $15-35.
Tips: "It's rewarding for us to find a freelancer who reads and understands a set of writer's guidelines, but it is annoying when writers fail to submit supporting photography."

OTTAWA MAGAZINE, Ottawa Magazine Inc., 192 Bank St., Ottawa, Ontario K2P 1W8 Canada. (613)234-7751. Editor: Heather Loucks. 80% freelance written. Prefers to work with published/established writers. Magazine, published 11 times/year, covering life in Ottawa and environs. "*Ottawa Magazine* reflects the interest and lifestyles of its readers who tend to be married, ages 35-55, upwardly mobile and urban." Circ. 50,000. **Pays on acceptance.** Publishes ms an average of 6 months after acceptance. Byline given. "Kill fee depends on agreed-upon fee; very seldom used." Buys first North American serial rights and second serial (reprint) rights. Simultaneous queries and previously published submissions OK. Reports in 2 months. Sample copy $1.
Nonfiction: Book excerpts (by local authors or about regional issues); exposé (federal or regional government, education); general interest; interview/profile (on Ottawans who have established national or international reputations); photo feature (for recurring section called Freezeframe); and travel (recent examples are Brazil, Trinidad & Tobago, Copenhagen). "No articles better suited to a national or special interest publication." Buys 100 mss/year. Query with published clips. Length: 2,000-3,500 words. Pays $500/1,000 (Canadian).
Tips: "A phone call to our associate editor is the best way to assure that queries receive prompt attention. Once a query interests me the writer is assigned a detailed 'treatment' of the proposed piece which is used to determine viability of story. We will be concentrating on more issue-type stories with good, solid fact-researched base, also doing more fluffy pieces—best and worst of Ottawa—that sort of stuff. Harder for out-of-town writers to furnish. The writer should strive to inject a personal style and avoid newspaper-style reportage. *Ottawa Magazine* also doesn't stoop to boosterism and points out the bad along with the good. Good prospects for U.S. writers are interiors (house and garden type), gardening (for Northern climate), leisure/lifestyles. Second rights OK."

‡SOUTHENDER MAGAZINE, Graphic Advocate Company, Ltd., 1869 Upper Water St., 3rd Floor Collins Bank Building, Halifax, Nova Scotia B3H 2W3 Canada. (902)422-4990. Editor: Bob LeDrew. 80% freelance written. Monthly community magazine covering Halifax. Estab. 1983. Circ. 15,000. Pays on publication. Publishes ms an average of 1 month after acceptance. Byline given. Offers variable kill fee. Buys first North American serial rights or one-time rights. Submit seasonal/holiday material 4 months in advance. Previously published submissions OK. Query for electronic submissions. Reports in 1 month on queries. Sample copy for 9 × 12 SAE with 4 first class Canadian stamps or 4 IRC's.

Nonfiction: General interest, historical/nostalgic, interview/profile, travel. "We are by definition a *community* magazine. Any material I publish *must* have a Halifax aspect to it." Buys 150 mss/year. Query with published clips. Length: 150-1,200 words. Pays $25-100 for assigned articles; $25-75 for unsolicited articles. Sometimes pays expenses of writers on assignment.

Photos: State availability of photos with submission. Reviews negatives and prints. Offers negotiable payment. Captions and identification of subjects required. Buys one-time rights.

Tips: "We are small, but growing. Give me a well-focused, lively query that tells me why my readers will read the story. Don't send me anything that doesn't have some relationship to Halifax. And *follow up* your queries. I appreciate professionalism in attitude. New writers are most welcome."

TORONTO LIFE, 59 Front St. E., Toronto, Ontario M5E 1B3 Canada. (416)364-3333. Editor: Marq de Villiers. 95% freelance written. Prefers to work with published/established writers. Monthly magazine emphasizing local issues and social trends, short humor/satire, and service features for upper income, well educated and, for the most part, young Torontonians. Uses some fiction. **Pays on acceptance.** Publishes ms an average of 3-4 months after acceptance. Byline given. Buys first North American serial rights. Pays 50% kill fee "for commissioned articles only." Phone queries OK. Reports in 3 weeks. Sample copy $2.50 with SAE and IRCs.

Nonfiction: Uses most types of articles. Buys 17 mss/issue. Query with published clips. Buys about 40 unsolicited mss/year. Length: 1,000-5,000 words. Pays $800-3,000.

Photos: State availability of photos. Uses good color transparencies and clear, crisp b&w prints. Seldom uses submitted photos. Captions and model release required.

Columns/Departments: "We run about five columns an issue. They are all freelanced, though most are from regular contributors. They are mostly local in concern and cover politics, money, fine art, performing arts, movies and sports." Length: 1,800 words. Pays $1,500.

‡**WESTENDER MAGAZINE**, Graphic Advocate Company, Ltd., 1869 Upper Water St., 3rd Floor, Collins' Bank Building, Halifax, Nova Scotia B3H 2W3 Canada. (902)422-4990. Editor: Bob LeDrew. 80% freelance written. Monthly community magazine covering Halifax. Estab. 1989. Circ. 15,000. Pays on publication. Publishes ms an average of 1 month after acceptance. Byline given. Offers variable kill fee. Buys first North American serial rights, one-time rights or second serial (reprint) rights. Submit seasonal/holiday material 4 months in advance. Previously published submissions. Query for electronic submissions. Reports in 1 month. Sample copy for 9 × 12 SAE with 4 first class Canadian stamps or 4 IRC's.

Nonfiction: Essays, general interest, historical/nostalgic, humor, interview/profile, travel. "Nothing without a Halifax angle except travel pieces." Buys 120 mss/year. Query with or without published clips, or send complete ms. Length: 150-1,200 words. Pays $25-100 for assigned articles; $25-80 for unsolicited articles. Sometime pays expenses of writers on assignment.

Photos: State availability of photos with submission. Reviews prints (any). Offers negotiable payment per photo. Captions and identification of subjects required. Buys one-time rights.

Tips: "We are small, but growing. Give me a well-focused, lively query that tells me why my readers will read the story. Don't send anything that doesn't have some relationship to Halifax. And follow up your queries. I appreciate professional attitudes. New writers are most welcome."

WESTERN PEOPLE, Supplement to the Western Producer, Western Producer Publications, Box 2500, Saskatoon, Saskatchewan S7K 2C4 Canada. (306)665-3500. Managing Editor: Michael Gillgannon. Weekly farm newspaper supplement covering rural Western Canada. "Our magazine reflects the life and people of rural Western Canada both in the present and historically." Estab. 1978. Circ. 135,000. **Pays on acceptance.** Publishes ms an average of 6 months after acceptance. Byline given. Buys first rights. Submit seasonal/holiday material 3 months in advance. Reports in 2 weeks on queries; 6 weeks on mss. Sample copy for 9 × 12 SAE and 3 IRC's; writer's guidelines for #10 SAE and 2 IRC's.

Nonfiction: General interest, historical/nostalgic, humor, interview/profile, personal experience and photo feature. Buys 450 mss/year. Send complete ms. Length: 500-2,500 words. Pays $80-250.

Photos: Send photos with submission. Reviews transparencies and prints. Offers $5-25 per photo. Captions and identification of subjects required. Buys one-time rights.

Fiction: Adventure, historical, humorous, mainstream, mystery, novel excerpts, romance, serialized novels, suspense and western stories reflecting life in rural Western Canada. Buys 50 mss/year. Send complete ms. Length: 1,000-2,000 words. Pays $80-150.

Poetry: Free verse, traditional, haiku and light verse. Buys 75 poems/year. Submit maximum 3 poems. Length: 4-50 lines. Pays $15-50.

Tips: "Western Canada is geographically very large. The approach for writing about an interesting individual is to introduce that person *neighbor-to-neighbor* to our readers."

THE WESTERN PRODUCER, Western Producer Publications, Box 2500, 2310 Millar Ave., Saskatoon, Saskatchewan S7K 2C4 Canada. (306)665-3500. FAX: (306)653-1255. Editor: Keith Dryden. Managing Editor: Garry Fairbairn. 30% freelance written. Weekly newspaper covering agriculture and rural life. Publishes "informative material for 135,000 western Canadian farm familes." **Pays on acceptance.** Byline given. Kill fee varies. Not copyrighted. Buys one-time rights. Submit seasonal/holiday material 2 months in advance. Simultaneous and previously published submissions OK. Query for electronic submissions. Reports in 1 week on queries; 3 weeks on mss. Sample copy for 11 × 14 SAE with IRC; writer's guidelines for #10 SAE.

Nonfiction: General interest, historical/nostalgic, how-to (on farm machinery or construction), humor, new product, technical and rural cartoons. Special supplement (spring and fall) on livestock. Nothing "non-Canadian, over 1,500 words." Buys 600 mss/year. Query. Length: 2,000 words. Pays $100-400 for assigned articles; pays $150 maximum for unsolicited articles. Sometimes pays the expenses of writers on assignment.

Photos: Send photos with submission. Reviews contact sheets, negatives, transparencies and prints. Offers $15-50 per photo. Captions required. Buys one-time rights.

Columns/Departments: Michael Gillgannon, editor. Western People (magazine insert focusing on Western Canadian personalities, hobbies, history, fiction), 500-2,000 words. Buys 350 mss/year. Query. Length: 500-2,000 words. Pays $50-500.

Fiction: Ethnic, historical, humorous, slice-of-life vignettes, western and rural settings. No non-western Canadian subjects. Buys 40 mss/year. Query. Length: 500-2,000. Pays $50-500.

Poetry: Free verse, light verse and traditional. Buys 20 poems/year. Length: 10-100 lines. Pays $10-100.

Tips: "Use CP/AP/UPI style and a fresh ribbon." Areas most open to freelancers are "cartoons, on-farm profiles, rural Canadian personalities."

WHERE VICTORIA/ESSENTIAL VICTORIA, Key Pacific Publishers Co. Ltd., 3rd Fl., 1001 Wharf St., Victoria, British Columbia V8W 1T6 Canada. (604)388-4324. FAX: (604)388-6166. Editor: Janice Strong. 40% freelance written. Monthly magazine on Victoria and Vancouver Island. Estab. 1977. Circ. 30,000. Pays on publication. Publishes ms an average of 1-2 months after acceptance. Byline given. Buys first North American serial rights and all rights. Query for electronic submissions. Reports in 3 months. Free sample copy.

Nonfiction: General interest and travel. Essential Victoria. Buys 30 mss/year. Query with published clips. Length: 500-2,500 words. Pays 20-40¢/word.

Photos: State availability of photos with submission. Reviews contact sheets, transparencies and prints. Offers $50-150 per photo. Model releases and identification of subjects required. Buys one-time rights.

‡WINDSOR THIS MONTH MAGAZINE, Box 1029, Station A, Windsor, Ontario N9A 6P4 Canada. (519)966-7411. Publisher: J.S. Woloschak. 75% freelance written. "*Windsor This Month* is mailed out in a system of controlled distribution to 24,000 households in the area. The average reader is a university graduate, of middle income, and active in leisure areas." Circ. 24,000. Pays on publication. Buys first North American serial rights. Submit seasonal/holiday material 4 months in advance. Query for electronic submissions. Reports in 1 month.

Nonfiction: Windsor-oriented editorial: issues, answers, interviews, lifestyles, profiles, photo essays and opinion. How-to accepted if applicable to readership. Special inserts: design and decor, gourmet and travel featured periodically through the year. Buys 5 mss/issue. Query (phone queries OK). Buys 15 unsolicited mss/year. Length: 500-5,000 words. Pays $64.

Photos: State availability of photos with query. Pays $25. Captions preferred. Buys all rights.

Tips: "If experienced, arm yourself with published work and a list of ten topics that demonstrate knowledge of the Windsor market, and query the editor."

‡THE YUKON READER, World-Yukon Publications Ltd., P.O. Box 4306, Whitehorse, Yukon Y1A 3T3 Canada. (403)668-2355. FAX: (403)667-2737. Editor: Sam Holloway. 90% freelance written. Bimonthly magazine covering the Northwest (Alaska, Yukon, Northern B.C., N.W.T.) History and personality profiles. Estab. 1989. Circ. 25,000. Pays 25% on acceptance, balance on publication. Byline given. Buys first North American serial rights. Submit seasonal/holiday material 2 months in advance. Simultaneous and previously published submissions accepted. Query for electronic submissions. Reports in 3 weeks on queries; 5 weeks on manuscripts. Free sample copy.

Nonfiction: book excerpts, essays, exposé, general interest, historical/nostalgic, humor, inspirational, interview/profile, personal experience, photo feature. "The ultimate submission would be an unpublished diary of an adventure in Alaska or Yukon, 1850 to 1990! No free verse, political treatises."

Buys 25 mss/year. Send complete ms. Length: 500-6,500 words. $100-500 for unsolicited articles. Pays ballads—6 magazines plus $50.
Photos: State availability of photos with submnission. Send photos with submission. Reviews prints. Offers $10-25 per photo. Identification of subjects required. Buys one-time rights.

Relationships

These publications focus on lifestyles and relationships. These magazines are read and often written by single people, gays and lesbians and those interested in these lifestyles or in alternative outlooks. They may offer writers a forum for unconventional views or serve as a voice for particular audiences or causes.

ATLANTA SINGLES MAGAZINE, Hudson Brooke Publishing, Inc., 1780 Century Circle, Suite 2, Atlanta GA 30345, or P.O. Box 49286, Atlanta GA 30359. (404)636-2260. FAX: (404)636-2366. Editor: Margaret Anthony. Associate Editor: Diana Porter. 10% freelance written. Works with a small number of new/unpublished writers each year. A bi-monthly magazine for single, widowed or divorced adults, medium to high income level, many business and professionally oriented; single parents, ages 25 to 55. Estab. 1977. Circ. 15,000. Pays on publication. Publishes ms an average of 6 months after acceptance. Byline given. Buys one-time rights, second serial (reprint) rights and simultaneous rights. Submit seasonal/holiday material 6 months in advance. Simultaneous and previously published submissions OK. Sample copy $2; writer's guidelines for #10 SASE.
Nonfiction: General interest, humor, personal experience, photo feature and travel. No pornography. Buys 5 mss/year. Send complete ms. Length: 600-1,200 words. Pays $50-150 for unsolicited articles; sometimes trades for personal ad.
Photos: Send photos with submission. Cover photos also considered. Reviews prints. Offers no additional payment for photos accepted with ms. Model releases and identification of subjects required. Buys one-time rights.
Columns/Departments: Will consider ideas. Query. Length: 600-800 words. Pays $50-150 per column/department.
Tips: No fiction. "We are open to articles on *any* subject that would be of interest to singles, i.e., travel, autos, movies, love stories, fashion, investments, real estate, etc. Although singles are interested in topics like self-awareness, being single again, and dating, they are also interested in many of the same subjects that married people are, such as those listed."

BAY WINDOWS, New England's Largest Gay and Lesbian Newspaper, Bay Windows, Inc.. 1523 Washington St., Boston MA 02118. (617)266-6670. FAX: (617)266-5973. Editor: Jeff Epperly; Arts Editor: Ruby Kikel. 30-40% freelance written. A weekly newspaper of gay news and concerns. "*Bay Windows* covers predominantly news of New England, but will print non-local news and features depending on the newsworthiness of the story. We feature hard news, opinion, news analysis, arts reviews and interviews." Estab. 1983. Publishes ms within 2 months of acceptance, pays within 2 weeks of publication. Byline given. Offers 50% kill fee. Rights obtained varies, usually first serial rights. Simultaneous submissions accepted if other submissions are outside of New England. Submit seasonal-holiday material 3 months in advance. Sample copies $4; writer's guidelines for #10 SASE.
Nonfiction: Hard news, general interest with a gay slant, interview/profile, opinion and photo features. Publishes 200 mss/year. Query with published clips, or send complete ms. Length: 500-1,500 words. Pay varies: $25-100 news; $10-60 arts.
Photos: $25 per published photo, b&w photos only. Model releases and identification of subjects required.
Columns/Departments: Film, music, dance, books, art. Length: 500-1,500 words. Buys 200 mss/year. Pays $10-100.
Poetry: All varieties. Publishes 50 poems per year. Length: 10-30 lines. No payment.
Tips: "Too much gay-oriented writing is laden with the clichés and catch phrases of the movement. Writers must have intimate knowledge of gay community; however, this should not mean that standard English usage is not required. We look for writers with new—even controversial perspectives on the lives of gay men and lesbians. While we assume gay is good, we will print stories which examine problems within the community and movement. No pornography or erotica."

CHANGING MEN, Issues in Gender, Sex and Politics, Feminist Men's Publications, 306 N. Brooks St., Madison WI 53715. Editor: Rick Cote. Managing Editor: Michael Birnbaum. 80% freelance written. Works with a small number of new/unpublished writers each year. A feminist men's journal published two times a year. "We are a forum for anti-sexist men and women to explore the politics of gender, the complexities of sexual relations, and the expressions of love in a changing world." Estab. 1979. Circ. 4,000. Publishes ms an average of 1 year after acceptance. Byline given. Buys one-time rights. Simultaneous queries and simultaneous and previously published submissions OK. Reports in 2 months. Sample copy $6; writer's guidelines for #10 SASE.

Nonfiction: Submit nonfiction to: Rick Cote, P.O. Box 639, Durham NH 03824-0639. Book excerpts, humor, interview/profile, opinion, personal experience and photo feature. Plans special issues on male/female intimacy. Future issues expected to focus on fathering, men's spirituality, feminism, divorce, prisons. No theoretical articles. Query with published clips. Length: 3,500 words maximum. Pays $25 maximum.

Columns/Departments: Men and War (focus on masculinity and how culture shapes male values), Sports (with a feminist slant), and Book Reviews (focus on sexuality and masculinity). Query with published clips. Length: 500-1,500 words. Pays $15 maximum.

Fiction: Submit fiction to: Jeff Kirsch, fiction editor, Department of Spanish and Portugese, Tulane University, New Orleans LA 70118. Erotica, ethnic, experimental, humorous and novel excerpts. Buys 2 mss/year. Query with published clips. Length: 3,500 words maximum. Pays $20 maximum.

Poetry: Free verse, haiku and light verse. Submit maximum 3 poems. Length: 50 lines maximum. No payment for poetry.

Fillers: Clippings, jokes and newsbreaks. Length: 300 words. No payment for fillers.

COLUMBUS BRIDE & GROOM MAGAZINE, National Bridal Publications, Inc., 303 East Livingston Ave., Columbus OH 43215. (614)224-1992. Editor: Marvin Brown. Managing Editor: Jill Vishey. 5% freelance written. Semiannual magazine on weddings. Estab. 1985. Circ. 13,000. Pays on publication. Publishes ms an average of 4 months after acceptance. Byline given. Offers 50% kill fee. Buys all rights. Submit seasonal/holiday material 6 months in advance. Reports in 1 month. Sample copy $1.50.

Nonfiction: General interest (within our specialized field), how-to (plan and execute a wedding and take up married life), humor and inspirational. "No articles promoting a specifically named product and/or service." Buys 4-5 mss/year. Query. Length: 250-1,500 words. Pays $40-250 for assigned articles; $25-150 for unsolicited articles. Sometimes pays expenses of writers on assignment.

Photos: State availability of photos with submission. Reviews contact sheets, 35mm and up transparencies and 5×7 and up prints. Captions and model releases required. Buys one-time rights.

Fillers: Anecdotes, facts, newsbreaks and short humor. Length: 40-200 words.

‡DRUMMER, Desmodus, Inc., Box 11314, San Francisco CA 94101. (415)864-3456. Editor: A.F. De-Blase. 80% freelance written. Gay male leather and related fetish erotica/news. Monthly magazine publishes "erotic aspects of leather and other masculine fetishes for gay men." Circ. 60,000. Pays on publication. Publishes ms an average of 3 months after acceptance. Byline given. Buys first North American serial rights or makes work-for-hire assignments. Submit seasonal/holiday material 9 months in advance. Previously published submissions OK. Reports in 1 month on queries; in 3 months on mss. Sample copy $6; writer's guidelines for #10 SASE.

Nonfiction: Book excerpts, essays, historical/nostalgic, how-to, humor, interview/profile, new product, opinion, personal experience, photo feature, technical and travel. No feminine slanted pieces. Buys 25 mss/year. Query with or without published clips, or send complete ms. Length: 1,000-15,000 words. Pays $50-200 for assigned articles; $50-100 for unsolicited articles. Rarely pays expenses of writers on assignment.

Photos: Send photos with submission (photocopies OK). Reviews contact sheets and transparencies. Offers $10-100 per photo. Model releases and identification of subjects required. Buys one-time rights or all rights.

Fiction: Adventure, erotica, ethnic, fantasy, historical, horror, humorous, mystery, novel excerpts, science fiction, slice-of-life vignettes, suspense and western. Must have gay "macho" erotic elements. Buys 60-75 mss/year. Send complete ms. Length: 1,000-20,000 words. Occasionally serializes stories. Pays $100.

Fillers: Anecdotes, facts, gags, cartoons and newsbreaks. Buys 50/year. Length: 10-100 words. pay $10-50.

Tips: "All they have to do is write—but they must be knowledgeable about some aspect of the scene. While the magazine is aimed at gay men, we welcome contributions from straight men and from straight, bisexual and gay women who understand leather and s/m and kinky erotic fetishes. Fiction is most open to freelancers."

‡DUNGEON MASTER, Desmodus Inc., Box 11314, San Francisco CA 94101. (415)978-5377. Editor: T.A. Feldwebel. 50% freelance written. Quarterly magazine covering gay male erotic s/m. "Safety is emphasized. This is not a fantasy magazine but is for real how-to articles on equipment, techniques, etc." Circ. 6,000. Most articles are unpaid—except by complimentary subscriptions, ads, etc. Byline given. Buys first North American serial rights, one-time rights, simultaneous rights or makes work-for-hire assignments. Previously published submissions OK. Sample copy $5; writer's guidelines for #10 SASE.

Nonfiction: Book excerpts, essays, historical/nostalgic, how-to (mainly), humor, interview/profile, new product, opinion, personal experience, photo feature (may be paid), technical, travel and safety. No fiction or unsafe practices. Buys 40 mss/year. Query with or without published clips, or send complete ms. Length: no limit. Pays $25-200 for assigned articles. Usually pays writers with contributor copies or other premiums rather than a cash payment. Rarely pays expenses of writers on assignment.

Photos: Send photos with submission. Photocopies OK. Reviews contact sheets and transparencies. Offers $10-100/photo. Model releases and identification of subjects required. Buys one-time rights or all rights.

Fillers: Anecdotes, facts, gags to be illustrated and newbreaks. Buys 10/year. Pays $5-25.

Tips: "Must be knowledgeable in specialized field. While the publication is aimed at gay men, submission by straight men and straight and gay women are welcome."

FIRST HAND, Experiences For Loving Men, Firsthand, Ltd., 310 Cedar Lane, Teaneck NJ 07666. (201)836-9177. Editor: Bob Harris. Publisher: Jackie Lewis. 75% freelance written. Eager to work with new/unpublished writers. Monthly magazine of homosexual erotica. Estab. 1980. Circ. 70,000. Pays 8 months after acceptance or on publication, whichever comes first. Publishes ms an average of 8 months after acceptance. Byline given. Buys all rights (exceptions made) and second serial (reprint) rights. Submit seasonal/holiday material 10 months in advance. Reports in 2 months. Sample copy $5; writer's guidelines for #10 SASE.

Nonfiction: "We seldom use nonfiction except for our 'Survival Kit' section."

Columns/Departments: Survival Kit (short nonfiction articles, up to 1,000 words, featuring practical information on safe sex practices, health, travel, books, video, psychology, law, fashion, and other advice/consumer/lifestyle topics of interest to gay or single men). "These should be written in the second or third person." Query. "For this section, we sometimes also buy reprint rights to appropriate articles previously published in local gay newspapers around the country." Pays $35 to $70, depending on length, if original; if reprint, pays half that rate.

Fiction: Erotic fiction up to 5,000 words in length, average 2,000-3,000 words. "We prefer fiction in the first person which is believable—stories based on the writer's actual experience have the best chance. We're not interested in stories which involve underage characters in sexual situations. Other taboos include bestiality, rape—except in prison stories, as rape is an unavoidable reality in prison—and heavy drug use. Writers with questions about what we can and cannot depict should write for our guidelines, which go into this in more detail. We print mostly self-contained stories; we will look at novel excerpts, but only if they stand on their own."

Poetry: Free verse and light verse. Buys 12/year. Submit maximum 5 poems. Length: 10-30 lines. Pays $25.

Tips: "*First Hand* is a very reader-oriented publication for gay men. Half of each issue is comprised by letters from our readers describing their personal experiences, fantasies and feelings. Our readers are from all walks of life, all races and ethnic backgrounds, all classes, all religious and political affiliations, and so on. They are very diverse, and many live in far-flung rural areas or small towns; for some of them, our magazines are the primary source of contact with gay life, in some cases the only support for their gay identity. Our readers are very loyal and save every issue. We return that loyalty by trying to reflect their interests—for instance, by striving to avoid the exclusively big-city bias so common to national gay publications. So bear in mind the diversity of the audience when you write."

‡GENRE, Magazine for the "Gay Nineties," #261, 8033 Sunset Bl., Los Angeles CA 90046. (213)461-1444. Editor: Richard Settles. Managing Editor: Charles Isherwood. 50% freelance written. Quarterly magazine for gay men—lifestyle. "Intelligent and up-beat articles for an intelligent and hip readership." Estab. 1990. Circ. 100,000. Pays on publication. Byline sometimes given. Offers 10% kill fee. Buys all rights. Submit seasonal/holiday material 3 months in advance. Simultaneous and previously published submissions OK. Query for electronic submissions. Reports in 1 month. Sample copy $3.95. Free writer's guidelines.

Nonfiction: Book excerpts, exposé, historical, how-to (dress, meet men), humor, inspirational, interview/profile, new product, opinion (does not mean letters to the editor), personal experience, photo feature, religious, travel. Buys 1 mss/year. Send complete ms. Length: 500-1,500 words. Pays 10¢ per word. Pays in contributor's copies or other premiums.

Photos: Send photos with submission. Offers no additional payment for photos accepted with ms. Model releases required. Buys all rights.

Columns/Departments: Buys 2 mss/year. Send complete ms. Length: 200-500 words. Pays 10¢ per word.

Fillers: Gags to be illustrated by cartoonist. Buys 2/year. Pays $25.

Tips: "Send resume and samples—call first. Gay issues are important to us."

‡**THE GUIDE, To The Gay Northeast,** Fidelity Publishing. Box 593, Boston MA 02199. (617)266-8557. FAX: (617)266-1125. Editor: French Wall. 50% freelance written. A monthly magazine on the gay and lesbian community. Circ. 22,000. **Pays on acceptance.** Publishes ms an average of 2 months after acceptance. Kill fee negotiable. Buys all rights. Submit seasonal/holiday material 2 months in advance. Simultaneous and photocopied submissions OK. Sample copy for 9×12 SAE with 8 first class stamps; writer's guidelines for #10 SASE.
Nonfiction: Book excerpts (if yet unpublished), essays, exposé, general interest, historical/nostalgic, humor, interview/profile, opinion, personal experience, photo feature and religious. Buys 48 mss/year. Query with or without published clips, or send complete ms. Length: 500-5,000 words. Pays $50-180. Send photos with submission. Reviews contact sheets. Offers no additional payment for photos accepted with ms/negotiable. Captions, model releases, identification of subjects prefered; releases required sometimes. Buys one-time rights.
Fiction: Adventure, erotica, ethnic, experimental, fantasy, historical, humorous, novel excerpts, religious, romance, science fiction, slice-of-life vignettes and suspense. Query with published clips. Length: 500-4,000 words. Pays $90.
Tips: "Brevity, humor and militancy appreciated."

IN TOUCH FOR MEN, In Touch Publications International, Inc., 7216 Varna, North Hollywood CA 91605. (818)764-2288. FAX: (818)782-2307. Editor: A.C. Wagner. 80% freelance written. Works with a small number of new/unpublished writers each year. A monthly magazine covering the gay male lifestyle, gay male humor and erotica. Circ. 70,000. Pays on publication. Byline given. Buys one-time rights. Simultaneous submissions OK. Reports in 2 weeks on queries; 6 weeks on mss. Sample copy $5.95; writer's guidelines for #10 SAE.
Nonfiction: Buys 36 mss/year. Send complete ms. Length: 3,000-3,500 words. Pays $25-75.
Photos: State availability of photos with submission. Reviews contact sheets, transparencies, and prints. Offers $35/photo. Captions, model releases and identification of subjects required. Buys one-time rights.
Fiction: Erotica; all must be gay male erotica. No "heterosexual, heavy stuff." Buys 36 mss/year. Send complete ms. Length: 3,000-3,500 words. Pays $75 maximum.
Fillers: Short humor. Buys 12/year. Length: 1,500-3,500 words. Pays $50-75.
Tips: "Our publication features male nude photos plus two fiction pieces, several articles, cartoons, humorous comments on items from the media, photo features. We try to present the positive aspects of the gay lifestyle, with an emphasis on humor. Humorous pieces may be erotic in nature. We are open to all submissions that fit our gay male format; the emphasis, however, is on humor and the upbeat. We receive many fiction manuscripts but not nearly enough articles and humor."

METRO SINGLES LIFESTYLES, Metro Publications, P.O. Box 28203, Kansas City MO 64118. (816)436-8424. Editor: Robert L. Huffstutter. 40% freelance written. Eager to work with new/unpublished writers and photographers. A tabloid appearing 6 times/year covering singles lifestyles. Estab. 1984. **Pays on acceptance.** Publishes ms an average of 2 months after acceptance. Byline given with photo optional. Buys one-time rights and second serial (reprint) rights. Submit seasonal/holiday material 3 months in advance. Reports in 6 weeks. Sample copy $2 and 9×12 SAE with 5 first class stamps.
Nonfiction: Essay, general interest, how-to (on meeting the ideal mate, recovering from divorce, etc.), inspirational, interview/profile, personal experience and photo feature. Buys 6-12 mss/year. Send complete ms. Length: 700-1,200 words. Pays $100 maximum for assigned articles; pays $20-50 for unsolicited articles. Will pay in copies or other if writer prefers.
Photos: Pays up to $100 for photo layouts (10-12 photos). Subject matter suggested includes swimwear fashion, recreational events, "day in the life of an American single," etc. Reviews 3×5 and 8×10 color or b&w prints. Model releases of close-up or fashion shots required. Buys one-time and reprint rights. **Pays on acceptance.**
Columns/Departments: Movie Reviews, Lifestyles, Singles Events, and Book Reviews (about singles), all 400-1,000 words. Buys 9-12 mss/year. Send complete ms. Pays $20-50.
Fiction: Confession, humorous, romance and slice-of-life vignettes. Buys 6-12 mss/year. Send complete ms. Length: 700-1,200 words. Pays $20-50.
Poetry: Free verse and light verse. Buys 40-60 poems/year. Submit maximum 3 poems. Length: 21 lines. Pays in complimentary copies and subscriptions for poetry. Byline given.
Tips: "A freelancer can best approach and break in to our publication with positive articles, photo features about singles and positive fiction about singles. Photos and short bios of singles (blue collar, white collar, and professional) at work needed. Photos and a few lines about singles enjoying recreation (swimming, sports, chess, etc.) always welcome. Color photos, close-up, are suitable."

MOM GUESS WHAT NEWSPAPER, New Helvetia Communications, 1725 L St., Sacramento CA 95814. (916)441-6397. Editor: Linda Birner. 80% freelance written. Works with small number of new/unpublished writers each year. Biweekly tabloid covering gay rights and gay lifestyles. Estab. 1978.

Circ. 21,000. Publishes ms an average of 3 months after acceptance. Byline given. Buys all rights. Submit seasonal/holiday material 3 months in advance. Reports in 2 months. Sample copy $1; writer's guidelines for 8½×11 SAE with 3 first class stamps.
Nonfiction: Interview/profile and photo feature of international, national or local scope. Buys 8 mss/ year. Query. Length: 200-1,500 words. Payment depends on article. Pays expenses of writers on special assignment.
Photos: State availability of photos with submission. Reviews 5×7 prints. Offers no additional payment for photos accepted with ms. Captions and identification of subjects required. Buys one-time rights.
Columns/Departments: News, Restaurants, Political, Health, and Film, Video and Book Reviews. Buys 12 mss/year. Query. Payment depends on article.

SINGLELIFE MAGAZINE, SingleLife Enterprises, Inc., 606 W. Wisconsin Ave., Milwaukee WI 53203. (414)271-9700. FAX: (414)271-5263. Editor: Leifa Butrick. 40% freelance written. Prefers to work with published/established writers; works with a small number of new/unpublished writers each year. Bimonthly magazine covering single lifestyles. Estab. 1982. Circ. 22,000. Pays on publication. Publishes ms an average of 4 months after acceptance. Byline given. Buys one-time rights, second serial (reprint) rights and simultaneous rights. Submit seasonal material 4 months in advance. Simultaneous and previously published submissions OK. Reports in 3 weeks. Sample copy and writer's guidelines for $3.50 and 9×11 SASE; writer's guidelines for #10 SAE with 1 first class stamp.
Nonfiction: Upbeat and in-depth articles on significant areas of interest to single people such as male/female relationships, travel, health, sports, food, single parenting, humor, finances, places to go and things to do. Prefers third person point of view and ms to query letter. Our readers are between 25 and 50. Length: 1,000-3,000 words. Pays $50-150. Sometimes pays expenses of writers on assignment.
Fiction and Poetry: Buys 3-4 stories or poems per year, which are well written and cast a new light on what being single means. Length: not over 2,500 words. Submit any number of poems that pertain to being single. Pays $25-50.
Tips: "The easiest way to get in is to write something light, unusual, but also well-developed."

TORSO, Varsity Communications, 462 Broadway, New York NY 10013. (212)966-8400. Editor: Stan Leventhal. 75% freelance written. Works with a small number of new/unpublished writers each year. A monthly magazine for gay men. "Divergent viewpoints are expressed in both feature articles and fiction, which examine values and behavior patterns characteristic of a gay lifestyle. *Torso* has a continuing commitment to well-documented investigative journalism in areas pertaining to the lives and well-being of homosexuals." Circ. 60,000. Pays on publication. Publishes ms an average of 5 months after acceptance. Byline given. Buys first North American serial rights. Submit seasonal/holiday material 6 months in advance. No simultaneous submissions accepted. Reports in 2 weeks on queries; 1 month on mss. Sample copy $5; writer's guidelines for #10 SASE.
Nonfiction: Exposé, general interest, humor, interview/profile, opinion, personal experience, photo feature and travel. "*Torso* also regularly reports on cultural and political trends, as well as the arts and entertainment, often profiling the people and personalities who affect them. The tone must be positive regarding the gay experience." Buys 12 mss/year. Query with or without published clips or send complete ms (typewritten and double-spaced). Length: 2,000-4,000 words. Pays $150.
Fiction: Erotica, adventure, fantasy, humorous, novel excerpts and romance. "No long, drawn-out fiction with no form, etc." Buys 35 mss/year. Query with or without published clips or send complete ms. Length: 2,000-4,000 words. Pays $100.
Tips: "Write about what is happening—what you as a gay male (if you are) would care to read."

THE WASHINGTON BLADE, Washington Blade, Inc., 8th Floor, 724 9th St. NW, Washington DC 20001. (202)347-2038. FAX: (202)393-6510. Senior Editor: Lisa M. Keen. 20% freelance written. Weekly news tabloid covering the gay/lesbian community. "Articles (subjects) should be written from or directed to a gay perspective." Estab. 1969. Circ. 27,500. Pays in 1 month. Publishes ms an average of 1 month after acceptance. Byline given. Offers $15 kill fee. Buys first North American serial rights. Submit seasonal/holiday material 1 month in advance. Sample copy and writer's guidelines for 8½×11 SASE and $1.
Nonfiction: Exposé (of government, private agency, church, etc., handling of gay-related issues); historical/nostalgic; interview/profile (of gay community/political leaders; persons, gay or nongay, in positions to affect gay issues; outstanding achievers who happen to be gay; those who incorporate the gay lifestyle into their professions); photo feature (on a nationally or internationally historic gay event); and travel (on locales that welcome or cater to the gay traveler). *The Washington Blade* basically covers two areas: news and lifestyle. News coverage of D.C. metropolitan area gay community, local and federal government actions relating to gays, as well as national news of interest to gays. Section also includes features on current events. Special issues include: Annual gay pride issue (early June). No sexually explicit material. Articles of interest to the community must include and be written for both

gay men and lesbians. Buys 30 mss/year, average. Query with published clips and resume. Length: 500-1,500 words. Pays 5-10¢/word. Sometimes pays the expenses of writers on assignment.

Photos: "A photo or graphic with feature/lifestyle articles is particularly important. Photos with news stories are appreciated." State availability of photos. Reviews b&w contact sheets and 5×7 glossy prints. Pays $25 minimum. Captions preferred; model releases required. On assignment, photographer paid mutually agreed upon fee, with expenses reimbursed. Publication retains all rights.

Tips: "Send good examples of your writing and know the paper before you submit a manuscript for publication. We get a lot of submissions which are entirely inappropriate. We're looking for more features, but fewer AIDS-related features." Greatest opportunity for freelancers resides in current events, features, interviews and book reviews.

THE WEEKLY NEWS, The Weekly News Inc., 901 NE 79th St., Miami FL 33138. (305)757-6333. Editor: Jay Vail. Managing Editor: Bill Watson. 40% freelance written. Weekly gay tabloid. Circ. 32,000. Pays on publication. Byline given. Buys one-time rights. Submit seasonal/holiday material 2 months in advance. Simultaneous and previously published submissions OK. Sample copy for 9½×12½ SAE with $1.50 postage.

Nonfiction: Exposé, humor and interview/profile. Buys 8 mss/year. Send complete ms. Length: 1,000-5,000 words. Pays $25-125. Sometimes pays the expenses of writers on assignment.

Photos: State availability of photos with submission. Reviews 3×5 prints. Offers $5-20/photo. Buys first and future use.

Columns/Departments: Send complete ms. Length: 900 words maximum. Pays $15-30.

Religious

Religious magazines focus on a variety of subjects, styles and beliefs. Fewer religious publications are considering poems and personal experience articles, but many emphasize special ministries to singles, seniors and deaf people. Such diversity makes reading each magazine essential for the writer hoping to break in. Educational and inspirational material of interest to church members, workers and leaders within a denomination or religion is needed by the publications in this category. Publications intended to assist professional religious workers in teaching and managing church affairs are classified in Church Administration and Ministry in the Trade section. Religious magazines for children and teenagers can be found in the Juvenile and Teen and Young Adult classifications.

AGLOW, For the Spirit-Renewed Christian Woman, Aglow Publications, Box 1548, Lynnwood WA 98046-1557. (206)775-7282. Editor: Gwen Weising. 66% freelance written. Works with a small number of new/unpublished writers each year. Bimonthly nondenominational Christian charismatic magazine for women. **Pays on acceptance.** Publishes ms an average of 6 months to 1 year after acceptance. Byline given. Buys first North American serial rights, and reprint rights for use in *Aglow* magazine in other countries. Submit seasonal/holiday material 8 months in advance. Simultaneous queries OK. Reports in 2 months. Sample copy for 9×12 SAE and 2 first class stamps; writer's guidelines for #10 SASE.

Nonfiction: Contact Gloria Chisholm, Acquisitions Editor. Christian women's spiritual experience articles (first person) and some humor. "Each article should be either a personal experience of or teaching about Jesus as Savior, as Baptizer in the Holy Spirit, or as Guide and Strength in everyday circumstances." Queries only. "We would like to see material about 'Women of Vision' who have made and are making an impact on their world for God." Length: 1,000-2,000 words. Pays up to 10¢/word. Sometimes pays expenses of writers on assignment.

‡**AMERICA,** 106 W. 56th St., New York NY 10019. (212)581-4640. Editor: Rev. George W. Hunt. Published weekly for adult, educated, largely Roman Catholic audience. Estab. 1909. **Pays on acceptance.** Byline given. Usually buys all rights. Reports in 2-3 weeks. Free writer's guidelines.

Nonfiction: "We publish a wide variety of material on politics, economics, ecology, and so forth. We are not a parochial publication, but almost all of our pieces make some moral or religious point. We are not interested in purely informational pieces or personal narratives which are self-contained and have no larger moral interest." Articles on literature, current political and social events. Length: 1,500-2,000 words. Pays $50-100.

Poetry: Length: 15-30 lines. Address to poetry editor, Patrick Samway, S.J.

‡**THE ANNALS OF SAINT ANNE DE BEAUPRE,** Redemptorist Fathers, 9795 St. Anne Blvd., St. Anne De Beaupre, Quebec G0A 3C0 Canada. (418)827-4538. FAX: (418)827-4530. Editor: Bernard Mercier. Managing Editor: Roch Achard. 80% freelance written. Works with a small number of new/

unpublished writers each year. "Anyone can submit manuscripts. We judge." Monthly magazine on religion. "Our aim is to promote devotion to St. Anne and Christian family values." Circ. 45,000. **Pays on acceptance.** Publishes ms an average of 1 year after acceptance. Byline given. Buys first North American serial rights. Submit seasonal/holiday material 2½ months in advance. Simultaneous queries and photocopied submissions OK. Reports in 2 weeks. Free sample copy and writer's guidelines.

Nonfiction: Exposé, general interest, inspirational and personal experience. No articles without spiritual thrust. Buys 30 mss/year. Send complete ms. Length: 500-1,200 words. Pays 3-4¢/word.

Fiction: Religious. Buys 15 mss/year. Send complete ms. Length: 500-1,200 words. Pays 3-4¢/word.

Poetry: Traditional. Buys 12/year. Submit maximum 2-3 poems. Length: 12-20 lines. Pays $5-8.

Tips: "Write something educational, inspirational, objective and uplifting. Reporting rather than analysis is simply not remarkable."

THE ASSOCIATE REFORMED PRESBYTERIAN, Associate Reformed Presbyterian General Synod, 1 Cleveland St., Greenville SC 29601. (803)232-8297. Editor: Ben Johnston. 5% freelance written. Works with a small number of new/unpublished writers each year. A Christian publication serving a conservative, evangelical and Reformed denomination, most of whose members are in the Southeast U.S. Estab. 1976. Circ. 6,700. **Pays on acceptance.** Publishes ms an average of 4 months after acceptance. Byline given. Not copyrighted. Buys first rights, one-time rights, or second serial (reprint) rights. Submit seasonal/holiday material 4 months in advance. Simultaneous submissions and previously published submissions OK. Reports in 1 month. Sample copy $1.50; writer's guidelines for #10 SASE.

Nonfiction: Book excerpts, essays, inspirational, opinion, personal experience and religious. Buys 10-15 mss/year. Query. Length: 400-2,000 words. Pays $50 maximum.

Photos: State availability of photos with submission. Reviews 5 × 7 reprints. Offers $25 maximum per photo. Captions and identification of subjects required. Buys one-time rights. Sometimes pays expenses of writers on assignment.

Fiction: Religious and children's. Pays $50 maximum.

Tips: "Feature articles are the area of our publication most open to freelancers. Focus on a contemporary problem and offer Bible-based solutions to it. Provide information that would help a Christian struggling in his daily walk. Writers should understand that we are denominational, conservative, evangelical, Reformed and Presbyterian. A writer who appreciates these nuances would stand a much better chance of being published here than one who does not."

AXIOS, 800 S. Euclid St., Fullerton CA 92632. (714)526-4952. Computer number for Axios BBS (714)526-2387. Editor: Daniel John Gorham. 10% freelance written. Eager to work with new/unpublished writers. Monthly journal seeking spiritual articles mostly on Orthodox Christian background, either Russian, Greek, Serbian, Syrian or American. Estab. 1980. Circ. 8,789. Pays on publication. Publishes ms an average of 6 months after acceptance. Byline given. Offers 50% kill fee. Buys all rights. Submit seasonal/holiday material 4 months in advance. Simultaneous queries, and simultaneous and previously published submissions OK. Query for electronic submissions. Reports in 1 month. Sample copy for $2 and 9 × 12 SAE with 50¢ postage.

Nonfiction: Book excerpts; exposé (of religious figures); general interest; historical/nostalgic; interview/profile; opinion; personal experience; photo feature; and travel (shrines, pilgrimages). Special issues include the persecution of Christians in Iran, Russia or in Arab lands; Roman Catholic interest in the Orthodox Church. Nothing about the Pope or general "all-is-well-with-Christ" items. Buys 14 mss/year. Send complete ms. Length: 1,000-3,000 words. Pays 4¢/word minimum.

Columns/Departments: Reviews religious books and films. Buys 80 mss/year. Query.

Tips: "We need some hard hitting articles on the 'political' church—the why, how and where of it and why it lacks the timelessness of the spiritual. Here in *Axios* you can discuss your feelings, your findings, your needs, your growth; give us your outpouring. Don't mistake us for either Protestant or Roman Catholic; we are the voice of Catholics united with the Eastern Orthodox Church, also referred to as the Greek Orthodox Church. We are most interested in the western rite within eastern Orthodoxy; and the return of the Roman Catholic to the ancient universal church. Very interested in the old calendar."

BAPTIST LEADER, Valley Forge PA 19482-0851. (215)768-2153. Editor: Linda Isham. For pastors, teachers and leaders in churches. 5% freelance written. Works with several new/unpublished writers each year. Quarterly. Estab. 1939. **Pays on acceptance.** Publishes ms an average of 8 months after acceptance. Deadlines are 8 months prior to date of issue. Sample copy for $1.25; writer's guidelines for #10 SASE.

Nonfiction: Educational topics. How-to articles for local church teachers and leaders. Length: 1,500-2,000 words. Pays $25-75.

Tips: "We're planning more emphasis on Christian education administration and planning and articles for all church leaders."

CATHOLIC NEAR EAST MAGAZINE, Catholic Near East Welfare Association, 1011 1st Ave., New York NY 10022-4195. (212)826-1480. FAX: (212)838-1344. Editor: Thomas McHugh. 50% freelance written. Quarterly magazine. For a Roman Catholic audience with interest in the Near East, particularly its current religious, cultural and political aspects. Circ. 150,000. Pays on publication. Publishes ms an average of 4 months after acceptance. Byline given. Buys all rights. Photocopied submissions OK if legible. Reports in 1 month. Sample copy and writer's guidelines for 9½ × 6½ SAE with 2 first class stamps.

Nonfiction: "Cultural, territorial, devotional, political, historical material on the Near East, (especially the Eastern forms of Catholicism and the Church). Style should be simple, factual, concise. Articles must stem from personal acquaintance with subject matter, or thorough up-to-date research." Length: 1,200-1,800 words. Pays 15¢/word.

Photos: "Photographs to accompany manuscript are welcome; they should illustrate the people, places, ceremonies, etc. which are described in the article. We prefer color transparencies but occasionally use black and white. Pay varies depending on use of—scale from $75-200."

Tips: "Writers: we are interested in current events in the regions listed above as they affect the cultural, political and religious lives of people."

CHICAGO STUDIES, Box 665, Mundelein IL 60060. (708)566-1462. Editor: Rev. George J. Dyer. 50% freelance written. Magazine published 3 times/year. For Roman Catholic priests and religious educators. Estab. 1962. Circ. 8,200. **Pays on acceptance.** Buys all rights. Reports in 2 months. Sample copy $5; free writer's guidelines.

Nonfiction: Nontechnical discussion of theological, Biblical and ethical topics. Articles aimed at a nontechnical presentation of the contemporary scholarship in those fields. Submit complete ms. Buys 30 mss/year. Length: 3,000-5,000 words. Pays $35-100.

THE CHRISTIAN CENTURY, 407 S. Dearborn St., Chicago IL 60605. (312)427-5380. Editor: James M. Wall. Senior Editors: Martin E. Marty and Dean Peerman. Managing Editor: David Heim. 70% freelance written. Eager to work with new/unpublished writers. Weekly magazine for ecumenically-minded, progressive church people, both clergy and lay. Circ. 37,000. Pays on publication. Publishes ms an average of 2 months after acceptance. Usually buys all rights. Reports in 1 month. Sample copy available for $1.50. All queries, mss should be accompanied by SASE.

Nonfiction: "We use articles dealing with social problems, ethical dilemmas, political issues, international affairs, and the arts, as well as with theological and ecclesiastical matters. We focus on concerns that arise at the juncture between church and society, or church and culture." Query appreciated, but not essential. Length: 2,500 words maximum. Payment varies, but averages $30/page.

CHRISTIAN HERALD, 40 Overlook Dr., Chappaqua NY 10514. (914)769-9000. Editor: Bob Chuvala. 50% freelance written. Bimonthly magazine for evangelical Protestants. Estab. 1877. Circ. 165,000. **Pays on acceptance.** Byline given. Offers ⅓ kill fee. Buys first North American serial rights or second serial (reprint) rights. Submit seasonal/holiday material 8 months in advance. Reports in 2 month. Sample copy for 9 × 12 SAE with 3 first class stamps; writer's guidelines for #10 SASE.

Nonfiction: Diane M. Logan, Editorial Assistant. Humor, interview/profile, personal experience and religious. "No articles that tell the reader what to do or how to live." Buys 50 mss/year. Query with published clips, or send complete ms. Length: 100-2,500 words. Pays 10-15¢/word. Sometimes pays the expenses of writers on assignment. Include SASE for return manuscript or reply.

Photos: Peter Gross, art director. Send photos with submission. Reviews contact sheets, transparencies and prints. Captions, model releases and identification of subjects required. Buys one-time rights.

Columns/Departments: Kids of the Kingdom (enlightening moments in the course of parenting or teaching children), up to 200 words; Crossroads (the story of your salvation or spiritual turning point), up to 1,200 words; One Last Word (personal experiences that pointed out something eternal), up to 1,000 words. Buys 30 mss/year. Send complete ms. Pays 10-15¢/word.

Fiction: "Will consider *excellent* short stories."

Tips: "Look around for people who are demonstrating their faith, not just talking about it."

CHRISTIAN HOME & SCHOOL, Christian Schools International, 3350 East Paris Ave. SE, P.O. Box 8709, Grand Rapids MI 49508. (616)957-1070. Editor: Gordon L. Bordewyk. Associate Editor: Judy Zylstra. 30% freelance written. Works with a small number of new/unpublished writers each year. Magazine published 6 times/year covering family life and Christian education. "The magazine is designed for parents who support Christian education. We feature material on a wide range of topics of interest to parents." Estab. 1922. Pays on publication. Publishes ms an average of 4 months after acceptance. Byline given. Buys first North American serial rights. Submit seasonal/holiday material 4 months in advance. Simultaneous queries OK. Reports in 3 weeks on queries; 1 month on mss. Sample copy for 9 × 12 SAE and 4 first class stamps; writer's guidelines for #10 SASE.

Nonfiction: Book excerpts, interview/profile, opinion, personal experience and articles on parenting and school life. "We publish features on issues which affect the home and school and profiles on interesting individuals, providing that the profile appeals to our readers and is not a tribute or eulogy of that person." Buys 40 mss/year. Send complete ms. Length: 500-2,000 words. Pays $50-110. Sometimes pays the expenses of writers on assignment.

Photos: "If you have any black-and-white photos appropriate for your article, send them along."

Tips: "Features are the area most open to freelancers. We are publishing articles that deal with contemporary issues which affect parents; keep that in mind. Use an informal easy-to-read style rather than a philosophical, academic tone. Try to incorporate vivid imagery and concrete, practical examples from real life."

CHRISTIAN SINGLE, Family Ministry Dept., Baptist Sunday School Board, 127 9th Ave. N., Nashville TN 37234. (615)251-2277. Editor: Cliff Allbritton. 50-70% freelance written. Prefers to work with published/established writers; works with a small number of new/unpublished writers each year. Monthly magazine covering items of special interest to Christian single adults. "*Christian Single* is a contemporary Christian magazine that seeks to give substantive information to singles for living the abundant life. It seeks to be constructive and creative in approach." Circ. 85,000. Pays on acceptance "for immediate needs"; on publication "for unsolicited manuscripts." Publishes ms 1-2 years after acceptance. Byline given. Buys all rights; makes work-for-hire assignments. Submit seasonal/holiday material 1½ years in advance. Reports in 2 months. Sample copy and writer's guidelines for 9 × 12 SASE with 98¢ postage.

Nonfiction: Humor (good, clean humor that applies to Christian singles); how-to (specific subjects which apply to singles; query needed); inspirational (of the personal experience type); high adventure personal experience (of single adults); photo feature (on outstanding Christian singles; query needed); well researched financial articles targeted to single adults (query needed). No "shallow, uninformative mouthing off. This magazine says something, and people read it cover to cover." Buys 120-150 unsolicited mss/year. Query with published clips. Length: 300-1,200 words. Pays 5½¢/word.

‡CHRISTIAN SOCIAL ACTION, 100 Maryland Ave. NE, Washington DC 20002. (202)488-5632. Editor: Lee Ranck. 2% freelance written. Works with a small number of new/unpublished writers each year. Monthly for "United Methodist clergy and lay people interested in in-depth analysis of social issues, with emphasis on the church's role or involvement in these issues." Circ. 3,500. May buy all rights. Pays on publication. Publishes ms an average of 2 months after acceptance. Rights purchased vary with author and material. Returns rejected material in 4-5 weeks. Reports on material accepted for publication in several weeks. Free sample copy and writer's guidelines for #10 SASE.

Nonfiction: "This is the social action publication of the United Methodist Church published by the denomination's General Board of Church and Society. Our publication tries to relate social issues to the church—what the church can do, is doing; why the church should be involved. We only accept articles relating to social issues, e.g., war, draft, peace, race relations, welfare, police/community relations, labor, population problems, drug and alcohol problems." No devotional, 'religious,' superficial material, highly technical articles, personal experiences or poetry. Buys 25-30 mss/year. "Query to show that writer has expertise on a particular social issue, give credentials, and reflect a readable writing style." Query or submit complete ms. Length: 2,000 words maximum. Pays $75-100. Sometimes pays the expenses of writers on assignment.

Tips: "Write on social issues, but not superficially; we're more interested in finding an expert who can write (e.g., on human rights, alcohol problems, peace issues) than a writer who attempts to research a complex issue."

CHRISTIANITY & CRISIS, 537 W. 121st St., New York NY 10027. (212)662-5907. Editor: Leon Howell. Managing Editor: Vivian Lindermayer 10% freelance written. Works with a small number of new/unpublished writers each year. Biweekly Protestant journal of opinion. "We are interested in foreign affairs, domestic, economic and social policy, and theological developments with social or ethical implications, e.g., feminist, black and liberation theologies. As an independent religious journal it is part of *C&C's* function to discuss church policies from a detached and sometimes critical perspective. We carry no 'devotional' material but welcome solid contemplative reflections. Most subscribers are highly educated, well-informed." Estab. 1941. Circ. 14,000. Pays on publication. Publishes ms an average of 2 months after acceptance. Byline given. Offers variable kill fee. Submit seasonal/holiday material 2 months in advance. Simultaneous queries OK. Reports in 1 month. Sample copy $1.75 with 9 × 12 SAE and 2 first class stamps; writer's guidelines for #10 SASE.

Nonfiction: Buys 150 mss/year. Query with or without published clips. Length: 1,000-4,000 words. Pays 3¢/word. Rarely pays expenses of writers on assignment.

Tips: "We have been publishing more international stories and need to build up reporting on U.S. issues."

CHRISTIANITY TODAY, 465 Gundersen Dr., Carol Stream IL 60188. 80% freelance written. Works with a small number of new/unpublished writers each year. Emphasizes orthodox, evangelical religion. Semimonthly magazine. Circ. 180,000. Publishes ms an average of 6 months after acceptance. Usually buys first serial rights. Submit seasonal/holiday material at least 8 months in advance. Reports in 2 months. Sample copy and writer's guidelines for 9 × 12 SAE and 3 first class stamps.

Nonfiction: Theological, ethical, historical and informational (not merely inspirational). Buys 4 mss/issue. *Query only.* Unsolicited mss not accepted and not returned. Length: 1,000-4,000 words. Pays negotiable rates. Sometimes pays the expenses of writers on assignment.

Columns/Departments: The Arts (Christian review of the arts). Buys 12 mss/year. Send complete ms. Length: 800-900 words. Pays negotiable rates.

Tips: "We are developing more of our own manuscripts and requiring a much more professional quality of others. Queries without SASE will not be answered and manuscripts not containing SASE will not be returned."

CHRISTMAS, The Annual of Christmas Literature and Art, Augsburg Fortress, Publishers, 426 S. 5th St., P.O. Box 1209, Minneapolis MN 55440. (612)330-3442. Editor: Jennifer Huber. 100% freelance written. "An annual literary magazine that celebrates Christmas focusing on the effect of the Christmas love of God on the lives of people, and how it colors and shapes traditions and celebrations." Estab. 1931. **Pays on acceptance.** Byline given. Buys first rights, one-time rights and all rights; makes work-for-hire assignments. Submit seasonal/holiday material 18 months in advance. Reports in 1 month on queries; 3 months on mss. Sample copy $10.95 plus postage.

Nonfiction: Historical/nostalgic (on Christmas customs); inspirational, interview/profile, personal experience and travel. Focusing on more family-oriented articles with stories for children and young adults. Articles on art and music with Christmas relationships. Buys 3-4 mss/year. Query with published clips, or send complete ms. Length: 2,500-2,700 words. Pays $200-450 for assigned articles; pays $150-300 for unsolicited articles.

Photos: State availability of photos with submission. Reviews transparencies. Offers $15-100 per photo. Captions and identification of subjects required. Buys one-time rights.

Fiction: Ethnic, historical and slice-of-life vignettes. "No stories of fictionalized characters at the Bethlehem stable. Fiction should show the effect of God's love on the lives of people." Buys 3-4 mss/year. Send complete ms. Length: 5,000 words maximum. Pays $150-300.

Poetry: Free verse, light verse and traditional. No poetry dealing with Santa Claus. Buys 2-3 poems/year. Submit maximum 3 poems. Pays $35-40.

CHRYSALIS, Journal of the Swedenborg Foundation, 139 East 23rd St., New York NY 10010. FAX: (804)983-1074. Send inquiries and manuscripts directly to the editorial office: Route 1, Box 184, Dillwyn VA 23936. Editor: Carol S. Lawson. Managing Editor: Susanna van Rensselaer. 50% freelance written. A literary magazine published 3 times per year on spiritually related topics. *It is very important to send for writer's guidelines and sample copies before submitting.* "Content of fiction, articles, reviews, poetry, etc., should be directly focused on that issue's theme and directed to the educated, intellectually curious reader." Estab. 1985. Circ. 1,200. Pays at page-proof stage. Publishes ms an average of 9 months after acceptance. Byline given. Buys first rights and makes work-for-hire assignments. Reports in 2 weeks on queries; 2 months on mss. Sample copy and writer's guidelines for 9 × 12 SAE and $3.50. Writer's guidelines and copy deadlines for SASE. Upcoming Themes: Spring 1992: "Science and Spirituality"; Summer 1992: "The Future of Human Nature"; Autumn 1992: "Crossroads"; Spring 1993: "Time"; Summer 1993: "Work"; and Autumn 1993: "Family."

Nonfiction: Essays and interview/profile. Buys 15 mss/year. Query. Length: 750-2,500 words. Pays $50-250 for assigned articles. Pays $50-150 for unsolicited articles.

Photos: Send suggestions for illustrations with submission. Offers no additional payment for photos accepted with ms. Captions and identification of subjects required. Buys original artwork for cover and inside copy, $25-150. Buys one-time rights.

Columns/Departments: Vital Issues (articles and material related to practical psychology, health, healing), 750-2,000 words; Patterns (philosophical inquiry into the underlying patterns found within reality), 750-2,000 words; Currents (articles and material on the fine and visionary arts); 750-2,000 words; and Fringe Benefits (book, film, art, video reviews relevant to *Chrysalis* subject matter), 350-500 words. Buys 12 mss/year. Length: 350-2,000. Pays $50-250.

Fiction: Phoebe Loughrey, fiction editor. Adventure, experimental, historical, mainstream, mystery and science fiction, related to theme of issue. Buys 6 mss/year. Query. Length: short more likely to be published, 500-2,000 words. Pays $50-150.

Poetry: Avante-garde and traditional. Buys 10 poems/year. Pays $25. Submit maximum 6.

CHURCH & STATE, Americans United for Separation of Church and State, 8120 Fenton St., Silver Spring MD 20910. (301)589-3707. Managing Editor: Joseph Conn. 10% freelance written. Prefers to work with published/established writers. Monthly magazine. Emphasizes religious liberty and church/

state relations matters. Readership "includes the whole spectrum, but is predominantly Protestant and well-educated." Estab. 1947. Circ. 33,000. **Pays on acceptance.** Publishes ms an average of 2 months after acceptance. Buys all rights. Simultaneous and previously published submissions OK. Reports in 1 month. Sample copy and writer's guidelines for 9×12 SAE and 3 first class stamps.
Nonfiction: Expose, general interest, historical and interview. Buys 11 mss/year. Query. Length: 3,000 words maximum. Pays negotiable fee.
Photos: State availability of photos with query. Pays negotiable fee for b&w prints. Captions preferred. Buys one-time rights.

COLUMBIA, 1 Columbus Plaza, New Haven CT 06507. Editor: Richard McMunn. Monthly magazine for Catholic families. Caters particularly to members of the Knights of Columbus. Estab. 1921. Circ. 1.5 million. **Pays on acceptance.** Buys first serial rights. Free sample copy and writer's guidelines.
Nonfiction: Fact articles directed to the Catholic layman and his family dealing with current events, social problems, Catholic apostolic activities, education, ecumenism, rearing a family, literature, science, arts, sports and leisure. Color glossy prints, transparencies or contact prints with negatives are required for illustration. Articles without ample illustrative material are not given consideration. Pays up to $500, including photos. Buys 30 mss/year. Query. Length: 1,000-1,500 words.

‡COMMENTS, From the Friends, Box 840, Stoughton MA 02072. Editor: David A. Reed. 20% freelance written. A quarterly Christian newsletter written especially for "Jehovah's Witnesses, ex-Jehovah's Witnesses and persons concerned about Jehovah's Witness, relatives, friends, and neighbors." Circ. 1,500. Pays on publication. Publishes ms an average of 3 months after acceptance. Byline sometimes given. Buys second serial (reprint) and simultaneous rights. Submit seasonal/holiday material 4 months in advance. Simultaneous, photocopied and previously published submissions OK. Query for electronic submissions. Reports in 1 month on mss. Sample copy $1; writer's guidelines for #10 SAE with 2 first class stamps.
Nonfiction: Book excerpts, essays, exposé, how-to (witnessing tips), humor, inspirational, interview/profile, personal experience, religious and book reviews of books on cults only. Special issue topic will be The Next Watchtower President (replacing Fred Franz). "No general religious material not written specifically for our unique readership." Buys 8 mss/year. Send complete ms. Length: 200-1,000 words. Pays $2-20. May pay with contributor copies rather than a cash payment "when a writer contributes an article as a gift to this ministry."
Columns/Departments: Witnessing Tips (brief, powerful and effective approaches), 250-300 words; and News Briefs (current events involving Jehovah's Witnesses and ex-Jehovah's Witnesses), 60-240 words. Buys 4 mss/year. Send complete ms. Length: 60-300 words. Pays $2-10.
Fillers: Facts, newsbreaks and quotes. Buys 4/year. Length: 10-50 words. Pays $1-5.
Tips: "Acquaint us with your background that qualifies you to write in this field. Write well-documented, germane articles in layman's language."

CONFIDENT LIVING, P.O. Box 82808, Lincoln NE 68501. (402)474-4567. Editor: Jan Reeser. 40% freelance written. Monthly interdenominational magazine for adults, mostly age 50 and up. Estab. 1944. Circ. 85,000. **Pays on acceptance.** Buys first serial rights or first North American serial rights, or second serial (reprint) rights. Submit seasonal material at least 1 year in advance. Reports in 5 weeks. Sample copy $1.95; writer's guidelines with SASE.
Nonfiction: Jan E. Reeser, managing editor. Articles which will help the reader learn and apply Christian Biblical principles to his life from the writer's or the subject's own experience. Writers are required "to affirm agreement with our doctrinal statement. We are especially looking for true, personal experience 'salvation,' church, 'how to live the Christian life' articles, reports and interviews regarding major and interesting happenings and people in fundamental, evangelical Christian circles." Nothing rambling or sugary sweet, or without Biblical basis. Details or statistics should be authentic and verifiable. Style should be conservative but concise. Buys approximately 100 mss/year. Length: 1,500 words maximum. Pays 7-12¢/word, unassigned; 10-15¢/word, assigned; 3¢/word reprint.
Photos: Pays $25 maximum for b&w glossies; $50 maximum for transparencies inside, $85 cover. Photos paid on publication.
Tips: "The basic purpose of the magazine is to explain the Bible and how it is relevant to life because we believe this will accomplish one of two things—to present Christ as Savior to the lost or to promote the spiritual growth of believers, so don't ignore our primary purposes when writing for us. Nonfiction should be Biblical and timely; at the least Biblical in principle. Use illustrations of your own experiences or of someone else's when God solved a problem similar to the reader's. Be so specific that the meanings and significance will be crystal clear to all readers."

CONSCIENCE, A Newsjournal of Prochoice Catholic Opinion, Catholics for a Free Choice, Suite 301, 1436 U St., NW, Washington DC 20009-3916. (202)638-1706. Editor: Nancy H. Evans. 80% freelance written. Eager to work with new/unpublished writers. Bimonthly newsjournal covering reproductive rights, specifically abortion rights in area of church and church and government in U.S. and worldwide. "A feminist, prochoice perspective is a must, and knowledge of Christianity and specifically Catholicism is helpful." Circ. 10,000. Pays on publication. Publishes ms an average of 4 months after acceptance. Byline given. Buys first North American serial rights; makes work-for-hire assignments. Submit seasonal/holiday material 4 months in advance. Simultaneous queries and previously published submissions OK. Query for electronic submissions. Reports in 2 months; free sample copy for #10 SAE with 2 first class stamps; free writer's guidelines for #10 SASE.

Nonfiction: Book excerpts, interview/profile, opinion and personal experience. Especially needs "expose/refutation of antichoice misinformation and specific research into the implications of new reproductive technology and fetal personhood bills/court decisions." Buys 8-12 mss/year. Query with published clips or send complete ms. Length: 1,000-3,500 words. Pays $25-100. "Writers should be aware that we are a nonprofit organization." A substantial number of articles are contributed without payment by writers. Sometimes pays the expenses of writers on assignment.

Photos: State availability of photos with query or ms. Prefers 5×7 b&w prints. Identification of subjects required. Buys all rights.

Columns/Departments: Book reviews. Buys 6-10 mss/year. Send complete ms. Length: 1,000-2,000 words. Pays $25.

Fillers: Clippings and newsbreaks. Uses 6/year. Length: 25-100 words. No payment.

Tips: "Say something new on the abortion issue. Thoughtful, well-researched and well-argued articles needed. The most frequent mistakes made by writers in completing an article for us are untimeliness and wordiness. When you have shown you can write thoughtfully, we may hire you for other types of articles."

CORNERSTONE, Jesus People USA, 939 W. Wilson, Chicago IL 60640. Editor: Dawn Herrin. 10% freelance written. Works with a small number of new/unpublished writers each year; eager to work with new/unpublished writers. A bimonthly magazine covering contemporary issues in the light of Evangelical Christianity. Estab. 1972. Circ. 50,000. Pays after publication. Publishes ms an average of 4-6 months after acceptance. Byline given. Buys first serial rights. Submit seasonal/holiday material 6 months in advance. Simultaneous and previously published submissions OK. Reports in 6-8 weeks. Sample copy and writer's guidelines for 12×16 SAE with 6 first class stamps.

Nonfiction: Essays, personal experience, religious. Buys 3-4 mss/year. Query. Length: 2,700 words maximum. Pays negotiable rate. Sometimes pays the expenses of writers on assignment.

Photos: Send photos with accompanying ms. Reviews 8×10 b&w and color prints and 35mm slides. Identification of subjects required. Buys negotiable rights.

Columns/Departments: Music (interview with artists, mainly rock, focusing on artist's world view and value system as expressed in his/her music); Current Events; Personalities; Film and Book Reviews (focuses on meaning as compared and contrasted to Biblical values). Buys 2-6 mss/year. Query. Length: 100-2,500 words (negotiable). Pays negotiable rate.

Fiction: "Articles may express Christian world view but should not be unrealistic or 'syrupy.' Other than porn, the sky's the limit. We want fiction as creative as the Creator." Buys 1-4 mss/year. Send complete ms. Length: 250-2,500 words (negotiable). Pays negotiable rate.

Poetry: Avant-garde, free verse, haiku, light verse and traditional. No limits *except* for epic poetry ("We've not the room!"). Buys 10-50 poems/year. Submit maximum 5 poems. Payment negotiated.

Tips: "A display of creativity which expresses a biblical world view without clichés or cheap shots at non-Christians is the ideal. We are known as one of the most avant-garde magazines in the Christian market, yet attempt to express orthodox beliefs in language of the '90s. *Any* writer who does this may well be published by *Cornerstone*. Creative fiction is begging for more Christian participation. We anticipate such contributions gladly. Interviews where well-known personalities respond to the gospel are also strong publication possibilities. Please address all submissions to: Nanci Fahey, submissions editor."

THE COVENANT COMPANION, Covenant Publications of the Evangelical Covenant Church, 5101 N. Francisco Ave., Chicago IL 60625. (312)784-3000. FAX: (312)784-4366. Editor: James R. Hawkinson. 10-15% freelance written. "As the official monthly organ of The Evangelical Covenant Church, we seek to inform, stimulate and gather the denomination we serve by putting Covenants in touch with each other and assisting them in interpreting contemporary issues. We also seek to inform them on events in the church. Our background is evangelical and our emphasis is on Christian commitment and life." Circ. 23,500. Publishes ms an average of 2 months after acceptance. Byline given. Buys first or all rights. Submit seasonal/holiday material 4 months in advance. Simultaneous and previously published submissions OK. Query for electronic submissions. Sample copy $2.25; writer's guidelines for #10 SASE. Unused mss only returned if accompanied by SASE.

Nonfiction: Humor, inspirational and religious. Buys 10-15 mss/year. Send complete ms. Length: 500-2,000 words. Pays $15-50 for assigned articles; pays $15-35 for unsolicited articles.

Photos: Send photos with submissions. Reviews prints. Offers no additonal payment for photos accepted with ms. Identification of subjects required. Buys one-time rights.

Poetry: Traditional. Buys 10-15 poems/year. Submit maximum 10 poems. Pays $10-15.

Tips: "Seasonal articles related to church year and on national holidays are welcome."

DAILY MEDITATION, Box 2710, San Antonio TX 78299. Editor: Ruth S. Paterson. Quarterly. Byline given. Rights purchased vary. **Pays on acceptance.** Submit seasonal material 6 months in advance. Sample copy 50¢.

Nonfiction: "Inspirational, self-improvement and nonsectarian religious articles, 750-1,600 words, showing the path to greater spiritual growth." Pays 1½-2¢/word.

Fillers: Length: 400 words maximum.

Poetry: Inspirational. Length: 16 lines maximum. Pays 14¢/line.

Tips: "All our material is freelance submission for consideration except our meditations, which are staff written. We buy approximately 250 manuscripts per year. We must see finished manuscripts; no queries, please. Checking copy is sent upon publication."

DECISION, Billy Graham Evangelistic Association, 1300 Harmon Place, Minneapolis MN 55403-1988. (612)338-0500. FAX: (612)338-6014. Editor: Roger C. Palms. 25% freelance written. Works each year with small number of new/unpublished writers, as well as a solid stable of experienced writers. A magazine, published 11 times per year, "to set forth to every reader the Good News of salvation in Jesus Christ with such vividness and clarity that he or she will be drawn to make a commitment to Christ; to encourage, teach and strengthen Christians." Circ. 2 million. Pays on publication. Byline given. Buys first rights and assigns work-made-for-hire manuscripts, articles, projects. Include telephone number with submission. Submit seasonal/holiday material 10 months in advance; other mss published up to 1 year after acceptance. No simultaneous submissions. No unsolicited poetry. Reports in 2 months on mss. Sample copy for 8½ × 11 SAE and 4 first class stamps; writer's guidelines for #10 SASE.

Nonfiction: How-to, motivational, personal experience and religious. "No personality-centered articles or articles which are issue oriented or critical of denominations." Buys approximately 50 mss/year. Send complete ms. Length: 400-1,800 words. Pays $30-225. Pays expenses of writers on assignment.

Photos: State availability of photos with submission. Reviews prints. Captions, model releases and identification of subjects required. Buys one-time rights.

Tips: "We are seeking personal conversion testimonies and personal experience articles which show how God intervened in a person's daily life and the way in which Scripture was applied to the experience in helping to solve the problem. The conversion testimonies describe in first person what author's life was like before he/she became a Christian, how he/she committed one's life to Christ and what tangible difference He has made since that decision. We also are looking for vignettes on various aspects of personal evangelism. SASE required with submissions."

DISCIPLESHIP JOURNAL, NavPress, a division of The Navigators, P.O. Box 6000, Colorado Springs CO 80934. (719)548-9373 ext. 291. FAX: (719)598-7128. Editor: Susan Maycinik. 90% freelance written. Works with a small number of new/unpublished writers each year. Bimonthly magazine on Christian discipleship. "The mission of *Discipleship Journal* is to help believers develop a deeper relationship with Jesus Christ, and to provide practical help in understanding the scriptures and applying them to daily life and ministry." Estab. 1981. Circ. 95,000. **Pays on acceptance.** Publishes ms an average of 6 months after acceptance. Byline given. Buys first North American serial rights and second serial (reprint) rights. Submit seasonal/holiday material 6 months in advance. Simultaneous queries, and previously published submissions OK. Query for electronic submissions. Reports in 1 month. Sample copy and writer's guidelines for 9 × 12 SAE and 7 first class stamps.

Nonfiction: Book excerpts (rarely); how-to (grow in Christian faith and disciplines; help others grow as Christians; serve people in need; understand and apply the Bible); inspirational; interview/profile (focusing on one aspect of discipleship); and interpretation/application of the Bible. No personal testimony; humor; anything not directly related to Christian life and faith; politically partisan articles. Buys 80 mss/year. Query with published clips or send complete ms. Length: 500-3,000 words. Pays 3¢/word reprint; 15¢/word first rights. Pays the expenses of writers on assignment.

Tips: "Our articles are meaty, not fluffy. Study writer's guidelines and back issues and try to use similar approaches. Don't preach. Polish before submitting. About half of the articles in each issue are related to one theme. Freelancers should write to request theme list. We are looking for more practical articles on ministering to others and more articles dealing with world missions."

‡THE DOOR, Box 530 , Yreka CA 96097. (916)842-2701. Contact: Bob Darden. (817)752-1468. 40% freelance written. Works with a small number of new/unpublished writers each year. Bimonthly magazine for men and women connected with the church. Circ. 11,000. Pays on publication. Publishes ms an average of 1 year after acceptance. Buys first rights. Reports in 3 months.

Nonfiction: Satirical articles on church renewal, Christianity, and organized religion. Few book reviews. Buys about 30 mss/year. Submit complete ms. Length: 1,500 words maximum, 750-1,000 preferred. Pays $200. Sometimes pays expenses of writers on assignments.

Tips: "We look for someone who is clever, on our wave length, and has some savvy about the evangelical church. We are very picky and highly selective. The writer has a better chance of breaking in with our publication with short articles and fillers since we are a bimonthly publication with numerous regular features and the magazine is only 40 pages. The most frequent mistake made by writers is that they do not understand satire. They see we are a humor magazine and consequently come off funny/cute (like *Reader's Digest*) rather than funny/satirical (like *National Lampoon*)."

EVANGEL, Free Methodist Publishing House, P.O. Box 535002, Indianapolis IN 46253-5002. (219)267-7161. Editor: Vera Bethel. 100% freelance written. Weekly magazine. Audience is 65% female, 35% male; married, 25-31 years old, mostly city dwellers, high school graduates, mostly nonprofessional. Estab. 1897. Circ. 35,000. Pays on publication. Publishes ms an average of 1 year after acceptance. Buys simultaneous rights, second serial (reprint) rights or one-time rights. Submit seasonal/holiday material 3 months in advance. Reports in 1 month. Sample copy and writer's guidelines for 6 × 9 SAE with 2 first class stamps.

Nonfiction: Interview (with ordinary person who is doing something extraordinary in his community, in service to others); profile (of missionary or one from similar service profession who is contributing significantly to society); and personal experience (finding a solution to a problem common to young adults; coping with handicapped child, for instance, or with a neighborhood problem. Story of how God-given strength or insight saved a situation). Buys 100 mss/year. Submit complete ms. Length: 300-1,000 words. Pays $10-25.

Photos: Purchased with accompanying ms. Captions required. Send prints. Pays $10 for 8 × 10 b&w glossy prints.

Fiction: Religious themes dealing with contemporary issues dealt with from a Christian frame of reference. Story must "go somewhere." Buys 50 mss/year. Submit complete ms. Length: 1,200 words. Pays $45.

Poetry: Free verse, haiku, light verse, traditional and religious. Buys 50 poems/year. Submit maximum 6 poems. Length: 4-24 lines. Pays $10.

Tips: "Seasonal material will get a second look (won't be rejected so easily) because we get so little. Write an attention grabbing lead followed by a body of article that says something worthwhile. Relate the lead to some of the universal needs of the reader—promise in that lead to help the reader in some way. Remember that everybody is interested most in himself. Lack of SASE brands author as a nonprofessional; I seldom even bother to read the script. Prefers non-justified righthand margin. If dot-matrix is used, 24-pin is required."

THE EVANGELICAL BEACON, 901 E. 78th St., Minneapolis MN 55420. (612)854-1300. Editor: Carol Madison. 30% freelance written. Works with a small number of new/unpublished writers each year. Denominational magazine of the Evangelical Free Church of America—evangelical Protestant readership; published 12 times/year. Estab. 1930. Pays on publication. Publishes ms an average of 6 months after acceptance. Rights purchased vary with author and material. Buys first rights or all rights, and some reprints. Sample copy and writer's guidelines for $1.

Nonfiction: Articles on the church, Christ-centered human interest and personal testimony articles, well researched on current issues of religious interest. No queries. Desires crisp, imaginative, original writing—not sermons on paper. Length: 250-2,000 words. Pays 7¢/word for original articles; 3¢/word for reprints.

Photos: Prefers 8 × 10 b&w photos. Pays $10 minimum.

Poetry: Very little poetry used.

Tips: "Articles need to be helpful to the average Christian—encouraging, challenging, instructive. Also needs material presenting reality of the Christian faith to non-Christians. Some tie-in with the Evangelical Free Church of America is helpful but not required. Follow writer's guidelines/themes for the year. Our articles are all theme-related."

EVANGELIZING TODAY'S CHILD, Child Evangelism Fellowship Inc., Warrenton MO 63383. (314)456-4321. Editor: Elsie Lippy. 75% freelance written. Prefers to work with published/established writers. Bimonthly magazine. "Our purpose is to equip Christians to win the world's children to Christ and disciple them. Our readership is Sunday school teachers, Christian education leaders and children's workers in every phase of Christian ministry to children up to 12 years old." Estab. 1942. Circ. 22,000. Pays within 90 days of acceptance. Publishes ms an average of 6 months after acceptance. Byline given. Pays a kill fee if assigned. Buys first serial rights. Submit seasonal/holiday material 6 months in advance. Simultaneous queries OK. Reports in 3 weeks on queries; 2 months on mss. Free sample copy; writer's guidelines with SASE.

Nonfiction: Unsolicited articles welcomed from writers with Christian education training or current experience in working with children. Buys 25 mss/year. Query. Length: 1,200-1,500. Pays 6-8¢/word.
Photos: Submissions of photos on speculation accepted. Needs photos of children or related subjects. Pays $30 for 8×10 b&w glossy prints; $35 for inside color prints or transparencies $100 for cover transparencies.

THE FAMILY, Daughters of St. Paul, 50 St. Paul's Ave., Boston MA 02130. (617)522-8911. Editor: Sr. Mary Lea Hill. Managing Editor: Sr. Donna William Giaimo. Monthly magazine on Catholic family life. "*The Family* magazine stresses the special place of the family within society as an irreplaceable center of life, love and faith. Articles on timely, pertinent issues help families approach today's challenges with a faith perspective and a spirit of commitment to the Gospel of Jesus Christ." Estab. 1953. Pays on publication. Publishes ms an average of 6 months after acceptance. Byline given. Buys first and second serial (reprint) rights. Reimbursement for reprints varies. Submit seasonal/holiday material 5 months in advance. Previously published submissions OK. Sample copy $1.75 with 8½×11 SAE with 5 first class stamps. Writer's guidelines for #10 SASE.
Nonfiction: Humor, inspirational, interview/profile, religious. Buys 70 mss/year. Send complete ms. Length: 500-1,500 words. Pays $50-150. Also may pay in contributor's copies.
Photos: Send photos with submission. Reviews 4×5 transparencies. Captions, model releases and identification of subjects required. Buys one-time rights.
Fiction: Humorous, religious, slice-of-life vignettes, family. Buys 12 mss/year. Send complete ms. Length: 1,000-2,000 words. Pays $50-150.
Fillers: Anecdotes, short humor. Buys 30/year. Length: 100-300 words. Pays $10-30.

GROWING CHURCHES, 127 9th Ave., N., Nashville TN 37234. (615)251-2062. FAX: (615)251-3866. Editor: Gary Hardin. 30% freelance written. Works with new/unpublished writers. Quarterly. For Southern Baptist pastors, staff and volunteer church leaders. Uses some freelance material. **Pays on acceptance.** Publishes ms an average of 1 year after acceptance. Byline given. Buys all rights. Free sample copy and writer's guidelines for SAE with 2 first class stamps.
Nonfiction: "This is a magazine that focuses on practical church growth ideas for Southern Baptists." Length: 1,200-1,800 words. Pays 5½¢/word.
Tips: "Send query letter. Articles must be targeted to Southern Baptist churches and their leaders. Type at 54 characters per line, 25 lines per page, double-spaced. Not responsible for manuscripts not accompanied by return postage."

GUIDEPOSTS MAGAZINE, 747 3rd Ave., New York NY 10017. Editor: Van Varner. 30% freelance written. "Works with a small number of new/unpublished writers each year, and reads all unsolicited manuscripts. *Guideposts* is an inspirational monthly magazine for people of all faiths, in which men and women from all walks of life tell in first-person narrative how they overcame obstacles, rose above failures, handled sorrow, learned to master themselves and became more effective people through faith in God." Estab. 1945. Publishes ms an "indefinite" number of months after acceptance. Pays 25% kill fee for assigned articles. Byline given. "Most of our stories are ghosted articles, so the writer would not get a byline unless it was his/her own story." Buys all rights and second serial (reprint) rights.
Nonfiction and Fillers: Articles and features should be written in simple, anecdotal style with an emphasis on human interest. Short mss of approximately 250-750 words (pays $50-200) would be considered for such features as Quiet People and general one-page stories. Full-length mss, 750-1,500 words, pays $200-400. All mss should be typed, double-spaced and accompanied by a stamped, self-addressed envelope. Annually awards scholarships to high school juniors and seniors in writing contest. Buys 40-60 unsolicited mss/year. Pays expenses of writers on assignment.
Tips: "Study the magazine before you try to write for it. Each story must make a single spiritual point. The freelancer would have the best chance of breaking in by aiming for a one-page or maybe two-page article. That would be very short, say two and a half pages of typescript, but in a small magazine such things are very welcome. Sensitively written anecdotes are extremely useful. And it is much easier to just sit down and write them than to have to go through the process of preparing a query. They should be warm, well written, intelligent and upbeat. We like personal narratives that are true and have some universal relevance, but the religious element does not have to be driven home with a sledge hammer. A writer succeeds with us if he or she can write a true article in short-story form with scenes, drama, tension and a resolution of the problem presented." Address short items to Rick Hamlin.

HICALL, Gospel Publishing House, 1445 Boonville Ave., Springfield MO 65802. (417)862-2781, ext. 4349. Editor: Deanna Harris. Mostly freelance written. Eager to work with new/unpublished writers. Assemblies of God (denominational) weekly magazine of Christian fiction and articles for church-oriented teenagers, 12-17. Circ. 85,000. **Pays on acceptance.** Publishes ms an average of 15 months after acceptance. Byline given. Buys first North American serial rights, one-time rights, simultaneous rights and second serial (reprint) rights. Submit seasonal/holiday material 18 months in advance. Simultaneous and previously published submissions OK—if typed, double-spaced, on 8½ × 11 paper. Reports in 6 weeks. Sample copy for 8 × 11 SAE and 2 first class stamps; writer's guidelines for SAE.

Nonfiction: Book excerpts; historical; general interest; how-to (deal with various life problems); humor; inspirational; and personal experience. Buys 80-100 mss/year. Send complete ms. Length: 500-1,500 words. Pays 2-3¢/word.

Photos: Photos purchased with or without accompanying ms. Pays $25/8 × 10 b&w glossy print; $35/35mm.

Fiction: Adventure, humorous, mystery, romance, suspense and religious. Buys 80-100 mss/year. Send complete ms. Length: 500-1,500 words. Pays 2-3¢/word.

Poetry: Free verse, light verse and traditional. Buys 30 poems/year. Length: 10-40 lines. Pays 25¢/line, minimum of $5 (first rights).

Fillers: Puzzles. Buys 10/year. Pays 2-3¢/word.

‡**HINDUISM TODAY,** Himalayan Academy, Box 157, Hanamaulu HI 96715. (808)822-7032. Publisher: H.H. Sivaya Subramniya-Swami. Editor: Rev. Palaniswami. Managing Editor: Rev. Arumugaswami. 25% freelance written. Monthly tabloid covering Hindu spirituality and related areas. "Our philosophy is to inform and inspire Hindus worldwide, dispel myths, illusions and disinformation about Hinduism, protect, preserve and promote Hindu religion." Estab. 1979. Circ. 150,000. Pays 30 days after publication. Publishes ms an average of 2 months after acceptance. Byline given. $25 kill fee. Buys all rights. Previously published submissions OK. Query for electronic submissions. Reports in 3 months. Free sample copy and writer's guidelines.

Nonfiction: Book excerpts, essays, exposé, general interest, historical/nostalgic, humor, inspirational, interview/profile, personal experience, photo feature, religious. "Nothing that is all politics." Buys 60 mss/year. Query with published clips. Length: 500-2,000 words. Pays 6¢/word. Sometimes pays expenses of writers on assignment.

Photos: Send photos with submission. Reviews 4 × 6 prints. Offers $10 minimum; negotiable maximum per photo. Captions and identification of subjects required. Buys all rights.

Fillers: Anecdotes, facts, newsbreaks. Buys 80/year. Length: 30-200 words. Pays $5-20.

Tips: "We need people who can do first-hand reports on events and people of interest to Hindus and spiritual seekers drawn toward Eastern traditions. Feature articles are most open to freelancers."

‡**HOME TIMES,** (formerly *Sun and Sonlight Christian Newspaper*), "A Good Little Newspaper—For God and Country," Neighbor News, Inc., 4118 10th Ave. N, Lake Worth FL 33461. (407)439-3509. Editor: Dennis Lombard. 80% freelance written. Weekly tabloid covering conservative Christian and Jewish news and views on world, national and local scales. Estab. 1988. Circ. 10,000. Pays on publication. Publishes ms an average of 2 months after acceptance. Byline given. No kill fee. Buys one-time rights, second serial (reprint) rights, makes work-for-hire assignments locally. Submit seasonal/holiday material 2 months in advance. Simultaneous and previously published submissions OK. Reports in 1 week on manuscripts. No queries please! Sample copy $2; or (we suggest) three consecutive issues, $3; SAE appreciated. Writer's guidelines for #10 SASE.

Nonfiction: Book excerpts, essays, how-to, humor, inspirational, interview/profile, opinion, personal experience, photo feature, religious. Buys 30 mss/year. Send complete ms. Length 500-1,000 words. Pays $5-50. Sometimes pays the expenses of writers on assignment.

Photos: Send photos with submission. Reviews contact sheets and prints (any size). Offers $5-10 per photo. Captions, model releases and identification of subjects required. Buys one-time rights.

Columns/Departments: "Open to new column ideas." Buys 20 mss/year. Send complete ms. Length: 300-900 words. Pays $5-25.

Fiction: Humorous, religious. Buys 10 mss/year. Send complete ms. Length 300-1,200 words. Pays $5-50.

Poetry: Free verse, light verse and traditional. Buys 6 poems/year. Submit maximum 3 poems. Lines: 2-48 lines. Pays $3-10.

Fillers: "We accept and use but do not pay."

Tips: "We are very open to new writers. You must see and read the paper (we suggest three consecutive issues) to get the flavor of our conservative, Christian, Jewish, pro-family, pro-American slants. Writers have the best chance selling us Op Eds (200-500 words), how-to and fiction (religious but not preachy, doctrinal or denominational)." If you specialize in poetry of fiction (or whatever) ask for sample issues with some in them. Or send $6 for 3 samples plus writer's subscription (13 issues).

INTERLIT, David C. Cook Foundation, Cook Square, Elgin IL 60120. (708)741-2400, ext. 316. Editor: Tim Bascom. 80% freelance written on assignment. Works with a small number of new/unpublished writers each year. Quarterly journal emphasizing sharpening skills in Christian journalism and publishing. Especially for editors, publishers and writers in the third world (developing countries). Also goes to missionaries, broadcasters and educational personnel in the U.S. Circ. 6,000. **Pays on acceptance.** Publishes ms an average of 6 months after acceptance. Buys all rights. Reports in 6 weeks. Free sample copy.

Nonfiction: Technical and how-to articles about all aspects of publishing, writing and literacy. "Please study publication and query before submitting manuscripts." Buys 7 mss/issue, mostly on assignment. Length: 500-1,500 words. Pays 8-10¢/word.

Photos: Purchased with accompanying ms only. Uses b&w. Query or send prints. Captions required.

THE JEWISH WEEKLY NEWS, Bennett-Scott Publications Corp., 99 Mill St., P.O. Box 1569, Springfield MA 01101. (413)739-4771. 25% freelance written. Jewish news and features, secular and non-secular; World Judaism; arts (New England based). Estab. 1945. Circ. 2,500. Pays on publication. Publishes ms an average of 2 months after acceptance. Byline given. Not copyrighted. Buys first North American serial rights and second serial (reprint) rights. Submit seasonal/holiday material 2 months in advance. Simultaneous and previously published submissions OK. Query for electronic submissions. Sample copy for 9 × 12 SAE with 5 first class stamps.

Nonfiction: Interview/profile, religious and travel. Special issues include Jewish New Year (September); Chanukah (December); Home Issues (March); Bar/Bat Mitzvahs (May). Buys 61 mss/year. Query with published clips. Length: 300-1,000 words. Pays $5.

Photos: Send photos with submission. Reviews 5 × 7 prints. Offers no additional payment for photos accepted with ms. Identification of subjects required.

Columns/Departments: Jewish Kitchen (Kosher recipes), 300-500 words. Buys 10 mss/year. Query with published clips. Length: 300-5,000 words. Pays 50¢/inch.

Fiction: Sheila Thompson, editor. Slice-of-life vignettes. Buys 5 mss/year. Query with published clips. Length: 750-1,000 words. Pays 50¢/inch.

LIGHT AND LIFE MAGAZINE, Free Methodist Church of North America, P.O. Box 535002, Indianapolis IN 46253-5002. FAX: (317)244-1247. Editor: Bob Haslam. 35% freelance written. Works with a small number of new/unpublished writers each year. Monthly magazine. Emphasizes evangelical Christianity with Wesleyan slant for a cross section of adults. Estab. 1868. Circ. 35,000. Pays on publication. Publishes ms an average of 6 months after acceptance. Byline given. Prefers first serial rights; rarely buys second serial (reprint) rights. Submit seasonal/holiday material 6 months in advance. Reports in 6 weeks. Sample copy and guidelines $1.50; writer's guidelines for SASE.

Nonfiction: "Each issue includes a theme (4 or 5 articles addressing contemporary topics such as entertainment media, personal relationships, Christians as citizens), so freelancers should request our schedule of theme topics. We also need fresh, upbeat articles showing the average layperson how to be Christlike at home, work and play." Submit complete ms. Buys 50-60 unsolicited ms/year. Pays 4¢/word.

Photos: Purchased without accompanying ms. Send prints. Pays $5-35 for b&w photos. Offers additional payment for photos accepted with accompanying ms.

LIGUORIAN, Liguori MO 63057. FAX: (314)464-8449. Editor: Rev. Allan Weinert. Managing Editor: Francine M. O'Connor. 25% freelance written. Prefers to work with published/established writers; works with a small number of new/unpublished writers each year. Monthly. For families with Catholic religious convictions. Estab. 1913. Circ. 430,000. **Pays on acceptance.** Publishes ms an average of 3-4 months after acceptance. Byline given "except on short fillers and jokes." Buys all rights but will reassign rights to author *after* publication upon written request. Submit seasonal material 6 months in advance. Query for electronic submissions. Reports in 6 weeks. Sample copy and writer's guidelines for 6 × 9 SAE with 3 first class stamps.

Nonfiction: "Pastoral, practical and personal approach to the problems and challenges of people today. No travelogue approach or unresearched ventures into controversial areas. Also, no material found in secular publications—fad subjects that already get enough press, pop psychology, negative or put-down articles." Buys 60 unsolicited mss/year. Buys 12 fiction mss/year. Length: 400-2,000 words. Pays 10-12¢/word. Sometimes pays expenses of writers on assignment.

Photos: Photographs on assignment only unless submitted with and specific to article.

LIVE, 1445 Boonville Ave., Springfield MO 65802. (417)862-2781. 100% freelance written. Works with several new/unpublished writers each year. Weekly. For adults in Assemblies of God Sunday schools. Circ. 180,000. **Pays on acceptance.** Publishes ms an average of 1 year after acceptance. Not copyrighted. Submit seasonal material 1 year in advance; do not mention Santa Claus, Halloween or Easter bunnies. Submissions held for consideration require more time. Free sample copy and writer's guidelines for 7½ × 10½ SASE and 40¢ postage. Letters without SASE will not be answered.

Nonfiction: In the narrative mode emphasizing some phase of Christian living presented in a down-to-earth manner. Biography or missionary material using narrative techniques. Historical, scientific, nature, humorous material with spiritual lesson. "Be accurate in detail and factual material. Writing for Christian publications is a ministry. The spiritual emphasis must be an integral part of your material." Prefers not to see material on highly controversial subjects but would appreciate stories on contemporary issues and concerns (e.g. substance abuse, AIDS, euthanasia, cults, integrity, etc.). Buys about 12 mss/year. Length: 1,000-1,600 words. Pays 3¢/word for first serial rights; 2¢/word for second serial (reprint) rights, according to the value of the material and the amount of editorial work necessary.

Photos: Color photos or transparencies purchased with mss, or on assignment. Pay open.

Fiction: "Present believable characters working out their problems according to Bible principles; in other words, present Christianity in action without being preachy. The stories (fictional or true) should tell themselves without moral lessons tacked on. We want multinational, ethnic, urban and intercultural characters. Use action, suspense, humor! Stories should be true to life but not what we would feel is a sinful pattern for living. Stories should not put parents, teachers, ministers or other Christian workers in a bad light. Setting, plot and action should be realistic, with strong motivation. Characterize so that the people will live in your story. Construct your plot carefully so that each incident moves naturally and suspensfully toward crisis and conclusion. *An element of conflict is necessary in fiction.* We do not accept fiction based on incidents in the Bible." Length: 1,200-1,600 words. Buys 120 mss/year. Pays 3¢/word for first serial rights; 2¢/word for second serial (reprint) rights.

Poetry: Traditional, free and blank verse. Length: 12-20 lines. "Please do not send large numbers of poems at one time." Pays 25¢/line.

Fillers: Brief and humorous, usually containing an anecdote, and always with a strong evangelical emphasis. Length: 200-600 words.

LIVING WITH TEENAGERS, Baptist Sunday School Board, 127 9th Ave. N., Nashville TN 37234. (615)251-2273. Editor: Jimmy Hester. 50-75% freelance written. Works with a number of new/unpublished writers each year. Quarterly magazine about teenagers for Baptist parents of teenagers. Estab. 1978. Circ. 50,000. Pays within 2 months of acceptance. Publishes ms an average of 18 months after acceptance. Buys all rights. Submit seasonal material 1 year in advance. Reports in 2 months. Sample copy for 9×12 SAE with 4 first class stamps; writer's guidelines for #10 SASE.

Nonfiction: "We are looking for a unique Christian element. We want a genuine insight into the teen/parent relationship." General interest (on communication, emotional problems, growing up, drugs and alcohol, leisure, sex education, spiritual growth, working teens and parents, money, family relationships and church relationships); inspirational; and personal experience. Buys 60 unsolicited mss/year. Query with clips of previously published work. Length: 600-2,000 words. Pays 5½¢/published word.

Fiction: Humorous and religious, but must relate to parent/teen relationship. "No stories from the teen's point of view." Buys 2 mss/issue. Query with clips of previously published work. Length: 600-2,000 words. Pays 5½¢/published word.

Poetry: Free verse, light verse, traditional and devotional inspirational; all must relate to parent/teen relationship. Buys 3 mss/issue. Submit 5 poems maximum. Length: 35 lines maximum. Pays $2.10 plus $1.25/line for 1-7 lines; $5.40 plus 75¢/line for 8 lines minimum.

Tips: "A writer can meet our needs if they have something to say to parents of teenagers concerning an issue the parents are confronting with the teenager."

THE LOOKOUT, 8121 Hamilton Ave., Cincinnati OH 45231. (513)931-4050. Editor: Simon J. Dahlman. 50-60% freelance written. Eager to work with new/unpublished writers. Weekly for adults and young adults attending Sunday schools and Christian churches. Estab. 1892. **Pays on acceptance.** Publishes ms an average of 5 months after acceptance. Byline given. Buys first serial rights, one-time rights, second serial (reprint) rights, or simultaneous rights. Simultaneous submissions OK. Reports in 2 months, sometimes longer. Sample copy and writer's guidelines 50¢. Guidelines only for #10 SASE.

Nonfiction: "Seeks stories about real people or Sunday school classes; items that are helpful in practical Christian living (how-to's); items that shed Biblical light on matters of contemporary controversy; and items that motivate, that lead the reader to ask, 'Why shouldn't I try that?' or 'Why couldn't our Sunday school class accomplish this?' Articles should tell how real people are involved for Christ. In choosing topics, *The Lookout* considers timeliness, the church and national calendar, and the ability of the material to fit the above guidelines. Tell us about ideas that are working in your Sunday school and in the lives of its members. Remember to aim at laymen." Submit complete ms. Length: 1,200-2,000 words. Pays 4-7¢/word. We also use inspirational short pieces. "About 600-800 words is a good length for these. Relate an incident that illustrates a point without preaching." Pays 4-6¢/word.

Fiction: "A short story is printed in many issues; it is usually between 1,200-1,800 words long and should be as true to life as possible while remaining inspirational and helpful. Use familiar settings and situations. Most often we use stories with a Christian slant." Pays 5-6¢/word.

Photos: Reviews b&w prints, 4×6 or larger. Pays $25-35. Pays $75-150 for color transparencies for covers and inside use. Needs photos of people, especially adults in a variety of settings. Send to Photo Editor, Standard Publishing, at the above address.

THE LUTHERAN, Magazine of the Evangelical Lutheran Church in America, Evangelical Lutheran Church in America, 8765 W. Higgins Rd., Chicago IL 60631. (312)380-2540. FAX: (312)380-1465. Editor: Edgar R. Trexler. Managing Editor: Roger R. Kahle. 30% freelance written. Biweekly magazine. "Audience is lay people in church. News and activities of the Evangelical Lutheran Church in America, news of the world of religion, ethical reflections on issues in society, personal Christian experience." Estab. 1988. Circ. 1.1 million. **Pays on acceptance.** Publishes ms an average of 3 months after acceptance. Byline given. Offers ½ kill fee. Buys first rights. Submit seasonal/holiday material 4 months in advance. Query for electronic submissions. Reports in 3 weeks on queries; 6 weeks on mss. Free sample copy and writer's guidelines.
Nonfiction: David L. Miller. Inspirational, interview/profile, personal experience, photo feature, religious. "No articles unrelated to the world of religion." Buys 40 mss/year. Query with published clips. Length: 300-2,000 words. Pays $400-1,000 for assigned articles; $50-400 for unsolicited articles. Pays expenses of writers on assignment.
Photos: Send photos with submission. Reviews contact sheets, transparencies and prints. Offers $10-50 per photo. Captions and identification of subjects required. Buys one-time rights.
Columns/Departments: Lite Side (humor—church, religious), 25-100 words. Send complete ms. Length: 25-100 words. Pays $5.
Tips: "Writers have the best chance selling us feature articles."

LUTHERAN FORUM, P.O. Box 327, Delhi NY 13753. (607)746-7511. Editor: Dr. Paul R. Hunlicky. Works with a small number of new/unpublished writers each year. Quarterly magazine. For church leadership, clerical and lay. Circ. 4,000. Pays on publication. Publishes ms an average of 6 months after acceptance. Byline given. Rights purchased vary with author and material; buys all rights, first North American serial rights, second serial (reprint) rights and simultaneous rights. Will consider simultaneous submissions. Reports in 9 weeks. Sample copy $1.50, SAE and 4 first class stamps; writer's guidelines for #10 SASE.
Nonfiction: Articles about important issues and developments in the church's institutional life and in its cultural/social setting. No purely devotional/inspirational material. Buys 2-3 mss/year. Query or submit complete ms. Length: 1,000-3,000 words. Informational, how-to, interview, profile, think articles and exposé. Length: 500-3,000 words.
Photos: Purchased with ms and only with captions. Prefers 4×5 prints. Pays $15 minimum.

‡THE LUTHERAN JOURNAL, 7317 Cahill Rd., Edina MN 55435. Editor: Rev. Armin U. Deye. Quarterly magazine. Family magazine for Lutheran Church members, middle age and older. Estab. 1936. Circ. 136,000. Pays on publication. Byline given. Will consider photocopied and simultaneous submissions. Reports in 2 months. Free sample copy.
Nonfiction: Inspirational, religious, human interest and historical articles. Interesting or unusual church projects. Informational, how-to, personal experience, interview, humor and think articles. Buys 25-30 mss/year. Submit complete ms. Length: 1,500 words maximum; occasionally 2,000 words. Pays 1-3¢/word.
Photos: B&w and color photos purchased with accompanying ms. Captions required. Payment varies.
Fiction: Mainstream, religious and historical fiction. Must be suitable for church distribution. Length: 2,000 words maximum. Pays 1-1½¢/word.
Poetry: Traditional poetry, blank verse and free verse, related to subject matter.

MENNONITE BRETHREN HERALD, 3-169 Riverton Ave., Winnipeg, Manitoba R2L 2E5 Canada. FAX: (204)654-1865. Contact: Editor. 25% freelance written. Family publication "read mainly by people of the Mennonite faith, reaching a wide cross section of professional and occupational groups, but also including many homemakers. Readership includes people from both urban and rural communities." Biweekly. Estab. 1962. Circ. 13,500. Pays on publication. Publishes ms an average of 4-6 months after acceptance. Not copyrighted. Byline given. Sample copy for $1 with 9×12 SAE and IRCs. Reports in 6 months.
Nonfiction: Articles with a Christian family orientation; youth directed, Christian faith and life, and current issues. Wants articles critiquing the values of a secular society, attempting to relate Christian living to the practical situations of daily living; showing how people have related their faith to their vocations. Length: 1,500 words. Pays $30-40. Pays the expenses of writers on assignment.
Photos: Photos purchased with mss; pays $5.

THE MESSENGER OF THE SACRED HEART, Apostleship of Prayer, 661 Greenwood Ave., Toronto, Ontario M4J 4B3 Canada. (416)466-1195. Editor: Rev. F.J. Power, S.J. For "Canadian and U.S. Catholics interested in developing a life of prayer and spirituality; stresses the great value of our ordinary actions and lives." 20% freelance written. Monthly. Estab. 1891. Circ. 17,500. Buys first rights only. Byline given. **Pays on acceptance.** Submit seasonal material 5 months in advance. Reports in 1 month. Sample copy $1 and 7½×10½ SAE; writer's guidelines for #10 SASE.

Fiction: Religious/inspirational. Stories about people, adventure, heroism, humor, drama. Buys 12 mss/year. Send complete ms with SAE and IRCs. Unsolicited manuscripts, unaccompanied by return postage, will not be returned. Length: 750-1,500 words. Pays 4¢ word.

Tips: "Develop a story that sustains interest to the end. Do not preach, but use plot and characters to convey the message or theme. Aim to move the heart as well as the mind. Before sending, cut out unnecessary or unrelated words or sentences. If you can, add a light touch or a sense of humor to the story. Your ending should have impact, leaving a moral or faith message for the reader."

‡**THE MIRACULOUS MEDAL**, 475 E. Chelten Ave., Philadelphia PA 19144. FAX: (215)848-1014. Editorial Director: Rev. Robert P. Cawley, C.M. 40% freelance written. Quarterly. **Pays on acceptance.** Publishes ms an average of 2 years after acceptance. Buys first North American serial rights. Buys articles only on special assignment. Sample copy for 6×9 SAE with 2 first class stamps.

Fiction: Should not be pious or sermon-like. Wants good general fiction—not necessarily religious, but if religion is basic to the story, the writer should be sure of his facts. Only restriction is that subject matter and treatment must not conflict with Catholic teaching and practice. Can use seasonal material; Christmas stories. Length: 2,000 words maximum. Occasionally uses short-shorts from 750-1,250 words. Pays 2¢/word minimum.

Poetry: Maximum of 20 lines, preferably about the Virgin Mary or at least with religious slant. Pays 50¢/line minimum.

MOODY MAGAZINE, (formerly *Moody Monthly*), Moody Bible Institute, 820 N. LaSalle Dr., Chicago IL 60610. (312)329-2163. FAX: (312)329-2144. Senior Editor: Andrew Scheer. 40% freelance written. A monthly magazine for evangelical Christianity. "Our readers are conservative, evangelical Christians highly active in their churches and concerned about family living." Estab. 1900. Circ. 160,000. **Pays on acceptance.** Publishes ms an average of 6-9 months after acceptance. Byline given. Offers $50 kill fee. Buys first North American serial rights. Submit seasonal/holiday material 9 months in advance. Query for electronic submissions. Reports in 1 month on queries; 2 months on mss. Sample copy for 10×13 SASE; writer's guidelines for #10 SASE.

Nonfiction: How-to (on living the Christian life), personal experience. Buys 60 mss/year. Query. Length: 750-2,000 words. Pays 10-15¢/word for assigned articles. Sometimes pays the expenses of writers on assignment.

Photos: State availability of photos with submission. Offers $35-50 per photo. Buys one-time rights.

Columns/Departments: First Person (the only article written for non-Christians; a personal conversion testimony written by the author [we will accept 'as told to's']; the objective is to tell a person's testimony in such a way that the reader will understand the gospel and want to receive Christ as Savior), 800-1,000 words; Just for Parents (provides practical anecdotal guidance for parents, solidly based on biblical principles), 1,300-1,500 words. Buys 30 mss/year. Query. Pays 10-15¢/word.

MY DAILY VISITOR, Our Sunday Visitor, Inc., 200 Noll Plaza, Huntington IN 46750. (219)356-8400. Editors: Catherine and William Odell. 99% freelance written. Bimonthly magazine on spirituality and scripture meditations. Circ. 30,000. **Pays on acceptance.** Publishes ms an average of 1 year after acceptance. Byline given. Not copyrighted. Buys one-time rights. Reports in 2 months. Sample copy and writer's guidelines for #10 SAE with 2 first class stamps. "Guest editors write on assignment basis only."

Nonfiction: Inspirational, personal experience, religious. Buys 12 mss/year. Query with published clips. Length: 150-160 words times number of days in month. Pays $200 for one month (28-31) of meditations. Sometimes pays writers 25 gratis copies.

NATIONAL CHRISTIAN REPORTER, Box 222198, Dallas TX 75222. (214)630-6495. Editor/Chief Executive: Spurgeon M. Dunnam III. Managing Editor: John A. Lovelace. 5% freelance written. Prefers to work with published/established writers. Weekly newspaper for an interdenominational national readership. Circ. 25,000. Pays on publication. Publishes ms an average of 1 month after acceptance. Byline given. Not copyrighted. Free sample copy and writer's guidelines.

ALWAYS submit unsolicited manuscripts or queries with a self-addressed, stamped envelope (SASE) within your country or a self-addressed envelope with International Reply Coupons (IRC) purchased from the post office for other countries.

Nonfiction: "We welcome short features, approximately 500 words. Articles need to have an explicit 'mainstream' Protestant angle. Write about a distinctly Christian response to human need or how a person's faith relates to a given situation. Include evidence of participation in a local Protestant congregation." Send complete ms. Pays 4¢/word. Sometimes pays the expenses of writers on assignment.

Photos: Purchased with accompanying ms. "We encourage the submission of good action photos (5×7 or 8×10 b&w glossy prints) of the persons or situations in the article." Pays $10.

Poetry: "Good poetry welcomed on a religious theme." Length: 4-20 lines. Pays $2.

OBLATES, Missionary Association of Mary Immaculate, 15 S. 59th St., Belleville IL 62223-4694. (618)233-2238. Managing Editor: Jacqueline Lowery Corn. 30-50% freelance written. Prefers to work with published writers but will work with new/unpublished writers. Bimonthly inspirational magazine for Christians; audience mainly older adults. Circ. 750,000. **Pays on acceptance.** Usually publishes ms within 2 years after acceptance. Byline given. Buys first North American serial rights. Submit seasonal/holiday material 8 months in advance. Reports in 2 months. Sample copy and writer's guidelines for 6×9 or larger SAE with 52¢ in postage.

Nonfiction: Inspirational and personal experience with positive spiritual insights. No preachy, theological or research articles. Avoid current events and controversial topics. Send complete ms. Length: 500 words. Pays $75.

Poetry: Light verse — reverent, well written, perceptive, with traditional rhythym and rhyme. "Emphasis should be on inspiration, insight and relationship with God." Submit maximum 2 poems. Length: 8-16 lines. Pays $25.

Tips: "Our readership is made up mostly of mature Americans who are looking for comfort, encouragement, and a positive sense of applicable Christian direction to their lives. Focus on sharing of personal insight to problem (i.e. death or change), but must be positive, uplifting. We have well-defined needs for an established market, but are always on the lookout for exceptional work."

THE OTHER SIDE, 300 W. Apsley St., Philadelphia PA 19144-4221. Editor: Mark Olson. Associate Editor: Dee Dee Risher. 50% freelance written. Prefers to work with published/established writers; works with a small number of new/unpublished writers each year. Magazine published bimonthly, focusing on "peace, justice and economic liberation from a radical Christian perspective." Circ. 15,000. **Pays on acceptance.** Publishes ms an average of 1-6 months after acceptance. Byline given. Buys all or first serial rights. Query for electronic submissions. Reports in 6 weeks. Sample copy $4.50; free writer's guidelines with #10 SASE.

Nonfiction: Doug Davidson, assistant editor. Current social, political and economic issues in the U.S. and around the world: personality profiles, interpretative essays, interviews, how-to's, personal experiences and investigative reporting. "Articles must be lively, vivid and down-to-earth, with a radical Christian perspective." Length: 500-6,000 words. Pays $25-300. Sometimes pays expenses of writers on assignment.

Photos: Cathleen Boint, art director. Photos or photo essays illustrating current social, political, or economic reality in the U.S. and Third World. Pays $15-75 for b&w and $50-300 for color.

Fiction: Barbara Moorman, fiction editor. "Short stories, humor and satire conveying insights and situations that will be helpful to Christians with a radical commitment to peace and justice." Length: 300-4,000 words. Pays $25-250.

Poetry: Rod Jellema, poetry editor. "Short, creative poetry that will be thought-provoking and appealing to radical Christians who have a strong commitment to spirituality, peace and justice." Length: 3-50 lines. No more than 4 poems may be submitted at one time by any one author. Pays $15-20.

Tips: "We're looking for tightly written pieces (1,000-1,500 words) on interesting and unusual Christians (or Christian groups) who are putting their commitment to peace and social justice into action in creative and useful ways. We're also looking for provocative analytical and reflective pieces (1,000-4,000 words) dealing with contemporary social issues in the U.S. and abroad."

OUR FAMILY, Oblate Fathers of St. Mary's Province, P.O. Box 249, Battleford, Saskatchewan S0M 0E0 Canada. (306)937-7771. FAX: (306)937-7644. Editor: Nestor Gregoire. 60% freelance written. Prefers to work with published/established writers; works with a small number of new/unpublished writers each year. Monthly magazine for average family men and women with high school and early college education. Estab. 1949. Circ. 14,265. **Pays on acceptance.** Publishes ms an average of 6 months after acceptance. Byline given. Offers 100% kill fee. Generally purchases first North American serial rights; also buys all rights, simultaneous rights, second serial (reprint) rights or one-time rights. Submit seasonal/holiday material 4 months in advance. Simultaneous and previously published submissions OK. Reports in 1 month. Sample copy $2.50 in postage and 9×12 SAE; writer's guidelines for #10 SAE and 46¢ (Canadian funds). U.S. postage cannot be used in Canada.

Nonfiction: Humor (related to family life or husband/wife relations); inspirational (anything that depicts people responding to adverse conditions with courage, hope and love); personal experience (with religious dimensions); and photo feature (particularly in search of photo essays on human/religious themes and on persons whose lives are an inspiration to others). Phone queries OK. Buys 72-88 unsolicited mss/year. Pays expenses of writers on assignment.

Photos: Photos purchased with or without accompanying ms. Pays $35 for 5×7 or larger b&w glossy prints and color photos (which are converted into b&w). Offers additional payment for photos accepted with ms (payment for these photos varies according to their quality). Free photo spec sheet with SASE.

Poetry: Avant-garde, free verse, haiku, light verse and traditional. Buys 4-10 poems/issue. Length: 3-30 lines. Pays 75¢-$1/line. Must have a religious dimension.

Fillers: Jokes, gags, anecdotes and short humor. Buys 2-10/issue.

Tips: "Writers should ask themselves whether this is the kind of an article, poem, etc. that a busy housewife would pick up and read when she has a few moments of leisure. We are particularly looking for articles on the spirituality of marriage. We will be concentrating more on recent movements and developments in the church to help make people aware of the new church of which they are a part."

OUR SUNDAY VISITOR MAGAZINE, Our Sunday Visitor, Inc., Noll Plaza, Huntington IN 46750. (219)356-8400. Publisher: Robert P. Lockwood. Editor: Gregory R. Erlandson. 5% freelance written. Works with small number of new/unpublished writers each year. Weekly magazine for general Catholic audience. Circ. 160,000. **Pays on acceptance.** Publishes ms an average of 2 months after acceptance. Byline given. Submit seasonal material 2 months in advance. Query for electronic submissions. Reports in 3 weeks. Free sample copy with SASE.

Nonfiction: Uses articles on Catholic-related subjects. Should explain Catholic religious beliefs in articles of human interest; articles applying Catholic principles to current problems, Catholic profiles, etc. Payment varies depending on reputation of author, quality of work, and amount of research required. Buys 25 mss/year. Query. Length: 1,000-1,200 words. Minimum payment for features is $100. Pays expenses of writers on assignment.

Photos: Purchased with mss; with captions only. Reviews b&w glossy prints and transparencies. Pays minimum of $200/cover photo story; $125/b&w story; $25/color photo; $10/b&w photo.

PARISH FAMILY DIGEST, Our Sunday Visitor, Inc., 200 Noll Plaza, Huntington IN 46750. (219)356-8400. Editor: Corine B. Erlandson. 100% freelance written. Works with small number of new/unpublished writers each year. Bimonthly magazine. "*Parish Family Digest* is geared to the Catholic family and to that family as a unit of the parish." Circ. 150,000. **Pays on acceptance.** Publishes ms an average of 6 months-1 year after acceptance. Byline given. Buys first North American rights. Submit seasonal/holiday material 6 months in advance. Reports in 3 weeks on queries and on mss. Sample copy and writer's guidelines for 6½×9½ SAE and 2 first class stamps.

Nonfiction: General interest, historical, inspirational, nostalgia (if related to overall parish involvement) and profile. Send complete ms. Buys 60 unsolicited mss/year. Length: 750-1,000 words maximum. Pays 5¢/word.

Photos: State availability of photos with ms. Pays $10 for 3×5 b&w prints. Buys one-time rights. Captions preferred; model releases required.

Fillers: Anecdotes and short humor. Buys 3/issue. Length: 100 words maximum.

Tips: "If an article does not deal with some angle of Catholic family life, the writer is wasting time in sending it to us. We rarely use reprints; we prefer fresh material that will hold up over time and is not tied to an event in the news. We are more oriented to families with kids and the problems such families face in the Church and society, in particular, the struggle to raise good Catholic kids in a secular society. Articles on how to overcome these, and other family problems will be welcomed."

PENTECOSTAL EVANGEL, The General Council of the Assemblies of God, 1445 Boonville, Springfield MO 65802. (417)862-2781. FAX: (417)862-8558. Editor: Richard G. Champion. 33% freelance written. Works with a small number of new/unpublished writers each year. Weekly magazine. Emphasizes news of the Assemblies of God for members of the Assemblies and other Pentecostal and charismatic Christians. Estab. 1913. Circ. 280,000. **Pays on acceptance.** Publishes ms an average of 4-6 months after acceptance. Byline given. Buys first serial rights, a few second serial (reprint) rights or one-time rights. Submit seasonal/holiday material 6 months in advance. Reports in 3 months. Free sample copy and writer's guidelines.

Nonfiction: Informational (articles on homelife that convey Christian teachings); inspirational; and personal experience. Buys 5 mss/issue. Send complete ms. Length: 500-1,500 words. Pays 6¢/word maximum. Sometimes pays the expenses of writers on assignment.

Photos: Photos purchased without accompanying ms. Pays $7.50-15 for 8 × 10 b&w glossy prints; $10-35 for 35mm or larger transparencies. Total purchase price for ms includes payment for photos.
Poetry: Religious and inspirational. Buys 1 poem/issue. Submit maximum 6 poems. Pays 20-40¢/line.
Tips: "Break in by writing up a personal experience. We publish first-person articles concerning spiritual experiences; that is, answers to prayer for help in a particular situation, of unusual conversions or healings through faith in Christ. All articles submitted to us should be related to religious life. We are Protestant, evangelical, Pentecostal, and any doctrines or practices portrayed should be in harmony with the official position of our denomination (Assemblies of God)."

‡**THE PENTECOSTAL MESSENGER**, Messenger Publishing House, 4901 Pennsylvania, P.O. Box 850, Joplin MO 64802. (417)624-7050. FAX: (417)624-7102. Editor: Don Allen. Managing Editor: Peggy Lee Allen. 25% freelance written. Works with small number of new/unpublished writers each year. Monthly (excluding July) magazine covering Pentecostal Christianity. "*The Pentecostal Messenger* is the official organ of the Pentecostal Church of God. Goes to ministers and church members." Estab. 1919. Circ. 8,000. Pays on publication. Publishes ms an average of 6 months after acceptance. Byline given. Buys second serial (reprint) rights or simultaneous rights. Submit seasonal/holiday material 4 months in advance. Simultaneous and previously published submissions OK. Reports in 4 weeks on mss. Sample copy for 9 × 12 SAE and 4 first class stamps; free writer's guidelines.
Nonfiction: Inspirational, personal experience and religious. Buys 35 mss/year. Send complete ms. Length: 1,800 words. Pays 1½¢/word.
Photos: Send photos with submission. Reviews 2¼ × 2¼ transparencies and prints. Offers $10-25 per photo. Captions and model releases required. Buys one-time rights.
Tips: "Articles need to be inspirational, informative, written from a positive viewpoint, not extremely controversial."

PIME WORLD, (formerly *Catholic Life*), 35750 Moravian Dr., Fraser MI 48026. FAX: (313)791-8204. Editor-in-Chief: Fr. John J. Majka, PIME. 10% freelance written. Monthly (except July or August) magazine. Emphasizes foreign missionary activities of the Catholic Church in Burma, India, Bangladesh, the Philippines, Hong Kong, Africa, etc., for an adult audience, interested in current issues in the missions. Audience is largely high school educated (on the average), conservative in both religion and politics. Estab. 1954. Circ. 25,200. Pays on publication. Publishes ms an average of 3 months after acceptance. Buys all rights. Byline given. Submit seasonal/holiday material 4 months in advance. Simultaneous submissions OK. Reports in 2 weeks.
Nonfiction: Informational and inspirational foreign missionary activities of the Catholic Church. Buys 5-10 unsolicited mss/year. Query or send complete ms. Length: 1,000-3,000 words. Pays 5¢/word; $5 per color photo.
Tips: Submit articles dealing with current issues of social justice, evangelization and pastoral work in Third World countries. Interviews of missionaries accepted. Good quality color photos greatly appreciated.

PRAIRIE MESSENGER, Catholic Weekly, Benedictine Monks of St. Peter's Abbey, P.O. Box 190, Muenster, Saskatchewan S0K 2Y0 Canada. (306)682-5215. FAX: (306)682-5285. Editor-in-Chief: Andrew Britz. Editor: Art Babych. Associate Editors: Emily Greter and Marian Noll. 10% freelance written. A weekly Catholic journal with strong emphasis on social justice, Third World and ecumenism. Estab. 1905. Circ. 11,000. Pays on publication. Publishes ms an average of 2-3 months after acceptance. Byline given. Offers 70% kill fee. Not copyrighted. Buys first North American serial rights, first rights, one-time rights, second serial (reprint) rights or simultaneous rights. Submit seasonal/holiday material 3 months in advance. Query for electronic submissions. Sample copy for 9 × 12 SAE with 80¢ Canadian postage; writers guidelines for 9 × 12 SAE with 80¢ first class Canadian stamps.
Nonfiction: Interview/profile, opinion, and religious. "No articles on abortion or homosexuality." Buys 30 mss/year. Send complete ms. Length: 250-600 words. Pays $40-60. Sometimes pays expenses of writers on assignment.
Photos: Send photos with submission. Reviews 3 × 5 prints. Offers $10/photo. Captions required. Buys all rights.

PRESBYTERIAN RECORD, 50 Wynford Dr., Don Mills, Ontario M3C 1J7 Canada. (416)444-1111. FAX: (416)441-2825. 50% freelance written. Eager to work with new/unpublished writers. Monthly magazine for a church-oriented, family audience. Circ. 68,000. Buys 35 mss/year. Pays on publication. Publishes ms an average of 4 months after acceptance. Buys first serial rights, one-time rights, simultaneous rights. Submit seasonal material 3 months in advance. Reports on ms accepted for publication in 2 months. Returns rejected material in 3 months. Sample copy and writer's guidelines for 9 × 12 SAE with $1 Canadian postage or IRCs.

Nonfiction: Material on religious themes. Check a copy of the magazine for style. Also, personal experience, interview, and inspirational material. No material solely or mainly American in context. When possible, black-and-white photos should accompany manuscript; i.e., current events, historical events and biographies. Buys 15-20 unsolicited mss/year. Query. Length: 1,000-2,000 words. Pays $45-55 (Canadian funds). Sometimes pays expenses of writers on assignment.

Photos: Pays $15-20 for b&w glossy photos. Uses positive transparencies for cover. Pays $50. Captions required.

Tips: "There is a trend away from maudlin, first-person pieces redolent with tragedy and dripping with simplistic pietistic conclusions."

PRESBYTERIAN SURVEY, Presbyterian Publishing House, Inc., 100 Witherspoon St., Louisville KY 40202-1396. (502)569-5079. Editor: Vic Jameson. Managing Editor: Catherine Cottingham. 65% freelance written. Prefers to work with published/established writers; works with a small number of new/unpublished writers each year; willing to work with new/unpublished writers. Denominational magazine published 10 times/year covering religion, denominational activities and public issues for members of the Presbyterian Church (U.S.A.). **Pays on acceptance.** Publishes ms an average of 9 months after acceptance. Byline given. Offers variable kill fee. Buys first North American serial rights. Submit seasonal/holiday material 8 months in advance. Simultaneous submissions OK. Reports in 2 weeks on queries; 1 month on mss. Sample copy and writer's guidelines for 10×13 SAE and $1.

Nonfiction: Inspirational and Presbyterian programs, issues, people; any subject from a Christian viewpoint. No secular subjects. Buys 30 mss/year. Send complete ms. Length: 800-1,500 words. Pays $50-200.

Photos: State availability of photos. Reviews color transparencies and 8×10 b&w prints. Pays $15-25 for b&w; $25-50 for color. Identification of subjects required. Buys one-time rights.

Columns/Departments: "The only column not by a regular columnist is an op ed page for readers of the magazine (As I See It)." Accepts 10 mss/year. Send complete ms. Length: 600-750 words. No payment.

PURPOSE, 616 Walnut Ave., Scottdale PA 15683-1999. (412)887-8500. Editor: James E. Horsch. 95% freelance written. Weekly magazine "for adults, young and old, general audience with interests as varied as there are people. My readership is interested in seeing how Christianity works in difficult situations." Estab. 1908. Circ. 18,225. **Pays on acceptance.** Publishes ms an average of 8 months after acceptance. Byline given. Buys one-time rights. Submit seasonal material 6 months in advance. Simultaneous submissions OK. Submit complete ms. Reports in 2 months. Free sample copy and writer's guidelines for 6×9 SAE with 2 first class stamps.

Nonfiction: Inspirational articles from a Christian perspective. "I want stories that go to the core of human problems in family, business, politics, religion, gender and any other areas — and show how the Christian faith resolves them. I want material that's upbeat. *Purpose* is a magazine which conveys truth either through quality fiction or through articles that use the best story techniques. Our magazine accents Christian discipleship. Christianity affects all of life, and we expect our material to demonstrate this. I would like to see story-type articles about individuals, groups and organizations who are intelligently and effectively working at some of the great human problems such as overpopulation, hunger, poverty, international understanding, peace, justice, etc., because of their faith." Buys 175-200 mss/year. Submit complete ms. Length: 900 words maximum. Pays 5¢/word maximum. Buys one-time rights only.

Photos: Photos purchased with ms. Pays $5-25 for b&w (less for color), depending on quality. Must be sharp enough for reproduction; requires prints in all cases. Can use color prints. Captions desired.

Fiction: Humorous, religious and historical fiction related to discipleship theme. "Produce the story with specificity so that it appears to take place somewhere and with real people. It should not be moralistic."

Poetry: Traditional poetry, blank verse, free verse and light verse. Length: 12 lines maximum. Pays $5-15 per poem depending on length and quality. Buys one-time rights only.

Fillers: Anecdotal items from 200-600 words. Pays 4¢/word maximum.

Tips: "We are looking for articles which show the Christian faith working at issues where people hurt; stories need to be told and presented professionally. Good photographs help place material with us."

QUEEN OF ALL HEARTS, Montfort Missionaries, 26 S. Saxon Ave., Bay Shore NY 11706. (516)665-0726. Managing Editor: Roger Charest, S.M.M. 50% freelance written. Bimonthly magazine covering Marian doctrine and devotion. "Subject: Mary, Mother of Jesus, as seen in the sacred scriptures, tradition, history of the church, the early Christian writers, lives of the saints, poetry, art, music, spiritual writers, apparitions, shrines, ecumenism, etc." Estab. 1950. Circ. approx 6,000. **Pays on acceptance.** Publishes ms an average of 6 months after acceptance. Byline given. Not copyrighted. Submit seasonal/holiday material 6 months in advance. Reports in 6 weeks. Sample copy $2.50

Nonfiction: Essays, inspirational, personal experience and religious. Buys 25 ms/year. Send complete ms. Length: 750-2,500 words. Pays $40-60. Sometimes pays writers in contributor copies or other premiums "by mutual agreement. Poetry paid by contributor copies."

Photos: Send photos with submission. Reviews transparencies and prints. Offers variable payment per photo. Buys one-time rights.

Fiction: Religious. Buys 6 mss/year. Send complete ms. Length: 1,500-2,500 words. Pays $40-60.

Poetry: Joseph Tusiani, poetry editor. Free verse. Buys approximately 10 poems/year. Submit 2 poems maximum at one time. Pays in contributor copies.

REFORM JUDAISM, Union of American Hebrew Congregations, 838 5th Ave., New York NY 10021. (212)249-0100. Editor: Aron Hirt-Manheimer. Managing Editor: Joy Weinberg. 20% freelance written. Quarterly magazine of Reform Jewish issues. "*Reform Judaism* is the official voice of the Union of American Hebrew Congregations, linking the institutions and affiliates of Reform Judaism with every Reform Jew. RJ covers developments within the Movement while interpreting events and Jewish tradition from a Reform perspective." Pays on publication. Publishes ms an average of 3 months after acceptance. Byline given. Offers negotiable kill fee. Buys first North American serial rights. Submit seasonal/holiday material 3 months in advance. Photocopied and previously published submissions OK. Reports in 2 weeks on queries; 3 weeks on mss. Sample copy $2.50.

Nonfiction: Book excerpt (reviews), expose, general interest, historical/nostalgic, inspirational, interview/profile, opinion, personal experience, photo feature and travel. Buys 60 mss/year. Submit complete ms. Length: 600-1800 words. Pays 10¢/word. Sometimes pays expenses of writers on assignment.

Photos: Send photos with ms. Prefers 8×10/color and b&w prints. Pays $25-75. Identification of subjects required. Buys one-time rights.

Fiction: Ethnic, humorous, mainstream and religious. Buys 4 mss/year. Send complete ms. Length: 600-1800 words. Pays 10¢/word.

THE REPORTER, (formerly *ORT Reporter*), Women's American ORT, Inc., 315 Park Ave. So., New York NY 10010. (212)505-7700. Editor: Eve Jacobson. 85% freelance written. Nonprofit journal published by Jewish women's organization. Quarterly magazine covering "Jewish topics, social issues, education, Mideast and women." Estab. 1966. Circ. 112,000. Payment time varies. Publishes ms ASAP after acceptance. Byline given. Buys first North American serial rights. Submit seasonal/holiday material 6 months in advance. Reports "as soon as possible." Free sample copy with 9×12 SASE.

Nonfiction: Book excerpts, essays, general interest, humor, opinion. Buys approximately 40 mss/year. Send complete ms. Length: 500-3,000. Pays varies.

Photos: Send photos with submission. Reviews 5×7 prints. Offers $35-85 per photo. Identification of subjects required. Purchases "whatever rights photographer desires."

Columns/Departments: Books, Film, Stage, TV. Buys 4-10 mss/year. Send complete ms. Length: 200-2,000 words. Pay varies.

Fiction: Jewish novel excerpts. Buys 2 ms/year. Send complete ms. Pays 15¢/word, less for reprints.

Tips: "Simply send ms; do not call. First submission must be 'on spec.' Open Forum (opinion section) is most open to freelancers, although all are open. Looking for well-written essay on relevant topic that makes its point strongly – evokes response from reader."

REVIEW FOR RELIGIOUS, 3601 Lindell Blvd., Room 428, St. Louis MO 63108. (314)535-3048. Editor: David L. Fleming, S.J. 100% freelance written. "Each ms is judged on its own merits, without reference to author's publishing history." Bimonthly. For Roman Catholic priests, brothers and sisters. Estab. 1942. Pays on publication. Publishes ms an average of 9 months after acceptance. Byline given. Buys first North American serial rights and rarely second serial (reprint) rights. Reports in 2 months.

Nonfiction: Articles on ascetical, liturgical and canonical matters only; not for general audience. Length: 2,000-8,000 words. Pays $6/page.

Tips: "The writer must know about religious life in the Catholic Church and be familiar with prayer, vows and problems related to them."

ST. ANTHONY MESSENGER, 1615 Republic St., Cincinnati OH 45210. Editor-in-Chief: Norman Perry. 55% freelance written. "Willing to work with new/unpublished writers if their writing is of a professional caliber." Monthly magazine for a national readership of Catholic families, most of which have children in grade school, high school or college. Circ. 370,000. **Pays on acceptance.** Publishes ms an average of 9 months after acceptance. Byline given. Buys first North American serial rights. Submit seasonal/holiday material 6 months in advance. Query for electronic submissions. Sample copy and writer's guidelines for 9×12 SASE.

Nonfiction: How-to (on psychological and spiritual growth, problems of parenting/better parenting, marriage problems/marriage enrichment); humor; informational; inspirational; interview; personal experience (if pertinent to our purpose); personal opinion (limited use; writer must have special qualifications for topic); and profile. Buys 35-50 mss/year. Length: 1,500-3,500 words. Pays 14¢/word. Sometimes pays the expenses of writers on assignment.

Fiction: Mainstream and religious. Buys 12 mss/year. Submit complete ms. Length: 2,000-3,500 words. Pays 14¢/word.

Tips: "The freelancer should ask why his or her proposed article would be appropriate for us, rather than for *Redbook* or *Saturday Review*. We treat human problems of all kinds, but from a religious perspective. Get authoritative information (not merely library research); we want interviews with experts. Write in popular style. Word length is an important consideration."

ST. JOSEPH'S MESSENGER & ADVOCATE OF THE BLIND, Sisters of St. Joseph of Peace, St. Joseph's Home, P.O. Box 288, Jersey City NJ 07303. Editor-in-Chief: Sister Ursula Maphet. 30% freelance written. Eager to work with new/unpublished writers. Quarterly magazine. Estab. 1898. Circ. 25,000. **Pays on acceptance.** Publishes ms an average of 3 months after acceptance. Buys first serial rights and second serial (reprint) rights, but will reassign rights back to author after publication asking only that credit line be included in next publication. Submit seasonal/holiday material 3 months in advance (no Christmas issue). Simultaneous and previously published submissions OK. Reports in 3 weeks. Sample copy and writer's guidelines 8½ × 11 SAE with 45¢ postage.

Nonfiction: Humor, inspirational, nostalgia, personal opinion and personal experience. Buys 24 mss/year. Submit complete ms. Length: 300-1,500 words. Pays $3-15.

Fiction: Romance, suspense, mainstream and religious. Buys 30 mss/year. Submit complete ms. Length: 600-1,600 words. Pays $6-25.

Poetry: Light verse and traditional. Buys 25 poems/year. Submit maximum 10 poems. Length: 50-300 words. Pays $5-20.

Tips: "It's rewarding to know that someone is waiting to see freelancers' efforts rewarded by 'print'. It's annoying, however, to receive poor copy, shallow material or inane submissions. Human interest fiction, touching on current happenings, is what is most needed. We look for social issues — woven into story form. We also seek non-preaching articles that carry a message that is positive."

SCP JOURNAL AND SCP Newsletter, Spiritual Counterfeits Project, P.O. Box 4308, Berkeley CA 94704. (415)540-0300. Editors: Cal Brooke and Brooks Alexander. 5% freelance written. Prefers to work with published/established writers. "The *SCP Journal* and *SCP Newsletter* are occasional publications that analyze new religious movements and spiritual trends from a Christian perspective. Their targeted audience is the educated lay person." Estab. 1975. Circ. 16,500. Pays on publication. Publishes ms an average of 6 months after acceptance. Byline given. Simultaneous and previously published submissions OK. Sample copy for 8½ × 11 SAE and 4 first class stamps.

Nonfiction: Book excerpts, essays, exposé, interview/profile, opinion, personal experience and religious. Buys 10 mss/year. Query with published clips. Length: 2,500-3,500 words. Pays $20-35/typeset page.

Photos: State availability of photos with submission. Reviews contact sheets and prints. Offers no additional payment for photos accepted with ms. Captions, model releases and identification of subjects required. Buys one-time rights.

Tips: "The area of our publication most open to freelancers is reviews of books relevant to subjects covered by *SCP*. These should not exceed 6 typewritten, double-spaced pages, 1,500 words. Send samples of work that are relevant to the *SCP's* area of interest."

‡SEEK, Standard Publishing, 8121 Hamilton Ave., Cincinnati OH 45231. (513)931-4050, ext. 365. Editor: Eileen H. Wilmoth. 98% freelance written. Prefers to work with published/established writers; works with a small number of new/unpublished writers each year. Sunday school paper. Quarterly, in weekly issues for young and middle-aged adults who attend church and Bible classes. Circ. 45,000. **Pays on acceptance.** Publishes ms an average of 1 year after acceptance. Byline given. Buys first serial rights and second serial (reprint) rights. Buys 150-200 mss/year. Submit seasonal material 1 year in advance. Reports in 6 weeks. Sample copy and writer's guidelines for 6 × 9 SAE and 2 first class stamps.

Nonfiction: "We look for articles that are warm, inspirational, devotional, of personal or human interest; that deal with controversial matters, timely issues of religious, ethical or moral nature, or first-person testimonies, true-to-life happenings, vignettes, emotional situations or problems; communication problems and examples of answered prayers. Article must deliver its point in a convincing manner but not be patronizing or preachy. It must appeal to either men or women, must be alive, vibrant, sparkling and have a title that demands the article be read. We always need stories about families, marriages, problems on campus and life testimonies." No poetry. Buys 150-200 mss/year. Submit complete ms. Length: 400-1,200 words. Pays 3¢/word.

Photos: B&w photos purchased with or without mss. Pays $20 minimum for good 8 × 10 glossy prints.
Fiction: Religious fiction and religiously slanted historical and humorous fiction. Length: 400-1,200 words. Pays 3¢/word.
Tips: Submit mss which tell of faith in action or victorious Christian living as central theme. "We select manuscripts as far as one year in advance of publication. Complimentary copies are sent to our published writers immediately following printing."

SHARING THE VICTORY, Fellowship of Christian Athletes, 8701 Leeds Rd., Kansas City MO 64129. (816)921-0909. FAX: (816)921-8755. Editor: John Dodderidge. Assistant Editor: Dana J. King. Managing Editor: Don Hilkemeier. 60% freelance written. Prefers to work with published/established writers, but works with a growing number of new/unpublished writers each year. A bimonthly magazine. "We seek to encourage and enable athletes and coaches at all levels to take their faith seriously on and off the 'field.' " Estab. 1959. Circ. 50,000. Pays on publication. Publishes ms an average of 4 months after acceptance. Byline given. Buys first rights. Submit seasonal/holiday material 3 months in advance. Reports in 1 week on queries; 2 weeks on manuscripts. Sample copy $1 with 9 × 12 SAE and 3 first class stamps; free writer's guidelines for #10 SASE.
Nonfiction: Humor, inspirational, interview/profile (with "name" athletes and coaches solid in their faith), personal experience, and photo feature. No "sappy articles on 'I became a Christian and now I'm a winner.' " Buys 5-20 mss/year. Query. Length: 500-1,000 words. Pays $100-200 for unsolicited articles, more for the exceptional profile.
Photos: State availability of photos with submission. Reviews contact sheets. Pay depends on quality of photo but usually a minimum $100. Model releases required for "name" individuals. Buys one-time rights.
Poetry: Free verse. Buys 3 poems/year. Pays $50.
Tips: "Profiles and interviews of particular interest to coed athlete, primarily high school and college age. Our graphics and editorial content appeal to youth. The area most open to freelancers is profiles on or interviews with well-known athletes or coaches (male, female, minorities); and offbeat but interscholastic team sports."

‡**SIGNS OF THE TIMES,** Pacific Press Publishing Association, Box 7000, Boise ID 83707. (208)465-2500. FAX: (208)465-2531. Editor: Kenneth J. Holland. Managing Editor: B. Russell Holt. 40% freelance written. Works with a small number of new/unpublished writers each year. Monthly magazine on religion. "We are a Christian publication encouraging the general public to put into practice the principles of the Bible." Establ 1874. Circ. 400,000. **Pays on acceptance.** Publishes ms an average of 5 months after acceptance. Byline given. Offers $100 kill fee. Buys first North American serial rights and simultaneous rights. Submit seasonal/holiday material 8 months in advance. Simultaneous queries and submissions, and previously published submissions OK. Reports in 2 weeks on queries; 1 month on mss. Free sample copy and writer's guidelines.
Nonfiction: General interest (home, marriage, health—interpret current events from a Biblical perspective); how-to (overcome depression, find one's identity, answer loneliness and guilt, face death triumphantly); humor; inspirational (human interest pieces that highlight a Biblical principle); interview/profile; personal experience (overcome problems with God's help); and photo feature. "We want writers with a desire to share the good news of reconciliation with God. Articles should be people-oriented, well-researched and should have a sharp focus and include anecdotes." Buys 150 mss/year. Query with or without published clips, or send complete ms. Length: 500-3,000 words. Pays $100-400. Sometimes pays the expenses of writers on assignment.
Photos: Ed Guthero, photo editor. Send photos with query or ms. Reviews b&w contact sheets; 35mm color transparencies; 5 × 7 or 8 × 10 b&w prints. Pays $35-300 for transparencies; $20-50 for prints. Model releases and identification of subjects required (captions helpful). Buys one-time rights.
Tips: "One of the most frequent mistakes made by writers in completing an article assignment for us is trying to cover too much ground. Articles need focus, research and anecdotes. We don't want essays."

SISTERS TODAY, The Liturgical Press, St. John's Abbey, Collegeville MN 56321. Editor-in-Chief: Sister Mary Anthony Wagner, O.S.B. Associate Editor: Sister Mary Elizabeth Mason, O.S.B. Review Editor: Sister Stefanie Weisgram, O.S.B. 80% freelance written. Prefers to work with published/established writers; works with a small number of new/unpublished writers each year. Magazine, beginning with January 1990, will be published bimonthly, exploring the role of women and the Church, primarily. Circ. 8,000. Pays on publication. Publishes ms 1-2 years after acceptance. Byline given. Buys first rights. Submit seasonal/holiday material 4 months in advance. Reports in 3 months. Sample copy $2.

Nonfiction: How-to (pray, live in a religious community, exercise faith, hope, charity etc.); informational; and inspirational. Also articles concerning religious renewal, community life, worship, and the role of sisters in the Church and in the world today. Buys 50-60 unsolicited mss/year. Query. Length: 500-2,500 words. Pays $5/printed page.
Poetry: Free verse, haiku, light verse and traditional. Buys 3 poems/issue. Submit maximum 4 poems. Pays $10.
Tips: "Some of the freelance material evidences the lack of familiarity with *Sisters Today*. We would prefer submitted articles not to exceed eight or nine pages."

SOCIAL JUSTICE REVIEW, 3835 Westminister Place, St. Louis MO 63108. (314)371-1653. Contact: Rev. John H. Miller, C.S.C. 25% freelance written. Works with a small number of new/unpublished writers each year. Bimonthly. Estab. 1908. Publishes ms an average of 6-12 months after acceptance. Not copyrighted; "however special articles within the magazine may be copyrighted, or an occasional special issue has been copyrighted due to author's request." Buys first serial rights.
Nonfiction: Wants scholarly articles on society's economic, religious, social, intellectual and political problems with the aim of bringing Catholic social thinking to bear upon these problems. Query w/ SASE. Length: 2,500-3,500 words. Pays about 2¢/word.

‡SOUTH TEXAS CATHOLIC, Bishop Rene H. Gracida/Catholic Diocese of Corpus Christi, 1200 Lantana, Corpus Christi TX 78407. (512)289-6501. Editor: Rachelle Ramon. 10% freelance written. Weekly tabloid covering news and features about the Catholic Church. "The South Texas Catholic is the official publication of the Catholic Church in South Texas. We run local, national and international news as well as features and columns." Estab. 1966. Circ. 31,000. Pays on publication. Byline given. Offers no kill fee. Not copyrighted. Buys simultaneous rights. Submit seasonal/holiday material 1 month in advance. Simultaneous and previously published submissions OK. Query for electronic submissions. Reports in 2 weeks on queries; 1 month on mss. Free sample copy.
Nonfiction: Inspirational, interview/profile, personal experience, religious. "No non-religious or non-inspirational. The material in our newspaper should have a message of hope for our readers about the world they live in." Buys 10 mss/year. Query with or without published clips, or send complete ms. Length: 800 words. Pays $25-100 for assigned articles; $25-70 for unsolicited articles. Sometimes pays expenses of writers on assignment.
Photos: State availability of photos with submission. Offers $10 per photo. Captions and identification of subjects required. Buys all rights.
Columns/Departments: Book reviews (books of interest to Catholic readers), 600; Christian family life, 600; Humorous anecdotes about life in a Catholic parish, 600. Buys 15 mss/year. Query. Length: 600 words. Pays $25-70.
Fiction: Religious. Buys 5 mss/year. Query. Length: 800 words. Pays $70.
Tips: "As mentioned previously, a writer must have a working knowledge of (and obviously what would be beneficial is a love of) the Catholic Church. General columns or stories about strong morals and values (such as family values) are also acceptable."

SPIRIT, Lectionary-based Weekly for Catholic Teens, Editorial Development Associates, 1884 Randolph Ave., St. Paul MN 55434. (612)690-7005. Editor: Joan Mitchell, CSJ. Managing Editor: Therese Sherlock, CSJ. 50% freelance written. Weekly newsletter for religious education of high schoolers. "We want realistic fiction and nonfiction that raises current ethical and religious questions and conflicts in multi-racial contexts." Estab. 1988. Circ. 26,000. Pays on publication. Publishes ms an average of 6 months after acceptance. Byline given. Buys all rights. Submit seasonal/holiday material 4-6 months in advance. Simultaneous submissions OK. Reports in 2 weeks on queries; 6 weeks on mss. Free sample copy and writer's guidelines.
Nonfiction: Interview/profile, personal experience, photo feature (homelessness, illiteracy), religious, Roman Catholic leaders, human interest features, social justice leaders, projects, humanitarians. "No Christian confessional pieces." Buys 12 mss/year. Query. Length: 1,100-1,200 words. Pays $135-150 for articles; $75 for one-page articles.
Photos: State availability of photos with submission. Reviews contact sheets, transparencies and prints. Offers $25-35 per photo. Identification of subjects required. Buys one-time rights.
Fiction: Fantasy and slice-of-life vignettes. "We want realistic pieces for and about teens—nonpedantic, nonpious." Buys 12 mss/year. Query. Length: 1,100-1,200 words. Pays $150.
Tips: "Query to receive call for stories, spec sheet, sample issues."

SPIRITUAL LIFE, 2131 Lincoln Rd. NE, Washington DC 20002. (202)832-6622. Editor: Rev. Steven Payne, O.C.D. 80% freelance written. Prefers to work with published/established writers; works with a small number of new/unpublished writers each year. Quarterly. "Largely Catholic, well-educated, serious readers. A few are nonCatholic or nonChristian." Circ. 14,000. **Pays on acceptance.** Publishes ms an average of 1 year after acceptance. Buys first North American serial rights. "Brief autobiographi-

cal information (present occupation, past occupations, books and articles published, etc.) should accompany article." Reports in 6 weeks. Sample copy and writer's guidelines for SASE (9×6 or larger) with 4 first class stamps.
Nonfiction: Serious articles of contemporary spirituality. High quality articles about our encounter with God in the present day world. Language of articles should be college level. Technical terminology, if used, should be clearly explained. Material should be presented in a positive manner. Sentimental articles or those dealing with specific devotional practices not accepted. Buys inspirational and think pieces. No fiction or poetry. Buys 20 mss/year. Length: 3,000-5,000 words. Pays $50 minimum. "Five contributor's copies are sent to author on publication of article." Book reviews should be sent to Rev. Steven Payne, O.C.D.

‡**SPIRITUALITY TODAY**, 3642 Lindell Blvd., St. Louis MO 63108. Regina Siegfried, ASC. 25% freelance written. Works with a small number of new/unpublished writers each year. Magazine "for those interested in a more integral and fuller Christian life in the contemporary world." Pays on publication. Publishes ms an average of 14 months after acceptance. Byline given. Buys first North American serial rights only. Sample copy $2 and 6½×9½ SAE; free writer's guidelines.
Nonfiction: Articles that seriously examine important issues concerning the spiritual life, or Christian life, in the context of today's world. Scriptural, biographical, doctrinal, liturgical and ecumenical articles are acceptable. No poetry. Generally Catholic readership, but ecumenically open. Buys 5-7 unsolicited mss/year. Query only. Length: 4,000 words. Pays 1½¢/word.
Tips: "Examine the journal. It is not a typical devotional or inspirational magazine. Given its characteristics, the style of writing required is deeper and richer than regular freelance writers usually employ."

STANDARD, Nazarene International Headquarters, 6401 The Paseo, Kansas City MO 64131. (816)333-7000, ext. 555. FAX: (816)333-1683. Editor: Beth A. Watkins. 95% freelance written. Works with a small number of new/unpublished writers each year. Weekly inspirational paper with Christian reading for adults. Estab. 1938. Circ. 170,000. **Pays on acceptance.** Publishes ms an average of 15 months after acceptance. Byline given. Buys one-time rights and second serial (reprint) rights. Submit seasonal/holiday material 12-14 months in advance. Reports in 8-10 weeks. Free sample copy; writer's guidelines for SAE with 2 first class stamps.
Nonfiction: How-to (grow spiritually); inspirational; social issues; and personal experience (with an emphasis on spiritual growth). Buys 400 mss/year. Send complete ms. Length: 300-1,500 words. Pays 3½¢/word for first rights; 2¢/word for reprint rights.
Photos: Pays $25-45 for 8×10 b&w prints. Buys one-time rights. Accepts photos with ms.
Fiction: Adventure, religious, romance and suspense—all with a spiritual emphasis. Buys 400 mss/year. Send complete ms. Length: 500-1,500 words. Pays 3½¢/word for first rights; 2¢/word for reprint rights.
Poetry: Free verse, haiku, light verse and traditional. Buys 50 poems/year. Submit maximum 5 poems. Length: 50 lines maximum. Pays 25¢/line.
Fillers: Jokes, anecdotes and short humor. Buys 52/year. Length: 300 words maximum. Pays same as nonfiction and fiction.
Tips: "Articles should express Biblical principles without being preachy. Setting, plot and characterization must be realistic. Fiction articles should be labeled 'Fiction' on the manuscript. True experience articles may be first person, 'as told to,' or third person."

SUNDAY DIGEST, David C. Cook Publishing Co., 850 N. Grove Ave., Elgin IL 60120. Editor: Ronda Oosterhoff. 75% freelance written. Prefers to work with established writers. Issued weekly to Christian adults in Sunday School. "*Sunday Digest* provides a combination of original articles and reprints, selected to help adult readers better understand the Christian faith, to keep them informed of issues within the Christian community, and to challenge them to a deeper personal commitment to Christ." Estab. 1886. **Pays on acceptance.** Publishes ms an average of 15 months after acceptance. Buys first or reprint rights. Reports in 3 months. Sample copy and writer's guidelines for 6½×9½ SAE with 2 first class stamps.
Nonfiction: Needs articles applying the Christian faith to personal and social problems, articles on family life and church relationships, inspirational self-help, personal experience; how-to and interview articles preferred over fiction. Length: 400-1,700 words. Pays $40-200, less for reprints.
Tips: "It is crucial that the writer is committed to quality Christian communication with a crisp, clear writing style. Christian message should be woven in, not tacked on."

SUNDAY SCHOOL COUNSELOR, General Council of the Assemblies of God, 1445 Boonville, Springfield MO 65802. (417)862-2781. Editor: Sylvia Lee. 60% freelance written. Works with small number of new/unpublished writers each year. Monthly magazine on religious education in the local church—the official Sunday school voice of the Assemblies of God channeling programs and help to local, primarily lay, leadership. Estab. 1939. Circ. 35,000. **Pays on acceptance.** Publishes ms an average of 9 months after acceptance. Byline given. Offers variable kill fee. Buys first North American serial rights, one-time rights, all rights, simultaneous rights, first serial rights, or second serial (reprint) rights; makes work-for-hire assignments. Submit seasonal/holiday material 7 months in advance. Simultaneous and previously published submissions OK. Reports in 2 weeks on queries; 1 month on mss. Free sample copy and writer's guidelines for SASE.

Nonfiction: How-to, inspirational, interview/profile, personal experience and photo feature. All related to religious education in the local church. Buys 100 mss/year. Send complete ms. Length: 300-1,800 words. Pays $25-90. Sometimes pays expenses of writers on assignment.

Photos: Send photos with ms. Reviews b&w and color prints. Model releases and identification of subjects required. Buys one-time rights.

TEACHERS INTERACTION, A Magazine Church School Workers Grow By, Concordia Publishing House, LCMS, 1333 S. Kirkwood Rd., St. Louis MO 63122-7295. Editor: Martha Streufert Jander. 20% freelance written. Published 7 times/year of practical, inspirational, theological articles for volunteer church school teachers. Material must be true to the doctrines of the Lutheran Church—Missouri Synod. Estab. 1960. Circ. 20,400. Pays on publication. Publishes ms an average of 1 year after acceptance. Byline given. Buys first rights. Submit seasonal/holiday material 7 months in advance. Query for electronic submissions. Reports in 3 months on queries; 6 months on mss. Sample copy $1; writer's guidelines for 9×12 SAE (with sample copy); for #10 SAE (without sample copy).

Nonfiction: How-to (practical helps/ideas used successfully in own classroom); inspirational (to the church school worker—must be in accordance with LCMS doctrine); and personal experience (of a Sunday school classroom nature—growth). No theological articles. Buys 6 mss/year. Send complete ms. Length: 750-1,500 words. Pays $35.

Fillers: Cartoons. Buys 14/year. "*Teachers Interaction* buys short items—activities and ideas planned and used successfully in a church school classroom." Buys 40/year. Length: 100 words maximum. Pays $10.

Tips: "Practical, or 'it happened to me' experiences articles would have the best chance. Also short items—ideas used in classrooms; seasonal and in conjunction with our Sunday school material, Our Life in Christ. Our format includes all volunteer church school teachers, not just Sunday school teachers. Because of backlog, accepting little freelance material."

THIS PEOPLE MAGAZINE, Exploring LDS issues and personalities, Utah Alliance Publishing Co., Box 2250, Salt Lake City UT 84110. (801)538-2262. FAX: (801)364-1510. Editor: William B. Smart. 75% freelance written. Quarterly magazine covering Mormon issues and personalities. "This magazine is aimed at Mormon readers and examines Mormon issues and people in an upbeat, problem-solving way." Estab. 1979. Circ. 30,000. Pays on publication. Publishes an average of 6 months after acceptance. Byline given. Offers 15% kill fee. Buys first rights. Submit seasonal/holiday material 6 months in advance. Query for electronic submissions. Reports in 2 months. Sample copy 8½×11 SAE with 4 first class stamps. Writer's guidelines for #10 SAE with 1 first class stamp.

Nonfiction: Essays, historical/nostalgic, humor, inspirational, interview/profile, personal experience, photo feature and travel—all Mormon oriented. No poetry, cartoons, fiction. Buys 15-20 mss/year. Query with or without published clips, or send complete ms. Length: 1,000-3,500 words. Pays $150-400 for assigned articles; $100-400 for unsolicited articles. Sometimes pays expenses of writers on assignment.

Photos: State availability of photos with submission. Model releases and identification of subjects required. Buys all rights.

Tips: "I prefer query letters that include the first 6-8 paragraphs of an article plus an outline of the article. Clips and credits of previous publications are helpful."

THE UNITED CHURCH OBSERVER, 85 St. Clair Ave. E., Toronto, Ontario M4T 1M8 Canada. (416)960-8500. Acting Editor: Muriel Duncan. 40% freelance written. Prefers to work with published/established writers. A 60-page monthly newsmagazine for people associated with The United Church of Canada. Deals primarily with events, trends and policies having religious significance. Most coverage is Canadian, but reports on international or world concerns will be considered. Pays on publication. Publishes ms an average of 4 months after acceptance. Byline usually given. Buys first serial rights and occasionally all rights.

Nonfiction: Occasional opinion features only. Extended coverage of major issues usually assigned to known writers. No opinion pieces, poetry. Submissions should be written as news, no more than 1,200 words length, accurate and well-researched. Queries preferred. Rates depend on subject, author and work involved. Pays expenses of writers on assignment "as negotiated."

Photos: Buys photographs with mss. B&w should be 5×7 minimum; color 35mm or larger format. Payment varies.

Tips: "The writer has a better chance of breaking in at our publication with short articles; it also allows us to try more freelancers. Include samples of previous *news* writing with query. Indicate ability and willingness to do research, and to evaluate that research. The most frequent mistakes made by writers in completing an article for us are organizational problems, lack of polished style, short on research, and a lack of inclusive language."

UNITED METHODIST REPORTER, Box 660275, Dallas TX 75266-0275. (214)630-6495. Editor/General Manager: Spurgeon M. Dunnam, III. Managing Editor: John A. Lovelace. Weekly newspaper for a United Methodist national readership. Circ. 475,000. Pays on publication. Byline given. Not copyrighted. Free sample copy and writer's guidelines.

Nonfiction: "We accept occasional short features, approximately 500 words. Articles need not be limited to a United Methodist angle but need to have an explicit Protestant angle, preferably with evidence of participation in a local congregation. Write about a distinctly Christian response to human need or how a person's faith relates to a given situation." Send complete ms. Pays 4¢/word.

Photos: Purchased with accompanying ms. "We encourage the submission of good action photos (5×7 or 8×10 b&w glossy prints) of the persons or situations in the article." Pays $10.

UNITY MAGAZINE, Unity School of Christianity, Unity Village MO 64065. (816)524-3550. Editor: Philip White. 90% freelance written. Monthly magazine on the metaphysical. Interested in working with authors who are skilled at writing in the metaphysical Christian/New Thought/spiritual development persuasion. Circ. 250,000. **Pays on acceptance.** Publishes ms an average of 1 year after acceptance. Byline given. Buys first North American serial rights. Submit seasonal/holiday material 9 months in advance. Query for electronic submissions. Reports in 3 weeks on queries; 2 months on mss. Free sample copy and writer's guidelines.

Nonfiction: Inspirational, personal experience, biblical interpretation, self-help, holistic health, prosperity, religious. Buys 200 mss/year. Send complete ms. Length: 1,000-1,800 words. Pays 8¢/word minimum; varies with quality of ms.

Photos: State availability of photos with submission. Reviews transparencies and prints. Offers $35-200/photo. Model release and identification of subjects required. Buys one-time rights.

Poetry: Inspirational, religious, seasonal. Buys 100 poems/year. Submit maximum 10 poems. Length: 30 lines maximum. Pays $20 minimum.

VENTURE AND VISIONS, Lectionary-based weeklies for Catholic youth, Pflaum/Editorial Development Associates, 1884 Randolph Ave., St. Paul MN 55105. (612)690-7010. Editor: Joan Mitchell, CSJ. Managing Editor: Therese Sherlock, CSJ. 40% freelance written. Weekly newsletter on religious education for intermediate and junior high students. "We want realistic fiction and nonfiction that raises current ethical and religious questions and conflicts in multiracial contexts to which intermediate and junior high youth can relate." Estab. 1980. Circ. 140,000. Pays on publication. Byline given. Publishes ms an average of 6 months after acceptance. Buys all rights. Submit seasonal/holiday material 4-6 months in advance. Simultaneous submissions OK. Reports in 2 weeks on queries; 2 months on mss. Free sample copy. Writer's guidelines for #10 SASE.

Nonfiction: Marianne W. Nold. General interest (human interest features), interview/profile, personal experience, photo feature (students in other countries), religious, Roman Catholic leaders, humanitarians and social justice projects. "No Christian confessional pieces." Buys 14 mss/year. Length: 900-1,100 words. Pays $100-125 for assigned articles; $75-125 for unsolicited articles.

Photos: State availability of photos with submission. Reviews contact sheets, transparencies and prints. Offers $15-50 per photo. Identification of subjects required. Buys one-time rights.

Fiction: Fantasy, religious and slice-of-life-vignettes. "No 'Christian'. We want realistic pieces for and about intermediate and junior-high aged students—non-pedantic, non-pious." Buys 30-40 mss/year. Query. Length: 900-1,100 words. Pays $100-125.

Tips: "Query to receive call for stories, spec sheet, sample issues."

VIRTUE, The Christian Magazine for Women, 548 Sisters Pkwy, P.O. Box 850, Sisters OR 97759. (503)549-8261. FAX: (503)549-0153. Editor: Marlee Alex. Managing Editor: Jeanette Thomason. 75% freelance written. Works with small number of new/unpublished writers each year. Bimonthly magazine that "shows through features and columns the depth and variety of expression that can be given to femininity and faith." Estab. 1978. Circ. 175,000. **Pays on acceptance.** Publishes ms an average of 4 months after acceptance. Byline given. Buys first North American serial rights. Submit seasonal/holiday material 9 months in advance. Reports in 6 weeks on queries; 2 months on mss. Sample copy $3; writer's guidelines for #10 SASE.

Nonfiction: Book excerpts, how-to, humor, inspirational, interview/profile, opinion, personal experience and religious. Buys 70 mss/year. Query. Length: 600-1,800 words. Pays 15-25¢/word. Sometimes pays the expenses of writers on assignment.
Photos: State availability of photos with submission.
Columns/Departments: In My Opinion (reader editorial); One Woman's Journal (personal experience); Equipped for Ministry (Christian service potpourri); Working Smart—Not Harder (the best ideas in home management); Women Like Us (doing the extraordinary). Buys 25 mss/year. Query. Length: 1,000-1,500. Pays 15-25¢/word.
Fiction: Humorous and religious. Buys 4-6 mss/year. Send complete ms. Length: 1,500-1,800 words. Pays 15-25¢/word.
Poetry: Free verse, haiku and traditional. Buys 7-10 poems/year. Submit maximum 3 poems. Length: 3-30 lines. Pays $15-50.

VISTA, Wesleyan Publishing House, P.O. Box 50434, Indianapolis IN 46250-0434. Editor: Rebecca Higgins. 95% freelance written. Eager to work with new/unpublished writers—"quality writing a must, however." Weekly publication of The Wesleyan Church for adults. Circ. 40,000. **Pays on acceptance.** Publishes ms an average of 10 months after acceptance. Byline given. Not copyrighted. Buys first rights, simultaneous rights, second rights and reprint rights. Submit seasonal/holiday material 10 months in advance. Reports in 2 months. Sample copy for 9×12 SASE. Writer's guidelines for #10 SASE.
Nonfiction: Testimonies, how-to's, humor, interviews, opinion pieces from conservative Christian perspective. Length: 500-1,200 words.
Photos: Pays $20-40 for 5×7 or 8×10 b&w glossy print natural-looking close-ups of faces in various emotions, groups of people interacting. Various reader age groups should be considered.
Fiction: Believable, quality articles, no Sunday "soaps." Length: 500-1,200 words. Pays 2-4¢/word.
Tips: "Read the writer's guide carefully before submitting."

‡VITAL CHRISTIANITY, Warner Press, Inc., 1200 E. 5th St., Anderson IN 46018. (317)644-7721. Editor-in-Chief: Arlo F. Newell. Managing Editor: Richard L. Willowby. 20-25% freelance written. Prefers to work with published/established writers; works with small number of new/unpublished writers each year. Monthly magazine covering Christian living for people attending local Church of God congregations. Estab. 1907. Circ. 26,000. **Pays on acceptance.** Byline given. Offers kill fee. Buys one-time rights. Submit seasonal/holiday material 6 months in advance. Query for electronic submissions. Reports in 6 weeks. Sample copy and writer's guidelines for SASE (with postage for 7 ounces).
Nonfiction: Humor (with religious point); inspirational (religious—not preachy); interview/profile (of church-related personalities); opinion (religious/theological); and personal experience (related to putting one's faith into practice). Buys 125 mss/year. Query. Length: 1,000 words maximum. Pays $10-100.
Photos: State availability of photos. Pays $50-300 for 5×7 color transparencies; $20-40 for 8×10 b&w prints. Identification of subjects (when related directly to articles) required. Buys one-time rights. Reserves the right to reprint material it has used for advertising and editorial purposes (pays second rights for editorial re-use).
Fiction: Fiction with a religious message. "It should show reality from a Christian point of view."
Tips: "Fillers, personal experience, personality interviews, profiles and good holiday articles are areas of our magazine open to freelancers. Writers should request our guidelines and list of upcoming topics of interest to determine if they have interest or expertise in writing for us. Always send SASE."

THE WESLEYAN ADVOCATE, The Wesleyan Publishing House, P.O. Box 50434, Indianapolis IN 46250-0434. (317)576-1313. FAX: (317)842-9188. Editor: Dr. Wayne E. Caldwell. 10% freelance written. A biweekly magazine by the Wesleyan Church. Estab. 1842. Circ. 20,000. Pays on publication. Publishes ms an average of 1 year after acceptance. Byline given. Buys first rights or simultaneous rights. Submit seasonal/holiday material 1 year in advance. Simultaneous submissions OK. Query for electronic submissions. Reports in 2 weeks. Sample copy for $2; writer's guidelines for #10 SASE.
Nonfiction: Humor, inspirational and religious. Buys 5 mss/year. Send complete ms. Length: 250-650 words. Pays $10-40 for assigned articles; $5-25 for unsolicited articles.
Photos: Send photos with submission. Reviews transparencies. Buys one-time rights.
Tips: "Write for a guide."

‡WOMAN'S TOUCH, Assemblies of God Women's Ministries Department (GPH), 1445 Boonville, Springfield MO 65802-1894. (417)862-2781. Editor: Sandra Goodwin Clopine. Associate Editor: Aleda Swartzendruber. 75-90% freelance written. Eager to work with new/unpublished writers. A bimonthly inspirational magazine for women. "Articles and contents of the magazine should be compatible with Christian teachings as well as human interests. The audience is women, both homemakers and those who are career-oriented." Estab. 1977. Circ. 21,000. **Pays on acceptance.** Byline given. Buys one-time rights. Submit seasonal/holiday material 8 months in advance. Photocopied and previously published submissions OK. Reports in 6 weeks. Sample copy 9½x11 SAE with 85¢ postage; writer's guidelines for #10 SASE.

Nonfiction: General interest, how-to, inspirational, personal experience, religious and travel. Buys 75 mss/year. Send complete ms. Length: 500-1,000 words. Pays $10-35 for unsolicited articles.

Photos: State availability of photos with submission. Reviews negatives, transparencies and 4x6 prints. Offers no additional payment for photos accepted with ms. Identification of subjects required. Buys one-time rights.

Columns/Departments: An Added Touch (special crafts, holiday decorations, family activities); A Personal Touch (articles relating to personal development such as fashion accents, skin care, exercises, etc.). "We've added 'A Final Touch' for short human interest articles—home and family or career-oriented." Buys 10 mss/year. Query with published clips. Length: 500-800 words. Pays $20-35.

Poetry: Free verse, light verse and traditional. Buys 10 poems/year. Submit maximum 4 poems. Length: 4-50 lines. Pays $5-20.

Fillers: Facts. Buys 5/year. Length: 50-200. Pays $5-15.

Retirement

Retirement magazines have changed to meet the active lifestyles of their readers and editors dislike the kinds of stereotypes people have of retirement magazines. More people are retiring in their 50s, while others are starting a business or traveling and pursuing hobbies. These publications give readers specialized information on health and fitness, medical research, finances and other topics of interest, as well as general articles on travel destinations and recreational activities.

ALIVE! A Magazine for Christian Senior Adults, Christian Seniors Fellowship, P.O. Box 369, West Chester OH 45069. (513)825-3681. Editor: J. David Lang. Office Editor: A. June Lang. 60% freelance written. Quarterly magazine for senior adults ages 55 and older. "We need timely articles about Christian seniors in vital, productive lifestyles, travels or ministries." Estab. 1988. **Pays on acceptance.** Byline given. Buys first or second serial (reprint) rights. Submit seasonal/holiday material 6 months in advance. Previously published submissions OK. Reports in 6 weeks. Sample copy for 8½ × 11 SAE with $1 postage; writer's guidelines for #10 SASE.

Nonfiction: General interest, humor, inspirational, interview/profile, photo feature, religious, travel. Buys 25 mss/year. Send complete ms. Length: 600-1,800 words. Pays $18-75. Organization membership may be deducted from payment at writer's request.

Photos: State availability of photos with submission. Offers $10-25. Model releases and identification of subjects required. Buys one-time rights.

Columns/Departments: Heart Medicine (humorous personal anecdotes; prefer grandparent/grandchild stories or anecdotes re: over 55 persons), 10-100 words; Games n' Stuff (word games, puzzles, word search), 200-500 words. Buys 50 mss/year. Send complete ms. Pays $2-25.

Fiction: Adventure, humorous, religious, romance (if it fits age group), slice-of-life vignettes, motivational/inspirational. Buys 12 mss/year. Send complete ms. Length: 600-1,500 words. Pays $20-60.

Fillers: Anecdotes, facts, gags to be illustrated by cartoonist, short humor. Buys 15/year. Length: 50-500 words. Pays $2-15.

Tips: "Include SASE. If second rights, list where article has appeared and if ms is to be returned or tossed."

‡THE ELDER STATESMAN, For Today's Times, The Elder Statesman Publishing Co., Suite 301, 1201 W. Pender St., Vancouver, British Columbia V6E 2V2 Canada. (604)683-1344. Editor: Elizabeth Carroll. 40% freelance written. Monthly tabloid for people over 50. Estab. 1958. Circ. 30,000. Pays 30 days after publication. Byline given. Offers 25% kill fee. Buys first rights. Submit seasonal/holiday material 6 months in advance. Query for electronic submissions. Reports in 2 months. Sample copy $1; free writer's guidelines.

Nonfiction: General interest (for 50+), historical/nostalgic, humor, personal experience, travel. Only articles that relate to 50+ readers who live in British Columbia. Buys 50 mss/year. Query with published clips. Length: 350-600 words. Pays $75-100 for assignment articles; $50-100 for unsolicited articles (all Canadian dollars).

Photos: State availability of photos with submission. Reviews prints. Offers no additional payment for photos accepted with ms. Buys one-time rights.

Tips: "Put word length on first page and when sending SASE remember Canada has its own postal system and is not an offshoot of US. We cannot use US stamps. Best departments for freelancers are travel, nostalgia, retirement housing. Remember 50+ is a broad spectrum."

FIFTY-SOMETHING MAGAZINE, For the Fifty-or-Better Mature Adult, Media Trends Publications, Unit E, 8250 Tyler Blvd., Mentor OH 44060. (216)974-9594. Editor: Linda L. Lindeman. 40% freelance written. Bimonthly magazine on aging, travel, relationships, money, health, hobbies. "We are looking for a positive and upbeat attitude on aging. Proving that 50 years old is *not* over-the-hill but instead a prime time of life." Estab. 1989. Circ. 25,000. Pays on publication. Publishes ms an average of 2 months after acceptance. Byline given. Buys all rights. Submit seasonal/holiday material 4 months in advance. Simultaneous and previously published submissions OK. Query for electronic submissions. Reports in 2 months. Send SASE for guidelines (29¢) or 9 × 12 SASE for sample copy ($1) postage.

Nonfiction: Book excerpts, essays, expose, general interest, historical/nostalgic, how-to (sports), humor, inspirational, interview/profile, opinion, personal experience, photo feature, religious, travel, health, employment. Buys 6 mss/year. Query with published clips, or send complete ms. Length: 100-1,000 words. Pays $25-500 for assigned articles; $25-100 for unsolicited articles. Sometimes pays expenses of writers on assignment.

Photos: Send photos with submission. Reviews contact sheets, negatives, transparencies, and 5 × 7 prints. Offers $25-100 per photo. Captions, model releases and identification of subjects required. Buys one-time or all rights.

Columns/Departments: Book Review (50 and over market); Movie/Play Review (new releases); Sports (for the mature adult); Travel (for the mature adult). Buys 50 mss/year. Send complete ms. Length: 100-1,000 words. Pays $25-500.

Fiction: Adventure, condensed novels, ethnic, experimental, fantasy, historical, humorous, mainstream, mystery, novel excerpts, religious, romance, slice-of-life vignettes, suspense. Buys 25 mss/year. Send complete ms. Length: 100-1,000 words. Pays $25-500.

Poetry: Avant-garde, free verse, light verse and traditional. Buys 15 poems/year. Length: 25-150 lines. Pays $25-100.

Fillers: Anecdotes, facts, gags to be illustrated by cartoonist, newsbreaks, short humor. Buys 100/year. Length: 25-150 words. Pays $25-100.

Tips: "We are a regional publication in northeast Ohio. All areas are open. If you are 50 or more, write as if you are addressing your peers. If you are younger, take a generic approach to age. You don't have to be 50 to address this market."

GOLDEN YEARS MAGAZINE, Golden Years Senior News, Inc., 233 E. New Haven Ave., Melbourne FL 32902-0537. (407)725-4888. FAX: (407)724-0736. Editor: Carol Brenner Hittner. 50% freelance written. Prefers to work with published/established writers. Bimonthly national magazine covering the needs and interests of our fastest growing generation. Editorial presented in a positive, uplifting, straightforward manner. Estab. 1978. Circ. 407,513. Pays on publication. Publishes ms an average of 7 months after acceptance. Byline given. Buys first serial rights and first North American serial rights. Submit seasonal/holiday material 1 year in advance. Simultaneous queries OK. SASE for return of ms *required* for acceptance. Sample copy for 9 × 12 SAE and $2; writer's guidelines for #10 SASE.

Nonfiction: Profile (senior celebrities), travel, second careers, hobbies, retirement ideas and real estate. Limited need for poetry and cartoons. Nostalgia articles generally not accepted. Buys 100 mss/year. Query with published clips or send complete ms. Length: 600 words maximum. Pays 10¢/word.

Photos: "We like to include a lot of photos." Send photos with query or ms. Pays $25 for transparencies. Captions, model releases, and identification of subjects required. Buys one-time rights. Pays $10 per each b&w photo.

Tips: "Our magazine articles are short and special—that's why we are successful."

MATURE LIVING, A Christian Magazine for Senior Adults, Sunday School Board of the Southern Baptist Convention, 127 9th Ave. N., Nashville TN 37234. (615)251-2274. Assistant Editor: Judy Pregel. 70% freelance written. A monthly leisure reading magazine for senior adults 60 and older. Estab. 1892. Circ. 350,000. **Pays on acceptance.** Byline given. Buys all rights and sometimes one-time rights. Submit seasonal/holiday material 18 months in advance. Reports in 3 months. Sample copy for 9 × 12 SAE with 89¢ postage; writer's guidelines for #10 SASE.

Nonfiction: General interest, historical/nostalgic, how-to, humor, inspirational, interview/profile, personal experience, photo feature, crafts, and travel. No pornography, profanity, occult; liquor, dancing, drugs, gambling; no book reviews. Buys 100 mss/year. Send complete ms. Length: 1,475 words maximum, prefers 950 words. Pays 5½¢/word (accepted).

Photos: State availability of photos with submission. Offers $10-15/photo. Pays on publication. Buys one-time rights.

Fiction: Humorous, mainstream and slice-of-life vignettes. No reference to liquor, dancing, drugs, gambling; no pornography, profanity or occult. Buys 12 mss/year. Send complete ms. Length: 900-1,475 words. Pays 5½¢/word.

Poetry: Light verse and traditional. Buys 50 poems/year. Submit maximum 5 poems. Length: open. Pays $5-24.

Fillers: Anecdotes, facts and short humor. Buys 15/issue. Length: 50 words maximum. Pays $5.

MATURE OUTLOOK, Meredith Corp., 1716 Locust St., Des Moines IA 50336. Editor: Marjorie P. Groves, Ph.D. 80% freelance written. A bimonthly magazine and newsletter on travel, health, nutrition, money and garden for over-50 audience. They may or may *not* be retired. Circ. 870,000. **Pays on acceptance.** Publishes ms an average 3 months after acceptance. Byline given. Offers 20% kill fee. Buys all rights or makes work-for-hire assignments. Submit seasonal/holiday material 9 months in advance. Query for electronic submissions. Reports in 2 weeks. Sample copy $1. Writer's guidelines for #10 SASE.

Nonfiction: How-to, interview/profile, technical and travel. No humor, personal experience or poetry. Buys 50-60 mss/year. Query with published clips. Length: 500-2,000 words. Pays $200-1,000 for assigned articles. Pays telephone expenses of writers on assignment.

Photos: State availability of photos with submission.

Tips: "Please query. Please don't call."

MATURE YEARS, 201 8th Ave., S., P.O. Box 801, Nashville TN 37202. Editor: Marvin W. Cropsey. 30% freelance written. Prefers to work with published/established writers; works with a small number of new/unpublished writers each year. Quarterly magazine for retired persons and those facing retirement; persons seeking help on how to handle problems and privileges of retirement. Estab. 1968. **Pays on acceptance.** Publishes ms an average of 14 months after acceptance. Rights purchased vary with author and material; usually buys first North American serial rights. Submit seasonal material 14 months in advance. Query for electronic submissions. Reports in 6 weeks. Sample copy for 9 × 12 SAE and $2; writer's guidelines for #10 SASE.

Nonfiction: "*Mature Years* is different from the secular press in that we like material with a Christian and church orientation. Usually we prefer materials that have a happy, healthy outlook regarding aging. Advocacy (for older adults) articles are at times used; some are freelance submissions. We need articles dealing with many aspects of pre-retirement and retirement living, and short stories and leisure-time hobbies related to specific seasons. Give examples of how older persons, organizations, and institutions are helping others. Writing should be of interest to older adults, with Christian emphasis, though not preachy and moralizing. No poking fun or mushy, sentimental articles. We treat retirement from the religious viewpoint. How-to, humor and travel are also considered." Buys 24 unsolicited mss/year. Submit complete ms (include SASE and Social Security number with submissions). Length: 1,200-1,500 words.

Photos: 8 × 10 b&w glossy prints, color prints or transparencies purchased with ms or on assignment.

Fiction: "We buy fiction for adults. Humor is preferred. No children's stories and no stories about depressed situations of older adults." Length: 1,000-1,500 words. Payment varies, usually 4¢/word.

Tips: "We like writing to be meaty, timely, clear and concrete."

MODERN MATURITY, American Association of Retired Persons, 3200 E. Carson, Lakewood CA 90712. (213)496-2277. Editor: J. Henry Fenwick. 50% freelance written. Prefers to work with published/established writers. Bimonthly magazine for readership of persons 50 years of age and over. Circ. 22,450,000. **Pays on acceptance.** Publishes ms an average of 4-6 months after acceptance. Byline given. Buys first North American serial rights. Submit seasonal/holiday material 6 months in advance. Query for electronic submissions. Reports in 8-10 weeks. Free sample copy and writer's guidelines.

Nonfiction: Careers, workplace, practical information in living, financial and legal matters, personal relationships, and consumerism. Query first. Length: up to 2,000 words. Pays up to $3,000. Sometimes pays expenses of writers on assignment.

Photos: Photos purchased with or without accompanying ms. Pays $250 and up for color and $150 and up for b&w.

Fiction: Very occasional short fiction.

Tips: "The most frequent mistake made by writers in completing an article for us is poor follow-through with basic research. The outline is often more interesting than the finished piece. We do not accept unsolicited manuscripts."

‡**PRIME**, Sunlife, Inc., #101, 5300 W. Sahara Ave., Las Vegas NV 89102. (702)871-6780. Editor: Colin McKinlay. 60% freelance written. Monthly magazine for retirees. "Prime covers activities of active, interesting persons who have retired and are doing interesting things, activities for retired persons, travel, profiles, life styles." Estab. 1988. Circ. 18,000. Pays on publication. Publishes ms an average of 3 months after acceptance. Byline given. Offers no kill fee. Not copyrighted. Buys one-time rights. Submit seasonal/holiday material 6 months in advance. Reports in 2 weeks. Sample copy $1.

Nonfiction: General interest, historical/nostalgic, interview/profile, personal experience and travel. Buys 10 mss/year. Query. Length: 1,000-2,000 words. Pays $2/column inch for features. Pays 10¢/word for cover stories. Pays $50 minimum. Sometimes pays expenses of writers on assignment. State availability of photos with submission.

Columns/Departments: Real People (active retired persons with interesting activities to keep busy), 300-500 words. Buys 20 mss/year. Query. Pays $50 minimum.

Tips: "We are most open to people profiles and feature stories of interesting things for retired persons to do in the four-state area of Nevada, SW Utah, NW Arizona and SE California. Articles should involve things that retired people can do, or places to go."

PRIME TIMES, Grote Publishing, Suite 120, 2802 International Ln., Madison WI 53704. Executive Editor: Rod Clark. 80% freelance written. Prefers to work with published/established writers. Quarterly magazine "for people who are in prime mid-life or at the height of their careers and planning a dynamic retirement lifestyle or second career." Estab. 1980. Circ. 75,000. Pays on publication. Buys first North American serial rights and second serial (reprint) rights. Publishes ms an average of 6 months after acceptance. Submit seasonal material 6 months in advance. Previously published submissions OK as long as they were not in another national maturity-market magazine. Reports in 2 months. Sample copy for $2.50, 9 × 12 SAE and 5 first class stamps; writer's guidelines for #10 SASE. Query first.

Nonfiction: Investigative journalism, new research and updates (related to financial planning methods, consumer activism, preventive health and fitness, travel, and careers/dynamic lifestyle after retirement); opinion; profile; travel; popular arts; self-image; personal experience; humor; and photo feature. "No rocking-chair reminiscing." Articles on health and medical issues and research *must* be founded in sound scientific method and must include current, up-to-date data. "Health-related articles are an easy sale, but you must be able to document your research. Don't waste your time or ours on tired generalizations about how to take care of the human anatomy. If you've heard it before, so have we. We want to know who is doing new research, what the current findings may be, and what scientists on the cutting edge of new research say the future holds, preferably in the next one to five years. Give us the facts, only the facts, and all of the facts. Allow the scientists and our audience to draw their own conclusions." Buys 30-40 mss/year, about half from new talent. Query with published clips. Length: 1,000-3,000 words. Pays $50-1,000. "Be sure to keep a photocopy." Sometimes pays the expenses of writers on assignment.

Photos: Payment is based on one-time publication rights; $75 for less than ½ page, $125 for ½ page and $250 for full page. Cover photos, spreads, multiple purchases to be negotiated. Payment on publication. Photo release is necessary to prove ownership of copyright. No standard kill fee. "Do not send irreplaceable *anything*."

Tips: "Query should reflect writing style and skill of the author. Special issues requiring freelance work include publications on adult relationships and developmental transitions such as mid-life and 'empty-nest' passages and couple renewal; mid-life women's issues; health and medical research and updates; second careers; money management; continuing education; consequences of the ongoing longevity revolution; and the creation of new lifestyles for prime-life adults (ages 40-70 primarily) who are well-educated, affluent, and above all, *active*. About 55% of our readers are women. All are active and redefining the middle years with creative energy and imagination. Age-irrelevant writing is a must. The focus of *Prime Times* in 1992 will be on presenting readers with refreshing and newsworthy material for dynamic mid-lifers, people who have a forever-forty mentality."

SENIOR, California Senior Magazine, 3565 S. Higuera St., San Luis Obispo CA 93401. (805)544-8711. FAX: (805)544-4450. Editor: George Brand. Associate Editor: Herb Kamm, R. Judd. 90% freelance written. Monthly magazine covering senior citizens to inform and entertain the "over-50" audience. Estab. 1982. Circ. 340,000. Pays on publication. Byline given. Publishes ms an average of 1 month after acceptance. Not copyrighted. Buys first rights or second rights. Submit seasonal/holiday material 2 months in advance. Reports in 2 weeks. Sample copy for 9 × 11 SAE and 6 first class stamps; writer's guidelines for SASE.

Nonfiction: Historical/nostalgic, humor, inspirational, personal experience and travel. Special issue features War Years (November); Christmas (December); and Travel (April). Buys 30-75 mss/year. Query. Length: 300-900 words. Pays $1.50/inch.

Photos: Send photos with submission. Reviews 8 × 10 b&w prints only. Offers $10-25 per photo. Captions and identification of subjects required. Buys one-time rights.

Columns/Departments: Finance (investment); Taxes; Auto; Medicare, Health. Length: 300-900 words. Pays $1.50/inch.

‡SENIOR EDITION USA/COLORADO and COLORADO OLD TIMES, Suite 218, 1385 S. Colorado Blvd., Denver CO 80222-3312. (303)758-4040. Managing Editor: Rose Beetem. 15% freelance written. Monthly tabloid. "Colorado newspaper for seniors (with national distribution) emphasizing legislation, opinion and advice columns, local and national news, features and local calendar aimed at over-55 community." Estab. 1972. Circ. 35,000. Pays on publication. Publishes ms an average of 1-6 months after acceptance. Byline given. Offer 25-50% kill fee for assigned stories only. Buys first North American serial rights and simultaneous rights. Submit seasonal/holiday material 3 months in advance. Reports in 1-3 months. Sample copy $1; writer's guidelines for SASE.

Nonfiction: Historical/nostalgic, humor, opinion, personal experience and travel. Does not want "anything aimed at less than age 55-plus market; anything patronizing or condescending to seniors." Buys 3-6 mss/year. Buys over 70 mss/year in nostalgia. Query with or without published clips, or send complete ms. Length: 50-1,000 words. Pays $5-30 for assigned articles; $5-25 for unsolicited articles. Sometimes pays expenses of writers on assignment.

Photos: Send photos with submission (or photocopies of available pictures). Offers $3-10 per photo. Identification of subjects required. Buys one-time rights.

Columns/Departments: Senior Overlook (opinions of seniors about anything they feel strongly about: finances, grandkids, love, life, social problems, etc. May be editorial, essay, prose or poetry). Buys 12 mss/year. Send complete ms. Length: 50-1,000 words. Pays $10 maximum.

Fillers: Short humor. Buys 4/year. Length: 300 words maximum. Pays $10 maximum.

Tips: Areas most open to freelancers are "Opinion: have a good, reasonable point backed with personal experience and/or researched data. Diatribes, vague or fuzzy logic or overworked themes not appreciated. Advice: solid information and generic articles accepted. We will not promote any product or business unless it is the only one in existence. Must be applicable to senior lifestyle."

SENIOR SPOTLITE NEWSPAPERS, INC., The Paper of Choice for People Over 50, 5601 Olde Wadsworth Blvd., Arvada CO 80002. (303)421-8171. Editor: JoAnn L. Jones. 10% freelance written. Monthly tabloid covering anything of interest to seniors—health issues, travel, legislation, etc. Estab. 1986. Circ. 100,000. Pays on publication. Byline given. Buys one-time rights. Submit seasonal/holiday material 3 months in advance. Simultaneous submissions OK. Reports in 3 months. Sample copy $1 with 9×12 SAE and 2 first class stamps.

Nonfiction: General interest, historical/nostalgic, humor, inspirational, interview/profile, religious. No poetry. Buys 5 mss/year. Send complete ms. Length: 200-1,000 words. Pays $1 per column inch. Pays in contributor copies or other premiums if asked.

Photos: State availability of photos with submission or send photos with submission. Offers no additional payment for photos accepted with ms. Model releases and identification of subjects required.

SENIOR WORLD NEWS MAGAZINE, (formerly *Senior World of California*), Californian Publishing Co., P.O. Box 1565, 1000 Pioneer Way, El Cajon CA 92022. (619)593-2910. Executive Editor: Laura Impastato. Travel Editor: Jerry Goodrum. Entertainment Editor: Iris Neal. Health Editor: Arlene Holmes. Lifestyle Editor: Sandy Pasqua. 10% freelance written. Prefers to work with published/established writers. Monthly tabloid newspaper for active older adults living in San Diego, Orange, Los Angeles, Santa Barbara, Ventura, Riverside and San Bernardino counties. Estab. 1973. Circ. 525,000. Pays on publication. Publishes ms an average of 3 months after acceptance. Buys first serial rights. Simultaneous submissions OK. Reports in 2 months. Sample copy $2; free writer's guidelines.

Nonfiction: "We are looking for stories on health, stressing wellness and prevention; travel—international, domestic and how-to; profiles of senior celebrities and remarkable seniors; finance and investment tips for seniors; and interesting hobbies." Send query or complete ms. Length: 500-1,000 words. Pays $30-100.

Photos: State availability of photos with submission. Need b&w with model release. Will pay extra for photos. Buys all rights to photos selected to run with a story.

Columns/Departments: Most of our columns are local or staff-written. We will consider a query on a column idea accompanied by a sample column.

Tips: "No pity the poor seniors material. Remember that we are primarily a news publication and that our content and style reflect that. Our readers are active, vital adults 55 years of age and older." No telephone queries.

‡VANTAGE, Montgomery Ward Signature Group, Cade Communications, 11 E. Illinois St., 4th Fl., Chicago IL 60611. (312)644-4485. Editor: Ann Cade. 50% freelance written. Bimonthly magazine for people in their fifites and up. "Our readers are members of Montgomery Ward's Y.E.S. Club." Estab. 1984. Pays on publication. Publishes ms 6 months after acceptance. Byline given. Buys first North American serial rights. Query for electronic submissions. Reports in 6 months on mss.

Nonfiction: How-to, photo feature. Send complete ms. Length: 1,000-1,500 words. Pays $200-500.

Photos: Reviews contact sheets and transparencies. Model releases and identification of subjects required. Buys one-time rights.

Tips: "We are looking for articles on money, household fix-it projects, decorating, fashion and other general interest consumer topics. We are also looking for photos of people in their 50s or so—engaged in activities."

Romance and Confession

Listed here are publications that need stories of romance ranging from ethnic and adventure to romantic intrigue and confession. Each magazine has a particular slant; some are written for young adults, others to family-oriented women. Some magazines also are interested in general interest nonfiction on related subjects.

AFFAIRE DE COEUR, Suite B, 1555 Washington Ave., San Leandro CA 94577. (415)357-5665. Editor: Louise Snead. Publisher: Barbara Keenan. 56% freelance written. Monthly magazine of book reviews, articles and information on publishing for romance readers and writers. Circ. 115,000. Pays on publication. Publishes ms an average of 6-12 months after acceptance. Byline given. Buys one-time rights. Submit seasonal/holiday material 3 months in advance. Simultaneous and previously published submissions OK. Reports in 4 months. Sample copy $10.
Nonfiction: Book excerpts, essays, general interest, historical/nostalgic, how-to, interview/profile, personal experience and photo feature. Buys 2 mss/year. Query. Length: 500-2,200 words. Pays $5-15. Sometimes pays writers with contributor copies or other premiums.
Photos: State availability of photos with submission. Review prints. Identification of subjects required. Buys one-time rights.
Columns/Departments: Reviews (book reviews). Bios and articles, 2,000 word or less.
Fiction: Historical, mainstream and romance. Pays $15.
Poetry: Light verse. Buys 2 poems/year. Submit 1 poem. Does not pay.
Fillers: Newsbreaks. Buys 2/year. Length: 50-100 words. Does not pay.
Tips: "Please send clean copy. Do not send material without SASE. Do not expect a return for 2-3 months. Type all information. Send some sample of your work."

‡BLACK SECRETS, Lexington Library Inc., 355 Lexington Ave., New York NY 10017. (212)973-3200. Editor: D. Boyd. See *Intimacy/Black Romance.*
Fiction: "This is our most romantic magazine of the five. We use one longer story between 20-24 pages for this book, and sometimes we feature it on the cover. Save your harsh, sleazy stories for another magazine. Give us your softest, dreamiest, most imaginative, most amorous story with a male love interest we can't help but fall in love with. Make sure your story has body and not just bodies. Our readers love romance, but they also require substance."
Tips: "Please request a sample and guidelines before submitting. Enclose a 9×12 SASE with five first class stamps."

BRONZE THRILLS, Lexington Library, Inc., 355 Lexington Ave., New York NY 10017. (212)949-6850. FAX: (212)986-5926. Editor: D. Boyd. Estab. 1982. See *Intimacy/Black Romance.* "Stories can be a bit more extraordinary and uninhibited than in the other magazines but still they have to be romantic. For example, we might buy a story about a woman who finds out her husband is a transsexual in *Bronze Thrills,* but not for *Jive* (our younger magazine). The stories for this magazine tend to have a harder, more adult edge of reality than the others."

‡INTIMACY/BLACK ROMANCE, 355 Lexington Ave., New York NY 10017. (212)949-6850. FAX: (212)986-5926. Editor: D. Boyd. 100% freelance written. Eager to work with new/unpublished writers. A bimonthly magazine covering romance and love. Estab. 1982. Circ. 100,000. Pays on publication. Publishes ms an average of 6 months after acceptance. Byline given on articles only. Buys all rights. Submit seasonal/holiday material 6 months in advance. Reports in 2 months on queries; 3-6 months on mss. Sample copy for 9×12 SASE with 5 first class stamps; writer's guidelines for #10 SASE with 3 first class stamps.
Nonfiction: How-to (relating to romance and love); and feature articles on any aspect of relationships. Buys 100 mss/year. Query with published clips, or send complete ms. Length: 3-5 typed pages. Pays $100.
Photos: Send photos with submission. Reviews contact sheets, negatives, transparencies.
Fiction: Confession and romance. "I would not like to see anything that stereotypes Black people. Stories which are too sexual in content and lack romance are unacceptable." Buys 300 mss/year. Accepts stories which are a bit more romantic than those written for *Jive, Black Confessions* or *Bronze Thrills.* Send complete ms (17-19 typed pages). Pays $75-100.
Tips: "I still get excited when I read a manuscript by an unpublished writer whose use of language is magical and fresh. I'm always looking for that diamond in the fire. Send us your *best* shot. Writers who are careless, sloppy and ungrammatical are an immediate turn-off for me. Please do your homework first. Is it the type of story we buy? Is it written in manuscript format? Does it make one want to read it?"

JIVE, Lexington Library, Inc., 355 Lexington Ave., New York NY 10017. (212)949-6850. FAX: (212)986-5926. Editor: D. Boyd. 100% freelance written. Eager to work with new/unpublished writers. A bimonthly magazine covering romance and love. Estab. 1982. Circ. 100,000. Pays on publication. Publishes ms an average of 3 months after acceptance. Byline given on articles only. Buys all rights. Submit seasonal/holiday material 6 months in advance. Reports in 2 months on queries; 3-6 months on mss. Sample copy for 9×12 SASE with 5 first class stamps; free writer's guidelines.
Nonfiction: How-to (relating to romance and love); and feature articles on any aspect of relationships. "We like our articles to have a down-to-earth flavor. They should be written in the spirit of sisterhood, fun and creativity. Come up with an original idea our readers may not have thought of but will be dying to try out." Buys 100 mss/year. Query with published clips, or send complete ms. Length: 3-5 typed pages. Pays $100.
Columns/Departments: Fashion, health, beauty currently handled by assignment. Unsolicited articles will be returned.
Fiction: Confession and romance. "We would not like to see anything that stereotypes Black people. Stories which are too sexual in content and lack romance are unacceptable. However, all stories must contain one or two love scenes that are romantic, not lewd." All love scenes should not show the sex act, but should allude to it through the use of metaphors and tags. Buys 300 mss/year. Send complete ms (17-19 typed pages). Pays $75-100.
Tips: "We are leaning toward more romantic writing styles as opposed to the more graphic stories of the past. We reach an audience that is comprised mostly of women who are college students, high school students, housewives, divorcees and older women. For this magazine, however, our audience is largely teenagers and geared toward teenage issues. The audience is mainly Black. The stories should reinforce Black pride. Our philosophy is to show our experiences in as positive a light as possible without promoting any of the common stereotypes that are associated with Black men, love-making prowess, penile size, etc. Stereotypes of any kind are totally unacceptable. The fiction section which accepts romance stories and confession stories about love and romance are most open to free-lancers. Also, our special features section is very open. We would also like to see stories that are set outside the U.S.—perhaps they could be set in the Caribbean, Europe, Africa, etc. Women should be shown as being professional, assertive, independent, but should still enjoy being romanced and loved by a man. We'd like to see themes that are reflective of things happening around us in the 90's—abortion, AIDS, alienation, surrogate mothers, etc. But we also like to see stories that transcend our contemporary problems and can give us a moment of pleasure, warmth, joy and relief. The characters should be anywhere from teenage to 30's but not the typical 'country bumpkin girl who was turned out by a big city pimp' type story. Please, writers who are not Black, research your story to be sure that it depicts Black people in a positive manner. Do not make a Black character a caricature of a non-Black character. This is totally unacceptable. Read contemporary Black fiction to ensure that your dialogue and speech idioms are natural to the Black vernacular."

JIVE/BLACK CONFESSIONS, Lexington Library, Inc., 355 Lexington Ave., New York NY 10017. (212)949-6850. FAX: (212)986-5926. Editor: D. Boyd. Estab. 1982. See *Jive*.

MODERN ROMANCES, Macfadden Women's Group, Inc., 233 Park Ave. South, New York NY 10003. Editor: Cherie Clark King. 100% freelance written. Monthly magazine for family-oriented women, ages 18-65 years old. Circ. 200,000. Pays the last week of the month of issue. Buys all rights. Submit seasonal/holiday material at least 6 months in advance. Reports in 9 months. Writer's guidelines for #10 SASE.
Nonfiction: Confession stories with reader identification and a strong emotional tone. No third-person material. Buys 12 mss/issue. Submit complete ms. Length: 2,500-12,000 words. Pays 5¢/word.
Poetry: Light, romantic poetry, and seasonal/holiday subjects. Length: 24 lines maximum. Pay depends on merit.

TRUE CONFESSIONS, Macfadden Holdings, Inc., 233 Park Ave. South, New York NY 10003. (212)979-4800. Editor: H. Marie Atkocius. 90% freelance written. Eager to work with new/unpublished writers. For high-school-educated, blue-collar women, teens through maturity. Monthly magazine. Circ. 250,000. Buys all rights. Byline given on some articles. Pays during the last week of month of issue. Publishes ms an average of 4 months after acceptance. Submit seasonal material 6 months in advance. Reports in 6-8 months. Submit complete ms. No simultaneous submissions.
Stories, Articles, and Fillers: Timely, exciting, emotional first-person stories on the problems that face today's women. The narrators should be sympathetic, and the situations they find themselves in should be intriguing, yet realistic. Many stories may have a strong romantic interest and a high moral tone; however, personal accounts or "confessions," no matter how controversial the topic, are encouraged and accepted. Careful study of a current issue is suggested. Length: 2,000-6,000 words; 5,000-word stories preferred; also book lengths of 8,000-10,000 words. Pays 5¢/word. Also publishes articles poetry, recipes and mini-stories (1,200 words maximum).

TRUE LOVE, Macfadden Women's Group, 233 Park Ave. South, New York NY 10003. (212)979-4800. Editor: Marcia Pomerantz. 100% freelance written. Monthly magazine. For young, blue-collar women, teens through mid-30's. Confession stories based on true happenings, with reader identification and a strong emotional tone. No third-person material; no simultaneous submissions. Circ. 200,000. Pays the last week of the month of the issue. Buys all rights. Submit seasonal material 6 months in advance. Reports within 2 months. Sample copy for 9 × 12 SAE and $2. Writer's guidelines for #10 SASE.

Nonfiction and Fiction: Confessions, true love stories; problems and solutions; health problems; marital and child-rearing difficulties. Avoid graphic sex. Stories dealing with reality, current problems, everyday events, with emphasis on emotional impact. Buys 10 stories/issue. Submit complete ms. Length: 2,000-10,000 words. Pays 3¢/word.

Columns/Departments: "The Life I Live," $100; "How I Know I'm In Love," 700 words or less; $75; "Pet Shop," $50.

Poetry: Light romantic poetry. Length: 24 lines maximum. Pay depends on merit.

Tips: "The story must appeal to the average blue-collar woman. It must deal with her problems and interests. Characters—especially the narrator—must be sympathetic. Focus is especially on teenagers, young working (or student) women."

TRUE ROMANCE, Macfadden Women's Group, 233 Park Ave. South, New York NY 10003. (212)979-4800. Editor: Jean Sharbel. Monthly magazine. 100% freelance written. Readership primarily young, blue-collar women, teens through mid-30's. Confession stories based on true happenings, with reader identification and strong emotional tone. No third-person material; no simultaneous submissions. Estab. 1923. Circ. 225,000. Pays 1 month after publication. Buys all rights. Submit seasonal/holiday material at least 5 months in advance. Reports in 3 months.

Nonfiction and Fiction: Confessions, true love stories; problems and solutions; dating and marital and child-rearing difficulties. Realistic stories dealing with current problems, everyday events, with strong emotional appeal. Buys 14 stories/issue. Submit complete ms. Length 1,500-7,500 words. Pays 3¢/word; slightly higher rates for short-shorts. Informational and how-to articles. Byline given. Length: 250-800 words. Pays 5¢/word minimum.

Poetry: Light romantic poetry. Buys 100/year. Length: 24 lines maximum. Pay depends on merit.

Tips: "A timely, well-written story that is told by a sympathetic narrator who sees the central problem through to a satisfying resolution is all important to break into *True Romance*. We are always looking for good emotional, identifiable stories."

Rural

Readers may be conservative or liberal, but these publications draw them together with a focus on rural lifestyles. Surprisingly, many readers are from urban centers who dream of or plan to build a house in the country.

‡ALBERTA FARM AND RANCH, Alberta's Foremost Rural Magazine, North Hill Publications, 4000 19th Street N.E., Calgary Alberta T2E 6P8 Canada. (403)250-6633. FAX: (403)291-0502. Editor: Mike Steele. 10-30% freelance written. Monthly magazine covering rural and agricultural issues in Alberta. Estab. 1983. Circ. 80,000. Pays on publication. Publishes ms an average of 4 months after acceptance. Byline given. Buys First Canadian Rights. Submit seasonal/holiday material 6 months in advance. Reports in 1 month. Sample copy for 8 × 10 SAE with 2 first class Canadian stamps or IRC's. Writer's guidelines for #10 SASE with Canadian postage or SAE with 1 IRC.

Nonfiction: General interest, historical/nostalgic, humor, interview/profile, technical. "September's issue always features Women in Agriculture and related issues. No non-relevant articles or articles not of interest to rural Albertans." Buys 20-30 mss/year. Query with published clips. Length: 1,000-2,000 words. Pays $50-200 for assigned articles; $50-100 for unsolicited articles.

Photos: Reviews 4 × 6 prints. Offers $5-10 per photo. Captions and identification of subjects required.

Columns/Departments: "Columnists work on annual contracts only."

Tips: "While *AF&R* seldom accepts unsolicited manuscripts, we always encourage writers to send in queries before going to the time and expense of completing a story. The best way to break into our magazine is with a unique story idea with specific interest to rural Albertans. Stories looking at unique personalities, insightful material on ag related issues and stories of issues concerning the family tend to fill most pages. For new writers trying to solicit their material with little publishing experience, I suggest the submission of typed manuscripts in lieu of tearsheets. Caution: the fastest way to get a rejection is to spell words incorrectly or with glaring grammatical errors. Also, superficial stories that do not entice reading or leave extensive informational gaps tend to be overlooked. I would rather see penned in corrections than errors left unchecked."

COUNTRY JOURNAL, P.O. Box 8200, Harrisburg PA 17105. FAX: (717)657-9526. Editor: Peter V. Fossel. 90% freelance written. Works with a small number of new/unpublished writers each year. Bimonthly magazine featuring country living for people who live in rural areas or who are thinking about moving there. Estab. 1974. Circ. 200,000. Average issue includes 6-8 feature articles and 10 departments. **Pays on acceptance.** Rates range from 30-50¢/word. Byline given. Buys first North American serial rights. Submit seasonal material 1 year in advance. Reports in 2 months. Sample copy $4; writer's guidelines for SASE.

Nonfiction: Book excerpts; general interest; opinion (essays); profile (people who are outstanding in terms of country living); how-to; issues affecting rural areas; and photo feature. Query with published clips with SASE. Length: 2,000-3,500 words. Pays 30-50¢/word. Pays the expenses of writers on assignment.

Photos: Sheryl O'Connell, art director. State availability of photos. Reviews b&w contact sheets, 5×7 and 8×10 b&w glossy prints and 35mm or larger transparencies with SASE. Captions, model release, and identification of subjects required. Buys one-time rights.

Columns/Departments: Listener (brief articles on country topics, how-to's, current events and updates). Buys 5 mss/issue. Query with published clips with SASE. Length: 200-400 words. Pays approximately $75.

Poetry: Free verse, light verse and traditional. Buys 1 poem/issue. Pays $50/poem. Include SASE.

Tips: "Be as specific in your query as possible and explain why you are qualified to write the piece (especially for how-to's and controversial subjects). The writer has a better chance of breaking in at our publication with short articles."

ELECTRIC CONSUMER, Indiana Statewide Assn. of Rural Electric Cooperatives, Inc., P.O. Box 24517, Indianapolis IN 46224. (317)248-9453. Editor: Emily Born. Associate Editor: Richard G. Biever. Monthly tabloid covering rural electric cooperatives (relevant issues affecting members). News/feature format for electric cooperative members in Indiana. Among regular featured departments are: gardening, food, poetry, health and humor. Estab. 1951. Circ. 278,000. Pays on publication. Byline given. Buys one-time rights. Submit seasonal/holiday material 2 months in advance. Simultaneous submissions OK. Reports in 1 month. Free sample copy and writer's guidelines.

Nonfiction: General interest and humor. Buys 25 mss/year. Send complete ms. Considers any length. Pays $25-150. Pays expenses of writers on assignment.

Photos: State availability of photos with submission. Offers $10 per photo. Captions, model releases and identification of subjects required. Buys one-time rights.

Columns/Departments: Humor (personal experiences usually, always "clean" family-oriented), 2,000 words. Buys 10-12 mss/year. Send complete ms. Considers any length. Pays $75.

Poetry: Light verse and traditional. "We don't pay for poems we publish."

Tips: "We receive the majority of our freelance submissions for our humor department although we're happy to look at submissions of other types as well. Keep in mind that our readers are rural/suburban, generally conservative and have the common bond of electric cooperative membership."

FARM & RANCH LIVING, Reiman Publications, 5400 S. 60th St., Greendale WI 53129. (414)423-0100. Editor: Bob Ottum. 80% freelance written. Eager to work with new/unpublished writers. A bimonthly lifestyle magazine aimed at families that farm or ranch full time. "*F&RL* is *not* a 'how-to' magazine – it deals with people rather than products and profits." Estab. 1970. Circ. 380,000. **Pays on acceptance.** Publishes ms an average of 1 year after acceptance. Byline given. Offers 20% kill fee. Buys first serial rights and one-time rights. Submit seasonal/holiday material 6 months in advance. Previously published submissions OK. Reports in 6 weeks. Sample copy $2; writer's guidelines for #10 SASE.

Nonfiction: Interview/profile, photo feature, historical/nostalgic, humor, inspirational and personal experience. No how-to articles or stories about "hobby farmers" (doctors or lawyers with weekend farms); no issue-oriented stories (pollution, animal rights, etc.). Buys 50 mss/year. Query first with or without published clips; state availability of photos. Length: 1,000-3,000 words. Pays $150-500 for text-and-photos package. Pays expenses of writers on assignment.

Photos: Scenic. Pays $75-200 for 35mm color slides. Buys one-time rights.

Fillers: Jokes, anecdotes and short humor with farm or ranch slant. Buys 150/year. Length: 50-150 words. Pays $20 minimum.

Tips: "In spite of poor farm economy, most farm families are proud and optimistic, and they especially enjoy stories and features that are upbeat and positive. *F&RL*'s circulation continues to increase, providing an excellent market for freelancers. A freelancer must see *F&RL* to fully appreciate how different it is from other farm publications – ordering a sample is strongly advised (not available on newsstands). Query first – we'll give plenty of help and encouragement if story looks promising, or we'll explain why if it doesn't. Photo features (about interesting farm or ranch families) and personality profiles are most open to freelancers. We can make separate arrangements for photography if writer is unable to provide photos."

FARM FAMILY AMERICA, Fieldhagen Publishing, Inc., Suite 121, 333 On Sibley, St. Paul MN 55101. (612)292-1747. Editor: George Ashfield. 75% freelance written. A quarterly magazine published by American Cyanamid and written to the lifestyle, activities and travel interests of American farm families. Circ. 295,000. **Pays on acceptance.** Publishes ms an average of 2 months after acceptance. Byline given. Offers 25% kill fee. Buys first or second serial (reprint) rights. Submit seasonal/holiday material 6 months in advance. Simultaneous submissions OK. Query for electronic submissions. Reports in 6 weeks. Writer's guidelines for #10 SASE.

Nonfiction: General interest and travel. Buys 24 mss/year. Query with published clips. Length: 1,000-1,800 words. Pays $300-650. Sometimes pays the expenses of writers on assignment.

Photos: State availability of photos with submission. Reviews 35mm transparencies and prints. Offers $160-700 per photo. Model releases and identification of subjects required. Buys one-time rights.

HARROWSMITH COUNTRY LIFE, Ferry Road, Charlotte VT 05445. (802)425-3961. FAX: (802)425-3307. Editor: James M. Lawrence. Bimonthly magazine covering country living, gardening, shelter, food, and environmental issues. "*Harrowsmith Country Life* readers are generally college educated country dwellers, looking for good information." Estab. 1986. Circ. 250,000. Pays 30-45 days after acceptance. Byline given. Offers 25% kill fee. Buys first North American periodical rights. Reports in 6 weeks. Sample copy $4; writer's guidelines for #10 SASE.

Nonfiction: Book excerpts, essays, exposé (environmental issues), how-to (gardening/building), humor, interview/profile, opinion. Buys 36 mss/year. Query with published clips. Length: 500-5,000 words. Pays $500-1,500. Pays expenses of writers on assignment.

Photos: State availability of photos with submission. Reviews 35mm transparencies. Offers $100-325/photo. Model releases and identification of subjects required. Buys one-time rights.

Columns/Departments: Sourcebank (ideas, tips, tools, techniques relating to gardening, the environment, food, health), 50-400 words; Gazette (brief news items). Buys 30 mss/year. Query with published clips. Length: 40-400 words. Pays $25-150.

Tips: "While main feature stories are open to freelancers, a good way for us to get to know the writer is through our Screed (essays), Sourcebank (tips and ideas) and Gazette (brief news items) departments. Articles should contain examples, quotations and anecdotes. They should be fairly detailed and factual. Please submit material to Suzanne Seibel, Assistant Editor."

HARROWSMITH MAGAZINE, Camden House Publishing, Ltd., Camden East, Ontario K0K 1J0 Canada. (613)378-6661. Editor: Michael Webster. 75% freelance written. Published 6 times/year "for those interested in country life, nonchemical gardening, energy, self-sufficiency, small-stock husbandry, owner-builder architecture and alternative styles of life." Circ. 154,000. **Pays on acceptance.** Publishes ms an average of 4 months after acceptance. Byline given. Buys first North American serial rights. Submit seasonal/holiday material 6 months in advance. Reports in 6 weeks. Sample copy $5; free writer's guidelines.

Nonfiction: Exposé, how-to, general interest, humor, environmental and profile. "We are always in need of quality gardening articles geared to northern conditions. No articles whose style feigns 'folksiness.' No how-to articles written by people who are not totally familiar with their subject. We feel that in this field simple research does not compensate for lack of long-time personal experience." Buys 10 mss/issue. Query. Length: 500-4,000 words. Pays $150-1,250 but will consider higher rates for major stories.

Photos: State availability of photos with query. Pays $50-250 for 35mm or larger transparencies. Captions required. Buys one-time rights.

Tips: "We have standards of excellence as high as any publication in the country. However, we are by no means a closed market. Much of our material comes from unknown writers. We welcome and give thorough consideration to all freelance submissions. Our magazine is read by Canadians who live in rural areas or who hope to make the urban to rural transition. They want to know as much about the realities of country life as the dreams. They expect quality writing, not folksy clichés."

RURAL HERITAGE, P.O. Box 516, Albia IA 52531. (515)932-5084. Publisher: D.H. Holle. 98% freelance written. Works with a small number of new/unpublished writers each year. Quarterly magazine covering individuals dedicated to preserving traditional American life. Estab. 1975. Circ. 10,000. Pays on publication. Publishes ms an average of 1 year after acceptance. Byline given. Buys first North American rights. Submit seasonal/holiday material 1 year in advance. Reports in 3 months. Sample copy $4.50; writer's guidelines #10 SASE.

Nonfiction: Essays; historical/nostalgic; how-to (all types of crafting and farming); interview/profile (especially people using draft animals); photo feature; and travel (emphasizing our theme, "rural heritage"). No articles on *modern* farming. Buys 100 mss/year. Send complete ms. Length: 500-1,500 words. Pays $15-400.

Photos: Send photos with ms. (B&w 5×7 or larger.) No negatives. Pays $5-40. Captions, model releases and identification of subjects (if applicable or pertinent) required. Buys one-time rights.
Columns/Departments: Self-Sufficiency (modern people preserving traditional American lifestyle), 500-1,500 words; Drafter's Features (draft horses and mules used for farming, horse shows and pulls — their care), 500-2,000 words; and Crafting (new designs and patterns), 500-1,500 words. Buys 75 mss/ year. Send complete ms. Pays $15-125.
Poetry: Traditional. Pays $5-25.
Fillers: Anecdotes and short humor. Pays $15-25.
Tips: "Profiles/articles on draft horses and draft horse shows and pulling events are *very* popular with our readers."

Science

These publications are published for laymen interested in technical and scientific develop-ments and discoveries, applied science and technical or scientific hobbies. Publications of interest to the personal computer owner/user are listed in the Personal Computers section. Journals for scientists and engineers are listed in Trade in various sections.

AD ASTRA, 922 Pennsylvania Ave. SE, Washington DC 20003-2140. (202)543-3991. FAX: (202)546-4189. Editor-in-Chief: A. Royce Dalby. Managing Editor: A.R. Hogan. 80% freelance written. A monthly magazine covering the space program. "We publish non-technical, lively articles about all aspects of international space programs, from shuttle missions to planetary probes to plans for the future." Estab. 1989. Circ. 42,000. Pays on publication. Byline given. Buys first North American serial rights. Simultaneous, photocopied and previously published submissions OK. Query for electronic submissions. Reports in 6 weeks on queries; 1 month on mss. Sample copy for 9×12 SAE; writer's guidelines for #10 SAE. "Strongly prefer manuscripts to be accompanied by ASCII or Word Perfect 4.2 floppy disk."
Nonfiction: Book excerpts, essays, exposé, general interest, historical/nostalgic, interview/profile, opinion, personal experience, photo feature and technical. No science fiction or UFO stories. Query with published clips. Length: 1,200-3,000 words. Pays $150-250 for features.
Photos: State availability of photos with submission. Reviews 4×5 color transparencies and b&w prints. Negotiable payment. Identification of subjects required. Buys one-time rights.
Columns/Departments: Mission Control (news about space from around the world), 100-400 words; Space Ed (information for educators), 700-750 words; Reviews (reviews of books or other media); Enterprises (commercial space activities); and Touchdown (opinion pieces). Query with published clips. Pay $35-100.

ARCHAEOLOGY, Archaeological Institute of America, 15 Park Row, New York NY 10038. (212)732-5154. FAX: (212)732-5707. Editor: Peter A. Young. 5% freelance written. "We generally commission articles from professional archaeologists." Bimonthly magazine on archaeology. "The only magazine of its kind to bring worldwide archaeology to the attention of the general public." Estab. 1949. Circ. 140,000. Pays on publication. Byline given. Offers kill fee of ¼ of agreed upon fee. Buys first North American serial rights. Submit seasonal/holiday material 6 months in advance. Simultaneous submis-sions OK. Query preferred. Free sample copy and writer's guidelines.
Nonfiction: Essays and general interest. Buys 6 mss/year. Length: 1,000-3,000 words. Pays $750 maxi-mum. Sometimes pays expenses of writers on assignment.
Photos: Send photos with submission.

‡ASTRONOMY, Kalmbach Publishing, 21027 Crossroads Circle, P.O. Box 1612, Waukesha WI 53187. (414)796-8776. Editor: Richard Berry. Managing Editor: Rhoda I. Sherwood. 75% freelance written. Monthly magazine covering astronomy—the science of and hobby of. "Half of our magazine is for hobbyists (who may have little interest in the heavens in a scientific way); the other half is directed toward armchair astronomers who may be intrigued by the science." Estab. 1976. Circ. 165,000. **Pays on acceptance.** "This varies. We are governed by what is happening in the space program and the heavens. It can be up to a year." Byline given. Buys first North American serial rights, one-time rights, and all rights. Query for electronic submissions. Reports in 1 month on queries; 2 months on mss. Free writer's guidelines.
Nonfiction: Senior editor: Robert Burnham. Book excerpts, c. space and astronomy, how-to for astro hobbyists, humor (in the viewpoints column and about astro), new product, photo feature and techni-cal. Buys 100-200 mss/year. Query. "To propose ideas, also write to Robert Burnham, senior editor." Length: 500-4,500 words. Pays $50-100. Send photos with submission. Reviews transparencies and prints. Pays $10/photo. Captions, model releases and identification of subjects required.

Fillers: "Submitting to *Astronomy* could be tough. (Take a look at how technical astronomy is.) But if someone is a physics teacher (or math or astronomy), he or she might want to study the magazine for a year to see the sorts of subjects and approaches we use and then submit a proposal to Robert Burnham."

‡DISCOVER, Family Media Inc., 3 Park Ave., New York NY 10016. (212)779-6200. Editor: Gill Rosen. 50% freelance written. Monthly magazine. **Pays on acceptance.** Publishes ms an average of 4 months after acceptance. Kill fee varies according to articles assigned. Buys first and one-time rights. Reports in 5 months.
Nonfiction: Prefers to see articles containing hard science. Query. Length and payment vary with article and writer.

THE ELECTRON, CIE Publishing, 1776 E. 17th St., Cleveland OH 44114-3679. (216)781-9400. (216)781-0331. Managing Editor: Janice Weaver. 80% freelance written. Bimonthly tabloid on electronics and high technology. Circ. 60,000. Pays on publication. Publishes ms an average of 2 months after acceptance. Byline given. Buys all rights. Simultaneous queries and previously published submissions OK. Reports in 1 month or earlier. Free sample copy and writer's guidelines.
Nonfiction: Technical (tutorial and how-to), technology news and feature, photo feature, career/educational. All submissions must be electronics/technology-related. Query with letter/proposal and published clips. Pays $50-500.
Photos: State availability of photos. Reviews 8×10 and 5×7 b&w prints. Captions and identification of subjects required.
Tips: "We would like to receive educational electronics/technical articles. They must be written in a manner understandable to the beginning-intermediate electronics student. We are also seeking news/feature-type articles covering timely developments in high technology."

FINAL FRONTIER, The Magazine of Space Exploration, Final Frontier Publishing, Suite 312, 1422 West Lake St., Minneapolis MN 55408. (612)822-9600. FAX: (612)822-9647 for editorial submissions. Editor: Jeremiah Creedon. 95% freelance written. Bimonthly magazine on space exploration. "We are not a technical journal nor a science fiction magazine. We're looking for well-told, factual articles about the people, events and exciting possiblities of the world's space programs." Estab. 1988. Circ. 100,000. **Pays on acceptance.** Byline given. Pays 33% kill fee. Buys first North American serial rights. Submit seasonal/holiday material 6 months in advance. Simultaneous submissions OK. Query for electronic submissions. Reports in 2 months. Sample copy for $3 and a 9×12 SAE with 6 first class stamps. Writer's guidelines for #10 SASE.
Nonfiction: Book excerpts, essays, expose, general interest, historical/nostalgic, humor, interview/profile, new product, personal experience, photo feature. No technical papers, no science fiction or UFOs. Buys 60 mss/year. Query with published clips. Length: 1,000-3,000 words. Pays $600-800 per feature. Sometimes pays expenses of writers on assignment.
Photos: State availability of photos with submission. Offers no additional payment for photos accepted with ms "except as agreed ahead of time."
Column/Departments: Boundaries (the cutting edge of exploration); The Private Vector (space businesses); Earthly Pursuits (spinoffs of space technology); Global Currents (international space happenings); Reviews (books, films, videos, computer programs), all 800 words; Notes from Earth (miscellaneous short items), 200-250 words. Buys 120 mss/year. Query with published clips. Pays $50-150.
Tips: "Look for fresh approaches to familiar subjects. Rather than simply suggesting a story on the space shuttle or Mars exploration, we need a tie-in to a specific project or personality. Think behind-the-scenes. 'Notes from Earth' is a grab-bag of short, quick stories—no more than 250 words. Send your ideas!"

OMNI, 1965 Broadway, New York NY 10023-5965. Editor: Keith Ferrell. 75% freelance written. Prefers to work with published/established writers; works with a small number of new/unpublished writers each year. Monthly magazine of the future covering science fact, fiction, and fantasy for readers of all ages, backgrounds and interests. Estab. 1978. Circ. 750,000. Average issue includes 2-3 nonfiction feature articles and 1-2 fiction articles; also numerous columns. **Pays on acceptance.** Publishes ms an average of 5 months after acceptance. Offers 25% kill fee. Buys exclusive worldwide and exclusive first English rights and rights for *Omni* anthologies. Submit seasonal material 4-6 months in advance.

 The double dagger before a listing indicates that the listing is new in this edition. New markets are often more receptive to freelance submissions.

Reports in 6 weeks. Free writer's guidelines with SASE (request fiction or nonfiction).

Nonfiction: "Feature articles for *Omni* cover all branches of science with an emphasis on the future: What will this discovery or technique mean to us next year, in five years, or even by the year 2025? People want to know and understand what scientists are doing and how scientific research is affecting their lives and their future. *Omni* publishes articles about science in language that people can understand. We seek very knowledgeable science writers who are ready to work with scientists and futurists to produce articles that can inform, interest and entertain our readers with the opportunity to participate in many ground breaking studies." Send query/proposal. Length: 1,500-3,000 words. Pays $2,500-4,500, plus reasonable expenses.

Photos: Frank DeVino, graphic director. State availability of photos. Reviews 35mm slides and 4x5 transparencies. Pays the expenses of writers on assignment.

Columns/Departments: Explorations (unusual travel or locations on Earth); Mind (psychiatry and psychology, neurology, the brain); Earth (environment); Space (technology); Arts (theatre, music, film, technology); Interview (of prominent person); Continuum (newsbreaks); Antimatter and UFO Update (unusual newsbreaks, paranormal); Stars (astronomy); First/Last Word (editorial/humor); Artificial Intelligence (computers, etc.); The Body (medical); Digs (anthropology, archaeology, paleontology, etc.); Books (technology, profiles—no reviews); Transportation (technology); First Word (editorial commissioned, no queries); Last Word (humor, submit ms, no queries). Query with clips of previously published work. Length: 750 words. Pays $1,200; $200 for Continuum and Antimatter items.

Fiction: Contact Ellen Datlow. Fantasy and science fiction. Buys 2 mss/issue. Send complete ms. Length: 10,000 words maximum. Pays $1,250-2,000.

Tips: "To get an idea of the kinds of fiction we publish, check recent back issues of the magazine."

POPULAR SCIENCE, 2 Park Ave., New York NY 10016. FAX: (212)779-5468. Editor-in-Chief: Fred Abatemarco. 50% freelance written. Prefers to work with published/established writers. Monthly magazine. For the well-educated adult, interested in science, technology, new products. Estab. 1872. Circ. 1.8 million. **Pays on acceptance.** Publishes ms an average of 4 months after acceptance. Byline given. Buys all rights. Pays negotiable kill fee. Any electronic submission OK. Reports in 4 weeks. Query. Writer's guidelines for #10 SASE.

Nonfiction: "*Popular Science* is devoted to exploring (and explaining) to a nontechnical but knowledgeable readership the technical world around us. We cover all of the sciences, engineering and technology, and above all, products. We are largely a 'thing'-oriented publication: things that fly or travel down a turnpike, or go on or under the sea, or cut wood, or reproduce music, or build buildings, or make pictures. We are especially focused on the new, the ingenious and the useful. We are consumer-oriented and are interested in any product that adds to the enjoyment of the home, yard, car, boat, workshop, outdoor recreation. Some of our 'articles' are only a picture and caption long. Some are a page long. Some occupy 4 or more pages. Contributors should be as alert to the possibility of selling us pictures and short features as they are to major articles. Freelancers should study the magazine to see what we want and avoid irrelevant submissions." Buys several hundred mss/year. Uses mostly color photos. Pays expenses of writers on assignment.

Tips: "Probably the easiest way to break in here is by covering a news story in science and technology that we haven't heard about yet. We need people to be acting as scouts for us out there and we are willing to give the most leeway on these performances. We are interested in good, sharply focused ideas in all areas we cover. We prefer a vivid, journalistic style of writing, with the writer taking the reader along with him, showing the reader what he saw, through words. Please query first."

SCIENTIFIC AMERICAN, 1415 Madison Ave., New York NY 10017. Did not want to be listed.

TECHNOLOGY REVIEW, The Association of Alumni and Alumnae of the Massachusetts Institute of Technology, W59-200, Massachusetts Institute of Technology, Cambridge MA 02139. 30% freelance written. Emphasizes technology and its implications for scientists, engineers, managers and social scientists. Magazine published 8 times/year. Estab. 1890. Circ. 85,000. Pays on publication. Publishes ms an average of 3-6 months after acceptance. Buys first rights and some exclusive rights. Phone queries OK but *much* prefer written queries. Submit seasonal/holiday material 6 months in advance. No simultaneous submissions. Reports in 6 weeks. Sample copy $2.50; writer's guidelines for #10 SASE. "Please send two copies of all submissions and a self-addressed stamped envelope for return of manuscripts. Please double-space everything!"

Nonfiction: General interest, interview, photo feature and technical. Buys 5-10 mss/year. Query. Length: 1,000-6,000 words. Pays $50-750. Sometimes pays the expenses of writers on assignment.

Columns/Departments: Book Reviews; Trends; Technology and Economics; and Prospects (guest column). Also special reports on other appropriate subjects. Query. Length: 750-4,000 words. Pays $50-1,500.

Science Fiction, Fantasy and Horror

Additional science fiction, fantasy and horror markets are in the Literary and "Little" section.

ABORIGINAL SCIENCE FICTION, Absolute Entertainment Inc., P.O. Box 2449, Woburn MA 01888. Editor: Charles C. Ryan. 99% freelance written. A bimonthly science fiction magazine. "We publish short, lively and entertaining science fiction short stories and poems, accompanied by full-color art." Estab. 1985. Circ. 31,000. Pays on publication. Publishes ms an average of 8-12 months after acceptance. Byline given. Buys first North American serial rights, non-exclusive options on other rights. Query for electronic submissions. Sample copy $3.50, 9 × 12 SAE and $1.05 postage; writer's guidelines for #10 SASE.

Fiction: Science fiction of all types. "We do not use fantasy, horror, sword and sorcery or 'Twilight Zone' type stories." Buys 36 mss/year. Send complete ms. Length: 2,000-6,000 words. Pays $250.

Poetry: Science and science fiction. Buys 8-12 poems/year.

Tips: "Read science fiction novels and other science fiction magazines. Do not rely on science fiction movies or TV. We are open to new fiction writers who are making a sincere effort."

AMAZING® Stories, TSR, Inc., P.O. Box 111, Lake Geneva WI 53147. (414)248-3625. FAX: (414)248-0389. Editor: Mr. Kim Mohan. 95% freelance written. Monthly magazine of science fiction, fantasy and horror short stories. "We are looking for stories and articles that truly live up to the magazine's name—imaginative, trend-setting, thought-provoking pieces of work that will hold a reader's attention and live in his or her memory long after the reading experience is over." Accepts manuscript submissions from new/unpublished writers as well as those with professional credentials. Circ. 15,000 and rising. **Pays on acceptance.** Publishes ms an average of 6 months after acceptance. Byline given. Buys first worldwide serial rights in the English language only; nonexclusive reuse option (with additional pay). No simultaneous or previously published submissions. Reports in 3 months. Sample copy $5; writer's guidelines for #10 SASE.

Nonfiction: Science-fact articles of interest to science fiction audience; essays and opinion pieces by authorities in some area of science or speculative fiction. No true-life experiences, no "soap box" pieces about invalidated theories. Buys 6-12 mss/year. Query first, with published clips if available. Length: 1,000-5,000 words. Pays 10-12¢/word.

Fiction: Science fiction; contemporary and ethnic fantasy; horror. "We want science fiction stories to dominate the magazine's content, but will not turn away any well-written piece of speculative fiction. Horror has the best chance of selling if it has a science-fictional or fantastic setting. Stay away from predictable plot lines and rehashes of old themes—show us *new* ideas." Buys 100-120 mss/year. Send complete ms. Length: 1,000-25,000 words. Pays 6-10¢/word, with shorter stories earning higher rates.

Tips: "Although a large portion of each magazine is devoted to stories from established writers, we are also committed to finding new talent and being a place where unpublished authors can get a start. Nevertheless, we are *very* discriminating about what we purchase. Do not expect to succeed with cliché ideas, stereotypical characters or obtuse 'literary' rambling. Hard science fiction is especially in demand, but any such story must be based on a *plausible* extrapolation from real science. Be familiar with the magazine, and have a copy of our guidelines in hand, before sending us something to review."

ANALOG SCIENCE FICTION/SCIENCE FACT, 380 Lexington Ave., New York NY 10017. Editor: Dr. Stanley Schmidt. 100% freelance written. Eager to work with new/unpublished writers. For general future-minded audience. Monthly. Estab. 1930. Buys first North American serial rights and nonexclusive foreign serial rights. **Pays on acceptance.** Publishes ms an average of 6-10 months after acceptance. Byline given. Reports in 1 month. Sample copy $2.50 and 6 × 9 SASE; writer's guidelines for #10 SASE.

Nonfiction: Illustrated technical articles dealing with subjects of not only current but future interest, i.e., topics at the present frontiers of research whose likely future developments have implications of wide interest. Buys about 13 mss/year. Query. Length: 5,000 words. Pays 6¢/word.

Fiction: "Basically, we publish science fiction stories. That is, stories in which some aspect of future science or technology is so integral to the plot that, if that aspect were removed, the story would collapse. The science can be physical, sociological or psychological. The technology can be anything from electronic engineering to biogenetic engineering. But the stories must be strong and realistic, with believable people doing believable things—no matter how fantastic the background might be." Buys 60-100 unsolicited mss/year. Send complete ms on short fiction; query about serials. Length: 2,000-80,000 words. Pays 4¢/word for novels; 5-6¢/word for novelettes; 6-8¢/word for shorts under 7,500 words; $450-550 for intermediate lengths.

Tips: "In query give clear indication of central ideas and themes and general nature of story line— and what is distinctive or unusual about it. We have no hard-and-fast editorial guidelines, because science fiction is such a broad field that I don't want to inhibit a new writer's thinking by imposing

'Thou Shalt Not's.' Besides, a really good story can make an editor swallow his preconceived taboos. I want the best work I can get, regardless of who wrote it—and I need new writers. So I work closely with new writers who show definite promise, but of course it's impossible to do this with *every* new writer. No occult or fantasy."

ISAAC ASIMOV'S SCIENCE FICTION MAGAZINE, Davis Publications, Inc., 380 Lexington Ave., New York NY 10168-0035. (212)557-9100. Editor-in-Chief: Gardner Dozois. 98% freelance written. Works with a small number of new/unpublished writers each year. Emphasizes science fiction. 13 times a year magazine, including two double issues. Estab. 1977. Circ. 100,000. **Pays on acceptance.** Buys first North American serial rights, nonexclusive foreign serial rights and occasionally reprint rights. No simultaneous submissions. Reports in 6 weeks. Sample copy for 6½ × 9½ SAE and $3; writer's guidelines for #10 SASE.
Nonfiction: Science. Query first.
Fiction: Science fiction primarily. Some fantasy and poetry. "It's best to read a great deal of material in the genre to avoid the use of some *very* old ideas." Buys 10 mss/issue. Submit complete ms. Length: 100-20,000 words. Pays 5-8¢/word except for novel serializations at 4¢/word.
Tips: Query letters not wanted, except for nonfiction.

BEYOND . . .,Science Fiction and Fantasy, Other World Books, P.O. Box 136, New York NY 10024. Editor: Shirley Winston. Managing Editor: Roberta Rogow. 80% freelance written. Eager to work with new/unpublished writers. A science fiction and fantasy magazine published 4 times a year. "Our audience is mostly science fiction fans." Estab. 1985. Circ. 300. Pays on publication. Publishes ms an average of 6-9 months after acceptance. Byline given. Buys first North American serial rights. Submit seasonal/holiday material 6 months in advance. Query for electronic submissions. Reports in 3 weeks. Sample copy $4.50 and 9 × 12 SAE; writer's guidelines for #10 SASE.
Nonfiction: Essays and humor. Buys 3 mss/year. Send complete ms. Length: 500-1,500 words. Pays $1.25-3.75 and 1 copy.
Columns/Departments: Reviews (of books and periodicals in science fiction and fantasy area), 500-1,500 words. Buys 3 mss/year. Send complete ms. Length: 500-1,500 words. Pays $1.25-3.75.
Fiction: Fantasy and science fiction only. "We enjoy using stories with a humorous aspect. No horror stories, excessive violence or explicit sex; nothing degrading to women or showing prejudice based on race, religion, or planet of origin. No predictions of universal destruction; we prefer an outlook on the future in which the human race survives and progresses." Buys 20 mss/year. Send complete ms. Length: 500-8,000 words; prefers 4,000-5,000 words. Pays $1.25-20 and 1 copy.
Poetry: Free verse, haiku, light verse and traditional. "Poetry should be comprehensible by an educated reader literate in English, take its subject matter from science fiction or fantasy, need not rhyme but should fall musically on the ear." No poetry unrelated to science fiction or fantasy. Buys 18 poems/year. Submit maximum 3 poems. Length: 4-65 words. Pays 2¢/line and 1 copy.
Tips: Fiction and poetry are most open to freelancers.

MARION ZIMMER BRADLEY'S FANTASY MAGAZINE, Marion Zimmer Bradley Ltd., P.O. Box 245-A, Berkeley CA 94701. Editor: Marion Z. Bradley. 100% freelance written. Quarterly magazine of fantasy fiction. Estab. 1988. **Pays on acceptance.** Publishes ms an average of 3-6 months after acceptance. Byline given. Offers $25 kill fee. Buys first North American serial rights. Sample copy $4.
Nonfiction: Humor, personal experience (writers), technical. "We rarely buy except on assignment from known writers." Buys 1-2 mss/year. Query with or without published clips. Length: 5,000 words maximum.
Fiction: Fantasy. No science fiction, very little horror. Buys 55-60 mss/year. Send complete ms. Length: 300-7,500 words. Pays 2-10¢/word.
Tips: "Do not submit without first reading guidelines."

HAUNTS, Nightshade Publications, P.O. Box 3342, Providence RI 02906. (401)781-9438. Editor: Joseph K. Cherkes. 98% freelance written. Prefers to work with published/established writers; works with small number of new/unpublished writers each year. "We are a literary quarterly geared to those fans of the 'pulp' magazines of the 30's, 40's and 50's, with tales of horror, the supernatural, and the bizarre. We are trying to reach those in the 18-35 age group." Estab. 1984. Circ. 1,200. Pays on publication. Publishes ms an average of 9 months after acceptance. Byline given. Buys first North American serial rights. Reports in 3 weeks on queries; 3 months on mss. Sample copy $3.95 plus $1 postage; writer's guidelines for #10 SASE.
Fiction: Fantasy, horror and suspense. "No fiction involving blow-by-blow dismemberment, explicit sexual scenes or pure adventure." Buys 36 fiction mss/year. Query. Length: 1,500-8,000 words. Pays $5-50.

Poetry: Free verse, light verse and traditional. Buys 12-16 poems/year. Submit maximum 3 poems. Offers contributor's copies.
Tips: "Market open from June 1 to December 1 inclusive. How the writer handles revisions often is a key to acceptance."

HOBSON'S CHOICE, (formerly *Starwind*), The Starwind Press, P.O. Box 98, Ripley OH 45167. (513)392-4549. Editors: David F. Powell and Susannah C. West. 75% freelance written. Eager to work with new/unpublished writers. A monthly magazine "for older teenagers and adults who have an interest in science and technology, and who also enjoy reading well-crafted science fiction and fantasy." Estab. 1974. Circ. 2,500. Pays on publication. Publishes ms an average of 1 year after acceptance. Byline given. Rights vary with author and material; negotiated with author. Usually first serial rights and second serial reprint rights (nonfiction). Query for electronic submissions. "In fact, we encourage disposable submissions; easier for us and easier for the author. Just enclose SASE for our response. We prefer non-simultaneous submissions." Reports in 3 months. Sample copy for $1.75 and 9 × 12 SAE; writer's guidelines for #10 SASE.
Nonfiction: How-to (technological interest, e.g., how to build a robot eye, building your own radio receiver, etc.); interview/profile (of leaders in science and technology fields); and technical ("did you know" articles dealing with development of current technology). "No speculative articles, dealing with topics such as the Abominable Snowman, Bermuda Triangle, etc. At present, most nonfiction is staff-written or reprinted from other sources. We hope to use more freelance written work in the future." Query. Length: 1,000-7,000 words. Pays 1-4¢/word.
Photos: Send photos with accompanying query or ms. Reviews b&w contact sheets and prints. Model releases and identification of subjects required. "If photos are available, we prefer to purchase them as part of the written piece." Buys negotiable rights.
Fiction: Fantasy and science fiction. "No stories whose characters were created by others (e.g. *Lovecraft, Star Trek, Star Wars* characters, etc.)." Buys 15-20 mss/year. Send complete ms. Length: 2,000-10,000 words. Pays 1-4¢/word. "We prefer previously unpublished fiction." No query necessary. We don't publish horror, poetry, novel excerpts or serialized novels.
Tips: "Our need for nonfiction is greater than for fiction at present. Almost all our fiction and nonfiction is unsolicited. We rarely ask for rewrites, because we've found that rewrites are often disappointing; although the writer may have rewritten it to fix problems, he/she frequently changes parts we liked, too."

‡THE MAGAZINE OF FANTASY & SCIENCE FICTION, Mercury Press, P.O. Box 11526, Eugene OR 97440. Editor: Kristine Kathryn Rusch. 100% freelance written. Monthly fantasy fiction and science fiction magazine. Estab. 1949. Circ. 53,000. **Pays on acceptance.** Byline given. Buys first North American serial rights and foreign serial rights. Submit seasonal/holiday material 8 months in advance. Reports in 1 month on mss. Writer's guidelines for #10 SASE.
Fiction: Fantasy, horror, science fiction. Send complete ms. Length: 2,000-20,000 words. Pays 5-7¢/word.

‡MIDNIGHT ZOO, Experiences Unlimited, 544 Ygnacio Valley Rd, #A273, P.O. Box 8040, Walnut Creek CA 94596. (415)942-5116. Editor: Jon L. Herron. Bimonthly magazine of horror, science fiction, fantasy and science fact. "All articles and stories must have a H/SF/F slant. Science fact must be hard science. No explicit sex or blood and guts. Audience 12-100 years old." Estab. 1990. Circ. 3,000. Pays on publication. Publishes ms an average of 2 months after acceptance. Byline given. Buys one-time rights, second serial (reprint) rights, simultaneous rights and telephone rights. Submit seasonal/holiday material 6 months in advance. Simultaneous and previously published submissions OK. Query for electronic submissions. Reports in 1 month on queries; 2 months on mss. Sample copy $4.95 with 9 × 12 SAE and 4 first class stamp. Writer's guidelines for #10 SASE.
Nonfiction: Articles editor: Elizabeth Gilligan. Book excerpts, essays, general interest (SF/H/F), humor, interview/profile (SF/H/F), new product, opinion, personal experience (psychic, occult, strange), technical (science), book video, movie reviews poems, writers interest. Buys 30 mss/year. Query with or without published clips or send complete ms. Length: 1,000-3,000 words. Pays $5-30 for assigned articles; copy-$15 for unsolicited articles. "Pays in copies for some unsolicited articles."
Photos: Send photos with submission. Reviews 3 × 5 b&w prints *only*. Offers $3-5 per photo. Model releases and identification of subjects required. Buys one-time rights.
Columns/Departments: Elizabeth Gilligan. Strange Happenings (occult, strange, supernatural, psychic, etc.), 1-1,300 words; Scientific Scene (hard science, new discoveries, etc.), 1-3,000 words; Interviews (H/SF/F writers, artists, stars), 2,500-4,000 words; Writer's Corner (tips for writers), 1-3,000 words; Reviews (movie, video, book, magazine), 200-1,000 words. Buys 25 mss/year. Query with published clips. Pays $5-30.

Fiction: Jon L. Herron. Fantasy, horror, mystery (with horror/Sci-Fi), science fiction. "No formula stories. All must have sci-fi, horror, fantasy slant. No work based on creations of others." Buys 250 mss/year. Send complete ms. Length: 1,000-7,000 words. Pays $5-70.

Poetry: Dianne Anderson. Avant-garde, free verse, light verse, traditional. "No haiku, please." Buys 150 poems/year. Submit maximum 10 poems. Length: 10-100 lines. Pays $3-10.

Fillers: Stephen Mitchell. Anecdotes, facts, gags to be illustrated by cartoonist, newsbreaks and short humor. Length: 20-100 words. Pays $3-10.

Tips: "Submit original ideas. No formula stories. We cater to unpublished and underpublished writers. Writers have their best chance with fiction and poems."

NEW BLOOD MAGAZINE, Suite 3730, 540 W. Foothill Blvd., Glendora CA 91740. Editor: Chris B. Lacher. 90% freelance written. Quarterly magazine that uses fiction considered too strong or bizarre for ordinary periodicals. "*NB* is an outlet for work that is otherwise unpublishable because of content, view, opinion, or other. We reach all readers—horror, fantasy, sci-fi, mystery/suspense, erotic—because we do not print generic forms of fiction." Estab. 1986. Circ. 15,000. Pays half on acceptance, half on publication. Publishes ms an average of 6 months after acceptance. Byline given. Offers 50% kill fee. All rights revert to author upon publication. Submit seasonal/holiday material 6 months in advance. Previously published submissions OK. No simultaneous submissions. Reports in 1 month. "Please do not market accepted articles while awaiting publication." Sample copy $4. Writer's guidelines for #10 SASE.

Nonfiction: Book excerpts (query), essays, exposé, humor, interview/profile, new product, opinion and photo feature. Buys 8-12 mss/year. Query or send complete ms. Length: 500-3,000 words. Pays 6¢/word for assigned articles.

Photos: State availability of photos with submission. Reviews contact sheets. Sometimes offers additional payment for photos accepted with ms. Model releases required. Buys one-time rights.

Columns/Departments: Shelf-Life (book reviews), 100-500 words; Prose & Conversation (novel excerpt/opinion), 1,000-5,000 words. Buys 12-24 mss/year. Query or send complete ms. Pays 6¢/word.

Fiction: Adventure, erotica, experimental, fantasy, horror/gore, humorous, mainstream, mystery, novel excerpts, science fiction, slice-of-life vignettes and suspense. Open to all subjects, except libelous fiction, fiction that portrays children in pornographic situations. Buys 50-100 mss/year. Send complete ms. Length: 750-5,000 words. Pays 6¢/word; higher for special.

Fillers: Anecdotes, facts, gags to be illustrated by cartoonist, newsbreaks and short humor. Buys 10-25/year. Pays $5 minimum.

Tips: "I support you by answering your submission personally—always, with no exceptions—so I hope you will support me by buying a sample copy of the publication. *NB* was created as an outlet not only for the unpublishable, but also for the beginning or less established author, hence the title. I try not to discourage any contributor—if you're brave enough and dedicated enough to submit your work professionally, I believe you will eventually become successful. Don't get discouraged. I submitted my work for 8 years before I made my first sale, so be persistent."

‡OWLFLIGHT, Science Fiction & Fantasy, Unique Graphics, 1025 55th St., Oakland CA 94608. Editor: Millea Kenin. 99% freelance written. Irregularly published magazine offering science fiction and fantasy. "*Owlflight* publishes science fiction and fantasy fiction of fully professional quality that has failed to find publication in commercial markets." Estab. 1982. Circ. 1,500. Pays on publication. Publishes ms over one year after acceptance. Byline given. Buys first North American serial rights or second serial (reprint) rights (rarely). Query for electronic submissions. Reports in 3 weeks on queries; 6 weeks on manuscripts. Sample copy $2.50. Writer's guidelines for #10 SASE.

Photos: State availability of photos with submission. Reviews prints of any size, b&w *Only*!!! Offers negotiable payment. Buys one-time rights.

Fiction: Experimental (F/SF genre), fantasy, science fiction. "Nothing that lacks intrinsic and necessary fantasy/science fiction themes. No horror, media SF (eg. Star Trek) or anything else using characters/settings copyright by anyone other than the author. No short-shorts. Send for guidelines before first submission, then send complete ms if it fits theme and does not fall into a category in which we are backlogged. Never describe the plot or theme of a submission in a query or cover letter." Length 2,500-8,000 words. Pays $25-80.

Poetry: "Nothing that lacks a SF/Fantasy theme—but this can be broadly interpreted for poetry. Also, don't send ye olde tyme language!" Length 100 maximum lines. Pays 1¢ word, $1 minimum.

Tips: "Never submit anything without having seen guidelines, and without having queried within 6 months to find out if we are overstocked, since we often are. If you have our phone number and leave a message by phone, include address for reply! We do not answer phone calls from strangers outside the 415 area code."

PANDORA, 2844 Grayson, Ferndale MI 48220. Editors: Meg MacDonald, Polly Vedder (art), Ruth Berman (poetry). 99% freelance written. Works with a number of new/unpublished writers each year. Anthology published 2 times/year covering science fiction and fantasy. Anticipate quarterly status in 1992/93. Estab. 1978. Circ. 1,000. Pays on publication. Publishes ms an average of 6-12 months after acceptance. Byline given. Buys first North American serial rights and second serial (reprint) rights; one-time rights on some poems. Reports in 6 weeks. Sample copy $5, ($10 overseas); writer's guidelines for #10 SASE. Foreign contributors, please use enough IRC's to cover return of manuscript or letter.

Columns/Departments: "We buy short reviews of science fiction and fantasy books that a reader feels truly exemplify fine writing and will be of interest and use to other writers. Small press titles as well as major press titles are welcome." Query with specific idea or send complete ms. Length: under 500 words. Pays $5 and up.

Fiction: Fantasy, science fiction. "No pun stories. No Lucifer stories or deals with the devil stories. Nothing x-rated (no vulgar language, gratuitous violence, sex, racisim, etc.). No inaccurate science and no horror of the chainsaw variety. Scarey stories, ghost stories OK. No occult material, however." Buys 20 mss/year. Send complete ms. Length: under 5,000 words. Longer work must be exceptional. Pays 1-2¢/word.

Poetry: Ruth Berman, poetry editor. 2809 Drew Ave. S., Minneapolis MN 55417. Buys 10-15 poems/year. Payment starts at $4. Length: open. No romance, occult or horror.

Tips: "We still want stories about characters our readers can sympathize with and care about. Then give them convincing, relevant problems that they must overcome. Stories about people and their difficulties, victories, and losses are of more interest to us than stories about futuristic gadgets. What impact does the gadget have on society? *That's* what we want to know. Stories must have a point—not just a pun. Happy endings aren't necessary, but we urge authors to leave the reader with a sense that no matter the outcome, something has been accomplished between the first and last pages. Reading our magazine is the best way to determine our needs, and we strongly recommend all contributors read at least one sample. Always send for guidelines before submitting as well. We like to see whole stories, the shorter the better, and we will make attempts to respond personally with a critique. Stories which support the existance of a higher authority than man are welcome. We like fantasy and don't see enough of it. Highly descriptive, but not overwritten, language is a plus. Take us on a magical journey—through time, through space, through the 'looking glass'—we want to see your work, and we want to publish as much as we can. Anticipate quarterly status and may pay on acceptance in 1992/93. Also anticipate payment increase. Query."

QUANTUM—SCIENCE FICTION AND FANTASY REVIEW, Thrust Publications, 8217 Langport Terrace, Gaithersburg MD 20877. (301)948-2514. Editor: D. Douglas Fratz. 20-40% freelance written. Prefers to work with published/established writers; works with small number of new/unpublished writers each year. A quarterly literary review magazine covering science fiction and fantasy literature. "*QUANTUM—Science Fiction and Fantasy Review* is the highly acclaimed, Hugo-Award-nominated magazine about science fiction and fantasy. Since 1973, *QUANTUM* has been featuring in-depth interviews with science fiction's best known authors and artists, articles and columns by the field's most outspoken writers, and reviews of current science fiction books. *QUANTUM* has built its reputation on never failing to take a close look at the most sensitive and controversial issues concerning science fiction and continues to receive the highest praise and most heated comments from professionals and fans in the science fiction field." Estab. 1973. Circ. 1,800. Pays on publication. Publishes ms an average of 6 months after acceptance. Byline given. Buys first North American serial rights, one-time rights and second serial (reprint) rights. Submit seasonal/holiday material 3-6 months in advance. Simultaneous queries, and simultaneous and previously published submissions OK. Query for electronic submissions. Reports in 2 weeks on queries; 2 months on mss. Sample copy for $3.00 ($3.50 foreign).

Nonfiction: Humor, interview/profile, opinion, personal experience and book reviews. Buys 50-100 mss/year. Query or send complete ms. Length: 200-10,000 words. Pays 1-2¢/word.

Photos: "We publish only photos of writers being interviewed." State availability of photos. Pays $2-15 for smaller than 8×10 b&w prints. Buys one-time rights.

Columns/Departments: Uses science fiction and fantasy book reviews and film reviews. Buys 40-90 mss/year. Send complete ms. Length: 100-1,000 words. Pays 1¢/word. (Reviews usually paid in subscriptions, not cash.)

Tips: "Reviews are best way to break into *QUANTUM*. Must be on current science fiction and fantasy books. The most frequent mistake made by writers in completing articles for us is writing to a novice audience; *QUANTUM*'s readers are science fiction and fantasy experts."

THE SCREAM FACTORY, The Magazine of Horrors, Past, Present, and Future, Deadline Publications, 145 Tully Rd., San Jose CA 95111. Editors: Peter Enfantino, Joe Lopez, Bob Morrish and John Scoleri. 75% freelance written. Quarterly literary magazine about horror in films and literature. Estab. 1988. Circ. 1,000. **Pays on acceptance.** Publishes ms an average of 6 months after acceptance. Buys first North American serial rights. Submit seasonal/holiday material 6 months in advance. No simultaneous submissions or reprints. Reports in 2 weeks on queries, 1 month on ms. Sample copy $6 (please make checks payable to Joe Lopez); writer's guidelines for #10 SASE.

Nonfiction: Book excerpts (from published novelists), essays, historical/nostalgic, interview/profile, new product and personal experience. Buys 35-50 mss/year. Query or send complete ms. Pays 1/2¢/word.

Photos: Send photos with submission. Reviews prints. Offers no additional payment for photos accepted with ms. Captions required. Buys one-time rights.

Columns/Departments: Book reviews of horror novels/collections; Writer's Writing (what horror authors are currently working on); A Tale of Wyrmwood (fiction saga about haunted town). Query or send complete ms. Pays 1/2¢/word.

Fillers: Facts, newsbreaks. Pays 1/2¢/word.

Tips: "Looking for reviews of horror fiction, especially the lesser known authors. News on the horror genre, interviews with horror authors and strong opinion pieces. No unsolicited fiction accepted."

‡**THE STANDING STONE,** #312, 120 Perth Ave., Toronto, Ontario M6P 4E1 Canada. Editor: Gordon R. Menzies. 100% freelance written. Quarterly magazine of fantasy and horror literature. Estab. 1990. **Pays on acceptance.** No kill fee. Buys first North American serial rights. Submit seasonal/holiday material 1-3 months in advance. Simultaneous submissions OK. Reports in 1 week on queries; 1 month on manuscripts. Sample copy $3. Writer's guidelines for #10 SAE with 1 first class stamp—use Canadian postage.

Fiction: Fantasy, horror. Buys 12-20 mss/year. Send complete ms. Length: 500-3,000 words, pays maximum $15, 1/2¢/word (Canadian funds).

Poetry: Avant-garde, free verse, haiku, light verse, traditional. "No cryptic. Do not want to see poems that only the poet can understand." Buys 12-20 poems/year. Submit maximum 3-5 poems. Length: 1 pg. Pays 10¢/line, minimum $1 (Canadian funds). All cheques to: Ebenrock Enterprises (publisher).

STARLOG MAGAZINE, The Science Fiction Universe, Starlog Group, 475 Park Ave. S., 8th Floor, New York NY 10016. (212)689-2830. FAX: (212) 889-7933. Editor: David McDonnell. 85% freelance written. Very eager to work with new/unpublished writers. Monthly magazine covering "the science fiction-fantasy-adventure genre: its films, TV, books, art and personalities." Estab. 1976. "We concentrate on interviews with actors, directors, screenwriters, producers, special effects technicians and others. Be aware that 'sci-fi' and 'Trekkie' are seen as derogatory terms by our readers and by us." Pays on publication. Publishes ms an average of 4 months after acceptance. Byline given. Offers kill fee "only to mss *written* or interviews *done*." Buys all rights and second serial (reprint) rights to certain other material. Submit seasonal/holiday material 6 months in advance. Simultaneous queries and submissions OK if noted. Reports in 1 month on queries; 6 weeks on mss. "We provide an assignment sheet and contract to *all* writers with deadline and other info, thus authorizing a queried piece." Sample copy ($4.50). Writer's guidelines for 8½ × 11 SAE with 3 first class stamps. Writer's guidelines for #10 SASE.

Nonfiction: Interview/profile (actors, directors, screenwriters who've made science fiction films, and science fiction novelists); photo features; special effects how-tos (on filmmaking only); retrospectives of famous SF films and TV series; coverage of science fiction fandom, conventions, etc. "We also sometimes cover animation (especially Disney and WB) SF-based and comics." No personal opinion think pieces/essays. *No* first person. "We prefer article format as opposed to Q&A interviews." Buys 150 mss/year. Query first with published clips. "We prefer queries by mail to phone or fax." Length: 500-3,000 words. Pays $35 (500-word pieces); $50-75 (sidebars); $125-225 (1,000-word and up pieces). Avoids articles on horror films/creators.

Photos: State availability of photos. Pays $10-25 for slide transparencies and 8 × 10 b&w prints depending on quality. "No separate payment for photos provided by film studios." Captions, model releases, identification of subjects and credit line on photos required. Photo credit given. Buys all rights.

Columns/Departments: Fan Network (articles on fandom and its aspects—mostly staff-written); Booklog (book reviews, $10 each, by assignment only); Medialog (news of upcoming science fiction films and TV projects and mini-interviews with those involved, $35); Videolog (videocassette and disk releases of genre interest, staff-written). Buys 18-20 mss/year. Query with published clips. Length: 300-500 words. No kill fee.

Tips: "Absolutely *no fiction*. We throw fiction mistakenly sent to us in the nearest wastebasket. Nonfiction only please!! A writer can best break in to *Starlog* with short news pieces or by getting an unusual interview or by *out-thinking* us and coming up with something *new* on a current film or book *before* we can think of it. We are always looking for *new* angles on *Star Trek: The Next Generation, Star Wars*, the original *Star Trek, Doctor Who* and seek features on series that remain very popular: *Starman, Beauty & the Beast, Lost in Space, Space 1999, Battlestar Galactica, The Twilight Zone, The Outer Limits*. Know your subject before you try us. Most full-length major assignments go to freelancers with whom we're already dealing. But if we like your clips and ideas, we'll be happy to give *you* a chance. We're fans of this material—and a prospective writer must be, too—but we were *also* freelancers. And if you love science fiction, we would love to *help* you break in to print as we've done with many others in the past."

2 AM MAGAZINE, P.O. Box 6754, Rockford IL 61125. Editor: Gretta M. Anderson. 100% freelance written. A quarterly magazine of fiction, poetry, articles and art for readers of fantasy, horror and science fiction. Estab. 1986. Circ. 1,000. **Pays on acceptance.** Publishes ms an average of 9 months after acceptance. Byline given. Buys first North American serial rights. Submit seasonal/holiday material 1 year in advance. Reports in 1 month on queries; 3 months on mss. Sample copy $5.95; writer's guidelines for #10 SAE with 1 first class stamp.

Nonfiction: How-to, interview/profile, opinion, also book reviews of horror, fantasy or SF recent releases. "No essays originally written for high school or college courses." Buys 5 mss/year. Query with or without published clips or send complete ms. Length: 500-2,000 words. Pay ½-1¢/word.

Photos: State availability of photos with submission. Offers no additional payment for photos accepted with ms. Identification of subjects required. Buys one-time rights.

Fiction: Fantasy, horror, mystery, science fiction and suspense. Buys 50 mss/year. Send complete ms. Length: 500-5,000 words. Pays ½-1¢/word.

Poetry: Free verse and traditional. "No haiku/zen or short poems without imagery." Buys 20 poems/year. Submit up to 5 poems at one time. Length: 5-100 lines. Pays $1-5.

Tips: "We are looking for taut, imaginative fiction. Please use proper manuscript format; all manuscripts must include a SASE to be considered. We suggest to Canadian and foreign writers that they send disposable manuscripts with one IRC and one #10 SAE for response, if U.S. postage stamps are unavailable to them."

VISIONS, the intercollegiate magazine of speculative fiction and fantasy, Visions Magazine, Inc., 409 College Ave., Ithaca NY 14850. (607)272-2000. Editor: Shelly Nichols. 95% freelance written. Quarterly literary magazine of imaginative fiction by college authors. "Authors must be college students (graduate or undergrad) and write imaginative, speculative fiction for an international audience of fellow students." Estab. 1986. Circ. 12,000 U.S./U.K./Canada. Publishes ms an average of 5 months after acceptance. Byline given. Buys first North American serial rights or first USSR serial rights. Simultaneous submissions. Query for electronic submissions. Reports in 1 month on queries; 3 months on mss. Sample copy $4. Writer's guidelines for #10 SAE with 1 first class stamp.

Fiction: Adventure, experimental, fantasy, horror, novel excerpts, science fiction. "No pulp or space opera (except camp farce), sexist/racist overtones or gritty *New Yorker*-style realism." Buys 50 mss/year. Send complete ms with SASE.

Tips: "Avoid excessive use of capital letters! Tell human stories about alien conditions rather than the other way around. Know your science and get it right—pseudo science won't make it. Fiction should be snappy and avoid clichés. Grammar and style must be polished, though we do work with authors whose manuscripts can be revised to printable quality. Still looking for U.S. fantasy or magical realism."

Sports

A variety of sports magazines, from general interest to sports medicine, are covered in this section. For the convenience of writers who specialize in one or two areas of sport and outdoor writing, the publications are subcategorized by the sport or subject matter they emphasize. Publications in related categories (for example, Hunting and Fishing; Archery and Bowhunting) often buy similar material. Writers should read through this entire category to become familiar with the subcategories. Publications on horse breeding and hunting dogs are classified in the Animal category, while horse racing is listed here. Publications dealing with automobile or motorcycle racing can be found in the Automotive and Motorcycle category. Markets interested in articles on exercise and fitness are listed in the Health and Fitness section. Outdoor publications that promote the preservation of nature, placing only secondary emphasis on nature as a setting for sport, are in the Nature, Conservation and Ecology category. Regional magazines are frequently interested in sports material with a local angle. Camping publications are classified in the Travel, Camping and Trailer category.

Archery and Bowhunting

BOW AND ARROW HUNTING, Box HH/34249 Camino Capistrano, Capistrano Beach CA 92624. Editorial Director: Roger Combs. 80% freelance written. Eager to work with new/unpublished writers. Bimonthly magazine for bowhunters. **Pays on acceptance.** Publishes ms an average of 6 months after acceptance. Buys first serial rights. Byline given. Reports in 2 months. Author must have some knowledge of archery terms.

Nonfiction: Articles: bowhunting, techniques used by champs, how to make your own tackle and off-trail hunting tales. Likes a touch of humor. "No dead animals or 'my first hunt.'" Also uses one technical and how-to article per issue. Submit complete ms. Length: 1,500-2,500 words. Pays $150-300.

Photos: Purchased as package with ms; 5×7 minimum. Pays $100 for cover chromes, 35mm or larger.
Tips: "Subject matter is more important than style—that's why we have editors and copy pencils. Good b&w photos are of primary importance. We staff-write our shorter pieces."

BOWHUNTER, The Magazine for the Hunting Archer, Cowles Magazines, 2245 Kohn Rd., Box 8200, Harrisburg PA 17105-8200. (717)540-8192. FAX (717) 657-9526. Editor: M.R. James. Editorial Director: Dave Canfield. 85% freelance written. Bimonthly magazine (with two special issues) on hunting big and small game with bow and arrow. "We are a special interest publication, produced by bowhunters for bowhunters, covering all aspects of the sport. Material included in each issue is designed to entertain and inform readers, making them better bowhunters." Estab. 1971. Circ. 250,000. **Pays on acceptance.** Publishes ms an average of 10-12 months after acceptance. Byline given. Kill fee varies. Buys first North American serial rights and one-time rights. Submit seasonal/holiday material 8 months in advance. Reports in 1 month on queries; 5 weeks on mss. Sample copy $2. Free writer's guidelines.

Nonfiction: General interest, how-to, interview/profile, opinion, personal experience and photo feature. "We publish a special 'Big Game' issue each Fall (September) but need all material by mid-March. Our annual publication, *Whitetail Bowhunter*, is staff written or by assignment only. We don't want articles that graphically deal with an animal's death. And, please, no articles written from the animal's viewpoint." Buys 100 plus mss/year. Query. Length: 250-2,500 words. Pays $500 maximum for assigned articles; $25-500 for unsolicited articles. Sometimes pays expenses of writers on assignment.
Photos: Send photos with submission. Reviews 35mm and 2¼×2¼ transparencies and 5×7 and 8×10 prints. Offers $35-200 per photo. Captions required. Buys one-time rights.
Columns/Departments: Would You Believe (unusual or offbeat hunting experiences), 250-1,000 words. Buys 6-8 mss/year. Send complete ms. Pays $25-100.
Tips: "A writer must know bowhunting and be willing to share that knowledge. Writers should antici-pate *all* questions a reader might ask, then answer them in the article itself or in an appropriate sidebar. Articles should be written with the reader foremost in mind; we won't be impressed by writers seeking to prove how good they are—either as writers or bowhunters. We care about the reader and don't need writers with 'I' trouble. Features are a good bet because most of our material comes from freelancers. The best advice is: Be yourself. Tell your story the same as if sharing the experience around a campfire. Don't try to write like you think a writer writes."

BOWHUNTING WORLD, Ehlert Publishing Group, Suite 101, 319 Barry Ave. S., Wayzata MN 55391. (612)476-2200. Editor: Tim Dehn. 70% freelance written. A magazine published 11 times/year and written for bowhunting and archery enthusiasts who participate in the sport year-round. Estab. 1951. Circ. 250,000. **Pays on acceptance.** Publishes manuscripts an average of 5 months after acceptance. Byline given. Buys first rights. Reports in 3 weeks on queries, 6 weeks on manuscripts. Sample copy for 9×12 SAE and $2 postage; free writer's and photographers guidelines.
Nonfiction: Hunting adventure and scouting and hunting how-to features, primarily from a first-person point of view. Also interview/profile pieces, historical articles, humor and do-it-yourself pieces. Buys 60 mss/year. Query or send complete ms. Length: 1,500-3,000 words. Pays from less than $200 to more than $500.
Photos: Send photos with submission. Reviews 35mm transparencies and b&w or color prints. Captions required. Buys one-time rights. Send for separate photo guidelines.
Tips: "We look for a combination of good writing and good information. Although we've expanded our focus in recent years to include all North American big and small game typically hunted with bow and arrow, nearly half the articles we buy are about bowhunting for deer. Many freelancers are submitting slides only because that allows magazines to reproduce photos in either b&w or color. Our experience shows that detail is lost converting the slides and that we typically buy additional freelance color to support the article. For that reason, we now encourage authors with access to high quality, b&w print developing services to send b&w illustrations with their packages."

INTERNATIONAL BOWHUNTER MAGAZINE, International Bowhunting Publications, Inc., Rt. 1, Box 41E, P.O. Box 67, Pillager MN 56473-0067. (218)746-3333. FAX: (218)746-3333. Editor: Johnny E. Boatner. 95% freelance written. Magazine publishes seven issues per year on bowhunting. "We are interested in any kind of articles that deal with bowhunting. We pride ourselves as a magazine written by hunter/writers, rather than writer/hunters. We are not interested in articles that just fill pages, we like each paragraph to say something." Estab. 1983. Circ. 57,000. Pays on publication. Publishes ms an average of 1 or 2 months after acceptance. Byline sometimes given. Buys first rights. Submit seasonal/holiday material 4 months in advance. Reports in 1 week on queries; 6 weeks on mss. Free sample copy and writer's guidelines.

Nonfiction: Historical/nostalgic, how-to, humor, interview/profile, new product, personal experience, photo feature, technical, travel; bowhunting and archery related. "No commercials of writers' pet products; articles including bad ethics, gory, target archery." Buys 75 mss/year. Send complete ms. Length: 600-3,500 words. Pays $25 minimum for assigned articles; $25-150 for unsolicited articles. Sometimes pays in contributor copies or other premiums (trade ads for articles). Sometimes pays expenses of writers on assignments.

Photos: Send photos with submission. Reviews transparencies and prints. Offers no additional payment for photos accepted with ms. Captions and identification of subjects required. Buys one-time rights.

Fiction: Adventure (bowhunting related) and historical (bowhunting). Send complete ms. Length: 600-3,500 words. Pays $25-150.

Fillers: Anecdotes, facts, gags to be illustrated by cartoonist, newsbreaks and short humor. Buys 10/year. Length: 100-500 words. Pays $10-25.

Tips: "We do mainly first person accounts as long as they relate to hunting with the bow and arrow. If you have a bowhunting story you want to tell, then type it up and send it in. We probably publish more first time writers than any other bowhunting magazine today. Keep the articles clean, entertaining and informative. We do a few how-tos, but mainly want articles about bowhunting and the great outdoors that relate to bowhunting."

Baseball

‡BASEBALL AMERICA, "Baseball News You Can't Get Anywhere Else," American Sports Publishing Inc., P.O. Box 2089, Durham NC 27702. (919)682-9635. Editor: Allan Simpson. Senior Associate Editor: John Royster. 5% freelance written. Biweekly tabloid covering baseball. "We cover every aspect of baseball: the majors, the minors, Japanese and Mexican leagues, colleges, high schools, amateurs, etc. with an emphasis on player development." Estab. 1981. Circ. 70,000. Pays on publication. No kill fee. Buys first rights or second serial (reprint) rights. Query for electronic submissions. Free sample copy.

Nonfiction: Book excerpts, essays, exposé, general interest, historical/nostalgic, humor, interview/profile, opinion, personal experience, photo feature and technical. Buys 12 mss/year. Query with published clips or send complete ms. Length: 100-2,000 words. Pays $25-150. Sometimes pays expenses of writers on assignment.

Photos: State availability of photos with submission. Reviews contact sheets, negatives, normal slides and 5×7 prints. Offers $25-100/photo. Identification of subjecs required. Rights purchased vary.

Tips: "The sections most open to freelancers include the Minor League Notebook and the College Notebook. We look for short (100-250 words, sometimes longer), catchy notes and usually pay $25. That's how we often discover future correspondents."

Bicycling

BICYCLE GUIDE, Raben Publishing Co., 711 Boylston St., Boston MA 02116. (617)236-1885. FAX: (617) 267-1849. Editor: Theodore Costantino. 25% freelance written. "We're equally happy working with established writers and new writers." Magazine published 9 times/year covering "the world of high-performance cycling. We cover racing, touring and mountain biking from an enthusiast's point of view." Estab. 1984. Circ. 165,000. Pays on publication. Publishes ms an average of 4 months after acceptance. Byline given. Offers kill fee. Buys first North American serial rights. Submit seasonal/holiday material 6 months in advance. Simultaneous submissions OK. Reports in 3 weeks on queries; 1 month on mss. Sample copy for 8½×11 SAE with 2 first class stamps; writer's guidelines for #10 SASE.

Nonfiction: Humor, interview/profile, new product, opinion, photo feature, technical, and travel (short rides in North America only). Buyers' annual published in April. "We need 'how-to-buy' material by preceding November." No entry-level how-to on repairs or projects; long overseas tours; puff pieces on sports medicine; or 'my first ride' articles." Buys 18 mss/year. Query. Length: 900-3,500 words. Pays $200-600. Sometimes pays expenses of writers on assignment.

Photos: Send photos with submissions. Reviews transparencies and 5 × 8 b&w prints. Offers $50-250/photo. Captions, model releases, and identification of subjects required. Buys one-time rights.

Columns/Departments: What's Hot (new product reviews, personalities, events), 100-200 words; Fat Tracks (mountain bike news and events), 100-200 words. Buys 30 mss/year. Query. Pays $25-450.

Tips: "Freelancers should be cyclists with a thorough knowledge of the sport. Areas most open to freelancers are Training Methods (cover specific routines); Rides (75-100-mile loop rides over challenging terrain in continental U.S.); and Technical Pages (covers leading edge, technical innovations, new materials)."

BICYCLING, Rodale Press, Inc., 33 E. Minor St., Emmaus PA 18098. FAX: (215)965-6069. Editor and Publisher: James C. McCullagh. 20-25% freelance written. Prefers to work with published/established writers. Publishes 10 issues/year (8 monthly, 2 bimonthly); 104-250 pages. Estab. 1978. Circ. 385,000. Pays on acceptance or publication. Publishes ms an average of 6 months after acceptance. Byline given. Buys all rights. Submit seasonal/holiday material 5 months in advance. Query for electronic submissions. Writer's guidelines for SASE.

Nonfiction: How-to (on all phases of bicycle touring, bike repair, maintenance, commuting, new products, clothing, riding technique, nutrition for cyclists, conditioning). Fitness is more important than ever. Also travel (bicycling must be central here); photo feature (on cycling events of national significance); and technical (component review—query). "We are strictly a bicycling magazine. We seek readable, clear, well-informed pieces. We rarely run articles that are pure humor or inspiration but a little of either might flavor even our most technical pieces. No poetry or fiction." Buys 1-2 unsolicited mss/issue. Send complete ms. Length: 1,500 words average. Pays $25-1,200. Sometimes pays expenses of writers on assignment.

Photos: State availability of photos with query letter or send photo material with ms. Pays $15-50 for b&w prints and $35-250 for transparencies. Captions preferred; model release required.

Fillers: Anecdotes and news items for Paceline section.

Tips: "We're alway seeking interesting accounts of cycling as a lifestyle."

BIKE MIDWEST MAGAZINE, Peter Wray, Publisher, Suite C, 2099 W. Fifth Ave., Columbus OH 43212. (614)481-7723. FAX: (614)481-8261. Editor: Lynne Barst. 50% freelance written. Monthly tabloid on bicycling in the state of Ohio. "All aspects of adult bicycling covering both racing and recreational riding." Estab. 1987. Circ. 35,000. Pays on publication. Byline given. Buys first rights and second serial (reprint) rights. Simultaneous submissions OK. Query for electronic submissions. Sample copy and writer's guidelines for 10 × 13 SAE with 75¢ postage. Writer's guidelines for #10 SASE.

Nonfiction: How-to (athletics), humor (bicycle related), interview/profile (bicycle related), new product (bicycle related), personal experience (bicycle related) and photo feature (bicycle related). Buys 10 mss/year. Query. Length: 500-2,500 words. Pays $25-50. Sometimes pays expenses of writers on assignment.

Photos: Send photos with submission. Reviews contact sheets and 5 × 7 prints. Offers no additional payment for photos accepted with ms. Identification of subjects required. Buys one-time rights.

Tips: "Consult with editor. Looking for reports of racing/riding events, previews, interviews with personalities. Inclusion of art is very important."

BIKEREPORT, Bikecentennial, Inc., The Bicycle Travel Association, Box 8308, Missoula MT 59807. (406)721-1776. FAX: (406)721-8754. Editor: Daniel D'Ambrosio. 75% freelance written. Works with a small number of new/unpublished writers each year. Bicycle touring magazine for Bikecentennial members published 9 times yearly. Circ. 20,000. Pays on publication. Publishes an average of 8 months after acceptance. Byline given. Include short bio with manuscript. Buys first serial rights. Submit seasonal/holiday material 3 months in advance. Simultaneous queries OK. Query for electronic submissions. Reports in 2 weeks on queries; 1 month on mss. Sample copy and guidelines for 9 × 12 SAE with $1 postage.

Nonfiction: Historical/nostalgic (interesting spots along bike trails); how-to (bicycle); humor (touring); interview/profile (bicycle industry people); personal experience ("my favorite tour"); photo feature (bicycle); technical (bicycle); travel ("my favorite tour"). Buys 20-25 mss/year. Query with published clips or send complete ms. Length: 800-2,500 words. Pays 3¢/word and up.

Photos: Bicycle, scenery, portraits. State availability of photos. Model releases and identification of subjects required.

Fiction: Adventure, experimental, historical, humorous. Not interested in anything that doesn't involve bicycles. Query with published clips or send complete ms. Length: 800-2,500 words. Pays 3¢/word and up.

Tips: "We don't get many good essays. Consider that a hint. But we are still always interested in travelogs."

‡**BMX PLUS MAGAZINE**, Daisy/Hi-Torque Publishing Co., Inc., 10600 Sepulveda Blvd., Mission Hills CA 91345. (818)545-6012. FAX: (818)361-4512. Editor: Karl Rothe. Monthly magazine covering the sport of bicycle motorcross for a youthful readership (95% male, aged 8-25). 3% freelance written. Prefers to work with published/established writers. Estab. 1978. Circ. 54,000. Pays on publication. Byline given. Buys one-time rights. Submit seasonal/holiday material 4 months in advance. Simultaneous queries and manuscripts OK. Reports in 2 months. Publishes ms an average of 3 months after acceptance. Sample copy $3; writer's guidelines for #10 SASE.

Nonfiction: Historical/nostalgic, how-to, humor, interview/profile, new product, photo feature, technical, travel. "No articles for a general audience; our readers are BMX fanatics." Buys 20 mss/year. Send complete ms. Length: 500-1,500 words. Pays $30-250.

Photos: "Photography is the key to our magazine. Send us some exciting and/or unusual photos of hot riders in action." Send photos with ms. Pays $40-50 for color photo published; $25 for b&w photos. Reviews 35mm color transparencies and b&w negatives and 8×10 prints. Captions and identification of subjects required.

Tips: "We would like to receive more material on hot freestylers from areas other than California. Photo/story submissions would be welcomed. We also need more material about racing and freestyle from foreign countries. The sport of BMX is young. The opportunities for talented writers and photographers in this field are open. Send us a good interview or race story with photos. Race coverage is the area that's easiest to break in to. It must be a *big* race, preferably national or international in scope. Submit story within one week of completion of race."

CYCLING USA, The Official Publication of the U.S. Cycling Federation, 1750 E. Boulder St., Colorado Springs CO 80909. (719)578-4581. FAX: (719)578-4628. Editor: Steve Penny. 50% freelance written. Monthly magazine covering reportage and commentary on American bicycle racing, personalities and sports physiology, for USCF licensed cyclists. Circ. 32,000. Pays on publication. Publishes ms an average of 2 months after acceptance. Byline given. Simultaneous queries and previously published submissions OK. Reports in 2 weeks. Sample copy for 10×12 SAE and 60¢ postage.

Nonfiction: How-to (train, prepare for a bike race); interview/profile; opinion; personal experience; photo feature; technical; and race commentary on major cycling events. No comparative product evaluations. Buys 15 mss/year. Query with published clips. Length: 500-2,000 words. Pays 10¢/word.

Photos: State availability of photos. Pays $10-25 for 5×7 b&w prints; $100 for transparencies used as cover. Captions required. Buys one-time rights.

Columns/Departments: Athlete's Kitchen, Nuts & Bolts, Coaches Column.

Tips: "A background in bicycle racing is important because the sport is somewhat insular, technical and complex. Most major articles are generated inhouse. Race reports are most open to freelancers. Be concise, informative and anecdotal. The most frequent mistake made by writers in completing an article for us is that it is too lengthy; our format is more compatible with shorter (500-800-word) articles than longer features."

‡**DIRT RAG, For the Mountain Biker of the East**, A.K.A. Productions, 460 Maple Ave., Springdale PA 15144. (412)274-4529. Publisher: Maurice Tierney. Managing Editor: Elaine Tierney. 75% freelance written. Mountain biking magazine published every 6 weeks. "Dirt Rag is regional (not national). The style is much looser and more fun than national (glossy) magazines on the same subject. Avante garde, humorous, off-beat." Estab. 1989. Circ. 5,000. Pays on publication. Byline given. No kill fee. Buys one-time rights. Simultaneous and previously published submissions OK. Query for electronic submissions. Sample copy for 5 first class stamps, writer's guidelines for SASE.

Nonfiction: Book excerpts, essays, exposé, general interest, historical/nostalgic, how-to (bike maintenance, bike technique), humor, interview/profile, new product, opinion, personal experience, photo feature, technical, travel (places to ride). Buys 24 mss/year. Query. Pays $10-50. Sometimes pays expenses of writers on assignment.

Photos: Send photos with or without submission. Reviews contact sheets and/or prints (any). Offers no additional payment for photos accepted with ms. $35 cover. Captions required. Buys one-time rights. Always looking for good photography and art regardless of subject.

Columns/Departments: Place to Ride (anywhere in Eastern States—must have map!), 500-2,000 words; Trialsin (coverage of the sport), 50-500 words; Race Reports (coverage of race events), 50-250 words. Buys 14 mss/year. Query. Pays $10-50.

Fiction: Adventure, fantasy, historical, humorous, mainstream, slice-of-life vignettes. Buys 1-5 mss/year. Query. Pays $10-50.

Poetry: Avant-garde, free verse, light verse, traditional. Pays $10-50.

Fillers: Anecdotes, facts, gags, newsbreaks, short humor. Buys 20/year. Pays $0-50.

VELONEWS, The Journal of Competitive Cycling, 1830 55th St, Boulder CO 80301-2700. (303)440-0601. FAX: (303)444-6788. Managing Editor: Tim Johnson. 60% freelance written. Monthly tabloid September-February, biweekly March-August covering bicycle racing. Estab. 1972. Circ. 35,000. Pays on publication. Publishes ms an average of 1 month after acceptance. Byline given. Buys one-time rights. Simultaneous queries and submissions OK. Electronic submissions OK; call first. Reports in 3 weeks. Sample copy for 9×12 SAE plus $2.13 postage.

Nonfiction: In addition to race coverage, opportunities for freelancers include reviews (book and videos) and health-and-fitness departments. Buys 100 mss/year. Query. Length: 300-2,000 words. Pays up to 10¢/word.

Photos: State availability of photos. Pays $16.50-41.50 for b&w prints. Pays $150 for color used on cover. Captions and identification of subjects required. Buys one-time rights.

Boating

BOAT JOURNAL, 2100 Powers Ferry Rd., Atlanta GA 30339. (404)955-5656. FAX: (404)952-0669. Editor: Richard Lebovitz. Managing Editor: John Weber. 95% freelance written. Bimonthly magazine covering recreational boating. "*Boat Journal* focuses on the use and enjoyment of all types of power-boats up to 30 feet in length. Topics include cruising areas and adventures, boat evaluations, and helpful tips for upgrading, maintaining and safely handling small powerboats." Estab. 1979. Circ. 65,000. Pays on publication. Publishes ms an average of 6 months after acceptance. Byline given. Offers 50% kill fee. Buys first rights. Submit seasonal/holiday material 6 months in advance. No simultaneous submissions. Query for electronic submissions. Reports in 2-3 weeks. Sample copy for 8½×11 SAE with 7 first class stamps; writer's guidelines for #10 SASE.

Nonfiction: Historical/nostalgic, how-to (repair, maintenance and improvements), humor, interview/profile, personal experience, photo feature, technical, and travel. Plans special issues on electronics, engines, fishing boats and equipment. Buys 60 mss/year. Query with or without published clips, or send complete ms. Length: 800-3,000 words. Pays $150-600 for assigned articles; pays $75-400 for unsolicited articles. Sometimes pays the expenses of writers on assignment.

Photos: Send photos with submission. Reviews contact sheets, transparencies and prints. Offers $15-200 per photo. Buys one-time rights.

Columns/Departments: Seamanship (boating safety, piloting and navigation), 1,400 words; Custom Boat (ideas for improving a boat), 1,400 words; Engines (selection and maintenance of engines), 1,400 words; Electronics (selection and maintenance), 1,400 words. Buys 20 mss/year. Query with published clips. Length: 900-2,500 words. Pays $50-400.

Tips: "Our best stories provide comprehensive, in-depth information about a particular boating subject. *BJ*'s readers are experienced and sophisticated boating enthusiasts—most own more than one type of boat—and expect well-researched articles with a practical, how-to slant. Excellent photos are a must, as are stories with engaging tales drawn from the author's experience." Most open to freelancers are "topics related to cruising, personal adventures, seamanship, engine maintenance and repair, boat handling, hull maintenance and repair, trailering, and electronics."

‡BOAT PENNSYLVANIA, Pennsylvania Fish Commission, Box 1673, Harrisburg PA 17105. (717)657-4520. Editor: Art Michaels. 60-80% freelance written. Quarterly magazine covering motorboating, sailing, canoeing, water skiing, kayaking and rafting in Pennsylvania. Prefers to work with published/established contributors, but works with a few unpublished writers and photographers every year. Pays 6-8 weeks after acceptance. Publishes ms an average of 8 months after acceptance. Byline given. Buys variable rights. Submit seasonal/holiday material 8 months in advance. Reports in 2 weeks on queries; 2 months on manuscript. Writer's guidelines for #10 SASE.

Nonfiction: How-to, photo feature, technical and historical/nostalgic, all related to water sports in Pennsylvania. No saltwater material. Buys 40 mss/year. Query. Length: 300-3,000 words. Pays $25-300.

Photos: Send photos with submission. Reviews 35mm and larger color transparencies and 8×10 b&w prints. Captions, model releases and identification of subjects required.

CANOE MAGAZINE, Canoe Associates, Box 3146, Kirkland WA 98083. (206)827-6363. FAX: (206)827-1893. Editor: Les Johnson. 80-90% freelance written. A bimonthly magazine on canoeing, whitewater kayaking and sea kayaking. Circ. 60,000. Pays on publication. Publishes ms an average of 9-12 months after acceptance. Byline given. Buys right to reprint in annuals; author retains copyright. Submit seasonal/holiday material 4 months in advance. Query for electronic submissions. Reports in 1 month. Free sample copy and writer's guidelines for 9×12 SASE.

Nonfiction: Essays, general interest, historical/nostalgic, how-to, humor, interview/profile, new product, opinion, personal experience, photo feature, technical and travel. Plans a special entry-level guide to canoeing and kayaking. No "trip diaries." Buys 60 mss/year. Query with or without published clips, or send complete ms. Length: 500-2,200 words. Pays $5/column inch. Pays the expenses of writers on assignment.

Photos: State availability of photos with submission or send photos with submission. "Good photos help sell a story." Reviews contact sheets, negatives, transparencies and prints. "Some activities we cover are canoeing, kayaking, canoe fishing, camping, canoe sailing or poling, backpacking (when compatible with the main activity) and occasionally inflatable boats. We are not interested in groups of people in rafts, photos showing disregard for the environment, gasoline-powered, multi-horsepower engines unless appropriate to the discussion, or unskilled persons taking extraordinary risks." Offers $50-150/photo. Model releases and identification of subjects occasionally required. Buys one-time rights.

Columns/Departments: Continuum (essay); Counter Currents (environmental) both 1,500 words; Put-In (short interesting articles); Short Strokes (destinations), 1,000-1,500 words. Buys 60 mss/year. Pays $5/column inch.

Fiction: Uses very little fiction.

Fillers: Anecdotes, facts and newsbreaks. Buys 20/year. Length: 500-1,000 words. Pays $5/column inch.

Tips: "Start with Put-In articles (short featurettes) of approximately 500 words, book reviews, or short, unique equipment reviews. Or give us the best, most exciting article we've ever seen—with great photos. Short Strokes is also a good entry forum focusing on short trips on good waterways accessible to lots of people. Focusing more on technique and how-to articles."

‡COASTAL CRUISING. Nautilus Publishing, Inc., P.O. Box 444, Beaufort NC 28516. (919)247-4185. Editor: Ted Jones. 75% freelance written. Semi-monthly magazine. A boating and yachting travelogue for North America covering cruising/racing/cruising grounds. Estab. 1985. Circ. 20,000. Pays on acceptance or publication. Publishes ms an average of 6 months after acceptance. Byline given. Buys one-time rights or second serial (reprint) rights. Submit seasonal/holiday material 6 months in advance. Simultaneous, photocopied and previously published submissions OK. Query for electronic submissions. Free sample copy and writer's guidelines.

Nonfiction: How-to (technical items dealing with boating—both power and sail), humor, new product (boating items), personal experience, photo feature, technical and travel. "I do not read anything that does not deal with boating and/or travel along our waterways and coastline." Buys 25 mss/year. Send complete ms. Length: 500-3,000 words (6,000 if it is a 2-part series). Pays $75-100. Sometimes pays expenses of writers on assignment.

Photos: Send photos with submission. Reviews transparencies and 3×5 or 5×7 prints. Offers no additional payment for photos accepted with ms (except for certain assignments). Model releases and identification of subjects required. Buys one-time rights.

Columns/Departments: Scuttlebutt (club news, upcoming boating events, boat shows, etc.); and New Products (new product information on boating gear, products, equipment, etc.), all 100-800 words.

Fiction: Adventure and humorous. "Nothing that does not deal with boating." Buys 2 ms/year. Send complete ms. Length: 500-3,000 words. Pays $50-100.

CRUISING WORLD, Cruising World Publications, Inc., 5 John Clarke Rd., Newport RI 02840. (401)847-1588. Editor: Bernadette Brennan. 70% freelance written. Monthly magazine for all those who cruise under sail. Circ. 136,000. **Pays on acceptance.** Publishes ms an average of 8 months after acceptance. Offers variable kill fee, $50-150. Buys first North American periodical rights or first world periodical rights. Reports in about 2 months. Query for electronic submissions. Free writer's guidelines.

Nonfiction: Book excerpts, how-to, humor, inspirational, opinion and personal experience. "We are interested in seeing informative articles on the technical and enjoyable aspects of cruising under sail. Also subjects of general interest to seafarers." Buys 135-140 unsolicited mss/year. Submit complete ms. Length: 500-3,500 words. Pays $150-800.

Photos: 35mm slides purchased with accompanying ms. Captions and identification of subjects required. Buys one-time rights.

Columns/Departments: People & Food (recipes for preparation aboard sailboats); Shoreline (sailing news, vignettes); and Workbench (projects for upgrading your boat). Send complete ms. Length: 150-500 words. Pays $25-150.

Tips: "Cruising stories should be first-person narratives. In general, authors must be sailors who read the magazine. Color slides always improve a ms's chances of acceptance. Technical articles should be well-illustrated."

CURRENTS, Voice of the National Organization for River Sports, 314 N. 20th St., Colorado Springs CO 80904. (719)473-2466. Editor: Eric Leaper. Managing Editor: Mary McCurdy. 25% freelance written. Quarterly magazine covering whitewater river running (kayaking, rafting, river canoeing). Estab. 1979. Circ. 10,000. Pays on publication. Publishes ms an average of 6 months after acceptance. Byline given. Offers 25% kill fee. Buys first North American serial rights, first rights and one-time rights. Submit seasonal/holiday material 2 months in advance. Simultaneous queries, and simultaneous and previously published submissions OK. "Please let us know if this is a simultaneous submission or if the article has been previously published." Reports in 2 weeks on queries; in 1 month on mss. Sample copy for $1 and 9×12 SAE with 3 first class stamps; writer's guidelines for #10 SASE.

Nonfiction: How-to (run rivers and fix equipment); in-depth reporting on river conservation and access issues and problems; humor (related to rivers); interview/profile (any interesting river runner); new product; opinion; personal experience; technical; travel (rivers in other countries). "We tell river runners about river conservation, river access, river equipment, how to do it, when, where, etc." No trip accounts without originality; no stories about "my first river trip." Buys 20 mss/year. Query with or without clips of published work. Length: 500-2,500 words. Pays $35-150.

Photos: State availability of photos. Pays $35-50. Reviews b&w or color prints or slides; b&w preferred. Captions and identification of subjects (if racing) required. Buys one-time rights. Captions must include names of the river and rapid.

Columns/Departments: Book and film reviews (river-related). Buys 5 mss/year. Query with or without clips of published work or send complete ms. Length: 100-500 words. Pays $25.

Fiction: Adventure (river). Buys 2 mss/year. Query. Length: 1,000-2,500 words. Pays $35-75. "Must be well-written, on well-known river and beyond the realm of possibility."

Fillers: Clippings, jokes, gags, anecdotes, short humor, newsbreaks. Buys 5/year. Length: 25-100 words. Pays $5-10.

Tips: "We need more material on river news—proposed dams, wild and scenic river studies, accidents, etc. If you can provide brief (300-500 words) on these subjects, you will have a good chance of being published. Material must be on whitewater rivers. Go to a famous river and investigate it; find out something we don't know—especially about rivers that are *not* in Colorado or adjacent states—we already know about the ones near us."

HEARTLAND BOATING, Inland Publications, Inc., P.O. Box 1067, Martin TN 38237. (901)587-6791. FAX: (901)587-6893. Editor: Molly Lightfoot Blom. 40% freelance written. Bimonthly magazine on boating. "Magazine is devoted to both power and sail boating enthusiasts throughout middle America; houseboats are included. The focus is on the freshwater inland rivers and lakes of the Heartland; primarily the Tennessee, Cumberland, Ohio and Mississippi rivers and the Tennessee-Tombigbee Waterway. No Great Lakes or salt water material wil be considered unless it applies to our area." Estab. 1988. Circ. 13,000. Pays on publication. Publishes ms an average of 3 months after acceptance. Byline given. Buys first North American serial rights and sometimes second serial (reprint) rights. Submit seasonal/holiday material 6 months in advance. Simultaneous submissions OK. Query for electronic submissions. Reports in 1 month. Sample copy $3; free writer's guidelines.

Nonfiction: General interest, historical/nostalgic, how-to, humor, interview/profile, new product, personal experience, photo feature, technical, travel. Buys 20-30 mss/year. Query with or without published clips, or send complete ms. Length: 800-2,000 words. Pays 5-25¢/word.

Photos: Send photos with query. Reviews contact sheets, transparencies. Buys one-time rights.

Columns/Departments: Buys 10 mss/year. Query. Pays 5-25¢/word.

HOT BOAT, LFP Publishing, Suite 300, 9171 Wilshire Blvd., Beverly Hills CA 90210. (213)858-7155. FAX: (213)274-7985. Editor: Kevin Spaise. 50% freelance written. A monthly magazine on performance boating (16-35 feet), water skiing and water sports in general. "We're looking for concise, technically oriented 'how-to' articles on performance modifications; personality features on interesting boating-oriented personalities, and occasional event coverage." Circ. 90,000. Pays 1 month after acceptance. Publishes ms an average of 2 months after acceptance. Byline given. Offers 40% kill fee. Buys all rights; also reprint rights occasionally. Submit seasonal/holiday material 3 months in advance. Reports in 3 weeks on queries; 1 month on mss. Sample copy for $3, and 9×12 SAE with $1.35 postage.

Nonfiction: How-to (increase horsepower, perform simple boat related maintenance), humor, interview/profile (racers and manufacturers), new product, personal experience, photo feature, technical. "Absolutely no sailing—we deal strictly in powerboating." Buys 30 mss/year. Query with published clips. Length: 500-2,000 words. Pays $75-450. Sometimes pays expenses of writers on assignment.

Photos: Send photos with submission. Reviews transparencies. Captions, model releases and identification of subjects required. Buys all rights.

Tips: "We're always open to new writers. If you query with published clips and we like your writing, we can keep you on file even if we reject the particular query. It may be more important to simply establish contact. Once we work together there will be much more work to follow."

LAKELAND BOATING, The magazine for Great Lakes boaters, O'Meara-Brown Publications, Suite 500, 1600 Orrington Ave., Evanston IL 60201. (708)869-5400. FAX: (708)869-5989. Editor: Sarah Wortham. 50% freelance written. Monthly magazine covering Great Lakes boating. Estab. 1945. Circ. 60,000. **Pays on acceptance.** Byline given. Offers 25% kill fee. Buys first North American serial rights. Query for electronic submissions. Sample copy for $5.50 with 9×12 SAE and 6 first class stamps. Writer's guidelines for #10 SAE with 1 first class stamp.

Nonfiction: Book excerpts, historical/nostalgic, how-to, interview/profile, personal experience, photo feature, technical and travel. No humor, inspirational, religious, exposé or poetry. Must relate to boating in Great Lakes. Buys 20-30 mss/year. Query. Length: 800-3,500 words. Pays $100-600 for assigned articles. Sometimes pays expenses of writers on assignment.

Photos: State availability of photos. Reviews transparencies, prefers 35mm. Captions required. Buys one-time rights.

Columns/Departments: Bosun's Locker (technical or how-to pieces on boating), 100-1,000 words. Buys 40 mss/year. Query. Pays $30-100.

‡**LONG ISLAND POWER & SAIL**, 403 Main St., Port Washington NY 11050. (516)944-8654. Editor: Kathleen Yasas. 80% freelance written. Bimonthly magazine covering boating on Long Island. "*LIP&S* is a service magazine, geared to improving the sport of boating on Long Island." Estab. 1989. Circ. 35,000. Pays on publication. Publishes ms an average of 6 months after acceptance. Byline given. Offers $100 kill fee. Buys first rights. Submit seasonal material 6 months in advance. Query for electronic submissions. Reports in 2 months. Sample copy $4. Writer's guidelines for SAE and 1 first class stamp.

Nonfiction: Historical/nostalgic, how-to, humor, interview/profile, personal experience, photo feature, technical and travel. Buys 40 mss/year. Send complete ms. Length: 900-2,000 words.

Columns/Departments: LIPService (service articles/how-to); 950 words; Dockside Dining (restaurant review/on Long Island), 950 words; Profile (people of interest in boating industry), 1500 words; Angler's Corner (fishing), 1000 words. Send complete ms. Length: 950-1,500 words. Pays $150-300.

Tips: "All areas open to freelancers. Facts are important. If our checking department finds more than a few errors, writer will not be used again."

‡**MOTOR BOATING & SAILING**, 224 W. 57th St., New York NY 10019. (212)649-3068. FAX: (212)649-3065. Editor: Peter A. Janssen. Monthly magazine covering powerboats and sailboats for people who own their own boats and are active in a yachting lifestyle. Estab. 1907. Circ. 135,056. **Pays on acceptance.** Byline given. Buys one-time rights. Reports in 3 months.

Nonfiction: General interest (navigation, adventure, cruising), and how-to (maintenance). Buys 5-6 mss/issue. Average issue includes 8-10 feature articles. Query. Length: 2,000 words.

Photos: Reviews 5×7 b&w glossy prints and 35mm or larger color transparencies. Offers no additional payment for photos accepted with ms. Captions and model releases required.

PLEASURE BOATING MAGAZINE, Graphcom Publishing, Inc., Suite 107, 1995 NE 150th St., N. Miami FL 33181. (305)945-7403. FAX: (305)947-6410. Publisher: Robert Ulrich. Executive Editor: Don Zern. 60% freelance written. Monthly magazine covering boating around Florida, The Bahamas and Caribbean. Estab. 1971. Circ. 25,000. Pays on publication. Publishes ms an average of 2 months after acceptance. Byline given. Kill fee varies. Buys first rights. Reports in 1 month on queries. Free sample copy and writer's guidlines.

Nonfiction: General interest (motor boating), how-to (boating travel, safety and navigation), personal experience (boating adventure), travel (cruising in boat). No silly humor; pornographic stuff. Buys 35-40 mss/year. Query with published clips. Length: 1,200-2,000 words. Pays $200 minimum; maximum amount varies. Sometimes pays the expenses of writers on assignment.

Photos: Send photos with submission. Reviews negatives. Offers no additional payment for photos accepted with ms. Identification of subjects required. Buys one-time rights.

Tips: "Know the region we cover, offer fresh perspectives and be flexible with editors."

‡**POWER BOATING CANADA**, CRU Publications, 2077 Dundas St. E, Mississauga, Ontario L4X 1M2 Canada. (416)624-8218. Editor: Darryl Simmons. 40% freelance written. Bimonthly magazine covering power boating. Estab. 1984. Circ. 50,000. Pays on publication. Publishes ms an average of 3 months after acceptance. Byline given. Offers no kill fee. Not copyrighted. Buys first North American serial rights in English and French or second serial (reprint) rights. Simultaneous and previously published submissions OK. Query for electronic submissions.

Nonfiction: "Any articles related to the sport of power boating, especially boat tests." Travel (boating destinations). No personal anecdotes. Buys 20 mss/year. Query. Length: 1,000-2,500 words. Pays $150-300.

Photos: State availability of photos with submission. Send photos with submission. Reviews contact sheets, negatives, transparencies and prints. Offers no additional payment for photos accepted with ms. Identification of subjects required. Buys one-time rights.

SAIL, Charlestown Navy Yard, 100 First Ave., Charlestown MA 02129-2097. (617)241-9500. FAX: (617)241-7968. Editor: Patience Wales. Managing Editor: Amy Ullrich. 50% freelance written. Works with a small number of new/unpublished writers each year. Monthly magazine for audience that is "strictly sailors, average age 42, above average education." Estab. 1970. Pays on publication. Publishes ms an average of 10 months after acceptance. Buys first North American rights. Submit seasonal or special material at least 6 months in advance. Reports in 10 weeks. Writer's guidelines for 1 first class stamp.

Nonfiction: Amy Ullrich, managing editor. Wants "articles on sailing: technical, techniques and feature stories." Interested in how-to, personal experience, profiles, historical and new products. "Generally emphasize the excitement of sail and the human, personal aspect. No logs." Special issues: "Cruising issues, chartering issues, fitting-out issues, special race issues (e.g., America's Cup), boat show issues." Buys 100 mss/year (freelance and commissioned). Length: 1,500-2,800 words. Pays $300-800. Sometimes pays the expenses of writers on assignment.

Photos: Offers additional payment for photos. Uses b&w glossy prints or Kodachrome 64 transparencies. Pays $600 if photo is used on the cover.

Tips: Request an articles specification sheet.

‡**SAILING MAGAZINE**, 125 E. Main St., Port Washington WI 53074. (414)284-3494. FAX: (414)284-0067. Editor and Publisher: William F. Schanen, III. Monthly magazine. For readers ages 25-44, majority professionals. About 75% of them own their own sailboat. Estab. 1966. Circ. 35,000. Pays on publication. Simultaneous submissions OK. Reports in 6 weeks. Sample copy for 12×15 SAE and $1 postage; writer's guidelines for #10 SASE.

Nonfiction: Micca Leffingwell Hutchins, editor. "Experiences of sailing, whether cruising, racing or learning. We require no special style. We're devoted exclusively to sailing and sailboat enthusiasts, and particularly interested in articles about the trend toward cruising in the sailing world." Informational, personal experience, profile, historical, travel and book reviews. Buys 24 mss/year. Query or submit complete ms. Length: open. Payment negotiable. Must be accompanied by photos.

Photos: B&w and color photos purchased with or without accompanying ms. Captions required. Pays flat fee for article.

SAILING WORLD, N.Y. Times Magazine Group, 5 John Clarke Rd., Newport RI 02840. FAX: (401)848-5048. Editor: John Burnham. 40% freelance written. Magazine published 12 times/year. Estab. 1962. Circ. 61,000. Pays on publication. Publishes ms an average of 4 months after acceptance. Buys first North American world serial rights. Byline given. Query for electronic submissions. Sample copy $2.50.

Nonfiction: How-to for racing and performance-oriented sailors, photo feature, profile, regatta reports, and charter. No travelogs. Buys 5-10 unsolicited mss/year. Query. Length: 500-1,500 words. Pays $150-200/page text.

Tips: "Send query with outline and include your experience. The writer may have a better chance of breaking in with short articles and fillers such as regatta news reports from his or her own area."

SANTANA, The So-Cal Sailing Rag, Santana Publications, Inc., #211, 4911 Warner Ave., Huntington Beach CA 92649. (714)893-3432. Editor: David Poe. Managing Editor: Kitty James. 50% freelance written. A monthly magazine on sailing. "We publish conversationally written articles of interest to Southern California sailors, including technical, cruising, racing, fiction, etc." Estab. 1988. Circ. 25,000. Pays on publication. Publishes ms an average of 2 months after acceptance. Byline given. Publication not copyrighted. Buys first North American serial rights or second serial (reprint) rights. Submit seasonal/holiday material 3 months in advance. Previously published submissions OK. Reports in 1 month. Sample copy for 9×12 SAE with 5 first class stamps.

Nonfiction: Essays, general interest, historical/nostalgic, how-to (technical articles), humor, interview/profile, personal experience. Buys 50 mss/year. Query with or without published clips or send complete ms. Length: 1,000-4,000 words. Pays $50-150.

Photos: State availability of photos with submission. Reviews contact sheets, negatives, transparencies (35mm) and prints (5×7 or 8×10). Offers $10/photo. Captions and identification of subjects required. Buys one-time rights.

Tips: "Our style tends towards conversational, frequently irreverent, but we are also interested in technical articles. Virtually the entire range of topics covered is open to freelance submissions. Articles must have Southern California angle."

SEA, The Magazine of Western Boating for 82 years, Duncan McIntosh Co., Inc., Suite C, 2nd Floor, 17782 Cowan, Irvine CA 92714. FAX: (714)660-6172. Editor and Publisher: Duncan McIntosh Jr. Executive Editor: Linda Yuskaitis. 70% freelance written. A monthly magazine covering recreational power boating, offshore fishing and coastal news of the West Coast, from Alaska to Hawaii. Also includes separate regional sections on Southern California, the Pacific Northwest and sailing. Estab. 1908. Circ. 70,000, all regional editions combined. Pays on publication. Publishes ms an average of 4 months after acceptance. Byline given. Buys first North American serial rights or second serial (reprint) rights. Reports in 1 month on queries; 6 weeks on mss. Free writer's guidelines, deadline schedule and sample copy with 9×12 SASE.

Nonfiction: General interest (on boating and coastal topics); how-to (tips on maintaining a boat, engine, and gear); interview/profile (of a prominent boating personality); travel (West Coast cruising or fishing destination). Buys 150 mss/year. Query with published clips, or send complete ms. Length: 250 (news items) to 2,500 (features) words. Pays $35 (news items) to $275 (features). Some assignment expenses covered if requested in advance.

Photos: Stories accompanied by photos are preferred. Transparencies only; no color negatives or prints. Pays $35 (inside b&w) to $250 (color cover) for photos. Identification of photo subjects required. Buys one-time rights.

Columns/Departments: West Coast Focus (boating and fishing news with color photos); National Focus (national boating news with color photos); Southern California Focus (boating and fishing news from Ventura to San Diego with b&w photos); Northwest Focus (boating and fishing news in Alaska, Washington and Oregon with b&w photos); Sportfishing (sportfishing tips); Mexico Report (short features on boating and fishing destinations in Mexico).

Tips: "*Sea*'s editorial focus is on West Coast boating and sportfishing. We are not interested in stories about the East Coast, Midwest or foreign countries. First-time contributors should include resume or information about themselves that identifies their knowledge of subject. Written queries required. No first-person 'what happened on our first cruise' stories. No poetry, fiction or cartoons."

SEA KAYAKER, Sea Kayaker, Inc., 6327 Seaview Ave. NW., Seattle WA 98107. (206)789-1326. FAX: (206)789-6392. Editor: Christopher Cunningham. 80% freelance written. Works frequently with new/unpublished writers each year. A quarterly magazine on the sport of sea kayaking. Estab. 1984. Circ. 12,000. Pays on publication. Publishes ms an average of 6 months after acceptance. Byline given. Offers 10% kill fee. Buys first North American serial rights or second serial (reprint) rights. Submit seasonal material 6 months in advance. Reports in 2 months. Sample copy $4.60; free writer's guidelines.

Nonfiction: Essays, historical, how-to (on making equipment), humor, profile, opinion, personal experience, technical and travel. Buys 40 mss/year. Query with or without published clips, or send complete ms. Length: 750-4,000 words. Pays 5-10¢/word. Sometimes pays the expenses of writers on assignment.

Photos: Send photos with submission. Reviews contact sheets. Offers $15-35/photo. Captions required. Buys one-time rights.

Columns/Department: History, Safety, Environment and Journey. Length: 750-4,000 words. Pays 5-10¢/word.

Fiction: Adventure, fantasy, historical, humorous, mainstream, slice-of-life vignettes. Send complete ms. Length: 750-4,000 words. Pays 5-10¢/word.

Tips: "We consider unsolicited mss that include a SASE, but we give greater priority to brief (several paragraphs) descriptions of proposed articles accompanied by at least two samples—published or unpublished—of your writing. Enclose a statement as to why you're qualified to write the piece and indicate whether photographs or illustrations are available to accompany the piece."

SOUTHERN BOATING MAGAZINE, The South's Largest Boating Magazine, Southern Boating & Yachting, Inc., 1766 Bay Rd., Miami Beach FL 33139. (305)538-0700. Editor: Skip Allen, Sr. Editorial Director: Andree Conrad. 50% freelance written. Monthly magazine on cruising and fishing in the Southeastern U.S. "Our readers are long-time boat owners who spend a good deal of their time on the water. They have an interest in everything from diesel maintenance to one-design sailboat racing. Above all, they are interested in new and accurate information about cruising destinations." Estab. 1973. Circ. 26,000. Pays on publication. Publishes ms an average of 3-6 months after acceptance (depends, some issues have themes). Byline given. Buys first North American serial rights, first rights, or one-time rights. Submit seasonal/holiday material 4 months in advance. Simultaneous and previously published submissions OK. Query for electronic submissions. Sample copy $4; writer's guidelines for #10 SASE.

Nonfiction: Book excerpts (occasionally), new products, photo features, technical and travel. "Write for editorial calendar. No personal experience or disasters aboard boats." Buys 50 ms/year. Query with or without published clips, or send complete ms. Length: 750-2,500 words. Pays $100-200 for assigned articles; $75-150 for unsolicited articles. Sometimes pays expenses of writers on assignment.

Photos: Send photos with submission. Reviews transparencies (both slides and larger formats). Offers no additional payment for photos accepted with ms. Captions, model releases, and identification of subjects required. Buys one-time rights.

Tips: "Anyone who has plans to or has already taken a cruise in Southeastern or Carribean waters, and can adequately convey the kind of information other cruising yachtsmen need to decide whether they want to undertake a similar cruise, should contact us. We ask for excellent color pictures, preferably slides in Kodachrome or Fujichrome, 35mm or larger. We do not publish stories without photos. Maps are appreciated by all of our readers. Freelancers have the best chance with feature articles.

We are also looking for writers with the ability to write technical information on engines, electronics and other topics of interest intelligibly."

TRAILER BOATS MAGAZINE, Poole Publications, Inc., 20700 Belshaw Ave., Carson CA 90746-3510. (213)537-6322. FAX: (213)537-8735. Editor: Wiley Poole. 30-40% freelance written. Works with a small number of new/unpublished writers each year. Monthly magazine (November/December issue combined). Emphasizes legally trailerable boats and related powerboating activities. Circ. 80,000. Pays on publication. Publishes ms 2-6 months after acceptance. Byline given. Buys all rights. Submit seasonal/holiday material 3 months in advance. Query for electronic submissions. Reports in 1 month. Sample copy $1.25; writer's guidelines for #10 SASE.

Nonfiction: General interest (trailer boating activities); historical (places, events, boats); how-to (repair boats, installation, etc.); humor (almost any boating-related subject); nostalgia (same as historical); personal experience; photo feature; profile; technical; and travel (boating travel on water or highways). No "How I Spent My Summer Vacation" stories, or stories not even remotely connected to trailerable boats and related activities. Buys 18-30 unsolicited mss/year. Query or send complete ms. Length: 500-2,000 words. Pays expenses of writers on assignment.

Photos: Send photos with ms. Pays $10-75 for 8×10 b&w prints; $25-350 for color transparencies. Captions required.

Columns/Departments: Boaters Bookshelf (boating book reviews); Over the Transom (funny or strange boating photos); and Patent Pending (an invention with drawings). Buys 2/issue. Query. Length: 100-500 words. Mini-Cruise (short enthusiastic approach to a favorite boating spot). Need map and photographs. Length: 500-750 words. Pays $100. Open to suggestions for new columns/departments.

Fiction: Adventure, experimental, historical, humorous and suspense. "We do not use too many fiction stories but we will consider them if they fit the general editorial guidelines." Query or send complete ms. Length: 500-1,500 words. Pays $50 minimum.

Tips: "Query should contain short general outline of the intended material; what kind of photos; how the photos illustrate the piece. Write with authority covering the subject like an expert. Frequent mistakes are not knowing the subject matter or the audience. Use basic information rather than prose, particularly in travel stories. The writer may have a better chance of breaking in at our publication with short articles and fillers if they are typically hard to find articles. We do most major features inhouse."

WATERWAY GUIDE, Communication Channels, Inc., 6255 Barfield Rd., Atlanta GA 30328. (404)256-9800. FAX: (404)256-3116. Editor: Judith Powers. 90% freelance written. Quarterly magazine on intracoastal waterway travel for recreational boats. "Writer must be knowledgeable about navigation and the areas covered by the guide." Estab. 1947. Circ. 45,000. Pays on publication. Publishes ms an average of 3 months after acceptance. Byline given sometimes. Kill fee varies. Buys all rights. Reports in 2 month on queries; 3 months on mss. Sample copy $27.95 and $3 postage.

Nonfiction: Historical/nostalgic, how-to, photo feature, technical and travel. "No personal boating experiences." Buys 25 mss/year. Query with or without published clips, or send complete ms. Length: 200 words minimum. Pays $50-3,000 for assigned articles. Pays in contributor copies or other premiums for helpful tips and useful information.

Photos: Send photos with submission. Reviews 3×5 prints. Offers $25 per b&w photo, $600 for color photos used on the cover. Identification of subjects required. Buys one-time rights.

Fillers: Facts. Buys 6/year. Length: 250-1,000 words. Pays $50-150.

Tips: "Must have on-the-water experience and be able to provide new and accurate information on geographic areas covered by Waterway Guide."

WOODENBOAT MAGAZINE, The Magazine for Wooden Boat Owners, Builders, and Designers, WoodenBoat Publications, Inc., P.O. Box 78, Brooklin ME 04616. (207)359-4651. FAX: (207)359-8920. Editor: Jon Wilson. Executive Editor: Jennifer Elliott. Senior Editor: Mike O'Brien. 50% freelance written. Works with a small number of new/unpublished writers each year. Bimonthly magazine for wooden boat owners, builders, and designers. "We are devoted exclusively to the design, building, care, preservation, and use of wooden boats, both commercial and pleasure, old and new, sail and power. We work to convey quality, integrity, and involvement in the creation and care of these craft, to entertain, to inform, to inspire, and to provide our varied readers with access to individuals who are deeply experienced in the world of wooden boats." Estab. 1974. Circ. 106,000. Pays on publication. Publishes ms an average of 6-12 months after acceptance. Byline given. Offers variable kill fee. Buys first North American serial rights. Simultaneous queries and submissions (with notification) and previously published submissions OK. Query for electronic submissions. Reports in 3 weeks on queries; 4 weeks on mss. Sample copy $4.50; writer's guidelines for SASE.

Nonfiction: Technical (repair, restoration, maintenance, use, design and building wooden boats). No poetry, fiction. Buys 50 mss/year. Query with published clips. Length: 1,500-5,000 words. Pays $6/column inch. Sometimes pays expenses of writers on assignment.

Photos: Send photos with query. Negatives must be available. Pays $15-75 for b&w; $25-350 for color. Identification of subjects required. Buys one-time rights.

Columns/Departments: On the Waterfront pays for information on wooden boat-related events, projects, boatshop activities, etc. Buys 25/year. "We use the same columnists for each issue." Send complete information. Length: 250-1,000 words. Pays $5-50 for information.

Tips: "We appreciate a detailed, articulate query letter, accompanied by photos, that will give us a clear idea of what the author is proposing. We appreciate samples of previously published work. It is important for a prospective author to become familiar with our magazine first. It is extremely rare for us to make an assignment with a writer with whom we have not worked before. Most work is submitted on speculation. The most common failure is not exploring the subject material in enough depth."

YACHTING, Times-Mirror, 2 Park Ave., New York NY 10016. (212)779-5000. FAX: (212)725-1035. Publishing Director: Oliver S. Moore III. Senior Editor: Cynthia Taylor. 50% freelance written. "The magazine is written and edited for experienced, knowledgeable yachtsmen." Estab. 1907. Circ. 155,000. Pays on publication. Byline given. Buys first rights. Submit seasonal/holiday material 6 months in advance. Reports in 2 weeks on queries; 1 month on mss.

Nonfiction: Book excerpts, personal experience, photo feature and travel. No cartoons, fiction, poetry. Query with published clips. Length: 250-2,500 words. Pays $250-1,000 for assigned articles. Pays expenses of writers on assignment.

Photos: Send photos with submission. Reviews 35mm transparencies. Offers no additional payment for photos accepted with ms. Captions, model releases and identification of subjects required.

Columns/Departments: Cruising Yachtsman (stories on cruising; contact Cynthia Taylor, managing editor); Racing Yachtsman (stories about sail or power racing; contact Lisa Gosselin); Yacht Yard (how-to and technical pieces on yachts and their systems; contact Charles Barthold, executive editor). Buys 30 mss/year. Send complete ms. Length: 750 words maximum. Pays $250-500.

Tips: "We require considerable expertise in our writing because our audience is experienced and knowledgeable. Vivid descriptions of quaint anchorages and quainter natives are fine, but our readers want to know how the yachtsmen got there, too. They also want to know how their boats work."

Bowling

BOWLERS JOURNAL, 101 E. Erie St., Chicago IL 60611. (312)266-7171. Editor-in-Chief: Mort Luby. Managing Editor: Jim Dressel. 30% freelance written. Prefers to work with published/established writers; works with a small number of new/unpublished writers each year. Monthly magazine emphasizing bowling. Circ. 22,000. **Pays on acceptance.** Publishes ms an average of 2 months after acceptance. Buys all rights. Submit seasonal/holiday material 3 months in advance of issue date. Reports in 6 weeks. Sample copy $2.

Nonfiction: General interest (stories on top pros); historical (stories of old-time bowlers or bowling alleys); interview (top pros, men and women); and profile (top pros). "We publish some controversial matter, seek outspoken personalities. We reject material that is too general; that is, not written for high average bowlers and bowling proprietors who already know basics of playing the game and basics of operating a bowling alley." Buys 15-20 unsolicited mss/year. Query, phone queries OK. Length: 1,200-3,500 words. Pays $75-200.

Photos: State availability of photos with query. Pays $5-15 for 8 × 10 b&w prints; and $15-25 for 35mm or 2¼ × 2¼ color transparencies. Buys one-time rights.

‡BOWLING, 5301 S. 76th St., Greendale WI 53129. (414)421-6400, ext. 230. Editor: Dan Matel. 15% freelance written. Official publication of the American Bowling Congress. Monthly. **Pays on acceptance.** Publishes ms an average of 2 months after acceptance. Byline given. Rights purchased vary with author and material; usually buys all rights. Reports in 1 month.

Nonfiction: "This is a specialized field and the average writer attempting the subject of bowling should be well-informed. However, anyone is free to submit material for approval." Wants articles about unusual ABC sanctioned leagues and tournaments, personalities, etc., featuring male bowlers. Nostalgia articles also considered. No first-person articles or material on history of bowling. Length: 500-1,200 words. Pays $100-300 per article. No poems.

Photos: Pays $10-15/photo.

Tips: "Submit feature material on bowlers, generally amateurs competing in local leagues, or special events involving the game of bowling. Should have connection with ABC membership. Queries should be as detailed as possible so that we may get a clear idea of what the proposed story would be all about. It saves us time and the writer time. Samples of previously published material in the bowling or general sports field would help. Once we find a talented writer in a given area, we're likely to go back to him in the future. We're looking for good writers who can handle assignments professionally and promptly." No articles on professionals.

‡BOWLING MAGAZINE, American Bowling Congress, 5301 S. 76th St., Greendale WI 53129. (414)421-6400. Editor: Bill Vint. 20% freelance written. Bimonthly magazine covering bowling. "*Bowling* Magazine features unusual bowling feats worthy of national recognition and profiles of national bowling figures." Estab. 1934. Circ. 120,000. **Pays on acceptance.** Publishes ms an average of 3-4 months after acceptance. Byline given. Offers $30 kill fee. Buys first North American serial rights. Submit seasonal/holiday material 4 months in advance. Reports in 1 month on queries; 6 weeks on mss. Free sample copy and writer's guidelines.
Nonfiction: Articles Editor: Rory Gillespie. General interest, historical/nostalgic, humor, interview/profile, opinion, personal experience and photo feature. "No 'Local bowler shoots 300 game' stories. There are 10,000 perfect games a year. Unless it is something unusual or the bowler is special, send it to your local newspaper." Buys 6-10 mss/year. Query. Length: 500-1,500 words. Pays $100-350 for assigned articles; $100-350 for unsolicited articles. Send photos with submission. Reviews contact sheets, negatives, transparencies (35mm or 2¼×2¼), or 5×7 or 8×10 prints. Offers $25-50/photo. Captions and identification of subjects required. Buys one-time rights.
Columns/Departments: Spare Shots (unusual bowling items—e.g. house for sale with bowling lane in basement.), 100 words. Buys 6-10 mss/year. Send complete ms. Length: 50-100 words. Pays $15-50.
Tips: "Learn the terminology. Bowling is great fun but, do not assume that bowlers like to be made fun of. Query, query, query. Once we have published you, we will repeat business."

WOMAN BOWLER, 5301 S. 76th St., Greendale WI 53129. (414)421-9000. FAX: (414)421-3013. Editor: Karen Sytsma. 3% freelance written. Works with a small number of new/unpublished writers each year. Published eight times a year with combined March/April, May/June, August/September, November/December issues. Circ. 150,000. Emphasizes bowling for women bowlers, ages 18-90. Buys all rights. **Pays on acceptance.** Publishes ms an average of 3 months after acceptance. Byline given "except on occasion, when freelance article is used as part of a regular magazine department. When this occurs, it is discussed first with the author." Submit seasonal/holiday material 2 months in advance. Previously published submissions OK. Reports in 1 month. Free sample copy and writer's guidelines.
Nonfiction: Interview; profile; and spot news. Buys 25 mss/year. Query. Length: 1,500 words maximum (unless by special assignment). Pays $25-100.
Photos: Purchased with accompanying ms. Query. Pays $25-100 for b&w glossy prints. Model releases and identification of subjects required.

Gambling

CASINO PLAYER, Nation's Largest Gaming Guide, (formerly *The Player*), Player's Intl./ACE Marketing, 2524 Arctic Ave., Atlantic City NJ 08401. (609)344-9000. FAX: (609)345-3239. Publisher: Glenn Fine. Editor: Roger Gros. 15% freelance written. Monthly tabloid on gambling. "We cover any issue that would interest the gambler, from table games to sports betting, to slot machines. Articles should be light, entertaining and give tips on how to win." Estab. 1985. Circ. 210,000. Pays on publication. Byline sometimes given. Buys all rights. Submit seasonal/holiday material 3 months in advance. Sample copy $2 with 9×12 SAE and 5 first class stamps.
Nonfiction: How-to (win!) and new product (gaming equipment). "No articles dependent on statistics/no travelogues. No first person gambling stories." Query with published clips. Length: 500-1,000 words. Pays $50-250 for assigned articles; $50-100 for unsolicited articles. Sometimes pays expenses of writers on assignment.
Photos: Send photos with submission. Reviews contact sheets and 5×7 prints. Offers $10 per photo. Captions and identification of subjects required. Buys all rights.
Columns/Departments: Table Games (best ways to play, ratings); Slots (new machines, methods, casino policies); Nevada (what's new in state, properties); Tournaments (reports on gaming, tournaments) and Caribbean (gaming in the islands), all 500 words. Buys 10 mss/year. Query with published clips. Pays $50-100.
Fillers: Facts and gags to be illustrated by cartoonist. Buys 5/year. Length: 25-100 words. Pays $25-100.
Tips: "Writer must understand the gambler: why he gambles, what his motivations are. The spread of legalized gaming will be an increasingly important topic in the next year. Write as much to entertain as to inform. We try to give the reader information they will not find elsewhere."

WINNING!, NatCom, Inc., 15115 S. 76th East Ave., Bixby OK 74008. (918)366-4441. FAX: (918)366-6250. Managing Editor: Simon P. McCaffery. 30% freelance written. Monthly magazine covering gaming/travel. How-to-win articles addressing all aspects of legal gaming-casinos, high-stakes bingo,

contests and sweepstakes and so on." Estab. 1976. Circ. 150,000. Pays 30 days after acceptance. Publishes ms an average of 3 months after acceptance. Byline given. Buys first rights. No simultaneous submissions. Query for electronic submissions. Reports in 1 week on queries; 1-2 weeks on mss. Sample copy for 9 × 12 SAE with 5 first class stamps. Writer's guidelines for #10 SAE with 1 first class stamp.
Nonfiction: How-to (gaming-casino, etc. bingo, sweepstakes and contests), interview/profile, new product, travel. "No negative profiles of casino performers/how-to-cheat gaming articles." Buys 24-30 mss/year. Query. Length: 400-1,200 words. Pays $75-200 for articles; $5-50 for short items and fillers.

General Interest

HIGH SCHOOL SPORTS, Suite 2000, 1230 Avenue of the Americas, New York NY 10020. (212)765-3300. FAX: (212)265-7278. Editor: Joe Guise. Associate Editors: Scott Brodeur and John Shabe. Assistant Editor: Susan Vinella. 80% freelance written. Bimonthly magazine. "We are the only national magazine in America that focuses exclusively on the efforts and achievements of high school athletes. Features are on individuals, teams or issues (steroids, small school basketball)." Estab. 1985. Circ. 500,000. **Pays on acceptance.** Publishes ms an average of 2 months after acceptance. Byline given. Offers 25% kill fee. Buys first rights. Simultaneous and previously published submissions OK. Query for electronic submissions. Sample copy $2 with 8½ × 11 SAE and 90¢ in postage. Writer's guidelines for #10 SASE.
Nonfiction: Buys approximately 35 mss/year. Query with published clips. Length: 1,500-2,000. Pays $400-750. Sometimes pays expenses of writers on assignment.
Photos: State availability of photos with submission. Reviews 35mm transparencies. Most photos are assigned. Buys one-time rights.
Columns/Departments: Dateline: USA (2-page round-up of news in different areas of the country), 250 words; Coach's Clinic (how-to on single subject, i.e., vision training, concentration); Time Out (unusual high school activities); Sneak Previews (a look at the nation's brightest new starts); Retrospect (a high profile sports figure looks back at his/her high school days); Great Rivalries (a look at some of the more emotional, long-running series between teams in a variety of sports). Buys 35 mss/ year. Query with published clips. Length 300-750. Pays $75-350.

‡**INSIDE SPORTS**, Century Publishing Co., 990 Grove St., Evanston IL 60201. (708)491-6440. Editor-in-Chief: Michael Herbert. 90% freelance written. Monthly magazine. Pays on publication. Publishes ms an average of 4 months after acceptance. Offers 100% kill fee. Rights are negotiated individually. Reports on queries and mss "as soon as we can; sometimes it will be the same day; sometimes it will be weeks."
Nonfiction: Query with or without published clips, or send complete ms. Length of article and payment vary with each article and writer.

OUTDOOR CANADA MAGAZINE, Suite 202, 703 Evans Ave., Toronto, Ontario M9C 5E9 Canada. (416)695-0311. FAX: (416)695-0382. Editor-in-Chief: Teddi Brown. 70% freelance written. Works with a small number of new/unpublished writers each year. Emphasizes noncompetitive outdoor recreation in Canada *only*. Magazine published 9 times/year. Estab. 1972. Circ. 141,000. Pays on publication. Publishes ms an average of 6-8 months after acceptance. Buys first rights. Submit seasonal/holiday material 1 year in advance of issue date. Byline given. *Enclose SASE or IRCs or material not returned.* Reports in 1 month. Mention *Writer's Market* in request for editorial guidelines.
Nonfiction: Fishing, hunting, adventure, outdoor issues, exploring, outdoor destinations in Canada, some how-to. Buys 35-40 mss/year, usually with photos. Length: 1,000-2,500 words. Pays $100 and up.
Photos: Emphasize people in the outdoors. Pays $35-225 for 35mm transparencies; and $400/cover. Captions and model releases required.
News: Short news pieces. Buys 70-80/year. Length: 200-500 words. Pays $6/printed inch.

OUTSIDE, Mariah Publications Corp., 1165 N. Clark St., Chicago IL 60610. (312)951-0990. Editor: Mark Bryant. Managing Editor: Beth Greenfield. 90% freelance written. Monthly magazine on outdoor recreation and travel. "*Outside* is a monthly national magazine for active, educated, upscale adults who love the outdoors and are concerned about its preservation." Estab. 1977. Circ. 325,000. **Pays on acceptance.** Publishes ms an average of 3 months after acceptance. Byline given. Offers 25% kill fee. Buys first North American serial rights. Submit seasonal/holiday material 4-5 months in advance. Electronic submission OK for solicited materials; not for unsolicited. Reports in 1 month on queries; 6 weeks on mss. Sample copy $4 with 8½ × 11 SAE and $2.40 postage. Writer's guidelines for SASE.
Nonfiction: Book excerpts, essays, reports on the environment, outdoor sports and expeditions, general interest, how-to, humor, inspirational, interview/profile (major figures associated with sports, travel, environment, outdoor), opinion, personal experience (expeditions; trying out new sports),

photo feature (outdoor photography), technical (reviews of equipment; how-to) and travel (adventure, sports-oriented travel). All should pertain to the outdoors: Bike section; Downhill Skiing; Cross-country Skiing; Adventure Travel. Do not want to see articles about sports that we don't cover (basketball, tennis, golf, etc.). Buys 40 mss/year. Query with published clips and SASE. Length: 1,500-4,000 words. Pays 50¢/word. Pays expenses of writers on assignment.

Photos: "Do not send photos; if we decide to use a freelancer's story, we may request to see the writer's photos." Reviews transparencies. Offers $180 minimum per photo. Captions and identification of subjects required. Buys one-time rights.

Columns/Departments: Dispatches, contact Dan Coyle, (news, events, short profiles relevant to outdoors), 200-1,000 words; Destinations, contact Lisa Chase, (places to explore, news, and tips for adventure travelers), 250-400 words; Review, contact Matthew Childs, (evaluations of products), 200-1,500 words. Buys 180 mss/year. Query with published clips. Length: 200-2,000 words. Pays 50¢/word.

Tips: "Prospective writers should study the magazine before querying. Look at the magazine for our style, subject matter and standards." The departments are the best areas for freelancers to break in.

REFEREE, Referee Enterprises, Inc., P.O. Box 161, Franksville WI 53126. (414)632-8855. Editor: Tom Hammill. For well-educated, mostly 26- to 50-year-old male sports officials. 20-25% freelance written. Eager to work with new/unpublished writers; works with a small number of new/unpublished writers each year. Monthly magazine. Estab. 1976. Circ. 42,000. Pays on acceptance of completed manuscript. Publishes ms an average of 3-6 months after acceptance. Rights purchased varies. Submit seasonal/holiday material 6 months in advance. Previously published submissions OK. Reports in 2 weeks. Sample copy for 10×13 SAE and $2 postage; writer's guidelines for #10 SASE.

Nonfiction: How-to, informational, humor, interview, profile, personal experience, photo feature and technical. Buys 54 mss/year. Query. Length: 700-3,000 words. Pays 4-10¢/word. "No general sports articles."

Photos: Purchased with or without accompanying ms or on assignment. Captions preferred. Send contact sheet, prints, negatives or transparencies. Pays $20 for each b&w used; $35 for each color used; $100 for color cover.

Columns/Departments: Arena (bios); Law (legal aspects); Take Care (fitness, medical). Buys 24 mss/year. Query. Length: 200-800 words. Pays 4¢/word up to $100 maximum for Law and Take Care. Arena pays about $15 each, regardless of length.

Fillers: Jokes, gags, anecdotes, puzzles and referee shorts. Query. Length: 50-200 words. Pays 4¢/word in some cases; others offer only author credit lines.

Tips: "Queries with a specific idea appeal most to readers. Generally, we are looking more for feature writers, as we usually do our own shorter/filler-type material. It is helpful to obtain suitable photos to augment a story. Don't send fluff—we need hard-hitting, incisive material tailored just for our audience. Anything smacking of public relations is a no sale. Don't gloss over the material too lightly or fail to go in-depth looking for a quick sale (taking the avenue of least resistance)."

‡SPORT, Petersen Publishing Co., 8490 Sunset Blvd., Los Angeles CA 90069. (213)854-2222. Editor: Mr. Kelly Garrett. 30% freelance written. Monthly magazine. **Pays on acceptance.** Publishes ms an average of 3 months after acceptance. Offers 25% kill fee. Buys first North American serial rights or all rights. Reports in 3 months.

Nonfiction: "Prefers to see articles on professional, big-time sports: basketball, football, baseball, with some boxing and hockey. The articles we buy must be contemporary pieces, not a history of sports or a particular sport." Query with published clips. Length: News briefs, 200-300 words; Departments, 1,400 words; Features, 2,000-3,000 words. Averages 50¢/word for articles.

‡THE SPORTING NEWS, Times Mirror Co., 1212 N. Lindbergh Blvd., Box 56, St. Louis MO 63132. (314)997-7111. Editor: John Rawlings. 50-60% freelance written. Weekly tabloid. Pays on publication. Publishes ms an average of 2-3 months after acceptance. Offers 50% kill fee. Buys first or one-time and second serial rights. Reports in 3 weeks

Nonfiction: "Prefers to see trend stories, perspective stories, trend analysis of major spectator sports." Prefers to see complete ms, but may query with published clips. Length: 100-2,000 words. Pays $100-200.

SPORTS ILLUSTRATED, Time & Life Bld., Rockefeller Center, New York NY 10020-1393. Did not want to be listed.

SPORTS PARADE, Meridian Publishing Co., Inc., P.O. Box 10010, Ogden UT 84409. (801)394-9446. 65% freelance written. Works with a small number of new/unpublished writers each year. A monthly general interest sports magazine distributed by business and professional firms to employees, customers, clients, etc. Readers are predominantly upscale, mainstream, family oriented. **Pays on acceptance.** Publishes ms an average of 8 months after acceptance. Byline given. Buys first rights, second serial (reprint) rights or nonexclusive reprint rights. Submit seasonal/holiday material 6 months in advance. Simultaneous and previously published submissions OK. Reports in 6 weeks. Sample copy $1 with 9×12 SAE; writer's guidelines for #10 SASE.

Nonfiction: General interest and interview/profile. "General interest articles covering the entire sports spectrum, personality profiles on top flight professional and amateur sports figures. *Sports Parade* is now combined with *People in Action*. We are looking for articles on well-known athletes in the top 10% of their field. We are still looking at articles and profiles of well-known celebrities." Buys 20 mss/year. Query. Length: 1,200-1,580 words. Pays 15¢/word.

Photos: Send with query or ms. Pays $35 for transparencies; $50 for cover. Captions and model releases required.

Tips: "I will be purchasing more articles based on personalities—today's stars."

WOMEN'S SPORTS AND FITNESS MAGAZINE, Women's Sports and Fitness, Inc., Suite 421, 1919 14th St., Boulder CO 80302. (303)440-5111. FAX: (303)440-3313. Editor: Marjorie McCloy. 90% freelance written. Works with a small number of new/unpublished writers each year. Magazine published 8 times yearly; 68-125 pages. Emphasizes women's sports, fitness and health. Estab. 1975. Circ. 200,000. Pays on publication. Publishes ms an average of 3 months after acceptance. Buys first North American serial rights. Submit seasonal/holiday material 3 months in advance. Reports in 2 months. Sample copy $2.50 with 9×12 SAE and 2 first class stamps; writer's guidelines for SASE.

Nonfiction: Profile, service piece, interview, how-to, historical, personal experience, personal opinion, new product. "All articles should have the latest information from knowledgeable sources. All must be of national interest." Buys 5 mss/issue. Length: 500-2,000 words. Query with published clips. Pays $300-1,000 for features, including expenses.

Photos: State availability of photos. Pays about $50-300 for b&w prints; $50-500 for 35mm color transparencies. Buys one-time rights.

Columns/Departments: Buys 8-10/issue. Query with published clips. Length: 200-750 words. Pays $100-400.

Tips: "If the writer doesn't have published clips, best advice for breaking in is to concentrate on columns and departments (the Fast Breaks and Personal Best departments) first. Query letters should tell why our readers—active women (with an average age in the mid thirties) who partake in sports or fitness activities six times a week—would want to read the article. We're especially attracted to articles with a new angle, fresh information, or difficult-to-get information. We go after the latest in health, nutrition and fitness research, or reports about lesser-known women in sports who are on the threshold of greatness. We also present profiles of the best athletes and teams. We want the profiles to give insight into the person as well as the athlete. We have a cadre of writers who we've worked with regularly, but we are always looking for new writers."

Golf

GOLF DIGEST, 5520 Park Ave., Trumbull CT 06611. (203)373-7000. Editor: Jerry Tarde. 30% freelance written. Emphasizes golfing. Monthly magazine. Circ. 1.3 million. **Pays on acceptance.** Publishes ms an average of 6 weeks after acceptance. Buys all rights. Byline given. Submit seasonal/holiday material 4 months in advance. Reports in 6 weeks.

Nonfiction: Lisa Sweet, editorial assistant. How-to, informational, historical, humor, inspirational, interview, nostalgia, opinion, profile, travel, new product, personal experience, photo feature and technical; "all on playing and otherwise enjoying the game of golf." Query. Length: 1,000-2,500 words. Pays $150-1,500 depending on length of edited mss.

Photos: Nick DiDio, art director. Purchased without accompanying ms. Pays $75-150 for 5×7 or 8×10 b&w prints; $100-300/35mm transparency. Model release required.

Poetry: Lois Hains, assistant editor. Light verse. Buys 1-2/issue. Length: 4-8 lines. Pays $25.

Fillers: Lois Hains, assistant editor. Jokes, gags, anecdotes and cutlines for cartoons. Buys 1-2/issue. Length: 2-6 lines. Pays $10-25.

GOLF ILLUSTRATED, Family Media, Inc., 3 Park Ave., New York NY 10016. (212)779-6200. Editor-in-Chief: Al Barkow. Executive Editor: David Gould. Managing Editor: Hal Goodman. 50% freelance written. Eager to work with new/unpublished writers. A monthly magazine covering personalities and developments in the sport of golf. Circ. 500,000. Pays on acceptance or publication. Publishes ms an average of 2 months after acceptance. Offers 10% kill fee. Submit seasonal/holiday material 6 months in advance. Query for electronic submissions. Reports in 3 weeks on queries; 6 weeks on manuscripts.

Nonfiction: Essays, historical/nostalgic, how-to, humor, interview/profile, opinion, personal experience, photo feature and travel. Buys 50 mss/year. Query with published clips. Length: 750-1,750 words. Pays $500-1,500 for assigned articles; pays $250-1,000 for unsolicited articles. Usually pays the expenses of writers on assignment.

Photos: State availability of photos with submission. Reviews contact sheets and transparencies. Offers $50-500/photo. Captions and identification of subjects required. Buys one-time rights.

Columns/Departments: Health and Fitness, Food and Opinion (all related to golf), approximately 750 words. Query with published clips. Pays $500-1,000.

Fillers: Anecdotes, facts, gags to be illustrated by cartoonist and short humor. Buys 30/year. Length: 100-500 words. Pays $25-300.

Tips: "A freelancer can best break in to our publication by following the personalities—the PGA, LPGA and PGA Senior tour pros and the nature of the game in general."

GOLF MAGAZINE, Times-Mirror Magazines, 2 Park Ave., New York NY 10016. (212)779-5000. Editor: James A. Frank. Senior Editors: David Barrett and Mike Purkey. 40% freelance written. Monthly magazine on golf, professional and amateur. Circ. 1.05 million. **Pays on acceptance.** Publishes ms an average of 2-4 months after acceptance. Byline sometimes given. Offers 20% kill fee. Buys first North American serial rights. Submit seasonal/holiday material 3-4 months in advance. Query for electronic submissions. Reports in 1 month on queries; 2 weeks on mss. Free writer's guidelines.

Nonfiction: General interest, historical/nostalgic, how-to, humor, interview/profile. Buys 10-20 mss/year. Query or query with published clips. Length: 100-2,500 words. Pays $100-2,500. Sometimes pays expenses of writers on assignment.

Photos: State availability of photos with submission or send photos with submission. Offers standard page rate. Captions, model releases and identification of subjects required. Buys one-time rights.

Columns/Departments: See magazines for columns. Buys 5-10 mss/year. Query, query with published clips or send complete ms. Length: 100-1,200 words. Pays $100-1,000.

Fillers: Newsbreaks and short humor. Buys 5-10/year. Length: 50-100 words. Pays $50-100.

Tips: "Be familiar with the magazine and with the game of golf."

‡SCORE, Canada's Golf Magazine, Canadian Controlled Media Communications, 287 MacPherson Ave., Toronto, Ontario M4V 1A4 Canada. (416)928-2909. FAX: (416)928-1357. Managing Editor: John Gordon. 70% freelance written. Works with a small number of new/unpublished writers each year. Magazine published 6 times/year covering golf. "*Score* magazine provides seasonal coverage of the Canadian golf scene, professional, amateur, senior and junior golf for men and women golfers in Canada, the U.S. and Europe through profiles, history, travel, editorial comment and instruction." Circ. 110,000 audited. **Pays on acceptance.** Byline given. Offers negotiable kill fee. Buys all rights and second serial (reprint) rights. Submit seasonal/holiday material 8 months in advance. Reports within 1 month. Sample copy for $2 (Canadian), 9 × 12 SAE and IRCs; writer's guidelines for #10 SAE and IRC.

Nonfiction: Book excerpts (golf); historical/nostalgic (golf and golf characters); interview/profile (prominent golf professionals); photo feature (golf); and travel (golf destinations only). The yearly April/May issue includes tournament results from Canada, the U.S., Europe, Asia, Australia, etc., history, profile, and regular features. "No personal experience, technical, opinion or general-interest material. Most articles are by assignment only." Buys 25-30 mss/year. Query with published clips. Length: 700-3,500 words. Pays $140-800.

Photos: Send photos with query or ms. Pays $50-100 for 35mm color transparencies (positives) or $30 for 8 × 10 or 5 × 7 b&w prints. Captions, model release (if necessary), and identification of subjects required. Buys all rights.

Columns/Departments: Profile (historical or current golf personalities or characters); Great Moments ("Great Moments in Canadian Golf"—description of great single moments, usually game triumphs); New Equipment (Canadian availability only); Travel (golf destinations, including "hard" information such as greens fees, hotel accommodations, etc.); Instruction (by special assignment only; usually from teaching golf professionals); The Mental Game (psychology of the game, by special assignment only); and History (golf equipment collections and collectors, development of the game, legendary figures and events). Buys 17-20 mss/year. Query with published clips or send complete ms. Length: 700-1,700 words. Pays $140-400.

Tips: "Only writers with an extensive knowledge of golf and familiarity with the Canadian golf scene should query or submit in-depth work to *Score*. Many of our features are written by professional people who play the game for a living or work in the industry. All areas mentioned under Columns/Departments are open to freelancers. Most of our *major* features are done on assignment only."

Guns

AMERICAN HANDGUNNER, Publishers' Development Corp., Suite 200, 591 Camino de la Reina, San Diego CA 92108. (619)297-5352. FAX: (619)297-5353. Editor: Cameron Hopkins. 90% freelance written. A bimonthly magazine covering handguns, handgun sports and handgun accessories. "Semi-technical publication for handgun enthusiasts of above-average knowledge/understanding of handguns. Writers must have ability to write about technical designs of handguns as well as ability to write intelligently about the legitimate sporting value of handguns." Circ. 150,000. Pays on publication. Publishes ms an average of 5-9 months after acceptance. Byline given. Offers $50 kill fee. Buys all world rights for text, first North American for photos. Submit seasonal/holiday material 7 months in advance. All submissions must be on computer disk. Reports in 3 weeks. Free sample copy and writer's guidelines.

Nonfiction: How-to, interview/profile, new product, photo feature, technical and "iconoclastic think pieces." Special issue is the *American Handgunner Annual*. No handgun competition coverage. Buys 60-70 mss/year. Query. Length: 500-3,000 words. Pays $175-600 for assigned articles; pays $100-400 for unsolicited articles. Sometimes pays the expenses of writers on assignment.

Photos: Send photos with submission. Reviews contact sheets, 35mm and 4×5 transparencies and 5×7 b&w prints. Offers no additional payment for b&w photos accepted with ms; offers $50-250/color photo. Captions and identification of subjects required. Buys first North American serial rights.

Tips: "We are always interested in 'round-up' pieces covering a particular product line or mixed bag of different product lines of the same theme. If vacation/travel takes you to an exotic place, we're interested in, say, 'The Guns of Upper Volta.' We are looking more closely at handgun hunting."

‡**AMERICAN RIFLEMAN**, National Rifle Association of America, Suite 1000, 470 Spring Park Place, Herndon VA 22070. (703)481-3340. Editor: William F. Parkerson, III. Managing Editor: Ron Keysor. 25% freelance written. Monthly magazine covering firearms. "We are a member magazine devoted to the history, use, manufacturing, development and care of all types of portable small arms. We have a relatively sophisticated audience and international readership in this subject area." Estab. 1871. Circ. 1.4 million. **Pays on acceptance.** Publishes ms an average of 3-5 months after acceptance. Byline given. Offers no kill fee. Buys first North American serial rights. Submit seasonal/holiday material 3 months in advance. Query for electronic submissions. Reports in 1 week on queries; 3 weeks on mss. Free writer's guidelines.

Nonfiction: Historical/nostalgic (firearms), how-to (firearms making/repair), technical (firearms related). "No fiction, poetry, essays, pure hunting tales or anything unrelated to firearms." Buys 30-35 mss/year. Query. Length: 5,000 words maximum. Pays $500 maximum. Sometimes pays expenses of writers on assignment.

Photos: Send photos with submission. Offers no additional payment for photos accepted with ms. Captions and identification of subjects required. Buys one-time rights.

Columns/Departments: From The Bench (articles on reloading ammunition or how-to firearms-related pieces), 2-3,000 words. Buys 12 mss/year. Query. Pays $400 maximum.

Tips: "For starters, it is unlikely that any of our potential authors are unfamiliar with this magazine. Well illustrated, high-quality gunsmithing articles are needed, as well as innovative material on reloading, any of the shooting sports, historical topics, etc. We have an abundance of scholarly material on the gun control issue, but we have bought the occasional thoughtful piece. Aside from our 'From The Bench' column we purchase only feature articles. We do accept unpaid submissions called 'In My Experience' that might introduce authors to us, but most are from long-time readers."

GUN DIGEST, DBI Books, Inc., 4092 Commercial Ave., Northbrook IL 60062. (312)272-6310. Editor-in-Chief: Ken Warner. 50% freelance written. Prefers to work with published/established writers and works with a small number of new/unpublished writers each year. Annual journal covering guns and shooting. Estab. 1944. **Pays on acceptance.** Publishes ms an average of 20 months after acceptance. Byline given. Buys all rights. Reports in 1 month.

Nonfiction: Buys 50 mss/issue. Query. Length: 500-5,000 words. Pays $100-600; includes photos or illustration package from author.

Photos: State availability of photos with query letter. Reviews 8×10 b&w prints. Payment for photos included in payment for ms. Captions required.

Tips: Award of $1,000 to author of best article (juried) in each issue.

GUN WORLD, 34249 Camino Capistrano, Box HH, Capistrano Beach CA 92624. Editorial Director: Jack Lewis. 50% freelance written. For ages that "range from mid-teens to mid-60s; many professional types who are interested in relaxation of hunting and shooting." Monthly. Estab. 1960. Circ. 128,000. Buys 80-100 unsolicited mss/year. **Pays on acceptance.** Publishes ms an average of 6 months after acceptance. Buys first rights and sometimes all rights, but rights reassigned on request. Byline given. Submit seasonal material 5 months in advance. Reports in 6 weeks. Copy of editorial requirements for SASE.

Nonfiction: General subject matter consists of "well-rounded articles—not by amateurs—on shooting techniques, with anecdotes; hunting stories with tips and knowledge integrated. No poems or fiction. We like broad humor in our articles, so long as it does not reflect upon firearms safety. Most arms magazines are pretty deadly, and we feel shooting can be fun. Too much material aimed at pro-gun people. Most of this is staff-written and most shooters don't have to be told of their rights under the

Constitution. We want articles on new developments; off-track inventions, novel military uses of arms; police armament and training techniques; do-it-yourself projects in this field." Buys informational, how-to, personal experience and nostalgia articles. Pays up to $300, sometimes more.

Photos: Purchases photos with mss and captions required. Wants 5×7 b&w photos. Sometimes pays the expenses of writers on assignment.

Tips: "The most frequent mistake made by writers in completing an article for us is surface writing with no real knowledge of the subject. To break in, offer an anecdote having to do with proposed copy."

‡**GUNS & AMMO,** Petersen Publishing Co., 8490 Sunset Blvd., #204, Los Angeles CA 90069. (213)854-2160. Editor: Red Bell. Managing Editor: Karen Dunbar Enzer. 5% freelance written. Monthly magazine covering firearms. "Our readers are enthusiasts of handguns, rifles, shotguns and accessories." Circ. 650,000. **Pays on acceptance.** Publishes ms 6 months after acceptance. Byline given. Buys all rights. Submit seasonal material 6 months in advance. Query for electronic submissions. Free writer's guidelines.

Nonfiction: Opinion. Buys 12 mss/year. Send complete ms. Length: 1,000-2,500 words. Pays $125-500.

Photos: Send photos with submissions. Review 7×9 prints. Offers no additional payment for photos accepted with ms. Captions, model releases and identification of subjects required. Buys all rights.

Columns/Departments: RKBA (opinion column on right to keep and bear arms). Send complete ms. Length: 1,000-2,500 words. Pays $125-500.

‡**GUNS & AMMO ANNUAL,** Petersen Publishing Co., 8490 Sunset Blvd. #204, Los Angeles CA 90069. (213)854-2160. Editor: Bill O'Brien. Managing Editor: Karen Dunbar Enzer. 20% freelance written. Annual magazine covering firearms. "Our audience consists of enthusiasts of firearms, shooting sports and accessories." **Pays on acceptance.** Publishes ms an average of 9-12 months after acceptance. Byline given. Buys all rights.

Nonfiction: Buys 10 mss/year. Send complete ms. Length: 2,000-4,000 words. Pays $250-350.

Photos: Send photos with submission. Reviews 8×10 prints. Offers no additional payment for photos accepted with ms. Captions, model releases and identification of subjects required. Buys all rights.

Tips: "We need feature articles on firearms and accessories. See current issue for examples."

‡**GUNS MAGAZINE,** 591 Camino de la Reina, San Diego CA 92108. (619)297-5352. Editor: Jerome Lee. 50% freelance written. Monthly magazine for firearms enthusiasts. Circ. 200,000. Pays on publication for first North American rights. Publishes manuscripts 4-6 months after acceptance. Free sample copy and writer's guidelines.

Nonfiction: Test reports on new firearms; round-up articles on firearms types; guns for specific purposes (hunting, target shooting, self-defense); custom gunmakers; history of modern guns. Buys approximately 25 ms/year. Length: 1,000-2,500 words. Pays $100-350.

Photos: Major emphasis on quality photography. Additional payment of $50-200 for color, 4×5 or 2¼×2¼ preferred.

‡**PETERSEN'S HANDGUNS for Sport & Defense,** Petersen Publishing Company, 8490 Sunset Blvd., #204, Los Angeles CA 90069. (213)854-6891. Editor: Mr. Jane M. Libourel. Managing Editor: Karen Dunbar-Enzer. 60% freelance written. Monthly magazine covering handguns and handgun accessories. Estab. 1986. Circ. 130,000. **Pays on acceptance.** Byline given. No kill fee. Buys all rights. Reporting time varies. Free sample copy and writer's guidelines.

Nonfiction: General interest, historical, how-to, Profile, new product and technical. "No articles not germane to established topics of magazine." Buys 72 mss/year. Send complete ms. Pays $300-450.

Photos: Send photos with submission. Reviwes contact sheets, 5×7 prints. Offers no additional payment for photos accepted with ms. Captions, model releases and identification of subjects required. Buys all rights.

Tips: "Send manuscript after querying editor by telephone and establishing acceptability. We are most open to feature stories. Be guided by published examples appearing in the magazine."

WOMEN & GUNS, SAF Periodicals Group, P.O. Box 488, Station C, Buffalo NY 14209. (716)885-6408. Editor: Sonny Jones. 50% freelance written. Monthly magazine covering "all aspects of women's involvement with firearms, including self-defense, competition, hunting, and target shooting, as well as related legal and legislative issues." Estab. 1989. Circ. 10,000. Pays within 60 days of publication. Publishes ms an average of 3 months after acceptance. Byline given. Buys first North American serial rights or second serial (reprint) rights. Submit seasonal/holiday material 3 months in advance. Previously published submissions OK. Query for electronic submissions. Reports in 1 month on queries; 2 months on mss. Free sample copy and writer's guidelines.

Nonfiction: How-to, interview/profile, new product, photo feature, and technical. Buys 20-30 mss/year. Query with or without published clips, or send complete ms. Length: 500-2,500 words. Pays $50-100 for assigned articles; $25-50 for unsolicited articles.

Photos: Send photos with submission. Reviews transparencies and 5 × 7 color and b&w prints. Offers no additional payment for photos accepted with ms. Captions, model releases and identification of subjects required. Buys one-time rights.

Columns/Departments: Query. Length: 250-500 words. Pays $10-50.

Fillers: Anecdotes, facts, gags to be illustrated by cartoonist, newsbreaks and short humor. Buys 10/year. Length: 10-100 words. Pays $5-10.

Tips: "Writers must possess superior working knowledge of firearms and insight into related issues."

Horse Racing

THE BACKSTRETCH, 19899 West 9 Mile Rd., Southfield MI 48075. (313)354-3232. FAX: (313)354-3157. Editor: Harriet Randall. 50% freelance written. Works with a small number of new/unpublished writers each year. Bimonthly magazine for Thoroughbred horse trainers, owners, breeders, farm managers, track personnel, jockeys, grooms and racing fans who span the age range from very young to very old. Publication of United Thoroughbred Trainers of America, Inc. Estab. 1962. Circ. 12,000. Publishes ms an average of 3 months after acceptance. Sample copy $3.

Nonfiction: "*Backstretch* contains mostly general information. Articles deal with biographical material on trainers, owners, jockeys, horses and their careers on and off the track, historical track articles, etc. Unless writer's material is related to Thoroughbreds and Thoroughbred racing, it should not be submitted. Opinion on Thoroughbreds should be qualified with expertise on the subject. Articles accepted on speculation basis—payment made after material is used. If not suitable, articles are returned if SASE is included. Articles that do not require printing by a specified date are preferred. There is no special length requirement and amount paid depends on material. It is advisable to include photos, if possible. Articles should be original copies and should state whether presented to any other magazine, or whether previously printed in any other magazine. Submit complete ms. We do not buy crossword puzzles, cartoons, newspaper clippings, fiction or poetry."

HOOF BEATS, United States Trotting Association, 750 Michigan Ave., Columbus OH 43215. (614)224-2291. FAX: (614)228-1385. Editor: Dean A. Hoffman. 35% freelance written. Works with a small number of new/unpublished writers each year. Monthly magazine covering harness racing for the participants of the sport of harness racing. "We cover all aspects of the sport—racing, breeding, selling, etc." Estab. 1933. Circ. 24,000. Pays on publication. Publishes ms an average of 3 months after acceptance. Byline given. Buys negotiable rights. Submit seasonal/holiday material 3 months in advance. Reports in 3 weeks. Free sample copy, postpaid.

Nonfiction: General interest, historical/nostalgic, humor, inspirational, interview/profile, new product, personal experience, photo feature. Buys 15-20 mss/year. Query. Length: open. Pays $100-400. Pays the expenses of writers on assignment "with approval."

Photos: State availability of photos. Pays variable rates for 35mm transparencies and prints. Identification of subjects required. Buys one-time rights.

Fiction: Historical, humorous, interesting fiction with a harness racing theme. Buys 2-3 mss/year. Query. Length: open. Pays $100-400.

‡THE QUARTER RACING JOURNAL, American Quarter Horse Association, P.O. Box 32470, Amarillo TX 79120. (806)376-4811. Editor: Jim Jennings. Executive Editor: Audie Rackley. 10% freelance written. Monthly magazine; the official racing voice of The American Quarter Horse Association. "We promote quarter horse racing. Articles include training, breeding, nutrition, sports medicine, health, history, etc." Estab. 1988. Circ. 12,000. **Pays on acceptance.** Publishes ms an average of 3 months after acceptance. Offers no kill fee. Buys first North American serial rights. Submit seasonal/holiday material 3 months in advance. Reports in 2 weeks on queries. Free sample copy and writer's guidelines.

Nonfiction: Historical (must be on quarter horses or people associated with them), how-to (training), nutrition, health, breeding, opinion. "We welcome submissions year around. No fiction or personality profiles." Query. Length: 700-2,500 words. Pays 5-8¢/word.

Photos: Send photos with submission. Offers no additional payment for photos accepted with ms. Captions and identification of subjects required.

Tips: "Query first—must be familiar with quarter horse racing and be knowledgeable of the sport. If writing on nutrition, it must be applicable. Most open to features covering nutrition, health care. Use a knowledgeable source with credentials."

‡**SPUR**, P.O. Box 85, Middleburg VA 22117. (703)687-6314. FAX: (703)687-3925. Editor: Cathy Laws. 80% freelance written. Prefers to work with published/established writers; works with a small number of new/unpublished writers each year. Bimonthly magazine covering thoroughbred horses and the people who are involved in the business and sports of flat racing, steeplechasing, hunter/jumper showing, dressage, driving, foxhunting and polo. Estab. 1964. Circ. 15,000. Pays on publication. Publishes ms an average of 3 months after acceptance. Byline given. Buys first North American rights. Reports in 1 month on mss and queries. Sample copy $5; writer's guidelines for #10 SASE.
Nonfiction: Historical/nostalgic, thoroughbred care, personality profile, farm, special feature, regional, photo essay, steeplechasing and polo. Buys 50 mss/year. Query with clips of published work, "or we will consider complete manuscripts." Length: 300-4,000 words. Payment negotiable. Sometimes pays the expenses of writers on assignment.
Photos: State availability of photos. Reviews color and b&w contact sheets. Captions, model releases and identification of subjects required. Buys all rights "unless otherwise negotiated."
Columns/Departments: Query or send complete ms to Editorial Dept. Length: 100-500 words. Pays $50 and up.
Tips: "Writers must have a knowledge of horses, horse owners, breeding, training, racing, and riding — or the ability to obtain this knowledge from a subject."

Hunting and Fishing

ALABAMA GAME & FISH/GAME & FISH PUBLICATIONS, INC., P.O. Box 741, Marietta GA 30061. Editor: Jimmy Jacobs. See *Game & Fish Publications*.

AMERICAN HUNTER, Suite 1000, 470 Spring Park Pl., Herndon VA 22070. Editor: Tom Fulgham. 90% freelance written. For hunters who are members of the National Rifle Association. Circ. 1.3 million. Buys first North American serial rights. Byline given. Free sample copy for 9×12 SAE with $1.44 postage; writer's guidelines for #10 SASE.
Nonfiction: Factual material on all phases of hunting. Not interested in material on fishing or camping. Prefers queries. Length: 2,000-3,000 words. Pays $250-450.
Photos: No additional payment made for photos used with mss. Pays $25 for b&w photos purchased without accompanying mss. Pays $50-300 for color.

ARKANSAS SPORTSMAN, Game & Fish Publications, Inc., P.O. Box 741, Marietta GA 30061. (404)953-9222. Editor: Bob Borgwat. 90-95% freelance written. Works with a small number of new/unpublished writers each year. Monthly how-to, where-to and when-to hunting and fishing magazine covering Arkansas. Estab. 1980. Pays 3 months before publication. Byline given. Buys one-time rights. Submit seasonal material 8 months in advance. Simultaneous queries and submissions OK. Reports in 2 months. Sample copy for $2.50 and 10×12 SAE; writer's guidelines for SASE.
Nonfiction: How-to (hunting and fishing *only*); humor (on limited basis); interview/profile (of successful hunter/angler); personal experience (hunting or fishing adventure). No hiking, backpacking or camping. No "my first deer" articles. Buys 60 mss/year. Query with or without published clips. Length: 2,200-2,500 words. Pays $150.
Photos: State availability of photos. Pays $75 for inside color for covers; $250 for covers; $25 for b&w photos not submitted as part of story package. Captions and identification of subjects required. Buys one-time rights.

BASSIN', 15115 S. 76th E. Ave., Bixby OK 74008. (918)366-4441. FAX: (918)366-4439. Managing Editor: Gordon Sprouse. 90% freelance written. Magazine published 8 times/year covering freshwater fishing with emphasis on black bass. Estab. 1985. Circ. 220,000. Publishes ms an average of 8 months after acceptance. Pays within 30 days of acceptance. Byline given. Buys first serial rights. Submit seasonal material 8 months in advance. Prefers queries but will examine mss accompanied by SASE. Query for electronic submissions. Reports in 3 weeks. Sample copy $3; writer's guidelines for #10 SASE.
Nonfiction: How-to and where-to stories on bass fishing. Prefers completed ms. Length: 1,200-1,500 words. Pays $275-400 on acceptance.
Photos: Send photos with ms. Pays $300 for color cover; $100 for color cover inset. Send b&w prints or transparencies. Buys one-time rights. Photo payment on publication.
Tips: "Reduce the common fishing slang terminology when writing for *Bassin'*. This slang is usually regional and confuses anglers in other areas of the country. Good strong features will win me over more quickly than short articles or fillers. Absolutely no poetry. We also need stories on fishing tackle and techniques for catching all species of freshwater bass."

‡**BASSMASTER MAGAZINE**, B.A.S.S. Publications, 5845 Carmichael Pkwy., Montgomery AL 36117. (205)272-9530. Editor: Dave Precht. 80% freelance written. Prefers to work with published/established writers. Magazine (10 issues/year) about largemouth, smallmouth, spotted bass for dedicated beginning and advanced bass fishermen. Circ. 550,000. **Pays on acceptance.** Publication date of ms after acceptance "varies—seasonal material could take years"; average time is 8 months. Byline given. Buys all rights. Submit seasonal material 6 months in advance. Reports in 1 month. Sample copy $2; writer's guidelines for #10 SASE.

Nonfiction: Historical; interview (of knowledgable people in the sport); profile (outstanding fishermen); travel (where to go to fish for bass); how-to (catch bass and enjoy the outdoors); new product (reels, rods and bass boats); and conservation related to bass fishing."No 'Me and Joe Go Fishing' type articles." Query. Length: 400-2,100 words. Pays 20¢/word.

Columns/Departments: Short Cast/News & Views (upfront regular feature covering news-related events such as new state bass records, unusual bass fishing happenings, conservation, new products and editorial viewpoints); 250-400 words.

Photos: "We want a mixture of b&w and color photos." Pays $50 minimum for b&w prints. Pays $300-350 for color cover transparencies. Captions required; model releases preferred. Buys all rights.

Fillers: Anecdotes, short humor and newsbreaks. Buys 4-5 mss/issue. Length: 250-500 words. Pays $50-100.

Tips: "Editorial direction continues in the short, more direct how-to article. Compact, easy-to-read information is our objective. Shorter articles with good graphics, such as how-to diagrams, step-by-step instruction, etc., will enhance a writer's articles submitted to *Bassmaster Magazine*. The most frequent mistakes made by writers in completing an article for us are poor grammar, poor writing, poor organization and superficial research."

BC OUTDOORS, OP Publishing, 202-1132 Hamilton St., Vancouver, British Columbia V6B 2S2 Canada. (604)687-1581. FAX: (604)687-1925. Editor: George Will. 80% freelance written. Works with a small number of new/unpublished writers each year. Outdoor recreation magazine published 7 times/year. *BC Outdoors* covers fishing, camping, hunting, and the environment of outdoor recreation. Estab. 1934. Circ. 55,000. **Pays on acceptance.** Publishes ms an average of 3 months after acceptance. Byline given. Offers negotiable kill fee. Buys first North American serial rights. Query for electronic submissions. Reports in 1 month on queries; 2 months on mss. Sample copy and writer's guidelines for 8 × 10 SAE with $2 postage.

Nonfiction: How-to (new or innovative articles on outdoor subjects); personal experience (outdoor adventure); and outdoor topics specific to British Columbia. "We would like to receive how-to, where-to features dealing with hunting and fishing in British Columbia and the Yukon." Buys 80-90 mss/year. Query. Length: 1,500-2,000 words. Pays $300-500. Sometimes pays the expenses of writers on assignment.

Photos: State availability of photos with query. Pays $25-75 on publication for 5 × 7 b&w prints; $35-150 for color contact sheets and 35mm transparencies. Captions and identification of subjects required. Buys one-time rights.

Tips: "More emphasis on saltwater angling and less emphasis on self-propelled activity, like hiking and canoeing will affect the types of freelance material we buy. Subject must be specific to British Columbia. We receive many manuscripts written by people who obviously do not know the magazine or market. The writer has a better chance of breaking in at our publication with short, lesser-paying articles and fillers, because we have a stable of regular writers in constant touch who produce most main features."

‡**CALIFORNIA ANGLER, The Magazine For Fresh and Saltwater Fishing**, Outdoor Ventures, Ltd., Suite 3-N, 1921 E. Carnegie Ave., Santa Ana CA 92705. (714)262-9779. FAX: (714)261-9853. Editor: John Skrabo. 90% freelance written. A sportfishing magazine published monthly, devoted to the affluent, serious California angler. Circ. 30,000. Pays one month prior to publication. Publishes ms 2-4 months after acceptance. Byline given. Purchases one-time rights. Sample copy and writer's guidelines available upon request.

Nonfiction: How-to and where-to with emphasis on California destinations and techniques. Monthly stories on Baja, Mexico. Columns include: Travel, Tactics, Flyfishing, Boating, Longrange, Conservation, News, Product Reviews, Baja Bite, Mexico Mainland and Bass. All open to freelancers. "We're working 6 months in advance so query accordingly. Pays $400 for a 1,800-word feature with 35mm transparencies and two short sidebars. Columns get $200-300, 1,000 to 1,400 words. Illustrations are great and we buy 20 or more a year. Cover photos earn $300. Annual specials and themes include: Canada (Jan.), Bass (Feb.), Baja (March), Eastern Sierra (April), San Diego Longrage (May), Colorado River (June), Alaska (Dec.). We prefer first-hand stories that are well researched."

Photos: Send photos with submissions and queries, 35mm transparencies.
Tips: "We're always looking for talented young writers. Remember, our name is California Angler, so the emphasis is on Golden State destinations. However, our readers are wide travelers so new, unpublished destination stories are welcomed."

CALIFORNIA GAME & FISH, Game & Fish Publications, Inc., Box 741, Marietta GA 30061. Editor: Burt Carey. See *Game & Fish Publications.*

DEER AND DEER HUNTING, The Stump Sitters, Inc., P.O. Box 1117, Appleton WI 54912. (414)734-0009. FAX: (414)734-2919. Editors: Al Hofacker and Rob Wegner. 80% freelance written. Prefers to work with published/established writers. Magazine (8 issues annually) covers deer hunting for individuals who hunt with bow, gun or camera. Estab. 1977. Circ. 160,000. **Pays on acceptance.** Publishes ms an average of 6 months after acceptance. Byline given. Offers $50 kill fee. Buys first North American serial rights and second serial (reprint) rights. Submit seasonal/holiday material 8 months in advance. Reports in 2 weeks. Sample copy for 9×12 SAE with 7 first class stamps; writer's guidelines for #10 SASE.
Nonfiction: Historical/nostalgic; how-to (hunting techniques); opinion; personal experience; photo feature; technical. "Our readers desire factual articles of a technical nature that relate deer behavior and habits to hunting methodology. We focus on deer biology, management principles and practices, habitat requirements, natural history of deer, hunting techniques and hunting ethics." No hunting "Hot Spot" or "local" articles. Buys 70 mss/year. Query with clips of published work. Length: 1,000-3,000 words. Pays $150-350.
Photos: Pays $75-250 for 35mm transparencies; $500 for front cover; $50 for 8×10 b&w prints. Captions and identification of subjects required. Buys one-time rights. Prefers action shots, as opposed to "portraits" of deer. Also need hunter photos.
Columns/Departments: Deer Browse (unusual observations of deer behavior). Buys 20 mss/year. Length: 200-600 words. Pays $10-50.
Fillers: Clippings, anecdotes, newsbreaks. Buys 20/year. Length: 200-800 words. Pays $10-40.
Tips: "Break in by providing material of a technical nature, backed by scientific research, and written in a style understandable to the average deer hunter. We focus primarily on white-tailed deer."

MIKE EASTMAN'S OUTDOORSMEN, P.O. Box 231, Thermopolis WY 82443. (307)864-3405. Editor: Mike Eastman. 75% freelance written. Quarterly magazine on big game hunting in the West. "All readers are avid hunters, wanting helpful information on hunting big game out West. Writers must know the sport of big game hunting." Estab. 1987. Circ. 2,000. Pays on publication. Publishes ms an average of 3 months after acceptance. Byline given. Buys first rights. Submit seasonal/holiday material 6 months in advance. Query for electronic submissions. Reports in 2 months on queries. Sample copy for 9×12 SAE and 5 first class stamps. Writer's guidelines for #10 SASE.
Nonfiction: Exposé, general interest, humor, interview/profile, personal experience, photo feature, technical. Buys 12 mss/year. Send outline ms. Length: 200-1,000 words. Pays 8¢/word maximum for assigned articles; 8¢/word maximum for unsolicited articles.
Photos: Send photos with submission. Reviews 3×4 prints. Captions required. Buys one-time rights.
Columns/Departments: How-To (informative—hunting product use or technique), 500 words; Area Focus (thoroughly researched hot hunting area in a Western state), 200 words. Buys 4-8 mss/year. Length: 200-1,000 words. Pays 8¢/word maximum.
Fillers: Anecdotes, facts, newsbreaks, short humor. Buys 12-16/year. Length: 200-1,000 words. Pays 8¢/word maximum.
Tips: "Send us your qualifications as a writer and a knowledgable person in the hunting field. Give the reader enough information that he feels he has learned something useful he can apply out in the field."

FIELD & STREAM, 2 Park Ave., New York NY 10016. Editor: Duncan Barnes. 50% freelance written. Eager to work with new/unpublished writers. Monthly. Estab. 1895. Buys first rights. Byline given. Reports in 6 weeks. Query. Writer's guidelines for 8×10 SAE with 1 first class stamp.
Nonfiction and Photos: "This is a broad-based service magazine for the hunter and fisherman. Editorial content ranges from very basic how-to stories detailing a useful technique or a device that sportsmen can make to articles of penetrating depth about national hunting, fishing, and related activities. Also humor and personal essays, nostalgia and 'mood pieces' on the hunting or fishing experience." Prefers color photos to b&w. Query first with photos. Length: 1,000-2,000 words. Payment varies depending on the quality of work, importance of the article. Pays $750 and up for major features. *Field & Stream* also publishes regional sections with feature articles on hunting and fishing in specific areas of the country. The sections are geographically divided into Northeast, Midwest, Far West, West and South, and appear 12 months a year. Usually buys photos with mss. When purchased separately, pays $450 minimum for color. Buys first rights to photos.

Fillers: Buys "how it's done" fillers of 250-750 words. Must be unusual or helpful subjects. Pays $250 on acceptance. Also buys "Field Guide" pieces, short (750-word maximum) articles on natural phenomena as specifically related to hunting and fishing; and "Myths and Misconceptions," short pieces debunking a commonly held belief about hunting and fishing. Pays $500.

THE FISHERMAN, LIF Publishing Corp., 14 Ramsey Rd., Shirley NY 11967-4704. (516)345-5200. FAX: (516)345-5304. Editor: Fred Golofaro. Senior Editor: Pete Barrett. 5 regional editions: *Long Island*, *Metropolitan New York*, Fred Golofaro, editor; *New England*, Tim Coleman, editor; *New Jersey*, Dusty Rhodes, editor; and *Delaware-Maryland-Virginia*, Keith Kaufman, editor, *Florida*, Jim Oldham, editor. 75% freelance written. A weekly magazine covering fishing with an emphasis on saltwater. Combined circ. 110,000. Pays on publication. Byline given. Offers variable kill fee. Buys all rights. Articles may be run in one or more regional editions by choice of the editors. Submit seasonal/holiday material 2 months in advance. Reports in 3 weeks. Free sample copy and writer's guidelines.
Nonfiction: Send submission to editor of regional edition. General interest, historical/nostalgic, how-to, interview/profile, personal experience, photo feature, technical and travel. Special issues include Trout Fishing (April), Bass Fishing (June), Offshore Fishing (July), Surf Fishing (September), Tackle (October) and Electronics (November). "No 'me and Joe' tales. We stress how, where, when, why." Buys approx. 300 mss/year, each edition. Length: 1,200-2,000 words. Pays $100-150 for unsolicited feature articles.
Photos: Send photos with submission; also buys single photos for cover use. Offers no additional payment for photos accepted with ms. Identification of subjects required.
Tips: "Focus on specific how-to and where-to subjects within each region."

FISHING WORLD, 51 Atlantic Ave., Floral Park NY 11001. FAX: (516)437-6841. Editor: Keith Gardner. 100% freelance written. Estab. 1955. Bimonthly. Circ. 300,000. **Pays on acceptance.** Buys first North American serial rights. Publishes ms an average of 6 months after acceptance. Reports in 2 weeks. Free sample copy; writer's guidelines for #10 SASE.
Nonfiction: "Destination-oriented boat-fishing feature articles should range from 1,200-1,500 words with the shorter preferred. A good selection of transparencies must accompany each submission. Subject matter should be a hot fishing site, either freshwater or salt. Where-to articles should be accompanied by sidebars covering how to make reservations and arrange transportation, how to get there, where to stay. Angling methods should be developed in clear detail, with accurate and useful information about tackle and boats. Pay is at the rate of $250 if the article runs in one of four regional editions, $300 if it runs in two regionals, etc. Transparencies selected for cover use pay an additional $300. Brief queries accompanied by photos are preferred."
Photos: "Cover shots are purchased separately, rather than selected from those accompanying mss. The editor favors boat-fishing drama rather than serenity in selecting cover shots."
Tips: Looking for "quality photography and more West Coast fishing."

FLORIDA GAME & FISH, Game & Fish Publications, Inc., Box 741, Marietta GA 30061. (404)953-9222. Editor: Jimmy Jacobs. See *Game & Fish Publications*.

FLORIDA SPORTSMAN, Wickstrom Publishers Inc., 5901 SW 74th St., Miami FL 33143. (305)661-4222. Editor: Vic Dunaway. Managing Editor: Biff Lampton. 80% freelance written. Eager to work with new/unpublished writers. A monthly magazine covering fishing, boating and related sports— Florida and Caribbean only. Circ. 100,000. Pays on publication. Publishes ms an average of 6 months after acceptance. Byline given. Offers 50% kill fee. Buys first North American serial rights. Submit seasonal/holiday material 6 months in advance. Reports in 1 week on queries; 1 month on mss. Free sample copy; writer's guidelines for #10 SASE.
Nonfiction: Essays (environment or nature); how-to (fishing, hunting, boating); humor (outdoors angle); personal experience (in fishing, etc.); and technical (boats, tackle, etc., as particularly suitable for Florida specialties). "We use reader service pieces almost entirely—how-to, where-to, etc. One or two environmental pieces per issue as well. Writers *must* be Florida based, or have lengthy experience in Florida outdoors. All articles must have strong Florida emphasis. We do not want to see general how-to-fish-or-boat pieces which might well appear in a national or wide-regional magazine." Buys 120 mss/year. Query with or without published clips, or send complete ms. Length: 2,000-3,000 words. Pays $300-400 for assigned articles; pays $150-300 for unsolicited articles.
Photos: Send photos with submission. Reviews 35mm transparencies and 4x5 and larger prints. Offers no additional payment for photos accepted with ms. Buys one-time rights.
Columns/Departments: Sportsman Scene (news-feature items on outdoors subjects), 100-500 words. Buys 25 mss/year. Send complete ms. Pays $15-100.
Tips: "Feature articles are most open to freelancers; however there is little chance of acceptance unless contributor is an accomplished and avid outdoorsman *and* a competent writer-photographer with considerable experience in Florida."

FLORIDA WILDLIFE, Florida Game & Fresh Water Fish Commission, 620 S. Meridian St., Tallahassee FL 32399-1600. (904)488-5563. FAX: (904)488-6988. Editor: Andrea H. Blount. About 30% freelance written. Bimonthly state magazine covering hunting, natural history, fishing, endangered species and wildlife conservation. "In outdoor sporting articles we seek themes of wholesome recreation. In nature articles we seek accuracy and conservation purpose." Estab. 1947. Circ. 29,000. Pays on publication. Publishes ms 2 months to 2 years after acceptance. Byline given. Buys first North American serial rights and occasionally second serial (reprint) rights. Submit seasonal/holiday material 6 months in advance. Simultaneous queries, and simultaneous and previously published submissions OK. "Inform us if it is previously published work." Reports in 6 weeks on queries; variable on mss. Sample copy $1.25; free writer's/photographer's guidelines for SASE.

Nonfiction: General interest (bird watching, hiking, camping, boating); how-to (hunting and fishing); humor (wildlife related; no anthropomorphism); inspirational (conservation oriented); personal experience (wildlife, hunting, fishing, outdoors); photo feature (Florida species: game, nongame, botany); and technical (rarely purchased, but open to experts). "We buy general interest hunting, fishing and nature stories. No stories that humanize animals, or opinionated stories not based on confirmable facts." Buys 30-40 mss/year. Send slides/manuscript. Length: 500-1,500 words. Generally pays $50/published page; including use of photos.

Photos: State availability of photos with story query. Prefer 35mm color slides of hunting, fishing, and natural science series of Florida wildlife species. Pays $20-50 for inside photos; $100 for front cover photos, $50 for back cover. "We like short, specific captions." Buys one-time rights.

Fiction: "We rarely buy fiction, and then only if it is true to life and directly related to good sportsmanship and conservation. No fairy tales, erotica, profanity, or obscenity." Buys 2-3 mss/year. Send complete mss and label "fiction." Length: 500-1,200 words. Generally pays $50/published page.

Tips: "Read and study recent issues for subject matter, style and examples of our viewpoint, philosophy and treatment. We look for wholesome recreation, ethics, safety, and good outdoor experience more than bagging the game in our stories. We usually need well-written hunting and freshwater fishing articles that are entertaining and informative and that describe places to hunt and fish in Florida."

FLY FISHERMAN, Cowles Magazines Inc., 2245 Kohn Rd., P.O. Box 8200, Harrisburg PA 17105. (717)657-9555. Editor and Publisher: John Randolph. Associate Editor: Philip Hanyok. 85-90% freelance written. Magazine published 6 times/year on fly fishing. Circ. 140,000.

FUR-FISH-GAME, 2878 E. Main, Columbus OH 43209. Editor: Mitch Cox. 65% freelance written. Works with a small number of new/unpublished writers each year. Monthly magazine. For outdoorsmen of all ages who are interested in hunting, fishing, trapping, dogs, camping, conservation and related topics. Estab. 1900. Circ. 150,000. **Pays on acceptance.** Publishes ms an average of 7 months after acceptance. Byline given. Buys first serial rights or all rights. Prefers non-simultaneous submissions. Reports in 6 weeks. Query. Sample copy for $1 and 8×11 SAE. Writer's guidelines for #10 SASE.

Nonfiction: "We are looking for informative, down-to-earth stories about hunting, fishing, trapping, dogs, camping, boating, conservation and related subjects. Nostalgic articles are also used. Many of our stories are 'how-to' and should appeal to small-town and rural readers who are true outdoorsmen. Some recent articles have told how to train a gun dog, catch big-water catfish, outfit a bowhunter and trap late-season muskrat. We also use personal experience stories and an occasional profile, such as an article about an old-time trapper. 'Where-to' stories are used occasionally if they have broad appeal." Length: 1,500-3,000 words. Pays $75-150 depending upon quality, photo support, and importance to magazine. Short filler stories pay $35-80.

Photos: Send photos with ms. Photos are part of ms package and receive no additional payment. Prefer b&w but color prints or transparencies OK. Prints can be 5×7 or 8×10. Caption information required.

Tips: "We are always looking for quality articles that tell how to hunt or fish for game animals or birds that are popular with everyday outdoorsmen but often overlooked in other publications, such as catfish, bluegill, crappie, squirrel, rabbit, crows, etc. We also use articles on standard seasonal subjects such as deer and pheasant, but like to see a fresh approach or new technique. Trapping articles, especially instructional ones based on personal experience, are useful all year. Articles on gun dogs, ginseng and do-it-yourself projects are also popular with our readers. An assortment of photos and/ or sketches greatly enhances any ms, and sidebars, where applicable, can also help."

GAME & FISH PUBLICATIONS, INC., Suite 110, 2250 Newmarket Parkway, Marietta GA 30067. (404)953-9222. FAX: (404)933-9510. Editorial Director: Ken Dunwoody. Publishes 30 different monthly outdoor magazines, each one covering the fishing and hunting opportunities in a particular state or region (see individual titles and editors). 90% freelance written. Total circ. 400,000. Pays 75 days prior to cover date of issue. Publishes ms an average of 6 months after acceptance. Byline given. Offers negotiable kill fee. Buys first North American serial rights. Submit seasonal material at least 8 months in advance. Editors prefer to hold queries until that season's material is assigned. Reports in 3 months on mss. Sample copy for $2.50 and 9×12 SAE; writer's guidelines for #10 SASE.

Nonfiction: Prefer queries over unsolicited ms. Article lengths either 1,500 or 2,500 words. Pays separately for articles and accompanying photos. Manuscripts pay $125-250, cover photos $250, inside color $75 and b&w $25. Reviews transparencies and b&w prints. Prefers captions and identification of species/subjects. Buys one-time rights to photos.

Fiction: Buys some humor and nostalgia stories pertaining to hunting and fishing. Pays $125-250. Length 1,500-2,500 words.

Tips: "Our readers are experienced anglers and hunters, and we try to provide them with useful, entertaining articles about where, when and how to enjoy the best hunting and fishing in their state or region, as well as covering topics concerning game and fish management, conservation and environmental issues. Most articles should be aimed at outdoorsmen in one particular state. After familiarizing themselves with our magazine(s), writers should query the appropriate state editor (see individual listings) or send to Ken Dunwoody."

GEORGIA SPORTSMAN, Game & Fish Publications, Box 741, Marietta GA 30061. (404)953-9222. Editor: Jimmy Jacobs. See *Game & Fish Publications*.

GREAT LAKES FISHERMAN, Outdoor Publishing Co., 1432 Parsons Ave., Columbus OH 43207. Editor: Dan Armitage. 95% freelance written. Eager to work with new/unpublished writers. Monthly magazine covering how, when and where to fish in the Great Lakes region. Estab. 1976. Circ. 50,000. Pays on 15th of month prior to issue date. Publishes ms an average of 8 months after acceptance. Byline given. Offers $40 kill fee. Buys first North American serial rights. Submit seasonal/holiday material 8-12 months in advance. Reports in 5 weeks. Free sample copy and writer's guidelines for 9×12 SAE with 5 first class stamps.

Nonfiction: How-to (where to and when to freshwater fish). "No 'me and Joe' or subject matter outside the Great Lakes region." Buys 84 mss/year. Query with clips of published work. "Letters should be tightly written, but descriptive enough to present no surprises when the ms is received. Prefer b&w photos to be used to illustrate ms with query." Length: 1,000-1,500 words. Pays $135-200. Sometimes pays telephone expenses of writers on assignment.

Photos: Send photos with ms. "Black and white photos are considered part of manuscript package and as such receive no additional payment. We consider b&w photos to be a vital part of a ms package. We look for four types of illustration with each article: scene (a backed off shot of fisherman); result (not the typical meat shot of angler grinning at camera with big stringer but in most cases just a single nice fish with the angler admiring the fish); method (a lure shot or illustration of special rigs mentioned in the text); and action (angler landing a fish, fighting a fish, etc.). Illustrations (line drawings) need not be finished art but should be good enough for our artist to get the idea of what the author is trying to depict." Prefers cover shots to be verticals with fish and fisherman action shots. Pays $200 for 35mm transparencies. Captions, model releases and identification of subjects required. Buys one-time rights.

Tips: "Our feature articles are 95% freelance material. The magazine is circulated in the eight states bordering the Great Lakes, an area where one-third of the nation's licensed anglers reside. All of our feature content is how, when or where, or a combination of all three covering the species common to the region. Fishing is an age-old sport with countless words printed on the subject each year. A fresh new slant that indicates a desire to share with the reader the author's knowledge is a sale. We expect the freelancer to answer any anticipated questions the reader might have (on accommodations, launch sites, equipment needed, etc.) within the ms. We publish an equal mix each month of both warm- and cold-water species articles."

‡GREAT PLAINS GAME & FISH, Game & Fish Publications, Box 741, Marietta GA 30061. (404)953-9222. Editor: Nick Gilmore. See *Game & Fish Publications*.

GULF COAST FISHERMAN, Harold Wells Gulf Coast Fisherman, Inc., 401 W. Main St., Port Lavaca TX 77979. (512)552-8864. Publisher/Editor: Gary M. Ralston. 95% freelance written. A quarterly magazine covering Gulf Coast saltwater fishing. "All editorial material is designed to expand the knowledge of the Gulf Coast angler and promote saltwater fishing in general." Estab. 1979. Circ 15,000. Pays on publication. Publishes ms an average of 2 months after acceptance. Byline given. Buys first North American serial rights. Submit seasonal/holiday material 2 months in advance. Submissions of manuscripts on Macintosh 3½″ diskette most preferred. Sample copy and writer's guidelines for 9×12 SAE and 5 first class stamps.

Nonfiction: How-to (any aspect relating to saltwater fishing that provides the reader specifics on use of tackle, boats, finding fish, etc.); interview/profile; new product; personal experience; and technical. Buys 25 mss/year. Query with or without published clips, or send complete ms. Length: 900-1,800 words. Pays $100-275.

Photos: State availability of photos with submission. Offers no additional payment for photos accepted with ms. Captions and identification of subjects required. Buys one-time rights.
Tips: "Features are the area of our publication most open to freelancers. Subject matter should concern some aspect of or be in relation to saltwater fishing in coastal bays or offshore."

HOOKED ON FISHING MAGAZINE, Southeast Outdoors, Inc., 604 Jefferson, P.O. Box 682, Cape Girardeau MO 63702-0682. (314)651-3638. Editorial Director: Ron Pobst. Editor: Sheri Robertson. 95% freelance written. Bimonthly magazine covering fishing in: MO, IL, KY, TN, AR, IN, MS. "*Hooked on Fishing* is a family-oriented magazine. 50% of our readers have some college or are college graduates. We emphasize the family aspect of fishing in our region, and our purpose is to educate and entertain." Estab. 1988. Circ. 10,000. Pays on publication. Publishes ms an average of 3-4 months after acceptance. Byline given. Buys first and one-time rights. Submit seasonal/holiday material 4-6 months in advance. Reports in 2 weeks. Sample copy for 9×12 SAE with 5 first class stamps. Free writer's guidelines.
Nonfiction: How-to (fishing techniques), humor, interview/profile, new product, opinion, personal experience, photo feature, technical, travel. Special November-December Christmas issue. We are a family-oriented magazine. We do not accept "booze, broads, beards, bellies and belt buckles" type of articles (the "good old boy" slant). Buys 30 mss/year. Query with published clips. Length: 1,800-2,500 words. Pays $75-125 for assigned articles; $50-100 for unsolicited articles.
Photos: Send photos with submission. Reviews standard transparencies and 5×7 prints. Offers $5-50 per photo. Captions, model releases and identification of subjects required. Buys one-time rights.
Columns/Departments: Buyer's Guide (new fishing gear/products), open length—about 1 column; Club News (for fishing clubs in 7-state area), open; Conservation Dept. (opinion is welcome—ecology, regulations, etc. Also factual information [news]), open. Buys 18 mss/year. Query with published clips. Pays $30-80.
Fiction: Humorous, slice-of-life vignettes on fishing in the 7-state area. No good old boy fiction. Buys 4-8 mss/year. Query with published clips. Length: 1,800-2,500 words. Pays $50-100.
Fillers: Anecdotes, facts, newsbreaks, short humor. Pays $20-30.
Tips: "We are looking for fishing articles that keep a family approach to the sport in mind, but with a certain aesthetic appeal beyond hard facts and technical jargon. Articles *must* have photo or illustrative support and maps if applicable. Ms submissions must include SASE."

ILLINOIS GAME & FISH, Game & Fish Publications, Inc., Box 741, Marietta GA 30061. (404)953-9222. Editor: Bill Hartlage. See *Game & Fish Publications*.

INDIANA GAME & FISH, Game & Fish Publications, Inc., Box 741, Marietta GA 30061. (404)953-9222. Editor: Ken Freel. See *Game & Fish Publications*.

IOWA GAME & FISH, Game & Fish Publications, Inc., Box 741, Marietta GA 30061. (404)953-9222. Editor: Nick Gilmore. See *Game & Fish Publications*.

KENTUCKY GAME & FISH, Game & Fish Publications, Inc., Box 741, Marietta GA 30061. (404)953-9222. Editor: Bill Hartlage. See *Game & Fish Publications*.

LOUISIANA GAME & FISH, Game & Fish Publications, Inc., Box 741, Marietta GA 30061. (404)953-9222. Editor: Bob Borgwat. See *Game & Fish Publications*.

MARLIN, The International Sportfishing Magazine, EBSCO Industries, Inc., P.O. Box 12902, Pensacola FL 32576. (904)434-5571. FAX: (904)433-6303. Editor: Dave Lear. 90% freelance written. Bimonthly magazine on big game fishing. "*Marlin* covers the sport of big game fishing (billfish, tuna, sharks, dorado and wahoo). Our readers are sophisticated, affluent and serious about their sport— they expect a high-class, well-written magazine that provides information and practical advice." Estab. 1982. Circ. 30,000. **Pays on acceptance.** Publishes ms an average of 3 months after acceptance. Byline given. Buys first North American serial rights. Submit seasonal/holiday material 2-3 months in advance. Query for electronic submissions. Free sample copy and writer's guidelines.
Nonfiction: General interest, how-to (bait-rigging, tackle maintenance, etc.), new product, personal experience, photo feature, technical and travel. "No freshwater fishing stories. No 'me & Joe went fishing' stories, unless top quality writing." Buys 30-50 mss/year. Query with published clips. Length: 800-2,200 words. Pays $250-500.
Photos: State availability of photos with submission. Reviews negatives, transparencies and prints. Offers $25-300 per photo. $300 is for a cover. Buys one-time rights.
Columns/Departments: Tournament Reports (reports on winners of major big game fishing tournaments), 300-600 words; Blue Water Currents (news features), 300-900 words. Buys 25 mss/year. Query. Pays $100-250.

Tips: "Tournament reports are a good way to break in to *Marlin*. Make them short but accurate, and provide photos of fishing action (*not* dead fish hanging up at the docks!). We always need how-tos and news items. Our destination pieces (travel stories) emphasize where and when to fish, but include information on where to stay also. For features: crisp, high action stories—nothing flowery or academic. Technical/how-to: concise and informational—specific details. News: Again, concise with good details—watch for legislation affecting big game fishing, outstanding catches, new clubs and organizations, new trends and conservation issues."

MICHIGAN OUT-OF-DOORS, P.O. Box 30235, Lansing MI 48909. (517)371-1041. FAX: (517)371-1505. Editor: Kenneth S. Lowe. 50% freelance written. Works with a small number of new/unpublished writers each year. Emphasizes outdoor recreation, especially hunting and fishing, conservation and environmental affairs. Monthly magazine. Estab. 1947. Circ. 130,000. **Pays on acceptance.** Publishes ms an average of 6 months after acceptance. Byline given. Buys first North American serial rights. Phone queries OK. Submit seasonal/holiday material 6 months in advance. Reports in 1 month. Sample copy $2; free writer's guidelines.
Nonfiction: Exposé, historical, how-to, informational, interview, nostalgia, personal experience, personal opinion, photo feature and profile. No humor or poetry. "Stories *must* have a Michigan slant unless they treat a subject of universal interest to our readers." Buys 8 mss/issue. Send complete ms. Length: 1,000-3,000 words. Pays $75 minimum for feature stories. Pays expenses of writers on assignment.
Photos: Purchased with or without accompanying ms. Pays $15 minimum for any size b&w glossy prints; $100 maximum for color (for cover). Offers no additional payment for photos accepted with accompanying ms. Buys one-time rights. Captions preferred.
Tips: "Top priority is placed on true accounts of personal adventures in the out-of-doors—well-written tales of very unusual incidents encountered while hunting, fishing, camping, hiking, etc. The most rewarding aspect of working with freelancers is realizing we had a part in their development. But it's annoying to respond to queries that never produce a manuscript."

MICHIGAN SPORTSMAN, Game & Fish Publications, Inc., Box 741, Marietta GA 30061. (404)953-9222. Editor: Dennis Schmidt. See *Game & Fish Publications*.

MID WEST OUTDOORS, Mid West Outdoors, Ltd., 111 Shore Drive, Hinsdale (Burr Ridge) IL 60521. (708)887-7722. FAX: (708)887-1958. Editor: Gene Laulunen. Emphasizes fishing, hunting, camping and boating. Monthly tabloid. 100% freelance written. Estab. 1967. Circ. 43,814. Pays on publication. Buys simultaneous rights. Byline given. Submit seasonal material 2 months in advance. Simultaneous and previously published submissions OK. Reports in 3 weeks. Publishes ms an average of 3 months after acceptance. Sample copy $1; free writer's guidelines with #10 SASE.
Nonfiction: How-to (fishing, hunting, camping in the Midwest) and where-to-go (fishing, hunting, camping within 500 miles of Chicago). "We do not want to see any articles on 'my first fishing, hunting or camping experiences,' 'Cleaning My Tackle Box,' 'Tackle Tune-up,' or 'Catch and Release.' " Buys 1,800 unsolicited mss/year. Send complete ms. Length: 1,000-1,500 words. Pays $15-30.
Photos: Offers no additional payment for photos accompanying ms unless used as covers; uses b&w prints. Buys all rights. Captions required.
Columns/Departments: Fishing, Hunting. Open to suggestions for columns/departments. Send complete ms. Pays $25.
Tips: "Break in with a great unknown fishing hole or new technique within 500 miles of Chicago. Where, how, when and why. Know the type of publication you are sending material to."

‡**MID-ATLANTIC GAME & FISH**, Game & Fish Publications, Inc., Box 741, Marietta GA 30061. (404)953-9222. Editor: Ken Freel. See *Game & Fish Publications*.

MINNESOTA SPORTSMAN, Game & Fish Publications, Inc., Box 741, Marietta GA 30061. (404)953-9222. Editor: Dennis Schmidt. See *Game & Fish Publications*.

MISSISSIPPI GAME & FISH, Game & Fish Publications, Inc., Box 741, Marietta GA 30061. (404)953-9222. Editor: Bob Borgwat. See *Game & Fish Publications*.

Always check the most recent copy of a magazine for the address and editor's name before you send in a query or manuscript.

MISSOURI GAME & FISH, Game & Fish Publications, Inc., Box 741, Marietta GA 30061. (404)953-9222. Editor: Bill Hartlage. See *Game & Fish Publications*.

NEW ENGLAND GAME & FISH, Game & Fish Publications, Inc., Box 741, Marietta GA 30061. (404)953-9222. Editor: Kim Leighton. See *Game & Fish Publications*.

NEW YORK GAME & FISH, Game & Fish Publications, Inc., Box 741, Marietta GA 30061. (404)953-9222. Editor: Kim Leighton. See *Game & Fish Publications*.

NORTH AMERICAN FISHERMAN, Official Publication of North American Fishing Club, Suite 260, 12301 Whitewater Dr., Minnetonka MN 55343. (612)936-0555. Editor: Mark LaBarbera. Managing Editor: Steve Pennaz. 75% freelance written. Bimonthly magazine on fresh- and saltwater fishing across North America. Estab. 1988. Circ. 200,000. **Pays on acceptance.** Publishes ms an average of 4 months after acceptance. Offers $150 kill fee. Buys first North American serial rights, one-time rights and all rights. Submit seasonal/holiday material 6 months in advance. Reports in 3 weeks. Sample copy $5 with 9 × 12 SAE and 6 first class stamps. Prefers queries by phone.
Nonfiction: How-to (species–specific information on how-to catch fish), news briefs on fishing from various state agencies and travel (where to information on first class fishing lodges). Buys 35-40 mss/year. Query (preferably by phone). Length: 700-2,100. Pays $100-325.
Photos: Send photos with submission. Offers no additional payment for photos accepted with ms. Captions and identification of subjects required. Buys one-time rights.
Fillers: Facts and newsbreaks. Buys 60/year. Length: 50-100. Pays $35-50.
Tips: "We are looking for news briefs on important law changes, new lakes, etc. Areas most open for freelancers are: full-length features, cover photos and news briefs. Know what subject you are writing about. Our audience of avid fresh and saltwater anglers know how to fish and will see through weak or dated fishing information. Must be on cutting edge for material to be considered."

NORTH AMERICAN HUNTER, Official Publication of the North American Hunting Club, North American Hunting Club, P.O. Box 3401, Minnetonka MN 55343. (612)936-9333. FAX: (612)944-2687. Publisher: Mark LaBarbera. Editor: Bill Miller. 60% freelance written. A bimonthly magazine for members of the North American Hunting Club covering strictly North American hunting. "The purpose of the NAHC is to enhance the hunting skill and enjoyment of its 240,000 members." Circ. 240,000. **Pays on acceptance.** Publishes ms an average of 6-10 months after acceptance. Byline given. Buys first North American serial rights, first rights, one-time rights, second serial (reprint) rights or all rights. Submit seasonal/holiday material 1 year in advance. Query for electronic submissions. Reports in 3 weeks. Sample copy $5; writer's guidelines for #10 SASE.
Nonfiction: Exposé (on hunting issues); how-to (on hunting); humor; interview/profile; new product; opinion; personal experience; photo feature and where-to-hunt. No fiction or "Me and Joe." Buys 18-24 mss/year. Query. Length: 1,000-2,500 words. Pays $200-325 for assigned articles; pays $25-325 for unsolicited articles.
Photos: Send photos with submissions. Reviews transparencies and 5 × 7 or 8 × 10 prints. Offers no additional payment for photos accepted with ms. Captions and identification of subjects required. Buys one-time rights.
Tips: "Write stories as if they are from one hunting friend to another."

NORTH AMERICAN WHITETAIL, The Magazine Devoted to the Serious Trophy Deer Hunter, Game & Fish Publications, Inc., Suite 110, 2250 Newmarket Parkway, Marietta GA 30067. (404)953-9222. FAX: (404)933-9510. Editor: Gordon Whittington. 70% freelance written. Magazine, published 8 times/year, about hunting trophy-class white-tailed deer in North America, primarily the U.S. "We provide the serious hunter with highly sophisticated information about trophy-class whitetails and how, when and where to hunt them. We are not a general hunting magazine or a magazine for the very occasional deer hunter." Estab. 1982. Pays 75 days prior to cover date of issue. Publishes ms an average of 6 months after acceptance. Byline given. Offers negotiable kill fee. Buys first North American serial rights. Submit seasonal/holiday material 10 months in advance. Reports in 3 months on mss. Editor prefers to keep queries on file, without notification, until the article can be assigned or author informs of prior sale. Sample copy $3 with 9 × 12 SAE and 7 first class stamps. Writer's guidelines for #10 SASE.
Nonfiction: How-to, interview/profile. Buys 50 mss/year. Query. Length: 1,400-3,000 words. Pays $150-400.
Photos: Send photos with submission. Reviews 2 × 2 transparencies and 8 × 10 prints. Offers no additional payment for photos accepted with ms. Captions and identification of subjects required. Buys one-time rights.

Columns/Departments: Trails and Tails (nostalgic, humorous or other entertaining styles of deer-hunting material, fictional or nonfictional), 1,400 words. Buys 8 mss/year. Send complete ms. Pays $150.

Tips: "Our articles are written by persons who are deer hunters first, writers second. Our hard-core hunting audience can see through material produced by non-hunters or those with only marginal deer-hunting expertise. We have a continual need for expert profiles/interviews. Study the magazine to see what type of hunting expert it takes to qualify for our use, and look at how those articles have been directed by the writers. Good photography of the interviewee and his hunting results must accompany such pieces."

NORTH CAROLINA GAME & FISH, Game & Fish Publications, Inc., Box 741, Marietta GA 30061. (404)953-9222. Editor: Jeff Samsel. See *Game & Fish Publications.*

OHIO FISHERMAN, Ohio Fisherman Publishing Co., 1432 Parsons Ave., Columbus OH 43207. (614)445-7507. Editor: Dan Armitage. 95% freelance written. Works with a small number of new/unpublished writers each year. Monthly magazine covering the how, when and where of Ohio fishing. Estab. 1976. Circ. 45,000. Pays on 15th of month prior to issue date. Publishes ms an average of 4-6 months after acceptance. Byline given. Offers $40 kill fee. Buys first rights. Submit seasonal/holiday material 6-8 months in advance. Reports in 5 weeks. Sample copy and writer's guidelines for 9 × 12 SAE and 5 first class stamps.

Nonfiction: How-to (also where-to and when-to fish). "Our feature articles are 95% freelance material, and all have the same basic theme—sharing fishing knowledge. No 'me and Joe' articles." Buys 84 mss/year. Query with clips of published work. Letters should be "tightly written, but descriptive enough to present no surprises when the ms is received. Prefer b&w photos to be used to illustrate ms with query." Length: 1,000-1,500 words. Pays $135-200.

Photos: "Need cover photos constantly." Pays $200 for 35mm transparencies (cover use); buys b&w prints as part of ms package—"no additional payments." Captions and identification of subjects required. Buys one-time rights.

Tips: "The specialist and regional markets are here to stay. They both offer the freelancer the opportunity for steady income. Fishing is an age-old sport with countless words printed on the subject each year. A fresh new slant that indicates a desire to share with the reader the author's knowledge is a sale. We expect the freelancer to answer any anticipated questions the reader might have (on accommodations, launch sites, equipment needed, etc.) within the ms."

OHIO GAME & FISH, Game & Fish Publications, Inc., Box 741, Marietta GA 30061. (404)953-9222. Editor: Ken Freel. See *Game & Fish Publications.*

OKLAHOMA GAME & FISH, Game & Fish Publications, Box 741, Marietta GA 30061. (404)953-9222. FAX: (404)933-9510. Editor: Nick Gilmore. See *Game & Fish Publications.*

OUTDOOR LIFE, Times Mirror Magazines, Inc., 2 Park Ave., New York NY 10016. (212)779-5000. Editor: Vin T. Sparano. Executive Editor: Gerald Bethge. 95% freelance written. A monthly magazine covering hunting and fishing. Estab. 1890. Circ. 1.5 million. **Pays on acceptance.** Publishes ms an average of 6-12 months after acceptance. Byline given. Buys first North American serial rights. Submit seasonal/holiday material 6 months in advance. Previously published submissions OK on occasion. Reports in 1 month on queries; 2 months on mss. Writer's guidelines for SASE.

Nonfiction: Book excerpts; essays; how-to (must cover hunting, fishing or related outdoor activities); humor; interview/profile; new product; personal experience; photo feature; technical; and travel. Special issues include Bass and Freshwater Fishing Annual (March), Deer and Big Game Annual (Aug.), and Hunting Guns Annual (Sept.). No articles that are too general in scope—need to write specifically. Buys 400 mss/year. Query or send ms—"either way, photos are *very important.*" Length: 800-3,000 words. Pays $350-600 for 1,000-word features and regionals; pays $900-1,200 for 2,000-word or longer national features. "We receive and encourage queries over CompuServe."

Photos: Send photos with submission. Reviews 35mm transparencies and 8 × 10 b&w prints. Offers variable payment. Captions and identification of subjects required. Buys one-time rights. "May offer to buy photos after first use if considered good and have potential to be used with other articles in the future (file photos)." Pay for freelance photos is $100 for ¼ page color to $800 for 2-page spread in color; $1,000 for covers. All photos must be stamped with name and address.

Columns/Departments: This Happened to Me (true-to-life, personal outdoor adventure, harrowing experience), approximately 300 words. Buys 12 mss/year. Pays $50.

Fillers: National and International newsbreaks (200 words max.). Newsbreaks and do-it-yourself for hunters and fishermen. Buys unlimited number/year. Length: 1,000 words maximum. Payment varies.

Tips: "It is best for freelancers to break in by writing features for one of the regional sections—East, Midwest, South, West. These are where-to-go oriented and run from 800-1,500 words. Writers must send one-page query with photos."

‡PANFISHERMAN'S, Fishing Line, CLM Enterprize, P.O. Box 641, Charlotte TN 37036. (615)789-5421. Editor: Larry Irons. 60% freelance written. Monthly magazine covering fishing (all species) and boating. Pays on publication. Byline given. No kill fee. Buys first North American serial rights. Submit seasonal/holiday material 2 months in advance. Reports in 6 weeks on queries; 2 months on manuscripts. Free sample copy and writer's guidelines.
Nonfiction: General interest, how-to, humor, new product, personal experience. Buys 70 mss/year. Send complete ms. Length 750-2,000 words. Pays $25-125 for unsolicited articles. Sometimes pays expenses of writers on assignment.
Photos: Send photos with submission. Reviews transparencies and prints. Captions required. Buys all rights.

PENNSYLVANIA ANGLER, Pennsylvania Fish Commission, P.O. Box 1673, Harrisburg PA 17105-1673. (717)657-4518. Editor: Art Michaels. 60-80% freelance written. Prefers to work with published/established writers but works with a few unpublished writers every year. A monthly magazine covering fishing and related conservation topics in Pennsylvania. Circ. 50,000. Pays 6-8 weeks after acceptance. Publishes ms an average of 7-9 months after acceptance. Byline given. Rights purchased vary. Submit seasonal/holiday material 8 months in advance. Reports in 2 weeks on queries; 2 months on mss. Sample copy for 9×12 SAE with 4 first class stamps; writer's guidelines for #10 SASE.
Nonfiction: Historical/nostalgic, how-to, where-to and technical. No saltwater or hunting material. Buys 120 mss/year. Query. Length: 300-3,000 words. Pays $25-300.
Photos: Send photos with submission. Reviews 35mm and larger transparencies and 8×10 b&w prints. Offers no additional payment for photos accepted with ms. Captions, model releases and identification of subjects required.
Tips: "Our mainstays are how-tos, where-tos, and conservation pieces, but we seek more top-quality fiction, first-person stories, humor, reminiscenses and historical articles. These pieces must have a strong, specific Pennsylvania slant."

PENNSYLVANIA GAME & FISH, Game & Fish Publications, Inc., Box 741, Marietta GA 30061. (404)953-9222. Editor: Kim Leighton. See *Game & Fish Publications*.

‡PENNSYLVANIA GAME NEWS, Pennsylvania Game Commission, 2001 Elmerton Ave., Harrisburg PA 17110-9797. (717)787-3745. Editor: Bob Mitchell. 60% freelance written. Works with a small number of new/unpublished writers each year. "We have a large inventory; nevertheless, we read everything that comes in." Monthly magazine covering hunting and outdoors in Pennsylvania. Emphasizes sportsmanlike actions of hunters. Estab. 1930. Circ. 150,000. **Pays on acceptance.** Publishes ms an average of 8-10 months after acceptance. Byline given. Buys all rights; "we return unused rights after publication." Submit seasonal/holiday material 8 months in advance. Reports in 3 weeks on queries; 6 weeks on mss. Free sample copy and writer's guidelines.
Nonfiction: General interest and personal hunting experiences. "We consider material on any outdoor subject that can be done in Pennsylvania *except* fishing and boating." Buys 60 mss/year. Query. Length: 2,500 words maximum. Pays $250 maximum.
Photos: Send photos with submission. Offers $5-20/photo. Captions required. Buys all rights.
Fiction: Must deal with hunting or outdoors; no fishing. Buys very few mss/year. Send complete ms.
Tips: "True hunting experiences—'me and Joe' stuff—are best chances for freelancers. Must take place in Pennsylvania."

PENNSYLVANIA SPORTSMAN, Northwoods Publications Inc., P.O. Box 90, Lemoyne PA 17043. (717)761-1400. Editor: Lou Hoffman. Managing Editor: Sherry Ritchey. 50% freelance written. Magazine appears 8 times a year on region—state of Pennsylvania hunting, fishing sports. Circ. 68,575. **Pays on acceptance.** Publishes ms an average of 4 months after acceptance. Byline given. Buys one-time or first North American serial rights. Simultaneous submissions OK. Reports in 2 weeks on queries; 3 weeks on mss. Sample copy $2. Free writer's guidelines for #10 SASE.
Nonfiction: How-to, new product, personal experience and photo feature. September—Hunting annual; March—Fishing annual. Buys 80 mss/year. Query. Length: 600-1,800 words. Sometimes pays the expenses of writers on assignment.
Photos: Send photos with submissions. Reviews negatives (slides). Offers no additional payment for photos accepted with ms. Captions required. Buys one-time rights.
Fiction: Mainstream and slice-of-life vignettes. Buys 10 mss/year. Query. Length: 600-1,500 words.
Fillers: Facts and newsbreaks. Buys 10/year. Length: 300-600 words.

‡PETERSEN'S HUNTING, Petersen's Publishing Co., 8490 Sunset Blvd., Los Angeles CA 90069. (213)854-2184. Editor: Craig Boddington. Managing Editor: Denise LaSalle. 40% freelance written. Works with a small number of new/unpublished writers each year. A monthly magazine covering sport hunting. "We are a 'how-to' magazine devoted to all facets of sport hunting, with the intent to make our readers more knowledgeable, more successful and safer hunters." Circ. 325,000. **Pays on acceptance.** Publishes ms an average of 9 months after acceptance. Byline given. Offers $50 kill fee. Buys all rights. Submit seasonal/holiday material 9 months in advance. Reports in 2 weeks. Free sample copy and writer's guidelines.

Nonfiction: General interest; historical/nostalgic; how-to (on hunting techniques); humor; and travel. Special issues include Hunting Annual (August) and the Deer Hunting Annual (September). Buys 50 mss/year. Query. Length: 2,000-3,000 words. Pays $350 minimum.

Photos: Send photos with submission. Reviews 35mm transparencies and 8×10 b&w prints. Offers no additional payment for b&w photos accepted with ms; offers $50-250/color photo. Captions, model releases and identification of subjects required. Buys one-time rights.

ROCKY MOUNTAIN GAME & FISH, Game & Fish Publications, Inc., Box 741, Marietta GA 30061. Editor: Burt Carey. See *Game & Fish Publications*.

SAFARI MAGAZINE, The Journal of Big Game Hunting, Safari Club International, 4800 W. Gates Pass Rd., Tucson AZ 85745. (602)620-1220. FAX: (602)622-1205. Editor: William R. Quimby. 90% freelance written. Bimonthly club journal covering international big game hunting and wildlife conservation. Circ. 18,000. Pays on publication. Publishes ms an average of 12-18 months after acceptance. Byline given. Offers $100 kill fee. Buys all rights. Submit seasonal/holiday material 1 year in advance. Reports in 2 weeks on queries; up to 6 weeks on mss. Sample copy $3.50; writer's guidelines for SAE.

Nonfiction: Doug Fulton; articles editor. Photo feature (wildlife); and technical (firearms, hunting techniques, etc.). Buys 48 mss/year. Query or send complete ms. Length: 1,500-2,500 words. Pays $200.

Photos: State availability of photos with query or ms, or send photos with query or ms. Payment depends on size in magazine. Pays $45 for b&w; $50-150 color. Captions, model releases and identification of subjects required. Buys one-time rights.

Tips: "Study the magazine. Send manuscripts and photo packages with query. Make it appeal to knowledgable, world-travelled big game hunters. Features on conservation contributions from big game hunters around the world are open to freelancers. We have enough stories on first-time African safaris and North American hunting. We need South American and Asian hunting stories, plus stories dealing with hunting and conservation."

SALT WATER SPORTSMAN, 280 Summer St., Boston MA 02210. (617)439-9977. FAX: (617)439-9357. Editor-in-Chief: Barry Gibson. Emphasizes saltwater fishing. 85% freelance written. Works with a small number of new/unpublished writers each year. Monthly magazine. Circ. 150,000. **Pays on acceptance.** Publishes ms an average of 5 months after acceptance. Byline given. Buys first North American serial rights. Offers 100% kill fee. Submit seasonal material 8 months in advance. Reports in 1 month. Sample copy and writer's guidelines for 8½×11 SAE with $2.90 postage.

Nonfiction: How-to, personal experience, technical and travel (to fishing areas). "Readers want solid how-to, where-to information written in an enjoyable, easy-to-read style. Personal anecdotes help the reader identify with the writer." Prefers new slants and specific information. Query. "It is helpful if the writer states experience in salt water fishing and any previous related articles. We want one, possibly two well-explained ideas per query letter—not merely a listing." Buys 100 unsolicited mss/ year. Length: 1,200-1,500 words. Pays $350 and up. Sometimes pays the expenses of writers on assignment.

Photos: Purchased with or without accompanying ms. Captions required. Uses 5×7 or 8×10 b&w prints and color slides. Pays $600 minimum for 35mm, 2¼×2¼ or 8×10 transparencies for cover. Offers additional payment for photos accepted with accompanying ms.

Columns: Sportsman's Workbench (how to make fishing or fishing-related boating equipment), 100-300 words.

Tips: "There are a lot of knowledgeable fishermen/budding writers out there who could be valuable to us with a little coaching. Many don't think they can write a story for us, but they'd be surprised. We work with writers. Shorter articles that get to the point which are accompanied by good, sharp photos are hard for us to turn down. Having to delete unnecessary wordage—conversation, clichés, etc.—that writers feel is mandatory is annoying. Often they don't devote enough attention to specific fishing information."

SOUTH CAROLINA GAME & FISH, Game & Fish Publications, Inc., Box 741, Marietta GA 30061. (404)953-9222. Editor: Jeff Samsel. See *Game & Fish Publications*.

SOUTH CAROLINA WILDLIFE, P.O. Box 167, Rembert Dennis Bldg., Columbia SC 29202. (803)734-3972. Editor: John Davis. Managing Editor: Linda Renshaw. For South Carolinians interested in wildlife and outdoor activities. 75% freelance written. Bimonthly magazine. Estab. 1954. Circ. 69,000. Byline given. **Pays on acceptance.** Publishes ms an average of 6 months after acceptance. Buys first rights. Free sample copy. Reports in 6 weeks.

Nonfiction: Articles on outdoor South Carolina with an emphasis on preserving and protecting our natural resources. "Realize that the topic must be of interest to South Carolinians and that we must be able to justify using it in a publication published by the state wildlife department—so if it isn't directly about hunting, fishing, a certain plant or animal, it must be somehow related to the environment and conservation. Readers prefer a broad mix of outdoor related topics (articles that illustrate the beauty of South Carolina's outdoors and those that help the reader get more for his/her time, effort, and money spent in outdoor recreation). These two general areas are the ones we most need. Subjects vary a great deal in topic, area and style, but must all have a common ground in the outdoor resources and heritage of South Carolina. Review back issues and query with a one-page outline citing sources, giving ideas for graphic design, explaining justification and giving an example of the first two paragraphs." Does not need any column material. Generally does not seek photographs. The publisher assumes no responsibility for unsolicited material. Buys 25-30 mss/year. Length: 1,000-3,000 words. Pays an average of $200-400 per article depending upon length and subject matter. Sometimes pays the expenses of writers on assignment.

Tips: "We need more writers in the outdoor field who take pride in the craft of writing and put a real effort toward originality and preciseness in their work. Query on a topic we haven't recently done. The most frequent mistakes made by writers in completing an article are failure to check details and go in-depth on a subject."

SOUTHERN OUTDOORS MAGAZINE, B.A.S.S. Publications, 5845 Carmichael Rd., Montgomery AL 36117. Editor: Larry Teague. Emphasizes Southern outdoor activities, including hunting, fishing, boating, shooting, camping. 90% freelance written. Prefers to work with published/established writers. Published 9 times/year. Estab. 1952. Circ. 257,000. **Pays on acceptance.** Publishes ms an average of 6 months to 1 year after acceptance. Buys all rights. Reports in 2 months. Sample copy for 9 × 12 SAE, 5 first class stamps, and $2.50.

Nonfiction: Articles should be service-oriented, helping the reader excel in outdoor sports. Emphasis is on techniques, trends and conservation. Some "where-to" stories purchased on Southern hunting and fishing destinations. Buys 120 mss/year. Length: 2,500 words maximum. Pays 15¢/word.

Photos: Usually purchased with manuscripts. Pays $50-75 for 35mm transparencies without ms, and $400 for covers.

Fillers: Humorous or thought-provoking pieces (1,200-1,500 words) appear in each issue's S.O. Essay feature.

Tips: "It's easiest to break in with short articles on 'how-to' fishing and hunting topics. We buy very little first-person. Stories most likely to sell: bass fishing, deer hunting, other freshwater fishing, inshore saltwater fishing, bird and small-game hunting, shooting, camping and boating."

‡SPORT FISHING, The Magazine of Offshore Fishing, 330 W. Canton Ave., Winter Park FL 32803. (407)628-4802. Editor: Albia Dugger. Managing Editor: Connie Sue White. 60% freelance written. Magazine covering offshore sport fishing. Estab. 1986. Circ. 85,000. Pays within 6 weeks of acceptance. Byline given. Offers $100 kill fee. Buys first North American serial rights or one-time rights. Submit seasonal/holiday material 2 months in advance. Simultaneous submission OK. Query for electronic submissions. Reports in 1 month. Free sample copy and writer's guidelines.

Nonfiction: How-to (sport fishing/techniques), humor, new product, personal experience, photo feature, technical, travel (on sport fishing). Buys 32-40 mss/year. Query with or without published clips or send complete ms. Length: 1,500-4,500 words. Pays $150-500 for assigned articles.

Photos: Send photos with submission. Reviews transparencies. Offers $50-400 per photo. Identification of subjects required. Buys one-time rights.

Columns/Departments: Fish Tales (humorous sport fishing anecdotes), 800-1,500 words; Rigging (how-to rigging for sport fishing), 800-1,500 words; Technique (how-to technique for sport fishing), 800-1,500 words. Buys 8-24 mss/year. Send complete ms. Pays $150-250.

SPORTS AFIELD, 250 W. 55th St., New York NY 10019. (212)649-4000. Editor: Tom Paugh. Executive Editor: Fred Kesting. 20% freelance written. Eager to work with new/unpublished writers. For people of all ages whose interests are centered around the out-of-doors (hunting and fishing) and related subjects. Monthly magazine. Estab. 1887. Circ. 518,010. Buys first North American serial rights for features. **Pays on acceptance.** Publishes ms an average of 6 months after acceptance. Byline given. "Our magazine is seasonal and material submitted should be in accordance. Fishing in spring and summer; hunting in the fall; camping in summer and fall." Submit seasonal material 6 months in advance. Reports in 2 months. Query or submit complete ms. Sample copy for $1; writer's guidelines for 1 first class stamp.

Nonfiction: "Informative how-to articles with emphasis on product and service and personal experiences with good photos on hunting, fishing, camping, boating and subjects such as conservation, environment and some where-to-go related to hunting and fishing. We want first-class writing and reporting." Buys 15-17 unsolicited mss/year. Length: 500-2,500 words. Pays $750 minimum, depending on length and quality.

Photos: Photos purchased with or without ms. Pays $50 minimum for 8 × 10 b&w glossy prints. Pays $50 minimum for 35mm or larger transparencies. Sometimes pays the expenses of writers on assignment.

Fiction: Adventure, humor (if related to hunting and fishing).

Fillers: Send to *Almanac* editor. *Almanac* pays $25 and up depending on length, for newsworthy, unusual, how-to and nature items. Payment on publication. Buys all rights.

Tips: "We seldom give assignments to other than staff. Top-quality 35mm slides to illustrate articles a must. Read a recent copy of *Sports Afield* so you know the market you're writing for." No typewritten ms.

TENNESSEE SPORTSMAN, Game & Fish Publications, Box 741, Marietta GA 30061. (404)953-9222. Editor: Bill Hartlage. See *Game & Fish Publications*.

TEXAS SPORTSMAN, Game & Fish Publications, Inc., Box 741, Marietta GA 30061. (404)953-9222. Editor: Nick Gilmore. See *Game & Fish Publications*.

TURKEY CALL, Wild Turkey Center, Box 530, Edgefield SC 29824. (803)637-3106. Editor: Gene Smith. 50-60% freelance written. Eager to work with new/unpublished writers and photographers. An educational publication for members of the National Wild Turkey Federation. Bimonthly magazine. Estab. 1973. Circ. 65,000. Buys one-time rights. Byline given. **Pays on acceptance.** Publishes ms an average of 6 months after acceptance. Reports in 1 month. No queries necessary. Submit complete package. Wants original ms only. Sample copy $3 with 9 × 12 SAE. Writer's guidelines for #10 SASE.

Nonfiction: Feature articles dealing with the hunting and management of the American wild turkey. Must be accurate information and must appeal to national readership of turkey hunters and wildlife management experts. No poetry or first-person accounts of unremarkable hunting trips. May use some fiction that educates or entertains in a special way. Length: up to 3,000 words. Pays $35 for items, $65 for short fillers of 600-700 words, $200-350 for illustrated features.

Photos: "We want quality photos submitted with features." Art illustrations also acceptable. "We are using more and more inside color illustrations." For b&w, prefer 8 × 10 glossies, but 5 × 7s OK. Transparencies of any size are acceptable. No typical hunter-holding-dead-turkey photos or setups using mounted birds or domestic turkeys. Photos with how-to stories must make the techniques clear (example: how to make a turkey call; how to sculpt or carve a bird in wood). Pays $20 minimum for one-time rights on b&w photos and simple art illustrations; up to $75 for inside color, reproduced any size. Covers: Most are donated. Any purchased are negotiated.

Tips: The writer "should simply keep in mind that the audience is 'expert' on wild turkey management, hunting, life history and restoration/conservation history. He/she *must know the subject*. We are buying more third-person, more fiction, more humor—in an attempt to avoid the 'predictability trap' of a single subject magazine."

VIRGINIA GAME & FISH, Game & Fish Publications, Inc., Box 741, Marietta GA 30061. (404)953-9222. Editor: Jeff Samsel. See *Game & Fish Publications*.

WASHINGTON-OREGON GAME & FISH, Game & Fish Publications, Inc., Box 741, Marietta GA 30061. Editor: Burt Carey. See *Game & Fish Publications*.

WEST VIRGINIA GAME & FISH, Game & Fish Publications, Inc., Box 741, Marietta GA 30061. (404)953-9222. Editor: Ken Freel. See *Game & Fish Publications*.

WESTERN OUTDOORS, 3197-E Airport Loop, Costa Mesa CA 92626. (714)546-4370. Editor: Jack Brown. 75% freelance written. Works with a small number of new/unpublished writers each year. Emphasizes hunting, fishing, camping, boating for 11 Western states only, Baja California, Canada, Hawaii and Alaska. Publishes 9 issues/year. Estab. 1961. Circ. 138,000. **Pays on acceptance.** Publishes ms an average of 6 months after acceptance. Buys first North American serial rights. Query (in writing). Submit seasonal material 4-6 months in advance. Reports in 6 weeks. Sample copy $1.75; writer's guidelines for #10 SASE.

Nonfiction: Where-to (catch more fish, bag more game, improve equipment, etc.); how-to informational; photo feature. "We do not accept fiction, poetry, cartoons." Buys 50-60 assigned mss/year. Query. Length: 1,000-1,500 words maximum. Pays $300-500.

Photos: Purchased with accompanying ms. Captions required. Uses 8 × 10 b&w glossy prints; prefers Kodachrome II 35mm slides. Offers no additional payment for photos accepted with accompanying ms. Pays $200-250 for covers.

Tips: "Provide a complete package of photos, map, trip facts and manuscript written according to our news feature format. Excellence of color photo selections make a sale more likely. The most frequent mistake made by writers in completing an article for us is that they don't follow our style. Our guidelines are quite clear."

WESTERN SPORTSMAN, P.O. Box 737, Regina, Saskatchewan S4P 3A8 Canada. (306)352-2773. FAX: (306)565-2440. Editor: Roger Francis. 90% freelance written. For fishermen, hunters, campers and others interested in outdoor recreation. "Note that our coverage area is Alberta, Saskatchewan and Manitoba." Bimonthly magazine. Estab. 1968. Circ. 31,000. Rights purchased vary with author and material. May buy first North American serial rights or second serial (reprint) rights. Byline given. Pays on publication. Publishes ms an average of 2-8 months after acceptance. "We try to include as much information as possible on all subjects in each edition. Therefore, we usually publish fishing articles in our winter issues along with a variety of winter stories. If material is dated, we would like to receive articles 4 months in advance of our publication date." Reports in 1 month. Sample copy $4; free writer's guidelines.
Nonfiction: "It is necessary that all articles can identify with our coverage area of Alberta, Saskatchewan and Manitoba. We are interested in mss from writers who have experienced an interesting fishing, hunting, camping or other outdoor experience. We also publish other informational pieces as long as they can relate to our coverage area. We are more interested in articles which tell about the average guy living on beans, guiding his own boat, stalking his game and generally doing his own thing in our part of Western Canada than a story describing a well-to-do outdoorsman traveling by motorhome, staying at an expensive lodge with guides doing everything for him except catching the fish, or shooting the big game animal. The articles that are submitted to us need to be prepared in a knowledgeable way and include more information than the actual fish catch or animal or bird kill. Discuss the terrain, the people involved on the trip, the water or weather conditions, the costs, the planning that went into the trip, the equipment and other data closely associated with the particular event in a factual manner. We're always looking for new writers." Buys 60 mss/year. Submit complete ms and SASE or IRC's. Length: 1,500-2,000 words. Pays up to $400. Sometimes pays the expenses of writers on assignment.
Photos: Photos purchased with ms with no additional payment. Also purchased without ms. Pays $30-50/5×7 or 8×10 b&w print; $175-250/35mm or larger transparency for front cover.

WISCONSIN SPORTSMAN, Game & Fish Publications, Inc., Box 741, Marietta GA 30061. Editor: Dennis Schmidt. See *Game & Fish Publications.*

Martial Arts

BLACK BELT, Rainbow Publications, Inc., 24715 Ave. Rockefeller, Valencia CA 91355. (818)843-4444. FAX: (805)257-3028. Executive Editor: Jim Coleman. 80-90% freelance written. Works with a small number of new/unpublished writers each year. Emphasizes martial arts for both practitioner and layman. Monthly magazine. Estab. 1961. Circ. 100,000. Pays on publication. Publishes ms an average of 3-5 months after acceptance. Buys first North American serial rights, retains right to republish. Submit seasonal/holiday material 6 months in advance. Reports in 3 weeks.
Nonfiction: Exposé, how-to, informational, interview, new product, personal experience, profile, technical and travel. Buys 8-9 mss/issue. Query or send complete ms. Length: 1,200 words minimum. Pays $100-300.
Photos: Very seldom buys photos without accompanying mss. Captions required. Total purchase price for ms includes payment for photos. Model releases required.
Fiction: Historical and modern day. Buys 1-2 mss/year. Query. Pays $100-150.
Tips: "We also publish an annual yearbook and special issues periodically. The yearbook includes our annual 'Black Belt Hall of Fame' inductees."

INSIDE KARATE, The Magazine for Today's Total Martial Artist, Unique Publications, 4201 Vanowen Pl., Burbank CA 91505. (818)845-2656. FAX: (818)845-7761. Editor: John Steven Soet. 90% freelance written. Works with a number of new/unpublished writers each year. Monthly magazine covering the martial arts. Circ. 120,000. Publishes ms an average of 3 months after acceptance. Byline given. Buys first North American serial rights. Reports in 3 weeks on queries; in 6 weeks on mss. Sample copy $2.50, 9×12 SAE and 5 first class stamps; free writer's guidelines for #10 SASE.
Nonfiction: Book excerpts; exposé (of martial arts); historical/nostalgic; humor; interview/profile (with approval only); opinion; personal experience; photo feature; and technical (with approval only). *Inside Karate* seeks a balance of the following in each issue: tradition, history, glamor, profiles and/or interviews (both by assignment only), technical, philosophical and think pieces. Not interested in 'tough guys,' self-serving pieces, or movie-star wannabes. Buys 70 mss/year. Query. Length: 1,000-2,500 words; prefers 10-12 page mss. Pays $25-125.

Photos: Send photos with ms. Prefers 3×5 bordered b&w. Captions and identification of subjects required. Buys one-time rights.

Tips: "In our publication, writing style and/or expertise is not the determining factor. Beginning writers with martial arts expertise may submit. Trends in magazine publishing that freelance writers should be aware of include the use of less body copy, better (and interesting) photos to be run large with 'story' caps. If the photos are poor and the reader can't grasp the whole story by looking at photos and copy, forget it."

INSIDE KUNG-FU, The Ultimate In Martial Arts Coverage!, Unique Publications, 4201 Vanowen Pl., Burbank CA 91505. (818)845-2656. FAX: (818)845-7761. Editor: Dave Cater. 75% freelance written. Monthly magazine covering martial arts for those with "traditional, modern, athletic and intellectual tastes. The magazine slants toward little-known martial arts, and little-known aspects of established martial arts." Estab. 1973. Circ. 100,000. Pays on publication. Publishes ms an average of 6 months after acceptance. Byline given. Buys first North American serial rights. Submit seasonal/holiday material 4 months in advance. Simultaneous queries and submissions OK. Reports in 3 weeks on queries; 1 month on mss. Sample copy $2.50 with 9×12 SAE and 5 first class stamps; free writer's guidelines for #10 SASE.

Nonfiction: Exposé (topics relating to the martial arts); historical/nostalgic; how-to (primarily technical materials); cultural/philosophical; interview/profile; personal experience; photo feature; and technical. "Articles must be technically or historically accurate." No "sports coverage, first-person articles or articles which constitute personal aggrandizement." Buys 120 mss/year. Query or send complete ms. Length: 8-10 pages, typewritten and double-spaced.

Photos: Send photos with accompanying ms. Reviews b&w contact sheets, b&w negatives and 8×10 b&w prints. "Photos are paid for with payment for ms." Captions and model release required.

Fiction: Adventure, historical, humorous, mystery and suspense. "Fiction must be short (1,000-2,000 words) and relate to the martial arts. We buy very few fiction pieces." Buys 2-3 mss/year.

Tips: "The writer may have a better chance of breaking in at our publication with short articles and fillers since smaller pieces allow us to gauge individual ability, but we're flexible—quality writers get published, period. The most frequent mistakes made by writers in completing an article for us are ignoring photo requirements and model releases (always number one—and who knows why? All requirements are spelled out in writer's guidelines)."

M.A. TRAINING, Rainbow Publications, P.O. Box 918, Santa Clarita CA 91380-9018. (805)257-4066. FAX: (805)257-3028. Contact: Marian K. Castinado. 75% freelance written. Works with many new/unpublished writers each year. Bimonthly magazine about martial arts training. Estab. 1961. Circ. 60,000. Pays on publication. Publishes ms an average of 3-6 months after acceptance. Buys all North American serial rights. Submit seasonal material 4 months in advance, but best to send query letter first. Reports in 6 weeks. Writer's guidelines for SASE.

Nonfiction: How-to: want training related features. Buys 30-40 unsolicited mss/year. Send query or complete ms. Length: 1,500-2,500 words. Pays $150.

Photos: State availability of photos. Most ms should be accompanied by photos. Reviews 5×7 and 8×10 b&w glossy prints. Can reproduce prints from negatives. Will use illustrations. Offers no additional payment for photos accepted with ms. Model releases required. Buys all rights. Photos are not purchased without accompanying manuscript.

Tips: "I'm looking for how-to, nuts-and-bolts training stories which are martial arts related. Our magazine covers fitness and conditioning, not the martial arts techniques themselves."

Miscellaneous

BALLOON LIFE, Balloon Life Magazine, Inc., 2145 Dale Ave., Sacramento CA 95815. (916)922-9648. Editor: Glen Moyer. 75% freelance written. Monthly magazine for sport of hot air ballooning. Estab. 1986. Circ. 3,500. Pays on publication. Byline given. Offers 50-100% kill fee. Buys first North American serial rights or second serial (reprint) rights. Submit seasonal/holiday material 3-4 months in advance. Previously published submissions OK. Query for electronic submissions. Reports in 3 weeks on queries; 2 weeks on mss. Sample copy for 9×12 SAE with $2 postage. Writer's guidelines for letter SASE.

Nonfiction: Book excerpts, general interest, how-to (flying hot air balloons, equipment techniques), interview/profile, new product, letters to the editor, technical. Buys 150 mss/year. Query with or without published clips or send complete ms. Length: 800-5,000 words. Pays $50-75 for assigned articles; $25-50 for unsolicited articles. Sometimes pays expenses of writers on assignment.

Photos: Send photos with submission. Reviews transparencies and prints. Offers $15-50 per photo. Identification of subjects required. Buys one-time rights.
Columns/Departments: Hangar Flying (real life flying experience that others can learn from), 800-1,500 words; Preflight (a news and information column), 100-500 words; Logbook (recent balloon events—events that have taken place in last 3-4 months), 300-500 words. Buys 60 mss/year. Send complete ms. Pays $15-50.
Fiction: Humorous. Buys 3-5 mss/year. Send complete ms. Length: 800-1,500 words. Pays $50.
Tips: "This magazine slants toward the technical side of ballooning. We are interested in articles that help to educate and provide safety information. Also stories with manufacturers, important individuals and/or of historic events and technological advances important to ballooning. The magazine attempts to present articles that show "how-to" (fly, business opportunities, weather, equipment). Both our Feature Stories section and Logbook section are where most mss are purchased."

BALLS AND STRIKES, Amateur Softball Association, 2801 NE 50th St., Oklahoma City OK 73111. (405)424-5266. Senior Editor: Bill Plummer III. Editor: Larry Floyd. Production/Design Director: Mary Randerson. 20% freelance written. Works with a small number of new/unpublished writers each year. "Only national monthly tabloid covering amateur softball." Circ. 300,000. Pays on publication. Publishes ms an average of 2 months after acceptance. Buys first rights. Byline given. Reports in 3 weeks. Free sample copy.
Nonfiction: General interest, historical/nostalgic, interview/profile and technical. Query. Length: 2-3 pages. Pays $50-75.
Tips: "We generally like shorter features because we try to get as many different features as possible in each issue."

‡FANTASY BASEBALL, Krause Publications, 700 E. State St., Iola WI 54990. FAX: (715)445-4087. Editor: Kit Kiefer. 65% freelance written. A bimonthly magazine for players of Rotisserie and fantasy baseball, other fantasy and Rotisserie sports and tabletop and computer sports games. Readers are 21- to 45-year-old game players. Estab. 1990. Circ. 145,000. Sample copy for 8½ × 11 SASE with $1.25 postge. Pays on publication. Publishes ms an average of 4 months after acceptance. Byline given. Buys first North American and second serial (reprint) rights. Submit seasonal/holiday material 6 months in advance. Reports in 1 month. Writer's guidelines for #10 SASE.
Nonfiction: How-to articles on strategies and tactics, league histories, explanations of different games and methods of playing, some reviews, some humor, some statistical analysis and Bill James-style writing and reporting. If you don't know who Bill James and Glen Waggoner are you shouldn't be writing for this magazine. Buys 36-50 mss/year. Query. Length: 1,000-2,500 words. Pays up to $800.
Photos: Send photos with submission. Reviews contact sheets and transparencies. Payment negotiated. Identification of subjects required.
Tips: We aim to be a great baseball magazine, but one with a very specific focus. In-depth knowledge of baseball and a distinct writing style are musts. If you haven't seen the magazine before, please read through a copy before querying.

HOCKEY ILLUSTRATED, Lexington Library, Inc., 355 Lexington Ave., New York NY 10017. (212)391-1400. FAX: (212)986-5926. Editor: Stephen Ciacciarelli. 90% freelance written. Published 3 times in season. Magazine covering NHL hockey. "Upbeat stories on NHL superstars—aimed at hockey fans, predominantly a younger audience." **Pays on acceptance.** Publishes ms an average of 1-2 months after acceptance. Byline given. Buys first North American serial rights. Reports in 2 weeks. Sample copy $1.95 with 9 × 12 SAE with 3 first class stamps.
Nonfiction: Inspirational and interview/profile. Buys 40-50 mss/year. Query with or without published clips, or send complete ms. Length: 1,500-3,000 words. Pays $75-125.
Photos: State availability of photos with submission. Reviews transparencies and prints. Offers no additional payment for photos accepted with ms. Identification of subjects required. Buys one-time rights.

INSIDE TEXAS RUNNING, 9514 Bristlebrook Dr., Houston TX 77083. (713)498-3208. Editor: Joanne Schmidt. 50% freelance written. A monthly tabloid covering running, cycling and triathloning. "Our audience is made up of Texas runners and triathletes who may also be interested in cross training with biking and swimming." Estab. 1977. Circ. 10,000. **Pays on acceptance.** Publishes ms an average of 1-2 months after acceptance. Byline given. Buys first rights, one-time rights, second serial (reprint) rights, exclusive Texas and all rights. Submit seasonal/holiday material 2 months in advance. Previously published submissions OK. Reports in 1 month on queries; 6 weeks on mss. Sample copy $1.50; writer's guidelines for #10 SASE.
Nonfiction: Book excerpts, exposé, historical/nostalgic, humor, interview/profile, opinion, photo feature, technical and travel. "We would like to receive controversial and detailed news pieces that cover both sides of an issue: for example, how a race director must deal with city government to put on an

event. Problems seen by both sides including cost, traffic congestion, red tape, etc." No personal experience such as "Why I Love to Run," "How I Ran My First Marathon." Buys 18 mss/year. Query with published clips, or send complete ms. Length: 500-2,500 words. Pays $100 maximum for assigned articles; $50 maximum for unsolicited articles. Sometimes pays the expenses of writers on assignment.
Photos: Send photos with submission. Offers $25 maximum/photo. Captions required. Buys one-time rights.
Tips: "We are looking for specific pieces that cite names, places, costs and references to additional information. Writers should be familiar with the sport and understand race strategies, etc. The basic who, what, where, when and how also applies. The best way to break in to our publication is to submit brief (3 or 4 paragraphs) write-ups on road races to be used in the Results section. We also need more cycling articles for new biking section."

INTERNATIONAL GYMNAST, Sundby Sports, Inc., 225 Brooks St., Box 2450, Oceanside CA 92051. (619)722-0030. Editor: Dwight Normile. 50% freelance written. Monthly magazine on gymnastics. "*IG* is dedicated to serving the gymnastics community with competition reports, personality profiles, training and coaching tips and innovations in the sport." Circ. 25,000. Pays on publication. Publishes ms an average of 3 months after acceptance. Byline given. Buys one-time rights. Submit seasonal/holiday material 3 months in advance. Sample copy $3.25. Writer's guidelines for #10 SASE.
Nonfiction: How-to (coaching/training/ business, i.e. running a club), interview/profile, opinion, photo feature (meets or training sites of interest, etc.), competition reports and technical. "Nothing unsuitable for young readers." Buys 25 mss/year. Send complete ms. Length: 500-2,250 words. Pays $15-25. Pays in contributor copies or other premiums when currency exchange is not feasible i.e., foreign residents.
Photos: Send photos with submission. Reviews transparencies and prints. Offers $5-40 per photo published. Identification of subjects required. Buys one-time rights.
Columns/Departments: Innovations (new moves, new approaches, coaching tips); Nutrition (hints for the competitive gymnast); Dance (ways to improve gymnasts through dance, all types); Club Corner (business hints for club owners/new programs, etc.) and Book Reviews (reviews of new books pertaining to gymnastics). Buys 10 mm/year. Send complete ms. Length: 750-1,000. Pays $15-25.
Fiction: Humorous, anything pertaining to gymnastics, nothing inappropriate for young readers. Buys 1-2 ms/year. Send complete ms. Length: 1,500 words maximum. Pays $15-25.
Tips: "To *IG* readers, a lack of knowledge sticks out like a sore thumb. Writers are generally coaches, ex-gymnasts and 'hardcore' enthusiasts. Most open area would generally be competition reports. Be concise, but details are necessary when covering gymnastics. Again, thorough knowledge of the sport is indispensable."

NATIONAL MASTERS RUNNING NEWS, Gain Publications, P.O. Box 2372, Van Nuys CA 91404. (818)785-1895. FAX: (818)782-1135. Editor: Al Sheahen. 50% freelance written. Monthly tabloid. "The only national publication devoted exclusively to runners age 40 and over. We feature results of track meets and road races, profiles, stories, health articles, training advice, etc. for the masters competitive athlete." Estab. 1977. Circ. 5,300. Pays on publication. Byline given. Not copyrighted. Buys one-time rights. Submit seasonal/holiday material 1 month in advance. Simultaneous and previously published submissions OK. Reports in 1 week on queries; 3 weeks on mss. Free sample copy.
Nonfiction: General interest, how-to (training), inspirational, interview/profile, opinion, photo feature. Buys 8 mss/year. Send complete ms. Length: 100-1,500 words. Pays $25-100. Pays writers with contributor copies or other premiums rather than a cash payment by "mutual agreement."
Photos: State availability of photos with submission. Offers $7.50-15 per photo. Identification of subjects required. Buys one-time rights.
Columns/Departments: Health & Fitness (how to keep fit); Training Advice (how to improve performance); Profile (individual profile); Speakers Corner (general interest), all 750-1,000 words. Buys 2 mss/year. Send complete ms. Length: 500-1,500 words. Pays $25-100.
Fillers: Facts, newsbreaks, short humor. Pays $5-25.

NEW YORK RUNNING NEWS, New York Road Runners Club, 9 E. 89th St., New York NY 10128. (212)860-2280. FAX: (212)860-9754. Editor: Raleigh Mayer. Managing Editor: Don Mogelefsky. 75% freelance written. A bimonthly regional sports magazine covering running, racewalking, nutrition and fitness. Material should be of interest to members of the New York Road Runners Club. Estab. 1958. Circ. 45,000. Pays on publication. Time to publication varies. Byline given. Offers ⅓ kill fee. Buys first North American serial rights. Submit seasonal/holiday material 4 months in advance. Simultaneous and previously published submissions OK. Reports in 1 month. Sample copy for 9×12 SASE with $1.75 postage; writer's guidelines for #10 SASE.
Nonfiction: Running and marathon articles. Special issues include N.Y.C. Marathon (submissions in by August 1). No non-running stories. Buys 25 mss/year. Query. Length: 750-1,750 words. Pays $50-250. Pays documented expenses of writers on assignment.

Photos: Send photos with submission. Reviews 8×10 b&w prints. Offers $35-300/photo. Captions, model releases and identification of subjects required. Buys one-time rights.
Columns/Departments: Essay (running-related topics). Query. Length: 750 words. Pays $50-125.
Fiction: Running stories. Query. Length: 750-1,750 words. Pays $50-150.
Tips: "Be knowledgeable about the sport of running. Write like a runner."

‡**OLYMPIAN MAGAZINE,** U.S. Olympic Committee, 1750 E. Boulder St., Colorado Springs CO 80909. (719)578-4529. Editor: Bob Condron. 50% freelance written. Monthly magazine covering olympic sports and athletes. Estab. 1974. Circ. 50,000. Pays on publication. Byline given. Offers 100% kill fee. Query for electronic submissions. Free writer's guidelines.
Nonfiction: Photo feature, feature/profiles of athletes in olympic sports. Query. Length: 1,500-2,500 words. Pays $300 for assigned articles. Sometimes pays expenses of writers on assignment.
Photos: State availability of photos with submission. Reviews transparencies and prints. Offers $50-250 per photo. Captions, model releases and identification of subjects required. Buys one-time rights.

RUNNER'S WORLD, Rodale Press, 33 E. Minor St., Emmaus PA 18098. (215)967-5171. Senior Editor: Bob Wischnia. 25% freelance written. Monthly magazine on running, mainly long-distance running. "The magazine for and about distance running, training, health and fitness, injury precaution, race coverage, personalties of the sport." Estab. 1966. Circ. 450,000. Pays on publication. Publishes ms an average of 2-3 months after acceptance. Byline given. Buys one-time rights. Submit seasonal/holiday material 6 months in advance. Query for electronic submissions. Reports in 1 month. Writer's guidelines for #10 SAE with 1 first class stamp.
Nonfiction: How-to (train, prevent injuries), interview/profile, personal experience. No "my first marathon" stories. Buys 30 mss/year. Query. Pays the expenses of writers on assignment.
Photos: State availability of photos with submission. Identification of subjects required. Buys one-time rights.
Columns/Departments: Christina Negron. Finish Line (personal experience—humor); Training Log (training of well-known runner). Buys 15 mss/year. Query.

‡**RUNNING TIMES, The National Calendar Magazine for Runners,** 18 Azalea Ave., Fairfax CA 94930. (415)258-0883. FAX: (415)258-0231. Editor: Bob Cooper. 90% freelance written. Monthly magazine on running. "*Running Times* readers range from recreational enthusiasts to world-class marathoners; but whether turtles or hounds, they share a conviction that running is an important part of their lives." Circ. 61,000. Pays on publication. Publishes ms an average of 2 months after acceptance. Byline given. Offers 50% kill fee. Buys one-time rights and makes work-for-hire assignments. Submit seasonal/holiday material 4 months in advance. Reports in 10 weeks. Sample copy $2.95 with 9×12 SAE and 7 first class stamps.
Nonfiction: Essays, interview/profile, photo feature. "We have no need for rehashed advice, cute humor, slick or glitzy profiles or anything lacking in real depth, humor or authenticity." Query or send complete ms. Length: 100-3,000 words. Pays $50-650 for assigned and unsolicited articles. Sometimes pays expenses of writers on assignment.
Photos: State availability of photos with submission or send photos with submission. Reviews any color transparencies or b&w prints. Buys one-time rights.
Fillers: Anecdotes, facts. Buys 50/year. Length: 50-200 words. Pays $20-50.
Tips: "Our greatest needs are for short anecdotes or news pieces on current trends, offbeat occurrences, issues or phenomena of interest to runners; and well-researched expositions on cutting-edge developments in the scientific and medical aspects of distance running. These types of submissions, if well written, have a high probability of acceptance."

SIGNPOST MAGAZINE, Suite 512, 1305 4th Ave., Seattle WA 98101. Publisher: Washington Trails Association. Editor: Ann L. Marshall. 10% freelance written. "We will consider working with both previously published and unpublished freelancers." Monthly about hiking, backpacking and similar trail-related activities, mostly from a Pacific Northwest viewpoint. Estab. 1966. Will consider any rights offered by author. Buys 12 mss/year. Pays on publication. Publishes ms an average of 6 months after acceptance. Reports in 6 weeks. Query or submit complete ms. Sample copy and writer's guidelines for SASE.
Nonfiction and Photos: "Most material is donated by subscribers or is staff-written. Payment for purchased material is low, but a good way to break in to print and share your outdoor experiences."
Tips: "We cover only *self-propelled* backcountry sports and won't consider manuscripts about trail bikes, snowmobiles, or power boats. We *are* interested in articles about modified and customized equipment, food and nutrition, and personal experiences in the backcountry (primarily Pacific Northwest, but will consider nation- and world-wide)."

Close-up

Bob Wischnia
Senior Editor
Runner's World

"If you're a runner, you know *Runner's World*," says Senior Editor Bob Wischnia. "We dominate the market to such a degree that I don't think there are too many runners in this country who, at the very least, haven't heard of us." Established in 1966 as a mimeographed tabloid, *Runner's World* has evolved into the nation's largest and most successful long-distance running magazine.

Wischnia joined the magazine in 1978 in the midst of the running boom, and was witness to the "ups and downs" it would encounter in the following years. *Runner's World* faced its most significant difficulty in the late 1970s when it fell into disrepute, losing circulation and advertising. This changed in 1985 when the magazine was sold to Rodale Press. "Rodale quickly turned things around by pumping money, enthusiasm and professionalism back into the magazine," he says.

Runner's World is unique among running magazines in that it is the only international magazine that covers the sport of distance running from a competitive and recreational standpoint. It not only provides race results and upcoming races, but also features articles on races, prominent runners, training techniques, shoes, health and fitness topics written by some of the best writers in the business. "Our audience is the recreational runner/ racer," says Wischnia. "We try to do many things, but essentially it boils down to presenting in a graphic, well-written, entertaining manner all that matters to a distance runner. That entails training stories, nutrition, injury prevention, newsy items, personal essays and columns by well-known writers."

Runner's World is a highly specialized market. Wischnia advises freelancers to read the magazine thoroughly for several months before submitting manuscripts in order to thoroughly acquaint themselves with its audience. "Our readership is very specialized, well educated and sophisticated when it comes to running knowledge and background," he says. "We never write down to our readers. We get a lot of unsolicited material from our readers and if it does get published, it's usually in our Finish Line column (personal essays), Human Race column (short vignettes about notable runners), or Warmups column (news items)." Wischnia advises writers to query before submitting material to *Runner's World*. Neatness and concision do count. He dislikes poor typing jobs and long, detailed cover letters, and looks for well-written, thoroughly researched and well-attributed stories that have a point as well as a beginning, middle and end to them.

"I don't know if the simile is correct," he says, "but our readers are so loyal (the magazine's renewal rate is over 70% and the average reader has been subscribing for seven years), that they almost believe they 'own' the magazine. If we do anything they don't like, they let us know where we went wrong with a great deal of passion. Our readers keep coming back to our magazine for a lot of reasons—training, race information, stories to keep them healthy—but what we try to never forget is that we have to entertain our readers for 30-45 minutes a month."

—Roseann Shaughnessy

SKYDIVING, Box 1520, DeLand FL 32721. (904)736-9779. Editor: Michael Truffer. 25% freelance written. Works with a small number of new/unpublished writers each year. Monthly tabloid featuring skydiving for sport parachutists, worldwide dealers and equipment manufacturers. Circ. 8,600. Average issue includes 3 feature articles and 3 columns of technical information. Pays on publication. Publishes ms an average of 3 months after acceptance. Byline given. Buys one-time rights. Simultaneous and previously published submissions OK, if so indicated. Query for electronic submissions. Reports in 1 month. Sample copy $2; writer's guidelines with 9 × 12 SAE and 4 first class stamps.

Nonfiction: "Send us news and information on equipment, techniques, events and outstanding personalities who skydive. We want articles written by people who have a solid knowledge of parachuting." No personal experience or human-interest articles. Query. Length: 500-1,000 words. Pays $25-100. Sometimes pays the expenses of writers on assignment.

Photos: State availability of photos. Reviews 5 × 7 and larger b&w glossy prints. Offers no additional payment for photos accepted with ms. Captions required.

Fillers: Newsbreaks. Length: 100-200 words. Pays $25 minimum.

Tips: "The most frequent mistake made by writers in completing articles for us is that the writer isn't knowledgeable about the sport of parachuting."

‡TAVERN SPORTS INTERNATIONAL, National Bowlers Journal Inc., Suite 850 101 E. Erie St., Chicago IL 60611. (312)266-9499. FAX: (312)266-7215. Managing Editor: Jocelyn Hathaway. 50% freelance written. Bimonthly magazine reporting on the business and trends of recreational entertainment and coin-operated games. "*TSI* serves as the only information source for the emerging market between the coin-op music/amusement and hospitality industries. Primary readers are location owners/managers and operator vendors. Editorial coverage features successful league/even promotion and marketing case studies, as well as analyzing legislative issues and market trends." Estab. 1988. Circ. 20,500. Pays on publication. Publishes ms an average of 2-4 months after acceptance. Byline usually given. Offers $25 kill fee. Buys first North American serial rights. Submit seasonal/holiday material 4 months in advance. Simultaneous, photocopied and previously published submissions OK. Reports in 2-4 weeks. Sample copy for 9 × 12 SAE with $1.25 in postage. Free writer's guidelines.

Nonfiction: Trade news analyses, marketing techniques, game historical/nostalgic, promotion how-to, interview/profile, photo feature and tournament coverage. Buys 20-30 mss/year. Query with (preferred) or without clips, or send complete ms. Length 1,000-2,000. Pays $125.

Photos: Send photos with submission. Reviews contact sheets, negatives, transparencies and prints (color slides preferred). Offers $5-50 per photo. Identification of subjects required. Buys all rights.

Tips: "Extensive knowledge of promotion and/or marketing of recreational entertainment and related areas is most desired, but not required. Letters addressed to the managing editor detailing proposed topic are preferred. Enclosing published clips and daytime telephone number is helpful."

‡TRIATHLETE, Triathlons, Duathlons, Multi-Sport Events, Suite 303, 1415 Third St., Santa Monica CA 90291. (213)394-1321. Editor: Richard Graham. 60% freelance written. Multi-sport events magazine published 11 times per year. Estab. 1983. Circ. 75,000. Pays on the 15th of the month of publication. Byline given. Offers 50% kill fee. Buys first North American serial rights. Submit seasonal/holiday material 3-6 months in advance. Query for electronic submissions. Reports in 2 months. Free writer's guidelines.

Nonfiction: How-to (swim, bike, run faster), humor, inspirational, interview/profile, new product (occasionally), opinion, personal experience and technical. "Nothing unrelated to *multi*-sport events, such as bike rides and marathons." Buys 20 mss/year. Query with published clips. Length: 800-3,000 words. Pays $125-600 for assigned articles. Sometimes pays expenses of writers on assignment.

Photos: State availability of photos with submission. Reviews 35mm transparencies. Offers $35-300 per photo. Buys one-time rights.

Columns/Departments: Swim, Bike, Run, Perspective (opinion), Sports Health (nutrition, physiology, massage, etc.). Buys 50 mss/year. Query with published clips. Length: 1,000-1,500 words. Pays $125-200.

Tips: "The areas most open to freelancers are columns and race features."

USA GYMNASTICS, United States Gymnastics Federation, Suite 300, 201 S. Capitol Ave., Pan American Plaza, Indianapolis IN 46225. (317)237-5050. FAX: (317)237-5069. Editor: Luan Peszek. 20% freelance written. Bimonthly magazine covering gymnastics—national and international competitions. Designed to educate readers on fitness, health, safety, technique, current topics, trends and personalities related to the gymnastics/fitness field. Readers are between the ages of 7 and 18, parents and coaches. Estab. 1981. Circ. 63,000. Pays on publication. Publishes ms an average of 3-4 months after acceptance. Byline given. Buys all rights. Submit seasonal/holiday material 4 months in advance. Simultaneous submissions OK. Reports in 1 month. Sample copy $3.

Nonfiction: General interest, how-to (related to fitness, health, gymnastics), inspirational, interview/ profile, new product, opinion (Open Floor section), photo feature. Buys 5 mss/year. Query. Length: 2,000 words maximum. Payment to be negotiated.

Photos: Send photos with submission. Offers no additional payment for photos accepted with ms. Identification of subjects required. Buys all rights.

Columns/Departments: Open Floor (opinions—regarding gymnastics/nutrition related topic), up to 1,000 words; Letter to the Editor; New Product, up to 300 words. Buys 2 mss/year. Query or send complete ms. Donated—nonprofit organization.

Tips: "Any articles of interest to gymnasts (men, women and rhythmic gymnastics) coaches, judges and parents, are what we're looking for. This includes nutrition, toning, health, safety, current trends, gymnastics techniques, timing techniques etc. The sections most open to freelancers are Open Floor— opinions on topics related to gymnasts, and features on one of the above mentioned items."

Skiing and Snow Sports

AMERICAN SKATING WORLD, Independent Publication of the American Ice Skating Community, Business Communications Inc., 2545-47 Brownsville Rd., Pittsburgh PA 15210. (412)885-7600. FAX: (412)885-7617. Editor: Robert A. Mock. Magazine Editor: H. Kermit Jackson. 70% freelance written. Eager to work with new/unpublished writers. Monthly tabloid on figure skating. Estab. 1981. Circ. 15,000. Pays on publication. Publishes ms an average of 2-3 months after acceptance. Byline given. Buys first North American serial rights and occasionally second serial rights. Submit seasonal/ holiday material 3 months in advance. Reports in 3 months. Sample copy and writer's guidelines $2.

Nonfiction: Expose; historical/nostalgic; how-to (technique in figure skating); humor; inspirational; interview/profile; new product; opinion; personal experience; photo feature; technical and travel. Special issues include recreational (July), classic skaters (August), annual fashion issue (September), Industry (May). No fiction. AP Style Guidelines are the primary style source. Short, snappy paragraphs desired. Buys 200 mss/year. Send complete ms. "Include phone number; response time longer without it." Length: 600-1,000 words. Pays $25-100.

Photos: Send photos with query or ms. Reviews transparencies and b&w prints. Pays $5 for b&w; $15 for color. Identification of subjects required. Buys all rights for b&w; one-time rights for color.

Columns/Departments: Buys 60 mss/year. Send complete ms. Length: 500-750 words. Pays $25-50.

Fillers: Clippings and anecdotes. No payment for fillers.

Tips: "Event coverage is most open to freelancers; confirm with managing editor to ensure event has not been assigned. Questions are welcome; call managing editor EST, 10 a.m.-4 p.m., Monday-Friday."

‡AMERICAN SKIER, American Ski Association, 64 Inverness Dr. E., Englewood CO 80112. (303)397-7676. Editor: Valerie Rogers. Managing Editor: Todd Runestad. 75% freelance written. Quarterly magazine covering skiing and snowboarding. "The magazine is distributed to members of the American Ski Association. Articles focus on skiing at 300 North American ski resorts. Snowboarding is also a focus, as well as travel, lodging and ski equipment and accesories." Estab. 1976. Circ. 150,000. **Pays on acceptance.** Byline given. Offers ⅓ kill fee. Buys first North American serial rights. Submit seasonal/ holiday material 4 months in advance. Query for electronic submissions. Reports in 1 month. Sample copy $1 with 9 × 12″ SAE.

Nonfiction: How-to, interview/profile, new product, travel and recreational. Buys 15 mss/year. Query with published clips or send complete ms. Length: 300-2,000 words. Pays $75-500.

Photos: Send photos with submission. Reviews transparencies. Offers $50-500/photo. Model releases and identification of subjects are required. Buys one-time rights.

SKATING, United States Figure Skating Association, 20 First St., Colorado Springs CO 80906. (719)635-5200. Editor: Kim Mutchler. Published 10 times a year—monthly except August/September. Estab. 1923. Circ. 35,000. Official publication of the USFSA. Pays on publication. Publishes ms an average of 3 months after acceptance. Buys all rights. Byline given.

Nonfiction: Historical; humor; informational; interview; photo feature; historical biographies; profile (background and interests of national-caliber amateur skaters); technical; and competition reports. Buys 4 mss/issue. All work by assignment.

Photos: Photos purchased with or without accompanying ms. Pays $15 for 8 × 10 or 5 × 7 b&w glossy prints and $35 for color prints or transparencies. Query.

Columns/Departments: Ice Abroad (competition results and report from outside the U.S.); Book Reviews; People. Buys 4 mss/issue. All work by assignment. Length: 500-2,000 words.

Tips: "We want sharp, strong, intelligent writing by experienced persons knowledgeable in the technical and artistic aspects of figure skating with a new outlook on the development of the sport. Knowledge and background in technical aspects of figure skating are essential to the quality of writing expected. We would also like to receive articles on former competitive skaters. No professional skater material."

SKI MAGAZINE, 2 Park Ave., New York NY 10016. (212)779-5000. Editor: Dick Needham. Executive Editor: Steve Cohen. 15% freelance written. A monthly magazine on snow skiing. "*Ski* is a ski-lifestyle publication written and edited for recreational skiers. Its content is intended to help them ski better (technique), buy better (equipment and skiwear), and introduce them to new experiences, people and adventures." Estab. 1936. Circ. 430,000. **Pays on acceptance.** Publishes ms an average of 3 months after acceptance. Byline given. Offers 15% kill fee. Buys first North American serial rights. Submit seasonal/holiday material 8 months in advance. Reports in 1 week on queries; 2 weeks on ms. Sample copy for 8½×11 SAE and 5 first class stamps.
Nonfiction: Essays, historical/nostalgic, how-to, humor, interview/profile and personal experience. Buys 5-10 mss/year. Send complete ms. Length: 1,000-3,500 words. Pays $500-1,000 for assigned artiicles; pays $300-700 for unsolicited artiicles. Pays the expenses of writers on assignment.
Photos: Send photos with submission. Offers $75-300/photo. Captions, model releases and identification of subjects required. Buys one-time rights.
Columns/Departments: Ski Life (interesting people, events, oddities in skiing), 150-300 words; Going Places (items on new or unique places, deals or services available to skiers); Discoveries (special products or services available to skiers that are out of the ordinary), 100-200 words; and It Worked for Me (new ideas invented by writer that make his skiing life easier, more convenient, more enjoyable), 50-150 words. Buys 20 mss/year. Send complete ms. Length: 100-300 words. Pays $50-100.
Fillers: Facts and short humor. Buys 10/year. Length: 60-75 words. Pays $50-75.
Tips: "Writers must have an extensive familiarity with the sport and know what concerns, interests and amuses skiers. Ski Life, Discoveries, Going Places and It Worked for Me are most open to freelancers."

SKIING, Times Mirror Magazines, Inc., 2 Park Ave., New York NY 10016. Did not want to be listed.

SNOW GOER, For Active Snowmobilers, Ehlert Publishing Group, Inc. 319 Barry Ave., Wayzata, MN 55391. (612)476-2200. FAX: (612)476-8065. Editor: Dick Hendricks. Managing Editor: John Sandberg. Seasonal (Dec-Jan-Feb-March) magazine providing active snowmobilers with more information during the heart of the season. Estab. 1990. Circ. 100,000. Pays on publication. Byline given. Buys first North American serial rights. Submit seasonal/holiday material 2 months in advance. Query for electronic submissions. Reports in 3 weeks. Free writer's guidelines.
Nonfiction: How-to, new product, personal experience, technical, travel. Buys 12 mss/year. Query. Length: 1,000-5,000 words. Pays $100-500. Sometimes pays expenses of writers on assignment.
Photos: Send photos with submission. Reviews 35mm transparencies and 5×7 b&w prints. Offers no additional payment for photos accepted with ms. Captions and identification of subjects required. Buys one-time rights.

‡SNOWBOARDER, The Magazine, For Better Living Communications, P.O. Box 1028, Danapoint CA 92629. (714)496-5922. Editor: Douglas C. Palladini. Managing Editor: Steve Casimiro. 50% freelance written. Magazine covering snowboarding; published 5 times during September-February. Estab. 1987. Circ. 75,000. Pays on publication. Publishes ms an average of 4 months after acceptance. Byline given. 25% kill fee. Buys first North American serial rights. Query for electronic submissions. Reports in 1 month on queries. Sample copy $1 with 1 first class stamp. Free writer's guidelines.
Nonfiction: How-to, personal experience, photo feature, technical and travel. No fiction. Buys 7-10 mss/year. Query with published clips. Length: 100-1,200 words. Pays $50-750. Sometimes pays expenses of writers on assignment.
Photos: State availability of photos with submissions. Reviews transparencies. Offers $50-600. Identification of subjects required. Buys one-time rights.

SNOWMOBILE MAGAZINE, Ehlert Publishing Group, Inc., Suite 101, 319 Barry Ave., Wayzata MN 55391. (612)476-2200. FAX: (612)476-8065. Editor: Dick Hendricks. 25% freelance written. A seasonal magazine (September, October and November) covering recreational snowmobiling. Estab. 1980. Circ. 500,000. Pays on publication. Byline given. Buys first North American serial rights. Submit seasonal/holiday material 5 months in advance. Reports in 1 month. Sample copy $2.50; free writer's guidelines.
Nonfiction: How-to, interview/profile, new product, photo feature and travel. Buys 5-6 mss/year. Query. Length: 300-1,000 words. Pays $150-500. Sometimes pays the expenses of writers on assignment.
Photos: Send photos with submission. Reviews 35mm transparencies and 3×5 prints. Offers no additional payment for photos accepted with ms. Captions and identification of subjects required. Buys one-time rights.

Tips: The areas most open to freelancers include "travel and tour stories (with photos) on snowmobiling and snowmobile resorts and event coverage (races, winter festivals, etc.)."

Soccer

‡SOCCER AMERICA, Box 23704, Oakland CA 94623. (415)528-5000. FAX: (415)528-5177. Editor-in-Chief: Lynn Berling-Manuel. 10% freelance written. Works with a small number of new/unpublished writers each year. Weekly tabloid for a wide range of soccer enthusiasts. Estab. 1971. Circ. 25,000. Pays on publication. Publishes ms an average of 2 months after acceptance. Buys all rights. Byline given. Submit seasonal/holiday material 30 days in advance. Query for electronic submissions. Reports in 2 months. Sample copy and writer's guidelines $1.

Nonfiction: Expose (why a pro franchise isn't working right, etc.); historical; how-to; informational (news features); inspirational; interview; photo feature; profile; and technical. "No 'Why I Like Soccer' articles in 1,000 words or less. It's been done. We are very much interested in articles for our 'special issues': fitness, travel, and college selection process." Buys 1-2 mss/issue. Query. Length: 200-1,500 words. Pays 50¢/inch minimum.

Photos: Photos purchased with or without accompanying ms or on assignment. Captions required. Pays $12 for 5×7 or larger b&w glossy prints. Query.

Tips: "Freelancers mean the addition of editorial vitality. New approaches and new minds can make a world of difference. But if they haven't familiarized themselves with the publication it is a total waste of my time and theirs."

Tennis

‡RACQUET, Heather & Pine, Inc. 1202 42 W. 38th, New York NY 10018. (212)768-8360. Editor: Mark L. Stewart. 30% freelance written. Bimonthly tennis/lifestyle magazine. "*Racquet* celebrates the lifestyle of tennis." Estab. 1978. Circ. 145,000. Pays on publication. Publishes ms an average of 2-3 months after acceptance. Byline given. Offers negotiable kill fee. Rights purchased negotiable. Submit seasonal/holiday material 4-5 months in advance. Simultaneous submissions OK. Query for electronic submissions. Reports in 1 month. Sample copy $4.

Nonfiction: Essays, exposé, historical/nostalgic, humor, interview/profile, opinion, personal experience, travel. "No instruction or poetry." Buys 15-20 mss/year. Query. Length: 1,000-6,500 words. Pays $200-750 for assigned articles; $100-300 for unsolicited articles. Pays in contributor copies or other negotiable premiums. Sometime pays expenses of writers on assignment.

Photos: State availability of photos with submission. Offers no additional payment for photos accepted with ms. Rights negotiable.

Columns/Departments: "Courtside" (personal experience—fun facts), 500-2,500 words; "Business of Tennis" (financial side of tennis and related industries), 2,000-2,500 words. Buys 5-10 mss/year. Query. Pays $100-300.

Fillers: Steve Tucker. Anecdotes and short humor. Buys 5/year. Length: 250-750 words. Pays $50-150.

Tips: "Get a copy, understand how we approach tennis, submit article written to style and follow-up. We are always looking for innovative or humorous ideas."

TENNIS, 5520 Park Ave., Trumbull CT 06611. Publisher: Mark Adorney. Editor: Donna Doherty. 10% freelance written. Works with a small number of new/unpublished writers each year. For persons who play tennis and want to play it better and who follow tennis as fans. Monthly magazine. Estab. 1965. Circ. 755,000. Buys all rights. Byline given. Pays on publication. Publishes ms an average of 6 months after acceptance.

Nonfiction and Photos: Emphasis on instructional and reader service articles, but also seeks lively, well-researched features on personalities and other aspects of the game, as well as humor. Query. Length varies. Pays $200 minimum/article, considerably more for major features. Pays $60 and up/ 8×10 b&w glossies; $120 and up/transparencies.

Tips: "When reading our publication the writer should note the depth of the tennis expertise in the stories and should note the conversational, informal writing styles that are used."

WORLD TENNIS, Family Media, 3 Park Ave., New York NY 10016. (212)779-6200. Executive Editor: Peter M Coan. Editor: Steve Flink. Managing Editor: Cindy Shemerler. Monthly tennis magazine. "We are a magazine catering to the complete tennis player." Circ. 500,000. **Pays on acceptance.** Byline given. Offers 25% kill fee. Buys all rights. Submit seasonal/holiday material 3 months in advance. Query for electronic submissions. Query for electronic submissions. Reports in 2 weeks on queries; 1 month on manuscripts. Sample copy for 8×11 SAE and 5 first class stamps.

Nonfiction: Book excerpts (tennis, fitness, nutrition), essays, interview/profile, new product, personal experience, photo feature, travel (tennis resorts). No instruction, poetry or fiction. Buys 30-40 mss/year. Query with published clips. Length: 750-3,000 words. Pays $100 and up. Sometimes pays expenses of writers on assignment.

Photos: State availability of photos with submission. Reviews contact sheets. Payment varies. Requires captions and identification of subjects. Buys one-time rights.

Columns/Departments: My Ad (personal opinion on hot tennis topics); all 200-1,000 words. Buys 25-30 mss/year. Query with published clips. Pays $100 and up.

Fillers: Anecdotes, facts, people/player news, international tennis news. Buys 10-15/year. Length: 750-1,000 words. Pays $100.

Water Sports

‡BODY BOARDING, Western Empire Publications, Suite C, 950 Calle Amanecer, P.O. Box 3010, San Clemente CA 92672. (714)492-7873. Editor: Bill Dellefield. Associate Editor: Sean O'Brien. 60% freelance written. Published 8 times/year. Magazine covering bodyboarding (a.k.a. boogieboarding; surfing on a small foam board). "We cover all aspects of the sport of bodyboarding, focusing equally on the lifestyle and the professional/competitive side. We also provide instruction and information on the equipment bodyboarders need and use. Avg. age of our readers: 18. Primarily (92%) male." Estab. 1985. Circ. 52,000. Pays 2 weeks after publication. Publishes ms an average of 2.5 months after acceptance. Byline given. Offers 25% kill fee. Buys first North American serial rights. Submit seasonal/holiday material 6 months in advance. Accepts previously published submissions depending upon the publication. Reports in 4 weeks. Sample copy $5. Writer's guidelines for SAE with 1 first class stamp.

Nonfiction: Essays (that take a provocative and/or humorous standpoint), general interest (of g.i. to bodyboarders), historical/nostalgic (the "old days," i.e., the 70s and early 80s), how-to (everything but maneuvers, which we assign to pro riders), humor (true stories and humorous renderings of g.i. stories, general interest), interview/profile, new product, opinion (does not mean letters to the editor), personal experience ("heavy" surf stories welcome), photo feature, travel. Product Review in production Dec. '91; Summer Special—in production Feb. '92. No fiction, poetry. Buys approximately 30 mss/year. Query with or without published clips, or send complete ms. Length: 200-2,000 words. Pays 10-20¢/word. Sometimes pays expenses of writers on assignment.

Photos: Send photos with submission. Reviews transparencies. Offers $5-200 per photo. Captions, model releases and identification of subjects required. Buys one-time rights.

Columns/Departments: Hot Tips (how-to article), 1,500 words; Viewpoint (opinion/point of view on various subjects concerning bodyboarding and bodyboarders), 1,500 words; Boarderline (interesting, funny, relevant current events stories), 100-500 words; Surf Lore (amazing and/or funny but true surf stories), 150-1,000 words. Buys 16 mss/year. Query with published clips. Send complete ms. Pays 10-15¢/word.

Fillers: Anecdotes, facts, gags, newsbreaks and cartoons, Buys 5/year. Length: 50-150 words. Pays $10-50.

Tips: "Know bodyboarding experientially/intimately. If you live the surf life it will show in your writing and our readers will recognize it and appreciate it. No flowery or heavy, metaphysical writing; 'hardcore,' insider voices are a must."

‡DIVER, Seagraphic Publications, Ltd., 10991 Shellbridge Way, Richmond, British Columbia V6X 3C6 Canada. (604)273-4333. Editor/Publisher: Peter Vassilopoulos. 75% freelance written. Emphasizes scuba diving, ocean science and technology (commercial and military diving) for a well-educated, outdoor-oriented readership. Published 9 times/year. Circ. 25,000. Payment "follows publication." Buys first North American serial rights. Byline given. Query (by mail only). Submit seasonal/holiday material 3 months in advance of issue date. Send SAE with IRCs. Reports in 6 weeks. Publishes ms an average of 2 months after acceptance. "Articles are subject to being accepted for use in supplement issues on tabloid."

Nonfiction: How-to (underwater activities such as photography, etc.); general interest (underwater oriented); humor; historical (shipwrecks, treasure artifacts, archeological); interview (underwater personalities in all spheres—military, sports, scientific or commercial); personal experience (related to diving); photo feature (marine life); technical (related to oceanography, commercial/military diving, etc.); and travel (dive resorts). No subjective product reports. Buys 40 mss/year. Submit complete ms. Length: 800-1,500 words. Pays $2.50/column inch.

Photos: "Features are mostly those describing dive sites, experiences, etc. Photo features are reserved more as specials, while almost all articles must be well illustrated with b&w prints supplemented by color transparencies." Submit original photo material with accompanying ms. Pays $7 minimum for 5×7 or 8×10 b&w glossy prints; $15 minimum for 35mm color transparencies. Captions and model releases required. Buys one-time rights.

Columns/Departments: Book reviews. Submit complete ms. Length: 200 words maximum. Pays $2.50/column inch.

Fillers: Anecdotes, newsbreaks and short humor. Buys 8-10/year. Length: 50-150 words. Pays $2.50/column inch.

Tips: "It's rewarding finding a talented writer who can make ordinary topics come alive. But dealing with unsolicited manuscripts that don't even come close to being suitable for *Diver* is the most frustrating aspect of working with freelancers."

THE DIVER, Diversified Periodicals, P.O. Box 313, Portland CT 06480. (203)342-4730. Editor: Bob Taylor. 50% freelance written. Magazine published 6 times/year for divers, coaches and officials. Estab. 1978. Circ. 1,500. Pays on publication. Byline given. Submit material at least 2 months in advance. Simultaneous queries and simultaneous and previously published submissions OK. Reports in 2 weeks on queries; 1 month on mss. Sample copy for 9×12 SAE and 85¢ postage.

Nonfiction: Interview/profile (of divers, coaches, officials); results; tournament coverage; any stories connected with platform and springboard diving; photo features and technical. Buys 35 mss/year. Query. Length: 500-2,500 words. Pays $15-40.

Photos: Pays $5-25 for b&w prints. Captions and identification of subjects required. Buys one-time rights.

Tips: "We're very receptive to new writers."

PACIFIC DIVER, Western Outdoors Publications, 3197-E Airport Loop Dr., Costa Mesa CA 92626. (714)546-4370. FAX: (714)662-3486. Editor: John Brumm. Send all mss and queries to Editor, *Pacific Diver*, P.O. Box 6218, Huntington Beach CA 92615. (714)536-7252. 75% freelance written. Bimonthly magazine on scuba diving. "Aimed at scuba diving in the Pacific, covering events, destinations and activities from the Pacific Coast to Mexico and as far as the South Pacific. Aimed at all divers interested in Pacific diving." Estab. 1988. Circ. 32,000. **Pays on acceptance.** Publishes mss an average of 2 months after acceptance. Byline given. Offers $50 kill fee. Buys first North American serial rights and one-time rights. Submit seasonal/holiday material 3 months in advance. Query for electronic submissions. Reports in 3 weeks. Sample copy $2. Free writer's guidelines.

Nonfiction: General interest, historical/nostalgic, how-to, humor, interview/profile, new product, opinion, personal experience, photo feature, technical and travel; all must relate to scuba diving in the Pacific. "No poems, fiction." Buys 60 mss/year. Query or send complete ms. Length: 1,500-2,000. Pays $150-350.

Photos: Send photos with submission. Reviews 35mm transparencies. Offers no additional payment for photos accepted with ms. Captions and identification of subjects required. Buys one-time rights.

SWIM MAGAZINE, Sports Publications, Inc., P.O. Box 45497, Los Angeles CA 90045. (213)674-2120. Editor: Kim A. Hansen. 50% freelance written. Prefers to work with published/selected writers. Bimonthly magazine. "*Swim Magazine* is for adults interested in swimming for fun, fitness and competition. Readers are fitness-oriented adults from varied social and professional backgrounds who share swimming as part of their lifestyle. Readers' ages are evenly distributed from 25 to 90, so articles must appeal to a broad age group." Estab. 1984. Circ. 9,390. Pays approximately 1 month after publication. Publishes ms an average of 4 months after acceptance. Byline given. Submit seasonal/holiday material 4 months in advance. Simultaneous queries OK. Reports in 1 month on queries; 3 months on mss. Sample copy for $3 prepaid and 9×12 SAE with 11 first class stamps. Free writer's guidelines.

Nonfiction: How-to (training plans and techniques); interview/profile (people associated with fitness and competitive swimming); new product (articles describing new products for fitness and competitive training). "Articles need to be informative as well as interesting. In addition to fitness and health articles, we are interested in exploring fascinating topics dealing with swimming for the adult reader." Send complete ms. Length: 1,000-3,500 words. Pays $3/published column inch. "No payment for articles about personal experiences."

Photos: Send photos with ms. Offers no additional payment for photos accepted with ms. Captions, model releases, and identification of subjects required.

Tips: "Our how-to articles and physiology articles best typify *Swim Magazine*'s projected style for fitness and competitive swimmers. *Swim Magazine* will accept medical guidelines and exercise physiology articles only by M.D.s and Ph.Ds."

UNDERCURRENT, Box 1658, Sausalito CA 94966. FAX: (415)461-4563. Managing Editor: Ben Davison. 20-50% freelance written. Works with a small number of new/unpublished writers each year. Monthly consumer-oriented *scuba diving newsletter*. Circ. 15,000. Pays on publication. Publishes ms an average of 2 months after acceptance. Buys first rights. Pays $50 kill fee. Byline given. Simultaneous (if to other than diving publisher) and previously published submissions OK. Reports in 6 weeks. Free sample copy and writer's guidelines; mention *Writer's Market* in request.

Nonfiction: Equipment evaluation, how-to, general interest, new product and travel review. Buys 2 mss/issue. Query with brief outline of story idea and credentials. Will commission. Length: 2,000 words maximum. Pays 10-20¢/word. Sometimes pays the expenses of writers on assignment.

Wrestling

‡**BODY BUILDING LIFESTYLES,** World Wrestling Federal, 1241 E. Main St., Stamford CT 06905. (203)352-8600. Editor-in-Chief: Tom Emanuel. 75% freelance written. Monthly magazine. **Pays on acceptance.** Publishes ms an average of 2-3 months after acceptance. Offers varying kill fee. Buys first North American or one-time rights. Reports in 6 weeks.
Nonfiction: "Wants to see anything pro world body building, federal, training techniques, personal care and hygiene, interviews with body builders and wrestlers." Query or send complete ms. Length: 1,000-14,000 words. Pays varying rates.

WRESTLING WORLD, Lexington Library Inc., 355 Lexington Ave., New York NY 10017. (212)949-6850. FAX: (212)986-5926. Editor: Stephen Ciacciarelli. 100% freelance written. Magazine published bimonthly. "Professional wrestling fans are our audience. We run profiles of top wrestlers and managers and articles on current topics of interest on the mat scene." Circ. 100,000. **Pays on acceptance.** Byline given. Buys first North American serial rights. Reports in 2 weeks. Sample copy $3.
Nonfiction: Interview/profile and photo feature. "No general think pieces." Buys 100 mss/year. Query with or without published clips or send complete ms. Length: 1,500-2,500 words. Pays $75-125.
Photos: State availability of photos with submision. Reviews 35mm transparencies and prints. Offers $25-50/photo package. Pays $50-150 for transparencies. Identification of subjects required. Buys one-time rights.
Tips: "Anything topical has the best chance of acceptance. Articles on those hard-to-reach wrestlers stand an excellent chance of acceptance."

‡**WWF MAGAZINE,** World Wrestling Federation, 1241 E. Main St., Stamford CT 06905. (203)352-8600. Editor: Edward R. Ricciute. 50% freelance written. Monthly magazine. **Pays on acceptance.** Offers varying kill fee. Buys first North American or one-time rights. Reports in 3 weeks.
Nonfiction: "Prefers to see anything connected with WWF television shows—feuds, pro WWF wrestlers, etc." Query with published clips or send complete ms. Length: 200-1,5000 words. Payment varies depending on photos used.

‡**WWF SUPERSTARS,** 1241 E. Main St., Stamford CT 06905. (203)352-8600. Editor: Edward R. Ricciute. 50% freelance written. Annual magazine. **Pays on acceptance.** Pays varying kill fee. Buys first North American or one-time rights. Reports in 3 weeks.
Nonfiction: "Prefers to see articles from writers with a general feel for World Wrestling." Query with published clips or send complete ms. Length: 200-1,500 words. Pay varies with length of article.

‡**WWF WRESTLING SPOTLIGHT MAGAZINE,** 1241 E. Main St., Stamford CT 06905. (203)352-8600. Editor: Edward R. Ricciute. 35% freelance written. Quarterly magazine. **Pays on acceptance.** Offers varying kill fees. Buys first North American or one-time rights. Reports in 3 weeks.
Nonfiction: "Prefers the writer to have a good knowledge of events in WWF. We also spotlight careers of athletes." Query with published clips or send complete ms. Length: 200-1,500 words. Pay varies according to word length and photos used.

Teen and Young Adult

The publications in this category are for young people ages 13-19. Publications for college students are listed in Career, College and Alumni. Those for younger children are listed in the Juvenile category.

‡**BREAD,** Nazarene Publishing House, 6401 The Paseo, Kansas City MO 64131. (816)333-7000. Editor: Karen DeSollar. 20% freelance written. Works with a small number of new/unpublished writers each year. A monthly magazine for Nazarene teens. Circ. 26,000. **Pays on acceptance.** Publishes ms an average of 8 months after acceptance. Byline given. Buys one-time rights. Submit seasonal/holiday material 10 months in advance. Simultaneous, photocopied, and previously published submissions OK. Reports in 6 weeks on queries; 2 months on mss. Must receive SASE or material will not be returned. Sample copy and writer's guidelines for 9 × 12 SAE and $1 with 2 first class stamps.
Nonfiction: How-to and personal experience, both involving teens and teen problems and how to deal with them. Buys 25 mss/year. Send complete ms. Length: 800-1,500 words. Pays 3-3½¢/word.
Fiction: Adventure, humorous and romance, all demonstrating teens living out Christian commitment in real life.

CAREERS, The Magazine for Today's Young Achievers, E.M. Guild, Inc., 1001 Avenue of the Americas, New York NY 10018. (212)354-8877. Editor: Mary Dalheim. 75% freelance written. Works with a small number of new/unpublished writers each year. A magazine published 4 times a year covering life-coping skills, career choices, and educational opportunities for high school juniors and seniors. "*Careers* is designed to offer a taste of the working world, new career opportunities, and stories covering the best ways to reach those opportunities—through education, etc." Circ. 600,000. Pays 30 days after acceptance. Publishes ms an average of 2-3 months after acceptance. Byline given. Offers 25% kill fee. Buys first North American serial rights. Submit seasonal/holiday material 6 months in advance. Sometimes accepts previously published submissions. Reports in 2 months on queries. Sample copy $2.50; writer's guidelines for #10 SAE with 1 first class stamp.

Nonfiction: Book excerpts, how-to, interview/profile, photo feature, travel, humor. Buys 25 mss/year. Query with published clips. Length: 1,000-1,500 words. Pays $250. Sometimes pays the expenses of writers on assignment.

Photos: State availability of photos with submission. Reviews contact sheets and transparencies. Offers $100 minimum/photo. Captions, model releases, and identification of subjects required. Buys one-time rights.

Columns/Departments: Money-Wise, College Hotline, Career Watch, Tech Talk, Global Views, High Achievers and Life After High School. Buys 15 mss/year. Length: 1,000-1,500 words. Pays $250.

EXPLORING MAGAZINE, Boy Scouts of America, 1325 W. Walnut Hill Ln., P.O. Box 152079, Irving TX 75015-2079. (214)580-2365. FAX: (214)580-2079. Executive Editor: Scott Daniels. 85% freelance written. Prefers to work with published/established writers. Magazine published 4 times/year—January, March, May, September. Covers the educational teen-age Exploring program of the BSA. Estab. 1970. Circ. 350,000. **Pays on acceptance.** Publishes ms an average of 6 months after acceptance. Byline given. Buys first rights. Submit seasonal/holiday material 6 months in advance. Simultaneous queries OK. Reports in 2 weeks. Sample copy for 9×12 SAE and 4 first class stamps; writer's guidelines for #10 SASE. Write for guidelines and "What is Exploring?" fact sheet.

Nonfiction: General interest, how-to (achieve outdoor skills, organize trips, meetings, etc.); interview/profile (of outstanding Explorer); travel (backpacking or canoeing with Explorers). Buys 15-20 mss/year. Query with clips. Length: 800-1,600 words. Pays $350-500. Pays expenses of writers on assignment.

Photos: Brian Payne, photo editor. State availability of photos with query letter or ms. Reviews b&w contact sheets and 35mm transparencies. Captions required. Buys one-time rights.

Tips: "Contact the local Exploring Director in your area (listed in phone book white pages under Boy Scouts of America). Find out if there are some outstanding post activities going on and then query magazine editor in Irving, Texas. Strive for shorter texts, faster starts and stories that lend themselves to dramatic photographs."

‡FLIP, "The Official Magazine of *Dance Party USA*," Drake Publishers, Suite 1404, 801 2nd Ave., New York NY 10017. (212)986-5100. Editor: Sue Kossoy. Managing Editor: Mary Anne Cassata. 50% freelance written. Consumer publication. Magazine covering *Dance Party USA* TV Show, "Teen" stars, dance music; published 10 times/year. "Magazine for teenagers, mostly girls. We seek to entertain while maintaining a positive self-image by offering role models. Focus on popular music acts, plus TV and movie stars, teens, love!" Estab. 1990. Circ. 200,000. **Pays on acceptance.** Publishes ms an average of 2 months after acceptance. Byline sometimes given. Offers 50% kill fee. Buys all rights and makes work-for-hire assignments. Submit seasonal/holiday material 6 months in advance. Query for electronic submissions. Reports in 1 month. Free sample copy. Writer's guidelines for 1 SAE with 1 first class stamp.

Nonfiction: Interview/profile (By query only! Popular TV, music and movie stars with teen appeal), (By query only interviews/profiles with teens of outstanding achievement). "No 'service' articles, personal experience, anything downbeat." Buys 60 mss/year. Query with published clips. Length 250-900 words. Pays $25-125 for assigned articles. (*No* unsolicited). We have *kids* review games—they keep game.

Photos: Send photos with submission. Reviews b/w contact sheets, color transparencies and b/w prints. Model releases and identification of subjects required.

Tips: "Know your subject matter and have experience doing celeb interviews. Try watching the *Dance Party USA* program (USA network)—it's a good way to see the kind of energy and subjects we like."

FREEWAY, P.O. Box 632, Glen Ellyn IL 60138. Editor: Kyle L. Olund. For "young Christian adults of high school and college age." 80% freelance written. Eager to work with new/unpublished writers. Weekly. Estab. 1967. Prefers one-time rights but buys some reprints. Purchases 100 mss/year. Byline given. Reports on material accepted for publication in 2 months. Publishes ms an average of 1 year after acceptance. Returns rejected material in 2 months. Free sample copy and writer's guidelines with SASE.

Nonfiction: "*FreeWay*'s greatest need is for personal experience stories showing how God has worked in teens' lives. Stories are best written in first-person, 'as told to' author. Incorporate specific details, anecdotes, and dialogue. Show, don't tell, how the subject thought and felt. Weave spiritual conflicts and prayers into entire manuscript; avoid tacked-on sermons and morals. Stories should show how God has helped the person resolve a problem or how God helped save a person from trying circumstances (1,000 words or less). Avoid stories about accident and illness; focus on events and emotions of everyday life. Short-short stories are needed as fillers. We also need self-help or how-to articles with practical Christian advice on daily living, and trend articles addressing secular fads from a Christian perspective. We do not use devotional material, or fictionalized Bible stories." Pays 7-10¢/word for assigned articles, 5-8¢ for unsolicited or reprints. Some poetry ($20-50). Sometimes pays the expenses of writers on assignment.

Photos: Whenever possible, provide clear 8 × 10 or 5 × 7 b&w photos to accompany mss (or any other available photos). Payment is $5-30.

Fiction: "We use little fiction, unless it is allegory, parable, or humor."

Tips: "Study our 'Tips to Writers' pamphlet and sample copy, then query or send complete ms. In your cover letter, include information about who you are, writing qualifications, and experience working with teens. Include SASE."

GUIDE, 55 W. Oak Ridge Dr., Hagerstown MD 21740. FAX: (301)791-7012. Editor: Jeannette Johnson. 50% freelance written. Works with a small number of new/unpublished writers each year. A journal for junior youth and early teens. "Its content reflects Christian beliefs and standards." Weekly magazine. Estab. 1953. Circ. 40,000. Buys first serial rights, simultaneous rights, and second serial (reprint) rights to material originally published elsewhere. **Pays on acceptance.** Publishes ms an average of 6-9 months after acceptance. Byline given. Submit seasonal/holiday material 6 months in advance. Query for electronic submissions. Reports in 3 weeks. Free sample copy.

Nonfiction: Wants nonfiction stories of character-building and spiritual value. Should emphasize the positive aspects of living, obedience to parents, perseverance, kindness, etc. "We use a number of stories dealing with problems common to today's Christian youth, such as peer pressure, parents' divorce, chemical dependency, etc. We can always use 'drama in real life' stories that show God's protection and seasonal stories—Christmas, Thanksgiving, special holidays. We do not use stories of hunting, fishing, trapping or spiritualism." Buys about 300 mss/year. Send complete ms (include word count and Social Security number). Length: up to 1,200 words. Pays 3-4¢/word.

Tips: "Typical topics we cover in a yearly cycle include choices (music, clothes, friends, diet); friend-making skills; school problems (cheating, peer pressure, new school); death; finding and keeping a job; sibling relationships; divorce; step-families; drugs; communication; and suicide. We often buy short fillers, and an author who does not fully understand our needs is more likely to sell with a short-short. Our target age is 10-14. Our most successful writers are those who present stories from the viewpoint of a young teen-ager. Stories that sound like an adult's sentiments passing through a young person's lips are *not* what we're looking for. Use believable dialogue."

HIGH SCHOOL I.D., (formerly *Lighted Pathway*), Pathway Press, 922 Montgomery Ave., P.O. Box 2250, Cleveland TN 37320-2250. (615)476-4512. Editor: Lance Colkmire. 8% freelance written. A weekly take-home paper emphasizing Christian living for high schoolers. **Pays on acceptance.** Publishes ms an average of 1 year after acceptance. Byline given. Buys first North American serial rights and one-time rights. Submit seasonal/holiday material 1 year in advance. Simultaneous queries, and simultaneous, and previously published submissions OK. Reports in 2 weeks on queries; 1 month on mss. Free sample copy and writer's guidelines for SASE.

Nonfiction: Inspirational, interview/profile, personal experience and other nonfiction. "Our primary objective is to show how teens can live a Christian life in a secular world." Buys 6-10 mss/year. Length: 500-1,000 words. Pays 3-5¢/word.

Tips: "Write to conservative, pentecostal audience about current subjects involving young people today." Human interest stories, especially first-person experiences, are most open to freelancers.

KEYNOTER, Key Club International, 3636 Woodview Trace, Indianapolis IN 46268. Executive Editor: Tamara P. Burley. 65% freelance written. Works with a small number of new/unpublished writers each year, and is eager to work with new/unpublished writers willing to adjust their writing styles to *Keynoter*'s needs. A youth magazine published monthly Oct.-May (Dec./Jan. combined issue), distributed to members of Key Club International, a high school service organization for young men and women. Estab. 1946. Circ. 130,000. **Pays on acceptance.** Publishes ms an average of 5 months after acceptance. Byline given. Buys first North American serial rights. Submit seasonal/holiday material 7 months in advance. Simultaneous queries and submissions (if advised), and previously published submissions OK. Reports in 1 month. Sample copy for 9 × 12 SAE and 3 first class stamps; writer's guidelines for #10 SASE.

Nonfiction: Book excerpts (may be included in articles but are not accepted alone); general interest (must be geared for intelligent teen audience); historical/nostalgic (generally not accepted); how-to (if it offers advice on how teens can enhance the quality of lives or communities); humor (accepted very infrequently; if adds to story, OK); interview/profile (rarely purchased, "would have to be on/ with an irresistible subject"); new product (only if affects teens); photo feature (if subject is right, might consider); technical (if understandable and interesting to teen audience); travel (sometimes OK, but must apply to club travel schedule); subjects that entertain and inform teens on topics that relate directly to their lives. "We would also like to receive self-help and school-related nonfiction on leadership, community service, and teen issues. Please, no first-person confessions, no articles that are written down to our teen readers." Buys 10-15 mss/year. Query. Length: 1,500-2,500 words. Pays $125-250. Sometimes pays the expenses of writers on assignment.

Photos: State availability of photos. Reviews b&w contact sheets and negatives. Identification of subjects required. Buys one-time rights. Payment for photos included in payment for ms.

Tips: "We want to see articles written with attention to style and detail that will enrich the world of teens. Articles must be thoroughly researched and must draw on interviews with nationally and internationally respected sources. Our readers are 13-18, mature and dedicated to community service. We are very committed to working with good writers, and if we see something we like in a well-written query, we'll try to work it through to publication."

‡THE MAGAZINE FOR CHRISTIAN YOUTH! The United Methodist Publishing House, 201 Eighth Ave. S., Box 801, Nashville TN 37202. (615)749-6463. FAX: (615)749-6078 or 749-6079. Editor: Christopher B. Hughes. Monthly magazine. Circ. 40,000. **Pays on acceptance.** Publishes ms an average of 6 months after acceptance. Byline given. Buys one-time and all rights. Submit seasonal/holiday material 1 year in advance. Photocopied and previously published submissions OK. Writer's guidelines for SASE.

Nonfiction: Book excerpts; general interest; how-to (deal with problems teens have); humor (on issues that touch teens' lives); inspirational; interview/profile (well-known singers, musicians, actors, sports); personal experience; religious and travel (include teen culture of another country). Buys 5-10 mss/year. Queries welcome. Length: 700-2,000 words. Pays $80-110 for assigned articles; 4¢/word for unsolicited articles.

Photos: State availability of photos with submission. Reviews transparencies and 8×10 prints. Offers $25-150/photo. Captions and model releases required. Buys one-time rights.

Fiction: (From teens only) adventure, ethnic, fantasy, historical, humorous, mainstream, mystery, religious, romance, science fiction, suspense and western. No stories where the plot is too trite and predictable—or too preachy. Send complete ms. Length: 700-2,000 words. Pays 4¢/word.

Fillers: Gags to be illustrated by cartoonists and short humor. Buys 6-8/year. Length: 10-75 words. Pays $15-80.

Tips: "Stay current with the youth culture so that your writing will reflect an insight into where teenagers are. Be neat, and always proofread and edit your own copy. Use faith language in a natural manner."

THE NEW ERA, 50 E. North Temple, Salt Lake City UT 84150. (801)240-2951. Managing Editor: Richard M. Romney. 60% freelance written. "We work with both established writers and newcomers." Monthly magazine. For young people of the Church of Jesus Christ of Latter-day Saints (Mormon); their church leaders and teachers. Estab. 1971. Circ. 180,000. **Pays on acceptance.** Publishes ms an average of 1 year after acceptance. Byline given. Buys all rights. Submit seasonal material 1 year in advance. Query for electronic submissions. Reports in 1 month. Query preferred. Sample copy $1 and 9×12 SAE; writer's guidelines for SASE.

Nonfiction: Material that shows how the Church of Jesus Christ of Latter-day Saints is relevant in the lives of young people today. Must capture the excitement of being a young Latter-day Saint. Special interest in the experiences of young Mormons in other countries. No general library research or formula pieces without the *New Era* slant and feel. Uses informational, how-to, personal experience, interview, profile, inspirational, humor, historical, think pieces, travel and spot news. Length: 150-3,000 words. Pays 3-12¢/word. *For Your Information* (news of young Mormons around the world). Pays expenses of writers on assignment.

Photos: Uses b&w photos and transparencies with mss. Payment depends on use in magazine, but begins at $10.

Fiction: Adventure, science fiction and humorous. Must relate to young Mormon audience. Pays minimum 3¢/word.

Poetry: Traditional forms, blank verse, free verse, light verse and all other forms. Must relate to editorial viewpoint. Pays minimum 25¢/line.

Tips: "The writer must be able to write from a Mormon point of view. We're especially looking for stories about successful family relationships. We anticipate using more staff-produced material. This means freelance quality will have to improve."

PURPLE COW Newspaper for Teens, Suite 415, Piedmont Rd. NE, Atlanta GA 30305. (404)239-0642. FAX: (404)237-8232. Editor: Todd Daniel. 5% freelance written. A monthly tabloid circulated to Atlanta area high schools. Estab. 1977. Circ. 50,000. Pays on publication. Buys one-time rights. "Manuscripts are accepted on a 'space-available' basis. If space becomes available, we publish the manuscript under consideration 1-12 months after receiving." Byline given. Simultaneous queries and previously published submissions OK. Sample copy for $1 with 9×12 SAE and 2 first class stamps; writer's guidelines for #10 SASE.

Nonfiction: At this time we are only accepting articles for our Career and College sections. Acceptable topics: babysitting, part-time jobs, college admissions, careers, scholarships, college life, freshman year. No fiction. Buys 7-10 mss/year. Send complete ms. Length: 1,000 words maximum. Pays $10-25.

Cartoons and Photos: Must be humorous, teen-related, up-to-date with good illustrations. Buys 12/year. Send photos with ms. Buys one-time rights. Pays $5.

Tips: "A freelancer can best break in to our publication with articles which help teens. Examples might be how to secure financial aid for college or how to survive your freshman year of college."

SENIOR HIGH I.D., David C. Cook Publishing Co., 850 N. Grove, Elgin IL 60120. (708)741-2400. Editor: Doug Schmidt. 75% freelance written. Prefers to work with published/established writers and works with a small number of new/unpublished writers each year. Quarterly magazine. "A take-home paper used in senior high Sunday School classes. We encourage Christian teens to write to us." **Pays on acceptance.** Publishes ms an average of 15 months after acceptance. Buys all rights. Reports in 3 months. Sample copy and writer's guidelines for SASE.

Nonfiction: How-to (Sunday School youth projects); humor (from Christian perspective); inspirational and personality (nonpreachy); personal teen experience (Christian); poetry written by teens and photo feature (Christian subject). "Nothing not compatible with a Christian lifestyle." Submit complete ms. Length: 500-1,000 words. Pays $100; $40 for short pieces.

Fiction: Adventure (with religious theme); humorous; and religious. Submit complete ms. Length: 500-1,000 words. Pays $100. "No preachy experiences."

Photos: Ruth Corcoran, photo editor. Photos purchased with or without accompanying ms or on assignment. Send contact sheets, prints or transparencies. Pays $25-40 for 8½×11 b&w photos; $50 minimum for transparencies. "Photo guidelines available."

Tips: "Our demand for manuscripts should increase, but most of these will probably be assigned rather than bought over-the-transom. Our features are always short. A frequent mistake made by writers in completing articles for us is misunderstanding our market. Writing is often not Christian at all, or it's too 'Christian,' i.e. pedantic, condescending and moralistic."

SEVENTEEN, 850 3rd Ave., New York NY 10022. Editor-in-Chief: Midge Turk Richardson. Managing Editor: Mary Anne Baumgold. 80% freelance written. Works with a small number of new/unpublished writers each year. Monthly. Circ. 1.9 million. Buys one-time rights for nonfiction and fiction by adult writers and work by teenagers. Pays 25% kill fee. **Pays on acceptance.** Publishes ms an average of 6 months after acceptance. Byline given. Reports in 6 weeks.

Nonfiction: Roberta Anne Myers, articles editor. Articles and features of general interest to young women who are concerned with the development of their lives and the problems of the world around them; strong emphasis on topicality and helpfulness. Send brief outline and query, including a typical lead paragraph, summing up basic idea of article. Also like to receive articles and features on speculation. Query with tearsheets or copies of published articles. Length: 1,200-2,000 words. Pays $50-150 for articles written by teenagers but more to established adult freelancers. Articles are commissioned after outlines are submitted and approved. Fees for commissioned articles $650-1,500. Sometimes pays the expenses of writers on assignment.

Photos: Anna Demchick, art director. Photos usually by assignment only.

Fiction: Adrian LeBlanc, fiction editor. Thoughtful, well-written stories on subjects of interest to young women between the ages of 12 and 20. Avoid formula stories—"My sainted Granny," "My crush on Brad," etc.—heavy moralizing, condescension of any sort. Humorous stories and mysteries are welcomed. Best lengths are 1,000-3,000 words. Pays $500-1,500.

Poetry: Contact teen features editor. By teenagers only. Pays $15. Submissions are nonreturnable unless accompanied by SASE.

Tips: "Writers have to ask themselves whether or not they feel they can find the right tone for a *Seventeen* article—a tone which is empathetic yet never patronizing; lively yet not superficial. Not all writers feel comfortable with, understand or like teenagers. If you don't like them, *Seventeen* is the wrong market for you. The best way for beginning teenage writers to crack the *Seventeen* lineup is for them to contribute suggestions and short pieces to the Voices section, a literary format which lends itself to just about every kind of writing: profiles, essays, exposes, reportage, and book reviews."

STRAIGHT, Standard Publishing Co., 8121 Hamilton Ave., Cincinnati OH 45231. (513)931-4050. Editor: Carla J. Crane. 90% freelance written. Estab. 1866 (publishing house). "Teens, age 13-19, from Christian backgrounds generally receive this publication in their Sunday School classes or through subscriptions." Weekly (published quarterly) magazine. **Pays on acceptance.** Publishes ms an average of 1 year after acceptance. Buys first rights, second serial (reprint) rights or simultaneous rights. Byline given. Submit seasonal/holiday material 1 year in advance. Reports in 6 weeks. Include Social Security number on ms. Free sample copy; writer's guidelines with #10 SASE and 2 first class stamps.

Nonfiction: Religious-oriented topics, teen interest (school, church, family, dating, sports, part-time jobs), humor, inspirational, personal experience. "We want articles that promote Christian values and ideals." No puzzles. Query or submit complete ms. "We're buying more short pieces these days; 12 pages fill up much too quickly." Length: 800-1,500 words.

Fiction: Adventure, humorous, religious and suspense. "All fiction should have some message for the modern Christian teen." Fiction should deal with all subjects in a forthright manner, without being preachy and without talking down to teens. No tasteless manuscripts that promote anything adverse to the Bible's teachings. Submit complete ms. Length: 1,000-1,500 words. Pays 3-7¢/word.

Photos: May submit photos with ms. Pays $25-40 for 8 × 10 b&w glossy prints and $75-125 for color slides. Model releases should be available. Buys one-time rights.

Tips: "Don't be trite. Use unusual settings or problems. Use a lot of illustrations, a good balance of conversation, narration, and action. Style must be clear, fresh—no sermonettes or sickly-sweet fiction. Take a realistic approach to problems. Be willing to submit to editorial policies on doctrine; knowledge of the *Bible* a must. Also, be aware of teens today, and what they do. Language, clothing, and activities included in mss should be contemporary. We are becoming more and more selective about freelance material and the competition seems to be stiffer all the time."

TEEN BEAT, MacFadden Holdings, 233 Park Ave. S., New York NY 10003. Staff written. Did not want to be listed.

TEEN DREAM, Starline Publications, 63 Grand Ave., River Edge NJ 07661. (201)487-6124. FAX: (201)487-6390. Editor: Anne Raso. 20% freelance written. Bimonthly magazine of teen entertainment. Estab. 1988. Circ. 180,000. Pays on publication. Byline given. Offers 50% kill fee. Buys all rights. Submit seasonal/holiday material 3 months in advance. Reports in 2 months. Sample copy $3. No fiction or poetry.

Nonfiction: Photo feature. Buys 50 mss/year. Call editor about ms. Length: 500-1,000 words. Pays $50-100 for assigned articles. Sometimes pays expenses of writers on assignment.

Photos: State availability of photos with submission or send photos with submission. Reviews color slides and 8 × 10 b&w prints. Offers $25-125 per photo. Captions required. Buys one-time rights.

'TEEN MAGAZINE, 8490 Sunset Blvd., Hollywood CA 90069. (212)854-2222. Editor: Roxanne Camron. 20-30% freelance written. Prefers to work with published/established writers. For teenage girls. Monthly magazine. Circ. 1.1 million. Publishes ms an average of 6 months after acceptance. Buys all rights. Reports in 4 months. Sample copy and writer's guidelines for 8½ × 11 SAE and $2.50.

Fiction: Dealing specifically with teenage girls and contemporary teen issues. More fiction on emerging alternatives for young women. Suspense, humorous and romance. "Young love is all right, but teens want to read about it in more relevant settings." Length: 2,500-4,000 words. Pays $100. Sometimes pays the expenses of writers on assignment.

Tips: "No fiction with explicit language, casual references to drugs, alcohol, sex, or smoking; no fiction with too depressing outcome."

‡TEENS TODAY, Church of the Nazarene, 6401 The Paseo, Kansas City MO 64131. (816)333-7000. Editor: Karen De Sollar. 25% freelance written. Eager to work with new/unpublished writers. For junior and senior high teens, to age 18, attending Church of the Nazarene Sunday School. Weekly magazine. Circ. 55,000. **Pays on acceptance.** Publishes ms an average of 14 months after acceptance. Byline given. Buys first rights and reprint rights. Submit seasonal/holiday material 10 months in advance. Simultaneous, photocopied and previously published submissions OK. Submissions not returned without SASE. Reports in 2 months. Sample copy and writer's guidelines for 50¢ and SAE with 2 first class stamps.

Photos: Pays $10-30 for 8 × 10 b&w glossy prints.

Fiction: Adventure (if Christian principles are apparent); humorous; religious; and romance (keep it clean). Buys 1 ms/issue. Send complete ms. Length: 1,000-1,500 words. Pays 3½¢/word, first rights; 3¢/word, second rights.

Poetry: "We accept poetry written by teens—no outside poetry accepted." Buys 10 poems/year.

Tips: "We look for quality fiction dealing with teen issues: peers, self, parents, vocation, Christian truths related to life, etc. We do not condone dancing, drinking, drugs or premarital sex. Avoid overused themes."

‡TEXAS TEEN!, Texas Teen Publications, P.O. Box 5787, Denton TX 76203. (817)566-1659. Editor: D.J. Norman-Cox. 85% freelance written. Monthly magazine. *"Texas Teen!* is written for and about 15-18-year-old guys and girls who are academically capable, competitive and not allergic to excellence. All content is about teenagers who accomplish major feats. Estab. 1991. Circ. 25,000. Pays on publication. Publishes ms an average of 2 months after acceptance. Byline sometimes given. Buys all rights or second serial (reprint) rights. Submit seasonal/holiday material 4 months in advance. Previously published submissions OK. Reports in 2 weeks on queries; 5 weeks on mss. Sample copy $2 with 9 × 12 SAE and 4 first class stamps. Writer's guidelines for #10 SASE.
Nonfiction: Essays, expose, general interest, how-to (apply for college, find a job, plan group trips, etc.), humor, interview/profile. May issue features a salute to the respective year's graduating class. November issue features information for the college-bound. "No rock or movie star gossip; no beauty queen tips; no 'ain't it awful' stories." Buys 40 mss/year. Query with or without published clips, or send complete ms. Length: 600-900 words. Pays $50-100. Pays in copies for poetry.
Photos: State availability of photos withy submission. Reviews contact sheets. Offers $10 per photo. Captions, model releases and identification of subjects required. Buys all rights.
Columns/Departments: Rodeo stuff (stories about teenage rodeo participants—Texans only), 75-150 words; Sports Report (articles about teenagers in sports—Texans only), 75-150 words. Buys 20 mss/year. Send complete ms. Pays $15-25.
Fiction: Adventure, humorous, mystery, religious, science fiction, suspense, western. Mysteries are the only type of fiction purchased from adults. All other types are accepted from Texas teenagers only. "No erotica, stories with profane language or excessive gore, or stories with adults or small children as main character." Buys 10/year. Send complete ms. Length: 600-900 words. Pays $25-100.
Poetry: Free verse. Poetry is acquired from Texas teenagers only. Buys 30 poems/year. Submit maximum 4 poems at one time. Length: open. Pays in copies.
Fillers: Anecdotes, facts, short humor. Buys 30/year. Length: 75 words maximum. Pays $5.
Tips: "Talk with high school students (especially males). If they seem excited about the subject and would like to know more, send it in. Look for truly unique and fascinating subjects. Be conversational, informative and fun."

TQ (TEEN QUEST), The Good News Broadcasting Association, Inc., P.O. Box 82808, Lincoln NE 68501. (402)474-4567. FAX: (402)474-4519. Editor-in-Chief: Woodrow Kroll. Managing Editor: Win Mumma. 50% freelance written. Works with a small number of new/unpublished writers each year. Monthly magazine emphasizing Christian living for Protestant church-oriented teens, ages 14-17. Circ. 50,000. Buys first serial rights or second serial (reprint) rights. Publishes ms an average of 8 months after acceptance. Byline given. Submit seasonal/holiday material 1 year in advance. Previously published submissions OK. Reports in 2 months. Sample copy and writer's guidelines for 9 × 12 SAE with 4 first class stamps.
Nonfiction: Interviews with Christian sports personalities and features on teens making unusual achievements or involved in unique pursuits—spiritual emphasis a must. "Articles on issues of particular importance to teens—drugs, pregnancy, school, jobs, recreational activities, etc. Christian element not necessary on morally neutral issues." Buys 1-3 mss/issue. Query or send complete ms. No phone queries. Length: 500-1,800 words. Pays 7-10¢/word for unsolicited mss; 10-15¢ for assigned articles. Sometimes pays expenses of writers on assignment.
Fiction: Needs stories involving problems common to teens (dating, family, alcohol and drugs, peer pressure, school, sex, talking about one's faith to non-believers, standing up for convictions, etc.) in which the resolution (or lack of it) is true to our readers' experiences. "In other words, no happily-ever-after endings, last-page spiritual conversions, or pat answers to complex problems. We are interested in the everyday (though still profound) experiences of teen life. If the story was written just to make a point, or grind the author's favorite axe, we don't want it. Most of our stories feature a protagonist 14-17 years old. The key is the spiritual element—how the protagonist deals with or makes sense of his/her situation in light of Christian spiritual principles and ideals, without being preached to or preaching to another character or to the reader." Buys 30 mss/year. Send complete ms. Length: 800-1,800 words. Pays 7-10¢/word for unsolicited mss; 10-15¢/word for assigned fiction.
Tips: "Articles for *TQ* need to be written in an upbeat style attractive to teens. No preaching. Writers must be familiar with the characteristics of today's teenagers in order to write for them."

WITH MAGAZINE, Faith and Life Press and Mennonite Publishing House, 722 Main St., Box 347, Newton KS 67114. (316)283-5100. Coeditors: Eddy Hall, Carol Duerksen, Cynthia Linscheid. 30% freelance written. Monthly magazine for teenagers. "We approach Christianity from an Anabaptist-

For explanation of symbols, see the Key to Symbols and Abbreviations on Page 5. For unfamiliar words, see the Glossary.

Mennonite perspective. Our purpose is to disciple youth within congregations." Circ. 6,500. **Pays on acceptance.** Byline given. Buys one-time rights. Submit seasonal/holiday material 6 months in advance. Simultaneous and previously published submissions OK. Query for electronic submissions. Reports in 6 weeks on queries; 4 months on mss. Sample copy free with 9×12 SAE and 98¢ postage. Writer's guidelines for #10 SASE.

Nonfiction: Humor, personal experience, religious, youth. Buys 15 mss/year. Send complete ms. Length: 400-1,500 words. Pays 4¢/word for simultaneous rights; 2¢/word for reprint rights for unsolicited articles.

Photos: Sometimes pays the expenses of writers on assignment. Send photos with submission. Reviews 8×10 prints. Offers $10-50 per photo. Identification of subjects required. Buys one-time rights.

Fiction: Humorous, religious, youth. Buys 12 mss/year. Send complete ms. Length: 500-1,500 words. Payment same as nonfiction.

Poetry: Avant-garde, free verse, haiku, light verse, traditional. Buys 20-25 poems. Pays $10-35.

Tips: "We're looking for more wholesome humor, not necessarily religious—fiction, nonfiction, cartoons, light verse. We're eager to see reprints from today's top writers for Christian teens."

YOUNG SALVATIONIST, The Salvation Army, 799 Bloomfield Ave., Verona NJ 07044. (201)239-0606. Editor: Capt. Robert R. Hostetler. 75% freelance written. Works with a small number of new/unpublished writers each year. Monthly Christian magazine for high school teens. "Only material with a definite Christian emphasis or from a Christian perspective will be considered." Circ. 48,000. **Pays on acceptance.** Publishes ms an average of 10 months after acceptance. Byline given. Buys first North American serial rights, first rights, one-time rights or second serial (reprint) rights. Submit seasonal/holiday material 6 months in advance. Reports in 2 weeks on queries; 1 month on mss. Sample copy for 8½×11 SAE with 3 first class stamps; writer's guidelines for #10 SASE.

Nonfiction: Inspirational, how-to (Bible study, workshop skills), humor, interview/profile, personal experience, photo feature, religious. "Articles should deal with issues of relevance to teens today; avoid 'preachiness' or moralizing." Buys 60 mss/year. Send complete ms. Length: 500-1,200 words. Pays 5¢/word for unsolicited mss; 6¢/word for assigned articles.

Columns/Departments: SALSpots (media-related news and human interest from a Christian perspective, book and record reviews). Buys 10-12 mss/year. Send complete ms. Length: 50-200 words. Pays 5¢/word.

Fiction: Adventure, fantasy, humorous, religious, romance, science fiction—all from a Christian perspective. Length: 500-1,200 words. Pays 5-6¢/word.

Tips: "Study magazine, familiarize yourself with the unique 'Salvationist' perspective of *Young Salvationist*; learn a little about the Salvation Army; media, sports, sex and dating are strongest appeal."

YOUTH UPDATE, St. Anthony Messenger Press, 1615 Republic St., Cincinnati OH 45210. (513)241-5615. Editor: Carol Ann Morrow. 90% freelance written. Monthly newsletter of faith life for teenagers. Designed to attract, instruct, guide and challenge Catholics of high school age by applying the Gospel to modern problems/situations. Circ. 38,000. **Pays on acceptance.** Publishes ms an average of 6 months after acceptance. Byline given. Reports in 2 months. Sample copy and writer's guidelines for #10 SASE.

Nonfiction: Inspirational, practical self-help and spiritual. Buys 12 mss/year. Query. Length: 2,200-2,300 words. Pays $350-400. Sometimes pays expenses of writers on assignment.

‡ZING, Teen Throbs, Tempo Publications, Suite 2201, 475 Park Ave. South, New York NY 10016. (212)213-8620. Editor: Anne Raso. Monthly magazine covering teen entertainers. "*Zing* is a fanzine for teens with a light and fluffy style." Estab. 1986. Circ. 150,000. Pays 2 months after publication. Byline sometimes given. No kill fee. Buys first rights. Submit seasonal/holiday material 4 months in advance. Simultaneous submissions OK. Free sample copy.

Nonfiction: Interview/profile, photo feature. One-shots on hot teen music stars and shows. "No articles about newcomers—we can get those interviews ourselves." Query with published clips. Length: 250-1,000 words. Pays $50-100.

Photos: State availability of photos with submission. Reviews transparencies (standard size) and 5×7 or 8×10 prints. Offers $25-150. Captions required. Buys one-time rights.

Columns/Departments: Hollywood Connection (teen star gossip), 1,000; Foxy Finds (newcomer teen stars), 1,000 words. Buys 2 mss/year. Query. Length: 500-1,000 words. Pays $50-100.

Tips: "Call or write with a letter stating ideas for story. We are most open to general feature stories on teen stars—like New Kids on the Block or Paula Abdul."

Travel, Camping and Trailer

Travel magazines give travelers indepth information about destinations, detailing the best places to go, attractions in the area and sites to see—but they also keep them up-to-date about potential negative aspects of these destinations. Publications in this category tell tourists and campers the where-tos and how-tos of travel. This category is extremely competitive, demanding quality writing, background information and professional photography. Each has its own slant and should be studied carefully before sending submissions.

AAA GOING PLACES, Magazine for Today's Traveler, AAA Auto Club South, 1515 No. Westshore Blvd., Tampa FL 33607. (813)289-5923. Editor: Phyllis Zeno. Managing Editor: Milana Petty. 50% freelance written. Bimonthly magazine on auto news, driving trips or tips and travel. Estab. 1982. Circ. 845,000. Pays on publication. Publishes ms an average of 3-6 months after acceptance. Byline given. Buys one-time rights. Submit seasonal/holiday material 9 months in advance. Simultaneous submissions OK. Reports in 2 months. Sample copy for 8 × 10 SAE with $1 postage. Free writer's guidelines.
Nonfiction: Historical/nostalgic, how-to, humor, interview/profile, personal experience, photo feature, travel. Special issues include Cruise Guide and Europe Issue. Buys 15 mss/year. Send complete ms. Length: 500-1,500 words. Pays $15 per printed page.
Photos: State availability of photos with submission. Reviews 2 × 2 transparencies. Offers no additional payment for photos accepted with ms. Captions required.
Columns/Departments: AAAway We Go (local attractions in Florida, Georgia or Tennessee.)

ACCENT, Meridian Publishing Inc., 1720 Washington, P.O. Box 10010, Ogden UT 84409. (801)394-9446. 60-70% freelance written. Works with a small number of new/unpublished writers each year. A monthly inhouse travel magazine distributed by various companies to employees, customers, stockholders, etc. "Readers are predominantly upscale, mainstream, family oriented." Circ. 110,000. **Pays on acceptance.** Publishes ms an average of 8 months after acceptance. Byline given. Buys first rights, second serial (reprint) rights and nonexclusive reprint rights. Simultaneous and previously published submissions OK. Reports in 6 weeks. Sample copy $1 and 9 × 12 SAE; writer's guidelines for #10 SASE.
Nonfiction: "We want upbeat pieces slanted toward the average traveler, but we use some exotic travel. Resorts, cruises, hiking, camping, health retreats, historic sites, sports vacations, national or state forests and parks are all featured. No articles without original color photos, except with travel tips. We also welcome pieces on travel tips and ways to travel." Buys 40 mss/year. Query. Length: 1,200 words. Pays 15¢/word.
Photos: Send photos with ms. Pays $35 for color transparencies; $50 for cover. Captions and model releases required. Buys one-time rights.
Tips: "Write about interesting places. We are inundated with queries for stories on California and the southeastern coast. Excellent color transparencies are essential. Most rejections are because of poor quality photography or the writer didn't study the market. We are using three times as many domestic pieces as foreign because of our readership. Address queries to Attention: Editor."

ADVENTURE ROAD, 560 Lexington Ave., 19th Floor, New York NY 10022. (212)756-7640. Editor: Marilyn Holstein. 100% freelance written. Bimonthly magazine that features domestic, general interest travel articles that stimulate reader to travel. Circ. 1.5 million. **Pays on acceptance.** Publishes ms an average of 4 months after acceptance. Byline given. Offers 25% kill fee. Buys first North American serial rights. Simultaneous and previously published submissions OK. Sample for 9 × 12 SAE. Writer's guidelines for #10 SASE.
Nonfiction: Travel. "No first-person articles." Buys 21 mss/year. Query with published clips. Length: 800-1,800 words. Pays $300-750. Sometimes pays expenses of writers on assignment.
Photos: State availability of photos with submission. (Do not send unsolicited transparencies). Offers $200 minimum per photo. Captions required. Buys one-time rights.
Columns/Departments: Calendar (events listing, domestic), 90 entries; Weekend Wanderer (3-day trips from a major city), 1,000 words; Motor Talk (automotive tips), 800 words and Certicare Adviser (Q&A from readers), 800 words. Buys 30 mss/year. Query with published clips. Pays $300-450.

AMOCO TRAVELER, K.L. Publications, Suite 105, 2001 Killebrew Dr., Bloomington MN 55425. Editor: Mary Lou Brooks. 80% freelance written. A quarterly magazine published for the Amoco Traveler Club. Circ. 55,000. Pays on acceptance by client. Byline given. Buys various rights. "This publication is a mix of original and reprinted material." Previously published submissions OK. Submit seasonal/holiday material 8 months in advance. Simultaneous submissions OK. Reports in 1 month. Sample copy for 9 × 12 SAE with 3 first class stamps. Writer's guidelines for #10 SASE.
Nonfiction: Focus is on U.S. destinations by car, although occasionally will use a foreign destination. Traveler Roads showcases a North American city or area, its attractions, history and accomodations; Traveler Focus features a romantic, getaway destination for the armchair traveler; Traveler Weekends focuses on an activity-oriented destination. Length: 1,200-1,500 words. Pays $325-425 for originals; $100-150 for reprints.

Columns/Departments: Healthwise (travel-related health tips). Length: 500-600 words. Pays $175. **Photos:** Reviews 35mm transparencies. No b&w. Pay varies.

ASU TRAVEL GUIDE, ASU Travel Guide, Inc., 1525 E. Francisco Blvd., San Rafael CA 94901. (415)459-0300. FAX: (415)459-0494. Managing Editor: Christopher Gil. 90% freelance written. Quarterly guidebook covering international travel features and travel discounts for well-traveled airline employees. Estab. 1970. Circ. 60,000. Payment terms negotiable. Publishes ms an average of 18 months after acceptance. Byline given. Buys first North American serial rights, first and second rights to the same material, and second serial (reprint) rights to material originally published elsewhere. Makes work-for-hire assignments. Submit seasonal/holiday material 6 months in advance. Simultaneous queries and simultaneous and previously published submissions OK. Reports in 1 month. Writer's guidelines for #10 SASE.
Nonfiction: International travel articles "similar to those run in consumer magazines." Not interested in amateur efforts from inexperienced travelers or personal experience articles that don't give useful information to other travelers. Buys 17 ms/year. Destination pieces only; no "Tips On Luggage" articles. "We will be accepting fewer manuscripts and relying more on our established group of freelance contributors." Unsolicited mss or queries without SASE will not be acknowledged. No telephone queries. Length: 1,200-1,500 words. Pays $200.
Photos: "Interested in clear, high-contrast photos; we prefer not to receive material without photos." Reviews 5×7 and 8×10 b&w prints. "Payment for photos is included in article price; photos from tourist offices are acceptable."
Tips: "Query with samples of travel writing and a list of places you've recently visited. We appreciate clean and simple style. Keep verbs in the active tense and involve the reader in what you write. Avoid 'cute' writing, coined words and stale cliches. The most frequent mistakes made by writers in completing an article for us are: 1) Lazy writing—using words to describe a place that could describe any destination such as 'there is so much to do in (fill in destination) that whole guidebooks have been written about it'; 2) Including fare and tour package information—our readers make arrangements through their own airline."

BACKPACKER, Rodale Press, Inc., 33 E. Minor St., Emmaus PA 18098. (215)967-8296. Editor: John Viehman. Managing Editor: Tom Shealey. 25% freelance written. 8 times/year magazine covering wilderness travel. Estab. 1973. Circ. 190,000. **Pays on acceptance.** Byline given. Offers 25% kill fee. Buys one-time rights or all rights. Reports in 2 months. Writer's guidelines for #10 SAE with 1 first class stamp.
Nonfiction: Essays, exposé, historical/nostalgic, how-to (expedition planner), humor, inspirational, interview/profile, new product, opinion, personal experience, technical and travel. No step-by-step accounts of what you did on your summer vacation: stories that chronicle every rest stop and gulp of water. Query with published clips and SASE. Length: 740-3,000 words. Pays $400. Sometimes pays (pre-determined) expenses of writers on assignment.
Photos: State availability of photos with submission. Amount varies—depends on size of photo used. Buys one-time rights or all rights.
Columns/Departments: What we want are features that let us and the readers "feel" the place, and experience your wonderment, excitement, disappointment or other emotions encountered "out there." If we feel like we've been there after reading your story, you've succeeded. Footnotes "News From All Over" (adventure, environment, wildlife, trails, techniques, organizations, special interests—well-written, entertaining, short, newsy item) 50-500 words; Geosphere (essay about some biological, psychological or scientific aspect of the natural world, often takes a philosophical approach, should offer the reader a fresh perspective on the natural world) 750-1,200 words; Body Language (in-the-field column) 750-1,200 words; Moveable Feast (food-related aspects of wilderness: nutrition, cooking techniques, recipes, products and gear), 500-750 words; Weekend Wilderness (three brief but detailed guides to wilderness areas, providing thorough trip-planning information, only enough anecdote to give a hint, then the where/when/hows) 500-750 words; Technique (ranging from beginner to expert focus, written by people with solid expertise, details ways to improve performance, how-to-do-it instructions, information on equipment manufacturers and places readers can go), 750-1,500 words; and Backcountry (personal perspectives, quirky and idiosyncratic, humorous critiques, manifestos and misadventures, interesting angle, lesson, revelation or moral), 750-1,200 words. Buys 25-50 mss/year. Query with published clips. Pays $25-350. No phone calls regarding story ideas. Written queries only.
Tips: "Our best advice is to read the publication—most freelancers don't know the magazine at all. The best way to break in is with an article for the Backcountry, Weekend Wilderness or Footnotes Department."

BAJA TIMES, Editorial Playas De Rosarito, S.A., P.O. Box 5577, Chula Vista CA 91912-5577. Editor: John W. Utley. 90% freelance written. Monthly tourist and travel publication on Baja California, Mexico. "Oriented to the Baja California, Mexico aficionada—the tourist and those Americans who are living in Baja California or have their vacation homes there. Articles should be slanted to Baja." Pays on publication. Publishes ms an average of 8 months after acceptance. Byline given. Buys first rights. Submit seasonal/holiday material 4 months in advance. Sample copy for 9×12 SAE with 4 first class stamps; free writer's guidelines.

Nonfiction: General interest, historical/nostalgic, humor, personal experience, photo feature, travel. All with Baja California slant. "Nothing that describes any negative aspects of Mexico (bribes, bad police, etc.). We are a positive publication." Query with or without published clips, or submit complete ms. Length: 750-2,100 words. Pays $50-100 for assigned articles; $35-50 for unsolicited articles. Sometimes pays expenses of writers on assignment.

Photos: Send photos with submission. Reviews 5×7 prints. Captions and identification of subjects required. Buys one-time rights.

Tips: "Take a chance—send in that Baja California related article. We guarantee to read them all. Over the years we have turned up some real winners from our writers—many who do not have substantial experience. The entire publication is open. We buy an average of 6 freelance each issue. Virtually any subject is acceptable as long as it has a Baja California slant. Remember Tijuana, Mexico (on the border with San Diego, CA) is the busiest border crossing in the world. We are always interested in material relating to Tijuana, Rosarito, Ensenada, San Felipe, LaPaz."

‡BRIO, The Magazine of Costa Cruise Lines, Cruise Passenger Network, Suite 245, 2001 W. Main St., Stamford CT 06902. (203)359-8626. Editorial Director: Barbara Coats. 80% freelance written. Magazine published 3 times/year covering the Caribbean. The magazine does not cover cruising, but is meant as an enhancement of the cruise/port experience (arts, culture, natural history). Estab. 1989. Circ. 150,000. **Pays on acceptance.** Publishes ms an average of 3 months after acceptance. Byline given. Offers 25% kill fee. Buys first rights. Submit seasonal/holiday material 6 months in advance. Query for electronic submissions. Reports in 1 month. Sample copy for 9×12 SAE.

Nonfiction: Book excerpts, general interest, historical, interview/profile, new product, photo feature, arts, nature. Buys 30-40 mss/year. Query with published clips. Length: 300-1,500 words. Pays $300-1,000 for assigned articles. Sometimes pays expenses of writers on assignment.

Photos: State availability of photos with submission. Reviews contact sheets. Offers no additional payment for photos accepted with ms. Identification of subjects required. Buys one-time rights.

Columns/Departments: Collecting (collectors' items, who collects, why), Perspective (interview with celebrity on newsworthy subject), and Ultimate Traveler (essay on interesting travel "truth"). Query with published clips. Length: 650 words maximum. Pays $300-600.

CAMPING & RV MAGAZINE, Camping Voice of Midwest, Joe Jones Publishing, P.O. Box 337, Iola WI 54945. (715)445-5000. FAX: (715)445-4053. Editor: Barbara Case. 75% freelance written. Monthly magazine on camping in the Midwest states. "We accept both casual and technical articles dealing with camping, and destination pieces from our coverage area." Estab. 1985. Circ. 25,000. Pays on publication. Publishes ms an average of 6 months after acceptance. Byline given. Buys first rights, one-time rights or second serial (reprint) rights. Submit seasonal/holiday material 3 months in advance. Previously published submissions OK. Free sample copy and writer's guidelines.

Nonfiction: General interest, how-to, personal experience, photo feature, technical, and travel. "No articles of destinations out of our coverage area." Buys 60 mss/year. Send complete ms. Length: 1,000-2,000 words. Pays 5¢/word.

Photos: State availability of photos with submission. Reviews prints. Pays $5 per photo. Identification of subjects required. Buys one-time rights.

Columns/Departments: Living on Wheels; Camping Comforts; RV Wife and Care of RV (hints, suggestions, general interest, technical, equipment care), 1,000 words. Buys 50 mss/year. Query. Pays 5¢/word.

Fillers: Anecdotes and facts. Buys 12/year. Length: 500-1,000 words. Pays 3-5¢/word.

Tips: "Write from a campground background—be knowledgeable about how and where to camp as well as camping related activities."

CAMPING TODAY, Official Publication of National Campers & Hikers Association, 126 Hermitage Rd., Butler PA 16001. (412)283-7401. Editors: DeWayne and June Johnston. 30% freelance written. Prefers to work with published/established writers. The monthly official membership publication of the NCHA, "the largest nonprofit family camping and RV organization in the United States and Canada. Members are heavily oriented toward RV travel, both weekend and extended vacations. A small segment is interested in hiking. Concentration is on member activities in chapters. Group is also interested in conservation and wildlife. The majority of members are retired." Circ. 27,500. Pays on publication. Publishes ms an average of 6 months after acceptance. Byline given. Buys one-time rights. Submit seasonal/holiday material 3 months in advance. Simultaneous and previously published submissions OK. Reports in 1 month. Sample copy and guidelines for 4 first class stamps or writer's guidelines for #10 SASE.

Nonfiction: Travel (interesting places to visit by RV, camping); humor (camping or travel related, please, no "our first campout stories"); interview/profile (interesting campers); new products and technical (RVs related). Buys 20-25 mss/year. Send complete ms with photos. Length: 750-2,000 words. Pays $50-150.

Photos: Send photos with ms. Need b&w or sharp color prints inside (we can make prints from slides) and vertical transparencies for cover. Captions required.

Tips: "Freelance material on RV travel, RV maintenance/safety, and items of general camping interest throughout the United States and Canada will receive special attention."

CARIBBEAN TRAVEL AND LIFE, Suite 830, 8403 Colesville Rd., Silver Spring MD 20910. (301)588-2300. Editor: Veronica Gould Stoddart. 90% freelance written. Prefers to work with published/established writers. A bimonthly magazine covering travel to the Caribbean, Bahamas and Bermuda. Estab. 1985. Circ. 100,000. Pays on publication. Publishes ms an average of 3 months after acceptance. Byline given. Offers 25% kill fee. Buys first North American serial rights. Submit seasonal/holiday material 6 months in advance. Reports in 2 months. Sample copy for 9×12 SAE with 5 first class stamps; writer's guidelines for #10 SASE.

Nonfiction: General interest, how-to, interview/profile, culture, personal experience and travel. No "guidebook rehashing; superficial destination pieces or critical exposes." Buys 30 mss/year. Query with published clips. Length: 2,000-2,500 words. Pays $550.

Photos: Send photos with submission. Reviews 35mm transparencies. Offers $75-400 per photo. Captions and identification of subjects required. Buys one-time rights.

Columns/Departments: Resort Spotlight (in-depth review of luxury resort); Tradewinds (focus on one particular kind of water sport or sailing/cruising); Island Buys (best shopping for luxury goods, crafts, duty-free); Island Spice (best cuisine and/or restaurant reviews with recipes); all 1,000-1,500 words; Caribbeana (short items on great finds in travel, culture, and special attractions), 500 words. Buys 36 mss/year. Query with published clips or send complete ms. Length: 500-1,250 words. Pays $75-200.

Tips: "We are especially looking for stories with a personal touch and lively, entertaining anecdotes, as well as strong insight into people and places being covered. Also prefers stories with focus on people, i.e, colorful personalities, famous people, etc. Writer should demonstrate why he/she is the best person to do that story based on extensive knowledge of the subject, frequent visits to destination, residence in destination, specialty in field."

‡COAST TO COAST MAGAZINE, A Publication for the Members of Coast to Coast Resorts, 64 Inverness Drive E., Denver CO 80112. (303)790-2267. FAX: (303)397-7657. Editor: Valerie Rogers. Associate Editor: Todd Runestad. 80% freelance written. Travel magazine for members of Coast to Coast Resorts; published 8 times/year. Estab. 1972. Circ. 300,000. **Pays on acceptance.** Publishes ms an average of 3 months after acceptance. Byline given. Offers ⅓ of amount kill fee. Buys first North American serial rights. Submit seasonal/holiday material 5 months in advance. Query for electronic submissions. Reports in 1 month on queries; 2 months on mss. Sample copy $2 with 9×12 SASE.

Nonfiction: Book excerpts, essays, general interest, historical/nostalgic, how-to, humor, inspirational, interview/profile, new product, opinion (does not mean letters to the editor), personal experience, photo feature, technical, travel. Buys 35 mss/year. Query with published clips, or send complete ms. Length: 500-2,500 words. Pays $75-500.

Photos: Send photos with submission. Reviews transparencies. Offers $50-600 per photo. Identification of subjects required. Buys one-time rights.

Columns/Departments: Buys 15 mss/year. Query with published clips. Send complete ms. Length: 1,000-1,800 words. Pays $200-400.

Fiction: Adventure, novel excerpts, slice-of-life vignettes.

Tips: "Send published clips or mss relating to North American travel that are lively and fun to read, informational and insightful."

THE COOL TRAVELER, The Rome Cappucino Review, P.O. Box 11975, Philadelphia PA 19145. (215)440-8257. Editor: Bob Moore. Managing Editor: MaryBeth Feeney. 100% freelance written. Quarterly publication covering travel. "Our audience has a zest for travel. Our readers usually have a college education and travel to experience different places and people. We do not emphasize affluence but rather the joy of travel." Estab. 1988. Circ. 750-1,250. Pays on publication. Publishes ms an average of 2-3 months after acceptance. Byline given. Buys one-time rights. Submit seasonal/holiday material 2 months in advance. Simultaneous and previously published submissions OK. Query for electronic submissions. Reports in 4 weeks. Free writer's guidelines.

Nonfiction: Personal experience, travel, art history. Christmas Issue, International Festival Issue. "We don't want a listing of names and prices but personal experiences and unusual experiences." Buys 10 mss/year. Send complete ms. Length: 2,500 words maximum. Pays $5-20 for unsolicited articles.

Columns/Departments: Seasonal (material pertaining to a certain time of year: like a winter festival or summer carnival), 2,500 words maximum. Pays $5-20.

Poetry: Avant-garde, free verse, haiku, light verse, traditional. No poetry that is too sentimental. Buys 10 poems/year. Submit maximum 10 poems. Length: 5-75 lines. Pays $5-20.

Tips: "Writer should have firsthand knowledge and experience of their topic or topics and be able to give the reader a feeling of being there through cultural, artistic and visual references. All areas are open to freelancers. The same tips apply toward seasonal material. The writer should connote to the reader a feeling of personal experience through the usage of cultural, artistic and visual references." Articles should be written in first person.

CRUISE TRAVEL MAGAZINE, World Publishing Co., 990 Grove St., Evanston IL 60201. (708)491-6440. Editor: Robert Meyers. Managing Editor: Charles Doherty. 95% freelance written. A bimonthly magazine on cruise travel. "This is a consumer oriented travel publication covering the world of pleasure cruising on large cruise ships (with some coverage of smaller ships), including ports, travel tips, roundups." Estab. 1979. **Pays on acceptance.** Publishes ms an average of 5 months after acceptance. Byline given. Offers ½ kill fee. Buys first North American serial rights, one-time rights, or second serial (reprint) rights. Simultaneous and previously published submissions OK. Sample copy $3 with 9 × 12 SAE and 6 oz. first class postage. Writer's guidelines for #10 SASE.

Nonfiction: General interest, historical/nostalgic, interview/profile, personal experience, photo feature, travel. "No daily cruise 'diary', My First Cruise, etc." Buys 72 mss/year. Query with or without published clips or send complete ms. Length: 500-2,000 words. Pay $100-400.

Photos: Send photos with submission. Reviews transparencies and prints. "Must be color, 35m preferred (other format OK); color prints second choice." Offers no additional payment for photos accepted with ms "but pay more for well-illustrated ms." Captions and identification of subjects required. Buys one-time rights.

Fillers: Anecdotes, facts. Buys 3 mss/year. Length: 300-700 words. Pays $75-200.

Tips: "Do your homework. Know what we do and what sorts of things we publish. Know the cruise industry—we can't use novices. Good, sharp, bright color photography opens the door fast."

‡CURRENTS, The Magazine Published for Carnival Passengers, Cruise Passenger Network, Suite 245, 2001 W. Main St., Stamford CT 06902. (203)359-8626. Editorial Director: Barbara Coats. 80% freelance written. Magazine published 3 times/year covering the Caribbean. The magazine does not cover cruising but is meant as an enhancement of the cruise/port experience (arts, culture, natural history of the islands). Estab. 1987. Circ. 544,000. **Pays on acceptance.** Publishes ms an average of 3 months after acceptance. Offers 25% kill fee. Buys first rights. Submit seasonal/holiday material 6 months in advance. Query for electronic submissions. Reports in 1 month. Sample copy for 9 × 12 SAE.

Nonfiction: Book excerpts, general interest, historical, inteview/profile, new product, photo feature, arts, nature. Buys 30-40 mss/year. Query with published clips. Length: 300-1,500 words. Pays $300-1,000 for assigned articles. Sometimes pays expenses of writers on assignment.

Photos: State availability of photos with submission. Reviews contact sheets. Offers no additional payment of photos accepted with ms. Identification of subjects required. Buys one-time rights.

Columns/Departments: Profile (Caribbean personality; ship captain), Travel Essay (on a universally recognized travel phenomenon), First Person (an adventure in the Caribbean, i.e. diving, parasailing). Buys 20 mss/year. Query with published clips. Length: 500 words. Pays $300-600.

‡DESTINATION WASHINGTON, The Official Washington State Travelers' Guide, GTE Discovery Publications, Inc., Suite 101, 22026 20th Ave. SE, Bothell WA 98021. (206)487-6100. Managing Editor: Karen D. Parkin. 50% freelance written. Annual magazine covering consumer travel. "*Destination Washington* is the state's official travel publication that provides an overview of the state's nine tourism regions. Copy is subject to review by editor, regional tourism chairs, and the Washington State Tourism Development Division." Estab. 1987. Circ. 325,000. **Pays on acceptance.** Publishes ms an average of 6 months after acceptance. Byline given sometimes. Kill fee varies, usually 25%. Buys first rights and world-wide reprint rights. Query for electronic submissions. Free sample copy, depending on availability.

Nonfiction: Essays (travel-related), personal experience (travel-related), photo feature and travel. Query with published clips. Length: 100-400 words. Pays $1 per word.

Photos: State availability of photos with submission. Reviews contact sheets, negatives, standard transparencies. No prints. Model releases and identification of subjects required. Payment set by photo editor. Buys one-time rights.

Fillers: Facts. Buys 6/year. Length: 100-250 words. Pays $1 per word.

Tips: "Send samples of published clips. We are looking for anything related to travel in Washington state. Please do not call."

ENDLESS VACATION, Endless Vacation Publications, Inc., P.O. 80260, Indianapolis IN 46280. (317)871-9500. Editor: Helen W. O'Guinn. Prefers to work with published/established writers. A 10 times per year magazine covering travel destinations, activities and issues that enhance the lives of vacationers. Estab. 1974. Circ. 800,000. **Pays on acceptance.** Publishes ms an average of 6 months after acceptance. Byline given. Buys first worldwide serial rights. Simultaneous submissions OK. Reports in 1 month on queries and manuscripts. Sample copy $5; writer's guidelines for SAE with 1 first class stamp.

Nonfiction: Contact Manuscript Editor. Travel. Buys 24 mss/year (approx). Most are from established writers already published in *Endless Vacation. Accepts very few unsolicited pieces.* Query with published clips. Length: 1,000-2,000 words. Pays $500-1,000 for assigned articles; pays $250-800 for unsolicited articles. Sometimes pays the expenses of writers on assignment.

Photos: State availability of photos with submissions. Reviews 4×5 transparencies and 35mm slides. Offers $100-500/photo. Model releases and identification of subjects required. Buys one-time rights.

Columns/Departments: Healthy Traveler (vacation health-related topics); Weekender (on domestic weekend vacation travel). Query with published clips. Length: 800-1,000 words. Pays $150-300. Sometimes pays the expenses of writers on assignment. Also news items for Facts, Fads and Fun Stuff column on new travel news, products or problems. Length: 100-200 words, $50 per item.

Tips: "We will continue to focus on travel trends and resort and upscale destinations. Articles must be packed with pertinent facts and applicable how-tos. Information — addresses, phone numbers, dates of events, costs — must be current and accurate. We like to see a variety of stylistic approaches, but in all cases the lead must be strong. A writer should realize that we require first-hand knowledge of the subject and plenty of practical information. For further understanding of *Endless Vacation*'s direction, the writer should study the magazine and guidelines for writers."

‡FAMILY MOTOR COACHING, Official Publication of the Family Motor Coach Association, 8291 Clough Pike, Cincinnati OH 45244-2796. (513)474-3622. FAX: (513)474-2332. Editor: Pamela Wisby Kay. Associate Editor: Robbin Maue. 80% freelance written. "We prefer that writers be experienced RVers." Emphasizes travel by motorhome, motorhome mechanics, maintenance and other technical information. Monthly magazine. Estab. 1963. Circ. 90,000. **Pays on acceptance.** Publishes ms an average of 8 months after acceptance. Buys first North American serial rights. Byline given. Submit seasonal/holiday material 4 months in advance. Reports in 2 months. Sample copy $2.50; writer's guidelines for #10 SASE.

Nonfiction: Motorhome travel and living on the road; travel (various areas of country accessible by motor coach); how-to (modify motor coach features); bus conversions; humor; interview/profile; new product; technical; and nostalgia. Buys 15-20 mss/issue. Query with published clips . Length: 1,000-2,000 words. Pays $100-500.

Photos: State availability of photos with query. Offers no additional payment for b&w contact sheets, 35mm or 2¼×2¼ color transparencies. Captions and model releases required. Buys one-time rights.

Tips: "The greatest number of contributions that we receive are travel; therefore that area is the most competitive. However, it also represents the easiest way to break in to our publication. Articles should be written for those traveling by self-contained motor home. The destinations must be accessible to RV travelers and any peculiar road conditions should be mentioned."

GREAT EXPEDITIONS, P.O. Box 8000-411, Sumas WA 98295; or P.O. Box 8000-411, Abbotsford, British Columbia V2S 6H1 Canada. Editor: Craig Henderson. 90% freelance written. Eager to work with new/unpublished writers. Quarterly magazine covering "off-the-beaten-path" destinations, outdoor recreation, cultural discovery, budget travel, socially-responsible tourism and working abroad. Estab. 1978. Circ. 8,000. Pays on publication. Buys first and second (reprint) rights. Simultaneous queries, and simultaneous and previously published submissions OK. Send SASE for return of article and photos. Reports in 2 months. Sample copy $4; free writer's guidelines.

Nonfiction: Articles range from very adventurous (living with an isolated tribe in the Philippines) to mildly adventurous (Spanish language school vacations in Guatemala and Mexico). We also like to see "how-to" pieces for adventurous travelers (i.e., How to Sail Around the World for Free, Swapping Homes with Residents of Other Countries, How to Get in on an Archaeological Dig). Buys 30 mss/year. Pays $60 maximum. Length 1,000-3,000 words.

Photos: B&w photos, color prints or slides should be sent with article. Captions required.

Tips: "It's best to send for a sample copy for a first-hand look at the style of articles we are looking for. If possible, we appreciate practical information for travelers, either in the form of a sidebar or incorporated into the article, detailing how to get there, where to stay, specific costs, where to write for visas or travel information."

‡HIDEAWAYS GUIDE, Hideaways International, 15 Goldsmith St., Littleton MA 01460. FAX: (508)486-8525. Editor: Michael Thiel. Managing Editor: Gail Richard. 10% freelance written. Magazine published 2 times/year—February, August. Also publishes 4 quarterly newsletters. Features travel/leisure and real estate information for upscale, affluent, educated, outdoorsy audience. Deals with unique vacation opportunities: vacation home renting, buying, exchanging, yacht/houseboat charters, adventure vacations, country inns and small resorts. Estab. 1979. Circ. 12,000. Pays on publication. Publishes ms an average of 4 months after acceptance. Byline given. Buys first North American serial rights, one-time rights and second serial (reprint) rights. Submit seasonal/holiday material 6 months in advance. Previously published submissions OK. Query for electronic submissions. Reports in 1 month on queries; 2 months on mss. Sample copy $15; writer's guidelines for #10 SASE.

Nonfiction: How-to (with focus on personal experience: vacation home renting, exchanging, buying, selling, yacht and house boat chartering); travel (intimate out-of-the-way spots to visit). Articles on "learning" vacations: scuba, sailing, flying, cooking, shooting, golf, tennis, photography, etc. Buys 5-10 mss/year. Query. Length: 800-1,500 words. Pays $75-150.

Photos: State availability of photos with query letter or ms or send photos with accompanying query or ms. Reviews transparencies. Pays negotiable fee. Captions and identification of subjects required. Buys one-time rights.

Tips: "The most frequent mistakes made by writers in completing an article for us are that they are too impersonal with no photos and not enough focus or accommodations."

HOME & AWAY, AAA Home & Away Inc., P.O. Box 3535, Omaha NE 68103. Did not want to be listed.

‡LEISURE WHEELS MAGAZINE, Murray Publications Ltd., Box 7302, Station "E", Calgary, Alberta, T3C 3M2 Canada. (403)263-2707. Editor: Murray Gimbel. 75% freelance written. Works with a small number of new/unpublished writers each year; eager to work with new/unpublished writers. Bimonthly magazine covering Canadian recreational vehicle travel. Circ. 47,700. Pays on publication. Publishes ms an average of 2 months after acceptance. Byline given. Buys second serial (reprint) rights. Submit seasonal/holiday material 2 months in advance. Sample copy 75¢; free writer's guidelines.

Nonfiction: Travel and outdoor leisure-time hobbies. Buys 12 mss/year. Query with published clips. Length: 1,000-2,000 words. Pays $135-200. Sometimes pays the expenses of writers on assignment.

Photos: State availability of photos. Pays $15-25 for 5x11 color prints; $10-20 for b&w 5x11 prints. Identification of subjects required. Buys one-time rights.

Columns/Departments: Buys 12 mss/year. Query with or without published clips. Length: 750-1,000 words. Pays $110-150.

Fiction: Adventure and humorous (relating to travel). Buys 6 mss/year. Query with or without published clips. Length: 1,000-1,500 words. Pays $135-150.

Fillers: Jokes and anecdotes. Buys 6 mss/year. Length: 500-700 words. Pays $50-70.

‡LEISUREWAYS, Canada Wide Magazines Ltd., Suite 1707, 2 Carlton St., Toronto, Ontario M5B 1J3 Canada. (416)595-5007. Editor: Deborah Milton. 80% freelance written. Bimonthly member magazine for CAA covering travel and leisure. "*Leisureways* goes to 580,000 members of Canadian Automobile Association in Ontario. Primarily travel articles plus auto-related material." Circ. 580,000. **Pays on acceptance.** Byline given. Offers 50% kill fee. Buys all rights. Query for electronic submission. Free sample copy. Writer's guidelines for SAE.

Nonfiction: Interview/profile, photo feature, travel. Buys 70 mss/year. Query with published clips or send complete ms. Length: 300-1,800 words. Pays $350-1,000 for unsolicited articles (Canadian funds).

Photos: State availability of photos with submission. Reviews 35mm or any transparencies. Offers no additional payment for photos accepted with ms. Captions and identification of subjects required. Buys one-time rights.

Columns/Departments: Great Cities (profile of major cities), 1,000 words; Traveling Health (information for travelers on various health subjects), 1,000 words; Automotive (general interest), 500-1,500 words. Buys 25 mss/year. Query with published clips or send complete ms. Pays $350-750.

Tips: "We look for stories with interesting angles—a bit out of the ordinary. Travel pieces aimed at the mature traveler are particularly good for our readership. We have enough material for the next 6 issues."

THE MATURE TRAVELER, Travel Bonanzas for 49ers-Plus, GEM Publishing Group, Box 50820, Reno NV 89513. (702)786-7419. Editor: Gene E. Malott. 30% freelance written. Monthly newsletter on senior citizen travel. Circ. 2,200. **Pays on acceptance.** Publishes ms an average of 3 months after acceptance. Byline given. Offers 25% kill fee. Buys one-time rights. Submit seasonal/holiday material 3 months in advance. Simultaneous ("if we know about it") and previously published submissions OK. Reports in 2 weeks. Sample copy for $1 and #10 SAE with 45¢ postage. Writer's guidelines for SAE with 45¢ postage.

Nonfiction: Travel for seniors. "General travel and destination pieces should be senior-specific, aimed at 49ers +." Query. Length: 600-1,200 words. Pays $50-100.

Photos: State availability of photos with submission. Reviews contact sheets and b&w (only) prints. Captions required. Buys one-time rights.

Tips: "Read the guidelines and write stories to our readers' needs—not to the general public."

MEXICO WEST, Mexico West Travel Club, Inc., Suite 107, 3450 Bonita Rd., Chula Vista CA 91910. (619)585-3033. FAX: (619)421-6002. Editor: Shirley Miller. 50% freelance written. Monthly newsletter on Baja California; Mexico as a travel destination. "Yes, our readers are travelers to Mexico, especially Baja California. They are knowledgeable but are always looking for new places to see." Estab. 1975. Circ. 5,000. Pays on publication. Publishes an average of 2 months after acceptance. Byline given. Buys first North American serial rights. Submit seasonal/holiday material 3 months in advance. Previously published submissions OK. Free sample copy. Writer's guidelines for #10 SAE with 2 first class stamps.

Nonfiction: Historical, humor, interview, personal experience and travel. Buys 36-50 mss/year. Send complete ms. Length: 900-1,500 words. Pays $50.

Photos: State availability of photos with submission. Reviews 3×5 prints. Offers no additional payment for photos accepted with ms. Captions required. Buys one-time rights.

‡MICHIGAN LIVING, AAA Michigan, 1 Auto Club Dr., Dearborn MI 48126. (313)336-1211. Editor: Len Barnes. 50% freelance written. Emphasizes travel and auto use. Monthly magazine. Circ. 1 million. **Pays on acceptance.** Publishes ms an average of 6 months after acceptance. Buys first North American serial rights. Offers 100% kill fee. Byline given. Submit seasonal/holiday material 3 months in advance. Reports in 6 weeks. Free sample copy and writer's guidelines.

Nonfiction: Travel articles on U.S. and Canadian topics. Buys 50-60 unsolicited mss/year. Send complete ms. Length: 200-1,000 words. Pays $88-315.

Photos: Photos purchased with accompanying ms. Captions required. Pays $367 for cover photos; $50-220 for color transparencies; total purchase price for ms includes payment for b&w photos.

Tips: "In addition to descriptions of things to see and do, articles should contain accurate, current information on costs the traveler would encounter on his trip. Items such as lodging, meal and entertainment expenses should be included, not in the form of a balance sheet but as an integral part of the piece. We want the sounds, sights, tastes, smells of a place or experience so one will feel he has been there and knows if he wants to go back."

‡THE MIDWEST MOTORIST, AAA Auto Club of Missouri, 12901 North Forty Dr., St. Louis MO 63141. (314)576-7350. Editor: Michael J. Right. Managing Editor: Debbie Reinhardt. Associate Editor: Jill Beaverson. 70% freelance written. Bimonthly magazine on travel and auto-related topics. Primarily focuses on travel throughout the world; prefers stories that tell about sights and give solid travel tips. Circ. 375,000. **Pays on acceptance.** Publishes ms an average of 8 months after acceptance. Byline given. Not copyrighted. Buys one-time rights, simultaneous rights (rarely), and second serial (reprint) rights. Submit seasonal/holiday material 6-8 months in advance. Simultaneous queries, and simultaneous, photocopied and previously published submissions OK. Query for electronic submissions. Reports in 1 month when query is accompanied by SASE. Sample copy for 9×12 SAE and 4 first class stamps. Writer's guidelines for #10 SASE.

Nonfiction: General interest; historical/nostalgic; how-to; humor (with motoring or travel slant); interview/profile; personal experience; photo feature; technical (auto safety or auto-related); and travel (domestic and international), all travel-related or auto-related. March/April annual European travel issue; November/December annual cruise issue. No religious, philosophical arguments or opinion not supported by facts. Buys 25 mss/year. Query with published clips. Length: 500-2,000 (1,500 preferred) words. Pays $50-200.

Photos: State availability of photos. Prefers color slides and b&w with people, sights, scenery mentioned. Reviews 35mm transparencies and 8×10 prints. Payment included in ms purchase. Captions, model releases and identification of subjects required. Buys one-time rights.

Tips: "Query should be informative and entertaining, written with as much care as the lead of a story. Feature articles on travel destinations and tips are most open to freelancers."

MOTORHOME, TL Enterprises, Inc., 29901 Agoura Rd., Agoura CA 91301. (818)991-4980. FAX: (818)991-8102. Editor: Bob Livingston. Managing Editor: Gail Harrington. 60% freelance written. A monthly magazine covering motorhomes. "*MotorHome* is exclusively for motorhome enthusiasts. We feature road tests on new motorhomes, travel locations, controversy concerning motorhomes, how-to and technical articles relating to motorhomes." Estab. 1953. Circ. 150,000. **Pays on acceptance.** Publishes ms an average of 4 months after acceptance. Byline given. Buys first North American serial rights. Submit seasonal/holiday material 8 months in advance. Query for electronic submissions. Reports in 3 weeks on queries; up to 2 months on mss depending on work load. Free sample copy and writer's guidelines.

Nonfiction: General interest; historical/nostalgic; how-to (do it yourself for motorhomes); humor; new product; photo feature; and technical. Buys 80 mss/year. Query with published clips. Length: 1,000-2,000 words. Pays $250-600 for assigned articles; pays $200-500 for unsolicited articles. Sometimes pays expenses of writers and/or photographers on assignment.

Photos: Send photos with submission. Reviews contact sheets and 35mm/120/4×5 transparencies. Offers no additional payment for photos accepted with ms except for use on cover. Captions, model releases and identification of subjects required. Buys first North American serial rights.

Tips: "If a freelancer has an idea for a good article it's best to send a query and include possible photo locations to illustrate the article. We prefer to assign articles and work with the author in developing a piece suitable to our audience. We are in a specialized field with very enthusiastic readers who appreciate articles by authors who actually enjoy motorhomes. The following areas are most open: Travel—places to go with a motorhome, where to stay, what to see etc.; we prefer not to use travel articles where the motorhome is secondary; and How-to—personal projects on author's motorhomes to make travel easier, etc., unique projects, accessories. Also articles on unique personalities, motorhomes, humorous experiences."

MOTORLAND, California State Automobile Assn., 150 Van Ness Ave., San Francisco CA 94101. Did not want to be listed.

NEWSDAY, NEW YORK NEWSDAY, 235 Pinelawn Rd., Melville NY 11747. (516)454-2980. Travel Editor: Marjorie K. Robins. Assistant Travel Editor: Barbara Shea. Travel Writer: Stephen Williams. 20% freelance written. For general readership of Sunday newspaper travel section. Estab. 1940. Circ. 700,000. Buys all rights for New York area only. Buys 45-60 mss/year. Pays on publication, $75-350, depending on space allotment. FAX submissions not encouraged. Prefer typewritten manuscripts. Simultaneous submissions considered if others are being made outside the New York area.

Nonfiction: No assignments to freelancers. No query letters. Only completed manuscripts accepted on spec. All trips must be paid for in full by writer. Proof required. Service stories preferred. Destination pieces must be for the current year. Length: 1,200 words maximum.

Photos: Color slides and black and white photos accepted: $50-250, depending on size of photo used.

NORTHEAST OUTDOORS, Northeast Outdoors, Inc., P.O. Box 2180, Waterbury CT 06722. (203)755-0158. FAX: (203)755-3480. Editor: Jean Wertz. 30% freelance written. Works with a small number of new/unpublished writers each year, and is eager to work with new/unpublished writers. A monthly tabloid covering family camping in the Northeastern U.S. Circ. 14,000. Pays on publication. Publishes ms an average of 8 months after acceptance. Byline given. Buys first rights, one-time rights, and regional rights. Submit seasonal/holiday material 5 months in advance. Query for electronic submissions. Reports in 1 month. Sample copy for 9×12 SAE with 6 first class stamps; writer's guidelines for #10 SASE.

Nonfiction: Book excerpts; general interest; historical/nostalgic; how-to (on camping); humor; new product (company and RV releases only); personal experience; photo feature; and travel. "No diaries of trips, dog stories, or anything not camping and RV related." Length: 300-1,500 words. Pays $40-80 for articles with b&w photos; pays $30-75 for articles without art.

Photos: Send photos with submission. Reviews contact sheets and 5×7 prints or larger. Captions and identification of subjects required. Buys one-time rights.

Columns/Departments: Mealtime (campground cooking), 300-900 words. Buys 12 mss/year. Query or send complete ms. Length: 750-1,000 words. Pays $25-50.

Fillers: Camping related anecdotes, facts, newsbreaks and short humor. Buys few fillers. Length: 25-200 words. Pays $5-15.

Tips: "We most often need material on private campgrounds and attractions in New England. We are looking for upbeat, first-person stories about where to camp, what to do or see, and how to enjoy camping."

‡ONTARIO MOTOR COACH REVIEW, Naylor Communications Ltd., 6th Fl., 920 Yonge St., Toronto, Ontario M4W 3C7 Canada. (416)961-1028. FAX: (416)924-4408. Editor: Greg Kero. 50% freelance written. Annual magazine on travel and tourist destinations. Circ. 3,000. Pays 30 days from deadline. Byline given. Offers 33⅓ kill fee. Buys first North American serial rights and all rights. Submit seasonal/holiday material 2 months in advance. Simultaneous and photocopied submissions OK. Query for electronic submissions. Free sample copy and writer's guidelines.

Nonfiction: General interest, historical, interview/profile, new product, personal experience (related to motor coach travel), photo feature, technical and travel. Buys 5-10 mss/year. Query with published clips. Length: 500-3,000 words. Pays 20-25¢/word. Pays expenses of writers on assignment.

Photos: State availability of photos with submission. Reviews transparencies and prints. Offers $25-200 per photo. Identification of subjects required.

‡**RV TIMES MAGAZINE**, Royal Productions, Inc., Box 6294, Richmond VA 23230. (804)288-5653. Editor: Alice Posner Supple. 75% freelance written. Prefers to work with published/established writers; works with a small number of new/unpublished writers each year. Published 11 times a year. Monthly except December. "We supply the camping public with articles and information on outdoor activities related to camping. Our audience is primarily families that own recreational vehicles." Circ. 35,000. Pays on publication. Publishes ms an average of 4-6 months after acceptance. Byline given. Buys one-time rights, second serial (reprint) rights or simultaneous rights. Submit seasonal/holiday material 2 months in advance. Simultaneous, photocopied and previously published submissions OK. Query for electronic submissions. Reports in 2 months. Sample copy and writer's guidelines for 9 × 12 SAE with $1.67 postage.
Nonfiction: How-to and travel; information on places to camp and fishing articles. Also "tourist related articles. Places to go, things to see. Does not have to be camping related." Buys 80 mss/year. Query with or without published clips, or send complete ms. Length: 500-2,000 words. Sometimes pays the expenses of writers on assignment.
Tips: "All areas of *RV Times* are open to freelancers. We will look at all articles and consider for publication. Return of unsolicited mss is not guaranteed; however, every effort is made to return photos."

RV WEST MAGAZINE, Outdoor Publications, Inc., Suite 226, 2033 Clement Ave., Alameda CA 94501. (415)769-8338. FAX: (415)769-8330. Editor: Dave Preston. 85% freelance written. Works with a small number of new/unpublished writers each year. A monthly magazine for Western recreational vehicle owners. Circ. 30,000. Pays on publication. Publishes ms an average of 6 months after acceptance. Byline given. Buys one-time rights. Submit seasonal/holiday material 6 months in advance. Simultaneous and previously published submissions OK. Query for electronic submissions. Reports in several weeks on queries; several months on mss. Free writer's guidelines.
Nonfiction: Historical/nostalgic; how-to (fix your RV); new product; personal experience (particularly travel); technical; and travel (destinations for RVs). No non-RV travel articles. Buys 36 mss/year. Query with or without published clips. Length: 750-2,000 words. Pays $1.50/inch.
Photos: Send photos with submissions. Reviews contact sheets, negatives, transparencies and prints. Prefers b&w prints. Offers $5 minimum/photo. Identification of subjects required.
Tips: "RV travel/destination stories are most open to freelancers. Include all information of value to RVers, and reasons why they would want to visit the location (12 Western states)."

‡**SAILAWAY**, Travel Agents International, P.O. Box 31005, St. Petersburg FL 33731-8905. (813)895-8241. FAX: (813)894-6318. Editor: Bill Bickler. Managing Editor: Matthew Wiseman. 75% freelance written. Consumer publication. Monthly magazine covering travel and cruises. "Cruise-related travel stories." Estab. 1988. Circ. 50,000. Pays on publication. Byline given. No kill fee. Not copyrighted. Length: 200-1,500 words. Pays $10-100. Reviews prints (any). Offers $2-10 per photo. Captions required. Buys one-time rights.
Columns/Departments: General (cruise stories), 500. Buys 10 mss/year. Query. Length: 200-1,800 words. Pays $5-100. Buys one-time rights. Submit seasonal/holiday material 2 months in advance. Simultaneous and previously published submissions OK. Query for electronic submissions. Reports in 2 weeks. Sample copy for 9 × 12 SAE with 2 first class stamps. Writer's guidelines for 9 × 12 SAE with 2 first class stamps.
Nonfiction: Essays, general interest, humor, new product, personal experience, photo feature, travel. "Send SASE for publication calendar." "Nonegative articles." Buys 12 mss/year. Query.
Fillers: Anecdotes, facts, short humor. Buys 10/year. Length: 100-500 words. Pays $5-25.
Tips: "Send SASE for guidelines. Emphasis on cruises."

TEXAS HIGHWAYS MAGAZINE, Official Travel Magazine for the State of Texas, State Dept. of Highways and Public Transportation, 11th and Brazos, Austin TX 78701. (512)463-8581. FAX: (512)483-3672. Editor: Tommie Pinkard. Managing Editor: Jack Lowry. 85% freelance written. Prefers to work with published/established writers. A monthly tourist magazine covering travel and history for Texas only. **Pays on acceptance.** Publishes ms an average of 10 months after acceptance. Byline given. Offers $100 kill fee. Buys one-time rights. Submit seasonal/holiday material 1 year in advance. Simultaneous queries and submissions OK. Query for electronic submissions. Reports in 2 weeks on queries; 1 month on mss. Sample copy and writer's guidelines for 9 × 12 SAE and 3 first class stamps.
Nonfiction: Historical/nostalgic, photo feature, travel. Must be concerned with travel in Texas. Send material on "what to see, what to do, where to go in *Texas*." Material must be tourist-oriented. "No disaster features." Buys 75 mss/year. Query with published clips. Length: 1,200-1,600 words. Pays $400-700. Sometimes pays expenses of writers on assignment "after we have worked with them awhile."

Photos: Bill Reaves, photo editor. Send photos with query or ms. Pays $80 for less than half a page, $120 for half page, $170 for a full page, $400 for cover, $300 for back cover. Accepts 4x5, 2¼ × 2¼, 35mm color transparencies. Captions and identification of subjects required. Buys one-time rights.
Tips: "We are looking for outdoor features this year, such as state parks, lakes, beaches, and dude ranches. We have too many historical homes and buildings stories now."

TOURS & RESORTS, The World-Wide Vacation Magazine, World Publishing Co., 990 Grove St., Evanston IL 60201-4370. (708)491-6440. Editor/Associate Publisher: Bob Meyers. Managing Editor: Ray Gudas. 90% freelance written. A bimonthly magazine covering world-wide vacation travel. Circ. 250,000. Byline given. Buys first North American serial rights. Submit seasonal/holiday material 6 months in advance. Previously published submissions acceptable, dependent upon publication—local or regional OK. Reports in 3 weeks on queries; 6 weeks on mss. Sample copy $3.50 with 9 × 12 SASE.
Nonfiction: Primarily destination-oriented travel articles, "Anatomy of a Tour" features, and resort/hotel profiles and roundups, but will consider essays, how-to, humor, company profiles, nostalgia, etc.—if travel-related. "It is best to study current contents and query first." Buys 75 mss/year. Average length: 1,500 words. Pays $150-500.
Photos: Top-quality original color slides preferred. Captions required. Buys one-time rights. Prefers photo feature package (ms plus slides), but will purchase slides only to support a work in progress.
Columns/Departments: Travel Views (travel tips; service articles). Buys 6 mss/year. Query or send complete ms. Length: 800-1,500 words. Pays $125-250.
Tips: "Travel features and the Travel Views department are most open to freelancers. Because we are heavily photo-oriented, superb slides are our foremost concern. The most successful approach is to send 2-3 sheets of slides with the query or complete ms. Include a list of other subjects you can provide as a photo feature package."

TRAILER LIFE, TL Enterprises, Inc., 29901 Agoura Rd., Agoura CA 91301. (213)991-4980. Editor: Bill Estes. Managing Editor: Sherry McBride. Editorial Director: Barbara Leonard. 60% freelance written. A monthly magazine covering the RV lifestyle, and RV travel and products. "Readers of *Trailer Life* are owners of recreational vehicles who spend a median 37.8 days traveling on the road. Articles should have a distinctive focus on the needs, entertainment and issues of the RV traveler." Estab. 1941. Circ. 310,000. **Pays on acceptance.** Byline given. Offers 30% kill fee. Buys first North American serial rights. Submit seasonal/holiday material 6 months in advance. Free sample copy and writer's guidelines.
Nonfiction: General interest, historical/nostalgic, how-to, humor, interview/profile, new product, guest editorials, personal experience, photo essay, technical and travel, all with RV focus. Query with or without published clips, or send complete ms. Length: 1,000-2,000 words. Pays $50-500. Sometimes pays the expenses of writers on assignment, under special circumstances.
Photos: Reviews contact sheets, 35mm transparencies (or larger), and 8 × 10 b&w prints. Offers no additional payment for photos accepted with ms, but also buys photos independent of articles. Captions, model releases and identification of subjects required. Buys one-time rights.
Columns/Departments: People on the Move (short RV-related people items with black-and-white photos or 35mm transparencies, can include events, humorous news items), 200-500 words; and RV Bulletin (news items specific to the RV industry/consumer or public lands), 100 words. Send complete ms. Pays $75-150.
Tips: "First-hand experience with recreational vehicles and the RV lifestyle makes the writer's material more appealing. Although the writer need not own an RV, accurate information and a knowledge of the RV lifestyle will lend desired authenticity to article submissions. People on the Move, travel features, how-to articles are areas most open to freelancers. Vehicle evaluations of home-built or home-modified trailers, campers or motorhomes are open to freelancers."

TRANSITIONS ABROAD, 18 Hulst Rd., P.O. Box 344, Amherst MA 01004. (413)256-0373. Editor/Publisher: Prof. Clayton A. Hubbs. 80-90% freelance written. Eager to work with new/unpublished writers. The resource magazine for low-budget international travel with an educational or work component. Bound magazine. Estab. 1977. Circ. 13,000. Pays on publication. Buys first rights and second (reprint) rights to material originally published elsewhere. Byline given. Written queries only. Reports in 2 months. Sample copy $3.50; writer's guidelines and topics schedule for #10 SASE. Manuscript returned only when postage is provided.
Nonfiction: How-to (find courses, inexpensive lodging and travel); interview (information on specific areas and people); personal experience (evaluation of courses, special interest and study tours, economy travel); and travel (what to see and do in specific areas of the world, new learning and travel ideas). Foreign travel only. Few destination ("tourist") pieces. Emphasis on information and on interaction with people in host country. Buys 20 unsolicited mss/issue. Query with credentials. Length: 500-2,000 words. Pays $25-150. Include author's bio with submissions.

Photos: Send photos with ms. Pays $10-25 for prints (color acceptable, b&w preferred), $125 for covers (b&w only). Photos increase likelihood of acceptance. Buys one-time rights. Captions and ID on photos required.

Columns/Departments: Study/Travel Program Notes (evaluation of courses or programs); Traveler's Advisory/Resources (new information and ideas for offbeat independent travel); Jobnotes (how to find it and what to expect); and World-wide travel bargains. Buys 8/issue. Send complete ms. Length: 1,000 words maximum. Pays $20-50.

Fillers: Info Exchange (information, preferably first-hand—having to do with travel, particularly offbeat educational travel and work or study abroad). Buys 10/issue. Length: 1,000 words maximum. Pays $20-50.

Tips: "We like nuts and bolts stuff, practical information, especially on how to work, live and cut costs abroad. Our readers want usable information on planning their own travel itinerary. Be specific: names, addresses, current costs. We are particularly interested in educational travel and study abroad for adults and senior citizens. More and more readers want information not only on work but retirement possibilities. We have a new department on exchange programs, homestays, and study/tours for precollege students. *Educational Travel Directory and Travel Planner* published each year in July provides descriptive listings of resources and information sources on work, study, and independent travel abroad along with study/travel programs abroad for adults."

‡TRAVEL À LA CARTE, Interpress Inc., Suite 404, 1200 Eglinton Ave. E., Toronto, Ontario M3C 1H9 Canada. (416)444-3633. Editor: Heather Kerrigan. 80% freelance written. Bimonthly travel magazine. "Lighthearted entertaining articles on travel destinations worldwide, with a focus on the places and people visited. Our audience is travellers, airline, train and car." Pays on publication. Byline given. Offers no kill fee. Not copyrighted. Buys first North American rights and one-time rights. Submit seasonal/holiday material 4 months in advance. Simultaneous submissions OK. Free sample copy and writer's guidelines.

Nonfiction: Travel. Buys 25-30 mss/year. Query with published clips. Length: 1,500-2,000 words. Pays $250-400. Sometimes pays expenses of writers on assignment.

Photos: Send photos with submission. Reviews transparencies or slides. Offers no additional payment for photos accepted with ms. Identification of subjects required. Buys one-time rights.

Tips: "Send a list of travel destinations and samples of writing and photography. Do not send off-the-beaten path articles for destinations that require flight changes followed by train, canoe and treks to remote areas."

TRAVEL & LEISURE, American Express Publishing Corp., 1120 Avenue of the Americas, New York NY 10036. (212)382-5600. Editor-in-Chief: Ila Stanger. Executive Editor: Susan Crandell. Managing Editor: Maria Shaw. 80% freelance written. Monthly magazine. Circ. 1.2 million. **Pays on acceptance.** Byline given. Offers 25% kill fee. Buys first world and foreign edition rights. Reports in 3 weeks. Sample copy $5. Free writer's guidelines.

Nonfiction: Travel. Buys 200 mss/year. Query. Length open. Payment varies. Pays the expenses of writers on assignment.

Photos: Discourages submission of unsolicited transparencies. Payment varies. Captions required. Buys one-time rights.

Tips: "Read the magazine. Regional sections are best places to start."

‡TRAVEL NEWS, Travel Agents International, Inc., St. Petersburg FL 33731-8905. (813)895-8241. Editor: Charlene Gunn. Managing Editor: Matthew Wiseman. 100% freelance written. Monthly travel tabloid. "Travel stories written to praise a particular trip. We want readers to consider taking a trip themselves." Estab. 1982. Circ. 250,000. Pays on publication. Publishes ms an average of 2 months after acceptance. Byline given. No kill fee. Not copyrighted. Buys simultaneous rights. Submit seasonal/holiday material 2 months in advance. Simultaneous and previously published submissions OK. Query for electronic submissions. Reports in 2 weeks. Sample copy for 9×12 SAE with 2 first class stamps. Writer's guidelines for 9×12 SAE with 2 first class stampls.

Nonfiction: Essays, general interest, historical/nostalgic, humor, new product, personal experience, photo feature, travel. "Each issue focuses on one travel category. We will accept submissions anytime but prefer SASE for publication calendar. No negative articles that would discourage travel." Buys 20 mss/year. Query with or without published clips, or send complete ms. Length: 200-3,000 words. Pays $10-300 for assigned articles; $10-200 for unsolicited articles.

 The double dagger before a listing indicates that the listing is new in this edition. New markets are often more receptive to freelance submissions.

Photos: State availability of photos with submission. Reviews prints (any). Captions required. Buys one-time rights or all rights.
Columns/Departments: General (travel—positive articles), 800-1,500. Buys 12 mss/yaer. Query. Length: 300-1,500 words. Pays $5-100.
Fillers: Anecdotes, facts, newsbreaks, short humor. Buys 20/year. Length: 50-300 words. Pays $5-25.
Tips: "Send SASE for publication calendar and submission requirements. Call or write well in advance of a trip to see what angle we would like the story to take."

‡TRAVEL PAPERS, Carousel Press/The Family Travel Guides Catalogue, P.O. Box 6061, Albany CA 94706. (415)527-5849. Editor: Carole T. Meyers. 100% freelance written. Consumer publication. Annual newsletter covering family travel. "We publish articles that help families plan successful vacations. Helpful detail is important." Estab. 1987. Circ. 50,000. "We pay royalties on articles ordered by customers—once each year in January." Byline given. No kill fee. Not copyrighted. Author retains copyright. Buys second serial (reprint) rights. Previously published submissions OK. Reports in 1 month. Sample copy and writer's guidelines for #10 SAE and 52¢ first class stamps.
Nonfiction: Travel. Buys 10 mss/year. Send complete ms. Length: 1,000-2,500 words. Pays 10% royalty.

TRAVEL SMART, Communications House, Inc., Dobbs Ferry NY 10522. (914)693-4208. Editor/Publisher: H.J. Teison. Managing Editor: Deborah Gaines. Covers information on "good-value travel." Monthly newsletter. Estab. 1976. Pays on publication. Buys all rights. Reports in 6 weeks. Sample copy and writer's guidelines for #10 SAE with 3 first class stamps.
Nonfiction: "Interested primarily in bargains or little-known deals on transportation, lodging, food, unusual destinations that won't break the bank. Also information on trends in industry. No destination stories on major Caribbean islands, London, New York, no travelogs, my vacation, poetry, fillers. No photos or illustrations. Just hard facts. We are not part of 'Rosy fingers of dawn ...' school." Write for guidelines, then query. Length: 100-1,000 words. Pays "up to $100."
Tips: "When you travel, check out small hotels offering good prices, little known restaurants, and send us brief rundown (with prices, phone numbers, addresses). Information must be current. Include your phone number with submission, because we sometimes make immediate assignments."

‡THE TRAVELER, The Ardmont Publishing Group Inc., Suite 220, 4200 S. I-10 Service Road, Metairie LA 70001. (504)456-2220. Editor: Maria Ward McIntosh. 90% freelance written. Annual hardback magazine covering travel in Baton Rouge LA, Columbus OH and Memphis TN. "The *Traveler*, placed in hotel rooms in Baton Rouge and Memphis, is designed to acquaint the visitor with local attractions, restaurants, etc." Estab. 1985. Circ. 22,000. Pays on publication. Publishes ms an average of 3 months after acceptance. Byline given. No kill fee. Buys first rights. Submit seasonal/holiday material 6 months in advance. Reports in 1 month.
Nonfiction: General interest, historical/nostalgic, photo feature, travel. Buys 10 mss/year per market. Query with published clips. Length: 800-1,500 words. Pays $150-250 for assigned articles. "Each writer receives 2 comp copies in addition to fee." Sometimes pays expenses of writers on assignment.
Photos: State availability of photos with submission. Reviews transparencies. Offers $25-135 per photo. Captions, model releases and identification of subjects required. Buys one-time rights.

TRAVEL-HOLIDAY, Reader's Digest, 28 W. 23rd St., New York NY 10010. Did not want to be listed.

TRAVELORE REPORT, Suite #100, 1512 Spruce St., Philadelphia PA 19102. (215)735-3838. Editor: Ted Barkus. For affluent travelers; businessmen, retirees, well-educated readers; interested in specific tips, tours, and bargain opportunities in travel. Monthly newsletter. Estab. 1974. Buys all rights. Pays on publication. Submit seasonal material 2 months in advance. Sample copy $2; writer's guidelines for #10 SASE.
Nonfiction: "Brief insights (25-200 words) with facts, prices, names of hotels and restaurants, etc., on offbeat subjects of interest to people going places. What to do, what not to do. Supply information. We will rewrite if acceptable. We're candid—we tell it like it is with no sugar coating. Avoid telling us about places in United States or abroad without specific recommendations (hotel name, costs, rip-offs, why, how long, etc.). No destination pieces which are general with no specific 'story angle' in mind, or generally available through PR departments." Buys 10-20 mss/year. Pays $5-20.
Tips: "Destinations confronted with political disturbances should be avoided. We'll put more emphasis on travel to North American destinations and Caribbean, and/or South Pacific, while safety exists. We're adding more topics geared to business-related travel and marketing trends in leisure-time industry."

‡TRIP & TOUR, Allied Publications, Inc., 1776 Lake Worth Rd., Lake Worth FL 33460. (407)582-2099. Associate Editor: Karl H. Meyer. 85% freelance written. Bimonthly magazine covering foreign travel. *Trip & Tour* is devoted to foreign (not domestic) travel and places of interest that are unknown to most tourists. Canada and Mexico qualify as foreign destinations. Estab. 1945. Circ. (combined) 105,000. Pays on publication. Publishes ms an average of 6 months after acceptance. Byline given. Offers no kill fee. Buys one-time rights and second serial (reprint) rights. Submit seasonal/holiday material 6-8 months in advance. Simultaneous and previously published submissions OK. Query for electronic submissions. Reports in 2 weeks on queries; 2 weeks-3 months on mss. Sample copy $1. Writer's guidelines for #10 SAE with 1 first class stamp.

Nonfiction: "No highly technical or cutesy material. No vulgar or obscene language. No jeremiads. Think positively." Buys 216 mss/year. Query with or without published clips, or send complete ms. "I often reject query and purchase clips submitted." Length: 300-1,500 words. Pays 30¢/published line. Offers contributor copies or other premiums only if author requests.

Photos: State availability of photos with submission. Photos almost a necessity; 35mm slides to 4×5 transparencies or sharp b&w. Offers $5 per photo. Model releases and identification of subjects required. Photographer must have model releases on file; do not send.

Tips: "All areas of magagzine are open to freelancers. I enjoy working with new writers, and have been the first to publish the work of many new writers who show skill at handling words and ideas, and who are receptive to my ideas."

VISTA/USA, P.O. Box 161, Convent Station NJ 07961-0161. (201)538-7600. FAX: (201)538-9509. Editor: Kathleen M. Caccavale. Managing Editor: Martha J. Mendez. 90% freelance written. Will consider ms submissions from *unpublished* writers. Quarterly magazine of Exxon Travel Club. "Our publication uses articles on North American areas. We strive to help our readers gain an in-depth understanding of cities, towns and areas as well as other aspects of American culture that affect the character of the nation." Estab. 1965. Circ. 900,000. **Pays on acceptance.** Publishes ms an average of 1 year after acceptance. Buys first North American serial rights. Query about seasonal subjects 18 months in advance. Reports in 6 weeks. Sample copy for a 9×12 or larger SAE with 5 first class stamps; writer's and photographer's guidelines for #10 SASE.

Nonfiction: Geographically oriented articles on North America focused on the character of an area or place; photo essays (recent examples include slot canyons, sand sculptures, kites); and some articles dealing with nature, Americana, crafts and collecting. Usually one activity-oriented article per issue. "We buy feature articles on the U.S., Canada, Mexico and the Caribbean that appeal to a national audience and prefer that destination queries have a hook or angle to them that give us a clear, solid argument for covering the average subject 'soon' rather than 'anytime.' " No feature articles that mention driving or follow routes on a map. Uses 7-15 mss/issue. Query with outline and clips of previously published work. Length: 1,200-2,000 words. Pays $450 minimum for features. Pays the expenses of writers on assignment.

Columns/Departments: "MiniTrips are point to point or loop driving tours of from 50 to 350 miles covering a healthy variety of stops along the way. 'Close Focus' covers openings or changing aspects of major attractions, small or limited attractions not appropriate for a feature article (800-1,000 words). 'American Vignettes' covers anything travel related that also reveals a slice of American life, often with a light or humorous touch, such as asking directions from a cranky New Englander, or the phenomenon of vanity plates. 'Information Please' provides practical information on travel safety, and health trends, tips; a service column."

Photos: Contact: photo researcher. Send photos with ms. Pays $100 minimum for color transparencies. Captions preferred. Buys one-time rights.

Tips: "We are looking for readable pieces with good writing that will interest armchair travelers as much as readers who may want to visit the areas you write about. Queries about well-known destinations should have something new or different to say about them, a specific focus or angle. Articles should have definite themes and should give our readers an insight into the character and flavor of an area or topic. Stories about personal experiences must impart a sense of drama and excitement or have a strong human-interest angle. Stories about areas should communicate a strong sense of what it feels like to be there. Good use of anecdotes and quotes should be included. Study the articles in the magazine to understand how they are organized, how they present their subjects, the range of writing styles, and the specific types of subjects used. Afterwards, query and enclose samples of your best writing. We continue to seek department shorts and inventory articles of a general, nonseasonal nature (1,500 to 1,800 words)."

VOYAGER/SUN SCENE, K.L. Publications, Suite 105, 2001 Killebrew Dr., Bloomington MN 55425. Editor: Mary Lou Brooks. Quarterly magazine published for Gulf Motor Club/Sun Travel Club. 80% freelance written. Estab. 1973. Circ. 114,000. Pays on acceptance by client. Byline given. Considers mostly previously published articles. Submit seasonal/holiday material 6-8 months in advance. Reports in 1 month. Sample copy for 9×12 SAE with 3 first class stamps; writer's guidelines for #10 SASE.

Nonfiction: Travel (U.S. destinations by car and some foreign destinations), lifestyle, how-to (travel-related), historical/nostalgic. Length: 500-1,500 words. Pays $75-125.

Photos: Reviews 35mm transparencies. Color only. Pay varies.

WESTERN RV NEWS, Suite B, 1350 SW Upland Dr., Portland OR 97221. (503)222-1255. Editor: James E. Hathaway. Managing Editor: Elsie P. Hathaway. 20% freelance written. Magazine published 12 times/year for owners of recreational vehicles. Estab. 1966. Pays on publication. Publishes ms an average of 3-6 months after acceptance. Byline sometimes given. Publication not copyrighted. Buys first North American serial rights. Simultaneous and previously published submissions OK. Reports in 1 month on queries; 3 weeks on mss. Free sample copy and writer's guidelines.

Nonfiction: How-to (RV oriented, purchasing considerations, maintenance), humor (RV experiences), new product (with ancillary interest to RV lifestyle), personal experiences (varying or unique RV lifestyles), technical (RV systems or hardware), and travel. "No articles without an RV slant." Buys 40 mss/year. Submit complete ms. Length: 250-1,500 words. Pays $150 maximum for assigned articles; $15-150 for unsolicited articles.

Photos: Send b&w photos with submission. Reviews 3 × 5 prints. Offers $5-15/photo. Captions, model releases, and identification of subjects required. Buys one-time rights.

Columns/Departments: Jim Schumock, features editor. Tips 'n Techniques (practical advice or specific information about processes or products), 100-250 words. Buys 25-30 mss/ year. Send complete ms. Pays $5-25.

Fillers: Jim Schumock, features editor. Anecdotes, gags to be illustrated by cartoonist, and short humor. Buys 10/year. Length: 50-150 words. Pays $5-25.

Tips: "Highlight the RV lifestyle! All areas open, but primarily interested in Western travel articles that include information about the availability of RV sites, dump stations, RV parking and accessibility. Thorough research and a pleasant, informative writing style are paramount. Read other RV publications. No folksy, generic writing. Technical, how-to, and new product writing is also of great interest to us. Photos definitely enhance the possibility of article acceptance."

Women's

Women have an incredible variety of publications available to them these days—about 50 appear on newsstands in an array of specialties. A number of titles in this area have been redesigned during the past year to compete in the crowded marketplace. Many of the fashion magazines are also following the European trend of putting models in casual minimal settings, especially out-of-doors. Magazines that also use material slanted to women's interests can be found in the following categories: Business and Finance; Child Care and Parental Guidance; Contemporary Culture; Food and Drink; Health and Fitness; Hobby and Craft; Home and Garden; Relationships; Religious; Romance and Confession; and Sports.

BRIDAL GUIDE, The How-To For I Do, Globe Communications Corp., 441 Lexington Ave., New York NY 10017. (212)949-4040. FAX: (212)286-0072. Editor: Deborah Harding. Articles Editor: Mary McHugh. 80% freelance written. Prefers to work with experienced/published writers. A bimonthly magazine covering wedding planning, fashion, beauty, contemporary relationship articles, honeymoon travel and planning for the first home. Sample copy for 9 × 12 SAE and $2.90 postage (1st class), or $1.50 postage (3rd class); writer's guidelines for #10 SASE.

Nonfiction: The editors prefer queries rather than actual manuscript submissions. All correspondence accompanied by a SASE will be answered (response is usually within 1 month). Length: 800-1,600 words. Pays $200-600 on acceptance. Buys 120 mss/year. Offers 20% kill fee. Buys first North American serial rights. Sample copy for $4.50.

Photos: Derek Burton, design director. Cartoons and photography submissions should be handled through the Art Department.

Columns/Departments: Regular departments include Finance, Sex, Remarriage, and Advice for the Groom.

BRIDAL TRENDS, Meridian Publishing, Inc., Box 10010, Ogden UT 84409. (801)394-9446. 65% freelance written. Monthly magazine with useful articles for today's bride. Circ. 60,000. **Pays on acceptance.** Publishes ms an average of 10 months after acceptance. Byline given. Buys first rights, second serial (reprint) rights and non-exclusive reprint rights. Simultaneous and previously published submissions OK. Reports in 6 weeks. Sample copy for $1 and 9 × 12 SAE; writer's guidelines for #10 SASE. All requests for sample copies and guidelines should be addressed Attn: Editor.

Nonfiction: "General interest articles about traditional and modern approaches to weddings. Topics include all aspects of ceremony and reception planning; flowers; invitations; catering; wedding apparel and fashion trends for the bride, groom, and other members of the wedding party, etc. Also featured are honeymoon destinations, how to build a relationship and keep romance alive, and adjusting to married life." Buys approximately 15 mss/year. Query. Length: 1,200 words. Pays 15¢/word for first rights plus non-exclusive reprint rights. Payment for second rights is negotiable.

Photos: State availability of photos with query letter. Color transparencies and 5×7 or 8×10 prints are preferred. Pays $35 for inside photo. Captions, model release, and identification of subjects required.

Tips: "We publish articles that detail each aspect of wedding planning: invitations, choosing your flowers, deciding on the style of your wedding, and choosing a photographer and caterer."

BRIDE'S, Conde Nast Bldg., 350 Madison Ave., New York NY 10017. (212)880-8800. Editor-in-Chief: Barbara D. Tober. 40% freelance written. Eager to work with new/unpublished writers. A bimonthly magazine for the first- or second-time bride, her family and friends, the groom and his family and friends. Circ. 479,335. **Pays on acceptance.** Publishes ms an average of 2 months after acceptance. Buys all rights. Also buys first and second serial rights for book excerpts on marriage, communication, finances. Offers 20% kill fee, depending on circumstances. Buys 40 unsolicited mss/year. Byline given. Reports in 2 months. Address mss to Features Department. Writer's guidelines for #10 SASE.

Nonfiction: "We want warm, personal articles, optimistic in tone, with help offered in a clear, specific way. All issues should be handled within the context of marriage. How-to features on all aspects of marriage: communications, in-laws, careers, money, sex, housing, housework, family planning, marriage after having a baby, religion, interfaith marriage, step-parenting, second marriage, reaffirmation of vows; informational articles on the realities of marriage, the changing roles of men and women, the kind of troubles in engagement that are likely to become big issues in marriage; stories from couples or marriage authorities that illustrate marital problems and solutions to men and women; book excerpts on marriage, communication, finances, sex; and how-to features on wedding planning that offer expert advice. Also success stories of marriages of long duration. We use first-person pieces and articles that are well researched, relying on quotes from authorities in the field, and anecdotes and dialogues from real couples. We publish first-person essays on provocative topics unique to marriage." Query or submit complete ms. Article outline preferred. Length: 1,000-3,000 words. Pays $300-800.

Columns/Departments: The Love column accepts reader love poems, for $25 each. The Something New section accepts reader wedding planning and craft ideas; pays $25.

Tips: "Since marriage rates are up and large, traditional weddings are back in style, and since more women work than ever before, do *not* query us on just living together or becoming a stay-at-home wife after marriage. Send us a query or a well-written article that is both easy to read and offers real help for the bride or groom as she/he adjusts to her/his new role. No first-person narratives on wedding and reception planning, home furnishings, cooking, fashion, beauty, travel. We're interested in unusual ideas, experiences, and lifestyles. No 'I used baby pink rose buds' articles."

CHATELAINE, 777 Bay St., Toronto, Ontario M5W 1A7 Canada. (416)596-5425. Editor-in-Chief: Mildred Istona. 75% freelance written. Prefers to work with published/established writers. Monthly general-interest magazine for Canadian women, from age 20 and up. "*Chatelaine* is read by one woman in three across Canada, a readership that spans almost every age group but is concentrated among those 25 to 45 including homemakers and working women in all walks of life." Circ. over 1 million. **Pays on acceptance.** Publishes ms an average of 3 months after acceptance. Byline given. Reports within 2 weeks. All mss must be accompanied by a SASE (IRCs in lieu of stamps if sent from outside Canada). Sample copy $2 and postage; free writer's guidelines.

Nonfiction: Elizabeth Parr, senior editor, articles. Submit an outline or query first. Full-length major pieces run from 1,500 to 2,500 words. Pays minimum $1,250 for acceptable major article. Buys first North American serial rights in English and French (the latter to cover possible use in *Chatelaine*'s sister French-language edition, edited in Montreal for French Canada). "We look for important national Canadian subjects, examining any and all facets of Canadian life, especially as they concern or interest women. Upfront columns include stories about relationships, health, nutrition, fitness and parents and kids. Submit outline first. Pays $350 for about 500 words. Prefers queries for nonfiction subjects on initial contact plus a resume and writing samples. Also seeks full-length personal experience stories with deep emotional impact. Pays $750. Pays expenses of writers on assignment.

Tips: Features on beauty, food, fashion and home decorating are supplied by staff writers and editors, and unsolicited material is not considered.

COMPLETE WOMAN, For All The Women You Are, Associated Publications, Inc., 1165 N. Clark, Chicago IL 60610. (312)266-8680. Editor: Bonnie L. Krueger. Managing Editor: Susan Handy. 90% freelance written. Bimonthly magazine of general interest for women. Areas of concern are love life, health, fitness, emotions, etc. Estab. 1980. Circ. 150,000. Pays on publication. Publishes ms an average of 5 months after acceptance. Byline given. Buys first North American serial rights, second serial (reprint) rights, simultaneous rights. Submit seasonal/holiday material 5 months in advance. Simultaneous submissions OK. Reports in 1 month. Writer's guidelines with SASE.

Nonfiction: Book excerpts, general interest, how-to, humor, inspirational, interview/profile, new product, personal experience, photo feature. No recipes or how to build a closet or sewing! Buys 60-100 mss/year. Query with or without published clips, or send complete ms. Length: 800-2,000 words. Pays $80-400. Sometimes pays expenses of writers on assignment.

Photos: Send photos with submission. Reviews 2¼ or 35mm transparencies and 5×7 prints. Offers $35-75 per photo. Captions, model releases and identification of subjects required. Buys one-time rights.

Poetry: Avant-garde, free verse, light verse, traditional. Nothing over 30 lines. Buys 50 poems/year. Submit maximum 5 poems. Pays $10.

COSMOPOLITAN, The Hearst Corp., 224 W. 57th St., New York NY 10019. Exec. Editor: Roberta Ashley. 90% freelance written. Monthly magazine about 18- to 35-year-old single, married, divorced—all working. **Pays on acceptance.** Byline given. Offers 10% kill fee. Buys all magazine rights and occasionally negotiates first North American rights. Submit seasonal/holiday material 6 months in advance. Previously published submissions in minor publications OK. Reports in 1 week on queries; 3 weeks on mss. Sample copy $2.50. Writer's guidelines for #10 SASE.

Nonfiction: Book excerpts, how-to, humor, opinion, personal experience and anything of interest to young women. Buys 350 mss/year. Query with published clips or send complete ms. Length: 500-3,500 words. Pays expenses of writers on assignment.

Fiction: Betty Kelly. Condensed novels, humorous, novel excerpts, romance and original short stories with romantic plots. Buys 18 mss/year. Query. Length: 750-3,000 words.

Poetry: Free verse and light verse. Buys 30 poems/year. No maximum number. Length: 4-30 lines.

Fillers: Irene Copeland. Facts. Buys 240/year. Length: 300-1,000 words.

COUNTRY WOMAN, Reiman Publications, P.O. Box 643, Milwaukee WI 53201. (414)423-0100. Managing Editor: Kathy Pohl. 75-85% freelance written. Willing to work with new/unpublished writers. Bimonthly magazine on the interests of country women. "*Country Woman* is for contemporary rural women of all ages and backgrounds and from all over the U.S. and Canada. It includes a sampling of the diversity that makes up rural women's lives—love of home, family, farm, ranch, community, hobbies, enduring values, humor, attaining new skills and appreciating present, past and future all within the content of the lifestyle that surrounds country living." Estab. 1970. Circ. 700,000. **Pays on acceptance.** Publishes ms an average of 1 year after acceptance. Byline given. Buys first North American serial rights, one-time rights, and second serial (reprint) rights; makes some work-for-hire assignments. Submit seasonal/holiday material 4-5 months in advance. Previously published (on occasion) submissions OK. Reports in 1 month on queries; 2 months on mss. Sample copy for $2.50; writer's guidelines for #10 SASE.

Nonfiction: General interest, historical/nostalgic, how-to (crafts, community projects, family relations, self-improvement, decorative, antiquing, etc.); humor; inspirational; interview/profile; personal experience; photo/feature packages profiling interesting country women; all pertaining to a rural woman's interest. Articles must be written in a positive, light and entertaining manner. Buys 100 mss/year. Query or send complete ms. Length: 1,000 words maximum.

Photos: Send color photos with query or ms. Reviews 35mm or 2¼ transparencies. Uses only excellent quality color photos. No b&w. "We pay for photo/feature packages." Captions, model releases and identification of subjects required. Buys one-time rights.

Columns/Departments: Why Farm Wives Age Fast (humor), I Remember When (nostalgia), Country Decorating, and Shopping Comparison (new product comparisons). Buys 20 mss (maximum)/year. Query or send complete ms. Length: 500-1,000 words. Pays $75-125.

Fiction: Main character *must* be a country woman. All fiction must have a country setting. Fiction must have a positive, upbeat message. Includes fiction in every issue. Would buy more fiction if stories suitable for our audience were sent our way. Query or send complete ms. Length: 750-1,000 words. Pays $90-125.

Poetry: Traditional and light verse. "Poetry must have rhythm and rhyme! It must be country-related. Always looking for seasonal poetry." Buys 40 poems/year. Submit maximum 6 poems. Length: 5-24 lines. Pays $10-40.

Fillers: Jokes, anecdotes, short humor and consumer news (e.g. safety, tips, etc.). Buys 40/year. Length: 40-250 words. Pays $25-40.

Tips: "We have recently broadened our focus to include 'country' women, not just women on farms and ranches. This allows freelancers a wider scope in material. Write as clearly and with as much zest and enthusiasm as possible. We love good quotes, supporting materials (names, places, etc.) and strong leads and closings. Readers relate strongly to where they live and the lifestyle they've chosen. They want to be informed and entertained, and that's just exactly why they subscribe. Readers are busy—not too busy to read—but when they do sit down, they want good writing, reliable information and something that feels like a reward. How-to, humor, personal experience and nostalgia are areas most open to freelancers. Profiles, to a certain degree, are also open. We are always especially receptive to short items—250 words, 400 words and so on. Be accurate and fresh in approach."

ENTREPRENURIAL WOMAN, Entrepreneur Group Inc., 2392 Morse Ave., Irvine CA 92714. (714)261-2325. Editor: Rieva Lesonsky. Managing Editors: Maria Anton and Maria Johnson. 70% freelance written. Monthly magazine for women business owners. Estab. 1989. Circ. 200,000. **Pays on acceptance.** Publishes ms an average of 5-6 months after acceptance. Byline given. Pays 20% kill fee. Buys first rights or all rights. Submit seasonal/holiday material 6-7 months in advance. Reports in 2 months. Sample copy $3. Writer's guidelines for #10 SASE.
Nonfiction: How-to, interview/profile, or any information to assist women running a business. Buys 75 mss/year. Query with published clips. Length: 500-2,000 words. Pays $250-700.
Photos: State availability of photos with submission or send photos with submission. Reviews transparencies. Payment and rights vary. Identification of subjects required.
Columns/Departments: Who's Hot (short profiles of women entrepreneurs), 500 words; Management Smarts and Building Blocks (how-to advice for running a business), 1,300-1,400 words; Healthy Outlook (specific health-related topics), 1,300 words. Buys 50 mss/year. Query with published clips. Pays $250-400.
Tips: "Submit well-written queries clearly detailing what you'd like to cover in an article. Do not query without reading our guidelines and a sample copy first. The first step to getting an assignment is understanding who the entrepreneurial woman is. We are seeking excellent writers who can take deep, psychological issues and see more than one side of the story."

ESSENCE, 1500 Broadway, New York NY 10036. Editor-in-Chief: Susan L. Taylor. Editor: Stephanie Stokes Oliver. Executive Editor: Valerie Wilson Wesley. Monthly magazine. Circ. 850,000. **Pays on acceptance.** Makes assignments on work-for-hire basis. 3 month lead time. Pays 25% kill fee. Byline given. Submit seasonal/holiday material 6 months in advance. Reports in 2 months. Sample copy $1.50; free writer's guidelines.
Features: Valerie Wilson Wesley, senior editor. "We're looking for articles that inspire and inform Black women. The topics we include in each issue are provocative. Every article should move the *Essence* woman emotionally and intellectually. We welcome queries from good writers on a wide range of topics; general interest, health and fitness, historical, how-to, humor, self-help, relationships, work, personality interview, personal experience, political issues, business and finances and personal opinion." Buys 200 mss/year. Query only; word length will be given upon assignment. Pays $500 minimum.
Photos: Marlowe Goodson, art director. State availability of photos with query. Pays $100 for b&w page; $300 for color page. Captions and model release required. "We particularly would like to see photographs for our travel section that feature Black travelers."
Columns/Departments: Query department editors: Contemporary Living (home, food, lifestyle, travel, consumer information): Harriette Cole; Arts: Benilde Little; Health & Working: Linda Villarosa; Money: Andrea R. Davis. Query only; word length will be given upon assignment. Pays $100 minimum.
Tips: "Please note that *Essence* no longer accepts unsolicited mss for fiction, poetry or nonfiction, except for the Brothers and Back Talk Interiors columns. So please only send query letters for nonfiction story ideas."

FAIRFIELD COUNTY WOMAN, FCW, Inc., 15 Bank St., Stamford CT 06901. (203)323-3105. Editor: Joan Honig. 75% freelance written. A women's regional monthly tabloid focusing on careers, education, health, relationships and family life. Estab. 1982. Circ. 40,000. Pays 60 days after publications. Byline given. Buys first rights. Submit seasonal/holiday material 3 months in advance. Simultaneous and previously published submissions OK. Query for electronic submissions. Sample copy for 10 × 13 SAE with $1.50 postage.
Nonfiction: Book excerpts, essays, general interest, how-to, humor, and local interview/profile. Buys 125 mss/year. Query with published clips. Length: 800-2,000 words. Pays $35-100 for assigned articles; $25-75 for unsolicited articles. Sometimes pays expenses of writers on assignment.
Photos: State availability of photos with submission. Reviews 5 × 7 prints. Offers no additional payment with ms. Buys one-time rights.
Columns/Departments: Health, auto, finance and home. Length: 1,200 words. Buys 50 mss/year. Query with published clips. Pays $25-50.

FAMILY CIRCLE MAGAZINE, 110 Fifth Ave., New York NY 10011. (212)463-1000. Editor-in-Chief: Jacqueline Leo. 70% freelance written. For women. Published 17 times/year. Usually buys all print rights. Offers 20% kill fee. Byline given. **Pays on acceptance.** "We are a national women's magazine which offers advice, fresh information and entertainment to women. Query should stress the unique aspects of an article and expert sources; we want articles that will help our readers or make a difference in how they live." Reports in 1 month.

Nonfiction: Susan Ungaro, executive editor. Women's interest subjects such as family and personal relationships, children, physical and mental health, nutrition, self-improvement and profiles of ordinary women doing extraordinary things for her community or the nation from 'Women Who Make a Difference' series. "We look for well-written, well-reported stories told through interesting anecdotes and insightful writing. We want well-researched service journalism on all subjects." Query. Length: 1,000-2,500 words. Pays $1/word.

Tips: Query letters should be "concise and to the point." Also, writers should "keep close tabs on *Family Circle* and other women's magazines to avoid submitting recently run subject matter."

FIRST FOR WOMEN, Bauer Publishing Co., P.O. Box 1648, 270 Sylvan Ave., Englewood Cliffs NJ 07632. Did not want to be listed.

GLAMOUR, Conde Nast, 350 Madison Ave., New York NY 10017. (212)880-8800. Editor-in-Chief: Ruth Whitney. 75% freelance written. Works with a small number of new/unpublished writers each year. For college-educated women, 18-35 years old. Monthly. Estab. 1939. Circ. 2.3 million. **Pays on acceptance.** Offers 20% kill fee. Publishes ms an average of 6-12 months after acceptance. Byline given. Reports in 2 months. Writer's guidelines for #10 SASE.

Nonfiction: Lisa Bain, articles editor. "Editorial approach is 'how-to' with articles that are relevant in the areas of careers, health, psychology, interpersonal relationships, etc. We look for queries that are fresh and include a contemporary, timely angle. Fashion, beauty, decorating, travel, food and entertainment are all staff-written. We use 1,000-word opinion essays for our Viewpoint section. Pays $500. Our His/Hers column features generally stylish essays on relationships or comments on current mores by male and female writers in alternate months." Pays $1,000 for His/Hers mss. Buys first North American serial rights. Buys 10-12 mss/issue. Query "with letter that is detailed, well-focused, well-organized, and documented with surveys, statistics and research, personal essays excepted." Short articles and essays (1,500-2,000 words) pay $1,000 and up; longer mss (2,500-3,000 words) pay $1,500 minimum on acceptance. Sometimes pays the expenses of writers on assignment.

Tips: "We're looking for sharply focused ideas by strong writers and are constantly raising our standards. We are interested in getting new writers, and we are approachable, mainly because our range of topics is so broad. We've increased our focus on male-female relationships."

GOOD HOUSEKEEPING, Hearst Corp., 959 8th Ave., New York NY 10019. (212)649-2000. Editor-in-Chief: John Mack Carter. Executive Editor: Mina Mulvey. Managing Editor: Mary Fiore. Prefers to work with published/established writers. Monthly. Circ. 5 million. **Pays on acceptance.** Buys all rights. Pays 25% kill fee. Byline given. Submit seasonal/holiday material 6 months in advance. Reports in 6 weeks. Sample copy $2. Free writer's guidelines with SASE.

Nonfiction: Joan Thursh, articles editor. Medical; informational; investigative stories; inspirational; interview; nostalgia; personal experience; and profile. Buys 4-6 mss/issue. Query. Length: 1,500-2,500 words. Pays $1,500 on acceptance for full articles from new writers. Regional Editor: Shirley Howard. Pays $250-350 for local interest and travel pieces of 2,000 words. Pays the expenses of writers on assignment.

Photos: Herbert Bleiweiss, art director. Photos purchased on assignment mostly. Some short photo features with captions. Pays $100-350 for b&w; $200-400 for color photos. Query. Model releases required.

Columns/Departments: Light Housekeeping & Fillers, edited by Rosemary Leonard. Humorous short-short prose and verse. Jokes, gags, anecdotes. Pays $25-50. The Better Way, edited by Erika Mark. Ideas and in-depth research. Query. Pays $250-500. "Mostly staff written; only outstanding ideas have a chance here."

Fiction: Lee Quarfoot, fiction editor. Uses romance fiction and condensations of novels that can appear in one issue. Looks for reader identification. "We get 1,500 unsolicited mss/month—includes poetry; a freelancer's odds are overwhelming—but we do look at all submissions." Send complete mss. Manuscripts will not be returned. Only responds on acceptance. Length: 1,500 words (short-shorts); novel according to merit of material; average 5,000-word short stories. Pays $1,000 minimum for fiction short-shorts; $1,250 for short stories.

Poetry: Arleen Quarfoot, poetry editor. Light verse and traditional. "Presently overstocked." Poems used as fillers. Pays $5/line for poetry on acceptance.

Tips: "Always send an SASE. We prefer to see a query first. Do not send material on subjects already covered in-house by the Good Housekeeping Institute—these include food, beauty, needlework and crafts."

HOMEMAKER'S, Telemedia Publishing, 50 Holly St., Toronto, Ontario MIK 5W9 Canada. Did not want to be listed.

THE JOYFUL WOMAN, For and About Bible-believing Women Who Want God's Best, The Joyful Woman Ministries, Inc., Business Office: P.O. Box 90028, Chattanooga TN 37412. (615)698-7318. Editor: Elizabeth Handford, 118 Shannon Lake Circle, Greenville SC 29615. 50% freelance written. Works with small number of new/unpublished writers each year. Bimonthly magazine covering the role of women in home and business. *"The Joyful Woman* hopes to encourage, stimulate, teach, and develop the Christian woman to reach the full potential of her womanhood." Estab. 1978. Circ. 12,000. Pays on publication. Publishes ms an average of 4 months after acceptance. Byline given. Buys first rights and reprint rights. Submit seasonal/holiday material 4 months in advance. Reports in 3 months. Sample copy for 9 × 12 SAE with 4 first class stamps; writer's guidelines for #10 SASE.
Nonfiction: Book excerpts, how-to (housekeeping, childrearing, career management, etc.); inspirational; interview/profile (of Christian women); and personal experience. "We publish material on every facet of the human experience, considering not just a woman's spiritual needs, but her emotional, physical, and intellectual needs and her ministry to others." Buys 80-100 mss/year. Send complete ms. Length: 700-2,500 words. Pays about 2¢/word.
Tips: "The philosophy of the woman's liberation movement tends to minimize the unique and important ministries God has in mind for a woman. We believe that being a woman and a Christian ought to be joyful and fulfilling personally and valuable to God, whatever her situation—career woman, wife, mother, daughter."

LADIES' HOME JOURNAL, Meredith Corporation, 100 Park Ave., New York NY 10017. (212)953-7070. Publishing Director and Editor-in-Chief: Myrna Blyth. Executive Editor: Lynn Langway. 50% freelance written. A monthly magazine focusing on issues of concern to women. *"LHJ* reflects the lives of the contemporary mainstream woman and provides the information she needs and wants to live in today's world." Circ. 5 million. **Pays on acceptance.** Publishes ms an average of 3 months after acceptance, but varies according to needs. Byline given. Offers 25% kill fee. Rights bought vary with submission. Submit seasonal/holiday material 6 months in advance. Reports in 6 weeks. Query for sample copy rates. Free writer's guidelines.
Nonfiction: Lynn Langway, executive editor, oversees the entire department and may be queried directly. In addition, submissions may be directed to Jane Farrell, articles editor, and on the following subjects to the editors listed for each: Relationships (psychology editor Pam Guthrie O'Brien); medical/health (Nelly Edmondson Gupta); investigative reports or new related features (senior editor Jane Farrell); and celebrities (executive editor Lynn Langway). Travel pieces for Prime Shopper may be sent to Copy Director Linda Fears. Query with published clips. Length: 1,500-3,500 words. Fees vary; average is between $1,000 and $3,500. Pays expenses of writers on assignment.
Photos: State availability of photos with submission. Offers variable payment for photos accepted with ms. Captions, model releases and identification of subjects required. Rights bought vary with submissions.
Columns/Departments: Query the following editors for column ideas. A Woman Today (Shana Aborn, associate editor); Parents' Journal (Mary Mohler, managing editor); and Pet News (Nina Keilin).
Fiction: Sofia Marchant, books and fiction editor. "We consider any short story or novel that is submitted by an agent or publisher that we feel will work for our audience." Buys 12 mss/year. Length: 4,000 words. Fees vary with submission.

‡LADY'S CIRCLE, Lopez Publications, Inc., 111 East 35th St., New York NY 10016. (212)689-3933. FAX: (212)729-2235. Editor: Mary F. Bemis. 50% freelance written. Bimonthly magazine. "Midwest homemakers. Christian. Middle to low income. A large number of senior citizens read *Lady's Circle."* Circ. 200,000. Pays on publication. Byline given. Submit seasonal/holiday material 6 months in advance. Photocopied and previously published submissions OK. Reports in 2 months on queries; 3 months on mss. Sample copy for 9 × 12 SAE with $1.25 postage. Writer's guidelines for #10 SASE.
Nonfiction: Historical/nostalgic, how-to (crafts, cooking, hobbies), humor, inspirational, interview/profile, opinion, personal experience and religious. No travel. Buys 50-75 mss/year. Query. Pays $125 for unsolicited articles. Sometimes pays expenses of writers on assignment.
Photos: State availability of photos with submission. Reviews negatives, transparencies and prints. Offers $10/photo. Model releases and identification of subjects required.
Columns/Departments: Sound Off (pet peeves) 250 words; Readers' Cookbook (readers send in recipes); and Helpful Hints (hints for kitchen, house, etc.) 3-4 lines per hint. Send complete ms. Pays $5-10.
Fiction: Humorous, mainstream, religious, romance, and slice-of-life vignettes. Nothing experimental. No foul language. Buys 3 mss/year. Send complete ms. Pays $125.
Fillers: Contact Adrian B. Lopez. Anecdotes and short humor. Buys 35/year. Length: 100 words. Pays $5-25.
Tips: "Write for guidelines. A good query is always appreciated. Fifty percent of our magazine is open to freelancers."

LEAR'S, Lear Publishing Inc., 655 Madison Ave., New York NY 10021. (212)888-0007. Editor: Myra Appleton. Executive Editor: Audreen Buffalo Ballard. Articles Editor: Nelson W. Aldrich, Jr. Monthly magazine for women. Circ. 450,000. **Pays on acceptance.** Byline given. Offers ¼ kill fee. Buys first North American serial rights. Reports in 8 weeks.
Nonfiction: Book excerpts, essays, general interest, interview/profile, opinion, personal experience, travel. Query with published clips. Length: 800-1,200 words. Pays $1 per word.
Columns/Departments: Self-Center, Money & Worth, Health and Features. Query with published clips. Length: 800-1,000 words. Pays $1 per word.

McCALL'S, 230 Park Ave., New York NY 10169. (212)551-9500. Editor: Anne Mollegen Smith. Executive Editor: Lisel Eisenheimer. 90% freelance written. "Study recent issues." Our publication "carefully and conscientiously services the needs of the woman reader—concentrating on matters that directly affect her life and offering information and understanding on subjects of personal importance to her." Monthly. Circ. 5 million. **Pays on acceptance.** Publishes ms an average of 6 months after acceptance. Offers 20% kill fee. Byline given. Buys first or exclusive North American rights. Reports in 2 months. Writer's guidelines for SASE.
Nonfiction: Andrea Thompson, articles editor. No subject of wide public or personal interest is out of bounds for *McCall's* so long as it is appropriately treated. The editors are seeking meaningful stories of personal experience, fresh slants for self-help and relationship pieces, and well-researched articles and narratives dealing with social problems concerning readers. *McCall's* buys 200-300 articles/year, many in the 1,000- to 1,500-word length. Pays variable rates for nonfiction. Helen Del Monte and Andrea Thompson are editors of nonfiction books, from which *McCall's* frequently publishes excerpts. These are on subjects of interest to women: personal narratives, celebrity biographies and autobiographies, etc. Almost all features on food, household equipment and management, fashion, beauty, building and decorating are staff-written. Query. "All manuscripts must be submitted on speculation, and *McCall's* accepts no responsibility for unsolicited manuscripts." Sometimes pays the expenses of writers on assignment.
Columns/Departments: The Mother's Page; true first-person stories of solving parenting problems.
Fiction: Jane Ciabattari, department editor. Not encouraging unsolicited fiction. "Again the editors would remind writers of the contemporary woman's taste and intelligence. Most of all, fiction can awaken a reader's sense of identity, deepen her understanding of herself and others, refresh her with a laugh at herself, etc. *McCall's* looks for stories which will have meaning for an adult reader of some literary sensitivity. *McCall's* principal interest is in short stories; but fiction of all lengths is considered." Length: about 3,000 words average. Length for short-shorts: about 2,000 words. Payment begins at $1,500.
Tips: "Except for humor, query first. We are interested in holiday-related pieces and personal narratives. We rarely use essays. We don't encourage an idea unless we think we can use it." Preferred length: 750-2,000 words. Address submissions to articles editor unless otherwise specified.

MADEMOISELLE, 350 Madison Ave., New York NY 10017. (212)880-8800. Articles Editor: Liz Logan. 95% freelance written. Prefers to work with published/established writers. Columns are written by columnists; "sometimes we give new writers a 'chance' on shorter, less complex assignments." Directed to college-educated, unmarried working women 18-34. Circ. 1.1 million. Reports in 1 month. Buys first North American serial rights. **Pays on acceptance**; rates vary. Publishes ms an average of 1 year after acceptance.
Nonfiction: Particular concentration on articles of interest to the intelligent young woman, including personal relationships, health, careers, trends, and current social problems. Send health queries to Ellen Tien, health editor. Send entertainment queries to Debbie Wise, entertainment editor. Query with published clips. Length: 1,500-3,000 words.
Art: Kay Spear, art director. Commissioned work assigned according to needs. Photos of fashion, beauty, travel. Payment ranges from no-charge to an agreed rate of payment per shot, job series or page rate. Buys all rights. Pays on publication for photos.
Fiction: Eileen Schnerr, fiction and books editor. Quality fiction by both established and unknown writers. "We are interested in encouraging and publishing new writers and welcome unsolicited fiction manuscripts. However we are not a market for formula stories, genre fiction, unforgettable character portraits, surprise endings or oblique stream of consciousness sketches. We are looking for well-told stories that speak in fresh and individual voices and help us to understand ourselves and the world we live in. Stories of particular relevance to young women have an especially good chance, but stories need not be by or from the point of view of a woman—we are interested in good fiction on any theme from any point of view." Buys first North American serial rights. Pays $1,500 for short stories (10-25 pages); $1,000 for short shorts (7-10 pages). Allow 3 months for reply. SASE required. In addition to year-round unqualified acceptance of unsolicited fiction manuscripts, *Mademoiselle* conducts a once-a-year fiction contest open to unpublished writers, male and female, 18-30 years old. First prize is $1,000 plus publication in *Mademoiselle*; second prize, $500 with option to publish. Watch magazine

for announcement, usually in January or February issues, or send SASE for rules, after Jan 1.
Tips: "We are looking for timely, well-researched manuscripts."

MODERN BRIDE, 475 Park Ave., South, New York NY 10016. (212)779-1999. Editor: Cele Lalli. Managing Editor: Mary Ann Cavlin. **Pays on acceptance.** Offers 25% kill fee. Buys first periodical rights. Previously published submissions OK. Reports in 1 month.
Nonfiction: Book excerpts, general interest, how-to, personal experience. Buys 70 mss/year. Query with published clips. Length: 500-2,000 words. Pays $600-1,200.
Columns/Departments: Geri Bain, editor. Travel.
Poetry: Free verse, light verse and traditional. Buys very few. Submit maximum 6 poems.

MS. MAGAZINE, Lang Communications, Inc., 230 Park Ave., 7th Floor, New York NY 10169. (212)551-9595. Editor: Robin Morgan. Managing Editor: Helen Zia. Executive Editor: Mary Thom. 75% freelance written. Monthly magazine on women's issues and news. Estab. 1972. Circ. 100,000. Pays on publication. Byline given. Offers 20% kill fee. Buys all rights. Submit seasonal material 6 months in advance. Reports in 8 weeks. Sample copy $5. Writer's guidelines for #10 SASE.
Nonfiction: International and national (U.S.) news, the arts, books, popular culture, feminist theory and scholarship, ecofeminism, women's health, spirituality, and political and economic affairs. Photo essays. Runs fiction and poetry but does not accept, acknowledge, or return unsolicited fiction or poetry. Does not discuss queries on the phone. Query with published clips. Length: 300-4,000 words. Pays $150-1500 for assigned articles; $150-1,000 for unsolicited articles. Pays expenses of writers on assignment.
Photos: State availability of photos with submission. Offers $75-200 per photo. Model releases and identification of subjects required. Buys one-time rights.

RADIANCE, The Magazine for Large Women, Box 31703, Oakland CA 94604. (415)482-0680. Editor: Alice Ansfield. 95% freelance written. "A quarterly magazine that encourages and supports women all sizes of large to live fully now, to stop putting their lives on hold until they lose weight." Estab. 1984. Circ. 30,000. Pays on publication. Publishes ms an average of 3 months after acceptance. Byline given. Offers $15 kill fee. Buys one-time and second serial (reprint) rights. Submit seasonal/holiday material 6 months in advance. Simultaneous and previously published submissions OK. Query for electronic submissions. Reports in 1½ months. Sample copy $3.50; writer's guidelines for #10 SASE.
Nonfiction: Book excerpts (related to large women), essays, expose, general interest, historical/nostalgic, how-to (on health/well-being/growth/awareness/fashion/movement, etc.), humor, inspirational, interview/profile, new product, opinion, personal experience, photo feature and travel. Future issues will focus on children and weight, interviews with large men, fashion update, emerging spirituality, women and the arts, and women in the media. "No diet successes or articles condemning people for being fat." Query with published clips. Length: 1,000-2,000 words. Pays $35-100. Sometimes pays writers with contributor copies or other premiums—"negotiable with writer and us."
Photos: State availability of photos with submission. Offers $15-50 per photo. Captions and identification of subjects preferred. Buys one-time rights.
Columns/Departments: Up Front and Personal (personal profiles of women in all areas of life); Health and Well-Being (physical/emotional well-being, self care, research); Images (designer interviews, color/style/fashion, features); Inner Journeys (spirituality awareness and growth, methods, interviews); Perspectives (cultural and political aspects of being in a larger body). Buys 60 mss/year. Query with published clips. Length: 1,000-2,000 words. Pays $50-100.
Fiction: Condensed novels, ethnic, fantasy, historical, humorous, mainstream, novel excerpts, romance, science fiction, serialized novels and slice-of-life vignettes relating somehow to large women. Buys 15 mss/year. Query with published clips. Length: 800-1,500 words. Pays $35-100.
Poetry: Nothing "too political or jargony." Buys 30 poems/year. Length: 4-45 lines. Pays $20-50.
Tips: "We need talented, sensitive and openminded writers. We profile women from all walks of life who are all sizes of large, of all ages and from all ethnic groups and lifestyles. We welcome writers' ideas on successful and interesting large women from their local areas. We're an open, light-hearted magazine that's working to help women feel good about themselves now, whatever their body size. *Radiance* is one of the major forces working for size acceptance. We want articles to address all areas of vital importance in their lives."

REDBOOK MAGAZINE, 224 W. 57th St., New York NY 10019. Senior Editor: Diane Salvatore. Health Editor: Jean Maguire. Fiction Editor: Dawn Raffel. 80% freelance written. Monthly magazine. Estab. 1903. Circ. 3.9 million. **Pays on acceptance.** Publishes ms an average of 1-2 years after acceptance. Rights purchased vary with author and material. Reports in 2-3 months. Writer's guidelines for SASE.

Nonfiction: *"Redbook* addresses young mothers between the ages of 25 and 44. Most of our readers are married with children 12 and under; more than half work outside the home. The articles entertain, educate and inspire our readers. Many pieces stress 'how-to,' the ways a woman can solve the problems in her everyday life. Article subjects of interest: social issues, parenting, sex, marriage, humor. Please enclose sample of previously published work with articles or unsolicited manuscripts. Length: articles, 2,500-3,000 words; short articles, 1,000-1,500 words.

Columns/Departments: "We are interested in stories for the Young Mother series offering the dramatic retelling of an experience involving you, your husband or child. Possible topics: how you have handled a child's health or school problem, or conflicts within the family. For each 1,500-2,000 words accepted for publication as Young Mother's Story, we pay $750. Mss accompanied by a 9×12 SASE, must be signed, and mailed to: Young Mother's Story, c/o *Redbook Magazine.* Young Mother's reports in 6 months."

Fiction: "Of the 20,000 unsolicited manuscripts that we receive annually, we buy about 20 or more stories/year. We also find many more stories that are not necessarily suited to our needs but are good enough to warrant our encouraging the author to send others. *Redbook* looks for fresh, well-crafted stories that reflect some aspect of the experiences and interests of our readers; it's a good idea to read several issues to get a feel for what we buy. No unsolicited novels or novellas, please. Payment begins at $1,000 for short stories."

Tips: "Shorter, front-of-the-book features are usually easier to develop with first-time contributors, especially the Young Mother's stories. Most *Redbook* articles require solid research, full, well-developed anecdotes from real people and clear, substantial quotes from established experts in a field."

SELF, Conde Nast, 350 Madison Ave., New York NY 10017. (212)880-8834. FAX: (212)880-8110. Editor-in-Chief: Alexandra Penney. Managing Editor: Lisa Shelkin. 50% freelance written. "We prefer to work with writers—even relatively new ones—with a degree, training or practical experience in specialized areas from psychology to health to nutrition." Monthly magazine emphasizing self improvement of emotional and physical well-being for women of all ages. Circ. 1 million. Average issue includes 12-20 feature articles and 4-6 columns. **Pays on acceptance.** Publishes ms an average of 6 months after acceptance. Byline given. Offers 25% kill fee. Buys first North American serial rights. Submit seasonal material 4 months in advance. Simultaneous submissions OK. Reports in 1 month. Writer's guidelines for SASE.

Nonfiction: Well-researched service articles on self improvement, health, careers, nutrition, fitness, fashion and beauty, medicine, male/female relationships and money. "We try to translate major developments and complex information in these areas into practical, personalized articles." Buys 6-10 mss/issue. Query with clips of previously published work. Length: 1,000-2,500 words. Pays $1,000-2,000. "We are always looking for any piece that has a psychological or behavioral side. We rely heavily on freelancers who can take an article on contraceptive research, for example, and add a psychological aspect to it. Everything should relate to the whole person." Pays the expenses of writers on assignment "with prior approval."

Photos: Submit to art director. State availability of photos. Reviews 5×7 b&w glossy prints.

Columns/Departments: Work (800-1,200 words on career topics); and Money (800-1,200 words on finance topics); others, such as Entertaining, Man's View. Buys 4-6 mss/issue. Query. Pays $800-2,000.

Tips: "Original ideas backed up by research open our doors. We almost never risk blowing a major piece on an untried-by-us writer, especially since these ideas are usually staff-conceived. It's usually better for everyone to start small, where there's more time and leeway for re-writes. The most frequent mistakes made by writers in completing an article for us are swiss-cheese research (holes all over it which the writer missed and has to go back and fill in) and/or not personalizing the information by applying it to the reader, but just reporting it."

‡SKYLANDER MAGAZINE, Jjade Associate, 202 Church St., Hackettstown NJ 07840. (201)850-6688. Editor-in-Chief: Alicia Nordquist. Managing Editor: Wendie Blanchard. Estab. 1990. Circ. 20,000. Pays on publication. Publishes ms an average of 2-3 months after acceptance. Byline given. Offers 25% kill fee. Buys first North American serial rights, first rights or one-time rights. Submit seasonal/holiday material 6 months in advance. Query for electronic submissions. Reports in 2 weeks on queries; 1 month on mss. Sample copy $3 with 9×12 SAE and $2.40 first class stamps. Writer's guidelines for #10 SAE with 1 first class stamp.

Nonfiction: General interest, historical/nostalgic, humor, interview/profile, personal experience, photo feature. Bridal issue, financial, year in review, growth and development, holiday/gift guide, local writer travel, home & garden, summer camps, education, dining out. "No reflectives, inspirational, religious, technical, opinions." Buys 20-25 mss/year. Query with or without published clips, or send complete ms. Length: 850-2,000 words. Pays $125. Pays with contributor's copies or other premiums rather than cash payment at author's request.

Photos: State availability of photos with submission. Reviews contact sheets, transparencies and prints. Offers $10-25 per photo. Captions, model releases and identification of subjects required. Buys one-time rights.

Fiction: Adventure, fantasy, humorous, slice-of-life vignettes. Send complete ms. Length: 850-1,000 words.

Tips: "Most open to features pertaining to NW New Jersey/Eastern PA—in-depth but focused on beauty, season, recreational aspects, environmental concerns specific to the area."

TODAY'S CHRISTIAN WOMAN, 465 Gundersen Dr., Carol Stream IL 60188. (708)260-6200. FAX: (708)260-0114. Managing Editor: Julie A. Talerico. 25% freelance written. Works with a small number of new/unpublished writers each year. A bimonthly magazine for Christian women of all ages, single and married, homemakers and career women. Estab. 1979. Circ. 190,000. **Pays on acceptance.** Publishes ms an average of 3 months after acceptance. Byline given. Buys first rights only. Submit seasonal/holiday material 9 months in advance. Sample copy $3.50; writer's guidelines for #10 SASE.

Nonfiction: How-to, narrative and inspirational. Query only; no unsolicited mss. "The query should include article summary, purpose and reader value, author's qualifications, suggested length and date to send, availability of photos if applicable." Pays 10-15¢/word.

Tips: "Nature of the articles are: relational, psychological or spiritual. All articles should be highly anecdotal, personal in tone, and universal in appeal."

VICTORIA, Hearst Corp., 1700 Broadway 28th Fl., New York NY 10019. Did not want to be listed.

‡WEST COAST WOMAN, GDP Media, Inc., P.O. Box 3047, Sarasota FL 34230. (813)954-3300. Editor: Louise Bruderle. 50% freelance written. Biweekly tabloid for women on the west coast of Florida. "*West Coast Woman* is a lifestyle publication." Estab. 1988. Circ. 42,000. **Pays on acceptance.** Byline given. Offers ½ kill fee. Buys first rights or one-time rights. Submit seasonal/holiday material 2 months in advance. Reports in 1 month on queries. Sample copy $3.50. Writer's guidelines for #10 SASE.

Nonfiction: Real estate, gardening, how-to, health, beauty, book reviews, seniors, car care, home design, fitness, photo feature, technical , travel, sports, fashion, money/finance, nutrition, cooking, food/wine. "Special issues: Bridal issue-January, Health & Fitness-January, Careers-October, Aids-November. No humor, slice-of-life, essays, poems, poetry or comics/cartoons." Buys 130 mss/year. Query with published clips. Length: 750-3,000 words. Pays $35-65 for 750 words. Also makes ad trades for promotional tie-ins.

Photos: State availability of photos with submission. Reviews contact sheets, 35mm transparencies. Model releases required. Buys one-time rights.

Columns/Departments: Money/Finance. Buys 130 mss/year. Query with published clips. Length: 750-3,000 words. Pays $35-65 for 750 words.

‡WOMAN BEAUTIFUL, Allied Publications, Inc., 1176 Lake Worth Rd., Lake Worth FL 33460. (407)582-2099. Associate Editor: Karl H. Meyer. 85% freelance written. Bimonthly magazine covering fashions, hair, beauty, health and cosmetics. "Most readers are 17-30 yrs. We need good how-to pieces on cosmetics, styling, health, clothes, lifestyles. Don't overlook male-oriented articles, but not strictly unisex fashions." Estab. 1945. Circ. (combined) 105,000. Pays on publication. Publishes ms an average of 6 months after acceptance. Byline given. Offers no kill fee. Buys one-time rights and second serial (reprint) rights. Submit seasonal/holiday material 6-8 months in advance. Simultaneous and previously published submissions OK. Query for electronic submissions. Reports in 2 weeks on queries; 2-12 weeks on mss. Sample copy $1. Writer's guidelines for #10 SAE with 1 first class stamp.

Nonfiction: "No highly technical or cutesy material. No vulgar or obscene language. No jeremiads. Think positively." Buys 216 mss/year. Query with or without publshed clips, or send complete ms. "I often reject query and purchase clips submitted." Length: 300-1,500 words. Pays $25 maximum for unsolicited articles at 30¢ per published line. Pays in contributor copies or other premiums only if author requests.

Photos: State availability of photos with submission. Offers $5 per photo. Model releases and identification of subjects required. Photographer must have model releases on file; do not send.

Tips: "Study an issue or two, then write and submit. If rejected, it's not because I don't like you, or even your writing. I might love it, but have no place for it for some reason (usually does not fit with other articles). Write something else and submit. *Do not* call me on phone one month after you submit to check status—it will be returned pronto! All areas of magazine are open to freelancers. I enjoy working with new writers, and have been the first to publish the work of many new writers who show skill at handling words and ideas, and who are receptive to my ideas."

WOMAN'S DAY, 1633 Broadway, New York NY 10019. (212)767-6000. Articles Editor: Rebecca Greer. 75% or more of articles freelance written. 15 issues/year. Circ. 6 million. Pays negotiable kill fee. Byline given. **Pays on acceptance.** Reports in 1 month on queries; longer on mss. Submit detailed queries.

Nonfiction: Uses articles on all subjects of interest to women—marriage, family life, childrearing, education, homemaking, money management, careers, family health, work and leisure activities. Also interested in fresh, dramatic narratives of women's lives and concerns. "These must be lively and fascinating to read." Length: 500-2,500 words, depending on material. Payment varies depending on length, type, writer, and whether it's for regional or national use, but rates are high. Pays the expenses of writers on confirmed assignment."

Fiction: Eileen Jordan, department editor. Not considering unsolicited fiction.

Fillers: Neighbors and Tips to Share columns also pay $75/each for brief practical suggestions on homemaking, childrearing and relationships. Address to the editor of the appropriate section.

Tips: "Our primary need is for ideas with broad appeal that can be featured on the cover. We're buying more short pieces. Writers should consider Quick section which uses factual pieces of 100-500 words."

WOMAN'S WORLD, The Woman's Weekly, Heinrich Bauer North American, Inc., 270 Sylvan Ave., Englewod Cliffs NJ 07632. (201)569-0006. Editor-in-Chief: Dena Vane. 95% freelance written. Weekly magazine covering "controversial, dramatic, and human interest women's issues" for women across the nation. **Pays on acceptance.** Publishes ms an average of 4 months after acceptance. Byline given. Offers kill fee. Buys first North American serial rights. Submit seasonal/holiday material 4 months in advance. Simultaneous queries, simultaneous, and previously published submissions OK. Reports in 6 weeks on queries; 2 months on mss. Sample copy $1 and self-addressed mailing label; writer's guidelines for #10 SASE.

Nonfiction: Well-researched material with "a hard-news edge and topics of national scope." Reports of 1,000 words on vital trends and major issues such as women and alcohol or teen suicide; dramatic, personal women's stories; articles on self-improvement, medicine and health topics; and the economics of home, career and daily life. Features include In Real Life (true stories); Turning Point (in a woman's life); Families (highlighting strength of family or how unusual families deal with problems); True Love (tender, beautiful, touching and unusual love stories). Other regular features are Report (1,500-word investigative news features with national scope, statistics, etc.); Scales of Justice (true stories of 1,000-1,200 words on women and crime "if possible, presented with sympathetic" attitude; Between You and Me (600-word humorous and/or poignant slice-of-life essays); and Relationships (800 words on pop psychology or coping). Queries should be addressed to Ester Dowitz, senior editor. We use no fillers, but all the Between You and Me pieces are chosen from mail. Sometimes pays the expenses of writers on assignment.

Fiction: Jeanne Muchnick, fiction editor. Short story, romance and mainstream of 3,400 words and mini-mysteries of 1,300 words. "Each of our stories has a light romantic theme with a protagonist no older than forty. Each can be written from either a masculine or feminine point of view. Women characters may be single, married or divorced. Plots must be fast moving with vivid dialogue and action. The problems and dilemmas inherent in them should be contemporary and realistic, handled with warmth and feeling. The stories must have a positive resolution." Not interested in science fiction, fantasy, historical romance or foreign locales. No explicit sex, graphic language or seamy settings. Humor meets with enthusiasm. Specify "short story" on envelope. Always enclose SASE. Reports in 2 months. No phone queries. Pays $1,000 on acceptance for North American serial rights for 6 months. "The mini-mysteries, at a length of 1,600 words, may feature either a 'whodunnit' or 'howdunnit' theme. The mystery may revolve around anything from a theft to a murder. However, we are not interested in sordid or grotesque crimes. Emphasis should be on intricacies of plot rather than gratuitous violence. The story must include a resolution that clearly states the villain is getting his or her come-uppance." Pays $500 on acceptance. Pays approximately 50¢ a published word on acceptance. Buys first North American serial rights. Queries with clips of published work are preferred; accepts complete mss. Specify "mini mystery" on envelope. Enclose SASE. Stories slanted for a particular holiday should be sent at least 6 months in advance. No phone queries.

Photos: State availability of photos. "State photo leads. Photos are assigned to freelance photographers." Buys one-time rights.

Tips: "Come up with good queries. Short queries are best. We have a strong emphasis on well-researched material. Writers must send research with manuscript including book references and phone numbers for double checking. The most frequent mistakes made by writers in completing an article for us are sloppy, incomplete research, not writing to the format, and not studying the magazine carefully enough beforehand."

WOMEN'S CIRCLE, Box 299, Lynnfield MA 01940-0299. Editor: Marjorie Pearl. 100% freelance written. Bimonthly magazine for women of all ages. Buys all rights. **Pays on acceptance.** Byline given. Publishes ms an average of 6 months to 1 year after acceptance. Submit seasonal material 8 months in advance. Reports in 3 months. Sample copy $2. Writer's guidelines for #10 SASE.

Nonfiction: Especially interested in stories about successful, home-based female entrepreneurs with b&w photos or transparencies. Length: 1,000-2,000 words. Also interesting and unusual money-making ideas. Welcomes good quality crafts and how-to directions in any media—crochet, fabric, etc.

WORKING MOTHER MAGAZINE, Lang Communications, 230 Park Ave., New York NY 10169. (212)551-9500. Editor: Judsen Culbreth. Executive Editor: Mary McLaughlin. 90% freelance written. Prefers to work with published/established writers; works with a small number of new/unpublished writers each year. For women who balance a career with the concerns of parenting. Monthly magazine. Circ. 700,000. **Pays on acceptance.** Publishes ms an average of 4 months after acceptance. Byline given. Buys first North American Serial Rights and all rights. Pays 20% kill fee. Submit seasonal/holiday material 6 months in advance. Reports in 6 weeks. Sample copy $1.95; writer's guidelines for SASE.
Nonfiction: Service, humor, child development, material pertinent to the working mother's predicament. "Don't just go out and find some mother who holds a job and describe how she runs her home, manages her children and feels fulfilled. Find a working mother whose story is inherently dramatic." Send query to attention of *Working Mother Magazine.* Buys 9-10 mss/issue. Length: 750-2,000 words. Pays $300-1,800. "We pay more to people who write for us regularly." Pays the expenses of writers on assignment.
Tips: "We are looking for pieces that help the reader. In other words, we don't simply report on a trend without discussing how it specifically affects our readers' lives and how they can handle the effects. Where can they look for help if necessary?"

First Bylines

by Roseann Shaughnessy

For many writers, the first byline provides the greatest impetus to continue writing. Although a writer may persist in his craft out of pure love for it, he still needs occasional affirmation to retain confidence in what he is doing. The three writers profiled in this article agree that their first bylines were turning points in their careers as writers. They were finally able to call themselves *published* writers. One is a full-time writer, and two write part-time. They share the backgrounds on their first bylines and offer advice to writers working toward first bylines of their own.

J.L. Lauinger
"Happy Day," *Lost Creek Letters*

J.L. Lauinger began writing as a college student for a creative writing class. He resolved then that if he could complete 10 short stories, he could consider himself a writer and begin submitting work for publication. Upon completion of the stories, he sent them out to the magazines that most every writer dreams of appearing in, such as the *The New Yorker*.

When rejections swiftly appeared, Lauinger became discouraged, unaware that he had simply failed to target the appropriate markets for an emerging writer. "The issue of getting published was never paramount. The act of creating was what mattered. I guess I was just too impractical—I never thought of specific markets for my stories and just wrote them as they came."

Upon the advice of a friend, he took a different approach to having his stories published. "Someone had told me that if I wanted to have short stories published, it would be important to have a novel written. So, I devoted myself somehow to the writing of a novel, and that took years. I managed to finish it, and then I had a novel on my hands. What do you do with a novel? I was fairly sure that no one would look at it without an agent, so I tried to find an agent, with little success. Several editors have seen it, but it has not been published. An unofficial agent sent it to Random House. The editor was very encouraging and asked to see some of my short stories and suggested that I try to get those published."

In an ironic twist, Lauinger found himself facing his initial goal of getting his short stories published. He began submitting them again, this time to "little" literary magazines seeking work from new writers. The most immediate response he received was from the editor of *Lost Creek Letters*, to whom he had submitted the story, "Happy Day," an ultimately humorous account of a young boy who is called upon to assist a Catholic priest in administering a sacrament. "It was stunning," says Lauinger. "The editor, Pamela Montgomery, responded right away saying that I had made her day. The first thing she mentioned was the story's humor. She said she had read a lot of manuscripts that day and all had been about dying. Since she was not about to turn *Lost Creek Letters* into a death publication, she was very happy to have it." "Happy Day" appeared in the Summer 1990 issue of *Lost Creek Letters* and was followed by the publication of "Retreatmaster" in the Fall 1990 issue.

With that experience, Lauinger had found a niche – an audience for his work that could not be found by submitting work arbitrarily. "I did have luck in that Pamela Montgomery liked my work and not only published it, but sent me very careful remarks showing how well she had read the story and encouraged me to write. In that encouragement, she also suggested names of other publications that may be interested in my work. Every writer should be so lucky."

Lauinger admits that, while he enjoys experimenting with other forms of writing such as plays and novellas, he is primarily concerned with improving his short story writing. The encouragement of his first byline has helped. "I think a writer needs all he can get, because so few people read or rely on reading anymore. In a way, this seems to suggest that writers read each other's work, and if you can get into that little group, that group may become wider and wider. Ultimately, I think that will help *me* as a writer because I will know who is reading my work. It is very difficult to write in a vacuum."

Liz Curtis Higgs
"The Pumpkin Parable," *The Lookout*
"What Makes Women Laugh?," *The Ireland Report*

Liz Curtis Higgs' writing career began at the age of 10 when she composed a mystery story in the style of a Nancy Drew mystery novel, using her own characters. Her desire to write professionally materialized in 1978 when she began writing copy for a radio station where she was a broadcaster. However, she still yearned to have an article published. In January 1989, she resolved to publish that article by the year's end.

She began work on "The Pumpkin Parable," a short tale about a family that discovers Christian significance in the traditional Halloween pumpkin-carving ritual. She submitted the story to a few large Christian magazines without luck. Discouraged, she set the story aside until the following summer when she took a course in magazine writing. She applied her learning to "The Pumpkin Parable," revising it until she felt it was ready for re-submission. In August 1989, she sent it to *The Lookout*. "This made the most sense to me because it is not a widely distributed publication, and it is connected with my own church association."

Higgs' work paid off when she received a letter from the magazine stating that the story had been accepted for publication, and a check for $90 was forthcoming. "It was very exciting," she says, "because I was finally a published author. I was really fired up to continue writing."

Although her first published piece was a work of fiction, Higgs admits that she is primarily interested in writing nonfiction pertaining to her work as An Encourager®. "I am a humorist by nature. I go around the country speaking and making people feel good. In the course of my presentations, I began to notice that men and women laugh at different things." This intrigued Higgs, and she began to collect data on it. At the time when "The Pumpkin Parable" was published, she received a call from the editor of *The Ireland Report*, a magazine covering women's health marketing. The editor was aware of Higgs' work as An Encourager®, and stated that she was looking for an article on women's health that was somewhat "light" in nature. Higgs described her research, and the editor said it would make an appropriate article. The article, "What Makes Women Laugh?" was published in the November/December 1990 issue of *The Ireland Report*.

Unlike the publication of "The Pumpkin Parable," the publication of "What Makes Women Laugh?" brought Higgs no financial reward. However, both articles meant success to Higgs. The former gave her tremendous confidence to continue writing; the latter gave her greater exposure as a writer and speaker. In both cases, she attributes her success to the strong convictions she had about the topics she was addressing, which translated into her writing.

"I think this experience shows that if you pursue what really interests you in your writing, not always focusing on what will sell, you will eventually find success," says Higgs. "There is a lot of creativity that I can channel into my career as a speaker. But there is something about writing that is a satisfaction level of its own like nothing else. Writing has such a permanence about it that neither radio nor speaking does."

Brian Rohan
"Spreading the Light: Jack Healy of Amnesty International," *Irish America*

Photo by James Higgins

Brian Rohan has pursued his career as a writer/reporter in a consistently innovative manner. The 22-year-old Bronx native has already established himself in the New York writing community. While still a high school student, he and friend Timothy Monaghan co-founded *The Ledge*, an independent poetry and prose magazine, to create a forum for their work, as well as the work of other writers. In addition, Rohan took his writing "to the streets," giving occasional readings in Greenwich Village.

By that time, Rohan had determined that he wanted to be a writer. He decided, however, that he did not wish to limit himself exclusively to the writing of poetry and fiction. "For me, writing fiction and poetry is far more demanding than writing nonfiction. It takes a lot out of me because it involves a more personal commitment." Rohan has since left *The Ledge*, but the magazine is still published by Monaghan and available in several New York City bookstores.

As a student at Fordham University, Rohan served as a summer intern at the *Irish Voice*, a leading Irish-American newspaper. The editor of the paper was pleased with his performance and invited him to stay on fulltime after graduation in May 1990. During that time, Rohan considered writing an article about Jack Healy, executive director of Amnesty International, for possible publication in *Irish America*, the sister publication of the *Irish Voice*. "I felt that the article would be relevant to *Irish America* because it would highlight a very important Irish American," he says.

Rohan queried editor Patricia Harty with his idea and arranged an interview when she expressed interest in the piece. The article, "Spreading the Light: Jack Healy of Amnesty International," appeared in the December 1990 issue of *Irish America* and brought Rohan $300 for his work.

Today, as a regular contributor to both the *Irish Voice* and *Irish America*, Rohan can enjoy seeing his work in print every week. In addition, he utilizes his Irish-American journalism connections as a New York correspondent for the Dublin-based *Irish Times*. He advises writers to take an aggressive approach to getting articles published: "To make it you simply have to keep sending material so that people there get familiar with you and start calling *you* to solicit articles. Now, even the secretaries at the *Irish Times* know me, and I've managed to make some good money there."

Other Consumer Publications

The following consumer publications were listed in the 1991 edition but do not have listings in this edition of *Writer's Market*. The majority did not respond to our request to update their listings or return a questionnaire for a new listing. If a reason was given for their exclusion, we have included it in parentheses after the listing name.

Action Digest (ceased publication)

After Hours (asked to be deleted for one year)

Aglow

Air Alaska

American Brewer (asked to be deleted)

American Fitness (asked to be deleted)

American Health Magazine, Fitness of Body and Mind

American History Illustrated

American Newspaper Carrier

American West (unable to contact)

Ann Arbor Magazine (ceased publication)

Antiques & Auction News

Arete, Forum for Thought (ceased publication)

The Athenian

Away (unable to contact)

Balance (ceased publication)

Bay Area Parent

Better Nutrition for Today's Living

Birder's World

Boat (ceased publication)

Boston Magazine

Boston Woman Magazine

Bowbender

Business New Hampshire Magazine

Business Today

California Basketball Magazine (ceased publication)

California Football Magazine (ceased publication)

Camping Canada (now staff written)

Campus Life Magazine (unable to contact; mail returned)

Capital Magazine

Car Collector/Car Classics

Carolina Quarterly

Cat Companion

The Catholic Answer

Catholic Digest

Catholic Forester

Central Coast Parent (asked to be deleted)

Central Florida Magazine

Charlotte (uses only local writers)

Chattanooga Life & Leisure (ceased publication)

Child Life

Christian Outlook (ceased publication)

Classic Auto Restorer

Coast

Coast & Country Magazine

College Outlook and Career Opportunities

The Companion of St. Francis and St. Anthony

Comico the Comic Company

Computer Gaming World, the Definitive Computer Game Magazine

Computing Now!

Conceive Magazine (ceased publication)

Consumers Digest Magazine

Contemporanea

Cook's (bought by *Gourmet* and no longer published)

Corpus Christi Magazine (unable to contact; mail returned)

Country Roads Quarterly (backlogged with submissions)

Crafting Today

Crafts 'n' Things

CV (ceased publication)

Denton Today Magazine (unable to contact; mail returned)

Detective Files (includes Detective Dragnet, Detective Cases, Headquarters Detective, Startling Detective and True Police Cases; unable to contact for verification)

Dialogue

Discoveries

Discovery

East West

El Palacio

The Elks Magazine

Entrepreneur Magazine

The Equine Market

Equinews

Fighting Woman News, Martial Arts, Self-Defense, Combative Sports Quarterly

Figment (temporarily suspended publication; new information not available at press time)

Fine Gardening

Florida Business/Southwest

Folio Weekly

Follow Me

Forest Notes (asked to be deleted)

4-Wheel & Off-Road

The Franklin Mint Almanac

The Florida Horse

Games Special Edition

Garden Magazine

Garden State Home & Garden

GBH Magazine (moved to 376 Boylston St., Boston MA 02116. Updated information not available.)

Gem Show News

The Gem

Gent

Globe

Good Taste/Menus Magazine

Gorezone

Gray Panther Network (asked to be deleted)

Great Lakes Sailor

Group Magazine

Group's Junior High Ministry Magazine

Guide to the Florida Keys, Humm's

Hadassah Magazine

Harvard Magazine (accepts minimal, specialized freelance material)

Health & Faith Digest (no longer accepts unsolicited freelance material)

Heddle Magazine

High Country News

Home & Country Ideas Holiday Cookbook (ceased publication)

Home Business News

Horseman Magazine

Horseplay

Horses West

Hudson Valley Magazine

Hustler Busty Beauties

Ideals Magazine

In Touch (ceased publication)

Income Opportunities

Insights

International Wine Review (ceased publication)

The Island Grower

Jacksonville Today

Junior Trails

Kentucky Happy Hunting Ground

Key Horizons

Kids & Parents

Knucklehead Press (does not pay for freelance material)

L.A. Style

Leatherneck

Legacy Magazine

Life in the Times

Link-Up

The Listen Again Music Newsletter

Lone Star Horse Report

Lone Star Humor

Long Island Monthly

Lutheran Woman Today

The Macintosh Buyer's Guide (ceased publication)

Magazine of the Midlands (ceased publication)

The Maine Sportsman

Marian Helpers Bulletin

Marriage & Family (ceasing publication)

Metropolitan Home
Midwest Poetry Review (unable to contact; mail returned)
Military Lifestyle
Military Living R&R Report (now staff written)
Minnesota Ink
Mississippi State University Alumnus
Model Railroader
Modern Liturgy
Modern Short Stories (ceased publication)
Monitoring Times
Monterey Life Magazine
Montana Magazine (backlogged with material)
The Mother Earth News
Motorboat
Movieline Magazine
Muir's Original Log Home Guide for Builders & Buyers
Music Magazine
Musky Hunter Magazine
Nanny Times
National Forum
National Geographic Traveler (asked to be deleted)
Natural Body & Fitness
Near West Gazette
The Nevadan (ceased publication)
New Age Journal
New England Travel (asked to be deleted)
The New Hampshire Alumnus (asked to be deleted; works mostly with freelancers who are graduates of their journalism program)
New Realities, Oneness of Self, Mind, and Body
New Jersey Reporter
New Ways
Nine
Nissan Discovery (publication suspended during format change; new information unavailable at press time)
Noah's Ark
North American Voice of Fatima
Northcoast View (temporarily suspended publication)
Northern Virginian Magazine
Northwest Magazine (asked to be deleted)
The Note
Nova Scotia Business Journal
Nugget
Oceanus (no longer uses freelance material)
O'Liners
On Your Way (ceased publication)
The Optimist Magazine
Palmer Video News
Palo Alto Weekly
Parents and Teenagers
PC Laptop Computers

The Pennsylvania Review
Performing Arts in Canada (ceased publication)
Performing Arts Magazine
Personal Computing Magazine (ceased publication)
Perspective
Pet Health News (ceased publication)
Phillysport (unable to contact; mail returned)
Phoenix Home & Garden
Plate World
Pleasure Quest
Prime Time Sports & Fitness
Psychology Today (ceased publication)
Pulse!
The Pun
Purrrrr!
Queen's Quarterly
Read Me (ceased publication)
Relix Magazine
Retirement Lifestyles (asked to be deleted; revamping and unsure of future publication)
Right On!
Ripon Forum
The Rock Hall Reporter
Rod & Custom (no longer accepts unsolicited freelance material)
Room of One's Own
The Rotarian
RV West Magazine
Sagebrush Journal
Savvy Woman (ceased publication)
Scholastic Scope (no longer accepts unsolicited freelance material)
School Mates (no longer accepts unsolicited freelance material; 95% staff written)
Sea Power
Secrets (magazine sold; updated information unavailable)
Senior Life Magazine
The $ensible Sound
Sewanee Review
Shareware Magazine
Sh-Boom (ceased publication)
Shofar Magazine
Silent Sports
Snow Country
Song Hits (ceased publication)
Sound Business (ceased publication)
The Southeastern Review
Southern Prestigious Homes & Interiors
Southern Woman to Woman
Spa Vacations Magazine
Sport Detroit Magazine (unable to contact; mail returned)
Star*Line
Starshore (ceased publication)
Start! (ceased publication)
The Strain (does not pay for

freelance material)
STV Guide
Sunday Magazine (no longer accepts unsolicited freelance material)
Super Ford
Tallahassee Magazine
Tattoo Advocate Journal
Thedamu
Thinking Families (no longer accepts unsolicited freelance material)
Third World
Today's Parish
Town and Country
Treasure Search/Found (ceased publication)
The Turkey Hunter
TV Entertainment
U.S. Art
UFO Universe
United Evangelical Action (no longer accepts unsolicited freelance material)
The Unspeakable Visions of the Individual Inc. (ceased publication)
Vermont Vanguard Press
Viajando/Traveling (ceased publication)
The Virginia Quarterly Review
Visio Magazine (ceased publication)
Vision
Volkswagon World
War Cry
Washington Jewish Singles Newsletter
The Washington Opera
Washington
The Water Skier
The Weekend Gardener (ceased publication)
The West Texas Sun (ceased publication)
The Western Boatman (ceased publication)
Western Humanities Review
Western New York Magazine
Westways
What's New Magazine
Wisconsin Visitor (ceased publication)
Woman's Enterprise for Entrepreneurs
Women's Chronicle (unable to contact for verification; mail returned)
Women's Circle Counted Cross-Stitch
Working Woman (no longer accepts unsolicited freelance material)
Yacht Vacations Magazine
York Magazine
Young American
The Young Soldier (ceased publication)
Your Health
Your Home
Youth Focus
Zyzzyva

Trade, Technical and Professional Journals

Often overlooked by writers in favor of consumer magazines, trade journals offer excellent freelance opportunities. Our placing them after Consumer Publications should not suggest that trade journals are a second-choice market. Indeed, they offer many advantages over their consumer counterparts.

Some consumer magazines are high profile, pay extremely well, and are recognizable to our non-writing friends. These are the vast minority among the entire population, though. On the whole, they tend to go out of business more frequently — and sooner after start-up (even top-budget, high-hope slicks). Payment also varies greatly: a few pay $1 per word or more, but a number also pay 1¢ per word or *less*. Finally, it is generally more challenging to become a regular contributing writer to consumer publications, because many want to maintain variety in writing.

Perhaps because they are often overlooked, trade journals offer writers more security. They tend to be more stable markets, not bought or sold as much, and continue to publish after achieving an acceptable level of success in their niche. Payment is rarely as high as $1 per word, but it is also rarely less than 10¢ per word. Also, trade journals are often actively seeking freelancers to add to their stables of regularly contributing writers.

Consequently, trade journals do not deserve a second-choice status among writers. Sure, maybe our non-writing friends will not be as greatly impressed by a clip from a trade journal. A professional writer, however, will recognize it for what it is: a published article that earns income and builds credentials. The stability, rate of pay and opportunity for regular contribution offered by trade journals make them a market too good to be over-looked.

Trade journal is the general term for all publications focusing on a particular occupation or industry. Other terms used to describe the different types of trade publications are business, technical and professional journals. "Trade magazines help readers do their jobs better," says one editor. Many technical journals are written for industrial and science trades and publish articles focusing on new technology or research. Professional journals contain articles from practitioners but focus on all aspects of an occupation. Physicians, educators and lawyers have their own professional journals.

Study several trade journals in the field to get a feel for trends and popular topics. "We look for writers who can recognize the cutting-edge of their industry," says an editor of a graphic design magazine. Newspapers are another good source of information. Changes in tax legislation and government regulations may affect several industries. Local news can be expanded into articles for regional, national and special interest magazines.

Writing for the trades is similar to writing for consumer magazines in many ways. Trade publication editors, like their consumer counterparts, seek professionally-presented sub-missions aimed specifically at their readers. An editor of a business journal says, "Our style is down-to-earth and terse. We pack a lot of information into short articles. Our readers are busy executives who want information dispatched quickly and without embroidery."

Most trade articles are shorter than consumer features, however, and trade journals tend to use more fillers, newsbreaks and short pieces. "We're looking for shorter, news-you-can-use articles," says one editor. "The writer should keep it interesting, but at the same time, stay solidly on track," says another. Trade journals are also more likely to buy all rights than consumer magazines, but their pay rates for sole rights to articles tend to be higher.

Photos help increase the value of most stories for trade. If you can provide photos, mention that in your query, or even send copies. Like consumer magazines, trade publications have become more visual. The availability of computer graphics has also increased the use of charts, graphs and other explanatory visuals.

Training or experience in a particular field is a definite plus. For some trade publications, it is essential. With others, it may be enough to provide the necessary information from a reliable and knowledgeable source. Access to experts is absolutely required for highly technical information. In fact, many trade journal editors will ask for a list of sources in order to verify information. Keep this in mind when querying and provide names of experts you talked with or plan to contact. Professionals will often consider a co-author arrangement—their expertise, your writing ability. Many professionals are willing interview subjects, eager to talk about trends or important developments in their fields.

One way to break into the trade field and to increase your income at the same time is to rewrite a consumer story to fit a trade publication. While working on a consumer story, you may also uncover a good trade story lead, such as an interesting new business or a manager with innovative ideas about increasing productivity. Remember to be alert for problem-solving material; readers want to know how they can apply this information to their own situations.

Query a trade journal as you would a consumer magazine. Most trade editors like to discuss an article idea with a writer first and will sometimes offer names of helpful sources. Some will provide a list of questions they want you to ask an interview subject. Mention any direct experience you may have in the industry in your cover letter. Send a resume and include clips if they show you have some background or related experience in the specific subject area. Don't forget to include a SASE with your query or manuscript and read the listing carefully for additional submission guidelines.

New magazines start up almost daily. Writers should watch for new publications in *Publishers Weekly*, *Folio*, *Magazine Week* and *Advertising Age*, as well as several other publications that stay abreast of the publishing industry.

This section contains about 600 listings for trade, technical and professional publications. Another source for trade publications is *The Business Publication Volume*, published by the Standard Rate and Data Service (SRDS). Designed primarily for buyers of ads, the volume provides the names and addresses of thousands of trade journals, listed by subject matter. The volume is updated monthly and should be available at most libraries.

For information on additional trade publications not listed in *Writer's Market*, see Other Trade Publications at the end of this section.

Advertising, Marketing and PR

Trade journals for advertising executives, copywriters and marketing and public relations professionals are listed in this category. Those whose main focus is the advertising and marketing of specific products, such as home furnishings, are classified under individual product categories. Journals for sales personnel and general merchandisers can be found in the Selling and Merchandising category.

ADVERTISING AGE, 740 N. Rush, Chicago IL 60611-2590. (312)649-5200. Managing Editor: Valerie Mackie. Managing Editor/Special Reports; Edward L. Fitch. Executive Editor: Dennis Chase. Deputy Editor: Larry Doherty. New York office: 220 E. 42 St., New York NY 10017. (212)210-0100. Editor: Fred Danzig. Currently staff-produced. Includes weekly sections devoted to one topic (i.e. marketing in Southern California, agribusiness/advertising, TV syndication trends). Much of this material is done freelance—on assignment only. Pays kill fee "based on hours spent plus expenses." Byline given "except short articles or contributions to a roundup."

AMERICAN DEMOGRAPHICS, American Demographics, Inc., P.O. Box 68, Ithaca NY 14851. (607)273-6343. FAX: (607)273-3196. Editor-in-Chief: Brad Edmondson. Managing Editor: Caroline Arthur. 25% freelance written. Works with a small number of new/unpublished writers each year. For business executives, market researchers, media and communications people, public policymakers. Monthly magazine. Estab. 1978. Circ. 35,000. Pays on publication. Publishes ms an average of 6 months after acceptance. Buys all rights. Submit seasonal/holiday material 6 months in advance. Query for electronic submissions. Reports in 1 month. Include self-addressed stamped postcard for return word that ms arrived safely. Sample copy for $5 with 9 × 11 SAE. Writer's guidelines for #10 SASE.
Nonfiction: General interest (on demographic trends, implications of changing demographics, profile of business using demographic data); and how-to (on the use of demographic techniques, psychographics, understand projections, data, apply demography to business and planning). No anecdotal material or humor. Sometimes pays the expenses of writers on assignment.
Tips: "Writer should have clear understanding of specific population trends and their implications for business and planning. The most important thing a freelancer can do is to read the magazine and be familiar with its style and focus."

‡ART DIRECTION, Advertising Trade Publications, Inc., 6th Floor, 10 E. 39th St., New York NY 10016. (212)889-6500. FAX: (212)889-6104. Editor: Hedi Levine. 10% freelance written. Prefers to work with published/established writers. Emphasis on advertising design for art directors of ad agencies (corporate, in-plant, editorial, freelance, etc.). Monthly magazine. Circ. 12,000. Pays on publication. Buys one-time rights. Reports in 3 months. Sample copy $4.
Nonfiction: How-to articles on advertising campaigns. Pays $100 minimum.

‡BARTER COMMUNIQUE, Full Circle Marketing Corp., P.O. Box 2527, Sarasota FL 33578. (813)349-3300. Editor-in-Chief: Robert J. Murely. 100% freelance written. Emphasizes bartering for radio and TV station owners, cable TV, newspaper and magazine publishers and select travel and advertising agency presidents. Semiannual tabloid. Circ. 50,000. Pays on publication. Publishes ms an average of 3 months after acceptance. Rights purchased vary with author and material. Phone queries OK. Simultaneous and previously published submissions OK. Query for electronic submissions. Reports in 1 month. Free sample copy and writer's guidelines.
Nonfiction: Articles on "barter" (trading products, goods and services, primarily travel and advertising). Length: 1,000 words. "Would like to see travel mss on southeast U.S. and the Bahamas, and unique articles on media of all kinds. Include photos where applicable. No manuscripts on barter for products, goods and services—primarily travel and media—but also excess inventory of business to business." Pays $30-50.
Tips: "Computer installation will improve our ability to communicate."

THE COUNSELOR MAGAZINE, Advertising Specialty Institute, NBS Bldg., 1120 Wheeler Way, Langhorne PA 19047. (215)752-4200. FAX: (215)752-9758. Editor: Daniel B. Cartledge. 25% freelance written. Works with a small number of new/unpublished writers each year. For executives, both distributors and suppliers, in the ad specialty industry. Monthly magazine. Estab. 1954. Circ. 6,000. Pays on publication. Publishes ms an average of 3 months after acceptance. Buys first rights only. No phone queries. Submit seasonal/holiday material 4 months in advance. Simultaneous, and previously published submissions OK. Reports in 3 months. Sample copy for 9 × 12 SAE with 3 first class stamps.
Nonfiction: Contact managing editor. How-to (promotional case histories); interview (with executives and government figures); profile (of executives); and articles on specific product categories. "Articles almost always have a specialty advertising slant and quotes from specialty advertising practitioners." Buys 30 mss/year. Length: open. Query with samples. Pays according to assigned length. Sometimes pays the expenses of writers on assignment.
Photos: State availability of photos. B&w photos only. Prefers contact sheet(s) and 5 × 7 prints. Offers some additional payment for original only photos accepted with ms. Captions and model releases required. Buys one-time rights.
Tips: "If a writer shows promise, we can help him or her modify his style to suit our publication and provide leads. Writers must be willing to adapt or rewrite their material for a specific audience. If an article is suitable for 5 or 6 other publications, it's probably not suitable for us. The best way to break in is to write for *Imprint*, a quarterly publication we produce for the clients of ad specialty counselors."

IDENTITY For Specifiers and Customers of Sign and Corporate Graphics, ST Publications, 407 Gilbert Ave., Cincinnati OH 45202. (513)421-2050. FAX: (513)421-5144. Editor: Lynn Baxter. 10% freelance written. Quarterly trade magazine on corporate identity. "We cover the design and implementation of corporate identity, sign programs and architectural graphics for environmental graphics designers, architects and their clients. We stress signage as a part of the total corporate identity program." Estab. 1988. Circ. 13,800. **Pays on acceptance.** Byline given. Offers 30% kill fee. Buys all rights. Query for electronic submission. Reports in 2 weeks. Free sample copy and writer's guidelines.

Nonfiction: How-to, interview/profile, opinion and technical. "No histories or profiles of design firms or manufacturers." Buys 4-10 mss/year. Query with or without published clips, or send complete ms. Length: 1,000-3,000. Pays $250-400. Sometimes pays expenses of writers on assignment.

Photos: Send photos with submission. Reviews 35mm to 4×5 transparencies. "We *sometimes* pay for photo rights from professional photographers." Identification of subjects required. Buys one-time rights.

Tips: "The best approach is a telephone or written query. Ours is a completely 4/color publication geared to graphically sophisticated audience, requiring professional photography and specific information about design solutions, fabrication and management of corporate identity programs. We prefer a case-history approach, but may accept some theoretical articles on the use of corporate identity, the value of signs, etc. Most open are feature stories written for designers (design, fabrication details) or buyers (value, costs, management of national programs). The more specific, the better. The more 'advertorial,' the less likely to be accepted. Unusual design solutions, unusual use of materials and breadth of design scope make stories more of interest."

‡IMPRINT, The Magazine of Specialty Advertising Ideas, Advertising Specialty Institute, 1120 Wheeler Way, Langhorne PA 19047. (215)752-4200. Managing Editor: Arn Bernstein. 25% freelance written. Works with a small number of new/unpublished writers each year. Quarterly magazine covering specialty advertising. Estab. 1967. Circ. 60,000. Pays on publication. Publishes ms an average of 6 months after acceptance. Byline given. Buys one-time rights. Submit seasonal/holiday material 6 months in advance. Simultaneous queries OK. Query for electronic submissions. Reports in 3 months. Sample copy for 9×12 SAE with 3 first class stamps.

Nonfiction: How-to (case histories of specialty advertising campaigns); and features (how ad specialties are distributed in promotions). "Emphasize effective use of specialty advertising. Avoid direct-buy situations. Stress the distributor's role in promotions. No generalized pieces on print, broadcast or outdoor advertising." Buys 10-12 mss/year. Query with published clips. Length: varies. Payment based on assigned length. "We pay authorized phone, postage, etc."

Photos: State availability of 5×7 b&w photos. Pays "some extra for *original* photos *only*." Captions, model release and identification of subjects required.

Tips: "The predominant cause of midsirected articles is the fact that many new writers simply don't understand the medium of specialty advertising, or our target audience—end-users. Writers are urged to investigate the medium a bit before attempting an article or suggesting an idea for one. We can also provide additional leads and suggestions. All articles, however, are specifically geared to specialty advertising (or premium) use."

‡MEDIA INC., Pacific Northwest media, marketing and creative services news, P.O. Box 24365, Seattle WA 98124. (206)382-9220. Editor: Gordon Todd. 10% freelance written. Monthly tabloid covering Northwest U.S. media, advertising, marketing and creative-service industries. "Audience is Northwest ad agencies, marketing professionals, media and creative-service professionals." Estab. 1987. Circ. 14,000. Byline given.

Tips: "It is best if writers live in the Pacific Northwest and can report on local news and events in Media Inc.'s areas of business coverage."

MORE BUSINESS, 11 Wimbledon Court, Jericho NY 11753. Editor: Trudy Settel. 50% freelance written. "We sell publications material to business for consumer use (incentives, communication, public relations)—look for book ideas and manuscripts." Monthly magazine. Estab. 1975. Circ. 10,000. **Pays on acceptance.** Publishes ms an average of 1 month after acceptance. Buys all rights. Reports in 1 month.

Nonfiction: General interest, how-to, vocational techniques, nostalgia, photo feature, profile and travel. Reviews new computer software. Buys 10-20 mss/year. Word length varies with article. Payment negotiable. Query. Pays $4,000-7,000 for book mss.

SIGNCRAFT, The Magazine for the Commercial Sign Shop, SignCraft Publishing Co., Inc., P.O. Box 06031, Fort Myers FL 33906. (813)939-4644. Editor: Tom McIltrot. 20% freelance written. Bimonthly magazine of the sign industry. "Like any trade magazine, we need material of direct benefit to our readers. We can't afford space for material of marginal interest." Estab. 1980. Circ. 20,500. Pays on publication. Publishes ms an average of 9 months after acceptance. Byline given. Offers negotiable kill fee. Buys first North American serial rights or all rights. Previously published submissions OK. Reports in 1 month. Sample copy and writer's guidelines for $2 and 5 first class stamps.

Nonfiction: Interviews and profiles. "All articles should be directly related to quality commercial signs. If you are familiar with the sign trade, we'd like to hear from you." Buys 20 mss/year. Query with or without published clips. Length: 500-2,000 words. Pays up to $250.

SIGNS OF THE TIMES, The Industry Journal Since 1906, ST Publications, 407 Gilbert Ave., Cincinnati OH 45202. (513)421-2050. FAX: (513)421-5144. Editor: Tod Swormstedt. Managing Editor: Wade Swormstedt. 15-30% freelance written. "We are willing to use more freelancers." Magazine published 13 times/year; special buyer's guide between November and December issue. Estab. 1906. Circ. 18,000. Pays on publication. Publishes ms an average of 3 months after acceptance. Byline given. Buys variable rights. Simultaneous queries, and simultaneous and previously published submissions OK. Reports in 3 months. Free sample copy. Writer's guidelines "flexible."
Nonfiction: Historical/nostalgic (regarding the sign industry); how-to (carved signs, goldleaf, etc.); interview/profile (usually on assignment but interested to hear proposed topics); photo feature (query first); and technical (sign engineering, etc.). Nothing "nonspecific on signs, an example being a photo essay on 'signs I've seen.' We are a trade journal with specific audience interests." Buys 15-20 mss/year. Query with clips. Pays $150-500. Sometimes pays the expenses of writers on assignment.
Photos: Send photos with ms. "Sign industry-related photos only. We sometimes accept photos with funny twists or misspellings."
Fillers: Open to queries; request rates.

VM + SD (Visual Merchandising and Store Design), ST Publications, 407 Gilbert Ave., Cincinnati OH 45202. (513)421-2050. FAX: (513)421-5144. Editor: Ms. P.K. Anderson. Managing Editor: Janet Groeber. 30% freelance written. Emphasizes store design and merchandise presentation. Monthly magazine. Circ. 20,000. Pays on publication. Buys first and second rights to the same material. Simultaneous and previously published submissions OK. Reports in 1 month. Publishes ms an average of 3 months after acceptance. Sample copy for 9×12 SAE with $2.70. Writer's guidelines for #10 SASE.
Nonfiction: How-to (display); informational (store design, construction, merchandise presentation); interview (display directors and store owners, industry personalities); profile (new and remodeled stores); new product; photo feature (window display); and technical (store lighting, carpet, wallcoverings, fixtures). No "advertorials" that tout a single company's product or product line. Buys 24 mss year. Query or submit complete ms. Length: 500-3,000 words. Pays $250-500.
Photos: Purchased with accompanying ms or on assignment.
Tips: "Be fashion and design conscious and reflect that in the article. Submit finished manuscripts with photos or slides always. Look for stories on department and specialty store visual merchandisers and store designers (profiles, methods, views on the industry, sales promotions and new store design or remodels). The size of the publication could very well begin to increase in the year ahead. And with a greater page count, we will need to rely on an increasing number of freelancers."

Art, Design and Collectibles

The businesses of art, art administration, architecture, environmental/package design and antiques/collectibles are covered in these listings. Art-related topics for the general public are located in the Consumer Art and Architecture category. Antiques and collectibles magazines for enthusiasts are listed in Consumer Hobby and Craft. (Listings of markets looking for freelance artists to do art work can be found in *Artist's Market* – see Other Books of Interest).

ANTIQUEWEEK, Mayhill Publications Inc., 27 N. Jefferson St., P.O. Box 90, Knightstown IN 46148. (317)345-5133. Managing Editor: Tom Hoepf. 80% freelance written. Weekly tabloid on antiques, collectibles and genealogy. *AntiqueWeek* publishes two editions: Eastern and Central. "*AntiqueWeek* has a wide range of readership from dealers and auctioneers to collectors, both advanced and novice. Our readers demand accurate information presented in an entertaining style." Estab. 1968. Circ. 60,000. Pays on publication. Publishes ms an average of 1-2 months after acceptance. Byline given. Buys first and second serial (reprint) rights. Submit seasonal/holiday material 1 month in advance. Reports in 1 month. Free sample copy and writer's guidelines.
Nonfiction: Historical/nostalgic, how-to, interview/profile, opinion, personal experience, antique show and auction reports, feature articles on particular types of antiques and collectibles. Buys 400-500 mss/year. Query with or without published clips, or send complete ms. Length: 1,000-2,000 words. Pays $25-150.
Photos: Send photos with submission. Reviews 3½×5 prints. Offers $10-15 per photo. Identification of subjects required. Buys one-time rights.
Columns/Departments: Insights (opinions on buying, selling and collecting antiques), 500-1,000 words; Your Ancestors (advice, information on locating sources for genealogists), 1,500-2,000 words. Buys 150 mss/year. Query. Length: 500-1,000 words. Pays $25-50.
Tips: "Writers should know their topic thoroughly to write about it. Feature articles must be well-researched and clearly written. An interview and profile article with a knowledgeable collector might be the break for a first-time contributor. As we move toward the year 2000, there is much more interest

in 20th-century collectibles. *Antiqueweek* also seeks articles that reflect the current popularity of Victorian-era antiques."

‡APPLIED ARTS QUARTERLY, Suite 324, 885 Don Mills Rd., Toronto, Ontario M3C 1V9 Canada. (416)510-0909. Editor: Peter Giffen. 70% freelance written. Quarterly magazine covering graphic design, advertising, photography and illustration. Estab. 1986. Circ. 12,000. **Pays on acceptance.** Byline given. Buys first North American serial rights. Query for electronic submissions. Reports in 1 month on queries. Sample copy for 10 × 13 SAE with $1.70 Canadian postage or 4 IRC's.
Nonfiction: Interview/profile, opinion, photo feature, technical (computers and the applied arts) and trade articles about graphic design, advertising, photography and illustration. Buys 20-30 mss/year. Query with published clips. Length: 500-2,500 words. Pays 60¢ (Canadian) per word.
Photos: Offers no additional payment for photos accepted with ms. Buys one-time rights.
Tips: "It helps if writers have some familiarity with the communication arts field. Writers should include a solid selection of published articles. Writers have the best chance selling us articles on graphic design and advertising. Look at what we've published before to see how we've handled stories in these areas in the past."

THE APPRAISERS STANDARD, New England Appraisers Assocation, 5 Gill Terrace, Ludlow VT 05149. (802)228-7444. Editor: Linda L. Tucker. 75% freelance written. Works with a small number of new/unpublished writers each year. Monthly publication on the appraisals of antiques, art, collectibles, jewelry, coins, stamps and real estate. "The writer should be extremely knowledgeable on the subject, and the article should be written with appraisers in mind with prices quoted for objects, good pictures and descriptions of articles being written about." Estab. 1980. Circ. 1,300. Pays on publication. Publishes ms an average of 2 months after acceptance. Byline given, with short biography to establish writer's credibility. Buys first rights, second serial (reprint) rights, and simultaneous rights. Submit seasonal/holiday material 2 months in advance. Simultaneous and previously published submissions OK. Reports in 1 week on queries; 3 weeks on mss. Sample copy for 9 × 12 SAE with 2 first class stamps; writer's guidelines for #10 SASE.
Nonfiction: Interview/profile, personal experience, technical and travel. "All articles must be geared toward professional appraisers." Query with or without published clips, or send complete ms. Length: 700 words. Pays $50.
Photos: Send photos with submission. Reviews negatives and prints. Offers no additional payment for photos accepted with ms. Identification of subjects required. Buys one-time rights.
Tips: "Interviewing members of the Association for articles, reviewing art books, shows and large auctions are all ways for writers who are not in the field to write articles for us."

ART BUSINESS NEWS, Myers Publishing Co., P.O. Box 3837, Stamford CT 06905. (203)356-1745. Editor: Jean Marie Angelo. Managing Editor: Fergus Reid. 25% freelance written. Prefers to work with published/established writers. Monthly trade tabloid covering news relating to the art and picture framing industry. Circ. 30,000. Pays on publication. Publishes ms an average of 3 months after acceptance. Byline given. Buys first-time rights. Submit seasonal/holiday material 2 months in advance. Simultaneous submissions OK. Reports in 3 months. Sample copy for 12 × 16 SAE and $4.
Nonfiction: News in art and framing field; interview/marketing profiles (of dealers, publishers in the art industry); new products; articles focusing on small business people—framers, art gallery management, art trends; and how-to (occasional article on "how-to frame" accepted). Buys 8-20 mss/year. Length: 1,000 words maximum. Query first. Pays $75-250. Sometimes pays the expenses of writers on assignment. "Useful if writer can photograph."

ARTS MANAGEMENT, 408 W. 57th St., New York NY 10019. (212)245-3850. Editor: A.H. Reiss. For cultural institutions. Published 5 times/year. 2% freelance written. Estab. 1962. Circ. 6,000. Pays on publication. Byline given. Buys all rights. Mostly staff-written; uses very little outside material. Query. Reports in "several weeks." Writer's guidelines for #10 SASE.
Nonfiction: Short articles, 400-900 words, tightly written, expository, explaining how art administrators solved problems in publicity, fund raising and general administration; actual case histories emphasizing the how-to. Also short articles on the economics and sociology of the arts and important trends in the nonprofit cultural field. Must be fact-filled, well-organized and without rhetoric. Payment is 2-4¢/word. No photographs or pictures.

CADALYST, Professional Management of AutoCAD Systems, P.O. Box 10460, Eugene OR 97440. (503)343-1200. Senior Editor: David Cohn. Managing Editor: Colleen McLaughlin. Monthly trade journal covering AutoCAD (computer-aided design). Estab. 1984. Circ. 45,000. Pays on publication. Publishes ms an average of 3-6 months after acceptance. Byline given. Offers $100 kill fee. Buys first North American serial rights. Submit seasonal/holiday 6 months in advance. Query for electronic submissions. Reports in 2 weeks on queries. Free writer's guidelines.

Nonfiction: Book excerpts (AutoCAD texts), expose, how-to (AutoCAD method articles, short tips), humor (AutoCAD person-in-the-trenches viewpoint), new product (press releases), opinion (guest editorial), personal experience, photo feature (Animator and other presentation graphics specific to AutoCAD), and technical (reviews of hardware and software). "No PR promotional articles on specific products or services. Buys 120 mss/year. Query. Length: 500-2,500 (can be longer for multiple product comparisons). Pays $100-1,000."

Photos: Send color photos with submission. Reviews negatives, transparencies ($2\frac{1}{4} \times 2\frac{1}{4}$), and prints ($8 \times 10$). Offers no additional payment for photos accepted with ms. Captions and identification of subjects required. Buys one-time rights.

Fillers: Anecdotes, facts, gags to be illustrated by cartoonist, newsbreaks, and short humor. Buys 30/year. Length: 50-500 words. Pays $100-300.

Tips: "We are only interested in people with an AutoCAD background in architecture/engineering/industrial design/surveying/construction industry. We are more interested in technical content than style. All areas are open. Please telephone or E-mail us on Compuserve first so we can assign you an article or chat about your story proposals."

CALLIGRAPHY REVIEW, 1624 24th Ave. SW, Norman OK 73072. (405)364-8794. Editor: Karyn L. Gilman. 98% freelance written. Eager to work with new/unpublished writers with calligraphic expertise and language skills. A quarterly magazine on calligraphy and related book arts, both historical and contemporary in nature. Estab. 1982. Circ. 5,500. Pays on publication. Publishes ms an average of 9 months after acceptance. Byline given. Offers 20% kill fee. Buys first rights. Query for electronic submissons. Sample copy for 9×12 SAE with 7 first class stamps; free writer's guidelines.

Nonfiction: Interview/profile, opinion, contemporary and historical. Buys 50 mss/year. Query with or without published clips, or send complete ms. Length: 1,000-2,000 words. Pays $50-200 for assigned articles; pays $25-200 for unsolicited articles. Sometimes pays the expenses of writers on assignment.

Photos: State availability of photos with submission. Reviews contact sheets, negatives, transparencies and prints. Pays agreed upon cost. Captions and identification of subjects required. Buys one-time rights.

Columns/Departments: Book Reviews, Viewpoint (critical), 500-1,500 words; Ms. (discussion of manuscripts in collections), 1,000-2,000 words; and Profile (contemporary calligraphic figure), 1,000-2,000 words. Query. Pays $50-200.

Tips: "*Calligraphy Review*'s primary objective is to encourage the exchange of ideas on calligraphy, its past and present as well as trends for the future. Practical and conceptual treatments are welcomed, as are learning and teaching experiences. Third person is preferred, however first person will be considered if appropriate. Writer should realize that this is a specialized audience."

THE CRAFTS REPORT, The Newsmonthly of Marketing, Management and Money for Crafts Professionals, The Crafts Report Publishing Co., 87 Wall St., 2nd Floor, Seattle WA 98121. (206)441-3102. FAX: (206)441-3203. Editor: Christine Yarrow. 50% freelance written. A monthly tabloid covering business subjects for crafts professionals. Estab. 1974. Circ. 18,000. Pays on publication. Byline given. Offers $50 kill fee. Buys first rights. Previously published submissions OK. Query for electronic submissions. Reports in 2 weeks. Sample copy $2.50

Nonfiction: Business articles for crafts professionals. No articles on art or crafts techniques. Buys approximately 70 mss/year. Query with published clips. Length: 800-1,200 words. Pays $100-150.

Photos: State availability of photos with submission or send photos with submission. Reviews 5×7 b&w prints, color prints and transparencies. Identification of subjects required. Buys one-time rights.

HOW, Ideas and Techniques in Graphic Design, F&W Publications, Inc., 1507 Dana Ave., Cincinnati OH 45207. (513)531-2222. Editor: Laurel Harper. 75% freelance written. Bimonthly graphic design and illustration business journal. "*HOW* gives a behind-the-scenes look at not only *how* the world's best graphic artists and designers conceive and create their work, but *why* they did it that way. We also focus on the *business* side of design—how to run a profitable studio." Estab. 1985. Circ. 35,000. **Pays on acceptance.** Byline given. Buys first North American serial rights. Query for electronic submission. Reports in 6 weeks. Sample copy for $8.50. Writer's guidelines for #10 SASE.

Nonfiction: Interview/profile, business tips and new products. Special issues—Sept/Oct: Self-Promotion Annual; Nov/Dec: Business Annual. No how-to articles for beginning artists or fine-art-oriented articles. Buys 40 mss/year. Query with published clips and samples of subject's work (artwork or design). Length: 1,200-2,500 words. Pays $250-600. Sometimes pays expenses of writers on assignment.

Photos: State availability of artwork with submission. Reviews 35mm or larger transparencies. May reimburse mechanical photo expenses. Captions are required. Buys one-time rights.

Columns/Departments: Marketplace (focuses on lucrative fields for designers/illustrators); Design Talk (Q&A interviews with top designers); Target Tactics (discusses self-promotion methods through successful case histories); and Production (ins, outs and tips on production). Buys 20 mss/year. Query with published clips. Length: 1,000-1,800 words. Pays $150-400.

Tips: "We look for writers who can recognize graphic designers on the cutting-edge of their industry, both creatively and business-wise. Writers must have an eye for detail, and be able to relay *HOW*'s step-by-step approach in an interesting, concise manner—without omitting any details. Showing you've done your homework on a subject—and that you can go beyond asking 'those same old questions'—will give you a big advantage."

MANHATTAN ARTS MAGAZINE, Renee Phillips Associates, Suite 26L, 200 East 72 St., New York NY 10021. (212) 472-1660. Editor: Renee Phillips. Managing Editor: Michael Jason. 100% freelance written. Monthly magazine covering fine art. Audience is comprised of art professionals, artists and emerging collectors. Educational, informative, easy-to-read style, making art more accessible. Highly promotional of new artists. Estab. 1983. Circ. 50,000. Pays on publication. Publishes ms an average of 1 month after acceptance. Byline given. Makes work for hire assignments. Submit seasonal/holiday material 3 months in advance. Simultaneous submissions OK. Sample copy $2.50, payable to Renée Phillips Associates (no postage or envelope required.)
Nonfiction: Book excerpts (art), essays (art world), general interest (collecting art), inspirational (artists success stories), interview/profile (major art leaders), new product (art supplies), technical (art business). Buys 100 mss/year. Query with published clips. Length: 150-500 words. Pays $25-100. New writers receive byline and promotion, art books. Sometimes pays expenses of writers on assignment.
Photos: Send photos with submission. Offers no additional payment for photos accepted with ms. Captions, model releases and identification of subjects required.
Columns/Departments: Reviews/Previews (art critiques of exhibitions in galleries and museums), 150-250 words; Artists/Profiles (features on major art leaders), 250-500 words; The New Collector (collectibles, interviews with dealers, collectors), 250-500 words; Artopia (inspirational features, success stories), 250-500 words; Art Books, Art Services, 150-500 words. Buys 100 mss/year. Query with published clips. Pays $25-100.
Tips: "A knowledge of the current, contemporary art scene is a must. An eye for emerging talent is an asset."

THE MIDATLANTIC ANTIQUES MAGAZINE, Monthly Guide to Antiques, Art, Auctions & Collectibles, The Henderson Daily Dispatch Company, Inc., P.O. Box 908, Henderson NC 27536. (919)492-4001. FAX: (919)430-0125. Editor: Lydia Tucker. 65% freelance written. Monthly tabloid that covers antiques, art, auctions and collectibles. "The *MidAtlantic* is a monthly trade publication that reaches dealers, collectors, antique shows and auction houses primarily on the east coast, but circulation includes 48 states and Europe." Estab. 1984. Circ. 12,000. Pays on publication. Byline given. Buys first rights, second serial (reprint) rights or simultaneous rights (noncompeting markets). Submit seasonal/holiday material 3 months in advance. Simultaneous and previously published submissions OK. Reports in 1 month on queries; 2 months on mss. Free sample copy and writer's guidelines.
Nonfiction: Book excerpts, historical/nostalgic, how-to (choose an antique to collect; how to sell your collection; how to identify market trends), interview/profile, personal experience, photo feature, and technical. Buys 96-120 mss/year. Query. Length: 800-2,000 words. Pays $50-150. Trade for advertising space. Rarely pays expenses of writers on assignment.
Photos: Send photos with submission. Offers no additional payment for photos accepted with ms. Identification of subjects required. Buys one-time rights.
Columns/Departments: Ask An Appraiser, Knock on Wood, Rinker on Collectibles, Lindquist on Antiques and Collecting For Fun (Insights on buying, selling, collecting antiques, art, collectibles, *not* looking for columnists at this time.), 800-2,000 words. Buys 96 mss/year. Query with published clips. Pays $3-50.
Tips: "Please contact by mail first, but a writer may call with specific ideas after initial contact. Looking for writers who have extensive knowledge in specific areas of antiques. Articles should be educational in nature. We are also interested in how-to articles, i.e., how to choose antiques to collect; how to sell your collection and get the most for it; looking for articles that focus on future market trends. We want writers who are active in the antiques business and can predict good investments. (Articles with photographs are given preference.) We are looking for people who are not only knowledgeable, but can write well."

‡**PROGRESSIVE ARCHITECTURE,** 600 Summer St., P.O. Box 1361, Stamford CT 06904. FAX: (203)348-4023. Editor: John M. Dixon. 5-10% freelance written. Prefers to work with published/established writers. Monthly. Estab. 1920. **Pays on acceptance.** Publishes ms an average of 4 months after acceptance. Buys all rights for use in architectural press. Query for electronic submissions.
Nonfiction: "Articles of technical, professional interest devoted to architecture, interior design, and urban design and planning and illustrated by photographs and architectural drawings. We also use technical articles which are prepared by technical authorities and would be beyond the scope of the lay writer. Practically all the material is professional, and most of it is prepared by writers in the field

who are approached by the magazine for material." Pays $150-400. Sometimes pays the expenses of writers on assignment.

Photos: Buys one-time reproduction rights to b&w and color photos.

Auto and Truck

These publications are geared to automobile, motorcycle and truck dealers; professional truck drivers; service department personnel; or fleet operators. Publications for highway planners and traffic control experts are listed in the Government and Public Service category.

AUTO GLASS JOURNAL, Grawin Publications, Inc., Suite 101, 303 Harvard E., P.O. Box 12099, Seattle WA 98102-0099. (206)322-5120. Editor: Burton Winters. 45% freelance written. Prefers to work with published/established writers. Monthly magazine on auto glass replacement. International publication for the auto glass replacement industry. Includes step-by-step glass replacement procedures for current model cars as well as shop profiles, industry news and trends. Estab. 1953. Circ. 5,700. **Pays on acceptance.** Publishes ms an average of 5 months after acceptance. No byline given. Buys all rights. Query for electronic submissions. Reports in 2 weeks. Sample copy for 6×9 SAE and 3 first class stamps. Writer's guidelines for #10 SASE.

Nonfiction: How-to (install all glass in a current model car); and interview/profile. Buys 22-36 mss/year. Query with published clips. Length: 2,000-3,500 words. Pays $75-250, with photos.

Photos: State availability of photos. Reviews b&w contact sheets and negatives. Payment included with ms. Captions required. Buys all rights.

‡THE BATTERY MAN, Independent Battery Manufacturers Association, Inc., 100 Larchwood Dr., Largo FL 34640. (813)586-1409. FAX: (813)586-1400. Editor: Celwyn E. Hopkins. 20% freelance written. Emphasizes SLI battery manufacture, applications and new developments. For battery manufacturers and retailers (garage owners, servicemen, fleet owners, etc.). Monthly magazine. Estab. 1959. Circ. 5,200. **Pays on acceptance.** Publishes ms an average of 1 year after acceptance. Buys all rights. Submit seasonal/holiday material 4 months in advance. Simultaneous and previously published submissions OK. Query for electronic submissions. Reports in 2 months. Send SASE for return of manuscript. Sample copy $3 and 9×12 SAE. Writer's guidelines for #10 SASE.

Nonfiction: Technical articles. "Articles about how a company is using batteries as a source of uninterruptable power supply for its computer systems or a hospital using batteries for the same (photos with article are nice) purpose as well as for life support systems, etc." Submit complete ms. Buys 19-24 unsolicited mss/year. Recent article examples: "State-of-the-Art Ventilation Engineering Principles of Laminar Flow and Recirculation in the Battery Industry" (April 1989); "North American SLI Battery Market Review and Forecast" (January 1989). Length: 750-1,200 words. Pays 6¢/word.

Tips: "Most writers are not familiar enough with this industry to be able to furnish a feature article. They try to palm off something that they wrote for a hardware store, or a dry cleaner, by calling everything a 'battery store.' We receive a lot of manuscripts on taxes and tax information (such as U.S. income tax) and mss on business management in general and managing a family-owned business. Since this is an international publication, we try to stay away from such subjects, since U.S. tax info is of no use or interest to overseas readers."

BRAKE & FRONT END, 11 S. Forge St., Akron OH 44304. (216)535-6117. FAX: (216)535-0874. Group Publisher: Jack Hone. Editor: Mary DellaValle. 5% freelance written. Works with a small number of new/unpublished writers each year. For owners of automotive repair shops engaged in brake, suspension, driveline, exhaust and steering repair, including: specialty shops, general repair shops, new car and truck dealers, gas stations, mass merchandisers and tire stores. Monthly magazine. Estab. 1931. Circ. 28,000. Pays on publication. Publishes ms an average of 3-4 months after acceptance. Byline given. Buys first North American serial rights. Reports immediately. Sample copy and editorial schedule $3; guidelines for SASE.

Nonfiction: Specialty shops taking on new ideas using new merchandising techniques; growth of business, volume; reasons for growth and success. Expansions and unusual brake shops. Prefers no product-oriented material. Query. Length: about 800-1,500 words. Pays 7-9¢/word. Sometimes pays expenses of writers on assignment.

Photos: Pays $8.50 for b&w glossy prints purchased with mss.

EASTERN AFTERMARKET JOURNAL, Stan Hubsher Inc., P.O. Box 373, Cedarhurst NY 11516. (516)295-3680. Editor: Stan Hubsher. 100% freelance written. Bimonthly magazine for automotive parts wholesaler buyers at the warehouse and jobber level, on the Eastern seaboard. "Audience operates stores and warehouses that handle replacement parts for automobiles. No technical knowl-

edge necessary. Profiles of owners/buyers, how they operate in highly competitive market that accounts for 40% of the entire country's aftermarket business." Estab. 1956. Circ. 8,500. Pays on publication. No byline. Buys all rights. Submit material 2 months in advance. Free sample copy and writer's guidelines.
Nonfiction: Buys 6-8 mss/year. Query. Length: 2,000 words. Pays $150 minimum to negotiable maximum. Sometimes pays expenses of writers on assignment.
Photos: Send photos with submission. Offers no additional payments for photos accepted with ms. Captions and identification of subjects required. Buys one-time rights.

‡JOBBER TOPICS, 7300 N. Cicero Ave., Lincolnwood IL 60646. (708)674-7300. FAX: (708)674-7015. Articles Editor: Peggy Person. 30% freelance written. Prefers to work with published/established writers, works with a small number of new/unpublished writers each year. "A magazine dedicated to helping its readers—auto parts jobbers and warehouse distributors—succeed in their business via better management and merchandising techniques and a better knowledge of industry trends, sales activities and local or federal legislation that may influence their business activities." Monthly. Estab. 1922. Pays on publication. Buys First North American serial rights. Sample copy and writer's guidelines for 8½×11 SASE.
Nonfiction: "Articles with unusual or outstanding automotive jobber procedures, with special emphasis on sales, merchandising and machine shop; any phase of automotive parts and equipment sales and distribution. Especially interested in merchandising practices and machine shop operations. Most independent businesses usually have a strong point or two. We like to see a writer zero in on that strong point(s) and submit an outline (or query), advising us of those points and what he/she intends to include in a feature. We will give him, or her, a prompt reply." Length: 2,500 words maximum. Pay based on quality and timeliness of feature. Pays the expenses of writers on assignment.
Photos: 5×7 b&w glossies or 35mm color transparencies purchased with mss.

MODERN TIRE DEALER, 110 N. Miller Rd., P.O. Box 3599, Akron OH 44313-3599. (216)867-4401. FAX: (216)867-0019. Editor: Lloyd Stoyer. 15-20% freelance written. Prefers to work with published/established writers. For independent tire dealers. Monthly tabloid, plus 2 special emphasis issue magazines. Published 14 times annually. Estab. 1919. Buys all rights. Reports in 1 month. Publishes ms an average of 2 months after acceptance. Sample copy $5.
Nonfiction: "How independent tire dealers sell tires, accessories and allied services such as brakes, wheel alignment, shocks and mufflers. The emphasis is on merchandising and management. We prefer the writer to zero in on some specific area of interest. Avoid shotgun approach." Query. Length: 1,500 words. Pays $300 and up. Sometimes pays the expenses of writers on assignment.
Photos: 8×10, 4×5, 5×7 b&w glossy prints purchased with mss.
Tips: "Changes in the competitive situation among tire manufacturers and/or distributors will affect the types of freelance material we buy. We want articles for or about tire dealers, not generic articles adapted for our publication."

‡OVERDRIVE, The Publication of the Independent Truckers, Randall Publishing Co./Overdrive, Inc., Box 3187, Tuscaloosa AL 35403. (205)349-2990. Editor: Steve Sturgess. Associate Editor: Debi Pennington. 50% freelance written. Monthly magazine for independent truckers. Estab. 1934. Circ. 90,000. Pays on publication. Publishes ms an average of 2 months after acceptance. Byline given. 10% kill fee. Buys first North American serial rights. Reports in 2 weeks on queries; 1 month on mss. Sample copy for 9×12 SAE.
Nonfiction: Essays, expose, how-to (truck maintenance and operation), interview/profile (successful independent truckers), new product, personal experience, photo feature, technical. All must be related to independent trucker interest. Buys 60+ mss/year. Query with or without published clips or send complete ms. Length: 500-2,000 words. Pays $100-600 for assigned articles; $50-500 for unsolicited articles.
Photos: Send photos with submission. Reviews transparencies and 5×7 prints. Offers $25-50 per photo. Identification of subjects required. Buys one-time rights.
Fiction: Humorous (short pieces with trucking theme), slice-of-life vignettes (illustrate a lesson about trucking business, safety, driving, etc.). Buys 2 mss/year. Send complete ms. Length: 500-1,500 words. Pays $50-200.
Tips: "Talk to independent truckers. Develop a good knowledge of their concerns as small business owners, truck drivers and individuals. We prefer articles that quote experts, people in the industry and truckers to first-person expositions on a subject. Get straight facts. Look for good material on truck safety, on effects of government regulations, and on rates and business realtionships between independent truckers, brokers, carriers and shippers."

SOUTHERN MOTOR CARGO, Wallace Witmer Co., 1509 Madison, Memphis TN 38104. (901)276-5424. FAX: (901)276-5400. Managing Editor: Randy Duke. 15% freelance written. Monthly trade publication providing useful information to trucking fleet managers and maintenance supervisors with emphasis on equipment, safety, shipping and trucking operations management. Estab. 1944. Circ. 61,000. **Pays on acceptance.** Publishes ms an average of 2 months after acceptance. Byline sometimes given. Buys all rights. Submit seasonal/holiday material 2 months in advance. Free sample copy.

Nonfiction: Interview/profile, new product, technical, industry news and other safety related articles. "We do not want articles about drivers or owner operators." Buys 10 mss/year. Send complete ms. Length: 500-2,500 words. Pays min. 10-15¢/word. Pays expenses of writers on cleared assignments.

Photos: Send photos with submission. Reviews contact sheets and negatives. Pays for film and processing. Captions, model releases and identification of subjects required. Buys all rights.

Columns/Departments: Southern Trucking (articles that affect the writer's region. Consists of state news which deals with trucking). Industry News (deals with company expansions, closings, etc.). Send complete ms. Length: 300-1,500 words. Pays 10-15¢/word.

Tips: "We have recently begun publishing *regional* sections. We *need* freelancers in the Atlantic, West South Central, and East South Central regions. These writers will report on truck news in their city and surrounding area."

TOW-AGE, Kruza Kaleidoscopix, Inc., P.O. Box 389, Franklin MA 02038. Editor: J. Kruza. For readers who run their own towing service business. 5% freelance written. Prefers to work with published/established writers. Published every 6 weeks. Circ. 18,000. Buys all rights; usually reassigns rights. Buys about 18 mss/year. **Pays on acceptance.** Simultaneous submissions OK. Reports in 1 month. Sample copy $3; free writer's guidelines for #10 SASE.

Nonfiction: Articles on business, legal and technical information for the towing industry. "Light reading material; short, with punch." Informational, how-to, personal, interview and profile. Query or submit complete ms. Length: 600-800 words. Pays $50-150. Spot news and successful business operations. Length: 300-800 words. Technical articles. Length: 400-1,000 words. Pays expenses of writers on assignment.

Photos: Buys up to 8×10 b&w photos purchased with or without mss, or on assignment. Pays $25 for first photo; $10 for each additional photo in series. Captions required.

‡TRUCKING DIGEST, Hammond Communications, Suite 221, 3387 Poplar, Memphis TN 38111. (901)458-5263. Editor: Pearce W. Hammond. Managing Editor: Connie White Mills. 25% freelance written. Monthly trade journal covering trucking industry. "*Trucking Digest* is distributed monthly to owners, operators, buyers, sellers and users of all types of truck trailers and medium and heavy duty trucks in the United States. Additional copies go to truck and trailer manufacturers and other industry suppliers." Estab. 1990. Circ. 30,000. Pays on publication. Byline sometimes given. No kill fee. Buys all rights. Query for electronic submissions. Reports in 3 weeks on queries. Free writer's guidelines.

Nonfiction: General interest, how-to, interview/profile, new product, technical. "No articles that are not related to the trucking industry." Query with published clips, or send complete ms. Length: 300-1,500 words. Pays 10-25¢/word for assigned articles; 10-20¢/word for unsolicited articles.

Photos: State availability of photos with submission. Reviews contact sheets, 35mm transparencies and 3×5 prints. Offers $5-20 per photo. Identification of subjects required. Buys one-time rights.

Columns/Departments: Buys 3 mss/year. Query. Length: 300-500 words. Pays 10-20%/word.

Fillers: Facts, newsbreaks. Buys 6/year. Length: 20-50 words. Pays $5-15.

Tips: "Be familiar with the trucking industry. Visit truck and trailer dealers and find out what is going on concerning the buying and selling of equipment. Visit trucking companies in their local area. Find out about new products available for trucks and trailers."

‡VEHICLE LEASING TODAY, National Vehicle Leasing Association, Suite 225, 3710 S. Robertson, P.O. Box 2349, Culver City CA 90232. (213)838-3170. Editor: Lorraine Alkire. 15% freelance written. A bimonthly magazine on vehicle leasing. "We cover critical issues for vehicle lesors, financial lending institutions, and computer software vendors with lessor programs." Estab. 1985. Circ. 6,000. Pays on publication. Publishes ms an average of 2 months after acceptance. Byline given. Negotiable kill fee. Buys one-time rights. Submit seasonal/holiday material 3 months in advance. Photocopied and previously published submissions OK. Computer printout submissions OK; no dot-matrix. Sample copy $5; free writer's guidelines.

Nonfiction: How-to (anything relating to a vehicle lessor business), interview/profile, new product, technical. Buys 5 mss/year. Query. Length: 1,000-2,000 words. Pays $50-250 for assigned articles; $50-200 for unsolicited articles. Sometimes pays expenses of writers on assignment.

Photos: State availability of photos with submission. Reviews 5×7 prints. Offers no additional payment for photos accepted with ms. Model releases required. Buys one-time rights.

Columns/Departments: Financial Institutions, Lessor Issues, 500-1,000 words; New Products and Services, 500 words. Buys 3 mss/year. Send complete ms. Length: 300-1,000 words. Pays $25-100.

WARD'S AUTO WORLD, % 28 W. Adams, Detroit MI 48226. (313)962-4433. FAX: (313)962-4456. Editor: Edward K. Miller. Managing Editor: Marjorie A. Sorge. 10% freelance written. Prefers to work with published/established writers; works with a small number of new/unpublished writers each year. For top and middle management in all phases of auto industry. Also includes heavy-duty vehicle coverage. Monthly magazine. Estab. 1970. Circ. 100,000. Pays on publication. Pay varies for kill fee. Byline given. Buys all rights. Phone queries OK. Query for electronic submissions. Reports in 2 weeks. Publishes ms an average of 1 month after acceptance. Free sample copy and writer's guidelines.

Nonfiction: Expose, general interest, international automotive news, interview, new product and technical. Few consumer type articles. No "nostalgia or personal history stories (like 'My Favorite Car')." Buys 4-8 mss/year. Query. Length: 700-2,500 words. Pays $200-750. Sometimes pays the expenses of writers on assignment.

Photos: Assignment only.

Tips: "Don't send poetry, how-to and 'My Favorite Car' stuff. They don't stand a chance. This is a business newsmagazine and operates on a news basis just like any other newsmagazine. We like solid, logical, well-written pieces with *all* holes filled. Most surprises over the transom turn out to be exactly what we don't want. If you have questions, save yourself some headaches and use your phone."

Aviation and Space

In this section are journals for aviation business executives, airport operators and aviation technicians. Publications for professional and private pilots can be found in the Consumer Aviation section.

AIR LINE PILOT, Magazine of Professional Flight Crews, Air Line Pilots Association, 535 Herndon Parkway, Box 1169, Herndon VA 22070. (703)689-4176. Editor: Esperison Martinez, Jr. 10% freelance written. Prefers to work with published/established writers. A monthly magazine for airline pilots covering "aviation industry information—economics, avionics, equipment, systems, safety—that affects a pilot's life in professional sense." Also includes information about management/labor relations trends, contract negotiations, etc. Circ. 60,000. **Pays on acceptance.** Publishes ms an average of 6 months after acceptance. Offers 35% kill fee. Buys first serial rights and makes work-for-hire assignments. Submit seasonal/holiday material 6 months in advance. Query for electronic submissions. Reports in 2 months. Sample copy $2 with 9 × 12 SAE; writer's guidelines for #10 SASE.

Nonfiction: Historical/nostalgic, humor, interview/profile, photo feature and technical. "We are backlogged with historical submissions and prefer not to receive unsolicited submissions at this time." Buys 20 mss/year. Query with or without published clips, or send complete ms. Length: 1,000-3,000 words. Pays $100-800 for assigned articles; pays $50-500 for unsolicited articles.

Photos: Send photos with submission. Reviews contact sheets, 35mm transparencies and 8 × 10 prints. Offers $10-25/photo. Identification of subjects required. Buys one-time rights.

Tips: "For our feature section, we seek aviation industry information that affects the life of a professional airline pilot from a career standpoint. We also seek material that affects his life from a job security and work environment standpoint. Historical material that addresses the heritage of the profession or the advancement of the industry is also sought. Any airline pilot featured in an article must be an Air Line Pilots Association member in good standing."

‡CAREER PILOT, FAPA, 4959 Massachusetts Blvd., Atlanta GA 30337. (404)997-8097. Editor: Teresa Greer. Director of Editorial/Publications: Carol Vernon. 80% freelance written. Monthly magazine covering aviation. "A career advisory magazine as a service to FAPA members. Readers largely are career pilots who are working toward their professional goals. Articles cover topics such as recent developments in aviation law and medicine, changes in the industry, job interview techniques and how to get pilot jobs." Estab. 1983. Circ. 17,486. Pays on acceptance. Publishes ms an average of 3-4 months after acceptance. Byline given. Offers 50% kill fee. Buys all rights. Simultaneous submissions and previously published submissions. Query for electronic submissions. Reports in 6 weeks.

Nonfiction: How-to (get hired by an airline), interview/profile (aviation related), personal experience (aviation related). Special issues: October-Corporate aviation, January-Helicopters. "No humor, cartoons or fiction." Buys 60 mss/year. Send query. Length: 2,000-2,500 words. "Pays 18¢/word with $50 bonus for meeting deadlines." Sometimes pays expenses of writers on assignment.

Photos: State availability of photos with submission. Reviews prints. Offers no additional payment for photos accepted with ms. Captions and identification of subjects required.

Tips: "Send articles and clips that are aviation/business related. Express your interest in writing for our publication on a semi-regular basis. Writers have a good chance selling us how to get started articles; and airline profiles."

Beverages and Bottling

Manufacturers, distributors and retailers of soft drinks and alcoholic beverages read these publications. Publications for bar and tavern operators and managers of restaurants are classified in the Hotels, Motels, Clubs, Resorts and Restaurants category.

AMERICAN BREWER, P.O. Box 510, Hayward CA 94541. (415)538-9500 (a.m. only). FAX: (415)537-0948. Publisher: Bill Owens. 100% freelance written. Quarterly magazine covering micro-breweries. Estab. 1986. Circ. 4,000. Pays on pubilcation. Publishes ms an average of 4 months after acceptance. Byline given. Buys one-time rights. Previously published submissions OK. Reports in 2 weeks on queries. Sample copy for $5.
Nonfiction: Humor, opinion and travel. Query. Length: 1,500-2,500 words. Pays $50-250 for assigned articles.

BEER WHOLESALER, Beverage Management Associates, Inc., Suite 4, 11460 W. 44th Ave., Wheat Ridge CO 80033. (303)425-4668. FAX: (303)425-4701. Editor: Daniel Morales Brink. 20% freelance written. Bimonthly magazine covering beverage wholesaling. *Beer Wholesaler* is edited for those in the beer distribution field. Editorial covers management, current sales promotions, national conventions, legal news, news on imported beers and various phases of the business activities of interest to the beer wholesaler. Also included are special features on warehouses, truck fleet management, beer consumption trends, computers/data processing systems, and other features pertinent to the beer distributor. *Beer Wholesaler* provides articles on individual wholesale operations as well as interpretive analysis of the industry. Estab. 1968. Circ. 3,217. Pays on acceptance. Byline given. Offers expenses plus 50% kill fee. Buys first North American serial rights. Submit seasonal/holiday material 3 months in advance. Simultaneous and previously published submissions OK. Query for electronic submissions. Reports in 2 weeks. Sample copy for $2. Free writer's guidelines.
Nonfiction: Special upcoming issues: Import issue (May); European Imports Issue (January, 1991); and Transportation Issue (September). Buys 6 mss/year. Query with published clips. Length: 300-3,000 words. Pays $50 minimum for assigned articles; $30-300 for unsolicited articles. Pays expenses of writers on assignment.
Photos: Send photos with submission. Reviews contact sheets and 35mm and 5×7 transparencies. Offers $20-100 per photo. Captions and identification of subjects required. Buys one-time rights.
Columns/Departments: Sales and Marketing Retail (retailer/wholesaler interface). Buys 2 mss/year. Query with published clips. Length: 250-1,500 words. Pays $15-150.
Fillers: Anecdotes, facts, gags to be illustrated by cartoonist, newsbreaks and short humor. Buys 10/year. Length: 10-300 words. Pays $5-50.
Tips: "We appreciate suggestions for possible stories submitted by the writer in his/her areas of expertise or interest. Writers have the best chance breaking in with industry interviews/profiles, emphasis on human interest stories and details of growth in business."

BEVERAGE WORLD, Keller International Publishing Corp., 150 Great Neck Rd., Great Neck NY 11021. (516)829-9210. Editor: Alan Wolf. Monthly magazine on the beverage industry. Estab. 1882. Circ. 35,000. **Pays on acceptance.** Publishes ms an average of 2 months after acceptance. Byline given. Buys all rights. Submit seasonal/holiday material 2 months in advance. Simultaneous submissions OK. Free sample copy and writer's guidelines.
Nonfiction: How-to (increase profit/sales), interview/profile and technical. Buys 15 mss/year. Query with published clips. Length:1,000-2,500 words. Pays $200-600. Sometimes pays expenses of writers on assignment.
Photos: State availability of photos with submission. Reviews contact sheets. Captions required. Buys one-time rights.
Columns/Departments: Buys 5 mss/year. Query with published clips. Length: 750-1,000 words. Pays $150-400.
Tips: "Requires background in beverage production and marketing. Business and/or technical writing experience *a must*. Do not call. This is a small staff that does not have much time for phone queries. Proof your queries carefully. Poor spelling/grammar is a turn-off."

LA BARRIQUE, Kylix Media Inc., Suite 414, 5165 Sherbrooke St. W., Montreal, Quebec H4A 1T6 Canada. (514)481-5892. Editor: Nicole Barette-Ryan. 20% freelance written. A magazine on wine published 7 times/year. "The magazine, *written in French*, covers wines of the world specially written for the province of Québec consumers and restaurant trade. It covers wine books, restaurants, vintage reports and European suppliers." Estab. 1972. Pays on publication. Publishes ms an average of 2 months after acceptance. Byline given. Buys first North American serial rights. Submit seasonal/holiday material 6 months in advance. Simultaneous submissions OK. Reports in 6 weeks on queries.
Nonfiction: General interest, how-to, humor, interview/profile, new product, opinion and travel. Knowledge of wines given primary consideration. Length: 500-1,500 words. Pays $25-100 for unsolicited articles.

Photos: Send photos with submission. Reviews transparencies and prints. Offers $25-100 per photo. Identifiction of subjects required. Buys one-time rights.

MID-CONTINENT BOTTLER, 10741 El Monte, Overland Park KS 66207. (913)341-0020. FAX: (913)341-3025. Publisher: Floyd E. Sageser. 5% freelance written. Prefers to work with published/ established writers. For "soft drink bottlers in the 20-state Midwestern area." Bimonthly. Estab. 1970. Not copyrighted. **Pays on acceptance.** Publishes ms an average of 2 months after acceptance. Buys first rights only. Reports "immediately." Sample copy for 9 × 12 SAE and 10 first class stamps; guidelines for #10 SASE.
Nonfiction: "Items of specific soft drink bottler interest with special emphasis on sales and merchandising techniques. Feature style desired." Buys 2-3 mss/year. Length: 2,000 words. Pays $15-100. Sometimes pays the expenses of writers on assignment.
Photos: Photos purchased with mss.

SOUTHERN BEVERAGE JOURNAL, 13225 SW 88th Ave., Miami FL 33176. (305)233-7230. FAX: (305)252-2580. Editor: Jackie Preston. 60% freelance written. Works with a small number of new/ unpublished writers each year, and is eager to work with new/unpublished writers. A monthly magazine for the alcohol beverage industry. Readers are personnel of bars, restaurants, package stores, night clubs, lounges and hotels—owners, managers and salespersons. Estab. 1945. Circ. 30,000. **Pays on acceptance.** Publishes ms an average of 3-4 months after acceptance. Byline given. Buys first rights. Submit seasonal/holiday material 3 months in advance. Query for electronic submissions. Reports in 1 month.
Nonfiction: General interest, historical, personal experience, interview/profile and success stories. Info on legislation (state) affecting alcohol beverage industry. No canned material. Buys 6 mss/year. Send complete ms. Length: 1,000-2,000 words. Pays 10¢/word for assigned articles.
Photos: State availability of photos with submission. Reviews 7 × 8 or 4 × 5 transparencies and 3 × 5 prints. Offers $15 maximum/photo. Identification of subjects required. Buys one-time rights.
Tips: "We are interested in legislation having to do with our industry and also views on trends, drinking and different beverages."

TEA & COFFEE TRADE JOURNAL, Lockwood Book Publishing Co., 130 W. 42nd St., New York NY 10036. (212)661-5980. FAX: (212)827-0945. Editor: Jane Phillips McCabe. 50% freelance written. Prefers to work with published/established writers. A monthly magazine covering the international coffee and tea market. "Tea and coffee trends are analyzed; transportation problems, new equipment for plants and packaging are featured." Estab. 1901. Circ. 5,000. Pays on publication. Publishes ms an average of 2 months after acceptance. Byline given. Makes work-for-hire assignments. Submit seasonal/holiday material 1 month in advance. Simultaneous submissions OK. Free sample copy.
Nonfiction: Exposé, historical/nostalgic, interview/profile, new product, photo feature and technical. Special issue includes the Coffee Market Forecast and Review (January). "No consumer related submissions. I'm only interested in the trade." Buys 60 mss/year. Query. Length: 750-1,500 words. Pays $5.50/published inch 4 months after publication.
Photos: State availability of photos with submission. Reviews contact sheets, negatives, transparencies and prints. Pays $5.50/published inch. Captions and identification of subjects required. Buys one-time rights.
Columns/Departments: Specialties (gourmet trends); and Transportation (shipping lines). Buys 36 mss/year. Query. Pays $5.50/published inch.

VINEYARD & WINERY MANAGEMENT, 103 3rd St., P.O. Box 231, Watkins Glen NY 14891. (607)535-7133. FAX: (607)535-2998. Editor: J. William Moffett. 80% freelance written. A bimonthly trade journal on the management of winemaking and grape growing. Estab. 1975. Circ. 4,500. Pays on publication. Byline given. Buys first North American serial rights and occasionally simultaneous rights. Electronic submissions preferred. Query for formats. Reports in 3 weeks on queries; 1 month on mss. Free sample copy; writer's guidelines for #10 SASE.

ALWAYS submit unsolicited manuscripts or queries with a self-addressed, stamped envelope (SASE) within your country or a self-addressed envelope with International Reply Coupons (IRC) purchased from the post office for other countries.

Nonfiction: How-to, interview/profile and technical. Buys 30 mss/year. Query. Length: 300-5,000 words. Pays $30-750 for assigned articles; pays $30-500 for unsolicited articles. Pays some expenses of writers on some assignments.

Photos: State availability of photos with submission. Reviews contact sheets, negatives and transparencies. Identification of subjects required. "Black and white often purchased for $20 each to accompany story material; 35mm and/or 4×5 transparencies for $50 and up; 6 per year of vineyard and/or winery scene related to story. Query."

Fiction: Occasional short, humorous fiction related to vineyard/winery operation.

Tips: "We're looking for long term relationships with authors who know the business and write well."

WINES & VINES, 1800 Lincoln Ave., San Rafael CA 94901. FAX: (415)453-2517. Editor: Philip E. Hiaring. 10-20% freelance written. Works with a small number of new/unpublished writers each year. For everyone concerned with the grape and wine industry including winemakers, wine merchants, growers, suppliers, consumers, etc. Monthly magazine. Estab. 1919. Circ. 4,500. Buy first North American serial rights or simultaneous rights. **Pays on acceptance.** Publishes ms an average of 3 months after acceptance. Submit special material (outlook, January; vineyard, February; Man-of-the-Year, March; Brandy, April; export-import, May; enological, June; statistical, July; merchandising, August; marketing, September; equipment and supplies, November; champagne, December) 3 months in advance. Reports in 2 weeks. Sample copy for 11×14 SAE with $2.05 postage; free writer's guidelines.

Nonfiction: Articles of interest to the trade. "These could be on grape growing in unusual areas; new winemaking techniques; wine marketing, retailing, etc." Interview, historical, spot news, merchandising techniques and technical. No stories with a strong consumer orientation as against trade orientation. Author should know the subject matter, i.e., know proper grape growing/winemaking terminology. Buys 3-4 ms/year. Query. Length: 1,000-2,500 words. Pays 5¢/word. Sometimes pays the expenses of writers on assignment.

Photos: Pays $10 for 4×5 or 8×10 b&w photos purchased with mss. Captions required.

Tips: "Ours is a trade magazine for professionals. Therefore, we do not use 'gee-whiz' wine articles."

Book and Bookstore

Publications for book trade professionals from publishers to bookstore operators are found in this section. Journals for professional writers are classified in the Journal and Writing category.

THE FEMINIST BOOKSTORE NEWS, P.O. Box 882554, San Francisco CA 94188. (415)626-1556. Editor: Carol Seajay. Managing Editor: Christine Chia. 10% freelance written. Works with a small number of new/unpublished writers each year. A bimonthly magazine covering feminist books and the women-in-print industry. "*Feminist Bookstore News* covers 'everything of interest' to the feminist bookstores, publishers and periodicals, books of interest and provides an overview of feminist publishing by mainstream publishers." Estab. 1976. Circ. 700. Pays on publication. Publishes ms an average of 2 months after acceptance. Byline sometimes given. Buys one-time rights. Simultaneous submissions OK. Reports in 3 weeks. Sample copy $6.

Nonfiction: Essays, exposé, how-to (run a bookstore); new product; opinion; and personal experience (in feminist book trade only). Special issues include Sidelines issue (July) and University Press issue (fall). No submissions that do not directly apply to the feminist book trade. Query with or without published clips, or send complete ms. Length: 250-2,000 words. Pays in copies when appropriate.

Photos: State availability of photos with submission. Model release and identification of subjects required. Buys one-time rights.

Fillers: Anecdotes, facts, newsbreaks and short humor. Length: 100-400 words. Pays $5-15.

Tips: "The writer must have several years experience in the feminist book industry. We publish very little by anyone else."

THE HORN BOOK MAGAZINE, The Horn Book, Inc., 14 Beacon St., Boston MA 02108. (617)227-1555. Editor: Anita Silvey. 25% freelance written. Prefers to work with published/established writers. Bimonthly magazine covering children's literature for librarians, booksellers, professors, and students of children's literature. Estab. 1924. Circ. 22,000. Pays on publication. Publishes ms an average of 4 months after acceptance. Byline given. Buys one-time rights. Submit seasonal/holiday material 6 months in advance. Simultaneous queries, and simultaneous and photocopied submissions OK. Computer printout submissions acceptable; no dot-matrix. Reports in 6 weeks on queries; 2 months on mss. Free sample copy; writer's guidelines upon request.

Nonfiction: Interview/profile (children's book authors and illustrators). Buys 20 mss/year. Query or send complete ms. Length: 1,000-2,800 words. Pays $25-250.

Tips: "Writers have a better chance of breaking in to our publication with a query letter on a specific article they want to write."

Brick, Glass and Ceramics

These publications are read by manufacturers, dealers and managers of brick, glass and ceramic retail businesses. Other publications related to glass and ceramics are listed in the Consumer Art and Architecture and Consumer Hobby and Craft sections.

AMERICAN GLASS REVIEW, P.O. Box 2147, Clifton NJ 07015. (201)779-1600. FAX: (201)779-3242. Editor-in-Chief: Donald Doctorow. 10% freelance written. Monthly magazine. Pays on publication. Estab. 1888. Byline given. Phone queries OK. Buys first time rights. Submit seasonal/holiday material 2 months in advance of issue date. Reports in 3 weeks. Free sample copy and writer's guidelines; mention *Writer's Market* in request.

Nonfiction: Glass plant and glass manufacturing articles. Buys 3-4 mss/year. Query. Length: 1,500-3,000 words. Pays $200.

Photos: State availability of photos with query. No additional payment for b&w contact sheets. Captions preferred. Buys one-time rights.

‡GLASS MAGAZINE, For the Architectural Glass Industry, National Glass Association, Suite 302, 8200 Greensboro Drive, McLean VA 22102. (703)442-4890. FAX: (703)442-0630. Editor-in-Chief: Nicole Harris. 25% freelance written. Prefers to work with published/established writers; works with a small number of new/unpublished writers each year. A monthly magazine covering the architectural glass industry. Circ. 18,000. **Pays on acceptance.** Publishes ms an average of 3-6 months after acceptance. Byline given. Offers varying kill fee. Buys first rights only. Reports in 1 month. Sample copy for $5 and 10x13 SAE with $2.40 postage; free writer's guidelines.

Nonfiction: Interview/profile (of various glass businesses; profiles of industry people or glass business owners); and technical (about glazing processes). Buys 30 mss/year. Query with published clips. Length: 1,200 words minimum. Pays $150-350.

Photos: State availability of photos.

Tips: Do *not* send in general glass use stories. Research the industry first, then query.

PROFESSIONAL STAINED GLASS, The Edge Publishing Group, Inc., Rt. 6 at Dingle Ridge Rd., P.O. Box 69, Brewster NY 10509. (914)279-7399. FAX: (914)279-7361. Editor: Julie L. Sloan. 90% freelance written. Monthly trade magazine on decorative glass. "We are a technical journal although freelancers can write by interviewing industry professionals and extrapolating from there. We also run profiles and fillers easily written by freelancers." Estab. 1980. Circ. 15,700. Pays on publication. Publishes ms an average of 2 months after acceptance. Byline given. Offers $25 kill fee. Buys first North American serial rights. Query for electronic submissions. Reports in 2 weeks. Free sample copy and writer's guidelines.

Nonfiction: Technical articles (glassworking techniques) and profiles of successful glass artists doing credible work. "We do not want fluffy newspaper pieces with series of quotes strung together. There is plenty of work here for the freelancer willing to interview, do a modest amount of research and put together a tight article." Buys 60 mss/year. Query. Length: 1,000-3,000 words. Pays $100-200.

Photos: State availability of photos with submission. Reviews contact sheets, 35mm transparencies and prints. Offers no additional payment for photos accepted with ms. Identification of subjects required. Buys one-time rights.

Columns/Departments: Profile (personality profile of industry artists and the work they do), 1,500 words; and Notable Works (brief introduction to unknown artist executing worthy work), 250 words. Buys 12 mss/year. Query.

Tips: "Writers should read our guidelines before writing anything and should discuss their article with an industry professional—not a hobbyist. If that person likes the idea, chances are we will too."

Building Interiors

Owners, managers and sales personnel of floor covering, wall covering and remodeling businesses read the journals listed in this category. Interior design and architecture publications may be found in the Consumer Art, Design and Collectibles category. For journals aimed at other construction trades see the Construction and Contracting section.

REMODELING, Hanley-Wood, Inc., Suite 475, 655 15th St. NW, Washington DC 20005. (202)737-0717. FAX: (202)737-2439. Editor: Wendy Jordan. 5% freelance written. A monthly magazine covering residential and light commercial remodeling. "We cover the best new ideas in remodeling design, business, construction and products." Estab. 1985. Circ. 92,000. Pays on publication. Publishes ms an average of 3 months after acceptance. Byline given. Offers 5¢/word kill fee. Buys first North American serial rights. Query for electronic submissions. Reports in 1 month. Free sample copy and writer's guidelines.

Nonfiction: Interview/profile, new product and technical. Buys 4 mss/year. Query with published clips. Length: 250-1,000 words. Pays 20¢/word. Sometimes pays the expenses of writers on assignment.

Photos: State availability of photos with submission. Reviews slides, 4×5 transparencies, and 8×10 prints. Offers $25-100/photo. Captions, model releases, and identification of subjects required. Buys one-time rights.

Tips: "The areas of our publication most open to freelancers are news and new product news."

‡**REMODELING NEWS**, DPH Communications, Inc., 2269 Saw Mill River Rd., Elmsford NY 10523. (914)347-3000. Editor: Liz Wagner. 80% freelance written. Monthly tabloid covering professionally installed home remodeling and light construction. "The magazine is written for people actively engaged in professional home remodeling. Articles must be geared toward professional tradespeople, not do-it-yourselfers." Estab. 1987. Circ. 90,000. **Pays on acceptance.** Publishes ms an average of 3 months after acceptance. Byline given. Offers 25% kill fee. Buys first North American serial rights, second serial (reprint) rights or all rights. Submit seasonal/holiday material 6 months in advance. Simultaneous and previously published submissions OK. Query for electronic submissions. Reports in 2 months. Sample copy for 12×15½" SAE with 8 first class stamps. Free writer's guidelines.

Nonfiction: How-to for professional remodelers. Must be more in-depth than how-to articles for do-it-yourselfers. "Do not submit article for consumers or do-it-yourselfers." Query with published clips. Do not submit manuscripts without prior authorization. Unsolicited manuscripts will not be returned. Length: 600-3,000 words. Pays $75-500 for assigned articles; $50-200 for reprints.

Photos: State availability of photos with submission. Reviews transparencies. Captions, model releases and identification of subjects required. Buys all rights.

Columns/Departments: Business Tips (How to run a remodeling business more successfully), 800-1,000; Show Case (Before and after and step-by-step tours of unique remodeling projects), 1,000-1,500; The Tool Belt (Reviews of new or unique tools), 1,500-2,500; Contractor's Lawyer (Legal aspects and problems in the remodeling business), 800-1,000. Buys 30 mss/year. Query. Length: 600-1,500 words. Pays $50-300.

Fillers: Facts, newsbreaks, short humor. Buys 20/year. Length: 200-600 words. Pays $50-150.

Tips: "We are interested in stories that cover situations or problems with which professional contractors deal on a regular basis. These may be customer relations, installation problems, running a contracting business, labor concerns, etc. Writers have the best chance selling us feature articles. A writer must be able to provide in-depth stories about the many aspects of the remodeling business. It is important that the writer be able to speak a contractor's language."

WALLS & CEILINGS, 8602 N. 40th St., Tampa FL 33604. (813)989-9300. FAX: (813)980-3982. Managing Editor: Melissa Wells. 10% freelance written. Prefers to work with published/established writers, and works with a small number of new/unpublished writers each year. For contractors involved in lathing and plastering, drywall, acoustics, fireproofing, curtain walls, movable partitions together with manufacturers, dealers, and architects. Monthly magazine. Estab. 1938. Circ. 15,000. Pays on publication. Publishes ms an average of 4-6 months after acceptance. Buys first North American serial rights. Byline given. Phone queries OK. Submit seasonal/holiday material 3 months in advance. Query for electronic submissions. Reports in 3 weeks. Sample copy with 9×12 SAE and $2 postage.

Nonfiction: How-to (drywall and plaster construction and business management); and interview. Buys 12 mss/year. Query. Length: 200-1,500 words. Pays $50-150 maximum. Sometimes pays the expenses of writers on assignment.

Photos: State availability of photos with query. Pays $5 for 8×10 b&w prints. Captions required. Buys one-time rights.

Tips: "We would like to receive wall and ceiling finishing features about unique designs and applications in new buildings (from high-rise to fast food restaurants), fireproofing, and acoustical design with photography (b&w and color)."

Business Management

These publications cover trends, general theory and management practices for business owners and top-level business executives. Publications that use similar material but have a less technical slant are listed in the Consumer Business and Finance section. Journals for middle management, including supervisors and office managers, appear in the Management and Supervision section. Those for industrial plant managers are listed under Industrial Operations and under sections for specific industries, such as Machinery and Metal. Publications for office supply store operators are included in the Office Environment and Equipment section.

CHIEF EXECUTIVE, 233 Park Ave. S., New York NY 10003. (212)979-4810. FAX: (212)979-7431. Editor: J.P. Donlon. Written by and for CEOs. Limited freelance opportunity. Published 9 times/year. Circ. 35,000. **Pays on acceptance.** Publishes ms an average of 2-3 months after acceptance. Byline given. Offers kill fee. Buys world serial rights. Free writer's guidelines. Query required for all departments. Unsolicited manuscripts will not be returned. Pays $300-800. Pays previously agreed upon expenses of writers on assignment.

Photos: State availability of photos with submission. Reviews 4-color transparencies and slides. Offers $100 maximum per photo. Captions required. Buys one-time rights.

Column/Departments: N.B. (profile of CEO/Chairman/President of mid- to large-size company), 400-500 words; Amenities, 1,000-1,500 words; CEO-At-Leisure, 1,000-1,500 words; Business Travel (provides CEOs with *key names* and information on business/government inner network for city/area being visited—who to know to get things done) 1,000-1,500 words.

COMMUNICATION BRIEFINGS, Encoders, Inc., Suite 110, 700 Black Horse Pike, Blackwood NJ 08012. (609)232-6380. FAX: (609)232-8229. Executive Editor: Frank Grazian. 15% freelance written. Prefers to work with published/established writers. A monthly newsletter covering business communication and business management. "Most readers are in middle and upper management. They comprise public relations professionals, editors of company publications, marketing and advertising managers, fund raisers, directors of associations and foundations, school and college administrators, human resources professionals, and other middle managers who want to communicate better on the job." Estab. 1980. Circ. 42,000. **Pays on acceptance.** Publishes ms an average of 2-3 months after acceptance. Byline given sometimes on Bonus Items and on other items if idea originates with the writer. Buys one-time rights. Submit seasonal/holiday material 2 months in advance. Previously published submissions OK, "but must be rewritten to conform to our style." Reports in 1 month. Sample copy and writer's guidelines for #10 SAE and 2 first class stamps.

Nonfiction: "Most articles we buy are of the 'how-to' type. They consist of practical ideas, techniques and advice that readers can use to improve business communication and management. Areas covered: writing, speaking, listening, employee communication, human relations, public relations, interpersonal communication, persuasion, conducting meetings, advertising, marketing, fund raising, telephone techniques, teleconferencing, selling, improving publications, handling conflicts, negotiating, etc. Because half of our subscribers are in the nonprofit sector, articles that appeal to both profit and nonprofit organizations are given top priority." *Short Items:* Articles consisting of one or two brief tips that can stand alone. Length: 40-70 words. *Articles:* A collection of tips or ideas that offer a solution to a communication or management problem or that show a better way to communicate or manage. Examples: "How to produce slogans that work," "The wrong way to criticize employees," "Mistakes to avoid when leading a group discussion," and "5 ways to overcome writer's block." Length: 125-150 words. *Bonus Items:* In-depth pieces that probe one area of communication and cover it as thoroughly as possible. Examples: "Producing successful special events," "How to evaluate your newsletter," and "How to write to be understood." Length: 1,300 words. Buys 30-50 mss/year. Pays $15-35 for 40- to 150-word pieces; Bonus Items, $200. Pays the expenses of writers on assignment.

Tips: "Our readers are looking for specific and practical ideas and tips that will help them communicate better both within their organizations and with outside publics. Most ideas are rejected because they are too general or too elementary for our audience. Our style is down-to-earth and terse. We pack a lot of useful information into short articles. Our readers are busy executives and managers who want information dispatched quickly and without embroidery. We omit anecdotes, lengthy quotes and long-winded exposition. The writer has a better chance of breaking in at our publication with short articles and fillers since we buy only six major features (bonus items) a year. We require queries on longer items and bonus items. Writers may submit short tips (40-70 words) without querying. The most frequent mistakes made by writers in completing an article for us are failure to master the style of our publication and to understand our readers' needs."

‡COMPUTERS IN ACCOUNTING, Warren, Gorham & Lamont, 1 Penn Plaza, New York NY 10119. (212)971-5000. FAX: (212)971-5025. Editor: Theodore Needleman. 80% freelance written. Business journal publishes 10 times/year, covering the use of computers in accounting practices. "*Computers in Accounting* is dedicated to showing the accounting professional how to get the most out of computers, both in their own practices and in their client's businesses. Our slant is how any particular piece of hardware or software package is useful in the above context, and our approach is very 'how-to.' "

Estab. 1984. Circ. 25,000. Pays 1 month after acceptance, "unless other arrangements are made on assignment." Publishes ms an average of 4 months after acceptance. Byline given. Offers 25% kill fee. Buys first North American serial rights and second serial (reprint) rights. Query for electronic submissions. Reports in 2 months. Free sample copy and writer's guidelines.

Nonfiction: How-to, technical, spreadsheet templates. "All using computer hardware/software in the practice of accounting. Not interested in application articles (i.e.—How Joe made a million dollars with 'Product X'). We also do not accept unsolicited product reviews." Buys 30 mss/year. Query with published clips. Length: 2,000 minimum. No maximum words "Product Reviews are 1,000 words." Pays $150 minimum; no set maximum for assigned articles. Sometimes pays expenses of writers on assignment.

‡CONVENTION SOUTH, Covey Communications Corp., 2001 W. 1st St., P.O. Box 2267, Gulf Shores AL 36547. (205)968-5300. FAX: (205)968-4532. Editor: J.Talty O'Connor. 50% freelance written. Trade journal on planning meetings and conventions in the South. Estab. 1983. Circ. 7,000. Pays on publication. Byline given. Buys first rights or second serial (reprint) rights. Submit seasonal/holiday material 2 months in advance. Simultaneous and previously published submissions OK. Query for electronic submissions. Reports in 2 months on queries. Free sample copy.

Nonfiction: How-to (relative to meeting planning/travel), photo feature and travel. Buys 20 mss/year. Query. Length: 1,250-3,000 words. Pays $75. Pays in contributor copies or other premiums if arranged in advance. Sometime pays expenses of writers on assignment.

Photos: Send photos with submission. Reviews 5×7 prints. Offers no additional payment for photos accepted with ms. Captions and identification of subjects required. Buys one-time rights.

EARLY CHILDHOOD NEWS, Peter Li, Inc., 2451 E. River Rd., Dayton OH 45439. (513)294-5785. FAX: (513)294-7840. Editor: Janet Coburn. 75% freelance written. Bimonthly trade journal on child care centers. "Our publication is a news and service magazine for owners, directors and administrators of child care centers serving children from age 6 weeks to 2nd grade." Estab. 1988. Circ. 30,000. Pays on publication. Publishes ms an average of 3-4 months after acceptance. Copyright pending. Buys first rights. Submit seasonal/holiday material 5-6 months in advance. Query for electronic submissions. Sample copy $4 with 9×12 SAE and 2 first class stamps.

Nonfiction: How-to (how I solved a problem other center directors may face), interview/profile personal experience and business aspects of child care centers. "No articles directed at early childhood teachers or lesson plans." Buys 15 mss/year. Query with or without published clips, or send complete ms. Length: 500-1,500 words. Pays $50-150.

Photos: Send photos with submission if available. Reviews 35mm and 4×5 transparencies and 5×7 prints. Captions, model releases and identification of subjects required. Buys one-time rights.

Fillers: Facts and newsbreaks. Length: 100-250 words. Pays $10-25.

Tips: "Send double-spaced typed mss and pay attention to grammar and punctuation. Enclose SASE for faster reply. No scholarly pieces with footnotes and bibliography. No activities/lesson plans for use with kids. We need short, easy-to-read articles written in popular style that give child care center owners information they can use right away to make their centers better, more effective, more efficient, etc. Feature stories and fillers are most open to freelancers. Be specific and concrete; use examples. Tightly focused topics are better than general 'The Day Care Dilemma' types."

FARM STORE, Miller Publishing, P.O. Box 2400, Minneapolis MN 55343. (612)931-0211. FAX: (612)931-0217. Editor: Jan Johnson. 10% freelance written. Eager to work with new/unpublished writers. A monthly magazine for business owners and managers who sell to farmers. Estab. 1886. Primary business lines are bulk and bagged feed, animal health products, grain storage, agricultural chemicals. Pays on publication. Publishes ms an average of 3 months after acceptance. Byline given. Buys one-time rights. Simultaneous and previously published submissions OK. Reports in 3 months. Free sample copy and writer's guidelines.

Nonfiction: How-to (subjects must be business-oriented, credit, taxes, inventory, hiring, firing, etc.); interview/profile (with successful agribusiness dealers or industry leaders); opinion (on controversial industry issues). Buys 6 mss/year. Query. Length: 500-2,000 words. Pays $100-300 for assigned articles; pays $50-150 for unsolicited articles. Sometimes pays the expenses of writers on assignment.

Photos: State availability of photos with submission. Reviews contact sheets, 2×4 transparencies and 5×7 prints. Offers $10-50 per photo. Identification of subjects required. Buys one-time rights.

Tips: "The area of our publication most open to freelancers is features on successful farm store dealers. Submit two to three black and white photos or color slides. Keep the article under 2,000 words and don't get bogged down in technical details. Tell what sets their business apart and why it works. General business articles also are needed, especially if they have a business slant."

FINANCIAL EXECUTIVE, Financial Executives Institute, 10 Madison Ave., Morristown NJ 07962-1938. FAX: (201)898-4649. Editor: Catherine M. Coult. Managing Editor: Robin L. Couch. 5% freelance written. A bimonthly magazine for corporate financial management. "*Financial Executive* is published for senior financial executives of major corporations and explores corporate accounting and treasury related issues without being anti-business." Circ. 18,000. Pays on publication. Byline given. Buys all rights. Reports in 1 month on queries; 2 months on mss. Sample copy $5; writer's guidelines for #10 SASE.

Nonfiction: Analysis, based on interviews, of accounting, finance, and tax developments of interest to financial executives. Buys 3 mss/year. Query with published clips. Length: 1,500-2,500 words. Pays $500-1,000.

Tips: "Most article ideas come from editors, so the query approach is best. (Address correspondence to Robin L. Couch.) We use business or financial articles that follow a *Wall Street Journal* approach— a fresh idea, with its significance (to financial executives), quotes, anecdotes and an interpretation or evaluation. Our content will follow developments in market volatility, M&A trend, information management, regulatory changes, tax legislation, Congressional hearings/legislation, re business and financial reporting. There is a growing interest in employee benefits, international business and impact of technology. We have very high journalistic standards."

‡**HOME SWEET HOME,** P.O. Box 1254, Milton WA 98354. (206)922-5941. Editor: Mark and Laurie Sleeper. 15% freelance written. Quarterly magazine covering home business and home life. Estab. 1989. Circ. 640. Pays on publication. Publishes ms an average of 4 months after acceptance. Byline given. No kill fee. Buys first rights. Simultaneous and previously published submissions OK. Query for electronic submissions. Reports in 2-4 months. Sample copy $6. Writer's guidelines for SAE with 1 first class stamp.

Nonfiction: Book excerpts, general interest, how-to, interview/profile, personal experience (on home business and home medicine and home life, home management, home education), Paraprofessional Home Businesses, Indoor Gardening (Greenhouses, mushrooms, sprouts), Baking Home Business and Music. Buys 60 mss/year. Send complete ms. Length: 500-2,500 words. Pays 2¢/word. Pays writers with contributor copies or other premiums rather than a cash payment "when requested."

Photos: Send photos with submission. Reviews prints. Offers no additional payment for photos accepted with ms.

Columns/Departments: Home Medicine (practical, documented, personal accounts, home remedies), 500-2,500; Home Education (personal experience of veteran home schoolers), 500-2,500; Home Life (advice on interpersonal relations in busy households), 500-2,500; Home Management (hints, tips, tricks, etc. to organize and manage day to day), 500-2,500. Buys 30 mss/year. Send complete ms. Length 500-2,500 words. Pays 2¢/word.

Poetry: Light verse, traditional. Buys 6 poems/year. Pays $5-10.

‡**LOOKING FIT, The Magazine for Health Conscious Tanning & Toning Centers,** Virgo Publishing, Inc., P.O. Box C-5400, Scottsdale AZ 85261. (602)483-0014. FAX: (602)483-1247. Editor: Nancy Bercaw. 15% freelance written. A monthly magazine on issues related to the indoor tanning and toning industries. "*Looking Fit* is interested in material dealing with any aspect of operating a tanning or toning salon. Preferred style is light whenever subject matter doesn't preclude it. Technical material should be written in a manner interesting and intelligible to the average salon operator." Estab. 1985. Circ. 28,000. Pays 1 month after publication. Byline given. Buys all rights. Submit seasonal/holiday material 3 months in advance. Simultaneous submissions OK. Query for electronic submissions. Reports in 1 month. Sample copy for 10×13 SAE and $2.50.

Nonfiction: How-to (operational—how to choose a location, buy equipment, etc.), humor, new product and technical. Buys 10-20 mss/year. Query with or without published clips, or send complete ms. Length: 1,500-9,000 words. Pays $50-175 for assigned articles. Pays $50-150 for unsolicited articles.

Photos: Send photos with submission. Reviews contact sheets, transparencies (2×4) and prints (2×4). Offers no additional payment for photos accepted with ms. Model releases and identification of subjects required.

Columns/Departments: Clublines (profiles of unusual/successful salons), 750-1,500 words; Profiles (profiles of unusual/successful manufacturers/distributors), 1,000-2,500 words. Buys 5-10 mss/year. Query or send complete ms. Length: 750-2,500 words. Pays $25-75.

Tips: "The best way to break in is to call or write with a good story idea. If it's workable, we'll have the writer do it. Unsolicited manuscripts are welcome, but may not fit into the magazine's goals. We're happy to offer direction or style angles by phone. In general, *Looking Fit* follows Associated Press style. Full-length (1,500-7,500 words) features are what we most often buy. For best results, contact us with story ideas and we can supply the names and numbers of industry contacts."

MAY TRENDS, George S. May International Company, 303 S. Northwest Hwy., Park Ridge IL 60068. (312)825-8806. Editor: John E. McArdle. 20% freelance written. Works with a small number of new/ unpublished writers each year. For owners and managers of small and medium-sized businesses, hospitals and nursing homes, trade associations, Better Business Bureaus, educational institutions and newspapers. Magazine published without charge 3 times a year. Estab. 1967. Circ. 30,000. Buys all rights. Byline given. Buys 10-15 mss/year. **Pays on acceptance.** Publishes ms an average of 4-6 months after acceptance. Returns rejected material immediately. Query or submit complete ms. Reports in 2 weeks. Sample copy available on request for 9 × 12 SAE with 2 first class stamps.

Nonfiction: "We prefer articles dealing with how to solve problems of specific industries (manufacturers, wholesalers, retailers, service businesses, small hospitals and nursing homes) where contact has been made with key executives whose comments regarding their problems may be quoted. We want problem solving articles, *not* success stories that laud an individual company. We like articles that give the business manager concrete suggestions on how to deal with specific problems—i.e., '5 steps to solve . . .,' '6 key questions to ask when . . .,' and '4 tell-tale signs indicating . . . .' " Focus is on marketing, economic and technological trends that have an impact on medium- and small-sized businesses, not on the "giants"; automobile dealers coping with existing dull markets; and contractors solving cost-inventory problems. Will consider material on successful business operations and merchandising techniques. Length: 2,000-3,000 words. Pays $150-250.

Tips: Query letter should tell "type of business and problems the article will deal with. We specialize in the problems of small (20-100 employees, $500,000-3,000,000 volume) businesses (manufacturing, wholesale, retail and service), plus medium and small health care facilities. We are now including nationally known writers in each issue—writers like the Vice Chairman of the Federal Reserve Bank, the U.S. Secretary of the Treasury; names like George Bush and Malcolm Baldridge; titles like the Chairman of the Joint Committee on Accreditation of Hospitals; and Canadian Minister of Export. This places extra pressure on freelance writers to submit very good articles. Frequent mistakes: 1) Writing for big business, rather than small, 2) using language that is too academic."

THE MEETING MANAGER, Meeting Planners International, Suite 5018, 1950 Stemmons, Dallas TX 75207. (214)746-5222. FAX: (214)746-5248. Editor: Tina Berres Filipski. 50% freelance written. Monthly association magazine for the meetings/hospitality/travel industries. Estab. 1980. Circ. 10,000. **Pays on acceptance.** Publishes ms an average of 2 months after acceptance. Byline given. Query. Reports in 1 month. Free sample and writer's guidelines.

Nonfiction: How-to, trends, interview/profile, personal development, opinion and personal experience. Query with published clips. Length: 500-2,500 words. Pays $300-450.

Photos: State availability of photos with submission. Reviews contact sheets and transparencies. Offers no additional payment for photos accepted with ms. Captions required.

MEETING NEWS, News, Education and Ideas for Better Meetings, Gralla Publications, 1515 Broadway, New York NY 10036. (212)869-1300. FAX: (212)302-6273. Publisher: Peter Johnsmeyer. Editor: Anthony Rutigliano. A monthly business travel magazine covering news, facts, ideas and methods in meeting planning and special events; hospitality, industry developments, airline, hotel and business tax legislation, hotel development and acquisitions, new labor contracts, business practices and costs for meeting planners. Estab. 1976. Circ. 75,000. **Pays on acceptance.** Byline given. Buys first rights. Reports in 1 month on queries; 2 weeks on mss. Free sample copy.

Nonfiction: Travel and specifics on how a group improved its meetings or trade shows, saved money or drew more attendees. "Stress is on business and travel articles—facts and figures." Special issues and sections cover specific meeting destinations—Florida/Canada/Texas/California/New York and Arizona. No general or philosophical pieces. Buys 50-75 mss/year. Query with published clips. Length: varies. Pays variable rates.

Tips: "Special issues focusing on certain states as meeting sites are most open. Best suggestion—query in writing, with clips, on any area of expertise about these states that would be of interest to people planning meetings there. Example: food/entertainment, specific sports, group activities, etc."

‡NATION'S BUSINESS, Chamber of Commerce of the United States, 1615 H St. NW, Washington DC 20062. (202)463-5650. Editor: Robert Gray. Deputy Editor: Ripley Hotch. 50% freelance written. Monthly magazine of useful information for business people about managing a business. Audience includes owners and managers of businesses of all sizes, but predominantly smaller to medium-sized businesses. Estab. 1912. Circ. 850,000. **Pays on acceptance.** Publishes ms an average of 6 months after acceptance. Byline given. Kill fee negotiable. Buys all rights. Submit seasonal/holiday material 6 months in advance. Simultaneous queries and submissions OK, but only for exclusive use upon acceptance. Query for electronic submissions. Reports in 2 months on queries; 3 months on mss. Sample copy for 9 × 12 SAE and $3; free writer's guidelines.

Nonfiction: How-to (run a business); interview/profile (business success stories; entrepreneurs who successfully implement ideas); and business trends stories. Buys 40 mss/year. Query. Length: 250-3,000 words. Pays $100-2,000. Sometimes pays expenses of writers on assignment.

Tips: "Ask for guidelines and read them carefully before making any approach."

‡OUTSIDE BUSINESS, Mariah Publications, a Division of Burke Communication Industries, 1165 N. Clark St., Chicago IL 60610. (312)951-0990. Editor: Charles Plueddeman. 60% freelance written. Monthly magazine on retailing of outdoor recreational products. "Our readers are retailers of upscale equipment and apparel used for outdoor activities. Writers must be familiar with the business issues involved in retailing, or with the products themselves, or both." Estab. 1985. Circ. 14,500. Pays on publication. Publishes ms an average of 3 months after acceptance. Byline given. Buys first rights, second serial (reprint) rights and makes work-for-hire assignments. Query for electronic submissions. Reports in 2 months on queries. Sample copy for 9×12 SAE with $2.40 postage.

Nonfiction: Interview/profile, technical (equipment and/or apparel round-ups) and business issues (affecting retailing). "Not responsible for unsolicited manuscripts." Buys 40-48 mss/year. Query. Length: 1,500-3,000 words. Pays $400-1,000 for assigned articles. Sometimes pays expenses of writers on assignment.

Photos: State availability of photos with submission. Reviews 35mm transparencies. Captions, model releases and identification of subjects required. Buys one-time rights.

Columns/Departments: Management, Advertising/Promotion, Merchandising, and Financial Planning: all written for retail audience and all 1,500 words. Buys 24 mss/year. Query. Pays $300-350.

Tips: "We value knowledge of outdoor equipment and apparel, *and* familiarity with business issues affecting retailers."

RECORDS MANAGEMENT QUARTERLY, Association of Records Managers and Administrators, Inc., P.O. Box 4580, Silver Spring MD 20914. Editor: Ira A. Penn, CRM, CSP. 10% freelance written. Eager to work with new/unpublished writers. Quarterly professional journal covering records and information management. Estab. 1967. Circ. 11,000. Pays on publication. Publishes ms an average of 6 months after acceptance. Byline given. Buys all rights. Simultaneous submissions OK. Reports in 1 month on mss. Sample copy $14; free writer's guidelines.

Nonfiction: Professional articles covering theory, case studies, surveys, etc. on any aspect of records and information management. Buys 20-24 mss/year. Send complete ms. Length: 2,500 words minimum. Pays $50-200 "stipend"; no contract.

Photos: Send photos with ms. Does not pay extra for photos. Prefers b&w prints. Captions required.

Tips: "A writer *must* know our magazine. Most work is written by practitioners in the field. We use very little freelance writing, but we have had some and it's been good. A writer must have detailed knowledge of the subject he/she is writing about. Superficiality is not acceptable."

SECURITY DEALER, PTN Publishing Co., 445 Broad Hollow Rd., Melville NY 11747. (516)845-2700. FAX: (516)845-7109. Editor: Susan A. Brady. 25% freelance written. A monthly magazine for electronic alarm dealers; burglary and fire installers, with technical, business, sales and marketing information. Circ. 25,000. Pays 3 weeks after publication. Publishes ms an average of 4 months after acceptance. Byline given sometimes. Buys first North American serial rights. Simultaneous and previously published submissions OK. Prefer computer disk to accompany.

Nonfiction: How-to, interview/profile and technical. No consumer pieces. Query or send complete ms. Length: 1,000-3,000 words. Pays $300 for assigned articles; pays $100-200 for unsolicited articles. Sometimes pays the expenses of writers on assignment.

Photos: State availability of photos with submission. Reviews contact sheets and transparencies. Offers $25 additional payment for photos accepted with ms. Captions and identification of subjects required.

Columns/Departments: Closed Circuit TV, and Access Control (both on application, installation, new products), 500-1,000 words. Buys 25 mss/year. Query. Pays $100-150.

Tips: "The areas of our publication most open to freelancers are technical innovations, trends in the alarm industry and crime patterns as related to the business as well as business finance and management pieces."

SELF-EMPLOYED AMERICA, The News Publication for your Small Business, National Association for the Self-Employed, P.O. Box 612067, DFW Airport TX 75261. Editor: Karen C. Jones. 90% freelance written. Published 6 times/year for association members. "Keep in mind that the self-employed don't need business news tailored to meet needs of what government considers 'small business'. We reach those with few, if any, employees. Our readers are independent business owners going it alone—and in need of information." Estab. 1988. Circ. 300,000. Pays on publication. Byline given. Offers 10% kill fee. Buys full rights only and makes work-for-hire assignments. Submit seasonal/holiday material 6 months in advance. Query for electronic submissions. Reports in 2 months on queries; 6 weeks on mss. Sample copy for 9×12 with 2 first class stamps. Writer's guidelines for #10 SASE.

Nonfiction: Book excerpts, how-to and travel (how to save money on travel or how to combine business and personal travel). "No big-business or how to claw your way to the top stuff. Generally my readers are happy as small businesses." Buys 50-60 mss/year. Query with published clips. First article accepted many times on spec only. Length: 150-700 words. Pays $200-350 for assigned articles; $100-250 for unsolicited articles. Sometimes pays expenses of writers on assignment.

Photos: State availability of photos with submission. Reviews 3×5 prints. Offers $25-50 per photo. Captions, model releases and identification required. Buys one-time rights.

Columns/Departments: Tax Tips. Send complete ms. Length: 200-300. Pays $50-100. Touch of Success profiles. Pays $70 for 125 words. Tight writing, concise.

Fillers: Anecdotes, facts, newsbreaks and short humor. Buys 50/year. Length: 75-125 words. Pays $25-50.

Tips: "Keep in mind reader demographics show 300,000 people with nothing in common except the desire to be independent. Be inventive with your subject matter proposed. We've covered the basics of small business already."

THE SERVICING DEALER, The Communications Group, Suite 108, 3703 N. Main St., Rockford IL 61103-1677. (815)633-2680. FAX: (815)633-6880. Editor: Craig Wyatt. 15% freelance written. Trade journal, published 10 times/year, on outdoor power equipment retailing and service. "Editorial is basic retail management oriented. Readers are servicing dealers of lawn and other outdoor power equipment. They're good mechanics but not-so-good businessmen." Estab. 1987. Circ. 23,000. Pays on publication. Publishes ms an average of 2 months after acceptance. Byline given. Offers 20% kill fee. Buys one-time rights and exclusive rights within industry. Submit seasonal/holiday material 4 months in advance. Simultaneous and previously published submissions OK. Query for electronic submissions. Sample copy $3. Writer's guidelines for #10 SASE.

Nonfiction: How-to (marketing, personnel management and financial management) and technical (dealing with small air-cooled engines and lawn equipment repair). Buys 6-10 mss/year. Query with published clips. Length: 600-1,200 words. Pays $150-300 for assigned articles; $50-250 for unsolicited articles. Sometimes pays expenses of writers on assignment.

Photos: Send photos with submission. Reviews contact sheets, transparencies and prints. Offers no additional payment for photos accepted with ms. Captions and identification of subjects required.

Columns/Departments: Sales Tips (basic sales methods and suggestions); Out Back (personnel management topics for small business); Greenbacks (financial management) and Ad-Visor (advertising and promotion for small business). Buys 7 mss/year. Query with published clips. Length: 450-675 words. Pays $50-250.

Tips: "Any prior knowledge of the outdoor power equipment industry, retail management topics, small engine repair is a plus. Read our magazine and other industry magazines. Small business management is a plus. Use electronic media to transfer directly into our Mac system. Give readers something they can walk away with and use the minute they put the magazine down."

SIGN BUSINESS, National Business Media Inc., 1008 Depot Hill Rd., P.O. Box 1416, Broomfield CO 80020. (303)469-0424. FAX: (303)469-5730. Editor: Glen Richardson. 15% freelance written. Trade journal on the sign industry—electric, commercial, architectural. "This is business-to-business writing; we try to produce news you can use, rather than human interest." Circ. 20,500. Pays on publication. Publishes ms an average of 1-2 months after acceptance. Byline given. Buys first North American serial rights. Submit seasonal/holiday material 4 months in advance. Query for electronic submissions. Reports in 1 week on queries; 2 weeks on mss. Sample copy $2.50. Free writer's guidelines for #10 SASE.

Nonfiction: How-to (sign-painting techniques, new uses for computer cutters, plotters lettering styles); interview/profile (sign company execs, shop owners with *unusual*; work etc.) and other (news on sign codes, legislation, unusual signs, etc.). "No humor, human interest, generic articles with sign replacing another industry, no first person writing, no profiles of a sign shop just because someone nice runs the business." Buys 20 mss/year. Query with published clips. Length: 500-3,000 words. Pays $125-200.

Photos: Send photos with submission. Reviews 3×5 transparencies and 3×5 prints. Offers $5-10 per photo. Identification of subjects required. Buys one-time rights and/or reprint rights.

Tips: "Find a sign shop, or sign company, and take some time to learn the business. The sign business is easily a $5 billion-plus industry every year in the United States, and we treat it like a business, not a hobby. If you see a sign that stops you in your tracks, find out who made it; if it's a one-in-10,000 kind of sign, chances are good we'll want to know more. Writing should be factual and avoid polysyllabic words that waste a reader's time. I'll work with writers who may not know the trade, but can write well."

TOBACCO REPORTER, Specialized Agricultural Publications, Inc., Suite 300, 3000 Highwoods Blvd., Raleigh NC 27625. (919)872-5040. FAX: (919)876-6531. Editor/Publisher: Dayton Matlick. Managing Editor: Colleen Zimmerman. 30% freelance written. Monthly magazine covering the international tobacco industry. "Though we are not aligned with any tobacco manufacturers, we provide the most timely, accurate and interesting coverage of the tobacco industry worldwide. Our readership consists primarily of presidents, VPs, and CEOs of tobacco products manufacturers, leaf processors, and suppliers." Estab. 1873. Circ. 6,000. Pays on publication. Publishes ms an average of 5 months after acceptance. Byline usually given. Offers 20% kill fee on commissioned work. Buys all rights. Submit seasonal/holiday material 4 months in advance. Responds in 1 month on queries; 6 weeks on mss. Sample copy for $5 plus P/H.

Nonfiction: Editorial calendar available on request; we publish features and country profiles each month. We can use clippings from major publications; we do not accept articles written from an antitobacco perspective. No personal testimonials. Buys 8-15 mss/year. Query with or without published clips, or send complete ms. Length: 500-3,000 words. Pays 72¢ per published line. May pays expenses of writers on assignment.

Photos: Send photos with submission, transparencies and 5×7 prints or larger. Offers $25-50 per photo. Captions, model releases and identification of subjects required. Buys one-time rights.

Columns/Departments: International News (crop reports, tobacco/cigarette prices, industry and corporate news, legislation), 50-300 words; and Topline (late-breaking news, acquisitions, financial news), 30-100 words. Buys 50 mss/year. Pays 72¢ per published line.

Fillers: Newsbreaks. Buys 10/year. Length: 30-100 words. Pays 72¢ per published line.

Tips: "Usually, someone who has had some involvement with the tobacco industry will be atuned to the needs of our magazine. No antagonistic articles will be accepted. We would like to see articles relating to the international tobacco industry and its issues. The sections most open to freelancers are International News and features. Freelancers must communicate with us to discover what we need in the way of country spotlights, industry issues, news ideas."

‡**VIDEO BUSINESS**, 825 7th Ave., New York NY 10019-6001. FAX: (212)887-8484. 35% freelance written. A monthly magazine on video software retailing. *"Video Business* covers trends in marketing and videocassette programming for 40,000 retailers of all sizes. All articles should be written with the intent of providing information that a retailer can apply to his/her business immediately." Estab. 1981. Byline given. Buys first rights. Submit seasonal/holiday material 2 months in advance. Query for electronic submissions. Reports in 2 weeks. Free sample copy and writer's guidelines.

Nonfiction: Historical/nostalgic (movie genres), interview/profile, new product and technical. Query with published clips. Pays 25-35¢/word. Sometimes pays the expenses of writers on assignment.

Photos: State availability of photos with submission. Reviews negatives. Offers additional payment for photos accepted with ms. Buys one-time rights.

WOMEN IN BUSINESS, The ABWA Co., Inc.. 9100 Ward Parkway, Kansas City MO 64114. (816)361-6621. Editor: Wendy Myers. 30% freelance written. A bimonthly magazine for members of the American Business Women's Association. "We publish articles of interest to the American working woman." Estab. 1949. Circ. 110,000. **Pays on acceptance.** Publishes ms an average of 2 months after acceptance. Byline given. Kill fee negotiable. Buys all rights. Submit seasonal/holiday material 4 months in advance. Reports in 1 week. Sample copy for 9×12 SAE with 4 first class stamps. Writer's guidelines for #10 SASE.

Nonfiction: "We cannot use success stories about individual businesswomen." Buys 30 mss/year. Query with published clips or send complete ms. Length: 1,000-3,000 words. Pays 15¢/word.

Photos: State availability of photos with submission. Offers no additional payment for photos accepted with ms. Identification of subjects required.

Columns/Departments: Holly Oeltjen, column/department editor. Working Capital (personal finance for women), 1,500 words; Health Scope (health topics for women); Moving Up (advice for the up-and-coming woman manager); Business Basics (for women small business owners). Buys 18 mss/year. Query with published clips or send complete ms. Length: 1,000-1,500 words. Pays 15¢/word.

Tips: "It would be very difficult to break into our columns. We have regular contributing freelance writers for those. But we are always on the look out for good feature articles and writers. We are especially interested in writers who provide a fresh, new look to otherwise old topics, such as time management etc."

Church Administration and Ministry

Publications in this section are written for clergy members, church leaders and teachers. Magazines for lay members and the general public are listed in the Consumer Religious section.

THE CHRISTIAN MINISTRY, The Christian Century Foundation, Suite 1405, 407 S. Dearborn St., Chicago IL 60605. (312)427-5380. Editor: James M. Wall. Managing Editor: Mark R. Halton. 80% freelance written. Bimonthly magazine for parish clergy. "Most of our articles are written by parish clergy, describing parish situations. Our audience is comprised of mainline church ministers who are looking for practical ideas and insights concerning the ministry." Estab. 1969. Circ. 12,000. Pays on publication. Publishes ms an average of 6 months after acceptance. Byline given. Offers $20 kill fee.

Buys all rights. Submit seasonal/holiday material 4 months in advance. Simultaneous submissions OK. Reports in 3 weeks. Sample copy for $2 plus 9 × 12 SAE with 3 first class stamps. Writer's guidelines for #10 SASE.

Nonfiction: Book excerpts (forthcoming books), essays, how-to (parish subjects), religious and preached sermons. No articles with footnotes or inspirational poetry. Buys 60 mss/year. Send complete ms. Length: 1,000-3,000 words. Pays $50-100 for assigned articles; $40-75 for unsolicited articles. Pays in contributor copies for book reviews.

Photos: State availability of photos with submission. Reviews 8 × 10 b&w prints. Offers $20-50 per photo. Model releases preferred. Buys one-time rights.

Columns/Departments: Reflection on ministry (discusses an instance in which the author reflects on his or her practice of ministry), 2,500 words; From the Pulpit (preached sermons), 2,500 words. Buys 18 mss/year. Send complete ms. Length: 2,000-2,500 words. Pays $50-75.

Fillers: Newsbreaks and short humor. Buys 30/year. Length: 150-300 words. Pays $10.

Tips: "Send us finished manuscripts—not rough drafts. Freelancers have the best chance selling us articles on spec. Issues affecting parish clergy."

CHURCH ADMINISTRATION, 127 9th Ave. N., Nashville TN 37234. (615)251-2062. FAX: (615)251-3866. Editor: Gary Hardin. 15% freelance written. Works with a small number of new/unpublished writers each year. Monthly. For Southern Baptist pastors, staff and volunteer church leaders. Uses limited amount of freelance material. Estab. 1953. **Pays on acceptance.** Publishes ms an average of 1 year after acceptance. Byline given. Buys all rights. Free sample copy and writer's guidelines for SAE with 2 first class stamps.

Nonfiction: "Ours is a journal for effectiveness in ministry, including leadership, church programming, organizing, and staffing; administrative skills; church financing; church food services; church facilities; communication; and pastoral ministries and community needs." Length: 1,800-2,000 words. Pays 5½¢/word.

Tips: "Send query letter. Writers should be familiar with the organization and policy of Southern Baptist churches. Articles should be practical, how-to articles that meet genuine needs faced by leaders in SBC churches. Type at 54 characters per line, 25 lines per page, double-spaced. Send originals, not copies. Not responsible for manuscripts not accompanied by return postage."

CHURCH EDUCATOR, Creative Resources for Christian Educators, Educational Ministries, Inc., 2861-C Saturn St., Brea CA 92621. (714)961-0622. Editor: Robert G. Davidson. Managing Editor: Linda S. Davidson. 80% freelance written. Works with a small number of new/unpublished writers each year. A monthly magazine covering religious education. Estab. 1976. Circ. 5,200. Pays on publication. Publishes manuscript an average of 4 months after acceptance. Byline given. Buys first rights, second serial (reprint) rights, or all rights. "We prefer all rights." Submit seasonal/holiday material 4 months in advance. Simultaneous submissions OK. Reports in 3 months. Sample copy for 9 × 12 SAE and 3 first class stamps; free writer's guidelines.

Nonfiction: General interest; how-to (crafts for Church school) programs for church school, adult education study classes. "Our editorial lines are very middle of the road—mainline Protestant. We are not seeking extreme conservative or liberal theology pieces." No testimonials. Buys 100 mss/year. Send complete ms. Length: 100-2,000 words. Pays 2-4¢/word.

Photos: Send photos with submissions. Reviews 5 × 7 b&w prints. Offers $5-10/photo. Captions required. Buys one-time rights.

Fiction: Mainstream, religious and slice-of-life vignettes. Buys 15 mss/year. Send complete ms. Length: 100-2,000 words. Pays 2-4¢/word.

Fillers: Anecdotes and short humor. Buys 15/year. Length: 100-700 words. Pays 2-4¢/word.

Tips: "Send the complete manuscript with a cover letter which gives a concise summary of the manuscript. We are looking for how-to articles related to Christian education. That would include most any program held in a church. Be straightforward and to the point—not flowery and wordy. We're especially interested in youth programs. Give steps needed to carry out the program: preparation, starting the program, continuing the program, conclusion. List several discussion questions for each program."

‡CIRCUIT RIDER, A Journal for United Methodist Ministers, United Methodist Publishing House, Box 801, Nashville TN 37202. (615)749-6137. FAX: (615)749-6079. Editor: Keith I. Pohl. Editorial Director: J. Richard Peck. 60% freelance written. Works with a small number of new/unpublished writers each year. A monthly magazine covering professional concerns of clergy. Estab. 1789. Circ. 40,000. **Pays on acceptance.** Publishes ms an average of 1 year after acceptance. Byline given. Buys all rights. Submit seasonal/holiday material 6 months in advance. Reports in 3 weeks. Sample copy for 8½ × 11 SAE with $1 postage. Writer's guidelines for #10 SASE.

Nonfiction: How-to (improve pastoral calling, preaching, counseling, administration, etc.). No personal experience articles; no interviews. Buys 50 mss/year. Send complete ms. Length: 600-2,000 words. Pays $30-150.

Photos: State availability of photos. Pays $25-100 for 8 × 10 b&w prints. Model release required. Buys one-time rights.

Tips: "Know the concerns of a United Methodist pastor. Be specific. Think of how you can help pastors."

THE CLERGY JOURNAL, Church Management, Inc., P.O. Box 162527, Austin TX 78716. (512)327-8501. Editor: Manfred Holck, Jr. 20% freelance written. Eager to work with new/unpublished writers. Monthly (except June and December) covering religion. Readers are Protestant clergy. Estab. 1924. Circ. 30,000. Pays on publication. Publishes ms an average of 4 months after acceptance. Byline given. Offers 50% kill fee. Buys all rights. Submit seasonal/holiday material 6 months in advance. Reports in 2 weeks on queries; 1 month on mss. Sample copy for $3 and 9 × 12 SAE with 8 first class stamps.
Nonfiction: How-to (be a more efficient and effective minister/administrator). No devotional, inspirational or sermons. Buys 20 mss/year. Query. Length: 500-1,500 words. Pays $25-40.

LEADER, Board of Christian Education of the Church of God, P.O. Box 2458, Anderson IN 46018-2458. (317)642-0257. Editor: Joseph L. Cookston. 50% freelance written. Works with a small number of new/unpublished writers each year. A bimonthly magazine covering local Sunday school teaching and administrating, youth work, worship, family life and other local church ministries. Estab. 1939. Circ. 4,000. Pays on publication. Publishes ms an average of 10 months after acceptance. Byline given. Buys first rights and second serial (reprint) rights. Submit seasonal/holiday material 6 months in advance. Simultaneous queries OK. Reports in 4 months. Sample copy and writer's guidelines for 9 × 12 SAE with 3 first class stamps.
Nonfiction: General interest, how-to, inspirational, personal experience, guidance for carrying out programs for special days, continuing ministries and short-short ministry ideas. No articles that are not specifically related to local church leadership. Buys 20 mss/year. Send complete ms, brief description of present interest in writing for church leaders, background and experience. Length: 300-800 words. Pays 2¢/word ($10 minimum).
Tips: "How-to articles related to Sunday school teaching, program development and personal teacher enrichment or growth, and program and teaching ideas are most open to freelancers."

LEADERSHIP, A Practical Journal for Church Leaders, Christianity Today, Inc., 465 Gundersen Dr., Carol Stream IL 60188. (312)260-6200. Editor: Marshall Shelley. 75% freelance written. Works with a small number of new/unpublished writers each year. A quarterly magazine covering church leadership. Writers must have a "knowledge of and sympathy for the unique expectations placed on pastors and local church leaders. Each article must support points by illustrating from real life experiences in local churches." Estab. 1980. Circ. 90,000. **Pays on acceptance.** Publishes ms an average of 6 months after acceptance. Byline given. Buys first North American serial rights. Submit seasonal/holiday material 6 months in advance. Previously published submissions OK. Reports in 6 weeks on queries; 2 months on mss. Sample copy $3; free writer's guidelines.
Nonfiction: How-to, humor and personal experience. "No articles from writers who have never read our journal." Buys 50 mss/year. Send complete ms. Length: 100-5,000 words. Pays $30-300. Sometimes pays the expenses of writers on assignment.
Photos: State availability of photos with submission. Offers no additional payment for photos accepted with ms. Identification of subjects required. Buys one-time rights.
Columns/Departments: People in Print (book reviews with interview of author), 1,500 words. To Illustrate (short stories or analogies that illustrate a biblical principle), 100 words. Buys 25 mss/year. Send complete ms. Pays $25-100.

PASTORAL LIFE, Society of St. Paul, Route 224, Canfield OH 44406. Editor: Anthony Chenevey, SSP. 66% freelance written. Eager to work with new/unpublished writers. Emphasizes priests and those interested in pastoral ministry. Monthly magazine. Circ. 3,000. Buys first rights only. Byline given. Pays on publication. Publishes ms an average of 6 months after acceptance. Query with a outline before submitting ms. "New contributors are expected to include, in addition, a few lines of personal data that indicate academic and professional background." Reports within 2 weeks. Free sample copy and writer's guidelines.
Nonfiction: "*Pastoral Life* is a professional review, principally designed to focus attention on current problems, needs, issues and all important activities related to all phases of pastoral work and life." Buys 30 unsolicited mss/year. Length: 2,000-3,400 words. Pays 4¢/word minimum.

Always check the most recent copy of a magazine for the address and editor's name before you send in a query or manuscript.

THE PREACHER'S MAGAZINE, Nazarene Publishing House, E. 10814 Broadway, Spokane WA 99206. Editor: Randal E. Denny. Assistant Editor: Cindy Osso. 15% freelance written. Works with a small number of new/unpublished writers each year. Quarterly magazine of seasonal/miscellaneous articles. "A resource for ministers; Wesleyan-Arminian in theological persuasion." Circ. 18,000. **Pays on acceptance.** Publishes ms an average of 9 months after acceptance. Byline given. Buys first serial rights, second serial (reprint) rights and simultaneous rights. Submit seasonal/holiday material 9 months in advance. Simultaneous queries OK. Writer's guidelines for #10 SASE.

Nonfiction: How-to, humor, inspirational, opinion and personal experience, all relating to aspects of ministry. No articles that present problems without also presenting answers to them; things not relating to pastoral ministry. Buys 48 mss/year. Send complete ms. Length: 700-2,500 words. Pays 3½¢/word.

Photos: Send photos with ms. Reviews 35mm transparencies and 35mm b&w prints. Pays $25-35. Model release and identification of subjects required. Buys one-time rights.

Columns/Departments: Today's Books for Today's Preacher—book reviews. Buys 24 mss/year. Send complete ms. Length: 300-400 words. Pays $7.50.

Fillers: Anecdotes and short humor. Buys 10/year. Length: 400 words maximum. Pays 3½¢/word.

Tips: "Writers for the *Preacher's Magazine* should have insight into the pastoral ministry, or expertise in a specialized area of ministry. Our magazine is a highly specialized publication aimed at the minister. Our goal is to assist, by both scholarly and practical articles, the modern-day minister in applying Biblical theological truths."

PREACHING, Preaching Resources, Inc., 1529 Cesery Blvd., Jacksonville FL 32211. (904)743-5994. Editor: Dr. Michael Duduit. 75% freelance written. Bimonthly magazine for the preaching ministry. "All articles must deal with preaching. Most articles used offer practical assistance in preparation and delivery of sermons, generally from an evangelical stance." Estab. 1985. Circ. 10,000. Pays on publication. Publishes ms an average of 1 year after acceptance. Byline given. Buys first rights. Submit seasonal/holiday material 1 year in advance. Query for electronic submissions. Reports in 2-4 months. Sample copy $2.50; writer's guidelines for SASE.

Nonfiction: How-to (preparation and delivery of sermon; worship leadership). Special issues include Personal Computing in Preaching (September-October); materials/resources to assist in preparation of seasonal preaching (November-December, March-April). Buys 18-24 mss/year. Query. Length: 1,000-2,000 words. Pays $35-50.

Photos: Send photos with submission. Reviews prints. Offers no additional payment for photos accepted with ms. Captions, model releases and identification of subjects required. Buys one-time rights.

Fillers: Buys 10-15/year. "Buys only completed cartoons." Art must be related to preaching. Pays $25.

Tips: "Most desirable are practical, 'how-to' articles on preparation and delivery of sermons."

Clothing

‡APPAREL INDUSTRY MAGAZINE, Shore Communications, Suite 300-North, 180 Allen Rd., Atlanta GA 30328. FAX: (404)252-4436. Editor: Meg Thornton. Managing Editor: Gary Fong. 30% freelance written. Monthly magazine for executive management in apparel companies with interests in equipment, fabrics, licensing, distribution, finance, management and training. Estab. 1946. Circ. 18,700. Pays on publication. Publishes ms an average of 4 months after acceptance. Byline given. Buys first serial rights. Query for electronic submissions. Reports in 1 month. Sample copy $3; writer's guidelines for #10 SASE.

Nonfiction: Articles dealing with equipment, manufacturing techniques, training, finance, licensing, fabrics, quality control, etc., related to the industry. "Use concise, precise language that is easy to read and understand. In other words, because the subjects are often technical, keep the language comprehensible. Material must be precisely related to the apparel industry. We are not a retail or fashion magazine." Informational, interview, profile, successful business operations and technical articles. Buys 30 mss/year. Query. Length: 3,000 words maximum. Pays 20¢/word. Sometimes pays expenses of writers on assignment.

Photos: Pays $5/photo with ms.

Tips: "Frequently articles are too general due to lack of industry-specific knowledge by the writer."

ATI, America's Textiles International, Billian Publishing Co., 2100 Powers Ferry Rd., Atlanta GA 30339. (404)955-5656. FAX: (404)952-0669. Editor: Monte G. Plott. Associate Editor: Rolf Viertel. 10% freelance written. Monthly magazine covering textiles, apparel, and fibers. "We cover the business of textile, apparel, and fiber industries with considerable technical focus on products and processes. No puff pieces pushing a particular product." Pays on publication. Byline sometimes given. Buys first North American serial rights. Query for electronic submissions.

Nonfiction: Technical, business. "No PR, just straight technical reports." Buys 10 mss/year. Query. Length: 500 words minimum. Pays $100/published page. Sometimes pays expenses of writers on assignment.

Photos: Send photos with submission. Reviews prints. Offers no additional payment for photos accepted with ms. Captions required. Buys one-time rights.

‡CHRISTIAN RETAILING, Strang Communications, 600 Rinehart Road, Lake Mary FL 32746. (407)333-0600. Editor: Brian Peterson. 60% freelance written. Monthly magazine covering issues and products of interest to Christian vendors and retail stores. "Our editorial is geared to help retailers run a successful business. We do this with product information, industry news and feature articles." Estab. 1958. Circ. 9,500. Pays on publication. Publishes ms an average of 5 months after acceptance. Bylines sometimes given. Kill fee varies with writer, length of article. Buys all rights. Submit seasonal/holiday material 5 months in advance. Previously published submissions OK. Reports in 2 months. Sample copy $3. Writer's guidelines for #10 SASE.

Nonfiction: How-to (any articles on running a retail business—books, gifts, music, video, clothing of interest to Christians), new product, religious, technical. Buys 36 mss/year. Send complete ms. Length: 700-2,300 words. Pays 12¢/word minimum for assigned articles; 10¢/word minimum for unsolicited articles. Sometimes pays expenses of writers on assignment.

Photos: State availability of photos with submission. Reviews contact sheets, transparencies (any) and prints (any). Usually offers no additional payment for photos accepted with ms. Captions required. Buys one-time rights.

Columns/Departments: Book News; Music Notes; Video Talk; Gift Rap. Pays 12¢/word minimum; no maximum.

Fillers: Anecdotes, facts, gags to be illustrated by cartoonist, short humor. Buys 5/year. Length: 50-300 words. Pays 12¢/word minimum.

Tips: "Visit Christian bookstores and see what they're doing—the products they carry, the issues that concern them. Then write about it!"

SPECIALTY STORE SERVICE, Vanguard Publications, Inc., 6604 W. Saginaw Hwy., Lansing MI 48917. (517)321-0671. Editor: Ralph D. Ward. 70% freelance written. Monthly newsletter for women's independent clothing stores. Estab. 1978. Circ. 1,400. **Pays on acceptance.** Publishes ms an average of 3 months after acceptance. Byline given. Buys first North American serial rights and second serial (reprint) rights. Submit seasonal/holiday material 5 months in advance. Simultaneous submissions OK. Query for electronic submissions. Reports in 6 weeks. Free sample copy and writer's guidelines for SASE.

Nonfiction: How-to (retail sales, inventory management, retail promotion); Specializing (fresh ideas from various women's specialty retailing areas); Store Business/Your Business (personal/money and lifestyle management for store owners). No color analysis. Buys 60 mss/year. Query with published clips and areas of expertise. Length: 900-1,200 words. Pays 11¢/word.

Tips: Writers with retail or fashion experience preferred. Knowledge of industry vital.

‡T-SHIRT RETAILER AND SCREEN PRINTER, WFC, Inc., 3000 Hadley Rd., S. Plainfield NJ 07080. (908)769-1160. FAX: (908)769-1171. Editor: Bruce Sachenski. 10% freelance written. A monthly magazine for persons in imprinted garment industry and screen printing. Circ. 27,000. Pays on publication. Publishes ms an average of 3 months after acceptance. Byline given. Buys one-time rights. Submit seasonal/holiday material 3 months in advance. Photocopied and previously published submissions OK. Reports in 1 month. Sample copy $5.

Nonfiction: How-to, new product, photo feature, technical and business. Buys 6 mss/year. Send complete ms. Length: 1,500-3,500 words. Pays $100-200 for assigned articles.

Photos: Send photos with submission. Reviews contact sheets. Offers no additional payment for photos accepted with ms. Identification of subjects required.

Columns/Departments: Query. Length: 1,000-2,000 words. Pays $50-150.

Tips: "We need general business stories: equipment, advertising, store management, etc."

Coin-Operated Machines

AMERICAN COIN-OP, 500 N. Dearborn St., Chicago IL 60610. (312)337-7700. FAX: (312)337-8654. Editor: Ben Russell. 30% freelance written. Monthly magazine for owners of coin-operated laundry and dry cleaning stores. Estab. 1960. Circ. 20,100. Rights purchased vary with author and material but are exclusive to the field. Pays two weeks prior to publication. Publishes ms an average of 4 months after acceptance. Byline given for frequent contributors. Reports as soon as possible; usually in 2 weeks. Free sample copy.

Nonfiction: "We emphasize store operation and use features on industry topics: utility use and conservation, maintenance, store management, customer service and advertising. A case study should emphasize how the store operator accomplished whatever he did—in a way that the reader can apply to his own operation. Manuscript should have a no-nonsense, business-like approach." Uses informational, how-to, interview, profile, think pieces and successful business operations articles. Length: 500-3,000 words. Pays 7½¢/word minimum.

Photos: Pays $7.50 minimum for 5×7 b&w glossy photos purchased with mss. (Contact sheets with negatives preferred.)

Fillers: Newsbreaks and clippings. Length: open. Pays $10 minimum.

Tips: "Query about subjects of current interest. Be observant of coin-operated laundries—how they are designed and equipped, how they serve customers and how (if) they advertise and promote their services. Most general articles are turned down because they are not aimed well enough at our audience. Most case histories are turned down because they lack practical purpose (nothing new or worth reporting). A frequent mistake is failure to follow up on an interesting point made by the interviewee—probably due to lack of knowledge about the industry."

PLAY METER MAGAZINE, Skybird Publishing Co., Inc., P.O. Box 24970, New Orleans LA 70184. FAX: (504)488-7083. Publisher: Carol Lally. Editor: Valerie Cognevich. 25% freelance written. "We will work with new writers who are familiar with the amusement industry." Monthly trade magazine for owners/operators of coin-operated amusement machine companies, e.g., pinball machines, video games, arcade pieces, jukeboxes, etc. Estab. 1974. Circ. 6,500. Pays on publication. Publishes ms an average of 2 months after acceptance. Byline given. Buys all rights. Submit seasonal/holiday material 2 months in advance. Previously published submissions OK. Query answered in 2 months. Sample copy $5; free writer's guidelines.

Nonfiction: How-to (get better locations for machines, promote tournaments, evaluate profitability of route, etc.); interview (with industry leaders); new product. "Our readers want to read about how they can make more money from their machines, how they can get better tax breaks, commissions, etc. Also no stories about *playing* pinball or video games. Also, submissions on video-game technology advances; technical pieces on troubleshooting videos, pinballs and novelty machines (all coin-operated); trade-show coverage (query) submissions on the pay-telephone industry. Our readers don't play the games per se; they buy the machines and make money from them." Buys 48 mss/year. Submit complete ms. Length: 250-3,000 words. Pays $30-215. Sometimes pays expenses of writers on assignment.

Photos: "The photography should have news value. We don't want 'stand 'em up-shoot 'em down' group shots." Pays $15 minimum for 5×7 or 8×10 b&w prints. Captions preferred. Buys all rights. Art returned on request.

Tips: "We need feature articles more than small news items or featurettes. Query first. We're interested in writers who either have a few years of reporting/feature-writing experience or who know the coin-operated amusement industry well but are relatively inexperienced writers."

VENDING TIMES, 545 8th Ave., New York NY 10018. FAX: (212)564-0196. Editor: Arthur E. Yohalem. Monthly. For operators of vending machines. Estab. 1960. Circ. 14,700. Pays on publication. Buys all rights. "We will discuss in detail the story requirements with the writer." Sample copy $4.

Nonfiction: Feature articles and news stories about vending operations; practical and important aspects of the business. "We are always willing to pay for good material." Query.

Confectionery and Snack Foods

These publications focus on the bakery, snack and candy industries. Journals for grocers, wholesalers and other food industry personnel are listed in Groceries and Food Products.

CANDY INDUSTRY, Edgell Communications, Inc., 7500 Old Oak Blvd., Cleveland OH 44130. (216)891-2612. FAX: (216)819-2651. Editor: Susan Tiffany. 5% freelance written. Monthly. Prefers to work with published/established writers. For confectionery manufacturers. Publishes ms an average of 4 months after acceptance. Buys all rights. Reports in 1 month. Writer's guidelines for #10 SASE.

Nonfiction: "Feature articles of interest to large scale candy manufacturers that deal with activities in the fields of production, packaging (including package design), merchandising; and financial news (sales figures, profits, earnings), advertising campaigns in all media, and promotional methods used to increase the sale or distribution of candy." Length: 1,000-1,250 words. Pays 15¢/word; "special rates on assignments."

Photos: "Good quality glossies with complete and accurate captions, in sizes not smaller than 5×7." Pays $15 b&w; $20 for color.

Fillers: "Short news stories about the trade and anything related to candy." Pays 5¢/word; $1 for clippings.

PACIFIC BAKERS NEWS, Suite F, 1818 Mt. Diablo Blvd., Walnut Creek CA 94596. (415)932-1256. Publisher: C.W. Soward. 30% freelance written. Eager to work with new/unpublished writers. Monthly business newsletter for commercial bakeries in the western states. Estab. 1961. Pays on publication. No byline given; uses only one-paragraph news items.

Nonfiction: Uses bakery business reports and news about bakers. Buys only brief "boiled-down news items about bakers and bakeries operating only in Alaska, Hawaii, Pacific Coast and Rocky Mountain states. We welcome clippings. We need monthly news reports and clippings about the baking industry and the donut business. No pictures, jokes, poetry or cartoons." Length: 10-200 words. Pays 10¢/word for news and 6¢ for clips (words used).

‡**SNACK FOOD**, Edgell Communications, Inc., 131 W. 1st St., Duluth MN 55802. (218)723-9343. Editor-in-Chief: Jerry L. Hess. 15% freelance written. For manufacturers and distributors of snack foods. Monthly magazine. Circ. 10,000. **Pays on acceptance.** Publishes ms an average of 2 months after acceptance. Buys first serial rights. Occasional byline given. Phone queries OK. Reports in 2 months. Free sample copy and writer's guidelines.
Nonfiction: Informational, interview, new product, nostalgia, photo feature, profile and technical articles. "We use an occasional mini news feature or personality sketch." Length: 300-600 words for mini features; 750-1,200 words for longer features. Pays 15-18¢/word. Sometimes pays the expenses of writers on assignment.
Photos: Purchased with accompanying ms. Captions required. Pays $20 for 5×7 b&w photos. Total purchase price for ms includes payment for photos when used. Buys all rights.
Tips: "Query should contain specific lead and display more than a casual knowledge of our audience. The most frequent mistakes made by writers are not writing to our particular audience, and lack of a grasp of certain technical points on how the industry functions."

Construction and Contracting

Builders, architects and contractors learn the latest industry news in these publications. Journals targeted to architects are also included in the Consumer Art and Architecture category. Those for specialists in the interior aspects of construction are listed under Building Interiors.

ACCESS CONTROL, 6255 Barfield Rd., Atlanta GA 30328. (404)256-9800. FAX: (404)256-3116. Editor/Associate Publisher: Steven Lasky. 50% freelance written. Prefers to work with published/established writers. Monthly tabloid for end users and installers of access control equipment. Estab. 1955. Circ. 24,000. Pays on publication. Publishes ms an average of 2 months after acceptance. Buys all rights. Query for electronic submissions. Reports in 3 months. Free sample copy for 8×10 SASE; writer's guidelines for #10 SASE.
Nonfiction: Case histories, large-scale access control "systems approach" equipment installations. A format for these articles has been established. Query for details. Buys 10-12 unsolicited mss/year. Query. Length: 4,500 words maximum.
Columns/Departments: Also take technical or practical application features for following monthly columns dealing with perimeter security fencing and accessories, gate systems, sensor technology card access systems, and CCTV technology. Length: 2,000 words maximum.
Photos: Pays $10 for 5×7 b&w photos purchased with mss. Captions required.
Tips: "We will place more focus on access control installations."

‡**ATLANTIC CONSTRUCTION**, Naylor Communications Ltd., 6th Fl., 920 Yonge St., Toronto, Ontario M4W 3C7 Canada. (416)961-1028. FAX: (416)924-4408. Editor: C. Winslow Pettingill. 50% freelance written. Annual trade journal for the construction industry in region of Atlantic Canada. "*Construction Atlantic* focuses on issues of interest to the members of four provincial construction associations. A topical and informed style is sought from all writers supplying material." Circ. 5,000. Pays 30 days "from deadline." Byline given. Offers 33⅓% kill fee. Buys first North American serial rights. Submit seasonal/holiday material 2 months in advance. Simultaneous and previously published submissions OK. Query for electronic submissions.
Nonfiction: General interest, historical, interview/profile, new product, photo feature and technical. "Our publishing date is normally mid-November each year. Articles or ideas for same should be looked at in summer months and as late as September. No promotional, inspirational or personal fluff." Buys 10 mss/year. Query with published clips. Length: 500-2,500 words. Pays 20-25¢/word. Pays expenses of writers on assignment.
Photos: State availability of photos with submission or send photos with submission. Reviews transparencies and prints. Offers $25-200 per photo. Identification of subjects required. Buys all rights.
Tips: "Query with examples of work. I always respond to every inquiry even if it's to say we're not interested. Major tip: Research facts and quote experts in particular fields."

AUTOMATED BUILDER, CMN Associates, Inc., P.O. Box 120, Carpinteria CA 93014. (805)684-7659. FAX: (805)684-1765. Editor-in-Chief: Don Carlson. 15% freelance written. Monthly magazine specializing in management for industrialized (manufactured) housing and volume home builders. Circ.

25,000. Pays on acceptance. Publishes ms an average of 3 months after acceptance. Buys first North American serial rights. Phone queries OK. Reports in 2 weeks. Free sample copy and writer's guidelines.
Nonfiction: Case history articles on successful home building companies which may be 1) production (big volume) home builders; 2) mobile home manufacturers; 3) modular home manufacturers; 4) prefabricated home manufacturers; 5) house component manufacturers; or 6) special unit (in-plant commercial building) manufacturers. Also uses interviews, photo features and technical articles. "No architect or plan 'dreams'. Housing projects must be built or under construction." Buys 15 mss/year. Query. Length: 500-1,000 words maximum. Pays $300 minimum.
Photos: Purchased with accompanying ms. Query. No additional payment for 4×5, 5×7 or 8×10 b&w glossies or 35mm or larger color transparencies (35mm preferred). Captions required.
Tips: "Stories often are too long, too loose; we prefer 500 to 750 words. We prefer a phone query on feature articles. If accepted on query, article usually will not be rejected later."

‡**BUILDER INSIDER**, P.O. Box 191125, Dallas TX 75219-1125. (214)871-2913. Editor: Mike Anderson. 18% freelance written. Works with a small number of new/unpublished writers each year. Covers the entire north Texas building industry for builders, architects, contractors, remodelers and homeowners. Circ. 8,000. Publishes ms an average of 2 months after acceptance. Free sample copy.
Nonfiction: "What is current in the building industry" is the approach. Wants "advertising, business builders, new building products, building projects being developed and helpful building hints localized to the Southwest and particularly to north Texas." Submit complete ms. Length: 100-900 words. Pays $30-50.

CONSTRUCTION COMMENT, Naylor Communications Ltd., 6th Fl., 920 Yonge St., Toronto, Ontario M4W 3C7 Canada. (416)961-1028. FAX: (416)924-4408. Editor: C. Winslow Pettingell. 50% freelance written. Semiannual magazine on construction industry in Ottawa. "*Construction Comment* reaches all members of the Ottawa Construction Association and most senior management of firms relating to the industry." Circ. 3,000. Pays 30 day after deadline. Byline given. Offers ⅓ kill fee. Buys first North American serial rights. Submit seasonal/holiday material 2 months in advance. Simultaneous submissions OK. Query for electronic submissions.
Nonfiction: General interest, historical, interview/profile, new product, photo feature and technical. "We publish a spring/summer issue and a fall/winter issue. Submit correspondingly or inquire two months ahead of these times." Buys 20 mss/year. Query with published clips. Length: 500-2,500 words. Pays 20-25¢/word. Pays expenses of writers on assignment.
Photos: State availability of photos with submission. Send photos with submission. Reviews transparencies and prints. Offers $25-200 per photo. Identification of subjects required.
Tips: "Please send copies of work and a general query. I will respond as promptly as my deadlines allow. Company publications also include *Toronto Construction News* a bimonthly magazine on construction industry in Toronto reaching all members of the Toronto Construction Association, and *The Generals*, a quarterly magazine for general contractors in Ontario, reaching all members of the Ontario General Contractors Association."

CONSTRUCTION SPECIFIER, 601 Madison St., Alexandria VA 22314. (703)684-0300. FAX: (703)684-0465. Publisher: Jack Reeder. 50% freelance written. Works with a small number of new/unpublished writers each year. Monthly professional society magazine for architects, engineers, specification writers and project managers. Monthly. Estab. 1949. Circ. 19,000. Pays on publication. Publishes ms an average of 4 months after acceptance. Deadline: 60 days preceding publication on the 1st of each month. Buys North American serial rights. Query for electronic submissions. "Call or write first." Model release, author copyright transferral requested. Reports in 3 weeks. Sample copy for 9×12 SAE and 6 first class stamps. Writer's guidelines for #10 SASE.
Nonfiction: Articles on selection and specification of products, materials, practices and methods used in commercial (nonresidential) construction projects, specifications as related to construction design, plus legal and management subjects. Query. Length: 3,000-5,000 words maximum. Pays up to 15¢/published word (negotiable), plus art. Pays minor expenses of writers on assignment, to an agreed upon limit.
Photos: Photos desirable in consideration for publication; line art, sketches, diagrams, charts and graphs also desired. Full color transparencies may be used. 8×10 glossies, 3¼ slides preferred. Payment negotiable.
Tips: "We need more good technical articles."

FINE HOMEBUILDING, The Taunton Press, Inc., 63 S. Main St., P.O. Box 5506, Newtown CT 06470. (203)426-8171. Editor: Mark Feirer. Less than 5% freelance written. Bimonthly magazine covering house building, construction, design for builders, architects and serious amateurs. Estab. 1976. Circ. 245,000. Pays advance, balance on publication. Publishes ms an average of 6-12 months after acceptance. Byline given. Offers negotiable kill fee. Buys first rights and "use in books to be published." Query for electronic submissions. Reports as soon as possible. Free writer's guidelines.

Nonfiction: Technical (techniques in design or construction process). Query. Length: 2,000-3,000 words. Pays $150-1,200.

Columns/Departments: Tools and Materials (products or techniques that are new or unusual); Great Moments in Building History (humorous, embarrassing, or otherwise noteworthy anecdotes); Reviews (short reviews of books on building or design) and Reports and Comment (essays, short reports on construction and architecture trends and developments). Query. Length: 300-1,000 words. Pays $50-250.

HOME BUILDER, Work-4 Projects Ltd., P.O. Box 400, Victoria Station, Westmount, Quebec H3Z 2V8 Canada. (514)489-4941. FAX: (514)489-5505. Publisher: Nachmi Artzy. Editor: Frank O'Brien. 80% freelance written. Magazine covers new home construction, published 6 times annually. "*Home Builder* reports on builders, architects, mortgage, sub-trades, associations and government. We keep the readers' concerns in the forefront, not the advertisers." Estab. 1976. Circ. 12,000. Pays on publication. Publishes ms an average of 4 months after acceptance. Byline sometimes given. Buys all rights. Simultaneous submissions OK. Reports in 3 weeks on queries. Free sample copy.

Nonfiction: Exposé, how-to (builders, administration, production, etc.), interview/profile, new product and technical. Buys 20-30 mss/year. Query with published clips. Length: 100-500 words. Pays 10-20¢/word. Pays in contributor copies or other premiums "if suitable for both parties." Sometimes pays expenses of writers on assignment.

Photos: Send photos with submission. Reviews transparencies and prints. Offers expense-$300 per photo. Captions and identification of subjects required. Buys all rights.

Columns/Departments: Perspective (general news of importance to audience), 100-300 words; and Industry News (specific company information of relevance—not sales pitch), 75-300 words. Buys 20 mss/year. Query with published clips. Pays 10-20¢/word.

Fillers: Facts and gags. Buys 5/year. Length: 5-50 words. Pays 10¢/word-$25.

Tips: "Keep audience in mind. Give them something that will affect them, not something they will forget five minutes after reading it. Keep in mind Canadian content."

INLAND ARCHITECT, The Midwestern Building Arts Magazine, Inland Architect Press, 10 West Hubbard St., P.O. Box 10394, Chicago IL 60610. (312)321-0583. FAX: (312)467-7051. Senior Editor: Barbara K. Hower. 80% freelance written. Prefers to work with published/established writers. Bimonthly magazine covering architecture and urban planning. "*Inland Architect* is a critical journal covering architecture and design in the midwest for an audience primarily of architects. *Inland* is open to all points of view, providing they are intelligently expressed and of relevance to architecture." Estab. 1957. Circ. 7,000. Pays on publication. Publishes ms an average of 2 months after acceptance. Byline given. Offers 60% kill fee. Buys first rights. Reports in 1 month on queries; 2 months on mss. Sample copy $9 includes shipping and handling.

Nonfiction: Book excerpts, essays, historical/nostalgic, interview/profile, criticism and photo feature of architecture. Every summer *Inland* focuses on a midwestern city, its architecture and urban design. Call to find out 1992 city. No new products, "how to run your office," or technical pieces. Buys 40 mss/year. Query with or without published clips, or send complete ms. Length: 750-3,500 words. Pays $100-300 for assigned articles; pays $75-250 for unsolicited articles. Sometimes pays the expenses of writers on assignment.

Photos: Send photos with submission. Reviews 4×5 transparencies, slides and 8×10 prints. Offers no additional payment for photos accepted with ms. Identification of subjects required. Buys one-time rights.

Columns/Departments: Books (reviews of new publications on architecture, design and, occasionally, art), 250-1,000 words. Buys 10 mss/year. Query. Length: 250-1,000 words. Pays $25-100.

Tips: "Propose to cover a lecture, to interview a certain architect, etc. Articles must be written for an audience primarily consisting of well-educated architects. If an author feels he has a 'hot' timely idea, a phone call is appreciated."

MIDWEST CONTRACTOR MAGAZINE, 3170 Mercier, Box 419766, Kansas City MO 64141. (816)931-2080. FAX: (816)753-1106. 5% freelance written. Biweekly magazine covering the public works and engineering construction industries in Iowa, Nebraska, Kansas and western and northeastern Missouri. Estab. 1901. Circ. 8,426. Pays on publication. Byline given depending on nature of article. Reports in 1 month. Sample copy for 11×15 SAE with first class stamps.

Nonfiction: How-to, photo feature, technical, "nuts and bolts" construction job-site features. "We seek two- to three-page articles on topics of interest to our readership, including marketing trends, tips, and construction job-site stories. Providing concise, accurate and original news stories is another freelance opportunity." Buys 4 mss/year. Query with three published clips. Length: 175 typewritten lines, 35 character count, no maximum. Pays $50/published page.

Tips: "We need writers who can write clearly about our specialized trade area. An engineering/construction background is a plus. The most frequent mistake made by writers is that they do not tailor their article to our specific market—the nonresidential construction market in Nebraska, Iowa, Kansas and Missouri. We are not interested in what happens in New York unless it has a specific impact in the Midwest."

PACIFIC BUILDER & ENGINEER, Vernon Publications Inc.. Suite 200, 3000 Northup Way, Bellevue WA 98004. (206)827-9900. FAX: (206)822-9372. Editor: John M. Watkins. Editorial Director: Michele Dill. 20% freelance written. A biweekly magazine on heavy construction. "We cover non-residential construction in Washington, Oregon, Idaho, Montana and Alaska." Estab. 1902. Circ. 12,000. Pays on publication. Byline given. Buys first North American serial rights. Submit seasonal material 2 months in advance. Reports in 3 weeks on queries; 6 weeks on mss.
Nonfiction: How-to (construction), interview/profile and technical (construction). Buys 10 mss/year. Query with published clips. Length: 1,000-2,500 words. Pays $100-200. Does not pay for unsolicited manuscripts. Sometimes pays the expenses of writers on assignment.
Photos: Send photos with submission. Reviews contact sheets, transparencies (35mm) and prints (8×10). Payment is by the page. Buys North American rights.

ROOFER MAGAZINE, D&H Publications, 12120 Amedicus Ln., Ft. Myers FL 33907. (813)275-7663. Editor: Kaerrie A. Simons. 10% freelance written. Eager to work with new/unpublished writers. Monthly magazine covering the roofing industry for roofing contractors. Estab. 1981. Circ. 17,000. Pays on publication. Publishes ms an average of 5 months after acceptance. Byline given. Buys first serial rights and second serial (reprint) rights. Submission must be exclusive to our field. Submit seasonal/holiday material 4 months in advance. Reports in 2 weeks on queries; 1 month on mss. Sample copy and writer's guidelines for SAE and 6 first class stamps.
Nonfiction: Historical/nostalgic; how-to (solve application problems, overcome trying environmental conditions); interview/profile; and technical. "Write articles directed toward areas of specific interest; don't generalize too much." Buys 10 mss/year. Query in writing. Length: 1,000-1,500 words. Pays $125-250.
Photos: Send photos with completed mss; color slides are preferred. Identification of subjects required. Buys all rights. Always searching for photos of unusual roofs or those with a humorous slant.
Tips: "We prefer substantial articles (no fillers please). Slant articles toward roofing contractors. We have little use for generic articles that can appear in any business publication and give little consideration to such material submitted. The tone of articles submitted to us needs to be authoritative but not condescending. We are eager to review material with a humorous slant. Authors of successful freelance articles know the roofing industry." Freelance writers should keep in mind that we most frequently purchase contractor profiles on roofing contractors around the globe (very explicit guidelines for these articles are available upon request).

SOUTHWEST CONTRACTOR, McGraw Hill Publishing Co., #1, 2050 E. University, Phoenix AZ 85034. (602)258-1641. FAX: (602)495-9407. Editor: Elaine M. Beall. 20% freelance written. Monthly magazine about construction industry/engineering. "Problem-solving case histories of projects in Arizona, New Mexico, Nevada and West Texas emphasizing engineering, equipment, materials and people." Estab. 1938. Circ. 6,200. Pays on publication. Byline given. Buys first rights and makes work-for-hire assignments. Submit seasonal/holiday material 3 months in advance. Previously published submissions OK. Sample $3 with 9×12 SAE and 4 first class stamps. Writer's guidelines for #10 SASE.
Nonfiction: Interview/profile and technical. Buys 12 mss/year. Query. Length: 1,000-3,000 words. Pays $4/column inch at 14 picas wide. Sometimes pays expenses of writers on assignment.
Photos: State availability of photos with submission. Reviews 3x5 prints. Offers $10 maximum per photo. Captions and identification of subjects required. Buys one-time rights.
Columns/Departments: People, Around Southwest (general construction activities), Association News (all associations involved with industry), Manufacturer's News, Legal News (construction only). Contracts awarded (construction only).

Dental

DENTAL ECONOMICS, Penwell Publishing Co., P.O. Box 3408, Tulsa OK 74101. (918)835-3161. FAX: (918)831-9497. Editor: Dick Hale. 50% freelance written. A monthly dental trade journal. "Our readers are actively practicing dentists who look to us for current practice-building, practice-administrative and personal finance assistance." Estab. 1911. Circ. 110,000. **Pays on acceptance.** Publishes ms an average of 3-4 months after acceptance. Byline given. Buys first rights. Submit seasonal/holiday material 6 months in advance. Reports in 3 weeks on queries; 1 month on mss. Free sample copy and writer's guidelines.

Nonfiction: General interest, how-to and new product. "No human interest and consumer-related stories." Buys 40 mss/year. Query. Length: 750-3,500 words. Pays $150-500 for assigned articles; pays $75-350 for unsolicited articles. Sometimes pays the expenses of writers on assignment.

Photos: State availability of photos with submission. Reviews contact sheets. Offers no additional payment for photos accepted with ms. Model releases and identification of subjects required. Buys one-time rights.

Columns/Departments: Ron Combs, editor. Tax Q&A (tax tips for dentists), 1,500 words; Capitolgram (late legislative news—dentistry), 750 words; and Econ Report (national economic outlook), 750 words. Buys 36 mss/year. Pays $50-300.

Tips: "How-to articles on specific subjects such as practice-building, newsletters and collections should be relevant to a busy, solo-practice dentist."

PROOFS, The Magazine of Dental Sales and Marketing, P.O. Box 3408, Tulsa OK 74101. (918)835-3161. FAX: (918)831-9497. Publisher: Dick Hale. Editor: Mary Elizabeth Good. 10% freelance written. Magazine published 10 times/year; combined issues July/August, November/December. Estab. 1926. Pays on publication. Byline given. Reports in 2 weeks. Free sample copy.

Nonfiction: Uses short articles, chiefly on selling to dentists. Must have understanding of dental trade industry and problems of marketing and selling to dentists and dental laboratories. Query. Pays about $125.

Tips: "The most frequent mistakes made by writers are having a lack of familiarity with industry problems and talking down to our audience."

RDH, The National Magazine for Dental Hygiene Professionals, Stevens Publishing Corp., 225 N. New Rd., Waco TX 76714. (817)776-9000. Editor: Laura Albrecht. 65% freelance written. Eager to work with new/unpublished writers. Monthly magazine, covering information relevant to dental hygiene professionals as business-career oriented individuals. "Dental hygienists are highly trained, licensed professionals; most are women. They are concerned with ways to develop rewarding careers, give optimum service to patients and to grow both professionally and personally." Circ. 63,210. Usually pays on publication; sometimes on acceptance. Publishes ms an average of 8 months after acceptance. Byline given. Buys first serial rights. Reports in 2 weeks on queries; 2 months on mss. Sample copies and writer's guidelines available.

Nonfiction: Essays, general interest, interview/profile, personal experience, photo feature and technical. "We are interested in any topic that offers broad reader appeal, especially in the area of personal growth (communication, managing time, balancing career and personal life). No undocumented clinical or technical articles; how-it-feels-to-be-a-patient articles; product-oriented articles (unless in generic terms); anything cutesy-unprofessional." Length: 1,500-3,000 words. Pays $100-350 for assigned articles; pays $50-200 for unsolicited articles. Sometimes pays expenses of writers on assignment.

Photos: Covers are shot on location across U.S.

Tips: "Freelancers should have a feel for the concerns of today's business-career woman—and address those interests and concerns with practical, meaningful and even motivational messages. We want to see good-quality manuscripts on both personal growth and lifestyle topics. For clinical and/or technical topics, we prefer the writers be members of the dental profession. New approaches to old problems and dilemmas will always get a close look from our editors. *RDH* is also interested in manuscripts for our feature section. Other than clinical information, dental hygienists are interested in all sorts of topics—finances, personal growth, educational opportunities, business management, staff/employer relations, communication and motivation, office rapport and career options. Other than clinical/technical articles, *RDH* maintains an informal tone. Writing style can easily be accommodated to our format."

Drugs, Health Care and Medical Products

THE APOTHECARY, Health Care Marketing Services, #200, 95 First St., P.O. Box AP, Los Altos CA 94023. (415)941-3955. FAX: (415)941-2303. Editor: Jerold Karabensh. Publication Director: Janet Goodman. 100% freelance written. Prefers to work with published/established writers who possess some knowledge of pharmacy and business/management topics. Quarterly magazine. "*The Apothecary* aims to provide practical information to community retail pharmacists." Estab. 1888. Circ. 60,000. **Pays on acceptance.** Publishes ms an average of 5 months after acceptance. Byline given. Buys all rights. Submit seasonal material 8 months in advance. Simultaneous queries OK. Reports in 2 months on queries; 5 months on mss. Sample copy for 9 × 12 SAE with 4 first class stamps. Writer's guidelines for #10 SASE.

Nonfiction: How-to (e.g., manage a pharmacy); opinion (of registered pharmacists); and health-related feature stories. "We publish only those general health articles with some practical application for the pharmacist as business person. No general articles not geared to our pharmacy readership; no fiction." Buys 4 mss/year. Query with published clips. Length: 750-3,000 words. Pays $100-300.

Columns/Departments: Commentary (views or issues relevant to the subject of pharmacy or to pharmacists). Send complete ms. Length: 750-1,000 words. "This section is unpaid; we will take submissions with byline."

Tips: "Submit material geared to the *pharmacist* as *business person*. Write according to our policy, i.e., business articles with emphasis on practical information for a community pharmacist. We suggest reading several back issues and following general feature story tone, depth, etc. Stay away from condescending use of language. Though our articles are written in simple style, they must reflect knowledge of the subject and reasonable respect for the readers' professionalism and intelligence."

CANADIAN PHARMACEUTICAL JOURNAL, 1785 Alta Vista Dr., Ottawa, Ontario K1G 3Y6 Canada. (613)523-7877. FAX: (613)523-0445. Editor: Jane Dewar. Clinical Editor: Mary MacDonald-LaPrade. News and Features Editor: Diana Gibbs. 40% freelance written. Works with a small number of new/ unpublished writers each year. Monthly journal for pharmacists. Estab. 1868. Circ. 12,500. Pays after editing. Publishes ms an average of 3 months after acceptance. Buys first serial rights. Reports in 2 months. Free sample copy and writer's guidelines.

Nonfiction: Relevant to Canadian pharmacy. Publishes exposés (pharmacy practice, education and legislation); how-to (pharmacy business operations); historical (pharmacy practice, Canadian legislation, education). Length: 200-400 words (for news notices); 800-1,500 words (for articles). Query. Payment is contingent on value. Sometimes pays expenses of writers on assignment.

Photos: Color and b&w (5×7) glossies purchased with mss. Captions and model release required.

Tips: "Query with complete description of proposed article, including topic, sources (in general), length, payment requested, suggested submission date, and whether photographs will be included. It is helpful if the writer has read a *recent* copy of the journal; we are glad to send one if required. References should be included where appropriate (this is vital where medical and scientific information is included). Send 3 copies of each ms. Author's degree and affiliations (if any) and writing background should be listed."

HEALTH SYSTEMS REVIEW, (formerly *FAHS Review*), Suite 308, 1405 N. Pierce St., Little Rock AR 72207. (501)661-9555. FAX: (501)663-4903. Editor: John Herrmann. 10% freelance written. Bimonthly trade journal on health care issues and health care politics (federal and state). "*Health Systems Review* publishes articles concerning the politics of health care, covers legislative activities and broad grass roots stories involving particular hospitals or organizations and their problems/solutions. Goes to health care managers, executives, to all members of the Congress, its staffs, the Administration and staff." Estab. 1967. Circ. 35,000. **Pays on acceptance.** Byline given. Offers $100 kill fee. Buys first North American serial rights and second serial (reprint) rights. Submit seasonal/holiday material 4-5 months in advance. Simultaneous submissions OK. Query for electronic submissions. Reports in 1 week on queries; 1 month on mss. Sample copy for 9×12 SAE with 5 first class stamps.

Nonfiction: Essays, interview/profile, opinion and personal experience. "No articles about health care or medical procedures. No new products pieces. No articles about health care and the stock market." Buys 2-4 mss/year. Query with published clips. Length: 1,500-3,500 words. Pays $200-750. "Articles by health care leaders, members of Congress and staff and legal columns generally not paid." Pays expenses of writers on assignment.

Photos: Send photo with submission. Reviews contact sheets, transparencies and prints. Offers no additional payment for photos accepted with ms. Captions and identification of subjects required. Buys one-time rights and all rights.

Columns/Departments: Jennifer L. Smith. Health Care Financing (business issues in health care), 1,500-3,500 words; Health Law Perspectives (written in-house); and Supply Side (health care suppliers news update), 1,500-3,500 words. Buys 2 mss/year. Query with published clips. Pays $100-200.

Tips: "Any specific information on Medicare/Medicaid problems; a good large multi-hospital group business story (failure or success); good contacts with state or federal senators and representatives and/or their staff members for close-ups, profiles. No writing in supply side that sells the supplier or its products but, rather, how it sees current issues from its perspective."

JEMS, A Journal of Emergency Medical Services, Jems Communications, Suite 200, 1947 Camino Vida Roble, Carlsbad CA 92008. (619)431-9797. FAX: (619)431-8176. Executive Editor: Keith Griffiths. Managing Editor: Diane Lofshult. 25% freelance written. Monthly magazine of emergency medical services—all phases. Our writings are directed to the personnel who service the emergency medicine world: paramedics, EMTs, emergency physicians and nurses, administrators, EMS consultants, etc. Estab. 1980. Circ. 35,000. Pays on publication. Publishes ms an average of 3 months after acceptance. Byline given. Buys first North American serial rights. Submit seasonal/holiday material 6 months in advance. Query for electronic submissions. Reports in 1 month on queries; 1 week on mss with acknowledgement letter. Free sample copy and writer's guidelines.

Nonfiction: Essays, general interest, how-to (prehospital care), humor, interview/profile, new product, opinion, photo feature, technical. Buys 18 mss/year. Query. Length: 900-3,600 words. Pays $150-350.

Photos: State availability of photos with submission. Offers no additional payment for photos accepted with ms. Buys one-time rights.

Columns/Departments: Diane Lofshult, managing editor. Teacher Talk (directed toward EMS instructors), 2,400 words; Pediatric Notebook (emergency care of the child), 2,400 words.

Tips: Feature articles are most open to freelancers. We have guidelines available upon request and of course, manuscripts must be geared toward our specific EMS audience.

PHARMACY TIMES, Romaine Pierson Publishers, 80 Shore Rd., Port Washington NY 11050. (516)883-6350. FAX: (516)883-6609. Publisher/Editor-in-Chief: Raymond A. Gosselin, R.Ph. Executive Editor: Joseph Cupolo. 15% freelance written. Monthly magazine on the pharmaceutical industry. Estab. 1897. Circ. 95,000. Pays on publication. Publishes ms an average of 4 months after acceptance. Byline given. Buys one-time rights. Submit seasonal/holiday material 6 months in advance. Query for electronic submissions. Reports in 3 weeks on queries; 6 weeks on mss. Free sample copy and writer's guidelines.

Nonfiction: Interview/profile, new product, opinion, personal experience, photo feature, technical and travel. Buys 12-15 mss/year. Send complete ms. Length: 800-1,500 words. Pays $250-400 for assigned articles; $100-250 for unsolicited articles. Pays in contributor copies or other premiums "per author request or for reprinted material."

Photos: State availability of photos with submission. Reviews negatives and 3×5 prints. Offers no additional payment for photos accepted with ms. Captions, model releases and identification of subjects required. Buys one-time rights.

Education and Counseling

Professional educators, teachers, coaches and counselors—as well as other people involved in training and education—read the journals classified here. Many journals for educators are nonprofit forums for professional advancement; writers contribute articles in return for a byline and contributor's copies. *Writer's Market* includes only educational journals that pay freelancers for articles. Education-related publications for students are included in the Consumer Career, College and Alumni and Teen and Young Adult sections.

ARTS & ACTIVITIES, Publishers' Development Corporation, Suite 200, 591 Camino de la Reina, San Diego CA 92108. (619)297-5352. FAX: (619)297-5353. Editor: Dr. Leven C. Leatherbury. Managing Editor: Maryellen Bridge. 95% freelance written. Eager to work with new/unpublished writers. Monthly (except July and August) art education magazine covering art education at levels from pre-school through college for educators and therapists engaged in arts and crafts education and training. Estab. 1932. Circ. 25,433. Pays on publication. Publishes ms an average of 6 months after acceptance. Byline given. Buys first North American rights. Submit seasonal/holiday material 4 months in advance. Reports in 2 months. Sample copy for 9×12 envelope and 8 first class stamps; writer's guidelines for #10 SASE.

Nonfiction: Historical/nostalgic (arts activities history); how-to (classroom art experiences, artists' techniques); interview/profile (of artists); opinion (on arts activities curriculum, ideas on how to do things better); personal experience in the art class room ("this ties in with the how-to, we like it to be *personal*, no recipe style"); and articles on exceptional art programs. Buys 50-80 mss/year. Length: 200-2,000 words. Pays $35-150.

Tips: "Frequently in unsolicited manuscripts, writers obviously have not studied the magazine to see what style of articles we publish. Send for a sample copy to familiarize yourself with our style and needs. The best way to find out if his/her writing style suits our needs is for the author to submit a manuscript on speculation."

BEAUTY EDUCATION, (formerly *National Beauty Education Journal*), Milady Publishing Corp., 220 White Plains Rd., Tarrytown NY 10591. (914)332-4800. Editor: Sheila Furjanic. Associate Editor: Catherine Frangie. 75% freelance written. Works with a small number of new/unpublished writers each year. A monthly magazine serving beauty educators, trainers and professionals. Each issue presents content-rich articles that provide information, skills and techniques on a variety of subjects including hairstyling, makeup, nail care, hair extensions, aromatherapy, salon training, retailing, skincare, hair coloring, perming, massage, salon management, communication, beauty careers and health and sanitation. Estab. 1949. Circ. 8,900 schools. Pays on publication. Publishes ms an average of 2 months after acceptance. Byline given. Buys first rights. Submit seasonal/holiday material 3 months in advance. Simultaneous submissions OK. Free sample copy and editorial calendar with writer's guidelines.

Nonfiction: Articles should provide detailed, comprehensive information and techniques for the professional or soon-to-be professional. Articles should be easy to read, yet informative and challenging. They should be written to correspond with the monthly theme as specified by the editorial calendar. Buys 24 mss/year. Query with published clips, or send complete ms. Length: 1,000-2,500 words. Pays $150 if published.

Photos: Send photos with submissions. Reviews 5×7 b&w prints. Offers no additional payment for photos accepted with ms. Identification of subjects required. Buys first rights; make sure reprint permission is granted.

Columns Departments: Buys 6 mss/year; willing to start new departments. Length: 500-1,000 words. Pays $150.

Tips: "Take time to research the various aspects of the subject you're writing on. Don't assume that one school owner or instructor can give you enough information for an article. Dig in and have fun discovering the information that will inform your readers."

‡COMPUTERS IN EDUCATION, Moorshead Publications, 1300 Don Mills Rd., North York, Toronto, Ontario M3B 3M8 Canada. (416)445-5600. FAX: (416)445-8149. Editor: John Swinimer. 90% freelance written. Eager to work with new/unpublished writers. Magazine published 10 times/year. Articles of interest to teachers, computer consultants and administrators working at the kindergarten to post secondary level. Estab. 1977. Circ. 16,000. Pays on publication. Publishes ms an average of 2 months after acceptance. Byline given. Buys first serial rights, first North American serial rights, one time rights, second serial (reprint) rights, and all rights. Phone queries OK. Query for electronic submissions. Sample copy and writer's guidelines with SASE or IRC.

Nonfiction: Use of computers in education and techniques of teaching using computers; lesson plans, novel applications, anything that is practical for the teacher. Does not want overviews, "Gee Whizzes," and reinventions of the wheel. Length 750-1000 words. Pays 10¢/word.

Photos: Photos and/or artwork all but mandatory. Captions required.

Tips: "We are looking for practical articles by working teachers. Nothing too general, no overviews, or the same thing that has been said for years."

COTTONWOOD MONTHLY, Cottonwood Press, Suite 398, 305 W. Magnolia, Ft. Collins CO 80521. (303)493-1286. Editor: Cheryl Thurston. 25% freelance written. Monthly, Sept.-May newsletter for language arts teachers, grades 5 and up. "The *Cottonwood Monthly* publishes ideas, activities, lessons, games and assignments for language arts teachers to use in the classroom. Our emphasis is upon practical materials that a teacher can photocopy and use tomorrow. We also like to use material with a humorous slant." Estab. 1986. Circ. 300. Pays on publication. Publishes ms an average of 3 months after acceptance. Byline sometimes given. Buys all rights. Submit seasonal/holiday material 4 months in advance. Simultaneous submissions OK. Sample copy $1 with SASE.

Nonfiction: How-to (practical ideas on anything that can make a teacher's life easier), humor, (games lessons, activities, assignments for language arts classes grades 5 and up). "Nothing theoretical. We want only practical material teachers can actually *use* in their classrooms." Buys 20 mss/year. Send complete ms. Length: 250-1,000 words. Pays $20-25 for unsolicited articles.

Columns/Departments: Teacher Tips (practical tips on anything of concern to language arts teachers: discipline, stress management, school programs, motivating students, grading papers, communicating with parents, etc.). Buys 9 mss/year. Send complete ms. Length: 75-200 words. Pays $10.

Tips: "Show us that you know kids, real life kids. If your material will appeal to modern-day students, we are interested and flexible. We don't like to see dry, textbook-like material. We are interested in material that takes a lighter, humorous, even offbeat approach to language arts."

INSTRUCTOR MAGAZINE, Scholastic, Inc., 730 Broadway, New York NY 10003. Editor-in-Chief: John Lent. Executive Editor: Debra Martorelli. Eager to work with new/unpublished writers, "especially teachers." Monthly magazine. Emphasizes elementary education. Circ. 300,000. **Pays on acceptance.** Publishes ms an average of 1 year after acceptance. Byline given. Buys all rights. Submit seasonal/holiday material 6 months in advance. Query for electronic submissions. Reports in 1 month on queries; 2 months on mss. Send a SASE for a free writer's guidelines; mention *Writer's Market* in request.

Nonfiction: How-to articles on elementary classroom practice—practical suggestions and project reports. Occasionally publishes first-person accounts of classroom experiences. Buys 100 mss/year. Query. Length: 400-2,000 words. Pays $15-75 for short items; $125-400 for articles and features. Send all queries to Attention: manuscripts editor.

Photos: Send photos with submission. Reviews 4×5 transparencies and prints. Offers no additional payment for photos accepted with ms. Model releases and identification of subjects required. Buys all rights.

Columns/Departments: Teachers Express (quick teacher tips and ideas); Planner (seasonal activities, bulletin boards and crafts); Whole K Catalog (teaching ideas for primary grades); Partnerships (teacher-initiated school/business partnerships). Buys 100 mss/year. Query with SASE. Length: 50-1,000 words. Pays $30-100.

Fiction: Occasionally buys plays and read-aloud stories for children. Length: 500-2,500 words. Pays $75-200.

Tips: "How-to articles should be kept practical, with concrete examples whenever possible. Writers should keep in mind that our audience is elementary teachers."

JOURNAL OF CAREER PLANNING & EMPLOYMENT, College Placement Council, Inc., 62 Highland Ave., Bethlehem PA 18017. (215)868-1421. FAX: (215)868-0208. Associate Editor: Bill Beebe. 25% freelance written. Published Nov., Jan., March and May. A magazine for career development professionals who counsel and/or hire college students, graduating students, employees and job-changers. Estab. 1940. Circ. 4,200. **Pays on acceptance.** Publishes ms an average of 4 months after acceptance. Byline given. Buys first rights. Reports in 1 month on queries; 2 months on mss. Free writer's guidelines for #10 SASE.

Nonfiction: Book excerpts, how-to, interview/profile, opinion, photo feature, new techniques/innovative practices and current issues in the field. **No articles that speak directly to job candidates.** Buys 7-10 mss/year. Query with published clips, or send complete ms. Length: 3,000-4,000 words. Pays $200-400.

Tips: "A freelancer can best break into our publication by sending query with clips of published work, by writing on topics that aim directly at the journal's audience—professionals in the college career planning, placement and recruitment field—and by using an easy-to-read, narrative style rather than a formal, thesis style. The area of our publication most open to freelancers is nonfiction feature articles only. Topics should directly relate to the career planning and employment of the college educated and should go beyond the basics of career planning, job hunting and hiring issues, since *Journal* readers are well-versed in those basics."

‡LEARNING 92, 1111 Bethlehem Pike, Springhouse PA 19477. Editor: Charlene F. Gaynor. 45% freelance written. Published monthly during school year. Emphasizes elementary and junior high school education topics. Circ. 275,000. **Pays on acceptance.** Buys all rights. Submit seasonal/holiday material 9 months in advance. Reports in 3 months. Sample copy $3; free writer's guidelines.

Nonfiction: "We publish manuscripts that describe innovative, practical teaching strategies." How-to (classroom management, specific lessons or units or activities for children—all at the elementary and junior high level, and hints for teaching in all curriculum areas): personal experience (from teachers in elementary and junior high schools); and profile (with teachers who are in unusual or innovative teaching situations). Strong interest in articles that deal with discipline, teaching strategy, motivation and working with parents. Buys 250 mss/year. Query. Length: 1,000-3,500 words. Pays $50-350.

Photos: State availability of photos with query. Model release required. "We are also interested in series of photos that show step-by-step projects or tell a story that will be of interest."

Tips: "We're looking for practical, teacher-tested ideas and strategies as well as first-hand personal accounts of dramatic successes—or failures—with a lesson to be drawn. We're also interested in examples of especially creative classrooms and teachers. Emphasis on professionalism will increase: top teachers telling what they do best and others can also."

LOLLIPOPS, The Magazine for Early Childhood Educators, Good Apple, Inc., 1204 Buchanan, Box 299, Carthage IL 62321. (212)357-3981. Editor: Jerry Aten. 20% freelance written. A magazine published 5 times a year providing easy-to-use, hands-on practical teaching ideas and suggestions for early childhood education. Circ. 20,000. Pays on publication. Months until publication vary. Buys all rights. Submit seasonal/holiday material 6 months in advance. Sample copy for 9 × 12 SAE with 3 first class stamps; writer's guidelines for #10 SAE with 2 first class stamps.

Nonfiction: How-to (on creating usable teaching materials). Buys varying number of mss/year. Query with or without published clips, or send complete ms. Length: 200-1,000 words. Pays $25-100 for assigned articles; pays $10-30 for unsolicited articles. Writer has choice of cash or Good Apple products worth twice the contract value.

Photos: State availability of photos with submission. Reviews contact sheets and transparencies. Offers $10 minimum/photo. Model releases and identification of subjects required. Buys all rights.

Columns/Departments: Accepts material dealing with the solving of problems encountered by early childhood education. Buys varying number of mss/year. Query with published clips. Length: varies. Pays $25-100.

Fiction: Adventure and fantasy (for young children). Query with published clips.

Poetry: Light verse. Buys varying number of poems/year.

Tips: "I'm always looking for something that's new and different—something that works for teachers of young children."

MEDIA & METHODS, American Society of Educators, 1429 Walnut St., Philadelphia PA 19102. (215)563-3501. Editor/Director: Michele Sokoloff. Bimonthly trade journal published during the school year about educational products, media technologies and programs for schools and universities. Readership: Librarians and media specialists. Estab. 1963. Circ. 40,000. Pays on publication. Publishes ms an average of 3 months after acceptance. Byline given. Buys first North American serial rights. Free sample copy and writer's guidelines.

Nonfiction: How-to, practical, new product, personal experience, technical. Must send query letter, outline or call editor. Do not send ms. Length: 600-1,200 words. Pays $75-200.

Photos: State availability of photos with submission. Reviews 3×5 prints. Offers no additional payment for photos accepted with ms. Captions and identification of subjects required. Buys one-time rights.

MEDIA PROFILES: The Health Sciences Edition, Olympic Media Information, P.O. Box 190, West Park NY 12493-0190. (914)384-6563. Publisher: Walt Carroll. 100% freelance written. For hospital education departments, nursing schools, schools of allied health, paramedical training units, colleges, community colleges, local health organizations. Serial, in magazine format, published quarterly. Circ. 1,000. Pays on publication. Publishes ms an average of 6 months after acceptance. Buys all rights. Buys 160 mss/year. Electronic submissions OK. "Sample copies and writer's guidelines sent on receipt of resume, background, and mention of audiovisual hardware you have access to. Enclose $5 for writer's guidelines and sample issue. (Refunded with first payment upon publication)." Reports in 1 month. Query.

Nonfiction: "Reviews of all kinds of audiovisual media. We are the only review publication devoted exclusively to evaluation of audiovisual aids for medical and health training. We have a highly specialized, definite format that must be followed in all cases. Samples should be seen by all means. Our writers should first have a background in health sciences; second, have some experience with audiovisuals; and third, follow our format precisely. Writers with advanced degrees and teaching affiliations with colleges and hospital education departments given preference. We are interested in reviews of media materials for nursing education, in-service education, continuing education, personnel training, patient education, patient care and medical problems. We will assign audiovisual aids to qualified writers and send them these to review for us. Unsolicited mss not welcome." Pays $15/review.

MOMENTUM, National Catholic Educational Association, 1077 30th St. NW, Washington DC 20007. Editor: Patricia Feistritzer. 10% freelance written. Quarterly magazine. For Catholic administrators and teachers, some parents and students, in all levels of education (preschool, elementary, secondary, higher). Estab. 1970. Circ. 25,000. Pays on publication. Buys first serial rights. Reports in 3 months. Free sample copy. Send SASE.

Nonfiction: Articles concerned with educational philosophy, psychology, methodology, innovative programs, teacher training, research, financial and public relations programs and management systems—all applicable to nonpublic schools. Book reviews on educational/religious topics. Avoid general topics or topics applicable *only* to public education. "We look for a straightforward, journalistic style with emphasis on practical examples, as well as scholarly writing and statistics. All references must be footnoted, fully documented. Emphasis is on professionalism." Buys 28-36 mss/year. Length: 1,500-2,000 words. Pays 2¢/word.

SCHOOL ARTS MAGAZINE, 50 Portland St., Worcester MA 01608. FAX: (508)753-3834. Editor: Kent Anderson. 85% freelance written. Monthly, except June, July and August. Serves arts and craft education profession, kindergarten-12, higher education and museum education programs. Written by and for art teachers. Estab. 1901. Pays on publication. Publishes ms an average of 3 months "if timely; if less pressing, can be 1 year or more" after acceptance. Buys first serial rights and second serial (reprint) rights. Reports in 3 months. Free sample copy and writer's guidelines.

Nonfiction: Articles, with photos, on art and craft activities in schools. Should include description and photos of activity in progress as well as examples of finished art work. Query or send complete ms. Length: 600-1,400 words. Pays $20-100.

Tips: "We prefer articles on actual art projects or techniques done by students in actual classroom situations. Philosophical and theoretical aspects of art and art education are usually handled by our contributing editors. Our articles are reviewed and accepted on merit and each is tailored to meet our needs. Keep in mind that art teachers want practical tips, above all. Our readers are visually, not verbally, oriented. Write your article with the accompanying photographs in hand." The most frequent mistakes made by writers are "bad visual material (photographs, drawings) submitted with articles, or a lack of complete descriptions of art processes; and no rationale behind programs or activities. It takes a close reading of *School Arts* to understand its function and the needs of its readers. Some writers lack the necessary familiarity with art education."

SCHOOL SHOP/TECH DIRECTIONS, Prakken Publications, Inc., P.O. Box 8623, Ann Arbor MI 48107. FAX: (313)769-8383. Editor: Susanne Peckham. 100% freelance written. Eager to work with new/unpublished writers. A monthly (except June and July) magazine covering issues, trends and projects of interest to industrial, vocational, technical and technology educators at the secondary and postsecondary school levels. Estab. 1941. Circ. 45,000. Buys all rights. Pays on publication. Publishes ms an average of 8-12 months after acceptance. Byline given. Prefers authors who have direct connection with the field of industrial and/or technical education. Simultaneous queries, and simultaneous and previously published submissions OK. Reports in 2 months. Free sample copy and writer's guidelines.
Nonfiction: Uses articles pertinent to the various teaching areas in industrial and technology education (woodwork, electronics, drafting, machine shop, graphic arts, computer training, etc.). "The outlook should be on innovation in educational programs, processes or projects that directly apply to the industrial/technical education area." Buys general interest, how-to, opinion, personal experience, technical and think pieces, interviews, humor, and coverage of new products. Buys 135 unsolicited mss/year. Length: 200-2,000 words. Pays $25-150.
Photos: Send photos with accompanying query or ms. Reviews b&w and color prints. Payment for photos included in payment for ms.
Columns/Departments: Shop Kinks (brief items which describe short-cuts or special procedures relevant to the industrial arts classroom). Buys 30 mss/year. Send complete ms. Length: 20-100 words. Pays $15 minimum.
Tips: "We are most interested in articles written by industrial, vocational and technical educators about their class projects and their ideas about the field. We need more and more technology-related articles."

TEACHING TODAY, 6112-102 Ave., Edmonton, Alberta T6A 0N4 Canada. (403)465-2990. Editor: Betty Coderre. Managing Editor: Max Coderre. 90% freelance written. Educational magazine published 5 times per year. Estab. 1983. Circ. 12,000. Pays on publication. Publishes ms an average of 6-24 months after acceptance. Mss must be accompanied by SASE with IRC's for return. Byline given. Buys first rights, one-time rights or all rights. Simultaneous submissions OK. Query for electronic submissions. Sample copy $3 (check or money order addressed to *Teaching Today*.)
Nonfiction: How-to (related to teaching), humor (related to education), inspirational, interview/profile (publicly visible people's views on education), personal experience (if related to teaching), communication skills and professional development (teacher). Buys 40-50 mss/year. Query with published clips. Length: 150-1,500 words. Pays $20-225 for assigned articles; $15-150 for unsolicited articles. Sometimes pays expenses of writers on assignment.
Photos: Send photos with submission. Reviews 4×5 prints. Offers $15-100 per photo. Model releases and identification of subjects required. Buys one-time rights.
Fillers: Anecdotes and gags to be illustrated by cartoonist. Buys 20/year. Length: 20-100 words. Pays $5-25.
Tips: "A freelancer can best break into our magazine with articles, cartoons, fillers related to education. Articles primarily that will *help* educators personally or professionally."

TECHNOLOGY & LEARNING, (formerly *Classroom Computer Learning*), Suite A4, 2169 Francisco Blvd. E., San Rafael CA 94901. FAX: (415)457-4378. Editor-in-Chief: Holly Brady. 50% freelance written. Works with a small number of new/unpublished writers each year. Monthly magazine published during school year emphasizing elementary through high school educational technology topics. Estab. 1980. Circ. 83,000. **Pays on acceptance.** Publishes ms an average of 8 months after acceptance. Buys all rights or first serial rights. Submit seasonal/holiday material 6 months in advance. Reports in 2 months. Writer's guidelines for #10 SASE; sample copy for 8×10 SAE and 6 first class stamps.
Nonfiction: "We publish manuscripts that describe innovative ways of using technology in the classroom as well as articles that discuss controversial issues in computer education." Interviews, brief technology-related activity ideas and longer featurettes describing fully developed and tested classroom ideas. Buys 50 mss/year. Query. Length: 500 words or less for classroom activities; 1,500-2,500 words for major articles. Pays $25 for activities; payment varies from $200 or more for articles. Educational Software Reviews: Assigned through editorial offices. "If interested, send a letter telling us of your areas of interest and expertise as well as the microcomputer(s) and other equipment you have available to you." Pays $75 per review. Pays expenses of writers on assignment.
Photos: State availability of photos with query.
Tips: "The talent that goes into writing our shorter hands-on pieces is different from that required for features (e.g., interviews, issues pieces, etc.) Write whatever taps your talent best. A frequent mistake is taking too 'novice' or too 'expert' an approach. You need to know our audience well and

Close-up

Holly Brady
Editor
Technology & Learning

In a step toward keeping in tune with the 90s, *Classroom Computer Learning* is now *Technology & Learning*.

According to Editor Holly Brady, the magazine started in 1980 as a grassroots newsletter edited for and by teachers in order to keep in step with the then-burgeoning trend of computers in the classroom. Since then, the magazine's horizons have broadened and *Classroom Computer Learning* is no longer a definitive title. "It started out talking just about computers," says Brady. "Now we're talking about all different types of technologies (in addition to computers), such as educational television, video cameras, telecommunications and modems." Also, "we wanted to drop the 'classroom' part of the title because we are now dealing with all different types of educators." Besides classroom teachers, the magazine also targets administrators, librarians and coordinators at the school and district levels.

Brady, once a teacher herself, admits she has no formal training in computers. But the man who hired her for the job didn't want a computer guru. "He wanted someone with a strong educational background, but who was relatively naive about computers in order not to be 'wowed' by the technology alone," she says.

Brady's main priority for the magazine is to concentrate on the educational value of the content. "The chief thing we try to do is take the technological jargon and make it understandable to our readership. It's very similar to what the *Wall Street Journal* does every day when it talks about the economy—making macroeconomics clear to the average reader."

Technology & Learning, now owned by Peter Li Publications, usually generates story ideas inhouse or through long-term freelancers who know the magazine well, says Brady. However, she won't rule out potential contributors contacting her. "The most fruitful way (for freelancers to break in to this market) is for them to jot down four or five short ideas and send them to me, along with a writing sample. They need to let us know what they are interested in writing about."

Brady says she considers three elements when judging freelancers: computer know-how, writing ability and educational expertise. She notes the latter is weighed the most, and it is imperative the writer understand what happens in schools and classrooms and how technology is being used. She says she receives many query letters and unsolicited articles with a "gee whiz, isn't technology great" slant. "Our readers are well beyond reading articles saying 'aren't computers neat in the classroom.' They need much more detail. People who want to write for us often underestimate the sophistication of our readers."

Finally, Brady says freelancers who do make it through *Technology & Learning*'s door should be aware of the magazine's specific needs. "Many freelancers have a chip on their shoulder because they're worried we might not treat them well. Be understanding and flexible. Understand we have parameters in which we have to work too. If we need a re-write, do it with some grace."

—Lisa Carpenter

to understand how much they know about computers. Also, too many manuscripts lack a definite point of view or focus or opinion. We like pieces with clear, strong, well thought out opinions."

TODAY'S CATHOLIC TEACHER, 2451 E. River Rd., Dayton OH 45439-1597. (513)294-5785. FAX: (513)294-7840. Editor: Stephen Brittan. 40% freelance written. Works with a small number of new/unpublished writers each year. For administrators, teachers and parents concerned with Catholic schools, both parochial and CCD. Estab. 1967. Circ. 60,000. Pays after publication. Publishes ms an average of 3 months after acceptance. Byline given. Buys all rights. Phone queries OK. Submit seasonal/holiday material 3 months in advance. Sample copy $3; writer's guidelines for #10 SASE; mention *Writer's Market* in request.
Nonfiction: How-to (based on experience, particularly in Catholic situations, philosophy with practical applications); interview (of practicing educators, educational leaders); personal experience (classroom happenings); and a few profiles (of educational leader). Buys 40-50 mss/year. Submit complete ms. Length: 800-2,000 words. Pays $15-175.
Photos: State availability of photos with ms. Offers no additional payment for 8×10 b&w glossy prints. Buys one-time rights. Captions preferred; model release required.
Tips: "We prefer articles that are of interest or practical help to educators—teaching ideas, curriculum-related material, administration suggestions, resource guides, articles teachers can use in classroom to teach current topics, etc. We use many one-page features."

Electronics and Communication

These publications are edited for broadcast and telecommunications technicians and engineers, electrical engineers and electrical contractors. Included are journals for electronic equipment designers and operators who maintain electronic and telecommunication systems. Publications for appliance dealers can be found in Home Furnishings and Household Goods.

AMERICAN ELECTRONICS ASSOCIATION UPDATE, The business and management publication for electronics executives, American Electronics Association, P.O. Box 54990, Santa Clara CA 95056-9060. (408)987-4200. FAX: (408)970-8565. Editor: April Neilson. 40-50% freelance written. Monthly tabloid covering electronics industry trends, new technologies, finance, marketing, manufacturing, public affairs, task forces and business networking. Pays 10-15 working days after acceptance. U.S. circulation 31,000; mostly executives and managers in large and small electronics companies nationwide.
Nonfiction: Industry event coverage, public policy reporting, international trade, technology education, (company profiles); pays 20-35¢/word for assigned articles. Query with published clips. Buys 30 mss/year. Length: 500-1,500 words. Query for electronic submissions.
Columns/Departments: Public Affairs, Industry Trends, Education and Science Policy, Campus Research Report, Small Business, Management, Regional Councils.
Tips: "We require specialty in writing about the electronics industry and the ability to meet 1 to 1½ week deadlines. Unsolicited work not accepted."

BROADCAST TECHNOLOGY, P.O. Box 420, Bolton, Ontario L7E 5T3 Canada. (416)857-6076. FAX: (416)857-6045. Editor-in-Chief: Doug Loney. 50% freelance written. Monthly (except August, December) magazine. Emphasizes broadcast engineering. Estab. 1975. Circ. 9,000. Pays on publication. Byline given. Buys all rights. Phone queries OK.
Nonfiction: Technical articles on developments in broadcast engineering, especially pertaining to Canada. Query. Length: 500-1,500 words. Pays $100-300.
Photos: Purchased with accompanying ms. Black and white or color. Captions required.
Tips: "Most of our outside writing is by regular contributors, usually employed full-time in broadcast engineering. The specialized nature of our magazine requires a specialized knowledge on the part of a writer, as a rule."

BUSINESS RADIO, National Association of Business and Educational Radio, 1501 Duke St., Alexandria VA 22314. (703)739-0300. Editor: Amy Goetz. Assistant Editor: Chris Bryum. 25% freelance written. Magazine is published 10 times/year on two-way radio communications. "Magazine is for land mobile equipment users, dealers, service shop operators, manufacturers, communications technicians, SMR owners and operators. To acquaint members with the diversity of uses to which land mobile radio can be applied. To identify and discuss new and developing areas of RF technology and their application." Circ. 6,000. **Pays on acceptance.** Publishes ms an average of 3 months after acceptance. Byline given. Buys first rights. Previously published submissions OK. Query for electronic submissions.

Reports in 1 month. Sample copy for 9 × 12 SAE with 5 first class stamps. Writer's guidelines for 9 × 12 SASE.

Nonfiction: General interest, interview/profile, new product, technical, and general — small business or management articles all related to two-way (land mobile) communications. Buys 5 mss/year. Query with or without published clips, or send complete ms. Length: 2,500-4,000 words. Pays $100-300 for unsolicited articles. Sometimes pays expenses of writers on assignment.

Photos: Send photos with submission. Reviews contact sheets, negatives, transparencies and prints. Offers no additional payment for b&w photos accepted with ms. Offers $200-250 per photo if color used for cover. Captions, model releases and identification of subjects required. Buys one-time rights.

Columns/Departments: Management Notebook (small business, general management), 2,000-3,000 words. Buys 8 mss/year. Query or send complete ms. Pays $50-150.

Tips: "Many people use two-way radios. Any of them could be the subject of a potential article."

CABLE COMMUNICATIONS MAGAZINE, Canada's Authoritative International Cable Television Publication, Ter-Sat Media Publications Ltd., 4 Smetana Dr., Kitchener, Ontario N2B 3B8 Canada. (519)744-4111. FAX: (519)744-1261. Editor: Udo Salewsky. 33% freelance written. Prefers to work with published/established writers. Monthly magazine covering the cable television industry. Estab. 1934. Circ. 8,119. **Pays on acceptance.** Publishes ms an average of 2 months after acceptance. Byline given. Buys all rights. Submit seasonal/holiday material 1 month in advance. Query for electronic submissions. Reports in 2 weeks on queries; 1 month on mss. Free writer's guidelines; sample copy for 9 × 12 SAE and $3.50 in IRCs.

Nonfiction: Expose, how-to, interview/profile, opinion, technical articles, and informed views and comments on topical, industry related issues. Also, problem solving-related articles, new marketing and operating efficiency ideas. No fiction. Buys 50 mss/year. Query with published clips or send complete ms. Length: 1,000-4,000 words. Pays $250-1,000. Pays expenses of writers on assignment.

Columns/Departments: Buys 48 items/year. Query with published clips or send complete ms. Length: 1,000-1,500 words. Pays $250-375.

Tips: "Forward manuscript and personal resume. We don't need freelance writers for short articles and fillers. Break in with articles related to industry issues, events and new developments; analysis of current issues and events. Be able to interpret the meaning of new developments relative to the cable television industry and their potential impact on the industry from a growth opportunity as well as a competitive point of view. Material should be well supported by facts and data. Insufficient research and understanding of underlying issues are frequent mistakes."

ELECTRONIC SERVICING & TECHNOLOGY, CQ Communications, 76 N. Broadway, Hicksville NY 11801. (516)681-2922. FAX: (516)681-2926. Editorial Office: P.O. Box 12487, Overland Park KS 66212. Phone/FAX (913)492-9310. Editor: Conrad Persson. Associate Editor: Jeffrey Uschok. 90% freelance written. Eager to work with new/unpublished writers. Monthly magazine for professional servicers and electronic enthusiasts who are interested in buying, building, installing and repairing consumer electronic equipment (audio, video, microcomputers, electronic games, etc.) Estab. 1950. Circ. 38,000. **Pays on acceptance.** Publishes ms an average of 6 months after acceptance. Byline given. Buys all rights. Simultaneous queries OK. Reoprts in 2 weeks on queries; 1 month on mss. Free samply copy and writer's guidelines.

Nonfiction: How-to (service, build, install and repair home entertainment; electronic testing and servicing equipment). "Explain the techniques used carefully so that even hobbyists can understand a how-to article. Buys 36 mss/year. Send complete ms. Length: 1,500 words minimum. Pays $100-300.

Photos: Send photos with ms. Reviews color and b&w transparencies and b&w prints. Captions and identification of subjects required. Buys all rights. Payment included in total ms package.

Columns/Departments: Jeff Uschok, associate editor. Troubleshooting Tips: Buys 12 mss/year. Send complete ms. Length: open. Pays $25.

Tips: "In order to write for *ES&T* it is almost essential that a writer have an electronics background: technician, engineer or serious hobbyist. Our readers want nuts-and-bolts information on electronics."

INFORMATION TODAY, Learned Information Inc., 143 Old Marlton Pike, Medford NJ 08055. (609)654-6266. FAX: (609)654-4309. Publisher: Thomas H. Hogan. Editor: Patricia Lane. 30% freelance written. A tabloid for the users and producers of electronic information services, published 11 times per year. Estab. 1979. Circ. 10,000. Pays on publication. Publishes ms an average of 1 month after acceptance. Byline given. Buys first North American serial rights. Submit seasonal/holiday material 2 months in advance. Reports in 2 weeks. Free sample copy and writer's guidelines.

Nonfiction: Book reviews; interview/profile and new product; technical (dealing with computerized information services); and articles on library technology, artificial intelligence, online databases and services." We also cover software and optical publishing (CD-ROM). More focus on coverage of integrated online library systems." Buys approximately 25 mss/year. Query with published clips or send complete ms on speculation. Length: 500-1,500 words. Pays $90-220.

Photos: State availability of photos with submission.
Tips: "We look for clearly-written, informative articles dealing with the electronic delivery of information. Writing style should not be jargon-laden or heavily technical."

MICROWAVES & RF, 611 Route #46 W., Hasbrouck Heights NJ 07604. (201)393-6293. FAX: (201)393-6297. Chief Editor: Jack Browne. 20% freelance written. Monthly magazine emphasizing radio frequency design. "Qualified recipients are those individuals actively engaged in microwave and RF research, design, development, production and application engineering, engineering management, administration or purchasing departments in organizations and facilities where application and use of devices, systems and techniques involve frequencies from HF through visible light." Estab. 1964. Circ. 65,000. Pays on publication. Publishes ms an average of 6 months after acceptance. Buys all rights. Phone queries OK. Query for electronic submissions. Reports in 1 month. Free sample copy and writer's guidelines; mention *Writer's Market* in request.
Nonfiction: "We are interested in material on research and development in microwave and RF technology and economic news that affects the industry." How-to (circuit design), new product, opinion, and technical. Buys 100 mss/year. Query. Pays $100.

OUTSIDE PLANT, P.O. Box 183, Cary IL 60013. (312)639-2200. FAX: (312)639-9542. Editor: John H. Saxtan. 50% freelance written. Prefers to work with published/established writers. Trade publication focusing exclusively on the outside plant segment of the telephone industry. Readers are end users and/or specifiers at Bell and independent operating companies, as well as long distance firms whose chief responsibilities are construction, maintenance, OSP planning and engineering. Readership also includes telephone contracting firms. Publishes an average of 12 issues/year. Estab. 1982. Circ. 18,000. Buys first rights. Pays on publication. Publishes ms an average of 3 months after acceptance. Reports in 1 month. Free sample copy and guidelines for #10 SASE.
Nonfiction: Must deal specifically with outside plant construction, maintenance, planning and fleet vehicle subjects for the telephone industry. "Case history application articles profiling specific telephone projects are best. Also accepts trend features, tutorials, industry research and seminar presentations. Preferably, features should be by-lined by someone at the telephone company profiled." Pays $35-50/published page, including photographs; pays $35 for cover photos.
Departments: OSP Tips & Advice (short nuts-and-bolts items on new or unusual work methods); and OSP Tommorrow (significant trends in outside plant), 300-600 word items. Pays $5-50. Other departments include new products, literature, vehicles and fiber optics.
Tips: Submissions should include author bio demonstrating expertise in the subject area.

‡PRO SOUND NEWS, International News Magazine for the Professional Sound Production Industry, 2 Park Ave., New York NY 10016. (212)213-3444. Editor: Debra A. Pagan. 20% freelance written. Works with a small number of new/unpublished writers each year. Monthly tabloid covering the music recording, concert sound reinforcement, TV and film sound industry. Circ. 18,000. Pays on publication. Publishes ms an average of 1 month after acceptance. Byline given. Buys first serial rights. Simultaneous queries and previously published submissions OK. Query for electronic submissions. Reports in 2 weeks.
Nonfiction: Query with published clips. Pays $150-300 for assigned articles (approximately 1,000 words). Sometimes pays the expenses of writers on assignment.

‡RADIO WORLD INTERNATIONAL, Industrial Marketing Advisory Services, Suite 310, 5827 Columbia Pike, Falls Church VA 22041. (703)998-7600. FAX: (703)998-2966. Editor: Alan Carter. Assistant Editor: Debra Green. 50% freelance written. Monthly trade newspaper for radio broadcasting. "Covers radio station technology, regulatory news and business developments outside the U.S. Articles should be geared toward engineers, producers and managers." Estab. 1990. Circ. 18,000. Pays on publication. Byline given. Offers 50% kill fee. Buys serial rights. Query for electronic submissions. Reports in 3 weeks. Free sample copy and writer's guidelines.
Nonfiction: New product, technical, regulatory news. No programming or non-technical management pieces. Buys 100 mss/year. Query with published clips. Length: 750-1,000 words. Pays 20¢/word. Sometimes pays expenses of writers on assignment.
Photos: Send photos with submission. Captions and identification of subjects required. Buys all rights.
Columns/Departments: User reports (field reports from engineers on specific equipment), 750-1,000 words. Buys 50/year. Query. Pays 20¢/word.
Fillers: Newsbreaks. Buys 50/year. Length: 100-500 words.
Tips: "Our news and feature sections are the best bets for freelancers. Focus on radio station operations and the state of the industry worldwide."

RADIO WORLD NEWSPAPER, Industrial Marketing Advisory Services, Suite 310, 5827 Columbia Pike, Falls Church VA 22041. (703)998-7600. FAX: (703)998-2966. Editor: Alex Zavistovich. News Editor: John Gatski. 50% freelance written. Bimonthly newspaper on radio station technology and regulatory news. "Articles should be geared toward radio station engineers, producers, technical people and managers wishing to learn more about technical subjects. The approach should be more how-to than theoretical, although emerging technology may be approached in a more abstract way." Estab. 1976. Pays on publication. Publishes ms an average of 1-2 months after acceptance. Byline given. Buys first North American serial rights plus right to publish in monthly international and annual directory supplements. Submit seasonal/holiday material 2 months in advance. Query for electronic submissions. Reports in 2 months.

Nonfiction: Exposé, historical/nostalgic, how-to (radio equipment maintenance and repair), humor, interview/profile, new product, opinion, personal experience, photo feature and technical. "No general financial, or vogue management concept pieces." Buys 24-40 mss/year. Query. Length: 750-1,250 words. Pays $75-200. Pays in contributor copies or other premiums "if they request it, and for one special feature called Workbench." Sometimes pays expenses of writers on assignment.

Photos: Send photos with submission. Reviews 3×5 or larger prints. Offers no additional payment for photos accepted with ms. Identification of subjects required. Buys one-time rights.

Columns/Departments: Charles Taylor, Buyers Guide editor. Buyers Guide User Reports (field reports from engineers on specific pieces of radio station equipment). Buys 100 mss/year. Query. Length: 750-1,250 words. Pays $25-125.

Fillers: Newsbreaks and short humor. Buys 6/year. Length: 500-1,000 words. Pays $25-75.

Tips: "I frequently assign articles by phone. Sometimes just a spark of an idea can lead to a story assignment or publication. The best way is to have some radio station experience and try to think of articles other readers would benefit from reading."

‡RETAILING, Martin Stanley Publishing Inc., 248 W. Cerritos Ave., Anaheim CA 92805. (714)635-9774. Publisher: Martin Barsky. 5-10% freelance written. Prefers to work with published/established writers. Monthly tabloid covering consumer electronics and major appliances. For retailers of consumer electronics and major appliances, primarily in the West, but also the rest of the nation." Circ. 9,500. Pays on publication. Publishes ms an average of 2 months after acceptance. Byline given. Buys all rights. Submit seasonal/holiday material 3 months in advance. Simultaneous submissions OK. Sample copy for 12×16 SAE with $2.40 postage.

Nonfiction: Interview/profile. Query with published clips. Length: 800-1,500 words. Pays $125-175 for assigned articles. Pays expenses of writers on assignment.

Photos: Send photos with submission. Reviews 4×6 prints. Offers no additional payment for photos accepted with ms. Captions and identification of subjects required. Buys all rights.

SATELLITE RETAILER, Triple D Publishing, Inc., P.O. Box 2384, Shelby NC 28151. (704)482-9673. FAX: (704)484-8558. Editor: David B. Melton. 75% freelance written. Monthly magazine covering home satellite TV. "We look for technical, how-to, marketing, sales, new products, product testing, and news for the satellite television dealer." Estab. 1981. Circ. 12,000. Pays on publication. Byline given. 30% kill fee. Buys all rights. Submit seasonal/holiday material 3 months in advance. Simultaneous submissions OK. Query for electronic submissions. Free sample copy and writer's guidelines.

Nonfiction: How-to, new product, personal experience, photo feature, technical. Buys 24 mss/year. Query with or without published clips, or send complete ms. Length: 1,800-3,600 words. Pays $150-400. Sometimes pays expenses of writers on assignment.

Photos: Send photos with submission. Reviews contact sheets, transparencies (135 to 4×5). Captions, model releases and identification of subjects required. Buys all rights.

Tips: "Familiarity with electronics and television delivery systems is a definite plus."

SHOPTALK, National Association of Business and Educational Radio, 1501 Duke St., Alexandria VA 22314. (703)739-0300. Editor: A. E. Goetz. Managing Editor: Christine W. Bryum. 25% freelance written. Monthly newsletter about two-way radios. "Newsletter targeted toward dealers, service shop owners and manufacturers of two-way radio. Newsletter supplies information to help readers manage businesses better." Circ. 1,000. **Pays on acceptance.** Publishes ms an average of 2 months after acceptance. Byline given. Buys first rights. Previously published submissions OK. Query for electronic submissions. Reports in 1 month. Sample copy for #10 SAE with 2 first class stamps. Writer's guidelines for #10 SASE.

Nonfiction: Book excerpts, essays, how-to, new product and technical, all small business or two-way radio related. Buys 9 mss/year. Query with or without published clips, or send complete ms. Length: 1,000-1,500 words. Pays $100-200 for unsolicited articles.

Photos: Send photos with submission. Reviews contact sheets. Offers no additional payment for photos accepted with ms. Captions, model releases and identification of subjects required. Buys one-time rights.

Tips: "All material should be written clearly and simply. Sidebars are helpful."

TECHTALK, National Association of Business and Educational Radio, 1501 Duke St., Alexandria VA 22314. (703)739-0300. Editor: A. E. Goetz. Managing Editor: Christine W. Bryum. Bimonthly newsletter on two-way radio communications. "Newsletter is for technicians in communications field, especially two-way radio. Material relates to technical changes in the industry, installation procedures, testing and repair methods and self-improvement." Circ. 2,500. **Pays on acceptance.** Publishes ms an average of 2 months after acceptance. Byline given. Buys first rights. Previously published submissions OK. Query for electronic submissions. Reports in 1 month. Sample copy for #10 SAE with 2 first class stamps. Writer's guidelines for #10 SASE.
Nonfiction: Book excerpts, essays, how-to, new product and technical, all dealing with communications. Query with or without published clips, or send complete ms. Length: 1,000-1,500 words. Pays $50-125.
Photos: Send photos with submission. Reviews contact sheets. Offers no additional payment for photos accepted with ms. Captions, model releases and identification of subjects required.
Tips: "Writer needs a technical background such as tech school training and/or experience in communications, especially land-mobile."

‡**VOICE PROCESSING MAGAZINE**, Information Publishing Corp., Suite 100, 3721 Briarpark, Box 42382, Houston TX 77242. (713)974-6637. FAX: (713)974-6272. Editor: Kim Wilson. Managing Editor: Sara Stephens. 10% freelance written. Monthly magazine about the voice processing industry. Estab. 1989. Pays on publication. Publishes ms an average of 2 months after acceptance. Byline given. Offers $100 kill fee. Buys one-time rights. Simultaneous submissions OK. Query for electronic submissions. Free sample copy.
Nonfiction: How-to select a voice messaging system, interview/profile, new product and technical. Buys 8-10 mss/year. Query. Length: 2,000-2,400 words. Pays 15¢/word. "Doesn't pay industry insiders for contributions."
Photos: Send photos with submission. Offers no additional payment for photos accepted with ms. Captions required. Buys one-time rights.

Energy and Utilities

People who supply power to homes, businesses and industry read the publications in this section. This category includes journals covering the electric power, natural gas, petroleum, solar and alternative energy industries.

ALTERNATIVE ENERGY RETAILER, Zackin Publications, Inc., P.O. Box 2180, Waterbury CT 06722. (203)755-0158. FAX: (203)755-3480. Editorial Director: John Florian. 5% freelance written. Prefers to work with published/established writers. Monthly magazine on selling alternative energy products— chiefly solid fuel burning appliances. "We seek detailed how-to tips for retailers to improve business. Most freelance material purchased is about retailers and how they succeed." Estab. 1980. Circ. 10,000. Pays on publication. Publishes ms an average of 2 months after acceptance. Buys first North American serial rights. Submit seasonal/holiday material 4 months in advance. Reports in 2 weeks on queries. Sample copy for 9×12 SAE with 4 first class stamps; writer's guidelines for #10 SASE.
Nonfiction: How-to (improve retail profits and business know-how); and interview/profile (of successful retailers in this field). No "general business articles not adapted to this industry." Buys 10 mss/ year. Query. Length: 1,000 words. Pays $200.
Photos: State availability of photos. Pays $25-125 maximum for 5×7 b&w prints. Reviews color slide transparencies. Identification of subject required. Buys one-time rights.
Tips: "A freelancer can best break in to our publication with features about readers (retailers). Stick to details about what has made this person a success."

ELECTRICAL APPARATUS, The Magazine of the Electromechanical & Electronic Application & Maintenance, Barks Publications, Inc., 400 N. Michigan Ave., Chicago IL 60611-4198. (312)321-9440. Editorial Director: Elsie Dickson. Managing Editor: Kevin N. Jones. Prefers to work with published/ established writers. Uses very little freelance material. A monthly magazine for persons working in electrical maintenance, chiefly in industrial plants, who install and service electrical motors, transformers, generators, controls and related equipment. Estab. 1967. Circ. 17,000. **Pays on acceptance.** Publishes ms an average of 2-3 months after acceptance. Byline given. Buys all rights unless other arrangements made. Prefer copy on DOS disk. Reports in 1 week on queries; 1 month on mss. Sample copy $4.
Nonfiction: Technical. Buys very few mss/year. Query essential, along with letter outlining credentials. Length: 1,500-2,500. Pays $250-500 for assigned articles only. Pays the expenses of writers on assignment by advance arrangement. Prefer freelance writers who are interested in becoming regular contributors.

Photos: Send photos with submission. "Photos are important to most articles. We prefer 35mm color slides, but sometimes use color or b&w prints." Offers additional payments, depending on quality and number. Captions and identification of subjects required. Buys one-time rights. "If we reuse photos, we pay residual fee."

Columns/Departments: Electrical Manager (items on managing businesses, people), 150-600 words; and Electropix (photo of interest with electrical slant), brief captions. Pays $50-100.

Tips: "Queries are essential. Technical expertise is absolutely necessary, preferably an E.E. degree, or practical experience. We are also book publishers and some of the material in *EA* is now in book form, bringing the authors royalties. Also publishes an annual directory, subtitled *ElectroMechanical Bench Reference*."

ELECTRICAL CONTRACTOR, 7315 Wisconsin Ave., Bethesda MD 20814. (301)657-3110. Editor: Tom Nabor. 10% freelance written. Monthly. For electrical contractors. Circ. 67,000. Publishes ms an average of 3 months after acceptance. Buys first serial rights, second serial (reprint) rights or simultaneous rights. Usually reports in 1 month. Byline given. Free sample copy.

Nonfiction: Management articles of interest to the owners of electrical construction and (transmission) line construction companies. Query. Length: 800-2,500 words. Pays $100/printed page, including photos and illustrative material.

Photos: Photos should be sharp, reproducible b&w glossies or color slides.

NATIONAL PETROLEUM NEWS, 950 Lee St., Des Plaines IL 60016. (708)296-0770. FAX: (708)803-3328. Editor-in-Chief: Peggy Smedley. 3% freelance written. Prefers to work with published/established writers. For businessmen who make their living in the oil marketing industry, either as company employees or through their own business operations. Monthly magazine. Estab. 1909. Circ. 14,000. Rights purchased vary with author and material. Usually buys all rights. Pays on acceptance if done on assignment. Publishes ms an average of 2 months after acceptance. "The occasional freelance copy we use is done on assignment." Query.

Nonfiction: Material related directly to developments and issues in the oil marketing industry and "how-to" and "what-with" case studies. "No unsolicited copy, especially with limited attribution regarding information in story." Buys 3-4 mss/year. Length: 2,000 words maximum. Pays $50-150/printed page. Sometimes pays the expenses of writers on assignment.

Photos: Pays $150/printed page. Payment for b&w photos "depends upon advance understanding."

PIPELINE & UNDERGROUND UTILITIES CONSTRUCTION, Oildom Publishing Co. of Texas, Inc., Box 22267, Houston TX 77027. Editor: Oliver Klinger. 5% freelance written. Prefers to work with published/established writers. Monthly magazine covering oil, gas, water, and sewer pipeline construction for contractors and construction workers who build pipelines. Circ. 22,000. No byline given. Not copyrighted. Buys first North American serial rights. Publishes ms an average of 3 months after acceptance. Simultaneous queries OK. Reports in 2 weeks on queries; 3 weeks on mss. Sample copy for $1 and 9×12 SAE.

Nonfiction: How-to. Query with published clips. Length: 1,500-2,500 words. Pays $100/printed page "unless unusual expenses are incurred in getting the story." Sometimes pays the expenses of writers on assignment.

Photos: Send photos with ms. Reviews 5×7 and 8×10 prints. Captions required. Buys one-time rights.

Tips: "We supply guidelines outlining information we need." The most frequent mistake made by writers in completing articles is unfamiliarity with the field.

PUBLIC POWER, 2301 M St. NW, Washington DC 20037. (202)467-2948. Editor/Publisher: Jeanne Wickline LaBella. 20% freelance written. Prefers to work with published/established writers. Bimonthly. Estab. 1942. **Pays on acceptance.** Publishes ms an average of 3 months after acceptance. Byline given. Query for electronic submissions. Free sample copy and writer's guidelines.

Nonfiction: Features on municipal and other local publicly owned electric systems. Payment negotiable.

Photos: Uses b&w glossy and color slides.

UTILITY AND TELEPHONE FLEETS, Practical Communications, Inc., 37 W. Main, Box 183, Cary IL 60013. (312)639-2200. FAX: (312)639-9542. Editor: Alan Richter. 5% freelance written. Magazine published 8 times/year for fleet managers and maintenance supervisors for electric gas and water utilities; telephone, interconnect and cable TV companies, public works departments and related contractors. "We seek case history/application features covering specific fleet management and maintenance projects/installations. Instructional/tutorial features are also welcome." Circ. 18,000. Pays on publication. Publishes ms an average of 1 month after acceptance. Byline given. 20% kill fee. Buys all rights. Submit seasonal/holiday material 2 months in advance. Reports in 2 weeks. Free sample copy and writer's guidelines.

Nonfiction: How-to (ways for performing fleet maintenance/improving management skills/vehicle tutorials), technical, case history/application features. No advertorials in which specific product or company is promoted. Buys 2-3 ms/year. Query with published clips. Length: 1,000-2,800 words. Pays $50/page.

Photos: Send photos with submission. Reviews contact sheets, negatives, transparencies (3×5) and prints (3×5). Offers no additional payment for photos accepted with ms. Captions required. Buys one-time rights.

Columns/Departments: Vehicle Management and Maintenance Tips (nuts-and-bolts type items dealing with new or unusual methods for fleet management, maintenance and safety). Buys 2 mss/year. Query with published clips. Length: 100-400 words. Pays $10-20.

Tips: "Working for a utility or telephone company and gathering information about a construction, safety or fleet project is the best approach for a freelancer."

Engineering and Technology

Engineers and professionals with various specialties read the publications in this section. Publications for electrical, electronics and telecommunications engineers are classified separately under Electronics and Communication. Magazines for computer professionals are in the Information Systems section.

AMERICAN MACHINIST, Penton Publishing, 826 Broadway, 4th Floor, New York NY 10003. (212)477-6420. FAX: (212)477-6457. Editor: Joseph Jablonowski. A monthly magazine about durable-goods manufacturing. Circ. 82,000. **Pays on acceptance.** Publishes ms an average of 4 months after acceptance. Sometimes byline given. Makes work-for-hire assignments. Query for electronic submissions. Reports in 2 months on queries; 3 months on mss. Free sample copy.

Nonfiction: Technical. Query with or without published clips, or send complete ms. Length: 1,500-4,000 words. Pays $300-1,500. Pays the expenses of writers on assignment.

Photos: Send photos with submission. Offers no additional payment for photos accepted with ms. Buys all rights.

Tips: "Articles that are published are probably 85% engineering details. We're interested in feature articles on technology of manufacturing in the metalworking industries (automaking, aircraft, machinery, etc.). Aim at instructing a 45-year-old degreed mechanical engineer in a new method of making, say, a pump housing."

BIONICS, P.O. Box 1553, Owosso MI 48867. Editor: Ben Campbell. Managing Editor: Val Kluge. 50% freelance written. Quarterly newsletter on bionics. Estab. 1988. Circ. 1,500. Pay on publication. Buys first North American serial rights, first rights, one-time rights, second serial (reprint) rights and simultaneous rights. Submit seasonal/holiday material 3 months in advance. Simultaneous and previously published submissions OK. Reports in 2 weeks on queries. Sample copy $10. Free writer's guidelines.

Nonfiction: Book excerpts, how-to, interview/profile, new product, opinion, personal experience and technical. Buys 24 mss/year. Query with or without published clips, or send complete ms. Length: 50-5,000 words. Pays 3-5¢/words. Sometimes pays expenses of writers on assignment.

Photos: Send photos with submission. Reviews negatives and 5×8 transparencies. Offers $10-50 per photo. Model releases required. Buys one-time rights.

Columns/Departments: Bionics, Bi-sensors, Bio-Medical and Robotics. Buys 24 mss/year. Send complete ms. Length: 50-1,000 words.

Fiction: Ethnic, experimental and novel excerpts. Buys 12 mss/year. Query. Length: 50-5,000 words.

Fillers: Facts and newsbreaks. Buys 36/year. Length: 50-200 words.

Tips: "Consult with industry experts. Read the latest magazine articles."

CANADIAN LABORATORY, Sentry Communications, Suite 500, 245 Fairview Mall Dr., Willowdale, Ontario M2J 4T1 Canada. (416)490-0220. FAX: (416)490-0119. Editor: Sally Praskey. 60% freelance written. Bimonthly magazine on hard sciences at Ph.D. level. Circ. 28,000. **Pays on acceptance.** Publishes ms an average of 3 months after acceptance. Byline given. Buys first North American serial rights and one-time rights. Query for electronic submissions. Sample copy $4.

Nonfiction: How-to (science techniques), new product, opinion and technical. Buys 50 mss/year. Query. Length: 150-1,500 words. Pays 23¢/word or agreed-upon flat rate. Sometimes pays expenses of writers on assignment.

Photos: Send photos with submission. Reviews transparencies and prints. Offers $25 per photo. Captions, model releases and identification of subjects required. Buys one-time rights.

Fillers: Facts and newsbreaks. Buys 50/year. Length: 50-200 words. Pays 23¢/word or agreed-upon flat rate.

Tips: "Tightly written, and *scientifically accurate*! We also publish *Canadian Clinical Laboratory* for hospital and private labs (6 times/year). Same info applies, but articles focus on clinical diagnostics and related issues."

‡**DESIGN MANAGEMENT**, Communication Channels, Inc., 6255 Barfield Rd., Atlanta GA 30328. (404)256-9800. FAX: (404)256-3116. Editor: Eric Torrey. 10% freelance written. Works with a small number of new/unpublished writers each year. A monthly magazine covering design graphics in the architecture, engineering and construction community. Estab. 1977. Circ. 41,500. Pays on publication. Publishes ms an average of 2 months after acceptance. Byline given. Buys all rights. Submit seasonal/holiday material 3 months in advance. Reports in 1 month on queries; 2 weeks on mss. Sample copy for 10×13 SAE.

Nonfiction: How-to, interview/profile, new product and technical. "Articles should be knowledgeable, informative and written for professional architects, engineers and designers." No product sales information, brand- or product-specific information features. Buys 8 mss/year. Query with published clips. Length: 500-2,000 words. Pays $50-500 for assigned article. Sometimes pays the expenses of writers on assignment.

Photos: Send photos with submission. Reviews 2×2 transparencies and 5×7 prints. Offers no additional payment for photos accepted with ms. Identification of subjects required. Buys all rights.

Tips: "Writers should be capable of dropping consumer-prose writing styles and adopt more technical language and usage."

‡**GRADUATING ENGINEER**, Peterson's/COG Publishing, Suite 560, 16030 Ventura Blvd., Encino CA 91436. (818)789-5371. Editor-in-Chief: Charlotte Chandler Williams. 90% freelance written. Prefers to work with published/established writers. Published September-March "to help graduating engineers make the transition from campus to the working world." Circ. 83,000. Pays 30 days after acceptance. Publishes ms an average of 2 months after acceptance. Byline given. Buys first North American serial rights. Reports in 3 weeks. Writer's guidelines available.

Nonfiction: General interest (on management, human resources); and career entry, interpersonal skills, job markets, careers, career trends. Special issues include Minority, Women and High Technology. Buys 100 mss/year. Query. Length: 2,000-3,000 words. Pays $300-700.

Photos: State availability of photos, illustrations or charts. Reviews 35mm color transparencies, 8×10 b&w glossy prints. Captions and model release required.

Tips: "We're generating new types of editorial. We closely monitor economy here and abroad so that our editorial reflects economic, social, and global trends."

HIGH TECHNOLOGY CAREERS, %Writers Connection, Suite 180, 1601 Saratoga-Sunnyvale Rd., Cupertino CA 95014. (408)973-0227. FAX: (408)973-1219. Managing Editor: Meera Lester. 100% freelance written. Monthly tabloid on high technology industries. "Articles must have a high technology tie-in and should be written in a positive and lively manner. The audience includes managers, engineers and other professionals working in the high technology industries." Circ. 348,000. Pays on publication. Publishes ms an average of 3 months after acceptance. Byline given. Offers 25% kill fee. Buys all rights. Query for electronic submissions. Reports in 3 weeks. Free sample copy; writer's guidelines for #10 SASE.

Nonfiction: General interest (with high tech tie-in), technical. Publishes five regular 800 word columns (career-oriented) and two 1,500 word features each issue. Buys 50-60 mss/year. Query with or without published clips, or send complete ms. Length: 1,500-2,000 words. Pays 17½¢/word. Sometimes pays expenses of writers on assignment.

Photos: State availability of photo with submission.

LASER FOCUS WORLD MAGAZINE, 1 Technology Park Dr., P.O. Box 989, Westford MA 01886. (508)692-0700. FAX: (508)692-0525. Publisher: Dr. Morris R. Levitt. Editor-in-Chief: Dr. Lewis M. Holmes. Managing Editor: Barbara Murray. Less than 1% freelance written. A monthly magazine for physicists, scientists and engineers involved in the research and development, design, manufacturing and applications of lasers, laser systems and all other segments of electro-optical technologies. Estab. 1964. Circ. 60,000. Publishes ms an average of 6 months after acceptance. Byline given unless anonymity requested. Retains all rights. Query for electronic submissions. Free sample copy and writer's guidelines.

Nonfiction: Lasers, laser systems, fiberoptics, optics, imaging and other electro-optical materials, components, instrumentation and systems. "Each article should serve our reader's need by either stimulating ideas, increasing technical competence or improving design capabilities in the following

areas: natural light and radiation sources, artificial light and radiation sources, light modulators, optical materials and components, image detectors, energy detectors, information displays, image processing, information storage and processing, subsystem and system testing, support equipment and other related areas." No "flighty prose, material not written for our readership, or irrelevant material." Query first "with a clear statement and outline of why the article would be important to our readers."
Photos: Send photos with ms. Reviews 8×10 b&w glossies or 4×5 color transparencies. Drawings: Rough drawings acceptable, are finished by staff technical illustrator.
Tips: "The writer has a better chance of breaking in at our publication with short articles because shorter articles are easier to schedule, but must address more carefully our requirements for technical coverage. Most of our submitted materials come from technical experts in the areas we cover. The most frequent mistake made by writers in completing articles for us is that the articles are too commercial, i.e., emphasize a given product or technology from one company. Also articles are not the right technical depth, too thin or too scientific."

MACHINE DESIGN, Penton Publishing Inc., 1100 Superior Ave., Cleveland OH 44114. (216)696-7000. FAX: (216)696-0177. Editor: Ronald Khol. Executive Editor: Richard Beercheck. 1-2% freelance written. Works with a small number of new/unpublished writers each year. A bimonthly magazine covering technical developments in products or purchases of interest to the engineering community. Estab. 1929. Circ. 180,000. Pays on publication. Publishes ms an average of 2 months after acceptance. Byline given. Buys first rights. Reports in 1 month. Free sample copy.
Nonfiction: General interest; how-to (on using new equipment or processes); and new product. No non-technical submissions. Buys 10-15 mss/year. Query. Length and payment for articles must be negotiated in advance. Sometimes pays the expenses of writers on assignment.
Photos: State availability of photos with submission. Offers negotiable payment. Captions, model releases, and identification of subjects required.
Columns/Departments: Design International (international news), captions; Backtalk (technical humor) and Personal Computers in Engineering (use of personal computers), both have negotiable word length. Buys 50-200 items/year. Query. Pays $20 minimum.
Tips: "The departments of our publication most open to freelancers are Back Talk, News Trends and Design International. Those without technical experience almost never send in adequate material."

MECHANICAL ENGINEERING, American Society of Mechanical Engineers, 345 E. 47th St., New York NY 10017. (212)705-7782. Editor: Jay O'Leary. Managing Editor: Alexander Wolfe. 30% freelance written. A monthly magazine on mechanical process and design. "We publish general interest articles for graduate mechanical engineers on high-tech topics." Circ. 135,000. **Pays on acceptance.** Sometimes byline given. Kill fee varies. Buys first rights. Submit seasonal material 4 months in advance. Reports in 6 weeks. Free writer's guidelines.
Nonfiction: Historical, interview/profile, new product, photo feature and technical. Buys 25 mss/year. Query with or without published clips, or send complete ms. Length: 1,500-3,500 words. Pays $500-1,500.
Photos: Send photos with submission. Reviews transparencies and prints. Offers no additional payment for photos accepted with ms. Captions and identification of subjects required. Buys one-time rights.

THE MINORITY ENGINEER, An Equal Opportunity Career Publication for Professional and Graduating Minority Engineers, Equal Opportunity Publications, Inc., 44 Broadway, Greenlawn NY 11740. (516)261-8917. FAX: (516)261-8935. Executive Editor: James Schneider. 60% freelance written. Prefers to work with published/established writers. Magazine published 4 times/year covering career guidance for minority engineering students and professional minority engineers. Estab. 1969. Circ. 16,000. Pays on publication. Publishes ms an average of 3-6 months after acceptance. Byline given. Buys first rights. "Deadline dates: fall, June 1; winter, September 15; spring, January 15; April/May, March 1." Simultaneous and previously published submissions OK. Sample copy and writer's guidelines for 9×12 SAE with 5 first class stamps.
Nonfiction: Book excerpts; articles (on job search techniques, role models); general interest (on specific minority engineering concerns); how-to (land a job, keep a job, etc.); interview/profile (minority engineer role models); new product (new career opportunities); opinion (problems of ethnic minorities); personal experience (student and career experiences); and technical (on career fields offering opportunities for minority engineers). "We're interested in articles dealing with career guidance and job opportunities for minority engineers." Query or send complete ms. Length: 1,000-1,500 words. Sometimes pays the expenses of writers on assignment. Pays 10¢/word.
Photos: Prefers 35mm color slides but will accept b&w. Captions and identification of subjects required. Buys all rights. Pays $15. Cartoons accepted. Pays $25.
Tips: "Articles should focus on career guidance, role model and industry prospects for minority engineers. Prefer articles related to careers, not politically or socially sensitive."

NATIONAL DEFENSE, American Defense Preparedness Association, 2101 Wilson Blvd, Arlington VA 22201-3061. (703)522-1820. FAX: (703)522-1885. Editor: F. Clifton Berry, Jr. Managing Editor: Vincent P. Grimes. A magazine covering all facets of the North American defense industrial base published 11 times/year. "Interest is on articles offering a sound analysis of new and ongoing patterns in procurement, research and development of new technology, and budgeting trends." Estab. 1920. Circ. 40,000. Pays on publication. Byline given. Buys all rights. Requires electronic submission. Reports in 3 weeks on queries. Free sample copy and writer's guidelines.
Nonfiction: Feature and photos. Buys 12-15 mss/year. Query first. Length: 1,200-1,500 words. Pays negotiated fees, up to $600. Pays expenses of writers on assignment "with prior arrangement."
Photos: Send photos with submission. Reviews contact sheets, negatives, transparencies and prints. Offers no additional payment for photos accepted with ms. Captions required. Buys all rights.

WOMAN ENGINEER, An Equal Opportunity Career Publication for Graduating Women and Experienced Professionals, Equal Opportunity Publications, Inc., 44 Broadway, Greenlawn NY 11740. (516)261-8917. Editor: Anne Kelly. 60% freelance written. Works with a small number of new/unpublished writers each year. Magazine published 4 times/year (fall, winter, spring, April/May) covering career guidance for women engineering students and professional women engineers. Circ. 16,000. Pays on publication. Publishes ms 3-12 months after acceptance. Byline given. Buys all rights. Free sample copy and writer's guidelines.
Nonfiction: "Interested in articles dealing with career guidance and job opportunities for women engineers. Looking for manuscripts showing how to land an engineering position and advance professionally. Wants features on job-search techniques, engineering disciplines offering career opportunities to women, companies with affirmative action and career advancement opportunities for women, problems facing women engineers and how to cope with such problems, in addition to role-model profiles of successful women engineers, especially in government, military and defense-related industries." Query. Length: 1,000-2,500 words. Pays 10¢/word.
Photos: Prefers color slides but will accept b&w. Captions, model release and identification of subjects required. Buys all rights. Pays $15.
Tips: "We will be looking for shorter manuscripts (800-1,000 words) on job-search techniques, and first-person Endpage Essay."

Entertainment and the Arts

The business of the entertainment/amusement industry in arts, film, dance, theater, etc. is covered by these publications. Journals that focus on the people and equipment of various music specialties are listed in the Music section, while art and design business publications can be found in Art, Design and Collectibles. Entertainment publications for the general public can be found in the Consumer Entertainment section.

‡AMUSEMENT BUSINESS, Billboard Publications, Inc., P.O. Box 24970, Nashville TN 37202. (615)321-4269. FAX: (615)327-1575. Managing Editor: Lisa Zhito. 25% freelance written. Works with a small number of new/unpublished writers each year. Weekly tabloid emphasizing hard news of the amusement, sports business, and mass entertainment industry. Read by top management. Circ. 15,000. Pays on publication. Publishes ms an average of 3 weeks after acceptance. Byline sometimes given; "it depends on the quality of the individual piece." Buys all rights. Submit seasonal/holiday material 3 weeks in advance. Phone queries OK. Sample copy for 11x14 SAE with 5 first class stamps.
Nonfiction: How-to (case history of successful advertising campaigns and promotions); interviews (with leaders in the areas we cover highlighting appropriate problems and issues of today, i.e. insurance, alcohol control, etc.). Likes lots of financial support data: grosses, profits, operating budgets and per-cap spending. Also needs in-depth looks at advertising and promotional programs of carnivals, circuses, amusement parks, fairs: how these facilities position themselves against other entertainment opportunities in the area. No personality pieces or interviews with stage stars. Publishes profiles of key industry leaders, but must be well-known within the entertainment industry. Buys 500-1,000 mss/year. Query. Length: 400-700 words. Pays $3/published inch. Sometimes pays the expenses of writers on assignment.
Photos: State availability of photos with query. Pays $3-5 for 8×10 b&w glossy prints. Captions and model release required. Buys all rights.
Columns/Departments: Auditorium Arenas; Fairs, Fun Parks; Food Concessions; Merchandise; Promotion; Shows (carnival and circus); Talent; Tourist Attractions; Management Changes; ProAm/Athletics; Profile; Eye On Legislation; Commentary and International News.
Tips: There will be more and more emphasis on financial reporting of areas covered. "Submission must contain the whys and whos, etc. and be strong enough that others in the same field will learn from it and not find it naive. We will be increasing story count while decreasing story length."

BOXOFFICE MAGAZINE, RLD Publishing Corp., Suite 710, 1800 N. Highland Ave., Hollywood CA 90028. (213)465-1186. FAX: (213)465-5049. Editor: Harley W. Lond. 5% freelance written. Monthly business magazine about the motion picture industry for members of the film industry: theater owners, film producers, directors, financiers and allied industries. Estab. 1920. Circ. 10,000. Pays on publication. Publishes ms an average of 2-4 months after acceptance. Byline given. Buys one-time rights. Submit seasonal material 2 months in advance. Simultaneous and previously published submissions OK. Reports in 2 months. Sample copy for 9 × 12 SAE with 6 first class stamps.
Nonfiction: Investigative, interview, profile, new product, photo feature and technical. "We are a general news magazine about the motion picture industry and are looking for stories about trends, developments, problems or opportunities facing the industry. Almost any story will be considered, including corporate profiles, but we don't want gossip or celebrity stuff." Query with published clips. Length: 1,500-2,500 words. Pays $100-150.
Photos: State availability of photos. Pays $10 maximum for 8 × 10 b&w prints. Captions required.
Tips: "Request a sample copy, indicating you read about *Boxoffice* in *Writer's Market*. Write a clear, comprehensive outline of the proposed story and enclose a resume and clip samples. We welcome new writers but don't want to be a classroom. Know how to write. We look for 'investigative' articles."

‡CABLECASTER, Southam Business Communications Inc., 1450 Don Mills Rd., Don Mills, Ontario M3B 2X7 Canada. (416)445-6641. FAX: (416)442-2213. Editor: Bruce Parkinson. Monthly magazine on the cable industry. "National magazine for the Canadian cable industry. Focus on management/technical regulatory issues." Estab. 1989. Pays on publication. Offers 50% kill fee. Buys all rights. Reports in 3 weeks on queries; 2 weeks on mss. Free sample copy.
Nonfiction: General interest, interview/profile and new product. Buys 20 mss/year. Query with published clips. Length: 1,000-2,000 words. Pays $150-300 per article. Pays expenses of writers on assignment.
Photos: Send photos with submission. Reviews 8 × 10 prints.
Tips: "Focus must be on the Canadian cable industry—the people, issues and technology that drive the industry."

THE HOLLYWOOD REPORTER, 6715 Sunset Blvd., Hollywood CA 90028. (213)464-7411. President: Robert J. Dowling. Publisher: Tichi Wilkerson Kassel. Editor: Teri Ritzer. Emphasizes entertainment industry, film, TV and theatre and everything to do with financial news in these areas. 15% freelance written. Daily entertainment trade publication: 25-100 pages. Circ. 25,000. Publishes ms an average of 1 week after acceptance. Send queries first. Reports in 1 month. Sample copy $1.
Tips: "Short articles fit our format best. The most frequent mistake made by writers in completing an article for us is that they are not familiar with our publication. We are a business publication, we don't want celebrity gossip."

LOCATION UPDATE, Suite 612, 6922 Hollywood Blvd., Hollywood CA 90028. (213)461-8887. FAX: (213)469-3711. Managing Editor: Lee Thomas. Bimonthly entertainment industry magazine covering all aspects of filming on location. "*Location Update* communicates the issues, trends, problems, solutions and business matters that affect productions working on location. Features include interviews with industry professionals, controversial issues, regional spotlights, hard-to-find or difficult locations, etc. Audience is made up of producers, directors, production managers, location managers—any person who works on location for film, TV, commercials and videos." Estab. 1985. Circ. 30,000. Pays on publication. Publishes ms an average of 2 months after acceptance. Byline given. Offers 50% kill fee. Publication not copyrighted. Buys first North American serial rights. Query for electronic submissions. Reports in 3 weeks. Sample copy for 9 × 12 SAE with 7 first class stamps; free writer's guidelines.
Nonfiction: Exposé, general interest, historical/nostalgic, interview/profile, new product, opinion, photo feature, technical and features about productions on location. No fluffy or glitzy "Hollywood" slants. Buys 75 mss/year. Query with published clips. Length: 1,000-2,500 words. Pays $100-300 for assigned articles; $50-100 for unsolicited articles. Sometimes pays expenses of writers on assignment.
Photos: State availability of photos with submission. Reviews contact sheets, 35mm, 2¼ × 2¼ transparencies and 8 × 10 prints. Offers no additional payment for photos accepted with ms. Identification of subjects required. Buys one-time rights.
Columns/Departments: Locations (hard to find or difficult locations and how to use them), 1,000-1,500 words; Supporting Roles (support services used on location: security companies, catering, etc.), 1,000-1,500 words; Newsreel (short news briefs on location-related issues), 250 words. Buys 25-30 mss/year. Query with published clips. Pays $25-100.
Tips: "The best way to break in is to query with story ideas and to be familiar with film, TV, video and commercials. Know the workings of the entertainment industry and the roles of producers, directors and location managers. Articles about locations are most open to freelance writers. Everything is a possible location for productions. Every state has a film commission that can help with who is where and how to go about using particular locations."

MIDDLE EASTERN DANCER, Mideastern Connection, Inc., P.O. Box 181572, Casselberry FL 32718-1572. (407)831-3402. Editor: Karen Kuzsel. Managing Editor: Jeanette Spencer. 60% freelance written. Eager to work with new/unpublished writers. A monthly magazine covering Middle Eastern dance and culture (belly dancing). "We provide the most current news and entertainment information available in the world. We focus on the positive, but don't shy away from controversy. All copy and photos must relate to Middle Eastern dance and cultural activities. We do not get into politics." Estab. 1979. Circ. 2,500. **Pays on acceptance.** Publishes ms an average of 4 months after acceptance, usually sooner, but it depends on type of article and need for that month. Byline given. Buys first rights, simultaneous rights or second serial (reprint) rights. Submit seasonal/holiday material 3 months in advance. Simultaneous and previously published submissions OK, unless printed in another belly dance publication. Reports in 2 weeks on queries; 3 weeks on mss. Sample copy for 9 × 12 SAE with 4 first class stamps; writer's guidelines for #10 SASE.

Nonfiction: Essays; general interest; historical/nostalgic; how-to (on costuming, putting on shows, teaching and exercises); humor; inspirational; interview/profile; personal experience; photo features; travel (to the Middle East or related to dancers); and reviews of seminars, movies, clubs, restaurants and museums. Special issues include costuming (March); and anniversary issue (October). No politics. Buys 60 mss/year. Query. Pays $20 for assigned articles; pays $10 for unsolicited articles. Sometimes pays the expenses of writers on assignment.

Photos: Send photos with submission. Offers $5 additional payment for each photo accepted with ms. Identification of subjects required. Buys one-time rights.

Columns/Departments: Critic's Corner (reviews of books, videotapes, records, movies, clubs and restaurants, museums and special events); Helpful Hints (tips for finding accessories and making them easier or less); Putting on the Ritz (describes costume in detail with photo); and Personal Glimpses (autobiographical) and Profiles (biographical — providing insights of benefit to other dancers). Query.

Fiction: Open to fiction dealing with belly dancers as subject.

Poetry: Avant-garde, free verse, light verse and traditional. Buys 5 poems/year. Submit maximum 3 poems. Pays $5 maximum.

Tips: "It's easy to break in if you stick to belly dancing related information and expect little money. Although we are the leader in the world in this field, we're still small."

OPPORTUNITIES FOR ACTORS & MODELS, A Guide to Working in Cable TV-Radio-Print Advertising, Copy Group, Suite 315, 1900 N. Vine St., Hollywood CA 90068. FAX: (213)465-5161. Editor: Len Miller. 50% freelance written. Works with a small number of new/unpublished writers each year. A monthly newsletter "serving the interests of those people who are (or would like to be) a part of the cable-TV, radio, and print advertising industries." Estab. 1969. Circ. 10,000. **Pays on acceptance.** Publishes ms an average of 3 months after acceptance. Byline given. Buys all rights. Simultaneous queries OK. Reports in 3 weeks. Free sample copy and writer's guidelines for #10 SASE.

Nonfiction: How-to, humor, inspirational, interview/profile, local news, personal experience, photo feature and technical (within cable TV). Coverage should include the model scene, little theatre, drama groups, comedy workshops and other related events and places. "Detailed information about your local cable TV station should be an important part of your coverage. Get to know the station and its creative personnel." Buys 120 mss/year. Query. Length: 100-950 words. Pays $50 maximum.

Photos: State availability of photos. Model release and identification of subjects required. Buys one-time or all rights.

Columns/Departments: "We will consider using your material in a column format with your byline." Buys 60 mss/year. Query. Length: 150-450 words. Pays $50 maximum.

Tips: "Good first person experiences, interviews and articles, all related to modeling, acting, little theater, photography (model shots) and other interesting items are needed."

‡**THE PRODUCTION RESOURCE**, 5535 Rockefeller Center, New York NY 10185. (212)518-4616. Editor: Laura Kerr. Managing Editor: Wladimir Vostrikov. 40% freelance written. Monthly trade journal for the film industry. Also publishes an annual magazine. "*The Production Resource* is a publication for film-makers and anyone interested in getting *behind* the movie screen and scene. It's *not* a fanzine!" Estab. 1990. Circ. 50,000. Pays on publication. Publishes ms an average of 2 months after acceptance. Byline given. Offers 25% kill fee. Buys first North American and second serial (reprint) rights; also makes work-for-hire assignments. Submit seasonal/holiday material 4 months in advance. Previously published submissions OK. Query for electronic submissions. Reports in 2 weeks on queries; 1 month on mss. Sample copy $1; includes guidelines.

Nonfiction: Book excerpts, essays, historical/nostalgic, interview/profile, new product, photo feature, technical. The annual handbook is a yearbook reflecting on the year in film and a sourcebook of resources producers and directors require in filming. "We are not interested in movie and videotape reviews from readers/writers; reviews are staff-written. Not interested in 'I met' pieces." Buys 120 mss/year. Query with published clips. Length: 1,000-10,000 words. Pays $150-2,500 for assigned articles. Pays $50-1,500 for unsolicited articles. Pays expenses of writers on assignment.

Photos: Send photos with submission. Reviews contact sheets, 3×3 transparencies and 8x10 prints. Offers $25-150 for photos. Captions, model releases and identification of subjects required. Buys one-time rights.

Columns/Departments: Various columns open; specifics included in writer's guidelines. Buys 200/year. Query with published clips. Length: 400-750 words. Pays $25-200.

Fillers: "We are considered a trade publication, but we aren't high-brow or technical. We keep it conversational and word-of-mouth. Easiest way to break in is with fillers or items for various columns and it is best to submit two or three at a time."

‡**STRIPPER MAGAZINE, Magazine for Exotic Dancing Industry,** 4C, 344 W. 49th St., New York NY 10019. (212)262-9697. Editor: Duncan Dexter. 75% freelance written. Bimonthly magazine covering the exotic dance industry. Estab. 1989. Circ. 20,000. Pays on publication. Publishes ms an average of 1 month after acceptance. Byline given. Offers 50% kill fee. Buys all rights. Submit seasonal material 3 months in advance. Simultaneous and previously published submissions OK. Query for electronic submissions. Reports in 2 weeks on queries; 1 month on mss. Free sample copy.

Nonfiction: Book excerpts, essays, exposé, general interest, historical/nostalgic, how-to, humor, inspirational, interview/profile, new product, opinion, personal experience, photo feature, technical and travel (all related to exotic dancing). Buys 20 mss/year. Query. Length: 750-2,000 words. Pays 10¢/word. Pays in contributor copies or other premiums if requested. Pays expenses of writers on assignment.

Photos: State availability of photos with submission. Reviews contact sheets. Payment is "flexible." Model releases and identification of subjects required. Buys all rights.

Farm

The successful farm writer focuses on the business side of farming. For technical articles, editors feel writers should have a farm background or agricultural training, but there are opportunities for the general freelancer too. The following farm publications are divided into seven categories, each specializing in a different aspect of farming: agricultural equipment; crops and soil management; dairy farming; livestock; management; miscellaneous and regional.

Agricultural Equipment

CUSTOM APPLICATOR, Little Publications, Suite 540, 6263 Poplar Ave., Memphis TN 38119. (901)767-4020. FAX: (901)767-4026. Editor: Rob Wiley. 50% freelance written. Works with a small number of new/unpublished writers each year. For "firms that sell and custom apply agricultural fertilizer and chemicals." Estab. 1957. Circ. 16,100. Pays on publication. Publishes ms an average of 2 months after acceptance. Buys all rights. "Query is best. The editor can help you develop the story line regarding our specific needs." Free sample copy and writer's guidelines.

Nonfiction: "We are looking for articles on custom application firms telling others how to better perform jobs of chemical application, develop new customers, handle credit, etc. Lack of a good idea or usable information will bring a rejection." Length: 1,000-1,200 words "with 3 or 4 b&w glossy prints." Pays 20¢/word.

Photos: Accepts b&w glossy prints. "We will look at color slides for possible cover or inside use."

Tips: "We don't get enough shorter articles, so one that is well-written and informative could catch our eyes. Our readers want pragmatic information to help them run a more efficient business; they can't get that through a story filled with generalities."

Crops and Soil Management

ONION WORLD, Columbia Publishing, 111C S. 7th Ave., P.O. Box 1467, Yakima WA 98907. (509)248-2452. FAX: (509)248-4056. Editor: D. Brent Clement. 90% freelance written. A monthly magazine covering "the world of onion production and marketing" for onion growers and shippers. Estab. 1975. Circ. 5,500. Pays on publication. Publishes ms an average of 1 month after acceptance. Byline given. Not copyrighted. Buys first North American serial rights. Submit seasonal/holiday material 1 month in advance. Simultaneous submissions OK. Reports in several weeks. Sample copy for 9×12 SAE with 4 first class stamps.

Nonfiction: General interest, historical/nostalgic and interview/profile. Buys 60 mss/year. Query. Length: 1,200-1,500 words. Pays $75-150 for assigned articles.

Photos: Send photos with submission. Offers no additional payment for photos accepted with ms unless cover shot. Captions and identification of subjects required. Buys all rights.

Tips: "Writers should be familiar with growing and marketing onions. We use a lot of feature stories on growers, shippers and others in the onion trade—what they are doing, their problems, solutions, marketing plans, etc."

SINSEMILLA TIPS, Domestic Marijuana Journal, New Moon Publishing, 215 SW 2nd, P.O. Box 1027, Corvallis OR 97339. (503)757-8477. FAX: (503)757-0028. Editor: Tom Alexander. 50% freelance written. Eager to work with new/unpublished writers. Quarterly magazine tabloid covering the domestic cultivation of marijuana. Estab. 1980. Circ. 15,000. Pays on publication. Publishes ms an average of 3 months after acceptance. Byline given. "Some writers desire to be anonymous for obvious reasons." Buys first serial rights and second serial (reprint) rights. Submit seasonal/holiday material 2 months in advance. Query for electronic submissions. Reports in 2 months. Sample copy $6; writer's guidelines for #10 SASE.

Nonfiction: Book excerpts and reviews; expose (on political corruption); general interest; how-to; interview/profile; opinion; personal experience; and technical. Send complete ms. Length: 500-2,000 words. Pays 2½¢/word. Sometimes pays the expenses of writers on assignment.

Photos: Send photos with ms. Pays $10-20 for b&w prints; $20-50 color inside print; $50-75 color cover photo. Captions optional; model release required. Buys all rights.

Tips: "Writers have the best chance of publication if article is *specifically* related to the American marijuana industry."

‡SOYBEAN DIGEST, Box 41309, 540 Maryville Centre Dr., St. Louis MO 63141-1309. (314)576-2788. FAX: (314)576-2786. Editor: Gregg Hillyer. 75% freelance written. Works with a small number of new/unpublished writers each year. Emphasizes soybean production and marketing. Published monthly except semi-monthly in February and March, and bimonthly in June/July and August/September. Estab. 1941. Circ. 205,000. **Pays on acceptance.** Buys all rights. Byline given. Phone queries OK. Submit seasonal material 2 months in advance. Query for electronic submissions. Reports in 3 weeks. Sample copy $3; mention *Writer's Market* in request. Free writer's guidelines.

Nonfiction: How-to (soybean production and marketing); and new product (soybean production and marketing). Buys 100 mss/year. Query or submit complete ms. Length: 1,000 words. Pays $50-350. Sometimes pays the expenses of writers on assignment.

Photos: State availability of photos with query. Pays $25-100 for 5×7 or 8×10 b&w prints, $50-350 for 35mm color transparencies, and up to $600 for covers. Captions and/or ms required. Buys all rights.

Dairy Farming

BUTTER-FAT, Fraser Valley Milk Producers' Cooperative Association, P.O. Box 9100, Vancouver, British Columbia V6B 4G4 Canada. (604)420-6611. Editor: Grace Chadsey. Managing Editor: Carol A. Paulson. Eager to work with new/unpublished writers. 20% freelance written. Quarterly magazine emphasizing this dairy cooperative's processing and marketing operations for dairy farmers and dairy workers in British Columbia. Estab. 1923. Circ. 2,500. **Pays on acceptance.** Publishes ms an average of 8 months after acceptance. Byline given. Buys first rights. Makes work-for-hire assignments. Phone queries preferred. Submit seasonal material 4 months in advance. Simultaneous and previously published submissions OK. Reports in 1 week on queries; 1 month on mss. Free sample copy.

Nonfiction: Interview (character profile with industry leaders); British Columbian nostalgia; opinion (of industry leaders); and profile (of association members and employees).

Photos: Reviews 5×7 b&w negatives and contact sheets and color photos. Offers $10/published photo. Captions required. Buys all rights.

Columns/Departments: "We want articles on the people, products, business of producing, processing and marketing dairy foods in this province." Query first. Buys 3 mss/year. Length: approx. 1,000 words. Pays 7¢/word.

Fillers: Jokes, short humor, quotes, cartoons. Buys 5 mss/year. Pays $15.

Tips: "Make an appointment to come by and see us!"

 The double dagger before a listing indicates that the listing is new in this edition. New markets are often more receptive to freelance submissions.

THE DAIRYMAN, P.O. Box 819, Corona CA 91718. (714)735-2730. FAX: (714)735-2460. Editor: Dennis Halladay. 10% freelance written. Prefers to work with published/established writers, but also works with a small number of new/unpublished writers each year. Monthly magazine dealing with large herd commercial dairy industry. Estab. 1922. Circ. 33,000. Pays on acceptance or publication. Publishes ms an average of 2-3 months after acceptance. Byline given. Buys first North American serial rights. Submit seasonal material 3 months in advance. Reports in 2 weeks. Sample copy for 9×12 SAE with 4 first class stamps.

Nonfiction: Humor, interview/profile, new product, opinion, and industry analysis. Special issues: Computer issue (February); Herd Health issue (August); Feeds and Feeding (May); and Barns and Equipment (November). No religion, nostalgia, politics or 'mom and pop' dairies. Query or send complete ms. Length: 300-5,000 words. Pays $10-200.

Photos: Send photo with query or ms. Reviews b&w contact sheets and 35mm or 2¼×2¼ transparencies. Pays $10-25 for b&w; $25-100 for color. Captions and identification of subjects required. Buys one-time rights.

Columns/Departments: Herd health, computers, economic outlook for dairying. Buys 25/year. Query or send complete ms. Length: 300-2,000 words. Pays $25-200.

Tips: "Pretend you're an editor for a moment; would you want to buy a story without any artwork? Neither would I. Writers often don't know modern commercial dairying and they forget they're writing for an audience of *dairymen*. Publications are becoming more and more specialized. You've really got to know who you're writing for and why they're different."

Livestock

ANGUS JOURNAL, Angus Publications, Inc., 3201 Frederick Blvd., St. Joseph MO 64506. (816)233-0508. FAX: (816)233-0508, ext. 112. Editor: Jerilyn Johnson. 10% freelance written. Monthly (except June/July, which are combined) magazine. "Must be Angus-related or beef cattle with no other breeds mentioned." Circ. 17,500. **Pays on acceptance.** Byline given. Buys first North American serial rights, second serial(reprint) rights, simultaneous rights and makes work-for-hire assignments. Submit seasonal/holiday material 3 months in advance. Simultaneous and previously published submissions OK. Reports in 2 weeks. Samples copy $1.50 wtih 10×13 SAE and 4 first class stamps.

Nonfiction: Historical/nostalgic, how-to, humor, interview/profile and photo feature. Nothing without an Angus slant. Buys 6 mss/year. Send complete ms. Length: 1,000-2,000 words. Pays $225.

Photos: Send photos with submission. Review contact sheets and transparencies. Offers no additional payment for photos accepted with ms. Identification of subjects required. Buys one-time rights.

Columns/Departments: The Grazier (pasture, fencing, range management). Send complete ms. Length: 500-1,000 words. Pays $25-75.

Poetry: Light verse and traditional. Nothing without an Angus or beef cattle slant. Submit up to 4 poems at one time. Length: 4-20 lines. Pays $25.

Tips: Areas most open to freelancers are "farm and ranch profiles—breeder interviews."

BEEF, The Webb Co., 7900 International Dr., Minneapolis MN 55425. (612)851-4668. Editor-in-Chief: Paul D. Andre. Managing Editor: Joe Roybal. 5% freelance written. Prefers to work with published/established writers. Monthly magazine for readers who have the same basic interest—making a living feeding cattle or running a cow herd. Estab. 1964. Circ. 107,000. **Pays on acceptance.** Publishes ms an average of 4 months after acceptance. Buys all rights. Byline given. Submit seasonal material 3 months in advance. Reports in 2 months.

Nonfiction: How-to and informational articles on doing a better job of producing, feeding cattle, market building, managing, and animal health practices. Material must deal with beef cattle only. Buys 8-10 mss/year. Query. Length: 500-2,000 words. Pays $25-300. Sometimes pays the expenses of writers on assignment. Articles and photos returned only if accompanied by SASE.

Photos: B&w glossies (8×10) and color transparencies (35mm or 2¼×2¼) purchased with or without mss. Query or send contact sheet, captions and/or transparencies. Pays $10-50 for b&w; $25-100 for color. Model release required.

Tips: "Be completely knowledgeable about cattle feeding and cowherd operations. Know what makes a story. We want specifics, not a general roundup of an operation. Pick one angle and develop it fully. The most frequent mistake is not following instructions on an angle (or angles) to be developed."

BEEF TODAY, Farm Journal, Inc., 230 W. Washington Sq., Philadelphia PA 19105. (215)829-4700. Editor: Bill Miller. 10% freelance written. Monthly magazine on cattlemen and the beef-cattle industry. "The audience is comprised of larger-scale cattlemen. We emphasize current industry trends, innovative production practices, finances and other business subjects, but also run humor and profiles." Estab. 1985. Circ. 200,000. **Pays on acceptance.** Publishes ms an average of 2 months after acceptance. Byline given. Offers $150 kill fee. Buys all rights. Submit seasonal/holiday material 3 months in advance. Reports in 2 weeks. Sample copy for 9×12 SAE with 2 first class stamps; free writer's guidelines.

Nonfiction: How-to (do a better job of running a ranch or feed lot), humor, interview/profile and photo feature. "No articles explaining the cattle industry to the general public." Query with published clips. Length: 500-2,500 words. Pays $300-650 for assigned articles; $150-600 for unsolicited articles. Pays expenses of writers on assignment.

Photos: State availability of photos with submissions or send photos with submissions—preferred. Reviews transparencies. Offers $100-200 per photo. Captions and identification of subjects required. Buys one-time rights.

Tips: "Authors should include details in their queries and mention what sort of expertise they bring to the subject. Most of the unsolicited manuscripts that we've accepted have been on lighter subjects—personality profiles and humor, for instance. But even here, freelance writers should remember that we're a business magazine and that our readers are working cattlemen who already know their business. They (and we) want specifics—numbers, results, problems, etc.—rather than a general introduction. Reports from abroad can be slightly more introductory, though."

HOG FARM MANAGEMENT, Miller Publishing Co., Suite 160, 12400 Whitewater Dr., Box 2400, Minneapolis MN 55343. (612)931-2900. Editor: Steve Marbery. 25% freelance written. A monthly trade journal on hog production. "Specialized management-oriented features on hog production: feeding, health, finances." Circ. 45,000. Pays on publication. Publishes ms an average of 2 months after acceptance. Byline given. Offers $25 kill fee. Buys all rights. Submit seasonal/holiday material 3 months in advance. Reports in 2 weeks on queries. Sample copy $1; free writer's guidelines.

Nonfiction: General interest, how-to, interview/profile and new product. No humor or excerpts of any kind. Buys 6-8 mss/year. Query with or without published clips, or send complete ms. Length: 200-1,000 words. Pays $150-350.

Photos: State availability of photos with submission. Reviews contact sheets. Offers $10-40 per photo. Model releases and identification of subjects required. Buys all rights.

LLAMAS MAGAZINE, The International Camelid Journal, Clay Press, Inc., P.O. Box 100, Herald CA 95638. (916)448-1668. FAX: (916)448-1668. Editor: Cheryl Dal Porto. Magazine published 8 times per year covering llamas, alpacas, camels, vicunas and guanacos. Estab. 1979. Circ. 5,500. **Pays on acceptance.** Publishes ms an average of 4 months after acceptance. Byline given. Buys first rights, second serial (reprint) rights and makes work-for-hire assignments. Submit seasonal/holiday material 6 months in advance. Simultaneous and previously published submissions OK. Reports in 2 weeks. Sample copy for 4 first class stamps; writer's guidelines for #10 SASE.

Nonfiction: How-to (on anything related to raising llamas), humor, interview/profile, opinion, personal experience, photo feature and travel (to countries where there are camelids). "All articles must have a tie in to one of the camelid species." Buys 30 mss/year. Query with published clips. Length: 1,000-5,000 words. Pays $50-300 for assigned articles; pays $50-150 for unsolicited articles. May pay new writers with contributor copies. Sometimes pays the expenses of writers on assignment.

Photos: State availability of photos with submission or send photos with submission. Reviews transparencies and 5×7 prints. Offers $25-100 per photo. Captions, model releases and identification of subjects required. Buys one-time rights.

Fillers: Anecdotes, gags and short humor. Buys 25/year. Length: 100-500 words. Pays $25-50.

Tips: "Get to know the llama folk in your area and query us with an idea. We are open to any and all ideas involving llamas, alpacas and the rest of the camelids. We are always looking for good photos. You must know about camelids to write for us."

NATIONAL CATTLEMEN, National Cattlemen's Association, 5420 S. Quebec St., Englewood CO 80111. (303)694-0305. Editor: Scott R. Cooper. 15% freelance written. Monthly trade journal on the beef-cattle industry. "We deal extensively with animal health, price outlook, consumer demand for beef, costs of production, emerging technologies, developing export markets, marketing and risk management." Estab. 1985. Circ. 40,000. Pays on publication. Byline given. Buys all rights. Sample copy for 11×15 SAE.

Nonfiction: How-to (cut costs of production, risk management strategies), new product (emerging technologies), opinion, and technical (emerging technologies, animal health, price outlook). Upcoming issue will focus on state of the industry. Buys 10 mss/year. Query with published clips. Length: 1,500-1,750 words. Sidebars encouraged. Pays $250-300 for assigned articles. Pays expenses of writers on assignment.

Photos: Send photos with submission. Reviews negatives and transparencies. Identification of subjects required.

Columns/Departments: My View (opinions dealing with the beef cattle industry), 750 words. Query. Pays $250-300.

POLLED HEREFORD WORLD, 11020 NW Ambassador Dr., Kansas City MO 64153. (816)891-8400. FAX: (816)333-7365. Editor: Ed Bible. 1% freelance written. For "breeders of Polled Hereford cattle—about 80% registered breeders, 5% commercial cattle breeders; remainder are agribusinessmen in related fields." Monthly. Estab. 1947. Circ. 11,500. Not copyrighted. Buys "no unsolicited mss at present." Pays on publication. Publishes ms an average of 2 months after acceptance. Submit seasonal material "as early as possible: 2 months preferred." Reports in 1 month. Query first for reports of events, activities and features. Free sample copy.
Nonfiction: "Features on registered or commercial Polled Hereford breeders. Some on related agricultural subjects (pastures, fences, feeds, buildings, etc.). Mostly technical in nature; some human interest. Our readers make their living with cattle, so write for an informed, mature audience." Buys informational articles, how-to's, personal experience articles, interviews, profiles, historical and think pieces, nostalgia, photo features, coverage of successful business operations, articles on merchandising techniques, and technical articles. Length: "varies with subject and content of feature." Pays about 5¢/word ("usually about 50¢/column inch, but can vary with the value of material").
Photos: Purchased with mss, sometimes purchased without mss, or on assignment; captions required. "Only good quality b&w glossies accepted; any size. Good color prints or transparencies." Pays $2 for b&w, $2-25 for color. Pays $50 for color covers.

SHEEP! MAGAZINE, Rt. 1, Box 78, Helenville WI 53137. (414)593-8385. FAX: (414)593-8385. Editor: Dave Thompson. 50% freelance written. Prefers to work with published/established writers, but works with a small number of new/unpublished writers each year. Monthly magazine. "We're looking for clear, concise, useful information for sheep raisers who have a few sheep to a 1,000 ewe flock." Estab. 1980. Circ. 15,000. Pays on publication. Byline given. Offers $30 kill fee. Buys all rights. Makes work-for-hire assignments. Submit seasonal/holiday material 3 months in advance. Free sample copy and writer's guidelines.
Nonfiction: Book excerpts; information (on personalities and/or political, legal or environmental issues affecting the sheep industry); how-to (on innovative lamb and wool marketing and promotion techniques, efficient record-keeping systems or specific aspects of health and husbandry). Health and husbandry articles should be written by someone with extensive experience or appropriate credentials (i.e., a veterinarian or animal scientist); profiles (on experienced sheep producers who detail the economics and management of their operation); features (on small businesses that promote wool products and stories about local and regional sheep producer's groups and their activities); new products (of value to sheep producers; should be written by someone who has used them); and technical (on genetics, health and nutrition). First person narratives. Buys 80 mss/year. Query with published clips or send complete ms. Length: 750-2,500 words. Pays $45-250. Pays the expenses of writers on assignment.
Photos: "Color—vertical compositions of sheep and/or people—for our cover. Use only b&w inside magazine. B&w, 35mm photos or other visuals improve your chances of a sale." Pays $100 maximum for 35mm color transparencies; $20-50 for 5 × 7 b&w prints. Identification of subjects required. Buys all rights.
Tips: "Send us your best ideas and photos! We love good writing!"

Management

‡**AGWAY COOPERATOR**, P.O. Box 4933, Syracuse NY 13221. (315)477-6231. Editor: Jean Willis. 2% freelance written. For farmers. Published 9 times/year. Estab. 1964. **Pays on acceptance.** Publishes ms an average of 6 months after acceptance. Time between acceptance and publication varies considerably. Usually reports in 1 week. Free sample copy.
Nonfiction: Should deal with topics of farm or rural interest in the Northeastern U.S. Length: 1,200 words maximum. Pays $100-150, depending on length, illustrations.
Tips: "We prefer an Agway tie-in, if possible. Fillers don't fit into our format. We do not assign freelance articles."

FARM JOURNAL, 230 W. Washington Square, Philadelphia PA 19105. Editor: Earl Ainsworth. "The business magazine of American agriculture" is published 14 times/year with many regional editions. Material bought for one or more editions depending upon where it fits. Buys all rights. Byline given "except when article is too short or too heavily rewritten to justify one." **Pays on acceptance.** Payment is the same regardless of editions in which the piece is used.
Nonfiction: Timeliness and seasonableness are very important. Material must be highly practical and should be helpful to as many farmers as possible. Farmers' experiences should apply to one or more of these 8 basic commodities: corn, wheat, milo, soybeans, cotton, dairy, beef and hogs. Technical material must be accurate. No farm nostalgia. Query to describe a new idea that farmers can use. Length: 500-1,500 words. Pays 10-20¢/published word.

Photos: Much in demand either separately or with short how-to material in picture stories and as illustrations for articles. Warm human-interest-pix for covers—activities on modern farms. For inside use, shots of homemade and handy ideas to get work done easier and faster, farm news photos, and pictures of farm people with interesting sidelines. In b&w, 8×10 glossies are preferred; color submissions should be 2¼×2¼ for the cover, and 35mm for inside use. Pays $50 and up for b&w shot; $75 and up for color.

Tips: *"Farm Journal* now publishes in hundreds of editions reflecting geographic, demographic and economic sectors of the farm market."

FARM SHOW MAGAZINE, 20088 Kenwood Trail, P.O. Box 1029, Lakeville MN 55044. (612)469-5572. FAX: (612)469-5575. Editor: Mark A. Newhall. 10% freelance written. A bimonthly trade journal covering agriculture. Estab. 1977. Circ. 150,000. **Pays on acceptance.** Publishes ms an average of 4 months after acceptance. Byline sometimes given. Buys one-time and second serial (reprint) rights. Previously published submissions OK. Reports in 1 week. Free sample copy.

Nonfiction: How-to and new product. No general interest, historic or nostalgic articles. Buys 90 mss/year. Send complete ms. Length: 100-2,000 words. Pays $50-300.

Photos: Send photos with submission. Reviews any size color or b&w prints. Offers no additional payment for photos accepted with ms. Captions required. Buys one-time rights.

Tips: "We're looking for first-of-its-kind, inventions of the nuts-and-bolts variety for farmers."

FFA NEW HORIZONS, 5632 Mt. Vernon Memorial Highway, Alexandria VA 22309. (703)360-3600. FAX: (703)360-5524. Editor-in-Chief: Wilson W. Carnes. 20% freelance written. Prefers to work with published/established writers, but is eager to work with new/unpublished writers. Bimonthly magazine for members of the National FFA Organization who are students of agriculture in high school, ranging in age from 14-21 years; major interest in careers in agriculture/agribusiness and other youth interest subjects. Circ. 400,000. **Pays on acceptance.** Publishes ms an average of 4 months after acceptance. Buys all rights. Byline given. Submit seasonal/holiday material 4 months in advance. Query for electronic submissions. Usually reports in 1 month. Free sample copy and writer's guidelines.

Nonfiction: How-to for youth (outdoor-type such as camping, hunting, fishing); and informational (getting money for college, farming; and other help for youth). Informational, personal experience and interviews are used only if FFA members or former members are involved. "Science-oriented material is being used more extensively as we broaden people's understanding of agriculture." Buys 15 unsolicited mss/year. Query or send complete ms. Length: 1,000 words maximum. Pays 4-6¢/word. Sometimes pays the expenses of writers on assignment.

Photos: Purchased with mss (5×7 or 8×10 b&w glossies; 35mm or larger color transparencies). Pays $15 for b&w; $30-40 for inside color; $100 for cover.

Tips: "Find an FFA member who has done something truly outstanding that will motivate and inspire others, or provide helpful information for a career in farming, ranching or agribusiness. We've increased emphasis on agriscience and marketing. We're accepting manuscripts now that are tighter and more concise. Get straight to the point."

FORD NEW HOLLAND NEWS, P.O. Box 1895, New Holland PA 17557. Editor: Gary Martin. 50% freelance written. Works with a small number of new/unpublished writers each year. Magazine on agriculture; published 8 times/year; designed to entertain and inform farm families. Estab. 1960. **Pays on acceptance.** Publishes ms an average of 9 months after acceptance. Byline given. Offers negotiable kill fee. Buys first North American serial rights, one-time rights and second serial (reprint) rights. Submit seasonal/holiday material 6 months in advance. Simultaneous queries and previously published submissions OK. Reports in 1 month. Sample copy and writer's guidelines for 9×12 SASE and 2 first class stamps.

Nonfiction: "We need strong photo support for articles of 1,200-1,700 words on farm management and farm human interest." Buys 40 mss/year. Query. Pays $400-600. Sometimes pays the expenses of writers on assignment.

Photos: Send photos with query when possible. Reviews color transparencies. Pays $50-300. Captions, model release and identification of subjects required. Buys one-time rights.

Tips: "We thrive on good article ideas from knowledgeable farm writers. The writer must have an emotional understanding of agriculture and the farm family and must demonstrate in the article an understanding of the unique economics that affect farming in North America. We want to know about the exceptional farm managers, those leading the way in agriculture. We want new efficiencies and technologies presented through the real-life experiences of farmers themselves. Use anecdotes freely. Successful writers keep in touch with the editor as they develop the article."

HIGH PLAINS JOURNAL, The Farmer's Paper, High Plains Publishers, Inc., P.O. Box 760, Dodge City KS 67801. (316)227-7171. Editor: Galen Hubbs. 5% freelance written. Weekly tabloid with news, features and photos on all phases of farming and livestock production. Estab. 1884. Circ. 64,000. Pays on publication. Publishes ms an average of 1 month after acceptance. Byline given. Not copyrighted. Buys first serial rights. Submit seasonal/holiday material 1 month in advance. Simultaneous queries OK. Reports in 3 weeks on queries; 1 month on mss. Sample copy for $2.

Nonfiction: General interest (agriculture); how-to; interview/profile (farmers or stockmen within the High Plains area); and photo feature (agricultural). No rewrites of USDA, extension or marketing association releases. Buys 10-20 mss/year. Query with published clips. Length: 10-40 inches. Pays $1/column inch. Sometimes pays the expenses of writers on assignment.

Photos: State availability of photos. Pays $5-10 for 4×5 b&w prints. Captions and complete identification of subjects required. Buys one-time rights.

Tips: "Limit submissions to agriculture. Stories should not have a critical time element. Stories should be informative with correct information. Use quotations and bring out the human aspects of the person featured in profiles. Stories are too long or are too far from our circulation area to be beneficial."

MISSOURI FARM MAGAZINE, Total Concept Small Farming, Gardening, and Rural Living, Missouri Farm Publishing, Ridge Top Ranch, 3903 W. Ridge Trail Rd., Clark MO 65243. (314)687-3525. Editor: Ron Macher. 50% freelance written. Bimonthly magazine on small farms. "Magazine for small farmers and small-acreage landowners interested in diversification, direct marketing, alternative crops, minor breeds of livestock, exotics, home-based business, gardening, vegetable and small fruit crops, horses, draft horses and small stock." Estab. 1984. Circ. 5,000. Pays on publication. Publishes ms an average of 2 months after acceptance. Byline given. Buys first rights and second serial (reprint) rights to material in the magazine, for use in anthologies. Submit seasonal/holiday material 3 months in advance. Reports in 2 weeks on queries. Sample copy $2. Writer's guidelines for #10 SASE.

Nonfiction: How-to (small farming, gardening, alternative crops/livestock). "No political opinions, depressing articles." Buys 70 mss/year. Query with or without published clips. Please do *not* send completed mss without querying first. Length: 500-2,500 words. Pays $10-75. Pays in contributor copies or other premiums by individual negotiation.

Photos: Send photos with submission. Reviews contact sheets (b&w only), negatives and 3×5 and larger prints. Offers $4-10 per photo. Captions required. Buys one-time rights and nonexclusive reprint rights (for anthologies).

Tips: "We like upbeat, how-to articles on anything pertaining to the small farm. Come up with a good idea that we or competing publications haven't done before, and query. Good black and white photos are also a plus. Probably the best thing for freelancers to do is find people who lives on a small farm and are successful at something (raising hogs, bees, raspberries, etc.), then interview the people and get as much 'how-to' information about their operation as possible. We don't run just profiles: all of our stories have a 'how-to' angle, even if they feature one particular operation as an example. All manuscripts must be accompanied by a list of sources contacted. Lists of sources for more information (books, associations, etc.) for sidebars are also appreciated. The stories don't have to be about Missouri small farmers, just about successful small farmers."

PROGRESSIVE FARMER, Southern Progress Corp., 2100 Lakeshore Dr., Birmingham AL 35209. (205)877-6401. Editorial Director: Tom Curl. Editor: Jack Odle. 3% freelance written. Monthly agriculture trade journal. Country people, farmers, ranchers are our audience. Estab. 1886. Circ. 865,000. **Pays on acceptance.** Publishes ms an average of 4 months after acceptance. Byline sometimes given. Buys all rights. Reports in 3 weeks. Free sample copy and writer's guidelines.

Nonfiction: How-to (agriculture and country related), humor (farm related) and technical (agriculture). Buys 30-50 mss/year. Query with published clips. Length: 2,000 words maximum. Pays $100 minimum. Sometimes pays expenses of writers on assignment.

Photos: Send photos with submission. Reviews negatives and transparencies. Payment negotiable. Captions and identification of subjects required. Rights depend on assignment.

Columns/Departments: Handy Devices (need photos and short text on the little shop ideas that make farm work easier and rural living more enjoyable). Buys 70 mss/year Send complete ms. Length: 20-75 words. Pays $50.

Tips: Query with ideas compatible with basic tone of magazine.

SUCCESSFUL FARMING, 1716 Locust St., Des Moines IA 50336. (515)284-2897. Managing Editor: Gene Johnston. 3% freelance written. Prefers to work with published/established writers. Magazine for farm families that make farming their business. Published 12 times/year. Estab. 1902. Circ. 500,000. Buys all rights. **Pays on acceptance.** Publishes ms an average of 2 months after acceptance. Reports in 2 weeks. Sample copy for SAE and 5 first class stamps.

Nonfiction: Semitechnical articles on all aspects of farming, including production, business, country living and recreation with emphasis on how to apply this information to one's own farm family. Also articles on interesting farm people and activities. Buys 30 unsolicited mss/year. Query with outline. Length: about 1,000 words maximum. Pays $250-600. Sometimes pays the expenses of writers on assignment.

Photos: Jim Galbraith, art director. Prefers color with transparencies, not prints. Buys exclusive rights. Assignments are given, and sometimes a guarantee, provided the editors can be sure the photography will be acceptable.

Tips: "A frequent mistake made by writers in completing articles is that the focus of the story is not narrow enough and does not include enough facts, examples, dollar signs and a geographic and industry perspective. Greatest need is for short articles and fillers that are specific and to the point."

Miscellaneous

GLEANINGS IN BEE CULTURE, P.O. Box 706, Medina OH 44258. FAX: (216)725-5624. Editor: Mr. Kim Flottum. 50% freelance written. For beekeepers and those interested in the natural science of honey bees. Publishes environmentally oriented articles relating to honey bees or pollination. Monthly. Estab. 1873. Buys first North American serial rights. Pays on both publication and acceptance. Publishes ms an average of 4 months after acceptance. Reports in 1 month. Sample copy for 9 × 12 SAE and 5 first class stamps; free writer's guidelines.

Nonfiction: Interested in articles giving new ideas on managing bees. Also looking for articles on honey bee/environment connections or relationships. Also uses success stories about commercial beekeepers. No "how I began beekeeping" articles. No highly advanced, technical and scientific abstracts or impractical advice. Length: 2,000 word average. Pays $30-50/published page — on negotiation.

Photos: Sharp b&w photos (pertaining to honey bees, honey plants or related to story) purchased with mss. Can be any size, prints or enlargements, but 4 × 5 or larger preferred. Pays $7-10/picture.

Tips: "Do an interview story on commercial beekeepers who are cooperative enough to furnish accurate, factual information on their operations. Frequent mistakes made by writers in completing articles are that they are too general in nature and lack management knowledge."

UNITED CAPRINE NEWS, Double Mountain Press, Drawer A, Rotan TX 79546. (915)735-2278. Editor: Kim Pease. Managing Editor: Jeff Klein. 80% freelance written. A monthly tabloid covering dairy pygmy and angora goats. Estab. 1976. Circ. 5,000. Pays on publication. Publishes ms an average of 3 months after acceptance. Byline given. Buys first rights and makes work-for-hire assignments. Reports in 1 month. Sample copy $1.

Nonfiction: Interview/profile, new product, photo feature and technical — articles directed to all phases of goat keeping: management, showing, breeding and products. Buys 50 mss/year. Send complete ms. Length: open. Pays 25¢/column inch.

Photos: Send photos with submission. Reviews 5 × 7 prints. Offers 25¢/column inch. Captions required. Buys first rights.

Fillers: Facts and newsbreaks. Buys 25/year. Pays 25¢/column inch.

Tips: "We will consider any articles of an informative nature relating to goats that will benefit professional goat breeders. Most acceptable would be features on goat dairies or farms, technical data on health care and state-of-art topics related to breeding and genetics."

Regional

AG ALERT, California Farm Bureau Federation, 1601 Exposition Blvd., Sacramento CA 95815. (916)924-4140. Editor: Steve Adler. Managing Editor: Don Myrick. 10% freelance written. Weekly farm newspaper covering agriculture. Estab. 1978. Circ. 50,000. **Pays on acceptance.** Publishes ms an average of 1-2 months after acceptance. Byline given. Publication not copyrighted. Buys first North American serial rights. Query for electronic submissions. Reports in 3 weeks on queries; 6 weeks on mss. Free sample copy and writer's guidelines.

Nonfiction: How-to, technical, and news, all farm related. Special issue on irrigation each Sept. Buys 30-40 mss/year. Query. Length: 1,000-1,500 words. Pays $25-300. Sometimes pays expenses of writers on assignment.

Photos: State availability of photos with submission. Reviews contact sheets, negatives and transparencies. Offers no additional payment for photos accepted with ms. Captions required. Buys one-time rights.

Tips: "We need feature articles on farmers who are doing the job better than their neighbors. Articles must be specific to California. Be sure to query before sending mss."

‡**AGRI-TIMES NORTHWEST**, J/A Publishing Co., 206 S.E. Court, P.O. Box 189, Pendleton OR 97801. (503)276-7845. FAX: (503)276-7964. Editor: Virgil Rupp. Managing Editor: Jim Eardley. 50% freelance written. Weekly newspaper on agriculture in western Idaho, eastern Oregon and eastern Washington. "News, features about regional farmers/agribusiness *only*." Estab. 1983. Circ. 5,200. Pays 15th of month after publication. Publishes ms an average of 1 month after acceptance. Byline given. Buys

one-time rights. Submit seasonal/holiday material 1 month in advance. Simultaneous and previously published submissions OK. Sample 50¢ with 8×10 SAE and 4 first class stamps. Writer's guidelines for #10 SAE with 1 first class stamp.

Nonfiction: How-to (farming and ranching *regional*), humor (regional farming and ranching), interview/profile (regional farmers/ ranchers), photo feature (regional agriculture) and technical (regional farming and ranching). Buys 100 mss/year. Query with or without published clips, or send complete ms. Length: 750 words maximum. Pays 75¢ per column inch.

Photos: Send photos with submission. Reviews contact sheets, negatives and prints. Offers $5-10 per photo. Captions and identification of subjects required. Buys one-time rights.

Columns/Departments: Agri-Talk (quips, comments of farmers/ranchers). Buys 50 mss/year. Send complete ms. Length: 100 words maximum. Pays 75¢ per column inch.

Tips: "Focus on our region's agriculture. Be accurate."

ARKANSAS FARM & COUNTRY, Arkansas' Only Agricultural Journal, AgCom, Inc., 912 S. Grand, Stuttgart AR 72160. (501)673-3276/673-6283. Editor: Jeffrey Tennant. 20% freelance written. Monthly tabloid covering agriculture. Commercial farmers and ranchers doing business in Arkansas. Estab. 1985. Circ. 11,700. Pays on publication. Byline given. Negotiable kill fee. Buys one-time rights. Submit seasonal/holiday material 1 month in advance. Query for electronic submissions. Reports in 3 weeks on queries; 1 month on mss. Sample copy for 9×13 SAE with 3 first class stamps.

Nonfiction: How-to (farming or ranching only), humor (country or rural oriented), inspirational, interview/profile (farmer, rancher, agribusiness or legislator), new product, technical (farm oriented products or method). No general interest pieces without relevance to farming or country living. Buys 15-20 mss/year. Query with or without published clips, or send complete ms. Length: 125-3,000 words. Pays $1/printed inch.

Photos: State availability of photos with submission. Reviews contact sheets and 3×5 or larger prints. Offers $5-20 per photo. Captions and identification of subjects required. Buys one-time rights.

Tips: Query with good ideas that will be of interest to Arkansas farmers and ranchers. We serve their interests *only*. Keep mss short (15-40 inches maximum). Photos are helpful.

THE FARMER/DAKOTA FARMER, Webb Division/Intertec Publishing, 7900 International Dr., Minneapolis MN 55425. (612)851-9329. Editor: Tom Doughty. Managing Editor: David Hest. 20% freelance written. Magazine is published 19 times a year about agriculture in the Upper Midwest (MN, ND, SD). *"The Farmer/Dakota Farmer* provides timely indepth information on crop and livestock production, farm business, governmental affairs/policy and farm lifestyle—all tailored to our 3-state area of MN, ND and SD." Estab. 1882. Circ. 115,000. **Pays on acceptance.** Byline given. Buys first rights or one-time rights. Query for electronic submissions. Reports in 3 weeks on mss. Sample copy for 8×10 SAE.

Nonfiction: How-to (make money farming/ranching in the Upper Midwest) and personal experience (success stories on agriculture). Buys 15-25 mss/year. Query. Length: 300-1,200 words. Pays $100-500 for assigned articles; $100-300 for unsolicited articles. Sometimes pays expenses of writers on assignment.

Photos: Send photos with submission. Reviews contact sheets and transparencies. Offers no additional payment for photos accepted with ms. Captions and identification of subjects required. Buys one-time rights.

FARMWEEK, Mayhill Publications, Inc. 27 N. Jefferson, P.O. Box 90, Knightstown IN 46148. (317)345-5133. FAX: (317)345-5133, ext. 198. Editor: Nancy Searfoss. 5% freelance written. Agriculture newspaper that covers agriculture in Indiana, Ohio and Kentucky. Estab. 1955. Circ. 28,000. Pays on publication. Byline given. Buys first rights or second serial (reprint) rights. Submit seasonal/holiday material 1 month in advance. Simultaneous submissions OK. Reports on queries. Free sample copy and writer's guidelines.

Nonfiction: General interest (agriculture), interview/profile (ag leaders), new product, opinion (ag issues) and photo feature (Indiana, Ohio, Kentucky agriculture). "We don't want first person accounts or articles from states outside Indiana, Kentucky, Ohio (unless of general interest to all farmers and agribusiness)." Number of mss/year varies. Query with published clips. Length: 500-1,500 words. Pays $50 maximum. Sometimes pays expenses of writers on assignment.

Photos: State availability of photos with submission. Reviews contact sheets and 4×5 and 5×7 prints. Offers $5 maximum per photo. Identification of subjects required. Buys one-time rights.

Tips: "We want feature stories about farmers and agribusinessmen in Indiana, Ohio and Kentucky. How do they operate their business? Keys to success, etc.? Best thing to do is call us first with idea, or write. Could also be a story about some pressing issue in agriculture nationally that affects farmers everywhere."

‡IOWA REC NEWS, Suite 48, 8525 Douglas, Urbandale IA 50322. (515)276-5350. Editor: Karen Howe. Managing Editor: Jody Garlock. 5% freelance written. Emphasizes energy issues for residents of rural Iowa. Monthly magazine. Circ. 115,000. Pays on publication. Publishes ms an average of 3 months after acceptance. Buys first serial rights and second serial (reprint) rights. Not copyrighted. Simultaneous and previously published submissions OK.

Nonfiction: General interest, historical, humor, farm issues and trends, rural lifestyle trends, energy awareness features and photo feature. Send complete ms. Pays $40-60.

Tips: "The easiest way to break into our magazine is: research a particular subject well, include appropriate attributions to establish credibility, authority and include a couple paragraphs about the author. Reading and knowing about rural people is important. Stories that touch the senses or can improve the lives of the readers are highly considered, as are those with a strong Iowa angle. We prefer to tailor our articles to Iowa REC readers and use our staff's skills. Freelancers have the advantage of offering subject matter that existing staff may not be able to cover. Often, however, many articles lack evidence of actual research—they provide lots of information but do not include any sources to give the story any credibility. (Rarely is the author a renowned expert on the subject he's written about.) Inclusion of nice photos is also a plus. The most frequent mistakes made by writers are: lots of typos in copy, uncorrected; story too long, story too biased; no attribution to any source of info; and not relevant to electric consumers, rural living."

MAINE ORGANIC FARMER & GARDENER, Maine Organic Farmers & Gardeners Association, RR 2, Box 594, Lincolnville ME 04849. (207)622-3118. Editor: Jean English. 40% freelance written. Prefers to work with published/established writers. Bimonthly magazine covering organic farming and gardening for urban and rural farmers and gardeners and nutrition-oriented, environmentally concerned readers. "*MOF&G* promotes and encourages sustainable agriculture and environmentally sound living. Our primary focus is organic farming, gardening and forestry, but we also deal with local, national and international agriculture, food and environmental issues." Circ. 10,000. Pays on publication. Publishes ms an average of 8 months after acceptance. Byline and bio given. Buys first North American serial rights, one-time rights, first serial rights, or second serial (reprint) rights. Submit seasonal/holiday material 9 months in advance. Simultaneous queries, and simultaneous or previously published submissions OK. Reports in 2 months. Sample copy $2; free writer's guidelines.

Nonfiction: Humor; book reviews; how-to information can be handled as first person experience, technical/research report, or interview/profile focusing on farmer, gardener, food plant, forests, livestock, weeds, insects, trees, renewable energy, recycling, nutrition, health, non-toxic pest control, organic farm management. We use profiles of New England organic farmers and gardeners and news reports (500-1,000 words) dealing with U.S./international sustainable ag research and development, rural development, recycling projects, environmental problem solutions, organic farms with broad impact, cooperatives, community projects, American farm crisis and issues, food issues. Buys 30 mss/year. Query with published clips or send complete ms. Length: 1,000-3,000 words. Pays $20-100. Sometimes pays expenses of writers on assignment.

Photos: State availability of photos with query; send photos or proof sheet with manuscript. Prefer b&w but can use color slides or negatives in a pinch. Captions, model releases and identification of subjects required. Buys one-time rights.

Tips: "We are a nonprofit organization. Our publication's primary mission is to inform and educate. Our readers want to know how to, but they also want to enjoy the reading and know the source/expert/writer. We don't want impersonal how-to articles that sound like Extension bulletins or textbooks. As consumers' demand for organically grown food increases, we are increasingly interested in issues about certification of organic food, legislation that affects organic growers, and marketing of organic food."

NEW ENGLAND FARM BULLETIN & GARDEN GAZETTE, Jacob's Meadow, Inc., P.O. Box 147, Cohasset MA 02025. Editor-in-Chief: V.A. Lipsett. Managing Editor: M.S. Maire. 5% freelance written. Works with a small number of new/unpublished writers each year. A biweekly newsletter covering New England farming and gardening. Estab. 1976. Circ. 11,000. Pays on publication. Publishes ms an average of 2 months after acceptance. Byline given. Buys first North American serial rights. Submit seasonal/holiday material 6 months in advance. Reports in 1 week. Sample copy and writer's guidelines for #10 SAE and $1.25.

Nonfiction: Essays (farming/agriculture), general interest, historical, how-to, personal experience and technical. All articles must be related to New England farming. Buys 6-12 mss/year. Query or send complete ms. Length: 500-1,000 words.

Tips: "We would probably require the writer to live in New England or to have an unmistakable grasp of what New England is like; must also know farmers." Especially interested in general articles on New England crops/livestocks, specific breeds, crop strains and universal agricultural activity in New England.

NEW ENGLAND FARMER, Northeast Farm Publications, P.O. Box 8, 96 Targosh Rd., Candor NY 13743. (607)659-4326. Editor: Alan Knight. 75% freelance written. Monthly farm publication covering New England agriculture for farmers. Estab. 1822. Circ. 18,000. **Pays on acceptance.** Byline given. Buys all rights and makes work-for-hire assignments. Submit material 2 months in advance. Reports as soon as possible. Free sample copy.

Nonfiction: How-to, interview/profile, opinion and technical. No romantic views of farming. "We use on-the-farm interviews with good black and white photos that combine technical information with human interest. Also need short news items expressly about New England farming, agricultural issues relevant to New England farmers." Buys 150 mss/year. Send complete ms. Pays $75-200. Sometimes pays the expenses of writers on assignment.

Photos: Send photos with ms. Payment for photos is included in payment for articles. Reviews b&w contact sheets and 8 × 10 b&w prints.

Tips: "Good, accurate stories needing minimal editing, with art, of interest to commercial farmers in New England are welcome. A frequent mistake made by writers is sending us items that do not meet our needs; generally, they'll send stories that don't have a New England focus. Writers with farm background are particularly appreciated. Writers from out of the region have slim chance."

THE OHIO FARMER, 1350 W. 5th Ave., Columbus OH 43212. (614)486-9637. Editor: Andrew Stevens. 10% freelance written. "We are backlogged with submissions and prefer not to receive unsolicited submissions at this time." For Ohio farmers and their families. Biweekly magazine. Circ. 81,000. Usually buys all rights. Pays on publication. Publishes ms an average of 2 months after acceptance. Reports in 2 weeks. Query for electronic submissions. Sample copy $1; free writer's guidelines.

Nonfiction: Technical and on-the-farm stories. Buys informational, how-to and personal experience. Buys 5 mss/year. Submit complete ms. Length: 600-700 words. Pays $30.

Photos: Photos purchased with ms with no additional payment, or without ms. Pays $5-25 for b&w; $35-100 for color. 4 × 5 b&w glossies; and transparencies or 8 × 10 color prints.

Tips: "We are now doing more staff-written stories. We buy very little freelance material."

PENNSYLVANIA FARMER, Harcourt Brace Jovanovich Publications, 704 Lisburn Rd., Camp Hill PA 17011. (717)761-6050. Editor: John Vogel. 10% freelance written. A monthly farm business magazine "oriented to providing readers with ideas to help their businesses and personal lives." Estab. 1877. Circ. 68,000. Pays on publication. Publishes ms an average of 3 months after acceptance. Byline sometimes given. Buys first-time rights. Submit seasonal/holiday material 3 months in advance. Simultaneous submissions OK. Reports in 2 weeks. Writer's guidelines for #10 SASE.

Nonfiction: Humor, inspirational and technical. No stories without a strong tie to Mid-Atlantic farming. Buys 15 mss/year. Query. Length: 500-1,000 words. Pays $50-150. Sometimes pays the expenses of writers on assignment.

Photos: Send photos with submission. Reviews contact sheets, 35mm transparencies and 5 × 7 prints. $25-50 for each b&w photo accepted with ms. Captions and identification of subjects required. Buys one-time rights.

WYOMING RURAL ELECTRIC NEWS, P.O. Box 380, Casper WY 82602. (307)234-6152. Editor: Jack Rollison. 25% freelance written. For audience of small town rural people, farmers and ranchers. Monthly magazine. Estab. 1950. Circ. 30,000. Not copyrighted. Byline given. Pays on publication. Publishes ms an average of 3 months after acceptance. Buys first serial rights. Will consider simultaneous submissions. Submit seasonal material 2 months in advance. Reports in 1 month. Free sample copy for SAE and 3 first class stamps.

Nonfiction and Fiction: Wants energy-related material, "people" features, historical pieces about Wyoming and the West, and things of interest to Wyoming's rural people. Buys informational, humor, historical, nostalgia and photo mss. Submit complete ms. Buys 25-30 mss/year. Length for nonfiction and fiction: 800-1,500 words. Pays $25-50. Buys some experimental, western, humorous and historical fiction. Pays $25-50. Sometimes pays the expenses of writers on assignment.

Photos: Photos purchased with accompanying ms with additional payment, or purchased without ms. Captions required. Pays up to $50 for cover photos. Color only.

Tips: "Study an issue or two of the magazine to become familiar with our focus and the type of freelance material we're using. Submit entire manuscript. Don't submit a regionally set story from some other part of the country and merely change the place names to Wyoming. Photos and illustrations (if appropriate) are always welcomed."

Finance

These magazines deal with banking, investment and financial management. Publications that use similar material but have a less technical slant are listed under the Consumer Business and Finance section.

THE BOTTOM LINE, The News and Information Publication for Canada's Financial Professionals, Bottom Line Publications Inc., 75 Clegg Rd., Markham, Ontario L3R 9V6 Canada. (416)474-9532. FAX: (416)474-9803. Editor: Gundi Jeffrey. 35% freelance written. Monthly tabloid on accounting/ finance/ business. "Reaches 80% of all Canadian accountants. Information should be news/commentary/analysis of issues or issues of interest to or about accountants." Estab. 1985. Circ. 48,000. Pays on publication. Publishes ms an average of 2 weeks to 4 months after acceptance. Byline given. Buys first rights. Query for electronic submissions. Free sample copy.

Photos: State availability of photos with submission. Offers $50 maximum per photo. Buys one-time rights.

CHEKLIST, Magazine for Check Cashers, Chek-Mate, 450 Main St., Springfield MA 01105. (413)736-2517. Editor: A.J. Bonavita. 100% freelance written. Quarterly magazine. The majority of our readers are owners of check cashing stores. The rest have an interest in or sell to these stores. They look to the magazine for advice, news, items of interest, advertisements. Estab. 1989. Circ. 3,400. Pays on publication. Publishes ms an average of 1 month after acceptance. Byline given. Buys one-time rights. Submit seasonal/holiday material 3 months in advance. Simultaneous and previously published submissions OK. Query for electronic submissions. Reports in 1 week on queries; 1 month on mss. Sample copy for 9 × 12 SAE with 5 first class stamps. Free writer's guidelines.

Nonfiction: David S. Rosen, marketing director. Book excerpts, exposé, general interest, historical/nostalgic, humor, inspirational, interview/profile, new product, opinion (does not mean letters to the editor), personal experience, photo feature, technical. Buys 20-30 mss/year. Query with or without published clips, or send complete ms. Length: 500 words minimum. Pays $100-300 for assigned articles; $50 minimum for unsolicited articles.

Photos: Send photos with submission. Reviews prints. Offers no additional payment for photos accepted with ms. Identification of subjects required. Buys one-time rights.

Columns/Departments: New Products/Series (generic analysis of new technologies), 500-1,000 words; Profile (person in or near industry), 500-1,500 words. Buys 10-15 mss/year. Query. Pays $100-300.

Fillers: Anecdotes, facts, short humor.

Tips: "Reading really is the best way, but we do our best to outline methods in guidelines. The feature story is the most open. This can range from a phase of the business to a story about related industries or items."

‡CONSUMER LENDING REPORT, Warren Gorham & Lamont, 40th Floor, One Penn Plaza, New York NY 10119. (212)971-5000. FAX: (212)971-5025. Editor: Natalie Baumer. 75% freelance written. A monthly trade journal covering all aspects of consumer lending. Circ. 3,000. Pays on publication. No byline given. Free sample copy available.

Nonfiction: How-to (market, analyze, retail banking services); strategic planning and trends; developments in banking technology. Query with or without published clips, or send complete ms. Length: 120-150 lines. Pays $1.50/line.

EQUITIES, OTC Review, Inc., 37 E. 28th St., Suite 706, New York NY 10016. (212)685-6244. Editor: Robert J. Flaherty. 50% freelance written. A monthly magazine covering publicly owned middle market and emerging growth companies. "We are a financial magazine covering the fastest-growing companies in the world. We study the management of companies and act as critics reviewing their performances. We aspire to be 'The Shareholder's Friend.' " Estab. 1951. Circ. 27,000. Pays on publication. Publishes ms an average of 2 months after acceptance. Byline given. Buys first rights or reprint rights. Sample copy for 9 × 12 SAE with 5 first class stamps.

Nonfiction: New product and technical. Buys 30 mss/year. "We must know the writer first as we are careful about whom we publish. A letter of introduction with résumé and clips is the best way to introduce yourself. Financial writing requires specialized knowledge and a feel for people as well, which can be a tough combination to find." Query with published clips. Length: 300-1,500 words. Pays $150-750 for assigned articles, more for very difficult or investigative pieces. Carries guest columns by famous money managers who are not writing for cash payments, but to showcase their ideas and approach. Pays expenses of writers on assignment.

Photos: Send photos with submission. Reviews contact sheets, negatives, transparencies and prints. Offers no additional payment for photos accepted with ms. Identification of subjects required.

Columns/Departments: Pays $25-75 for assigned items only.

Tips: "Anyone who enjoys analyzing a business and telling the story of the people who started it, or run it today, is a potential *Equities* contributor. But to protect our readers and ourselves, we are careful about who writes for us. Business writing is an exciting area and our stories reflect that. If a writer relies on numbers and percentages to tell his story, rather than the individuals involved, the result will be numbingly dull."

THE FEDERAL CREDIT UNION, National Association of Federal Credit Unions, P.O. Box 3769, Washington DC 20007. (703)522-4770. Editor: Patrick M. Keefe. 25% freelance written. "Looking for writer with financial, banking or credit union experience, but will work with inexperienced (unpublished) writers based on writing skill." Bimonthly magazine covering credit unions. Circ. 8,200. Pays on publication. Publishes ms an average of 3 months after acceptance. Byline sometimes given. Buys first North American serial rights. Submit seasonal/holiday material 5 months in advance. Simultaneous submissions OK. Query for electronic submissions. Reports in 1 month. Writer's guidelines for #10 SASE.

Nonfiction: How-to, interview/profile, new product, legal, technical and credit union operations innovations. Special issues include Technology for Financial Institutions (summer); Purchasing (winter). Query with published clips. Length: 3,000-6,000 words. Pays $200-1,000 for assigned articles.

Photos: Send photos with submission. Reviews 35mm transparencies and 5×7 prints. Offers no additional payment for photos accepted with ms. Model releases and identification of subjects required. Buys all rights.

Tips: "Provide resume or listing of experience pertinent to subject. We seek tips on better ways for credit unions to operate." Areas most open to freelancers are "technical articles/how-to/reports on credit union operations, innovation."

‡FINANCIAL TECHNOLOGY NEWS, #2030, 150 Nassau St., New York NY 10038. (212)267-7709. Editor: Phil Hall. Associate Editor: John Sullivan. 50% freelance written. Monthly tabloid covering technology and automation within the financial services industry. Estab. 1990. Circ. 10,000. Pays on publication. Byline given. No kill fee. Submit seasonal/holiday material 3 months in advance. Simultaneous submissions accepted. Reports in 3 weeks on queries. Free sample copy.

Nonfiction: Interview/profile, new product, opinion and technical. Buys 15 mss/year. Query. Length: 800-3,000 words. Pays $5/column inch for assigned articles. Sometimes pays expenses of writers on assignment.

Photos: State availability of photos with submission. Reviews 5×7 prints. Additional payment for photos accepted with ms "negotiable." Captions required. Buys all rights.

FINANCIAL WOMAN TODAY, Suite 1400, 500 N. Michigan Ave., Chicago IL 60611. (312)661-1700. FAX: (312)661-0769. Managing Editor: Stacy Day. 10-15% freelance written. Monthly newspaper for members of *Financial Women International* and paid subscribers covering banking, insurance, financial planning, diversified financials, credit unions, thrifts, investment banking and other industry segments. Circ. 22,000. Publishes ms an average of 2 months after acceptance. Byline given. Buys all rights. Submit seasonal material 2 months in advance. Simultaneous queries OK. Reports in approximately 1 month. Sample copy $1.

Nonfiction: "We are looking for articles in the general areas of financial services, career advancement, businesswomen's issues and management. Because the financial services industry is in a state of flux at present, articles on how to adapt to and benefit from this fact, both personally and professionally, are particularly apt." Query with resume and clips of published work. Length: 500-3,000 words. Pays variable rates.

Photos: "Photos and other graphic material can make an article more attractive to us." Captions and model release required.

Tips: "We're looking for writers who can write effectively about the people who work in the industry and combine that with hard data on how the industry is changing. We're especially interested in how companies are dealing with workforce issues such as childcare, productivity, customer service, pay equity and training."

ILLINOIS BANKER, Illinois Bankers Association, Suite 1111, 111 N. Canal, Chicago IL 60606. (312)876-9900. FAX: (312)876-3826. Vice President, Public Affairs: Martha Rohlfing. Production: Cindy Altman. Monthly magazine about banking for top decision makers and executives, bank officers, title and insurance company executives, elected officials and individual subscribers interested in banking products and services. Estab. 1916. Circ. 3,000. Pays on publication. Publishes ms an average of 4 months after acceptance. Byline given. Buys first serial rights. Phone queries OK. Submit material 6 weeks prior to publication. Simultaneous submissions OK. Free sample copy, writer's guidelines and editorial calendar.

Nonfiction: Interview (ranking government and banking leaders); personal experience (along the lines of customer relations); and technical (specific areas of banking). "The purpose of the publication is to educate, inform and guide its readers on public policy issues affecting banks, new ideas in management and operations, and banking and business trends in the Midwest. Any clear, fresh approach geared to a specific area of banking, such as agricultural bank management, credit, lending, marketing and trust is what we want." Send complete ms. Length: 825-3,000 words. Pays $75-100.

INDEPENDENT BANKER, Independent Bankers Association of America, P.O. Box 267, Sauk Centre MN 56378. (612)352-6546. Editor: Norman Douglas. 15% freelance written. Works with a small number of new/unpublished writers each year. Monthly magazine for the administrators of small, independent banks. Estab. 1950. Circ. 10,000. **Pays on acceptance.** Publishes ms an average of 3 months after acceptance. Byline given. Not copyrighted. Buys all rights. Reports in 1 week. Sample copy and writer's guidelines for 9×12 SAE and 5 first class stamps.

Nonfiction: How-to (banking practices and procedures); interview/profile (popular small bankers); technical (bank accounting, automation); and banking trends. "Factual case histories, banker profiles or research pieces of value to bankers in the daily administration of their banks." No material that ridicules banking and finance or puff pieces on products and services. Buys 12 mss/year. Query. Length: 2,000-2,500 words. Pays $300 maximum.

Tips: "In this magazine, the emphasis is on material that will help small banks compete with large banks and large bank holding companies. We look for innovative articles on small bank operations and administration."

Photos: State availability of photos with submission. Reviews 3¾ transparencies and 5×7 prints. Offers no additional payment for photos accepted with ms. Identification of subjects required. Buys one-time rights.

Tips: "Freelancers should know the major players in the market they are trying to crack, and how those players relate to the market."

RESEARCH MAGAZINE, Ideas for Today's Investors, Research Services, 2201 3rd St., San Francisco CA 94107. (415)621-0220. Editor: Anne Evers. 50% freelance written. Monthly business magazine of corporate profiles and subjects of interest to stockbrokers. Estab. 1977. Circ. 80,000. Pays on publication. Publishes ms an average of 2 months after acceptance. Byline given. Offers 20% kill fee. Buys first North American serial rights or second serial (reprint) rights. Query for electronic submissions. Reports in 1 month. Sample copy for 9×12 SAE with 4 first class stamps; writer's guidelines for #10 SASE.

Nonfiction: How-to (sales tips), interview/profile, new product, financial products. Buys approx. 50 mss/year. Query with published clips. Length: 1,000-3,000 words. Pays 300-900. Sometimes pays expenses of writers on assignment.

Tips: "Only submit articles that fit our editorial policy and are appropriate for our audience. *Only the non-corporate profile section is open to freelancers.* We use local freelancers on a regular basis for corporate profiles."

SECONDARY MARKETING EXECUTIVE, LDJ Corporation, P.O. Box 2330, Waterbury CT 06722. (203)755-0158. FAX: (203)755-3480. Editorial Director: John Florian. 30% freelance written. A monthly tabloid on secondary marketing. "The magazine is read monthly by executives in financial institutions who are involved with secondary marketing, which is the buying and selling of mortgage loans and servicing rights. The editorial slant is toward how-to and analysis of trends, rather than spot news." Estab. 1968. Circ. 27,000. **Pays on acceptance.** Publishes ms an average of 1 month after acceptance. Byline given. 30% kill fee. Buys first rights. Submit seasonal/holiday material 4 months in advance. Query for electronic submissions. Reports in 1 week. Free sample copy and writer's guidelines.

Nonfiction: How-to (how to improve secondary marketing operations and profits) and opinion. Buys 20 mss/year. Query. Length: 800-1,200 words. Pays $200-400.

Photos: State availability of photos with submission. Reviews contact sheets. Offers $25 per photo. Captions, model releases and identification of subjects required. Buys one-time rights.

THE TRADER, (formerly *The Futures and Options Trader*), DeLong–Western Publishing Co., 13618 Scenic Crest Dr., Yucaipa CA 92399. (714)797-3532. Editor: Kent DeLong. Managing Editor: Jeanne Johnson. 50% freelance written. Monthly newspaper covering futures and other speculative investments. Publishes "basic descriptions of trading systems or other regarding speculative investments, information which would be useful to traders. No hype or sales-related articles." Estab. 1986. Circ. 20,000. **Pays on acceptance.** Publishes ms an average of 1 month after acceptance. Not copyrighted. Buys various rights. Simultaneous submissions OK. Query for electronic submissions. Free sample copy and writer's guidelines. Any description of reasonable speculative investments.

Nonfiction: Technical and general trading-related articles; any description of reasonable speculative investments. Buys 35 mss/year. Send complete ms. Length: 250-1,000 words. Pays $10-100 for unsolicited articles.

Columns/Departments: Options Trader; Spread Trader (futures and options spread and arbitrage trading); Precious Metals Trader; and Index Trader (stock index trading) and The Speculator. Buys

35 mss/year. Send complete ms. Length: 250-1,000 words. Pays $10-100.
Tips: "Authors should be active in the markets."

Fishing

PACIFIC FISHING, Salmon Bay Communications, 1515 NW 51st St., Seattle WA 98107. (206)789-5333. FAX: (206)784-5545. Editor: Steve Shapiro. 75% freelance written. Eager to work with new/unpublished writers. Monthly business magazine for commercial fishermen and others in the West Coast commercial fishing industry. *Pacific Fishing* views the fisherman as a small businessman and covers all aspects of the industry, including harvesting, processing and marketing. Estab. 1979. Circ. 10,000. Pays on publication. Publishes ms an average of 2 months after acceptance. Byline given. Offers 10-15% kill fee on assigned articles deemed unsuitable. Buys one-time rights. Queries highly recommended. Reports in 1 month. Free sample copy and writer's guidelines.
Nonfiction: Interview/profile and technical (usually with a business hook or slant). "Articles must be concerned specifically with *commercial* fishing. We view fishermen as small businessmen and professionals who are innovative and success-oriented. To appeal to this reader, *Pacific Fishing* offers four basic features: technical, how-to articles that give fisherman hands-on tips that will make their operation more efficient and profitable; practical, well-researched business articles discussing the dollars and cents of fishing, processing and marketing; profiles of a fisherman, processor or company with emphasis on practical business and technical areas; and in-depth analysis of political, social, fisheries management and resource issues that have a direct bearing on West Coast commercial fishermen." Buys 20 mss/year. Query noting whether photos are available, and enclosing samples of previous work. Length: 1,500-2,500 words. Pays 10-15¢/word. Sometimes pays the expenses of writers on assignment.
Photos: "We need good, high-quality photography, especially color, of West Coast commercial fishing. We prefer 35mm color slides. Our rates are $150 for cover; $50-100 for inside color; $25-50 for b&w and $10 for table of contents."
Tips: "Because of the specialized nature of our audience, the editor strongly recommends that freelance writers query the magazine in writing with a proposal. Most of our shorter items are staff written. Our freelance budget is such that we get the most benefit by using it for feature material. The most frequent mistakes made by writers are not keeping to specified length and failing to do a complete job on statistics that may be a part of the story."

‡WESTCOAST FISHERMAN, Westcoast Publishing Ltd., 1496 West 72 Ave., Vancouver, British Columbia V6P 3C8 Canada. (604)266-8611. Editor: David Rahn. 50% freelance written. Monthly trade journal covering commercial fishing in B.C. "We're a non-political non-aligned magazine dedicated to the people in the B.C. commercial fishing industry. Our publication reflects and celebrates the individuals and communities that collectively constitute B.C. fishermen." Pays on publication. Byline given. Buys first rights and one-time rights. Previously published submissions OK. Query for electronic submission. Reports in 1 month on queries and mss. Free writer's guidelines.
Nonfiction: Interview/profile, photo feature, technical. Buys 40-50 mss/year. Query with or without published clips, or send complete ms. Length: 250-2,500 words. Pays $40-700.
Photos: Send photos with submission. Reviews contact sheets, negatives, 24×36 transparencies and 5×7 prints. Offers $5-100 per photo. Identification of subjects required. Buys one-time rights.
Poetry: Avant-garde, free verse, Haiku, light verse and traditional. "We use poetry written by or for west coast fishermen." Buys 6 poems/year. Length: 1 page. Pay is same as editorial copy.

Florists, Nurseries and Landscaping

Readers of these publications are involved in growing, selling or caring for plants, flowers and trees. Magazines geared to consumers interested in gardening are listed in the Consumer Home and Garden section.

FLORAL & NURSERY TIMES, XXX Publishing Enterprises Ltd., P.O. Box 699, Wilmette IL 60091. (708)256-8777. FAX: (708)256-8791. Editor: Barbara Gilbert. 10% freelance written. A bimonthly trade journal covering wholesale and retail horticulture and floriculture. Estab. 1979. Circ. 17,500. Pays on publication. Byline given. Buys simultaneous rights. Submit seasonal/holiday material 3 months in advance. Simultaneous submissions OK. Reports in 2 weeks. Sample copy for 9×12 SAE and $3; writer's guidelines for #10 SASE.

Nonfiction: General interest and technical. Buys 20 mss/year. Query with or without published clips, or send complete ms. Payment is negotiable.
Photos: State availability of photos with submission. Reviews prints. Offers no additional payment for photos accepted with ms. Captions and identification of subjects required. Buys simultaneous rights.
Columns/Departments: Care & Handling (horticultural products). Query. Payment negotiable.

FLORIST, Florists' Transworld Delivery Association, 29200 Northwestern Hwy., Box 2227, Southfield MI 48037. (313)355-9300. Editor-in-Chief: William P. Golden. Managing Editor: Susan L. Nicholas. 1% freelance written. For retail florists, floriculture growers, wholesalers, researchers and teachers. Monthly magazine. Circ. 28,000. **Pays on acceptance.** Publishes ms an average of 2 months after acceptance. Buys one-time rights. Pays 10-25% kill fee. Byline given "unless the story needs a substantial rewrite." Phone queries OK. Submit seasonal/holiday material 4 months in advance. Simultaneous and previously published submissions OK. Reports in 1 month.
Nonfiction: How-to (more profitably run a retail flower shop, grow and maintain better quality flowers, etc.); general interest (to floriculture and retail floristry); and technical (on flower and plant growing, breeding, etc.). Buys 5 unsolicited mss/year. Query with published clips. Length: 1,200-3,000 words. Pays 20¢/word.
Photos: "We do not like to run stories without photos." State availability of photos with query. Pays $10-25 for 5×7 b&w photos or color transparencies. Buys one-time rights.
Tips: "Send samples of published work with query. Suggest several ideas in query letter."

FLOWER NEWS, 549 W. Randolph St., Chicago IL 60661. (312)236-8648. FAX: (312)236-8891. Editors: M. Karen Baldwin and Rosemary C. Martin. For retail, wholesale florists, floral suppliers, supply jobbers and growers. Weekly newspaper. Estab. 1946. Circ. 18,000. **Pays on acceptance.** Byline given. Submit seasonal/holiday material at least 2 months in advance. Previously published submissions OK. Reports "immediately." Sample copy for 10×13 SAE and 10 first class stamps.
Nonfiction: How-to (increase business, set up a new shop, etc.; anything floral related without being an individual shop story); informational (general articles of interest to industry); and technical (grower stories related to industry, but not individual grower stories). Submit complete ms. Length: 3-5 typed pages. Payment varies.
Photos: "We do not buy individual pictures. They may be enclosed with manuscript at regular manuscript rate (b&w only)."

GARDEN SUPPLY RETAILER, Chilton Publishing, 1 Chilton Way, Radnor PA 19089. (215)964-4327. Editor: Jan Brenny. 5% freelance written. Prefers to work with published/established writers but "quality work is more important than experience of the writer." Monthly magazine for lawn and garden retailers. Estab. 1950. Circ. 41,000. Pays on acceptance in most cases. Publishes ms an average of 3-4 months after acceptance. Buys first serial rights, and occasionally second serial (reprint) rights. Previously published submissions "in different fields" OK as long as not in overlapping fields such as hardware, nursery growers, etc. Reports in 1 month on rejections, acceptance may take longer. Sample copy for 9×12 SAE and $1 postage.
Nonfiction: "We aim to provide retailers with management, merchandising, tax planning and computer information. No technical advice on how to care for lawns, plants and lawn mowers. Articles should be of interest to *retailers* of garden supply products. Stories should tell retailers something about the industry that they don't already know; show them how to make more money by better merchandising or management techniques; address a concern or problem directly affecting retailers or the industry." Buys 6-7 mss/year. Send complete ms or rough draft plus clips of previously published work. Length: 800-1,000 words. Pays $150-200.
Photos: Send photos with ms. Reviews color negatives and transparencies, and 5×7 b&w prints. Captions and identification of subjects required.
Tips: "We will not consider manuscripts offered to 'overlapping' publications such as the hardware industry, nursery growers, etc. Query letters outlining an idea should include at least a partial rough draft; lists of titles are uninteresting. We want business-oriented articles specifically relevant to interests and concerns of retailers of lawn and garden products. We seldom use filler material. Freelancers submitting articles to our publication will find it increasingly difficult to get acceptance as we will be soliciting stories from industry experts and will not have much budget for general freelance material."

For explanation of symbols, see the Key to Symbols and Abbreviations on Page 5. For unfamiliar words, see the Glossary.

THE GROWING EDGE, New Moon Publishing Inc., Suite 201, 215 SW 2nd, P.O. Box 1027, Corvallis OR 97339. (503)757-2511. FAX: (503)757-0028. Editor: Don Parker. 60% freelance written. Eager to work with new or unpublished writers. Quarterly magazine signature covering indoor and outdoor high-tech gardening techniques and tips. Estab. 1980. Circ. 25,000. Pays on publication. Publishes ms an average of 3 months after acceptance. Byline given. Buys first serial rights and reprint rights. Submit seasonal/holiday material at least 6 months in advance. Query for electronic submissions. Sample copy $6.

Nonfiction: Book excerpts and reviews relating to high-tech gardening, general interest, how-to, interview/profile, personal experience and technical. Query first. Length: 500-2,500 words. Pays 7½¢/word.

Photos: Pays $50/color cover photos; $10-30/color inside photo; $10-20/b&w inside photos; $50-150/text/photo package. Pays on publication. Credit line given. Buys first and reprint rights. Simultaneous and previously published submissions OK.

Tips: Looking for information which will give the reader/gardener/farmer the "growing edge" in high-tech gardening and farming on topics such as hydroponics, high intensity grow lights, water conservation, drip irrigation, advanced organic fertilizers, new seed varieties and greenhouse cultivation.

INTERIOR LANDSCAPE INDUSTRY, The Magazine for Designing Minds and Growing Businesses, American Nurseryman Publishing Co., Suite 545, 111 N. Canal St., Chicago IL 60606. (312)782-5505. FAX: (312)782-3232. Editor: Brent C. Marchant. 10% freelance written. Prefers to work with published/established writers. "Willing to work with freelancers as long as they can fulfill the specifics of our requirements." Monthly magazine on business and technical topics for all parties involved in interior plantings, including interior landscapers, growers and allied professionals (landscape architects, architects and interior designers). "We take a professional approach to the material and encourage our writers to emphasize the professionalism of the industry in their writings." Estab. 1984. Circ. 3,000. Pays on publication. Publishes ms an average of 5 months after acceptance. Byline given. Buys all rights. Submit material 2½ months in advance. Query for electronic submissions. Reports in 3 weeks on queries; 2 weeks on mss. Free sample copy and writer's guidelines.

Nonfiction: How-to (technical and business topics related to the audience); interview/profile (companies working in the industry); personal experience (preferably from those who work or have worked in the industry); photo feature (related to interior projects or plant producers); and technical. No shallow, consumer features. Buys 30 mss/year. Query with published clips. Length: 3-15 ms pages double spaced. Pays $2/published inch. Sometimes pays expenses of writers on assignment.

Photos: Send photos with ms. Reviews b&w contact sheet, negatives, and 5×7 prints; standard size or 4×5 color transparencies. Pays $5-10 for b&w; $15 for color. Identification of subjects required. Buys all rights.

Tips: "Demonstrate knowledge of the field—not just interest in it. Features, especially profiles, are most open to freelancers."

TURF MAGAZINE, P.O. Box 391, 50 Bay St., St. Johnsbury VT 05819. (802)748-8908. FAX: (802)748-1866. Editors and Publishers: Francis Carlet and Dan Hurley. 40% freelance written. "Primarily focused on the professional turf grass applicators and users: superintendents of grounds for golf courses, cemeteries, athletic fields, parks, recreation fields, lawn care companies, landscape contractors/architects." Estab. 1977. Four regional editions, North, South, Central and West; with a combined national circulation of 88,000. Pays on publication. Byline given. Buys all rights or makes work-for-hire assignments. Submit seasonal/holiday material 2 months in advance. Reports in 3 months. Free sample copy.

Nonfiction: How to, interview/profile, opinion and technical. We use on-the-job type interviews with good b&w photos that combine technical information with human interest. "No poetics!" Buys 150 mss/year. Send complete ms. Pays $75-150. Sometimes pays the expenses of writers on assignment.

Photos: Send photos with ms. Payment for photos is included in payment for articles. Reviews b&w contact sheets and 8×10 b&w prints.

Tips: "Good, accurate stories needing minimal editing, with art, of interest to commercial applicators east of the Mississippi are welcomed."

Government and Public Service

Listed here are journals for people who provide governmental services at the local, state or federal level or for those who work in franchised utilities. Journals for city managers, politicians, bureaucratic decision makers, civil servants, firefighters, police officers, public administrators, urban transit managers and utilities managers are listed in this section. Those for private citizens interested in government and public affairs are classified in the Consumer Politics and World Affairs category.

THE CALIFORNIA FIRE SERVICE, The Official Publication of the California State Firefighters' Association, 3246 Ramos Circle, Sacramento CA 95827-2513. FAX: (916)368-8191. Editor: Gary Giacomo. 60% freelance written. Monthly fire service trade journal. Estab. 1927. Circ. 31,000. Pays on publication. Publishes ms an average of 2 months after acceptance. Byline given. Buys first North American serial rights. Submit seasonal/holiday material 4 months in advance. Simultaneous submissions OK. Reports in 1 month. Sample copy for $1.50; writer's guidelines for #10 SASE.

Nonfiction: Expose (circumvention of fire regulations), historical/nostalgic (California slant), how-to (fight specific types of fires), interview/profile (innovative chiefs and/or departments and their programs), new product (fire suppression/fire prevention), opinion (current issues related to the fire service), personal experience (fire or rescue related), photo features (large or dramatic fires in California), technical (fire suppression/fire prevention). Special issues include: January 1992: firefighter's wages survey. For this issue we will be looking for submissions dealing with wages and benefits of firefighters and privitization. April 1992: training. "No political submissions." Buys 24 mss/year. Query with or without published clips, or send complete ms. Length: 400-1,200 words. Pays $55-100 for assigned articles; $35-55 for unsolicited articles. Pays in contributor's copies for opinion pieces and book reviews.

Photos: State availability or send photos with submission. Reviews contact sheets, trasparencies and 5×7 prints. Captions and identification of subjects required. Buys one-time rights. Pays $10.

Columns/Departments: Opinion (essay related to an issue facing the modern fire service. Some examples: AIDS and emergency medical services; hazardous materials cleanup and cancer) 400-700 words. Buys 9 mss/year. Send complete ms. Pays in contributor's copies.

Fillers: Anecdotes, facts, newsbreaks. Buys 60 fillers/year. Length: 30-180. Pays $2.

Tips: "Send for writer's guidelines, an editorial calendar and sample issue. Study our editorial calendar and submit appropriate articles as early as possible. We are always interested in articles that are accompanied by compelling fire or firefighting photographs. Articles submittted with quality photographs, graphs or other illustrations will receive special consideration. Also, if you're a good photojournalist and you submit photographs with complete information there is a good chance you can develop into a regular contributor. Remember that we have readers from all over California—from urban as well as forestry and rural departments."

‡THE CALIFORNIA HIGHWAY PATROLMAN, California Association of Highway Patrolmen, 2030 V Street, Sacramento CA 95818-1730. (916)452-6751. Editor: Carol Perri. 80% freelance written. Monthly magazine covering CHP info; transportation; history of vehicles and/or transportation. "Our readers are either uniformed officers or pro-police oriented." Estab. 1937. Circ. 20,000. Pays on publication. Publishes ms an average of 6-9 months after acceptance. Byline given. No kill fee. Buys one-time rights. Submit seasonal/holiday material 6 months in advance. Simultaneous and previously published submissions OK. (Let me know where it's been published.) Query for electronic submissions. Reports in 1 month on queries; up to 3 months on mss. Sample copy for 9×12 SAE with 4 first-class stamps. Writer's guidelines for letter-size SAE with 1 first-class stamp.

Nonfiction: General interest, historical/nostalgic, humor, interview/profile, photo feature, technical, travel. "No 'how you felt when you received a ticket (or survived an accident)!' No fiction." Buys 80-100 mss/year. Query with or without published clips, or send complete ms. Length: 750-3,000 words. Pays $50 minimum.

Photos: State availability of photos with submission. Send photos (or photocopies of available photos) with submission. Reviews prints. Offers $5 per photo. Captions and identification of subjects required. Buys one-time rights.

Tips: "We are not a technical or strictly 'police' publication. We are most open to travel (in the West) to out-of-the-way places. Historical pieces about little-known California history. Consumer pieces—relatively short—such as how to buy a carpet (the new fibers, etc.) or what questions to ask when hiring a contractor (roofer, cement, etc.)."

CANADIAN DEFENCE QUARTERLY, Revue Canadienne de Défense, Baxter Publications Inc., 310 Dupont St., Toronto, Ontario M5R 1V9 Canada. (416)968-7252. FAX: (416)968-2377. Editor: John Marteinson. 90% freelance written. Professional bimonthly journal on strategy, defense policy, military technology, history. "A professional journal for officers of the Canadian Forces and for the academic community working in Canadian foreign and defense affairs. Articles should have Canadian or NATO applicability." Pays on publication. Byline given. Offers $150 kill fee. Buys all rights. Simultaneous submissions OK. Reports in 1 month. Free sample copy and writer's guidelines.

Nonfiction: Historical, new product, opinion, technical and military strategy. Buys 45 mss/year. Query with or without published clips, or send complete ms. Length: 2,500-4,000 words. Pays $150-300.

Photos: State availability of photos with submission. Offers no additional payment for photos accepted with ms. Buys one-time rights.

Tips: "Submit a well-written manuscript in a relevant field that demonstrates an original approach to the subject matter. Manuscripts *must* be double-spaced, with good margins."

CHIEF OF POLICE MAGAZINE, National Association of Chiefs of Police, 3801 Biscayne Blvd., Miami FL 33137. (305)573-0070. Editor-in-Chief: Jim Gordon. A bimonthly trade journal for law enforcement commanders (command ranks). Circ. 13,500. **Pays on acceptance.** Publishes ms an average of 4-6 months after acceptance. Byline given. Full payment kill fee offered. Buys first rights. Submit seasonal/holiday material 6 months in advance. Simultaneous and previously published submissions OK. Reports in 2 weeks. Sample copy for $3, 9×12 SAE and 5 first class stamps; writer's guidelines for #10 SASE.

Nonfiction: General interest, historical/nostalgic, how-to, humor, inspirational, interview/profile, new product, personal experience, photo feature, religious and technical. "We want stories about interesting police cases and stories on any law enforcement subject or program that is positive in nature. No exposé types. Nothing anti-police." Buys 50 mss/year. Send complete ms. Length: 600-2,500 words. Pays $25-75 for assigned articles; pays $10-50 for unsolicited articles. Sometimes (when pre-requested) pays the expenses of writers on assignment.

Photos: Send photos with submission. Reviews 5×6 prints. Pays $5-10 for b&w; $10-25 for color. Captions required. Buys one-time rights.

Columns/Departments: New Police (police equipment shown and tests), 200-600 words. Buys 6 mss/year. Send complete ms. Pays $5-25.

Fillers: Anecdote, short humor and law-oriented cartoons. Buys 100/year. Length: 100-1,600 words. Pays $5-25.

Tips: "Writers need only contact law enforcement officers right in their own areas and we would be delighted. We want to recognize good commanding officers from sergeant and above who are involved with the community. Pictures of the subject or the department are essential and can be snapshots. We are looking for interviews with police chiefs and sheriffs on command level with photos."

FIREHOUSE MAGAZINE, PTN Publishing, Suite 21, 445 Broad Hollow Rd., Melville NY 11747. (516)845-2700. FAX: (516)845-7109. Executive Editor: Tom Rahilly. 85% freelance written. Works with a small number of new/unpublished writers each year. Monthly magazine covering fire service. "*Firehouse* covers major fires nationwide, controversial issues and trends in the fire service, the latest firefighting equipment and methods of firefighting, historical fires, firefighting history and memorabilia. Fire-related books, firefighters with interesting avocations, fire safety education, hazardous materials incidents and the emergency medical services are also covered." Estab. 1976. Circ. 110,000. Pays on publication. Byline given. Exclusive submissions only. Query for electronic submissions. Reports ASAP. Sample copy for 8½×11 SAE with 7 first class stamps; free writer's guidelines.

Nonfiction: Book excerpts (of recent books on fire, EMS and hazardous materials); historical/nostalgic (great fires in history, fire collectibles, the fire service of yesteryear); how-to (fight certain kinds of fires, buy and maintain equipment, run a fire department); interview/profile (of noteworthy fire leader, centers, commissioners); new product (for firefighting, EMS); personal experience (description of dramatic rescue, helping one's own fire department); photo feature (on unusual apparatus, fire collectibles, a spectacular fire); technical (on almost any phase of firefighting, techniques, equipment, training, administration); and trends (controversies in the fire service). No profiles of people or departments that are not unusual or innovative, reports of nonmajor fires, articles not slanted toward firefighters' interests. Buys 100 mss/year. Query with or without published clips, or send complete ms. Length: 500-3,000 words. Pays $50-400 for assigned articles; pays $50-300 for unsolicited articles. Sometimes pays the expenses of writers on assignment.

Photos: Tom Rahilly, executive editor. Send photos with query or ms. Pays $15-45 for 8×10 b&w prints; $20-200 for transparencies and 8×10 color prints. Captions and identification of subjects required.

Columns/Departments: Command Post (for fire service leaders); Training (effective methods); Book Reviews; Fire Safety (how departments teach fire safety to the public); Communicating (PR, dispatching); Arson (efforts to combat it); Doing Things (profile of a firefighter with an interesting avocation, group projects by firefighters). Buys 50 mss/year. Query or send complete ms. Length: 750-1,000 words. Pays $100-300.

Tips: "Read the magazine to get a full understanding of the subject matter, the writing style and the readers before sending a query or manuscript. Send photos with manuscript or indicate sources for photos. Be sure to focus articles on firefighters."

‡FOREIGN SERVICE JOURNAL, 2101 E St. NW, Washington DC 20037. (202)338-4045. Editor: Anne Stevenson-Yang. 80% freelance written. For Foreign Service personnel and others interested in foreign affairs and related subjects. Monthly. Pays on publication. Publishes ms an average of 3 months after acceptance. Byline given. Buys first North American serial rights. Sample copy $2.50.

Nonfiction: Uses articles on "diplomacy, professional concerns of the State Department and Foreign Service, diplomatic history and articles on Foreign Service experiences. Much of our material is contributed by those working in the profession. Informed outside contributions are welcomed, however." Query. Buys 5-10 unsolicited mss/year. Length: 1,000-4,000 words. Offers honoraria.

Tips: "We're more likely to want your article if it has something to do with diplomacy or diplomats."

GRASSROOTS FUNDRAISING JOURNAL, Klein & Honig, Partnership, P.O. 11607, Berkeley CA 94601. Editors: Kim Klein and Lisa Honig. A bimonthly newsletter covering grassroots fund raising for small social change and social service nonprofit organizations. Estab. 1981. Circ. 3,000. Pays on publication. Byline given. Buys first serial rights. Submit seasonal/holiday material 2 months in advance. Simultaneous queries, simultaneous and (occasionally) previously published submissions OK. Reports in 2 weeks on queries; 2 months on mss. Sample copy $3.
Nonfiction: Book excerpts; how-to (all fund raising strategies); and personal experience (doing fund raising). Buys 10 mss/year. Query. Length: 2,000-20,000 words. Pays $35 minimum.

LAW AND ORDER, Hendon Co., 1000 Skokie Blvd., Wilmette IL 60091. (312)256-8555. Editor: Bruce W. Cameron. 90% freelance written. Prefers to work with published/established writers. Monthly magazine covering the administration and operation of law enforcement agencies, directed to police chiefs and supervisors. Estab. 1952. Circ. 30,000. Pays on publication. Publishes ms an average of 6 months after acceptance. Byline given. Buys first North American serial rights. Submit seasonal/holiday material 3 months in advance. No simultaneous queries. Query for electronic submissions. Can accept manuscripts via compuserve: #71171, 1344. Reports in 1 month. Sample copy for 9×12 SAE; free writer's guidelines.
Nonfiction: General police interest; how-to (do specific police assignments); new product (how applied in police operation); and technical (specific police operation). Special issues include Buyers Guide (January); Communications (February); Training (March); International (April); Administration (May); Small Departments (June); Police Science (July); Equipment (August); Weapons (September); Mobile Patrol (November); and Community Relations (December). No articles dealing with courts (legal field) or convicted prisoners. No nostalgic, financial, travel or recreational material. Buys 100 mss/year. Length: 2,000-3,000 words. Pays 10¢/word.
Photos: Send photos with ms. Reviews transparencies and prints. Identification of subjects required. Buys all rights.
Tips: "*L&O* is a respected magazine that provides up-to-date information that chiefs can use. Writers must know their subject as it applies to this field. Case histories are well received. We are upgrading editorial quality—stories *must* show some understanding of the law enforcement field. A frequent mistake is not getting photographs to accompany article."

‡NATIONAL POLICE UNION NEWS, Delta Publishing Company, 3022 Harrison Ave., Cincinnati OH 45211. (513)481-9457. Editor: Krista Swan Welsh. Managing Editor: M.C. Munson. 10% freelance written. Quarterly magazine covering law enforcement. "This magazine is an interchange of ideas and information, a joining or uniting for the purpose of being more a professional and a better law enforcement officer. It is a sharing of information and an effort dedicated to providing the citizens of our great nation a better place to live." Estab. 1990. Circ. 20,000. **Pays on acceptance.** Publishes ms an average of 6 months after acceptance. No kill fee. Buys one-time rights. Submit seasonal/holiday material 6 months in advance. Simultaneous and previously published submissions OK. Query for electronic submissions. Reports in 6 weeks on mss. Sample copy $1.
Nonfiction: Exposé, general interest, historical/nostalgic, humor, inspirational, interview/profile, new product, personal experience, photo feature, technical, travel. "We do not use fiction. We do not accept any articles critical of specific police departments or associations, or enforcement in general." Send complete ms. Length: 200-1,000 words. Pays $10-100 for unsolicited articles.
Photos: Send photos with submission. Reviews contact sheets, 3×5 prints, b&w only. Captions, model releases and identification of subjects required. Buys one-time rights.
Columns/Departments: On the Lighter Side (humorous, real-life anecdotes), 200-500 words; Unsolved Cases (cases that baffle police), 500-1,000 words; Everyday Heroes (law enforcement personnel who have saved lives/risked life), 200-500 words. Buys 12 mss/year. Send complete ms. Length: 200-1,000 words. Pays $10-100.
Poetry: Traditional. Buys 4 poems/year. Submit maximum 3 poems. Length: 10-25 lines. Pays $10-30.
Fillers: Anecdotes, facts. Length: 50-100 words. Pays $10-30.
Tips: Writers should have an intricate knowledge of field of law enforcement and police work, as well as personal experience with specific types of equipment.

‡9-1-1 MAGAZINE, Official Publications, Inc. 18201 Weston Pl., Tustin CA 92680. (714)544-7776. FAX: (714)838-9233. Editor: Alan Burton. 85% freelance written. Bimonthly magazine for knowledgeable emergency response personnel and those associated with those respective professions. *9-1-1 Magazine* is published to provide information valuable to all those interested in this dangerous, exciting and rewarding profession. Estab. 1988. Circ. 30,000. Pays on publication. Publishes ms an average of 2 months after acceptance. Byline given. Offers 20% kill fee. Buys one-time rights and second serial (reprint) rights. We prefer queries, but will look at manuscripts on speculation. Most positive responses to queries are to considered on spec, but occasionally we will make assignments. Submit seasonal/ holiday material well in advance. Simultaneous and previously published submissions OK. Query for electronic submissions. Reports in 1 month on queries; 3 months on mss. Must be accompanied by SASE if to be returned. Sample copy for 9×12 SAE with 5 first class stamps. Writer's guidelines for #10 SASE.

Nonfiction: Incident report, new product, photo feature, technical and travel. Buys 10 mss/year. Send complete ms. Length: 1,000-3,000 words. Pays $100-300 for unsolicited articles.

Photos: Send photos with submission. Reviews color transparencies and b&w prints. Offers $25-300 per photo. Captions and identification of subjects required. Buys one-time rights.

Fillers: Cartoons. Buys 10/year. Pays $25-50.

Tips: "What we don't need are 'My first call' articles, or photography of a less-than-excellent quality. We seldom use poetry of fiction. *9-1-1- Magazine* is published for a knowledgeable, up-scale audience. Our primary considerations in selecting material are: quality, appropriateness of material, brevity, knowledge of our readership, accuracy, accompanying photography, originality, wit and humor, a clear direction and vision, and proper use of the language."

PLANNING, American Planning Association, 1313 E. 60th St., Chicago IL 60637. (312)955-9100. Editor: Sylvia Lewis. 25% freelance written. Emphasizes urban planning for adult, college-educated readers who are regional and urban planners in city, state or federal agencies or in private business or university faculty or students. Monthly. Circ. 30,000. Pays on publication. Publishes ms an average of 3 months after acceptance. Buys all rights or first rights. Byline given. Previously published submissions OK. Reports in 2 months. Sample copy and writer's guidelines for 9×12 SAE.

Nonfiction: Exposé (on government or business, but on topics related to planning, housing, land use, zoning); general interest (trend stories on cities, land use, government); how-to (successful government or citizen efforts in planning; innovations; concepts that have been applied); and technical (detailed articles on the nitty-gritty of planning, zoning, transportation but no footnotes or mathematical models). Also needs news stories up to 500 words. "It's best to query with a fairly detailed, one-page letter. We'll consider any article that's well written and relevant to our audience. Articles have a better chance if they are timely and related to planning and land use and if they appeal to a national audience. All articles should be written in magazine feature style." Buys 2 features and 1 news story/issue. Length: 500-2,000 words. Pays $100-750. "We pay freelance writers and photographers only, not planners."

Photos: "We prefer that authors supply their own photos, but we sometimes take our own or arrange for them in other ways." State availability of photos. Pays $25 minimum for 8×10 matte or glossy prints and $200 for 4-color cover photos. Caption material required. Buys one-time rights.

POLICE AND SECURITY NEWS, Days Communications, Inc.. 15 Thatcher Rd., Quakertown PA 18951. (215)538-1240. FAX: (215)538-1208. Editor: James Devery. 40% freelance written. A bimonthly tabloid on public law enforcement and private security. "Our publication is designed to provide educational and entertaining information directed toward management level. Technical information written for the expert in a manner that the non-expert can understand." Estab. 1985. Circ. 20,640. Pays on publication. Publishes ms an average of 2 months after acceptance. Byline given. Buys first North American serial rights. Submit seasonal/holiday material 2 months in advance. Simultaneous and previously published submissions OK. Free sample copy and writer's guidelines.

Nonfiction: Al Menear, articles editor. Exposé, historical/nostalgic, how-to, humor, interview/profile, opinion, personal experience, photo feature and technical. Buys 12 mss/year. Query. Length: 200-4,000 words. Pays $50-200. Sometimes pays in trade-out of services.

Photos: State availability of photos with submission. Reviews prints (3×5). Offers $10-50 per photo. Buys one-time rights.

Fillers: Facts, newsbreaks and short humor. Buys 6/year. Length: 200-2,000 words. Pays $50-150.

SUPERINTENDENT'S PROFILE & POCKET EQUIPMENT DIRECTORY, Profile Publications, 220 Central Ave., P.O. Box 43, Dunkirk NY 14048. (716)366-4774. Editor: Robert Dyment. 60% freelance written. Prefers to work with published/established writers. Monthly magazine covering "outstanding" town, village, county and city highway superintendents and Department of Public Works Directors throughout New York state only. Estab. 1978. Circ. 2,600. Publishes ms an average of 4 months after acceptance. Pays within 90 days. Byline given for excellent material. Buys first serial rights. Submit seasonal/holiday material 3 months in advance. Simultaneous queries OK. Reports in 2 weeks on queries; 1 month on mss. Sample copy for 9×12 SAE and 4 first class stamps.

Nonfiction: John Powers, articles editor. Interview/profile (of a highway superintendent or DPW director in NY state who has improved department operations through unique methods or equipment); and technical. Special issues include winter maintenance profiles. No fiction. Buys 20 mss/year. Query. Length: 1,500-2,000 words. Pays $150 for a full-length ms. "Pays more for excellent material. All manuscripts will be edited to fit our format and space limitations." Sometimes pays the expenses of writers on assignment.

Photos: John Powers, photo editor. State availability of photos. Pays $5-10 for b&w contact sheets; reviews 5×7 prints. Captions and identification of subjects required. Buys one-time rights.

Poetry: Buys poetry if it pertains to highway departments. Pays $5-15.

Tips: "We are a widely read and highly respected state-wide magazine, and although we can't pay high rates, we expect quality work. Too many freelance writers are going for the exposé rather than the meat-and-potato type articles that will help readers. We use more major features than fillers. Frequently writers don't read sample copies first. We will be purchasing more material because our page numbers are increasing."

TRANSACTION/SOCIETY, Rutgers University, New Brunswick NJ 08903. (201)932-2280, ext. 83. FAX: (201)932-3138. Editor: Irving Louis Horowitz. 10% freelance written. Prefers to work with published/ established writers. For social scientists (policymakers with training in sociology, political issues and economics). Published every 2 months. Circ. 45,000. Buys all rights. Byline given. Pays on publication. Publishes ms an average of 6 months after acceptance. No simultaneous submissions. Query for electronic submissions; "manual provided to authors." Reports in 1 month. Query. Sample copy and writer's guidelines for 9×12 SAE and 5 first class stamps.

Nonfiction: Brigitte M. Goldstein, managing editor. "Articles of wide interest in areas of specific interest to the social science community. Must have an awareness of problems and issues in education, population and urbanization that are not widely reported. Articles on overpopulation, terrorism, international organizations. No general think pieces." Payment for articles is made only if done on assignment. *No payment for unsolicited articles.*

Photos: Douglas Harper, photo editor. Pays $200 for photographic essays done on assignment or accepted for publication.

Tips: "Submit an article on a thoroughly unique subject, written with good literary quality. Present new ideas and research findings in a readable and useful manner. A frequent mistake is writing to satisfy a journal, rather than the intrinsic requirements of the story itself. Avoid posturing and editorializing."

VICTIMOLOGY: An International Journal, 2333 N. Vernon St., Arlington VA 22207-4036. (703)528-3387. Editor-in-Chief: Emilio C. Viano. "We are the only magazine specifically focusing on the victim, on the dynamics of victimization; for social scientists, criminal justice professionals and practitioners, social workers and volunteer and professional groups engaged in prevention of victimization and in offering assistance to victims of rape, spouse abuse, child abuse, incest, abuse of the elderly, natural disasters, etc." Quarterly magazine. Circ. 2,500. Pays on publication. Buys all rights. Byline given. Reports in 2 months. Sample copy $5; free writer's guidelines.

Nonfiction: Exposé, historical, how-to, informational, interview, personal experience, profile, research and technical. Buys 10 mss/issue. Query. Length: 500-5,000 words. Pays $50-150.

Photos: Purchased with accompanying ms. Captions required. Send contact sheet. Pays $15-50 for 5×7 or 8×10 b&w glossy prints.

Poetry: Avant-garde, free verse, light verse and traditional. Length: 30 lines maximum. Pays $10-25.

Tips: "Focus on what is being researched and discovered on the victim, the victim/offender relationship, treatment of the offender, the bystander/witness, preventive measures, and what is being done in the areas of service to the victims of rape, spouse abuse, neglect and occupational and environmental hazards and the elderly."

YOUR VIRGINIA STATE TROOPER MAGAZINE, Virginia State Police Association, 6944 Forest Hill Ave., Richmond VA 23225. Editor: Rebecca V. Jackson. 70% freelance written. Triannual magazine covering police topics for troopers (state police), libraries, legislators and medical offices. Estab. 1974. Circ. 10,000. **Pays on acceptance.** Publishes ms an average of 3 months after acceptance. Byline given. Buys first North American serial rights and all rights on assignments. Submit seasonal/holiday material 2 months in advance. Simultaneous submissions OK. Reports in 2 months.

Nonfiction: Exposé (consumer or police-related); general interest; fitness/health; tourist (VA sites); financial planning (tax, estate planning tips); historical/nostalgic; how-to; book excerpts/reports (law enforcement related); humor, interview/profile (notable police figures); technical (radar) and other (recreation). Buys 55-60 mss/year. Query with clips or send complete ms. Length: 2,500 words. Pays $250 maximum/article (10¢/word). Sometimes pays expenses of writers on assignment.

Photos: Send photos with ms. Pays $50 maximum for several 5×7 or 8×10 b&w glossy prints to accompany ms. Cutlines and model releases required. Buys one-time rights.

Cartoons: Send copies. Pays $15; $20 if customized per request. Buys one-time rights. Buys 20 cartoons/year.

Fiction: Adventure, humorous, mystery, novel excerpts and suspense. Buys 3 mss/year. Send complete ms. Length: 2,500 words minimum. Pays $250 maximum (10¢/word) on acceptance.

Tips: In addition to items of interest to the VA State Police, general interest is stressed.

Groceries and Food Products

In this section are publications for grocers, food wholesalers, processors, warehouse own-ers, caterers, institutional managers and suppliers of grocery store equipment. See the section on Confectionery and Snack Foods for bakery and candy industry magazines.

AUTOMATIC MERCHANDISER, Edgell Communications, 7500 Old Oak Blvd., Cleveland OH 44130. (216)243-8100. FAX: (216)891-2683. Editor: Mark L. Dlugoss. Managing Editor: Elizabeth C. Mesz-aros. 10% freelance written. Prefers to work with published/established writers. A monthly trade journal covering vending machines, contract foodservice and office coffee service. "*AM's* readers are owners and managers of these companies; we profile successful companies and report on market trends." Circ. 13,250. **Pays on acceptance.** Publishes ms an average of 3 months after acceptance. Byline sometimes given. Buys first North American serial rights, all rights or makes work-for-hire assignments. Submit seasonal/holiday material 4 months in advance. Free sample copy and writer's guidelines.
Nonfiction: Buys 30 mss/year. Query. Length: 1,000-6,000 words. Pays $150-600. Sometimes pays the expenses of writers on assignment.
Photos: Send photos with submission. Reviews contact sheets, transparencies and prints. Offers $50 maximum per photo. Buys all rights.

CANADIAN GROCER, Maclean-Hunter Ltd., Maclean Hunter Building, 777 Bay St., Toronto, Ontario M5W 1A7 Canada. (416)596-5772. Editor: George H. Condon. 10% freelance written. Prefers to work with published/established writers. Monthly magazine about supermarketing and food retailing for Canadian chain and independent food store managers, owners, buyers, executives, food brokers, food processors and manufacturers. Estab. 1886. Circ 18,500. Pays on publication. Publishes ms an average of 2 months after acceptance. Byline given. Buys first Canadian rights. Phone queries OK. Submit seasonal material 2 months in advance. Reports in 1 month. Sample copy $5.
Nonfiction: Interview (Canadian trendsetters in marketing, finance or food distribution); technical (store operations, equipment and finance); and news features on supermarkets. "Freelancers should be well versed on the supermarket industry. We don't want unsolicited material. Writers with business and/or finance expertise are preferred. Know the retail food industry and be able to write concisely and accurately on subjects relevant to our readers: food store managers, senior corporate executives, etc. A good example of an article would be 'How a dairy case realignment increased profits while reducing prices, inventory and stock-outs.'" Buys 14 mss/year. Query with clips of previously published work. Pays 30¢/word. Sometimes pays the expenses of writers on assignment.
Photos: State availability of photos. Pays $10-25 for prints or slides. Captions preferred. Buys one-time rights.
Tips: "Suitable writers will be familiar with sales per square foot, merchandising mixes and direct product profitability."

CANDY WHOLESALER, National Candy Wholesalers Association, Suite 1120, 1120 Vermont Ave. NW, Washington DC 20005. (202)463-2124. Publisher: Shelley Estersohn. Editor: Kevin Settlage. 35% freelance written. A monthly magazine for distributors of candy/tobacco/snacks/groceries and other convenience-store items. "*Candy Wholesaler* magazine is published to assist the candy/tobacco/snack food distributor in improving his business by providing a variety of relevant operational information. Serves as the voice of the distributor in the candy/tobacco/snack industry." Circ. 11,419. **Pays on acceptance.** Publishes ms an average of 4 months after acceptance. Byline given. Offers $50 kill fee. Buys all rights. Submit seasonal/holiday material 6 months in advance. Query for electronic submis-sions. Reports in 1 month. Sample copy for 9 × 12 SAE with 6 first class stamps.
Nonfiction: Historical/nostalgic, how-to (related to distribution), interview/profile, photo feature, technical (data processing) and (profiles of distribution films/or manufacturers). "No simplistic pieces with consumer focus that are financial, tax-related or legal." Buys 30-35 mss/year. Query with or without published clips, or send complete ms. Length: 8-12 double-spaced typewritten pages. Pays $750-1,000 for assigned articles. Pays $250-500 for unsolicited articles. Sometimes pays copies to industry members who author articles. Pays the expenses of writers on assignment.
Photos: Send photos with submission. Reviews contact sheets, transparencies and prints. Offers $5-10 per photo. Captions and identification of subjects required. Buys all rights.
Fillers: Kevin Settlage, fillers editor. Anecdotes, facts and short humor. Length: 50-200 words. Pays $10-20.
Tips: "Talk to wholesalers about their business—how it works, what their problems are, etc. We need writers who understand this industry. Company profile feature stories are open to freelancers. Get into the nitty gritty of operations and management. Talk to several key people in the company."

‡**FLORIDA GROCER,** Florida Grocer Publications, Inc., P.O. Box 430760, South Miami FL 33243. (305)441-1138. Editor: Dennis Kane. 5% freelance written. *"Florida Grocer* is a 16,000 circulation monthly trade newspaper, serving members of the Florida food industry. Our publication is edited for chain and independent food store owners and operators as well as members of allied industries." Estab. 1956. Circ. 16,000. **Pays on acceptance.** Byline given. Buys all rights. Submit seasonal/holiday material 3 months in advance. Sample copy for #10 SAE with 6 first class stamps.
Nonfiction: Book excerpts, expose, general interest, humor, features on supermarkets and their owners, new product, new equipment, photo feature and video. Buys variable number of mss/year. Query with or without published clips, or send complete ms. Length: varies. Payment varies. Sometimes pays the expenses of writers on assignment.
Photos: State availability of photos with submission. Terms for payment on photos "included in terms of payment for assignment."
Tips: "We prefer feature articles on new stores (grand openings, etc.), store owners, operators; Florida based food manufacturers, brokers, wholesalers, distributors, etc. We also publish a section in Spanish and also welcome the above types of materials in Spanish (Cuban)."

‡**FOOD & SERVICE,** Texas Restaurant Association, P.O. Box 1429, Austin TX 78767. (512)444-6543 (in Texas, 1-800-395-2872). FAX: (512)444-7811. Editor: Steve Greenhow. 50% freelance written. Magazine published 11 times/year providing business solutions to Texas restaurant owners and operators. Estab. 1940. Circ. 5,000. Written queries required. Reports in 1 month. Byline given. Not copyrighted. Buys first rights. Simultaneous queries, photocopied submissions OK. No previously published submissions. Query for electronic submissions. Sample copy and editorial calendar for 9 × 12 SAE and 6 first class stamps. Free writer's guidelines. Pays on acceptance; rates vary.
Nonfiction: Features must provide business solutions to problems in the restaurant and food service industries. Topics vary but always have business slant; particular to Texas. No restaurant critiques, human interest stories or seasonal copy. Quote members of the Texas Restaurant Association; substantiate with facts and examples. Query. Length: 2,000-2,500 words, features; shorter articles sometimes used; product releases, 300-word maximum. Payment rates vary.
Photos: State availability of photos, but photos usually assigned.
Columns/Departments: Written in-house only.

FOOD PEOPLE, Olson Publications, Inc., P.O. Box 1208, Woodstock GA 30188. (404)928-8994. Managing Editor: Ms. Johnnie Nelson. 75% freelance written. Prefers to work with published/established writers, but works with a small number of new/unpublished writers each year. Always willing to consider new writers, but they must have a basic command of their craft. Monthly tabloid covering the retail food industry. Estab. 1981. Circ. 30,000. Pays on publication. Publishes ms an average of 1 month after acceptance. Byline given. Buys all rights. Will reassign subsidiary rights after publication and upon request. Submit seasonal/holiday material 6 weeks in advance. Computer modem submissions encouraged. Reports in 6 weeks. Sample copy for 9 × 12 SAE with 5 first class stamps; writer's guidelines for #10 SASE.
Nonfiction: Interview/profile (of major food industry figures), photo features of ad campaigns, marketing strategies, important new products and services. "We would like to receive feature articles about people and companies that illustrate trends in the food industry. Articles should be informative, tone is upbeat. Do not send recipes or how-to shop articles; we cover food as a business." Buys 250-300 mss/year. Query or send complete ms. Length: 500-1,500 words. Pays $3/published inch minimum. Pays the expenses of writers on assignment.
Photos: "Photos of people. Photos of displays, or store layouts, etc., that illustrate points made in article are good, too. But stay away from storefront shots." State availability of photos with query or send photos with ms. Pays $10 plus expenses for 5 × 7 b&w prints; and $25 plus expenses for color transparencies. Captions required. Buys one-time rights.
Columns/Departments: Company news, People, Organizations, New Products, and Morsels . . . a Smorgasbord of Tidbits in the National Stew. Send complete ms. Pays $3/inch.
Tips: "Begin with an area news event—store openings, new promotions. Write that as news, then go further to examine the consequences. We are staffing more conventions, so writers should concentrate on features about people, companies, trends, new products, innovations in the food industry in their geographic areas and apply these to a national scope when possible. Talk with decision makers to get 'hows' and 'whys.' We now are more feature than news oriented. We look for contributors who work well, quickly and always deliver. We are now buying some international material."

FOODSERVICE DIRECTOR, Bill Communications, 633 3rd Ave., New York NY 10017. (212)984-2356. FAX: (212)983-3198. Editor: Walter J. Schruntek. Managing Editor: Karen Weisberg. 20% freelance written. Monthly tabloid on non-commercial foodservice operations for operators of kitchens and dining halls in schools, colleges, hospitals/health care, office and plant cafeterias, military, airline/transportation, correctional institutions. Estab. 1988. Circ. 45,000. Pays on publication. Byline given sometimes. Offers 25% kill fee. Buys all rights. Submit seasonal/holiday material 2-3 months in advance. Simultaneous submissions OK. Free sample copy.

Nonfiction: How-to, interview/profile. Buys 60-70 mss/year. Query with published clips. Length: 700-900 words. Pays $250-500. Sometimes pays the expenses of writers on assignment.

Photos: Send photos with submission. Reviews transparencies. Offers no additional payment for photos accepted with ms. Identification of subjects required. Buys all rights.

Columns/Departments: Equipment (case studies of kitchen/serving equipment in use), 700-900 words; Food (specific category studies per publication calendar), 750-900 words. Buys 20-30 mss/year. Query. Length: 400-600 words. Pays $150-250.

‡**THE GOURMET RETAILER MAGAZINE,** Sterling Southeast Inc., 1450 NE 123 St., N. Miami FL 33161. (305)893-8771. FAX: (305)893-8783. Executive Editor: Nancy Moore. 30% freelance written. Monthly magazine covering gourmet and specialty foods and housewares. "Our readers are owners and managers of specialty food and upscale housewares retail units. Writers must know the trade exceptionally well and must know their subjects well. Numerous interviews required for each article." Estab. 1979. Circ. 18,000. Pays on publication. Publishes ms an average of 3 months after acceptance. Byline sometimes given. No kill fee. Buys all rights. Submit seasonal/holiday material 6 months in advance. Query for electronic submissions. Reports in 2 months on queries. Free sample copy and writer's guidelines.

Nonfiction: Interview/profile (corporate profile; we choose subject), features on specialty foods. "Do not send unsolicited manuscripts; queries only." Buys 12 mss/year. Query with published clips. Length: 1,500-2,200 words. Pays $300 for assigned articles plus pre-approved expenses such as phone and mail.

Photos: State availability of photos with submission. Reviews negatives, 5×7 transparencies, 8×10 prints. Offers $15-25 per photo. Identification of subjects required. Buys one-time rights.

Tips: "If you are already in the specialty food or housewares industry as a writer and do not write for my competition, I would be interested in hearing from you. We offer exposure for the consumate professional. We are the leading book in our industry."

HEALTH FOODS BUSINESS, Howmark Publishing Corp., 567 Morris Ave., Elizabeth NJ 07208. (908)353-7373. FAX: (908)353-8221. Editor: Gina Geslewitz. 40% freelance written. Eager to work with new/unpublished writers if competent and reliable. For owners and managers of health food stores. Monthly magazine. Circ. 11,000. Pays on publication. Publishes ms an average of 4 months after acceptance. Byline given "if story quality warrants it." Buys first North American serial rights; "also exclusive rights in our trade field." Phone queries OK. "Query us about a good health food store in your area. We use many store profile stories." Simultaneous submissions OK if exclusive to their field. Previously published work OK, but please indicate where and when material appeared previously. Reports in 1 month. Sample copy $3 plus $2 for postage and handling; writer's guidelines for #10 SASE.

Nonfiction: Exposé (government hassling with health food industry); how-to (unique or successful retail operators); interview (must be prominent person in industry or closely related to the health food industry or well-known or prominent person in any arena who has undertaken a natural diet/lifestyle). Buys 1-2 mss/issue. Query for interview and photo features. Length: long enough to tell the whole story without padding. Pays $50 and up for feature stories, $100 and up for store profiles.

Photos: "Most articles must have photos included;" negatives and contact sheet OK. Captions required. No additional payment.

Tips: "A writer may find that submitting a letter with a sample article he/she believes to be closely related to articles read in our publication is the most of expedient way to determine the appropriateness of his/her skills and expertise."

‡**MEAT BUSINESS MAGAZINE,** 9701 Gravois Ave., St. Louis MO 63123. (314)638-4050. FAX: (314)638-3880. Editor: Louise King. 10% freelance written. Prefers to work with published/established writers; works with a small number of new/unpublished writers each year. For meat processors, retailers, locker plant operators, freezer provisioners, portion control packers, meat dealers and food service (food plan) operators. Monthly. Pays on publication. Publishes ms an average of 6 months after acceptance. Computer printout submissions acceptable. Reports in 2 weeks.

Nonfiction and Fillers: Buys feature-length articles and shorter subjects pertinent to the field. Length: 1,000-1,500 words for features. Pays 10¢/word. Sometimes pays the expenses of writers on assignment.

Photos: Pays $5 for photos.

MINNESOTA GROCER, Official Publication of the Minnesota Grocers Association, Minnesota Grocers Council, Inc., 533 St. Clair Ave., St. Paul MN 55102. (612)228-0973. FAX: (612)228-1949. Editor: Randy Schubring. 25% freelance written. Bimonthly magazine on the retail grocery industry in Minnesota. Estab. 1951. Circ. 4,800. Pays on publication. Publishes ms an average of 1-2 months after acceptance. Byline given. Buys all rights. Submit seasonal/holiday material 3 months in advance. Previously published submissions OK. Reports in 1 month on queries; 2 weeks on mss. Free sample copy and writer's guidelines.

Nonfiction: How-to better market, display and sell food, and other items in a grocery store. How to find new markets. Interview/profile and new products. Special issues: "We do an economic forecast in Jan/Feb. issue." Buys 6 mss/year. Query with published clips. Length: 300-1,500 words. Pays $100-500 for assigned articles. Sometimes pays expenses of writers on assignment.

Photos: State availability of photos with submission. Reviews contact sheets and 5×7 prints. Captions, model releases and identification of subjects required. Buys all rights.

Columns/Departments: Query with published clips.

Tips: "The best way to be considered for a freelance assignment is first and foremost to have a crisp journalistic writing style on clips. Second it is very helpful to have a knowledge of the issues and trends in the grocery industry. Because we are a regional trade publication, it is crucial that articles be localized to Minnesota."

PRODUCE NEWS, 2185 Lemoine Ave., Fort Lee NJ 07024. FAX: (201)592-0809. Editor: Gordon Hochberg. 10-15% freelance written. Works with a small number of new/unpublished writers each year. For commercial growers and shippers, receivers and distributors of fresh fruits and vegetables, including chain store produce buyers and merchandisers. Weekly. Estab. 1897. Circ. 10,000. Pays on publication. Publishes ms an average of 2 weeks after acceptance. Deadline is Tuesday afternoon before Thursday press day. Free sample copy and writer's guidelines.

Nonfiction: News stories (about the produce industry). Buys profiles, spot news, coverage of successful business operations and articles on merchandising techniques. Query. Pays minimum of $1/column inch for original material. Sometimes pays the expenses of writers on assignment.

Photos: B&w glossies. Pays $8-10 for each one used.

Tips: "Stories should be trade-oriented, not consumer-oriented. As our circulation grows in the next year, we are interested in stories and news articles from all fresh fruit-growing areas of the country. Looking especially for writers in California and lower Rio Grande Valley of Texas."

QUICK FROZEN FOODS INTERNATIONAL, E.W. Williams Publishing Co., Suite 305, 2125 Center Ave., Fort Lee NJ 07024-5898. (201)592-7007. FAX: (201)592-7171. Editor: John M. Saulnier. 20% freelance written. Works with a small number of new/unpublished writers each year. Quarterly magazine covering frozen foods around the world—"every phase of frozen food manufacture, retailing, food service, brokerage, transport, warehousing, merchandising. Especially interested in stories from Europe, Asia and emerging nations." Circ. 13,500. Pays on publication. Publishes ms an average of 3 months after acceptance. Byline given. Offers kill fee; "if satisfactory, we will pay promised amount. If bungled, half." Buys all rights, but will relinquish any rights requested. Submit seasonal/holiday material 6 months in advance. Sample copy $8.

Nonfiction: Book excerpts, general interest, historical/nostalgic, interview/profile, new product (from overseas), personal experience, photo feature, technical and travel. No articles peripheral to frozen food industry such as taxes, insurance, government regulation, safety, etc. Buys 20-30 mss/year. Query or send complete ms. Length: 500-4,000 words. Pays 5¢/word or by arrangement. "We will reimburse postage on articles ordered from overseas." Sometimes pays the expenses of writers on assignment.

Photos: "We prefer photos with all articles." State availability of photos or send photos with accompanying ms. Pays $10 for 5×7 b&w prints (contact sheet if many shots). Captions and identification of subject required. Buys all rights. Release on request.

Columns/Departments: News or analysis of frozen foods abroad. Buys 20 columns/year. Query. Length: 500-1,500 words. Pays by arrangement.

Fillers: Newsbreaks. Length: 100-500 words. Pays $5-20.

Tips: "We are primarily interested in feature materials, (1,000-3,000 words with pictures). We are now devoting more space to frozen food company developments in Pacific Rim and East European countries. Stories on frozen food merchandising and retailing in foreign supermarket chains in Europe, Japan and Australia/New Zealand are welcome. National frozen food production profiles are also in demand worldwide. A frequent mistake is submitting general interest material instead of specific industry-related stories."

SEAFOOD LEADER, Waterfront Press Co., 1115 NW 45th St., Seattle WA 98107. (206)789-6506. FAX: (206)548-9346. Editor: Peter Redmayne. Managing Editor: Wayne Lee. 20% freelance written. Works with a small number of new/unpublished writers each year. A trade journal on the seafood business published 6 times/year. Estab. 1980. Circ. 15,000. Pays on publication. Publishes ms an average of 3 months after acceptance. Byline given. Buys first rights and second serial (reprint) rights. Simultaneous and previously published submissions OK. Query for electronic submissions. Reports in 1 month on queries; 2 months on mss. Sample copy $3 with 9×12 SAE.

Nonfiction: General seafood interest, marketing/business, historical/nostalgic, interview/profile, opinion and photo feature. Each of *Seafood Leader's* six issues has a slant: Whole Seafood Catalog (Jan/Feb), Buyer's Guide (Mar/Apr), International (May/June), Foodservice/Restaurant (July/Aug), Retail/Aquaculture (Sep/Oct) and Shrimp (Nov/Dec). Each issue also includes stories outside of the particular focus, particularly shorter features and news items. No recreational fishing; no first person articles. Buys 12-15 mss/year. Query with or without published clips, or send complete ms. Length: 1,000-2,500 words. Pay rate is 15-20¢/word published depending upon amount of editing necessary. Sometimes pays the expenses of writers on assignment.

Photos: State availability of photos with submission. Reviews contact sheets and transparencies. Offers $50 per inside color photo, $100 for cover. Buys one-time rights.

Fillers: Newsbreaks. Buys 10-15/year. Length: 100-250 words. Pays $50-100.

Tips: *"Seafood Leader* is steadily increasing in size and has a growing need for full-length feature stories and special sections. Articles on innovative, unique and aggressive people or companies involved in seafood are needed. Writing should be colorful, tight and fact-filled, always emphasizing the subject's formula for increased seafood sales. Readers should feel as if they have learned something applicable to their business."

THE WISCONSIN GROCER, Wisconsin Grocers Association, Suite 203, 802 W. Broadway, Madison WI 53713. (608)222-4515. Editor: Dianne Calgaro. Eager to work with new/unpublished writers. Bimonthly magazine covering grocery industry of Wisconsin. Estab. 1900. Circ. 1,500. Pays on publication. Publishes ms an average of 3 months after acceptance. Byline given. Not copyrighted. Buys first North American serial rights, second serial (reprint) rights or simultaneous rights. Submit seasonal/holiday material 5 months in advance. Simultaneous and previously published submissions OK. Reports in 2 weeks on queries; 2 months on mss. Sample copy for 9×12 SAE with 3 first class stamps.

Nonfiction: How-to (money management, employee training/relations, store design, promotional ideas); interview/profile (of WGA members and Wisconsin politicans only); opinion; technical (store design or equipment). No articles about grocers or companies not affiliated with the WGA. Buys 6 mss/year. Query. Length: 500-2,000 words. Pays $15 minimum. Pays in copies if the writer works for a manufacturer or distributor of goods or services relevant to the grocery industry, or if a political viewpoint is expressed.

Photos: Send photos with submission. Reviews 5×7 prints. Offers no additional payment for photos accepted with ms. Identification of subjects required. Buys one-time rights.

Columns/Departments: Security (anti-shoplifting, vendor thefts, employee theft, burglary); Employee Relations (screening, training, management); Customer Relations (better service, corporate-community relations, buying trends); Money Management (DPP programs, bookkeeping, grocery—specific computer applications); Merchandising (promotional or advertising ideas), all 1,000 words. Buys 6 mss/year. Query. Length: 500-1,500 words.

Fillers: Facts and newsbreaks. Buys 6/year. Length: 50-250 words.

Tips: "How-tos are especially strong with our readers. They want to know how to increase sales and cut costs. Cover new management techniques, promotional ideas, customer services and industry trends."

Hardware

Journals for general and specialized hardware wholesalers and retailers are listed in this section. Journals specializing in hardware for a certain trade, such as plumbing or automotive supplies, are classified with other publications for that trade.

‡BLADE TRADE, (See *Blade*, Consumer Publications, Hobby and Craft).

CHAIN SAW AGE, Hatton-Brown Publisher, P.O. Box 2268, Montgomery AL 36102-2268. (205)834-1170. Editor: Rich Donnell. 1% freelance written. "We will consider any submissions that address pertinent subjects and are well-written." For "chain saw dealers (retailers); small businesses—usually family-owned, typical ages, interests and education." Monthly. Circ. 20,000. Pays on acceptance or publication. Publishes ms an average of 4 months after acceptance. Free sample copy.

Nonfiction: "Must relate to chain saw use, merchandising, adaptation, repair, maintenance, manufacture or display." Buys informational articles, how-to, personal experience, interview, profiles, inspirational, personal opinion, photo feature, coverage of successful business operations, and articles on merchandising techniques. Buys very few mss/year. Query first. Length: 500-1,000 words. Pays $20-50 "5¢/word plus photo fees." Sometimes pays the expenses of writers on assignment.

Photos: Photos purchased with or without mss, or on assignment. For b&w glossies, pay "varies." Captions required.

Tips: "Frequently writers have an inadequate understanding of the subject area."

HARDWARE AGE, Chilton Co., 1 Chilton Way, Radnor PA 19089. (215)964-4275. Editor-in-Chief: Terry Gallagher. Managing Editor: Rick Carter. 2% freelance written. Emphasizes retailing, distribution and merchandising of hardware and building materials. Monthly magazine. Circ. 71,000. Buys first North American serial rights. No guarantee of byline. Simultaneous, and previously published submissions OK, if exclusive in the field. Reports in 2 months. Sample copy for $1; mention *Writer's Market* in request.

Nonfiction: Rick Carter, managing editor. How-to more profitably run a hardware store or a department within a store. "We particularly want stories on local hardware stores and home improvement centers, with photos. Stories should concentrate on one particular aspect of how the retailer in question has been successful." Also wants technical pieces (will consider stories on retail accounting, inventory management and business management by qualified writers). Buys 1-5 unsolicited mss/year. Submit complete ms. Length: 1,500-3,000 words. Pays $75-200.

Photos: "We like store features with b&w photos. Usually use b&w for small freelance features." Send photos with ms. Pays $25 for 4×5 glossy b&w prints. Captions preferred. Buys one-time rights.

Columns/Departments: Retailers' Business Tips; Wholesalers' Business Tips; and Moneysaving Tips. Query or submit complete ms. Length: 1,000-1,250 words. Pays $100-150. Open to suggestions for new columns/departments.

Home Furnishings and Household Goods

Readers rely on these publications to learn more about new products and trends in the home furnishings and appliance trade. Magazines for consumers interested in home furnishings are listed in the Consumer Home and Garden Section.

APPLIANCE SERVICE NEWS, 110 W. Saint Charles Rd., P.O. Box 789, Lombard IL 60148. Editor: William Wingstedt. For professional service people whose main interest is repairing major and/or portable household appliances. Their jobs consist of service shop owner, service manager or service technician. Monthly "newspaper style" publication. Estab. 1950. Circ. 51,000. Buys all rights. Byline given. Pays on publication. Will consider simultaneous submissions. Reports in about 1 month. Sample copy $2.

Nonfiction: James Hodl, associate editor. "Our main interest is in technical articles about appliances and their repair. Material should be written in a straightforward, easy-to-understand style. It should be crisp and interesting, with high informational content. Our main interest is in the major and portable appliance repair field. We are not interested in retail sales." Query. Length: open. Pays $200-300/feature.

Photos: Pays $20 for b&w photos used with ms. Captions required.

‡BEDROOM MAGAZINE, Bobit Publishing, 2512 Artesia Blvd. Redondo Beach CA 90278. (213)376-8788. Editor: Kathy Knoles. 10% freelance written. Prefers to work with published/established writers. A monthly magazine covering bedroom furniture, mattresses, linens and accessories for specialty shop owners, furniture stores, sleep shops and bedroom furniture manufacturers, distributors. Circ. 18,200. Pays on publication. Publishes ms an average of 2 months after acceptance. Byline given. Buys first rights or second serial (reprint) rights. Submit seasonal/holiday material 3 months in advance. Reports in 2 weeks. Sample copy for 10×13 SAE with 5 first class stamps.

Nonfiction: Book excerpts; essays (health benefits of waterbeds); historical/nostalgic; how-to (business management, display techniques, merchandising tips); humor (if in good taste); interview/profile; new product; personal experience; photo feature; technical; and general features depicting bedroom furniture in a positive way. No articles depicting furniture or mattresses in a negative manner. Query with published clips. Length: 1,000-5,000 words. Pays $60-250 for assigned articles; pays $50-200 for unsolicited articles. Sometimes pays the expenses of writers on assignment.

Photos: Send photos with submission. Reviews contact sheets, transparencies and 8×10 prints. Offers $25-100/photo. Captions and identification of subjects required. Buys one-time rights.

Tips: "We need profiles on successful bedroom furniture retailers in all parts of the country. If a large, full-line furniture store in your area also sells waterbeds, we are interested in profiles on those stores and owners as well. We are also always looking for interviews with doctors, chiropractors and other health professionals who recommend waterbeds for their patients. Most of our freelance articles concern store management. Stores that do an excellent job with display and promotions are of special interest when accompanied by good photos. We need articles on obtaining credit, display techniques, merchandising, how to be a successful salesperson, attracting new customers, creating effective advertising, how to put togehter an attractive store window display, hiring employees, etc. Anything that could benefit a salesperson or store owner."

CHINA GLASS & TABLEWARE, Doctorow Communications, Inc., P.O. Box 2147, Clifton NJ 07015. (201)779-1600. FAX: (201)779-3242. Editor-in-Chief: Amy Stavis. 60% freelance written. Works with a small number of new/unpublished writers each year. Monthly magazine for buyers, merchandise managers and specialty store owners who deal in tableware, dinnerware, glassware, flatware and other tabletop accessories. Estab. 1892. Pays on publication. Publishes ms an average of 3-4 months after acceptance. Buys one-time rights. Byline given. Phone queries OK. Submit seasonal/holiday material 3 months in advance. Reports in 3 weeks. Free sample copy for 9×12 SAE and writer's guidelines; mention *Writer's Market* in request.

Nonfiction: General interest (on store successes, reasons for a store's business track record); interview (personalities of store owners, how they cope with industry problems, why they are in tableware); and technical (on the business aspects of retailing china, glassware and flatware). "Bridal registry material always welcomed." No articles on how-to or gift shops. Buys 2-3 mss/issue. Query. Length: 1,500-3,000 words. Pays $50/page. Sometimes pays the expenses of writers on assignment.

Photos: State availability of photos with query. No additional payment for b&w or color contact sheets. Captions required. Buys first serial rights.

Tips: "Show imagination in the query; have a good angle on a story that makes it unique from the competition's coverage and requires less work on the editor's part for rewriting a snappy beginning."

FLOORING MAGAZINE, 7500 Old Oak Blvd., Cleveland OH 44130. FAX: (216)891-2683. Editor: Mark S. Kuhar. 10-20% freelance written. Prefers to work with published/established writers. Monthly magazine for floor covering retailers, wholesalers, contractors, specifiers and designers. Estab. 1931. Circ. 25,000. **Pays on acceptance.** Publishes ms an average of 3 months after acceptance. Byline given. Buys all rights. Query for electronic submissions. "Send letter with writing sample to be placed in our freelance contact file." Editorial calendar available on request. Send #10 SASE.

Nonfiction: "Mostly staff written. Buys a small number of manuscripts throughout the year. Needs writers with 35mm photography skills for local assignments. Study our editorial calender and send a concise query."

GIFT & STATIONERY, 1515 Broadway, New York NY 10036. (212)869-1300. Editor: Joyce Washnik. 10% freelance written. Prefers to work with published/established writers. Monthly for "merchants (department store buyers, specialty shop owners) engaged in the resale of giftware, china and glass, stationery and decorative accessories." Monthly. Circ. 40,000. Buys all rights. Pays on publication. Publishes ms an average of 2 months after acceptance. Query for electronic submissions.

Nonfiction: "Retail store success stories. Describe a single merchandising gimmick. We are a tabloid format—glossy stock. Descriptions of store interiors are less important than sales performance unless display is outstanding. We're interested in articles on aggressive selling tactics. We cannot use material written for the consumer." Buys coverage of successful business operations and merchandising techniques. Query or submit complete ms. Length: 1,200 words maximum. Sometimes pays the expenses of writers on assignment.

Photos: Purchased with mss and on assignment; captions required. "Individuals are to be identified." Reviews b&w glossy prints (preferred) and color transparencies.

Tips: "All short items are staff produced. The most frequent mistake made by writers is that they don't know the market. As a trade publication, we require a strong business slant, rather than a consumer angle."

‡HAPPI, (*Household and Personal Products Industry*), P.O. Box 555, 17 S. Franklin Turnpike, Ramsey NJ 07446. FAX: (201)825-0553. Editor: Hamilton C. Carson. 5% freelance written. For "manufacturers of soaps, detergents, cosmetics and toiletries, waxes and polishes, insecticides, and aerosols." Circ. 18,000. Not copyrighted. Pays on publication. Publishes ms an average of 2 months after acceptance. Submit seasonal material 2 months in advance. Query.

Nonfiction: "Technical and semitechnical articles on manufacturing, distribution, marketing, new products, plant stories, etc., of the industries served. Some knowledge of the field is essential in writing for us." Buys informational interview, photo feature, spot news, coverage of successful business operations, new product articles, coverage of merchandising techniques and technical articles. No articles slanted toward consumers. Query with published clips. Buys 3 to 4 mss a year. Length: 500-2,000 words. Pays $25-300. Sometimes pays expenses of writers on assignment.

Photos: 5×7 or 8×10 b&w glossies purchased with mss. Pays $10.

Tips: "The most frequent mistakes made by writers are unfamiliarity with our audience and our industry; slanting articles toward consumers rather than to industry members."

HOME LIGHTING & ACCESSORIES, P.O. Box 2147, Clifton NJ 07015. (201)779-1600. FAX: (201)779-3242. Editor: Peter Wulff. 5% freelance written. Prefers to work with published/established writers. For lighting stores/departments. Monthly magazine. Estab. 1923. Circ. 10,000. Pays on publication.

Publishes ms an average of 4-6 months after acceptance. Buys all rights. Submit seasonal/holiday material 6 months in advance. Free sample copy.

Nonfiction: Interview (with lighting retailers); personal experience (as a businessperson involved with lighting); profile (of a successful lighting retailer/lamp buyer); and technical (concerning lighting or lighting design). Buys less than 10 mss/year. Query. Pays $60/published page. Sometimes pays the expenses of writers on assignment.

Photos: State availability of photos with query. Offers no additional payment for 5×7 or 8×10 b&w glossy prints. Pays additional $90 for color transparencies used on cover. Captions required.

Tips: "We don't need fillers—only features."

‡**RETAILER AND MARKETING NEWS**, P.O. Box 191105, Dallas TX 75219-1105. (214)871-2930. Editor: Michael J. Anderson. Monthly for retail dealers and wholesalers in appliances, TVs, furniture, consumer electronics, records, air conditioning, housewares, hardware, and all related businesses. Circ. 10,000. Free sample copy.

Nonfiction: "How a retail dealer can make more profit" is the approach. Wants "sales promotion ideas, advertising, sales tips, business builders and the like, localized to the Southwest and particularly to north Texas." Submit complete ms. Length: 100-900 words. Pays $30.

Hospitals, Nursing and Nursing Homes

In this section are journals for medical and nonmedical nursing home personnel, clinical and hospital staffs and medical laboratory technicians and managers. Journals publishing technical material on medical research and information for physicians in private practice are listed in the Medical catetory.

‡**AMERICAN JOURNAL OF NURSING**, 555 West 57th St., New York NY 10019. (212)582-8820. Editor: Mary B. Mallison, RN. 2% freelance written. Eager to work with new/unpublished writers. Monthly magazine covering nursing and health care. Estab. 1900. Circ. 235,000. Pays on publication. Publishes ms an average of 6 months after acceptance. Byline given. Simultaneous queries OK. Reports in 3 weeks on queries, 4 months on mss. Sample copy $3; free writer's guidelines.

Nonfiction: How-to, satire, new product, opinion, personal experience, photo feature and technical. No material other than nursing care and nursing issues. "Nurse authors mostly accepted for publication." Query. Length: 1,000-1,500 words. Payment negotiable. Pays the expenses of writers on assignment.

Photos: Forbes Linkhorn, art editor. Reviews b&w and color transparencies and prints. Model release and identification of subjects required. Buys variable rights.

Columns/Departments: Buys 20 mss/year. Query with or without clips of published work.

‡**HOSPITAL RISK MANAGEMENT**, American Health Consultants, P.O. Box 740059, Atlanta GA 30374. (404)262-7436. Editor: Cheli Brown. 10% freelance written. A monthly newsletter on health care risk management. Circ. 2,500. Pays on publication. Publishes ms an average of 1 month after acceptance. Byline given. Buys all rights. Reports in 1 month. Free sample copy and writer's guidelines.

Nonfiction: How-to (pertaining to hospitals' legal liability management). Nothing analytical. Buys 10-12 mss/year. Query. Length: 600 words. Pays $50-150.

HOSPITAL SUPERVISOR'S BULLETIN, Bureau of Business Practice, 24 Rope Ferry Rd., Waterford CT 06386. Editor: Michele Dunaj. 40% freelance written. Works with a small number of new/unpublished writers each year. For non-medical hospital supervisors. Semimonthly newsletter. Circ. 3,300. **Pays on acceptance.** Publishes ms an average of 5 months after acceptance. Buys all rights. No byline. Submit seasonal/holiday material 6 months in advance. Reports in 1 month. Sample copy and writer's guidelines for SAE with 2 first class stamps.

Nonfiction: Publishes interviews with non-medical hospital department heads. "You should ask supervisors to pinpoint current problems in supervision, tell how they are trying to solve these problems and what results they're getting—backed up by real examples from daily life." Also publishes interviews on people problems and good methods of management. People problems include the areas of training, planning, evaluating, counseling, discipline, motivation, supervising the undereducated, getting along with the medical staff, dealing with change, layoffs, etc. No material on hospital volunteers. "We prefer six- to eight-page typewritten articles. Articles must be interview-based." Pays 12-15¢/word after editing.

Tips: "Often stories lack concrete examples explaining general principles. I want to stress that freelancers interview supervisors (not high-level managers, doctors, or administrators) of non-medical departments. Interviews should focus on supervisory skills or techniques that would be applicable in any hospital department. The article should be conversational in tone: not stiff or academic. Use the second person to address the supervisor/reader."

NURSING92, Springhouse Corporation, 1111 Bethlehem Pike, Springhouse PA 19477. (215)646-8700. Editor: Maryanne Wagner. Managing Editor: Jane Benner. 100% freelance written. Monthly magazine on the nursing field. "Our articles are written by nurses for nurses; we look for practical advice for the working nurse that reflects the author's experience." Estab. 1971. Circ. 500,000. Pays on publication. Publishes ms an average of 10-12 months after acceptance. Byline given. Offers 50% kill fee. Buys all rights. Submit seasonal/holiday material 6-8 months in advance. Query for electronic submissions. Reports in 2 weeks on queries; 10-12 weeks on mss. Sample copy for $3 with 9 × 12 SAE. Free writers' guidelines.
Nonfiction: Book excerpts, exposé, how-to (specifically as applies to nursing field), inspirational, new product, opinion, personal experience and photo feature. No articles from patients' point of view; humor articles, poetry, etc. Buys 100 mss/year. Query. Length: 100 words minimum. Pays $50-400.
Photos: State availability of photos with submission. Offers no additional payment for photos accepted with ms. Model releases required. Buys all rights.

Hotels, Motels, Clubs, Resorts and Restaurants

These publications offer trade tips and advice to hotel, club, resort and restaurant managers, owners and operators. Journals for manufacturers and distributors of bar and beverage supplies are listed in the Beverages and Bottling section.

BARTENDER MAGAZINE, Foley Publishing, Box 158, Liberty Corner NJ 07938. (908)766-6006. FAX: (908)766-6607. Publisher: Raymond P. Foley. Editor: Jaclyn M. Wilson. Emphasizes liquor and bartending for bartenders, tavern owners and owners of restaurants with full-service liquor licenses. 100% freelance written. Prefers to work with published/established writers; eager to work with new/unpublished writers. Magazine published 4 times/year. Circ. 140,000. Pays on publication. Publishes ms an average of 3 months after acceptance. Buys first serial rights, first North American serial rights, one-time rights, second serial (reprint) rights, all rights, and simultaneous U.S. rights. Byline given. Phone queries OK. Submit seasonal/holiday material 3 months in advance. Simultaneous and previously published submissions OK. Reports in 2 months. Sample copies for 9 × 12 SAE with $2.50 for postage.
Nonfiction: General interest, historical, how-to, humor, interview (with famous bartenders or ex-bartenders); new products, nostalgia, personal experience, unique bars, opinion, new techniques, new drinking trends, photo feature, profile, travel and bar sports or bar magic tricks. Send complete ms. Length: 100-1,000 words. Sometimes pays the expenses of writers on assignment.
Photos: Send photos with ms. Pays $7.50-50 for 8 × 10 b&w glossy prints; $10-75 for 8 × 10 color glossy prints. Caption preferred and model release required.
Columns/Departments: Bar of the Month; Bartender of the Month; Drink of the Month; New Drink Ideas; Bar Sports; Quiz; Bar Art; Wine Cellar; Tips from the Top (from prominent figures in the liquor industry); One For The Road (travel); Collectors (bar or liquor-related items); Photo Essays. Query. Length: 200-1,000 words. Pays $50-200.
Fillers: Clippings, jokes, gags, anecdotes, short humor, newsbreaks and anything relating to bartending and the liquor industry. Length: 25-100 words. Pays $5-25.
Tips: "To break in, absolutely make sure that your work will be of interest to all bartenders across the country. Your style of writing should reflect the audience you are addressing. The most frequent mistake made by writers in completing an article for us is using the wrong subject."

FLORIDA HOTEL & MOTEL JOURNAL, The Official Publication of the Florida Hotel & Motel Association, Accommodations, Inc., P.O. Box 1529, Tallahassee FL 32302. (904)224-2888. Editor: Mrs. Jayleen Woods. 10% freelance written. Prefers to work with published/established writers. Monthly magazine for managers in the lodging industry (every licensed hotel, motel and resort in Florida). Estab. 1978. Circ. 6,800. Pays on publication. Publishes ms an average of 2 months after acceptance. Byline given. Offers $50 kill fee. Buys all rights and makes work-for-hire assignments. Submit seasonal/holiday material 3 months in advance. Reports in 1 month. Sample copy and writer's guidelines for 9 × 12 SAE and 5 first class stamps.

For information on setting your freelance fees, see How Much Should I Charge? in the Business of Writing section.

Nonfiction: General interest (business, finance, taxes); historical/nostalgic (old Florida hotel reminiscences); how-to (improve management, housekeeping procedures, guest services, security and coping with common hotel problems); humor (hotel-related anecdotes); inspirational (succeeding where others have failed); interview/profile (of unusual hotel personalities); new product (industry-related and non brand preferential); photo feature (queries only); technical (emerging patterns of hotel accounting, telephone systems, etc.); travel (transportation and tourism trends only—no scenics or site visits); and property renovations and maintenance techniques. Buys 10-12 mss/year. Query with proposed topic and clips of published work. Length: 750-2,500 words. Pays $75-250 "depending on type of article and amount of research." Sometimes pays the expenses of writers on assignment.
Photos: Send photos with ms. Pays $25-100 for 4 × 5 color transparencies; $10-15 for 5 × 7 b&w prints. Captions, model release and identification of subjects required.
Tips: "We prefer feature stories on properties or personalities holding current membership in the Florida Hotel and Motel Association. Membership and/or leadership brochures are available (SASE) on request. We're open to articles showing how hotel management copes with energy systems, repairs, renovations, new guest needs and expectations. The writer may have a better chance of breaking in at our publication with short articles and fillers because the better a writer is at the art of condensation, the better his/her feature articles are likely to be."

FLORIDA RESTAURATEUR, Florida Restaurant Association, 2441 Hollywood Blvd., Hollywood FL 33020. (305)921-6300. FAX: (305)925-6381. Editor: Hugh P. (Mickey) McLinden. 15% freelance written. Monthly magazine for food service and restaurant owners and managers—"deals with trends, legislation, training, sanitation, new products, spot news." Estab. 1946. Circ. 18,200. Pays on publication. Publishes ms an average of 1 month after acceptance. Byline given. Buys one-time rights. Submit seasonal/holiday material 3 months in advance. Simultaneous submissions OK. Reports in 1 week on queries; 2 weeks on mss.
Nonfiction: How-to, general interest, interview/profile, new product, personal experience and technical. Query. Length: 500-2,000 words. Pays $200-300 for assigned articles; $150-250 for unsolicited articles.
Photos: State availability of photos with submission. Reviews transparencies and 5 × 7 prints. Offers $50-250 per photo. Model releases and identification of subjects required. Buys one-time rights.

HOTEL AMENITIES IN CANADA, Encove Publishing Inc., Unit 5, 24 Hayes Ave., P.O. Box 1747, Guelph, Ontario N1H 7A1 Canada. (519)824-6842. FAX: (519)824-7533. Editor: Jayne Guild. 30% freelance written. Bimonthly magazine covering the lodging hospitality industry. *"Hotel Amenities in Canada* is a publication dedicated to the promotion of amenities and essential supplies and services in the Canadian hospitality industry." Estab. 1987. Circ. 4,500. Pays on publication. Publishes ms an average of 2 months after acceptance. Byline given. Buys first North American serial rights. Submit seasonal/holiday material 3 months in advance. Simultaneous and previously published submissions OK. Reports in 6 weeks. Sample copy for 8 × 10 SAE with Canadian postage or International Reply Coupon.
Nonfiction: New product, company feature. *"Hotel Amenities in Canada* is aimed primarily at the lodging hospitality industry so we do not need foodservice articles." Buys 12 mss/year. Query with published clips. Length: 500-1,500 words. Pays up to $100.
Photos: State availability of photos with submission. Reviews 5 × 7 prints. Offers $5/photo. Identification of subjects required. Buys one-time rights.
Columns/Departments: Products and Services (new products). Length 50-100 words. Pays up to $10.
Tips: "Research the amenities trend in the hospitality industry."

INNKEEPING WORLD, P.O. Box 84108, Seattle WA 98124. FAX: (206)362-7847. Editor/Publisher: Charles Nolte. 75% freelance written. Eager to work with new/unpublished writers. Emphasizes the hotel industry worldwide. Published 10 times a year. Estab. 1979. Circ. 2,000. **Pays on acceptance.** Publishes ms an average of 4 months after acceptance. Buys all rights. No byline. Submit seasonal/holiday material 1 month in advance. Reports in 1 month. Sample copy and writer's guidelines for 9 × 12 SAE with 3 first class stamps.
Nonfiction: Managing—interviews with successful hotel managers of large and/or famous hotels/resorts (600-1,200 words); Marketing—interviews with hotel marketing executives on successful promotions/case histories (300-1,000 words); Sales Promotion—innovative programs for increasing business (100-600 words); Bill of Fare—outstanding hotel restaurants, menus and merchandising concepts (300-1,000 words); and Guest Relations—guest service programs, management philosophies relative to guests (200-800 words). Pays $100 minimum or 15¢/word (whichever is greater) for main topics. Other topics—advertising, creative packages, cutting expenses, frequent guest profile, guest comfort, hospitality, ideas, public relations, reports and trends, special guestrooms, staff relations. Length: 50-500 words. Pays 15¢/word. "If a writer asks a hotel for a complimentary room, the article will not be accepted, nor will *Innkeeping World* accept future articles from the writer."

Tips: "We need more in-depth reporting on successful case histories — results-oriented information."

LODGING HOSPITALITY MAGAZINE, Penton Publishing, 1100 Superior Ave., Cleveland OH 44114. (216)696-7000. FAX: (216)696-7658. Editor: Edward Watkins. 10% freelance written. Prefers to work with published/established writers. A monthly magazine covering the lodging industry. "Our purpose is to inform lodging management of trends and events which will affect their properties and the way they do business. Audience: owners and managers of hotels, motels, resorts." Estab. 1949. Circ. 50,000. **Pays on acceptance.** Publishes ms an average of 2 months after acceptance. Byline given. Buys first rights. Submit seasonal/holiday material 2 months in advance. Reports in 1 month.
Nonfiction: General interest, how-to, interview/profile and travel. Special issues include technology (January); interior design (April); foodservice (May); investments (June); franchising (July); marketing (September); and state of the industry (December). "We do *not* want personal reviews of hotels visited by writer, or travel pieces. All articles are geared to hotel executives to help them in their business." Buys 25 mss/year. Query. Length: 700-2,000 words. Pays $150-600. Sometimes pays the expenses of writers on assignment.
Photos: State availability of photos with submission. Reviews contact sheets and transparencies. Offers no additional payment for photos accepted with ms. Captions and identification of subjects required. Buys one-time rights.
Columns/Departments: Budget Line, Suite Success, Resort Report, Executive on the Spot, Strategies Marketwatch, Report from Washington, Food for Profit, Technology Update — all one-page reports of 700 words. Buys 25 mss/year. Query. Pays $150-250.

PIZZA TODAY, The Professional Guide To Pizza Profits, ProTech Publishing and Communications, Inc., P.O. Box 114, Santa Claus IN 47579. (812)937-4464. FAX: (812)937-4688. Editor: Paula Werne. 30% freelance written. Prefers to work with published/established writers. A monthly magazine for the pizza industry, covering trends, features of successful pizza operators, business and management advice, etc. Estab. 1983. Circ. 550,000. Pays on publication. Publishes ms an average of 2 months after acceptance. Byline given. Offers 10-30% kill fee. Buys all rights and negotiable rights. Submit seasonal/holiday material 3 months in advance. Simultaneous and previously published submissions OK. Query for electronic submissions. Reports in 2 weeks on queries; 3 weeks on manuscripts. Sample copy and writer's guidelines for 10×13 SAE with 6 first class stamps. No phone calls, please.
Nonfiction: Interview/profile, new product, entrepreneurial slants, time management, pizza delivery and employee training. No fillers, fiction, humor or poetry. Buys 40-60 mss/year. Query with published clips. Length: 750-2,500 words. Pays $50-125/page. Sometimes pays the expenses of writers on assignment.
Photos: Send photos with submission. Reviews contact sheets, negatives, 4×5 transparencies, color slides and 5×7 prints. Offers $5-25/photo. Captions required.
Tips: "We would like to receive nutritional information for low-cal, low-salt, low-fat, etc. pizza. Writers must have strong business and foodservice background."

RESTAURANT HOSPITALITY, Penton Publishing, 1100 Superior Ave., Cleveland OH 44114. (216)696-7000. FAX: (216)696-0836. Editor-in-Chief: Michael DeLuca. 30% freelance written. Works exclusively with published/established writers. Monthly magazine covering the foodservice industry for owners and operators of independent restaurants, hotel foodservices, executives of national and regional restaurant chains. Estab. 1919. Circ. 100,000. Average issue includes 5-10 features. **Pays on acceptance.** Publishes ms an average of 3 months after acceptance. Byline given. Buys first North American rights. Reports in 3 weeks. Sample copy for 9×12 SAE and with 10 first class stamps.
Nonfiction: General interest (articles that advise operators how to run their operations profitably and efficiently); interview (with operators); and profile. Stories on psychology, consumer behavior, managerial problems and solutions, design elements. No restaurant reviews. Buys 50-60 mss/year. Query with clips of previously published work and a short bio. Length: 500-1,500 words. Pays $125/published page. Pays the expenses of writers on assignment.
Photos: Send color photos with manuscript. Captions required.
Tips: "We would like to receive queries for articles on food and management trends. We need new angles on old stories, and we like to see pieces on emerging trends and technologies in the restaurant industry. Our readers don't want to read how to open a restaurant or why John Smith is so successful."

VACATION INDUSTRY REVIEW, Worldex Corp., P.O. Box 431920, South Miami FL 33243. (305)285-2200. FAX: (305)665-2546. Managing Editor: George Leposky. 10% freelance written. Prefers to work with published/established writers. A quarterly magazine covering leisure lodgings (timeshare resorts, fractionals, condo hotels, and other types of vacation ownership properties). Estab. 1982. Circ. 10,000. Pays on publication. Publishes ms an average of 3-6 months after acceptance. Byline given. Buys all rights and makes work-for-hire assignments. Submit seasonal/holiday material 6 months in advance.

"Electronic submissions—query for details." Reports in 1 month. Sample copy $3; writer's guidelines with #10 SASE.

Nonfiction: How-to, interview/profile, new product, opinion, personal experience, technical and travel. No consumer travel or non-vacation real-estate material. Buys 5 mss/year. Query with published clips. Length: 1,000-2,500 words. Pays $75-175. Pays the expenses of writers on assignment, if previously arranged.

Photos: Send photos with submission. Reviews contact sheets, 35mm transparencies, and 5×7 or larger prints. Offers no additional payment for photos accepted with ms. Captions and identification of subjects required. Buys one-time rights.

Tips: "We want articles about the business aspects of the vacation industry: entrepreneurship, project financing, design and construction, sales and marketing, operations, management—in short, anything that will help our readers plan, build, sell and run a quality vacation property that satisfies the owners/ guests while earning a profit for the proprietor. Our destination pieces are trade-oriented, reporting the status of tourism and the development of various kinds of leisure lodging facilities in a city, region or country. We're interested in homeowners associations at vacation ownership resorts (not residential condos). You can discuss things to see and do in the context of a resort located near an attraction, but that shouldn't be the main focus or reason for the article."

Industrial Operations

Industrial plant managers, executives, distributors and buyers read these journals. Some industrial management journals are also listed under the names of specific industries. Publications for industrial supervisors are listed in Management and Supervision.

CHEMICAL BUSINESS, Schnell Publishing Company, 80 Broad St., New York NY 10004-2203. FAX: (212)248-4901. Editor: Arthur R. Kavaler. Executive Editor: J. Robert Warren. 90% freelance written. A monthly magazine covering chemicals and related process industries such as plastics, paints, some minerals, essential oils, soaps, detergents. Publishes features on the industry, management, financial (Wall Street), marketing, shipping and storage, labor, engineering, environment, research, international and company profiles. Estab. 1875. Circ. 40,000. **Pays on acceptance.** Publishes ms an average of 3 months after acceptance. Byline given. Offers $100 kill fee. Buys all rights. Call before submitting seasonal/holiday material. Previously published book excerpts OK. Free sample copy and writer's guidelines.

Nonfiction: No broad, general industrial submissions on how-to. Buys 35 mss/year. Query. Length: 1,200-1,500 words. Pays $500 for assigned articles. Pays the expenses of writers on assignment.

Photos: Send photos with submission. Reviews contact sheets, negatives and 35mm or 70mm ("almost any size") transparencies. No pay for company photos; offers $10-25/photo taken by writer. Model releases required. Buys all rights.

COMPRESSED AIR, 253 E. Washington Ave., Washington NJ 07882. Editor/Publications Manager: S.M. Parkhill. 75% freelance written. Emphasizes applied technology and industrial management subjects for engineers and managers. Publishes 8 times per year. Estab. 1896. Circ. 150,000. Buys all rights. Publishes ms an average of 4 months after acceptance. Reports in 6 weeks. Free sample copy; mention *Writer's Market* in request.

Nonfiction: "Articles must be reviewed by experts in the field." Buys 56 mss/year. Query with published clips. Pays negotiable fee. Sometimes pays expenses of writers on assignment.

Photos: State availability of photos in query. Payment for slides, transparencies and glossy prints is included in total purchase price. Captions required. Buys all rights.

Tips: "We are presently looking for freelancers with a track record in industrial/technology/management writing. Editorial schedule is developed in the summer before the publication year and relies heavily on article ideas from contributors. Resume and samples help. Writers with access to authorities preferred; and prefer interviews over library research. The magazine's name doesn't reflect its contents. We suggest writers request sample copies."

CPI PURCHASING, The Magazine About Buying in the Chemical and Process Industries, Cahners Publishing, 275 Washington St., Newton MA 02158. (617)558-4224. Editor: Kevin R. Fitzgerald. 5% freelance written. A monthly magazine covering the chemical and process industries. Estab. 1983. Circ. 40,000. **Pays on acceptance.** Publishes ms an average of 2 months after acceptance. Byline given. Offers 50% kill fee. Buys all rights. Sample copy $10.

Nonfiction: "We assign stories, usually on chemical market developments. Our readers are buyers of chemicals and related process equipment, packaging, transportation and environmental services. Freelancers should not submit *anything* on spec." Query. Length: 1,000-3,000 words. Pays $300-1,500 for assigned articles. Pays the expenses of writers on assignment.

Photos: State availability of photos.
Tips: "We prefer writers with some background in chemicals or equipment. Houston/Gulf Coast residents are especially welcome, but, please no PR writers."

MANUFACTURING SYSTEMS, The Management Magazine of Integrated Manufacturing, Hitchcock Publishing Co., 191 S. Gary Ave., Carol Stream IL 60188. (708)665-1000. FAX: (708)462-2225 (staff). Editor: Tom Inglesby. Executive Editor: Mary Emrich. Managing Editor: Barbara Dutton. Associate Editor: Carol Smith. 10-15% freelance written. A monthly magazine covering computers/information in manufacturing for upper and middle-level management in manufacturing companies. Estab. 1982. Circ. 115,000. **Pays on acceptance.** Publishes ms an average of 4 months after acceptance. Byline given. Offers 35% kill fee on assignments. Buys all rights. Simultaneous submissions OK. Exclusive submissions do receive more consideration. Query for electronic submissions. Reports in 6 weeks. Free sample copy and writer's guidelines.
Nonfiction: Book excerpts, essays, general interest, interview/profile, new product, opinion, technical, case history—applications of system. "Each issue emphasizes some aspect of manufacturing. Editorial schedule available, usually in September, for next year." Buys 6-8 mss/year. Query with or without published clips, or send complete ms. Length: 500-2,500 words. Pays $150-600 for assigned articles; pays $50/published page for unsolicited articles. Sometimes pays limited, pre-authorized expenses of writers on assignment.
Photos: State availability of photos with submission. Reviews contact sheets, negatives, 2×2 and larger transparencies and 5×7 and larger prints. Offers no additional payment for photos accepted with ms. Captions and identification of subjects required. Buys one-time rights.
Columns/Departments: Forum (VIP-to-VIP, bylined by manufacturing executive), 1,000-1,500 words. Buys 1-2 mss/year. Query. Sometimes pays $100-200. "These are *rarely* paid for but we'd consider ghost written pieces bylined by 'name.' "
Tips: "We are moving more toward personal management issues and away from technical articles—how to manage, not what tools are available. Check out success stories of companies winning against overseas competition in international marketplace. New trends in manufacturing include application of artificial intelligence (expert systems); standards for computer systems, networks, operating systems; computer trends, trade, taxes; movement toward "lights-out" factory (no human workers) in Japan and some U.S. industries; desire to be like Japanese in management style; more computer power in smaller boxes. Features are the most open area. We will be happy to provide market information, reader profile and writer's guidelines on request. We are moving to 'require' submission in electronic form—diskette, MCI-mail. Rekeying ms into our word processing system is more work (and cost)."

PLANT, Suite 500, 245 Fairview Mall Dr., Willowdale/Ontario, Ontario M2J 4T1 Canada. FAX: (416)490-0220. Editor: Ron Richardson. 10% freelance written. Prefers to work with published/established writers. For Canadian plant managers and engineers. Monthly magazine. Estab. 1941. Circ. 52,000. **Pays on acceptance.** Publishes ms an average of 2 months after acceptance. Buys first Canadian rights. Reports in 3 weeks. Free sample copy.
Nonfiction: How-to, technical and management technique articles. Must have Canadian slant. No generic articles that appear to be rewritten from textbooks. Buys fewer than 20 unsolicited mss/year. Query. Pays 22¢/word minimum. Sometimes pays the expenses of writers on assignment.
Photos: State availability of photos with query. Pays $25-50 for b&w prints; $50-100 for 2¼×2¼ or 35mm transparencies. Captions required. Buys one-time rights.
Tips: "Increased emphasis on the use of computers and programmable controls in manufacturing will affect the types of freelance material we buy. Read the magazine. Know the Canadian readers' special needs. Case histories and interviews only—no theoretical pieces. We have gone to tabloid-size format, and this means shorter (about 800 word) features."

QUALITY ASSURANCE BULLETIN, (formerly *Quality Control Supervisor's Bulletin*), Bureau of Business Practice, 24 Rope Ferry Rd., Waterford CT 06386. (800)243-0876. FAX: (203)434-3341. 80% freelance written. Biweekly newsletter for quality assurance supervisors and managers. **Pays on acceptance.** No byline given. Buys all rights. Reports in 2 weeks on queries; 1 month on mss. Free sample copy and writer's guidelines.
Nonfiction: Interview and articles with a strong how-to slant that make use of direct quotes whenever possible. Query before writing your article. Length: 800-1,500 words. Pays 8-15¢/word.
Tips: Write for freelancer guidelines and follow them closely.

‡**QUALITY DIGEST,** QCI International, P.O. Box 1503, 1425 Vista Way, Red Bluff CA 96080. (916)527-8875. Editor: Scott M Paton. 75% freelance written. Monthly trade magazine covering quality improvement. Estab. 1981. Circ. 10,000. **Pays on acceptance.** Byline given. Buys all rights. Submit material 4 months in advance. Accepts simultaneous and previously published submissions. Query for electronic submissions. Reports in 2 weeks. Free sample copy and writer's guidelines.

Nonfiction: Book excerpts, how-to implement quality programs, etc., interview/profile, opinion, personal experience, technical. Buys 25 mss/year. Query with or without published clips, or send complete ms. Length: 1,000-6,000 words. Pays $25-350. Pays with contributor copies or other premiums for unsolicited manuscripts. Sometimes pays expenses of writers on assignment.

Photos: Send photos with submisison. Reviews any size prints. Offers no additional payment for photos accepted with ms. Captions, model releases and identification of subjects required. Buys one-time rights.

Tips: "Please be specific in your articles. Explain what the problem was, how it was solved and what the benefits are. Tell the reader how the technique described will benefit him or her."

WEIGHING & MEASUREMENT, Key Markets Publishing Co., P.O. Box 5867, Rockford IL 61125. (815)229-1818. FAX: (815)229-4086. Editor: David M. Mathieu. For users of industrial scales and meters. Bimonthly magazine. Estab. 1914. Circ. 15,000. **Pays on acceptance.** Buys all rights. Pays 20% kill fee. Byline given. Reports in 2 weeks. Sample copy $1.

Nonfiction: Interview (with presidents of companies); personal opinion (guest editorials on government involvement in business, etc.); profile (about users of weighing and measurement equipment); and technical. Buys 25 mss/year. Query on technical articles; submit complete ms for general interest material. Length: 750-1,500 words. Pays $125-200.

Information Systems

These publications give computer professionals more data about their field. Consumer computer publications are listed under Personal Computers.

‡ACCESS TO WANG, The Independent Magazine for Wang System Users, Data Base Publications, Suite 385, 8310 Capital of Texas Hwy., Austin TX 78731. (512)343-9066. Editor: Anne M. Heinen. 80% freelance written. Monthly trade journal about Wang Laboratories, their products and related topics. Estab. 1983. Circ. 26,000. Pays on publication. Publishes ms an average of 2 months after acceptance. Byline given. No kill fee. Buys first rights. Query for electronic submissions. Reports in 2 weeks. Sample copy for 8×11 SAE with 65¢. Free writer's guidelines.

Nonfiction: Technical. "We have a revolving schedule of special reports." No product promotions. Buys 70 mss/year. Query with published clips or send complete ms. Length: 100-2,000 words. Pays $75-400 for assigned articles. Sometimes pays expenses of writers on assignment.

Tips: "A thorough knowledge of the computer world is necessary."

ATUNC NEWSLETTER, Apple Three Users of Northern California, P.O. Box 16427, San Francisco CA 94116. (415)731-0829. Editor: Li Kung Shaw. 50% freelance written. Monthly newsletter of AIII technology, life and stories of all users. Technical and human aspects of AIII and its users in the world. Estab. 1984. Circ. 150. Pays on publication. Buys first rights. Submit seasonal/holiday material 2 months in advance. Simultaneous and previously published material OK. Query for electronic submissions. Reports in 1 month. Free sample copy.

Nonfiction: Anything related to AIII or its users. Buys 12 mss/year. Query. Length: 500-3,000 words. Pays $10-100. Pays in contributor copies or other premiums under mutual agreement.

Photos: Send photos with submission. Reviews contact sheets. Offers no additional payment for photos accepted with ms. Buys one-time rights.

Fiction: "No fiction except those related to AIII and its users."

Poetry: "No poems except those related to AIII or its users."

Fillers: "No fillers except those related to AIII or its users."

COMMUNIXATIONS, Uniform Association, Suite 201, 2901 Tasman Dr., Santa Clara CA 95054. (408)986-8840. FAX: (408)986-1645. Publications Director: Jordan Gold. Managing Editor: Jeffrey Bartlett. 80% freelance writtten. Monthly trade journal covering UNIX. "Writers must have a sound knowledge of the UNIX operating system." Estab. 1981. Circ. 10,000. **Pays on acceptance.** Publishes ms an average of 2 months after acceptance. Byline given. Offers 30% kill fee. Buys all rights. Query for electronic submissions. Reports in 6 weeks. Free sample copy and writer's guidelines.

Nonfiction: Interview/profile, opinion, and technical. Buys 35 mss/year. Query with or without published clips. Length: 1,000-3,500 words. Pays $0-1,200. Sometimes pays in other premiums or contributors copies "when article is written by industry member." Pays expenses of writers on assignment. International writers actively sought.

Photos: Send photos with submission. "Photos are required with ms, but offers no additional payment." Buys one-time rights.

Columns/Departments: UNIX for Beginners, 700-1,200 words; Programming Tips (technical issues), 700-1,500 words; Career Corner (career tips), 700-800 words; Reseller Update, 700-800 words. Buys 12 mss/year. Query. Pays $0-250.

‡**COMPUTER LANGUAGE**, Miller Freeman Publications, 500 Howard St., San Francisco CA 94105. (415)397-1881. Editor: Larry O'Brien. Managing Editor: Brett Warren. 75% freelance written. A monthly trade journal on software development. *"Computer Language* editorial contains practical information on programming and design for programmers and software developers." Circ. 65,000. Pays on publication. Publishes ms an average of 6 months after acceptance. Byline given. Buys first or second rights. Query for electronic submissions. Reports in 1 month on queries; 2 months on mss. Free writer's guidelines. "Writer's guidelines, editorial calendar and other information may be obtained by calling (415)905-2501."
Nonfiction: Interview/profile, technical. Buys 70 mss/year. Query. Length: 2,500-5,000 words. Pays $200-600.
Tips: Emphasis will be on programming design and techniques with emphasis on Windows, C, and object-oriented programming.

DATA BASED ADVISOR, The Database Management Systems Magazine, Data Based Solutions, Inc., Suite 200, 4010 Morena Blvd., San Diego CA 92117. (619)483-6400. FAX: (619)483-9851. Executive Editor: John L. Hawkins. Managing Editor: Dian Schaffhauser. 90% freelance written. Monthly magazine covering database management systems for microcomputers. *Data Based Advisor*'s mission is to provide information to users and prospective users of microcomputer database management systems. Estab. 1983. Circ. 40,642. Pays on publication. Publishes ms an average of 4 months after acceptance. Byline given. Offers 25% kill fee. Buys all rights. Query for electronic submissions. Reports in 3 months. Free sample copy and writer's guidelines.
Nonfiction: How-to, interview/profile and technical. "We don't like to see articles that cover database managers superficially. Other computer magazines do this all too well—'What's a database manager?' 'How do you use it?' 'How do you automate your inventory?' Our writers understand their subjects intimately and provide detailed instructions for their products of choice. We also don't like to see queries for software reviews. These are assigned by the editorial staff." Buys 240 mss/year. Query with published clips. Length: 400-3,000 words. Pays $50-650 for assigned articles; $50-350 for unsolicited articles. Sometimes pays expenses of writers on assignment.
Columns/Departments: Fast Takes (reviews of products and books, *always assigned*), 300-1,000 words. Buys 80 mss/year. Query. Pays $25-200.
Tips: "Write a concise query that summarizes who will read the article, why you're the best person to handle the job, and what the article will consist of. Then be *very* patient with us. 'Fast Takes' is a great way to break into the magazine. Query us with your areas of interest and we'll try to make an assignment based on your expertise."

‡**DBMS**, M&T Publishing, Inc., 501 Galveston Dr., Redwood City CA 94063. (415)366-3600. Editor: Kevin Strehlo. Managing Editor: Steve Wilent. 60% freelance written. Monthly magazine covering database applications and technology. "Our readers are database developers, consultants, VARs, programmers in MIS/DP departments, and serious users." Estab. 1988. Circ. 55,000. **Pays on acceptance.** Publishes ms 3 months after acceptance. Byline given. Offers 33% kill fee. Buys all rights. Query for electronic submissions. Reports in 6 weeks on queries. Sample copy for 9 × 12 SAE with 8 first class stamps.
Nonfiction: Technical. Buys 40-50 mss/year. Query with published clips. Length: 750-6,000 words. Pays $800.
Photos: Send photos with submission. Offers no additional payment for photos accepted with ms. Captions, model releases and identification of subjects required. Buys all rights.
Tips: "New writers should submit clear, concise queries of specific article subjects and ideas. *Read the magazine* to get a feel for the kind of articles we publish. This magazine is written for a highly technical computer database developer, consultant and user readership. We need technical features that inform this audience of new trends, software, hardware and techniques, including source code, screen caps, and procedures."

DEVELOPERS' INSIGHT, (formerly *Programmer's Update*) SDC Communications, 90 Industrial Park Rd., Hingham MA 02043. (617)740-0135. FAX: (617)740-2620. Editor: Michael Kei Stewart. 75% freelance written. Monthly magazine of PC programming trends and strategies. Write to enlighten professional software developers, provide perspective on practices and trends; support with concrete examples and useful information. Emphasize *impact* of every subject on programmers. Estab. 1990. Pays on publication. Publishes ms an average of 1 month after acceptance. Byline given. Buys first and second rights. Submit seasonal/holiday material 1 month in advance. Previously published material OK. Query for electronic submissions. Reports in 1 week. Free sample copy.
Nonfiction: General interest, how-to (programming techniques, tool use and *impact*, user story, interview/profile, new product (if first in category), opinion (industry, technical trends), technical (development strategies and comparisons). No how-to's that don't say "why-to" or reviews (unless new category of product). Buys 15-20 mss/year. Query with or without published clips, or send complete ms. Length:

1,000-4,000 words. Pays $1-100/published page. Pays in contributor copies or other premiums if writer works for company that has vested interest in article topic.
Photos: State availability of photos with submission. Offers no additional payment for photos accepted with ms.
Fillers: Cartoons. Buys up to 5/year. Pays $1-50.
Tips: "Call and get acquainted *if you have a definite idea*. Write a letter with an idea. Send ms with SASE. Writers have the best chance selling us features. Check topic first with us, then make sure tech content is accurate, complete and relevant."

DG REVIEW, For Data General and Compatible Users, Data Base Publications, Suite 385, 8310 Capital of Texas Hwy., Austin TX 78731. (512)343-9066. FAX: (512)345-1935. Editor: Cynthia Kurkowski. 50% freelance written. Works with a small number of new/unpublished writers each year. A monthly magazine covering Data General computer systems. "*DG Review* is the primary independent source of technical and market-specific information for people who use Data General computer systems or sell to the Data General market." Estab. 1981. Circ. 15,000. Pays on publication. Publishes ms an average of 3 months after acceptance. Byline given. Buys first North American serial rights and second serial (reprint) rights. Submit seasonal/holiday material 3 months in advance. Query for electronic submissions. Reports in 1 month. Free sample copy and writer's guidelines.
Nonfiction: How-to, new product (computer-related), and technical all specific to Data General systems. No articles which cannot be related to Data General. Buys 25 mss/year. Query with published clips. Length: 1,000-3,500 words. Pays $100-300 for assigned articles.
Photos: State availability of photos with submission. Reviews contact sheets, transparencies and 5×7 prints. Offers $0-25/photo. Captions, model releases, and identification of subjects required. Buys first serial rights.
Columns/Departments: Technical columns (instructive articles on Data General computer hardware and software, including reviews by users), 1,000-2,500 words. Query with published clips. Pays $0-300.
Tips: "Feature articles are the area of our publication most open to freelancers."

‡DR. DOBB'S JOURNAL, Software Tools for Advanced Programmers, M&T Publishing, Inc., 501 Galveston Dr., Redwood City CA 94063. (415)366-3600. FAX: (415)366-1685. Editor: Jon Erickson. Managing Editor: Monica Berg. 60% freelance written. Eager to work with new/unpublished writers. Monthly magazine on computer programming. Circ. 85,000. Pays on publication. Publishes ms an average of 5 months after acceptance. Byline given. Buys all rights. Query for electronic submissions. Reports in 1 month on queries; 9 weeks on mss. Writer's guidelines for #10 SASE.
Nonfiction: How-to and technical. Buys 70 mss/year. Send complete ms. Word length open. Pays $75-1,000.
Tips: "We are happy to look at outlines or queries to see if an author is suitable. They may also obtain writer's guidelines. We are a 'hot rodding' magazine for experienced programmers. Our articles show how to write faster, yet smaller, code. Almost all articles are programmers talking to programmers."

‡FLEXLINES, Data Access Corp., 14000 SW 199 Ave., Miami FL 33186. (305)238-0012. Managing Editor: Beverly Horning-Gore. 40% freelance written. Bimonthly magazine covering Data Flex software. "Publication is for users, developers and sellers of Data Flex software." Estab. 1976. Circ. 10,000. Pays on publication. Pubilshes ms an average of 2 months after acceptance. Byline given. Negotiable kill fee. Buys all rights. Query for electronic submissions. Reports in 2 weeks. Sample copy $2 with 9×12 SAE. Free writer's guidelines.
Nonfiction: New product, technical (about Data Flex). Buys 12 mss/year. Send complete ms. Length: 500-5,000 words. Pays $100-250.
Photos: Send photos with submission. Reviews prints (any). Offers no additional payment for photos accepted with ms. Captions and model releases required. Buys one-time rights.
Columns/Departments: Unix (Data Flex with Unix), 500-5,000 words; User Groups (Dada Flex user group profiles), 500-5,000 words. Send complete ms. Length: 500-5,000 words. Pays $100-250.
Tips: "Know Data Flex as an expert."

‡INFORM, The Magazine of Information and Image Management, Association for Information and Image Management, 1100 Wayne Ave., Silver Spring MD 20910. (301)587-8202. FAX: (301)587-2711. Editor: Gregory E. Kaebnick. 30% freelance written. Prefers to work with writers with business/high tech experience. A monthly trade magazine on information and image processing. "Specifically we feature coverage of micrographics, electronic imaging and developments in storage and retrieval technology like optical disk, computer-assisted retrieval." Circ. 10,000. Pays on publication. Publishes ms an average of 3 months after acceptance. Byline given. Offers $50 kill fee. Buys first North American serial and second serial (reprint) rights. Submit seasonal/holiday material 2 months in advance. Simultaneous submissions OK. Free sample copy and writer's guidelines.

Nonfiction: Interview/profile, new product, photo feature and technical. Buys 4-12 mss/year. Query. Length: 1,500-4,000 words. Pays $200-500 for assigned articles. Sometimes pays the expenses of writers on assignment.

Photos: State availability of photos with submission. Reviews negatives, 4x5 transparencies and prints. Offers no additional payment for photos accepted with ms. Captions and identification of subjects required. Buys all rights.

Columns/Departments: Trends (developments across industry segments); Technology (innovations of specific technology); Management (costs, strategies of managing information), all 500-1,500 words. Query. Length: 500-1,500 words. Pays $250.

Fillers: Facts and newsbreaks. Length: 150-500 words. Pays $50-250.

Tips: "We would encourage freelancers who have access to our editorial calendar to contact us regarding article ideas, inquiries, etc. We also cover numerous trade shows during the year, and the availability of freelancers to cover these events would be valuable to us. Our feature section is the area where the need for quality freelance coverage of our industry is most desirable. The most likely candidate for acceptance is someone who has a proven background in business writing, and/or someone with demonstrated knowledge of high-tech industries as they relate to information management."

INFORMATION WEEK, CMP Inc., 600 Community Dr., Manhasset NY 11030. (516)365-4600. FAX: (516)562-5474. Contact: Elliot Kass. Assistant Managing Editor: John McCormick. 20% freelance written. Weekly magazine covering strategic use of information systems and telecom. "Our readers are busy executives who want excellent information or thoughtful opinion on making computers and associated equipment improve the competitiveness of their companies." Circ. 170,000. Pays on publication. Publishes ms an average of 1 month after acceptance. Byline given. Offers 25% kill fee. Buys first North American serial rights and second serial (reprint) rights. Submit seasonal/holiday material 2 months in advance. Previously published submissions rarely OK. Query for electronic submissions. Reports in 3 weeks on queries; 2 week on mss. Sample copy for 8 × 11 SAE.

Nonfiction: Book excerpts (information management); exposé (government computing, big vendors); humor (850 word piece reflecting on our information era and its people); and interview/profile (corporate chief information officers). No software reviews, product reviews, no "gee whiz—computers are wonderful" pieces. Buys 20-30 mss/year. Query with or without published clips. Length: 500-3,500 words. Pays $300-1,500. Pays expenses of writers on assignment.

Photos: Send photos with submission. Reviews negatives and transparencies. Pays negotiable rates. Captions, model releases and identification of subjects required. Buys one-time rights.

Columns/Departments: Final Word (a humorous or controversial personal opinion page on high-level computer-oriented business), 850 words; Chiefs (interview, portrait of chief information officer in Fortune 500 Company), 2,000-3,000 words. Buys 100 mss/year. Query. Length: 800-900 words. Pays $100-1,500.

Tips: "We appreciate a *one-paragraph* lead, a headline, a deck and a very brief outline. This evokes the quickest response. Humor is the most difficult thing to create and the one we crave the most. Humor is especially difficult when the subject is management information systems. Good humor is an easy sell with us."

NETWORK WORLD, Network World Publishing, 161 Worcester Rd., Framingham MA 01701. (508)875-6400. FAX: (508)820-3467. Editor: John Gallant. Features Editor: Paul Strauss. 25% freelance written. A weekly tabloid covering data, voice and video communications networks (including news and features on communications management, hardware and software, services, education, technology and industry trends) for senior technical managers at large companies. Estab. 1986. Circ. 150,000. **Pays on acceptance.** Byline given. Offers negotiable kill fee. Buys all rights. Submit all material 2 months in advance. Query for electronic submissions. Reports in 3 weeks. Free sample copy and writer's guidelines.

Nonfiction: Exposé, general interest, how-to (build a strong communications staff, evaluate vendors, choose a value-added network service), humor, interview/profile, opinion and technical. Editorial calendar available. "Our readers are users: avoid vendor-oriented material." Buys 100-150 mss/year. Query with published clips. Length: 500-2,500 words. Pays $600 minimum—negotiable maximum for assigned or unsolicited articles.

Photos: Send photos with submission. Reviews 35mm, 2¼ and 4 × 5 transparencies and b&w prints (prefers 8 × 10 but can use 5 × 7). Captions, model releases and identification of subjects required. Buys one-time rights.

Tips: "We look for accessible treatments of technological, managerial or regulatory trends. It's OK to dig into technical issues as long as the article doesn't read like an engineering document. Feature section is most open to freelancers. Be informative, stimulating, controversial and technically accurate."

RESELLER MANAGEMENT, Elsevier Communications, Inc., P.O. Box 650, Morris Plains NJ 07950-0650. (201)292-5100. Editor: Tom Farre. 50% freelance written. Eager to work with new/unpublished writers if they know the field. Monthly management and technology magazine for computer resellers, including dealers, VARs and systems integrators. Estab. 1978. Circ. 55,000. Pays on publication. Publishes ms an average of 3 months after acceptance. Buys all rights. Query for electronic submissions.

Nonfiction: Management issues for resellers. "Writers must know microcomputer hardware and software and be familiar with computer *reselling*—our readers are computer-industry professionals in an extremely competitive field." Buys 3-6 mss/issue. Query with published clips. Length: 400-2,000 words. Sometimes pays the expenses of writers on assignment.

Photos: B&w or color.

Columns/Departments: Solicited by editor. "If the writer has an idea, query by mail to the editor, with clips."

Tips: "All articles must have a heavy managerial slant, while still covering the microcomputer industry for resellers."

SOFTWARE MAINTENANCE NEWS, Suite 5F, 141 Saint Mark's Place, Staten Island NY 10301. (718)816-5522. FAX: (718)816-9038. 75% freelance written. Monthly magazine covering software maintenance. Estab. 1983. Circ. 7,000. Pays on publication. Publishes ms an average of 3 months after acceptance. Byline given. Buys one-time rights. Simultaneous submissions OK. Query for electronic submissions. Reports in 1 week. Free sample copy.

Nonfiction: New product, technical. "No how-to or user stories." Buys 36 mss/year. Query or send complete ms. Length: 100-2,400 words. Pays about 4¢/word.

Photos: State availability of photos with submission. Offers no additional payment for photos accepted with ms. Captions required. Buys one-time rights.

Columns/Departments: Bug/People (experiences with software), 600 words. Buys 10 mss/year. Query or send complete ms. Length: 600 words minimum. Pays $35 minimum.

Fiction: We *are* looking for fiction. Must be about software. Buys 1 ms/year. Query or send complete ms. Length: 600-2,400 words. Pays about 4¢/word.

Poetry: Haiku, light verse. Must be about software! Buys 2 poems/year. Pays about 4¢/word.

Tips: "Call first. Show familiarity with field."

SUNWORLD, (formerly *Suntech Journal*), IDGC/Peterborough, 80 Elm St., Peterborough NH 03458. (603)924-0100. Editor-in-chief: John Barry. Managing Editor: Joseph J. Fatton. 75% freelance written. Monthly magazine that covers computer workstations. "*SunWorld* covers the technical and application issues relating to Sun and SPARC computers and the UNIX operating system." Buys first rights. Simultaneous and previously published submissions OK. Query for electronic submissions. Reports in 2 weeks on queries; 3 weeks on mss. Free sample copy and writer's guidelines.

Nonfiction: How-to (e.g., write a RISC compiler), new product and technical. "Marketing-oriented articles are taboo. Technical audience must be kept in mind." Buys 24-30 mss/year. Query. Length: 2,000-4,000 words. Pays $500-1,000 for assigned articles. Sometimes pays expenses of writers on assignment.

Photos: Send figures, charts and program listings with submission. Offers no additional payment for photos accepted with ms. Captions and identification of subjects required. Buys all rights except advertising.

Columns/Departments: Synergy ("success" story of technical application), 750-1,500 words. Reviews (product evaluations), 750-1,500 words. Writers of review articles must be in intimately familiar with a given product area (databases, for example) and must be unbiased. Query. Pays $300-500. Buys 8 mss/year. Query. Pays $400 maximum.

Tips: "Writers should be technically sophisticated. *SunWorld* readers are some of the most technically astute people in the world, which is why their companies/universities give them the powerful computers from Sun to work with. Do not try to fool them with PR-hype. User profiles are the best entry into *SunWorld*. Some of the most interesting scientists and engineers in the world use Sun equipment, (e.g., those monitoring Voyager II; those who found the *Titanic*, etc.). This work makes for exciting reading when handled by a fine writer."

SYSTEMS 3X/400, Hunter Publishing, 950 Lee St., Des Plaines IL 60016. (708)296-0770. FAX: (708)803-3328. Editor: Bob Mueller. 10% freelance written. Works with a small number of new/unpublished writers each year. Monthly magazine covering applications of IBM minicomputers (S/34/36/38/ and AS/400) in business. Estab. 1973. Circ. 55,000. Pays on publication. Publishes ms an average of 3 months after acceptance. Byline given. Buys all rights. Submit seasonal material 4 months in advance. Query for electronic submissions. Reports in 2 weeks on queries. Sample copy for 9×12 SAE and 4 first class stamps; writer's guidelines for #10 SASE.

Nonfiction: How-to (use the computer in business); and technical (organization of a data base or file system). "A writer who submits material to us should be an expert in computer applications. No material on large-scale computer equipment." No poetry. Buys 8 mss/year. Query. Length: 2,000-4,000 words. Sometimes pays expenses of writers on assignment.
Tips: "Frequent mistakes are not understanding the audience and not having read the magazine (past issues)."

UNIX WORLD, McGraw-Hill's Magazine of Open Systems Computing, McGraw-Hill Inc., 444 Castro St., Mountain View CA 94041. (415)940-1500. Editor-in-Chief: David L. Flack. 20% freelance written. Mostly freelancers are used for product reviews. Monthly magazine directed to people who use, make or sell UNIX products, particularly in an open systems environment. Readers are employed in management, engineering, and software development. Circ. 70,000. Pays 1 month after publication. Publishes ms an average of 4 months after acceptance. Byline given. Offers kill fee. Buys all rights. Electronic submissions only. Reports in 1 month. Sample copy $3. Writer's guidelines sent. Ask for editorial calendar so query can be tailored to the magazine's need; send SASE with 2 first class stamps.
Nonfiction: Tutorials (technical articles on the Unix system or the C language); new products; technical overviews; and product reviews. Query by phone or with cover letter and published clips. Length: 2,500-3,000 words. Pays $100-1,000. Sometimes pays the expenses of writers on assignment.
Tips: "We are shifting more toward a business and commercial focus and would appreciate knowledge in that area. The best way to get an acceptance on an article is to consult our editorial calendar and tailor a pitch to a particular story."

‡WORKSTATION, Independent Magazine for Hewlett-Packard Apollo Workstation Users, Wilson Publications, Inc., 12416 Hymeadow Dr., Austin TX 78750. (512)250-5518. FAX: (512)331-6779. Editor-in-Chief: Ron Seybold. 30% freelance written. Willing to work with new/unpublished writers. A monthly magazine covering Hewlett-Packard and Apollo workstation computers and instruments. "*Workstation* contains material covering the use of HP computers running the HP-UX, Dowain, Rocky Mountain Boise and OSF/1 opearting systems. This includes features on current technology issues, HP news, tutorials, reviews and new product announcements. Writers must be technically concise and coherent about their subject. Freelance articles must include HP slant." Estab. 1985. Circ. 20,000. Pays on publication. Publishes ms an between 2-4 months after acceptance. Byline given. Offers negotiable percentage of promised payment as kill fee. Buys first North American serial rights. Query for electronic submissions. Reports in 3 weeks on queries; 5 weeks on mss. Sample copy for 8½×11 SASE.
Nonfiction: How-to (on hardware and software applications), application stories (case studies), and hands-on evaluations of hardware and software, tested on HP workstation plot forms and technical. Submissions must be directly related to HP 9000, computers or peripherals. May consider company profiles, in-depth pieces on firms working with HP in new or contemporary technologies and markets. Buys 30 mss/year. Query with outline with or without published clips. Can send complete ms. Length: 750-2,500. Pays 10-15¢/word. Sometimes pays the expenses of writers on assignment.
Photos: State availability of photos with submission. Reviews contact sheets, negatives, transparencies and prints. Captions required.
Tips: Eager to establish writers as evaluators. "Accepting more pieces that acknowledge the person behind the equipment—targeting more articles to vertical applications, i.e. the use of HP equipment in aerospace, automotive and manufacturing industries. Writer need not be an engineer or computer scientist, but must have thorough grasp of subject. Accepting more articles concerning industry standards, but copy should reflect writer's work experience with such standards; i.e.," How OSF network standards helped out site." Let us know what your expertise is and how it will make you the right person to cover the proposed topic. Write for the system administrator or the workstation end-user. Tell how to get the most out of hardware/software. Let readers know of unusual uses for equipment. Be as lively as possible, but technically complete. Don't write in manual style."

Insurance

FLORIDA UNDERWRITER, National Underwriter Company, Suite 115, 1345 S. Missouri Ave., Clearwater FL 34616. (813)442-9189. FAX: (813)443-2479. Editor: James E. Seymour. Managing Editor: Garry Baumgartner. 20% freelance written. Monthly magazine about insurance. "*Florida Underwriter* covers insurance for Florida insurance professionals: producers, executives, risk managers, employee benefit administrators. We want material about any insurance line, Life & Health or Property & Casualty, but *must* have a Florida tag—Florida authors preferred." Estab. 1984. Circ. 10,000. Pays on publication. Publishes ms an average of 2-3 months after acceptance. Byline given. Buys all rights. Submit seasonal/holiday material 3 months in advance. Simultaneous and previously published submissions OK (notification of other submission, publications required). Query for

electronic submissions. Reports in 3 weeks. Free sample copy and writer's guidelines.
Nonfiction: Essay, exposé, historical/nostalgic, how-to, interview/profile, new product, opinion and technical. "We don't want articles that aren't about insurance for insurance people or those that lack Florida angle. No puff pieces." Buys 6 mss/year. Query with or without published clips, or send complete ms. Length: 500-1,500 words. Pays $50-150 for assigned articles; $25-100 for unsolicited articles. "Industry experts contribute in return for exposure." Sometimes pays expenses of writers on assignment.
Photos: State availability of photos with submission. Send photos with submission. Reviews 5×7 prints. Offers no additional payment for photos accepted with ms. Identification of subjects required.

GEICO DIRECT, K.L. Publications, Suite 105, 2001 Killebrew Dr., Bloomington MN 55425. Editor: Eileen Kuehn. 60% freelance written. Semiannual magazine published for the Government Employees Insurance Company (GEICO) policyholders. Circ. 1.5 million. Pays on acceptance by client. Byline given. Buys first North American serial rights. Query for electronic submissions.
Nonfiction: Americana, home and auto safety, car care, financial, lifestyle and travel. Query with published clips. Length: 1,000 words. Pays $350-600.
Photos: Reviews 35mm transparencies. Payment varies.
Columns/Departments: Moneywise, 50+, Your Car. Query with published clips. Length: 500-600 words. Pays $175-350.
Tips: "We prefer work from published/established writers, especially those with specialized knowledge of the insurance industry, safety issues and automotive topics."

INSURANCE REVIEW, Insurance Information Institute, 110 William St., New York NY 10038. (212)669-9200. Editor: Olga Badillo-Sciortino. Managing Editor: Kenneth M. Coughlin. 100% freelance written. A monthly magazine covering property and casualty insurance for agents, brokers, insurers, risk managers, educators, lawyers, financial analysts and journalists. Estab. 1940. Circ. 70,000. **Pays on acceptance.** Publishes ms an average of 2 months after acceptance. Byline given. Offers 25% kill fee. Buys first North American serial rights; rights returned to author 90 days after publication. "We retain right to reprint." Query for electronic submissions. Reports in 1 month. Free sample copy and writer's guidelines.
Nonfiction: How-to (improve agency business), interview/profile, opinion, industry issues, technical and business articles with insurance information. Buys 75 mss/year. Query with published clips. Length: 750-2,500 words. Pays $350-1,200 for assigned articles. Pays phone and postage expenses.
Photos: Send photos with submission. Reviews contact sheets and transparencies. Captions, model releases and identification of subjects required.
Columns/Departments: By Line (analysis of one line of p/c business), Analysis (financial aspects of p/c industry); Technology (innovative uses for agents or insurers); Agency Profitability; Agency Business. Query. Length: 750-1,500 words. Pays $350-1,000.
Tips: "Become well-versed in issues facing the insurance industry. Identify provocative topics worthy of in-depth treatment. Profile successful or unusual agents or brokers."

THE LEADER, Fireman's Fund Insurance Co., 777 San Marin Dr., Novato CA 94998. (415)899-2109. FAX: (415)899-2126. Editor: Jim Toland. 70% freelance written. Bimonthly magazine on insurance. "*The Leader* contains articles and information for Fireman's Fund employees and retirees about special offices and employees nationwide—emphasizing the business of insurance and the unique people who work for the company." Estab. 1863. **Pays on acceptance.** Publishes ms an average of 3 months after acceptance. Byline given. Buys one-time rights. Simultaneous submissions OK. Reports in 1 month on mss. Free sample copy.
Nonfiction: Interview/profile, new products and employees involved in positive activities in the insurance industry and in the communities where company offices are located. Query with published clips. Length: 200-2,500 words. Pays $50-300.
Photos: Reviews contact sheets and prints. Sometimes buys color slides. Offer $25-50 per photo for b&w, up to $100 for color. Buys one-time rights.
Tips: "It helps to work in the insurance business and/or know people at Fireman's Fund. Writers with business reporting experience are usually most successful—though we've published many first time writers. Research the local Fireman's Fund branch office (not sales agents who are independents). Look for newsworthy topics. Strong journalism and reporting skills are greatly appreciated."

PROFESSIONAL AGENT MAGAZINE, The magazine of the National Association of Professional Insurance Agents, 400 N. Washington St., Alexandria VA 22314. (703)836-9340. FAX: (703)836-1279. Editor: John S. DeMott. 85% freelance written. Monthly magazine covering insurance/small business for independent insurance agents, legislators, regulators and others in the industry. Estab. 1937. Circ. 30,000. **Pays on acceptance.** Publishes ms an average of 1 month after acceptance. Byline given. Buys exclusive rights in the industry. Prefers electronic submissions. Reports ASAP. Sample copy for SASE.

Nonfiction: Insurance management for small businesses and self-help. Special issues on life insurance and computer interface. Buys 36 mss/year. Query with published clips or send complete ms. Length: 2,000-4,000 words. Pays $700-1,200. Pays the expenses of writers on assignment.

Tips: "We prefer to work with established magazine writers. Query by phone, then send clips or mss. We prefer submissions by modem or disk, with hard copy accompanying by mail."

International Affairs

These publications cover global relations, international trade, economic analysis and philosophy for business executives and government officials involved in foreign affairs. Publications for the general public on related subjects appear in Consumer Politics and World Affairs.

FOREIGN AFFAIRS, 58 E. 68th St., New York NY 10021. (212)734-0400. Editor: William G. Hyland. Primarily freelance written. For academics, businessmen (national and international), government, educational and cultural readers especially interested in international affairs of a political nature. Published 5 times/year. Circ. 100,000. Pays on publication. Byline given. Query for electronic submissions. Reports in 2 months.

Nonfiction: "Articles dealing with international affairs; political, educational, cultural, economic, scientific, philosophical and social sciences. Develop an original idea in depth, with a strong thesis usually leading to policy recommendations. Serious analyses by qualified authors on subjects with international appeal." Buys 25 unsolicited mss/year. Submit complete ms, double-spaced. Length: 5,000 words. Pays approximately $750.

Tips: "We like the writer to include his/her qualifications for writing on the topic in question (educational, past publications, relevant positions or honors), and a clear summation of the article: the argument (or area examined), and the writer's policy conclusions."

JOURNAL OF DEFENSE & DIPLOMACY, Defense and Diplomacy, Inc., Suite 200, 6849 Old Dominion Dr., MacLean VA 22101. (703)448-1338. FAX: (703)448-1841. Editor-in-Chief: Wm. Chaze. 75% freelance written. Eager to work with new/unpublished writers. "Publication credentials not necessary for consideration." Monthly publication covering international affairs and defense. "The *Journal* is a sophisticated, slick publication that analyzes international affairs for decision-makers—heads of state, key government officials, defense industry executives—who have little time to pore through all the details themselves." Estab. 1983. Circ. 20,000. Pays on publication. Publishes ms an average of 2 months after acceptance. Byline given. Offers 10% kill fee. Buys first rights and second serial (reprint) rights. Simultaneous queries, and simultaneous and previously published submissions OK. Reports in 1 month on queries; 2 months on mss. Sample copy $5 (includes postage); writer's guidelines for #10 SASE.

Nonfiction: Book excerpts, general interest (strategy and tactics, diplomacy and defense matters), interview/profile, opinion and photo feature. "Decision-makers are looking for intelligent, straightforward assessments. We want clear, concise writing on articles with international appeal. While we have accepted articles that deal with U.S. decisions, there is always an international aspect to the subject." No articles that focus solely on the United States. Buys 24 mss/year. Send complete ms. Length: 2,000-4,000 words. Pays $900-1,000.

Photos: Reviews color and b&w photos. No additional payment is offered for photos sent with ms.

Columns/Departments: Speaking Out (1,000 to 2,000-word "point of view" piece analyzing any current topic of widespread interest); Materiel (a technical discussion of current and upcoming weapons systems); Books (reviews of books on world politics, history, biography and military matters); interview ("We constantly need interviews with important international figures. We are always looking for the non-U.S. interview."). Buys 12 mss/year. Query with published clips. Length: 1,500-3,000 words. Pays $100-250.

Tips: "We depend on experts in the field for most of the articles that we use. As long as a manuscript demonstrates that the writer knows the subject well, we are willing to consider anyone for publication. The most frequent mistake made by writers in completing an article for us is writing in too technical

Market conditions are constantly changing! If this is 1993 or later, buy the newest edition of Writer's Market at your favorite bookstore or order directly from Writer's Digest Books.

or too official a style. We want to be very readable. We are looking for writers who are able to digest complex subjects and make them interesting and lively. We need writers who can discuss complicated and technical weapons systems in clear non-technical ways."

Jewelry

THE DIAMOND REGISTRY BULLETIN, #806, 580 5th Ave., New York NY 10036. (212)575-0444. FAX: (212)575-0722. Editor-in-Chief: Joseph Schlussel. 25% freelance written. Monthly newsletter. Estab. 1969. Pays on publication. Buys all rights. Submit seasonal/holiday material 1 month in advance. Simultaneous and previously published submissions OK. Reports in 3 weeks. Sample copy $5.

Nonfiction: Prevention advice (on crimes against jewelers); how-to (ways to increase sales in diamonds, improve security, etc.); and interview (of interest to diamond dealers or jewelers). Submit complete ms. Length: 50-500 words. Pays $25-150.

Tips: "We seek ideas to increase sales of diamonds."

THE ENGRAVERS JOURNAL, P.O. Box 318, 26 Summit St., Brighton MI 48116. (313)229-5725. FAX: (313)229-8320. Co-Publisher and Managing Editor: Michael J. Davis. 15% freelance written. "We are eager to work with published/established writers as well as new/unpublished writers." A bimonthly magazine covering the recognition and identification industry (engraving, marking devices, awards, jewelry, and signage.) "We provide practical information for the education and advancement of our readers, mainly retail business owners." Estab. 1975. **Pays on acceptance.** Publishes ms an average of 1 year after acceptance. Byline given "only if writer is recognized authority." Buys all rights (usually). Query with published clips and resume. Previously published submissions OK. Query for electronic submissions. Reports in 2 weeks. Free writer's guidelines; sample copy to "those who send writing samples with inquiry."

Nonfiction: General interest (industry-related); how-to (small business subjects, increase sales, develop new markets, use new sales techniques, etc.); interview/profile; new product; photo feature (a particularly outstanding signage system); and technical. No general overviews of the industry. Buys 12 mss/year. Query with writing samples "published or not," or "send samples and resume to be considered for assignments on speculation." Length: 1,000-5,000 words. Pays $75-250, depending on writer's skill and expertise in handling subject.

Photos: Send photos with query. Reviews 8×10 prints. Pays variable rate. Captions, model release and identifiction of subjects required.

Tips: "Articles should always be down to earth, practical and thoroughly cover the subject with authority. We do not want the 'textbook' writing approach, vagueness, or theory—our readers look to us for sound practical information."

FASHION ACCESSORIES, S.C.M. Publications, Inc., 65 W. Main St., Bergenfield NJ 07621-1696. (201)384-3336. FAX: (201)384-6776. Managing Editor: Samuel Mendelson. Monthly newspaper covering costume or fashion jewelry. "Serves the manufacturers, manufacturers' sales reps., importers and exporters who sell exclusively through the wholesale level in ladies' fashion jewlery, mens' jewelry, gifts and boutiques and related novelties." Estab. 1951. Circ. 8,000. **Pays on acceptance.** Byline given. Not copyrighted. Buys first rights. Submit seasonal/holiday material 3 months in advance. Sample copy for $2 and 9×12 SAE.

Nonfiction: Essays, general interest, historical/nostalgic, how-to, humor, interview/profile, new product and travel. Buys 20 mss/year. Query with published clips. Length: 1,000-2,000 words. Pays $100-300. Sometimes pays the expenses of writers on assignment.

Photos: Send photos with submission. Reviews 4×5 prints. Offers no additional payment for photos accepted with ms. Identification of subjects required. Buys one-time rights.

Columns/Departments: Fashion Report (interviews and reports of fashion news), 1,000-2,000 words.

Tips: "We are interested in anything that will be of interest to costume jewelry buyers at the wholesale level."

Journalism and Writing

Journalism and writing magazines cover both the business and creative sides of writing. Writing publications offer inspiration and support for professional and beginning writers. Although there are many valuable writing publications that do not pay, we only have space to list those writing publications that pay for articles.

BOOK DEALERS WORLD, North American Bookdealers Exchange, Box 606, Cottage Grove OR 97424. (503)942-7455. Editorial Director: Al Galasso. Senior Editor: Judy Wiggins. 50% freelance written. Quarterly magazine covering writing, self-publishing and marketing books by mail. Circ. 20,000. Pays on publication. Publishes ms an average of 3 months after acceptance. Byline given. Buys first serial rights and second serial (reprint) rights. Simultaneous and previously published submissions OK. Reports in 1 month. Sample copy for $3.

Nonfiction: Book excerpts (writing, mail order, direct mail, publishing); how-to (home business by mail, advertising); and interview/profile (of successful self-publishers). Positive articles on self-publishing, new writing angles, marketing, etc. Buys 10 mss/year. Send complete ms. Length: 1,000-1,500 words. Pays $25-50.

Columns/Departments: Print Perspective (about new magazines and newsletters); Small Press Scene (news about small press activities); and Self-Publisher Profile (on successful self-publishers and their marketing strategy). Buys 20 mss/year. Send complete ms. Length: 250-1,000 words. Pays $5-20.

Fillers: Fillers concerning writing, publishing or books. Buys 6/year. Length: 100-250 words. Pays $3-10.

Tips: "Query first. Get a sample copy of the magazine."

BRILLIANT IDEAS FOR PUBLISHERS, Creative Brilliance Associates, P.O. Box 44237, Madison WI 53744-4237. (608)233-2669. Editor: Naomi K. Shapiro. 2% freelance written. A bimonthly magazine covering the newspaper and shopper industry. "We provide business news and ideas to publishers of the daily, weekly, community, surburban newspaper and shopper publishing industry." Estab. 1982. Circ. 17,000. Pays on publication. Publishes ms an average of 4 months after acceptance. Byline given. Buys all rights. Query for electronic submissions. Reports in 3 weeks. Sample copy for 9 × 12 SAE with 4 first class stamps.

Nonfiction: *Only submit articles related to the newspaper industry*, i.e., sales, marketing or management. General interest, historical/nostalgic, how-to (tips and hints regarding editorial, production, etc.), humor, interview/profile, new product and opinion. *"The writer has to know and understand the industry."* No general writing or editing articles. Buys 3 mss/year. Query. Length: 200 words maximum. Pays $10-50 for unsolicited articles. May pay writers with contributor copies or other premiums if writer requests.

Photos: State availability of photos with submission. Offers no additional payment for photos accepted with ms. Captions, model releases and identification of subjects required. Buys all rights.

Columns/Departments: "Any books or brochures related to sales, marketing, management, etc. can be submitted for consideration for our BIFP Press department." Buys 3 mss/year. Query. Length: 200 words maximum. Pays $10-50.

Tips: "We are interested in working with any writer or researcher who has good, solid, documented pieces of interest to this specific industry."

BYLINE, P.O. Box 130596, Edmond OK 73013. (405)348-5591. Executive Editor/Publisher: Marcia Preston. Managing Editor: Kathryn Fanning. 80-90% freelance written. Eager to work with new/unpublished writers. Monthly magazine for writers and poets. "We stress encouragement of beginning writers." Estab. 1981. Publishes ms an average of 3 months after acceptance. Byline given. Buys first North American serial rights. Reports within 1 month. Sample copy and guidelines for $3.

Nonfiction: How-to, humor, inspirational, personal experience, *all* connected with writing and selling. Read magazine for special departments. Buys approximately 72 mss/year. Prefers queries; will read complete mss. Length: 1,500-2,000 words. Usual rate for features is $50, on acceptance. Needs short humor on writing (400-800 words). Pays $35.

Fiction: General fiction. Writing or literary slant preferred, but not required. Send complete ms: 2,000-3,000 words preferred. Pays $50 on acceptance.

Poetry: Any style, on a writing theme. Preferred length: 4-30 lines. Pays $5-10 on publication plus free issue.

CANADIAN AUTHOR & BOOKMAN, Canadian Authors Association, Suite 104, 121 Avenue Rd., Toronto, Ontario M5R 2G3 Canada. Contact: Editor. 95% freelance written. Prefers to work with published/established writers. "For writers—all ages, all levels of experience." Quarterly magazine. Estab. 1919. Circ. 3,000. Pays on publication. Publishes ms an average of 6 months after acceptance. Buys first Canadian rights. Byline given. Written queries only. Sample copy for $5; writer's guidelines for #10 SASE.

Nonfiction: How-to (on writing, selling; the specifics of the different genres—what they are and how to write them); informational (the writing scene—who's who and what's what); interview (on writers, mainly leading ones, but also those with a story that can help others write and sell more often); and opinion. No personal, lightweight writing experiences; no fillers. Query with immediate pinpointing of topic, length (if ms is ready), and writer's background. Length: 1,000-2,500 words. Pays $30/printed page.

Photos: "We're after an interesting-looking magazine, and graphics are a decided help." State availability of photos with query. Offers $10/photo for b&w photos accepted with ms. Buys one-time rights.

Poetry: High quality. "Major poets publish with us—others need to be as good." Buys 60 poems/year. Pays $15.

Tips: "We dislike material that condescends to its reader and articles that advocate an adversarial approach to writer/editor relationships. We agree that there is a time and place for such an approach, but good sense should prevail. If the writer is writing to a Canadian freelance writer, the work will likely fall within our range of interest."

CANADIAN WRITER'S JOURNAL, Gordon M. Smart Publications, P.O. Box 6618, Depot 1, Victoria, British Columbia V8P 5N7 Canada. (604)477-8807. Editor: Gordon M. Smart. Quarterly magazine for writers. Estab. 1985. Circ. 350. 75% freelance written. Will accept well-written articles by inexperienced writers. Pays on publication, an average of 3-9 months after acceptance. Byline given. Sample copy for $3 plus $1 postage; writer's guidelines for #10 SASE.

Nonfiction: How-to articles for writers. Buys 50-55 mss/year. Query optional. Length: 500-1,000 words.

Fiction: Fiction: Occasional short story to 1,000 words; tie-in to writing or publishing preferred. Pays about $5 (Canadian) per published magazine page.

Tips: "We prefer short, tightly written, informative how-to articles. U.S. writers note that U.S. postage cannot be used to mail from Canada. Obtain Canadian stamps, use IRC's or tape coins to a card."

COLUMBIA JOURNALISM REVIEW, 700 Journalism Bldg., Columbia University, New York NY 10027. (212)854-1881. Managing Editor: Gloria Cooper. "We welcome queries concerning media issues and performance. *CJR* also publishes book reviews. We emphasize in-depth reporting, critical analysis and good writing. All queries are read by editors."

THE COMICS JOURNAL, THE Magazine of News and Criticism, Fantagraphics, Inc., 7563 Lake City Way, Seattle WA 98115. (206)524-1967. Managing Editor: Helena G. Harvilicz. Editor: Gary Groth. 90% freelance written. A monthly magazine covering the comic book industry. "Comic books can appeal intellectually and emotionally to an adult audience, and can express ideas that other media are inherently incapable." Circ. 11,500. Pays on publication. Publishes ms an average of 2 months after acceptance. Byline given. Buys first rights. Submit seasonal/holiday material 5 months in advance. Reports in 2 weeks. Sample copy $3.50.

Nonfiction: Essays, news, exposé, historical, interview/profile, opinion and magazine reviews. Buys 120 mss/year. Send complete ms. Length: 500-3,000 words. Pays 1.5¢/word; writers may request trade for merchandise. Pays the expenses of writers on assignment.

Photos: Send photos with submission. Offers additional payment for photos accepted with ms. Identification of subjects required. Buys one-time rights.

Columns/Departments: Opening Shots (brief commentary, often humorous), 1,000 words; Newswatch (in depth reporting on the industry, U.S. and foreign news); The Comics Library (graphic review), and Ethics (examining the ethics of the comic-book industry), both 3,000 words. Buys 60 mss/year. Send complete ms. Pays 1.5¢/word; more for news items.

Tips: "Have an intelligent, sophisticated, critical approach to writing about comic books."

EDITOR & PUBLISHER, 11 W. 19th St., New York NY 10011. Editor: Robert U. Brown. Managing Editor: John Consoli. 10% freelance written. Weekly magazine. For newspaper publishers, editors, executives, employees and others in communications, marketing, advertising, etc. Circ. 29,000. Pays on publication. Publishes ms an average of 2 weeks after acceptance. Buys first serial rights. Sample copy $1.

Nonfiction: Uses newspaper business articles and news items; also newspaper personality features and printing technology. Query.

THE EDITORIAL EYE, Focusing on Publications Standards and Practices, Editorial Experts, Inc., Suite 200, 66 Canal Center Plaza, Alexandria VA 22314-1538. (703)683-0683. FAX: (703)683-4915. Editor: Ann R. Molpus. Managing Editor: Linda Jordenson. 5% freelance written. Prefers to work with published/established writers. Monthly professional newsletter on editorial subjects: writing, editing, graphic design, production, proofreading and levels of editing. "Our readers are professional publications people. Use journalistic style." Circ. 3,000. **Pays on acceptance.** Publishes ms an average of 6 months after acceptance. Byline given. Kill fee determined for each assignment. Buys first North American serial rights. "We retain the right to use articles in our training division and in an anthology of collected articles." Reports in 1 month. Sample copy for 6 × 9 SAE and 2 first-class stamps; writer's guidelines for #10 SASE.

Nonfiction: Editorial and production problems, issues, standards, practices and techniques; publication management; publishing technology; style, grammar and usage. No word games, vocabulary building, language puzzles, or jeremiads on how the English language is going to blazes. Buys 12 mss/year. Query. Length: 300-1,200. Pays $40-120.

Tips: "We seek mostly lead articles written by people in the publications field about the practice of publications work. Our style is journalistic with a light touch (not cute). We are interested in submissions on the craft of editing, levels of editing, editing by computer, publications management, indexing, lexicography, usages, proofreading. Our back issue list provides a good idea of the kinds of articles we run."

EDITORS' FORUM, Editors' Forum Publishing Company, P.O. Box 411806, Kansas City MO 64141. (913)236-9235. Managing Editor: William R. Brinton. 50% freelance written. Prefers to work with published/established but works with a small number of new/unpublished writers each year. A monthly newsletter geared toward communicators, particularly those involved in the editing and publication of newsletters and company publications. Estab. 1980. Circ. 900. Pays on publication. Publishes ms an average of 4 months after acceptance. Byline given. Offers 25% kill fee. Buys first North American serial rights, second serial (reprint) rights and makes work-for-hire assignments. Previously published submissions OK depending on content. Reports in 2 weeks on queries. Sample copy for 9 × 12 SAE and 2 first class stamps. Writer's guidelines for #10 SASE.

Nonfiction: How-to on editing and writing, etc. "With the advent of computer publishing, *EF* is running a regular high tech column on desk top publishing, software, etc. We can use articles on the latest techniques in computer publishing. Not interested in anything that does not have a direct effect on writing and editing newsletters. This is a how-to newsletter." Buys 22 mss/year. Query. Length: 250-1,000 words. Pays $20/page maximum.

Photos: State availability of photos/illustrations with submission. Reviews contact sheets. Offers $5/photo. Captions, model releases and identification of subjects required. Buys one-time rights.

Tips: "We are necessarily interested in articles pertaining to the newsletter business. That would include articles involving writing skills, layout and makeup, the use of pictures and other graphics to brighten up our reader's publication, and an occasional article on how to put out a good publication inexpensively."

‡FAIRBANKS ARTS MAGAZINE, Fairbanks Arts Association, P.O. Box 72786, Fairbanks AK 99707. (907)456-6485. Editor: LeAnn Lowe. 100% freelance written. Bimonthly publication promoting excellence in contemporary and traditional arts. **Pays on acceptance.** Byline given. Reports in 3 weeks. Sample copy and writer's guidelines for $3.

Nonfiction: How-to, humor, inspirational, personal experience (pertaining to writing, marketing, lifestyles, etc.). Query or send complete ms. Buys 12-15 mss/year. Length: 800-1,300 words. Pays $75.

Tips: "Studying sample copy highly recommended."

FREELANCE WRITER'S REPORT, Cassell Communications Inc., P.O. Box 9844, Fort Lauderdale FL 33310. (305)485-0795. FAX: (305)485-0806. Editor: Dana K. Cassell. 35% freelance written. Prefers to work with published/established writers. Monthly newsletter covering writing and marketing advice for established freelance writers. Estab. 1982. Pays on publication. Publishes ms an average of 6 months after acceptance. Byline given. Buys one-time rights. Submit seasonal/holiday material 2 months in advance. Simultaneous queries, and simultaneous and previously published submissions OK. Reports in 1 month. Sample copy $4 current issue; $2.50 past issue. No writer's guidelines; refer to this listing.

Nonfiction: Book excerpts (on writing profession); how-to (market, write, research); interview (of writers or editors); new product (only those pertaining to writers); photojournalism; promotion and administration of a writing business. No humor, fiction or poetry. Buys 72 mss/year. Query or send complete ms. Length: 500 words maximum. Pays 10¢/edited word.

Tips: "Write in terse newsletter style, eliminate flowery adjectives and edit mercilessly. Send something that will help writers increase profits from writing output—must be a proven method. We're targeting more to the established writer, less to the beginner."

HOUSEWIFE-WRITER'S FORUM, P.O. Box 780, Lyman WY 82937. (307)786-4513. Editor: Diane Wolverton. 90% freelance written. Bimonthly newsletter and literary magazine for women writers. "We are a support network and writer's group on paper directed to the unique needs of women who write and juggle home life." Estab. 1988. Circ. 1,200. **Pays on acceptance.** Publishes ms an average of 6-12 months after acceptance. Byline given. Buys one-time rights. Submit seasonal/holiday material 6 months in advance. Simultaneous and previously published submissions OK. Reports in 1 month on queries; 2 months on mss. Sample copy $4; writer's guidelines for #10 SASE.

Nonfiction: Essays, how-to, humor, interview/profile, opinion, personal experience. Buys 60-100 mss/year. Query with or without published clips, or send complete ms. Length: 2,000 words maximum, 400-750 words preferred. Pays 1¢ per word.

Columns/Departments: Confessions of Housewife-Writers (essays pertaining to our lives as women, writers, our childhoods, etc.), 25-800 words; Reviews (books, reference texts, products for housewife writers), 50-300 words. Buys 6-20 mss/year. Send complete ms. Length: 25-800 words. Pays 1¢ per word.

Fiction: Confession, experimental, fantasy, historical, horror, humorous, mainstream, mystery, romance, science fiction, slice-of-life vignettes, suspense. No pornography. Buys 6-12 mss/year. Send complete ms. Length: 2,000 words maximum. Pays 1¢ per word.

Poetry: Avant-garde, free verse, haiku, light verse, traditional, humorous. Buys 30-60 poems/year. Submit maximum 5 poems at one time. Pays $2 maximum.

Fillers: Anecdotes, facts, short humor, hints on writing and running a home. Length: 25-300 words. Pays $2 maximum.

Tips: "We consider ourselves a beginner's market for women who want to write for the various major women's markets. Like any woman, I like to laugh and I love a good cry. I also like to be educated. More importantly, I want to know about you as a person. My goal is to help each other become the best writers we can be. Everything is open to freelancers."

‡**THE ILLINOIS PUBLISHER,** Illinois Press Association, 701 South Grand Ave., West, Springfield IL 62704. (217)523-5092. FAX: (217)523-5103. Editor: David Porter. 50% freelance written. Quarterly magazine covering newspapers, especially Illinois. "We have a sophisticated, statewide audience that includes lawmakers, judges and other community leaders as well as publishers and editors of Illinois newspapers. Humor must be well done and be relative to topic." Estab. 1939. Circ. 2,500. **Pays on acceptance.** Publishes ms an average of 2 months after acceptance. Byline given. Offers 20% kill fee. Buys one-time rights, all rights or makes work-for-hire assignments. Submit seasonal/holiday material 6 months in advance. Simultaneous and previously published submissions OK. Query for electronic submissions. Reports in 6 weeks. Sample copy $2. Free writer's guidelines.

Nonfiction: Essays, historical/nostalgic, how-to (anything relating to newspapers, production or editorial or advertising), humor, interview/profile, opinion (does not mean letters to the editor), personal experience, photo feature, technical. No poetry. Buys 12-14 mss/year. Query with published clips. Length: 500-3,000 words. Pays $75-175 for assigned articles; $50-150 for unsolicited articles. No cash payment for columns. Sometimes pays expenses of writers on assignment.

Photos: State availability of photos with submission. Offers no additional payment for photos accepted with ms. Model releases and identification of subjects required.

Columns/Departments: Initial Insights (current, often first-person accounts on newspapering like trends—recycling. 1st amendment,etc.), 500; Parting Shots (like initial insights but often tongue-in-cheek), 500; On the Law (current legal issues pertaining to newspapers), 500. Buys 10-12 mss/year. Send complete ms. Length: 450-600 words. Pays copies.

Fiction: Experimental, humorous. "For us, fiction is best used to illustrate a point, like a fable. Humor is okay. Fiction that is written as if it were true is *not* accepted." Buys 2-4 mss/year. Query with published clips. Length: 500-3,000 words. Pays $50-175.

Tips: "We try to utilize Illinois writers, especially those affiliated with a newspaper. Other writers are encouraged, though. On the law column is good to break into as well as technical or how-to nonfiction articles. Query with idea and *clips*."

MAGAZINE ISSUES, Serving Under 500,000 Circulation Publications, Feredonna Communications, Drawer 9808, Knoxville TN 37940. Editor: Michael Ward. 50% freelance written. Quarterly magazine covering magazine publishing. Circulated to approximately 10,000 publishers, editors, ad managers, circulation managers, production managers and art directors of magazines. Estab. 1982. Circ. 10,000. Publishes ms an average of 2 months after acceptance. Byline given. Submit seasonal/holiday material 6 months in advance. Query for electronic submissions. Reports in 2 months on queries. Sample copy $5. Writer's guidelines available for SASE.

Nonfiction: How-to (write, sell advertising, manage production, manage creative and sales people, etc.); interview/profile (*only* after assignment—must be full of "secrets" of success and how-to detail); personal experiences; new product (no payment); and technical (aspects of magazine publishing). "Features deal with every aspect of publishing, including: creating an effective ad sales team; increasing ad revenue; writing effective direct-mail circulation promotion; improving reproduction quality; planning and implementing ad sales strategies; buying printing; gathering unique information; writing crisp, clear articles with impact; and designing publications with visual impact." No general interest. "Everything must be keyed directly to our typical reader—a 39 year-old publisher/editor producing a trade magazine for 30,000 or more readers." Buys 18-24 mss/year. Query. Length: 900-3,000 words.

Photos: Send photos with ms.

Tips: "Articles must present practical, useful, new information in how-to detail, so readers can do what the articles discuss. Articles that present problems and discuss how they were successfully solved also are welcome. These must carry many specific examples to flesh out general statements. We don't care who you are, just how you write."

NEW WRITER'S MAGAZINE, Sarasota Bay Publishing, P.O. Box 5976, Sarasota FL 34277. (813)953-7903. Editor: George J. Haborak. 95% freelance written. Bimonthly magazine for new writers. "*New Writer's Magazine* believes that *all* writers are *new* writers in that each of us can learn from one another. So, we reach *pro* and non-pro alike." Estab. 1986. Circ. 5,000. Pays on publication. Byline given. Buys first rights. Query for electronic submissions. Reports in 2 weeks on queries; 1 month on mss. Sample copy $2. Writer's guidelines for #10 SASE.

Nonfiction: General interest, how-to (for new writers), humor, interview/profile, opinion and personal experience (with *pro* writer). Buys 50 mss/year. Send complete ms. Length: 300-850 words. Pays $5-50 for assigned articles; $5-25 for unsolicited articles. Pays in contributor copies or other premiums for short items, poetry, fillers, etc.

Photos: Send photos with submission. Reviews 5×7 prints. Offers no additional payment for photos accepted with ms. Captions required. Buys one-time rights.

Fiction: Experimental, historical, humorous, mainstream and slice-of-life vignettes. "Again, we do *not* want anything that does not have a tie-in with the writing life or writers in general." Buys 2-6 mss/year. "We offer a special fiction contest held each year with cash prizes." Send complete ms. Length: 750-1,500 words. Pays $5-20.

Poetry: Free verse, light verse and traditional. Does not want anything *not* for writers. Buys 10-20 poems/year. Submit maximum 3 poems. Length: 8-20 lines. Pays $5 maximum.

Fillers: Anecdotes, facts, illustrated cartoons, newsbreaks and short humor. Buys 5-15/year. Length: 20-100 words. Pays $5 maximum.

Tips: "Any article *with photos* has a good chance, especially an *up close & personal* interview with an established professional writer offering advice, etc."

RIGHTING WORDS, The Journal of Language and Editing, Feredonna Communications, Drawer 9808, Knoxville TN 37940. (615)584-1918. Editor: Michael Ward. 80% freelance written. Eager to work with new/unpublished writers. A quarterly magazine on language usage, trends and issues. "Our readers include copy editors, book and magazine editors, and journalism and English teachers—people interested in the changing ways of the language and in ways to improve their editing and writing skills." Estab. 1987. Pays on publication. Publishes an average of 1 month after acceptance. Byline given. Buys first North American serial rights. Query for electronic submissions. Reports only on accepted ms. "Allow one month for reply before sending ms elsewhere." Sample copy $5 with 9×12 SAE and 3 first class stamps; writer's guidelines for #10 SASE.

Nonfiction: Buys 30 mss/year. Send complete ms. Length: 3,000 words. Pays $100 minimum for assigned articles.

Tips: "Our contributors have included Rudolf Flesch and Willard Espy, but we welcome freelance submissions on editing and language topics that are well-written, contain hard information of value to editors, and that display wit and style. Yes, the editor reads *all* submissions, and often suggests approaches to writers whose material may be good but whose approach is off. No book reviews, please; other than that, all parts of the magazines are open to freelancers."

RISING STAR, 47 Byledge Rd., Manchester NH 03104. (603)623-9796. Editor: Scott E. Green. 50% freelance written. A bimonthly newsletter on science fiction and fantasy markets for writers and artists. Estab. 1980. Circ. 150. Pays on publication. Publishes an average of 3 months after acceptance. Byline given. Not copyrighted. Buys first rights. Simultaneous and previously published submissions OK. Reports in 2 weeks on queries. Sample copy $1.50 with #10 SASE; free writer's guidelines. Subscription $7.50 for 6 issues, payable to Scott Green.

Nonfiction: Book excerpts, essays, interview/profile and opinion. Buys 8 mss/year. Query. Length: 500-900 words. Pays $3 minimum.

ST. LOUIS JOURNALISM REVIEW, 8380 Olive Blvd., St. Louis MO 63132. (314)991-1699. FAX: (314)997-1898. Editor/Publisher: Charles L. Klotzer. 50% freelance written. Prefers to work with published/established writers. Monthly tabloid newspaper critiquing St. Louis media, print, broadcasting, TV and cable primarily by working journalists and others. Also covers issues not covered adequately by dailies. Occasionally buys articles on national media criticism. Estab. 1970. Circ. 6,500. Buys all rights. Byline given. Sample copy $2.

Nonfiction: "We buy material which analyzes, critically, St. Louis metro area media and, less frequently, national media institutions, personalities or trends." No taboos. Payment depends. Pays the expenses of writers on assignment subject to prior approval.

SCAVENGER'S NEWSLETTER, 519 Ellinwood, Osage City KS 66523. (913)528-3538. Editor: Janet Fox. 15% freelance written. Eager to work with new/unpublished writers. A monthly newsletter covering markets for science fiction/fantasy/horror materials especially with regard to the small press. Estab. 1984. Circ. 1,000. Publishes ms an average of 8 months after acceptance. Byline given. Not copyrighted. Places copyright symbol on title page; rights revert to contributor on publication. Buys one-time rights.

Simultaneous and previously published submissions OK. Reports in 2 weeks. Sample copy $1.50; writer's guidelines for #10 SASE.

Nonfiction: Essays; general interest; how-to (write, sell, publish sf/fantasy/horror); humor; interview/profile (writers, artists in the field); and opinion. Buys 12-15 mss/year. Send complete ms. Length: 1,000 words maximum. Pays $4 on acceptance.

Poetry: Avant-garde, free verse, haiku and traditional. All related to science fiction/fantasy/horror genres. Buys 48 poems/year. Submit maximum 3 poems. Length: 10 lines maximum. Pays $2 on acceptance.

Tips: "Because this is a small publication, it has occasional overstocks. We're especially looking for sf/fantasy/horror commentary as opposed to writer's how-to's."

SCIENCE FICTION CHRONICLE, P.O. Box 2730, Brooklyn NY 11202-0056. (718)643-9011. Editor: Andrew Porter. 3% freelance written. Works with a small number of new/unpublished writers each year. Monthly magazine about science fiction, fantasy and horror publishing for readers, editors, writers, et al., who are interested in keeping up with the latest developments and news. Publication also includes market reports, UK news, letters, reviews, columns. Estab. 1963. Circ. 5,600. Buys first serial rights. Pays on publication. Publishes ms an average of 2 months after acceptance. Submit seasonal material 4 months in advance. Reports in 1 month. Sample copy for 9×12 SAE and 5 first class stamps.

Nonfiction: New product and photo feature. No articles about UFOs, or "news we reported six months ago." Buys 10 unsolicited mss/year. Send complete ms. Length: 200-500 words. Pays 3-5¢/word.

Photos: Send photos with ms. Pays $5-15 for 4×5 and 8×10 b&w prints. Captions preferred. Buys one-time rights.

Tips: "News of publishers, booksellers and software related to sf, fantasy and horror is most needed from freelancers. *No fiction.* This is a news magazine, like *Publishers Weekly* or *Writer's Digest.* (I still get 10-20 story mss a year, which are returned, unread.)"

SMALL PRESS, The Magazine of Independent Publishing, Small Press Inc., Colonial Hill, RFD #1, Mt. Kisco NY 10549. (914)666-0069. FAX: (914)666-9384. Editor: Wendy Reid Crisp. 90% freelance written. Quarterly magazine on independent publishers/independent publishing. "The writers and reviewers of *Small Press,* in cooperation with the publishers, editors, booksellers and trade participants, work to create a periodical that affirms and nurtures independent-press publishing and that epitomizes the ideology and strength of our industry." Estab. 1983. Circ. 5,400. Pays on publication. Publishes ms an average of 2-6 months after acceptance. Byline given. Makes work-for-hire assignments. Submit seasonal/holiday material 3-6 months in advance. "While *Small Press* does, occasionally, reprint articles, we strive to publish only original material; articles of particular relevance to the trade are accepted on other bases with the editor's approval." Query for electronic submissions. Reports in 6 weeks on queries; 2 months on mss. Free sample copy and writer's guidelines.

Nonfiction: Essays, general interest to the trade, how-to (practical applications), interview/profile, new product, technical, use of computers, legal/financial strategies, promotion and marketing. "Interested parties should write for an editorial calendar. Such a calendar is available upon request, and there is no charge. Editorial agenda is fixed to a degree, but certain items are subject to change. NO FICTION!! I prefer not to receive blind submissions. Please inquire before mailing. Articles of a strictly personal nature—not genre-oriented—are discouraged. Articles must relate to the independent-press industry." Buys 10-12 mss/year. Query with published clips or send complete ms. Length: 250-4,000 words. Pays $45-65/page. Book reviewers receive only the title sent for review and a copy of the issue in which the review appears. Sometimes pays expenses of writers on assignment.

Photos: Send photos with submission. Offers no additional payment for photos accepted with ms. Captions, model releases and identification of subjects required.

Columns/Departments: "Columns are assigned to contributing editors. Only practical/advice for trade articles are available to freelance writers at this time." Practical and advisory articles on technical, legal, financial, promotional strategies [e.g., marketing to independent bookstores, tax advice for publishers, non-traditional marketing techniques, implementation of graphics with computer systems, etc.], 250-2,000 words. Buys 30-50 mss/year. Query with published clips. Send complete ms. Pays $45-65/page.

Fillers: Facts and newsbreaks. Buys 6/year. Length: 250-1,500 words. Pays $65 maximum.

Tips: "Please familiarize yourself with the independent-press industry. I neither want nor need writers who have neither knowledge nor appreciation of the industry *Small Press* serves. Writing skills are not sufficient qualification. Genre-oriented articles are sought and preferred. Filler articles on a variety of subjects of practical advice to the trade are the most open to freelance writers. I am amenable to submissions of feature articles relating to publishers, inventories, traditional, and desktop-publishing systems, trade events (London Book Fair, Frankfurt, ABA, etc.), publishing trends, regional pieces (with a direct relationship to the independent-press industry), production issues, business-oriented advice, promotion and marketing strategies, interviews with industry participants."

SMALL PRESS REVIEW, Box 100, Paradise CA 95967. Editor: Len Fulton. Monthly for "people interested in small presses and magazines, current trends and data; many libraries." Circ. 3,500. Byline given. "Query if you're unsure." Reports in 2 months. Free sample copy.
Nonfiction: News, short reviews, photos, short articles on small magazines and presses. Uses how-to, personal experience, interview, profile, spot news, historical, think, photo, and coverage of merchandising techniques. Accepts 50-200 mss/year. Length: 100-200 words.

WEST COAST REVIEW OF BOOKS, Rapport Publishing Co., Inc., 5265 Fountain Ave., Upper Terrace #6, Los Angeles CA 90029. (213)660-0433. Editor: D. David Dreis. Bimonthly magazine for book consumers. "Provocative articles based on specific subject matter, books and author retrospectives." Circ. 80,000. Pays on publication. Byline given. Offers kill fee. Buys one-time rights and second serial (reprint) rights to published author interviews. Sample copy $2.
Nonfiction: General interest, historical/nostalgic and profile (author retrospectives). "No individual book reviews." Buys 25 mss/year. Query. Length: open.
Tips: "There must be a reason (current interest, news events, etc.) for any article here. Example: 'The Jew-Haters' was about anti-semitism which was written up in six books; all reviewed and analyzed under that umbrella title. Under no circumstances should articles be submitted unless query has been responded to." No phone calls.

THE WRITER, 120 Boylston St., Boston MA 02116. Editor-in-Chief/Publisher: Sylvia K. Burack. 20-25% freelance written. Prefers to buy work of published/established writers. Monthly. Estab. 1887. **Pays on acceptance.** Publishes ms an average of 6-8 months after acceptance. Buys first serial rights. Sample copy $3.
Nonfiction: Practical articles for writers on how to write for publication, and how and where to market manuscripts in various fields. Will consider all submissions promptly. No assignments. Length: 2,000 words maximum.
Tips: "New types of publications and our continually updated market listings in all fields will determine changes of focus and fact."

‡WRITERS CONNECTION, Suite 180, 1601 Saratoga-Sunnyvale Rd., Cupertino CA 95014. (408)973-0227. Editor: Jan Stiles. 60% freelance written. Works with new/unpublished writers each year. Monthly magazine covering writing and publishing. Estab. 1983. Circ. 2,500. Pays in services on acceptance. Publishes ms an average of 7 months after acceptance for articles, much less for column updates. Byline given. Buys first serial rights or second serial (reprint) rights. Submit seasonal/holiday material 4 months in advance. Simultaneous queries, and simultaneous, and previously published submissions OK. Prefers complete manuscript. Sample copy free on request, and writer's guidelines for #10 SASE.
Nonfiction: Book excerpts (on writing/publishing); how-to (write and publish, market your writing); interview/profile (writers and publishers with how-to slant); new product (books, videotapes, etc. on writing and publishing); and writing for business and technical fields. "All types of writing from technical to romance novels and article writing are treated." No personal experience or profiles without a strong how-to slant. Buys 25-32 mss/year. Length: 1,200-2,200 words, occasional shorter pieces. Pays $12-80; "pay is in credit for Writers Connection memberships, seminars, subscriptions and advertising only."
Columns/Departments: Markets, contests, events, etc. are staff-written. Send information or announcements 6 weeks in advance of issue date for free listings in our newsletter; space available basis.
Tips: "We are currently seeking how-to articles that will benefit writers working for business and high-tech companies. The focus for these articles should appeal to the working professional writer. Also, find and report on new markets freelancers can break in to, new ways to succeed in the business. Provide new techniques or ideas for writing fiction or nonfiction; present your ideas in a lively, but practical style. No parodies or sarcasm, please."

WRITER'S DIGEST, F&W Publications, Inc., 1507 Dana Ave., Cincinnati OH 45207. (513)531-2222. Submissions Editor: Peter Blocksom. 90% freelance written. Monthly magazine about writing and publishing. "Our readers write fiction, poetry, nonfiction, plays and all kinds of creative writing. They're interested in improving their writing skills, improving their sales ability, and finding new outlets for their talents." Estab. 1921. Circ. 225,000. **Pays on acceptance.** Publishes ms an average of 1 year after acceptance. Buys first North American serial rights for one-time editorial use, microfilm/microfiche use and magazine promotional use. Pays 20% kill fee. Byline given. Submit seasonal/holiday material 8 months in advance. Previously published submissions OK. Query for electronic submissions. "We're able to use electronic submissions only for accepted pieces/and will discuss details if we buy your work. We'll accept computer printout submissions, of course—but they *must* be readable. We strongly recommend letter-quality. If you don't want your manuscript returned, indicate that on the first page of the manuscript or in a cover letter." Reports in 2 weeks. Sample copy $3; writer's guidelines for #10 SASE.

Nonfiction: "Our mainstay is the how-to article—that is, an article telling how to write and sell more of what you write. For instance, how to write compelling leads and conclusions, how to improve your character descriptions, how to become more efficient and productive. We like plenty of examples, anecdotes and $$$ in our articles—so other writers can actually see what's been done successfully by the author of a particular piece. We like our articles to speak directly to the reader through the use of the first-person voice. Don't submit an article on what five book editors say about writing mysteries. Instead, submit an article on how you cracked the mystery market and how our readers can do the same. But don't limit the article to your experiences; include the opinions of those five editors to give your article increased depth and authority." General interest (about writing); how-to (writing and marketing techniques that work); humor (short pieces); inspirational; interview and profile (query first); new product; and personal experience (marketing and freelancing experiences). "We can always use articles on fiction and nonfiction technique, and solid articles on poetry or scriptwriting are always welcome. No articles titled 'So You Want to Be a Writer,' and no first-person pieces that ramble without giving a lesson or something readers can learn from in the sharing of the story." Buys 90-100 mss/year. Queries are preferred, but complete mss are OK. Length: 500-3,000 words. Pays 10¢/word minimum. Sometimes pays expenses of writers on assignment.

Photos: Used only with interviews and profiles. State availability of photos or send contact sheet with ms. Pays $25 minimum for 5×7 or larger b&w prints. Captions required.

Columns/Departments: Chronicle (first-person narratives about the writing life; length: 1,200-1,500 words; pays 10¢/word); The Writing Life (length: 50-800 words; pays 10¢/word); Tip Sheet (short, unbylined items that offer solutions to writing- and freelance business-related problems that writers commonly face; pays 10¢/word); and My First Sale (an "occasional" department; a first-person account of how a writer broke into print; length: 1,000 words; pays 10¢/word). "For First Sale items, use a narrative, anecdotal style to tell a tale that is both inspirational and instructional. Before you submit a My First Sale item, make certain that your story contains a solid lesson that will benefit other writers." Buys approximately 200 articles/year for Writing Life section, Tip Sheet and shorter pieces. Send complete ms.

Poetry: Light verse about "the writing life"—joys and frustrations of writing. "We are also considering poetry other than short light verse—but related to writing, publishing, other poets and authors, etc." Buys 2-3/issue. Submit poems in batches of 1-8. Length: 2-20 lines. Pays $10-50/poem.

Fillers: Anecdotes and short humor, primarily for use in The Writing Life column. Uses 4/issue. Length: 50-250 words. Pays 10¢/word.

WRITER'S FORUM, (formerly *WDS Forum*), Writer's Digest School, F&W Publications, Inc., 1507 Dana Ave., Cincinnati OH 45207. (513)531-2222. Editor: Tom Clark. 100% freelance written. Quarterly newsletter covering writing techniques and marketing for students of courses in fiction and nonfiction writing offered by Writer's Digest School. Estab. 1970. Circ. 13,000. **Pays on acceptance.** Publishes ms an average of 6 months after acceptance. Byline given. Pays 25% kill fee. Buys first serial rights and second serial (reprint) rights. Submit seasonal/holiday material 4 months in advance. Simultaneous and previously published submissions OK. Query for electronic submissions. Reports in 3 weeks. Free sample copy.

Nonfiction: How-to (write or market short stories, articles, novels and nonfiction books); and interviews (with well-known authors of fiction and nonfiction). Buys 12 mss/year. "Query by mail, please, not phone." Length: 500-1,000 words. Pays $10-25.

WRITER'S GUIDELINES, (formerly *Guidelines Magazine*), P.O. Box 608, Pittsburg MO 65724. Editor: Susan Salaki. 97% freelance written. Full-size bimonthly. *WGM* is a roundtable forum for writers and editors. *WGM* is published by Writers Corporation of America a nonprofit organization. "We are interested in what writers on both sides of the desk have to say about the craft of writing." Estab. 1988. Circ. 1,000. Pays on publication. Byline given. Rights to the original work revert to contributors after publication. Reports in 1 month. Sample copy $4; SASE for writer's guidelines and themes for upcoming issues.

Nonfiction: General interest, historical articles on writers/writing, psychological aspects of being a writer, how-to, interview/profile, personal experience, humor and fillers. Buys 20 mss/year. Prefer disposable photocopy submissions complete with SASE. May use both sides of each sheet of paper to save postage costs. Include SASE with all correspondence. Length: 50-1,500 words. Pays 1¢/word.

Fiction: Accepts short fiction (800 words max) on any subject. All accepted fiction published in *WGM* automatically becomes eligible for nomination and publication in *Street Songs: New Voices in Fiction*, an annual anthology of the 20 best stories of 1991. Pays in copies.

Poetry: Short poetry, any form, having to do with writing or editing. Submit minimum of 3 poems. Pays 1 copy. Length: up to 20 lines "unless it is exceptional."

Fillers: Facts about writing or writers, short humor and cartoons,"wide-open to any facts of interest to writers or editors." No payment for Fillers.

Tips: "If you believe what you have to say about writing or editing has needed to be said for some time now, then I'm interested. If you say it well, I'll buy it. This is a unique publication in that we offer original guidelines for over 300 magazine and book publishers and because of this service, writers and editors are linked in a new and exciting way—as correspondents. Articles that help to bridge the gap which has existed between these two professions have the best chance of being accepted. Publishing background does not matter. Writers should query for theme list. Include a short biography and cover letter with your submissions. All contributors receive a copy of the issue in which their work appears."

WRITER'S INFO, Box 1870, Hayden ID 83835. (208)772-6184. Editor: Linda Hutton. 90% freelance written. Eager to work with new/unpublished writers. Monthly newsletter on writing. "We provide helpful tips and advice to writers, both beginners and old pros." Circ. 200. **Pays on acceptance.** Publishes ms an average of 6 months after acceptance. Byline given. Buys first North American serial rights and second serial (reprint) rights. Submit seasonal/holiday material 9 months in advance. Simultaneous queries and simultaneous and previously published submissions OK. Reports in 1 month. Sample copy for #10 SAE and 2 first class stamps; writer's guidelines for #10 SASE.

Nonfiction: How-to, humor and personal experience, all related to writing. No interviews or rehashes of articles published in other writers magazines. Buys 50-75 mss/year. Send complete ms. Length: 300 words. Pays $1-10.

Poetry: Free verse, light verse and traditional. No avant-garde or shaped poetry. Buys 40-50/year. Submit maximum 6 poems. Length: 4-20 lines. Pays $1-10.

Fillers: Jokes, anecdotes and short humor. Buys 3-4/year. Length: 100 words maximum. Pays $1-10.

Tips: "Tell us a system that worked for you to make a sale or inspired you to write. All departments are open to freelancers."

WRITER'S JOURNAL, Minnesota Ink, Inc., 27 Empire Dr., St. Paul MN 55103. (612)225-1306. Publisher/Managing Editor: Valerie Hockert. Poetry Editor: Esther M. Leiper. 40% freelance written. Monthly. Circ. 37,000. Pays on publication. Publishes ms an average of 4 months after acceptance. Byline given. Buys first North American serial rights. Submit seasonal/holiday material 6 months in advance. Simultaneous queries OK. Query for electronic submissions. Reports in 1 month on queries; 6 weeks on mss. Sample copy $3; writer's guidelines for #10 SASE.

Nonfiction: How-to (on the business and approach to writing); motivational; interview/profile; opinion. "*Writer's Journal* publishes articles on style, technique, editing methods, copy writing, research, writing of news releases, writing news stories and features, creative writing, grammar reviews, marketing, the business aspects of writing, copyright law and legal advice for writers/editors, independent book publishing, interview techniques, and more." Also articles on the use of computers by writers and a book review section. Buys 30-40 mss/year. Send complete ms. Length: 700-1,000 words. Pays to $50.

Poetry: Avant-garde, free verse, haiku, light verse and traditional. "The *Writer's Journal* runs two poetry contests each year in the spring and fall: Winner, 2nd, 3rd place and 10 honorable mentions." Buys 20-30 poems/year. Submit maximum 5 poems. Length: 25 lines maximum. Pays 25¢ line.

Tips: "Articles must be *well* written and slanted toward the business (or commitment) of writing and/or being a writer. Interviews with established writers should be in-depth, particularly reporting interviewee's philosophy on writing, how he or she got started, etc." The *Writer's Journal* now incorporates *Minnesota Ink. Minnesota Ink* is 80% freelance written and contains fiction and poetry.

THE WRITER'S NOOK NEWS, 38114 3rd St. #181, Willoughby OH 44094-6140. (216)975-8965. FAX: (216)354-6403. Editor: Eugene Ortiz. 100% freelance written. A quarterly newsletter for professional writers. "We don't print fluff, anecdotes or platitudes. Articles must be specific, terse, pithy and contain information readers can put to immediate, practical use. Every article should be the kind you want to cut out and tape to your desk somewhere." Estab. 1985. Circ. 5,000. **Pays on acceptance.** Publishes ms an average of 5 months after acceptance. Byline given. Publication is not copyrighted. Buys first North American serial rights. Reports within 3 months. Sample copy $4. Writer's guidelines for 9 × 12 SAE with 52¢ postage.

Nonfiction: How-to and interview/profile (writing and marketing). "No essays, poetry, fiction, ruminations or anecdotes." Buys 100 mss/year. Send complete ms with credits and short bio. Length: 100-400 words. Pays 6¢/word.

Photos: Send photos with submission. Reviews b&w prints. Offers $5 maximum per photo. Identification of subjects required. Buys one-time rights.

Columns/Departments: Book Bench (short reviews of books related to writing), 400 words; Conferences & Klatches (listings of conferences and gatherings), 400-1,200 words; Contests & Awards (listings of contests and awards), 400 words; Writer's Rights (latest information on what's happening on Capitol Hill), 400 words; Markets (listings of information on markets for writers), 400 words. Buys 20 mss/year. Query with published clips and short bio. Length: 400 words. Pays 6¢/word.

Fillers: Facts and newsbreaks. Buys 20/year. Length: 20-100 words. Pays 6¢/word.

Tips: "Take the writer's guidelines very seriously. 90% of the best submissions are still about 25% fluff. Don't tell me how hard or impossible it is to write anything of worth in only 400 words. This is not a market for beginners. Particularly looking for genre tips. Any genre. I need more helpful information for established writers, on alternative ways of earning money as a writer, songwriting, playwriting and screenwriting. We also publish a quarterly series of bulletins: The Nook News Market Bulletin; Nook News Conferences & Klatches Bulletin; Nook News Contests & Awards Bulletin; and the Nook News Review of Writers Publications. All publications, including the Nook News, cost $4 for a sample copy and $14.40 for a one-year subscription."

WRITER'S YEARBOOK, F&W Publications, Inc., 1507 Dana Ave., Cincinnati OH 45207. Submissions Editor: Peter Blocksom. 90% freelance written. Newsstand annual for freelance writers, journalists and teachers of creative writing. "Please note that the *Yearbook* is currently using a 'best of' format. That is, we are reprinting the best of writing about writing published in the last year: articles, fiction, and book excerpts. The *Yearbook* now uses little original material, so do not submit queries or original manuscripts to the *Yearbook*. We will, however, consider already-published material for possible inclusion." Estab. 1929. Buys reprint rights. Pays 20% kill fee. Byline given. **Pays on acceptance.** Publishes ms an average of 6 months after acceptance. "If you don't want your manuscript returned, indicate that on the first page of the manuscript or in a cover letter."

Nonfiction: "In reprints, we want articles that reflect the current state of writing in America. Trends, inside information and money-saving and money-making ideas for the freelance writer. We try to touch on the various facets of writing in each issue of the *Yearbook*—from fiction to poetry to playwriting, and any other endeavor a writer can pursue. How-to articles—that is, articles that explain in detail how to do something—are very important to us. For example, you could explain how to establish mood in fiction, how to improve interviewing techniques, how to write for and sell to specialty magazines, or how to construct and market a good poem. We are also interested in the writer's spare time—what she/he does to retreat occasionally from the writing wars; where and how to refuel and replenish the writing spirit. 'How Beats the Heart of a Writer' features interest us, if written warmly, in the first person, by a writer who has had considerable success. We also want interviews or profiles of well-known bestselling authors, always with good pictures. Articles on writing techniques that are effective today are always welcome. We provide how-to features and information to help our readers become more skilled at writing and successful at selling their writing." Buys 10-15 mss (reprints only)/year. Length: 750-4,500 words. Pays 2½¢/word minimum.

Photos: Interviews and profiles must be accompanied by high-quality photos. Reviews b&w photos only, depending on use; pays $20-50/published photo. Captions required.

Law

While all of these publications deal with topics of interest to attorneys, each has a particular slant. Be sure that your subject is geared to a specific market—lawyers in a single region, law students, paralegals, etc. Publications for law enforcement personnel are listed under Government and Public Service.

ABA JOURNAL, American Bar Association, 750 N. Lake Shore Dr., Chicago IL 60611. (312)988-5000. FAX: (312)988-6014. Editor: Gary A. Hengstler. Managing Editor: Robert Yates. 35% freelance written. Prefers to work with published/established writers. Monthly magazine covering law and laywers. "The content of the *Journal* is designed to appeal to the association's diverse membership with emphasis on the general practitioner." Circ. 400,000. **Pays on acceptance.** Publishes ms an average of 2 months after acceptance. Byline given. "Editor works with writer until article is in acceptable form." Buys all rights. Submit seasonal/holiday material 3 months in advance. Simultaneous queries and submissions OK. Query for electronic submissions. Reports in 3 weeks. Free sample copy and writer's guidelines.

Nonfiction: Book excerpts; general interest (legal); how-to (law practice techniques); interview/profile (law firms and prominent individuals); and technical (legal trends). "The emphasis of the *Journal* is on the practical problems faced by lawyers in general practice and how those problems can be overcome. Articles should emphasize the practical rather than the theoretical or esoteric. Writers should avoid the style of law reviews, academic journals or legal briefs and should write in an informal, journalistic style. Short quotations from people and specific examples of your point will improve an article." Special issues have featured women and minorities in the legal profession. Buys 30 mss/year. Query with published clips or send complete ms. Length: 3,000 words. Pays $1,000-2,000. Pays expenses of writers on assignment.

Tips: "Write to us with a specific idea in mind and spell out how the subject would be covered. Full length profiles and feature articles are always needed. We look for practical information. If *The New York Times* or *Wall Street Journal* would like your style, so will we."

THE ALTMAN WEIL PENSA REPORT TO LEGAL MANAGEMENT, Altman Weil Pensa Publications, P.O. Box 625, Newtown Square PA 19073. (215)359-9900. Editor: Linda Iannelli. 15-20% freelance written. Works with a small number of new/unpublished writers each year. Monthly newsletter covering law office purchases (equipment, insurance services, space, etc.), technology and law office management. Circ. 2,200. Pays on publication. Publishes ms an average of 3-6 months after acceptance. Byline given. Buys all rights; sometimes second serial (reprint) rights. Previously published submissions OK. Query for electronic submissions. Reports in 1 month on queries; 6 weeks on mss. Sample copy for #10 SASE.

Nonfiction: How-to (buy, use, repair), interview/profile and new product. Buys 6 mss/year. Query. Submit a sample of previous writing. Length: 500-2,500 words. Pays $125/published page.

Photos: State availability of photos. Reviews b&w prints; payment is included in payment for ms. Captions and model release required. Buys one-time rights.

BARRISTER, American Bar Association Press, 750 N. Lake Shore Dr., Chicago IL 60611. (312)988-6047. Editor: Vicki Quade. 60% freelance written. Prefers to work with published/established writers. For young lawyers who are members of the American Bar Association concerned about practice of law, career trends, public service, social issues, personalities. Quarterly magazine. Estab. 1971. Circ. 175,000. Pays on acceptance. Publishes ms an average of 3-6 months after acceptance. Buys all rights, first serial rights or simultaneous rights. Query for electronic submissions. Reports in 6-8 weeks. Sample copy $5.

Nonfiction: "All areas of law are fair game, but stories should have a young lawyer tie-in. Readers interested in career stories (such as what to do when you lose your job), social issues (such as free speech and hate crimes), and personality profiles of innovative or prominent young lawyers. Rarely use humor. No political opinion pieces." Length: 2,500-3,000 words; pays $450-850 and reasonable expenses. Must query with outline. Buys 12 mss/year. Special summer issue features "20 Young Lawyers Whose Work Makes a Difference," 700-1,000 words; $250 payment. Buys 15 mss/year. Query.

Photos: Donna Tashjian, photo editor. B&w photos and color transparencies purchased without accompanying ms. Pays $35-150.

Tips: "The biggest mistake writers make is to think of us as a law review journal. We are a general interest magazine with a focus on young lawyers. We want cutting-edge topics written in a crisp journalistic style."

BENCH & BAR OF MINNESOTA, Minnesota State Bar Association, Suite 403, 430 Marquette Ave., Minneapolis MN 55401. (612)333-1183. FAX: (612)333-4927. Editor: Judson Haverkamp. 10% freelance written. A magazine on the law/legal profession published 11 times/year. "Audience is mostly Minnesota lawyers. *Bench & Bar* seeks reportage, analysis, and commentary on developments in the law and the legal profession, especially in Minnesota. Preference to items of practical/human interest to professionals in law." Estab. 1931. Circ. 13,000. Pays on acceptance. Publishes ms an average of 3 months after acceptence. Byline given. Buys first North American serial rights and makes work-for-hire assignments. Reports in 1 month. Sample copy for 9 × 12 SAE and 4 first class stamps; free writer's guidelines.

Nonfiction: General interest, historical/nostalgic, how-to (how to handle particular types of legal, ethical problems in office management, representation, etc.), humor, interview/profile and technical/legal. "We do not want one-sided opinion pieces or advertorial." Buys 4-5 mss/year. Query with published clips, or send complete ms. Length: 1,500-3,000 words. Pays $300-800. Sometimes pays expenses of writers on assignment.

Photos: State availability of photos with submission. Reviews 5 × 7 or larger prints. Offers $25-100 per photo upon publication. Model releases and identification of subjects required. Buys one-time rights.

CALIFORNIA LAWYER, 1016 Fox Plaza, 1390 Market St., San Francisco CA 94102. (415)558-9888. Editor: Ray Reynolds. Managing Editor: Tom Brom. 80% freelance written. Monthly magazine of law-related articles and general interest subjects of appeal to lawyers and judges. Estab. 1928. Circ. 133,000. Pays on acceptance. Publishes ms an average of 3 months after acceptance. Byline given. Buys first rights; publishes only original material. Simultaneous queries and submissions OK. Reports in 2 weeks on queries; 3 weeks on mss. Sample copy and writer's guidelines on request.

Nonfiction: General interest, new and feature articles on law-related topics. "We are interested in concise, well-written and well-researched articles on recent trends in the legal profession, legal aspects of issues of current concern, as well as general interest articles of potential appeal and benefit to the state's lawyers. We would like to see a description or outline of your proposed idea, including a list of possible sources." Buys 36 mss/year. Query with published clips if available. Length: 500-3,000 words. Pays $200-1,500.

Photos: Max Ramirez, director of photography. State availability of photos with query letter or manuscript. Reviews prints. Identification of subjects and releases required.

Columns/Departments: Legal Technology, Law Office Management, Marketing, Ethics, Books. Query with published clips if available. Length: 750-1,500 words. Pays $200-600.

COMPUTER USER'S LEGAL REPORTER, Computer Law Group, Inc., Box 375, Charlottesville VA 22902. (804)977-6343. Editor: Charles P. Lickson. 20% freelance written. Prefers to work with published/established writers or "experts" in fields addressed. Newsletter published quarterly featuring legal issues, alternate dispute resolution and considerations facing users of computer and processed data. "The *Computer User's Legal Reporter* is written by a fully qualified legal and technical staff for essentially nonlawyer readers. It features brief summaries on developments in such vital areas as computer contracts, insurance, mediation, arbitration, warranties, crime, proprietary rights and privacy. Each summary is backed by reliable research and sourcework." Circ. 1,000. Pays on publication. Publishes ms an average of 1 month after acceptance. Offers 50% kill fee. Buys first North American serial rights. Simultaneous queries and submissions OK. Reports in 2 weeks. Sample copy for $10 with #10 SAE and 2 first class stamps.

Nonfiction: Book excerpts; expose; how-to (protect ideas, resolve problems); humor "Computer law . . . according to Murphy"; interview/profile (legal or computer personality); and technical. No articles not related to high-tech and society. Buys 4-6 mss/year. Query with published clips. Length: 250-1,000 words. Pays $50; $150 for scenes.

Columns/Departments: Computer Law . . . according to Murphy (humorous "laws" relating to computers, definitions, etc.). The editor buys all rights to Murphyisms which may be included in his book, *Computer Law . . . According to Murphy.* Buys 10 mss/year. Length: 25-75 words. Pays $10-50.

Tips: "Send materials with a note on your own background and qualifications to write what you submit. We invite intelligently presented and well-argued controversy within our field. Our audience is primarily non-lawyers. We are looking for new ways to resolve disputes."

THE DOCKET, National Association of Legal Secretaries, Suite 550, 2250 E. 73rd St., Tulsa OK 74136. (918)493-3540. Editor: Debora L. Riggs. 20% freelance written. Bimonthly magazine that covers continuing legal education for legal support staff. "*The Docket* is written and edited for legal secretaries, legal assistants and other non-attorney personnel. Feature articles address general trends and emerging issues in the legal field, provide practical information to achieve proficiency in the delivery of legal services, and offer techniques for career growth and fulfillment." Circ. 20,000. Pays on publication. Publishes ms an average of 3-6 months after acceptance. Byline given. Offers 25-35% of original commission fee as kill fee. Buys first North American serial rights. Simultaneous and previously published submissions OK. Reports in 1 month.

Nonfiction: How-to (enhance the delivery of legal services or any aspect thereof), new product (must be a service or equipment used in a legal office), personal experience (legal related) and technical (legal services and equipment). Buys 20-25 mss/year. Query about specific subjects/articles or send complete ms. Length: 500-2,500 words. Pays $50-250.

Photos: State availability of photos with submission. Reviews contact sheets, negatives, transparencies and prints. Offers no additional payment for photos accepted with ms. Buys one-time rights.

LAW PRACTICE MANAGEMENT, (formerly *Legal Economics*), A magazine of the section of Law Practice Management of the American Bar Association, P.O. Box 11418, Columbia SC 29211. Managing Editor/Art Director: Delmar L. Roberts. 10% freelance written. For the practicing lawyer and law practice administrator. Magazine published 8 times/year. Estab. 1975. Circ. 23,113 (BPA). Rights purchased vary with author and material. Usually buys all rights. Byline given. Pays on publication. Publishes ms an average of 8 months after acceptance. Query. Free writer's guidelines; sample copy $7 (make check payable to American Bar Association). Returns rejected material in 90 days, if requested.

Nonfiction: "We assist the practicing lawyer in operating and managing his or her office by providing relevant articles and departments written in a readable and informative style. Editorial content is intended to aid the lawyer by conveying management methods that will allow him or her to provide legal services to clients in a prompt and efficient manner at reasonable cost. Typical topics of articles include fees and billing; client/lawyer relations; computer hardware/software; mergers; retirement/disability; marketing; compensation of partners and associates; legal data base research; and use of paralegals." No elementary articles on a whole field of technology, such as, "why you need computers in the law office." Pays $100-350.

Photos: Pays $50-60 for b&w photos purchased with mss; $50-100 for color; $150-200 for cover transparencies.

Tips: "We have a theme for each issue with two to three articles relating to the theme. We also publish thematic issues occasionally in which an entire issue is devoted to a single topic. The November/December issue each year is devoted to new office technology."

THE LAWYER'S PC, A Newsletter for Lawyers Using Personal Computers, Shepard's/McGraw-Hill, Inc., P.O. Box 1108, Lexington SC 29071. (803)359-9941. Editor: Robert P. Wilkins. Managing Editor: Daniel E. Harmon. 50% freelance written. A biweekly newsletter covering computerized law firms. "Our readers are lawyers who want to be told how a particular microcomputer program or type of program is being applied to a legal office task, such as timekeeping, litigation support, etc." Estab. 1983. Circ. 5,500. Pays end of the month of publication. Publishes ms an average of 1-2 months after acceptance. Byline given. Buys first North American serial rights and the right to reprint. Submit seasonal/holiday material 5 months in advance. Query for electronic submissions. Reports in 1 month on queries; 2 months on mss. Sample copy for 9×12 SAE with 3 first class stamps; free writer's guidelines.

Nonfiction: How-to (applications articles on law office computerization) and software reviews written by lawyers who have no compromising interests. No general articles on why lawyers need computers or reviews of products written by public relations representatives or vending consultants. Buys 30-35 mss/year. Query. Length: 500-2,500 words. Pays $25-125. Sometimes pays the expenses of writers on assignment.

Tips: "Most of our writers are lawyers. If you're not a lawyer, you need to at least understand why general business software may not work well in a law firm. If you understand lawyers' specific computer problems, write an article describing how to solve one of those problems, and we'd like to see it."

THE LAWYERS WEEKLY, The Newspaper for the Legal Profession in Canada, Butterworth (Canada) Inc., Suite 201, 423 Queen St. W., Toronto, Ontario M5V 2A5 Canada. (416)598-5211. FAX: (416)598-5659. Assignments Editor: Don Brillinger. 20% freelance written. "We will work with any *talented* writer of whatever experience level." A 48 times/year tabloid covering law and legal affairs for a "sophisticated up-market readership of lawyers and accountants." Circ. 41,000. Pays on publication. Publishes ms an average of 1 month after acceptance. Byline given. Offers 50% kill fee. Usually buys all rights. Submit seasonal/holiday material 6 weeks in advance. Simultaneous queries and submissions OK. Query for electronic submissions. Electronic submissions on PC compatible disks, WordStar or WordPerfect. Printout backup a must. Reports in 1 month. Sample copy $6.50 Canadian funds and 9×12 SAE.

Nonfiction: Expose; general interest (law); historical/nostalgic; how-to (professional); humor; interview/profile (lawyers and judges); opinion; technical; news; and case comments. "We try to wrap up the week's legal events and issues in a snappy informal package with lots of visual punch. We especially like news stories with photos or illustrations. We are always interested in feature or newsfeature articles involving current legal issues, but contributors should keep in mind our audience is trained in *English/Canadian common law* – not U.S. law. That means most U.S. constitutional or criminal law stories will generally not be accepted. Special Christmas issue. No routine court reporting or fake news stories about commercial products. Buys 200-300 mss/year. Query or send complete ms. Length: 700-1,500 words. Pays $25 minimum, negotiable maximum (have paid up to $500 in the past). Payment in Canadian dollars. Sometimes pays the expenses of writers on assignment.

Photos: State availability of photos with query letter or ms. Reviews b&w and color contact sheets, negatives, and 5×7 prints. Identification of subjects required. Buys one-time rights.

Columns/Departments: Buys 90-100 mss/year. Send complete ms or Wordstar or WordPerfect disk. Length: 500-1,000 words. Pays negotiable rate.

Fillers: Clippings, jokes, gags, anecdotes, short humor and newsbreaks. Cartoon ideas will be drawn by our artists. Length: 50-200 words. Pays $10 minimum.

Tips: "Freelancers can best break into our publication by submitting news, features, and accounts of unusual or bizarre legal events. A frequent mistake made by writers is forgetting that our audience is intelligent and learned in law. They don't need the word 'plaintiff' explained to them." No unsolicited

ALWAYS submit unsolicited manuscripts or queries with a self-addressed, stamped envelope (SASE) within your country or a self-addressed envelope with International Reply Coupons (IRC) purchased from the post office for other countries.

mss returned without SASE (or IRC to U.S. or non Canadian destinations).

‡**THE LAWYER'S WORD**, A Newsletter for Lawyers Using Microsoft Word and Other Microsoft Products, Shepard's/McGraw-Hill, P.O. Box 1108, Lexington SC 29071. (803)359-9941. Editor: Robert P. Wilkins. Managing Editor: Daniel E. Harmon. 35% freelance written. A monthly newsletter demonstrating how computerized law offices can use Microsoft Word and related software products for legal-specific office tasks. Estab. 1991. Pays end of the month of publication. Publishes ms an average of 2 months after acceptance. Byline given. Buys first North American serial rights and reprint rights. Submit seasonal material 5 months in advance. Query for electronic submissions. Reports in 1 month on queries; 2 months on mss. Sample copy for 9×12 SAE with 3 first class stamps; free writer's guidelines.
Nonfiction: How-to and applications articles on law office computerization with Microsoft Word, Windows and related products. Query. Pays $25-100.

THE PENNSYLVANIA LAWYER, Pennsylvania Bar Association, 100 South St., P.O. Box 186, Harrisburg PA 17108. (717)238-6715. Executive Editor: Marcy Carey Mallory. Managing Editor: Donald C. Sarvey. 25% freelance written. Prefers to work with published/established writers. Magazine published 6 times/year as a service to the legal profession. Estab. 1895. Circ. 27,000. **Pays on acceptance.** Publishes ms an average of 3-6 months after acceptance. Byline given. Buys negotiable serial rights; generally first rights, occasionally one-time rights or second serial (reprint) rights. Submit seasonal/holiday material 6 months in advance. Simultaneous submissions are discouraged. Reports in 6 weeks. Free sample copy and writer's guidelines.
Nonfiction: General interest, how-to, interview/profile, new product, law-practice management and personal experience. All features *must* relate in some way to Pennsylvania lawyers or the practice of law in Pennsylvania. Buys 10-12 mss/year. Query. Length: 600-1,500 words. Pays $75-350. Sometimes pays the expenses of writers on assignment.

THE PERFECT LAWYER, A Newsletter for Lawyers Using WordPerfect Products, Shepard's/McGraw-Hill Inc., P.O. Box 1108, Lexington SC 29071. (803)359-9941. Editor: Robert P. Wilkins. Managing Editor: Daniel E. Harmon. 50% freelance written. Monthly newsletter covering the use of WordPerfect Corporation related products in law offices. Estab. 1990. Circ. 3,900. Pays at end of the month after publication. Publishes ms an average of 2-3 months after acceptance. Byline given. Buys first North American serial rights and the right to reprint. Submit seasonal/holiday material 5 months in advance. Query for electronic submissions. Reports in 1 month on queries; 2 months on mss. Sample copy for 9×12 SAE with 4 first class stamps; free writer's guidelines.
Nonfiction: How-to computer articles. Must be law office specific. Occasional reviews of WordPerfect related products for law firms. Buys 25-35 mss/year. Query. Length: 500-2,500 words. Pays $25-200. Sometimes pays expenses of writers on assignment.
Tips: "Writers should understand the specific computer needs of law firms. Our readers are interested in howto solve office automation problems with computers and WordPerfect or related software products."

‡**SHEPARD'S ELDER CARE/LAW NEWSLETTER**, Shepard's/McGraw-Hill, Inc., P.O. Box 1108, Lexington SC 29071. (803)359-9941. Editor: Robert P. Wilkins. Managing Editor: Daniel E. Harmon. 40% freelance written. A monthly newsletter for lawyers and other professionals who work with older clients, focusing on legal and related issues of concern to the aging community. Estab. 1991. Pays end of the month of publication. Publishes ms an average of 2 months after acceptance. Byline given. Buys first North American serial rights and reprint rights. Submit seasonal material 5 months in advance. Query for electronic submissions. Reports in 1 month on queries; 2 months on mss. Sample copy for 9×12 SAE with 3 first class stamps; free writer's guidelines.
Nonfiction: Informational articles about legal issues, pending and new legislation, organizations and other resources of interest to lawyers who work with aging clients and their families. Query. Pays $25-200.

‡**STUDENT LAWYER**, American Bar Association, 750 N. Lake Shore Dr., Chicago IL 60611. (312)988-6048. Editor: Sarah Hoban. Managing Editor: Miriam R. Krasno. 95% freelance written. Works with a small number of new/unpublished writers each year. Monthly (September-May) magazine. Estab. 1972. Circ. 35,000. Pays on publication. Buys first serial rights and second serial (reprint) rights. Pays negotiable kill fee. Byline given. Submit seasonal/holiday material 4 months in advance. Reports in 6 weeks. Publishes ms an average of 3 months after acceptance. Sample copy $4; free writer's guidelines.
Nonfiction: Exposé (government, law, education and business); profiles (prominent persons in law-related fields); opinion (on matters of current legal interest); essays (on legal affairs); interviews; and photo features. Query. Length: 3,000-5,000 words. Pays $250-800 for main features. Covers some writer's expenses.

Columns/Departments: Briefly (short stories on unusual and interesting developments in the law); Legal Aids (unusual approaches and programs connected to teaching law students and lawyers); Esq. (brief profiles of people in the law); End Note (short pieces on a variety of topics; can be humorous, educational, outrageous); Pro Se (opinion slot for authors to wax eloquent on legal issues, civil rights conflicts, the state of the union); and Et Al. (column for short features that fit none of the above categories). Buys 4-8 mss/issue. Length: 250-1,000 words. Pays $75-250.

Fiction: "We buy fiction only when it is very good and deals with issues of law in the contemporary world or offers insights into the inner workings of lawyers. No mystery, poetry or science fiction accepted."

Tips: "*Student Lawyer* actively seeks good new writers. Legal training definitely not essential; writing talent is. The writer should not think we are a law review; we are a feature magazine with the law (in the broadest sense) as the common denominator. Past articles concerned gay rights, prison reform, the media, pornography, capital punishment, and drug education. Find issues of national scope and interest to write about; be aware of subjects the magazine—and other media—have already covered and propose something new. Write clearly and well."

Leather Goods

SHOE RETAILING TODAY, National Shoe Retailers Association, 9861 Broken Land Pkwy., Columbia MD 21046. (301)381-8282. FAX: (301)381-1167. Editor: Cynthia Emmel. 10% freelance written. Bimonthly newsletter covering footwear/accessory industry. Looks for articles that are "informative, educational, but with wit, interest, and creativity. I hate dry, dusty articles." Estab. 1972. Circ. 4,000-5,000. Byline given. Buys one-time rights. Submit seasonal/holiday material 3 months in advance. Reports in 2 weeks. Free sample copy and writer's guidelines.

Nonfiction: How-to, interview/profile, new product and technical. January and July are shoe show issues. Buys 6 mss/year. Length: 450 words. Pays $125 for assigned articles. Pays up to $200 for "full-fledged research—1,000 words or more on assigned articles."

Photos: State availability of photos with submission. Offers no additional payment for photos accepted with ms. Buys one-time rights.

Columns/Departments: Query. Pays $50-125.

Tips: "We are a trade magazine/newsletter for the footwear industry. Any information pertaining to our market is helpful: advertising/display/how-tos."

SHOE SERVICE, SSIA Service Corp., 5024-R Campbell Blvd., Baltimore MD 21236. (301)931-8100. FAX: (301)931-8111. Editor: Mitchell Lebovic. 50% freelance written. "We want well-written articles, whether they come from new or established writers." Monthly magazine for business people who own and operate small shoe repair shops. Estab. 1921. Circ. 17,000. Pays on publication. Publishes ms an average of 3 months after acceptance. Byline given. Buys first serial rights, first North American serial rights, and one-time rights. Submit seasonal/holiday material 3 months in advance. Simultaneous queries and previously published submissions OK. Reports in 6 weeks. Sample copy $2 and 9 × 12 SAE; free writer's guidelines.

Nonfiction: How-to (run a profitable shop); interview/profile (of an outstanding or unusual person on shoe repair); and business articles (particularly about small business practices in a service/retail shop). Buys 12-24 mss/year. Query with published clips or send complete ms. Length: 500-2,000 words. Pays 5¢/word.

Photos: "Quality photos will help sell an article." State availability of photos. Pays $10-30 for 8 × 10 b&w prints. Uses some color photos, but mostly uses b&w glossies. Captions, model release, and identification of subjects required.

Tips: "Visit some shoe repair shops to get an idea of the kind of person who reads *Shoe Service*. Profiles are the easiest to sell to us if you can find a repairer we think is unusual."

Library Science

Librarians read these journals for advice on promotion and management of libraries, library and book trade issues and information access and transfer. Be aware of current issues such as censorship, declines in funding and government information policies. For journals on the book trade see Book and Bookstore.

AMERICAN LIBRARIES, 50 E. Huron St., Chicago IL 60611. (312)280-4216. FAX: (312)440-0901. Editor: Thomas Gaughan. 5-10% freelance written. Works with a small number of new/unpublished writers each year. Magazine published 11 times/year for librarians. "A highly literate audience. They are for the most part practicing professionals with a down-to-earth interest in people and current trends." Estab. 1907. Circ. 53,000. Buys first North American serial rights. Publishes ms an average of 4 months after acceptance. Pays negotiable kill fee. Byline given. Submit seasonal material 6 months in advance. Reports in 10 weeks.

Nonfiction: "Material reflecting the special and current interests of the library profession. Nonlibrarians should browse recent journals in the field, available on request in medium-sized and large libraries everywhere. Topic and/or approach must be fresh, vital or highly entertaining. Library memoirs and stereotyped stories about old maids, overdue books, fines, etc., are unacceptable. Our first concern is with the American Library Association's activities and how they relate to the 50,000 reader/members. Tough for an outsider to write on this topic, but not to supplement it with short, offbeat or significant library stories and features." No fillers. Buys 2-6 freelance mss/year. Pays $15 for news tips used, and $25-300 for briefs and articles.

Photos: "Will look at color transparencies and bright color prints for inside and cover use." Pays $50-200 for photos.

Tips: "You can break in with a sparkling, 300-word report on a true, offbeat library event, use of new technology, or with an exciting color photo and caption. Though stories on public libraries are always of interest, we especially need arresting material on academic and school libraries."

CHURCH MEDIA LIBRARY MAGAZINE, 127 9th Ave. N., Nashville TN 37234. (615)251-2752. Editor: Floyd B. Simpson. Quarterly magazine. For adult leaders in church organizations and people interested in library work (especially church library work). Estab. 1891. Circ. 16,000. Pays on publication. Buys all rights, first serial rights and second serial (reprint) rights. Byline given. Phone queries OK. Submit seasonal/holiday material 14 months in advance. Previously published submissions OK. Reports in 1 month. Free sample copy and writer's guidelines.

Nonfiction: "We are primarily interested in articles that relate to the development of church libraries in providing media and services to support the total program of a church and in meeting individual needs. We publish how-to accounts of services provided, promotional ideas, exciting things that have happened as a result of implementing an idea or service; human interest stories that are library-related; and media training (teaching and learning with a media mix). Articles should be practical for church library staffs and for teachers and other leaders of the church." Buys 10-15 mss/issue. Query. Pays 5½¢/word.

EMERGENCY LIBRARIAN, Dyad Services, P.O. Box 46258, Stn. G, Vancouver, British Columbia V6R 4G6 Canada. FAX: (604)734-0221. Editor: Ken Haycock. Publishes 5 issues/year. Estab. 1979. Circ. 6,500. Pays on publication. No multiple submissions. Reports in 6 weeks. Free writer's guidelines.

Nonfiction: Emphasis is on improvement of library service for children and young adults in school and public libraries. Also annotated bibliographies. Buys 3 mss/issue. Query. Length: 1,000-3,500 words. Pays $50.

Columns/Departments: Five regular columnists. Also Book Reviews (of professional materials in education, librarianship). Query. Length: 100-300 words. Payment consists of book reviewed.

THE LIBRARY IMAGINATION PAPER, Carol Bryan Imagines, 1000 Byus Dr., Charleston WV 25311. (304)345-2378. 30% freelance written. Quarterly newspaper covering public relations education for librarians. Clip art included in each issue. Estab. 1978. Circ. 3,000. Pays on publication. Publishes ms an average of 6 months after acceptance. Byline given. Buys one-time rights. Submit seasonal/holiday material 3 months in advance. Simultaneous and previously published submissions OK. Reports in 6 weeks on queries; 3 weeks on mss. Sample copy $5; writer's guidelines for SASE.

Nonfiction: How-to (on "all aspects of good library public relations both mental tips and hands-on methods. We need how-to and tips pieces on all aspects of PR, for library subscribers—both school and public libraries. In the past we've featured pieces on taking good photos, promoting an anniversary celebration, working with printers, and producing a slide show.") No articles on "what the library means to me." Buys 4-6 mss/year. Query with or without published clips, or send complete ms. Length: 500-2,200 words. Pays $35.

Photos: Send photos with submission. Reviews 5×7 prints. Offers $5 per photo. Captions required. Buys one-time rights.

Tips: "Someone who has worked in the library field and has first-hand knowledge of library PR needs, methods and processes will do far better with us. Our readers are people who cannot be written down to—but their library training has not always incorporated enough preparation for handling promotion, publicity and the public."

THE NEW LIBRARY SCENE, Library Binding Institute, 8013 Centre Park Dr., Austin TX 78754. (512)836-4141. FAX: (512)836-4849. 50% freelance written. A bimonthly magazine on library book binding and conservation. Estab. 1970. Circ. 3,000. **Pays on acceptance.** Publishes ms an average of 2 months after acceptance. Byline given. Buys first North American serial rights. Reports in 1 month on queries. Sample copy for 9×12 SAE and 4 first class stamps and writer's guidelines for #10 SASE.

Nonfiction: How-to (libraries, book binding, conservation), interview/profile and technical. Buys 6-10 mss/year. Query. Pays $100.
Photos: State availability of photos with submission. Reviews contact sheets and prints (3 × 5 or 5 × 7). Offers no additional payment for photos accepted with ms. Identification of subjects required. Buys one-time rights.

WILSON LIBRARY BULLETIN, 950 University Ave., Bronx NY 10452. (212)588-8400 ext. 2245. FAX: (212)681-1511. Editor: Mary Jo Godwin. 75% freelance written. Monthly (September-June) for professional librarians and those interested in the book and library worlds. Estab. 1914. Circ. 14,000. Pays on publication. Publishes ms an average of 2 months after acceptance. Buys first North American serial rights. Sample copies may be seen on request in most libraries. "Manuscript must be original copy, double-spaced; additional photocopy is appreciated." Deadlines are a minimum 2 months before publication. Reports in 3-6 months. Free sample copy and writer's guidelines.
Nonfiction: Uses articles "of interest to librarians and information professionals throughout the nation and around the world. Style must be lively, readable and sophisticated, with appeal to modern professionals; facts must be thoroughly researched. Subjects range from the political to the comic in the world of media and libraries, with an emphasis on the human as well as the technical aspects of any story. No condescension: no library stereotypes." Buys 20 mss/year. Send complete ms. Length: 2,500-6,000 words. Pays about $100-400, "depending on the substance of article and its importance to readers." Sometimes pays the expenses of writers on assignment.
Tips: "The best way you can break in is with a first-rate black and white or color photo and caption information on a library, library service or librarian who departs completely from all stereotypes and the commonplace. Libraries have changed. You'd better first discover what is now commonplace."

Lumber

CANADIAN FOREST INDUSTRIES WEST, Southam Communications Ltd., 4285 Canada Way, Burnaby, British Columbia V5G 1H2 Canada. (604)433-6125. Editor: Rollin Milrow. 10% freelance written. Monthly magazine. "*Canadian Forest Industries West* covers all facets of the logging and sawmilling sectors of the forest industry." Estab. 1880. Circ. 22,000. **Pays on acceptance.** Byline given. Buys first rights. Previously published submissions OK. Reports in 6 weeks on queries; 1 month on mss. Free writer's guidelines.
Nonfiction: Humor, interview/profile, new product and technical. "We do not want fiction." Buys 6 mss/year. Query with published clips. Length: 800-1,500 words. Payment varies. Sometimes pays expenses of writers on assignment.
Photos: State availability of photos with submission. Reviews transparencies. Payment varies. Buys one-time rights.

NORTHERN LOGGER AND TIMBER PROCESSOR, Northeastern Loggers' Association, P.O. Box 69, Old Forge NY 13420. (315)369-3078. FAX: (315)369-3736. Editor: Eric A. Johnson. 40% freelance written. Monthly magazine of the forest industry in the northern U.S. (Maine to Minnesota and south to Virginia and Missouri). "We are not a purely technical journal, but are more information oriented." Estab. 1952. Circ. 13,600. Pays on publication. Publishes ms an average of 3 months after acceptance. Byline given. Buys all rights. Submit seasonal/holiday material 3 months in advance. Previously published submissions OK. Reports in 2 weeks. Free sample copy and writer's guidelines.
Nonfiction: Expose, general interest, historical/nostalgic, how-to, interview/profile, new product and opinion. "We only buy feature articles, and those should contain some technical or historical material relating to the forest products industry." Buys 12-15 mss/year. Query. Length: 500-2,500 words. Pays $50-250.
Photos: Send photos with ms. Pays $35 for 35mm color transparencies; $15 for 5 × 7 b&w prints. Captions and identification of subjects required.
Tips: "We accept most any subject dealing with this part of the country's forest industry, from historical to logging, firewood, and timber processing."

SOUTHERN LUMBERMAN, Greysmith Publishing, Inc., P.O. Box 681629, Franklin TN 37068. (615)791-1961. FAX: (615)790-6188. Editor: Nanci P. Gregg. 20-30% freelance written. Works with a small number of new/unpublished writers each year. A monthly trade journal for the sawmill industry. Estab. 1881. Circ. 12,000. Pays on publication. Publishes ms an average of 3 months after acceptance. Byline given. Not copyrighted. Buys first North American rights. Submit seasonal/holiday material 6 months in advance. Query for electronic submissions. Reports in 1 month on queries; 2 months on mss. Sample copy $2 with 9 × 12 SAE and 5 first class stamps; writer's guidelines for #10 SASE.

Nonfiction: How to sawmill better, interview/profile, equipment analysis, technical. Sawmill features. Buys 10-15 mss/year. Query with or without published clips, or send complete ms. Length: 500-2,000 words. Pays $150-350 for assigned articles; pays $100-250 for unsolicited articles. Sometimes pays the expenses of writers on assignment.
Photos: Send photos with submission. Reviews transparencies and 4×5 b&w prints. Offers $10-25 per photo. Captions and identification of subjects required.
Tips: "Like most, we appreciate a clearly-worded query listing merits of suggested story—what it will tell our readers they need/want to know. We want quotes, we want opinions to make others discuss the article. Find an interesting sawmill operation owner and start asking questions—I bet a story idea develops. We need b&w photos too. Most open is what we call the Sweethart Mill stories. We publish at least one per month, and hope to be printing two or more monthly in the immediate future. We're interested in new facilities, better marketing, improved production."

Machinery and Metal

‡AUTOMATIC MACHINING, 100 Seneca Ave., Rochester NY 14621. (716)338-1522. Editor: Donald E. Wood. For metalworking technical management. Buys all rights. Byline given.
Nonfiction: "This is not a market for the average freelancer. A personal knowledge of the trade is essential. Articles deal in depth with specific job operations on automatic screw machines, chucking machines, high production metal turning lathes and cold heading machines. Part prints, tooling layouts always required, plus written agreement of source to publish the material. Without personal background in operation of this type of equipment, freelancers are wasting time. No material researched from library sources." Query. Length: no limit. Pays $20/printed page.
Tips: "In the year ahead there will be more emphasis on plant and people news so less space will be available for conventional articles."

CANADIAN MACHINERY & METALWORKING, 777 Bay St., Toronto, Ontario M5W 1A7 Canada. (416)596-5714. Editor: James Barnes. 10% freelance written. Monthly. Circ. 17,000. Buys first North American rights. **Pays on acceptance.** Query. Publishes ms an average of 6 weeks after acceptance.
Nonfiction: Technical and semi-technical articles dealing with metalworking operations in Canada and in the U.S., if of particular interest to Canadian readers. Accuracy and service appeal to readers is a must. Pays minimum 30¢ (Canadian)/word.
Photos: Purchased with mss and with captions only. Pays $10 minimum for b&w features.

MODERN MACHINE SHOP, 6600 Clough Pike, Cincinnati OH 45244. FAX: (513)231-2818. Editor: Ken Gettelman. 25% freelance written. Monthly. Estab. 1928. Pays 1 month following acceptance. Publishes ms an average of 6 months after acceptance. Byline given. Query for electronic submissions. Reports in 5 days. Writer's guidelines for #10 SASE.
Nonfiction: Uses articles dealing with all phases of metal working, manufacturing and machine shop work, with photos. No general articles. "Ours is an industrial publication, and contributing authors should know the metalworking industry." Buys 10 unsolicited mss/year. Query. Length: 1,000-3,500 words. Pays current market rate. Sometimes pays the expenses of writers on assignment.

NICKEL, The magazine devoted to nickel and its applications, Nickel Development Institute, Suite 402, 15 Toronto St., Toronto, Ontario M5C 2E3 Canada. (416)362-8850. Editor: Desmond M. Chorley. 30% freelance written. Quarterly magazine covering the metal nickel and all of its applications. Estab. 1985. Circ. 30,000. **Pays on acceptance.** Publishes ms an average of 3 months after acceptance. Byline given. Buys first rights. Free sample copies and writer's guidelines from Nickel Development Institute Librarian.
Nonfiction: Semi technical. Buys 20 mss/year. Query. Length: 50-450 words. Pays competitive rates, by negotiation. Sometimes pays expenses of writers on assignment.
Photos: State availability of photos with submission. Offers competitive rates by negotiation. Captions, model releases and identification of subjects required.
Tips: "Write to Librarian, Nickel Development Institute, for two free copies of *Nickel* and study them. Know something about nickel's 300,000 end uses. Be at home in writing semitechnical material. Then query the Editor with a story *idea* in a one-page letter—no fax queries or phone calls. Complete magazine is open, except Technical Literature column."

Maintenance and Safety

CLEANING BUSINESS, (formerly *Cleaning*), 1512 Western Ave., Seattle WA 98101. (206)622-4241. Publisher: William R. Griffin. Associate Editor: Jim Saunders. 80% freelance written. Quarterly magazine covering technical and management information relating to cleaning and self-employment. "We cater to those who are self-employed in any facet of the cleaning and maintenance industry and seek to be top professionals in their field. *Cleaning Business* is published for self-employed cleaning professionals, specifically carpet, upholstery and drapery cleaners, janitorial and maid services, window washers, odor, water and fire damage restoration contractors. Our readership is small but select. We seek concise, factual articles, realistic but definitely upbeat." Circ. 6,000. Pays 1 month after publication. Publishes ms an average of 3 months after acceptance. Byline given. Buys first serial rights, second serial (reprint) rights, and all rights; makes work-for-hire assignments. Submit seasonal/holiday material 4 months in advance. Simultaneous queries and previously published work (rarely) OK. Reports in 3 months. Sample copy for $3, 8 × 10 SAE and 3 first class stamps; writer's guidelines for #10 SASE.

Nonfiction: Exposé (safety/health business practices); how-to (on cleaning, maintenance, small business management); humor (clean jokes, cartoons); interview/profile; new product (must be unusual to rate full article—mostly obtained from manufacturers); opinion; personal experience; and technical. Special issues include "What's New?" in Feb. No "wordy articles written off the top of the head, obviously without research, and needing more editing time than was spent on writing." Buys 40 mss/year. Query with or without published clips. Length: 500-3,000 words. Pays $5-80. ("Pay depends on amount of work, research and polishing put into article much more than on length.") Pays expenses of writers on assignment with prior approval only.

Photos: State availability of photos or send photos with ms. Pays $5-25 for "smallish" b&w prints. Captions, model release, and identification of subjects required. Buys one-time rights and reprint rights. "Magazine size is 7 × 8½—photos need to be proportionate."

Columns/Departments: "Ten regular columnists now sell four columns per year to us. We are interested in adding a Safety & Health column (related to cleaning and maintenance industry). We are also open to other suggestions—send query." Buys 36 columns/year; department information obtained at no cost. Query with or without published clips. Length: 500-1,500 words. Pays $15-85.

Fillers: Jokes, gags, anecdotes, short humor, newsbreaks and cartoons. Buys 40/year. Length: 3-200 words. Pays $1-20.

Tips: "We are constantly seeking quality freelancers from all parts of the country. A freelancer can best break in to our publication with fairly technical articles on how to do specific cleaning/maintenance jobs; interviews with top professionals covering this and how they manage their business; and personal experience. Our readers demand concise, accurate information. Don't ramble. Write only about what you know and/or have researched. Editors don't have time to rewrite your rough draft. Organize and polish before submitting."

CLEANING MANAGEMENT, The Magazine for Today's Building Cleaning Maintenance/Housekeeping Executive, National Trade Publications, Inc., 13 Century Hill Dr., Latham NY 12110-2197. (518)783-1281. FAX: (518)783-1386. Editor: Thomas H. Williams. Monthly national trade magazine covering building cleaning maintenance/housekeeping operations in larger institutions such as hotels, schools, hospitals, office buildings, industrial plants, recreational and religious buildings, shopping centers, airports, etc. Articles must be aimed at managers of on-site building/facility cleaning staffs or of owners/managers of contract cleaning companies. Estab. 1981. Circ. 45,000. **Pays on acceptance**, with invoice. Byline given. Buys all rights. Reports in 2 weeks. Free sample copy and writer's guidelines.

Nonfiction: Articles on: how-to discussions of custodial operations/cleaning tasks; the organization of cleaning tasks on an institution-wide basis; recruitment, training, motivation and supervision of building cleaning employees; the cleaning of buildings or facilities of unusual size, type, design, construction or notoriety; interesting case studies; or advice for the successful operation of a contract cleaning business. Buys 6-12 mss/year. Length: 800-2,000 words. Pays $50-300. Please query.

Photos: State availability of photos. Prefer color or b&w prints, rates negotiable. Captions, model releases and identification of subjects required.

Tips: Chances of acceptance are directly proportional to the article's relevance to the professional, on-the-job needs and interests of custodial managers or contract building cleaners.

PEST CONTROL MAGAZINE, 7500 Old Oak Blvd., Cleveland OH 44130. (216)243-8100. FAX: (216)826-2832. Editor: Jerry Mix. For professional pest control operators and sanitarians. Monthly magazine. Estab. 1933. Circ. 15,000. Buys all rights. Buys 12 mss/year. Pays on publication. Submit seasonal material 2 months in advance. Reports in 1 month. Query or submit complete ms.

Nonfiction: Business tips, unique control situations, personal experience (stories about 1-man operations and their problems) articles. Must have trade or business orientation. No general information type of articles desired. Buys 3 unsolicited mss/year. Length: 1,000 words. Pays $150 minimum. Regular columns use material oriented to this profession. Length: 2,000 words.

Photos: No additional payment for photos used with mss. Pays $50-150 for 8×10 color or transparencies.

SAFETY COMPLIANCE LETTER, with OSHA Highlights, Bureau of Business Practice, 24 Rope Ferry Rd., Waterford CT 06386. (203)442-4365. Editor: Margot Loomis. Managing Editor: Many Schantz. 80% freelance written. Bimonthly newsletter covering occupational safety and health. Publishes interview-based 'how-to' and 'success' stories for personnel in charge of safety and health in manufacturing/industrial environments. Estab. 1915. Circ. 8,000. Pays on acceptance after editing. Publishes ms an average of 3-6 months after acceptance. No byline given. Buys all rights. Submit seasonal/holiday material 4 months in advance. Reports in 1 week on queries; 1 month on mss. Free sample copy and writer's guidelines.
Nonfiction: How-to (implement an occupational safety/health program), changes in OSHA regulations and examples of safety/health programs. No articles that aren't based on an interview. Buys 48 mss/year. Query. Length: 750-1,200 words. Pays 10¢-15¢/word. Sometimes pays the expenses of writers on assignment.

‡**SANITARY MAINTENANCE,** Trade Press Publishing Co., 2100 W. Florist Ave., Milwaukee WI 53209. (414)228-7701. FAX: (414)228-1134. Managing Editor: Austin Weber. Associate Editor: Susan M. Netz. 7-8% freelance written. Prefers to work with published/established writers, although all will be considered. A monthly magazine for the sanitary supply industry covering "trends in the sanitary supply industry; offering information concerning the operations of janitor supply distributors and building service contractors; and helping distributors in the development of sales personnel." Estab. 1943. Circ. 15,000. Pays on publication. Publishes ms an average of 5 months after acceptance. Byline given. Buys first North American serial rights. Query for electronic submissions. Free sample copy and writer's guidelines.
Nonfiction: How-to (improve sales, profitability as it applies to distributors, contractors); and technical. No product application stories. Buys 8-12 mss/year. Query with published clips. Length: 1,500-3,000 words. Pays $75-300.
Photos: State availability of photos with query letter or ms. Reviews 5×7 prints. Payment for photos included in payment for ms. Identification of subjects required.
Tips: Articles on sales and financial information for small businesses are open to freelancers.

‡**UTILITY CONSTRUCTION AND MAINTENANCE,** Practical Communications, Inc., 37 W. Main, Box 183, Cary IL 60013. (312)639-2200. FAX: (312)639-9542. Editor: Alan Richter. 5% freelance written. Quarterly magazine for equipment managers and maintenance supervisors for electric, gas and water utilities; interconnect and cable TV companies, public works departments and related contractors. "We seek case history/application features covering specific equipment management and maintenance projects/installations. Instructional/tutorial features are also welcome." Circ. 25,000. Pays on publication. Publishes ms an average of 1 month after acceptance. Byline given. 20% kill fee. Buys all rights. Submit seasonal/holiday material 2 months in advance. Reports in 2 weeks. Free sample copy and writer's guidelines.
Nonfiction: How-to (ways for performing fleet maintenance/improving management skills/vehicle tutorials), technical, case history/application features. No advertorials in which specific product or company is promoted. Buys 2-3 ms/year. Query with published clips. Length: 1,000-2,800 words. Pays $50/page.
Photos: Send photos with submission. Reviews contact sheets, negatives, tranparencies (3×5) and prints (3×5). Offers no additional payment for photos accepted with ms. Captions required. Buys one-time rights.

Management and Supervision

This category includes trade journals for middle management business and industiral managers, including supervisors and office managers. Journals for business executives and owners are classified under Business Management. Those for industrial plant managers are listed in Industrial Operations.

‡**DATA TRAINING,** Weingarten Publications, Inc. 38 Chauncy St., Boston MA 02111. (617)542-0146. Editor: Douglas W. Roberts. 50% freelance written. A monthly magazine on computer training and training management. "*Data Training* is aimed at people who teach other people how to use computers within corporations. We try to help our readers advance in their profession by including information on management and business." Circ. 10,000. **Pays on acceptance.** Publishes ms an average of 3 months after acceptance. Byline given. Query for electronic submissions. Free sample copy; writer's guidelines for #10 SASE.

Nonfiction: How-to, interview/profile, opinion, technical. Buys 24 mss/year. Query with or without published clips or send complete ms. Length: 500-5,000 words. Pays $100-600. Sometimes pays expenses of writers on assignment.
Photos: State availability of photos with submission.
Tips: "Most articles are contributed by training professionals in data processing or end user computing. Freelancers should be familiar with computers and/or training. A query, with clips, is a good idea."

EMPLOYEE RELATIONS AND HUMAN RESOURCES BULLETIN, Bureau of Business Practice, 24 Rope Ferry Rd., Waterford CT 06386. FAX: (203)434-3078. Senior Editor: Barbara Kelsey. 40% freelance written. Works with a small number of new/unpublished writers each year. For personnel, human resources and employee relations managers on the executive level. Semimonthly newsletter. Estab. 1940. Circ. 5,500. **Pays on acceptance.** Publishes an average of 3 months after acceptance. Buys all rights. No byline. Phone queries OK. Submit seasonal/holiday material 6 months in advance. Reports in 1 month. Free sample copy and writer's guidelines.
Nonfiction: Interviews about all types of business and industry such as banks, insurance companies, public utilities, airlines, consulting firms, etc. Interviewee should be a high level company officer—human resources executive, president, industrial relations manager, etc. Writer must get signed release from person interviewed showing that article has been read and approved by him/her, before submission. Some subjects for interviews might be productivity improvement, communications, compensation, labor relations, safety and health, grievance handling, human relations techniques and problems, etc. No general opinions and/or philosophy of good employee relations or general good motivation/morale material. Buys 2 mss/issue. Query is mandatory. Length: 1,500-2,000 words. Pays 8-18¢/word after editing. Sometimes pays the telephone expenses of writers on assignment. Modem transmission available by prior arrangement with editor.

‡HUMAN RESOURCE EXECUTIVE, Axon Group, 747 Dresher Rd., P.O. Box 980, Dresher PA 19044. (215)784-0860. Editor: David Shadovitz. 30% freelance written. A monthly magazine for human resource professionals/executives. "The magazine serves the information needs of chief human resource executives in companies, government agencies and nonprofit institutions with 500 or more employees." Estab. 1987. Circ. 45,000. **Pays on acceptance.** Publishes ms an average of 2 months after acceptance. Byline given. Offers 50% kill fee. Buys first rights and second serial (reprint) rights. Query for electronic submissions. Reports in 1 month. Sample copy for 13 × 10 SAE with 2 first class stamps. Writer's guidelines for #10 SAE with 1 first class stamp.
Nonfiction: Book excerpts, interview/profile. Buys 16 mss/year. Query with published clips. Length: 1,700-2,400 words. Pays $200-700. Sometimes pays expenses of writers on assignment.
Photos: State availability of photos with submission. Reviews contact sheets. Offers no additional payment for photos accepted with ms. Identification of subjects required. Buys first and repeat rights.

INDUSTRY WEEK, The Industry Management Magazine, Penton Publishing Inc., 1100 Superior Ave., Cleveland OH 44114. (216)696-7000. FAX: (216)696-7670. Editor: Charles R. Day, Jr. Associate Mangaging Editors: Dale W. Sommer, John H. Carson. 15% freelance written. Industrial management magazine published on the first and third Monday of each month. "*Industry Week* is designed to help its audience—mid- and upper-level managers in industry—manage and lead their organizations better. Every article should address this editorial mission." Estab. 1921. Circ. 288,000. **Pays on acceptance.** Publishes ms an average of 2-4 months after acceptance. Byline given. Buys first North American serial rights. Free sample copy and writer's guidelines. "An SAE speeds replies."
Nonfiction: Interview/profile. "Any article submitted to *Industry Week* should be consistent with its mission. We suggest authors contacting us before submitting anything." Buys 15-20 mss/year. Query with or without published clips, or send complete ms. Length: 750-2,500 words. Pays $350 minimum. "We pay *routine* expenses; we do *not* pay for travel unless arranged in advance." Manuscripts and queries should be directed to Michael A. Verespej, Associate Editor.
Photos: State availability of photos with submission. Send photo with submission. Reviews contact sheets, transparencies and prints. Payment arranged individually. Captions and identification of subjects required. Buys one-time rights.
Tips: "Become familiar with *Industry Week*. We're after articles about managing in industry, period. While we do not use freelancers too often, we do use some. The stories we accept are written with an understanding of our audience, and mission. We prefer multi-source stories that offer lessons for all managers in industry."

MANAGE, 2210 Arbor Blvd., Dayton OH 45439. (513)294-0421. FAX: (513)294-2374. Editor-in-Chief: Douglas E. Shaw. 60% freelance written. Works with a small number of new/unpublished writers each year. Quarterly magazine. For first-line and middle management and scientific/technical managers. Estab. 1925. Circ. 75,000. **Pays on acceptance.** Publishes ms an average of 6 months after acceptance. Buys North American magazine rights with reprint privileges; book rights remain with the author.

Reports in 1 month. Free sample copy for 9×12 SAE; free writer's guidelines.

Nonfiction: "All material published by *Manage* is in some way management oriented. Most articles concern one or more of the following categories: communications, executive abilities, human relations, job status, leadership, motivation and productivity and professionalism. Articles should be specific and tell the manager how to apply the information to his job immediately. Be sure to include pertinent examples, and back up statements with facts and, where possible, charts and illustrations. *Manage* does not want essays or academic reports, but interesting, well-written and practical articles for and about management." Buys 6 mss/issue. Phone queries OK. Submit complete ms. Length, 600-2,000 words. Pays 5¢/word.

Tips: "Keep current on management subjects; submit timely work."

PERSONNEL ADVISORY BULLETIN, Bureau of Business Practice, 24 Rope Ferry Rd., Waterford CT 06386. (203)442-4365, ext. 778. Editor: Jill Whitney. 75% freelance written. Eager to work with new/unpublished writers. Emphasizes all aspects of personnel practices for personnel managers in all types and sizes of companies, both white collar and industrial. Semimonthly newsletter. **Pays on acceptance.** Publishes ms an average of 5 months after acceptance. Buys all rights. Submit seasonal/holiday material 4 months in advance. Reports in 2 weeks. Free sample copy and writer's guidelines for 10×13 SAE and 2 first class stamps.

Nonfiction: Interviews with personnel managers or human resource professionals on topics of current interest in the personnel field. Buys 30 mss/year. Query with brief, specific outline. Length: 1,500-1,800 words.

Tips: "We're looking for concrete, practical material on how to solve problems. We're providing information about trends and developments in the field. We don't want filler copy. It's very easy to break in. Include your phone number with your query so we can discuss the topic. Send for guidelines first, though, so we can have a coherent conversation."

PERSONNEL JOURNAL, The business magazine for leaders in human resources, ACC Communications Inc., 245 Fischer Ave., B-2, Costa Mesa CA 92626. (714)751-1883. FAX: (714)751-4106. Editor: Allan Halcrow. 10% freelance written. Monthly magazine. "*Personnel Journal* is targeted to senior human resources executives in companies with 500 or more employees. The editorial content is aimed at helping readers define and improve corporate policy on personnel issues, as well as to identify trends and issues in the field and provide case examples of successful personnel programs." Estab. 1922. Circ. 30,000. **Pays on acceptance.** Publishes ms an average of 2 months after acceptance. Byline given. Offers kill fee of ½ original fee plus expenses. Buys all rights (can be negotiable). Reports in 3 weeks on queries; 1 month on mss. Free sample copy and writer's guidelines.

Nonfiction: How-to (explanation of a personnel-related program or system), opinion (informed commentary on some aspect of personnel management), personal experience (case study detailing a personnel program's development and implementation) and technical (how to use computers in the personnel department; analysis of recent legislation or court decisions). "We do not want literature surveys (a round-up of all published thought on a topic, such as performance appraisals). We do not want anything written to or for employees." Buys 6-8 mss/year. Query with published clips. Length: 1,200-3,500 words. Pays $700-3,000 for assigned articles; $500-2,000 for unsolicited articles. Pays with contributor copies when articles submitted by practitioners (not writers) and when terms are understood up-front. Pays expenses of writers on assignment.

Photos: State availability of photos with submission. Reviews 35mm transparencies. Offers $50-200 per photo. Model releases are required. Buys one-time rights.

Tips: "The best way to get into *Personnel Journal* is to base material in reality. Too many writers present management theory with no evidence it has been tried or write a how-to that does not include examples. Be specific—*why* was a program developed, *how* (step-by-step) was it implemented. Also, it's best to assume readers have some sophistication—they do not need basic techniques defined; they want *new* ideas."

PRODUCTION SUPERVISOR'S BULLETIN, Bureau of Business Practice, 24 Rope Ferry Rd., Waterford CT 06386. (800)243-0876. FAX: (203)434-3341. 75% freelance written. Biweekly newsletter. "The audience is primarily first-line production supervisors and managers. Articles are meant to address a common workplace issue faced by such a supervisor, (absenteeism, low productivity, improving quality, ensuring safety, etc.) and explain how interviewee dealt with the issue." **Pays on acceptance.** Publishes ms an average of 4 months after acceptance. Byline not given. Buys all rights. Reports in 2 weeks on queries; 3 weeks on mss. Free sample copy and writer's guidelines.

Nonfiction: How-to (on managing people, solving workplace problems, improving productivity). No high-level articles aimed at upper management. Buys 60-70 mss/year. Query. Length: 800-1,500 words. Pays 9-15¢/word.

Tips: Freelancers may call the editor at (800)243-0876. Prospective writers are strongly urged to send for writer's guidelines. Sections of publication most open to freelancers are lead story; inside stories (generally 3 to 4 per issue); and Production Management Clinic (in every other issue). Include concrete, how-to steps for dealing effectively with the topic at hand.

SALES MANAGER'S BULLETIN, The Bureau of Business Practice, 24 Rope Ferry Rd., Waterford CT 06386. Editor: Paulette S. Kitchens. 33% freelance written. Prefers to work with published/established writers. Newsletter published twice/month. For sales managers and salespeople interested in getting into sales management. Estab. 1917. **Pays on acceptance.** Publishes ms an average of 3-6 months after acceptance. Written queries only except from regulars. Submit seasonal/holiday material 6 months in advance. Original interview-based material only. Buys all rights. Reports in 2 weeks. Sample copy and writer's guidelines only when request is accompanied by SAE with 2 first clas stamps.
Nonfiction: How-to (motivate salespeople, cut costs, create territories, etc.); interview (with working sales managers who use innovative techniques); and technical (marketing stories based on interviews with experts). No articles on territory management, saving fuel in the field, or public speaking skills. Break into this publication by reading the guidelines and sample issue. Follow the directions closely and chances for acceptance go up dramatically. One easy way to start is with an interview article ("Here's what sales executives have to say about . . ."). Query is vital to acceptance: "send a simple note explaining briefly the subject matter, the interviewees, slant, length, and date of expected completion, accompanied by a SASE. Does not accept unqueried mss." Length: 800-1,000 words. Pays 10-15¢/word.
Tips: "Freelancers should always request samples and writer's guidelines, accompanied by SASE. Requests without SASE are discarded immediately. Examine the sample, and don't try to improve on our style. Write as we write. Don't 'jump around' from point to point and don't submit articles that are too chatty and with not enough real information. The more time a writer can save the editors, the greater his or her chance of a sale and repeated sales, when queries may not be necessary any longer. We will focus more on selling more product, meeting intense competiton, while spending less money to do it."

‡**SECURITY MANAGEMENT: PROTECTING PROPERTY, PEOPLE & ASSETS,** Bureau of Business Practice, 24 Rope Ferry Rd., Waterford CT 06386. Editor: Alex Vaughn. 75% freelance written. Eager to work with new/unpublished writers. Semimonthly newsletter. Emphasizes security for industry. "All material should be slanted toward security directors, primarily industrial, retail and service businesses, but others as well." Circ. 3,000. **Pays on acceptance.** Buys all rights. Phone queries OK. Reports in 2 weeks. Free sample copy and writer's guidelines.
Nonfiction: Interview (with security professionals only). "Articles should be tight and specific. They should deal with new security techniques or new twists on old ones." Buys 2-5 mss/issue. Query. Length: 750-1,000 words. Pays 15¢/word.

‡**SUPERVISION,** 424 N. 3rd St., P.O. Box 1, Burlington IA 52601-0001. FAX: (319)752-3421. Publisher: Michael S. Darnall. Editorial Supervisor: Doris J. Ruschill. Editor: Barbara Boeding. 95% freelance written. Monthly magazine for first-line foremen, supervisors and office managers. Estab. 1939. Circ. 5,402. Pays on publication. Publishes ms an average of 6 months after acceptance. Buys all rights. Reports in 3 weeks. Sample copy and writer's guidelines for 9×12 SAE with 4 first class stamps; mention *Writer's Market* in request.
Nonfiction: How-to (cope with supervisory problems, discipline, absenteeism, safety, productivity, goal setting, etc.); and personal experience (unusual success story of foreman or supervisor). No sexist material written from only a male viewpoint. Include biography and/or byline with ms submissions. Author photos requested. Buys 12 mss/issue. Query. Length: 1,500-1,800 words. Pays 4¢/word.
Tips: "Following AP stylebook would be helpful." Uses no advertising. Send correspondence to Editor.

SUPERVISOR'S BULLETIN, Bureau of Business Practice, 24 Rope Ferry Rd., Waterford CT 06386. (203)442-4365. FAX: (203)434-3078. Editor: April L. Katz. 50-75% freelance written. "We work with both new and established writers, and are always looking for fresh talent." Bimonthly newsletter for manufacturing supervisors wishing to improve their managerial skills. Estab. 1915. **Pays on acceptance.** Publishes ms on average of 2 months after acceptance. No byline given. Buys all rights. Reports in 2 weeks on queries, 6 weeks on mss. Free sample copy and writer's guidelines.
Nonfiction: How-to (solve a supervisory problem on the job); and interview (of top-notch supervisors). Sample topics could include: how-to increase productivity, cut costs, achieve better teamwork." No filler or non-interview based copy. Buys 72 mss/year. Query first. "Strongly urge writers to study guidelines and samples." Length: 750-1,000 words. Pays 8-16¢/word.
Tips: "We need interview-based articles that emphasize direct quotes. Define a problem and show how the supervisor solved it. Write in a light, conversational style, talking directly to supervisors who can benefit from putting the interviewee's tips into practice."

TRAINING, The Magazine of Human Resources Development, Lakewood Publications, 50 S. Ninth St., Minneapolis MN 55402. (612)333-0471. Editor: Jack Gordon. Managing Editor: Chris Lee. 10% freelance written. A monthly magazine covering training and employee development in the business world. "Our core readers are managers and professionals who specialize in employee training and development (e.g., corporate training directors, VP-human resource development, etc.). We have a large secondary readership among managers of all sorts who are concerned with improving human performance in their organizations. We take a businesslike approach to training and employee education." Estab. 1964. Circ. 52,000. **Pays on acceptance.** Publishes ms an average of 3 months after acceptance. Byline given. Buys first North American serial rights and second serial (reprint) rights. Simultaneous submissions OK. Reports in 2 weeks on queries; 6 weeks on mss. Sample copy for 9×12 SAE with 4 first class stamps. Writer's guidelines for #10 SASE.
Nonfiction: Essay; exposé; how-to (on training, management, sales, productivity improvement, etc.); humor; interview/profile; new product; opinion; photo feature; and technical (use of audiovisual aids, computers, etc.). "No puff, no 'testimonials' or disguised ads in any form, no 'gee-whiz' approaches to the subjects." Buys 10-12 mss/year. Query with or without published clips, or send complete ms. Length: 200-3,000 words. Pays $50-650.
Photos: State availability of photos or send with submission. Reviews contact sheets and prints. Offers no additional payment for photos accepted with ms. Identification of subjects required. Buys one-time rights and reprint rights.
Columns/Departments: Training Today (news briefs, how-to tips, reports on pertinent research, trend analysis, etc.), 200-800 words. Buys 6 mss/year. Query or send complete ms. Pays $50-75.
Tips: "We would like to develop a few freelancers to work with on a regular basis. We almost never give firm assignments to unfamiliar writers, so you have to be willing to hit us with one or two on spec to break in. Short pieces for our Training Today section involve least investment on your part, but also are less likely to convince us to assign you a feature. When studying the magazine, freelancers should look at our staff-written articles for style, approach and tone. Do not concentrate on articles written by people identified as consultants, training directors, etc."

WAREHOUSING SUPERVISOR'S BULLETIN, Bureau of Business Practice, 24 Rope Ferry Rd., Waterford CT 06386. (203)442-4365. FAX: (203)434-3078. Editor: April L. Katz. 75-90% freelance written. "We work with a wide variety of writers, and are always looking for fresh talent." Biweekly newsletter covering traffic, materials handling and distribution for warehouse supervisors "interested in becoming more effective on the job." **Pays on acceptance.** Publishes ms an average of 3 months after acceptance. No byline given. Buys all rights. Reports in 2 weeks on queries; 6 weeks on mss. Free sample copy and writer's guidelines.
Nonfiction: How-to (increase efficiency, control or cut costs, cut absenteeism or tardiness, increase productivity, raise morale); and interview (of warehouse supervisors or managers who have solved problems on the job). No noninterview articles, textbook-like descriptions, union references or advertising of products. Buys 50 mss/year. Query. "A resumé and sample of work are helpful." Length: 1,580-2,900 words. Pays 10-15¢/word. Sometimes pays the expenses of writers on assignment.
Tips: "All articles must be interview-based and emphasize how-to information. They should also include a reference to the interviewee's company (location, size, products, function of the interviewee's department and number of employees under his control). Focus articles on one problem, and get the interviewee to pinpoint the best way to solve it. Write in a light, conversational style, talking directly to warehouse supervisors who can benefit from putting the interviewee's tips into practice."

Marine and Maritime Industries

NORTHERN AQUACULTURE, Harrison House Publishers, 4611 William Head Rd., Victoria, British Columbia V8X 3W9 Canada. (604)478-9209. FAX: (604)478-1184. Editor: Peter Chettleburgh. 50% freelance written. Works with a small number of new/unpublished writers each year. A bimonthly magazine covering aquaculture in Canada and the northern United States. Estab. 1985. Circ. 4,500. Pays on publication. Publishes ms an average of 3 months after acceptance. Byline given. Buys first North American serial rights. Submit seasonal/holiday material 5 months in advance. Reports in 3 weeks. Free sample copy for 9×12 SAE with $2 IRCs.; free writer's guidelines.
Nonfiction: How-to, interview/profile, new product, opinion and photo feature. Buys 20-24 mss/year. Query. Length: 200-1,500 words. Pays 10-20¢/word for assigned articles; pays 10-15¢/word for unsolicited articles. May pay writers with contributor copies if writer requests. Sometimes pays the expenses of writers on assignment.
Photos: Send photos with submission. Reviews 5×7 prints. Captions required. Buys one-time rights.

PROCEEDINGS, U.S. Naval Institute, Annapolis MD 21402. (301)268-6110. Editor: Fred H. Rainbow. Managing Editor: John G. Miller. 95% freelance written. Eager to work with new/published writers. Monthly magazine covering naval and maritime subjects. Circ. 100,000. **Pays on acceptance.** Publishes ms an average of 5 months after acceptance. Byline given. Buys all rights. Submit seasonal/holiday material 3 months in advance. Reports in 2 weeks on queries; 1 month on mss. Free sample copy and writer's guidelines.

Nonfiction: Essays, exposé, general interest, historical/nostalgic, how-to (related to sea service professional subjects), humor, interview/profile, new product, opinion, personal experience, photo feature and technical. "*Proceedings* is an unofficial, open forum for the discussion of naval and maritime topics." Special issues include International Navies (March) and Naval Review (May). Buys 250 mss/year. Query or send complete ms. Length: up to 3,500 words. Pays $50-600. Sometimes pays writers with contributor copies or other premiums "if author desires." Sometimes pays the expenses of writers on assignment.

Photos: Send photos with submission. Reviews contact sheets, negatives, transparencies and prints. Offers $10-100 per photo. Buys one-time rights.

Columns/Departments: Book Reviews, Nobody Asked Me But . . ., and Crossword Puzzles (all with naval or maritime slants), all 500-2,000 words. Buys 90 mss/year. Query. Pays $50-200.

Fiction: Adventure, historical and humorous. Buys 4 mss/year. Query. Length: 500-3,000 words. Pays $50-600.

Fillers: Anecdotes. Buys 50/year. Length: 1,000 words maximum. Pays $25-150.

Tips: "Write about something you know about, either from first-hand experience or based on primary source material. Our letters to the editor column is most open to freelancers."

‡**SEA'S INDUSTRY WEST, The Western Marine Industry Magazine,** Duncan McIntosh Co. Inc., Suite C, 17782 Cowen, 2nd Floor, Irvine CA 92714. (714)660-6150. Editor: Linda Yuskaitis. 30% freelance written. Quarterly magazine covering recreational boating industry in the 13 western states. "*Sea's Industry West* covers news and trends that directly affect the western marine industry. Articles are aimed directly at industry professionals, offering them the information they need to make the most of their business." Estab. 1990. Circ. 12,375. Pays on publication. Publishes ms an average of 4 months after acceptance. Byline given. Buys first North American serial rights or second serial (reprint) rights. Query for electronic submissions. Reports in 1 month on queries; 6 weeks on mss. Sample copy and writer's guidelines for SASE.

Nonfiction: Interview/profile, new product, West Coast industry trend features. "No cartoons, poetry, fiction or features aimed at consumers instead of marine business people." Buys 25 mss/year. Query with published clips or send complete ms. Length: 250-2,000 words. Pays $35-275. "Some expenses covered if requested in advance, in writing."

Photos: State availability of photos with submission or send photos with submission. Reviews any size color transparencies. Offers $35-250 per photo. Identification of subjects required. Buys one-time rights.

Columns/Departments: Business Briefs (short news items about changes, developments at Western Marine companies); Legislative Update (new bills, laws and court decisions affecting the marine industry in the west); New products (boating accessories and services available for sale by Western marine distributors/retailers). Query with published clips or send complete ms. Length: 250 words. Pays $35.

WORKBOAT, P.O. Box 1348, Mandeville LA 70470. (504)626-0298. FAX: (504)624-5801. Senior Editor: Marilyn Barrett. 60% freelance written. Bimonthly magazine on all working boats: commerical inland and near shore. Target work boat owners, boat captains, operators, service companies and related businesses." Estab. 1943. Pays on acceptance or publication. Publishes ms average of 2 months after acceptance. Byline given. Offers negotiable kill fee. Buys first time rights. Query for electronic submissions. Sample copy for 9 × 12 SAE and $3; writer's guidelines for #10 SASE.

Nonfiction: General interest, how-to, interview/profile and technical. Query or query with published clips. Sometimes pays expenses of writers on assignment.

Photos: State availability of photos with submission. Reviews contact sheets and transparencies, prefers color. Pay negotiable. Identification of subjects required. Buys one-time rights.

Tips: "Learn all you can about tugs, barges, supply boats, passenger vessels (excursion and ferry), dredges, fire boats, patrol boats and any vessel doing business on America's inland waterways, harbors and close to shore. Also, familiarity with issues affecting the maritime industry is a plus."

Medical

Through these journals physicians, pharmacists, therapists and mental health professionals learn how other professionals help their patients and manage their medical practices. Publications for nurses, laboratory technicians and other medical personnel are listed in the Hospitals, Nursing and Nursing Home section. Publications for drug store managers and drug wholesalers and retailers, as well as hospital equipment suppliers, are listed with

Drugs, Health Care and Medical Products. Publications for consumers that report trends in the medical field are found in the Consumer Health and Fitness categories.

AMERICAN MEDICAL NEWS, American Medical Association, 516 N. State St., Chicago IL 60610. (312)464-5000. Editor: Barbara Bolsen. 5-10% freelance written. "Prefers writers already interested in the health care field—not clinical medicine." Weekly tabloid providing nonclinical information for physicians—information on socio-economic, political and other developments in medicine. "*AMN* is a specialized publication circulating to physicians, covering subjects touching upon their profession, practices and personal lives. This is a well-educated, highly sophisticated audience." Circ. 375,000 physicians. **Pays on acceptance.** Publishes ms an average of 2 months after acceptance. Byline given. Offers variable kill fee. Buys all rights. Rights sometimes returnable on request after publication. Simultaneous queries OK. Reports in 1 month. Sample copy for 9×12 SAE and 2 first class stamps. Free writer's guidelines.

Nonfiction: Flora Johnson Skelly, assistant executive editor for outside contributions. Interview/profile (occasional); opinion (mainly from physicians); and news and interpretive features. Special issues include "Year in Review" issue published in January. No clinical articles, general-interest articles physicians would see elsewhere, or recycled versions of articles published elsewhere. Buys 200 mss/year. Query. Length: 200-4,000 words. Pays $400-750 for features; $50-100 for opinions and short news items. "We have limited travel budget for freelancers; we pay minimal local expenses."

Tips: "We are trying to create a group of strong feature writers who will be regular contributors."

CARDIOLOGY WORLD NEWS, Medical Publishing Enterprises, P.O. Box 1548, Marco Island FL 33969. (813)394-0400. Editor: John H. Lavin. 75% freelance written. Prefers to work with published/established writers. Monthly magazine covering cardiology and the cardiovascular system. "We need short news articles *for doctors* on any aspect of our field—diagnosis, treatment, risk factors, etc." Estab. 1985. **Pays on acceptance.** Publishes ms an average of 2 months after acceptance. Byline given "for special reports and feature-length articles." Offers 20% kill fee. Buys first North American serial rights. Query for electronic submissions. Reports in 1 month. Sample copy $1; free writer's guidelines with #10 SASE.

Nonfiction: New product and technical (clinical). No fiction, fillers, profiles of doctors or poetry. Query with published clips. Length: 250-1,500 words. Pays $50-300; $50/column for news articles. Pays expenses of writers on assignment.

Photos: State availability of photos with query. Pays $50/published photo. Rough captions, model release and identification of subjects required. Buys one-time rights.

Tips: "Submit written news articles of 250-500 words on speculation with basic source material (not interview notes) for fact-checking. We demand clinical or writing expertise for full-length feature. Clinical cardiology conventions/symposia are the best source of news and feature articles."

CINCINNATI MEDICINE, Academy of Medicine, 320 Broadway, Cincinnati OH 45202. (513)421-7010. Executive Editor: Susan J. Clarke. 40-50% freelance written. Works with a small number of new/unpublished writers each year. Quarterly membership magazine for the Academy of Medicine of Cincinnati. "We cover socio-economic and political factors that affect the practice of medicine in Cincinnati. For example: How will changes in Medicare policies affect local physicians and what will they mean for the quality of care Cincinnati's elderly patients receive. (Ninety-nine percent of our readers are Cincinnati physicians.)" Estab. 1978. Circ. 3,500. **Pays on acceptance.** Publishes ms an average of 3-6 months after acceptance. Byline given. Makes work-for-hire assignments. Simultaneous queries OK. Reports in 6 weeks on queries; 1 month on mss. Sample copy for $3 and 9×12 SAE and 7 first class stamps; writer's guidelines for #10 SASE.

Nonfiction: Historical/nostalgic (history of, or reminiscences about, medicine in Cincinnati); interview/profile (of nationally known medical figures or medical leaders in Cincinnati); and opinion (opinion pieces on controversial medico-legal and medico-ethical issues). "We do not want: scientific-research articles, stories that are not based on good journalistic skills (no seat-of-the-pants reporting), or why my 'doc' is the greatest guy in the world stories." Buys 10-12 mss/year. Query with published clips or send complete ms. Length: 800-2,500 words. Pays $125-300. Sometimes pays expenses of writers on assignment.

Always check the most recent copy of a magazine for the address and editor's name before you send in a query or manuscript.

Photos: State availability of photos with query or ms. Captions and identification of subjects required. Buys one-time rights.

Tips: "Send published clips; do some short features that will help you develop some familiarity with our magazine and our audience; and show initiative to tackle the larger stories. First-time writers often don't realize the emphasis we place on solid reporting. We want accurate, well-balanced reporting or analysis. Our job is to *inform* our readers."

CONSULTANT PHARMACIST, American Society of Consultant Pharmacists, Suite 515, 2300 S. 9th St., Arlington VA 22204. (703)920-8492. FAX: (703)892-2084. Editor: L. Michael Posey. Managing Editor: Joanne Kaldy. 10% freelance written. A monthly magazine on consultant pharmacy. "We do not promote drugs or companies but rather ideas and information." Circ. 10,000. **Pays on acceptance.** Publishes ms an average of 2 months after acceptance. Byline given. Buys first North American serial rights. Query for electronic submissions. Reports in 2 weeks. Sample copy for 9 × 12 SAE with 4 first class stamps. Writer's guidelines for #10 SASE.
Nonfiction: How-to (related to consultant pharmacy), interview/profile, technical. Buys 10 mss/year. Query with published clips. Length: 750-2,000 words. Pays $300-1,200. Sometimes pays expenses of writers on assignment.
Photos: Send photos with submission. Offers $100/per photo session. Captions, model releases, identification of subjects required. Buys one-time rights.
Tips: "This journal is devoted to consultant pharmacy, so articles must relate to this field."

DIAGNOSTIC IMAGING, Miller Freeman, 600 Harrison St., San Francisco CA 94107. Publisher: Vicki Masseria. Editor: Peter Ogle. 10% freelance written. Monthly news magazine covering radiology, nuclear medicine, magnetic resonance, and ultrasound for physicians in diagnostic imaging professions. Estab. 1979. Circ. 24,000. Average issue includes 4-5 features. **Pays on acceptance.** Publishes ms an average of 2-3 months after acceptance. Byline given. Buys all rights. No phone queries. "Written query should be well-written, concise and contain a brief outline of proposed article and a description of the approach or perspective the author is taking." Submit seasonal material 1 month in advance. Simultaneous submissions OK. Query for electronic submissions. Reports in 2 weeks. Free sample copy.
Nonfiction: "We are interested in topical news features in the areas of radiology, magnetic resonance imaging, nuclear medicine and ultrasound, especially news of state and federal legislation, new products, insurance, regulations, medical literature, professional meetings and symposia and continuing education." Buys 10-12 mss/year. Query with published clips. Length: 1,000-2,000 words. Pays 30¢/ word minimum.
Photos: Reviews 5 × 7 b&w glossy prints and 35mm and larger color transparencies. Offers $20 for photos accepted with ms. Captions required. Buys one-time rights.

DOCTORS SHOPPER, Marketing Communications, Inc., 1086 Remsen Ave., Brooklyn NY 11236. (718)257-8484. FAX: (718)257-8845. Publisher: Ralph Selitzer. 35% freelance written. Quarterly magazine on medical business, travel, finances, lifestyle articles for doctors. Circ. 211,000. Pays on publication. Byline given. Buys one-time rights. Submit seasonal/holiday material 6 months in advance. Previously published submissions OK. Reports in 1 month. Free sample copy for 9 × 12 SAE and 12 first class stamps. Writer's guidelines for #10 SASE.
Nonfiction: General interest, new product, photo feature, technical, travel and financial. Buys 8 mss/ year. Send complete ms. Length: 250-2,000 words. Pays $250-500 for assigned articles; $125-250 for unsolicited articles.
Photos: State availability of photos with submission. Reviews contact sheets and 2 × 2 transparencies. Offers no additional payment for photos accepted with ms. Captions, model releases and identification of subjects required. Buys one-time rights.
Columns/Departments: CME Travel (travel articles for doctors attending continuing education conferences), 500-1,000 words. Buys 4 mss/year. Pays $125-250.
Fillers: Anecdotes, facts, gags to be illustrated by cartoonist, all *medical*. Buys 8/year. Length: 100-500 words. Pays $25-50.
Tips: "Contribute self help articles for physicians on serving patients better, run a more efficient practice, enjoy leisure time, travel, etc. Travel articles, new medical office methods, actual physician case histories are areas most open to freelancers."

EMERGENCY, The Journal of Emergency Services, 6300 Yarrow Drive, Carlsbad CA 92009. (619)438-2511. FAX: (619)931-5809. Editor: Rhonda L. Foster. 100% freelance written. Works with a small number of new/unpublished writers each year. A monthly magazine covering pre-hospital emergency care. "Our readership is primarily composed of EMTs, paramedics and other EMS personnel. We prefer a professional, semi-technical approach to pre-hospital subjects." Estab. 1969. Circ. 29,000. **Pays on acceptance.** Publishes ms an average of 4 months after acceptance. Byline given. Buys all rights, (revert back to author after 90 days). Submit seasonal/holiday material 6 months in advance. Reports in 2 months. Sample copy $3; writer's guidelines for #10 SASE.

Nonfiction: Semi-technical exposé, how-to (on treating pre-hospital emergency patients), interview/profile, new techniques, opinion and photo feature. "We do not publish cartoons, term papers, product promotions disguised as articles or overly technical manuscripts." Buys 60 mss/year. Query with published clips. Length 1,500-3,000 words. Pays $100-400.

Photos: Send photos with submission. Reviews color transparencies and b&w prints. Offers no additional payment for photos accepted with ms. Offers $30/photo without ms.; $100 for cover photos. Captions and identification of subjects required.

Columns/Departments: Open Forum (opinion page for EMS professionals), 500 words. Trauma Primer (pre-hospital care topics, treatment of injuries, etc.), 1,000-2,000 words. Drug Watch (focus on one particular drug a month). Buys 10 mss/year. Query first. Pays $50-250.

Fillers: Facts and newsbreaks. Buys 10/year. Length: no more than 500 words. Pays $0-75.

Tips: "Writing style for features and departments should be knowledgeable and lively with a clear theme or story line to maintain reader interest and enhance comprehension. The biggest problem we encounter is dull, lifeless term-paper-style writing with nothing to pique reader interest. Keep in mind we are not a textbook. Accompanying photos are a plus.We appreciate a short, one paragraph biography on the author."

FACETS, American Medical Association Auxiliary, Inc., 515 N. State St., Chicago IL 60610. (312)464-4470. FAX: (312)464-4184. Editor: Kathleen T. Jordan. Work with both established and new writers. For physicians' spouses. 30% freelance written. Magazine published 6 times/year. Estab. 1965. Circ. 90,000. **Pays on acceptance.** Publishes ms an average of 6 months after acceptance. Buys first rights. Simultaneous, and previously published submissions OK. Reports in 6 weeks. Free sample copy and writer's guidelines.

Nonfiction: All articles must be related to the experiences of physicians' spouses. Current health issues; financial topics; physicians' family circumstances; business management; volunteer leadership how-to's. Buys 20 mss/year. Query with clear outline of article—what points will be made, what conclusions drawn, what sources will be used. No personal experience or personality stories. Length: 1,000-2,500 words. Pays $300-800. Pays expenses of writers on assignment.

Photos: State availability of photos with query. Uses 8×10 glossy b&w prints and $2\frac{1}{4} \times 2\frac{1}{4}$ transparencies.

Tips: Uses "articles only on specified topical matter with good sources, not hearsay or personal opinion. Since we use only nonfiction and have a limited readership, we must relate factual material."

GERIATRIC CONSULTANT, Medical Publishing Enterprises, P.O. Box 1548, Marco Island FL 33969. (813)394-0400. Editor: John H. Lavin. 70% freelance written. Prefers to work with published/established writers. Bimonthly magazine for physicians covering medical care of the elderly. "We're a clinical magazine directed to doctors and physician assistants. All articles must *help* these health professionals to help their elderly patients. We're too tough a market for nonmedical beginners." Estab. 1982. Circ. 97,500. **Pays on acceptance.** Publishes ms an average of 3-6 months after acceptance. Byline given. Offers 20% kill fee. Buys first North American serial rights. Simultaneous queries OK. Query for electronic submissions. Reports in 1 month. Sample copy for $1; writer's guidelines for #10 SASE.

Nonfiction: How-to (diagnosis and treatment of health problems of the elderly) and technical/clinical. No fiction or articles directed to a lay audience. Buys 20 mss/year. Query. Length: 750-3,000 words. Pays $200-350 for features; $50-100 for 250 word-plus news articles. Pays expenses of writers on assignment.

Photos: State availability of photos. (Photos are not required.) Model release and identification of subjects required. Buys one-time rights.

Tips: "Many medical meetings are now held in the field of geriatric care. These offer potential sources and subjects for us."

‡HEALTHCARE PROFESSIONAL PUBLISHING, Division of TM Marketing, Inc., 105 Main Street, Hackensack NJ 06701. (201)342-6511. Write to Editorial Director. 45% freelance written. "Produces single-sponsored publications. Work is made on assignment only. An ability to work with specialized scientific material and condense it into tightly written news stories for physicians is important." **Pays on acceptance.** Publishes ms an average of 1-2 months after acceptance. Byline sometimes given. Makes work-for-hire assignments.

‡THE MAYO ALUMNUS, Mayo Clinic, 200 SW 1st St., Rochester MN 55905. (507)284-8565. Editor: Rosemary Cashman. 10% freelance written. "We usually use our own staff for writing, and only occasionally use freelancers." For physicians, scientists and medical educators who trained at the Mayo Clinic. Quarterly magazine. Circ. 13,500. **Pays on acceptance.** Publishes ms an average of 3 months after acceptance. Buys all rights. Free sample copy; mention *Writer's Market* in request. Writer's guidelines available on request.

Nonfiction: "We're interested in seeing interviews with members of the Mayo Alumni Association — stories about Mayo-trained doctors/educators/scientists/researchers who are interesting people doing interesting things in medicine, surgery or hobbies of interest, etc." Query with clips of published work. Length: 1,500-3,000 words. Payment negotiable. Sometimes pays the expenses of writers on assignment.

Photos: "We need art and must make arrangements if not provided with the story." State availability of photos with query. Captions preferred. Buys all rights.

Tips: "I keep a file of freelance writers, and when I need an alumnus covered in a certain area of the country, I contact a freelancer from that area. Those who suit my needs are the writers in the right place at the right time or those who have a story about an interesting alumnus."

THE NEW PHYSICIAN, 1890 Preston White Dr., Reston VA 22091. Editor: Richard Camer. 50% freelance written. For medical students, interns and residents. Published 9 times/year. Circ. 30,000. Buys first serial rights. Pays on publication. Publishes features an average of 2 months after acceptance. Will consider simultaneous submissions. Reports in 2 months. Sample copy for 10×13 SAE with 5 first class stamps; writer's guidelines for SASE.

Nonfiction: Articles on social, political, economic issues in medicine/medical education. "We want skeptical, accurate, professional contributors to do well-researched, comprehensive, incisive reports and offer new perspectives on health care problems. Not interested in highly technical or clinical material. Humorous articles and cartoons welcome." Buys about 12 features/year plus 6 departments. Query or send complete ms. Length: 500-3,500 words. Pays $100-1,000 with higher fees for selected pieces. Pays expenses of writers on assignment.

Tips: "We need more practically oriented articles for physicians-in-training — how-to's for young doctors starting out. We are not however, *Medical Economics.* They must be authoritative, and from objective sources, not a consultant trying to sell his services. Our magazine demands sophistication on the issues we cover. We are a professional magazine for readers with a progressive view on health care issues and a particular interest in improving the health care system. Freelancers should be willing to look deeply into the issues in question and not be satisfied with a cursory review of those issues."

THE NEW YORK DOCTOR, Chase Communications, P.O. Box 9001, Mt. Vernon NY 10552. (914)699-2020. FAX: (212)964-9885. Editor: Michelle Eldrige. Monthly news and city magazine for physicians in the five boroughs, Long Island and Westchester. "Our magazine covers AIDS, nursing shortages, malpractice and legislative issues affecting New York-area doctors." Estab. 1985. Circ. 15,000. **Pays on acceptance.** Byline given. No kill fee. Buys first North American serial rights or second rights. Query for electronic submissions. Reports in 1 month on mss. Sample copy for 8×10 SAE with 3 first class stamps.

Nonfiction: "We do not want anything too clinical or technical." Accepts very little freelance material. Buys 35-60 mss/year. Query with published clips. Length: 250-1,500 words. Pays $25-350 for assigned articles.

Photos: State availability of photos with submission. Reviews contact sheets, negatives and prints. Payment varies. Captions and identification of subjects required.

Columns/Departments: Query. Inside-talk (hospitals, government, pharmaceutical companies), Medicare, The Environment/Medical Waste Management, After Hours (New York area physicians' hobbies, life-styles), Recruitment (trends at hospitals, managed-care companies, pharmaceutical companies), Malpractice, Office Labs, Op-Ed (by health-care experts), Research (human-interest behind the effort).

THE PHYSICIAN AND SPORTSMEDICINE, McGraw-Hill, 4530 W. 77th St., Edina MN 55435. (612)835-3222. Features Editor: Amber Stenger. Managing Editor: Terry Monahan. 30% freelance written. Prefers to work with published/established writers. Monthly magazine covering medical aspects of sports and exercise. "We look for feature articles or subjects of practical interest to our physician audience." Estab. 1973. Circ. 130,000. **Pays on acceptance.** Publishes ms an average of 2 months after acceptance. Byline given. Generally buys all rights. Reports in 1 month. Sample copy for $4; writer's guidelines for #10 SASE.

Nonfiction: Interview (persons active in this field); and technical (new developments in sports medicine). Query. Length: 250-2,500 words. Pays $150-900.

Photos: Shelly Fling, photo editor. State availability of photos. Buys one-time rights.

PHYSICIAN'S MANAGEMENT, Edgell Communications Health Care Publications, 7500 Old Oak Blvd., Cleveland OH 44130. (216)243-8100. FAX: (216)891-2683. Editor-in-Chief: Bob Feigenbaum. Prefers to work with published/established writers. Monthly magazine emphasizes finances, investments, malpractice, socioeconomic issues, estate and retirement planning, small office administration, practice management, computers, and taxes for primary care physicians in private practice. Estab. 1960. Circ. 120,000. **Pays on acceptance.** Publishes ms an average of 6 months after acceptance. Buys first North American rights. Submit seasonal or holiday material 5 months in advance. Query for electronic submissions. Reports in 1 month. Sample copy $3.50. Writer's guidelines for #10 SASE.

Nonfiction: *"Physician's Management* is a practice management/economic publication, not a clinical one." Publishes how-to articles (limited to medical practice management); informational (when relevant to audience); and personal experience articles (if written by a physician). No fiction, clinical material or satire that portrays MD in an unfavorable light; or soap opera, "real-life" articles. Length: 2,000-2,500 words. Query with SASE. Pays $125/3-column printed page. Use of charts, tables, graphs, sidebars and photos strongly encouraged. Sometimes pays expenses of writers on assignment.

Tips: "Talk to doctors first about their practices, financial interests, and day-to-day nonclinical problems and then query us. Also, the ability to write a concise, well-structured and well-researched magazine article is essential. Freelancers who think like patients fail with us. Those who can think like MDs are successful. Our magazine is growing significantly. The opportunities for good writers will, therefore, increase greatly."

PODIATRY MANAGEMENT, P.O. Box 50, Island Station NY 10044. (212)355-5216. Publisher: Scott C. Borowsky. Editor: Barry Block, D.P.M. Managing Editor: M.J. Goldberg. Business magazine published 9 times/year for practicing podiatrists. "Aims to help the doctor of podiatric medicine to build a bigger, more successful practice, to conserve and invest his money, to keep him posted on the economic, legal and sociological changes that affect him." Estab. 1982. Circ. 11,000. Pays on publication. Byline given. Buys first North American serial rights and second serial (reprint) rights. Submit seasonal/holiday material 4 months in advance. Simultaneous queries, and simultaneous and previously published submissions OK. Reports in 2 weeks. Sample copy $2 with 9×12 SAE; free writer's guidelines for #10 SASE.

Nonfiction: General interest (taxes, investments, estate planning, recreation, hobbies); how-to (establish and collect fees, practice management, organize office routines, supervise office assistants, handle patient relations); interview/profile about interesting or well-known podiatrists; and personal experience. "These subjects are the mainstay of the magazine, but offbeat articles and humor are always welcome." Buys 25 mss/year. Query. Length: 1,000-2,500 words. Pays $150-350.

Photos: State availability of photos. Pays $15 for b&w contact sheet. Buys one-time rights.

RESCUE, Jems Communications, P.O. Box 2789, Carlsbad CA 92018. (619)431-9797. FAX: (619)431-8176. Executive Editor: Keith Griffiths. Managing Editor: Lee Reeder. 60% freelance written. Bimonthly magazine covering basic life support and technical areas of interest for providers and administrators of emergency care. Estab. 1988. Circ. 12,000. Pays on publication. Byline given. Buys first North American serial and one-time rights. Submit seasonal/holiday material 6 months in advance. Query for electronic submissions. Reports in 3 weeks on queries; 2 months on mss. Sample copy and writer's guidelines for $1.41.

Nonfiction: Book excerpts, how-to, humor, new product, opinion, photo feature and technical. Special issues include "Vehicle Extrication, rescue training, mass-casualty incidents, water rescue and wilderness rescue. No 'I was saved by a ranger' " articles. Buys 15-20 mss/year. Query with or without published clips, or send complete ms. Length: 1,000-3,000 words. Pays $125-200. Sometimes pays the expenses of writers on assignment.

Photos: Send photos with submission. Reviews contact sheets, negatives, 2×2 transparencies and 5×7 prints. Offers $50-125 per photo. Buys one-time rights.

Tips: "Read our magazine, spend some time with a rescue team. We will begin to focus on all aspects of rescue, including basic life support, vehicle extrication, transport and treatment, in addition to the specialized rescue we have been covering. Emphasis on techniques and new technology, with more color photos as support."

SENIOR PATIENT, McGraw-Hill, 4530 W. 77th St., Edina MN 55435. (612)835-3222. Managing Editor: Terry Monahan. Assistant Managing Editor: Kathleen Kimball-Baker. Monthly magazine covering the health care needs of the elderly. "As the American population ages, doctors need more information to help them better care for the psychosocial—as well as the medical—needs of the elderly." 20-50% freelance written. Estab. 1989. Circ. 135,000. **Pays on acceptance.** Publishes ms an average of 4 months after acceptance. Byline given. (Sometimes byline shared with physician.) Buys limited rights. Send seasonal/holiday material 6 months in advance. Query for electronic submissions. Reports in 6 weeks. Sample copy for $5; writer's guidelines for #10 SASE.

Nonfiction: Articles include journalistic features (Special Reports) on political, economic and social issues of interest to physicians who treat older adults; "not-exactly-medical" features (Features) that share one doctor's experiences about managing senior patients; and short news stories (Currents) with up-to-date information on Medicare policies, ethical concerns and recent studies that have immediate applicability to our readers' practices. Query. Length: 100-2,500 words. Pays $50-1,000.

Photos: Tina Adamek, photo editor. State availability of photos. Buys one-time rights.

STRATEGIC HEALTH CARE MARKETING, Health Care Communications, 11 Heritage Ln., P.O. Box 594, Rye NY 10580. (914)967-6741. Editor: Michele von Dambrowski. 40% freelance written. Prefers to work with published/established writers. "Will only work with unpublished writer on a 'stringer' basis initially." A monthly newsletter covering health care services marketing in a wide range of settings including hospitals and medical group practices, home health services and ambulatory care centers. Emphasizes strategies and techniques employed within the health care field and relevant applications from other service industries. Estab. 1984. Pays on publication. Publishes ms an average of 2 months after acceptance. Byline given. Offers 25% kill fee. Buys first North American serial rights. Reports in 1 month. Sample copy for 9 × 12 SAE and 3 first class stamps; guidelines sent with sample copy only.
Nonfiction: How-to, interview/profile, new product and technical. Buys 25 mss/year. Query with published clips. No unsolicited mss accepted. Length: 700-2,000 words. Pays $100-400. Sometimes pays the expenses of writers on assignment with prior authorization.
Photos: State availability of photos with submissions. (Photos, unless necessary for subject explanation, are rarely used.) Reviews contact sheets. Offers $10-30/photo. Captions and model releases required. Buys one-time rights.
Tips: "Writers with prior experience on business beat for newspaper or newsletter will do well. This is not a consumer publication—the writer with knowledge of both health care and marketing will excel. Interviews or profiles are most open to freelancers. Absolutely no unsolicited manuscripts; any received will be returned or discarded unread."

‡**SURGICAL ROUNDS,** Romaine Pierson Publishers, Inc., 80 Shore Rd., Port Washington NY 11050. (516)883-6350. FAX: (516)883-6609. Editor: Bernard M. Jaffe, M.D. Executive Editor: Susan Reckling. Monthly magazine for surgeons and surgical specialists throughout the country, including interns and residents, all surgical faculty in medical schools, plus full-time hospital and private practice surgeons and operating room supervisors. Estab. 1978. Circ. 50,000. **Pays on acceptance.** Byline given. Buys all rights. Reports in 1 month. Sample copy $8; free writer's guidelines.
Nonfiction: How-to (practical, everyday clinical applications). "Articles for 'The Surgeon's Laboratory' should demonstrate a particular procedure step-by-step and be amply and clearly illustrated with intraoperative color photographs and anatomical drawings." Buys 80 mss/year. Query with published clips. Length: 1,500-2,000 words.

Music

Publications for musicians and for the recording industry are listed in this section. Other professional performing arts publications are classified under Entertainment and the Arts. Magazines featuring music industry news for the general public are listed in the Consumer Entertainment and Music sections. (Markets for songwriters can be found in *Songwriter's Market*—see Other Books of Interest).

THE CHURCH MUSICIAN, 127 9th Ave. N., Nashville TN 37234. (615)251-2961. Editor: William Anderson. 30% freelance written. Works with a small number of new/unpublished writers each year; eager to work with new/unpublished writers. Southern Baptist publication for Southern Baptist church music leaders. Quarterly. Circ. 16,000. Buys all rights. **Pays on acceptance.** Publishes ms an average of 1 year after acceptance. No query required. Reports in 2 months. Free sample copy.
Nonfiction: Leadership and how-to features, success stories and articles on Protestant church music. "We reject material when the subject of an article doesn't meet our needs. And they are often poorly written, or contain too many 'glittering generalities' or lack creativity. We're interested in success stories; a 'this-worked-for-me' type of story." Length: maximum 1,300 words. Pays up to 5½¢/word.
Photos: Purchased with mss; related to mss content only. "We are going to full color in April, 1991."
Fiction: Inspiration, guidance, motivation and morality with Protestant church music slant. Length: to 1,300 words. Pays up to 5½¢/word.
Poetry: Church music slant, inspirational. Length: 8-24 lines. Pays $5-15.
Fillers: Short humor. Church music slant. No clippings. Pays $5-15.
Tips: "I'd advise a beginning writer to write about his or her experience with some aspect of church music; the social, musical and spiritual benefits from singing in a choir; a success story about their instrumental group; a testimonial about how they were enlisted in a choir—especially if they were not inclined to be enlisted at first. A writer might speak to hymn singers—what turns them on and what doesn't. Some might include how music has helped them to talk about Jesus as well as sing about Him. We would prefer most of these experiences be related to the church, of course, although we include many articles by freelance writers whose affiliation is other than Baptist. A writer might relate his

experience with a choir of blind or deaf members. Some people receive benefits from working with unusual children – retarded, or culturally deprived, emotionally unstable, and so forth."

THE INSTRUMENTALIST, Instrumentalist Publishing Company, 200 Northfield Rd., Northfield IL 60093. (708)446-5000. FAX: (708)446-6263. Managing Editor: Anne Driscoll. Approximately 95% freelance written. A monthly magazine covering instrumental music education for school band and orchestra directors, as well as performers and students. Estab. 1944. Circ. 22,000. Pays on publication. Publishes ms an average of 6-9 months after acceptance. Byline given. Buys all rights "but willing to permit authors to sell articles again to noncompeting publications." Submit seasonal/holiday material 6 months in advance. Reports in 1 month. Sample copy for 9 × 12 SAE and $2.50; free writer's guidelines.
Nonfiction: Book excerpts (rarely); essays (on occasion); general interest (on occasion, music); historical/nostalgic (music); how-to (teach, repair instruments); humor (on occasion); interview/profile (performers, conductors, composers); opinion; personal experience; photo feature; and travel. Buys 100 mss/year. Send complete ms. Length: 750-1,750 words. Pays $30-45/published page.
Photos: State availability of photos with submission. Reviews slides and 5 × 7 prints (photo guidelines available upon request). Payment varies. Captions and identification of subjects required. Buys variable rights.
Columns/Departments: Personal Perspective (opinions on issues facing music educators), 500-750 words; Idea Exchange ('how-tos' from educators), 250-500 words. Send complete ms. Length: 250-500 words. Pays $30-45.
Fillers: Anecdotes and short humor. Buys 5/year. Length: 250 words maximum. Pays $25-45.
Tips: "Know the music education field, specifically band and orchestra. Interviews with performers should focus on the person's contribution to education and opinions about it. We are interested in interviews and features that focus on ideas rather than on personalities. Writers must have a strong educational background in classical music."

INTERNATIONAL BLUEGRASS, International Bluegrass Music Association, 326 St. Elizabeth St., Owensboro KY 42301. (502)684-9025. Editor: Dan Hays. All editorial submissions should be directed to Dan Hays. 30% freelance written. Bimonthly newsletter covering bluegrass music industry. "We are the business publication for the bluegrass music industry. IBMA believes that our music has growth potential. We are interested in hard news and features concerning how to reach that potential and how to conduct business more effectively." Estab. 1985. Circ. 3,000. Pays on publication. Publishes ms an average of 2 months after acceptance. Byline given. Not copyrighted. Buys one-time rights. Submit seasonal/holiday material 4 months in advance. Simultaneous and previously published submissions OK. Query for electronic submissions. Reports in 1 month on queries; 6 weeks on mss. Sample copy for 6 × 9 SAE and 2 first class stamps.
Nonfiction: Book excerpts, essays, how-to (conduct business effectively within bluegrass music), new product and opinion. No interview/profiles of performers (rare exceptions) or fans. Buys 6 mss/year. Query with or without published clips, or send complete ms. Length: 300-1,200 words. Pays $25 maximum for assigned articles. Pays in contributor's copies unless payment in cash agreed at assignment.
Photos: Send photos with submission. Reviews 5 × 8 prints. Offers no additional payment for photos accepted with ms. Captions and identification of subjects required. Buys one-time rights.
Columns/Departments: At the Microphone (opinion about the bluegrass music industry). Buys 6 mss/year. Send complete ms. Length: 300-1,200 words. Pays $0-25.
Fillers: Anecdotes, facts and newsbreaks.
Tips: "The easiest break-in is to submit an article about an organizational member of IBMA – such as a bluegrass associate, instrument manufacturer or dealer, or performing venue. We're interested in a slant strongly toward the business end of bluegrass music. At the Microphone is the most open to freelancers. We're especially looking for material dealing with audience development and how to book bluegrass bands outside of the existing market."

OPERA NEWS, 70 Lincoln Center Plaza, New York NY 10023-6593. FAX: (212)769-7007. Editor: Patrick J. Smith. 75% freelance written. Monthly magazine (May-November); biweekly (December-April). For people interested in opera; the opera professional as well as the opera audience. Estab. 1936. Circ. 120,000. Pays on publication. Publishes ms an average of 3 months after acceptance. Buys

ALWAYS submit unsolicited manuscripts or queries with a self-addressed, stamped envelope (SASE) within your country or a self-addressed envelope with International Reply Coupons (IRC) purchased from the post office for other countries.

first serial rights only. Pays negotiable kill fee. Byline given. Sample copy $2.50.

Nonfiction: Most articles are commissioned in advance. Monthly issues feature articles on various aspects of opera; in biweekly issues many articles relate to the weekly broadcasts from the Metropolitan Opera. Emphasis is on high quality writing and an intellectual interest to the opera-oriented public. Informational, personal experience, interview, profile, historical, think pieces, personal opinion and opera reviews. Query; no telephone inquiries. Length: 2,500 words maximum. Pays 13¢/word minimum for features; 11¢/word minimum for reviews. Rarely pays the expenses of writers on assignment.

Photos: Pays minimum of $25 for photos purchased on assignment. Captions required.

Office Environment and Equipment

GEYER'S OFFICE DEALER, 51 Madison Ave., New York NY 10010. (212)689-4411. FAX: (212)683-7929. Editor: Robert D. Rauch. 20% freelance written. For independent office equipment and stationery dealers, and special purchasers for store departments handling stationery and office equipment. Monthly. Buys all rights. Byline given. Estab. 1877. Pays on publication. Publishes ms an average of 3 months after acceptance. Reports "immediately."

Nonfiction: Articles on dealer efforts in merchandising and sales promotion; programs of stationery and office equipment dealers. Problem-solving articles related to retailers of office supplies, social stationery items, office furniture and equipment and office machines. Must feature specific stores. Query. Length: 300-1,000 words. Pays $175 minimum but quality of article is real determinant.

Photos: Black and white and color glossies are purchased with accompanying ms with no additional payment.

MODERN OFFICE TECHNOLOGY, Penton Publishing, 1100 Superior Ave., Cleveland OH 44114. (216)696-7000. FAX: (216)696-7658. Associate Publisher and Editorial Director: John Dykeman. Editor: Lura K. Romei. Production Manager: Gina Runyon. 5-10% freelance written. A monthly magazine covering office automation for corporate management and personnel, financial management, administrative and operating management, systems and information management, managers and supervisors of support personnel and purchasing. Estab. 1956. Circ. 157,000. Pays on publication. Publishes ms an average of 6 months after acceptance. Byline given. Buys first and one-time rights. Query for electronic submissions. Reports in 1 month. Sample copy and writer's guidelines for 9×12 SAE and 2 first class stamps.

Nonfiction: New product, opinion and technical. Query with or without published clips, or send complete ms. Length: open. Pays $250-500 for assigned articles; pays $250-400 for unsolicited articles. Pays expenses of writers on assignment.

Photos: Send photos with submission. Reviews contact sheets, 4×5 transparencies and prints. Additional payment for photos accepted with ms. Consult editorial director. Captions and identification of subjects required. Buys one-time rights.

Tips: "Submitted material should alway present topics, ideas, on issues that are clearly and concisely defined. Material should describe problems and solution. Writer should describe benefits to reader in tangible results whenever possible."

Paper

‡BOXBOARD CONTAINERS, Maclean Hunter Publishing Co., 29 N. Wacker Dr., Chicago IL 60606-3298. (312)726-2802. FAX: (312)726-2574. Editor: Charles Huck. Managing Editor: Christopher Howes. A monthly magazine covering box and carton manufacturing for corrugated box, folding carton, setup box manufacturers internationally. Emphasizes technology and management. Circ. 14,000. Pays on publication. Byline given. Buys first North American serial rights. Submit seasonal/holiday material 2 months in advance. Query for electronic submissions. Reports in 1 month. Free sample copy.

Nonfiction: How-to, interview/profile, new product, opinion, personal experience, photo feature and technical. Buys 10 mss/year. Query. Length: 2,000-6,000 words. Pays $75-350 for assigned articles; pays $50-200 for unsolicited articles. Sometimes pays the expenses of writers on assignment.

Photos: Send photos with submission. Reviews 35mm, 4×5 and 6×6 transparencies and 8×10 prints. Offers no additional payment for photos accepted with ms. Captions, model releases and identification of subjects required. Buys one-time rights.

Tips: Features are most open to freelancers.

PULP & PAPER CANADA, Southam Business Communications Inc., Suite 410, 3300 Côte Vertu, St. Laurent, Quebec H4R 2B7 Canada. (514)339-1399. FAX: (514)339-1396. Editor/Associate Publisher: Peter N. Williamson. Managing Editor: Graeme Rodden. 5% freelance written. Prefers to work with published/established writers. Monthly magazine. Estab. 1903. Circ. 9,309. **Pays on acceptance.** Publishes ms "as soon as possible" after acceptance. Byline given. Offers kill fee according to prior agreement. Buys first North American serial rights. Reports in 3 weeks. Free sample copy and writer's guidelines.
Nonfiction: How-to (related to processes and procedures in the industry); interview/profile (of Canadian leaders in pulp and paper industry); and technical (relevant to modern pulp and/or paper industry). No fillers, short industry news items, or product news items. Buys 10 mss/year. Query first with published clips or send complete ms. Articles with photographs (b&w glossy) or other good quality illustrations will get priority review. Length: 1,500-2,000 words (with photos). Pays $160 (Canadian funds)/published page, including photos, graphics, charts, etc. Sometimes pays the expenses of writers on assignment.
Tips: "Any return postage must be in either Canadian stamps or International Reply Coupons *only*."

Pets

Listed here are publications for professionals in the pet industry—pet product wholesalers, manufacturers, suppliers, and retailers, and owners of pet specialty stores, grooming businesses, aquarium retailers and those interested in the pet fish industry. The Veterinary section lists journals for animal health professionals. Publications for pet owners are listed in the Consumer Animal section.

GROOM & BOARD, Incorporating "Groomers Gazette Kennel News," H.H. Backer Associates Inc., Suite 504, 207 S. Wabash Ave., Chicago IL 60604. (312)663-4040. FAX: (312)663-5676. Editor: Karen Long MacLeod. 10% freelance written. Magazine about grooming and boarding pets published 9 times/year. "*Groom & Board* is the only national trade publication for professional pet groomers and boarding kennel operators. It provides news, technical articles and features to help them operate their businesses more successfully." Estab. 1980. Circ. 16,000. **Pays on acceptance.** Publishes ms an average of 6 months after acceptance. Byline given. Buys first North American serial rights, one-time rights, all rights or exclusive to industry. Submit seasonal/holiday material 6 months in advance. Previously published submissions OK (rarely). Query for electronic submissions. Reports in 2 months on queries; 1 month on mss. Sample copy $2.50 plus $3.50 shipping and handling (total $6); writer's guidelines for #10 SASE.
Nonfiction: How-to (groom specific breeds of pets, run business, etc.), interview/profile (successful grooming and/or kennel operations) and technical. "We do not want consumer-oriented articles or stories about a single animal (animal heroes, grief, etc.)." Buys 3-6 mss/year. Query with or without published clips, or send complete ms. Length: 1,000-3,000 words. Pays $90 minimum for assigned articles; $65-200 for unsolicited articles. Sometimes pays expenses of writers on assignment.
Photos: Send photos with submission. Reviews contact sheets, transparencies and prints. Offers $7 per photo. Captions and identification of subjects required. Buys one-time or all rights.

PET AGE, The Largest Circulation Pet Industry Trade Publication, H.H. Backer Associates, Inc., 207 S. Wabash Ave., Chicago IL 60604. (312)663-4040. FAX: (312)663-5676. Editor: Karen Long MacLeod. 20-30% freelance written. Prefers to work with published/established writers. Monthly magazine for pet/pet supplies retailers, covering the complete pet industry. Estab. 1971. Circ. 18,026. **Pays on acceptance.** Publishes ms an average of 3-6 months after acceptance. Byline given. Buys first North American serial rights, one-time rights, all rights or exclusive industry rights. Submit seasonal/holiday material 6 months in advance. Query for electronic submissions. Reports in 2 months on queries; 1 month on mss. Sample copy for $2.50 plus $3.50 shipping and hangling (total $6); writer's guidelines for #10 SASE.
Nonfiction: Book excerpts, profile (of a successful, well-run pet retail operation); how-to; interview; photo feature; and technical—all trade-related. Query first with published clips. Buys 6-12 mss/year. "Query as to the name and location of a pet operation you wish to profile and why it would make a good feature. No general retailing articles or consumer-oriented pet articles." Length: 1,000-3,000 words. Pays $75-300 for assigned articles; $50-150 for unsolicited articles. Sometimes pays the expenses of writers on assignment.
Photos: Reviews 5×7 b&w glossy prints. Captions and identification of subjects required. Offers $7 (negotiable) for photos. Buys one-time rights or all rights.
Tips: "Our readers already know about general animal care and business practices. This is a business publication for busy people, and must be very informative in easy-to-read, concise style. The type of article we purchase most frequently is the pet shop profile, a story about an interesting/successful pet

shop. We need queries on these (we get references on the individual shop from our sources in the industry). We supply typical questions to writers when we answer their queries."

‡PET BUSINESS, P.O. Box 2300, Miami FL 33243. (305)667-4402. Editor: Karen Payne. 20% freelance written. Eager to work with new/unpublished writers. "Our monthly news magazine reaches retailers, distributors and manufacturers of companion animals and pet products. Groomers, veterinarians and serious hobbyists are also represented." Estab. 1973. Circ. 17,000. Pays on publication. Publishes ms an average of 2 months after acceptance. Byline sometimes given. Buys first rights. Submit seasonal/ holiday material 3 months in advance. Sample copy $3. Writer's guidelines for SASE.

Nonfiction: "Articles must be newsworthy and pertain to animals routinely sold in pet stores (dogs, cats, fish, birds, reptiles and small animals). Research, legislative and animal behavior reports are of interest. All data must be attributed. No fluff!" Buys 15-20 mss/year. Send complete ms. "No queries—the news gets old quickly." Length: 50-800 words. Pays $5 per column inch.

Photos: Send photos (slides or prints) with submission. Offers $10-20 per photo. Buys one-time rights.

Tips: "We are open to national and international news written in standard news format. Buys cartoons; pays $10 each on publication."

THE PET DEALER, Howmark Publishing Corp., 567 Morris Ave., Elizabeth NJ 07208. (908)353-7373. FAX: (908)353-8221. Editor: Donna Eastman. 55% freelance written. Prefers to work with published/ established writers, but is eager to work with new/published writers. "We want writers who are good reporters and clear communicators." Monthly magazine. Emphasizes merchandising, marketing and management for owners and managers of pet specialty stores, departments, and pet groomers and their suppliers. Estab. 1949. Circ. 16,000. Pays on publication. Publication "may be many months between acceptance of a manuscript and publication." Byline given. Phone queries OK. Submit seasonal/holiday material 4 months in advance. Reports in 6 weeks. Sample copy for 8 × 10 SAE and $5.

Nonfiction: How-to (store operations, administration, merchandising, marketing, management, promotion and purchasing). Consumer pet articles—lost pets, best pets, humane themes—*not* welcome. "We *are* interested in helping—dog, cat, monkey, whatever stories tie in with the human/animal bond." Emphasis is on *trade* merchandising and marketing of pets and supplies. Buys 6-8 unsolicited mss/ year. Length: 800-1,500 words. Pays $100-125.

Photos: Submit undeveloped photo material with ms. No additional payment for 5 × 7 b&w glossy prints. Buys one-time rights. Will give photo credit for photography students.

Fillers: "Will buy some cartoons ($20 each) if they are absolutely hilarious. Will publish poetry (unpaid) as fillers in directory issue."

Tips: "We're interested in store profiles outside the New York, New Jersey, Connecticut and Pennsylvania metro areas. Photos are of key importance. Articles focus on new techniques in merchandising or promotion. Want to see more articles from retailers and veterinarians. Submit query letter first, with writing background summarized; include samples. We seek one-to-one, interview-type features on retail pet store merchandising. Indicate the availability of the proposed article, your willingness to submit on exclusive or first-in-field basis, and whether you are patient enough to await payment on publication."

Photography Trade

Journals for professional photographers are listed in this section. Magazines for the general public interested in photography techniques are in the Consumer Photography section. (For listings of markets for freelance photography use *Photographer's Market*—see Other Books of Interest).

AMERICAN CINEMATOGRAPHER, A.S.C. Holding Corp., Box 2230, Hollywood CA 90078. (213)876-5080. FAX: (213)876-4973. Editor: George Turner. 50% freelance written. Monthly magazine. An international journal of film and video production techniques "addressed to creative, managerial, and technical people in all aspects of production. Its function is to disseminate practical information about the creative use of film and video equipment, and it strives to maintain a balance between technical sophistication and accessibility." Circ. 28,000. Pays on publication. Publishes ms an average of 3 months after acceptance. Buys all rights. Phone queries OK. Simultaneous submissions OK. Query for electronic submission. Sample copy for 9 × 12 SAE with $1 postage; writer's guidelines for #10 SASE.

Nonfiction: Jean Turner, associate editor. Descriptions of new equipment and techniques or accounts of specific productions involving unique problems or techniques; historical articles detailing the production of a classic film, the work of a pioneer or legendary cinematographer or the development of a significant technique or type of equipment. Also discussions of the aesthetic principles involved in

production techniques. Length 2,000-2,500 words. Pays according to position and worth. Negotiable. Sometimes pays the expenses of writers on assignment.
Photos: B&w and color purchased with mss. No additional payment; rate covers ms and photo package.
Tips: "No unsolicited articles. Call first. Doesn't matter whether you are published or new. Queries must describe writer's qualifications and include writing samples. We expect expansion of videography."

PHOTO MARKETING, Photo Marketing Assocation Intl., 3000 Picture Place, Jackson MI 49201. (517)788-8100. FAX: (517)788-8371. Managing Editor: Margaret Hooks. 2% freelance written. A monthly magazine for photo industry retailers, finishers and suppliers. "Articles must be specific to the photo industry and cannot be authored by anyone who writes for other magazines in the photo industry. We provide management information on a variety of topics as well as profiles of successful photo businesses and analyses of current issues in the industry." Estab. 1925. Circ. 22,000. **Pays on acceptance.** Publishes ms an average of 2 months after acceptance. Byline given. Buys one-time rights and exclusive photo magazine rights. Simultaneous submissions OK. Reports in 2 weeks. Free sample copy and writer's guidelines.
Nonfiction: Interview/profile (anonymous consumer shops for equipment); personal experience (interviews with photo retailers); technical (photofinishing lab equipment); new technology (still electronic video). Buys 5 mss/year. Send complete ms. Length: 1,000-2,300 words. Pays $150-350.
Photos: State availability of photos with submission. Reviews negatives, 5×7 transparencies and prints. Offers $25-35 per photo. Buys one-time rights.
Columns/Departments: Anonymous Consumer (anonymous shopper shops for equipment at photo stores) 1,800 words. Buys 5 mss/year. Query with published clips. Length: 1,800 words. Pays up to $200.
Tips: "All main sections use freelance material: business tips, promotion ideas, employee concerns, advertising, co-op, marketing. But they must be geared to and have direct quotes from members of the association."

‡**THE PHOTO REVIEW**, 301 Hill Ave., Langhorne PA 19047. (215)757-8921. Editor: Stephen Perloff. 50% freelance written. A quarterly magazine on photography with reviews, interviews and articles on art photography. Estab. 1976. Circ. 1,000. Pays on publication. Publishes ms an average of 3 months after acceptance. Byline given. Buys one-time rights. Simultaneous and previously published submissions OK. Reports in 3 weeks on queries; 2 months on mss. Sample copy for 8½×11 SAE with 6 first class stamps. Writer's guidelines for #10 SASE.
Nonfiction: Essays, historical/nostalgic, interview/profile and opinion. No how-to articles. Buys 10-15 mss/year. Query. Pays $25-200.
Photos: Send photos with submission. Reviews 8×10 prints. Offers no additional payment for photos accepted with ms. Captions and identification of subjects required. Buys one-time rights.

PHOTOLETTER, PhotoSource International, Pine Lake Farm, Osceola WI 54020. (715)248-3800. FAX: (715)248-7394. Editor: Lynette Layer. Managing Editor: H.T. White. 10% freelance written. A monthly newsletter on marketing photographs. "The *Photoletter* pairs photobuyers with photographers' collections." Estab. 1976. Circ. 780. **Pays on acceptance.** Publishes ms an average of 6 months after acceptance. Byline given. Buys one-time rights and simultaneous rights. Submit seasonal/holiday material 3 months in advance. Simultaneous and previously published submissions OK. Query for electronic submissions. Reports in 2 weeks on queries. Sample copy $3; writer's guidelines for #10 SASE.
Nonfiction: How-to market photos and personal experience in marketing photos. "Our readers expect advice in how-to articles." No submissions that do not deal with selling photos. Buys 6 mss/year. Query. Length: 300-850 words. Pays $50-100 for unsolicited articles.
Columns/Departments: Jeri Engh, columns department editor. "We welcome column ideas." Length: 350 words. Pays $45-75.
Fillers: Facts. Buys 20/year. Length: 30-50 words. Pays $10.
Tips: "Columns are most open to freelancers. Bring an *expertise* on marketing photos or some other aspect of aid to small business persons."

PROFESSIONAL PHOTOGRAPHER, The Business Magazine of Professional Photography, Professional Photographers of America, Inc., 1090 Executive Way, Des Plaines IL 60018. (708)299-8161. FAX: (708)299-2685. Editor: Alfred DeBat. 80% freelance written. Monthly magazine of professional portrait, wedding, commercial, corporate and industrial photography. Describes the technical and business sides of professional photography—successful photo techniques, money-making business tips, legal considerations, selling to new markets, and descriptions of tough assignments and how completed. Estab. 1907. Circ. 32,000. Publishes ms an average of 6-9 months after acceptance. Byline given. Buys one-time rights. Submit seasonal/holiday material 6 months in advance. Simultaneous queries and previously published submissions OK. Reports in 2 months. Sample copy $5; free writer's guidelines.

Nonfiction: How-to. Professional photographic techniques: How I solved this difficult assignment, How I increased my photo sales, How to buy a studio, run a photo business, etc. Special issues include February: Portrait Photography; April: Wedding Photography; May: Commercial Photography; and August: Industrial Photography. Buys 8-10 ms/issue. Query. Length: 1,000-3,000 words. "We seldom pay, as most writers are PP of A members and want recognition for their professional skills, publicity, etc."

Photos: State availability of photos. Reviews color transparencies and 8×10 unmounted prints. Captions and model release required. Buys one-time rights.

‡**PTN**, PTN Publishing Corp, 210 Crossways Park Dr., Woodbury NY 11797. (516)496-8000. FAX: (516)496-8013. Editor: Bill Schiffner. 20-25% freelance written. A semimonthly magazine about the photographic/video and photofinishing industries. Circ. 15,000. Pays on publication. Publishes ms an average of 2 months after acceptance. Byline given. Buys first North American serial rights. Submit seasonal/holiday material 3 months in advance. Simultaneous and previously published submissions OK. Reports in 2 weeks on queries; 3 weeks on mss. Free sample copy and writer's guidelines.

Nonfiction: Interview/profile, technical. Buys 50 mss/year. Send complete ms. Length: 750-1,500 words. Pays $75-300. Sometimes pays expenses of writers on assignment.

Photos: Send photos with submission. Reviews 5×7 prints. Offers no additional payment for photos accepted with ms. Captions and identification of subjects required. Buys one-time rights.

Tips: "Know the photo and video and photofinishing industries."

‡**THE RANGEFINDER**, 1312 Lincoln Blvd., Santa Monica CA 90406. (213)451-8506. FAX: (213)395-9058. Editor: Arthur C. Stern. Associate Editor: Carolyn Ryan. Monthly magazine; 80 pages. Emphasizes professional photography. Circ. 55,000. Pays on publication. Publishes ms an average of 3-6 months after acceptance. Byline given. Buys first North American serial rights. Phone queries OK. Submit seasonal material 4 months in advance. Reports in 6 weeks. Sample copy $2.50; writer's guidelines for SASE.

Nonfiction: How-to (solve a photographic problem; such as new techniques in lighting, new poses or set-ups); profile; and technical. "Articles should contain practical, solid information. Issues should be covered in depth. Look thoroughly into the topic." Buys 5-7 mss/issue. Query with outline. Length: 800-1,200 words. Pays $60/published page.

Photos: State availability of photos with query. Captions preferred; model release required.

Tips: "Exhibit knowledge of photography. Introduce yourself with a well-written letter and a great story idea."

Plumbing, Heating, Air Conditioning and Refrigeration

HEATING, PLUMBING, AIR CONDITIONING, 1450 Don Mills Rd., Don Mills, Ontario M3B 2X7 Canada. (416)445-6641. FAX: (416)442-2077. Editor: Ronald H. Shuker. 20% freelance written. Monthly. For mechanical contractors; plumbers; warm air and hydronic heating, refrigeration, ventilation, air conditioning and insulation contractors; wholesalers; architects; consulting and mechanical engineers who are in key management or specifying positions in the plumbing, heating, air conditioning and refrigeration industries in Canada. Estab. 1923. Circ. 16,500. Pays on publication. Publishes ms an average of 3 months after acceptance. Reports in 2 months. For a prompt reply, "enclose a sheet on which is typed a statement either approving or rejecting the suggested article which can either be checked off, or a quick answer written in and signed and returned." Free sample copy.

Nonfiction: News, technical, business management and "how-to" articles that will inform, educate, motivate and help readers to be more efficient and profitable who design, manufacture, install, sell, service, maintain or supply all mechanical components and systems in residential, commercial, institutional and industrial installations across Canada. Length: 1,000-1,500 words. Pays 25¢/word. Sometimes pays expenses of writers on assignment.

Photos: Photos purchased with ms. Prefers 4×5 or 5×7 glossies.

Tips: "Topics must relate directly to the day-to-day activities of *HPAC* readers in Canada. Must be detailed, with specific examples, quotes from specific people or authorities—show depth. We specifically want material from other parts of Canada besides southern Ontario. Not really interested in material from U.S. unless specifically related to Canadian readers' concerns. We primarily want articles that show *HPAC* readers how they can increase their sales and business step-by-step based on specific examples of what others have done."

SNIPS MAGAZINE, 407 Mannheim Rd., Bellwood IL 60104. (708)544-3870. FAX: (708)544-3884. Editor: Nick Carter. 2% freelance written. Monthly. For sheet metal, warm air heating, ventilating, air conditioning and roofing contractors. Estab. 1932. Publishes ms an average of 3 months after acceptance. Buys all rights. "Write for detailed list of requirements before submitting any work."
Nonfiction: Material should deal with information about contractors who do sheet metal, warm air heating, air conditioning, ventilation and roofing work; also about successful advertising campaigns conducted by these contractors and the results. Length: "prefers stories to run less than 1,000 words unless on special assignment." Pays 5¢/word for first 500 words, 2¢/word thereafter.
Photos: Pays $5 each for small snapshot pictures, $10 each for usable 8×10 pictures.

Printing

‡HIGH VOLUME PRINTING, Innes Publishing Co., P.O. Box 368, Northbrook IL 60062. (708)564-5940. FAX: (708)564-8361. Editor: Catherine M. Stanulis. 20% freelance written. Eager to work with new/unpublished writers. Bimonthly magazine for book, magazine printers, large commercial printing plants with 20 or more employees. Aimed at telling the reader what he needs to know to print more efficiently and more profitably. Circ. 36,500. Pays on publication. Publishes ms an average of 9 months after acceptance. Byline given. Buys first and second serial rights. Simultaneous queries OK. Query for electronic submissions. Reports in 2 weeks. Writer's guidelines, sample articles provided.
Nonfiction: How-to (printing production techniques); new product (printing, auxiliary equipment, plant equipment); photo feature (case histories featuring unique equipment); technical (printing product research and development); shipping; and publishing distribution methods. No product puff. Buys 12 mss/year. Query. Length: 700-3,000 words. Pays $50-300.
Photos: Send photos with ms. Pays $25-150 for any size color transparencies and prints. Captions, model release, and identification of subjects required.
Tips: "Feature articles covering actual installations and industry trends are most open to freelancers. Be familiar with the industry, spend time in the field, and attend industry meetings and trade shows where equipment is displayed. We would also like to receive clips and shorts about printing mergers."

PRINT & GRAPHICS, 911 N. Fillmore St., Arlington VA 22201. (703)525-4800. FAX: (703)525-4805. Publisher: Geoff Lindsay. 5% freelance written. Eager to work with new/unpublished writers. Monthly tabloid of the commercial printing industry for owners and executives of graphic arts firms. Circ. 20,000. **Pays on acceptance.** Publishes ms an average of 1 month after acceptance. Byline given. Buys one-time rights. Simultaneous queries, and simultaneous and previously published submissions OK. Electronic submissions OK via standard protocols, but requires hard copy also. Reports in 1 week. Sample copy for $2.
Nonfiction: Book excerpts, historical/nostalgic, how-to, interview/profile, new product, opinion, personal experience, photo feature and technical. "All articles should relate to graphic arts management or production." Buys 20 mss/year. Query with published clips. Length: 750-2,000 words. Pays $100-250.
Photos: State availability of photos. Pays $25-75 for 5×7 b&w prints. Captions and identification of subjects required.

QUICK PRINTING, The Information Source for Commercial Copyshops and Printshops, Coast Publishing, 1680 SW Bayshore Blvd., Port St. Lucie FL 34984. (407)879-6666. FAX: (407)879-7388. Publisher: Cyndi Schulman. Editor: Bob Hall. 50% freelance written. A monthly magazine covering the quick printing industry. "Our articles tell quick printers how they can be more profitable. We want figures to illustrate points made." Estab. 1977. Circ. 57,000. **Pays on acceptance.** Publishes ms an average of 4 months after acceptance. Byline given. Buys first North American serial rights, all rights. Submit seasonal/holiday material 6 months in advance. Rarely uses previously published submissions. Query for electronic submissions. Reports in 1 month. Sample copy for $3 and 9×12 SAE with 7 first class stamps; writer's guidelines for #10 SASE.
Nonfiction: How-to (on marketing products better or accomplishing more with equipment); new product; opinion (on the quick printing industry); personal experience (from which others can learn); technical (on printing). No generic business articles, or articles on larger printing applications. Buys 75 mss/year. Send complete ms. Length: 1,500-3,000 words. Pays $75 and up.
Photos: State availability of photos with submission. Reviews transparencies and prints. Offers no payment for photos. Captions and identification of subjects required.
Columns/Departments: Viewpoint/Counterpoint (opinion on the industry); QP Profile (shop profiles with a marketing slant); Management (how to handle employees and/or business strategies); and Marketing Impressions, all 500-1,500 words. Buys 10 mss/year. Send complete ms. Pays $75.
Tips: "The use of electronic publishing systems by quick printers is of increasing interest. Show a knowledge of the industry. Try visiting your local quick printer for an afternoon to get to know about us. When your articles make a point, back it up with examples, statistics, and dollar figures. We need

good material in all areas, but avoid the shop profile. Technical articles are most needed, but they must be accurate. No puff pieces for a certain industry supplier."

SCREEN PRINTING, 407 Gilbert Ave., Cincinnati OH 45202. (513)421-2050. FAX: (513)421-5144. Editor: Susan Venell. 30% freelance written. Works with a small number of new/unpublished writers each year. Monthly magazine for the screen printing industry, including screen printers (commercial, industrial and captive shops), suppliers and manufacturers, ad agencies and allied professions. Estab. 1953. Circ. 15,000. Pays on publication. Publishes ms an average of 3-4 months after acceptance. Byline given. Buys all rights. Reporting time varies. Free sample copy and writer's guidelines.
Nonfiction: "Because the screen printing industry covers a broad range of applications and overlaps other fields in the graphic arts, it's necessary that articles be of a significant contribution, preferably to a specific area of screen printing. Subject matter is fairly open, with preference given to articles on administration or technology; trends and developments. We try to give a good sampling of technical business and management articles; articles about unique operations. We also publish special features and issues on important subjects, such as material shortages, new markets and new technology breakthroughs. While most of our material is nitty-gritty, we appreciate a writer who can take an essentially dull subject and encourage the reader to read on through concise, factual, 'flairful' and creative, expressive writing. Interviews are published after consultation with and guidance from the editor." Interested in stories on unique approaches by some shops. No general, promotional treatment of individual companies. Buys 6-10 mss/year. Query. Unsolicited mss not returned. Length: 1,500-3,500 words. Pays minimum of $150 for major features. Sometimes pays the expenses of writers on assignment.
Photos: Cover photos negotiable; b&w or color. Published material becomes the property of the magazine.
Tips: "If the author has a working knowledge of screen printing, assignments are more readily available. General management articles are rarely used."

Real Estate

AREA DEVELOPMENT MAGAZINE, 400 Post Ave., Westbury NY 11590. (516)338-0900. Editor-in-Chief: Tom Bergeron. 50% freelance written. Prefers to work with published/established writers. Emphasizes corporate facility planning and site selection for industrial chief executives worldwide. Monthly magazine. Estab. 1964. Circ. 33,000. Pays when edited. Publishes ms an average of 2 months after acceptance. Buys first rights only. Byline given. Reports in 3 weeks. Free sample copy. Writer's guidelines for #10 SASE.
Nonfiction: How-to (experiences in site selection and all other aspects of corporate facility planning); historical (if it deals with corporate facility planning); interview (corporate executives and industrial developers); and related areas of site selection and facility planning such as taxes, labor, government, energy, architecture and finance. Buys 100 mss/yr. Query. Pays $30-50/ms page; rates for illustrations depend on quality and printed size. Sometimes pays the expenses of writers on assignment.
Photos: State availability of photos with query. Prefer 8×10 or 5×7 b&w glossy prints or color transparencies—35mm OK. Captions preferred.
Tips: "Articles must be accurate, objective (no puffery) and useful to our industrial executive readers. Avoid any discussion of the merits or disadvantages of any particular areas or communities. Writers should realize we serve an intelligent and busy readership—they should avoid 'cute' allegories and get right to the point."

BUSINESS FACILITIES, Group C Communications, Inc., 121 Monmouth St., P.O. Box 2060, Red Bank NJ 07701. (908)842-7433. FAX: (908)758-6634. Editor: Eric Peterson. Managing Editor: James Picerno. 20% freelance written. Prefers to work with published/established writers. A monthly magazine covering economic development and commercial and industrial real estate. "Our audience consists of corporate site selectors and real estate people; our editorial coverage is aimed at providing news and trends on the plant location and corporate expansion field." Estab. 1967. Circ. 32,000. Pays on publication. Publishes ms an average of 3 months after acceptance. Byline given. Buys all rights. Previously published submissions OK. Reports in 2 weeks. Free sample copy and writer's guidelines.
Nonfiction: General interest, how-to, interview/profile and personal experience. No news shorts or clippings; feature material only. Buys 12-15 mss/year. Query. Length: 1,000-3,000 words. Pays $200-1,000 for assigned articles, pays $200-600 for unsolicited articles. Sometimes pays the expenses of writers on assignment.
Photos: State availability of photos with submission. Reviews contact sheets, negatives, transparencies and 8×10 prints. Payment negotiable. Captions and identification of subjects required. Buys one-time rights.

Tips: "First, remember that our reader is a corporate executive responsible for his company's expansion and/or relocation decisions and our writers have to get inside that person's head in order to provide him with something that's helpful in his decision-making process. And second, the biggest turnoff is a telephone query. We're too busy to accept them and must require that all queries be put in writing. Submit major feature articles only; all news departments, fillers, etc., are staff prepared. A writer should be aware that our style is not necessarily dry and business-like. We tend to be more upbeat and a writer should look for that aspect of our approach. We are currently overstocked, however, and for the near future will be accepting fewer pieces."

FINANCIAL FREEDOM REPORT, 2450 Fort Union Blvd., Salt Lake City UT 84121. (801)943-1280. FAX: (801)942-7489. Chairman of the Board: Mark O. Haroldsen. Managing Editor: Carolyn Tice. 25% freelance written. Eager to work with new/unpublished writers. For "professional and nonprofessional investors and would-be investors in real estate—real estate brokers, insurance companies, investment planners, truck drivers, housewives, doctors, architects, contractors, etc. The magazine's content is presently expanding to interest and inform the readers about other ways to put their money to work for them." Monthly magazine. Estab. 1976. Circ. 50,000. Pays on publication. Publishes ms an average of 3 months after acceptance. Buys all rights. Phone queries OK. Simultaneous submissions OK. Query for electronic submissions. Reports in 2 weeks. Sample copy $3; free writer's guidelines.

Nonfiction: How-to (find real estate bargains, finance property, use of leverage, managing property, developing market trends, goal setting, motivational); and interviews (success stories of those who have relied on own initiative and determination in real estate market or related fields). Buys 25 unsolicited mss/year. Query with clips of published work or submit complete ms. Length: 1,500-3,000 words. "If the topic warranted a two- or three-parter, we would consider it." Pays 5-10¢/word. Sometimes pays the expenses of writers on assignment.

Photos: Send photos with ms. Uses 8×10 b&w or color matte prints. Makes additional payment for photos accepted with ms. Captions required.

Tips: "We would like to find several specialized writers in our field of real estate investments. A writer must have had some hands-on experience in the real estate field."

REAL ESTATE COMPUTING, Real Estate Software Company, Inc., Suite D, 10622 Montwood Dr., El Paso TX 79935. (915)598-2435. Editor: Ralph Tutor. 25% freelance written. Bimonthly tabloid on computers and computerization of/for real estate professionals. Circ. 85,000. Pays on publication. Publishes ms an average of 2 months after acceptance. Byline given. Offers 25% kill fee. Buys first rights, one-time rights, or second serial (reprint) rights. Submit seasonal/holiday material 3 months in advance. Previously published submissions OK. Query for electronic submissions. Reports in 3 weeks on queries.

Nonfiction: Book excerpts, how-to (computerize, increase production with computers), interview/profile (real estate pros, computer experts, opinion (on real estate computerization trends, needs, state of), photo feature, technical and real estate sales and management success secrets. "No articles on competing companies or products or articles which do not involve both computers and real estate. We don't want articles that involve Apple or other non-IBM-compatible computers." Query. Length: 500-1,500 words. Pays $50-150 for assigned articles; $25-100 for unsolicited articles. Sometimes pays expenses of writers on assignment.

Photos: State availability of photos with submission. Reviews contact sheets and prints. Offers $10-35 per photo. Model releases and identification of subjects required. Buys one-time rights.

Tips: "Although originally produced to keep in touch with users of our software products, the strong response from non-users has let us to greatly expand our editorial aim. We now mail to every real estate broker in the USA. Our readers are not technical wizards; they're busy real estate professionals and residential property managers. They look to us for plain-English solutions to their everyday computerization problems. Our publication is colorful and illustrated with graphs, charts and 'button-by-button examples'. We like interviews with agents who've successfully implemented computers into their offices. We expect facts to be researched and well documented."

‡SOUTHWEST REAL ESTATE NEWS, Communication Channels, Inc., Suite 240, 18601 LBJ Freeway, Mesquite TX 75150. (214)270-6651. FAX: (214)681-8391. Publisher: Beth Santo. Associate Publisher/Editor: Jim Mitchell. 40% freelance written. Prefers to work with published/established writers. Tabloid newspaper published 6 times/year about commercial and industrial real estate for professional real estate people, including realtors, developers, mortgage bankers, corporate real estate executives, architects, contractors and brokers. Estab. 1972. Circ. 15,000. Average issue includes 4 columns, 10-20 short news items, 2-5 special articles and 2-10 departments. Pays on publication. Publishes ms an average of 2 months after acceptance. Byline given. Buys all rights. Phone queries OK. Submit seasonal/holiday material 2 months in advance. Reports in 4-6 weeks. Sample copy for 12×16½ SAE with 3 first class stamps.

Nonfiction: "We're interested in hearing from writers in major cities in the states that we cover, which are TX, OK, CO, NM, LA, AZ, AR, NV and CA. We are particularly interested in writers with newspaper experience and real estate background. Assignments are made according to our editorial schedule which we will supply upon request. Most open to freelancers are city reviews. Contact the staff to discuss ideas first. No unsolicited material." Buys 2-4 mss/issue. Query. Pays $100-500.

Columns/Departments: Offices, Shopping Centers, Industrials, Multi-Use, Leasing Update, Sales and Purchases, Financial, Realty Operations, Residentials, and People. No newspaper clippings.

Tips: "We retain resumes from writers for possible future use—particularly in the states we cover. Call us and submit a sample of previous work."

Resources and Waste Reduction

GROUND WATER AGE, National Trade Publications, 13 Century Hill Dr., Latham NY 12110. (518)783-1281. Editor: Gregg Norton. 30% freelance written. Monthly magazine that covers water well drilling and pump installation. "We want good, solid writing, accurate facts and up-to-date information on technical subjects." Estab. 1966. Circ. 20,000. **Pays on acceptance.** Publishes ms an average of 3-4 months after acceptance. Byline given. Buys first North American serial rights. Submit seasonal/holiday material 6 months in advance. Simultaneous and previously published submissions OK. Reports in 2 weeks on queries; 1 month on mss. Sample copy for 9 × 12 SAE with 5 first class stamps.

Nonfiction: Historical/nostalgic, interview/profile, new product, photo feature and technical. Buys 5-10 mss/year. Query with published clips. Length: 750-3,000 words. Pays $50-350 for assigned articles; $50-250 for unsolicited articles. "Trades articles for advertising, on occasion and when desirable." Sometimes pays expenses of writers on assignment.

Photos: State availability of photos with submission. "We need quality photos of water well drillers, monitoring well contractors or pump installers in action, on the job." Reviews contact sheets, negatives, transparencies and prints. Offers no additional payment for photos accepted with ms. Identification of subjects required. Buys one-time rights.

Columns/Departments: Down the Hole (technical, how-to aspects of water well or monitoring well drilling); Pumps and Water Systems (technical aspects of water well pumps, tanks, valves and piping for domestic well systems); business topics (for improving productivity, marketing, etc.). 300-1,000 words. Buys 6-10 mss/year. Query first by phone or mail. Pays $50-150.

‡**THE PUMPER**, COLE Publishing Inc., Drawer 220, Three Lakes WI 54562. (715)546-3347. Production Manager: Ken Lowther. 50% freelance written. Eager to work with new/unpublished writers. A monthly tabloid covering the liquid waste hauling industry (portable toilet renters, septic tank pumpers, industrial waste haulers, chemical waste haulers, oil field haulers, and hazardous waste haulers). "Our publication is read by companies that handle liquid waste and manufacturers of equipment." Estab. 1979. Circ. 15,000. Pays on publication. Publishes ms an average of 1 month after acceptance. Byline given. Buys first serial rights. Submit seasonal/holiday material 3 months in advance. Simultaneous queries, and simultaneous and previously published submissions OK. Query for electronic submissions. Reports in 1 month. Free sample copy and writer's guidelines.

Nonfiction: Exposé (government regulations, industry problems, trends, public attitudes, etc.); general interest (state association meetings, conventions, etc.); how-to (related to industry, e.g., how to incorporate septage or municipal waste into farm fields, how to process waste, etc.); humor (related to industry, especially septic tank pumpers or portable toilet renters); interview/profile (including descriptions of business statistics, type of equipment, etc.); new product; personal experience; photo feature; and technical (especially reports on research projects related to disposal). "We are looking for quality articles that will be of interest to our readers; length is not important. We publish trade journals. We need articles that deal with the trade. Studies on land application of sanitary waste are of great interest." Query or send complete ms. Pays 7½¢/word.

Photos: Send photos with query or ms. Pays $15 for b&w and color prints that are used. No negatives. "We need good contrast." Captions "suggested" and model release required. Buys one-time rights.

Tips: "Material must pertain to liquid waste-related industries listed above. We hope to expand the editorial content of our monthly publications. We also have publications for sewer and drain cleaners with the same format as *The Pumper*; however, *The Cleaner* has a circulation of 18,000. We are looking for the same type of articles and pay is the same."

‡**RECYCLING TODAY**, Municipal Market Edition, GIE Inc., 4012 Bridge Ave., Cleveland OH 44113. (216)961-4130. Editor: Jeff Solomon-Hess. 50% freelance written. Monthly trade magazine covering recycling programs for municipalities. *Recycling Today* serves recycling coordinators at the state, county and municipal levels, as well as private companies providing information and services to government. Estab. 1990. Circ. 10,000. Pays on publication. Publishes ms an average of 2 months after acceptance.

Byline given. No kill fee. Buys all rights (will reassign). Submit seasonal/holiday material 3 months in advance. Simultaneous submissions OK. Sample copy for 8½×11 SAE with 6 first class stamps.

Nonfiction: Profiles of innovative recycling programs, solutions to current recycling challenges. Buys 40 mss/year. Query with published clips. Length: 2,000-3,000 words. Pays $200-300. Sometimes pays expenses of writers on assignment.

Photos: Send photos with submission. Reviews contact sheets, 2×3 slide or transparencies or 3×5 prints. Offers no additional payment for photos accepted with ms. Captions and identification of subjects required. Buys all rights (will reassign).

RESOURCE RECYCLING, North America's Recycling Journal, Resource Recycling, Inc., P.O. Box 10540, Portland OR 97210. (503)227-1319. FAX: (503)227-6135. Editor-in-Chief: Jerry Powell. Editor: Meg Lynch. 10% freelance written. Eager to work with new/unpublished writers. A trade journal published 12 times/year, covering recycling of paper, plastics, metals, glass and other materials. Estab. 1982. Circ. 12,000. Pays on publication. Publishes ms an average of 3-9 months after acceptance. Byline given. Buys first rights. Simultaneous and previously published submissions OK. Query for electronic submissions. Reports in 1 month on queries. Sample copy and writer's guidelines for 9×12 SAE with 7 first class stamps.

Nonfiction: "No non-technical or opinion pieces." Buys 10-15 mss/year. Query with published clips. Length: 1,200-1,800 words. Pays $100-250. Pays with contributor copies "if writers are more interested in professional recognition than financial compensation." Sometimes pays the expenses of writers on assignment.

Photos: State availability of photos with submission. Reviews contact sheets, negatives and prints. Offers $5-50. Identification of subjects required. Buys one-time rights.

Tips: "Overviews of one recycling aspect in one state (e.g., oil recycling in Alabama) will receive attention. We will increase coverage of yard waste composting."

Selling and Merchandising

Sales personnel and merchandisers interested in how to sell and market products successfully consult these journals. Publications in nearly every category of Trade also buy salesrelated materials if it is slanted to the product or industry with which they deal.

THE AMERICAN SALESMAN, 424 N. 3rd St., P.O. Box 15, Burlington IA 52601-0001. FAX: (319)752-3421. Publisher: Michael S. Darnall. Editorial Supervisor: Doris J. Ruschill. Editor: Barbara Boeding. 95% freelance written. Prefers to work with published/established writers, but works with a small number of new/unpublished writers each year. Monthly magazine for distribution through company sales representatives. Estab. 1955. Circ. 1,625. Pays on publication. Publishes ms an average of 4 months after acceptance. Buys all rights. Sample copy and writer's guidelines for 8×10 SAE and 2 first class stamps; mention *Writer's Market* in request.

Nonfiction: Sales seminars, customer service and follow-up, closing sales, sales presentations, handling objections, competition, telephone usage and correspondence, managing territory and new innovative sales concepts. No sexist material, illustration written from a salesperson's viewpoint. No ms dealing with supervisory problems. Length: 900-1,200 words. Pays 3¢/word. Uses no advertising. Follow AP Stylebook. Include biography and/or byline with ms submissions. Author photos used. Send correspondence to Editor.

ART MATERIAL TRADE NEWS, The Journal of All Art, Craft, Engineering and Drafting Supplies, Communication Channels Inc., 6255 Barfield Rd., Atlanta GA 30328. (404)256-9800. Editor: Tom C. Cooper. 15% freelance written. Works with a small number of new/unpublished writers each year. Monthly magazine on art materials. "Our editorial thrust is to bring art materials retailers, distributors and manufacturers information they can use in their everyday operations." Estab. 1949. Circ. 12,000. Pays on publication. Publishes ms an average of 3 months after acceptance. "All assigned manuscripts are published." Buys first serial rights. Submit seasonal/holiday material 3 months in advance. Reports in 6 weeks. Sample copy for 9×12 SAE and 4 first class stamps. Writer's guidelines for #10 SASE.

Nonfiction: How-to (sell, retail/wholesale employee management, advertising programs); interview/profile (within industry); and technical (commercial art drafting/engineering). "We encourage a strong narrative style where possible. We publish an editorial 'theme' calendar at the beginning of each year."

For explanation of symbols, see the Key to Symbols and Abbreviations on Page 5. For unfamiliar words, see the Glossary.

Buys 15-30 mss/year. Query with published clips. Length: 1,000-3,000 words (prefers 2,000 words). Pays $75-300.

Photos: State availability of photos. Pays $10 maximum for b&w contact sheets. Identification of subjects required.

ASD/AMD TRADE NEWS, Associated Surplus Dealers/Associated Merchandise Dealers, 1666 Corinth Ave., Los Angeles CA 90025. (213)477-2556. FAX: (213)479-5736. Editor: Jay Hammeran. 75% freelance written. Monthly trade newspaper on trade shows and areas of interest to surplus/merchandise dealers. "Many of our readers have small, family-owned businesses." Estab. 1967. Circ. 80,000. **Pays on acceptance.** Publishes ms an average of 1-2 months after acceptance. Byline given. Negotiable kill fee. Buys all rights. Submit seasonal/holiday material 3 months in advance. Simultaneous submissions OK. Query for electronic submissions. Reports in 2 weeks on queries; 1 month on mss. Free sample copy and writer's guidelines.

Nonfiction: How-to (merchandise a store more effectively), interview/profile (dealers/owners), personal experience (of dealers and merchandisers), photo feature (ASD/AMD trade shows), and general business articles of interest. "Jan. and July are the largest issues of the year. We generally need more freelance material for those two issues. No articles that are solely self-promotion pieces or straight editorials. We also need articles that tell a small business owner/manager how to handle legal issues, personnel questions and business matters, such as accounting." Buys 100 mss/year. Query with or without published clips, or send complete ms. Length: 500-1,250 words. Pays $50-75. Pays expenses of writers on assignment.

Photos: State availability of photos with submission. Reviews 3½×5 prints. Payment depends on whether photos were assigned or not. Identification of subjects required. Buys all rights.

Columns/Departments: Business & News Briefs (summarizes important news/business news affecting small businesses/dealers/merchandisers), 500 words; ASD Profile (interview with successful dealer), 1,000-1,250 words; Merchandising Tips (how to better merchandise a business), 750-1,000. Buys 40 mss/year. Query or send complete ms. Length: 500-1,250 words. Pays $50-75.

Fillers: Facts and newsbreaks. Buys 10/year. Length: 50-300 words. Pays $25-45.

Tips: "Talk to retailers. Find out what their concerns are, and the types of wholesalers/merchandisers they deal with. Talk to those people and learn what they're looking for. Write articles to meet those needs. It's as simple as that. The entire publication is open to freelance writers who can write good articles."

‡**BEDROOM MAGAZINE,** Bobit Publishing, 2512 Artesia Blvd. Redondo Beach CA 90278. (213)376-8788. Editor: Kathy Knoles. 10% freelance written. Prefers to work with published/established writers. A monthly magazine covering bedroom furniture, mattresses, linens and accessories for specialty shop owners, furniture stores, sleep shops and bedroom furniture manufacturers, distributors. Circ. 18,200. Pays on publication. Publishes ms an average of 2 months after acceptance. Byline given. Buys first rights or second serial (reprint) rights. Submit seasonal/holiday material 3 months in advance. Reports in 2 weeks. Sample copy for 10×13 SAE with 5 first class stamps.

Nonfiction: Book excerpts; essays (health benefits of waterbeds); historical/nostalgic; how-to (business management, display techniques, merchandising tips); humor (if in good taste); interview/profile; new product; personal experience; photo feature; technical; and general features depicting bedroom furniture in a positive way. No articles depicting furniture or mattresses in a negative manner. Query with published clips. Length: 1,000-5,000 words. Pays $60-250 for assigned articles; pays $50-200 for unsolicited articles. Sometimes pays the expenses of writers on assignment.

Photos: Send photos with submission. Reviews contact sheets, transparencies and 8×10 prints. Offers $25-100/photo. Captions and identification of subjects required. Buys one-time rights.

Tips: "We need profiles on successful bedroom furniture retailers in all parts of the country. If a large, full-line furniture store in your area also sells waterbeds, we are interested in profiles on those stores and owners as well. We are also always looking for interviews with doctors, chiropractors and other health professionals who recommend waterbeds for their patients. Most of our freelance articles concern store management. Stores that do an excellent job with display and promotions are of special interest when accompanied by good photos. We need articles on obtaining credit, display techniques, merchandising, how to be a successful salesperson, attracting new customers, creating effective advertising, how to put togehter an attractive store window display, hiring employees, etc. Anything that could benefit a salesperson or store owner."

CASUAL LIVING, Columbia Communications, 370 Lexington Ave., New York NY 10164. (212)532-9290. FAX: (212)779-8345. Publisher/Editor: Eileen Robinson Smith. A monthly magazine covering outdoor furniture for outdoor furniture specialists, including retailers, mass merchandisers and department store buyers. Estab. 1957. Circ. 14,000. Pays on publication. Buys first North American serial rights. Submit seasonal/holiday material 2 months in advance. Reports in 1 month. Sample copy for 9×12 SAE with 2 first class stamps.

Nonfiction: Interview/profile (case histories of retailers in the industry); new product; opinion; and technical. Buys 7-8 mss/year. Query with clips, then follow up with phone call. Length: 1,000 words average. Pays $150-400.

Photos: State availability of photos with query letter or ms. Reviews b&w contact sheets and color prints. Payment for photos usually a package deal with ms. Buys all rights.

Tips: "Know the industry, trades and fashions, and what makes a successful retailer."

‡**FOOD & DRUG PACKAGING,** 7500 Old Oak Blvd., Cleveland OH 44130. FAX: (216)891-2735 or 2683. Editor: Sophia Dilberakis. 5% freelance written. Prefers to work with published/established writers. For packaging decision makers in food, drug and cosmetic firms. Monthly. Circ. 82,012. Rights purchased vary with author and material. **Pays on acceptance.** Publishes ms an average of 2-4 months after acceptance. Query for electronic submissions.

Nonfiction and Photos: "Looking for news stories about local and state (not federal) packaging legislation, and its impact on the marketplace. Newspaper style." Query only. Length: 1,000-2,500 words; usually 500-700. Payments vary.

Photos: Photos purchased with mss. 5 × 7 glossies preferred. Sometimes pays the expenses of writers on assignment.

Tips: "Get details on local packaging legislation's impact on marketplace/sales/consumer/retailer reaction; etc. Keep an eye open to *new* packages. Query when you think you've got one. New packages move into test markets every day, so if you don't see anything new this week, try again next week. Buy it; describe it briefly in a query."

INCENTIVE, Bill Communications, 633 3rd Ave., New York NY 10017. (212)986-4800. FAX: (212)867-4395. Editor: Bruce Bolger. Executive Editor: Todd Englander. Monthly magazine covering sales promotion and employee motivation: managing and marketing through motivation. Estab. 1905. Circ. 41,000. **Pays on acceptance.** Publishes ms an average of 3 months after acceptance. Byline sometimes given. Buys all rights. Query for electronic submissions. Reports in 1 month on queries; 2 months on mss. Sample copy for 9 × 12 SAE; writer's guidelines for #10 SAE.

Nonfiction: General interest (motivation, demographics), how-to (types of sales promotion, buying product categories, using destinations), interview/profile (sales promotion executives); corporate case studies; and travel (incentive-oriented). Buys up to 48 mss/year. Query with 2 published clips. Length: 1,000-2,000 words. Pays $250-700 for assigned articles; pays $0-100 for unsolicited articles. Pays expenses of writers on assignment.

Photos: Send photos with submission. Reviews contact sheets and transparencies. Offers no additional payment for photos accepted with ms. Identification of subjects required.

Tips: "Read the publication, then query."

‡**INFO FRANCHISE NEWSLETTER,** Box 670, 9 Duke St., St. Catharines, Ontario L2R 6W8 Canada or Box 550, 728 Center St., Lewiston NY 14092. (716)754-4669. Editor-in-Chief: E.L. Dixon, Jr. Managing Editor: Denise Muir. Monthly newsletter. Circ. 5,000. Pays on publication. Buys all rights. Reports in 1 month.

Nonfiction: "We are particularly interested in receiving articles regarding franchise legislation, franchise litigation, franchise success stories, and new franchises. Both American and Canadian items are of interest. We do not want to receive any information which is not fully documented or articles which could have appeared in any newspaper or magazine in North America. An author with a legal background who could comment upon such things as arbitration and franchising or class actions and franchising, would be of great interest to us." Expose, how-to, informational, interview, profile, new product, personal experience and technical. Buys 10-20 mss/year. Length: 25-1,000 words. Pays $10-300.

PROFESSIONAL SELLING, 24 Rope Ferry Rd., Waterford CT 06386. (203)442-4365. FAX: (203)434-3078. Editor: Paulette S. Kitchens. 33% freelance written. Prefers to work with published/established writers, but works with a small number of new/unpublished writers each year. Bimonthly newsletter in two sections for sales professionals covering industrial, wholesale, high-tech and financial services sales. "*Professional Selling* provides field sales personnel with both the basics and current information that can help them better perform the sales function." Estab. 1917. **Pays on acceptance.** Publishes ms an average of 4-6 months after acceptance. No byline given. Buys all rights. Submit seasonal/holiday material 4 months in advance. Reports in 2 weeks. Sample copy and writer's guidelines for #10 SAE and 2 first class stamps.

Nonfiction: How-to (successful sales techniques); and interview/profile (interview-based articles). "We buy only interview-based material." Buys 12-15 mss/year. No unsolicited manuscripts; written queries only. Length: 1,000-1,200 words.

Tips: *"Professional Selling* includes a 4-page clinic devoted to a single topic of major importance to sales professionals. Only the lead article for each section is open to freelancers. Lead article must be based on an interview with an actual sales professional. Freelancers may occasionally interview sales managers, but the slant must be toward field sales, *not* management."

Sport Trade

Retailers and wholesalers of sports equipment and operators of recreation programs read these journals. Magazines about general and specific sports are classified in the Consumer Sports section.

AMERICAN BICYCLIST, Suite 305, 80 8th Ave., New York NY 10011. (212)206-7230. FAX: (212)633-0079. Editor: Konstantin Doren. 40% freelance written. Prefers to work with published/established writers. Monthly magazine for bicycle sales and service shops. Estab. 1879. Circ. 11,200. Pays on publication. Publishes ms an average of 4 months after acceptance. Only staff-written articles are bylined, except under special circumstances. Buys all rights.
Nonfiction: Typical story describes (very specifically) unique traffic-builder or merchandising ideas used with success by an actual dealer. Articles may also deal exclusively with moped sales and service operation within conventional bicycle shops. Emphasis on showing other dealers how they can follow similar pattern and increase their business. Articles may also be based entirely on repair shop operation, depicting efficient and profitable service systems and methods. Buys 12 mss/year. Query. Length: 1,000-2,800 words. Pays about 13¢/word, plus bonus for outstanding manuscript. Pays expenses of writers on assignment.
Photos: Reviews relevant b&w photos illustrating principal points in article purchased with ms; 5×7 minimum. Pays $10/photo. Captions required. Buys all rights.
Tips: "A frequent mistake made by writers is writing as if we are a book read by consumers instead of professionals in the bicycle industry."

AMERICAN FIREARMS INDUSTRY, AFI Communications Group, Inc., 2801 E. Oakland Park Blvd., Ft. Lauderdale FL 33306. FAX: (305)561-4129. 10% freelance written. "Work with writers specifically in the firearms trade." Monthly magazine specializing in the sporting arms trade. Estab. 1973. Circ. 30,000. Pays on publication. Publishes ms an average of 4 months after acceptance. Buys all rights. Reports in 2 weeks.
Nonfiction: R.A. Lesmeister, articles editor. Publishes informational, technical and new product articles. No general firearms subjects. Query. Length: 900-1,500 words. Pays $250-500. Sometimes pays the expenses of writers on assignment.
Photos: Reviews 8×10 b&w glossy prints. Manuscript price includes payment for photos.

AMERICAN FITNESS, The Official Publication of the Aerobics and Fitness Association of America, Suite 310, 15250 Ventura Blvd., Sherman Oaks CA 91403. (818)905-0040. FAX: (818)990-5468. Editor-at-Large: Peg Jordan, R.N. Managing Editor: Rhonda J. Wilson. 80% freelance written. Eager to work with new/unpublished writers. Bimonthly magazine covering exercise and fitness, health and nutrition. "We need timely, in-depth informative articles on health, fitness, aerobic exercise, sports nutrition, sports medicine and physiology." Circ. 25,100. Pays 4-6 weeks after publication. Publishes ms an average of 6 months after acceptance. Byline given. Buys first North American serial rights and simultaneous rights (in some cases). Submit seasonal/holiday material 4 months in advance. Simultaneous queries and simultaneous and previously published submissions OK. Query for electronic submissions. Reports in 2 weeks. Sample copy for $1 or SAE with 6 first class stamps; writer's guidelines for SAE.
Nonfiction: Book excerpts (fitness book reviews); exposé (on nutritional gimmickry); historical/nostalgic (history of various athletic events); humor (personal fitness profiles); inspirational (sports leader's motivational pieces); interview/profile (fitness figures); adventure (treks, trails and global challenges); strength (the latest breakthroughs in weight training); new product (plus equipment review); clubscene (profiles and highlights of the fitness club industry); personal experience (successful fitness story); photo feature (on exercise, fitness, new sport); and travel (spas that cater to fitness industry). No articles on unsound nutritional practices, popular trends or unsafe exercise gimmicks. Buys 18-25 mss/year. Query. Length: 800-2,500 words. Pays $80-120. Sometimes pays expenses of writers on assignment.
Photos: Sports, action, fitness, aerobic competitions and exercise classes. Pays $10 for b&w prints; $35 for transparencies. Captions, model release, and identification of subjects required. Buys one-time rights; other rights purchased depend on use of photo.

Columns/Departments: Fitness Industry News (shorts on health, fitness and beauty). Buys 50 mss/year. Query with published clips or send complete ms. Length: 50-150 words. Pays 1¢/word.
Fillers: Cartoons, clippings, jokes, short humor and newsbreaks. Buys 12/year. Length: 75-200 words. Pays $35.
Tips: "Cover an athletic event, get a unique angle, provide accurate and interesting findings, and write in a lively, intelligent manner. We are looking for new health and fitness reporters and writers. *A&F* is a good place to get started. I have generally been disappointed with short articles and fillers submissions due to their lack of force. Cover a topic with depth."

ARCHERY BUSINESS, Ehlert Publishing Group, Suite 101, 319 Barry Ave. S., Wayzata MN 55391. Editor: Tim Dehn. 20% freelance written. Bimonthly trade magazine written for dealers, distributors, sales reps and manufacturers of archery and bowhunting equipment. Estab. 1976. Controlled circulation. Pays on publication. Reports in 3 weeks on queries; 6 weeks on mss. Free writer's guidelines. Sample copy for 9×12 SAE and 10 first class stamps.
Nonfiction: Buys clear and concise articles written to help small retailers improve their profit picture. Articles must be specific to this industry and should use actual examples. Length: 1,500-3,000 words. Pays from less than $200 to more than $400.

BICYCLE BUSINESS JOURNAL, 1904 Wenneca, Box 1570, Fort Worth TX 76101. FAX: (817)870-0341. Editor: Rix Quinn. Works with a small number of new/unpublished writers each year. 10% freelance written. Monthly. Circ. 10,000. **Pays on acceptance.** Publishes ms an average of 3 months after acceptance. Buys all rights. Sample copy for 8×10 SAE and 2 first class stamps.
Nonfiction: Stories about dealers who service what they sell, emphasizing progressive, successful sales ideas in the face of rising costs and increased competition. Length: 750 words. Sometimes pays the expenses of writers on assignment.
Photos: B&w or color glossy photo a must; vertical photo preferred. Query.

GOLF COURSE MANAGEMENT, Golf Course Superintendents Association of America, 1421 Research Park Dr., Lawrence KS 66049-3859. (913)832-4490. FAX: (913)832-4466. Editor: Clay Loyd. 20% freelance written. Monthly magazine covering golf course and turf management. Estab. 1926. Circ. 22,000. Byline given. Buys first-time rights. Submit seasonal/holiday material 6 months in advance. Publishes ms an average of 3 months after acceptance. Simultaneous queries and submissions OK. Reports in 2 weeks on queries; 1 month on mss. Writer's guidelines for #10 SASE; sample copy for $3.
Nonfiction: Book excerpts, historical/nostalgic, interview/profile, personal experience and technical. "All areas that relate to the golf course superintendent—whether features or scholarly pieces related to turf/grass management. We currently lean toward technical mss." Special issues include January "conference issue"—features on convention cities used each year. Buys 50 mss/year. Query with clips of published work. Length: 1,500-3,000 words. Pays $100-300 or more. Sometimes pays the expenses of writers on assignment.
Photos: Send photos with ms. Pays $50-250 for color, slides or transparencies preferred. Captions, model release and identification of subjects required. Buys one-time rights.
Tips: "Call publications department (913)832-4490, offer idea, follow with outline and writing samples. Response from us is immediate."

GOLF SHOP OPERATIONS, 5520 Park Ave., Trumbull CT 06611. (203)373-7232. Editor: Mike Schwanz. 20% freelance written. Works with a small number of new/unpublished writers each year. Magazine published 9 times/year for golf professionals and shop operators at public and private courses, resorts, driving ranges and golf specialty stores. Circ. 16,000. Pays on publication. Publishes ms an average of 2 months after acceptance. Byline given. Submit seasonal material (for Christmas and other holiday sales, or profiles of successful professionals with how-to angle emphasized) 4 months in advance. Reports in 1 month. Sample copy free.
Nonfiction: "We emphasize improving the golf retailer's knowledge of his profession. Articles should describe how pros are buying, promoting, merchandising and displaying wares in their shops that might be of practical value. Must be aimed only at the retailer." How-to, profile, successful business operation and merchandising techniques. Buys 15-20 mss/year. Written queries preferred. Pays $500 maximum for assigned articles. Sometimes pays expenses of writers on assignment.
Columns/Departments: Shop Talk (interesting happenings in the golf market), 250 words; Roaming Range (new and different in the driving range business), 500 words. Buys 4 mss/year. Send complete ms. Pays $50-150.

IDEA TODAY, The Association for Fitness Professionals, Suite 204, 6190 Cornerstone Court E., San Diego CA 92121. (619)535-8979. Editor: Patricia A. Ryan. Senior Editor: Mary Monroe. 70% freelance written. A trade journal published 10 times/year for the dance-exercise and personal training industry.

"All articles must be geared to fitness professionals—aerobics instructors, one-to-one trainers and studio and health club owners—covering topics such as aerobics, nutrition, injury prevention, entrepreneurship in fitness, fitness-oriented research and exercise programs." Estab. 1984. Circ. 19,000. **Pays on acceptance.** Publishes ms an average of 4 months after acceptance. Byline given. Buys all rights. Simultaneous submissions OK. Reports in 6 weeks on queries. Sample copy $4.

Nonfiction: How-to, technical. No general information on fitness; our readers are pros who need detailed information. Buys 15 mss/year. Query. Length: 1,000-3,000 words. Pays $100-300.

Photos: State availability of photos with submission. Offers no additional payment for photos with ms. Model releases required. Buys all rights.

Columns/Departments: Exercise Technique (detailed, specific info; must be written by expert), 750-1,500 words; Industry News (short reports on research, programs and conferences), 150-300 words; Student Handout (exercise and nutrition info for participants), 750 words; Program Spotlight (detailed explanation of specific exercise program), 1,000-1,500 words. Buys 80 mss/year. Query. Length: 150-1,500 words. Pays $15-150.

Tips: "We don't accept fitness information for the consumer audience on topics such as why exercise is good for you. Industry News (column) is most open to freelancers. We're looking for short reports on fitness-related conferences and conventions, research, innovative exercise programs, trends, news from other countries and reports on aerobics competitions. Writers who have specific knowledge of, or experience working in the fitness industry have an edge."

NSGA RETAIL FOCUS, National Sporting Goods Association, Suite 700, 1699 Wall St., Mt. Prospect IL 60056. (708)439-4000. FAX: (708)439-0111. Publisher: Thomas G. Drake. Editor: Larry Weindruch. 75% freelance written. Works with a small number of new/unpublished writers each year. *NSGA Retail Focus* serves as a monthly trade journal for presidents, CEOs and owners of more than 21,000 retail sporting goods firms. Estab. 1948. Circ. 9,000. Pays on publication. Publishes ms an average of 1 month after acceptance. Byline given. Offers 50% kill fee. Buys first and second serial (reprint) rights. Submit seasonal/holiday material 3 months in advance. Query for electronic submissions. Sample copy for 9 × 12 SAE with 5 first class stamps.

Nonfiction: Essays, interview/profile and photo feature. "No articles written without sporting goods retail businessmen in mind as the audience. In other words, no generic articles sent to several industries." Buys 50 mss/year. Query with published clips. Pays $75-500. Sometimes pays the expenses of writers on assignment.

Photos: State availability of photos with submission. Reviews contact sheets, negatives, transparencies and 5 × 7 prints. Payment negotiable. Buys one-time rights.

Columns/Departments: Personnel Management (succinct tips on hiring, motivating, firing, etc.); Tax Advisor (simplified explanation of how tax laws affect retailer); Sales Management (in-depth tips to improve sales force performance); Retail Management (detailed explanation of merchandising/ inventory control); Advertising (case histories of successful ad campaigns/ad critiques); Legal Advisor; Computers; Store Design; Visual Merchandising; all 1,500 words. Buys 50 mss/year. Query. Length: 1,000-1,500 words. Pays $75-300.

POOL & SPA NEWS, Leisure Publications, 3923 W. 6th St., Los Angeles CA 90020. (213)385-3926. FAX: (213)383-1152. Editor-in-Chief: J. Field. 25-40% freelance written. Semimonthly magazine emphasizing news of the swimming pool and spa industry for pool builders, pool retail stores and pool service firms. Circ. 15,000. Pays on publication. Publishes ms an average of 1-2 months after acceptance. Buys all rights. Query for electronic submissions. Reports in 2 weeks. Sample copy for 9 × 12 SAE and 10 first class stamps; writer's guidelines for #10 SASE.

Nonfiction: Interview, new product, profile and technical. Phone queries OK. Length: 500-2,000 words. Pays 10-12¢/word. Pays expenses of writers on assignment.

Photos: Pays $10 per b&w photo used.

PROFESSIONAL BOATBUILDER MAGAZINE, WoodenBoat Publications Inc., P.O. Box 78, Naskeag Rd., Brooklin ME 04616. (207)359-4651. FAX: (207)359-8920. Editor: Chris Cornell. 75% freelance written. Bimonthly magazine on boat building companies, repair yards, naval architects, and marine supervisors. Estab. 1989. Circ. 20,000. Pays 45 days after acceptance. Byline given. Offers 20% kill fee. Buys first North American serial rights. Free sample copy and writer's guidelines.

Nonfiction: How-to, new product, opinion, technical. No information better directed to consumers. Buys 20 mss/year. Query with or without published clips or send complete ms. Length: 1,000-4,000 words. Pays 20¢/word. Sometimes pays expenses of writers on assignment.

Photos: State availability of photos with submission. Reviews slide transparencies and 8 × 10 b&w. Offers $15-200 per photo. $350 for color cover. Identification of subjects and full captions required. Buys one-time rights.

Columns/Departments: Barbara Walsh, Assistant editor. Tools of the Trade (new tools/machinery of interest to boat builders), 100-500 words; Work in Progress (new and reconstruction of vessels; 10'-200' in length—emphasize materials and methods and machinery), 100 words. Buys 12 mss/year. Query with published clips. Pays $25-100.

SPORT STYLE, Fairchild Publication, 7 W. 34th St., New York NY 10001. (212)630-3750. Editor: Dusty Kidd. 10% freelance written. Biweekly tabloid that covers all sports. "Submit material on product technology, business and marketing trends that are helpful for sports *retailers* in selling and running their stores." Estab. 1979. Circ. 30,000. **Pays on acceptance.** Publishes ms an average of 1 month after acceptance. Byline given. Buys all rights. Submit seasonal/holiday material 1 month in advance. Query for electronic submissions. Free sample copy and writer's guidelines.
Nonfiction: Interview/profile, new product, photo feature, technical and marketing information. Buys 20 mss/year. Query with published clips. Length: 300-1,500 words. Pays $100-500. Sometimes pays expenses of writers on assignment.
Photos: State availability of photos with submission. Reviews contact sheets and negatives. Offers negotiable payment. Identification of subjects required. Buys one-time rights.
Columns/Departments: Scoreboard (sports events—unusual first-time marketing oriented), up to 300 words; and Sport Seen (photo essay on trends). Buys 20 mss/year. Query with published clips. Length: 500-1,200 words. Pays $300-500.

THE SPORTING GOODS DEALER, 1212 N. Lindbergh Blvd., St. Louis MO 63132. (314)997-7111. FAX: (314)993-7726. President/CEO: Richard Waters. Editor: Steve Fechter. 20% freelance written. Prefers to work with published/established writers. For members of the sporting goods trade: retailers, manufacturers, wholesalers and representatives. Monthly magazine. Estab. 1899. Circ. 30,000. Buys second serial (reprint) rights. Buys about 15 mss/year. Pays on publication. Publishes ms an average of 3 months after acceptance. Query. Sample copy $4 (refunded with first ms).
Nonfiction: "Articles about specific sporting goods retail stores, their promotions, display techniques, sales ideas, merchandising, timely news of key personnel; expansions, new stores, deaths—all in the sporting goods trade. Specific details on how individual successful sporting goods stores operate and what is new and different. We would also be interested in features dealing with stores doing an outstanding job in retailing of exercise equipment, athletic footwear, athletic apparel, baseball, fishing, golf, tennis, camping, firearms/hunting and allied lines of equipment. Query on these." Successful business operations and merchandising techniques. Does not want to see announcements of doings and engagements. Length: open. Rates negotiated by assignment.
Columns/Departments: Inside Retail (store news); Selling Slants (store promotions); and Open for Business (new retail sporting goods stores or sporting goods departments). All material must relate to specific sporting goods stores by name, city and state; general information is not accepted.
Photos: Pays minimum of $3.50 for sharp clear b&w photos; size not important. These are purchased with or without mss. Captions optional, but identification requested.
Fillers: Clippings. These must relate directly to the sporting goods industry. Pays 2¢/published word.
Tips: "The writer has to put himself or herself in our readers' position and ask: Does my style and/or expertise help retailers run their business better?"

‡SWIMMING POOL/SPA AGE, Communication Channels, Inc., 6255 Barfield Rd., Atlanta GA 30328. (404)256-9800. FAX: (404)256-3116. Editor: Terri Simmons. 30% freelance written. Works with a small number of new/unpublished writers each year. Monthly tabloid emphasizing pool, spa and hot tub industry. Estab. 1926. Circ. 17,500. Pays on publication. Publishes ms an average of 3 months after acceptance. Buys all rights. Submit seasonal/holiday material 3 months in advance. Query for electronic submissions.
Nonfiction: How-to (installation techniques, service and repairs, tips, etc.); interview (with people and groups within the industry); photo feature (pool/spa/tub construction or special use); technical (should be prepared with expert within the industry); industry news; and market research reports. Also, comparison articles exploring the same type of products produced by numerous manufacturers. Buys 1-3 unsolicited mss/year. Query. Length: 250-2,500 words. Pays 10¢/word. Sometimes pays the expenses of writers on assignment.
Photos: Purchased with accompanying ms or on assignment. Query or send contact sheet. Will accept 35mm transparencies of good quality. Captions required.
Tips: "If a writer can produce easily understood technical articles containing unbiased, hard facts, we are definitely interested. We will be concentrating on technical and how-to articles because that's what our readers want."

TENNIS BUYER'S GUIDE, New York Times Magazine Group, 5520 Park Ave., Trumbull CT 06611. (203)373-7232. FAX: (203)373-7033. Managing Editor: Sandra Dolbow. 5% freelance written. A bi-monthly tabloid on the tennis industry. "We publish for the tennis retailer. We favor a business angle, providing information that will make our readers better tennis professionals and better business people." Estab. 1985. Circ. 11,000. Pays on publication. Publishes ms an average of 3 months after acceptance. Byline given. Offers 15% kill fee. Buys one-time rights. Submit seasonal/holiday material 6 months in advance. Simultaneous submissions OK. Reports in 6 weeks on queries. Free sample copy and writer's guidelines.

Nonfiction: How-to, interview/profile, new product, photo feature, technical and travel. No professional tennis tour articles. Buys 8 mss/year. Send complete ms. Length: 500-2,000 words. Pays $75-300 for assigned articles. Pays $50-300 for unsolicited articles. Sometimes pays the expenses of writers on assignment.

Photos: Reviews transparencies and prints (35mm). Captions, model releases and identification of subjects required. Buys one-time rights.

Tips: "Express an interest and knowledge in tennis or a business management field and an understanding of retail business."

WOODALL'S CAMPGROUND MANAGEMENT, Woodall Publishing Co., 28167 N. Keith Dr., Lake Forest IL 60045. (708)362-6700. Editor: Mike Byrnes. 10% freelance written. A monthly tabloid covering campground management and operation for managers of private and public campgrounds throughout the U.S. Estab. 1970. Circ. 16,000. Pays after publication. Publishes ms an average of 8 months after acceptance. Byline given. Buys all rights. Will reassign rights to author upon written request. Submit seasonal/holiday material 4 months in advance. Simultaneous queries OK. Reports in 1 month on queries; 2 months on mss. Free sample copy and writer's guidelines.

Nonfiction: How-to, interview/profile and technical. "Our articles tell our readers how to maintain their resources, manage personnel and guests, market, develop new campground areas and activities, and interrelate with the major tourism organizations within their areas. 'Improvement' and 'profit' are the two key words." Buys 14 mss/year. Query. Length: 500 words minimum. Pays $50-200.

Photos: Send contact sheets and negatives. "We pay for each photo used."

Tips: "The best type of story to break in with is a case history approach about how a campground improved its maintenance, physical plant or profitability."

Stone, Quarry and Mining

COAL PEOPLE MAGAZINE, Al Skinner Productions, 629 Virginia St. W., P.O. Box 6247, Charleston WV 25362. (304)342-4129. FAX: (304)343-3124. Editor: Al Skinner. Managing Editor: Gary Stuber. 50% freelance written. A monthly magazine with stories about coal people, towns and history. "Most stories are historical—either narrative or biographical about all levels of coal people, past and present—from coal execs down to grass roots miners. Most stories are upbeat—showing warmth of family or success from underground up!" Estab. 1976. Circ. 10,000. Pays on publication. Publishes ms an average of 3 months after acceptance. Byline given. Buys first rights, second serial (reprint) rights and makes work-for-hire assignments. Submit seasonal/holiday material 2 months in advance. Previously published submissions OK. Reports in 3 months. Sample copy for 9×12 SAE and 5 first class stamps.

Nonfiction: Book excerpts (and film if related to coal), historical/nostalgic (coal towns, people, lifestyles), humor (including anecdotes and cartoons), interview/profile (for coal personalities), personal experience (as relates to coal mining), photo feature (on old coal towns, people, past and present). January issue every year is calendar issue for more than 300 annual coal shows, assocation meetings, etc. July issue is always surface mining/reclamation award issue. December issue is Christmas in Coal Country issue. No poetry, no fiction or environmental attacks on the coal industry. Buys 32 mss/year. Query with published clips. Length: 5,000 words. Pays $35.

Photos: Send photos with submission. Reviews contact sheets, transparencies, and 5×7 prints. Captions and identification of subjects required. Buys one-time rights and one-time reprint rights.

Columns/Departments: Editorials (anything to do with current coal issues); Mine'ing Our Business (bull pen column—gossip—humorous anecdotes), Coal Show Coverage (freelance photojournalist coverage of any coal function across the U.S.). Buys 10 mss/year. Query. Length: 300-500 words. Pays $5.

Fillers: Anecdotes. Buys 10/year. Length: 300 words. Pays $5.

Tips: "We are looking for good feature articles on coal people, towns, companies—past and present, color slides (for possible cover use) and b/w photos to complement stories. Could also use a few news writers to take photos and do journalistic coverage on coal events across the country."

DIMENSIONAL STONE, Dimensional Stone Institute, Inc., Suite 400, 20335 Ventura Blvd., Woodland Hills CA 91364. (818)704-5555. FAX: (818)704-6500. Editor: John Maynard. 25% freelance written. Magazine covering dimensional stone use for managers of producers, importers, contractors, fabricators and specifiers of dimensional stone published 10 times/year. Estab. 1979. Circ. 15,849. Pays on publication. Publishes ms an average of 2 months after acceptance. Byline given. Buys first rights or second serial (reprint) rights. Previously published submissions OK. Sample copy for 9×12 SAE and 11 first class stamps; writer's guidelines for #10 SASE.

Nonfiction: Interview/profile and technical, only on users of dimensional stone. Buys 6-7 mss/year. Send complete ms. Length: 1,000-3,000 words. Pays $100 maximum. Sometimes pays the expenses of writers on assignment.

Photos: Send photos with submission. Reviews any size prints. Offers no additional payment for photos accepted with ms. Identification of subjects required.

Tips: "Articles on outstanding uses of dimensional stone are most open to freelancers."

GOLD PROSPECTOR, Gold Prospectors Association of America, P.O. Box 507, Bonsall CA 92003. (619)728-6620. Editor-in-Chief: George Massie. Managing Editor: Perry Massie. Production Editor: Tom Kraak. 60% freelance written. Eager to work with new/unpublished writers. Bimonthly magazine covering gold prospecting and mining. "*Gold Prospector* magazine is the official publication of the Gold Prospectors Association of America. The GPAA is an international organization of more than 25,000 members who are interested in recreational prospecting and mining. Our primary audience is people of all ages who like to take their prospecting gear with them on their weekend camping trips, and fishing and hunting trips. Our readers are interested not only in prospecting, but camping, fishing, hunting, skiing, backpacking, etc. We try to carry stories in each issue pertaining to subjects besides prospecting." Estab. 1965. Circ. 50,000. Pays on publication. Publishes ms an average of 6 months after acceptance. Byline given. Buys first North American serial rights and second serial (reprint) rights. Submit seasonal/holiday material 6 months in advance. Simultaneous queries and previously published submissions OK. Reports in 6 weeks. Sample copy for $2; writer's guidelines for #10 SASE.

Nonfiction: Historical/nostalgic; how-to (prospecting techniques, equipment building, etc.); humor; new product; personal experience; technical; and travel. "One of our publishing beliefs is that our audience would rather experience life than watch it on television—that they would like to take a rough and tumble chance with the sheer adventure of taking gold from the ground or river after it has perhaps lain there for a million years. Even if they don't, they seem to enjoy reading about those who do in the pages of *Gold Prospector* magazine." Buys 75-100 mss/year. Query with or without published clips if available or send complete ms. Length: 1,000-3,000 words. Pays 75¢/column inch (photos and illustrations are measured the same as type).

Photos: State availability of photos with query or ms. Pays 75¢/column inch for photos, transparencies or reflective art. Buys all rights.

Tips: "Articles must be slanted to interest a prospector, miner, or treasure hunter. For example, a first-aid article could address possible mining accidents. Any subject can be so tailored."

‡ROCK PRODUCTS, Maclean Hunter Publishing Co., 29 N. Wacker Dr., Chicago IL 60606. (312)726-2802. FAX: (312)726-2574. Editor: Richard S. Huhta. 1-5% freelance written. Monthly magazine of the nonmetallic mining industry for producers of cement, lime, sand, gravel, crushed stone and lightweight aggregate. Estab. 1896. Circ. 23,000. Pays on publication. Publishes ms an average of 3-6 months after acceptance. Byline given. Buys first serial rights. Query for electronic submissions. Reports in 2 weeks.

Nonfiction: Technical. "All pieces must relate directly to our industry. No general business articles." Buys 5-6 mss/year. Query. Length: 2,000-4,000 words. Pays variable fee. Pays expenses of writers on assignment.

Photos: No restrictions. Color transfer a plus. No additional fee for ms accompanied by photos.

STONE REVIEW, National Stone Association, 1415 Elliot Place NW, Washington DC 20007. (202)342-1100. FAX: (202)342-0702. Editor: Frank Atlee. Bimonthly magazine covering quarrying and supplying of crushed stone. "Designed to be a communications forum for the crushed stone industry. Publishes information on industry technology, trends, developments and concerns. Audience are quarry operations/management, and manufacturers of equipment, suppliers of services to the industry." Estab. 1985. Circ. 4,000. Pays on publication. Publishes ms an average of 3 months after acceptance. Byline given. Negotiable kill fee. Buys one-time rights. Simultaneous and previously published submissions OK. Reports in 1 month. Sample copy sent upon request.

Nonfiction: Technical. Query with or without published clips, or send complete ms. Length: 1,000-2,500 words. "Note: We have no budget for freelance material, but I'm willing to secure payment for right material."

Photos: State availability of photos with query, then send photos with submission. Reviews contact sheets, negatives, transparencies and prints. Offers no additional payment for photos accepted with ms. Identification of subjects required. Buys one-time rights.

Tips: "At this point, most features are written by contributors in the industry, but I'd like to open it up. Articles on unique equipment, applications, etc. are good, as are those reporting on trends (e.g., there is a strong push on now for environmentally sound operations). Also interested in stories on family-run operations involving three or more generations."

STONE WORLD, Tradelink Publishing Company, 320 Kinderkamack Rd., Oradell NJ 07649. (201) 599-0136. FAX: (201)599-2378. Editor: John Sailer. Associate Editor: Susan Springstead. A monthly magazine on natural building stone for producers and users of granite, marble, limestone, slate, sandstone, onyx and other natural stone products. Circ. 15,000. Pays on publication. Publishes ms an average of 2 months after acceptance. Byline given. Buys first rights or second serial (reprint) rights. Submit seasonal/holiday material 4 months in advance. Previously published submissions OK. Reports in 2 weeks on queries; 1 month on mss. Free sample copy.
Nonfiction: How-to (fabricate and/or install natural building stone), interview/profile, photo feature, technical, architectural design, artistic stone uses, statistics, factory profile, equipment profile and trade show review. Buys 5 mss/year. Query with or without published clips, or send complete ms. Length: 600-3,000 words. Pays $75-150. Pays the expenses of writers on assignment.
Photos: State availability of photos with submission. Reviews transparencies and prints. Offers no additional payment for photos accepted with ms. Captions and identification of subjects required. Buys one-time rights.
Columns/Departments: News (pertaining to stone or design community); New Literature (brochures, catalogs, books, videos, etc. about stone); New Products (stone products); New Equipment (equipment and machinery for working with stone); Calendar (dates and locations of events in stone and design communities). Query or send complete ms. Length: 300-600 words. Pays $25-50.
Tips: "Articles about architectural stone design accompanied by professional photographs and quotes from designing firms are often published, as are articles about new techniques of quarrying and/or fabricating natural building stone."

Toy, Novelty and Hobby

Publications focusing on the toy and hobby industry are listed in this section. For magazines for hobbyists see the Consumer Hobby and Craft section.

MINIATURES DEALER MAGAZINE, 21027 Crossroads Circle, P.O. Box 1612, Waukesha WI 53186. FAX: (414)796-0126. Editor: Geraldine Willems. 50% freelance written. Eager to work with new/unpublished writers. For "retailers in the dollhouse/miniatures trade. Our readers are generally independent, small store owners who don't have time to read anything that does not pertain specifically to their own problems." Monthly magazine. Circ. 1,300. Pays on publication. Publishes ms an average of 3 months after acceptance. Buys all rights. Byline given. Phone queries OK. Submit seasonal/holiday material 4 months in advance. Previously published and simultaneous submissions (if submitted to publications in different fields) OK. Reports in 1 month. Sample copy $1.50; writer's guidelines for SASE.
Nonfiction: How-to (unique articles—e.g., how to finish a dollhouse exterior—are acceptable if they introduce new techniques or ideas; show the retailer how learning this technique will help sell dollhouses); profiles of miniatures shops; and business information pertaining to small store retailers. Buys 2-4 mss/issue. Query or send complete ms. "In query, writer should give clear description of intended article, when he could have it to me plus indication that he has studied the field, and is not making a 'blind' query. Availability of b&w photos should be noted." Pay negotiable.
Photos: "Photos must tie in directly with articles." State availability of photos. Pays $7 for each photo used. Prefers 5×7 b&w glossy prints (reviews contact sheets). Captions and model release preferred.
Tips: "We are interested in articles on full-line miniatures stores. The best way for a freelancer to break in is to study several issues of our magazine, then try to visit a miniatures shop and submit an *MD* Visits . . . article. This is a regular feature that can be written by a sharp freelancer who takes the time to study and follow the formula this feature uses. Also, basic business articles for retailers—inventory control, how to handle bad checks, etc., that are written with miniatures dealers in mind, are always needed. *MD* is extremely interested in good business articles."

PLAYTHINGS, Geyer-McAllister, 51 Madison Ave., New York NY 10010. (212)689-4411. FAX: (212)683-7929. Editor: Frank Reysen, Jr. Executive Editor: Eugene Gilligan. 20-30% freelance written. A monthly merchandising magazine covering toys and hobbies aimed mainly at mass market toy retailers. Estab. 1903. Circ. 15,000. **Pays on acceptance.** Publishes ms an average of 3 months after acceptance. Byline sometimes given. Buys one-time rights. Submit seasonal/holiday material 3 months in advance. Simultaneous submissions OK. Reports in 2 weeks. Free sample copy and writer's guidelines.

Nonfiction: Interview/profile, photo feature and retail profiles of toy and hobby stores and chains. Annual directory published in May. Buys 10 mss/year. Query. Length: 900-2,500 words. Pays $100-350. Sometimes pays the expenses of writers on assignment.

Photos: Send photos with submission. Captions and identification of subjects required. Buys one-time rights.

Columns/Departments: Buys 5 mss/year. Query. Pays $50-100.

THE STAMP WHOLESALER, P.O. Box 706, Albany OR 97321. FAX: (503)967-7262. Executive Editor: Dane S. Claussen. 80% freelance written. Newspaper published 28 times/year for philatelic business-men; many are part-time and/or retired from other work. Circ. 6,000. Pays on publication. Byline given. Buys all rights. Reports in 10 weeks. Free sample copy and writer's guidelines.

Nonfiction: How-to information on how to deal more profitably in postage stamps for collections. Emphasis on merchandising techniques and how to make money. Does not want to see any so-called "humor" items from nonprofessionals. Buys 60 ms/year. Submit complete ms. Length: 1,000-1,500 words. Pays $35 and up/article.

Tips: "Send queries on business stories. Send manuscript on stamp dealer stories. We need stories to help dealers make and save money."

Transportation

These publications are for professional movers and people involved in transportation of goods. For magazines focusing on trucking see also Auto and Truck.

AMERICAN MOVER, American Movers Conference, 2200 Mill Rd., Alexandria VA 22314. (703)838-1938. FAX: (703)838-1925. Editor: Ann S. Dinerman. 10% freelance written. Works with a small number of new/unpublished writers each year. A monthly trade journal on the moving and storage industry for moving company executives. Estab. 1945. Circ. 2,200. Pays on publication. Publishes ms an average of 3 months after acceptance. Byline given. Offers $100 kill fee. Buys first North American serial rights. Submit seasonal/holiday material 3 months in advance. Query for electronic submissions. Reports in 3 weeks on queries. Free sample copy and writer's guidelines.

Nonfiction: How-to, interview/profile, new product, personal experience, photo feature, technical and small business articles. "No fiction or articles geared toward consumers." Buys 6 mss/year. Query with published clips. Length: 1,000-5,000 words. Pays $100-200 for assigned articles. Pays contributor copies at writer's request.

Photos: Send photos with submission. Reviews 5×7 prints. Offers no additional payment for photos accepted with ms. Captions required. Buys one-time rights.

Tips: "We have an editorial calendar available that lists topics we'll be covering. Articles on small business are helpful. Feature articles are most open to freelancers. Articles must slant toward moving business-related issues. Timely topics are safety, deregulation, drug testing, computers, insurance, tax reform and marketing."

‡BUS RIDE, Friendship Publications, Inc., P.O. Box 1472, Spokane WA 99210. (509)328-9181. FAX: (509)325-5396. Editor: William A. Luke. Magazine published 8 times/year covering bus transportation. Estab. 1965. Circ. 13,000. Byline given. Not copyrighted. Sample copy $3.50; free writer's guidelines.

Nonfiction: How-to (on bus maintenance, operations, marketing); new product; and technical. Only bus transportation material is acceptable. Query. Length: 500-1,500 words. No payment from publication; "writer may receive payment from company or organization featured."

Photos: State availability of photos. Reviews b&w 8×10 prints. Captions required.

Fillers: Newsbreaks. Length: 50-100 words.

Tips: "A freelancer can contact bus companies, transit authorities, suppliers and products for the bus industry to write articles which would be accepted by our publication."

BUS WORLD, Magazine of Buses and Bus Systems, Stauss Publications, P.O. Box 39, Woodland Hills CA 91365. (818)710-0208. Editor: Julian Wolinsky. 75% freelance written. Quarterly trade journal covering the transit and intercity bus industries. Estab. 1978. Circ. 5,000. Pays on publication. Sample copy with writer's guidelines $2.

Photos: "We buy photos with manuscripts under one payment."

Fillers: Cartoons. Buys 4-6/year. Pays $10.

Tips: "No tourist or travelog viewpoints. Be employed in or have a good understanding of the bus industry. Be enthusiastic about buses—their history and future—as well as current events. Acceptable material will be held until used and will not be returned unless requested by sender. Unacceptable and excess material will be returned only if accompanied by suitable SASE."

INBOUND LOGISTICS, Thomas Publishing Co., 5 Penn Plaza, 8th Fl., New York NY 10001. (212)629-1560. FAX: (212)629-1584. Publisher: Keith Biondo. 20% freelance written. Prefers to work with published/established writers. Monthly magazine covering the transportation industry. *"Inbound Logistics* is distributed to people who buy, specify, or recommend inbound freight transportation services and equipment. The editorial matter provides basic explanations of inbound freight transportation, directory listings, how-to technical information, trends and developments affecting inbound freight movements, and expository, case history feature stories." Circ. 43,000. Pays on publication. Publishes ms an average of 3 months after acceptance. Byline given. Buys all rights. Simultaneous queries, and simultaneous submissions OK. Reports in 2 weeks. Sample copy and writer's guidelines for 9×12 SAE and 5 first class stamps.

Nonfiction: How-to (basic help for purchasing agents and traffic managers) and interview/profile (purchasing and transportation professionals). Buys 15 mss/year. Query with published clips. Length: 750-1,000 words. Pays $300-1,200. Pays expenses of writers on assignment.

Photos: Emily Sloves, photo editor. State availability of photos with query. Pays $100-500 for b&w contact sheets, negatives, transparencies and prints; $250-500 for color contact sheets, negative transparencies and prints. Captions and identification of subjects required.

Columns/Departments: Viewpoint (discusses current opinions on transportation topics). Query with published clips.

Tips: "Have a sound knowledge of the transportation industry; educational how-to articles get our attention."

Travel

Travel professionals read these publications to keep up with trends, tours and changes in transportation. Magazines about vacations and travel for the general public are listed in the Consumer Travel section.

BUS TOURS MAGAZINE, The Magazine of Bus Tours and Long Distance Charters, National Bus Trader, Inc., 9698 W. Judson Rd., Polo IL 61064. (815)946-2341. FAX: (815)946-2347. Editor: Larry Plachno. Editorial Assistant: Carol Merbach. 80% freelance written. Eager to work with new/unpublished writers. Bimonthly magazine for bus companies and tour brokers who design or sell bus tours. Estab. 1977. Circ. 9,306. Pays as arranged. Publishes ms an average of 6 months after acceptance. Byline given. Not copyrighted. Buys rights as arranged. Submit seasonal/holiday material 9 months in advance. Simultaneous queries OK. Reports in 1 month. Free sample copy and writer's guidelines.

Nonfiction: Historical/nostalgic, how-to, humor, interview/profile, new product, professional, personal experience and travel; all on bus tours. Buys 10 mss/year. Query. Length: open. Pays negotiable fee.

Photos: State availability of photos. Reviews 35mm transparencies and 6x9 or 8×10 prints. Caption, model release and identification of subjects required.

Columns/Departments: Bus Tour Marketing; and Buses and the Law. Buys 15-20 mss/year. Query. Length: 1-1½ pages.

Tips: "Most of our feature articles are written by freelancers under contract from local convention and tourism bureaus. Specifications sent on request. Writers should query local bureaus regarding their interest. Writer need not have extensive background and knowledge of bus tours."

NATIONAL BUS TRADER, The Magazine of Bus Equipment for the United States and Canada, 9698 W. Judson Rd., Polo IL 61064. (815)946-2341. FAX: (815)946-2347. Editor: Larry Plachno. 25% freelance written. Eager to work with new/unpublished writers. Monthly magazine for manufacturers, dealers and owners of buses and motor coaches. Estab. 1977. Circ. 7,354. Pays on either acceptance or publication. Publishes ms an average of 3 months after acceptance. Byline given. Not copyrighted. Buys rights "as required by writer." Simultaneous queries, simultaneous and previously published submissions OK. Reports in 1 month. Free sample copy.

Nonfiction: Historical/nostalgic (on old buses); how-to (maintenance repair); new products; photo feature; and technical (aspects of mechanical operation of buses). "We are finding that more and more firms and agencies are hiring freelancers to write articles to our specifications. We are more likely to run them if someone else pays." No material that does *not* pertain to bus tours or bus equipment. Buys 3-5 unsolicited mss/year. Query. Length varies. Pays variable rate. Sometimes pays the expenses of writers on assignment.

Photos: State availability of photos. Reviews 5 × 7 or 8 × 10 prints and 35mm transparencies. Captions, model release and identification of subjects required.

Columns/Departments: Bus maintenance; Buses and the Law; Regulations; and Bus of the Month. Buys 20-30 mss/year. Query. Length: 250-400 words. Pays variable rate.

Tips: "We are a very technical publication. Writers should submit qualifications showing extensive background in bus vehicles. We're very interested in well-researched articles on older bus models and manufacturers, or current converted coaches. We would like to receive history of individual bus models prior to 1953 and history of GMC 'new look' models. Write or phone editors with article concept or outline for comments and approval."

RV BUSINESS, TL Enterprises, Inc., 29901 Agoura Rd., Agoura CA 91301. (818)991-4980. FAX: (818)991-8102. Executive Editor: Katherine Sharma. 60% freelance written. Prefers to work with published/established writers. Semi-monthly magazine covering the recreational vehicle and allied industries for people in the RV industry—dealers, manufacturers, suppliers, campground management, and finance experts. Estab. 1950. Circ. 25,000. **Pays on acceptance.** Publishes ms an average of 2 months after acceptance. Byline given. Offers 50% kill fee. Buys first North American serial rights. Submit seasonal/holiday material 6 months in advance. Query for electronic submissions. Reports in 3 weeks on queries; 6 weeks on mss. Sample copy for 9 × 12 SAE and 3 first class stamps.

Nonfiction: Technical, financial, legal or marketing issues; how-to (deal with any specific aspect of the RV business); specifics and verification of statistics required—must be factual; and technical (photos required, 4-color preferred). General business articles may be considered. Buys 75 mss/year. Query with published clips. Send complete ms—"but only read on speculation." Length: 1,000-1,500 words. Pays variable rate up to $500. Sometimes pays expenses of writers on assignment.

Photos: State availability of photos with query or send photos with ms. Reviews 35mm transparencies and 8 × 10 b&w prints. Captions, model release, and identification of subjects required. Buys one-time or all rights; unused photos returned.

Columns/Departments: Guest editorial; News (50-500 words maximum, b&w photos appreciated); and RV People (color photos/4-color transparencies; this section lends itself to fun, upbeat copy). Buys 100-120 mss/year. Query or send complete ms. Pays $10-200 "depending on where used and importance."

Tips: "Query. Phone OK; letter preferable. Send one or several ideas and a few lines letting us know how you plan to treat it/them. We are always looking for good authors knowledgable in the RV industry or related industries. Change of editorial focus requires more articles that are brief, factual, hard hitting, business oriented and in-depth. Will work with promising writers, published or unpublished."

STAR SERVICE, (formerly *ABC Star Service*), Reed Travel Group, 131 Clarendon St., Boston MA 02116. (617)262-5000. FAX: (617)421-9353. Publisher: Steven R. Gordon. "Eager to work with new/ unpublished writers as well as those working from a home base abroad, planning trips that would allow time for hotel reporting, or living in major ports for cruise ships." Worldwide guide to accommodations and cruise ships founded in 1960 (as *Sloane Travel Agency Reports*) and sold to travel agencies on subscription basis. Pays 15 days after publication. Buys all rights. Query should include details on writer's experience in travel and writing, clips, specific forthcoming travel plans, and how much time would be available for hotel or ship inspections. Buys 5,000 reports/year. Pays $18/report used. Sponsored trips are acceptable. General query statement should precede electronic submission. Writer's guidelines and list of available assignments for #10 SASE.

Nonfiction: Objective, critical evaluations of hotels and cruise ships suitable for international travelers, based on personal inspections. Freelance correspondents ordinarily are assigned to update an entire state or country. "Assignment involves on-site inspections of all hotels we review; revising and updating published reports; and reviewing new properties. Qualities needed are thoroughness, precision, perseverance and keen judgment. Solid research skills and powers of observation are crucial. Travel and travel writing experience are highly desirable. Reviews must be colorful, clear, and documented with hotel's brochure, rate sheet, etc. We accept no hotel advertising or payment for listings, so reviews should dispense praise and criticism where deserved."

Tips: "We may require sample hotel or cruise reports on facilities near freelancer's hometown before giving the first assignment. No byline because of sensitive nature of reviews."

Veterinary

Journals for veterinarians and pet health professionals are located in this section. For publications targeted to pet shop and grooming business managers and the pet supply industry see the Pets section. For magazines for pet owners see the Consumer Animal section.

NEW METHODS, The Journal of Animal Health Technology, P.O. Box 22605, San Francisco CA 94122-0605. (415)664-3469. Managing Editor: Ronald S. Lippert, AHT. *"New Methods* is an educational and informational newsletter about animal health technology." Estab. 1976. Circ. 5,600. Pays on publication. Byline given. Buys simultaneous rights. Submit seasonal/holiday material 2 months in advance. Simultaneous submissions OK. Reports in 2 weeks. Sample copy for $2, #10 SAE and 2 first class stamps; writer's guidelines for #10 SASE.
Nonfiction: How-to (technical), new product and technical. Buys 1 ms/year. Query. Pays in contributor copies or other premiums. Sometimes pays expenses of writers on assignment.
Photos: State availability of photos with submission. Reviews contact sheets. Offers variable payment. Captions, model releases and identification of subjects required. Buys one-time rights.
Columns/Departments: Buys 12 mss/year. Query. Length and payment variable.
Poetry: We do not want unrelated subject matter, very long or abstract poetry. Buys 2 poems/year. Submit maximum 1 poem. Length and payment variable.
Fillers: Facts and newsbreaks. Buys 12/year.
Tips: "Contact *New Methods* in writing with an SASE before writing or submitting any finished material; ideas first. Could use individual(s) to write and submit press releases."

VETERINARY ECONOMICS MAGAZINE, 9073 Lenexa Dr., Lenexa KS 66215. (913)492-4300. FAX: (913)492-4157. Editor: Rebecca R. Turner. 75% freelance written. Prefers to work with published/established writers but will work with several new/unpublished writers each year. Monthly business magazine for all practicing veterinarians in the U.S. Estab. 1960. Buys exclusive rights in the field. Pays on publication. Publishes ms 3-6 months after acceptance. Free sample copy and writer's guidelines.
Nonfiction: Publishes non-clinical articles on business and management techniques that will strengthen a veterinarian's private practice. Also interested in articles on financial problems, employee relations, marketing and similar subjects of particular interest to business owners. "We look for carefully researched articles that are specifically directed to our field." Pays negotiable rates. Pays expenses of writers on assignment.
Tips: "Our articles focus on nuts-and-bolts practice management techniques prescribed by experts in the practice management field and applied by successful veterinarians. Articles must be useful and appeal to a broad section of our readers."

Other Trade, Technical and Professional Journals

The following trade journals were listed in 1991 but do not have listings in this edition of *Writer's Market*. The majority did not respond to our request to update their listings or return a questionnaire for a new listing. If a reason was given for their exclusion, we have included it in parentheses after the listing name.

Ag-Pilot International Magazine
Airport Services Magazine
Alumni-News
Automation
American Paint & Coatings Journal (asked to be deleted)
American Hockey Magazine
Auto Laundry News
Automotive Executive
Awards & Engraving Business Magazine
Balloons Today Magazine
Bank Operations Report
The Best Report (no longer accepts unsolicited freelance material)
Bobbin
BPME Image
The Brahman Journal
Building Services Contractor
Cable Marketing
Cable TV Business
California Nursing Review
Canadian Computer Dealer News
Christian Education Today

Clavier
Citrus & Vegetable Magazine, and the Florida Farmer
CMAA
Commerce Magazine
Compass
Concrete Construction Magazine
The Concrete Trader
Condominium Times
Construction Supervision & Safety Letter
Copy Magazine
Cost Cuts
Cutting Tool Engineering
Dance Teacher Now
Defense & Foreign Affairs
Deli-Dairy
Dentist
Discipleship Training
Educational Dealer
The Electric Weenie
Family Therapy News
Farm Pond Harvest
The Financial Manager (ceased publication)
Fitness Management
Florida Grower & Rancher

Florida Nursing News
Food Business (asked to be deleted)
The Front Striker Bulletin
Fur Trade Journal of Canada
Futures Magazine
General Dentistry (does not use freelance writing)
Giftware News
Glass Art
Gourmet Today
Group Practice Journal (no longer accepts unsolicited freelance material)
Ham Radio Magazine
Heavy Truck Salesman (no longer accepts unsolicited freelance material)
ID Systems
Ideas
Industrial Fabric Products Review
Jet Cargo News
The Journal
Lawyers Monthly (ceased publication)
The Lone Star Comedy Monthly

Los Angeles Lawyer (asked to be deleted)
Midwest Purchasing Management and Purchasing Management (only accepts freelance articles on a non-paying basis)
The Mini-Storage Messenger
Modern Cartooning
Multichannel News (unable to contact; mail returned)
The Music & Computer Educator
National Wool Grower
New England Antiques Journal
New Mexico Business Journal
Nurseweek
The Paralegal
Pension World
Perinatal Press

Photo Lab Management
Printing News Midwest
Pro Trucker and Over the Road
Prorodeo Sports News
Purchasing World
Recognition & Promotions Business
RSI, Roofing/Siding/Insulation
Sales & Marketing Management in Canada
Shipping Digest
Shopping Center World
Ski Business
Sound Management
Souvenirs & Novelties Magazine
Specialty Retailer
The Successful Dealer
The Successful Hotel Marketer
Travel Life

Travelage MidAmerica
Travelage West
Teaching/K-8
Television Broadcast (now staff written)
Texas Architect
Tile World
Tourist Attractions & Parks Magazine
Truck World
Trucks Magazine (asked to be deleted)
UPB Magazine (ceased publication)
Utility Supervision
Western & English Fashions
Wings West
The Wisconsin Restaurateur
Your Church

Scriptwriting

by Kerry Cox

As a writer, you'll encounter several myths about scriptwriting. Scriptwriting is *not*: 1) Easier than writing a book. 2) A great way to make tons of money. 3) Only a viable pursuit if you live in Hollywood.

Scriptwriting *is*: 1) A craft. 2) A business. 3) A unique, challenging form of writing with a wide range of career opportunities.

To write an effective script is to master the art of storytelling in such a way that you utilize the full potential of the medium. "Think visually" is the advice heard over and over, whether writing for the big screen or corporate video, and it's wise to tell as much of your story through visuals as possible. Audio scripts (such as radio advertising, motivational or instructional audiotapes, etc.) require skillful use of dialogue and sound effects.

Whatever form of scriptwriting you undertake, the importance of crisp, concise dialogue cannot be overemphasized. Nothing gets an audience snoozing faster than a droning narrator or an endless barrage of chatter. Use your dialogue to move the script along from point to point, each word contributing to the forward momentum.

Because of the variety of markets for the scriptwriter, it is necessary to become familiar with a number of formats. Sitcom format is different from feature format, which is roughly the same as animation format, which is different from video format, which looks pretty much like multi-image format, which is wholly different from stage play format. To learn the proper way to lay out your page, consult some of the books currently available, or get some sample scripts as models. You can obtain scripts from production houses or from one of several script vendors that advertise in writer's magazines.

Because scripts are needed by advertising agencies, local television stations, stand-up comics, public speakers, independent video producers and many others, scriptwriting is not something you can only do if you live next door to the Hollywood sign. There are opportunities everywhere, as you can see from the following listings. And one more thing: if you're an aspiring screenwriter, don't turn up your nose at business or education writing, or if you're a playwright, don't consider yourself above penning a TV spec script. Any kind of scriptwriting you can do is beneficial in the long run. The more you do, the more you master the form, and the better your chances of success.

Business and educational writing

It's probably safe to say that most writers who dream of writing The Perfect Script aren't envisioning a 10-minute feature on the Health Insurance Benefits for XYZ Corporation.

But maybe they ought to.

Scriptwriting for the corporate, business and industrial arena can not only be lucrative and challenging; it can also provide a realistic alternative to those who want to write scripts for a living but haven't been able to crack the formidable barriers to Hollywood success.

No, it's not glamorous. The majority of work will consist of task-oriented training videos, promotional or marketing pieces, corporate image shows, educational modules and

Kerry Cox is a Los Angeles writer with more than ten years of experience in television, motion picture, theater and business/educational scriptwriting. He is the co-author (with Jurgen Wolff) of Successful Scriptwriting *(Writer's Digest Books), and is editor and publisher of* Hollywood Scriptwriter, *a newsletter for scriptwriters throughout the U.S. and Canada.*

straightforward informational presentations. Does this mean it will, by its very nature, have to be mundane and boring? Absolutely not. In fact, the most successful corporate and industrial scriptwriters rely heavily on humor, drama, and creative conceptualization to bring entertainment value to their scripts.

The challenge comes in finding ways to add some life to a dry subject, without forcing or shoehorning that subject into a premise that simply doesn't work. Another challenge: staying away from corporate cliches. Just about every writer of business scripts (yours truly included) has, at one time or another, fallen back on the Bogart/Private Eye premise; the Siskel and Ebert premise; the Twilight Zone premise (done to death!); and the Wide World of Sports premise. They have all been done before, and they'll no doubt be done again. But before you use them, try to stretch a bit and come up with something new.

Writing for this market demands a knowledge of two-column format, since most video producers work with this format. It's fairly simple: Video is single-spaced, usually all caps, on the left side of the page, Audio is double-spaced, upper-lower case, on the right. Timing usually runs about 45 produced seconds per page, but of course this can vary.

As a freelancer, your work will come from any number of sources. Production companies specializing in industrial work will very often rely solely on a core group of freelancers for their writing needs. Companies with in-house production teams will occasionally use freelancers to handle some of the writing load. Advertising agencies are often called upon to assist in the production of industrials and are a good contact for the business scriptwriter. Virtually any business with a budget for promotional events or sales conventions likes to use "meeting openers," and these become a viable market for the enterprising freelancer.

Budgets in this field are strictly adhered to and can be quite limited, so it behooves the writer to be very familiar with the approximate costs of production. A good business scriptwriter will be skilled in crafting scripts with a minimum number of actors, special effects and locations.

What does this kind of writing pay? It depends on your experience, the budget for the production and how hungry you are for the work. Some things to check before setting your fee: Roughly how many meetings will you have to attend? How many drafts are expected? What is the intended length of the show? How will the show be used? How extensive will production be? Answers to these questions will enable you to approximate the budget of the show (and its importance to the client) and can help you arrive at a fair price. The most important factor to consider, though, is how long it will take you to write the script, and what you feel your time is worth. General rule of thumb: $100 per finished minute (actual running time) of script, with a $500-1,000 minimum.

For more business and education markets, see Other Scriptwriting Markets at the end of the Screenwriting section.

ABS & ASSOCIATES, P.O. Box 5127, Evanston IL 60204. (708)982-1414. President: Alan Soell. "We produce material for all levels of corporate, medical, cable and educational institutions for the purposes of training and development, marketing and meeting presentations. We also are developing programming for the broadcast areas. 75% freelance written. We work with a core of three to five freelance writers from development to final drafts." All scripts published are unagented submissions. Buys all rights. Previously produced material OK. Reports in 2 weeks on queries. Catalog for 9×12 SAE and 6 first class stamps.
Needs: Videotape, 16mm films, silent and sound filmstrips, multimedia kits, overhead transparencies, realia, slides, tapes and cassettes, and television shows/series. Currently interested in "sports instructional series that could be produced for the consumer market on tennis, gymnastics, bowling, golf, aerobics, health and fitness, cross-country skiing and cycling. Also motivational and self-improvement type videos and film ideas to be produced. These could cover all ages '6-60'; and from professional to blue collar jobs. These two areas should be 30 minutes and be timeless in approach for long shelf life." Sports audience, age 25-45; home improvement, 25-65. "Cable TV needs include the two groups of programming detailed here. We are also looking for documentary work on current issues, nuclear power, solar power, urban development, senior citizens—but with a new approach." Query or submit synopsis/outline and resume. Pays by contractual agreement.

Tips: "I am looking for innovative approaches to old problems that just don't go away. The approach should be simple and direct so there is immediate audience identification with the presentation. I also like to see a sense of humor used. Trends in the audiovisual field include interactive video with disk — for training purposes."

‡**THE ALLAGASH GROUP**, 55 Wheeler St., Cambridge MA 02138. (617)492-8923. Project Development: Jacki Roche. Estab. 1990. Buys 3-5 scripts/year. Buys all rights. No previously produced material. **Needs:** Films (35mm). Submit synopsis/outline, completed script and resume. Pays in accordance with Writers Guild standards.
Tips: "We are a feature film production company looking for full-length screenplays. Psychological suspense/thrillers."

ARNOLD AND ASSOCIATES PRODUCTIONS, INC., 2159 Powell St., San Francisco CA 94133. (415)989-3490. President: John Arnold. Executive Producers: Deirdre Say, James W. Morris and Peter Dutton. Produces material for the general public (entertainment/motion pictures) and for corporate clients (employees/customers/consumers). Buys 10-15 scripts/year. Works with 3 writers/year. Buys all rights. Previously produced material OK. Reports in 1 month.
Needs: Films (35mm) and videotape. Looking for "upscale image and marketing programs." Dramatic writing for "name narrators and post scored original music; and motion picture. $5-6 million dollar budget. Dramatic or horror." Query with samples or submit completed script. Makes outright purchase of $1,000.
Tips: Looking for "upscale writers who understand corporate image production, and motion picture writers who understand story and dialogue."

A/V CONCEPTS CORP., 30 Montauk Blvd., Oakdale NY 11769. (516)567-7227. FAX: (516)567-5908. Contact: P. Solimene or L. Solimene. Produces material for elementary-high school students, either on grade level or in remedial situations. Estab. 1971. 100% freelance written. Buys 25 scripts/year from unpublished/unproduced writers. Employs filmstrip, book and personal computer media. Reports on outline in 1 month; on final scripts in 6 weeks. Buys all rights.
Needs: Interested in original educational computer (disk-based) software programs for Apple +, 48k. Main concentration in language arts, mathematics and reading. "Manuscripts must be written using our lists of vocabulary words and meet our reading ability formula requirements. Specific guidelines are devised for each level. Length of manuscript and subjects will vary according to grade level for which material is prepared. Basically, we want material that will motivate people to read." Pays $300 and up.
Tips: "Writers must be highly creative and highly disciplined. We are interested in high interest-low readability materials."

‡**BENENSON PRODUCTIONS**, #209, 321 Hampton Dr., Venice CA 90291. (213)399-7793. Director of Development: Tracy J. Brown. Estab. 1980. "For intelligent adults. We purchase roughly two scripts/year, with 3-10 projects in development at once." Buys film rights. No previously published material. Reports in 5 weeks on queries; 6 weeks on submissions.
Needs: Films. "We are interested in true historical stories; stories based on fact or on classic literature. Scripts, 100-140 pages. We also occasionally look at serious scripts that don't fit the above description." Query with synopsis (short synopsis). "Option and purchase and deferred payment depends on material and probable budget."
Tips: "Do not send a script — it will be returned unopened. No comedy; sci-fi; action-adventure. Interesting human dramas will get our attention."

‡**BOSUSTOW VIDEO**, 3000 Olympic Blvd., Santa Monica CA 90404. (213)315-4888. Owner: Tee Bosustow. Estab. 1983. Produces material for corporate, PBS and home video clients. Worked with 6 writers on videos in 1990. No previously produced material. Reports in 2 weeks on queries.
Needs: Tapes, cassettes and videotapes. "Unfortunately, no one style, etc. exists. We produce a variety of products." Submit synopsis/outline and resume only. Pays agreed upon fee.
Tips: "Bear with us; we aren't ready for scripts yet. Our writers usually come via our clients . . . companies."

CLEARVUE, INC., 6465 N. Avondale Ave., Chicago IL 60631. (312)775-9433. President: William T. Ryan. Produces material for educational market — grades kindergarten-12. 90% freelance written. Prefers to work with published/established writers. Buys 20-50 scripts/year from previously unpublished/unproduced writers. Buys all rights. Previously produced material OK. Query for electronic submissions. Reports in 2 weeks on queries; 3 weeks on submissions. Free catalog.

Needs: Videos, filmstrips (sound), multimedia kits and slides. "Our filmstrips and videos are 35 to 100 frames—8 to 30 minutes for all curriculum areas." Query. Makes outright purchase, $100-5,000. Sometimes pays the expenses of writers on assignment.
Tips: "Our interests are in video for the elementary and high school markets on all subjects."

‡**COMARK**, 1636 Abbot Kinney Blvd., Venice CA 90291. FAX: (213)450-5393. Vice President: Stan Ono. Produces material for corporate/industrial audience. Buys 18 scripts/year. Buys all rights. No previously produced material. Also brochures, collateral print material.
Needs: "Video training, sales/marketing, retail, financial and food services." Produces 16mm film, multimedia kits, slides and video. Submit résumé and samples. Makes outright purchase.

‡**COMPASS FILMS/VIDEO**, 921 Jackson Dr., Cleveland WI 53015. Executive Producer: Robert Whittaker. Produces material for educational, industrial and general adult audiences. Specializes in Marine films, stop motion and special effects with a budget . . . and national and worldwide filming in difficult locations. 60% freelance written. Works with 3 writers/year. Buys 2-4 scripts/year. 100% of scripts are unagented submissions. Buys all rights. Query with samples or submit resume with SASE.
Needs: Scriptwriters for 5- to 30-minute business films and general documentaries. "We would like to review writers to develop existing film treatments and ideas with strong dialogue." Also needs ghostwriters, editors and researchers. Produces 16mm and 35mm films and videotape products. Payment negotiable, depending on experience. Pays expenses of writers on assignment.
Tips: Writer/photographers receive higher consideration "because we could also use them as still photographers on location and they could double-up as rewrite men . . . and ladies. Experience in videotape editing supervision an asset. We are producing more high 'fashion-tech' industrial video."

COMPRO PRODUCTIONS, Suite 114, 2080 Peachtree Ind. Ct., Atlanta GA 30341. (404)455-1943. FAX: (404)455-3356. Producers: Nels Anderson and Steve Brinson. Estab. 1977. Audience is general public and specific business audience. Buys 10-25 scripts/year. Buys all rights. No previously produced material. No unsolicited material; submissions will not be returned because "all work is contracted."
Needs: "We solicit writers for corporate films/video in the areas of training, point purchase, sales, how-to, benefit programs, resorts and colleges." Produces 16-35mm films and videotapes. Query with samples. Makes outright purchase or pays cost per minute.

CONTINENTAL FILM PRODUCTIONS CORPORATION, P.O. Box 5126, 4220 Amnicola Hwy., Chattanooga TN 37406. (615)622-1193. FAX: (615)629-0853. Executive Vice President: James L. Webster. Estab. 1951. Produces "AV and video presentations for businesses and nonprofit organizations for sales, training, public relations, documentation, motivation, etc." Works with many writers annually. Buys all rights. No previously produced material. Unsolicited submissions not returned. Reports in 1 week.
Needs: "We do need new writers of various types. Please contact us by mail with samples and resume." Produces slides, filmstrips, motion pictures, multi-image presentations and videos. Query with samples and resume. Outright purchase: $250 minimum.
Tips: Looks for writers whose work shows " technical understanding, humor, common sense, practicality, simplicity, creativity, etc. Important for writers to adapt script to available production budget." Suggests writers "increase use of humor in training films." Also seeking scripts on "human behavior in industry."

NICHOLAS DANCY PRODUCTIONS, INC., 333 W. 39th St., New York NY 10018. President: Nicholas Dancy. Produces media material for corporate communications, the health care field, general audiences, employees, members of professional groups, members of associations and special customer groups. 60% freelance written. Prefers to work with published/established writers. Buys 5-10 scripts/year; works with 5-10 writers/year. None of scripts is unagented. Buys all rights. Query for electronic submissions. Reports in 1 month.
Needs: "We use scripts for videotapes or films from 5 minutes to 1 hour for corporate communications, sales, orientation, training, corporate image, medical and documentary." Format: videotape, occasionally 16mm films. Query with résumé. "No unsolicited material. Our field is too specialized." Pays by outright purchase of $800-5,000. Pays expenses of writers on assignment.
Tips: "Writers should have a knowledge of business and industry and professions, an ability to work with clients and communicators, a fresh narrative style, creative use of dialogue, good skills in accomplishing research and a professional approach to production. New concept trends are important in business. We're looking for new areas. The cautious loosening of FDA processes will create an even sharper need for skilled and talented scriptwriters in the medical field."

‡DELTA MAX PRODUCTIONS, P.O. Box 7188, Newport Beach CA 92660. (714)760-9638. President: Robert Swanson. Estab. 1983. Produces material for feature film audience. Buys 1-5 scripts/year. Works with 10-20 writers/year. Buys all rights or other rights depending on material. Reports in 2 weeks on queries.

Needs: Film loops (35mm), films (35/70mm), tapes and cassettes and videotapes. "We are seeking feature film scripts; proper format, 2 hour length. All subjects, particularly comedy, action-adventure, drama, sci/fi." Submit completed script. Pays outright purchase; in accordance with Writers Guild standards; a varied amount of options, with money.

Tips: "Get the script in as complete a form as possible before submitting; submit with release form, agent's letter or attorney letter; include a SASE if you want it returned; include *where* you have sent the project and *to whom* it was sent; do not ask for constructive criticism—it will be given if appropriate."

EDUCATIONAL IMAGES LTD., P.O. Box 3456, Elmira NY 14905. (607)732-1090. Executive Director: Dr. Charles R. Belinky. Produces material (videos, sound filmstrips, multimedia kits and slide sets) for schools, kindergarten through college and graduate school, public libraries, parks, nature centers, etc. Also produces science-related software material. Buys 50 scripts/year. Buys all AV rights. Free catalog.

Needs: Videos, slide sets and filmstrips on science, natural history, anthropology and social studies. "We are looking primarily for complete AV programs; we will consider slide collections to add to our files. This requires high quality, factual text and pictures." Query with a meaningful sample of proposed program. Pays $150 minimum.

Tips: The writer/photographer is given high consideration. "Once we express interest, follow up. Potential contributors lose many sales to us by not following up on initial query. Don't waste our time and yours if you can't deliver. The market seems to be shifting to greater popularity of video and computer software formats."

EDUCATIONAL INSIGHTS, 19560 S. Rancho Way, Dominguez Hills CA 90220. (213)637-2131. FAX: (213)605-5048. VP/Director of Development: Dennis J. Graham. Estab. 1962. Produces material for elementary schools and retail "home-learning" markets. Works with 10 writers/year. Buys all rights. Previously produced material OK. Reports in 2 weeks. Catalog for 9 × 12 SAE with 2 first class stamps.

Needs: Charts, models, multimedia kits, study prints, tapes and cassettes, and teaching machine programs. Query with samples. Pays varied royalties or makes outright purchase.

Tips: "Keep up-to-date information on educational trends in mind. Study the market before starting to work. We receive 20 manuscripts per week—all reviewed and returned, if rejected."

EDUCATIONAL VIDEO NETWORK, 1401 19th St., Huntsville TX 77340. (409)295-5767. President: Dr. Kenneth L. Russell. Produces material for junior high, senior high, college and university audiences. Buys "perhaps 20 scripts/year." Buys all rights or pays royalty on gross retail and wholesale. Previously produced material OK. Reports in 1 week on queries; in 1 month on submissions. Free catalog.

Needs: "Video for educational purposes. Photographs on 2×2 slides must have good saturation of color." Query. Royalty varies.

Tips: Looks for writers with the "ability to write and illustrate for educational purposes. Schools are asking for more curriculum oriented live-action video. Recent trends include more emphasis on video; less emphasis on filmstrips."

EFFECTIVE COMMUNICATION ARTS, INC., 221 W. 57th St., New York NY 10019. (212)333-5656. FAX: (212)333-7748. Vice President: W.J. Comcowich. Estab. 1965. Produces films, videotapes and interactive videodisks for physicians, nurses and medical personnel. Prefers to work with published/established writers. 80% freelance written. Buys approximately 20 scripts/year. Query for electronic submissions. Buys all rights. Reports in 1 month.

Needs: Multimedia kits, television shows/series, videotape presentations and interactive videodisks. Currently producing about 15 videotapes for medical audiences; 6 interactive disks for medical audience; 3 interactive disks for point-of-purchase. Submit complete script and resume. Makes outright purchase. Pays expenses of writers on assignment.

Tips: "Videotape scripts on technical subjects are becoming increasingly important. Explain what the film accomplishes—how it is better than the typical."

‡EURO COMMUNICATION ENTERTAINMENT GROUP, 223 Strand St., Santa Monica CA 90405. (213)399-1101. Producer: Liliane Pelzmau. Estab. 1983. Produces material for ages 17-44. Buys all rights. No previously published material. Does not return submissions.

Needs: Videotapes. Pays royalty in accordance with Writers Guild standards.

FLIPTRACK LEARNING SYSTEMS, Division of Mosaic Media, Inc., Suite 200, 999 Main St., Glen Ellyn IL 60137. (708)790-1117. FAX: (708)790-1196. Publisher: F. Lee McFadden. Contact: Natalie Young. Estab. 1976. Produces training courses for microcomputers and business software. Works with a small number of new/unpublished writers each year. 35% freelance written. Buys 3-5 courses/year; 1-2 from unpublished/unproduced writers. All courses published are unagented submissions. Works with 3-5 writers/year. Buys all rights. Query for electronic submissions. Reports in 3 weeks. Free product literature; sample copy for 9×12 SAE.

Needs: Training courses on how to use personal computers/software, video or audio geared to the adult student in a business setting and usually to the novice user; a few courses at advanced levels. Primarily audio, also some reference manuals, video and feature articles on personal computers. Query with resume and samples if available. Pays negotiable royalty or makes outright purchase.

Tips: "We prefer to work with Chicago-area writers with strong teaching/training backgrounds and experience with microcomputers. Writers from other regions are also welcome. We also need feature/journalism writers with strong microcomputer interest and experience."

HAYES SCHOOL PUBLISHING CO., INC., 321 Pennwood Ave., Wilkinsburg PA 15221. (412)371-2373. FAX: (412)371-6408. President: Clair N. Hayes, III. Estab. 1940. Produces material for school teachers, principals, elementary through high school. Also produces charts, workbooks, teacher's handbooks, posters, bulletin board material and reproducible blackline masters (grades kindergarten through 12). 25% freelance written. Prefers to work with published/established writers. Buys 5-10 scripts/year from unpublished/unproduced writers. 100% of scripts produced are unagented submissions. Buys all rights. Query for electronic submissions. Catalog for 3 first class stamps; writer's guidelines for #10 SAE and 2 first class stamps.

Needs: Educational material only. Particularly interested in educational material for elementary school level. Query. Pays $25 minimum.

‡INTERACTIVE ARTS, 3200 Airport Ave., Santa Monica CA 90405. (213)390-9466. Vice President: David Schwartz. Estab. 1985. Audience is general public; theme parks; museums; college and high school students; corporate and industrial clients. Buys 4-5 scripts and 10 treatments/year; works with 5-6 writers/year. Buys all rights. Reports in 2 weeks.

Needs: Theme park films, videotapes, interactive videodiscs, multimedia (computer), educational/science documentaries. "Our needs vary from consumer multimedia titles to museum projects and from theme park projects to educational/scientific documentaries." Queries desired from California residents only.

DAVID JACKSON PRODUCTIONS, 1020 N. Cole St., 3rd Floor, Hollywood CA 90038. (213)465-3810. FAX: (213)465-1096. President: David Jackson. Estab. 1985. We have feature, corporate, commercial and educational audiences. Buys 3-10 scripts/year. Buys all rights. Reports on queries in 1 week; 1 month on submissions.

Needs: Models, phonograph records, tapes and cassettes, videotapes. "We are looking for video format—instructional, educational and film format—commercial." Query. Pays in accordance with Writers Guild standards.

Tips: "We are interested in both fantasy and real life writings."

JACOBY/STORM PRODUCTIONS INC., 22 Crescent Road, Westport CT 06880. (203)227-2220. Contact: Doris Storm. Produces material for business people, students, professionals (e.g. medical). Works with 4-6 writers annually. Buys all rights. No previously produced material. Reports in 2 weeks.

Needs: "Short dramatic films on business subjects, educational films on varied subjects, sales and corporate image films." Produces 16mm films, slides, tapes and cassettes, videotapes and videodisks. Query. Usually makes outright purchase.

Tips: "Prefers local people. Looks for experience, creativity, dependability, attention to detail, enthusiasm for project, ability to interface with client. Wants creative approaches to material."

KIMBO EDUCATIONAL-UNITED SOUND ARTS, INC., 10-16 N. 3rd Ave., Box 477, Long Branch NJ 07740. (201)229-4949. Contact: James Kimble or Amy Laufer. Produces materials for the educational market (early childhood, special education, music, physical education, dance, and preschool children 6 months and up). 50% freelance written. Buys approximately 6 scripts/year; works with approximately 6 writers/year. Buys 3 scripts/year from unpublished/unproduced writers. Most scripts are unagented submissions. Buys all rights or first rights. Previously produced material OK "in some instances." Reports in 1 month. Free catalog.

Needs: "For the next two years we will be concentrating on general early childhood songs and movement oriented products, new albums in the fitness field and more. Each will be an album/cassette with accompanying teacher's manual and, if warranted, manipulatives." Phonograph records and cassettes, "all with accompanying manual or teaching guides." Query with samples and synopsis/outline or completed script. Pays 5-7% royalty on lowest wholesale selling price, and by outright purchase. Both negotiable.

Tips: "We look for creativity first. Having material that is educationally sound is also important. Being organized is certainly helpful. The early childhood market and fitness is growing rapidly in popularity and will always be a necessary thing. Children will always need to be taught the basic fine and gross motor skills. Capturing interest while reaching these goals is the key."

MARSH MEDIA, P.O. Box 8082, Shawnee Mission KS 66208. (816)523-1059. FAX: (816)333-7421. President: Joan K. Marsh. Estab. 1969. Produces software and video and filmstrips for elementary and junior/senior high school students. 100% freelance written. Works with a small number of new/unpublished writers each year. Buys 8-16 scripts/year. All scripts produced are unagented submissions. Buys all rights.

Needs: 50-frame; 15-minute scripts for video or sound filmstrips. Query only. Pays by outright purchase of $250-500/script.

Tips: "We are seeking generic, curriculum-oriented educational scripts suitable for interactive video disk development."

‡MIRIMAR ENTERPRISES, P.O. Box 4621, N. Hollywood CA 91617. (818)784-4177. CEO: Mirk Mirkin. Estab. 1967. "Audience is varied, sophisticated and intelligent." Buys 4-6 scripts/year. Buys all rights or first rights (in some cases). Accepts previously published material (in rare cases). Reports in 1 month on queries; 2 months on submissions.

Needs: Films (35mm), slides, tapes and cassettes, and videotapes. "We are seeking travel topics — particularly exotic, rarely visited places. 1st person, in-depth experiences, with some visuals to show them in situ." Query with synopsis and resume. Pays in accordance with Writers Guild standards.

Tips: "Be honest in your approach. Don't be over-flowery in language unless you can back it up. Writers should express themselves in a down-to-earth manner. Not raw or crude, but in graphic terms that are real."

‡MOTIVATION MEDIA, INC., 1245 Milwaukee Ave., Glenview IL 60025. (708)297-4740. FAX: (708)297-6829. Creative Director: Ken Lewis. Produces customized meeting, training and marketing material for presentation to salespeople, customers, corporate/industrial employees and distributors. 90% freelance written. Buys 100 scripts/year from unpublished/unproduced writers. Prefers to work with published/established writers. All scripts produced are unagented submissions. Buys all rights. Reports in 1 month.

Needs: Material for all audiovisual media — particularly marketing-oriented (sales training, sales promotional, sales motivational) material. Produces 16mm films, multimedia sales meeting programs, videotapes, cassettes and slide sets. Software should be AV oriented. Query with samples. Pays $150-5,000. Pays the expenses of writers on assignment.

OMNI COMMUNICATIONS, Suite 103, 655 W. Carmel Drive, P.O. Box 302, Carmel IN 46032. (317)844-6664. Vice President: Dr. Sandra M. Long. Estab. 1976. Produces commercial, training, educational and documentary material. Buys all rights. No previously produced material.

Needs: "Educational, documentary, commercial, training, motivational." Produces slides, shows and multi-image shows and videotapes. Query. Makes outright purchase.

Tips: "Must have experience as writer and have examples of work. Examples need to include print copy and finished copy of videotape if possible. A résumé with educational background, general work experience and experience as a writer must be included. Especially interested in documentary-style writing. Writers' payment varies, depending on amount of research needed, complexity of project, length of production and other factors."

OUR SUNDAY VISITOR, INC., Religious Education Dept., 200 Noll Plaza, Huntington IN 46750. (219)356-8400. Estab. 1913. Produces print and video material for students (pre-K through 12th grade), adult religious education groups and teacher trainees. "We are very concerned that the materials we produce meet the needs of today's church." Free catalog.

Needs: "Proposals for projects should be no more than 2 pages in length, in outline form. Programs should display up-to-date techniques and cohesiveness. Broadly speaking, material should deal with religious education, including liturgy and daily Christian living, as well as structured catechesis. It must not conflict with sound Catholic doctrine and should reflect modern trends in education." Produces educational books, charts and videos. "Work-for-hire and royalty arrangements possible."

‡PALARDO PRODUCTIONS, Suite 4, 1807 Taft Ave., Hollywood CA 90028. (213)469-8991. Director: Paul Ardolino. Estab. 1971. Produces material for youth ages 13-35. Buys 3-4 scripts/year. Buys all rights. Reports in 2 weeks on queries; 1 month on mss.

Needs: Multimedia kits, tapes and cassettes, videotapes. "We are seeking ideas relating to virtual reality, comedy scripts involving technology and coming of age; rock'n'roll bios." Submit synopsis/outline and resume. Pays in accordance with Writers Guild standards.

Tips: "Do not send a complete script—only synopsis of 4 pages or less *first.*"

PC ADVISOR, Mosaic Media Inc., Suite 200, 999 Main St., Glen Ellyn IL 60137. FAX: (708)790-1196. Publisher: F. Lee McFadden. Contact: Al Henderson, Managing Editor. Estab. 1977. Published monthly in a 90-minute audiocassette format for PC users and those who supervise PC users in an office environment. Subscribers have varying degrees of technical expertise and interest. Buys all rights. Electronic submissions preferred. Query first.

Needs: 4- to 8-minute scripts on hardware, software, systems and training. Most scripts are distillations of existing print materials, but we will consider original materials from writers with name recognition in the PC field.

Tips: "We prefer to work with writers who are accustomed to writing for a non-technical, business audience. Experience in writing for the ear rather than the eye is preferred. Technical expertise and name recognition are an asset."

PHOTO COMMUNICATION SERVICES, INC., 6410 Knapp NE, Ada MI 49301. (616)676-1499 or (616)676-2429. President: Lynn Jackson. Produces commercial, industrial, sales, training material etc. 95% freelance written. No scripts from unpublished/unproduced writers. 100% of scripts produced are unagented submissions. Buys all rights and first serial rights. Query for electronic submissions. Reports in 1 month.

Needs: Multimedia kits, slides, tapes and cassettes, and video presentations. Primarily interested in 35mm multimedia and video. Query with samples or submit completed script and résumé. Pays in outright purchase or by agreement.

PREMIER VIDEO FILM & RECORDING CORP., 3033 Locust, St. Louis MO 63103. (314)531-3555. Secretary/Treasurer: Grace Dalzell. Estab. 1931. Produces material for the corporate community, religious organizations, political arms, and hospital and educational groups. 100% freelance written. Prefers to work with published/established writers. Buys 50-100 scripts/year. All scripts are unagented submissions. Buys all rights; "very occasionally the writer retains rights." Previously produced material OK; "depends upon original purposes and markets." Reports "within a month or as soon as possible."

Needs: "Our work is all custom produced with the needs being known only as required." 35mm film loops, super 8mm and 35mm films, silent and sound filmstrips, multimedia kits, overhead transparencies, phonograph records, slides, and tapes and cassettes. Produces TV, training and educational scripts for video. Submit complete script and resume. Pays in accordance with Writers Guild standards or by outright purchase of $100 or "any appropriate sum." Sometimes pays the expenses of writers on assignment.

Tips: "Always place without fail *occupational pursuit,* name, address and phone number in upper right hand corner of resume. We're looking for writers with creativity, good background and a presentable image."

BILL RASE PRODUCTIONS, INC., 955 Venture Ct., Sacramento CA 95825. (916)929-9181. FAX: (916)929-4751. President: Bill Rase. Produces material for business education and mass audience. Buys about 20 scripts/year. Buys all rights. Reports "when an assignment is available."

Needs: Produces multimedia, slides, cassettes and video productions. Submit resume and sample page or two of script, and description of expertise. Pays negotiable rate in 30 days.

Tips: "Call and ask for Bill Rase personally. Must be within 100 miles and thoroughly professional."

RHYTHMS PRODUCTIONS, P.O. Box 34485, Los Angeles CA 90034. President: Ruth White. Estab. 1955. Produces children's musically oriented educational cassettes/books. Buys all rights. Previously published material OK "if it is suitable for our market and is not now currently on the market. We look for tapes that have been produced and are ready for publication." Reports on mss in 2 months. Catalog for 9×12 SAE and 3 first class stamps.

Needs: Phonograph records and tapes and cassettes. "Looking for children's stories or ideas with musical treatments. Must have educational content or values and must be ready for publication (complete with musical treatments as per above)." Query with samples. Payment is negotiable.

Tips: "SASE required for return of materials."

ALWAYS submit unsolicited manuscripts or queries with a self-addressed, stamped envelope (SASE) within your country or a self-addressed envelope with International Reply Coupons (IRC) purchased from the post office for other countries.

SPENCER PRODUCTIONS, INC., 234 5th Ave., New York NY 10001. (212)697-5895. General Manager: Bruce Spencer. Executive Producer: Alan Abel. Produces material for high school students, college students and adults. Occasionally uses freelance writers with considerable talent.
Needs: 16mm films, prerecorded tapes and cassettes. Satirical material only. Query. Pay is negotiable.

TALCO PRODUCTIONS, 279 E. 44th St., New York NY 10017. (212)697-4015. President: Alan Lawrence. Vice President: Marty Holberton. Produces variety of material for TV, radio, business, trade associations, nonprofit organizations, etc. Audiences range from young children to senior citizens. 20-40% freelance written. Buys scripts from published/produced writers only. All scripts produced are unagented submissions. Buys all rights. No previously published material. Reports in 3 weeks on queries. *Does not accept unsolicited mss.*
Needs: Films (16-35mm), slides, radio tapes and cassettes and videotape. "We maintain a file of writers and call on those with experience in the same general category as the project in production. We do not accept unsolicited manuscripts. We prefer to receive a writer's resume listing credits. If his/her background merits, we will be in touch when a project seems right." Makes outright purchase/project and in accordance with Writers Guild standards (when appropriate). Sometimes pays the expenses of writers on assignment.
Tips: "Concentration is now in TV productions. Production budgets will be tighter. *Productions will be of shorter length to save money.*"

TEL-AIR INTERESTS, INC., 1755 N.E. 149th St., Miami FL 33181. (305)944-3268. President: Grant H. Gravitt. Produces material for groups and theatrical and TV audiences. Buys all rights. Submit resume.
Needs: Documentary films on education, travel and sports. Produces films and videotape. Pays by outright purchase.

‡TRANSTAR PRODUCTIONS, INC., Suite C, 9520 E. Jewell Ave., Denver CO 80231. (303)695-4207. Producer/Director: Doug Hanes. Produces primarily industrial material. 10% freelance written. Buys 1-2 scripts/year from unpublished/unproduced writers. 100% of scripts are unagented submissions. Buys all rights. No previously produced material. Computer printout submissions acceptable; prefers letter-quality. Reporting time varies.
Needs: 16mm films, slides, tapes and cassettes, and videotape presentations. Also produces scripts for industrial sales and training. Submit resume. Pays negotiable rate.

‡TRI VIDEO TELEPRODUCTION—Lake Tahoe, P.O. Box 8822, Incline Village NV 89450-8822. (702)323-6868. Production Manager: Beth Davidson. Produces material primarily for corporate targets (their sales, marketing and training clients). Works with 1-2 writers each year developing contracted material. Could work with more, and could produce more programs if the right material were available. Buys all rights or negotiable rights. No previously produced material. Does not return material unless requested.
Needs: "Will have a need for writing contract projects; would consider other projects which are either sold to a client and need a producer, or which the writer wishes to sell and have produced. In all cases, corporate sales, marketing and training materials in the fields of health and the environment." Produces videtapes only. Query. Makes outright purchase in accordance with Writers Guild standards.
Tips: "We are strong on production skill; weak on sales, so if your idea needs to be sold to an end user before it is produced, we may not be the right avenue. However, give us a try. We might be able to put the right people together." Looks for "creativity, of course, but solid understanding of the buying market. We don't go in for highly symbolic and abstract materials."

TROLL ASSOCIATES, 100 Corporate Dr., Mahwah NJ 07430. (201)529-4000. Contact: M. Schecter. Produces material for elementary and high school students. Buys approximately 200 scripts/year. Buys all rights. Reports in 3 weeks. Free catalog.
Needs: Produces multimedia kits, tapes and cassettes, and (mainly) books. Query or submit outline/synopsis. Pays royalty or by outright purchase.

‡UNIVERSITY OF WISCONSIN-STOUT TELEPRODUCTION CENTER, 820 S. Broadway, Menomonie WI 54751. (715)232-2624. Center Director: Rosemary Jacobson. Produces instructional TV programs for primary, secondary, post secondary and specialized audiences. 10% freelance written. All scripts produced are unagented submissions. "We produce instructional TV programs for national, regional and state distribution to classrooms around the U.S. and Canada." Buys all rights. Computer printout submissions acceptable; prefers letter-quality.
Needs: "Our clients fund programs in a 'series' format which tend to be 8-12 programs each." Produces with 1" and BETACAM broadcast quality. "We have a need for writers in Wisconsin and Minnesota whom we can call on to write single or multi-program/series in instructional television." Query with resume and samples of TV scripts. Sometimes pays the expenses of writers on assignment.

Tips: "Freelance writers should be aware of the hardware advances in broadcast and nonbroadcast. There are new avenues for writers to pursue in adult learning, computer-assisted programming and interactive programming. Our focus is moving from K-12 to post-secondary and adult education."

VISUAL HORIZONS, 180 Metro Park, Rochester NY 14623. (716)424-5300. FAX: (716)424-5313. President: Stanley Feingold. Produces material for general audiences. Buys 5 programs/year. Reports in 5 months. Free catalog, 48 pages.
Needs: Business, medical and general subjects. Produces silent and sound filmstrips, multimedia kits, slide sets and videotapes. Query with samples. Payment negotiable.

Playwriting

There is probably no more exhilarating—or humbling—experience than seeing your words and story brought to life before an audience, within the intimate confines of a local theater. To hear the people laugh right where you expected them to, cry when you hoped they would and applaud just the way they did in your dreams—well, that's magic. On the other hand, nothing sounds quite so empty as what you thought were your best lines when they echo around a silent, unresponsive audience. It's the fastest, and sometimes the most painful, way to learn that what worked on the page doesn't always work on the stage.

Writers love the theater, though, hailing it as the last bastion of respect for their craft. Traditionally, the theater is the one place where the writer still has the final say, where script changes are not arbitrarily made, but are done in consultation with the playwright. That's not the case in writing for movies, and is pretty much unheard of in television writing.

In some ways, writing for the stage can be very liberating, in that there is a great deal of room for experimentation and storytelling innovation. On the other hand, the playwright labors under some very definite restrictions, all of which are usually related to budget.

For example, the beginning playwright, who will probably be seeking to get his or her work produced at a small, local theater, must keep a tight rein on the size of the cast required by the script, the number of set changes, the amount of physical space necessary, the complexity of action, the amount and types of props and any special effects such as weather or fire. Local theaters generally operate with a repertory cast and severe budget constraints, so the simpler the production values of your script, the better chance you have of getting it produced.

There is one exception: in writing plays for children, particularly plays that will be used by schools, it's desirable to call for a large number of characters in order to involve as many kids as possible. However, the main action and dialogue should be carried by a few core characters, so small schools can still mount a production.

Plays can be of varying lengths. One-act plays will generally run no more than an hour; full-length plays about two hours, with one or two intermissions. There seems to be more demand for full-length plays, although many times local theaters will present a group of related one-acts instead.

To learn more about the restrictions of stage plays, try to become active in production. Work the lights, get on the stage crew, whatever—it will serve to strengthen your writing. In fact, many writers find that doing a turn on stage as an actor is very beneficial (though sometimes terrifying), helping them hone their dialogue skills and discover how to "direct" the action on the page.

The aspiring playwright must become a produced playwright through his or her own efforts; agents for playwrights only handle proven (meaning successfully produced) talent. Therefore, it's up to you to contact the artistic directors at the theaters and ask if they're willing to look at new material. They may be able to offer some tips on what they'll be looking for in the future or steer you to other theaters that might be open to your project.

Turnover of artistic directors is high, so keep up with the business through such trade publications as the newsletter published by The Dramatists Guild, 234 W. 44th St., New York NY 10036.

For more playwriting markets, see Other Scriptwriting Markets at the end of the Screenwriting section.

A.D. PLAYERS, 2710 W. Alabama, Houston TX 77098. (713)526-2721. Artistic Director: Jeannette Clift George. Estab. 1967. Produces 4-6 plays/year. "These are professional productions that are performed either in our mainstage season or on tour. On tour the performance arenas vary. The full-length road show productions are performed in civic auditoriums, theaters, opera houses. The one-act and revue shows are performed in various settings; churches. Our audiences are primarily family-oriented, a majority come from a church affiliation." Query and synopsis or submit complete ms. Please send materials to Ragan Courtney, Dramaturge. Reports in 6 weeks. Pays per performance.
Needs: "We produce one-act and full-length plays, any style. As a professional Christian repertory company, we produce shows that express a Christian world view, i.e. God's reality in everyday life. This can range from Biblical to contemporary to anything in between. We produce two children's shows a season and do a lot of touring performances for high school age groups. We are looking for plays that have no more than 14 characters. We have the limitation of a proscenium stage with no fly space."
Tips: "Because of our specific signature as a Christian repertory company we would not be interested in plays that have no reference to the reality of God or man's search for spiritual significance in his world."

ACTORS THEATRE OF LOUISVILLE, 316 W. Main St., Louisville KY 40202. (502)584-1265. Producing Director: Jon Jory. Estab. 1964. Produces approximately 30 new plays of varying lengths/year. Professional productions are performed for subscription audience from diverse backgrounds. Agented submissions only for full-length plays; open submissions to National Ten-Minute Play Contest. Reports in 6-9 months on submissions. Buys variable rights. Offers variable royalty.
Needs: "We are interested in full-length, one-act and ten-minute plays. They should address contemporary issues."

‡ALBUNDEGUS ALL-STARS, 709 13th St., Greeley CO 80631. Artistic Director: Michael Baczuk. Estab. 1989. Produces 4-6 plays/year. "We are a nonprofit theater group formed for the purpose of developing new and original works by Colorado playwrights. Performances are in Greeley and sometimes tour around Colorado." Submit complete ms with synopsis. Reports in 2 months. Buys exclusive rights in Colorado area for 6 months; rights revert to author after this period. Writer, actors and technicians divide 50-70% of gross ticket sales.
Needs: "We're not concerned about genre, style or topic so long as it's well written. Prefer play length no longer than 2 hours. Case size of no more than 7. Try to keep the set and props simple."
Tips: "We want to see plays by Colorado playwrights *only* at this time."

ALLEY THEATRE, 615 Texas Ave., Houston TX 77002. Literary Director: Christopher Baker. A resident professional theatre: large stage seating 824; arena stage seating 296.
Needs: Plays and musicals (synopsis and cassette); plays for young audiences; adaptations and translations. Makes variable royalty arrangements. No unsolicited scripts accepted. Send description/synopsis and letter of inquiry. Reports in 6 months. Produces 6-8 plays/year.

‡AMELIA MAGAZINE, 329 "E" St., Bakersfield CA 93304. (805)323-4064. Editor: Frederick A. Raborg, Jr. Estab. 1983. Publishes 1 play/year. Submit complete ms. Reports in 2 months. Buys first North American serial rights only. Pays $150 plus publication as winner of annual Frank McClure One-act Play Award.
Needs: "Plays with virtually any theme or concept. We look for excellence within the one-act, 45 minutes running time format. We welcome the avant garde and experimental. We do not object to the erotic, though not pornographic. Fewer plays are being produced on Broadway, but the regionals seem to be picking up the slack. That means fewer equity stages and more equity waivers."

‡THE AMERICAN PLACE THEATRE, 111 W. 46th St., New York NY 10036. (212)840-2960. Artistic Director: Wynn Handman. Estab. 1963. Produces 6 plays/year in New York City off-Broadway. Send query and synopsis. Reports in 3 months.
Needs: Full-length plays or performance pieces by American writers, especially minorities. "Small cases (fewer than 8) and minimal set requirements are desirable."
Tips: "No musicals, no conventional 'well-made' plays. Material should cut deeply into American life."

AMERICAN STAGE, 211 3rd St. So., P.O. Box 1560, St. Petersburg FL 33731. (813)823-1600. Artistic Director: Victoria Holloway. Estab. 1978. Produces 5 plays/year. Plays performed on "our mainstage, in the park (Shakespeare) or on tour in schools." Submit query and synopsis. Reports in 4 months. Payment varies.
Needs: New American plays for small cast. No musicals.

‡AMERICAN STAGE FESTIVAL, P.O. Box 225, Milford NH 03055. Producing Director: Richard Rose. Estab. 1975. "The ASF is a central New England professional theater (professional equity company) with a 3-month summer season (June-August)" for audience of all ages, interests, education and sophistication levels. Query with synopsis. Produces musicals (20%) and nonmusicals (80%). 5 are mainstage and 10 are children's productions; 40% are originals. Royalty option and subsequent amount of gross: optional. Reports in 3 months.
Needs: "The Festival can do comedies, musicals and dramas. However, the most frequent problems are bolder language and action than a general mixed audience will accept. Prefer not to produce plays with strictly urban themes. We have a 40-foot proscenium stage with 30-foot wings, but no fly system. Festival plays are chosen to present scale and opportunities for scenic and costume projects far beyond the 'summer theater' type of play." Length: mainstage: 2-3 acts; children's productions: 50 minutes.
Recent Productions: *Woody Guthrie's American Song*, adapted by Peter Slazer, and *Starmites*, music & lyric by Barry Keating, book by Stuart Ross & Barry Keating.
Tips: Writers could improve submissions with "dramatic action, complexity, subplot and a unique statement. Try to get a staged reading of the script before submitting the play to us. Our audiences prefer plays that deal with human problems presented in a conventional manner."

AN CLAIDHEAMH SOLUIS/CELTIC ARTS CENTER, 5651 Hollywood Blvd., Hollywood CA 90028. (213)462-6844. Artistic Director: S. Walsh. Estab. 1985. Produces 6 plays/year. Equity waiver. Query and synopsis. Reports in 6 weeks. Rights acquired vary. Pays $25-50.
Needs: Scripts of Celtic interest (Scottish, Welsh, Irish, Cornish, Manx, Breton). "This can apply to writer's background or subject matter. We are particularly concerned with works that relate to the survival of cultures and traditions."

THE ARKANSAS ARTS CENTER CHILDREN'S THEATRE, P.O. Box 2137, MacArthur Park, Little Rock AR 72203. (501)372-4000. Artistic Director: Bradley Anderson. Produces 6 mainstage plays, 3 tours/year. Mainstage season plays performed at The Arkansas Arts Center for Little Rock and surrounding area; tour season by professional actors throughout Arkansas and surrounding states. Mainstage productions perform to family audiences in public performances; weekday performances for local schools in grades kindergarten through senior high school. Tour audiences generally the same. Accepts unsolicited scripts. Prefers synopsis and letter of inquiry. Reports in several months. Buys negotiable rights. Pays $250-1,500 or negotiable commission.
Needs: Original adaptations of classic and contemporary works. Also original scripts. "This theater is defined as a children's theater; this can inspire certain assumptions about the nature of the work. We would be pleased if submissions did not presume to condescend to a particular audience. We are not interested in 'cute' scripts. Submissions should simply strive to be good theater literature."
Tips: "We would welcome scripts open to imaginative production and interpretation. Also, scripts that are mindful that this children's theater casts adults as adults and children as children. Scripts that are not afraid of contemporary issues are welcome."

‡ARKANSAS REPERTORY THEATRE, P.O. Box 110, Little Rock AR 72203-0110. (501)378-0445. Artistic Director: Cliff Fannin Baker. Estab. 1976. Produces 8 full productions, 4 staged readings, 1 educational tour, 1 workshop. "Professional productions, with optional transfers for a subscriber base, plus individuals in the state and community. One MainStage show tours the region and our educational tour travels the state." Send query and synopsis. Reports in up to 3 months. Rights purchased vary. Pays royalty or per performance; "this also varies per show."
Needs: "We are open to all styles, all genres, and full lengths." Casts under 10 (except musicals).

ARROW ROCK LYCEUM, Main St., Arrow Rock MO 65320. (816)837-3311. Artistic Director: Michael Bollinger. Produces 8 plays/year. "Lyceum has two main projects: a 31-year-old summer season, performing seven plays in repertory in the historic village of Arrow Rock and a Holiday Festival Production, based in a much larger house in Columbia, Missouri. The Lyceum is a regional repertory theater and employs professional actors." Query and synopsis throughout year, or (submit complete ms with synopsis and résumé for contest subs). Also sponsors the National Playwrights Contest. "Lyceum and original artistic staff to get future credit, and Lyceum to retain 5% of author's gross commissions for first 5 years only. Lyceum either commissions w/separate deals, or simply pays a flat fee to National Playwrights Contest winners, which also receive full-scale world premiere."

Needs: The repertory season includes seven diverse plays, including musicals, classic, comedy, drama, world premiere. Generally each season will feature one world premiere, contest winner or a commissioned work. "I would suggest plays with casts not exceeding 12, and one set, or rather open space with various locales."

Tips: "Who knows—if it works, anything can go! However, keeping budgets in mind, etc., works that have a bit of flexibility are best—could be produced with all 20 characters, or could be produced with six actors doubling supporting roles. Also, keep in mind set. Generally two or three realistic sets in one play could hinder original chances; one set or open staging could help. I do feel it is important for professional theaters to be 'theatrical creators' as well as mere 'consumers'!"

‡ART EXTENSIONS THEATRE, 11144 Weddington, N. Hollywood CA 91601. (818)760-8675. Artistic Director: Maureen Kennedy Samuels. Estab. 1989. Produces 2 plays/year. Equity waiver productions for general audiences. Query and synopsis or submit complete ms. Reports in 3 weeks. Buys rights to produce play for 6-week run. Pays 2-10% royalty.

Needs: One acts, full-length plays and musicals: Comedy or drama particularly interested in plays with strong female characters, plays for children, plays with dance. Staging should be one set and as simple as possible.

Tips: "We are looking for positive themes presented beautifully and in good taste. In most of the plays I have seen so far there are too many vulgar words and negative themes. Also, I have not seen an ear for dialogue in many submissions."

ARTREACH TOURING THEATRE, 3074 Madison Rd., Cincinnati OH 45209. (513)871-2300. Director: Kathryn Schultz Miller. Produces 6 plays/year to be performed nationally in theaters and schools. "We are a professional company. Our audience is primarily young people in schools and their families." Submit complete ms. Reports in 6 weeks. Buys exclusive right to produce for 9 months. Pays $10/show (approximately 1,000 total performances through the year).

Needs: Plays for children and adolescents. Serious, intelligent plays about contemporary life or history/legend. "Limited sets and props. Can use scripts with only 3 actors; 45 minutes long. Should be appropriate for touring." No clichéd approaches, camp or musicals.

Tips: "We look for opportunities to create innovative stage effects using few props, and we like scripts with good acting opportunities."

BAILIWICK REPERTORY, 3212 N. Broadway, Chicago IL 60657-3515. (312)883-1091. Artistic Director: David Zak. Estab. 1982. Produces: 5 mainstage plays (classic and newly comissioned) each year (submit by Nov. 1); 5 new full-length in New Directions series; 50 1-act in annual Directors Festival (submit by Dec. 1); gay and lesbian festival (community outreach program); includes full-length, one-act, poetry, workshops, and staged adaptations of prose. Submit by Jan. 1. Our audience is a typical Chicago market. Our plays are highly theatrical and politically aware. Submit complete ms. One acts should be submitted *before* Dec. 1. (One-act play fest runs March-April). Reports in 3 months. Pays 8% royalty.

Needs: We need daring scripts that break the mold. Large cast or musicals are OK. Creative staging solutions are a must.

Tips: "Know the rules, then break them creatively and *boldly*! Please send SASE for Manuscript Submission Guidelines before you submit."

BAKER'S PLAY PUBLISHING CO., 100 Chauncy St., Boston MA 02111. FAX: (617)482-7613. Editor: John B. Welch. Estab. 1845. 80% freelance written. Plays performed by amateur groups, high schools, children's theater, churches and community theater groups. "We are the largest publisher of chancel drama in the world." 90% of scripts are unagented submissions. Works with 2-3 unpublished/unproduced writers annually. Submit complete script. Submit complete cassette of music with musical submissions. Publishes 18-25 straight plays and musicals; all originals. Pay varies; outright purchase price to split in production fees. Reports in 4 months.

Needs: "We are finding strong support in our new division—plays for young adults featuring contemporary issue-oriented dramatic pieces for high school production."

‡MARY BALDWIN COLLEGE THEATRE, Mary Baldwin College, Staunton VA 24401. (703)887-7192. Artistic Director: Terry K. Southerington. Produces 5 plays/year. 10% freelance written. 75% of scripts are unagented. Works with 0-1 unpublished/unproduced writer annually. An undergraduate women's college theater with an audience of students, faculty, staff and local community (adult, conservative). Query with synopsis. Query for electronic submissions. Reports in 6 months. Buys performance rights only. Pays $10-50/performance.

Needs: Full-length and short comedies, tragedies, musical plays, particularly for young women actresses, dealing with women's issues both contemporary and historical. Experimental/studio theater not suitable for heavy sets. Cast should emphasize women. No heavy sex; minimal explicit language.

Close-up

Thom Atkinson
Playwright

Although he's been writing for more than a decade, Thom Atkinson is fairly new to playwriting. Before his first play, *Clear Liquor and Coal Black Nights*, was produced in 1986, he'd already had several short stories and some poetry published. Making the transition from fiction to playwriting was not hard to make, he says. In fact, while he continues to write fiction, he feels playwriting better suits his style.

"One reason playwriting comes fairly naturally to me is because the strength of my fiction has always been dialogue and images—the two most important elements of a play."

In a novel or short story, he says, you have the luxury of being able to look into a character's head, but in a play—as in real life—the only way you know what a person is thinking is by what they say and what they do.

"Don't forget the doing. Many beginning playwrights, and even some experienced ones, make the mistake of thinking all they have to work with in a play are words. They tend to forget deeds speak louder than words," Atkinson says. "If you've done a good job with a scene, the audience will stick with you when people stop talking. I've learned not to fear quiet time. In a way, I try to earn it."

Playwrights also worry about how much direction to include in a play and what to leave to a director's discretion. Although there's a great deal of give and take on this subject and he's heard of directors who ignore all but the dialogue, Atkinson writes in as much direction as possible.

Keeping track of the action is a difficult part of the playwriting process, he admits. "One thing I do even before I start to write is make a detailed diagram of my ideal set. It's not only important to me in terms of keeping track of the visual images and action, but the diagram helps me establish a place in my mind. It helps me get back into the work each day—like looking at a snapshot."

After he's written a first draft, Atkinson invites local actors to read through the work for him. That way he can see what works and what needs to be changed before the final draft. "To me the writing is only half of the process. You really have to see a play to know if everything works."

Building a relationship with actors in your area and with your community theater group is very important for any playwright. When looking for markets for your work, community theater provides an excellent opportunity for new playwrights and new works. "Not only are the financial risks low, but they're always looking for a chance to do something that has not been performed hundreds of times before."

The hardest part about marketing your plays, he says, is the waiting. "Even when things are going well it can be two years between productions." In the meantime, he advises writers to keep busy by starting on the next project. Atkinson is working on a third play while his second is making the rounds. Although he now considers himself a playwright, he continues to explore other genres. In fact, he's also working on a novel. Working in other genres has taught him a lot about playwriting, he says. Most importantly, he says, "I've learned to appreciate what each form does best."

—Robin Gee

Tips: "A perfect play for us has several roles for young women, few male roles, minimal production demands, a concentration on issues relevant to contemporary society, and elegant writing and structure."

BARTER THEATRE, P.O. Box 867, Abingdon VA 24210. (703)628-2281. Artistic Director: Rex Partington. Estab. 1933. Produces 10 plays/year. Play performed in residency at our two facilities, a 400-seat proscenium theater and a smaller 150-seat thrust theater. "Our plays are intended for diversified audiences of all ages." Submit complete ms. Reports in 6 months. Pays 4-7% royalty.
Needs: "We are looking for good plays, comedies and dramas, that entertain and are relevant; plays that comment on the times and mankind; plays that are universal. We prefer casts of 4-12, single or unit set."
Tips: "No silly, obscene or totally irrelevant material, lacking in wit or humor. Writers should be mindful of, and avoid a lack of the use of good understandable language and a tendency to resort to grunts and incomplete phrases."

BERKSHIRE PUBLIC THEATRE, 30 Union St., P.O. Box 860, Pittsfield MA 01202. (413)445-4631. Artistic Director: Frank Bessell. Literary Manager: Linda Austin. Estab. 1976. Produces 10 plays/year. Year-round regional theater. Professional, non-Equity. Special Interests: Contemporary issues; works dealing with ethics and morality; global concerns. Query and synopsis or submit complete ms. Reports in 3 months. Various payment arrangements.

BERKSHIRE THEATRE FESTIVAL, INC., E. Main St., Stockbridge MA 01262. Artistic Director: Richard Dunlap. 25% original scripts. Produces 7-8 plays a year (4 are mainstage and 4 are second spaces). Submissions by agents only.

‡BILINGUAL FOUNDATION OF THE ARTS, 421 N. Ave., #19, Los Angeles CA 90031. (213)225-4044. Artistic Director: Margarita Galban. Estab. 1973. Produces 3-5 plays/year. "Productions are presented at home theater in Los Angeles, California. Our audiences are largely Hispanic and all productions are performed in English and Spanish. The Bilingual Foundation of the Arts produces plays in order to promote the rich heritage of Hispanic history and culture. Though our plays must be Hispanic in theme, we reach out to the entire community." Submit complete ms. Reports in 2 months. Rights negotiable. Pays royalty.
Needs: "Plays must be Hispanic in theme. We do not produce extreme violence or outrageous sexual work. Comedy, drama, light musical, children's theater, etc. are accepted for consideration. Theater is 99-seater, no flies."

BOARSHEAD THEATER, 425 S. Grand Ave., Lansing MI 48933. (517)484-7800. Artistic Director: John Peakes. Estab. 1966. Produces 7-9 plays/year. Mainstage Actors' Equity Association company; also Youth Theater—touring to schools by our intern company. Query, synopsis, cast list (with descriptions), 5-10 pages of representative dialogue, SASE postcard. "Reports on query and synopsis in 1 week. Full manuscripts (when requested by us) in 4-8 months." Pays royalty.
Needs: Thrust stage. Cast usually 8 or less; ocassionally up to 12-14. Prefer staging which depends on theatricality rather than multiple sets.

BOSTON POST ROAD STAGE COMPANY, 25 Powers Ct., Westport CT 06880. (203)227-1290. FAX: (203)222-9027. Artistic Director: Douglas Moser. Literary Manager: Burry Fredrik. Produces 6 plays/year. "LOA (Equity) theater playing to audiences in Fairfield County. Audiences are adult, seniors and interested students." Submit complete ms. Reports in 6 months. Right to produce a 4-week run of the play with an option for several months following conclusion of run to explore further production possibilities. Pays 4-5% royalty.
Needs: Off-Broadway in Connecticut. Emphasis on originality of script. We will take risks if the play is good. We produce a wide range of plays, comedy, drama, musical (small). Budgetary considerations are our limitations. Maximum seven characters; we prefer fewer, however. We are eligible for grants to develop new plays if something were to strike us which was more expensive than our budget would allow.
Tips: "We're tired of NYC apartment tirades and moot-point 'true' biographies. No obviously large cast or panoramic history plays. The dramatic structure of a play must stimulate an audience. Foul language acceptable only when inherent to the dramatic situation; no headline plays that cannot transcend the ordinary details of everyday life. Even a 'slice-of-life' play must inform us about life, not just illustrate it. Energy, guts, vision and the ability to pull it all together. Those are the well written, stimulating playwrights and plays which will get the most of our attention."

BRISTOL RIVERSIDE THEATRE, P.O. Box 1250, Bristol PA 19007. (215)785-6664. Producing Artistic Director: Susan D. Atkinson. Estab. 1986. Produces 5 mainstage, 3 workshops, and 15 readings plus children's theater/year. "We are a professional regional theater company; we produce new works exclusively in our workshop and reading series. The intention is to develop the works for mainstage productions. Our audience is drawn from Bucks County, Philadelphia, Trenton, Princeton and surrounding New Jersey areas. We also plan a two-show, popular, summer program." Submit complete ms. Reports in 10 months. "Since we are a developmental company and spend a great deal of time on each work selected for reading and/or workshop, we request a percentage of author's revenues for a given period of time and recognition of the theater and key individuals on subsequent productions, after the reading phase of the development is completed." Offers variable royalty.

Needs: "We produce all types from dramas, comedies to musicals and operas. We also produce one-acts. We would prefer smaller shows with limited costs, but we have never shied away from larger shows. The quality, not the quantity, is the determining factor in all cases."

Tips: "We are not interested in plays that have as their only goal entertainment. We would hope all works would have this quality, but if there is no other value sought, we would not be interested. We are a company in search of the new mainstream of theater in America. We aim to entertain, enlighten and elevate our audience. We have a holiday show for special events. And we are seeking authors who are interested in developing their works, not just presenting them; we view theater as a process."

CALIFORNIA THEATER CENTER, P.O. Box 2007, Sunnyvale CA 94110. (408)245-2978. Literary Manager: Will Huddleston. Produces 15 plays/year. Plays are for young audiences in both our home theater and for tour. Query and synopsis. Reports in 3 months. We negotiate a set fee.

Needs: All plays must be suitable for young audiences, must be under one hour in length. Cast sizes vary. Sets must be able to tour easily.

‡CASA MANANA MUSICALS, INC., 3101 W. Lancaster, Fort Worth TX 76107. (817)332-9319. FAX: (817)332-5711. Executive Producer/General Manager: Van Kaplan. Administrative Director: Steven C. Peterson. "All performances are staged at Casa Manana Theatre and are community funded." Query. Produces 6 summer stock musicals (uses Equity people only), theater-in-the-round. Children's playhouse theater produces 8 children's shows in the winter season.

Needs: Scripts of all kinds; cassettes acceptable.

CENTER STAGE, 700 N. Calvert St., Baltimore MD 21202. (301)685-3200. Resident dramaturg: Mona Heinze. Produces 6-9 plays/year. "Professional LORT 'B' company; audience is both subscription and single-ticket. Wide-ranging audience profile." Query with synopsis and resumé or submit through agent. Reports in 3 months. Rights and payment negotiated.

Needs: Produces "dramas and comedies, occasional musicals. No restrictions on topics or styles, though experimental work is encouraged. Casts over 20 would give us pause. Be inventive, theatrical, not precious; we like plays with vigorous language and stage image. Domestic naturalism is discouraged; strong thematic, political, or social interests are encouraged."

Tips: "We are interested in reading adaptations and translations as well as original work."

THE CHANGING SCENE THEATER, 1527½ Champa St., Denver CO 80202. Director: Alfred Brooks. Year-round productions in theater space. Cast may be made up of both professional and amateur actors. For public audience; age varies, but mostly youthful and interested in taking a chance on new and/or experimental works. No limit to subject matter or story themes. Emphasis is on the innovative. "Also, we require that the playwright be present for at least one performance of his work, if not for the entire rehearsal period. We have a small stage area, but are able to convert to round, semi-round or environmental. Prefer to do plays with limited sets and props." One-act, two-act and three-act.

Needs: Produces 8-10 nonmusicals a year; all are originals. 90% freelance written. 65% of scripts produced are unagented submissions. Works with 3-4 unpublished/unproduced writers annually. "We do not pay royalties or sign contracts with playwrights. We function on a performance-share basis of payment. Our theater seats 76; the first 50 seats go to the theater; the balance is divided among the participants in the production. The performance-share process is based on the entire production run and not determined by individual performances. We do not copyright our plays." Send complete script. Reporting time varies; usually several months.

Recent Title: *Hyaena*, by Ross MacLean.

Tips: "We are experimental: open to young artists who want to test their talents and open to experienced artists who want to test new ideas/explore new techniques. Dare to write 'strange and wonderful' well-thought-out scripts. We want upbeat ones. Consider that we have a small performance area when submitting."

CHILDREN'S STORY SCRIPTS, Baymax Productions, Suite 130, 2219 W. Olive Ave., Burbank CA 91506. (818)563-6105. FAX: (818)563-2968. Editor: Deedra Bebout. Estab. 1990. Publishes 20-30 scripts/year. "Our audience consists of children, grades K-8 (5-13 year olds)." Send complete ms. Reports in 1 month. Licenses all rights to story; author retains copyright. Pays graduated royalty based on sales.

Needs: We will publish almost any topic. Stories with a purpose that can be discussed afterwards work well. Stories that dovetail with classroom studies also work well. Scripts blend narration and dialogue. They are not meant to be memorized. Cast is stationary, readers theater-style.

Tips: "The scripts are not like theatrical scripts. They read like prose. If a writer shows promise, we'll work with him or her. Our most important goal is to benefit children. Send business-sized SASE for guidelines with samples."

‡CINCINNATI PLAYHOUSE IN THE PARK, P.O. Box 6537, Cincinnati OH 45206. (513)421-5440. Contact: Artistic Director. Estab. 1960. Produces 2 original works, 8 or 9 previously produced plays. "Nonprofit LORT theater, producing in two spaces—a 629-seat thrust stage and a 220-seat three/sided arena. The audience is a broad cross-section of people from all over the Ohio, Kentucky and Indiana areas, from varied educational and financial bases." Agented submissions only. Unrepresented authors eligible for the Lois and Richard Rosenthal New Play Prize. Reports in 6 months. Pays royalty, $1,500 stipend and residency expenses for winner of Rosenthal competition.

CIRCUIT PLAYHOUSE/PLAYHOUSE ON THE SQUARE, 51 S. Cooper, Memphis TN 38104. (901)725-0776. Artistic Director: Jackie Nichols. Produces 16 plays/year. 100% freelance written. Professional plays performed for the Memphis/Mid-South area. Member of the Theatre Communications Group. 100% of scripts are unagented submissions. Works with 1 unpublished/unproduced writer annually. A play contest is held each fall. Submit complete ms. Reports in 3 months. Buys "percentage of royalty rights for 2 years." Pays $500.

Needs: All types; limited to single or unit sets. Cast of 20 or fewer.

Tips: "Each play is read by three readers through the extended length of time a script is kept. Preference is given to scripts for the southeastern region of the U.S."

‡CITIARTS THEATRE, 1950 Parkside Dr., Concord CA 94519. (415)671-3065. Contact: Richard Elliott. Estab. 1978. Produces 7 plays/year. Professional production during subscription season (Aug-June). Approximate audience of 5,500, San Francisco Bay Area. Submit complete ms with SASE and resumé. Reports in 2 months. "Obtains negotiable, various rights." Pays negotiable royalty.

Needs: "We need smaller (9 person or less) musicals (no revues), contemporary dramas dealing with urban issues and contemporary comedy—all styles. We have no flyspace, and prefer unit or platform sets, using 9 people or less."

Tips: "No gay revues. No dramatizations of Russian military figures. We'll read almost anything. We are seeking thoughtful, carefully composed works incorporating performance art, electronic media with strong narrative, blends of different styles. It's best to submit plays by November 1 for the folowing subscription season."

CITY THEATRE COMPANY, 315 S. Bellefield Ave., Pittsburgh PA 15260. Scott T. Cummings, Resident Dramaturg. Produces 4 full productions and 6 readings/year. "We are a small professional theater, operating under an Equity contract, and committed to twentieth-century American plays. Our seasons are innovative and challenging, both artistically and socially. We perform in a 117-seat thrust stage, playing usually 6 times a week, each production running 5 weeks or more. We have a committed audience following." Query and synopsis or submit through agent. Obtains no rights. Pays 5-6% royalty.

Needs: "No limits on style or subject, but we are most interested in theatrical plays that have something to say about the way we live. No light comedies or TV-issue dramas." Normal cast limit is 8. Plays must be appropriate for small space without flies.

Tips: "Our emphasis is on new and recent American plays. Our staged reading series of 6 plays a year looks for scripts that challenge the dramatic medium and that are asking for further development."

I.E. CLARK, INC., Saint John's Rd., P.O. Box 246, Schulenburg TX 78956. (409)743-3232. Estab. 1956. Publishes 15 plays/year for educational theater, children's theater, religious theater, regional professional theater and amateur community theater. 20% freelance written. 3-4 scripts published/year are unagented submissions. Works with 2-3 unpublished writers annually. Submit complete script—but only one script at a time. Manuscript will not be returned without a SASE. Reports in 6 months or more. Buys all available rights; "we serve as an agency as well as a publisher." Pays standard book and performance royalty, "the amount and percentages dependent upon type and marketability of play." Catalog for $1.50; writer's guidelines for #10 SASE.

Needs: "We are interested in plays of all types—short or long. Audiotapes of music or videotapes of a performance are requested with submissions of musicals. We require that a play have been produced (directed by someone other than the author); photos and reviews of the production are helpful. No limitations in cast, props, staging, etc. Plays with only one or two characters are difficult to sell. We insist on literary quality. We like plays that give new interpretations and understanding of human nature. Correct spelling, punctuation and grammar (befitting the characters, of course) impress our editors."

Tips: "Entertainment value and a sense of moral responsibility seem to be returning as essential qualities of a good play script. The era of glorifying the negative elements of society seems to be fading rapidly. Literary quality, entertainment value and good craftsmanship rank in that order as the characteristics of a good script in our opinion. 'Literary quality' means that the play must—in beautiful, distinctive, and un-trite language—say something; preferably something new and important concerning man's relations with his fellow man; and these 'lessons in living' must be presented in an intelligent, believable and creative manner. Plays for children's theater are tending more toward realism and childhood problems rather than fantasy or dramatization of fairy tales."

THE CLEVELAND PLAY HOUSE, 8500 Euclid Ave., Cleveland OH 44106. (216)795-7010. FAX: (216)795-7005. Artistic Director: Josephine Abady. Literary Manager: Roger T. Danforth. Produces 12 plays/year. Resident LORT theater. Audience: subscribers and single ticket buyers; three different theaters with different audience needs/requirements: 160-experimental, 499 and 615-mainstage subscription theaters. Agented submissions only. Reports in 6 months. Negotiated rights. Pay negotiable.

Needs: Full length; emphasis on American realism; all styles and topics given full consideration, however. Musicals also welcome.

Tips: "No translations of foreign works. No previously produced works that received national attention."

CONTEMPORARY DRAMA SERVICE, Meriwether Publishing Ltd., P.O. Box 7710, Colorado Springs CO 80933. (303)594-4422. FAX: (719)594-9916. Editor-in-Chief: Arthur Zapel. Estab. 1969. Publishes 50-60 plays/year. "We publish for the secondary school market and colleges. We also publish for mainline liturgical churches—drama activities for church holidays, youth activities and fundraising entertainments. These may be plays or drama-related books." Query with synopsis or submit complete ms. Reports in 5 weeks. Obtains either amateur or all rights. Pays 10% royalty or outright negotiated purchase.

Needs: "Most of the plays we publish are one-acts, 15 to 45 minutes in length. We occasionally publish full-length three-act plays. We prefer comedies in the longer plays. Musical plays must have name appeal either by prestige author, prestige title adaptation or performance on Broadway or TV. Comedy sketches, monologues and 2-character plays are welcomed. We prefer simple staging appropriate to high school, college or church performance. We like playwrights who see the world positively and with a sense of humor. Offbeat themes and treatments are accepted if the playwright can sustain a light touch and not take himself or herself too seriously. In documentary or religious plays we look for good research and authenticity. We will be publishing more textbooks on the theatrical arts than trade books."

‡THE COTERIE, 2450 Grand Ave., Kansas City MO 64108. (816)474-6785. Artistic Director: Jeff Church. Estab. 1979. Produces 7-8 plays/year. "Plays produced at Hallmark's Crown Center in downtown Kansas City in the Coterie's resident theater (capacity 240). A typical performance run is one month in length." Submit query and synopsis or complete ms only if an established playwright in youth theater field. Reports in 2-4 months. "We retain rights only on commissioned plays." Pays royalty, per performance and flat fee.

Needs: "We produce plays which are universal in appeal; they may be original or adaptations of classic or contemporary literature. Typically, not more than 12 in a cast—prefer 5-9 in size. No fly space or wing space."

Tips: "No couch plays. Prefer plays by seasoned writers who have established reputations. Groundbreaking and exciting scripts from the youth theater field welcome. It's prefectly fine if your play is a little off center." Trends in the field that writers should be mindful of: "Make certain your submitted play to us is *very* theatrical and not cinematic. Writers need to see how far the field of youth and family theater has come—the interesting new areas we're going—before sending us your query or manuscript."

‡CREATIVE PRODUCTIONS, INC., 2 Beaver Pl., Aberdeen NJ 07747. (908)566-6985. Artistic Director: Walter L. Born. Produce 4 musicals/year. Amateur, year-round productions. "We use plays/musicals with folks with disabilities and the older performers in addition to 'normal' performers, for the broad spectrum of viewers." Submit query and synopsis. Reports in 2 weeks. Buys rights to perform play for specified number of performances. Pays $75-150 per performance.

Needs: Plays/musicals about people with disabilities where they are actually used as performers; unusual subjects out of ordinary human experiences plus music. Limitations: Cast: maximum 12, sets can't "fly," facilities are schools, no mammoth sets and multiple scene changes.

Tips: No blue material; pornographic; obscene language. Submit info on any performances plus pix of set and actors in costume. Demo tape (musicals); list of references on users of their material to confirm bio info.

‡CREEDE REPERTORY THEATRE, P.O. Box 269, Creede CO 81130. (719)658-2541. Artistic Director: Richard Baxter. Estab. 1966. Produces 6 plays/year. Plays performed for a summer audience. Submit query and synopsis. Reports in 10 months. Pays 5% royalty.
Needs: One-act children's scripts; special consideration given to topics of Western history.
Tips: "No avant garde or experimental work. We seek new adaptations of classical or older works as well as original scripts."

DEEP ELLUM THEATRE GROUP/UNDERMAIN THEATRE, P.O. Box 141166, Dallas TX 75214. (214)748-3082. Artistic Directors: Raphael Parry and Katherine Owens. Estab. 1983. Produces 5 plays/year. Submit query and synopsis with dialogue sample. Reports in 1 month. Pays 6% royalty.
Needs: "We generally produce plays experimental or avant-garde in style. They are usually under 2 hours in length. We draw an intelligent audience with a wide age range, who seek to be challenged and provoked. We are also drawn to writing poetic or impressionist in style. We work with a resident acting company of 6. We are non-equity. Our stage setup is flexible, thrust proscenium etc. We seat approximately 80."
Tips: "No plays resembling family dramas, soap opera styles, television sit-com styles. The Undermain Company is small and young (under 40). We have great difficulty in casting older parts."

DELAWARE THEATRE COMPANY, P.O. Box 516, Wilmington DE 19899. (302)594-1104. Artistic Director: Cleveland Morris. Estab. 1978. Produces 5 plays/year. 10% freelance written. "Plays are performed as part of a five-play subscription season in a 300-seat auditorium. Professional actors, directors and designers are engaged. The season is intended for a general audience." 10% of scripts are unagented submissions. Works with 1 unpublished/unproduced writer every two years. Query with synopsis. Reports in 6 months. Buys variable rights. Pays 5% (variable) royalty.
Needs: "We present comedies, dramas, tragedies and musicals. All works must be full length and fit in with a season composed of standards and classics. All works have a strong literary element. Plays showing a flair for language and a strong involvement with the interests of classical humanism are of greatest interest. Single-set, small-cast works are likeliest for consideration." Recent trend toward "more economical productions."

DENVER CENTER THEATRE COMPANY, 1050 13th St., Denver CO 80204. (303)893-4200. FAX: (303)893-2860. Artistic Director: Donovan Marley. Estab. 1979. Produces 12 plays/year. "Denver Center Theater Company produces an annual New Plays Festival, entitled US West Theatre Fest. 8-10 new scripts are rehearsed and presented in staged readings. From this festival, 4 are selected for full production in the following DCTC Theatre season." Submit complete ms. Reports in 6 weeks. Theatre Fest submittals must be previously unproduced. DCTC negotiates for production rights on scripts selected for full presentation but does not hold rights on Theatre Fest scripts. Royalty to be negotiated.
Needs: Full-length unproduced scripts. "We do not accept one-acts, adaptations, children's plays, or musicals at this time."

‡DISCOVERY '92, Paul Mellon Arts Center, P.O. Box 788, Wallingford CT 06492. (203)269-1113. Artistic Director: Terrence Ortwein. Estab. 1984. Produces 3-5 plays/year. "Choate Rosemary Hall in Wallingford, Connecticut, will host its eighth summer theater program committed to the discovery and development of new scripts written specifically for secondary school production. Students with an interest in theater from around the country will join directors and writers-in-residence in order to rehearse and perform new works in July. Playwrights will have the opportunity to hear, see and rewrite their scripts during three-week residencies. Public workshop performances will provide audience reactions to the works-in-progress and will enable the playwrights to further develop their scripts for future productions." Submit complete ms. Reports in 3 months. Playwrights selected must agree to be in residence at Choate Rosemary Hall from July 12-August 1. Room, board and a stipend will be given each playwright selected. The workshop productions, script-in-hand so that the playwright will have every opportunity to rewrite during every step of his *discovery*, will be the responsibility of Choate Rosemary Hall.
Tips: The content should appeal strongly and directly to teenagers. Although all the characters don't have to be teenagers, the actors will be. In most high schools, more girls than boys participate in drama. Most high schools have limited technical resources and limited budgets. Although we will look at full-length scripts, the real need and interest is in the one-act and hour-length play. This program is established to help playwrights develop scripts, not to produce already finished scripts. *Only unproduced and unpublished scripts may be submitted.*

‡**DOUGLAS COLLEGE**, P.O. Box 2503, New Westminster, British Columbia V3L 1X1 Canada. (604)527-5293. Editor: Dale Zieroth. Estab. 1970. Publishes 1-3 plays/year. "We have a literary audience." Submit complete ms. Reports in 4 months. Buys first North American serial rights. Pays $20 per page.
Needs: "We are looking for one acts."
Tips: "Please make certain to enclose sufficient IRC's with U.S. submissions."

THE DRAMATIC PUBLISHING CO., 311 Washington St., Woodstock IL 60098. (815)338-7170. FAX: (815)338-8981. Estab. 1885. Publishes about 30 new shows per year. 60% freelance written. 40% of scripts published are unagented submissions. "Current growth market is in plays and musicals for children, plays and small-cast musicals for stock and community theater." Also has a large market for plays and musicals for schools and other amateur theater groups. Works with 2-6 unpublished/unproduced writers annually. Reports in 2-6 months. Buys stock and amateur theatrical rights. Pays by usual royalty contract, 10 free scripts and 30% discount on script purchases.
Tips: "Avoid stereotype roles and situations. Submit cassette tapes with musicals whenever possible. Always include SASE if script is to be returned. Only one intermission (if any) in a show running up to two hours."

‡**DRAMATICS MAGAZINE**, 3368 Central Pkwy., Cincinnati OH 45225. (513)559-1996. Editor: Don Corathers. Estab. 1929. Publishes 5 plays/year. For high school theater students and teachers. Submit complete ms. Reports in 2 months. Buys first North American serial rights only. Purchases one-time publication rights only for $100-400.
Needs: "We are seeking one-acts to full-lengths that can be produced in an educational theater setting. We don't publish musicals."
Tips: "No melodrama, farce, children's theatre, or cheap knock-offs of TV sit-coms to movies. Fewer writers are taking the time to learn the conventions of theatre—what makes a piece work on stage, as opposed to film and television—and their scripts show it."

EAST WEST PLAYERS, 4424 Santa Monica Blvd., Los Angeles CA 90029. (213)660-0366. Artistic Director: Nobu McCarthy. Dramaturg: Dick Dotterer. 75% freelance written. Produces 4-6 plays/year. Original plays, translations, adaptations, musicals, youth theatre. Professional Equity company performing under the Equity 99-seat theater plan for all audiences. Produces 2-3 new plays annually. Also has play reading series and writer's laboratory for selected projects. Query with letter, synopsis and 10 pages of dialogues (preferred); or submit complete ms. Reports in 5-6 weeks on query and synopsis; up to 6 months for complete ms. "High majority" of scripts produced are unagented submissions. Standard Dramatist's Guild contract rights offerd.
Needs: "Our acting company is 98% Asian-American/Pacific/Asian, so the majority of important roles should be playable by Asian-American actors. We emphasize plays dealing with Asian-American experiences and themes. A script with one or two minor roles for Asian actors does not make it suitable for our theater."
Tips: "East West Players was founded by a group of Asian-American actors weary of playing stereotypes in theater and film. Writers should bear this in mind and refrain from wallowing in 'exoticism.' There is a burgeoning of interest in Asian-American writers and themes—witness David Henry Hwang's success on the East Coast, the emergence of Philip Kan Gotanda in regional theaters, Amy Tan and Maxine Hong Kingston in fiction and Bette Bao Lord in nonfiction; continuing success and influence of East West Players on the West Cost and the development of Asian-American materials in a number of established regional theaters."

ELDRIDGE PUBLISHING CO., P.O. Box 216, Franklin OH 45005. (513)746-6531. Estab. 1906. Publishes 15-20 plays/year. For middle school, junior high, senior high, church and community audience. Query with synopsis (acceptable) or submit complete ms (preferred). Please send cassette tapes with any operettas. Reports in 2 months. Buys all rights. Pays 35% royalty (three-act royalties approximately $50/$35). Outright purchase from $100-300 or offers 10% of copy sale receipts. Writer's guidelines for #10 SASE.
Needs: "We are always on the lookout for Xmas plays (religious for our church market or secular for the public school market). Also lighthearted one-acts and three-acts. We do like some serious, high caliber plays reflective of today's sophisticated students. Also operettas for jr/sr high school and more limited middle school (fourth grade and above) market. We prefer larger casts for our three-acts and

The double dagger before a listing indicates that the listing is new in this edition. New markets are often more receptive to freelance submissions.

operettas. Staging should be in keeping with school budgets and expertise. We are *not* interested in plays that are highly sexually suggestive or use abusive language."

Tips: "We're especially interested in large cast, full-length plays and musicals for our school market and Easter plays for our religious market for 1992. Submissions are welcomed at any time but during our fall season, response will definitely take 2 months. Authors are paid royalties twice a year. They receive complimentary copies of their published plays, the annual catalog and 50% discount if buying additional copies."

THE EMPTY SPACE, P.O. Box 1748, Seattle WA 98111-1748. (206)587-3737. Artistic Director: Kurt Beattie. Estab. 1970. Produces 6 plays/year. 100% freelance written. Professional plays for subscriber base and single ticket Seattle audience. 1 script/year is unagented submission. Works with 5-6 unpublished/unproduced writers annually. Query with synopsis before sending script. Response in 4 months. LOA theater.
Needs: "Other things besides linear, narrative realism, but we are interested in that as well. No restriction on subject matter. Generally we opt for broader, more farcical comedies and harder-edged, uncompromising dramas. We like to go places we've never been before."

ENCORE PERFORMANCE PUBLISHING, P.O. Box 692, Orem UT 84057. (801)225-0605. Editor: Michael C. Perry. Estab. 1979. Publishes 8-12 plays/year. "Our audience consists of all ages with emphasis on the family; educational institutions from elementary through college/university, community theaters and professional theaters." Query and synopsis or complete ms. Reports in 3 months. Buys publishing and revival performance rights. Pays 50% royalty.
Needs: "We are looking for plays with strong message about or for families, plays with young actors among cast any length, all genres. We prefer scripts with at least close or equal male/female roles, could lean to more female roles." Plays must have had at least 1 professional or 2 amateur productions.
Tips: "No performance art pieces or plays with overtly sexual themes or language."

‡THE ENSEMBLE STUDIO THEATRE, 549 W. 52nd St., New York NY 10019. (212)247-4982. FAX: (212)664-0041. Artistic Director: Curt Dempster. Literary Manager: Christopher Smith. Estab. 1971. Produces 15-20 plays/year for off-off Broadway theater. 100-seat house, 60-seat workshop space. Do not FAX ms or résumés. Submit complete ms. Reports in 3 months. Standard production contract: mini contract with Actors' Equity Association or letter of agreement. Pays $80-1,000.
Needs: Full-lengths and one-acts with strong dramatic actions and situations. No musicals, verse-dramas or elaborate costume dramas.
Tips: Submit work September through April.

‡ENSEMBLE THEATRE OF CINCINNATI, 1127 Vine St., Cincinnati OH 45210. (513)421-3556. Artistic Director: David A. White II. Estab. 1986. Produces 6 plays/year. "ETC is a franchised theater of the Actors' Equity Association. Our audiences tend to be serious theater people, with an interest in new works." Submit complete ms. Reports in 3 months. Pays 7% royalty or $1,000-10,000 outright purchase.
Needs: "We have discovered that good comedies are hard to come by. We are also interested in socially relevant material. We prefer a simple set with 6 or fewer actors."
Tips: "No AIDS or 'Thirty-Something' material."

RICHARD FICARELLI, P.O. Box 23548, Fort Lauderdale FL 33307-3548. Produces 1-2 plays/year. Plays are Equity productions performed in New York, Broadway and off-Broadway theaters. Regional possibilities. Submit query and synopsis. Reports in 6 weeks. Acquires Dramatist's Guild (standard) rights. Pays standard royalty.
Needs: Situation comedies *only*. Prefers cast of fewer than 14. No dramas.
Tips: "Stronger possibilities for regional and dinner theater productions as well as Broadway and off-Broadway."

THE FIREHOUSE THEATRE, 514 S. 11th St., Omaha NE 68102. (402)346-6009. Artistic Director: Dick Mueller. Produces 7 plays/year. Has produced 4 unagented submissions in 14 years.
Needs: "We produce at the Firehouse Theatre in Omaha. Our interest in new scripts is the hope of finding material that can be proven here at our theater and then go on to find its audience." Submit complete ms. Reporting times vary; depends on workload. Buys negotiable rights. Pays $100/week or negotiable rates.
Tips: "We are a small theater. Certainly size and cost are a consideration. Quality is also a consideration. We can't use heavy drama in this theater. We might, however, consider a production if it were a good script and use another theater."

THE FREELANCE PRESS, P.O. Box 548, Dover MA 02030. (508)785-1260. Managing Editor: David Downing. Publishes 4 plays/year for children/young adults. Send copy of script and SASE. Reports in 2 months. Pays 2-3% royalty. Pays 10% of the price of each script and score.

Needs: "Publish original musical theater for young people, dealing with issues of importance to them, also adapt 'classics' into musicals for 8-16-year-old age groups to perform." Large cast; flexible, simple staging and props.

SAMUEL FRENCH, INC., 45 W. 25th St., New York NY 10010. Editor: Lawrence Harbison. 100% freelance written. "We publish about 80-90 new titles a year. We are the world's largest publisher of plays. 10-20% are unagented submissions. In addition to publishing plays, we occasionally act as agents in the placement of plays for professional production—eventually in New York. Pays on royalty basis. Submit complete ms (bound). Always type your play in the standard, accepted stageplay manuscript format used by all professional playwrights in the U.S. If in doubt, send $3 to the attention of Lawrence Harbison for a copy of 'Guidelines.' We require a minimum of two months to report."
Needs: "We are willing at all times to read the work of freelancers. Our markets prefer simple-to-stage, light, happy romantic comedies or mysteries. If your work does not fall into this category, we would be reading it for consideration for agency representation. No 25-page 'full-length' plays; no children's plays to be performed *by* children; no puppet plays; no adaptations of public domain children's stories; no verse plays; no large-cast historical (costume) plays; no seasonal and/or religious plays; no television, film or radio scripts; no translations of foreign plays."

GEORGETOWN PRODUCTIONS, 7 Park Ave., New York NY 10016. Producer: Gerald van de Vorst. Literary Manager: George Grec. Estab. 1972. Produces 1-2 plays/year for a general audience. Works with 2-3 unpublished/unproduced writers annually. Submit complete ms only. Standard Dramatists Guild contract.
Needs: Prefers plays with small casts and not demanding more than one set. Interested in new unconventional scripts dealing with contemporary issues, comedies, mysteries, musicals or dramas. No first drafts, outlines or one-act plays.
Tips: "The current trend is toward light entertainment, as opposed to meaningful or serious plays."

‡**EMMY GIFFORD CHILDREN'S THEATER,** 3504 Center St., Omaha NE 68105. (402)345-4849. Artistic Director: James Larson. Produces 6 plays/year. "Our target audience is children, preschool-jr. high and their parents." Query with synopsis with SASE. Reports in 9 months. Royalty negotiable.
Needs: "Plays must be geared to children and parents (PG rating). Titles recognized by the general public have a stronger chance of being produced." Cast limit: 25 (8-10 adults). No adult scripts.
Tips: "Previously produced plays may be accepted only after a letter of inquiry (familiar titles only!)."

‡**GREATWORKS PLAY SERVICE,** P.O. Box 3148, Shell Beach CA 93448. (805)773-3419. Editor: Richard Sharp. Publishes 30 plays/year. All professional, community theatre and college; some high school. Query and synopsis. Reports in 6 months. Buys exclusive rights to publish and represent play for purposes/leasing production rights. Pays variable royalty. Submissions with SASE returned.
Needs: "We specialize in translations from other languages and adaptation for the stage from other forms—especially recognized works of literature. No material that has not already been produced."

‡**HARTFORD STAGE COMPANY,** 50 Church St., Hartford CT 06103. (203)525-5601. Artistic Director: Mark Lamos. Estab. 1964. Produces 6 plays/year. Professional regional theater with subscriber base. Query with synopsis. Reports in 8 months. Buys only one-time production rights. Pays royalty.
Needs: Full-length plays, translations, adaptations. Limitations are figured on a per-season, rather than per-script basis.
Tips: No one-acts, work for children.

HONOLULU THEATRE FOR YOUTH, 2846 Ualena St., Honolulu HI 96819. (808)839-9885. FAX: (808)839-7018. Artistic Director: Pam Sterling. Produces 6 plays/year. 50% freelance written. Plays are professional productions in Hawaii, primarily for young audiences (aged 2 to 20). 80% of scripts are unagented submissions. Works with 2 unpublished/unproduced writers annually. Reports in 4 months. Buys negotiable rights.
Needs: Contemporary subjects of concern/interest to young people; adaptations of literary classics; fantasy including space, fairy tales, myth and legend. "HTY wants well-written plays, 60-90 minutes in length, that have something worthwhile to say and that will stretch the talents of professional adult actors." Cast not exceeding 8; *no* technical extravaganzas; *no* full-orchestra musicals; simple sets and props, costumes can be elaborate. No plays to be enacted by children or camp versions of popular fairytales. Query with synopsis. Pays $1,000-2,500.
Tips: "Young people are intelligent and perceptive; if anything, more so than lots of adults, and if they are to become fans and eventual supporters of good theater, they must see good theater while they are young. Trends on the American stage that freelance writers should be aware of include a growing awareness that we are living in a world community. We must learn to share and understand other people and other cultures."

‡**HORIZON THEATRE COMPANY,** P.O. Box 5376, Station E, Atlanta GA 30307. (404)584-7450. Artistic Director: Lisa Adler. Estab. 1983. Produces 4 plays/year. Professional productions for young professionals. Query and synopsis with resume. Reports in 1-2 years. Buys rights to produce in Atlanta area. Pays 6-8% royalty or $50-75 per performance.
Needs: "We produce contemporary plays with realistic base, but which utilize heightened visual or language elements. Interested in comedy satire, plays that are entertaining, but also thought provoking." No more than 10 in cast.
Tips: "No plays about being in theater or film; no plays without hope; no plays that include playwrights as leading characters; no all-male casts; no plays with all older (50+) characters."

WILLIAM E. HUNT, 801 West End Ave., New York NY 10025. Estab. 1947. Interested in reading scripts for stock production, off-Broadway and even Broadway production. "Small cast, youth-oriented, meaningful, technically adventuresome; serious, funny, far-out. Must be about people first, ideas second. No political or social tracts." No one-act, anti-Black, anti-Semitic or anti-gay plays. "I do not want 1920, 1930 or 1940 plays disguised as modern by 'modern' language. I do not want plays with 24 characters, plays with 150 costumes, plays about symbols instead of people. I do not want plays that are really movie or television scripts." Works with 2-3 unpublished/unproduced writers annually. Pays royalties on production. Off-Broadway, 5%; on Broadway, 5%, 7½% and 10%, based on gross. No royalty paid if play is selected for a showcase production. Reports in "a few weeks." Must have SASE or script will not be returned.
Tips: "Production costs and weekly running costs in the legitimate theater are so high today that no play (or it is the very rare play) with more than six characters and more than one set, by a novice playwright, is likely to be produced unless that playwright will either put up or raise the money him or herself for the production."

‡**IMPULSE THEATRE COMPANY,** 8815 Selkirk St., Vancouver, British Columbia V6P 4J7 Canada. (604)263-3315. Artistic Director: David L. Young. Estab. 1987. Produces 6-8 plays/year. "Semi-professional and professional productions take place in our multi-purpose theater and performing arts facility. Most of our productions take place between May and October, and are supported by a wide range of Vancouver's theater-going public. We are also in the formative stages of fostering a new lunch-time theater program." Submit complete ms (typed on near letter-quality computer printer). Reports in 2 months. Buys "full production right of the piece within a 250-mile radius." Pays royalty or by honorarium (average amount ranges from $100 (Canadian) to $500 (Canadian).
Needs: "ANYTHING GOES!!! We prefer to see pieces that can be played in an intimate theater venue, however, larger production constraints can and will be considered. I think the playwright/author *must* use some personal discretion as to what they feel an alternate or 'fringe' theater company might produce. Playwrights/authors should keep away from creating busy sets, with overly zealous and gratuitous stage business."
Tips: "Please don't send television melodramatic fluff. Theater (in the Canadian context) is moving away from television reality and spectacle, and going more in the direction of human reality for self-initiated actors and theater companies to produce. *All* material will be looked at, read and considered . . . and will receive a short critique from our play-search/adjudication committee."

JEWEL BOX THEATRE, 3700 N. Walker, Oklahoma City OK 73118. (405)521-1786. Artistic Director: Charles Tweed. Estab. 1988. Produces 6 plays/year. Amateur productions. Intended for 3,000 season subscribers and general public. Submit complete ms. Reports in 3 months. "We would like to have first production rights and 'premiere' the play at Jewel Box Theatre." Pays $500 contest prize.
Needs: "Write theater for entry form during September-October. We produce dramas, comedies and musicals. Only two- or three-act plays can be accepted. Our theater is in-the-round, so we adapt plays accordingly." Deadline: middle of January.

JEWISH REPERTORY THEATRE, 344 E. 14th St., New York NY 10003. (212)674-7200. Artistic Director: Ran Avni. Estab. 1974. Produces 5 plays, 15 readings/year. New York City professional off-Broadway production. Submit complete ms. Reports in 1 month. 1st production/option to move to Broadway or off-Broadway. Pays royalty.
Needs: Full-length only. Straight plays and musicals. Must have some connection to Jewish life, characters, history. Maximum 10 characters. Limited technical facilities.
Tips: No biblical plays.

LONG ISLAND STAGE, P.O. Box 9001, Rockville Centre NY 11571-9001. (516)456-4600. FAX: (516)867-3066. Artistic Director: Clinton J. Atkinson. Estab. 1974. Produces 6 plays/year. We are a fully professional company, operating under at LORT agreement with all theatrical unions; our audience is a subscription audience of mature adults of conservative bent. Query and synopsis. Reports in 3 months. Pays royalty.

Needs: "We are interested in contemporary materials, small casts, occasional translations, small sets. We have no parameters on materials, etc. The smaller the cast, props, and staging, the better."
Tips: "We rarely do musicals. Writers should write what they feel and want to; let trends take care of themselves."

‡**MAGIC THEATRE, INC.,** Bldg. D, Fort Mason, San Francisco CA 94123. (415)441-8001. Artistic Director: Harvey Seifter. Estab. 1966. Produces 8 plays/year. Regional theater. Submit query and synopsis. Reports in 3 months. Pays royalty or per performance fee.
Needs: "We are looking for plays with a poetic bent; serials, in-depth comedies and dramas, experimental and multi-cultural works. Staging should be small, preferably."
Tips: "No mainstream materialism plays, please."

MAGNUS THEATRE COMPANY, 137 N. May St., Thunder Bay, Ontario P7C 3N8 Canada. (807)623-5818. Artistic Director: Michael McLaughlin. Produces 6 plays/year. Professional stock theater produced in 197-seat facility and performed for a demographically diverse general audience.
Needs: "Fairly general in genres, but with a particular emphasis on new plays, must be full-length. Smaller (i.e., up to seven) casts are viewed favorably; some technical limitations. Always, budget limitations. Also produces one-act theater-in-education scripts for all age ranges, with emphasis on socially and curriculum-relevant material."
Tips: "Thunder Bay is a very earthy, working city, and we try to reflect that sensibility in our choice of plays. Beyond that, however, Magnus has gained a national reputation for its commitment to the development and production of new plays, including, where possible, workshops. Scripts should be accessible to Canadian audiences in theme; should be produceable within realistic budget limitations."

MANHATTAN THEATRE CLUB, 453 W. 16th St., New York NY 10011. Director of the Script Department: Kate Loewald. Produces 9 plays/year. All freelance written. A two-theater performing arts complex classified as off-Broadway, using professional actors. No unsolicited scripts. Query with synopsis. Reports in 6 months. Payment is negotiable.
Needs: "We present a wide range of new work, from this country and abroad, to a subscription audience. We want plays about contemporary problems and people. Comedies are welcome. Heavy set shows or multiple detailed sets are discouraged. We present shows with casts of not more than 15; average cast is 8. No skits."

MERRIMACK REPERTORY THEATRE, P.O. Box 228, Lowell MA 01853. (508)454-6324. Artistic Director: David G. Kent. Produces 7 plays/year. Professional LORT D. Agented submissions and letters of inquiry only. Reports in 6 months.
Needs: All styles and genres. "We are a small 386-seat theater—with a modest budget. Plays should be good stories, with strong dialogue, real situations and human concerns. Especially interested in plays about American life and culture."

MIAMI BEACH COMMUNITY THEATRE, 2231 Prairie Ave., Miami Beach FL 33139. (305)532-4515. FAX: (305)531-9209. Artistic Director: Jay W. Jensen. Produces 5 plays/year. "Amateur productions performed during the year for the Miami Beach community." Send query and synopsis or submit complete ms. Reports in 3 weeks. Pays $35-75/performance (if published work); does not pay for unpublished plays.
Needs: "All types. Interested in Spanish themes—Latin American plots, etc. Interested in new plays dealing with AIDS and short plays dealing with AIDS that could be used in junior highs and senior highs for motivation—about 30 minutes long. Avoid sex."

MILL MOUNTAIN THEATRE, Market Square, Center in Square, Roanoke VA 24011. (703)342-5730. Executive Director: Jere Lee Hodgin. Produces 8 established plays, 10 new one-acts and 2 new full-length plays/year. "Some of the professional productions will be on the main stage and some in our alternative theater B." Submit complete ms. Reports in 8 months. Payment negotiable on individual play. Send SASE for guidelines; cast limit 15 for play and 24 for musicals. Do not include loose stamps or money.
Needs: "We are interested in plays with racially mixed casts, but not to the exclusion of others. We are constantly seeking one-act plays for 'Centerpieces', our Lunch Time Program of Script-in-Hand Productions. Playing time should be between 25-35 minutes. Cast limit 6."
Tips: "Subject matter and character variations are open, but gratuitous language and acts are not acceptable. A play based on large amounts of topical reference or humor has a very short life. Be sure you have written a play and not a film script."

‡**MILWAUKEE REPERTORY THEATER,** 108 E. Wells St., Milwaukee WI 53202. (414)224-1761. Artistic Director: John Dillon. Estab. 1955. Produces 16 plays/year. "We perform in a LORT, professional theater. The Powerhouse Theater (700 seats), thrust stage, the Stiemeke Theater (199 seat) black box,

The Stackner Cabaret (106 seats) cabaret space. Audience includes subscribers and single ticket buyers." Query and synopsis or professional recommendation. Reports in 4 months. Rights negotiable. Pays royalty; all negotiated with individual writer.
Needs: "We produce an eclectic mix of plays. We are interested in plays that illuminate the human condition. We cast in non-traditional style. We are specifically looking for plays and cabaret pieces, small cast with few musicians, running about an hour. Full musicals usually stand little chance."

MISE EN SCÈNE THEATRE, 5110 Tujunga #4, North Hollywood CA 91601. (818)763-3101. Artistic Director: Herb Rodgers. Produces 6-16 plays/year at two theaters. For Los Angeles audiences, casting directors, agents and producers. Equity 99-seat plan. Submit complete ms. Reports in 2 months. Payment negotiable.
Needs: "Only original, unproduced, full-lengths and one-acts. Any genre, topic, style." Stage has 28-foot opening, 21-foot depth.
Tips: "No previously produced plays. Our objective is to give playwrights the opportunity to work in production with the directors and actors, to better prepare the play for professional productions. Our plays are reviewed by the *Los Angeles Times*, *Variety*, *Hollywood Reporter* and other local papers. Productions are videotaped."

MISSOURI REPERTORY THEATRE, 4949 Cherry St., Kansas City MO 64110. (816)276-2727. Contact: Mary Guaraldi, Director of Second Stage. Estab. 1963. Produces 7 plays/year on the mainstage; 2 productions, 7 readings on the second stage. Regional professional theater. Query and synopsis.
Needs: Well-known contemporary American, classics with an emphasis on Shakespeare, and new plays for development.

MIXED BLOOD THEATRE COMPANY, 1501 S. 4th St., Minneapolis MN 55454. (612)338-0937. Artistic Director: Jack Reuler. Estab. 1975. Produces 5 plays/year. Equity productions in 200-seat theatre. General audiences. Submit query and synopsis. No unsolicited scripts unless intended for "Mixed Blood Versus America." Annual playwriting contest.
Needs: In the past we have produced high-tech spectacles, original musicals, wild satires as well as regional and American premieres.
Tips: "The best means for submitting new work to our theatre is through our annual playwriting contest Mixed Blood Versus America; a copy of guidelines is available by sending an SASE to our theatre attn: David Kunz. *Otherwise we accept query letters with play synosis ONLY.*"

‡MODERN INTERNATIONAL DRAMA, Theater Dept. S.U.N.Y., P.O. Box 6000, Binghamton NY 13902-6000. (607)777-2704. Managing Editor: George E. Wellwarth. Estab. 1967. Publishes 5-6 plays/ year. "Audience is academic and professional." Submit query and synopsis or complete ms. Reports in 2 months. "Rights remain with author and translator." Pays complimentary copies (3).
Needs: Publishes plays of ideas; 20th century; any style and any length; translations of previously untranslated plays from any language *only*.
Tips: "No (popular) theater."

‡MUSICAL THEATRE WORKS, INC., 440 Lafayette St., 4th Floor, New York NY 10003. (212)677-0040. Artistic Director: Anthony Stimac. Estab. 1983. Produces 4 mainstage productions; 6 workshops; 10 readings. "MTW musicals are professionally produced and presented in an off-Broadway New York City theater and intended for a well-rounded, sophisticated, theater-going audience. Additionally, 50% of all MTW MainStage productions have gone on to engagements on Broadway and in 12 states across the country." Submit complete ms with audiotape. Reports in 2 months. Buys 1% future gross; on fully-produced works. Pays negotiable royalty.
Needs: "MTW only produces full-length works of musical theater and is interested not only in those classically written, but has a keen interest in works which expand the boundaries and subject matter of the artform. MTW is a small, but prolific, organization with a limited budget. It is, therefore, necessary to limit production costs. Authors should take note."
Tips: "The dramatic stage of recent years has successfully interpreted societal problems of the day, while the musical theater has grown in spectacle and foregone substance. Since the musical theater traditionally incorporated large themes and issues it is imperative that we now marry these two ideas — large themes and current issues — to the form. Send a neat, clean, typewritten manuscript with a well marked, clear audiotape, produced as professionally as possible, to the attention of the Literary Manager."

NATIONAL MUSIC THEATER CONFERENCE, EUGENE O'NEILL THEATER CENTER, Suite 901, 234 W. 44th St., New York NY 10036. (212)382-2790. FAX: (212)921-5538. Artistic Director: Paulette Haupt. Estab. 1978. Paying audiences drawn from local residents, New York and regional theater professionals and others. Conference takes place each August at center in Waterford, Connecticut.

Send #10 SASE after September 15 to request application guidelines. Application deadline: February 1, subject to change. Pays stipend plus room and board during conference.

Needs: "We develop new music theater works of all forms, traditional and non-traditional. Singing must play a dominant role. Works are given minimally staged readings, script in hand, no props or lighting, piano only."

Tips: Works not considered eligible are those that have been fully produced by a professional company and adapted works for which rights have not been obtained. Writers and composers must be U.S. citizens or permanent residents.

NECESSARY ANGEL THEATRE, #400, 553 Queen St. W., Toronto, Ontario M5V 2B6 Canada (416)365-0533. Dramaturg: D. D. Kugler. Estab. 1978. Produces 2 plays/year. Plays are Equity productions in various Toronto theaters and performance spaces for an urban audience between 20-55 years of age. Submit synopsis only. Please include SASE (international postal coupon if from the U.S.) if you would like your synopsis returned. Reports in 6 months. Obtains various rights "based on the manuscript (original, translation, adaptation) and the playwright (company member, etc.)." Pays 10% royalty.

Needs: "We are open to new theatrical ideas, environmental pieces, unusual acting styles and large casts. The usual financial constraints exist, but they have never eliminated a work to which we felt a strong commitment." No "TV-influenced sit-coms or melodramas."

Tips: "All submissions are considered for long-term script/playwright development, including one-day readings and one-week workshops, leading to company productions. Playwrights should be aware of our interdisciplinary approach to performance (music, dance and visual arts that support the text)."

‡THE NEW AMERICAN THEATER, 118 N. Main St., Rockford IL 61101. (815)963-9454. Producing Director: J.R. Sullivan. Produces a spectrum of American and international work in 10-month season. "The New American Theater is a professional resident theater company performing on a thrust stage with a 270-seat house. It is located in a predominantly middle-class Midwestern town." Submit synopsis and SASE. *Do not* send full manuscript. Pays royalty based on number of performances.

Needs: No limitations, prefer serious themes, contemporary pieces. Open to format, etc. No opera.

Tips: "We look for new work that addresses contemporary issues; we do not look for work of any one genre or production style. We encourage experimentation."

THE NEW CONSERVATORY CHILDREN'S THEATRE COMPANY AND SCHOOL, Zephyr Theater Complex, 25 Van Ness, Lower Level, San Francisco CA 94102. (415)861-4814. Artistic Director: Ed Decker. Produces 4-5 plays/year. "The New Conservatory is a children's theater school (ages 4 to 19) and operates year-round. Each year we produce several plays, for which the older students (usually 11 and up) audition. These are presented to the general public at the Zephyr Theatre Complex San Francisco (50-350 seats). Our audience is approximately age 10 to adult." Send query and synopsis. Reports in 2 months. Royalty negotiable.

Needs: "We emphasize works in which children play *children*, and prefer relevant and controversial subjects, although we also do musicals. We have a commitment to new plays. Examples of our shows are: Mary Gail's *Nobody Home* (world premiere; about latchkey kids); Brian Kral's *Special Class* (about disabled kids), and *The Inner Circle*, by Patricia Loughrey (commissioned scripts about AIDS prevention for kids). As we are a nonprofit group on limited budget, we tend not to have elaborate staging; however, our staff is inventive—includes choreographer and composer. Write innovative theater that explores topics of concern/interest to young people, that takes risks. We concentrate more on ensemble than individual roles, too. We do *not* want to see fairytales or trite rehashings of things children have seen/heard since the age of 2. See theater as education, rather than 'children being cute'."

Tips: "It is important for young people and their families to explore and confront issues relevant to growing up in the '90s. Theatre is a marvelous teaching tool that can educate while it entertains."

NEW PLAYS INCORPORATED, P.O. Box 5074, Charlottesville VA 22905. (804)979-2777. Publisher: Patricia Whitton. Estab. 1964. Publishes an average of 4 plays/year. Publishes for producers of plays for young audiences and teachers in college courses on child drama. Query with synopsis. Reports in 2 months. Agent for amateur and semi-professional productions, exclusive agency for script sales. Pays 50% royalty on productions; 10% on script sales. Free catalog.

Needs: Plays for young audiences with something innovative in form and content. Length: usually 45-90 minutes. "Should be suitable for performance by adults for young audiences." No skits, assembly programs, improvisations or unproduced manuscripts.

NEW PLAYWRIGHTS' PROGRAM, THE UNIVERSITY OF ALABAMA, P.O. Box 870239, Tuscaloosa AL 35487-0239. (205)348-9032. Director and Dramaturg: Dr. Paul C. Castagno. Estab. 1982. Produces at least 1 new play/year. Mainstage and second stage. Collaborations with Stillman College and Theatre Tuscaloosa, University Theatre, The University of Alabama. Submit complete ms. Playwrights may submit potential workshop ideas for consideration. Reports in 3 months. Accepts scripts in various forms: New dramaturgy to traditional. Also radio plays.

‡**NEW TUNERS THEATRE**, 1225 W. Belmont Ave., Chicago IL 60657. (312)929-7367. Literary Manager: Allan Chambers. Produces 3-4 new musicals/year. 66% freelance written. "Nearly all" scripts produced are unagented submissions. Plays performed in a small off-Loop theater seating 148 for a general theater audience, urban/suburban mix. Submit complete ms and cassette tape of the score, if available. Reports in 6 months. Buys exclusive right of production within 80-mile radius. "Submit first, we'll negotiate later." Pays 5-10% of gross. "Authors are given a stipend to cover a residency of at least two weeks."

Needs: "We're interested in traditional forms of musical theater as well as more innovative styles. We have less interest in operetta and operatic works, but we'd look at anything. At this time, we have no interest in nonmusical plays unless to consider them for possible adaptation—please send query letter first. Our production capabilities are limited by the lack of space, but we're very creative and authors should submit anyway. The smaller the cast, the better. We are especially interested in scripts using a younger (35 and under) ensemble of actors. We mostly look for authors who are interested in developing their script through workshops, rehearsals and production. No interest in children's theater. No casts over 15. No one-man shows."

Tips: "Freelance writers should be aware that musical theater can be more serious. The work of Sondheim and others who follow demonstrates clearly that musical comedy can be ambitious and can treat mature themes in a relevant way. Probably 90% of what we receive would fall into the category of 'fluff.' We have nothing against fluff. We've had some great successes producing it and hope to continue to offer some pastiche and farce to our audience; however, we would like to see the musical theater articulating something about the world around us, rather than merely diverting an audience's attention from that world."

NEW YORK SHAKESPEARE FESTIVAL/PUBLIC THEATER, 425 Lafayette St., New York NY 10003. (212)598-7100. Producer: Joseph Papp. Director, Plays & Musicals Department: Gail Merrifield. Literary Manager: Jason Fogelson. Estab. 1954. Interested in plays, musicals, translations, adaptations. No restriction as to style, form, subject matter. Produces classics, new American and international works year-round at the Public Theater complex housing 5 theaters (100-300 seat capacity): Newman, Anspacher, Shiva, LuEsther Hall, Martinson. Also at Delacorte 2,100-seat amphitheater in Central Park. Transfers to Broadway, film and television. Unsolicited and unagented submissions accepted. All scripts: include cast of characters with age and brief description; musical works: submit cassette with at least 3 songs. Standard options and production agreements. Response in 4 months. Include SASE with all submissions.

‡**NEW YORK STATE THEATRE INSTITUTE**, formerly Empire State Institute for the Performing Arts, 1400 Washington Ave., Albany NY 12222. (518)442-5399. Acting Artistic Director: Ed Lange. Literary Manager: James Farrell. Produces 4-5 plays/year. Professional regional productions for adult and family audiences. Query with synopsis. Reports in 3 months. Pay varies.

NEW YORK THEATRE WORKSHOP, 220 W. 42 St., 18th Fl., New York NY 10036. (212)302-7737. Artistic Director: James C. Nicola. Literary Associate: Christopher Ashley. Estab. 1979. Produces 6 full productions; approximately 50 readings per year. Plays are performed off-Broadway, Equity mini-contract theater. Audience is New York theatergoing audience and theater professionals. Query with synopsis and 10 pg. sample scene. Reports in 5 months. Option to produce commercially; percentage of box office gross from commercial productions within a specified time limit from our original production; percentage of author's net subsidiary rights within specified time limit from our original production. Pays fee because of limited run, with additional royalty payments; for extensions, $1,500-2,000 fee range.

Needs: Full-length plays, one-acts, translations/adaptations, music theater pieces; proposals for performance projects. Large issues, socially relevant issues, innovative form and language, minority issues. Plays utilizing more than 8 actors usually require outside funding.

Tips: No overtly commercial, traditional Broadway-type "musicals."

JACKIE NICHOLS, 51 S. Cooper, Memphis TN 38104. Artistic Director: Jackie Nichols. Produces 16 plays/year. Professional productions at Playhouse on the Square. Submit complete ms. Reports in 5 months. Pays $500.

Needs: All types. "Small cast, single or unit set."

Tips: "Playwrights from the South will be given preference. South is defined as the following states: Alabama, Florida, Georgia, Kentucky, Louisiana, Mississippi, Missouri, North Carolina, South Carolina, Tennessee, Texas, Virginia and West Virginia. This means we will read all shows and when final decisions are made, if every other aspect of the plays are equal, we will choose a Southern author."

NO EMPTY SPACE THEATRE, 568 Metropolitan Ave., Staten Island NY 10301-3431. Producing Director: James E. Stayoch. Estab. 1986. Produces 3 plays/year. Performed locally on S.I., usually Equity Showcase, intended for NYC audience. Submit complete ms. Reports in 3 months from deadline. Buys one-time production rights. Award - $500. Also sponsors contest beginning again in 1992. No restrictions on type, size, content, etc. Send SASE for application.

THE NORTH CAROLINA BLACK REPERTORY COMPANY, P.O. Box 95, Winston-Salem NC 27102. (919)723-2266. Artistic Director: Larry Leon Hamlin. Estab. 1979. Produces 4-6 plays/year. Plays produced primarily in North Carolina, New York City, and the North and Southeast. Submit complete ms. Reports in 5 months. Obtains negotiable rights. Negotiable payment.
Needs: "Full-length plays and musicals: mostly African-American with special interest in historical or contemporary *statement* genre. A cast of 10 would be a comfortable limit; we discourage multiple sets."
Tips: "The best time to submit manuscript is between September and February."

ODYSSEY THEATRE ENSEMBLE, 2055 S. Sepulveda Blvd., Los Angeles CA 90025. (213)826-1626. Literary Manager: Jan Lewis. Estab. 1969. Produces 12 plays/year. Plays performed in a 3-theater facility. "All three theaters are Equity 99-seat theater plan. We have a subscription audience of 2,000 who subscribe to a six-play main season and a 3-4 play lab season, and are offered a discount on our remaining non-subscription plays. Remaining seats are sold to the general public." Query with resume, synopsis, cast breakdown and 8-10 pages of sample dialogue. Scripts must be securely bound. Reports in 1 month on queries; 6 months on scripts. Buys negotiable rights. Pays 5-7% royalty. "We will *not* return scripts without SASE."
Needs: Full-length plays only with "either an innovative form or extremely provocative subject matter. We desire more theatrical pieces that explore possibilities of the live theater experience. We are seeking full-length musicals. We are not reading one-act plays or light situation comedies. We are seeking Hispanic material for our resident Hispanic unit."

OLD GLOBE THEATRE, P.O. Box 2171, San Diego CA 92112. (619)231-1941. Literary Manager: Mark Hofflund. Produces 12 plays/year. "We are a LORT B+ institution with 3 theaters: 581-seat mainstage, 225-seat arena, 621-seat outdoor. Our plays are produced for a single-ticket and subscription audience of 250,000 patrons from a large cross-section of southern California, and including visitors from throughout the U.S." Submit complete ms through agent only. Send one-page letter or synopsis if not represented. Reports in 6 months. Buys negotiable rights. Royalty varies.
Needs: "We are looking for plays of strong literary and theatrical merit, works that display an accomplished sense of craft, and pieces that present a detailed cultural vision. All submissions must be full-length plays or musicals."
Tips: "Pursue every opportunity to reach your public, to listen to them, to embrace them in all their contradictions. Hence lies your wealth of experience, and perhaps a glimpse of something universal."

EUGENE O'NEILL THEATER CENTER'S NATIONAL PLAYWRIGHTS CONFERENCE and NEW DRAMA FOR TELEVISION PROJECT, Suite 901, 234 W. 44th St., New York NY 10036. (212)382-2790. Artistic Director: Lloyd Richards. Administrator: Peggy Vernieu. Estab. 1965. Develops staged readings of 10-12 stage plays, 2-3 teleplays/year for a general audience. "We accept unsolicited mss with no prejudice toward either represented or unrepresented writers. Our theater is located in Waterford, Connecticut, and we operate under an Equity LORT contract. We have 3 theaters: Barn-250 seats, Amphitheater-300 seats, Instant Theater-150. Send #10 SASE in the fall for submission guidelines. Complete bound, unproduced, original plays are eligible (no adaptations). Decision by late April. Pays stipend plus room, board and transportation. We accept script submissions from Sept. 15-Dec. 1 of each year. Conference takes place during four weeks in July each summer."
Needs: "We use modular sets for all plays, minimal lighting, minimal props and no costumes. We do script-in-hand readings with professional actors and directors. Our focus is on new play/playwright development."

THE OPEN EYE: NEW STAGINGS, 270 W. 89th St., New York NY 10024. (212)769-4143. Artistic Director: Amie Brockway. Estab. 1972. Produces 3-4 full-length plays/year plus a series of readings and workshop productions of one-acts. "The Open Eye is a professional, Equity LOA and TYA 115-seat, off-off Broadway theater. Our audiences include a broad spectrum of ages and backgrounds." Submit complete ms in clean, bound copy with SASE for its return. Reports in 6 months. Playwright fee for mainstage varies.

Needs: "New Stagings is particularly interested in one-act and full-length plays that take full advantage of the live performance situation. We tend not to do totally realistic plays. We especially like plays that appeal to young people and adults alike."

OREGON SHAKESPEARE FESTIVAL ASSOCIATION, P.O. Box 158, Ashland OR 97520. (503)482-2111. Literary Manager: Cynthia White. Estab. 1935. Produces 16 plays/year. The Angus Bowmer Theater has a thrust stage and seats 600. The Black Swan is an experimental space and seats 150; The Elizabethan Outdoor Theatre seats 1,200 (stages almost exclusively Shakespearean productions there—mid-June through September). OSFA also produces a separate five-play season at the Portland Center for The Performing Arts in a 725-seat proscenium theater. Producing director of OSFA Portland Center Stage: Dennis Bigelow. Query with synopsis plus 10 pages of dialogue from unsolicited sources/also resume. Complete scripts from agents only. Reports in 9 months. Negotiates individually for rights with the playwright's agent. "Most plays run within our 10-month season for 6-10 months, so royalties are paid accordingly."
Needs: "A broad range of classic and contemporary scripts. One or two fairly new scripts per season. Also a play readings series which focuses on new work. Plays must fit into our 10-month rotating repertory season. Black Swan shows usually limited to 6 actors." No one-acts or musicals.
Tips: "Send your work through an agent if possible. Send the best examples of your work rather than all of it. Don't become impatient or discouraged if it takes 6 months or more for a response. Don't expect detailed critiques with rejections. As always, I want to see plays with heart and soul, intelligence, humor and wit. I also think theater is a place for the *word*. So, the word first, then spectacle and high-tech effects."

PAPER MILL PLAYHOUSE, Brookside Dr., Millburn NJ 07041. (201)379-3636. Literary Advisor: Maryan F. Stephens. Estab. 1934. Produces 4 musicals, 2 plays/year. Paper Mill Playhouse is an artistically oriented nonprofit theatre. More than 370 performances are scheduled annually for nearly 400,000 patrons (including a record 43,000 subscribers). Our audience could be classified as "mainstream." For our mainstage we seat 1,192, proscenium stage with flyloft and orchestra pit. Submit complete ms and include a cassette tape with musicals. Reports in 6 months.
Needs: Paper Mill produces full-length plays (drama, comedy, farce), musicals and operettas. Please do not submit children's plays/musicals or one-acts.
Tips: Playwrights should remember they are writing for the stage, not television or film. We are looking for well crafted new American plays and musicals with strong commercial appeal. Paper Mill Playhouse has a development program, Musical Theatre Project. A series of staged readings are given each season, of plays and musicals, with the intention of giving one or more new work full-production. Submissions should have no previous history of professional production.

THE PASSAGE THEATRE COMPANY, P.O. Box 967, Trenton NJ 08605-0967. Artistic Director: Veronica Brady. Estab. 1985. Produces 3 plays/year. "Passage is a professional theater company. Most of our work is performed at the Mill Hill Playhouse in Trenton, New Jersey. Our work is intended for all audiences, culturally and artistically." Query with synopsis or submit complete ms. Reports in 3 months. Pays royalty.
Needs: "We are committed to producing only new American plays. 1-3-act plays (this is general, based on previous experience) dealing with social, cultural and artistic issues. We also do workshops and readings of plays. We work actively with the writers in developing their work. Passage Theatre has a strong propensity towards plays with multi-ethnic themes and utilizing inter-racial casting."

PCPA THEATERFEST, P.O. Box 1700, Santa Maria CA 93456. (805)928-7731. Artistic Director: Jack Shouse. Estab. 1967. Produces 14 plays/year. "We have year-round theater: the Marian Theatre seats 500, the Interim Theatre seats 160; Backstage Theatre is 130 seats; the Festival Theatre m Solvang is open-air, seats 750 and is for summer only. Our audience is broad spectrum." Accept only letter, synopsis with cast list, playwright's resume, production history. No unsolicited scripts. If script is requested, reports within 9 months. Rights negotiaged with each playwright on an individual basis. Pay negotiable.
Needs: All genres. All topics. All styles. Full length only. No children's plays. "We have 2 distinct play series in winter—one for large scale productions, the other for smaller scale, more contemporary/experimental.
Tips: "No formulaic writing or television-style writing. Works *should be theatrical*, using the elements that make theater a distinctive art form. Works should *say* something moving, interesting, thought-provoking and entertaining about the human condition. We want fresh voices. Originality, not repetition is key here. We are looking for top-quality plays with fresh insights/approaches. Musicals should have top-quality music, lyrics and book."

WOULD YOU USE THE SAME CALENDAR YEAR AFTER YEAR?

Of course not! If you scheduled your appointments using last year's calendar, you'd risk missing important meetings and deadlines, so you keep up-to-date with a new calendar each year. Just like your calendar, *Writer's Market*® changes every year, too. Many of the editors move or get promoted, rates of pay increase, and even editorial needs change from the previous year. You can't afford to use an out-of-date book to plan your marketing efforts!

So save yourself the frustration of getting your work returned in the mail, stamped MOVED: ADDRESS UNKNOWN. And of NOT submitting your work to new listings because you don't know they exist. **Make sure you have the most current marketing information by ordering *1993 Writer's Market* today.** All you have to do is complete the attached post card and return it with your payment or charge card information. Order now, and there's one thing that won't change from your *1992 Writer's Market* - the price! That's right, we'll send you the 1993 edition for just $25.95. *1993 Writer's Market* will be published and ready for shipment in September 1992.

Let an old acquaintance be forgot, and toast the new edition of *Writer's Market*. Order today!

(See other side for more books to help you get published)

SAVE 15%
ON THESE NEW WRITING BOOKS!

Close-up

Lloyd Richards
Artistic Director
National Playwrights Conference

The Eugene O'Neill Theater Center, located in Waterford, Connecticut, is one of the nation's great meeting places for playwrights, composers, lyricists and other performing arts professionals. The center was established in 1964 in conjunction with the National Playwrights Conference, which is dedicated to providing talented writers the opportunity to develop their plays in the company of other theater artists. Lloyd Richards, dean of the Yale School of Drama, serves as the artistic director of the conference.

Richards, whose background includes work on- and off-Broadway, television, regional and community theater and radio, has been directing plays for more than 40 years. Having been involved with the National Playwrights Conference since its formation, Richards has witnessed the development of this unique playwriting project, conducted over a four-week period each July. "The conference is unique both in terms of its longevity, the quality of artists who continually participate who support the development of new playwrights, and the success and proliferation of its systems of work," he says.

The selection process for plays to be featured at the conference begins each fall when the office receives approximately 1,400 manuscripts. From these, up to 15 plays are selected over a period of seven months. The writers of the chosen works are invited to participate in a Pre-Conference Weekend at the O'Neill Center, at which time they give readings of their works to the artistic staff of the conference, as well as to their peers. They then meet with the artistic director, director, dramaturg and designer to determine how their plays may be improved and refined. Scripts are selected on the basis of talent and not, as Richards points out, on the basis of commercial potential. "Scripts are not selected simply because they are believed to be next year's off-Broadway or Broadway hit. We search for a unique voice, an original voice, a talent for the theater, and we attempt to accomplish that through the work we do."

During the actual conference, playwrights remain at the O'Neill Center, free to discuss and revise their works as necessary. Plays are given four to five days of rehearsal and two staged readings before visitors, the public and the regular conference staff. Richards advises writers to develop their scripts as far as they can before submitting them to the conference. All full-length plays are eligible, including plays with music. Musicals and operas should be submitted to the National Music Theater Conference (write to the "Music Theater Conference" at the O'Neill Center's New York office). Adaptations and previously produced plays are not eligible.

While "a great deal of intensive work is done in a very short time," the conference program is a successful one, and is emulated internationally. All playwrights holding American citizenship or permanent residency in the U.S. are encouraged to submit their work. "Everyone has an opportunity," says Richards. "We invite playwrights to submit and respect the fact that they are guests as a consequence of that invitation."

—Roseann Shaughnessy

PEOPLE'S LIGHT & THEATRE COMPANY, 39 Conestoga Rd., Malvern PA 19355. (215)647-1900. Producing Director: Danny S. Fruchter. Produces 5 full-length plays/year; no more than 1 new play/year. "LORT D Actors' Equity plays are produced in Malvern 30 miles outside Philadelphia in 350-seat mainstage and 150-seat Steinbright Stage. Our audience is mainly suburban, some from Philadelphia." Query with synopsis and cast list. Reports in 10 months. No scripts returned without SASE. Buys "rights to production in our theater, sometimes for local touring." Pays 2-5% royalty.
Needs: "We will produce anything that interests us." Prefers single set, maximum cast of 12 (for full length), fewer for one-act. No musicals, mysteries, domestic comedies.
Tips: "Writers should be aware of trend away from naturalistic family drama and trend toward smaller cast size."

PHILADELPHIA FESTIVAL THEATRE FOR NEW PLAYS, 3900 Chestnut St., Philadelphia PA 19104. (215)222-5000. Artistic Director: Dr. Carol Rocamora. Estab. 1981. Produces 4-6 plays/year. Professional productions (LORT D contract), subscriber series. Submit complete ms with SASE and $5 processing fee. Reports in 6 months.
Needs: A wide variety of new works without previous professional production.

PIER ONE THEATRE, P.O. Box 894, Homer AK 99603. (907)235-7333. Artistic Director: Lance Petersen. Estab. 1973. Produces 5-8 plays/year. "Plays to various audiences for various plays—e.g. children's, senior citizens, adult, family, etc. Plays are produced on Kemai Peninsula." Submit complete ms. Reports in 2 months. Pays $25-125/performance.
Needs: "No restrictions—willing to read *all* genres." No stock reviews, hillbilly or sit-coms.
Tips: "There are slightly increased opportunities for new works. Don't start your play with a telephone conversation. New plays ought to be risky business; they ought to be something the playwright feels is terribly important."

PIONEER DRAMA SERVICE, P.O. Box 22555, Denver CO 80222. (303)759-4297. FAX: (303)759-0475. Publisher: Steven Fendrich. Estab. 1963. 10% freelance written. Plays are performed by high school, junior high and adult groups, colleges, churches and recreation programs for audiences of all ages. "We are one of the largest full-service play publishers in the country in that we handle straight plays, musicals, children's theater and melodrama." Publishes 15 plays/year; 20% musicals and 80% straight plays. Query only; no unsolicited manuscripts. Buys all rights. Reports in 2 months. Pays on royalty basis with some outright purchase.
Needs: "We use the standard two-act format, two-act musicals, religious drama, comedies, mysteries, drama, melodrama and plays for children's theater (plays to be done by adult actors for children)." Length: two-act musicals and two-act comedies up to 90 minutes; and children's theater of 1 hour. Prefer many female roles, one simple set. Currently overstocked on one-act plays.

☐**PLAYERS PRESS, INC.,** P.O. Box 1132, Studio City CA 91604. Senior Editor: Robert W. Gordon. "We deal in all entertainment areas and handle publishable works for film and television as well as theater. Performing arts books, plays and musicals. All plays must be in stage format for publication." Also produces scripts for video and material for cable television. 80% freelance written. 20-30 scripts/year are unagented submissions; 5-15 books are also unagented. Works with 1-10 unpublished/unproduced writers annually. Submit query. "Include one #10 SASE, reviews and proof of production. All play submissions must have been produced and should include a flyer and/or program with dates of performance." Reports in 3 months. Buys negotiable rights. "We prefer all area rights." Pays variable royalty "according to area; approximately 10-75% of gross receipts." Also pays in outright purchase of $100-25,000 or $5-5,000/performance.
Needs: "We prefer comedies, musicals and children's theater, but are open to all genres. We will rework the ms after acceptance. We are interested in the quality, not the format. Performing Arts Books that deal with theater how-to are of strong interest."
Tips: "Send only material requested. Do not telephone."

PLAYS, The Drama Magazine for Young People, 120 Boylston St., Boston MA 02116. Editor: Sylvia K. Burack. Estab. 1941. Publishes approximately 75 one-act plays and dramatic program material each school year to be performed by junior and senior high, middle grades, lower grades. Mss should follow the general style of *Plays*. Stage directions should not be typed in capital letters or underlined. No incorrect grammar or dialect. Desired lengths for mss are: junior and senior high—18-20 double-

☐ *Open box preceding a listing indicates a cable TV market.*

spaced ms pages (25 to 30 minutes playing time). Middle grades—10 to 15 pages (15 to 20 minutes playing time). Lower grades—6 to 10 pages (8 to 15 minutes playing time). Pays "good rates on acceptance." Query first for adaptations. Reports in 2-3 weeks. Sample copy $3.50; send SASE for mss specification sheet.

Needs: "Can use comedies, farces, melodramas, skits, mysteries and dramas, plays for holidays and other special occasions, such as Book Week; adaptations of classic stories and fables; historical plays; plays about black history and heroes; puppet plays; folk and fairy tales; creative dramatics; and plays for conservation, ecology or human rights programs."

THE PLAYWRIGHTS' CENTER, 2301 Franklin Ave. E., Minneapolis MN 55406. (612)332-7481. Director of Public Relations: Lisa Stevens. Estab. 1971. "Midwest Playlabs is a 2-week developmental workshop for new plays. The program is held in Minneapolis and is open by script competition. It is an intensive two-week workshop focusing on the development of a script and the playwright. 4-6 new plays are given rehearsed public readings at the site of the workshop." Announcements of playwrights by end of April. Playwrights receive honoraria, travel expenses, room and board.

Needs: "We are interested in playwrights with talent, ambitions for a sustained career in theater and scripts which could benefit from an intensive developmental process involving professional dramaturgs, directors and actors. U.S. citizens, only; no musicals or children's plays. Participants must attend all or part of conference depending on the length of their workshop. Full lengths only. No previously produced materials. Call or write for application. Submission deadline: January 14.

Tips: "We do not buy scripts or produce them. We are a service organization that provides programs for developmental work on scripts for members."

PLAYWRIGHTS PREVIEW PRODUCTIONS, #304, 1160 5th Ave., New York NY 10029. Artistic Director: Frances Hill. Estab. 1983. Produces 4-6 plays/year. Professional productions off or off off-broadway, 1 production Kennedy Center—throughout the year. General audience. Submit complete ms. Reports in 4 months. If produced, option for 6 months. Pays royalty.

Needs: Both one-act and full-length; generally one set or styled playing dual. Good imaginative, creative writing. Cast limited to 3-7.

Tips: "We tend to reject 'living-room' plays. We look for imaginative settings. Be creative and interesting with intellectual content."

PLAYWRIGHTS THEATRE OF NEW JERSEY, 33 Green Village Rd., Madison NJ 07940. (201)514-1787. Artistic Director: Buzz McLaughlin. Estab. 1986. Produces 3 productions/6 staged readings/12 sit-down readings/year. "We operate under a small professional theater contract with Actors' Equity Association for all productions and readings." Submit complete ms. Short bio and production history required. Reports in 2 months. "For productions we ask the playwright to sign an agreement that gives us exclusive rights to the play for the production period and for 30 days following. After the 30 days we give the rights back with no strings attached, except for commercial productions. We ask that our developmental work be acknowledged in any other professional productions." Pays $100 for productions and staged readings plus living expenses.

Needs: Any style or length; full-length, one-acts, musicals.

Tips: "No plays that simply reflect the world's chaos. We are interested in developing plays that illuminate the human spirit. We're looking for plays that are in their early stages of development."

PRIMARY STAGES COMPANY, INC., 584 9th Ave., New York NY 10036. (212)333-7471. Artistic Director: Casey Childs. Estab. 1983. Produces 4 plays, 3 workshops, over 100 readings/year. All of the plays are produced professionally off-Broadway at the 45th Street Theatre, 354 West 45th St. Query and synopsis. Reports in 3 months. "If Primary Stages produces the play, we ask for the right to move it for up to 6 months after the closing performance." Writers paid "same as the actors."

Needs: "We are looking for highly theatrical works that were written exclusively with the stage in mind. We do not want TV scripts or strictly realistic plays."

Tips: No "living room plays, disease-of-the-week plays, back-porch plays, father/son work-it-all-out-plays, etc."

THE QUARTZ THEATRE, P.O. Box 465, Ashland OR 97520. (503)482-8119. Artistic Director: Dr. Robert Spira. Estab. 1973. Produces 5 plays/year. "Semi-professional mini-theater. General audience." Send 3-page dialogue and personal bio. Reports in 2 weeks. Pays 5% royalty after expenses.

Needs: "Any length, any subject, with or without music. We seek playwrights with a flair for language and theatrical imagination."

Tips: "We look at anything. We do not do second productions unless substantial rewriting is involved. Our theater is a stepping stone to further production. Our playwrights are usually well-read in comparative religion, philosophy, psychology, and have a comprehensive grasp of human problems. We seek the 'self-indulgent' playwright who pleases him/herself first of all."

RADIO REPERTORY COMPANY, INC., P.O. Box 23179, Cincinnati OH 45223. President: Jon C. Hughes. Estab. 1988. Produces 6 plays/year. Public radio. Query before submitting manuscript. Buys first rights. Payment depends on non-profit funding. Authors' honorarium $400.
Needs: Genres: dramatic adaptations of classical and contemporary short stories. Length: 24-27 minutes (about 20 pages). No more than 10 characters.
Tips: "The ms must be in the appropriate format. Request free copy of guidelines and format before submitting ms. Enclose SASE."

‡RIVER ARTS REPERTORY, P.O. Box 1166, Woodstock NY 12498. (914)679-5899. Artistic Director: Lawrence Sacharon. Estab. 1979. Produces 6 plays/year. Plays are performed at Bearsville Theatre, a professional summer theater. Submit query and synopsis. Reports in 6 months. Buys negotiable rights. Pays 6% royalty.
Needs: Original, unproduced full-length plays.

THE ROAD COMPANY, P.O. Box 5278 EKS, Johnson City TN 37603. (615)926-7726. Artistic Director: Robert H. Leonard. Literary Manager: Christine Murdock. Estab. 1975. Produces 3 plays/year. "Our professional productions are intended for a general adult audience." Query and synopsis. Reports in 4 months. Pays royalty. "When we do new plays we generally try to have the playwright in residence during rehearsal for 3-4 weeks for about $1,000 plus room and board."
Needs: We like plays that experiment with form, that challenge, inform and entertain. We are a small ensemble based company. We look for smaller cast shows of 4-6."
Tips: "We are always looking for 2-character (male/female) plays. We are interested in plays set in the South. We are most interested in new work that deals with new forms. We write our own plays using improvisational techniques which we then tour throughout the Southeast. When funding permits, we include one of our own new plays in our home season."

SHAW FESTIVAL, P.O. Box 774, Niagara-on-the-Lake, Ontario L0S 1J0 Canada. FAX: (416)468-5438. Artistic Director: Christopher Newton. Estab. 1972. Produces 10 plays/year. "Professional summer festival operating three theaters (Festival: 861 seats, Court House: 370 seats and Royal George: 350 seats). We also host some music and some winter rentals. Mandate is based on the works of G.B. Shaw and his contemporaries. We prefer to hold rights for Canada and northeastern U.S., also potential to tour." Pays 5-6% royalty. Submit with SASE or SAE and IRCs, depending on country of origin.
Needs: "We operate an acting ensemble of up to 75 actors; this includes 14 actor/singers and we have sophisticated production facilities. We run some winter seasons in Toronto for the production of new works. During the summer season (April-October) the Academy of the Shaw Festival organizes several workshops of new Canadian plays."

‡THE SHAZZAM PRODUCTION COMPANY, 418 Pier Ave., Santa Monica CA 90405. Artistic Director: Edward Blackoff. Estab. 1980. Produces 2 plays/year. Equity-waiver productions for adult audience. Query with complete ms and synopsis. Reports in 6 weeks. Obtains negotiable rights. Pays $15-25/ performance.
Needs: "Full-length plays dealing with important contemporary social and political human issues. Limit of 2 sets and requiring no more than 12 actors. No musicals or drawing-room farces."

‡AUDREY SKIRBALL-KENIS THEATRE, Suite 308, 9478 W. Olympic Blvd., Beverly Hills CA 90212. (213)284-8965. Program Director: Dennis Clontz. Estab. 1989. Produces 40 stage readings and workshop productions/year. "We utilize 3 theater facilities in the Los Angeles area with professional director and casts. Our stage readings and workshop productions are offered year-round. Our audience is the general public *and* theater professionals." Submit query and synopsis. Reports in 3 months. Obtains no rights. Pays $100 for stage readings; $500 for workshop productions.
Needs: "We need full-length original plays that have not been produced in the Los Angeles area and from which the playwright would benefit from a stage reading or workshop production as a means to either further develop the play or attract possible producing entities."
Tips: "No screenplays disguised as stage plays or domestic dramas about dysfunctional families. We are a nonprofit organization dedicated to new plays and playwrights. We do not produce plays for commercial runs, nor do we request any future commitment from the playwright should their play find a production by virtue of our stage reading or workshop programs."

SOUTH COAST REPERTORY, P.O. Box 2197, Costa Mesa CA 92628. (714)957-2602. Dramaturg: Jerry Patch. Literary Manager: John Glore. Estab. 1964. Produces 6 plays/year on mainstage, 5 on second stage. A professional nonprofit theater; a member of LORT and TCG. "We operate in our own facility which houses a 507-seat mainstage theater and a 161-seat second stage theater. We have a combined subscription audience of 24,000." Submit query and synopsis; manuscripts considered if submitted by agent. Reports in 4 months. Acquires negotiable rights. Pays negotiable royalty.

Needs: "We produce full-lengths. Our only iron-clad restriction is that a play be well written. We prefer plays that address contemporary concerns and are dramaturgically innovative. A play whose cast is larger than 15-20 will need to be extremely compelling and its cast size must be justifiable."
Tips: "We don't look for a writer to write for us—he or she should write for him or herself. We look for honesty and a fresh voice. We're not likely to be interested in writers who are mindful of *any* trends. Originality and craftsmanship are the most important qualities we look for."

SOUTHEAST PLAYWRIGHTS PROJECT, 353 Elmira Pl. NE, Atlanta GA 30307. (404)523-1368. Executive Director: Jim Grimsley. Estab. 1976. Produces approximately 30 readings/workshops/year and provides career development services, including ongoing Writers' Lab, newsletter and workshops. Write (including SASE) for general membership applications.
Needs: General membership open to any playwright who lives, or has lived in the Southeast. Associate member must have had public reading of one full-length or two one-act plays. Full Member must have had at least one full production of a full-length play or be Associate Member. Selection is competitive.
Tips: "We aim at becoming a regional type of New Dramatists organization. Selection committee is looking for a distinctive voice, imaginative use of the stage, not just TV movies or sitcoms in play form."

SOUTHERN APPALACHIAN REPERTORY THEATRE (SART), Mars Hill College, P.O. Box 620, Mars Hill NC 28754-0620. (704)689-1384. Artistic Director: James W. Thomas. Estab. 1975. Produces 5 plays/year. "Since 1975 the Southern Appalachian Repertory Theatre has produced 742 performances of 81 plays and played to over 100,000 patrons in the 152-seat Owen Theatre on the Mars Hill College campus. The theater's goals are quality, adventurous programming and integrity, both in artistic form and in the treatment of various aspects of the human condition. SART is a professional summer theater company whose audiences range from students to senior citizens." Also conducts an annual Southern Appalachian Playwrights' Conference in which five playwrights are invited for informal readings of their new scripts. Deadline for submission is Dec. 1 and conference is held the last weekend in January. If script is selected for production during the summer season, an honorarium is paid to the playwright in the amount of $500.
Needs: "Since 1975, one of SART's goals has been to produce at least one original play each summer season. To date, 27 original scripts have been produced. Plays by southern Appalachian playwrights or about southern Appalachia are preferred, but by no means exclusively. Complete new scripts welcomed."

STAGE ONE: The Louisville Children's Theatre, 425 W. Market St., Louisville KY 40202. (502)589-5946. Producing Director: Moses Goldberg. Estab. 1946. Produces 6-7 plays/year. 20% freelance written. 15-20% of scripts produced are unagented submissions (excluding work of playwright-in-residence). Plays performed by an Equity company for young audiences aged 4-18; usually does different plays for different age groups within that range. Submit complete ms. Reports in 4 months. Pays negotiable royalty or $25-50/performance.
Needs: "Good plays for young audiences of all types: adventure, fantasy, realism, serious problem plays about growing up or family entertainment." Cast: ideally, 10 or less. "Honest, visual potentiality, worthwhile story and characters are necessary. An awareness of children and their schooling is a plus. No campy material or anything condescending to children. No musicals unless they are fairly limited in orchestration."

STAGE WEST, 821 W. Vickery, Fort Worth TX 76104. (812)332-6238. Artistic Director: Jerry Russell. Estab. 1979. Produces 8 plays/year. "We stage professional productions at our own theater for a mixed general audience." Query and synopsis. Reports in 3 months. Rights are negotiable. Pays 7% royalty.
Needs: "We want full-length plays that are accessible to a mainstream audience but possess traits that are highly theatrical. Cast size of 10 or less and single or unit set are desired."

STEPPENWOLF THEATRE COMPANY, 1650 N. Halsted, Chicago IL 60614. (312)335-1888. Artistic Director: Randall Arney. Estab. 1976. Produces 5 plays/year.
Needs: We look mostly for contemporary comedies.

CHARLES STILWILL, Managing Director, Community Playhouse, P.O. Box 433, Waterloo IA 50704. (319)235-0367. Estab. 1917. Plays performed by Waterloo Community Playhouse with a volunteer cast. Produces 12 plays (7 adult, 5 children's); 1-2 musicals and 10-12 nonmusicals/year; 1-4 originals. 17% freelance written. Most scripts produced are unagented submissions. Works with 1-4 unpublished/unproduced writers annually. "We are one of few community theaters with a commitment to new scripts. We do at least one and have done as many as four a year. We have 4,300 season members." Average attendance at main stage shows is 3,300; at studio shows 2,000. "We try to fit the play to the theater. We do a wide variety of plays. Our public isn't going to accept nudity, too much sex, too much strong language. We don't have enough Black actors to do all-Black shows." Theater has done plays with as few as two characters, and as many as 98. "On the main stage, we usually pay between $300 and $500. In our studio, we usually pay between $50 and $500. We also produce children's theater. Send complete script. "Please, no loose pages." "Reports negatively within 1 year, but acceptance sometimes takes longer because we try to fit a wanted script into the balanced season. We sometimes hold a script longer than a year if we like it but cannot immediately find the right slot for it. We just did the Midwest premier of *Even in Laughter* which was written in 1981 and last year we did the world premiere of *Veranda*, which we'd had since 1986."

Needs: "We are looking for good adaptations of name children's shows and very good shows that don't necessarily have a name. We produce children's theater with both adult and child actors. We also do a small (2-6 actors) cast show that tours the elementary schools in the spring. This can only be about 45 minutes long."

STREET PLAYERS THEATRE, P.O. Box 2687, Norman OK 73070. (405)364-0207. Artistic Director: Robert Woods. Estab. 1980. Produces 6 play/year. Professional productions performed for Midwestern university community. One children's theater piece is toured throughout the region. Submit complete ms. Reports in 6 months. Limited production rights.
Needs: Produces previously unproduced work; slight preference given to Oklahoma and Southwest regional writers. Full-length plays preferred; all styles and topics considered. Small cast (5-6), single set preferred. Storefront-type theater, which holds up to 99 people. Fall Festival Contest pays $250, no guarantee of production; deadline: June 30 each year. New Plays Series and children's 50-minute piece: Negotiated average: $250.

THEATER ARTISTS OF MARIN, P.O. Box 150473, San Rafael CA 94915. (415)454-2380. Artistic Director: Charles Brousse. Estab. 1980. Produces 3 plays/year. Professional showcase productions for a general adult audience. Submit complete ms. Reports in 3 months. Assists in marketing to other theaters.
Needs: "All types of scripts: comedy, drama, farce. Prefers contemporary setting, with some relevance to current issues in American society. Will also consider 'small musicals,' reviews or plays with music." No children's shows, domestic sitcoms, one-man shows or commercial thrillers.

THEATER LUDICRUM, INC., Suite 83, 64 Charlesgate E., Boston MA 02215. (617)424-6831. Contact: Director. Estab. 1985. Produces 2-3 plays/year. Plays are performed in a small, non-equity theater in Boston. "Our audience includes minority groups (people of color, gays, women)." Submit complete ms. Reports in 4 months. Rights revert to author after production. Pays $15-30/performance.
Needs: "As a small theater with a small budget, we look for scripts with minimal sets, costumes, props and expense in general. We are interested in scripts that emphasize the word and acting."

THE THEATER OF NECESSITY, 11702 Webercrest, Houston TX 77048. (713)733-6042. Artistic Director: Philbert Plumb. Estab. 1981. Produces 4 plays/year. Our plays are produced in a small professional theater. Submis complete ms. Reports in 6 months. Buys performance rights. Pays standard royalties based on size of house for small productions or individual contracts for large productions (average $500/run). We usually keep mss on file unless we are certain we will never use script. Send SASE for script and #10 SASE for response.
Needs: Any play in a recognizable genre must be superlative in form and intensity. Experimental plays are given an easier read. We move to larger venue if the play warrants the expense.
Tips: "We are trying to buck some of the trends toward certain hits, and have been taking chances since our founding in 1981. The longer it takes us to respond, the more likely we will be producing your play."

THEATRE CALGARY, 220 9th Ave. SE, Calgary, Alberta T2G 5C4 Canada. (403)294-7440. FAX: (403)294-7493. Artistic Director: Brian Rintoul. Estab. 1970. Produces 6-8 plays/year. Professional productions. Reports in 3 months. Buys production rights usually, "but it can vary with specific contracts." Payments and commissions negotiated under individual contracts.
Needs: "Theatre Calgary is a major Canadian regional theater."
Tips: "Theatre Calgary still accepts unsolicited scripts, but does not have a significant script development program at the present time. We cannot guarantee a quick return time, and we will not return scripts without pre-paid envelopes."

THEATRE DE LA JEUNE LUNE, P.O. Box 25170, Minneapolis MN 55458. (612)332-3968. Artistic Directors: Barbra Berlovitz Desbois, Vincent Garcieux, Robert Rosen, Dominique Serrand. Estab. 1979. Produces 4 plays/year. Professional nonprofit company producing September-May for general audience. Query and *synopsis*. Reports in 2 months. Pays royalty or per performance. No unsolicited scripts, please.

Needs: "All subject matter considered, although plays with universal themes are desired; plays that concern people of today. We are constantly looking for plays with large casts. Generally *not* interested in plays with 1-4 characters. No psychological drama or plays that are written alone in a room without the input of outside vitality and life."
Tips: "We are an acting company that takes plays and makes them ours; this could mean cutting a script or not heeding a writer's stage directions. We are committed to the performance in front of the audience as the goal of all the contributing factors; therefore, the actors' voice is extremely important."

THEATRE ON THE MOVE, 1000 Murray Ross Parkway, North York, Ontario M3J 2P3 Canada. (416)665-8824. Artistic Director: Anne Hines. Produces 4 plays/year for families and young audiences—elementary and high schools and special venues (museums, etc.). Uses professional, adult, union actors. Submit query and synopsis or complete ms. Reports in 2 months. Acquires exclusive rights to Ontario, usually for a minimum of 1 year. Pays royalty or commission for works-in-progress.
Needs: Musicals or dramas for small casts (limit 4 actors) which deal with current topics of interest to children and families. Uncomplicated, "tourable" sets.
Tips: "Our shows have to educate the audience about some aspect of modern life, as well as entertain. The trend is away from fairy tales, etc."

THEATRE PROJECT COMPANY, 634 N. Grand, #10-H, St. Louis MO 63103. (314)531-1315. FAX: (314)533-3345. Artistic Director: William Freimuth. Estab. 1975. Produces 5 full-length adult plays for adventurous audience, plus one family show in 250-seat theater. Tours with three 50-minute children's plays that tour schools in Illinois and Missouri. Query and synopsis. Reports in 6 weeks. Pays 4-8% royalty.
Needs: "We are leaning toward an overt theatricality. We produce more comedy than drama; Shakespeare to Ionesco to Ludlam; one world premiere per year. We prefer casts of 8 or fewer. No big period costume shows."
Tips: "No 'people sitting around a New York apartment talking,' hopeless angst or historical drama."

THEATREWORKS, University of Colorado, P.O. Box 7150, Colorado Springs CO 80933. (719)593-3232. FAX: (719)593-3362. Producing Director: Whit Andrews. Estab. 1975. Produces 4 full-length plays/year and two new one-acts. "New full-length plays produced on an irregular basis. Casts are semi-professional and plays are produced at the university." Submit query and synopsis. No unsolicited manuscripts. One-act plays are accepted as Playwrights' Forum competition entries—submit complete ms. Deadline: Dec. 1; winners announced March 1. Two one-act competition winners receive full production, cash awards and travel allowances. Acquires exclusive regional option for duration of production. Full rights revert to author upon closing. Pays $300-1,200.
Needs: Full-lengths and one-acts—no restrictions on subject. "Cast size should not exceed 20; stage area is small with limited wing and fly space. Theatreworks is interested in the exploration of new and inventive theatrical work. Points are scored by imaginative use of visual image. Static verbosity and staid conventionalism not encouraged." No melodrama or children's plays.
Tips: "Too often, new plays seem far too derivative of television and film writing. We think theater is a medium which an author must specifically attack. The standard three-act form would appear to be on the way out. Economy, brevity and incisiveness are favorably received."

THEATREWORKS/USA, 890 Broadway, New York NY 10003. (212)677-5959. Artistic Director: Jay Harnick. Literary Manager: Barbara Pasternack. Produces 3 new musical plays/season. Produces professional musicals that primarily tour (TYA contract) but also play at an off-Broadway theater for a young audience. Submit query and synopsis or sample song. Reports in 8 months. Buys all rights. Pays 6% royalty; offers $1,500 advance against future royalties for new, commissioned plays.
Needs: Musicals and plays with music. Historical/biographical themes (ages 8-15), classic literature, fairy tales, and issue-oriented themes and material suitable for young people ages 5-10. Five person cast, minimal lighting. "We like well-crafted shows with good dramatic structure—a protagonist who wants something specific, an antagonist, a problem to be solved—character development, tension, climax, etc. No Saturday Afternoon Special-type shows, shows with nothing to say or 'kiddie' theater shows or fractured fairy tales. We do not address high school audiences."
Tips: "Writing for kids is just like writing for adults—only better (clearer, cleaner). Kids will not sit still for unnecessary exposition and overblown prose. Long monologues, soliloquies and 'I Am' songs and ballads should be avoided. Television, movies and video make the world of entertainment highly competitive. We've noticed lately how well popular children's titles, contemporary and in public domain, sell. We are very interested in acquiring adaptations of this type of material."

TRINITY SQUARE ENSEMBLE, P.O. Box 1798, Evanston IL 60204. (312)328-0330. Managing Director: Kathleen A. Martin. Estab. 1981. Tours 6-8 plays/year. "Professional non-equity company, member of League of Chicago Theatres, ensemble, company of artists. We look for scripts adapted from classics suited to our ensemble as well as new works. Writers are encouraged to research our company. We produce new children's pieces—must blend stories with school curriculum." Send query and synopsis. "We do not want full ms submissions. If we request, then we'll return." Reports in 6-18 months. Obtains negotiated percentage of rights, usually 10%.

Needs: Cast: prefer 3-4, no more than 10. Set: preferably simple for touring shows.

Tips: "We are particularly interested in producing 45-60 minute youth oriented scripts that address topical issues, such as self-esteem and ecology as well as curriculum-enhancing theater pieces. Also, scripts which can be easily expanded with music and movement to full-length mainstage productions."

‡**UNDERMAIN THEATRE**, P.O. Box 141166, Dallas TX 75214. (214)748-3082. Artistic Directors: Raphael Parry and Katherine Owens. Estab. 1984. Produces 4-5 plays/year. "We are intended for a general audience. We are a professional theater with a resident ensemble." Submit complete ms. Writer must include SASE. Reports in 6 months. Buys limited restricted professional rights exclusive to a 100-mile radius. Pays $500-1,000 outright purchase.

Needs: "We produce 1-2-act modern works. The majority of the plays produced are avant-garde or alternative plays with a strong emphasis on surreal, post-modern and expressionistic." Cast limit of 10; minimal props; sets minimal.

Tips: "No kitchen dramas or naturalistic family dramas. Theater must strive to be different from television and film. There needs to be something that the audience receives that they can only receive from live theater."

UNICORN THEATRE, 3820 Main St., Kansas City MO 64111. (816)531-PLAY. Producing Artistic Director: Cynthia Levin. Estab. 1980. Produces 8 plays/year. "We are a professional Equity Theatre. Typically, we produce contemporary plays." Query and synopsis and sample dialogue. Will not consider unsolicited mss. Reports in 2 weeks.

Needs: Prefers contemporary (post-1950) scripts. Does not accept musicals, one-acts, or historical plays. When a manuscript is requested, include a brief synopsis, a bio, a character breakdown, SASE if manuscript is to be returned, a self-addressed, stamped post card for acknowledgement of receipt is desired. A royalty/prize of $1,000 will be awarded the playwright of any play selected through this process, The National Playwright Award. This script shall receive production as part of the Unicorn's regular season.

‡**UNIVERSITY OF HAWAII PRESS/HAWAII REVIEW**, 1733 Donagho Rd., Honolulu HI 96822. (808)956-8548. Artistic Director: Galatea Maman. Estab. 1963. Publishes 3 plays/year. "For a general audience, literary types." Submit complete ms. Reports in 1-3 months. Buys copyright, reverts to author on publication. Pays honorarium, $5/page. SASE.

Needs: "Besides all types of plays, we accept fiction, poetry and nonfiction. Nothing too avant-garde."

Tips: "No obscene, disjointed, performance material. Audiences are changing to include more of a broader representation of classes, ethnic backgrounds and ages, necessitates universality of themes. Originality is a must; plays still need to aim at touching the heart, the emotions of reader/audience."

UNIVERSITY OF MINNESOTA, DULUTH THEATRE, 10 University Dr., Duluth MN 55812. (218)726-8562. Artistic Director: Ann Bergeron. Produces 12 plays/year. Plays are performed at the University Theatre, American College Theatre Festival and the Minnesota Repertory Theatre (summer). Submit query and synopsis only. Reports in 3 weeks. Acquires performance rights. Pays $35-100/performance.

Needs: All genres. Prefers younger casting requirements and single set or unit setting shows. No previously produced work or one-act plays.

Tips: "We are a very active undergraduate theater program that is very interested in producing new work. We annually produce a new play for the American College Theatre Festival in which there are several major playwriting awards."

‡**VIRGINIA STAGE COMPANY**, P.O. Box 3770, Norfolk VA 23514. (804)627-6988. Artistic Director: Charles Towers. Estab. 1979. Produces 6 plays/year. 20% freelance written. Only agent submitted or professionally recommended work accepted. A professional regional theater serving the 1 million people of the Hampton Roads area. Plays are performed in LORT C proscenium mainstage or LORT D flexible second stage. Works with 2 writers annually. Query with synopsis only; "sample scene or dialogue may be included." Negotiates rights and payment.

Needs: "Primarily full-length dramas and comedies that address contemporary issues within a study of broader themes and theatricality. Material must be inherently theatrical in use of language, staging or character. We do not want to see material that offers simplistic solutions to complex concerns, or is more easily suited for television or film."

WALNUT STREET THEATRE, 9th and Walnut Streets, Philadelphia PA 19107. (215)574-3550. Executive Director: Bernard Havard. Literary Manager: Alexa Kelly. Produces 5 mainstage and 4 studio plays/year. "Our plays are performed in our own space. WST has 3 theaters—a proscenium (main-

stage), audience capacity: 1,052; 2 studios, audience capacity: 79-99. We have a subscription audience, second largest in the nation." Query with synopsis and 10 pages. Reports in 5 months. Rights negotiated per project. Pays royalty (negotiated per project) or outright purchase.
Needs: "Full-length dramas and comedies, musicals, translations, adaptations and revues. The studio plays must be small cast, simple sets."
Tips: "We will consider anything. Bear in mind that on the mainstage we look for plays with mass appeal, Broadway-style. The studio spaces are our Off-Broadway. No children's plays. Our mainstage audience goes for work that is entertaining and light. Our studio season is when we look for plays that have bite and are more provocative."

WEST COAST ENSEMBLE, P.O. Box 38728, Los Angeles CA 90038. (213)871-8673. Artistic Director: Les Hanson. Estab. 1982. Produces 6 plays/year. Plays will be performed in one of our two theaters in Hollywood in an Equity-waiver situation. Submit complete ms. Reports in 5 months. Obtains the exclusive rights in southern California to present the play for the period specified. All ownership and rights remain with the playwright. Pays $25-45/performance.
Needs: Prefers a cast of 6-12.
Tips: "Submit the manuscript in acceptable dramatic script format."

WESTBETH THEATRE CENTER, INC., 151 Bank St., New York NY 10014. (212)691-2272. FAX: (212)924-7185. Producing Director: Arnold Engelman. Estab. 1977. Produces 10 readings and 6 productions/year. Professional off-Broadway theater. Submit complete ms with SASE and allow 90 days for response. Obtains rights to produce as showcase with option to enter into full option agreement.
Needs: "Contemporary full-length plays. Production values (i.e. set, costumes, etc.) should be kept to a minimum." No period pieces. Limit 10 actors; doubling explained.

THE WESTERN STAGE, 156 Homestead Ave., Salinas CA 93901. Dramaturg: Joyce Lower. Estab. 1990.
Needs: The Steinbeck Playwriting Prize for playwrights whose works are in the spirit of John Steinbeck. One winner will be chosen following staged readings of three finalists to receive a $1,000 cash award, support during the revision process (up to $4,000), a full production and royalties for the production. Submissions accepted June 1-August 31 only. Response by September 30. An application must accompany each submission. For an application and the complete submission guidelines, contact Joyce Lower at The Western Stage.

THE WOMEN'S PROJECT AND PRODUCTIONS, 220 W. 42nd St., 18th Fl., New York NY 10036. (212)382-2750. Artistic Director: Julia Miles. Estab. 1978. Produces 3 plays/year. Professional off-Broadway productions. Submit query and synopsis. Reports in 3 weeks on queries.
Needs: "We are looking for full-length plays, written by women only. No plays by male authors."

‡WOOLLY MAMMOTH THEATRE COMPANY, 1401 Church St. NW, Washington DC 20005. (202)393-3939. Artistic Director: Howard Shalwitz. Literary Manager: Greg Tillman. Produces 5 plays/year. 50% freelance written. Produces professional productions for the general public in Washington, DC. 2-3 scripts/year are unagented submissions. Works with 1-2 unpublished/unproduced writers annually. Accepts unsolicited scripts; reports in 6 weeks on scripts; very interesting scripts take much longer. Buys first- and second- class production rights. Pays 5% royalty.
Needs: "We look only for plays that are highly unusual in some way. Apart from an innovative approach, there is no formula. One-acts are not used." Cast limit of 8.

WORCESTER FOOTHILLS THEATRE COMPANY, 074 Worcester Center, Worcester MA 01608. (508)754-3314. Artistic Director: Marc P. Smith. Literary Manager: Greg DeJarnett. Estab. 1974. Produces 7 plays/year. Full time professional theater, general audience. Query and synopsis. Reports in 3 weeks. Pays royalty.
Needs: "Produce plays for general audience. No gratuitous violence, sex or language. Prefer cast under 10 and single set. 30' proscenium with apron but no fly space."

Screenwriting

It's probably a good bet that last year a lot of writers took a look at the most recent check they received for a magazine article, compared it to the $3 million price tag commanded by Joe Eszterhas' script called *Basic Instinct*, and decided that the time was ripe for a career change.

There is no doubt that the payoff can be big. But don't let the big numbers hypnotize you into thinking that the payoff is easy. The competition is fierce, and not just from other writers. For some reason, nearly everyone who has ever seen a movie considers himself capable of writing a script. Folks who would never consider sitting down and writing a novel are convinced that they can write something a lot better than the stuff they see on television or in the theaters.

The result is an overwhelming flood of mostly unsuitable material that must be dealt with on a daily basis by agents, producers and studio readers. Their challenge is to filter through this mess and somehow discover the gold nuggets that remain, and the rules they've set and the process they rely on has left many would-be screenwriters frustrated and bitter.

The serious writer must accept these rules and play by them in order to win. There are certain required tools: 1) At least two *really good* spec scripts (scripts written "on speculation"); 2) A professional approach to the craft; and 3) Patience and perseverence.

The marketplace has changed over the past couple of years. It used to be that a writer would be brought on as something akin to a hired gun and asked to simply execute an idea already in development. Or, a writer might verbally pitch a story and receive a development deal in which everyone on a producer's or studio's development staff would have a voice in the writing process.

Recently, though, the spec script has become the hot item on the market. The above-mentioned *Basic Instinct* was written on spec, as was *Flatliners*, which brought a $400,000 fee to first-time screenwriter Peter Filardi. *Jacob's Ladder*, Bruce Joel Rubin's horrific thriller, was a spec effort that made the rounds for years before being produced. Twenty-three-year-old Kathy McWorter sold her spec, *The Cheese Stands Alone*, (unproduced at this writing) for a cool million. The list goes on and on.

What does this mean to the writer? It means the emphasis is back on the written word, not on the verbal pitch. And that means that writers everywhere, regardless of what part of the country they call home, have a chance to see their stories end up on the big screen. But first, they need to have those spec scripts in hand – at least two of them, because agents (yes, you'll probably need an agent) will want to see that you aren't just a One-Script Wonder, but are in this for the long haul.

You can send scripts to production companies without using an agent. You'll need a release form, (a generic one is supplied in *Successful Scriptwriting*, Writer's Digest Books) which you can usually obtain from the production company. Many writers are concerned about release forms, worried that is is a license to steal. Forget about that. You can't sell your work unless someone reads it, and no one will read it without a release form (due to the proliferation of so-called "nuisance lawsuits"). This is one of the rules you have to follow if you want to play the game. You can take steps toward protecting your work by registering it with The Writers Guild, 8955 Beverly Blvd., Los Angeles CA 90048.

On the other hand, if you want to write for television, it is virtually impossible to break in without an agent. Production companies rely on agents to screen out the chaff and to provide a modicum of legal protection. So, write a couple of spec scripts for quality shows currently on the air – don't write a pilot for an original show – and contact agents willing to consider new writers. You can obtain a list of all Guild-sanctioned agents through the Writers Guild, and *The Hollywood Scriptwriter* newsletter features an Annual Agency Review for its subscribers, which surveys open agencies (*The Hollywood Scriptwriter*, 1626 N. Wilcox #385, Hollywood CA 90028, (818)991-3096). *Guide to Literary Agents and Art/Photo Reps* (Writer's Digest Books) also includes a section of script agents.

If you've never written a script before, take the time to learn the form. There are some very definite guidelines to follow in terms of format, structure, exposition, character development, and a host of do's and don'ts you need to be cognizant of if you are going to approach the marketplace as a professional. There are a number of books available on the subject, many of which explore not only the craft but the business of screenwriting as well. Rent some tapes of successful movies, and outline the scenes as they appear – it's a great way to study structure and pacing. Another tip: Tape record the dialogue and play it back without the picture. You'll be amazed at how succinct, even sparse, screen dialogue is.

Once your script is written, you'll approach agents with a query letter. This is your sales pitch. It should be no more than a page long and should include any writing credits you may have. If you have no credits, don't point that out—just devote the page to a compact, powerful description of your script. Don't tell the agent how rich he will become thanks to your script, and don't warn the agent that you've registered, copyrighted and mailed copies of the script to your next of kin. Just describe the script, ask if they'd like to see it and enclose a SASE if you expect any response.

Stay in touch with the business. Trade publications such as *Daily Variety* or *Hollywood Reporter* keep you up-to-date with who's who and what's happening; specialty newsletters such as *Hollywood Scriptwriter* offer tips from top professionals, instructional articles and general advice.

Finally, heed the words of Jim Cash (*Batman, Top Gun*) who advises writers to "accept failure as a temporary state—however long that state may be—and simply outlast it." In other words, don't stop after the first or second script. Almost without exception, those "overnight success" stories you read about have a whole other story behind them—a story of years of toil on scripts that will never see the light of day, scripts that were just a part of the learning and dues-paying process all writers must endure.

For more screenwriting markets, see Other Scriptwriting Markets at the end of the Screen-writing section.

ANGEL'S TOUCH PRODUCTIONS, 10445 Chandler Blvd., North Hollywood CA 91601. Director of Develpment: Phil Nemy. Professional screenplays and teleplays. Send script and/or synopsis. Reports in 6 months. Rights negotiated between production company and author. Payment negotiated.
Needs: All types, all genres, only full-length teleplays and screenplays—no one-acts or pieces involving homosexuality.
Tips: "We are now only seeking feature film screenplays, television screenplays, episodic and sitcom teleplays."

BLAZING PRODUCTIONS, INC., Suite 286, 4712 Avenue N, Brooklyn NY 11234. Contact: David Krinsky. Estab. 1985. Produces material for "major and independent studios." Buys 1-3 scripts/year. Buys all rights. No books, no treatments, no articles. *Only* completed movie scripts and television movie scripts. Reports in 6 weeks on queries.
Needs: Commercial, well written, high concept scripts in the drama, comedy, action and thriller genres. No other scripts. Submit a one-page synopsis along with a query letter regarding the material. Include SASE. *Do not send any scripts unless requested.*
Tips: "Can always use a *good* comedy. Writers should be flexible and open to suggestions. Material with interest (in writing) from a known actor/director is a *major plus* in the consideration of the material. We also need sexy thrillers."

‡ANTHONY CARDOZA ENTERPRISES, Box 4163, North Hollywood CA 71617. (818)985-5550. President: Anthony Cardoza. Produces material for "theater, TV and home." Buys one screenplay/year. Buys all rights. No previously produced material. Reports in 1 month.
Needs: Feature films. Submit completed script. Outright purchase.

‡□THE CHAMBA ORGANIZATION, 230 W. 105th St., #2-A, New York NY 10025. President: St. Clair Bourne. Produces material for "the activist-oriented audience; the general audience (PG), and in the educational film market we aim at high school and adult audiences, especially the so-called 'minority' audiences. Assignments are given solely based upon our reaction to submitted material. The material is the credential." 100% freelance written. 100% of scripts produced are unagented submissions. Buys 2-4 scripts/year. Works with 3 unpublished/unproduced writers annually.
Needs: "I concentrate primarily on feature film projects and unique feature-length documentary film projects. We prefer submission of film treatments first. Then, if the idea interests us, we negotiate the writing of the script." Also needs scripts for music videos and material (film) for cable television. Query with a brief description of plot, thumbnail descriptions of principal characters and any unusual elements. Payment negotiable according to Writers Guild standards.
Tips: Trends in screen include "a critical examination of traditional American values and dissatisfaction with 'yuppie ideology.' "

CINE/DESIGN FILMS, INC., P.O. Box 6495, Denver CO 80206. (303)777-4222. Producer/Director: Jon Husband. Produces educational material for general, sales-training and theatrical audiences. 75% freelance written. 90% of scripts produced are unagented submissions. "Original, solid ideas are encouraged." Rights purchased vary.
Needs: "Motion picture outlines in the theatrical and documentary areas. We are seeking theatrical scripts in the low-budget area that are possible to produce for under $1 million. We seek flexibility and personalities who can work well with our clients." Produces 16mm and 35mm films. Send an 8-10-page outline before submitting ms or script. Pays $100-200/screen minute on 16mm productions. Theatrical scripts negotiable.
Tips: "Understand the marketing needs of film production today. Materials will not be returned."

CTS ENTERPRISES, 1000 S. Westgate Ave., Los Angeles CA 90049. Artistic Director/President: Mitchell Nestor. Estab. 1985. Shares all rights. Reports in 3 months on submissions.
Needs: 35mm films projects and small cast plays. "We are now starting to work on plays to be made into films: "Dance of the Ghosts," "The Husband," and "Lone Eagle and Juliet." Jackson Pollock. Submit synopsis/outline and resume. Charges $150 fee for a critique. Must include SASE. Negotiates financial arrangements.

HARRY DELIGTER PRODUCTIONS, 3866 Keeshen Dr., Los Angeles CA 90066. (213)398-4949. President: Harry DeLigter. We have a theatrical motion pictures and television audience. Buys film, TV, worldwide and all media rights. Reports in 1 month.
Needs: Films, scripts, and videotapes. Query with synopsis.
Tips: "Remember we're offering entertainment. Upbeat, uplifting themes inventively presented reach bigger audiences. A sense of humor and good characters are important. Fragmented market means we're competing even more for audiences. Pitch/synopsis should include a simple to grasp one-line hook that might attract audiences in advertisement or in film trailers."

ENTERTAINMENT PRODUCTIONS, INC., #714, 2210 Wilshire Blvd., Santa Monica CA 90403. (213)456-3143. Producer: Edward Coe. Estab. 1971. Produces films for theatrical and television (worldwide) distribution. Reports in 1 month (only if SASE is enclosed for reply and/or return or material).
Needs: Screenplays. Only unencumbered originals. Query with synopsis. Pays outright purchase for all rights. Price negotiated on a project-by-project basis.
Tips: "Learn your trade. Be flexible."

ESTEBAN FILMS INC., 250 W. 57th St., New York NY 10107. (212)489-1491. FAX: (212)489-4954. Estab. 1988. We have a general audience. Buys all rights. Accepts previously published material. Reports in 1 week on queries; 3 months on submissions. Catalog for #10 SASE.
Needs: 35mm films, tapes and cassettes, and videotapes. We need feature films and music videos. Submit synopsis/outline, completed script and resume. Payment to be discussed personally with writer.

‡FURMAN FILMS, INC., P.O. Box 1769, Venice CA 90291. (213)306-2700. Vice President: Norma Doane. Estab. 1967. Produces material for the general public. Buys 2-3 scripts/year. Buys all rights. No previously produced material. Reports in 2 weeks on queries; 6 weeks on submissions.
Needs: Films (16mm) and videotapes. Looking for general film and video projects—8-30 minutes; corporate. Also looking for TV series—60 minutes each. Query or query with synopsis. Pays in accordance with Writers Guild standards.

‡EDWARD D. HANSEN, INC., 437 Harvard Dr., Arcadia CA 91006. (818)447-3168. President: Edward D. Hansen. Estab. 1973. Theatrical, television and home video markets comprise our audience. Buys 3-6 scripts/year. Buys all rights. Reporting time varies.
Needs: Films (35mm) and videotapes. We are looking for feature films, movies of the week, dramatic teleplays of varying lengths, and home videos. Query with synopsis. Pays in accordance with Writers Guild standards.
Tips: "What comes around goes around. Don't go with the trends."

‡INTERNATIONAL HOME ENTERTAINMENT INC., Suite 350, 1440 Veteran Ave., Los Angeles CA 90024. (213)460-4545. Assistant to the President: Jed Leland, Jr. Estab. 1976. Buys first rights. Reports in 2 months. Query. Pays in accordance with Writers Guild standards.

‡JLP PICTURES, P.O. Box 5155, Beverly Hills CA 90210. (213)276-8196. Development/Production Executive: John Dunbar. Estab. 1985. Produces material for feature TV, general audience, network, some TV documentary, and some sponsored films. Buys 8-10 scripts/year. Buys motion picture rights, some publishing rights. Accepts previously published material. Reports in 2 months.

Needs: Films (35mm) and videotapes. "We are seeking film/TV writers for various projects." Query with synopsis/outline and resume. Pays in accordance with Writers Guild standards or negotiates deal above WGA standard.

☐**LEE MAGID PRODUCTIONS**, P.O. Box 532, Malibu CA 90265. (213)463-5998. President: Lee Magid. Produces material for all markets: adult, commercial — even musicals. 90% freelance written. 70% of scripts produced are unagented submissions. Works with "many" unpublished/unproduced writers. Buys all rights or will negotiate. No previously produced material. Does not return unsolicited material.

Needs: Films, sound filmstrips, phonograph records, television shows/series, videotape presentations. Currently interested in film material, either for video (television) or theatrical. "We deal with cable networks, producers, live-stage productions, etc." Works with musicals for cable TV. Prefers musical forms for video comedy. Submit synopsis/outline and resume. Pays in royalty, in outright purchase, in accordance with Writers Guild standards, or depending on author.

Tips: "We're interested in comedy material. Forget drug-related scripts."

‡**MARATHON ENTERTAINMENT PRODUCERS**, #215, 10202 W. Washington BC, Culver City CA 90232. (213)280-8243. Development Executive: David King. Estab. 1985. "Audience is the movie going public." "We generally work on 5-10 projects per year with more than 10 writers." Buys film rights. Previously produced material OK. SASE. Reports in 1 week on queries; 2 months on submissions.

Needs: Films (35mm). Query with synopsis or submit completed script. Pays in accordance with Writers Guild standards.

☐**MEDIACOM DEVELOPMENT CORP.**, P.O. Box 1926, Simi Valley CA 93062. (818)594-4089. Director/Program Development: Felix Girard. Estab. 1978. 80% freelance written. Buys 10-20 scripts annually from unpublished/unproduced writers. 50% of scripts produced are unagented submissions. Query with samples. Reports in 1 month. Buys all rights or first rights.

Needs: Produces charts, sound filmstrips, 16mm films, multimedia kits, overhead transparencies, tapes and cassettes; slides and videotape with programmed instructional print materials, broadcast and cable television programs. Publishes software ("programmed instruction training courses"). Negotiates payment depending on project.

Tips: "Send short samples of work. Especially interested in flexibility to meet clients' demands, creativity in treatment of precise subject matter. We are looking for good, fresh projects (both special and series) for cable and pay television markets. A trend in the audiovisual field that freelance writers should be aware of is the move toward more interactive video disk/computer CRT delivery of training materials for corporate markets."

MERIWETHER PUBLISHING LTD. (Contemporary Drama Service), 885 Elkton Dr., Colorado Springs CO 80907. Editor: Arthur Zapel. Estab. 1969. "We publish how-to materials in book and video formats. We are interested in materials for high school and college level students only. Our Contemporary Drama Service division publishes 60-70 plays/year." 80% written by unpublished writers. Buys 40-60 scripts/year from unpublished/unproduced writers. 90% of scripts are unagented submissions. Reports in 1 month on queries; 2 months on full-length submissions. Query should include synopsis/outline, resume of credits, sample of style and SASE. Catalog available for $2 postage. Offers 10% royalty or outright purchase.

Needs: Book mss on theatrical arts subjects. Christian activity book mss also accepted. We will consider elementary level religious materials and plays, but no elementary level children's secular plays. Query. Pays royalty; buys some mss outright.

Tips: "We publish a wide variety of speech contest materials for high school students. We are publishing more reader's theater scripts and musicals based on classic literature or popular TV shows, provided the writer includes letter of clearance from the copyright owner. Our educational books are sold to teachers and students at college and high school levels. Our religious books are sold to youth activity directors, pastors and choir directors. Our trade books are directed at the public with a sense of humor. Another group of buyers is the professional theater, radio and TV category."

THE MERRYWOOD STUDIO, 137 E. 38th St., New York NY 10016-2650. Creative Director: Raul da Silva. 20% freelance written. Estab. 1984. Produces animated motion pictures for entertainment audiences. No children's material sought or produced.

Needs: Proprietary material only. Human potential themes woven into highly entertaining drama, high adventure, comedy. This is a new market for animation with only precedent in the illustrated novels published in France and Japan. Cannot handle unsolicited mail/scripts and will not return mail. Open to credit sheets, concepts and synopses only. Profit sharing depending upon value of concept and writer's following. Will pay at least Writer's Guild levels or better, plus expenses.

Tips: "This is not a market for beginning writers. Established, professional work with highly unusual and original themes is sought. If you love writing, it will show and we will recognize it and reward it in every way you can imagine. We are not a 'factory' and work on a very high level of excellence."

‡**MONAREX HOLLYWOOD CORPORATION,** 9421½ West Pico Blvd., Los Angeles CA 90035. (213)552-1069. FAX: (213)552-1724. Chairman: Chris D. Nebe. Estab. 1978. Produces material for international theatrical and television motion pictures. We are producers and distributors. Buys 5-6 scripts/year. Buys all rights. Accepts previously produced material. Reports in 2 months. Free catalog.
Needs: Films (35mm) and videotapes. "We are seeking action, comedy and character-oriented love stories, dance films, anything commercial for theatrical or television production. Also, horror and dramatic screenplays." Submit synopsis/outline and completed script. Pays in accordance with Writers Guild standards.
Tips: "We look for strong visuals with strong characters and a unique plot."

NORTHSTAR ENTERTAINMENT GROUP, 1000 Centerville Turnpike, Virginia Beach VA 23463. (804)424-7777. Director of Development: Matt Sommer. Produces family-oriented material (made-for-TV movies, films and TV series). Query first and ask for a release form before submitting a short (two-or-three pages) synopsis of your script. Letter-quality please." Reports in 2 months.
Tips: "We are interested in very creative stories that explore Judeo-Christian themes in unique, imaginative ways. Compelling historical pieces and characters are welcome."

PACE FILMS, INC., 411 E. 53rd St., PHC, New York NY 10022. (212)755-5486. President: R. Vanderbes. Estab. 1965. Produces material for a general theatrical audience. Buys all rights. Reports in 2 months.
Needs: Theatrical motion pictures. Produces and distributes 35mm motion pictures for theatrical, TV and videocassettes. Query with synopsis/outline and writing background/credits. Completed scripts should be submitted together with an outline and SASE. Pays in accordance with Writers Guild standards.

‡**PARALLEL PICTURES,** P.O. Box 985, Hollywood CA 90078. (213)654-6113. New Projects Executive: Rick Tyler. Estab. 1988. "For a general audience, ages 16-31; depends on project. We produce for domestic as well as overseas audiences." Works with 5 writers/year. Buys all rights. No previously published material. Reports in 3 weeks on queries; 4 months on submissions.
Needs: Films (35mm). "We are looking for feature-length screenplays—action, comedy, low budget. We accept all genres—very openminded. We love rare and new ideas." Submit completed script. Buys by outright purchase.
Tips: "Take risks. I see too many replicas and poor development. If I don't see a plan of action or direction by the first 30 pages, something is wrong. Plots make the movie. That doesn't mean having many plots. You can keep it simple. Also, 80 pages is not feature length."

□ **TOM PARKER MOTION PICTURES,** 3491 S. Bristol, #285, Santa Anna CA 92704. (714)545-2887. FAX: (714)545-9775. President: Tom Parker. Produces and distributes feature-length motion pictures worldwide (Member AFMA) for theatrical, home video, pay and free TV. Works with 5-10 scripts per year. Previously produced and distributed "Wackiest Wagon Train in the West," (Rated G); "S S Girls," (Rated R); and "Initiation" (Rated R). Will acknowledge receipt of material and report within 90 days. "Follow the instructions herein and do not phone for info or to inquire about your script."
Needs: Completed scripts *only* for low budget (under $1 million) "R" or "PG" rated action/thriller, action/adventure, comedy, adult romance (R), sex comedy (R), family action/adventure to be filmed in 35mm film for the theatrical and home video market (do not send TV movie scripts, series, teleplays, stage plays). *Very limited dialogue.* Scripts should be action-oriented and fully described. Screen stories or scripts OK, but no camera angles please. No heavy drama, documentaries, social commentaries, dope stories, weird or horror. Violence or sex OK, but must be well motivated with strong story line. Submit synopsis and description of characters with finished scripts. Outright purchase: $5,000-25,000. Will consider participation, co-production.
Tips: "Absolutely will not return scripts or report on rejected scripts unless accompanied by SASE."

QUICKSILVER PRODUCTIONS, Suite 315, 12021 Wilshire Blvd., Los Angeles CA 90025. (213)826-7766. Vice President: Bret Carr. Estab. 1986. We have a motion picture audience. Buys all rights. Reports in 3 weeks.

□ *Open box preceding a listing indicates a cable TV market.*

Close-up

Bruce Joel Rubin
Screenwriter

Photo by Chuck Hashbarger

Bruce Joel Rubin, whose credits include "Ghost," (for which he won an Academy Award), and the surreal thriller "Jacob's Ladder," is a soft-spoken, articulate midwestern native who always wanted to write movies. A graduate of NYU Film School in 1965, Rubin recalls, "I thought I would leave film school and be immediately successful in the business. Nobody told me it would take 20 years to get a movie made. But I've learned that that is something not altogether uncommon; in fact, what is more common is to never get a movie made at all."

But after two decades of writing industrial films and teaching part-time at the University of Illinois, Rubin finally experienced the kind of success he'd been dreaming of. "I really wanted to be a Hollywood screenwriter," he says, "and in order to do that, you have to write a lot of screenplays." And that's what he did, including many that will never see the light of day, much less the light from a projector. But Rubin feels that it's all part of the learning process. "If you want to write a feature film, you have to write one. It has a very defined form. It's like writing a sonnet; you can't write a six-line sonnet, because that's not a sonnet. There is structure and flow to learn, and while you have great freedom within that, you have to obey the structure. And learning the structure of film is the essence of writing a screenplay."

Another key to quality writing, says Rubin, is to write about something that interests or moves you, instead of just telling a story. Certainly both of Rubin's major films reflect his intense personal fascination with the Ultimate Question. "My writing has always come from the same space inside of me. It's really a metaphysical world view, and my best writing has always been motivated and inspired by that. It is a postulation of a vision of life that is not bookended by the experience of birth or death. It's a bigger experience, a bigger world, than we perceive, and I feel drawn to addressing those issues."

It's that purpose that drives Rubin to write. But with that purpose, does the writing come easily? Not at all, says Rubin. "Writing, ultimately, is the battle with myself, and it is a struggle. Sure, sometimes it flows beautifully, but more often I find I've gone in the wrong direction, or the material hasn't coalesced the way I wanted it to, or I've written five degrees lower than I was aiming for. And when that happens, I enter into a kind of sacrificial moment, and there follows a terrible bloodletting where I go in and do terrible damage to my material. I slash it to pieces. I've done that many times, and it seems to me that it is that moment when the movie truly becomes mine."

If you write a superficial movie, Rubin believes, you get a superficial script. "And I can't be happy with that." But don't confuse "superficial" with "commercial," because Rubin avers that they are not the same thing at all. "I just want to write an entertaining movie. I don't mind being commercial. My themes are hopefully buried within some sort of commercial pill that you can swallow, so the message might detonate inside you later, or even during the movie. I'm always trying to get at something inside people, and I love to be commercially successful in doing it."

—Kerry Cox

Needs: Filmstrips, sound and videotapes. Submit completed script. Pays in accordance with Writers Guild standards.

‡**SAFARI**, P.O. Box 480865, Los Angeles CA 90048. Contact: Script Dept. Estab. 1981. Produces material for PG-R audience. Buys 3-4 scripts/year. Buys all rights. Reports in 1 month.
Needs: Films. Looking for full-length feature scripts. Submit synopsis or completed script. Pays in accordance with Writers Guild standards; "depends on individual situation."
Tips: "We are looking for topical, character-driven scripts with lead characters in their late 20's or early 30's."

‡**SPI ENTERTAINMENT**, 279 S. Beverly Dr., Beverly Hills CA 90212. (213)827-4229. President/Producer: Michael Sourapas. Estab. 1987. We have a feature film audience. Buys 6-8 scripts/year. Buys all rights or other options. Reports in 2 months.
Needs: Feature films. Submit completed script with brief outline only. Pays royalty or makes outright purchase, "depending on the situation."
Tips: "See all movies. Pay attention to grosses and what stays in the theaters. Then pitch finished scripts as though we were going to the movies to see them. Be brief with cast and keep the director in mind. We are looking for entertaining, fast paced, universal themes with a twist."

☐ **TELEVISION PRODUCTION SERVICES CORP.**, Box 1233, Edison NJ 08818. (201)287-3626. Executive Director/Producer: R.S. Burks. Produces video music materials for major market distributor networks, etc. Buys 50-100 scripts/year. Buys all rights. Reports in 2 weeks.
Needs: "We do video music for record companies, MTV, HBO, etc. We use treatments of story ideas from the groups' management. We also do commercials for over-the-air broadcast and cable. We are now doing internal in-house video for display on disk or internally distributed channels, and need good script writers." Submit synopsis/outline or completed script, and resume; include SASE for response or materials will not be returned.
Tips: Looks for rewrite flexibility and availability. "We have the capability of transmission electronically over the phone modem to our printer or directly onto disk for storage. We commission or contract out all scripts."

‡**THEME SONG: A Musical and Literary Production House**, 396 Watchogue Rd., Staten Island NY 10314. (718)698-4178. Director: Lawrence Nicastro. Estab. 1980. Produces material for theater (stage/ screen); radio; television (entertainment/educational documentary). Buys 50 scripts/year. Buys first rights. Previously published material OK, if a revision is sought. Reports in 1 month.
Needs: Phonograph records, tapes and cassettes and ¾" videotape. Query. "I'll answer each query individually. We enjoy newsworthy subjects and investigative/collaborative themes." Pays negotiable royalty.
Tips: "I am interested in political lyrics/songs/parodies, ballads, religious hymns, satirical sketches, folk-work songs, short drama, epic poetry, and concrete criticism of American life, with prescriptive institutional changes necessary to improve our condition; also, international themes or cooperative themes. I am a member of The Dramatists Guild and The Songwriters Guild. I re-write artistic works and seek to collaborate and network writers. I am interested in dramatic dialogue suitable for comic strips and cartoon books. We have a stable of artists and illustrators on board."

UNIFILMS, INC., 22931 Sycamore Creek Dr., Valencia CA 91354-2050. (805)297-2000. Vice President, Development: Jack Adams. Estab. 1984. We buy 0-5 scripts/year. Reports in 2 weeks on queries; 2 months on submissions.
Needs: Feature films *only*. We are looking for feature film screenplays, current format, 100-120 pages long; commercial but not stupid, dramatic but not "artsy," funny but not puerile. **Query with synopsis with SASE.** We do not accept unsolicited scripts. Save your postage; if you send us a script we'll return it unopened.
Tips: "If you've taken classes, read books, attended seminars and writers workshops all concerned with scriptwriting and read hundreds of produced screenplays *prior* to seeing the film and you're still convinced you've got a saleable script, we might want to see it. If you've got someone else in the entertainment industry to recommend your script, we would be more interested in seeing it. But if you waste our time with a project that's not yet ready to be seen, we're not going to react well. Your first draft is not usually the draft you're going to show to the industry. *Get a professional opinion first,* then rewrite before you submit to us. Very few people care about synopses, outlines or treatments as a starting point. THE SCRIPT is the basic blueprint, and everyone in the country is working on a script. Ideas are a dime a dozen. If you can *execute* that idea well and get people *excited* about that

idea, you've got something. But most writers are wanna-bes, who submit scripts that need a lot of work just to get to the "promising" stage. Scripts are *always* rewritten. If you can't convince us you're a *writer*, we don't care. But if you *can* write and you've got a *second* idea we might talk."

Other Scriptwriting Markets

The following scriptwriting publications were listed in the 1991 edition but do not have listings in this edition of *Writer's Market*. The majority did not respond to our request to update their listings or return a questionnaire for a new listing. If a reason was given for their exclusion, we have included it in parentheses after the listing name.

Actors' Stock Company

Amas Repertory Theatre, Inc.

American Motion Pictures (asked to be deleted for one year)

Animation Arts Associates, Inc.

Arena Stage (no longer accepts unsolicited manuscripts)

Artzco Pictures, Inc.

Art Craft Publishing Co.

Asolo Center for the Performing Arts

At the Foot of the Mountain Theater (asked to be deleted)

Avila College, Department of Theatre

Samuel R. Blate Associates

Lee Caplin Productions

Carey-It-Off Productions

Chelsea Stage, Inc./Hudson Guild Theatre

The Chicago Board of Rabbis Broadcasting Commission

Colony Studio Theatre

Company One (no longer accepts unsolicited manuscripts)

The Cricket Theatre

Cutting Edge Productions

(backlogged with material)

Dorset Theatre Festival

Florida Studio Theatre

Paul French & Partners, Inc.

George Street Playhouse

Gessler Publishing Co., Inc.

Griffin & Boyle

Guthrie Theater (no longer accepts unsolicited manuscripts)

Brad Hager

Image Innovations

International Home Entertainment

Invisible Theatre

Kumu Kahua

David Lancaster Productions (no longer accepts unsolicited manuscripts)

Linnenas Publishing Co.

Mad River Theater Works

The Wilton Marks Studio

Nine O'Clock Players

Numan Films (unable to contact; mail returned)

Oldcastle Theatre Company

Pacific West Entertainment Group (backlogged with material)

Pennsylvania Stage Company

Perseverance Theatre

Quaigh Theatre

The Road Company

Peter Schleger Company

Seattle Group Theatre Co.

Shenandoah Playwrights Retreat

Frank Silvera Writers' Workshop

The Snowmass Aspen Repertory Theatre

South Fork Productions (asked to be deleted)

SPI Entertainment

Stop-Gap (no longer accepts unsolicited manuscripts)

Storefront Theatre

Theatre Tesseract

Theatre Virginia

Bob Thomas Productions, Inc.

Unity Pictures Corp.

Vigilante Players, Inc.

Dimitri Villard Productions

Washington State University Theatre (no longer accepts unsolicited manuscripts)

Whole Theatre (unable to contact; mail returned)

YMAM/Academy of Performing Arts

Syndicates

Although it continues to be a highly competitive industry, syndication is an excellent money-making alternative for your columns and features. While sports, humor and political commentary columns in newspapers are generally reserved for marquee names such as Jim Murray, Jim Davis and George Will, columns covering fashion, cooking and gardening by less known writers are often syndicated. The past year has seen the development of more focused columns on working women, careers and coping with economic recession.

It is important to think of syndication as a building process. Begin the process by writing feature articles for local newspapers. When you are confident that you have developed a good collection of clips representative of your best writing, approach a syndicate. In many cases, the process of selection by a syndicate can take several submissions over a period of years. Writers often submit work for consideration, continue to compile clips and re-submit new work after a year or so.

Most syndicates distribute a variety of columns, cartoons and features. Specialized syndicates—those that deal with a single area such as business—often sell to magazines, trade journals and business publications, as well as to newspapers.

Keep in mind that syndicated material must compete with staff-written material, particularly in newspapers. Often, existing material must give way to a new syndicated piece to accommodate a publication's budget. Before an editor will make this sacrifice, he must be convinced of your ability to consistently produce a column that is appealing and fresh and has lasting value.

Study the popular syndicated columnists to see how successful columns are structured. For example, most columns are short—from 500 to 750 words—so columnists learn how to make every word count. Don't make the mistake of imitating a well-known columnist—newspapers do not want more of the same. This applies to subject matter, as well. Keep abreast of trends, but make certain you do not submit a column on a subject already covered by that syndicate. The more unique the topic, the greater your chances at syndication, but choose a subject that interests you and one you know well.

Editors look for writers with unique viewpoints on lifestyle or political topics, but they also seek how-to columns and one-shot features on a variety of subjects. One-shot features tend to be longer than columns and can be tied to a news peg or event. Other one-shot items include puzzles, cartoons and graphics.

Most syndicate editors prefer a query letter and about six sample columns or writing samples and a SASE. If you have a particular field of expertise, be sure to mention this in your letter and back it up by sending related material. For highly specialized or technical matter, provide some credentials to show you are qualified to handle the topic.

In essence, syndicates act as agents or brokers for the material they handle. Writing material is usually sold as a package. The syndicate will promote and market the work and keep careful records of sales. Writers usually receive 40-60% of gross receipts. Syndicates may also pay a small salary or a flat fee for one-shot items.

Syndicates usually aquire all rights to accepted material, although a few are now offering writers and artists the option of retaining ownership. When selling all rights, writers give up all ownership and future use of their creations. Sale of all rights is not the best deal for the writer and has been the reason writers choose to work with syndicates that buy less restrictive rights. Some choose to self-syndicate their work so they can retain these rights.

Writers who syndicate their own work have all the freedom of a business owner, but must also act as their own managers, marketing team and sales force. Payment is usually negotiated on a case-by-case basis. Small newspapers may offer only $10-20 per column, but larger papers may pay up to $50. The number of papers you deal with is only limited by your marketing budget and sales ability.

If you self-syndicate you should be aware that some newspapers are not copyrighted, so you should copyright your own material. It's less expensive to copyright columns as a collection, rather than individually. For more information on copyright procedures see Copyrighting Your Writing in the Business of Writing section.

For information on column writing and syndication see *How to Write & Sell a Column*, by Julie Raskin and Carolyn Males (Writer's Digest Books). Additional information on newspaper markets can be found in *The Gale Directory of Publications* (available in most libraries). *The Editor & Publisher Syndicate Directory* (11 W. 19th St., New York NY 10011) has a list of syndicates, contact names and features; the weekly magazine also has news articles about syndicates and can provide you with information about trends in the industry.

For information on syndicates not included in *Writer's Market*, see Other Syndicates at the end of this section.

ADVENTURE FEATURE SYNDICATE, 329 Harvery Dr., Glendale CA 91206. (818)247-1721. Editor: R.E. Davio. Reports in 1 month. Buys all rights, first North American serial rights and second serial (reprint) rights. Free cartoonist's guidelines.
Needs: Fiction (spies) and fillers (adventure/travel), action/adventure comic strips and graphic novels. Submit complete ms.

ALLIED FEATURE SYNDICATE, P.O. Drawer 48, Joplin MO 64802-0048. (417)673-2860. Editor Robert J. Blanset. Estab. 1940. 70% written by writers on contract; 30% freelance by writers on a one-time basis. Works with 36 writers/year. Works with 30-40 previously unpublished writers/year. Syndicates to newspapers (60%); magazines (30%); in-house organs (10%). Submissions will be returned "only on request." Reports in 6 weeks. Buys all rights.
Needs: "We will consider all materials." Buys one-shot features and articles series. Query with clips of published work. Pays 50% author's percentage "after production costs" or 5¢/word. Currently syndicates "A Little Prayer," by Mary Alice Bennett (religious filler); "Murphy's Law of Electronics," by Nic Frising (cartoon panel); "Selling in the Year 2000," by Dick Meza (marketing column).
Tips: "Allied Feature Syndicate is one of very few agencies syndicating electronics manufacturing targeted materials and information."

AMERICA INTERNATIONAL SYNDICATE, 1324 N. 3rd St., St. Joseph MO 64501. (816)233-8190. FAX: (816)279-9315. Executive Director: Gerald A. Bennett. Associate Director (London office): Paul Eisler. 100% freelance written by cartoonists on contract. "We sell to newspapers, trade magazines, puzzle books and comic books." Reports in 6 weeks. Buys all rights.
Needs: Short fictional crime story "You Are The Detective" for magazines, books and comics; also comic strips of adventure, western or family type. Children's features and games also needed. Scientific or unusual features with art and written text needed. Send 6-8 samples with SASE. Pays 50% of gross sales. Currently syndication features: "Alfonso," "Silent Sam," "Tex Benson," "Double Trouble," "Buccaneers," "A.J. Sowell," "Figment," "Adventures in Nature," and "Dad's Place" (comic strips). Panel features are "Stacey," "Girls," and "The Edge."
Tips: "Keep the art simple and uncluttered as possible: Know your subject and strive for humor."

‡AMERICAN NEWS FEATURES SYNDICATE, P.O. Box 46004, Bedford OH 44146. (216)232-7771. Executive Editor: T.S. Peric. Estab. 1988. Syndicates one-shot feature articles to a wide variety of newspapers throughout the country.
Needs: "We are unusual in that we pay for ideas as well as for writing an article. We are only interested in stories that have been covered before. Submit the idea, but we must know and see the source. We are constantly on the lookout for articles that have appeared in local papers that might have national appeal. You must send us a good photocopy of the article. If interested, we will either pay for the idea outright or assign the article. We are looking for government waste, how-to, profile/interview, human interest, consumerism, women's interest, medical, especially breakthrough, celebrities, inspirational." No first person or fiction. Pays $35-200 for an idea; up to $400 for a 1,000-word article. Idea and writer's guidelines request *must* include SASE. Reports in 1 month.

Tips: "We need articles that are newsy, breezy, emotional, and can be written with a punchy lead. *Forget* ideas/articles that have appeared in major magazines, newspapers, wire service stories such as AP, UPI or the tabloids. But if it happened in your town and was covered only by the local paper, then you have a real shot. Be sure to include your name, addresses and daytime phone number on the back of the photocopy. Do not send us completed mss. If you want the article returned you must include a SASE."

AMERICAN NEWSPAPER SYNDICATE, 9 Woodrush Dr., Irvine CA 92714. (714)559-8047. Executive Editor: Susan Smith. Estab. 1988. 50% regular columns by writers under contract; 50% freelance articles and series by writers on a one-time basis. Plan to syndicate up to 7 new U.S. and Canadian columnists this year. Plan to buy 20 one-time articles/series per year. Syndicates to U.S. and Canadian medium-to-large general interest and special interest newspapers. Works with previously unpublished and published writers. Pays 50% of net sales, salary on some contracted columns. Buys first North American serial rights. Reports in 3 weeks. Writer's guidelines for SASE.
Needs: Newspaper columns and one-time articles/series on travel, entertainment, how-to, human interest, business, personal finance, lifestyle, health, legal issues. "Practical, money-saving information on everyday needs such as medicine, insurance, automobiles, education, home decoration and repairs, and travel is always in great demand by newspapers." Will not return material without SASE. Columns should be 700 words in length; one-time articles should be 1,500 words.
Tips: "We seek fresh, innovative material that may be overlooked by the other syndicates. Because we know the newspaper syndication market, we feel we can find a place for the previously-unpublished writer if the material is well-executed. Be sure to research your idea thoroughly. This is a very tough business to penetrate—but the rewards can be great for those who are successful."

‡AMPERSAND COMMUNICATIONS, 2311 S. Bayshore Dr., Miami FL 33133. (305)285-2200. Editor: George Leposky. Estab. 1982. 100% written by writers on contract. "We syndicate only our own material at present, but we will consider working with others whose material is exceptionally good. Novices need not contact us." Syndicates to magazines and newspapers. Query for electronic submissions. Reports in 3 months. Buys all rights. Writer's guidelines for $2 and SASE.
Needs: Newspaper columns, travel, business, science and health, regional cuisine, natural foods, environment, typically 500-750 words, rarely up to 1,500 words. Material from other writers must complement, not compete with, our own travel, business, environment and health columns. Query with clips of published work and submit complete ms—samples of proposal columns. Pays 50% of net after production. "Note: For columns requiring photos, the writer must supply to us the required number of images and quantity of each image at his/her expense. We are not in the photo duplication business and will not provide this service." Currently syndicates Traveling the South, by George and Rosalie Leposky (travel); Business Insights, by Lincoln Avery (business); HealthScan, by George Leposky (health); EnviroScan, by George Leposky (environment).
Tips: "Be an *excruciatingly* good writer; good alone isn't enough. Find a niche that doesn't seem to be covered. Do research to cover your topics in-depth, but in few words. The reader's attention span is shriveling, and so are ad lineage and column inches available for syndicated features."

ARKIN MAGAZINE SYNDICATE INC., 1817 NE 164th St., North Miami Beach FL 33162. Editor: Joseph Arkin. Estab. 1958. 20% freelance written by writers on contract; 70% freelance written by writers on a one-time basis. "We regularly purchase articles from several freelancers for syndication in trade and professional magazines." Previously published submissions OK, "if all rights haven't been sold." Reports in 3 weeks. Buys all North American magazine and newspaper rights.
Needs: Magazine articles (nonfiction, 750-2,200 words), directly relating to business problems common to several different types of businesses; and photos (purchased with written material). "We are in dire need of the 'how-to' business article." Will not consider article series. Submit complete ms; "SASE required with all submissions." Pays 3-10¢/word; $5-10 for photos; "actually, line drawings are preferred instead of photos." **Pays on acceptance.**
Tips: "Study trade magazines to learn style, needs and other facets of the field."

BUDDY BASCH FEATURE SYNDICATE, 771 West End Ave., New York NY 10025-5572. (212)666-2300. Editor/Publisher: Buddy Basch. 10% written by writers on contract; 2% freelance written by writers on a one-time basis. Buys 10 features/year; works with 3-4 previously unpublished writers annually. Syndicates to print media: newspapers, magazines, giveaways, house organs, etc. Reports in 2 weeks. Buys first North American serial rights.
Needs: Magazine features, newspaper features, and one-shot ideas that are really different. "Try to make them unusual, unique, real 'stoppers,' not the usual stuff." Will consider one-shots and article series on travel, entertainment, human interest—"the latter, a wide umbrella that makes people stop and read the piece. Different, unusual and unique are the key words, not what the *writer* thinks is, but which has been done nine million times before." Query. Pays 20-50% commission. Additional payment

for photos $10-50. Currently syndicates It Takes a Woman by Frances Scott (woman's feature), Travel Whirl, Scramble Steps (puzzle) and others.

Tips: "Never mind what your mother, fiancé or friend thinks is good. If it has been done before and is old hat, it has no chance. Do some research and see if there are a dozen similar items in the press. Don't just try a very close 'switch' on them. You don't fool anyone with this. There are fewer and fewer newspapers, with more and more people vying for the available space. But there's *always* room for a really good, *different* feature or story. Trouble is few writers (amateurs especially) know a good piece, I'm sorry to say. Read *Writer's Market*, carefully, noting which syndicate might be interested in the type feature you are offering."

‡BONAT'S DIVERSIFIED, INC., #206, 19351 Seahorse Ln., Huntington Beach CA 92648. (714)969-4006. FAX: (714)854-8025. Editor: Teresa Carlton and Natalie Carlton. Estab. 1978. 75% written by writers on contract; 10% freelance written by writers on a one-time basis. "Our syndicate does not purchase material, we syndicate to our clients worldwide." Works with 25 previously unpublished writers/year. Syndicates to magazines, newspapers and tabloids. Reports in 2 weeks. Buys first North American serial rights and second serial (reprint) rights. Free writer's guidelines.

Needs: Fiction (short stories or novels); fillers (helpful hints, beauty hints, exercise); magazine columns and features, newspapers columns and features (beauty, exercise, diet). "I do not purchase material . . . syndication only." Query with clips of published work or submit complete ms. Pays 70% author's percentage. "Payment remains 70%; articles with photos or transparencies usually command a higher fee." Currently syndicates Late Show, by Natalie Carlton (trivia quiz); Beauty Round-Up, by Patricia Canole (beauty Q&A); Star Interviews, by Gloria Grale (entertainment).

Tips: "Well-written and researched articles, depending upon timely markets, sell in the women's magazines. Material should be submitted at least six months before anticipated published interest, that is, summer articles in December, Christmas material in June, etc. Also, subjects should be universal."

BUSINESS FEATURES SYNDICATE, P.O. Box 9844, Ft. Lauderdale FL 33310. (305)485-0795. FAX: (305)485-0806. Editor: Dana K. Cassell. Estab. 1976. 100% freelance written. Buys about 100 features a year. Syndicates to trade journal magazines, business newspapers and tabloids. Buys exclusive rights while being circulated. Writer's guidelines for #10 SASE. Reports in 1 month.

Needs: Buys single features aimed at the independent retailer, small service business owner, consultant or professional on any of these marketing topics: advertising, public relations, promotion, self-promotion, display, merchandising, packaging, written communications. Length: 1,000-2,500 words. Complete ms preferred. Computer DOS disk, filed in ASCii, *must* accompany manuscript printout. Pays 50% commission.

Tips: "Material must be written for and of value to more than one field, for example: jewelers, drug store owners and sporting goods dealers. We aim at retail trade journals; our material is more how-to business oriented than that bought by other syndicates."

CHRONICLE FEATURES, Suite 1011, 870 Market St., San Francisco CA 94102. (415)777-7212. General Manager: Stuart Dodds. Buys 3 features/year. Syndicates to daily newspapers in the U.S. and Canada with representation overseas. Reports in 1 month.

Needs: Newspaper columns and features. "In choosing a column subject, the writer should be guided by the concerns and aspirations of today's newspaper reader. We look for originality of expression and, in special fields of interest, exceptional expertise." Preferred length: 500-700 words. Submit complete ms. Pays 50% revenue from syndication. Offers no additional payment for photos or artwork accompanying ms. Currently syndicates Bizarro, by Dan Piraro (cartoon panel); Earthweek, by Steve Newman (planetary diary); Home Entertainment, by Harry Somerfield (audiovisual equipment advice and reviews); Streetwise, by Herb Greenberg (up-to-the-minute business column); and First Person Singular, by Ruthe Stein (singles column).

Tips: "We are seeking features that will be ongoing enterprises, not single articles or news releases. Examples of a proposed feature are more welcome than a query letter describing it."

CONTINENTAL FEATURES/CONTINENTAL NEWS SERVICE, Suite 265, 341 W. Broadway, San Diego CA 92101. (619)492-8696. Editor: Gary P. Salamone. Estab. 1981. 100% written by writers on contract; 30% freelance written by writers on a one-time basis. "Writers who offer the kind and quality of writing we seek stand an equal chance regardless of experience." Syndicates to the print media. Reports in 1 month. Writer's guidelines for #10 SASE.

Needs: Magazine features, newspaper features. "Feature material should fit the equivalent of one-quarter to one-half standard newspaper page, and Continental News considers an ultra-liberal or ultra-conservative slant inappropriate." Query. Pays 70% author's percentage. Currently syndicates News and Comment by Charles Hampton Savage (general news commentary/analysis); Continental Viewpoint, by staff (political and social commentary); Portfolio, by William F. Pike (cartoon/caricature art); FreedomWatch, by Glenn Church; Travelers Checks by Anne Hattes √√√ and Middle East Cable, by Mike Maggio.

Tips: "Continental News seeks country profiles/background articles that pertain to foreign countries. Writers who possess such specific knowledge/personal experience stand an excellent chance of acceptance, provided they can focus the political, economic and social issues. We welcome them to submit their proposals. We foresee the possibility of diversifying our feature package by representing writers and feature creators on more one-shot projects."

COPLEY NEWS SERVICE, P.O. Box 190, San Diego CA 92112. (619)293-1818. Editorial Director: Nanette Wiser. Buys 85% of work from contracted stringers; 15% from freelancers on a one-time basis. Offers 200 features/week. Sells to magazines, newspapers, radio. Reports in 1-2 months. Buys all rights or second serial (reprint) rights (sometimes).

Needs: Fillers, magazine columns, magazine features, newspaper columns and newspaper features. Subjects include interior design, outdoor recreation, fashion, antiques, real estate, pets and gardening. Buys one-shot and articles series. Query with clips of published work. Pays $50-100 flat rate or $400 salary/month.

CREATIVE SYNDICATION SERVICES, P.O. Box 40, Eureka MO 63025. (314)938-9116. FAX: (314)343-0966. Editor: Debra Holly. Estab. 1977. 10% written by writers on contract; 50% freelance written by writers on a one-time basis. Syndicates to magazines, newspapers and radio. Query for electronic submissions. Reports in 1 month. Buys all rights. Currently syndicates The Weekend Workshop, by Ed Baldwin; Woodcrafting, by Ed Baldwin (woodworking) and Classified Clippers, a feature exclusive for the Classified Section of newspapers.

CREATORS SYNDICATE, INC., Suite 700, 5777 W. Century Blvd., Los Angeles CA 90045. (213)337-7003. Columns President: Richard Newcombe. Estab. 1987. Syndicates to newspapers. Reports in 2 months. Buys negotiable rights. Reports in 2 months. Writer's guidelines for SASE.

Needs: Newspaper columns and features. Query with clips of published work or submit complete ms. Author's percentage: 50%. Currently syndicates Ann Landers (advice) B.C. (comic strip) and Herblock (editorial cartoon). Please write "Cartoon Submissions" on lower left of appropriate envelope.

Tips: "Syndication is very competitive. Writing regularly for your local newspaper is a good start."

CRICKET COMMUNICATIONS, INC., (formerly The Cricket Letter, Inc.), P.O. Box 527, Ardmore PA 19003. (215)789-2480. Editor: J.D. Krickett. Estab. 1975. 10% written by writers on contract; 10% freelance written by writers on a one-time basis. Works with 2-3 previously unpublished writers annually. Syndicates to trade magazines and newspapers. Reports in 3 weeks. Buys all rights.

Needs: Magazine columns, magazine features, newspaper columns, newspaper features and news items—all tax and financial-oriented (700-1,500 words); newspaper columns, features and news items directed to small business. Query with clips of published work. Pays $50-500. Currently syndicates Hobby/Business, by Mark E. Battersby (tax and financial); Farm Taxes, by various authors; and Small Business Taxes, by Mark E. Battersby.

CROWN SYNDICATE, INC., P.O. Box 99126, Seattle WA 98199. President: L.M. Boyd. Estab. 1967. Buys countless trivia items, cartoons and panel gag lines. Syndicates to newspapers, radio. Reports in 1 month. Buys first North American serial rights. Free writer's guidelines.

Needs: Filler material used weekly, items for trivia column, gaglines for specialty comic strip (format guidelines sent on request). Pays $1-5/item, depending on how it's used, i.e., trivia or filler service or comic strip. Offers no additional payment for photos accompanying ms. Currently syndicates columns, puzzle panels and comic strips.

EDITORIAL CONSULTANT SERVICE, P.O. Box 524, West Hempstead NY 11552. Editorial Director: Arthur A. Ingoglia. Estab. 1964. 40% written by writers on contract; 25% freelance written by writers on a one-time basis. "We work with 75 writers in the U.S. and Canada." Previously published writers only. Adds about 5 new columnists/year. Syndicates material to an average of 60 newspapers, magazines, automotive trade and consumer publications, and radio stations with circulation of 50,000-575,000. Buys all rights. Writer's guidelines for #10 SASE. Reports in 3 weeks.

Needs: Magazine and newspaper columns and features, news items and radio broadcast material. Prefers carefully documented material with automotive slant. Also considers automotive trade features. Will consider article series. No horoscope, child care, lovelorn or pet care. Query. Author's percentage varies; usually averages 50%. Additional payment for 8×10 b&w and color photos accepted with ms. Submit 2-3 columns. Currently syndicates Let's Talk About Your Car, by R. Hite.

Tips: "Emphasis is placed on articles and columns with an automotive slant. We prefer consumer-oriented features, how to save money on your car, what every woman should know about her car, how to get more miles per gallon, etc."

‡**ENTERTAINMENT NEWS SYNDICATE**, 155 E. 55th St., New York NY 10022. (212)223-1821. FAX: (212)223-3737. Editor: Lee Canaan. Estab. 1970. 10% written by writers on contract. Syndicates to newspapers and magazines. Reports in 1 month. Buys all rights. Free writer's guidelines.
Needs: Fillers, magazine and newspaper features, and news on travel and entertainment. No single (one-shot) features. Query. Payment negotiable. Currently syndicates Cruise Callings, Hotels & Spas and Tour Treats, by L. Canaan (column).

‡**EUROPA PRESS NEWS SERVICE**, Clasificador 5, Tajamar Providencia, Santiago, Chile. (562)40044. FAX: (562)2351731. Editor: Renato Campodonico. Estab. 1963. 50% freelance written by writers on a one-time basis. Syndicates to magazines and newspapers. Reports in 3 months. Buys second serial rights for Latin America and other customers in Europe, Far East.
Needs: Magazine features (science, technology, celebrities: interviews with candid shots), newspaper features, recipes, handiworks, etc. with color photos. Buys one-shot features and article series. "Travel, adventure, human-interest stories with pictures. Query with clips of published work or submit complete ms. Pays 50% author's percentage. Currently syndicates Moda al dia, by Claudia Moda (color photos with captions); Household Advice, by Penny Orchard (column with illustrations); and The World Today, by London Express (articles with b&w pictures).
Tips: "We are seeking good, up-to-date articles about technology, science, medicine, business, marketing; also, interviews with celebrities in show business, politics, sports preferably with color photos."

FEATURE ENTERPRISES, 33 Bellwood, Northport AL 35476. Editor: Maury M. Breecher. Estab. 1979. 10% written by writers on contract; 90% freelance written by writers on a one-time basis. Syndicates 100 mss/year. Works with 10-20 previously unpublished writers/year. Syndicates to magazines and newspapers. Reports in 1 month. Buys first North American serial rights and second serial (reprint) rights. Writer's guidelines for $2.
Needs: No columns. Need one-shot features, popular psychology, medical breakthroughs and celebrity interviews. Payment on 50/50 standard syndicate split. SASE required for return of material.
Tips: "Use lots of direct, to-the-point quotes. Completely identify experts with full title and affiliation. Supply contact numbers."

‡**FNA NEWS**, P.O. Box 11999, Salt Lake City UT 84147. (801)355-0005. Editor: R.N. Goldberger. 5% written by writers on contract; 95% freelance written by writers on one-time basis. Works with 10 freelance writers/year. Syndicates to magazines and newspapers. Usually reports in 1 month. Buys all rights, first North American serial rights or second serial (reprint) rights.
Needs: Quality fiction, fillers, magazine columns, magazine features, newspaper columns, newspaper features, news items and radio broadcast material. Buys one-shot features and articles series. Query with published clips. Payment negotiated separately.
Tips: "Be very clear. Do not use unnecessary words. Write to be comfortably read." Also offers a private writing consultation service.

FOTOPRESS, INDEPENDENT NEWS SERVICE INTERNATIONAL, P.O. Box 1268, Station Q, Toronto, Ontario M4T 2P4 Canada. (416)841-4486. FAX: (416)841-2283. Estab. 1983. 50% written by writers on contract; 25% freelance written by writers on a one-time basis. Works with 30% previously unpublished writers. Syndicates to domestic and international magazines, newspapers, radio, TV stations and motion picture industry. Reports in 6 weeks. Buys variable rights. Writer's guidelines for $3 in IRCs.
Needs: Fillers, magazine columns, magazine features, newspaper columns, newspaper features, news items, radio broadcast material, documentary, the environment, travel and art. Buys one-shot and article series for international politics, scientists, celebrities and religious leaders. Query or submit complete ms. Pays 50-75% author's percentage. Offers $5-150 for accompanying ms.
Tips: "We need all subjects from 500-3,000 words. Photos are purchased with or without features. All writers are regarded respectfully—their success is our success."

(GABRIEL) GRAPHICS NEWS BUREAU, P.O. Box 38, Madison Square Station, New York NY 10010. (212)254-8863. Cable: NOLNOEL. Editor: J. G. Bumberg. 25% freelance written by writers on contract; 50% freelance written by writers on one-time basis. Custom-syndicates for clients to weeklies (selected), suburbans and small dailies. Reports in 1 month. Buys all rights for clients, packages. Writer's guidelines for SASE.
Needs: Magazine features, newspaper columns, fillers and features and news items for PR clients, custom packages. Pays 15% from client. Also has consulting/conceptualizing services in communications/graphics/management.

GENERAL NEWS SYNDICATE, 147 W. 42nd St., New York NY 10036. (212)221-0043. Estab. 1940. 25% written by writers on contract; 12% freelance written by writers on a one-time basis. Works with 12 writers/year; 5 previously unpublished writers annually. Syndicates to an average of 12 newspaper and radio outlets averaging 20 million circulation; buys theater and show business people columns (mostly New York theater pieces). Reports on *accepted* material in 3 weeks. Buys one-time rights.

Needs: Entertainment-related material.

Tips: Looking for "short copy (250-500 words)."

GOODWIN & ASSOCIATES, Drawer 54-6661, Surfside FL 33154. FAX: (305)531-5490. Editor: Dave Goodwin. 70% written by writers on contract; 10% freelance written by writers on a one-time basis. Buys about 25 features a year from freelancers. Works with 2 previously unpublished writers annually. Rights purchsed vary with author and material. May buy first rights or second serial (reprint) rights or simultaneous rights. Will handle copyrighted material. Query for electronic submissions. Query or submit complete ms. Reports in 3 weeks.

Nonfiction: "Money-saving information for consumers: how to save on home expenses; auto, medical, drug, insurance, boat, business items, etc." Buys article series on brief, practical, down-to-earch items for consumer use or knowledge. Rarely buys single features. Currently handling Insurance for Consumers. Length: 300-5,000 words. Pays 50% on publication. Submit 2-3 columns.

‡GSM FEATURES, P.O. Box 104, Oradell NJ 07649. (201)385-2000. Editor: Bob Nesoff. Estab. 1968. 100% written by writers on contract. Buys 300 pieces/year. Syndicates to newspapers. Reports in 3 weeks. Buys first North American serial rights. Writer's guidelines for SASE.

Needs: Newspaper columns and features. Does not purchase single (one-shot) features. Query only with SASE. Pays flat rate $25-100. Currently syndicates Traveling, by Bob and Sandy Nesoff (weekly travel column); Cooking, by Janine Draizin (recipes); Powder Trails, by Wendy and Barbara Nesoff (18-30 yr. old audience ski column); Books, by Ross Warren (book review column).

Tips: "Trend toward more family-oriented and less expensive activities."

HISPANIC LINK NEWS SERVICE, 1420 N St. NW, Washington DC 20005. (202)234-0280. Publisher: Charles A. Ericksen. Editor: Felix Perez. Estab. 1980. 50% freelance written by writers on contract; 50% freelance written by writers on a one-time basis. Buys 156 columns and features/year. Works with 50 writers/year; 5 previously unpublished writers. Syndicates to 150 newspapers and magazines with circulations ranging from 5,000 to 300,000. Reports in 2 weeks. Buys second serial (reprint) or negotiable rights. Free writer's guidelines.

Needs: Newspaper columns and features. One-shot features and article series. "We prefer 650-700 word op/ed or features geared to a general national audience, but focus on issue or subject of particular interest to Hispanic Americans. Some longer pieces accepted occasionally." Query or submit complete ms. Pays $25-100. Syndicates Hispanic Link, (opinion and/or feature columns).

Tips: "We would especially like to get topical material and vignettes relating to Hispanic presence and progress in the United States. Provide insights on Hispanic experience geared to a general audience. Eighty-five to 90% of the columns we accept are authored by Hispanics; the Link presents Hispanic viewpoints and showcases Hispanic writing talent through its subscribing newspapers and magazines. Copy should be submitted in English. We syndicate in English and Spanish."

HOLLYWOOD INSIDE SYNDICATE, P.O. Box 49957, Los Angeles CA 90049. (714)678-6237. FAX: (714)678-6237. Editor: John Austin. Estab. 1968. 10% written by writers on contract; 40% freelance written by writers on a one-time basis. Purchases entertainment-oriented mss for syndication to newspapers in San Francisco, Philadelphia, Detroit, Montreal, London, Sydney, Manila, South Africa, etc. Works with 2-3 previously unpublished writers annually. Previously published submissions OK, if published in the U.S. and Canada only. Reports in 6 weeks. Negotiates for first rights or second serial (reprint) rights.

Needs: News items (column items concerning entertainment—motion picture—personalities and jet setters for syndicated column; 750-800 words). Also considers series of 1,500-word articles; "suggest descriptive query first. We are also looking for off-beat travel pieces (with pictures) but not on areas covered extensively in the Sunday supplements. We can always use pieces on 'freighter' travel. Not luxury cruise liners but lower cost cruises. We also syndicate nonfiction book subjects—sex, travel, etc., to overseas markets. No fiction. Must have b&w photo with submissions if possible." Also require 1,500-word celebrity profiles on internationally recognized celebrities." We *stress* "internationally." Query or submit complete ms. Pay negotiable. Currently syndicates Books of the Week column.

Tips: "Study the entertainment pages of Sunday (and daily) newspapers to see the type of specialized material we deal in. Perhaps we are different from other syndicates, but we deal with celebrities. No 'I' journalism such as 'when I spoke to Cloris Leachman.' Many freelancers submit material from the 'dinner theater' and summer stock circuit of 'gossip type' items from what they have observed about the 'stars' or featured players in these productions—how they act off stage, who they romance, etc. We use this material."

‡**HYDE PARK MEDIA,** Chicago Metro News Services, Suite 2, 1314 Howard St., Chicago IL 60626. 10% freelance written by writers on a one-time basis. Syndicates to midwestern newspapers and magazines. Reports in 2 weeks. Buys first and second serial rights.
Needs: Unusual, off-beat magazine features (1,500-3,000 words) and newspaper features with a regional hook (750-1,500 words). Buys single (one-shot) features only. Send SASE with query. Pays 50% commission on sale.
Tips: "Please read 'Needs' graph before sending material. Why waste anyone's time?"

‡**INTERMEDIA NEWS AND FEATURE SERVICE,** 434 Avenue of the Americas, Box 691, New York NY 10011. Editor: Pat Mason. Estab. 1980. 20% written by writers on contract: 5% freelance written by writers on a one-time basis. Buys 30 ms/year. Syndicates to magazines and newspapers. Reports in 2 months. Buys first North American serial rights.
Needs: Fillers (for magazines only), newspaper columns and features. Buys one-shot features and article series. Query with clips of published work. Pays flat rate and the opportunity for publishing. Currently syndicates Best Buys, by staff (reviews); Books in Review, by staff (reviews); Music on Record, Tape, Disc (reviews).
Tips: "We need precise information and objective opinion to guide our audience."

INTERPRESS OF LONDON AND NEW YORK, 400 Madison Ave., New York NY 10017. (212)832-2839. Editor: Jeffrey Blyth. Estab. 1971. 50% freelance written by writers on contract; 50% freelance written by writers on a one-time basis. Works with 3-6 previously unpublished writers annually. Buys British and European rights mostly, but can handle world rights. Previously published submissions OK "for overseas." Pays on publication or agreement of sale. Reports as soon as possible.
Needs: "Unusual nonfiction stories and photos for British and European press. Picture stories, for example, on such 'Americana' as a 5-year-old evangelist; the 800-pound 'con-man'; the nude-male calendar; tallest girl in the world; interviews with pop celebrities such as Yoko Ono, Michael Jackson, Bill Cosby, Tom Selleck, Cher, Priscilla Presley, Cheryl Tiegs, Eddie Murphy, Liza Minelli, also news of stars on such shows as 'Dynasty'/'Dallas'; cult subjects such as voodoo, college fads, anything amusing or offbeat. Extracts from books such as Earl Wilson's *Show Business Laid Bare*, inside-Hollywood type series ('Secrets of the Stuntmen'). Real life adventure dramas ('Three Months in an Open Boat,' 'The Air Crash Cannibals of the Andes'). No length limits—short or long, but not too long. Query or submit complete ms. Payment varies; depending on whether material is original, or world rights. Pays top rates, up to several thousand dollars, for exclusive material."
Photos: Purchased with or without features. Captions required. Standard size prints. Pay $50-100, but no limit on exclusive material.
Tips: "Be alert to the unusual story in your area—the sort that interests the American tabloids (and also the European press)."

INTERSTATE NEWS SERVICES, INC., 237 S. Clark Ave., St. Louis MO 63135. (314)522-1300. Editor: Michael J. Olds. Estab. 1985. 50% of material from freelancers on one-time basis. Purchases 1,200 mss/year. "Interstate acts as the local news bureau for newspapers that are too small to operate their own state capital bureau." Buys all rights and makes work-for-hire assignments. Call for information.
Needs: Hard news emphasis, concentrating on local delegations, tax money and local issues. Query with clips of published work. Negotiates with writers under contract.
Tips: "We deal only with freelancers who work with us regularly and in selected states (MO, IL, AR, TX, VA, DC, MD). We do not buy unsolicited mss."

JEWISH TELEGRAPHIC AGENCY, 330 7th Ave., New York NY 10001-5010. (212)643-1890. Editor: Mark Joffe. Managing Editor: Elli Wohlgelernter. 40% written by writers on contract; 40% freelance written by writers on a one-time basis. Buys 40 features/year. Syndicates to newspapers. Query for electronic submissions. Submissions with SASE will not be returned. Reports in 2 months. Buys second serial (reprint) rights.
Needs: Fillers, magazine features, newspaper features and news items. "Anything of Jewish interest, 500-1,000 words. Can be first-person or op-ed; news stories should be balanced." Buys one-shot features and article series. Submit complete ms. Pays $25-50-75 flat rate. Currently syndicates Commentary, by Rabbi Marc Tanenbaum.
Tips: "Simply put, good writing will get published. Anything of Jewish interest, nationally or worldwide, will be considered. I'm looking for good stories on trends in Jewish life."

JSA PUBLICATIONS, P.O. Box 37175, Oak Park MI 48237. (313)546-9123. Director: Joe Ajlouny. Editor: Paul Ammar. Estab. 1982. Alternative features syndicate and humor/trade book packager; 50% of requirements bought from freelance submissions; 40% from writers and illustrators under contract; 10% self-generated. "Please don't send general/family comic strips. We prefer contemporary and thematic single panels. Truly unique puzzles only." Always query first with samples and SASE.

Reports in 2 months. Buys some rights, prefers licensing agreements. Guidelines for SASE.
Needs: Features capable of book length and other adaptations, such as greeting cards, postcards and booklets. Humorous or clever concepts, articles and illustrations. Will accept magazine articles, nonfiction, only after query with SASE. Pays standard royalties on syndication contracts. Purchased illustrations between $30-700; magazine humor or nonfiction articles between $110-400. Currently syndicated: Party Ranks, The Bob Zone, Future Features, Off the Wall. Packaged: "The Name is Trump," "The Official Handbook of Cold War Nostalgia." Always query first, please enclose SASE.

KING FEATURES SYNDICATE, INC., 235 E. 45th St., New York NY 10017. (212)455-4000. Director of Editorial Projects: Merry Clark. Syndicates material to newspapers. Submit brief cover letter with six samples of column or 24 daily comic strips with comic proposal. Reports in 2 weeks by letter.
Needs: "We are looking for original ideas for columns and first-rate writing. Check *Editor & Publisher Annual Directory of Syndicated Services* before you submit a column idea."

LOS ANGELES TIMES SYNDICATE, Times Mirror Square, Los Angeles CA 90053. (213)237-3700. Executive Editor: Steven Christensen. Special Articles Editor: Dan O'Toole. Syndicates to U.S. and worldwide markets. Usually buys first North American serial rights and world rights, but rights purchased can vary. Submit seasonal material 6 weeks in advance. Material ranges from 800-2,000 words.
Needs: Reviews continuing columns and comic strips for U.S. and foreign markets. Send columns and comic strips to Steven Christensen. Also reviews single articles, series, magazine reprints, and book serials. Send these submissions to Dan O'Toole. Send complete mss. Pays 50% commission. Currently syndicates Art Buchwald, Dr. Henry Kissinger, Dr. Jeane Kirkpatrick, William Pfaff, Paul Conrad and Lee Iacocca.
Tips: "We're dealing with fewer undiscovered writers but still do review material."

‡MEGALO MEDIA, P.O. Box 678, Syosset NY 11791. (212)535-6811. Editor: J. Baxter Newgate. Estab. 1972. 50% written by writers on contract; 50% freelance written by writers on a one-time basis. Works with 5 previously unpublished writers/year. Syndicates to newspapers. Query for electronic submissions. Reports in 1 month. Buys all rights. Free writer's guidelines.
Needs: Crossword puzzles. Buys one-shot features. Submit complete ms. Pays flat rate of $150 for Sunday puzzle. Currently syndicates National Challenge, by J. Baxter Newgate (crossword puzzle); Crossword Puzzle, by J. Baxter Newgate.

NEW YORK TIMES SYNDICATION SALES CORP., 130 5th Ave., New York NY 10011. (212)645-3000. FAX: (212)645-3949. Managing Editor: Barbara Gaynes. Syndicates numerous one-shot articles. Buys second serial (reprint) rights or all rights.
Needs: Magazine and newspaper features. "On syndicated articles, payment to author is varied. We only consider articles that have been previously published. Send tearsheets of articles published." Photos are welcome with articles.
Tips: "Topics should cover universal markets and either be by a well-known writer or have an off-beat quality. Quizzes are welcomed if well researched."

NEWS FLASH INTERNATIONAL, INC., Division of the Observer Newspapers, 2262 Centre Ave., Bellmore NY 11710. (516)679-9888. Editor: Jackson B. Pokress. 25% written by writers on contract; 25% freelance written by writers on a one-time basis. Supplies material to Observer newspapers and overseas publications. Works with 10-20 previously unpublished writers annually. "Contact editor prior to submission to allow for space if article is newsworthy." Pays on publication.
Nonfiction: "We have been supplying a 'ready-for-camera' sports page (tabloid size) complete with column and current sports photos on a weekly basis to many newspapers on Long Island, as well as pictures and written material to publications in England and Canada. Payment for assignments is based on the article. Payments vary from $20 for a feature of 800 words. Our sports stories feature in-depth reporting as well as book reviews on this subject. We are always in the market for good photos, sharp and clear, action photos of boxing, wrestling, football, baseball and hockey. We cover all major league ball parks during the baseball and football seasons. We are accredited to the Mets, Yanks, Jets and Giants. In winter we cover basketball, hockey and all sports events at the Nassau Coliseum."
Photos: Purchased on assignment; captions required. Uses "good quality 8 × 10 b&w glossy prints; good choice of angles and lenses." Pays $7.50 minimum for b&w photos.
Tips: "Submit articles which are fresh in their approach on a regular basis with good quality black and white glossy photos if possible; include samples of work. We prefer well-researched, documented stories with quotes where possible. We are interested in profiles and bios on woman athletes. There is a big interest in this in the foreign market. Women's boxing, volleyball and basketball are major interests."

NEWSPAPER ENTERPRISE ASSOCIATION, INC., 200 Park Ave., New York NY 10166. (212)692-3700. Editorial Director: David Hendin. Director, International Newspaper Operations: Sidney Goldberg. Deputy Editorial Director: Diana Loevy. Director of Comics: Sarah Gillespie. 100% written by writers on contract. "We provide a comprehensive package of features to mostly small- and medium-sized newspapers." Reports in 6 weeks. Buys all rights.

Needs: "Any column we purchase must fill a need in our feature lineup and must have appeal for a wide variety of people in all parts of the country. We are most interested in lively writing. We are also interested in features that are not merely copies of other features already on the market. The writer must know his or her subject. Any writer who has a feature that meets all of those requirements should send a few copies of the feature to us, along with his or her plans for the column and some background material on the writer." Current columnists include Bob Wagman, Chuck Stone, Dr. Peter Gott, Tom Tiede, Ben Wattenberg and William Rusher. Current comics include Born Loser, Frank & Ernest, Eek & Meek, Kit 'n' Carlyle, Berry's World, Arlo and Janis, and Snafu.

Tips: "We get enormous numbers of proposals for first person columns—slice of life material with lots of anecdotes. While many of these columns are big successes in local newspapers, it's been our experience that they are extremely difficult to sell nationally. Most papers seem to prefer to buy this sort of column from a talented local writer."

‡PACIFIC NEWS SERVICE, 450 Market St., Room 506, San Francisco CA 94105-2505. (415)243-4364. Editor: Sandy Close. Estab. 1969. 50% written by writers on contract; 50% freelance written by writers on a one-time basis. Buys 350 articles annually. "We use about 10% of all submissions." Syndicates to magazines and newspapers. Reports in 2 weeks. Buys first North American rights. Writer's guidelines for SASE.

Needs: Newspaper and news features (700-900 words). Buys one-shot features. Query with clips of published work or submit complete ms. Pays flat rate of $100-150. "We do not regularly syndicate *anyone*. We distribute individual articles daily via wire, then compile weekly packet."

‡PEN SYNDICATED FICTION PROJECT, P.O. Box 15650, Washington DC 20003. Director: Caroline Marshall. Estab. 1982. 100% freelance written by writers on a one-time basis. Buys 50-60 short stories (short fiction of 2,500 words or less) per year. Outlets: newspapers, regional magazines, literary quarterly *American Short Fiction*, and radio (NPR, BBC). Receives submissions only in January each year; replies by early May. Buys all rights for 3 years. Free writer's guidelines.

Needs: Fiction (short stories of 2,500 words or fewer). Submit complete ms (Jan. only). "Please write to Project for guidelines first." Pays flat rate of $500 for purchase of rights, $100 per print publication thereafter, $100 if used in print or audio anthology.

Tips: "We're looking for stories with a 'high narrative profile' (principally because they work best on radio). We see a lot of stories that don't 'tell' much. They're well-written, capably crafted, but there's no real story—news—there. I call them empty house—a la the current construction boom—that no one has yet moved in to. I think writers need to look at their work to see if it's emotionally trenchant. Ask the same question reporters need to ask: why is this important compelling? This is an especially important dimension of fiction for us because we try to place it in the mass media, in the context of news, so for business as well as artistic/aesthetic reasons, it's an important question."

ROYAL FEATURES, P.O. Box 58174, Houston TX 77258. (713)280-0777. Executive Director: Fay W. Henry. Estab. 1984. 80% written by writers on contract; 10% freelance written by writers on one-time basis. Syndicates to magazines and newspapers. Reports in 2 months. Buys all rights or first North American serial rights.

Needs: Magazine and newspaper columns and features. Buys one-shot features and article series. Query with or without published clips. Send SASE with unsolicited queries or materials. Pays authors percentage, 40-60%.

‡SCRAMBL-GRAM INC., 1772 State Rd., Cuyahoga Falls OH 44223. Editor: C. R. Elum. Estab. 1972. 40% freelance written by writers on a one-time basis. Buys several hundred features yearly. Works with 50-100 previously unpublished writers/year. "5 of our puzzle features are appearing in 200-plus newspapers across the U.S. and Canada." Reports back in 3 weeks. Buys all rights. Writer's guidelines for SASE.

Needs: Newspaper features, word puzzles and games. Buys one-shot features. Submit complete puzzle and solution with SASE. Pays $10-50 per puzzle or game. "We sell a complete constructor's kit with grids, how-to course, tips for making money with puzzles, lists of potential markets, etc.—$37.50 check or money order to Scramble-Gram Inc.—includes guidelines." Currently syndicates Kwikcross Crossword, by various authors; Wonder in Words, by various authors.

‡SENIOR WIRE, Clear Mountain Communications, 2377 Elm St., Denver CO 80207. (303)355-3882. Editor: Allison St. Claire. Estab. 1988. 100% freelance written. Monthly news, information and feature syndication service to various senior publications, general interest publications, and companies interested in senior market. Circulation nationwide, varies per article depending on which articles are bought for publication. Pays 50% of fee for each use of manuscript (fees range from $5-50). Pays on publication. Buys first North American serial rights and simultaneous rights. Submit seasonal/holiday material 3 months in advance. Prefers manuscripts, queries only with. SASE. No payment for photos but they help increase sales. Reports in 2-4 weeks. Writer's guidelines for $1 and SASE. Query for electronic submissions. Please indicate on top of ms if available on 5¼" floppy disk or by modem.

Needs: Does not want "anything aimed at less than age 55-plus market; anything patronizing or condescending to seniors." Manuscripts requested include: Seasonal features, especially those with a nostalgic angle (750-1,000 words); older celebrity profiles, photos required (900-1,100 words); travel tips (no more than 500-750 words); personal travel experiences as a mature traveler, photos are a must (1,000 words); humorous fillers or poems (100-500 words); or miscellaneous other material of universal interest to seniors. Accepts 12 mss in each category per year, 25-50 fillers/year.

Tips: "All areas open to freelancers. Sometimes give assignments to proven, reliable freelancers whose work has sold well through the syndication. Want fresh approach to senior issues, overworked themes not appreciated. Solid informational and generic articles accepted. We will not promote any product or business unless it is the only one in existence. Must be applicable to senior lifestyle."

SINGER MEDIA CORPORATION, 1030 Calle Cordillera, Unit #106, San Clemente CA 92672. (714)498-7227. FAX: (714)498-2162. Editors: Kurt Singer and Dorothy Rosati. Estab. 1940. 25% written by writers on contract; 25% freelance written by writers on a one-time basis. Syndicates to magazines, newspapers, cassettes and book publishers. Reports in 3 weeks. Rights negotiable, world rights preferred. Writer's guidelines for #10 SAE and $1.

Needs: Short stories, crosswords, puzzles, quizzes, interviews, entertainment and psychology features, cartoons, books for serialization and foreign reprints. Syndicates one-shot features and article series on celebrities. Query with clips of published work or submit complete ms. Pays 50% author's percentage. Currently syndicates Solve a Crime, by B. Gordon (mystery puzzle) and Hollywood Gossip, by June Finletter (entertainment).

Tips: "Good interviews with celebrities, men/women relations, business and real estate features have a good chance with us. Aim at world distribution and therefore have a universal approach."

THE SOUTHAM SYNDICATE, 20 Yorks Mills Rd., Toronto, Ontario M2P 2C2 Canada. (416)222-8000. Editor: Jeffrey McBain. Estab. 1986. 90% written by writers on contract; 5% freelance written by writers on a one-time basis. Buys 10 features/year. Works with 3-4 previously unpublished writers/year. Syndicates to newspapers. Query for electronic submissions. Reports in 2 months. Buys Canadian rights.

Needs: Fillers (400-500 words), newspaper columns (700-800 words, self help) and newspaper features (1,000 words). Buys one-shot features and article series. Query with clips of published work. Pays 50% author's percentage. Currently syndicates Claire Hoy, William Johnson, Ben Wicks and David Suzuki.

SPORTS FEATURES SYNDICATE/WORLD FEATURES SYNDICATE, 1005 Mulberry, Marlton NJ 08053. (609)983-7688. Editor: Ronald A. Sataloff. Estab. 1981. 1-5% written by freelance on one-time basis. Nearly all material is syndicated to daily newspapers and the Associated Press's supplemental sports wire. Reports in 2 months. Buys all rights.

Needs: Currently syndicates Sports Lists, by staff; No Kidding?, by Karl Van Asselt; Mr. Music, by Jerry Osborne.

Tips: "No surprise—space is at a premium and one wishing to sell a column is at a disadvantage unless he is an expert in a chosen field and can relate that area of expertise in layman's language. Concentrate on features that take little space and that are helpful to the reader as well as interesting. *USA Today* has revolutionized newspapering in the sense that it is no longer a sin to be brief. That trend is here for a long time, and a writer should be aware of it. Papers are also moving toward more reader-oriented features, and those with an ability to make difficult subjects easy reading have an advantage. No one-shots!"

TEENAGE CORNER, INC., 70-540 Gardenia Ct., Rancho Mirage CA 92270. President: Mrs. David J. Lavin. Buys 122 items/year for use in newspapers. Submit complete ms. Reports in 1 week. Material is not copyrighted.

Needs: 500-word newspaper features. Pays $25.

UNITED MEDIA/UNITED FEATURE SYNDICATE, 200 Park Ave., New York NY 10166. (212)692-3700. Editorial Director: David Hendon. Deputy Editorial Director: Diana Loevy. VP Director of Comic Art: Sarah Gillespie. 100% written by writers on contract. Syndicates to newspapers. Reports in 6 weeks. Writer's guidelines for #10 SASE.

Close-up

Caroline Marshall
Director
PEN Syndicated Fiction Project

Photo by E.J. Morris

"Each year six or seven short stories seem to capture the spirit of our times," says PEN Syndicated Fiction Project Director Caroline Marshall. "These stories fit in extremely well with our format as they will likely appear in the supplement pages of Sunday newspapers." The stories are quite different than those aspiring to publication in literary magazines. "Topical stories do well for us," says Marshall. "We tend to look for stories with news value even as literature."

Created in 1982 by the National Endowment for the Arts, the PEN Syndicated Fiction Project reflected the resurgence of interest in the short story. Syndicated fiction in the color supplements of Sunday newspapers dates back to the fiction of Mark Twain, Charles Dickens and Arthur Conan Doyle but its popularity has waxed and waned over the years.

By 1960 syndicated fiction had been dropped by most newspapers. Publishers were competing with television and other entertainment media. Interest began to turn around again, however, in the early 1980s. The NEA spent five years studying the feasibility of syndicated fiction, and in 1982 made a seed grant in conjunction with PEN, the international writers' organization, to launch the project. Marshall has been the director of the project from the beginning, after working as a reporter, teacher and a poet in the schools for various foundations. "It's the only thing I've ever done that calls on everything I've done before."

Twelve newspapers were signed up at the outset. "We had as many as 60 papers in 1986," says Marshall. "Since then there has been a gradual decline in that outlet." Sunday supplements are not the only market, however. In 1985 Richard Harthise helped develop "The Sound of Writing," which features two short stories and commentary, broadcast by National Public Radio. "Because all of the stories we accept will be done on the radio show, we also look for a high narrative profile and stories that track well," says Marshall. "Extremely experimental stories don't work well for the radio, so we tend to avoid them."

A third outlet has surfaced recently. In 1990 *American Short Fiction*, a new literary magazine published by the University of Texas Press, sealed an agreement with the PEN Syndicated Fiction Project so *American Short Fiction* has the first option to publish anything accepted by the project. Writers receive $500 upon being selected by the project and $100 each time a story is reprinted in a newspaper. "With all of these markets for syndicated fiction," Marshall says, "a writer has a realistic potential to earn $1,000."

Manuscripts are accepted only in January of every year. Despite that small window, the project took in more than 3,000 stories in 1991. Preliminary readers make first round cuts and a panel of judges decides the final 52 selections. Final selections are announced in May. Stories must not be longer than 2,500 words or 10 pages. "We are glad to get shorter stories, too," says Marshall. "I recommend that everyone write for the guidelines first. It's the best way to send appropriate manuscripts."

— Mark Kissling

Needs: Newspaper columns and newspaper features. Query with photocopied clips of published work. "Authors under contract have negotiable terms." Currently syndicates Miss Manners, by Judith Martin (etiquette); Dr. Gott, by Peter Gott, M.D. (medical); Supermarket Shopper, by Martin Sloane (coupon clipping advice); Jack Anderson and Dale van Atta (investigative reporting).
Tips: "We include tips in our guidelines. We buy very few of the hundreds of submissions we see monthly. We are looking for the different feature as opposed to new slants on established columns."

‡**UNIVERSAL PRESS SYNDICATE,** 4900 Main Street, Kansas City MO 64112. Estab. 1970. Buys syndication rights. Reports normally in 1 month. Return postage required.
Nonfiction: Looking for features—columns for daily and weekly newspapers. Distributes one-shot articles (profiles, lifestyle pieces, etc). "Any material suitable for syndication in daily newspapers." Currently handling James J. Kilpatrick, Dear Abby, Erma Bombeck and others. Payment varies according to contract.

WASHINGTON POST WRITERS GROUP, 1150 15th St. NW, Washington DC 20071. (202)334-6375. Editor/General Manager: Alan Shearer. Estab. 1973. Currently syndicates 32 features (columns and cartoons). A news syndicate that provides features for newspapers nationwide. Responds in 2 weeks. Buys all rights.
Needs: Newspaper columns (editorial, lifestyle, humor), and newspaper features (comic strips, political cartoons). Query with clips of published work and samples of proposed column. Pays combination of salary and percentage. Currently syndicates George F. Will column (editorial); Ellen Goodman column (editorial). Writers Group will not consider single (freelance) articles or stories.
Tips: "At this time, The Washington Post Writers Group will review editorial page and lifestyle page columns, as well as political cartoons and comic strips. Will not consider games, puzzles, or similar features. Send sample columns to the attention of Alan Shearer, general manager. Send sample cartoons or comic strips (photocopies—no original artwork, please) to the attention of Alan Shearer. Enclose a SASE for the return and response."

WHITEGATE FEATURES SYNDICATE, 71 Faunce Dr., Providence RI 02906. (401)274-2149. Contact: Eve Green. Editor: Ed Isaac. Estab. 1987. Buys 100% of material from freelance writers. Syndicates to newspapers; planning to begin selling to magazines and radio. Query for electronic submissions. Reports in 3 months. Buys all rights.
Needs: Fiction for Sunday newspaper magazines; magazine columns and features, newspaper columns and features, cartoon strips. Buys one-shots and article series. Query with clips of published work. For cartoon strips, submit samples. Pays 50% author's percentage on columns. Additional payment for photos accepted with ms. Currently syndicates Indoor Gardening, by Jane Adler; Looking Great, by Gloria Lintermans; Strong Style, by Hope Strong; On Marriage and Divorce, by Dr. Melvyn A. Berke.
Tips: "Please aim for a topic that is fresh. Newspapers seem to want short text pieces, 400-800 words. Please include SASE. We like to know a little about author's or cartoonist's background. We prefer people who have already been published. Plese send material to Eve Green."

Other Syndicates

The following syndicates were listed in the 1991 edition but do not have listings in this edition of *Writer's Market*. The majority did not respond to our request to update their listings or return a questionnaire for a new listing. If a reason was given for their exclusion, we have included it in parentheses after the listing name.

AP Newsfeatures
Arthur's International
Black Conscience Syndication
 Inc.

International Photo News
National News Bureau
News USA Inc.
North America Syndicate

Syndicated Writers & Artists
 Inc. (asked to be deleted)
Tribune Media Services

Greeting Card Publishers

Greetings cards continue to serve as one of the most viable means of communication in the active 1990s. While we have always sent cards to commemorate holidays and other special days, today we use them to express innumerable sentiments. Thus the market, though competitive, remains strong for the innovative freelancer with fresh ideas. Because the market is continually growing and changing with consumers' needs, it is important to keep abreast of trends in the industry. Most significantly, familiarize yourself with the differences among lines of cards by visiting card racks. If a particular line appeals to you, write to that company requesting its market list, catalog or submission guidelines (often available for a SASE or small fee). In addition, trade magazines such as *Greetings* (Mackay Publishing Corp., 309 5th Ave., New York NY 10016) can keep you apprised of changes and occurrences within the field, including seminars and trade shows.

Although new trends and areas of growth arise each year, certain factors remain constant and should be considered. Women continue to comprise the majority of card buyers. And the three basic card categories—traditional, studio (or contemporary) and alternative—have remained the same for a number of years.

The popularity of alternative cards continues to grow as smaller companies expand their lines to accommodate issues relevant to today's consumers. For example, cards commemorating new jobs and salary raises are top sellers, as are cards dealing with more sensitive issues such as divorce, terminal illness and substance abuse. In particular, greeting cards directed at people suffering or recovering from alchohol and drug addictions have become an important market. These cards often incorporate the language of 12-step programs, including addiction, denial, codependency and healing the "inner child." Gibson Greetings has created one such line, entitled Hopelines, in conjunction with the Minnesota-based Hazelden Foundation.

With regard to traditional and nontraditional cards, personal, expressive verse is still preferred over rhymed verse. Most editors are looking for a conversational tone relevant to today's consumers.

The relationship between artwork and copy is always important. It is crucial to think visually—to plan the card as an entire product—even if you are not artistically inclined. Although most editors do not want to see artwork unless it is professional, they do appreciate suggestions from writers who have a concept for the card. If your verse depends on an illustration to make its point or if you have an idea for a unique card shape or foldout, include a dummy card with your writing samples.

Payment for greeting card verse varies, but most firms pay per card or per idea; a handful pay small royalties. Some card companies prefer to test a card first and will pay a small fee for a test card idea.

Greeting card companies will also buy ideas for gift products and may plan to use card material for a number of subsequent items. Licensing—the sale of rights to a particular character for a variety of products from mugs to T-shirts—is a growing part of the greetings industry. Because of this, however, note that most card companies buy all rights. Many companies also require writers to provide a release form, guaranteeing the material submitted is original and has not been sold elsewhere. Before signing a release form or a contract to sell all rights, be sure you understand the terms.

Submission requirements may vary slightly from company to company, so send a SASE for writer's guidelines if they are available. To submit conventional card material, type or neatly print your verses on 8½×11, 4×6 or 3×5 slips of paper or index cards. The usual submission includes from five to 15 cards and an accompanying cover letter. For studio cards, or cards with pop-outs or attachments also send a mechanical dummy card. For more help on card submissions see the samples in *The Writer's Digest Guide to Manuscript Formats* (Writer's Digest Books).

Because you will be sending out many samples, you may want to label each sample. Establish a master card for each verse or idea and record where and when each was sent and whether it was rejected or purchased. Keep all cards sent to one company in a batch and give each batch a number. Write this number on the back of your return SASE to help you match up your verses as they are returned.

For information on greeting card companies not included in *Writer's Market*, see Other Greeting Card Publishers at the end of this section.

AMBERLEY GREETING CARD CO., 11510 Goldcoast Dr., Cincinnati OH 45249-1695. (513)489-2775. Editor: Ned Stern. Estab. 1966. 90% freelance written. Bought 200 freelance ideas/samples last year; receives an estimated 25,000 submissions annually. Reports in 1 month. Material copyrighted. Buys all rights. **Pays on acceptance.** Writer's guidelines for #10 SASE. Market list is regularly revised.
Needs: Humorous, informal and studio. No seasonal material or poetry. Prefers unrhymed verses/ideas. Humorous cards sell best. Pays $50/card idea.
Tips: "Amberley publishes specialty lines and humorous studio greeting cards. We accept freelance ideas, including risque and nonrisque. Make it short and to the point. Include SASE (with correct postage) for return of rejects."

AMCAL, 1050 Shary Ct., Concord CA 94518. (415)689-9930. Product Development Manager: Jennifer DeCristoforo. 80% of material is freelance written. Buys 10 freelance ideas/samples per year; receives 60 submissions annually. Reports in 3 weeks. Rights negotiable. **Pays on acceptance.** Writer's guidelines/market list for SASE.
Needs: Conventional, informal, sensitive and soft line. Prefers generally unrhymed. Submit 12 ideas/batch.
Other Product Lines: Calendars and gift products.
Tips: Our target audience is female, ages 20-50. Direct, thoughtful sentiments sell the best. Generally short.

AMERICAN GREETINGS, 10500 American Rd., Cleveland OH 44144. (216)252-7300. Director of Conventional Concept Development: Kathleen McKay. No unsolicited material. "We like to receive a letter of inquiry describing education or experience, or a resume first. We will then screen those applicants and request samples from those that interest us." Reports in 3 months. Buys all rights. **Pays on acceptance.** Guidelines for #10 SASE.
Tips: "Our target audience is the mass-market retail crowd, so we generally purchase the more conventional forms of verse, prose and humorous writing."

‡ARGUS COMMUNICATIONS, 1 DLM Park, Allen TX 75002. (214)248-6300. FAX: (214)727-2175. Editorial Coordinator: Lori Potter. 90% freelance written. Interested in everyday material for cards and posters. Reports in 2 months. Buys all rights. **Pays on acceptance.** Submission guidelines available for #10 SASE.
Needs: Posters: At-a-glance messages that are succinct and memorable. An "about me" statement that represents an attitude or image that the buyer wants to be identified with. Humorously captioned with brief text. Strong editorial and trendy styling which reflect today's lifestyles and concerns are our focus. Focusing on the 16-22 year old age group.
Other Product Lines: Greeting cards, postcards and calendars.
Tips: "Posters capture your attention with a creative mixtue of humorous dynamic and motivational editorial. We encourage you to be funny, to be inspirational, but to be brief. Target audience is teenagers (both male and female) and women."

BLUE MOUNTAIN ARTS, INC., Dept. WM, P.O. Box 1007, Boulder CO 80306. Contact: Editorial Staff. Estab. 1971. Buys 50-75 items/year. Reports in 3-6 months. **Pays on acceptance.**
Needs: "Primarily need sensitive and sensible writings about love, friendships, families, philosophies, etc.—written with originality and universal appeal." Also poems and writings for specific holidays (Christmas, Valentine's Day, etc.), and special occasions, such as birthdays, get well, and sympathy. Seasonal writings should be submitted at least 4 months prior to the actual holiday. For worldwide,

exclusive rights we pay $200 per poem; for one-time use in anthology, we pay $25.
Other Product Lines: Calendars, gift books and greeting books. Payment varies.
Tips: "Get a feel for the Blue Mountain Arts line prior to submitting material. Our needs differ from other card publishers; we do not use rhymed verse, preferring instead a more honest, person-to-person style. Have a specific person or personal experience in mind as you write. We use unrhymed, sensitive poetry and prose on the deep significance and meaning of life and relationships. A very limited amount of freelance material is selected each year, either for publication on a notecard or in a gift anthology, and the selection prospects are highly competitive. But new material is always welcome and each manuscript is given serious consideration."

‡BLUE Q, 46 Waltham St., Boston MA 02118. (617)482-7576. FAX: (617)482-6710. Editor: Mitch Nash. Estab. 1988. 20% of material is freelance written. Buys 10 freelance ideas/samples per year; receives 20 submissions annually. Submit seasonal/holiday material 8 months in advance. Pays on publication. Free writer's guidelines/market list. Market list is regularly revised.
Needs: Humorous and studio. "Irreverent, cutting edge, nutty-wack-o." Prefers unrhymed verse. Submit 20 ideas/batch.
Other Product Lines: Bumper stickers ($100-500), calendars ($100-500), gift books ($100-500), greeting books ($100-500), postcards ($100-500) and any creative paper products. "Humorous, funky, cutting-edge humor. Target audience is upscale, young urban. Creative card formats are becoming as important as creative copy and imagery."

BRILLIANT ENTERPRISES, 117 W. Valerio St., Santa Barbara CA 93101. Contact: Editorial Dept. Buys all rights. Submit words and art in black on $3\frac{1}{2} \times 3\frac{1}{3}$ horizontal, thin white paper in batches of no more than 15. Reports "usually in 2 weeks." Catalog and sample set for $2.
Needs: Postcards. Messages should be "of a highly original nature, emphasizing subtlety, simplicity, insight, wit, profundity, beauty and felicity of expression. Accompanying art should be in the nature of oblique commentary or decoration rather than direct illustration. Messages should be of universal appeal, capable of being appreciated by all types of people and of being easily translated into other languages. Because our line of cards is highly unconventional, it is essential that freelancers study it before submitting. No topical references, subjects limited to American culture or puns." Limit of 17 words/card. Pays $50 for "complete ready-to-print word and picture design."

THE CALLIGRAPHY COLLECTION, 2604 NW 74th Place, Gainesville FL 32606. (904)378-0748. Editor: Katy Fischer. Reports in 6 months. Buys all rights. Pays on publication.
Needs: "Ours is a line of framed prints of watercolors with calligraphy." Conventional, humorous, informal, inspirational, sensitivity and soft line. Prefers unrhymed verse, but will consider rhymed. Submit 3 ideas/batch. Pays $50-100/framed print idea.
Other Product Lines: Gift books, greeting books and plaques.
Tips: Sayings for friendship are difficult to get. Bestsellers are humorous, sentimental and inspirational ideas—such as for wedding and family and friends. "Our audience is women 20 to 50 years of age. Write something they would like to give or receive as a lasting gift."

CHIPPENDALES, 2115 Pico Blvd., Santa Monica CA 90405. (213)396-4045. FAX: (213)396-9912. Editor: Steve Cadena. Estab. 1980. 50% of material is freelance written. Submit seasonal/holiday material 1 year in advance. Reports in 1 month. Pays on publication. Free writer's guidelines/market list. Market list is regularly revised.
Needs: Humorous, informal, invitations, sensitivity and soft line. Submit 12 ideas/batch.
Tips: Our target audience requires cards for birthdays, ages 14-40.

‡CITY MERCHANDISE INC., 750 8th Ave., New York NY 10036. (212)944-6592. FAX (212)944-6621. President: Jack Gindi. Estab. 1986. Reports in 1 month. Rights purchased "depends on deal." Pays on publication. Free writer's guidelines/market list. Market list is regularly revised.
Needs: NY cartoon postcards.
Other Product Lines: Bumper stickers ($25-50), postcards ($50-150).

COMSTOCK CARDS, Suite 15, 600 S. Rock, Reno NV 89502. FAX: (702)333-9406. Owner: Patti P.Wolf. Art Director: David Delacroix. Estab. 1986. 35% freelance written. Buys 50 freelance ideas/samples per year; receives 500 submissions annually. Submit seasonal/holiday material 1 year in advance. Reports in 5 weeks. Buys all rights. **Pays on acceptance.** Writer's guidelines/market list for SASE. Market list issued one time only.
Needs: Humorous, informal, invitations and "puns, put-downs, put-ons, outrageous humor aimed at a sophisticated, adult female audience. No conventional, soft line or sensitivity hearts and flowers, etc." Prefers to receive 25 cards/batch. Pays $50-75/card idea.

Other Product Lines: Notepads.

Tips: "Always keep holiday occasions in mind and personal me-to-you expressions that relate to today's occurrences. Ideas must be simple and concisely delivered. A combination of strong image and strong gag line make a successful greeting card. Consumers relate to themes of work, sex and friendship combined with current social, political and economic issues."

CONTEMPORARY DESIGNS, 213 Main St., Gilbert IA 50105. (515)232-5188. FAX: (515)232-3380. Editor: S. Abelson. Estab. 1977. 25% of written material is freelance. Submit seasonal/holiday material 1 year in advance. Reports in 1 month. Buys all rights. **Pays on acceptance.**
Needs: Invitations and memo pads. Unrhymed verse.
Other Product Lines: Activity books, gift books, mugs, tote bags, aprons and pillow cases.

CONTENOVA GIFTS, P.O. Box 69130, Postal Station K, Vancouver, British Columbia V5K 4W4 Canada. (604)253-4444. FAX: (604)253-4014. Editor: Jeff Sinclair. Estab. 1965. 100% freelance written. Bought over 100 freelance ideas last year; receives an estimated 15,000 submissions annually. Submit ideas on 3×5 cards or small mock-ups in batches of 10-15. Buys world rights. **Pays on acceptance.** Current needs list for SAE and IRC.
Needs: Humorous and studio. Both risqué and nonrisqué. "Short gags with good punch work best." Birthday, belated birthday, get well, anniversary, thank you, congratulations, miss you, new job, etc. Seasonal ideas needed for Christmas, Valentine's Day, Mother's Day, Father's Day. Pays $50.
Tips: "Not interested in play-on-words themes. We're leaning toward more 'cute risqué' and no longer using drinking themes. Put together your best ideas and submit them. One great idea sent is much better than 20 poor ideas filling an envelope. We are always searching for new writers who can produce quality work. You need not be previously published. Our audience is 18-65 – the full spectrum of studio card readers. We do *not* use poetry."

CREATE-A-CRAFT, P.O. Box 330008, Fort Worth TX 76163-0008. (817)292-1855. Editor: Mitchell Lee. Estab. 1967. 5% freelance written. Buys 2 freelance ideas/samples per year; receives 300 submissions annually. Submit seasonal/holiday material 1 year in advance. Submissions not returned even if accompanied by SASE – "not enough staff to take time to package up returns." Buys all rights. Sample greeting cards are available for $2.50 and a #10 SASE.
Needs: Announcements, conventional, humorous, juvenile and studio. "Payment depends upon the assignment, amount of work involved, and production costs involved in project."
Tips: No unsolicited material. "Send letter of inquiry describing education, experience, or resume with one sample first. We will screen applicants and request samples from those who interest us."

DIGRESSIONS, INC., (formerly Eldercards, Inc.), P.O. Box 202, Piermont NY 10968. (914)359-7137. Editors: Steve Epstein and Lenore Benowitz. 10% of material is freelance written. Receives 20 submissions annually. Submit seasonal/holiday material 3 months in advance. Reports in 1 month. Pays royalties.
Needs: Funny birthdays and buttons, informal, invitations, sensitivity and studio. Prefers unrhymed verse. Submit 24 ideas/batch. Pays $10-200.
Tips: "Market is contemporary, upbeat, humorous, for 20-50 years old. Writers should be mindful of babies and the baby boom, singles (young and old) but mostly birthdays and anniversaries and get well."

‡EARTH CARE PAPER INC., Box 14140, Madison WI 53714. (608)277-2920. Editor: Barbara Budig. Submit seasonal/holiday material 1 year in advance. Prefers to keep on file rather than return by SASE. Reports in 2 months. Buys card rights. **Pays on acceptance for use.** Free writer's guidelines.
Needs: Humorous, informal, brief, sensitivity, soft line. Prefers unrhymed verse, but will consider rhymed. Pays $50/minimum.
Tips: "Our company features cards printed on recycled paper. We are interested in humor relating to nature, environmental protection or social issues. Submit illustration ideas with verse."

‡FOTOFOLIO, INC., 536 Broadway, New York NY 10012. (212)226-0923. FAX: (212)226-0072. Editors: Julie Galant and Ron Schick. Estab. 1976. Submit seasonal/holiday material one year in advance (visuals only). Reports in 1 month. Pays on publication.
Other Product Lines: Postcards, notecards, posters.
Tips: "We specialize in high quality fine art photography."

FREEDOM GREETING CARD CO., P.O. Box 715, Bristol PA 19007. (215)945-3300. FAX: (215)547-0248. Editor: J. Levitt. Estab. 1969. 90% freelance written. Submit seasonal/holiday material 1 year in advance. Reports in 2 weeks. **Pays on acceptance.** Free writer's guidelines/market list. Market list available to writer on mailing list basis.

Needs: Announcements, conventional, humorous, inspirational, invitations, juvenile and sensitivity. Payment varies.

Tips: "General and friendly cards sell best. Freedom is looking for a sensitive verse that conveys the special message between family members and friends. We have found that it is becoming more and more difficult to find this type of message in the greeting card stores and we are beginning to target these areas with our prose."

‡**FULLMOON CREATIONS INC.**, 74 South Hamilton St., Doylestown PA 18901. Editor: Lisa Gingras. Estab. 1986. 30-80% of material is freelance written. Buys 10 freelance ideas/samples per year; receives 20 submissions annually. Submit seasonal/holiday material 2 months in advance. Reports in 1 month. Pays on publication. Market list is regularly revised.

Needs: Announcements, humorous, inspirational, juvenile and studio. Prefers unrhymed verse. Submit 20 ideas/batch.

Other Product Lines: Promotions.

GIBSON GREETINGS, 2100 Section Rd., Cincinnati OH 45237. Did not want to be listed.

HALLMARK CARDS, INC., P.O. Box 419580, 2501 McGee, Mail Drop 276, Kansas City MO 64141. Contact: Carol King with letter of inquiry only; no sample. Reports in 2 months. Request guidelines if not on current Hallmark freelance roster; include SASE.

Needs: Humorous, studio cards, and conversational prose.

Tips: "Purchasing writing for everyday and seasonal greeting cards. Because Hallmark has an experienced and prolific writing staff, freelance writers must show a high degree of skill and originality to interest editors who are used to reading the very best."

INDUSTRIAL WHIMSY CO., P.O. Box 1330, Cedar Ridge CA 95924. (916)272-5062. Editor: J. Thom. Helsom. Estab. 1988. 75% of material is freelance written. Buys 50 freelance ideas/samples per year; receives 1,000 submissions monthly. Submissions will be returned only if requested at time of submission. Reports in 3 months if accepted. Buys all rights. **Pays on acceptance.** Writer's guidelines for #10 SASE.

Needs: No greeting cards. Bumper stickers, calendars, plaques, postcards and posters.

INNOVISIONS, INC., 445 W. Erie St., #B3, Chicago IL 60610. (312)642-4871. Editor: Jay Blumenfeld. Estab. 1980. 100% of material freelance written. Buys 50 freelance ideas/samples per year; receives 400 submissions annually. Submit seasonal/holiday material 1 year in advance. Reports in 3 weeks. Buys all rights. Pays within 30 days of publication. Market list issued one time only.

Needs: Humorous. Prefers unrhymed verse. Submit any amount/batch.

Tips: Looks for "off-the-wall humor and novelty cards (small 'joke' items that are the punch line)."

KALAN, INC., 97 S. Union Ave., Lansdowne PA 19050. (215)623-1900. Contact: Editor. 80% freelance written. Buys 150 freelance ideas/samples per year; receives 1,000 submissions annually. Submit seasonal/holiday material 10 months in advance. Reports in 1 month. Buys all rights. **Pays on acceptance.** Writer's guidelines for #10 SASE. Foreign submissions must include at least 2 IRC's. Submit ideas on 3×5 cards or small mock-ups. If artwork is necessary for the understanding of the gag, it may be described briefly for our art department.

Needs: Risque and non-risque knock-'em-dead funny messages for birthday, friendship, love, Christmas and Valentine's Day studio greeting cards. Our x-rated line uses humorous gags with the artwork usually completing the gag.

Other Product Lines: For our key rings and buttons, we seek funny non-risque and risque one-liners about school dating, money, life, sex, etc. Payment is $75/purchased idea. "Put Attn: Editor on submissions envelope." Payment for new product ideas is negotiable.

Tips: "Send for guidelines and samples before submitting. Write for a specific occasion: birthday, celebrating love, good-bye, Christmas, etc. Once you've decided on an occasion, write with a specific person in mind—lover, mother, coworker, etc. This tends to produce specific, funny copy able to be sent to many different types of people."

‡**LIFE GREETINGS**, Box 468, Little Compton RI 02837. (401)635-8535. Editor: Kathy Brennan. Buys 50% of material from freelancers; bought 400 samples in past year. Submit seasonal/holiday material 6 months in advance. Reports in 2 weeks. Buys all rights. **Pays on acceptance.** Free guidelines sheet.

Needs: Humorous, inspirational, sensitivity.

Tips: Our cards are marketed mainly through Christian bookstores.

‡**MAGIC MOMENTS**, 10 Deanna Ct., Deer Park NY 11729. (516)595-2300. FAX: (516)254-3922. Editor: David Braunstein. Estab. 1938. 30% of material is freelance written. Submit seasonal/holiday material 12-18 months in advance. Reports in 1 month. Material not copyrighted. Pays on acceptance. Writer's guidelines/market list for SASE.

Needs: Conventional, humorous, inspirational, juvenile, sensitivity, soft line and studio.

Tips: Conventional cards sell best.

MERLYN GRAPHICS, P.O. Box 9087, Canoga Park CA 91309. (818)349-2775. Editor: Bettie Galling. Estab. 1987. 50% of material bought is freelance written. Bought 50 freelance ideas last year; receives 2,000 submissions annually. Submit seasonal/holiday material 1 year in advance. Reports in 1 month. Buys all rights. Pays on publication. Writer's guidelines for #10 SASE.

Needs: "Humorous everyday cards: birthday, friendship, get well, miss you. The only holiday/occasion cards we are currently publishing are Christmas and Valentine's. We want *very* funny, clever, witty, slightly twisted, belly-busting lines that lend themselves to a very strong visual. We do not want sentimental, 'hearts & flowers,' or cute traditional material. Neither do we want vulgar or 'x-rated' material. Go for clever 'double entendre' and unpredictable punch lines."

Tips: "Please send for and really study our guidelines. Suggested visuals are OK but not required. Only once have we used a writer's suggested visual. However, you must think visually! Remember that you are not writing for 'stand-up comedy.' You should also ask yourself if the card is 'sendable.' Who would you send it to and why? Always remember that most cards (93%) are purchased by women! Our cards are 100% photographic, and almost exclusively photographed in a studio setting. They are 5×7, with the photo on the front and the punchline on the inside, with little or no set-up on the front. Stay away from outlandish 'flying dinosaurs' type concepts. We are not currently accepting outside photography or artwork. We do not guarantee the return of your submissions, so please keep copies. We publish two or three times annually in groups of 36 designs. As a result, when we find material we want to use we may hold it for as long as six months before publishing it. You may write or submit material as often as you wish, but please, no phone calls or certified mail. We provide samples of the finished cards at no charge to the writers, and we give a writer's credit line on the back of the card."

NEW BOUNDARY DESIGNS, INC., 1453 Park Rd., Chanhassen MN 55317. (612)474-0924. FAX: (612)474-9525. Estab. 1979. 5% freelance written. Buys 9 freelance ideas/samples per year; receives 100 submissions annually. Submit seasonal/holiday material 1 year in advance. Reports in 2 weeks. Pays on publication.

Needs: Inspirational, juvenile and sensitivity. Prefers unrhymed verse.

NOBLEWORKS, 113 Clinton St., Hoboken NJ 07030. (800)346-6253. Editor: Christopher Noble. Estab. 1982. 35% freelance written. Buys about 50 submissions/year; received about 10,000 last year. Submit seasonal/holiday material 1 year in advance for Christmas; 8-9 months for other holidays. Reports in 2 months. Buys greeting card rights only. Pays initial fee no later than publication and a royalty up to a specified amount. Guidelines for SASE. Market list is regularly updated.

Needs: Humorous. Prefers to receive 12-24 card ideas/batch.

Tips: "Through many years of trial and error, we have found that very humorous, silly, irreverent and outrageously humorous cards are what we sell. Our cards are aimed at a sophisticated urban market with humor that is unexpected and off-center (though not sleazy and sexual). Our humor is modern, on the edge and takes risks! A card must be instantly understandable. Though an idea may be clever, it will never fly if the reader must complete the thought in order to get at the gist of the joke. Satire, political and social, is very popular if applied correctly."

OATMEAL STUDIOS, P.O. Box 138W3, Rochester VT 05767. (802)767-3171. Creative Director: Helene Lehrer. Estab. 1979. 85% freelance written. Buys 200-300 greeting card lines/year. **Pays on acceptance.** Reports in 2 months. Current market list for #10 SASE.

Needs: Birthday, friendship, anniversary, get well cards, etc. Also Christmas, Chanukah, Mother's Day, Father's Day, Easter, Valentine's Day, etc. Will review concepts. Humorous material (clever and *very* funny) year-round. "Humor, conversational in tone and format, sells best for us." Prefers unrhymed contemporary humor. Current pay schedule available with guidelines.

For explanation of symbols, see the Key to Symbols and Abbreviations on Page 5. For unfamiliar words, see the Glossary.

Other Product Lines: Notepads.
Tips: "The greeting card market has become more competitive with a greater need for creative and original ideas. We are looking for writers who can communicate situations, thoughts, and relationships in a funny way and apply them to a birthday, get well, etc., greeting and we are willing to work with them in targeting our style. We will be looking for material that says something funny about life in a new way."

OUTREACH PUBLICATIONS, P.O. Box 1010, Siloam Springs AR 72761. (501)524-9381. Editor: David Taylor. Estab. 1971. Submit seasonal/holiday material 1 year in advance. Reports in 2 months. **Pays on acceptance.** Guidelines for #10 SASE.
Needs: Calendars, announcements, invitations, all major seasonal and special days, all major everyday cards—birthday, anniversary, get well, friendship, etc. Material must be usable for the Christian market.
Tips: "Study our line, DaySpring Greeting Cards, before submitting. We are looking for sentiments with relational, inspirational messages that minister love and encouragement to the receiver." Prefer unrhymed verse.

PARAMOUNT CARDS INC., 400 Pine St., Pawtucket RI 02860. Editorial Director: Elizabeth Gordon. Estab. 1906. Buys 200 greeting card ideas per year. Submit seasonal/material at least 6 months in advance. Reports in 1 month. Buys all rights. **Pays on acceptance.** Writer's guidelines for SASE.
Needs: All types of conventional verses. Fresh, inventive humorous verses, especially family birthday cards. Would also like to see more conversational prose, especially in family titles such as Mother, Father, Sister, Husband, Wife, etc. Submit in batches of 10-15. Would not like to see tired, formulaic rhymes.
Tips: "Study the market! Go to your local card shops and analyze what you see. Ask the storekeepers which cards are selling. Then apply what you've learned to your own writing. The best cards (and we buy only the best) will have mass appeal and yet, in the consumer's eyes, will read as though they were created exclusively for her. A feminine touch is important, as 90% of all greeting cards are purchased by women."

‡PLUM GRAPHICS INC., P.O. Box 136, Prince Station, New York NY 10012. (212)966-2573. Editor: Yvette Cohen. Estab. 1983. Buys 100% of material from freelancers; purchased 21 samples in past year. Does not return samples unless accompanied by SASE. Reports in 3-4 months. Buys greeting card and stationery rights. Pays on publication. Guidelines sheet for SASE. "Sent out about twice a year in conjunction with the development of new cards."
Needs: Humorous. "We don't want general submissions. We want them to relate to our next line." Prefers unrhymed verse. Greeting cards pay $20-40, depending on series and strength of line. Pays $50 for very good lines.
Tips: "Sell to all ages. Humor is always appreciated. Wants short to-the-point lines."

‡PORTAL PUBLICATIONS, 770 Tamalpias Dr., Corte Madera CA 94925. (415)924-5652. Creative Director: Mike Dowdall. 50% of material is freelance written. Buys 100 freelance ideas/samples per year; receives 200 submissions annually. Reports in 2 months. Pays on publication. Free writer's guidelines/market list.
Needs: Conventional, humorous, informal, soft line and studio. Prefers unrhymed verse. Submit 12 ideas/batch.
Other Product Lines: Calendars and posters.
Tips: "Upscale, cute, humorous cards for bookstores and college bookstores."

RED FARM STUDIO, 1135 Roosevelt Ave., P.O. Box 347, Pawtucket RI 02862. (401)728-9300. FAX: (401)728-0350. Art Director: Lisa Halter Saunders. Estab. 1955. Buys 50 ideas/samples per year. Reports in 2 weeks. Buys all rights. **Pays on acceptance.** Market list for #10 SASE.
Needs: Conventional, inspirational, sensitivity and soft line cards. "We cannot use risqué or insult humor." Submit no more than 10 ideas/samples per batch. Pays $3 per line of copy. Prose, short and long.
Tips: "Write verses that are direct and honest. Flowery sentiments are not in fashion right now. It is important to show caring and sensitivity, however. Our audience is middle to upper middle class adults of all ages."

ROCKSHOTS, INC., 632 Broadway, New York NY 10012. (212)420-1400. FAX: (212)353-8756. Editor: Bob Vesce. Estab. 1979. "We buy 75 greeting card verse (or gag) lines annually." Submit seasonal/holiday material 1 year in advance. Reports in 2 months. Buys rights for greeting-card use. Writer's guidelines for SASE.

Needs: Humorous ("should be off-the-wall, as outrageous as possible, preferably for sophisticated buyer"); soft line; combination of sexy and humorous come-on type greeting ("sentimental is not our style"); and insult cards ("looking for cute insults"). No sentimental or conventional material. "Card gag can adopt a sentimental style, then take an ironic twist and end on an off-beat note." Submit no more than 10 card ideas/samples per batch. Send to attention: Submissions. Pays $50 per gagline. Prefers gag lines on 8×11 paper with name, address, and phone and social security numbers in right corner, or individually on 3×5 cards.

Tips: "Think of a concept that would normally be too outrageous to use, give it a cute and clever wording to make it drop-dead funny and you will have commercialized a non-commercial message. It's always good to mix sex and humor. Our emphasis is definitely on the erotic. Hard-core eroticism is difficult for the general public to handle on greeting cards. The trend is toward 'light' sexy humor, even cute sexy humor. 'Cute' has always sold cards, and it's a good word to think of even with the most sophisticated, crazy ideas. 80% of our audience is female. Remember that your gag line will be illustrated by a photographer. So try to think visually. If no visual is needed, the gag line *can* stand alone, but we generally prefer some visual representation. It is a very good idea to preview our cards at your local store if this is possible to give you a feeling of our style."

SANGAMON, INC., Box 410, Taylorville IL 62568. (217)824-2261. Estab. 1931. 90% freelance written. Buys all rights. **Pays on acceptance.** Writer's guidelines or market list for SASE. Market list is regularly revised.
Needs: Conventional, humorous, inspirational, juvenile, sensitivity and studio. We offer a balance of many styles. Submit 15 ideas maximum/batch.
Other Product Lines: Calendars and promotions.
Tips: "We only request submissions based on background and writing experience. We work 12-18 months ahead of a season and only accept material on assignment."

‡SCANDECOR INC., 430 Pike Rd., Southampton PA 18966. (215)355-2410. FAX: (215)364-8737. Creative Director: Lauren B. Harris. Estab. 1970. 40% of material is freelance written. Buys 46 freelance ideas/samples per year; receives 700 submissions annually. Reports in 2 months. Buys poster rights.
Needs: Humorous, inspirational, juvenile, sensitivity, soft line and studio. Rhymed and unrhymed OK.
Other Product Lines: Posters ($150-1,000).
Tips: "Our posters are our main product in the US. Our target audience is mother-child, 0-8, teen market, 8-22 and adult."

MARCEL SCHURMAN CO., INC., 2500 N. Watney Way, Fairfield CA 94533. Editor: Lynnea Washburn. Estab. 1950. 20% freelance written. Buys 50 freelance ideas per year; receives 500 submissions per year. Reports in 1 month. **Pays on acceptance.** Writer's guidelines for #10 SASE.
Needs: Conventional, light humor, informal, juvenile, sensitivity, conversational, seasonal and everyday categories. Prefers unrhymed verse, but on juvenile cards rhyme is OK. Submit 10-15 cards in one batch.
Tips: "Historically, our nostalgic and art museum cards sell best. However, we are moving toward more contemporary cards and humor. Target market: upscale, professional, well-educated; average age 40; more female."

SCOTT CARDS INC., P.O. Box 906, Newbury Park CA 91319. Editor: Larry Templeman. Estab. 1985. 95% of material is freelance written. Buys 75 freelance ideas/samples per year. Not printing seasonal/holiday cards at present. Reports in 3 months. **Pays on acceptance.** Writer's guidelines/brochure for SAE and 2 first class stamps.
Needs: Conventional, humorous and sensitivity.
Tips: "New ways to say 'I love you' always sell if they aren't corny or too obvious. Humor helps, especially if there is a twist. We are looking for non-traditional sentiments that are sensitive, timely and sophisticated. Our cards have a distinct flavor, so before submitting your work, write for our guidelines and sample brochure."

‡SECOND NATURE LTD., 10 Malton Rd., London W10 5UP England. (800)233-0092. Editor: Rod Shrager. Estab. 1980. Submit seasonal/holiday material 18 months in advance. Reports in 6 weeks. **Pays on acceptance.** Market list is regularly revised.
Needs: Humorous, informal, inspirational and soft line. Rhymed and unrhymed verse OK.

SILVER VISIONS, P.O. Box 49, Newton Highlands MA 02161. (617)244-9504. Editor: B. Kaufman. Estab. 1981. Submit seasonal/holiday material 9 months to 1 year in advance. Reports in 2 months. Pays on publication. Guidelines are available for SASE.

Needs: Humorous, humorous Jewish, contemporary occasion for photography line. Copy must work with a photograph. Send 10-16 card ideas/batch.

‡**THESE THREE, INC.**, 120 E. 9th Ave., Homestead PA 15120. (412)461-5525. FAX: (412)461-5653. Editor: Jean Bridgers. Estab. 1987. 10% of material is freelance written. Buys 10 freelance ideas/samples per year; receives 100 submissions annually. Submit seasonal/holiday material 8 months in advance. Reports in 2 months. Pays on publication.
Needs: Conventional, humorous, informal, juvenile, sensitivity and soft line. Prefers unrhymed verse. Submit 20 ideas/batch.
Tips: "We are looking for fine art and juvenile material."

TRISAR, INC., 121 Old Springs Rd., Anaheim CA 92808. (714)282-2626. FAX: (714)282-1370. Editor: Randy Harris. Estab. 1979. 10% freelance written. Buys 12 freelance ideas/samples per year. Submit seasonal/holiday material 9 months in advance. Reports in 1 month. **Pays on acceptance.**
Needs: Humorous, studio and age-related adult feelings about turning 40, 50, 60. Prefers unrhymed verse.
Other Product Lines: T-shirts and mugs.
Tips: "Our audience is over the hill: Birthdays for adults turning 30, 40, 50 etc. Thoughts on growing older but not wanting to grow up."

VAGABOND CREATIONS, INC., 2560 Lance Dr., Dayton OH 45409. (513)298-1124. Editor: George F. Stanley, Jr. 10% freelance written. Buys 10-15 ideas annually. Submit seasonal/holiday material 6 months in advance. Reports in 1 week. Buys all rights. Ideas sometimes copyrighted. **Pays on acceptance.** Writer's guidelines for #10 SASE. Market list issued one time only.
Needs: Cute, humorous greeting cards (illustrations and copy) often with animated animals or objects in people-situations with short, subtle tie-in message on inside page only. No poetry. Pays $15-25/card idea.

‡**VINTAGE IMAGES**, (formerly Wildwood Design Group), P.O. Box 228, Lorton VA 22199. (703)550-1881. Editor: Brian Smolens. Estab. 1986. 5% of material is freelance written. Reports in 1 month. Buys all rights. Pays on publication. Writer's guidelines/market list for 8½ × 11 SAE with 3 first class stamps. Must submit samples with request for guidelines.
Needs: Humorous only. "We supply pictures—caption must be written to match." Submit 10 ideas/batch.
Other Product Lines: Post cards ($5-20) and posters ($10-50).

WARNER PRESS, INC., P.O. Box 2499, Anderson IN 46018. (317)644-7721. Product Editor: Cindy Maddox. 50% freelance written. Request guidelines for scheduled reading times. Reports in 5 weeks. Buys all rights. **Pays on acceptance.** Writer's guidelines and portfolio for #10 SASE with two first class stamps.
Needs: Conventional, informal, inspirational, juvenile, sensitivity and verses of all types with contemporary Christian message and focus. No off-color humor. "Cards with a definite Christian perspective that is subtly stressed, but not preachy, sell best for us." Uses both rhymed and unrhymed verses/ideas but moving more toward prose. Pays $20-35 per card idea.
Other Product Lines: Pays $60-150 for calendars; $20-50 for plaques; $20-50 for posters; $20-50 for short meditations; negotiates payment for coloring books.
Tips: "An estimated 75% of purchases are Christian in focus; 25% good conventional verses. Our best sellers are short poems or sensitivity verses that are unique, meaningful and appropriate for many people. We do not purchase verses written specifically to one person (such as relative or very close friend) but rather for boxed assortments. We are now requiring all freelance writers to successfully complete a short portfolio to receive permission to submit. No unsolicited material without the proper code numbers will be accepted."

WEST GRAPHICS, 238 Capp St., San Francisco CA 94110. (415)621-4641. FAX: (415)621-8613. Editor: Carol West. Estab. 1980. 60% freelance written. Buys 200 freelance ideas/samples per year; receives 1,000 submissions annually. Reports in 6 weeks. Buys greeting card rights. Pays 30 days after publication. Writer's guidelines/market list for #10 SASE.
Needs: Humorous and studio. Prefers unrhymed verse. Submit 10-30 ideas/batch. Pays $100.
Other Product Lines: Gift books (open), notepads, gift bags, t-shirts and calendars.
Tips: "The majority of our audience are women in their 30's and 40's and respond to fresh ideas on the cutting edge."

WESTERN GREETING, INC., P.O. Box 81056, Las Vegas NV 89180. Editor: Barbara Jean Sullivan. Estab. 1986. 100% of material is freelance written. Buys 15 freelance ideas/samples per year. Reports in 1 month. Buys all rights. **Pays on acceptance.** Writer's guidelines/market list for #10 SASE.

Needs: Humorous, sensitivity, soft line, Western and Indian and Southwest themes. Considers rhymed and unrhymed verse for Christmas only.
Tips: "Our cards are produced from Western and Southwest art. Subjects include the cowboy, mountain man, Indian, cowgirl, western still-life and landscape. We furnish the art and ask for verse based on this art. We have found that much unsolicited material does not fit our cards."

CAROL WILSON FINE ARTS, INC., P.O. Box 17394, Portland OR 97217. FAX: (503)287-2217. Editor: Gary Spector. Estab. 1983. 90% freelance written. Buys 100 freelance ideas/samples per year; receives thousands annually. Submit seasonal/holiday material 1 year in advance. Reports in 6 weeks. Buys negotiable rights. Whether payment is made on acceptance or publication varies, with type of agreement. Writer's guidelines/market list for #10 SASE.
Needs: Humorous and unrhymed. Pays $50-100 per card idea. "Royalties could be considered for a body of work."
Other Product Lines: Postcards.
Tips: "We are looking for laugh-out-loud, unusual and clever ideas for greeting cards. All occasions are needed but most of all birthday cards are needed. It's OK to be outrageous or risque. Cards should be 'personal'—ask yourself—is this a card that someone would buy for a specific person?"

Other Greeting Card Publishers

The following greeting card publishers were listed in the 1991 edition but do not have listings in this edition of *Writer's Market*. The majority did not respond to our request to update their listings or return a questionnaire for a new listing. If a reason was given for their exclusion, we have included it in parentheses after the listing name.

Carolyn Bean Publishing, Ltd.
Fravessi-Lamont, Inc.
Gallant Greetings
Knockouts Publishing, Inc.

Maine Line Co. (asked to be deleted)
Minneapolis Gift Mart (asked to be deleted)

Popshots, Inc.
Sunrise Publications, Inc.
Wizworks (backlogged with material)

Resources

Contests and Awards

Contests and awards offer writers the opportunity to distinguish themselves among their peers. Prize money and publication or production are nice rewards, but many writers get more satisfaction from being recognized as the best in a particular writing area. Winning a contest or award could also be the catalyst for launching a successful writing career.

The competition is often very strong, especially for the better paying and higher profile contests. Several writers may be selected for publication in a particular journal, but in most cases, only one will win the prize. Writers should, therefore, approach contests and awards with a different philosophy and plan of action.

Like submission for publication, a writer should send only professional, finished work. Contest directors often comment on the high percentage of submissions they receive that never have a chance of winning. Often this is because the submissions are not suited to the precise subject area. Another first round disqualifier is unpolished, amateurish work. Writers must consider carefully what they send out.

Some contests are more specific than others. For example, many contests reward a "best poem." However, some seek to recognize the best type of poem: haiku, narrative or sonnet, to name three. Also, some reward excellence in writing on a specific subject matter, such as a historical figure or a particular sport. This year there are contests and awards listed for the best one-act play, the best science journalism article and the best first book of poetry. In addition to contests for poetry, short stories and journalism, we've included competitions for plays, novels, books of nonfiction, children's books, translations, film and radio scripts, and even writing about bowling.

Not every contest is for every writer. Eligibility may be based on the writer's age, geographic location or whether the work has been previously published or unpublished. Read the contest rules and requirements carefully to avoid submitting to a contest for which you are not qualified. In addition, writers should be aware that more and more contests, particularly those sponsored by "little" literary magazines, are charging entry fees.

Always send a self-addressed, stamped envelope (SASE) to the contact person in the listings before entering a contest. Response with rules and guidelines will not only provide specific instructions, it will also confirm for you the simple but important fact that the award is still being offered. Also, if you have a question about the contest, its rules or regulations, make it a pointed one in your query with SASE. Contest directors have no time to answer lengthy letters.

Some contests and awards require nomination by a publisher. If this is required, just ask. Most publishers welcome the opportunity to promote a work this way. Be certain the publisher has plenty of time before the deadline to nominate your work.

Included in this section are also grants, scholarships, residencies and fellowship programs. Information on funding for writers is available in most large public libraries. See the *Annual Register of Grant Support* (National Register Publishing Co., 3004 Glenview Rd., Wilmette IL 60091); *Foundation Grants to Individuals* (Foundation Center, 79 5th Ave., New York NY 10003) and *Grants and Awards Available to American Writers* (PEN American

Center, 568 Broadway, New York NY 10012). For more listings of contests and awards for fiction writers, see *Novel & Short Story Writer's Market*; see *Poet's Market* for more contests and awards available to poets (both by Writer's Digest Books). Two more good sources for literary contests and awards are *Poets & Writers* (72 Spring St., New York NY 10012), and the *Associated Writing Programs Newsletter* (Old Dominion University, Norfolk VA 23529). Journalists should look into the annual Journalism Awards Issue of *Editor & Publisher* magazine (11 W. 19th St., New York NY 10011), published in the last week of December. Playwrights should be aware of the newsletter put out by The Dramatists Guild, (234 W. 44th St., New York NY 10036).

The contests in this section are listed by title, address, contact person, type of competition and deadline. Deadlines that state a range—for example, July to September—will only accept entries within that period. For information on contests not included here, see Other Contests and Awards at the end of this section.

‡**AAAS PRIZE FOR BEHAVIORAL SCIENCE RESEARCH**, American Association for the Advancement of Science, Directorate for Education and Human Resources Programs, 1333 H. St. NW, 11th Floor, Washington DC 20005. Prize for anthropology, psychology, social sciences, sociology. Published in peer-reviewed journals only. Deadline: July 1.

‡**AAAS-WESTINGHOUSE SCIENCE JOURNALISM AWARDS**, American Association for the Advancement of Science, 1333 H St. NW, Washington DC 20005. (202)326-6431. FAX: (202)289-4021. Contact: Nan Broadbent. Annual award for previously published work (between July 1, 1990 and June 30, 1991). "Purpose is to reward excellence in reporting on science and its applications in daily newspapers with circulation over 100,000; newspapers with circulation under 100,000; general circulation magazines; radio; television." Deadline: July 14. Award: $2,500, plaque, trip to AAAS Annual Meeting.

‡**ACTORS' GUILD OF LEXINGTON NEW THEATRE FESTIVAL**, 161 N. Mill, Lexington KY 40507. (606)233-0663. Artistic Manager: Vic Chaney. Annual festival for previously unpublished plays. Special interest in works addressing contemporary social, political and personal dilemmas; prefers small cast, simple set; 2- submission limit. Deadline Aug. 1. Guidelines for #10 SASE. Prizes: 3 awards of $300.

HERBERT BAXTER ADAMS PRIZE, Committee Chairman, American Historical Association, 400 A St. SE, Washington DC 20003. European history (first book). Deadline: June 15.

JANE ADDAMS CHILDREN'S BOOK AWARD, Jane Addams Peace Association and Women's International League for Peace and Freedom, 980 Lincoln Pl., Boulder CO 80302. Award Director: Jean Gore. Estab. 1953. Book published previous year that promotes peace, social justice, and the equality of the sexes and races. Deadline: April 1.

ADRIATIC AWARD, International Society of Dramatists, Box 1310, Miami FL 33153. (305)531-1530. Award Director: A. Delaplaine. Full-length play either unproduced professionally, *or* with one professional production (using Equity actors). Deadline: Nov. 1. Query. Prize: $250.

AIM MAGAZINE SHORT STORY CONTEST, P.O. Box 20554, Chicago IL 60620. (312)874-6184. Publisher: Ruth Apilado. Estab. 1975. Unpublished short stories (4,000 words maximum) "promoting brotherhood among people and cultures." Deadline: Aug. 15.

AJL REFERENCE BOOK AWARD, Association of Jewish Libraries, YIVO Institute for Jewish Research, 1048 5th Ave., New York NY 10028. (212)535-6700. FAX: (212)879-9763. Contact: Zachary Baker. Outstanding reference book published during the previous year in the field of Jewish studies.

‡**NELSON ALGREN SHORT STORY AWARDS**, Chicago Tribune, 435 N. Michigan Ave., Chicago IL 60611. Previously unpublished submissions. Deadline: Feb. 1. "Write to Tribune—SASE *not* necessary for information." Prize: $5,000-1st prize, $1,000-each to 3 runners-up. Must be stories between 2,500 and 10,000 words by American writers.

ALLEGHENY REVIEW LITERARY AWARDS, *Allegheny Review*, P.O. Box 32 Allegheny College, Meadville PA 16335. (814)332-4343. Contact: Review's Editors. Estab. 1983. Unpublished short fiction and poetry by undergraduate college students. Deadline: January 15.

AMBERGRIS ANNUAL FICTION AWARD, *Ambergris* Magazine, P.O. Box 29919, Cincinnati OH 45229. Editor: Mark Kissling. Estab. 1988. Previously unpublished fiction. No simultaneous submissions. Prefers works of 5,000 words or fewer. Winner is chosen from all works submitted during the year. Writer's guidelines for #10 SASE. Award: $100 and nomination to *The Pushcart Prize*.

AMELIA STUDENT AWARD, *Amelia Magazine*, 329 E St., Bakersfield CA 93304. (805)323-4064. Editor: Frederick A. Raborg, Jr. Previously unpublished poems, essays and short stories by high school students. Deadline: May 15.

AMERICAN ASSOCIATION OF UNIVERSITY WOMEN AWARD, NORTH CAROLINA DIVISION, North Carolina Literary and Historical Association, 109 E. Jones St., Raleigh NC 27601-2807. (919)733-7305. Previously published juvenile literature by a North Carolina resident. Deadline: July 15.

‡AMERICAN FICTION AWARDS, Birch Lane Press, Springfield College, Springfield MA 01109. (413)731-1669. Editor: Michael White. Unpublished submissions. Award "to recognize *previously unpublished* work by both new and emerging writers." Deadline: April 1. SASE for guidelines. Charges $7.50 *per* story; "multiple stories welcome." Prize: $1,000, $500, $250; $50 payment; 20-25 finalists published.

AMERICAN-SCANDINAVIAN FOUNDATION/TRANSLATION PRIZE, American-Scandinavian Foundation, 725 Park Ave., New York NY 10021. (212)879-9779. Contact: Publishing Division. Contemporary Scandinavian fiction and poetry translations. Deadline: June 3. Award: $2,000, bronze medallion, publication of an excerpt in the *Scandinavian Review*.

AMERICAN SOCIETY OF JOURNALISTS & AUTHORS EXCELLENCE AWARDS, Room 302, 1501 Broadway, New York NY 10036. (212)997-0947. FAX: (212)768-7414. Executive Director: Alexandra Cantor. Estab. 1948. Author, article and magazine awards. Nominations accepted after February 1 for May 31 deadline each year. Write or call for official nomination forms.

AMERICAN SPEECH-LANGUAGE-HEARING ASSOCIATION (ASHA), NATIONAL MEDIA AWARDS, 10801 Rockville Pike, Rockville MD 20852. (301)897-5700. FAX: (301)571-0457. Estab. 1925. Speech-language pathology and audiology (radio, TV, newspaper, magazine). Deadline: June 30.

AMWA MEDICAL BOOK AWARDS COMPETITION, American Medical Writers Association, 9650 Rockville Pike, Bethesda MD 20814. (301)493-0003. Contact: Book Awards Committee. Previously published and must have appeared in print previous year. Contest is to honor the best medical book published in the previous year in each of three categories: Books for Physicians, Books for Allied Health Professionals and Trade Books. Deadline April 1. Charges $10 fee.

AMWA VIDEO AND FILM FESTIVAL, American Medical Writers Association, 9650 Rockville Pike, Bethesda MD 20814. (301)493-0003. Contact: Video and Film Festival Chair. Previously published medical films in professional education, patient education, public information and general information. Deadline: April 30. Charges $75 AMWA member, $125 nonmember.

AMY WRITING AWARDS, The Amy Foundation, P.O. Box 16091, Lansing MI 48901. (517)323-3181. President: James Russell. Estab. 1985. Articles communicating Biblical truth previously published in the secular media. Deadline: Jan. 31.

‡ANNUAL ASSOCIATESHIP, Rocky Mountain Women's Institute, 7150 Montview Blvd., Denver CO 80220. (303)871-6923. Contact: Cheryl Bezio-Gorham. "The Rocky Mountain Women's Institute offers Associateships for artists, writers and scholars to concentrate on a one year project in the arts and humanities. Associates are provided with a work space, small stipend, support and pormotional services within the community of creative individuals in a wide variety of disciplines." Deadline: March 15. SASE for guidelines. "Guidelines are sent so each person can determine if they have a project with which to apply. They are asked to send a $5 application fee to the RMWI at the above address to obtain the application materials." Prize: A furnished work space, small stipend (usually under $1,000), support services i.e. telephone, computer, photocopying, library and university access and promotional events. "Ability to be in Denver metro area for one year is essential."

‡ANNUAL FICTION AND POETRY CONTEST, Rambunctious Press, 1221 W. Pratt, Chicago IL 60626. (312)338-2439. Contest/Award Director: Mary Dellutri. Estab. 1982. Unpublished short stories and poems. Deadline varies. Charges $3 per story, $2 per poem.

‡**ANNUAL GRANT AWARD PROGRAM**, Witter Bynner Foundation for Poetry, Inc., P.O. Box 2188, Santa Fe NM 87504. (505)988-3251. Contact: Steven Schwartz. "Grants through nonprofit organizations in the following categories: individual poets, uses of poetry, developing the poetry audience and translation and the process of translation." Deadline Feb. 1. "Please send 1 adhesive mailing label with query. No SASE's." Poet must be sponsored by nonprofit fiscal agent.

‡**ANNUAL INTERNATIONAL NARRATIVE CONTEST**, Poets and Patrons, Inc., 1206 Hutchings, Glenview IL 60025. Contact: Constance Vogel. Unpublished poetry. Deadline: Sept. 1. Prizes: $75, 1st prize; $25, 2nd.

‡**ANNUAL POETRY CONTEST**, National Federation of State Poetry Societies, 3520 State Rt. 56, Mechanicsburg OH 43044. (513)834-2666. Chairperson: Amy Jo Zook. Estab. 1959. Previously unpublished poetry. "There are fifty categories. Entrant must have flyer to see them all." Deadline March 15. Guidelines for #10 SASE. Charges entry fees. See guidelines for fees and prizes.

ANNUAL POETRY/FICTION/NONFICTION AWARDS, *Sonora Review*, Department of English, University of Arizona, Tucson AZ 85721. (602)626-8383. For previously unpublished poetry, fiction and nonfiction. Deadlines: April 15, poetry; November 15, fiction and nonfiction. Charges $2 entry fee.

‡**THE ARCHER MAGAZINE POETRY AWARDS**, Pro Poets of Salem, Oregon, 2285 Rogers Ln., Salem OR 97304. (503)363-0712. Contact: Winifred Layton. Previously unpublished poetry. "Categories: cinquain, sonnet, light verse, any form with sea bird theme, 5 lines or fewer, and any form with nature theme." Deadline June 1. Guidelines for #10 SASE. Charges $1 per poem; limit 1 poem per category. Prizes: $25 in each category.

ARIZONA AUTHORS' ASSOCIATION ANNUAL NATIONAL LITERARY CONTEST, Arizona Authors' Association, Suite 117WM, 3509 E. Shea Blvd., Phoenix AZ 85028-3339. (602)996-9706. Contact: Velma Cooper. Previously unpublished poetry, short stories, essays. Deadline: July 29. Charges $4 for poetry; $6 for short stories and essays.

‡**ARKANSAS POETRY AWARD**, The University of Arkansas Press, 201 Ozark Ave., Fayetteville AR 72701. (501)575-3246. FAX: (501)575-6044. Award Director: David Sanders. Estab. 1990. Previously unpublished poetry. The purpose is to recognize living U.S. poets whose works have not been previously published or accepted for publication in book form and thus forward the Press's stated mission of "disseminating the fruits of creative activity." Deadline May 1. Guidelines for #10 SASE. Award: publication of the collection by the University of Arkansas Press, $500 advance against royalties.

‡**ARTIST PROJECTS**, Rhode Island State Council on the Arts, Suite 103, 95 Cedar St., Providence RI 02903. (401)277-3880. Contact: Edward Holgate. Previously published or unpublished submissions. "Artist Project grants enable an artist to create new work and/or complete works-in-progress by providing direct financial assistance. By encouraging significant development in the work of an individual artist, these grants recognize the central contribution artists make to the creative environment of Rhode Island." Deadline: October 1. Send 9×12 SASE for guidelines. Prize: non-matching grants of $2,000-5,000. Open only to RI residents, age 18 or older. Students not eligible. Consult program director.

‡**ARTISTS FELLOWSHIP GRANTS**, Oregon Arts Commission, 835 Summer St. NE, Salem OR 97301. (503)378-3625. Assistant Director: Vincent K. Dunn. Award offered every two years. "Grants for advancement in the field of literature." Deadline: Sept. 1, 1992; only offered in even numbered years. Contact Oregon Arts Commission for details. Prize: $3,000 fellowships and $10,000 Masters awards. Open only to Oregon residents. Students are not eligible.

‡**ARTISTS FELLOWSHIPS**, Illinois Arts Council, Suite 10-500, 100 W. Randolph, Chicago IL 60601. (312)814-6750. FAX: (312)814-1471. Contact: Richard Gage. Previously published or unpublished work. "Work needs to have been completed four years prior to deadline date. Non-matching Fellowships in fixed amounts of $5,000, $10,000 and $15,000 and Finalist Awards of $500 are awarded to Illinois artists of exceptional talent to enable them to pursue their artistic goals. Artists Fellowships are granted to creative individuals in recognition of their outstanding work and commitment within the arts. Individuals can apply in poetry or prose (fiction or creative nonfiction)." Deadline: September 1. Send 9×12" SASE for guidelines. Prize: a check.

ARTIST'S FELLOWSHIPS, New York Foundation for the Arts, 5 Beekman St., New York NY 10038. (212)233-2900 ext. 217. Contact: Penelope Dannenberg. "Artists' Fellowships are awarded in 15 disciplines. They are awarded to artists based upon the recommendations of panels comprised of professionals in each field. They are not project support and may be used by each recipient as she/he sees fit. In literature four disciplines are reviewed individually. They are fiction, nonfiction, playwriting/screenwriting and poetry." Deadline: September 6. "We re-evaluate our process and make necessary changes." SASE. Prizes: $6,500 plus $500 for a public service event. "All applicants must be at least 18 years old and a New York state resident for 2 years. The New York Foundation of the Arts supports artists at all stages of their careers and from diverse backgrounds."

‡ARTS INDIANA CRITICAL WRITING COMPETITION, Arts Indiana, Inc. Suite 701, 47 S. Pennsylvania, Indianapolis IN 46204. (317)632-7894. Executive Director: Mary Anna Hunt. Articles previously published in *Arts Indiana* are not eliible. "Arts Indiana, Inc. and its magazine, *Arts Indiana*, offer this competition to promote critical writing about the performing, visual and literary arts related to Indiana. Manuscripts will be considered on the basis of the author's quality of writing and ability to analyze the relevant issues and to inform the work with a critical perspective." Deadline: Feb. 1. SASE for guidelines. Prize: $500 in cash awards—one or two awards left to the discretion of the jurors. Writers must reside in Indiana during competition year.

‡ARTS INDIANA LITERARY SUPPLEMENT 1992, Arts Indiana, Inc., Suite 701, 47 S. Pennsylvania, Indianapolis IN 46204. (317)632-7894. Publisher and CEO: Ann M. Stack. New work will be given first consideration. Previously published work will not be eligible for payment. "The Arts Indiana Literary Supplement is Arts Indiana, Inc.'s sole forum for fiction and poetry. The 32-page supplement is published in magazine format and included in the September issue of *Arts Indiana* as a benefit to its members. Approximately 7 short stories and 35 poems will be printed." Deadline: March 22. SASE for guidelines. Prize: $125 for each accepted short story and $20 for each poem. Two Awards of Excellence of $500 for poem and short story. Writers must currently reside in Indiana.

‡ARTS RECOGNITION AND TALENT SEARCH, National Foundation for Advancement in the Arts, 3915 Biscayne Blvd., Miami FL 33137. (305)573-0490. FAX: (305)573-4870.Vice President, Programs: Dr. William Banchs. Estab. 1981. For achievements in dance, music, theater, visual arts and writing. Students fill in and return the application, available at every public and private high school around the nation. Deadline: early-June 1, regular-October 1. Charges $25 registration fee.

‡ASSISTANCE TO ESTABLISHED WRITERS, Nova Scotia Dept. of Tourism and Culture, Cultural Affairs Division, P.O. Box 456, Halifax, Nova Scotia B3J 2R5 Canada. (902)424-6389. FAX: (902)424-2668. Offered twice annually for unpublished submissions. "Objective: To assist the professional writer with the costs of completing the research or manuscript preparation for a project in which a trade publisher has expressed serious interest." Deadline: April 1 and October 1. Prize: Maximum of $2,000 Canadian. Applicant must be a Canadian citizen or landed immigrant and must have had their principal residence in Nova Scotia for 12 consecutive months at the time of application. Applicant must be an experienced writer who writes for print or broadcast media, film or stage, who has been consistently published and/or produced in the media.

ASSOCIATION FOR EDUCATION IN JOURNALISM AWARDS, Department of Communication, University of Akron, Guzzetta Hall, Akron OH 44325-1003. Contact: Kathleen L. Endres. Awards to enrolled college students for nonfiction article written for consumer or business/trade magazine article, research paper on magazine journalism or new magazine prospectus.

VINCENT ASTOR MEMORIAL LEADERSHIP ESSAY CONTEST, U.S. Naval Institute, Preble Hall, U.S. Naval Academy, Annapolis MD 21402. (301)268-6110. Award Director: James A. Barber, Jr. Essays on the topic of leadership (junior officers and officer trainees). Deadline: February 15.

THE ATHENAEUM OF PHILADELPHIA LITERARY AWARD, The Athenaeum of Philadelphia, 219 S. 6th St., Philadelphia PA 19106. (215)925-2688. Award Director: Lea C. Sherk. Estab. 1814. Nominated book by a Philadelphia resident. Deadline: Dec. 31.

AVON FLARE YOUNG ADULT NOVEL COMPETITION, Avon Books, 105 Madison Ave., New York NY 10016. FAX: (212)532-2172. Editorial Director: Ellen Krieger. Unpublished novel written by an author 13-18 years old. Manuscript should be 150-200 pages, and appeal to readers 13-18. Deadline: Jan. 1-Aug. 31. Contest held every other year.

‡AWA AWARDS OF EXCELLENCE, Aviation/Space Writers Association, Suite 1200, 17 S. High St., Columbus OH 43215. (614)221-1900. FAX: (614)221-1989. Executive Director: Madeline Field. Previously published (between October 1 and September 30) work. "The Aviation/Space Writers Association annually recognizes the outstanding contributions in aviation and aerospace communications of each preceding year through its Awards of Excellence program." Deadline: Nov. 30. SASE for guide-

lines. Charges a fee for entry. "Entries must have been published, broadcast, televised or otherwise presented to the public in final form for the first time during Jan. 1, 1991 and Sept. 30, 1991. Entries must be submitted in English."

‡**AWARD FOR LITERARY TRANSLATION**, American Translators Association, % Anne Cordero, 3818 N. Ridgeview Rd., Arlington VA 22207. (914)941-1500. Contact: Chair, Honors & Awards. Previously published book translated from German to English. In even years, Lewis Galentière Prize awarded for translations other than German to English. Deadline: March 15.

‡**AWARDS FOR EXCELLENCE IN BUSINESS AND FINANCIAL JOURNALISM**, John Hancock Financial Services and Fordham University (New York), John Hancock Pl., P.O. Box 111, Boston MA 02117. (617)572-6384. FAX: (617)572-6451. Contact: Richard P. Bevilacqund. Annual award for previously published (between January 1 and December 31) work. "To award writers for their expertise in writing business and financial articles." Deadline: January 15. SASE for guidelines. Award: $5,000 cash prize to each winner in one of 7 categories. Open to freelancers.

AWP ANNUAL AWARD SERIES, Associated Writing Programs, Old Dominion University, Norfolk VA 23529-0079. (804)683-3839. Contact: Beth Jarock. Annual award series for book length mss in poetry, short fiction, nonfiction and novel. Deadline: Feb. 28. Charges $10 per ms.

THE MARGARET BARTLE PLAYWRITING AWARD, Community Children's Theatre of Kansas City, 8021 E. 129th Terrace, Grandview MO 64030. (816)761-5775. Award Director: E. Blanche Sellens. Estab. 1951. Unpublished play for elementary school audiences. Deadline: Jan. 29.

THE ELIZABETH BARTLETT AWARD, 2875 Cowley Way-1302, San Diego CA 92110. (619)276-6199. Contest/Award Director: Elizabeth Bartlett. Estab. 1990. For best unpublished 12-tone poem. Award $100.

‡**MRS. SIMON BARUCH UNIVERSITY AWARD**, United Daughters of the Confederacy, 4373 Wieuca Rd., NE, Atlanta GA 30342. (404)255-0549. Award offered every two years (even years). Unpublished work for the purpose of encouraging research in Southern history, the United Daughters of the Confederacy offers as a grant-aid of publication the Mrs. Simon Baruch University Award of Two Thousand Dollars. Deadline: May 1. Authors and publishers interested in the Baruch Award contest should ask for a copy of these rules. All inquiries should be addressed to the Chairman of the Mrs. Simon Baruch University Award Committee, United Daughters of the Confederacy, 328 North Boulevard, Richmond VA 23220. Award: $2,000 plus $500. Invitation to participate in the contests is extended (1) to anyone who has received a Master's, Doctoral, or other advanced degree within the past fifteen years, from a university in the United States: and (2) to any graduate student whose thesis or dissertation has been accepted by such an institution. Manuscripts must be accompanied by a statement from the registrar giving dates of attendance, and by full biographical data together with passport photograph of the authors.

GEORGE BENNETT FELLOWSHIP, Phillips Exeter Academy, Exeter NH 03833. Estab. 1968. Annual award of stipend, room and board "to provide time and freedom from material considerations to a person seriously contemplating or pursuing a career as a writer. Applicants should have a manuscript in progress which they intend to complete during the fellowship period." Send SASE for application form and details. Deadline: Dec. 1. Charges $5 fee. Residence at the Academy during the Fellowship period required.

BEST OF *HOUSEWIFE-WRITER'S FORUM*: THE CONTESTED WILLS TO WRITE, *Housewife-Writer's Forum*, P.O. Box 780, Lyman WY 82937. (307)786-4513. Contest Director: Diane Wolverton. Estab. 1988. Unpublished prose and poetry categories. Deadline: April 15. Charges $4 for prose; $2 for poetry.

ALBERT J. BEVERIDGE AWARD, Committee Chairman, American Historical Association, 400 A St. SE, Washington DC 20003. American history of U.S., Canada and Latin America (book). Deadline: June 15.

THE BEVERLY HILLS THEATRE GUILD-JULIE HARRIS PLAYWRIGHT AWARD COMPETITION, 2815 N. Beachwood Drive, Los Angeles CA 90068. (213)465-2703. Playwright Award Coordinator: Marcella Meharg. Estab. 1978. Original full-length plays, unpublished, unproduced and not currently under option. Application required, available upon request with SASE. Deadline: Nov. 1.

IRMA SIMONTON BLACK AWARD, Bank Street College of Education, 610 W. 112th St., New York NY 10025. (212)222-6700. Award Director: Linda Greengrass. Annual award. Estab. 1972. Purpose of the award: "The award is given each spring for a book for young children, published in the previous year, for excellence of both text and illustrations." Entries must bave been published during the previous calendar year. Deadline for entries: January after book is published.

BLACK WARRIOR REVIEW LITERARY AWARDS, *Black Warrior Review*, P.O. Box 2936, Tuscaloosa AL 35486. (205)348-4518. Estab. 1974. Submit work for possible publication to the appropriate genre editor. Awarded annually to the best poetry and fiction published in the *BWR* the previous volume year. Winners are announced in the Fall/Winter issue.

SUSAN SMITH BLACKBURN PRIZE, 3239 Avalon Place, Houston TX 77019. (713)654-4484. FAX: (713)654-8184. Director: Emilie S. Kilgore. Annual prize for woman playwright. Deadline: third Monday in September. Nomination by artistic directors or theater professionals only.

HOWARD W. BLAKESLEE AWARDS, American Heart Association, 7320 Greenville Ave., Dallas TX 75231. (214)706-1340. Award Director: Howard L. Lewis. Estab. 1953. Previously published or broadcast reports on cardiovascular diseases. Deadline: Feb. 1.

BOSTON GLOBE-HORN BOOK AWARDS, *The Boston Globe*, Boston MA 02107. Children's Book Editor: Stephanie Loer. Fiction, nonfiction and illustrated book. Deadline: May 1.

BOWLING WRITING COMPETITION, American Bowling Congress Publications, 5301 S. 76th St., Greendale WI 53129. FAX: (414)421-1194. Director: Rory Gillespie, Publications Manager. Estab. 1935. Feature, editorial and news. Deadline: December 1.

BRITTINGHAM PRIZE IN POETRY, University of Wisconsin Press, 114 N. Murray, Madison WI 53715. (608)262-6438. Contest Director: Ronald Wallace. Estab. 1985. Unpublished book-length manuscript of original poetry. Deadline: Submissions must be *received* by the press *during* the month of September (postmark is irrelevant) and must be accompanied by a SASE for contest results. Manuscripts will *not* be returned. Charges $10 fee, payable to University of Wisconsin Press. Results in February.

‡THE HEYWOOD BROUN AWARD, The Newspaper Guild (AFL-CIO, CLC), 8611 Second Ave., Silver Spring MD 20910. (301)585-2990. Contact: Phillip M. Kadis. Previously published (between Jan. 1 and Dec. 31) work. Deadline: approx. Jan. 7. Rules and entry forms for SASE. Prize: $2,000 and a guild citation. "Entries become the property of the award committee unless return is requested. Contest open to news writers, broadcasters, cartoonists, etc."

ARLEIGH BURKE ESSAY CONTEST, U.S. Naval Institute, Preble Hall, U.S. Naval Academy, Annapolis MD 21402. (301)268-6110. FAX: (301)269-7940. Award Director: James A. Barber, Jr. Estab. 1873. Essay that advances professional, literary or scientific knowledge of the naval and maritime services. Deadline: Dec. 1.

BUSH ARTIST FELLOWSHIPS, The Bush Foundation, E-900 First Natl. Bank Bldg., 332 Minnesota St., St. Paul MN 55101. (612)227-5222. Contact: Sally F. Dixon. Award for Minnesota, North Dakota, South Dakota, and western Wisconsin residents "to buy 6-18 months of time for the applicant to do his/her own work." Up to 15 fellowships annually. $26,000 stipend each plus additional $7,000 for production and travel. Deadline: late October.

BYLINE MAGAZINE CONTESTS, P.O. Box 130596, Edmond OK 73013. (405)348-5591. Publisher: Marcia Preston. Estab. 1981. Unpublished short stories, poems and other categories. Several categories offered each month which are open to anyone. Deadline on annual award, which is for subscribers only, Dec. 1. Send #10 SASE for information. Charges fee of $5 for short story; $2 for poems on annual award.

‡GERALD CABLE POETRY CHAPBOOK COMPETITION, Silverfish Review, P.O. Box 3541, Eugene OR 97403. (503)344-5060. Contact: Rodger Moody. Previously unpublished work. Purpose is to publish a poetry chapbook by a deserving author. Deadline: October 15 (scheduling demands sometimes change). SASE for guidelines. Charges $6 fee. Prize: $300 and 25 copies (press run of 750).

‡CALIFORNIA PLAYWRIGHTS COMPETITION, South Coast Repertory, P.O. Box 2197, Costa Mesa CA 92628. (714)957-2602. Contact: John Glore. Previously unpublished submissions. "Competition is used as a means to find plays for our annual spring California Play Festival, which features readings and two or more full productions." Deadline: usually Oct. 31 or Nov. 15. Guidelines and application form available after September 1; writers must phone or write for complete guidelines and application form. Prize: $5,000 first prize; $3,000 2nd prize. "Writer must maintain principal residence in California."

CALIFORNIA WRITERS' CLUB CONFERENCE CONTEST, 2214 Derby St., Berkeley CA 94705. (415)841-1217. Unpublished adult fiction, adult nonfiction, juvenile fiction or nonfiction, poetry and scripts. "Our conference is biennial, next being in 1993." Deadline: varies in spring. Charges fee.

CANADIAN AUTHOR & BOOKMAN STUDENT CREATIVE WRITING AWARDS, Canadian Authors Association, 121 Avenue Rd., Toronto, Ontario M5R 2G3 Canada. (416)926-8084. Contact: Contest Editor of Canadian Author & Bookman. Estab. 1919. Contest is to encourage creative writing of unpublished fiction, nonfiction and poetry at the secondary school level. Deadline: Mid-February. Must purchase fall or winter issue of CA&B and use tearsheet entry form. Must be secondary school student and nominated by his/her instructor.

CANADIAN FICTION MAGAZINE, Contributor's Prize. P.O. Box 946, Station F, Toronto, Ontario M4Y 2N9 Canada. Contact: Editor-in-Chief. Estab. 1971. Best story of year in French or English. Canadian citizens only. Deadline: Sept. 15. Prize: $500.

MELVILLE CANE AWARD, Poetry Society of America, 15 Gramercy Park S., New York NY 10003. (212)254-9268. Contact: Award Director. Published book of poems or prose work on a poet or poetry submitted by the publisher. Deadline: Dec. 31.

BILL CASEY AWARD, *San José Studies*, San José State University, San José CA 95192. (408)924-4476. Editor: Fauneil J. Rinn. Estab. 1975. Offered annually. Best published article, short story, poem in previous volume of *San José Studies*. Prize: $100 and full–page notice in spring issue of the following year.

‡**CATHOLIC PRESS ASSOCIATION JOURNALISM AWARDS**, Catholic Press Association, 119 N. Park Ave., Rockville Centre NY 11570. (516)766-3400. FAX: (516)766-3416. Contact: Owen McGovern. To recognize quality work of journalists published between January and December of previous year who work for a Catholic publication. There are numerous categories for newspapers and magazines. Deadline: Mid-February. Charges $30 fee. Only journalists who are published in Catholic publications are eligible.

CEC NATIONAL CHILDREN'S THEATRE PLAYWRITING CONTEST, Columbia Entertainment Company, 309 Parkade Blvd., Columbia MO 65202. (314)874-5628. Contact: Betsy Phillips. Annual award for "top notch unpublished scripts for theater school use, to challenge and expand the talents of our students, ages 10-15. The entry should be a full length play with speaking roles for 20 to 30 characters of all ages and with at least 10 roles developed in some detail." Deadline: June 30. Production and some travel expenses for 1st and 2nd place winners, plus cash award for 1st place.

RUSSELL L. CECIL ARTHRITIS WRITING AWARDS, Arthritis Foundation, 1314 Spring St. NW, Atlanta GA 30309. (404)872-7100. FAX: (404)872-0457. Contact: Public Relations Department. Estab. 1948. Medical and features (news stories, articles and radio/TV scripts) published or broadcast for general circulation during the previous calendar year. Deadline: Feb. 15.

CELEBRATION OF ONE-ACTS, West Coast Ensemble, P.O. Box 38728, Los Angeles CA 90038. Artistic Director: Les Hanson. Estab. 1984. Unpublished (in Southern California) one-act plays. Deadline: Nov. 15. "Up to 3 submissions allowed for each playwright." Casts should be no more than 6 and plays no longer than 35 minutes.

PAULETTE CHANDLER AWARD, Council for Wisconsin Writers, P.O. Box 55322, Madison WI 53705. (608)233-0531. Estab. 1964. "For a Wisconsin poet or short story writer based on need and ability." Deadline: Jan. 15. Poets in even years (1992); short story writers in odd years (1993). Applications do not open until November.

‡**CHAPBOOK COMPETITION**, Maine Arts Commission, State House #25, Augusta ME 04333. (207)289-2724. Contact: David Cadigan. Previously unpublished submissions. "In alternate years, a juror selects either the best poetry or best fiction for publication, a run of 500, paid for by the commission." Deadline: early August. SASE for guidelines. Prize: $350 plus publication of 500 copies. Must be a resident of Maine at least 8 months/year.

Your Guide to
Getting Published

Learn to write publishable material and discover the best-paying markets for your work. Subscribe to *Writer's Digest*, the magazine that has instructed, informed and inspired writers since 1920. Every month you'll get:

- Fresh markets for your writing, including the names and addresses of editors, what type of writing they're currently buying, how much they pay, and how to get in touch with them.
- Insights, advice, and how-to information from professional writers and editors.
- In-depth profiles of today's foremost authors and the secrets of their success.
- Monthly expert columns about the writing and selling of fiction, nonfiction, poetry and scripts.

Plus, a $16.00 discount. Subscribe today through this special introductory offer, and receive a full year (12 issues) of Writer's Digest for only $17.00—that's a $16.00 savings off the $33 newsstand rate. Enclose payment with your order, and we will add an extra issue to your subscription, absolutely **free**.

Detach postage-free coupon and mail today!

Subscription Savings Certificate
Save $16.00

Yes, I want professional advice on how to write publishable material and sell it to the best-paying markets. Send me 12 issues of Writer's Digest for just $17...a $16 discount off the newsstand price. Outside U.S. add $7 (includes GST in Canada) and remit in U.S. funds.

☐ Payment enclosed (send me an extra issue *free*—13 in all).
☐ Please bill me.

Writer's® DIGEST

Guarantee: If you are not satisfied with your subscription at any time, you may cancel it and receive a full refund for all unmailed issues due you.

Name (please print)

Address   Apt.

City

State   Zip

Basic rate, $24.   VVWM0

Writer's®
DIGEST

How would you like to get:

- up-to-the-minute reports on new markets for your writing
- professional advice from editors and writers about what to write and how to write it to maximize your opportunities for getting published
- in-depth interviews with leading authors who reveal their secrets of success
- expert opinion about writing and selling fiction, nonfiction, poetry and scripts
- ...all at a $16.00 discount?

Share in the discovery of America's best new fiction

Subscribe to STORY, the magazine that made literary history by discovering some of the best-known writing talents of this century. Favorites like Salinger, Cheever, McCullers, Saroyan, Capote, and Mailer are among those writers first published in STORY, and that legacy continues today. After a 22-year interim, STORY was revived in 1989 with its original mission intact: to showcase the country's finest new writing talents.

Each quarterly issue brings you 128 pages of memorable short stories chosen for their strong narratives, engaging styles and challenging subject matter— good fiction that touches the reader long after the final page is turned... fiction that will inspire you as a writer.

Be on hand for the next STORY discovery, and start your subscription to the most widely circulated literary magazine published in America.

The first issues of STORY were cranked out on an old mimeograph machine in 1931 by two American newspaper correspondents in Vienna. Editors Whit Burnett and his wife Martha Foley had no money—just a vision to create a forum for outstanding short stories, regardless of their commercial appeal. The magazine was an instant literary success, and was hailed "The most distinguished short story magazine in the world."

Now STORY returns with the same commitment to publishing the best new fiction written today. It will also provide a workshop for new material from established writers such as Joyce Carol Oates and Madison Smartt Bell. And each issue features a STORY Classic, a story that launched the career of a distinguished writer, reprinted from an early issue of STORY.

Printed on heavy premium paper, each is meant to be read and cherished for years to come. (Those first mimeographed copies of STORY are collector's items today!)

One of the most talked-about revival in magazine publishing...

BUSINESS REPLY MAIL
FIRST CLASS MAIL   PERMIT NO. 125   MT. MORRIS, IL

POSTAGE WILL BE PAID BY ADDRESSEE

STORY

P O BOX 396
MT MORRIS IL 61054-7910

NO POSTAGE
NECESSARY
IF MAILED
IN THE
UNITED STATES

‡**THE CHELSEA AWARDS FOR POETRY AND SHORT FICTION**, Chelsea Associates, Inc., P.O. Box 1040, York Beach ME 03910. Associate Editor: Richard Foerster. Previously unpublished submissions. "Two prizes awarded for the best work of short fiction and for the best group of 4-6 poems selected by the editors in anonymous competitions." Deadline: June 15 for fiction; Dec. 15 for poetry. SASE for guidelines. Charges $10 (entrants will receive a free subscription to *Chelsea*). Checks made payable to Chelsea Associates, Inc. Prize: $500; winning entries published in *Chelsea*. Include a SASE for notification of competition results. Manuscripts will not be returned.

‡**CHICANO/LATINO LITERARY CONTEST**, Dept of Spanish and Portuguese, UCI, Irvine CA 92717. (714)856-5702. Contact: Juan Bruce-Novoa. "To promote the dissemination of unpublished Chicano/ Latino literature, and to encourage its development. The call for entries will be genre specific, rotating through four categories: novel (1991), short story (1992), poetry (1993), and drama (1994)." Deadline: May 31. "Interested parties may call or write for entry procedures." The contest is open to all citizens or permanent residents of the United States.

THE CHRISTOPHER AWARD, The Christophers, 12 E. 48th St., New York NY 10017. (212)759-4050. Award Director: Peggy Flanagan. Estab. 1949. Outstanding books published during the calendar year that "affirm the highest values of the human spirit."

CINTAS FELLOWSHIP, Arts International Institute of International Education, 809 United Nations Pl., New York NY 10017-3580. (212)984-5370. "Cintas Fellowships are intended to acknowledge demonstrated creative accomplishment and to encourage the professional development of talented, previously published or unpublished creative artists in the fields of architecture, visual arts, music composition and literature." Deadline: March 1. Eligibility is limited to professionals living outside Cuba, who are of Cuban citizenship or direct lineage and who have completed their academic and technical training. The fellowships are not awarded toward the furtherance of academic study, research on writing, nor to performing artists."

GERTRUDE B. CLAYTOR MEMORIAL AWARD, Poetry Society of America, 15 Gramercy Park S., New York NY 10003. (212)254-9628. Contact: Award Director. Poem in any form on the American scene or character. Deadline: Dec. 31. Members only.

CLEVELAND STATE UNIVERSITY POETRY CENTER PRIZE, Cleveland State University Poetry Center, Cleveland OH 44115. (216)687-3986. FAX: (216)687-9366. Editor: Leonard Trawick. To identify, reward and publish the best unpublished book-length poetry manuscript submitted. Submissions accepted only Dec.-Feb. Deadline: Postmarked on or before March 1. Charges $10 fee. "Submission implies willingness to sign contract for publication if manuscript wins." Two of the other finalist manuscripts are also published for standard royalty (no prize). Send SASE for guidelines and entry form.

COLLEGIATE POETRY CONTEST, *The Lyric*, 307 Dunton Dr. SW, Blacksburg VA 24060. Editor: Leslie Mellichamp. Estab. 1921. Unpublished poems (36 lines or less) by fulltime undergraduates in U.S. or Canadian colleges. Deadline: June 1. Send SASE for rules.

‡**COMMONWEALTH CLUB OF CALIFORNIA BOOK AWARDS**, 595 Market St., San Francisco CA 94105. (415)597-6700. Contact: Book Awards Jury. Previously published books from each year. "For books of exceptional literary merit by a California resident." Deadline Jan. 31. Guidelines for #10 SASE. Prizes: gold and silver medals.

COMMONWEALTH OF PENNSYLVANIA COUNCIL ON THE ARTS LITERATURE FELLOWSHIPS, 216 Finance Bldg., Harrisburg PA 17120. (717)787-6883. Award Director: Peter Carnahan. Estab. 1966. Fellowships for Pennsylvania writers of fiction and poetry. Deadline: Oct 1.

‡**COMPUWRITE**, The Writers Alliance, P.O. Box 2014, Setauket NY 11733. Contest Director: Kiel Stuart. Estab. 1982. Previously unpublished poems. "We want an expressive, clever poem (up to 30 lines) on the act of writing with a personal computer." Deadline Jan. 15. Guidelines for #10 SASE. Charges $2 per poem. First prize: $25, publication.

‡**THE BERNARD F. CONNERS PRIZE FOR POETRY**, *The Paris Review*, 541 E. 72nd St., New York NY 10021. Poetry Editor: Editorial Office. Unpublished poetry over 300 lines. Deadline: April 1.

COUNCIL FOR WISCONSIN WRITERS, INC. ANNUAL AWARDS COMPETITION, P.O. Box 55322, Madison WI 53705. Contact: Awards committee. Estab. 1964. Book-length fiction, short fiction, short nonfiction, poetry, play, juvenile books, children's picture books and outdoor writing by Wisconsin residents published preceding year. Deadline: Jan. 15. Applications do not open until November.

‡CREATIVE ARTISTS GRANT, Michigan Council for the Arts, 1200 Sixth Ave., Detroit MI 18226. (313)256-3719. Individual Artist Coordinator: Martha Gibiser Shea. Grants of up to $10,000 for Michigan creative artists. Deadline: generally March or April. Check for specific yearly deadline.

CREATIVE ARTS CONTEST, Woman's National Auxiliary Convention, Free Will Baptists, P.O. Box 5002, Antioch TN 37011-5002. Contact: Lorene Miley. Estab. 1973. Unpublished articles, plays, poetry, programs and art from Auxiliary members. Deadline: March 1.

CREATIVITY FELLOWSHIP, Northwood Institute Alden B. Dow Creativity Center, Midland MI 48640-2398. (517)837-4478. Award Director: Carol B. Coppage. Ten-week summer residency for individuals in any field who wish to pursue a new and different creative idea that has the potential of impact in that field. Deadline: Dec. 31.

GUSTAV DAVIDSON MEMORIAL AWARD, Poetry Society of America, 15 Gramercy Park S., New York NY 10003. (212)254-9628. Contact: Award Director. Sonnet or sequence in traditional forms. Deadline: Dec. 31. Members only.

MARY CAROLYN DAVIES MEMORIAL AWARD, Poetry Society of America, 15 Gramercy Park S., New York NY 10003. (212)254-9628. Contact: Award Director. Unpublished poem suitable for setting to music. Deadline: December 31. Members only.

DE LA TORRE BUENO PRIZE, Dance Perspectives Foundation, 29 E. 9th St., New York NY 10003. (212)777-1594. Open to writers or their publishers who have published an original book of dance scholarship within the year. Deadline: Dec. 31.

DEEP SOUTH WRITERS CONTEST, Deep South Writers Conference, P.O. Box 44691, University of Southwestern Louisiana, Lafayette LA 70504. (318)231-6908. Contact: Contest Clerk. Estab. 1960. Unpublished works of short fiction, nonfiction, novels, poetry, drama and French literature. Deadline: July 15. Charges $25 fee for novels; $15 for full-length plays; $5 for other submissions. Also: Special Columbus Quincentennial play contest; no entry fee; deadline: November 15, 1991. No manuscripts are returned except novels and full-length plays if accompanied by SASE.

DELACORTE PRESS PRIZE FOR A FIRST YOUNG ADULT NOVEL, Delacorte Press, 666 5th Ave., New York NY 10103. (212)765-6500. Contest Director: Lisa Oldenburg. Estab. 1963. Previously unpublished young adult fiction. Submissions: Labor Day through December 31 only. Send for complete rules enclosing SASE.

BILLEE MURRAY DENNY POETRY CONTEST, Lincoln College, 300 Keokuk St., Lincoln IL 62656. (217)732-3155 ext. 201. Contest/Award Director: Valecia Crisafulli. Estab. 1981. Unpublished poetry. Deadline: May 31. Charges $2 fee per poem (limit 3). Enclose SASE with request for entry form.

MARIE-LOUISE D'ESTERNAUX STUDENT POETRY CONTEST, The Brooklyn Poetry Circle, 2550 Independence Ave., #3U, Bronx NY 10463. Contest Chairman: Ruth Fowler. Poetry by students between 16 and 21 years of age. Deadline: April 15.

‡DEXTER PRIZE, Society for the History of Technology, Social Sciences, Michigan Tech Univ., 1400 Townsend Dr., Houghton MI 49931-1295. (906)487-2459. FAX: (906)487-2468. Contact: Society Secretary. Previously published (previous three years: for 1991–1988 to 1990). "Award given to the best book in the history of technology." Deadline: April 1. SASE for guidelines. Prize: $2,000 and a plaque from the Dexter Chemical Company.

ALICE FAY DI CASTAGNOLA AWARD, Poetry Society of America, 15 Gramercy Park S., New York NY 10003. (212)254-9628. Contact: Award Director. Manuscript in progress: poetry, prose (on poetry) or verse-drama. Deadline: Dec. 31. Members only.

EMILY DICKINSON AWARD, Poetry Society of America, 15 Gramercy Park S., New York NY 10003. (212)254-9628. Contact: Award Director. Poem inspired by Emily Dickinson. Deadline: Dec. 31. Members only.

GORDON W. DILLON/RICHARD C. PETERSON MEMORIAL ESSAY PRIZE, American Orchid Society, Inc., 6000 S. Olive Ave., West Palm Beach FL 33405. (407)585-8666. FAX: (407)585-0654. Contact: Dr. Alec M. Pridgeon. Estab. 1932. "To honor the memory of two outstanding former editors of the

American Orchid Society Bulletin. Annual themes of the essay competitions are announced by the Editor of the *A.O.S. Bulletin* in the May issue. Themes in past years have included Orchid Culture, Orchids in Nature and Orchids in Use. The contest is open to all individuals with the exception of A.O.S. employees and their immediate families."

DISCOVERY/THE NATION, The Poetry Center of the 92nd Street YM-YWCA, 1395 Lexington Ave., New York NY 10128. (212)415-5760. Estab. 1973. Open to poets who have not published a book of poems (chapbooks, self-published books included). Deadline: Early February. Write or call for competition guidelines.

DIVERSE VISIONS REGIONAL GRANTS PROGRAM, Intermedia Arts, 425 Ontario St. SE, Minneapolis MN 55414. (612)627-4444. Director of Artist Programs: Al Kosters. Estab. 1986. Regional (IA, KS, MN, NE, ND, SD, WI) writers' grants. Deadline: Spring.

‡FRANK NELSON DOUBLEDAY MEMORIAL AWARD, Wyoming Arts Council, 2320 Capitol Ave., Cheyenne WY 82002. (307)777-7742. Literature Coordinator: Doug Black. Estab. 1989. "This award honors a woman writer of exceptional talent in any genre." Writers may call WAC office for guidelines, which also appear in Wyoming Arts Council's free monthly *All Arts Newsletter*. Applicants must have been Wyoming residents for one year prior to entry deadline, must be women writers, and neither full-time students nor tenured faculty. Deadline usually May 1; may vary year to year.

DRURY COLLEGE ONE-ACT PLAY CONTEST, Drury College, 900 N. Benton Ave., Springfield MO 65802. (417)865-8731. Contact: Sandy Asher. Estab. 1986. Contest is offered every two years, even years only. Plays must be unpublished and professionally unproduced. One play per playwright. Deadline: Dec. 1. Send SASE for complete guidelines.

DUBUQUE FINE ARTS PLAYERS, 569 S. Grandview Ave., Dubuque IA 52001. (319)582-5558. Coordinator: Sally T. Ryan. Estab. 1977. Produces 3 one acts, plays/year. Only original material accepted. Obtains first productions rights. Winning plays produced in September. Deadline: Jan. 31. Charges: $5 fee. Contest rules available for legal SASE, results reports by June 30. Script Readers' Evaluation sheets returned with ms. Only scripts of 45 minutes running time (or less) will be considered for production. Travel stipend for winning playwrights often available. Cash prizes of $200, $150, $100 to top 3 winners.

JOHN H. DUNNING PRIZE IN AMERICAN HISTORY, Committee Chairman, American Historical Association, 400 A St. SE, Washington DC 20003. Annual award for U.S. history monograph/book. Deadline: June 15.

EATON LITERARY ASSOCIATES LITERARY AWARDS PROGRAM, P.O. Box 49795, Sarasota FL 34230-6795. (813)366-6589. Vice President: Richard Lawrence. Estab. 1984. Previously unpublished short stories and book-length manuscripts. Deadline: March 31 (short story); Aug. 31 (book length).

EDITORS' BOOK AWARD, Pushcart Press, Box 380, Wainscott NY 11975. (516)324-9300. President: Bill Henderson. Unpublished books. Deadline: Sept. 15. "All manuscripts must be nominated by an editor in a publishing house."

‡DAVID JAMES ELLIS MEMORIAL AWARD, Theatre Americana, Box 245, Altadena CA 91001. (818)397-1740. Director: Elaine Hamilton, Playreading Committee. Offered annually. Previously unpublished work. "To produce original plays of Americana background and history or by American authors." Deadline: January 31. "No entry necessary but we will send guidelines, as enclosed, on request and with SASE." Prize: $500. Judges: 3 judges (different every year) selected by chairperson of board.

EMERGING PLAYWRIGHT AWARD, Playwrights Preview Productions, 1160 5th Ave. #304, New York NY 10029. (212)289-2168. Contact: Jennifer Johnson. Submissions required to be unpublished. Awards are announced in the Spring/Fall. Submissions accepted year-round.

LAWRENCE S. EPSTEIN PLAYWRITING AWARD, 280 Park Ave. S., New York NY 10010. (212)979-0865. Contact: Lawrence Epstein. Unpublished submissions. Deadline: October. Published in Dramatist's Guild and other newsletters.

DAVID W. AND BEATRICE C. EVANS BIOGRAPHY AWARD, Mountain West Center for Regional Studies, Utah Sate University, University Hill, Logan UT 84322-0735. (801)750-3630. FAX: (801)750-1092. Contact: F. Ross Peterson or Shannon L. Haskins. Estab. 1986. Submissions to be published or unpublished. To encourage the writing of biography about people who have played a role in Mormon Country. (Not the religion, the country i.e., Intermountain West with parts of Southwestern Canada and Northwestern Mexico.) Deadline: March. Publishers or author may nominate book. Criteria for consideration: Work must be a biography or autobiography on "Mormon Country"; must be submitted for consideration for publication year's award; new editions or reprints are not eligible; manuscripts are accepted. Submit 5 copies.

‡**EVE OF ST. AGNES POETRY COMPETITION,** *Negative Capability*, 62 Ridgelawn Dr. E, Mobile AL 36608. (205)460-6146. Contact: Sue Walker. Previously unpublished poetry. "To recognize and support poets." Deadline Dec. 1. Guidelines for #10 SASE. Charges $3 per poem. Prize: $800 plus publication.

EYSTER PRIZE, *New Delta Review*, % Department of English, Louisiana State University, Baton Rouge LA 70803-5001. (504)388-4079. Editor: Janet Wondra. Estab. 1983. Semiannual award for best works of poetry and fiction in each issue. Deadline: April 15, spring/summer issue; Oct. 15, fall/winter issue.

JOHN K. FAIRBANK PRIZE IN EAST ASIAN HISTORY, American Historical Association, 400 A St. SE, Washington DC 20003. Contact: Committee Chariman. Book on East Asian history. Deadline: June 15.

FALL FESTIVAL OF PLAYS, Street Players Theatre, 771 Asp, Norman OK 73069. Contact: Robert R. Woods. Estab. 1980. Unproduced plays.

NORMA FARBER FIRST BOOK AWARD, Poetry Society of America, 15 Gramercy Park S., New York NY 10003. (212)254-9628. Contact: Award Director. Book of original poetry. Deadline: Dec. 31. Charges $5 entry fee for non-members. Publishers only.

VIRGINIA FAULKNER AWARD FOR EXCELLENCE IN WRITING, *Prairie Schooner*, 201 Andrews, University of Nebraska, Lincoln NE 68588-0334. (402)472-3191. Editor: Hilda Raz. Estab. 1988. All genres eligible for consideration. The winning piece must have been published in *Prairie Schooner* during that calendar year.

‡**FELLOWSHIP IN LITERATURE,** Rhode Island State Council on the Arts, Suite 103, 95 Cedar St., Providence RI 02903. (401)277-3880. Contact: Edward Holgate. Previously published or unpublished submissions. "Fellowships encourage the creative development of artists by enabling them to set aside time to pursue their work and achieve specific career goals. Fellowships provide funds for the purchase of materials and supplies." Deadline: April 1. Send 9 × 12 SASE with 75¢ postage for guidelines. Prize: $3,000 fellowship. Open only to RI residents, age 18 or older. Students not eligible. Consult program director.

‡**FELLOWSHIP-LITERATURE,** Alabama State Council on the Arts. One Dexter Ave., Montgomery AL 36130. (205)242-4076. FAX: (205)240-3269. Contact: Randy Shoults. Previously published or unpublished. "To set aside time to create and to improve skills." Deadline: May 1. Guidelines available. Prize: $10,000, $5,000 or $2,500. Two year Alabama residency requirement.

FELLOWSHIPS FOR CREATIVE WRITERS, Pennsylvania Council on the Arts, 216 Finance Bldg., Harrisburg PA 17120. (717)787-6883. Literature Program Director: Peter M. Carnahan. Annual fellowships for Pennsylvania residents.

FELLOWSHIPS TO ASSIST RESEARCH AND ARTISTIC CREATION, John Simon Guggenheim Memorial Foundation, 90 Park Ave., New York NY 10016. (212)687-4470. Annual. The fellowships assist scholars and artists to engage in research in any field of knowledge and creation in any of the arts, under the freest possible conditions and irrespective of race, color, or creed.

FEMINIST WRITERS' CONTEST, Dept. WD, P.O. Box 2440, Des Plaines IL 60018. Contact: Clara Johnson for rules; SASE required. Estab. 1990. Categories: Fiction and nonfiction (5,000 or fewer words). Work should reflect feminist perspectives (should not endorse or promote sexism, racism, ageism, anti-lesbianism, etc.) Deadline: Aug. 30. Charge $10 fee. Cash awards.

THE FESTIVAL OF EMERGING AMERICAN THEATRE, The Phoenix Theatre, 749 N. Park Ave., Indianapolis IN 46202. (317)635-7529. Contact: Bryan Fonseca. Annual playwriting competition. Deadline: April 30.

FICTION WRITERS CONTEST, *Mademoiselle Magazine*, 350 Madison Ave., New York NY 10017. Contest Director: Eileen Schnurr. Short stories by unpublished writers aged 18-30. Deadline: March 15. Unsolicited mss will not be returned.

‡**FIRST BOOK AWARD**, Montana Arts Council, 48 N. Last Chance Gulch, Helena MT 59620. (406)444-6430. Contact: Julie Smith. Award offered every two years for unpublished submissions. Full manuscripts must be unpublished; individual works may have been published in magazines, etc. "Purpose of award is to encourage and rework talented young writers in Montana who have not yet published a separate volume of writing." Deadline: April 20. SASE for guidelines. Award: Publication of the manuscript. Writers must be residents of the state of Montana; writers must not have had a full volume of their work published in the past; writers must be at least 18 years old and not be a degree-seeking student.

ROBERT L. FISH MEMORIAL AWARD, Mystery Writers of America, Inc., 236 W. 27th St., New York NY 10001. (212)255-7005. Contact: Priscilla Ridgway. Annual award for the best first mystery or suspense short story published during the previous year. Deadline: Dec. 1.

WILLIAM FLANAGAN MEMORIAL CREATIVE PERSONS CENTER, Edward F. Albee Foundation, 14 Harrison St., New York NY 10013. (212)226-2020. Annual contest/award. Either previously published or unpublished. One month residency at "The Barn" in Montauk, New York offers writers privacy and a peaceful atmosphere in which to work. Deadline: April 1. Prize: Room only; writers pay for food and travel expenses. Judging by panel of qualified professionals.

‡**FLORIDA INDIVIDUAL ARTIST FELLOWSHIPS**, Florida Department of State, Bureau of Grants Services, Division of Cultural Affairs, The Capitol, Tallahassee FL 32399-0250. (904)487-2980. Director: Peyton Fearington. Fellowship for Florida writers only. Award: $5,000 each for fiction, poetry and children's literature. Deadline: mid-February.

‡**FLORIDA POETRY CONTEST**, Zetaxi Chapter of Sigma Tau Delta, Dept. of English, University of Central Florida, Orlando FL 32816. (407)823-2212. Contact: Jonathan Harrington. Previously unpublished poetry. Deadline: May 1. Charges $1/poem. Prize: $500 first prize; $100 second prize.

‡**FMCT'S BIENNIAL PLAYWRIGHTS COMPETITION (MID-WEST)**, Fargo-Moorhead Community Theatre, P.O. Box 644, Fargo ND 58107. (701)235-1901. Contact: Richard Jordan. Estab. 1988. Contest offered every two years (next contest will be held 1991-92). Submissions required to be unpublished. Deadline: Dec. 1.

FOLIO, Department of Literature, American University, Washington DC 20016. Estab. 1984. Fiction, poetry, essays, interviews and b&w artwork. Published twice anually. Manuscripts read Aug.-April.

CONSUELO FORD AWARD, Poetry Society of America, 15 Gramercy Park S., New York NY 10003. (212)254-9628. Contact: Award Director. Unpublished lyric. Deadline: Dec. 31. Members only.

THE 49th PARALLEL POETRY CONTEST, The Signpost Press Inc., 1007 Queen St., Bellingham WA 98226. (206)734-9781. Contest Director: Knute Skinner. Estab. 1977. Unpublished poetry. Submission period: Sept. 15-Dec. 1. Charges $3/poem. Anyone submitting 3 or more poems will receive a complimentary 1-year subscription to *The Bellingham Review*. Awards: $150, first prize; $100, second prize; $50, third prize.

‡**MILES FRANKLIN LITERARY AWARD**, Arts Management Pty. Ltd., 50 Kellett St., Potts Point, NSW 2011 Australia. Annual award for previously published novels or plays about Australian life. Deadline: Dec. 31. Guidelines for #10 SAE and 1 IRC. Prize: $20,000 (Australian dollars).

GEORGE FREEDLEY MEMORIAL AWARD, Theatre Library Association, New York Public Library at Lincoln Center, 111 Amsterdam Ave., New York NY 10023. (212)870-1638. FAX: (212)787-3852. Contact: Award Committee Chair. Estab. 1968. Published books related to performance in theatre. Deadline: Feb. 1.

DON FREEMAN MEMORIAL GRANT-IN-AID, Society of Children's Book Writers, P.O. Box 66296, Mar Vista, Los Angeles CA 90066. To enable picture-book artists to further their understanding, training and/or work. Members only. Deadline: Feb. 15. Grants: $1,000 and $500 runner-up grant.

FULBRIGHT SCHOLAR PROGRAM, Council for International Exchange of Scholars, Suite 5M, 3007 Tilden St. NW,Washington DC 20008. (202)686-7877. Estab. 1947. "Approximately 1,000 awards are offered annually in virtually all academic disciplines for university lecturing or research in over 100 countries. The opportunity for multicountry research also exists in many areas. Grant duration ranges from 2 months to an academic year." Deadlines are: June 15 – Australasia, South Asia, Latin America, USSR and Aug. 1 – Africa, Asia, Western Europe, East Europe and the Middle East. Eligibility criteria include U.S. citizenship at the time of application; M.F.A., Ph.D or equivalent professional qualifications; for lecturing awards, university teaching experience.

‡**FUND FOR NEW AMERICAN PLAYS**, J.F. Kennedy Ctr., American Express & President's Committee on Arts & Humanities, % Kennedy Center, Washington DC 20566. (202)416-8024. FAX: (202)416-8026. Contact: Deborah G. Dixon. Previously unpublished work. "Program objectives: to ensure the continued vitality of the nation's theatrical heritage; to encourage playwrights to write and nonprofit professional theaters to produce new American plays; to ease the financial burdens of nonprofit professional theater organizations producing new plays; to stimulate and foster the development of plays or plays with music; to provide a playwright with a better production of the play than the producing theater would normally be able to accomplish without the grant; to give direct financial support to the playwright so that there will be a greater opportunity to create a production of a much higher quality at a theatre of the playwright's choice." Deadline: Changes from year to year. "Writers or nonprofit theatre organizations can mail in name and address to be placed on the mailing list." Prize: $10,000 for playwrights and depends on what the theatre needs. Open only to a producing theatre.

‡**LEWIS GALANTIÈRE PRIZE FOR LITERARY TRANSLATION**, American Translators Association, 3818 N. Ridgeview Rd., Arlington VA 22207. Contact: Chair.: Dr. Anne Cordero. Award offered in even years recognizing the outstanding translation of a previously published work from languages other than German published in the United States." Deadline: March 15.

‡**GALLERY PLAYERS PLAYWRITING CONTEST**, 1125 College Ave., Columbus OH 43209. (614)231-2731. FAX: (614)231-8222. Contact: Harold M. Eisenstein. Offered every two years for previously unpublished work. "The purpose of the contest is to encourage and stimulate artistic growth in the area of dramatic literature." Deadline: "Deadlines of previous contests have varied because of script availabilities." SASE for guidelines. Prize: $1,000. The Leo Yassenoff Jewish Community Center (LYJCC) will reserve the right to produce the winning play as part of Gallery Players' 1992-93 season. "The contest is open to any playwright who is a United States citizen and resides in the state of Ohio (including students of Ohio colleges and universities). The subject matter may be on any topic. Any treatment of the play will be accepted, except musicals. All manuscripts must be typewritten, double-spaced on one side of page. Manuscript should be well-bound."

‡**GAP (GRANTS FOR ARTIST PROJECTS); FELLOWSHIP**, Artist Trust, Suite 512, 1331 3rd Ave, Seattle WA 98101. (206)467-8734. Executive Director: David Mendoza. Fellowship offered as announced. Either published or unpublished works. "The GAP is awarded to about 15 artists, including writers, per year. The award is meant to help finance a specific project, which can be in very early stages or near completion. The Fellowship is awarded to eight artists per year; the award is made on the basis of work of the past five years. It is 'no-strings-attached' funding." SASE for guidelines. Prize: GAP: up to $750. Fellowship: $5,000. Full-time students not eligible. *Only Washington state residents are eligible.*

JOHN GASSNER MEMORIAL PLAYWRITING AWARD, The New England Theatre Conference, 50 Exchange St., Waltham MA 02154. (617)893-3120. Estab. 1952. Unpublished one-act plays. Deadline: April 15. Charges $5 fee; free for members of New England Theatre Conference.

THE CHRISTIAN GAUSS AWARD, The Phi Beta Kappa Society, 1811 Q St. NW, Washington DC 20009. (202)265-3808. Contact: Administrator, Phi Beta Kappa Book Awards. Estab. 1950. Works of literary criticism or scholarship published in the U.S. during the 12-month period preceding the entry deadline, and submitted by the publisher. Deadline: April 30.

GAVEL AWARDS, American Bar Association, 750 N. Lake Shore Dr., Chicago IL 60611. (312)988-6137. FAX: (312)988-6281. Contact: Peggy O'Carroll. Estab. 1957. Previously published, performed or broadcast works that promote "public understanding of the American system of law and justice." Deadline: Feb. 1.

‡**GERMAN PRIZE FOR LITERARY TRANSLATION**, American Translators Association, 3818 N. Ridgeview Rd., Arlington VA 22207. (914)941-1500. Chair.: Dr. Anne Cordero. Prize offered every two years. Submissions must be previously published and appeared in print between January, two years previous and March 15, current year in odd-numbered calendar. "Recognizes outstanding translations of a literary work from German published in the United States." Deadline March 15.

‡**JOHN GLASSCO TRANSLATION PRIZE**, Literary Translators' Association of Canada, Bureau 510, 1030 rue Cherrier, Montreal, Quebec H2L 1H9 Canada. Estab. 1981. Annual award for a translator's *first* book-length literary translation into French or English, published in Canada during the previous

calendar year. The translator must be a Canadian citizen or landed immigrant. Eligible genres include fiction, creative nonfiction, poetry, published plays, children's books. Deadline: March 15. Write for application form. Award: $500.

GOLDEN GATE NATIONAL PLAYWRIGHTING CONTEST, American Theatre Ventures, Inc., 580 Constanzo St., Stanford CA 94305. (415)326-0336. Contact: David Arrow, John Goodman. Estab. 1980. Playwrighting contest held to seek out and develop scripts from previously published or unpublished (cannot be produced previously in an Equity contract) American writers. Its goal is to encourage and stimulate the writing of new and original plays." Contest and dates will vary. For application send SASE.

GOLDEN KITE AWARDS, Society of Children's Book Writers (SCBW), P.O. Box 66296 Mar Vista Station, Los Angeles CA 90066. (818)347-2849. Coordinator: Sue Alexander. Estab. 1973. Calendar year published children's fiction, nonfiction and picture illustration books by a SCBW member. Deadline: Dec. 15.

GOLF WRITER'S CONTEST, Golf Course Superintendents Association of America, GCSAA, 1421 Research Park Dr., Lawrence KS 66049. Public Relations Manager: Scott Smith. Previously published work pertaining to golf course superintendents. Must be a member of Golf Writers Association of America.

GOODMAN AWARD, Thorntree Press, 547 Hawthorn Lane, Winnetka IL 60093. (708)446-8099. Contact: Eloise Bradley Fink. Estab. 1985. Imagery is important. For our $400, $200 and $100 Goodman Awards Jan. 1-Feb. 14, in odd-numbered years only we will be selecting three poets for our next Troika. Contestants are asked to submit a stapled group of ten pages of unpublished poetry, single or double spaced, photocopied, with a $4 reader's fee. Manuscripts will not be returned. SASE for winners' names.

GOVERNOR GENERAL'S LITERARY AWARDS, Canada Council, Communications Section, 99 Metcalf St., P.O. Box 1047, Ottawa, Ontario K1P 5V8 Canada. (613)598-4365. Contact: Lise Rochon. Awards are for best book of the year in categories of fiction, nonfiction, poetry, drama, children's literature (text and illustration). Guidelines for #10 SASE with Canadian postage (IRC). Canadian writers only.

THE GREAT AMERICAN TENNIS WRITING AWARDS, Tennis Week, 124 E. 40th St., New York NY 10016. (212)808-4750. FAX: (212)983-6302. Publisher: Eugene L. Scott. Estab. 1986. Category 1: unpublished manuscript by an aspiring journalist with no previous national byline. Category 2: unpublished manuscript by a non-tennis journalist. Category 3: unpublished manuscript by a tennis journalist. Categories 4-6: published articles and one award to a book. Deadline: Dec. 15.

‡**GREAT PLATTE RIVER PLAYWRIGHTS FESTIVAL**, Kearney State College Theatre Department, 905 W. 25th St., Kearney NE 68849. (308)234-8406. FAX: (308)234-8665. Contact: Charles Davies. Unpublished submissions. "Purpose of award is to develop original dramas and encourage playwrights to work in regional settings. There are five catagories: 1) Adult 2) Youth (Adolescent) 3) Children's 4) Musical Theater 5) Native American Drama. Entries may be drama or comedy." Deadline: March 1. Awards: $500-First, $300-Second, $200-Third, plus free lodging and a travel stipend. "The Festival reserves the rights to development and premiere production of the winning plays without payment of royalties." Contest opent to entry by any writer "provided that the writer submits playscripts to be performed on stage-works in progress also acceptable. Works involving the Great Plains will be most favored. More than one entry may be submitted."

THE GREENSBORO REVIEW LITERARY AWARD IN FICTION AND POETRY, *The Greensboro Review*, English Department, UNCG, Greensboro NC 27412. (919)334-5459. Editor: Jim Clark. Estab. 1966. Annual award for fiction and poetry; recognizes the best work published in the winter issue of *The Greensboro Review*. Deadline: Sept. 15.

‡**GROLIER POETRY PRIZE**, Grolier Poetry Book Shop, Inc. & Ellen LaForge Memorial Poetry Foundation, Inc., 6 Plympton St., Cambridge MA 02138. (617)547-4648. Contact: Ms. Louisa Solano. Previously unpublished work. The primary purpose of the Prize is to encourage and recognize developing writers. Open to all poets who have not published with either a vanity, small press, trade, or chapbook of poetry. Deadline: April 2. SASE for guidelines. Charges $5 fee. Prize: honorarium of $150 for two poets. Also 4 poems of each winner will be chosen for publication in the Grolier Poetry Prize Annual.

HACKNEY LITERARY AWARDS, Writing Today, Box A-3/Birmingham-Southern College, Birmingham AL 35254. (205)226-4921. Contact: Dr. Myra Crawford. Annual award for unpublished novel, short story and poetry. Deadline: Sept. 30 for novels and Dec. 31 for short stories and poetry. Must send for guidelines to enter.

SARAH JOSEPHA HALE AWARD, Trustees of the Richards Library, 58 N. Main, Newport NH 03773. (603)863-3430. Contact: Award Administrator. Estab. 1956. The award is to a New England author for the full body of his/her work. Open only to New England authors. May not be applied for.

‡HARVARD OAKS CAREER GUIDANCE AWARD, Suite 802, 80 River Oaks Ctr., Calumet City IL 60409. Award Director: William A. Potter. "Quarterly award to writers of published articles covering relevant topics in career selection and job search strategies." Deadlines: March 31, June 30, Sept. 30, Dec. 31. Guidelines for #10 SASE.

‡HEADLANDS RESIDENCY, North Carolina Arts Council/Headlands Center for the Arts, Dept. of Cultural Resources, Raleigh NC 27601-2807. (919)733-2111. Contact: Deborah McCill. "To provide writers an opportunity for concentrated work and a chance to explore the source material in the Marsh Headlands, a 13,000-acre park northwest of San Francisco." Deadline: mid-August. SASE for guidelines. Prize: two-month residency at Headlands Center for the Arts; round-trip airfare; $200/week stipend. "Writer must have been a resident of N.C. for at least a year prior to application and may not be enrolled in a degree-granting program."

DRUE HEINZ LITERATURE PRIZE, University of Pittsburgh Press, 127 N. Bellefield Ave., Pittsburgh PA 15260. (412)624-4110. FAX: (412)624-7380. Estab. 1936. Collection of short fiction. Award open to writers who have published a book-length collection of fiction or a minimum of three short stories or novellas in commercial magazines or literary journals of national distribution. We are unable to return any manuscripts for this contest. Deadline: July-August.

ERNEST HEMINGWAY FOUNDATION AWARD, PEN American Center, 568 Broadway, New York NY 10012. Contact: John Morrone. First-published novel or short story collection by an American author. Submit 3 copies. Deadline: Dec. 31.

HEMINGWAY SHORT STORY COMPETITION, (formerly *Short Story Writers Competition*), Hemingway Days Festival, P.O. Box 4045, Key West FL 33041. (305)294-4440. Coordinator: Lorian Hemingway. Estab. 1981. Unpublished short stories. Deadline: early July. Charges $10 fee. Send SASE for rules, specific deadline, and entry form. Prize: $1,000 cash, first prize; two $500 runner-up awards.

CECIL HEMLEY MEMORIAL AWARD, Poetry Society of America, 15 Gramercy Park S., New York NY 10003. (212)254-9628. Contact: Award Director. Unpublished lyric poem on a philosophical theme. Deadline: Dec. 31. Members only.

O. HENRY FESTIVAL SHORT STORY CONTEST, O. Henry Festival, Inc., P.O. Box 29484, Greensboro NC 27429. Estab. 1985. Contest offered every other year to encourage unpublished writing of literary quality short fiction. No children's stories. Deadline date is August of even-numbered years. Charges $7 per story.

‡HIGH SCHOOL PLAYWRITING CONTEST, Baker's Plays, 100 Chauncy St., Boston MA 02111. (617)482-1280. FAX: (617)482-7613. Contest Director: Raymond Pape. Annual contest for previously unpublished plays. "We must continue to commit ourselves to the future of American Theater by encouraging and supporting those who are its cornerstone: young playwrights." Deadline is usually the last week of January. Guidelines for #10 SASE. Prizes: 1st place: $500, and the play will be published under *Best Plays from the High School* series by Baker's Plays; 2nd place: $250 and an Honorable Mention; Third place: $100 and an Honorable Mention. "Open to any high school student. Plays must be accompanied by the signature of a sponsoring high school drama or English teacher, and it is recommended that the play receive a production or a public reading prior to the submission."

HIGHLIGHTS FOR CHILDREN **FICTION CONTEST,** *Highlights for Children*, 803 Church St., Honesdale PA 18431. Editor: Kent L. Brown, Jr. Estab. 1946. Stories for children ages 2-12, category varies each year. Write for guidelines. Stories should be limited to 900 words for older readers, 600 words for younger readers. No crime or violence, please. Specify that your manuscript is a contest entry. All entries must be postmarked between Jan. 1 and Feb. 28.

‡THE CLARENCE HOLTE LITERARY PRIZE, The Schomburg Center for Research in Black Culture and the Phelps Stokes Fund, 515 Malcom X Blvd., New York NY 10037-1801. (212)491-2229. FAX: (212)491-6760. Contact: Howard Dodson. Award made every two years. The prize will be awarded to a living writer in recognition of a significant contribution to the cultural heritage of Africa and the African diaspora made through published writings in the humanities. Guidelines for #10 SASE. Awards made up to $7,500.

‡HOUGHTON MIFFLIN LITERARY FELLOWSHIP, Houghton Mifflin Co., 2 Park St., Boston MA 02108. Open—not awarded every year. Unpublished submissions. The Houghton Mifflin Literary Fellowship is designed to reward American authors for a first adult trade book (fiction or nonfiction) of outstanding literary merit. Only books accepted for publication by HM Co. are eligible. We ask that applicants follow our standard submission procedure. Please provide: (1) a letter describing the project and your background; (2) a sample chapter; (3) a stamped, self-addressed envelope for the return of the material if necessary. The awards are $10,000 each, $7,500 of which is to be considered an advance against royalties. The royalty rate is 10% of the invoice price on the first 7,500 copies sold, 12½% on the next 5,000 copies and 15% thereafter. (Note: Poetry and drama are not eligible and will not be read. Queries regarding juvenile submissions should be directed to the Children's Department; textbook proposals to the School or College Division.)

‡DARRELL BOB HOUSTON PRIZE, 1931 Second Ave., Seattle WA 98101. (206)441-6239. Journalism published within the previous year in Washington State which shows "some soul, some color, some grace, robustness, mirth and generosity," to honor the memory of writer Darrell Bob Houston. Deadline: contact for exact date, usually in May.

THE ROY W. HOWARD AWARDS, Scripps Howard Foundation, P.O. Box 5380, Cincinnati OH 45201. (513)977-3035. Estab. 1972. Public service reporting by a newspaper.

HTC ONE-ACT PLAYWRITING COMPETITION, Henrico Recreation and Parks, P.O. Box 27032, Richmond VA 23273. (804)672-5100. Contact: J. Larkin Brown. Estab. 1986. Annual unpublished one-act play or musical.

L. RON HUBBARD'S WRITERS OF THE FUTURE CONTEST, P.O. Box 1630, Los Angeles CA 90078. (213)466-3310. Award Director: Rachel Denk. Estab. 1983. Unpublished science fiction and fantasy.

HUTTON FICTION CONTESTS, Hutton Publications, P.O. Box 83835, Hayden ID 83835. (208)772-6184. Contact: Linda Hutton. Quarterly awards for beginning and published writers. Deadline: first or fifteenth. Charges from no fee up to $2. Send #10 SASE for rules.

IDAHO WRITER IN RESIDENCE, Idaho Commission on the Arts, 304 W. State, Boise ID 83720. (208)334-2119. Program Coordinator: Cort Conley. Estab. 1982. Previously published works by Idaho writers; award of $10,000 offered every two years.

INDEPENDENT SCHOLARS, LOWELL, MARRARO, SHAUGHNESSY AND MILDENBERGER AWARDS, MLA, 10 Astor Place, New York NY 10003. (212)614-6406. Contact: Richard Brod. Mildenberger Prize: research publication on teaching foreign languages and literatures. Shaughnessy Prize: research publication on teaching English. Lowell Prize: previously published literary, linguistic study or critical edition or biography. Marraro Prize: scholarly book or essay on Italian literature. Independent Scholars: published research in modern languages and literature. Lowell and Marraro awards only open to MLA members in good standing.

INDIVIDUAL ARTIST FELLOWSHIP AWARD, Montana Arts Council, 48 N. Last Chance Gulch, Helena MT 59620. (406)444-6430. Contact: Julie Smith. Award made every two years to Montana residents. Deadline: May 1.

‡INDIVIDUAL ARTISTS FELLOWSHIPS, Nebraska Arts Council, 1313 Farnam on-the-Mall, Omaha NE 68102-1873. (402)595-2122. FAX: (402)595-2217. Contact: Suzanne Wise. Offered every two years (literature alternates with performing arts). Previously unpublished work preferred, not mandated. "The Individual Artists Fellowship program recognizes exemplary achievements by originating artists in their fields of endeavor and supports the contributions made by Nebraska artists to the quality of life in this state." Deadline: Nov. 1. Prize: one $3,500 master award, four $1,000 merit awards. Must be a resident of Nebraska for at least two years prior to submission date; 18 years of age; not enrolled in an undergraduate, graduate or certificate-granting program in English, creative writing, literature, or related field.

INTERNATIONAL FILM & FILM LITERATURE AWARDS, International Film & Film Literature Society, P.O. Box 12193, La Jolla CA 92039. Previously published or unpublished. To encourage excellence in films and the literature of film production, pre-production and post-production. Deadline: Dec. 20. No screenplays.

‡INTERNATIONAL HAIKU CONTEST, The North Carolina Haiku Society, 132 Penny Rd., High Point NC 27265. (919)882-2460. Contest Director: Rebecca Rust. Previously unpublished poetry. "To foster the reading, writing, sharing of haiku and to improve the quality of haiku writing." Deadline Dec. 31. Guidelines for #10 SASE. Charges $1 per entry. Prizes: $50 first place, $25 second place, $15 third place.

‡INTERNATIONAL READING ASSOCIATION CHILDREN'S BOOK AWARD, International Reading Association, P.O. Box 8139, 800 Barksdale Rd., Newark DE 19714-8139. (302)731-1600. Director: IRA Children's Book Award Subcommittee. The IRA Children's Book Awards will be given for a first or second book, either fiction or nonfiction, by an author who shows unusual promise in the children's book field. Two categories: younger readers, ages 4-10; older readers, ages 10-16+. Deadline: Dec 1.

INTERNATIONAL READING ASSOCIATION PRINT MEDIA AWARD, International Reading Association, 800 Barksdale Rd., P.O. Box 8139, Newark DE 19714-8139. (302)731-1600. FAX: (302)731-1057. Contact: Wendy L. Russ. Estab. 1956. Reports by professional journalists from newspapers, magazines and wire services on reading and literacy activities and programs. Deadline: Jan. 15.

‡ISLAND LITERARY AWARDS, Prince Edward Island Council of the Arts, P.O. Box 2234, Chardotte-town, Prince Edward Island C1A 8B9 Canada. (902)368-4410. Award Director: Judy K. MacDonald. Previously unpublished works. Offers 5 awards: poetry, short fiction, historical work, children's literature and student writing. Deadline Feb. 15. Guidelines for #10 SASE with Canadian postage or #10 SAE with 1 IRC. Charges $5 fee.

JOSEPH HENRY JACKSON/JAMES D. PHELAN LITERARY AWARDS, The San Francisco Foundation, Suite 910, 685 Market St., San Francisco CA 94105. (415)543-0223. Awards Coordinator: Liela Greiman. Jackson Award: unpublished, work-in-progress — fiction (novel or short story), nonfiction or poetry by author age 20-35, with 3-year consecutive residency in N. California or Nevada prior to submission. Phelan: unpublished, work-in-progress fiction, nonfiction, short story, poetry or drama by California-born author age 20-35. Deadline: Jan. 15.

1992 JAPAN-U.S. FRIENDSHIP COMMISSION PRIZE FOR THE TRANSLATION OF JAPANESE LITERATURE, Donald Keene Center of Japanese Culture, 407 Kent Hall, Columbia University, New York NY 10027. (212)854-5036. FAX: (212)854-7480. Estab. 1979. Book-length works of any period or genre of Japanese literature by a not widely recognized American translator. Deadline: Dec. 1.

JEWEL BOX THEATRE PLAYWRIGHTING COMPETITION, Jewel Box Theatre, 3700 N. Walker, Oklahoma City OK 73118. (405)521-1786. Contact: Charles Tweed. Only two or three acts accepted. Deadline: Jan. 15. Prize: $500.

ANSON JONES AWARD, % Texas Medical Association, 1801 N. Lamar Blvd., Austin TX 78701. (512)477-6704. Estab. 1957. Health (Texas newspaper, magazine — trade, commercial, association, chamber or company — radio and TV). Deadline: Jan. 15.

THE CHESTER H. JONES NATIONAL POETRY COMPETITION, P.O. Box 498, Chardon OH 44024. Estab. 1982. An annual competition for persons in the U.S., Canada and U.S. citizens living abroad. Winning poems plus others, called "commendations," are published in a chapbook available from the foundation. Deadline: March 31. Charges $1/poem, maximum 10 entries, no more than 32 lines each; must be unpublished.

‡THE JUNIPER PRIZE, University of Massachusetts Press, % Mail Office, University of Massachusetts, Amherst MA 01003. (413)545-2217. Second or subsequent book of poetry. Deadline: Sept. 1. Charges $10 fee.

‡JURIED COMPETITION, Florida Literary Foundation, 2516 Ridge Ave., Sarasota FL 34235. (813)388-2378. FAX: (813)954-5083. Contest Director: Patrick J. Powers. Previously unpublished poetry, fiction and nonfiction. "Will accept previously published poetry if poet has copyright." Deadlines June 30 and Dec. 15. Guidelines for #10 SASE. Charges fee. Prize: Publication; cash award.

‡JUVENILE BOOK AWARDS, Friends of American Writers, 15237 Redwood, Libertyville IL 60048. (312)362-3782. Contest is offered annually. Submissions are required to be published in the previous year. Author must be a native or current resident (5 years) of the following states: AR, IL, IN, IA, KS, MI, MN, MO, NE, ND, OH, SD or WI. Writer cannot have published more than 3 prior books.

THE JANET HEIDINGER KAFKA PRIZE, English Department, Susan B. Anthony Center, 538 Lattimore Hall, University of Rochester, Rochester NY 14627. (716)275-8318. Attention: Director SBA Center. Book-length fiction (novel, short story or experimental writing) by U.S. woman citizen submitted by publishers.

‡KALTENBORN FOUNDATION, 349 Seaview, Palm Beach FL 33480. Contact: Dr. Rolf Kaltenborn. Offered annually for previously unpublished work. Grants up to $1,500 for scholarly, publishable, studies (articles, books) in communications—including radio, TV, film/press, etc. Prize: $1,500 grant.

KANSAS QUARTERLY/KANSAS ARTS COMMISSION AWARDS, SEATON AWARDS, Department of English, Kansas State University, Manhattan KS 66506. (913)532-6716. Editor: Ben Nyberg, et al. Estab. 1968. *KQ/KAC* awards for poetry and fiction published in *KQ*; Seaton awards for Kansas writers whose poetry, fiction and prose appear in *KQ*.

‡ROBERT F. KENNEDY BOOK AWARD, 1031 31st St. NW, Washington DC 20007. (202)333-1880. Executive Director: Frederick Grossberg. Estab. 1980. Fiction or nonfiction published in the U.S. in 1991. Book which reflects "concern for the poor and the powerless, justice, the conviction that society must assure all young people a fair chance and faith that a free democracy can act to remedy disparities of power and opportunity." Deadline: Jan. 7. Charges $20 entry fee.

‡ROBERT F. KENNEDY JOURNALISM AWARDS, 1031 31st St. NW, Washington DC 20007. (202)333-1880. FAX: (202)333-4903. Director: John Bourgeois. Estab. 1968. Previously published entries on problems of the disadvantaged. Deadline: Jan. 31.

‡KENTUCKY ARTS COUNCILS FELLOWSHIPS IN WRITING, Kentucky Arts Council, Berry Hill Mansion, Frankfort KY 40601. (502)564-3757. FAX: (502)564-3256. Contact: Irwin Pickett. Award offered every two years for previously published or unpublished work for development/artist's work. Deadline: July every other year. Rules and entry form for SASE (3 months before deadline). Award: $5,000. Must be Kentucky resident.

GEORGE R. KERNODLE ONE-ACT PLAYWRITING COMPETITION, University of Arkansas, Department of Drama, 406 Kimpel Hall, Fayetteville AR 72701. (501)575-2953. Contact: Kent R. Brown. Submissions to be unpublished and unproduced (workshop productions acceptable). Deadline: June 1. Charges $3 fee per submission. Three submission limit. Open to entry to all playwrights residing in the United States and Canada.

DONALD KEYHOE JOURNALISM AWARD, Fund for UFO Research, P.O. Box 277, Mt. Rainier MD 20712. (703)684-6032. FAX: (703)684-6032. Contact: Executive Committee, Fund for UFO Research. Estab. 1979. Annual awards for the best article or story published or broadcast in a newspaper, magazine, TV or radio news outlet during the previous calendar year. Separate awards for print and broadcast media. Also makes unscheduled cash awards for published works on UFO phenomena research or public education.

AGA KHAN PRIZE FOR FICTION, *The Paris Review*, 541 E. 72nd St., New York NY 10021. Director: George Plimpton. Estab. 1953. Unpublished fiction less than 10,000 words. Must include self-addressed stamped envelope. Deadline: May 1-June 1.

MARC A. KLEIN PLAYWRITING AWARD FOR STUDENTS, Department of Theatre, Case Western Reserve University, 2070 Adelbert Rd., Cleveland OH 44106. (216)368-2858. Chair, Reading Committee: John Orlock. Unpublished, professionally unproduced full-length plays, or substantial one-act play by student in American college or university. Deadline: April 1.

KUMU KAHUA/UHM THEATRE DEPARTMENT PLAYWRITING CONTEST, Kumu Kahua/UHM Theatre Dept. 1770 East-West Rd., Honolulu HI 96822. (808)948-7677. Contact: Dennis Carroll. Annual award for unpublished plays in two divisions: one for Hawaiian themes, one for residents of Hawaii only. Deadline: Jan. 1.

RUTH LAKE MEMORIAL AWARD, Poetry Society of America, 15 Gramercy Park S., New York NY 10003. (212)254-9628. Contact: Award Director. Unpublished poem of retrospection. Deadline: Dec. 31. Charges $5 fee.

LAMONT POETRY SELECTION, The Academy of American Poets, 177 E. 87th St., New York NY 10128. (212)427-5665. Award Director: Beth McCabe. Second book of unpublished poems by an American citizen, submitted by publisher in manuscript form. Deadline: April 15. Contact the Academy office for guidelines and official entry form.

LAWRENCE FOUNDATION AWARD, *Prairie Schooner,* 201 Andrews, University of Nebraska, Lincoln NE 68588-0334. (402)472-3191. FAX: (402)472-4636. Editor: Hilda Raz. Estab. 1978. Annual award for the best short story published in *Prairie Schooner.* Winner announced in the spring issue of the following year.

STEPHEN LEACOCK MEMORIAL AWARD FOR HUMOUR, Stephen Leacock Associates, P.O. Box 854, Orillia, Ontario L3V 6K8 Canada. (705)325-6546. Contest Director: Jean Dickson. Estab. 1947. Previously published book of humor by a Canadian author. Include 10 books each entry and a b&w photo with bio. Deadline: Dec. 31. Charges $25 fee. Prize: Stephen Leacock Medal and J.P. Wiser cash award of $3,500.

LEAGUE OF CANADIAN POETS AWARDS, National Poetry Contest, Gerald Lampert Memorial Award, and Pat Lowther Memorial Award. 24 Ryerson Ave., Toronto, Ontario M5T 2P3 Canada. (416)363-5047. FAX: (416)860-0826. Executive Director: Angela Rebeiro. Submissions to be published in the preceding year (awards), or previously unpublished (poetry contest). To promote new Canadian poetry/poets and also to recognize exceptional work in each category. Awards and Contest Deadline: Jan. 31. Enquiries from publishers welcome. Charge: $5 per poem for contest *only.* Open to Canadians living at home and abroad. The candidate must be a Canadian citizen or landed immigrant, although publisher need not be Canadian. For complete contest rules, contract Dolores Ricketts, at address above.

ELIAS LIEBERMAN STUDENT POETRY AWARD, Poetry Society of America, 15 Gramercy Park S., New York NY 10003. (212)254-9628. Contact: Award Director. Unpublished poem by student (grades 9-12). Deadline: Dec. 31. Charges $5 fee.

THE RUTH LILLY POETRY PRIZE, The Modern Poetry Association and The American Council for the Arts, 60 W. Walton St., Chicago IL 60610. Contact: Joseph Parisi. Estab. 1986. Annual prize to poet "whose accomplishments in the field of poetry warrant extraordinary recognition." No applicants or nominations are accepted. Deadline varies.

LINCOLN MEMORIAL ONE-ACT PLAYWRITING CONTEST, International Society of Dramatists, Box 1310, Miami FL 33153. (305)531-1530. Award Director: A. Delaplaine. Unpublished one-act plays, any type, any style. Awards and reading, and possible future production. Deadline: Jan. 15.

‡THE LINCOLN PRIZE AT GETTYSBURG COLLEGE, Lincoln & Soldiers Institute, Gettysburg College, Campus Box 435, Gettysburg PA 17325. (717)337-6590. FAX: (717)337-6596. Chairman of the Board: Gabor S. Boritt. Previously published works appearing in print between Jan. 1 and Dec. 31 each year. Prize to be awarded February of the following year. "To recognize annually the finest scholarly work on Abraham Lincoln, the Civil War soldier, or on the American Civil War. All things being equal, preference will be given to work on Lincoln, the Civil War soldier and work that addresses the literate general public. In rare instances the Prize may go to a work of fiction, poetry, drama and beyond." Deadline: October 1, July 1 (for spring publications). Guidelines for #10 SASE. Prize: $50,000 cash award and sculpture. "Ten copies of the published entry must be submitted by the appropriate deadline, accompanied by a brief letter stating the author, title of work and publication date."

‡LITERARY ARTS AWARDS, Arts Branch, Dept of Tourism, Recreation and Heritage, P.O. Box 12345, Fredericton, New Brunswick E3B 5C3 Canada. (506)453-2555. FAX: (506)453-2416. Contact: Arts Branch. Annual awards: Excellence Award, Creation Grant, Artist-in-Residence program, and travel program. Guidelines for 9×12 SAE with 3 Canadian first class stamps.

‡LITERATURE FELLOWSHIPS, D.C. Commission on the Arts and Humanities, 410 8th St, N.W., 5th Fl., Washington DC 20004. (202)724-5613. FAX: (202)927-4135. TDD: (202)727-3148. Contact: Literature Staff Liaison. "Annual fellowships to support individual artists (writers of creative fiction, nonfiction, poetry, prose, novels, etc.)." Deadline: spring. Guidelines for #10 SASE. Fellowship: $5,000 per year.

‡LIVE OAK THEATRE NEW PLAY AWARDS, Live Oak Theatre, 311 Nueces St., Austin TX 78701. (512)472-5143. Contact: Mari Marchbanks. Annual awards for previously unpublished plays. Deadline: Aug. 1. Guidelines for #10 SASE. Award: $1,000 and possible production.

‡LOCAL 7's ANNUAL POETRY COMPETITION, Santa Cruz/Monterey Local 7, National Writers Union, P.O. Box 2409, Aptos CA 95002. (408)427-2950. Coordinator: Steve Turner. Previously unpublished poetry. "To encourage the writing of poetry and to showcase unpublished work of high quality. Proceeds support the work of Local 7 of the National Writers Union." Deadline varies. Guidelines for #10 SASE. Charges $3 per poem. Prizes: $150 first; $100 second; $50 third.

LOCKERT LIBRARY OF POETRY IN TRANSLATION, Princeton University Press, 41 William St., Princeton NJ 08540. (609)452-4900. Literature Editor: Robert E. Brown. Book-length poetry translation of a single poet.

‡**THE GERALD LOEB AWARDS**, G. and R. Loeb Foundation, Inc., 405 Hilgard Ave., Los Angeles CA 90024-1481. (213)206-1877. FAX: (213)206-9830. Contact: Fran Spears. Previously published during the previous calendar year. "To recognize writers who make significant contributions to the understanding of business, finance and the economy." Deadline: Feb. 15 "unless it lands on a holiday." Charges $20 fee per entry. Winners in each category receive $1,000. Honorable mentions, when awarded, receive $500.

LOFT CREATIVE NONFICTION RESIDENCY PROGRAM, The Loft, Pratt Community Center, 66 Malcolm Ave., S.E., Minneapolis MN 55414-3551. Program Director: Carolyn Holbrook-Montgomery. Estab. 1974. Opportunity to work in month-long seminar with resident writer and cash award to six creative nonfiction writers. "Must live close enough to Minneapolis to participate fully." Deadline: April.

LOFT-McKNIGHT WRITERS AWARD, The Loft, Pratt Community Center, 66 Malcolm Ave., S.E., Minneapolis MN 55414-3551. Program Director: Carolyn Holbrook-Montgomery. Eight awards of $7,500 and two awards of distinction at $10,000 each for Minnesota writers of poetry and creative prose. Deadline: November.

LOFT-MENTOR SERIES, The Loft, Pratt Community Center, 66 Malcolm Ave. S.E., Minneapolis MN 55414-3551. Program Director: Lois Vossen. Estab. 1974. Opportunity to work with four nationally known writers and cash award available to six winning poets and fiction writers. "Must live close enough to Minneapolis to participate fully in the series." Deadline: May.

‡**THE REVA AND DAVID LOGAN GRANTS IN SUPPORT OF NEW WRITING ON PHOTOGRAPHY**, The Photographic Resource Center, 602 Commonwealth Ave., Boston MA 02215. (617)353-0700. FAX: (617)353-1662. Contact: Dan Younger. "Intended to support new and outstanding writing on photographic criticism, history, aesthetics theory, and issues of contemporary importance to the field." Deadline: March 15. SASE for guidelines. Prize: a total of $7,000 which is broken down for different categories of proposals, and $3,000 for commissioned essays. "Applicants must be 18 years of age, citizens or legal residents of USA. Students of degree programs as of the application deadline are ineligible, as are members and affiliates of the PRC staff; previous recipients of the grant within the past 5 years are also ineligible."

LOUISIANA LITERARY AWARD, Louisana Library Association, P.O. Box 3058, Baton Rouge LA 70821. (504)342-4928. FAX: (504)342-3547. Contact: Literary Award Committee. Estab. 1909. Submissions to be previously published. "Must be related to Louisiana. Write for details."

LOUISIANA LITERATURE PRIZE FOR POETRY, Louisiana Literature, P.O. Box 792, Southeastern Louisiana University, Hammond LA 70402. Contest Director: Dr. Tim Gautreaux. Estab. 1985. Unpublished poetry. Deadline: Feb. 15. Write for rules. Prize: $300.

‡**LOVE CREEK ANNUAL SHORT PLAY FESTIVAL**, Love Creek Productions, % Granville, 42 Sunset Dr., Croton NY 10520-2821. Festival Manager: Cynthia Granville. Annual festival for previously unpublished and unproduced plays. "We believe that a script is incomplete as a work of art until it is performed. As an encouragement to playwrights and an enrighment opportunity for Love Creek's over 100 member artists, administrators and technicians, we have therefore established the Festival as a playwriting competition in which scripts are judged on their merits in performance." Deadline: Oct. 1. Guidelines for #10 SASE. "Finalists receive a mini-showcase production in New York City—winner receives $300 prize."

‡**LOVE CREEK MINI FESTIVALS**, Love Creek Productions, % Granville, 42 Sunset Dr., Croton NY 10520-2821. Festival Literary Manager: Cynthia Granville. "The Mini Festivals are an outgrowth of our annual Short Play Festival in which we produce scripts concerning a particular issue or theme which our artistic staff selects according to current needs, interests and concerns of both our members and playwrights submitting to out Short Play Festival throughout the year." Guidelines for #10 SASE. Finalists receive a mini-showcase production in New York City. Winner receives a $200 prize.

‡**AMY LOWELL POETRY TRAVELLING SCHOLARSHIP**, % Choate, Hall & Stewart, Exchange Pl. 35th Fl., Boston MA 02109. (617)227-5020. FAX: (617)227-7566. Award Director: F. Davis Dassori, Jr., Trustee. "Annual award to support an American-born poet whose work would benefit from a year

spent outside of North America." Deadline: Oct. 15. Guidelines for #10 SASE. Prize: $27,000 (amount varies as it is a portion of income of a portfolio) to be paid in quarterly installments.

‡McLAREN MEMORIAL COMEDY PLAYWRITING COMPETITION, Midland Community Theatre, 2000 W. Wadley, Midland TX 79705. (915)682-2544. FAX: (915)682-6136. Contact: Mary Lou Cassidy. Contest offered annually for unpublished work. "Entry must be a comedy. Can be one- or two-act. Number of characters or subject is not limited. Make us laugh." Deadline: Jan. 31. Rules and entry form for SASE. Prize: $400, Reader's Theatre Performance, airfare and hotel for 1 week rehearsal and performance.

THE LENORE MARSHALL/NATION PRIZE FOR POETRY, The New Hope Foundation and *The Nation* Magazine, 72 5th Ave., New York NY 10011. (212)242-8400. Administrator: Peter Meyer. Book of poems published in the United States during the previous year and nominated by the publisher. Cash award of $10,000. Deadline: June 1. Books must be submitted *directly* to judges. Query *The Nation* for addresses of judges.

WALTER RUMSEY MARVIN GRANT, Ohioana Library Association, Room 1105 State Departments Bldg., 65 S. Front St., Columbus OH 43215. (614)466-3831. Director: Linda Hengst. Award given every 2 years, (even years). Applicant must have been born in Ohio or have lived in Ohio for 5 years or more, must be 30 years of age or younger, and not have published a book. Deadline Jan. 31.

JOHN MASEFIELD MEMORIAL AWARD, Poetry Society of America, 15 Gramercy Park S., New York NY 10003. (212)254-9628. Contact: Award Director. Unpublished narrative poem in English. No translations. Deadline: Dec. 31. Charges $5 fee.

MASSACHUSETTS ARTISTS FELLOWSHIP, Artists Foundation, 8 Park Plaza, Boston MA 02116. (617)227-2787. Director: Kathleen Brandt. Award offered every two years for fiction, nonfiction, playwriting and poetry to enhance the careers of individual artists in Massachusetts. Call the Artists Foundation for application. Award: $10,000 Fellowship; $1,000 finalist. All applicants must be residents of Massachusetts, over age 18 and not a student. Deadline December 6.

‡EDGAR LEE MASTERS AWARDS, Caravan Press, 343 S. Broadway, Los Angeles CA 90013. (818)377-4301. Contact: Ms. Sana Cain. Annual awards for previously published and unpublished poetry, fiction and creative nonfiction. Guidelines for #10 SASE. Charges fee. Three awards of $2,500, plus publication.

LUCILLE MEDWICK MEMORIAL AWARD, Poetry Society of America, 15 Gramercy Park S., New York NY 10003. (212)254-9628. Contact: Award Director. Original poem on a humanitarian theme. Deadline: Dec. 31. Members only.

THE EDWARD J. MEEMAN AWARDS, Scripps Howard Foundation, P.O. Box 5380, Cincinnati OH 45201. (513)977-3035. Estab. 1967. Environmental reporting by a newspaper.

MELCHER BOOK AWARD, Unitarian Universalist Association, 25 Beacon St., Boston MA 02108. FAX: (617)523-4123. Staff Liaison: Judith Meyer. Estab. 1964. Previously published book on religious liberalism. Deadline: Dec. 31.

MENCKEN AWARDS, Free Press Association, P.O. Box 15548, Columbus OH 43215. FPA Executive Director: Michael Grossberg. Estab. 1981. Honoring defense of human rights and individual liberties, or exposes of governmental abuses of power. Categories: News Story or Investigative Report, Feature Story, Editorial or Op-Ed Column, Editorial Cartoon, Book and Defense of First Amendment. Entries *must* have been published or broadcast during previous calendar year. Deadline: April 1 (for work from previous year). Fee: $4 per entry. Late deadline May 1 with extra fee. *Must* send SASE for entry form.

ALWAYS submit unsolicited manuscripts or queries with a self-addressed, stamped envelope (SASE) within your country or a self-addressed envelope with International Reply Coupons (IRC) purchased from the post office for other countries.

‡THE MENTOR AWARD, Mentor Newsletter, P.O. Box 4382, Overland Park KS 66204. Award Director: Maureen Waters. Estab. 1989. Award offered quarterly. "To promote and encourage mentoring through feature articles, essays, book/movie reviews, interviews or short stories." Deadlines: March 31, June 30, Sept. 30, Dec. 31. Guidelines for #10 SASE. Charges $4 fee. Writer must be 18 years old.

MIDLAND AUTHORS AWARD, Society of Midland Authors, % Bowman, 152 N. Scoville, Oak Park IL 60302. (708)383-7568. FAX: (708)524-9233. Estab. 1915. Annual awards for previously published drama, fiction, nonfiction, poetry, biography, children's fiction and children's nonfiction. Authors must reside in the states of Indiana, Iowa, Kansas, Michigan, Minnesota, Missouri, Nebraska, North Dakota, South Dakota, Wisconsin or Ohio. Deadline: Dec. 15.

MILITARY LIFESTYLE FICTION CONTEST, *Military Lifestyle Magazine*, Suite 710, 4800 Montgomery Lane, Bethesda MD 20814-5341. (301)718-7600. FAX: (301)718-7652. Editor-in-Chief: Hope Daniels. Annual award for short stories featuring U.S. military families. Deadline: March 31.

‡MILKWEED EDITIONS NATIONAL FICTION PRIZE, Milkweed Editions, P.O. Box 3226, Minneapolis MN 55403. (612)332-3192. FAX: (612)332-6248. Contest Director: Emilie Buchwald. "To find, publish and promote exceptional new voices in American Literature." Submit mss May 1-August 15. "Writers *must* send SASE for complete guidelines or risk having entry disqualified." Charges $5 fee. Prize: $3,000 advance against royalties and publication by Milkweed Editions. "Open to writers who have previously published a book-length collection of fiction, or a minimum of three short stories or novellas in commercial or literary journals with national distribution."

MILL MOUNTAIN THEATRE NEW PLAY COMPETITION, Mill Mountain Theatre, Center in the Square, 1 Market Sq., Roanoke VA 24011. (703)342-5730. Literary Manager: Jo Weinstein. Estab. 1985. Previously unpublished and unproduced plays for up to 10 cast members. Deadline: Jan. 1. Send SASE for guidelines.

MINNESOTA INK FICTION CONTEST, Minnesota Ink, Inc., 27 Empire Dr., St. Paul MN 55103. (612)225-1306. Contact: Valerie Hockert. Previously unpublished fiction. Deadline: Dec. 31. Charges $5 fee.

MINNESOTA INK SEMI-ANNUAL POETRY CONTEST, Minnesota Ink, Inc., 27 Empire Dr., St. Paul MN 55103. (612)225-1306. Contact: Anthoney Stomski. Offered winter and summer. Unpublished. Deadline: Feb. 28; Aug. 15. Charges $2 for first poem; $1 each poem thereafter.

MINNESOTA VOICES PROJECT COMPETITION, New Rivers Press, #910, 420 N. 5th St., Minneapolis MN 55401. (612)339-7114. Editor/Publisher: C.W. Truesdale. Annual award for new and emerging writers of poetry, prose, essays, and memoirs (as well as other forms of creative prose) from Wisconsin, Minnesota, Iowa and the Dakotas, to be published in book form for the first time. Deadline: April 1.

‡MINORITY SCREENWRITERS DEVELOPMENT AND PROMOTIONAL PROGRAM, American Film Institute Alumni Assoc. Writers Workshop, P.O. Box 69799, Los Angeles CA 90069. (213)559-4512. FAX: (213)559-3251. Founder Director: Willard Rodgers. Estab. 1990. Previously unproduced scripts. "To bring ethnic minority writers to the attention of the motion picture industry, where they are severely under represented." Deadline varies. Guidelines for #10 SASE. Charges $25 fee. Prize: $500 and exposure to the motion picture industry.

‡MIRRORS INTERNATIONAL TANKA AWARD, AHA Books P.O. Box 1250, Gualala CA 95445. (707)882-2226. Editor: Jane Reichhold. Estab. 1990. "The purpose of the contest is to acquaint writers with the Japanese poetry form, tanka. By choosing 30 winners for publication in a chapbook, it is hoped that standards and examples will be set, re-evaluated, changed and enlarged. The genre is one of Japan's oldest, but the newest to English." Deadline: Nov. 30. Guidelines for #10 SASE. The first entry is free. Unlimited entries cost either $1 or one IRC each. Prize: $200 in 1991. Grand prize with 30 winning entries published in *Tanka Splendor*.

MISSISSIPPI VALLEY POETRY CONTEST, P.O. Box 3188, Rock Island IL 61204. (309)788-8041. Director: Sue Katz. Estab. 1971. Unpublished poetry: adult general, student division, Mississippi Valley, senior citizen, religious, rhyming, humorous, haiku, history, ethnic and traditional jazz. Deadline: Sept. 15. Charges $3 to enter contest. Up to 5 poems may be submitted without line limitation.

MIXED BLOOD VERSUS AMERICA, Mixed Blood Theatre Company, 1501 S. 4th St., Minneapolis MN 55454. (612)338-0984. Contact: David B. Kunz. Estab. 1975. "Mixed Blood Versus America" encourages and seeks out the emerging playwright. Mixed Blood is not necessarily looking for scripts that have multi-racial casts, rather good scripts that will be cast with the best actors available." Open to all playwrights who have had at least one of their works produced or workshopped (either professionally or educationally). Only unpublished unproduced plays are eligible for contest. Limit two submissions per playwright. No translations or adaptations. Send SASE for copy of guidelines. Deadline: March 15, 1992.

MORSE POETRY PRIZE, Northeastern University English Deptment, 406 Holmes Hall, Boston MA 02115. (617)437-2512. Contact: Guy Rotella. Previously published poetry, book-length mss. Charges $10/entry. Prize: Publication of mss by Northeastern University Press and a $500 cash award.

FRANK LUTHER MOTT-KAPPA TAU ALPHA RESEARCH AWARD IN JOURNALISM, University of Missouri, School of Journalism, Columbia MO 65205. (314)882-7685. Executive Director, Central Office: Dr. Keith Sanders. For "best researched book in journalism." 5 copies required. No forms required. Deadline: Jan. 15. Award: $1,000.

‡MRTW ANNUAL RADIO SCRIPT CONTEST, Midwest Radio Theatre Workshop, 915 E. Broadway, Columbia MO 65201. (314)874-5676. Contact: Diane Huneke. "The purpose of the award is to encourage the writing of radio scripts and to showcase both well established and emerging radio playwrights. Some winning works are produced for radio and all winning works are published in the annual MRTW Scriptbook. Our scriptbook is the only one of it's kind in this country." Deadline: July 30. Rules and entry form for SASE. "A cash award of $900 is split among the top 2-4 entries, depending on recommendation of the jurors. Winners receive free workshop registration. Those who receive honorable mention, as well as award winning plays, are included in the scriptbook; a total of 10-16 are published annually. We acquire the right to publish the script in the scriptbook, which is distributed at cost and the right to produce the script for air; all other rights retained by the author."

MULTICULTURAL PLAYWRIGHTS' FESTIVAL, The Seattle Group Theatre Company, 3940 Brooklyn Ave. NE, Seattle WA 98105. (206)685-4969. Estab. 1984. One-act and full-length plays by African-American, Native American, Hispanic and Asian playwrights. Honorarium, airfare and housing for 2 playwrights plus workshop productions. 4-6 playwrights receive readings. Deadline: Nov. 15.

‡LA NAPOULE RESIDENCY, North Carolina Arts Council, Dept. of Cultural Resources, Raleigh NC 27601-2807. (919)733-2111. Contact: Deborah McGill. "To provide an international experience and time to work for writers who live in North Carolina." Deadline: Feb. 1. SASE for guidelines. Prize: 3-month stay at the La Napoule Foundation in southern France; round trip air fare; room and board; materials subsidy of $500; $1,000 for additional living expenses. Writer must have been a resident of the state for at least a year prior to application and may not be enrolled in a degree-granting program.

NATIONAL ARCHIVES ONE-ACT PLAYWRITING COMPETITION, National Archives and Records Administration, Education Branch, NEE-E, Washington DC 20408. Contact: Cynthia A. Hightower. To educate playwrites about the vast resources within the records of the National Archives. Script must be unpublished and based on events, episodes pertaining to the United States' involvement during World War II from 1941 to 1946 such as the homefront, sabotage, O.S.S., Pearl Harbor, propaganda, rationing, WACs, etc. Scripts must be based on records held by the National Archives in Washington, DC and/or its regional archives, and/or any of the presidential libraries. Deadline: Jan. 15. Open to all except the employees of the National Archives and Records Administration, its field branches and the presidential libraries.

‡NATIONAL AWARDS FOR EDUCATION REPORTING, Education Writers Association, 1001 Connecticut Ave. NW, Washington DC 20036. (202)429-9680. FAX: (202)872-4050. Submissions to be previously published, previous year. There are 17 categories; write for more information. Deadline, mid-January. Charges $30 for first entry, $20 for each additional.

‡NATIONAL CANADIAN ONE ACT PLAYWRITING COMPETITION, Ottawa Little Theatre, 400 King Edward Ave., Ottawa, Ontario K1N 7M7 Canada. (613)233-8948. Director: Lorraine St. Laurent. "To encourage literary and dramatic talent in Canada." Submit Jan.-May. Rules and regulations for #10 SASE with Canadian postage or #10 SAE with 1 IRC. Prizes: $1,000, $500, $300.

‡NATIONAL CHILDREN'S THEATRE PLAYWRITING CONTEST, Columbia Entertainment Co. (a community theatre), 309 Parkade, Columbia MO 65202. (314)874-5628. Contact: Betsy Phillips. Offered annually for previously unpublished work. "We are seeking large cast plays for full-scale production by students in our theatre school, aged 10-15. Plays should be full-length (1 to 1½ hours) with speaking roles for 20-30 characters of all ages, and with at least 10 roles developed in some detail. Plays should be challenging and enjoyable for students to act in, and entertaining for audiences of all ages to attend." Deadline: June 30. Guidelines for SASE. Prize: $250 1st prize, full scale production, partial travel expenses for author to attend. 2nd prize (if warranted), full-scale production and partial travel expenses. Right to produce 1st place and 2nd place winners by theatre school students without royalty payment, during that year's season.

NATIONAL ENDOWMENT FOR THE ARTS: ARTS ADMINISTRATION FELLOWS PROGRAM/FELLOWSHIP, National Endowment for the Arts, 1100 Pennsylvania Ave., NW, Washington DC 20506. (202)682-5786. Contact: Anya Nykyforiak. Estab. 1973. Offered three times each year: Spring, Summer and Fall. "The Arts Administration Fellowships are for arts managers and administrators in the nonprofit literary publishing field or writers' centers. Fellows come to the NEA for a 11-week residency to acquire an overview of this Federal agency's operations." Deadline: Jan./April/July. Guidelines may be requested by letter or telephone.

NATIONAL JEWISH BOOK AWARD—AUTOBIOGRAPHY/MEMOIR, Sandra Brand and Arik Weintraub Award, 15 E. 26th St., New York NY 10010. (212)532-4949. Director: Paula G. Gottlieb. Given to an author of an autobiography or a memoir of the life of a Jewish person.

NATIONAL JEWISH BOOK AWARD—CHILDREN'S LITERATURE, Shapolksy Family Award, Jewish Book Council, 15 E. 26th St., New York NY 10010. (212)532-4949. Director: Paula G. Gottlieb. Children's book on Jewish theme. Deadline: Nov. 20.

NATIONAL JEWISH BOOK AWARD—CHILDREN'S PICTURE BOOK, Marcia and Louis Posner Award, Jewish Book Council, 15 E. 26th St., New York NY 10010. (212)532-4949. Director: Paula G. Gottlieb. Author and illustrator of a children's book on a Jewish theme. Deadline: Nov. 20.

NATIONAL JEWISH BOOK AWARD—CONTEMPORARY JEWISH LIFE, Muriel and Phil Berman Award, 15 E. 26th St., New York NY 10010. (212)532-4949. Contact: Paula G. Gottlieb. Nonfiction work dealing with the sociology of modern Jewish life.

NATIONAL JEWISH BOOK AWARD—FICTION, William and Janice Epstein Award, 15 E. 26th St., New York NY 10010. (212)532-4949. Director: Paula G. Gottlieb. Jewish fiction (novel or short story collection). Deadline: Nov. 20.

NATIONAL JEWISH BOOK AWARD—HOLOCAUST, Leon Jolson Award, Jewish Book Council, 15 E. 26th St., New York NY 10010. (212)532-4949. Contact: Paula G. Gottlieb. Nonfiction book concerning the Holocaust. Deadline: Nov. 20.

NATIONAL JEWISH BOOK AWARD—ISRAEL, Morris J. and Betty Kaplun Memorial Award, Jewish Book Council, 15 E. 26th St., New York NY 10010. (212)532-4949. Director: Paula G. Gottlieb. Nonfiction work about the State of Israel. Deadline: Nov. 20.

NATIONAL JEWISH BOOK AWARD—JEWISH HISTORY, Gerrard and Ella Berman Award, Jewish Book Council, 15 E. 26th St., New York NY 10010. (212)532-4949. Director: Paula G. Gottlieb. Book of Jewish history. Deadline: Nov. 20.

NATIONAL JEWISH BOOK AWARD—JEWISH THOUGHT, Jewish Book Council, 15 E. 26th St., New York NY 10010. (212)532-4949. Director: Paula G. Gottlieb. Book dealing with some aspect of Jewish thought, past or present. Deadline: Nov. 20.

NATIONAL JEWISH BOOK AWARD—SCHOLARSHIP, Sarah H. and Julius Kushner Memorial Award, Jewish Book Council, 15 E. 26th St., New York NY 10010. (212)532-4949. Director: Paula G. Gottlieb. Book which makes an original contribution to Jewish learning. Deadline: Nov. 20.

NATIONAL JEWISH BOOK AWARD—VISUAL ARTS, Leon L. Gildesgame Award, Jewish Book Council, 15 E. 26th St., New York NY 10010. (212)532-4949. Director: Paula G. Gottlieb. Book about Jewish art. Deadline: Nov. 20.

‡NATIONAL LOOKING GLASS AWARD FOR A SINGLE POEM, *Pudding Magazine*, 60 N. Main St., Johnstown OH 43031. (614)967-6060. Contest Director: Jennifer Bosveld. Previously unpublished poems. "To identify and publish the finest work reflecting the editorial slant of *Pudding Magazine*: Applied Poetry. We recommend subject matter in the area of social justice, ecology and humans impact, human relations and *artistic* work from a therapeutic process." Deadline Sept. 30. Guidelines for #10 SASE. Charges $1 per poem. Number of entries unlimited. Prize: $500 total in cash prizes.

‡**NATIONAL LOOKING GLASS POETRY CHAPBOOK COMPETITION,** *Pudding Magazine,* 60 N. Main St., Johnstown OH 43031. (614)967-6060. Contest Director: Jennifer Bosveld. "To publish a collection of poems that represents our magazine's editorial slant: Applied Poetry. Poems might be themed or not." Deadline: June 30. Guidelines for #10 SASE. Charges $9 fee. Prize: $100 and publication of the book.

NATIONAL ONE-ACT PLAYWRITING COMPETITION, Little Theatre of Alexandria, 600 Wolfe St., Alexandria VA 22314. (703)683-5778. Contact: Chairman Playreading Committee. Estab. 1978. To encourage original writing for theatre. Criteria: submissions must be original, unpublished, unproduced one-act stage plays. Deadline: March 31. Send SASE for guidelines. Prize: $350 first; $250 second; $150 third.

‡**NATIONAL PLAY AWARD,** National Repertory Theatre Foundation, Suite 405, 630 N. Grand Ave., Los Angeles CA 90012. Contact: Lloyd Steele. Offered every two years. "Award is for unproduced original full-length play—no translations, adaptations, musicals." Deadline: Jan. 1. SASE for guidelines. Prize: $7,500 grant to writer, $5,000 to first professional production.

‡**NATIONAL PLAYWRIGHTS' AWARD,** Unicorn Theatre, 3820 Main St., Kansas City MO 64111. (816)531-7529. Literary Manager: Jan Kohl. Offered annually for previously unpublished work. "We produce contemporary original scripts, preferring scripts that deal with social concerns. However, we accept (and have produced) comedies." SASE for guidelines. Prize: $1,000 in royalty/prize fee and a mainstage production at the Unicorn as part of its regular season.

NATIONAL PLAYWRIGHTS COMPETITION ON THEMES OF "THE AMERICAN DREAM," Arrow Rock Lyceum Theatre, Main St., Arrow Rock MO 65320. Contact: Michael Bollinger. Offered every two years to unpublished full length plays dealing with the reality and/or myth of "the American dream." Submit between Aug. and Dec. of 1992, for summer-1993 production.

‡**NATIONAL POETRY COMPETITION,** 21 Earls Court Square, London SW5 9DE England. (071)373-7861. Contest Organizer: Betty Redpath. Annual contest for unpublished poetry. Deadline: first week of November. Guidelines available for 6×9 SAE with 2 IRC's. Charges entry fee. Prizes: £2,000, £1,000, £500.

‡**NATIONAL POETRY SERIES,** 26 W. 17th St., New York NY 10128. Coordinator: Suzanne Fox. Annual prize for previously unpublished poetry in book form. "Our goal is to publish 5 books of poetry annually through a series of participating publishers." Open competition, Jan. 1-Feb. 15, annually. Guidelines for #10 SASE. Charges $15 fee. Award: book publication.

NATIONAL TEN-MINUTE PLAY CONTEST, Actors Theatre of Louisville, 316 W. Main St., Louisville KY 40202. (502)584-1265. Literary Manager: Michael Bigelow Dixon. Previously unproduced (professionally) ten-minute plays (10 pages or less). "Entries must *not* have had an Equity or Equity-waiver production." Deadline: Dec. 1.

‡**LARRY NEAL WRITERS' COMPETITION,** D.C. Commission on the Arts and Humanities, 410 8th St. NW, 5th Fl., Washington DC 20004. Contact: Literature Staff Liaison. "Annual competition to encourage and reward Washington writers *and* honor the legacy of Larry Neal." Deadline: spring. Guidelines for #10 SASE. Prize: $500.

‡**NEGATIVE CAPABILITY SHORT FICTION CONTEST,** *Negative Capability,* 62 Ridgelawn Dr. E, Mobile AL 36608. (205)460-6146. Contact: Sue Walker. Previously unpublished short fiction."To recognize and support fiction writers." Deadline Dec. 1. Guidelines for #10 SASE. Reading fee $10 per story. Prize: $1,000 plus publication.

NEUSTADT INTERNATIONAL PRIZE FOR LITERATURE, 110 Monnet Hall, Norman OK 73019. (405)325-4531. Estab. 1969. Previously published fiction, poetry and drama. Nominations are made only by members of the jury, which changes every two years.

ALLAN NEVINS PRIZE, Society of American Historians, 603 Fayerweather Hall, Columbia University, New York NY 10027. Sec./Treas.: Prof. Kenneth T. Jackson. American history (nominated doctoral dissertations on arts, literature, science and American biographies). Deadline: Dec. 31. Prize: $1,000, certificate and publication.

‡**NEW CHRISTIAN PLAYS COMPETITION,** Colorado Christian University, 180 S. Garrison St., Lakewood CO 80226. (303)238-5386. Theater Coordinator: Patrick Rainville Dorn. Offered annually for unpublished work. "To encourage the development of Christian plays and playwrights, and help make

scripts available to producers of Christian plays." Deadline: Jan. 31. SASE for guidelines. Prize: $200 cash prize for overall first place. Staged reading/workshop production for top four finalists. "Finalists will be requested to give photocopy and production permission and approval to pass the script along to other producing/publishing organizations."

‡NEW HAMPSHIRE INDIVIDUAL ARTISTS' FELLOWSHIPS, New Hampshire State Council on the Arts, 40 N. Main St., Concord NH 03301. (603)271-2789. Coordinator: Audrey V. Sylvester. Previously published entries of not more than 5 years since completion. "To recognize artistic excellence and professional commitment." Deadline: May 1. Contest/award rules and entry forms available with SASE or call for application. Prize: $1,000-2,000. Applicant must be over 18; not enrolled as full-time student; have resided in NH for at least one year prior to application and may not have been a fellow in preceding year.

NEW LETTERS LITERARY AWARDS, University of Missouri-Kansas City, Kansas City MO 64110. FAX: (816)235-5191. Awards Coordinator: Glenda McCrary. Estab. 1986. Unpublished fiction, poetry and essays. Deadline: May 15. Charges $10 fee.

NEW PLAY COMPETITION, Contemporary Arts Center, P.O. Box 30498, New Orleans LA 70190. (504)523-1216. FAX: (504)528-3828. Contact: Julie Hebert. Estab. 1986. Writers must be resident of Alabama, Arkansas, Georgia, Louisiana or Mississippi. Only unproduced, unpublished scripts are eligible. Full-length only. Limit two scripts per writer. Deadline: Nov. 1.

NEW YORK STATE HISTORICAL ASSOCIATION MANUSCRIPT AWARD, P.O. Box 800, Cooperstown NY 13326. (607)547-2508. Director of Publications: Dr. Wendell Tripp. Estab. 1973. Unpublished book-length monograph on New York State history. Deadline: Feb. 20.

JOHN NEWBERY MEDAL, Association for Library Service to Children/American Library Association, 50 E. Huron St., Chicago IL 60611. (312)280-2163. Award Director: Susan Roman. For children's literature published in the previous year.

NHS BOOK PRIZE, National Historical Society, 2245 Kohn Rd., P.O. Box 8200, Harrisburg PA 17105. (717)657-9555. Estab. 1972. NHS Book Prize for first book published by author. Prize awarded annually. Books pubilshed in previous year only. Deadline: July 31.

DON AND GEE NICHOLL FELLOWSHIPS IN SCREENWRITING, Academy of Motion Picture Arts & Sciences, 8949 Wilshire Blvd., P.O. Box 5511, Beverly Hills CA 90209. (213)278-8990. Director: Greg Beal. Estab. 1985. Unproduced screenplays; up to five $20,000 fellowships awarded each year. Deadline: June 1. Charges $25 fee. Send SASE for application form.

CHARLES H. AND N. MILDRED NILON EXCELLENCE IN MINORITY FICTION AWARD, University of Colorado at Boulder and Fiction Collective Two, University of Colorado, Campus Box 494, Boulder CO 80309. Contact: Donald Laing. Estab. 1989. Unpublished book-length fiction, 200 pp. minimum. Only mss. from protected minority authors will be considered.

NIMROD, ARTS AND HUMANITIES COUNCIL OF TULSA PRIZES, 2210 South Main, Tulsa OK 74114. (918)584-3333. Editor: Francine Ringold. Unpublished fiction (Katherine Anne Porter prize) and poetry (Pablo Neruda Prize). Deadline: April 15. Fee $10, for which you receive an issue of *Nimrod*. (Writers entering both fiction and poetry contest need only pay once.) Send #10 SASE for complete guidelines.

NMMA DIRECTORS AWARD, National Marine Manufacturers Association, 353 Lexington Ave., New York NY 10016. (212)684-6622. FAX: (212)683-7074. Contribution to boating and allied water sports through newspaper, magazine, radio, television, film or book as a writer, artist, broadcaster, editor or photographer. Nomination must be submitted by a representative of a member company of National Marine Manufacturers Association. Deadline: Nov. 30.

‡NO EMPTY SPACE THEATRE BIANNUAL CONTEST, No Empty Space Theatre, 568 Metropolitan Ave., Staten Island NY 10301. (718)273-5923. Contact: Maria Palma. Offered every two years for unpublished work. Award for the discovery of new and emerging contemporary American playwrights. "Normally, Dec. 31 every 2 years, depending on our season and workload." Prize: $500, and possibility of full-scale production if winning entry is financially producible. Signature required which offers N.E.S.T. the right to procure winning script within 1 year. No restrictions per type size of cast, number of acts, etc. "We are looking for the best scripts."

NORTHERN NEW ENGLAND PLAYWRIGHTS AWARD, Valley Players, P.O. Box 441, Waitsfield VT 05673. (802)583-3203. Contact: Howard Chapman. Estab. 1982. Contest offered annually for unpublished scripts. Non-musical, full length play suitable for production by a community theater group. Any northern New England (Vermont, New Hampshire, Maine) resident may submit a play (or plays) as long as it has not been produced or published before. Deadline: August 1.

NUTS TO US!, New Hope Press, 304 S. Denton St., Dothan AL 36301. (205)792-2331. Contact: Sue Cronkite. Estab. 1989. Short stories, tales and poems which touch upon peanuts in some way. Deadline: July 31. Charges $15 fee first entry; $7 each additional entry. No limit to number of entries. Prize: $100 first prize in each of the 3 categories; $25 second; $10 third. — and publication for winners and runners-up.

THE FLANNERY O'CONNOR AWARD FOR SHORT FICTION, The University of Georgia Press, Terrell Hall, Athens GA 30602. (404)542-2830. FAX: (404)542-0601. Series Editor: Charles East. Estab. 1981. Submission period: June-July 31. Charges $10 fee. Manuscripts will not be returned.

O'CONNOR PRIZE FOR FICTION, *Descant*, Texas Christian University, P.O. Box 32872, Fort Worth TX 76129. (817)921-7240. An annual award for the best short story in the *Descant* volume; writer of the story receives a $500 prize given through the magazine by an anonymous donor.

SCOTT O'DELL AWARD FOR HISTORICAL FICTION, 1100 E. 57th St., Chicago IL 60637. (312)702-8293. Director: Zena Sutherland. Estab. 1981. Previously published historical fiction book for children set in the Americas. Entries must have appeared in print during previous year. Deadline: Dec. 31.

OGLEBAY INSTITUTE/TOWNGATE THEATRE PLAYWRITING, Oglebay Institute, Oglebay Park, Wheeling WV 26003. (304)242-4200. FAX: (304)242-4203. Contact: Debbie Hynes. Estab. 1976. Deadline: Jan. 1. All full-length *non*-musical plays that have never been professionally produced or published are eligible.

OHIO ARTS COUNCIL INDIVIDUAL ARTISTS FELLOWSHIP, Ohio Arts Council, 727 E. Main St., Columbus OH 43205. (614)466-2613. Contact: Susan Dickson. Estab. 1965. Contest/award offered annually. Intended to recognize and support Ohio's creative artists. Deadline: Jan. 15. Writer should call or write and request guidelines and an application form. SASE is not required. Prize: $5,000 or $10,000. Panel of experts, (writers, critics, editors) judge. Writers must be a residents of the State of Ohio for at least one year prior to the application deadline and the applicant cannot be enrolled in a degree or certificate-granting program of any kind.

OHIOANA BOOK AWARDS, Ohioana Library Association, Room 1105, Ohio Departments Bldg., 65 S. Front St., Columbus OH 43215. (614)466-3831. Director: Linda Hengst. Books published within the past 12 months by Ohioans or about Ohio and Ohioans. Submit two copies of book on publication.

ONES AT EIGHT, City of Virginia Beach, 800 Monmouth Ln., Virginia Beach VA 23464. (804)474-8492. Contact: Ann Hicks. Annual award for unpublished plays. Deadline: Nov. 1, 1991 for production in January 1992. Three scripts chosen for production and plaque presented to finalists.

THE C.F. ORVIS WRITING CONTEST, The Orvis Company, Inc., Historic Route 7A, Manchester VT 05254. (802)362-3622. Contest/Award Director: Doug Truax. Outdoor writing about upland bird hunting and fly fishing (magazine and newspaper). Deadline: April 1.

PANHANDLER POETRY CHAPBOOK COMPETITION, *The Panhandler Magazine*, English Dept. University of West Florida, Pensacola FL 32514. (904)474-2923. Editor: Michael Yots. Estab. 1979. Individual poems may have been published. To honor excellence in the writing of short collections of poetry. Two winning manuscripts are published each year. Submit between Oct. 15 and Jan. 15. Charges $7 (includes copy of winning chapbooks).

‡FRANCIS PARKMAN PRIZE, Society of American Historians, 603 Fayerweather Hall, Columbia University, New York NY 10027. Contact: Professor Kenneth T. Jackson. Colonial or national U.S. history book. Deadline: Jan. 15.

‡ALICIA PATTERSON JOURNALISM FELLOWSHIP, Alicia Patterson Foundation, #1250, 1001 Pennsylvania Ave. NW, Washington DC 20004. (202)393-5995. Contact: Margaret Engel. Offered annually for previously published submissions. Purpose is "to give 5-7 print journalists a year of in-depth research and reporting. Applicants must have 5 years of professional print journalism experience and be U.S. citizens. Fellows write four, magazine-length pieces for the *Alicia Patterson Reporter*, a quarterly magazine, during their fellowship year. Fellows must take a year's leave from their jobs, but may do other freelance articles during the year." Deadline: Oct. 1. SASE not required for contest guidelines. "Journalists should write or call for applications." Prize: $30,000 stipend for calendar year.

WILLIAM PEDEN PRIZE IN FICTION, *Missouri Review*, 1507 Hillcrest Hall, Columbia MO 65211. (314)882-4474. Contact: Greg Michalson. Awarded annually to best piece of fiction published in *MR* in a given volume year. All work published in *MR* automatically eligible. No other guidelines available.

PEN CENTER USA WEST AWARDS, PEN Center USA West, 1100 Glendon Ave., Los Angeles CA 90024. (213)824-2041. FAX: (213)824-1679. Estab. 1952. Award offered for previously published work in a calendar year. Deadline: Dec. 31. Open to writers living west of the Mississippi River whose books have been published in the calendar year.

PEN MEDAL FOR TRANSLATION, PEN American Center, 568 Broadway, New York NY 10012. (212)334-1660. FAX: (212)334-2181. Translators nominated by the PEN Translation Committee. Given every 3 years.

PEN PUBLISHER CITATION, PEN American Center, 568 Broadway, New York NY 10012. (212)334-1660. FAX: (212)334-2181. "Awarded every two years to a publisher who has throughout his career, given distinctive and continuous service." Nominated by the PEN Executive Board.

PEN WRITING AWARDS FOR PRISONERS, PEN American Center, 568 Broadway, New York NY 10012. (212)334-1660. FAX: (212)334-2181. "Awarded to the authors of the best poetry, plays, short fiction and nonfiction received from prison writers in the U.S." Deadline variable.

PEN/BOOK-OF-THE-MONTH CLUB TRANSLATION PRIZE, PEN American Center, 568 Broadway, New York NY 10012. Contact: John Morrone. One award to a literary book-length translation into English published in 1991. (No technical, scientific or reference.) Deadline: Dec. 31.

PEN/JERARD FUND, PEN American Center, 568 Broadway, New York NY 10012. (212)334-1660. FAX: (212)334-2181. Contact: John Morrone. Estab. 1986. Biennial grant for American woman writer of nonfiction for a booklength work in progress in odd-numbered years. Next award: 1993. Deadline: Jan. 15.

PEN/MARTHA ALBRAND AWARD FOR NONFICTION, PEN American Center, 568 Broadway, New York NY 10012. (212)334-1660. FAX: (212)334-2181. Coordinator: John Morrone. Eligible books must have been published in the calendar year under consideration. Authors must be American citizens or permanent residents. Although there are no restrictions on the subject matter of titles submitted, non-literary books will not be considered. Books should be of adult nonfiction for the general or academic reader. For a first-published book of general nonfiction distinguished by qualities of literary and stylistic excellence. Deadline: Dec. 31. Publishers, agents and authors themselves must submit *three* copies of each eligible title. $1,000 prize.

PEN/REVSON FOUNDATION FELLOWSHIPS, PEN American Center, 568 Broadway, New York NY 10012. (212)334-1660. FAX: (212)334-2131. Contact: John Morrone. "A candidate for the fellowship will be a writer in 'early-mid career' whose body of work to date (normally no more than two books) has been marked by singular talent but has not been sufficiently recognized by the literary community and the reading public. The Fellowship is intended to assist the writer at a point in the candidate's career where monetary support and critical encouragement may be particularly needed. Deadline for poetry submissions is Jan. 15, 1993. Deadline for fiction submissions is Jan. 15, 1992. Candidates must be nominated by an editor or a fellow writer. It is strongly recommended that the nominator write a letter of support, describing the literary quality of the candidate's work and explaining in some detail why the candidate's published work has not yet met with the recognition it merits. Three copies of no more than fifty pages of current work, intended as part of a new book, must be submitted."

PEN/SPIELVOGEL-DIAMONSTEIN AWARD, PEN American Center, 568 Broadway, New York NY 10012. (212)334-1660. FAX: (212)334-2181. Coordinator: John Morrone. For the best previously un-published collection of essays on any subject by an American writer. The $5,000 prize is awarded to preserve the dignity and esteem that the essay form imparts to literature. Authors must be American citizens or permanent residents. The essays included in books submitted may have been previously published in magazines, journals or anthologies, but must not have collectively appeared before in book form. Books will be judged on the basis of the literary character and distinction of the writing. *Three* copies of each eligible title may be submitted by publishers, agents, or the authors themselves. Deadline: Dec. 31.

PERKINS PLAYWRITING CONTEST, International Society of Dramatists, Box 1310, Miami FL 33153. (305)531-1530. Award Director: A. Delaplaine. Unproduced full-length plays, any genre, any style. Awards plus staged reading and possible future production. Travel and expenses. Deadline: Dec. 6.

PHI BETA KAPPA BOOK AWARDS, The Phi Beta Kappa Society, 1811 Q St. NW, Washington DC 20009. (202)265-3808. Contact: Linda Surles. Estab. 1776. "Annual award to recognize and honor outstanding scholarly books published in the United States in the fields of the humanities, the social sciences, and the natural sciences and mathematics." Deadline: April 30. "Authors may request information, however it is requested that books be submitted by the publisher." Entries must be the works of authors who are U.S. citizens or residents.

‡ROBERT J. PICKERING AWARD FOR PLAYWRIGHTING EXCELLENCE, Coldwater Community Theater, % 89 Division, Coldwater MI 49036. (517)279-7963. Committee Chairperson: J. Richard Colbeck. Previously unproduced monetarily. "To encourage playwrights to submit their work, to present a previously unproduced play in full production." Deadline: end of November. Guidelines for #10 SASE. Prize: 1st prize, $200, 2nd prize $50, 3rd prize, $25. "We reserve right to produce winning manuscript."

PLAYWRIGHTS' CENTER JEROME PLAYWRIGHT-IN-RESIDENCE FELLOWSHIP, The Playwrights' Center, 2301 Franklin Ave. E, Minneapolis MN 55406. (612)332-7481. Estab. 1976. To provide emerging playwrights with funds and services to aid them in the development of their craft. Deadline: Jan. 15, 1992. Open to playwrights only—may not have had more than 2 fully staged productions of their works by professional theaters. Must spend fellowship year in Minnesota at Playwrights' Center. U.S. citizens only.

PLAYWRIGHTS' CENTER McKNIGHT FELLOWSHIP, The Playwrights' Center, 2301 Franklin Ave. E, Minneapolis MN 55406. (612)332-7481. Estab. 1982. Recognition of playwrights whose work has made a significant impact on the contemporary theater. Deadline: Dec. 16. Open to playwrights only. Must have had a minimum of two fully staged productions by professional theaters. Must spend 1 or 2 months at Playwrights' Center. U.S. citizens only.

THE PLAYWRIGHTS' CENTER MIDWEST PLAYLABS, The Playwrights' Center, 2301 Franklin Ave. E, Minneapolis MN 55406. (612)332-7481. Assists in the development of unproduced or unpublished new plays. Deadline: Dec. 2. Playwrights only; no one acts, musicals or childrens plays; and must be available for entire pre-conference and conference.

‡PLAYWRIGHTS' FORUM AWARDS, Theatreworks/Colorado, Box 7150, Colorado Springs CO 80933-7150. (719)593-3232. Producing Director: Whit Andrews. Submissions to be unpublished. To recognize excellence in playwriting in the one-act form. Deadline: Dec. 1.

‡PLAYWRIGHT'S-IN-RESIDENCE GRANTS, c/o HPRL, INTAR Hispanic-American Theater, P.O. Box 788, New York NY 10108. (212)695-6134. Estab. 1980. Residency grant for Hispanic-American playwrights. Deadline: June 30.

PLAYWRIGHTS PROJECT, P.O. Box 2068, San Diego CA 92112. (619)232-6188. Contact: Deborah Salzer. Estab. 1985. For Californians under 19 years of age. Every writer receives an individualized script critique if requested in cover letter; selected scripts receive professional productions. Deadline varies from May to June. Request for poster is sufficient. For California residents under 19 years of age.

EDGAR ALLAN POE AWARD, Mystery Writers of America, Inc. 236 W. 27th St. #600, New York NY 10001. (212)255-7005. Entries must be copyrighted or produced/published in the year they are submitted. Deadline: Dec. 1. Entries for the book categories are usually submitted by the publisher but may be submitted by the author or his agent.

‡POET HUNT, *The MacGuffin* and Schoolcraft College, 18600 Haggerty Rd., Livonia MI 48152. (313)462-4400 ext. 5292. Contest Director: Arthur J. Lindenberg. Previously unpublished poems. Submit Nov. 30-Feb. 10. Guidelines for #10 SASE. Charges 75¢ per poem. Prizes: 1st place $100, 2nd place $50, 3rd place $25 and publication.

POETRY ARTS PROJECT CONTEST, United Resource Press, Suite 388, 4521 Campus Drive, Irvine CA 92715. Director: Charlene B. Brown. Poetry with social commentary. Prizes awarded in US Savings Bonds. Deadline: April 15. Send SASE for entry form. Must sign release. Charges $3 per poem jury fee.

‡**THE POETRY CENTER BOOK AWARD**, The Poetry Center, San Francisco State University, 1600 Holloway Ave., San Francisco CA 94132. (415)338-2227. Award Director: Ashley McNeely. Estab. 1980. Previously published books of poetry and chapbooks, appearing in year of the prize. "Prize given for an extraordinary book of American poetry." Deadline Dec. 31. Guidelines for #10 SASE. Charges $5 per book. Prize: $500 and an invitation to read in The Poetry Center Reading Series.

‡**POETRY CONTEST**, The Poet Band Co. P.O. Box 2648, Newport News VA 23609. (804)874-2428. Contest Director: Arthur C. Ford. Estab. 1984. Semi-annual contest for previously unpublished poetry. Deadlines in Sept. and March. Guidelines for #10 SASE. Charges $3 per poem.

POETRY MAGAZINE POETRY AWARDS, 60 W. Walton St., Chicago IL 60610. (312)280-4870. Editor: Joseph Parisi. Estab. 1912. All poems published in *Poetry* are automatically considered for prizes.

POETS AND PATRONS, INC. INTERNATIONAL NARRATIVE POETRY CONTEST, 1206 Hutchings, Glenview IL 60025. Director: Constance Vogel. Deadline: Sept. 1. *Must* send for rules after March 1.

POETS CLUB OF CHICAGO INTERNATIONAL SHAKESPEAREAN SONNET CONTEST, 2930 Franklin St., Highland IN 46332. Chairman: June Shipley. Deadline: Sept. 1. Rules available after March 1. SASE required.

RENATO POGGIOLI TRANSLATION AWARD, PEN American Center, 568 Broadway, New York NY 10012. (212)334-1660. FAX: (212)334-2181. "Given to encourage a beginning and promising translator who is working on a first book length translation from Italian into English." Deadline: Jan. 15.

‡**FELIX POLLAK/CHRIS O'MALLEY PRIZES IN POETRY AND FICTION**, *The Madison Review*, Dept. of English, 600 N. Park St., Madison WI 53706. (608)263-3374. Director: Ronald Kuka. Offered annually for previously unpublished work. "The Felix Pollak contest awards $500 to the best poems submitted, out of a field of around 500 submissions yearly. The purpose of the prize is to award good poets. Submissions must consist of three poems. The Chris O'Malley prize in Fiction of $250 is awarded to the best piece of fiction." Deadline: Sept. 30. Prize: poetry $500; fiction $250; plus publication in the spring issue of *The Madison Review*. All contest entries are considered as submissions to *The Madison Review*, the literary journal sponsoring the contest. No simultaneous submissions to other publications."

PRAIRIE SCHOONER BERNICE SLOTE AWARD, *Prairie Schooner*, 201 Andrews, University of Nebraska, Lincoln NE 68588-0334. (402)472-3191. FAX: (402)472-4636 Editor: Hilda Raz. Estab. 1984. Work by a beginning writer previously published in *Prairie Schooner*. Annual award given for best work by a beginning writer from that year's volume.

PRAIRIE SCHOONER STROUSSE AWARD, *Prairie Schooner*, 201 Andrews, University of Nebraska, Lincoln NE 68588-0334. (402)472-3191. FAX: (402)472-2410. Editor: Hilda Raz. Estab. 1977. Poem or group of poems previously published in *Prairie Schooner*. Annual award given for the best poem or group of poems in that year's volume.

‡**PRISM INTERNATIONAL FICTION CONTEST**, *Prism International*, University of British Columbia, Buch E462, 1866 Main Mall, Vancouver British Columbia V6T 1W5 Canada. (604)228-2514. Contest Director: Pierre Stolte. Previously unpublished fiction. Deadline: Dec. 1. Guidelines for #10 SASE with Canadian postage or #10 SAE with 1 IRC. Charges $10 plus per story submitted. Prizes: $2,000 first prize, 5 honorable mentions of $200 each.

PRIX ALVINE-BELISLE, ASTED, 1030 Cherrier, Bureau 505, Montreal, Quebec H2L 1H9 Canada. FAX: (514)521-9561. Agent: Johanne PeTel. Estab. 1974. French-Canadian literature for children submitted by the publisher.

‡**PROFESSIONAL DEVELOPMENT GRANTS**, RI State Council on the Arts, Suite 103, 95 Cedar St., Providence RI 02903. (401)277-3880. Contact: Edward Holgate. Twice-yearly application deadline. "Travel Grants provide funds to an individual artists for an impending out-of-state travel opportunity that will significantly impact upon the artist's work and/or art career." Deadline: April 1, October 1. Send 9 × 12 SASE for contest guidelines. Prize: non-matching grants of $100-1,000.

PULITZER PRIZES, The Pulitzer Prize Board, 702 Journalism, Columbia University, New York NY 10027. (212)854-3841. Secretary: Robert C. Christopher. Awards for journalism in U.S. newspapers (published daily or weekly), and in literature, drama and music by Americans. Deadline: Feb. 1 (journalism); March 14 (music); March 1 (drama); July 1 and Nov. 1 (letters).

PULP PRESS INTERNATIONAL 3-DAY NOVEL WRITING CONTEST, Pulp Press Book Publishers Ltd., 100-1062 Homer St., Vancouver, British Columbia V6B 2W9 Canada. (604)687-4233. Contact: Brian Lam. Estab. 1972. Best novel written in three days; specifically, over the Labor Day weekend. Entrants return finished novels to Pulp Press for judging. Deadline: Friday before Labor Day weekend. Charges $7 fee.

PURE-BRED DOGS AMERICAN KENNEL GAZETTE FICTION CONTEST. The American Kennel Club, 51 Madison Ave., New York NY 10010. Cash prize to top three winners. First place receives $500 and publication. Guidelines for #10 SASE.

ERNIE PYLE AWARD, Scripps Howard Foundation, P.O. Box 5380, Cincinnati OH 45201. (513)977-3035. Estab. 1953. Human-interest reporting by a newspaper man or woman.

‡**QRL POETRY SERIES**, *Quarterly Review of Literature*, 26 Haslet Ave., Princeton NJ 08540. (609)921-6976. Contact: Renée Weiss. An open competition that awards $1,000, plus 100 copies and publication to each winner for a book of miscellaneous poems, a single long poem, a poetic play, a book of translation. Submission May and October *only*. $20 subscription to the series. Send SASE for complete information.

‡**READER RITER POLL**, *Affaire de Coeur*, 1555 Washington Ave., San Leandro CA 94577. (415)357-5665. Director: Barbara N. Keenan. Awards for previously published material in five categories appearing in magazine. Deadline: March 15.

‡**THE BYRON HERBERT REECE INTERNATIONAL POETRY AWARDS**, Georgia State Poetry Society, Inc., 2233 Drew Valley Rd. NE, Atlanta GA 30319. (404)939-1924. Contest Director: Virginia Cole Veal. Estab. 1987. Previously unpublished poetry. "To honor the late Georgia poet, Byron Herbert Reece." Deadline in Jan. Guidelines for #10 SASE. Charges $5 for the first poem; $1 for each additional poem. Prizes: First: $250, Second: $100, Third: $50.

‡**REUBEN AWARD**, National Cartoonists Society, Suite 904, 157 W. 57th St., New York NY 10019. (212)333-7606. "Outstanding Cartoonist of the Year" chosen from National Cartoonists Society membership.

‡**RHODE ISLAND STATE COUNCIL ON THE ARTS FELLOWSHIP**, Suite 103, 95 Cedar St., Providence RI 02903. (401)277-3880. Award Director: Edward Holgate. Poetry, fiction or play, must be a resident of Rhode Island and cannot be a student in a degree—or certificate—granting program of study. Deadline: April 1.

RHYME TIME CREATIVE WRITING COMPETITION, *Rhyme Time/Story Time*, Box 1870, Hayden ID 83835. (208)772-6184. Award Director: Linda Hutton. Rhymed poetry, fiction and essays. Deadline: first and fifteenth of each month. Send #10 SASE for rules.

THE HAROLD U. RIBALOW PRIZE, *Hadassah Magazine*, 50 W. 58th St., New York NY 10019. Executive Editor: Alan M. Tigay. English-language book of fiction on a Jewish theme. Deadline: Feb/March. "Books published in a given year will be eligible for the following year's prize. For example, books published in 1991 will be eligible for the 1992 Ribalow prize."

MARY ROBERTS RINEHART FUND, English Department, George Mason University, 4400 University Dr., Fairfax VA 22030-4444. (703)323-2396. Contact: Roger Lathbury. Grants by nomination to unpublished creative writers for fiction, poetry, drama, biography, autobiography or history with a strong narrative quality. Submissions are accepted for fiction and poetry in odd years, and nonfiction and drama in even years. Deadline: Nov. 30.

‡*RIVER CITY* **WRITING AWARDS IN FICTION**, *River City* and Memphis State University, *River City*, Dept. of English, Memphis TN 38152. (901)678-4509. Editor: Sharon Bryan. Estab. 1980. Previously unpublished fiction. *River City* receives right of first refusal to publish any manuscript entered in contest. Deadline usually first week in Dec. Guidelines for #10 SASE. Charges $6 fee. "The $6 fee may be applied toward a subscription to *River City*. Subscribers do not have to pay fee." Prizes: first: $2,000, second: $500, third: $300.

ROBERTS WRITING AWARDS, H.G. Roberts Foundation, Inc., P.O. Box 1868, Pittsburg KS 66762. (316)231-2998. Contact: Stephen Meats. Estab. 1988. Competitions in unpublished poetry, short fiction, and informal essays. No limitations on subject matter or form. Deadline: Sept. 15. Charges $6 for 1-5 poems; additional poems $1 each. Short fiction, essays, $6 each. Open to English language works by any writers. SASE for guidelines and entry form.

THE LOIS AND RICHARD ROSENTHAL NEW PLAY PRIZE, Cincinnati Playhouse in the Park, Box 6537, Cincinnati OH 45206. (513)421-5440. Unpublished plays. "Scripts must not have received a full-scale professional production." Deadline: Oct. 15-Jan. 15.

‡**WILLIAM B. RUGGLES JOURNALISM SCHOLARSHIP**, National Right to Work Committee, Suite 500, 8001 Braddock Rd., Springfield VA 22160. (703)321-9820. FAX: (703)321-7342. Contact: Director, Public Relations. "To honor the late William B. Ruggles, editor emeritas of the Dallas Morning News, who coined the phrase 'Right to Work.' " Deadline: Jan. 1 through March 31. Prize: 1- $2,000 scholarship. "We do reserve the right to reprint the material/excerpt from the essay in publicizing the award. Applicant must be a graduate of undergraduate student majoring in journalism in institutions of higher learning throughout the U.S."

‡**ST. LOUIS LITERARY AWARD**, Associates of St. Louis University Libraries, 40 N. Kingshighway, St. Louis MO 63108. (314)361-1616. Contact: Award Committee. Estab. 1967. Annual award. Works are nominated by committee.

‡**THE CARL SANDBURG LITERARY ARTS AWARDS**, The Friends of the Chicago Public Library, 78 E. Washington St., Chicago IL 60602. (312)269-2922. Chicago writers of published fiction, nonfiction, poetry and children's literature.

‡**THE BARBARA SAVAGE "MILES FROM NOWHERE" MEMORIAL AWARD**, The Mountaineers Books, Suite 107, 1011 SW Klickitat Way, Seattle WA 98134. (800)553-4453. Award Director: Donna DeShazo. Award offered every two years for previously unpublished prose. Acceptable subjects include personal narratives involving hiking, mountain climbing, bicycling, paddle sports, skiing, snow-shoeing, nature, conservation, ecology and adventure travel not involving public transport. Deadline: Feb. 1. Guidelines for #10 SASE. Prize: $3,000 cash award, a $12,000 guaranteed advance against royalties and publication by The Mountaineers.

SCHOLASTIC WRITING AWARDS, Scholastic Inc., 730 Broadway, New York NY 10003. (212)505-3566. Estab. 1923. Fiction, nonfiction, poetry and drama (for students in grades 7-12 only). Write for complete information. Cash prizes, equipment prizes and scholarships. Deadline: August-December.

THE CHARLES M. SCHULZ AWARD, Scripps Howard Foundation, P.O. Box 5380, Cincinnati OH 45201. (513)977-3035. Estab. 1980. For a student cartoonist at a college newspaper or magazine.

THE SCIENCE AWARD, The Phi Beta Kappa Society, 1811 Q St. NW, Washington DC 20009. (202)265-3808. Contact: Administrator, Phi Beta Kappa Book Awards. Estab. 1959. Interpretations of the physical or biological sciences or mathematics published in the U.S. during the 12-month period preceding the entry deadline, and submitted by the publisher. Books that are exclusively histories of science are *not* eligible, nor are biographies of scientists in which a narrative emphasis predominates. Works of fiction are not eligible. Deadline: April 30.

‡**SCIENCE IN SOCIETY JOURNALISM AWARDS**, National Association of Science Writers, Box 294, Greenlawn NY 11740. (516)757-5664. Contact: Diane McGurgan. Newspaper, magazine and broadcast science writing. Deadline: July 1 for work published June 1-May 31 of previous year.

SCIENCE-WRITING AWARD IN PHYSICS AND ASTRONOMY, American Institute of Physics, 335 E. 45th St., New York NY 10017. (212)661-9404. Contact: Public Information Division. Previously published articles, booklets or books "that improve public understanding of physics and astronomy." Deadline: Jan. 10 for professional writers; May 10 for physicists, astronomers or members of AIP member and affililated societies; Oct. 10 for articles or books intended for children preschool to 15 years old.

CHARLES E. SCRIPPS AWARD, Scripps Howard Foundation, P.O. Box 5380, Cincinnati OH 45201. (513)977-3035. Estab. 1986. Combatting illiteracy, by a newspaper, television, cable and/or radio station.

THE EDWARD WILLIS SCRIPPS AWARD, Scripps Howard Foundation, P.O. Box 5380, Cincinnati OH 45201. (513)977-3035. Estab. 1976. Service to the First Amendment by a newspaper.

SENIOR AWARD, International Society of Dramatists, Box 1310, Miami FL 33153. Award Director: A. Delaplaine. Previously unpublished scripts (any media or length) written by college students. Award plus staged reading and possible future production. Deadline: May 1.

SEVENTEEN MAGAZINE FICTION CONTEST, 850 3rd Ave., New York NY 10022. Estab. 1948. Previously unpublished short stories from writers 13-21 years old. Deadline: March 31.

SHELLEY MEMORIAL AWARD, Poetry Society of America, 15 Gramercy Park S., New York NY 10003. (212)254-9628. Contact: Award Director. Deadline: Dec. 31. By nomination only to a living American poet.

SHIRAS INSTITUTE/MILDRED & ALBERT PANOWSKI PLAYWRITING AWARD, (formerly Forest A. Roberts Playwriting Award), Forest A. Roberts Theatre, Northern Michigan University, Marquette MI 49855-5364. (906)227-2553. Award Director: Dr. James A. Panowski. Estab. 1978. Unpublished, unproduced plays. Scripts must be *received* on or before Nov. 22.

SHORT STORY CONTEST, *Japanophile*, P.O. Box 223, Okemos MI 48864. (517)249-1795. Contact: Earl Snodgrass. Annual award for unpublished fiction "that leads to a better understanding of Japanese culture. We prefer a setting in Japan and at least one Japanese and one non-Japanese character." Entry fee: $5. Deadline: Dec. 31.

SIENA COLLEGE PLAYWRIGHTS' COMPETITION, Siena College Theatre Program, Department of Fine Arts, Loudonville NY 12211. (518)783-2381. Director of Theatre: Mark A. Heckler. Contest offered during even numbered years to recognize unpublished and unproduced works of playwrights, professional and amateur. Winning playwright required to participate in six-week residency on college campus to prepare play for production. Deadline: Feb. 1 - June 30. $2,000 prize plus $1,000 in living expenses for residency. Write for contest guidelines.

SIERRA REPERTORY THEATRE, P.O. Box 3030, Sonora CA 95370. (209)532-3120. Estab. 1980. Full-length plays. Deadline: May 15.

‡**SILVER BRIDLE NATIONAL PLAYWRIGHTS COMPETITION**, ProRodeo Hall of Fame, P.O. Box 392, Manitou Springs CO 80829. Contact: Director. "To increase the general appreciation of the heritage of the frontier and to provide an outlet for an under-developed area of historical theater." Deadline Jan. 31. Guidelines for 9×14 SAE with 2 first class stamps. Prize: $500, performance and royalties.

DOROTHY SILVER PLAYWRITING COMPETITION, (formerly JCC Theatre of Cleveland Playwriting Competition), Jewish Community Center, 3505 Mayfield Rd., Cleveland Heights OH 44118. (216)382-4000, ext. 275. FAX: (216)382-5401. Contact: Elaine Rembrandt. Estab. 1948. All entries must be original works, not previously produced, suitable for a full-length presentation; directly concerned with the Jewish experience. Deadline: Dec. 15.

CHARLIE MAY SIMON AWARD, Arkansas State Dept. of Education, University of Central Arkansas, P.O. Box 4918, Conway AR 72032. (501)450-3177. Chair: Dr. Jody Charter. Award for books published three years previous to award year that allows Arkansas children in grades 4-6 to vote for their favorite book from a list selected by a committee designated by Elementary Council, Arkansas DOE Books for committee's reading selected in June each year. Nominations are collected in the spring from schools or other interested parties.

SMALL PRESS PUBLISHER OF THE YEAR, Quality Books Inc., 918 Sherwood Dr., Lake Bluff IL 60044-2204. (312)295-2010. FAX: (708)295-1556. Contact: Tom Drewes. Estab. 1964. "Each year a publisher is named that publishes titles we stock and has demonstrated ability to produce a timely and topical title, suitable for libraries, attains "quality bestseller status and supports their distributor." Title must have been selected for stocking by Quality Books Inc. QBI is the principal nationwide distributor of small press titles to libraries.

‡**THE JOHN BEN SNOW PRIZE**, Syracuse University Press, 1600 Jamesville Ave., Syracuse NY 13244. (315)443-5534. FAX: (315)443-5545. Contact: Charles Backus. Offered annually for unpublished submissions. The John Ben Snow Prize, inaugurated in 1978, is given annually by Syracuse University Press to the author of a nonfiction manuscript dealing with some aspect of New York State. The purpose of the award is to encourage the writing of books of genuine significance and literary distinction that will augment knowledge of New York State and appreciation for its unique physical, historical and cultural characteristics. A manuscript based on direct, personal experience will receive the same consideration as one relying on scholarly research. The criteria are authenticity, accuracy, readability

and importance. Deadline: Dec. 31. Prize: $1,500 to the author and publication by Syracuse University Press. Send for contest rules and entry forms.

‡SOCIETY OF MIDLAND AUTHORS AWARD, Society of Midland Authors, % Bowman, 152 N. Scoville, Oak Park IL 60302-2642. (708)383-7568. FAX: (708)524-9233. Contact: Award Director. Award offered annually for previously published (between Jan. 1 and Dec. 31) work. "Award for the creation of a closer association among writers of the Middle West, and the stimulation of creative literary effort. 7 categories: poetry, adult fiction, adult nonfiction, biography, juvenile fiction, juvenile nonfiction, drama." Deadline: Dec. 15. SASE for award guidelines. Money (upwards of $300) and plaque given at annual dinner, Drake Hotel, Chicago, in May.

C.L. SONNICHSEN BOOK AWARD, Texas Western Press of the University of Texas at El Paso, El Paso TX 79968-0633. (915)747-5688. Press Director: Dale L. Walker. Estab. 1952. Previously unpublished nonfiction manuscript dealing with the history, literature or cultures of the Southwest. Deadline: March 1.

‡SOUTH CAROLINA NEW PLAY FESTIVAL, Trustus Theatre, P.O. Box 11721, Columbia SC 29211. (803)254-9732. Contact: Jim Thigpen. Offered annually for previously unpublished work. "Playwright must be SC native or current or former resident, or have attended school in SC. Full-length plays, one-acts, plays for young audiences accepted. No musicals, cast limit 8." Deadline: April 1. Contact by phone between 1-6 pm. Prize: 1st place $1,000, full production, travel and housing for rehearsals; 2nd place $500 plus staged reading.

‡SOUTHERN PLAYWRIGHTS COMPETITION, Center for Southern Studies/Jacksonville State University, Pelham Rd., Jacksonville AL 36265. (205)782-5412. FAX: (205)782-5291. Contact: Steven J. Whitton. Offered annually for previously unpublished/unproduced work. "The Center for Southern Studies seeks to identify and encourage the best of Southern Playwrighting." Deadline: Feb. 15. SASE for contest guidelines. Prize: $1,000 and a production of the play. Playwrights must be native to or resident of AL, AR, FL, GA, KY, LA, MS, NC, SC, TN, TX, VA, or WV.

SOUTHERN PLAYWRITING COMPETITION, Festival of Southern Theatre, Dept. of Theatre Arts Univ. of Mississippi, University MS 38677. (601)232-5816. Contact: Scott McCoy. Competiton for unpublished and unproduced original full-length scripts for the theatre by a Southern writer or a work with a markedly Southern theme. Deadline: Dec. 1. Three winners annually are awarded $1,000 each and full professional production.

THE SOUTHERN REVIEW/LOUISIANA STATE UNIVERSITY SHORT FICTION AWARD, Louisiana State University, 43 Allen Hall, Baton Rouge LA 70803. (504)388-5108. Selection Committee Chairman: Warren Eyster. First collection of short stories by an American published in the U.S. during previous year. Deadline: Jan. 31. A publisher or an author may submit an entry by mailing two copies of the collection to *The Southern Review* Short Story Award.

SOUTHWEST REVIEW AWARDS, Southern Methodist University, 6410 Airline Rd., Dallas TX 75275. (214)373-7440. Annual awards for fiction, nonfiction and poetry published in the magazine. The $1,000 John H. McGinnis Memorial Award is given each year for fiction and nonfiction that has been published in the *Southwest Review* in the previous year. Stories or articles are not submitted directly for the award, but simply for publication in the magazine. The Elizabeth Matchett Stover Award, an annual prize of $150 is awarded to the author of the best poem or group of poems published in the magazine during the preceding year.

‡SOVEREIGN AWARD OUTSTANDING NEWSPAPER STORY, OUTSTANDING FEATURE STORY, The Jockey Club of Canada, P.O. Box 156, Rexdale, Ontario M9W 5L2 Canada. (416)675-7756. Contact: Nigel P.H. Wallace. Estab. 1975. To recognize outstanding achievement in the area of Canadian thoroughbred racing of work published in the previous year. Newspaper Story: Appeared in a newspaper by a racing columnist on Canadian Racing subject matter. Outstanding Feature Story: Appeared in a magazine book or newspaper, written as feature story on Canadian Racing subject matter. Deadline: Oct. 31. There is no nominating process other than the writer submitting no more than two entries per category. Special Criteria: Must be published between Nov. 1 and Oct. 31 and be of Canadian racing content.

‡THE SOW'S EAR POETRY PRIZE, The Sow's Ear Poetry Journal, 245 McDowell St., Bristol TN 37620. (615)764-1625. Contest Director: Errol Hess. Estab. 1988. Previously unpublished poetry. Submit Sept.-Oct. Guidelines for #10 SASE. Charges $2 fee per poem. Prize: $500 and publication. All submissions considered for publication.

BRYANT SPANN MEMORIAL PRIZE, History Dept., Indiana State University, Terre Haute IN 47809. Estab. 1980. Social criticism in the tradition of Eugene V. Debs. Deadline: April 30. SASE required. Prize: $1,000.

‡**SPECIAL LIBRARIES ASSOCIATION PUBLIC RELATIONS AWARD**, Special Libraries Association, 1700 18th St., NW, Washington DC 20009. (202)234-4700. FAX: (202)265-9317. Director, Communications: Mary Zimmermann. Estab. 1987. SLA's Public Relations Award is presented to a writer who develops an outstanding feature story on the special libraries profession published previous calendar year. The article must appear in a general-circulation magazine or newspaper. (Library journal magazine articles or submissions from librarians are not eligible.) Deadline: Dec. 31.

‡**SPUR AWARDS (WESTERN WRITERS OF AMERICA, INC.)**, WWA, P.O. Box 823, Sheridan WY 82801. (307)672-0889. Director: Barbara Ketcham. Estab. 1954. Ten categories of western: novel, historical novel, nonfiction book, juvenile nonfiction, juvenile fiction, nonfiction article, fiction short story, best TV script, movie screenplay, cover art. Also, Medicine Pipe Bearer's Award for best first novel. Deadline: Dec. 31. Submissions must be published in the calendar year they are submitted.

‡**SSSS STUDENT RESEARCH GRANT**, The Society for the Scientific Study of Sex, P.O. Box 208, Mount Vernon IA 52314. (319)895-8407. FAX: (319)895-6203. Contact: Patricia B. Koch, Ph.D. Offered twice a year. The Society for the Scientific Study of Sex will award two grants of $500 to a student doing research in the area of human sexuality. The purpose of the research can be a masters thesis or doctoral dissertation, but this is not a requirement. Applicants must be enrolled in a degree-granting program. Deadline: Feb. 1 and Sept. 1. SASE. Prize: $500.

‡**ANN STANFORD POETRY PRIZE**, Southern California Anthology, % Master of Professional Writing Program, WPH 404, U.S.C., Los Angeles CA 90089-4034. (213)740-3252. Contest Director: Dr. James Ragan. Estab. 1988. Previously unpublished poetry. "To honor excellence in poetry in memory of poet and teacher Ann Stanford." Deadline: March 15. Guidelines for #10 SASE. Charges $10 fee. First Prize $750, Second Prize $250, Third Prize $100. Winning poems are published in *The Southern California Anthology*.

STANLEY DRAMA AWARD, Wagner College, Staten Island NY 10301. (212)390-3256. Estab. 1957. Unpublished and nonprofessionally produced full-length plays, musicals or related one-acts by American playwrights. Submissions must be accompanied by completed application and written recommendation by theatre professional or drama teacher. First prize: $2,000, possibility of production. Deadline: Sept. 1.

THE AGNES LYNCH STARRETT POETRY PRIZE, University of Pittsburgh Press, 127 N. Bellefield Ave., Pittsburgh PA 15260. (412)624-4110. FAX: (412)624-7380. Estab. 1936. First book of poetry for poets who have not had a full-length book published. Deadline: March and April only. Write for complete guidelines for manuscript submission.

STEGNER FELLOWSHIP, Stanford Creative Writing Program, Stanford University, Stanford CA 94305-2087. (415)723-2637. Contact: Prof. Nancy Packer. Annual fellowships include all tuition costs and a living stipend (four in fiction and four in poetry) for writers to come to Stanford for a period of two years to attend workshop to develop their particular writing. Deadline: Jan. 1. Charges $20 fee.

I.F STONE AWARD FOR STUDENT JOURNALISM, *The Nation*, 72 5th Ave., New York NY 10011. (212)242-8400. Director: Peter Meyer. Annual award "to recognize excellence in student journalism." Deadline: June 30.

THE WALKER STONE AWARDS, Scripps Howard Foundation, P.O. Box 5380, Cincinnati OH 45201. (513)977-3035. Estab. 1973. Editorial writing by a newspaper man or woman.

‡**STORY TIME SHORT STORY CONTEST**, Hutton Publications, P.O. Box 1870, Hayden ID 83835. (208)772-6184. Contest Director: Linda Hutton. Quarterly contest for previously published or unpublished short fiction. "To encourage beginning short story writers." Deadlines vary. Guidelines for #10 SASE.

‡**STUDENT GRANT-IN-AID**, American Translators Association, % Dr. Anne Cordero, 3818 N. Ridgeview Rd., Arlington VA 22207 (914)941-1500. Contact: Chair, Honors & Awards Committee. Support is granted for a promising project to an unpublished student enrolled in a translation program at a U.S. college or university. Deadline: Feb. 28. Open to any student enrolled in a translation program at a U.S. college or university. Must be sponsored by a faculty member.

‡**AMAURY TALBOT PRIZE FUND FOR AFRICAN ANTHROPOLOGY,** Charitable Will Trust, Trust Management Office, 61 Group, Octagon House, Gadbrook Park, Northwich CW9 7RE England. Annual award for previously published nonfiction (between Jan. 1 and December 31). Deadline: March 31. Guidelines for #10 SAE and 1 IRC.

‡**TANTALUS POETRY SOCIETY COMPETITION,** P.O. Box 39675, Atwater Village CA 90039. (818)242-7519. Contest Director: Harry Crosby. Estab. 1989. Quarterly competition for previously unpublished poetry. "To give support to poets of talent, whose works possess substance and may or may not be widely known. All themes, types of poetry, and use of language are welcome." Deadlines: March 1, June 1, Sept. 1, Dec. 1. Guidelines for #10 SASE. Charges $5 for up to three poems. Prizes: First $250; two Seconds $125; three Thirds $50.

MARVIN TAYLOR PLAYWRITING AWARD, Sierra Repertory Theatre, P.O. Box 3030, Sonora CA 95370. (209)532-3120. Producing Director: Dennis C. Jones. Estab. 1980. Full-length plays. Deadline: May 15.

THE TEN BEST "CENSORED" STORIES OF 1991, Project Censored — Sonoma State University, Rohnert Park CA 94928. (707)664-2500. FAX: (707)664-2505. Award Director: Carl Jensen, Ph.D. Estab. 1976. Current published, nonfiction stories of national social significance that have been overlooked or under-reported by the news media. Deadline: Nov. 1.

‡**THE TENNESSEE WILLIAMS/NEW ORLEANS LITERARY FESTIVAL ONE-ACT PLAY AWARD,** Box 70495, New Orleans LA 70172. (504)522-9958. Contact: Dr. W. Kenneth Holditch. Offered annually. "The purpose of the contest is primarily to honor Tennessee Williams, who first made his name as a writer of one-act plays. Because there are few markets for such plays these days, we decided to honor this genre and its writers. Also, of course, we hope to turn up very good writers and very good plays and to offer them an opportunity to have their work showcased." Deadline: Feb. 1. SASE for guidelines. Charges $5 fee.

THE THEATRE LIBRARY ASSOCIATION AWARD, Theatre Library Association, New York Public Library at Lincoln Center, 111 Amsterdam Ave., New York NY 10023. (212)870-1638. Awards Committee Chair: Stephen M. Vallillo. Estab. 1973. Book published in the United States in the field of recorded performance, including motion pictures and television. Deadline: Feb. 1.

THEATRE MEMPHIS NEW PLAY COMPETITION, Theatre Memphis, P.O. Box 240117, Memphis TN 38124-0117. (901)682-8323. Estab. 1984. Award offered every 3 years "To promote new playwrights' works and new works by established playwrights." No musicals. Bound scripts only. Deadline for script entry: Sept. 1, 1993. Include SASE if scripts are to be returned.

TOWSON STATE UNIVERSITY PRIZE FOR LITERATURE, College of Liberal Arts, Towson State University, Towson MD 21204. (301)830-2128. Award Director: Dean Annette Chappell. Estab. 1979. Book or book-length manuscript that has been accepted for publication, written by a Maryland author of no more than 40 years of age. Deadline: May 15.

THE JOHN TRAIN HUMOR PRIZE, *The Paris Review,* 541 E. 72nd St., New York NY 10021. Contest/Award Director: George Plimpton. Estab. 1953. Unpublished humor — fiction, nonfiction or poetry, 10,000 words or less. Deadline: March 31.

THE TRANSLATION CENTER AWARDS, The Translation Center, 412 Dodge Hall, Columbia University, New York NY 10027. (212)854-2305. FAX: (212)749-0397. Executive Director: Frank MacShane. Awards are grants to a translator for an outstanding translation of a substantial part of a book length literary work from other languages into English. Deadline: Jan. 15. Award: $1,000-2,000.

UCROSS FOUNDATION RESIDENCY, 2836 U.S. Highway 14-16E, Clearmont WY 82835. (307)737-2291. Contact: Elizabeth Guheen. Four concurrent positions open for artists-in-residence in various disciplines (includes writers, visual artists, music, humanities) extending from 2 weeks-4 months. No charge for room, board or studio space. Deadline: March 1 for August-December program; Oct. 1 for January-May program.

UNDERGRADUATE ANNUAL PAPER COMPETITION IN CRYPTOLOGY, *Cryptologia,* Rose-Hulman Institute of Technology, Terre Haute IN 47803. Contact: Editor. Unpublished papers on cryptology. Deadline: Jan. 1.

‡**U.S. WEST FEST,** Denver Center Theatre Company, 1050 13th St., Denver CO 80204. (303)893-4200. FAX: (303)893-2860. Contest/Award Director: Barbara Sellers. Offered annually for unpublished work. "US West Fest is a new plays contest. Unproduced, full length plays are read and considered for the annual contest. Eight scripts are selected each year. Four of these scripts are then taken into full production in the following theatre season." Deadline: Dec. 31. Rules and entry form for SASE. A financial stipend awarded to the selected playwrights.

UNIVERSITY OF ALABAMA NEW PLAYWRIGHTS PROGRAM, Box 870239, Tuscaloosa AL 35487-0239. (205)348-9032. Director and Dramaturg: Dr. Paul C. Castagno. Estab. 1982. Full-length plays for mainstage; experimental plays for B stage. Workshops and radio plays can be proposed. SASE. Up to 6 months assessment time.

DANIEL VAROUJIAN AWARD, New England Poetry Club, Lois Ames, 285 Marlborough Rd., Sudbury MA 01776. Contact: Diana DerHovanessian. Unpublished poems in duplicate. Send SASE for rules. Deadline: June 30. Charges $2 per poem; no charge for New England Poetry Club members.

‡**VERVE POETRY CONTEST,** *VERVE* Magazine, P.O. Box 3205, Simi Valley CA 93093. Contest Director: Ron Reichick. Estab. 1989. Contest offered twice annually for previously unpublished poetry. "Fund raiser for *VERVE* Magazine which receives no grants and has no ties with any institutions." Deadlines: May 18 and Nov. 17. Guidelines for #10 SASE. Charges $2 per poem. Prizes: First $75, Second $20, Third $25, plus publication and copy of issue.

CELIA B. WAGNER AWARD, Poetry Society of America, 15 Gramercy Park St. S., New York NY 10003. (212)254-9628. Contact: Award Director. Unpublished poem. "Poem worthy of the tradition of the art in any style." Deadline: Dec. 31. Charges $5 fee.

EDWARD LEWIS WALLANT BOOK AWARD, Mrs. Irving Waltman, 3 Brighton Rd., West Hartford CT 06117. Published fiction with significance for the American Jew (novel or short stories) by an American writer. Book must have been published during current year. Deadline: Dec. 31.

THEODORE WARD PRIZE FOR PLAYWRITING, Columbia College Theater/Music Center, 72 E 11th St., Chicago IL 60605. Contact: Chuck Smith. Estab. 1985. "To uncover and identify new unpublished African American plays that are promising and produceable." Deadline: August 1. All rights for music or biographies must be secured prior to submission. All entrants must be of African American descent and residing within the U.S. Only one completed script per playwright will be accepted.

‡**THE WASHINGTON PRIZE,** The Word Works, P.O. Box 42164, Washington DC 20015. (202)543-1868. Contest Director: Beth McGrath. Estab. 1974. Previously unpublished poetry. Deadline March 1. Guidelines for #10 SASE. Charges $10 fee. Prize: $1,000 and publication.

WASHINGTON PRIZE FOR FICTION, Larry Kaltman Literary Agency, 1301 S. Scott St., Arlington VA 22204. (703)920-3771. Estab. 1989. Fiction, previously unpublished, of at least 65,000 words. Deadline: Nov. 30. Charges $25 fee. Prizes: $500, $250 and $100.

L. ARNOLD WEISSBERGER PLAYWRITING AWARD, New Dramatists, 424 W. 44th St., New York NY 10036. (212)757-6960. FAX: (212)581-4483. Contest/Award Director: Scott Stohler. Estab. 1984. Unpublished full-length plays; no musicals or children's plays. Accepting applications: Sept. 15-Feb. 1.

‡**WELLSPRING'S SHORT FICTION CONTEST,** Costalia Bookmakers, Inc., 770M Tonkawa Rd., Long Lake MN 55356. (612)471-9259. Contest Director: Maureen LaJoy. Estab. 1988. Contest offered twice annually for previously unpublished short fiction. "To encourage the writing of well-crafted and plotted, meaningful short fiction." Deadlines Jan. 1 and July 1. Guidelines for #10 SASE. Charges $5 fee. Prizes: $100, $75, $25.

WEST COAST ENSEMBLE FULL-PLAY COMPETITION, CELEBRATION OF ONE-ACTS, West Coast Ensemble, P.O. Box 38728, Los Angeles CA 90038. Artistic Director: Les Hanson. Estab. 1982. Unpublished (in Southern California) plays. No musicals or children's plays for full-play competition. No

Always check the most recent copy of a magazine for the address and editor's name before you send in a query or manuscript.

restrictions on subject matter for one-acts. Deadline: Nov. 15 for one-act plays; Dec. 31 for full-length plays.

WESTERN STATES BOOK AWARDS, Western States Arts Federation, 236 Montezuma Ave., Santa Fe NM 87501. (505)988-1166. Estab. 1984. Unpublished fiction, poetry or creative nonfiction, that has been accepted for publication in the award year, by a press in a Western States Arts Federation member state. Deadline: spring of the year preceding the award year. Open to authors in Alaska, Arizona, California, Colorado, Idaho, Montana, Nevada, New Mexico, Oregon, Utah, Washington, and Wyoming. Manuscript duplication and return postage fee of $10.

WHITING WRITERS' AWARDS, Mrs. Giles Whiting Foundation, Rm. 3500, 30 Rockefeller Plaza, New York NY 10112. Director: Gerald Freund. "For writers of poetry, fiction, nonfiction and plays. The awards place special emphasis on exceptionally promising emerging talent." Direct applications and informal nominations are not accepted by the Foundation.

WHITNEY-CARNEGIE AWARD, American Library Association Publishing Services, 50 E. Huron, Chicago IL 60611. (312)280-5416. FAX: (312)944-2641. Contact: Edgar S. McLarin. Submissions to be unpublished. "The grants are awarded to individuals for the preparation of bibliographic aids for research. The aids must be aimed at a scholarly audience but have a general applicability. Products prepared under this project must be offered to ALA Publishing Services for first consideration." Maximum award: $5,000. Deadline: Sept. 15.

WICHITA STATE UNIVERSITY PLAYWRITING CONTEST, Wichita State University Theatre, WSU, Box 31, Wichita KS 67208. (316)689-3185. Contest Director: Professor Bela Kiralyfalvi. Estab. 1974. Two or three short, unpublished, unproduced plays or full-length Gerald Freund. Estab. 1985. "For writers of poetry, fiction, nonfiction and plays. The awards place special emphasis on exceptionally promising emerging talent." Direct applications and informal nominations are not accepted by the Foundation.

BELL I. WILEY PRIZE, National Historical Society, 2245 Kohn Rd., P.O. Box 8200, Harrisburg PA 17105. (717)657-9555. Estab. 1981. Civil War and Reconstruction nonfiction (book). Biennial award. Deadline: July 31.

WILLIAM CARLOS WILLIAMS AWARD, Poetry Society of America, 15 Gramercy Park S., New York NY 10003. (212)254-9628. Contact: Award Director. Deadline: Dec. 31. Small press, nonprofit, or university press book of poetry submitted by publisher.

L.L. WINSHIP BOOK AWARD, *The Boston Globe*, 135 Morissey Blvd., Boston MA 02107. For a New England-related book. Deadline: June 30.

‡WISCONSIN ARTS BOARD INDIVIDUAL ARTIST PROGRAM, 131 W. Wilson St., #301, Madison WI 53705. (608)266-0190. Contact: Program Coordinator. Estab. 1973. Literary awards for Wisconsin writers in the categories of poetry, drama, fiction and essay/criticism. Deadline: Sept. 15.

WITTER BYNNER FOUNDATION FOR POETRY, INC. GRANTS, P.O. Box 2188, Santa Fe NM 87504. (505)988-3251. Executive Director: Steven D. Schwartz. Estab. 1972. Grants for poetry and poetry-related projects. Deadline: Feb. 1.

‡WOMEN IN THEATRE NEW PLAY GRANT, Women in Theatre, P.O. Box 3718, Hollywood CA 90078. (213)465-5567. Award Director: Nancy McFarland. "Annual grant to encourage the production of new plays written by emerging female playwrights." Deadline: Nov. Award: $1,000. "Contest is open to producing theaters, theater groups or independent producers. Playwrights *cannot* apply directly."

‡WOMEN'S WORDS WRITING COMPETITION, Still Waters Press, 112 W. Duerer St., Galloway Township NJ 08201-9402. Contest Director: Shirley A. Warren. Estab. 1989. "Purpose is the discovery and cultivation of short, but significant women's works in poetry, the essay and fiction." Deadline Dec. 31. Guidelines for #10 SASE. Charges $10 fee. Prize: 25 copies to the author, professional publicity package (press releases, review copy distribution), 50% discount on additional copies, royalties on second and subsequent press runs.

WORK-IN-PROGRESS GRANT, Society of Children's Book Writers and Judy Blume, P.O. Box 66296 Mar Vista, Los Angeles CA 90069. Write *SCBW* at preceding address. Two grants—one designated specifically for a contemporary novel for young people—to assist SCBW members in the completion of a specific project. Deadline: June 1.

WORK-IN-PROGRESS GRANT, Society of PLAY GRANT, Women in Theatre, P.O. Box 3718, Hollywood CA 90078. (213)465-5567. Award Director: Nancy McFarland. "Annual grant to encourage the production of new plays written by emerging female playwrights." Deadline: Nov. Award: $1,000. "Contest is open to producing theaters, theater groups or independent producers. Playwrights *cannot* apply directly."

WORLD'S BEST SHORT STORY CONTEST, English Department, Writing Program, Florida State University, Tallahassee FL 32306. (904)644-4230. Contact: Jerome Stern. Estab. 1986. Annual award for unpublished short short story (no more than 250 words). Send SASE for rules. Deadline: Feb. 15.

WRITER-IN-RESIDENCE PROGRAM, The Syvenna Foundation, Rt 1, Box 193, Linden TX 75563. (903)835-8252. Contact: Sylva Billue. Opportunity for beginning and intermediate women writers to have a cottage rent and utilities free for 2 or 3 months to pursue their craft. Four terms available each year. A $300/month stipend is also provided. All types of writing are considered. Deadline: Aug. 1, Oct. 1, Dec. 1., April 1.

‡**WRITERS AND ARTIST CONTEST**, *Midnight Zoo* Magazine, 544 Ygnacio Valley Rd., #A273, Walnut Creek CA 94596. (415)942-5116. FAX: (415)933-3801. Publisher: Jon L. Herron. Estab. 1990. Annual contest for unpublished works. Deadline Nov. 15. Guidelines #10 SASE. "All stories which are published by *Midnight Zoo* during that year are eligible for prizes except stories of staff members." Various prizes. No entry fee.

WRITERS DIGEST **WRITING COMPETITION**, *Writer's Digest Magazine*, F&W Publications, Inc., 1507 Dana Ave., Cincinnati OH 45207. (513)531-2222. Contest Director: Peter Blocksom. Submissions to be unpublished. Deadline: May 31.

‡**WRITERS FELLOWSHIPS**, NC Arts Council, Dept. of Cultural Resources, Raleigh NC 27601-2807. (919)733-2111. Literature Director: Deborah McGill. Offered annually. "To serve writers of fiction and poetry in North Carolina and to recognize the contribution they make to this state's creative environment." Deadline: Feb. 1. SASE for guidelines. We offer five $8,000 grants each year. Writer must have been a resident of NC for at least a year and may not be enrolled in any degree-granting program at the time of application.

‡**WRITERS GUILD OF AMERICA WEST AWARDS**, Writers Guild of America West, 8955 Beverly Blvd., West Hollywood CA 90048. Scripts (screen, TV and radio). Members only. Deadline: September.

‡**WYOMING ARTS COUNCIL LITERARY FELLOWHIPS**, Wyoming Arts Council, 2320 Capitol Ave. Cheyenne WY 82002. (307)777-7742. Literature Coordinator: Doug Black. Estab. 1986. Fellowships to honor the most outstanding previously published or unpublished new work by Wyoming writers (all genres: poetry, fiction, nonfiction, drama). Deadline: August 1, subject to change subsequent years. Writers may call WCA office; guidelines are also printed in monthly *All Arts Newsletter*. Applicants must have been Wyoming residents for one year prior to entry deadline – and must remain so for one year following – and may not be fulltime students.

Y.E.S. NEW PLAY FESTIVAL, Northern Kentucky University, 207FA, Department of Theatre, Highland Heights KY 41071. (606)572-6303. FAX: (606)572-5566. Artistic Director: Joe Conger. Estab. 1981. Deadline: August 25-Thanksgiving 1992 for scripts. Full-length plays, one-acts and musicals.

‡**YALE SERIES OF YOUNGER POETS**, Yale University Press, 92A Yale Station, New Haven CT 06520. Contact: Charles Grench. Previously unpublished poetry. Submit during Feb. Guidelines for #10 SASE. Charges $8 fee. "Winning ms is published by Yale University Press. The author receives the usual royalties."

‡**ANNA ZORNIO MEMORIAL THEATRE FOR YOUTH PLAYWRITING AWARD**, U of NH Youth Drama Program /TRY, Paul Creative Arts, Durbam NH 03824. (603)862-2150. Contact: Carol Lucha-Burns. To bring quality unpublished plays and musicals (45 minutes-1 hour in length) to young audiences. Deadline: May 1. Production is planned.

‡**ZUZU'S PETALS POETRY CONTEST**, P.O. Box 4476, Allentown PA 18105. (215)821-1324. Contest Director: T. Dunn. Contest offered 4 times per year for previously unpublished poetry. Deadlines: March 1, June 1, Sept. 1, Dec. 1. Guidelines for #10 SASE. Charges $1 per poem. Prize: top 3 winners share 40% of "Zuzu's" proceeds.

Other Contests and Awards

The following contests and awards were listed in the 1991 edition but do not have listings in this edition of *Writer's Market*. The majority did not respond to our request to update their listings or return a questionnaire for a new listing. If a reason was given for their exclusion, we have included it in parentheses after the listing name.

Alabama Artists Fellowship Awards

The Annual Nissan Focus Awards

Artist Assistance Fellowship, Minnesota State Arts Board

Aspirations

Best Private Eye Novel Contest

Bitterroot Magazine Poetry Contest (contest discontinued)

Brody Arts Fund Fellowship

Canadian Booksellers Association Author of the Year Award

Career Opportunity Grants

Chicago Women in Publishing Awards

Creative Fellowships, Colorado Council on the Arts & Humanities

The Dobie-Paisano Fellowship

The Ralph Waldo Emerson Award

Fellowship Awards, Vermont Council on the Arts

Fellowship/New Jersey State Council on the Arts

Festival of Firsts

Foster City Annual Writers Contest

French-American Foundation Translation Prize

Gallaudet Journalism Award

Great Lakes Colleges Association New Writers Award

Guideposts Magazine Youth Writing Contest

The Headlands Project

Sidney Hillman Prize Award

Hoover Annual Journalism Awards

Indiviual Artist Program, Wisconsin Arts Board

Iowa Arts Council Literary Awards

Jamestown Prize

Louisa Kern Award (contest discontinued)

Jack Kerouac Literary Prize

The Harold Morton Landon Translation Prize (unable to contact; mail returned)

The Peter I.B. Lavan Younger Poets Award (unable to contact; mail returned)

Linden Lane Magazine English-Language Poetry Contest

Joseph W. Lippincott Award

McLemore Prize

The Mayflower Society Cup Competition

Felix Morley Memorial Prizes

Most Outstanding Self-Published Book Competition (asked to be deleted)

National Book Awards

National Journalism Awards Program (contest discontinued)

National Psychology Awards for Excellence in the Media

The Nebraska Review Awards in Fiction and Poetry

New American Voices Poetry/Short Story Contest (contest discontinued)

New Play Competition

New Playwrights Competition and Festival

Eli M. Oboler Memorial Award

Off-Off-Broadway Original Short Play Festival

Ommation Press Book Contest

The Other Side Magazine Short Fiction Award (contest discontinued)

The Paper Bag Short Fiction Contest

PEN/Roger Klein Award for Editing

Playboy College Fiction Contest

Playwriting Competition for Young Audiences

Quarterly West Novella Competition

Sir Walter Raleigh Award

Roanoke-Chowan Award for Poetry

SFWA Nebula Awards

Southeastern Theatre of Conference New Play Project

The Stand Magazine Short Story Competition

Elizabeth Matchett Stover Memorial Award

Texas Bluebonnet Award

The Turner Tomorrow Award (not sponsored for 1992)

Warehouse Theatre One-Act Competition

Western Heritage Award

Laura Ingalls Wilder Award

H.W. Wilson Library Periodical Award

Woodbine House Award (contest discontinued)

World Fantasy Awards

Writers' Journal Annual Short Story Contest

Writers' Journal Semi-Annual Poetry Contest

Young Playwrights Program

Organizations of Interest

Writing can be a lonely occupation, but there are many organizations to keep you in touch with other writers, with developments in writing and publishing, and with opportunities to market your work.

We have listed only national organizations here. The majority of these have newsletters and other publications that can provide you with useful information for your writing career. Numerous local organizations and writers' clubs also exist. Often information about them is available at your local library or through a local college writing program.

Some of the following national organizations also have chapters in various cities. Write to the organization for information about their membership requirements, individual chapters and programs for writers.

American Society of Journalists and Authors
Suite 302, 1501 Broadway
New York NY 10036

Associated Writing Programs
Old Dominion University
Norfolk VA 23529

The Authors Guild
330 W. 42nd St.
New York NY 10036

The Dramatists' Guild
234 W. 44th St.
New York NY 10036

Freelance Editors Association
P.O. Box 835
Cambridge MA 02238

International Society of Dramatists
P.O. Box 1310
Miami Fl 33153

International Womens' Writing Guild
P.O. Box 810
Gracie Station
New York NY 10028

Mystery Writers of America
236 W. 27th St.
New York NY 10001

National Association of Greeting Card Publishers
#300, 600 Pennsylvania Ave.
Washington DC 20003

National Writers Club
Suite 620, 1450 S. Havana
Aurora CO 80012

National Writers Union
13 Astor Pl.
New York NY 10003

PEN American Center
568 Broadway
New York NY 10012

Poetry Society of America
15 Gramercy Park S.
New York NY 10003

Poets & Writers
72 Spring St.
New York NY 10012

Romance Writers of America
#315, 13700 Veterans Memorial Dr.
Houston TX 77014

Science Fiction Writers of America
P.O. Box 4335
Spartanburg SC 29305

Society of American Travel Writers
Suite 500
1155 Connecticut Ave. NW
Washington DC 20036

Society of Children's Book Writers
P.O. Box 66296
Mar Vista Station
Los Angeles CA 90066

Society of Professional Journalists
P.O. Box 77
Greencastle IN 46135

Writers Connection
Suite 180
1601 Saratoga-Sunnyvale Rd.
Cupertino CA 95014

Writers Guild of America (East)
555 W. 57th St.
New York NY 10019

(West)
8955 Beverly Blvd.
Los West Hollywood CA 90048

Publications of Interest

In addition to newsletters and publications from local and national organizations, several trade publications, books and directories offer valuable information to help in writing, in marketing your manuscripts and in understanding the business side of publishing.

Trade magazines

DAILY VARIETY, 5700 Wilshire Blvd., Los Angeles CA 90036. *Trade publication on the entertainment industry, with helpful information for screenwriters.*

FOLIO, 6 River Bend, P.O. Box 4949, Stamford Ct 06907. *Monthly magazine covering the magazine publishing industry.*

MAGAZINE WEEK, 432 Park Ave., New York NY 10016. *Weekly magazine of the magazine publishing industry.*

POETS & WRITERS, 72 Spring St., New York NY 10012. *Monthly magazine, primarily for literary writers and poets.*

PUBLISHERS WEEKLY, 205 W. 42nd St., New York NY 10017. *Weekly magazine covering the book publishing industry.*

THE WRITER, 120 Boylston St., Boston MA 02116. *Monthly magazine for writers.*

WRITER'S DIGEST, 1507 Dana Ave., Cincinnati OH 45207. *Monthly magazine for writers.*

EDITOR & PUBLISHER, 11 W. 19th St., New York NY 10011. *Weekly magazine covering the newspaper publishing industry.*

Books and directories

THE COMPLETE BOOK OF SCRIPTWRITING, by J. Michael Straczynski, Writer's Digest Books, 1507 Dana Ave., Cincinnati OH 45207.

THE COMPLETE GUIDE TO SELF PUBLISHING, by Marilyn and Tom Ross, Writer's Digest Books, 1507 Dana Ave., Cincinnati OH 45207.

DRAMATISTS SOURCEBOOK, edited by Angela E. Mitchell and Gilliam Richards, Theatre Communications Group, Inc., 355 Lexington Ave., New York NY 10017.

THE GUIDE TO WRITERS CONFERENCES, Shaw Associates, Suite 1406, Biltmore Way, Coral Gables FL 33134.

HOW TO WRITE IRRESISTIBLE QUERY LETTERS, by Lisa Collier Cool, Writer's Digest Books, 1507 Dana Ave., Cincinnati OH 45207.

THE INSIDER'S GUIDE TO BOOK EDITORS & PUBLISHERS, by Jeff Herman, Prima Publishing & Communications, Box 1260, Rocklin CA 95677-1260.

INTERNATIONAL DIRECTORY OF LITTLE MAGAZINES & SMALL PRESSES, edited by Len Fulton, Dustbooks, P.O. Box 100, Paradise CA 95967.

LITERARY MARKET PLACE and **INTERNATIONAL LITERARY MARKET PLACE**, R.R. Bowker Co., 121 Chanlon Rd., New Providence NJ 07974.

PROFESSIONAL WRITER'S GUIDE, edited by Donald Bower and James Lee Young, National Writers Press, Suite 620, 1450 S. Havana, Aurora CO 80012.

THE WRITER'S GUIDE TO SELF-PROMOTION AND PUBLICITY, by Elane Feldman, Writer's Digest Books, 1507 Dana Ave., Cincinnati OH 45207.

THE WRITER'S LEGAL COMPANION, by Brad Bunnin and Peter Beren, Addison-Wesley, 1 Jacob Way, Reading MA 01867.

Glossary

Key to symbols and abbreviations is on page 5.

Advance. A sum of money that a publisher pays a writer prior to the publication of a book. It is usually paid in installments, such as one-half on signing the contract; one-half on delivery of a complete and satisfactory manuscript. The advance is paid against the royalty money that will be earned by the book.

Advertorial. Advertising presented in such a way as to resemble editorial material. Information may be the same as that contained in an editorial feature, but it is paid for or supplied by an advertiser and the word "advertisement" appears at the top of the page.

All rights. See Rights and the Writer in the Business of Writing article.

Anthology. A collection of selected writings by various authors or a gathering of works by one author.

Assignment. Editor asks a writer to do a specific article for a certain price to be paid upon completion.

Auction. Publishers sometimes bid for the acquisition of a book manuscript that has excellent sales prospects. The bids are for the amount of the author's advance, guaranteed dollar amounts, advertising and promotional expenses, royalty percentage, etc.

B&W. Abbreviation for black and white photographs.

Backlist. A publisher's list of its books that were not published during the current season, but that are still in print.

Belles lettres. A term used to describe fine or literary writing—writing more to entertain than to inform or instruct.

Bimonthly. Every two months. See also *semimonthly*.

Bionote. A sentence or brief paragraph about the writer. Also called a "bio," it can appear at the bottom of the first or last page of a writer's article or short story or on a contributor's page.

Biweekly. Every two weeks.

Boilerplate. A standardized contract. When an editor says "our standard contract," he means the boilerplate with no changes. Writers should be aware that most authors and/or agents make many changes on the boilerplate.

Book auction. Selling the rights (e.g. paperback, movie, etc.) of a hardback book to the highest bidder. A publisher or agent may initiate the auction.

Book packager. Draws all elements of a book together, from the initial concept to writing and marketing strategies, then sells the book package to a book publisher and/or movie producer. Also known as book producer or book developer.

Business size envelope. Also known as a #10 envelope, it is the standard size used in sending business correspondence.

Byline. Name of the author appearing with the published piece.

Caption. Originally a title or headline over a picture, but now a description of the subject matter of a photograph; includes names when appropriate. Also called cutline.

Category fiction. A term used to include all various labels attached to types of fiction. See also *genre*.

Chapbook. A small booklet, usually paperback, of poetry, ballads or tales.

Clean copy. A manuscript free of errors, cross-outs, wrinkles or smudges.

Clippings. News items of possible interest to trade magazine editors.

Clips. Samples, usually from newspapers or magazines, of your *published* work.

Coffee table book. An oversize book, heavily illustrated, for display on a coffee table.

Column inch. All the type contained in one inch of a typeset column.

Commercial novels. Novels designed to appeal to a broad audience. These are often broken down into categories such as western, mystery and romance. See also *genre*.

Commissioned work. See *assignment*.

Compatible. The condition which allows one type of computer/word processor to share information or communicate with another type of machine.

Concept. A statement that summarizes a screenplay or teleplay—before the outline or treatment is written.

Contributor's copies. Copies of the issues of magazines sent to the author in which the author's work appears.

Cooperative publishing. See *co-publishing*.

Co-publishing. Arrangement where author and publisher share publication costs and profits of a book. Also known as *cooperative publishing*. See also *subsidy publisher*.

Copyediting. Editing a manuscript for grammar, punctuation and printing style, not subject content.

Copyright. A means to protect an author's work. See Copyrighting Your Writing in the Business of Writing section.

Cover letter. A brief letter, accompanying a complete manuscript, especially useful if responding to an editor's request for a manuscript. A cover letter may also accompany a book proposal. (A cover letter is *not* a query letter; see Approaching Markets in the Business of Writing section.

Cutline. See *caption*.

Derivative works. A work that has been translated, adapted, abridged, condensed, annotated or otherwise produced by altering a previously created work. Before producing a derivative work, it is necessary to secure the written permission of the author or copyright owner of the original piece.

Desk-top publishing. A publishing system designed for a personal computer. The system is capable of typesetting, some illustration, layout, design and printing—so that the final piece can be distributed and/or sold.

Disk. A round, flat magnetic plate on which computer data may be stored.

Docudrama. A fictional film rendition of recent newsmaking events and people.

Dot-matrix. Printed type where individual characters are composed of a matrix or pattern of tiny dots. Near letter quality (see *NLQ*) dot-matrix submissions are generally acceptable to editors.

Electronic submission. A submission made by modem or computer disk.

El-hi. Elementary to high school.

Epigram. A short, witty sometimes paradoxical saying.

Erotica. Fiction or art that is sexually-oriented.

ESL. Abbreviation for English as a second language.

Fair use. A provision of the copyright law that says short passages from copyrighted material may be used without infringing on the owner's rights.

Fanzine. A noncommercial, small circulation magazine dealing with fantasy or science fiction literature and art.

FAX. A communication system used to transmit documents over telephone lines.

Feature. An article giving the reader information of human interest rather than news. Also used by magazines to indicate a lead article or distinctive department.

Filler. A short item used by an editor to "fill" out a newspaper column or magazine page. It could be a timeless news item, a joke, an anecdote, some light verse or short humor, puzzle, etc.

First chapter novel. A book for children that is roughly the size of an adult novel's first chapter.

First North American serial rights. See Rights and the Writer in the Business of Writing article.

Formula story. Familiar theme treated in a predictable plot structure—such as boy meets girl, boy loses girl, boy gets girl.

Galleys. The first typeset version of a manuscript that has not yet been divided into pages.

Genre. Refers either to a general classification of writing, such as the novel or the poem, or to the categories within those classifications, such as the problem novel or the sonnet. Genre fiction describes commercial novels, such as mysteries, romances and science fiction. (Also called category fiction.).

Ghostwriter. A writer who puts into literary form an article, speech, story or book based on another person's ideas or knowledge.

Glossy. A black and white photograph with a shiny surface as opposed to one with a non-shiny matte finish.

Gothic novel. A fiction category or genre in which the central character is usually a beautiful young girl, the setting an old mansion or castle, and there is a handsome hero and a real menace, either natural or supernatural.

Graphic novel. A term to describe an adaptation of a novel in graphic form, long comic strip or heavily illustrated story, of 40 pages or more, produced in paperback form.

Hard copy. The printed copy of a computer's output.

Hardware. All the mechanically-integrated components of a computer that are not software. Circuit boards, transistors and the machines that are the actual computer are the hardware.

Hi-Lo. Abbreviation for high interest, low reading level, as pertains mostly to beginning adult readers.

Honorarium. Token payment—small amount of money, or a byline and copies of the publication.

Illustrations. May be photographs, old engravings, artwork. Usually paid for separately from the manuscript. See also *package sale*.

Imprint. Name applied to a publisher's specific line or lines of books (e.g., Delacorte Press is an imprint of Dell Publishing).

Interactive fiction. Works of fiction in book or computer software format in which the reader determines the path the story will take. The reader chooses from several alternatives at the end of a "chapter," and thus determines the structure of the story. Interactive fiction features multiple plots and endings.

Invasion of privacy. Writing about persons (even though truthfully) without their consent.

Kill fee. Fee for a complete article that was assigned but which was subsequently cancelled.

Lead time. The time between the acquisition of a manuscript by an editor and its actual publication.

Letter-quality submission. Computer printout that looks typewritten.

Libel. A false accusation or any published statement or presentation that tends to expose another to public contempt, ridicule, etc. Defenses are truth; fair comment on a matter of public interest; and privileged communication—such as a report of legal proceedings or client's communication to a lawyer.

Little magazine. Publications of limited circulation, usually on literary or political subject matter.

LORT. An acronym for League of Resident Theatres. Letters from A to D follow LORT and designate the size of the theater.

Mainstream fiction. Fiction that transcends popular novel categories such as mystery, romance and science fiction. Using conventional methods, this kind of fiction tells stories about people and their conflicts with greater depth of characterization, background, etc., than the more narrowly focused genre novels.

Mass market. Nonspecialized books of wide appeal directed toward an extremely large audience.

Microcomputer. A small computer system capable of performing various specific tasks with data it receives. Personal computers are microcomputers.

Midlist. Those titles on a publisher's list that are not expected to be big sellers, but are expected to have limited sales. Midlist books are mainstream, not literary, scholarly or genre, and are usually written by new or unknown writers.

Model release. A paper signed by the subject of a photograph (or the subject's guardian, if a juvenile) giving the photographer permission to use the photograph, editorially or for advertising purposes or for some specific purpose as stated.

Modem. A small electrical box that plugs into the serial card of a computer, used to transmit data from one computer to another, usually via telephone lines.

Monograph. A detailed and documented scholarly study concerning a singular subject.

MOW. Movie of the week.

Multiple submissions. Sending more than one poem, gag or greeting card idea at the same time. This term is often used synonymously with simultaneous submission.

Net receipts. A royalty payment based on the amount of money a book publisher receives on the sale of a book after booksellers' discounts, special sales discounts and returns.

New Age. A generic term for works linked by a common interest in metaphysical, spiritual, holistic and other alternative approaches to living. It embraces astrology, psychic phenomena, spiritual healing, UFOs, mysticism—anything that deals with reality beyond everyday material perception.

Newsbreak. A brief, late-breaking news story added to the front page of a newspaper at press time or a magazine news item of importance to readers.

NLQ. Near letter-quality print required by some editors for computer printout submissions. See also *dot-matrix*.

Novelette. A short novel, or a long short story; 7,000 to 15,000 words approximately. Also known as a novella.

Novelization. A novel created from the script of a popular movie, usually called movie "tie-ins" and published in paperback.

Offprint. Copies of an author's article taken "out of issue" before a magazine is bound and given to the author in lieu of monetary payment. An offprint could be used by the writer as a published writing sample.

On spec. An editor expresses an interest in a proposed article idea and agrees to consider the finished piece for publication "on speculation." The editor is under no obligation to buy the finished manuscript.

One-shot features. As applies to syndicates, single feature article for syndicate to sell; as contrasted with article series or regular columns syndicated.

One-time rights. See Rights and the Writer in the Business of Writing article.

Outline. A summary of a book's contents in five to 15 double-spaced pages; often in the form of chapter headings with a descriptive sentence or two under each one to show the scope of the book. A screenplay's or teleplay's outline is a scene-by-scene narrative description of the story (10-15 pages for a ½-hour teleplay; 15-25 pages for a 1-hour teleplay; 25-40 pages for a 90-minute teleplay; 40-60 pages for a 2-hour feature film or teleplay).

Over-the-transom. Unsolicited material submitted by a freelance writer.

Package sale. The editor buys manuscript and photos as a "package" and pays for them with one check.

Page rate. Some magazines pay for material at a fixed rate per published page, rather than per word.

Payment on acceptance. The editor sends you a check for your article, story or poem as soon as he reads it and decides to publish it.

Payment on publication. The editor doesn't send you a check for your material until it is published.

Pen name. The use of a name other than your legal name on articles, stories or books when you wish to remain anonymous. Simply notify your post office and bank that you are using the name so that you'll receive mail and/or checks in that name. Also called a pseudonym.

Photo feature. Feature in which the emphasis is on the photographs rather than on accompanying written material.

Photocopied submissions. Submitting *photocopies* of an original manuscript is acceptable to the majority of editors instead of the author sending the original manuscript. Do not assume that an editor who accepts photocopies will also accept multiple or simultaneous submissions.

Plagiarism. Passing off as one's own the expression of ideas and words of another writer.

Potboiler. Refers to writing projects a freelance writer does to "keep the pot boiling" while working on major articles—quick projects to bring in money with little time or effort. These may be fillers such as anecdotes or how-to tips, but could be short articles or stories.

Proofreading. Close reading and correction of a manuscript's typographical errors.

Proscenium. The area of the stage in front of the curtain.

Prospectus. A preliminary written description of a book or article, usually one page in length.

Pseudonym. See *pen name*.

Public domain. Material that was either never copyrighted or whose copyright term has expired.

Publication not copyrighted. Publication of an author's work in such a publication places it in the public domain and it cannot subsequently be copyrighted. See Copyrighting Your Writing in the Business of Writing article.

Query. A letter to an editor intended to raise interest in an article you propose to write.

Rebus. Stories, quips, puzzles, etc., in juvenile magazines that convey words or syllables with pictures, objects or symbols whose names resemble the sounds of intended words.

Realia. Activities that relate classroom study to real life.

Release. A statement that your idea is original, has never been sold to anyone else and that you are selling the negotiated rights to the idea upon payment.

Remainders. Copies of a book that are slow to sell and can be purchased from the publisher at a reduced price. Depending on the author's book contract, a reduced royalty or no royalty is paid on remainder books.

Reporting time. The time it takes for an editor to report to the author on his/her query or manuscript.

Reprint rights. See Rights and the Writer in the Business of Writing article.

Round-up article. Comments from, or interviews with, a number of celebrities or experts on a single theme.

Royalties, standard hardcover book. 10% of the retail price on the first 5,000 copies sold; 12½% on the next 5,000; 15% thereafter.

Royalties, standard mass paperback book. 4 to 8% of the retail price on the first 150,000 copies sold.

Royalties, trade paperback book. No less than 6% of list price on the first 20,000 copies; 7½% thereafter.

Scanning. A process through which letter-quality printed text (see *NLQ*) or artwork is read by a computer scanner and converted into workable data.

Screenplay. Script for a film intended to be shown in theaters.

Self-publishing. In this arrangement, the author keeps all income derived from the book, but he pays for its manufacturing, production and marketing.

Semimonthly. Twice per month.

Semiweekly. Twice per week.

Serial. Published periodically, such as a newspaper or magazine.

Sidebar. A feature presented as a companion to a straight news report (or main magazine article) giving sidelights on human-interest aspects or sometimes elucidating just one aspect of the story.

Simultaneous submissions. Sending the same article, story or poem to several publishers at the same time. Some publishers refuse to consider such submissions. No simultaneous submissions should be made without stating the fact in your letter.

Slant. The approach or style of a story or article that will appeal to readers of a specific magazine. For example, a magazine may always use stories with an upbeat ending.

Slice-of-life vignette. A short fiction piece intended to realistically depict an interesting moment of everyday living.

Slides. Usually called transparencies by editors looking for color photographs.

Slush pile. The stack of unsolicited or misdirected manuscripts received by an editor or book publisher.

Software. Programs and related manuals for use with a particular computer system.

Speculation. The editor agrees to look at the author's manuscript with no assurance that it will be bought.

Style. The way in which something is written—for example, short, punchy sentences or flowing narrative.

Subsidiary rights. All those rights, other than book publishing rights included in a book contract—such as paperback, book club, movie rights, etc.

Subsidy publisher. A book publisher who charges the author for the cost to typeset and print his book, the jacket, etc. as opposed to a royalty publisher who pays the author.

Syndication rights. See Rights and the Writer in the Business of Writing article.

Synopsis. A brief summary of a story, novel or play. As part of a book proposal, it is a comprehensive summary condensed in a page or page and a half, single-spaced. See also *outline*.

Tabloid. Newspaper format publication on about half the size of the regular newspaper page, such as the *National Enquirer*.

Tagline. A caption for a photo or a comment added to a filler.

Tearsheet. Page from a magazine or newspaper containing your printed story, article, poem or ad.

Trade. Either a hardcover or paperback book; subject matter frequently concerns a special interest. Books are directed toward the layperson rather than the professional.

Transparencies. Positive color slides; not color prints.

Treatment. Synopsis of a television or film script (40-60 pages for a 2-hour feature film or teleplay).

Unsolicited manuscript. A story, article, poem or book that an editor did not specifically ask to see.

User friendly. Easy to handle and use. Refers to computer hardware and software designed with the user in mind.

Vanity publisher. See *subsidy publisher*.

Word processor. A computer that produces typewritten copy via automated typing, text-editing and storage and transmission capabilities.

Work-for-hire. See Copyrighting Your Writing in the Business of Writing article.

YA. Young adult books.

Book Publishers Subject Index

This index will help you find publishers that consider books on specific subjects — the subjects you choose to write about. Remember that a publisher may be listed here under a general subject category such as Art and Architecture, while the company publishes *only* art history or how-to books. Be sure to consult each company's detailed individual listing, its book catalog and several of its books before you send your query or manuscript.

Fiction

Adventure. Access Publishers; Advocacy Press; Atheneum Children's Books; Avalon Books; Avanyu Publishing Inc.; Avon Books; Avon Flare Books; Bantam Books; Bethel Publishing; Branden Publishing Co., Inc..; British American Publishing; Camelot Books; Capstone Press, Inc.; Carol Publishing; Clarion Books; Cook Publishing Co., David C.; Davenport, Publishers, May; Dial Books For Young Readers; Dutton Children's Books; Evergreen Communications, Inc.; Fine, Inc., Donald I.; Gallaudet University Press; Harian Creative Books; HarperCollins Publishers; Info Net Publishing; Innovatia Press; Kar-Ben Copies Inc.; Library Research Associates, Inc.; Lodestar Books; Mother Courage Press; Mountaineers Books, The; New Victoria Publishers; Overlook Press; Permanent Press/Second Chance Press, The; Pippin Press; Presidio Press; QED Press; Random House, Inc.; Random House, Inc. Juvenile Books; Soho Press, Inc.; Starburst Publishers; Stemmer House Publishers, Inc.; Unlimited Publishing Co.; Villard Books; Walker and Co.; Wayfinder Press; Wilderness Adventure Books; Willowisp Press, Inc.; Woodsong Graphics, Inc.; Yankee Books; Zebra Books; Whitman and Co., Albert.

Confession. British American Publishing; Carol Publishing; Permanent Press/Second Chance Press, The; Random House, Inc.; Zebra Books.

Erotica. Carroll & Graf Publishers, Inc.; Devonshire Publishing Co.; Gay Sunshine Press and Leyland Publications; New Victoria Publishers; Yankee Books.

Ethnic. Atheneum Children's Books; Avon Flare Books; Branden Publishing Co., Inc..; China Books & Periodicals, Inc.; City Lights Books; Coffee House Press; Coteau Books; Cuff Publications Ltd., Harry; Faber & Faber, Inc.; Gallaudet University Press; Gay Sunshine Press and Leyland Publications; Guernica Editions; Kar-Ben Copies Inc.; Overlook Press; Permanent Press/Second Chance Press, The; QED Press; Soho Press, Inc.; Spinsters Book Company; Stemmer House Publishers, Inc.; University of Illinois Press; Vesta Publications, Ltd..

Experimental. Atheneum Children's Books; British American Publishing; China Books & Periodicals, Inc.; Coach House Press; Coffee House Press; Coteau Books; Devonshire Publishing Co.; Faber & Faber, Inc.; Gay Sunshine Press and Leyland Publications; Harian Creative Books; Permanent Press/Second Chance Press, The; QED Press; Random House, Inc.; Unlimited Publishing Co.; Woodsong Graphics, Inc..

Fantasy. Access Publishers; Ace Science Fiction; Atheneum Children's Books; Avon Books; Bantam Books; British American Publishing; Camelot Books; Capstone Press, Inc.; Carol Publishing; Carroll & Graf Publishers, Inc.; Coteau Books; Crossway Books; Davenport, Publishers, May; DAW Books, Inc.; Del Rey Books; Dial Books For Young Readers; Dutton Children's Books; Fine, Inc., Donald I.; Gallaudet University Press; HarperCollins Publishers; Imagine, Inc.; Innovatia Press; Intervarsity Press; Iron Crown Enterprises; Kar-Ben Copies Inc.; Lion Publishing Corporation; Lodestar Books; Mother Courage Press; New Victoria Publishers; Overlook Press; Permanent Press/Second Chance Press, The; Pippin Press; QED Press; Random House, Inc.; Random House, Inc. Juvenile Books; TOR Books; TSR, Inc.; Whitman and Co., Albert; Willowisp Press, Inc.; Woodsong Graphics, Inc..

Feminist. Black Sparrow Press; British American Publishing; China Books & Periodicals, Inc.; Coach House Press; Coteau Books; Firebrand Books; Mercury Press, The; Mother Courage Press; QED Press; Soho Press, Inc..

Gay/Lesbian. Alyson Publications, Inc.; Bantam Books; Black Sparrow Press; Cleis Press; Firebrand Books; Gay Sunshine Press and Leyland Publications; Knights Press, Inc.; Los Hombres Press; Mother Courage Press; Naiad Press, Inc., The; Spinsters Book Company.

Gothic. Atheneum Children's Books; HarperCollins Publishers; Woodsong Graphics, Inc.; Zebra Books.

Hi-Lo. Access Publishers; Afcom Publishing; Capstone Press, Inc.; Carroll & Graf Publishers, Inc.; Catbird Press; China Books & Periodicals, Inc.; Fearon/Janus Publishers; Info Net Publishing; Peachtree Publishers, Ltd.; Picadilly Books; Sunflower University Press.

Historical. Access Publishers; Advocacy Press; Atheneum Children's Books; Avanyu Publishing Inc.; Avon Books; Bantam Books; Berkley Publishing Group, The; Bradbury Press; Branden Publishing Co., Inc..; British American Publishing; Capstone Press, Inc.; Carolrhoda Books, Inc.; Cook Publishing Co., David C.; Cuff Publications Ltd., Harry; Dial Books For Young Readers; Fine, Inc., Donald I.; Gallaudet University Press; Gay Sunshine Press and Leyland Publications; Guernica Editions; HarperCollins Publishers; Harvest House Publishers; Houghton Mifflin Co.; Innovatia Press; Kar-Ben Copies Inc.; Leisure Books; Library Research Associates, Inc.; Lion Publishing Corporation; Lodestar Books; Macmillan of Canada; Mother Courage Press; Nautical & Aviation Publishing Co., The; New Victoria Publishers; Overlook Press; Pelican Publishing Company; Permanent Press/Second Chance Press, The; Pineapple Press, Inc.; Pippin Press; Poseidon Press; Presidio Press; QED Press; Random House, Inc.; Random House, Inc. Juvenile Books; Soho Press, Inc.; Stemmer House Publishers, Inc.; TOR Books; Unlimited Publishing Co.; Villard Books; Wayfinder Press; Whitman and Co., Albert; Wilderness Adventure Books; Winston-Derek Publishers, Inc.; Woodsong Graphics, Inc.; Ye Galleon Press; Zebra Books.

Horror. Atheneum Children's Books; Bantam Books; British American Publishing; Carol Publishing; Carroll & Graff Publishers; Fine, Inc., Donald I.; Random House, Inc.; Random House, Inc. Juvenile Books; TOR Books; TSR, Inc.; Villard Books; Willowisp Press, Inc.; Zebra Books.

Humor. Access Publishers; Atheneum Children's Books; Avon Flare Books; British American Publishing; Camden House Publishing; Camelot Books; Capstone Press, Inc.; Carol Publishing; Clarion Books; Coteau Books; Cuff Publications Ltd., Harry; Fine, Inc., Donald I.; Gallaudet University Press; Harian Creative Books; Innovatia Press; Intervarsity Press; Lodestar Books; New Victoria Publishers; Once Upon a Planet, Inc.; Pelican Publishing Company; Permanent Press/Second Chance Press, The; Random House, Inc. Juvenile Books; Unlimited Publishing Co.; Willowisp Press, Inc.; Wyrick & Company; Yankee Books; Zebra Books.

Juvenile. Afcom Publishing; Archway/Minstrel Books; Atheneum Children's Books; Bantam Books; Blue Heron Publishing; Boyds Mills Press; Bradbury Press; Camelot Books; Capstone Press, Inc.; Carolrhoda Books, Inc.; Chronicle Books; Concordia Publishing House; Coteau Books; Crossway Books; Denison & Co., Inc., T.S.; Dutton Children's Books; Evergreen Communications, Inc.; Faber & Faber, Inc.; Farrar, Straus and Giroux, Inc.; Fawcett Juniper; Gallaudet University Press; Grosset & Dunlap Publishers; Harbinger House, Inc.; Harcourt Brace Jovanovich; HarperCollins Children's Books Pacific Northwest; Hendrick-Long Publishing Co., Inc.; Houghton Mifflin Co.; Knowledge Book Publishers; Lion Publishing Corporation; Lothrop, Lee & Shepard Books; Morrow Junior Books; Pelican Publishing Company; St. Paul Books and Media; Scribner's Sons, Charles; Shoe Tree Press; Silver Press; Starburst Publishers; Tidewater Publishers; Walker and Co.; Whitman and Co., Albert; Willowisp Press, Inc.; Winston-Derek Publishers, Inc..

Literary. Applezaba Press; Bantam Books; Black Sparrow Press; Carol Publishing; Catbird Press; China Books & Periodicals, Inc.; City Lights Books; Coach House Press; Coffee House Press; Coteau Books; Fine, Inc., Donald I.; Gallaudet University Press; Godine, Publisher, Inc., David; HarperCollins Publishers; Houghton Mifflin Co.; Hounslow Press; Little, Brown and Co., Inc.; Longstreet Press, Inc.; Louisiana State University Press; Macmillan of Canada; Mercury Press, The; Peachtree Publishers, Ltd.; Pineapple Press, Inc.; Poseidon Press; QED Press; Soho Press, Inc.; Stormline Press; Three Continents Press; University of Arkansas Press, The; University of Pittsburgh Press; Vesta Publications, Ltd.; Villard Books; Willowisp Press, Inc.; Wyrick & Company; Zoland Books, Inc..

Mainstream/Contemporary. Access Publishers; Atheneum Children's Books; Avalon Books; Avon Flare Books; Bantam Books; Berkley Publishing Group, The; Blair, Publisher, John F.;

Bradbury Press; Branden Publishing Co., Inc..; British American Publishing; Camelot Books; Capstone Press, Inc.; Carroll & Graf Publishers, Inc.; Catbird Press; Chelsea Green; Citadel Press; City Lights Books; Clarion Books; Cook Publishing Co., David C.; Coteau Books; Cuff Publications Ltd., Harry; Crossway Books; Down East Books; Dutton, E. P.; Ediciones Universal; Eriksson, Publisher, Paul S.; Fawcett Juniper; Fine, Inc., Donald I.; Gallaudet University Press; Harian Creative Books; Houghton Mifflin Co.; International Publishers Co., Inc.; Intervarsity Press; Little, Brown and Co., Inc.; Lodestar Books; Longstreet Press, Inc.; Macmillan of Canada; Mercury Press, The; Morrow and Co., William; Overlook Press; Pantheon Books; Peachtree Publishers, Ltd.; Pelican Publishing Company; Permanent Press/Second Chance Press, The; Perspectives Press; Pineapple Press, Inc.; QED Press; Random House, Inc.; St. Luke's Press; St. Martin's Press; Simon & Schuster; Soho Press, Inc.; Starburst Publishers; Stemmer House Publishers, Inc.; Ticknor & Fields; University of Iowa Press; University of Nevada Press; University Press of Mississippi; Villard Books; Watts, Inc., Franklin; Willowisp Press, Inc.; Woodsong Graphics, Inc.; Wyrick & Company; Zebra Books.

Military. British American Publishing.

Mystery. Access Publishers; Atheneum Children's Books; Avon Books; Avon Flare Books; Bantam Books; British American Publishing; Camelot Books; Capstone Press, Inc.; Carol Publishing; Carroll & Graf Publishers, Inc.; Clarion Books; Cliffhanger Press; Cook Publishing Co., David C.; Countryman Press, Inc., The; Dial Books For Young Readers; Doubleday Books; Evergreen Communications, Inc.; Fine, Inc., Donald I.; Gallaudet University Press; Gay Sunshine Press and Leyland Publications; Godine, Publisher, Inc., David R.; Guernica Editions; HarperCollins Publishers; Harvest House Publishers; Innovatia Press; Library Research Associates, Inc.; Lodestar Books; Macmillan of Canada; Mother Courage Press; Mysterious Press, The; Overlook Press; Permanent Press/Second Chance Press, The; Pippin Press; Pocket Books; QED Press; Random House, Inc.; Random House, Inc. Juvenile Books; Scholastic, Inc.; Soho Press, Inc.; TOR Books; TSR, Inc.; Unlimited Publishing Co.; Villard Books; Walker and Co.; Watts, Inc., Franklin; Wayfinder Press; Whitman and Co., Albert; Willowisp Press, Inc.; Woodsong Graphics, Inc..

Occult. Berkley Publishing Group, The.

Picture Books. Advocacy Press; Bradbury Press; Capstone Press, Inc.; Chronicle Books; Coteau Books; Dutton Children's Books; Gallaudet University Press; Grosset & Dunlap Publishers; Harbinger House, Inc.; Harcourt Brace Jovanovich; Lodestar Books; Lothrop, Lee & Shepard Books; Pippin Press; Random House, Inc. Juvenile Books; Silver Press; Wayfinder Press; Whitman and Co., Albert; Willowisp Press, Inc.; Yankee Books.

Plays. Anchorage Press, Inc.; City Lights Books; Coteau Books; Drama Book Publishers; French, Inc., Samuel; Gallaudet University Press; Guernica Editions; Players Press, Inc.; Zoland Books, Inc..

Poetry. Applezaba Press; Blue Dolphin Publishing, Inc.; Boyds Mills Press; Chatham Press; China Books & Periodicals, Inc.; Christopher Publishing House, The; Cleveland State University Poetry Center; Daniel and Company, Publishers, John; Dante University Of America Press, Inc.; Ediciones Universal; Firebrand Books; HarperCollins Children's Books Pacific Northwest; International Publishers Co., Inc.; Los Hombres Press; Louisiana State University Press; Mark Publishing; Mercury Press, The; Morrow and Co., William; Overlook Press; Paragon House Publishers; QED Press; Sheep Meadow Press, The; Sparrow Press; Spinsters Book Company; Star Books Inc.; Sunstone Press; Three Continents Press; University of Arkansas Press, The; University of California Press; University of Iowa Press; University of Massachusetts Press; University of Pittsburgh Press; Vesta Publications, Ltd.; Wake Forest University Press; Wilderness Adventure Books; Winston-Derek Publishers, Inc..

Regional. Blair, Publisher, John F.; Borealis Press; Cuff Publications Ltd., Harry; Down East Books; Faber & Faber, Inc.; Sunstone Press; Texas Christian University Press.

Religious. Accent Books; Bethany House Publishers; Bethel Publishing; Bookcraft, Inc.; British American Publishing; China Books & Periodicals, Inc.; Cook Publishing Co., David C.; Evergreen Communications, Inc.; Harvest House Publishers; Herald Press; Innovatia Press; Intervarsity Press; Kar-Ben Copies Inc.; St. Bede's Publications; St. Paul Books and Media; Standard Publishing; Star Books Inc.; UAHC Press; Victor Books; Winston-Derek Publishers, Inc..

Romance. Access Publishers; Atheneum Children's Books; Avalon Books; Avon Books; Avon Flare Books; Bantam Books; Berkley Publishing Group, The; Branden Publishing Co., Inc..; Capstone Press, Inc.; Dial Books For Young Readers; Doubleday Books; Evans and Co., Inc., M.; Evergreen

Communications, Inc.; Harian Creative Books; Leisure Books; Mother Courage Press; Pocket Books; Scholastic, Inc.; Silhouette Books; Walker and Co.; Willowisp Press, Inc.; Woodsong Graphics, Inc.; Zebra Books.

Science Fiction. Access Publishers; Ace Science Fiction; Atheneum Children's Books; Avon Books; Bantam Books; Capstone Press, Inc.; Carol Publishing; Carroll & Graf Publishers, Inc.; Crossway Books; DAW Books, Inc.; Del Rey Books; Devonshire Publishing Co.; Fine, Inc., Donald I.; Gallaudet University Press; Gay Sunshine Press and Leyland Publications; HarperCollins Publishers; Imagine, Inc.; Intervarsity Press; Iron Crown Enterprises; Lodestar Books; Mother Courage Press; New Victoria Publishers; Overlook Press; Pocket Books; QED Press; Random House, Inc. Juvenile Books; TOR Books; TSR, Inc.; Villard Books; Watts, Inc., Franklin; Willowisp Press, Inc.; Woodsong Graphics, Inc..

Short Story Collections. Applezaba Press; Black Sparrow Press; British American Publishing; Camden House Publishing; Chronicle Books; Coach House Press; Coffee House Press; Coteau Books; Daniel and Company, Publishers, John; Dutton Children's Books; Faber & Faber, Inc.; Harian Creative Books; Innovatia Press; International Publishers Co., Inc.; Louisiana State University Press; Mercury Press, The; QED Press; University of Arkansas Press, The; University of Illinois Press; Wayfinder Press; Willowisp Press, Inc.; Zoland Books, Inc..

Spiritual (New Age, etc.). Graywolf Press.

Suspense. Access Publishers; Atheneum Children's Books; Avon Books; Avon Flare Books; Bantam Books; Berkley Publishing Group, The; Bethel Publishing; British American Publishing; Capstone Press, Inc.; Carroll & Graf Publishers, Inc.; Clarion Books; Cliffhanger Press; Dial Books For Young Readers; Doubleday Books; Fine, Inc., Donald I.; Gallaudet University Press; HarperCollins Publishers; Hounslow Press; Library Research Associates, Inc.; Lodestar Books; Mysterious Press, The; Overlook Press; Permanent Press/Second Chance Press, The; Pippin Press; Pocket Books; QED Press; Random House, Inc.; Random House, Inc. Juvenile Books; Soho Press, Inc.; Villard Books; Walker and Co.; Willowisp Press, Inc.; Winston-Derek Publishers, Inc.; Woodsong Graphics, Inc.; Zebra Books.

Western. Access Publishers; Atheneum Children's Books; Avalon Books; Avanyu Publishing Inc.; Avon Books; Bantam Books; Berkley Publishing Group, The; Capstone Press, Inc.; Evans and Co., Inc., M.; Fine, Inc., Donald I.; HarperCollins Publishers; Lodestar Books; New Victoria Publishers; Pocket Books; Walker and Co.; Willowisp Press, Inc.; Woodsong Graphics, Inc..

Young Adult. Access Publishers; Advocacy Press; Archway/Minstrel Books; Bantam Books; Berkley Publishing Group, The; Bethel Publishing; Blue Heron Publishing; Boyds Mills Press; Cook Publishing Co., David C.; Crossway Books; Dutton Children's Books; Evergreen Communications, Inc.; Farrar, Straus and Giroux, Inc.; Fawcett Juniper; Fearon/Janus Publishers; Gallaudet University Press; Harcourt Brace Jovanovich; HarperCollins Children's Books Pacific Northwest; Herald Press; Houghton Mifflin Co.; Lodestar Books; McElderry Books, Margaret K.; Morrow and Co., William; Random House, Inc. Juvenile Books; St. Paul Books and Media; Scholastic, Inc.; Starburst Publishers; Texas Christian University Press; Wilderness Adventure Books; Willowisp Press, Inc..

Nonfiction

Agriculture/Horticulture. Alaska Northwest Books; Between the Lines; Camden House Publishing; Camino Books, Inc.; Hartley & Marks, Inc.; Interstate Publishers, Inc. The; Kumarian Press, Inc.; Lyons & Burford, Publishers, Inc.; Michigan State University Press; Pruett Publishing; Stipes Publishing Co.; Stormline Press; University of Nebraska Press; Warner Mills Press; Woodbridge Press.

Americana. Alaska Northwest Books; Ancestry Incorporated; Atheneum Children's Books; Avanyu Publishing Inc.; Bantam Books; Blair, Publisher, John F.; Boston Mills Press; Bowling Green State University Popular Press; Branden Publishing Co., Inc..; Camino Books, Inc.; Capstone Press, Inc.; Carol Publishing; Caxton Printers, Ltd., The; Christopher Publishing House, The; Clarion Books; Clark Co., Arthur H.; Creative Publishing Co.; Crown Publishing Group; Denali Press, The; Devin-Adair Publishers, Inc.; Down East Books; Durst Publications Ltd.; Eriksson, Publisher, Paul S.; Faber & Faber, Inc.; Filter Press; Glenbridge Publishing Ltd.; Globe Pequot Press, Inc., The; Godine, Publisher, Inc., David R.; Hancock House Publishers Ltd.; Harian Creative Books; HarperCollins Publishers; Herald Publishing House; Heyday Books; Hippocrene Books Inc.; International Publishers Co., Inc.; Interurban Press/Trans Anglo Books; Knowledge Book Publishers; Lexikos; Library Research Associates, Inc.; Longstreet Press, Inc.; Lyons & Burford, Publishers,

Inc.; McFarland & Company, Inc., Publishers; Madison Books; Media Publishing/Midgard Press; Monitor Book Co., Inc.; Mosaic Press Miniature Books; Mountain Press Publishing Company; Mustang Publishing Co.; Oregon Historical Society Press; Overlook Press; Pacific Books, Publishers; Paragon House Publishers; Pelican Publishing Company; Permanent Press/Second Chance Press, The; Peter Pauper Press, Inc.; Pruett Publishing; QED Press; Scarborough House/Publisher; Schiffer Publishing Ltd.; Seven Locks Press, Inc.; Shoe String Press, The; Silver Burdett Press; Smith, Publisher, Gibbs; Stemmer House Publishers, Inc.; Sterling Publishing; Sunflower University Press; Texas Christian University Press; Transaction Books; University of Alaska Press; University of Arizona Press; University of Arkansas Press, The; University of Illinois Press; University of Nebraska Press; University of North Carolina Press, The; University of Oklahoma Press; University of Pennsylvania Press; University Press of Kentucky; University Press of Mississippi; University Press of New England; Utah State University Press; Vesta Publications, Ltd.; Warner Books, Inc.; Washington State University Pess; Watts, Inc., Franklin; Wayfinder Press; Webb Research Group; Westernlore Press; Wilderness Adventure Books; Winston-Derek Publishers, Inc.; Woodbine House; Yankee Books; Ye Galleon Press.

Animals. Alaska Northwest Books; Alpine Publications Inc.; Archway/Minstrel Books; Atheneum Children's Books; Barron's Educational Series, Inc.; Beaver Pond Publishing & Printing; Blockbuster Books, Inc.; Boxwood Press, The; Camden House Publishing; Canadian Plains Research Center; Capstone Press, Inc.; Carol Publishing; Carolrhoda Books, Inc.; Crown Publishing Group; Denlingers Publishers, Ltd.; Dillon Press, Inc.; Dutton Children's Books; Eriksson, Publisher, Paul S.; Faber & Faber, Inc.; Half Halt Press, Inc.; HarperCollins Publishers; Hay House, Inc.; Homestead Publishing; Hounslow Press; Kesend Publishing, Ltd., Michael; Krieger Publishing Co.; Lone Pine Publishing; Lucent Books; Lyons & Burford, Publishers, Inc.; Mosaic Press Miniature Books; Northland Publishing Co., Inc.; Pineapple Press, Inc.; Pippin Press; Pruett Publishing; Random House, Inc. Juvenile Books; Sandhill Crane Press, Inc.; Scarborough House/Publisher; Sierra Club Books; Silver Press; Stemmer House Publishers, Inc.; Stormline Press; TAB Books; University of Alaska Press; Warner Books, Inc.; Whitman and Co., Albert; Wilderness Adventure Books; Williamson Publishing Co.; Willowisp Press, Inc.; Wilshire Book Co.; Yankee Books.

Anthropology/Archaeology. Alaska Northwest Books; Avanyu Publishing Inc.; Bantam Books; Beacon Press; Blue Dolphin Publishing, Inc.; Bowling Green State University Popular Press; Cambridge University Press; City Lights Books; Dee, Inc., Ivan R.; Denali Press, The; Dundurn Press Ltd.; Filter Press; Guernica Editions; Inner Traditions International; Insight Books; Johnson Books; Kent State University Press; Kodansha International U.S.; Kumarian Press, Inc.; Lone Pine Publishing; Louisiana State University Press; Marketscope Books; Milkweed Editions; Northland Publishing Co., Inc.; Pennsylvania Historical and Museum Commission; Pruett Publishing; QED Press; Routledge, Chapman & Hall, Inc.; Scarborough House/Publisher; Stanford University Press; Sunflower University Press; University of Alabama Press; University of Alaska Press; University of Arizona Press; University of Iowa Press; University of Michigan Press; University of Nevada Press; University of New Mexico Press; University of Pennsylvania Press; University of Pittsburgh Press; University of Tennessee Press, The; University of Texas Press; University Press of Kentucky; Westernlore Press; White Cliffs Media Company; Whitman and Co., Albert; Wilderness Adventure Books; Wyrick & Company; Yankee Books.

Art/Architecture. Abrams, Inc. Harry N.; Alaska Northwest Books; Architectural Book Publishing Co., Inc.; Art Direction Book Company; Atheneum Children's Books; Avanyu Publishing Inc.; Barron's Educational Series, Inc.; Beacon Press; Bowling Green State University Popular Press; Branden Publishing Co., Inc.; Bucknell University Press; Cambridge University Press; Camino Books, Inc.; C&T Publishing; Caratzas, Publisher, Aristide D.; Carol Publishing; Carolrhoda Books, Inc.; Chelsea Green; Chicago Review Press; China Books & Periodicals, Inc.; Christopher Publishing House, The; Clarkson Potter; Coach House Press; Consultant Press, The; Coteau Books; Crisp Publications, Inc.; Crown Publishing Group; Davenport, Publishers, May; Davis Publications, Inc.; Dee, Inc., Ivan R.; Distinctive Publishing Corporation; Durst Publications Ltd.; Eriksson, Publisher, Paul S.; Fairleigh Dickinson University Press; Family Album, The; Fitzhenry & Whiteside; Forman Publishing, Inc.; Godine, Publisher, Inc., David R.; Gower Publishing Co.; HarperCollins Publishers; Hartley & Marks, Inc.; Homestead Publishing; Hounslow Press; Hudson Hill Press, Inc.; Inner Traditions International; Insight Books; Intervarsity Press; Iowa State University Press; Kent State University Press; Kodansha International U.S.; Lang Publishing, Peter; Lone Pine Publishing; Louisiana State University Press; Loyola University Press; Lyons & Burford,

Publishers, Inc.; McFarland & Company, Inc., Publishers; Mark Publishing; Meeramma Publications; Mercury Press, The; Milkweed Editions; Morrow and Co., William; Mosaic Press Miniature Books; Museum of Northern Arizona Press; North Light Books; Northland Publishing Co., Inc.; Ohio State University Press; Oregon Historical Society Press; PBC International, Inc. ; Pennsylvania Historical and Museum Commission; Prakken Publications, Inc.; Prentice Hall Press; Preservation Press, The; Press at California State University, Fresno, The; Princeton Architectural Press; Professional Publications, Inc.; Random House, Inc.; Rosen Publishing Group, The; Sasquatch Books; Schiffer Publishing Ltd.; Semaphore Press; Simon & Schuster; Smith, Publisher, Gibbs; ST Publications, Inc.; Starrhill Press; Stemmer House Publishers, Inc.; Sterling Publishing; Stormline Press; Sunstone Press; TAB Books; Twayne Publishers; University of Alaska Press; University of California Press; University of Massachusetts Press; University of Michigan Press; University of New Mexico Press; University of Pittsburgh Press; University of Tennessee Press, The; University of Texas Press; University Press of America, Inc.; University Press of New England; Walch, Publisher, J. Weston; Washington State University Pess; Western Producer Prairie Books; Whitman and Co., Albert; Whitson Publishing Co., The; Yankee Books; Zoland Books, Inc.

Astrology/Psychic/New Age. ACS Publications, Inc.; Bear and Co., Inc.; Blue Dolphin Publishing, Inc.; Cassandra Press; Delta Books; Humanics Publishing Group; McFarland & Company, Inc., Publishers; Newcastle Publishing Co., Inc.; Prentice Hall Press; Theosophical Publishing House, The; Whitford Press; Wingbow Press.

Audiocassettes. Abingdon Press; Chatham Press; Craftsman Book Company; Devin-Adair Publishers, Inc.; Gower Publishing Co.; Human Kinetics Publishers, Inc.; Humanics Publishing Group; Interstate Publishers, Inc. The; Kar-Ben Copies Inc.; Metamorphous Press; Muir Publications, John; National Textbook Co.; Peterson's; Potentials Development for Health & Aging Services; Price Stern Sloan, Inc.; Professional Publications, Inc.; Rainbow Books; St. Anthony Messenger Press; St. Bede's Publications; Stemmer House Publishers, Inc.; Troubador Press; Utah State University Press; Walch, Publisher, J. Weston; Wilshire Book Co.; Winston-Derek Publishers, Inc..

Autobiography. Berkley Publishing Group, The; Clarkson Potter; Daniel and Company, Publishers, John; Poseidon Press; Soho Press, Inc.

Bibliographies. Borgo Press, The; Chosen Books Publishing Co.; CQ Inc.; Family Album, The; Klein Publications, B.; Permanent Press/Second Chance Press, The; Scarecrow Press, Inc.; Whitson Publishing Co., The.

Biography. Addison-Wesley Publishing Co., Inc.; Advocacy Press; Architectural Book Publishing Co., Inc.; Arden Press, Inc.; Atheneum Children's Books; Atheneum Publishers; Avanyu Publishing Inc.; Avon Books; Baker Book House Company; Bantam Books; Berkley Publishing Group, The; Binford & Mort Publishing; Blair, Publisher, John F.; Blue Dolphin Publishing, Inc.; Bonus Books, Inc.; Borgo Press, The; Bosco Multimedia, Don; Bowling Green State University Popular Press; Boxwood Press, The; Branden Publishing Co., Inc..; British American Publishing; Camino Books, Inc.; Canadian Plains Research Center; Carol Publishing; Carolrhoda Books, Inc.; Carolrhoda Books, Inc.; Carroll & Graf Publishers, Inc.; Catholic University of America Press; Chelsea Green; China Books & Periodicals, Inc.; Christopher Publishing House, The; Citadel Press; Clarion Books; Clark Co., Arthur H.; Clarkson Potter; Contemporary Books, Inc.; Creative Publishing Co.; Crown Publishing Group; Cuff Publications Ltd., Harry; Daniel and Company, Publishers, John; Dante University Of America Press, Inc.; Dee, Inc., Ivan R.; Delta Books; Dillon Press, Inc.; Dundurn Press Ltd.; Dutton, E. P.; Ediciones Universal; Eriksson, Publisher, Paul S.; Faber & Faber, Inc.; Family Album, The; Fine, Inc., Donald I.; Fitzhenry & Whiteside; Fromm International; Gallaudet University Press; Gaslight Publications; Globe Pequot Press, Inc., The; Godine, Publisher, Inc., David R.; Gospel Publishing House; Great Northwest Publishing and Distributing Company, Inc.; Guernica Editions; Hancock House Publishers Ltd.; Harper San Francisco; HarperCollins Publishers; Hay House, Inc.; Hendrick-Long Publishing Co., Inc.; Here's Life Publishers, Inc.; Homestead Publishing; Houghton Mifflin Co.; Hounslow Press; ILR Press; Inner Traditions International; Innovatia Press; Insight Books; International Publishers Co., Inc.; Iowa State University Press; Kent State University Press; Kesend Publishing, Ltd., Michael; Kodansha International U.S.; Lang Publishing, Peter; Lawrence Books, Merloyd; Library Research Associates, Inc.; Little, Brown and Co., Inc.; Lone Pine Publishing; Longstreet Press, Inc.; Louisiana State University Press; Loyola University Press; Macmillan of Canada; Madison Books; Marketscope Books; Masters Press; Media Forum International, Ltd.; Media Publishing/Midgard Press; Mercury Press, The; Monitor Book Co., Inc.; Morrow and Co., William; Mosaic Press Miniature Books; Mother

Courage Press; Motorbooks International Publishers & Wholesalers; National Press, Inc.; Naval Institute Press; New Leaf Press, Inc.; New Victoria Publishers; Noble Press, Incorporated, The; Northland Publishing Co., Inc.; Ohio State University Press; Oregon Historical Society Press; Oregon State University Press; Pacific Press Publishing Association; Paragon House Publishers; Pelican Publishing Company; Permanent Press/Second Chance Press, The; Picadilly Books; Pineapple Press, Inc.; Pippin Press; Pocket Books; Poseidon Press; Presidio Press; Press at California State University, Fresno, The; Prima Publishing and Communications; Pruett Publishing; QED Press; Quill; Random House, Inc.; Random House, Inc. Juvenile Books; Routledge, Chapman & Hall, Inc.; Rutledge Hill Press; St. Martin's Press; St. Paul Books and Media; Scarborough House/Publisher; Schirmer Books; Scribner's Sons, Charles; Semaphore Press; Seven Locks Press, Inc.; Shoe String Press, The; Shoe Tree Press; Simon & Schuster; Smith, Publisher, Gibbs; Soho Press, Inc.; Stemmer House Publishers, Inc.; Stormline Press; Sunflower University Press; Thunder's Mouth Press; Times Books; Transaction Books; Twayne Publishers; University of Alabama Press; University of Alaska Press; University of Arkansas Press, The; University of Illinois Press; University of Massachusetts Press; University of Nebraska Press; University of Nevada Press; University of New Mexico Press; University of Pennsylvania Press; University of Pittsburgh Press; University Press of Kansas; University Press of Kentucky; University Press of Mississippi; University Press of New England; Unlimited Publishing Co.; Utah State University Press; Vesta Publications, Ltd.; VGM Career Horizons; Walker and Co.; Warner Books, Inc.; Washington State University Pess; Watts, Inc., Franklin; Wayfinder Press; Webb Research Group; Westernlore Press; Westport Publishers, Inc.; White Cliffs Media Company; Whitman and Co., Albert; Wilderness Adventure Books; Winston-Derek Publishers, Inc.; Woodsong Graphics, Inc.; Wyrick & Company; Yankee Books; Ye Galleon Press; Zebra Books; Zoland Books, Inc.; Zondervan Corp., The.

Business/Economics. Abbott, Langer & Associates; Adams, Inc., Bob; Addison-Wesley Publishing Co., Inc.; Afcom Publishing; Allen Publishing Co.; Almar Press; Amacom Books; American Business Consultants, Inc.; American Hospital Publishing, Inc.; Asher-Gallant Press; Atheneum Children's Books; Avery Publishing Group; Avon Books; Bantam Books; Barron's Educational Series, Inc.; Berkley Publishing Group, The; Betterway Publications, Inc.; Between the Lines; Blockbuster Books, Inc.; BNA Books; Bonus Books, Inc.; Brevet Press, Inc.; Brick House Publishing Co.; British American Publishing; Business & Legal Reports, Inc.; Cambridge University Press; Canadian Plains Research Center; Career Press Inc., The; Carol Publishing; Cassell Publications; Cato Institute; China Books & Periodicals, Inc.; Christopher Publishing House, The; Cleaning Consultant Services, Inc.; Conari Press; Consultant Press, The; Contemporary Books, Inc.; Crisp Publications, Inc.; Dee, Inc., Ivan R.; Devin-Adair Publishers, Inc.; Devonshire Publishing Co.; Durst Publications Ltd.; Enterprise Publishing Co., Inc.; Eriksson, Publisher, Paul S.; Facts On File, Inc.; Fairleigh Dickinson University Press; Fiesta Books Inc.; Financial Sourcebooks; Fitzhenry & Whiteside; Forman Publishing, Inc.; Fraser Institute; Glenbridge Publishing Ltd.; Gower Publishing Co.; Gulf Publishing Co.; HarperCollins Publishers; Hay House, Inc.; Health Administration Press; HRD Press, Inc.; Humanics Publishing Group; ILR Press; Industrial Press, Inc.; Info Net Publishing; Inner Traditions International; Insight Books; Intercultural Press, Inc.; International Foundation Of Employee Benefit Plans; International Publishers Co., Inc.; Iowa State University Press; Klein Publications, B.; Knowledge Industry Publications, Inc.; Kodansha International U.S.; Kumarian Press, Inc.; Lang Publishing, Peter; Liberty Hall Press; Liberty Publishing Company, Inc.; Library Research Associates, Inc.; Lone Pine Publishing; Longman Publishing Group; Loompanics Unlimited; Lucent Books; McFarland & Company, Inc., Publishers; Menasha Ridge Press, Inc.; Metamorphous Press; MGI Management Institute, Inc., The; Michigan State University Press; Mosaic Press Miniature Books; National Press, Inc.; National Textbook Co.; NavPress; NTC Publishing Group; Overlook Press; Pelican Publishing Company; Pfeiffer & Company; Pilot Books; Poseidon Press; Prentice Hall Press; Press at California State University, Fresno, The; Prima Publishing and Communications; Probus Publishing Co.; Professional Publications, Inc.; PSI Research; QED Press; R&E Publishers; Random House, Inc.; Regnery/Gateway, Inc.; Ronin Publishing; Ross Books; Routledge, Chapman & Hall, Inc.; Roxbury Publishing Co.; Russell Sage Foundation; Seven Locks Press, Inc.; Shapolsky Publishers; Shelby Publishing Co.; Slawson Communications, Inc.; Starburst Publishers; Sterling Publishing; Stipes Publishing Co.; Success Publishing; Sunflower University Press; TAB Books; Ten Speed Press; Times Books; Transaction Books; Trend Book Division; Twin Peaks Press; Union Square Press; University of Illinois Press; University of Michigan Press; University of Pennsylvania Press; University of Pittsburgh Press;

ARE YOU SERIOUS?

About learning to write better? Getting published? Getting paid for what you write? If you're dedicated to your writing, **Writer's Digest School** can put you on the fast track to writing success.

You'll Study With A Professional

Writer's Digest School offers you more than textbooks and assignments. As a student you'll correspond <u>directly with a professional writer</u> who is currently writing **and selling** the kind of material that you want to write. You'll learn from a pro who knows from personal experience, what it takes to get a manuscript written and published. A writer who can guide you as you work to achieve the same thing. A true mentor.

Work On Your Novel, Short Story, Nonfiction Book, Or Article

Writer's Digest School offers five courses: The Novel Writing Workshop, the Nonfiction Book Workshop, Writing to Sell Fiction (Short Stories), Writing to Sell Nonfiction (Articles), and the Science Fiction and Fantasy Workshop. Each course is described on the reverse side.

If you're serious about your writing, you owe it to yourself to check out **Writer's Digest School**. Mail the coupon below today for FREE information! Or call **1-800-759-0963**. (Outside the U.S., call (513) 531-2222.) Writer's Digest School, 1507 Dana Avenue, Cincinnati, Ohio 45207-1005.

- -

Here are five **Writer's Digest School** courses to help you write better and sell more:

Novel Writing Workshop. A professional novelist helps you iron out your plot, develop your main characters, write the background for your novel, and complete the opening scene and a summary of your novel's complete story. You'll even identify potential publishers, write a query letter, and get practical advice on the submission process.

Nonfiction Book Workshop. You'll work with your mentor to create a book proposal that you can send directly to a publisher. You'll develop and refine your book idea, write a chapter-by-chapter outline of your subject, line up your sources of information, write sample chapters, identify potential publishers, and complete your query letter.

Writing to Sell Fiction. Learn the basics of writing/selling short stories: plotting, characterization, dialogue, theme, conflict, and other elements of a marketable short story. Course includes writing assignments and one complete short story (and its revision).

Writing to Sell Nonfiction. Master the fundamentals of writing/selling nonfiction articles: finding article ideas, conducting interviews, writing effective query letters and attention-getting leads, targeting your articles to the right publication, and other important elements of a salable article. Course includes writing assignments and one complete article manuscript (and its revision).

Science Fiction and Fantasy Workshops. Explore the exciting world of science fiction and fantasy with one of our professional science fiction writers as your guide. Besides improving your general writing skills, you'll learn the special techniques of creating worlds, science and magic, shaping time and place. And how to get published in <u>this</u> world. Choose Short Story or Novel Writing.

Mail this card today for **FREE** information!

University Press of America, Inc.; Unlimited Publishing Co.; VGM Career Horizons; Wadsworth Publishing Company; Walch, Publisher, J. Weston; Walker and Co.; Warner Books, Inc.; Washington State University Press; Williamson Publishing Co.; Windsor Books.

Child Guidance/Parenting. Abbey Press; ALA Books; Avery Publishing Group; Baker Book House Company; Bantam Books; Barron's Educational Series, Inc.; Blockbuster Books, Inc.; Blue Bird Publishing; British American Publishing; Calgre Press; Cambridge Career Products; Camino Books, Inc.; Career Press Inc., The; Carol Publishing; Center for Applied Linguistics; Concordia Publishing House; Delta Books; Distinctive Publishing Corporation; Evergreen Communications, Inc.; Fiesta Books Inc.; Gallaudet University Press; Gardner Press, Inc.; Harbinger House, Inc.; Harvest House Publishers; Health Communications, Inc.; Hensley, Inc., Virgil W.; Hounslow Press; HRD Press, Inc.; Human Services Institute, Inc.; Inner Traditions International; Insight Books; Lawrence Books, Merloyd; Lion Publishing Corporation; Macmillan of Canada; Marketscope Books; Mills & Sanderson, Publishers; Muir Publications, John; National Press, Inc.; NavPress; Pruett Publishing; QED Press; R&E Publishers; Scarborough House/Publisher; Skidmore-Roth Publishing; Starburst Publishers; Victor Books; Walker and Co.; Warner Books, Inc.; Westport Publishers, Inc.; Williamson Publishing Co.; Woodbine House; Yankee Books.

Coffee Table Book. Bantam Books; Bentley, Inc., Robert; Blockbuster Books, Inc.; Bonus Books, Inc.; Camden House Publishing; Camino Books, Inc.; Canadian Plains Research Center; C&T Publishing; Caxton Printers, Ltd., The; China Books & Periodicals, Inc.; Dundurn Press Ltd.; Evergreen Communications, Inc.; Gallaudet University Press; Harian Creative Books; Homestead Publishing; Hounslow Press; Howell Press, Inc.; Ideals Publishing Corp.; Imagine, Inc.; Inner Traditions International; Lexikos; Lone Pine Publishing; Longstreet Press, Inc.; Macmillan of Canada; Mark Publishing; Multnomah Press; Museum of Northern Arizona Press; Northland Publishing Co., Inc.; Northwood Press, Inc.; Pelican Publishing Company; Pennsylvania Historical and Museum Commission; Press at California State University, Fresno, The; Pruett Publishing; Schiffer Publishing Ltd.; Taylor Publishing Company; Tidewater Publishers; Western Producer Prairie Books; Westport Publishers, Inc.; Willow Creek Press; Wyrick & Company; Yankee Books; Zoland Books, Inc.

Communications. Beacon Press; Longman Publishing Group; TAB Books; Union Square Press; Univelt, Inc.

Community/Public Affairs. Jalmar Press, Inc.; Pfeiffer & Company; Taylor Publishing Company; University of Alabama Press.

Computers/Electronics. Addison-Wesley Publishing Co., Inc.; Afcom Publishing; ALA Books; Amacom Books; Arcsoft Publishers; Bantam Books; Boyd & Fraser Publishing Company; Branden Publishing Co., Inc..; Career Publishing, Inc.; Carol Publishing; Center for Applied Linguistics; Computer Science Press; Entelek; Erlbaum Associates, Inc., Lawrence; Financial Sourcebooks; Gifted Education Press; Grapevine Publications, Inc.; Industrial Press, Inc.; Lucent Books; Macmillan of Canada; MGI Management Institute, Inc., The; Microtrend Books; Osborne/McGraw-Hill; PSI Research; Que Corporation; R&E Publishers; Ross Books; Slawson Communications, Inc.; Sybex, Inc.; TAB Books; Teachers College Press; Technical Communications Associates, Inc.; University of Pennsylvania Press; Walch, Publisher, J. Weston; White Cliffs Media Company; Whitman and Co., Albert.

Consumer Affairs. Almar Press; Beacon Press; Brick House Publishing Co.; International Foundation Of Employee Benefit Plans; Menasha Ridge Press, Inc.; Pharos Books.

Cooking/Foods/Nutrition. Addison-Wesley Publishing Co., Inc.; Alaska Northwest Books; Applezaba Press; Atheneum Children's Books; Atheneum Publishers; Avery Publishing Group; Bantam Books; Barron's Educational Series, Inc.; Better Homes and Gardens Books; Betterway Publications, Inc.; Blockbuster Books, Inc.; Blue Dolphin Publishing, Inc.; Bonus Books, Inc.; Briarcliff Press Publishers; Bristol Publishing Enterprises, Inc.; British American Publishing; Bull Publishing Co.; Cambridge Career Products; Camden House Publishing; Camino Books, Inc.; Carol Publishing; Cassandra Press; Chatham Press; Chicago Review Press; China Books & Periodicals, Inc.; Christopher Publishing House, The; Chronicle Books; Clarkson Potter; Consumer Reports Books; Contemporary Books, Inc.; Countryman Press, Inc., The; Crossing Press, The; Crown Publishing Group; DCI Publishing; Down East Books; Durst Publications Ltd.; Ediciones Universal; Eriksson, Publisher, Paul S.; Evans and Co., Inc., M.; Facts On File, Inc.; Filter Press; Fine, Inc., Donald I.; Fisher Books; Forman Publishing, Inc.; Globe Pequot Press, Inc., The; Godine, Publisher, Inc., David R.; Golden West Publishers; Hancock House Publishers Ltd.; Harian Creative Books; HarperCollins Publishers; Hartley & Marks, Inc.; Harvard Common Press, The; Hawkes Publishing, Inc.; Hay House, Inc.; Hounslow Press; Info Net Publishing; Inner Traditions International; Jonathan David Publishers; Liberty Publishing Company, Inc.; Little, Brown and Co., Inc.; Lone Pine Publishing; Longstreet Press, Inc.; Lyons & Burford, Publishers, Inc.; McCutchan Publishing Corporation; Macmillan of Canada; Media Forum International, Ltd.; Morrow and Co., William; Mosaic Press Miniature Books; National Press, Inc.; NordicPress; Northland Publishing Co., Inc.; Pacific Press Publishing Association; Peachtree Publishers, Ltd.; Pelican Publishing Company; Pennsylvania Historical and Museum Commission; Pocket Books; Prentice Hall Press; Prevention Health Books; Prima Publishing and Communications; Pruett Publishing; QED Press; R&E Publishers; Random House, Inc.; Richboro Press; Rutledge Hill Press; Sasquatch Books; Scarborough House/Publisher; Starburst Publishers; Stemmer House Publishers, Inc.; Sterling Publishing; Taylor Publishing Company; Ten Speed Press; Tidewater Publishers; Times Books; Twin Peaks Press; University of North Carolina Press, The; Unlimited Publishing Co.; Warner Books, Inc.; Wayfinder Press; Westport Publishers, Inc.; Whitman and Co., Albert; Williamson Publishing Co.; Wine Appreciation Guild, Ltd.; Woodbridge Press; Woodsong Graphics, Inc.; Yankee Books.

Counseling/Career Guidance. Adams, Inc., Bob; Almar Press; Career Publishing, Inc.; Jist Works, Inc.; National Textbook Co.; Octameron Associates; Peterson's; Pilot Books; Teachers College Press; VGM Career Horizons; Williamson Publishing Co..

Crafts. Barron's Educational Series, Inc.; Better Homes and Gardens Books; Briarcliff Press Publishers; Davis Publications, Inc.; Down East Books; Naturegraph Publishers, Inc.; Four Walls Eight Windows; Kumarian Press, Inc.; University of Nevada Press.

Educational. Advocacy Press; Afcom Publishing; ALA Books; Amacom Books; American Catholic Press; Anchorage Press, Inc.; Barron's Educational Series, Inc.; Between the Lines; Blue Bird Publishing; Blue Dolphin Publishing, Inc.; Bosco Multimedia, Don; British American Publishing; Bull Publishing Co.; Calgre Press; Cambridge Career Products; Canadian Institute of Ukranian Studies Press; Career Press Inc., The; Cato Institute; Center for Applied Linguistics; Crisp Publications, Inc.; Dante University Of America Press, Inc.; Denison & Co., Inc., T.S.; Dillon Press, Inc.; Distinctive Publishing Corporation; Duquesne University Press; Education Associates; EES Publications; Entelek; Erlbaum Associates, Inc., Lawrence; ETC Publications; Fairleigh Dickinson University Press; Fearon/Janus Publishers; Gallaudet University Press; Gardner Press, Inc.; Garrett Park Press; General Hall, Inc.; Gifted Education Press; Gospel Publishing House; Harian Creative Books; Hay House, Inc.; Hollowbrook Publishing; Humanics Publishing Group; Insight Books; Intercultural Press, Inc.; Interstate Publishers, Inc. The; Ishiyaku Euroamerica, Inc.; Jalmar Press, Inc.; Kent State University Press; Knopf, Inc., Alfred A.; Lang Publishing, Peter; Longman Publishing Group; McCutchan Publishing Corporation; Metamorphous Press; Morehouse Publishing Co.; Naturegraph Publishers, Inc.; Noble Press, Incorporated, The; NTC Publishing Group; Octameron Associates; Ohio State University Press; Open Court Publishing Co.; Peterson's; Pfeiffer & Company; Pilot Books; Porter Sargent Publishers, Inc.; Prakken Publications, Inc.; Preservation Press, The; PSI Research; Que Corporation; R&E Publishers; Reference Service Press; Routledge, Chapman & Hall, Inc.; Russell Sage Foundation; Scarborough House/Publisher; Speech Bin, Inc., The; Standard Publishing; Teachers College Press; University of Alaska Press; University Press of America, Inc.; University Press of Colorado; Walch, Publisher, J. Weston; Warner Books, Inc.; Whitaker House; White Cliffs Media Company; Williamson Publishing Co.; Woodbine House.

Entertainment/Games. Borgo Press, The; Broadway Press; Citadel Press; Delta Books; Drama Book Publishers; Faber & Faber, Inc.; Fairleigh Dickinson University Press; Focal Press; McFarland & Company, Inc., Publishers; Speech Bin, Inc., The; Standard Publishing; Sterling Publishing; University of Nevada Press.

Ethnic. Alaska Northwest Books; Avanyu Publishing Inc.; Between the Lines; Camino Books, Inc.; Canadian Institute of Ukranian Studies Press; Carol Publishing; China Books & Periodicals, Inc.; Coteau Books; Denali Press, The; Fairleigh Dickinson University Press; Filter Press; Garrett Park Press; General Hall, Inc.; Herald Press; Hill Books, Lawrence; Indiana University Press; Inner Traditions International; Insight Books; International Publishers Co., Inc.; Judson Press; Kar-Ben Copies Inc.; Kodansha International U.S.; Louisiana State University Press; Luramedia; Media Forum International, Ltd.; Noble Press, Incorporated, The; Oregon Historical Society Press; Pruett Publishing; QED Press; R&E Publishers; Reference Service Press; Scarborough House/Publisher; Semaphore Press; Silver Press; Stormline Press; Sunflower University Press; Temple

University Press; University of Alaska Press; University of Massachusetts Press; University of New Mexico Press; University of Oklahoma Press; University of Pittsburgh Press; University of Tennessee Press, The; University of Texas Press; University Press of America, Inc.; University Press of Mississippi; Vesta Publications, Ltd.; White Cliffs Media Company; Whitman and Co., Albert.

Feminism. Crossing Press, The; Firebrand Books; New Victoria Publishers.

Film/Cinema/Stage. Focal Press; French, Inc., Samuel; Gaslight Publications; Imagine, Inc.; Indiana University Press; Knowledge Industry Publications, Inc.; Lone Eagle Publishing Co.; McFarland & Company, Inc., Publishers; Media Forum International, Ltd.; Players Press, Inc.; Prentice Hall Press; Schirmer Books; Starrhill Press; TAB Books; Teachers College Press; University of Michigan Press; University of Texas Press; University Press of America, Inc.; Vestal Press, Ltd., The; VGM Career Horizons.

Gardening. Alaska Northwest Books; Better Homes and Gardens Books; Briarcliff Press Publishers; Camden House Publishing; Camino Books, Inc.; China Books & Periodicals, Inc.; Fisher Books; Globe Pequot Press, Inc., The; Godine, Publisher, Inc., David R.; Hartley & Marks, Inc.; Hay House, Inc.; Kodansha International U.S.; Lone Pine Publishing; Longstreet Press, Inc.; Lyons & Burford, Publishers, Inc.; Macmillan of Canada; Naturegraph Publishers, Inc.; Pineapple Press, Inc.; Prentice Hall Press; Pruett Publishing; Richboro Press; Sasquatch Books; Scarborough House/Publisher; Stackpole Books; Taylor Publishing Company; Ten Speed Press; Timber Press, Inc.; University of North Carolina Press, The; Warner Books, Inc.; Western Producer Prairie Books; Whitman and Co., Albert; Williamson Publishing Co.; Woodbridge Press; Wyrick & Company.

Gay/Lesbian. Alyson Publications, Inc.; Bantam Books; Between the Lines; Carol Publishing; City Lights Books; Cleis Press; Crossing Press, The; Firebrand Books; Gay Sunshine Press and Leyland Publications; General Hall, Inc.; Hay House, Inc.; Knights Press, Inc.; Los Hombres Press; Marketscope Books; Publishers Associates; Ten Speed Press.

General Nonfiction. Atheneum Publishers; Avon Flare Books; Beacon Press; Evans and Co., Inc., M.; Indiana University Press; Johnson Books; Jonathan David Publishers; Kent State University Press; Knopf, Inc., Alfred A.; Lang Publishing, Peter; Leisure Books; Lothrop, Lee & Shepard Books; Media Publishing/Midgard Press; Mills & Sanderson, Publishers; Morrow and Co., William; Norton Co., Inc., W.W.; Ohio State University Press; Pacific Books, Publishers; Pantheon Books; Peachtree Publishers, Ltd.; Pocket Books; Potentials Development for Health & Aging Services; Rainbow Books; Renaissance House Publishers; St. Anthony Messenger Press; St. Martin's Press; Scholastic, Inc.; Shaw Publishers, Harold; Shoe String Press, The; Ticknor & Fields; Time-Life Books Inc.; Twayne Publishers; University of Wisconsin Press; Writer's Digest Books.

Government/Politics. Addison-Wesley Publishing Co., Inc.; Arden Press, Inc.; Atheneum Publishers; Avon Books; Bantam Books; Beacon Press; Between the Lines; Bonus Books, Inc.; Borgo Press, The; Branden Publishing Co., Inc.; British American Publishing; Bucknell University Press; C Q Press; Camino Books, Inc.; Canadian Institute of Ukranian Studies Press; Canadian Plains Research Center; Carol Publishing; Cato Institute; China Books & Periodicals, Inc.; Christopher Publishing House, The; Cleis Press; CQ Inc.; Crown Publishing Group; Cuff Publications Ltd., Harry; Dee, Inc., Ivan R.; Denali Press, The; Devin-Adair Publishers, Inc.; Dutton, E. P.; Ediciones Universal; Eriksson, Publisher, Paul S.; Fairleigh Dickinson University Press; Financial Sourcebooks; FPMI Communications, Inc.; Fraser Institute; General Hall, Inc.; Glenbridge Publishing Ltd.; Gower Publishing Co.; HarperCollins Publishers; Health Administration Press; Hill Books, Lawrence; Humanities Press International, Inc.; Indiana University Press; Intercultural Press, Inc.; International Publishers Co., Inc.; Kodansha International U.S.; Kumarian Press, Inc.; Lang Publishing, Peter; Library Research Associates, Inc.; Lone Pine Publishing; Longman Publishing Group; Loompanics Unlimited; Louisiana State University Press; Lucent Books; Macmillan of Canada; Media Publishing/Midgard Press; Mercury Press, The; Michigan State University Press; Milkweed Editions; National Press, Inc.; Noble Press, Incorporated, The; Open Court Publishing Co.; Oregon Historical Society Press; Paragon House Publishers; Pelican Publishing Company; Pennsylvania Historical and Museum Commission; Permanent Press/Second Chance Press, The; Poseidon Press; Press at California State University, Fresno, The; Prima Publishing and Communications; Publishers Associates; QED Press; R&E Publishers; Regnery/Gateway, Inc.; Russell Sage Foundation; St. Martin's Press; Sasquatch Books; Scarborough House/Publisher; Seven Locks Press, Inc.; Shoe String Press, The; Stanford University Press; Starburst Publishers; Sunflower

University Press; Teachers College Press; Temple University Press; Thunder's Mouth Press; Transaction Books; Trend Book Division; University of Alabama Press; University of Alaska Press; University of Arkansas Press, The; University of Illinois Press; University of North Carolina Press, The; University of Pittsburgh Press; University Press of Kansas; University Press of Kentucky; University Press of Mississippi; University Press of New England; Utah State University Press; Vesta Publications, Ltd.; Walch, Publisher, J. Weston; Warner Books, Inc.; Washington State University Pess; Watts, Inc., Franklin; Wayfinder Press; Yankee Books.

Health/Medicine. Addison-Wesley Publishing Co., Inc.; Almar Press; America West Publishers; American Hospital Publishing, Inc.; Atheneum Children's Books; Avery Publishing Group; Avon Books; Bantam Books; Barron's Educational Series, Inc.; Berkley Publishing Group, The; Between the Lines; Blue Dolphin Publishing, Inc.; Bonus Books, Inc.; Branden Publishing Co., Inc.; Briarcliff Press Publishers; British American Publishing; Bull Publishing Co.; Cambridge Career Products; Camden House, Inc.; Carol Publishing; Cassandra Press; Cato Institute; Christopher Publishing House, The; Cleaning Consultant Services, Inc.; Consumer Reports Books; Contemporary Books, Inc.; Crisp Publications, Inc.; Crossing Press, The; Crown Publishing Group; DCI Publishing; Dee, Inc., Ivan R.; Devin-Adair Publishers, Inc.; Distinctive Publishing Corporation; EES Publications; Elysium Growth Press; Eriksson, Publisher, Paul S.; Erlbaum Associates, Inc., Lawrence; Evans and Co., Inc., M.; Facts On File, Inc.; Fiesta Books Inc.; Fisher Books; Fitzhenry & Whiteside; Forman Publishing, Inc.; Gallaudet University Press; Gardner Press, Inc.; Government Institutes, Inc.; Green, Inc., Warren H.; HarperCollins Publishers; Hartley & Marks, Inc.; Hawkes Publishing, Inc.; Hay House, Inc.; Health Administration Press; Houghton Mifflin Co.; Hounslow Press; Human Kinetics Publishers, Inc.; Humanics Publishing Group; In Depth Publishers; Inner Traditions International; Insight Books; International Foundation Of Employee Benefit Plans; Iowa State University Press; Ishiyaku Euroamerica, Inc.; Kesend Publishing, Ltd., Michael; Knowledge Book Publishers; Kodansha International U.S.; Krieger Publishing Co.; Lawrence Books, Merloyd; Leisure Press; Luramedia; McFarland & Company, Inc., Publishers; Macmillan of Canada; Marketscope Books; Meeramma Publications; Menasha Ridge Press, Inc.; Metamorphous Press; Mills & Sanderson, Publishers; Mosaic Press Miniature Books; Mother Courage Press; Naturegraph Publishers, Inc.; Newcastle Publishing Co., Inc.; NordicPress; Pacific Press Publishing Association; Pelican Publishing Company; Perspectives Press; Plenum Publishing; Prevention Health Books; Prima Publishing and Communications; QED Press; R&E Publishers; Random House, Inc.; Rosen Publishing Group, The; Scarborough House/Publisher; Scribner's Sons, Charles; Sierra Club Books; Skidmore-Roth Publishing; Slawson Communications, Inc.; Speech Bin, Inc., The; Starburst Publishers; Sterling Publishing; Sunflower University Press; TAB Books; Temple University Press; Ten Speed Press; Theosophical Publishing House, The; Times Books; Transaction Books; Twin Peaks Press; Ultralight Publications, Inc.; University of Alaska Press; University of Pennsylvania Press; University of Pittsburgh Press; VGM Career Horizons; Walch, Publisher, J. Weston; Walker and Co.; Warner Books, Inc.; Weiser, Inc., Samuel; Whitaker House; Whitman and Co., Albert; Williamson Publishing Co.; Wilshire Book Co.; Winston-Derek Publishers, Inc.; Woodbine House; Woodbridge Press; Zebra Books.

Hi-Lo. Cambridge Career Products; Fearon/Janus Publishers; National Textbook Co.; New Readers Press; Rosen Publishing Group, The; University of Michigan Press.

History. Academy Chicago; Addison-Wesley Publishing Co., Inc.; Alaska Northwest Books; Ancestry Incorporated; Appalachian Mountain Club Books; Architectural Book Publishing Co., Inc.; Arden Press, Inc.; Atheneum Children's Books; Atheneum Publishers; Avanyu Publishing Inc.; Avery Publishing Group; Avon Books; Beacon Press; Binford & Mort Publishing; Blair, Publisher, John F.; Borgo Press, The; Boston Mills Press; Bowling Green State University Popular Press; Boxwood Press, The; Branden Publishing Co., Inc.; Brevet Press, Inc.; Bucknell University Press; Camino Books, Inc.; Canadian Institute of Ukranian Studies Press; Canadian Plains Research Center; Capstone Press, Inc.; Caratzas, Publisher, Aristide D.; Carol Publishing; Carolrhoda Books, Inc.; Carroll & Graf Publishers, Inc.; Catholic University of America Press; Chatham Press; China Books & Periodicals, Inc.; Christopher Publishing House, The; Citadel Press; Clark Co., Arthur H.; Countryman Press, Inc., The; Creative Publishing Co.; Crossway Books; Crown Publishing Group; Cuff Publications Ltd., Harry; Dee, Inc., Ivan R.; Denali Press, The; Devin-Adair Publishers, Inc.; Devonshire Publishing Co.; Dillon Press, Inc.; Down East Books; Dundurn Press Ltd.; Eerdmans Publishing Co., William B.; Eriksson, Publisher, Paul S.; Facts On File, Inc.; Fairleigh Dickinson University Press; Family Album, The; Fine, Inc., Donald I.; Fitzhenry & Whiteside;

Flores Publications, J.; Fromm International; Gallaudet University Press; Gaslight Publications; Glenbridge Publishing Ltd.; Globe Pequot Press, Inc., The; Globe Press Books; Godine, Publisher, Inc., David R.; Golden West Publishers; Gospel Publishing House; Guernica Editions; Hancock House Publishers Ltd.; HarperCollins Publishers; Hawkes Publishing, Inc.; Heart Of The Lakes Publishing; Herald Publishing House; Heritage Books, Inc.; Heyday Books; Hippocrene Books Inc.; Hollowbrook Publishing; Homestead Publishing; Houghton Mifflin Co.; Hounslow Press; Howell Press, Inc.; Humanities Press International, Inc.; ILR Press; Indiana University Press; Info Net Publishing; Inner Traditions International; Innovatia Press; International Publishers Co., Inc.; Interurban Press/Trans Anglo Books; Intervarsity Press; Iowa State University Press; Kent State University Press; Kesend Publishing, Ltd., Michael; Kinseeker Publications; Kodansha International U.S.; Krieger Publishing Co.; Lang Publishing, Peter; Lexikos; Library Research Associates, Inc.; Little, Brown and Co., Inc.; Lone Pine Publishing; Longman Publishing Group; Longstreet Press, Inc.; Louisiana State University Press; Loyola University Press; Lucent Books; Macmillan of Canada; Madison Books; Media Publishing/Midgard Press; Mercury Press, The; Michigan State University Press; Milkweed Editions; Morehouse Publishing Co.; Morrow and Co., William; Mosaic Press Miniature Books; Motorbooks International Publishers & Wholesalers; National Press, Inc.; Nautical & Aviation Publishing Co., The; Naval Institute Press; New Victoria Publishers; Noble Press, Incorporated, The; Northern Illinois University Press; Northland Publishing Co., Inc.; Oddo Publishing, Inc.; Ohio State University Press; Oregon Historical Society Press; Oregon State University Press; Overlook Press; Paragon House Publishers; Peachtree Publishers, Ltd.; Pennsylvania Historical and Museum Commission; Permanent Press/Second Chance Press, The; Pineapple Press, Inc.; Poseidon Press; Preservation Press, The; Presidio Press; Press at California State University, Fresno, The; Pruett Publishing; Publishers Associates; Quill; R&E Publishers; Random House, Inc.; Russell Sage Foundation; St. Bede's Publications; St. Martin's Press; Sasquatch Books; Scarborough House/Publisher; Schiffer Publishing Ltd.; Semaphore Press; Seven Locks Press, Inc.; Shaw Publishers, Harold; Shoe String Press, The; Sierra Club Books; Silver Burdett Press; Silver Press; Simon & Schuster; Smith, Publisher, Gibbs; Southfarm Press; Stanford University Press; Starburst Publishers; Stemmer House Publishers, Inc.; Stormline Press; Sunflower University Press; Sunstone Press; Teachers College Press; Temple University Press; Texas A&M University Press; Texas Western Press; Three Continents Press; Timber Press, Inc.; Times Books; Transaction Books; Transportation Trails; Trend Book Division; Twayne Publishers; University of Alabama Press; University of Alaska Press; University of Arkansas Press, The; University of Illinois Press; University of Iowa Press; University of Massachusetts Press; University of Michigan Press; University of Nebraska Press; University of Nevada Press; University of New Mexico Press; University of North Carolina Press, The; University of Oklahoma Press; University of Pennsylvania Press; University of Pittsburgh Press; University of Tennessee Press, The; University of Texas Press; University Press of America, Inc.; University Press of Kansas; University Press of Kentucky; University Press of Mississippi; University Press of New England; Vestal Press, Ltd., The; Wadsworth Publishing Company; Walch, Publisher, J. Weston; Walker and Co.; Washington State University Pess; Watts, Inc., Franklin; Wayfinder Press; Webb Research Group; Westernlore Press; Wilderness Adventure Books; Woodbine House; Yankee Books; Ye Galleon Press; Zebra Books.

Hobby. Afcom Publishing; Alaska Northwest Books; Almar Press; Ancestry Incorporated; Arcsoft Publishers; Atheneum Children's Books; Beaver Pond Publishing & Printing; Betterway Publications, Inc.; C&T Publishing; Camden House Publishing; Capstone Press, Inc.; Carstens Publications, Inc.; Collector Books; Crown Publishing Group; Devonshire Publishing Co.; Dundurn Press Ltd.; Durst Publications Ltd.; Eriksson, Publisher, Paul S.; Facts On File, Inc.; Filter Press; Hartley & Marks, Inc.; Hawkes Publishing, Inc.; Interurban Press/Trans Anglo Books; Interweave Press; Kalmbach Publishing Co.; Kesend Publishing, Ltd., Michael; Klein Publications, B.; Kodansha International U.S.; Liberty Publishing Company, Inc.; Mark Publishing; Marketscope Books; Menasha Ridge Press, Inc.; Mosaic Press Miniature Books; Mustang Publishing Co.; Picadilly Books; Prentice Hall Press; QED Press; Scarborough House/Publisher; Schiffer Publishing Ltd.; Semaphore Press; Silver Press; Stackpole Books; Sterling Publishing; Success Publishing; Sunstone Press; TAB Books; Travel Keys; Ultralight Publications, Inc.; University of North Carolina Press, The; Unlimited Publishing Co.; Vestal Press, Ltd., The; Williamson Publishing Co.; Wilshire Book Co.; Woodbine House; Woodsong Graphics, Inc..

How-to. AASLH; Abbott, Langer & Associates; Accent Books; Addison-Wesley Publishing Co., Inc.;

Afcom Publishing; Allen Publishing Co.; Almar Press; Alpine Publications Inc.; Amacom Books; American Business Consultants, Inc.; American Correctional Association; Amherst Media; Ancestry Incorporated; Andrews and McMeel; Appalachian Mountain Club Books; Arman Publishing, Inc., M.; Aronson, Inc., Jason; Art Direction Book Company; Asher-Gallant Press; Atheneum Children's Books; Avery Publishing Group; Avon Books; Bantam Books; Beaver Pond Publishing & Printing; Bentley, Inc., Robert; Berkley Publishing Group, The; Better Homes and Gardens Books; Betterway Publications, Inc.; Bicycle Books, Inc.; Blockbuster Books, Inc.; Blue Bird Publishing; Blue Dolphin Publishing, Inc.; Bonus Books, Inc.; Briarcliff Press Publishers; Brick House Publishing Co.; British American Publishing; Bull Publishing Co.; Calgre Press; Cambridge Career Products; Camden House Publishing; Camino Books, Inc.; C&T Publishing; Career Press Inc., The; Carol Publishing; Cassandra Press; Cassell Publications; Chicago Review Press; China Books & Periodicals, Inc.; Chosen Books Publishing Co.; Christopher Publishing House, The; Clarkson Potter; Cleaning Consultant Services, Inc.; Consumer Reports Books; Contemporary Books, Inc.; Cornell Maritime Press, Inc.; Countryman Press, Inc., The; Craftsman Book Company; Crisp Publications, Inc.; Crossing Press, The; Crown Publishing Group; Denlingers Publishers, Ltd.; Devin-Adair Publishers, Inc.; Distinctive Publishing Corporation; Durst Publications Ltd.; Education Associates; EES Publications; Eriksson, Publisher, Paul S.; Evergreen Communications, Inc.; Fiesta Books Inc.; Filter Press; Fisher Books; Flores Publications, J.; Focal Press; Forman Publishing, Inc.; Gay Sunshine Press and Leyland Publications; Gifted Education Press; Globe Pequot Press, Inc., The; Grapevine Publications, Inc.; Graphic Arts Technical Foundation; Great Northwest Publishing and Distributing Company, Inc.; Half Halt Press, Inc.; Hamilton Institute, Alexander; Hancock House Publishers Ltd.; Harper San Francisco; HarperCollins Publishers; Hartley & Marks, Inc.; Harvard Common Press, The; Harvest House Publishers; Hawkes Publishing, Inc.; Hay House, Inc.; Here's Life Publishers, Inc.; Heritage Books, Inc.; Heyday Books; Hounslow Press; Human Kinetics Publishers, Inc.; Imagine, Inc.; In Depth Publishers; Info Net Publishing; Intercultural Press, Inc.; International Wealth Success; Interweave Press; Jist Works, Inc.; Kalmbach Publishing Co.; Kesend Publishing, Ltd., Michael; Klein Publications, B.; Knowledge Book Publishers; Leisure Press; Liberty Hall Press; Liberty Publishing Company, Inc.; Library Research Associates, Inc.; Linch Publishing, Inc.; Little, Brown and Co., Inc.; Llewellyn Publications; Lone Eagle Publishing Co.; Lone Pine Publishing; Loompanics Unlimited; Macmillan of Canada; Mark Publishing; Marketscope Books; Media Publishing/Midgard Press; Menasha Ridge Press, Inc.; Metamorphous Press; MGI Management Institute, Inc., The; Morrow and Co., William; Mother Courage Press; Motorbooks International Publishers & Wholesalers; Mountaineers Books, The; Muir Publications, John; Mustang Publishing Co.; Naturegraph Publishers, Inc.; Newcastle Publishing Co., Inc.; Noble Press, Incorporated, The; NordicPress; North Light Books; Northland Publishing Co., Inc.; Northwood Press, Inc.; Ohara Publications, Inc.; Overlook Press; Pacific Press Publishing Association; Pelican Publishing Company; Pennsylvania Historical and Museum Commission; Perspectives Press; Picadilly Books; Pineapple Press, Inc.; Prevention Health Books; Prima Publishing and Communications; Princeton Book Company, Publishers; Probus Publishing Co.; PSI Research; QED Press; Que Corporation; R&E Publishers; Resource Publications, Inc.; Richboro Press; Ronin Publishing; Ross Books; Scarborough House/Publisher; Schiffer Publishing Ltd.; Semaphore Press; Shapolsky Publishers; Shelby Publishing Co.; Sierra Club Books; Speech Bin, Inc., The; ST Publications, Inc.; Standard Publishing; Starburst Publishers; Sterling Publishing; Stoeger Publishing Company; Success Publishing; Sunstone Press; TAB Books; Ten Speed Press; Thomas Publications; Tidewater Publishers; Twin Peaks Press; Ultralight Publications, Inc.; Union Square Press; Unlimited Publishing Co.; Weiser, Inc., Samuel; Whitaker House; Whitford Press; Wilderness Adventure Books; Wilderness Press; Williamson Publishing Co.; Wilshire Book Co.; Windsor Books; Wine Appreciation Guild, Ltd.; Woodsong Graphics, Inc.; Yankee Books; Zebra Books.

Humanities. Asian Humanities Press; Duquesne University Press; Indiana University Press; Roxbury Publishing Co.; Stanford University Press; Whitson Publishing Co., The.

Humor. Andrews and McMeel; Atheneum Children's Books; Baker Book House Company; Bale Books; Bantam Books; Blue Dolphin Publishing, Inc.; British American Publishing; C.S.S. Publishing Co.; Camino Books, Inc.; Carol Publishing; CCC Publications; Citadel Press; Clarion Books; Clarkson Potter; Cliffs Notes, Inc.; Contemporary Books, Inc.; Coteau Books; Crown Publishing Group; Cuff Publications Ltd., Harry; Ediciones Universal; Eriksson, Publisher, Paul S.; Faber & Faber, Inc.; Fine, Inc., Donald I.; Harian Creative Books; HarperCollins Publishers; Hay House,

Inc.; Hounslow Press; Innovatia Press; Jonathan David Publishers; Longstreet Press, Inc.; Macmillan of Canada; Marketscope Books; Media Forum International, Ltd.; Mosaic Press Miniature Books; Mustang Publishing Co.; Once Upon a Planet, Inc.; Peachtree Publishers, Ltd.; Pelican Publishing Company; Pharos Books; Picadilly Books; Price Stern Sloan, Inc.; QED Press; R&E Publishers; Random House, Inc.; Random House, Inc. Juvenile Books; Ronin Publishing; Rutledge Hill Press; Sterling Publishing; Stormline Press; Success Publishing; Taylor Publishing Company; University of Arkansas Press, The; Unlimited Publishing Co.; Warner Books, Inc.; Western Producer Prairie Books; Whitman and Co., Albert; Willow Creek Press; Woodsong Graphics, Inc.; Wyrick & Company; Yankee Books.

Illustrated Book. Abrams, Inc. Harry N.; Atheneum Children's Books; Avanyu Publishing Inc.; Bantam Books; Bear and Co., Inc.; Betterway Publications, Inc.; Boston Mills Press; Branden Publishing Co., Inc..; Canadian Plains Research Center; Carol Publishing; Chronicle Books; Cleaning Consultant Services, Inc.; Coach House Press; Coteau Books; Davis Publications, Inc.; Dial Books For Young Readers; Elysium Growth Press; Flores Publications, J.; Gallaudet University Press; Godine, Publisher, Inc., David R.; Graphic Arts Center Publishing Co.; Harvest House Publishers; Homestead Publishing; Hounslow Press; Howell Press, Inc.; Imagine, Inc.; Inner Traditions International; Kesend Publishing, Ltd., Michael; Lexikos; Longstreet Press, Inc.; Lothrop, Lee & Shepard Books; Metamorphous Press; Milkweed Editions; Mosaic Press Miniature Books; Multnomah Press; Noble Press, Incorporated, The; Northland Publishing Co., Inc.; Northwood Press, Inc.; Once Upon a Planet, Inc.; Pelican Publishing Company; Pennsylvania Historical and Museum Commission; Prentice Hall Press; Princeton Architectural Press; Pruett Publishing; R&E Publishers; Random House, Inc.; Random House, Inc. Juvenile Books; Schiffer Publishing Ltd.; Semaphore Press; Speech Bin, Inc., The; Stemmer House Publishers, Inc.; Stormline Press; Sunflower University Press; Tidewater Publishers; UAHC Press; University of New Mexico Press; Unlimited Publishing Co.; Warner Books, Inc.; Wayfinder Press; Western Producer Prairie Books; Whitman and Co., Albert; Wilderness Adventure Books; Williamson Publishing Co.; Willow Creek Press; Willowisp Press, Inc.; Woodsong Graphics, Inc.; Wyrick & Company; Yankee Books.

Juvenile Books. Abingdon Press; Advocacy Press; Archway/Minstrel Books; Atheneum Children's Books; Baker Book House Company; Bantam Books; Barron's Educational Series, Inc.; Beacon Press; Behrman House Inc.; Betterway Publications, Inc.; Bosco Multimedia, Don; Boyds Mills Press; Branden Publishing Co., Inc..; Cambridge Career Products; Camden House Publishing; Camino Books, Inc.; Carolrhoda Books, Inc.; Charlesbridge Publishing; Chronicle Books; Clarion Books; Clarkson Potter; Concordia Publishing House; Consumer Reports Books; Coteau Books; Davenport, Publishers, May; Denison & Co., Inc., T.S.; Dial Books For Young Readers; Dillon Press, Inc.; Dundurn Press Ltd.; Dutton Children's Books; Education Associates; Evergreen Communications, Inc.; Fawcett Juniper; Fitzhenry & Whiteside; Gallaudet University Press; Godine, Publisher, Inc., David R.; Greenhaven Press, Inc.; Grosset & Dunlap Publishers; Guernica Editions; Harbinger House, Inc.; Harcourt Brace Jovanovich; HarperCollins Children's Books Pacific Northwest; Harvest House Publishers; Hay House, Inc.; Hendrick-Long Publishing Co., Inc.; Herald Press; Homestead Publishing; Houghton Mifflin Co.; HRD Press, Inc.; Ideals Publishing Corp.; Kar-Ben Copies Inc.; Knowledge Book Publishers; Lone Pine Publishing; Lothrop, Lee & Shepard Books; Lucent Books; McElderry Books, Margaret K.; Metamorphous Press; Morehouse Publishing Co.; Morrow and Co., William; Morrow Junior Books; Muir Publications, John; Multnomah Press; NavPress; Northwood Press, Inc.; Oddo Publishing, Inc.; Oregon Historical Society Press; Pacific Press Publishing Association; Pelican Publishing Company; Perspectives Press; Players Press, Inc.; Price Stern Sloan, Inc.; Random House, Inc. Juvenile Books; Review and Herald Publishing Association; St. Paul Books and Media; Shaw Publishers, Harold; Shoe String Press, The; Shoe Tree Press; Sierra Club Books; Silver Burdett Press; Silver Press; Speech Bin, Inc., The; Standard Publishing; Stemmer House Publishers, Inc.; Sterling Publishing; Stormline Press; Texas Christian University Press; Tidewater Publishers; Troubador Press; UAHC Press; Victor Books; Western Producer Prairie Books; Willowisp Press, Inc.; Woodsong Graphics, Inc.; Yankee Books.

Labor/Management. Abbott, Langer & Associates; ALA Books; BNA Books; Drama Book Publishers; Enterprise Publishing Co., Inc.; FPMI Communications, Inc.; Gulf Publishing Co.; Hamilton Institute, Alexander; ILR Press; International Publishers Co., Inc.; MGI Management Institute, Inc., The; Pfeiffer & Company; Teachers College Press.

Language and Literature. Alaska Northwest Books; Anchorage Press, Inc.; Asian Humanities Press; Baker Book House Company; Bantam Books; Barron's Educational Series, Inc.; Beacon

Press; Black Sparrow Press; Bowling Green State University Popular Press; British American Publishing; Camden House, Inc.; Canadian Institute of Ukranian Studies Press; Caratzas, Publisher, Aristide D.; Cassell Publications; Catholic University of America Press; Center for Applied Linguistics; Chicago Review Press; China Books & Periodicals, Inc.; Clarion Books; Clarkson Potter; Coach House Press; Coteau Books; Crossing Press, The; Daniel and Company, Publishers, John; Dante University Of America Press, Inc.; Dee, Inc., Ivan R.; Dundurn Press Ltd.; Facts On File, Inc.; Family Album, The; Gallaudet University Press; Godine, Publisher, Inc., David R.; Harian Creative Books; Hippocrene Books Inc.; Hollowbrook Publishing; Indiana University Press; Insight Books; Intervarsity Press; Kent State University Press; Kodansha International U.S.; Lang Publishing, Peter; Longstreet Press, Inc.; Louisiana State University Press; Macmillan of Canada; Mercury Press, The; Michigan State University Press; Milkweed Editions; Modern Language Association of America; National Textbook Co.; New Readers Press; NTC Publishing Group; Ohio State University Press; Oregon State University Press; Pippin Press; QED Press; Roxbury Publishing Co.; Scarborough House/Publisher; Shoe String Press, The; Silver Press; Stanford University Press; Sunflower University Press; Three Continents Press; Twayne Publishers; University of Alabama Press; University of Alaska Press; University of Arkansas Press, The; University of California Press; University of Illinois Press; University of Iowa Press; University of Michigan Press; University of Nebraska Press; University of Nevada Press; University of North Carolina Press, The; University of Oklahoma Press; University of Pittsburgh Press; University of Texas Press; University Press of America, Inc.; University Press of Mississippi; Utah State University Press; Vesta Publications Ltd.; Wake Forest University Press; Walch, Publisher, J. Weston; Warner Books, Inc.; Writer's Digest Books; Wyrick & Company; Yankee Books; Zoland Books, Inc..

Law. Almar Press; Anderson Publishing Co.; Banks-Baldwin Law Publishing Co.; BNA Books; Durst Publications Ltd.; EES Publications; Enterprise Publishing Co., Inc.; Government Institutes, Inc.; Hamilton Institute, Alexander; Liberty Hall Press; Linch Publishing, Inc.; McCutchan Publishing Corporation; Monitor Book Co., Inc.; Ohio State University Press; Transaction Books; Trend Book Division; University of Michigan Press; University of North Carolina Press, The; University of Pennsylvania Press.

Literary Criticism. Barron's Educational Series, Inc.; Borgo Press, The; Bucknell University Press; Dundurn Press Ltd.; ECW Press; Fairleigh Dickinson University Press; Firebrand Books; Gaslight Publications; Graywolf Press; Lang Publishing, Peter; Mysterious Press, The; Northern Illinois University Press; Routledge, Chapman & Hall, Inc.; Texas Christian University Press; Three Continents Press; University of Alabama Press; University of Massachusetts Press; University of Pennsylvania Press; University of Tennessee Press, The; University Press of Mississippi.

Marine Subjects. Binford & Mort Publishing; Cornell Maritime Press, Inc.; Flores Publications, J.; TAB Books; Transportation Trails.

Military/War. Avery Publishing Group; Avon Books; Bantam Books; Beau Lac Publishers; Cato Institute; Crown Publishing Group; Dee, Inc., Ivan R.; Fine, Inc., Donald I.; Flores Publications, J.; Hippocrene Books Inc.; Howell Press, Inc.; Info Net Publishing; Innovatia Press; Kodansha International U.S.; Louisiana State University Press; Lucent Books; Macmillan of Canada; Nautical & Aviation Publishing Co., The; Naval Institute Press; Prentice Hall Press; Presidio Press; Quill; Reference Service Press; Scarborough House/Publisher; Schiffer Publishing Ltd.; Shoe String Press, The; Southfarm Press; Stackpole Books; Starburst Publishers; Sterling Publishing; Sunflower University Press; Texas A&M University Press; University of Alaska Press; University Press of Kansas; Warner Books, Inc.; Webb Research Group; Zebra Books.

Money/Finance. Allen Publishing Co.; Almar Press; Bale Books; Bantam Books; Better Homes and Gardens Books; Blockbuster Books, Inc.; Bonus Books, Inc.; Briarcliff Press Publishers; Brick House Publishing Co.; Cambridge Career Products; Career Press Inc., The; Carol Publishing; Cato Institute; Consumer Reports Books; Contemporary Books, Inc.; Crisp Publications, Inc.; Enterprise Publishing Co., Inc.; Financial Sourcebooks; Hancock House Publishers Ltd.; Hay House, Inc.; Hensley, Inc., Virgil W.; Hounslow Press; Insight Books; International Wealth Success; Liberty Hall Press; Liberty Publishing Company, Inc.; Macmillan of Canada; National Press, Inc.; NavPress; Pilot Books; Probus Publishing Co.; PSI Research; QED Press; R&E Publishers; Scarborough House/Publisher; Shelby Publishing Co.; Slawson Communications, Inc.; Starburst Publishers; Success Publishing; Sunflower University Press; Ten Speed Press; ULI, The Urban Land Institute; United Resource Press; Vesta Publications, Ltd.; Warner Books, Inc.; Wilshire Book Co.; Windsor Books.

Music and Dance. American Catholic Press; Atheneum Children's Books; Bantam Books; Betterway Publications, Inc.; Branden Publishing Co., Inc..; Bucknell University Press; Camden House, Inc.; Carol Publishing; Carolrhoda Books, Inc.; Dance Horizons; Davenport, Publishers, May; Delta Books; Distinctive Publishing Corporation; Drama Book Publishers; Faber & Faber, Inc.; Fairleigh Dickinson University Press; Fromm International; Glenbridge Publishing Ltd.; Godine, Publisher, Inc., David R.; Guernica Editions; HarperCollins Publishers; Hollowbrook Publishing; Inner Traditions International; Kodansha International U.S.; Krieger Publishing Co.; Lang Publishing, Peter; Louisiana State University Press; McFarland & Company, Inc., Publishers; Mercury Press, The; Mosaic Press Miniature Books; Pelican Publishing Company; Pendragon Press; Pippin Press; Press at California State University, Fresno, The; Prima Publishing and Communications; Princeton Book Company, Publishers; Quill; R&E Publishers; Random House, Inc.; Resource Publications, Inc.; Rosen Publishing Group, The; Scarecrow Press, Inc.; Schirmer Books; Semaphore Press; Stipes Publishing Co.; Sunflower University Press; TAB Books; Timber Press, Inc.; Transaction Books; University of Illinois Press; University of Michigan Press; University of Pittsburgh Press; University Press of America, Inc.; Vestal Press, Ltd., The; Wadsworth Publishing Company; Walch, Publisher, J. Weston; Walker and Co.; White Cliffs Media Company; Writer's Digest Books.

Nature and Environment. Abrams, Inc. Harry N.; Alaska Northwest Books; Appalachian Mountain Club Books; Asian Humanities Press; Atheneum Children's Books; Avery Publishing Group; Backcountry Publications; Beacon Press; Bear and Co., Inc.; Beaver Pond Publishing & Printing; Binford & Mort Publishing; Blue Dolphin Publishing, Inc.; BNA Books; Boxwood Press, The; Brick House Publishing Co.; Camden House Publishing; Carol Publishing; Carolrhoda Books, Inc.; Charlesbridge Publishing; Chelsea Green; China Books & Periodicals, Inc.; Clarion Books; Clarkson Potter; Countryman Press, Inc., The; Crown Publishing Group; Devin-Adair Publishers, Inc.; Devonshire Publishing Co.; Down East Books; Dutton Children's Books; Elysium Growth Press; Eriksson, Publisher, Paul S.; Facts On File, Inc.; Forman Publishing, Inc.; Godine, Publisher, Inc., David R.; Government Institutes, Inc.; Grosset & Dunlap Publishers; Hancock House Publishers Ltd.; Harbinger House, Inc.; HarperCollins Publishers; Hartley & Marks, Inc.; Hay House, Inc.; Heyday Books; Homestead Publishing; Houghton Mifflin Co.; Inner Traditions International; Insight Books; Johnson Books; Kesend Publishing, Ltd., Michael; Kodansha International U.S.; Kumarian Press, Inc.; Lawrence Books, Merloyd; Lexikos; Llewellyn Publications; Lone Pine Publishing; Longstreet Press, Inc.; Lucent Books; Lyons & Burford, Publishers, Inc.; Marketscope Books; Milkweed Editions; Mosaic Press Miniature Books; Mountain Press Publishing Company; Mountaineers Books, The; Museum of Northern Arizona Press; Noble Press, Incorporated, The; Northland Publishing Co., Inc.; Northwood Press, Inc.; Oregon Historical Society Press; Overlook Press; Pacific Press Publishing Association; Pennsylvania Historical and Museum Commission; Pineapple Press, Inc.; Pippin Press; Prentice Hall Press; Pruett Publishing; QED Press; R&E Publishers; Random House, Inc. Juvenile Books; Review and Herald Publishing Association; Sandhill Crane Press, Inc.; Sasquatch Books; Scribner's Sons, Charles; Seven Locks Press, Inc.; Shoe String Press, The; Sierra Club Books; Silver Burdett Press; Stemmer House Publishers, Inc.; Sunflower University Press; Taylor Publishing Company; Ten Speed Press; Texas A&M University Press; Timber Press, Inc.; University of Alaska Press; University of Arizona Press; University of Arkansas Press, The; University of California Press; University of Nebraska Press; University of North Carolina Press, The; University of Texas Press; University Press of Colorado; University Press of Mississippi; University Press of New England; Unlimited Publishing Co.; Walker and Co.; Warner Books, Inc.; Washington State University Pess; Wayfinder Press; Whitman and Co., Albert; Wilderness Adventure Books; Wilderness Press; Williamson Publishing Co.; Woodbridge Press; Yankee Books; Zoland Books, Inc.

Philosophy. Asian Humanities Press; Atheneum Children's Books; Baker Book House Company; Bantam Books; Beacon Press; Bucknell University Press; Carol Publishing; Cassandra Press; Catholic University of America Press; Christopher Publishing House, The; City Lights Books; Ediciones Universal; Eerdmans Publishing Co., William B.; Elysium Growth Press; Facts On File, Inc.; Fairleigh Dickinson University Press; Gifted Education Press; Glenbridge Publishing Ltd.; Globe Press Books; Gower Publishing Co.; Guernica Editions; Harper San Francisco; HarperCollins Publishers; Hay House, Inc.; Hollowbrook Publishing; Humanities Press International, Inc.; Indiana University Press; Inner Traditions International; Insight Books; Intercultural Press, Inc.; International Publishers Co., Inc.; Intervarsity Press; Kodansha International U.S.; Krieger Publishing Co.; Lang

Publishing, Peter; Larson Publications/PBPF; Lone Pine Publishing; Loompanics Unlimited; Louisiana State University Press; Meeramma Publications; Michigan State University Press; Noble Press, Incorporated, The; Northern Illinois University Press; Ohio State University Press; Open Court Publishing Co.; Paragon House Publishers; Paulist Press; Permanent Press/Second Chance Press, The; QED Press; R&E Publishers; Routledge, Chapman & Hall, Inc.; St. Bede's Publications; Shoe String Press, The; Sierra Club Books; Simon & Schuster; Teachers College Press; Temple University Press; Theosophical Publishing House, The; Transaction Books; University of Alabama Press; University of Massachusetts Press; University of Pittsburgh Press; University Press of America, Inc.; University Press of Kansas; Vesta Publications, Ltd.; Wadsworth Publishing Company; Washington State University Pess; Weiser, Inc., Samuel; Wingbow Press; Winston-Derek Publishers, Inc.; Wizards Bookshelf; Woodsong Graphics, Inc.

Photography. Alaska Northwest Books; Amherst Media; Atheneum Children's Books; Avanyu Publishing Inc.; Beaver Pond Publishing & Printing; Bowling Green State University Popular Press; Branden Publishing Co., Inc..; Camden House Publishing; Carstens Publications, Inc.; Clarion Books; Clarkson Potter; Coach House Press; Consultant Press, The; Coteau Books; Crown Publishing Group; Cuff Publications Ltd., Harry; Elysium Growth Press; Focal Press; Godine, Publisher, Inc., David R.; Homestead Publishing; Hounslow Press; Hudson Hill Press, Inc.; Longstreet Press, Inc.; Louisiana State University Press; Milkweed Editions; Motorbooks International Publishers & Wholesalers; Northland Publishing Co., Inc.; NTC Publishing Group; Oregon Historical Society Press; PBC International, Inc. ; Pennsylvania Historical and Museum Commission; Prentice Hall Press; Random House, Inc.; Sasquatch Books; Sierra Club Books; Sterling Publishing; Stormline Press; Sunflower University Press; TAB Books; Temple University Press; University of Iowa Press; University of Nebraska Press; University of New Mexico Press; Wake Forest University Press; Wayfinder Press; Whitman and Co., Albert; Writer's Digest Books; Wyrick & Company; Yankee Books; Zoland Books, Inc.

Psychology. Conari Press; DIC Publishing; Dutton, E.P.; Fisher Books; Guernica Editions; Hartley & Marks, Inc.; Hay House, Inc.; Health Communications, Inc.; HRD Press, Inc.; Inner Traditions International; Kodansha International U.S.A.; Larson Publications/PBPF; Lawrence Books, Macmillan of Canada; Meeramma Publications; Merloyd; Twayne Publishers; Warner Books, Inc..

Real Estate. Contemporary Books, Inc.; Government Institutes, Inc.; Liberty Hall Press; Linch Publishing, Inc.; ULI, The Urban Land Institute.

Recreation. Abrams, Inc. Harry N.; Afcom Publishing; Alaska Northwest Books; Appalachian Mountain Club Books; Atheneum Children's Books; Backcountry Publications; Beaver Pond Publishing & Printing; Bicycle Books, Inc.; Binford & Mort Publishing; Bonus Books, Inc.; Cambridge Career Products; Camden House Publishing; Carol Publishing; Chatham Press; Chicago Review Press; Countryman Press, Inc., The; Crown Publishing Group; Denali Press, The; Down East Books; Elysium Growth Press; Eriksson, Publisher, Paul S.; Facts On File, Inc.; Falcon Press Publishing Co.; Gardner Press, Inc.; Globe Pequot Press, Inc., The; Golden West Publishers; Hancock House Publishers Ltd.; Harian Creative Books; Hay House, Inc.; Heyday Books; Info Net Publishing; Johnson Books; Kalmbach Publishing Co.; Liberty Publishing Company, Inc.; McFarland & Company, Inc., Publishers; Macmillan of Canada; Marketscope Books; Masters Press; Menasha Ridge Press, Inc.; Mountain Press Publishing Company; Mountaineers Books, The; Muir Publications, John; Mustang Publishing Co.; NordicPress; Overlook Press; Peachtree Publishers, Ltd.; Pelican Publishing Company; Picadilly Books; Pruett Publishing; Random House, Inc. Juvenile Books; Sasquatch Books; Scarborough House/Publisher; Semaphore Press; Sierra Club Books; Sterling Publishing; Stipes Publishing Co.; Sunflower University Press; Ten Speed Press; Twin Peaks Press; Warner Books, Inc.; Wayfinder Press; Webb Research Group; Westport Publishers, Inc.; Whitman and Co., Albert; Wilderness Press; Willow Creek Press; Wilshire Book Co.; Yankee Books.

Reference. AASLH; Abbott, Langer & Associates; Adams, Inc., Bob; Afcom Publishing; ALA Books; Amacom Books; American Correctional Association; American Hospital Publishing, Inc.; Ancestry Incorporated; Andrews and McMeel; Appalachian Mountain Club Books; Architectural Book Publishing Co., Inc.; Arden Press, Inc.; Arman Publishing, Inc., M.; Aronson, Inc., Jason; Asher-Gallant Press; Asian Humanities Press; Avanyu Publishing Inc.; Avery Publishing Group; Backcountry Publications; Baker Book House Company; Banks-Baldwin Law Publishing Co.; Behrman House Inc.; Bethany House Publishers; Bethel Publishing; Betterway Publications, Inc.; Binford & Mort Publishing; Blue Bird Publishing; BNA Books; Borgo Press, The; Bowling Green

State University Popular Press; Branden Publishing Co., Inc..; Brick House Publishing Co.; Broadway Press; Business & Legal Reports, Inc.; Calgre Press; Cambridge University Press; Camden House, Inc.; Caratzas, Publisher, Aristide D.; Career Press Inc., The; Cassell Publications; Catbird Press; Christopher Publishing House, The; Clark Co., Arthur H.; Cleaning Consultant Services, Inc.; Computer Science Press; Consumer Reports Books; Contemporary Books, Inc.; Coteau Books; Crown Publishing Group; Cuff Publications Ltd., Harry; Dante University Of America Press, Inc.; Denali Press, The; Devonshire Publishing Co.; Distinctive Publishing Corporation; Drama Book Publishers; Durst Publications Ltd.; Dustbooks; ECW Press; Ediciones Universal; Eerdmans Publishing Co., William B.; EES Publications; Evans and Co., Inc., M.; Evergreen Communications, Inc.; Facts On File, Inc.; Fairleigh Dickinson University Press; Ferguson Publishing Company, J.G.; Financial Sourcebooks; Focal Press; Gallaudet University Press; Gardner Press, Inc.; Garrett Park Press; Gaslight Publications; Genealogical Publishing Co., Inc.; Glenbridge Publishing Ltd.; Government Institutes, Inc.; Gower Publishing Co.; Graphic Arts Technical Foundation; Gulf Publishing Co.; Harper San Francisco; HarperCollins Publishers; Harvard Common Press, The; Harvest House Publishers; Hay House, Inc.; Health Administration Press; Here's Life Publishers, Inc.; Heritage Books, Inc.; Heyday Books; Hippocrene Books Inc.; Homestead Publishing; HRD Press, Inc.; Human Kinetics Publishers, Inc.; Hunter Publishing, Inc.; ILR Press; Imagine, Inc.; Indiana University Press; Industrial Press, Inc.; Info Net Publishing; Intercultural Press, Inc.; International Foundation Of Employee Benefit Plans; International Publishers Co., Inc.; Ishiyaku Euroamerica, Inc.; Jist Works, Inc.; Jonathan David Publishers; Kinseeker Publications; Klein Publications, B.; Krieger Publishing Co.; Lang Publishing, Peter; Leisure Press; Liberty Publishing Company, Inc.; Libraries Unlimited; Library Research Associates, Inc.; Lone Eagle Publishing Co.; Longstreet Press, Inc.; Loompanics Unlimited; McFarland & Company, Inc., Publishers; Macmillan of Canada; Madison Books; Media Forum International, Ltd.; Menasha Ridge Press, Inc.; Metamorphous Press; Michigan State University Press; Modern Language Association of America; Monitor Book Co., Inc.; Muir Publications, John; Museum of Northern Arizona Press; Mysterious Press, The; Nautical & Aviation Publishing Co., The; Noble Press, Incorporated, The; Octameron Associates; Oregon Historical Society Press; Our Sunday Visitor, Inc.; Overlook Press; Pacific Books, Publishers; Paragon House Publishers; Pendragon Press; Pennsylvania Historical and Museum Commission; Pharos Books; Pineapple Press, Inc.; Pocket Books; Porter Sargent Publishers, Inc.; Princeton Book Company, Publishers; Professional Publications, Inc.; PSI Research; Que Corporation; Rainbow Books; R&E Publishers; Reference Service Press; Rosen Publishing Group, The; Routledge, Chapman & Hall, Inc.; Rutledge Hill Press; St. Martin's Press; Sandhill Crane Press, Inc.; Scarborough House/Publisher; Scarecrow Press, Inc.; Schiffer Publishing Ltd.; Schirmer Books; Seven Locks Press, Inc.; Shaw Publishers, Harold; Shelby Publishing Co.; Shoe String Press, The; Speech Bin, Inc., The; ST Publications, Inc.; Standard Publishing; Starrhill Press; Sterling Publishing; Sunflower University Press; Technical Communications Associates, Inc.; Ten Speed Press; Thomas Publications; Tidewater Publishers; Transaction Books; Trend Book Division; Twin Peaks Press; Union Square Press; United Resource Press; University of Alaska Press; University of Illinois Press; University of Michigan Press; University of Pittsburgh Press; University Press of Kentucky; University Press of New England; Unlimited Publishing Co.; Utah State University Press; Vesta Publications, Ltd.; Victor Books; Walker and Co.; Warner Books, Inc.; Wayfinder Press; Webb Research Group; Westport Publishers, Inc.; Westport Publishers, Inc.; Whitford Press; Whitson Publishing Co., The; Wingbow Press; Woodsong Graphics, Inc.; Writer's Digest Books; Yankee Books; Zondervan Corp., The.

Regional. Abbey Press; Alaska Northwest Books; Almar Press; Appalachian Mountain Club Books; Avanyu Publishing Inc.; Binford & Mort Publishing; Blair, Publisher, John F.; Borealis Press; Boston Mills Press; Bowling Green State University Popular Press; Boxwood Press, The; British American Publishing; Camden House Publishing; Camino Books, Inc.; Carol Publishing; Caxton Printers, Ltd., The; Chatham Press; Chicago Review Press; Coteau Books; Countryman Press, Inc., The; Creative Publishing Co.; Cuff Publications Ltd., Harry; Denali Press, The; Dillon Press, Inc.; Distinctive Publishing Corporation; Down East Books; Dundurn Press Ltd.; ECW Press; Eerdmans Publishing Co., William B.; Faber & Faber, Inc.; Family Album, The; Fiesta Books Inc.; Filter Press; Fitzhenry & Whiteside; Gallaudet University Press; Globe Pequot Press, Inc., The; Golden West Books; Golden West Publishers; Great Northwest Publishing and Distributing Company, Inc.; Gulf Publishing Co.; Hancock House Publishers Ltd.; Harian Creative Books; Heart Of The Lakes Publishing; Hendrick-Long Publishing Co., Inc.; Herald Publishing House; Heritage Books,

Inc.; Heyday Books; Hippocrene Books Inc.; Indiana University Press; Interurban Press/Trans Anglo Books; Johnson Books; Kent State University Press; Lexikos; Longstreet Press, Inc.; Louisiana State University Press; Marketscope Books; Milkweed Editions; Mountain Press Publishing Company; Museum of Northern Arizona Press; National Press, Inc.; Northern Illinois University Press; Northland Publishing Co., Inc.; Oregon Historical Society Press; Pacific Books, Publishers; Pacific Press Publishing Association; Pennsylvania Historical and Museum Commission; Pruett Publishing; QED Press; R&E Publishers; Renaissance House Publishers; Schiffer Publishing Ltd.; Stormline Press; Sunflower University Press; Sunstone Press; Syracuse University Press; Taylor Publishing Company; Temple University Press; Texas A&M University Press; Texas Christian University Press; Texas Western Press; Tidewater Publishers; Timber Press, Inc.; Trend Book Division; University of Alaska Press; University of Arizona Press; University of Michigan Press; University of Nevada Press; University of Pittsburgh Press; University of Tennessee Press, The; University of Texas Press; University Press of Colorado; University Press of Kansas; University Press of Mississippi; University Press of New England; Utah State University Press; Vestal Press, Ltd., The; Washington State University Press; Wayfinder Press; Westernlore Press; Westport Publishers, Inc.; Wilderness Adventure Books; Wyrick & Company; Yankee Books; Zoland Books, Inc.

Religion. Abingdon Press; Accent Books; Aglow Publications; Alban Institue, Inc., The; American Catholic Press; Aronson, Inc., Jason; Asian Humanities Press; Atheneum Children's Books; Baker Book House Company; Bantam Books; Beacon Hill Press of Kansas City; Beacon Press; Bear and Co., Inc.; Behrman House Inc.; Berkley Publishing Group, The; Bethany House Publishers; Bethel Publishing; Blockbuster Books, Inc.; Blue Dolphin Publishing, Inc.; Bookcraft, Inc.; Bosco Multimedia, Don; Bowling Green State University Popular Press; Bucknell University Press; C.S.S. Publishing Co.; Canadian Institute of Ukranian Studies Press; Caratzas, Publisher, Aristide D.; Cassandra Press; Catholic University of America Press; Chalice Press; China Books & Periodicals, Inc.; Chosen Books Publishing Co.; Christopher Publishing House, The; College Press Publishing Co.; Concordia Publishing House; Crossway Books; Dee, Inc., Ivan R.; Eerdmans Publishing Co., William B.; Evergreen Communications, Inc.; Facts On File, Inc.; Fraser Institute; Gardner Press, Inc.; Gospel Publishing House; Guernica Editions; Harper San Francisco; HarperCollins Publishers; Harvest House Publishers; Hay House, Inc.; Hendrickson Publishers Inc.; Hensley, Inc., Virgil W.; Herald Press; Herald Publishing House; Here's Life Publishers, Inc.; Howell Press, Inc.; Human Kinetics Publishers, Inc.; Indiana University Press; Inner Traditions International; Innovatia Press; Insight Books; Intervarsity Press; Jalmar Press, Inc.; Judson Press; Kodansha International U.S.; Kumarian Press, Inc.; Lang Publishing, Peter; Larson Publications/PBPF; Lion Publishing Corporation; Loyola University Press; Macmillan of Canada; Marketscope Books; Meeramma Publications; Michigan State University Press; Morehouse Publishing Co.; Morrow and Co., William; Multnomah Press; NavPress; Nelson Publishers, Thomas; New Leaf Press, Inc.; Newcastle Publishing Co., Inc.; Open Court Publishing Co.; Our Sunday Visitor, Inc.; Pacific Press Publishing Association; Paragon House Publishers; Paulist Press; Pelican Publishing Company; Pennsylvania Historical and Museum Commission; Peter Pauper Press, Inc.; Pilgrim Press, The; Publishers Associates; QED Press; Random House, Inc.; Regal Books; Religious Education Press; Resource Publications, Inc.; Review and Herald Publishing Association; St. Anthony MessengerPress; St. Bede's Publications; St. Paul Books and Media; St. Vladimir's Seminary Press; Servant Publications; Seven Locks Press, Inc.; Shapolsky Publishers; Shoe String Press, The; Standard Publishing; Star Books Inc.; Starburst Publishers; Sunflower University Press; Theosophical Publishing House, The; UAHC Press; University of Alabama Press; University of North Carolina Press, The; University of Tennessee Press, The; University Press of America, Inc.; Vesta Publications, Ltd.; Victor Books; Wadsworth Publishing Company; Webb Research Group; Weiser, Inc., Samuel; Whitaker House; Whitman and Co., Albert; Wingbow Press; Winston-Derek Publishers, Inc.; Yankee Books; Zondervan Corp., The.

Scholarly. Cambridge University Press; Canadian Plains Research Center; Hollowbrook Publishing; Humanities Press International, Inc.; McFarland & Company, Inc., Publishers; Michigan State University Press; Oregon State University Press; Pacific Books, Publishers; Press at California State University, Fresno, The; Religious Education Press; St. Vladimir's Seminary Press; Schirmer Books; Stanford University Press; Texas Christian University Press; Texas Western Press; Three Continents Press; Transaction Books; Twayne Publishers; University of Alabama Press; University of Arizona Press; University of California Press; University of Illinois Press; University of North

Carolina Press, The; University of Pennsylvania Press; University of Tennessee Press, The; University of Texas Press; University of Wisconsin Press; University Press of America, Inc.; University Press of Kansas; University Press of Kentucky; University Press of Mississippi; Utah State University Press; Washington State University Press; Westernlore Press; Whitson Publishing Co., The.

Science/Technology. Abbott, Langer & Associates; Abrams, Inc. Harry N.; Alaska Northwest Books; American Astonautical Society; Arcsoft Publishers; Bantam Books; Bear and Co., Inc.; Boxwood Press, The; Cambridge University Press; Capstone Press, Inc.; Carol Publishing; Charlesbridge Publishing; Chicago Review Press; Crown Publishing Group; Delta Books; Dillon Press, Inc.; Dutton Children's Books; Dutton, E. P.; Erlbaum Associates, Inc., Lawrence; Focal Press; Gallaudet University Press; Grapevine Publications, Inc.; Green, Inc., Warren H.; Gulf Publishing Co.; HarperCollins Publishers; Hay House, Inc.; Hollowbrook Publishing; Houghton Mifflin Co.; HRD Press, Inc.; Industrial Press, Inc.; Insight Books; Interstate Publishers, Inc. The; Iowa State University Press; Johnson Books; Knowledge Book Publishers; Kodansha International U.S.; Krieger Publishing Co.; Little, Brown and Co., Inc.; Lucent Books; Lyons & Burford, Publishers, Inc.; Macmillan of Canada; Metamorphous Press; Mountain Press Publishing Company; Museum of Northern Arizona Press; Naturegraph Publishers, Inc.; Oddo Publishing, Inc.; Oregon State University Press; Plenum Publishing; Quill; R&E Publishers; Random House, Inc. Juvenile Books; Ross Books; Routledge, Chapman & Hall, Inc.; St. Martin's Press; Scarborough House/Publisher; Scribner's Sons, Charles; Sierra Club Books; Silver Burdett Press; Simon & Schuster; Stackpole Books; Stanford University Press; Sunflower University Press; Technical Communications Associates, Inc.; Ten Speed Press; Theosophical Publishing House, The; Times Books; Transaction Books; Union Square Press; Univelt, Inc.; University of Alaska Press; University of Arizona Press; University of Pennsylvania Press; University of Texas Press; University Press of New England; Walker and Co.; Warner Books, Inc.; Whitman and Co., Albert; Willowisp Press, Inc.; Woodbine House.

Self-Help. Abbey Press; Accent Books; Adams, Inc., Bob; Advocacy Press; Afcom Publishing; Aglow Publications; Allen Publishing Co.; Almar Press; Amacom Books; Atheneum Children's Books; Avon Books; Baker Book House Company; Bantam Books; Betterway Publications, Inc.; Blockbuster Books, Inc.; Blue Dolphin Publishing, Inc.; Bonus Books, Inc.; British American Publishing; Bull Publishing Co.; C.S.S. Publishing Co.; Calgre Press; Cambridge Career Products; Career Press Inc., The; Carol Publishing; Cassandra Press; CCC Publications; China Books & Periodicals, Inc.; Chosen Books Publishing Co.; Christopher Publishing House, The; Chronicle Books; Clarkson Potter; Cleaning Consultant Services, Inc.; Cliffs Notes, Inc.; Conari Press; Consumer Reports Books; Contemporary Books, Inc.; Crisp Publications, Inc.; Crown Publishing Group; DCI Publishing; Distinctive Publishing Corporation; Dutton, E. P.; Elysium Growth Press; Enterprise Publishing Co., Inc.; Eriksson, Publisher, Paul S.; Evergreen Communications, Inc.; Fiesta Books Inc.; Fine, Inc., Donald I.; Fisher Books; Flores Publications, J.; Forman Publishing, Inc.; Gallaudet University Press; Gardner Press, Inc.; Globe Press Books; Gospel Publishing House; Grapevine Publications, Inc.; Hancock House Publishers Ltd.; Harbinger House, Inc.; Harian Creative Books; Harper San Francisco; HarperCollins Publishers; Hartley & Marks, Inc.; Harvard Common Press, The; Harvest House Publishers; Hawkes Publishing, Inc.; Hay House, Inc.; Health Communications, Inc.; Herald Press; Herald Publishing House; Here's Life Publishers, Inc.; Hounslow Press; HRD Press, Inc.; Human Kinetics Publishers, Inc.; Human Services Institute, Inc.; Humanics Publishing Group; Info Net Publishing; Inner Traditions International; Insight Books; Intercultural Press, Inc.; International Wealth Success; Kesend Publishing, Ltd., Michael; Klein Publications, B.; Larson Publications/PBPF; Liberty Hall Press; Liberty Publishing Company, Inc.; Llewellyn Publications; Lone Eagle Publishing Co.; Loompanics Unlimited; Luramedia; Macmillan of Canada; Marketscope Books; Media Publishing/Midgard Press; Meeramma Publications; Menasha Ridge Press, Inc.; Metamorphous Press; Mills & Sanderson, Publishers; Mother Courage Press; Multnomah Press; Mustang Publishing Co.; Nelson Publishers, Thomas; New Leaf Press, Inc.; Newcastle Publishing Co., Inc.; Noble Press, Incorporated, The; NordicPress; Pacific Press Publishing Association; Paulist Press; Pelican Publishing Company; Perspectives Press; Picadilly Books; Poseidon Press; Prentice Hall Press; Prevention Health Books; Prima Publishing and Communications; Princeton Book Company, Publishers; PSI Research; QED Press; Rainbow Books; R&E Publishers; Random House, Inc.; Rosen Publishing Group, The; St. Martin's Press; St. Paul Books and Media; Scarborough House/Publisher; Scribner's Sons, Charles; Semaphore Press; Shaw Publishers, Harold; Skidmore-Roth Publishing; Spinsters Book Company; Starburst Publishers; Success Publishing; Taylor Publishing Company; Ten Speed Press; Theosophical Publishing House, The; Tidewater Publishers; Twin Peaks Press; Ultralight Publications, Inc.; United Resource Press; Unlimited Publishing Co.; Victor Books; Walker and Co.; Warner Books, Inc.; Wayfinder Press; Weiser, Inc., Samuel; Whitford Press; Williamson Publishing Co.; Wilshire Book Co.; Wingbow Press; Woodbridge Press; Woodsong Graphics, Inc.; Yankee Books; Zebra Books; Zondervan Corp., The.

Social Sciences. Borgo Press, The; C Q Press; Caratzas, Publisher, Aristide D.; Catholic University of America press; Chelsea Green; Duquesne University Press; Eerdmans Publishing Co., William B.; Indiana University Press; International Publishers Co., Inc.; Longman Publishing Group; Madison Books; Northern Illinois University Press; Routledge, Chapman & Hall, Inc.; Roxbury Publishing Co.; Stanford University Press; Teachers College Press; University of California Press; Wadsworth Publishing Company; Walch, Publisher, J. Weston; Whitson Publishing Co., The.

Sociology. Atheneum Children's Books; Avanyu Publishing Inc.; Baker Book House Company; Bantam Books; Beacon Press; Bowling Green State University Popular Press; Branden Publishing Co., Inc..; Bucknell University Press; Canadian Institute of Ukranian Studies Press; Canadian Plains Research Center; Cato Institute; China Books & Periodicals, Inc.; Christopher Publishing House, The; Cleis Press; Cuff Publications Ltd., Harry; Dee, Inc., Ivan R.; Devonshire Publishing Co.; Distinctive Publishing Corporation; Edicones Universal; Eerdmans Publishing Co., William B.; Elysium Growth Press; Eriksson, Publisher, Paul S.; Faber & Faber, Inc.; Fairleigh Dickinson University Press; Fraser Institute; Gallaudet University Press; Gardner Press, Inc.; General Hall, Inc.; Glenbridge Publishing Ltd.; Gower Publishing Co.; Harbinger House, Inc.; HarperCollins Publishers; Harrow And Heston; Hay House, Inc.; Health Administration Press; Humanics Publishing Group; Humanities Press International, Inc.; ILR Press; Insight Books; Intercultural Press, Inc.; Intervarsity Press; Kodansha International U.S.; Kumarian Press, Inc.; Lang Publishing, Peter; Libra Publishers, Inc.; Longman Publishing Group; Louisiana State University Press; McFarland & Company, Inc., Publishers; Madison Books; Marketscope Books; Mercury Press, The; Metamorphous Press; Mother Courage Press; Noble Press, Incorporated, The; Ohio State University Press; Pendragon Press; Perspectives Press; Plenum Publishing; QED Press; R&E Publishers; Random House, Inc.; Roxbury Publishing Co.; Russell Sage Foundation; Semaphore Press; Seven Locks Press, Inc.; Stanford University Press; Sunflower University Press; Teachers College Press; Temple University Press; Thomas Publications; Transaction Books; Twayne Publishers; Twin Peaks Press; University of Arkansas Press, The; University of Illinois Press; University of Massachusetts Press; University of North Carolina Press, The; University of Pittsburgh Press; University Press of America, Inc.; University Press of Kansas; University Press of Kentucky; University Press of New England; Unlimited Publishing Co.; Wadsworth Publishing Company; Walch, Publisher, J. Weston; Wall & Emerson, Inc.; Warner Books, Inc.; Washington State University Pess; Wayfinder Press; White Cliffs Media Company; Woodbine House.

Software. Anderson Publishing Co.; Arcsoft Publishers; Barron's Educational Series, Inc.; Branden Publishing Co., Inc..; Career Publishing, Inc.; Chronicle Books; Devin-Adair Publishers, Inc.; Family Album, The; Grapevine Publications, Inc.; Heinle & Heinle Publishers, Inc.; HRD Press, Inc.; Interstate Publishers, Inc. The; Jist Works, Inc.; Libraries Unlimited; Macmillan of Canada; National Textbook Co.; NavPress; Osborne/McGraw-Hill; Pacific Press Publishing Association; Peterson's; Que Corporation; R&E Publishers; Richboro Press; Ross Books; SAS Institute Inc.; Schirmer Books; Slawson Communications, Inc.; Sybex, Inc.; TAB Books; Technical Communications Associates, Inc.; Wadsworth Publishing Company; White Cliffs Media Company; Windsor Books; Wine Appreciation Guild, Ltd.

Sports. Afcom Publishing; Alaska Northwest Books; Archway/Minstrel Books; Atheneum Children's Books; Atheneum Publishers; Avon Books; Backcountry Publications; Bantam Books; Bentley, Inc., Robert; Bicycle Books, Inc.; Blockbuster Books, Inc.; Bonus Books, Inc.; Bowling Green State University Popular Press; Briarcliff Press Publishers; British American Publishing; Bull Publishing Co.; Cambridge Career Products; Capstone Press, Inc.; Carol Publishing; Contemporary Books, Inc.; Crown Publishing Group; Denali Press, The; Devin-Adair Publishers, Inc.; Eriksson, Publisher, Paul S.; Facts On File, Inc.; Fine, Inc., Donald I.; Gallaudet University Press; Gardner Press, Inc.; Hancock House Publishers Ltd.; HarperCollins Publishers; Howell Press, Inc.; Human Kinetics Publishers, Inc.; Hungness Publishing, Carl; Info Net Publishing; Jonathan David Publishers; Kesend Publishing, Ltd., Michael; Leisure Press; Liberty Publishing Company, Inc.; Little, Brown and Co., Inc.; Lone Pine Publishing; Longstreet Press, Inc.; Lucent Books; Lyons & Burford,

Publishers, Inc.; McFarland & Company, Inc., Publishers; Macmillan of Canada; Masters Press; Menasha Ridge Press, Inc.; Milkweed Editions; Mosaic Press Miniature Books; Motorbooks International Publishers & Wholesalers; Mountaineers Books, The; Muir Publications, John; Mustang Publishing Co.; National Press, Inc.; Ohara Publications, Inc.; Overlook Press; Pennsylvania Historical and Museum Commission; Picadilly Books; Prentice Hall Press; Prevention Health Books; Pruett Publishing; Random House, Inc.; Random House, Inc. Juvenile Books; Sasquatch Books; Scarborough House/Publisher; Scribner's Sons, Charles; Semaphore Press; Sierra Club Books; Stackpole Books; Sterling Publishing; Stoeger Publishing Company; Sunflower University Press; Taylor Publishing Company; Temple University Press; Times Books; Twin Peaks Press; University of Illinois Press; University of Nebraska Press; Warner Books, Inc.; Watts, Inc., Franklin; Whitman and Co., Albert; Wilderness Adventure Books; Willow Creek Press; Willowisp Press, Inc.; Yankee Books.

Technical. Abbott, Langer & Associates; Almar Press; American Correctional Association; American Hospital Publishing, Inc.; American Society of Civil Engineers; Arcsoft Publishers; Arman Publishing, Inc., M.; Aronson, Inc., Jason; Bentley, Inc., Robert; Bicycle Books, Inc.; Boxwood Press, The; Branden Publishing Co., Inc..; Brevet Press, Inc.; Brick House Publishing Co.; Broadway Press; Camden House, Inc.; Canadian Plains Research Center; C&T Publishing; Caratzas, Publisher, Aristide D.; Cleaning Consultant Services, Inc.; Computer Science Press; Cornell Maritime Press, Inc.; Craftsman Book Company; Cuff Publications Ltd., Harry; Denlingers Publishers, Ltd.; Distinctive Publishing Corporation; EES Publications; Erlbaum Associates, Inc., Lawrence; Financial Sourcebooks; Focal Press; FPMI Communications, Inc.; Gallaudet University Press; Government Institutes, Inc.; Gower Publishing Co.; Grapevine Publications, Inc.; Graphic Arts Technical Foundation; Hartley & Marks, Inc.; Human Kinetics Publishers, Inc.; ILR Press; Industrial Press, Inc.; Info Net Publishing; International Foundation Of Employee Benefit Plans; Interweave Press; Iowa State University Press; Knowledge Book Publishers; Krieger Publishing Co.; Leisure Press; Library Research Associates, Inc.; Lone Eagle Publishing Co.; McFarland & Company, Inc., Publishers; Metamorphous Press; MGI Management Institute, Inc., The; Michigan State University Press; Microtrend Books; Museum of Northern Arizona Press; Osborne/McGraw-Hill; Pacific Books, Publishers; Pennsylvania Historical and Museum Commission; Probus Publishing Co.; Professional Publications, Inc.; Que Corporation; R&E Publishers; Religious Education Press; Sandhill Crane Press, Inc.; SAS Institute Inc.; Shelby Publishing Co.; Skidmore-Roth Publishing; Slawson Communications, Inc.; ST Publications, Inc.; Sterling Publishing; Stipes Publishing Co.; Sybex, Inc.; TAB Books; Technical Communications Associates, Inc.; Texas Western Press; Tidewater Publishers; Transaction Books; ULI, The Urban Land Institute; Ultralight Publications, Inc.; Union Square Press; Univelt, Inc.; University of Alaska Press; Unlimited Publishing Co.; Vestal Press, Ltd., The; Wayfinder Press; White Cliffs Media Company; Windsor Books.

Textbook. AASLH; Abingdon Press; Afcom Publishing; Amacom Books; American Correctional Association; American Hospital Publishing, Inc.; Anchorage Press, Inc.; Arden Press, Inc.; Arman Publishing, Inc., M.; Art Direction Book Company; Asian Humanities Press; Avery Publishing Group; Baker Book House Company; Barron's Educational Series, Inc.; Beacon Hill Press of Kansas City; Behrman House Inc.; Bosco Multimedia, Don; Bowling Green State University Popular Press; Boxwood Press, The; Boyd & Fraser Publishing Company; Branden Publishing Co., Inc..; C Q Press; Cambridge University Press; Camden House, Inc.; Canadian Plains Research Center; Caratzas, Publisher, Aristide D.; Career Publishing, Inc.; Charlesbridge Publishing; China Books & Periodicals, Inc.; Christopher Publishing House, The; Cleaning Consultant Services, Inc.; Cliffs Notes, Inc.; College Press Publishing Co.; Computer Science Press; Cuff Publications Ltd., Harry; Distinctive Publishing Corporation; Drama Book Publishers; Education Associates; Eerdmans Publishing Co., William B.; EES Publications; Elysium Growth Press; Erlbaum Associates, Inc., Lawrence; ETC Publications; Financial Sourcebooks; Fitzhenry & Whiteside; Focal Press; Fromm International; Gallaudet University Press; Gardner Press, Inc.; Glenbridge Publishing Ltd.; Gower Publishing Co.; Grapevine Publications, Inc.; Graphic Arts Technical Foundation; Harrow And Heston; Health Administration Press; Heinle & Heinle Publishers, Inc.; Hendrick-Long Publishing Co., Inc.; Human Kinetics Publishers, Inc.; ILR Press; Inner Traditions International; Intercultural Press, Inc.; International Foundation Of Employee Benefit Plans; International Publishers Co., Inc.; Interstate Publishers, Inc. The; Intervarsity Press; Iowa State University Press; Jist Works, Inc.; Krieger Publishing Co.; Libraries Unlimited; Longman Publishing Group; Loyola University Press; McCutchan Publishing Corporation; Media Publishing/Midgard Press; Metamorphous

Press; National Textbook Co.; Nelson-Hall Publishers; NTC Publishing Group; Oddo Publishing, Inc.; Pacific Press Publishing Association; Porter Sargent Publishers, Inc.; Princeton Architectural Press; Princeton Book Company, Publishers; Professional Publications, Inc.; Pruett Publishing; PSI Research; Publishers Associates; Que Corporation; R&E Publishers; Religious Education Press; Rosen Publishing Group, The; Routledge, Chapman & Hall, Inc.; Roxbury Publishing Co.; St. Bede's Publications; St. Martin's Press; Sandhill Crane Press, Inc.; SAS Institute Inc.; ddSchiffer Publishing Ltd.; Schirmer Books; Semaphore Press; Seven Locks Press, Inc.; Skidmore-Roth Publishing; ST Publications, Inc.; Standard Publishing; Stanford University Press; Stipes Publishing Co.; Technical Communications Associates, Inc.; Thomas Publications; Tidewater Publishers; Transaction Books; Trend Book Division; UAHC Press; University of Alaska Press; University of Michigan Press; University of Pittsburgh Press; University Press of America, Inc.; Utah State University Press; VGM Career Horizons; Wadsworth Publishing Company; White Cliffs Media Company.

Translation. Alaska Northwest Books; Alyson Publications, Inc.; Architectural Book Publishing Co., Inc.; Arcsoft Publishers; Asian Humanities Press; Barron's Educational Series, Inc.; Blue Dolphin Publishing, Inc.; Bosco Multimedia, Don; Briarcliff Press Publishers; Canadian Institute of Ukranian Studies Press; Chatham Press; China Books & Periodicals, Inc.; Citadel Press; City Lights Books; Clarion Books; Clarkson Potter; Cleis Press; Dante University Of America Press, Inc.; Davis Publications, Inc.; Devin-Adair Publishers, Inc.; Drama Book Publishers; Ediciones Universal; ETC Publications; Fromm International; Gallaudet University Press; Gardner Press, Inc.; Godine, Publisher, Inc., David R.; Guernica Editions; Hartley & Marks, Inc.; Hounslow Press; Indiana University Press; Intercultural Press, Inc.; Iowa State University Press; Johnson Books; Kodansha International U.S.; Lang Publishing, Peter; Motorbooks International Publishers & Wholesalers; Northern Illinois University Press; Open Court Publishing Co.; Pacific Books, Publishers; Paulist Press; Porter Sargent Publishers, Inc.; QED Press; Resource Publications, Inc.; Ross Books; Semaphore Press; Sybex, Inc.; TAB Books; Theosophical Publishing House, The; Three Continents Press; Timber Press, Inc.; University of Alabama Press; University of Massachusetts Press; University of Texas Press; Wake Forest University Press; Wizards Bookshelf; Zoland Books, Inc.

Transportation. Arman Publishing, Inc., M.; Bentley, Inc., Robert; Boston Mills Press; Carstens Publications, Inc.; Golden West Books; Interurban Press/Trans Anglo Books; Iowa State University Press; Transportation Trails; Ultralight Publications, Inc..

Travel. Academy Chicago; Alaska Northwest Books; Almar Press; APA Publications; Appalachian Mountain Club Books; Atheneum Children's Books; Bantam Books; Barron's Educational Series, Inc.; Bicycle Books, Inc.; Binford & Mort Publishing; Blair, Publisher, John F.; Briarcliff Press Publishers; British American Publishing; Camden House Publishing; Camino Books, Inc.; Capstone Press, Inc.; Caratzas, Publisher, Aristide D.; Carol Publishing; Chatham Press; Chelsea Green; Chicago Review Press; China Books & Periodicals, Inc.; Christopher Publishing House, The; Countryman Press, Inc., The; Denali Press, The; Devin-Adair Publishers, Inc.; Eerdmans Publishing Co., William B.; Elysium Growth Press; Eriksson, Publisher, Paul S.; Falcon Press Publishing Co.; Fiesta Books Inc.; Filter Press; Gallaudet University Press; Globe Pequot Press, Inc., The; Godine, Publisher, Inc., David R.; Golden West Publishers; HarperCollins Publishers; Harvard Common Press, The; Heyday Books; Hippocrene Books Inc.; Homestead Publishing; Hunter Publishing, Inc.; Info Net Publishing; Inner Traditions International; Intercultural Press, Inc.; Interurban Press/Trans Anglo Books; Johnson Books; Kesend Publishing, Ltd., Michael; Kodansha International U.S.; Liberty Publishing Company, Inc.; Lone Pine Publishing; Loompanics Unlimited; Lyons & Burford, Publishers, Inc.; Marlor Press, Inc.; Menasha Ridge Press, Inc.; Mills & Sanderson, Publishers; Moon Publications, Inc.; Mosaic Press Miniature Books; Mountain Press Publishing Company; Mountaineers Books, The; Muir Publications, John; Mustang Publishing Co.; NTC Publishing Group; Passport Press; Peachtree Publishers, Ltd.; Pelican Publishing Company; Pennsylvania Historical and Museum Commission; Peterson's; Pilot Books; Prentice Hall Press; Pruett Publishing; R&E Publishers; Sasquatch Books; Scarborough House/Publisher; Sierra Club Books; Soho Press, Inc.; Transportation Trails; Travel Keys; Trend Book Division; Twin Peaks Press; Umbrella Books; University of Alaska Press; Unlimited Publishing Co.; Wayfinder Press; Webb Research Group; Whitman and Co., Albert; Wilderness Adventure Books; Wine Appreciation Guild, Ltd.; Woodbine House; Wyrick & Company; Zoland Books, Inc.

Women's Issues/Studies. Addison-Wesley Publishing Co., Inc.; Advocacy Press; Alaska Northwest

Books; Arden Press, Inc.; Baker Book House Company; Beacon Press; Between the Lines; Bonus Books, Inc.; Bowling Green State University Popular Press; C&T Publishing; Camden House Publishing; Carol Publishing; Chicago Review Press; China Books & Periodicals, Inc.; City Lights Books; Cleis Press; Conari Press; Contemporary Books, Inc.; Coteau Books; Crossing Press, The; Dee, Inc., Ivan R.; Erlbaum Associates, Inc., Lawrence; Evergreen Communications, Inc.; Fairleigh Dickinson University Press; Gardner Press, Inc.; General Hall, Inc.; Harbinger House, Inc.; Hay House, Inc.; Hensley, Inc., Virgil W.; Hill Books, Lawrence; Hollowbrook Publishing; Human Services Institute, Inc.; Indiana University Press; Inner Traditions International; Insight Books; International Publishers Co., Inc.; Kumarian Press, Inc.; Llewellyn Publications; Longstreet Press, Inc.; Louisiana State University Press; Lucent Books; Luramedia; McFarland & Company, Inc., Publishers; Macmillan of Canada; Meeramma Publications; Mercury Press, The; Milkweed Editions; Mother Courage Press; Multnomah Press; NavPress; Noble Press, Incorporated, The; Oregon Historical Society Press; Peter Pauper Press, Inc.; Publishers Associates; QED Press; R&E Publishers; Reference Service Press; Routledge, Chapman & Hall, Inc.; Russell Sage Foundation; Scarecrow Press, Inc.; Spinsters Book Company; Sunflower University Press; Temple University Press; Texas A&M University Press; Times Books; Twayne Publishers; University of Massachusetts Press; University of Michigan Press; University of Tennessee Press, The; Victor Books; Warner Books, Inc.; Whitaker House; Wingbow Press; Zoland Books, Inc.

World Affairs. Carroll & Graf Publishers, Inc.; Dillon Press, Inc.; Family Album, The; Fraser Institute.

Young Adult. Atheneum Children's Books; Bale Books; Barron's Educational Series, Inc.; Cliffs Notes, Inc.; Davenport, Publishers, May; Dial Books For Young Readers; Dillon Press, Inc.; Education Associates; Falcon Press Publishing Co.; Fitzhenry & Whiteside; Houghton Mifflin Co.; McElderry Books, Margaret K.; Rosen Publishing Group, The; Silver Burdett Press.

Index

A

A.D. Players 838
AAA Going Places 644
AAAS Prize for Behavioral Science Research 898
AAAS-Westinghouse Science Journalism Awards 898
AASLH 58
ABA Journal 781
Abbey Press 58
Abbott, Langer & Associates 59
ABC Star Service (See Star Service 825)
Abingdon Press 59
Aboard 410
Aboriginal Science Fiction 583
Above The Bridge Magazine 511
Abrams, Inc. Harry N. 59
ABS & Associates 829
Absolute Sound, The 458
Academy Chicago 59
Accent 644
Accent Books 59
Accent on Living 358
Access Control 704
Access Publishers 60
Access to Wang 763
Ace Science Fiction 60
ACM 427
Acorn Publishing 236
ACS Publications, Inc. 61
Actors' Guild of Lexington New Theatre Festival 898
Actors Theatre of Louisville 838
Ad Astra 580
Adams, Inc., Bob 60
Adams Prize, Herbert Baxter 898
Adcom Magazine 292
Addams Children's Book Award, Jane 898
Addison-Wesley Publishing Co., Inc. 61
Adirondack Life 518
Adriatic Award 898

Adventure Feature Syndicate 875
Adventure Road 644
Adventures in Hell 427
Advertising Age 676
Advocacy Press 61
Aegina Press Inc. 253
Afcom Publishing 61
Affaire de Coeur 575
Africa Abroad 331
Africa Report 479
African-American Heritage 331
AG Alert 735
Aglow 543
Aglow Publications 61
Agri-Times Northwest 735
Agway Cooperator 732
Ahsahta Press 236
Aim 297
Aim Magazine 332
Aim Magazine Short Story Contest 898
Air and Space/Smithsonian Magazine 285
Air Line Pilot 286
AJL Reference Book Award 898
ALA Books 61
Alabama Game & Fish/Game & Fish Publications, Inc. 610
Alabama Heritage 487
Alaska 488
Alaska Northwest Books 62
Alaska Outdoors Magazine 488
Alaska Quarterly Review 427
Alban Institue, Inc., The 62
Alberta Farm and Ranch 577
Albundegus All-Stars 838
Alcalde 297
Alfred Hitchcock's Mystery Magazine 464
Algren Short Story Awards, Nelson 898
Alive! 570
Allagash Group, The 830
Allegheny Review Literary Awards 898

Allen Publishing Co. 62
Alley Theatre 838
Allied Feature Syndicate 875
Almar Press 63
Aloha 501
Alpine Publications Inc. 63
Alternative Energy Retailer 720
Altman Weil Pensa Report to Legal Management, The 782
Alyson Publications, Inc. 63
Amacom Books 63
Amazing Computing 473
Amazing Heroes 313
Amazing® Stories 583
Ambergris Annual Fiction Award 899
Amberley Greeting Card Co. 888
AMCAL 888
Amelia Magazine (Literary and "Little") 428
Amelia Magazine (Playwriting) 838
Amelia Student Award 899
America 543
America International Syndicate 875
America West Airlines Magazine 410
America West Publishers 64
American Art Journal, The 265
American Association of University Women Award, North Carolina Division 899
American Astronautical Society 64
American Atheist 344
American Baby Magazine 305
American Bicyclist 816
American Brewer 687
American Business Consultants, Inc. 64
American Catholic Press 64
American Cinematographer 806

American Citizen Italian Press, The 332
American Coin-Op 702
American Collectors Journal, The 373
American Correctional Association 65
American Dane 332
American Demographics 677
American Electronics Association Update 716
American Fiction Awards 899
American Film Magazine 323
American Firearms Industry 816
American Fitness 816
American Forests 464
American Glass Review 690
American Greetings 888
American Handgunner 606
American Heritage 365
American Horticulturist 399
American Hospital Publishing, Inc. 65
American Hunter 610
American Indian Art Magazine 265
American Jewish World 333
American Journal of Nursing 757
American Legion Magazine, The 344
American Libraries 786
American Machinist 722
American Medical News 797
American Motorcyclist 278
American Mover 823
American News Features Syndicate 875
American Newspaper Syndicate 876
American Photo 478
American Photographer (See American Photo 478)
American Place Theatre, The 838
American Rifleman 607
American Salesman, The 813
American-Scandinavian Foundation/Translation Prize 899
American Scholar, The 344
American Short Fiction 428
American Skating World 631
American Skier 631

American Society of Civil Engineers 65
American Society of Journalists & Authors Excellence Awards 899
American Speech-Language-Hearing Association (ASHA), National Media Awards 899
American Squaredance 323
American Stage 839
American Stage Festival 839
American Survival Guide 453
American Visions 333
American Voice, The 429
American Way 410
American Woman Magazine 278
American Woman Road Riding (See American Woman Magazine 278)
Americana Magazine 366
Americas 484
America's Civil War 366
Amherst Media 65
Amicus Journal, The 465
Amoco Traveler 644
Ampersand Communications 876
Amusement Business 725
AMWA Medical Book Awards Competition 899
AMWA Video and Film Festival 899
Amy Writing Awards 899
An Claidheamh Soluis/Celtic Arts Center 839
Analog Science Fiction/Science Fact 583
Ancestry Incorporated 65
Ancestry Newsletter 366
Anchorage Press, Inc. 66
Anderson Publishing Co. 66
Andrews and McMeel 66
Angel's Touch Productions 867
Anglo-American Spotlight 345
Angus Journal 730
Animal House Magazine 256
Animal Tales 256
Animals 256
Ann Arbor Observer 511
Annals of Saint Anne De Beaupre, The 543

Annual Associateship 899
Annual Fiction and Poetry Contest 899
Annual Grant Award Program 900
Annual International Narrative Contest 900
Annual Poetry Contest 900
Annual Poetry/Fiction/Nonfiction Awards 900
Antaeus 429
Antietam Review 429
Antioch Review 429
Antique Review 373
Antique Trader Weekly, The 373
Antiqueweek 679
APA Publications 217
Apothecary, The 708
Appalachian Mountain Club Books 66
Appalachian Trailway News 465
Appaloosa Journal 257
Apparel Industry Magazine 701
Applause 324
Applezaba Press 66
Appliance Service News 755
Applied Arts Quarterly 680
Appraisers Standard, The 680
Aquarian Press 217
Aquarium Fish Magazine 257
Arabian Horse Times 257
Ararat 333
Archaeology 580
Archer Magazine Poetry Awards, The 900
Archery Business 817
Archetype Press, Inc. 249
Archipelago 465
Architectural Book Publishing Co., Inc. 67
Architectural Digest 399
Archway/Minstrel Books 67
Arcsoft Publishers 67
Arden Press, Inc. 67
Ardor Publishing 236
Area Development Magazine 810
Argus Communications 888
Arizona Authors' Association Annual National Literary Contest 900
Arizona Highways 488

Can't find a listing? Check the end of each section: Book Publishers, page 253; Consumer Publications, pg. 673; Trade Journals, page 826; Scriptwriting Markets, page 873; Syndicates, page 886; Greeting Card Publishers, page 896; and Contests, page 937.

Arkansas Arts Center Children's Theatre, The 839
Arkansas Farm & Country 736
Arkansas Poetry Award 900
Arkansas Repertory Theatre 839
Arkansas Sportsman 610
Arkansas Times 489
Arkin Magazine Syndicate Inc. 876
Arman Publishing, Inc., M. 67
Armenian International Magazine 334
Army Magazine 453
Arnold and Associates Productions, Inc. 830
Aronson, Inc., Jason 68
Arrow Rock Lyceum Theatre 839
Art Business News 680
Art Direction 677
Art Direction Book Company 68
Art Extensions Theatre 840
Art Material Trade News 813
Art Times 266
Arthritis Today 320
Artilleryman, The 367
Artist Projects 900
Artists Fellowship Grants 900
Artists Fellowships (IL) 900
Artist's Fellowships (NY) 900
Artist's Magazine, The 266
Artreach Touring Theatre 840
Arts & Activities 710
Arts Indiana 506
Arts Indiana Critical Writing Competition 901
Arts Indiana Literary Supplement 1992 901
Arts Journal, The 267
Arts Management 680
Arts Recognition and Talent Search 901
ASD/AMD Trade News 814
Asher-Gallant Press 68
Asian Humanities Press 68
Asia-Pacific Defense Forum 453
Asimov's Science Fiction Magazine, Isaac 584
Aspen Magazine 494
Assistance to Established Writers 901
Associate Reformed Presbyterian, The 544
Association Executive, The 270

Association for Education in Journalism Awards 901
Astarte Shell Press 236
Astor Memorial Leadership Essay Contest, Vincent 901
Astronomy 580
ASU Travel Guide 645
Atari Explorer 473
Athenaeum of Philadelphia Literary Award, The 901
Atheneum Children's Books 69
Atheneum Publishers 69
ATI 701
Atlanta Singles Magazine 538
Atlantic City Magazine 516
Atlantic Construction 704
Atlantic Monthly, The 345
Atlantic Salmon Journal, The 466
Atticus Press 249
ATUNC Newsletter 763
Audubon 466
Authors' Unlimited 253
Auto Book Press 236
Auto Glass Journal 683
Automated Builder 704
Automatic Machining 789
Automatic Merchandiser 750
Automobile 279
A/V Concepts Corp. 830
Avalon Books 69
Avanyu Publishing Inc. 69
Avery Publishing Group 70
Avon Books 70
Avon Flare Books 70
Avon Flare Young Adult Novel Competition 901
AWA Awards of Excellence 901
Award for Literary Translation 902
Awards for Excellence in Business and Financial Journalism 902
AWP Annual Award Series 902
Axios 544

B

Back Home In Kentucky 507
Backcountry Publications 70
Backpacker 645
Backstretch, The 609
Backwoods Home Magazine 399
Bad Haircut 429
Bailiwick Repertory 840
Baja Times 645

Baker Book House Company 71
Baker's Play Publishing Co. 840
Baldwin College Theatre, Mary 840
Bale Books 71
Ballantine 71
Balloon Life 625
Balls and Strikes 626
Baltimore Magazine 509
BAM 459
Banjo Newsletter 459
Bank Note Reporter 373
Banks-Baldwin Law Publishing Co. 71
Bantam Books 71
Bantam Doubleday Dell 72
Baptist Leader 544
Barefoot Reporter 496
Barn Owl Books 236
Barrister 782
Barron's 287
Barron's Educational Series, Inc. 72
Bartender Magazine 758
Barter Communique 677
Barter Theatre 842
Bartle Playwriting Award, The Margaret 902
Bartlett Award, The Elizabeth 902
Barton & Brett, Publishers, Inc. 236
Baruch University Award, Mrs. Simon 902
Basch Feature Syndicate, Buddy 876
Baseball America 591
Baseball Cards 374
Bassin' 610
Bassmaster Magazine 611
Battery Man, The 683
Bay Windows 538
BC Outdoors 611
Beacon Hill Press of Kansas City 72
Beacon Magazine 522
Beacon Press 72
Bear and Co., Inc. 72
Beau Lac Publishers 73
Beauty Education 710
Beaver Pond Publishing & Printing 73
Beckett Baseball Card Monthly 374
Beckett Basketball Monthly 374
Beckett Focus on Future Stars 375

Beckett Football Monthly 375
Beckett Hockey Monthly 376
Bedroom Magazine 755
Beef 730
Beef Today 730
Beer Wholesaler 687
Behrman House Inc. 73
Bench & Bar of Minnesota 782
Bend of the River Magazine 522
Benenson Productions 830
Bennett Fellowship, George 902
Bentley, Inc., Robert 73
bePuzzled 342
Berkley Publishing Group, The 73
Berkshire Public Theatre 842
Berkshire Theatre Festival, Inc. 842
Berkshire Traveller Press 236
Best of Housewife-Writer's Forum: The Contested Wills to Write 902
Best Recipes Magazine 339
Bethany House Publishers 74
Bethel Publishing 74
Better Health 358
Better Homes and Gardens 400
Better Homes and Gardens Books 74
Better Life for You, A 345
Betterway Publications, Inc. 74
Between the Lines Inc. 217
Beverage World 687
Beveridge Award, Albert J. 902
Beverly Hills Theatre Guild-Julie Harris Playwright Award Competition, The 902
Beyond . . . 584
Bicycle Books, Inc. 75
Bicycle Business Journal 817
Bicycle Guide 591
Bicycling 592
Bike Midwest Magazine 592
Bikeport 592
Bilingual Foundation of the Arts 842
Binford & Mort Publishing 75
Bionics 722

Bird Talk 258
Bird Watcher's Digest 466
Birder's World 467
Black Award, Irma Simonton 903
Black Bear Publications 236
Black Belt 624
Black Collegian, The 297
Black Mountain Review 430
Black Secrets 575
Black Sparrow Press 75
Black Tie Press 236
Black Warrior Review 430
Black Warrior Review Literary Awards 903
Blackbirch Graphics, Inc. 249
Blackburn Prize, Susan Smith 903
Blade Magazine, The 376
Blade Trade 754
Blair, Publisher, John F. 75
Blakeslee Awards, Howard W. 903
Blazing Productions, Inc. 867
Blockbuster Books, Inc. 76
Bloomsbury Review 430
Blue Bird Publishing 76
Blue Dolphin Publishing, Inc. 76
Blue Heron Publishing 76
Blue Mountain Arts, Inc. 888
Blue Q 889
Blue Ridge Country 484
Bluegrass Unlimited 459
BMX Plus Magazine 593
BNA Books 77
B'nai B'rith International, The 334
Boarshead Theater 842
Boat Journal 594
Boat Pennsylvania 594
Boca Raton Magazine 497
Body Boarding 634
Body Building Lifestyles 636
Body, Mind & Spirit 275
Boing-Boing 431
Bonat's Diversified, Inc. 877
Bonus Books, Inc. 77
Book Dealers World 772
Bookcraft, Inc. 77
Bookworks, Inc. 249
Borealis Press, Ltd. 217
Borgo Press, The 78
Bosco Multimedia, Don 78
Boston Business Journal 292

Boston Globe Magazine 510
Boston Globe-Horn Book Awards 903
Boston Mills Press, The 218
Boston Post Road Stage Company 842
Boston Review 316
Bostonia 510
Bosustow Video 830
Bottom Line, The 739
Boulder County Business Report 293
Boulevard 431
Bow and Arrow Hunting 590
Bowhunter 590
Bowhunting World 590
Bowlers Journal 601
Bowling 601
Bowling Green State University Popular Press 78
Bowling Magazine 602
Bowling Writing Competition 903
Boxboard Containers 804
Boxoffice Magazine 726
Boxwood Press, The 78
Boyd & Fraser Publishing Company 79
Boyds Mills Press 79
Boys' Life 413
Bradbury Press 79
Bradley's Fantasy Magazine, Marion Zimmer 584
Brake & Front End 683
Branden Publishing Co., Inc.. 79
Bread 636
Brevet Press, Inc. 80
Briarcliff Press Publishers 80
Brick House Publishing Co. 80
Bridal Guide 658
Bridal Trends 658
Bride's 659
Brilliant Enterprises 889
Brilliant Ideas for Publishers 772
Brio 646
Bristol Publishing Enterprises, Inc. 81
Bristol Riverside Theatre 842
British American Publishing 81
British Car 279
British Heritage 334

Can't find a listing? Check the end of each section: Book Publishers, page 253; Consumer Publications, pg. 673; Trade Journals, page 826; Scriptwriting Markets, page 873; Syndicates, page 886; Greeting Card Publishers, page 896; and Contests, page 937.

Brittingham Prize in Poetry 903
Broadcast Technology 716
Broadview Press Ltd. 218
Broadway Press 81
Bronze Thrills 575
Broun Award, The Heywood 903
Brunswick Publishing Co. 253
Bucknell University Press 81
Buffalo Spree Magazine 518
Builder Insider 705
Bull Publishing Co. 81
Burke Essay Contest, Arleigh 903
Bus Ride 823
Bus Tours Magazine 824
Bus World 823
Bush Artist Fellowships 903
Business & Legal Reports, Inc. 82
Business Facilities 810
Business Features Syndicate 877
Business Radio 716
Business to Business Magazine 288
Business Week 288
Butter-Fat 729
Buzzworm 467
Byline 772
Byline Magazine Contests 903
Byte Magazine 473

C

C Q Press 82
C.S.S. Publishing Co. 82
CAA's Autopinion Annual 279
Cable Communications Magazine 717
Cable Poetry Chapbook Competition, Gerald 903
Cablecaster 726
CADalyst 680
Calgre Press 82
California Angler 611
California Business 293
California Fire Service, The 745
California Game & Fish 612
California Highway Patrolman 270
California Highway Patrolman, The 745
California Horse Review 258
California Journal 480
California Lawyer 782
California Magazine 490

California Playwrights Competition 903
California Quarterly 431
California Theater Center 843
California Writers' Club Conference Contest 904
Calligraphy Collection, The 889
Calligraphy Review 681
Calliope 413
Cambridge Career Products 83
Cambridge University Press 83
Camden House, Inc. 83
Camden House Publishing 218
Camelot Books 83
Camera & Darkroom Magazine 478
Camino Books, Inc. 84
Camping & RV Magazine 646
Camping Today 646
Canadian 411
Canadian Author & Bookman 772
Canadian Author & Bookman Student Creative Writing Awards 904
Canadian Defense Quarterly 745
Canadian Dimension 318
Canadian Fiction Magazine 432
Canadian Forest Industries West 788
Canadian Geographic 534
Canadian Grocer 750
Canadian Indie Star 335
Canadian Institute of Ukrainian Studies Press 218
Canadian Laboratory 722
Canadian Literature 432
Canadian Machinery & Metalworking 789
Canadian Pharmaceutical Journal 709
Canadian Plains Research Center 219
Canadian West 367
Canadian Workshop, The Do-It-Yourself Magazine 400
Canadian Writer's Journal 773
Candy Industry 703
Candy Wholesaler 750
Cane Award, Melville 904
Canoe Magazine 594

C&T Publishing 84
Cape Cod Home & Garden 510
Cape Cod Life 510
Capper's 345
Capstone Press, Inc. 84
Car And Driver 279
Car Audio and Electronics 280
Car Craft 280
Caratzas, Publisher, Aristide D. 84
Cardiology World News 797
Cardoza Enterprises, Anthony 867
Career Focus 298
Career Pilot 286
Career Press Inc., The 84
Career Publishing, Inc. 85
Career Woman 298
Careers & the Disabled 320
Careers 637
Caribbean Travel and Life 647
Carlton Press, Inc. 253
Carnegie Mellon Magazine 298
Carol Publishing 85
Carolrhoda Books, Inc. 85
Carousel Press 237
Carpenter Publishing House 250
Carroll & Graf Publishers, Inc. 85
Carstens Publications, Inc. 86
Cartoon World 313
Casa Manana Musicals, Inc. 843
Cascades East 524
Casey Award, Bill 904
Casino Player 602
Cassandra Press 86
Cassell Publications 86
Casual Living 814
Cat Fancy 258
Catbird Press 86
Catholic Forester 346
Catholic Life (See PIME World 560)
Catholic Near East Magazine 545
Catholic Press Association Journalism Awards 904
Catholic University of America Press 87
Cato Institute 87
Cats Magazine 259
Cavalier 448
Caxton Printers, Ltd., The 87
CBP (See Chalice Press 88)

CCC Publications 87
CD Review 459
CEC National Children's Theatre Playwriting Contest 904
Cecil Arthritis Writing Awards, Russell L. 904
Celebrate Life! 483
Celebration of One-Acts 904
Center for Applied Linguistics 87
Center Stage 843
Chain Saw Age 754
Chakra 432
Chalice Press 88
Challenger Press 237
Chamba Organization, The 867
Champaign-Urbana Magazine 503
Chandler Award, Paulette 904
Changes 358
Changing Men 538
Changing Scene Theater, The 843
Changing Times 314
Chapbook Competition 904
Chariton Review, The 432
Charlesbridge Publishing 88
Charleston Magazine 527
Chatelaine 659
Chatham Press 88
Cheklist 739
Chelsea Awards for Poetry and Short Fiction, The 905
Chelsea Green 88
Chemical Business 761
Chesapeake Bay Magazine 509
Chess Life 343
Chevy High Performance 280
Chic Magazine 449
Chicago History 367
Chicago Life 503
Chicago Magazine 503
Chicago Review Press 89
Chicago Studies 545
Chicago Tribune Magazine, The 504
Chicano/Latino Literary Contest 905
Chickadee Magazine 414
Chief Executive 692
Chief of Police Magazine 746

Children's Album, The 414
Children's Digest 414
Children's Playmate 415
Children's Story Scripts 843
Chile Pepper 339
China Books & Periodicals, Inc. 89
China Glass & Tableware 756
Chippendales 889
Chosen Books Publishing Co., Ltd. 90
Christian Century, The 545
Christian Herald 545
Christian Home & School 545
Christian Ministry, The 698
Christian Parenting Today 306
Christian Retailing 702
Christian Science Monitor, The 346
Christian Single 546
Christian Social Action 546
Christianity & Chrisis 546
Christianity Today 547
Christmas 547
Christopher Award, The 905
Christopher Publishing House, The 90
Chronicle Books 90
Chronicle Features 877
Chronicle of the Horse, The 259
Chrysalis 547
Church Administration 699
Church & State 547
Church Educator 699
Church Media Library Magazine 787
Church Musician, The 802
Cincinnati Magazine 522
Cincinnati Medicine 797
Cincinnati Playhouse in the Park 844
Cineaste 324
Cine/Design Films, Inc. 868
Cinefantastique Magazine 324
Cintas Fellowshiop 905
Circle K Magazine 299
Circuit Playhouse/Playhouse on the Square 844
Circuit Rider 699
Citadel Press 90
Citiarts Theatre 844
City Guide Magazine 518

City Lights Books 91
City Limits 518
City Merchandise Inc. 889
City, The, San Francisco's Magazine 490
City Theatre Company 844
Civil War Times Illustrated 367
Clarion Books 91
Clarity Press Inc. 237
Clark Co., Arthur H. 91
Clark, Inc., I.E. 844
Clarkson Potter 91
Classroom Computer Learning (See Technology & Learning 714)
Claytor Memorial Award, Gertrude B. 905
Cleaning (See Cleaning Business 789)
Cleaning Business 789
Cleaning Consultant Services, Inc. 91
Cleaning Management 790
Clearvue, Inc. 830
Cleis Press 92
Clergy Journal, The 700
Cleveland Play House, The 845
Cleveland State University Poetry Center 92
Cleveland State University Poetry Center Prize 905
Cliffhanger Press 92
Cliffs Notes, Inc. 93
Clifton Magazine 347
Clockwatch Review 433
Closing the Gap, Inc. 473
Clothespin Fever Press 237
Clubhouse 415
Coach House Press 219
Coal People Magazine 820
Coast to Coast Magazine 647
Coastal Cruising 595
Cobblestone 416
Coffee House Press 93
Coin Enthusiast's Journal, The 377
Coins 377
Collector Books 93
Collector Editions 377
Collectors News & The Antique Reporter 377
Collectors' Showcase 378
College Monthly 299

Can't find a listing? Check the end of each section: Book Publishers, page 253; Consumer Publications, pg. 673; Trade Journals, page 826; Scriptwriting Markets, page 873; Syndicates, page 886; Greeting Card Publishers, page 896; and Contests, page 937.

College Press Publishing Co., Inc. 93
College Preview 299
Collegiate Poetry Contest 905
Colonial Homes 400
Colorado Associated University Press (See University Press of Colorado 202)
Colorado Homes & Lifestyles 400
Colorado Review 433
Colormore Inc. 237
Columbia 548
Columbia Journalism Review 773
Columbus Bride & Groom Magazine 539
Columbus Monthly 523
Comark 831
Comedy Writers Association Newsletter 271
Comics Journal, The 773
Comics Scene 313
Comments 548
Commonwealth Club of California Book Awards 905
Commonwealth of Pennsylvania Council on the Arts Literature Fellowships 905
Communication Briefings 692
Communixations 763
Compass Films/Video 831
Complete Woman 659
Compressed Air 761
Compro Productions 831
Computer Language 474
Computer Language 764
Computer Science Press 93
Computer User's Legal Reporter 783
Computercraft 474
Computers in Accounting 692
Computers in Education 711
Computoredge 474
CompuWrite 905
Comstock Cards 889
Conari Press 94
Concordia Publishing House 94
Confident Living 548
Confrontation 433
Congress Monthly 335
Connecticut Magazine 494
Connecticut Poetry Review 433
Conners Prize for Poetry, The Bernard F. 905
Connoisseur, The 347
Conscience 548

Construction Comment 705
Construction Specifier 705
Consultant Pharmacist 798
Consultant Press, The 94
Consumer Action News 315
Consumer Lending Report 739
Consumer Reports Books 94
Consumer Sense 288
Contemporary Books, Inc. 95
Contemporary Designs 890
Contemporary Drama Service 845
Contenova Gifts 890
Continental Features/Continental News Service 877
Continental Film Productions Corporation 831
Convention South 693
Cook Publishing Co., David C. 95
Cooking Light 340
Cool Traveler, The 647
Copley News Service 878
Coral Springs Monthly 497
Corkscrew Press 237
Cornell Maritime Press, Inc. 95
Cornerstone 549
Corporate Cleveland 293
Cosmopolitan 660
Coteau Books 219
Coterie, The 845
Cottage Life 401
Cottonwood Monthly 711
Council for Wisconsin Writers, Inc. Annual Awards Competition 905
Counselor Magazine, The 677
Country America 324
Country Home 401
Country Journal 578
Country Living 401
Country Music 460
Country Woman 660
Countryman Press, Inc., The 95
Covenant Companion, The 549
CPI Purchasing 761
CQ Inc. 81
Crafts Magazine 378
Crafts Report, The 681
Craftsman Book Company 95
Crain's Detroit Business 294
Crazyhorse 433
Create-a-Craft 890
Creative Artists Grant 906
Creative Arts Contest 906

Creative Productions, Inc. 845
Creative Publishing Co. 96
Creative Syndication Services 878
Creative With Words Publications 237
Creative Woodworks & Crafts 378
Creativity Fellowship 906
Creators Syndicate, Inc. 878
Creede Repertory Theatre 846
Cricket 416
Cricket Communications, Inc. 878
Crisis Magazine 318
Crisp Publications, Inc. 96
Crochet Fantasy 378
Cross Stitch Sampler 379
Crossing Press, The 96
Cross-Stitch Plus 379
Crossway Books 96
Crown Publishing Group 97
Crown Syndicate, Inc. 878
Cruise Travel Magazine 648
Cruising World 595
Crusader Magazine 416
CTS Enterprises 868
Cuff Publications Limited, Harry 219
Current Comedy 408
Current Health 1 417
Current World Leaders 480
Currents (Sports) 595
Currents (Travel) 648
Custom Applicator 728
Cycle 280
Cycle World 280
Cycling USA 593

D

"D" Magazine 528
Daedalus Press 237
Daily Meditation 550
Dairyman, The 730
Dakota Outdoors 528
Dallas Life Magazine 529
Dance Connection 325
Dance Horizons 97
Dance Magazine 325
Dancy Productions, Inc., Nicholas 831
D&B Reports 288
Daniel and Company, Publishers, John 97
Dante University Of America Press, Inc. 97
Darkroom & Creative Camera Techniques 478

Darkroom Photography Magazine (See Camera & Darkroom Magazine 478)
Data Based Advisor 764
Data Training 791
Davenport, Publishers, May 97
Davidson Memorial Award, Gustav 906
Davies Memorial Award, Mary Carolyn 906
Davis Publications, Inc. 98
DAW Books, Inc. 98
DBMS 764
DCI Publishing 98
De La Torre Bueno Prize 906
De Young Press 253
Decision 550
Decorating Remodeling 401
Decorative Artist's Workbook 379
Dee, Inc., Ivan R. 98
Deep Ellum Theatre Group/ Undermain Theatre 846
Deep South Writers Contest 906
Deer and Deer Hunting 612
Del Rey Books 98
Delacorte Press 99
Delacorte Press Prize for a First Young Adult Novel 906
Delaware Theatre Company 846
Deligter Productions, Harry 868
Dell Books 99
Delta Books 99
Delta Max Productions 832
Denali Press, The 99
Denison & Co., Inc., T.S. 99
Denlingers Publishers, Ltd. 99
Denny Poetry Contest, Billee Murray 906
Dental Economics 707
Denver Center Theatre Company 846
Denver Quarterly, The 434
Design Management 723
D'Esternaux Student Poetry Contest, Marie-Louise 906
Destination Washington 648

Detroit Free Press Magazine, The 511
Detroit Monthly 512
Developers' Insight 764
Devin-Adair Publishers, Inc. 99
Devonshire Publishing Co. 100
Dexter Prize 906
DG Review 765
Di Castagnola Award, Alice Fay 906
Diabetes Self-Management 321
Diagnostic Imaging 798
Dial Books For Young Readers 100
Diamond Press 237
Diamond Registry Bulletin, The 771
Dickinson Award, Emily 906
Digressions, Inc. 890
Dillon Press, Inc. 101
Dillon/Richard C. Peterson Memorial Essay Prize, Gordon W. 906
Dimensional Stone 820
Dimi Press 237
Directions 300
Dirt Rag 593
Discipleship Journal 550
Discover 581
Discovery '92 846
Discovery YMCA 271
Discovery/The Nation 907
Distinctive Publishing Corporation 101
Diver 634
Diver, The 635
Diverse Visions Regional Grants Program 907
Diversion 347
Diversity 347
Docket, The 783
Dr. Dobb's Journal 765
Doctors Shopper 798
Dog Fancy 260
Dolls 380
Dolphin Log, The 417
Door, The 550
Doubleday Books 101
Doubleday Memorial Award, Frank Nelson 907
Douglas College 847
Down East Books 101

Dragon® Magazine 343
Drama Book Publishers 102
Dramatic Publishing Co., The 847
Dramatics Magazine (Entertainment) 325
Dramatics Magazine (Scriptwriting) 847
Drummer 539
Drury College One-Act Play Contest 907
Dubuque Fine Arts Players 907
Dundurn Press Ltd. 220
Dungeon Master 539
Dunning Prize in American History, John H. 907
Duquesne University Press 102
Durst Publications Ltd. 102
Dustbooks 102
Dusty Dog Chapbook Series 237
Dutton Children's Books 102
Dutton, E. P. 103
Dutton/New American Library 103

E
Early American Life 380
Early Childhood News 693
Earth Care Paper Inc. 890
East End Lights 325
East West Players 847
Eastern Aftermarket Journal 683
Eastman's Outdoorsmen, Mike 612
Eating Well 340
Eaton Literary Associates Literary Awards Program 907
Ebony Magazine 335
Eclipse Comics 314
Economic Facts 315
ECW Press 220
Edges 380
Ediciones Universal 103
Editor & Publisher 773
Editorial Consultant Service 878
Editorial Eye, The 773
Editors' Book Award 907
Editors' Forum 774
Education Associates 103

Can't find a listing? Check the end of each section: Book Publishers, page 253; Consumer Publications, pg. 673; Trade Journals, page 826; Scriptwriting Markets, page 873; Syndicates, page 886; Greeting Card Publishers, page 896; and Contests, page 937.

Educational Images Ltd. 832
Educational Insights 832
Educational Video Network 832
Eerdmans Publishing Co., William B. 103
EES Publications 104
Effective Communication Arts, Inc. 832
Elder Statesman, The 570
Eldercards, Inc. (See Digressions, Inc. 890)
Eldridge Publishing Co. 847
Electric Consumer 578
Electrical Apparatus 720
Electrical Contractor 721
Electron, The 581
Electronic Composition and Imaging 475
Electronic Servicing & Technology 717
Ellery Queen's Mystery Magazine 464
Ellis Memorial Award, David James 907
Elysium Growth Press 104
Emergency 798
Emergency Librarian 787
Emerging Playwright Award 907
Emmy Magazine 326
Empire State Report 480
Employee Relations and Human Resources Bulletin 792
Empty Space, The 848
Encore Performance Pubishing 848
Endless Vacation 649
Engravers Journal, The 771
Ensemble Studio Theatre, The 848
Ensemble Theatre of Cincinnati 848
Entelek 104
Enterprise Publishing Co., Inc. 104
Entertainment News Syndicate 879
Entertainment Productions, Inc. 868
Entreprenurial Woman 661
Environment 468
Environmental Action 468
Epoch 434
Epstein Playwriting Award, Lawrence S. 907
Equal Opportunity 300
Equine Images 267
Equinox: The Magazine of

Canadian Discovery 348
Equities 739
Eriksson, Publisher, Paul S. 104
Erlbaum Associates, Inc., Lawrence 105
Erotic Fiction Quarterly 434
Esquire 449
Essence 661
Esteban Films Inc. 868
Etc Magazine 300
ETC Publications 105
Euro Communication Entertainment Group 832
Europa Press News Service 879
Europe 480
European Car 281
Evangel 551
Evangelical Beacon, The 551
Evangelizing Today's Child 551
Evans and Co., Inc., M. 105
Evans Biography Award, David W. and Beatrice C. 907
Eve of St. Agnes Poetry Competition 908
Event 434
Evergreen Communications, Inc. 106
Executive Female 288
Exhibit 267
Expecting 306
Exploring Magazine 637
Eyster Prize 908

F

Faber & Faber, Inc. 106
Facets 799
Facets of New York 519
Facts On File, Inc. 106
FAHS Review (See Health Systems Review 709)
Fairbank Prize in East Asian History, John K. 908
Fairbanks Arts Magazine 774
Fairfield County Woman 661
Fairleigh Dickinson University Press 106
Fairway Press 253
Falcon Press Publishing Co., Inc. 107
Fall Festival of Plays 908
Fallen Leaf Press 237
Family Album, The 107
Family Circle Magazine 661
Family Living 401
Family Magazine 454
Family Motor Coaching 649
Family, The 552

Fangoria 326
Fantasy Baseball 626
Farber First Book Award, Norma 908
Farm & Ranch Living 578
Farm Family America 579
Farm Journal 732
Farm Show Magazine 733
Farm Store 693
Farmer/Dakota Farmer, The 736
Farmweek 736
Farrar, Straus and Giroux, Inc. 107
Fashion Accessories 771
Fate 276
Faulkner Award for Excellence in Writing, Virginia 908
Fawcett Juniper 107
FDA Consumer 315
Fearon/Janus Publishers 107
Feature Enterprises 879
Fedco Reporter 271
Federal Credit Union, The 740
Fellowship in Literature 908
Fellowship-Literature 908
Fellowships for Creative Writers 908
Fellowships to Assist Research and Artistic Creation 908
Feminist Bookstore News, The 689
Feminist Writers' Contest 908
Ferguson Publishing Company, J.G. 107
Festival of Emerging American Theatre, The 908
FFA New Horizons 733
Fiberarts 381
Ficarelli, Richard 848
Fiction Quarterly 434
Fiction Writers Contest 908
Fiddlehead, The 435
Field & Stream 612
Fiesta Books Inc. 108
Fiesta City Publishers 237
Fifty-Something Magazine 571
Film Quarterly 326
Filter Press 108
Final Frontier 581
Financial Executive 693
Financial Freedom Report 811
Financial Sourcebooks 108
Financial Technology News 740

Financial Woman Today 740
Financial World 289
Fine Homebuilding 705
Fine, Inc., Donald I. 108
Fine Woodworking 381
Finescale Modeler 381
Finger Lakes Magazine 519
Firebrand Books 109
Firehouse Magazine 746
Firehouse Theatre, The 848
First Book Award 909
First for Women 662
First Hand 540
First Opportunity 301
Fish Memorial Award, Robert L. 909
Fisher Books 109
Fisherman, The 613
Fishing World 613
Fithian Press 253
Fitzhenry & Whiteside, Ltd. 220
Flanagan Memorial Creative Persons Center, William 909
Flexlines 765
Fling 449
Flip 637
Fliptrack Learning Systems 833
Flooring Magazine 756
Floral & Nursery Times 742
Flores Publications, J. 109
Florida Game & Fish 613
Florida Grocer 751
Florida Home & Garden 401
Florida Hotel & Motel Journal 758
Florida Individual Artist Fellowships 909
Florida Leader 301
Florida Living 497
Florida Poetry Contest 909
Florida Restaurateur 759
Florida Sportsman 613
Florida Trend 294
Florida Underwriter 768
Florida Wildlife 614
Florist 743
Flower and Garden Magazine 401
Flower News 743
Fly Fisherman 614
Flying 286
FMCT's Biennial Playwrights

Competition (Mid-West) 909
FNA News 879
Focal Press 109
Folio 909
Food And Service 751
Food & Wine 340
Food & Drug Packaging 815
Food People 751
Foodservice Director 751
Ford Award, Consuelo 909
Ford New Holland News 733
Ford Times 348
Ford-Brown & Co., Publishers 237
Fordham Magazine 301
Foreign Affairs 770
Foreign Service Journal 746
Forests & People 468
Forman Publishing, Inc. 109
49th Parallel Poetry Contest, The 909
Forum 450
Fotofolio, Inc. 890
Fotopress, Independent News Service 879
Four Walls Eight Windows 110
Four Wheeler Magazine 281
4-Wheel & Off-Road (See Petersen's 4-Wheel 283)
Fox Valley Living 504
FPMI Communications, Inc. 110
France Today 318
Frank: An International Journal of Contemporary Writing & Art 435
Franklin Literary Award, Miles 909
Fraser Institute, The 220
Freedley Memorial Award, George 909
Freedom Greeting Card Co. 890
Freedom Magazine 481
Freelance Press, The 848
Freelance Writer's Report 774
Freeman Memorial Grant-In-Aid, Don 909
Freeman, The 481
Freeway 637
French, Inc., Samuel (Book Publishers) 110

French, Inc., Samuel (Playwriting) 849
Friedman Publishing Group, Michael 250
Friend, The 417
Friendly Exchange 348
Frog in The Well 237
Fromm International 110
Front Row Experience 237
Frost Associates, Helena 250
Fulbright Scholar Program 909
Fullmoon Creations Inc. 891
Fund for New American Plays 910
Fur-Fish-Game 614
Furman Films, Inc. 868
Futures and Options Trader, The (See Trader, The 741)
Futurific Magazine 348

G

(Gabriel) Graphics News Bureau 879
Galantière Prize for Literary Translation, Lewis 910
Gallaudet University Press 111
Gallery Magazine 450
Gallery Players Playwriting Contest 910
Game & Fish Publications, Inc. 614
Gamut, The 435
GAP (Grants for Artist Projects); Fellowship 910
Garden Design 402
Garden Supply Retailer 743
Gardner Press, Inc. 111
Garrett Park Press 111
Gaslight Publications 112
Gassner Memorial Playwriting Award, John 910
Gauss Award, The Christian 910
Gavel Awards 910
Gay Sunshine Press and Leyland Publications 112
GEICO Direct 769
Genealogical Computing 475
Genealogical Publishing Co., Inc. 112
General Aviation News & Flyer 286
General Hall, Inc. 112

Can't find a listing? Check the end of each section: Book Publishers, page 253; Consumer Publications, pg. 673; Trade Journals, page 826; Scriptwriting Markets, page 873; Syndicates, page 886; Greeting Card Publishers, page 896; and Contests, page 937.

General News Syndicate 879
Genesis 450
Genre 540
Gentlemen's Quarterly 451
Georgetown Productions 849
Georgia Sportsman 615
Georgia Straight, The 534
Geriatric Consultant 799
German Prize for Literary Translation 910
Geyer's Office Dealer 804
Ghost Town Quarterly 368
Giant Crosswords 343
Gibson Greetings 891
Gifford Children's Theater, Emmy 849
Gift & Stationery 756
Gifted Education Press 113
Giniger Company, Inc., The K S 250
Glamour 662
Glass Magazine 690
Glassco Translation Prize, John 910
Gleanings in Bee Culture 735
Glenbridge Publishing Ltd. 113
Globe Pequot Press, Inc., The 113
Globe Press Books 113
GMS Publications 237
Godine, Publisher, Inc., David R. 113
Gold Prospector 821
Golden Gate National Playwrighting Contest 911
Golden Kite Awards 911
Golden Quill Press, The 253
Golden West Books 114
Golden West Publishers 114
Golden Years Magazine 571
Golf Course Management 817
Golf Digest 605
Golf Illustrated 605
Golf Magazine 606
Golf Shop Operations 817
Golf Writer's Contest 911
Good Housekeeping 662
Good Old Days 368
Good Reading 349
Goodman Award 911
Goodwin & Associates 880
Goose Lane Editions 221
Gospel Publishing House 114
Gourmet 341
Gourmet Retailer Magazine, The 752
Government Institutes, Inc. 114

Governor General's Literary Awards 911
Gower Publishing Co. 114
Graduating Engineer 723
Grand Rapids Magazine 512
Grapevine Publications, Inc. 115
Graphic Arts Center Publishing Co. 115
Graphic Arts Technical Foundation 115
Grassroots Fundraising Journal 747
Graywolf Press 115
Great American Tennis Writing Awards, The 911
Great Expeditions 649
Great Lakes Fisherman 615
Great Northwest Publishing and Distributing Company, Inc. 116
Great Plains Game & Fish 615
Great Platte River Playwrights Festival 911
Greater Phoenix Jewish News 335
Greater Portland Magazine 508
Greatworks Play Service 849
Green, Inc., Warren H. 116
Green Timber Publications 237
Greenhaven Press, Inc. 116
Greensboro Review Literary Award in Fiction and Poetry, The 911
Greyhound Review, The 260
Grit 349
Grolier Poetry Prize 911
Groom & Board 805
Grosset & Dunlap Publishers 116
Ground Water Age 812
Grove Wiedenfeld 117
Growing Churches 552
Growing Edge, The 744
Growing Parent 306
GSM Features 880
Guernica Editions 221
Guide 638
Guide, The 541
Guidelines Magazine (See Writer's Guidelines 779)
Guideposts Magazine 552
Guitar Player Magazine 460
Gulf Coast 498
Gulf Coast Fisherman 615
Gulf Publishing Co. 117
Gulfshore Life 498

Gun Digest 607
Gun World 607
Guns & Ammo Annual 608
Guns & Ammo 608
Guns Magazine 608
Gurze Books 237
Guys 451

H

Hackney Literary Awards 912
Hale Award, Sarah Josepha 912
Half Halt Press, Inc. 117
Hallmark Cards, Inc. 891
Hamilton Institute, Alexander 117
Hancock House Publishers Ltd. 117
Hands-On Electronics (See Popular Electronics 388)
Handwoven 382
Hansen, Inc., Edward D. 868
Hanson's 435
HAPPI 756
Harbinger House, Inc. 118
Harcourt Brace Jovanovich 118
Harcourt Brace Jovanovich, Children's Book Division 118
Hardware Age 755
Harlequin Enterprises, Ltd. 221
Harper San Francisco 118
HarperCollins Children's Books Pacific Northwest 118
HarperCollins Publishers 119
Harper's Magazine 350
Harris Music Co., Limited, The Frederick 224
Harrow And Heston 119
Harrowsmith Country Life 579
Harrowsmith Magazine 579
Hartford Monthly 495
Hartford Stage Company 849
Hartley & Marks 119
Harvard Common Press, The 120
Harvard Oaks Career Guidance Award 912
Harvest House Publishers 120
Haunts 584
Hawaii Magazine 501
Hawkes Publishing, Inc. 120
Hay House, Inc. 120
Hayes School Publishing Co., Inc. 833
Haypenny Press 238

Headlands Residency 912
Health Administration Press 121
Health Communications, Inc. 121
Health Foods Business 752
Health Systems Review 709
Healthcare Professional Publishing 799
Healthy Kids: Birth-3/ Healthy Kids: 4-10 307
Heart Of The Lakes Publishing 121
Heartland Boating 596
Heating, Plumbing, Air Conditioning 808
Heinle & Heinle Publishers, Inc. 121
Heinz Literature Prize, Drue 912
Helix Press 238
Hemingway Foundation Award, Ernest 912
Hemingway Short Story Competition 912
Hemingway Western Studies Series 238
Hemley Memorial Award, Cecil 912
Hendrick-Long Publishing Co., Inc. 121
Hendrickson Publishers Inc. 122
Henry Festival Short Story Contest, O. 912
Hensley, Inc., Virgil W. 122
Herald Press 122
Herald Press Canada 224
Herald Publishing House 122
Herb Companion, The 402
Herb Quarterly 402
Here's Life Publishers, Inc. 123
Heritage Books, Inc. 123
Heritage Florida Jewish News 336
Heyday Books 123
Hicall 552
Hideaways Guide 649
High Adventure 418
High Plains Journal 733
High Plains Literary Review 436
High School I.D. 638

High School Playwriting Contest 912
High School Sports 603
High Technology Careers 723
High Times 318
High Volume Printing 809
Highlander, The 336
Highlights for Children 418
Highlights for Children Fiction Contest 912
Hill Books, Lawrence 123
Hinduism Today 553
Hippocrene Books Inc. 124
Hispanic 336
Hispanic Link News Service 880
Hit Parader 460
Hobo Jungle 436
Hobson's Choice 585
Hockey Illustrated 626
Hog Farm Management 731
Hohm Press 238
Hollowbrook Publishing 124
Hollywood Inside Syndicate 880
Hollywood Magazine 327
Hollywood Reporter, The 726
Holt, Rinehart & Winston 124
Holte Literary Prize, The Clarence 912
Home 402
Home & Away 650
Home Builder 706
Home Education Magazine 307
Home Life 307
Home Lighting & Accessories 756
Home Magazine 403
Home Mechanix 382
Home Office Computing 475
Home Shop Machinist, The 382
Home Sweet Home 694
Home Times 553
Homemaker's 662
Homeowner 403
Homestead Publishing 124
Homeworking Mothers 289
Honolulu 502
Honolulu Theatre for Youth 849
Hoof Beats 609

Hooked on Fishing Magazine 616
Hopscotch 418
Horizon Theatre Company 850
Horn Book Magazine, The 689
Horsdal & Schubart Publishers Ltd. 224
Horse and Horseman 260
Horse Digest, The (See International Horse Digest 262)
Horse Illustrated 260
Horse World USA 261
Horsemen's Yankee Pedlar Newspaper 261
Horses All 261
Hospital Risk Management 757
Hospital Supervisor's Bulletin 757
Hot Boat 596
Hot Rod 281
Hotel Amenities in Canada 759
Houghton Mifflin Co. (Adult Trade Division) 124
Houghton Mifflin Co. (Children's Division) 125
Houghton Mifflin Literary Fellowship 913
Hounslow Press 225
Housewife-Writer's Forum 774
Houston Metropolitan Magazine 529
Houston Prize, Darrell Bob 913
HOW 681
Howard Awards, The Roy W. 913
Howell Press, Inc. 125
HRD Press, Inc. 125
HTC One-Act Playwriting Competition 913
Hubbard's Writers of the Future Contest, L. Ron 913
Hudson Hill Press, Inc. 125
Hudson Review, The 436
Human Kinetics Publishers, Inc. 126
Human Resource Executive 792

Can't find a listing? Check the end of each section: Book Publishers, page 253; Consumer Publications, pg. 673; Trade Journals, page 826; Scriptwriting Markets, page 873; Syndicates, page 886; Greeting Card Publishers, page 896; and Contests, page 937.

Human Services Institute, Inc. 126
Humanics Publishing Group 126
Humanities Press International, Inc. 126
Humpty Dumpty's Magazine 419
Hungness Publishing, Carl 126
Hunt, William E. 850
Hunter Publishing, Inc. 127
Hutton Fiction Contests 913
HW 495
Hyde Park Media 881

I

I.B. (Independent Business) 289
I Love Cats 262
Idaho Writer in Residence 913
Idea Today 817
Ideals Publishing Corp. 127
Identity 677
IEA Publishers (See Ishiyaku Euroamerica Inc. 133)
IEEE Press 127
IFMT Magazine (See Picture Perfect 303)
Illinois Banker 740
Illinois Entertainer 460
Illinois Game & Fish 616
Illinois Magazine 504
Illinois Publisher, The 775
Illuminations Press 238
ILR Press 127
Imagine, Inc. 127
Imprint 678
Impulse Theatre Company 850
In Depth Publishers 128
In Health 359
In Touch for Men 541
Inbound Logistics 824
Incentive 815
Income Plus Magazine 315
Independent Banker 741
Independent Living 321
Independent Scholars, Lowell, Marraro, Shaughnessy and Mildenberger Awards 913
India Currents 336
Indiana Business Magazine 294
Indiana Game & Fish 616
Indiana Review 436
Indiana University Press 128
Indianapolis Monthly 506

Individual Artist Fellowship Award 913
Individual Artists Fellowships 913
Individual Investor 290
Industrial Press, Inc. 128
Industrial Whimsy Co. 891
Industry Week 792
Info Franchise Newsletter 815
Info Net Publishing 128
Inform 765
Information Today 717
Information Week 766
Inland 485
Inland Architect 706
Inner Traditions International 129
Innkeeping World 759
InnoVisions, Inc. 891
Innovatia Press 129
Inside 337
Inside Chicago 505
Inside Detective 319
Inside Hollywood 327
Inside Karate 624
Inside Kung-Fu 625
Inside Sports 603
Inside Texas Running 626
Insight Books 129
Institute of Psychological Research, Inc./Institut de Recherches Psychologiques, Inc. 225
Instructor Magazine 711
Instrumentalist, The 803
Insurance Review 769
Interactive Arts 833
Intercultural Press, Inc. 130
Interior Landscape Industry 744
Interlit 553
Intermedia News and Feature Service 881
International Bluegrass 803
International Bowhunter Magazine 591
International Doll World 383
International Film & Film Literature Awards 913
International Foundation Of Employee Benefit Plans 130
International Gymnast 627
International Haiku Contest 914
International Home Entertainment Inc. 868
International Horse Digest, The 262

International Living 485
International Musician 461
International Publishers Co., Inc. 130
International Reading Association Children's Book Award 914
International Reading Association Print Media Award 914
International Self-Counsel Press, Ltd. 225
International Wealth Success 130
International Wildlife 468
Interpress of London and New York 881
Interstate News Services, Inc. 881
Interstate Publishers, Inc. The 131
Interurban Press/Trans Anglo Books 131
Intervarsity Press 131
Interweave Press 132
Intimacy/Black Romance 575
Inverted-A, Inc. 238
Iowa Game & Fish 616
Iowa Rec News 737
Iowa Review, The 438
Iowa State University Press 132
Irish American Magazine 337
Iron Crown Enterprises 132
Ishiyaku Euroamerica, Inc. 133
Island Life 498
Island Literary Awards 914
Islands 486
Islesboro Island News 508

J

Jack and Jill 419
Jackson Productions, David 833
Jackson/James D. Phelan Literary Awards, Joseph Henry 914
Jacoby/Storm Productions Inc. 833
Jalmar Press, Inc. 133
Jamenair Ltd. 238
James Books, Alice 238
Japanophile 438
Japan-U.S. Friendship Commission Prize For the Translation of Japanese Literature, 1992 914
Jason & Nordic Publishers 238

JEMS 709
Jesperson Press Ltd. 225
Jet 327
Jewel Box Theatre 850
Jewel Box Theatre Playwrighting Competition 914
Jewish Action 337
Jewish Repertory Theatre 850
Jewish Telegraphic Agency 881
Jewish Weekly News, The 554
Jist Works, Inc. 133
Jive 576
Jive/Black Confessions 576
JLP Pictures 868
Jobber Topics 684
Johnson Books 133
Jonathan David Publishers 134
Jones Award, Anson 914
Jones Foundation National Poetry Competition, The Chester H. 914
Journal of Career Planning & Employment 712
Journal of Defense & Diplomacy 770
Journal of Graphoanalysis 484
Journal, The 438
Journey 302
Joyful Woman, The 662
JSA Publications 881
Judson Press 134
Juggler's World 383
Juniper Prize, The 914
Juried Copmpetition 914
Juvenile Book Awards 914

K

Kafka Prize, The Janet Heidinger 915
Kalan, Inc. 891
Kaleidoscope 321
Kalmbach Publishing Co. 134
Kaltenborn Foundation 915
Kansas! 506
Kansas City Live! 514
Kansas Quarterly/Kansas Arts Commission Awards, Seaton Awards 915
Kar-Ben Copies Inc. 134
Kashrus Magazine 341

Kau Kau Kitchen Newsletter 502
Keepin' Track of Vettes 281
Kennedy Book Award, Robert F. 915
Kennedy Journalism Awards, Robert F. 915
Kent State University Press 135
Kentucky Arts Councils Fellowships in Writing 915
Kentucky Game & Fish 616
Kentucky Living 507
Kernodle One-Act Playwriting Competition, George R. 915
Kesend Publishing, Ltd., Michael 135
Keyhoe Journalism Award, Donald 915
Keynoter 638
Khan Prize for Fiction, Aga 915
Kid City™ 420
Kimbo Educational-United Sound Arts, Inc. 833
King Features Syndicate, Inc. 882
Kinseeker Publications 135
Kitplanes 383
Kiwanis 271
Klein Playwriting Award for Students, Marc A. 915
Klein Publications, B. 135
Knights Press, Inc. 135
Knopf, Inc., Alfred A. 136
Knowledege 350
Knowledge Book Publishers 136
Knowledge Industry Publications, Inc. 136
Kodansha International U.S. 136
KPBS On Air 327
Krieger Publishing Company 138
Kumarian Press, Inc. 138
Kumu Kahua/UHM Theatre Department Playwriting Contest 915

L

L.A. Parent 308
La Barrique 687
Ladies' Home Journal 663

Ladybug 420
Lady's Circle 663
Lahontan Images 238
Laing Communications Inc. 250
Lake Memorial Award, Ruth 915
Lake Superior Magazine 512
Lakeland Boating 596
Lamont Poetry Selection 915
Lamppost Press Inc. 250
Landmark Editions, Inc. 238
Lang Publishing, Peter 138
Larson Publications/PBPF 138
Laser Focus World Magazine 723
Latest Jokes 408
Lavender Tapes 238
Law and Order 747
Law Practice Management 783
LAWCO Ltd. 238
Lawrence Books, Merloyd 139
Lawrence Foundation Award 916
Lawyer's PC, The 784
Lawyers Weekly, The 784
Lawyer's Word, The 785
Leacock Memorial Award for Humour, Stephen 916
Leader 700
Leader, The 769
Leadership 700
League of Canadian Poets Awards 916
Learning 92 712
Lear's 664
Leather Crafters Journal, The 384
Lefthander Magazine 350
Legal Economics (See Law Practice Management 783)
Leisure Books 139
Leisure Press 139
Leisure Wheels Magazine 650
Leisure World 350
Leisureways 650
Let's Live Magazine 359
Lexikos 139
Liberty Bell Press 238
Liberty Hall Press 140

Can't find a listing? Check the end of each section: Book Publishers, page 253; Consumer Publications, pg. 673; Trade Journals, page 826; Scriptwriting Markets, page 873; Syndicates, page 886; Greeting Card Publishers, page 896; and Contests, page 937.

Liberty Publishing Company, Inc. 140
Libra Publishers, Inc. 140
Libraries Unlimited 140
Library Imagination Paper, The 787
Library Research Associates, Inc. 141
Lieberman Student Poetry Award, Elias 916
Life 352
Life Greetings 891
Light and Life Magazine 554
Lighted Pathway (See High School I.D. 638)
Lighthouse 438
Liguorian 554
Lily Poetry Prize, The Ruth 916
Linch Publishing, Inc. 141
Lincoln Memorial One-Act Playwriting Contest 916
Lincoln Prize at Gettysburg College, The 916
Lincoln Springs Press 238
Linn's Stamp News 384
Lintel 238
Lion Publishing Corporation 141
Lion, The 272
Literary Arts Awards 916
Literary Magazine Review 439
Literary Sketches 439
Literature Fellowships 916
Little, Brown and Co., Inc. 141
Live 554
Live Oak Theatre New Play Awards 916
Live Steam 384
Living With Children 308
Living With Preschoolers 308
Living With Teenagers 555
Llamas Magazine 731
Llewellyn Publications 142
Local 7's Annual National Poetry Competition 916
Location Update 726
Lockert Library of Poetry in Translation 917
Lodestar Books 142
Lodging Hospitality Magazine 760
Loeb Awards, The Gerald 917
Loft Creative Nonfiction Residency Program 917
Loft-McKnight Writers Award 917

Loft-Mentor Series 917
Log Home Living 403
Logan Grants in Support of New Writing on Photography, The Reva and David 917
Lollipops 712
Lone Eagle Publishing Co. 142
Lone Pine Publishing 225
Long Island Parenting News 309
Long Island Power & Sail 597
Long Island Stage 850
Longevity 359
Longman Publishing Group 143
Longstreet Press, Inc. 143
Looking Fit 694
Lookout, The 555
Loompanics Unlimited 143
Loose Change 385
Los Angeles Magazine 490
Los Angeles Reader 491
Los Angeles Times Book Review 439
Los Angeles Times Magazine 491
Los Angeles Times Syndicate 882
Los Hombres Press 143
Lost Creek Letters 439
Lost Treasure 385
Lothrop, Lee & Shepard Books 144
Louisana Literary Award 917
Louisana Literature Prize for Poetry 917
Louisiana Game & Fish 616
Louisiana Life Magazine 507
Louisiana State University Press 144
Love Creek Annual Short Play Festival 917
Love Creek Mini Festivals 917
Lowell Poetry Travelling Scholarship, Amy 917
Loyola University Press 144
Lucas-Evans Books 251
Lucent Books 144
Luramedia 145
Lutheran Forum 556
Lutheran Journal, The 556
Lutheran, The 556
Lyons & Burford, Publishers, Inc. 145

M

M.A. Training 625
McCall's 664
McClelland & Stewart Inc. 226
McCutchan Publishing Corporation 145
McElderry Books, Margaret K. 145
McFarland & Company, Inc., Publishers 145
McGraw-Hill Inc. 146
McGraw-Hill Ryerson Limited 226
Machine Design 724
McLaren Memorial Comedy Playwriting Competition 918
Maclean's 352
Macmillan Of Canada 226
Macmillan Publishing Company 146
Mad Magazine 408
Mademoiselle 664
Madison Books 146
Madison Magazine 533
Madwoman Press 238
Magazine for Christian Youth!, The 639
Magazine Issues 775
Magazine of Fantasy & Science Fiction, The 585
Magic Moments 892
Magic Theatre, Inc. 851
Magical Blend 276
Magid Productions, Lee 869
Magnus Theatre Company 851
Maine Motorist 508
Maine Organic Farmer & Gardener 737
Mainline Modeler & N-Scale 385
Mainstream 321
Malahat Review, The 439
Manage 792
Manhattan Arts Magazine 682
Manhattan Theatre Club 851
Manufacturing Systems 762
Manuscripts 385
Maradia Press 239
Marathon Entertainment Producers 869
Marine Corps Gazette 454
Mark Publishing 146
Marketscope Books 146
Markgraf Publications Group 239
Marlin 616

Marlor Press, Inc. 147
Marsh Media 834
Marshall/Nation Prize for Poetry, The Lenore 918
Marvel Comics 314
Marvin Grant, Walter Rumsey 918
Maryland Magazine 510
Masefield Memorial Award, John 918
Massachusetts Artists Fellowship 918
Massachusetts Review, The 440
Massage Magazine 360
Masters Awards, Edgar Lee 918
Masters Press 147
Mature Living 571
Mature Outlook 572
Mature Traveler, The 650
Mature Years 572
Maupin House Publishing 239
May Trends 694
Mayberry Gazette, The 328
Mayo Alumnus, The 799
Meat Business Magazine 752
Mechanical Engineering 724
Media & Methods 713
Media Forum International, Ltd. 147
Media History Digest 368
Media Inc. 678
Media Profiles 713
Media Publishing/Midgard Press 147
Mediacom Development Corp. 869
Meditation 276
Medwick Memorial Award, Lucille 918
Meeman Awards, The Edward J. 918
Meeramma Publications 147
Meeting Manager, The 695
Meeting News 695
Mega-Books of New York, Inc. 251
Megalo Media 882
Melcher Book Award 918
Memphis 528
Memphis Business Journal 295

Menasha Ridge Press, Inc. 148
Mencken Awards 918
Mennonite Brethren Herald 556
Men's Fitness 360
Men's Health 360
Mentor Award, The 919
Mercury Press, The 227
Meriwether Publishing Ltd. 869
Merlyn Graphics 892
Merrimack Repertory Theatre 851
Merry Men Press 239
Merrywood Studio, The 869
Messenger of the Sacred Heart, The 556
Metamorphous Press 148
Metro 491
Metro Singles Lifestyles 541
Metro Toronto Business Journal 295
Metropolis 267
Mexico West 651
Meyerbooks, Publisher 239
MGI Management Institute, Inc., The 148
MHQ 369
Miami Beach Community Theatre 851
Michigan Arts 360
Michigan Country Lines 512
Michigan Living 651
Michigan Natural Resources Magazine 469
Michigan Out-of-Doors 617
Michigan Quarterly Review 440
Michigan Sportsman 617
Michigan State University Press 148
Microage Quarterly 475
MICROpendium 476
Microtrend Books 148
Microwaves & RF 718
Mid West Outdoors 617
Mid-American Review 440
MidAtlantic Antiques Magazine, The 682
Mid-Atlantic Game & Fish 617
Mid-Continent Bottler 688
Middle Eastern Dancer 727
Midland Authors Award 919

Midnight Zoo 585
Midstream 337
Midway Magazine 411
Midwest Contractor Magazine 706
Midwest Living 403
Midwest Motorist, The 651
Military History 369
Military Images 369
Military Lifestyle Fiction Contest 919
Military Review 454
Milkweed Editions 149
Milkweed Editions National Fiction Prize 919
Mill Mountain Theatre 851
Mill Mountain Theatre New Play Competition 919
Mills & Sanderson, Publishers 149
Milwaukee Magazine 533
Milwaukee Repertory Theater 851
Miniature Quilts 386
Miniatures Dealer Magazine 822
Miniatures Showcase 386
Minnesota Grocer 752
Minnesota Ink (See Writer's Journal 780)
Minnesota Ink Fiction Contest 919
Minnesota Ink Semi-Annual Poetry Contest 919
Minnesota Sportsman 617
Minnesota Voices Project Competition 919
Minority Engineer, The 724
Minority Screenwriters Development and Promotional Program 919
Miraculous Medal, The 557
Mirimar Enterprises 834
Mirror, The 535
Mirrors International Tanka Award 919
Mise En Scene Theatre 852
Mississippi 513
Mississippi Game & Fish 617
Mississippi Rag, The 461
Mississippi Valley Poetry Contest 919
Missouri Farm Magazine 734
Missouri Game & Fish 618
Missouri Magazine 514

Can't find a listing? Check the end of each section: Book Publishers, page 253; Consumer Publications, pg. 673; Trade Journals, page 826; Scriptwriting Markets, page 873; Syndicates, page 886; Greeting Card Publishers, page 896; and Contests, page 937.

Missouri Repertory Theatre 852

Misty Hill Press 239

Mixed Blood Theatre Company 852

Mixed Blood Versus America 919

Modern Bride 665

Modern Drummer 461

Modern Electronics (See Computercraft 474)

Modern Gold Miner and Treasure Hunter 386

Modern International Drama 852

Modern Language Association of America 149

Modern Machine Shop 789

Modern Maturity 572

Modern Office 290

Modern Office Technology 804

Modern Romances 576

Modern Tire Dealer 684

Modern Woodmen, The 272

Mom Guess What Newspaper 541

Momentum 713

Monarex Hollywood Corporation 870

Money 290

Money Maker 290

Money World 291

Monitor Book Co., Inc. 149

Moody Magazine 557

Moody Monthly (See Moody Magazine 557)

Moon Publications, Inc. 149

Mopar Muscle 281

More Business 678

Morehouse Publishing Co. 150

Morrow and Company, Inc., William 150

Morrow Junior Books 150

Morse Poetry Prize 920

Mosaic Press Miniature Books 150

Mother Courage Press 151

Mother Jones Magazine 481

Motivation Media, Inc. 834

Motor Boating & Sailing 597

Motor Trend 282

Motorbooks International Publishers & Wholesalers 151

Motorhome 651

Motorland 652

Mott-Kappa Tau Alpha Research Award in Journalism, Frank Luther 920

Mount Ida Press 251

Mountain Automation Corporation 239

Mountain House Press 239

Mountain Press Publishing Company 151

Mountain States Collector 386

Mountaineers Books, The 152

Movie Marketplace 328

Mpls. St. Paul Magazine 513

MRTW Annual Radio Script Contest 920

Ms. Magazine 665

Muir Publications, John 152

Multicultural Playwrights' Festival 920

Multnomah Press 152

Muscle & Fitness 361

Muscle Mag International 361

Museum & Arts/Washington 268

Museum of Northern Arizona Press 152

Mushing 262

Music City News 461

Music Express 461

Musical America 462

Musical Theatre Works, Inc. 852

Musician 462

Mustang Monthly 282

Mustang Publishing Co. 153

My Daily Visitor 557

Mysterious Press, The 153

Mystic Seaport Museum 239

N

N.Y. Habitat 519

Naiad Press, Inc., The 153

Napoule Residency, La 920

NAR Publications 239

Nation, The 481

National Archives One-Act Playwriting Competition 920

National Awards for Education Reporting 920

National Beauty Education Journal (See Beauty Education 710)

National Bus Trader 824

National Canadian One Act Playwriting Competition 920

National Cattlemen 731

National Children's Theatre Playwriting Contest 920

National Christian Reporter 557

National Defense 725

National Dragster 282

National Endowment for the Arts: Arts Administration Fellows Program/Fellowship 921

National Gardening 403

National Geographic Magazine 352

National Jewish Book Award Autobiography/Memoir 921

National Jewish Book Award Children's Literature 921

National Jewish Book Award—Children's Picture Book 921

National Jewish Book Award—Contemporary Jewish Life 921

National Jewish Book Award—Fiction 921

National Jewish Book Award—Holocaust 921

National Jewish Book Award—Israel 921

National Jewish Award—Jewish History 921

National Jewish Book Award—Jewish Thought 921

National Jewish Book Award—Scholarship 921

National Jewish Book Award—Visual Arts 921

National Lampoon 409

National Looking Glass Award for a Single Poem 921

National Looking Glass Poetry Chapbook Competition 922

National Masters Running News 627

National Music Theater Conference, Eugene O'Neill Theater Center 852

National One-Act Playwriting Competition 922

National Parks 469

National Petroleum News 721

National Play Award 922

National Playwrights' Award 922

National Playwrights Competition on Themes of "The American Dream" 922

National Poetry Competition 922
National Poetry Series 922
National Police Union News 747
National Press, Inc. 153
National Publishing Company 239
National Review 482
National Ten-Minute Play Contest 922
National Textbook Co. 153
National Wildlife 469
Nation's Business 291
Native Peoples Magazine 338
Natural Food & Farming 341
Natural History 469
Naturegraph Publishers, Inc. 154
Nature's Design 239
Nautical & Aviation Publishing Co., The 154
Naval Institute Press 154
NavPress 154
Navy Times 455
Neal Writers' Competition, Larry 922
Necessary Angel Theatre 853
Negative Capability Short Fiction Contest 922
Neighborhood Works, The 272
Nelson Publishers, Thomas 155
Nelson-Hall Publishers 155
Netherlandic Press 227
Network World 766
Neustadt International Prize for Literature 922
Nevada Magazine 515
Nevins Prize, Allan 922
New American Theater, The 853
New Blood Magazine 586
New Body 361
New Boundary Designs, Inc. 892
New Business Opportunities 291
New Christian Plays Competition 922
New Conservatory Children's Theatre Company and School, The 853
New England Farm Bulletin

& Garden Gazette 737
New England Farmer 738
New England Game & Fish 618
New England Publishing Associates, Inc. 251
New England Review 440
New Era, The 639
New Hampshire Individual Artists' Fellowships 923
New Hampshire Life 515
New Hampshire Profiles 515
New Home 404
New Jersey Monthly 516
New Leaf Press, Inc. 155
New Letters Literary Awards 923
New Library Scene, The 787
New Methods 826
New Mexico Magazine 517
New Physician, The 800
New Play Competition 923
New Plays Incorporated 853
New Playwrights' Program, The University of Alabama 853
New Readers Press 155
New Renaissance, The 441
New Tuners Theatre 854
New Victoria Publishers 155
New Writer's Magazine 776
New York Alive 520
New York Antique Almanac, The 387
New York Daily News 520
New York Doctor, The 800
New York Game & Fish 618
New York Magazine 520
New York Nightlife 328
New York Running News 627
New York Shakespeare Festival/Public Theater 854
New York State Historical Association Manuscript Award 923
New York State Theatre Institute 854
New York Theatre Workshop 854
New York Times Syndication Sales Corp. 882
New Yorker, The 352
Newbery Medal, John 923
Newcastle Publishing Co., Inc. 156

NeWest Publishers Ltd. 227
News Flash International, Inc. 882
NewSage Press 239
Newsday 521
Newsday, New York Newsday 652
Newspaper Enterprise Association, Inc. 883
Newsweek 482
NHS Book Prize 923
Nicholl Fellowships in Screenwriting, Don and Gee 923
Nichols, Jackie 854
Nickel 789
Nightshade Press 239
Nilon Excellence in Minority Fiction Award, Charles H. and N. Mildred 923
Nimbus Publishing Limited 227
Nimrod, Arts and Humanities Council of Tulsa Prizes 923
9-1-1 Magazine 747
NMMA Directors Award 923
No Empty Space Theatre 855
No Empty Space Theatre Biannual Contest 923
Noble Press, Incorporated, The 156
Nobleworks 892
Nordicpress 156
North American Fisherman 618
North American Hunter 618
North American Review, The 441
North American Whitetail 618
North Carolina Black Repertory Company, The 855
North Carolina Game & Fish 619
North Georgia Journal 501
North Light Books 156
North Shore 505
Northeast Magazine 495
Northeast Outdoors 652
Norther Aquaculture 795
Northern California Home and Garden 404
Northern Illinois University Press 157

Can't find a listing? Check the end of each section: Book Publishers, page 253; Consumer Publications, pg. 673; Trade Journals, page 826; Scriptwriting Markets, page 873; Syndicates, page 886; Greeting Card Publishers, page 896; and Contests, page 937.

Northern Logger and Timber Processor 788
Northern New England Playwrights Award 924
Northland Publishing Co., Inc. 157
Northstar Entertainment Group 870
Northwest Airlines (See Skies America Publishing 411)
Northwest Living 532
Northwest Travel 524
Northwood Press, Inc. 157
Norton Co., Inc., W.W. 157
Notre Dame Magazine 302
Novascope 531
Now And Then 486
NSGA Retail Focus 818
NTC Publishing Group 157
Numismatist, The 387
Nursing92 758
Nuts to Us! 924
Nutshell News 387

O

Oatmeal Studios 892
Oblates 558
Ocean Realm 470
O'Connor Award for Short Fiction, The Flannery 924
O'Connor Prize for Fiction 924
Octameron Associates 158
Oddo Publishing, Inc. 158
O'Dell Award for Historical Fiction, Scott 924
Odyssey 421
Odyssey Theatre Ensemble 855
Off Duty Magazine 455
Oglebay Institute Towngate Theatre Playwriting 924
OH! Idaho 503
Ohara Publications, Inc. 158
Ohio Arts Council Individual Artists Fellowship 924
Ohio Farmer, The 738
Ohio Fisherman 619
Ohio Game & Fish 619
Ohio Magazine 523
Ohio Review, The 442
Ohio State University Press 158
Ohioana Book Awards 924
Oise Press 227
Oklahoma Game & Fish 619
Oklahoma Today 524
Old Cars News & Marketplace 387
Old Cars Weekly (See Old Cars News & Marketplace 387)
Old Globe Theatre 855
Old Mill News 370
Old Oregon, The Magazine of the University of Oregon 302
Olson & Co., C. 239
Olympian Magazine 628
Omni 581
Omni Communications 834
On The Line 421
On Track 282
On the Scene Magazine 517
Once Upon a Planet, Inc. 158
One Shot 462
1,001 Home Ideas 404
O'Neill Theater Center's National Playwrights Conference/New Drama for Television Project, Eugene 855
Ones at Eight 924
Onion, The 409
Onion World 728
Ontario Motor Coach Review 652
Ontario Out of Doors 535
Oolichan Books 228
Open Court Publishing Co. 159
Open Eye: New Stagings, The 855
Open Hand Publishing, Inc. 239
Open Wheel Magazine 283
Opera Canada 462
Opera News 803
Opportunities for Actors & Models 727
Options 451
Orange Coast Magazine 491
Orca Book Publishing Ltd. 228
Oregon Business 295
Oregon Coast 525
Oregon Coast Getaway Guide 525
Oregon Historical Society Press 159
Oregon Shakespeare Festival Association 856
Oregon State University Press 159
Organic Gardening 406
Original Art Report, The 268
Orlando Magazine 295
ORT Reporter (See The Reporter 562)
Orvis Writing Contest, The C.F. 924
Osborne/McGraw-Hill 159
Other Side, The 558
Ottawa Magazine 535
Ottenheimer Publishers, Inc. 251
Our Family 558
Our Sunday Visitor, Inc. (Book Publishers) 159
Our Sunday Visitor, Inc. (Scriptwriting) 834
Our Sunday Visitor Magazine 559
Our Town 521
Out West 352
Out West Publishing 239
Outdoor America 470
Outdoor Canada Magazine 603
Outdoor Life 619
Outreach Publications 893
Outside 603
Outside Business 695
Outside Plant 718
Overdrive 684
Overlook Press, The 160
Overseas! 455
Owl Magazine 421
Owlflight 586

P

P. I. Magazine 319
Pace Films, Inc. 870
Pacific Bakers News 703
Pacific Books, Publishers 160
Pacific Builder & Engineer 707
Pacific Discovery 470
Pacific Diver 635
Pacific Fishing 742
Pacific News Service 883
Pacific Northwest 532
Pacific Press Publishing Association 160
Paint Horse Journal 263
Palardo Productions 834
Palm Beach Life 498
Palm Springs Life 492
Pandora 587
Pan-Erotic Review 240
Panfisherman's 620
Panhandler Poetry Chapbook Competition, The 924
Pantex International Ltd. 240
Pantheon Books 160
Paper Collectors Marketplace 388
Paper Mill Playhouse 856
Papier-Mache Press 240

Parade 353
Paradise Publications 240
Paragon House Publishers 160
Parallel Pictures 870
Parameters: U.S. Army War College Quarterly 456
Paramount Cards Inc. 893
Paraplegia News 322
Parenting Magazine 309
Parents Care, Parents Count Newsletter 309
Parents Magazine 310
Parents' Press 310
Paris Review, The 442
Parish Family Digest 559
Parker Motion Pictures, Tom 870
Parkman Prize, Francis 924
Partners in Publishing 240
Passage Theatre Company, The 856
Passages North 442
Passport Press 162
Pastoral Life 700
Patterson Journalism Fellowship, Alicia 924
Paulist Press 162
PBC International, Inc. 162
PC Computing 476
PC Advisor 835
PC Press 240
PCM 476
PCPA Theaterfest 856
Peachtree Publishers, Ltd. 162
Peden Prize in Fiction, William 925
Pediatrics for Parents 310
Peel Productions 240
Peguis Publishers Limited 228
Pelican Publishing Company 163
Pen and Quill, The 388
PEN Center USA West Awards 925
PEN Medal for Translation 925
PEN Publisher Citation 925
PEN Syndicated Fiction Project 883
PEN Writing Awards for Prisoners 925
PEN/Book-of-the-Month

Club Translation Prize 925
Pendragon Press 163
Penguin USA 163
Peninsula Magazine 492
PEN/Jerard Fund 925
PEN/Martha Albrand Award for Nonfiction 925
Pennsylvania 525
Pennsylvania Angler 620
Pennsylvania Farmer 738
Pennsylvania Game & Fish 620
Pennsylvania Game News 620
Pennsylvania Heritage 526
Pennsylvania Historical and Museum Commission 163
Pennsylvania Lawyer, The 785
Pennsylvania Sportsman 620
Pennywhistle Press 422
PEN/Revson Foundation Fellowships 925
PEN/Spielvogel-Diamonstein Award 925
Pentecostal Evangel 559
Pentecostal Messenger, The 560
People Magazine 329
PeopleNet 322
People's Light & Theatre Company 858
Perfect Lawyer, The 785
Perfection Form, The 240
Periodical 456
Perivale Press & Agency 240
Perkins Playwriting Contest 926
Permanent Press/Second Chance Press, The 164
Persimmon Hill 370
Personal Fitness and Weight Loss 361
Personnel Advisory Bulletin 793
Personnel Journal 793
Perspectives Press 164
Pest Control Magazine 790
Pet Age 805
Pet Business 806
Pet Dealer, The 806
Peter Pauper Press, Inc. 164
Petersen's 4-Wheel 283
Petersen's Handguns 608
Petersen's Hunting 620

Peterson's 164
Pets Magazine 263
Pfeiffer & Company 165
Pharmacy Times 710
Pharos Books 165
Phi Beta Kappa Book Awards 926
Philadelphia Festival Theatre for New Plays 858
Philadelphia Magazine 526
Phoenix 488
Phoenix, The 362
Photo Communication Services, Inc. 835
Photo Marketing 807
Photo Review, The 807
Photo Traveler 478
Photoletter 807
Physician and Sportsmedicine, The 800
Physician's Management 800
Picadilly Books 165
Pickering Award for Playwrighting Excellence, Robert J. 926
Picture Perfect 303
Pier One Theatre 858
Pig Iron Magazine 442
Pilgrim Press, The 165
Pilot Books 165
PIME World 560
Pineapple Press, Inc. 166
Pinehurst Journal, The 442
Pioneer Drama Service 858
Pipeline & Underground Utilities Construction 721
Pippin Press 166
Pittsburgh Magazine 526
Pittsburgh Press Sunday Magazine, The 526
Pizza Today 760
Plain Dealer Magazine 523
Planning 748
Plant 762
Play Machine, The 329
Play Meter Magazine 703
Playbill 329
Playboy 451
Player, The (See Casino Player 602)
Players Press, Inc. (Book Publishers) 166
Players Press, Inc. (Scriptwriting) 858
Plays 858

Can't find a listing? Check the end of each section: Book Publishers, page 253; Consumer Publications, pg. 673; Trade Journals, page 826; Scriptwriting Markets, page 873; Syndicates, page 886; Greeting Card Publishers, page 896; and Contests, page 937.

Playthings 822
Playwrights Canada Press 229
Playwrights' Center Jerome Playwright-In-Residence Fellowship 926
Playwrights' Center McKnight Fellowship 926
Playwrights' Center Midwest Playlabs, The 926
Playwrights' Center, The 859
Playwrights' Forum Awards 926
Playwright's-in-Residence Grants 926
Playwrights Preview Productions 859
Playwrights Project 926
Playwrights Theatre of New Jersey 859
Pleasure Boating Magazine 597
Plenum Publishing 166
Ploughshares 443
Plum Graphics Inc. 893
Pocket Books 167
Pockets 422
Podiatry Management 801
Poe Award, Edgar Allan 926
Poet Hunt 926
Poetry 443
Poetry Arts Project Contest 926
Poetry Center Book Award, The 927
Poetry Contest 927
Poetry Magazine Poetry Awards 927
Poets and Patrons, Inc. International Narrative Poetry Contest 927
Poets Club of Chicago International Shakespearean Sonnet Contest 927
Poggioli Translation Award, Renato 927
Polestar Press Ltd. 229
Police and Security News 748
Polish American Journal 338
Polka-Dot Press (See Picadilly Books 165)
Pollak, Felix/Chris O'Malley Prizes in Poetry and Fiction 927
Polled Hereford World 732
Pool & Spa News 818
Popular Electronics 388
Popular Electronics Hobbyist's Handbook 388
Popular Mechanics 388
Popular Medicine Press 240

Popular Photography 479
Popular Science 582
Porcépic Books 229
Portable 100 476
Portal Publications 893
Porter Sargent Publishers, Inc. 167
Poseidon Press 167
Postcard Collector 389
Potentials Development for Health & Aging Services 167
Power Boating Canada 597
Practical Homeowner 406
Pragmatist, The 482
Prairie Journal, The 443
Prairie Messenger 560
Prairie Schooner Bernice Slote Award 927
Prairie Schooner Strousse Strousse Award 927
Prakken Publications, Inc. 167
Prarie Oak Press 240
Preacher's Magazine, The 701
Preaching 701
Premier Video Film & Recording Corp. 835
Premiere 329
Prentice-Hall Canada, Inc., College Division 229
Prentice Hall Canada, Inc., School Division 229
Prentice-Hall Canada, Inc., Trade Division 230
Prentice Hall Press 168
Presbyterian Record 560
Presbyterian Survey 561
Preservation News 370
Preservation Press, The 168
Presidio Press 168
Press At California State University, Fresno, The 169
Press Gang Publishers 230
Prevention Health Books 169
Price Stern Sloan, Inc., Publishers 169
Prima Publishing and Communications 169
Primary Stages Company, Inc. 859
Prime 572
Prime Times 573
Princeton Architectural Press 169
Princeton Book Company, Publishers 170
Print & Graphics 809
Prism International 443

Prism International Fiction Contest 927
Private Pilot 287
Prix Alvine-Belisle 927
Pro Sound News 718
Probus Publishing Co. 170
Proceedings 795
Produce News 753
Production Resource, The 727
Production Supervisor's Bulletin 793
Professional Agent Magazine 769
Professional Boatbuilder Magazine 818
Professional Development Grants 927
Professional Photographer 807
Professional Pilot 287
Professional Publications, Inc. 170
Professional Quilter, The 389
Professional Selling 815
Professional Stained Glass 690
Profit, The Magazine for Canadian Entrepreneurs 316
Programmer's Update (See Developers' Insight 764)
Progressive Architecture 682
Progressive Farmer 734
Progressive, The 482
Proofs 708
Pruett Publishing 170
PSI Research 171
PTN 808
Public Power 721
Publish 477
Publishers Associates 171
Publishers Syndication International 240
Puckerbrush Press 240
Pulitzer Prizes 927
Pulp & Paper Canada 805
Pulp Press International 3-Day Novel Writing Contest 928
Pumper, The 812
Purdue Alumnus, The 303
Pure-Bred Dogs American Kennel Gazette Fiction Contest 928
Pure-bred Dogs American Kennel Gazette 263
Purple Cow 640
Purpose 561
Putnam Berkley Group, The 171

Pyle Award, Ernie 928

Q
QED Press 171
QRL Poetry Series 928
QST 390
Quality Assurance Bulleting 762
Quality Digest 762
Quality Living 319
Quality Control Supervisor's Bulletin (See Quality Assurance Bulletin 762)
Quantum—Science Fiction and Fantasy Review 587
Quarry 444
Quarter Horse Journal, The 264
Quarter Racing Journal, The 609
Quartz Theatre, The 859
Que Corporation 172
Queen Of All Hearts 561
Quick & Easy Crafts 390
Quick Frozen Foods International 753
Quick Printing 809
Quicksilver Productions, Inc. 870
QuikRef Publishing 240
Quill 172
Quilt World 390
Quilter's Newsletter Magazine 390
Quilting International 391
Quilting Today Magazine 391

R
R & R Entertainment Digest (See R & R Shoppers News 456)
R & R Shoppers News 456
Racquet 633
R-A-D-A-R 422
Radiance 665
Radio Repertory Company, Inc. 860
Radio World International 718
Radio World Newspaper 718
Radio-Electronics 391
Railroad Model Craftsman 391
Rainbow Books 172
Rainbow City Express 277

Ranch & Coast 492
Randall Publisher, Peter 253
R&E Publishers 172
Random House, Inc. 173
Random House, Inc. Juvenile Books 173
Rangefinder, The 808
Ranger Rick 422
Rase Productions, Inc., Bill 835
RDH 708
Reader Riter Poll 928
Reader's Digest 354
Reader's Digest (Canada) 353
Readers Review 354
Real Estate Computing 811
Real People 354
Reason Magazine 482
Records Management Quarterly 696
Recreation News 273
Recycling Today 812
Red Alder Books 240
Red Deer College Press 230
Red Farm Studio 893
Redbook Magazine 665
Reece International Poetry Awards, The Byron Herbert 928
Referee 604
Reference Publications, Inc. 240
Reference Service Press 173
Reflected Images Publishers 253
Reform Judaism 562
Regal Books 173
Regardies: The Magazine of Washington Business 295
Regnery/Gateway, Inc. 174
Reidmore Books, Inc. 230
Religious Education Press 174
Remodeling 691
Remodeling News 691
Renaissance House Publishers 174
Renovated Lighthouse 444
Report on the Americas 483
Reporter, The 562
Reptile & Amphibian Magazine 264
Rescue 801
Research Magazine 741

Reseller Management 767
Resolution Business Press 240
Resource Publications, Inc. 174
Resource Recycling 813
Restaurant Hospitality 760
Retail Reporting Corp. 252
Retailer and Marketing News 757
Retailing 719
Retired Officer Magazine, The 457
Reuben Award 928
Review 273
Review and Herald Publishing Association 175
Review for Religious 562
Rhode Island Monthly 527
Rhode Island State Council on the Arts Fellowship 928
Rhombus Publishing Co. 240
Rhyme Time Creative Creative Writing Competition 928
Rhythms Productions 835
Ribalow Prize, The Harold U 928
Richboro Press 175
Richmond Surroundings 531
Righting Words 776
Rinehart Fund, Mary Roberts 928
Ripon College Magazine 303
Rising Star 776
River Arts Repertory 860
River City Writing Awards in Fiction 928
Rivercross Publishing, Inc. 253
Road Company, The 860
Road King Magazine 283
Roanoker, The 532
Robb Report, The 354
Roberts Writing Awards 928
Rochester Business Magazine 296
Rock & Roll Disc 463
Rock Products 821
Rockford Magazine 505
Rockshots, Inc. 893
Rocky Mountain Game & Fish 621
Ronin Publishing 175
Roofer Magazine 707

Can't find a listing? Check the end of each section: Book Publishers, page 253; Consumer Publications, pg. 673; Trade Journals, page 826; Scriptwriting Markets, page 873; Syndicates, page 886; Greeting Card Publishers, page 896; and Contests, page 937.

Rooster & the Raven, The 354
Rosen Publishing Group, The 175
Rosenthal New Play Prize, The Lois and Richard 929
Ross Books 176
Routledge, Chapman & Hall, Inc. 176
Roxbury Publishing Co. 176
Royal Features 883
Ruggles Journalism Scholarship, William B. 929
Runner's World 628
Running Times 628
Rural Heritage 579
Ruralite 487
Russell Sage Foundation 176
Rutgers Magazine 303
Rutledge Hill Press 176
RV Business 825
RV Times Magazine 653
RV West Magazine 653
Rydal Press, The 242

S

Sacramento Magazine 493
Safari 872
Safari Magazine 621
Safety Compliance Letter 791
Sail 597
Sailaway 653
Sailing Magazine 598
Sailing World 598
St. Anthony Messenger 562
St. Anthony Messenger Press 176
St. Bede's Publications 177
St. John's Publishing, Inc. 242
St. Joseph's Messenger & Advocate of the Blind 563
Saint Louis Journalism Review 776
St. Louis Literary Award 929
St. Louis Magazine 515
St. Luke's Press 177
St. Martin's Press 177
St. Paul Books and Media 178
St. Vladimir's Seminary Press 178
Sales Manager's Bulletin 794
Salt Lake City 529
Salt Water Sportsman 621
Sample Case, The 273
San Diego Publishing Company 253
San Francisco Bay Guardian 493
San Francisco Business Times 296

San Francisco Focus 493
San Gabriel Valley Magazine, The 493
Sand River Press 242
Sandburg Literary Arts Awards, The Carl 929
Sandhill Crane Press, Inc. 178
Sandlapper 527
Sandpaper, The 516
Sandpiper Press 242
Sangamon, Inc. 894
Sanitary Maintenance 791
Santana 598
SAS Institute Inc. 178
Sasquatch Books 179
Satellite Orbit 329
Satellite Retailer 719
Saturday Evening Post, The 354
Savage "Miles From Nowhere" Memorial Award, The Barbara 929
Scandecor Inc. 894
Scarborough House/Publisher 179
Scarecrow Press, Inc. 179
Scavenger's Newsletter 776
Schiffer Publishing Ltd. 179
Schirmer Books 180
Scholastic, Inc. 180
Scholastic Professional Books 180
Scholastic Writing Awards 929
School Arts Magazine 713
School Shop/Tech Directions 714
Schulz Award, The Charles M. 929
Schurman Co., Inc., Marcel 894
Science Award, The 929
Science Fiction Chronicle 777
Science in Society Journalism Awards 929
Science-Writing Award in Physics and Astronomy 929
Scientific American 582
Score 606
Scorecard 304
Scott Cards Inc. 894
Scott Stamp Monthly 392
Scottsdale Progress, The 489
Scouting 273
Scouting 423
SCP Journal and SCP Newsletter 563
Scrambl-Gram Inc. 883
Scream Factory, The 587

Screen Printing 810
Screw 452
Scribner's Sons, Charles 180
Scripps Award, Charles E. 929
Scripps Award, The Edward Willis 929
Sea 598
Sea Frontiers 471
Sea Kayaker 599
Seafood Leader 753
Sea's Industry West 796
Seattle Weekly, The 532
Seattle's Child 311
Second Nature Ltd. 894
Secondary Marketing Executive 741
Security Dealer 696
Security Management: Protecting Property, People & Assets 794
Seek 563
Selected Reading 355
Self 666
Self-Employed America 696
Semaphore Press 181
Senior 573
Senior Award 930
Senior Edition USA/Colorado 573
Senior High I.D. 640
Senior Patient 801
Senior Spotlite Newspapers, Inc. 574
Senior Voice of Florida 499
Senior Wire 883
Senior World News Magazine 574
Senior World of California (See Senior World News Magazine 574)
Servant Publications 181
Servicing Dealer, The 697
Sesame Street Magazine 311
Seven Locks Press, Inc. 181
Seventeen 640
Seventeen Magazine Fiction Contest 930
Sew News 392
SF 268
Shape Magazine 362
Shapolsky Publishers 181
Sharing the Victory 564
Shaw Festival 860
Shaw Publishers, Harold 181
Shazzam Production Company, The 860
Sheep! Magazine 732
Sheep Meadow Press, The 182

Shelby Publishing Co. 182
Shelley Memorial Award 930
Shepard's Elder Care/Law Newsletter 785
Shipmate 304
Shiras Institute/Mildred & Albert Panowski Playwriting Award 930
Shoe Retailing Today 786
Shoe Service 786
Shoe String Press, The 182
Shoe Tree Press 182
Shoptalk 719
Short Story Contest 930
Shuttle Spindle & Dyepot 392
Siena College Playwrights' Competition 930
Sierra 471
Sierra Club Books 182
Sierra Repertory Theatre 930
Sign Business 697
Signcraft 678
Signpost Magazine 628
Signs of the Times 564
Silex Publishing 253
Silhouette Books 183
Silver Bridle National Playwrights Competition 930
Silver Burdett Press 183
Silver Playwriting Competition, Dorothy 930
Silver Press 183
Silver Visions 894
Silvercat Publications 242
Simon & Pierre Publishing Co. Ltd. 230
Simon Award, Charlie May 930
Simon & Schuster 183
Sing Heavenly Muse! 444
Singer Media Corporation 884
Single Parent, The 311
Singlelife Magazine 542
Sinsemilla Tips 729
Sisters Today 564
Site Sound 269
Skating 631
Ski Magazine 632
Skidmore-Roth Publishing 184
Skies America Publishing 411
Skiing 632
Skirball-Kenis Theatre, Audrey 860

Sky 411
Skydiving 630
Skylander Magazine 666
Slawson Communications, Inc. 184
Small Press 777
Small Press Publisher of the Year 930
Small Press Review 778
Smith, Publisher, Gibbs 184
Smithsonian Magazine 355
Smooth Stone Press 242
Snack Food 704
Snips Magazine 809
Snow Goer 632
Snow Prize, The John Ben 930
Snowboarder, The Magazine 632
Snowmobile Magazine 632
Snowy Egret 471
Soap Opera Digest 329
Sober Times, The Recovery Magazine 362
Soccer America 633
Social Justice Review 565
Society of Midland Authors Award 931
Software Maintenance News 767
Soho Press, Inc. 184
Soldier of Fortune 457
Sonnichsen Book Award, C.L. 931
Sons of Norway Viking, The 274
Sound View Press 242
Soundtrack 463
South Carolina Game & Fish 621
South Carolina New Play Festival 931
South Carolina Wildlife 621
South Coast Repertory 860
South Florida 499
South Florida Poetry Review, The 444
South Texas Catholic 565
Southam Syndicate, The 884
Southeast Playwrights Project 861
Southender Magazine 535
Southern Accents 406
Southern Appalachian Rep-

ertory Theatre (SART) 861
Southern Beverage Journal 688
Southern Boating Magazine 599
Southern Exposure 522
Southern Homes, Atlanta's Magazine for Better Living 406
Southern Living 355
Southern Lumberman 788
Southern Motor Cargo 684
Southern Outdoors Magazine 622
Southern Playwrights Competition 931
Southern Playwriting Competition 931
Southern Review, The 445
Southern Review, The/Louisiana State University Short Fiction Contest 931
Southfarm Press 185
Southwest Art 269
Southwest Contractor 707
Southwest Profile 517
Southwest Real Estate News 811
Southwest Review 445
Southwest Review Awards 931
Sovereign Award, Outstanding Newspaper Story, Outstanding Feature Story 931
Sow's Ear Poetry Prize, The 931
Soybean Digest 729
Spann Memorial Prize, Bryant 932
Sparrow Press 185
Special Libraries Association Public Relations Award 932
Specialty Store Service 702
Spectrum 445
Speech Bin, Inc., The 185
Spencer Productions, Inc. 836
Spheric House 242
SPI Entertainment 872
Spin-Off 392
Spinsters Book Company 185
Spirit 565
Spiritual Life 565

Can't find a listing? Check the end of each section: Book Publishers, page 253; Consumer Publications, pg. 673; Trade Journals, page 826; Scriptwriting Markets, page 873; Syndicates, page 886; Greeting Card Publishers, page 896; and Contests, page 937.

Spirituality Today 566
Sport 604
Sport Fishing 622
Sport Style 819
Sporting Goods Dealer, The 819
Sporting News, The 604
Sports Afield 622
Sports Collectors Digest 393
Sports Features Syndicate/ World Features Syndicate 884
Sports Illustrated 604
Sports Illustrated for Kids 423
Sports 'n Spokes 323
Sports Parade 604
Springfield! Magazine 514
Sproutletter 407
Spur 610
Spur Awards (Western Writers of America, Inc.) 932
Spy 319
SSSS Student Research Grant 932
St. Louis Magazine 515
ST Publications, Inc. 186
Stackpole Books 186
Stage One 861
Stage West 861
Stamp Collector 393
Stamp Wholesaler, The 823
Standard 566
Standard Publishing 186
Standing Stone, The 588
Stanford Poetry Prize, Ann 932
Stanford University Press 186
Stanley Drama Award 932
Star Books Inc. 187
Star Service 825
Star, The 355
Starburst Publishers 187
Starlog Magazine 588
Starrett Poetry Prize, The Agnes Lynch 932
Starrhill Press 187
Starwind (See Hobson's Choice 585)
State, The 522
Stegner Fellowship 932
Stemmer House Publishers, Inc. 187
Steppenwolf Theatre Company 861
Stereo Review 463
Sterling Publishing 188
Stilwill, Charles 861
Stipes Publishing Co. 188

Stock Car Racing Magazine 284
Stoeger Publishing Company 188
Stone Award for Student Journalism, I.F. 932
Stone Awards, The Walker 932
Stone Bridge Press 242
Stone Review 821
Stone Soup 423
Stone Wall Press, Inc. 242
Stone World 822
Stormline Press 188
Story 446
Story Friends 424
Story Time Short Story Contest 932
Storytelling Magazine 446
Straight 641
Strategic Health Care Marketing 802
Street Players Theatre 862
Stripper Magazine 728
Student Grant-In-Aid 932
Student Lawyer 785
Student, The 304
Success Publishing 189
Successful Farming 734
Summit 472
Sun 356
Sun and Sonlight Christian Newspaper (See Home Times 553)
Sun, The 356
Sunday Advocate Magazine 508
Sunday Digest 566
Sunday Journal Magazine 487
Sunday School Counselor 566
Sunflower University Press 189
Sunset 487
Sunshine Artists USA 394
Sunshine Magazine 356
Sunshine: The Magazine of South Florida 499
Sunstone Press 189
Suntech Journal (See Sunworld 767)
Sunworld 767
Super Cycle 284
Superintendent's Profile & Pocket Equipment Directory 748
Supervision 794
Supervisor's Bulletin 794
Surgical Rounds 802
Swank 452
Swim Magazine 635

Swimming Pool/Spa Age 819
Sword & Quill 242
Sybex, Inc. 189
Syracuse University Press 190
Systems 3X/400 767

T

TAB Books 190
Talbot Prize Fund for African Anthropology, Amaury 933
Talco Productions 836
Tambra Publishing 242
Tampa Bay Life 500
Tampa Review 446
Tantalus Poetry Society Competition 933
Tapley, Publisher, Inc., Lance (See Yankee Books 214)
Tavern Sports International 630
Taylor Playwriting Award, Marvin 933
Taylor Publishing Company 190
TDC 330
TDR 330
Tea & Coffee Trade Journal 688
Teachers College Press 190
Teachers Interaction 567
Teaching Today 714
Technical Analysis of Stocks & Commodities 242
Technical Analysis of Stocks & Commodities 291
Technical Communications Associates, Inc. 191
Technology & Learning 714
Technology Review 582
TechTalk 720
Teddy Bear Review 394
Teen Beat 641
Teen Dream 641
'Teen Magazine 641
Teenage Corner, Inc. 884
Teens Today 641
Tel-Air Interests, Inc. 836
Television Production Services Corp. 872
Temple University Press 191
Ten Best "Censored" Stories of 1991, The 933
Ten Speed Press 191
Tennessee Magazine, The 528
Tennessee Sportsman 623
Tennessee Williams, The/ New Orleans Literary Fes-

tival One-Act Play Award 933

Tennis 633

Tennis Buyer's Guide 819

Tenth Avenue Editions 252

Tessera Publishing, Inc. 242

Texas A&M University Press 191

Texas Christian University Press 191

Texas Gardener 407

Texas Highways Magazine 653

Texas Sportsman 623

Texas Teen 642

Texas Western Press 192

Theater Artists of Marin 862

Theater Ludicrum, Inc. 862

Theater of Necessity, The 862

Theatre Arts Books 192

Theatre Calgary 862

Theatre De La Jeune Lune 862

Theatre Library Association Award, The 933

Theatre Memphis New Play Competition 933

Theatre on the Move 863

Theatre Project Company 863

Theatreworks 863

Theatreworks/USA 863

Thema 446

Theme Song 872

Theosophical Publishing House, The 192

These Three, Inc. 895

This People Magazine 567

Thistledown Press 231

Thomas Publications 192

Thorsons 231

Three and Four Wheel Action 285

Three Continents Press 193

Threepenny Review, The 447

3-2-1 Contact 424

Thunder's Mouth Press 193

Ticknor & Fields 193

Tidewater Publishers 193

Timber Press, Inc. 194

Time 356

Time-Life Books Inc. 194

Timeline 371

Times Books 194

Toastmaster, The 274

Tobacco Reporter 697

Today's Catholic Teacher 716

Today's Christian Woman 667

Toledo Magazine 523

TOR Books 194

Toronto Life 536

Torso 542

Total Health 362

Touch 424

Tours & Resorts 654

Tow-Age 685

Towers Club, USA Newsletter 316

Towson State University Prize for Literature 933

TQ (Teen Quest) 642

Traces of Indiana and Midwestern History 371

Trader, The 741

TradeWind 412

Tradition 464

Traditional Quilter 394

Traditional Quiltworks 394

Trafalgar Square Publishing 242

Trailer Boats Magazine 600

Trailer Life 654

Train Humor Prize, The John 933

Training 795

Transaction Books 194

Transaction/Society 749

Transformation Times 277

Transitions Abroad 654

Translation Center Awards, The 933

Transportation Trails 195

Transtar Productions, Inc. 836

Travel à la carte 655

Travel & Leisure 655

Travel Keys 195

Travel News 655

Travel Papers 656

Travel Smart 656

Traveler, The 656

Travel-Holiday 656

Travelore Report 656

Treasure 395

Treasure Chest 395

Trend Book Division 195

Tri Video Teleproduction 836

Triathlete 630

Trinity Square Ensemble 863

Trip & Tour 656

Triquarterly 447

Trisar, Inc. 895

Troll Associates 836

Tropic Magazine 500

Tropical Fish Hobbyist 264

Troudabor Press 195

Trucking Digest 685

True Confessions 576

True Love 577

True Romance 577

True West 371

Trumpeter, The 395

T-Shirt Retailer and Screen Printer 702

TSR, Inc. 195

Tucson Lifestyle 489

Tuff Stuff 396

Turf Magazine 744

Turkey Call 623

Turn-On Letters 452

Turtle Magazine for Preschool Kids 425

Tuttle Publishing Company, Inc., Charles E. 231

Twayne Publishers 196

TwentyOne® Magazine 408

Twin Peaks Press 196

Twins 312

2 AM Magazine 589

U

UAHC Press 196

UCLA-American Indian Studies Center 242

Ucross Foundation Residency 933

UFO Magazine 277

Ukrainian Weekly, The 338

ULI, The Urban Land Institute 196

Ultra 529

Ultralight Publications, Inc. 196

Umbrella Books 197

Undercurrent 635

Undergraduate Annual Paper Competition in Cryptology 933

Undermain Theatre 864

Unicorn Theatre 864

Unifilms, Inc. 872

Union Square Press 197

United Caprine News 735

United Church Observer, The 567

Can't find a listing? Check the end of each section: Book Publishers, page 253; Consumer Publications, pg. 673; Trade Journals, page 826; Scriptwriting Markets, page 873; Syndicates, page 886; Greeting Card Publishers, page 896; and Contests, page 937.

United Media/United Feature Syndicate 884
United Methodist Reporter 568
United Resource Press 197
U.S. West Fest 934
Unity Magazine 568
Univelt, Inc. 197
Universal Press Syndicate 886
University Associates, Inc. (See Pfeiffer & Company 165)
University of Alabama New Playwrights Program 934
University of Alabama Press 197
University of Alaska Press 198
University of Alberta Press, The 232
University of Arizona Press 198
University of Arkansas Press, The 198
University of Calgary Press, The 232
University of California Press 198
University of Hawaii Press/ Hawaii Review 864
University of Illinois Press 199
University of Iowa Press 199
University of Massachusetts Press 199
University of Michigan Press 199
University of Minnesota, Duluth Theatre 864
University of Nebraska Press 200
University of Nevada Press 200
University of New Mexico Press 200
University of North Carolina Press, The 200
University of Oklahoma Press 201
University of Ottawa Press, The 232
University of Pennsylvania Press 201
University of Pittsburgh Press 201
University of Tennessee Press, The 201
University of Texas Press 202
University of Toronto Quarterly 447

University of Windsor Review 447
University of Wisconsin Press 202
University of Wisconsin-Stout Teleproduction Center 836
University Press of America, Inc. 202
University Press of Colorado 202
University Press of Kansas 202
University Press of Kentucky 203
University Press of Mississippi 203
University Press of New England 203
UNIX World 768
Unlimited Publishing Co. 203
USA Gymnastics 630
USAir Magazine 412
Utah Holiday Magazine 530
Utah State University Press 204
Utility and Telephone Fleets 721
Utility Construction and Maintenance 791
Utne Reader 319

V

Vacation Industry Review 760
Vagabond Creations, Inc. 895
Valley Magazine 494
Vantage 574
Vantage Press 253
Vanwell Publishing Limited 232
Varoujian Award, Daniel 934
Vegetarian Journal 363
Vegetarian Times 363
Vehicle Leasing Today 685
Vehicule Press 233
VeloNews 593
Vending Times 703
Ventura County & Coast Reporter 494
Venture 425
Venture and Visions 568
Vermont Business Magazine 296
Vermont Life Magazine 530
Vermont Magazine 531
Verve Poetry Contest 934
Vesta Publications, Ltd. 233
Vestal Press, Ltd., The 204

Veterinary Economics Magazine 826
Vette Magazine 285
VFW Auxiliary Magazine 274
VFW Magazine 275
VGM Career Horizons 204
Vibrant Life 363
Victimology 749
Victor Books 204
Victoria 667
Victoria's Business Report 296
Victory Press 242
Video Business 698
Video Magazine 330
Videomaker™ 396
Videomania 330
Vietnam 458
Viking Penguin 205
Villard Books 205
Vim & Vigor 364
Vineyard & Winery Management 688
Vintage Images 895
Virginia Cavalcade 371
Virginia Game & Fish 623
Virginia Stage Company 864
Virtue 568
Visions 304
Visions 589
Vista 339
Vista 569
Vista/USA 657
Visual Horizons 837
Vital Christianity 569
VM +SD 679
Voice Processing Magazine 720
Vortex Communications 243
Voyager/Sun Scene 657

W

Wadsworth Publishing Company 205
Wagner Award, Celia B. 934
Wake Forest University Press 205
Walch, Publisher, J. Weston 205
Walker and Co. 206
Walking Magazine, The 364
Wall & Emerson, Inc. 233
Wallant Book Award, Edward Lewis 934
Walls & Ceilings 691
Walnut Street Theatre 864
Wang in the News 477
Ward Prize for Playwriting, Theodore 934
Ward's Auto World 685

Warehousing Supervisor's Bulletin 795
Warner Books 206
Warner Press, Inc. 895
Wasatch Publishers 243
Washington Blade, The 542
Washington Flyer Magazine 412
Washington Monthly 483
Washington Post, The 496
Washington Post Magazine, The 496
Washington Post Writers Group 886
Washington Prize for Fiction 934
Washington Prize, The 934
Washington State University Pess 206
Washingtonian Magazine, The 496
Washington-Oregon Game & Fish 623
Waterfront Books 243
Waterfront News 500
Waterway Guide 600
Watts, Inc., Franklin 207
Wayfarer Books 243
Wayfinder Press 207
WDS Forum (See Writer's Forum 779)
We Are The Weird 409
Webb Research Group 207
Webster Review 447
Wee Care for Kids 312
Wee Wisdom 426
Weekly News, The 543
Weighing & Measurement 763
Weight Watchers Magazine 364
Weigl Educational Publishers Ltd. 234
Weiser, Inc., Samuel 207
Weiss Associates, Inc., Daniel 252
Weissberger Playwriting Award, L. Arnold 934
Wellspring's Short Fiction Contest 934
Wesleyan Advocate, The 569
West Coast Ensemble 865
West Coast Ensemble Full-Play Competition 934

West Coast Review of Books 778
West Coast Woman 667
West Graphics 895
West Virginia Game & Fish 623
Westart 269
Westbeth Theatre Center, Inc. 865
Westcoast Fisherman 742
Westender Magazine 536
Western & Eastern Treasures 397
Western Greeting, Inc. 895
Western Horse, The 265
Western Horseman, The 265
Western Outdoors 623
Western People 536
Western Photo Traveler (See Photo Traveler 478)
Western Producer Prairie Books 234
Western Producer, The 537
Western Publishing 208
Western RV News 658
Western Sportsman 624
Western Stage, The 865
Western States Book Awards 934
Western Tanager Press 243
Westernlore Press 208
Westport Publishers, Inc. 208
What Makes People Successful 356
Wheetley Company, Inc., The 252
Where Victoria/Essential Victoria 537
Whitaker House 208
White Cliffs Media Company 208
Whitegate Features Syndicate 886
Whitford Press 208
Whiting Writers' Awards 935
Whitman and Co., Albert 209
Whitney-Carnegie Award 935
Whitston Publishing Co., The 209
Whole Chile Pepper, The (See Chile Pepper 339)
Wichita State University Playwriting Contest 935
Wieser & Wieser, Inc. 252
Wild West 372

Wilderness Adventure Books 209
Wilderness Press 210
Wildlife Art News 269
Wildlife Conservation 472
Wildlife Photography 479
Wiley & Sons, John 210
Wiley Prize, Bell I. 935
Williams Award, William Carlos 935
Williamson Publishing Co. 210
Willow Creek Press 210
Willowisp Press, Inc. 210
Wilshire Book Co. 211
Wilson Fine Arts, Inc., Carol 896
Wilson Library Bulletin 788
Windsor Books 211
Windsor This Month Magazine 537
Wine Appreciation Guild, Ltd. 211
Wine Enthusiast 342
Wine Spectator, The 342
Wine Tidings 342
Wines & Vines 689
Wingbow Press 211
Wingra Woods Press 252
Winning! 602
Winship Book Award, L.L. 935
Winston-Derek Publishers, Inc. 212
Wisconsin 534
Wisconsin Arts Board Individual Artist Program 935
Wisconsin Grocer, The 754
Wisconsin Sportsman 624
Wisconsin Trails 534
With Magazine 642
Witter Bynner Foundation for Poetry, Inc. Grants 935
Wizards Bookshelf 212
Woman Beautiful 667
Woman Bowler 602
Woman Engineer 725
Woman's Day 667
Woman's Touch 569
Woman's World 668
Women & Guns 608
Women Artists News 270
Women in Business 698
Women in Theatre New Play Grant 935

Can't find a listing? Check the end of each section: Book Publishers, page 253; Consumer Publications, pg. 673; Trade Journals, page 826; Scriptwriting Markets, page 873; Syndicates, page 886; Greeting Card Publishers, page 896; and Contests, page 937.

Women's Circle 668
Women's Household Crochet 397
Women's Project and Productions 865
Women's Sports and Fitness Magazine 605
Women's Words Writing Competition 935
Wonder Time 426
Wonderful West Virginia 533
Wood Lake Books, Inc. 234
Woodall's Campground Management 820
Woodbine House 212
Woodbridge Press 213
Woodenboat Magazine 600
Woodmen of the World Magazine 275
Woodshop News 397
Woodsong Graphics, Inc. 213
Woodwork 397
Woodworking Association of North America Monthly Bonus Packet 398
Woolly Mammoth Theatre Company 865
Worcester Foothills Theatre Company 865
WordPerfect, The Magazine 477
Workbasket, The 398
Workbench 398
Workboat 796
Working Mother Magazine 292
Working Mother Magazine 669
Work-In-Progress Grant (So-

ciety of Children's Book Authors) 935
Work-In-Progress Grant (Society of PLAY GRANT, Women in Theatre) 936
Workstation 768
World & I, The 357
World Coin News 398
World of Busines$ Kids, The 426
World Policy Journal 483
World Tennis 633
World War II 458
World's Best Short Short Story Contest 936
World's Fair 357
Worldwide Library 234
WPI Journal 305
Wrestling World 636
Writer, The 778
Writer-In-Residence Program 936
Writers and Artist Contest 936
Writers Connection 778
Writer's Digest 778
Writer's Digest Books 213
Writers Digest Writing Competition 936
Writers Fellowships 936
Writer's Forum 779
Writer's Guidelines 779
Writers Guild of America West Awards 936
Writer's Info 780
Writer's Journal 780
Writer's Nook News, The 780
Writer's Yearbook 781
WWF Magazine 636
WWF Superstars 636

WWF Wrestling Spotlight Magazine 636
Wyoming Arts Council Literary Fellowships 936
Wyoming Rural Electric News 738
Wyrick & Company 214

Y

Y.E.S. New Play Festival 936
Yachting 601
Yale Review, The 448
Yale Series of Younger Poets 936
Yankee Books 214
Ye Galleon Press 214
Yellow Silk 448
Yesterday's Magazette 372
Yesteryear 399
Yoga Journal, The 364
York Press Ltd. 235
Young Salvationist 643
Your Health & Fitness 365
Your Health 365
Your Virginia State Trooper Magazine 749
Youth Update 643
Yukon Reader, The 537

Z

Zebra Books 214
Zing 643
Zoland Books, Inc. 214
Zondervan Corp. The 215
Zornio Memorial Theatre for Youth Playwriting Award, Anna 936
Zuzu's Petals Poetry Contest 936

PROOFREADER'S MARKS

MARK	EXPLANATION	(In margin) EXAMPLE (In Text)	
e	Take out character indicated.	*e*	Your manuscript.
stet or ...	Let it stay.	*stet*	Your manuscript.
#	Put in space.	#	Yourmanuscript.
⌒	Close up completely.	⌒	Writer's Di gest School.
tr	Transpose; change places.	*tr*	Yuor manuscript.
caps or	Use capital letters.	*caps*	Writer's Digest School. / writer's digest school.
lc	Use lower-case letters.	*lc*	Your Manuscript.
bf or ~~~~	Use bold-face type.	*bf*	Writer's Digest School / Writer's Digest School
ital or ___	Use italic type.	*ital*	Writer's Digest.
ˇ	Put in apostrophe.	ˇ	Writers Digest School.
⊙	Put in period.	⊙	Your manuscript∧
'/	Put in comma.	'/	Your manuscript∧
:/	Put in colon.	:/	Your manuscript∧
;/	Put in semicolon.	;/	Writer's Digest School∧
ˇ ˇ	Put in quotation marks.	ˇ ˇ	He said, Yes.
?	Question to author.	? No hyphen OK	Free∧lance writer.
=/	Put in hyphen.	=/	Free∧lance writer.
!	Put in exclamation.	!	This is great∧
?	Put in question mark.	?	Are you starting∧
c/ɔ	Put in parenthesis.	(/)	Your first∧rough∧draft.
¶	Start paragraph.	¶	a writer.∫Learn to sell
‖	Even out lines	‖	⌐Writer's Digest and / Writer's Digest School.
⊏	Move the line left	⊏	Your manuscript.
⊐	Move the line right		Your manuscript. ⊐
No ¶	No paragraph; run together	*No ¶*	a writer.↰ / There are more needed
out, sc	Something missing, see copy.	*out, sc*	Writer's∧School.
spell out	Spell it out.	*spell out*	Your ms.

From *The Writer's Book of Checklists*, by Scott Edelstein (Writer's Digest Books).

Other Books of Interest

Annual Market Books

  Artist's Market, edited by Lauri Miller $21.95

  Children's Writer's & Illustrator's Market, edited by Lisa Carpenter (paper) $16.95

  Guide to Literary Agents & Art/Photo Reps, edited by Robin Gee $15.95

  Humor & Cartoon Markets, edited by Bob Staake (paper) $16.95

  Novel & Short Story Writer's Market, edited by Robin Gee (paper) $18.95

  Photographer's Market, edited by Sam Marshall $21.95

  Poet's Market, by Judson Jerome $19.95

  Songwriter's Market, edited by Brian Rushing $19.95

General Writing Books

  Beginning Writer's Answer Book, edited by Kirk Polking (paper) $13.95

  How to Write a Book Proposal, by Michael Larsen $10.95

  Make Your Words Work, by Gary Provost $17.95

  On Being a Writer, edited by Bill Strickland $19.95

  Pinckert's Practical Grammar, by Robert C. Pinckert (paper) $11.95

  The 29 Most Common Writing Mistakes & How To Avoid Them, by Judy Delton (paper) $9.95

  The Wordwatcher's Guide to Good Writing & Grammar, by Morton S. Freeman (paper) $15.95

  The Writer's Book of Checklists, by Scott Edelstein $16.95

  The Writer's Digest Guide to Manuscript Formats, by Buchman & Groves $18.95

  The Writer's Essential Desk Reference, edited by Glenda Neff $19.95

Nonfiction Writing

  The Complete Guide to Writing Biographies, by Ted Schwarz $19.95

  Creative Conversations: The Writer's Guide to Conducting Interviews, by Michael Schumacher $16.95

  How to Do Leaflets, Newsletters & Newspapers, by Nancy Brigham (paper) $14.95

  How to Sell Every Magazine Article You Write, by Lisa Collier Cool (paper) $11.95

  The Magazine Article: How To Think It, Plan It, Write It, by Peter Jacobi $17.95

Fiction Writing

  Characters & Viewpoint, by Orson Scott Card $13.95

  The Complete Guide to Writing Fiction, by Barnaby Conrad $17.95

  Cosmic Critiques: How & Why 10 Science Fiction Stories Work, edited by Asimov & Greenberg (paper) $12.95

  Creating Characters: How To Build Story People, by Dwight V. Swain $16.95

  Dialogue, by Lewis Turco $13.95

  The Fiction Writer's Silent Partner, by Martin Roth $19.95

  Handbook of Short Story Writing: Vol 1, by Dickson and Smythe (paper) $10.95

  Handbook of Short Story Writing: Vol. II, edited by Jean Fredette (paper) $12.95

  Manuscript Submission, by Scott Edelstein $13.95

  Mastering Fiction Writing, by Kit Reed $18.95

  Plot, by Ansen Dibell $13.95

  Revision, by Kit Reed $13.95

  Theme & Strategy, by Ronald B. Tobias $13.95

  Writing the Novel: From Plot to Print, by Lawrence Block (paper) $10.95

The Writing Business

  The Complete Guide to Self-Publishing, by Tom & Marilyn Ross (paper) $16.95

  The Writer's Friendly Legal Guide, edited by Kirk Polking $16.95

  A Writer's Guide to Contract Negotiations, by Richard Balkin (paper) $11.95

  The Writer's Guide to Self-Promotion & Publicity, by Elane Feldman $16.95

  Writing A to Z, edited by Kirk Polking $22.95

To order directly from the publisher, include $3.00 postage and handling for 1 book and $1.00 for each additional book. Allow 30 days for delivery.

Writer's Digest Books, 1507 Dana Avenue, Cincinnati, Ohio 45207

Credit card orders call TOLL-FREE

1-800-289-0963

Prices subject to change without notice.

Write to this same address for information on *Writer's Digest* magazine, *Story* magazine, Writer's Digest Book Club, Writer's Digest School, and Writer's Digest Criticism Service.

Canadian Postage by the Page

The following chart is for the convenience of Canadian writers sending domestic mail and other writers sending an envelope with International Reply Coupons (IRCs) or Canadian stamps for return of a manuscript from a Canadian publisher.

For complete postage assistance, use in conjunction with the U.S. Postage by the Page. Remember that manuscripts returning from the U.S. to Canada will take a U.S. stamped envelope although the original manuscript was sent with Canadian postage. This applies to return envelopes sent by American writers to Canada, too, which must be accompanied with IRCs or Canadian postage.

In a #10 envelope, you can have up to five pages for 40¢ (on manuscripts within Canada) or 46¢ (on manuscripts going to the U.S.). If you enclose a SASE, four pages is the limit. If you use 10×13 envelopes, send one page less than indicated on the chart.

IRC's are worth 46¢ Canadian postage but cost 95¢ to buy in the U.S. (Hint to U.S. writers: If you live near the border or have a friend in Canada, stock up on Canadian stamps. Not only are they more convenient than IRCs, they are cheaper.)

Canada Post designations for types of mail are:

Standard Letter Mail	Minimum size: 9cm × 14cm (3⅝″ × 5½″); Maximum size: 15cm × 24.5cm (6″ × 9⅝″); Maximum thickness: 5mm (³⁄₁₆″)
Oversize Letter Mail	Minimum size: 14cm × 24.5cm (5½″ × 9⅝″); Maximum size: 27cm × 38cm (10⅞″ × 15″); Maximum thickness: 2cm (¹³⁄₁₆″)
International Letter Mail	Minimum size: 9cm × 14cm (3⅝″ × 5½″); Maximum size: Length + width + depth 90cm (36″) Greatest dimension must not exceed 60cm (24″)

Insurance: To U.S. and within Canada – 45¢ for each $100 coverage to a maximum coverage of $1000. International – 65¢ for each $100 coverage to a maximum coverage of $1000.
Registered Mail: $2.70 plus postage (air or surface – any destination). Legal proof of mailing provided.
Priority Courier: Letter – $7.30 regional, $10.50 national. Pack – $8.10 regional, $11.55 national.